# Footprint Indi

*Matt Barrett and Annie Dare*

14th edition

*"All the convergent influences of the world run through this society: hindu, Moslem, Christian, secular, Stalinist, liberal, Maoist, democratic socialist, Gandhian. There is not a thought that is being thought in the West or East that is not active in some Indian mind."*

*Rabindranath Tagore: Poet and Dramatist,* Edward Thompson

**1 Delhi**
The capital city: Jama Masjid, the Qutb Minar and the chaos

**2 Corbett National Park**
Tiger country seen from a howdah

**3 Amritsar**
A golden temple sparkling in the dawn light

**4 Manali to Leh**
Terrifying but spectacular

**5 Agra**
The incomparable Taj Mahal

**6 Osian**
An extraordinary variety of temples surrounded by sand

**7 Jaisalmer**
Medieval city floating in a desert haze

**8 Orchha**
Palace and chhattris are quiet but very atmospheric

**9 Khajuraho**
Erotic temple architecture

**10 Sanchi**
Crowned on a hill, a key Buddhist site

**11 Udaipur**
Undeniably romantic with white palaces, blue lakes and green hills

**12 Juna Mahal, Dungarpur**
A fascinating glimpse of life in a royal palace 200 years ago

**13 Mandu**
Huge fort with fine Islamic buildings

# India Highlights

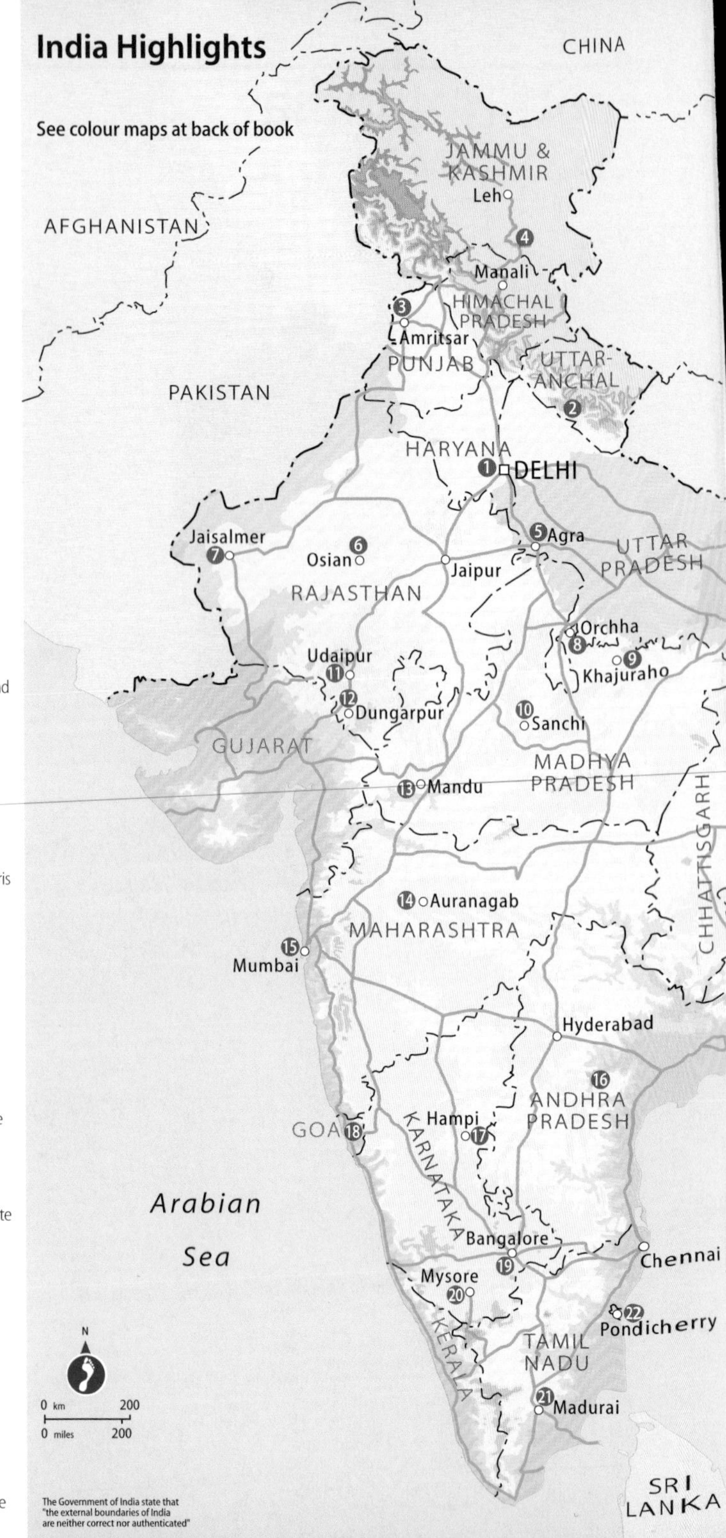

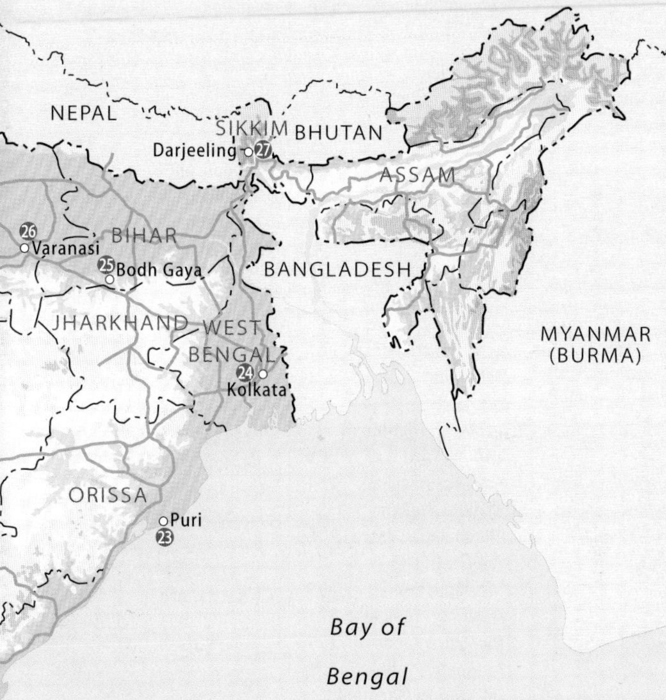


**14 Auranagab**
Visit the Ajanta and Ellora caves

**15 Mumbai**
Bollywood, tea at the Taj and Queen Victoria's necklace

**16 Nagarjuna-konda Island**
Board a boat to reach one of India's oldest Buddhist sites

**17 Hampi**
Hugely impressive ruins: home of the Vijayanagar kings

**18 Goa**
White sands, white-washed churches and formidable forts

**19 Bangalore**
At the heart of India's silicon valley

**20 Mysore**
Be there for the Dasara celebrations

**21 Madurai**
Temple elephants, flower sellers and musicians

**22 Pondicherry**
The old French enclave still retains a gallic flavour

**23 Puri**
A riot of colour and noise at the car festival

**24 Kolkata**
The intellectual capital of India

**25 Bodh Gaya**
Monlam festival is very atmospheric

**26 Varanasi**
India in the raw

**27 Darjeeling**
Tea gardens and trekking

# Contents



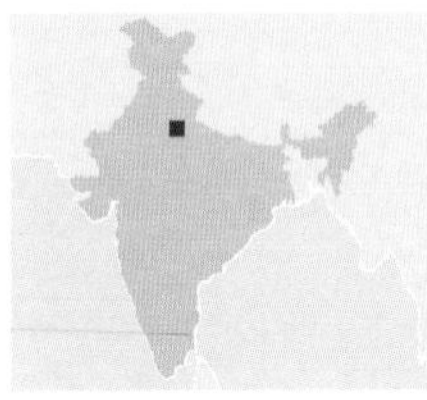

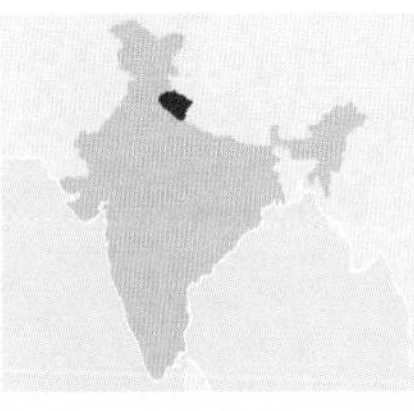



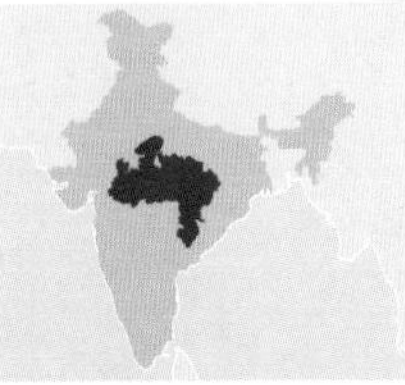



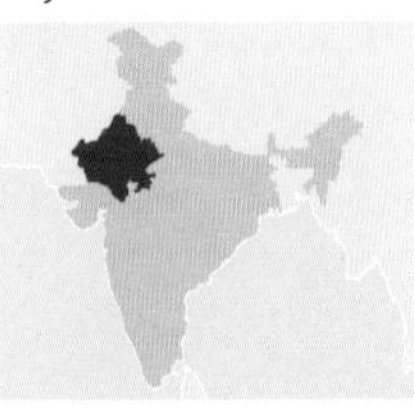

## Orissa

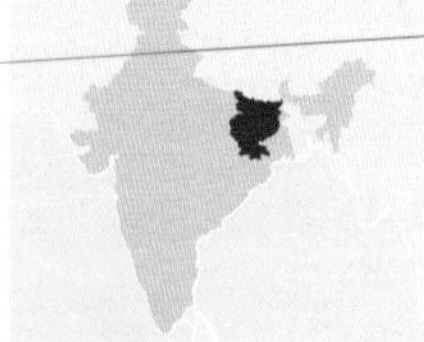



## Bihar & Jharkhand

## Andaman & Nicobar Islands



# South India 785

## Tamil Nadu

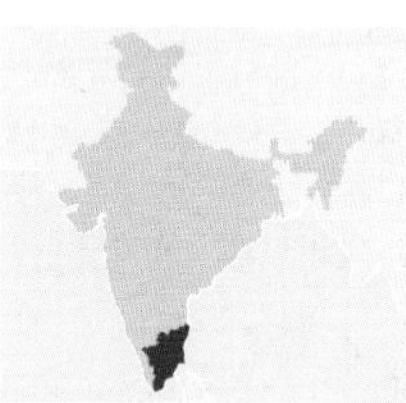



## Kerala

## Karnataka

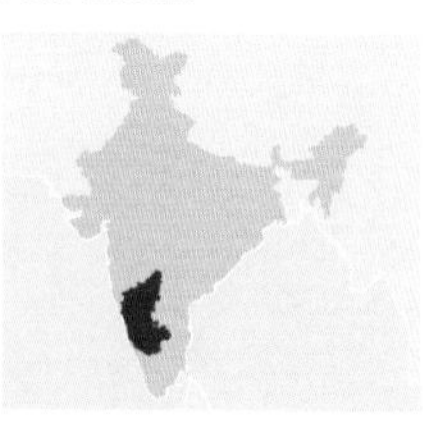

**Ebb and flow**

*Floating along the endlessly intersecting rivers, lagoons and tanks of Kerala's backwaters gives you a snail's pace window onto Keralite life on the waterfront.*

# A foot in the door

When VS Naipaul wrote, "there is little subtlety to India," it was itself an understatement. Whether in politics or cricket, this is a subcontinent built on passion. Those common western currencies of apathy, minimalism and restraint carry little weight here. Instead, the colours are richer, faith and festivals rushed into at fuller-tilt, the temples are older, the gods are painted more gaudily, the air is clouded with thicker incense, the politicians come more scandal- dogged and the cinema storylines are far more outlandish.

It's a place brimming with the type of extremes that make for easy, exaggerated contrasts. Twenty-first century India, in its anabolic-style sprint to embrace modernity, is all too acquainted with the imbalance between rich and poor. As Suketu Mehta puts it in his book on Bombay, "in the Bayview Bar of the Oberoi Hotel you can order a bottle of Dom Perignon for 1½ times the average annual income, this in a city where 40% of the houses lack safe drinking water."

Away from the tangled roads, jangling bazars and the unceasing humanity of its cities and towns the atavistic, eternal India remains, unswayed and undiminished by all the headline-grabbing of this modern land of biotech industries and nuclear tests. An azure blue sky hovers, as piercingly bright as ever, over Himalayan desert plains, populated by roaming yaks and punctuated by monasteries and mounds of holy rubble, where the fabric of Buddhist prayer flags slowly dissolves in the arid winds, offering beneficent wishes to passing travellers. These far off places still turn on their spiritual axis and continue, as they have for millennia, to inspire pilgrimage and to nurture meditation, philosophical thought and self-examination. In some parts of India, the 21st-century, as we know it, will have to wait.

## 10 From chaff to chip

India, blessed or cursed with an unimaginable 'human capital' – as its captains of industry call that one billion strong population – is emerging from over 50 years of stagnation post-Independence. Staring national bankruptcy in the face in 1991, the country was forced to open up to capitalism in a move that has made it the world's second fastest growing economy after China. The political and economic ambition is plain: to become a developed country, with mobile phones in every hand, broadband internet in every town and tractors replacing every plough. The textile mills, built by the British, now make perfect sites for multi-storied shopping emporia, crammed with businesses built to satisfy the ever-swelling middle-classes' voracious appetite for places to eat, drink and shop. India's refusal of help from the international community following the devastating tsunami that struck its southeast coastline in December 2004 is something of a statement of self-sufficient intent.

**24-hour rush hour**
*Home to over one billion and rising fast, there aren't many places in India's cities to get a moment to yourself. Allahabad is no exception.*

## Peasants revolt



However, India, some say, is becoming a rich country where poor people live. Some 40% of the world's poor are reckoned to live here. They exist on a near-constant dripfeed of Dolby-digital dreaming, beamed from 150 cable channels plus the la-la-land of Bollywood. And you ignore that aspirant rural poor at your peril. The Hindu nationalist and modernizing BJP's re-election campaign in 2004 rested heavily on the laurels of its perceived economic success in the shopping centre-strewn cities. There followed a democratic peasants revolt in which India's rural population, still 70% of the country's total, delivered a huge political upset by returning Gandhi's Congress Party to power. Although this was a clear vote of no confidence from the dispossessed villages, the Congress they voted in is a party that is fairly faithful to the aims of the apparatus it replaced: as Arundhati Roy has written "big dams, nuclear bombs and privatization." It is a party that also has to face the potential of a huge humanitarian crisis in India'a rates of HIV infection.

**Abodes of the gods**

*The shrines in the Garhwal Himalaya are visited by thousands of Hindu pilgrims each summer. One of the most important is the 18th-century granite temple of Gangotri.*

1
2
4
5
7
8
10
11

1 *India is home to much wildlife, including some wonderful bird species. Here, a couple of painted storks survey the scene below.* ▸▸ *See page 1347.*

2 *Superbly sited, this hill fort, overlooking the town of Gwalior, contains sculptures, temples and even a few palaces, yet few tourists make the journey.* ▸▸ *See page 269.*

3 *Hinduism is followed by over 80% of the population and its influence over daily life is omnipresent.* ▸▸ *See page 1322.*

4 *Festivals are celebrated with gusto; the throwing of powder paint over everyone makes for a colourful affair.* ▸▸ *See page 61.*

5 *The Brahmaputra, known here as the Siang River, enters Arunachal Pradesh from China, flows through a deeply cut valley.* ▸▸ *See page 676.*

6 *The food alone justifies a visit to India. The tropical climate in the south is ideal for growing papaya as well as other delicious fruits.* ▸▸ *See page 59.*

7 *There is a long tradition in India of performing: music, dance, snake charming, fire-eating.* ▸▸ *See page 1320.*

8 *The Tughluqabad ruins still convey a sense of the power and energy of the newly arrived Muslims in India.* ▸▸ *See page 108.*

9 *The Church of the Immaculate Conception in Panjim, Goa's capital, was built in Portuguese Baroque style.* ▸▸ *See page 1160.*

10 *On the dry, arid plateau of Ladakh, the Chang-la nomads bring colour and life to the landscape.* ▸▸ *See page 555.*

11 *The memorial to Swami Vivekananda draws thousands of Hindu pilgrims to Kanniyakumari.* ▸▸ *See page 886.*

12 *One of Rajasthan's many cities well worth visiting, Jodhpur.* ▸▸ *See page 381.*

## Set in stone

With human settlement stretching back 500,000 years, you have a dizzying choice ahead of you by way of architectural investigation from the crude relics of Stone Age civilizations to the intricacies of Islamic, Hindu, Jain and Buddhist archeological sites. The south yields the crumbling old homes of Pondicherry and the spice-sack wooden stalls of Cochi, while the north has princely forts and palaces that tower above the empty deserts. Stonemasonry of the highest order has long since been practised here: there's the delicate Buddhist-inspired carved gateways at Sanchi, the impossibly ornate windows at Fatehpur Sikri and the shimmering Golden Temple at Amritsar. The 17th-century masterpiece, the Taj Mahal, continues to render those who view it speechless. An icon of love and a perfect marriage of Indian Hindu and Persian Muslim architecture, its beauty is unmatched.

## Mother earth

From the icy peaks of the Himalaya to the warm waters of the Andaman Sea, the sub-continent has almost every landscape you could wish to see. When the snow melts from the high, vertiginous roads, visits to places like Ladakh, otherwise known as 'Little Tibet, are possible. After the North's gangetic plains, the southern landscape gives way to paddy fields, coconut thickets, mangrove swamps and spice plantations. Further south still are the coral atolls in the Arabian and Andaman sea filled with underwater forests. This diversity of landscape allows all kinds of different birds and beasts to survive. Lions, snow leopards, antelopes, monkeys, deer, elephants and tigers roam, many protected within the boundaries of national parks.

*Travellers to the Spiti Valley, in the rainshadow of the Himalaya, are met by this welcome gate. Lying ahead is a beautiful, barren landscape of deep valleys and jagged peaks.*

*One of the most holy cities in the world, Varanasi draws pilgrims from all over the globe to meditate, worship and bathe in the waters of the River Ganges.*

## Three hundred and thirty million gods

Worship is omnipresent: roadside shrines are daubed with potash and hung with marigolds, gods are balanced on dashboards, coconuts are smashed and incense is burnt. A testimony to the central role religion plays in India was the arrival of some 30 million visiting pilgrims for the Khumb Mela in 2001; the largest human gathering on earth. The sacred city of Varanasi, with its winding alleys and burning ghats, sees the daily flow of Hindu faithful making their way to the banks of the Ganges. At the other end of the spectrum are the hushed corridors of Old Goa's convents and the cool interiors of the white-washed churches that are dotted throughout the state. It's little wonder that the calendar is crammed with festivals that explode in riots of colour, sound and food. The ways to celebrate are as various as the reasons: bonfires lit, paint thrown, kites flown, gods drowned, goats sacrificed, food forsaken and chests beaten.

## Packed to the rafters

Nothing can wrong-foot you quite as fast as standing for the first time on the pavement of an Indian metropolis. Each point on the Indian compass has its headquarters. The north has New Delhi, the sober political capital of the subcontinent, India's answer to Washington. Bombay, on the other hand, has the sass and swagger of the economic and lifestyle capital New York. Calcutta in the east is the cultural capital, full of intellectualism, social reforms, striking colonial buildings and some of the most densely populated slums in the world. The southern city of Chennai is probably the most conservative, a sprawl of low-slung buildings and Indo-Saracenic architecture spread along the Marina beach.

**Camel country**

*The forbidding Thar desert, with its shifting sand dunes and crushingly high summer temperatures, is an inhospitable place.*

# Essentials

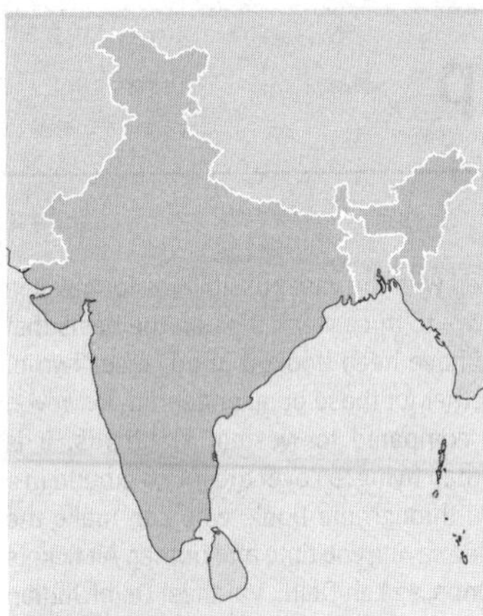



**Footprint features**

# Planning your trip

## Where to go

First time visitors are often at a loss when faced with the vast possibilities for travel in India. We have made a few suggestions for two- to three-week trips on the basis that some journeys will be flown and that tickets have been booked in advance. Two or three of these itineraries could be pieced together for those on a longer trip. However, since travelling times are often quite long compared to western standards, it is advisable to stick to a particular region rather than trying to cover too much ground in a short time. Reliable travel agencies are listed through the book, who can make the necessary arrangements for a relatively small fee saving you time and bother. Air tickets can be difficult to get at short notice for some trips, eg Leh-Delhi, Varanasi-Delhi. Indian railways are divided into regions, and despite computerized booking and the growing number of booking offices where all-India reservations can be made there are still places where it is impossible to book tickets in regions other than the one you are in. Allow more time if you are planning to travel entirely by road and rail. However, if you use overnight trains for longer journeys you can cover almost as much ground in the same time as flying. Figures in brackets are number of nights we suggest you spend.



### The Himalayan Foothills

**Two weeks** **Delhi** (2) has both the British built New Delhi and Shah Jahan's 17th-century capital. The city also provides access to some of the most beautiful sights in the Himalayan foothills and awe-inspiring mountain peaks. You can fly to **Shimla** (2), the British summer capital, then continue by road to **Dharamshala** (3) associated with the Dalai Lama and the Tibetan settlement. Spend a night in **Mandi** (1) en route to **Naggar** (2) and **Manali** (4) for some trekking. Fly back to **Delhi** from Kullu to visit **Agra** (1) for the Taj and the splendid fort on the fast *Shatabdi Express*.

**Three weeks** Between late June and September the tour could be altered to take in the Tibetan-Buddhist area of **Ladakh** (3) (instead of Dharamshala) by travelling to **Leh** (5) by the spectacular road from **Manali** (2).

### Central India

**Two weeks** This tour of is characterized by pre-history and palaces. It starts in the centre of Muslim influence in **Delhi** (2) and **Agra** (1), and passes through some of the great Rajput palaces and forts in **Gwalior** (3) visiting **Datia** and idyllic **Orchha** (2) via **Jhansi** en route to **Bhopal** (3). Around Bhopal are impressive prehistoric rock art at **Bhimbetka**, and early Hindu and Buddhist remains at **Bhojpur** and **Sanchi**. On the way to **Mumbai** (2) a brief diversion from **Indore** takes you to the quaint fortified site at **Mandu** (2) with its picturesque past.

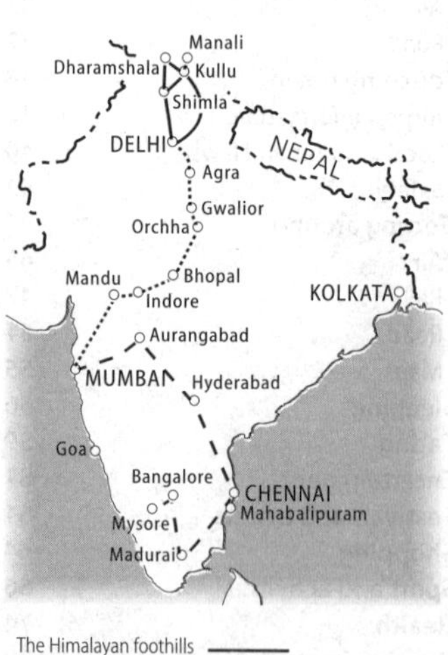

## South India

**Three weeks** The historical South India circuit starts at **Mumbai** (2) where you can first visit the rock-cut caves rich in frescoes and carvings at **Ajanta** and **Ellora** and the rugged **Daulatabad** fort near **Aurangabad** (3). Then on to **Hyderabad** (3), with the former capital of the Muslim Nizam with Golconda fort and the tombs nearby. You then visit centres of ancient Tamil culture at **Chidambaram, Gangaikondacholapuram** and **Thanjavur** (3) after **Chennai** (1) fitting in a visit to **Mahabalipuram's** shore temple (2). The tour returns through southern Karnataka via **Mysore** (3), visiting the exquisite carvings in the Hindu and Jain temples at **Belur** and **Halebid** from **Hassan** or **Chikmagalur** (2), and finally to **Bangalore** (2).

## The North West

**Three weeks** This route taking in Mughal and Rajput India starts in **Delhi** (2) and moves to **Agra** (2) and **Jaipur** (2). Relax at the sleeping village of **Samode** (2) before flying across the desert to **Jaisalmer** (3) and then head for **Jodhpur** (2). On the way to lakeside **Udaipur** (3) you can visit the exquisite Jain temples at **Ranakpur** and the impressive fort at **Kumbhalgarh** from restful **Deogarh** (2). As a bonus, you can sample the charming hospitality at heritage hotels in former palaces and forts in both Rajasthan and Gujarat. Stop at **Poshina Fort** (2) or **Balaram Palace** en route to **Ahmadabad** (2) with its architectural heritage and Calico Museum, before flying back.

## The Far South

**Three weeks** From **Chennai** (2) drive to **Swamimalai** (2) known for traditional bronze casting and continue south to the ancient Tamil temples at **Thanjavur** (2) and **Madurai** (2). A morning start allows a stop at **Padmanabhapuram Palace** on the way across to Kerala on the west coast to relax by the beach at **Kovalam** (3) near Thiruvananthapuram. Take a boat along the backwaters as you move to **Kochi** (3), a fascinating meeting point of Eastern and European cultures. Then drive across to the tea estates of **Munnar** (2), high in the Western Ghats before dropping to the Tamil plains to visit the ancient fort and temples at **Trichy** (2) and **Srirangam**. Before returning home from Chennai, stop by the sea for the rock-cut cave temples at **Mahabalipuram** (3).

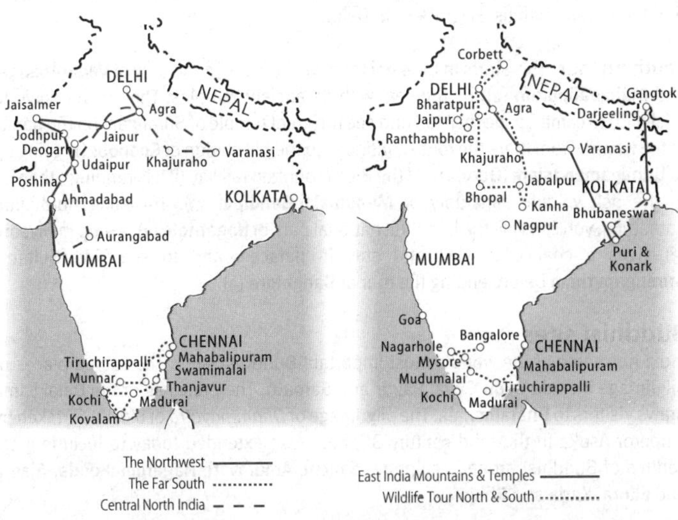

## Central North India

**Three weeks** Across the heart of central North India it is possible to see some of the best examples of Buddhist, Hindu and Muslim art and architecture. Travelling partly by road or rail, you also see a range of India's varied scenery and agriculture, going first across the Deccan plateau, with its rich black lava soils, then over Rajasthan and then Khajuraho on the northern edge of the Peninsula. **Mumbai** (2) - **Aurangabad** (3) for **Ajanta, Ellora** and **Daulatabad** fort - **Udaipur** (3) - **Deogarh** (2) visiting **Ranakpur** Jain temples and **Kumbhalgarh** Fort - **Jaipur** (2) - **Agra** (2) - **Khajuraho** (2) - **Varanasi** (3) - **Delhi** (2).

## East India

**Two weeks** This tour, characterized by mountains and temples, starts in **Kolkata** (2), a vibrant city which was once the capital of the Raj, and then takes you to the foothills of the Himalaya starting with **Darjeeling** (3), famous for its tea estates and magnificent views of Kanchengdzonga. Distant **Sikkim** (3) with its distinctive Buddhist influence is a fascinating side trip. Magnificent Orissan temples can be seen at **Bhubaneswar** (3) and **Konark** (with a possible beach diversion near the pilgrimage centre of **Puri** (3), and on to the holy city of **Varanasi** (2) to see India laid bare for the first time visitor. The tour winds up with a visit to see the fabulous carvings at **Khajuraho** (2) and concludes in **Delhi** (2) with a stop en route at **Agra** (1) to see the finest of the Mughal buildings, the Taj Mahal.

## Wildlife tours

Each region with its distinctive habitats and outstanding reserves offer many opportunities for seeing wildlife in some of India's 54 national parks and over 370 sanctuaries. The suggested tours take you to the most popular of these and also allow excursions to cultural sites. Camera/video fees, vehicle charges and guides, usually compulsory, can add a lot to the cost of the actual entry fee.

**Northern tour** This starts in **Delhi** (2) and goes via **Bhopal** (2) and **Jabalpur** (1) to **Kanha** (3), one of the most outstanding reserves in Central India, with very rich habitat and still little visited. It continues to **Khajuraho** (2), where there is a chance to see magnificent 10th-century temples, en route to **Agra**'s (2) magnificent Taj Mahal and the abandoned city of **Fatehpur Sikri** before arriving at the peaceful bird sanctuary at **Bharatpur** (2), excellent for waterside birds. Not far away, **Ranthambhore** (2), with the semi-arid environment of Rajasthan, is the habitat for a range of wildlife including tigers. Return to **Delhi** (1) via the pink city of **Jaipur** (1) and continue to **Corbett** (3) in the Himalayan foothills. Fly back from Delhi.

**Southern tour** This starts in **Chennai** (2) to visit the bird sanctuary of **Vedanthangal** and **Mahabalipuram** (2), by the sea, with its ancient temples. Then travel down to **Trichy** (2) to climb up the rock fort and see the great temple of Srirangam on the banks of the Kaveri. From there the route continues to the hill station of **Coonoor** (1) going up to **Udhagamandalam (Ooty)** (1) on the Blue Mountain railway (if it is running), then on to the rich wildlife sanctuary of **Mudumalai-Bandipur** (3). Travelling north into Karnataka, you can visit the beautiful national park of **Nagarhole** (3). A stop in **Mysore** (3) gives a chance to visit and stay in palaces, and to see Tipu Sultan's **Srirangapatnam** before ending the tour at **Bangalore** (3).

## Buddhist sites

India has some of the world's most important Buddhist sites. The sacred places of pilgrimage include **Bodh Gaya, Rajgir** and **Sarnath**. The presence of the Dalai Lama draws visitors to **Dharamshala**. The pilgrimage or *Dhammayatra* of old, undertaken by Emperor Asoka in the third century BC, has been extended today to include great centres of Buddhist art and sculpture. **Sanchi, Amaravati, Nagarjunakonda, Ajanta** and **Ellora, Karla** and **Bhaja.**

## Forts

A wealth of history awaits you in the forts and citadels of the subcontinent. There are those that still hold rich architectural treasures such as the red forts at **Delhi**, **Agra** and Meherangarh in **Jodhpur**; those with evocative remains of a bygone lifestyle as in **Gwalior**, **Orchha** and **Mandu** (Madhya Pradesh), **Kota**, **Bundi**, **Jaisalmer** in the desert (Rajasthan) and at **Gingee** (Tamil Nadu) and **Warangal** (Andhra Pradesh). There are desolate ruins at **Cabo de Rama** (Goa) and atmospheric **Hampi-Vijaynagar** (Karnataka) whilst there are marvellous examples of strategic defence at **Kumbhalgarh** (Rajasthan), **Daulatabad** (Maharashtra) and **Golconda** near Hyderabad (Andhra Pradesh). On a smaller scale, the tiny coastal outpost of **Tiracol** in Goa has been restored to accommodate guests. Add to these the numerous fortified 'palaces' now joining the Heritage hotels group in **Rajasthan** and **Gujarat** (Deogarh, Kuchaman, Poshina). Enthusiasts may want to explore the Sivaji forts in **Maharashtra** or the Chandela forts in **Madhya Pradesh**.



## When to go

*To check weather conditions try www.wunderground.com*

In most of India, by far the best time to visit is from the end of the monsoon in October to the end of March. However, there are important exceptions. The hill stations in the Himalaya and the Western Ghats are beautiful in the hot weather months of April to early June. Parts of the western Himalaya can be excellent through to September though it can be very cold and sometimes very wet in the spring. The chart over the page gives an idea of which states can be visited comfortably during any particular month, indicated by a tick.

| | North | | | | | | East | | | | | South | | | | West | | | |
|---|---|---|---|---|---|---|---|---|---|---|---|---|---|---|---|---|---|---|---|
| | Rajasthan | Uttar Pradesh | Punjab | Madhya Pradesh | Himachal | Ladakh | W Bengal | Orissa | Assam | Sikkim | Bihar | Tamil Nadu | Kerala | Karnataka | Andhra Pradesh | South coast | Maharashtra hills | Goa | Gujarat |
| **January** | ✓ | ✓ | ✓ | ✓ | ✓ | | ✓ | ✓ | ✓ | | ✓ | ✓ | ✓ | ✓ | ✓ | ✓ | ✓ | ✓ | ✓ |
| | Warm days (18-25°C), dry, cool nights; very cold and clear in the mountains | | | | | | Warm days (15-30°C) dry, cool nights | | | | | Hot days (30-40°C) dry, cool nights | | | | Hot days (25-35°C) dry, cool nights | | | |
| **February** | ✓ | ✓ | ✓ | ✓ | ✓ | | ✓ | ✓ | ✓ | | ✓ | ✓ | ✓ | ✓ | ✓ | ✓ | ✓ | ✓ | ✓ |
| | Warm days (18-25°C), dry, cool nights; very cold and clear in the mountains | | | | | | Warm days (20-30°C) dry, cool nights | | | | | Hot days (30-40°C) dry; cool and dry in hills | | | | Hot days (25-35°C) dry, cool nights | | | |
| **March** | ✓ | ✓ | ✓ | ✓ | ✓ | | ✓ | ✓ | ✓ | ✓ | ✓ | ✓ | ✓ | ✓ | ✓ | ✓ | ✓ | ✓ | ✓ |
| | Warm days (21-30°C), dry, cool nights; cold and clear in the mountains | | | | | | Cool warm days in hills (20-25°C); cool nights | | | | | Hot days (30-40°C) dry; warm and dry in hills by day, cold at night | | | | Hot days (25-35°C) dry, cool nights | | | |
| **April** | ✓ | ✓ | ✓ | ✓ | ✓ | | ✓ | ✓ | ✓ | ✓ | ✓ | ✓ | ✓ | ✓ | | ✓ | ✓ | ✓ | ✓ |
| | Hot days (30-40°C), dry, warm nights; coo and clear in the mountains | | | | | | Hot on plains (35-42°C); clear warm days in hills (20-25°C), cool nights | | | | | Hot (35-42°C) humid on coastal plains; cool and dry in hills | | | | Hot days (25-35°C) dry, cool nights | | | |
| **May** | | ✓ | | | ✓ | | ✓ | | ✓ | ✓ | | ✓ | ✓ | ✓ | | | ✓ | | |
| | Very hot days (40-50°C), dry, hot nights in plains; clear and warm in hills | | | | | | Very hot (35-45°C) and dry in plains; Warm days in hills (20-30°C), dry, cool nights | | | | | Very hot in plains (35-45°C); Warm (20-30°C), dry in hills | | | | Hot days (25-35°C) dry, cool nights | | | |
| **June** | | | | | ✓ | | ✓ | | | | | | | ✓ | | | ✓ | | |
| | Warm days (20-30°C) in hills, rains begins end June, hot (35-45°C) on plains | | | | | | Warm days in hills (20-30°C), dry, cool nights until rains; hot and wet on plains | | | | | Cool, wet, misty in hills, hot (30-35°C) and humid on plains, rains sweep west coast | | | | Hot, wet days (25-35°C), humid nights, coastal Goa and Maha-rastra have heavy monsoon | | | |
| **July** | | | | | ✓ | ✓ | | | | | | | | ✓ | | | ✓ | | |
| | Warm days (18-25°C), wet except in North and East | | | | | | Very hot and wet | | | | | Hot (30-40°C), showery; wet in hills | | | | Very warm (20-30°C) humid, often wet | | | |
| **August** | | | | | ✓ | ✓ | | | | | | | | ✓ | | | | | |
| | Warm days (18-25°C), cool nights at atitude | | | | | | Very hot and wet | | | | | Hot (30-40°C), showery; wet in hills | | | | Hot, humid, wet | | | |
| **September** | | | | | ✓ | ✓ | ✓ | ✓ | | | | ✓ | ✓ | ✓ | | | ✓ | ✓ | |
| | Warm days (18-25°C), dry, cool nights; very cold, clear and dry in mountains | | | | | | In hills warm days (20-25°C), sometimes wet; hotter on plains (35-40°C) | | | | | Hot (30-40°C), dry; cooler but still often wet in hills | | | | Hot and humid | | | |

**Essentials** Planning your trip

| | North | | | | | | East | | | | | South | | | | West | | | |
|---|---|---|---|---|---|---|---|---|---|---|---|---|---|---|---|---|---|---|---|
| | Rajasthan | Uttar Pradesh | Punjab | Madhya Pradesh | Himachal | Ladakh | W Bengal | Orissa | Assam | Sikkim | Bihar | Tamil Nadu | Kerala | Karnataka | Andhra Pradesh | South coast | Maharashtra hills | Goa | Gujarat |
| **October** | ✓ | ✓ | ✓ | ✓ | ✓ | | ✓ | ✓ | ✓ | ✓ | ✓ | | ✓ | ✓ | | ✓ | ✓ | ✓ | ✓ |
| | Hot days (30-40°C), warm nights; mountains getting much cooler | | | | | | Warm days (20-30°C), dry, cool nights | | | | | Hot (30-40°C), cool and dry in hills, monsoon in Tamil Nadu | | | | Hot days (25-35°C), dry, cool nights | | | |
| **November** | ✓ | ✓ | ✓ | ✓ | | | ✓ | ✓ | ✓ | | ✓ | | ✓ | ✓ | | ✓ | ✓ | ✓ | ✓ |
| | Warm days (18-25°C), dry, cool nights; cold, clear and dry in mountains | | | | | | Warm days (20-30°C), dry, cool nights | | | | | Cyclones in Andhra and Tamil Nadu; hot (30-40°C), hills cooling | | | | Hot days (25-35°C), dry, cool nights | | | |
| **December** | ✓ | ✓ | ✓ | ✓ | ✓ | | ✓ | ✓ | ✓ | | ✓ | | ✓ | ✓ | | ✓ | ✓ | ✓ | ✓ |
| | Warm days (18-25°C), dry, cool nights; very cold, clear and dry in mountains | | | | | | Warm days (20-30°C), dry, cool nights; cyclones in Orissa | | | | | Hot (30-40°C), dry, cool and dry in hills; cyclones early December in Andhra and Tamil Nadu | | | | Hot days (25-35°C), dry, cool nights | | | |

Some of the country's great festivals such as **Dasara** and **Diwali** across India and **Pongal** in Tamil Nadu are celebrated in the autumn and winter. In Rajasthan, local camel and cattle fairs and the **Desert Festival** among the dunes are added attractions during these seasons.

## Tour operators

You may choose to try an inclusive package holiday or let a specialist operator quote for a tailor-made tour. Out of season these can be worth exploring. The lowest prices quoted from the UK vary from about US$550 for a week (flights, hotel and breakfast) in the low season, to over US$3,000 for three weeks during the peak season. Most will chalk out individual itineraries and cover the major sights with small groups. Tour companies are listed here who arrange anything from general tours to wildlife safaris to ashram retreats. See page 71 for trekking operators and page 122 for operators in Delhi.

**Ace**, T01223 835055, ace@studytours.org. Cultural study tours, expert led.

**Adventures Abroad**, T0114 2473400; USA & Canada, T800 6653998, Australia T800 890790, info@adventures-abroad.org. Outward bound.

**Andrew Brock** (Coromandel), T01572 821330, abrock@aol.com. Special interest.

**Cox & Kings** (Taj Group), T020 78735000, www.coxandkings.co.uk.

**Discovery Initiatives**, T00185 643333, www.discoveryinitiatives.com. Wildlife safaris.

**Dragoman**, T0870 4994475, www.dragoman.co.uk. Overland, adventure, camping.

**Exodus**, T0870 244 5550, www.exodus.co.uk. Adventure holidays.

**Gateway to India**, T0870 4423204, tours@gateway-to-india.com. Tailor-made, off-the-beaten-track, local reps.

**Greaves Travels**, T020 74879111, www.greavesindia.com.
**Guerba Expeditions**, T01373 826611, iwww.guerba.co.uk. Adventure, treks.
**Ibex Expeditions**, Delhi, T+91-11-6912641, www.ibexexpeditions.com. Organizes tours, activities, accommodation and makes travel arrangements throughout India.
**Indian Magic**, T020-84274848, sales@indiamagic.co.uk. Homestays, small-scale.
**Master Travel**, T020-75016742, www.mastertravel.co.uk. History, ayurveda.
**Myths and Mountains**, USA T800-6706984, www.mythsandmountains.com. Culture, crafts, religion.
**on the go**, 68 North End Rd, West Kensington, London W14 9EP, T020-73711113, www.onthegotours.com. Legendary tours and tailormades at amazing prices.

**Palanquin Travels**, T020-75806700, www.palanquin.co.uk. Culture, wildlife.
**Paradise Holidays**, T-95, C L House, Adjacent Jetair House, T91-11-51644534, www.paradiseholidays.com. A whole raft of different tours from cultural to adventure to religious. Tailor made.
**Parul Tours & Travels**, 32 Lal Ghat, Udaipur 313 001, T0294 242 1697, www.rajasthan travelbycab.com. Ticketing, reservations, escorted tours, etc, throughout Rajasthan and South India.
**Pettitts**, T01892-515966, www.pettitts.co.uk. Unusual locations.
**Royal Expeditions**, R-184, Greater Kailash, New Delhi 110048, T91-11-26238545, www.royalexpeditions.com. Tailor-made tours: wildlife, photography, cultural, etc.
**Select Connections**, T01892 725555, www.selectconnections.co.uk. Excellent tailor-made breaks throughout India and Sri Lanka.
**Spirit of India**, USA T888-3676147, www.spirit-of-india.com. Focused, local experts.
**Steppes Travel**, 51 Castle St, Cirencester, GL7 1QD, UK, T01285-880980, www.steppeseast.co.uk. Tailor-made tours. ATOL protected. Recommended.
**Trans Indus**, 11 The Pavement, Popes Lane Ealing, London W5 4NG, T020-85662729, www.transindus.com. Activities, wildlife, etc.
**The Adventure Company**, 15 Turk St, Alton, Hampshire, GU34 1AG, T0870 794 1009, www.adventurecompany.co.uk. Adventure tours, small groups.
**Weeks Tours**, T12/1463A, Cochin, Kerala, weekstour@vsnl.net. Good tours.

## Finding out more

### Tourist offices

There are Government of India Tourist offices in Delhi and the state capitals, as well as State Tourist Offices (usually known as Tourism Development Corporations) in the major cities and a few important sites. See the Directory sections throughout the guide for contact details. In addition, some regions eg Kumaon (KMVN) and Garhwal (GMVN) in Uttaranchal, Darjeeling (DGHC) in West Bengal have their own offices. They produce their own tourist literature, either free or sold at a nominal price, and some also have lists of city hotels and paying guest options. The quality of material is improving though maps handed out are often inadequate. Many offer tours of the city, neighbouring sights and overnight and regional packages. Some run modest hotels and mid-way motels with restaurants, and may also arrange car hire and guides. The staff in the regional and local offices are usually helpful, although the standard of information can be widely variable from town to town. Don't take advice from unofficial 'Tourist Offices' at airports or railway stations.

#### Tourist offices overseas

**Australia** Level 1, 2 Picadilly, 210 Pitt St, Sydney, NSW 2000, T612-292644855, F92644860.
**Canada** 60 Bloor St, West Suite No 1003, Toronto, Ontario, T416-9623787, F9626279.
**France** 11-13 Bis Boulevard Hausmann, F75009, Paris T45233045, F45233345.
**Germany** Baserler St 48, 60329, Frankfurt AM-Main 1, T069-2429490, F24294977.
**Italy** Via Albricci 9, Milan 20122, T8053506.
**Japan** Pearl Building, 9-18 Chome Ginza, Chuo Ku, Tokyo 104, T33-5715196, F5715235.
**The Netherlands** Rokin 9-15, 1012 Amsterdam, T020-6208991, F6383059.
**Singapore** 20 Kramat Lane, 01-01A United House, Singapore 0922, T2353800, F2358677.
**Sweden** Sveavagen 9-11 1st floor, S-III 57 Stockholm 11157, T468-101187, F210186.
**Switzerland** 1-3 rue de Chantepoulet, 1201 Geneva, T41-227321813, F7315660.
**Thailand** 3rd floor, KFC Bldg, 62/5 Thaniya Rd, Bangkok 10500, T662-2352585, F2368411.
**UK** 7 Cork St, London W1X 2AB, T020-74373677, F74941048.
**USA** 3550 Wilshire Blvd, Room 204, Los Angeles, California 90010. T213-3808855, F3806111; Suite 1808, 1270 Avenue of Americas, New York, NY 10020, T212-5864901, F5823274.

### Websites

**www.123india.com** Wide-ranging current affairs and general India site.
**www.fco.gov** Advice to travellers from the Foreign Office, London.
**www.incredibleindia.org** Official tourist board website.
**www.indev.org** British Council site devoted to development issues in India.
**www.india.org** Contains excellent information on the structure of Indian government.
**www.indiagov.org** and **www.indiacurrent affairs.com** Regularly updated cuttings from Indian national dailies.
**www.indianrail.gov.in** Info on the railways.
**www.nic.in** Official government portal, with good state by state information.
**www.responsibletravel.com** Green tourism.
**www.tourindia.com** The official government promotional site with useful information but has no objective evaluation of problems and difficulties. 'India Travel Online' is informative and issued fortnightly.
**www.travel.indiamart.com** Details of online bookings for selected hotels.
**www.tourismindia.com** Yellow pages.
**www.travel-health.co.uk/index.html** and **www. tripprep.com** Health advice prior to travel.



## Language

Hindi, spoken as a mother tongue by over 400 million people, is India's official language. The use of English is also enshrined in the Constitution for a wide range of official purposes, notably communication between Hindi and non-Hindi speaking states. The most widely spoken Indo-Aryan languages are: Bengali (8.3%), Marathi (8%), Urdu (5.7%), Gujarati (5.4%), Oriya (3.7%) and Punjabi (3.2%). Among the Dravidian languages Telugu (8.2%), Tamil (7%), Kannada (4.2%) and Malayalam (3.5%) are the most widely used. Most of these languages have their own scripts. In all, there are 15 major and several hundred minor languages and dialects.

English now plays an important role across India. It is widely spoken in towns and cities and even in quite remote villages it is usually not difficult to find someone who speaks at least a little English. Other European languages are almost completely unknown. The accent in which English is spoken is often affected strongly by the mother tongue of the speaker and there have been changes in common grammar which sometimes make it sound unusual. Many of these changes have become standard Indian English usage, as valid as any other varieties of English used around the world. It is possible to study a number of Indian languages at language centres.

See the Footnotes chapter, page 1368, for Hindi words and phrases, food and drink and a glossary of terms.

## Disabled travellers

India is not geared up specially for making provisions for the physically handicapped or wheelchair bound traveller. Access to buildings, toilets (sometimes 'squat' type), pavements, kerbs and public transport can prove frustrating, but it is easy to find people to give a hand with lifting and carrying. Provided there is an able-bodied companion to scout around and arrange help, and so long as you are prepared to pay for at least mid-price hotels or guesthouses, private car-hire and taxis, India should be perfectly rewarding, even if in a somewhat limited way.

Some travel companies are beginning to specialize in exciting holidays, tailor-made for individuals depending on their level of disability. For those with

*Whilst it is true that India adopted the English language, the English also adopted some Indian words; pajama, shampoo and nincompoop to name a few.*

access to the internet, a Global Access – Disabled Travel Network Site is www.geocities.com/Paris/1502. It is dedicated to providing travel information for 'disabled adventurers' and includes a number of reviews and tips from members of the public. You might also want to read *Nothing Ventured*, edited by Alison Walsh (Harper Collins), which gives personal accounts of worldwide journeys by disabled travellers, plus advice and listings.

## Gay and lesbian travellers

Indian law forbids homosexual acts for men (but not women) and carries a maximum sentence of life imprisonment. Although it is common to see young males holding hands in public, it doesn't necessarily indicate a gay relationship and is usually an expression of friendship. Overt displays of affection between homosexuals (and hetrosexuals) give offence and should be avoided.

## Student travellers

Full time students qualify for an ISIC (International Student Identity Card) which is issued by student travel and specialist agencies (eg **STA**) at home. It allows certain travel concessions and acts as proof of student status within India which may allow ticket concessions into a few sites. Those intending to study in India may get a one year student visa, see page 30.

## Travelling with children

*For older kids, you can't go far wrong with a play station and two handsets.*

Children of all ages are widely welcomed, being greeted with a warmth in their own right which is often then extended to those accompanying them. However, care should be taken when travelling to remote areas where health services are primitive since children can become more rapidly ill than adults. It is best to visit India in the cooler months since you need to protect children from the sun, heat, dehydration and mosquito bites. Cool showers or baths help, and avoid being out during the hottest part of the day. Diarrhoea and vomiting are the most common problems, so take the usual precautions, but more intensively. Breastfeeding is best and most convenient for babies. In the big cities you can get safe baby foods and formula milk. It doesn't harm a baby to eat an unvaried and limited diet of familiar food carried in packets for a few weeks if the local dishes are not acceptable, but it may be an idea to give vitamin and mineral supplements. Wet wipes, always useful, are sometimes difficult to find in India as are disposable nappies. The biggest hotels provide babysitting. For further information see www.babygoes2.com.

## Women travellers

Although it is relatively safe for women to travel around India, most people find it an advantage to travel with a companion. Even then, privacy is rarely respected and there can be a lot of hassle, pressure and intrusion on your personal space, as well as some outright harassment. Backpackers setting out alone often meet like-minded travelling companions at budget hotels. If you are blonde, you are quite naturally likely to attract more attention. Some seasoned travellers find that dyeing their hair dark, helps. See also below and page 44. One way of dealing with people who hassle you on the street is to simply say "thank you", smile and walk away. If you show annoyance, it may result in more pestering or abusive language. Cases of rape in Goa have been reported at late or after late-night parties. It is best to walk in a group at night. **Independent Traveller,** T0870-7605001, www.independenttraveller.com, runs women-only tours to various destinations including India.

## Working in the country

It is best to arrange voluntary work well in advance with organizations in India (addresses are given in some towns, eg Delhi, Darjeeling, Dharamshala, Kolkata, Leh); alternatively, contact an organization abroad.

**Co-ordinating Committee for International Voluntary Service**, 1 rue Miollis, 75732 Paris, France, T01-45684936, www.unesco.org/ccivs.
**Council for International Programs**, 1101 Wilson Blvd Ste 1708, Arlington, VA 22209.
**International Voluntary Service**, 7 Upper Bow, Edinburgh EH1 2JN, UK, T0131-2266722, www.sci-ivs.org.
**VSO**, 317 Putney Bridge Rd, London SW15 2PN, UK, T020-87807200, www.vso.org.uk.
**Volunteer Work Information Service**, PO Box 2759, Lewes, BN7 1WU, UK, T01273-470015, www.workingabroad.com. Students in UK may spend part of their 'year off' helping in a school through 'GAP', teach English, or help with a conservation project through **'i to i' International Projects**, 1 Cottage Rd, Headingly, Leeds, LS6 4DD, T0800 985 4864, www.i-to-i.com.



# Before you travel

## Visas and immigration

Virtually all foreign nationals require a visa to enter India. Nationals of Bhutan and Nepal only require a suitable means of identification. The rules regarding visas change frequently and arrangements for application and collection also vary from town to town so it is essential to check details and costs with the relevant office. These remain closed on Indian national holidays. In London, applications are processed in an hour or two (0800-1200). Visitors from countries which do not have an Indian representation may apply to the resident British representative, or enquire at the **Air India** office. An application on the prescribed form should be accompanied by three passport photographs and your passport which should be valid for at least three months beyond the period of the visit.

Visa fees vary according to nationality. The following visas are available: **Transit** For passengers en route to another country (valid up to five days). **Tourist** Six-month visa, from the date of issue with multiple entry. Most visitors require this type. **Business** Up to one year from the date of issue. A letter from company giving the nature of business is required. **Five year** For those of Indian origin only, who have held Indian passports, and their spouses. **Student** Valid up to one year from the date of issue. Attach a letter of acceptance from Indian institution, and an AIDS test certificate. Allow up to three months for approval. **Visa extensions** Applications should be made to the Foreigners' Regional Registration Offices at New Delhi, Mumbai, Kolkata or Chennai, or an office of the Superintendent of Police in the District Headquarters. After six months, those with a tourist visa must leave India and apply for a new visa - the Nepal office is known to be difficult.

No foreigner needs to **register** within the 180 day period of their tourist visa. All foreign visitors who stay in India for more than 180 days are required to register at the nearest Foreigners' Registration Office and get an **income tax clearance** exemption certificate from the Foreign Section of the Income Tax Department in Delhi, Mumbai, Kolkata or Chennai.

## Embassies

**Australia**, 3-5 Moonah Place, Yarralumla, Canberra T2733999; Level 27, 25 Bligh St, Sydney T2239500; Melbourne T3840141.
**Austria**, Kärntner Ring 2, A-1015 Vienna, T01-5058666, indemb@eoivien.vienna.at.
**Bangladesh**, 2 Dhanmondi RA, House 129, Dhaka-2, T503606, Chittagong T654021.
**Belgium**, 217-Chaussée de Vleurgat, 1050 Brussels, T02-6409140, hoc@indembassy.be. Consulates: Ghent T09-263423, Antwerp T03-2341122.
**Bhutan**, India House Estate, Thimpu, T09752-322162, hocbht@druknet.bt.
**Canada**, 10 Springfield Rd, Ottawa, Ontario K1M 1C9, T613-7443751. Consulates: Toronto T416-9600751, Vancouver T604-6628811.
**Denmark**, Vangehusvej 15, 2100 Copenhagen, T31982888, F39270218, indemb@email.dk.
**Finland**, Satamakatu 2 A8, 00160 Helsinki-16, T00-358-9-2289910, eoihelsinki@indianembassy.fi.
**France**, 15 Rue Alfred Dehodencq, Paris, T01-40507070. Visas from consulate, 20 Rue Albéric Magnard, 75016 Paris, T01 40507171,eiparis.admin@wanadoo.fr, deposit passport 0930-1030, collect same day 1600-1700.
**Germany**, Tiergartenstrasse, visa at Pohlstr 20, 10785 Berlin, T030-4853002, chancery@ indianembassy. Consulates: Willy-Brandt Allee 16, 53113 Bonn T0228-540132, Friedrich Ebert Anlage 26, 60325 Frankfurt T069-271040, Raboisen 6, 20095 Hamburg T040-338036, Munich T089- 92562067, Stuttgart T0711-1530050.
**Ireland**, 6 Lesson Park, Dublin 6, T01-4970959, indembassy@eircom.net.
**Israel**, 4 Kaufmann St, Sharbat, Tel Aviv 68012, T03 5291999, indemtel@ind embassy.co.il.
**Italy**, Via XX Settembre 5, 00187 Rome, T06 4884642, admin.wing@indianembassy. it. Consulates: Milan T02-8690314, Genoa T010 54891.
**Japan**, 2-11, Kudan Minami 2-Chome, Chiyoda-ku, Tokyo 102, T03-32622391, indembjp@gol.com. Consulate: Kobe T078-2418116.
**Malaysia**, 19 Malacca St, Kuala Lumpur, T221766.
**Maldives**, Mafabbu Aage 37, Orchid Magu, Male 20-02, T323015.
**Nepal**, Lainchour, PO Box No 292, Kathmandu, T0891-410900, hocktm@mos.com.np.
**Netherlands**, Buitenrustweg 2, The Hague (2517KD), T070-3469771, fscultur@bart.nl.
**New Zealand**, 10th floor, Princess Tower, 180 Molesworth St (PO Box 4045), Wellington, T4736390.
**Norway**, 30 Niels Jules Gate, 0272 Oslo-2, T22443194.
**Pakistan**, G5 Diplomatic Enclave, Islamabad, T050-814731, Karachi T021-522275.
**Singapore**, 31 Grange Rd, Singapore 0923, T7376777.
**Spain**, Avda Pio XII 30-32, 28016 Madrid, T091-902901010, info@embassyindia. jazztel.es . Consulate: Barcelona T093-2120422.
**Sri Lanka**, 36-38 Galle Rd, Colombo 3, T01-421605 Kandy, T08-446430.
**Sweden**, Adolf Fredriks Kyrkogata 12, Box 1340, 11183 Stockholm, T08-107008, information@indianembassy.se.
**Switzerland**, Kirchenfeldstr 28, CH-3005 Bern, T031-3511100, India@spectraweb.ch .
**Thailand**, 46, Soi 23 (Prasarn Mitr) Sukhumvit 23, Bangkok 10110, T2580300, indiaemb@mozart.inet.co.th.
**UK**, India House, Aldwych, London WC2B 4NA, T020-78368484 (0930-1300, 1400-1730), www.hcilondon.org. Consulates: The Spencers, 20 Augusta St, Hockley, Birmingham, B18 6DS, T0121-2122782; Rutland Sq, Edinburgh EH1 2BB, T0131-2292144; 6th floor, 134 Renfrew St, Glasgow 3 7ST, T0141-3310777.
**USA**, 2107 Massachusetts Ave, Washington DC 20008, T0202-9397000, indembwash@ indiagov.org. Consulates: Houston, Texas, T7136262148, New Orleans T0504-5828105, New York T0212-7740600, San Francisco T0415-6680683, Chicago T0312-5950405.

## Restricted and protected areas

Some areas are politically sensitive. The border regions, tribal areas and Himalayan zones are subject to restrictions and special permits may be needed to visit them though the government is relaxing its regulations.

Currently the following require special permits: **Arunachal Pradesh**, **Manipur** (for five days), **Mizoram** and **Nagaland**. Apply to the Under Secretary, Ministry of Home Affairs, Foreigners Division, Lok Nayak Bhavan, Khan Market, New Delhi 110003 at least four weeks in advance. Special permission is no longer needed to visit Assam, Meghalaya and Tripura. For the **Andaman Islands**, permits are issued for 30 days to visit some of the islands on arrival at Port Blair, see page 766. Of the **Lakshadweep Islands**, foreigners may visit Bangaram and Suheli Islands only; permits from the Lakshadweep Administration, Willingdon Island, Harbour Road, Kochi 3. For **Sikkim**, permits for 15 days are issued by a large number of government offices.



## Work permits

Foreigners should apply to the Indian representative in their country of origin for the latest information about work permits.

## Liquor permits

Periodically some Indian states have tried to enforce prohibition. Some degree of prohibition is in force in Gujarat, Mizoram and Manipur. When applying for your visa you can ask for an All India Liquor Permit. Foreigners can also get the permit from any Govt of India Tourist Office in Delhi or the state capitals. Instant 'spot' permits are issued by some hotels.

# What to take

Travel light. Most essentials are available in the larger cities, items are cheap and laundry services are generally speedy. Here are some items you might find particularly helpful:

Loose-fitting, light cotton **clothes** are good for travelling almost anywhere at any time of year, being cool and comfortable with the added advantage of being quick drying. Pale colours may give some protection against mosquitoes. Sarongs are useful – they can be used as a skirt, towel, used to cover your shoulders, shade against the sun etc. Women should dress modestly at all times. Brief shorts and tight vest tops are best avoided, though on the beach 'modest' swimwear is fine. Locally bought, inexpensive and cool *kurta pyjama* for men, and *shalwar kameez* for women are excellent options on the plains but it can be cold in the north between December and February and also everywhere at heights above 1,500 m, where some heavier clothing is essential. Comfortable shoes, sandals or trainers are essential. Take high-factor sun screen and a sun hat.

*For a medical checklist see page 75.*

It is best to take a sufficient supply of personal **medicines** from home, including inhalers and anti-malarial drugs (Proguanil is not available from pharmacists). Most **toiletries**, contact lens cleaners, tampons and barrier contraceptives are available in the larger cities. Contact lens wearers may be affected by pollution in some large cities, so carry spectacles and a spare set plus your prescription.

Photocopies of essential **documents**, passport identification and visa pages, and spare photos are useful when applying for permits or in case of loss or theft.

Although good quality **films** are available in all major cities and tourist centres, it is best to take rolls of films from home and certainly any specialist camera batteries. In India, only buy films from a reputable shop since hawkers and roadside stalls may not be reliable; check the carton carefully as well as the expiry date. Whilst on the

subject, many monuments now charge a camera fee ranging from Rs 20-50 for still cameras, and as much as Rs 500 for video cameras (more for professionals). Special permits are needed from the Archaeological Survey of India, Delhi for using tripods and artificial lights.

Of use to **budget travellers** are the following: Nets are rarely provided in cheap hotels so try to take an impregnated mosquito net. A wedge-shaped one (for single-point fixing) is preferable. Earplugs come in handy when a hotel room is particularly noisy, especially during festivals when loudspeakers playing Hindi film music tend to work overtime. On overnight journeys, blocking out the perpetual light is effective with eyesmasks (given away by some airlines). Take a good padlock to secure your budget room too. Those with a secret combination number are recommended. A cotton, sheet sleeping bag which can cover a pillow; these are cheap and easy to get made at any tailor's shop. Toilet paper, soap, towel and the washbasin plug may all be missing so be prepared.



# Money

Prices in the handbook are quoted in Rupees, although top hotels often quote rates in US$. Very few people are familiar with international currencies apart from currency touts on city street corners. Visitors do best to think in Rupee terms. In April 2005, exchange rates were as follows: Australian $ = Rs 30, Euro € = Rs 50, Japanese Yen = Rs 0.40, New Zealand $ = Rs 29, United Kingdom = Rs 80, United States $ = Rs 45.

## Currency

Indian currency is the Indian Rupee (Re/Rs). It is **not** possible to purchase these before you leave. If you want cash on arrival it is best to get it at the airport bank. Rupee notes are printed in denominations of Rs 1000 (rarely seen), 500, 100, 50, 20, 10. The Rupee is divided into 100 Paise. Coins are minted in denominations of Rs 5, 2, 1, and 50, 25, 20, 10 and 5 Paise, though coins below 50 paise are rarely seen. Carry money, mostly as travellers' cheques, in a money belt worn under clothing. Have enough for daily requirements in an easily accessible place. The Rs 500 note is difficult to change outside the big cities, and it has also encouraged a wave of convincing forged copies. Avoid changing from unauthorised dealers.

## Banks and other dealers

If you cash sterling, make certain you have not been given Rupees at the dollar rate. The **State Bank of India** and several others in major towns are authorized to deal in foreign exchange. Some give cash against Visa/Master cards (eg **Standard Chartered Grindlays, Bank of Baroda** who print a list of their participating branches, **Andhra Bank**). **American Express** cardholders can use their cards to get either cash or TCs in the four major cities. They also have offices in Ahmadabad, Coimbatore, Goa, Guwahati, Hyderabad, Pune, Thiruvananthapuram and Vadodara. The larger cities and tourist centres have licensed money changers with offices usually in the commercial sector. Changing money through unauthorized dealers is illegal. There is virtually no currency black market now. Premiums on the street corner are very small and highly risky, especially with the influx of fake Rs 500 notes. Large **hotels** change money 24 hours a day for guests, but banks often give a substantially better rate of exchange than hotels.

You should be given a foreign currency **encashment certificate** when you change money through a bank or authorized dealer. Ask for one if it is not automatically given. It allows you to change Indian Rupees back to your own currency on departure, so ensure that you have a valid one at this time. It also enables you to use Rupees to pay

### Money matters

It can be difficult to use torn or very worn currency notes. Check notes when you are given them and refuse any that are damaged.

Request some Rs 100 and 50 notes. Rs 500 (can be mistaken for Rs 100) notes can reduce 'wallet bulge' but be difficult to change.

A good supply of small denomination notes always comes in handy for bus tickets, cheap meals and tipping. Remember that if offered a large note, the recipient will never have any change!

It can be worth carrying a few clean, new sterling or dollar notes for use where travellers' cheques and credit cards are not accepted. It is likely to be quite a while before Euro notes are widely accepted.

hotel bills or buy air or train tickets for which payment in foreign exchange may be required although in practice, those using mid-range or cheaper hotels rarely have to produce them. The certificates are only valid for three months.

## Travellers' cheques

Travellers' cheques (TCs) issued by **American Express** and **Thomas Cook** are accepted without difficulty in the major towns and tourist centres. Most banks, but not all, will accept US$ or £ sterling TCs, so it is a good idea to carry some of each. Other major currency TCs are also accepted in some larger cities. Euro currency notes may not be accepted in Indian banking for some time, so do not rely on them alone. TCs can be exchanged in banks, hotels or a growing number of private dealers, the latter often offering a faster service at a higher rate. They can be used directly for payment in the more expensive hotels and souvenir shops, as well as for purchasing airline tickets and foreign quota train tickets. Otherwise, ensure that you have enough cash to cover your needs. Your passport and visa must be shown. In banks, encashing any form of currency nearly always takes up to 30 minutes or longer, so it is worth taking larger denomination TCs and changing enough money to last for some days. If you are travelling to remote areas it can be worth buying Indian Rupee TCs from a major bank, as these are more widely accepted than foreign currency ones. If stolen, you must get a police report and be prepared to contact the issuing company with the numbers of the stolen cheques, your receipt and a plausible story! For some, the wait for replacement cheques can take weeks, so take great care of them!

## Credit cards and debit cards

Major credit cards are increasingly acceptable in the main centres, but with exceptions (eg Chennai does not give cash against **Amex**). In smaller cities and towns it is still rare to be able to pay by credit card. Payment by credit card can sometimes be more expensive than payment by cash, whilst some credit card companies charge a premium on cash withdrawals. **Visa** and **Mastercard** have a growing number of **ATMs** in major cities; try ICICI, HDFC and Centurion Banks. This is by the far easiest way to obtain cash against either a credit or debit card. Railway Reservation centres in 17 major cities are now taking payment for train tickets by Visa card which can be very quick as the queue is very short, although they cannot generally be used for Tourist Quota tickets! Websites that list locations of ATMs that are http://international.visa.com, www.mastercard.com and www.americanexpress.com.

## Transferring money to India

**Thomas Cook, American Express** and **Standard Chartered Grindlays** and others can make 'instant' transfers to their offices in India but charge a high fee (about US$30 or

15%). Sending a bank draft (up to US$1,000) by post (four to seven days by Speedpost) is the cheapest option. **Western Union** has a growing number of agents (check www.westernunion.com), while **Thomas Cook**, operates through international **Moneygram**, www.moneygram.com. 

### Cost of living

The cost of living in India remains well below that in the West. The average wage is about Rs 12,000 per month (US$240) for government employees according to government statistics – manual workers and unskilled labourers expect to earn at least Rs 100 per day; women are often paid less than men, and in some parts of rural India earn as little as Rs 30.

### Cost of travelling

Most food, accommodation and public transport, especially rail and bus, are exceptionally cheap. There is a widening range of moderately priced but clean hotels and restaurants outside the big cities, making it possible to get a great deal for your money. Budget travellers sharing a room, eating in local restaurants, and using the cheapest means of travel can expect to spend around Rs 450-500 (about US$10-12) a day, though you can each get by on less in the south. Those looking for the comfort of the occasional night in a simple a/c room, and using reserved seats on trains and luxury buses, should budget for about US$25-30 a day. However, if you travel alone and are looking for reasonably comfortable a/c rooms, use taxis and second class a/c train berths, expect to spend around US$70 a day. When shopping or hiring an unmetered vehicle, bargaining is expected, and essential.



# Getting there

## Air

India is accessible by air from virtually every continent. Most international flights arrive in Delhi, Mumbai,Chennai or Kolkata. There are also international airports in several other cities (eg Ahmadabad, Thiruvananthapuram, Goa), some of which allow customs formalities to be completed there although the flight may be routed through a principal airport. Some carriers permit 'open-jaw' travel, arriving in, and departing from, different cities in India. Some (eg **Air India, British Airways**) have convenient non-stop flights from Europe, eg from London to Delhi, takes only nine hours.

### Charter flights

Several tour operators from Europe, especially from Britain (eg **First Choice,** T0870-7500001, www.firstchoice.co.uk, **JMC,** T0870 7505711, www.jmc.com, **Jewel in the Crown,** T01293 533338, www.jewelholidays.com, **Manos,** T0870 7530530, www.manos.co.uk, **Somak,** T020 84233000, www.somak.co.uk, flying from Gatwick and Manchester, offer package holidays from October to April to Goa and Kerala. They are often great value (especially in November and from mid-January to mid-March).

The following rules apply:

**1** They are not available to Indian nationals.

**2** The deal must include accommodation. If you take the cheap 'dorm house' option, it may be necessary to change to a more comfortable room. It may be difficult to find a room during the peak Christmas and New Year period so it is worth paying a little extra on booking, to ensure accommodation of a reasonable standard.

3 Officially, charter passengers can only stay for a maximum of 45 days, although this restriction can be bent somewhat if you have a valid visa to cover the duration of your proposed extension. You may not travel on a non-charter international flight (eg to Sri Lanka) while in India.

## Stop-overs and Round-the-World tickets

You can arrange several stop-overs in India on Round-the-World and long-distance tickets. RTW tickets allow you to fly in to one and out from another international aiport. You may be able to arrange some internal flights using international carriers eg **Air India**, www.airindia.com, sometimes allows stop-overs within India for a small extra charge.



## Discounts

The cheapest fares from Europe tend to be with Central European, Central Asian or Middle Eastern airlines. With these airlines it pays to confirm your return flight as early as possible. You can also get good discounts from Australasia, Southeast Asia and Japan. If you plan to visit two or more South Asian countries within three weeks, you may qualify for a 30% discount on your international tickets. Ask your National Tourist office. International air tickets can be bought in India though payment must be made in foreign exchange.

## Ticket agents

Companies dealing in volume and taking reduced commissions for ticket sales can offer better deals than the airlines themselves. The national press carry their advertisements. **Trailfinders,** T0845 0585858, www.trailfinders.co.uk, has worldwide agencies; **STA,** T0870-1600599, www.statravel.co.uk, with over 100 offices worldwide, offers special deals for under-26s; **Travelbag,** T0800 082 5000, www.travelbag.co.uk, quotes competitive fares, part of ebookers. **General Sales Agents** (GSAs) for specific airlines can sometimes offer attractive deals: **Jet Air,** 188 Hammersmith Rd, London W6 7DJ, T020-89701555, for Gulf Air, Kuwait Airways etc and **Welcome Travels,** 58 Wells Street, London W1P 3RA, T020-74363011, for Air India.

## Airline security

International airlines vary in their arrangements and requirements for security, in particular the carrying of equipment like radios, lap-top computers and batteries. It is advisable to ring the airline in advance to confirm what their current regulations are.

## From the UK, Continental Europe and the Middle East

Expect to pay anything from £300 to £500 from London. The best deals are offered from the UK (try www.cheapflights.com, which also provides additional useful information). You can pick up attractive deals on **Air India** which flies direct to Delhi and Mumbai throughout the year. A few European airlines (eg **Lufthansa, KLM**) and several from the Middle East (eg **Emirates, Gulf Air, Kuwait Airways, Royal Jordanian**) offer good discounts to Mumbai and other Indian regional capitals from London, but fly via their hub cities, so adding to the journey time. **Virgin Atlantic** www.virgin-atlantic.com, now offer a three times weekly London-Delhi-London service. Good deals can be offered by General Sales Agents (GSAs), see above. Consolidators in UK quote competitive fares: **Bridge the World,** T0870 8144400, www.b-t-w.co.uk. **Flight bookers,** T0800 082 3000, www.ebookers.com. **North South Travel,** T01245 608291, www.northsouthtravel.co.uk (profits to charity).

## From Australasia via the Far East

**Qantas, Singapore Airlines, Thai Airways, Malaysian Airlines, Cathay Pacific** and **Air India** are the principal airlines connecting the continents. They fly to one of the Indian regional capitals. **STA** and **Flight Centre** offer discounted tickets from their branches in major cities in Australia and New Zealand. **Abercrombie & Kent, Adventure World, Peregrine** and **Travel Corporation of India,** organize tours. 

### From North America

From the east coast, it is best to fly direct to India from New York via London by **Air India** (18 hours), or pick up a direct charter from UK to Goa or Thiruvananthapuram but this will usually involve a stopover in London. Discounted tickets on **British Airways, KLM, Lufthansa, Gulf Air** and **Kuwait Airways** are sold through agents although they will invariably fly via their country's capital cities. From the west coast, it is best to fly via Hong Kong, Singapore or Bangkok to Delhi, Kolkata or Mumbai using one of those countries' national carriers. **Air Brokers International,** www.airbrokers.com, is competitive and reputable. **STA,** www.statravel.co.uk, has offices in many US cities, Toronto and Ontario. Student fares are also available from **Travel Cuts,** T0800-6672887, www.travelcuts.com, in Canada.



## Road

Crossings between India and its neighbours are affected by the political relations between them. Get your Indian visa in advance, before arriving at the border. Several road border crossings are open periodically, but permission to cross cannot be guaranteed. Those listed below are the main crossings which are normally open throughout the year to tourists. New direct 'friendship' buses have been introduced between Lahore and Delhi, and between Dhaka and Kolkata. Note also that you are not allowed to take any Indian currency from India into Pakistan. Indian Rupees can be changed on a 1:1 basis at the border.

### From Bangladesh

**To Kolkata** from Dhaka and Jessore. The Bangaon-Benapol crossing is the most reliable. On the Bangladesh side rickshaws are available from Benapol, while buses and minibuses go to Bangaon railway station from the border. **To Tripura** from Dhaka is only four hours by road from the border crossing just 2 km from the centre of Agartala, which has flights to Kolkata. The border post is efficient when open but arrive there before 1500, as the formalities often take time. Regulations are subject to change so find out in advance. In London, Bangladesh High Commission, T020-75840081.

### From Bhutan

**To Bagdogra,** the nearest airport is three to four hours' drive from Jaigaon, the rather untidy and unkempt Indian border town. The Indian Immigration checkpost is on the main street, about a kilometre from the 'Bhutan Gate' at the border town of Phuntsholing where it is possible to spend a night. Accommodation ranges from the simple **Central Hotel** to the moderate government run **Druk Hotel.** To enter Bhutan you need an Entry Permit and a Visa.

### From Nepal

Four crossings are in common use: **To Delhi via Banbassa** is the shortest direct route between Kathmandu and Delhi, via the Nepali town of Mahendranagar and Banbassa.

**To Varanasi via Gorakhpur** you must go to the **Sonauli-Bhairawa** crossing, the shortest and fastest route to Varanasi; many continue to Delhi from there. From Kathmandu or Pokhara you can get to Bhairawa, 6 km inside the Nepal border, Sonauli on the border itself, and Nautanwa on the Indian side. From there, buses take 3½ hours to Gorakhpur, with train connections for Delhi, or 5½ hours by bus to Varanasi, see page 194.

**To Patna via Raxaul-Birganj** several buses run daily from Raxaul to Patna (five to seven hours) but timings are unreliable and the buses are crowded and uncomfortable. Night buses from Patna reach the border in the early morning; morning buses from Patna connect with the night bus to Kathmandu. Either way you have to have at least one night bus journey unless you stay overnight at Birganj or Raxaul, which is not recommended. The bus journey between Kathmandu or Pokhara and the border takes about 11-12 hours. Even Express buses are slow and packed. Tourist minibuses are the only moderately comfortable option. For details see Patna, page 740.

**Kakarbhitta** (Kakarvita) is on the Nepalese side of a wide river which forms the border here between India and Nepal. A kilometre long road bridge links it to the Indian town of Raniganj on the east bank. Cycle rickshaws run between the two. A small notice and an Indian flag are all that mark the Indian Immigration checkpost which is in a shady grove of trees by the road. The larger Indian town of Bagdogra is 15 km away. For details see under Siliguri, page 623.



### From Pakistan

**Wagha border**, 23 km from Lahore, is the only crossing open. Vans from central Lahore take you to the border where you walk across through Pakistani and Indian immigration and customs. There are taxis and rickshaws on the Indian side to take you to Attari; buses from there go to **Amritsar** (see page 467). The only **train crossing** is an uncertain one. The Lahore to Amritsar train via the Wagha border post is scheduled to run twice weekly but it can take five hours to clear customs. It is normally much slower than the bus and is not recommended.

### From Europe

The reopening of Iran to travellers of most nationalities has reinstated the Istanbul-Teheran-Quetta route when the political situation in the region is stable. We highly recommend Footprint's *Pakistan Handbook* for anyone contemplating the journey.

# Touching down

## Airport information

### Duty-free allowance

Tourists are allowed to bring in all personal effects 'which may reasonably be required', without charge. The official customs allowance includes 200 cigarettes or 50 cigars, 0.95 litres of alcohol, a camera with five rolls of film and a pair of binoculars. Valuable personal effects or professional equipment must be registered on a Tourist Baggage Re-Export Form (TBRE), including jewellery, special camera equipment and lenses, lap-top computers, sound and video recorders. These forms require the serial numbers of such equipment. It saves considerable frustration if you know the numbers in advance and are ready to show the serial numbers on the equipment. In addition to the forms, details of imported equipment may be entered into your passport. Save time by completing the formalities while waiting for your baggage. **It is essential to keep these forms** for showing to the customs when leaving India, otherwise considerable delays are very likely at the time of departure.

### Currency regulations

There are no restrictions on the amount of foreign currency or travellers' cheques a tourist may bring into India. If you were carrying more than US$10,000 or its equivalent in cash or travellers' cheques you need to fill in a currency declaration form.

## Touching down

**Electricity** 220-240 volts AC. Some top hotels have transformers. There may be pronounced variations in the voltage, and power cuts are common. During power cuts, diesel generators are often used to provide power for essential equipment but this may not always cover air-conditioning. India uses round-pin plugs and socket sizes vary so you are advised to take a universal adaptor (available at most airports). Many hotels don't have electric razor sockets.

**Hours of business** **Banks:** 1030-1430, Monday-Friday; 1030-1230, Saturday. Top hotels sometimes have a 24-hour service. **Post offices:** Usually 1000-1700, Monday-Friday; Saturday mornings. **Government offices:** 0930-1700, Monday- Friday; 0930-1300, Saturday (some open on alternate Saturday). **Shops:** 0930-1800, Monday-Saturday. Bazars keep longer hours. There are regional variations.

**IDD** 91. A double ring repeated regularly means it is ringing. Equal tones with equal pauses means engaged.

**Official time** GMT +5½ hours throughout the year (USA, EST +10½ hours).

**Weights and measures** Metric system has come into universal use in the cities. In remote areas local measures are sometimes used. One lakh is 100,000 and 1 core is 10 million.

## Prohibited items

The import of dangerous drugs, live plants, gold coins, gold and silver bullion and silver coins not in current use are either banned or subject to strict regulation. It is illegal to import firearms into India without special permission. Enquire at consular offices abroad for details.

## Export restrictions

Export of gold jewellery purchased in India is allowed up to a value of Rs 2,000 and other jewellery (including settings with precious stones) up to a value of Rs 10,000. Export of antiquities and art objects over 100 years old is restricted. Ivory, skins of all animals, *toosh* wool, snake skin and articles made from them are banned, unless you get permission for export. For further information enquire at the Indian High Commission or consulate, or access the Government of India at www.indiagov.org.

## Documentation

The formalities on arrival in India have been increasingly streamlined during the last five years and the facilities at the major international airports greatly improved. However, arrival can still be a slow process. Disembarkation cards, with an attached customs declaration, are handed out to passengers during the inward flight. The immigration form should be handed in at the immigration counter on arrival. The customs slip will be returned, for handing over to the customs on leaving the baggage collection hall. The immigration formalities at both Delhi and Mumbai can be very slow. You may well find that there are delays of over an hour in processing passengers passing through immigration who need help with filling forms.

## Departure tax

Rs 500 is payable for all international departures other than those to neighbouring SAARC countries, when the tax is Rs 150. This must be paid in Rupees in India unless it

## First impressions

On arrival at any of India's major cities the first impressions can take you aback. The exciting images of an ancient and richly diverse culture which draw many visitors to India can be overwhelmed by the immediate sensations which first greet you...

**Pollution** All the cities seriously suffer.

**Noise** Many people also find India incredibly noisy, as radios, videos and loudspeakers seem to blare in unlikely places at **all** times.

**Smells** India has an almost baffling mixture of smells, from the richly pungent and unpleasant to the delicately subtle.

**Pressure** From stepping out of your hotel everybody seems to clamour to sell you their services. Taxi and rickshaw drivers are always there when you don't want them, much less often when you do. There often seems to be no sense of personal space or privacy. Young women are often stared at.

**Public hygiene** (or lack of it) It is common to see people urinating in public places and defecating in the open countryside.

These can all be daunting and make early adjustment to India difficult. Even on a short visit give yourself time and space to adjust.



is included in your international ticket; check when buying. Look for 'FT' in the tax column of your ticket. A domestic departure tax is payable on internal flights when the ticket has been paid for in Rupees. 'Security Check' your baggage for the hold before checking-in at Departure and identify them again outside the departure lounge. Cabin baggage should have a luggage tag for stamping after it has been security checked. Regulations are extra strict in sensitive border areas and at military airports (eg Leh, Ladakh and Dabolim, Goa).

### Public transport to and from airport

Detailed advice is given under international airports. Most major international airports have special bus services into the town centre from early morning to around midnight. **Pre-paid taxis** to the city are available at all major airports. Some airports have up to three categories, 'limousine', 'luxury' and ordinary. The first two usually have prominent counters, so you may have to insist if you want to use the standard service. Insist on being taken to your chosen destination even if the driver claims the city is unsafe, or there is a major festival and everywhere is full, or the hotel has closed down, etc...

## Local customs and laws

Most travellers experience great warmth and hospitality in India. You may however, be surprised that with the warm welcome comes an open curiosity about personal matters. Total strangers on a train, for example, may ask for details about your job, income and family circumstances, or discuss politics and religion.

### Conduct

Respect for the foreign visitor should be reciprocated by a sensitivity towards local customs and culture. How you dress is mostly how people judge you. Clean, modest clothes and a smile go a long way. Scanty, tight clothing draws unwanted attention. Nudity is not permitted on beaches in India and although there are some places where this ban is ignored, it causes much offence. Displays of intimacy are not considered suitable in public. You may at times be justifiably frustrated by delays, bureaucracy and inefficiency, but displays of anger and rudeness will not achieve anything positive, and often make things worse. The concept of time and punctuality is also rather vague so be prepared to be kept waiting.

**No smoking please**

Several state governments have passed a law banning smoking in all public buildings and transport but exempting 'open spaces'. To avoid fines, check for notices.

## Courtesy

It takes little effort to learn common gestures of courtesy and they are greatly appreciated. The **greeting** when meeting or parting, used universally among the Hindus across India, is the palms joined together as in prayer, sometimes accompanied with the word *namaste* (North and West), *namoshkar* (East) or *vanakkam* in Tamil. Muslims use the greeting *assalãm aleikum*, with the response *waleikum assalãm*, meaning 'peace be with you'; **'please'** is *mehrbani-se*; **'thank you'** is often expressed by a smile, or with the somewhat formal *dhannyabad*, *shukriya* (Urdu), and *nandri* in Tamil.

## Hands and eating

Traditionally, Indians use the right hand for eating, cutlery being alien at the table although westernized restaurants will always provide these. In rural India, don't expect table knives and forks though you might find small spoons. Use your right hand for giving, receiving, eating or shaking hands as the left is considered to be unclean since it is associated with washing after using the toilet.

## Women

Indian women in urban and rural areas differ in their social interactions with men. Certainly, to the westerner, Indian women may seem to remain in the background and appear shy when approached, often hiding their face and avoiding eye contact. Yet you will see them working in public, often in jobs traditionally associated with men in the West, in the fields, in construction sites or in the market place. Even from a distance, men should not photograph women without their consent.

Women do not, in general, shake hands with men since physical contact is not traditionally acceptable between acquaintances of the opposite sex. A westernized city woman, however, may feel free to shake hands with a foreign visitor. In traditional rural circles, it is still the custom for men to be offered food first, separately, so don't be surprised if you, as foreign guest (man or woman), are awarded this special status when invited to an Indian home, and never set eyes on your hostess.

## Visiting religious sites

Visitors to all religious places should be dressed in clean, modest clothes; shorts and vests are inappropriate. Always remove shoes before entering a temple or mosque (and all leather items in Jain temples). Sun-baked stone floors often call for thick socks to protect against the heat. Menstruating women are considered 'unclean' and should not enter places of worship. It is discourteous to sit with one's back to a temple or shrine. You will be expected to sit cross-legged on the floor – avoid pointing your feet at others when attending prayers at a temple.

*Walk clockwise around a shrine (keeping it to your right).*

Non-Hindus are sometimes excluded from the inner sanctum of **Hindu** temples and occasionally from the temple itself. Look for signs or ask. In certain temples, and on special occasions, men may only enter if they wear unstitched clothing such as a *dhoti*.

In **Buddhist** shrines, turn prayer wheels in a clockwise direction. In **Sikh** gurudwaras, everyone should cover their head, even if it is with a handkerchief.

Tobacco and cigarettes should not be taken in. In **Muslim** mosques, visitors should only have their face, hands and feet exposed; women should also cover their heads. Mosques may be closed to non-Muslims shortly before formal prayers.

Some temples have a register or a receipt book for **donations** which works like an obligatory entry fee. The money is normally used for the upkeep and services of the temple or monastery. In some pilgrimage centres, as at Pushkar, priests can become unpleasantly persistent. In general, if you wish to leave a donation, put money in the donation box; some priests and Buddhist monks do not handle money. It is not customary to shake hands with a priest or monk. **Alms** *Sanyasis* (holy men), and some pilgrims, depend on gifts of money.

## Guide fees

Guides at tourist sites vary considerably in their knowledge and ability. Government trained and licensed guides are covered by specified fees. Local temple and site guides should charge less. Approximate charges: for four people for half a day, Rs 280, for a full day, Rs 400; for five to 15 people for half a day Rs 400, for a full day, Rs 530. Rs 125 for a language other than English.



## Begging

Beggars are often found in busy street corners in large Indian cities, as well as at bus and train stations where they often target foreigners for special attention. Visitors usually find this very distressing, especially the sight of severely undernourished children or those displaying physical deformity. You may be particularly affected when some persist on making physical contact. You might find a firm "*Jaao*" (go away) works. In the larger cities, beggars are often exploited by syndicates which cream off most of their takings. Yet those seeking alms near religious sites are another matter, and you may see Indian worshippers giving freely to those less fortunate than themselves, since this is tied up with gaining 'merit'. How you deal with begging is a matter of personal choice but it is perhaps better to give to a recognized charity than to make largely ineffectual handouts to individuals. It is not helpful to hand out sweets, 'school pens' and money indiscriminately to open-palmed children who tag on to any foreigner. Some visitors prefer to give food to beggars.

Young people occasionally follow travellers around and attempt to exchange words in English. When you find this tiring, say "bye bye". If you wish to avoid shaking hands, use the Indian greeting and say *namaste.*

## Charitable giving

Some visitors like to support self-help co-operatives, orphanages, disabled or disadvantaged groups, or international charities which work with local partners, by either making a donation or by buying their products. Some of these are listed under the appropriate towns. A few (which also welcome volunteers) are listed here.

**Concern India Foundation**, 6K Dubash Marg, Mumbai, T022-2029707, www.concernindia.org, is an umbrella organization working with local charities.
**Oxfam**, Sushil Bhawan, 210 Shahpur Jat, New Delhi 110049, T011-6491774; 274 Banbury Rd, Oxford OX2 7D2, UK, www.oxfam.org (400 grassroots projects).
**SOS Children's Villages**, A-7 Nizamuddin (W), New Delhi 110013, T011-4647835, www.sos-childrensvillages.org (over 30 poor and orphaned children's projects in India.
**Trek-Aid**, 2 Somerset Cottages, Stoke Villages, Plymouth, Devon, PL3 4AZ, www.a38.com/trekaid, (health, education etc through self-help schemes for displaced Tibetan refugees).
**Save the Children India**, 4C Swapnalok, 47 LJ Mard, Mumbai 400036, www.savethechildrenindia.org.
**Urmul Trust**, Urmul Dairy, Ganganagar Rd, Bikaner, Rajasthan, T0151 2522139 (health care, education and rural crafts in Rajasthani villages).

**Very Special Arts India**, C 418 Defence Colony, New Delhi, T011 2613 4983, www.vsarts.org, promotes the creative power in people with disabilities and works to enrich their lives through remedial therapies.

### Tipping

A tip of Rs 10 to a bell-boy carrying luggage in a modest hotel (Rs 20 in a higher category) would be appropriate. In up-market restaurants, a 10% tip is acceptable when 'Service' is not already included, while in places serving very cheap meals, round off the bill with small change. Indians don't normally tip taxi drivers but a small extra amount over the fare is welcomed. Porters at airports and railway stations often have a fixed rate displayed but will usually press for more. Rs 10 per item carried would be fair. For tour guides, a tip of Rs 50 per day from each member of a coach group (or Rs 100 per person in a car) can safely be regarded as generous.

### Photography

When photographing people, it is polite to first ask – they will usually respond warmly with smiles, although the 'moment' may have been lost as they line up, military style! Visitors often promise to send copies of the photos – don't, unless you really mean to do so. Photography of airports, military installations, bridges and in tribal and 'sensitive border areas', is not permitted.

## Safety

### Personal security

In general the threats to personal security for travellers in India are remarkably small. In most areas it is possible to travel either individually or in groups without any risk of personal violence. However, care is necessary in some places, and basic common sense needs to be used with respect to looking after valuables.

Some parts of India are subject to political violence. The Vale of Kashmir and Jammu remains under tight military control. Even when the border area is relatively quiet, very few hotels are open in Srinagar and the army is massively deployed and on constant alert. Despite the promises of travel touts that Kashmir is completely safe, tourists who visit, do so at considerable risk and are subjected to regular curfews. There is no prospect of an early solution to the political problem or of a quick return to normality. Some areas have long been noted for banditry. However in the great majority of places visited by tourists, violent crime and personal attacks are extremely rare.

### Theft

Theft is not uncommon. It is best to keep travellers' cheques, passports and valuables with you at all times since you can't regard hotel rooms as automatically safe; even hotel safes don't guarantee secure storage. Avoid leaving valuables near open windows even when you are in the room. Use your own padlock in a budget hotel when you go out. Pickpockets and other thieves operate in the big cities. Crowded areas are particularly high risk. Take special care of your belongings when getting on or off public transport. Never accept food or drink from casual acquaintances; travellers have reported being drugged and then robbed.

### Confidence tricksters

These are particularly common where people are on the move, notably around railway stations or places where budget tourists gather. A common plea is some sudden and desperate calamity; sometimes a letter will be produced in English to back up the claim. The demands are likely to increase sharply if sympathy is shown. See also Shopping, page 64.

## Security on trains

It can be difficult to keep an eye on your belongings when travelling. Nothing of value should be left close to open train windows. First class a/c compartments are self-contained and normally completely secure. Second class a/c compartments are larger, allowing more movement of passengers but are not so secure so luggage should be chained to a seat for security overnight. Locks and chains are easily available at main stations and bazaars but they are better brought from home. Some travellers prefer to reserve upper berths which offer some added protection against theft and also have the benefit of allowing daytime sleeping.

## Police

If you have items stolen, they should be reported to the police as soon as possible. Keep a separate record of vital documents, including passport details and travellers' cheques numbers. Larger hotels will be able to assist in contacting and dealing with the police.

Dealings with the police can be very difficult and in the worst regions, such as Bihar, even dangerous. The paperwork involved in reporting losses can be time consuming and irritating, and your own documentation (eg passport and visas) may be demanded. In some states the police themselves sometimes demand bribes, though tourists should not assume, however, that if procedures move slowly they are automatically being expected to offer a bribe. If you face really serious problems, for example in connection with a driving accident, you should contact your consular office as quickly as possible. You should ensure you always have your International driving licence and motorbike or car documentation with you.



## Drugs

Certain areas have become associated with foreigners taking drugs such as Manali and Manikaran (Himachal), Puri (Orissa), Kovalam (Kerala), Gokarna and Hampi (Karnataka) and the beaches in Goa. Be aware that the government takes the misuse of drugs very seriously. Anyone charged with the illegal possession of drugs risks facing a fine of Rs 100,000 and a minimum 10 years' imprisonment.

## Women travellers

There are some simple precautions to take, particularly when travelling alone, to avoid both personal harassment and giving offence. Modest dress is always advisable; loose-fitting non-see-through clothes, covering the shoulders, and skirts, dresses or shorts of a decent length attract less attention. Many find the *shalwar-kameez*-scarf ideal. In mosques women should be covered from head to ankle. In Sikh temples everyone should cover their heads. Unaccompanied women are most vulnerable in major cities, crowded bazars, beach resorts and tourist centres where men may follow them and touch them. "Eve teasing" is the euphemism for physical harassment; some buses have seats reserved for women. If you are harassed, it can be effective to make a scene. Avoid travelling alone by rickshaw or taxi late at night. It is best to be accompanied by a friend while being measured for clothing in tailors' shops or when having an ayurvedic massage.

Be firm and clear if you don't wish to speak to someone. To deal with unwanted advances from men, one tip is to say that you are married (wearing a 'wedding' ring may help); having children also raises your level of respect. See also page 29.

## Advice

It is better to seek advice on security from your own embassy than from travel agencies. Before you travel you can contact:

**Australian Department of Foreign Affairs**, Canberra, Australia, T06-62613305, www.dfat.gov.au/consular/advice.html. Canadian official advice is on www.dfait-maeci.gc.ca/travelreport/menu_e.html.
**British Foreign and Commonwealth Office**, Travel Advice Unit, Consular Division, 1 Palace St, London SW1E 5HE, UK, T020-72384503, www.fco.gov.uk/travel.
**US State Department's Bureau of Consular Affairs**, Overseas Citizens Services, Room 4800, Department of State, Washington, DC 20520-4818, USA, T0202-6474225, www.travel.state.gov/travel_warnings.html.

# Getting around

## Air

India has a comprehensive network linking the major cities of the different states. In addition to **Indian Airlines** (the nationalized carrier), www.indian-airlines.nic.in, and its subsidiary **Alliance Air**, there are a few private airlines such as **Jet Airways**, www.jetairways.com, and **Sahara**, www.airsahara.net, which provide supplementary flights on several routes as well as filling gaps in a particular area, as with **Jagson**. Competition from the efficiently run private sector has, in general, improved the quality of services provided by the nationalized airlines. The Airports Authorities too have made efforts to improve handling on the ground. Although flying is expensive, for covering vast distances or awkward links on a route, it is an option worth considering, though delays and re-routing can be irritating. **Air Deccan** is a new-commer offering cheap flights if booked far in advance, at the moment covering the south mainly. For short distances, and on some routes (eg Delhi-Agra-Delhi), it makes more sense to travel by train.

### Air tickets

All the major airlines are connected to the central reservation system and there are local travel agents who will book your tickets for a fee if you don't want to spend precious time waiting in a queue. Remember that tickets are in great demand in the peak season on some sectors (eg Delhi-Leh-Delhi) so it is essential to get them months ahead. If you are able to pre-plan your trip, it is even possible to ask if the internal flights can be booked at the time you buy your international air ticket at home through an agent (eg **Trailfinders, SD Enterprises**, London) or direct (eg **Jet Airways**). You can also book internal flights on the internet and collect and pay for them on your arrival in India.

### Payment

Non-resident, foreign passport holders buying air tickets in India must pay the 'US dollar rate' (higher than published Rupee rates) and pay in foreign exchange (major credit cards, travellers' cheques accepted), or in rupees against an encashment certificate which will be endorsed accordingly. There is very little difference in prices quoted by competing airlines.

### Special fares

**Indian Airlines**, www.indian-airlines.nic.in, and **Jet Airways**, www.jetairways.com, offer special seven, 15 and 21 day unlimited travel, deals from around US$300-750 (some are limited to one sector) which represent good savings. **Youth fares** 25% discount is given on US$ fares for anyone between 12 and 30 years. **Night savers** 25% discount fares are being introduced on late night flights between some metropolitan cities.

## Approximate economy airfares on popular routes

| Sector | US$ |
|---|---|
| **From Agra to:** | |
| Delhi | 60 |
| Khajuraho | 90 |
| Varanasi | 110 |
| **From Ahmedabad to:** | |
| Bangalore | 225 |
| Kolkata[4] | 235 |
| Chennai | 250 |
| Delhi | 140 |
| Hyderabad | 170 |
| Jaipur | 110 |
| Mumbai | 90 |
| Vadodara | 40 |
| **From Amritsar to:** | |
| Delhi | 105 |
| **From Aurangabad to:** | |
| Delhi | 170 |
| Mumbai | 80 |
| **From Bagdogra for Darjeeling to:** | |
| Kolkata[4] | 85 |
| Delhi | 190 |
| Guwahati | 55 |
| **From Bangalore to:** | |
| Kolkata[4] | 270 |
| Chennai | 70 |
| Cochin[3] | 85 |
| Delhi | 260 |
| Goa | 110 |
| Hyderabad | 110 |
| Mumbai | 145 |
| Pune | 150 |
| Trivandrum[1] | 125 |
| **From Bhopal to:** | |
| Delhi | 125 |
| Mumbai | 135 |

| Sector | US$ |
|---|---|
| **From Bhubaneshwar to:** | |
| Kolkata[4] | 90 |
| Chennai | 205 |
| Delhi | 220 |
| Varanasi | 130 |
| **From Bhuj to:** | |
| Mumbai | 105 |
| **From Calicut[2] to:** | |
| Chennai | 95 |
| Mumbai | 145 |
| **From Chandigarh to:** | |
| Delhi | 80 |
| Leh | 75 |
| **From Chennai to:** | |
| Cochin[3] | 125 |
| Coimbatore | 95 |
| Delhi | 265 |
| Goa | 145 |
| Hyderabad | 110 |
| Madurai | 95 |
| Mangalore | 110 |
| Mumbai | 165 |
| Port Blair | 200 |
| Trichy | 85 |
| Trivandrum[1] | 110 |
| **From Cochin[3] to:** | |
| Goa | 130 |
| Mumbai | 160 |
| **From Delhi to:** | |
| Goa | 240 |
| Jodhpur | 110 |
| Khajuraho | 105 |
| Leh | 110 |
| Mumbai | 180 |
| Trivandrum[1] | 365 |
| Udaipur | 110 |

| Sector | US$ |
|---|---|
| **From Goa to:** | |
| Mumbai | 100 |
| **From Hyderabad to:** | |
| Mumbai | 125 |
| Nagpur | 115 |
| **From Jaipur to:** | |
| Jodhpur | 85 |
| Mumbai | 160 |
| Udaipur | 85 |
| **From Jammu to:** | |
| Leh | 75 |
| **From Jodhpur to:** | |
| Mumbai | 155 |
| **From Khajuraho:** | |
| Varanasi | 85 |
| **From Kolkata[4] to:** | |
| Chennai | 225 |
| Delhi | 205 |
| Guwahati | 75 |
| Jaipur | 225 |
| Lucknow | 160 |
| Mumbai | 235 |
| Patna | 105 |
| Port Blair | 200 |
| Visakhapatnam | 150 |
| **From Mangalore to:** | |
| Mumbai | 125 |
| **From Mumbai to:** | |
| Trivandrum[1] | 200 |

**Alternative names:**
[1] Thiruvananthapuram
[2] Kozhikode
[3] Kochi
[4] Calcutta

## Delays

Be prepared for delays, especially in North India during the winter. Nearly all northern routes originate in Delhi, where from early December through to February, smog has become an increasingly common morning hazard, sometimes delaying departures by several hours.

## Air travel tips

**Security** Indian airlines don't permit batteries in cabin baggage, and once confiscated, you may never see your batteries again. You may need to identify your baggage after they have been checked in and just before they are loaded onto the plane. All baggage destined for the hold must be X-rayed by security before checking in, so do this first on arrival at the airport.

**Telephone** There is a free telephone service at major airports (occasionally through the tourist office counter), to contact any hotel of your choice.



**Wait-lists** If you don't have a confirmed booking and are 'wait-listed' it pays to arrive early at the airport and be persistent in enquiring about your position.

# Rail

Trains can still be the cheapest and most comfortable means of travelling long distances saving you hotel expenses on overnight journeys. It gives access to booking station Retiring Rooms, which can be useful from time to time. Above all, you have an ideal opportunity to meet local travellers and catch a glimpse of life on the ground. Remember the dark glass fitted on a/c coaches does restrict vision. See also www.indianrail.gov.in.



## High-speed trains

There are over 170 air-conditioned 'high-speed' **Shatabdi** for day travel, and **Rajdhani Express** ('Capital City') for overnight journeys. These cover large sections of the network but as they are in high demand you need to book them up to 60 days ahead. Meals and drinks are usually included.

## Royal trains

You can travel like a maharaja on the **Palace on Wheels** which gives visitors an opportunity to see some of the 'royal' cities in Rajasthan during the winter months for around US$250 a day. A wonderful way to travel but time at the destinations is a little compressed for some. See www.palaceonwheels.net. A similar tour which also includes a part of Gujarat is **The Royal Orient** which uses the old royal carriages. The **Bauddha Parikrama Express** runs from Kolkata, covering important Buddhist locations.

## Steam

For rail enthusiasts, the steam-hauled narrow-gauge trains between Kurseong and Darjeeling in North Bengal (a World Heritage Site), and between Mettupalayam and Coonoor, and a special one between Ooty and Runnymede in the Nilgiris, are an attraction. **SD Enterprises** (address below) is recommended for tailor-made trips. The oldest working steam engine, **Fairy Queen**, built in 1855, runs a weekend tour to Sariska from Delhi in the winter.

## Classes

**A/c First Class**, available only on main routes and cheaper than flying, is very comfortable (bedding provided). It will also be possible for tourists to reserve special coaches (some a/c) which are normally allocated to senior railway officials only. **A/c Sleeper**, two and three-tier, are clean and comfortable and good value. **A/c Executive Class**, with wide reclining seats, are available on many *Shatabdi* trains at double the price of the ordinary **a/c Chair Car** which are equally comfortable. **1st Class** (non-a/c) is gradually being phased out (now rather run-down but still pleasant if you like open windows). **Sleeper Class** provides basic upholstered seats and is a 'Reserved' class though tickets are sometimes 'subject to available accomodation'. **2nd Class** (non-a/c) two and three-tier, provides exceptionally cheap travel but can be crowded and uncomfortable, and toilet facilities can be unpleasant. It is nearly always better to use the Indian style toilets as they are better maintained.

## Indrail passes

These allow travel across the network without having to pay extra reservation fees and sleeper charges but you have to spend a high proportion of your time on the train to make it worthwhile. However, the advantages of pre-arranged

## Riding the rails

High class, comfortable, and by Indian standards quick new Express trains have brought many journeys within daytime reach. But while they offer an increasingly functional means of covering long distances in comfort, it is the overnight trips which still retain something of the early feel of Indian train travel. The bedding carefully prepared – and now available on a/c Second Class trains – the early morning light illuminating another stretch of hazy Indian landscape, the spontaneous conversations with fellow travellers – these are still on offer, giving a value far beyond the still modest prices. Furthermore, India still has a complete guide to its rail timetables.



reservations and automatic access to 'Tourist Quotas' can tip the balance in their favour for some travellers.

Tourists (foreigners and Indians resident abroad) may buy these passes for periods ranging from seven to 90 days from the tourist sections of principal railway booking offices, and pay in foreign currency, major credit cards, travellers' cheques or rupees with encashment certificates. Rail-cum-air tickets are also to be made available.

Indrail passes can also conveniently be bought abroad from special agents. For most people contemplating a single long journey soon after arriving in India, the Half or One day Pass with a confirmed reservation is worth the peace of mind; two or four day passes are also sold. A White Pass allows first class a/c travel; a Green, a/c two-tier Sleepers and Chair Cars; and the Yellow, only second class travel. Passes for up to four days' duration are only sold abroad.

**Cost** A/c first class costs about double the rate for two-tier shown below, and non a/c second class about half. Children (five-12) travel at half the adult fare. The young (12-30) and senior citizens (65+) are allowed a 30% discount on journeys over 500 km (just show passport).

| Period | US$ A/c 2-tier | Period | US$ A/c 2-tier |
|---|---|---|---|
| ½ day | 26 | 21 days | 198 |
| 1 day | 43 | 30 days | 248 |
| 7 days | 135 | 60 days | 400 |
| 15 days | 185 | 90 days | 530 |

Fares for individual journeys are based on distance covered and reflect both the class and the type of train. Higher rates apply on the Mail and Express trains and the air conditioned *Shatabdi* and *Rajdhani Expresses.*

### Rail travel tips

**Bedding** Travelling at night in the winter can be very cold in North India and in a/c coaches. Bedding is provided on second-class a/c sleepers. On others it can be hired for Rs 20 from the Station Manager for first class.

**Berths** It is worth asking for upper berths, especially in second-class three-tier sleepers, as they can also be used during the day time when the lower berths are used as seats, and which may only be used for lying down after 2100.

**Credit cards** Some main stations now have separate credit card booking queues – even shorter than women's queues! A service charge of Rs 30 is levied.

**Delays** Always allow plenty of time for booking and for making connections. Delays are common on all types of transport. The special **Shatabdi** and **Rajdhani**

## The hazards of road travel

On most routes it is impossible to average more than 50-60 kph in a car. Journeys are often very long, and can seem an endless succession of horn blowing, unexpected dangers, and unforeseen delays. Villages are often congested – beware of the concealed spine-breaking speed bumps – and cattle, sheep and goats may wander at will across the road. Directions can also be difficult to find. Drivers frequently don't know the way, maps are often hopelessly inaccurate and map reading is an almost entirely unknown skill. Training in driving is negligible and the test often a farce. You will note a characteristic side-saddle posture, one hand constantly on the horn, but there can be real dangers from poor judgement, irresponsible overtaking and a general philosophy of 'might is right'.



**Express** are generally quite reliable. Ordinary Express and Mail trains have priority over local services and occasionally surprise by being punctual, but generally the longer the journey time, the greater the delay. Delays on the rail network are cumulative, so arrivals and departures from mid-stations are often several hours behind schedule. Allow at least two hours for connections, more if the first part of the journey is long distance.

**Food and drink** It is best to carry some though tea and snacks are sold on the platforms (through the windows). Carry plenty of small notes and coins on long journeys. Rs 50 and Rs 100 notes can be difficult to change when purchasing small food items. On long distance trains, the 'pantry' car is often near the upper class carriages (bogies).

**Getting a seat** It is usually impossible to make seat reservations at small 'intermediate' stations as they don't have an allocation. You can sometimes use a porter to get you a seat in a second-class carriage. For about Rs 20 he will take the luggage and ensure that you get a seat.

**Left-luggage** Bags left in station cloakrooms must be lockable. Don't leave any food in them. These are especially useful when there is time to sight-see before an evening train, although luggage can be left for up to 30 days.

**Ladies' compartments** A woman travelling alone, overnight, on an unreserved second-class train can ask if there is one of these.

**Ladies' queues** Separate (much shorter) ticket queues may be available for women.

**Overbooking** Passengers with valid tickets but no berth reservations are sometimes permitted to travel overnight, causing great discomfort to travellers occupying lower berths. Wait-listed passengers should confirm the status of their ticket in advance by calling enquiries at the nearest computerised reservation office. At the station, check the reservation charts (usually on the relevant platform) and contact the Station Manager or Ticket Collector.

**Porters** They can carry prodigious amounts of luggage. Rates vary from station to station but around Rs 10 per item of luggage (check board on the station platform) is fair. They can be quite aggressive particularly on the main tourist routes: be firm but polite and remember that they will always leave the train when it pulls out of the station!

**Pre-paid taxis** Many main stations have a pre-paid taxi (or rickshaw) service which offers a reliable, fair-price service. Give your receipt to the driver upon reaching the destination.

**Quotas** A large number of seats are technically reserved as 'quotas' for various groups of travellers (civil servants, military personnel, foreign tourists etc). In

## Train touts

Many railway stations – and some bus stations and major tourist sites – are heavily populated with touts. Self-styled 'agents' will board trains before they enter the station and seek out tourists, often picking up their luggage and setting off with words such as "Madam!/Sir! Come with me madam/sir! You need top class hotel ...". They will even select porters to take your luggage without giving you any say.

If you have succeeded in getting off the train or even in obtaining a trolley you will find hands eager to push it for you.

For a first time visitor such touts can be more than a nuisance. You need to keep calm and firm. Decide in advance where you want to stay. If you need a porter on trains, select one yourself and agree a price **before** the porter sets off with your baggage. If travelling with a companion one can stay guarding the luggage while the other gets hold of a taxi and negotiates the price to the hotel. It sounds complicated, and sometimes it feels it. The most important thing is to behave as if you know what you are doing!



addition, many stations have their own quota for particular trains so that a train may be 'fully booked' when there are still some tickets available from the special quota of other stations. These are only sold on the day of departure so wait-listed passengers are often able to travel at the last minute. Ask the Superintendent on duty to try the 'Special' or 'VIP Quota'. The 'Tatkal' system realeases a small percentage of seats at 0800 on the day before a train departs; you pay an extra Rs 50 to get on an otherwise heavily booked train.

**Reservations** Ask for the separate Tourist Quota counter at main stations, and while queuing fill up the Reservation Form which requires the number and name of the train, preferred class of travel, and the passenger's name, age and sex (for Tourist Quota you may need to mention the passport number and nationality); you can use one form for up to six passengers. If you don't have a reservation for a particular train but carry an Indrail Pass, you may get one by arriving about three hours early. Tourist Quota tickets must be paid for in foreign exchange, so have an exchange certificate handy if yu use Rupees. It is possible to buy tickets for trains on most routes countrywide at many of the 520 computerised reservation centres across India. A short cut is to buy an ordinary second-class ticket and try upgrading to a/c by paying the conductor.

**Security** Keep valuables close to you, securely locked, and away from windows. For security, carry a good lock and chain to attach your luggage. There are usually metal loops under the lower berth for this purpose.

**Tickets** By asking a travel agent to get yours for a small fee, usually around Rs 50, saves much time and effort. Non-Indrail Pass tickets can be bought over the counter. It is always best to book as far in advance as possible (usually up to 60 days). Avoid touts at the station offering tickets, hotels or money changing. Only 'General Quota' (ie second class) tickets are sold on the day of travel. All others must be reserved in advance. For last minute trips, buy a second-class ticket and request and pay for an upgrade from the Travelling Ticket Inspector (TTE) on board.

**Timetables** Regional timetables are available cheaply from station bookstalls; the monthly 'Indian Bradshaw' is sold in principal stations. The handy 'Trains at a Glance' (Rs 25) lists popular trains likely to be used by most foreign travellers and is available in UK from SD Enterprises Ltd (see Indrail).

# Road

Road travel is often the only choice for reaching many of the places of outstanding interest in which India is so rich. For the uninitiated, travel by road can also be a worrying experience because of the apparent absence of conventional traffic regulations and also in the mountains, especially during the rainy season when landslides are possible. Vehicles drive on the left - in theory. Routes around the major cities are usually crowded with lorry traffic, especially at night, and the main roads are often poor and slow. There are a few motorway- style expressways, but most main roads are single track. Some district roads are quiet, and although they are not fast they can be a good way of seeing the country and village life if you have the time.

## Bus

Buses now reach virtually every part of India, offering a cheap, if often uncomfortable, means of visiting places off the rail network. Very few villages are now more than 2 or 3 km from a bus stop. Services are run by the State Corporation from the State Bus Stand (and private companies which often have offices nearby). The latter allow advance reservation and though tickets prices are a little higher, they have fewer stops and are a bit more comfortable.

**Bus categories** **A/c luxury coaches**: though comfortable for sight-seeing trips, apart from the very best 'sleeper coaches', even these can be very uncomfortable for really long journeys. Often the air conditioning is very cold, so wrap up. Journeys over 10 hours can be extremely tiring so it is better to go by train if there is a choice. **Express buses**: run over long distances (frequently overnight), these are often called 'video coaches' and can be an appalling experience unless you appreciate loud film music blasting through the night. Ear plugs and eye masks may ease the pain. They rarely average more than 45 km per hour. **Local buses**: these are often very crowded, quite bumpy and slow and usually poorly maintained. However, over short distances, they can be a very cheap, friendly and easy way of getting about. Even where signboards are not in English someone will usually give you directions. Many larger towns have **minibus** services which charge a little more than the buses and pick up and drop passengers on request. Again very crowded, and with restricted headroom, they are the fastest way of getting about many of the larger towns.

**Bus travel tips** Some towns have different bus stations for different destinations. Booking on major long-distance routes is now computerized. Book in advance where possible and avoid the back of the bus where it can be very bumpy. If your destination is only served by a local bus you may do better to take the Express bus and 'persuade' the driver, with a tip in advance, to stop where you want to get off. You will have to pay the full fare to the first stop beyond your destination but you will get there faster and more comfortably. When an unreserved bus pulls into a bus station, there is usually an unholy scramble for seats, whilst those arriving have to struggle to get off! In many areas there is an unwritten 'rule of reservation' using handkerchiefs or bags thrust through the windows to reserve seats. Some visitors may feel a more justified right to a seat having fought their way through the crowd, but it is generally best to do as local people do and be prepared with a handkerchief or 'sarong'. As soon as it touches the seat, it is yours!

## Car

A car provides a chance to travel off the beaten track, and gives unrivalled opportunities for seeing something of India's great variety of villages and small towns. Until recently, the most widely used hire car was the Hindustan Ambassador.

 However, except for the newest model, they are often very unreliable, and although they still have their devotees, many find them uncomfortable for long journeys. For a similar price, Maruti cars and vans (Omni) are much more reliable and are now the preferred choice in many areas. Gypsy 4WDs and Jeeps are also available, especially in the hills, where larger Sumos have made an appearance. Maruti Esteems and Toyota Qualis are comfortable and have optional reliable a/c. A specialist operator can be very helpful in arranging itineraries and car hire in advance.

**Car hire** Car hire, with a driver, is generally cheaper than in the West. A car shared by three or four can be very good value. Be sure to check carefully the mileage at the beginning and end of the trip. Two or three-day trips from main towns can also give excellent opportunities for sightseeing off the beaten track in reasonable comfort. Local drivers often know their way much better than drivers from other states, so where possible it is a good idea to get a local driver who speaks the state language, in addition to being able to communicate with you. In the mountains, it is better to use a driver who knows the roads. Drivers may sleep in the car overnight, though hotels sometimes provide a bed for them. They are responsible for all their expenses, including their meals. Car (and auto) drivers increase their earnings by taking you to hotels and shops where they get a handsome commission (which you will pay for!). If you feel inclined, a tip at the end of the tour of Rs 100 per day in addition to their daily allowance is perfectly acceptable. Check beforehand if fuel and inter-state taxes are included in the hire charge.

Cars can be hired through private companies. International companies such as **Hertz, Europcar** and **Budget** operate in some major cities and offer reliable cars; their rates are generally higher than those of local firms (eg **Sal Service, Wheels**). The price of an imported car can be three times that of the Ambassador.

| Car with Driver Ambassador | Economy Maruti 800 Contessa | Regular A/C Maruti 800 Opel etc | Premium A/C Maruti 1000 Qualis | Luxury A/C Esteem |
|---|---|---|---|---|
| 8 hrs/80 km | Rs 800 | Rs 1,000 | Rs 1,400 | Rs 1,800+ |
| Extra km | Rs 4-7 | Rs 9 | Rs 13 | Rs 18 |
| Extra hour | Rs 40 | Rs 50 | Rs 70 | Rs 100 |
| Out of town | | | | |
| Per km | Rs 7 | Rs 9 | Rs 13 | Rs 18 |
| Night halt | Rs 100 | Rs 200 | Rs 250 | Rs 250 |

**Importing a car** Tourists may import their own vehicles into India with a Carnet de Passage (Triptyques) issued by any recognized automobile association or club affiliated to the Alliance Internationale de Tourisme in Geneva.

**Self-drive car hire** This is still in its infancy and many visitors may find the road conditions difficult and sometimes dangerous. If you drive yourself it is essential to take great care. Pedestrians, cattle and a wide range of other animals roam at will. This can be particularly dangerous when driving after dark especially as even other vehicles often carry no lights.

**Car travel tips** When booking emphasize the importance of good tyres and general roadworthiness. On main roads across India **petrol stations** are reasonably frequent, but some areas are poorly served. Some service stations only have diesel pumps though they may have small reserves of petrol. Always carry a spare can. Diesel is widely available and normally much cheaper than petrol. Petrol is rarely above 92 octane. Drivers must have third party **insurance**. This may have to be with an Indian insurer, or with a foreign insurer who has a national guarantor. You must also

## On the road on a motorbike

An experienced motorbiker writes: unless you bring your own bike (Carnet de passage, huge deposit) the only acceptable machine is the legendary Enfield Bullet 350 or 500 cc. Humming along the Indian roads or tracks this lovely four stroke classic machine is a must. Also available in diesel version (1.5 litres per 100 km and much cheaper fuel) the 500 cc is much better for travelling with luggage and easier to take home as brakes and 12v lights conform with EC regulations.

Expect a cruising speed of around 50 kph. Riding above 70 gets very tiring due to the lack of silent blocks and the nerve-wracking Indian roads. A good average distance is 200 km per day. Riding at night furthers the excitement – practise at home on a death race video first, but bear in mind that accidents can turn into a first-hand lynching experience! If you stop, prepare to settle quickly in cash, but while third party insurance is cheap (Rs 53 per year!) refunds are less than guaranteed.

**Buying** In Delhi, Karol Bagh is the biker's den, where you can have your second hand bike assembled to order. It's also good for arranging shipping (Rs 13,000 to Europe), and for spares and gear. You can now find good helmets at a fraction of the European price (Studds Rs 300-Rs 2,000 for a full face type), also goggles, sturdy panniers and extras. A Bullet will cost from Rs 25,000 to Rs 40,000 second hand, or Rs 50,000-Rs 60,000 new. Allow plenty of time to shop around.

**Papers** Many Indians and tourists don't bother changing the name on the ownership papers. If you are driving through more than one state this is rash, as it is essential to have the papers in your name, plus the NOC (No Objection Certificate) from the Motor Vehicles Department if you intend to export the vehicle home. Regardless of the dealer's assertions to the contrary, demand the NOC as otherwise you will have to apply for it in the state of origin. You have to allow 15 days.

**Spares** Before buying, negotiate the essential extras: mirrors, luggage carriers, better saddle, battery. Spares are cheap and readily available for the 350cc model. Take along a spare throttle and clutch cable, a handful of nuts and bolts, puncture repair kit and pump or emergency canister so you don't have to leave the bike unattended while hitching a lift to the nearest puncture wallah – and of course a full set of tools. Check the oil level daily. Finally, remember that for long distances you can load your bike on a night train (Rs 100 per 100 km). Just turn up at the parcel office with an empty petrol tank at least two hours before departure.

be in possession of an 'International Driving Permit', issued by a recognised driving authority in your home country (eg the AA in the UK, apply at least six weeks before leaving). **Asking the way** can be very frustrating as you are likely to get widely conflicting advice each time you stop to ask. On the main roads, 'mile' posts periodically appear in English and can help. Elsewhere, it is best to ask directions often and follow the 'average direction'! **Accidents** often produce large and angry crowds very quickly. It is best to leave the scene of the accident and report it to the police as quickly as possible thereafter. Ensure that you have adequate **provisions,** plenty of food and drink and a basic tool set in the car.

### Taxi

'Yellow-top' taxis in cities and large towns are metered, although tariffs change frequently. These changes are shown on a fare chart which should be read in conjunction with the meter reading. Increased night time rates apply in some cities, and there is a small charge for luggage, insist on the taxi meter being 'flagged' in your presence. If the driver refuses, the official advice is to call the police. This may not work, but it is worth trying. When a taxi doesn't have a meter, you will need to fix the fare before starting the journey. Ask at the hotel desk for a guide price.

At stations and airports it is often possible to share taxis to a central point. It is worth looking for fellow passengers who may be travelling in your direction and get a pre-paid taxi. At night, always have a clear idea of where you want to go and insist on being taken there. Taxi drivers may try to convince you that the hotel you have chosen 'closed three years ago', is 'completely full' or is an 'unsafe den'. Say that you have an advance reservation.



## Rickshaw

**Auto-rickshaws ('autos')** These are almost universally available in towns across India and are the cheapest convenient way of getting about. It is best to walk a short distance away from a hotel gate before picking up an auto to avoid paying an inflated rate. In addition to using them for short journeys it is often possible to hire them by the hour, or for a half or full day's sight-seeing. In some areas younger drivers who speak some English and know their local area well, may want to show you around. However, rickshaw drivers are often paid a commission by hotels, restaurants and gift shops, so advice is not always impartial. Drivers sometimes refuse to use a meter, quote a ridiculous price or attempt to stop short of your destination. If you have real problems it can help to threaten to go to the police. Beware of some rickshaw drivers who show the fare chart for taxis, especially in Mumbai.

**Cycle-rickshaws and horse-drawn tongas** These are more common in the more rustic setting of a small town or the outskirts of a large one. You will need to fix a price by bargaining. The animal attached to a tonga usually looks too undernourished to have the strength to pull the driver, leave alone passengers. Beware of some rickshaw drivers who show the fare chart for taxis, especially in Mumbai.

## Cycling

Cycling is an excellent way of seeing the quiet by-ways of India. It is easy to hire bikes in most small towns for about Rs 15-20 per day. Indian bikes are heavy and without gears, but on the flat they offer a good way of exploring comparatively short distances outside towns. In the more prosperous tourist resorts, mountain bikes are now becoming available, but at a higher hire charge. It is also quite possible to tour more extensively and you may then want to buy a cycle.

*You are usually not far from a 'puncture wallah' who can make minor repairs cheaply.*

There are shops in every town and the local Hero are considered the best, with Atlas and BSA good alternatives; expect to pay around Rs 1,200-1,500 for a second-hand Indian bike but remember to bargain. At the end of your trip you can usually sell it quite easily at half that price. Imported bikes have the advantage of lighter weight and gears, but are more difficult to get repaired, and carry the much greater risk of being stolen or damaged. If you wish to take your own, it is quite easy if you dismantle it and pack it in its original shipping carton; be sure to take all essential spares including a pump. It is possible to get Indian spares for 26" wheel cycles. All cyclists should take bungy cords (to strap down a backpack) and good lights from home, although cycling at night is not recommended; take care not to leave your machine parked anywhere with your belongings though. Bike repair shops are universal and charges are nominal.

It is possible to cover 50 to 80 km a day quite comfortably. A cyclist wrote in to say that the National Highways are manic but country roads, especially along the coast, can be idyllic, if rather dusty and bumpy. You can even put your bike on a boat for the backwater trip or on top of a bus. Should you wish to take your bike on the train, allow plenty of time for booking it in on the brake van at the Parcels office, and for filling in forms.

It is best to start a journey early in the morning, stop at midday and resume cycling in the late afternoon. Night-riding, though cooler, can be hazardous because of lack of lighting and poor road surfaces. Try to avoid the major highways as far as possible. Fortunately foreign cyclists are usually greeted with cheers, waves and smiles and truck drivers are sometimes happy to give lifts to cyclists (and their bikes). This is a good way of taking some of the hardship out of cycling round India.

## Motorcycling

Motorcycling across India is particularly attractive for bike enthusiasts. It is easy to buy new Indian-made motorcycles including the Enfield Bullet and an ever-increasing range of Japanese models, including Suzukis and Hondas made in collaboration with Indian firms, from 100-225cc. Buying new ensures greater reliability and fixed price - (Indian Rajdoots are less expensive but have a poor reputation for reliability). Buying second hand in Rupees takes more time but is quite possible; expect to get a 30-40% discount. You can get a broker to help with the paperwork involved (certificate of ownership, insurance etc) for a fee. They charge about Rs 5,000 for a 'No Objection Certificate' (NOC) which is essential for reselling; it is easier to have the bike in your name. When selling, don't be in a hurry, and only negotiate with "ready cash" buyers. A black bike is easier to sell than a coloured one! Repairs are usually easy to arrange and quite cheap. Bring your own helmet and an International Driving Permit.

*See under Car and Cycling above for general advice.*

**Adventuremoto**, www.aventuremoto.com, for biking in Rajasthan and Garhwal Himalaya.

**Chandertal Tours & Himalayan Folkways**, based in the UK, organizes Royal Enfield tours of the high Himalaya (Himachal and Ladakh) and Rajasthan. Contact: 20 The Fridays, East Dean, Eastbourne, East Sussex, BN20 0DH, UK, T0091-1323-422213, www.steali.co.uk/india.

**Peter and Friends Classic Adventures**, an Indo-German company based in Goa at Casa Tres Amigos, Socol Vado 425, Assagao (4 km east on Anjuna road), T0832-2682411, www.classic-bike-india.de, runs organized motorbike tours in Goa and the Himalaya with good back up. They are well organized, friendly and popular with Germans. They also hire out Enfield motorbikes in Goa (US$120-165/week).

**Royal Enfield Motors**, Chennai, T0445-243300. Tours with full back up. You can choose between Rajasthan, Himachal/Ladakh and South India (about US$1,200-1,600 for 14 days).

## Hitchhiking

Hitchhiking is uncommon, partly because public transport is so cheap. If you try, you are likely to spend a very long time on the roadside. However, getting a lift on scooters and on trucks in areas with little public transport can be worthwhile, whilst those riding motorbikes or scooters in Goa can be expected to pick up the occasional hitchhiking policeman! It is not recommended for women on their own.

# Maps

For anyone interested in the geography of India, or even simply getting around, trying to buy good maps is a depressing experience. For security reasons it is illegal to sell large scale maps of areas within 80 km of the coast or national borders.

*The export of large scale maps from India is prohibited. For trekking maps, see page 73.*

The **Bartholomew** 1:4 m map sheet of India is the most authoritative, detailed and easy to use map available. It can be bought worldwide. **GeoCenter World Map** 1:2 m, covers India in three regional sections and are clearly printed. **Nelles'** regional maps of India at the scale of 1:1.5 m offer generally clear route maps, though neither the road classifications nor alignments are wholly reliable. The same criticism applies to the attractively produced and easy to read **Lonely Planet Travel Atlas of India and Bangladesh** (2001, 162 pp).

State and town plans are published by the **TTK Company**. These are often the best available though they are not wholly reliable. For the larger cities they provide the most compact yet clear map sheets (generally 50 mm x 75 mm format). **Indian Map Service** publishes a limited number of maps of Rajasthan and Maharashtra.

**The Survey of India** publishes large scale 1:10,000 town plans of approximately 70 cities. These detailed plans are the only surveyed town maps in India, and some are over 20 years old. The Survey also has topographic maps at the scale of 1:25,000 and 1:50,000 in addition to its 1:250,000 scale coverage, some of which are as recent as the late 1980s. However, maps are regarded as highly sensitive and it is only possible to buy these from main agents of the Survey of India.

**Stanfords,** 12-14 Long Acre, London, WC2, T020 78361321, www.stanfords.co.uk, offers a mail order service.



# Sleeping

India has an enormously wide range of accommodation. You can stay safely and very cheaply by western standards right across the country. In all the major cities there are also high quality hotels, offering a full range of facilities. In small centres even the best hotels are far more variable. In Rajasthan and Gujarat, old Maharajas' palaces and forts have been privately converted into comfortable, unusual hotels. Hotels in beach resorts and hill-stations, because of their location and special appeal, often deviate from the description of our different categories. In the peak season (October to April for most of India) bookings can be extremely heavy in popular destinations. It is sometimes possible to book in advance by phone, fax or email, but double check your reservation, and always try to arrive as early as possible in the day.

## Price categories

They are **not** star ratings and individual facilities vary widely. Modest hotels may not have their own restaurant but will often offer 'room service', bringing in food from outside. In South and West India, and in 'temple towns', the restaurants may only serve vegetarian food. Many hotels operate a '24 hour check-out' system. Make sure that this means that you can stay 24 hours from the time of check-in. Expect to pay more in Delhi, Mumbai, and to a lesser extent in Chennai and Kolkata for all categories. Prices away from large cities tend to be lower for comparable hotels. Away from the metropolitan cities, in South India, room rates tend to be lower than the North, and the standard of cleanliness is higher.

Large reductions are made by hotels in all categories **out-of-season** in many resorts. Always ask if any is available. You may also request the 10-15% agent's commission to be deducted from your bill if you book direct. Clarify whether the agreed figure includes all taxes.

## Taxes

In general most hotel rooms rated at Rs 1,200 or above are subject to an expenditure tax of 10%. Many states levy an additional luxury tax of between 10-25%, and some hotels add a service charge of 10%. Taxes are not necessarily payable on meals, so it

## Hotel price codes explained

Prices are based on two people sharing, excluding taxes.

LL (US$250 plus) and L (US$150-249) These are exceptional hotels. They are in the metropolitan cities or in exclusive locations such as a commanding coastal promontory, a lake island or a scenic hilltop, with virtually nothing to fault them. They have high class business facilities, specialist restaurants and well-stocked bars, several pools, sports.

AL (US$100-149) and A (US$50-99) Most major towns have at least some in these categories which too reach high international standards but are less exclusive. Many quote an inflated 'dollar price' to foreigners.

B (US$25-49) Comfortable but not plush, choice of restaurants, pool, some have a gym. These are often aimed at the business client.

C (Rs 750-1200) In many small towns the best hotel is in this category, but they are not necessarily the best value. Some charge higher prices for a flash reception area, usually central a/c, restaurant, satellite TV, foreign exchange and travel desk.

D (Rs 400-749) These hotels often offer very good value though quality and cleanliness can vary widely. Most have some a/c rooms with bath, satellite TV, restaurants. They may have some rooms in the E price range, so if you are looking for good but cheap accommodation, start here!

E (Rs 200-399) Simple room with fan (occasionally air-cooler or a/c), often shared toilet and shower. May not have a restaurant or provide bed linen, towel etc.

F (Under Rs 200) Very basic, shared toilet (often 'squat'), bucket and tap, variable cleanliness and hygiene. E and F category hotels are often in busy parts of town. They may have some rooms for under Rs 100, and dormitory beds for under Rs 50. (Some only have four or six beds.)

is worth settling the meals bill separately from the room bill. Most hotels in the C category and above accept payment by credit card. Check your final bill carefully. Visitors have complained of **incorrect bills**, even in the most expensive hotels. The problem particularly afflicts groups, when last-minute extras appear mysteriously on some guests' bills. Check the evening before departure, and keep all receipts.

### Hotel facilities

You have to be prepared for difficulties which are uncommon in the West. It is best to inspect the room and check that all equipment (a/c, TV, water heater, flush) works before checking in at a modest hotel.

In some states **power cuts** are common, or hot water may be restricted to certain times of day. The largest hotels have their own generators but it is best to carry a good torch. Usually, only category B and above have **central a/c**. Elsewhere a/c rooms are cooled by individual units and occasionally by large 'air-coolers' which can be noisy and unreliable. When they fail to operate tell the management as it is often possible to get a rapid repair done, or to transfer to a room where the unit is working. During power cuts generators may not be able to cope with providing air-conditioning. Fans are provided in all but the cheapest of hotels. Apart from those in the A category and above, 'attached bath' does not necessarily refer to a bathroom with a bathtub. Most will provide a **bathroom** with a toilet, basin and a shower. In the lower priced hotels and outside large towns, a bucket and tap may replace the shower, and an Indian 'squat' toilet instead of a Western WC (squat toilets often cleaner). Mid-price hotels, which are clean and pleasant, don't always provide towels, soap and toilet paper.

In some regions **water supply** is rationed periodically. Keep a bucket filled to use for flushing the toilet during water cuts. Occasionally, tap water may be discoloured due to rusty tanks. During the cold weather and in hill stations, hot water will be available at certain times of the day, sometimes in buckets, but is usually very restricted in quantity. Electric water heaters may provide enough for a shower but not enough to fill a bath tub! For details on drinking water, see page 60.

**Laundry** can be arranged very cheaply (eg a shirt washed and pressed for Rs 15-20 in C-D category; but Rs 50 or more in luxury hotels) and quickly (in 12-24 hours). It is best not to risk delicate fibres, though luxury hotels can usually handle these and also dry-clean items.

At some times of the year and in some places **mosquitoes** can be a real problem, and not all hotels have mosquito-proof rooms or mosquito nets. In cheap hotels you need to be prepared for a wider range of insect life, including flies, cockroaches and ants. Poisonous insects are extremely rare in towns. Hotel managements are nearly always prepared with insecticide sprays. Few small hotels in mosquito-prone areas supply nets so it is best for budget travellers to take one from home. An impregnated, wedge-shaped one (for single-point fixing) is preferable, available in all good camping/outdoor shops. Remember to shut windows and doors at dusk. Electrical devices are now widely available, as are mosquito coils which burn slowly. Dusk and early evening are the worst times for mosquitoes so trousers and long-sleeved shirts are advisable, especially out of doors. At night, fans can be very effective in keeping mosquitoes off, and remember to tuck the net under the mattress all round. As well as insects, expect to find spiders larger and hairier than those you see at home; they are mostly harmless and more frightened of you than you are of them! You will be lucky to come across a scorpion in rural areas (always check shoes/boots before putting them on). You are more likely to have a resident gecko (a harmless house lizard) in your room. They are your friends as they keep the number of mosquitoes down.

Hotels close to temples can be very **noisy**, especially during festivals. Music blares from loudspeakers late at night and from very early in the morning, often making sleep impossible. Mosques call the faithful to prayers at dawn. Some find earplugs helpful.

## Tourist 'Bungalows'

The different State Tourism Development Corporations run their own hotels and hostels which are often located in places of special interest. These are very reasonably priced, though they may be rather dated, restaurant menus may be limited and service is often slow. Upkeep varies and in some states it is sadly well below standard.

## Railway and airport retiring rooms

Railway stations often have 'Retiring Rooms' or 'Rest Rooms' which may be hired for periods of between one and 24 hours by anyone holding an onward train ticket. They are cheap and simple though some stations have a couple of a/c rooms, which are often heavily booked. In general, you must contact the Ticket Collector on duty for available rooms/beds. They are convenient for short stops, though some can be very noisy. Some major airports (eg Delhi, Mumbai) have similar facilities.

## Government rest houses

Rest house may sometimes be available for overnight stays, particularly in remote areas. They are usually extremely basic, with a caretaker who can sometimes provide a simple meal, given sufficient notice. Check the room rate in advance as foreigners are sometimes overcharged. Government officials always take precedence, even over-booked guests.

### Indian style hotels

These, catering for Indian businessmen, are springing up fast in or on the outskirts of many small and medium sized towns. Most have some air-conditioned rooms and attached showers. They are variable in quality but it is increasingly possible to find excellent value accommodation even in remote areas.

### Hostels

The Department of Tourism runs 16 hostels, each with about 50 beds, usually organized into dormitory accommodation. The YHA have a few sites all over India. Travellers may also stay in religious hostels (*dharamshalas*) for up to three days. These are primarily intended for pilgrims, and are sometimes free of charge though voluntary offerings are always welcome. Usually only vegetarian food is permitted; smoking and alcohol are not.

### Camping

Mid-price hotels with large grounds are sometimes willing to allow camping. Regional tourist offices have details of new developments. For information on YMCA camping facilities contact: **YMCA,** The National General Secretary, National Council of YMCAs of India, PB No 14, Massey Hall, Jai Singh Rd, New Delhi 1.

# Eating

## Food

You find just as much variety in dishes and presentation crossing India as you would on an equivalent journey across Europe. Combinations of spices give each region its distinctive flavour.

*See page 1370 for a food glossary. Regional cuisine is covered in the introduction to each state.*

The larger hotels, open to non-residents, often offer **buffet** lunches with Indian, Western and sometimes Chinese dishes. These can be good value (Rs 250-300; but around Rs 450 in the top grades), and can provide a welcome, comfortable break in the cool. The health risks, however, of food kept warm for long periods in metal containers are considerable, especially if turnover at the buffet is slow. This can be the case even in five-star hotels.

It is essential to be very careful since food hygiene may be poor, flies abound and refrigeration in the hot weather may be inadequate and intermittent because of power cuts. It is best to eat only freshly prepared food by ordering from the menu (especially meat and fish dishes); avoid salads and cut fruit.

If you are unused to spicy food, go slow! Stick to Western or mild Chinese meals in good restaurants, and try the odd Indian dish to test your reaction. Those used to Indian spices may choose to be more adventurous. Popular local restaurants are obvious from the number of people eating in them. Try a traditional *thali*, which is a complete meal served on a large stainless steel plate (or very occasionally on a banana leaf). Several preparations, placed in small bowls, surround the central serving of wholewheat chapati and rice. A vegetarian *thali* would include *daal* (lentils), two or three curries (which can be quite hot), and crisp poppadums, although there are regional variations. A variety of pickles are offered – mango and lime are two of the most popular. These can be exceptionally hot, and are designed to

## Two masala dosai and a pot of tea!

One traveller to Ooty reported that a hotel bar had closed, apparently permanently. He found however that it was still possible to obtain alcoholic drinks from the restaurant. Having ordered and been served a beer, he was intrigued that when the bill came it was made out for "2 masala dosai". The price was, of course, correct for the beer!

Another traveller found that a well-known hotel in the heart of New Delhi also appeared to have been forced to adapt its attitude to serving alcohol to the prevailing laws. Asked in the early evening for a double whisky the barman was very happy to comply until he was asked to serve it in the garden. On being told that he could only drink it in the bar the visitor expressed great disappointment, on which the barman relented, whispering that if the visitor really wanted to drink it outside he would serve it to him in a tea pot!

If you are thirsting for alcohol in a prohibitionist area perhaps you need to order two masala dosai and a pot of tea.

be taken in minute quantities alongside the main dishes. Plain *dahi* (yoghurt) in the south, or *raita* in the north, usually acts as a bland 'cooler'. Simple *dhabas* (rustic roadside eateries) are an alternative experience for sampling authentic local dishes.

Many city restaurants offer some so-called **European options** such as toasted sandwiches, stuffed pancakes, apple pies, crumbles and cheese cakes. Italian favourites (pizzas, pastas) can be very different from what you are used to. Western confectionery, in general, is disappointing. Ice creams, on the other hand, can be exceptionally good (there are excellent Indian ones as well as international brands such as Cadbury'sand Walls.

India has many delicious tropical **fruits**. Some are highly seasonal (eg mangoes, pineapples and lychees), while others (eg bananas, grapes, oranges) are available throughout the year. It is safe to eat the ones you can wash and peel.

## Drink

**Drinking water** used to be regarded as one of India's biggest hazards. It is still true that water from the tap or a well should never be considered safe to drink since public water supplies are often polluted. Bottled water is now widely available (Rs 10-12 per litre) although most bottled water is not mineral water but simply purified water from an urban supply; it is, however, perfectly safe to drink. Buy from a shop or stall, check the seal carefully (some companies now add a second clear plastic seal around the bottle top) and avoid street hawkers; when disposing bottles, crush to prevent misuse. There is growing concern over the mountains of plastic bottles that are collecting and the waste of resources to produce them, so travellers are encouraged to use alternative methods of getting safe drinking water. In some towns (eg Dharamshala, Leh) purified water is now sold for refilling your own container. Travellers may wish to purify water themselves, see page 72. A portable water filter is a good option, carrying the drinking water in a plastic bottle in an insulated carrier. Always carry enough drinking water with you when travelling. It is important to use pure water for cleaning teeth.

**Tea** and **coffee** are safe and widely available. Both are normally served sweet, and with milk. If you wish, say 'no sugar' (*chini nahin*), 'no milk' (*dudh nahin*) when ordering. Alternatively, ask for a pot of tea, and milk and sugar to be brought separately. Freshly brewed coffee is a common drink in South India, but in the North, ordinary city restaurants will usually serve the instant variety.

Bottled **carbonated drinks** such as 'Coke', 'Pepsi', 'Teem' and 'Gold Spot' are universally available but always check the seal when you buy from a street stall. There are also several brands of fruit **juice** sold in cartons, including mango, pineapple and apple. Don't add ice cubes as the water source may be contaminated. Take care with fresh fruit juices or *lassis* as ice is often added.

Indians rarely drink **alcohol** with a meal, water being on hand. In the past wines and spirits were generally either imported and extremely expensive, or local and of poor quality. Now, the best Indian whisky, rum and brandy are widely accepted, as are good Champagnoise and other wines from Maharashtra. If you hanker after a bottle of imported wine, you will only find it in the top restaurants and have to pay Rs 800-1,000 at least. For the urban elite, cooling Indian beers are popular when eating out and so are widely available, though you may need to check the 'chill' value. The 'English Pub' has appeared in major cities, where the foreign traveller too would feel comfortable. Elsewhere, seedy, all male drinking dens in the larger cities are best avoided. Head for the better hotel bar instead. In rural India, local rice, palm, cashew or date juice *toddy* and *arak* should be treated with great caution. However, the Sikkimese *chhang* makes a pleasant change drunk out of a wooden tankard through a bamboo straw! Most states have alcohol free 'dry' days; a few enforce degrees of Prohibition. Some up-market restaurants may serve beer even if it's not listed so it's worth asking. For 'dry' states and Liquor Permits, see page 32.

# Entertainment

Despite an economic boom in cities like Delhi and Mumbai and the rapid growth of a young business class, India's nightlife remains meagre, focused on club discos in the biggest hotels. In Goa, beach raves and parties (associated with Goa Trance and the drug scene), which usually take place in make-shift venues, continue to attract large groups of foreigners particularly during Christmas and the New Year. More traditional, popular entertainment is widespread across Indian villages in the form of folk drama, dance and music, each region having its own styles, and open air village performance being common. The hugely popular Hindi film industry comes largely out of this tradition. It's always easy to find a cinema, but prepare for a long sitting with a standard story line and set of characters and lots of action. See also page 74 for spectator sports and page 1321 for cinema.

# Festivals and events

India has an extraordinary wealth of festivals with many celebrated nationwide, while others are specific to a particular state or community or even a particular temple. Many festivals fall on different dates each year depending on the Hindu lunar calendar so check with the tourist office.

## The Hindu Calendar

Hindus follow two distinct eras: The *Vikrama Samvat* which began in 57 BC and the *Salivahan Saka* which dates from 78 AD and has been the official Indian calendar since 1957. The *Saka* new year starts on 22 March and has the same length as the Gregorian calendar. The 29½ day lunar month with its 'dark' and 'bright' halves based on the new and full moons, are named after 12 constellations, and total a 354 day year. The calendar cleverly has an extra month (*adhik maas*) every 2½-3 years, to bring it in line with the solar year of 365 days coinciding with the Gregorian calendar of the West.

Some major national and regional festivals are listed below; details of these and others appear under the particular state or town. A few count as national holidays: **26 January: Republic Day; 15 August: Independence Day; 2 October: Mahatma Gandhi's Birthday; 25 December: Christmas Day.**

## Purnima (Full Moon)

Many religious festivals depend on the phases of the moon. Full moon days are particularly significant and can mean extra crowding and merrymaking in temple towns throughout India, and are sometimes public holidays.



## Major festivals and fairs

**1 January New Year's Day** is accepted officially when following the Gregorian calendar but there are regional variations which fall on different dates, often coinciding with spring/harvest time in March and April: **Losar** in Ladakh, **Naba Barsha** in Bengal (14 April), **Goru** in Assam, **Ugadi** in Andhra, **Vishu** in Kerala and **Jamshed Navroj** for the Parsi community. **14 January Makar Sankranti** marks the end of winter and is celebrated with kite flying, especially in Gujarat. **Pongal** is Tamil Nadu's harvest festival. **26 January Republic Day Parade** in New Delhi. Communist-style display of military strength.

**February Vasant Panchami,** the Spring festival when people wear bright yellow clothes to mark the advent of the season with singing, dancing and feasting. In Bengal it is also **Saraswati Puja** when the goddess of learning is worshipped. **Desert Festival** – Jaisalmer, Rajasthan. **Nagaur Camel Fair** – Rajasthan. **Surajkund Crafts Mela** – Haryana. **International Yoga Festival** – Rishikesh, Uttaranchal. **Elephanta Festival** – Maharashtra. **Konark Festival** – Orissa.

**February-March Maha Sivaratri** marks the night when Siva danced his celestial dance of destruction (*Tandava*) celebrated with feasting and fairs at Siva temples, but preceded by a night of devotional readings and hymn singing. **Carnival** – Goa. Spectacular costumes, music and dance, float processions and feasting mark the three-day event.

**March Ellora Festival of Classical Dance and Music** – Maharashtra. **Khajuraho Dance Festival** – Madhya Pradesh. **Gangaur Mela** – Rajasthan. **Holi,** the festival of colours, marks the climax of spring. The previous night bonfires are lit in parts of North India symbolizing the end of winter (and conquering of evil). People have fun throwing coloured powder and water at each other and in the evening some gamble with friends. If you don't mind getting covered in colours, you can risk going out but celebrations can sometimes get very rowdy (and unpleasant). Some worship Krishna who defeated the demon Putana.

**April Mahavir Jayanti. Baisakhi** – North India.

**April/May Buddha Jayanti,** the first full moon night in April/May marks the birth of the Buddha. **Pooram** – Thrissur, Kerala.

**June/July Rath Yatra** – Puri, Orissa. **Hemis Festival** – Leh, Ladakh. **Teej** – Jaipur, Rajasthan.

**July/August** **Raksha (or Rakhi) Bandhan** symbolizes the bond between brother and sister, celebrated mainly in North India at full-moon. A sister says special prayers for her brother and ties colouredthreads around his wrist to remind him of the special bond. He in turn gives a gift and promises to protect and care for her. Sometimes *rakshas* are exchanged as a mark of friendship. **Narial Purnima** on the same full-moon. Hindus, particularly in coastal areas of West and South India, make offerings of *narial* (coconuts) to the Vedic god Varuna (Lord of the waters) by throwing them into the sea. **15 August** is **Independence Day**, a national secular holiday is marked by special events, and in Delhi there is an impressive flag hoisting ceremony at the Red Fort. **Ganesh Chaturthi** was established just over 100 years ago by the Indian nationalist leader Tilak. The elephant-headed God of good omen is shown special reverence. On the last of the five-day festival after harvest, clay images of Ganesh are taken in procession with dancers and musicians, and are immersed in the sea, river or pond.

**August/September** **Janmashtami**, the birth of Krishna is celebrated at midnight at Krishna temples. Special festivities are held in Mathura his birth place and nearby at Vrindavan where Rasalilas (dance dramas) are performed through the night.

**September/October** **Dasara** has many local variations. In North India, celebrations for the nine nights *(navaratri)* are marked with **Ramlila**, various episodes of the Ramayana story (see page 1327) are enacted with particular reference to the battle between the forces of good and evil. In some parts of India it celebrates *Rama*'s victory over the Demon king *Ravana* of Lanka with the help of loyal *Hanuman* (Monkey). Huge effigies of *Ravana* made of bamboo and paper are burnt on the 10th day (*Vijaya dasami*) of **Dasara** in public open spaces. In other regions the focus is on Durga's victory over the demon *Mahishasura*. Bengal celebrates **Durga** puja. **Onam** – Kerala.

**October/November** **2 October Gandhi Jayanti**, Mahatma Gandhi's birthday, is remembered with prayer meetings and devotional singing. **Diwali/Deepavali** (Sanskrit *ideepa* lamp), the festival of lights, is celebrated particularly in North India. Some Hindus celebrate Krishna's victory over the demon *Narakasura*, some Rama's return after his 14 years' exile in the forest when citizens lit his way with oil lamps, see also page 1341. The festival falls on the dark *chaturdasi* (14th) night (the one preceding the new moon), when rows of lamps or candles are lit in remembrance, and *rangolis* are painted on the floor as a sign of welcome. Fireworks have become an integral part of the celebration which are often set off days before Diwali. Equally, Lakshmi, the Goddess of Wealth (as well as Ganesh) is worshipped by merchants and the business community who open the new financial year's account on the day. Most people wear new clothes; some play games of chance. In Bengal **Kali Puja** is celebrated the day before Diwali but is a wholly distinct festival. **Pushkar Fair** – Rajasthan. **Guru Nanak Jayanti** commemorates the birth of Guru Nanak. **Akhand Pat** (unbroken reading of the holy book) takes place and the book itself (*Granth*) is taken out in procession. **Sonepur Fair** – Bihar.

**December** **25 December Christmas Day** sees Indian Christians celebrate the birth of Christ in much the same way as in the West; many churches hold services/mass at midnight. There is an air of festivity in city markets which are specially decorated and illuminated. **31 December** Over **New Year's Eve** hotel prices peak and large supplements are added for meals and entertainment in the upper category hotels. Some churches mark the night with a Midnight Mass. **Shekhavati Festival** – Rajasthan. **Hampi-Vijaynagar Festival** – Karnataka.

## Muslim holy days

These are fixed according to the lunar calendar, see page 1338. According to the Gregorian calendar, they tend to fall 11 days earlier each year, dependent on the sighting of the new moon.

**Ramadan** is the start of the month of fasting when all Muslims (except young children, the very elderly, the sick, pregnant women and travellers) must abstain from food and drink, from sunrise to sunset.

**Id ul Fitr** is the three-day festival that marks the end of Ramadan.

**Id-ul-Zuha/Bakr-Id** is when Muslims commemorate Ibrahim's sacrifice of his son according to God's commandment; the main time of pilgrimage to Mecca (the Hajj). It is marked by the sacrifice of a goat, feasting and alms giving.

**Muharram** is when the killing of the Prophet's grandson, Hussain, is commemorated by Shi'a Muslims. Decorated *tazias* (replicas of the martyr's tomb) are carried in procession by devout wailing followers who beat their chests to express their grief. Hyderabad and Lucknow are famous for their grand *tazias*. Shi'as fast for the 10 days.



# Shopping

*Export of certain items is controlled or banned, see page 39.*

India excels in producing fine crafts at affordable prices through the tradition of passing down of ancestral skills. The country is a vast market place but there are regional specializations. If you are planning to travel widely, wait to find the best places to buy specific items. You can get handicrafts of different states from the government emporia in the major cities which guarantee quality at fixed prices (no bargaining), but many are poorly displayed, not helped by reluctant and unenthusiastic staff. Private upmarket shops and top hotel arcades offer better quality, choice and service but at a price. Vibrant and colourful local bazars are often a great experience but you must be prepared to bargain.

Bargaining can be fun and quite satisfying. It is best to get an idea of prices being asked by different stalls for items you are interested in, before taking the plunge. Some shopkeepers will happily quote twice the actual price to a foreigner showing interest, so you might well start by halving the asking price. On the other hand it would be inappropriate to do the same in an established shop with price-tags, though a plea for the 'best price' might reap results even here. Remain good humoured throughout. Walking away slowly might be the test to ascertain whether your custom is sought and you are called back!

Taxi/rickshaw/hire car drivers and tour guides sometimes insist on recommending certain shops where they expect a commission, but prices there are invariably inflated. Some shops offer to pack and post your purchases but small private shops can't always be trusted. Unless you have a specific recommendation from a person you know, only make such arrangements in government emporia or a large store. Don't enter into any arrangement to help 'export' marble items, jewellery etc which a shopkeeper may propose by making tempting promises of passing on some of the profits to you. Several have been cheated through misuse of their credit card accounts, and being left with unwanted purchases. Make sure that credit cards are not 'run off' more than once when making a purchase.

## Carpets and dhurries

The superb hand-knotted carpets of Kashmir, using old Persian designs woven in wool or silk or both, are hard to beat for their beauty and quality. Kashmiri traders can now be found throughout India, wherever there is hint of foreign tourism. Agra too has a long tradition of producing wool carpets and welcomes visitors to their factories. Tibetan refugees in Darjeeling and Gangtok produce excellent carpets which are less expensive but of very high quality. They will make carpets to order and parcel post them safely. Flat woven cotton dhurries in subtle colours are best seen in Rajasthan,

## Jewellery

Whether it is chunky tribal necklaces from the Himalaya, heavy 'silver' bangles from Rajasthan, fine Orissan filigree, legendary pearls from Hyderabad, Jaipuri uncut gems set in gold or semi-precious stones in silver, or glass bangles from Varanasi, the visitor is drawn to the arcade shop window as much as the way-side stall. It is best to buy from reputable shops as street stalls often pass off fake ivory, silver, gems, stones and coral as real. Make sure your knowledge is up to scratch if considering investing in gems or jewellery, and never be persuaded to buy for an unknown third-party.

## Metal work

The choice is vast – from brass, copper and white-metal plates and bowls in the North, with ornate patterns or plain polished surfaces, exquisite Jaipuri enamelled silver pill boxes, tribal lost-wax *dhokra* toys from Orissa, Bihar and Bengal, Nawabi silver-on-gun metal Bidri pieces from around Hyderabad, to exceptional copies of Chola bronzes cast near Thanjavur.

## Paintings

Coveted contemporary Indian art is exhibited in modern galleries in the state capitals often at a fraction of London or New York prices. Traditional 'Mughal' miniatures, sometimes using natural pigments on old paper (don't be fooled) and new silk, are reaching mass production levels in Rajasthan's back alleys. Fine examples can still be found in good crafts shops.

## Stoneware

Artisans in Agra inspired by the Taj Mahal continue the tradition of inlaying tiny pieces of gem stones on fine white marble, to produce something for every pocket, from a small coaster to a large table top. Softer soap stone is cheaper. Stone temple carvings are produced for sale in Tamil Nadu (try Mahabalipuram), Orissa (Puri, Konark) and Uttar Pradesh (near Hamirpur).

## Textiles

Handlooms produce rich shot silk from Kanchipuram, skillful *ikat* from Gujarat, Orissa and Andhra, brocades from Varanasi, golden *muga* from Assam, printed silks and batiks from Bengal or opulent *Himroo* shawls from Aurangabad. Sober handspun *khadi*, colourful Rajasthani block-printed cottons using vegetable dyes, tribal weaving from remote Himalayan villages, and tie-and-dye Gujarati *bandhni* are easier on the pocket. Kashmiri embroidery on wool, Lucknowi *chickan* shadow work on fine voil or *zari* (gold/silver thread) work on silk, produce unique pieces. The *pashmina* shawl and scarf from Kashmir have travelled to every continent and are available in dozens of colours at less inflated prices. They come in various widths and quality (often mixed with silk). See page 547. All trade in tush (toosh) wool is banned.

### Wood craft

Each region has its special wood – walnut in Kashmir, sandalwood in Mysore, rosewood in the South, sheesham in the North. Carving, inlay and lacquer work are specialities. The southern states produce fine carved wooden panels and images which are sold through the state emporia (they offer a posting service).

# Sport and activities

Opportunities in adventure sports are now being offered. Such thrills can be combined with more conventional sightseeing. Apart from the activities listed here, you can also try ballooning, heli-skiing, hang-gliding, mountain or rock climbing and even motor rallying. There are skiing resorts in Himachal Pradesh, namely Manali and Narkanda, but they do not compare with western resorts.



## Participation sports

### Biking

For those keen on moving faster along the road, discover the joys of travelling on the two wheels of a motorbike. The 350cc Enfield Bullets are particularly attractive. Vespa, Kinetic Honda and other makes of scooters in India are slower than motorbikes but comfortable for short hauls of less than 100 km and have the advantage of a 'dicky' for spares, and a spare tyre. See page 55.

### Bird watching

The country's diverse and rich natural habitats harbour over 1,200 species of birds of which around 150 are endemic. Visitors to all parts of the country can enjoy spotting Oriental species whether it is in towns and cities, in the country side or more abundantly in the national parks and sanctuaries. On the plains, the cooler months (November to March) are the most comfortable for a chance to see migratory birds from the hills, but the highlands themselves are ideal between May and June and again after the monsoons when visibility improves in October and November. Water bodies large and small draw visiting water fowl from other continents during the winter.

It is quite easy to get to some parks from the important tourist centres, for example Keoladeo Ghana (Bharatpur) in Rajasthan, Sultanpur in Haryana, Chilika, in Orissa, Pulicat and Vedanthangal in Tamil Nadu, Ranganathittoo in Karnataka, Tadoba, in Maharashtra and Nal Sarovar in Gujarat. *A Birdwatcher's Guide to India* by Krys Kazmierczak and Raj Singh, published by Prion Ltd, Sandy, Bedfordshire, UK, 1998, is well researched and comprehensive with helpful practical information and maps.

The government's **Salim Ali Centre for Ornithology and Natural History** (SACON) is in Coimbatore. Useful websites include www.orientalbirdclub.org, and biks@giasdl01.vsnl.net.in, for **Bird Link**, concerned with conservation of birds and their habitat.

### Camel safaris

Today's camel safaris try to recreate something of the atmosphere of the early camel trains. The Thar desert, in Rajasthan, with its vast stretches of sand, dotted with dunes and its own specially adapted shrubs and wildlife is ideal territory. The guides are expert navigators and the villages on the way add colour to an unforgettable experience, if you are prepared to sit out the somewhat uncomfortable ride, see page 398.

## Himalayan environment trust code of practice

**Deforestation** Make no open fires and discourage others making one for you. Limit use of firewood and heated water and use only permitted dead wood. Choose accommodation where kerosene or fuel-efficient wood burning stoves are used.

**Litter** Remove it. Burn or bury paper and carry away non-degradable litter. If you find other people's litter, remove their's too! Pack food in biodegradable containers.

**Water** Keep local water clean. Do not use detergents and pollutants in streams and springs. Where there are no toilets be sure you are at least 30 m away from water source and bury or cover. Do not allow cooks or porters to throw rubbish in nearby streams and rivers.

**Plants** Do not take cuttings, seeds and roots – it is illegal in all parts of the Himalaya.

**Begging** Giving to children can encourage begging. Donations to a project, health centre or school may be more constructive.

Be aware of **local traditions** and **cultures**; respect their **privacy**, and ask permission before taking photographs; respect their **holy places**, never touching or removing religious objects, and removing shoes before entering temples; be aware of local **etiquette**, dressing modestly particularly when visiting temples and shrines and while walking through villages avoiding shorts, skimpy tops and tight-fitting outfits. Do not hold hands and kiss in public.



## Cycling

Cycling offers a peaceful – not to mention healthy – alternative to cars, buses or trains. Touring on locally hired bicycles is possible along country roads in Rajasthan, Uttaranchal and South India – ideal if you want to see village life in India and the lesser known wildlife parks. Consult a good Indian agent for advice. For example, a week's cycling trip could cover about 250 km in the Garhwal foothills, starting in Rishikesh, passing through the Corbett and Rajaji National Parks over easy gradients, to finish in Ramnagar. Expert guides, cycles and support vehicle, accommodation in simple resthouses or tents, are included.

## Horse safaris

Gaining in popularity they are offered in Rajasthan, particularly in the Shekhawati area, and south of Jodhpur around Sodawas and Kumbhalgarh. Conditions are similar to camel safaris with grooms (and often the horse owner) accompanying. The best months are November to March when it is cooler in the day (and often cold at night). The trails chosen usually enable you to visit small villages, old forts and temples, and take you through a variety of terrain and vegetation including scrub covered arid plains to forested hills. The charges can be a lot higher than for a camel safari but the night stays are often in comfortable palaces, forts or *havelis*.

## Snooker

Invented in the hill station clubs of British India, snooker has become increasingly popular in major cities across the country. Snooker halls have tables available for hire by the hour, and are often crowded with young people. They can be dimly lit and have loud music, but they also attract young families. Arcade games, sometimes harking back to those popular in the West in the early 90s, have their own devotees among the young.

## Watersports

Sun, sand and warm waters for safe swimming are not the only attractions along the long stretches of unspoilt coastal India. Select beaches in Goa, and the crystal clear waters around the Andamans and the Laccadive islands, are excellent for diving. Snorkelling is possible more widely, as well as parasailing, wind surfing and water skiing. The scuba diving centres are on Miramar Beach and Bogmalo in Goa, on Havelock Island and the Marine National Park in the Andamans, and on Bangaram in the Lakshadweeps. Courses are well-run and cost around US$75 for an introductory dive, US$350 for four days, or US$600 for a two-week Dive Master course. To check details of approved courses contact **PADI International**, Head Office, Unit 6, Unicorn Park, Whitby Road, Bristol, BS4 4EX, T0117-9711717, general@Tadi.co.uk or **PADI Europe**, Oberwilerstrasse 3, CH-8442, Hettlingen, Switzerland, T052-3041414, admin@Tadi.ch In addition, coastal resorts in Kerala and Goa offer fishing trips and dolphin viewing during the season, sometimes combining these with a beach barbecue.



## Whitewater rafting

The snow-fed rivers which flow through Kashmir, Himachal, Uttaranchal and Sikkim offer excellent whitewater rafting. The popular waters range from grades II-III for amateurs (Zanskar, Indus) to the greater challenges of grades IV-VI for the experienced (eg Chenab, Beas, Sutlej, Rangit, Tons). The options range from a half-day trip to one lasting several days, and again allows a chance to see scenery, places and people off the beaten track. The trips are organized and managed by professional teams who have trained abroad. The rivers can sometimes be dangerous in August and September.

## Yoga and meditation

There has been a growing Western interest in the ancient life-disciplines in search of physical and spiritual wellbeing, as practised in ancient India. Yoga is supposed to regulate the nervous system and aims to attain perfect equilibrium through the practice of *asanas* (body postures), breath control, discipline, cleansing, contemplation and awareness. It seeks to achieve moral purification through abstinence and restraint (dietary and sexual). Meditation which complements yoga to relieve stress, increase awareness and bring inner peace prescribes *dhyana* (purposeful concentration) by withdrawing oneself from external distractions and focusing ones attention to consciousness itself. This leads ultimately to *samadhi* (release from worldly bonds). At the practical level *Hatha Yoga* has captured the Western imagination as it promises good health through postural exercises, while the search for inner peace and calm drive others to learn meditation techniques.

Centres across the country offer courses for beginners and practitioners. Some are at special resort hotels which offer all inclusive packages in idyllic locations, some advocate simple communal living in an ashram while others may require rigorous discipline in austere monastic surroundings. Whether you wish to embark on a serious study of yoga or sample an hour's introductory meditation session, India offers opportunities for all, though you may need to apply in advance for some popular courses. Popular centres in places frequented by travellers are listed thoughout the book. **International Yoga Festival** is held in Rishikesh in the Himalayan foothills, each February.

*As are the Irish to the English and the Belgians to the French, so are the Sikhs to rest of the Indian population. Harbhajan Singh, one of the Indian cricket team's most successful spin bowlers, and more commonly known as the 'Turbanator', is frequently lampooned in national advertising campaigns.*

# Trekking

The Himalaya offers unlimited opportunities to view not only the natural beauty of mountains and the unique flora and fauna, but also the diverse groups of people who live in the ranges and valleys, many of whom have retained unique cultural identities because of their isolation. The treks described in this Handbook are only for guidance. They try to give you a flavour of an area or a destination. Some trails fall within the 'Inner Line' for which special **permits** are required. Other parts of India offer attractive options for hikers. For more detailed information, see Footprint's Indian Himalaya Handbook. See also Books, page 1364.

*Always carry your passport. Without one you can be turned back or, if in a restricted area, be deported at one of the regular trekking permit inspection points.*

## Types of trekking

**Independent trekking** There are some outstandingly beautiful treks, though they are often not through the 'wilderness' sometimes conjured up. However, trekking alone is not recommended as you will be in unfamiliar territory where you may not be able to communicate with the local people and if injured you may not have help at hand. Independent trekkers should get a specialist publication with detailed route descriptions and a good map. Remember, mountain topography is subject to constant change, and tracks and crossings can be affected very rapidly. Speak to those who know the area well and have been trekking to the places you intend visiting.

**Backpacking camping** Hundreds of people arrive each year with a pack and some personal equipment, buy some food and set off trekking, carrying their own gear and choosing their own campsites or places to stay. Serious trekkers will need a framed backpack. Supplies of fuel wood are scarce and flat ground suitable for camping rare. It is not always easy to find isolated and 'private' campsites.

**Trekking without a tent** Although common in Nepal, only a few trails in India offer the ease and comfort of this option. Exceptions are the Singalila Ridge trail in the Darjeeling area, the Sikkim Kanchenjunga trek, the Markha Valley trek in Ladakh and some lower elevation trails around Shimla and Manali. On these, it is often possible to stay in 'trekking huts' or in simple village homes. You carry clothes and bedding, as with youth hostelling, and for a few rupees a night you get a space on the floor, a wooden pallet or a camp bed, or in the more luxurious inns, a room and shower. The food is simple, usually vegetable curry, rice and *daal* which although repetitive, is healthy and can be tasty. This approach brings you into more contact with the local population, the limiting factor being the routes where accommodation is available.

**Locally organized treks** Porters can usually be hired through an agent in the town or village at the start of a trek. Porters hired in the bazar may be cheaper than agency porters but may be unreliable. Make sure they are experienced in carrying loads over distances at high altitude. They will help carry your baggage, sometimes cook for you, and communicate with the local people. A good porter will know the area and some can tell you about local customs and point out interesting details en route. Away from roads, the footpath is the principal line of communication between villages. Tracks tend to be very good, well graded and in good condition. In remoter areas away from all habitation, tracks may be indistinct and a local guide is recommended. Although some porters speak a little English (or another foreign language) you may have communication problems and misunderstandings. Remember, you may be expected to provide your porter's warm clothing and protective wear including shoes, gloves and goggles on high altitude treks.

Hiring a *sardar* and crew is more expensive but well worthwhile since he will speak some English, act as a guide, take care of engaging porters and cooks, arrange for provisions and sort out all logistical problems. A *sardar* will cost more and although he may be prepared to carry a load, his principal function will be as a guide and overseer for the porters. Make sure your *sardar* is experienced in the area you will be travelling in and can show good references which are his own and not borrowed.

**Using a trekking agent** Trekking agents based in Delhi or at hill stations (eg Dehradun, Shimla, Manali, Dharamshala, Leh, Darjeeling, Gangtok) will organize treks for a fee and provide a *sardar*, porters, cooks, food and equipment, but it requires effort and careful thought on your part. This method can be excellent and is recommended for a group, preferably with some experience, that wants to follow a specific itinerary.

You have to follow a pre-arranged itinerary in some areas, as required by the government, and also as porters expect to arrive at certain points on schedule. You can make arrangements from abroad in advance; often a protracted business with faxes and emails. Alternatively, wait until you get to India but allow at least a week to make arrangements.

**Fully organized and escorted trek** A company or individual with local knowledge and expertise organizes a trip and sells it. Some or all camp equipment, food, cooking, planning the stages, decision-making based on progress and weather conditions, liaison with porters, shopkeepers etc are all taken care of. When operating abroad, the agency may take care of all travel arrangements, ticketing, visas and permits. Make sure that both you and the trekking company understand exactly who is to provide what equipment. This has the advantage of being a good, safe introduction to the country. You will be able to travel with limited knowledge of the region and its culture and get to places more easily which as an individual you might not reach, without the expense of completely kitting yourself out. You should read and follow any advice in the preparatory material you are sent, as your enjoyment greatly depends on it.

An escorted trek involves going with a group; you will camp together but not necessarily all walk together. If you are willing to trade some of your independence for careful, efficient organization and make the effort to ensure the group works well together, the experience can be very rewarding. Ideally there should be no more than 20 trekkers (preferably around 12). Companies have reputations to maintain and try to comply with western concepts of hygiene. Before booking, check the itinerary (is it too demanding, or not adventurous enough?), whether the leader is qualified and is familiar with the route, and what exactly is provided by way of equipment.

## Local agents

Tourist offices and government approved trekking agents in **Delhi** and the hill stations will organize fairly inexpensive treks (on some routes, it is compulsory to trek in this way). Tour operators and travel agents are listed in each town. The following are recommended:

**Ibex**, G-66 East of Kailash, T26912641, www.ibexexpeditions.com.

**Mountain Adventures**, A-51, SFS Mount Kailash, New Delhi, T011 2622 2202, www.mountainindia.com.

**NEI (Nature Expedition India)**, B-966 Ansals Palam Vihar, Gurgaon, New Delhi Suburb, T0124-2368601,www.himalaya-india.com

**Peak Adventure Tours**, T-305 DAV Building, DDA Shopping Complex, Magur Vihar Phase-1, T22713483, www.peakadventuretours.com

**Snow Leaopard Adventures**, T011 2612 2775, www.snowleopardadventures.com.

**Wanderlust**,G-18,2nd floor, Masjid Moth, Greater Kailash Part-II, New Delhi-110048 T0115163 9347, www.wanderlustindia.com.

The following government organizations can advise and organize treks:

**Garhwal Mandal Vikas Nigam**, Kailash Gate, By Pass Rd, Rishikesh, T01364 2430372.
**Himalayan Mountaineering Institutes**, in hill stations in Uttaranchal and Himachal and Darjeeling, West Bengal.
**Kumaon Mandal Vikas Nigam**, Secretariat, Mallital, Nainital, T/F05942 236209.

## Foreign operators

These offer relatively expensive trips to include food, porters, cooks, *sardar* (guide), mess and toilet tents.

**Australia and New Zealand**
**Adventure World**, Sydney, T99567766; Auckland, T5245118.
**Himalayan Travellers**, Wellington, T863325.
**Peregrine Adventures**, Melbourne, T96638661.

**UK**
**Exodus**, T0870 2405550, www.exodus.co.uk.
**Explore Worldwide**, T0870 333 4001, info@explore.co.uk.
**High Places**, T0114-2757500, www.highplaces.co.uk.
**Himalayan Kingdoms**, T0845 3308579, www.himalayankingdoms.com.
**KE Adventure**, T01768-773966, www.keadventure.com.
**Snow Lion Expeditions**, T0800-5258735, www.snowlion.com.

**USA**
**High Adventure Travel**, T1877 247 8735, www.airtreks.com.
**Mercury**, T0800-2231474.
**Mountain Travel Sobek**, T1 510 5946000, www.mtsobek.com.

## Trekking seasons

These vary with the area you plan to visit and the elevation. Autumn is best in most parts of the Himalaya though March to May can be pleasant. The monsoons (mid-June to end-September) can obviously be very wet and localized thunderstorms can occur at any time, particularly in the spring and summer. Start your trek early in the morning as the monsoon approaches. It often continues to rain heavily up to mid-October in the eastern Himalaya. The Kullu valley is unsuitable for trekking during the monsoons but areas beyond the central Himalayan range, eg Ladakh, Zanskar, Lahul and Spiti are largely unaffected. Be prepared for extremes in temperatures in all seasons so come prepared with light clothing as well as enough waterproof protection. Winters can be exceptionally cold; high passes can be closed and you need more equipment. Winter treks on all but a few low-altitude ones (up to 3,200 m) are only recommended for the experienced trekker accompanied by a knowledgeable local guide.

**West Himalaya: Garhwal and Kumaon Himalaya Uttaranchal** (pages 228-232) This area is an all-season trekking destination because of its variety of climate and terrain. It is perhaps best in May-June when days are cool and clear. Even with the onset of the monsoons when mist covers the mountains you may get breaks in the rain of three or four days. Clouds can lift to give you some good mountain views but equipment may feel a little damp. The mountains are best for flowers in July-August. Late September to mid-November is again good for trekking.
**Himachal** (pages 534-540) The best times are as in Garhwal and Kumaon. The monsoon (mid-July to mid-September) is generally very wet and offer no mountain views. Trekking is usually possible from May to October when most passes are open (the Parvati Pass may be blocked until early July). In July-September high altitude flowers are in bloom including summer rhododendrons.
**Kashmir** (Kashmir, currently risky because of the political situation, Ladakh, page 565 and Zanskar, page 568) Trekking is ideal between April-November. In Ladakh (the area open to trekkers), the motorable road from Manali to Leh is normally open from mid-June to October though flights to Leh from Delhi operate all year round. Most treks cross passes above 4,500 m and are passable from early July to September.
**East Himalaya: Darjeeling area** (pages 617-619) April-May has a chance of occasional showers but the rhododendrons and magnolias are in full bloom;

## Water purification

There are various ways of purifying water in order to make it safe to drink. Dirty water should first be strained through a filter bag, and then boiled or treated.

Bringing water to a rolling **boil** at sea level is sufficient to make water safe for drinking, but at higher altitudes you have to boil the water for longer to ensure that all the microbes are killed.

Various sterilizing methods can be used and there are propriety preparations containing **chlorine** (eg 'Puritabs') or **iodine** (eg 'Pota Aqua') compounds. Chlorine compounds generally do not kill protozoa (eg giardia). Prolonged usage of iodine compounds may lead to thyroid problems, although this is rare if used for less than a year.

There are a number of **water filters** now on the market, available both in personal and expedition size. There are two types of water filter, **mechanical** and **chemical**. Mechanical filters are usually a combination of carbon, ceramic and paper, although they can be difficult to use. Although cheaper, the disadvantage of mechanical filters is that they do not always remove viruses or protozoa. Chemical filters use a combination of an iodine resin filter and a mechanical filter. The advantage is that according to the manufacturers' claims, everything in the water will be killed. The disadvantage is that the filters need replacing, adding a third to the price.

October-November is usually dry with excellent visibility. Early December is possible but very cold.

**Sikkim** (page 650) Mid-February to late May and again October-early December are possible; April-May, October-November are best.

**Away from the Himalaya** Some hill stations offer opportunities for short treks. Generally, November to March is best.

**Satpura** (Madhya Pradesh) Pachmarhi to Mahadeo and Dhupgarh peaks.

**Aravallis** (Rajasthan) Mount Abu to Shikhar, Achalgarh and Gaumukh.

**Western Ghats: Karnataka** Madikere, Tala Cauvery, Igutappa, Tadiandamole, Virajpet, Ponnampet, Srimangala, Nagarhole.

**Kerala** On the Ghats, from Munnar and Ponmudi.

**Nilgiris** Udhagamandalam (Ooty), Coonoor, Pollachi, Topslip, Monamboli, Valparai, Grass Hills, Vaguvarai, Chanduvarai, Kilavarai, Kodaikkanal. The hills can be damp during November-December and are best from January to May.

## Trekking permits

Trekking is permitted in all areas other than those described as Restricted or Protected and within the **'Inner Line'**, so that you may not go close to the international boundary in many places. Often, destinations falling within these 'sensitive' zones which have recently been opened for trekking, require treks to be organized by a recognized Indian Travel Agent for groups of at least four, travelling on a specified route, accompanied by a representative/liaison officer. Sometimes there are restrictions on the maximum number of days, season and type of transport used. The 'Inner Line' runs parallel and 40 km inside the international boundary; Kaza (Himachal Pradesh), however, is now open to group trekkers though overnight stay is not allowed at Puh, Khabo or Sumdo. Other areas now open to tourists include Kalindi Khal (Garhwal), Milam Glacier (Kumaon), Khardung La, Tso Moriri and Pangong (Ladakh), Tsangu Lake, Lachung and Yumthang (Sikkim) and Kameng Valley (Arunachal Pradesh). On arrival in India, Government approved trekking agencies can obtain permits relatively easily, usually within three or four days. It can be much slower applying for trekking permits from abroad and may also slow down your visa application.Some restricted areas are still totally closed to foreigners. For other restricted areas, permits are issued at the Foreigners' Regional Registration Offices in Delhi, Mumbai, Kolkata and Chennai (and sometimes at a local FRRO), from Immigration officers at some points of entry, and sometimes at the District Magistrate's. There are also entrance fees for the various national parks and conservation areas which can be as much as Rs 350 for foreigners.

## Mountaineering courses

Information on mountaineering is available from: **Indian Mountaineering Federation**, Benito Juarez Marg, New Delhi.

Courses in mountaineering, skiing, high altitude trekking and mountain-rescue: **Garhwal Mandal Vikas Nigam** (GMVN), Muni-ki-Reti, Rishikesh.

**Himalayan Mountaineering Institute**, Nehru Hill, Darjeeling.

**Mountaineering Institute** and **Allied Sports Complex**, 1½ km out of Manali.

**The Nehru Institute of Mountaineering**, Uttarkashi.

## Equipment and clothing

If you have good equipment, it is worth taking it, especially your own boots. Mountaineering and trekking equipment can sometimes be hired from various hill stations. Ask the *Institutes of Mountaineering* and tourist offices there. Guard against cold, wet, sudden changes of temperature, strong sun and wind! Waterproof jacket with hood and over-trousers (windproof, waterproof and 'breather' type); warm sweater; 'fleece' jacket; tracksuit; hiking trousers or shorts (knee length but not cycling); cotton T shirts; cotton underwear; thermal underwear (vests, longjohns); gloves; balaclava or ski toque; sun hat; swimwear. Try to carry lightweight, quick-drying fabrics that can be easily washed in cold water streams. (After the trek, you might consider offering clothes you can part with to your porter.) Good lightweight walking boots with ankle support should be comfortable and well worn in, as blisters can ruin a trek; spare laces, good trainers (for resting the feet; also suitable for many low-level treks except in snow and off-the-trails); polypropylene undersocks, heavy walking socks. Sunglasses (with UV filter), snow glasses if you are planning to go above the snow line, high-factor sun block (15+), lip cream, a good sleeping bag (cheap ones from a local market are unsuitable above 4,000 m) plus cotton liner, a Thermarest pad or a double thickness foam sleeping mat, 2 m square plastic sheet (sold locally), torch (flashlight) with replacement batteries or a Petzl headtorch, a compass, binoculars, insulated bag water-bottle (to also take to bed!), a day pack, a tent (in certain areas). Those expecting to climb high, cross glaciers etc may need to hire crampons, ice axes, snow gaiters, ropes etc as well as a silver survival blanket and a reinforced plastic 'bivouac bag'. A kerosene stove and strong fuel container suitable for high altitudes (kerosene is widely available); water filter and containers; nesting cooking pots (at least two); enamel mug and spoon and bags for provisions. Be sure to eat a balanced diet. Local foods will be available along the trail, and in fact the porters' meal of *chapati* or rice, vegetables, daal and sweet milky tea is quite nutritious. Some shops stock limited amounts of dry goods for trekkers (noodles, chocolate bars, canned foods, fruit, nuts, porridge oats etc). You might prefer to take some freeze-dried packs of favourites from home. Remember to thoroughly boil the fresh (unpasteurized) local milk.

## Maps

Survey of India has started producing trekking maps, Scale 1:250,000; a few only are available covering the Himachal and Uttaranchal areas. For details see page 55. **Leomann** Indian Himalaya maps (1:200,000) cover Uttaranchal, Himachal Pradesh and Jammu and Kashmir in eight sheets (1987-1994), and give descriptive itineraries of trekking routes. The **US Army Series (AMS)** U502 at the scale of 1:250,000 are available from selected booksellers in the United States and Europe. Showing contours at 250 or 500 ft, the series was completed before 1960, so some features, notably roads, are out of date. However, they provide good topographic information.

## Spectator sports

### Cricket

India's greatest popular entertainment has become sport, with cricket in particular having a fanatical following across the country. Reinforced by satellite TV and radio, and a national side that enjoys high world rankings and much outstanding individual talent, stars have cult status, and you can see children trying to model themselves on their game on any and every open space. The national side's greatest moment was, arguably, winning the 1983 World Cup. When foreign national sides tour India, tickets are remarkably easy to come by (for Test matches at least), and are considerably cheaper than for corresponding fixtures back home. Tickets are often sold through local bank branches.

### Football (Soccer)

Football is increasing in popularity across India, notably in the professional leagues of Goa and West Bengal. The crowds generate tremendous fervour for the big matches, and standards are improving. African players are now featuring more frequently with Indian teams and monthly salaries have risen to over Rs 40,000 per month, a very good wage by Indian standards.

# Health

It should be no surprise that since parts of India remain poor that health services are basic and that communicable diseases are an ever-present threat. However, there is a thriving private sector – up to 70% of all health care. Health care in the region is varied: there are some decent private and government clinics/hospitals, which more often than not follow the more aggressive American style of medicine (where you will be referred straight to a specialist) but as with all medical care, first impressions count.

### Before you go

Ideally, you should see your GP or travel clinic at least six weeks before your departure for general advice on travel risks, malaria and vaccinations. Make sure you have travel insurance, get a dental check (especially if you are going to be away for more than a month), know your own blood group and if you suffer a long-term condition such as diabetes or epilepsy make sure someone knows or that you have a Medic Alert bracelet/necklace with this information on it.

| **Vaccination** | **Obligatory** | **Recommended** |
|---|---|---|
| **Polio** | | Yes if nil in last 10 years |
| **Tetanus** | Yes if nil in last 10 years (but after 5 doses you have had enough for life) | |
| **Typhoid** | | Yes if nil in last three years |
| **Rabies** | | Yes for most areas |
| **Hepatitis A** | | Yes - the disease can be caught easily from food/water |
| **BCG** | | Yes if staying for more than one month |

**Yellow Fever** does not exist in the country and the Indians want to keep it that way, and so require evidence of vaccination if you have recently travelled from Africa or South America.

**Malaria** India is a real medical advice conundrum for malaria. Malaria risk is mainly of the P.vivax type and exists throughout the year even in the major cities of Delhi, Mumbai and Kolkata. The deadly P.falciparum malaria also exists. Areas currently free of malaria include Kashmir, Sikkim, Jammu and Himachal Pradesh. The choice of malaria drug depends on where you will travel, which type of malaria you may be exposed to, and your medical/psychological history. However, it should be noted that the British and the US have different views of the level of resistance to chloroquine. The US believe the resistance is too high to recommend chloroquine but we still recommend it - this advice may change. Some countries advise early treatment rather than drug prophylaxis. Always check with your doctor or travel clinic for the most up to date advice.



## What to take

**Mosquito repellents**: remember that DEET (Di-ethyltoluamide) is the gold standard. Apply the repellent every four to six hours but more often if you are sweating heavily. If a non-DEET product is used check who tested it. Validated products (tested at the London School of Hygiene and Tropical Medicine) include Mosiguard, Non-DEET Jungle formula and non-DEET Autan. If you want to use citronella remember that it must be applied very frequently (ie hourly) to be effective. If you are popular target for insect bites or develop lumps quite soon after being bitten, carry an Aspivenin kit. This syringe suction device is available from many chemists and draws out some of the allergic materials and provides quick relief. **Sun block: Pain killers:** Remember that more than eight paractemol a day can lead to liver failure. **Ciproxin (Ciprofloxacin):** a useful antibiotic for some forms of travellers diarrhoea (see below). **Anti-malarials:** start times for the anti-malarials vary in that if you have never taken Lariam (Mefloquine) before it is advised to start it at least two to three weeks before the entry to a malarial zone (to help identify serious side-effects early). Chloroquine and Paludrine are often started a week before the trip to establish a pattern but Doxycycline and Malarone can be started only one-two days before entry to the malarial area. **Immodium (Pepto-Bismol** is similar and used a lot in USA): a great standby for those diarrhoeas that occur at awkward times (ie before a long coach/train journey or on a trek). It helps stop the flow of diarrhoea and in my view is of more benefit than harm. It was believed that letting the bacteria or viruses flow out had to be more beneficial. However, with Immodium they still come out, just in a more solid form. For longer trips involving jungle treks taking a clean **needle pack**, clean **dental pack** and **water filtration devices** are common-sense measures.

# An A-Z of health risks

The greater disease risk in India is caused by the greater volume of disease carriers in the shape of mosquitoes and sandflies. The key viral disease is Dengue fever, which is transmitted by a mosquito that bites during the day. The disease is like a very nasty form of the 'flu with two-three days of illness, followed by a short period of recovery, then a second attack of illness. Westerners very rarely get the worst haemorrhagic form of the disease. Bacterial diseases include tuberculosis (TB) and some causes of the more common traveller's diarrhoea. The parasitic diseases are many but the two key ones are malaria and Indian trypanosomiasis (known as Chagas Disease).

## Altitude Sickness

**Symptoms** This can creep up on you as just a mild headache with nausea or lethargy during your visit to the Himalayas. The more serious disease is caused by fluid collecting in the brain in the enclosed space of the skull and can lead to coma and death. There is also a lung disease version with breathlessness and fluid infiltration of the lungs.

**Cures** The best cure is to descend as soon as possible.

**Prevention** Get acclimatized. Do not try to reach the highest levels on your first few days of arrival. Try to avoid flying directly into the cities of highest altitude. Climbers like to take treatment drugs as protective measures but this can lead to macho idiocy and death. The peaks are still there and so are the trails, whether it takes you a bit longer than someone else does not matter as long as you come back down alive.



## Dengue fever

**Symptoms** This disease can be contracted throughout India and is an increasing problem. In travellers this can cause a severe 'flu-like illness which includes symptoms of fever, lethargy, enlarged lymph glands and muscle pains. It starts suddenly, lasts for two to three days, seems to get better for two to three days and then kicks in again for another two to three days. It is usually all over in an unpleasant week. The local children are prone to the much nastier haemorrhagic form of the disease, which causes them to bleed from internal organs, mucous membranes and often leads to their death.

**Cures** The traveller's version of the disease is self limiting and forces rest and recuperation.

**Prevention** The mosquitoes that carry the Dengue virus bite during the day unlike the malaria mosquitoes. Which sadly means that repellent application and covered limbs are a 24-hour issue. Check your accommodation for flower pots and shallow pools of water since these are where the dengue-carrying mosquitoes breed.

## Diarrhoea

**Symptoms** Diarrhoea can refer either to loose stools or an increased frequency; both of these can be a nuisance. It should be short lasting but persistence beyond two weeks, with blood or pain, require specialist medical attention.

**Cures** Ciproxin (Ciprofloxacin) is a useful antibiotic for bacterial traveller's diarrhoea. It can be obtained by private prescription in the UK which is expensive, or bought over the counter in Indian pharmacies. You need to take one 500 mg tablet when the diarrhoea starts and if you do not feel better in 24 hours, the diarrhoea is likely to have a non-bacterial cause and may be viral (in which case there is little you can do apart from keep yourself rehydrated and wait for it to settle on its own). The key treatment with all diarrhoeas is rehydration. Try to keep hydrated by taking the right mixture of salt and water. This is available as Oral Rehydration Salts (ORS) in ready-made sachets or can be made up by adding a teaspoon of sugar and a half teaspoon of salt to a litre of clean water. Drink at least one large cup of this drink for each loose stool. You can also use flat carbonated drinks as an alternative. Immodium and Pepto- Bismol provide symptomatic relief.

**Prevention** The standard advice is to be careful with water and ice for drinking. Ask yourself where the water came from. If you have any doubts then boil it or filter and treat it. There are many filter/treatment devices now available on the market. Food can also transmit disease. Be wary of salads (what were they washed in, who handled them), re-heated foods or food that has been left out in the sun having been cooked earlier in the day. There is a simple adage that says wash it, peel it, boil it or forget it. Also be wary of unpasteurised dairy products, these can transmit a range of diseases from brucellosis (fevers and constipation), to listeria (meningitis) and tuberculosis of the gut (obstruction, constipation, fevers and weight loss).

## Hepatitis

**Symptoms** Hepatitis means inflammation of the liver. Viral causes of the disease can be acquired anywhere in South America. The most obvious symptom is a yellowing of your skin or the whites of your eyes. However, prior to this all that you may notice is itching and tiredness.

**Cures** Early on, depending on the type of hepatitis, a vaccine or immunoglobulin may reduce the duration of the illness.

**Prevention** Pre-travel hepatitis A vaccine is the best bet. Hepatitis B (for which there is a vaccine) is spread through blood and unprotected sexual intercourse, both of these can be avoided. Unfortunately there is no vaccine for hepatitis C or the increasing alphabetical list of other Hepatitis viruses.

## Leishmaniasis

**Symptoms** A skin and a liver/kidney form of this disease occurs in India. If infected, you may notice a raised lump, which leads to a purplish discoloration on white skin and a possible ulcer. The parasite is transmitted by the bite of a sandfly. Sandflies do not fly very far and the greatest risk is at ground levels, so if you can avoid sleeping on the jungle floor, do so. There is another rarer form which is caused by a sub species of the parasite, this affects the musocal tissues such as lips and nose. Treatment and mode of transmission are the same.

**Cures** Several weeks treatment is required under specialist supervision.

**Prevention** Sleep above ground, under a permethrin treated net, use insect repellent and get a specialist opinion on any unusual skin lesions as soon as you can.

## Malaria and insect bite prevention

**Symptoms** Malaria can cause death within 24 hours. It can start as something just resembling an attack of flu. You may feel tired, lethargic, headachy; or worse, develop fits, followed by coma and then death. Have a low index of suspicion because it is very easy to write off vague symptoms, which may actually be malaria. Whilst abroad and on return get tested as soon as possible, the test could save your life.

**Cures** Treatment is with drugs and may be oral or into a vein depending on the seriousness of the infection. Remember ABCD: Awareness (of whether the disease is present in the area you are travelling in), Bite avoidance, Chemoprohylaxis, Diagnosis.

**Prevention** This is best summarized by the B and C of the ABCD, bite avoidance and chemoprophylaxis. Wear clothes that cover arms and legs and use effective insect repellents in areas with known risks of insect-spread disease. Use a mosquito net dipped in permethrin as both a physical and chemical barrier at night in the same areas. Guard against the contraction of malaria with the correct anti-malarials (see above). Some would prefer to take test kits for malaria with them and have standby treatment available. However, the field tests of the blood kits have had poor results: when you have malaria you are usually too ill to be able to do the tests correctly enough to make the right diagnosis. Standby treatment (treatment that you carry and take yourself for malaria) should still ideally be supervised by a doctor since the drugs themselves can be toxic if taken incorrectly. The Royal Homeopathic Hospital in the UK does not advocate homeopathic options for malaria prevention or treatment.

## Rabies

**Symptoms** Most of you will know when you have been bitten. It may take days or weeks before odd tingling sensations occur in the affected part, followed by a fear of drinking water and spasms which lead to death.

**Cures** There is no cure for rabies once it has hold of the Central Nervous System.

**Prevention** Avoid getting bitten. Dog lovers have to remember that this is a whole new ball game. A full course of rabies vaccine is 100% effective. If you get bitten you will need more vaccine and if you had no pre-exposure vaccine or an inadequate amount you will also need to be injected with something called immunoglobulin. It is always wise to wash the wound but animal bites should ideally not be stitched up in the early stages.

## Sexual health

The range of visible and invisible diseases is awesome. Unprotected sex can spread HIV, Hepatitis B and C, Gonorrhea (green discharge), chlamydia (nothing to see but may cause painful urination and later female infertility), painful recurrent herpes, syphilis and warts, just to name a few. You can cut down the risk by using condoms, a femidom or avoiding sex altogether.



## Sun protection

**Symptoms** White Britons are notorious for becoming red in hot countries because, generally, it is fair to say that they like to stay out longer than everyone else and do not use adequate sun protection. Long-term sun damage leads to a loss of elasticity of skin and the development of pre-cancerous lesions. Many years later a mild or a very malignant form of cancer may develop. The milder basal cell carcinoma, if detected early, can be treated by cutting it out or freezing it. The much nastier malignant melanoma may have already spread to bone and brain at the time that it is first noticed.

**Prevention** Sun screen. SPF stands for Sun Protection Factor. It is measured by determining how long a given person takes to 'burn' with and without the sunscreen product on. So, if it takes 10 times longer to burn with the sunscreen product applied, then that product has an SPF of 10. However, do not just use higher factors just to stay out in the sun longer. 'Flash frying' (desperate bursts of excessive exposure), is known to increase the risks of skin cancer. Aloe vera gel is a good pain reliever for sunburn.

## Tuberculosis (TB)

**Symptoms** Cough, blood in spit, weight loss, fever. If you drink unpasteurised milk you can get gut or pelvic TB which can lead to intestinal obstruction and infertility.

**Cures** At least three drugs are required and the treatment period is at least 6 months.

**Prevention** If staying for over one month have a skin test for TB followed by the BCG vaccine. Try to avoid people coughing on your face and if you have an unexplained illness on your return ask your doctor to think about TB.

## Underwater health

**Symptoms** If you go diving make sure that you are fit do so. **The British Scuba Association** (BSAC), Telford's Quay, South Pier Road, Ellesmere Port, Cheshire CH65 4FL, United Kingdom, T01513-506200, F506215, www.bsac.com, can put you in touch with doctors who do medical examinations. Protect your feet from cuts, beach dog parasites (larva migrans) and sea urchins. The latter are almost impossible to remove but can be dissolved with lime or vinegar. Keep an eye out for secondary infection.

**Cures** Antibiotics for secondary infections. Serious diving injuries may need time in a decompression chamber.

**Prevention** Check that the dive company know what they are doing, have appropriate certification from BSAC or Professional Association of Diving Instructors (PADI), Unit 7, St Philips Central, Albert Road, St Philips, Bristol, BS2 0TD, T0117-3007234, www.padi.com, and that the equipment is well maintained.

## Further information

**Centers for Disease Control and Prevention (USA) www.cdc.gov** This site from the US Government gives excellent advice on travel health, has useful disease maps and details of disease outbreaks.
**Department of Health Travel Advice (UK) www.doh.gov.uk/traveladvice** This excellent site is also available as a free booklet, the T6, from post offices.
It lists the vaccine advice requirements for each country.
**Medic Alert (UK) www.medicalalert.co.uk** This is the website of the foundation that produces bracelets and necklaces for those with existing medical problems. Once you have ordered your bracelet/necklace you write your key medical details on paper inside it, so that if you collapse, a medical person can identify you as someone with epilepsy or allergy to peanuts etc.
**NetDoctor (UK) www.Netdoctor.co.uk** This general health advice site has a useful section on travel and has an 'ask the expert', interactive chat forum.
**Public Health Laboratory Service (UK) www.phls.org.uk** This site has up-to-date malaria advice guidelines for travel around the world. It gives specific advice about the right drugs for each location. It also has useful information for those who are pregnant, suffering from epilepsy or planning to travel with children.
**Travel Screening Services (UK) www.travelscreening.co.uk** A private clinic dedicated to integrated travel health. The clinic gives vaccine, travel health advice, email and SMS text vaccine reminders and screens returned travellers for tropical diseases.
**Websites Foreign and Commonwealth Office (FCO) (UK) www.fco.gov.uk** This is a key travel advice site, with useful information on the country, people, climate and lists the UK embassies/consulates. The site also promotes the concept of 'Know Before You Go' and encourages travel insurance and appropriate travel health advice.

**Books**
**Expedition Medicine** (The Royal Geographic Society), editors David Warrell and Sarah Anderson ISBN 1 86197 040-4.
**International Travel & Health World Health Organisation**, Geneva ISBN 92 4 158026 7.
**The Travellers Good Health Guide** by Dr Ted Lankester by ISBN 0-85969-827-0.
**The World's Most Dangerous Places** by Robert Young Pelton, Coskun Aral and Wink Dulles ISBN 1-566952-140-9.

# Keeping in touch

## Communications

### Internet

Access is becoming increasingly available in major cities and tourist centres as cyber cafés mushroom and PCOs (Public Call Office) are beginning to offer the service, but in small towns the machines can be woefully slow. The web is spreading wider to reach remote areas, and is becoming faster year by year. As access improves, surfing charges fall ranging from Rs 100 per hour (US$2.50) in remote places and some hotels, to as little as Rs 25 (US$.50) in big towns. Alternatively, you can ask a hotel or a travel agent if they will allow you to use their system but hotel rates tend to be much higher.

### Post

The post is frequently unreliable, and delays are common. It is advisable to use a post office where it is possible to hand over mail for franking across the counter, or a top hotel post box. Valuable items should only be sent by **Registered Mail.** Government Emporia or shops in the larger hotels will send purchases home if the items are difficult to carry. **Airmail** service to Europe, Africa and Australia takes at least a week and a little longer for the Americas. **Speed post** (which takes about four days to the UK) is available from major towns. Specialist shippers deal with larger items, normally approximately US$150 per cubic metre. **Courier services** (eg DHL, ATS) are available in the larger towns. At some main post offices you can send small packages under 2 kg as Letter Post (rather than parcel post) which is much cheaper at Rs 220. 'Book Post' (for printed paper) is cheaper still, approximately Rs 170 for 5 kg. Book parcels must be sewn in cloth (best over see-through plastic) with a small open 'window' slit for contents to be seen.

Sending a **parcel** can take up to two hours. Check that the post office holds necessary customs declaration forms (two/three copies needed). Write 'No commercial value' if returning used clothes, books etc. Air mail is expensive; sea mail slow but reasonable (10 kg, Rs 800). 'Packers' outside post offices will do all necessary cloth covering, sealing etc for Rs 20-50; you address the parcel, obtain stamps from a separate counter; stick stamps and one customs form to the parcel with glue available (the other form/s must be partially sewn on). Post at the Parcels Counter and obtain a Registration slip. **Maximum dimensions:** height 1 m, width 0.8 m, circumference 1.8 m. Cost: sea mail Rs 775 for first kilogram, Rs 70 each extra kilogram. Air mail also Rs 775 first kilogram, Rs 200 each subsequent kilogram. Many people complain that private shops offering a postal service actually send cheap substitutes. It is usually too late to complain when the buyer finds out. It is best to buy your item and then get it packed and posted yourself.

**Poste restante facilities** are widely available in even quite small towns at the GPO where mail is held for one month. Ask for mail to be addressed to you with your surname in capitals and underlined. When asking for mail at Poste Restante check under surname as well as Christian name. Any special issue foreign stamps are likely to be stolen from envelopes in the Indian postal service and letters may be thrown away. Advise people who are sending you mail to India to use only definitive stamps (without pictures).



## Telephone

→ *International code: +91. Phone codes for towns are printed after the town name or in the listings of smaller towns*

International Direct Dialling is now widely available in privately run call 'booths', usually labelled on yellow boards with the letters 'PCO-STD-ISD'. You dial the call yourself, and the time and cost are displayed on a computer screen. They are by far the best places from which to telephone abroad. Cheap rate (2100-0600) means long queues may form outside booths. Telephone calls from hotels are usually much more expensive (check price before calling). Major global **mobile phone** companies have partner servers in India, but coverage remains uneven. You can buy a local "pay as you go card" if you are going to make heavy local use of the mobile. **Ringing tone:** double ring, repeated regularly; **Engaged:** equal length, on and off. Both are similar to UK ringing and engaged tones.

One disadvantage of the tremendous pace of the telecommunications revolution is the fact that millions of telephone numbers go out of date every year. Current telephone directories themselves are often out of date and some of the numbers given in the Handbook will have been changed even as we go to press. Directory enquiries, **197**, can be helpful but works only for the local area code.

*India is running out of phone numbers. The answer is to put an additional "2" on the front of existing numbers. Unfortunately some states seem to have implemented this, others not and some have reverted to the existing number. Our best advice is if the number in the text does not work, add a "2".*

**Fax** services are available from many PCOs and larger hotels, who charge either by the minute or per page.



## Media

### Newspapers and magazine

International newspapers (mainly English language) are sold in the bookshops of top hotels in major cities, and occasionally by booksellers elsewhere. India has a large English language press. They all have extensive analysis of contemporary Indian and some international issues. The major papers now have internet sites which are excellent for keeping daily track on events, news and weather. The best known are: **The Hindu** (www.thehindu.com), **The Hindustan Times** (www.hindustantimes.com), **The Independent, The Times of India** (www.timesofindia.com/) and **The Statesman** (www.thestatesman.org/). **The Economic Times** is possibly the best for independent reporting and world coverage. **The Telegraph** (www.telegraphindia.com/) has good foreign coverage. **The Indian Express** (www.expressindia.com/) has stood out as being consistently critical of the Congress Party and Government. **The Asian Age** gives good coverage of Indian and international affairs. Of the fortnightly magazines, some of the most widely read are **Sunday, India Today** and **Frontline**, all of which are current affairs journals on the model of Time or Newsweek.

### Television and radio

India's national radio and television network, **Doordarshan**, broadcasts in national and regional languages but things have moved on. The advent of satellite TV has hit even remote rural areas. The 'Dish' can help travellers keep in touch through **Star TV** from Hong Kong (accessing **BBC World, CNN** etc), **VTV** (music) and **Sport**, now available even in some modest hotels in the smallest of towns. The decision by the government to issue more licences to satellite broadcasters has resulted in up to 50 available channels from **MTV** to **Maharishi Veda Vision**!

## Media

### Newspapers and magazines

[illegible]

### Television and radio

[illegible]

# North India

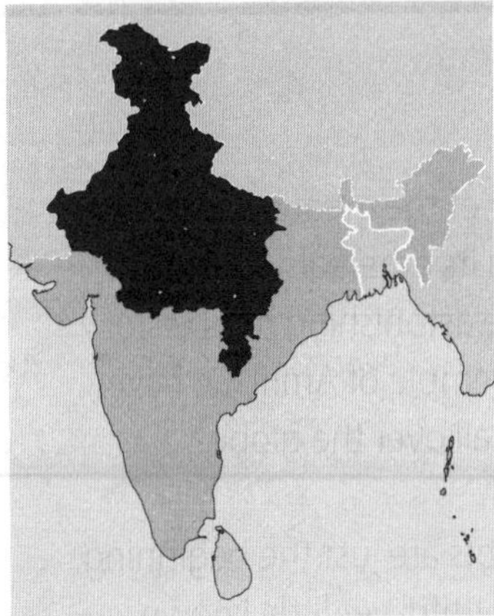

# Introduction

India's northern region has some of the greatest sights for travellers in the world. Agra, with its ethereal Taj Mahal, Rajasthan's royal palaces, and the astonishing temples of Khajuraho and the Sikh Golden Temple of Amritsar, have awed and charmed visitors from all over the globe.

But North India's well-known sights are just the beginning. Some of the Himalaya's most beautiful yet little known mountains are found north of Delhi in Hinduism's 'home of the gods', the Garhwal Himalaya. Still further north are former British hill stations like Shimla and Mussoorie, while beyond are the other worldly, high altitude deserts of the Tibetan borderlands, Spiti and Ladakh.

Then there are the lush green forests of Kanha and Bandhavgarh in Madhya Pradesh and the savanna grasslands of Ranthambhore, national parks home to some of the world's last remaining tigers. There are also the ancient and holy cities like Varanasi or Allahabad along the banks of India's holiest river, the Ganga. In contrast is Delhi, centrally located in the region and well connected with all parts of the country, with all the dynamism and facilities of a modern capital.

# Delhi

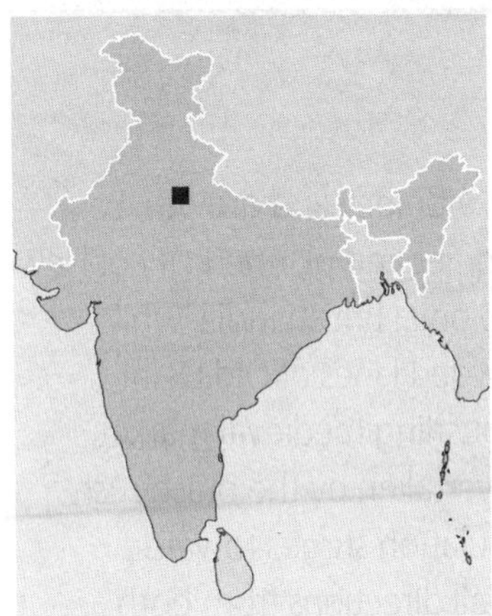



## Footprint features

# Introduction



Delhi can take you aback with its vibrancy and growth. Less than 60 years ago the spacious, quiet and planned city of New Delhi was still the pride of late colonial British India, while immediately to its north the crowded lanes of Old Delhi resonated with the sounds of a bustling medieval market. Today, both worlds have been overtaken by the brash rush of modernization. As Delhi's population surges towards 13 million its tentacles spread in all directions from both the ancient core of Shahjahan's city in the north and the late British capital of New Delhi to its south.

A daytime drive from the airport gives something of the feel of this dynamism, the roads often crowded with traffic, new highrise buildings transforming the spacious outlines of Lutyens' New Delhi with its broad tree-lined avenues, into a humming commercial hub centred around Connaught Place. Close to New Delhi Railway station, the hub of New Delhi's network to the rest of India, the cheap hotels and guesthouses of Paharganj, heart of backpackerland, squeeze between cloth merchants and wholesalers, cheek by jowl in the narrow lanes. In Old Delhi, further north, with the Red Fort and Jama Masjid, the old city is still a dense network of narrow alleys and tightly packed markets and houses. Your senses are bombarded by noise, bustle, smells and apparent chaos. A 'third city' comprises the remorselessly growing squatter settlements (jhuggies) which provide the only shelter for at least one-third of Delhi's total population. To the south is yet another, newer, chrome and glass city, the city of the modern suburbs and urban 'farms', where the rural areas of Gurgaon have become the preserve of the prosperous, with shopping malls, banks and private housing estates. Old and new, simple and sophisticated, traditional and modern, East and West are all juxtaposed.

## ★ Don't miss...

1 **Chandi Chowk to the Jama Masjid** Take a bicycle rickshaw down Chandi Chowk to the spice market and back through the bazaar to finish at Jama Masjid, page 89.

2 **Jama Masjid** The view from the minaret of sprawling Delhi is jaw dropping, page 96.

3 **India Gate at sunset** Crowds of Delhites come here to mill around, have an ice cream or go boating on the lakes, page 97.

4 **Gurudwara Bangla Sahib** A great chance to experience the serenity and hospitality of the Sikh religion, page 102.

5 **Lodi Gardens** Dotted with Moghul monuments and impeccably maintained, there's no better place to escape the mid-city madness, page 103.

6 **Qutb Minar complex** Travel back to the 12th century at the Qutb Minar complex with its impressive tower and even older gupta pillar, page 105.

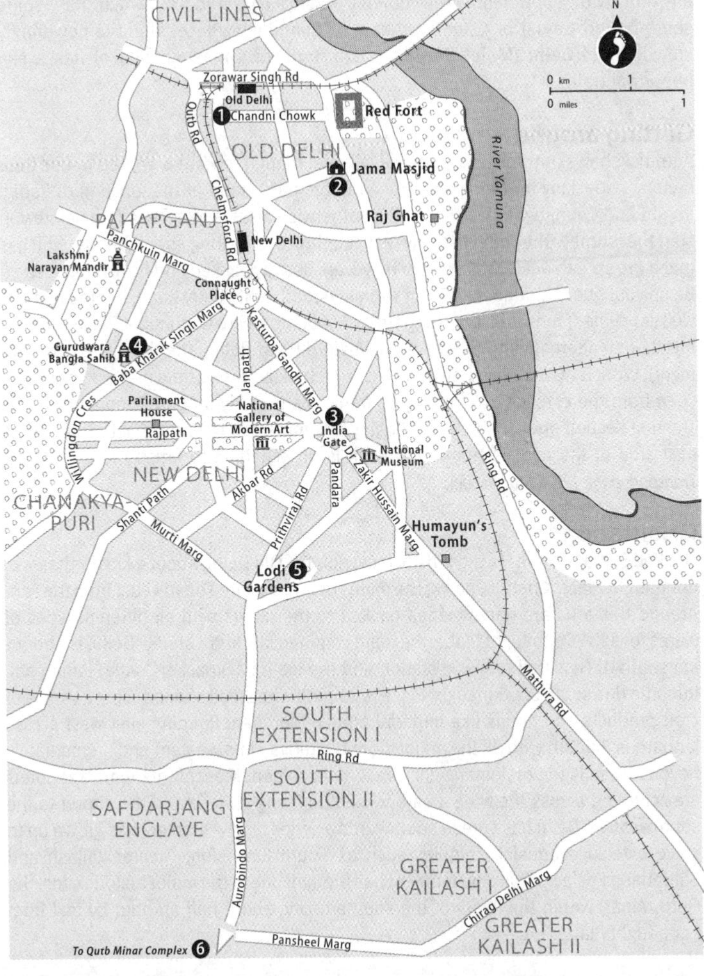

# Ins and outs

→ *Phone code: 011. Dial 1952, then old number, to get new phone number. Colour map 3, grid B2. Population: 12.8 mn. Area: 434 sq km.*

## Getting there

Delhi is served by **Indira Gandhi International (IGI) Airport**, which handles both international and domestic traffic. The Domestic Terminal 1, 15 km from the centre, handles flights from two separate sections: 'A', exclusively for **Indian Airlines** and 'B' for others. The International Terminal 2 is 23 km from the centre. During the day, it can take 30-45 minutes from the Domestic Terminal and 45 minutes to an hour from the International Terminal to get to the centre. A free shuttle runs between the terminals. To get to town take a pre-paid taxi or an airport coach or ask your hotel to collect.

The principal **Inter State Bus Terminus (ISBT)** is at Kashmir Gate, near the Red Fort, about 30 minutes by bus from Connaught Place. Services connect it to the other ISBTs.

There are three main railway stations. The busy **New Delhi** station, a 10-minute walk north of Connaught Place, can be maddeningly chaotic; you need to have all your wits about you. The quieter **Hazrat Nizamuddin** (which has some south-bound trains) is 5 km southeast of Connaught Place. The overpoweringly crowded **Old Delhi (Main) Station** (2 km north of Connaught Place) has a few important trains.

## Getting around

Auto-rickshaws and taxis are widely available, though few are prepared to use their meters, especially for foreigners – use the pre-paid stand at the junction of Radial Road 1 and Connaught Place if possible, otherwise be sure to agree a fare before you start the journey. They offer the only realistic choice for getting about the city, which is much too spread out to walk, as city buses are usually packed and have long queues. Be on your guard around New Delhi station. A road (State Entry Road, but the name is well concealed) runs from the southern end of platform 1 to Connaught Place. This is a hassle-free alternative to the main Chelmsford Road during the day (gate closed at night). Work is also well underway on a comprehensive metro train network, as can be seen from the extensive disruption to traffic, particularly around Connaught Place. The first section opened in 2004, bringing commuters to the centre of town from the east side of the river Yamuna, and work is on schedule to finish in 2008. ▸▸ *See Transport, page 122, for further details.*

## Orientation

The Red Fort and Jama Masjid are the focal point of Old Delhi, about 2 km northeast of Connaught Place. Chandi Chowk, the main commercial area heads east from the Fort. Around this area are narrow lanes packed to the rafters with all different types of wares for sale. Connaught Place, the main commercial centre of New Delhi, is about 1 km south of New Delhi railway station and the main backpackers' area, Paharganj. Running due south of Connaught Place is Janpath with small shops selling a variety of craft products and hotels like **Imperial** and **Le Meridien**. Running east west across Janpath is Rajpath with all the major state buildings at its western end. Immediately beyond them is the diplomatic enclave, Chanakyapuri. Most of the upmarket hotels are scattered across the wide area between Connaught Place and the airport to the southwest. As Delhi has spread southwards a series of new markets has grown up to serve extensive housing colonies such as South Extension, Greater Kailash and Safdarjang Enclave. This development has brought one of the major historic sites, the Qutb Minar, within the limits of the southern city, about half an hour by taxi from Connaught Place.

### Best time to visit

October-March are the best months, but December and January can get quite cold and foggy at night. Pollution can affect asthma sufferers. Monsoon lasts from the end of June to mid-September. May and June are very hot and dry.

## History

Delhi's present position as capital was only confirmed on 12 December 1911, when King George V announced at the Delhi Durbar that the capital of India was to move from Calcutta to Delhi. The new city, New Delhi, planned under the leadership of British architect Edwin Lutyens with the assistance of his friend Herbert Baker, was inaugurated on 9 February 1931.

The city was to accommodate 70,000 people and have boundless possibilities for future expansion. The King favoured something in form and flavour similar to the Mughal masterpieces but fretted over the horrendous expense that this would incur. A petition signed by eminent public figures such as Bernard Shaw and Thomas Hardy advocated an Indian style and an Indian master builder. Herbert Baker had made known his own views even before his appointment when he wrote "first and foremost it is the spirit of British sovereignty which must be imprisoned in its stone and bronze". Lutyens himself despised Indian architecture. "Even before he had seen any examples of it", writes Tillotson (architectural historian), "he pronounced Mughal architecture to be 'piffle', and seeing it did not disturb that conviction". Yet in the end, Lutyens was forced to settle for the compromise.

The Viceroy's House, the centrepiece of imperial proportions, was 1 km around the foundations, bigger than Louis XIV's palace at Versailles. It had a colossal dome surmounting a long colonnade and 340 rooms in all. It took nearly 20 years to complete, similar to the time it took to build the Taj Mahal. In the busiest year, 29,000 people were working on the site and buildings began to take shape. The project was surrounded by controversy from beginning to end. Opting for a fundamentally classical structure, both Baker and Lutyens sought to incorporate Indian motifs, many entirely superficial. While some claim that Lutyens achieved a unique synthesis of the two traditions, Tillotson asks whether "the sprinkling of a few simplified and classicized Indian details (especially *chhattris*) over a classical palace" could be called a synthesis.

# Sights

The sites of interest are grouped in three main areas. In the centre is the British built capital of **New Delhi**, with its government buildings and wide avenues. The heart of **Shah Jahanabad** (Old Delhi) is about 2 km north of Connaught Circus. Ten kilometres to the south is the **Qutb Minar** complex, with the old fortress city of **Tughluqabad**, 8 km to its east. You can visit each separately, or link routes together into a day-tour to include the most interesting sites. ▸▸ *For Sleeping, Eating and other listings, see pages 109-126.*

## Old Delhi

Shah Jahan (ruled 1628-1658) decided to move back from Agra to Delhi in 1638. Within 10 years the huge city of **Shahjahanabad**, now known as Old Delhi, was built. The plan of Shah Jahan's new city symbolized the link between religious authority enshrined in the Jama Masjid to the west, and political authority represented by the

## The peacock throne

In the centre of the Diwan-i-Khas (5) is a marble pedestal on which stood the Peacock Throne which Shah Jahan commissioned on his accession in 1627. It took seven years to make. The throne was designed with two peacocks standing behind with a parrot carved out of a single emerald between them. It was inlaid with a vast number of precious stones – sapphires, rubies, emeralds, pearls and diamonds. Over the top was a gem encrusted gold canopy edged with pearls, supported by 12 pillars.

The throne was carried off by Nadir Shah, a Turk, who after conquering Persia sacked Delhi in 1739. Soon after his occupation of Delhi a riot broke out in which 900 of his soldiers were killed. Nadir Shah himself rode through the streets of Delhi to assess the situation when some residents were rash enough to throw stones at him. Enraged, Nadir Shah ordered the entire population of Delhi to be massacred, resulting in 30,000 dead. In the evening the 'Great' Mughal (Mohammad Shah) begged for mercy, and such was Nadir Shah's control over his troops that he was able immediately to halt the carnage. The invaders took with them as much as they could extort from all the nobles. Bahadur Shah later replaced the throne with a poor copy. The Peacock Throne itself was broken up by Nadir Shah's assassins in 1747; some of the jewels are believed to have been incorporated into the late Shah of Iran's throne.

Diwan-i-Am in the Fort, joined by Chandni Chowk, the route used by the Emperor. The city was protected by rubble-built walls, some of which still survive. These walls were pierced by 14 main gates. The **Ajmeri Gate**, **Turkman Gate** (often referred to by auto-rickshaw wallahs as 'Truckman Gate'!), **Kashmir Gate** and **Delhi Gate** still survive.

### Chandi Chowk

Shahjahanabad was laid out in blocks with wide roads, residential quarters, bazars and mosques. Its principal street, Chandni Chowk, had a tree-lined canal flowing down its centre which quickly became renowned throughout Asia. The jumble of shops, labyrinthine alleys running off a main thoroughfare with craftsmen's workshops, hotels, mosques and temples, cause it to retain some of its magic, although the canal is long gone. A cycle rickshaw ride gives you a good feel of the place.

The impressive red sandstone façade of the **Diagambar Jain Mandir** (temple) standing at the eastern end of Chandni Chowk, faces the Red Fort. Built in 1656, it contains an image of Adinath. The bird hospital within this compound releases the birds on recovery (instead of returning them to their owners); many remain within the temple precincts.

### The Red Fort (Lal Qila)

ⓘ *Closed Mon, daily sunrise to sunset, US$2 foreigners, Rs 10 Indians, allow 1 hour. The entrance is through the Lahore Gate (nearest the car park) with the admission kiosk opposite. Keep your ticket as you will need to show it at the Drum House. The toilets are in Chatta Chowk and near Asad Burj but are best avoided.*

Between the new city and the river Yamuna, Shah Jahan built a fort. Most of it was built out of red (*lal*) sandstone, hence the name **Lal Qila** (Red Fort), the same as that at Agra on which the Delhi fort is modelled. Begun in 1639 and completed in 1648, it is said to have cost Rs 10 million, much of which was spent on the opulent marble palaces within. Visitors may be saddened by the neglected state of the once imposing fort – coloured marble-inlay is missing and the gardens are bare. However, despite the modern development of roads and shops and the never-ending traffic, that dominating impression is still immensely powerful.

**The approach** The entrance is by the Lahore Gate (make this clear to the rickshaw driver). The defensive barbican that juts out in front of the Lahore Gate was built by Aurangzeb, see page 1302. A common story suggests that Aurangzeb built the curtain wall at the entrance to save his nobles and visiting dignitaries from having to walk – and bow – the whole length of Chandni Chowk, for no one was allowed to ride in the presence of the Emperor. When the Emperor sat in the Diwan-i-Am he could see all the way down the Chowk, so the addition must have been greatly welcomed by his courtiers. The new entrance arrangement also made an attacking army more vulnerable to the defenders on the walls.

**Chatta Chowk** Inside is the 'Covered Bazar', quite exceptional in the 17th century. In Shah Jahan's time there were shops on both upper and lower levels. Originally they catered for the Imperial household and carried stocks of silks, brocades, velvets, gold and silverware, jewellery and gems. There were coffee shops too for nobles and courtiers. Walk through the left-hand archway and you will see a small building on your right near the Art Corner shop.

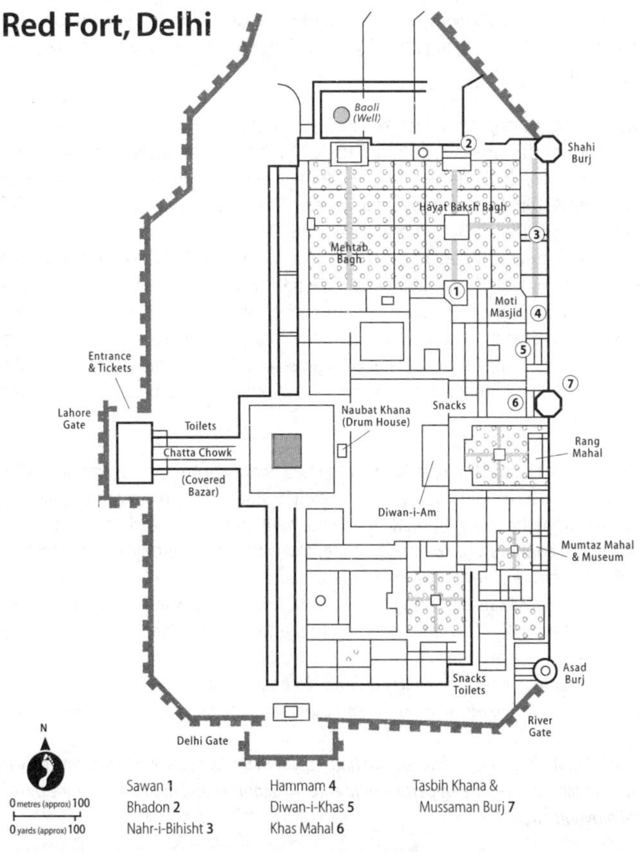

## A gift from Florence?

There are 318 Florentine pietra dura plaques in the niche behind the throne, showing flowers, birds and lions as well as the central figure of Orpheus, playing to the beasts. In between these Italian panels are Mughal pietra dura works with flowery arabesques and birds. Ebba Koch argues that the techniques employed by the Mughal artisans are exactly the same as the Italian ones, so there must have been a direct connection.

This is not to say that there was no independent development of Mughal inlay craftsmanship. Such a view has been described by Tillotson as the result of wishful thinking by Europeans, eager to claim a stake in the superb work. Infact the Mughals had an equally fine tradition of stone carving and of inlay work on which to draw as the Florentine princes, as can be seen from the work in the Jami Masjid in Ahmadabad, built in 1414.



**The Naubat Khana (Naqqar Khana)** The Naubat Khana (**Drum House** or music gallery), marked the entrance to the inner apartments of the fort. Here everyone except the princes of the royal family had to dismount and leave their horses or elephants (*hathi*), hence its other name of **Hathi Pol** (Elephant Gate). Five times a day ceremonial music was played on the kettle drum, shahnais (a kind of oboe) and cymbals, glorifying the emperor. In 1754 the Emperor Ahmad Shah was murdered here. The gateway with four floors is decorated with floral designs. You can still see traces of the original panels painted in gold or other colours on the interior of the gateway.

**Diwan-i-Am** Between the first inner court and the royal palaces at the heart of the fort, stood the Diwan-i-Am (Hall of Public Audience), the farthest point the normal visitor would reach. It has seen many dramatic events – the destructive whirlwind of the Persian Nadir Shah in 1739 and of Ahmad Shah the Afghan in 1756, and the trial of the last 'King of Delhi', **Bahadur Shah II** in 1858.

The well-proportioned hall was both a functional building and a showpiece intended to hint at the opulence of the palace itself. In Shah Jahan's time the sandstone was hidden behind a very thin layer of white polished plaster, *chunam*. This was decorated with floral motifs in many colours, especially gilt. Silk carpets and heavy curtains hung from the canopy rings outside the building, such interiors reminders of the Mughals' nomadic origins in Central Asia, where royal durbars were held in tents.

**The throne surround** At the back of the hall is a platform for the emperor's throne. Around this was a gold railing, within which stood the princes and great nobles separated from the lesser nobles (inside the hall) and minor officials from the general public in the courtyard (now the lawn). Behind the throne canopy are 12 marble inlaid panels. Figurative workmanship is very unusual in Islamic buildings, and this one panel is the only example in the Red Fort. Wherever you stand in the hall (everyone except the Emperor's favourite son had to stand), there is an uninterrupted view of the throne – a powerful psychological effect.

The business comprised official and domestic administration, reports from the provinces, tax and revenue matters and official appointments. On the personal side,

*Shah Jahan used to spend about two hours a day in the Diwan-i-Am. According to Bernier, the French traveller, the emperor would enter to a fanfare and mount the throne by a flight of movable steps.*

Shah Jahan would listen to accounts of illness, dream interpretations and anecdotes from his ministers and nobles. He usually retired to bed at around 2200 and liked to be read to, his particular favourite being the *Babur-i-nama*, the autobiography of his great-great-grandfather. 

Wednesday was the day of judgement. Sentences were often brutal but swift and sometimes the punishment of dismemberment, beating or death was carried out on the spot. The executioners were close at hand with axes and whips. On Friday, the Muslim holy day, there would be no business.

**Inner palace buildings** Behind the Diwan-i-Am is the private enclosure of the fort. Along the east wall, overlooking the River Yamuna, Shah Jahan set six small palaces (five survive). Also within this compound are the Harem, the Life-Bestowing Garden and the Nahr-i-Bihisht (Stream of Paradise). Leave the throne canopy area by the steps to your left, follow the path and carry on until you reach the white marble garden pavilion.



**Life-Bestowing Gardens (Hayat Baksh Bagh)** The original gardens were landscaped according to the Islamic principles of the Persian *char bagh*, with pavilions, fountains and water courses dividing the garden into various but regular beds. The two pavilions **Sawan** and **Bhadon**, named after the first two months of the rainy season (July-August), reveal something of the character of the garden. The garden used to create the effect of the monsoon and contemporary accounts tell us that in the pavilions, some of which were especially erected for the *Teej* festival which marks the arrival of the monsoon, the royal ladies would sit in silver swings and watch the rains. Water flowed from the back wall of the pavilion through a slit above the marble shelf and over the niches in the wall. Gold and silver pots of flowers were placed in these alcoves during the day whilst at night candles were lit to create a glistening and colourful effect. To the west is **Mehtab Bagh** which has a *baoli* (step well) to its northwest.

**Shahi Burj** From the pavilion next to the Shahi Burj ('Royal Tower') the canal known as the **Nahr-i-Bihisht** (Stream of Paradise) began its journey along the Royal Terrace. The three-storey octag- onal Tower, seriously damaged in 1857, is still unsafe. The lower storey contained a tank from which water was raised to flow into the garden. In Shah Jahan's time the Yamuna lapped the walls. Shah Jahan used the tower as his most private office and only his sons and a few senior ministers were allowed with him.

**Moti Masjid** To the right are the three marble domes of Aurangzeb's 'Pearl Mosque' (shoes must be removed). Bar the cupolas, it is completely hidden behind a wall of red sandstone, now painted white. Built in 1662 of polished white marble, it has some exquisite decoration. All the surfaces are highly decorated in a fashion similar to rococo, which was developed at the same time in Europe. Unusually the prayer hall is on a raised platform with inlaid outlines of individual 'prayer mats' (*musallas*) in black marble. While the outer walls were aligned to the cardinal points like all the other fort buildings, the inner walls were positioned so that the mosque would correctly face Mecca.

**Hammam** The Royal Baths have three apartments separated by corridors with canals to carry water to each room. The two flanking the entrance, for the royal children, had hot and cold baths. The room furthest away from the door has three basins for rose water fountains.

**Diwan-i-Khas** Beyond is the single-storeyed 'Hall of Private Audience', topped by four Hindu-style *chhattris* and built completely of white marble. The *dado* (lower part of the wall) on the interior was richly decorated with inlaid precious and semi-precious stones. The ceiling was silver but was removed by the Marathas in 1760. Outside, the hall used to have a marble pavement and an arcaded court. Both have gone.

This was the Mughal office of state. Shah Jahan spent two hours here before retiring for a meal, siesta and prayers. In the evening he would return to the Hall for more work before going to the harem. The hall's splendour moved the 14th-century

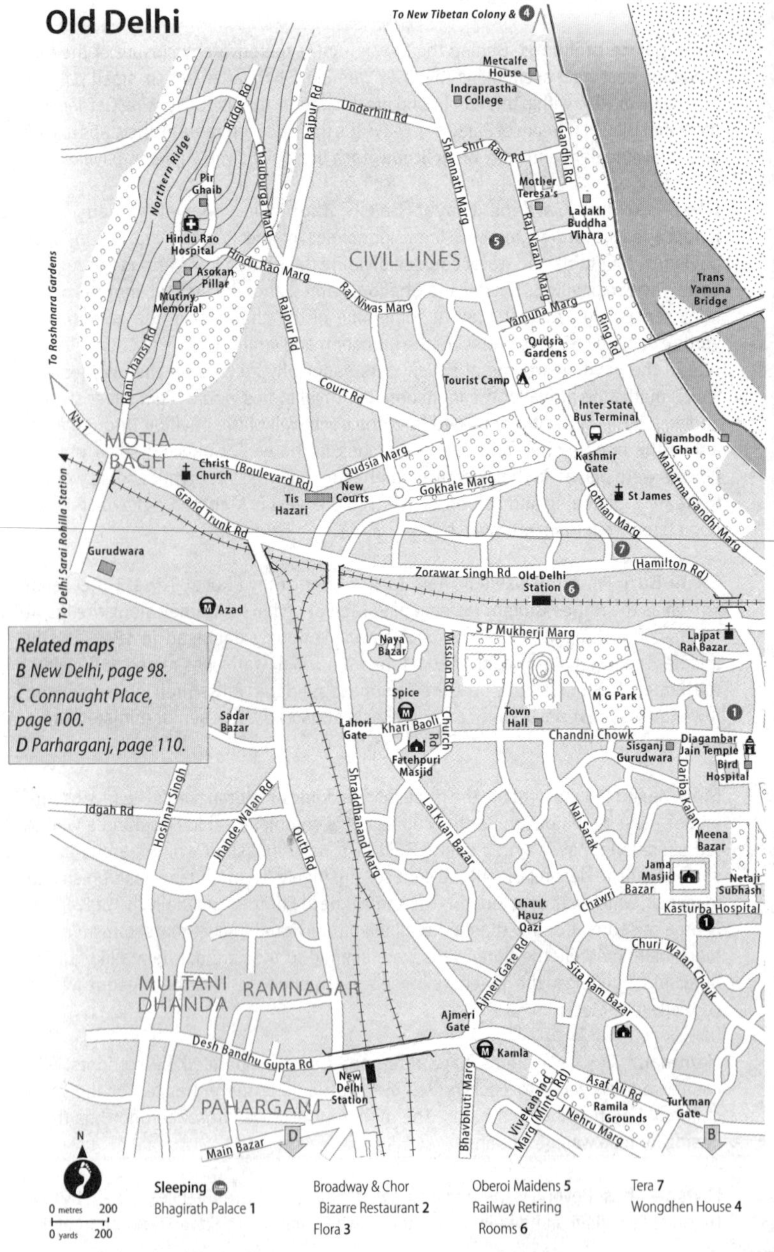

poet **Amir Khusrau** to write the lines inscribed above the corner arches of the north and south walls: "*Agar Firdaus bar rue Zamin-ast/Hamin ast o Hamin ast o Hamin ast*" (If there be a paradise on earth, it is here, it is here, it is here).

**Royal palaces** Next to the Diwan-i-Khas is the three-roomed **Khas Mahal** (Private Palace). Nearest the Diwan-i-Khas is the **Tasbih Khana** (Chamber for the Telling of Rosaries) where the emperor would worship privately with his rosary of 99 beads, one for each of the mystical names of Allah. In the centre is the Khwabgah (*'Palace of Dreams'*) which gives on to the octagonal **Mussaman Burj** tower. Here Shah Jahan would be seen each morning. A balcony was added to the tower in 1809 and here George V and Queen Mary appeared in their Coronation Durbar of 1911. The **Tosh Khana** (*Robe Room*), to the south, has a beautiful marble screen at its north end, carved with the scales of justice above the filigree grille. If you are standing with your back to the Diwan-i-Khas you will see a host of circulating suns (a symbol of royalty), but if your back is to the next building (the Rang Mahal), you will see moons surrounding the scales. All these rooms were sumptuously decorated with fine silk carpets, rich silk brocade curtains and lavishly decorated walls. After 1857 the British used the Khas Mahal as an officer's mess and sadly it was defaced.

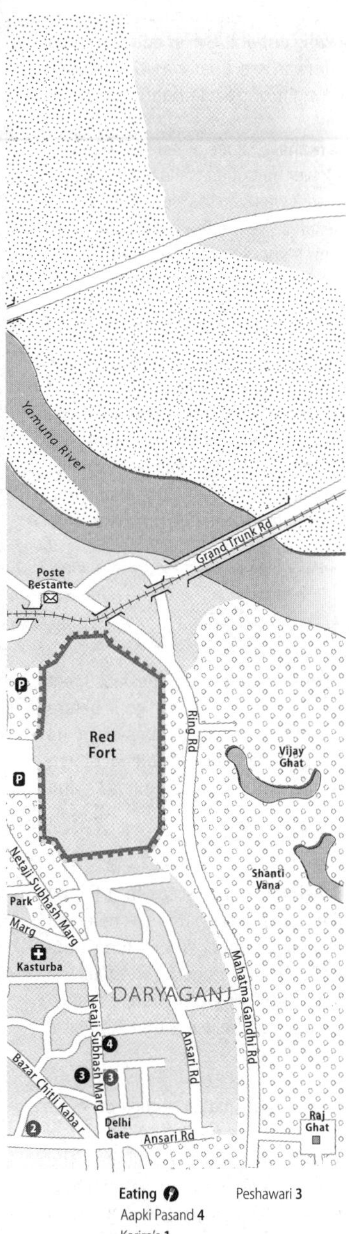


Beneath the Khas Mahal is the **Khirzi Gate**. This is neglected now, but was an important and convenient private entrance for the Emperor and his most senior nobles.

The **Rang Mahal** (Palace of Colours), the residence of the chief *sultana*, was also the place where the Emperor ate most of his meals. To protect the rich carpets, calico-covered leather sheets were spread out. It was divided into six apartments. Privacy and coolness were ensured by the use of marble *jali* screens. Like the other palaces it was beautifully decorated with a silver ceiling ornamented with golden flowers to reflect the water in the channel running through the building. The north and south apartments were both known as **Sheesh Mahal** (Palace of Mirrors) since into the ceiling were set hundreds of small mirrors. In the evening when candles were lit a starlit effect would be produced. This type of decoration was a favourite in Rajasthan before the Mughals arrived (see page 337 – Amber Fort). In the summer the ladies went to the water-cooled cellars underground (not accessible now).

❢ *The general public enter by the north gate. You must remove shoes and cover all exposed flesh from your shoulders to your legs.*

Through the palace ran the **Life-bestowing Stream** and at its centre is a lotus shaped marble basin which had an ivory fountain. As might be expected in such a cloistered and cossetted environment, the ladies sometimes got bored. In the 18th century the **Empress of Jahandar Shah** sat gazing out at the river and remarked that she had never seen a boat sink. Shortly afterwards a boat was deliberately capsized so that she could be entertained by the sight of people bobbing up and down in the water crying for help.

The southernmost of the palaces, the **Mumtaz Mahal** (Palace of Jewels) ⓘ *0900-1700, closed Fri,* was also used by the harem. The lower half of its walls are of marble and it contains six apartments. After the Mutiny of 1857 it was used as a guardroom and since 1912 it has been a museum with exhibits of textiles, weapons, carpets, jade and metalwork as well as works depicting life in the court. It should not be missed.



## Spice market

Outside of the Red Fort, cycle rickshaws offer a trip to the Spice Market, Jama Masjid and back through the bazar. You travel slowly westwards down Chandni Chowk passing the town hall. Dismount at Church Road and follow your guide into the heart of the market on Khari Baoli where wholesalers sell every conceivable spice. Ask to go to the roof for an excellent view over the market and back towards the Red Fort. The ride back through the bazar is equally fascinating – look up at the amazing electricity system. The final excitement is getting back across Netaji Subhash Marg. Panic not, the rickshaw wallahs know what they are doing. Negotiate for one hour and expect to pay about Rs 50. The spice laden air may irritate your throat.

## Jama Masjid (The Friday Mosque)

ⓘ *Visitors welcome from 30 mins after sunrise until 1200; and from 1345 until 30 mins before sunset, free, still or video cameras Rs 100, tower entry Rs 10.*

The magnificent Jama Masjid is the largest mosque in India and the last great architectural work of Shah Jahan, intended to dwarf all mosques that had gone before it. With the fort, it dominates Old Delhi. The mosque is much simpler in its ornamentation than Shah Jahan's secular buildings – a judicious blend of red sandstone and white marble, which are interspersed in the domes, minarets and cusped arches.

**The gateways** Symbolizing the separation of the sacred and the secular, the threshold is a place of great importance where the worshipper steps to a higher plane. There are three huge gateways, the largest being to the east. This was reserved for the royal family who gathered in a private gallery in its upper storey. Today, the faithful enter through the east gate on Fridays and for *Id-ul-Fitr* and *Id-ul-Adha*. The latter commemorates Abraham's (Ibrahim's) sacrificial offering of his son Ishmael (Ismail). Islam (unlike the Jewish and Christian tradition) believes that Abraham offered to sacrifice Ishmael, Isaac's brother.

**The courtyard** The façade has the main arch (*iwan*), five smaller arches on each side with two flanking minarets and three bulbous domes behind, all perfectly proportioned. The *iwan* draws the worshippers' attention into the building. The minarets have great views from the top; well worth the climb for Rs 10 (woman may not be allowed to climb alone). The **hauz**, in the centre of the courtyard, is an ablution tank placed as usual between the inner and outer parts of the building to remind the worshipper that it is through the ritual of baptism that one first enters the community of believers. The **Dikka**, in front of the ablution tank, is a raised platform. Muslim communities grew so rapidly that by the eighth century it sometimes became necessary to introduce a second *muballigh* (prayer leader) who stood on this platform and copied the postures and chants of the *imam* inside to relay them to a much larger congregation. With the introduction of the loudspeaker and amplification, the *dikka* and the *muballigh* became redundant. In the northwest corner of the masjid there is a small shed. For a small fee, the faithful are shown a hair from the beard of the prophet, as well as his sandal and his footprint in rock.

**The Kawthar Inscription** Set up in 1766, the inscription commemorates the place where a worshipper had a vision of the Prophet standing by the celestial tank in paradise. It is here that the Prophet will stand on Judgment Day. In most Islamic buildings, the inscriptions are passages from the Koran or Sayings of the Prophet. Shah Jahan, however, preferred to have sayings extolling the virtues of the builder and architect as well. The 10 detailed panels on the façade indicate the date of construction (1650-1656), the cost (10 lakhs – one million rupees), the history of the building, the architect (Ustad Khalil) and the builder (Nur Allah Ahmed, probably the son of the man who did most of the work on the Taj Mahal).



# New Delhi

## India Gate and around

A tour of New Delhi will usually start with a visit to India Gate. This war memorial is situated at the eastern end of **Rajpath**. Designed by Lutyens, it commemorates more than 70,000 Indian soldiers who died in the First World War. Some 13,516 names of British and Indian soldiers killed on the Northwest Frontier and in the Afghan War of 1919 are engraved on the arch and foundations. Under the arch is the Amar Jawan Jyoti, commemorating Indian armed forces' losses in the Indo-Pakistan War of 1971. The arch (43 m high) stands on a base of Bharatpur stone and rises in stages. Similar to the Hindu *chhattri* signifying regality, it is decorated with nautilus shells symbolizing British maritime power.

To the northwest of India Gate are two impressive buildings, **Hyderabad House** and **Baroda House**, built as residences for the Nizam of Hyderabad and the Gaekwar of Baroda. Now used as offices, both were carefully placed to indicate the paramountcy of the British Raj over the Princely States. The *Nizam*, reputed to be the richest man in the world, ruled over an area equal to that of France. The *Gaekwar* belonged to the top level of Indian Princes and both, along with the Maharajas of Mysore, Jammu and Kashmir and Gwalior were entitled to receive 21-gun salutes.

Rajpath leads west from India Gate towards **Janpath**. To the north are the **National Archives**. Formerly the Imperial Record Office, and designed by Lutyens, this was intended to be a part of a much more ambitious complex of public buildings. To the south is the National Museum (see below).

## National Gallery of Modern Art

ⓘ *Jaipur House, near India Gate, T23384640, closed Mon, 1000-1700, Rs 10, foreigners Rs 150.*

The excellent collection is housed in a former residence of the Maharaja of Jaipur. Some of the best exhibits are on the ground floor which is devoted to post-1930 works. To view the collections chronologically, begin on the first floor. Artists include: Amrita Shergil (ground floor): over 100 exhibits, synthesizing the flat treatment of Indian painting with a realistic tone; Rabindranath Tagore (ground floor): examples from a

# New Delhi

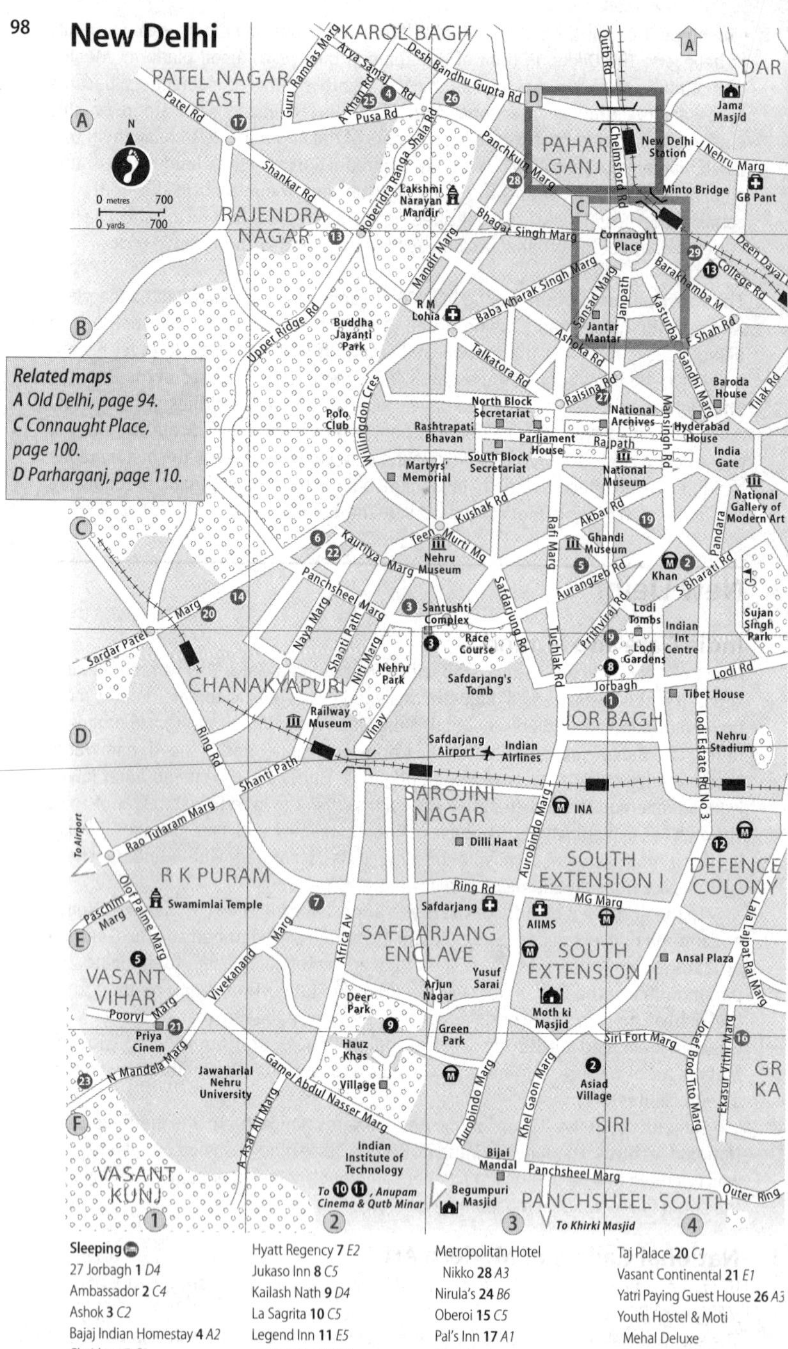


*Related maps*
*A Old Delhi, page 94.*
*C Connaught Place, page 100.*
*D Parharganj, page 110.*



**Sleeping**

27 Jorbagh **1** *D4*
Ambassador **2** *C4*
Ashok **3** *C2*
Bajaj Indian Homestay **4** *A2*
Claridges **5** *C3*
Diplomat **6** *C2*
Good Times **25** *A2*
Grand **23** *F1*
Grand Inter-Continental **29** *B4*
Hyatt Regency **7** *E2*
Jukaso Inn **8** *C5*
Kailash Nath **9** *D4*
La Sagrita **10** *C5*
Legend Inn **11** *E5*
Le Meridien **27** *B3*
Manor **12** *E6*
Master Paying Guesthouse **13** *B2*
Maurya Sheraton **14** *C1*
Metropolitan Hotel Nikko **28** *A3*
Nirula's **24** *B6*
Oberoi **15** *C5*
Pal's Inn **17** *A1*
Park Royal Intercontinental **27** *B3*
Rajdoot **16** *D5*
Surya (Crown Plaza) **18** *E6*
Taj Mahal **19** *C4*
Taj Palace **20** *C1*
Vasant Continental **21** *E1*
Yatri Paying Guest House **26** *A3*
Youth Hostel & Moti Mehal Deluxe Restaurant **22** *C2*

**Eating**

Ankur & Chopsticks **2** *F3*
Basil & Thyme **3** *D3*

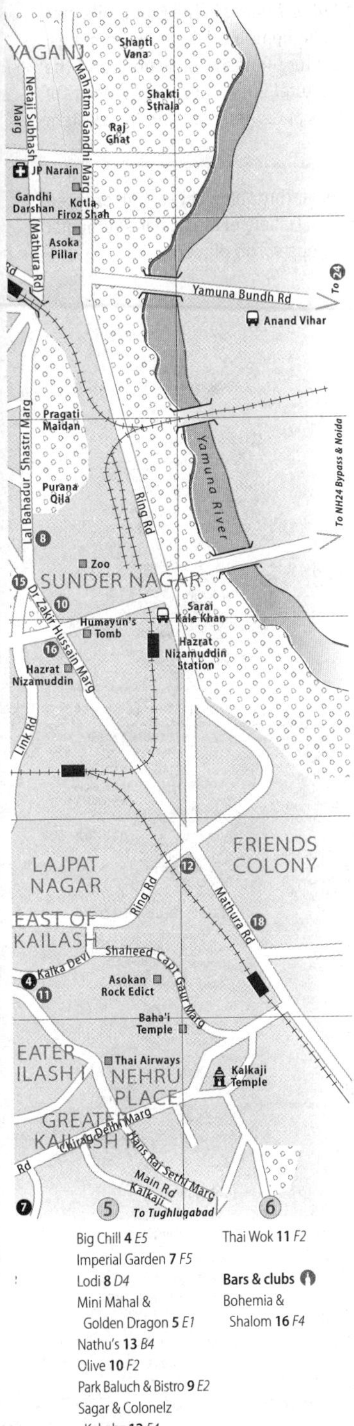


brief but intense spell in the 1930s; The Bombay School or Company School (first floor): includes Western painters who documented their visits to India. Realism is reflected in Indian painting of the early 19th century represented by the schools of Avadh, Patna, Sikkim and Thanjavur; The Bengal School (the late 19th-century Revivalist Movement): artists such as Abanindranath Tagore and Nandalal Bose have their works exhibited here. Western influence was discarded in response to the nationalist movement. Inspiration derived from Indian folk art is evident in the works of Jamini Roy and YD Shukla.

## National Museum

ⓘ *Janpath, T23019272, closed Mon, 1000-1700, Rs 10, foreigners Rs 150 (students Rs 1), camera Rs 300; free guided tours 1030, 1130, 1200, 1400, films are screened every day (1430), marble squat toilets, but dirty.*

The collection was formed from the nucleus of the Exhibition of Indian Art, London (1947). Now merged with the Asian Antiquities Museum it displays a rich collection of the artistic treasure of Central Asia and India including ethnological objects from prehistoric archaeological finds to the late Medieval period. Replicas of exhibits and books on Indian culture and art are on sale. There is a research library.

**Ground floor** Prehistoric: seals, figurines, toy animals and jewellery from the Harappan civilization (2400-1500 BC). Maurya Period: terracottas and stone heads from the Sunga period (third century BC) include the *chaturmukha* (four-faced) *lingam*. Gandhara School: stucco heads showing the Graeco Roman influence. Gupta terracottas (circa AD 400): include two life-size images of the river goddesses Ganga and Yamuna and the four-armed bust of Vishnu from a temple near Lal Kot. South Indian sculpture: from Pallava and early Chola temples and relief panels from Mysore. Tenth-century AD sculptures. Bronzes from the Buddhist monastery at Nalanda. Some of Buddha's relics were placed in the Thai pavilion in 1997.

**First floor** Illustrated manuscripts: include the *Babur-i-nama* in the Emperor's own handwriting and an autographed copy of Jahangir's memoirs. Miniature paintings: Include the 16th-century Jain School, the 18th-century Rajasthani School and the Pahari Schools of Garhwal, Basoli and Kangra. The Aurel Stein Collection consists of antiquities recovered by him during his explorations of Central Asia and the western borders of China at the turn of the century.

**Second floor** Pre-Columbian and Mayan artefacts: anthropological section devoted to tribal artefacts and folk arts. Sharad Rani Bakkiwal Gallery of Musical Instruments: displays over 300 instruments collected by the famous *sarod* player.



## Connaught Place

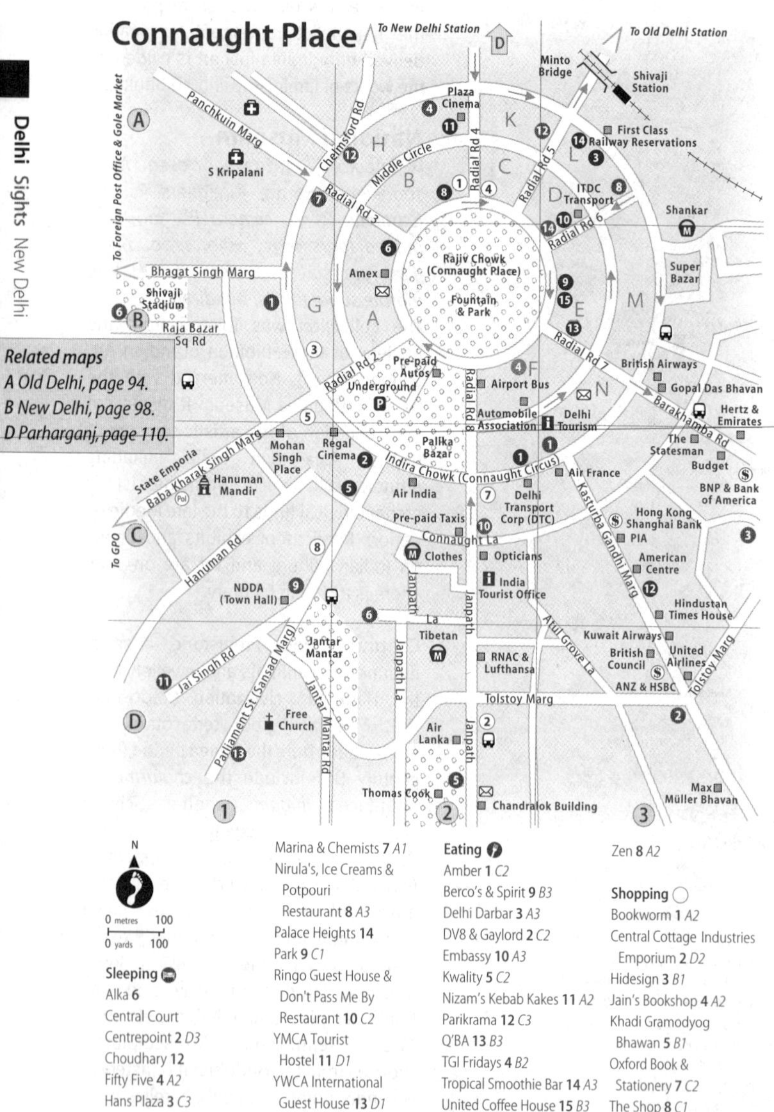


**Sleeping**
Alka 6
Central Court
Centrepoint 2 *D3*
Choudhary 12
Fifty Five 4 *A2*
Hans Plaza 3 *C3*
Imperial 5 *D2*
Marina & Chemists 7 *A1*
Nirula's, Ice Creams & Potpouri Restaurant 8 *A3*
Palace Heights 14
Park 9 *C1*
Ringo Guest House & Don't Pass Me By Restaurant 10 *C2*
YMCA Tourist Hostel 11 *D1*
YWCA International Guest House 13 *D1*

**Eating**
Amber 1 *C2*
Berco's & Spirit 9 *B3*
Delhi Darbar 3 *A3*
DV8 & Gaylord 2 *C2*
Embassy 10 *A3*
Kwality 5 *C2*
Nizam's Kebab Kakes 11 *A2*
Parikrama 12 *C3*
Q'BA 13 *B3*
TGI Fridays 4 *B2*
Tropical Smoothie Bar 14 *A3*
United Coffee House 15 *B3*
Wengers & Rodeo 6 *B2*
Zen 8 *A2*

**Shopping**
Bookworm 1 *A2*
Central Cottage Industries Emporium 2 *D2*
Hidesign 3 *B1*
Jain's Bookshop 4 *A2*
Khadi Gramodyog Bhawan 5 *B1*
Oxford Book & Stationery 7 *C2*
The Shop 8 *C1*

*Related maps*
*A Old Delhi, page 94.*
*B New Delhi, page 98.*
*D Parharganj, page 110.*

## The Secretariats

At the Secretariat and Rashtrapati Bhavan gates, the mounted and unmounted troops parade in full uniform on Saturdays at 1030 and are worth attending. Standing on either side of Raisina Hill, **North Block** houses the Home and Finance Ministries, **South Block** the Ministry of Foreign Affairs. These long classical buildings, topped by Baroque domes, designed by Baker, are similar to his Government Buildings of Pretoria, and were derived from Wren's Royal Naval College at Greenwich. The towers were originally designed to be twice the height of the buildings and to act as beacons guarding the way to the inner sanctum. Their height was reduced and with it their impact. The domes are decorated with lotus motifs and elephants, while the north and south gateways are Mughal in design. On the northern Secretariat building is the imperialistic inscription "Liberty will not descend to a people: a people must raise themselves to liberty. It is a blessing which must be earned before it can be enjoyed".

In the **Great Court** between the Secretariats are the four **Dominion Columns**, donated by the governments of Australia, Canada, New Zealand and South Africa – ironically, as it turned out. The resemblance of Baker's domes to his work in Pretoria is also striking and ironic! Each is crowned by a bronze ship sailing east, symbolizing the maritime and mercantile supremacy of the British Empire. In the centre of the court is the Jaipur column of red sandstone topped with a white egg, bronze lotus and six-pointed glass star of India (which has evolved into today's five-pointed star). Across the entrance to the Great Court is a 205 m wrought iron screen.



## Rashtrapati Bhavan and Nehru Memorial Museum

Once the Viceroy's House, Rashtrapati Bhavan is the official residence of the President of India. Designed by Lutyens, it combines western and eastern styles. Philip Davies describes it as a masterpiece of symmetry, discipline, silhouette and harmony. The Durbar Hall, 23 m in diameter, has coloured marble from all parts of India.

To the south is Flagstaff House, formerly the residence of the Commander-in-Chief. Renamed Teen Murti Bhawan it now houses the **Nehru Memorial Museum** ⓘ *Teen Murti Bhavan, closed Mon, museum 1000-1500 and planetarium 1130-1500, Library closed Sun, 0900-1900, free, T2301 4504*. Designed by Robert Tor Russell, in 1948 it became the official residence of India's first Prime Minister, Jawaharlal Nehru. Converted after his death (1964) into a national memorial, the reception, study and bedroom are intact. Note his extensive reading and wide interests. A *Jyoti Jawahar* (torch) symbolizes the eternal values he inspired, and a granite rock is carved with extracts from his historic speech at midnight 14-15 August 1947. A very informative and vivid history of the Independence Movement.

The **Martyr's Memorial**, at the junction of Sardar Patel Marg and Willingdon Crescent, is a magnificent 26-m long, 3-m high bronze sculpture by DP Roy Chowdhury. The 11 statues of national heroes are headed by Mahatma Gandhi.

## Gandhi Museum

ⓘ *Birla House, 5 Tees Jan Marg (near Claridges Hotel), closed Mon and 2nd Sat, 0930-1730, free, film at 1500, T2301 2843*, contains photos and memorabilia including his few possessions during his final days in the house. A monument marks where he fell. Definitely worth a visit. Others museums in the city related to Gandhi include **Gandhi Darshan** ⓘ *opposite Raj Ghat, closed Mon, 1000- 1700, T2331 1793*, has five pavilions – sculpture, photographs and paintings of Gandhi and the history of the *Satyagraha* movement, the philosophy of non-violence; **Gandhi Smarak Sangrahalaya** ⓘ *Raj Ghat, T3011480, closed Thu, 0930-1730*, displays some of Gandhi's personal belongings and a small library includes recordings of speeches; **Indira Gandhi Museum** ⓘ *1 Safdarjang Rd, T3010094, 0930-1700, closed Mon, free*, charts the phases of her life from childhood up to the moment of her death.

## Parliament House and around

Northeast of the Viceroy's House is the **Council House**, now **Sansad Bhavan**. Baker designed this and Lutyens suggested that it be circular (173 m diameter). Inside is the library and chambers for the Council of State, Chamber of Princes and Legislative Assembly – the **Lok Sabha**. Just opposite the Council House is the **Rakabganj Gurudwara** in Pandit Pant Marg. This 20th-century white marble shrine, which integrates the late Mughal and Rajasthani styles, marks the spot where the headless body of **Guru Tegh Bahadur**, the ninth Sikh Guru, was cremated in 1657. West of the Council House is the Cathedral **Church of the Redemption** (1927-1935) and to its north the Italianate Roman Catholic **Church of the Sacred Heart** (1930-1934), both conceived by Henry Medd whose designs won architectural competitions.

## Connaught Place and Connaught Circus

Connaught Place and its outer ring, Connaught Circus, comprise two-storey arcaded buildings, arranged radially. In 1995 they were re-named **Rajiv Chowk** and **Indira Chowk** respectively, but are still widely known by their original names. Designed by **Robert Tor Russell**, they have become the main commercial centre of Delhi. Sadly, the area also attracts bands of aggressive touts ready to take advantage of the unwary traveller by getting them into spurious 'official' or 'government' shops and travel agencies. The area (and Palika Bazar) is renowned for its shoe-shine tricksters. Large wadges of slime appear mysteriously on shoes and are then pointed out eagerly by attendant boys or men who offer to clean them off at a price. This can just be the start of 'necessary repairs' to the shoes for which bills of over Rs 300 are not unknown. If caught, insist politely but firmly that the dirt is cleaned off free of charge.

To the south in **Janpath** (the People's Way), the east and west Courts were hostels for the members of the newly convened Legislative Assembly. With their long colonnaded verandahs, these are Tuscan in character.

## Lakshmi Narayan Mandir

To the west of Connaught Circus is the Lakshmi Narayan **Birla Temple** in Mandir Marg. Financed by the prominent industrialist **Raja Baldeo Birla** in 1938, this is one of the most popular Hindu shrines in the city and one of Delhi's few striking examples of Hindu architecture. Dedicated to Lakshmi, the goddess of well-being, it is commonly referred to as **Birla Mandir**. The design is in the Orissan style with tall curved towers (*sikhara*) capped by large *amalakas*. The exterior is faced with red and ochre stone and white marble. Built around a central courtyard, the main shrine has images of Narayan and his consort Lakshmi while two separate cells have icons of Siva (the Destroyer) and his consort Durga (the 10-armed destroyer of demons). The temple is flanked by a *dharamshala* (rest house) and a Buddhist *vihara* (monastery).

East from the Birla Temple, down Kali Bari Marg to Baba Kharak Singh Marg (Irwin Road), is the **Hanuman Mandir**. This small temple (circa 1724) was built by Maharaja Jai Singh II of Jaipur. Of no great architectural interest, the temple is increasingly popular with devotees. **Mangal haat** (Tuesday Fair) is a popular market.

## Gurudwara Bangla Sahib

On Baba Kharak Singh Road is a fine example of Sikh temple architecture, featuring a large pool reminiscent of Amritsar's Golden Temple. The 24-hour reciting of the faith's holy book adds to the atmosphere, and there's free food on offer, although don't be surprised if you're asked to help out with the washing up! You must remove your shoes and cover your head to enter – suitable scarves are provided if you arrive without. There is no charge to enter.

## Jantar Mantar

Just to the east of the Hanuman Mandir in Sansad Marg (Parliament Street) is Jai Singh's observatory ('Jantar Mantar') ⓘ *sunrise-sunset, Rs 5, foreigners US$2*. The Mughal Emperor Mohammad Shah (ruled 1719-1748) entrusted the renowned astronomer Maharaja Jai Singh II with the task of revising the calendar and correcting the astronomical tables used by contemporary priests. Daily astral observations were made for years before construction began and plastered brick structures were favoured for the site instead of brass instruments. Built in 1725 it is slightly smaller than the later observatory at Jaipur.

## Memorial Ghats

Beyond Delhi Gate lies the **River Yamuna**, marked by a series of memorials to India's leaders. The river itself, a kilometre away, is invisible from the road, protected by a low rise and banks of trees. The most prominent memorial, immediately opposite the end of Jawaharlal Nehru Road, is that of Mahatma Gandhi at **Raj Ghat**. To its north is **Shanti Vana** ('Forest of Peace'), landscaped gardens where Prime Minister Jawaharlal Nehru was cremated in 1964, and subsequently his grandson Sanjay Gandhi in 1980, daughter **Indira Gandhi** in 1984 and elder grandson, Rajiv, in 1991. To the north again is **Vijay Ghat** ('Victory Bank') where Prime Minister Lal Bahadur Shastri was cremated.



# South Delhi

The spacious layout of New Delhi has been preserved despite the building on empty sites and the sub-division of previously large gardens. Still close to the centre, there are several attractive high-class residential areas such as Jor Bagh near the Lodi Gardens, while beyond the Ring Road are sprawling estates of flats and larger apartments and huge shopping and commercial centres.

## The Lodi Gardens

These beautiful gardens, with mellow stone tombs of the 15th- and 16th-century Lodi rulers, are popular for gentle strolls as much as for jogging. In the middle of the garden facing the east entrance from Max Mueller Rd is **Bara Gumbad** (Big Dome), a mosque built in 1494. The raised courtyard is provided with an imposing gateway and *mehman khana* (guest rooms). The platform in the centre appears to have had a tank for ritual ablutions.

**The Sheesh** (Shish) **Gumbad** (Glass Dome, late 15th-century) is built on a raised incline a few metres north of the Bara Gumbad and was once decorated with glazed blue tiles, painted floral designs and Koranic inscriptions. The façade gives the impression of a two-storeyed building, typical of Lodi architecture. **Mohammad Shah's tomb** (1450) is that of the third Sayyid ruler. It has sloping buttresses, an octagonal plan, projecting eaves and lotus patterns on the ceiling. **Sikander Lodi's tomb**, built by his son in 1517, is also an octagonal structure decorated with Hindu motifs. A structural innovation is the double dome which was later refined under the Mughals. The 16th-century **Athpula** (Bridge of Eight Piers) nearby, near the northeastern entrance, is attributed to Nawab Bahadur, a nobleman at Akbar's court.

## Safdarjang's tomb

ⓘ *Sunrise to sunset, Rs 5, foreigners Rs 100.*

Relatively little visited, Safdarjang's tomb was built by Nawab Shuja-ud-Daulah for his father Mirza Mukhim Abdul Khan, entitled Safdarjang, who was Governor of Oudh (1719-1748), and Wazir of his successor (1748-1754). Safdarjang died in 1754. With its high enclosure walls, *char bagh* layout of gardens, fountain and central domed mausoleum, it follows the tradition of Humayun's tomb. Typically, the real tomb is just below ground level. Flanking the mausoleum are pavilions used by Shuja-ud-Daulah as his family residence. Immediately to its south is the battlefield where Timur and his Mongol horde crushed Mahmud Shah Tughluq on 12 December 1398.

## Hazrat Nizamuddin

ⓘ *Dress ultra-modestly if you don't want to feel uncomfortable or cause offence.*
At the east end of the Lodi Road is Hazrat Nizamuddin Dargah. Nizamuddin 'village', now tucked away behind the residential suburb of Nizamuddin West, off Mathura Road, grew up around the shrine of Sheikh Nizamuddin Aulia (1236-1325), a Chishti saint. *Qawwalis* are sung at sunset after *namaaz* (prayers), and are particularly impressive on Thursdays.

West of the central shrine is the **Jama-at-khana Mosque** (1325). Its decorated arches are typical of the Khalji design also seen at the Ala'i Darwaza at the Qutb Minar. South of the main tomb and behind finely crafted screens is the grave of princess Jahanara, Shah Jahan's eldest and favourite daughter. She shared the emperor's last years when he was imprisoned at Agra Fort. The grave, open to the sky, is in accordance with the epitaph written by her "Let naught cover my grave save the green grass, for grass suffices as the covering of the lowly". Pilgrims congregate at the shrine twice a year for the *Urs* (fair) held to mark the anniversaries of Hazrat Nizamuddin Aulia and his disciple **Amir Khusrau**, whose tomb is nearby.



## Humayun's tomb

ⓘ *Sunrise to sunset, Rs 10, Rs 250 foreigners, video cameras Rs 25, located in Nizamuddin, 15 mins by taxi from Connaught Circus, allow 45 mins.*
Eclipsed later by the Taj Mahal and the Jama Masjid, this tomb is the best example in Delhi of the early Mughal style of tomb. Superbly maintained, it is well worth a visit, preferably before visiting the Taj Mahal. **Humayun**, the second Mughal Emperor, was forced into exile in Persia after being heavily defeated by the Afghan Sher Shah in 1540. He returned to India in 1545, finally recapturing Delhi in 1555. The tomb was designed and built by his senior widow and mother of his son Akbar, Hamida Begum. A Persian from Khurasan, after her pilgrimage to Mecca she was known as **Haji Begum**. She supervised the entire construction of the tomb (1564-1573), camping on the site.

**The plan** The tomb has an octagonal plan, lofty arches, pillared kiosks and the double dome of Central Asian origin, which appears here for the first time in India. Outside Gujarat, Hindu temples make no use of the dome, but the Indian Muslim dome had until now, been of a flatter shape as opposed to the tall Persian dome rising on a more slender neck. Here also is the first standard example of the garden tomb concept: the **char bagh** (garden divided into quadrants), water channels and fountains. This form culminated in the gardens of the Taj Mahal. However, the tomb also shows a number of distinctively Hindu motifs. Tillotson has pointed out that in Humayun's tomb, Hindu *chhattris* (small domed kiosks), complete with temple columns and *chajjas* (broad eaves), surround the central dome. The bulbous finial on top of the dome and the star motif in the spandrels of the main arches are also Hindu, the latter being a solar symbol.

**The approach** The tomb enclosure has two high double-storeyed gateways: the entrance to the west and the other to the south. A *baradari* occupies the centre of the east wall, and a bath chamber that of the north wall. Several Moghul princes, princesses and Haji Begum herself lie buried here. During the 1857 Mutiny **Bahadur Shah II**, the last Moghul Emperor of Delhi, took shelter here with his three sons. Over 80, he was seen as a figurehead by Muslims opposing the British. When captured he was transported to Yangon (Rangoon) for the remaining four years of his life. The tomb to the right of the approach is that of Isa Khan, Humayun's barber.

**The dome** Some 38-m high, the dome does not have the swell of the Taj Mahal and the decoration of the whole edifice is much simpler. It is of red sandstone with some white marble to highlight the lines of the building. There is some attractive inlay work, and some *jalis* in the balcony fence and on some of the recessed keel arch windows. The interior is austere and consists of three storeys of arches rising up to the dome. The Emperor's tomb is of white marble and quite plain without any inscription. The overall impression is that of a much bulkier, more squat building than the Taj Mahal. The cavernous space under the main tombs is an ideal home for great colonies of bats.

## Hauz Khas

ⓘ *1- hour cultural show, 1845, Rs 100 (check with Delhi Tourism).*

Immediately to the north again, and entered off either Aurobindo Marg on the east side or Africa Avenue on the west side, is Hauz Khas. Ala-ud-din Khalji (ruled 1296-1313) created a large tank here for the use of the inhabitants of **Siri**, the second capital city of Delhi founded by him. Fifty years later **Firoz Shah Tughluq** cleaned up the silted tank and raised several buildings on its east and south banks which are known as Hauz Khas or Royal Tank.

Firoz Shah's austere tomb is found here. The multi-storeyed wings, on the north and west of Firoz Shah's tomb, were built by him in 1354 as a *madrasa* (college). The octagonal and square *chhattris* were built as tombs, possibly to the teachers at the college. Hauz Khas is now widely used as a park for early morning recreation – walking, running and yoga exercises. Classical music concerts, dance performances and a *son et lumière* show are held in the evenings when monuments are illuminated by thousands of earthen lamps and torches.

## The Qutb Minar Complex

ⓘ *Sunrise-sunset, US$5 foreigners, Rs 10 Indians. Bus 505 from New Delhi Railway station (Ajmeri Gate), Super Bazar (east of Connaught Circus) and Cottage Industries Emporium, Janpath. Auto Rs 100, though drivers may be reluctant to take you.*

**Muhammad Ghuri** conquered northwest India at the very end of the 12th century. The conquest of the Gangetic plain down to Benares (Varanasi) was undertaken by Muhammad's Turkish slave and chief general, **Qutb-ud-din-Aibak**, whilst another general took Bihar and Bengal. In the process, temples were reduced to rubble, the remaining Buddhist centres were dealt their death blow and their monks slaughtered. When Muhammad was assassinated in 1206, his gains passed to the loyal Qutb-ud- din-Aibak. Thus the first sultans or Muslim kings of Delhi became known as the **Slave Dynasty** (1026-1290). For the next three centuries the Slave Dynasty and the succeeding Khalji (1290-1320), Tughluq (1320-1414), Sayyid (1414-1445) and Lodi (1451- 1526) dynasties provided Delhi with fluctuating authority. The legacy of their ambitions survives in the tombs, forts and palaces that litter Delhi Ridge and the surrounding plain. **Qutb-ud-din-Aibak** died after only four years in power, but he left his mark with the **Qutb Minar** and his **citadel**. Qutb Minar, built to proclaim the victory of Islam over the infidel (unbeliever), dominates the countryside for miles around. Visit the Minar first.

**Qutb Minar (1)** In 1199 work began on what was intended to be the most glorious tower of victory in the world and was to be the prototype of all *minars* (towers) in India. Qutb-ud-din-Aibak had probably seen and been influenced by the brick victory pillars in Ghazni in Afghanistan, but this one was also intended to serve as the minaret attached to the Might of Islam Mosque. From here the muezzin could call the faithful to prayer. Later every mosque would incorporate its minaret.

As a mighty reminder of the importance of the ruler as Allah's representative on earth, the Qutb Minar (literally 'axis minaret') stood at the centre of the community. A

## Gupta Pillar: the magic of iron

In the courtyard of the Quwwat-ul-Islam Mosque (2) is the fourth-century iron pillar. The Sanskrit inscription states that it was erected as a flagstaff in honour of Vishnu and in memory of the Gupta King Chandragupta II (375-413). Originally the pillar was topped by an image of Vishnu's vahana (carrier or vehicle) Garuda, the mythical half bird of prey, half man, and probably stood facing a Vishnu temple. The purity of its wrought iron (98%) is extraordinary, and it has survived 1,600 years virtually without blemish. A local tradition regards the pillar as having magical qualities. Anyone who can encircle it with their hands behind their back will have good fortune. This is difficult as the pillar is now fenced off!



pivot of Faith, Justice and Righteousness, its name also carried the message of Qutb-ud-din's ('Axis of the Faith') own achievements. The inscriptions carved in Kufi script tell that "the tower was erected to cast the shadow of God over both east and west". For Qutb-ud-din-Aibak it marked the eastern limit of the empire of the One God. Its western counterpart is the **Giralda Tower** built by Yusuf in Seville.

The Qutb Minar is 73 m high and consists of five storeys. The diameter of the base is 14.4 m and 2.7 m at the top. Qutb-ud-din built the first three and his son-in-law Iltutmish embellished these and added a fourth. This is indicated in some of the Persian and Nagari (North Indian) inscriptions which also record that it was twice damaged by lightning in 1326 and 1368. While repairing the damage caused by the second, Firoz Shah Tughluq added a fifth storey and used marble to face the red and buff sandstone. This was the first time contrasting colours were used decoratively, later to become such a feature of Mughal buildings. Firoz's fifth storey was topped by a graceful cupola but this fell down during an earthquake in 1803. A new one was added by a Major Robert Smith in 1829 but was so out of keeping that it was removed in 1848 and now stands in the gardens.

The original storeys are heavily indented with different styles of fluting, alternately round and angular on the bottom, round on the second and angular on the third. The beautifully carved honeycomb detail beneath the balconies is reminiscent of the Alhambra Palace in Spain. The calligraphy bands are verses from the Koran and praises to its patron builder.

**Quwwat-ul-Islam Mosque (2)** The Quwwat-ul-Islam Mosque (The Might of Islam Mosque), the earliest surviving mosque in India, is to the northwest of the Qutb Minar. It was begun in 1192, immediately after Qutb-ud-din's conquest of Delhi and completed in 1198, using the remains of no fewer than 27 local Hindu and Jain temples.

The architectural style contained elements that Muslims brought from Arabia, including buildings made of mud and brick and decorated with glazed tiles, *squinches* (arches set diagonally across the corners of a square chamber to facilitate the raising of a dome and to effect a transition from a square to a round structure), the pointed arch and the true dome. Finally, Muslim buildings came alive through ornamental calligraphy and geometric patterning. This was in marked contrast to indigenous Indian styles of architecture. Hindu, Buddhist and Jain buildings relied on the post-and-beam system in which spaces were traversed by corbelling, ie shaping flat-laid stones to create an arch. The arched screen that runs along the western end of the courtyard beautifully illustrates the fact that it was Hindu methods that still prevailed at this stage, for the 16-m high arch uses Indian corbelling, the corners being smoothed off to form the curved line.

**Screens (4)** Qutb-ud-din's screen formed the façade of the mosque and, facing in the direction of Mecca, became the focal point. The sandstone screen is carved in the Indo-Islamic style, lotuses mingling with Koranic calligraphy. The later screenwork and other extensions (1230) are fundamentally Islamic in style, the flowers and leaves having been replaced by more arabesque patterns. Indian builders mainly used stone, which from the fourth century AD had been intricately carved with representations of the gods. In their first buildings in India the Muslim architects designed the buildings and local Indian craftsmen built them and decorated them with typical motifs such as the vase and foliage, tasselled ropes, bells and cows.

**Iltutmish's extension** The mosque was enlarged twice. In 1230 Qutb-ud-din's son-in-law and successor **Shamsuddin Iltutmish** doubled its size by extending the colonnades and prayer hall – 'Iltutmish's extension'. This accommodated a larger congregation, and in the more stable conditions of Iltutmish's reign, Islam was obviously gaining ground. The arches of the extension are nearer to the true arch and are similar to the Gothic arch that appeared in Europe at this time. The decoration is Islamic. Almost 100 years after Iltutmish's death, the mosque was enlarged again, by **Ala-ud-din Khalji**. The conductor of tireless and bloody military campaigns, Ala-ud-din proclaimed himself 'God's representative on earth'. His architectural ambitions, however, were not fully realized, because on his death in 1316 only part of the north and east extensions were completed.



**Ala'i Minar (8) and the Ala'i Darwaza (9)** To the north of the Qutb complex is the 26-m **Ala'i Minar**, intended to surpass the tower of the Qutb, but not completed beyond the first storey. Ala-ud-din did complete the south gateway to the building, the **Ala'i Darwaza**; inscriptions testify that it was built in 1311 (Muslim 710 AH). He benefited from events in Central Asia. Since the early 13th century, Mongol hordes from Central Asia fanned out east and west, destroying the civilization of the Seljuk Turks in West Asia, and refugee artists, architects, craftsmen and poets fled east. They brought to India features and techniques that had developed in Byzantine Turkey, some of which can be seen in the Ala'i Darwaza.

The gate-house is a large sandstone cuboid, into which are set small cusped arches with carved *jali* screens. The lavish ornamentation of geometric and floral designs in red sandstone and white marble produced a dramatic effect when viewed against the surrounding buildings.

The inner chamber, 11 sq m has doorways and, for the first time in India, true arches. Above each doorway is an Arabic inscription with its creator's name and one of his self-assumed titles – 'The Second Alexander'. The north doorway, which is the main entrance, is the most elaborately carved. The dome, raised on squinched arches, is flat and shallow. Of the effects employed, the arches with their 'lotus-bud' fringes are Seljuk, as is the dome with the rounded finial and the façade. These now became trademarks of the **Khalji style**, remaining virtually unchanged until their further development in Humayun's tomb.

**Iltutmish's Tomb (3)** Built in 1235, Iltutmish's Tomb lies in the northwest of the compound, midway along the west wall of the mosque. It is the first surviving tomb of a Muslim ruler in India. Two other tombs also stand within the extended Might of Islam Mosque. The idea of a tomb was quite alien to Hindus, who had been practising cremation since around 400 BC. Blending Hindu and Muslim styles, the outside is relatively plain with three arched and decorated doorways. The interior carries reminders of the nomadic origins of the first Muslim rulers. Like a Central Asian *yurt* (tent) in its decoration, it combines the familiar Indian motifs of the wheel, bell, chain and lotus with the equally familiar geometric arabesque patterning. The west wall is inset with three *mihrabs* that indicate the direction of Mecca.

The tomb originally supported a dome resting on *squinches* which you can still see. The dome collapsed (witness the slabs of stone lying around) suggesting that the technique was as yet unrefined. From the corbelled squinches it may be assumed that the dome was corbelled too, as found in contemporary Gujarat and Rajput temples. The blocks of masonry were fixed together using the Indian technology of iron dowels. In later Indo-Islamic buildings lime plaster was used for bonding.

**Other tombs** To the southwest of the uncompleted Quwwat-ul-Islam mosque, an L-shaped ruin marks the site of **Ala-ud-din Khalji's tomb (6)** within the confines of a **madrasa** (college) **(7)**. This is the first time in India that a tomb and *madrasa* are found together, another custom inherited from the Seljuks. Immediately to the east of the Ala'i Darwaza stands the **tomb of Imam Zamin**, an early 16th-century *sufi* 'saint' from Turkestan. It is an octagonal structure with a plastered sandstone dome and has *jali* screens, a characteristic of the Lodi style of decoration.



## Tughluqabad

*ⓘ Sunrise-sunset, Rs 5, foreigners Rs 200, video camera Rs 25, allow 1 hr, for return rickshaws, turn right at entrance and walk 200 m.*

Tughluqabad's ruins, 7½ km east from Qutb Minar, still convey a sense of the power and energy of the newly arrived Muslims in India. From the walls you get a magnificent impression of the strategic advantages of the site. **Ghiyas'ud-Din Tughluq** (ruled 1321-1325), after ascending the throne of Delhi, selected this site for his capital. He built a massive fort around his capital city which stands high on a rocky outcrop of the Delhi Ridge. The fort is roughly octagonal in plan with a circumference of 6½ km. The vast size, strength and obvious solidity of the whole give it an air of massive grandeur. It was not until Babur (ruled 1526-1530) that dynamite was used in warfare, so this is a very defensible site.

*! The site is very deserted so don't go alone. As well as company, take plenty of water.*

East of the main entrance is the rectangular **citadel**. A wider area immediately to the west and bounded by walls contained the **palaces**. Beyond this to the north lay the **city**. Now marked by the ruins of houses, the streets were laid out in a grid fashion. Inside the citadel enclosure is the **Vijay Mandal** tower and the remains of several halls including a long underground passage. The fort also contained seven tanks.

A causeway connects the fort with the tomb of Ghiyas'ud-Din Tughluq, while a wide embankment near its southeast corner gave access to the fortresses of **Adilabad** about 1 km away, built a little later by Ghiyas'ud-Din's son Muhammad. The tomb is very well preserved and has red sandstone walls with a pronounced slope (the first Muslim building in India to have sloping walls), crowned with a white marble dome. This dome, like that of the Ala'i Darwaza at the Qutb, is crowned by an *amalaka*, a feature of Hindu architecture. Also Hindu is the trabeate arch at the tomb's fortress wall entrance. Inside are three cenotaphs belonging to Ghiyas'ud-Din, his wife and son Muhammad.

**Ghiyas'ud-Din Tughluq** quickly found that military victories were no guarantee of lengthy rule. When he returned home after a victorious campaign the welcoming pavilion erected by his son and successor, **Muhammad-bin Tughluq**, was deliberately collapsed over him. Tughluqabad was abandoned shortly afterwards and was thus only inhabited for five years. The Tughluq dynasty continued to hold Delhi until Timur sacked it and slaughtered its inhabitants. For a brief period Tughluq power shifted to Jaunpur near Varanasi, where the Tughluq architectural traditions were carried forward in some superb mosques.

*The Baha'i faith was founded by a Persian, Baha'u'llah (meaning 'glory of God'; 1817-1892), who is believed to be the manifestation of God for this age. His teachings were directed towards the unification of the human race, the establishment of a permanent universal peace.*

### Baha'i Temple (Lotus Temple)

*ⓘ 1 Apr-30 Sep 0900-1900, 1 Oct-31 Mar 0930-1730, closed Mon, free entry and parking, visitors are welcome to services, and at other times the temple is open for silent meditation and prayer. Audio visual presentations about the faith in English are at 1100, 1200, 1400 and 1530, remove your shoes before entering. Taxi or auto-rickshaw though Bus 433 from the centre (Jantar Mantar) goes to Nehru Pl, within walking distance (1½ km) of the temple at Kalkaji.*

Architecturally the Baha'i Temple is a remarkably striking building. Constructed in 1980-1981, it is built out of white marble and in the characteristic Baha'i temple shape of a lotus flower – 45 lotus petals form the walls – which internally creates a feeling of light and space (34 m high, 70 m in diameter). It is a simple design, brilliantly executed and very elegant in form. All Baha'i temples are nine sided, symbolizing 'comprehensiveness, oneness and unity'. The Delhi temple, which seats 1,300, is surrounded by nine pools, an attractive feature also helping to keep the building cool. It is particularly attractive when flood-lit. Baha'i temples are "dedicated to the worship of God, for peoples of all races, religions or castes. Only the Holy Scriptures of the Baha'i Faith and earlier revelations are read or recited".



## Sleeping

Avoid hotel touts. Airport taxis may pretend not to know the location of your chosen hotel so give full details and INSIST to be taken there. Hotel prices in Delhi are signifi- cantly higher than in most other parts of the country. Smaller **C**, **D** guesthouses away from the centre in South Delhi (eg Kailash, Safdarjang) or in Sunder Nagar, are quieter and often good value but may not provide food. Cheaper **E**, **F** accommodation is concentrated around Janpath and Paharganj (New Delhi), and Chandni Chowk (Old Delhi) – well patronized but basic and usually cramped yet good for meeting other backpackers. Some have dormitory beds for under Rs 100. Some city centre hotel rooms are windowless. Signs in some hotels warn against taking drugs as this is becoming a serious cause for concern. Police raids are frequent.

### Old Delhi *p89, map p94*

**L-AL Oberoi Maidens**, 7 Sham Nath Marg, T2397 5464, www.oberoihotels.com. 54 large well-appointed rooms, restaurant (slow), barbecue nights are excellent, coffee shop, old-style bar, attractive colonial style in quiet area, spacious gardens with excellent pool, friendly welcome, personal attention. Recommended.

**B Broadway**, 4/15A Asaf Ali Rd, T2327 3821, www.oldworldhospitality.com. 32 clean but slightly underwhelming rooms in an interestingly quirky hotel. **Chor Bizarre** restaurant and bar (see below) is highly regarded, as is the 'Thugs' pub – easily one of the best options in Old Delhi.

**C Flora**, Dayanand Rd, Daryaganj, T2327 3634. 24 small but clean a/c rooms centre 2 km, good restaurant.

**C-E Wongdhen House**, 15A New Tibetan Colony, Manju-ka-Tilla, T2381 6689, wongdhenhouse@hotmail.com. Very clean rooms, some with a/c and TV, safe, homely, good breakfast and Tibetan meals, an insight into Tibetan culture, peacefully located by the Yamuna River yet 15 mins by auto-rickshaw north from Old Delhi station, recommended.

**D Bhagirath Palace**, opposite Red Fort, Chandni Chowk, T2386 6223, hotbha@del3.vsnl.net.in. 12 rooms, some a/c, 1 km Old Delhi Railway, bar.

**E Tera**, 2802a Bazar, Kashmir Gate, T2391 1532. 42 rooms, some a/c, 500 m Old Delhi Railway, restaurant, coffee shop, TV.

**E-F Noor**, 421 Matia Mahal, Jama Masjid (1st left after **Flora's Restaurant**, then 3rd left), T2326 7791. 34 clean, quiet rooms, shared

*For an explanation of sleeping and eating price codes used in this guide, see inside the front cover. Other relevant information is found in Essentials, see pages 56-61.*

facilities (Indian WC), fans, rooftop views of Jama Masjid and fort, experience of Old Delhi.

## New Delhi *p97*

**Connaught Place** *p102, map p100*

**LL-L Park**, 15 Sansad Marg, T2374 3000, www.theparkhotels.com. 224 of the best contemporary-styled rooms in town, good views, friendly, award-winning restaurant and funky, modern bar, recommended.

**LL-AL Imperial**, Janpath, T2334 1234, www.theimperialindia.com. 263 rooms in supremely elegant Lutyens-designed 1933 hotel. Unparalleled location, great bar, gardens and secluded pool, slightly disappointing restaurants and service a bit fierce, but still quite an experience, highly recommended, check website for offers.

**L The Hans Plaza**, 15 Barakhamba Rd (16th-20th floor), T2331 6868, www.hanshotels.com. 67 slightly uninspired rooms, not a 'boutique hotel' as advertised but clean and quiet with superb views from the roomy rooftop restaurant.

**A Hotel Alka**, P Block, Connaught Circus, T2334 4328, hotelalka@vsnl.com. 21 well-appointed rooms in glitzy surroundings, including two spotless restaurants and a distinctively decorated bar.

**A Centrepoint**, 13 Kasturba Gandhi Marg, T2335 4304, www.thecentrepoint.com. Well-located, charming old building, although starting to show its age. 52 large, plainclean rooms, some with cramped bathrooms, smarter road side rooms can be noisy, restaurant lacks variety but reasonable breakfasts (included), reception 'willing but pushed', good exchange rate.

**A Marina**, G-59 Connaught Circus, T2332 4658, marina@nde.vsnl.net.in. 93 slightly old-fashioned but clean rooms (**A** suites),

bath with tubs, some large, others cramped but refurbished, attractive marble reception, good coffee shop, travel agent recommended, pleasant.

**A Nirula's**, L-Block, Connaught Circus, T2341 7419, www.nirulas.com. 31 small, plain, well-appointed rooms, good Potpourri restaurant, ice cream and pastry shops, internet, very central, clean, peaceful suites, efficient but not especially good value.

**B Fifty Five**, H-55 Connaught Pl, T2332 1244, bookings@hotel55.com. 15 small, clean, well-maintained rooms, darkish decor, central a/c, road can be a bit noisy, roof terrace for breakfast, helpful, very friendly staff, recommended.

**B-C Central Court**, N-Block, T23315013, F23317582. Simple hotel with basic 60s furniture, clean, very large doubles/suites with bath (small singles), windows in doors only, coffee shop, friendly staff, but no restaurant.

**B-C YMCA Tourist Hostel**, Jai Singh Rd, T2336 1915, www.delhiymca.com. 120 rooms, for both sexes, a/c rooms with bath (B-Block, non a/c and shared bath), some reported dirty, restaurant (breakfast included but disappointing), travel, peaceful gardens, tennis, good pool (Rs 100 extra), luggage stored (Rs 5 per day), pay in advance but check bill, reserve ahead, very professional.

**B-C YWCA International Guest House**, Sansad Marg (near Jantar Mantar), T2336 1561, www.ywcaindia.org. 24 clean, cozy, upgraded a/c rooms, centre 1 km, open to both sexes, restaurant (see below), handy internet in foyer, peaceful garden, convenient location, good value.

**C Choudhary**, H 35/3 Connaught Circus, T2332 2043, harsh@del3.vsnl.net.in. Tucked away but worth seeking out; 8 very clean rooms in a central location with a friendly manager who knows his stuff.

**C-D Hotel Palace Heights**, D Block, Connaught Pl, T2341 5419. 18 passable rooms, 6 with attached bathrooms and a/c on top floor with terrace and friendly staff.

**E-F Ringo Guest House**, 17 Scindia House (upstairs), off Kasturba Gandhi Marg, T2331 0605. Tiny rooms (some windowless) but no bugs, cheap crowded dorm (beds 15 cm apart) or beds on rooftop, hot showers, basic toilets, lockers, good restaurant (0700-2300), courtyard, friendly staff, backpackers' haunt (other hotel touts waylay travellers), superior to nearby **Sunny**, recommended at the price.

**Paharganj** *p97, map p110*

Rooms tend to be cheap, usually with shared baths, and the street-side rooms can be noisy. Though the packed bazars and crowded lanes can be dirty, Parharganj is where backpackers congregate. Sandwiched between the main sights and near the main railway station, it is convenient and on hand are plenty of shops selling souvenirs, travel agents, cheap hotels and cafés catering for Western tastes. For a more sedate, 'authentic' experience, you might like to try elsewhere. Avoid **Hotel Bright**.

**B-C Hotel Ajanta**, 36 Arakashan Rd, T2651 6097, www.hotelajanta.com. 60 well-maintained rooms, most a/c, good service and decent restaurant. Travel agency onsite.

**B-C Gold Regency**, 4350 Main Bazar, T2356 2101, www.goldregency.com. 40 good, clean, smallish a/c rooms, plus a moderately priced restaurant, disco and Cyber Café. Good facilities but some power problems.

**B-C Tourist Deluxe**, 7361 Qutb Rd, Ramnnagar, T2367 0985, touristdeluxe@ vsnl.net. 40 comfortable a/c rooms plus a few suites with tubs, vegetarian restaurant, on busy main road.

**C Tourist**, T2361 0334, tourist@schand.com. 65 rooms, 30 a/c, cleaner than Tourist Deluxe (and uncarpeted), vegetarian restaurant, rooms at rear quieter.

**C-D Rail Yatri Nivas**, behind New Delhi Railway Station (3-min walk from Ajmeri Gate, 8-storey building), T2323 3561. Only for transit train passengers holding a valid ticket. 36 cleanish rooms plus a dorm (rs135), all rates include breakfast. Phone ahead to book, very convenient location.

**C-D Shelton**, 5043 Main Bazar, T2358 0575. 36 clean, light rooms in a slightly grander hotel than its neighbours – it even has a lift!

**D Baba Deluxe**, 7795 Arakashan Rd, Ramnagar, T2354 8334, F3559858. 52 clean rooms, friendly staff, generator.

**D Rak International**, 820 Main Bazar, Chowk Bowli, T2358 6508. 27 basic but clean rooms in professionally run, quiet hotel with a rooftop restaurant and water feature and a friendly manager, recommended.

**D Royal Guest House**, 4464 Main Bazar, T2358 6176, royalguesthouse@yahoo.com. 17 spotless rooms, some a/c, in an exceptionally well-maintained, friendly hotel.

**D-E Bless Inn**, 2339-41, Rajguru Rd, Chuna Mandi, T2368 8400, narang_kelson@hotmail.com. 20 surprisingly smart rooms given unprepossessing exterior, but no character.

**D-E Hare Rama Guest House**, 298 Main Bazar, T2356 1301, harerama_2000@hotmail.com. 65 clean, tiled rooms, 24-hr hot water, many facilities, staff protective of female guests on their own, recommended.

**D-E Heritage Inn**, 2374 Raj Guru Rd, Chuna Mandi, T2358 8222. 20 simple, spotless rooms in brand new building with friendly staff.

**D-E Railway Retiring Rooms**, New (and Old) Delhi Railway Station. For 12 and 24 hrs, dorm beds (10 rooms, 6 a/c are usually pre-booked), only for train ticket-holders, basic, noisy, but convenient.

**D-E Star Palace**, 4590 Dal Mandi, off Main Bazar (lane opposite Khalsa Boots), T2358 4849, www.stargroupofhotels.com. 31 clean, well kept rooms (some a/c) with "fantastic showers", quiet, friendly, safe.

**D-E Starview**, 5136 Main Bazar, T2358 6810, www.stargroupofhotels.com. 23 small but adequate rooms, some with a/c, some triples.

**D-E Vivek**, 1534-1550, Main Bazar, T5154 1435, www.vivekhotel.com. 50 adequate rooms which are outshone by this hotel's impressive communal areas and a/c café. Plenty of facilities and friendly staff, good value, recommended.

**E Ajay's**, 5084a Main Bazar, T2358 3125, www.anupamhoteliersltd.com. 48 fairly clean (windowless) rooms with bath, dorm, good bakery, restaurant, friendly, popular backpackers' hangout.

**E Anoop**, 1566 Main Bazar, T5154 1390, www.anupamhoteliersltd.com. 43 rooms with bath, some with air-cooler, very clean though basic, noisy at times, safe, good 24-hr rooftop restaurant shared with Hare Krishna (waiters can 'forget' to give change).

**E Hare Krishna**, 1572 Main Bazar, T2352 9188, www.anupamhoteliersltd.com. 24 cleanish rooms with bath (some windowless, stuffy), friendly, travel, good rooftop restaurant.

**E-F Namaskar**, 917 Chandiwalan, Main Bazar, T2362 1234, namaskarhotel@yahoo.com. 32 small basic rooms (2-4 beds) with bath (bucket hot water), clean but some windowless, newer **D** a/c rooms (Rs 450) in extension, generator, safe, friendly service, good atmosphere, quiet at night, stores luggage, reserve ahead, unreliable travel information.

**Elsewhere in New Delhi** *p97, map p98*

**LL Grand Inter-Continental**, Barakhamba Ave, T2341 1001, www.intercontinental.com. 444 elegant, modern rooms in 28-storey hotel some find impersonal, others among best in its class, good patisserie, great views from rooftop restaurants.

**LL Le Meridien**, Windsor Pl, Janpath, T2371 0101, www.lemeridien-newdelhi.com. 355 rooms, visually striking space station interior, but otherwise disappointing, "too American, no soul".

**LL-L Metropolitan Hotel Nikko**, Bangla Sahib Rd, T5250 0200, www.nikkohotels.com. 167 classy, modern rooms (great bathrooms) in ultra-smart Japanese chain hotel. Excellent Japanese restaurant, highly professional staff, recommended.

**Outer New Delhi** *p97, map p98*

**LL Oberoi**, Dr Zakir Hussain Marg, T2436 3030, www.oberoihotels.com. 300 rooms, overlooking golf club, immaculate, quietly efficient, excellent all round but expensive Chinese restaurant disappointing.

**LL Park Royal Intercontinental**, Nehru Pl, T2622 3344, www.newdelhi.intercontinental.com. 224 light, modern and well-appointed rooms in a high class hotel, although location is not the best.

**LL Taj Mahal**, 1 Mansingh Rd, T2302 6162, www.tajhotels.com. 300 attractive, comfortable rooms, excellent restaurants and service (**Haveli** offers wide choice and explanations for the newcomer, **Ming House's** spicing varies), coffee shop pokey and disappointing, good Khazana shop, lavishly finished, friendly bar, good city views but lacks atmosphere.

**LL-L Maurya Sheraton Hotel** and **Towers**, Sardar Patel Marg, T2611 2233, www.welcomegroup.com. 516 rooms, those in premium block outstanding, excellent decor and service, splendid pool (solar heated), disco (noisy late at night, so avoid rooms nearby), good restaurants. See Eating.



**LL-L Taj Palace**, 2 Sardar Patel Marg, T2611 0202, www.tajhotels.com. 421 rooms, slightly dated bathrooms, standard 5-star facilities but well done, purpose-built for business travellers, generally excellent, **Orient Express** restaurant highly recommended (haute French), "service outstanding, food superb", 'Masala Art' Indian restaurant also good.

**L Claridges**, 12 Aurangzeb Rd, T2301 0211, www.claridges.com. 138 recently refurbished, classy rooms, art deco style interiors, colonial atmosphere, attractive restaurants (good **Jade Garden** Chinese), impeccable service, more atmosphere than most, recommended.

**AL Ambassador** (Taj), Sujan Singh Park, T2463 2600, www.tajhotels.com. 81 rooms in period property, no pool but pleasant garden, quirky bar and coffee shop, calm atmosphere, quiet and convenient location.

**AL Ashok** (ITDC), 50-B Chanakyapuri, T2611 0101, www.theashokg.com. 571 large rooms (some upgraded) in huge property, sunny coffee shop, 24-hr bank, smart new Lebanese restaurant, trendy **Ssteels** bar, quiet but overpriced.

**AL Diplomat**, 9 Sardar Patel Marg, T2301 0204, www.thehoteldiplomat.com. 25 rooms, all different, pleasant garden but no pool, quietly located, very popular.

**A Bajaj Indian Homestay**, 8A/34 WEA, Karol Bagh, T2573 6509, www.indianhomestay.com. Newish, Indian decor, all rooms different, mod cons, breakfast included, homely touches and atmosphere. At the lower end of the category.

**A Jukaso Inn**, 50 Sunder Nagar, T2435 0308, www.indiamart.com/jukasoinn. 50 a/c rooms, restaurant, room service, garden, pleasant, quiet, friendly staff, recommended.

**A Nirula's**, C-135 Sector 2, NOIDA, 15 km east of centre, T0120-2526512, www.nirulas.com (also Connaught Circus). Comfortable, friendly and helpful, pleasant atmosphere, good **Potpourri** restaurant and bar.

**A-B La Sagrita**, 14 Sunder Nagar, T2435 8572, www.lasagrita.com. 24 recently refurbished a/c rooms, modern bathrooms, phone, restaurant, helpful staff, quiet location.

**B Rajdoot**, Mathura Rd, T2431 6666, F2464 7442. 55 rooms, convenient location for Nizammuddin Railway, pool.

**B-C Good Times**, 8/7 WEA Karol Bagh, off Pusa Rd, T5100 5140, www.goodtimeshotel.com. 27 clean, modern rooms, friendly staff and a good rooftop restaurant.

**B-C Pal's Inn**, E Patel Nagar, Karol Bagh, T2578 5310, palsinn@del3vsnl.net. 16 rooms in new guest house, marble baths, clean, well kept, lobby café facing park (full break- fast included), good car hire (Rs 600 for 8 hrs), friendly and caring owner, attentive staff.

**C-D Master Paying Guesthouse**, R-500 New Rajendra Nagar (Shankar & GR Hospital Rds crossing), T2874 1089, www.master-guesthouse.com. 5 clean rooms (some **B** a/c), spotless shared facilities, rooftop for breakfast, evening *thalis*, warm welcome, personal attention, secure, recommended. Very knowledgeable owner also runs tours of 'hidden Delhi', which are recommended.

**C-D Yatri Paying Guest House**, corner of Panchkuin and Mandir Margs, T2362 5563, yatri@vsnl.com. 6 large clean rooms (some a/c) in family home, cold in winter, garden, mosquito problem, quiet, peaceful oasis, friendly, welcoming but can't stay long, discount during summer.

### Youth hostels

**D-F Youth Hostel**, 5 Naya Marg, Chanakyapuri, T2611 6285, www.yhaindia.org. Wide range of room from a/c doubles at Rs 700 to a basic dorm (Rs 50), breakfast, prefer International YHA members, popular, great location.

## South Delhi *p103*

**LL-L Hyatt Regency**, Bhikaiji Cama Pl, Ring Rd, T2679 1234, www.delhi.hyatt.com. 518 rooms, smart but tiny for price, restaurants good but expensive, glitzy but a little stuffy.

**LL-L Surya**, Crown Plaza, New Friends Colony, T2683 5070, www.suryadelhi.crowneplaza.com. 195 rooms, slightly isolated, good views, good service, renowned Chinese rooftop restaurant.

**LL-L Vasant Continental**, Vasant Vihar, T2614 8800, www.jaypeehtoels.com. 110 rooms in recently renovated, contemporary styled hotel, convenient for airports (free transfer), large pool and gardens near Basant Lok Market, good service, interesting range of restaurants, all with 'live' kitchens, recommended.

**LL-AL The Grand (formerly Hyatt)**, Nelson Mandela Rd, Vasant Kunj Phase II, T2677 1234, www.thegrandnewdelhi.com. 390 rooms, 25 suites in new, contemporary styled luxury hotel, choice of good restaurants, great pool, health club, tennis, golf (20 mins drive). Recommended.

**L Manor**, 77 Friends Colony, T2692 5151, www.themanordelhi.com. Contemporary styledboutique hotel with 10 stylish rooms, heavenly beds, polished stone surfaces and chrome, relaxing garden, a haven.

**B '27' Jorbagh**, 27 Jorbagh (2 mins from Lodi tombs), T2682 2763, www.jorbagh27.com. 20 a/c rooms, car hire, not plush but very quiet (Western food nearby), hassle free, book ahead. Highly recommended.

**B Kailash Nath**, 39 Prithviraj Rd, T2469 4523, F4635706. 15 a/c rooms in private guest-house in a bungalow, free airport pick-up/drop, full services, used by NGOs and foreign consultants.

**B Legend Inn**, E-4 East of Kailash, T2621 6111, www.thelegendinn.com. Comfortable a/c rooms, no restaurant but it does have a 40-ft climbing wall and adventure museum!

# Eating

The larger hotel restaurants are often the best for cuisine, decor and ambience. Buffets (lunch or dinner) cost Rs 500 or more. Others may only open around 1930 for dinner; some close on Sun. Alcohol is served in most top hotels, but only in some non-hotel restaur- ants eg **Amber**, **Ginza**, **Kwality**.

## Old Delhi *p89, map p94*

**TTT Chor Bizarre**, Broadway Hotel, Asaf Ali Rd, T2327 3821. *Tandoori* and Kashmiri cuisine (Wazwan, Rs 500). Comfortable if quirky decor, including salad bar that was vintage car.

**T Flora**, Daryaganj. North Indian, excellent kalmi chicken kebab, biryani and breads, dark and gloomy but good food, very popular.

Ÿ **Karim's**, Gali Kababiyan (south of Jama Masjid). Mughlai. Authentic, busy, plenty of local colour. The experience, as much as the food, makes this a must. Not much to tempt the vegetarian though.
Ÿ **Peshawari**, 3707 Subhash Marg, Daryaganj. Tiny, with tiled walls, serves delicious chicken, closed Tue.

## New Delhi *p97*

### Connaught Place *p102, map p100*

ŸŸŸ **Rodeo**, 12a, T2371 3780. Excellent Mexican (3-course and beer, Rs 350), Italian, continental. "Heavenly", fast service, fully-stocked bar, wild west decor.
ŸŸŸ **Zen**, B-25, T2335 7444. Stylish though a little impersonal but popular, generous portions for Chinese, more expensive Japanese and seafood.
ŸŸ **Amber**, N-Block, T3312092. High-class decor, lightly spiced Mughlai cuisine, beer.
ŸŸ **Berco's**, L-Block, T2331 8134. Chinese, Japanese. Generous helpings, fast service, very popular, quieter for dinner.
ŸŸ **DV8**, 13 Regal Building, T5150 0693, with smart and cosy pub below. Round the world meals, good buffet (Rs 250), á la carte (Rs 150+), good music, great Espresso coffee.
ŸŸ **Embassy**, D-11, T2341 6434. International. Mirrored, very popular, good food, long standing local favourite.
ŸŸ **Gaylord**, B16 Regal Building, T2374 4677. Multi cuisine menu takes back seat to original 1949 decor and old world ambience. Separate bar equally charming.
ŸŸ **Kwality**, Parliament St. International. Try spicy Punjabi dishes with various breads.
ŸŸ **Potpourri, Nirula's**, L-Block, T2331 6694. Indian and continental. Bright, clean and very popular – tasty light meals, snacks, ice creams, salad bar (safe!) Rs 143, beers, several branches including N-Block.
ŸŸ **Q'BA**, E-42 Connaught Pl, T5151 2888. Mystifying name but super-stylish decor and attractive menu should make this new venture a run away success.
ŸŸ **Spirit**, E-34 Connaught Pl, T5100 6603. Very chic Lebanese\Italian restaurant and bar, service and food outstanding.
ŸŸ **TGI Fridays**, F-16, T2371 1991. Western meals, Texmex, Americana style decor with 50s objects on walls, TV, Western music, 'Happy Hour' (1700-1930).
ŸŸ **United Coffee House**, E-15 Connaught Pl, T2341 1697. Recommended as much for the colonial-era cake-icing decor as for the fairly average food. Always attracts a mixed crowd, well worth a visit.
Ÿ **Don't Pass Me By**, by Ringos, 17 Scindia House. Chinese. Bit dingy, but good basic food and plenty of it, prompt, cooler upstairs.
Ÿ **Kake's**, H-block, Plaza Building, T2341 1580. Famous Punjabi dhaba. Handi dishes and delicious green masala fish, very cheap.
Ÿ **Nathu's**, Bengali Market (east of Connaught Place), T2371 7313. Sweet shops serving mainly vegetarian food. Good dosa, idli, utthapam and North Indian chana bathura, clean, functional canteen.
Ÿ **Nizam's Kathi Kebabs**, H-5 Plaza, T2371 3078. Very good, tasty filled parathas, good value, clean, excellent '3-D toilets' (note emergency button!).
Ÿ **Tropical Smoothie**, L-13 Connaught Pl Outer Circle, T5151 7021. Another great place for an escape to the West – fantastic smoothies, tasty wraps and a wonderfully cool interior.

### Paharganj *p97, map p110*

The rooftop restaurants are great locations for a bite to eat.
ŸŸ-Ÿ **Appetite**, 1575 Main Bazar, T2753 2079. Chinese, Nepali, Italian. Mouth-watering bakery, good lassis.
ŸŸ-Ÿ **Everest Bakery Cave**, Dal Mandi, near Star Palace Hotel. Fantastic momos, cakes and pies with an ambience to match. Highly recommended.
ŸŸ-Ÿ **Madan's**, 1601 Main Bazar. International. Egg and chips to *thalis*, not special but friendly, popular, good value.
ŸŸ-Ÿ **Malhotra's**, 1833 Laxmi Narayan St, T2358 9371. Good Indian and Chinese, wide choice, a/c section; also takeaway.
ŸŸ-Ÿ **Temptation**, at Chanakya, 4350 Main Bazar. Pleasant. Good western (veg burgers, cakes), internet, disco and bar.

*The old-fashioned 'tea on the lawns' is still served at the Imperial and in the Claridges. Aapki Pasand, on 15 Netaji Subhash Marg, is another unique tea-tasting, in high-class, extremely professional surroundings, quite an experience.*

**Elsewhere in New Delhi** *p97, map p98*

ΨΨΨ **Bukhara**, Maurya Sheraton, T2611 2233. Stylish Northwest Frontier cuisine. Amidst rugged walls draped with rich rugs (but uncomfortable seating), outstanding meat dishes but not much for the vegetarian.

ΨΨΨ **Chinese**, does great soups, "waiters treat beer bottles as fine wines!".

ΨΨΨ **Corbett's**, Claridge's Hotel, T2301 0211. Authentic North Indian. Animal park theme outdoor, straw huts, jungle soundtrack, hidden animals delight children, good value.

ΨΨΨ **Dum Phukt**, Maurya Sheraton, T2611 2233. North Indian. Slowly steam-cooked in sealed *handis* produces excellent melt-in-the-mouth Nawabi dishes. High quality service and decor. Expensive and a bit pretentious.

ΨΨΨ **La Rouchelle**, Oberoi, T2436 4084. High class French cuisine.

ΨΨΨ **Lodi**, Lodi Gardens, T4655054. Excellent lunchtime continental, dinner Indian in pleasant, Mediterranean style surroundings.

ΨΨΨ **Parikrama**, Kasturba Gandhi Marg, T2372 1616. International. Savour the rich food and the views as the restaurant slowly revolves – a quiet and relaxing way to see Delhi!

ΨΨΨ **Spice Route**, Imperial Hotel. Slightly disappointing, and definitely overpriced, Kerala, Thai, Vietnamese cuisines in extraordinary surroundings.

ΨΨ **Basil and Thyme**, Santushti Complex, Chanakyapuri, T2467 3322. Continental. Pleasant setting, simple decor, a/c, modestly priced Western snacks at lunch, fashionable meeting place (busy 1300-1400).

ΨΨ **Moti Mahal Deluxe**, Malcha Marg, Chanakyapuri (near *Diplomat*), T2611 8698. Excellent Mughlai, closed Tue, short on ambience but food makes up for it.

ΨΨ **Ten (YWCA International GH)**, Sansad Marg. Indian, Western. Good meals and snacks. New management, clean, modern, well run, recommended

Ψ **Andhra Bhavan**, near India Gate. South Indian (Chettinad).

Ψ **Karim's Nemat Kada**, Nizamuddin West. Mughlai. Good value.

## South Delhi *p103*

ΨΨΨ **Bistro**, Hauz Khas Village, a complex of restaurants, the pick of which is the open-air Mughlai on the rooftop, which boasts fantastic views over old ruins, hugely atmospheric by night.

ΨΨΨ **La Piazza**, Hyatt Regency, Bhikaji Cama Place, T2618 1234. Authentic Italian. Mon-Sat lunch buffet Rs 550. Try pizzas from wood-fired oven, good atmosphere.

ΨΨΨ **Olive**, Kalika Dass Marg, Mehrauli, T2664 5500. The city's best attempt at an upmarket Meditteranean restaurant, set in a lovely whitewashed building. Authentic menu and reliable, the bar is a great place to unwind.

ΨΨΨ **Orient Express**, Taj Palace Hotel, T2611 0202. Continental. Recreated luxury of the famous train carriages, formal dress code, expensive but different.

ΨΨΨ **Park Baluch**, inside Deer Park, Hauz Khas Village, T2685 9369. Highly praised cuisine in peaceful, understated surroundings.

ΨΨΨ **Thai Wok**, 1091/1 Ambavata Complex, Mehrauli, T2664 4289. Interesting Thai menu and outstanding views over the Qutab minar from the large terrace.

ΨΨ **Ankur**, Siri Fort Marg, Asiad Village. Mexican. Good food, especially the fajitas, agreeable bar and staff.

ΨΨ **The Big Chill**, F-38 East of Kailash (off Lala Lajpat Rai Path near Spring Meadows Hospital), also in Khan Market, 1230 till late. A bright, new café with a difference. A wide range of carefully prepared, wholesome light meals of grills, bakes, fresh pasta and salads, spectacularly successful homemade desserts. Great atmosphere (choose your own music).

ΨΨ **Chopsticks**, Siri Fort Marg, T2649 2348. Chinese, Thai. Good value, pleasant ambience, bar, weekend buffet lunches.

ΨΨ **Golden Dragon**, C Block, Vasant Vihar, T2614 1849. Very reliable Chinese, reasonably priced, long happy hours.

ΨΨ **Imperial Garden**, E3 Masjid Moth, Gt Kailash II, T2647 7798. Excellent Oriental, unusual menu, one of the best in town.

ΨΨ **Mini Mahal**, C-25A Vasant Vihar. North Indian. Popular with diplomats.

ΨΨ **Punjabi by Nature**, 11 Basant Lok, T5151 6666, for outstanding and very popular Punjabi dishes.

ΨΨ **O'Briens**, 32 Basant Lok, T5166 9166. An Irish sandwich bar franchise offering an unusual range of freshly-produced butties.

Ψ **Colonelz Kebabz**, Defence Colony Market. Tandoori. Excellent tikkas and kebabs. Several others, including RK Puram. and delicious, safe 'street food' 1000-2200.

Ỷ **Keraleeyam**, Yusuf Sarai. Malabar. Spicy unusual non-vegetarian dishes.
Ỷ **Moti Mahal**, South Extn II. Tandoori. Noisy and now very average food.
Ỷ **Naivedyam**, Haus Khas Village, T2696 0426. Very good south Indian, clean and cheap.
Ỷ **Sagar**, 18 Defence Colony Market, T2433 3110. Excellent South Indian. Cheap and 'amazing!' *thalis* and coffee, very hectic (frequent queues). (Others in Vasant Kunj, Malviya Nagar and NOIDA).
Ỷ **Sona Rupa**, 46 Janpath. Recommended for snacks (1030-2400).

## Bars and clubs

Many national holidays are 'dry' days. Normally hotel restaurants, bars and clubs serve alcohol. All top hotels have bars. Delhi's 'in' crowd is notoriously fickle, meaning that the hip place to be seen changes almost weekly; below is a selection of places which were popular in Sep 2004, but may not be for long!
**1911**, at **Imperial Hotel**, elegantly styled colonial bar, good snacks.
**Bohemia**, opposite **Shalom**, T2622 3328. Relaxed, contemporary bar, friendly staff plus a good Indian restaurant upstairs.
**Dublin at the Sheraton**, classic repro Irish bar, everything but Guiness.
**F Bar**, MG Rd. Trendy fashion bar cum club, but not a bad place for a boogie.
**Pegasus**, at **Nirula's**, N-Connaught Circus. English-style pub, very friendly.
**Pluto's**, Vasant Kunj. Proper nightclub, full of whistle-blowing, hands in the air teenagers, raving Delhi-style.
**RG's**, opposite Qutab Minar. One of the few nightclubs outside the 5 stars, expensive (Rs 2000 per couple) but drinks are included.
**Shalom**, 'N' Block Market, Greater Kailash 1, T98101 48084. Comfortable, stylish lounge bar serving Lebanese cuisine while the resident DJ plays ambient music at a pleasantly low volume.
**Ssteels**, at **Ashok Hotel**. Trendy, industrial decor, very crowded at weekends, good range of cocktails.

## Entertainment

*First City* monthly (Rs 20) with reviews, the free fortnightly weekly *Delhi City Info*, and the weekly *Delhi Diary*.

### Cinemas

**PVR Anupam**, Community Centre, Saket, T2686 5999. Good choice, phone reservations before 2000.
**Priya**, the 'young spot', Vasant Vihar, T2614 0048. Usual action movies.
**Satyam**, Patel Nagar, T2589 3322.
**Regal**, **PVR Plaza**, Connaught Place, usually screen Hindi movies.

### Clubs

**Delhi Gymkhana Club**, 2 Safdarjang Rd, T2301 5533. Mostly for government and defence personnel, squash, tennis, swimming, bar and restaurant.
**Habitat Centre**, Lodi Rd, T2468 2222, with good programme of lectures, exhibitions, excellent restaurant.

### Son et Lumière

**Red Fort**: Apr-Nov 1800-1900 (Hindi), 1930-2030 (English). Entry Rs 50. Tickets available after 1700. Take mosquito cream.

## Festivals and events

Consult the weekly *Delhi Diary* available at hotels and many shops and offices around town for exact dates. The following list gives an approximate indication of the dates.

### January

Lohri (**13**), the climax of winter is celebrated with bonfires and singing.

**Republic Day Parade** (**26**), Rajpath. A spectacular fly-past and military march-past, with colourful pageants and tableaux from every state, dances and music. Tickets through travel agents and most hotels, Rs 100. You can see the full dress preview free, usually 2 days before; week-long celebrations during which government buildings are illuminated. **Beating the Retreat** (**29**), Vijay Chowk, a stirring display by the armed forces' bands marks the end of the Republic Day celebrations. **Martyr's Day** (**30**), marks Mahatma Gandhi's death anniversary; devotional *bhajans* and Guard of Honour at Raj Ghat. **Kite Flying Festival** on Makar Sankranti above Palika Bazar, Connaught Pl.



## February

**Vasant Panchami** (**2**), celebrates the first day of spring. The Mughal Gardens are opened to the public for a month. **Delhi Flower Show**, Purana Qila. **Thyagaraja Festival**, South Indian music and dance, Vaikunthnath Temple.

## March

**Basant Ritu Sammelan**, North Indian music.

## April

**Amir Khusrau's Birth Anniversary**, a fair in Nizamuddin celebrates this with prayers and *qawwali* singing.

## May

Buddha Jayanti, the **first full moon night** in May marks the birth of the Buddha and prayer meetings are held at Ladakh Buddha Vihara, Ring Rd and Buddha Vihara, Mandir Marg.

## August

**Janmashtami** celebrates the birth of the Hindu god Krishna. Special *puja*, Lakshmi Narayan Mandir. **Independence Day** (**15**), impressive flag hoisting ceremony and Prime Ministerial address at the Red Fort. **Vishnu Digambar Sammelan**, North Indian music and dance festival.

## October-November

**Gandhi Jayanti** (**2**), Mahatma Gandhi's birthday; devotional singing at Raj Ghat. **Dasara**, with over 200 Ramlila performances all over the city recounting the Ramayana story (see p1316). **The Ramlila Ballet** at Delhi Gate (south of Red Fort) and Ramlila Ground, is performed for a month and is most spectacular. Huge effigies of Ravana are burnt on the **9th night**; noisy and flamboyant. **National Drama Festival**, Shri Ram Centre. **Diwali**, the festival of lights; lighting of earthen lamps, candles and firework displays. **National Drama Festival**, Rabindra Bhavan.

## December

**Christmas** (**25**). Special Christmas Eve entertainments at all major hotels and restaurants; midnight mass and services at all churches. **Ayyappa Temple Festival**, Ayyappa Swami Temple, Ramakrishnapuram; South Indian music. **New Year's Eve** (**31**), celebrated in most hotels and restaurants offering special food and entertainment. Muslim festivals of **Ramadan**, **Id-ul-Fitr**, **Id-ul-Zuha** and **Muharram** celebrated according to lunar calendar.

# Shopping

There are several state emporia around Delhi including the Cottage Industries Emporium (CIE), a huge department store of Indian handicrafts, and those along Baba Kharak Singh Marg. It is a convenient way of shopping; the choice being huge, as the shelves are packed with goods that are made all over India and everything has a fixed price. You may have to pay a little more for this.

Shops generally open from 1000-1930 (winter 1000-1900). Food stores, chemists stay open later. Most shopping areas are closed on Sun. Weekly *Free Ads* (Rs 5, Thu) lists 2nd-hand cameras, binoculars, etc.

## Art galleries

Galleries exhibiting contemporary art are listed in *Delhi Diary*.

**Delhi Art Gallery**, Hauz Khas Village. A newly expanded gallery with a good range of moderately priced contemporary art.

**Espace**, 16 Community Centre, New Friends Colony, T2683 0499. Group and solo shows by artists from all over India.

## Bookshops

Hotel booksellers often carry a good selection of imported books about India, though some charge inflated prices. Among those with specialist academic and art books focusing on India are: **Jainson's**, Janpath Hotel; **Krishan**, Claridges; **Khazana**, Taj Mahal and **Taj Palace** hotels (0900-2000).

**Bahri & Sons**, opposite Main Gate, Khan Market. Has a wide choice.

**The Bookshop**, Khan Market. Has a wide choice (also at Jor Bagh Market).

**Bookworm**, B-29, Connaught Place. Wide selection, including art, Indology, fiction.

**Central News Agency**, P 23/90, Connaught Place. Carries national and foreign newspapers and journals.

**ED Galgotia**, 17B, Connaught Place. Highly recommended.

**Jacksons**, 5106, Main Bazar, Paharganj, T5535 1083. Selection in many languages.

**Jain's Bookshop** C-Block, Connaught Place, the government book agency.

**New Book Depot**, 18B, Connaught Place. Highly recommended.

**Oxford Book and Stationery**, Scindia House, Connaught Place. Wide selection, including art, Indology, fiction.

**Manohar**, 4753/23 Ansar Rd, Daryaganj, Old Delhi. A real treasure trove for books on South Asia and India especially, most helpful, knowledgeable staff. Highly recommended.

**MI**, 15a, Khan Market. Has a wide choice.

**Motilal Banarsidass**, Nai Sarak, Chandni Chowk. Have books on Indology.

**Munshiram Manoharlal**, Nai Sarak, Chandni Chowk. Have books on Indology.

**People Tree**, 8 Regal Building, Parliament St, Connaught Place. Ecology oriented.

**Prabhu & Sons**, Hauz Khas Village, well-hidden on 1st floor balcony down side street, for antiquarian/second-hand books.

**Timeless**, 46 The Housing Society, 3rd floor and basement, Part 1, South extensions, full of coffee tables, art books and novels.

**Vintage**, next door to **Prabhu & Sons**, again selling antiquarian/second-hand books.

## Clothing shops

For inexpensive (Western and Indian) clothes, try shops along Janpath and between Sansad Marg and Janpath; you can bargain down 50%. Top quality clothes in the latest Western styles and fashionable fabrics are almost unobtainable. Having said that **Hauz Khas Village** and **Sunder Nagar Market** have some designer wear many for export to the West.

**Archana**, Gt Kailash I, has several boutiques.

**Central Cottage Industries Emporium**, good selection, also sells fabrics.

**Fab India**, 14N-Gt Kailash I (4 outlets in N Block and also in Vasant Kunj). Excellent shirts, Nehru jackets, *salwar kameez*, linen, furnishing fabrics and now furniture.

**Khadi shop**, near the Regal building, Janpath, for Indian wares.

**Palika Bazar**, Connaught Circus, underground, a/c, can be a hassle but has decent salwar kameez, leather jackets and trousers.

**The Shop**, Regal Building, Connaught Pl. Modest selection.

Tailoring at small shops charge around Rs 70-100 to copy a dress or shirt; trousers Rs 100-150. Nearly all big hotels have upmarket boutiques and also fabric/tailor's shops (some may allow fabric purchased elsewhere); allow 24 hrs for stitching.

**Delhi Cloth House**, fabric.

**Grover**, fabric.

**Khan Market**, several tailors and cloth stores.

**Shankar Market**, near Connaught Pl, has good suiting, corduroys, denim etc, and will suggest tailors.

## Food

**Assam**, excellent Indian teas.

**Bhim Sen's**, Bengali Market, end of Tansen Marg, near Connaught Pl. For ome of the best, freshest (hence safest) Indian sweets.

**Central Cottage Industries Emporium**, Janpath. Excellent Indian teas.

**Darjeeling Tea Bureau**, Kaka Nagar Market (opposite Delhi Golf Club), nathmulls@

goldentipstea.com. Charming, reliable and good selection. Highly recommended.
**Evergreen**, Green Park. Fresh *jelabies*.
**Khari Baoli**, Chandni Chowk, lined with colourful shops. Spices and dried fruit etc.
**Modern Bazar**, Vasant Vihar Market. Cold meats, cheeses, yoghurts, tea.
**Steak House**, Jorbagh Market. Cold meats, cheeses, yoghurts.
**W Bengal Emporia**, excellent Indian teas.

## Handicrafts

### Carpets

Carpets can be found in shops in most top hotels and a number round Connaught Pl, not necessarily fixed-price. If you are visiting Agra, check out the prices here first.

### Earthenware

Unglazed earthenware *khumba matkas* (water pots) are sold round New Delhi Rly Station (workshops behind the main road).

### Emporia

Most open 1000-1800 (close 1330-1400).
**Central Cottage Industries Emporium**, corner of Janpath and Tolstoy Marg, offers hassle-free shopping, exchange counter (spend at least 50% of amount to be cashed, take bills to till and use TCs/credit card to pay), gift wrapping, will pack and post overseas; best if you are short of time.
**Dilli Haat**, opposite INA Market, is a well-designed open-air complex with rows of brick alcoves for craft stalls from different states, changed periodically; local craftsmen's outlets (bargaining possible), occasional fairs (tribal art, textiles etc). (Also good regional food – hygienic, safe. Very pleasant, quiet, clean (no smoking) and uncrowded, no hassle. Rs 10, 1000-2230.
**Khadi Gramodyog Bhawan**, Regal Building, for inexpensive homespun cotton *kurta pajama* (loose shirt and trousers), cotton/silk waistcoats, fabrics and Jaipuri paintings.
**Khazana**, **Taj Mahal** and **Taj Palace** hotels (0900-2000; daily) is high class.
**Santushti**, Chanakyapuri, opposite **Hotel Samrat** has attractive a/c units in a garden setting, hassle free. Shops sell good quality clothes, crafts, linen, saris, silver etc (1000-1800, except Sun, some close for lunch), **Basil and Thyme** serves trendy western snacks (busy 1300-1400); **Anokhi**, near the entrance, has good household gifts and clothes; **IK** sells high quality silver gifts, jewellery and paintings.

### Jewellery

Traditional silver and goldsmiths in Dariba Kalan, off Chandni Chowk (north of Jama Masjid). Cheap bangles and along Janpath; also at Hanuman Mandir, Gt Kailash I, N-Block. Also Sundar Nagar market.
**Jewel Mine**, 12A Palika Bazar. Has silver, beads, semi-precious stones and fair prices.
**Silverline**, 18 Babar Rd, Bengali Market, T2335 0454. Contemporary silver jewellery at wholesale prices.

### Leather

Cheap sandals from Janpath (Rs 100).
**Baluja**, Connaught Pl. Shoes.
**Bata**, Connaught Pl. Shoes and bags.
**Bharat**, Connaught Pl, opposite **Nirula's**.
**Hidesign**, G49, Connaught Pl, high class.
**Khan Market**, goods and shoes.
**South Extension**, goods and shoes.

## Markets and malls

Beware of pickpockets in markets and malls.
**Ansal Plaza**, HUDCO, Khelgaon Marg (south of South Extension) is Delhi's first European style shopping mall. Very smart, lots of chains.
**Basant Lok**, Vasant Vihar, has a few upmarket shops attracting the young.
**Hauz Khas village** consists of authentic, old village houses converted into designer shops selling handicrafts, ceramics, antiques and furniture in addition to luxury wear. Many are expensive, but some are good value. You will also find art galleries and restaurants.
**Jorbagh, Gt Kailash Pt I-M**, Western travellers hankering for the familiar, and prepared to pay the price, will find a good range of eatables and toiletries.
**Main Bazar**, Paharganj, again a good range of food and toiletries for Westerners with enough cash.
**Santushti**, Chanakyapuri, see Handicrafts.
**Sarojini Nagar** sells daily necessities as well as cheap fabric and clothing.
**South Extension** is good for clothes, shoes, jewellery, music etc.
**Sunder Nagar** has a few shops selling Indian handicrafts and jewellery (precious and

semi-precious); some quite original. **Tibetan Market** stalls along Janpath have plenty of curios – most are new but rapidly aged to look authentic.



## Activities and tours

Local sightseeing tours can be arranged through approved travel agents and tour operators. For approved tourist guides/agencies contact India Tourist Office and travel agents. There are many small agents, eg opposite New Delhi Railway Station, seemingly offer unusual itineraries, but their standards can't be guaranteed and their rates are not significantly lower. Rates: Delhi only, half day Rs 90, full day Rs 160. **India Tourism Development Corporation** (ITDC) and **Delhi Tourism** both run city sightseeing tours. Combining Old and New Delhi tours on the same day can be very tiring. A/c coaches are particularly recommended during the summer months. The price includes transport and guide services, but all are whistle-stop tours. Check whether entrance fees to many sights are included in the price of the tour. A group of 3 or 4 people could consider hiring a car and doing the tour at their own pace. Another alternative is to hire an auto- rickshaw for the day (around Rs 200). It will entail visiting gift shops for the driver to get a commission, but you don't have to buy.



### Delhi Tourism Tours

Check time, T3314229. Book day in advance. Departure point: Delhi Tourism, Bombay Life Building, N-Block, Connaught Pl.
**New Delhi Tour** (0800-1400): Jantar Mantar, Qutb Minar, Lakshmi Narayan Temple, Safdarjang's Tomb, Diplomatic Enclave, India Gate.
**Old Delhi Tour** (1400-1700): Jama Masjid, Red Fort, Shanit Vana, Raj Ghat, Kotla Firoz Shah.
**Evening Tour** (1800-2200): Lakshmi Narayan Temple (evening prayer), India Gate, Purana Qila, son et lumière (Red Fort), Jama Masjid (dinner at a Mughlai restaurant). Both Rs 150.
**Museum Tour** (Sun only, check time): Air Force, Rail and Transport, and National Museums, Indira Gandhi Memorial, Nehru Planetarium, Museum of Natural History and Dolls Museum.

### ITDC Tours

Guides are generally good but tours are rushed, T2332 0331. Tickets can be booked from **Hotel Indraprastha**, T2334 4511.
**New Delhi Tour**: departs from L-1 Connaught Circus and **Hotel Indraprastha** (0800- 1330), Rs 125 (a/c coach): Jantar Mantar, Lakshmi Narayan Temple, India Gate,Nehru Pavilion, Pragati Maidan (closed Monday), Humayun's Tomb, Qutb Minar.
**Old Delhi Tour**: departs from **Hotel Indraprastha**. (1400-1700), Rs 100: Kotla Firoz Shah, Raj Ghat, Shantivana, Jama Masjid and Red Fort.

### Taj Mahal tours

Many companies offer coach tours to Agra (eg ITDC, from L1 Connaught Circus, 0630-2200 except Fri, Rs 600, a/c coach). However, travelling by road is slow and uncomfortable; by car, allow at least 4 hrs each way. Train is a better option; take either the *Shatabdi*, or *Taj Express*, but book early.

### Tour operators

There are many operators offering tours, ticketing, reservations, etc, for travel across India. Many are around Connaught Circus, Parharganj, Rajendra Place and Nehru Place. Most belong to special associations (IATA, PATA) for complaints.

**Creative Travel**, 27-30 Creative Plaza, Nanak Pura, Moti Bagh, T24679192, www.travel2 india.com. Efficient, reliable, helpful.

**Highland**, N-29 Middle Circus, Connaught Pl, T23318236, highlandtravels@usa.net. Friendly, competent and reasonable priced.

**Ibex Expeditions**, Delhi, T91-11-6912641, www.ibexexpeditions.com. Offers a wide range of tours,and ticketing, etc.

**Potala Tours & Travels**, 101 Antriksh Bhavan, 22 K Ghandi Marg, T23722552, www.potata tours.com. Excellent staff, car tours, ticketing. Recommended.

**Wanderlust Travels & Travels**, G-18, 2nd floor, Greater Kailash, New Delhi 110048, T3092 0231, www.wanderlustindia.com. Tailor-made tours throughout India, groups/individuals, ticketing, etc.

### Walking tours

**Chor Bizarre**, Hotel Broadway, T2327 3821 offers special walking tours of Old Delhi, with good lunch, 0930- 1330, 1300-1630, Rs 350 each, Rs 400 for both.

**Master Paying Guest House** (see Sleeping p109) offers walking tours twice a week which are highly recommended for a more intimate experience of Old Delhi.

# Transport

## Air

International flights arrive at the Indira Gandhi International Terminal. Enquiries T25622011; pre-recorded arrivals and departures, T144/5; reservations, T146. Palam Domestic Terminal; enquiries T23295121; pre-recorded arrivals and departures, T142/3, private airlines, T149, **Indian Airlines** reservations, T141. Delhi has daily connections (many direct) with the following domestic destinations. The number of flights, if more than 1, is shown in brackets.

**Airlines**: IC = Indian Airlines, **CD** Alliance, **JA** Jagson, **S2** Sahara, **9W** Jet Air, **AI** Air India, **BG** Bangladesh Biman, **RA** Royal Nepal, **TBA** Trans Bharat Aviation.

**Daily flights**: **Agra** (IC); **Ahmadabad** (IC 2, 9W); **Bagdogra** (for Darjeeling) (9W); **Bangalore** (IC 2, 9W); **Bhopal** (IC 2); **Bhubaneshwar**; **Kolkata** (IC 2, 9W); **Chandigarh** (9W); **Chennai (Madras)** (IC 2, 9W); **Cochin** (CD, IC); **Goa** (CD, IC, S2); **Guwahati** (IC, 9W); **Hyderabad** (IC 2, S2, 9W); **Jaipur** (9W); **Jammu** (IC, 9W); **Kathmandu** (IC, RA); **Khajuraho** (IC, 9W); **Kullu** (JA, TBA); **Lucknow** (S2, 9W); **Mumbai (Bombay)** (CD, IC 9, 9W 8, S2 3, AI); **Nagpur** (IC); **Patna** (IC); **Pune** (IC, 9W); **Raipur** (CD); **Rajkot**; **Ranchi** (IC); **Srinagar** (CD, 9W); **Trivandrum** (IC, 9W); **Udaipur** (IC, 9W); **Vadodara** (CD); **Varanasi** (IC, S2, 9W).

**Non-daily flights**: **Amritsar** (IC 3, AI 2); **Aurangabad** (IC 4); **Bagdogra** (for Darjiling) (IC 3, 9W 3); **Chandigarh** (IC, CD, JA); **Chennai (Madras)** (AI 3); **Dhaka** (BG 2); **Dibrugarh** (S2 3); **Guwahati** (IC 2, S2 2); **Gwalior** (CD 3, IC 4); **Indore** (CD 6, IC 6, 9W 6); **Imphal** (IC 2); **Jaipur** (CD 4, IC 8); **Jaisalmer** (CD, JA 3); **Jodhpur** (CD 3, JA 2); **Leh** (CD 4, CD 7); **Lucknow** (CD 3, IC 5); **Paro** (KP 2); **Shimla** (JA 3); **Srinagar** (IC 6); **Udaipur** (CD 6).

### Transport to and from the airport

There is a booth just outside 'Arrivals' at the International and Domestic terminals for the bus services. It is a safe, economical option. A free shuttle runs between the 2 terminals every 30 mins during the day. Some hotel buses leave from the Domestic terminal. **Bus 780** runs between the **airport** and **New Delhi Railway station**.

The International and Domestic terminals have **pre-paid taxi** counters outside the baggage hall (3 price categories) which ensure that you pay the right amount (give your name, exact destination and number of all items of luggage). Most expensive are white 'DLZ' **limousines** and then white 'DLY' **luxury taxis**. Cheapest are 'DLT' **ordinary Delhi taxis** (black with yellow top Ambassador/Fiat cars, often very old). 'DLY' taxis charge 3 times the DLT price, see page 40. A 'Welcome' desk by the baggage reclamation offers expensive taxis only. Take your receipt to the ticket counter outside to find your taxi and give it to the driver when you reach the destination; you don't need to tip (although they will ask!). From the International terminal DLT taxischarge about Rs 200 for the town-centre (Connaught Place area); night charges, double, 2300-0500. Rates from the Domestic terminal are slightly lower.

## Auto-rickshaw

Widely available at about half the cost of taxis (Rs 4 per km). Normal capacity for foreigners is 2 people! (3rd person extra); insist on using the metre or agree fare in advance. Expect to pay Rs 20 for the shortest journeys. Allow Rs 75 for 2 hrs' sight-seeing/shopping. It is best to walk away from tourist centres to look for an auto. Cycle-rickshaws are available in the Old City. Be prepared to bargain. New Delhi station to Jama Masjid Rs 20-25. They are not allowed into Connaught Place.

## Bus

### Local

The city bus service run by the **Delhi Transport Corporation (DTC)** connects all important points in the city. There are over 300 routes. Information is available at DTC assistance booths and at all major bus stops. Don't be afraid to ask conductors or fellow passengers. Buses are often hopelessly overcrowded so only use at off-peak.

### Long distance

Delhi is linked to most major centres in North India. Services are provided by Delhi Transport Corp (DTC) and State Roadways of neighbouring states from various **Inter-State Bus Termini (ISBT)**; these have bus services between them. Allow at least 30 mins for buying a ticket and finding the right bus.

**Kashmir Gate**, T22968709, has a restaurant, left luggage (Rs 5 per day), bank (1000-1400 Mon-Fri; 1000-1200 Sat), Post Office (0800-1700 Mon-Sat) and telephones (includes International calls). **DTC**, T2968836. For Manali: Himachal Roadways T2966725 (or Himachal Tourism which operate from various pick-up points), are better maintained than unregistered private buses.

**Ajmeri Gate**: **UP Roadways**, T22968709; to Almora (5 hrs), Dehradun, Haridwar, Mussoorie.

**Kingsway Camp**: Haryana Roadways, T22961262; daily to Agra (5-6 hrs, Rs 80, quicker by rail), Chandigarh (5 hrs), Jaipur (Rs 150, 6½ hrs), Mathura etc.

**Rajpur Rd**: Himachal Roadways, T2966725; twice daily to Dharamshala (12 hrs), Manali (15 hrs), Shimla (10 hrs) etc. **Jammu and Kashmir RTC**, Hotel Kanishka, T3324511; to Jammu; Yatri Niwas Hotel to Srinagar. **Punjab Roadways**, T2967842, to Amritsar, Chandigarh, Jammu, Pathankot. **Sarai Kale Khan Ring Rd** (near Nizamuddin Rly station): Terminal, T4638092. (Auto-rickshaws to Paharganj, Rs 50.) **Rajasthan Roadways**, T2961246, for Agra, 5-6 hrs (quicker by rail), Rs 58; via Mathura and Vrindavan, Ajmer, Alwar, Bharatpur (5 hrs), Bikaner (11 hrs), Gwalior, Jodhpur, Pushkar (10 hrs), Udaipur etc. **Anand Vihar**, Yamuna Bundh Rd, T2152431: **UP Roadways**, T2149089, to Dehradun (259 km, 6 hrs via Roorkee); Haridwar (5 hrs), Gorakhpur, Kanpur, Jhansi, Lucknow, Nainital, Varanasi. From **Bikaner House**, Pandara Rd (south of India Gate), T3383469; for several 'Deluxe' buses to Jaipur, 6 hrs, Rs 230 (a/c); ask for 'direct' bus (some buses stop at Amber for a tour of the fort). To Udaipur (via Ajmer), 1900; to Jodhpur (2120, 2200).

**To Nepal** Direct private buses run to Kathmandu, though the 36 hr journey is quite exhausting. A much shorter route to Nepal is to the Indian border town of **Banbassa** (see page 128) via Tanakpur and crossing to the western Nepal border town of Mahendranagar which has the Sukla Phanta Wildlife Reserve nearby. The onward journey to Kathmandu is about 20 hrs (the first section is over the very bumpy Mahindra Highway). It is best done in shorter stages via Royal Bardia National Park (5 hrs), or Nepalganj which has buses to Kathmandu and Pokhara (14 hrs). **UP Roadways** buses for Banbassa leave daily around 0730 from the **Tis-Hazari** Bus terminal and take under 8 hrs (but check details carefully).

**To Pakistan** A direct 'Friendship' bus

## Taxi tips

The first-time visitor can be vulnerable to exploitation by taxi drivers at the airport.

If arriving at night, you are very strongly advised to have a destination in mind and get a **pre-paid taxi**. Be firm about being dropped at the hotel of your choice and insist that you have a reservation; you can always change hotels the next day if you are unhappy. Don't admit to being a first-time visitor.

If you don't take a pre-paid taxi, the driver will demand an inflated fare. He may insist that the hotel you want to go to has closed or is full and will suggest one where he will get a commission (and you will be overcharged).

Sadly, some travellers have been told that the city was unsafe with street fighting, police barricades (which do exist) and curfews and have then been taken to Agra or Jaipur.



to Lahore runs on Tue, Wed, Sat and Sun, departing at 0600 from Ambedkar Stadium terminal, Old Delhi (reserve ahead, Rs 800, 14 hrs), for Indians with valid visas and relations in Pakistan, and for Pakistanis.

## Car

All road journeys in India are slow. Main roads out of Delhi are very heavily congested. Best time to leave is very early morning.

Delhi is well connected by road with major cities: by **NH2** to **Agra** (200 km), **Ajmer** (399 km); by **NH1** to **Amritsar** (446 km), **Bhopal** (741 km), **Chandigarh** (249 km), **Gwalior** (319 km); by **NH8** to **Jaipur** (261 km), **Jammu** (586 km), **Jodhpur** (604 km), **Kanpur** (490 km), **Kota** (505 km); by **NH24** to **Lucknow** (569 km), **Pathankot** (478 km), **Shimla** (368 km), **Srinagar** (876 km), **Udaipur** (635 km) and **Varanasi** (765 km).

### Car hire

An excellent way of getting about town either for sightseeing or if you have several journeys to make during the day.

Full day local use with driver (non a/c) is about Rs 700-800, 80 km/8 hrs, driver overnight *bata* Rs 150 per day; self-drive 24 hrs/150 km Rs 1,200. Airport to city centre Rs 400-500. To Jaipur, about Rs 3,000; return Rs 5,400. The Tourist Office, 88 Janpath, has a list of approved agents.

**Cozy Travels**, N1 BMC House, Middle Circle, Connaught Place, T2331 1593, cozytravels@vsnl.net.com, for Ambassador or similar, Rs 650 non-a/c, Rs 850 a/c.

**Metropole Tourist Service**, 244 Defence Flyover Market, T2431 2212, metropole@vsnl.com, car/jeep (US$30-40 per day), reliable and recommended.

**Mohindra Tourist Taxis**, corner of Poorvi/Paschimi Margs, Vasant Vihar, T2614 3188, "excellent service, safe driving".

**Western Court Tourist Taxis**, 36 Janpath, outside **Hotel Imperial**, T2332 1236. Helpful.

## Motorcycle

**Chawla Motorcycles**, 1770, Shri Kissan Dass Marg, Naiwali Gali, is very reliable, trustworthy, highly recommended for restoring classic bikes.

**Ess Aar Motors**, Jhandewalan Extn, west of Paharganj. Recommended for buying Enfields, very helpful.

**Nanna Motors**, 112 Press Rd (east of Connaught Circus), T23351769. Recommended for buying Enfields, very helpful.

## Taxi

Environment friendly taxis and autos with a green stripe run on compressed natural gas.

Yellow-top taxis are easily available at taxi stands or you can hail one on the road. Operated by meter, ask for the conversion card. Add 25% night charge (2300-0500) plus 50p for each piece of heavy luggage (over 20 kg).

## Train

'Trains at a glance' (Rs 25) lists important

trains across India. **Delhi Tourism**, Connaught Circus issues tickets on the spot. **New Delhi Railway Station** and **Hazrat Nizamuddin Station** (just north, and 5 km southeast of Connaught Place, respectively) connect Delhi with most major destinations. The latter has many important south-bound trains. **Old Delhi (Main) Station**, 6 km north of the centre, has broad and metre gauge trains. **Delhi Sarai Rohilla**, serves Rajasthan.

Enquiries T131, Tq3366177. Authorized porters (*coolies*), wear red shirts and white *dhotis;* agree the charge, before engaging one. For left luggage, you need a secure lock and chain.

Reservations T1330 or T23348686, Old Delhi T3975357, though generally for Northern Railway only (not all-India). Allow time (1-2 hrs) and be prepared to be very patient as it can be a nightmare, but don't be tempted to go to an unauthorized agent. The Central Booking Office has counters for paying by credit cards (although these cannot be used for booking tickets on the tourist quota).

Computerized reservation offices (in separate building in Connaught Circus); 0745-2100, Sun 0745-1400; fee Rs 20. May be quicker than ITB, but no advice offered. The Sarojini Nagar office is quick, hassle free (especially the credit card counter) and is well worth the detour. Alternatively, you can use a recommended travel agent for tickets/reservations and pay Rs 50-70 fee.

At **New Delhi Station**: **International Tourist Bureau (ITB)**, 1st Floor, Main Building, T3734164, F3343050, for foreigners, Mon-Fri 0930-1630; Sat 0930-1430; efficient and helpful if slow. You need your passport and visa; pay in US$, or rupees (with an encashment certificate). Those with Indrail passes, should confirm bookings. There is also a counter for foreigners and NRIs at Delhi Tourism, N-36 Connaught Pl, 1000-1700, Mon-Sat. The Airport counter (when open) is quick and efficient for air tickets and reservations. There is a pre-paid taxi and auto-rickshaw kiosks next to the taxi rank as you come out of the station.

Stations from which trains originate have codes: **OD** - Old Delhi, **ND** - New Delhi, **HN** - Hazrat Nizamuddin, **DSR** - Delhi Sarai Rohilla.

Some principal services are: **Agra**: *Shatabdi Exp, 2002*, ND 0600, 2 hrs; *Taj Exp, 2180*, HN, 0715, 2¾ hrs. **Ahmadabad**: *Rajdhani Exp, 2958, ND, 1935*, Tue, Thu, Sat, 14½ hrs. **Amritsar**: *Shatabdi Exp, 2013*, ND, 1630, 6 hrs; *New Delhi-Amritsar Exp, 4659*, ND, 1320, 8½ hrs; *Shane Punjab Exp, 2497*, ND, 0650, 7½ hrs. **Bangalore**: *Rajdhani Exp, 2430,* Mon, Tue, Fri, Sat, HN, 2050, 34 hrs; **Bhubaneswar**: *Rajdhani Exp, 2422*, ND, 1715, 24 hrs. **Bhopal**: *Shatabdi Exp, 2002*, ND, 0600, 8¾ hrs. **Bikaner**: *Bikaner Exp, 4789*, DSR, 0835, 10¼ hrs; *Bikaner Mail, 4791*, DSR, 2125, 11 hrs. **Kolkata**: *Rajdhani Exp, 2302*, ND, 1715, 17½ hrs (via Varanasi and Gaya; except Tue and Fri, *2306* via Patna, 19½ hrs); *Kalka-Howrah Mail, 2312*, OD, 0730, 23½ hrs. **Chandigarh**: *Shatabdi Exp, 2011*, ND, 0740, 3 hrs; *Shatabdi Exp, 2005,* ND, 1715, 3 hrs. **Chennai**: *Rajdhani Exp, 2434*, Wed, Fri, HN, 1530, 29 hrs; *GT Exp, 2616*, ND, 1840, 36¼ hrs; *Tamil Nadu Exp, 2622*, ND, 2230, 33¼ hrs; **Dehradun**: *Shatabdi Exp, 2017*, ND, 0700, 5¾ hrs. **Goa**: see Margao. **Guwahati**: *Rajdhani Exp, 2424,* ND, Tue, Wed, Sat, 1700, 28 hrs; *Rajdhani Exp, 2436, ND, Mon, Fri, 1240, 32 hrs*. **Gwalior**: *Shatabdi Exp, 2002*, ND, 0600, 3¼ hrs. **Haridwar**: *Shatabdi Exp*, 2017, ND, 0700, 4¼ hrs; *Mussoorie Exp, 4041*, OD, 2215, 7¾ hrs. **Jabalpur**: *Mahakoshal Exp, 1450*, HN, 1620, 18¼ hrs. **Jaipur**: *Shatabdi Exp, 2015*, daily except Sun, ND, 0615, 4¾ hrs; *Delhi-Jodhpur Exp, 4859,* OD, 1655, 5½ hrs. **Jammu**: *Malwa Exp, 9367*, ND, 0810, 10 hrs. *Rajdhani Exp, 2425*, ND, Fri, 2100, 9½ hrs. **Jhansi**: *Shatabdi Exp, 2002*, ND, 0600, 4½ hrs; *Lakshadweep Exp, 2618,* HN, 0955, 6 hrs. **Jodhpur**: *Mandore Exp, 2461*, OD, 2100, 11 hrs. **Kalka (for Shimla)**: *Shatabdi Exp, 2005*, ND, 1715, 4¾ hrs. **Kanpur**: *Shatabdi Exp, 2004*, ND, 0620, 5 hrs. **Lucknow**: *Shatabdi Exp, 2004*, ND, 0620, 6½ hrs. **Margao** (Goa): *Rajdhani Exp*, Wed, Thu, HN, 1100, 26 hrs. **Mathura**: *Taj Exp, 2180*, HN, 0715, 2 hrs. **Mumbai** (Central): *Rajdhani Exp, 2952*, ND, 1600, 17 hrs; *Paschim Exp, 2926*, ND, 1700, 22 hrs; *Golden Temple Mail, 2904*, ND, 0755, 22 hrs. **New Jalpaiguri** (for Darjeeling): *Rajdhani Exp, 2424,* Tue, Wed, Sat, ND, 1700, 21½ hrs. **Patna**: *NE Exp, 5622*, ND, 0645, 17 hrs. **Shimla**: *Howrah-Kalka Mail, 2311*, DSR, 2245 (change at **Kalka** to *101 railcar*), total 11 hrs (book sleeper ahead). From ND: *Himalayan Queen, 4095*, 0600 to Kalka, 5¼ hrs, change to narrow gauge *255*, 1105, total 13¼ hrs or *Shatabdi Exp, 2011*, 0740 to Chandigarh, 3¼ hrs leaving you an hour to reach Kalka for the narrow guage *255*, 1105, total 11 ½ hrs (see Shimla and Kalka, page 484). **Secunderabad** *Rajdhani Exp, 2430*, Mon, Tue, Fri, Sat, HN, 2050,

22 hrs. **Thiruvanantapuram**: *Rajdhani Exp*, HN, 0930, 31 hrs. **Udaipur**: *Chetak Exp, 9615*, DSR, 1410, 20¼ hrs; *Ahamadabad Exp, 9943*, DSR, 2100, 21 hrs. **Varanasi**: *Poorva Exp, 2382*, Mon, Tue, Fri, ND, 1615, 12¼ hrs; *Vishwanath Exp, 4258*, ND, 1330, 16 hrs.

For special steam *Fairy Queen* and the diesel *Palace on Wheels* tours see page 47 under Rajasthan. The latter departs from Delhi Cantonment every Wed Sep-Apr, US$270-325 each per night with 2 sharing a cabin.

## Directory

### Banks

Open Mon-Fri 1000-1400, Sat 1000-1200. Cash against Visa can take up to 1 hr; it is usually quicker to change foreign cash and TCs at hotels. ATMs for International Visa/ Plus card-holders using PIN at **HDFC, HSBC, Standard Chartered** and **Citibanks** all over Delhi. Foreign banks and money changers include: **American Express**, A-Block Connaught Pl, excellent; small branch in Pahar- ganj; **Standard Chartered Grindlays**, 15 KG Marg; **Thomas Cook**, Hotel Imperial, Janpath; New Delhi Railway station (24 hrs).

Indian banks (dealing in foreign exchange) open 24 hrs: **Central Bank of India**, Ashok Hotel, **State Bank of India**, Palam Airport.

Swift transfers from overseas through **Western Union**, SITA, F-12, Connaught Pl.

### Chemists

Many hospitals have 24-hr services: **Hindu Rao Hospital**, Sabzi Mandi; **Ram Manohar Lohia Hospital**, Willingdon Crescent; **S Kripalani Hospital**, Panchkuin Rd. In Connaught Pl: **Nath Brothers**, G-2, off Marina Arcade; **Chemico**, H-45.

### Embassies

Visas are easy (photo needed), collect passport next day. **Australia**, 1/50-G Shantipath, T5139 9900. **Canada**, 7-8 Shantipath, T5178 2000. **France**, 2/50-E Shantipath, T2611 8790. **Ireland**, 13 Jor Bagh, T2462 6733. **UK**, Shantipath, T2687 2161. **USA**, Shantipath, T2419 8000.

### Hospitals

Embassies and High Commissions have lists of recommended doctors and dentists. Doctors approved by IAMAT (International Association for Medical Assistance to Travellers) are listed in a directory. Casualty and emergency wards in both private and government hospitals are open 24 hrs. **Ram Manohar Lohia**, Willingdon Crescent, T2336 5525, 24 hr A&E. **Hindu Rao**, Sabzi Mandi, T2251 3355. **JP Narain**, J Nehru Marg, Delhi Gate, T2331 1621. **Safdarjang General**, Sri Aurobindo Marg, T2616 5060. **S Kripalani**, Panchkuin Rd, T2336 3788.

### Post

Stamps are often available from the reception in the larger hotels. **Speedpost** from 36 centres. Head post offices at **Sansad Marg**, 1000-1830 Mon-Sat, **Eastern Court**, Janpath, 24 hrs, **Connaught Place**, A-Block, 1000-1700 Mon-Sat (parcel packing service outside). New Delhi GPO at **Ashoka Place**, southwest of Connaught Pl, 24 hrs.

Poste restante is available; make sure senders specify 'New Delhi 110001'; collect from counter behind sorting office, 0900-1700, until 1300, Sat. Don't forget to take your passport.

### Tourist offices

Most are open 1000-1800, Mon-Fri. **Govt of India Tourist Office**, 88 Janpath, T23320008 (0900-1800, closed Sun). Helpful; issues permits for visits to Rashtrapati Bhavan and gardens. Also at International Airport. **Delhi Tourism**, N-36 Connaught Pl, T23315322, F23313637. For hotel, transport and tours: 18, DDA SCO Complex, Defence Colony, T24623782, Coffee Home Annexe, Baba Kharak Singh Marg, T23363607 (0700-2100); also at Airport Terminals; Maharana Pratap Inter-State Bus Terminal, T22962181; New Delhi Rly Station, T23732374; Old Delhi Railway Station, T22511083. **ITDC**, L-1 Connaught Circus, T23320331.

### Useful addresses

**Ambulance** (24 hrs): T102. **Fire**: T101. **Foreigners' Registration Office**: 1st floor, Hans Bhawan, Tilak Bridge, T2331 9489. **Police**: T100.

# Leaving Delhi

## Going south

### Surajkund

Surajkund (meaning sun pool) is a perennial lake surrounded by rock-cut steps, built by the Rajput king Surajpal Tomar. According to tradition this is where the Rajputs first settled near Delhi in the 11th century AD. At the head of the reservoir, to the east, are the ruins of what is believed to have been a sun temple. A little south is Siddha Kund, a pool of fresh water trickling from a rock crevice which is said to have healing properties.

The annual **Craft Mela**, held in February in the village complex, draws crafts people from all over India – potters, weavers, metal and stone workers, painters, printers, wood carvers, embroiderers.

### Sultanpur Bird Sanctuary

Beyond Gurgaon, 46 km from Delhi, is a small bird sanctuary with a *jheel* (shallow lake) with reeds and other waterside plants growing round the rim. The large and handsome Sarus, the only indigenous Indian crane, breed in the reed beds. The migratory demoiselle, the smallest member of the crane family, comes to the lakeside in huge flights late in the winter evenings. The greylag and bar-headed geese and most of the migratory duck species visit the jheel including the ruddy shelduck, mallard, teal and gadwall. Coots are common as are white (rosy) pelicans, flamingos and a variety of waders. Of the indigenous birds visiting Sultanpur, the grey pelican, cormorant, painted stork, grey and pond heron and egret, are all to be seen plus a few white ibis and the blacknecked stork. Take a blue Haryana bus to Gurgaon from Delhi (every 10 minutes from Dhaula Khan). At Gurgaon take a Chandu bus (three to four daily) and get off at Sultanpur.

### The Delhi Jaipur Road

The NH8 is the main route between Delhi and Jaipur but although it is very busy there are some attractive stops en route, notably at Neemrana, which allows an overnight stay between Delhi and Jaipur. **Tikli**, 8 km off the Sonah road (turn off at Badshapur), about an hour's drive from Delhi towards the Aravalli hills, is a gem of a rural escape lovingly conceived by an English couple who have architecturally combined the best of East and West, following Lutyens. The exclusive "farmhouse" stands in a flower and bird filled garden, has an inviting pool and is a place to spoil yourself. Ask for Manender Farm, Gairatpur Bass village. **Rewari**, 83 km from Delhi, was founded in AD 1000 by Raja Rawat but there are the ruins of a still older town east of the 'modern' walls. It has been a prosperous centre for the manufacture of iron and brass vessels. On a rocky outcrop just above an unspoilt village, is the beautiful **Neemrana Fort** built in 1464 by Prithvi Raj Chauhan III and converted into an exceptional hotel ① *T01494-6007, sales@neemrana.com*. With 42 rooms, it is quiet and peaceful (occasional loud chanting from village below!), full of character and beautifully furnished with collectors' pieces. Particularly recommended are Baag, Dakshin, Jharoka, Surya Mahals, though some (eg Moonga) are a testing climb up to the seventh level. Superb Rajasthani and French cuisine is served (non-residents Rs 350 which allows looking around), other visitors must pay Rs 100. It has a magical atmosphere, part-day rates, reservations essential. Highly recommended. The village with a step well, and the fort ruins above, are worth exploring.

## Going north

### Meerut → *Phone code: 0121. Population: 850,000.*

Meerut, known to this day as the place where the Indian Mutiny broke out in 1857, is a busy marketing, commercial and administrative town. It reputedly produces 80% of the world's cricket equipment, although Sialkot (in Pakistan) makes the same claim! Although the old city is compact, the cantonment to the north is typically spaced out with some attractive broad tree-lined streets.

On 10 May 1857 the first revolt that was to end the East India Company's rule and usher in the era of the British Indian Empire rocked the streets of Meerut. However, the town's history goes back as early as Asoka's time: the modern town contains various Hindu and Muslim buildings from the 11th century onwards. The British cantonment has a particularly fine Mall. The cemetery of St John's, the old garrison Church (1821) contains interesting memorials. The Baleshwar Nath Temple and several old Hindu shrines surround the Suraj Kund tank (1714) which is fed by a canal from the Ganga. The mausolea and mosques indicate strong Mughal influence. The Jama Masjid (1019, later restored by Humayun), is one of the oldest in India. The red sandstone Shah Pir Maqbara (1628) on Hapur Road was built by the Empress Nur Jahan and further west on Delhi Road is the Abu Maqbara, with a large tank. Qutb-ud-din Aibak is believed to have built the Maqbara of Salar Masa-ud Ghazi (1194). The **Nauchandi Mela** is held in March.

*The best time to visit is from November to February when there are northern migratory birds.*

The train takes 1½ hours, the bus takes two hours. The railway stations are to the west and the City bus stand nearly 2 km to the southeast.

## Going to Nepal

The road east from Delhi to the Nepal border gives access to some popular hill stations of the Uttaranchal Himalaya and to the Corbett National Park.

**Ghaziabad** is a modern satellite town for Delhi, with a population of 520,000, comprising tall blocks, low-rise buildings and low-cost housing, all made of brick or reinforced concrete, with little or no aesthetic appeal. Beyond Ghaziabad is countryside, an area where two crops are cultivated each year, mostly rice in the monsoon and wheat in winter, but also sugarcane. Countless bullock carts trundle along the highway and line up outside the refineries.

The small town of **Garmukhteswar**, with some typical North Indian temples, stands on the west bank of the Ganga, with riverside ghats. According to the Mahabharata, this is where King Santanu met the Goddess Ganga in human form. Each year at the full moon in October and November, thousands of pilgrims converge to bathe in the holy waters. From the road bridge you may see turtles swimming around in the waters below.

**Rampur** was fFounded in 1623 by two Afghan Rohillas who served under the Mughals. Subsequently, the Rohillas united and expanded their empire (Rohilkhand, see page 141), but in 1772 the region was invaded by the Marathas. The Nawab of Rampur remained loyal to the British during the Mutiny and supported them in the second Afghan War. There is an extensive palace and fort here. The State library has oriental manuscripts and an excellent collection of 16th- to 18th-century portraits, including a contemporary painting of Babur and a small book of Turkish verse with notes by both Babur and Shah Jahan.

**Banbassa** is a small town on the India-Nepal border with a large Nepali population has a friendly feel. It is the shortest route from Delhi to Nepal.

# Uttar Pradesh

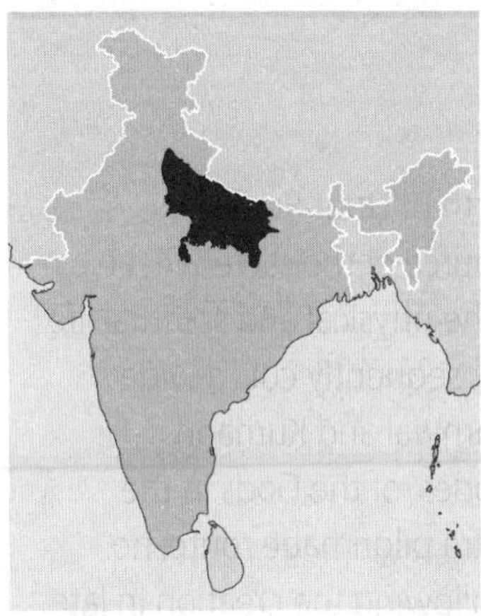



## Footprint features

# Introduction

Among the high peaks to the north of Uttar Pradesh, Himalayan springs provide the source of the sacred River Ganga – regarded by Hindus as the physical and spiritual life source of the country – which subsequently cuts a wide swathe through the state. The Garhwal and Kumaon Himalaya, as well as the 'holy abodes' of the Gods in the mountain shrines of the great Yatra pilgrimage route, no longer belong to Uttar Pradesh following the creation in late 2000 of the new state of Uttaranchal. However, Uttar Pradesh remains at the heart of much of India's religious, political and cultural life: the cradle of Hinduism and the cultural heartland of Indian Islam, a double identity symbolized by the presence of such contrasting sites as the Taj Mahal and the Mughal forts at Delhi and Agra, and the bathing ghats at Varanasi and Allahabad which attract millions of pilgrims. In the plains, historic cities such as Allahabad, Varanasi, Lucknow and Mathura are surrounded by a land transformed by great irrigation schemes.

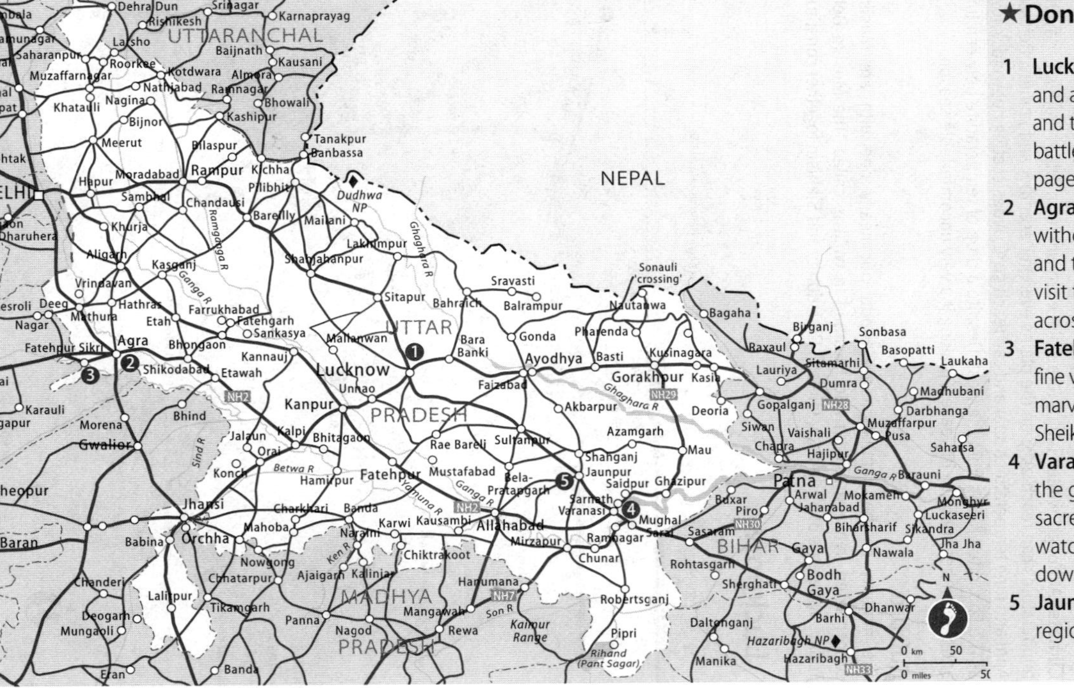


## ★ Don't miss...

1 **Lucknow** Purchase some fine chikan, zari and attar from the good craftsmen here and then visit one of the key battlegrounds of the 1857 Uprising, page 133.

2 **Agra** No visit to India is complete without visiting the show sites, Taj Mahal and the Red Fort, but also spare time to visit the baby Taj, I'timad-ud- Daulah, across the river, page 149.

3 **Fatehpur Sikri** Climb the Panch Mahal for fine views over Akbar's short-lived capital or marvel at the lattice work in the Tomb of Sheik Salim Chishti, page 162.

4 **Varanasi** Rise at dawn and go down to the ghats to watch pilgrims bathe in the sacred Ganga or hire a boat at sunset to watch leaf-boat lamps floating downstream, page 173.

5 **Jaunpur** Come and admire the fine regional Islamic architecture, page 182.

# Background → *Population: 166 mn. Area: 238,155 sq km. Languages: Hindi.*

## The land

**Geography** The landscapes of Uttar Pradesh ('Northern Province') are dominated by the flat alluvial plains of the Ganges and its tributaries. The north of the state runs along the southern margins of the **Shiwalik Hills**, which parallel the Himalaya, succeeded on their south by the often marshy, tropical **Terai**, which, until they were cleared for cultivation in the 1950s, formed a belt of jungle 65-km wide from the Ganga gorge at Haridwar to Bihar. The **Gangetic Plain** occupies most of the state, almost featureless and flat, stiflingly hot, dry and dusty in summer. To the south again are the northern margins of the Peninsula, including the outer slopes of the Vindhyan Mountains in the southeast which in places rise to more than 600 m.

**Climate** Although winter nights are cold everywhere in Uttar Pradesh, daytime temperatures can reach 25°C on the plains even in December and January. Between April and June temperatures soar and can reach 50°C. A desiccating hot wind, known as the Loo, often blows from the west. Despite a drop of temperature between June and September humidity increases, making it a very uncomfortable season.

## Culture

The majority of the population are Hindu but nearly one fifth are Muslim, concentrated between Aligarh and Faizabad in what is called 'The Muslim Belt'. Today, adherents of Buddhism, Jainism, Christianity and Sikhism together constitute



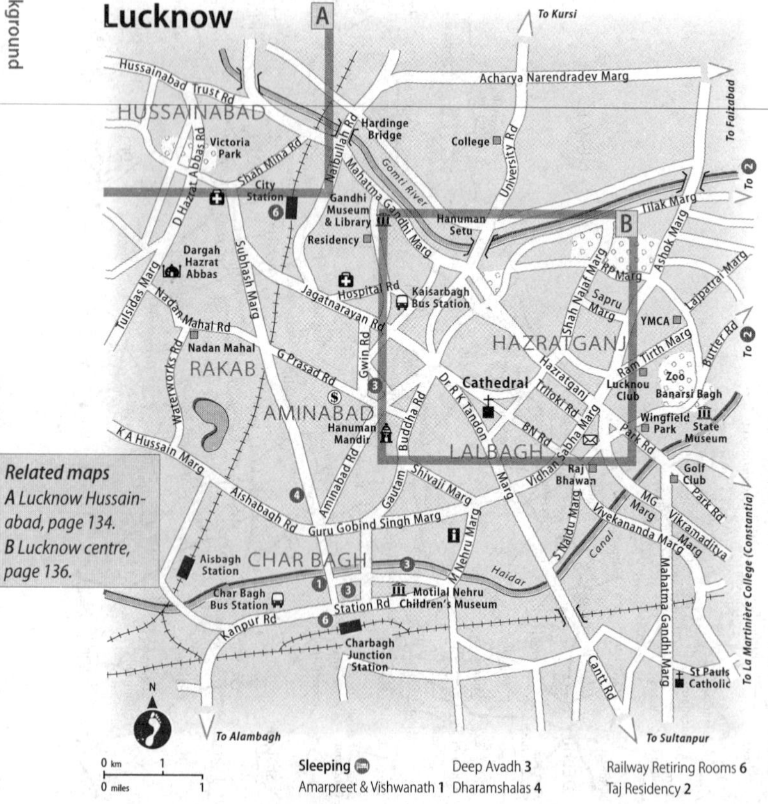


*Related maps*
*A Lucknow Hussainabad, page 134.*
*B Lucknow centre, page 136.*

less than three per cent of the state's population. Ethnically, the great majority of people on the plains are of Indo-Aryan stock. Most people speak Hindi, but Urdu is still quite widely used among Muslims. There are numerous local dialects. A broad division can be made between those on the plains and the *Pahari* (hill) dialects – one of the reasons given by the residents for the creation of the separate state of Uttaranchal in what was the Himalayan region of Uttar Pradesh (see page 197).

### Modern Uttar Pradesh

Uttar Pradesh has produced most of India's prime ministers since Independence, including Jawaharlal Nehru, his daughter Indira Gandhi and grandson Rajiv Gandhi. However, after three decades of Congress dominance, Uttar Pradesh politics has become like a frequently shaken kaleidoscope. Lower caste groups have become increasingly effectively mobilized, and have transferred their votes from the Congress to alternatives, mainly the Janata Party and the Bahujan Samaj Party. The rout of the Congress was completed by the emergence in the state of the BJP. Changing alliances, uncertainty and confusion have characterized much of the last five years. The state legislative assembly meets at Lucknow, the capital. Including those who now represent constituencies in Uttaranchal, but where there have not yet been new Parliamentary elections, UP has 85 seats in the Lok Sabha (Lower House) and 34 seats in the Rajya Sabha (Upper House), more than any other state. The BJP suffered a major reverse in the Assembly elections of 2002, with the the Samajwadi Party (SP) and the Bahujan Samaj Party (BSP) re-emerging as major forces in the State's legislative assembly.



# Lucknow

→ *Phone code: 0522. Colour map 3, grid A2. Population: 2,300,000.*

*In Kipling's Kim "no city – except Bombay, the queen of all – was more beautiful in her garish style than Lucknow". The capital of the state sprawls along the banks of the Gomti River in the heart of Uttar Pradesh. The ordered Cantonment area contrasts with the saffron-washed buildings of the congested city centre, dotted with an incredible variety of decaying mansions and historic monuments, the best of which are simply breathtaking. In the heart of the old city traditional craftsmen continue to produce the rich gold zari work, delicate chikan embroidery and strong attar perfume. The arts still flourish and the bookshops do brisk trade in serious reading. Veils have largely disappeared as progressive college girls speed along on their scooters weaving between cows, cars and rickshaws.* ▸▸ *For Sleeping, Eating and other listings, see pages 138-140.*

## Ins and outs

### Getting there

The modern airport, connected by direct flights to Delhi, Kolkata, Mumbai and Patna, is 14 km south of the city, about half an hour by taxi. Lucknow is well connected by train and road to other major cities of the north. The City Railway Station is in the southeast corner of the Hussainabad area, close to the historic sights, while the Charbagh Railway Station is to the south. The Kaiserbagh Bus Stand near the centre is for long-distance services, while local buses terminate at the Charbagh Station Bus Stand. ▸▸ *See Transport, page 140, for further details.*

### Getting around

The main sites are close enough to the centre to visit by cycle-rickshaw, or by hopping on a cheap shared tempo which run on fixed routes. However, the city is quite spread out and for extended sight-seeing it is worth hiring a taxi.

# Background

Today Lucknow is a major administrative centre and market city, growing rapidly on both sides of the Gomti River from its historic core along the river's right bank. Although the discovery of **Painted Grey Ware** and **Northern Black** pottery demonstrates the long period over which the site has been occupied, its main claim to fame is as the capital of the cultured Nawabs of **Oudh** (*Avadh*), and later the scene of one of the most remarkable episodes in the 'Uprising' of 1857. Lucknow developed rapidly under the Mughal Emperor Akbar's patronage in the 16th century. In the early 18th century, Nawab Saadat Khan Burhan-ul-Mulk, a Persian courtier founded the Oudh Dynasty. The city's growing reputation as a cultural centre attracted many others from Persia, leaving an indelible Shi'a imprint on the city's life. The builder of 'modern' Lucknow was Nawab Asaf-ud-Daula who shifted his capital here from Faizabad in 1775. In the attempt to build a wonderful city he emptied the regal coffers.

In the mid-1850s under **Lord Dalhousie**, the British annexed a number of Indian states. Percival Spear suggested that Dalhousie considered British rule so superior to Indian that the more territory directly administered by the British the better it would be for Indians. He evolved a policy of lapse whereby the states of Indian princes without direct heirs could be taken over on the ruler's death. Chronic mismanagement was also deemed just cause for takeover, the justification given for the annexation of Oudh. The novelist Premchand in the *Chess Players* attributes the fall of Oudh to the fact that "small and big, rich and poor, were dedicated alike to sensual joys ... song, dance and opium". History suggests that Nawab Wajid Ali Shah continued with his game of chess even as British soldiers occupied his capital. A strong British presence was established in the city as it became a key administrative and military centre. **Satyajit Ray's** film *'Satranj Ki Khilari (The Chess Players)'* is excellent.

When the **'Uprising'** (previously referred to as the Mutiny) broke in 1857, Sir Henry Lawrence gathered the British community into the Residency which rapidly became a fortress. The ensuing siege lasted for 87 days. When the relieving force under Sir Colin Campbell finally broke through, the once splendid Residency was a blackened ruin, its walls pockmarked and gaping with cannonball holes. Today it is a mute witness to a desperate struggle.



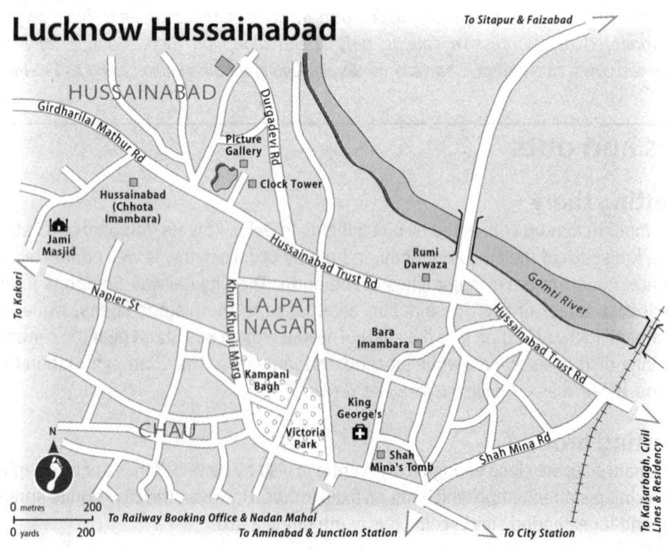

### Jobs for the boys?

In 1784 Lucknow and its region suffered an appalling famine, and thousands of starving people flocked into the city. In a spectacular example of 'food for work' – pre-Keynes Keynesian economics – Asaf-ud-Daula decided to build the Great Imambara. He offered work night and day, reputedly employing 22,000 men, women and children. However, in order to ensure that the task was not finished too quickly, he divided it into two parts. During the day, normal building proceeded. At night the workmen destroyed one quarter of what had been built the previous day. Nobles were allowed to work at night to spare them the embarrassment of being seen as having to labour to survive. To the labourers this was a life-saving act of charity, even if the building itself is widely reported as something of a monstrosity.

Under the **Nawabs**, Lucknow evolved specialized styles of dance, poetry, music and calligraphy. The Lucknowi *gharana* (house) of music and the exquisite crafts are reminders of its splendid past as it remains the regional cultural capital. Today, of the vintage modes of travel, only the *ekka* (one-horse carriage) has survived. To trace its Muslim heritage, visit the Bara and Chhota Imambaras, Shah Najaf Imambara and take a look at the Rumi Darwaza, Clock Tower and Chattar Manzil. Among the Colonial monuments, the Residency and Constantia are the most rewarding.

**Parivartan Chowk** and the black **Mayawati monument** which faces **Clarks Avadh Hotel** symbolize the spirit of 'change' (parivartan) which the 1997-1998 government of the fiery Chief Minister Mayawati hoped to encourage by giving increasing power to the scheduled castes. Recently Lucknow has been through periods of violent communal tension which is partly explained by the important BJP presence here. See Books, page 1362, for further reading.

## Sights

The original centre of the city is believed to be the high ground crowned by the Mosque of Aurangzeb on the right bank of the Gomti. Tillotson, an architectural historian, suggests that the major buildings of Asaf-ud-Daula, built after 1775 – the **Bara Imambara**, the **Rumi Darwaza** (Turkish Gate) and the **mosque** between them dramatically illustrate the 'debased Mughal' style of 'Indo-European' architecture in decline. The monuments have been divided into three main groups. They usually open between 0600 and 1700.

### North West and Hussainabad

Just south of the Hardinge Bridge was the **Machhi Bhavan** ('Fish House') enclosure. Safdarjang, Governor of Oudh (1719-1748), was permitted to use the fish insignia (a royal/Imperial symbol/crest) by the Mughal Emperor Akbar. The Machhi Bhavan itself, once a fort, was blown up by the British in 1857, the only surviving part being the *baoli* which escaped because it was sunk into the hillside. Allow two to three hours for the Hussainabad tour.

**Bara Imambara** ⓘ *Rs 300 foreigners, Rs 25 Indians for all buildings on the site*, on the western slope of the enclosure, is a huge vaulted hall which, like all *imambaras*, serves as the starting point for the Muharram procession, see page 64. The vast hall (50 m long and 15 m high), built by Asaf-ud-Daula to provide employment during a famine, is one of the largest in the world, unsupported by pillars. Note: "Spiting (sic), smoking and call of nature strictly prohibited"! The remarkable *bhul-bhulaya*, a maze of interconnecting passages above, is reached by stairs; a delightful diversion. One visitor spent over an hour trying to find his way out, though others have managed in less! Notice: "No gent with a lady visitor allowed... without a Trust employee/guide.". The five-storeyed *baoli* is connected directly with the River Gomti. Legends suggest that secret tunnels connect the lower steps, which are always under water, with a treasure stored beneath the Imambara itself.

At the end of the avenue leading up to the *imambara* from the river is the **Rumi Darwaza** (1784). Further along is the 19th-century gothic 67-m high Hussainabad **Clocktower** (1880s) designed by Roskell Payne, which contains the largest clock in India though three of the four faces have been smashed. Next to it is the attractive octagonal Hussainabad Tank (1837-1842), around which is the Taluqdar's Hall and the incomplete Satkhanda (1840) seven-storeyed watchtower. There are excellent views of Lucknow from the top.

**Hussainabad Imambara** (Chhota Imambara), with its golden dome and elaborate calligraphy and containing beautiful chandeliers, gilt edged mirrors and a silver throne (1837), is illuminated during Muharram. Further west is the extensively renovated **Jami Masjid** begun by Muhammad Shah and finished by his wife in the mid-1840s. **Victoria Park** (1890) with several British tombs is nearby. South of the park is the Chowk, the Old City bazar where there are some interesting old buildings including the **Dargah of Hazrat Abbas** which contains a relic, a metal crest from the battle at Kerbala. Nearby is **Nadan Mahal** (circa 1600), with the tomb of Shaikh Abdur Rahim, Akbar's Governor of Oudh, and son of Ibrahim Chishti. This is a fine building, built in the Mughal style and faced with red sandstone.



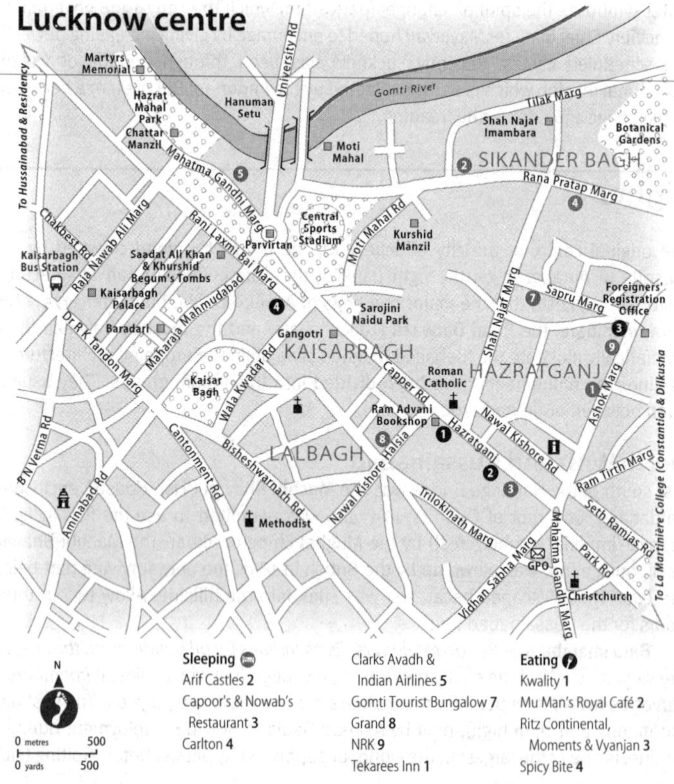

## Residency and Hazratganj area

The Residency's 3,000 mostly European occupants, hastily brought there by **Sir Henry Lawrence**, came under siege on the evening of 30 June 1857. Two days later Lawrence was fatally injured. After 90 days, Generals Sir Henry Havelock and Sir James Outram appeared through the battered walls with a column of Highlanders. However, the siege was intensified and sepoy engineers began tunnelling to lay mines to blow the place up. From quite early on, there was a shortage of food and disease spread. As rations dwindled, smallpox, cholera and scurvy set in. Havelock was slowly dying of dysentery. The heroic Irishman, Henry Kavanagh, had sat in the tunnels and shot mutineers as they wriggled forward to lay more mines. He then volunteered to run the gauntlet through the enemy lines to find Sir Colin Campbell's relieving force, which he did by swimming the Gomti. On 17 November, Lucknow was finally relieved. Of the 2,994 men, women and children who had taken refuge in the Residency, only 1,000 marched out.

**The Residency Compound**, inside the Residency's scarred walls, is now a historic monument. You enter through the Bailey Guard gate. The **Treasury** on your right served as an arsenal while the grand Banquet Hall next door housed the wounded during the 'Uprising'. On the lawn of **Doctor Fayrer's House** to your left, stands a marble cross to Sir Henry Lawrence. **Begum Kothi**, which belonged to Mrs Walters who married the Nawab of Oudh, can be reached through the long grass (popular with Indian courting couples!), but the old officers' mess has made way for flats and apartments.

The **Residency** (1800) ⓘ *Rs 5, foreigners Rs 100, cameras Rs25*, to the northeast, built by Saadat Ali Khan, has *tykhanas* (cool underground rooms for summer use) where there is a museum, the highlight of which is an 1873 model of the complex, which not only gives you a chance to get your bearings but also a good idea of how extensive and self-sufficient the original settlement was. At the time of the 'Uprising' the Residency was overlooked by high houses, now all destroyed, which gave cover to snipers firing into the compound. There are many etchings and records including Tennyson's "Relief of Lucknow". Suggestions of a wooden staircase for officers, an underground passage to the palace, a secret room hidden in the wall behind false doors, all conjure up images of the past. The graves of Lawrence, Neill and others are in the church **cemetery**. Women visitors should not visit the cemetery alone. Just outside the Residency on the banks of the Gomti is a white obelisk commemorating the 'Nationalist Insurgents' who lost their lives in 1857.

Southeast of the Residency, near the Hanuman Setu, is the Chattar Manzil (Umbrella Palace) now the Central Drug Research Institute, where the submerged basement provided natural air-conditioning. There are also the sad remains of the **Kaisarbagh Palace** (1850) conceived as a grand château. Better preserved are the almost twin **Tombs** of Saadat Ali Khan (1814) and Khurshid Begum and the restored Baradari housing a **Picture Gallery** (see below). To its east again are **Nur Bakhsh Kothi** and Tarawali Kothi (circa 1832), the observatory of the royal astronomer Colonel Wilcox, which is now the **State Bank of India**.

## Eastern Group

**Shah Najaf Imambara** (1814-1827), near the Gomti, free entry, has the tombs of Nawab Ghazi-ud-Din Haidar and his three wives, with its white dome and elaborate interior decorations, including a huge array of chandeliers. It was used by sepoy mutineers as a stronghold in 1857. Wajid Ali Shah's (ruled 1847-1856) pleasure garden **Sikander Bagh** to its east is now the Botanical Gardens.

To the south of these are **Wingfield Park**, laid out in the 1860s, which contains a marble pavilion and some statues. East of here is the **State Museum** ⓘ *Banarsi Bagh, T0522 220 6158, closed Mon, 1030-1630, Rs 5, foreigners Rs 10*, the oldest in Uttar Pradesh and one of the richest in India, now housing all archaeological material. First to 11th-century exhibits of Hindu, Buddhist and Jain works including stone sculptures from Mathura, busts and friezes from Allahabad and Garhwal. Also marble sculptures, paintings, natural history and anthropology (an Egyptian mummy). Relics of the British Raj, removed at the time of Independence, are in the backyard. **Christchurch** (1860), a memorial to the British killed during the 'Uprising' is nearby, along with the imposing Legislative Council Chamber (1928) and **Raj Bhawan** (Government House), enlarged in 1907.

To the east is Constantia, now **La Martinière College**, planned as the country residence of Major-General Claude Martin (1735-1800), a French soldier of fortune who is buried in the crypt. He ran highly successful indigo and money-lending businesses. The red-brick wedding cake of a building was completed after Martin's death from the endowment set aside by him for a school here and at Kolkata for 'Anglo-Indians' (Kipling's *Kim* being one of them). For the students' bravery during the siege of the Residency, the school was unique in being awarded Battle Honours. The chapel, historical photos and the crypt are interesting. You may ask to look around both outside and within. The office is at the east end.

Further south, **Dilkusha** (Heart's Delight), once a royal shooting lodge in what was a large deer park, is being restored. There are graves of soldiers who died here during the 'Uprising'. General Havelock died here; his grave obelisk is in Alam Bagh, 100 m northeast of the garden's main gateway (3 km southwest of Char Bagh station).



## Sleeping

**L Taj Residency**, Vipin Khand, Gomti Nagar, 5 km east of railway station, T0522 239 3939, ww.tajhotels.com. 110 rooms in elegant colonial style modern building, excellent restaurant, good pool, attractive gardens (transplanted mature palms!), city's most luxurious hotel and the only really quiet one.

**A Clarks Avadh**, 8 MG Marg, T0522 262 0131, www.clarksavadh.com. 98 rooms, good restaurants (see below), modern, clean, comfortable, efficient, attentive service. Recommended.

**A Park Inn**, 6 Shahnajaf Rd, T 0522 262 0220, www.parkinnlucknow.com. 50 contemporary styled rooms in modern, friendly chain hotel, very well maintained, attractive restarants, good location.

**B Arif Castles**, 4 Rana Pratap Marg, Hazratganj, T0522 261 1313, www.arifcastles.com. 52 rooms in good location, efficient.

**B-C Tekarees Inn**, 17/3 Ashok Marg, T0522 221 5409, www.tekareesinn.com. 16 high quality rooms in smart, newly built hotel, professional staff, Thai restaurant.

**B-D Vishwanath**, Subhash Marg, Charbagh, T0522 245 0879, vishwanath_04@yahoo.com. Similar rooms but better value than Amarpreet, also has restaurant and car parking plus friendly staff, recommended

**C Grand**, 4 Lalbagh, T0522 261 4022. 18 a/c rooms, modern, restaurant, good discounts.

**C-D Amarpreet**, Subhash Marg, Charbagh, T0522 2456626, www.hotelamarpreet.com. Modern but small rooms, restaurant and travel desk, not especially welcoming.

**C-D Capoor's**, 52 Hazratganj, T0522 222 3958, capoors@yahoo.com. 24 rooms, some a/c, some without windows, good restaurant, sports bar, old world charm, very central.

**C-D Carlton**, Rana Pratap Marg, T0522 223 1886. Charming ex-British residency with staff to match. Rooms are antiquated but large and full of character; there's also a huge lawn, a restaurant and a bar.

**C-D Deep Avadh**, 133/273 Aminabad Rd, T0522 268 4381, deepavadh@sify.com. 79 rooms, some a/c with TV, restaurant, travel desk, reasonable value, well run.

**C-D Gomti** (UP Tourism), 6 Sapru Marg, T0522 2220624, gomtiupt@sancharnet.in. 63 rooms covering a wide range of categories, some a/c, attractive restaurant, bar, clean, attentive service, looks better from inside than out!

**D NRK**, 17/2 Ashok Marg, Hazratganj, T0522 228 0380. 20 clean rooms with bath with hot water, some a/c, restaurant.

**D-E Shan Palace**, AP Sen Road, T0522 263 6300. Tatty but acceptable rooms in one of the only hotels close to the station which welcomes foreigners.

## Eating

The better hotels serve good Lucknowi food – rich *biryanis*, *roomali roti* and *kebabs* and *kulfis* to end the meal. Special *Dum Phukt* (steam cooked) dishes are worth trying. 1st and 7th of month and public holidays are 'dry' days.

¶¶¶ **Falaknuma**, on rooftop of **Clark's hotel**, T0522 262 0131. Serves tasty, spicy Nawabi cuisine by candle light, good views, beer available, attentive service and live ghazals of exceptionally high quality, recommended.

¶¶¶ **Taj Residency**: **Oudhyana**, T0522 239 3939. Special Avadhi food, lovely surroundings, the finest fine dining in town.

¶¶ **Chung Fa**, S-7 Gole Market, Mahanagar, T0522 237 3550. Good Chinese.

¶¶ **Kwality**, Mayfair Building, Hazratganj, T0522 222 3331. International. Cool.

¶¶ **Mu Man's Royal Café**, 51 Hazratganj, T0522 222 7070. Excellent Chinese. Live Indian music some nights. Recommended.

¶¶ **Nowab's** at **Capoor's Hotel**. Clean, good breakfasts, satisfactory dinners, kebab specialist, live music, attentive service, bar.

¶¶ **Ritz Continental**, Ashok Marg, opposite Jawahar Bhavan, Gole Market. Good vegetarian but "dismally slow".

¶¶ **Vyanjan**, Vinay Palace, Ashok Marg, T0522 228 0537. Good a/c vegetarian in family-friendly surroundings.

¶ **Moments**, corner of Ashok/Sapru Margs. Very good north Indian meat dishes, slightly gloomy interior

¶ **Tundey's**, Aminabad Chowk. Kebabs (named after one-armed ancestor) are sought after locally.

## Festivals and events

**Oct-Nov**: National Kite Flying Competition at the Patang Park, MG Marg the day after *Diwali*. **25 Nov-5 Dec every year**: Mahotsav **Festival** with emphasis on Indian classical music – song, drama and dance, processions, boating and *ekka* races, crafts and cuisine.

## Shopping

Lucknow is famous for fine floral *chikan* or 'shadow' embroidery in pastel colours, produced around the Chowk. You will also find gold *zari* and sequin work and prized *attar*. Shops usually open 1000-1930, markets up to 2000. Hazratganj, Janpath closed on Sun; Aminabad, Chowk, Sadar, Super Bazar on Thu. The following are in Hazratganj.

**Asghar Ali**, near Chowk, for *attar* perfume.

**Bhagwat Das**, Kusum Deep, Chowk. About Rs 600-900 for ladies 'Punjabi' outfits, or soft saris (5 m of fabric for dress making).

**Gangotri**, 31/29, handloom and crafts, and other Government emporia.

**Khazana**, at **Taj Mahal**, has high-class handicrafts (0900-2200, daily).

**Lal Behari Tandon**, 17 Ashok Marg, good quality chikan.

**Ram Advani**, Mayfair Cinema Building, next to British Council. Outstanding bookshop.

**Universal Booksellers**, Hazratganj. Large stock covering all subjects.

## Activities and tours

### Golf

Golf course at La Martinière Boys College, open to the public. The only golf course in India where one of the hazards is a tomb – that of Augustus Nayne, a British officer who fell in the 'Uprising' and was reputedly buried with his monocle still in place.

### Racing

Race course at Cantonment.

### Swimming

Pools at KD Singh Baba Stadium and **Hotel Clarks Avadh**.

### Tour companies

**Reception centre, and guides**: 4 hrs, Rs 200 or 8 hrs, Rs 600. Charbagh Railway Station, Main Hall, 1000-1700, T0522 263 6173.

**Regional (UP Tourism)**, 10/4 Station Rd, T0522 263 8105.

**Tornos**, C-2016 Indira Nagar, T0522 234 6965, www.tornosindia.com. Very reliable, reasonable prices.

**UP Tours**, 6 Sapru Marg, T0522 230 8916. For tours, car hire, air/rail tickets. **City Tours**: Shah Najaf Imambara, Picture Gallery, Rumi Darwaza, Shaheed Smarak (Martyrs' Memorial), Residency, Bara Imambara. Enjoyable and good value. Pick-up from Charbagh station 0830, **Gomti Hotel**, 0915, return 1335. Rs 130. Walking tours also arranged by appointment.

## Transport

### Air

**Amausi airport**, 14 km; pre-paid taxis available, Rs 160-200 to hotel. **Indian Airlines**, Clarks hotels, T0522 262 6623 (1000-1730, ticketing 1000-1300,1400-1630); airport T0522 243 5401 (1600-1830). Flights to **Delhi**, **Kolkata**, **Patna**, **Mumbai**. **Jet Airways**, 6 Park Rd, T0522 223 9612, Airport T0522 243 4009, to Delhi. **Sahara**, 7 Kapoorthala Complex, T0522 237 7675, airport T0522 237 2742; flies to Delhi. **Air India**, T0522 231 2409.

### Bus

**Local** Extensive network and cheap. UP Roadways bus stands are mostly local and some out-of-town from Char Bagh (opposite railway station), T0522 245 8096.

**Long distance** Out-of-town: UP Roadways, **Charbagh Bus Stand**, T0522 245 0988 (24-hr left luggage), 0600-2200, Rs 2-5 per piece. Bus to **Kanpur**, 2½ hrs. Kaisarbagh Bus Stand, T0522 222 2503. Bus to **Delhi**, 10-12 hrs.

### Rickshaw

Tempo-rickshaws on fixed routes are cheap (Rs 3 minimum), and easy to use (from station, cross the road and ask for a landmark nearby, eg GPO ). Cycle-rickshaws and horse tongas are widely available; Rs 10 for 2 km.

### Taxi

Unmetered. Private taxis from **Lucknow Car Taxi Owners Assoc**, Station Rd, and hotels and agencies. Full day a/c (8 hrs; 80 km), non-a/c Rs 500, a/c Rs 1,000.

### Train

Take special care of belongings at the railway station. Theft is common.

Lucknow is on the Northern and Northeastern railway. **Charbagh (Lucknow Junction)** Station is 3 km southwest of town centre. Computerized reservation is nearby (turn right from station; it is on the first street corner on the left). 24-hr left luggage across the road. Rest room, dormitory bed and locker (use your own lock), Rs 30 for 12 hrs. **Northern Railway**: enquiries T131 (Arrival T1331, Departures T1332); reservations Charbagh T0522 263 5841. **NE Rly**: enquiries T0522 263 5877. City Station: T242411; weekdays 0830-1530, 1600-1930, Sun 0830-1530. **Agra Fort**: *Lucknow Agra Fort Exp, 5313*, 1820, 15½ hrs. **Allahabad**: *Nauchandi Exp, 4512*, 0600, 4¾ hrs; *Ganga-Gomti Exp, 4216*, 1820, 3¼ hrs; *Kathgodham Mughalsarai Exp, 5016*, 2225, 8½ hrs. **Bhopal**: *Pushpak Exp, 2134*, 1920, 10½ hrs; *Lucknow Bhopal Exp, 1274*, 2235, Wed, Sat, 11½ hrs. **Gorakhpur** (for Nepal): Several, best are *Kathdogam Howrah Bagh Exp, 3020*, 0615, 7 hrs; *Lucknow Gorakhpur Exp, 5008*, 2300, 6¾ hrs. **Jabalpur** (for Kanha): *Chitrakoot Exp, 5010*, 1730, 15½ hrs. **Jhansi**: *Kushinagar Exp, 1016*, 0040, 6½ hrs; *Pushpak Exp, 2134*, 1920, 6½ hrs. **Kanpur**: *Gomti Exp, 2419*, 0535, except Sun, 1½ hrs; *Shatabdi Exp*, 2003, 1520, 1½ hrs; **Kolkata** (H): *Amritsar-Howrah Mail, 3006*, 1055, 20¾ hrs; *Doon Exp, 3010*, 0845, 22¼ hrs. **Lalkuan (for Nainital)**: *Nainital Exp, 5308*, 2120, 9¼ hrs. **New Delhi**: *Gomti Exp, 2419*, 0535, not Sun, 8 hrs; *Shatabdi Exp, 2003*, 1520, 6¼ hrs; *Lucknow New Delhi Mail, 4229*, 2200, 9¼ hrs. **Varanasi**: *Kashi Vishwanath Exp, 4258*, 2315, 6¼ hrs; *Varuna Exp, 4228*, 1800, 5¾ hrs.

## Directory

**Banks** Weekdays 1030-1430, Sat 1030-1230. **State Bank**, Hazratganj, T0522 222 7804, and **Punjab National Bank**, Ashok Marg change money. **Hospitals** **Balrampur**, Golaganj, T0522 222 4040. **Chhatrapati**, Chowk, T0522 226 6175 Sanjay Gandhi, Rai Bareli Rd, T0522 266 8700. **Internet** 30 Hazratganj. Rs 3 per hr, clean, fairly fast, plus several Sify outlets. **Post** GPO: Vidhan Sabha Marg, 0930-1730. Also in Chowk and Mahanagar. **Useful addresses** Ambulance: T0522222 4040. Fire: T101. Police: T100. Archaeological Survey of India: Amirud Daula Kothi, Kaisarbagh. Foreigners' Registration Office: 5th floor, Jawahar Bhavan, Ashok Marg. Passport Office: Nav Chetna Building, Ashok Marg, T0522 228 0520. Wildlife Office: 17 Rana Pratap Marg, T0522 220 6584.

# Around Lucknow

## Dudhwa National Park → *Colour map 3, grid A2. 220 km north of Lucknow.*

ⓘ *Open mid-Nov to mid-Jun. Rs 50 per day. Indians and students pay reduced rates. Camera free, video Rs 500. Road fees for light vehicles, Rs 150 per day. Night driving is not allowed in the park so arrive before sunset.*

A reserve since 1879, Dudhwa was designated a national park in 1977 and Project Tiger Reserve in 1988 by adding 200 sq km of the Kishanpur Sanctuary, 30 km away. Bordering the Sarda River in the Terai, it is very similar to the Corbett National Park. It has sal forest (in addition to sheesham, asna, khair and sagaun), tall savannah grasslands and large marshy areas watered by the Neora and Sohel rivers.

The swamps are the ideal habitat of the **barasingha** (swamp deer with 12 tined antlers, *Cervus duvanceli*), now numbering about 2,000, which are best seen in the Sathiana and Kakraha blocks. The tiger population is believed to be about 30 though they are rarely spotted. Dudhwa also has sambar, nilgai, some sloth bears (*Melursus ursinus*), the endangered hispid hare, fishing cats and a few leopards. The one-horned rhino was reintroduced from northeast India in 1985 but visitors are not allowed into the enclosure. The 400 species of avifauna includes Bengal floricans, pied and Great Indian hornbills, owls and king vultures. It also attracts a great variety of water birds (swamp partridge, eastern white stork) in addition to birds of prey (osprey, hawks, fishing eagles). Banke Tal is good for bird watching.

To view the wildlife you can hire a jeep or minibus (Rs 20-30 per km), from park office at Dudhwa. However, elephants are recommended and are available at Dudhwa only. Each carries four (Rs 50 per person for 2½ hours – minimum charge Rs 200). Book elephant ride on arrival at park.

The best time to visit is during February and April; from April to June it becomes very hot, dry and dusty, but is good for viewing big game. In summer the maximum is 35°C, minimum 10°C. Winter the maximum is 30°C, minimum 4°C. Annual rainfall is 1,500 mm; most June to September. Palia has a bank, a basic health centre and a post office. Dudhwa has a dispensary.

## Bareilly → *Phone code: 0581. Colour map 3, grid A2.*

Bareilly, the capital of Rohilkhand (an empire built by two Afghan Rohillas who served under the Moghals), was founded in 1537 by the Bas Deo and Barel Deo brothers (hence Bareilly) and traces of their fortress remain. It was ceded to the British in 1801 and later contributed to the drama of the 'Uprising'. There are three 17th-century mosques and two churches in town. Bareilly is known for its iron industry and its gold *zari* work. It is an important rail junction and its population numbers 700,000.

## Faizabad → *Phone code: 05278. Colour map 3, grid A3. Population: 160,000.*

Faizabad, 124 km east of Lucknow, is handy for visiting Ayodhya. It was once the capital of Oudh. Shuja-ud-Daula (1754-1775), the third Nawab of Oudh, built Fort Calcutta here after his defeat by the British at Buxar in 1764. The 42-m high white marble **Mausoleum of Bahu Begum** (circa 1816), his widow, is particularly fine. Gulab Bari (Mausoleum of Shuja-ud-Daula, circa 1775) nearby, contains the tombs of his mother and father.

## Ayodhya → *Phone code: 05276. Colour map 3, grid A3. Population: 50,000.*

Ayodhya, 9 km from Faizabad and meaning 'a place where battles cannot take place', also on the banks of the **Ghaghara River**, is one of the seven holy Hindu cities (others are Mathura, Haridwar, Varanasi, Ujjain, Dwarka and Kanchipuram). It is regarded by many Hindus as the birthplace of **Rama** and where he once reigned, though the

## Rama's birth

Rama's father, Dasaratha, unable to have children by any of his wives, was instructed to perform a great sacrifice in order that his wives might conceive. At the same time there was great trouble in the home of the gods, for Ravana, the king of the demons, had been assured by Brahma that he could never be harmed by a human, or by "devas and other supernatural beings". When the gods learned of this promise they turned to Vishnu and begged him to be born as a man so that he could put an end to Ravana. Vishnu agreed that he would be born as four sons of Dasaratha, who was then performing his sacrifice.

The sacred fire was lit and ghee poured on. Out of the flames emerged a startling figure. He held out a bowl of payasam (a milk dessert) to Dasaratha and said: "The gods are pleased with your sacrifice. If your wives drink this payasam they will be blessed with sons".

Dasaratha was overjoyed. He immediately gave the payasam to his wives. In due course all three became pregnant. Kausalya gave birth to Rama and Kaikeyi gave birth to Bharata. Sumitra, having taken two portions of the divine payasam, gave birth to the twins, Lakshmana and Satrughuna.



historian Romila Thapar stresses that there is no evidence for such a belief. Jains regard it as the birthplace of the first and fourth Tirthankars, and the Buddha is also thought to have stayed here.

The Archaeological Survey of India and the Indian Institute of Advanced Study began excavation in 1978. The ruins have a circumference of between 4 and 5 km, rising at some places to 10 m above the ground. According to Professor BB Lal, the site was occupied from at least the seventh century BC if not earlier, when both iron and copper were in use. Later finds include a Jain figure from the fourth to third century BC, possibly the earliest Jain figure found in India. Houses during this period were built in kiln-baked brick, and various coins have been found from periods up to the fourth century AD, some indicating extensive trade with East India. BB Lal goes on: "many of the now standing temples having been erected during the past two centuries only".

In accordance with Muslim practice elsewhere, a number of temples were razed and mosques were built on the site, often using the same building material. In recent years Ayodhya has become the focus of intense political activity by the *Vishwa Hindu Parishad*, an organization asserting a form of militant Hinduism, and the BJP, its leading political ally. They claim that Ayodhya was **'Ramajanambhumi'** (Rama's birthplace) and that this holy site is beneath the remains of the **Babri Mosque** built by **Babur**, deserted now for many years. On 6 December 1992, the mosque was destroyed by militant Hindus. This was followed by widespread disturbances resulting in over 2,500 deaths across the country. Ayodhya remains a potential flashpoint, so check conditions first if you plan to visit. The massacre of young Hindu activists returning from Ayodhya to Gujarat in February 2002 resulted in over 1,000 deaths in the following months. See further, page 1230.

Other sites include **Lakshmana Ghat**, 3 km from the station, where Rama's brother committed suicide. **Hanumangarh** takes its name from the Hanuman and Sita temple and the massive walls surrounding it.

## Gorakhpur → *Phone code: 0551. Colour map 3, grid A4. Population: 625,000.*

Gorakhpur, at the confluence of the Rapti and Rohini rivers, is the last major Indian town travellers bound for Nepal pass through. The British and the Gurkha armies clashed nearby in the early 18th century. Later it became the recruitment centre for Gurkha soldiers enlisting into the British and Indian armies. The **Gorakhnath Temple** attracts Hindu pilgrims, particularly *Kanfata sadhus* who have part of their ears cut. Unusual terracotta pottery figures and animals are made here.



## Kusinagara → *Colour map 3, grid A4.*

Kusinagara, 50 km east of Gorakhpur, is celebrated as the place where the Buddha died and was cremated and passed into *parinirvana*; the actual site is unknown. Originally known as Kushinara, it is one of four major Buddhist pilgrimage sites. See page 1339. Monasteries established after the Buddha's death flourished here until the 13th century.

In the main site, the core of the **Main Stupa** possibly dates from Asoka's time with the **Parinirvana Temple**. The restored 6-m recumbent sandstone figure of the dying Buddha in a shrine in front may have been brought from Mathura by the monk Haribala during King Kumargupta's reign (AD 413-455). The stupas, chaityas and viharas, however, were 'lost' for centuries. The Chinese pilgrims Fa Hien, Hiuen Tsang, and I Tsing, all recorded the decay and ruins of Kusinagara between 900 and 1,000 years after the Buddha's death. The stupa and the temple were rediscovered only in the 1880s. The **Mathakuar shrine** to the southwest has a large Buddha in the *bhumisparsha mudra* and marks the place where the Buddha last drank water. **Rambahar stupa** (Mukutabandhana), 1 km east, was built by the Malla Dynasty to house the Buddha's relics after the cremation. Some of the bricks (which have holes for easier firing) were carved to form figures.

Excavations were begun by the Archaeological Survey of India in 1904-1905, following clues left by the Chinese travellers. A shaft was driven through the centre of the Nirvana stupa "which brought to light a copper plate placed on the mouth of a relic casket in the form of a copper vessel with charcoal, cowries, precious stones and a gold coin of Kumaragupta I". The whole area was occupied until the 11th century. In all there are eight groups of monasteries, stupas and images, indicating that Kusinagara was a substantial community.

## Kanpur → *Phone code: 0512. Colour map 3, grid B2.*

With a population of over 2½ million people, Kanpur is the largest city of Uttar Pradesh and the most important industrial centre in the state. Cotton mills were first established in 1869, some of the first in India. It is now one of the major industrial cities in India with aviation, woollen and leather industries, cotton, flour and vegetable oil mills, sugar refineries and chemical works. As a result of this high level of industry, the city is extremely polluted, and has become one sprawling, congested market, with seemingly every street constantly choked with traffic. As an example of industry run riot it somehow has a perverse attraction, and perhaps needs to be experienced once in a lifetime.

The principal British monuments are in the southeast of the city in the old cantonment area. Stone posts mark the lines of the trenches near **All Soul's Memorial Church** (1862-1875), a handsome Gothic style building designed by Walter Granville. A tiled pavement outside marks the graves of those executed on 1 July 1857, soon after the Satichaura Ghat massacre. To the east, the **Memorial Garden** has a statue by Marochetti and a screen designed by Sir Henry Yule which were brought here after Independence. The infamous **Satichaura Ghat**, 1 km northeast of the church by the Ganga, has a small Siva temple. You can walk along the river from the Lucknow Road bridge (about 200 m, but dirty) which leads to the site of the boat massacre just upstream of the temple, where cannons were stationed on the high banks. The temple is altered but the landing ghats are still used by fishermen's boats and for washing clothes.

## The uprising in Kanpur

Kanpur was one of the most important British garrisons on the Ganga. During the 'Uprising' the insurgents rallied under Nana Sahib, who bore a grievance against the British because he had received only a small pension. They laid siege to the British community of around 400 men, women and children who had been gathered together under General Sir Hugh Wheeler. Inadequately protected and without enough food, after 18 days the defenders were severely reduced through gunshot wounds, starvation and disease. Nana Sahib then offered a truce and arranged for boats to take the survivors downstream to Allahabad. When they were boarding at Satichaura Ghat, they were raked with fire and hacked down by horsemen. One boat escaped. The survivors were either butchered and thrown down a well or died of cholera and dysentery. The reprisals were as horrible. General Sir James Neill "was seized with an Old Testamental vision of revenge" (Moorhouse). To break a man's religion and caste, pork and beef were stuffed down his throat, thus condemning him to eternal damnation. More often than not, suspected mutineers were bayoneted on sight. Nana Sahib escaped after pretending to commit suicide in the Ganga and is believed to have died in Nepal in 1859. See Further reading, page 1362, for recommended reading.

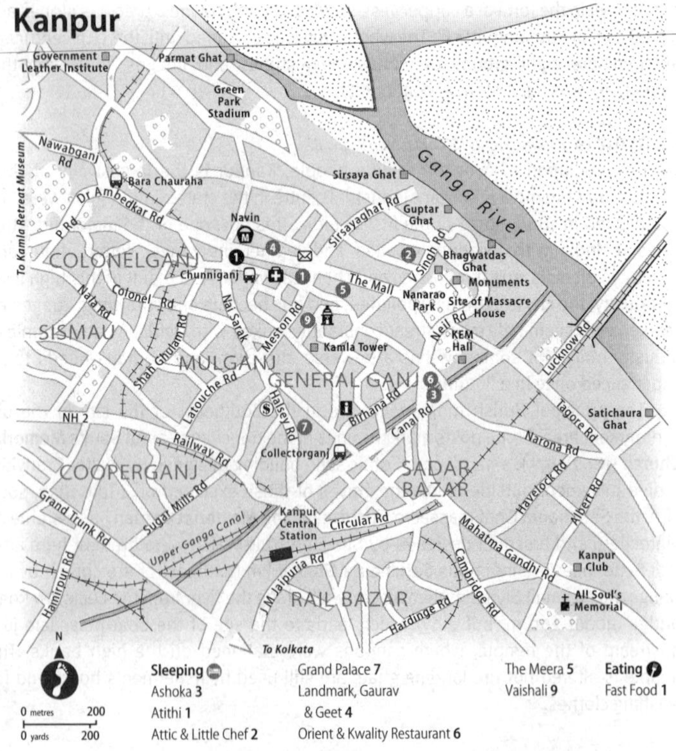

At the siege site, remains of the walls are still visible – as is the privy drain system and the well. The Massacre House was north of the canal about 250 m from the Ganga, and north of the Arms Factory, now marked by a statue of Nana Sahib. In the city centre there is the King Edward VII **Memorial (KEM) Hall** and **Christ Church** (1848). The higher grade hotels are along the Mall, some within reach of Meston Road with its interesting, faded, colonial architecture and cheap leather goods shops.

## Bithur

Nana Sahib's home town, 20 km north of Kanpur, has pleasant ghats by the Ganga. His opulent palace was destroyed by the British in 1857 and is now marked by a memorial bust. Ruins of a few large well heads survive in a park west of the main road into town from Kanpur. 'Enthusiasts' should allow two hours.

## Sleeping

**Dudhwa National Park** *p141*
All hotels are basic and foreigners pay more. Advance booking (15 days), and full payment (bank draft/postal order) is needed. Bedding is available at Dudhwa and Sathiana which have electricity; electricity generators on request at Sathiana, Sonaripur and Belrayan, at extra charge. For reservations at any of the places listed below, call Chief Wildlife Warden, UP, 17 Rana Pratap Marg, Lucknow, T0522-220 6584, for rest houses and Dy Director, Dudhwa Project Tiger, Palia, Lakhimpur Kheri, T05871-233485, for others.
**D Forest Resthouse**, Dudhwa, 5 suites, 1 a/c.
**D Forest Resthouse**, Sathiana, 2 suites.
**D-E Tiger Haven**, Palia. Lodges.
**E Forest Resthouse**, Bankatti, 4 suites.
**E Log huts**, Dudhwa, 2.
**E Log huts**, Sathiana, 6.
**E Tharu huts**, Dudhwa, 12.
**F** 25 dorm beds at Dudhwa. Reserve with Field Director, Dudhwa Project Tiger, Lakhimpur Kheri, T05872 252106.

**Bareilly** *p141*
**B Swarn Towers**, Station Rd, 5-min walk from station, T0581 2473143, www.hotelswarntowers.com. 29 rooms, clean, modern, friendly 'Cheers' bar for drinks and snacks, swimming pool and 3 restaurants.
**B-D Uberoi Anand**, 46 Civil Lines, T0581 257 0838, www.uberoianand.com. 88 rooms, some a/c or air-cooled, restaurant, exchange, terrace garden.
**E-F Civil and Military**, Station Rd, T0581 257 0879, hotlha@yahoo.com. 22 air-cooled rooms, dorm beds, central, restaurant, bar.
**F Railway Retiring Rooms**, 2 rooms, clean, hot and cold water, secure.

**Faizabad** *p141*
**C-E Shan-e-Avadh**, T05278 223586, F226545. Next door to **Tirupati**, 52 rooms with bath, hot water, good restaurant, clean.
**C-E Tirupati**, Main Rd, T05278 223231. Near Civil Lines Bus Stand, 35 rooms with bath (bucket hot water), some a/c, best upstairs at rear, good restaurant, modern.
**F Railway Retiring Rooms**. 2 rooms, dorm.

**Ayodhya** *p141*
Better hotels in Faizabad.
**E-F Pathik Niwas Saket** (UP Tourism), turn right from railway station, T05278 232435, rahisaket@up-tourism.com. Very clean, basic rooms, 1 a/c, simple restaurant, tourist information, friendly.

**Gorakhpur** *p142*
Budget hotels opposite the railway station can be noisy.
**C-D Ganges Delux**, Cinema Rd, T0551 233 6330. 10 comfortable a/c rooms.
**D Avantika**, Airport Rd (NH28), beyond cross-roads 3 km from railway station, T0551 220 0765. Modern, good rooms and restaurant.
**D Ganges**, Tarang Crossing, T0551 233 3530. Some a/c rooms, good restaurant and ice-cream parlour, well managed. Recommended.
**D President**, next door, T0551 233 7654. Best rooms, a/c with TV, 2 restaurants include pure veg.
**D-E Upvan**, Nepal Rd, T0551 233 8003. Ask rickshaw for **Bobina** next door. Some a/c or good air-cooled rooms, Indian restaurant, clean, efficient room service. Recommended.
**E Railway Retiring Rooms**, upstairs from Platform 1. Some a/c (best deluxe) and 3 dorms, restaurant, quiet. Recommended.

**E-F Kailash**, Nepal Rd, 1 km from railway station, T0551 233 6404. All air-cooled rooms, clean linen and bath, good management, no restaurants nearby.

**Kusinagara** *p143*
**E Pathik Niwas**, UP Tourism, near ASI office, T05564 271038, www.up-tourism.com. 8 rooms, tourist office.
**Dharamshalas**, the Chinese temple's new block, is recommended.

**Kanpur** *p143, map p144*
Some budget hotels are reluctant to take foreigners as it means filling up forms. Pools in hotels **Meghdoot, Grand Trunk** and **Landmark**.
**AL-A Landmark**, Som Datta Plaza, 10 The Mall, T0512 230 5305, lmknp@rediffmail.com. 131 plain but comfortable rooms, smart restaurants, casual coffee lounge, station/airport pickup, large pool and a huge games room including a 4-lane bowling alley.
**B-C Attic**, 15/198 V Singh Rd, Civil Lines, T0512 230 6691. 13 a/c rooms in a modern block behind a charming colonial house in a secluded setting and a beautifully kept garden. Probably the most peaceful place in town, recommended.
**C-D Ashoka**, 24/16 Birhana Rd, T0512 231 2742. 30 rooms on a relatively quiet backstreet but very centrally located.
**C-D Gaurav**, 18/54 The Mall, T0512 231 8532. 33 a/c rooms, restaurant, pleasant garden.
**C-D Geet**, 18/174-5 The Mall, T0512 231 1042. 40 a/c rooms, restaurant good, exchange. Slightly cheaper than **Gaurav**.
**C-D The Meera**, 37/19 The Mall, T0512 231 9972. 50 rooms, some a/c, restaurant (Indian snacks, drinks), clean and modern, friendly, good value, recommended.
**C-E Grand Palace**, 45/98 Moolganj Crossing, T0512 235 3405. 29 unexceptional rooms on busy main road, but the staff are extremely friendly and helpful.
**E-F Vaishali**, Meston Rd, Tilak Hall Lane, T0512 235 3404. 85 decent rooms, small baths.

## Eating

**Dudhwa National Park** *p141*
Only Dudhwa has a canteen serving meals and snacks. Other places have cooking facilities (crockery and utensils). Provisions must be brought in. Palia, 10 km away, has eating places.

**Faizabad** *p141*
**Gulnar**, Main Rd 'T' junction. Good curries.

**Gorakhpur** *p142*
**Bobi's**, over the road from **President Hotel**, tasty Indian and friendly staff. Hotel restaurants recommended including **Avantika, Ganges** and **President**. Also fast food outlets near Indira Children's Park.
**Ganesh**, pure veg, South Indian.

**Kanpur** *p143, map p144*
**Fu-Tu**, The Mall. For Chinese.
**Hot Trak**, The Mall, near **Landmark**. Fast food.
**Kabab Corner**, Sarvodaya Nagar. North Indian.
**Kwality**, The Mall, International, with bar.
**Little Chef**, specializes in outdoor catering, a little soulless but very hygienic.
**Sarovar**, Sarvodaya Nagar. For North Indian.
**Shalaka**, in shopping arcade opposite **Landmark**. For pizzas and South Indian snacks.
**Shanghai**, The Mall. Chinese.

## Festivals and events

**Kusinagara** *p143*
Buddha Jayanti (first full moon in **Apr/May**) marks the Buddha's birth. A huge fair is held when his relics (on public display at this time only) are taken out in procession.

## Shopping

**Kanpur** *p143, map p144*
Main shopping areas are The Mall, Birhana Rd and Navin Market. Kanpur is famous for cotton and leather products (along Meston Rd).

## Activities and tours

**Kanpur** *p143, map p144*
**Jet Air**, 24/1, LIC Building, 1st floor, The Mall, T0512 231 2559, yugesh@jetair.co.in (GSA for several foreign airlines). Very efficient. Recommended.
**Sita**, 18/53, T0512 235 2980, www.sitaindia.com. For **Indian Airlines** as well as several international airlines, plus package tours.

## Transport

### Dudhwa National Park *p141*

**Air**

Nearest airports are Lucknow (219 km) and Bareilly (260 km) in India, and Dhangari (35 km) in Nepal.

**Bus**

**UP Roadways** and private buses connect Palia with **Lakhimpur Kheri** and **Lucknow** (219 km), **Shahjahanpur** (107 km), **Bareilly** (260 km) and **Delhi** (420 km).

**Train**

Dudhwa is on the **Northeast Railway**, metre gauge line, and is connected with Lucknow and Moradabad, via Mailani (45 km from the park). A branch line from Mailani links places in the park. Transport is not always available at **Dudhwa Station**; best to get off at Palia (10 km) and take the hourly bus or taxi. The accommodation is 4 km from Dudhwa railway station, 10 km from Palia and 37 km from Mailani.

### Bareilly *p141*

**Bus**

Extensive connections with all major cities on the plains.

**Train**

The station is 3 km from the centre with frequent tempo transfer, Rs 5. **Dehra Dun**: *Doon Exp, 3009*, 2350, 7½ hrs; *Varanasi Dehra Dun Exp, 4265*, 0033, 8½ hrs. **Delhi (OD)**: *Avadh-Assam Exp, 5609*, 0923, 6½ hrs; *Bareilly Delhi Exp, 4555*, 1415, 7 hrs. **Delhi (ND)**: *Shramjeevi Exp, 2401*, 0010, 5½ hrs; *Kashi-Viswanath Exp, 4257*, 0100, 5¾ hrs; *Lucknow New Delhi Mail, 4229*, 0150, 5½ hrs. **Lucknow**: *Rohelkhand Exp, 5309*, 0800, 7¾ hrs. **Varanasi**: *Shramjeevi Exp, 2402*, 1745, 9 hrs; *Kashi-Viswanath Exp, 4258*, 1840, 10¾ hrs.

### Faizabad *p141*

**Bus** Bus Stand, T05278 222964, bus to **Lucknow**, 3 hrs, Rs 47; **Varanasi**, 0630, 6 hrs, Rs 156.

**Train** Railway station, T05278 244119.

### Ayodhya *p141*

**Train** T05278 232023. **Jodhpur, via Agra and Jaipur**: *Marudhar Exp, 4853*, 2040 (Mon, Wed, Sat), 9¼ hrs (Agra), 17½ hrs (Jaipur), 20¼ hrs (Jodhpur). **Varanasi**: *Marudhar Exp, 4854*, 0549 (Tue, Fri, Sun), 3¾ hrs.

### Gorakhpur *p142*

**Bus**

The bus station is a 3-min walk from the railway station. City buses meet most main trains. Services to **Lucknow** (6-7 hrs), **Varanasi**, 205 km (from Katchari Stand, 6 hrs), **Patna** (10 hrs), **Kusinagara** (55 km, on the hour) and others.

The usual route by bus is to go north to Nautanwa via Pharenda, crossing the Nepal border at Sonauli. (You can visit **Lumbini** (130 km) just across the Nepal border, the birthplace of the Buddha.) The bus stand is near the railway station. UP Govt buses (green and yellow) are 'Express' and depart close to schedule. Other private buses (sometimes deluxe a/c up to Kathmandu and Pokhara) leave from opposite the railway station. Services from 0500, for **Nautanwa** (95 km; 2½ hrs) or **Sonauli**, just beyond, on the border (102 km; Rs 40; 3 hrs). Buses to **Kathmandu** (Rs 100; 12 hrs), **Pokhara** (Rs 80; 10 hrs), **Nepalganj** (Rs 120) or **Narayanghat** (Rs 35 for National Park). Most depart at 0700. Local buses every 30 mins to **Lumbini** (Rs 10 for day trip) and **Butwal** (Rs 9). There are different bus stands depending on the destination. Beware of ticket touts in Gorakhpur (private buses opposite railway station) and Nepal border. Some overcharge and others demand excessive 'luggage charge'. When buying a ticket, make absolutely sure which bus, what is included in ticket (meals, overnight accommodation), when and from where it departs (may be 2 hrs delay). Avoid **International Tourism Agency** opposite railway station; its buses are very poorly maintained. Nepalese buses from Sonauli are alright.

At **Sonauli** you need to fill in a small blue form and get your Exit Visa stamp at the Indian Immigration office. You then proceed to the Nepalese Immigration counter to get your Entrance Visa stamp (starting date of visa noted); the counter is open from 0530-2100. If you leave Gorakhpur after 1400 you will arrive at Sonauli after 1700 and will probably do better to stay overnight on the Indian side (mosquito problem) and walk across or get a rickshaw for Rs 5 in the morning to maximize visa days. From there you can take a bus/jeep (Rs 5) to **Bhairawa** in Nepal (6 km) where onward buses to Kathmandu 235 km (0630, 0730, 0830, Rs 75) and flights are available. Indian rupees are exchanged on the Nepal side.

**Train**

**Gorakhpur Junc**, NE Rly HQ station, has tourist information, left luggage (only with padlocks, Rs 15 per piece) and computerized reservations; good waiting rooms. **Delhi:** *Barauni-Katihar Amritsar Exp, 5207*, 1245, 15½ hrs; *Assam Exp, 5609*, 2359, 16 hrs. **New Delhi**: *Vaishali Exp, 2553*, 1715, 13½ hrs (often longer, up to 20 hrs); several others. **Kolkata** (H): *Howrah Bagh Exp, 3020*, 1315, 22½ hrs. **Lucknow**: *Lucknow Exp, 5007*, 2300, 6¼ hrs. **Varanasi**: *Krishak Exp, 5001*, 0630, 5¾ hrs; *Manduadih Exp, 5103*, 1650, 5½ hrs; *Chauri Chaura Exp, 5004*, 2210, 6½ hrs. **Nautanwa**: the most convenient are 2 *Fast Passenger* trains, *95*, 0615, 2½ hrs (return departs Nautanwa, *96*, 0910); *93*, 1230, 3¼ hrs (return *94*, 1700). No need to book ahead (1st class, Rs 100; 2nd class, Rs 35). See above for bus services to Kathmandu and Pokhara from Nautanwa.

**Kusinagara** *p143*

Buses and taxis from Gorakhpur (30 mins).

**Kanpur** *p143, map p144*

**Air**

**Indian Airlines**, opposite MG College, Civil Lines, T0512 231 1430, www.indian-airlines.nic.in. TUP Roadways Bus Stand, Collectorganj, T0512 229 6657, for Lucknow, Allahabad etc; Chunniganj, T0512 253 0646, for Delhi, Agra.

**Bus**

City Bus Service has extensive network for getting around the city.

**Rickshaw**

Tempos, auto-rickshaws, cycle-rickshaws and horse tongas are available.

**Taxi**

Private taxis from Canal Rd taxi stand, hotels and agencies. Full day (8 hrs) about Rs 250.

**Train**

Kanpur is on the main broad gauge Delhi-Kolkata line and also has lines from Lucknow, Agra and Central India. **Central Station**, T131, T0512 232 8170; Anwarganj, T0512 254 5488. **Agra**: *Toofan Exp, 3007*, 0815, 7 hrs (Agra Cantt); *Link Exp, 5313A*, 2200, 11½ hrs (Agra Fort). **Kolkata (H)**: *Rajdhani Exp* (via Gaya), *2302/2422*, 2210, 12½ hrs; *Kalka-Howrah Mail, 2312*, 1440, 16¼ hrs. **Lucknow**: *Shatabdi Exp, 2004*, 1120, 1¼ hrs; *Pratapgarh Exp, 4124*, 1735, 1½ hrs. **New Delhi**: *Shatabdi Exp, 2003*, 1640, 5 hrs; *Rajdhani Exp, 2301/2305*, 0448, 5 hrs. **Patna**: *Rajdhani Exp, 2306/2310/2424*, 2155, 8 hrs; *Poorva Exp, 2304*, 2315, Wed, Thu, Sat, Sun, 8½ hrs; *Northeast Exp, 5622*, 1310, 9¼ hrs. **Varanasi**: *Lichhavi Exp 5206*, 2330, 6 hrs; *Farakka Exp, 3484/3414*, 0540, 9¾ hrs.

## Directory

**Dudhwa National Park** *p141*

**Tourist offices** Reception Centre, Dudhwa National Park, Lakhimpur Kheri, near Dist Magistrate's house, T05871-252106. Wildlife Warden, Dudhwa National Park, Palia, T05871-233485. Tours available in season.

**Gorakhpur** *p142*

**Telephone** ISD and fax services from **Door Sanchar**, The Target, opposite Vijay Cinema. **Tourist offices** Park Rd, Civil Lines, T0551 233 5450; counter on Platform 1, railway station. **Travel Bureau**, opposite railway station, **Hotel Elora Building**, T0551 220 2233.

**Kanpur** *p143, map p144*

**Banks** Usually open 1030-1430. **Standard Chartered Grindlays**, 16 MG Rd, T0512 236 8253. Changes TCs. **Allahabad Bank**, MG Rd. **Hospitals** Regency, T0512 229 5789. Dufferin, T0512 231 1510. KPM, T0512 235 8538. **Post** Head GPO: Bara Chauraha, The Mall, T0512 236 0493 (open 24 hrs). **Tourist offices** UP, 26/51 Birhana Rd, opposite Post office, T0512 235 8186. **Useful addresses** Police: T100.

# Agra and around

→ *Phone code: 0562. Colour map 3, grid A1. Population: 1.3 mn.*

*The romance of the world's most famous building still astonishes in its power. In addition to the Taj, Agra also houses the great monuments of the Red Fort and the I'timad-ud-Daulah, but to experience their beauty you have to endure the less attractive sides of one of India's least prepossessing towns. A big industrial city, the monuments are often covered in a haze of all too polluted air, while visitors may be subjected to a barrage of high power selling. Despite it all, the experience is still unmissable. The city is also the convenient gateway to the wonderful, abandoned capital of Fatehpur Sikri and some of Hinduism's most holy sites.* ⏩ *For Sleeping, Eating and other listings, see pages 167-172.*

## Ins and outs

**Getting there** By far the best way to arrive is by using the *Shatabdi Express* train. Considering waiting time and delays, it is usually faster than flying, and infinitely more comfortable than bus or car. There are frequent 'express' buses from Delhi and Jaipur, but it can take up to five tiring hours by bus or car.

**Getting around** Buses run a regular service between the station, bus stands and the main sites. See Entrances, page 152. Cycle-rickshaws and taxis can be hired to go further afield, or a bike if it's not too hot. ⏩ *See Transport, page 171, for further details.*

**Climate** Best time to visit is between November and March.

## History

With minor interruptions Agra alternated with Delhi as the capital of the Mughal Empire. **Sikander Lodi** seized it from a rebellious governor and made it his capital in 1501. He died in Agra but is buried in Delhi (see page 103). Agra was Babur's capital. He is believed to have laid out a pleasure garden on the east bank of the River Yamuna and his son Humayun built a mosque here in 1530. **Akbar** lived in Agra in the early years of his reign. Ralph Fitch, the English Elizabethan traveller, described a "magnificent city, with broad streets and tall buildings". He also saw Akbar's new capital at Fatehpur Sikri, 40 km west, describing a route lined all the way with stalls and markets. Akbar moved his capital again to Lahore, before returning to Agra in 1599, where he spent the last six years of his life. **Jahangir** left Agra for Kashmir in 1618 and never returned. Despite modifying the Red Fort and building the Taj Mahal, **Shah Jahan** too moved away in 1638 to his new city Shah Jahanabad in Delhi, though he returned in 1650 to spend his last days in Agra as his son Aurangzeb's prisoner. **Aurangzeb**, the last of the Great Mughals, moved the seat of government permanently to Delhi. In the 18th century it suffered at the hands of the Jats, was taken, lost and retaken by the Marathas who, in turn, were ousted by the British in 1803. It was the centre of much fighting in the 'Uprising' and was the administrative centre of the Northwest Provinces and Oudh until that too was transferred to Allahabad in 1877. See page 1302 for further details.

# Taj Mahal

ⓘ *Daily except Fri, 0600-1900, Rs 20, foreigners Rs750, includes still camera (video cameras not allowed). No photos inside the tomb (instant fines). Allow at least 1 hr.*

Of all the world's great monuments, the Taj Mahal is one of the most written about, photographed, televised and talked about. To India's Nobel Laureate poet, Tagore, the Taj was a "tear drop on the face of humanity", a building to echo the cry "I have not forgotten, I have not forgotten, O beloved" and its mesmerising power is such that still no one comes away disappointed.

Shah Jahan, fifth of the Great Mughals, was so devoted to his favourite wife, Mumtaz Mahal (Jewel of the Palace) that he could not bear to be parted from her and insisted that she always travel with him, in all states of health. While accompanying him on a military campaign, she died at the age of 39 giving birth to their 14th child. On her deathbed, it is said, that she asked the emperor to show the world how much they loved one another.



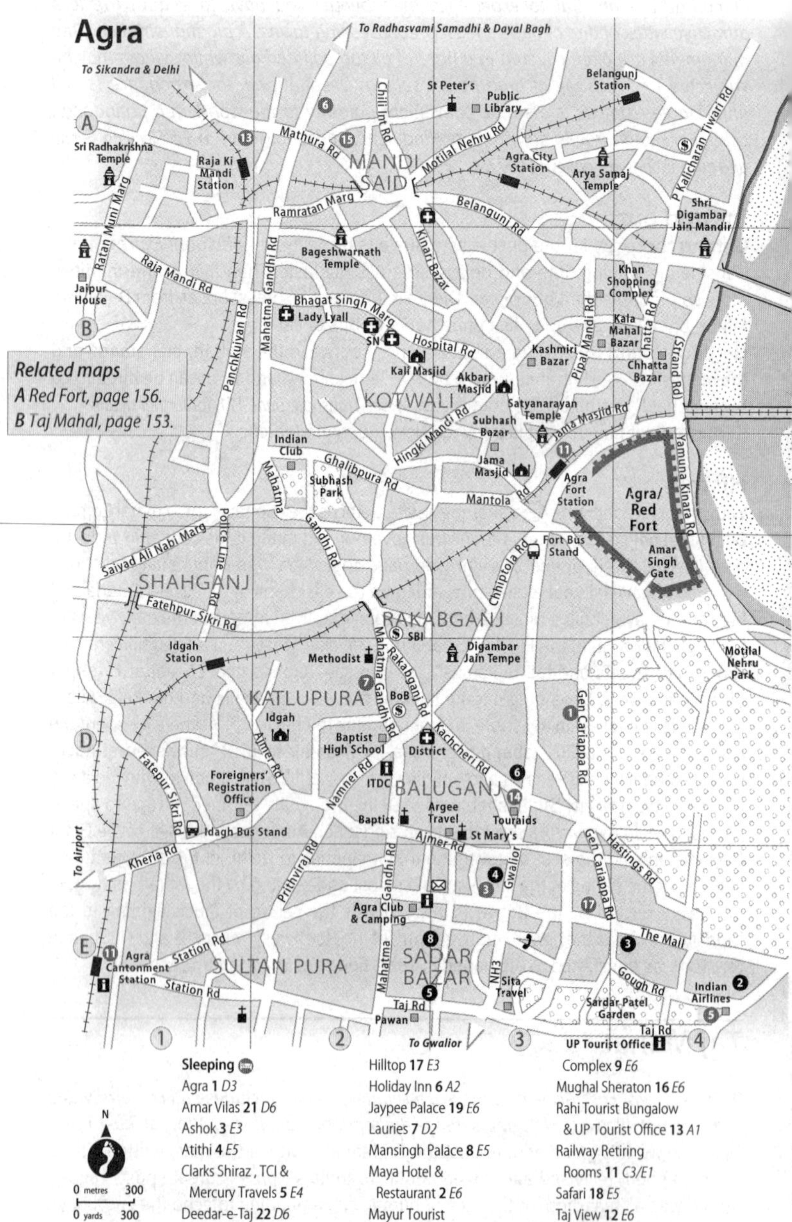


Related maps
A Red Fort, page 156.
B Taj Mahal, page 153.

The grief-stricken emperor went into mourning for two years. He turned away from the business of running the empire and dedicated himself to architecture, resolving to build his wife the most magnificent memorial on earth. On the right bank of the river Yamuna in full view of his fortress palace, it was to be known as the Taj-i-Mahal (The Crown of the Palace).

According to the French traveller Tavnier, work on the Taj commence in 1632 and took 22 years to complete, employing a workforce of 20,000. The red sandstone was available locally but the white marble was quarried at Makrana in Rajasthan and transported 300 km by a fleet of 1,000 elephants. Semi-precious stones for the inlay came from far and wide: red carnelian from Baghdad; red, yellow and brown jasper from the Punjab; green jade and crystal from China; blue lapis lazuli from Ceylon and Afghanistan; turquoise from Tibet; chrysolite from Egypt; amethyst from Persia; agates from the Yemen; dark green malachite from Russia; diamonds from Central India and mother-of-pearl from the Indian Ocean. A 3-km ramp was used to lift material up to the dome and, because of the sheer weight of the building; boreholes were filled with metal coins and fragments to provide suitable foundations. The resemblance of the exquisite double dome to a huge pearl is not coincidental; a saying of the Prophet describes the throne of God as a dome of white pearl supported by white pillars.

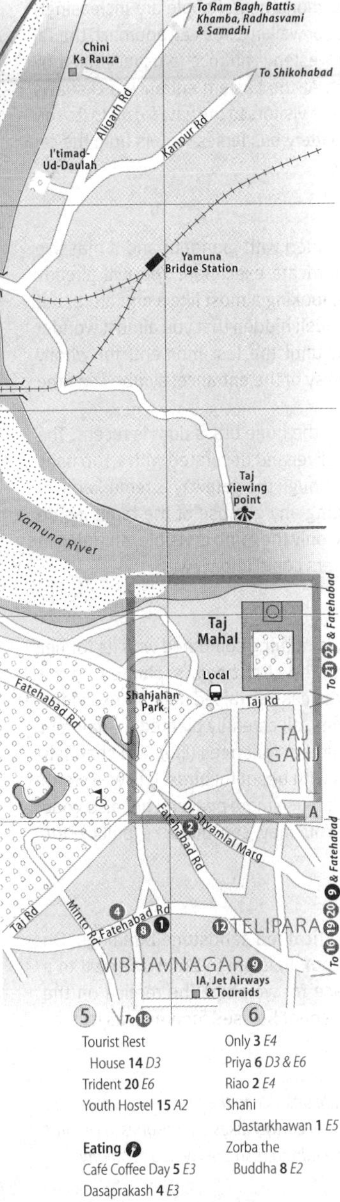


Myths and controversy surround the Taj Mahal. On its competition it is said that the Emperor ordered the chief mason's right hand to be cut off to prevent him from repeating his masterpiece. Another legend suggests that Shah Jahan intended to build a replica for himself in black marble on the other side of the river, connected to the Taj Mahal by a bridge built with alternate blocks of black and white marble. Some have asserted that architects responsible for designing this mausoleum must have come from Turkey, Persia or even Europe (because of the pietra dura work on the tomb). In fact, no one knows who drew the plans. What is certain is that in the Taj Mahal, the traditions of Indian Hindu and Persian Muslim architecture were fused together into a completely distinct and perfect art form.

## Viewing

The white marble of the Taj is extraordinarily luminescent and even on dull days seems bright. The whole building appears to change its hue according to the light in the sky. In winter (December-February), it is worth being there at sunrise. Then the mists that often lie over the river Yamuna lift as the sun rises and casts its golden rays over the pearl white tomb. Beautifully lit in the soft light, the Taj appears to float on air. At sunset, the view from across the river is equally wonderful. The Archaeological Survey of India explicitly asks visitors not to make donations to anyone including the custodians in the tomb who do ask for money.

## Entrances

To reduce damage to the marble by the polluted atmosphere, local industries are having to comply with strict rules now and vehicles emitting noxious fumes are not allowed within 2 km of the monument. People are increasingly using horse drawn carriages or walking. You can approach the Taj from three directions. The western entrance is usually used by those arriving from the fort. At the Eastern entrance, rickshaws and camel drivers offer to take visitors to the gate for up to Rs 100 each; however, an official battery bus ferries visitors from the car park to the gate for Rs 2 each.

*Visit at sunrise an sunset to avoid crowds and take photographs in peace (early morning can be misty). Hiring a guide isn't necessary.*



## The approach

In the unique beauty of the Taj, sudbtlety is blended with grandeur and a massive overall design is matched with immaculately intricate execution. You will already have seen the dome of the tomb in the distance, looking almost like a miniature, but as you go into the open square the Taj itself is so well hidden that you almost wonder where it can be. The glorious surprise is kept until the last moment, for wholly concealing it is the massive red sandstone gateway of the entrance, symbolizing the divide between the secular world and paradise.

The gateway was completed in 1648, though the huge brass door is recent. The original doors (plundered by the Jats) were solid silver and decorated with 1,100 nails whose heads were contemporary silver coins. Although the gateway is remarkable in itself, one of its functions is to prevent you getting any glimpse of the tomb inside until you are right in the doorway itself. From here only the tomb is visible, stunning in its nearness, but as you move forward the minarets come into view.

## The garden

The Taj garden, well kept though it is nowadays, is nothing compared with its former glory. The guiding principle is one of symmetry. The *char bagh*, separated by the watercourses (rivers of heaven) originating from the central, raised pool, were divided into 16 flower beds, making a total of 64. The trees, all carefully planted to maintain the symmetry, were either cypress (signifying death) or fruit trees (life). The channels were stocked with colourful fish and the gardens with beautiful birds. It is well worth wandering along the side avenues for not only is it much more peaceful but also good for framing photos of the tomb with foliage. You may see bullocks pulling the lawnmowers around!

## The mosque and its jawab

On the east and west sides of the tomb are identical red sandstone buildings. On the west (left-hand side) is a mosque. It is common in Islam to build one next to a tomb. It sanctifies the area and provides a place for worship. The replica on the other side is known as the **Jawab** (answer). This cannot be used for prayer as it faces away from Mecca.

*The four minarets at each corner of the plinth provide balance to the tomb – see how each slants outwards. Familiar with the disastrous effects of earthquakes on mosques in Gujarat to the south, the architects deliberately designed the minarets so they would fall away from the tomb, not onto it.*

## ❝❞ The white marble of the Taj is extraordinarily luminescent and even on dull days seems bright: the whole building appears to change its hue according to the light in the sky...

### The tomb

There is only one point of access to the **plinth** and tomb where, shoes must be removed (socks can be kept on; remember the white marble gets very hot) or cloth overshoes worn (Rs 2, though strictly free).

The **tomb** is square with bevelled corners. At each corner smaller domes rise while in the centre is the main dome topped by a brass finial. The dome is actually a double dome and this device, Central Asian in origin, was used to gain height. The resemblance of the dome to a huge pearl is not coincidental. The exterior ornamentation is calligraphy (verses of the Koran), beautifully carved panels in bas relief and superb inlay work.

The **interior** of the mausoleum comprises a lofty central chamber, a crypt (*maqbara*) immediately below this, and four octagonal corner rooms. The central chamber contains replica tombs, the real ones being in the crypt. The public tomb was originally surrounded by a jewel encrusted silver screen. Aurangzeb removed this, fearing it might be stolen, and replaced it with an octagonal screen of marble carved from one block of marble and inlaid with precious stones. It is an incredible piece of workmanship. This chamber is open at sunrise, but may close during the day.

Above the tombs is a **Cairene lamp** whose flame is supposed to never go out. This one was given by Lord Curzon, Governor General of India (1899-1905), to replace the original which was stolen by Jats. The tomb of Mumtaz with the 'female' slate, rests immediately beneath the dome. If you look from behind it, you can see how it lines up centrally with the main entrance. Shah Jahan's tomb is larger and to the side, marked by a 'male' pen-box, the sign of a cultured or noble person. Not originally intended to be placed there but squeezed in by Aurangzeb, this flaws the otherwise perfect symmetry of the whole complex. Finally, the acoustics of the building are superb, the domed ceiling being designed to echo chants from the Koran and musicians' melodies.

The **museum** ⓘ *1000-1700, closed Fri*, above the entrance has a small collection of Mughal memorabilia, photographs and miniatures of the Taj through the ages but has no textual information. Sadly, lights do not always work.

## Charbagh: The Mughal garden

In the Koran, the garden is repeatedly seen as a symbol for paradise. Islam was born in the deserts of Arabia. Muslims venerate water, without which plants will not grow - the old Persian word pairidaeza means 'garden'. It is no coincidence then that green is the colour of Islam.

Four main rivers of paradise are also specified: water, milk, wine and purified honey. This is the origin of the quartered garden (charbagh). The watercourses divided the garden into quadrats and all was enclosed behind a private wall. To the Muslim the beauty of creation and of the garden was held to be a reflection of God. The great Sufi poet **Rumi** used much garden imagery: "The trees are engaged in ritual prayer and the birds in singing the litany". Thus, the garden becomes as important as the tomb.



**Jami Masjid** (1648), near the Fort railway, is attributed to Shah Jahan's dutiful elder daughter Jahanara. The fine marble steps and bold geometric patterns on the domes are quite striking. The large gardens have deer, black buck and monkeys.

# Agra Fort (Red Fort)

ⓘ *0600-1830. Rs 15, foreigners Rs 300 (or Rs 50 if you've already been to the Taj), video Rs25. Allow a minimum of 1½ hrs for a visit.*

On the west bank of the River Yamuna, Akbar's magnificent fort dominates the centre of the city. Akbar erected the walls and gates and the first buildings inside. **Shah Jahan** built the impressive imperial quarters and mosque, while Aurangzeb added the outer ramparts. The outer walls, just over 20 m high and faced with red sandstone, tower above the outer moat. The fort is crescent-shaped with a long, nearly straight wall facing the river, punctuated at regular intervals by bastions. The main entrance used to be in the centre of the west wall, the Delhi Gate, facing the bazar. It led to the Jami Masjid in the city but is now permanently closed. You can only enter now from the Amar Singh gate in the south. Although only the southern third of the fort is open to the public, this includes nearly all the buildings of interest. You enter through the **Amar Singh Gate** having had to contend with vendors of cheap soapstone boxes and knick-knacks. If you want to buy something, bargain hard. Guides will offer their services – most are not particularly good. Rs 500 Development Authority 'tax' covers visits to all Agra and Fatehpur Sikri sites on the same day.

*The best route round is to start with the building on your right before going through the gate at the top of the broad 100 m ramp; the gentle incline made it suitable for elephants.*

## Fortifications

These tower above the 9-m wide, 10-m deep moat (still evident but containing stagnant water) formerly filled with water from the Yamuna. There is an outer wall on the riverside and an imposing 22 m high inner, main wall, giving a feeling of great defensive power. Although it served as a model for Shah Jahan's Red Fort in Delhi, its own model was the Rajput fort built by Raja Man Singh Tomar of Gwalior in 1500, see page 269. If an aggressor managed to get through the outer gate they would have to make a right hand turn and thereby expose their flank to the defenders on the inner wall. The inner gate is solidly powerful but has been attractively decorated with tiles. The similarities with Islamic patterns of the tilework are obvious, though the Persian blue was also used in the Gwalior Fort and may well have been imitated from that example. The incline up to this point and beyond was suitable for elephants and as you walk past the last gate and up the broad brick-lined ramp with ridged slabs, it is easy to imagine arriving on elephant back. At the top of this 100-m ramp is a **gate** with a map and description board on your left.

**Jahangiri Mahal (1)** Despite its name, this was built by Akbar (circa 1570) as women's quarters. It is all that survives of his original palace buildings. In front is a large **stone bowl** with steps both inside and outside, which was probably filled with fragrant rose water for bathing. Almost 75 m sq, the palace has a simple stone exterior. Tillotson has pointed out that the blind arcade of pointed arches inlaid with white marble which decorate the façade is copied from 14th-century monuments of the Khaljis and Tughluqs in Delhi. He notes that they are complemented by some features derived from Hindu architecture, including the balconies (*jarokhas*) protruding from the central section, the sloping dripstone in place of eaves (*chajja*) along the top of the façade, and the domed *chhattris* at its ends. The presence of distinctively Hindu features does not indicate a synthesis of architectural styles at this early stage of Mughal architecture, as can be seen much more clearly from inside the Jahangiri Mahal. Here most of the features are straightforwardly Hindu; square headed arches and extraordinarily carved capitals and brackets illustrate the vivid work of local Hindu craftsmen employed by Akbar without any attempt either to curb their enthusiasm for florid decoration and mythical animals nor to produce a fusion of Hindu and Islamic ideas. Tillotson argues that the central courtyard is essentially Hindu, in significant contrast with most earlier Indo-Islamic buildings. In these, an Islamic scheme was modified by Hindu touches. He suggests, therefore, that the Jahangiri Mahal marks the start of a more fundamental kind of Hinduization, typical of several projects during Akbar's middle period of rule, including the palace complex in Fatehpur Sikri. However, it did not represent a real fusion of ideas – something that only came under Shah Jahan – simply a juxtaposition of sharply contrasting styles.



**Jodh Bai's Palace (2)** On the south side, this is named after one of Jahangir's wives. On the east the hall court leads onto a more open yard by the inner wall of the fort. In contrast to other palaces in the fort, this is quite simple. Through the slits in the wall you can see the Taj.

## Shah Jahan's palace buildings

Turn left through to Shah Jahan's Khas Mahal (1636). The open tower allows you to view the walls and see to your left the decorated Mussaman Burj tower. The use of white marble transforms the atmosphere, contributing to the new sense of grace and light.

**Anguri Bagh (3)** (Vine Garden) The formal, 85 m sq, geometric gardens are on the left. In Shah Jahan's time the geometric patterns were enhanced by decorative flower beds. In the middle of the white marble platform wall in front is a decorative water slide. From the pool with its bays for seating and its fountains, water would drain off along channels decorated to mimic a stream. The surface was scalloped to produce a rippling waterfall, or inlaid to create a shimmering stream bed. Behind vertical water drops, there are little cusped arch niches into which flowers would be placed during the day and lamps at night. The effect was magical.

**Golden Pavilions (4)** The curved *chala* roofs of the small pavilions by the Khas Mahal are based on the roof shape of Bengali village huts constructed out of curved bamboo, designed to keep off heavy rain. The shape was first expressed in stone by the Sultans of Bengal. Originally gilded, these were probably ladies' bedrooms, with hiding places for jewellery in the walls. These pavilions are traditionally associated with Shah Jahan's daughters, Roshanara and Jahanara.

**Khas Mahal (5)** This was the model for the Diwan-i-Khas at the Red Fort in Delhi. Some of the original interior decoration has been restored (1895) and gives an impression of how splendid the painted ceiling must have been. The metal rings were probably used for *punkhas*. Underneath are cool rooms used to escape the summer heat. The Khas Mahal illustrates Shahs' original architectural contribution.

These buildings retain some distinctively Islamic Persian features – the geometrical planning of the pavilions and the formal layout of the gardens, for example. Tillotson points out that here "Hindu motifs are treated in a new manner, which is less directly imitative of the Hindu antecedents. The temple columns and corbel capitals have been stripped of their rich carving and turned into simpler, smoother forms ... the *chhattris* have Islamic domes. Through these subtle changes the indigenous motifs have lost their specifically Hindu identity; they therefore contrast less strongly with the Islamic components, and are bound with them into a new style. The unity is assisted by the use of the cusped arch and the *Bangladar* roof". Seen in this light, the Khas Mahal achieves a true synthesis which eluded Akbar's designs.



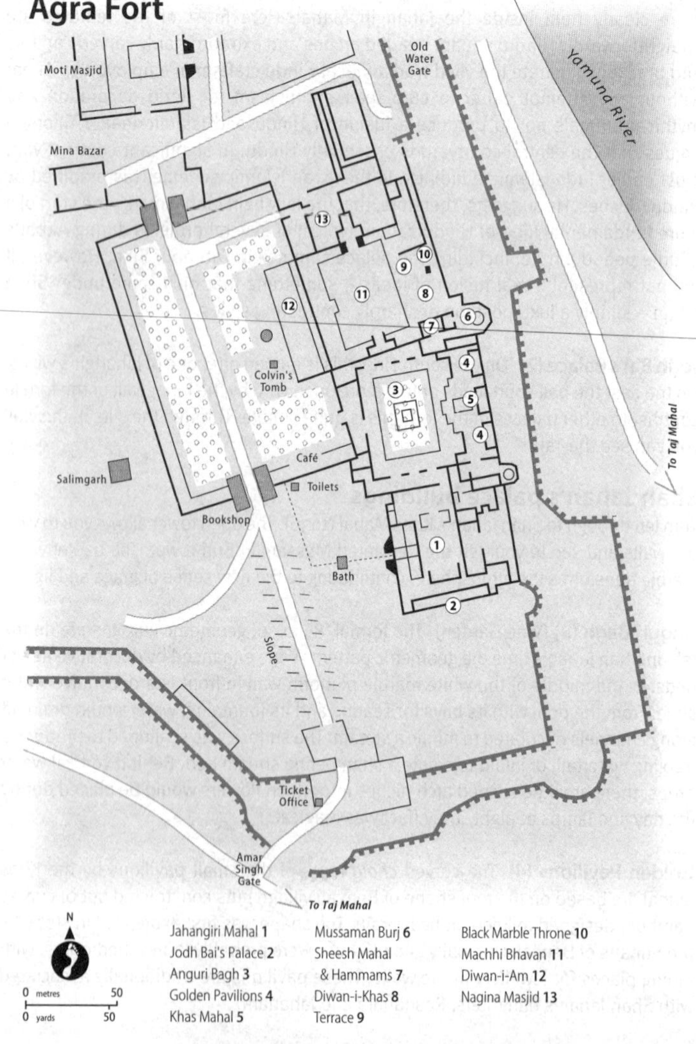

**Mussaman Burj (6)** On the left of the Khas Mahal is the Mussaman Burj (*Octagonal Tower*, though sometimes corrupted into Saman Burj, then translated as *Jasmine Tower*). It is a beautiful octagonal tower with an open pavilion. With its openness, elevation and the benefit of cooling evening breezes blowing in off the River Yamuna, this could well have been used as the emperor's bedroom. It has been suggested that this is where Shah Jahan lay on his deathbed, gazing at the Taj. Access to this tower is through a magnificently decorated and intimate apartment with a scalloped fountain in the centre. The inlay work here is exquisite, especially above the pillars. In front of the fountain is a sunken courtyard which could be filled by water carriers, to work the fountains in the pool.

**Sheesh Mahal (7)** (Mirror Palace) Here are further examples of decorative water engineering in the *hammams*; the water here may have been warmed by lamps. The mirrors which were more precious than marble were set into the walls, often specially chiselled to accommodate their crooked shape. The defensive qualities of the site and the fortifications are obvious. In the area between the outer rampart and the inner wall gladiatorial battles between man and tiger, or elephants were staged. The tower was the emperor's grandstand seat.

**Diwan-i-Khas (8)** (Hall of Private Audience, 1637) This is next to the Mussaman Burj, approached on this route by a staircase which brings you out at the side. The interior of the Diwan-i-Khas, a three-sided pavilion with a terrace of fine proportions, would have been richly decorated with tapestries and carpets. The double columns in marble inlaid with semi-precious stones in delightful floral patterns in *pietra dura* have finely carved capitals.

## Terrace and Machhi Bhavan

In front of the Diwan-i-Khas are two throne 'platforms' on a **terrace (9)**. Gascoigne recounts how Shah Jahan tried to trick a haughty Persian ambassador into bowing low as he approached the throne by erecting a fence with a small wicket gate so that his visitor would have to enter on hands and knees. The ambassador did so, but entered backwards, thus presenting his bottom first to the Emperor. The **black marble throne (10)** at the rear of the terrace was used by Jahangir when claiming to be Emperor at Allahabad. The emperor sat on the white marble platform facing the **Machhi Bhavan (11)** (Fish Enclosure), which once contained pools and fountains, waiting to meet visiting dignitaries.

**Diwan-i-Am (12)** Go down an internal staircase and you enter the Diwan-i-Am from the side. The clever positioning of the pillars gives the visitor arriving through the gates in the right and left hand walls of the courtyard an uninterrupted view of the throne. On the back wall of the pavilion are *jali* screens to enable the women of the court to watch without being seen. The open-sided, cusped arched hall built of plaster on red stone, is very impressive. The throne alcove of richly decorated white marble completed after seven years' work in 1634 used to house the Peacock Throne. Its decoration made it extraordinary: "the canopy was carved in enamel work and studded with individual gems, its interior was thickly encrusted with rubies, garnets and diamonds, and it was supported on 12 emerald covered columns" writes Tillotson. When Shah Jahan moved his capital to Delhi he took the throne with him to the Red Fort, only for it to be taken back to Persia as loot by Nadir Shah in 1739.

**Nagina Masjid (13)** From the corner opposite the Diwan-i-Khas two doorways lead to a view over the small courtyards of the *zenana* (harem). Further round in the next corner is the Nagina Masjid. Shoes must be removed at the doorway. Built by Shah Jahan, this was the private mosque of the ladies of the court. Beneath it was a *mina* bazar for the ladies to make purchases from the marble balcony above. Looking out of the Diwan-i-Am you can see the domes of the **Moti Masjid** (Pearl Mosque, 1646-1653), an extremely fine building closed to visitors because of structural problems. Opposite the Diwan-i-Am are the barracks and **Mina Bazar**, also closed to the public. In the paved area in front of the Diwan-i-Am is a large well and the tomb of **Mr John Russell Colvin**, the Lieutenant Governor of the Northwest Provinces who died here during the 1857 'Uprising'. Stylistically it is sadly out of place. The yellow buildings date from the British period.

### Jama Masjid

The mosque built in 1648, near the Fort railway, no longer connected to the Fort, is attributed to Shah Jahan's dutiful elder daughter Jahanara. Though in need of repair and not comparable to buildings within the fort, its symmetry has suffered since a small minaret fell in the 1980s. The fine marble steps and bold geometric patterns on the domes are quite striking. The large gardens have deer, black buck and monkeys.



## I'timad-ud-Daulah

ⓘ *0630-1830, Rs 10, foreigners Rs 110, video Rs 25.*
Sometimes called 'Baby Taj' set a startling precedent as the first Mughal building to be faced with white marble inlaid with contrasting stones. Unlike the Taj it is small, intimate and has a gentle serenity, but is just as ornate. The tomb was built for **Ghiyas Beg**, a Persian who had obtained service in Akbar's court, and his wife, see page 1302. On Jahangir's succession in 1605 he became *Wazir* (Chief Minister). Jahangir fell in love with his daughter, **Mehrunissa**, who at the time was married to a Persian. When her husband died in 1607, she entered Jahangir's court as a lady-in-waiting. Four years later Jahangir married her. Thereafter she was known first as **Nur Mahal** ('Light of the Palace'), later being promoted to **Nur Jahan** ('Light of the World'), see page 1302. Her niece Mumtaz married Shah Jahan

### The plan

Nur Jahan built the tomb for her father in the *char bagh* that he himself had laid out. It is beautifully conceived in white marble, mosaic and lattice. There is a good view from the roof of the entrance. Marble screens of geometric lattice work permit soft lighting of the inner chamber. The yellow marble caskets appear to have been carved out of wood. On the engraved walls of the chamber is the recurring theme of a wine flask with snakes as handles – perhaps a reference by Nur Jahan, the tomb's creator, to her husband Jahangir's excessive drinking. Stylistically, the tomb marks a change from the sturdy and manly buildings of Akbar's reign to softer, more feminine lines. The main chamber, **Pietra dura,** richly decorated with mosaics and semi-precious stones inlaid in the white marble, contains the tomb of I'timad-ud-Daulah ('Pillar of the goverment') and his wife. Some have argued that the concept and skill must have travelled from its European home of 16th-century Florence to India. However,Florentine *pietra dura* is figurative whereas the Indian version is essentially decorative and can be seen as a refinement of its Indian predecessor, the patterned mosaic. See also page 159.

## Sikandra

ⓘ *Sunrise-sunset. Indians Rs 10, foreigners Rs110, includes still camera, video Rs 25.*
Following the Timurid tradition, Akbar (ruled 1556-1605) had started to build his own tomb at Sikandra. He died during its construction and his son **Jahangir** completed it in 1613. The result is an impressive, large but architecturally confused tomb. A huge

gateway, the **Buland Darwaza**, leads to the great garden enclosure, where spotted deer run free on the immaculate lawns. The decoration on the gateway is strikingly bold, with its large mosaic patterns, a forerunner of the *pietra dura* technique. The white minarets atop the entrance were an innovation which reappear, almost unchanged, at the Taj Mahal. The walled garden enclosure is laid out in the *char bagh* style, with the mausoleum at the centre.

*Morning is the best time to visit when few others are likely to be around.*

A broad paved path leads to the 22.5-m high tomb with four storeys. The lowest storey, nearly 100 m sq and 9-m high, contains massive cloisters. The entrance on the south side leads to the tomb chamber. Shoes must be removed or cloth overshoes worn; hire Rs 2. In a niche opposite the entrance is an alabaster tablet inscribed with the 99 divine names of Allah. The sepulchre is in the centre of the room, whose velvety darkness is pierced by a single slanting shaft of light from a high window. The custodian, in expectation of a donation, makes 'Akbaaarrrr' echo around the chamber.

Four kilometres south of Sikandra, nearly opposite the high gateway of the ancient **Kach ki Sarai** building, is a sculptured horse, believed to mark the spot where Akbar's favourite horse died. There are also *kos minars* (marking a *kos*, about 4 km) and several other tombs on the way.

## Mathura

*Phone code: 0565. Colour map 2, grid A6. Population: 300,000.*

Mathura, 50 km from Agra on the west bank of the Yamuna, is one of the most sacred cities of Hinduism dating back to 600 BC. For Vaishnavites, it is perhaps the supremely sacred city of India, being the reputed birthplace of **Krishna**, the most human aspect of Vishnu. Krishna is widely seen as the embodiment of the ideal lover, soldier, statesman, as well as the adorable baby, or wayward child. Many places around are associated with episodes in his life. Mathura's ancient structures were mostly destroyed by Muslims but its religious association draws thousands of pilgrims. Today, it is also an important industrial city with much evidence of modernizing on the approach from the highway. The opening of a big oil refinery on the outskirts of the city in 1975 caused great concern among environmentalists that atmospheric pollution would irreversibly damage the Taj Mahal only 50 km away.

### History

Ptolemy mentioned the town and it assumed the importance of a capital city during the first to second century **Kushan Empire**. When the Chinese traveller Hiuen Tsang visited it in 634 AD it was an important Buddhist centre with several monasteries. However, **Mahmud of Ghazni** sacked the city and desecrated its temples in 1017, followed by **Sikander Lodi** in 1500, whilst the Mughal **Emperor Aurangzeb** used a local revolt in which his governor was killed as an excuse to destroy the main temples. Jats and Marathas fought over the city as the Mughal Empire declined, but at the beginning of the 19th century it came under British control. They laid out a cantonment in the south and left a cemetery and the Roman Catholic **Sacred Heart Cathedral** (1870).

### Sights

There are no pre-Muslim monuments of any significance, and some of the finest buildings have been badly scarred by decay, neglect and misuse. You enter Mathura by the finely carved **Holi Gate** and in the centre of the bustling old city is the **Jami Masjid** (1660-1661) with four minarets, which was built by Abd-un-Nadi, Aurangzeb's governor. It has a raised courtyard and above the façade which was once covered with brightly coloured enamel tiles, are the 99 names of Allah.

The **Katra** (500 m) contains a mosque built by Aurangzeb. This stands over the ruins of one of Mathura's most famous temples, the **Kesava Deo Mandir** which, in turn had been built on the ruins of a Buddhist monastery of the Kushan period. This is considered to be **Sri Krishna Janmabhumi** (Krishna's birthplace). The main statues are particularly serene and attractive but there may be difficulty in entering due to extra security at times since there is a mosque next to it. At the rear of this enclosure is a newer **Temple of Kesava**, built by Bir Singh of Orchha, see page 276. Nearby is the impressive **Potara Kund**, a stepped tank in which Krishna's baby clothes were washed. It is faced in the familiar local red sandstone with access for cattle and horses.

The river and its ghats are the focal point for Hindu pilgrims – a paved street runs their length, but recent developments have made the area very congested, and the two industrial-looking bridges which cross the river close to the ghats have taken away some of the charm. **Vishram Ghat** (rebuilt in 1814) is where Krishna rested after killing Kamsa. Cows, monkeys and turtles are fed when the *Arati* ceremony is performed, morning and evening which is best seen from a boat.

The **Sati Burj** (late 16th century), on the river, is a square, four-storey red sandstone tower with a plastered dome said to commemorate the *sati* by the wife of Rajbihari Mal of Amber. The **Kans Qila** fort was built by Raja Man Singh of Amber and



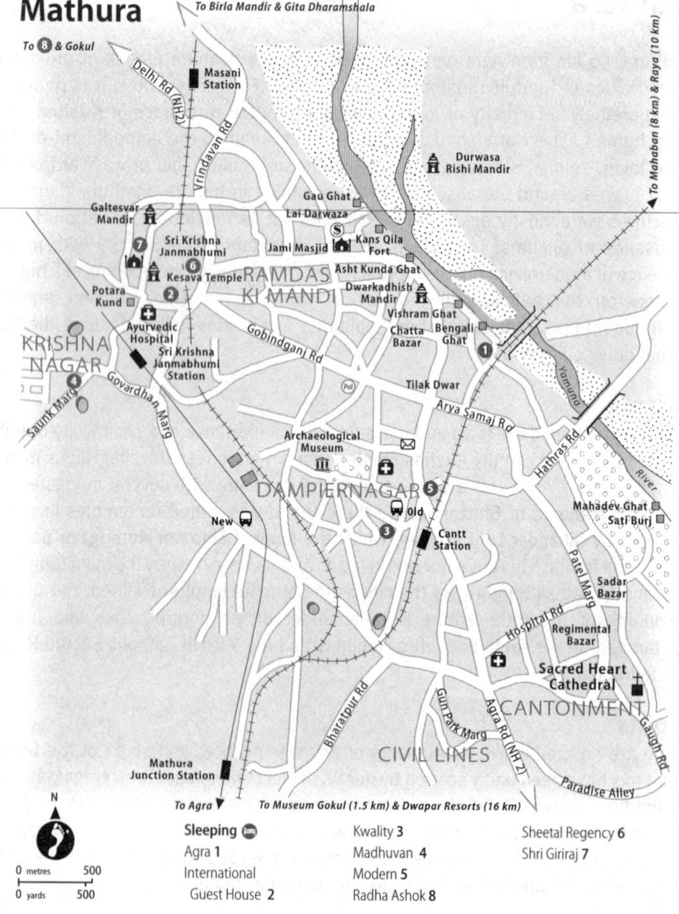

was rebuilt by Akbar but only the foundations remain. Nothing survives of Maharaja Jai Singh's, see page 326, observatory.

**Archaeological museum** ⓘ *Dampier Nagar, T0565 250 0847, 1030-1630, closed Mon, Rs 25 (foreigners), Rs 5 (Indians), camera Rs 20*, has an extensive and impressive collection of sculptures, terracottas, bronzes and coins housed in an octagonal red sandstone building. Also exhibited is the fifth-century 'Standing Buddha', numerous Gupta figures, a first-century headless Buddha, and Kushana sculptures and Gandhara pieces.

## Excursions

**Gokul**, 2 km away, is approached by a long flight of steps from the river. It is associated with very early Hindu legends, where Vishnu first appeared as Krishna. It is the headquarters of the Vallabhacharya Sect who built some large temples.

**Mahaban**, 9 km southeast of Mathura on the east bank of the Yamuna, means 'a great forest'. There is no forest now but in 1634 Shah Jahan is recorded as having killed four tigers in a hunt here. The town was sacked by Mahmud of Ghazni in the 11th century. Each year in August Vaishnavite pilgrims come to the Nanda Krishna **Palace** where Krishna was believed to have been secretly raised. His cradle stands in the hall, the hole in the wall is where the *gopis* hid his flute, and the place where his mother stood churning butter is marked by a polished pillar.

**Baradari of Sikander Lodi**, 28 km south of Mathura, is the 12 pillared pavilion of Sikander Lodi, one time King of Delhi, built in 1495, and the 1611 **Tomb of Mariam uz Zamani**, Akbar's Hindu Rajput wife who is said to have been converted to Christianity, though there is little supporting evidence. There are beautiful carvings on the red sandstone structure.

**Govardhan**, 26 km west of Mathura, lies in the narrow range of the Girraj Hills. In legend, when Indra caused a tremendous flood, Krishna raised these hills up above the flood for seven days so that people could escape. The **Harideva Temple**, by the Manasi Ganga River, was built by Raja Bhagwan Das in the reign of Akbar. On the opposite bank are the *chhattris* of Ranjit Singh and Balwant Singh, both rulers of Bharatpur. There are stone ghats on all sides, built in 1817. Krishna is believed to have ritually bathed at the temple to purify himself after killing the demon bull Arishta.

# Vrindavan → *Phone code: 0565. Colour map 2, grid A6.*

Vrindavan – 'Forest of Tulsi (basil) Plants' – is the most famous of the holy sites around Mathura. In Vrindavan, Krishna played with the *gopis* (cowgirls), stealing their clothes while they bathed. You are entering perhaps the most sacred region of India for Vaishnavite Hindus, where many of the stories surrounding **Krishna** are set, see page 1326). The town retains a tranquil, welcoming atmosphere, and offers an interesting mix of stunning temples, narrow medieval alleyways and beautiful river scenes, observed by an equally interesting mix of local Sadhus and international devotees of Hare Krishna.

*The temples are open morning and evening usually between 0900 and 1200 and 0800 and 2100 when you can attend worship.*

At the entrance to the town is the 16th-century temple of **Gobind Dev** (1590), the 'Divine Cowherd', Krishna. Built by Man Singh of Jaipur during Akbar's reign, it was severely damaged by the less tolerant Aurangzeb. Nearby there is a Dravidian style temple dedicated to **Sri Ranganathji** (Vishnu), with three *gopura*, each nearly 30 m high. There is an annual 10-day *Rath* (car) festival in March/April. The 16th-century **Madan Mohan** temple stands above a ghat on an arm of the river; there is a pavilion decorated with cobra carvings. Siva is believed to have struck Devi here and made it a place for curing snake bites. The octagonal tower is similar to the one on the 16th-century **Jagat Krishna** temple.

Other temples include **Jugal Kishor** (reputedly 1027) near Kesi Ghat, **Banke Behari** near Purana Bazar where great excitement builds up each time the curtain before the deity is opened for *darshan* and **Radha Ballabh**, partly demolished by Aurangzeb, close by. **ISKCON** (International Society for Krishna Consciousness) with the Shri Krishna Balaram Temple, has a modern marble memorial. The centre runs yoga and meditation courses.

## Fatehpur Sikri → *Phone code: 05613. Colour map 2, grid A6. Population: 29,000.*

The red sandstone capital of Emperor Akbar, one of his architectural achievements, spreads along a ridge. The great mosque and palace buildings, deserted after only 14 years are still a vivid reminder of his power and vision. Perfectly preserved, it conjures up the lifestyle of the Mughals at the height of their glory.

### History

The first two Great Mughals, Babur (ruled 1526-1530) and his son Humayun (ruled 1530-1540, 1555-1556) both won (in Humayun's case, won back) Hindustan at the end of their lives, and they left an essentially alien rule. Akbar, the third and greatest of the Mughals changed that. By marrying a Hindu princess, forging alliances with the Rajput leaders and making the administration of India a partnership with Hindu nobles and princes rather than armed foreign minority rule, Akbar consolidated his ancestors' gains, and won widespread loyalty and respect. Akbar had enormous magnetism. Though illiterate, he had great wisdom and learning as well as undoubted administrative and military skills. Fatehpur Sikri is testimony to this remarkable character.

Although he had many wives, the 26-year-old Akbar had no living heir; the children born to him had all died in infancy. He visited holy men to enlist their prayers for a son and heir. **Sheikh Salim Chishti**, living at Sikri, a village 37 km southwest of Agra, told the emperor that he would have three sons. Soon after, one of his wives,

the daughter of the Raja of Amber, became pregnant, so Akbar sent her to live near the sage. A son Salim was born, later to be known as **Jahangir**. The prophecy was fulfilled when in 1570 another wife gave birth to Murad and in 1572, to Daniyal. Salim Chishti's tomb is here.

Akbar, so impressed by this sequence of events, resolved to build an entirely new capital at Sikri in honour of the saint. The holy man had set up his hermitage on a low hill of hard reddish sandstone, an ideal building material, easy to work and yet very durable. The building techniques used imitated carvings in wood, as well as canvas from the Mughal camp (eg awnings). During the next 14 years a new city appeared on this hill – 'Fatehpur' (town of victory) added to the name of the old village, 'Sikri'. Later additions and alterations were made and debate continues over the function and dates of the various buildings. It is over 400 years old and yet perfectly preserved, thanks to careful conservation work carried out by the Archaeological Survey of India at the turn of the century. There are three sections to the City: 'The Royal Palace', 'Outside the Royal Palace' and the 'Jami Masjid'.

*Official guides can be good: Rs 100; Rs 30 off-season. Avoid main entrance (lots of hawkers); take right hand fork after passing through Agra gate to hassle-free 2nd entrance.*

When Akbar left, it was slowly abandoned to become ruined and deserted by the early 1600s. Some believe the emperor's decision was precipitated by the failure of the water supply, whilst local folklore claims the decision was due to the loss of the court singer Tansen, one of the "nine gems" of Akbar's court. However, there may well have been political and strategic motives. Akbar's change in attitude towards orthodox Islam and his earlier veneration of the Chishti saints supplanted by a new imperial ideology, may have influenced his decision. In 1585 he moved his court to Lahore and when he returned south again, it was to Agra. But it was at Fatehpur Sikri that Akbar spent the richest and most productive years of his 49-year reign.



## The entrance

ⓘ *Sunrise to sunset, Rs 5 Indians, foreigners US$5. It is best to visit early, before the crowds. Official guides are good (about Rs 100; Rs 30 off season) but avoid others. Allow 3 hrs and carry plenty of drinking water.*

You enter Fatehpur Sikri through the **Agra Gate**. The straight road from Agra was laid out in Akbar's time. If approaching from Bharatpur you will pass the site of a lake (32-km circumference) which provided one defensive barrier. On the other sides was a massive defensive wall with nine gates: Clockwise – Delhi, Lal, Agra, Bir or Suraj (Sun), Chandar (Moon), Gwaliori, Tehra (Crooked), Chor (Thief's) and Ajmeri. Sadly there are men with 'performing' bears along the road from Agra – they should be discouraged – avoid stopping to photograph and tip.

From the Agra Gate you pass the sandstone **Tansen's Baradari** on your right and go through the triple arched **Chahar Suq** with a gallery with two *chhattris* above which may have been a **Nakkar khana** (Drum House). The road inside the main city wall leading to the entrance would have been lined with bazars. Next on your right is the square, shallow-domed **Mint** with artisans' workshops or animal shelters, around a courtyard. Workmen still chip away at blocks of stone in the dimly lit interior.

## The Royal Palace

The **Diwan-i-Am** (Hall of Public Audience) was also used for celebrations and public prayers. It has cloisters on three sides of a rectangular courtyard and to the west, a pavilion with the emperor's throne, with *jali* screens on either side separating the court ladies. Some scholars suggest that the west orientation may have had the added significance of Akbar's vision of himself playing a semi-divine role.

This backed onto the private palace. In the centre of the courtyard behind the throne is the **Pachisi Board (1)** or Chaupar. It is said that Akbar had slave girls dressed in yellow, blue and red, moved around as 'pieces'!

The **Diwan-i-Khas** (Hall of Private Audience) to your right, is a two-storey building with corner kiosks. It is a single room with a unique circular throne platform. Here Akbar would spend long hours in discussion with Christians, Jains, Buddhists, Hindus and Parsis. They would sit along the walls of the balcony connected to the **Throne Pillar** by screened 'bridges', while courtiers could listen to the discussions from the ground floor. Decorative techniques and metaphysical labels are incorporated here – the pillar is lotus shaped (a Hindu and Buddhist motif), the Royal Umbrella (*chhattri*) is Hindu, and the Tree of Life, Islamic. The bottom of the pillar is carved in four tiers; Muslim, Hindu, Christian and Buddhist designs. The Throne Pillar can be approached by steps from the outside although there is no access to the upper floor. The design of the Hall deliberately followed the archaic universal pattern of establishing a hallowed spot from which spiritual influence could radiate. In his later years, Akbar developed a mystical cult around himself that saw him as being semi-divine.

An Archaeological Survey of India team recently discovered an "airconditioned palace" built for Akbar, while digging up steps leading down to a water tank set in the middle of the main palace complex. The subterranean chambers were found under the small quadrangle in sandstone, set in the middle of a water tank and connected on all four sides by narrow corridors. It's not yet open to the public.

In the **Treasury** in the northwest corner of the courtyard is the **Ankh Michauli** (Blind Man's Buff), possibly used for playing the game, comprising three rooms each protected by a narrow corridor with guards. The *makaras* on brackets are mythical sea creatures who guard the treasures under the sea. Just in front of the Treasury is **The Astrologer's Seat**, a small kiosk with elaborate carvings on the Gujarati 'caterpillar' struts which may have been used by the court astrologer or treasurer.



## Fatehpur Sikri

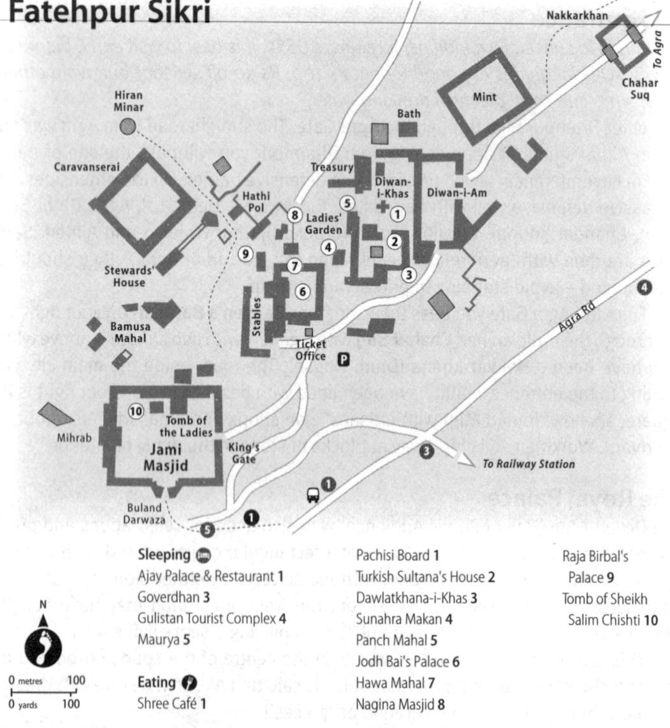


**Sleeping**
Ajay Palace & Restaurant **1**
Goverdhan **3**
Gulistan Tourist Complex **4**
Maurya **5**

**Eating**
Shree Café **1**

Pachisi Board **1**
Turkish Sultana's House **2**
Dawlatkhana-i-Khas **3**
Sunahra Makan **4**
Panch Mahal **5**
Jodh Bai's Palace **6**
Hawa Mahal **7**
Nagina Masjid **8**
Raja Birbal's Palace **9**
Tomb of Sheikh Salim Chishti **10**

The **Turkish Sultana's House (2)** or Anup Talao Pavilion is directly opposite, beyond the Pachisi Board. Sultana Ruqayya Begum was Akbar's favourite and her 'house', with a balcony on each side, is exquisitely carved with Islamic decorations. Scholars suggest this may have been a pleasure pavilion. The geometrical pattern on the ceiling is reminiscent of Central Asian carvings in wood while the walls may have been set originally with reflecting glass to create a Sheesh Mahal (Mirror Palace). In the centre of this smaller south courtyard is the **Anup Talao** where the Emperor may have sat on the platform, surrounded by perfumed water. The *Akbarnama* mentions the emperor's show of charity when he filled the Talao with copper, silver and gold coins and distributed them over three years.

**Dawlatkhana-i-Khas (3)**, the emperor's private chambers, are next to the rose-water fountain in the corner. There are two main rooms on the ground floor. One housed his library – the recesses in the walls were for manuscripts. Although unable to read or write himself, Akbar enjoyed having books read to him. Wherever he went, his library of 50,000 manuscripts accompanied him. The larger room behind was his resting area. On the first floor is the **Khwabgah** ('Palace of Dreams') which would have had rich carpets, hangings and cushions. This too was decorated with gold and ultramarine paintings. The southern window known as the Jharokha Darshan was where the Emperor showed himself to his people every morning.

Leaving the Dawlatkhana-i-Khas you enter another courtyard which contained the **Ladies' garden** for the *zenana*, and the **Sunahra Makan (4)** or the Christian wife **Maryam's** House, a two-storeyed affair for the Emperor's mother, which was embellished with golden murals in the Persian style. The inscriptions on the beams are verses by **Fazl**, Akbar's poet laureate, one of the '*Navaratna*' (Nine Jewels) of the Court. Toilets in the corner of the garden are quite clean.

The **Panch Mahal (5)** is an elegant, airy five-storeyed pavilion just north of this, each floor smaller than the one below, rising to a single domed kiosk on top. The horizontal line of this terraced building is emphasized by wide overhanging eaves (for providing shade), parapets broken by the supporting pillars of which there are 84 on the ground floor (the magic number of seven planets multiplied by 12 signs of the zodiac). The 56 carved columns on the second floor are all different and show Hindu influence. Originally dampened scented grass screens (*khuss*) which were hung in the open spaces, provided protection from the heat and sun, as well as privacy for the women who used the pavilion.

*From the upper storeys there is a fine view of the rest of Fatehpur Sikri and the adjoining countryside. The impression is that of an encampment in red stone.*

Jodh Bai, the daughter of the Maharaja of Amber, lived in Raniwas. The spacious **palace (6)** in the centre, assured of privacy and security by high walls and a 9-m high guarded gate to the east. Outside the north wall is the 'hanging' **Hawa Mahal (7)** (Palace of Winds) with beautiful *jali* screens facing the *zenana* garden which was once enclosed, and the bridge (a later addition) led to the Hathipol. Through the arch is the small **Nagina Masjid (8)**, the mosque for the ladies of the court. The *hammams* (baths) are to the south of the palace. The centre of the building is a quadrangle around which were the harem quarters, each section self-contained with roof terraces. The style, a blend of Hindu and Muslim (the lotus, chain and bell designs being Hindu, the black domes Muslim), is strongly reminiscent of Gujarati temples, possibly owing to the craftsmen brought in (see *jarokha* windows, niches, pillars and brackets). The upper pavilions north and south have interesting ceiling structure (imitating the bamboo and thatch roof of huts), here covered with blue glazed tiles, adding colour to the buildings of red sandstone favoured by Akbar. Jodh Bai's vegetarian kitchen opposite the Palace has attractive chevron patterns.

**Raja Birbal's Palace (9)** is a highly ornamented house to the northwest of Jodh Bai's Palace. It has two storeys – four rooms and two porches with pyramidal roofs below, and two rooms with cupolas and screened terraces above. Birbal, Akbar's

Hindu Prime Minister, was the brightest of Akbar's 'Nine Jewels'. Again the building combines Hindu and Islamic elements (note the brackets, eaves, *jarokhas*). Of particular interest is the insulating effect of the double-domed structure of the roofs and cupolas which allowed the rooms to remain cool, and the diagonal positioning of the upper rooms which ensured a shady terrace. Some scholars believe that this building, *Mahal-i-Ilahi*, was not for Birbal, but for Akbar's senior queens.

South of the Raja's house are the **stables**, a long courtyard surrounded by cells which probably housed zenana servants rather than the emperor's camels and horses, though the rings suggest animals may have been tied there.

## Jami Masjid

Leaving the Royal Palace you proceed across a car park to the Jami Masjid and the sacred section of Fatehpur Sikri. The oldest place of worship here was the **Stone Cutters' Mosque** (circa 1565) to the west of the Jami Masjid. It was built near Sheikh Salim Chishti's cell which was later incorporated into it by stonecutters who settled on the ridge when quarrying for the Agra Fort began. It has carved monolithic 'S' brackets to support the wide sloping eaves.

The **King's Gate** (Badshahi Darwaza) is the entrance Akbar used. Shoes must be left at the gate but there are strips of carpet cross the courtyard to save burning your feet. The porch is packed with aggressive salesmen. The two other gates on the south and north walls were altered by subsequent additions. Built in 1571-1572, this is one of the largest mosques in India. Inside is the congregational courtyard (132 x 111 m). To your right in the corner is the **Jamaat Khana Hall** and next to this the **Tomb of the Royal Ladies** on the north wall. The square nave carries the principal dome painted in the Persian style, with pillared aisles leading to side chapels carrying subsidiary domes. The **mihrab** in the centre of the west wall orientates worshippers towards Mecca. The sanctuary is adorned with carving, inlay work and painting.

The **Tomb of Sheikh Salim Chishti (10)**, a masterpiece in brilliant white marble, dominates the northern half of the courtyard. The Gujarati-style serpentine 'S' struts, infilled with *jali*, are highly decorative while the carved pillar bases and lattice screens are stunning pieces of craftsmanship. The canopy over the tomb is inlaid with mother of pearl. On the cenotaph is the date of the saint's death (1571) and the date of the building's completion (1580); the superb marble screens enclosing the verandah were added by Jahangir's foster brother in 1606. Around the entrance are inscribed the names of God, the Prophet and the four Caliphs of Islam. The shrine inside, on the spot of the saint's hermitage, originally had a red sandstone dome, which was marble veneered around 1806. Both Hindu and Muslim women pray at the shrine, tying cotton threads, hoping for the miracle of parenthood that Akbar was blessed with.

Next to it, in the courtyard, is the larger, red, sandstone tomb of **Nawab Islam Khan**, Sheikh Salim's grandson, and other members of the family.

**Buland Darwaza** (Triumphal Gate) dominates the south wall but it is a bit out of place. Built to celebrate Akbar's brilliant conquest of Gujarat (circa 1576), it sets the style for later gateways. The high gate is approached from the outside by a flight of steps which adds to its grandeur. The decoration shows Hindu influence, but is severe and restrained, emphasizing the lines of its arches with plain surfaces. You see an inscription on the right of a verse from the Qur'an:

*Said Jesus Son of Mary (on whom be peace):*
*The world is but a bridge;*
*pass over it but build no houses on it. He*
*who hopes for an hour, hopes for*
*Eternity. The world is an hour. Spend it*
*in prayer, for the rest is unseen.*

## Outside the Royal Palace



Between the Royal Palace and the Jami Masjid, a paved pathway to the northwest leads to the **Hathipol** (Elephant Gate). This was the ceremonial entrance to the palace quarters, guarded by stone elephants, with its *nakkar khana* and bazar alongside. Nearby are the **waterworks**, with a deep well which had an ingenious mechanism for raising water to the aqueducts above ridge height. The **caravanserai** around a large courtyard fits on the ridge side, and was probably one of a series built to accommodate travellers, tradesmen and guards. Down a ramp immediately beyond is the **Hiran Minar**, an unusual tower studded with stone tusks, thought to commemorate Akbar's favourite elephant, Hiran. However, it was probably an *Akash Diya* ('lamp to light the sky') or the 'zero point' for marking road distances in *kos*. You can climb up the spiral staircase inside it but take care as the top has no guard rail. This part of Fatehpur Sikri is off the main tourist track, and though less well preserved it is worth the detour to get the 'lost city' feeling, away from the crowds.

## Sleeping

**Agra** *p149, maps p150 and p153*

Most hotels are 5-10 km from the airport and 2-5 km from Agra Cantt Railway.

**LL Amar Vilas**, Taj East Gate End, T0562-223 1515, www.oberoihotels.com. 105 rooms, all Taj-facing. Absolutely mind-blowing. The modern-day equivalent of the most luxurious of maharaja's palaces, designed in strict adherence to the Mughal style. The most stunning swimming pool, superb rooms, extraordinary ambience. Reports of inattentive service. Prices start at $350.

**LL-AL Mughal Sheraton**, Fatehabad Rd, T0562-233 1701, www.sheraton.com. 285 rooms in various stages of renovation. Building beautifully designed in the Mughal tradition but is now in need of a face lift. Suites are stunning. Low-rise construction means only rooftop observatory offers good views of the Taj. Even has a dog kennel!

**L-AL Jaypee Palace**, Fatehabad Rd, T0562-233 0800, www.jaypeehotels.com. 350 rooms, enormous place, a little soulless. Aimed mainly at conference crowd, it boasts a leisure mall featuring a 2-lane bowling alley.

**L-AL Taj View** , Fatehabad Rd, T0562-223 2400, www.tajhotels.com. 100 rooms, vastly improved since recent overhaul. Tasteful Mughal-style interiors, good pool and friendly staff. Recommended.

**AL Trident** (Oberoi), Fatehabad Rd, T0562-233 1818, www.tridenthotels.com. 143 very comfortable rooms, good pool, beautiful gardens, polite, friendly staff. Recommended.

**A Ashok**, 6B Mall Rd, T0562-236 1223, moonagra@yahoo.com. 58 rooms, extensive renovation to be finished by 2004 end, relaxing atmosphere, good restaurant, large pool, good value. Recommended.

**A Clarks Shiraz**, 54 Taj Rd, T0562-222 6121, www.hotelclarksshiraz.com. 237 rooms. Opened 42 years ago as Agra's first 5-star, starting to show its age but is set in pleasant grounds and has a good rooftop restaurant.

**A Holiday Inn**, Sanjay Place, MG Rd, T0562-252 3460, www.holiday-inn.com. 94 rooms (148 by end of 2004). Situated in heart of business district, standard 5-star fare.

**A Mansingh Palace**, 181/2 Fatehabad Rd, T0562-223 0202, www.mansinghhotels.com. 97 comfortable rooms, 4th floor awaiting refurbishment, rather soulless, attractive bar and pool, slightly stuffy staff.

**B Atithi**, Fatehabad Rd, T0562-223 0040, hotelatithi@hotmail.com. 44 clean a/c rooms, attractive pool, friendly staff, good value.

**B Deedar-e-Taj**, Fatehabad Rd, T0562-309 0267, www.deedaretaj.net. 51 clean, good-sized rooms in modern, characterless building. Has Agra's only revolving restaurant, novel but overpriced.

**C Lauries**, MG Rd, T0562-236 4536, lauries hotel@hotmail.com. 28 rooms in 1880 building rich in history, including a 1961 visit from Queen Elizabeth II. A little rundown these days but retains an elegant air, and is set in beautiful surroundings.

**C Mayur Tourist Complex**, Fatehabad Rd, T0562-233 2302, mayur268@rediffmail.com. 24 a/c rooms in slightly rundown bungalows. Built in 1976, decor unchanged since; funky but dated. Restaurant, beer-only bar, large pool, relaxing garden setting.

**C-D Hotel Hilltop**, 21 The Mall, T0562-222 6836. 28 rooms undergoing major refurbishment, those finished are clean, modern and good value. Also has extensive lawns, great for camping.
**D Agra Hotel**, 165 F.M. Cariappa Rd, T0562-363 331, agrahotel@yahoo.co.in. 18 rooms in 1926 'British-time' bungalow. Basic, old fashioned, good food, pleasant garden.
**D Maya**, near Taj West Gate, Fatehabad Rd, T0562-233 2109, magicinmaya@hotmail.com. 6 rooms, 6 more by 2004 end. Exceptionally clean and well-maintained, tastefully decorated, very friendly manager. Highly recommended.
**D Rahi Tourist Bungalow** (UP Tourism), Station Rd, opposite Raja-ki-Mandi station, T0562-215 0120, uptdc1@sancharnet.in. 35 clean, well-equipped rooms. Friendly staff, good option if location suits.
**E Kamal**, Taj South Gate, T0562-233 0126, hotelkamal@hotmail.com. 18 clean rooms in unattractive prison-style arrangement, friendly manager and staff plus a good view from rooftop restaurant.
**E Hotel Sheela**, East Gate, 2 mins walk from Taj, T0562-233 1194, www.hotelsheelaagra.com. 25 decent rooms with bath, pleasant garden, good restaurant, clean, peaceful, reliable laundry, secure (ask for gates to be unlocked for sunrise or else climb over spiked railings!), very helpful manager, excellent value (no commission to rickshaws), reserve ahead. Recommended.
**E Tourists Rest House**, Kutchery Rd, Balugunj, T0562-236 3961, dontworry chickencurry@hotmail.com. 28 clean rooms, some a/c, vegetarian restaurant, fairly basic, a bit dog-eared but knowledgeable manager runs a good show and knows it, often full. Offers popular 2 week trips to Rajasthan.
**E-F Host**, West Gate, T0562-233 1010. 15 clean rooms with bath and hot water, rooftop restaurant with great view of Taj, better option than the nearby Siddartha.
**E-F Shah Jahan**, South Gate T0562-223 1784, shahjahanhotel@yahoo.co.in. 24 clean rooms, 3 of them a/c and very modern. Rooftop restaurant with obscured Taj view.
**F Youth Hostel**, Sanjay Pl, MG Rd, T0562-65812. 4 double rooms, 2 singles, 6 dorms. Clean if a little drab, good value but long way from Taj. Usual YHA rules apply.

**Mathura** *p159, map p160*

Hotels serve vegetarian food only. No alcohol.
**A-B Radha Ashok** (Best Western), Masani By-pass Rd, Chatikara, 4 km north of centre, T0565 2530395, www.mathura-vrindavan.com. 21 comfortable, spacious rooms (freezing a/c) in modern if bland hotel, good restaurant, pool.
**B-C Madhuvan**, Krishna Nagar, T0565 2420064, www.hotel-madhuvan.com. 28 clean, fragrant rooms, some a/c with bath, restaurant, exchange, travel, pool, a little gloomy but friendly
**B-C Sheetal Regency**, near Krishna Janam-bhoomi, Deeg Gate, Masani Road, T0565 240 4401, hotelsheetalregency @rediffmail.com. 28 passable rooms in friendly, modern hotel. Also changes money.
**C-D Dwaper Resorts**, at 162 km marker, NH2, 17 km south of Mathura on the Agra Rd, T0565 2480092. Restaurant, bar, attractive gardens, convenient rest stop but the rooms are in poor condition.
**C-D Mansarovar Palace**, State Bank Crossing, T0565 2408686. 22 rooms, most a/c, restaurant, noisy location.
**D Shri Giriraj Guest House**, near Potra Kund, Shri Krishna Janma Bhumi, T0565 242 3545. 11 basic rooms in quieter location than most.
**D-E Agra**, near Bengali Ghat, T0565 2403318. 15 clean, basic rooms, some a/c, traditional, friendly, well run.
**E-F Modern**, Near Old Bus Stand, T0565 240 4747. Basic rooms plus bar and restaurant.
**F International Guest House**, Katra Keshav Deo, T0565 2423888. Some air-cooled rooms, interesting place to stay.
**Railway Retiring Rooms**, at Cantt and Junction Stations.

**Vrindavan** *p161, map p162*

**B Ananda Krishna Van**, Parikrama Marg, near ISCKON, T0565 254 0878, www.ananda krishnavan.com. Sprawling new construction complete with waterfall, bathing pool, temple and restaurants, many rooms taken on timeshare basis, but some 4 bed a/c

*For an explanation of the sleeping and eating price codes used in this guide, see inside the front cover. Other relevant information is found in Essentials pages 56-61.*

rooms available to casual visitors, remarkable undertaking.

**C-D MVT Guest House**, next to ISCKON, 0565 254 0050. Comfortable rooms, some a/c, set around pleasant gardens plus a highly rated restaurant.

**E International Rest House** (ISKCON), Raman Reti, T0565 254 0022. Clean rooms, good, reasonably priced veg restaurant, very popular, book well ahead.

**E Shri Shri Radhashyam Palace**, signposted behind ISCKON, T0565 254 0729. 22 clean rooms in friendly, well located hotel.

**Fatehpur Sikri** *p162, map p164*

It is worth spending a night here to make an early start.

**C-D Gulistan Tourist Complex** (UP Tourism), Agra Rd, 1 km from Bus Stand, T05613 282490, www.up-tourism.com. Okay rooms with modern facilities, restaurant, bar, quiet, pleasant grounds, mixed reports on food and service.

**D-F Govardhan**, Buland Darwaza Rd Crossing, T05613 282643, www.hotelfatehpursikriviews.com. Rooms with clean common bath, air-cooled suites with fridge, summer camping (Rs 20), 40% university student discount, garden restaurant, pool, well maintained, lively and conscientious owner. Recommended.

**E-F Ajay Palace**, near Bus Stand, T05613 282950. Clean rooms in busy location overlooking market, mixed reports about food.

**E-F Maurya**, near Buland Darwaza, T05613 282 2348. Basic rooms (rock hard bed), some with bath (bucket hot water) in charming house in good location, rooftop restaurant..

## Eating

**Agra** *p149, maps p150 and p153*

Amongst the hotels, the restaurants at the **Clarks Shiraz** and the **Ashok** have good reputations, see Sleeping for details. See also **Amar Vilas** below.

**TTT Amar Vilas**, see Sleeping, is worth trying to get a table just to see the place, but do ring ahead to reserve.

**TT Only**, 45 Taj Rd, T0562 222 6834. Interesting menu, attractive outside seating, popular with tour groups, live entertainment.

**TT Priya**, near **Trident Hotel**, Fatehabad Rd, T0562 309 1957. Indian, Chinese, a/c, aimed primarily at tour groups, food has good reputation but restaurant lacks atmosphere despite live music, singing and magic shows.

**TT Riao**, next to **Clarks Shiraz**, 44 Taj Rd, T0562 309 2928. Good North Indian food, great garden and attitude.

**TT Shahi Dastarkhawan**, Fatehabad Rd, T0562 309 2534. A famous Delhi eaterie. Strictly for meat-lovers, a great range of Mughlai delicacies, ambience less special.

**TT Sonam**, 51 Taj Rd. Indian, Chinese. A/c, good food, well-stocked bar, large garden, popular with locals.

**TT Tin Tin**, near Taj. Chinese. Friendly owners.

**T Daawat**, Fatehabad Rd. Indian. Beer.

**T Dasaprakash**, Meher Theatre Complex, 1 Gwalior Rd, T0562 236 3535. Comprehensive range of South Indian offerings, *thalis* a speciality. Slightly sterile interior.

**T Joney's Place**, the original and, despite numerous similarly named imitators, still the best. Tiny place but the food is consistently good, and Joney's ability to produce Israeli and even Korean specialities is amazing. Recommended.

**T Lucky**, near Taj, good food, seasoned to your taste, pleasant, friendly.

**T Maya**, near Taj West Gate, Fatehabad Rd, T0562 233 2109. Varied menu, good Punjabi *thalis*, pasta, 'special tea', friendly, prompt service, hygienic, tasty, Moroccan style decor. Recommended.

**T Shankara Vegis**, Taj Ganj, vegetarian as name implies, food prepared in reassuringly clean, open kitchen. Rooftop seats have obscured view of Taj, vies with **Joney's Place** for claim to best lassi in Agra.

**T Shivam**, in **Raj Hotel** near Taj south gate. Quality Indian, clean.

**T Yash Café**, Indian/Western menu, cheap but freshly prepared, malai kofta very tasty.

**T Zorba the Buddha**, E-19 Sadar Bazaar, T0562 222 6091, zorbaevergreen@yahoo.com. Run by disciples of Osho, one of India's more popular, and most libidinous, gurus. Unusual menu (in a good way), naan breads a speciality, very clean , undersize furniture gives doll's house feel, an enjoyably quirky experience, opens 1200-1500, 1800-2100.

**Cafés**

**Café Coffee Day**, A7 Sadar Bazaar. Part of nationwide chain, good coffee and western snacks, nice escape.

**Park**, Taj Rd, Sadar Bazaar. Standard North Indian menu, decor and service above average.

## Festivals and events

**Agra** *p149, maps p150 and p153*
**18-27 Feb**: **Taj Mahotsav** is a celebration of the region's arts, crafts, culture and cuisine.
**Aug/Sep**: A **fair** at Kailash (14 km). A temple marks the place where Siva is believed to have appeared in the form of a stone lingam.

**Mathura** *p159, map p160*
**Mar**: **Rang Gulal**, the colourful Holi festival. Similar festivities at **Janmashtami. Banjatra** (Forest Pilgrimage). During the monsoon, episodes from Krishna's life are enacted.

## Shopping

**Agra** *p149, maps p150 and p153*
Agra specializes in jewellery, inlaid and carved marble, carpets and clothes. The main shopping areas are Sadar Bazar (closed Tue), Kinari Bazar, Gwalior Rd, Mahatma Gandhi Rd and Pratap Pura. Beware, you may order a carpet or an inlaid marble piece and have it sent later but it may not be what you ordered. Never agree to any export 'deals' and take great care with credit card slips (fiddles reported). Many rickshaws, taxi drivers and guides earn up to 40% commission by taking tourists to shops. Insist on not being rushed away from sights. To shop, go independ- ently. To get a good price you have to bargain hard anyway.

### Carpets
Silk/cotton/wool mix hand knotted carpets and woven *dhurries* are all made in Agra. High quality and cheaper than in Delhi.
**Kanu Carpet Factory**, Purani Mandi, Feteh-abad Rd, T0562 233 1307. A reliable source.
**Mughal Arts Emporium**, Shamshabad Rd. Also has marble. Artificial silk is sometimes passed off as pure silk.

### Handlooms and handicrafts
State Government emporia in arcade at Taj entrance.
**UP Handlooms** and **UPICA** at Sanjay Place, Hari Parbat.

### Marble
Delicately inlaid marble work is a speciality. Sometimes cheaper alabaster and soapstone is used and quality varies.
**Akbar International**, Fatehabad Rd. Good selection, inlay demonstration, fair prices.
**Handicrafts Inn**, 3 Gorg Niketan, Fatehabad Rd, Taj Ganj.
**Oswal**, 30 Munro Rd, Sadar Bazar, T0562 363240. Watch craftsmen working here, or at **Krafts Palace**, 506 The Mall.
**UP Handicrafts Palace**, 49 Bansal Nagar. Very wide selection from table tops to coasters, high quality and good value.

## Activities and tours

**Agra** *p149, maps p150 and p153*
### Swimming
Swimming pools in most **A** and **AL** hotels are open to non-residents.

### Tour companies
**ATS**, 48 MMIG, Shaheed Nagar, T0562 333357, atsagr@nde.vsnl.net.in. Tours to Khajuraho.
**Aargee**, Fatehabad Rd, T0562 360529.
**Mercury, Hotel Clarks Shiraz**, 54 Taj Rd, T/F0562 360282. Helpful and reliable.
**Sita**, Sadar Bazar, T0562 361429.
**TCI, Hotel Clarks Shiraz**, T0562 361121.
**Touraids**, 46 G Shivahare Rd, Sadar Bazar, T0562 363138.
**Travel Bureau**, near Taj View Hotel, T0562 330219.
**UP**, 64 Taj Rd, T0562 360517, and at Tourist Bungalow, Raja-ki-Mandi, T0562 350120, Agra Cantonment; T0562 368598. Rajasthan, T0562 360017 and Haryana, at Taj Mahal Shopping Arcade.
**UP Tourism**, Taj Khema, east Gate, Taj Mahal, T0562 330140.
**UP Tours**, T0562 351720. Tourist offices Govt of India, 191 The Mall, T0562 363377. Guides available (about Rs 100), helpful and friendly Director and staff. Kheria (Agra) Airport counter, during flight times. Coach tours: Fatehpur Sikri-Taj Mahal-Agra Fort (full day) 1000-1800, Rs 100 (including guide but not entry); Sikandra-Fatehpur Sikri (half day) 0930-1400, Rs 100 (excludes entry fees); Sikandra- Fatehpur Sikri-Taj Mahal-Agra Fort (full day), 0930-1800; Fatehpur Sikri (half day) 1030-1430 which only gives 45 mins at the

## Pedal power

To achieve a 'Greener', cleaner Agra by reducing pollution by vehicle emissions, a new model of cycle rickshaw has been developed by the Institute for Transportation and Development Policy, an Indian NGO, with help from the US Agency for International Development, after consulting local organizations and the men who will be pedalling them. The much lighter (and easier to operate), more comfortable and faster transport for two, is an attractive alternative to fume emitting engines. The concerned visitor can opt to hire one from outside a top hotel for around Rs 150, to be wheeled around the city to see the Taj, the Fort, sample local cuisine and also reduce approaches by hawkers and beggars.

site; not worthwhile, better take a taxi if you can afford it. Some tours start and finish at Agra Cantt Rly Station, T0562 368 598.

## Transport

**Agra** *p149, maps p150 and p153*

**Air**

**Kheria airport** is 7 km from city centre. Transport to town: airport bus to/from major hotels; auto-rickshaws charge about Rs 50; Taxis, Rs 75. **Indian Airlines**, Clarks Shiraz, airport T0562 302 274. Daily flights to **Delhi**. Long delays in flight departures and arrivals possible especially in winter when Agra and Delhi airports close for periods due to fog.

**Auto rickshaw**

Point-to-point rates, eg Idgah Bus Stand to Taj Ganj Rs 40.

**Bus**

**Local** City Bus Service covers most areas. Plenty leave from the Taj Mahal area and the Fort Bus Stand. Buses also go to main sites.
**Long distance** Most buses from Jaipur go on to a second stop near **Hotel Sakura**: closer to most hotels and where there is less hassle from touts; auto from first stop to Taj Ganj, Rs 25. **UPSRTC Roadways**, Bus Stand, Idgah, enquiry T0562 363 588; **Fort Bus Station** (opposite **Power House**), T056 236 0948; Ram Bagh Crossing (across river Yamuna). *Deluxe* buses from **Hotel Sheetal**, T0562 369 420. **Delhi** from tourist office, 0700, 1445, Deluxe, 4 hrs. Most long-distance services leave from the **Idgah Bus Stand** including daily Express buses to: **Fatehpur Sikri** (40 km away, about an hour). Others hourly, (1 hr), very bumpy.

**Cycle rickshaw**

Negotiate (pay more to avoid visiting shops); Taj Ganj to fort Rs 10; Rs 75-100 for visiting sights, PO, bank etc; Rs 150 for 10 hrs.

**Motorbike/bicycle hire**

**Firoz Motorcycle House**, Cariappa Rd, Enfield Bullets Rs 500 per day. Bike hire from Sadar Bazar, near Police station and near **Tourist Rest House**, Rs 20 per day.

**Taxi/car hire**

Tourist taxis from travel agents, remarkably good value for visiting nearby sights. Non-a/c car Rs 3 per km, full day Rs 400 (100 km), half day Rs 200 (45 km); a/c rates approximately double; to Fatehpur Sikri about Rs 650 return). **Budget** Rent-a-car, T0562 361771; **UP Tours**, T0562 351720.

**Train**

Train travel from Delhi is quicker and more reliable. Information and reservations: **Agra Cantt Railway Station**, enquiries T131, reservations T0562-236 4244, open 0800-2000. Foreigners' queue at Window 1. **Pre-paid taxi/auto rickshaw** kiosk outside the station. Railway Stations: **Agra Cantt**, T131, T0562-236 4516; **Agra Fort**, T132, T0562-236 9590.Trains mentioned arrive and depart from Agra Cantt southwest of the city, about 5 km from the Taj Mahal. From **New Delhi**: best is *Shatabdi Exp, 2002*, 0600, 2¼ hrs (meals included); *Punjab Mail, 2138*, 0530, 3 hrs; *Kerala Exp, 2626*, 1130, 2¾ hrs; from **New Delhi (HN)**: *Taj Exp, 2180*, 0715, 2½ hrs; *Lakshadweep Exp, 2618*, 0955, 2½ hrs; *Gondwana Exp, 2412*, 1430, 2½ hrs; *Goa Exp, 2780*, 1500, 2½ hrs; *Mahakoshal Exp, 1450*,

1620, 3 hrs. To **New Delhi**: *Shatabdi Exp, 2001*, 2018, 2½ hrs; to **New Delhi (HN)**: *Intercity Exp, 1103*, 0600, 3½ hrs (2nd class only); *Taj Exp, 2179*, 1835, 3¼ hrs (CC/II). To **Jaipur** *Howrah-Jodhpur/Bikaner Exp, 2307*, 2000, 8 hrs (from Fort); *Marudhar Exp, 4853/63*, 0715, 6¾ hrs. *Mumbai (CST)*: *Punjab Mail, 2138*, 0830, 23¼ hrs. **Sawai Madhopore** (for Ranthambore) at 0600, 0900, 1800.

**Mathura** *p159, map p160*

**Bus**

Frequent service to **Delhi**, **Jaipur** and neighbouring towns from the New Bus Stand opposite **Hotel Nepal**. Buses to **Govardhan** and **Agra** from Old Bus Stand near the railway station, T0565 240 6468.

**Taxi**

From opposite District Hospital. Also, buses, auto and cycle rickshaws.

**Train**

Mathura Junc is the main station, T0565 2405830. **Cantt Station** is at Bahadurganj (metre gauge). **Sri Krishna Janmabhumi** is at Bhuteshwar. For Delhi and Agra, the best is to **Agra Cantt**: *Taj Exp, 2180*, 0900, 47 mins. **New Delhi (HN)**: *Taj Exp, 2179*, 1930, 2¼ hrs. **Sawai Madhopur**: *Golden Temple Mail, 2904*, 1025, 3 hrs; *Bandra Exp, 9020*, 0140, 3½ hrs; *Janata Exp, 9024*, 1735, 4 hrs. **Vrindavan**: see below.

**Vrindavan** *p161, map p162*

To and from **Mathura**: buses, tempos and auto-rickshaws. Train services from Mathura Junction at 0627, 0850, 1457, 1655, 1925, takes 35 mins; returns from **Vrindavan** at 0725, 0940, 1610, 1740, 2015.

**Fatehpur Sikri** *p162, map p164*

**Bus**

Frequent buses from Agra Idgah Bus Stand (1 hr) Rs 16.

**Taxi**

From Agra include the trip in a day's sightseeing (about Rs 650 return).

**Train**

To **Sawai Madhopore** (for Ranthambore), departs 0600, 0900, 1800.

## Directory

**Agra** *p149, maps p150 and p153*

**Banks** Andhra Bank, Taj Rd, opposite Kwality's gives cash against card. Canara, Sadar Bazar and Sanjay Place, and others. **Internet** The Mall (24 hrs). At Taj Mahal and elsewhere, 1000-1700, closed Sun. Khurana Cyber Café, 805 Sadar Bazar, opposite Cantt Hospital, T0562-291562. **Hospital/Doctor** District, Chhipitola Rd/MG Rd, T0562-236 3043. **Dr VN**, Kaushal, opposite Imperial Cinema, T0562-236 3550. Recommended. **Post** GPO opposite India Tourist Office, with **Poste Restante**. **Useful addresses** Ambulance: T202. Fire: T201. Police: T200.

**Mathura** *p159, map p160*

**Hospitals** District Hospital, near Agra Rd, T0565 240 3006. **Methodist Hospital**, Vrindavan Rd, T0565 273 0043. **Tourist offices** **UP**, near Old Bus Stand, T0565 250 5351.

# Varanasi and around

→ *Phone code: 0542. Colour map 3, grid B4. Population: over 1.3 mn.*

*Perhaps the holiest of India's cities, Varanasi defies easy description. A highly congested maze of narrow alleys winding behind its waterfront ghats, at once highly sacred yet physically often far from clean. As an image, an idea and a symbol of Hinduism's central realities, the city draws pilgrims from around the world, to worship, to meditate, and above all to bathe. It is a place to be born and a place to die. In the cold mists of a winter's dawn, you can see life and death laid bare. For an outside observer it can be an uncomfortable, if unmissable experience, juxtaposing the inner philosophical mysteries of Hinduism with the practical complications of living literally and metaphorically on the edge.*

*More holy places surround Varanassi: Sarnath, one of Buddhism's major centres, Jaunpur, a city with a strong Islamic history, Allahabad, a sacred place for Hindus due to its position at the confluence of the Ganja and Jamuna rivers.* ▸▸ *For Sleeping, Eating and other listings, see pages 187-195.*

## Ins and outs

### Getting there

Several airlines link Varanasi with Delhi, Lucknow, Khajuraho, Kathmandu, Mumbai and other cities. From Babatpur airport, 22 km away, there is an airport bus which goes as far as the Indian Airlines office in the Cantonment area but not into the city centre. Alternatively, take a taxi. Most long-distance buses arrive at the bus stand near the crossroads 500 m northeast of the Junction Station. Most trains stop at the Junction Station near the Cantonment, about 3 km northwest of the Old City and the budget hotels. Some trains (eg Delhi-Kolkata *Rajdhani* and *Expresses* to New Jalpaiguri and Guwahati) do not pass through Varanasi itself but stop at Mughal Sarai, 16 km away, which is easily accessible by rail or road from Varanasi. A rickshaw to Assi Ghat costs around Rs 140.

### Getting around

The only way really to see the heart of the Old City is on foot, though no visit is complete without an early morning boat trip along the Ghats. Yet Varanasi is quite spread out: the university to the south is nearly 7 km from the spacious Cantonment area and the Junction Station to the north. Around town, cycle-rickshaws are common, while autos are usually shared. Buses are hopelessly crowded so you might consider hiring a bike if you are staying a few days. Unmetered taxis are best for longer sightseeing trips. The city has some of the disadvantages of pilgrimage centres, notably rickshaw drivers who seem determined to extort as much as possible from unsuspecting visitors. ▸▸ *See Transport, page 192, for further details.*

## Varanasi

The city's focus extends from Raj Ghat in the north, to Assi Ghat in the south. At dawn the riverbank's stone steps begin to hum with activity. Early risers immerse themselves in the water as they face the rising sun, boatmen wait expectantly on the waterside, pilgrims flock to the temples, flower sellers do brisk business, astrologers prepare to read palms and horoscopes while families carry the dead to their last rites by the holy river. A few steps away from the ghats, motor bikers speed through the lanes narrowly missing a motley band of wandering sadhus, hopeful beggars, curious visitors and wandering cows, while packs of stray dogs scavenge among the piles of rubbish.

### Background

Varanasi derives its name from two streams, the Varuna to the north and the Assi, a small trickle, on the south. **Banaras** is a corruption of Varanasi but it is also called **Kashi** ('The City of Light') by Hindus. As one of the seven sacred cities of Hinduism, see page 1324, it attracts well over one million pilgrims while about 50,000 Brahmins are permanant residents. The Jains too consider it holy because three *tirthankars* (seventh Suarsvanath, 11th Shyeyanshnath, 23th Parsvanath) were born here.

Varanasi is said to combine all the virtues of all other places of pilgrimage, and anyone dying within the area marked by the **Panch Kosi Road** is transported straight to heaven. Some devout Hindus move to Varanasi to end their days and have their ashes scattered in the holy Ganga. Every pilgrim, in addition to visiting the holy sites, must make a circuit of the Panch Kosi Road which runs outside and round the sacred territory of Varanasi. This starts at Manikarnika Ghat, runs along the waterfront to Assi Ghat, then round the outskirts in a large semi-circle to Barna Ghat. The 58-km route is

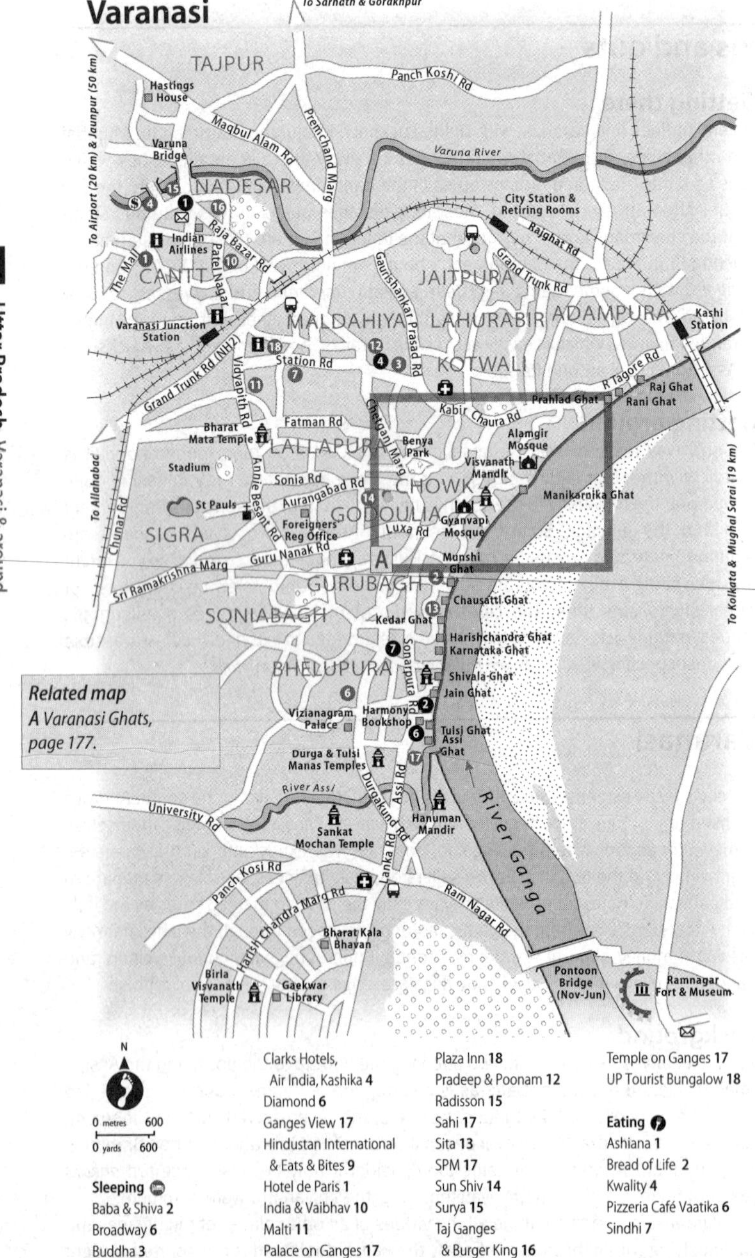


*Related map*
*A Varanasi Ghats, page 177.*

## Polluted Ganga purifies itself

All along the Ganga, the major problem of waste disposal (of human effluent and industrial toxins) has defied the best efforts of the Ganga Action Plan set up in 1986 to solve it. The diversion and treatment of raw sewage in seven main cities was planned. In Varanasi however, the 17th-century sewers, the inadequate capacity of the sewage works, the increased waterflow during the monsoons and the erratic electricity supply (essential for pumping) have all remained problems. In addition, although most Hindus are cremated, an estimated 45,000 uncremated or partially cremated bodies are put in the Ganga each year. A breed of scavenger turtles which dispose of rotting flesh was introduced down river but the turtles disappeared.

The Uttar Pradesh Water Board (Jal Nigam) has put forward a Ganga Action Plan II, but critics of the first failed scheme are proposing an alternative under the guidance of a Banaras Hindu University engineering professor Veer Bhadra Mishra. It remains to be seen whether his proposal of a massive educational programme backed by advanced engineering will help Varanasi purify the tide of filth that enters it every day.

Although the Ganga may be one of the world's most polluted rivers, like many tropical rivers it can cleanse itself quickly. Scientists had discovered the river's exceptional property in the last century. The cholera microbe did not survive three hours in Ganga water whereas in distilled water it survived 24 hours!



lined with trees and shrines and the pilgrimage is supposed to take six days, each day's walk finishing in a small village, equipped with temples and *dharamshalas*.

Varanasi was probably already an important town by the seventh century BC when Babylon and Nineveh were at the peak of their power. The Buddha visited it in 500 BC and it was mentioned in both the *Mahabharata* and the *Ramayana*. It became a centre of culture, education, commerce and craftsmanship but was raided by **Mahmud of Ghazni's** army in 1033 and by Qutb-ud-din Ghuri in 1194. **Ala-ud-din Khalji**, the King of Delhi (1294-1316), destroyed temples and built mosques on their sites. The Muslim influence was strong so even in the 18th century the city, for a brief period, was known as Mohammadabad. Despite its early foundation hardly any building dates before the 17th century, and few are more than 200 years old.

The city stands as the chief centre of **Sanskrit learning** in North India. Sanskrit, the oldest of the Indo-European languages, used for Hindu ritual has been sustained here long after it ceased to be a living language elsewhere. The Banaras Hindu **University** has over 150,000 rare manuscripts. Hindu devotional movements flourished here, especially in the 15th century under Ramananda, and **Kabir**, one of India's greatest poets, lived in the city. It was here that **Tulsi Das** translated the Ramayana from Sanskrit into Hindi.

### Old Centre

**Visvanath Temple** (1777) has been the main Siva temple in Varanasi for over 1,000 years. The original temple, destroyed in the 12th century, was replaced by a mosque. It was rebuilt in the 16th, and again destroyed within a century. The present **'Golden' temple** was built in 1777 by Ahilya Bai of Indore. The gold plating on the roof was provided by Maharaja Ranjit Singh in 1835. Its pointed spires are typically North Indian in style and the exterior is finely carved. Only Hindus are allowed inside. There are good views and photos from second floor of a silk shop across the road (pay about Rs 5) though 'guards' may object if you are seen taking photos. The

18th-century **Annapurna Temple** (*anna* food; *purna* filled) nearby, built by Baji Rao I, has shrines dedicated to Siva, Ganesh, Hanuman and Surya. Ask for directions as you make your way through the maze of alleys around the temples.

The **Gyan Kup** (Well of Knowledge) next door is said to contain the Siva lingam from the original temple – the well is protected by a stone screen and canopy. The **Gyanvapi Mosque** (Great Mosque of Aurangzeb) with 71-m high minarets shows evidence of the original Hindu temple, in the foundations, the columns and at the rear.

The 17th-century **Alamgir Mosque** (Beni Madhav ka Darera), imprssively situated on Panchganga Ghat, was Aurangzeb's smaller mosque. It was built on the original Vishnu temple of the Marathas, parts of which were used in its construction. You can climb on to the top for fantastic views (donation expected). Two minarets are missing – one fell and killed some people and the other was taken down by the government as a precaution.

## Back lanes

The maze of narrow lanes, or *galis*, along the ghats through the old quarters exude the smells and sounds of this holy city. They are fascinating to stroll through though easy to get lost in! Some find it all too over-powering. Near the Town Hall (1845) built by the Maharaja of Vizianagram, is the **Kotwali** (Police Station) with the Temple of **Bhaironath**, built by Baji Rao II in 1825. The image inside is believed to be of the Kotwal (Superintendent) who rides on a ghostly dog. Stalls sell sugar dogs to be offered to the image. In the temple garden of **Gopal Mandir** near the Kotwali is a small hut in which Tulsi Das is said to have composed the *Binaya Patrika* poem.

The **Bhelupura Temple** with a museum marks the birthplace of the 23rd Jain Tirthankar **Parsvanath** who preached non-violence. The **Durga Temple** (18th-century) to the south along Durga Kund Road, was built in the Nagara style. It is painted red with ochre and has the typical five spires (symbolizing the elements) merging into one (Brahma). Non-Hindus may view from rooftop nearby. Next door in a peaceful garden, the **Tulsi Manas Temple** (1964) in white marble commemorates the medieval poet Tulsi Das. It has walls engraved with verses and scenes from the *Ramcharitmanas*, composed in a Hindi dialect, instead of the conventional Sanskrit, and is open to all (closed 1130-1530). Good views from the second floor of 'Disneyland style' animated show. **Bharat Mata Temple**, south of Cantt Station, has a relief map of 'Mother India' in marble. Good bookshop, but not worth a detour.

## River front

The hundred and more **ghats** on the river are the main attraction for visitors to Varanasi. Visit them at first light before sunrise, 0430 in summer, 0600 in winter when Hindu pilgrims come to bathe in the sacred Ganga, facing the rising sun, or at dusk when synchronised pujas are performed, culminating in leaf-boat lamps being floated down the river, usually from 1800 (try Mir or Assi Ghat). Start the river trip at Dasasvamedha Ghat where you can hire a boat quite cheaply especially if you can share, bargain to about Rs 60-120 per hour for two to eight at dawn. You may go either upstream (south) towards Harishchandra Ghat or downstream to Manikarnika Ghat. You may prefer to have a boat on the river at sunset and watch the lamps floated on the river, or go in the afternoon at a fraction of the price quoted at dawn. For photographs, visit the riverside between 0700-0900. The foggy sunshine early in the morning often clears to produce a beautiful light.

**Kite flying** is a popular pastime, as elsewhere in India, especially all along the river bank. The serious competitors endeavour to bring down other flyers' kites and so fortify their twine by coating it with a mix of crushed light bulbs and flour paste to make it razor sharp! The quieter ghats, eg Panchganga, are good for watching the fun – boys in their boats on the river scramble to retrieve downed kites as trophies that can be re-used even though the kites themselves are very cheap.

**Dasasvamedha Ghat** Named as the 'Place of Ten Horse Sacrifices' performed here by **Brahma**, God of Creation. Some believe that in the age of the gods when the world was in chaos, **Divodasa** was appointed King of Kashi by Brahma. He accepted, on condition that all the gods would leave Varanasi. Even **Siva** was forced to leave but Brahma set the test for Divodasa, confident that he would get the complex ceremony wrong, allowing the gods back into the city. However, the ritual was performed flawlessly, and the ghat has thus become one of the holiest, especially at eclipses. Bathing here is regarded as being almost as meritorious as making the sacrifice.

*Photography is not permitted at the burning ghats but travellers are told that it is allowed and then a large fine is demanded. Other scams involve conmen collecting 'donations' to provide wood for burning the poor.*

**Moving south** You will pass **Munshi Ghat**, where some of the city's sizeable Muslim population (25%) come to bathe. The river has no religious significance for them. Close by is **Darbhanga Ghat** where the mansion had a hand-operated cable lift. Professional washermen work at the **Dhobi Ghat**; there is religious merit in having your clothes washed in the Ganga. Brahmins have their own washermen to avoid caste pollution. The municipality has built separate washing facilities away from the ghat.

**Narad** and **Chauki Ghats** are held sacred since the **Buddha** received enlightenment here under a *peepul* tree. Those who bathe together at Narad, supposedly go home and quarrel! The pink water tower here is for storing Ganga water. High water levels are recorded at **Raj Ghat**. The flood levels are difficult to imagine when the river is at its lowest in January/February. **Mansarovar Ghat** leads to



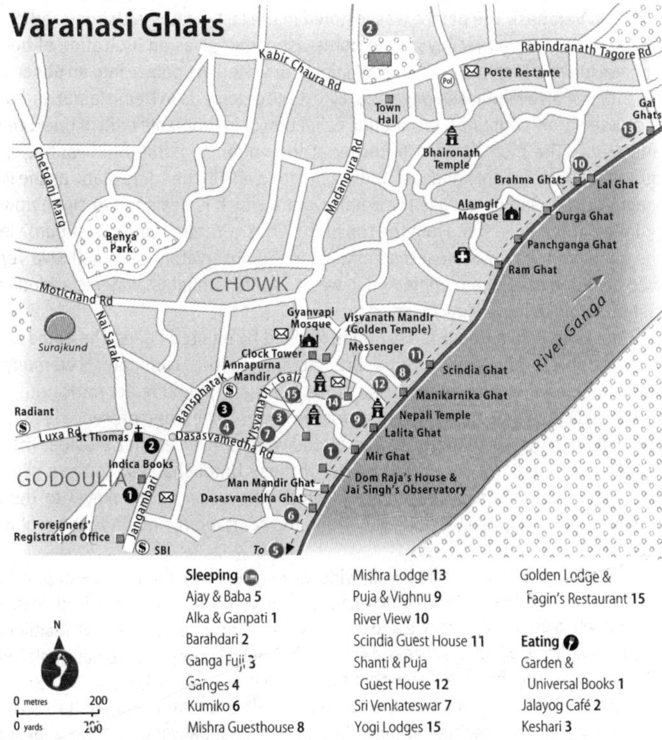


Sleeping
Ajay & Baba 5
Alka & Ganpati 1
Barahdari 2
Ganga Fuji 3
Ganges 4
Kumiko 6
Mishra Guesthouse 8
Mishra Lodge 13
Puja & Vighnu 9
River View 10
Scindia Guest House 11
Shanti & Puja Guest House 12
Sri Venkateswar 7
Yogi Lodges 15
Golden Lodge & Fagin's Restaurant 15

Eating
Garden & Universal Books 1
Jalayog Café 2
Keshari 3

 ruins of several temples around a lake. **Kedar Ghat** is named after Kedarnath, a pilgrimage site in the Uttaranchal, with a Bengali temple nearby.

The **Harishchandra Ghat** is particularly holy and is dedicated to King Harishchandra. It is now the most sacred *smashan* or cremation ghat although Manikarnika is more popular. Behind the ghat is a *gopuram* of a Dravidian style temple. The **Karnataka Ghat** is one of many regional ghats which are attended by priests who know the local languages, castes, customs and festivals.

The **Hanuman Ghat** is where Vallabha, the leader of a revivalist Krishna bhakti cult was born in the late 15th century. **Shivala Ghat** (Kali Ghat) is privately owned by the ex-ruler of Varanasi. **Chet Singh's Fort**, Shivala, stands behind the ghat. The fort, the old palace of the Maharajas, is where the British imprisoned him but he escaped by climbing down to the river and swimming away. **Anandamayi Ghat** is named after the Bengali saint Anandamayi Ma (died 1982) who received 'enlightenment' at 17 and spent her life teaching and in charitable work. **Jain Ghat** is near the birthplace of Tirthankar Shyeyanshnath. **Tulsi Ghat** commemorates the great saint-poet **Tulsi Das** who lived here (see Tulsi Manas Temple above). Furthest upstream is the **Assi Ghat**, where the river Assi meets the Ganga, one of the five that pilgrims should bathe from in a day. The order is Assi, Dasasvamedha, Barnasangam, Panchganga and Manikarnika. Upstream on the east bank is the Ramnagar Fort, the Maharaja of Varanasi's residence (see below). Here the boat will turn to take you back to Dasasvamedha Ghat.



**Moving north** Leaving from Dasasvamedha Ghat, you will pass the following: **Man Mandir Ghat** ⓘ *normally 0930-1730 but if you enquire locally you may be able to get in at dawn or dusk*, built by Maharajah Man Singh of Amber in 1600 and one of the oldest in Varanasi. The palace was restored in the last century with brick and plaster. The beautiful stone balcony on the northeast corner gives an indication of how the original looked. Maharaja Jai Singh of Jaipur converted the palace into an **observatory** in 1710, see also Jaipur, see page 326. Like its counterparts in Delhi, Jaipur and Ujjain, the observatory contains a fascinating collection of instruments built of brick, cement and stone. The most striking of these, at the entrance, is the Bhittiyantra, or wall quadrant, over 3 m high and just under 3 m broad and in the same plane as the line of longitude. Similarly placed is the Samratyantra which is designed to slope upwards pointing at the Pole Star. From the top of the Chakra Yantra there is a superb view of the ghats and the town. Near the entrance to the observatory is a small **Siva Temple** whose shrine is a lingam immersed in water. During droughts, water is added to the cistern to make it overflow for good luck.

The **Dom Raja's House** is next door, flanked by painted tigers. The **doms** are the 'Untouchables' of Varanasi who are integral to the cremation ceremony. As Untouchables they can handle the corpse, a ritually polluting act for Hindus. They also supply the flame from the temple for the funeral pyre. Their presence is essential and also lucrative since there are fees for the various services they provide. The Dom Raja is the hereditary title of the leader of these Untouchables. You can climb up through the astronomical observatory (which is overrun by monkeys) to the Raja Dom's Palace – a guide will take you round the court room, and on to the roof which has the best view of the river.

**Mir Ghat** leads to a sacred well; widows who dedicate themselves to prayer, are fed and clothed here. Then comes **Lalita Ghat** with the distinctive Nepalese style temple with a golden roof above and a Ganga mandir at water level. Above **Manikarnika Ghat** is a well into which Siva's dead wife Sati's earring is supposed to have fallen when Siva was carrying her after she committed suicide – see page 211. The Brahmins managed to find the jewel from the earring (*manikarnika*) and returned it to Siva who blessed the place. Offerings of *bilva* flowers, milk, sandalwood and sweetmeats are thrown into the tank where pilgrims come to bathe. Between the well and the ghat is

*Charanpaduka*, a stone slab with Vishnu's footprint. Boatmen may pursuade you to leave a 'private' offering to perform a puja (a ploy to increasing their earnings)!

The adjoining **Jalasayin Ghat** is the principal burning ghat of the city. The expensive scented sandalwood which the rich alone can afford is used sparingly; usually not more than two kilos. You may see floating bundles covered in white cloth; children, and those dying of 'high fever', or smallpox in the past, are not cremated but put into the river. This avoids injuring *Sitala* the goddess of smallpox.

**Scindia Ghat**, originally built in 1830, was so large that it collapsed. **Ram Ghat** was built by the Maharaja of Jaipur. Five rivers are supposed to meet at the magnificent **Panchganga Ghat** – the Ganga, Sarasvati, Gyana, Kirana and Dhutpapa. The stone column can hold around 1,000 lamps at festivals. The impressive flights of stone steps run up to the Alamgir Mosque (see above). At **Gai Ghat** there is a statue of a sacred cow whilst at **Trilochana Ghat** there is a temple to Siva in his form as the 'Three-eyed' (*Trilochana*); two turrets stand out of the water. **Raj Ghat** is the last on the boat journey. Excavations have revealed an eighth century BC site of a city on a grassy mound nearby. Raj Ghat was where the river was forded until bridges were built.

## Other sights

Varanasi is famous for ornamental brasswork, silk weaving and for its glass beads, exported all over the world. *Zari* work, whether embroidered or woven, once used silver or gold thread but is now done with gilded copper or brass. Visit the **Governmentt Weaving Centre** at Chauka Ghat to watch weavers at work. The significance of **silk** in India's traditional life is deep-rooted. Silk was considered a pure fabric, most appropriate for use on ceremonial and religious occasions. Its lustre, softness and richness of natural colour gave it precedence over all other fabrics. White or natural coloured silk was worn by the Brahmins and others who were 'twice born'. Women wore bright colours and the darker hues were reserved for the lowest caste in the formal hierarchy, few of whom could afford it. Silk garments were worn for ceremonials like births and marriages, and offerings of finely woven silks were made to deities in temples. This concept of purity may have given impetus to the growth of silk-weaving centres around ancient temple towns like Kanchipuram, Varanasi, Bhubaneswar and Ujjain, a tradition that is kept alive today, see page 583.

**Banaras Hindu University** (BHU) is one of the largest campus universities in India to the south of the city and enjoys a pleasant, relaxed atmosphere. Founded at the turn of the nineteenth century, it was originally intended for the study of Sanskrit, Indian art, music and culture and has the Bharat Kala Bhavan Museum (see below). The **New Visvanath Temple** (1966), one of the tallest in India, is in the university semi circle and was financed by the Birla family. It was planned by Madan Mohan Malaviya (1862-1942), Chancellor of the university, who believed in Hinduism without caste distinctions. The marble Shiva temple modelled on the old Visvanath Temple, is open to all.

The 17th-century **Ramnagar Fort** ⓘ *ferry Rs 10 return, rickshaws from centre, across a crumbling double-decker bridge, Rs 75, ask to wait or take a boat back or walk over the pontoon bridge*, across the river, was the home of the Maharaja of Varanasi; the Durbar Hall houses a **museum** (see below). Beautiful situation, surrounded by narrow, crowded streets, but the Fort is run down. *Ramlila* performances during Dasara.

**Bharat Kala Bhavan** ⓘ *BHU, T0542 230 7621, 1100-1630, closed Sun and holidays, Rs 40 for foreigners, Rs 5 Indians, Rs 10 camera (lockers at entrance)*, exhibits include sculptures from Mathura and Sarnath, excellent Mughal miniature paintings and Benarasi brocades. **Ramnagar Fort Museum** ⓘ *across the river, T0542 233 9322, summer 0900-1200, 1400-1700, winter 1000-1700, Rs 7 (includes Fort)*, has palanquins, elephant *howdahs*, costumes, arms and furniture gathering dust. See the amazing locally made astrological clock and single cylinder steam driven fan!

## Excursion

**Chunar**, 35 km southwest of Varanasi, is famous for Chunar sandstone, the material of the Asoka pillars, highly polished in a technique said to be Persian. The town is also noted for its **fort** built on a spur of the Kaimur Hills, 53 m above the surrounding plain. It was of obvious strategic importance and changed hands a number of times. The army occupies the fort today, but you can look around. There is an impressive well with steps leading down to a water gate; watch out for snakes. The British Cemetery below the fort overlooks the Ganga. Islamic tombs of Shah Kasim Suleiman and his son here, feature in paintings by Daniells and others. Buses from City Station, Varanasi take 1½ hours, Rs 75 return.

# Sarnath → *Phone code: 0542. Colour map 3, grid B4.*

Sarnath, 10 km northeast of Varanasi, is one of Buddhism's major centres in India. Given its great historic importance visitors may be disappointed to find the stupas neglected and the very limited collection in the museum, although it houses some superb pieces. Nevertheless, many find the deer park a place of peace and reflection despite distractions of loud transistor radios and young monks running around or playing cricket! » *For Sleeping, Eating and other listings, see pages 187-195.*



## History

When he had gained enlightenment at Bodh Gaya, the **Buddha** came to the deer park at Sarnath and delivered his first sermon (circa 528 BC), usually referred to as *Dharmachakra* (The Wheel of Law). Since then, the site has been revered. The Chinese traveller Hiuen Tsang described the *sangharama* (monastery) in AD 640 as having 1,500 monks, a 65-m high *vihara*, a figure of the Buddha represented by a wheel, a 22-m high stone stupa built by Asoka, a larger 90-m high stupa and three lakes. The remains here and the sculptures now at the Indian Museum, Kolkata and the National Museum, Delhi reveal that Sarnath was a centre of religious activity, learning and art, continuously from the fourth century BC until its abandonment in the ninth century AD and ultimate destruction by Muslim armies in 1197.

## Enclosure

A separate entrance leads to the enclosure on the far right. The statue on the right is of **Anagarika Dharmapala**, the founder of the Mahabodhi Society which has assumed responsibility for the upkeep of Sarnath and Bodh Gaya. The modern **Mulagandhakuti Vihara** (1929-31) contains frescoes by the Japanese artist Kosetsu Nosu depicting scenes from the Buddha's life. An urn in the ground is supposed to hold a Buddha relic obtained from Taxila (Pakistan). The **Bodhi tree** (*pipal, Ficus religiosa*) planted in 1931 is a sapling of the one in Sri Lanka which was grown from a cutting taken there circa 236 BC by Mahinda's sister Princess Sanghamitta.

Here is the **Dhamekh Stupa** (fifth to sixth century AD) ⓘ *Rs 5, foreigners US$2 or Rs100, video camera Rs 25*, or Dharma Chakra, the most imposing monument at Sarnath, built where the Buddha delivered his first sermon to his five disciples. Along with his birth, enlightenment and death, this incident is one of the four most significant. The stupa consists of a 28-m diameter stone plinth which rises to a height of 13 m. Each of the eight faces has an arched recess for an image. Above this base rises a 31-m high cylindrical tower. The upper part was probably unfinished. The central section has elaborate Gupta designs eg luxuriant foliation, geometric patterns, birds and flowers. The Brahmi script dates from sixth to ninth centuries. The stupa was enlarged six times and the well-known figures of a standing Boddhisattva and the Buddha teaching were found nearby.

## Other sights

The **deer park** is holy to Jains because **Shyeyanshnath**, the 11th Tirthankar, was born near the Dhamekh stupa. The temple to your left as you move between the stupas commemorates him; 'Sarnath' may be derived from his name. The monastery (fifth century onwards) in the southwest corner is one of four in the Deer Park. The others are along the north edge. All are of brick with cells off a central courtyard which are in ruins.

**Dharmarajika Stupa** was built by the Emperor Asoka to contain relics of the Buddha. It was enlarged on several occasions but was destroyed by Jagat Singh, Dewan of the Maharaja of Benares, in 1794, when a green marble casket containing human bones and pearls was found. The British Resident at the Maharaja's court published an account of the discovery thereby drawing the attention of scholars to the site.

The **Main shrine** is a rectangular building, 29 m by 27 m, with doubly recessed corners and is 5½-m high. The building, marking the place of the Buddha's meditation, is attributed to Asoka and the later Guptas. The concrete path and interior brick walls were added later to reinforce the building. To the rear is the 5 m lower portion of a polished sandstone **Asokan Column** (third century BC). The original was about 15 m high with a lion capital which is now in the Archaeological Museum. The four lions sitting back to back with the wheel of law below them is now the symbol of the Indian Union. The column was one of many erected by Asoka to promulgate the faith and this contained a message to the monks and nuns not to create any schisms and to spread the word.

## Sarnath

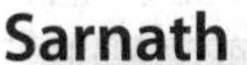

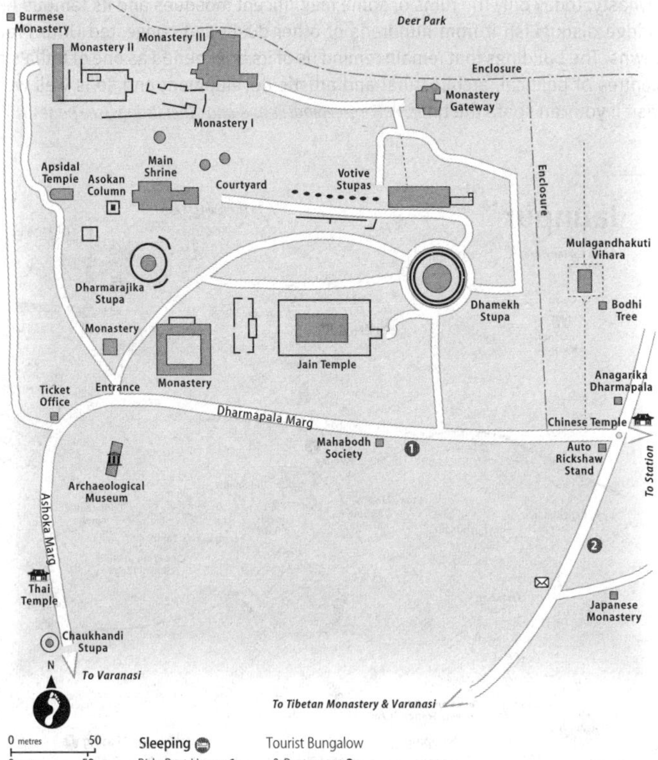


**Sleeping**
Birla Rest House **1**
Tourist Bungalow & Restaurant **2**

The modern **Burmese monastery** is worth the short detour from the road. It is very colourful and peaceful with no hawkers and hardly any tourists. Tibetan, Thai and Chinese monasteries have also been built around the old complex. The Central Institute of Higher Tibetan Studies, near the ruins, runs courses and carries out research. The library has a good collection of texts and manuscripts.

The **museum** ⓘ *closed Fri, 1030-1630*, has a well-displayed collection of pieces from the site, including the famous lion capital (Asokan Column), a Sunga Period (first century BC) stone railing, Kushana Period (second century AD) Boddhisattvas, Gupta Period (fifth century AD) figures, including the magnificent seated Buddha. Allow about one hour.Tickets are Rs 2 from across the road where Archaeological Survey booklets are for sale. Cameras and bags are not normally allowed.

**Chaukhandi**, 500 m south, has a fifth-century Stupa. On top of this is an octagonal brick tower built by Akbar in 1588 to commemorate the visit his father Humayun made to the site. The inscription above the doorway reads 'As Humayun, king of the Seven Climes, now residing in paradise, deigned to come and sit here one day, thereby increasing the splendour of the sun, so Akbar, his son and humble servant, resolved to build on this spot a lofty tower reaching to the blue sky'.



## Jaunpur → *Phone code: 05452. Colour map 3, grid B4. Population: 321,000.*

Jaunpur, 58 km from Varanasi, is a uniquely important centre of 14th- and 15th-century regional Islamic architecture. Once the short-lived capital of the Sharqi Dynasty, today only the ruins of some magnificent mosques and its famous Akbari Bridge distinguish it from hundreds of other dusty and congested Uttar Pradesh towns. The buildings that remain remind us of its brief period as one of India's main centres of political, architectural and artistic development and so is well worth a visit if you can spare the time. » *For Sleeping, Eating and other listings, see pages 187-195.*

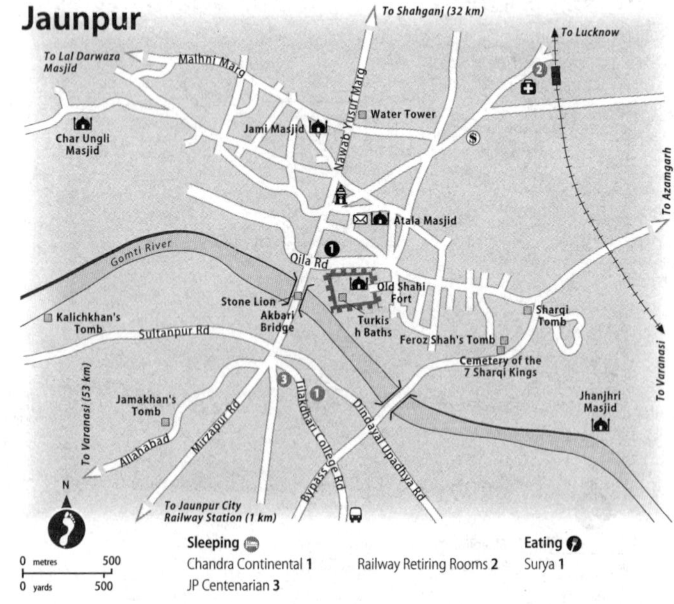

## History

Located at a strategic crossing point of the Gomti River, Jaunpur was established by Feroz Shah Tughluq in 1360 as part of his drive to the East. Earlier Hindu and Jain structures were destroyed to provide material for the mosques with which the Sharqi Dynasty rapidly embellished their capital. The Sharqi kings – named 'Kings of the East' by Feroz Shah – established effective independence from the Tughluqs who had been crushed in Timur's sack of Delhi in 1398. They maintained it until 1479, when Husain Shah, the last Sharqi king, was violently deposed by Ibrahim Lodi. Although all the secular buildings, including palaces and courts, were razed to the ground, Ibrahim Lodi spared at least some of the mosques. Some of the city's destruction visible today can be put down to much later events – floods in 1773 and 1871 and an earthquake in 1934. According to Rushbrook Williams this last catastrophe destroyed seven of the 15 arches in the great 200-m long Akbari Bridge, designed by the Afghan architect Afzal Ali and built between 1564-1568. The stone lion above an elephant at the end of the bridge marks the point from which distances from the city were measured.

## Sights

The **bridge** emphasized Jaunpur's role as the centre of a pre-Mughal trading network. In the 17th century the Gomti allowed ships up to 18 tons to navigate over 200 km upstream. Under the great king Shams-ud-din-Ibrahim (1402-1436) Jaunpur became a centre of the arts and university education. Today, however, it is the remains of the fort and the mosques which are most worth visiting.

The **Old Shahi Fort** ⓘ *Rs 2*, just north of the Akbari Bridge, is an irregular grassy quadrangle enclosed by ruined stone walls. It shelters the oldest **mosque** in Jaunpur (1377), a narrow arcade (40 m by 7 m) supported by carved pillars, named after its builder, Ibrahim Naib Barbak, Feroz Shah Tughluq's brother. In the mid-19th century Fergusson described some distinctive yellow and blue enamelled bricks on the fine 15 m high stone gateway, and an inscribed monolith (1766) at the entrance, still visible today. Of particular interest is the almost perfect model of a **hammam** (Turkish bath) which you can wander around.

Perhaps the most striking of the surviving mosques, the **Atala**, stands less than 400 m to the north of the fort. Built in 1408 on the site of the Hindu Atala Devi temple, it marks the triumphant beginning of Shams-ud-din-Ibrahim's reign and introduces unique features of Jaunpuri style. An arched gateway or 'pylon' fronts the sanctuary on the west side of the 50-m square court; the remaining three sides are spacious cloisters, two-storeyed and five aisles deep. The pylon has sloping sides, as in other Tughluq building, and its central arch is over 22 m high – along with the arch of the great Jami Masjid nearby, the highest in India. Other features borrowed from the Tughluq style are a recessed arch with its ornamented fringe, and tapering turrets on the west wall. Although artisans were brought in from Delhi, Jaunpur builders soon articulated their Tughluq traditions in a highly distinctive way. Note the beautiful sanctuary interior with its decorated nave and transepts, and the perforated stone screens. At the far end, the transepts are two-storeyed, with the upper section screened off for the zenana.

The same weakness applies to the 'most ambitious' of Jaunpur's mosques, the **Jami Masjid**, about 1 km north of the fort. Begun by Shah Ibrahim in 1438 it was completed by Husain Shah, the last Sharqi king, in 1470. Raised about 6 m on an artificial platform, the worshipper is forced to climb a steep flight of steps to enter the 60-m square courtyard. Built on an even grander scale than the Atala Mosque, the 25-m high central pylon dominates the sanctuary. Note the unsupported transept halls which create a remarkable clear covered open space. Despite the lack of pillars they have survived earthquakes as well as normal ageing. Allow three hours on foot for the main sights.

# Allahabad → *Phone code: 0532. Colour map 3, grid B3. Population: 1,015,000.*

The narrow spit of land at the confluence of the Ganges and Yamuna rivers, normally an almost deserted river beach of fine sand, becomes home for two weeks once every 12 years to the Kumbh Mela, when over 12 million pilgrims converge to bathe in the holy waters. The 2001 Kumbh Mela has been described as "the most spectacular ever", with live pictures shown on the internet! Allahabad has grown around this spot and is today a rapidly growing commercial and administrative city. It is particularly sacred for Hindus because it is at the confluence of the Ganga and the Jamuna. For the Muslims and the British too, this became a strategically vital centre; they have left their imprint on the landmarks of the city, making it an interesting city to wander around, particularly the Civil Lines area to the north. ▸▸ *For Sleeping, Eating and other listings, see pages 187-195.*

## Ins and outs

**Getting there** Bamrauli airport is 18 km west of town. The Civil Lines (MG Marg) Bus stand and the Leader Rd stand, near Junction station, are used by buses arriving from the north and west, while Zero Rd bus stand, half way between the Junction and City railway stations, serves local and southern routes, including Khajuraho. Just south of the Civil Lines, Allahabad Junction station is the main stop for Delhi and Kolkata trains. There are also direct trains from Mumbai and key cities of South India.

**Getting around** Many of the city's hotels are in Civil Lines, within easy reach of the Junction station (rear exit) and the bus stands. Although this centre is quite compact



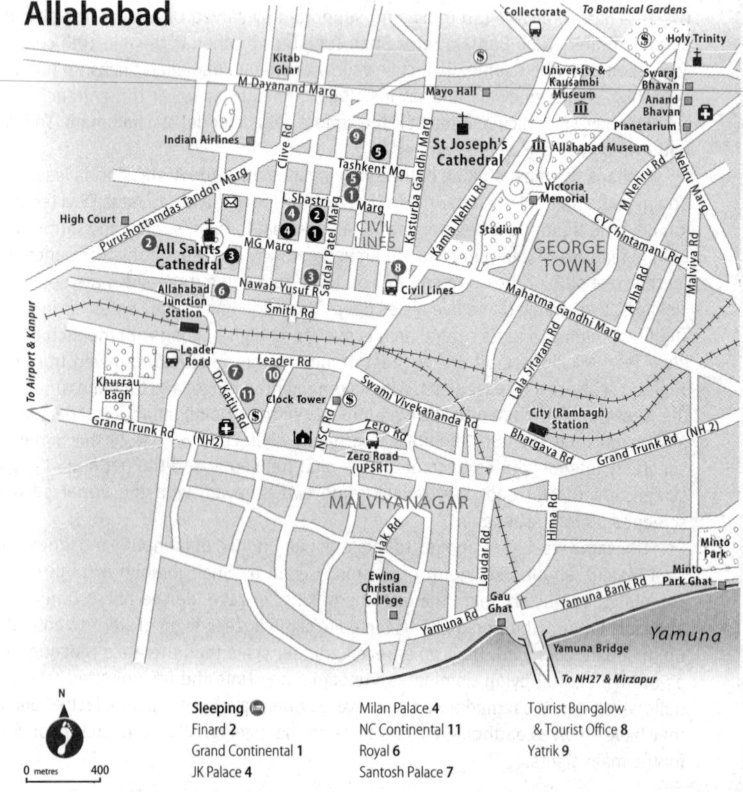

you need an auto-rickshaw to get to some of the main sights, including the Fort and the Sangam. Metered taxis and cycle-rickshaws are also easily available. ▸▸ *See Transport, page 194, for further details.*

## History

Ancient sites here point to Allahabad's early history. Draupadi Ghat has revealed signs of extensive habitation and quantities of pottery, Northern Black Polished Ware, dated between 1100 and 800 BC. Remains of the **The Kushans** were found on the Bharadwaj Ashram site. The Muslims first conquered it in 1194 and renamed it Allahabad in 1584. It later became the HQ of the British Government of the Northwest Provinces and Oudh, and here the transfer of government from the East India Company to the crown was announced by Lord Canning in 1858.

## Sights

**Prayag (The confluence)** The purifying power of a sacred river is strongest at a confluence. In addition, the mythical underground river **Sarasvati** is also said to surface here. Bathing here is auspicious at all times of the year, more so at **Magh Mela** which occurs every year for 15 days (January/February) and longer at the **Kumbh Mela** when pilgrims bathe at prayag to wash away a lifetime's sins. In legend, Hindu gods and demons vied for the pot (*kumbha*) that held the nectar of immortality (*amrit*). During the 12-day fight for possession, Vishnu spilt four drops of *amrit* which fell to earth, making four sacred places: Allahabad, Haridwar (Uttaranchal), Ujjain (MP) and Nasik (Maharashtra). Holiest of all is Allahabad, the site of the Maha (great) Kumbh Mela. This festival moves every three years returning to Allahabad every 12th year (last in 2001). There are still rows of tents at the prayag, which give a good indication of the sheer size of the Kumbh Mela, when the area becomes a canvas city, home to over a million people. **Boats** leave from nearby ghats, the nearest being the one by the fort.

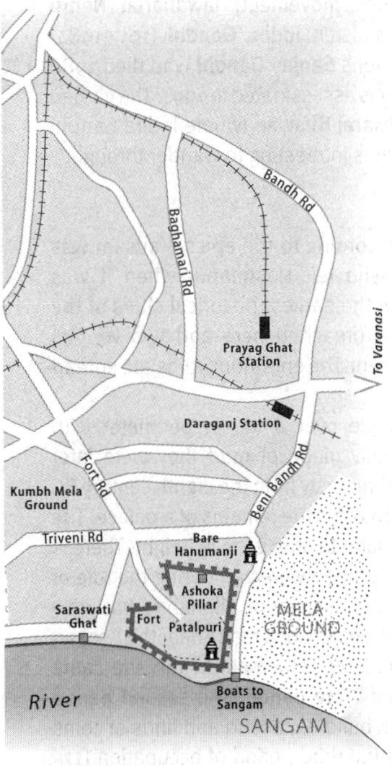

Bandh Rd
Baghamari Rd
Prayag Ghat Station
To Varanasi
Daraganj Station
Fort Rd
Beni Bandh Rd
Kumbh Mela Ground
Triveni Rd
Bare Hanumanji
Ashoka Pillar
Saraswati Ghat
Fort
Patalpuri
MELA GROUND
River
Boats to Sangam
SANGAM

**Eating**
Allahabad Regency **5**
El Chico **1**
Hot Stuff **2**
Jade Garden, Kwality & India Coffee House **3**
Kwality **4**

**Mughal Period** Allahabad has few monuments pre-dating the Muslim period. The **Fort**, begun in 1583, was the largest of **Akbar's** forts. It has three massive gateways and 7 m high walls, seen to advantage from across the river. The Marathas held it from 1739 to 1750, then the Pathans, and finally the British from 1801. Most of the fort is closed to visitors, including the third-century BC Asoka pillar, moved there from Kausambi under Akbar's orders. Under the fort's east wall is the **Undying Banyan Tree** (*Akshaivata*), an underground temple from which pilgrims threw themselves to achieve salvation in death. To see, ask for a permit at the Tourist Office.

**Khusrau Bagh** The typical Mughal garden enclosure houses the handsome tomb of **Prince Khusrau**. After staging an unsuccessful rebellion against his father **Jahangir** in 1607, Khusrau spent the next year in chains. When freed, he encouraged a plot to assassinate his father but was discovered. Partially blinded and kept a captive, he was murdered in 1615 by his own brother, later the **Emperor Shah Jahan** (ruled 1627-1658). The burial chamber is underground with decorative plasterwork. The tomb to the west is thought to be his sister's. Further west is the two-storey tomb of his Rajput mother.

**Buildings from the British Period** Canning Town, opposite Junction Railway Station, was laid out on a grid in the 1860s. Within it are the Old High Court and Public Offices, classical style buildings from the late 19th century including the Gothic style **All Saint's** Cathedral. At the east end of the Civil Lines is Alfred Park (now Chandra Sekhar Azad Park), north of which stands **Muir College**, a fine example of 'Indo-Saracenic' architecture. It was later established as the University of Allahabad. West of this is **Mayo Hall** with **St Joseph's Roman Catholic Cathedral** (1879) to its south. **Holy Trinity Church** (early 19th century) on J Nehru Marg, contains memorials from the Gwalior Campaign (1843) and the 'Uprising' (1857).

**The Allahabad Museum** ⓘ *Chandra Sekhar Azad Park, Kamla Nehru Rd, T0532 260 1200, closed Mon and second Sunday of month, 1000-1700, foreigners charged Rs100, Indians Rs5, 18 galleries.* Contains a wide range of stone sculptures (second century BC from Bharhut and Kausambi, first century AD Kushana from Mathura, fourth to sixth century Gupta and 11th-century carvings from Khajuraho). Also a fine collection of Rajasthani miniatures, terracotta figurines, coins and paintings by Nicholas Roerich. **Anand Bhavan** ⓘ *T0532 246 7071, 1000-1700, closed Mon, Rs 5*, is the former Nehru family home contains many interesting items relating to **Motilal Nehru** (1861-1931), active in the Independence movement, **Jawaharlal Nehru** (1889-1964), Independent India's first Prime Minister, **Indira Gandhi** (1917-1984) (Prime Minister 1966-1977, 1980-1984) and her sons **Sanjay Gandhi** who died 1980 and **Rajiv Gandhi** (Prime Minister 1984-89) who was assassinated in 1991. The garden (free) is pleasant to relax in. Next to it stands **Swaraj Bhawan** (where Indira Gandhi was born) ⓘ *closed Mon, 1000-1700, Rs 5*, which is interesting to wander through.



## Excursion

**Kausambi** is 44 km southwest of Allahabad. According to the epics, Kausam was founded by a descendant of the *Pandavas* who left Hastinapur when it was destroyed by floods from the Ganga. It is one of the earliest historical cities of the region. According to Hiuen Tsang the Buddha preached here and two *viharas* (monasteries) were built to commemorate the event.The enormous ruins are spread through several villages.

The ramparts form an approximate rectangle over 6 km in perimeter with bastions that tower up to nearly 23 m. Originally made of mud they were later surfaced with bricks. The town was occupied continuously from the eighth century BC to sixth century AD. In the southwest corner are possibly the remains of a palace. The main **stupa** (fifth century BC) measured 25 m in diameter and 25 m in height. There is also the damaged shaft of a sandstone column, probably erected during the rule of the Mauryan Emperor Asoka. GR Sharma of the University of Allahabad has now worked at four main areas on the site. The earliest excavations made near the Asokan pillar suggested that the first of the three periods of settlement of the site came immediately before the **Northern Black Polished Ware** period. The second period dated back to 300 BC and included the first brick building, a road and finds of coins with the typical Kausambi 'lanky bull' motifs. In the third period of occupation (175 BC-AD 325), the coins found testify to a succession of rulers; Mitras, followed by Kushan kings and then by Maghas. The road evidently continued in use up to about AD 300 and the site itself was occupied until about AD 400. Many of the coins and terracottas discovered here are now on display in the Allahabad City Museum and Kausambi Museum at the University of Allahabad.



## Sleeping

**Varanasi** *p173, maps p174 and p177*
Discounts in off-season (Jun-Jul). Be prepared for power cuts and carry a torch at night. Be aware that some insist on taking you to hotels where they get a commission. Hotels on the river front can be difficult to locate, particularly at night. Local people will often show you the way but may expect a commission from the hotel, thus increasing the rate you pay. Most **D** hotels have rooms with TV and attached baths. Rooms with river view are worth the extra.

**L-AL Taj Ganges**, Nadesar Palace Ground, T0542 250 3001, www.tajhotels.com. 130 rooms, good restaurants (spotless kitchen), pool, top-class facilities, busy, but efficient service, taxis from here overcharge.

**AL Radisson**, The Mall, T0542 250 1515, www.radisson.com. Impressively clean and bright, very modern interiors, 117 well equipped rooms, smart restaurant and coffee shop, very well run, recommended.

**A Clarks Tower**, The Mall, T0542 250 7899, www.clarkshotels.com. 58 decent rooms, clean pool, restaurant (beer Rs 170), some reports of unfriendly service.

**A Clarks Varanasi**, The Mall, T0542 250 1011, www.clarkshotels.com. 113 slightly musty rooms, pool (non-residents, Rs 200), large, bustling, quiet location, good facilities, good if buffet-biased restaurant but expensive drinks, beginning to feel a little outdated.

**A Hindustan International**, C 21/3 Maldahiya, T0542 241 1484, www.hhihotels.com. 85 rooms, modern, with the look of a multi-storeyed car park, slightly murky pool, clean and comfortable, good views from higher rooms, elegant restaurants.

**A Kashika** (Clarks), The Mall, connected to Clarks Tower by enclosed bridge, 5 km from centre, T0542 250 7899, www.clarkshotels.com. 40 very clean, well furnished rooms, limited Indian restaurant, friendly and helpful, plenty of light creates pleasant atmosphere, good value, shares facilities with other 2 Clarks hotels here.

**A Palace on Ganges**, B-1/158 Assi Ghat, T9542 231 5050, www.palaceonganges.com. 22 rooms (more coming), each decorated in the style of a different Indian state, in a converted old palace, plus a small rooftop restaurant and a health centre. The most luxurious hotel on the banks of the Ganga.

**B Ganges View**, Assi Ghat, T0542 231 3218, hotelgangesview@yahoo.com. Old patrician home converted into welcoming guest house with a tastefully decorated range of small rooms (noisy fan), very pleasant atmosphere, interesting clientele (artists, academics), lovely riverside verandas, vegetarian food, free yoga lessons, book ahead.

**B Hotel de Paris**, 15 The Mall, T0542 250 5131, hoteldeparis@indiananetwork.com. 42 fairly basic but spacious rooms in 100-year- old palace, very well kept lawns, not bad value.

**B India**, 59 Patel Nagar, Cantt, T0542 250 7593, www.hotelindiavns.com. 73 bright, modern a/c rooms, better in renovated building, restaurant (popular so service can be slow), bar, good rooftop garden, very clean, good value.

**C Diamond**, Bhelupura, T0542 227 6696, diamotel@satyam.net.in. 40 rooms, most a/c though regular rooms are just as good, restaurant, exchange, gardens, reasonable value.

**C Plaza Inn**, S.21/116H, Parade Kothi, Cantt, T0542 220 5504, www.hotelplazainn.com. 63 spacious, modern rooms, very professional staff, interesting Nawab restaurant and bar, reasonable value, recommended.

**C-D Ganges**, Dasasvamedha Rd, T0542 309 4005, bhataksun@yahoo.com. 24 rooms (1-6 bed), some with bath (**D** a/c), discounts given, cleanliness varies (inspect first), pleasantly old fashioned, good restaurant on 1st floor overlooks bazar, exchange, email, air/rail tickets plus two snooker tables.

**C-D Malti**, 31/3 Vidyapith Rd, T0542 222 3878, www.hotelmalti.com. 47 simple rooms, some a/c with balcony, restaurant,. Avoids early morning heat and includes transport to/from ghat north of Alamgir mosque, not bad value..

**C-D New Hotel Broadway**, near Vijaya Cinema Crossing, Bhelupur, T0542 227 7097, info@newhotelbroadway.com. 25 clean, modern rooms, can be noisy lower down, but very good service and Mughlai restaurant.

**C-D Pradeep**, Jagatganj, T0542 220 4963, hotelpradeep@satyam.net.in. 36 clean rooms, most a/c, near noisy junction, excellent **Poonam** restaurant (see below), very attractive roof top bar/restaurant with real lawn, friendly staff (nearby, a therapist offers 'Delusion Removal Conversation'!), not bad value, recommended

**C-D Temple on Ganges**, near Assi Ghat, T0542 236 6840, www.hoteltemple.com. 26 spartan rooms with bath (western toilets), views of sunrise over Ganga, **F** dorm, friendly, peaceful, clean, average rooftop veg restaurant (no alcohol), free yoga lessons, rail ticketing (Rs 50), boat rides (Rs 60, 2 hrs), mixed reports (poor laundry, little boys employed).

**C-D Vaibhav**, 56 Patel Nagar, Cantt, T0542 250 1359, hotelvaibhav@satyam.net.in. 60 clean rooms with bath (some excellent a/c), no mosquitoes, modern, restaurant good but dark, bar, good service and value though a bit soulless, discount deal offered at airport.

**C-E Alka**, Mirghat, T0542 240 1681, www.hotelalkavns.com. 31rooms, some deluxe a/c, some shared bath, clean, spacious, with good views of the river, good restaurant.

**C-E Sahi River View Guest House**, Asi Ghat, T0542 231 3695, sahi_rvgh@sify.com. 11 rooms (more coming), some a/c, great views from balcony, free local and received calls.

**C-E Sita Guest House**, D22/16 Chausatti Ghat, T0542 245 0061, sita_guest_house@yahoo.com. 20 rooms with river views, most with balconies, clean, rooftop restaurant, internet, good value.

**C-E Surya**, behind **Clarks**, Varuna Bridge Rd, Cantt, T0542 250 8465, www.hotelsuryavns.com. 60 rooms, modern and clean, some a/c rooms, internet, restaurant (unexciting but good food and filling) and bar, large relaxing garden, parking, excellent value, highly recommended

**C-F Ganga Fuji Home**, D7/21 Shakar Kand Gali, near Golden Temple, T0542 239 7333, raj327333@yahoo.com. 20 very clean rooms, some brand new deluxe a/c, some with common bath, very friendly family, a/c rooftop restaurant with interesting view of city, recommended.

**C-F Puja Guest House**, D1/45 Lalita Ghat (near Nepali Temple), T0542 240 5027, pujaguesthouse@hotmail.com.. 42 cleanish rooms, some a/c, gloomy but quiet, less touristy than most.Cheap rooftop restaurant, help with air, bus, train tickets, not recommended for single women.

**D Barahdari**, near GPO, Maidagin, T/F0542 244 0581. 16 large rooms, some a/c (check unit and water heater), veg restaurant, exchange, garden, simple, clean.

**D-E Buddha**, C26/35 Lahurabir (behind hotel Ayaya), T0542 220 3686, hotelbuddha@rediffmail.com. 22 large clean rooms hot showers, pleasant restaurant on veranda in the garden.

**D-E Tourist Bungalow** (UP Tourism), off Parade Kothi, opposite rly station, T0542 220 8413, F220 6638. 39 rooms, somea/c, with bath, 'deluxe suites' and dorm (Rs 75) in barrack-style 2-storey building, restaurant, bar, shady verandah, pleasant garden, simple, clean and efficient, very helpful Tourist Office. Auto-rickshaws may take you to the inferior private 'Tourist Bungalow' nearby which has no garden.

**D-F Ajay**, near Munshi Ghat, 0542 245 0970, sanjay560us@yahoo.com. Rooms on several levels, clean, rooftop restaurant with great views, good service, tasty food. Elena Hotel run by brother next door.

**D-F Ganpati**, next to Alka on Mir ghat, T0542 239 0059, www.ganpatiguesthouse.com. 19 rooms, 3 a/c, great views from rooftop restaurant, pleasant staff.

**D-F Shanti Guest House**, 8/129 Garwasi Tola, near Manikarnika Ghat , T0542 239 2568, varanasishanti@yahoo.com (discount on e-mail bookings). 31 rooms vary, some **D** a/c, open-air dorm, 24-hr rooftop restaurant serving tasty food, backpackers' haunt, free boat trips twice a day, motorbike hire, real effort being made, recommended.

**E Park Villa**, Rathayatra Crossing, T0542 235 7050. 14 rooms, atmospheric, decaying, interesting and friendly, food poor.

**E Radiant YMCA Tourist Hostel**, 28A Sampoornanand Nagar, Sigra, T0542 222 4951, radiant/varanasi@dartmail.dartnet.com. Internet, exchange.

**E Sun Shiv**, D 54/16-D Ravi Niketan, Jaddumandi Rd (off Aurangabad Rd), T0542 241 0468, hotelsunshiv@rediffmail.com. 16 modest but charming rooms with balconies in unusual, art deco inspired 1960s family house, room service, quiet, no commission to rickshaws. Highly engaging, multi-lingual owner, recommended.

**E-F Baba Guest House**, D20/15 Munshi Ghat, T0542 245 5452, babaguesthouse@yahoo.com. 23 basic rooms, some bath, dorm (rs40), very friendly family.

**E-F Golden Lodge**, D8/35 Kalika Gali, near Golden Temple, T0542 239 8788, www.goldenlodgetime.com. 14 cell-like clean rooms, some with bath (hot water), enthusiastic if pushy proprietor, a/c restaurant (**Fagin's**), some character, free washing machine, check-out 1030.

**E-F International Guest House**, C32/4 (opposite BHU), T0542 236 0912. Rooms, dorm, camping in garden.

**E-F Mishra Guest House**, near Manikarnika Ghat, T0542 240 1143, mgh_vns@yahoo.com. 43 rooms with bath in cool, quiet, haveli-style hotel, most with balcony, some with extra long beds, best with river view.

**E-F River View**, Brahma Ghat by Gai Ghat (approach from R Tagore Rd, inaccessible to rickshaws), T0542 311 3769. 15 rooms, most with hot bath, good view (watch the dawn from front rooms and dolphins from rooftop!), small restaurant, very peaceful, clean, friendly, and far from the main tourist area, recommended.

**E-F Sri Venkateswar Lodge**, D5/64 Dasaswamedh, T0542 239 2357, venlodge@yahoo.com. 28 clean rooms in calm, well-run hotel, all water solar heated.

**E-F Vishnu**, Pandey Ghat, T0542 245 0206. 18 okay rooms, pleasant café plus terrace restaurant, beware of similarly named imitations.

**F JPM**, behind Asi Ghat, T0542 236 7031, jpmguesthouse@rediffmail.com. 5 basic rooms in new guesthouse nicely tucked away in backstreets, friendly owner.

**F Kumiko**, riverside near Dasasvamedha Ghat, T0542 309 1356. Rooms and dorm, breakfast and dinner, Japanese spoken, very clean, friendly owner, if a bit paranoid (2000 curfew). Very welcoming, recommended.

**F Mishra Lodge**, Trilochan Ghat, T0542 243 6917. 8 basic rooms, some with great views, in very authentic unmodernised family home, well away from tourist area.

**F Shiva Guest House**, D20/14 Munshi Ghat, T0542 245 2108, shiva_guest_house@hotmail.com. 17 simple, clean rooms, some with hot bath, rooftop restaurant (good food), family run, friendly.

**F Yogi Lodge**, D8/29 Kalika Gali, near Golden Temple, T0542 239 2588, yogilodge@yahoo.com. 15 simple rooms (Rs 100), shared bath, dorm (Rs 50), meals on roof terrace or in pleasant courtyard, open kitchen, congested area, internet, friendly staff, recommended. Rickshaws don't get commission, so may take you to **Yogi** hotels which are poorer (take a non-English speaking rickshaw to Godoulia, then phone).

**F Railway Retiring Rooms** at Varanasi Cantt, some a/c rooms and dorm.

**Sarnath** *p180, map p181*

**D-E Hotel Mrigdava** (UP Tourism), T0542 259 5965, www.up-tourism.com. Rooms and dorm (Rs 70), Indian restaurant, tourist office, tours.

**E-F Golden Buddha Hotel**, T0542 258 7933, goldenbuddha@rediffmail.com. B Clean rooms, friendly owner, recommended.

**F Birla Rest House**, near Mulagandhakuti Vihara. Dorm (Rs 50).

**Jaunpur** *p182, map p182*

**D-E Hotel J.P.Centenarian**, Olandganj, T05452 268056. Cleanish rooms in central location, helpful staff.

**E Chandra Continental**, Tilakdhari College Rd, Olandganj, T05452 264388. 12 clean rooms.

**F Railway Retiring Rooms**, 2 rooms (Rs 35).

**Surya**, Qila Rd, for snacks, clean.

**Allahabad** *p184, map p184*

MG Marg is Mahatma Gandhi Marg.

**A-B Grand Continental**, Sardar Patel Marg, T0532 260 5888, www.birhotel.com. 34 modern rooms in smart hotel in very central location, attractive restaurant and bar, swimming pool, perhaps a little overpriced.

**B Kanha Shyam**, Civil Lines, T0532 256 0123, www.hotelkanhashyam.com. 85 comfortable rooms, pool, two huge restaurants, one on the rooftop next to the cozy bar, best in town.

*For an explanation of the sleeping and eating price codes used in this guide, see inside the front cover. Other relevant information is found in Essentials pages 56-61.*

**B Milan Palace**, 4/2 Strachy Road, T0532 262 1617, www.hotelmilanpalace.com. Very modern, lively hotel in good location, spotless rooms, contemporary styled restaurant and bar, professional staff, recommended.

**B Yatrik**, 33 Sardar Patel Marg, 1 km railway station, T0532 260 1509. 37 a/c rooms, smartened entrance, restaurant, lovely garden, good value, clean and comfortable, good service, pool (closed in winter).

**C JK Palace**, Tashkant Marg, T0532 260 8611. 35 spotless rooms in brand new hotel, very eager staff, good location.

**C-D Suncity**, 19/21 Leader Road, T0532 240 5130. 19 rooms in smart, modern hotel, very clean and comfortable, helpful staff, on busy road but recommended.

**C-D Tourist Bungalow** (UP Tourism), 35 MG Marg, T0532 260 1440, rahiilawart@up-tourism.com. Rooms vary, some clean, good size a/c with bath and hot water, restaurant, bar, pleasant garden but can be noisy, helpful staff.

**C-E Santosh Palace**, 100 Katju Rd, 1/F 0532 265 3976. Wide range of rooms, mostly clean but cheaper ones starting to look a bit tired.).

**D Finaro**, 8 Hastings Rd, opposite High Court, T0532 262 2452, imtindia@sanchar net.in. Simple but characterful rooms with bath (geyser) in old colonial style bungalow, pleasant small garden, near train station and Civil Lines shopping, excellent home cooking, very helpful owner. Recommended.

**D-E NC Continental**, Katju Road, T0532 265 2058. 70 reasonably well maintained rooms, helpful staff, one of better options in area.

**D-F Royal**, 24 South Rd, T0531 262 3285. Large, eclectically decorated old house with big rooms, very old fashioned, basic bath-rooms, restaurant, friendly, full of character.

**F Railway Retiring Rooms** and dorm.

## Eating

**Varanasi** *p173, maps p174 and p177*

Restaurants outside hotels tend to be vegetarian and are not allowed to serve alcohol. Dry days on the 1st and 7th of each month, and some public holidays. The locally made Melody chocolate ice-cream is reputed to taste like the best Belgian double chocolate! Top hotels have expensive restaurants.

**TTT Varanasi Ashok**, see Sleeping, does good Indian. Lacks ambience, but try chicken *Kebab-e-Kalni*, *Paneer Capsium Bhujia*, stuffed *Paratha*, and *Puri-Bhaji* for breakfast. Avoid buffet.

**TT Bread of Life**, B 3/322 Shivala, near Ratnakar Park. Great cakes, also burritos, pizza, pasta, coffee, friendly, profits go to charity, great for a quiet escape, recommended.

**TT Burger King**, Nai Bazar, Cantt (next to *Taj Ganges*) Veg only! Not a branch of the international chain. Good cheese burger, ice creams, also chow miens, soups etc, no seating but recommended, worth detour if you have a long wait for the train.

**TT Fagin's** (Golden Lodge), Kalika Gali. International. A/c, in a rather dark basement.

**TT Ganga Fuji**, Kalika Gali. International. Reasonable, safe food, tempered down for western palate, live classical music in the evenings, helpful and friendly owner, popular. Recommended for ambiance and hospitality.

**TT Gudiya**, 43 Cantonment (next to India Tourist Office). Chinese. Food OK but pricey.

**TT Haifa**, in pleasant garden, good Middle East dishes, great atmosphere.

**TT Keshari**, near Ganges Hotel, off Dasasvamedha Ghat. Excellent vegetarian *thalis*, "the longest menu in town", quick efficient service. Highly recommended.

**TT Monalisa**, Western favourites.

**TT Pizza Place**, a bit grubby but oven fresh pizzas, lasagnas.

**TT Pizzeria Café Vaatika**, wonderful terrace on the Ganga, friendly staff, Italian and Indian food, excellent coffee.

**TT Poonam**, in Pradeep Hotel. Indian. Good variety, clean, smart professional staff, order banana lassi, *masala* dishes and finish with *Shahi tukra* .

**TT Spicy Bites**. Western snacks are good. *Nachos* are a treat, friendly service, travellers' notice board and newspapers. Recommended.

**TT Shivan's Magna**, 5/15 Tripura Bhairavi, T321945. Clean, plush, good value.

**T Alka**, Mir Ghat. Very good vegetarian, clean kitchen, friendly management.

**T Ashiana**, Clark Rd, Varuna Bridge. Indian and Chinese.

**T Babla**, Yadav Katra, Godoulia. Vegetarian, excellent spring rolls.

**Coffee House**, Bhelapura. Decent South Indian.
**Eats & Bites**, C21/4 Shri Ram Complex, Maldahiya, next to **Hindustan International Hotel**. International. Great food, excellent service, moderate prices.
**Kerala**, Bhelupura. Good vegetarian.
**Garden**, opposite Sushil Cinema, Godoulia. Indian, Chinese and continental. Excellent food (if a bit slow), pleasant rooftop, friendly.
**Jalayog**, Godoulia. Good, traditional veg breakfast, cheap Indian snacks and sweets.
**Sindhi**, Bhelupura, next to Lalita Cinema. Excellent Indian vegetarian, difficult for foreigners to get fully-sugared Indian chai.
**Sona Rupa**, Indian veg and Chinese. Large tables, quiet, good prices and service, but 'too much chilli in everything' for some.
**Street View**, Gai Ghat. Good breakfast, 'Ayurvedic tea' recommended, friendly owners.

**Allahabad** *p184, map p184*
**Allahbad Regency**, Tashkant Rd. Dinner served in garden of former hotel, standard menu but great ambience, live music, chilled beer and friendly waiters, recommended.
**El Chico**, 24 MG Marg. Good quality and wide choice, with bakery next door,
**Jade Garden**, **Tepso Hotel**, MG Marg. For upmarket Chinese.
**Kwality**, MG Marg. New upmarket café.
**Hot Stuff**, 15 Elgin Rd. Smart, fast food, also good ices.
**Tripti**, Katju Rd. Indian.

## Entertainment

**Varanasi** *p173, maps p174 and p177*
**Clarks Cultural Centre**, Peshwa Palace, Raj Ghat, in an old Brahmin refectory. Enquire at **Clarks Varanasi**, The Mall, T0542 250 1011 or at travel agents. Evening entertainment begins at sunset with *Ganga aarti* with floating of lamps, performance of music and dance; US$20 including pick-up from hotels 1730, return 2030. At dawn, witness prayers with chanting and singing; provides a vantage point for photographs. A funfair with big-wheel etc (safety not up to international standards) near GPO by the roundabout.

**Allahabad** *p184, map p184*
**Prayag Sangeet Samiti** presents music and dance programmes in the evenings.

## Festivals and events

**Varanasi** *p173, maps p174 and p177*
**Jan**: **Parswanath Jayanti** has an elephant drawn *rath* from Belunala to Bhelupura.
**Feb**: **Ganga Water Rally**, organized by UP Tourism, is an international and national kayak get-together from Allahabad to Chunar Fort. A 40-km race from Chunar to Varanasi takes place on the final day (6-8 Feb 2005). Also International Yoga Week (9-15 Feb 2005).
**Late Feb/early Mar**: 3 days at Sivaratri, festival of Dhrupad music attracts performers from near and far, beginners and stars, in a very congenial atmosphere, a wonderful experience. **Mar/Apr**: **Holi** is celebrated with great fervour. **Apr**: pilgrims walk around 'Kashi', as laid down in the scriptures. Jain *Mahavir Jayanti*. **Apr/May**: **Sankat Mochan Music Festival**, Sankat Mochan Mandir. Non-stop temple music, open to all (28 Apr-2 May 2005). **May**: **Ganga Dasara** celebrates the day the waters of the Ganga reached Haridwar. **Oct/Nov**: **Dasara** Ramlila at Ramnagar. **Ganga Festival** is organized by UP Tourism alongside a 10 day craft fair (12-15 Nov 2005). **Nagnathaiya** draws up to 50,000 worshippers to Tulsi Ghat, re-enacting the story of Krishna jumping into the Yamuna to overcome *Kalija*, the King of the Serpents (5 Nov 2005). **Nakkataiya** A fair at Chetganj recalling Rama's brother, Lakshmana, cutting off Ravana's sister's nose when she attempted to force him into a marriage! At Nati Imli, **Bharat Milap**, the meeting of Rama and Bharat after 14 years' separation is celebrated – the Maharaja of Varanasi attends in full regalia on elephant back.
**Dec-Feb**: Music festivals.

**Sarnath** *p180*
**May**: on first full-moon, **Buddha Jayanti** marks the Buddha's birthday. A fair is held and relics which are not on public display at any other time are taken out in procession.

**Allahabad** *p184, map p184*
**Jan/Feb**: **Magh** and **Kumbh Mela** in 2013. Also International Yoga Week (22-28 Jan 2005).

## Shopping

**Varanasi** *p173, maps p174 and p177*
Varanasi is famous for silks including brocades (Temple Bazar, Visvanath Gali), brassware, gold jewellery, *sitar* making and hand block printed goods.The main shopping areas are Chowk, Godoulia, Visvanath Gali, Gyanvapi and Thatheri Bazar.

### Books

**Ashok Hotel** has new and second-hand (especially 'coffee-table') books.
**City Bookshop**, opposite **Indica Books**, sells new and secondhand, will also buy, good value and very helpful.
**Harmony**, B1/100 Assi Ghat. Good selection including travel guides.
**Indica Books**, D 40/18 Godoulia, near crossing. Specialist Indological bookshop.
**Universal Book Co**, D40/60 Godoulia, nearby. Wide range of English language books.

### Handloom and handicrafts

**Ali Handicrafts** (Workers Village), C 19/19 A-5 Lallapura (between Varuna Hospital and Muslim School), T0542 235 5676. Wholesale shop for silk scarves, saris, excellent and much cheaper than most, personal callers welcome.
**Bhagwan Stores**, in Visvanath Gali and K37/32 Golghar. Recommended.
**Brijraman Das**, in Visvanath Gali and K37/32 Golghar. Recommended.
**Ganga Handlooms**, D10/18 Kohli Katra, off Viswanath Gali, near Golden Temple (ask locally). 1100-2000. Large selection of beautiful cotton fabrics, *ikats*, vegetable dyes, good tailors, great patterns (western).
**Mohan Silks**, in Visvanath Gali and K37/32 Golghar. Recommended.
**Muslim Silk Weaving Centre** is next door.
**Oriental Arts Emporium**, 10/252 Maqbool Alam Rd, Chauki Ghat.

## Activities and tours

**Varanasi** *p173, maps p174 and p177*

### Swimming

Pools at hotels **Taj Ganges**, **Hindustan** and **Clarks Varanasi** (Rs 150-200 for non-residents).

### Tour companies

**Sita**, RH Tower Building, 53 The Mall, T0542 234 4692, vns@sitaindia.com.
**TCI**, Sri Das Foundation, S20/51-5 & S20/52-4, The Mall, T0542 2505928, tcivaranasi@tci.co.in. Highly recommended.
**Touraids**, Nadesar, T0542 234 5627.
**Travel Bureau**, The Mall, Cantt, T0542 234 5330. Highly recommended.
**UP Roadways** Tour I: River trip, temples, Benaras Hindu University. **Tour II**: Sarnath and Ramnagar Fort. Daily, summer 1430-1825, winter 1400-1755. Starts from Tourist Bungalow, picking up from Govt of India Tourist Office, The Mall. Tickets on bus.
**Varuna**, Pandey Haveli, near Bank of India (Old City), T0542 239 3568. All ticketing (Rs 200 for reconfirmation!); also tours.

### Yoga and meditation

**Vag Yoga Consciousness Society**, B3/13A Shivala, T0542 231 1706.
**Yoga Institute**, BHU, T0542 230 7208.

**Allahabad** *p184, map p184*
**Mayo Hall Complex**, one of the largest training centres in India for table tennis, basketball, badminton and volleyball.
**Krishna**, Bai-ka-Bagh, T0532 260 4121, tours.
**Varuna**, Civil Lines, T0532 2624323, tours.

## Transport

**Varanasi** *p173, maps p174 and p177*

### Air

Transport to town by bus to **Indian Airlines**, Tourist Office, top hotels and railway station. Tickets for bus from Arrival Hall, Rs 20, or from **Indian Airlines**, T0542 234 3746. Departs from tourist office 1030, 1200, 1430; from airport, 30-45 mins after each flight. Transfer by taxi, a/c Rs 300, non-a/c Rs 200. Some taxis offer free transfer and claim a commission from hotel on arrival. **Indian Airlines**, 52 Yadunath Marg, Cantt, T0542 234 5959, airport, T0542 234 3746, www.indian-airlines.nic.in, flies daily to **Delhi** via **Khajuraho** and **Agra**; to **Bhubaneswar**, Tue, Thu, Sat, Sun; to **Mumbai** via **Lucknow**, Mon, Wed, Fri. **Kathmandu**, daily. Indian Airlines flights originating in Delhi are subject to severe delays in Jan and Feb because of fog. Try to get a direct flight from Delhi. **Jet Airways**, S20/56D Kennedy Rd, The

Mall, T0542 250 6444 (airport T0542 262 2544), www.jetairways.com, flies to Delhi daily. **Sahara**, Mint House, opposite Taj Ganges, T0542 250 7572 (airport T0542 262 2334), www.airsahara.net, flies to and from **Delhi**, **Lucknow** and **Mumbai**, daily except Sun.

### Bicycle

Cycle and motorcycle hire: near **Hotel Hindustan International**, Maldahiya.

### Boat

This is the best way to enjoy Varanasi. It is necessary to bargain especially for the early morning ghats visit (1 hr): shared boat: Rs 50 per hr is the official rate for a small boat carrying up to 4 people, larger boats Rs 75. Ask around for others to share boat; river crossing about Rs 5. A boat ride at dusk is also recommended.

### Bus

Local buses cover most of Varanasi but crowded. UP Roadways Bus Stand, Sher Shah Suri Marg, is near the railway station, Cantt, open 24 hrs, T0542 2203476. Reservations for deluxe buses to Allahabad. Buses to **Sarnath**, 9 km, Rs 5 (see Excursions below). Frequent services to **Allahabad**, 122 km, 4 hrs; **Gorakhpur**, 7 hrs; **Jaunpur**, 1 hr, Rs 30. Also to **Delhi**, daily, via **Khajuraho and Agra**; **Lucknow** 286 km (0745, 1515), 9 hrs. Private buses stop opposite the railway station. **Khajuraho**: 565 km, 1600 bus to Rewa (night stop); next day change bus at Satna. **Gaya**: better by rail.

### Rickshaw

Tempos and auto-rickshaws usually run on fixed routes; those near hotel gates over-charge (fix the fare before hiring). They are not allowed in the narrow streets of the old city but will go to Godoulia in the centre or to Dasasvamedha Ghat, Rs 20-25 from station.

### Taxi

Unmetered taxis. Private taxis from agents and hotels. Full day (90 km; 8 hrs), a/c Rs 1000, non a/c Rs 600-800; basic rate per km about a/c Rs 86, non a/c Rs 64.

### Train

Beware: the large 'Tourist Information Counter' at Junction station run by travel agents adds large commissions to rail tickets.

Most trains stop at the **Junction (or Cantonment) Station**, T0542 234 8031 or 131 with 24-hr left luggage; to reach a Cantt hotel on foot, use the back exit. Can be very crowded; use a retiring room if you have a long wait. **Mughal Sarai** station, T0542 225 5703, has the Delhi/Kolkata *Rajdhani Exp* (though some go via Patna); see below. Get your tickets (preferably a day in advance) from the **Foreign Tourist Assistance** inside the main hall which is very helpful and efficient, passport required (0800-2200, Sun 0800-1400). When it is closed use the computerized railway reservations (0800-1400, 1430-2000). **Agra Fort**: *Marudhar Exp, 4853/4863*, 1725/1835, 12½ /11¼ hrs (book ahead); or go to Tundla from Mughal Sarai (see below). **Allahabad**: *Mahanagari Exp, 1094*, 1130, 3½ hrs; *Sarnath Exp, 4260*, 1230, 2¾ hrs; *Kamayani Exp, 1072*, 1550, 3¾ hrs. **Chennai**: *Ganga-Kaveri Exp, 6040*, 1745, Mon, Wed, 41 hrs, reserve early. **Dehra Dun**: *Varanasi Dehra Dun Exp, 4265*, 0840, 24¼ hrs. **Gaya**: *Dehra Dun Exp, 3010*, 1615, 5¼ hrs. **Gorakhpur** (for Nepal): *Krishak Exp, 5002*, 1630, 5½ hrs; *Manduadih Gorakhpur Exp*, 5104A, 0550, 5¼ hrs; **Jaunpur**: *Sutlej Doon Exp 3307*, 0640 1¼ hr; *Farakka Exp, 3483*, 1230, 50 mins. **Kanpur**: *Neelachal Exp, 8475*, 0742, Mon, Wed, Sat, 7¼ hrs; **Kolkata** (**H**): *Amritsar-Howrah Mail, 3006*, 1650, 14¾ hrs; *Doon Exp, 3010*, 1615, 14¾ hrs. **Lucknow**: *Varuna Exp, 4227*, 0510, 4¾ hrs; *Kashi-Visvanath Exp, 4257*, 1410, 6½ hrs. **Mahoba** (for *Khajuraho*): *Bundelkhand Exp, 1108*, 1330, 12¼ hrs (onward bus, 0600). **Satna** (for *Khajuraho*): *Satna Mahanagari Exp, 1094*, 1130, 6½ hrs (from Satna, bumpy bus next day, 4 hrs). **Mumbai** (CST): *Varanasi Lokmanya Tilak Exp, 1066*, 2025, Tue, Thu, Sun, 25¾ hrs. **New Delhi**: *Lichchavi Exp, 5205*, 1500, 13½ hrs; *Shramjeevi Exp, 2401*, 1520, 14¼ hrs. **Mughal Sarai** station (with retiring rooms and left luggage). Take a connecting train from Varanasi (45 mins), or allow plenty of time as you need to cross the Ganga and there are huge jams. Best to take a taxi from Varanasi as buses are not dependable and a rickshaw would feel very vulnerable next to the speeding juggernauts. **Agra**: *Marudhar Exp, 1725*, 13 hrs. **Kolkata (H)**: *Rajdhani Exp, 2302/2422*, 0235, 8-10 hrs; *Kalka Howrah Mail, 2312*, 2030, 10½ hrs. **New Delhi**: *Poorva Exp, 2381/2303*, 1910/2045, Wed, Thu, Sun, 13/11½ hrs; *Neelanchal Exp, 8475*, 0655, Mon, Wed, Sat, 14½ hrs; *Rajdhani Exp, 2301/5*, 0050, 9¼ hrs. **New Jalpaiguri** (for Darjeeling): *Mahananda Exp, 4084*, 2120, 18½ hrs; *NE Exp, 5622*, 1835, 16 hrs and to **Guwahati**, 24¼ hrs.

**Transport to Nepal**

Payment for Nepalese visa at border in cash only (preferably US dollars, but normally accept Indian or Nepalese); TCs are not accepted.

To **Kathmandu**, the journey requires an overnight stay near the border plus about 20 hrs on the road so can be tiring. UP Roadways buses go via **Gorakhpur** to **Sonauli**, depart 4 or 5 times per day, check for timings (usually early morning or night), 0300, 0400, 0930, 2130 (9-10 hrs), Rs 130; from Sonauli, 0600; (Lumbini is 386 km). Private buses (agents near UP *Tourist Bungalow*), often demand inclusive fares for hotel stay; you may prefer to opt for their deluxe buses to the border. Well organized bus service by **Paul Travels**, near *Tourist Bungalow*, Rs 400; departs 0800, overnight in basic hotel (breakfast); next morning, departs 0830 (10-11 hrs). See page 37.

**Sarnath** *p180, map p181*

Infrequent bus service; also included in coach tours. From Varanasi, bus from opposite railway station (Rs 5), sometimes stops opposite **Taj Hotel**. Auto-rickshaws (Rs 50), tempo seat (Rs 10). The road is bumpy; cycling is not recommended as trucks travel along it at great speed. Taxis take 30 mins (Rs 400 including wait).

**Jaunpur** *p182, map p182*

**Bus**

Frequent service along NH56 to/from **Varanasi** and **Lucknow** including *Express* (under 2 hrs). Ask to be dropped at the Akbari Bridge (crossroads north of the bus stand) where you can pick up a cycle rickshaw.

**Taxi**

From Varanasi, Rs 850 return.

**Train**

To **Varanasi** *Sutlej Exp, 3308*, 1820, 2 hrs; *Varuna Exp, 4228*, 2200.

**Allahabad** *p184, map p184*

**Bus**

UP Roadways and other state RTCs link Allahabad with **Delhi** (643 km), **Gwalior**, **Jaunpur**, **Jhansi** (375 km), **Kanpur**, **Lucknow** (204 km), **Meerut**, **Patna** (368 km), **Rewa**, **Sasaram** and **Varanasi** (122 km). **Roadways Bus Stands**: Civil Lines, T0532 2601257; Zero Rd, T0532 240 0192; Leader Rd (south gate of Junction station), T0532 261 5625. **Private** bus stands at Ram Bagh and Leader Rd for luxury coaches to **Lucknow** and **Varanasi**.

**Train**

Allahabad is on the major broad gauge route from Delhi to Kolkata but also has metre gauge trains. Allahabad Junction, T0532 260 0179, to avoid long queues use ticket booth on the north side. Prayag (broad gauge trains for Kanpur and Lucknow) with Left Luggage; **Allahabad City** T0532 260 6878(mostly for Varanasi); **Daraganj** (metre gauge). **Jabalpur**: *Patna Lokmanya Tilak Exp, 3201*, 0830, 6½ hrs; *Varanasi Lokmanya Tilak Exp, 2166*, 2330, Tue, Fri, Sun, 5½ hrs. **Jhansi**: *Bundelkhand Exp, 1108*, 1830, 12½ hrs. **Lucknow**: *Ganga-Gomti Exp, 2415*, 0600, 3½ hrs (2nd class only); *Nauchandi/Link Exp, 4011/4511*, 1730, 5 hrs. **Kolkata**: *Kalka-Howrah Mail, 2312*, 1730, 13¼ hrs; *Rajdhani Exp, 2302*, 0023, 10¼ hrs. **Mumbai** (CST): *Bombay Mail, 3003*, 1110, 24¼ hrs; *Mahanagiri Exp, 1094*, 1505, 24¼ hrs. (Lokmanya Tilak). **New Delhi**: *Prayagraj Exp, 2417*, 2130, 10½ hrs; *Poorva Exp, 2303/2381*, 2255, 9¼ hrs. **Patna**: *Magadh Exp, 2392*, 0500, 6¼ hrs; *Udyan Abha-Toofan Exp, 3008*, 2230, 7 hrs; *Howrah Quila Exp, 3112*, 1025, 8½ hrs. **Varanasi**: *Varanasi Kashi Exp, 1027*, 0845, 4 hrs; *Sarnath Exp, 4259*, 1305, 3 hrs; *Bundelkhand Exp, 1107*, 0640, 3¼ hrs.

## Directory

**Varanasi** *p173, maps p174 and p177*
**Banks** Most banks refuse to change money. Travellers are often stopped and asked for 'change'. **State Bank of India** at **Hotel Kashika** (Mon-Fri 1000-1400) T0542 234 3742, and **Godoulia** (near **Indica Books**), takes approximately 1 hr, changes Visa, TCs. Also at **Clarks Varanasi** and at airport. **Radiant Services**, D48/139A Misir Pokhra (by Mazda Cinema), Luxa Road, Godoulia, T0542 235 8852. Daily 0700-2200, changes TCs and 36 currencies, "long-winded but faster than a bank". Also has a 24-hr counter at **Shanti Guest House**, T0542 239 2017, and Cantt Office, above **Union Bank of India**, on the Mall, T0542 251 1052. Shops changing money offer a poor rate.
**Hospitals** **Chemists**: near hospitals. **Heritage Hospital, Lanka**, T0542 231 3977. Private hospital, out-patients 0830-2000. **BHU Hospital**, T0542 230 7542. **RK Mission Hospital**, Luxa, T0542 232 1727. **SSPG Hospital**, Kabir Chaura Rd, T0542 233 3723.
**Internet** In lane near Dasasvamedha Ghat, well signed. Several others, **The Messenger**, Temple Kashi Karvat, in the lanes. 7 terminals, Rs 30 per hr is recommended. **Astro Travel**, B1/108 Assi Ghat, for STD/ISD and email. **Post** **Head Post Office**: Bisheshwarganj (parcel packing outside). Post office in Cantt, post Mon-Sat 1000-1800, telegraph 0930-1630. A man offers to 'help' get a parcel posted for a fee (Rs 100), but you can do this yourself! A convenient PO is in an alley opposite **Garden Restaurant** in Godoulia. **Couriers**: **City Airlinkers**, Cantt, T0542 234 4214. **First Flight**, Jagatganj.
**Tourist offices** UP, Tourist Bungalow, Parade Kothi, T0542 220 8162. 1000-1700, closed Sun, very helpful, Japanese spoken. **Counter**, Cantt Railway Station, near 'Enquiry', T0542 234 6370. 0600-2000, very helpful information and map. **Govt of India**, 15B The Mall, Cantt, T/F0542 250 1784. 0900-1800, closed Sun, well run, very helpful manager and staff; **guides** available, about Rs 250 (half day), Rs 380 (full day) depending on group size. **Counter**, Babatpur Airport. **Bihar**, Englishiya Market, Cantt, T0542 222 3821. 0800-2000. **Useful addresses** **Ambulance**: T0542 233 3723. **Fire**: T101, T0542 232 2888. **Police**: T100. **Foreigners' Registration Office**: Sidh Giri Bagh (not easy to find), T0542 235 1968. **Language courses**: week long 'Tourist Hindi' courses, next to **Shanti Guest House**, Manikarnika Ghat.

**Allahabad** *p184, map p184*
**Banks** **Bank of India**, 10 Sardar Patel Marg, T0532 262 4834. **Hospitals** **Dufferin**, Hospital Chowk, T0532 265 1822. **Motilal Nehru**, Colvin, T0532 265 2141. **Tourist office** **Hotel Illawart**, 35 MG Marg, T0532 260 1440

# Uttaranchal

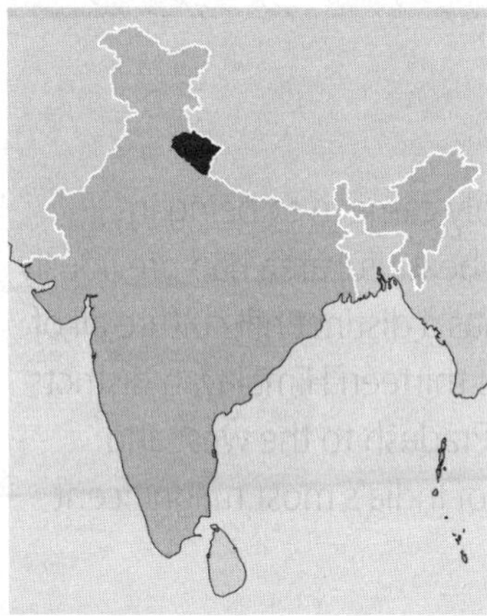



## Footprint features

# Introduction

Uttaranchal, India's 27th state, only came in to being in November 2000. This stunningly beautiful area had previously been part of Uttar Pradesh, but has a distinct hill culture all of its own. The new state comprises thirteen Himalayan districts sandwiched between Himachal Pradesh to the west and Nepal to the east, and has some of India's most magnificent mountain scenery.

It stretches from the densely populated foothills up to the heights of the Nanda Devi range, containing outstandingly beautiful yet relatively little-known trekking routes. Had it not been for the fact that this region of the Himalayas was closed in 1960 due to political troubles with China, it may well have become a trekking destination as popular as Nepal; the mountain scenery and routes on offer are certainly comparable.

The state also contains some of India's holiest shrines; Haridwar and Rishikesh have long attracted pilgrims from the world over, and many of the most beautiful treks are in fact age old pilgrimage routes, while Almora and Nanital offer cool holiday resorts in the hills, and Corbett National Park the chance to see tigers and elephants in the wild.

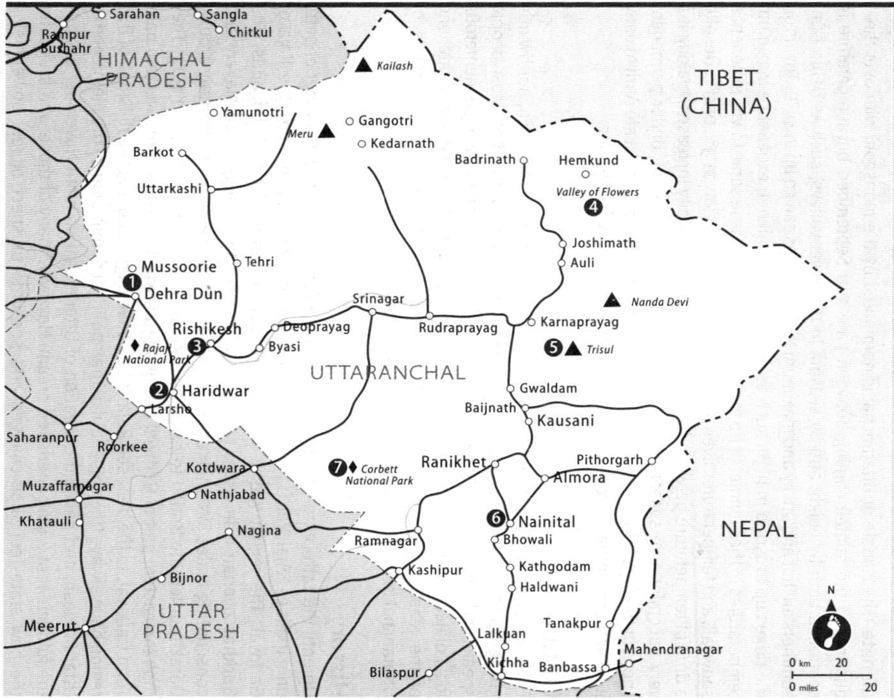

## ★Don't miss...

1 **Landour** Escape the heat of the plains by heading up to this hill station with its fresh, clean, pine-scented air, page 203.

2 **Haridwar** Watch priests performing spectacular Ganga aarti at sunset, said to be one of the oldest cities in the world, page 209.

3 **Rishikesh** Chill in an ashram and follow in the tracks of the Beatles and the Maharishi Mahesh Yogi, page 211.

4 **Valley of Flowers** If time is tight, trek this area, filled not only with flowers but waterfalls, wildlife, glaciers and forests too, page 224.

5 **Curzon Trail** Walk this incomparably beautiful trek. Taking 10 days, it crosses the Kuari Pass, said to be one of the finest vantage points in the Himalaya, page 234.

6 **Naintal** Have a few days rest at tis charming hill station and vist the atmospheric British cemetery, page 236.

7 **Corbett National Park** Unquestionably the highlight of the area, tiger-spotting, page 245.

# Background → *Population: 8½ mn. Area: 53,480 sq km.*

## The land

**Geography** The extraordinarily contorted geology of the Garhwal and Kumaon Himalaya reflects the fierce uplifting and the complex movements which have taken place since the Himalaya began to be formed. The outer ranges of the Siwaliks, generally less than 2500 m high, are a jumble of deeply dissected sediments. In places these are separated from the Lesser Himalayan ranges by great longitudinal valleys, or *duns*, such as Dehra Dun, while in the Lesser Himalaya immediately to their north, towns such as Mussoorie, Almora and Nainital offer coolness in the summer from the overpowering heat of the plains. Immediately to their north again the high peaks are surrounded by deep valleys, at their heads still some of the world's largest glaciers. Some meteorologists predict that the Himalaya will be glacier-free within 30 years or so. This is not the result of recent global warming, but the latest phase in the 10,000 year retreat of the latest northern hemisphere Ice Age. Glaciers such as the Milam, still several kilometres long, are covered in boulders, and float over the masses of material which have been dropped by glaciers too shrunk to move it any further. Forming a massive barrier to their north are the permanent snows and high peaks such as **Nanda Devi** (7,816 m), **Shivling** (6543 m) and other peaks over 6,000 m.



**Climate** The climate of Uttaranchal is dominated by the monsoon, with over three quarters of the rainfall coming between June and September, but temperature is controlled both by height and by season. In the lower valleys, such as Dehra Dun, summers are hot and sticky and maximum temperatures can go up to 45°C. Towns on the ridges up to 2,000 m high, such as Almora and Ranikhet, experience maximum temperatures in the summer of up to 34°C. Yet in winter these same towns experience snow fall, and temperatures even in the outer valleys are as low as 3°C or 4°C. Despite a drop of temperature between June and September humidity increases, making it a very uncomfortable season in the foothills. The high peaks are under permanent snow. In the higher hills the air is always fresh but can be very cold. Late April to early June and September-October are generally the best times for trekking.

## Culture

Ethnically, on the plains the inhabitants are largely of Indo-Aryan origin, northwards giving way to strong Mongoloid influences on the border with Tibet. Most people speak Hindi, but Urdu is still quite widely used among Muslims. There are numerous local dialects. In Uttaranchal Garhwali and Kumaoni (hill) dialects predominate, one of the reasons given by the residents for the creation of a separate state of Uttaranchal in the Himalayan region of Uttar Pradesh.

## History

Up until the 14th century Garhwal (Land of the Forts) comprised a number of petty principalities. Ajai Pal (1358-1370) consolidated these and became the Raja of Garhwal. The region was a popular plundering ground for Sikh brigands. The **Gurkhas** overran it in 1803, taking men, women and children into slavery and conscripting males into their army. Gurkha encroachments on the territory around Gorakhpur led the British to expel them from Garhwal and Kumaon in 1814. They took the eastern part of Garhwal as British Garhwal and returned the western part, Tehri Garhwal, to the deposed Raja. It has been suggested that the hillsmen of this region have always been resentful of their political domination by the plainsmen of Uttar Pradesh, and hence the creation of Uttaranchal on ninth November 2000 is the fulfillment of a long cherished dream. However, many of those who fought for the new state feel short-changed and see little prospect of real power being transferred to the hills people. Having realised their ambition for a separate 'Uttarakhand', the new state's name of Uttaranchal was a political decision by the ruling BJP party. The new State Assembly has been formed initially by the transfer of Members of the Uttar Pradesh Legislative Assembly who represent Uttaranchal constituencies. In the first state elections, held in February 2002, the Congress swept the BJP from power, and the veteran Congress leader ND Tiwari became Chief Minister. The question of the capital is still contentious. Dehra Dun has initially been given the status of 'interim capital', but there are still demands that it should be transferred to Gairsain, a hill town in the heart of the new state.

### Economy

Scattered farming villages among picturesque terraces present the skill with which Uttaranchal's mountain people have adapted to their hill environment. Agriculture is still by far the most important economic activity for people throughout the hills, often carried out with apparent simplicity but considerable sophistication, both of engineering and of cropping types. On many of the cultivated hillsides terracing is essential and wonderfully intricate, and a wide variety of crops are grown – paddy, wheat, barley and lentils on the low lying irrigated terraces, sugar cane, chillies, buckwheat and millets higher up. Market gardening and potato cultivation have spread around all the townships. Rotation of crops is widely practised and intensive use of animal manure helps to fertilise the soil. The terraces themselves, sometimes as high as 6-m, may have as many as 500 flights, and some villages have up to 6,000 individual terraces. Given that it takes one man a day to build a wall a 1-m high and 2-m long, it is easy to see what vast amounts of labour have gone into their construction, and how much care is lavished on their maintenance, for they are the peoples' security.

The forests also supply vital wealth. Apart from the timber itself resin is often a valuable export, and wood carving is a widely practised skill. Today tourism is an increasingly important source of income, and comprises of Indian visitors from the plains and foreigners seeking to experience something of the high Himalayan ranges. Tourism is believed to bring in approximately US$50 million a year, and horticulture, fruit cultivation and the production of medicinal plants are potentially of great value, though transport remains a huge problem. While the new state has massive hydroelectric potential its development is highly controversial. The Tehri Dam has been the focus of intense opposition from environmental campaigners for over 20 years, and while that project is now nearing completion other schemes may be very difficult to promote, despite the rapidly growing demand for electricity on the plains.

# The eastern hill stations

## Dehra Dun → *Phone code: 0135. Colour map 1, grid B4. Population: 370,000.*

Dehra Dun (dera – camp; dun – valley, pronounced 'doon'), lies in a wooded valley in the Shiwalik Hills. In Hindu legend the Dun Valley was part of Siva's stamping ground. Rama and his brother are said to have done penance for killing Ravana, and the five Pandavas stopped here on their way to the mountains. It makes a pleasant and relaxing stop on the way to the hills, and its mild climate has made it a popular retirement town. The cantonment, across the seasonal Bindal Rao River, is spacious and well wooded, while the Mussoorie road is lined with very attractive houses.

›› *For Sleeping, Eating and other listings, see pages 205-209.*

## Ins and outs

**Getting there** The railway station, off Haridwar Rd to the south of town, has trains from Delhi, Varanasi and Kolkata. Buses heading for the Mussoorie and the Garhwal hills use the Mussoorie Bus Stand outside the station, while those bound for the plains and the Kumaon hills use the Delhi Bus Stand near Hotel Drona, 500 m away. Share taxis operate services to the hills from the stand outside the railway station.

**Getting around** The City Bus Stand, also used by private buses, is just north of the Clock Tower in the busy town centre, about 10 mins on foot from the railway station. Although the town centre is compact it is best to get a taxi or auto-rickshaw for visiting the various sights which are between 4-8 km (10-20 minutes ride) away. » *See Transport, page 208, for further details.*

## History

A third-century BC Asoka rock inscription found near Kalsi suggests that the area was ruled by the emperor. During the 17th and 18th centuries Dehra Dun changed hands several times. The Gurkhas overran it on the westward expansion from Kumaon to Kangra, finally ceding it to the British in 1815 who developed it as a centre of education and research. It is still a major centre for government institutions like the Survey of India and for the Indian Army, and in November 2000 it became the



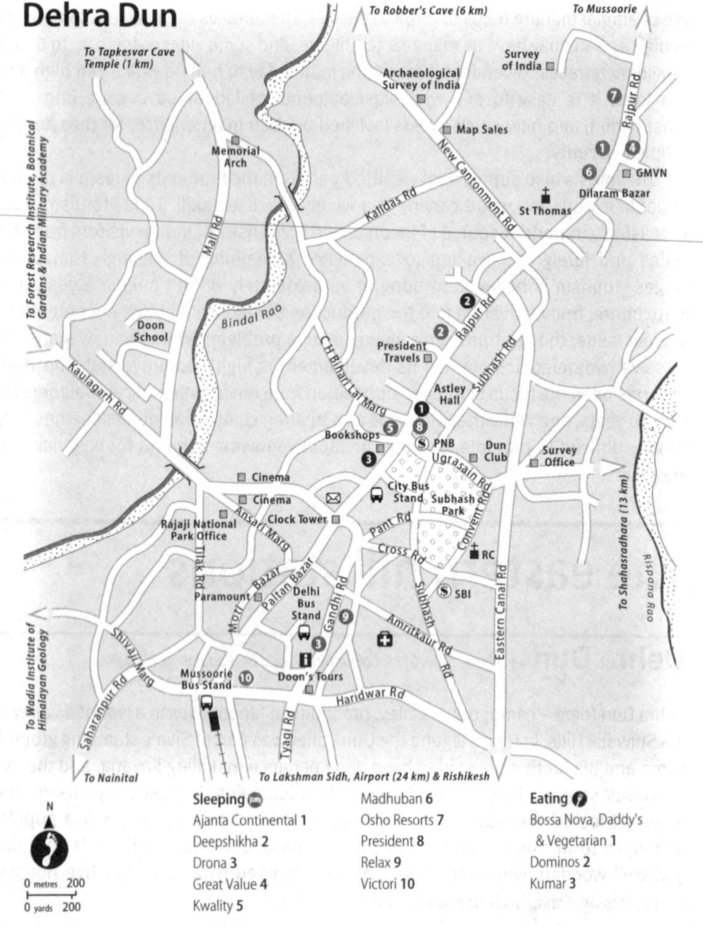

provisional state capital of Uttaranchal though many hill-dwellers consider it too close to sea-level to reflect the mountainous nature of the new state.



## Sights

The **Survey of India,** founded in 1767, has its headquarters on Rajpur Road, about 4 km from the Clock Tower. The **Doon School**, off Kaulagarh Road, India's first public school, is still one of its most prestigious. Further along, the highly regarded **Forest Research Institute** (1914), an impressive red-brick building which was designed by Lutyens, is surrounded by the fine lawns of the Botanical Gardens and forests. It has excellent museums which are open from 0900 to 1730 on weekdays. The **Royal Indian Military College** (1922), in quaint mock Tudor style and the Indian Military Academy (1932), which opened with 40 cadets now takes 1,200.

The **Tapkesvar Cave Temple** ⓘ *open sunrise to sunset, buses stop 500 m from the temple*, 5 km northwest, is in a pleasant setting with cool sulphur springs for bathing. There is a simple Indian café nearby.

**Robber's Cave** (8 km), **Lakshman Sidh** (12 km), the snows at **Chakrata** (9 km) and sulphur springs at **Shahasradhara** (14 km) are also within easy reach. The springs were threatened by limestone quarrying on the hills around until the High Court forced their closure. Replanting of the deforested hills has been allowing the water table and the springs to recover.

# Saharanpur

Saharanpur, 67 km south of Dehra Dun, actually in Uttar Pradesh, is famous for carved wood furniture. It was founded in 1340 as a summer retreat for the Mughals. During the British period it became an important military base but the Government also set out **Botanical Gardens** in 1817. The **Eastern Yamuna Canal,** one of the first great 19th-century canals to irrigate the Ganga-Yamuna doab, transformed the landscape of what had been a heavily overpopulated region. It has become a particularly important source of fruit trees for the whole of India. The **Mango Festival** is held in June/July when hundreds of varieties are displayed. Watch woodcarvers at work in Lakdi Bazar and the old market place.

# Mussoorie and Landour → *Phone code: 01362. Colour map 1, grid B4.*

*Population: 30,000. Altitude: 1,970 m.*

Mussoorie, named after the Himalayan shrub mansoor, has commanding views over the Doon Valley to the south and towards the High Himalaya to the north. It is spread out over 16 km along a horseshoe-shaped ridge up to which run a series of buttress-like subsidiaries. Being the nearest hill station to Delhi, it is very popular with Indian tourists though no longer as clean as it was once, and it has nothing over other hill stations. Landour, another 300 m higher and away from the crowds, by contrast has fresh, pine-scented air. ▸▸ *For Sleeping, Eating and other listings, see pages 205-209.*

## Ins and outs

**Getting there** Other than trekking in 7 km, the 30 km road from Dehra Dun (just under 1¾ hours away by bus) is the only way to the town, arriving at the library (west end of the long Mall) or the Masonic Lodge bus stand (east end). Buses from Delhi take six to seven hours.

**Getting around** Taxis are available for longer journeys, including the steep climb up to Landour but for local trips cycle rickshaws are available or you can hire a bike. ▸▸ *See Transport, page 208, for further details.*

## Sights

Captain Young 'discovered' Mussoorie in 1826 and it developed as an escape from the heat of the plains for the British troops. **Landour**, at 2,270 m, to the east has the old barracks area. The first British residence was built here which was followed by The Mall, Club, Christ Church (1837) and the library. It makes a really nice walk up through the woods and away from the pressing crowds of The Mall. There are good views, though the weather changes very quickly. 'Char Dukan' is a small junction in the cantonment area with two snack bar / shops and a very reliable post office; the road to the right leads to the **International Language School** and the one to the left to **Lal Tibba** – a nice view point with binoculars. The Woodstock School and the Language School are in a magnificent location, and some of the guesthouses have stunning views. To the west are Convent Hill, **Happy Valley** where Tibetan refugees have settled (the school there may welcome volunteers to teach English), and the pleasant **Municipal Garden**. Mall Road connects Kulri and Library Bazars. Camel's Back and Cart Roads also connect the two, but more circuitously.

## Walks

From the tourist office, **Lal Tibba** and nearby **Childe's Lodge** on the highest hill, are 5 km away. **Gun Hill**, where before Independence a midday gun fire enabled residents to set their watches, with a 400 m ropeway costing Rs 30 return, open from 0900-1900, can be reached by a bridle path in 20 minutes on horse back from the Kutchery on The Mall; the view of the snow-capped peaks is stunning and best at sunrise, although the mess of souvenir stalls, cafés and photographers later in the day may not appeal to all. The **Camel's Back Road**, from Kulri to the library, is a very pleasant 3-km walk.

## Excursions

**Kempty Falls**, 15 km on the Chakrata Road, is pretty and a popular picnic spot. A taxi is about Rs 250 with a one hour stop. Heading to **Dhanolti**, 25 km away, you can go on a

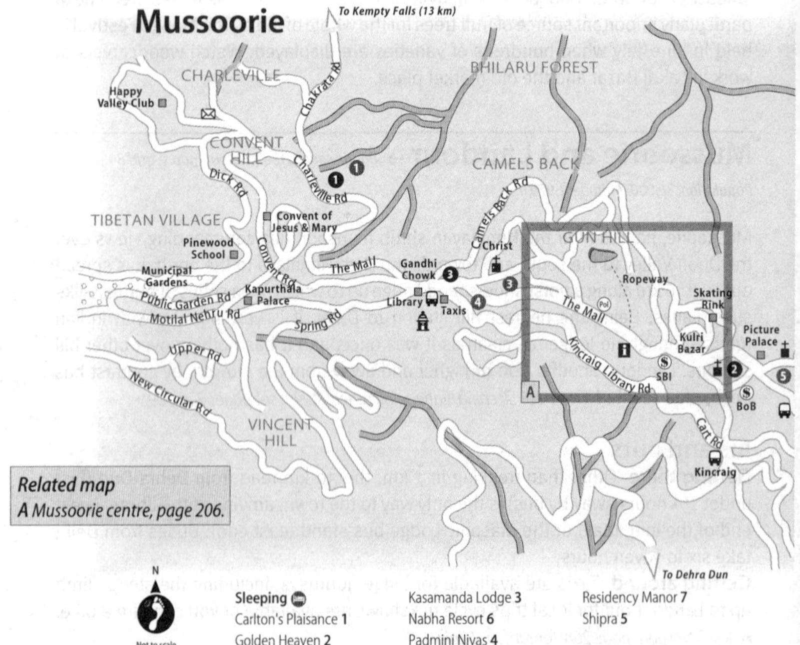


Related map
A Mussoorie centre, page 206.

further 3 km to find the **Surkhanda Devi Temple** at 3,030 m. There are superb views of several high peaks over 6,500 m. A taxi is Rs 600 with a two- to three-hour stop. Buses between Mussoorie and Chamba take you within 2 km of the hill top.

## Sleeping

### Dehra Dun *p201, map p202*

There are good discounts out of season (Aug-Feb). The cheaper hotels are near the station and the Clock Tower; the upmarket ones are north, along Rajpur Rd.

**A Madhuban** (Best Western), 97 Rajpur Rd, T0135 274 9990,www.hotelmadhuban.com. 60 rooms, good restaurants, pleasant garden, comfortable though rather characterless, but friendly staff, excellent views.

**A-B Great Value Dehradun** (Clarks), 74C Rajpur Rd, 4 km from the railway station, T0135 274 4086, www.greatvaluehotel.com. 53 pleasant a/c rooms (some upgraded), restaurant (Indian classical singing, evenings), business centre, modern, clean, good service, lives up to its name. Recommended.

**B Ajanta Continental**, 101 Rajpur Rd, T0135 274 9595, hotelajanta@hotmail.com. 29 rooms, good restaurant and bar, pool, pleasant ambience.

**B President**, 6 Astley Hall, Rajpur Rd, T0135 265 7082, prestrav@sancharnet.in. 22 a/c rooms, good restaurant, bar, coffee shop, exchange, travel, golf and riding arranged, pleasant service.

**B-C Osho Resorts**, 111 Rajpur Rd, T0135 274 9544, satish2@sancharnet.in. 20 clean, cottage rooms attached to the ashram, friendly staff.

**C Relax**, 7 Court Rd, T0135 265 7776, htl@nde.vsnl.net.in. 27 a/c or air-cooled rooms, all clean, okay restaurant, bar, operation overpriced.

**C-D Deepshikha**, 57/1 Rajpur Rd, T0135 265 9888, F271 0990. 22 rooms (some a/c), restaurant, pleasant, modern.

**D Kwality**, 19 Rajpur Rd, T0135 265 7001. 17 large rooms, some a/c, some singles, a bit ragged around the edges but OK, reasonable restaurant, bar.

**E-F Victoria**, opposite station, T0135 262 3486. 32 simple rooms, some with bath, clean linen, 24-hr check out, safe, friendly.

### Saharanpur *p203*

**C-D Taj**, near Clock Tower Chowk.

**D Swagat**, near Clock Tower Chowk, a modest business hotel.

### Mussoorie and Landour

*p203, maps p204 and p206*

Some hotels are old-fashioned but full of character. There are also a string of modern **B-C** hotels to the west of Gandhi Chowk on The Mall and Motilal Nehru Rd. The Mall is closed to cars and buses in the high season. You may have to walk to your hotel; porters are available at the bus stands. Prices are based on high-season tariffs, which are often quite ridiculous; most offer big off-season discounts, offering more realistic value for money. Most hotels check out at 1000. The options below are situated in Mussoorie unless stated in the address.

**AL Residency Manor**, Barlow Ganj, 4 km southeast of town, T0135 263 1800, www.jaypeehotels.com. Although a long walk, the 90 rooms are smart, large and impressive.

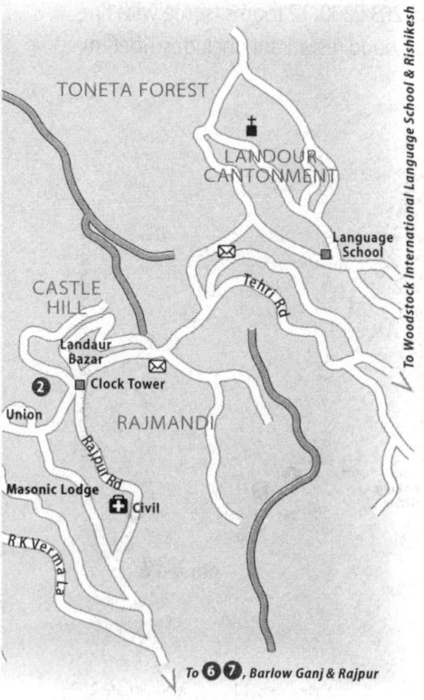

**Eating**
Coffee House 1
Tavern 2
Whispering Windows, Swiss Café & City Point 3

**AL-A Nabha Resort** (Claridge's), Airfield, Barlow Ganj Rd, 2 km town centre, T0135 263 1426, www.claridges.com. 22 rooms with verandah arranged around attractive garden in converted hill 'palace', superb views, excellent management, single storey, Raj style but with all modern comforts. Highly recommended.

**A-B Connaught Castle**, The Mall, T0135 263 2210. 29 comfortable rooms, restaurant, 50% off-season discount.

**A-B Kasamanda Palace Hotel** (Heritage), near The Mall, T0135 263 2424, www.welcomheritage.com. 14 comfortable rooms, once Basset Hall of the Christ Church complex (built 1836), a British sanatorium, then royal guesthouse from 1915, interesting furnishings (hunting trophies, bric-a-brac), 2 dining rooms, peaceful, spacious grounds (putting green, croquet), one of the better options but small off-season discount. Steep climb from Mall Rd so call for jeep transfer.

**B Filigree**, Camel's Back Rd, Kulri, T0135 263 2380, www.filigreehotel.com. 18 rooms, some well equipped, good restaurant, terrace with views. Uninspiring exterior but recommended.

**B Mall Palace**, The Mall, T0135 263 2097, mallpalace@rediffmail.com. 25 reasonable rooms with views, some tubs, clean, comfortable, friendly.

**B Padmini Nivas**, Library, The Mall, T0135 263 1093, www.hotelpadmininivas.com. 27 rooms in former palace with character, some with good views, also (**A**) cottages, not grand but pleasant ambience, good restaurant (pure veg Gujarati).

**B Shipra**, The Mall, T0135 263 2662, gmmussoorie@shiprahotel.com. 80 comfortable rooms in modern hotel, some with views, lift, restaurant.

**B-C Cloud End Forest Resort**, 7 km from town, T0135 263 2242, F263 0822. 7 rooms with bath in colonial period lodge. Home-cooked meals, rustic (bucket water), fabulous views.

**B-C Cherub Inn**, The Mall, T0135 263 2794. 19 reasonable rooms, no restaurant, modern, clean, best with views.

**B-C Golden Heaven**, near clock tower, Landour, T0135 263 3319. 12 rooms plus a cottage, reasonably clean, TV, hot water, good value off-season.

**C Dhanolti Breeze**, Rauslikhal, Kanatal, 5 km from the Surkhanda Devi Temple. Comfortable rooms.

**C Garhwal Terrace** (GMVN), The Mall near Ropeway, T0135 263 2682. 24 simple but clean rooms, dorm (Rs 130), restaurant, reasonable maintenance, excellent views.

**C-D Carlton's Plaisance**, Charleville Rd, T0135 263 2800. 12 rooms (some with fine views), good restaurant (includes Tibetan),

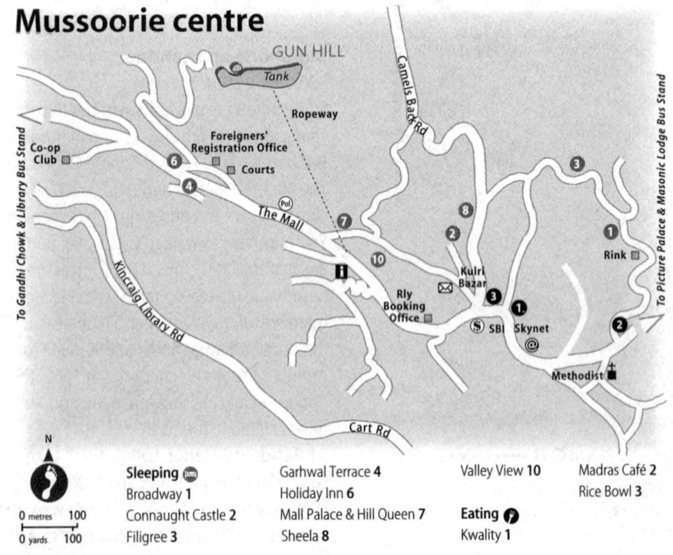

very Victorian with period furniture, peaceful orchard, spacious, charming and attentive service.

C-D **The Hermitage**, on a ridge near Surkhanda Devi Temple, 16 comfortable rooms, pleasant lawns and restaurant, nightly bonfire with music.

C-D **Valley View**, The Mall (Kulri) near Ropeway, T0135 263 2324. 14 clean rooms (some with kitchenette), restaurant, bakery, garden, friendly, good service.

E **Shalimar**, Charleville Rd, T0135 263 2410. 10 rooms, pleasant atmosphere.

E-F **Broadway**, Camel's Back Rd, next to rink, T0135 263 2243. 10 rooms with bath (bucket hot water), best with views and geyser, Indian meals, old hotel.

## Eating

**Dehra Dun** *p201, map p202*

ΨΨ **Kumar**, 15B Rajpur Rd (towards **Kwality**). Tasty Punjabi dishes, friendly staff.

Ψ **Bossa Nova**, Astley Hall. Ice creams and western snacks.

Ψ **Daddy's**, above **The Vegetarian**, serves travellers' favourites.

Ψ **Osho**, 111 Rajpur Rd. Good snacks in roadside café 'Rajneesh' atmosphere.

Ψ **Sheetal Restaurant**, west of town on canal bank, is in an attractive setting.

Ψ **The Vegetarian**, 3 Astley Plaza, Rajpur Rd. Non-veg.

### Bakeries

**Ellora**, Rajpur Rd, Paltan Bazar. Fresh bread, biscuits and local sticky toffees!

**Grand**, Rajpur Rd, Paltan Bazar. Fresh bread, biscuits and local toffees.

**Mussoorie and Landour**

*p203, maps p204 and p206*

Restaurants may be closed out-of-season, and to non-residents. Carlton's **Plaisance**, **Roselynn**, **Savoy** and **Valley View** have good restaurants. Some have a bar.

ΨΨΨ **Prakash**, Landour (above Woodstock School). Really good sandwiches, omelettes etc; also beer and cheese but at a silly price.

ΨΨ **Bhelpuri**, chaat, kababs, ice cream, also chicken curry with pulao, kulchas, dosas.

ΨΨ **Char Dukan**, Landour (above Woodstock School). Snacks. Really good sandwiches, omelettes etc.

ΨΨ **Coffee House**, Library, towards Happy Valley.

ΨΨ **Kwality**, above **Bank of Baroda**, Kulri. International. Dependable quality.

ΨΨ **Tavern**, Kulri. Dancing some nights.

ΨΨ **Whispering Windows**, Library. International. With a popular bar.

Ψ **Madras Café**, Kulri. Very good South Indian, friendly staff.

Ψ **Rice Bowl**, The Mall. Tibetan and Chinese.

### Cafés

**Swiss Café** and **City Point**, Gandhi Chowk. Reasonable fast food.

## Shopping

**Dehra Dun** *p201, map p202*

Shops around the Clock Tower, in Rajpur Rd, Paltan Bazar and Astley Hall, sell handwoven woollens, brassware and jewellery. For trekking equipment, try **Paramount**, 16 Moti Bazar (west of Paltan Bazar). For books, particularly natural history and related topics, try **The Green Bookshop**, on Rajpur Rd. Also **English Book Depot**, 15 Rajpur Rd, T0135 265 5192, www.englishbookdepot.com. Extensive collection of English fiction and non-fiction.

**Mussoorie and Landour**

*p203, maps p204 and p206*

The main areas are Library, Kulri and Landour Bazars and Shawfield Rd near Padmini Niwas.

### Crafts

**Banaras House**, The Mall. Silks.

**Baru Mal Janki Dass**, tribal silver jewellery.

**Inder Singh**, The Mall. Handcrafted sticks.

**Nirankari Cottage Industries**, The Mall. Handcrafted sticks.

**Star Walking Sticks**, The Mall. Handcrafted sticks.

### Photography

**Computerised Colour Lab**, The Mall.

**Mela Ram**, The Mall.

### Woollens

**Anand Gift Emporium**, near GPO.

**Garwhal Wool House**, near GPO.

**Natraj**, Picture Palace.

**Tibetan outdoor market**, near Padmini Nivas.

## Activities and tours

**Dehra Dun** *p201, map p202*
For tours to Chandrapuri Tent Camp and Auli Ski Resort, see page 225.
**GMVN**, Old Survey Chowk, 74/1 Rajpur Rd, T0135 265 6817, F265 4408.
**President Travel**, T0135 265 7082, prestrav@sancharnet.in. Ticketing and general travel arrangements.

**Mussoorie and Landour**
*p203, maps p204 and p206*
**Fishing**
In the Aglar and Yamuna rivers for mahseer and hill trout. Permit from Division Forest Officer, Yamuna Division is required.

**Horse riding**
1-hr ride (7 km) around Camel's Back Rd, Rs 250. Off-season, Rs 100.

**Paragliding**
Through Snowbird Flying Club, near the lake, T0135 263 1366; 1000-1700.

**Tour companies**
**Garhwal Alpine Tours**, Masonic Lodge, T0135 263 2507.
**Kulwant Travels**, Masonic Lodge Bus Stand, T0135 263 2717.

**Tours**
Operated by **GMVN**. Kempty Falls: Rs 50, season: 0900, 1200, 1500; off-season: 1000, 1300. Dhanolti, Surkhanda Devi Temple, Mussoorie Lake: full day (0900), Rs 130, season only. Tickets from KMVN and Uttaranchal Tourism.

## Transport

**Dehra Dun** *p201, map p202*
**Air**
Jolly Grant air strip (24 km), enquiry T0135 241 2412; limited flights to/ from **Delhi**.

**Bus**
**Local** From Rajpur Rd, near clocktower.
**Long distance** Delhi Bus Stand, Gandhi Rd, T0135 265 3797, for most hill destinations and the plains; Mussoorie Bus Stand, outside the railway station, T0135 262 3435. Half hourly to **Mussoorie**, 0600-2000, tickets from counter number 1, Rs 22. Private buses from City Bus Stand, Parade Ground. Regular services to **Mussoorie**, 1½ hrs; **Nainital**, 12 hrs; **Kullu**, 14 hrs; **Haridwar**, 1hrs. **From Shimla**: HP Roadways to Dehra Dun; deluxe buses, depart 0700, 0900, Rs 180; ordinary, last depart 1030 (10 hrs), Rs 140.

**Car**
Hire from Drona Travels (GMVN), T0135 265 6894, or Doon Tours & Travels, 16 Bhatt Shopping Complex, 1 Haridwar Rd, T0135 262 4520. Rs 750 per day, friendly and professional.

**Taxi and auto-rickshaw**
Taxi, T627877. Auto-rickshaw: the cheaper crowded Vikrams are easily available.

**Train**
Railway Station, T0135 262 2131. Reservations opposite, 0800-2000, Sun 0800-1400; book early for Haridwar. **New Delhi**: *Shatabdi Exp, 2018*, 1700, 5¾ hrs; **Delhi**: *Dehradun Bandra Exp, 9020*, 1035, 10 hrs; *Mussoorie Exp, 4042*, 2115, 9¾ hrs. **Allahabad**: *Link Exp, 4114*, 1315, 18¾ hrs. **Kolkata**: *Doon Exp, 3010*, 1945, 34½ hrs (via **Varanasi**, 19½ hrs). **Varanasi**: *Dehra Dun-Varanasi Exp, 4266*, 1815, 24 hrs.

**Mussoorie and Landour**
*p203, maps p204 and p206*
**Air**
Jolly Grant air strip, 60 km, limited flights to/from **Delhi** (see Dehra Dun above). 0800-1100, 1200-1500, Mon-Sat; 0800-1400, Sun.

**Bicycle**
Hire near Picture Palace.

**Bus**
Long-distance stands: Library (Gandhi Chowk), T0135 263 2258, Masonic Lodge (Kulri), T0135 263 2259. Frequent service to **Chamba**, scenic trip via Dhanolti, 3 hrs; **Dehra Dun** through Ghat roads, Rs 22, 1¾ hrs. From **Delhi** ISBT, dep 0515, 2230, 6-7 hrs, about Rs 90; stop for snacks at *Cheetal Grand*. Also buses from **Saharanpur Rly** and **Tehri**. Private buses to **Delhi**, are Rs 200-250 depending on a/c facility.

**Car**
Pay Rs 60 to drive on The Mall.

**Rickshaw**
Cycle rickshaws for the Mall, fixed fare chart from tourist office.

**Taxi**
Stand at Library, T0135 263 2115; Stand at Masonic Lodge, T0135 263 1407; **Kulwant Travels**, Masonic Lodge Bus Stand, T0135 263 2717. To Dehra Dun, Rs 350, Delhi Rs 2,200.

**Train**
See above for trains from Dehra Dun. **Railway Out Agency** (computerised all-India reservations), 0135 263 2846.

## Directory

**Dehra Dun** *p201, map p202*
**Banks** **Punjab National Bank**, Ashley Hall, Ugrasain Rd. Exchange on 1st floor, 1000-1400, 1500-1600, Sat 1000-1230; **State Bank of India**, Convent Rd, 1st floor. **President Travels**, 45 Rajpur Rd, changes TCs. **Hospital** Doon Hospital, Amrit Kaur Rd, T0135 265 9355. **Tourist offices** GMVN, 74/1 Rajpur Rd, T0135 265 3217; **Uttaranchal**, 45 Gandhi Rd, next to **Drona Hotel**, T0135 265 3217. Mon-Sat, 1000-1700. **Useful addresses** Rajaji National Park, 5/1 Ansari Marg, T0135 262 1669. The only office issuing permits for Rajaji. **Wildlife Institute of India**, PO Box 18, Chandrabani, T0135 264 0111, www.wii.gov.in.

**Mussoorie and Landour**
*p203, maps p204 and p206*
**Banks** Exchange can be difficult. **Bank of Baroda**, Kulri; or try Dehradun. **Hospitals** **Civil Hospital** at Landour, T0135 263 2053. **Community**, South Rd, T0135 263 2891. **St Mary's**, Gun Hill Rd, T0135 263 2891. **GPO**: Kulri. **Language schools** Landour, T0135 263 1467. Rs 100 per hr (less if sharing); maximum 4 lessons per day. Standard of teachers varies dramatically so try a few till you are happy. **Library** Gandhi Chowk, small fee. **Tourist offices** GMVN, Library Bus Stand and Tourist Bungalow, The Mall, T0135 263 2948. **Uttaranchal Tourism**, The Mall, T0135 263 2863. **Useful addresses** Ambulance: T0135 263 2829. **Fire**: T0135 263 2100. **Police**: Kotwali, T0135 263 2003.

# Haridwar, Rishikesh and around

## Haridwar → *Phone code: 0133. Colour map 1, grid C4. Population: 175,000.*

Haridwar, said to be one of the oldest cities in the world, lies at the base of the Shiwalik Hills where the River Ganga passes through its last gorge and begins a 2,000-km journey across the plains. Legend has sanctified it by placing Vishnu's footprint on the river bank, making Haridwar ('Vishnu's gate') one of the seven holy cities of Hinduism – see Hindu Holy Sites, page 1324. From sunrise, pilgrims come to bathe at the ghat to cleanse themselves of their sins. You will notice holy men in their huts dispensing wisdom to the willing, and wandering sadhus who have made make-shift shelters under trees. Here too, you can watch priests performing spectacular Ganga arati at sunset. Despite local opposition, Haridwar was included in the new state of Uttaranchal. ➤➤ *For Sleeping, Eating and other listings, see pages 213-218.*

*Only vegetarian food is available in town and there is no alcohol.*

### History
Various episodes from the *Mahabharata* are set in this ancient town which was mentioned by the Chinese traveller Hiuen Tsang. It attracted the attention of **Timur** who sacked it in 1399, see page 1298. The town, on the west bank of the river, centres

 on **Hari-ki-Pairi**, where **Vishnu** is believed to have left his footprint. At this point part of the Ganga has been diverted as irrigation water is drawn off for the Upper Ganga Canal system and for a hydro-electric power station.

## Sights

Near the steps at Hari-ki-Pairi is a modern clocktower and some temples, none particularly old. Further down, foodstalls and shrines line alleyways leading off into the bazar. There are six bridges to take you across the river, where it is quieter. A new footbridge leads directly to Hari-ki-Pairi. Foreign visitors are likely to be approached for donations for its construction and upkeep! There are many *ashrams* here like Shatikunj, Ananda Mayee Ma and Premnagar. Many have herb gardens producing ayurvedic medicines.

**Moti (Lower) bazar**, parallel to the Jawalapur-Haridwar Road, is interesting, colourful, invariably crowded and surprisingly clean and tidy. Stalls sell coloured powder piled high in carefully made cones (for *tikas*). Others sell saris, jewellery, brass and aluminium pots, sweets and snacks.

**Mansa Devi Temple** is worth visiting for the view. Set on the southernmost hill of the Shiwaliks, it is accessible on foot or by the crowded cable car, from 0630 to 2030 for Rs 31 return. A package ticket including Chandi Devi temple on the other side of the Ganga, 4 km away costs Rs 100. Towards Rishikesh, 5 km from Haridwar, are the newer temples: **Pawan Dham** with a Hanuman temple, its spectacular glittering glass interior and the seven-storey **Bharat Mata Mandir** to Mother India.

**Kankhal**, 3 km downstream, with the **Temple of Dakseshwara** is where Siva's wife, Sati, is believed to have burnt herself to death. Professor Wendy Doniger vividly



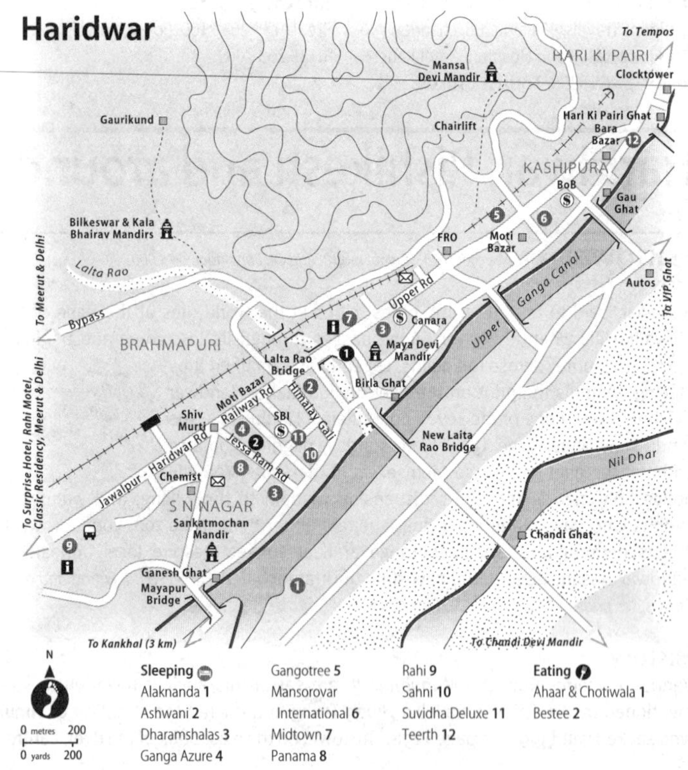

**From sunrise, pilgrims come to bathe at the ghat to cleanse themselves of their sins. You will notice holy men in their huts dispensing wisdom to the willing, and wandering sadhus who have made make-shift shelters under trees...**

summarizes the story as told in the *Puranas*: "**Daksa**, a son of Brahma, gave his daughter Sati in marriage to Siva, but he did not invite Siva to his grand sacrifice. Sati, in anger, burnt herself to death. Siva destroyed the sacrifice and beheaded Daksa, but when the gods praised Siva he restored the sacrifice and gave Daksa the head of a goat. When Siva learned that Sati had killed herself, he took up her body and danced in grief, troubling the world with his dance and his tears until the gods cut the corpse into pieces. When the *yoni* fell, Siva took the form of a *linga*, and peace was re-established in the universe". See also page 589.



## Rajaji National Park → *Colour map 1, grid B4. Altitude: 302-1,000 m.*

ⓘ *Permits from Haridwar office, Mohan's Adventure or at Chilla Park. Open 15 Nov-15 Jun between sunrise and sunset. Entry first 3 days Rs 350 (foreigners), Rs 40 (Indians). Additional day; Rs 150 and Rs 25. Camera, free; video, Rs 2,500. Elephant rides from Chilla, Rs 400 (foreigners), Rs 200 (Indians), 2 hrs. Chilla, 7 km from Haridwar, is the best for viewing. Car permit Rs 100. Jeep hire from Haridwar, Rishikesh or Dehradun.*

Uttaranchal's largest park, 820 sq km, is named after C Rajagopalachari, the only Indian to hold the post of Governor General. The Shiwaliks are rugged and dangerously steep slopes. The parks vegetation ranges from rich *sal, bhabbar* tracts, broad-leaf mixed forest to *Chir* pine forests interspersed with areas of scrub and pasture which provide a home for a wide variety of wildlife including over 23 mammal and 438 species of bird. On foot, however you are likely to see very little. Even by car or jeep many are disappointed as few animals are spotted.

*The park is accessible from Haridwar, Rishikesh and Dehra Dun*

A large number of **elephants**, together with the rarely-seen **tiger**, are at the northwest limit of their range in India. The elephants move up into the hills when the water holes are dry. A census taken in 2001 recorded 453 elephants, 30 tigers and 236 **leopards** in the park. Other animals include spotted deer, sambar, muntjac, nilgai and ghoral. Along the tracks, you may spot wild boar, langur and macaque; the Himalayan yellow-throated marten and civet are rare. Peacocks, jungle fowl and kaleej pheasants can be spotted in the drier areas, while waterbirds attracted by the Ganga and the Song rivers include many kinds of geese, ducks, cormorant, teal and spoonbill among others.

## Rishikesh → *Phone code: 01350. Colour map 1, grid B4. Population: 72,000.*

The Ganga, at this point still an astonishingly clear water river, links all the holy places of one of Hinduism's most sacred regions. Rishikesh stands tight-packed on the banks of the river as it runs swiftly through the southernmost ranges of the Shiwaliks on its way to the Plains. At Rishikesh the river begins to cut through the low foothills, which were once more densely forested than today. Those forests offered the prospect of quiet retreat, the original basis of the ashram ideal. Maharishi Mahesh Yogi had his ashram here and captured the imagination and attention of the Beatles in the 1960s. Today, however, the town has become heavily commercialized, full of ashrams, sadhus and visitors attending courses in yoga and meditation. Some find it disappointing and lacking in atmosphere, others thoroughly enjoy it and stay for weeks. It is surrounded by wonderful birdwatching territory. ▸▸ *For Sleeping, Eating and other listings, see pages 213-218.*

*A vegetarian temple town: meat and alcohol are prohibited; eggs are only eaten in private*

## Ins and outs

**Getting there** From Haridwar, buses are both quicker and far more frequent than trains. Buses from Delhi and Dehra Dun arrive at the main bus stand in the town centre and also stop south of Ram Jhula.

**Getting around** The centre near the bus stands and station is compact and is an easy walk to the river, less than a kilometre away. The ashrams are to the north. You can take a cycle-rickshaw or shared tempo (Rs 5-10) from the Bazar to the two suspension bridges and then walk across to the east side. You can also cross the river on a boat near Ram Jhula (Rs 4). ▸▸ *See Transport, page 217, for further details.*

## Sights

Rishikesh ('Hair of Sages') has a large number of ashrams. It is worth walking down to the river bank where pilgrims purify themselves by bathing in the Ganga at **Triveni**

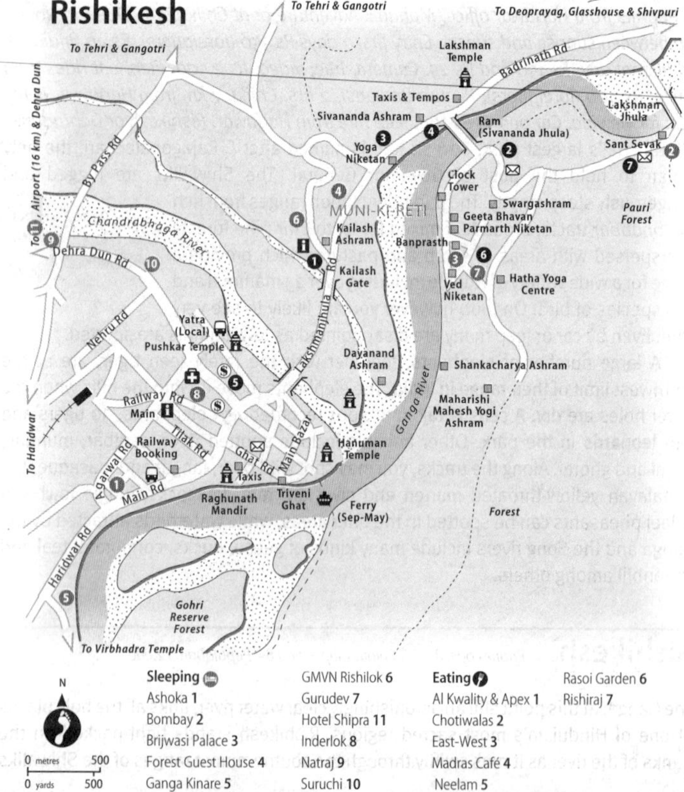

**Ghat** (which has some striking statues of Siva), offering milk and feeding the fish at dawn, and floating lamps after sunset for evening *aarati*. Many ashrams which offer the seeker a spiritual haven are on the east bank of the river at **Swargashram**. Some of them are bizarrely colourful, architectural curiosities leading Geoffrey Moorhouse to describe it as a cross between Blackpool and Lourdes. Several ashrams are seats of spiritual learning and meditation and offer courses (see below). **Muni-ki-Reti** is the area along the Chandrabhaga River which also has some temples. Be aware that not all in saffron/orange clothing are sadhus; some are con-men. If you walk northeast up the river you will find some secluded **beaches.**

There are two suspension bridges over the Ganga – **Ram (Sivananda) Jhula,** between Sivananda Ashram and Swargashram, and **Lakshman Jhula**. Music concerts are held in the Ram Jhula area on Sunday evenings but women should be careful. The Lakshman Jhula area is very picturesque with the best views though you may be troubled by rhesus monkeys.

Rishikesh is the base for several pilgrimages and treks, including the **Char Dham Pilgrimage,** see box page 222, or going to the Garhwal hills and Hemkund Sahib.

## Sleeping

**Haridwar** *p209, map p210*
There are over a 100 places to stay. Many offer off-season discounts outside Jun and Jul, up to 50% Nov-Feb.

**B Classic Residency**, Delhi-Haridwar Rd, Jwalapur Rd, 1.5 km south of town, T0133 442 8005, www.classichotelsindia.com. 44 a/c rooms, all facilities, shuttles to Hari-ki-Pairi, activity tours arranged.

**B-C Alaknanda** (UP Tourism), Belwala (east bank), By-pass Rd, T0133 242 6379, www.up-tourism.com. 32 rooms, best a/c with bath, dorm (Rs 150), restaurant (simple veg), small garden, on river bank, quiet.

**C-D Gautam Siddhartha**, Haridwar-Delhi Rd, Singh Dwar, T01334 224206. 14 rooms in a new comfortable hotel near the Ganga.

**C-D Mansarovar International**, Upper Rd, towards Hari-ki-Pairi, T01334 226501, hotel mansaroverinternational@rediff mail.com. 64 clean, simple rooms, dorm (Rs 100), restaurant.

**C-D Midtown**, Railway Rd, T01334 227507, F226049. 23 rooms, some a/c, modern, reasonably clean, fairly quiet.

**C-D Rahi** (Uttaranchal Tourism), opposite railway station, T01334 226430. 19 rooms (some a/c), restaurant, tourist information.

**C-D Suvidha Deluxe**, SN Nagar, T01334 227423, suvidha@aakashdeepgroup.com. 28 reasonably good rooms, some a/c, restaurant, modern, clean, central but quiet.

**D Gangotree**, Upper Rd, T01334 224407. 14 simple rooms, attached bath, bucket hot water.

**D-E Ganga Azure**, Railway Rd, T01334 227101, shyamco@vsnl.com. 32 adequate rooms, TV, hot water, some (**B**) a/c, decent restaurant.

**D-E Samrat**, Sadhubela Rd, T01334 227380. 14 good rooms with bath.

**D-E Teerth**, Subhash Ghat, Hari-ki-Pairi, T01334 242 5211. 32 reasonable rooms, some air-cooled, excellent central location, great views over ghats, high-quality cooking, friendly and helpful staff, good value.

**E Deep**, Sadhubela Rd,T01334 227609. 10 clean rooms. Recommended.

**E Sahni**, Niranjani Akhara Rd, SN Nagar, T01334 227906. 42 fairly clean, basic rooms, some with bath, some air-cooled (extra charge), hot water in buckets, helpful service.

**Rajaji National Park** *p211*
For reservation of a guesthouse, contact Rajaji National Park, 5/1 Ansari Marg, Dehra Dun, T0135 262 1669.

**C-E Forest Rest Houses** near all the gates. All have at least 2 suites. Those at Chilla (apparently best spot for wildlife) and Motichur cost Rs 1000. Others at Asarodi, Beribara, Kansrao, Kunnao, Phandowala, Ranipur and Satyanarain are Rs 600. All have electricity and water supply except Beribara and Kansrao. Very basic, self-catering

*For an explanation of the sleeping and eating price codes used in this guide, see inside the front cover. Other relevant information is found in Essentials pages 56-61.*

(utensils provided), not good value, 'concrete boxes'.

**C Tourist Bungalow**, Chilla, T951382 66678. With rooms, dorm (Rs 100) and tents. To stay in a tribal village, contact **Mohan's Adventure**, T01334 220910, see Haridwar.

**Rishikesh** *p211, map p212*

Most people prefer the peace across the river to the noisy, polluted atmosphere in town.

**LL Ananda-in-the-Himalayas**, The Palace, Narendranagar, T01378 227500, www.anandaspa.com. Exclusive heatlh resort with 75 rooms (some have original furniture), superb location and views, plus an amazing range of treatments. Fantastic place to spoil yourself, winner of many international awards.

**B Ganga Banks**, Shivpuri, contact Wanderlust in Delhi, T011 2687 5200, www.wanderlustindia.com, is a 'green' resort with 28 comfortable, eco-friendly cottages with bath, built with local raw materials, restaurant, pool, health spa, in natural surroundings employing recycling techniques (no plastics), solar heating, well placed for trekking, rafting, etc.

**B Ganga Kinare**, 16 Virbhadra Rd, on quiet riverside 2 km from centre, T0135 243 1658, F243 5243. 36 rooms (best face river), central a/c (heating inadequate in winter), pleasant restaurant, exchange, meditation, yoga (1-3 week courses), treks, boating Sep-Mar, rafting.

**B Natraj**, Dehra Dun Rd, T0135 243 1099, htnatraj@zyperway.com. 49 a/c rooms, restaurant (veg), large gardens, pool (Rs 250 for non-residents), modern, free airport transfer.

**C-D Inderlok**, Railway Rd, T0135 243 0555, F243 2855. 25 clean rooms, some a/c, with balconies, restaurant (veg), terrace lawn, older hotel but well kept and with pleasant ambience and mountain views.

**C-E Rishilok** (GMVN), Badrinath Rd, Muni-ki-Reti, T0135 243 0373, F243 0372. 46 clean rooms, some with bath in new cottages and 2-storey blocks, dorm (Rs 80), restaurant, pleasant garden, efficient service, above and away from Main Rd, peaceful.

**D Shikar**. Good clean a/c rooms, some with bath (order hot water), very good restaurant and superb views from rooftop.

**D Suruchi**, T0135 243 2269. Comfortable rooms (some air-cooled) and recommended restaurant.

**D-F Shipra**, Dehra Dun Rd, T0135 243 0533. 24 rooms in modern hotel, restaurant.

**E Banprasth**, next door to Hatha Yoga Centre, has clean rooms with bath in pleasant surroundings.

**E Hatha Yoga Centre**, 2 lanes beyond Green Hotel, very clean, tranquil and excellent value, occasional evening concert with local musicians on roof, yoga optional!

**E Phool Shanti**, 6 km on Neelkanth Rd (north of Lakshman Jhula), T0135 243 3174. Pleasant, quiet retreat by the Ganga.

**E-F Brijwasi Palace**, 1st right after Ram Jhula, 2nd left before Ved Niketan, T0135 243 5181, hotelbrijwasipalace@vsnl.com. 22 standard doubles with hot shower, some with geyser, clean, peaceful garden restaurant, yoga in basement, pleasant staff. Good value. Recommended.

**E-F Divya**, T0135 243 5998, www.laxmanjhula.com. 22 clean, but small rooms, attached hot bath, restaurant with travellers' favourites.

**F Ashoka**, away from noise of bus stand. 30 simple rooms, some attached.

**F Bombay Kshetra**, 20 basic rooms around a courtyard, clean common bath, popular.

**F Gurudev**, opposite Rishiraj. 7 clean rooms, some attached, roof terrace with good views, yoga, massage, ayurvedic meals.

Several **F** hotels near Main Bus Stand.

**Ashrams**

Ashrams are mostly on the east bank of the *jhulas*. Catering mainly for pilgrims; foreigners may need special permission. Some can be filthy; inspect first. They are always simple, rated **E-F** and hot water comes in buckets.

**Adanyanda** is very clean, with marble floors and tiled bathrooms.

**Eagles' Nest Retreat**, T09837100215. Popular for spiritual healing, yoga, reiki, sauna etc.

**Sant Sevak**, near Lakshman Jhula, T0135 243 0465, has large, fairly modern rooms.

## Eating

**Haridwar** *p209, map p210*

Cheap stalls on Railway Rd provide simple food for pilgrims.

**ΨΨ Aahar**, Railway Rd. Punjabi. Chinese and continental. Excellent meals.

¥¥ **Big Ben**, at Ganga Azure. Decent, large range of Indian, Chinese and continental.
¥ **Bestee**, Railway Rd. Mughlai and South Indian. Stuffed *parathas* are recommended.
¥ **Chotiwalas**, several (including on Railway Rd, opposite Tourist Office) of varying quality.

**Rishikesh** *p211, map p212*
Safe drinking water is sold to refill bottles near the Ram Jhula.
¥¥ **A1 Kwality**, near GMVN **Rishilok**. Varied.
¥¥ **Ganga View**, Lakshman Jhula. Western lunch, *thali* (1800-2000), snacks, pleasant location.
¥¥ **Midway**, 'resort' towards Haridwar (Rs 10 by tempo). For those desperate to replenish their protein intake, good tandoori and curries, washed down with chilled beer.
¥ **Chotiwalas**, Swargashram, east bank, near Ram Jhula. Crowded, plenty of atmosphere, inexpensive; one closer to the river is a bit cleaner, more spacious, nicer rooftop.
¥ **East-West**, west bank, Italian. Good breads and olive 'pizzas', but suspect hygiene.
¥ **Hill Top**, Lakshman Jhula. Wide choice with good views.
¥ **Madras Café**, by boat jetty. Mainly South Indian. Excellent service, cheese on brown toast to masala dosas.
¥ **Neelam**, near Yatra Bus Stand. Indian, Continental. Very good value.
¥ **Rasoi Garden**, Swargashram, 2-min walk behind **Green Hotel**. Excellent coffee, pizzas, pittas and hummus, peaceful.
¥ **Rishiraj**, near Lakshman Jhula. Italian.

## Festivals and events

**Haridwar** *p209, map p210*
Thousands of pilgrims visit the city, especially when the birth of the river (*Dikhanti*) is celebrated in spring. **Kumbh Mela**, held here every 12th year (next in Apr 2010), and **Ardha Kumbh** every 6 years (next also in 2010), attract millions of devotees who come to bathe in the confined area near Hari-ki-Pairi, see page 184.

**Rishikesh** *p211, map p212*
**Feb**: International Yoga week, an opportunity to learn yoga on the banks of the Ganga.

## Activities and tours

**Haridwar** *p209, map p210*
### Tour companies
**Ashwani Travels**, 3 Railway Rd, T01334 224581, ashwanitravels@hotmail.com. Official agent of GMVN, specializing in pilgrimage tours, also trekking.
**Mohan's Adventure**, next to Chitra Cinema, Railway Rd, T01334 220910, www.mohans adventure.com. Very reliable trips run by the experienced Sanjeev Mehta. Trekking, jeep safaris, rafting. Jungle trips into Rajaji National Park, with night stay in tribal village. Highly recommended.

### Tours
Daily, same day tours of Haridwar-Rishikesh, 0930, Rs 50; Dehra dun-Mussoorie, 0800, Rs 140; Rajaji National Park, 1000, 1430.

**Rishikesh** *p211, map p212*
### Boat rides
On the Ganga from Swargashram Ghat. Fix rates with local boatmen.

### Music
**Sivananda Ramesh**, towards Muni-ki-Reti Taxi Stand, T01334 437581. Lessons in tabla, sitar, santoor, singing etc.

### Rafting
Several whitewater rafting outfits on the Ganga, north of town. Best to book ahead.
**Himalayan River Runners**. Highly recommended, operates Mar-May, Sep-Oct, www.hrrindia.com, with an office in Delhi, T011 2685 2602.
**Shivpuri**, 18 km upstream, has a GMVN. **Mohan's Ganga River Camps** and **Garhwal Himalayan Exploration** offers rafting from Shivpuri: Rs 580 including lunch.
Mohan's 5-day Ganga Expedition includes whitewater, Rs 1,200 per day covers food and camping.
**Kaudiyala Resort**, 38 km away, has tents at Rs 100, beds at Rs 65, meals Rs 150. Rafting Rs 350 per day. Birdwatching. Contact **GMVN** Yatra Office, T0135 2431793. See also **Ganga Banks** under 'Sleeping' above.

### Swimming
Hotel **Natraj** pool (non-residents, Rs 250).

### Tour companies

**GMVN** (see below).

**Garhwal Himalayan Exploration**, PO Box 29, T0135 243 3478, www.garhwalhimalayas.com. Wide range of trekking and rafting trips.

**Triveni**, Haridwar Rd, T0135 243 0989, www.triveniindia.com. Recommended for rafting and trekking.

### Trekking

With guides, transport, camping; meals cost about Rs 1,500 per day through local agents.

### Yoga

Meditation courses and instruction in Vedanta. Most hotels can put you in touch.

**Onkarananda Ashram** (Durga Mandir) above Yoga Niketan, T0135 243 0883, good Iyengar yoga courses, also offers music and classical dance.

**Parmarth Niketan** and **Swargashram**, T0135 243 0252, are vast, and can be impersonal.

**Sivananda Ashram** (Divine Life Society), T0135 243 0040: short to 3-month courses (apply 1 month ahead); holds music classes and produces herbal medicines.

**Ved Niketan** has a flexible programme of yoga; also Hindi, Sanskrit, music and dance classes.

## Shopping

**Rishikesh** *p211, map p212*

Dehra Dun, Haridwar, Ghat and Railway rds have markets and curio shops. The latter are limited for choice and overpriced.

**Gandhi Ashram Khadi Bhandar**, Haridwar Rd.

**Ganga Emporium**, by Ram Jhula at the head of the bridge, especially spiritual texts, café attached – read, relax and sip a cool drink!

**Garhwal Wool and Craft**, opposite Yatra Office, Muni-ki-Reti.

**Photo Centre**, Dehra Dun Rd.

**UP Handlooms**, Dehra Dun Rd.

## Transport

**Haridwar** *p209, map p210*

### Bus

The long-distance bus stand is Roadways Bus Stand, Railway Station, T01334 227037; **Garhwal Motor Owners Union**, T01334 226886, also has buses. **Rishikesh** share taxis and buses (Rs 15 from bus stand, 45 mins). Share tempos from Bhimgoda tank (Rs 15-20, more for Lakshman Jhula); autos from across the river. Taxis, Rs 330. Buses to/from **Delhi**, hourly (4-5 hrs); **Dehra Dun** (1¼ hr); **Mathura** and **Vrindavan**, 10 hrs. **Rajasthan State Transport**, booth just inside bus station entrance, run deluxe buses to **Jaipur**, 0430, 0730, 1630, 1645, 1730, 1830, Rs 366, 12 hrs; also to **Udaipur** and **Pushkar**; several private buses to **Delhi**, Rs 120-150; **Ajmer/Pushkar**, 1300, 1500, 1600, 1700, Rs 270, 15 hrs; **Jaipur (via Delhi)**, same times as Ajmer, Rs 220, 15 hrs; **Jodhpur**, same timings, Rs 350, 15 hrs; **Nainital** (season only), 2000, Rs 220, 9 hrs; **Agra/Mathura**, 2000, Rs 180, 10-11 hrs.

### Rickshaw

Stands near railway station, fares negotiable.

### Taxi

Stands near railway station, fares negotiable. **Taxi Union**, T01334 227338. Rates for visiting the mountains are competitive; 4 day round trip, about Rs 4000.

### Train

Railway Station, T131. Reservation office 0800-2000. Three trains per day to **Rishikesh**, 0515, 0845, 1715, better to take road transport; **Allahabad**: *Link Exp, 4114*, 1445, 17¼ hrs. **Delhi (OD)**: *Dehra Dun Bandra Exp, 9020*, 1310, 7 hrs; *Mussoorie Exp, 4042*, 2300, 8 hrs (beware of thieves). **Delhi (ND)**: *Shatabdi Exp, 2018*, 1810, 4½ hrs. **Dehra Dun**: *Doon Exp, 3009*, 0535, 1¾ hrs; *Varanasi Dehra Dun Exp, 4265*, 0640, 2¼ hrs. hrs. **Varanasi**: *Dehra Dun Varanasi Exp, 4266*, 2010, 22 hrs. For **Nainital**: *Dehradun-Kathgodam Exp 4320*, 2230, 9 hrs. For **Shimla**, travel via Ambala and Kalka (trains better than bus).

**Rajaji National Park** *p211*

The park has 8 entry gates. From **Dehra Dun**: **Mohan** (25 km on Delhi-Dehra Dun highway, 5 hr drive from Delhi), **Ramgarh** (14 km, Delhi-Dehra Dun highway, via Clement Town) and **Lachhiwala** (18 km, Dehra Dun-Hardwar route, right turn before Doiwala). From **Haridwar**: **Chilla** (7 km, via private bus route to Rishikesh), **Motichur** (9 km, Haridwar-Rishikesh or Dehra Dun-Haridwar highways) and **Ranipur** (9 km, Haridwar-BHEL-Mohand Road). From

**Rishikesh**: Kunnao (6 km, via private bus route on Rishikesh-Pashulok route). From **Kotdwara**: Laldhang (25 km, via private bus route to Kotdwara to Chilla).

**Rishikesh** *p211, map p212*
Pilgrim centres of Badrinath (301 km); Gangotri (258 km); Kedarnath (228 km); Uttarkashi (154 km); Yamunotri (288 km).

**Bus**
Long-distance stand at Roadways or Main Bus Stand, Haridwar Rd, T0135 243 0066. Buses from Delhi finally stop by the Govind-Radha Mandir south of Ram Jhula, 15-min walk from the bridge. Reserve tickets at the Local (Yatra) Bus Stand from around 1600, the day before (especially during Yatra season, May-Nov); open 0400-1900. Various State Government bus services (DTC, Haryana Roadways, Himachal RTC, UP Roadways). **Chandigarh** (252 km), **Dehra Dun** (42 km), **Delhi** (238 km, 6 hrs, taxi 5 hrs). **Haridwar** (24 km); also share taxis from bus stand or auto rickshaws from Ram Jhula. **Mussoorie** (77 km), Patiala, Saharanpur. For **Shimla**: best to go to Dehra Dun and stay overnight and catch 0600 bus; or get a bus from Haridwar (0600, 1000, 1600, 2200) but it's a long hot journey (see 'Train' under Haridwar). From **Yatra (Local) Bus Stand**, Dehra Dun Rd, during the Yatra season, to **Char Dhams**: buses leave early for the very long routes to Hanuman Chatti (for Yamunotri), **Badrinath, Gangotri, Gaurikund** (for Kedarnath); best to take a 'Luxury' bus, and break your journey. For **Badrinath** and **Hemkund** stop overnight at Joshimath (after 1630 road to Govindghat is southbound only). Although the **Yatra season** ends in late Oct (Yamunotri, Gangotri, Kedarnath) to mid-Nov (Badrinath), bus frequency drops drastically during Oct. Even light rains can cause severe road blocks, mainly due to landslides. Bus for Badrinath dep from Private Bus Stand (100 m right from station), Rs 180, but noisy, crowded and uncomfortable. **Garhwal Motor Owners Union**, T0135 243 0076; **Tehri Garhwal MOU, Triveni**, Haridwar Rd, T0135 243 0989. From **Delhi**, best to get a bus to Haridwar and train from there (2nd class sleeper recommended) to Haridwar: *Shatabdi Exp, 2017*, 0700 (ND), 4½ hrs; *Mussoorie, 4042*, 2215 (OD) 2220, 7½ hrs. See Haridwar for departing trains. Reservations office, 0800-1800. For travelling north, cheapest are 'Newspaper taxis', eg Joshimath, Rs 140 per person; ask at **Sanjay News Agency**, Main Rd (before turn-off to Ghat Rd) or travel agent.

**Ferry**
Ferry boat from near Ram Jhula for river crossing, Rs 4; Rs 6 return.

**Jeep**
Hire for Badrinath (1-way), 1500-2000, is the best option. Book the evening before, for all.

**Motorbike**
Motorbike (Bullet) mechanic at **Bila**, opposite **Ganga View Hotel**, Lakshman Jhula.

**Rickshaw**
Cycle-rickshaw rates are negotiable. Constant shuttle between town centre and Lakshman Jhula.

**Taxi**
(Unmetered) from **Garhwal Mandal TCS**, Haridwar Rd or tour operators.

**Tempo**
Mostly fixed routes. From Ram Jhula shared, to Rishikesh Bazar Rs 3; from Lakshman Jhula Rs 5; to Haridwar Rs 15, 50 mins. Foreigners will probably be asked for more.

**Train**
There is a branch line from Haridwar to Rishikesh but the bus is quicker.

## Directory

**Haridwar** *p209, map p210*
**Banks** All close from Sat pm to Mon am. **State Bank of India**, Station Rd, 1030-1430. £ and $ cash only. **Bank of Baroda**, Upper Rd. Cash on Visa cards only. **Canara Bank**, Upper Rd. Changes TCs. **Hospitals** **District**, Upper Rd, T01334 226060. **RK Mission**, Kankhal, T01334 227141. **Chemists**: on Railway and Upper Rd. **Post** Railway Rd. 1000-1630. **Tourist offices** Uttaranchal, Motel Rahi, T01334 226430. 1000-1700 (Mon-Sat). **Lalta**

Rao Bridge, T01334 224240 (1000-1700). Ganga Sabha, near Hari-ki Pairi, T01334 227925. **Useful addresses** Police: T01334 227775. Rajaji National Park office: Dehradun, T0135 262 1669.

**Rishikesh** *p211, map p212*
**Banks** Bank of Baroda, Dehra Dun Rd, T0135 243 0653. Accepts Visa and Master Card. State Bank of India, Railway Rd. Mon-Fri 1000-1400, Sat 1000-1200. **Hospital** Govt Hospital, Dehra Dun Rd, T0135 243 0402. Nirmal Ashram, T0135 243 2215. Sivananda, Muni-ki-Reti, T0135 243 0040. **Internet** Several in town. Blue Hills Travels has best facilities in Ram Jhula area (Rs 50/hr), but queueing often necessary. Try Rana Tele Point at Jhula Restaurant, near taxi stand, Lakshman Jhula (Rs 30/hr) or several on the other bank. **Post** Open 0700-2200. GPO: at Harilal Marg, Lakshman Jhula and Muni-ki-Reti. Ghat Rd. Swargashram GPO by Chotiwalas. **Tourist offices** Garhwal Mandal Vikas Nigam (GMVN) & Yatra Office, Kailash Gate, By Pass Rd, T0135 243 1793, yatraoffice@sancharnet.in. Organizes trekking, mountaineering, rafting and Char Dham tour (12 days). Uttaranchal, 162 Rly Rd, T0135 243 0209. Helpful. Plans to move to the Tourist Bungalow. During Yatra season, only at Yatra Bus Stand. **Useful addresses** Ambulance: T102. Fire: T101. Police: T100.



# Garhwal and the Pilgrimage (Yatra)

*The shrines of Kedarnath, Yamunotri, Gangotri and Badrinath are visited by hundreds of thousands of Hindu pilgrims each summer. They come from all corners of the subcontinent to engage in what Dalrymple calls, "a modern-day Indian Canterbury Tales". Garhwal's fragmented political history gives no clue as to the region's religious significance. The sources of the Yamuna and the Ganga and some of Hinduism's holiest mountains lie in the heart of the region. Since the seventh-century Tamil saint Sankaracharya travelled north on his mission to reinvigorate Hinduism's northern heartland, some have been watched over permanently by South Indian priests. The most famous is the Rawal – head priest – at the Badrinath temple, who to this day comes from Kerala. Badrinath is one of the four* dhams *'holiest abodes' of the gods. Along with Dwarka, Puri and Ramesvaram, they mark the cardinal points of Hinduism's cultural geography. After a ritual purificatory bathe in the Ganga at Haridwar and, preferably, Rishikesh, the pilgrim begins the 301-km journey from Haridwar to Badrinath. The purpose is to worship, purify and acquire merit. Roads go all the way to Gangotri and Badrinath, and to within 14 km of Yamunotri and Kedarnath. The correct order for pilgrims is to visit the holy places from west to east: Yamunotri, Gangotri, Kedarnath and Badrinath.* ➤➤ *For Sleeping, Eating and other listings, see pages 225-227.*

## Ins and outs

Temples and trekking routes open from the end of April to mid-November (October for Badrinath). June is very crowded; heavy rains July to mid-September may trigger landslips. Best in May, mid-September to mid-October. Yatra tourists on public buses are required to register with the Yatra Office at the Yatra (Local) Bus Stand, Rishikesh (open 0600-2200). A current certificate covering immunization against cholera and typhoid is needed. In practice, 'Registration' is often waived, but the immunization certificate is checked. Accommodation prices are higher in this area.
➤➤ *For trekking, see page 227.*

# Yamunotri and Gangotri

Yamunotri can be reached from Rishikesh or from Dehra Dun via Yamuna Bridge and Barkot. The former is the more popular. From Rishikesh it is 83 km to Tehri, or 165 km via Deoprayag. Tehri, northeast of Rishikesh, the capital of the former princely state, will eventually be submerged by the waters behind the controversial and still unfinished Tehri Dam. New Tehri, 24 km from the original town, is a 'planned' town and the new district headquarters.

## Yamunotri → *Colour map 1, grid B4. Altitude: 3,291 m.*

Dominated by **Banderpunch** (6,316 m), Yamunotri, the source of the Yamuna, is believed to be the daughter of Surya, the sun, and the twin sister of Yama, the Lord of Death. Anyone who bathes in her waters will be spared an agonizing death.

To begin the trek to reach the temple take a jeep from **Hanuman Chatti** (large vehicles stop here and pick up) to **Janki Chatti**, 8 km further up, which is pleasanter and where you can leave luggage. The trek along the riverbank is exhilarating with the mountains rising up on each side, the last 5 km somewhat steeper. The source itself is a difficult 1-km climb from the 19th-century **Yamunotri Temple** ⓘ *0600-1200, 1400-2100*, with a black marble deity. The modern temple was rebuilt this century after floods and snow destroyed it. There are **hot springs** nearby (the most sacred being Surya Kund) in which pilgrims cook potatoes and rice tied in a piece of cloth. The meal, which takes only a few mins to cook is first offered to the deity and then distributed as *prasad*. On the return to Hanuman Chatti, you can visit the **Someshwar Temple** at **Kharsali**, 3 km across the river from Janki Chatti. The temple is one of the oldest and finest in the region and there are excellent views of the mountains.

## Uttarkashi → *Colour map 2, grid A2. Altitude: 3,140 m.*

This busy town, en route to Gangotri, 240 km from Rishikesh, has several places to stay but all are full during the season. The Nehru Institute of Mountaineering here offers courses and from here you can trek to **Dodital**. Porters can be hired locally and there are also tour operators, see below. The bazaar is near the bus stand and from here you can buy provisions. If you are in town on 14 January you will witness the **Makar Sankranti Garhwal festival** of music and dance.

## Gangotri and around → *Colour map 2, grid A2. Altitude: 3,140 m.*

Gangotri, 240 km from Rishikesh, is the second of the major shrines in the Garhwal Himalaya. A high bridge now takes the road across the Jad Ganga River joining the Bhagirathi which rushes through narrow gorges, so buses travel all the way. The 18th-century granite **temple** is dedicated to the Goddess **Ganga**, where she is believed to have descended to earth. It was built by a Gurkha commander, Amar Singh Thapa, in the early 18th century and later rebuilt by the Maharaja of Jaipur. Hindus believe that Ganga (here **Bhagirathi**) came down from heaven after **King Bhagirath's** centuries-long penance. He wanted to ensure his dead relatives' ascent to heaven by having their ashes washed by the sacred waters of the Ganga. When the tempestuous river arrived on earth, the force of her flow had to be checked by **Siva** who received her in the coils of his hair, lest she sweep all away. A submerged lingam is visible in the winter months.

**Rishikund**, 55 km from Uttarkashi, has hot sulphur springs near **Gangnani** suitable for bathing, and a 15th-century temple above. The **Gaurikund waterfall** here is one of the most beautiful in the Himalaya. Below Gangotri are **Bhojbasa** and **Gaumukh**, which are on a gradual but nevertheless scenically stunning trek. You can continue to trek another 6 km to Nandanvan (4,400 m), base camp for Bhagirathi peak, and continue 4 km to Tapovan (4,463 m), known for its meadows that encircle the base of Shivling peak. See page 229 for trekking information.

# From Rishikesh to Kedarnath

From Rishikesh the road follows the west bank of the Ganga and quickly enters forest. At the 23rd milestone, at **Gular-dogi village**, is the old orchard and garden of the Maharaja of Tehri Garhwal which is close to a white sand and rock beach, and is now home to a luxury hotel, see listings.

The section up to **Deoprayag** (68 km) is astonishingly beautiful. The folding and erosion of the hills can be clearly seen on the mainly uninhabited steep scarps on the opposite bank. Luxuriant forest runs down to the water's edge which in many places is fringed with silver sand beaches. In places the river rushes over gentle rapids. A few kilometres before Byasi is Vashisht Gufa (the cave where the saint meditated) which has an Ashram. About 5 km after **Byasi** the road makes a gradual ascent to round an important bluff. At the top, there are fine views down to the river. Villages now become more common. The way that small pocket handkerchief-sized fields have been created by terracing is marvellous. Jeep hire from here is easy, to Badrinath or Rishikesh.

*It is an offence to photograph sensitive installations, troop movements and bridges on most routes. Offenders can be treated very severely.*

**Deoprayag** is the most important of the hill *prayags* because it is at the junction of the Bhagirathi and Alaknanda rivers; Gangotri is the source of the Bhagirathi and Badrinath is near the source of the Alaknanda. Below Deoprayag, the river becomes the Ganga. The town tumbles down the precipitous hillside in the deeply cut 'V' between the junction of the two rivers, with houses almost on top of one another. Where the rivers meet is a pilgrims' bathing ghat, artificially made into the shape of India. From Deoprayag, the road is relatively flat as far as Srinagar (35 km) and for much of the way you pass through well-cultivated land. The Siva and Raghunath temples here attract pilgrims.

The old capital of Tehri Garhwal, **Srinagar** was devastated when the Gohna Lake dam was destroyed by an earthquake in the mid-19th century. The most attractive part of Srinagar, which is a university town, runs from the square down towards the river. There are some typical hill houses with elaborately carved door jambs. The 35-km route from Srinagar to **Rudraprayag**, at the confluence of the Mandakini and Alaknanda, is again mostly through cultivated areas. Roughly half way an enormous landslip indicates the fragility of the mountains. Approximately 5 km before reaching Rudrapayag, in a grove of trees by a village, is a tablet marking the spot where the 'man-eating leopard of Rudraprayag' was finally killed by Jim Corbett, see page 245. Rudraprayag with its temples is strung out along a fairly narrow part of the Alaknanda Valley.

For Kedarnath, leave the Pilgrim road at Rudraprayag, cross the Alaknanda River, and go through a tunnel before following the Mandakini Valley (the tributary) through terraced cultivation and green fields. The road goes past the first town **Tilwara**, 9 km, then **Kund**, to **Guptakashi** where Siva proposed to Parvati. If time permits and you have hired a jeep from Guptakachi, stop at **Sonprayag**, 26 km, a small village at the confluence of the Mandakini and Son Ganga rivers, to visit the **Triyuginarayan Temple** where the gods were married. Find the viewpoint here before continuing to **Gaurikund**, 4 km away, where the motorable road ends. Hundreds of pilgrims bathe in the hot sulphur springs in season. From here you either trek – early start recommended – or ride a mule to Kedarnath. It is 14 km away. The ascent, which is fairly steep at first, is through forests and green valleys to Jungle Ghatti and Rambara (over 1,500 m); the latter part goes through dense vegetation, ravines and passes beautiful waterfalls. Beyond **Rambara** the path is steep again. At intervals tea stalls sell refreshments.

# Kedarnath Temple and around → *Colour map 1, grid B5.*

The area around Kedarnath is known as Kedarkhand, the *Abode of Siva*. Kedarnath has one of the 12 *jyotirlingas* (luminous energy of Siva manifested at 12 holy places, miraculously formed lingams). In the *Mahabharata*, the **Pandavas** built the temple to atone for their sins after the battle at Kurukshetra, see page 453.

## Kedarnath Temple → *Altitude: 3,584 m. 77 km from Rudraparyag. Pujas at 0600 and 1800.*

The Kedarnath Temple is older and more impressive than Badrinath. Some claim it is originally over 800 years old. Built of stone, unpainted but carved outside, it comprises a simple, squat, curved tower and a wooden roofed *mandapa*. Set against an impressive backdrop of snow-capped peaks, the principal one being the Kedarnath peak (6,970 m), the view from the forecourt is ruined by ugly 'tube' lights. At the entrance to the temple is a large Nandi statue.

## Vasuki Tal → *A guide is necessary. Altitude: 4,235 m.*

Vasuki Tal, about 6 km away, the source of Son Ganga, is to the west up along a goat track. It has superb views of the Chaukhamba Peak (7,164 m). A short distance northwest is the beautiful Painya Tal where through the clear water you can see the rectangular rocks which form the lake bottom.

## Kedarnath Musk Deer Sanctuary

The area bounded by the Mandal-Ukhimath road and the high peaks to the north, (the Kedarnath Temple is just outside) was set aside in 1972 principally to protect the endangered Himalayan musk deer – the male carries the prized musk pod. There is a breeding centre at Khanchula Kharak about 10 km from Chopta. The diversity of the park's flora and fauna are particular attractions. Dense forested hills of chir pine, oak, birch and rhododendron and alpine meadows with the presence of numerous Himalayan flowering plants, reflect the diverse climate and topography of the area while 40% of the rocky heights remain under permanent snow. Wildlife includes jackal, black bear, leopard, snow leopard, sambar, *bharal* and Himalayan tarh, as well as 146 species of bird. A 2-km trek from Sari village near Chopta leads to Deoriatal, at 2,438 m, overlooking Chaukhamba Peak.

# The Panch Kedars

There are five temples visited by pilgrims: Kedarnath, Madhmaheswar, Tungnath, Rudranath and Kalpeshwar. These vary in altitude from 1,500-3,680 m in the Rudra Himalaya and make an arduous circuit. Kedarnath and Badrinath are only 41 km apart with a tiring *yatra* (pilgrim route) between the two; most pilgrims take the longer but easier way round by bus or car. The myth of the 'five Sivas' relates how parts of the shattered Nandi Bull fell in the five places – the humped back at Kedarnath, the stomach at Madhmaheswar, the legs at Tungnath, the face at Rudranath and the hair at Kalpeshwar. Since all but Kalpeshwar and Tungnath are inaccessible in the winter, each deity has a winter seat in a temple at Ukhimath where the images are brought down in the autumn. They are returned to their principal temples in the spring.

## Panch Kedar trek

If you wish to undertake the 170 km, 14-day trek, start at Rishikesh, visiting Kedarnath first (see above). Return to Guptakashi and proceed to Kalimath to start the 24-km trek to **Madhmaheswar** from Mansuna village. You can stop overnight at Ransi, 1 km southwest of Madhmaheswar, and continue following the Ganga through the

## Purification and piety

Bad karma (see page 1323), the impurity caused by bad actions in previous births, and death itself, are the focus of some of Hinduism's most important rituals. Rivers are believed to have great purifying power, stronger at the source, at their confluence, and at the mouth. There are five 'Prayags' (confluences) in the Himalayan section of the Ganga – Deoprayag, Rudraprayag, Karnaprayag, Nandaprayag and Vishnuprayag, called Trayagraj (King of Prayags). On the plains, Allahabad is the most important confluence of all, where the Yamuna, the Ganga and the mythical underground river, the Sarasvati, all meet.

**Piety** Hardship enhances the rewards of the yatra pilgrims. The really devout prostrate themselves either for the whole distance or around the temple, lying face down, stretching the arms forwards, standing up, moving up to where their fingertips reached and then repeating the exercise, each one accompanied by a chant. Most pilgrims today prefer to make the journey by bus or by car.



Kedarnath Musk Deer Sanctuary (see above). From near the temple at 3,030 m which has three streams flowing by it, you can see Chaukhamba Peak (7,164 m).

**Tungnath**, at 3,680 m the highest temple, is surrounded by the picturesque Nanda Devi, Neelkanth and Kedarnath mountains. You reach it by a 3-km trek from Chopta, on a driving route from Ukhimath to Gopeshwar, passing through villages, fields and wooded hills before reaching meadows with rhododendrons. The two-hour climb, though steep, is not difficult since it is along a good rocky path with occasional benches.

For **Rudranath**, at 3,030 m, get to Gopeshwar by road and then on to Sagar (5 km) for the 24-km trek covering stony, slippery ground through tall grass, thick oak and rhododendron forests. Landslides are quite common. The grey stone Rudranth temple has the Rudraganga flowing by it. The views of the Nandadevi, Trisul and Hathi Parbat peaks and down to the small lakes glistening in the surroundings are fantastic.

**Kalpeshwar**, at 2,100 m, near Joshimath, is the only one of the Panch Kedars accessible throughout the year. Its position, overlooking the Urgam Valley, offers beautiful views of the Garhwal's most fertile region with its terraced cultivation of rice, wheat and vegetables. Trekking across the Mandakini starts from Tangni.

# Rudraprayag to Badrinath

## The road to Joshimath

Along the Pilgrim Road, about midway between Rudraprayag and Karnaprayag, you pass **Gauchar**, famous locally for its annual cattle fair. The valley is wider here providing the local population with very good agricultural land. The beautiful Pindar River joins the Alaknanda at **Karnaprayag**, 17 km, while **Nandaprayag** is the confluence with the Mandakini River. All these places have GMVN accommodation. **Chamoli**, 40 km further on, is the principal market for the Chamoli district though the HQ is Gopeshwar on the hillside opposite. The valley walls are now much higher and steeper and the road twists and turns more. Troop movements up to the border with Tibet/China are common and military establishments are a frequent sight on the Pilgrim road. From Chamoli onwards the road is an impressive feat of engineering.

## Joshimath → *Phone code: 01389. Colour map 2, grid B3. Altitude: 1,875 m.*

Joshimath is at the junction of two formerly important trans-Himalayan trading routes. Travellers to Govindghat and beyond may be forced to spend a night here as the road closes to northbound traffic at 1630. Joshimath is now the base for India's longest and highest cable car route to Auli Ski Resort, with beautiful views of Nanda Devi, Kamet, Mana Parvat and Dunagiri peaks, all above 7,000 m. There is a restaurant in the meadow, see Eating below.

## Vishnuprayag

Vishnuprayag is at the bottom of the gorge at the confluence of the Alaknanda and Dhauliganga rivers. Some 12 km and a steep downhill stretch brings the road from Joshimath to the winter headquarters of the Rawal of Badrinath.

Buses for Badrinath, along the narrow hair-raising route start around 0600, the one-way flow regulated by police. You travel through precipitous gorges, past another Hanuman Chatti with a temple and climb above the treeline to reach the most colourful of the *Char Dhams*, in the valley.

**The Bhotias** (Bhutias), a border people with Mongoloid features and strong ties with Tibet live along these passes – see page 639. The women wear a distinctive Arab-like headdress. Like their counterparts in the eastern Himalaya, they used to combine high altitude cultivation with animal husbandry and trading, taking manufactured goods from India to Tibet and returning with salt and borax. When the border closed following the 1962 Indo-Chinese War, they were forced to seek alternative income and some were resettled by the government.

## Auli → *Colour map 2, grid B3. Altitude: 2,519 m. By road it is16 km from Joshimath, or a 5-km trek.*

The extensive meadows at Auli on the way to the Kauri Pass had been used for cattle grazing by the local herders. After the Indo-Chinese War (1962), a road was built from Joshimath to Auli and a Winter Craft Centre set up for the Border Police in the 1970s. With panoramic views of mountains, particularly Nanda Devi and others in the sanctuary, and Mana and Kamet on the Indo-Tibet border, and good slopes, Auli has been developed as a **ski** resort by GMVN and Uttaranchal Tourism operating from mid December to early March. There is a 500-m ski lift (Rs25) and 800-m chair lift (Rs 100). There is equipment available for hire, and you can stay at **Tourist Rest House**.



---

# Badrinath and around → *Phone code: 01389. Colour map 1, grid B5. Altitude: 3,150 m.*

According to Hindu Shastras, no pilgrimage is complete without a visit to Badrinath, the abode of Vishnu. Along with Ramesvaram, Dwarka and Puri, it is one of the four holiest places in India, see page 1324. Guarding it are the Nar and Narayan ranges and in the distance towers the magnificent pyramid-shaped peak of Neelkanth, at 6,558 m; a hike to its base takes two hours. Badri is derived from a wild fruit that Vishnu was said to have lived on when he did penance at Badrivan, the area which covers all five important temples including Kedarnath. Shankaracharya, the monist philosopher from South India, is credited with establishing the four great pilgrimage centres in the early ninth century AD, see page 1324.

## Badrinath Temple

The main Badrinath Temple is small and brightly painted in green, blue, pink, yellow, white, silver and red. The shrine is usually crowded with worshippers. The *Rawal* (Head Priest) always comes from a Namboodri village in Kerala, the birthplace of Shankaracharya. Badrinath is snowbound over winter, when the images are transferred to Pandukeshwar, and open from late April to October. Along with worshipping in the temple and dispensing alms to the official (sometimes wealthy) temple beggars outside, it is customary to bathe in **Tapt Kund**, a hot pool nearby below the temple. This is fed by a hot sulphurous spring in which **Agni** (the god of fire) resides by kind permission of Vishnu. The temperature is around 45°C. **Badrinath Festival** takes place from 3 to 10 June.

## Hemkund and the Valley of Flowers → *Colour map 1, grid B5.*

ⓘ *Permits to enter the national park are issued at the police post at the road head of Govindghat, Rs 350, plus camera fee, Rs 50; may be negotiable in the off-season. Camping overnight in the valley or taking back plants or flowers is prohibited.*

**Govindghat**, 20 km from Joshimath, is on the road to Badrinath. A bridle track leads to Ghangharia, for the Valley of Flowers, 19 km further on, and Hemkund Sahib. This trailhead is very crowded in the peak season (May-June). You can trek or hire mules for the two-day journey; there are several tea-stalls along the route.

**Ghangharia**, at 3,048 m, is a 14-km walk from Govindghat. May to June are very busy. Those arriving late without a reservation may only find floor space in the Gurudwara or must sleep in a field.

To reach **Hemkund** (6 km further on at 4,329 m) after 1 km from Ghangharia leave the main Valley of Flowers track, up a path to the right. **Guru Gobind Singh** is believed to have sat here in meditation during a previous incarnation, see page 1343. It is an important Sikh pilgrimage site. On the shore of the lake where pilgrims bathe in the icy cold waters, is a modern *gurudwara*; well worth the long trek though some may suffer from the high altitude. Hemkund is also a Hindu pilgrimage site, referred to as **Lokpal**. Lakshman, the younger brother of Rama, meditated by the lake and regained his health after being severely wounded by Ravana's son, Meghnath. A small Lakshman temple stands near the *gurudwara*. Despite its ancient connections, Hemkund/Lokpal was 'discovered' by a Sikh *Havildar*, Solan Singh, and only became a major pilgrimage centre after 1930.

The 14-km long trail from Govindghat to Ghangharia runs along a narrow forested valley past the villages of **Pulna** and **Bhiyundar**. **The Valley of Flowers** ⓘ *best season Jul-Aug 3,000-3,600 m*, is a further 5 km. Hathi Parbat (Elephant Peak), at 6,700 m, rises dramatically at the head of the narrow side valley. Close views of mountains can be seen from Bhiyundar. The trek has beautifully varied scenery. After crossing the Alaknanda River by suspension bridge the winding path follows the Laxman Ganga as its constant companion, passing dense forests and commanding panoramic views of the lovely Kak Bhusundi Valley on its way to the hamlet of **Ghangaria** (Govind Dham), the base for the Valley of Flowers, nestling amidst giant deodars. As the path from Ghangaria gradually climbs to the Valley of Flowers, glaciers, snow bridges, alpine flowers and wildlife appear at intervals. The 6-km long and 2-km wide 'U' shaped valley is laced by waterfalls. The River Pushpati and many other small streams wind across it, and its floor, carpeted with alpine flowers during the monsoons, is particularly beautiful. It is especially popular because of its accessibility. The Valley was popularized by **Frank Smythe**, the well-known mountaineer, in 1931. Local people had always kept clear of the Valley because of the belief that it was haunted, and any who entered it would be spirited away. A memorial stone to Margaret Legge, an Edinburgh botanist, who slipped and fell to her death in 1939 reads, "I will lift up mine eyes unto the hills from whence cometh my strength".

## Satopanth → *25 km from Badrinath. Take a guide.*

Satopanth, a glacial lake, takes a day to reach from Badrinath. You follow the track along the Alaknanda Valley, a gentle climb up to **Mana** village (6 km north) near the border, inhabited by Bhotias. Foreigners need to register here and sometimes deposit their cameras since they are not permitted to take photographs. Nearby is the cave where **Vyasa** is said to have written the epic *Mahabharata*. The track disappears and you cross a snowbridge, trek across flower-filled meadows before catching sight of the impressive 144-m **Vasudhara Falls**. The ascent becomes more difficult as you approach the source of the Alaknanda near where the Satopanth and Bhagirathi Kharak glaciers meet. The remaining trek takes you across the **Chakra Tirth** meadow and over the steep ridge of the glacier till you see the striking green Satopanth Lake. According to legend its three corners mark the seats of Brahma, Vishnu and Siva. The peaks of **Satopanth** (7,084 m) from which the glacier flows, **Neelkanth** (6,558 m) and **Chaukhamba** (7,164 m) make a spectacular sight.

## Sleeping

Contact GMVN, www.gmvnl.com, for reservations in their resthouse along the routes. Some have 'deluxe' rooms which are still basic, with toilet and hot water, dorm (Rs 100). They are **D-E**. There are also simple guesthouses in places. Reserve ahead. During Yatra season, GMVN places may only be available if you book their organized tour. Carry bottled water and take a good torch.

**Yamunotri** *p219*
There are other lodges and places to eat. Also dharamshalas and basic lodges.
**E Rest House**, Janki Chatti, GMVN. Closed Dec-March.
**E Rest House**, Yamunotri, GMVN, is on a hill.
**E Tourist Rest House**, by the river, Hanuman Chatti. GMVN, clean, simple rooms, dorm (Rs 100), hot water in buckets, the only decent place, closed Dec-Mar.

**Dodital** *p219*
**D-E Akash Ganga**.
**D-E Shivam**, T01374 222 525, some a/c.
**E Ceeway** short walk from bazar. Decent.
**E GMVN Tourist Bungalow**, near bridge, T01374 222 236. 33 rooms with bath, few a/c, vegetarian meals. Small.
**E-F** hotels are clustered near the bus stand.

**Gangotri** *p219*
**B Shikhar Nature Resort**, 5 km out of town, by the Bhagirathi River, T011-233 1 2444, www.shikhar.com. Luxury tents with mod cons in scenic setting.
**E Birla Niketan**, nearby, has rooms with bath. Other lodges have rooms without bath and electricity for under Rs 100.
**E Ganga Niketan**, across road bridge. Good rooms and a simple terrace restaurant.
**E Monal** is on the road to Gangotri.
**E Tourist Rest House**, across footbridge, 20 rooms and dorm, meals.

**From Rishikesh to Kedarnath** *p220*
**A Glasshouse on the Ganges**, Gular-dogi, 23 km north of Rishikesh on Badrinath Rd, T01378 269 224, www.neemranahotels.com. 16 rooms, best in the glass house itself, others in cottages in beautifully maintained gardens. Extremely peaceful location by the side of the river, wonderful place to relax.
**D New Tourist Bungalow**, on a hill, Rudraprayag, T01364 233 347, www.gmvnl.com. Has 25 rooms, deluxe with bath and dorm.
**D-E Tourist Rest House**, near bus stop in central square, Srinagar, T01388 252 199, www.gmvnl.com, has 90 rooms, deluxe with bath, cheaper cabins and dorm, restaurant, tourist office, clean and quiet.
**D-F Tourist Bungalow**, Guptakashi, T01364 267221, www.gmvnl.com. 6 basic but clean rooms, open all year.
**D-F Tourist Bungalow**, Gaurikund, T01364 269202, www.gmvnl.com.10 rooms, open May-Nov.
**E Alka** and **Menka**, opposite **Tourist Rest House**, Srinagar, among others in town.
**E Chandrapuri Camp**, north Rudraprayag, by the river, has 10 safari type tents for 4.
**E Tourist Bungalow**, 1½ km from main bazar and bus stand on a hillside, Deoprayag, T01378 266 013, www.gmvnl.com. 16 rooms, some with bath, meals.

**Kedarnath Temple** *p221*
**E Tourist Rest House**, T01364 263 228, has 16 rooms, some with bath, and dorm.

*For an explanation of the sleeping and eating price codes used in this guide, see inside the front cover. Other relevant information is found in Essentials pages 56-61.*

**The road to Joshimath** *p222*
**D-F Tourist Bungalow**, Gauchar, T01372 240 611, www.gmvnl.com. Open all year.
**D-F Tourist Bungalow**, Karnaprayag, T01363 244 210, www.gmvnl.com. Attractive setting, open all year.
**E-F Tourist Bungalow**, Nandaprayag, T01372 261 215, www.gmvnl.com. Small but clean rooms, open all year.

**Joshimath** *p223*
Hotel prices rise in high season.
**D-E Neelkantha Motel**, Upper Mall, by bus stand, T01389 222 226. 15 comfortable rooms, some deluxe with bath, dorm, restaurant (acceptable though limited menu), helpful staff (arrange jeep, porter), often full.
**E Kamet**, by Ropeway, Lower Mall. Rooms not great value but cheaper rooms in annexe facing main road.
**F Auli Paying Guest House**, opposite the police station, has an 8-bed dorm (Rs 100).
**F Nanda Devi**, between Upper and Lower Mall, in the bazar, T01389 222 170. Basic, cheap, porter agents.
**F Shailja**, behind **Neelkanth Motel**, is basic but friendly, good food but check bill.
**F Shivlok**, has basic doubles.

**Auli** *p223*
**C Tourist Bungalow**, 01389 223 208, www.gmvnl.com. Wide range of rooms including huts and a dorm (Rs150) plus a large restaurant.

**Badrinath** *p223*
**E Devlok** (GMVN), near Bus Stand, T01381 222 338, has 30 large rooms, a restaurant, and is the best option in the trekking area. For pilgrims: *dharamshalas* and *chattis* (resthouses), T01381 285 204.

**Hemkund and the Valley of Flowers** *p224*
**D-F Tourist Lodge**, Ghangharia, overpriced rooms, dorm (Rs 100), tent (Rs 60).
**E Bharat Lodge**, at the far end of Govindghat, with bucket hot water.
**E Merry Lodge**, rooms with bath.
**Forest Rest House** and **Govind Singh Gurudwara**, Govindghat, free beds and food to all (donations accepted) and reliable cloakroom service for trekkers.
**F Krishna**, Ghangharia, rooms with bath.
Free Gurudwara (Sikh religious complex), Ghangharia.

## Eating

**Dodital** *p219*
In the bazar serve vegetarian *thalis*.

**Gangotri** *p219*
Numerous tea and food stalls near the temple.

**Joshimath** *p223*
Several places serve veg meals.
**Pindari** serves delicious *thalis*.
**Paradise**, near **Pindari**.

## Activities and tours

**Dodital** *p219*
**Crystal Adventure**, Hotel Tapovan, near Tourist Bungalow, T01374 222 566.
**Mount Support**, Nautial Bhawan, Bhatwari Rd, near bus stand.

**Joshimath** *p223*
**Eskimo Travels**, next to GMVN, has also been recommended for trekking, climbing and skiing
**Garhwal Mountain Services**, T01389 222 288. For porters.
**Great Himalayan Expeditions** are trekking agents at **Nanda Devi Hotel**. Highly recommended for "local knowledge, good humour, high spirits and reliability".

## Transport

For further details of getting to the region, see Rishikesh transport section page 217.

**Yamunotri** *p219*
Early bus (0600) best from Rishikesh to Hanuman Chatti (210 km, 9 hrs).

**Dodital** *p219*
Frequent buses to Rishikesh (140 km) and Gangotri (100 km) during the *yatra* season. For a return trip in a taxi to Gangotri, Rs 1,300.

**Kedarnath** *p221*
Buses from Rishikesh to Rudraprayag and Gaurikund.

**Joshimath** *p223*
Frequent buses to Badrinath, 4 hrs, via **Govindghat**, 1 hr, Rs 7; to **Kedarprayag**, 1300, 4 hrs; **Rishikesh**, 0400, 0600, 10 hrs; **Rudraprayag**, 1100, 5 hrs.

**Auli** *p223*
A modern 25-seater cable car carries people from Joshimath. It costs Rs 300 in season, Rs 200 off return. Jeeps/taxis: between Joshimath and Auli. Regular buses from Rishikesh (253 km), Haridwar (276 km) up to Joshimath.

## Directory

**Joshimath** *p223*
**Tourist office** In annexe above Neekanth Motel, T01389 222 181; helpful.

# Trekking in the Garhwal and the Kumaon Himalaya

*This region contains some of the finest mountains in the Himalaya and is highly accessible and yet surprisingly very few westerners visit it, many preferring to go to Nepal. Of the many treks available, eight routes are included here. The scenic splendour of these mountains lies partly in the fact that the forests around the big peaks are still wonderfully untouched and the local population unaffected by the ravages of mass tourism. Also in Garhwal and Kumaon there are ranges that you can easily get among, enabling a greater feeling of intimacy with the alpine giants. The mountains have been described as "a series of rugged ranges tossed about in the most intricate confusion" (Walton, 1910).* ▸▸ *For Sleeping, Eating and other listings, see pages 225-227.*

## Ins and outs

Reliable local agents who will make all arrangements including accommodation and porters, are in Haridwar, Dehra Dun and Rishikesh (see pages 209, and 70). Porter agents in Uttarkashi, Joshimath, Munsiyari etc who act as trekking agents may not be as reliable; negotiate rates for specific services and insist on reliable porters. Different months offer different things: go in February and March, at lower altitudes, for the spectacular rhododendrons; April and May allows access to higher altitudes but can get very hot and views can be restricted due to large scale burning; July and August sees the monsoon and is good for alpine flowers but wet, humid and cloudy for much of the time. If the monsoon is heavy, roads and tracks can become impassable; in September the air is beautifully rainwashed, but early morning clear skies can give way by 1000 to cloud, and views may completely disappear; In October and November temperatures are lower, the skies clearer and the vegetation greener following the monsoon.

## Background

This region had been open since the British took over in 1815 but it was closed in 1960 due to political troubles with China, and during this period Nepal became popular with climbers and trekkers. Garhwal and Kumaon Himalaya have gradually been opened to explorers since 1975, though parts bordering Tibet remain closed. Much of the early Himalayan exploration was undertaken here. **Trisul**, 7,120 m, after it had been climbed by Doctor Tom Longstaff in 1906, remained the highest mountain climbed for the next 30 years.

## Trekking

Trekking in this region is not highly organized so you need to be well prepared. A good map for the area is Leomann's, Indian Himalya Sheet 8, Kumaon Garhwal. On most treks you need a tent (though not The Pindari Glacier trek, for example). Very few villagers speak English, but the rewards for the well-equipped trekker who has planned carefully are great, especially the feeling of being far from the madding crowd. If you are travelling in small groups of three to four persons it is often possible to get overnight accommodation in villagers' houses but despite their hospitality, this is uncomfortable. GMVN and KMVN lodges where available, provide rustic but clean rooms and some have deluxe rooms with bath. Caretakers cook simple meals. If you would like to leave logistics to someone else, hire a government recognized specialist tour operator, see page 71.

Around **Gangotri** and **Yamunotri** in Garhwal there are a number of good treks, some suitable for the independent or 'go-it-alone' trekker. **Nanda Devi** is the other area and this forms a ring that includes both Garhwal and Kumaon. There are many more treks than those indicated here. The lower part of the Niti Valley, and the Darma Valley, are open to groups of four with requisite permits. You are not allowed to go beyond Badrinath.

## Gangotri and Yamunotri area

### Gangotri to Gaumukh

The best known trek here is to Gaumukh (The Cow's Mouth) and, if desired, beyond onto the Gangotri Glacier. Gaumukh can easily be managed in three days with minimal equipment but carry provisions.

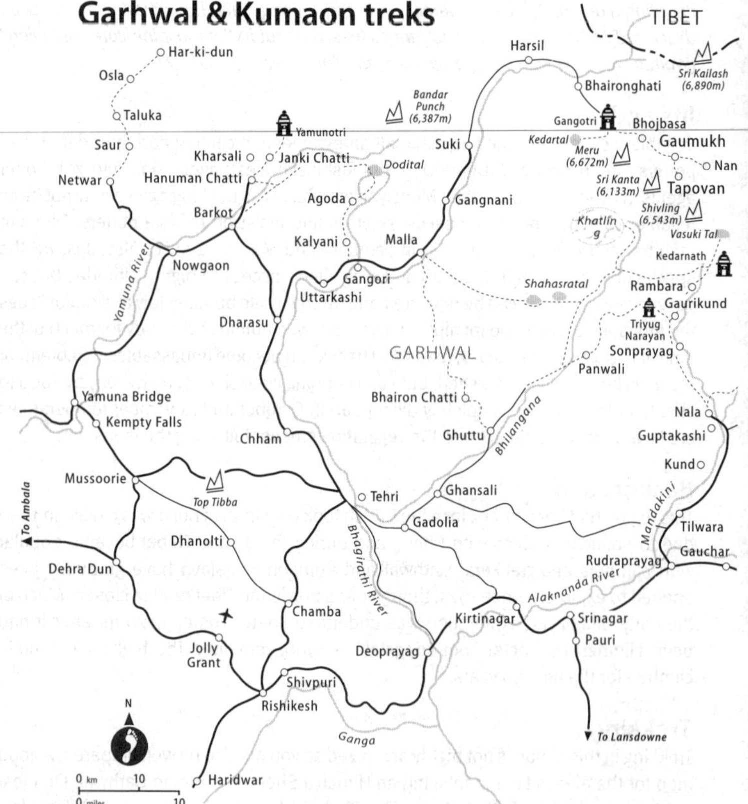

From Gangotri, at 3,046 m, follow the well-defined, gradually ascending path for 14 km to **Bhojbasa** at 3,792 m. It takes about five hours. There is a **Tourist Rest House** here which has fours rooms and a dorm without bedding. This is, however, often full. You may hire good value two-person tents for Rs 160 a night. There is also an *ashram* where trekkers and pilgrims can stay. There is also tented accommodation at Chirbasa, 5 km before Bhojbasa.

The 4 km to **Gaumukh**, the last kilometres across boulder scree and moraine, takes about one hour so it is quite feasible to go from Bhojbasa to Gaumukh, spend some time there, then return the same day. There are plenty of tea houses en route. Gaumukh, the present source of the Bhagirathi (Ganga) River, is at the mouth of the Gangotri Glacier where blocks of glacier ice fall into the river and pilgrims cleanse themselves in freezing water. There are breathtaking views. There is basic tent accommodation.

Beyond Gaumukh more care and camping equipment is required. The **Gangotri Glacier** is situated in an amphitheatre of 6,500-7,000 m peaks which include Satopanth (7,084 m), Vasuki (6,792 m), Bhagirathi (6,556 m), Kedar Dome and the prominent trio of Bhagirathi I, II and III; Shivling (6,543 m), standing alone, is one of the most spectacular peaks in the entire Himalaya.

## Tapovan → *Altitude: 4,463 m.*

In a breathtaking setting in a grassy meadow on the east bank of the Gangotri Glacier, this is the base camp for climbing expeditions to the stunningly beautiful **Shivling** (6,543 m), Siva's lingam and the 'Matterhorn of the Himalaya'. You can either return the same way or make a round trip by crossing over the glacier for 3 km to **Nandanvan**, at 4,400 m, and continuing upwards for a further 6 km to Vasuki Tal beneath **Vasuki** peak (6,792 m). Since the glacier crossing is fairly risky, it is recommended only for the experienced trekker. The return is via Nandanvan, the west bank of the Gangotri Glacier crossing the Raktvarn Glacier to Gaumukh-Raktvarn, so called because of the rust-coloured boulders in its moraine.

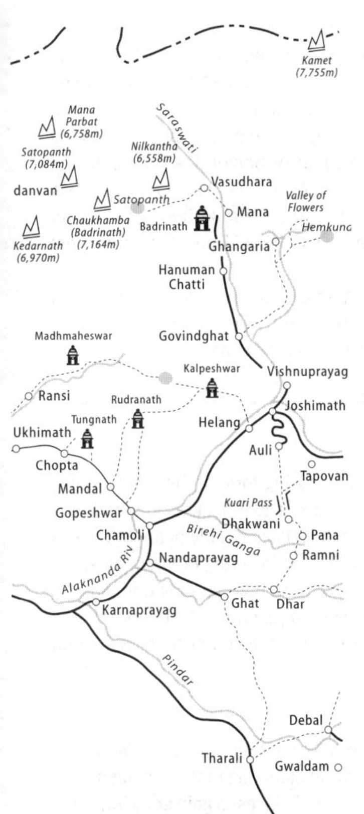


## Gangotri to Kedartal

This is an excellent short trek with scenic variety and spectacular views but be aware of the problems associated with altitude and allow time for acclimatization. It requires a tent, stove and food. It is 17 km to Kedartal (5,000 m), a small glacial lake surrounded by **Meru** (6,672 m), Pithwara (6,904 m) and Bhrigupanth (6,772 m).

Leaving Gangotri you proceed up the gorge of the Kedar Ganga (Siva's contribution to the Bhagirathi River). It is 8 km to Bhoj Kharak and then a further 4 km to Kedar Kharak, passing through some beautiful Himalayan birch forest en route. The bark from the trees (*bhoj* in Garhwali) was used by sages and hermits for manuscripts. From Kedar Kharak, where you can camp, it is a laborious 5-km ascent to Kedartal. Besides the peaks surrounding the lake you can also see the Gangotri range.

You return to Gangotri the same way. **Rudugaira Kharak** is the base camp for the peaks at the head of the Rudugaira Valley. Coming down towards Gangotri you must cross to the opposite bank near Patangnidhar to avoid the cliffs on the west bank. Nearer Gangotri cross back to the west bank.

## Gangori to Yamunotri via Dodital

This is a beautiful trek between Kalyani and Hanuman Chatti, a distance of 49 km. You can do a round trip from either end. It takes five days.

From **Uttarkashi** take a local bus to Kalyani via **Gangori**, 3 km away, or walk it. At **Kalyani**, 1,829 m, the recognized starting point of the trek, you take a track to the right. From here it gets steeper as the path climbs through forest to **Agoda** 5 km away. There is a suitable camping or halting place 2 km beyond Agoda. The next day carry on to **Dodital**, 16 km away at 3,024 m, picturesquely set in a forest of pine, deodar and oak. This is the source of the Asi Ganga and is stocked with trout. There is a dilapidated **Forest Rest House** and several cheap lodges. Above the lake there are fine views of Bandar Punch (Monkey's Tail, 6,387 m). To reach **Hanuman Chatti** at 2,400 m, walk for 6 km up to the Aineha Pass, 3,667 m, which also has splendid views. Then it is a 22-km walk down to Hanuman Chatti, the roadhead for Yamunotri.

## Har-ki-Dun Trek

Har-ki-Dun (God's Valley) nestles in the northwest corner of Garhwal near the Sutlej-Yamuna watershed. The people of the area have the distinction of worshipping **Duryodhana**, head of the crafty royal family in the *Mahabharata*, rather than siding with the pious Pandavas, see page 1316. The valley is dominated by Swargarohini (6,096 m) and Kalanag. From **Nowgaon**, 9 km south of Barkot, take a bus to the roadhead of **Sankri**. From here it is a gradual ascent over 12 km to **Taluka**, and **Osla** (2,559 m), 11 km further. Another 8 km and 1,000 m higher is **Har-ki-Dun** (3,565 m), an ideal base for exploring the valley. Allow three days to Har-ki-Dun. There are **Forest** and **Tourist Rest Houses** at all these places.

You can return to Nowgaon or, if properly equipped and provisioned, trek for 29 km on to **Yamunotri** via the Yamunotri Pass (5,172 m). You will need to allow time for acclimatization. The views from the pass are well worth the effort.



# Nanda Devi area

Nanda Devi (7,816 m), named after the all-encompassing form of the female deity, dominates the Garhwal and Kumaon Himalaya. With its two peaks separated by a 4-km long ridge, the second highest mountain in India is incredibly beautiful. She is also the most important of Garhwal's deities, protected by a ring of mountains, 112 km in circumference, containing 12 peaks over 6,400 m high. In only one place is this defensive ring lower than 5,500 m, at the **Rishi Gorge**, one of the deepest in the world. It is the place of ascetic sages (*rishis*). The Nanda Devi Sanctuary is a World Biosphere Reserve.

## Background

For half a century the problems which engaged the attention of many experienced explorers and mountaineers was not so much how to climb the mountain but how to get to it. Various attempts were made from a number of places to gain entry into what became known as the Nanda Devi Sanctuary. The riddle was finally solved by the

'Terrible Twins', Bill Tillman and Eric Shipton in a characteristically lightweight expedition (these two great mountaineers would agonize over whether to take one shirt or two on an expedition lasting a few months!). The way they discovered was up the Rishiganga and through the difficult Rishi Gorge. They made two trips into the Sanctuary during their five month expedition in the Garhwal Himalaya in 1934. Bill Tillman returned in 1936 (Shipton was on Hugh Rutledge's Everest Expedition) with a small climbing party and climbed the mountain with little real difficulty. See Books, page 1361, for recommended reading.



## Pindari Glacier Trek

This trek along the southern edge of the Sanctuary is an 'out and back' trek, ie you return by the same route. **KMVN Tourist Lodges** (www.kmvn.org,some with only four beds, none with telephones) are dotted along the route so this trek can be done with little equipment, although a sleeping bag is essential. Book accommodation early or take your own tent. The trek is 66 km from Song, which has the last bus terminus.

From **Bageshwar**, see page 240, get a local bus to **Bharari** at 1,524 m which has a **PWD Rest House**, a cheap hotel and **Tourist Bungalow** (T01372 260 465, www.gmvnl.com). Open all year.From here you can walk 16 km along the Sarju Valley to **Song** or take another bus. It is just over 1½ km further to **Loharkhet**, at 1,829 m, which also has a **PWD Bungalow** in the village and a basic **KMVN Tourist Rest House** overlooking it. Good views of the hillside opposite and the head of the Sarju Valley. It is 11 km from Loharkhet to **Dhakuri** via the Dhakuri Pass (2,835 m) which has a wonderful view of the south of the Nanda Devi Sanctuary including Panwali Dhar (6,683 m) and Maiktoli (6,803 m). The walk to the pass is mostly through forest on a well graded path. About 100 m below the pass on the north side is a clearing with a **PWD Bungalow** and a **KMVN Tourist Rest House**. Great views, especially at sunrise and sunset.

In the Pindar Valley you descend to **Khati** 8 km away at 2,194 m, first through rhododendron, then mixed forests dominated by stunted oak. Khati is a village with over 50 households situated on a spur that runs down to the river, some 200 m below. There is a **PWD Bungalow, KMVN Tourist Rest House** and a village hotel. You can buy biscuits, eggs and chocolate, brought in by mule from Bharari.

From Khati follow the Pindar 8 km to **Dwali**, 2,580 m, which is at the confluence of the Pindar and the Kaphini rivers. Here there is a **KMVN Travellers' Lodge** and a run down **PWD Bungalow**. If you have a tent, camp in front. The next halt 6 km on is **Phurkiya**, 3,260 m, which also has a **KMVN Travellers' Lodge**. This can be used as a base for going up to Zero Point (4,000 m), a view point from where the steep falling glacier can be seen (it is difficult for trekkers to go up to the snout of the glacier itself). On either side there are impressive peaks, including Panwali Dwar (6,683 m) and Nanda Kot (6,876 m). Return to Bharari the same way.

From Dwali, however, a side trip to the **Kaphini Glacier** is worthwhile. Alternatively, you could trek up to **Sundar Dhunga Glacier** from Khati. Including either of these, the trek can be accomplished in a week but for comfort allow nine days.

## Roopkund Trek → *Altitude: 4,800 m. Kund means lake in Garhwali.*

A legend relates Nanda Devi, the wife of Siva, to this small lake. When her sister Balpa accompanied her husband King Jasidhwal of the medieval Kingdom of Kanauj on a pilgrimage to Kailash (Mount Trisul), she delivered a child at Balpa de Sulera (adjoining Bhagwabasa), thus polluting the entire mountain. Nanda Devi's herald

*Famous mountaineers of the 1930s like Bill Tilman, Eric Shipton and Frank Smythe all marvelled at the beauty of the Garhwal and Kumaon Himalya region. Edmund Hillary's first Himalayan peak was Mukut Parbat. Later climbers like Chris Bonington, Peter Boardman, Joe Tasker, Dick Renshaw used alpine techniques to conquer Changabang and Dunagiri.*

 Latu (who has a temple at Wan), at the command of the Goddess, hurled the royal pilgrimage party into the small tarn called Roopkund; hence the remains of the 300 bodies found in the lake. Thirty years ago the Indian anthropologist DN Majumdar discovered a number of frozen bodies around this small mountain tarn, the remains of a party of pilgrims on a *yatra* who died when bad weather closed in. Carbon-dating suggests the bones are 600 years old.

This is a highly varied and scenic trek which can be undertaken by a suitably equipped party. A week is sufficient – nine days if you want to take it more comfortably with a rest day for acclimatization.The trek can start in Debal where you can pick up provisions, or at Bagrigarh (see below). You can usually get porters at Gwaldam or Debal.

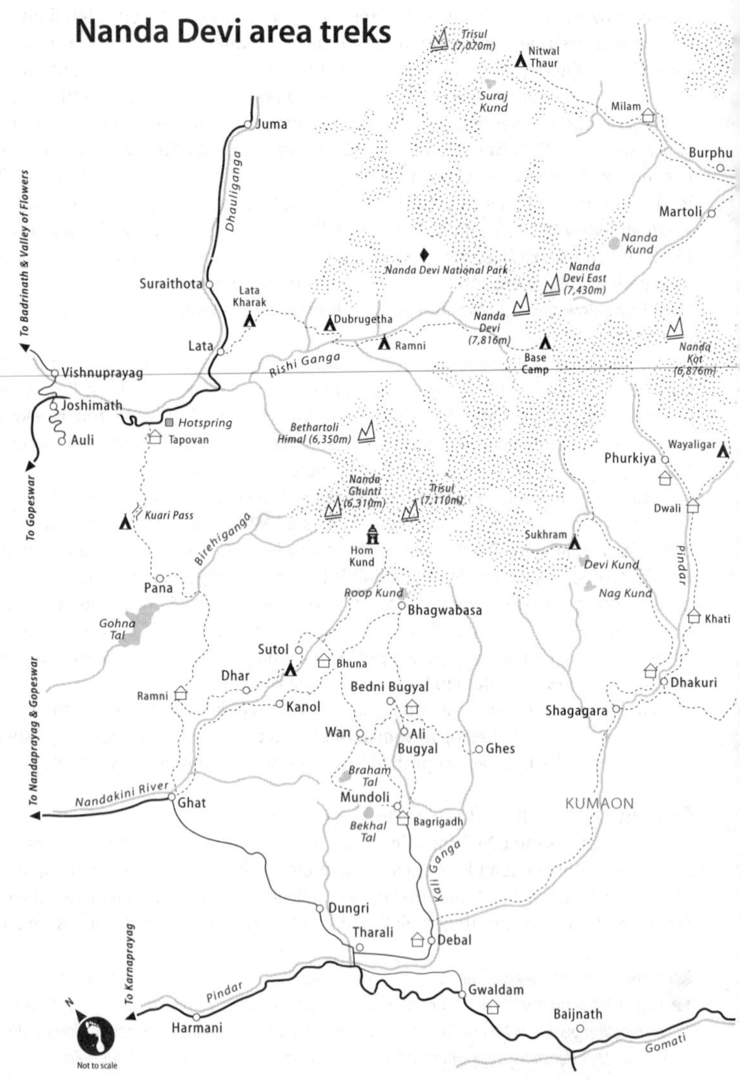

## Gwaldam → *Colour map 2, grid B3. Altitude: 1,950 m.*

Gwaldam is a small market strung out along a ridge surrounded by orchards. The British established tea plantations which have since been abandoned. **GMVN Tourist Bungalow** (T01363 274 244, www.gmvnl.com), has splendid views from the garden, especially at dawn and dusk, of Trisul (7,120 m) and Nanda Ghunti (6,310 m). Gwaldam, one of the starting points for the trek to Roopkund, see page 231, overlooks the beautiful Pindar River which the road follows down to its confluence with the Alaknanda River at **Karnaprayag**. The road joins the Pilgrim road which runs from **Rishikesh** and **Haridwar** to **Badrinath**, see page 222.

From Gwaldam, at 1,950 m, walk down through attractive pine forest, cross the River Pindar and continue 8 km to **Debal**, at 1,350 m, where there is a **KMVN Tourist Rest House**, a **Forest Rest House** and *dharamshalas*. From here you can either walk 12 km along a dirt road through villages with views of Trishul (6,855 m), or go by cramped jeep-taxi to **Bagrigad** which is 500 m below the **Lohajung Pass** (2,350 m) where there is an attractive **GMVN Travellers' Lodge** and two cheap lodges, right on the ridge beside a pretty shrine. The best option is **Patwal Tourist Lodge**, PO Mundoli, Chamoli, which has spotless, comfortable rooms, immaculate toilet and showers (bucket hot water), and treks arranged by a retired Army officer. Good views here of Nanda Ghunti. and Trisul from the terrace. If time is at a premium, you can save a day by going by bus from Gwaldam to Tharali, taking another bus to Debal, catching the jeep-taxi to Bagrigadh and walking up to Lohajung in one long day.

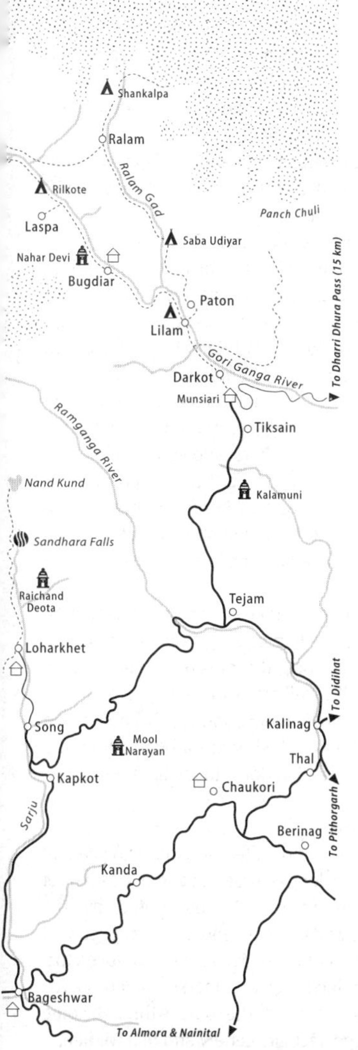


From **Lohajung** you walk down through stunted oak forest and along the *Wan Gad* (river) 12 km to the village of **Wan**, 2,400 m, which has a **Forest Rest House** and **GMVN Travellers' Lodge**. From Wan it is essentially wilderness travel as you make the ascent to Roopkund, first walking through thick forest to **Bedni Bugyal** (*bugyal* – meadow) which is used as summer pasture. This is at 3,550 m and has good views of Trisul, Nandaghunti and the Badrinath range to the north. There are some shepherds' stone huts which you may be able to use but it is better to take a tent.

From Bedni it is a gradual 7-km climb along a well defined path over the 4,500 m **Kalwa Vinayak** to more shepherds' huts at Bhagwabasa, at 4,000 m, the base for the final walk up to Roopkund. A stove is necessary for cooking and it can be very cold at night, but water is available about 150 m northeast and up the slope from the campsite. From here, it is two to three hours up to **Roopkund**. Immediately after the monsoon the views can disappear in cloud by 1000, so it is best to leave early. In the final steep part the ground can be icy. Roopkund Lake itself is small and unimpressive, but from the 4,900 m ridge approximately 50 m above Roopkund there is a magnificent view of the west face of Trisul rising over 3,500 m from the floor of the intervening hanging valley to the summit. Return to Gwaldam by the same route or via **Ali Bugyal** and village Didina which by-passes Wan.

## Curzon Trail

The Curzon Trail is an incomparably beautiful trek. However, rapid ascent follows equally steep descent from one valley to the next, and at no point does the trek get close to the high snow-covered peaks. It was the route followed by Tilman and Shipton on their way to the Rishi Gorge, and by other mountaineers en route to the peaks on the Indo-Tibetan border. The crossing of the Kuari Pass is a fitting conclusion to a trek that takes in three lesser passes and five major rivers – the Pindar, Kaliganga, Nandakini, Birehiganga and Dhauliganga. The trail was named after Lord Curzon, a keen trekker, and the path may have been specially improved for him. After 1947 it was officially renamed the 'Nehru Trail'. Take camping equipment. Some stopping off places have no suitable accommodation.

This trek begins at **Joshimath** via Auli, or at **Gwaldam** and ends at **Tapovan** in the Dhauliganga Valley on the Joshimath-Niti Pass road. It crosses the **Kuari Pass** (4,268 m), one of the finest vantage points in the Himalaya.

From Gwaldam proceed to **Wan** as in the previous trek. Then, go over the Kokinkhal Pass to **Kanol** (2,900 m) through thick mixed forest for 10 km to **Sutol**, at 2,100 m, in the Nandakini Valley. There is a good campsite by the river. The next two stages follow the Nandakini downstream 10 km to Padergaon, 2,500 m, via Ala. The trail to Tapovan leads up over the rhododendron forest clad **Ramni Pass** (3,100 m) with a good view of the Kuari Pass. The trail southwest of Ramni goes to the nearby road head at **Ghat**, from where you can also start the trek. To reach Tapovan from Ramni is a good three days' walk, down through lush forest to cross the Birehiganga River by an impressive suspension bridge, up around the horseshoe-shaped hanging valley around Pana Village, over an intervening spur and into the forested tributary valley of the Kuari nallah. There is no settlement in this area; *bharal* (mountain goats) and the rarely seen Himalayan black bear inhabit the rich forest. Waterfalls tumble down over steep crags. There is a camp and a cave (about one hour) before the Kuari pass at **Dhakwani** (3,200 m).

Leave early to get the full effect of sunrise over the peaks on the Indo-Tibetan border. Some of the peaks seen are Kamet, Badrinath (7,040 m), Dunagiri (7,066 m) and Changabang (6,863 m). There is a wonderful wooded campsite with marvellous views about 300 m below the pass. From here the trail drops down over 2,000 m to **Tapovan** and the Joshimath-Niti road. There is a hot sulpher spring (90°C) here and a bus service to **Joshimath**. Allow 10 days for the trek. A shorter trail leads from the campsite along a scenic ridge to Auli and a further 4 km down to Joshimath.

## Nanda Devi and Milam Glacier Trek

Much of this area was only reopened to trekkers in 1993 after more than 30 years of seclusion. The Milam Valley, incised by the 36-km long Gori Ganga gorge, was part of the old trade route between Kumaon and Tibet, only interrupted by the Indian-Chinese War of 1962. Milam, which once had 500 households, many occupied by wealthy traders and surrounded by barley and potato fields, has been reduced to a handful of occupied cottages. The trek is moderate, with some sustained steady walking but no really steep gradients or altitude problems. The route is through some of the remotest regions of the Himalaya with spectacular scenery and rich wildlife.

### Conquering Nanda Devi on apricot brandy

For half a century, the problem facing many experienced explorers and mountaineers was not so much how to climb the mountain but how to get to what became known as the Nanda Devi Sanctuary. The riddle was finally solved by Bill Tilman and Eric Shipton in a characteristically light-weight expedition. They discovered the way up the Rishiganga and through the difficult Rishi Gorge and made two trips into the sanctuary during their five-month expedition in 1934. Bill Tilman returned in 1936 with a small party and climbed the mountain with little real difficulty.

Tilman, a purist, wrote "mountaineering is in danger of becoming mechanized. It is therefore pleasing to record that in climbing Nanda Devi no climbing aids were used, apart, that is, from the apricot brandy we took. Our solitary oxygen apparatus was fortunately drowned, pitons were forgotten at base camp and crampons were solemnly carried up only to be abandoned" *The Ascent of Nanda Devi*.

In 1936 the monsoon was particularly heavy. The Pindar River rose dramatically. In the village of Tharali 40 lives were lost on 29 August, the day that Tilman's party reached the summit. Some say the anger of the Goddess was provoked by the violation of her sanctuary.

**Day 1** From **Munsiari** a 10-hour drive from Almora, takes you down to Selapani where the trail up the Milam Valley begins. **Lilam** (1,800 m) is an easy 7-km walk (2½ hours) where the tiny **Rest House** offers a convenient halt or camping ground for the first night. See page 240 for details about Munsiari.

**Day 2** (14 km; seven hours) From Lilam the trail enters the spectacular 25-km long gorge. Etched into the cliff face above the Gori Ganga the hillsides above are covered in dense bamboo thickets and mixed rain forest. After the junction of the Ralam and Gori Ganga rivers the track climbs to a tea shop at Radgari, then goes on to a small **Rest House** at **Bugdiar** (2,700 m). A memorial commemorates villagers and army personnel lost in the avalanche of 1989. Only a few houses remain on the edge of a wasteland.

**Day 3** (16 km; six hours) The valley opens up after climbing quite steeply to a huge overhanging cliff, which shelters a local deity. The route enters progressively drier terrain, but there are two waterfalls of about 100 m, one opposite a tea shop at Mapang. The track climbs to **Rilkote** (3,200 m).

**Day 4** (13 km; six hours) Passing deserted villages in the now almost arid landscape the track goes through the large village of **Burphu**, backed by the Burphu Peak (6,300 m). Nanda Devi East comes into view before reaching **Ganghar** village (3,300 m) where only three of the former 60 families remain. Some of the houses have beautiful carved wooden door and window frames; the carefully walled fields below are deserted.

**Day 5** (7 km; three hours) A steep narrow track leads into the **Pachhu Valley**, dominated by the northeast face of Nanda Devi East 3,800 m above the Pachhu Glacier. Dwarf rhododendron and birch, with anemones and primulas below, line the first section of the track before it emerges into alpine meadows below the debris of the glacier itself. **Tom Longstaff** came through this valley in his unsuccessful attempt to climb Nanda Devi East in 1905 before trying the parallel valley to the south of Pachhu via what is now known as Longstaff's Col. There is a campsite (3,900 m), 3 km from the base of Nanda Devi East, with both the col and the summit clearly visible in good weather.

**Day 6** Side treks are possible up to the Pachhu Glacier and along its edge to the glacial lake **Nanda Kund**.

**Day 7** (17 km; six hours) Returning via Ghanghar at Burfu, the track crosses the Gori Ganga on a wooden bridge then climbs to the former staging post of **Milam** (3,300 m).

**Day 8** Another 'excursion' (10 km; eight hours) is possible from Milam to the **Milam Glacier** (4,100 m). There are superb views of the clean ice uncovered by debris from the track which runs along the left bank of the Milam Glacier. Three tributary glaciers join the main Milam Glacier.

**Day 9** (13 km; five hours) The track runs along the left bank of the river via Tola village to the base of the 4,750 m Brijganga Pass, outside **Sumdu** village (3,400 m).

**Day 10** (12 km; seven hours) Superb views characterize this steady climb to the top of the pass. The razor sharp Panchulis dominate the south while the twin peaks of Nanda Devi are straight ahead. **Ralam** village is a steep drop below the pass (3,700 m).

**Day 11** (10 km; six hours) This can be a rest day or a day trek up to the Shankalpa Glacier along the watershed between the rarely visited Ralam and Darma valleys.

**Day 12-14** (six hours each day) The trek runs steadily down through the thickly forested Ralam valley, passing Marjhali, Bhujani, Buria, Sarpa and Besani villages.

**Day 15** (11 km; four hours) Return from Lilam to Munsiari via a number of villages.

### Darma Valley Trek

The easternmost of the Kumaon valleys, the Darma Valley is now also open to trekkers but you need permission. Separated from western Nepal by the Kaliganga River and with Tibet to the north, the valley is one of the least explored in the Himalaya. From the roadhead at **Dharchula** (on the India/Nepal border) it is possible to trek for four or five days up to Sipu and also to spend time exploring the numerous side valleys. Buses are available from Pithorgarh, see page 240, and Almora up to Dharchula from where it is often possible to get local transport for a further 32 km up to **Sobala**. Then it is a three to four days' trek up to Sipu, the northernmost point allowed under present regulations.

# Nainital and around

## Nainital → *Phone code: 05942. Colour map 1, grid C5. Population: 40,000. Altitude: 1,938 m.*

Set around a small lake, the charming hill station of Nainital has many villas, bungalows and fine houses with their well-kept lawns on the fairly steep tree covered hillsides. Overcrowded in summer, the resort is pleasanter out of season, with some attractive walks and only a few foreign tourists. It is more popular as an Indian family holiday centre. Congestion and pollution is taking its toll; the *tal*, now much reduced in size, is unable to cope with the increased tourist traffic. The pony riders, curio-sellers and snack stalls increase in number while the lake water becomes dirty and unable to support fish. Concerns that the lake contains excess amounts of toxic metals are exacerbated by the fact that it is the only source of the town's drinking water. It is best to drink bottled water here. It can be very cold in winter, and depressions sometimes bring cloud and rain obscuring the views of the mountains.

▸▸ *For Sleeping, Eating and other listings, see pages 241-244.*

## Ins and outs

**Getting there** The nearest railway station is 1¾ hrs away at Kathgodam, linked to Nainital by frequent buses. The climb from Kathgodam to Nainital is dramatic, rising 1,300 m over 30 km. The road follows the valley of the Balaya stream then winds up the hillsides through forests and small villages. After the long drive the town around the *tal* (lake) appears suddenly; the land south and on the plains-side fall away quite steeply so you only see the lake when you are at its edge. Buses from Delhi and the surrounding hill stations use the Tallital bus stand at the southern end of the lake, while some buses from Ramnagar (and Corbett National Park) use the Mallital bus stand at the northern end.

**Getting around** The Mall, pedestrianized at peak times, is the hub of Nainital's life. You can hire a cycle-rickshaw if the walk feels too much, or take a taxi for travelling further afield. ▸▸ *See Transport, page 243, for further details.*

## History

In 1839 the small hamlet of Nainital was 'discovered' by a Mr P Barron, a sugar manufacturer from Saharanpur. He was so impressed by the 1½ km long and 500 m wide lake that he returned with a sailing boat a year later, carried up in sections from the plains. In due course Nainital became the summer capital of the then United Provinces. An old legend of Siva and Sati, see page 210, associates the place as where Sati's eyes fell (hence *naini*). The *tal* (lake) is surrounded by seven hills, the *Sapta-Shring*. On 18 September 1880 disaster struck the town. At the north end of the lake, known now as Mallital (the southern part is Tallital) stood the **Victoria Hotel**. In two days nearly 1,000 mm of rain fell leading to a landslip which crushed some outhouses, burying several people. The cliff overhanging the hotel collapsed, burying the soldiers and civilians engaged in rescue work and making it impossible to save the 150 buried. Later the area was levelled, became known as The Flats, and was used for public meetings and impromptu games of football and cricket. Today it is more a bus park in the tourist season, though sports tournaments are held here in June, August and December.

## Sights

There is little of architectural interest other than the colonial style villas overlooking the lake (walking is the major attraction of this town). The **Church of St John in the Wilderness** (1846), one of the earliest buildings, is beyond Mallital, below the Nainital Club. The most distinctive building is **Government House** (1899, now the Secretariat) which was designed in stone by FW Stephens who was also responsible for VT (now CST) and Churchgate Stations in Mumbai (Bombay). Early in the season it is pleasant to walk round (the Lower Mall is pedestrianized) or take a boat across the lake; remember it can still be very cold in March.

**Naina (Cheena) Peak** (2,610 m) is a 5-km walk from the lake. From the top, there are stunning views of the Himalaya including **Nanda Devi** (7,816 m) and the mountains on the Tibetan border. In season there is a 'gondola' (Ropeway) which runs from the Mallital end of the lake to **Snow View** (2,270 m), another good vantage point for viewing the snow-capped peaks. It is also possible to make the 2-km steep climb up to the viewpoint from the north end of the lake, passing the small Tibetan gompa which has fluttering prayer flags marking it.

**Hanumangarh** with a small temple off Haldwani Road, and the **Observatory** (open evenings) further along the path (3 km from the lake), have lookouts for watching the sun set over the plains. The opposite side has only a few cottages and much higher up near the ridge are two private boys' schools – Sherwood College and St Joseph's. The atmospheric **British Cemetery** with its crumbling graves is about 3 km southeast of town. Take the minor road at the south end of the lake (not the Rampur Road); on the right side, the remains of the entrance gate are just visible behind some trees.

**Sat Tal**, 24 km away, has seven lakes including the jade green Garud Tal, the olive green Rama Tal and Sita Tal. **Naukuchiyatal**, 26 km away, is a lake with nine corners, hence the name. It is beautifully unspoilt, and quiet paddling round the lake allows you to see lots of birds; boats for hire. Tour buses stop around 1630.

**Pangot**, 15 km from Nainital via Kilbury, is in ideal birding territory where over 580 species have been recorded. **Jeolikote**, a small hamlet on the main road up from Ranpur, 18 km south of Nainital, is known for its health centre and butterflies, honey

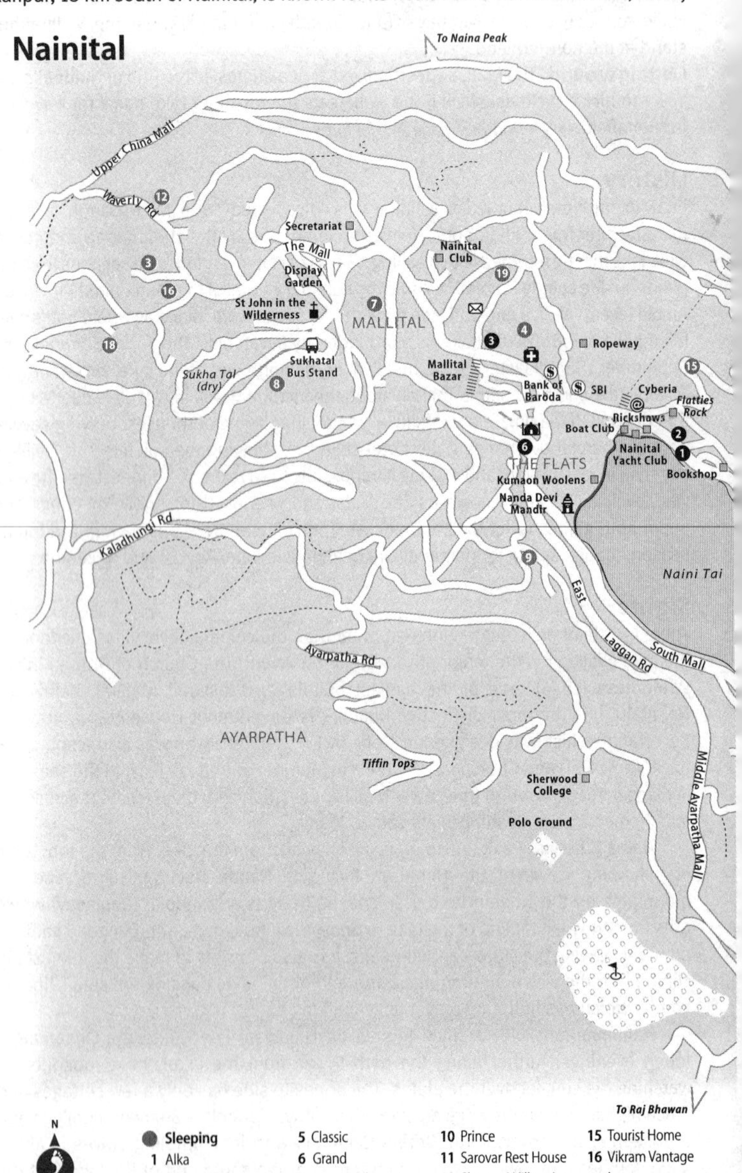


Sleeping
1 Alka
2 Alka Annexe
3 Balarampur House
4 Belvedere
5 Classic
6 Grand
7 Manu Maharani
8 Mount View Naina
9 Naina Retreat
10 Prince
11 Sarovar Rest House
12 Shervani Hilltop Inn
13 Silverton
14 Snow View
15 Tourist Home
16 Vikram Vantage Inn
17 YMCA
18 Youth Hostel

and mushrooms. It offers a peaceful weekend retreat. For Sleeping options around these areas, see the Nainital sleeping section.



## Around Nainital

### Almora and around

→ *Phone code: 05962. Colour map 1, grid C5. Population: 32,500. Altitude: 1,646 m.*

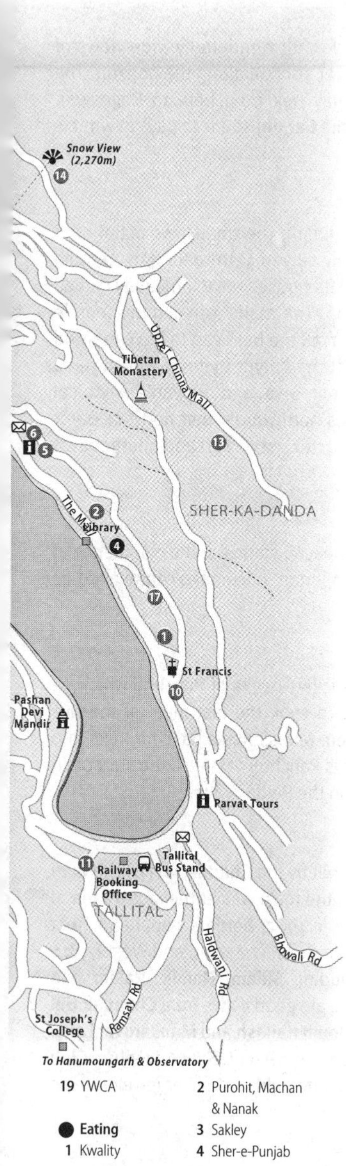


Like many hill towns, Almora occupies a picturesque horseshoe-shaped ridge. The Mall runs about 100 m below the ridge line, while the pedestrianized bazar above is jostling and colourful. The town was founded in 1560 by the Chand Dynasty who ruled over most of Kumaon, which comprises the present districts of Nainital, Almora and Pithoragarh. Overrun by the Gurkhas in 1798, it was heavily bombed by the British as they tried to expel them in the Gurkha Wars of 1814-1815. Traces of an old Chand fort, stone-paved roads, wooden houses with beautifully carved façades and homes decorated with traditional murals, reflect its heritage. Today it is an important market town and administrative centre and is also regarded as the cultural capital of the area.

Swami Vivekenanda came to Almora and gained enlightenment in a small cave at **Kasar Devi** on Kalimatiya Hill, 7 km northeast of town. This makes a pleasant walk and there are good views from the hill. Another vantage point for sunrise and sunset is Bright End Corner, 2½ km southwest of Mall Road, near All India Radio. The stone **Udyotchandesvar Temple**, above Mall Road, houses Kumaon's presiding deity, Nanda Devi, whose festival is in August/September. Almora's *Tamta* artisans still use traditional methods to work with copper. Copper metallurgy was known to the people here as early as the second century BC and is associated with the Kuninda Dynasty who traded in copper articles. The handbeaten copper pots are 'silver plated' in the traditional way (*kalhai*).

**Jageswar**, 34 km, in a serene wooded gorge famous for the 164 ornamented temples built by the Chand rajas, has one of the 12 *jyotirlingas*. The temples here and in nearby Gandeswar are very fine examples of early medieval hill temple architecture but are rarely visited by outsiders. The one dedicated to Jogeswar with finely carved pillars has a small museum; 6 km before Jageswar, a roadside sign points to stone-age **cave paintings**, about 50 m off the road. These are in red, white and black, depicting human figures, trees, animals and possibly water courses. Though several paintings were damaged by storage of cement bags during bridge building work nearby, many can be seen and are worth the short stop.

Once the capital of the Chand rajas, **Binsar** has a bird sanctuary sited at 2,410 m with superb views of valleys around and panoramic mountain views. It is 28 km away.

## Kausani → *Altitude: 1,892 m. 50 km north of Almora.*

Kausani sits on a narrow ridge among pine forests with wonderfully wide views of the **Nanda Devi** group of mountains stretching over 300 km along the horizon. The view is particularly stunning at sunrise. You may trek from here to Bageswar, Gwaldam and the Pindari Glacier. In 1929 **Mahatma Gandhi** spent 12 days at what is now Anashakti Ashram.

## Baijnath and Garur → *17 km northwest of Kausani.*

From Kausani, the road descends to Garur and Baijnath. The small town of Baijnath on the banks of the Gomti River has distinctively carved 12th- and 13th- century Katyuri temples. They are now mostly ruined, but its houses have intricately carved wooden doors and windows, see also page 497. The main 10th-century temple houses a beautiful image of **Parvati.** Siva and Parvati are believed to have married at the confluence of the Gomti and Garur Ganga. The Katyur Dynasty, which ruled the valley for 500 years, took their name from Siva and Parvati's mythical son, **Karttikeya**. **Garur** has plenty of buses/taxis northwards. Just north of Garur a road runs northwest to Gwaldam, see Roopkund trek, page 231, and another east to Bageshwar.



## Bageshwar

Bageshwar, meaning Siva as 'Lord of Eloquent Speech', stands at the confluence of the Gomti and Sarju rivers. It is Kumaon's most important pilgrimage centre and has several temples and two sacred pools.

## Munsiari → *Altitude: 2,300 m.*

This is a quiet hill town overlooked by the majestic five peaks of **Panchuli** which, in legend, served as the five *chulis* (stoves) used to cook the last meal of the five Pandava brothers before they ascended to heaven. Munsiari is a base for treks into the Milam, Ralam and Namik glaciers, and towards Panchuli. It is also the start of an easy trek (three to four days) via Namik to Dwali in the Pindar Valley.

## Pithorgarh

Sitting in a small valley with some fine temples built by the Chands, it is overlooked by a hill fort, 7 km away, dating from times when the town was at the crossroads of trade routes. The district, separated from Almora in 1962, borders Nepal and Tibet and has a number of high peaks such as Nanda Devi East (7,434 m) and West (7,816 m), and offers trekking to many glaciers including **Milam, Namik, Ralam** and **Panchuli**. See page 230 (no permit needed). There are good views from **Chandak Hill** (1,890 m), 7 km away. It is on the Pilgrim road to **Mount Kailash** and **Mansarovar Lake**. The Mount Kailash trek (Indian nationals only) starts from Askot. **Saur Adventure Club** is in Simalgher Bazar. The place is known for its fine gold and silver jewellery and bowls carved out of *sal* wood.

## Sleeping

**Nainital** *p236, map p238*
Peak rates (given here) can be high. Good off-season discounts are usual but may mean inadequate heating.

**AL-A Manu Maharani**, Grasmere, near Display Garden, T05942 237341, manu maharani@vsnl.com. 66 modern rooms, good views.

**A Naini Retreat**, Ayarpattha Slopes, 2 km from Mallital Bazar, T05942 235105, www.leisurehotels.co.in. 34 rooms, good restaurant, service and location.

**A Shervani Hilltop Inn**, Waverly Rd, T05942 236128, www.shervani hotels.com. 21 rooms in old royal home, some in cottages, peaceful, lovely garden, free jeep to centre.

**A-B Balarampur House**, Mallital, T05942 236236, balarampurhouse@rediffmail.com. 10 well-furnished rooms in a royal summer retreat converted to a luxury hotel, pleasant location.

**A-B Vikram Vintage Inn**, near ATI, Mallital, T05942 236177. 36 large, comfortable rooms, quiet wooded area but not all facilities (no pool).

**B Alka**, The Mall, Tallital, T05942 235220, www.alkahotel.com, and separate **Annexe** (closed in winter) nearby. 72 well-appointed, lake facing rooms, central heating, jungle theme, seasonal floating restaurant (good Indian). Recommended.

**B Belvedere** (WelcomHeritage), above **Bank of Baroda**, Mallital, T05942 237434, www.welcomheritage.com. 22 comfortable large rooms (good value family suite) with good lake views, in former Raja's summer palace – a colonial building with pleasant garden, restaurant, well located, quiet, friendly owners, helpful staff.

**B Cottage**, nestled on the hillside, Jeolikote, T05942 244413. Swiss chalet-style, has 3 beautiful spacious rooms with good valley views, meals included. Highly recommended.

**B-D Classic**, The Mall, T05942 237704, www.classichotelsindia.com. 25 pleasant rooms some with balcony, good restaurant, yoga.

**B-C Jungle Lore Lodge**, Pangot, has a cottage and hut with baths, 2 tents with shared facilities, meals included (from home-grown produce), library.

**C Grand**, The Mall, near Flatties Rock, T05942 235406, F235008. 31 basic but clean rooms, colonial style but faded, good food served on lake-facing verandah (order 3 hrs in advance), family run, friendly, good service. Recommended.

**C Lake Side**, Naukuchiyatal, T05942 247138. Well maintained and attractive. 12 rooms and dorm (Rs 60).

**C Sat Tal Camp**, Sat Tal, with pyramid tents, kayaking, mountain biking, rock climbing.

**C-D Prince**, The Mall, T05942 236817. 18 small, but comfortable rooms, decent room service.

**C-F Sarovar**, near Tallital Bus Stand, T05942 235570. 30 (**C**) rooms, 8-bed dorms (Rs 40), hot water, good value.

**D Silverton**, Sher-ka-Danda, 2½ km centre, T05942 235249. 27 rooms in 'chalets', some with good views, peaceful, veg restaurant.

**D-E KMVN Rest Houses**, www.kmvnl.com, are good value outside May to mid-Jul.

**E Damayanti**, Sat Tal, with 4 rooms.

**E-F Mount View Naina**, near Sukhatal Bus Stand, T05942 235400. 42 small, grubby rooms with bath, some with TV, restaurant, dorm (Rs 20), gardens, good value.

**F Youth Hostel**, west of Mallital Bazar, T05942 236353. 5 and 8-bed dorms, open to non-members (Rs 25), cheap meals, quiet, good, book 15 days ahead.

**Almora and around** *p239*
Most hotels give off-season discount of 50%. The options below are in Almora unless otherwise stated in the address.

**B Binsar Valley Resort**, Binsar, see Excursions, T1600 334539, www.clubmahindra.com, just outside the sanctuary, with 32 modern cottages, pleasant, clean, in spacious grounds, good food, exceptional service, good riding, river fishing and trekking.

**C-D Forest Rest House**, Binsar, see Excursions, T05962 280176, on a thickly

*For an explanation of the sleeping and eating price codes used in this guide, see inside the front cover. Other relevant information is found in Essentials pages 56-61.*

wooded spur near Nanda Devi, 1920s with 1930s cutlery and table linen lists still hanging on the walls! The furniture and decor are evocative of the Raj, and the caretaker may occasionally be persuaded to open the house for a few hours or for viewing.

C-D **Himsagar**, Mall Rd, T05962 230711, F230439. 18 comfortable rooms, best with view, hot water, TV, friendly.

C-E **Shikhar**, Mall Rd, near bus stand, T05962 230253, F230395. 55 rooms (vary widely), some with hot bath, good restaurant, fairly clean.

D **Nanda Devi**, in the heart of the sanctuary, Binsar, see Excursions, T05962 251110. Only filtered rainwater, electricity from solar batteries for few hours each evening.

D **Savoy**, above the GPO, T05962 230329. 17 good sized but basic rooms, some with hot bath, restaurant, pleasant terrace and quiet garden.

D **Snow View**, T05962 233650, sychem@ndf.vsnl.net.in. 15 rooms, some in cottages, great mountain views.

D-E **Holiday Home** (KMVN), 2 km southwest of bus stand, T05962 230250, www.kmvn.org. 14 simple cottages and 18 rooms with hot bath, dorm (Rs 60), restaurant, garden, good mountain views.

D-E **Jagnath** (KMVN), Jageswar, see Excursions, T05962 263028, www.kmvn.org, has rooms, dorm (Rs 60) and a restaurant.

D-E **Konark**, Mall Rd, T05962 231217. 13 clean rooms, TV, hot water in mornings, good views.

E **Shyam**, L R Shah Rd, T05962 235467, shyam2@nde.vsnl.net.in. 18 small but clean rooms, good terrace views.

F **Kailas**, up path opposite GPO, Mall Rd, T05962 230624, jawaharlalsah@India.com. 24 rooms all under Rs 100. Gloomy, dirty and poor food.

**Kausani** *p240*

B-D **Krishna Mountview**, near Gandhi Ashram, with 30 smart rooms, some with good views, fine location, credit cards accepted.

D-F **Trishul**, 2 km from town, with 6 basic cottages and dorm, restaurant, compass on the lawn to spot the peaks.

F **Uttarkhand Tourist Lodge** (View Point), near bus stand. Excellent value.

**Baijnath** *p240*

E Tourist Bungalow and Inspection House.

**Bageshwar** *p240*

C **Wayfarer Retreat**, 13 km before Chaukori

E **Bagnath**, 20 rooms, where you can hire trekking equipment, restaurant.

**Munsiari** *p240*

C **Wayfarer Mountain Resort**, 1 km beyond town. Comfortable Swiss tents, toilets, electricity, phone, Rs 1,200 including meals, forest walks, treks, trout fishing, jeeps, professionally run

D **Tourist Rest House**, main road just before the town, T05961 222 339. Comfortable, welcome hot showers, good value; also 2 other cheap lodges.

**Pithorgarh** *p240*

C **Rhythm Camp**, spacious tents with baths, meals included, views of valleys and peaks.

D-E **Ulka Devi**, T05964 222434, with restaurant. Others near the bus station are very basic.

## Eating

**Nainital** *p236, map p238*

Most restaurants are at the north of the lake, on the Mall. Some have a limited off-season menu.

ΨΨ **Kwality**, on the lake. Western and good Indian. Ideally located.

ΨΨ **Machan**, The Mall. Good Indian/Chinese and pizzas.

ΨΨ **Sakley**, The Mall, near GPO. Western dishes and confectionery.

Ψ **Sher-e-Punjab**, Mallital Bazar. Tasty, North Indian. Another half way to Tallital, with one serving very good local Kumaon dishes.

**Vegetarian**

**Kumaon Farm Products**, towards Ropeway, is good for snacks.

**Nanak** serves Western fast food.

**Purohit**, The Mall, opposite Kwality. Recommended for *thalis*.

**Almora** *p239*

Plenty of choice along the busy Mall Rd.

ΨΨ **Glory**, good North Indian, but a bit pricey.

Ψ **Madras Café**, beyond the bus stand. Good Indian meals and snacks.

**Kausani** *p240*
**Hill Queen**, above **Uttarkhand Tourist Lodge**, serves reasonably priced meals.

## Festivals and events

**Almora** *p239*
In **Sep-Oct Dasara** is celebrated with colourful Ramlila pageants. **Kumaon Festival of Arts.**

## Shopping

**Nainital** *p236, map p238*
Bazars sell local woollens and candles at Tallital and Mallital. Also souvenir shops on the Mall, Mallital, including **UP Handlooms, Gandhi Ashram**. Along the far edges of the Flats, Tibetan refugees sell wool and acrylic shawls; you can try steaming *momos* at a stall!
**Kumaon Woollens**, Mallital Bazar has locally made tweed – see also Almora, below.
**Narain's Bookshop**, The Mall (below Grand Hotel). A good selection.

**Almora** *p239*
**Ashok Traders**, LR Shah Rd, sells local copper articles.
**Kumaon Woollens**, just above the **KMVN Holiday Home**. Produces and sells 'Harris' type tweed. Locally knitted jumpers and the traditional Panchmarhi shawls ('five weave') in soft wool are popular.

### Photography

**Sangam**, Mall Road, opposite GPO. Slide, black and white films, lithium batteries available.

## Activities and tours

**Nainital** *p236, map p238*

### Boating

Peddle or sail on the lake, Rs 80 per hr; up and down Rs 60; pedal boat Rs 40.

### Fishing

Permits for the ake from Executive Officer, Nagar Palika. For other lakes Fisheries Officer, Bhimtal. Boat hire from Boat Club, Mallital.

### Mountaineering and trekking

Equipment can be hired from **Nainital Mountaineering Club**, T05942 222051, and KMVN, Tourist Office, Mallital, T05942 231 436. The Club organizes rock climbing at Barapathar, 3 km away.

### Pony hire

Snow View, Rs 40; Tiffin Top Rs 60; Naina (Chinna) Peak, Rs 150 (2½-3 hrs; can leave at 0500 to see sunrise from the top, but dress warmly); Naina Devi, Rs 30; horses are generally fit and well cared for. Horse Stand in Mallital, opposite **State Bank of India**.

### Tour companies

**Parvat Tours & Information** (KMVN), Dandi House, Tallital, near Rickshaw Stand, T05942 231 436, among others on the Mall. Day tours: Sat tal; Ranikhet; Mukteshwar (with the Veterinary Research Centre); Kaladhungi. 2-day trips: Kausani; Ranikhet/Almora; Corbett.
**Vibgyor**, 56 Tallital Bazar.

**Munsiari** *p240*
Nanda Devi Mountaineering Institution is in the SBI Building. In the main bazar is **Panchuli Trekking** and **Nanda Devi Trekking**, the former run by an elderly Milam tribal villager who has vast and accurate knowledge of the area.

**Almora** *p239*
**High Adventure**, Mall Rd, opposite the Post Office, T05962 232277. Organizes treks, cave tours, bus tickets.

## Transport

**Nainital** *p236, map p238*
Wherever possible, avoid night driving. The hill roads can be dangerous. Flat, straight stretches are rare, road lighting does not exist and villagers frequently drive their animals along them or graze them at the kerbside. During the monsoon (Jun-Sep) landslips are fairly common. Usually these are cleared promptly but in the case of severe slips requiring days to clear, bus passengers are transferred.
**Mall Road**: Access toll Rs 50. Access barred, May, Jun, Oct: heavy vehicles, 0800-1130, 1430-2230; light vehicles, 1800-2200; Nov-Apr: all vehicles, 1800-2000.

### Air

The nearest airport is Pantnagar (71 km) on the plains (flights suspended). **Parvat Tours** transfer coaches to Nainital (2 hrs). Open 1000-1600.

### Bus

**UP Roadways**, Tallital, for major inter-city services, T05942 235518, 0930-1200, 1230-1700; DTC, Hotel Ashok, Tallital, T35180. **Kumaon Motor Owners' Union** (KMOU), bus stand near Tourist Office, Sukhatal, Mallital, T05942 235451; used by private operators. Regular services to **Almora** (66 km, 3 hrs); **Dehra Dun** (390 km); **Delhi** (322 km), a/c night coach, 2100 (Rs 240, 8-9 hrs), or via Haldwani. **Haridwar** (390 km, 8 hrs); **Kausani** (120 km, 5 hrs); **Ranikhet** (60 km, 3 hrs) and **Ramnagar** for Corbett (66 km, 3½ hrs plus 3½ hrs).

### Rickshaw

Cycle-rickshaw and dandi about Rs 5-10 along The Mall.

### Ropeway

Cable-car/gondola, T05942 235772, from 'Poplars', Mallital (near GB Pant Statue) to Snow View, summer 0800-1830 in theory, but usually opens at 1000, winter 1000-1630, return fare Rs 65, advance booking recommended in season, tickets valid for a 1-hr halt at the top. Some claim its anchorage is weak.

### Taxi

From **Parvat Tours**, Tallital, T05942 231 436. Full day Rs 650 (120 km).

### Train

All India computerized reservation office, Tallital Bus Stand, T05942 235518. Mon-Fri, 0900-1200, 1400-1700, Sat, 0900-1200. The nearest railhead is **Kathgodam** (35 km), taxi, Rs 350 (peak season), bus Rs 24. **Delhi (OD)**: *Ranikhet Exp, 5014*, 2040, 8 hrs. Towards **Dehradun and Haridwar (OD)**: *Dehradun-Kathgodam Exp, 4321*, 2230, 9 hrs. **Kolkata (H) via Lucknow and Gorakhpur**, *Howrah Bagh Exp, 3020*, 1930, 64½ hrs. An alternative for **Lucknow** is the *Nainital Exp, 5307*, 2050, 9¼ hrs from **Lalkuan**, south of Kathgodam.

### Almora *p239*

### Bus

Connect Almora with **Kathgodam** (90 km, 3 hrs) for **rail** links, and with **Nainital** (3 hrs) and **Ranikhet** (2½ hrs). Hourly buses to **Kausani** (3 hrs). Direct buses go to **Banbassa** and the Nepal border, depart 0730 (6 hrs).

### Jeep

Share jeeps to **Ranikhet**, Rs 35. For **Nainital**, take **Haldwani** jeep as far as **Bhowali**, then bus or jeep to Nainital.

### Kausani *p240*

Buses from Almora and Ranikhet (2½-3½ hrs). Joshimath is a tough but spectacular 10-hr journey.

### Munsiari *p240*

Buses from Almora, change at Thal; from Haldwani or Nainital, take bus to Pithorgarh and change. To Almora (11 hrs) and Pithorgarh (8 hrs), 0500 and another for Pithorgarh in the afternoon.

## Directory

**Nainital** *p236, map p238*

**Banks** In Mallital: Bank of Baroda, below Belvedere Hotel. For cash against Visa card. State Bank of India for exchange. **Hospital** BD Pande Govt Hospital, Mallital, T05942 235012. **Internet** Try Cyberia, The Mall, near ropeway. Reasonably reliable connection if a bit pricy at Rs 2/min. **Library** The Library, The Mall, by the lake. Open weekdays (closed mid-morning to mid-afternoon). Pleasant for dropping in. **Post** Mallital. Branch at Tallital. **Tourist offices** KMVN: Information Centre, at Parvat Tours; at Secretariat, Mallital, T/F05942 231 436. Uttar Pradesh, Mall Rd, Mallital, T05942 235 337. Tourist Bungalow, T05942 235400. **Useful addresses** Ambulance: T05942 235022. Fire: T05942 235626. Police: T05942 235424 (Mallital), T05942 235525 (Tallital).

**Almora** *p239*

**Banks** State Bank of India, Mall Road. May change Amex TCs, but don't rely on this. Best to change in advance. **Hospitals** District Hospital, Chowk Bazar, T05962 230322. **Post** GPO on Mall Rd. **Tourist offices** KMVN, at Holiday Home, and Uttaranchal, opposite GPO, T05962 230180. 1000-1700.

# Corbett National Park

→ *Phone code: 05945. Colour map 1, grid C5. Altitude: 400-1,200 m.*

*The journey from Delhi to one of the finest wildlife parks in India offers excellent views of the almost flat, fertile and densely populated Ganga-Yamuna doab, one of the most prosperous agricultural regions of North India. Corbett is India's first national park and one of its finest. As well as rich and varied wildlife and birdlife it is also extremely picturesque with magnificent sub-montane and riverain views.* ▸▸ *For Sleeping, Eating and other listings, see pages 248-250.*

## Ins and outs

### Entry fees

Foreigners Rs 200, Indians Rs 30. Entrance permit for Dhikala is valid for three days (two nights), each additional day, Rs 150, Indians Rs 20. Otherwise permit is valid for a single visit each time the park is entered. Entrance permits are not transferable between gates (eg a morning visit to Bijrani and a night halt at Dhikala will entail payment of all entrance fees on both occasions). Car/jeep Rs 100 plus Rs 30 for driver. All visitors in cars or jeeps must have a guide, Rs 100 for the first four hours plus Rs 20 for each additional hour at Dhikala. In Bijrani, these fees are Rs 75 and Rs 15 respectively.

### Access

Day visits are allowed by entry at the Amdanda and Laldhang Gates for Bijrani and Jhirna respectively. A limit of 30 vehicles per day at each entrance is applied, half of which can be booked in advance. Prior reservation to enter is recommended for day visits, although not always necessary at dawn, when half the entry is determined on a first-come-first-served basis. You may be refused entry when the quota is filled. The main gate at Dhangarhi (for Dhikala) is approximately 16 km north of Ramnagar on the Ranikhet road. There is no entry to the park from the Kalagarh side. From 1 March until the monsoon all roads around Dhikala, except the main approach road, are closed between 1100-1500 when visitors are not allowed to move about the forest. A reservation at the Bijrani or Dhela **Forest Rest Houses** does not entitle visitors to enter by the Dhangari gate. Only visitors who are staying overnight may enter Dhikala. Closed 15 June-15 November.

### Climate

Rainfall is heavier in the higher hills, on average the valley receives 1,550 mm, the bulk from July to mid-September. Summer days are hot but the nights quite pleasant. Winter nights can get very cold and there is often a frost and freezing fog in the low lying tracts. January to mid-June; for birdwatching, December-February. Summer is the best time for seeing the larger mammals which are bolder in leaving the forest cover to come to the river and water holes; early summer for scenic charm and floral interest. Closed from 15 June to 15 November.

## Sights

### Wildlife

The park has always been noted for its **tigers**; there are around 80 but they are not easily spotted. About 10% of visitors see one – usually entering at the Bijrani gate.

 There are leopards too but they are seldom seen. Sambar, chital, para (hog deer) and muntjac (barking deer) are the main prey of the big cats and their population fluctuates around 20,000. Some like the chital are highly gregarious whilst the large sambar, visually very impressive with its antlers, is usually solitary. The two commonly seen monkeys of North India are the rhesus (a macaque – reddish face and brownish body) and the common langur (black face and silvery coat). Elephants are now permanent inhabitants since the Ramganga Dam has flooded their old trekking routes. There are now a few hundred and they are seen quite often. Other animals include porcupine, wild boar (often seen around Dhikala) – some can be quite dangerous, attacking unsuspecting visitors who have food with them. In total there are over 50 species of mammal alone, though the dam appears to have caused significant losses. The last Swamp deer was seen in March 1978, and the loss of habitat has been keenly felt by the cheetal, hog deer and porcupine, all of which appear to be declining.

There are 26 species of reptiles and seven of amphibians. In certain stretches of the river and in the Ramganga Lake are the common mugger crocodile, notice prohibits swimming – "Survivors will be prosecuted"!), the fish eating gharial, soft shelled tortoises in the streams, otters and river fish. The python is quite common.

The birdlife is especially impressive with over 600 species and this includes a wide range of water birds, birds of prey such as the crested serpent eagle, harriers, Pallas' fishing eagle, osprey, buzzards and vultures. Woodland birds include: Indian and Great Pied hornbills, parakeets, laughing thrushes, babblers and cuckoos.



## Corbett National Park

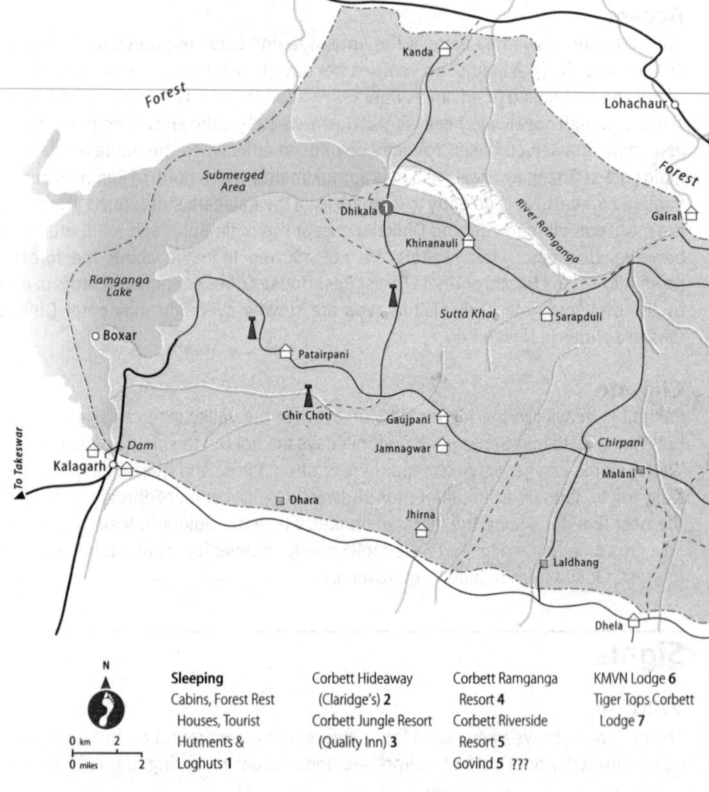

Doves, bee-eaters, rollers, bulbuls, warblers, finches, robins and chats are to be seen in the open scrub from the viewing towers. The rarer ibis bill is one of the main attractions for serious twitchers.

## Vegetation

There are 110 species of trees, 51 species of shrubs, three species of bamboos and 27 species of climbers. The valley floor is covered with tall elephant grass (*Nall* in the local terminology), lantana bushes and patches of *sal* and *sheesham* (*Dalbergia sissoo*) forest, whilst the enclosing hills on both sides are completely forest covered, with *sal*, *bakli*, *khair*, *jhingan*, *tendu*, *pula* and *sain*. *Charas* grows wild in the fields. Nullahs and ravines running deep into the forests are dry for much of the year, but there are swift torrents during the monsoon. These hold brakes of bamboo and thick scrub growth.

## Viewing

**Elephant rides** are available from Dhikala where there are about five animals, and three at Bijrani. Each elephant can carry four people. This is the best way to see the jungle and the wildlife. Morning and evening, two hours, Rs 200 per person (foreigner), Rs 100 (Indian); book at Dhikala or Bijrani Reception (whichever is relevant). Book as early as possible on arrival since these rides are very popular. **Cars** and **jeeps** may drive round part of the park. Check with Reception. Jeep safari (up to six persons), two to four hours, Rs 500; day hire Rs 800-1000 (negotiable) from Ramnagar. Apart from the immediate area within the complex at Dhikala, **don't go walking in the park**. Tiger and elephant attacks are not unknown. The two watch towers are good vantage points for spotting wildlife. Night driving is not allowed in the park.

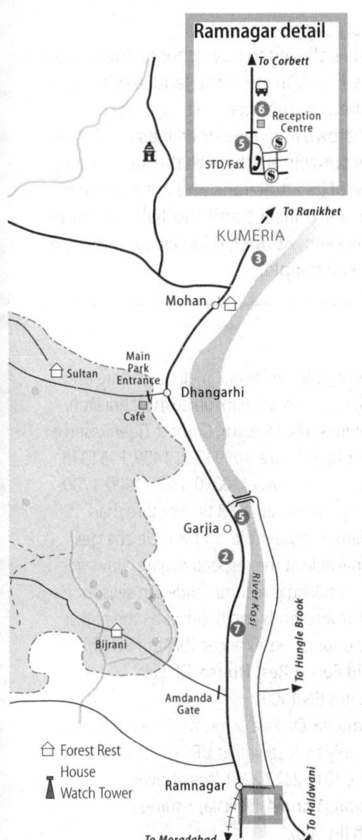


## Ramnagar

Ramnagar, with a railway station, 134 km from Moradabad, is 18 km from the Park boundary and 50 km from **Dhikala**. It is a noisy town with the Project Tiger Office for Corbett reservations, and provides a night halt. They will receive faxes and hold them.

## Kaladhungi

At Kaladhungi visit **Jim Corbett's house**, now a small museum, Rs 10. The area is an extension of the Tiger Reserve with equally good wildlife but minus the restrictions, and is also excellent for bird watching. If you turn up the road opposite and continue up into the hills, travelling along a delightful, metalled road that winds its way up the hillsides through *chir* pine forest and the occasional village, you'll see impressive views of the plains. You enter Nainital at the north end of the lake.

### Tiger, tiger, burning bright ...

Jim Corbett was born in 1875 into the large family of the postmaster at Nainital. From childhood he was fascinated by the jungles around Nainital. This developed into a considerable knowledge of the ecosystem's workings. He became a superb shot, killing his first leopard when he was eight. Tigers were his most sought after prey, followed by leopards which were difficult to sight, let alone shoot.

He continued to hunt during his working life in the Bengal Northeast Railway and later as an advisor to the army. But from the mid-1920s he turned to photography, tracking and killing only the man-eating leopards and tigers that terrorized the Kumaon hills from time to time. Later in life he recounted his exploits in a series of books about man-eaters and the jungle: *The Man-Eating Leopard of Rudrapayag*, *The Man-eaters of Kumaon* and *Jungle Lore*. For a biography of Corbett see *Carpet Sahib: The life of Jim Corbett* by Martin Booth.

Jim Corbett has always been an inspiration to India's conservationists. On 1 April 1973 Project Tiger was inaugurated in nine parks, the aim being to preserve the rapidly dwindling population of tigers in India. The scheme was later extended to over 18 reserves.



## Ranikhet → *Phone code: 05966. Colour map 1, grid C5.*

Rani Padmadevi, the queen of Raja Sudhardev is believed to have chosen the site of this scenic place, hence Ranikhet (The Queen's Field). In 1869 the land was bought from local villagers and the British established a summer rest and recreation settlement for their troops, made it a cantonment town and developed it as a quiet hill station. Set along a 1,800 m high ridge, Ranikhet sprawls out through the surrounding forest without having a proper centre. This is one of its attractions and there are many enjoyable walks. The views from the ridge are magnificent and the twin peaks of Nanda Devi (7,816 m and 7,434 m) can be clearly seen. At **Upat**, 6 km away, there is a beautifully located nine-hole golf course and a Kali temple.

## Sleeping

**Corbett National Park** *p245, map p246*
If you are travelling to the park without reserved accommodation, you must go to Ramnagar first to make a booking, see page 247. Dhikala is the park centre and has accommodation. Remember to get a clearance card from Dhikala from the office here before leaving in the morning. There is a decent restaurant (big portions). Also a small *dhaba* with cheaper food and basic necessities (biscuits, chocolate, soap etc).

**Within the park**
Reservations for all accommodation, except Annexe and Cabin 3 at Dhikala, can be booked at the Reception Centre in Ramnagar. The exceptions can at present only be booked in the UP/Uttaranchal Tourist Office in Delhi. Small quotas are also available from the Park office in Dehra Dun. Enquiries: The Director, Corbett Tiger Reserve Reception Centre, T05947-251489, F251376. Open 7 days a week, 0830-1300, 1500-1700. Foreigners pay about 3 times more than Indians. Entry permits and vehicle charges are payable at the respective gate. However, early booking is recommended in season and at weekends and holidays as the park is very popular, easily accessible from Delhi.

B **Old Forest Rest House**, Dhikala 5 suites (Rs 1500).

C **Annexe**, Dhikala, 7 rooms (Rs 900) (Rs 900) can only be reserved at UP Tourist Office, Delhi, T011 2332 2251 (see above).

C **Cabin 1 and 4**, Dhikala, 3 suites each (Rs 900).

**C Cabin 3**, Dhikala, with 2 suites (Rs 900) can only be reserved at UP Tourist Office, Delhi, T011 2332 2251 (see above).
**C New Forest Rest House**, Dhikala, 4 suites (Rs 900).
**D Tourist Hutment**, Dhikala, 6 3-bed suites (Rs 700).
**F Loghuts**, Dhikala, 24 bunks (Rs 100), separated into Indian and foreigner sections, but not noise-proof! Bedding is available, Rs 25. The restaurant is good with wonderful views, is reasonably priced but has limited choice.
A small *dhaba* provides a cheaper option.

**Outside the park**
In top resorts, meals and guided visits are included in the price.
**AL Infinity Resorts** (Infinity Resorts), T05947-251279, www.infinityresorts.com, 8 km north of Ramnagar. 24 rooms, pool, lawns, mango orchards, good food, old world feel, charming staff.
**A Jungle Brook**, Tera Village, T098110 95698 or Delhi T011 5516 6668, www.junglebrook.com. Choice of luxury tents or beautifully and originally designed cottages, whole place has innovative but friendly feel, all meals included, highly recommended.
**A Corbett Hideaway**, Garjia, above the river (10-min drive from gate), T05947 284132, www.leisurehotels.co.in. 30 upmarket lodges in orchard on riverside, 20 luxury tents, jeep transfer to park, good food, very good naturalist in Imran Khan, well run, own elephant for viewing, pool.
**A Corbett Jungle Resort (Quality Inn)**, Kumeria Reserve Forest, Mohan, about 13 km from the Dhangarhi entrance, T05947 251 230, www.qualityinn.com. Among mango and sal trees. 18 small cottages, imaginatively designed and built of natural materials, restaurant, elephant rides, jeeps, jungle walks, swimming in Kosi River, eco-friendly resort.
**A Corbett Ramganga Resort**, Jhamaria, 17 km from Dhangarhi, T011-2626 6650, www.welcomheritage.com. On the river. 10 well-appointed rooms in cottages, 8 Swiss cottage tents, safe spring water, river rafting, riding, rockclimbing and gliding, fishing (fighting fish in the river pools below), excellent pool and ground, friendly service, very picturesque position on the river edge.
**A Tiger Camp**, Dhikuli, T05974 287901, www.tiger-camp.com. 10 clean cottages (with 10 more to come) in Kumaoni Village style but modern interiors, rooms with fan and bath (**E**), tents (shared bath), electricity (plus generator), good food, lovely garden, jeep, hiking, friendly owner, recommended, contact **Asian Adventures**, Delhi, T0120-255 1963, tigercamp@indianwildlife.com.

**Ramnagar** *p247*
**C-D KMVN Lodge**T05947 251225. 12 rooms in 3 different categories.
**E Govind**, and 100 m down the road.
Also cheap, basic **F** guest houses in town.

**Kaladhungi** *p247*
**A Camp Corbett**, 25 km east of Corbett, T05942 242126, www.campcorbett.net. Cottages and tents, wonderful meals, an outstanding resort run by the hospitable Anand family, relaxing and totally hassle free, pick-up from Haldwani station arranged. Highly recommended.

**Ranikhet** *p248*
**B Chevron Rosemount**, The Mall (2 km centre), T05966 220191. Refurbished old colonial building, stylish, croquet lawn, tennis.
**B-D Parwati Inn**, above bus stand, T05966 220403. Good choice from 32 large rooms, restaurant, friendly staff, credit cards accepted, best in the town itself.
**C Moon**, Sadar Bazar, T05966 220382. 14 clean rooms plus 2 (**B**) cottages, TV, restaurant.
**C West View**, MG Rd, 5 km centre, T05966 220261. 19 rooms in an old-fashioned hotel, restaurant, exchange, large grounds, golf club nearby.
**D-E Himadri**, Chilia naula, 7 km west, T05966 220588. New unit next to the temple complex, rooms, dorm (Rs 50), restaurant.
**D-E Kalika**, T05966 220297. Pleasant rooms with bath, some 'super deluxe', restaurant (mostly Indian), attractive location in the upper cantonment with good views.

*For an explanation of the sleeping and eating price codes used in this guide, see inside the front cover. Other relevant information is found in Essentials pages 56-61.*

## Activities and tours

**Corbett National Park** *p245, map p246*
**GMVN** run 3-day tours from Delhi departing every Fri in season. Reservations: Uttar Pradesh Tourist Office, Chandralok Building, 36 Janpath, New Delhi, T011 2332 2251.
**Tigerland Safaris**, T05947-282122, www.tigerlandsafaris.com. Well-organised safaris, professional service. Recommended.

## Transport

**Corbett National Park** *p245, map p246*

**Air**
**Phoolbagh airport** at Pantnagar (130 km) has no flights at present.

**Bus**
The Delhi-Dhikala road (260 km) passes through Moradabad (turn left after Moradabad, towards Kashipur and Ramnagar), 5½-6 hrs – strewn with bus/lorry/car crashes.

Bus to **Ramnagar**, 1000 from Dhikala (after elephant ride), from Ramnagar, 1530, Rs 43, not reliable; several from Kumeria, Rs 12; several to **Moradabad** and **Ranikhet** (wait outside Dhangarhi gate, no need to return to Ramnagar). Also buses to **Delhi** (6½-7 hrs), and Lucknow.

**Jeep**
From near Ramnagar Park office; to Dhikala (return), Rs 500 one way; Rs 600-800 return, plus driver fee (Rs 30).

**Train**
Nearest station is at Ramnagar (50 km), for **Moradabad** and **Delhi**. From Old Delhi railway station, *Corbett Park Link Exp, 5016A*, 2245, 6 hrs; from Ramnagar, *5014A*, 2110, 7¼ hrs.

**Ranikhet** *p248*
Regular buses to **Ramnagar**, **Almora** and **Nainital** operated by KMOU, T20214, and UP Roadways (may change), T20516, with bus stands at each end of the Mall.

## Directory

**Ranikhet** *p248*
**Banks** State Bank of India, at the top end of The Mall. Changes Amex and Thomas Cook TCs only. **Hospital** Civil Hospital, near Bus Stand, T05966 220422. **Post** On The Mall. **Tourist office** Uttaranchal, The Mall, T05966 220227. 1000-1700.

# Madhya Pradesh and Chhattisgarh

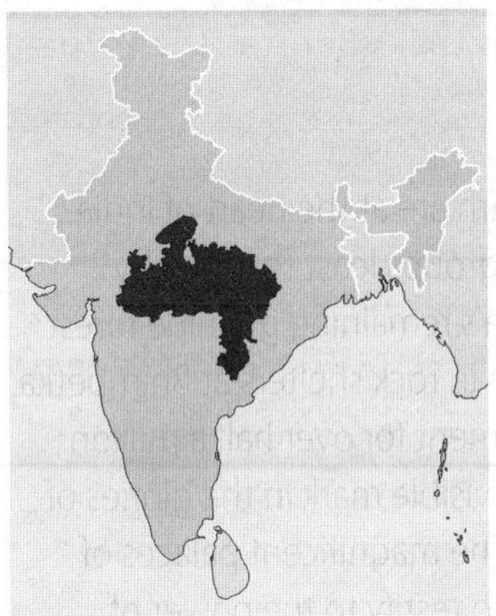



**Footprint features**

# Introduction

Madhya Pradesh and Chhattisgarh are at the heart of India. They contain many of the tribal groups least touched by modernization and most of India's remaining genuine forest. The magnificent paintings made in rock shelters at Bhimbetka illustrate the continuity of settlement for over half a million years, while Buddhism left a still visible mark in the glories of Sanchi's 2,000-year-old stupas. The magnificent palaces of Orchha and temples of Khajuraho testify to the power of Rajput dynasties for over a 1,000 years. Flowing westwards along the southern edge of the great Vindhyan ranges runs the Narmada, the site of one of the largest – and most controversial – dam development programmes in the world. Yet Madhya Pradesh remains largely unindustrialized and little visited, allowing the still dense forests and grasslands of the east to house two of India's best national parks at Kanha and Bandhavgarh.

On 1 November 2000 sixteen districts in the southeast of Madhya Pradesh were carved out to create the new state of Chhattisgarh. One of the least accessible areas of peninsular India, it is a largely tribal state.

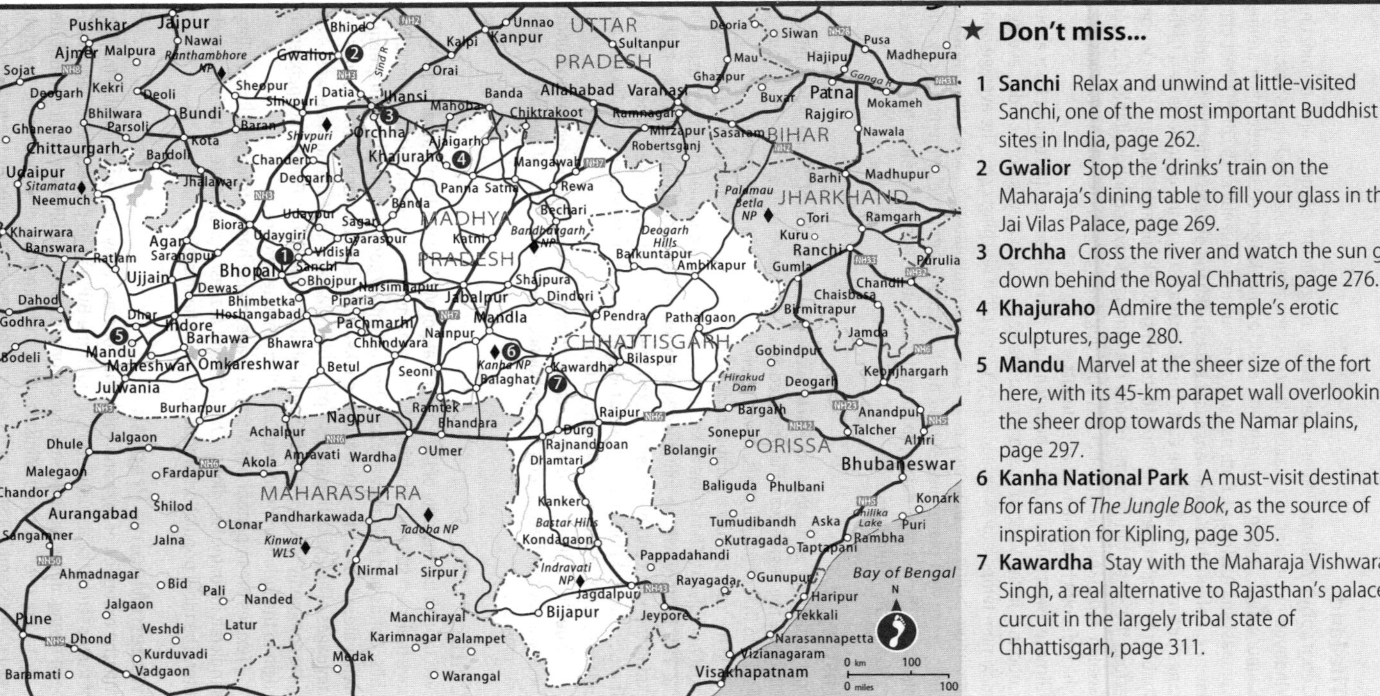


## ★ Don't miss...

1 **Sanchi** Relax and unwind at little-visited Sanchi, one of the most important Buddhist sites in India, page 262.

2 **Gwalior** Stop the 'drinks' train on the Maharaja's dining table to fill your glass in the Jai Vilas Palace, page 269.

3 **Orchha** Cross the river and watch the sun go down behind the Royal Chhattris, page 276.

4 **Khajuraho** Admire the temple's erotic sculptures, page 280.

5 **Mandu** Marvel at the sheer size of the fort here, with its 45-km parapet wall overlooking the sheer drop towards the Namar plains, page 297.

6 **Kanha National Park** A must-visit destination for fans of *The Jungle Book*, as the source of inspiration for Kipling, page 305.

7 **Kawardha** Stay with the Maharaja Vishwaraj Singh, a real alternative to Rajasthan's palace curcuit in the largely tribal state of Chhattisgarh, page 311.

# Background → *Population: 60.39 million. Area: 308,000 sq km.*

## The land

**Geography** Madhya Pradesh has some magnificent scenery. The dominating **Vindhyan** mountains run diagonally across the heart of Madhya Pradesh while the Kaimur range runs to the north and east, overlooking the Gangetic plain around Varanasi and Allahabad. Both rise to 600 m but are frequently cut by deep forest-clad ravines. Behind the Kaimur range is the **Baghelkhand plateau** while the Hazaribagh range juts into the state in the east. The **Narmada** rising in the east, flows west to the Arabian Sea, along with the Tapti to its south. Black volcanic soils are often visible across the state, but in some places the land is stony and inhospitable. Between Gwalior and Jhansi the Chambal River has dug deep gorges, creating a *badlands* area which **dacoits** have enjoyed as hideouts.

**Climate** Most rainfall comes between June and September, increasing from about 1,000 mm in the west to 2,000 mm in the east. March-May is hot and dry, average maximum temperatures exceeding 33°C and often reaching 44°C. The average daily maximum during the monsoon is 30°C and the minimum 19°C, when the landscape turns green and places like Mandu are particularly attractive. Winters are dry and pleasant. The average daily maximum temperature from November to February is 27°C and the minimum 10°C.



## History

Rock paintings and stone artefacts prove the existence of Stone Age cultures. Although the region was incorporated into successive states from the empire of Asoka to that of the Mughals, it was rarely the centre of a major power.

In the 10th century a number of dynasties controlled different parts of the region, most notably the Chandelas at Khajuraho. Gwalior was conquered by the Muslims in the 11th century, whose influence spread southeast under the Khaljis into Malwa during the 13th century. Akbar annexed this into his empire in the mid-16th century. The Scindia and Holkar Dynasties of Marathas ruled independently at Gwalior and Indore respectively during the 18th century.

Under the British the region became known as the Central Provinces and under the state re-organization after independence the modern state of Madhya Pradesh was created.

## Culture

Even though the majority of the former state of Madhya Pradesh's tribal people now have their own state of Chhattisgarh, MP remains the home of many tribals, including Bhils, Gonds and Baigas. Many have been painfully absorbed into the mainstream of Indian life. Hindi is the most widely spoken language. On each of the borders the languages of neighbouring states – particularly Marathi and Gujarati in the west – are quite commonly used. The Bhils speak **Bhili** and the Gonds **Gondi**, independent in origin to the Indo-European and Dravidian language groups.

Textiles are important but Madhya Pradesh also has a strong traditional village handicraft industry. Handloom *Chanderi* and *Maheshwar* silks are especially sought after. The tribal population produce attractive handicrafts.

## Modern Madhya Pradesh

With the exception of 1977 and 1989, the Congress Party held a comfortable majority of the Assembly seats until 2003, though the **BJP** and its predecessors had always been strong. In the last Lok Sabha elections in 2003, the BJP won , with Shri Babulal Gaur taking over as Chief Minister. With the formation of Chhattisgarh the state legislative assembly lost 90 of its seats to the new state, reducing the total to 230.

### Tribal traditions

In the last hundred years the Baigas of Central India have been forced to abandon shifting cultivation in favour of settled agriculture. Traditionally semi-nomadic, most tribals have now been settled but liquor and drug dependency are said to be common among the men. Over the centuries, tribal territory has gradually been nibbled away, and everywhere their way of life is under threat.

The Gonds, the largest of the tribes, managed to maintain their independence until the last century. From 1200 AD there were as many as four Gond Kingdoms. Some tribal traditions, mythology and folklore have been preserved, though they have been exposed to outside cultural influences. Today one of the biggest threats to the tribals comes from the dams across the Narmada River which will flood vast tracts of tribal forest land.

Under Digvijay Singh's leadership, the previous Chief Minister, Madhya Pradesh was been one of the first states to tackle its huge Government overspend problem. His cut backs on government jobs produced a strong reaction from the opposition, but by June 2002 the policy had led MP to being one of the first states to return to financial surplus.

# Central Madhya Pradesh

## Bhopal → *Phone code: 0755. Colour map 2, grid C6. Population: 1,450,000.*

Situated round two artificial lakes and on gently rolling hills, parts of Bhopal, the state capital of Madhya Pradesh, have a spacious feel with some pleasant parks, ambitious royal palaces and modern public buildings. The busy and rather dirty core of the Old City with its large mosques, as well as the crowded commercial centre in the New Market area of TT Nagar beyond the lakes to the southwest, are less attractive. ▸▸ *For Sleeping, Eating and other listings, see pages 265-268.*

### Ins and outs

**Getting there** Only seven hours by the *Shatabdi Express* train from Delhi, Bhopal is on the main line to South India. There are direct flights from Delhi, Gwalior and Bombay, and an extensive network of long-distance buses. The long-distance bus stand is on Hamidia Road, the main hotel area. The airport is about 20 minutes by bus from the town centre. ▸▸ *See Transport, page 267, for details.*

**Getting around** The town is quite spread out, and even from the Old City centre it takes about 15 minutes to walk from the railway station to the bus station. Local buses go to all parts of town but the best bet is an auto-rickshaw. A surcharge will be charged to go to the Shamla Hills or other points on the edge of town.

### History

Legend suggests that Bhopal stands on an 11th-century site created by Raja Bhoja, who is believed to have built a *pal* (dam) which created the lakes. The modern city was developed by **Dost Mohammad Khan**, one of Aurangzeb's Afghan governors, who planned to set out wide roads, adorn it with monuments and replant the gardens. After his death Bhopal remained almost an island state in Malwa. Loyal to the British throughout the 18th century, from 1857 until 1926, Bhopal was ruled by two Muslim women. It still retains a strong Muslim character. In 1984, the city hit international news headlines with the **Union Carbide** disaster when a poisonous gas escape killed and injured thousands of people.

## Sights

In 1878 Shah Jahan Begum (ruled 1868-1901), began work on the pink **Taj-ul Masjid**, one of the largest mosques in India, but it was left unfinished for over a century. It is a striking sight, with three white domes, two massive minarets and an impressive hall with attractive pillars. Today it is used as a religious school (madrassa). The main Chote Talao entrance, which has steps, is closed, so enter by the Lall Market gate. The smaller **Jama Masjid** (1837) in the bazar, with its minarets topped by gold spikes, was built by Qudsia Begum and the **Moti Masjid** (1860, based on the Jama Masjid in Delhi), was built by her daughter, Sikander Begum. At the entrance to the Chowk in the old city area is **Shaukat Mahal**, designed by a Frenchman, combining Post-Renaissance and Gothic styles. Nearby is the **Sadar Manzil**, the Hall of Public Audience of the former rulers of Bhopal. South of the Lower Lake is the modern **Lakshmi Narayan** (Birla) **Temple** (Vaishnavite), Arera Hills. There are good views from here and in the evening from Shamla Hills. There are pedalo and sailing boats for hire on the Upper Lake.

**State Archaeological Museum** ⓘ *Banganga Rd, closed Mon, 1000-1700, Rs 50, foreigner/Rs 10, camera Rs 10*, houses sculptures, antiquities and tribal

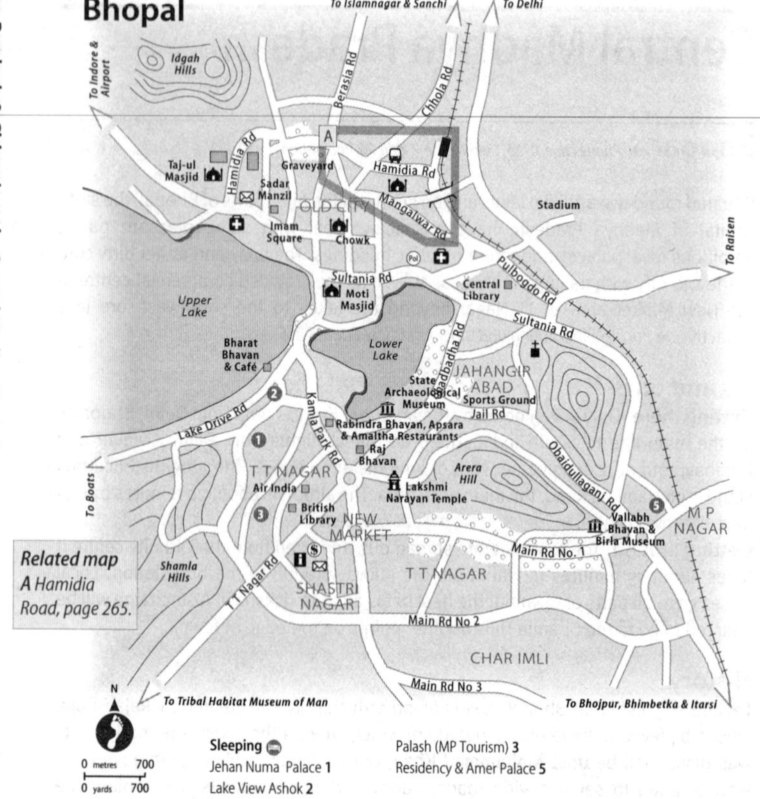

handicrafts, stone sculptures in gallery grounds and an interesting collection of 87 small Jain bronzes of the Paramar period (12th century) from a single site in Dhar District. **Birla Museum** ⓘ *closed Mon, 1000-1700, Rs 50 foreigners, Rs10 Indian*, by the Lakshmi Narayan Temple, complements the former. Small collection of well-displayed rare sculptures (seventh to 12th centuries) in Siva, Vishnu and Devi galleries. **Bharat Bhawan** ⓘ *1400-2000, closed Mon, Rs 5*, a centre for creative and performing arts, is in the Shamla Hills. Designed by the Indian architect Charles Correa in unobtrusive low-rise buildings, it houses an impressive collection of rural and tribal arts, a modern art gallery, crafts gallery, print maker's studio, library and theatre for performing arts, and a café. **Tribal Habitat (Museum of Man)** ⓘ *closed Mon, 1000-1800*, south of Shamla Hills, is an open-air permanent exhibition of tribal huts in typical settings from different parts of India showing details of interiors. A shop sells good tribal crafts.

## Excursions

**Islamnagar**, 11 km from the town centre on a drive north past the former Union Carbide factory, is an attractive little oasis of calm in a tiny village. The palace at the heart of the gardens was built by Dost Mohammad Khan, the early Afghan ruler of Bhopal. The pavilion pillars are decorated with floral patterns. The two-storeyed Rani Mahal and the baths (*hammam*) of the Chaman Mahal can also still be seen. The gardens are lovingly tended by the elderly chowkidar who, despite his limited English, is a very helpful guide. The gate is normally locked but as the village is very small it is usually easy to find him.

A cluster of sites to the northeast of Bhopal – **Sanchi, Vidisha, Gyaraspur**, the **Udaygiri caves** and **Udaypur** – can be visited on a day trip, see page 262. Equally, **Bhimbetka** to the south can be combined with **Bhojpur** 28 km from Bhopal. If you just have a day to spare, hire a car and visit Bhimbetka in the morning and Sanchi in the afternoon. If you have an afternoon, a four-hour excursion by taxi from Bhopal to Bhojpur and Bhimbetka will cost Rs 550 round trip and is the best way to visit.

# Bhojpur → *Colour map 2, grid C6.*

Bhojpur is famous for its Siva temple, sometimes referred to as the 'Somnath of the North', and for its dams, a testimony to the crucial importance of irrigation water for agriculture in this region. Both the religious and civil functions implicit in these buildings owed their origin to the 11th-century Paramar king of Dhar, **Raja Bhoj** (1010-1053), who was noted not only as a great builder but also as a scholar.

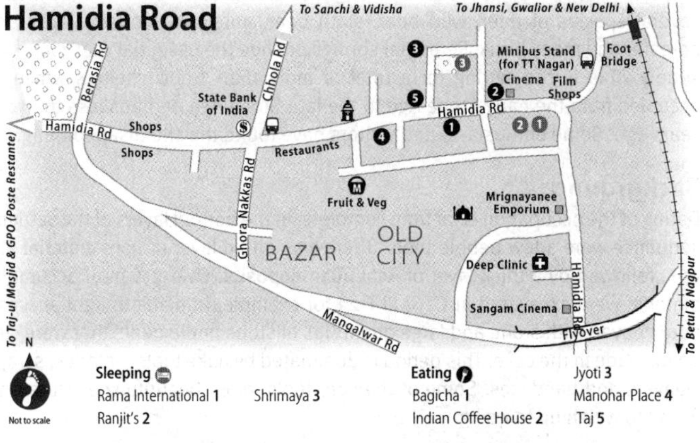

**Bhojeshwar Temple** is a simple square with sides of just over 20 m. Surmounted by a corbelled dome the lower doorposts are plain while the columns and upper sections inside are richly carved. Two ornamental figures guard the entrance. On a striking three-tiered sandstone platform over 6 m sq is a polished stone lingam 2.35-m high and nearly 6 m in circumference, the largest in India. The temple was never completed but the traditional medieval means of building the towering structures of great Hindu temples are still visible in the earth ramp, built as a temporary expedient to enable large stones to be raised to the height of the wall, yet in this case never cleared away. The gigantic patterns engraved on surrounding rocks, which are now protected by rails, suggest that the temple was part of a grand plan (note one of a Siva temple with pilgrims' footprints). Equally interesting are over 1,300 masons' marks that appear on and around the temple which would have been erased on completion. Stone masons can be seen working on site.

There is a white-washed **Jain shrine** nearby, behind a modern community centre, which encloses a 6-m high black statue of a Tirthankara flanked by two smaller ones. The inscription on the pedestal uses 11th-century script. A caretaker holds the keys.

The huge lake to the west once created by two massive stone and earth dams, has now disappeared. Built between two hills, the Cyclopean dams were up to 100 m wide at the base and retained a lake of over 700 sq km, but in 1430 Hoshang Shah of Malwa demolished the dams. The Gonds believe that it took three years to drain, and that the local climate underwent a major change as a result of its drying out.



## Bhimbetka Hill → *Colour map 2, grid C6.*

ⓘ *A taxi from Bhopal is the easiest way to visit the caves and Bhojpur temple. Alternatively, from Bhopal, take the Hoshangabad bus and ask to be dropped at the Bhimbetka turning (the caves are a 3-km walk). You may get a lift from a truck along the main road to Bhojpur. Or, from Bhopal take a bus to Obaidullaganj, 7 km north of the Bhimbetka turning, and hire a bicycle there. There is no obvious signpost in English to Bhimbetka on the main road. At a Hindi sign (on the left), a lane turns right with a railway crossing immediately after the turn. The caves are to the right, off this lane.*

Bhimbetka has South Asia's richest collection of prehistoric paintings and many other archaeological discoveries. The site was discovered by VS Wakanker of the Vikram University, Ujjain, in 1957. In the middle of a dense deciduous forest, there are over 30 species of trees with edible fruit, flower seeds and tubers – a vital food for tribal people even today. You may notice teak and *tendu*, the latter harvested in May and June to make *bidis* for smoking. The area is also rich in wildlife including several species of deer, wild boar, sloth bear, antelope, leopard, jackal, scaly anteater and many birds. Perennial springs provide the essential year-round water supply. This is the setting for a total of more than 1,000 shelters which were occupied from the early Stone Age to the late Stone Age perhaps less than 2,000 years ago. Some enthusiasts and visitors have found the site disappointing.

### Background

Dating of the occupation is far from complete. In the bottom layers of the settlement sequence were a few pebble tools. There was a thin layer of bare material above this, followed by a thick layer of **Acheulian deposits**. Over 2½ m of accumulated material were excavated in Cave III F-23 for example, bringing to light successive floors paved with stone and large quantities of stone implements that were clearly being made in the cave. This period is dominated by flake tools – blades, scrapers, cleavers and handaxes. Some of the core tools, often beautifully executed, were found to weigh up to 40 kg.

This level is followed in many caves by **Middle Palaeolithic** materials (approximately 40,000-12,000 BC), suggesting that this culture developed on the same site out of the preceding Acheulian culture. The same raw materials are used, although the tools are generally smaller. The **Upper Palaeolithic** period (approximately 12,000-5500 BC) was even shorter than the Middle, again growing out of it. Short thin blades made their appearance for the first time. It was in the **Mesolithic** period, immediately following the Upper Palaeolithic, that the largest number of caves were occupied. A Ghosh suggests that during this period there was a huge increase in population and some of the cave paintings can be correlated with this period. There may have been improvement in the climate, although there is evidence for climatic change even within the Mesolithic period, which at Bhimbetka has been Carbon-14 dated as running from 5500-1000 BC. A brand new technology was introduced. Tiny stone tools – microliths – were made: knives, arrow heads, spearheads and sickles. Hard, fine-grained rocks like chert and chalcedony were the basic material. The raw materials for the new industry had to be brought in – the nearest source is near Barkhera, 7 km to the southeast. The dead were buried in caves still occupied by the living, usually, though not always, in a crouched position with the head to the east. Grave goods like antlers and stone tools were buried alongside them. In the middle level of the deposits are copper tools and pottery. The site seems to have been largely deserted by the end of the first millennium BC. Several circular structures on the hills around have been interpreted as much later stupas, a view supported by Asokan inscription, found 20 km west of Bhimbetka.

## The caves

By far the most striking remains today, however, are the paintings covering walls and ceilings in over 500 shelters and in rocky hollows. Some are quite small, while some are as much as 10 m long. Red and white are the dominant colours used, but green and occasionally yellow are also found. These were obtained from manganese, haematite, soft red stone and charcoal, sometimes combined with animal fat and leaf extract. The site has been enclosed to allow visitors to be taken around nine representative caves by Archaeological Survey guides during daylight hours. The tour along a well-made path linking the major shelters takes about 45 minutes; allow longer if you wish to explore independently (there are about 130 caves along 4 km). The caretaker will expect a small tip. There are plans to provide a proper car park, picnic area and water supply with UNCF help. The **paintings** belong to three periods. The Upper Palaeolithic paintings, usually in white, dark red and green lines, depict large animals, eg bison, rhinoceros and tiger. The Mesolithic figures and animals, usually in red, are smaller but they lose their proportions and naturalism. Hunting is a common theme – 'stick men' appear; they are shown grazing, riding and hunting animals, dancing in groups. Women are sometimes seen with a child or appear pregnant. The later period, probably dating from the early centuries AD when green and yellow colours are also used, is quite different, showing battle scenes with men riding on elephants and horses, holding spears, shields, bows and arrows. Religious symbols, Ganesh and Siva, trees and flowers also appear. Some shelters were used over several periods and you can spot interesting details: Auditorium 3 has deer, peacock, leopard, old men and dancers; Rock Shelter 1 shows two elephants and a nilgai; No 8 has a garlanded king on horseback with hunters and a cheetah; No 9 has a flower pot, elephant and an old man; No 10 shows Ganesh, Siva lingam and a tree; No 7, stylized hunters on horseback based on simple crosses; No 6, drummer, group dancers, tree roots and branches, bisons.

*Take water if hot; there are no facilities. The area is often virtually deserted and it is not easy to find specific caves with worthwhile paintings outside the enclosure.*

# Pachmarhi → *Phone code: 07578. Colour map 3, grid C1. Population: 11,300. Altitude: 1,100 m.*

Pachmarhi is one of the most beautiful and friendly hill stations in Central India and rarely sees Western visitors. Except at the height of summer, the air remains pleasantly fresh and cool. The massive iron-rich sandstones which rise steeply from the trough of the Narmada Valley floor to form the Satpura Ranges offer plenty of scope for quiet, wooded walks, with several view points, waterfalls, rock pools and hills to climb within easy reach. The Gondwana series, known locally as Pachmarhi sandstones, are rich in plant fossils, notably of ferns. The area is also known for its ancient cave paintings. » *For Sleeping, Eating and other listings, see pages 265-268.*

## Ins and outs

**Getting there** Pachmarhi can easily be reached by bus in about 6 hrs. It is similarly accessible from Nagpur. Piparia (see below), between Jabalpur and Itarsi, is the nearest railway station. » *See Transport, page 268, for further details.*

**Getting around** The town is pleasant to walk around, most hotels being either near the bus stand or in the bazar. You can share a jeep to the major points of interest.

## History

In 1857 Captain Forsyth of the Bengal Lancers 'discovered' the spot on which Pachmarhi came to be built. He was said to have headed a column of troops but in fact was accompanied by just two others. The beautiful landscape of the plateau of the Satpura range impressed him with its tranquil forests of wild bamboo, *sal*, *yamun*, *amla* and *gular* trees, interspersed with deep pools fed by the streams that ran across the iron-stained sandstone hills. Later, the British developed Pachmarhi as a military sanatorium and hot weather resort.

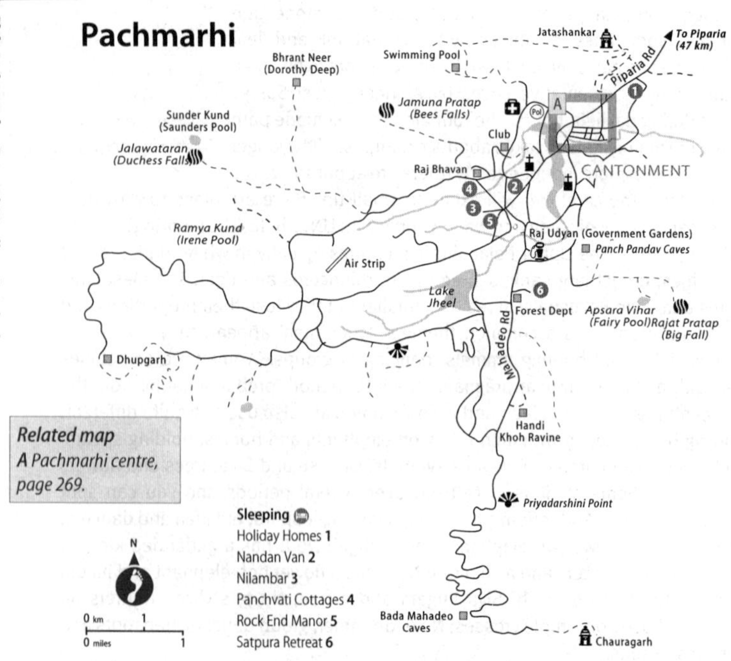


*Related map*
*A Pachmarhi centre, page 269.*

## Sights

The **Panch Pandav** 'caves', walking south from the bus stand beyond the Cantonment, are believed to have sheltered Buddhist monks in the first century BC; a fact confirmed by the recent discovery of the remains of a stupa from this period (6 m in circumference) at the caves. There are several delightful spots nearby. The small natural bathing pool **Apsara Vihar** is along a path to the left. The pool has a broad shallow edge, suitable for children to paddle. There is a short scramble from there to the top of **Rajat Pratap**, the 'big fall', over 110 m high.

There are other falls on the river which make attractive outings, including **Jalwataran** (Duchess Fall), 3 km along the path from Belle Vue. It is a strenuous 4-km walk to the base of the first cascade, perhaps the most attractive in Pachmarhi.

Short one-day treks are possible to Mahadeo and Dhupgarh peaks, and the spectacular hilltop temple of Chauragarh. The square-topped hill at **Chauragarh**, on the southern edge of the Pachmarhi plateau, is 10 km away. You follow the road past **Satpura Retreat** and head south. **Priyadarshini Point**, on the way, from which Captain Forsyth is said to have first set eyes on the Pachmarhi region, still gives a commanding view over the town and the region. You can look back at the **Handi Khoh** ravine from this vantage point. The ridge-top temple draws crowds of tribals and pilgrims for *Sivaratri* in February-March. It may owe its sanctity to the remarkable spring which flows out of the Cave of Mahadeo nearly 100 m inside the hillside. The temple is reached by 1,300 steps, and there are superb views from the top. It helps to have a bike to get there.

To the north of the bazar, a 3-km hike past some ancient rock shelters leads to the **Jatashankar Cave** where the Siva lingam bears the likeness of the god's coiled matted hair.

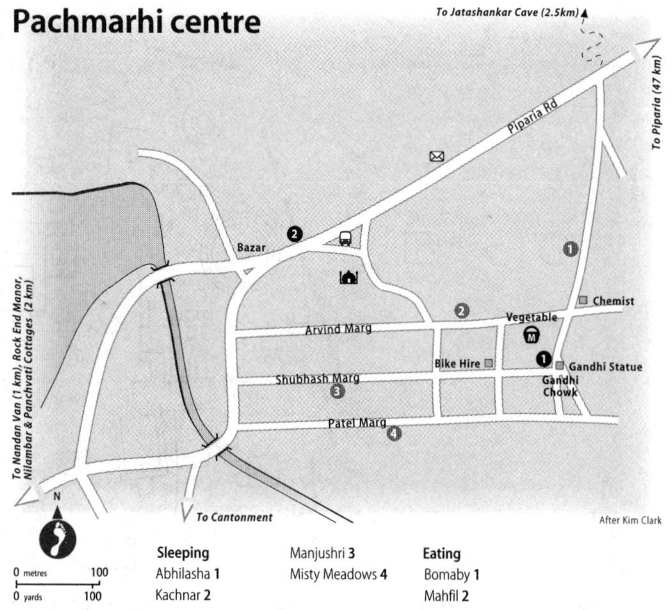

# Sanchi → *Phone code: 07482. Colour map 2, grid C6.*

A peaceful hill crowned by a group of stupas and abandoned monasteries are together one of the most important Buddhist sites in India. Although the Buddha himself never came to Sanchi it has a quiet stillness now, lost at many of the other famous places of religious pilgrimage, yet in keeping with the Buddhist faith. It was included on the World Heritage list in 1989. The imposing hilltop site has commanding views. Sitting under the trees in the bright sunshine, it is easy to be moved by the surroundings. Comparatively few people venture here so it is a good place to relax, unwind and explore the countryside. ⏩ *For Sleeping, Eating and other listings, see pages 265-268.*

## Ins and outs

**Getting there** Some 47 km northeast of Bhopal, Sanchi can easily be visited by car for a ½-day trip from Bhopal. The road out of Bhopal runs along the railway. Once in the countryside the Vindhya Hills lie to your right – the higher ground all covered in low scrub jungle, the flat lowland cultivated. ⏩ *See Transport, page 268, for further details.*

**Getting around** Entrance at Main Gate (bottom of hill). Museum 1000-1700, site open until sunset (usually 1800 in winter). Allow at least 1½ hours. If in a hurry, visit Stupas 1, 2 and 3, Gupta Temple (17), Temple 18, and Monasteries 45 and 51. The Stupa is within walking distance from the railway station.

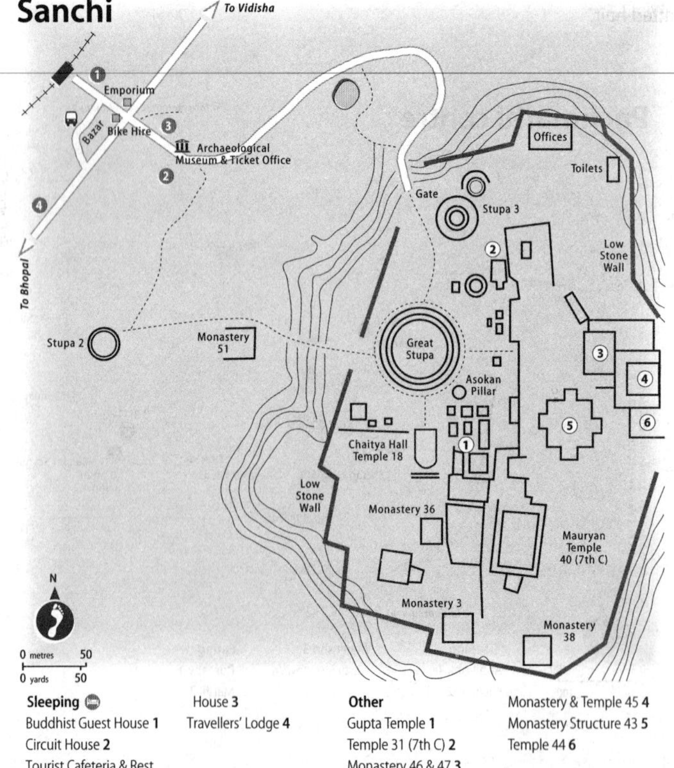

## Background



The first stupa was built during **Asoka's** reign in the third century BC, using bricks and mud mortar. Just over a century later it was doubled in size; a balcony/walkway and a railing were added. The gateways were built 75 years later. Finally in 450 AD four images of the Buddha (belonging to the later period), were placed facing each of the gateways. The entrances are staggered because it was commonly believed that evil spirits could only travel in a straight line. The wall was built for the same purpose. The **Great Stupa**, one of the largest in India (37 m in diameter, 16 m high), does not compare with the one at Anuradhapura in Sri Lanka. In India they became taller in proportion to their bases, in other countries the shape was modified further. Around the great stupas were lesser ones, often containing the ashes of monks famous for their piety and learning, plus a whole complex of buildings, eg monasteries, dining rooms, shrine-rooms, preaching halls and rest-houses for pilgrims. These can be seen at Sanchi.

From the 14th century Sanchi lay half buried, virtually forgotten and deserted until 'rediscovered' by General Taylor in 1818, the year before the Ajanta caves were found. Amateur archaeologists and treasure hunters caused considerable damage. Some say a local landholder, others say General Taylor, used the Asoka Pillar to build a sugarcane press, breaking it up in the process. Sir John Marshall, Director General of Archaeology from 1912-1919, ordered the jungle to be cut back and extensive restoration to be effected, restoring it to its present condition.

Originally, the brick and mortar domes were plastered and shone brilliant white in the tropical sun. The earliest decorative carving was done on wood and ivory but the craftsmen at Sanchi readily transferred their skills to the yellow sandstone here, which lends itself to intricate carving. The **carvings** illustrate scenes from the life of Buddha, events in the history of Buddhism and the *Jataka* stories (legends about the Buddha's previous lives). See Books, page 1362, for further reading.

## The site

**The Gateways** The basic model consists of two pillars joined by three architraves (cross beams), sculpted as if they actually passed through the upright posts. They are regarded as the finest of all Buddhist toranas. The **East Gate** shows the young prince Siddhartha Gautama, leaving his father's palace and setting off on his journey towards enlightenment, and the dream his mother had before Gautama's birth. The **West Gate** portrays the seven incarnations of the Buddha. The **North Gate**, crowned by a wheel of law, illustrates the miracles associated with the Buddha as told in the *Jatakas*. The **South Gate** reveals the birth of Gautama in a series of dramatically rich carvings. Just to the right of the south gate is the stump of the pillar erected by Asoka in the third century BC. The capital, with its four lion heads, is in the local museum. It recalls the one in the Sarnath Museum, of superior workmanship that was adopted as the national symbol of Independent India.

**Monastery 51** This is reached by steps opposite the west gateway of the Great Stupa. It is well preserved with thick stone walls faced with flat bricks and is typical in plan. A raised, pillared verandah with 22 monastic cells behind, surrounds a brick-paved courtyard. The discovery of charred wood suggested that roofs and pillars may have been constructed with wood. There was possibly a chapel at the centre of the west side; the massive 'bowl' beyond the west gate was caused by removal of a large boulder which you can see on your way to Stupa 2.

**Stupa 2** This stupa stands on a terrace down the slope. The original balustrade has been dated to the second century BC with later additions. The decoration, though interesting, is much simpler than on Stupa 1, especially when dealing with the human form. The relic chamber of the stupa contained valuable relics of 10 saints belonging to three generations after the Buddha's immediate disciples, which may explain the choice of this site, below the main terrace.

**The Gupta Temple** Constructed in the fifth century, this is one of the early structural temples of India, built of stone slabs with a flat roof. It has a square sanctuary and a pillared portico and shows the sombre decoration and symmetry typical of its style.

**Temple 18** Built in the seventh century, built on the site of an earlier apsidal temple, has only nine of its 12 pillars still standing which resemble those found in the Buddhist cave temples of western India.

**Monastery and Temple 45** ⓘ *closed Mon, 0900-1700, foreigners US $5.* On the eastern edge, built in seventh-11th centuries, this shows a more developed style of a North Indian temple. The monastery is built around a courtyard with a ruined temple of which only the core of the carved spire remains. The ornamental doorway and the Buddha image in the sanctuary with a decorative oval halo, are still visible.

**Museum Archaeological Museum** ⓘ *closed Fri, 0900-1700, foreigners US$5,* near entrance to monument. Exhibits include finds from the site (caskets, pottery, parts of gateway, images), dating from the Asokan period. Archaeological Survey guide books to the site and museum are available.



## Gupta sites near Sanchi

### Vidisha

In the fifth to sixth centuries BC Vidisha (known as Besnagar in Pali), located at the junction of the Betwa and Bes rivers, was an important trade centre of the Sunga Dynasty where Asoka was governor in the third century BC. The use of lime mortar in the construction of a shrine dedicated to Vishnu, dating from the second century BC, suggests this was one of the first structures in India to use 'cement'. The citizens of Vidisha were patrons of the monuments at Sanchi. Deserted after the sixth century AD, it came into prominence again as Bhilsa between the ninth to 12th centuries. It later passed on to the Malwa Sultans, the Mughals and the Scindias. The ruins of the Bijamandal Mosque and Gumbaz-ka Makbara both date from the Muslim period with remains of votive pillars nearby. The small museum contains some of Vidisha's earliest antiquities.

**Heliodorus Pillar**, the 'Khambha Baba', is a free-standing monolithic column, similar to Asokan pillars but much smaller, dated to 140 BC. It is 3 km after crossing the Betwa River. The inscription demonstrates that relations existed between the Greeks in the Punjab and the kings of this area and that Heliodorus had become a follower of Vishnu.

### Udaygiri Caves

ⓘ *From Vidisha take a tonga or auto-rickshaw (about Rs 40, includes waiting, or cycle from Bhopal and visit Vidisha and Udaygiri (an enjoyable 20 km each way).*

The group of rock-cut sanctuaries, 4 km north of Vidisha, are carved into the sandstone hillside, an inscription in one indicating that they were produced during the reign of **Chandragupta II** (AD 382-401). The caves possess all the distinctive features that gave Gupta art its unique vitality, vigour and richness of expression: the beautifully moulded capitals, the design of the entrance, and the system of continuing the architrave as a string-course around the structure. The caves have been numbered, probably in the sequence in which they were excavated.

**Cave 1** has a frontage created out of a natural ledge of rock. The row of four pillars bear the 'vase and foliage' pattern about which Percy Brown wrote: "the Gupta capital typifies a renewal of faith, the water nourishing the plant trailing from its brim, an allegory which has produced the vase and flower motif". The shrines become progressively more ornate. **Cave 5** depicts Vishnu in a massive carving in his Varaha (Boar) incarnation holding the earth goddess Prithvi aloft on one tusk. Another large sculpture is of the reclining Vishnu. Both reflect the grand vision and aspirations of the carvers. **Cave 19** is notable for its high pillars, its long portico and pillared hall.

## Udaypur

At Udaypur, 60 km north from Udaygiri, is the colossal **Neelkantheswara Temple**. The centrepiece, it is an outstanding example of 11th-century Paramara architecture. Built of red sandstone, it stands on a high platform and has a delicately carved, beautifully proportioned spire. **Basoda** is 24 km away and has accommodation, see page 266.

## Gyaraspur

Some 64 km northeast of Bhopal, Gyaraspur is an attractive and important site of medieval Jain and Hindu activity. The late ninth-century **Maladevi Temple**, on the hill above the village, is the most striking of the remains with the ruins of a stupa to its west. Partly rock cut (the sanctum conveniently set in a cave at the back), it has served as both a Hindu and a Jain shrine. There are ruins of an eight-pillared temple, *Athakhambe*, and a four-pillared *Chaukhambe*.

## Eran

Eran, north of Gyaraspur, has the only extant standing Gupta column (485 AD) near today's small village (once the fortified **Airikina**) which is reached by dusty tracks. The large (5-m long) late fifth-century Vishnu Varaha here (represented wholly as a boar) is carved with tiny figures of *sadhus* who are believed to have sheltered in its bristles during the Flood.

## Sleeping

**Bhopal** *p255, maps p256 and p257*
Mid-price hotels are in Hamidia Rd and Berasia Rd (15-min walk from bus and train station). Better hotels: in the quiet Shamla Hills, 5 km from railway, 2 km from centre. Most budget hotels are dire and infested with mosquitoes. Many refuse to take foreigners. There are cheap hotels on Station Rd (best avoided).

A **Jehan Numa Palace**, 157 Shamla Hill, T0755 2661100, www.hoteljehanumapalace.com. 60 pleasant rooms with verandah around courtyards, some in annexe, good restaurants, gardens, internet, good position but no lake view, friendly and efficient, pleasant atmosphere.

A **Noor-us-Sabah** (WelcomHeritage), VIP Rd, Koh-e-Fiza, T0755 5223333, www.noorussabahpalace.com. 39 comfortable modernized rooms in a 1920s palace, best in town.

A-B **Lake View Ashok** (ITDC), Shamla Hills, opposite TV Tower, T0755 26600980, hlva shok@sancharnet.in. Modern hotel, 45 comfortable but slightly shabby rooms (hot water erratic), good restaurant, competitive car hire, helpful staff, quiet location with views of Upper Lake.

B **Amer Palace**, 209 Zone 1, MP Nagar, T0755 2272110, oni@mantraonline.com. 60 a/c rooms, good restaurant, "best pastry shop in town", pleasant modern hotel.

B **Nisarga**, 211 Zone 1, MP Nagar, T0755 2555701, www.hotelnisarga.com. 41 rooms, very good restaurant (tasty Chinese), comfortable business style hotel.

B **Residency**, 208 MP Nagar, T0755 2556001, hoteltheresidency@yahoo.com, 48 a/c rooms, modern, clean rooms, excellent restaurant, pool.

C-D **Motel Shiraz**, Hamidia Rd, T0755 2552513. 22 rooms, some a/c in cottages, basic, 24-hrcheckout.

**C-D Palash**, near '45 Bungalows', TT Nagar, T0755 2553006, www.mptourism.com. 33 rooms (17 a/c, 1 **B**).
**D-E Rama International**, Radha Cinema Complex, T0755 2535542. 12 rooms, some a/c, little place tucked back, simple, rather dark but quiet.
**D-E Shrimaya**, No 3 Hamidia Rd, T0755 274 7401, shrimaya@sancharnet.in. 27 modern rooms, some a/c.
**E Sonali**, near Radha Talkies, Hamidia Rd, T0755 2740880, sonali@sancharnet.in, clean rooms (best a/c), good food (room service), professional and courteous staff. Recommended.
**E-F Ranjit's**, Hamidia Rd, T0755 2553006. Clean, simple rooms, attached bath (bucket hot water), TV, good restaurant.

**Pachmarhi** *p260, maps p260 and p261*
High season is May-Jun and Nov-Dec. Off-season discounts: 25% at MPT and SADA; 40-60% at private hotels.
**B Rock End Manor**, T07578 252079, www.mptourism.com. 6 deluxe rooms, 3 a/c, some with 6-m high ceilings in restored colonial building, lovely views of old golf course and polo fields. Recommended.
**B Satpura Retreat**, Mahadeo Rd, 2 km from centre, T07578 252097. 6 rooms, 2 a/c, attractive old bungalow with verandah, in pleasant setting.
**C Panchvati Cottages**, T07578 252096. Five 2-bedroom cottages, 5 huts, all with TV and hot water, reasonably priced restaurant, bar, quiet, well-maintained.
**D Kachnar**, Arvind Marg, T07578 252323. 12 spacious, clean, comfortable rooms with bath (bucket hot water), very friendly, helpful. Recommended.
**D Nilambar**, T07578 252039. 6 twinbed attractive cottages, hot water, good views.
**D-E Nandan Van** (SADA), T07578 252018. 12 cottages (hot water), in spacious peaceful gardens.
**D-F Misty Meadows**, Patel Marg, T07578 252136. Decent rooms, bucket hot water, beautiful garden, pleasant hotel.
**E-F Manjushri**, Shubhash Marg, T07578 252016. 24 rooms (bucket hot water), clean, friendly.
**E-F Natraj**, opposite Bus Stand, T07578 252151. 16 rooms, friendly.
**F Abhilasha**, T07578 252203. 10 rooms, bucket hot water, 24-hr check-out.
**F Panchali**, Main Rd, T07578 252223. 8 rooms, good restaurant.
**F Sapna**, Main Rd, T07578 252209. 7 rooms, clean.

**Sanchi** *p262, map p262*
**C Gateway Retreat**, T07482 266723, www.mptourism.com. 18 rooms, some a/c, plus bar and restaurant.
**C Travellers' Lodge**, T07482 266723. 10 clean, comfortable rooms, 4 a/c, restaurant, pleasant garden, at foot of stupa hill.
**D Tourist Cafeteria**, by the museum, T07482 266743. 2 basic but clean rooms.
**F Buddhist Guest House**, near railway station, T07482 266739. 20 clean, spartan but pleasant rooms (Rs 50), also dorm, contact Bhikku-in-charge, Mahabodhi Society, often full.
**F Railway Retiring Rooms**, 2 large rooms with shower and dressing room (Rs 100), busy line.
**F Rest House**, near Circuit House, eerie and run down, hospitable, Rs 130 each including breakfast and good veg dinner.

**Basoda** *p265*
**E-F Hotel Kumud Palace**, at Kala Bag, Bareth Rd, T07594 222223, with 16 clean air-cooled or a/c rooms, hot water, TV and a restaurant.

## Eating

**Bhopal** *p255, maps p256 and p257*
**TTT Jehan Numa Palace**, International, 3 restaurants, garden barbecues, 24-hr coffee shop with western snacks, excellent Indian. Very pleasant.
**TTT Lakeview Ashok**. International. Some excellent dishes, pleasant ambience but service can be slow.
**TT Bagicha**, 3 Hamidia Rd. Mughlai. 'Garden' restaurant and bar, good food, but pricey, and sometimes abysmal service.
**TT Kwality**, Hamidia Rd and New Market. Indian, Chinese, continental. Dark but cool and comfortable.

*For an explanation of the sleeping and eating price codes used in this guide, see inside the front cover. Other relevant information is found in Essentials pages 56-61.*

**Indian Coffee Houses** are in Hamidia Rd, Sivaji Nagar and New Market. Indian. Good *thalis* but poor *dosas*.
**Jyoti**, 53 Hamidia Rd. Indian. Spartan but excellent cheap vegetarian *thalis*.
**Taj**, 52 Hamidia Rd. Indian. Good food, pleasant roof garden.

### Cafés and fast food

**Manohar Place** (sign in Hindi), 6 Hamidia Rd. *Dosas* and snacks (fantastic *pakoras*), very reasonable, excellent sweets, delicious fresh fruit juices, an Indian café.

**Pachmarhi** *p260, maps p260 and p261*
MP Tourism hotels have bland restaurants serving Indian and a few Chinese dishes:
**Bombay**, Gandhi Chowk, serves excellent chicken and mutton.
**Satpura Retreat**, most pleasant.
**Mahfil**, one of several places near the Bus Stand, good.

**Sanchi** *p262, map p262*
**Kapil**, New Bus Stand. Good, cheap vegetarian food.
**Tourist Cafeteria** by the museum. Clean, pricey average meals, bit oily (suspicious shortage of change), small tidy garden.
**Travellers' Lodge**, Indian and Chinese. Non-residents with advance notice.

## Festivals and events

**Bhopal** *p255, maps p256 and p257*
**26-30 Jan**: Lok Rang features local crafts and cultural performances. **Feb**: **Bhopal** Mahotsav is similar. **Summer Festival**, Bharat Bhawan centre stages art exhibitions, theatre and music.

## Shopping

**Bhopal** *p255, maps p256 and p257*
Most shops open 0930-2000 and close on Sun (some Mon). **Chowk** and **New Market** are the main shopping centres.
**Handicrafts Emporium**, Hamidia Rd. Stock souvenirs and local handicrafts.
**MP State Emporium**, GTB Complex, TT Nagar. Specializes in local *chanderi* (cotton/silk mix, so sheer that Aurangzeb insisted that his daughter wear 7 layers of it!) as well as tussar and other raw silks.
**Mrignayanee Emporium**, 23 New Shopping Centre. Stock souvenirs and local handicrafts.

### Books

**Landmark**, Arera Colony. Also near water tower in the Old City.
**Variety Bookhouse**, GTB Complex, New Market, has an extensive choice in English.

## Activities and tours

**Bhopal** *p255, maps p256 and p257*
**MP Tourism**, 4th Floor, Gangotri, TT Nagar, T0755 2774340. **Bhopal Tours** on Sun, Tue and Thu, 0900-1600.

## Transport

**Bhopal** *p255, maps p256 and p257*

### Air

The airport is 11 km from centre. Transport to town by taxi, about Rs 200-250. **Indian Airlines** bus to the airport from City Office, 0700. **Air India**, GTB Complex, TT Nagar, T0755 2522 0666; **Indian Airlines**, Bhad Bhada Rd, T0755 2778434, airport T2646123, flies to Mumbai daily via Indore; also Delhi (2 via Gwalior). **Jet Airways**, T0755 2760371, airport T0755 2645676, to Mumbai.

### Bus

**Gwalior** 422 km, 0600, 1900; **Indore** 187 km, frequent, good a/c coach 0845, 1430, 4 hrs; **Sanchi** 45 km, 1½ hrs, hourly from Hamidia Rd Bus Stand. Nadara (State) Bus Stand, T540841, services include: **Agra** 541 km; **Jaipur** 572 km; **Khajuraho** 387 km, from Jhansi, bus 4½ hrs. **Mandu** 290 km, go to Indore and change; **Nagpur** 345 km; **Pachmarhi** 0230-1615; **Shivpuri**, 1130-1500. **Ujjain** bus to Devas (about 3 hrs; then jeep or bus to Ujjain).

### Car

Car hire tends to be more expensive than in other states; MP Tourism (Transport) a/c and non a/c cars; full day Rs 500-650 non-a/c, Rs 700-900 a/c. Out of town: Rs 5-12 per km, depending on type of vehicle, plus night halt charge, Rs 250.

### Taxi

(Unmetered). **Bhojpur** and **Bhimbetka** will cost around Rs 500 by taxi, 4 hrs round trip.

**Kanha** (540 km) is better visited from Jabalpur or Satna.

**Train**

City Booking T0755 2553599. Railway Station, enquiry T131, reservation T1335. Booking office and tourist information on Platform 1. **Agra Cantt**: see Delhi, and deduct 4-5 hrs. **Amritsar**: *Dadar Amritsar Exp, 1057*, 1510, 24¾ hrs. **Bangalore**: *Rajdhani Exp, 2430*, 0450, Mon, Tue, Fri, Sat, 26 hrs. **Chennai**: *Tamil Nadu Exp, 2622*, 0805, 23 hrs. **Delhi (ND)**: *Chhattisgarh Exp, 8237*, 0645, 13¾ hrs; *Punjab Mail, 2137*, 0920, 11 hrs; *Dadar Amritsar Exp, 1057*, 1510, 13¾ hrs; *GT Exp, 2615*, 1740, 11½ hrs; *AP Exp, 2723*, 2235, 10 hrs. **Gwailor**: *Punjab Mail, 2137*, 0920, 5½ hrs; *Dadar Amritsar Exp, 1057*, 1510, 6½ hrs. **Jabalpur**: *Narmada Exp Pass, 8233*, 2300, 7 hrs; *Amarkantak Exp, 8254*, 1600, Tue, Thu, Fri, Sat, 6 hrs. **Jalgaon (for Aurangabad)**: *Karnataka Exp, 2628*, 0705, 6½ hrs. **Kolkata**: *Shipra Exp, 9305*, 0225, Mon, Thu, Fri, 28 hrs. **Lucknow**: *Pushpak Exp, 2133*, 2205, 11½ hrs; *Kushi Nagar Exp, 1015*, 1420, 11½ hrs. **Mumbai (CST)**: *Punjab Mail, 2138*, 1650, 15 hrs; *Pushpak Exp, 2134*, 0605, 14½ hrs. **Ujjain**: *Narmada Exp, 8234*, 0535, 5½ hrs, continues to **Indore**.

**Pachmarhi** *p260, maps p260 and p261*

**4WD**

Most hotels can arrange 4WD Gypsys, Rs 900-1,000 per day.

**Bus**

Bus Stand, T07578 252058. Daily services to **Bhopal** 0530, 1500, 6 hrs; **Indore** 0630; **Khargon** 1830; **Nagpur** 0700, 1000, 12 hrs; **Piparia** 0700, 1000, 1300, 1½ hrs.

**Train**

The nearest station is Piparia, 47 km.

**Sanchi** *p262, map p262*

Frequent buses from Bhopal, Hamidia Rd, 0630-1930, 1½ hrs direct or over 2 hrs via Raisen; the latter is more attractive; also to **Vidisha**.

**Taxi**

Hire in Bhopal (or book in advance in Delhi); allow Rs 500 for visit and 1½ hrs each way.

**Train**

English timetable. Trains on the Jhansi-Itarsi section of the Central Railway, stop in Sanchi. *Pathankot Exp*, depart from Bhopal, 1530, 1 hr. The *Shatabdi Exp* does not stop at Sanchi; 1st class passengers travelling over 161 km and 2nd class passengers (minimum group of 10) travelling over 400 km may request a stop at Sanchi on the *Punjab Mail*. Enquire and arrange this in advance. For **Bhopal**, depart 0645, very slow; **Vidisha**, local train, 20 mins.

**Gupta sites near Sanchi** *p264*

Add on Rs 150 to the car hire from Bhopal to Sanchi to include **Vidisha** and **Udaygiri**. Bus from Sanchi regular service (Bhopal-Vidisha and Raisen-Vidisha), Rs 5. The train to Sanchi is 20 mins by local train. *Bhopal Dadar Exp, 1058*, 0950, 1½ hrs; *Punjab Mail 2138*, 1533, 1½ hrs (convenient for Jalgaon for Ajanta, 8 hrs, or Mumbai, 16 hrs).

For **Udaypur** from Bhopal: Pathankot Exp (1530) train to Basoda (1830; the station is Ganjbasoda), then bus (Rs 6) or tonga (Rs 25) to Udaypur.

## Directory

**Bhopal** *p255, maps p256 and p257*

**Banks** Indian Overseas Bank, near Surya Hotel for foreign exchange. **Cultural centres** British Council Library, GTB Complex, Roshanpura Naka, New Market, Tue-Sat, 1100-1900. English periodicals and newspapers in cool reading room. **Hospitals** Carewell, Mahadev Mandir Rd, T0755 2543983. **Mayo**, Shahjanabad, T0755 2535584. **Internet** Jehan Numa Palace Hotel (Rs 100 per hr). **Post** Central GPO: TT Nagar; Sultania Rd for Poste Restante. **Tourist offices** MP Tourism, Gangotri, 4th floor, TT Nagar, T0755 2774340, www.mptourism.com. Railway Station, T0755 2553599. **Useful addresses** Ambulance: T0755 2552222. Fire: T0755 2553333. Travel agents: Safari Travel, 2 Van Vihar Rd, T/F0755 2739997.

**Pachmarhi** *p260, maps p260 and p261*

Tourist Office T07578 252100, very helpful.

# Northern Madhya Pradesh

## Gwalior → *Phone code: 0751. Colour map 3, grid B1. Population: 827,000.*

Surrounded by attractive open plateau country immediately to the north of the Vindhyas, Gwalior is set in one of the state's driest regions. The majestic hill fort, formerly the key to control of the Central Provinces, dominates a ridge overlooking the town spread out below. It contains awe-inspiring Jain sculptures, Jain and Hindu temples and the charming sandstone palace. The Jai Vilas Palace, within its walls, bears testimony to the idiosyncratic tastes of the Scindia Maharajas. Much of the town, which sees few tourists, is very busy, noisy and crowded. » *For Sleeping, Eating and other listings, see pages 287-293.*

### Ins and outs

**Getting there** There are a few flights from Delhi and Mumbai, but the *Shatabdi Express* gives Gwalior excellent train connections with Agra and Delhi to the north and Jhansi and Bhopal to the south. The railway station and MP State Bus Stand are southeast of the fort. From there, it is 6 km along the dusty MLB Road to the Jayaji Chowk area of Lashkar, the New Town. » *See Transport, page 291, for further details.*
**Getting around** In addition to a tempo stand near the station there are unmetered autos and taxis. Gwalior is quite spread out and the fort is a stiff climb.

### History

In legend, Gwalior's history goes back to 8 AD when the chieftain **Suraj Sen** was cured of leprosy by a hermit saint, Gwalipa. In gratitude he founded and named the city after him. An inscription in the fort records that during the fifth-century reign of Mihiragula the Hun, a temple of the sun was erected here. Later, Rajput clans took and held the fort. Muslim invaders like **Qutb-ud-din-Aibak** (12th century) ruled Gwalior before it passed through a succession of Tomar Rajput, Mughal, Afghan and Maratha hands. During the 1857 **Mutiny**, the Maharaja remained loyal to the British but 6,500 of his troops mutinied on 14 June. The next year, there was fierce fighting round Gwalior, the rebels being led by Tantia Topi and the **Rani of Jhansi**. When the fort was taken by the British, the Rani was found, dressed in men's clothes, among the slain.

### The fort

ⓘ *1000-1700, US$5/Rs 250 for foreigners, may be cheaper at Urwahi Gate, allow 2-3 hrs, English speaking guides here expect Rs 200 (hotel guides charge more).*
The fort stands on a sandstone precipice 91m above the surrounding plain, 2.8km long and 200-850m wide. In places the cliff overhangs, elsewhere it has been steepened to make it unscaleable. The main entrance to the north comprised a twisting, easily defended approach. On the west is the **Urwahi Gorge** and another well guarded entrance. The fort's size is impressive but the eye cannot capture all of it at once. Apart from its natural defences, Gwalior had the advantage of an unlimited water supply with many tanks on the plateau.

**Approach** The fort is a long way to walk from the town. You may enter from the northeast by the Gwalior or Alamgiri Gate but it is quite a steep climb (and don't forget the interesting Jain sculptures on the west side). Mineral water is sold at the ticket counter; decline the booklet. Alternatively, take a taxi or an auto-rickshaw (cycle rickshaws often refuse to take you) and enter from the west by the Urwahi Gate. After visiting the temples and palaces, you can descend to the Gujari Mahal in the northeast and pick up an auto from the Gwalior Gate. Visitors to the fort (particularly young women) are sometimes hassled by boys who can be quite unpleasant.

**Western entrance** Above the **Urwahi Gate** there are 21 Jain sculptures dating from the seventh to 15th centuries, some up to 20m tall. An offended Babur ordered their faces and genitalia to be destroyed. Modern restorers have only repaired the faces. There is a paved terrace along one side (ask to be dropped near the steps to view the sculptures since vehicles may not park along the road).

**Northeast entrance** A 1-km steep, rough ramp, with good views, leads to the main palace buildings. You first pass through the **Gwalior Gate** (1660), the first of several gates, mostly built between 1486 and 1516. Next is the Badalgarh or **Hindola (1)** named because of the swing which was once here. It is (unusually) a true structural arch, flanked by two circular towers. Note the use of material from older buildings.

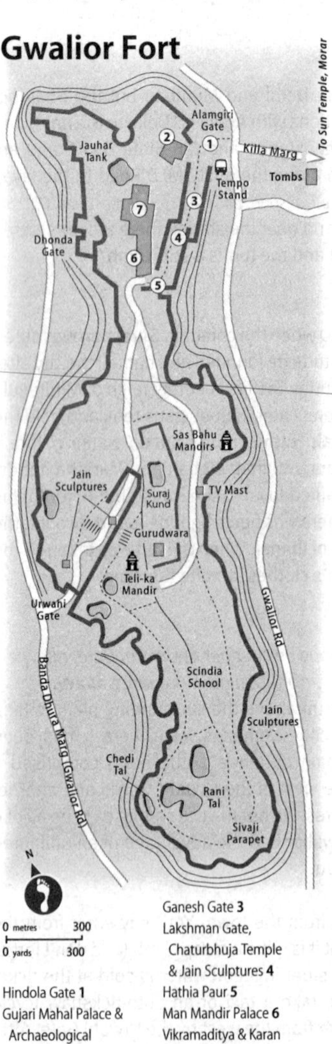


At the base of the ramp the **Gujari Mahal Palace** (circa 1510) containing the **Gujari Mahal Archaeological Museum (2)** ① *closed Mon, 1000-1700*. The pretty palace has an interesting collection including sculptures and archaeological pieces (second and first century BC), terracottas (Vidisha, Ujjain), coins and paintings andcopies of frescoes from the Bagh caves. Ask curator to see the beautiful 10th-century Shalbhanjika (Tree Goddess) miniature. Some museums and palaces are closed on Monday. Some distance from the fort above, this palace was built by Raja Man Singh for his Gujar queen Mrignayani. The exterior is well preserved. The 'Bhairon' gate no longer exists and the fourth is the simple **Ganesh (3)** with a *kabutar khana* (pigeon house) and a small tank nearby. The mosque beyond stands on the site of an old shrine to the hermit Gwalipa, the present temple having been built later with some of the original material. Before the **Lakshman Gate** (circa 14th century) is the ninth-century Vishnu **Chaturbhuja Temple (4)**, with later additions, in a deep gap. A Muslim tomb and the northeast group of Jain sculptures are nearby. **Hathia Paur (5)** (Elephant Gate, 1516), the last, is the entrance to the main Man Mandir palace which also had a Hawa gate, now demolished.

**Man Mandir Palace (6)** (1486-1516) Built by Raja Man Singh, this is the most impressive building in the fort. The 30-m high eastern retaining wall is a vast rock face on the cliff-side interrupted by large rounded bastions. The palace had ornamental parapets and cupolas, once brightly gilded, while blue, green and yellow tile-work with patterns of elephants, human figures, ducks, parrots, banana plants and flowers covered the exterior walls. The remarkable tiles, and the style of their inlay are probably derived from Chanderi (200 km south) or Mandu. The beautifully decorated little rooms arranged round two inner courts have small entrances, suggesting they were built for the royal ladies. The iron rings here were used for swings and decorative wall hangings.

*A torch is essential to explore the lower floors: there are holes in the floor, some of which are quite deep. Underground levels are infested with bats (easily disturbed) and so there is a revolting smell.*

Interestingly, in addition to the two storeys above ground there are two underground floors which provided refuge from hot weather and acted as circular dungeons when required; these should not be missed. **Guru Har Gobind** who was once detained here was freed at the behest of Nur Jahan – he was permitted to take out any others who could touch his shawl so he attached eight tassels which enabled 56 prisoners to be freed with him! On 24 June 1658 **Emperor Aurangzeb** took his elder brother **Murad** captive en route to Delhi and then transferred him to Gwalior fort to be imprisoned. In December of the same year Aurangzeb ordered his execution.

Angled ventilation ducts allowed in fresh air while pipes in the walls were used as 'speaking tubes'. You will find an octagonal bath which would have been filled with perfumed water – the water welled up through inlet holes in the floor which have now been blocked. The south wall which incorporates the arched Hathia Paur with its guardroom above is particularly ornate with moulded and colourfully tiled friezes. *Son et Lumière ⓘ Hindi at 1930, English at 2030 Rs 40/150 foreigner*, each evening well worth attending for stunning illumination of Man Mandir. A small **museum** *ⓘ closed Fri, 0800-1800, guides are around, especially for the underground floors (if you don't have a torch); give a small tip*, opposite the façade, has interesting archaeological pieces of Hindu deities.

**Vikramaditya Palace (7)** (1516) ⓘ *Tue-Sun 0800-1700 (1 Apr-30 Sep, 0700-1000, 1500-1800), free*. Located between Man Mandir and Karan Mandir, the palace is connected with them by narrow galleries. Inside is an open hall (*baradari*) with a domed roof. Opposite the Dhonda Gate is the **Karan Mandir (7)** (1454-1479), more properly called the Kirtti Mandir after its builder Raja Kirtti Singh. It is a long, two-storeyed building with a large, pillared hall and fine plaster moulding on ceilings of adjacent rooms. Just northwest is the **Jauhar Tank** where the Rajput women performed *jauhar* (mass suicide) just before the fort was taken by Iltutmish in 1232 (see page 1297), and also at Chittaurgarh (see page 371). The two unremarkable Muslim palaces, Jahangiri and Shah Jahan Mahals are further north. Moving south from Hathia Paur, towards the east wall, are the **Sas Bahu Mandirs**. Dedicated to Vishnu, the 11th-century 'Mother and Daughter-in-law' pair of temples built by Mahipala Kachhawaha (1093) still preserve fine carvings in places. The larger 12-sided is more interesting although only the *Mahamandapa* (Assembly Hall) remains. The smaller has an ornately carved base with a frieze of elephants, and a vaulted ceiling under the pyramidal roof. The wide ridged stone 'awning' is well preserved. An impressive modern marble **gurudwara** (1970) in memory of Sikh Guru Har Gobind (1595-1644), who had been imprisoned in the fort, is to its south. The Guru Granth Sahib is read right through the day while it provides a haven of cool respite for visitors. To its west is **Suraj Kund**, a large tank, first referred to in the fifth century, where Suraj Sen's leprosy was cured, though the water is now green and stagnant.

*The Maharaja (Scindia) of Gwalior was one of five Maharajas awarded a 21-gun salute by the British.*

**Teli-ka Mandir** Teli-ka Mandir probably means 'oil man's temple'. It is the earliest temple in Gwalior, and architecturally has more in common with some early Orissan temples than those in the south (though sometimes guides suggest a link with Telangana in modern Andhra Pradesh suggesting the fusion of Dravidian and North Indian architectural styles). This unique 25-m high Pratihara (mid-eighth century) Vishnu Temple is essentially a sanctuary with a *garuda* at the entrance. The oblong vaulted roof rather resembles a Buddhist *chaitya* and the Vaital Deul (Bhubaneswar). Tillotson records how after the 'Mutiny' "this great medieval temple, for example, was put to service as a soda-water factory and coffee shop. By such acts of desecration the British showed Indian rulers how the ancient Hindu heritage was then regarded by those who laid claim to power and authority". It was reconstructed in 1881-83. The Katora Tal behind was excavated when the fort was built, like many others here. The Ek-khamba Tal has a single stone column standing in it.

**Rani Tal (12)** further south was supposedly intended for the royal ladies; it is connected underground to the neighbouring **Chedi Tal**! Jain sculptures in the southeast corner can be seen from a path below the wall.

## The town

After Daulat Rao Scindia acquired Gwalior in 1809 he pitched camp to the south of the fort. The new city that arose was **Lashkar** (The Camp) with palaces, King George Park (now Gandhi Park) and the *chhattris* of the Maharajas. **Jayaji Chowk**, once an elegant square, dominated by late 19th- and early 20th-century buildings, notably the Regal Cinema, and the Chowk bazar can still be a pleasant place to watch people going about their business from one of the good little restaurants.

**Jai Vilas Palace** (1872-1874) ⓘ *closed Wed, 0930-1700, tickets at gate: Rs 25, foreigners Rs 175, camera Rs 25, video Rs 75, guided tours (1 hr) sometimes compulsory*, designed by Lt-Col Sir Michael Filose, resembles an Italian palazzo in places, using painted sandstone to imitate marble. Part of the palace is the present Maharaja's residence but 35 rooms house the **Scindia Museum**, an idiosyncratic



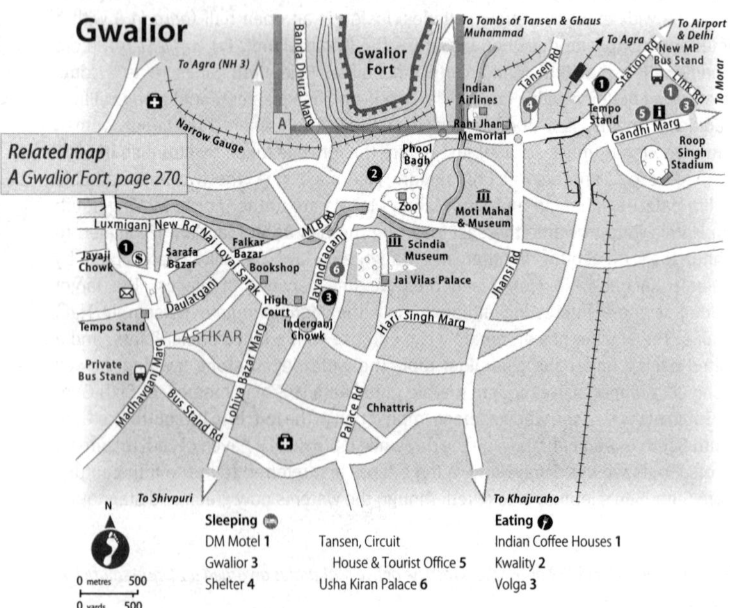


Related map
A Gwalior Fort, page 270.

collection of royal possessions, curiosities (eg 3-D mirror portraits), carpets (note the Persian rug with royal portraits) and interesting memorabilia.

In a separate building opposite (show ticket) is the extraordinary **Durbar Hall**. It is approached by a crystal staircase and in it hang two of the world's largest chandeliers each weighing 3½ tons; the ceiling was tested beforehand by getting 10 elephants to climb up a 2 km ramp! The gilding used 56 kilos of gold. Underneath is the dining room. The battery operated silver train set transported cigars, dry fruit and drinks round the table, after dinner. The lifting of a container or bottle would automatically reduce pressure on the track, and so stop the train! Southeast of the fort is the spot where **Rani Lakshmi Bai** of Jhansi was cremated, marked by a stirring statue.

The Royal **Chhattris**, south of town, are each dedicated to a Gwalior Maharaja. These ghostly pavilions are in various stages of neglect. The lighted images are still clothed and 'fed' daily. Be there at 1600 when they are shown again by the guardians after their afternoon nap.

In the crowded Hazira in the **Old Town**, northeast of the fort, is the **Tomb of Ghaus Muhammad**, a 16th-century Afghan prince who helped Babur to win the fort. It is in an early Mughal style with finely carved *jali* screens. Hindus and Muslims both make pilgrimage to the tomb. Nearby, in an attractive garden setting, is the **Tomb of Tansen**, the most famous musician of Akbar's court. It is the venue for the annual music festival (November/December). The present tamarind tree replaces the old one which was believed to have magical properties. Tansen was an exponent of the *dhrupad* style, and laid the foundations for what in the 19th century became the Gwalior *ghurana* style, noted for its stress on composition and forceful performance. One of the best known contemporary exponents is Amjad Ali Khan, a renowned sarod player. A recently built **Sun Temple** similar in style to Konark is at Morar, a few kilometres east of the tombs.

## Jhansi and around → *Phone code: 0517. Colour map 3, grid B1. Population: 405,000.*

Jhansi, in Uttar Pradesh, is best known for its fort and the involvement in the 1857 Mutiny of its queen Rani Lakshmi Bai. Today, it is a useful stop on the train from Delhi en route to visiting Khajuraho by road. There is plenty to explore nearby, though this is equally easily done from peaceful Orchha which offers a happy escape from the busy small town atmosphere. ⏩ *For Sleeping, Eating and other listings, see pages 287-293.*

### Jhansi

Jhansi was a small village until taken by the Marathas in 1742 who extended the old Fort. In 1853 it 'lapsed', see page 134, to the British when the Raja died without leaving a male heir. The fort was seized in 1857 by mutineers and most of the occupants slaughtered. The young Rani, who had been denied rule by the British, joined the rebels but had to retire to Gwalior. She continued her attempts to return after the British regained control of Jhansi. She was killed in action on 18 June 1858 at Kotah-ki-Sarai "dressed like a man ... holding her sword two-handed and the reins of her horse in her teeth ..." (Hibbert), see page 273. The British ceded the fort to the Maharaja of Scindia and exchanged it for Gwalior in 1866.

**Shankar Fort** ⓘ *0800-1700*, was built by Bir Singh Deo in 1613. The nucleus of the fort, which has concentric walls up to 9 m high with 10 gates, was breached by the British in 1858. There are good views from the walls. Rani Mahal, once Lakshmi Bai's home, is an **archaeological museum** (ninth-12th century). **Retribution Hill** ⓘ *closed Mon, 2nd Sun each month, 1030-1630 (6 Apr-30 Jun, 0730-1230), foreigners US$2*, marks the last stand of the Mutineers in 1858. The **State Museum** near the fort in a vast modern building has a good collection of stone sculptures in addition to weapons and ethnography.

## Barua Sagar

Some 24 km east along the Khajuraho road are the ruins of a historic fort where the Maratha Peshwas fought the Bundelas. The deserted sandstone fort has excellent views over the Sagar (lake) created by a dam across the Betwa river. The ninth-century early Pratihara temple, Jarai-ka-Math to Siva and Parvati, of red sandstone here is highly ornamented. Yet the place is rarely visited and is wonderfully peaceful; you can swim in the lake. Buses from Jhansi travelling to Khajuraho (0600, 0700, 1100) will stop here (one hour) on request. It is then a five-minute walk along a narrow tree-lined canal leads to the fort; ask locally for keys, to return, wave down any bus to Jhansi (frequent service).

## Datia → *75 km south of Gwalior, 34 km from Jhansi.*

Datia itself is not nearly as attractive as Orchha but is interesting to visit nevertheless, particularly as there is hardly a tourist in sight. The forgotten palace lies on the edge of the lively town with a significant Muslim population.

Bir Singh Deo's **Govind Mandir Palace** ⓘ *0800-1700, caretaker 'guide' (speaks little English but holds keys), expects Rs 50 for a tour*, (circa 1620), unlike other Bundelkhand palaces, was conceived as an integrated whole, its form and decoration blending Mughal and Rajput styles. Standing on an uneven rocky ridge, the palace has five storeys visible, while several cool underground floors excavated out of the rock, remain hidden. The lower floors are very dark – carry a torch. Dilapidated and deserted, it is still imposing and atmospheric. The Bundela chief Bir Singh Deo supported Salim (later Jahangir) against his father Akbar, and may have been responsible for robbing and killing Abul Fazl in an ambush. His successors, however, were loyal to the Mughals.

The main entrance is on the east side, approached through very narrow crowded streets, while the south overlooks the lake Karna Sagar. There is a profusion of arches, *chhattris*, ornamental *jali* screens, coloured tiling, balconies and oriel



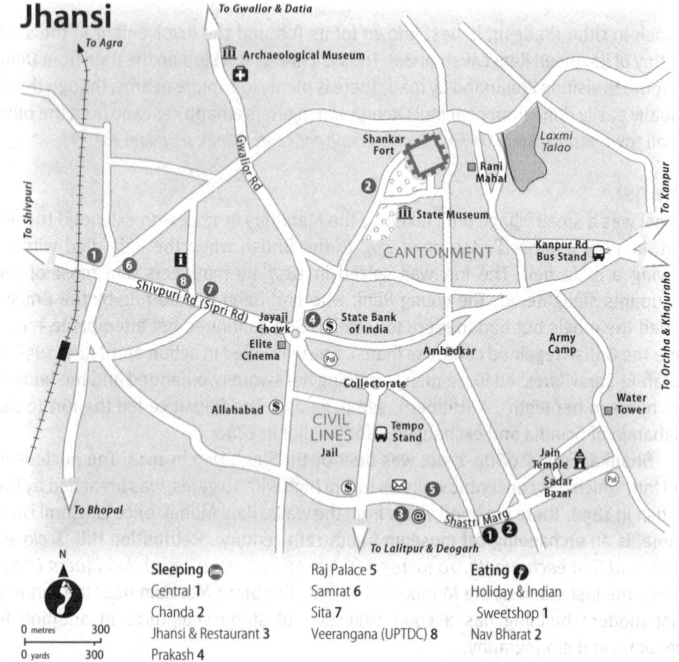

windows which open up delightful views. Within the square plan which surrounds the central courtyard, a separate five-storey 'tower' houses the royal apartments which itself is connected with the surrounding palace by four colonnaded flying bridges, completing this unusual architectural marvel. Strangely it was occupied only intermittently (possibly never by the royal family). The paintings – in deep red, orange and green – though few, are lovely. The first floor has a Dancing Room with stucco figures, the second floor the Queen's Room and a Dancing Room with beautiful wall and ceiling paintings of peacocks, elephants and kings, while the third floor has bridges and the Diwan-i-khas, for private audience (note the Mughal tomb in the corner). Keys are needed to go above this level. The King's Room on the fourth floor with its shallow dome has a beautifully sculpted ceiling with geometric designs of flower petals and stars while the roof parapet has remains of green and blue tiles. There are excellent views all round.

## Sonagiri

A few kilometres north of Datia, just off the main road, Sonagiri has 77 white Jain temples on a hill reached by a paved path. Some date from the 17th century, the one to Chatranatha is the best. It is a pilgrim site for *Digambara* Jains, see page 1342, many of whom attend the evening *arati* between 1800-2100.

## Shivpuri National Park → *Phone code: 07492. Colour map 3, grid B1.*

The dense forests of the Shivpuri or Madhav National Park, 114 km southwest of Gwalior, were the hunting grounds of the Mughal Emperors when great herds of elephants were captured for Emperor Akbar. Now mainly a deer park in forested hill territory, this was also where Maharajas of Gwalior once hunted.

The park is a 156-sq km dry deciduous forest, with Sakhya Sagar, a large perennial lake attracting a large number of migratory birds in the winter. Stop where the forest track crosses the stream from the Waste Wier. **George Castle** on high ground, once the Scindias' hunting lodge, and **Burah Koh** watchtower have good views over the lake at sunset. Animals include nilgai, chinkara, chowsingha, sambar, cheetal and wild pig. Chandpata Lake attracts numerous waterbirds including migratory pochard, pintail, teal, mallard, demoiselle crane and bar-headed geese which remain until May. The best time to visit is from January to March.

Near the Tourist Village, the pink **Madhav Vilas summer palace** ⓘ *1500-2000 (can be viewed from the boundary wall at other times), the palace is not open to visitors, evening prayers (*arati*) and concert of quality classical singing around 1900*, is now a government building. The impressive marble *chhattris* of the **Scindia** rulers, with fine *pietra dura* inlay and *jali* work, are set in formal Mughal gardens with flowering trees. They synthesize Hindu and Islamic styles with their *sikharas* and Mughal pavilions. Curiously, meals are still prepared for the past rulers! **Bhadaiya Kund** nearby has a spring rich in minerals.

## From Jhansi to Khajuraho

The route along the edge of the mainly agricultural hill region of Bundelkhand is on the northern edge of the Peninsula. The forested hill slopes are quite evident as you cross a number of rivers such as the Betwa and Dhasan as they flow off the plateau. Before Independence it was a land of small Rajput and Muslim states, struggling to maintain and expand their power against the greater forces from the plains to the north. Much is now open farmland with occasional scrub or forest, with outcropping rocks and hills. This very attractive route has very little traffic. For a stop-off, the **Tourist Cafeteria** in Nowgong, has a pleasant breezy restaurant in a pretty garden.

# Orchha → *Phone code: 07680. Colour map 3, grid B1. Population: 8,500.*

Highly picturesque, in the middle of nowhere, abandoned and somewhat neglected, Orchha pays rich rewards to the visitor and is an ideal stop between Gwalior and Khajuraho. Set on an island on a bend in the Betwa River, the fort palace from a bygone era is raised on a rocky promontory above the surrounding wooded countryside. This largely untouched island of peace and calm is approached by a remarkable early 17th-century granite bridge built by Bir Singh Deo, while all around, the forest encroaches on the tombs and monuments. » *For Sleeping, Eating and other listings, see pages 287-293.*

## Ins and outs

**Getting there** Orchha is quite easily reached by road from Jhansi. After travelling 9 km southeast along the Khajuraho Road, a minor road turns south for the remaining 7 km to Orchha. There are taxis, tempos or buses from Jhansi station, but it is best to travel during daylight hours, and book and enquire about return transport well ahead. **Getting around** The fort palace complex and the village are all easily seen on foot. The riverside is a 10-minute stroll away. If you are laden with luggage you can get a rickshaw from the village centre to your hotel. Women are advised not to wander around the site alone.

## History

The Bundela chief **Raja Rudra Pratap** (1501-1531) chose an easily defended and beautiful site for his capital. In the 11th century, a Rajput prince is said to have offered himself as a sacrifice to the mountain goddess Vrindavasini; she prevented his death and named him '*Bundela*' (one who offered blood). The dynasty ruled over the area between the Yamuna and Narmada rivers, having stepped into the vacuum left by the Tughlaqs and extended their power, moving their base to Orchha (meaning hidden). Raja Rudra Pratap threw a wall around the existing settlement and began work on the palace building (circa 1525-1531) and an arched bridge to it. This was completed by his successor Bharti Chand (1531-1554) who was installed in the Raj Mahal with great ceremony.

The continuing fortunes of the dynasty may have stemmed from the rulers' diplomatic skills. Though the third ruler, the religious **Madhukar Shah**, was defeated in battle by Akbar and was exiled in 1578 (died 1592), he nevertheless won the Mughal Emperor's friendship. Later Bir Singh Deo (1605-1627, see Datia below), while opposing Akbar, aligned himself with Prince Salim (Jahangir), who later rewarded him with the throne of Orchha, thus ensuring its ongoing prosperity. The Jahangir Mahal was built to commemorate the Emperor's visit to Orchha. However, Bir Singh's first son, Jhujan, ran foul of Shah Jahan and, ignoring orders, treacherously killed the neighbouring chief of Chauragarh. The imperial army routed Jhujan and Orchha was pillaged. In 1783 the Bundela capital was moved to Tikamgarh, leaving Orchha to the *dhak* forests, the Betwa River and its guardian eagles.

## The site

ⓘ *Rs 30 (Indians Rs 5); camera (no flash) Rs 20, video Rs 50; only available from ticket office at Palace entrance, 0800-1800. Allow about 2 hrs. Highly recommended.*
Orchha is a wonderful example of a medieval fort palace. Within the turreted walls are gardens, gateways, pavilions and temples, near the Betwa and Jamni rivers. On a moonlit night, the view across the palaces with their *chhattris* and ornamented battlements is enchanting. A suggested route is to visit the Raj Mahal with its Hall of Private Audience then go through the doorway to the Hall of Public Audience. From here go down the ramp and follow the path to the Rai Praveen Mahal. Continue along the path to the Jahangir Mahal, arriving back at the courtyard of the Sheesh Mahal.

**The Raj Mahal (1)**, to the right of the quadrangle, exemplifies Bundela Rajput architecture. There are two rectangular courtyards around which the floors rise in tiers (inspired by the Koshak Mahal in Chanderi, built a century earlier); typically there are cool chambers below ground and a fountain. Some of the original blue tile decoration remains on the upper outer walls. To the left of the first courtyard is the Hall of Private Audience which would have been covered with rich carpets and cushions (note floor-level windows). The Hall of the Public Audience has two quarter-size plaster elephants. Despite the neglected appearance of the royal chambers off the second courtyard, some have beautiful murals on the ceilings and walls. Representing both religious and secular themes, one series is devoted to the *Ramayana*, another to Vishnu's incarnations, others to scenes of court life – musicians, hunters, river excursions, fairground. Normally locked, but the caretaker

*The buildings are in a bad state of repair. If you go to the top take extra care. Carry a torch.*

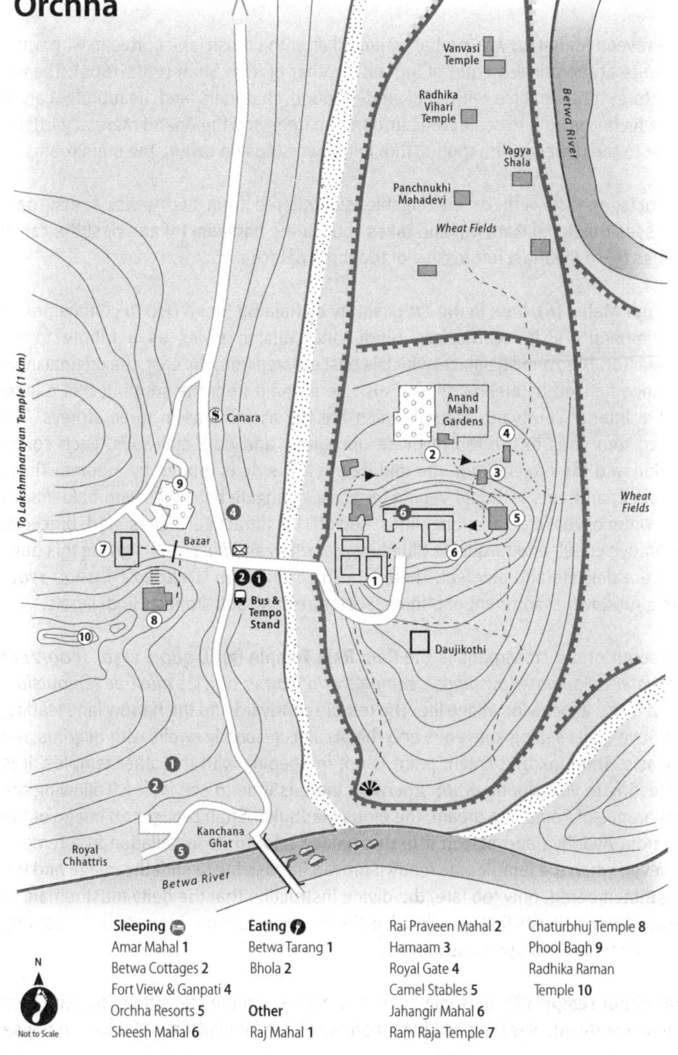

## ❝❞ There are good views of the nine palaces from the top, reached by the mini labyrinth of narrow corridors and steps. On the roof are langurs, wild bee hives and vultures nesting in corner towers...

will unlock some ground floor rooms. Don't miss Rooms 5 and 6 which have the best paintings but you will need a torch. There is a *Sheesh Mahal* upstairs as well as good views of other palaces and temples from the very top; watch your step though, especially in strong winds. In mid-2002, the Raj Mahal was being repaired.

**Rai Praveen Mahal (2)** was probably named after the musician-courtesan who was a favourite at the princely court of Indrajit, brother of Ram Shah (1592-1604). The low two-storey brick palace with cool underground chambers and beautifully carved stone niches is built to scale with surrounding trees and the Anand Mandal gardens. To get to the underground rooms, turn left down steps on exiting the main rooms.

The octagonal flowerbeds are ingeniously watered from two wells. A new path bypasses the **Royal Gate (4)**, and takes you via the **hamaam (3)** and past the **camel stables (5)** to the most impressive of the three palaces.

**Jahangir Mahal (6)**, built in the 17th century by Raja Bir Singh Deo to commemorate the Emperor's visit, synthesizes Hindu and Muslim styles as a tribute to his benefactor. The 70-m sq palace, which is best entered from the east, the original main entrance flanked by elephants, can also be entered from the south. It has a large square interior courtyard, around which are the apartments in three storeys. The guided tour goes to the top of these up narrow and dark stairways. Each corner bastion and the projection in the middle of each side is topped by a dome. These contain apartments with intervening terraces – hanging balconies with balustrades and wide eaves create strong lines set off by attractive arches and brackets, decorative cobalt and turquoise blue tiles, *chhattris* and *jali* screens giving this huge palace a delicate and airy feel. There is a small **museum** ⓘ *closed Fri, 1000-1700*, with a rundown assortment of photos, sculptures and *sati* stones; Hindi labels.

Just south of the crossroads is the **Ram Raja Temple (7)** ⓘ *0800-1230, 1900-2130 (1 hr later on summer evenings), cameras and leather articles must be left outside*, which forms a focus for village life. The temple courtyard and the narrow lane leading to it have stalls selling souvenirs and the area occasionally swells with pilgrims and sanyasis. The pink and cream paint is not in keeping with the other temples. It is interesting to visit during *arati*; otherwise there is little to see inside. Following the appearance of Rama in a dream, the pious Madhukar Shah brought an image of the god from Ayodhya and placed it in this palace prior to its installation in a temple. However, when the temple was ready it proved impossible to shift the image and the king remembered, only too late, the divine instruction that the deity must remain in the place where it was first installed. It is the only palace-turned-temple in the country where Rama is worshipped as king.

**Chaturbhuj Temple (8)** ⓘ *usually open 0800-1700*, up the steps from the Ram Raja Temple courtyard, was built by King Madhukar Shah for his Queen Kunwari to house the image of Rama brought from Ayodhya. Laid out in the form of a cross, a symbolic representation of the four-armed god Krishna, there is a triple-arched gate with attractive *jharokas* on the exterior. The tallest *sikhara* is over the *Garbagriha* shrine, to the left of which you will see a Ganesh and a set of kettle drums. The high arches and ceilings with vaulting and lotus domes painted in a rich red in places, are particularly striking. You can climb up any of the corner staircases, which lead up, by stages, to the very top of the temple. The second level gives access to tiny decorated balconies which provided privileged seating. There are good views of the nine palaces from the top, reached by the mini labyrinth of narrow corridors and steps. On the roof are langurs, wild bee hives and vultures nesting in corner towers.

A 1-km paved path links the Ram Raja with Bir Singh Deo's early 17th-century **Lakshminarayan Temple** ⓘ *0900-1700, 15-min walk, auto-rickshaws charge Rs 30 return, ticket attendant gives 'tour', naming characters illustrated, go up the tower-steep steps but very good views of entire area*, on a low hill, which incorporates elements of fort architecture. The typical village houses along the path are freshly white-washed at *Diwali*. The diagonal plan enclosing the central square temple structure is most unusual. The excellent murals (religious and secular), on the interior walls and ceilings of the four cool galleries around the temple here, are well-preserved examples of the Bundela school. The paintings in red, black, yellow, grey and turquoise portray Hindu deities, scenes from the epics, historical events including the early British period (note the interesting details of Lakshmi Bai's battle against the British), as well as giving an insight into the domestic pleasures of royalty.

**Phool Bagh (9)** is a formal garden and an eight-pillared pavilion which has a cool underground apartment. Well worth a visit.

Of the 15 **Royal Chhattris**, to former rulers grouped by the Kanchana Ghat by the river, about half are neglected and overgrown but pleasant for walking around in the late afternoon. A few are well-preserved; ask the watchman if you want to look inside. He will take you to the upper levels by some very narrow, dark stairs: good fun but take a torch and be careful. He will expect a small tip. The chhattris are best photographed from the opposite bank: take a stick as dogs can be a problem.

### Village bazar

The small but busy village bazar, with some interesting temples nearby, is about 10 minutes walk from the riverside where a series of royal *chhattris* still stand as sentinels. The riverside is ideal for lazing under a shady tree. Cross the bridge and head upstream for better spots for swimming (watch out for currents).

## Deogarh and Chanderi

→ *Colour map 3, grid B1.*

### Deogarh

On the Uttar Pradesh side of the Betwa River, the small village of Deogarh (Fort of the Gods), offers the chance to rest and enjoy cliff-top views of the Betwa River, go hiking and wildlife watching in the forest, and visit numerous temples. Impressive cliffs overlook the river with shrines and reliefs carved into the cliff walls. On the southern fringes of the great Gupta Empire (fourth to sixth century AD), its relative isolation has meant that some fine temples survive.

The temples were built of local stone (and occasionally granite), rather than the more easily destroyed brick. The sixth-century red sandstone, partly ruined but otherwise well preserved, **Dasavatara Temple** is the finest here. The central sanctum had four flat-roofed entrance porticoes in place of the normal one, and the first northern pyramidal temple *sikhara*, though little of it remains. There are fine sculptures on the three walls, of Vishnu legends and a doorway with carvings of Ganga and Yamuna. The remarkable Anantashayi Vishnu, in Harle's phrase, lies "dreaming another aeon into existence". While Lakshmi gently holds Vishnu, the sacred lotus with Brahma rises from his navel.

The dramatic **hilltop fort** encloses 31 Jain temples dating from the ninth to 10th centuries with sculpted panels, images and 'thousand image pillars'; the best examples are in temples 11 and 12. Nearby, the Sahu Jain Sangrahalaya has some fine 10th- to 11th-century carvings. A well marked path from the parking lot here leads to the river and the shrines; it is a fairly long walk.

## Chanderi

The road climbs steeply to approach Chanderi, 37 km west of Lalitpur, an important town under the Mandu sultans, which was dominated by a hill fort. It is attractively placed in an embayment in the hills overlooking the Betwa River and contains the 15th-century Koshak Mahal and other ruined palaces, market places, mosques and tombs. The old town, 8 km north and buried in jungle, has Jain temples dating from the 10th century. Chanderi is famous for very fine saris and brocades. There is a **Dak Bungalow.**



# Khajuraho → *Phone code: 07686. Colour map 3, grid B2. Population: 6,500.*

Khajuraho, home to what are now perhaps the most famous of India's temples on account of their remarkable erotic sculptures, lies in a rich, well-watered plain. Set miles from the nearest town in an open forested and cultivated landscape with the striking Vindhyan Hills as a backdrop, it is listed as a World Heritage Site. Sadly, this breeds very aggressive touts. The small village away from the tourist areas has a pleasant laid-back feel. The best time to visit is between October and March. From April to June it becomes very hot, dry and dusty. ›› *For Sleeping, Eating and other listings, see pages 287-293.*

## Ins and outs

**Getting there** Daily flights connect Khajuraho with Delhi, Agra and Varanasi. The airport is only 5 km from most hotels, with cycle-rickshaws and taxis available for transfer. Alternatively travel by bus or car from Jhansi across the open rolling northern plains of Madhya Pradesh, or come from the Varanasi direction via Satna or Mahoba. There are buses from other major cities in the north which come into the Main Bus Stand. ›› *See Transport, page 292, for further details.*

**Getting around** Khajuraho is still a small village though the temples are scattered over 8 sq km. Although some are within walking distance, hiring a bike is a good alternative to getting a cycle-rickshaw to visit the temples to the east and south.

## Background

Khajuraho was formerly the capital of the old kingdom of Jajhauti, the region now known as **Bundelkhand**. The name Khajuraho may be derived from *khajura* (date palm), which grows freely in the area and perhaps because there were two golden *khajura* trees on a carved gate here. The old name was Kharjuravahaka (scorpion bearer), the scorpion symbolizing poisonous lust.

Khajuraho's temples were built under later Chandela kings between 950 and 1050 AD in a truly inspired burst of creativity, but were 'lost' for centuries until they were accidentally 'discovered' by a British army engineer in 1839. Of the original 85 temples, the 20 surviving are among the finest in India.

Basham suggested that India's art came from secular craftsmen who, although they worked to instructions, loved the world they knew, their inspiration not so much a ceaseless quest for the absolute as a delight in the world as they saw it.

The Gods and demi-gods in temples all over India are young and handsome, their bodies rounded, often richly jewelled. They are often smiling and sorrow is rarely portrayed. Temple sculpture makes full use of the female form as a decorative motif. Goddesses and female attendants are often shown naked from the waist up, with tiny waists and large, rounded breasts, posing languidly – a picture of well-being and relaxation. See Books, page 1362, for further reading.

**Shakti worship and erotic sculptures** Although each temple here is dedicated to a different deity, each expresses its own nature through the creative energy of Shakti. Tantric beliefs within Hinduism led to the development of Shakti cults which stressed that the male could be activated only by being united with the female in which sexual expression and spiritual desire were intermingled. Since this could not be suppressed it was given a priestly blessing and incorporated into the regular ritual. Romila Thapar traces its origin to the persisting worship of the Mother Goddess (from the Indus Valley civilization, third millennium BC), which has remained a feature of religion in India. Until this century, many temples kept *devadasis* (literally, servants of God), women whose duty included being the female partner in these rituals.

The presence of erotic temple sculptures, even though they account for less than 10% of the total carvings, have sometimes been viewed as the work of a degenerate society obsessed with sex. Some believe they illustrate the Kama Sutra, the sensuality outside the temple contrasting with the serenity within. Yet others argue that they illustrate ritual symbolism of sexual intercourse in **Tantric belief**, see page 1329. The Chandelas were followers of the Tantric cult which believes that gratification of earthly desires is a step towards attaining the ultimate liberation or *moksha*.

Whatever the explanation, the sculptures are remarkable and show great sensitivity and warmth, reflecting society in an age free from inhibitions. They express the celebration of all human activity, displaying one aspect of the nature of Hinduism itself, a genuine love of life.

**Chandela Rajputs** The Chandela Rajputs claimed descent from the moon. **Hemwati**, the lovely young daughter of a Brahmin priest, was seduced by the Moon God while bathing in a forest pool. The child born of this union was **Chandravarman**, the founder of the dynasty. Brought up in the forests by his mother who sought refuge from a censorious society, Chandravarman, when established as ruler of the local area, had a dream visitation from his mother. She implored him to build temples that would reveal human passions and in doing so bring about a realization of the emptiness of desire.

The Chandelas, whose symbol recalls the 16-year-old king who slayed a lion bare-handed, developed into a strong regional power in the early 10th century. Under their patronage Jajhauti became prosperous, and the rulers decorated their kingdom with forts, palaces, tanks and temples, mainly concentrated in their strongholds of Mahoba, Kalinjar, Ajaigarh and also Dudhai, Chandpur, Madanpur and Deogarh (Jhansi District).

With the fading of Chandela fortunes, the importance of Khajuraho waned but temple building continued until the 12th century at a much reduced pace. Far removed from the political centres of the kingdom, the location of Khajuraho minimized the danger of external attack and symbolized its role as a celestial refuge.

## The temples

ⓘ *Sunrise to sunset. Foreigners US $5, camera Rs 25. Guides charge around Rs 250 for a small group (enquire at Raja's Café or Tourist Office). Choose carefully as some are push the new Cultural Centre, souvenir shop and puppet show (overpriced at*

*Rs 250) and others can be a little leary around the sculptures. Free guided tours are sometimes available in the peak season 0900-1430, except Fri and holidays, audio tours from 0900. Avoid the toilets. Son et lumière very evening at the Western group of temples, in English at 1900, Hindi at 2030, Rs 50/250 foreigners.*

The temples, built mostly of a fine sandstone from Panna and Ajaigarh – although granite was used in a few – can be conveniently divided into three groups: the **Western** (opposite bazar), **Eastern** (30 minutes away on foot) and **Southern**. The Western Group, which dominates the village, are the most impressive and the gardens the best kept. The temples in the other two groups are remarkable and pleasing in their own right but if you feel that temple fatigue is likely to set in, then the Western Group are the ones to see, especially the Lakshmana Temple. Allow a day (minimum five hours) for sightseeing.

The temples here are compact and tall, raised on a high platform with an ambulatory path around, but with no enclosure wall. Each follows an east-west axis and has the essential *garbha-griha* (sanctum) containing the chief image, joined to the hall for *mandapa* (worshippers) by a *antarala* (vestibule). The hall is approached through an ardha mandapa (porch); both have pyramidal towers. Larger temples have lateral transepts and balconied windows, an internal ambulatory and subsidiary shrines. The sanctuary is surmounted by a tall *sikhara* (tower), while smaller towers rise from other parts of the temple, imitating mountain peaks culminating in the highest. The sanctum is usually *sapta-ratha* (seven projections in plan and elevation), while the cubical section below the *sikhara* repeats the number, having seven bands, *sapta-bada*. The whole, studded with sculptured statues with clear lines of projections and recesses, makes most effective use of light and shade. The sculptures themselves are in the round or in high or medium relief depicting cult images, deities, celestial nymphs, secular figures and animals or mythical beasts.

*The temples are in a peaceful setting of a beautiful park. The area covered by the Western Group was originally a sacred lake – perhaps a reason for the high plinths.*

In India's medieval period of temple building, simple stonework techniques replaced previous wooden and brick work. Temples were heavily and ornately decorated. Heavy cornices, strong, broad pillars and the wide base of the tower (*sikhara*) give them the feeling of strength and solidity, only partly counteracted by the ornate friezes.

**Western Group** **Varaha Temple** (circa AD 900-925), a shrine dedicated to Vishnu in his third incarnation as **Varaha**, the boar (**Vishnu**, The Preserver), is usually depicted resting on a bed of serpents, until summoned to save the world from disaster. The rat-demon **Hiranyaksha** stole the earth and dragged it down to his underwater home. The Gods begged for Vishnu's help. The demon created 1,000 replicas of himself to confuse any pursuer, but Vishnu incarnated himself as a boar and was able to dig deep and seek out the real demon. Thus, Hiranyaksha was destroyed and the world saved. The 2.6-m long Varaha is of highly polished sandstone covered with 674 deities. He is the Lord of the Three Worlds – water, earth and heaven, and under him is the serpent *Sesha* and the feet of the broken figure of *Prithvi*, the earth goddess. The lotus ceiling shows superb relief carving.

**Lakshmana Temple** (circa AD 950) is the earliest and best preserves the architectural features that typify the larger temples here. The **platform** has friezes of hunting and battle scenes with soldiers, elephants and horses as well as scenes from daily life including the erotic. The **basement** again has bands of carvings – processional friezes showing animals, soldiers, acrobats, musicians, dancers, domestic scenes, festivities, ceremonies, loving couples and deities. The details differentiate between an Officer (beard), General (beard and belly) and Priest (beard, belly and stick). An ordinary soldier has none of these. You might spot the occasional error – a camel has legs jointed like a horse! Note the beautifully carved elephants at shoulder height, each one different. On the **walls** are the major sculptures of gods and goddesses in two rows, with *sura-sundaris* or *apsaras* in attendance on the raised sections and loving couples in the recesses. All the figures are relaxed, resting their weight on one leg, thus accentuating their curves. The bands are broken by ornate balconied windows with carved pillars and overhanging eaves. The nymphs shown attending to their toilet, bearing offerings, dancing, playing musical instruments or as sensual lovers, are executed with great skill. They are graceful and fluid (note the taut muscle or creased skin), with expressive faces and gestures. The best examples are seen in the recesses below the main tower. The **façades** are covered in superb sculpture. On the south façade are a couple of minstrels, their faces expressing devotional ecstasy, a dancing Ganesh, ladies attending to their toilet, and groups of lovers. Moving to the southwest, a *sura-sundari* applies vermilion while another plays with a ball. In the northwest corner is a nymph after her bath in her wet clothes. The south face of the northwest shrine has a fine Ganesh panel. On the north face, returning towards the porch, there is a group of *apsaras* accomplished in art and music (one plays the flute, another

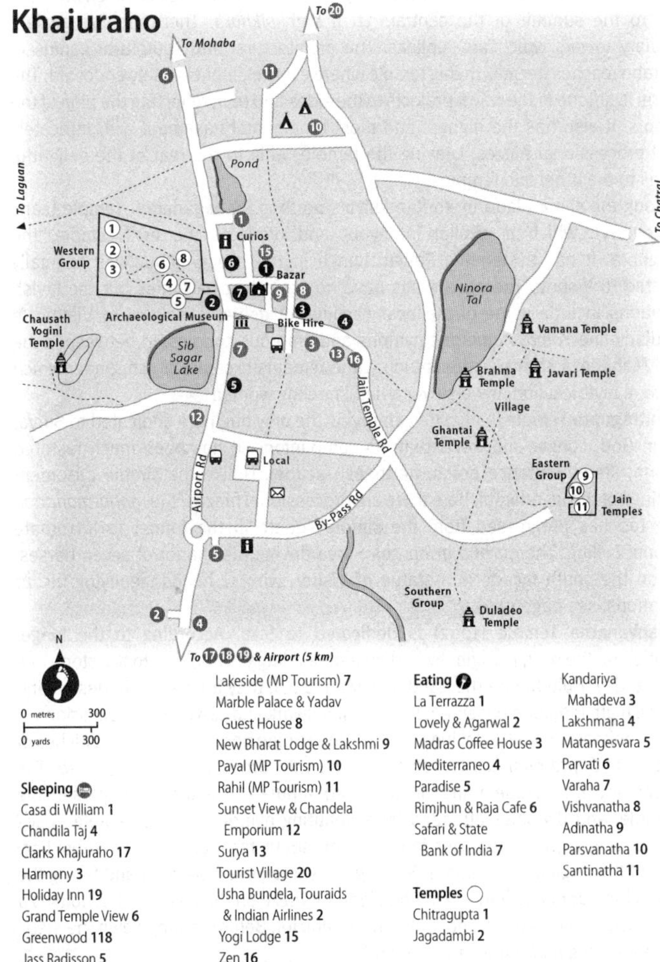

 paints, yet another writes a letter). The east face of the subsidiary shrine in the southeast corner has a master architect with his apprentices. Leave shoes at the entrance and enter **the interior** through a simple *makara-torana* flanked by gladiators. The circular ceiling of the porch (*ardha mandapa*) is a superbly carved open lotus blossom. In the hall (*mandapa*) is a raised platform possibly used for dancing and tantric rituals. At each corner of the platform are pillars with carved brackets with *apsaras* which are among the finest sculptures at Khajuraho. There are eight figures on each column, representing the eight sects of Tantra. The sanctum (*garba-griha*) doorway has a panel showing incarnations of Vishnu while the lintel has Lakshmi with Brahma and Siva on either side. A frieze above depicts the nine planets including *Rahu*, while Krishna legends and innumerable carvings of animals, birds and humans, appear on the wall. The *pancha-ratha* sanctum has a three-headed Vishnu as Vaikuntha, and around it are 10 incarnations and 14 forms of Vishnu.

**Kandariya Mahadeva Temple** (circa 1025-1050) is the most developed, the largest and tallest of the Khajuraho temples. Dedicated to **Siva**, the elaborately carved *makara torana* doorway leads to a porch with an ornate ceiling and a dark inner sanctum with a marble linga. The temple roof rises in a series of seven bands of peaks to the summit of the central, 31 m high *sikhara*. There are 84 smaller, subsidiary towers which are replicas. The architectural and sculptural genius of Khajuraho reaches its peak in this temple where every element is richly endowed. The platform is unique in the way it projects to the sides and rear, reflecting the plan of the transepts. It also has the highest and most ornamental basement with intricately carved processional friezes. Leaving the temple, walk to the rear of the delightful gardens to the other two temples.

Along the same platform, to Kandariya's north is the **Jagadambi Temple** (early 11th century), which is similar in layout and predates the next temple, the Chitragupta. It has a standing Parvati image in the sanctum but was originally dedicated to Vishnu. The outer walls have no projecting balconies but the lavish decorations include some of the best carvings of deities – several of Vishnu, a particularly fine *Yama*, numerous nymphs and amorous couples. In between is the ruined **Mahadeva shrine** (11th century). Little remains except a porch, under which *Sardula*, a mythical lion, towers over a half-kneeling woman.

**Chitragupta Temple** (early 11th century) is the only one here dedicated to Surya, the Sun God. Longer and lower than its companions, it has been much restored (platform, steps, entrance porch, northeast façade). Unlike the simple basement mouldings of the Jagadambi, here there are processional friezes; the *maha-mandapa* ceiling too has progressed from the simple square in the former to an ornate octagonal ceiling. The *garbha griha* has Surya driving his chariot of seven horses, while on the south façade is a statue of Vishnu with 11 heads signifying his 10 incarnations, see page 1326.

**Vishvanatha Temple** (1002) is dedicated to Siva. According to the longer inscription on the wall, it originally had an emerald linga in addition to the stone one present today. Built before the Kandariya Mahadeva, they are similar in design and plan. The high, moulded basement has fine scrollwork and carvings of processions of men and animals as well as loving couples. On the nine principal basement niches of both are the *Sapta-matrikas* (seven 'Mothers') with *Ganesha* and *Virabhadra*. The excellent carvings include a fine musician with a flute and amorous couples inside the temple, and divinities attended by enchanting nymphs in innumerable poses (one removing a thorn from her foot), on the south façade. Only two subsidiary shrines of the original four remain. Sharing the same raised platform and facing the temple is the **Nandi Pavilion** with a fine elephant frieze on the basement. It houses a 2.2-m polished sandstone Nandi bull (Siva's vehicle). Before coming down the steps note the sleeping *mahout* on an elephant!

Outside this garden complex of temples and next to the Lakshmana temple is the **Matangesvara Temple** (AD 900-925), simpler in form and decoration than its neighbour and unlike all the others, still in everyday use. It has an interesting circular interior which contains a large Siva linga.

**Chausath Yogini** (late ninth century) is a ruined Jain temple in coarse granite on a platform. It stands apart from the rest of the Western Group beyond the tank. Only 35 of the original *chausath* (64) shrines to the *yoginis* (attendants of Kali), of the 'open-air' temple, remain.

**Eastern Group** South of the village is the ruined **'Ghantai' Temple** (late 10th century). The fine carvings of chains-and-bells (*ghanta*) on the pillars, the richly ornamented doorway and ceiling of the entrance porch can only be seen from the road. Walk through Khajuraho village to the small **Javari Temple** (late 11th century), with its tall, slender *sikhara*. It has a highly decorative doorway and finely sculpted figures on the walls. About 200 m north is the **Vamana Temple** (late 11th century), with a four-armed Vamana incarnation of Vishnu in the sanctum. This is in the fully developed Chandela style and has a single tower and no ambulatory. The walls are adorned with sensuous *sura-sundaris*. Returning to the modern part of Khajuraho, you pass the early 10th-century so-called **Brahma Temple** on the bank of Ninora-tal. A Vishnu temple, wrongly attributed to Brahma, it has a sandstone *sikhara* on a granite structure.

Three **Jain temples** stand within an enclosure about 500 m southeast of the Ghantai Temple; others are scattered around the village. The **Parsvanatha Temple** (mid-10th century), is the largest and one of the finest. The curvilinear tower dominates the structure and is beautifully carved. There are no balconies but light enters through fretted windows. Although a Jain temple, there are numerous Vaishnav deities, many of them excellently carved on the three wall panels. Some of the best known non-erotic sculptures too are found here, particularly the graceful *sura-sundaris* (one applying kohl and another removing a thorn, on the south façade; one tying ankle-bells on the north façade), as well as the fine *Dikpalas* in the corners. The interior is richly carved with elephants, lions, sea goddesses and Jain figures. The temple was originally dedicated to Adinatha, but the modern black marble image of Parsvanatha was placed in the sanctum in 1860. Next, is the smaller and simpler **Adinatha Temple** (late 11th century), where only the sanctum (containing a modern image) and vestibule have survived – the porch is modern. The sculptures on three bands again depict attractive *sura-sundaris*, the niches have *yakshis*, the corners, *Dikpalas*. **Santinatha Temple** with its 4½-m statue of Adinatha is the main place of Jain worship. An inscription dating it at 1027-1028 is covered with plaster – the thoroughly renovated temple retains its ancient heart and medieval sculptures. The small sand coloured structures around the temples are reconstructions around remains of old shrines. There is also a small Jain museum and picture gallery here.

**Southern Group** The two temples stand on open land. The setting, attractive at sunset, lacks the overall ambience of the Western Group but the backdrop of the Vindhyas is impressive. **Duladeo Temple**, 800 m southwest of the Jain temples down a path off the road, is the last the Chandelas built here, when temple building was already in decline. There are 20 *apsara* brackets but the figures are often repetitive and appear to lack the quality of carving found in earlier temples. The shrine door and *mandapa* ceiling have some fine carving while the linga has 11 rows of 100 lingas. **Chaturbhuja Temple** (circa 1100), 3 km south of the village, anticipates the Duladeo but lacks erotic sculptures. The sanctum contains an exceptional 2.7 m four-armed *Dakshina-murti* Vishnu image while outside there are some fine *Dikpalas*, nymphs and mythical beasts in niches.

At **Rajgarh**, 5 km south, is the imposing ruined 19th-century hilltop fort-palace of the Maharaja which the Oberoi Group will convert to a heritage hotel. It is particularly interesting when villagers congregate for the Tuesday Market. Get there by auto-rickshaw or car. **Panna National Park** ⓘ *Nov to May, foreigners Rs 100 (with guide), camera Rs 100,* is accessed along the Satna Road with attractive waterfalls on the way. Ken River, parts of which have been declared a sanctuary for fish eating gharials, flows across the Panna National Park, which is a Project Tiger Reserve. The park, rich in biodiversity, covers dense forest, open meadows, plateaus and gorge with waterfalls, and supports chinkara, sambar, nilgai and the big cats. Although tiger sightings are rare, it is pleasant to visit in winter. There is little wildlife to be seen in the dry season (when the gharials are removed for their own protection). Access is easiest from Madla, 27 km from Khajuraho. Gypsy or motorbike hire from Khajuraho, or bus; tour of park can be arranged in Madla.

*Satna is down the road from the national park, a transport hub for the area.*

## Chandela Forts

The Chandela kings' main defensive bases were Mahoba and Kalinjar, but as the kingdom expanded these were complemented by other forts at Ajaigarh, Orchha, Datia, Deogarh and Chanderi. Like other kings, they donated villages to maintain the families of soldiers who had died in war. Heroic virtues were instilled into a child from birth and women admired men who fought well; *sati* became common practice throughout the region. After the mid-10th century the independent Chandelas joined a Hindu confederacy to repel Afghan invasions. **Mahmud of Ghazni**, the 'Idol Breaker', made at least 17 of his plunder raids into India between 1000-1027, ultimately taking the title, albeit briefly, Lord of Kalinjar. The forts suffered varied fortunes until the British took them over in the early 19th century. Now the area is being invaded by forests of teak and ebony but offer an insight into totally unspoilt territory. Ajaigarh and Kalinjar are quite 'primitive' but a visit, particularly to the former, is worthwhile. A tour of these and Chitrakoot is really worthwhile. Enlist a local guide to show you the best spots; Ajay Singh (see Khajuraho, Directory) is very knowledgeable and can organize jeep/motorbike. Carry water.

### Ajaigarh

Ajaigarh, 36 km north of Panna, surrounded by dense forest, stands on a granite outcrop crowned by a 15-m perpendicular scarp. Ajaigarh was a self-contained hill fort, intended to withstand long sieges and to house the entire population of the region, which accounts for its great size. Despite its inaccessibility and the difficult 250 m climb involved (allow about 40 minutes on the way up), the fort is worth visiting for its peaceful atmosphere and wonderful views. Two of the original five gates are accessible; the large stone steps here once helped elephants in their steep ascent. Encircling the hill, the fort wall encloses part-ruined temples; only four of the original 22 temples remain. Rock carvings, pillars and sculptures from Hindu and Jain temples, some later used by Muslims to reinforce the fortifications, today lie scattered amongst woodland. The old stone quarry now filled by a lake is said to have provided stone for Khajuraho.

*Some believe it is auspicious to eat here, hence the remains of bonfires and presence of picnickers.*

### Kalinjar

Some 20 km from Ajaigarh this fort stands on the last spur of the Vindhya hills overlooking the Gangetic plains, a plateau with a steep scarp on all sides. One of the most ancient sites in Bundelkhand (Ptolemy's Kanagora), it combines the sanctity of remote hilltops with natural defensive strength. One legend names Kalinjar after Siva, the Lord of Destruction (*kal* = death, *jar* = decay). The ancient hill has long been a place of pilgrimage and worship for Hindu sadhus, rishis and pilgrims. It is rarely visited by other travellers.

The design of the fort has a mystical significance. The only approach is from the north and entry is through **seven gates** with barbicans corresponding to the seven known planets and stations through which the soul must pass before being absorbed into Brahma. At the crest, crumbling Hindu and Muslim monuments stand side by side on the 1½-km long plateau. Beyond the last gate, a drop of about 3.6 m leads to **Sita Sej**, a stone couch set in a rock-cut chamber (fourth century). Beyond, a passage leads to Patalganga (underground Ganga), believed to run through Kalinjar. Koth Tirth at the centre of the fort is a 90-m long tank with ghats leading down to it. Numerous stone relics are scattered about the site; a dancing Ganesh, Nandi bulls, a model temple complete with figures like a miniature Khajuraho, a reclining Siva, Sati pillars and several *lingams* and *yonis* (fertility symbols).

### Mahoba

Some 63 km north of Khajuraho, Mahoba was reputedly founded by Raja Chandravarman, in 800 AD. Today, it is a small town with a fort on a low hill, several ancient tanks and a thriving 'Dariba' or betel market. The vines are grown under traditional shelters to produce high quality *paan* (betel leaf) for which the area is famous.

After winning Bundelkhand, the Chandela kings dedicated themselves not only to building temples for their gods, but also to bringing water to the land. They created large tanks by damming shallow valleys. Mahoba's oldest tank, **Rahila Sagar** (circa 900) has impressive ruins of a ninth-century granite Sun Temple. The 12th-century **Madan Sagar** has a granite Siva temple nearby and a ruined Vishnu temple on one of its rocky islets. Along its embankment is the old fort, **Qila Mismar** with ruins of palaces, Hindu temples and a tomb. In the fields, remains of Buddhist and Jain sculptures lie abandoned. Gokhar Hill, near Madan Sagar, with 24 Jain Tirthankaras figures carved out of sheer rock, is worth exploring. Two pools, Ram and Suraj Kund, lined with granite slabs, were originally intended for sacrificial fires. There is a *Tourist Bungalow* here with a restaurant and bar. The station is 3 km from the Bus Stand. To Jhansi (four hours); to Varanasi via Allahabad (11 hours).

## Chitrakoot

On the north flank of the Vindhyas where they dip gently beneath the Ganges Plains, 175 km from Khajuraho, Chitrakoot's forests and peaceful rivers were home to Rama and Sita in 11 of their 14 years of exile. **Ramghat**, the principal bathing ghat on the banks of the beautiful Mandakini River, is widely revered in India and the site of countless pilgrimages, though scarcely known to foreigners. Like the much more famous waters of the Yamuna at Allahabad or the Ganga at Varanasi, the River Mandakini is lined with temples. A good way to see the ghats is to hire a boat. Upstream from Ramghat the Mandakini passes through a beautiful stretch of wooded valley.

## Sleeping

**Gwalior** *p269, map p272*
There are several basic hotels with acceptable rooms, but some can be noisy.
**L Usha Kiran Palace** , Jayendraganj Lashkar, T0751 244 4000, www.tajhotels.com. 36 a/c rooms (some vast suites) in 120-year-old Maharaja's palace, recently refurbished, beautiful gardens, good restaurant, billiards, retains character of charming royal guesthouse, friendly. Recommended.
**B Gwalior Regency**, Link Rd, near New Bus Stand, T0751 234 0670, gregency@hotmail.

com. 51 modern rooms, smallish but well maintained, restaurant, coffee shop, pool.
**B-C Shelter**, Padav, T0751 232 6209, www.sheltergwalior.com. Modern clean rooms (some a/c), decorated to a high standard though bathrooms disappointing, good restaurant and bar, friendly staff.
**C-D Tansen**, 6A Gandhi Rd, T0751 234 0370, samsun@mantrafreenet. Undergoing renovation at time of research, but should be a good option when finished. 36 rooms, good restaurant, bar, garden, car hire, tourist information, camping, quiet location.
**E-F DM**, Link Rd, near New Bus Stand, T0751 234 2083. Rooms with bath (hot water), could be cleaner but good value and reasonably quiet.

**Jhansi** *p273, map p274*
It is better to stay at Orchha.
**B Sita**, Shivpuri Rd, T0517 2444690, F2444691. 29 smart, clean a/c rooms with bath, good restaurant, car hire, exchange.
**C Jhansi**, Shastri Marg, 3 km railway, T0517 2470360, F2470470. 28 overpriced rooms, restaurant, bar, exchange, very faded colonial feel, desperately needing overhaul yet garden well kept.
**C-D Chanda**, 365/1A Civil Lines, opposite Laxmi Bai Park, T0517 2450027. 24 comfortable a/c or air-cooled rooms with bath, restaurant.
**D-E Raj Palace**, Shastri Marg, T0517 2470554. 14 simple clean rooms with bath, a/c, air cooled, but overpriced.
**D-E Veerangana**, Shivpuri Rd, 1 km railway, Numaish Maidan, T0517 2442402, www.up-tourism.com. 20 rooms, 4 a/c, dorm (Rs 50), reasonable restaurant, bar, pleasant garden, mosquito infested.
**E Samrat**, Chitra Chauraha near railway station, T0517 2444943. Rooms with fan, mosquito mesh, rooftop preferable (No 210 best with shower, others have bucket), food brought to room, very friendly. Recommended.
**E Central**, 701 Civil Lines (500 m rly), T0517 2440509, F2445141. 39 rooms (some 4-bed), some air-cooled, with bath, Indian meals.
**F Railway Retiring Rooms** and 6-bed dorm. Other hotels near the station are dirty.

**Datia** *p274*
**C-D Datia Motel** (MP Tourism), 2 km from town on Gwalior Rd, T07522 238125, www.mptourism.com, overlooks the palace and lake. There are 4 spotless, airy, bright rooms and a restaurant.
**F Shri Raghunath Ganga Hotel**, Station Rd, opposite Pitambra Peeth Temple, T07522 236754. 9 air-cooled rooms, baths, clean, secure (Rs 200). Owners helpful and very welcoming.

**Shivpuri National Park** *p275*
**C Chinkara Motel**, NH3, 4 km south of Shivpuri, T07492 221297. 19 clean rooms, some a/c, restaurant.
**C Tourist Village** (MP Tourism), Jhansi Rd, 5 km east of town, Bhadaiya Kund, T07492 223760, www.mptourism.com. 19 rooms in cottages, 5 a/c, 2 4-bed, pleasant restaurant, attractive location overlooking lake, jeep hire, close to the park.
**D Delhi Hotel**, Madhav Chowk, A-B Rd, T07492 233093. 12 simple rooms with bath, some a/c, vegetarian restaurant.

**Orchha** *p276, map p277*
Hotels are best on the idyllic riverside.
**A Amar Mahal**, T07680 252102, www.amarmahal.com. Built in 2003, looks like a Maharaja palace, with 21 beautifully decorated rooms (12 more under construction) arranged around a central courtyard, comfy, friendly staff. Excellent but expensive restaurant with 24 carat gold-painted ceiling, pool and children's park on the way.
**A-B Orchha Resort**, Kanchanghat, on riverside, T07680 252222, www.orchharesort.com. 32 immaculate a/c rooms, 12 luxury a/c tents around tennis court, high standard, interesting decor (wall paintings, marble inlay), excellent restaurant (strict veg), friendly and attentive staff, exchange, gym, excellent outdoor pool (high wall along river for privacy), well-tended gardens, taxi to Khajuraho Rs 1600.
**A-C Sheesh Mahal**, inside Fort, uphill from Bus Stand, MP Tourism (must be booked in advance) T07680 252624. 8 rooms (2 **A** includes Royal Suite with terrace, antique fittings and furniture, huge marble

*For an explanation of the sleeping and eating price codes used in this guide, see inside the front cover. Other relevant information is found in Essentials pages 56-61.*

tub (for shower), panoramic view from toilet too), modernized within limits, restaurant, full of character, atmospheric, magnificent views, friendly staff, **C** rooms (no TV or a/c) great value.

**C-D Betwa Cottages**, overlooking river, 10-min walk from Bus Stand, MP Tourism (must be booked in advance), T07680 252618. 10 clean rooms in cottages, some a/c, well designed with rustic paintings, plus 10 luxury tents, spacious well-kept gardens, scattered ruins, nightly folk music and dance, average restaurant, pool and health club planned.

**C-E Ganpati**, T07680 252765. 10 airy rooms hot shower, 3 a/c, 5 more under construction, clean sheets, small courtyard, parking, great views of river, friendly and helpful owner.

**E Fort View**, just north of crossroads, T07680 252701. Retired school teacher's clean and friendly guesthouse, hot water in buckets, new dorm.

### Deogarh *p279*

**E Tourist Bungalow**, across the street from Dasavatara Temple. Clean air cooled rooms, water from nearby pump, kitchen. The caretaker, Mr Yadev, will prepare meals and escort you on hikes to half a dozen temples, 5 to 10 km away in the woods.

### Khajuraho *p280, map p283*

Most hotels are within 1 km of the western temples, notably along Jain Temple Rd. They are subject to frequent power cuts but top hotels have generators.

**AL Chandela** (Taj), Airport Rd, T07686 272355, www.tajhotels.com. 102 rooms (singles good value), some not spotless, expensive restaurants (slow service, ordinary food), best bookshop in town though pricey, predatory shopkeepers, small temple in pleasant garden.

**A Clarks Khajuraho**, T07686 274038, www.hotelclarks.com. Modern, 104 rooms, large grounds, pool and tennis.

**A Holiday Inn**, Airport Rd, T07686 272301, www.holiday-inn.com. Plush, 50 rooms, all facilities, bookshop.

**A Jass Radisson**, By-pass Rd, www.radisson.com. Undergoing conversion to Radisson group at time of research.

**A Usha Bundela**, Airport Rd, T07686 272386, www.ushashriramhotels.com. Comfortable rooms, well-managed, good pool.

**A-B Hotel Greenwood** (Best Western), opposite airport, T07686 274505, www.greenwoodhotels.com. 22 spotless rooms in brand new hotel, well maintained gardens, peaceful location.

**B Grand Temple View** , well located near Western temples, T07686 274024, www.ic hotelsgroup.com. Undergoing conversion to Grand group at time of research.

**C-D Lakeside**, by Sib Sagar Lake, T07686 274120. 18 functional rooms and dorm, clean but noisy, beautiful evening views.

**C-D Payal**, 10-min walk from centre, T07686 274076, mptkhaj@sancharnet.in. 25 decent rooms with bath, some a/c, restaurant (good breakfast and tea), bar, very quiet garden, helpful staff, good value.

**D Casa di William**, T07686 274244, hotel casadiwilliam@hotmail.com. 15 pleasant rooms with bath, some a/c, roof restaurant, Italian management.

**D-E Marble Palace**, opposite Gole Market, Jain Temples Rd, T07686 274353. 9 spacious rooms, dorm beds, interesting features – marble tiles, modern baths (tubs).

**D-E Rahil**, T07686 274062, mptrahil@sanch arnet.in. 12 rooms and dorm (Rs 90), restaurant, large gardens.

**D-E Surya**, Jain Temple Rd, T07686 274145. 20 small, clean and basic rooms, some a/c, veg restaurant, pleasant garden, helpful staff.

**D-E Tourist Village**, T07686 274128. 13 well-equipped attractive 2-room 'ethnic' huts, some with bath, outdoor restaurant, quiet, good value, bike useful, campsite nearby.

**D-F Sunset View**, south of Bazar, alongside Chandela Emporium, T07686 274077. Well located near Lake, 'unfinished' look with unimposing entrance, 12 simple rooms (6 air-cooled with tubs), fairly clean, pleasant terrace and garden, good value.

**E-F Zen**, Jain Temple Rd, T07686 274228, oshozen62@hotmail.com. 12 large and bright rooms, air cooler, clean attached bath (some tubs), **Ristorante Italiano** in garden.

**F New Bharat Lodge**, near Payal, T07686 274082. 12 refurbished rooms, some with small patio.

**F Yadav Guest House**, just east of **New Bharat Lodge**. Very cheap, basic but clean.

**F Yogi Lodge**, T07686 274158. Terrace, very well run, clean, internet, bike hire.

**Panna National Park** *p286*

**B Ken River Lodge**, T07732 275235, www.nivalink.com/kenriver. In a beautiful location with both cottages and 'Swiss' tents, tree-top restaurant, fishing, boating, swimming.

**D-E Giles' Treehouse**, 3 km from Madla, serves food (chilled beers are sent 20 m up a tree by a pulley system!). Camping possible, contact **Raja's Café**, Khajuraho.

**E Rest Houses**, ask at gate or park office, Panna. Carry provisions.

**Chitrakoot** *p287*

**F Tourist Bungalow**, near Bus Stand, T07670-265326, www.mptourism.com. 17 rooms (2a/c), restaurant (prior ordering).

**F Pitri Smriti Visram Grih**, Ramghat, Hathi Darwaza, T07670-265314. 16 basic rooms with bath (could be cleaner), friendly manager, pleasant place. Vegetarian; no alcohol.

## Eating

**Gwalior** *p269, map p272*

**TTT Usha Kiran Palace**, International. Good snacks, average meals, classical music, bar, attentive service, pleasant ambience.

**TT Kwality** south of the Fort. Mainly Indian and snacks. Rather dark but helpful staff.

**T Indian Coffee House**, in **India Hotel**; one just off Jayaji Chowk (upstairs). Great for South Indian breakfasts and snacks.

**T Volga**, near Inderganj Chowk. Indian. Popular locally.

**Jhansi** *p273, map p274*

Hotels **Sita** and **Samrat** are recommended.

**TT Holiday**, Shastri Marg. Indian and western. Clean, a/c, reasonably priced.

**T Nav Bharat**, Shastri Marg. Indian snacks.

**Orchha** *p276, map p277*

**TTT Orchha Resorts**, vegetarian. Pleasant décor, à la carte or buffet (breakfast Rs 200, lunch/dinner Rs 400).

**TT Betwa Tarang**, near Fort bridge (upstairs). Good food, pleasant roof terrace or indoor, clean toilets. Also 'picnic' meals by the riverside.

**TT Sheesh Mahal**. International, non-vegetarian served in a large foyer. Great north Indian, chilled beer, good service.

**T Bhola**, opposite post office. Basic but serves freshly cooked simple meals.

**Khajuraho** *p280, map p283*

Top hotels have very comfortable seating and good bars. Beer is expensive everywhere; Rs 100 minimum in hotels.

**TTT Mediterraneo**, opposite **Surya Hotel**. Italian. Good bruschetta, fresh pasta dishes, Indian/Italian owned.

**TT Paradise**, Main Rd, opposite Shiv Sagar Lake, T07686 272349. Western, Indian. Good meals reasonably priced (excellent banana pancakes), family run, friendly and inviting.

**TT Raja Café**, opposite Western Group. Western, Indian. Shady terrace with good view from top, bland food, pricey, often unfriendly service, undeservedly popular.

**TT Rimjhun**, opposite Vishvanatha Temple. International. Good food, attentive service, generous portions. Liquor stall has beer.

**TT La Terrazza**, near **Yogi Lodge**. Continental. Clean, good food, interesting trips to forts nearby (see below).

**T Agarwal**, nearby, does good Indian.

**T Lovely**, North Indian. Special *thali* (Rs 20), good curd, cheap, friendly.

**T Madras Coffee House**, Jain Temple Rd, does good *dosas*.

**T Ristorante Italiano**, **Zen Hotel**, has been recommended.

**T Safari**, bizarre array of menus, very good food, large helpings (Rs 35-40 dish), good lassi, amazing Indian muesli but slow service (breakfast can take 1 hr).

**Chitrakoot** *p287*

**Digbeah**, near bridge on Ramghat. Lunchtime *thalis* recommended.

## Entertainment

**Gwalior** *p269, map p272*

Winter evenings are chilly. Take a torch (seating on stepped terrace covered with mats).

**Son et Lumière** in front of Man Mandir Palace, Gwalior Fort, 45 min, 1830 in Hindi, 1930 in English (1 hr later in summer), Rs 40/ 150 foreigners. Colourful spectacle tracing the history of the site through interesting anecdotes. No bus; there is unlikely to be any transport available at the end of the show. Taxis, Rs 250 for return trip from hotels. Alternatively, visit the Fort last when hiring a car for the day in the summer (day hire covers only a single fort visit).

## Festivals and events

**Orchha** *p276, map p277*
Several annual events are celebrated including **Ram Vivah** (Rama's marriage) in late **Nov/Dec** when colourful processions draw crowds particularly as superbly trained horses perform extraordinary feats where one removes a horseman's eye make-up with a hoof!

**Khajuraho** *p280, map p283*
Dance Festival, **Feb-Mar**. Many of the country's most accomplished dancers perform in the spectacular setting of the Western Group. Tourist Office for details.

## Shopping

**Gwalior** *p269, map p272*
**Kothari**, Sarafa Bazar. Brocade, *chanderi* (light and flimsy cotton and silk material), silk saris.
**Ganpatlal Krishna Lal**, Sarafa Bazar. Jewellery and antiques. These close on Tue.
**Loyal**, near High Court, Nai Sarak. Books.
**MD Fine Arts**, Subhash Market. Paintings and objets d'art.
**MP Emporium**, Sarafa Bazar. Handlooms.
**MP Khadi Sangh**, Sarafa Bazar. Handlooms.
**Mrignayani's**, an MP State Emporium, in Patankar Bazar also recommended.

**Khajuraho** *p280, map p283*
Gift shops sell cheap stone and bronze sculptures, handicrafts and gems in the bazar near the Western Group (**Panna diamond mines**, the largest in the country, are nearby).
**Chandela Emporium**, near Sibsagar, has a large selection of gifts, crafts and jewellery.
**Ganesh Garments**, Jain Temples Rd. Reasonable western clothes (quick alterations).
**Karan Jewellers** for diamonds. Tuesday Market at Rajgarh (see Excursions above).
**MP Emporium** for fixed prices; small craft shops on way to Javeri temple cheaper than the bazar.

## Activities and tours

**Gwalior** *p269, map p272*
**SS Travels**, Usha Kiran Palace.
**Travel Bureau**, near Madhoganj Police, Lashkar, T/F0751 2340103, www.travelbureauagra.com.
Tours to **Orchha** and **Shivpuri**, Rs 1,200 (car for 5), same day return. City sights, Rs 400, contact tourist office at **Tansen Hotel**.

**Jhansi** *p273, map p274*
**Touraids**, Jai Complex, Civil Lines, T0517 2443490, helpful and reliable manager with a fleet of cars for hire.
**Travel Bureau**, 197 Chand Gate, Nai Basti, T0517 2449355, www.travelbureauagra.com.

**Khajuraho** *p280, map p283*
**Ajay Singh**, **La Terazza Restaurant**, opposite Western Group of Temples (or near Old Palace, Ajaigarh), recommended for tours, including Chandela forts and Chitrakoot (see below).
**ATS Tours**, Sevagram, T07686 274242, F272385, also Agra office.
**Bhavan Travel**, Raja Market, near Western Group, T07686 274275. Good guides.
**Touraids**, near **Usha Bundela**, reliable cars with drivers.
**Travel Bureau**, 84 Sevagram, T07686 274037, www.travelbureauagra.com.

## Transport

**Gwalior** *p269, map p272*

### Air
The airport is 9 km from town. **Indian Airlines**, T0751 2326872, airport T2470272, flies to **Delhi** and **Mumbai** via Bhopal and Indore, 3 weekly. Taxi to town, about Rs 120.

### Rickshaw
Unmetered tempos and auto-rickshaw available. Cycle-rickshaw charge around Rs 25 from the centre to the fort.

### Taxi
Charge about Rs 450 for 80 km per 8 hrs visiting all sights, once only; best to visit fort last and stay on for *Son et Lumière*. Evening visit to fort, Rs 250.

### Train
Tickets for the *Shatabdi Express* are usually sold in the separate, 'non- computerised' queue. Gwalior is on the Central Railways main Delhi-Mumbai and Chennai-Delhi lines. Rly station: enquiries T0751 222544/131, reservations T0751 225306/135. **Agra Cantt**:

*Lakshadweep Exp, 2617,* 1010, 1¾ hrs; *Punjab Mail, 2137,* 1500, 1¾ hrs; *Dadar Amritsar Exp, 1057,* 2150, 1¾ hrs. **Bhopal**: *Shatabdi Exp, 2002,* 0918, 5 hrs; *Punjab Mail, 2138,* 1025, 6¼ hrs; *Lakshadweep Exp, 2618,* 1415, 6 hrs. **Delhi**: *Lakshadweep Exp, 2617,* 1010, 6 hrs (HN); *Punjab Mail, 2137,* 1500, 5½ hrs (ND); *Taj Exp, 2179,* 1655, 5 hrs (HN). **Jabalpur (for Kanha)**: *Gondwana Exp, 2412,* 1838, 11 hrs; *Mahakoshal Exp, 1450,* 2110, 13¼ hrs. **Jhansi**: *Shatabdi Exp, 2002,* 0918, 1 hr; *Punjab Mail, 2138,* 1025, 1½ hrs; *Lakshadweep Exp, 2618,* 1415, 1½ hrs. **Lucknow**: *Gwailor Barauni Mail, 5224,* 1115, 9 hrs. **Mumbai (CST)**: *Punjab Mail, 2138,* 1025, 21¼ hrs, plus others to Dadar. **Varanasi**: *Bundelkhand Exp, 1107,* 1725, 17 hrs (calling at **Allahabad** 4 hrs earlier).

### Jhansi *p273, map p274*

#### Bus

To major North Indian cities from **Kanpur Rd Bus Stand**, 3 km east of railway station: **Gwalior** 0645-1800 via Datia; **Khajuraho**, so-called 'Deluxe' from railway station (fairly direct, bumpy but through attractive countryside), 1100 (tickets from booth on Platform 1, or on bus; Rs 85, plus luggage Rs 5, 5 hrs) picks up from bus stand around 1130, other buses 1700, 1800; **Lalitpur** 0730, 1025, 2100, 2300. **Shivpuri** 0500-1800. **Orchha**: buses from Kanpur Rd Bus Stand, half-hourly during daylight, take about 30 mins, Rs 5; quicker by **auto-rickshaw** from Jhansi railway station, Rs 125-175; return after sightseeing Rs 275-340; **taxis**: equally overpriced, about Rs 300-350; **tempos**: from bus stand 30 mins, Rs 10.

#### Car

Car hire with driver: about Rs 5 per km, minimum 200 km per day; night halt Rs 150. To **Khajuraho**, Hotel Sita; Touraids, Rs 2,100.

#### Rickshaw

Auto-rickshaws, Rs 20 from the railway station to hotel or bus stand; tempo, Rs 3 each from the station to main bus stand.

#### Train

Train porters are expensive: agree a price. **Agra Cantt**: see Delhi. **Bhopal**: *Shatabdi Exp, 2002,* 1032, 3¾ hrs; *Punjab Mail, 2138,* 1215, 4½ hrs; *Lakshadweep Exp, 2618,* 1547, 4¼ hrs. **Delhi**: *Lakshadweep Exp, 2617,* 0850, 7¼ hrs (HN); *Punjab Mail, 2137,* 1340, 6¾ hrs (ND); *Shatabdi Exp, 2001,* 1755, 5 hrs (HN). **Jabalpur (for Kanha)**: *Godwana Exp, 2412,* 2012, 9½ hrs. **Jalgaon (for Aurangabad)**: *Amritsar Dadar Exp, 1058,* 0545, 14¼ hrs; *Punjab Mail, 2138,* 1215, 11¾ hrs. **Lucknow**: *Kushi Nagar Exp, 1015,* 2000, 7 hrs (continues to **Gorakhpur**, 5¼ hrs); *Gwailor Barauni Mail, 5224,* 1315, 7 hrs, plus several non-daily services. **Mumbai**: *Punjab Mail, 2138,* 1215, 19½ hrs, plus several to Dadar. **Varanasi**: *Bundelkhand Exp, 1107,* 1920, 15 hrs.

### Datia *p274*

**Bus** Frequent from Jhansi (1 hr, Rs 10), and Gwalior (Rs 30).
**Rickshaw** Tempos and cycle-rickshaws run the 2 km between Datia station and the fort/palace (10 mins, Rs 20), and the 5 km between Sonagiri station and the temples.
**Train** Both are on the Delhi-Mumbai main line. From Gwalior: *Bundelkhand Exp, 1107,* 1725, 1¼ hrs. From Jhansi: *Bundelkhand Exp, 1108,* 0730, 21 mins; *Chappra-Gwalior Mail, 1144,* 1435, 21 mins. For return to **Jhansi**, *Chhattisgarh Exp, 8238,* depart Sonagiri 1210, Datia 1225.

### Shivpuri National Park *p275*

Nearest airport is at Gwalior (112 km). Nearest stations are at Jhansi and Gwalior. Regular bus services from Bhopal, Chanderi, Indore, Jhansi (101 km, 3 hrs by car) and Ujjain. Auto-rickshaws available at Bus Stand.

### Deogarh *p279*

Jakhlaun (13 km) is the nearest station, with buses to **Deogarh** and **Lalitpur**. Lalitpur (30 km away) has auto-rickshaws for transfer to Deogarh (1 hr, Rs 200). It also has trains to **Jhansi**: *Kushinagar Exp, 1015,* 1840, 1½ hrs; *Jhelum Exp, 1077,* 1230, 1½ hrs; *Amritsar Exp, 1457,* 1818, 1½ hrs. **Bina-Etawa**, south of Deogarh, is an important railway junction.

### Khajuraho *p280, map p283*

#### Air

Flights are heavily booked in season, confirm onward flight on arrival. The airport is 5 km south of the village centre. Transport to town: Taxi Rs 100, occasional auto-rickshaw Rs 50 (overpriced; difficult to bargain). **Indian Airlines**: Usha Bundela, T07686 274035, Airport T274036; credit cards not accepted.

Flies daily from **Delhi** to Khajuraho (2½ hrs) via **Agra**, returning the same route; also to **Varanasi**. Jet Airways: T07686 274406 (airport), daily to **Delhi** via **Varanasi**.

### Bicycle

Cycle hire behind museum, Jain Temples Rd; Rs 25 per day, recommended mode though not allowed in temple complex.

### Bus

Long-distance buses arrive at a newish bus stand 1½ km south of the main bazar on Airport Rd (which offers computerized reservations on buses and trains elsewhere). Daily buses to **Agra** 391 km, 0900 (10- 12 hrs); **Bhopal** 350 km, 0600, 0730; **Gwalior** 280 km (9 hrs); **Indore** 480 km, 0600; **Jabalpur** 210 km, 0730 via Satna; this bus connects with trains to Jabalpur, better than travelling all the way by bus – see Satna, 2100 (via Damoh); **Jhansi** 176 km, 0530- 1645 (4½-5 hrs), semi-deluxe via Orchha 1115; **Mahoba** (stops 3 km from the railway station), several 0700-1900 (3 hrs) and **Satna**, 0830, 0930, 1430, 1530, 4 hrs (very uncomfortable), Rs 55. UP Roadways runs a service to **Agra** via Gwalior, a long and tiring journey.

### Car

Car hire with driver to **Jhansi**, Rs 2,000 through Touraids, 3½ hrs. **Agra** or **Varanasi**, Rs 5,000, 8-9 hrs.

### Rickshaw and taxi

Cycle-rickshaws are expensive (Rs 30 for shortest journey), negotiate fare; Rs 75 per half day. Taxis are from MP Tourism or Touraids near Usha Hotel, but overpriced.

### Train

Railheads are **Jhansi** (176 km, for Agra, Delhi, Bhopal); **Satna** (117 km, best for Varanasi, see below); **Mahoba** (51 km, alternative for Varanasi, but few slow trains daily).

### Satna

Satna's only interest to visitors is as a transport link to Khajuraho.

### Bus

To **Amarkantak** 0750; for **Bandhavgarh**: daily bus to **Tala**, 0800, 4 hrs (Rs 28); **Chitrakoot** 0500, 1200, 1530; **Khajuraho**: very uncomfortable MPSRTC bus depart 0630-1530, 4 hrs (Rs 27); you can buy fruit from market towns en route. In Satna, it stops at the railway bridge which is a 2-km walk from the station (rickshaws charge Rs 10).

### Train

Reservations from office on right, outside main entrance. **Jabalpur-Kanha**: there are good connections with 0730 bus from Khajuraho (get off Khajuraho bus at railway bridge); bus also connects with Allahabad (4 hrs), Jabalpur, Lucknow, Chennai and Patna. **Kolkata** *Howrah Mumbai Mail, 3004*, 1705, 20¼ hrs. **Mumbai (CST)** *Howrah Mumbai Mail, 3003*, 1415, 21¼ hrs; *Mahanagri Exp, 1094*, 1800, 21¼ hrs. **Varanasi** *Sarnath Exp, 5159*, 0840, 7½ hrs; *5217/5219*, 0705, 7½ hrs; *Mahanagri Exp, 1093*, 2000, 8¼ hrs; plus many at awkward times, or certain days only.

### Chitrakoot *p287*

**Bus** Regular services to **Jhansi**, **Mahoba**, **Satna** and **Chhattarpur**.
**Train** The nearest station is Karwi (Chitrakoot Dham) with trains between **Delhi (HN)** and **Jabalpur** and to **Lucknow**, then tempo to **Chitrakoot**, 30 mins, Rs 10. **Delhi (HN)** via Agra: *Nizamuddin Mahakosal Exp*, 2033, 14 hrs (for Agra deduct 4½ hrs).

## Directory

**Gwalior** *p269, map p272*
**Post** GPO: Jayaji Chowk, Birla Nagar, Morar and Residency.

**Jhansi** *p273, map p274*
**Banks** State Bank of India, Jayaji Chowk week 1030-1430, Sat 1030-1230.

**Orchha** *p276, map p277*
**Banks** Orchha Resorts for residents; Canara Bank, main street, changes TCs.

**Khajuraho** *p280, map p283*
**Banks** State Bank of India, opposite Western Group, foreign exchange facilities, can be busy. **Post** Bus Stand, 0900-1700. **Tourist offices** Govt of India, opposite W Group, 0900-1730, Sat 0800-1230. Guides Rs 100 per day. **Useful addresses** Police: T07686 272032.

# Western Madhya Pradesh

## Indore ➔ *Phone code: 0731. Colour map 2, grid C5. Population: 1,600,000.*

A rapidly growing and rather characterless industrial city, Indore is on the banks of the rivers Sarasvati and Khan. A major centre for cotton textiles and the automobile industry, but the city is notable for Hindustani classical music. ▸▸ *For Sleeping, Eating and other listings, see pages 301-303.*

### Ins and outs

**Getting there** Indore has direct flights to Bhopal, Delhi, Gwalior and Mumbai. It is under five hours by the fastest train from Bhopal. The railway station and the Sarwate Bus Stand are near the town centre, but buses to Mandu go from the Gangwal Bus Stand, 10-min auto ride away. ▸▸ *See Transport, page 302, for further details.*
**Getting around** Indore is quite spread out so it is best to take an auto to visit the sights away from the centre. Some prefer to hire a bike.



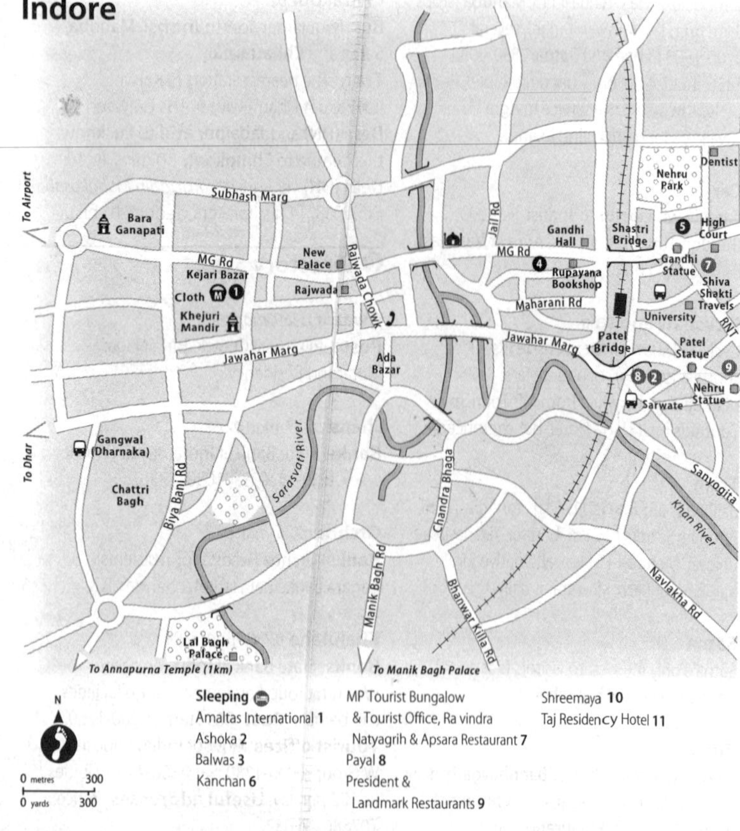

## History

The land on which Indore was built was given to **Malhar Rao Holkar** in 1733 by the Maratha Peshwas, see page 1076, in appreciation of his help in many of their battles. Malhar Rao left much of the statecraft in the highly gifted hands of his widowed daughter-in-law who succeeded him to the throne. The city was destroyed in 1801 but recovered and was the British headquarters of their Central India Agency. The ruling family of Indore, the **Holkars**, took the British side during the Mutiny in 1857. Indore was one of the first states to open temples, schools and public wells to *Harijans* (Untouchables), in support of Gandhi's campaign against untouchability.

## Sights

The **Rajwada** (Old Palace) with its seven-storeyed gateway, faces the main square. A third fire in 1984 destroyed most of it; now only the façade remains. On the north side is the **New Palace** and garden. In the streets are some good timber houses with deep recessed verandahs and carved pillars.

**Kanch Mandir** ⓘ *1000, allow 30 mins, shoes to be left at door*, is on Jawahar Marg next to **Hotel Sheesh Mahal**. Inside this Jain temple thousands of mirrors adorn the walls, floor and ceilings, supplemented by brightly patterned ceramic tiles, Chinese lantern-type glass lamps and cut glass chandeliers, all exquisitely crafted. There are about 50 murals depicting scenes of conversion to Jainism and 19th-century courtly life. The use of glass beads and raised figures produces a pleasing 3D effect. The image of the Mahavir is in plain black onyx. This mirrored palace is at variance with the austerity and simplicity of the Mahavira's supposed existence and teachings.

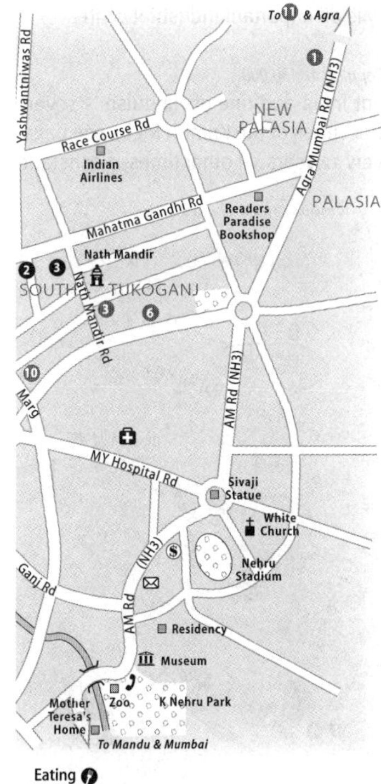


**Eating**

Café Udupi & Prithvilok **1**

Ding Ding **2**

Gypsy **3**

Indian Coffee House **4**

Statue **5**

**Chhattri Bagh**, on the banks of the Khan River, has seven memorials of the Holkar kings but the sanctums are locked. Although in a peaceful setting, the place is overgrown and unkempt, and hardly worth a special detour.

**Lal Bagh** (The Nehru Centre) ⓘ *closed Mon, 1100-1800, small entry fee*, southwest of town, once the residence of the Maharaja, built and decorated in a confusion of styles, is now a museum and cultural centre. The rooms have been restored and furnished to pleasing effect. Queen Victoria looks on to the main 'entrance portico' (you leave through this and enter through a side entrance). There are a number of sporting trophies including stuffed tigers. The Maharaja, a keen sportsman, is seen in photographs rowing on a lake, and flying in an early aeroplane. Both these are in fact 'backdrop paintings' with a hole for him to stand in to be photographed! There are

*If time is precious, visit this museum instead of the Cental Museum – riotously varied and fascinating.*

 also good prints of the Old Palace. The entrance hall is in marble and gilt rococo with a display of prehistoric artefacts. Two attractive rooms are predominantly 'Indian' and include Mughal exhibits. On the first floor is the coin collection which dates mostly from the Muslim period. Exhibits include miniatures, contemporary Indian sculptures and paintings, Italian sculptures and intricately inlaid boxes. The garden, though maintained, is dry and dusty.

**Central Museum** ⓘ *Agra-Mumbai Rd, near GPO, closed Mon, 1100-1800, free, guides available, allow 30 mins*, has two main galleries: **Gallery I** with artefacts from circa 50,000-4000 BC, some from west Malwa including stone tools, quartz sickles, ornaments. Also a model of the first Hindu temple at Bharhut (another is at Lal Bagh). **Gallery II** contains Hindu mythological carvings. Sculptures stand in the grounds, which were possibly a battlefield during the Mutiny.

# Around Indore

## Dewas

**EM Forster** 'worked' here in the court of the Raja of Dewas Senior in 1921, having visited it earlier in 1912. Forster came to regard his stay in this dusty town as the 'great opportunity' of his life and used this experience to good effect with the autobiographical *The Hill of Devi* and his most famous novel, *A Passage to India*. It is worth going up the 'Hill of Devi' overlooking the town for the views; you can drive all the way to the temple at the top. Dewas today is an important industrial centre.

## Ujjain → *Phone code: 0734. Colour map 2, grid C5. Population: 430,000.*

Ujjain, one of the best known cities of ancient India and one of Hinduism's seven sacred cities, see page 1324, is one of the four centres of the Kumbh Mela, see page 185, attracting about three million pilgrims every 12 years. At other times, a constant

stream come to bathe in the river Shipra and worship at the temples. Despite its sanctity and its age, it has few remarkable buildings. In its heyday, Ujjain was on a flourishing trade route to Mesopotamia and Egypt. Nowadays, it is little more than a provincial town. 

Many dynasties ruled over this prosperous city and it is said to have been the seat of the viceroyalty of Asoka in 275 BC. His sons were born here, and it was from here that they set out to preach Buddhism. The poet **Kalidasa**, one of the *Nava Ratna* (Nine Gems) of Hindu literature, wrote some of his works here. Ujjain stands on the **first meridian** of longitude for Hindu astronomers, who believed that the **Tropic of Cancer** also passed through the site. This explains the presence of the **Vedha Shala** observatory, southwest of town, built by Raja Jai Singh II of Jaipur around 1730 when he was the Governor of Malwa under the Mughals. Small, compared to the Jantar Mantars, it has only five instruments. Even today the *Ephemeris* tables (predicted positions of the planets), are published here.

**Mahakaleshwar Temple**, dedicated to Siva, was rebuilt by Marathas in the 18th century. The temple lingam is one of the 12 *jyotirlingas* (in India, believed to be *swayambhu* -- born of itself). The myths surrounding the 'linga of light' go back to the second century BC and were developed to explain and justify linga worship, see page 1329. The Chaubis Khambha Darwaza (circa 11th century) has 24 carved pillars which probably belonged to the medieval temple.

Close to the tank near Mahakaleshwar is a large sculpted image of Ganesh in the **Bade Ganeshji-ka Mandir**. A rock covered with turmeric is worshipped as the head of a legendary king Vikramaditya in the centre of the **Harsiddhi Mandir**. **Gopal Mandir** in the bazar contains a silver image of Krishna and an ornamental silver door. The **Bina-Niv-ki-Masjid** in Anantpeth, originally a Jain temple (see entrance porch), was converted to a mosque (circa 1400), by the first independent Sultan of Malwa. The **Chintamani Ganesh Temple** across the river is believed to have ancient medieval origins. There are other smaller temples and shrines along the river and the atmosphere at these is generally very restful and relaxed.



# Mandu (Mandav)

→ *Phone code: 07292. Colour map 2, grid C5. Population: 5,000.*

Architecturally, Mandu represents the best in a provincial Islamic style, restrained and lacking in elaborate external ornamentation. Fine buildings are spread over the naturally defensible plateau with a sheer drop towards the Namar plains to the south and waterfalls flowing into the Kakra Khoh gorge. You can visit Mandu from Indore on a long day excursion, but it is better to have a peaceful break here for a couple of days. ➤➤ *For Sleeping, Eating and other listings, see pages 301-303.*

## Ins and outs

**Getting there** Indore is the nearest centre for air, bus and train connections.

**Getting around** Everything worth visiting, spread across a few kilometres, can be reached on foot, bike or rickshaw. ➤➤ *See Transport, page 303, for further details.*

## History

Perched along the **Vindhya ranges**, Mandu was fortified as early as the sixth century. By 1261, King Jayavaram transferred the Paramara capital from Dhar to Mandu itself. The whole area fell to the Muslims in 1293, though Mandu remained under Hindu rule until 1305, when it came under the Khaljis in Delhi. The first of these Pathan sultans re-named **Mandu, Shadiabad** (City of Joy). Hoshang Shah (1405-35) made it his capital and as Mandu's strategic importance grew he embellished it with its most important civic buildings. Under his successor, the liberal Mahmud Khalji, a resurgence of art and literature followed, fostering Hindu, Jain as well as Muslim development. Mandu remained a prosperous centre of peace and stability under his son Ghiyasuddin until 1500. Several early Mughal rulers enjoyed visiting Mandu, but by the end of the Mughal period it had effectively been abandoned, and in 1732 it passed into Maratha hands.

## Sights

Most of the buildings date from 1401 to 1526 – some have stones salvaged from desecrated local Hindu temples. There are six groups of buildings at Mandu, the first three being the most important. The return trip taking in Roopmati's Pavilion is about 14 km. The 45-km parapet wall with 12 gates was built from rubble and boulders. Most notable is **Delhi Gate** (1405-7), the main entrance to the city. The approach is through a series of well fortified subsidiary gates such as Alamgir and Bhangi Darwaza (the only one now open). The present road is along this route.

**Royal Enclave Mosque of Dilwar Khan** (1405) ⓘ *Rs 2*, is the earliest Islamic building, comprising a central colonnaded courtyard. There are Hindu influences in the main entrances. **Hathi Pol** (Elephant Gate) is the main entrance to the royal enclosure. **Hindola Mahal** (Swing Palace, circa 1425), built on a 'T' plan, was the audience hall, acquiring its name from its inward sloping walls which give the impression of swaying. Behind and to the west of the Hindola Mahal is a jumble of ruins which was once the palace of the Malwa Sultans.

Here is the 6½-m deep **Champa Baoli**, an underground well (its water is said to have smelt like the *champak* flower), cool vaulted *tyhkhanas* (rooms for summer use), a *hammam* (hot bath) and a water pavilion.

The late 15th-century **Jahaz Mahal** (Ship Palace), reflects the spirit of romantic beauty characteristic of the palace life of the Muslim rulers of India. Built between two



## Mandu Fort

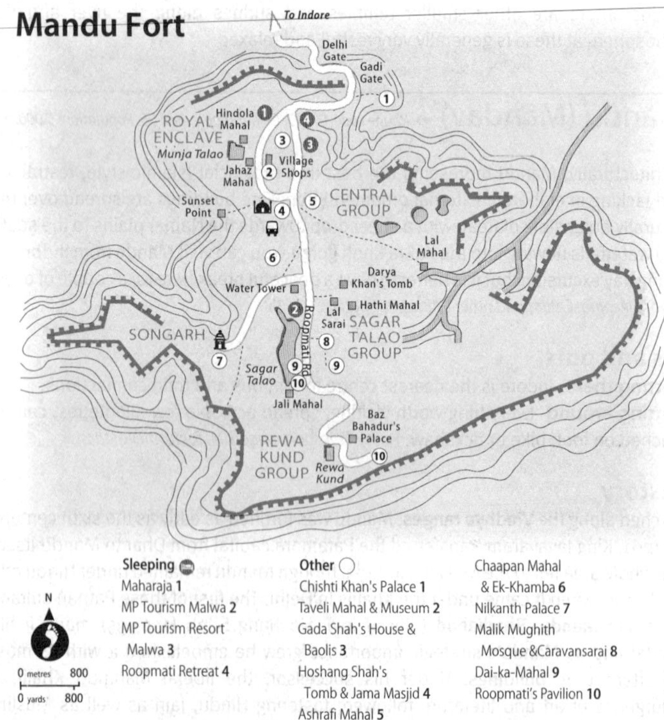

artificial lakes, Munj and Kapur Talaos, it is 122 m ng and only 15 m wide. Its shape and kiosks give it the impression of a stately shi Built to house Ghiyas'ud-Din's increasing *harem*, it was 'crewed' entirely by wom, some from as far off places as Turkey and Abyssinia, and consists of three great hlls with a beautiful bath.

Other places of interest in this enclave are **Taveli Mahal (2)** (stables and guardhouse), from which there is a wonderful panoma of the ruins of Mandu; it has a small **museum**. Two large wells – the *Ujala* (brigh and *Andheri* (dark) **baolis**, and **Gada Shah's House and Shop (3)**, Kesar Kasturi Maal are nearby. The last, in ruins, retains the romance of its second name – Gada Shahaking pity on a group of gypsies trying to sell their perfumed *kesar* and *kasturi* which ad been ruined by a downpour, bought their wares and then had to use it all in his place since it was unsaleable.

**Central Group** **Hoshang Shah's Tomb (4)** (circa 140) ⓘ *US$5 for foreigners*, in Mandu Bazar, is India's first marble monument, a refined example of Afghan architecture. It has a well-proportioned dome, delicate marble latticework and porticoed courts and towers. The square base of the interior changes to an octagon through being raised by arches to the next level, and then becomes 16-sided further up. Shah Jahan sent four of his architects, including Ustad Ahmed, who is associated with the Taj Mahal, to study it for inspiration. The adjoining **Jama Masjid (4)** (1454), which took three generations to complete, was inspired by the great mosque at Damascus. Conceived by Hoshang Shah on a grand scale, it is on a high plinth (4.6 m), with a large domed porch ornamented with jali screens and bands of blue enamel tiles set as stars. The courtyard is flanked by colonnades. The western one is the Prayer Hall and is the most imposing of all with numerous rows of arches and pillars which support the ceilings of the three great domes and the 58 smaller ones. The central niche (*mihrab*) is beautifully designed and ornamented along its sides with a scroll of interwoven Arabic letters containing quotations from the Koran.

**Ashrafi Mahal (5)** (Palace of gold coins, circa 1436-1440), now a ruin, was conceived as the first *madrassa* of Persian studies. Its builder Mahmud Shah Khilji (1436-1469) built the seven-storeyed tower to celebrate his victory over Rana Khumba of Mewar (Udaipur). Only one storey has survived. Also in ruins is the tomb, intended to be the largest building in Mandu.

**Sagar Talao Group** To the east of the road between the village and Sagar Talao is the **Hathi Mahal** (Elephant Palace). It takes its names from its stumpy pillars supporting the dome and was probably a *baradari* (pleasure pavilion), turned into a tomb with a mosque by it. The **Tomb of Darya Khan** (circa 1526), a red masonry mausoleum once embellished with rich enamel patterns, is nearby.

In the large group of monuments around the picturesque **Sagar Talao** (lake) is the **Malik Mughith Mosque (8)** built in 1432. It has a west wall retaining blue tile decoration in carved niches. In front is the **caravanserai** (also 1432), an open courtyard with two halls with rooms at both ends, probably for storage of goods while the halls provided living accommodation. The **Dai-ka-Mahal (9)** (Gumbad) to the south is a tomb which may first have been a house belonging to the wet-nurse of a Mandu Prince, and was later converted to her tomb. Alongside, the ruins of a pretty mosque has a fine octagonal base to the dome, decorated with small kiosks.

**Rewa Kund Group** **Rewa Kund**, 3.2 km south of the village, is a sacred tank whose waters were lifted to supply the **Palace of Baz Bahadur** (1508-1509), the musician prince, on the rising ground above. The palace was built before Baz Bahadur, the last Sultan of Malwa (1555), came to occupy it. The main portion of the palace consists of a spacious open court with halls and rooms on all sides and a beautiful cistern in its centre. On the terrace above are two *baradaris* (pavilions) from which there are lovely views.

On higher ground at the southern edge of the plateau is **Roopmati's Pavilion (10)**, originally built as a military observation post but later modified and added to as a palace, so that Baz Bahadur's mistress could have her *darshan* (view) of the sacred **Narmada River**, seen 305 m below winding like a white serpent across the plains. The shepherdess **Roopmati**, the story goes, so impressed Baz Bahadur with her singing that he captured her. She agreed to go to Mandu with Baz Bahadur when he promised that she would live in a palace within sight of her beloved river! He built the Rewa Kund so that she could practise her Hindu rites. The pavilions, square with hemispherical domes, are the latest additions.

**Other palaces** On the edge of the plateau is the **Lal Mahal** (Red/Ruby Palace) or Lal Bungalow, once used as a royal summer retreat. **Chishti Khan's Palace (1)**, used during the monsoon, is now in ruins but offers good views. West of Sagar Talao the Islamic **Nilkanth Palace (7)**, built for Akbar's Hindu wife, contains the Nilkanth (Siva) shrine. On the scarp of one of the great ravines, reached by steps and commanding a magnificent view of the valleys below, it was used by the Mughals as a water palace. On one of the outer room walls is an inscription recording Akbar's expeditions into the Deccan and the futility of temporal riches.

The **Lohani Caves** and temple ruins are near Hoshang Shah's Tomb. Approached by steep rock-cut steps, they are a maze of dark and damp caverns in the hillside. Panoramic views of the surroundings from **Sunset Point** in front of the caves.



## Maheshwar

On the north bank of the Narmada, Maheshwar has been identified as **Mahishmati**, the ancient capital of King Kartivirarjun, a spectacular temple city mentioned in the *Ramayana* and *Mahabharata* epics. The Holkar queen **Rani Ahilyabai of Indore** who died in 1795 was responsible for revitalizing the city by building temples and a fort complex. According to Sir John Malcolm, the queen was widely revered. She had "an almost sacred respect for native rights .. she heard every complaint in person". The palace inside the fort contains exhibits of the Holkar family treasures and memorabilia including the small shrine on a palanquin which is carried down from the fort during the annual *Dasara* ceremony. There is also a statue of the Rani seated on her throne.

The town is renowned for its *Maheshwar* saris woven in a unique way for over 200 years. Woven in cotton and silk, the 'body' of the sari may be plain, checked or striped. The **Ghats** on the river bank are interesting to visit and watch the daily rituals of ordinary villagers. Lining the banks are stone memorials to the *satis*. The temples to see are Kaleshwara, Rajarajeshwara, Vithaleshwara and Ahileshwar.

## Omkareshwar (Mandhata)

A sacred island shaped like the holy Hindu symbol 'Om' at the confluence of the Narmada and the Kaveri, Omkareshwar has drawn pilgrims for centuries. Over 2 km long and 1 km wide the island is divided north to south by a deep gully. The ground slopes gently along the north edge but in the south and east there are cliffs over 150 m high forming a gorge. The village spreads to the south bank from the island, now linked by a bridge. The river is reputedly very deep and has crocodiles.

**Sri Omkareshwar Mahadeo Temple** has one of the 12 *jyotirlingas* in India, natural rock features that are believed to be representations of Siva. The oldest temple is at the east end of the island. **Siddhnath Temple** on the hill is a fine example of early medieval temple architecture, its main feature being a frieze of elephants over 1½-m high carved on a stone slab at its outer perimeter. Craftsmen have carved elaborate figures on the upper portion of the temple and its roof. Encircling the shrine are verandahs with columns carved in circles, polygons and squares. A gigantic Nandi bull is carved in the hillside opposite the temple to **Gauri Somnath** at the west end of the island.

The temples were severely damaged after the Muslim invasions of **Mahmud of Ghazni**. Every dome was overturned and the sculptured figures mutilated. They became completely overgrown, and *Murray's Guide* records that when the Peshwa Baji Rao II wanted to repair the temple it could not be found, so he built a new one. Subsequently repairs were carried out to the part that was discovered.

## Sleeping

**Indore** *p294, map p294*
AM Rd, Agra-Mumbai Rd and RNT Marg is RN Tagore Marg.
**L-AL Fortune Landmark**, Meghdoot Gardens, T0731 2557700, www.fortuneindore.com. 80 very comfortable rooms, very good coffee shop.
**B President**, 163 RNT Marg, T0731 2528866, www.hotelpresidentindore.com. 65 comfortable a/c rooms, good south Indian restaurant, modern, friendly, good travel desk.
**B-C Mashal**, Jhoomerghat, Rasalpura, A-M Rd, T0731 5020301, www.hotelmashal.com. 36 comfortable a/c rooms on a hilltop out of town, gardens, pool, squash.
**C Balwas**, 30/2 S Tukoganj, T0731 2524934, balwasmp@sancharnet.in. 38 rooms, some a/c, good restaurant, popular with tours from Gulf, quiet, good value.
**C Kanchan Tilak**, 585/2 MG Rd, Palasia, T0731 2538606, kanchan@bom4.vsnl.net.in. 39 rooms, good restaurant, garden, clean, modern, family atmosphere, pleasant lobby, good service and value but noisy.
**C Shreemaya**, 12/1 RNT Marg (near railway), T0731 2515555, www.shreemaya.com. 52 a/c rooms with bath, very good popular cafeteria (South Indian), exchange, Indian style hotel, 0900 check-out.
**C-D Amaltas International**, A-M Rd, 2 RK Puram, T0731 2432631, amaltas_int@rediffmail.com. 30 small rooms, some a/c, restaurant claustrophobic but good value, bar, garden, far from centre.
**D Kanchan**, Kanchan Bagh, T0731 2518501, hotelkanchan@yahoo.co.in. 28 comfortable rooms, some a/c with bath, restaurant, bar, good value. Recommended.
**D Tourist Bungalow**, behind Ravindra Natya Griha, RNT Marg, T0731 2521818, www.mptourism.com. 6 rooms, 2 a/c with bath, Nos 4 and 5 larger, breakfast only, Tourist Office, safe, peaceful.
**E Ashoka**, T07331 2465991. Clean rooms (hot water).
**E Payal**, Chhoti Gwaltoli, opposite Sarawate bus station, T0731 2478460. Neat rooms with bath, some aircooled with TV.

**Ujjain** *p296, map p296*
**C Surana Palace**, 23 GDC Rd, southeast of Madhav Chowk, T0734 2530045, suranaujn@satyam.net.in. Comfy rooms, good eatery.
**C-D Shipra** (MP Tourism), University Rd, T0734 2551495, www.mptourism.com. 30 rooms (10 a/c), restaurant, beer bar, travel, garden, quiet but run down and major mosquito menace.
**D-F Yatri Niwas** (MP Tourism), LB Shastri Marg, 2½ km south of station, T0734 2511398, www.mptourism.com. 4 rooms, 60 dorm beds, canteen, clean, quiet.
**E-F Ajay**, opposite railway station, T0734 2550856. Some rooms air-cooled with bath.
**F Ayodhya Lodge**, Laxmi Bai Marg, is similar.
**F Ramkrishna**, Subhash Marg, T0734 2557012. Basic rooms, some with bath (check first), veg restaurant.

**Mandu** *p297, map p298*
Severe water shortage is likely before the monsoon – buckets are provided.
**C Malwa Resort** (MP Tourism), Roopmati Rd, 20-min walk from Bus Stand, T07292 263235, www.mptourism.com. 20 rooms (10 a/c), spacious cottages with small lounge, No 16 best a/c, No 18 best non-a/c (avoid 1, 2, 7 and 8), good restaurant, gardens, peaceful setting by Sagar Talao Lake.
**C-D Roopmati** (500 m beyond entrance), T07292 263270. 19 rooms, some a/c with balcony, decent showers, restaurant, beer.
**D-E Maharaja**, 500 m before Jahaz Mahal, T07292 263288. Well-kept rooms with bath (bucket hot water), courtyard, limited menu restaurant.

E Malwa Retreat (MP Tourism), get dropped before reaching bus stand, T07292 263221, www.mptourism. com. 8 rooms, restaurant (order ahead), bright, cheerful, very pleasant, excellent view of plateau. Reserve at MP Tourism, Bhopal or Indore.

## Eating

**Indore** *p294, map p294*
Several restaurants near bus stand and railway station serve Indian meals.
**TTT Fortune Landmark**, in hotel.
**TT Colonel's Fast Foods**, 2 MG Rd.
**TT Ding Ding**, 18/5 MG Marg. Open-air eating.
**TT Gypsy**, 17 MG Rd. Fast food. Good Western snacks, cakes and ices.
**TT Landmark**, RNT Marg, by **President**. Indian, Continental. Good ambience, unusual offerings.
**TT Pizza Hut**, 8B Silver Arcade, 56 Chhapan Dukan, New Palasia. Excellent pizzas, for free delivery T0731 2432625.
**TT Woodlands**, at **President**, 163 RNT Marg. Vegetarian. South Indian. A/c, bar, good food.
**T Apsara**, RNT Marg. Indian vegetarian. A/c and outdoors (evening).
**T Café Udupi**, Cloth Market. Indian.
**T Indian Coffee House**, off MG Rd. Indian. Light snacks, dated décor.
**T Prithvilok**, Cloth Market. Indian.
**T Statue**, 565 MG Rd. Indian veg. Large *thalis*.

**Ujjain** *p296, map p296*
**TT Ashnol**, University Rd. Indian vegetarian in pleasant a/c surroundings.
**TT Surana Palace**. Indian, some Chinese. Pleasant outdoor seating option, best in town.
**T 5 Star**, 1st floor, by Madhav Chowk Clock Tower. Mainly South Indian. Tasty snacks and meals, roof top pleasanter.
**T Kwality Ice Creams**, further south.
**T Sudama**, next to Ramkrishna, Subhash Marg. Good Indian meals.

## Festivals and events

**Ujjain** *p296, map p296*
**Kumbh Mela** takes place here every 12 years, see page 185. The next one is in 2016.
**Feb/Mar**: **Mahasivaratri Fair** is held at the Mahakaleshwar Temple. **Nov**: **Kartik Mela**, the month-long fair, draws large crowds from surrounding villages.

## Activities and tours

**Indore** *p294, map p294*
**MP Tourism**, T0731 2521818, tours Jul-Sep: Mandu Wed, Fri, Sat and Sun, Rs 100; **Omkareshwar** and **Maheshwar** Mon and Thu, Rs 75. Both depart from Tourist Bungalow, 0730, return 1900. Tours of **Mandu** from Vijayant, 165 RNT Marg, T0731 2430771, every Sun.

**Ujjain** *p296, map p296*
**MP Tourism**, T0734 2561544. **Ujjain** Darshan bus covers 11 temples and sights, Rs 100, 3½ hrs.

## Transport

**Indore** *p294, map p294*
**Air**
The airport is 9 km west of town; taxis charge Rs 150. **Indian Airlines** (Alliance Air), Race Course Rd, T0731 2531176; airport T2411758, www.indian-airlines.nic.in, flies to **Bhopal**, **Mumbai**, **Delhi** daily, and **Gwalior** (Mon, Fri). **Jet Airways**, G2 Vidyapathi, Race Course Rd, T0731 2544590, airport T2620819, www.jetairways.com, to **Delhi** and **Mumbai**. **Sahara**, to **Delhi**, **Bhopal**.

**Bus**
Timetables in Hindi only. Sarwate Bus Stand (south of railway station, through Exit 1), helpful enquiry desk, T0731 2465688. Gangwal Bus Stand (3 km west of town), T0731 2480688, has easy transfer by local bus or rickshaw to town centre. Private bus companies operate from east of the railway station. From **Sarwate**: (some return buses terminate at Gangwal): to **Bhopal** (187 km) 0800-2300, **Gwalior** 0500-1830 and **Ujjain** (55 km). For **Jhansi** 2100; **Khajuraho** 1700; **Omkareshwar** hourly; change at Omkareshwar Rd (6 hrs). **Pachmarhi** 2145; **Satna** 1415. From **Gangwal**: to **Ahmadabad**; **Aurangabad** (for Ajanta and Ellora caves) and **Amrawati**; **Dhar** (hourly) then **Mandu** (149 km, 6 hrs), 1 direct bus daily to Mandu from Indore at 1515.

**Train**
Indore is on a spur of the Mumbai-Delhi line to Ujjain. Station has pre-paid rickshaws. Enquiries, T131/132, Reservations, opposite,

in front of Rly Hospital, T0731 2430275. **Bhopal**: *Malwa Exp, 9367*, 1230, 5¼ hrs. **Kolkata** (H): *Shipra Exp, 9305*, 2030, Mon, Thu, Fri, 36½ hrs. **Delhi** (ND): *Malwa Exp, 9367*, 1230, 19¼ hrs; *Indore Nizamuddin Exp, 2415*, 1610, 14 hrs (HN). **Jaipur**: *Purna-Jaipur Exp, 9770*, 2200, 16 hrs. **Mumbai (Central)**: *Avantika Exp, 2962*, 1550, 14¾ hrs. **Ujjain**: *Intercity Exp, 9303*, 0600, not Sun, 1¾ hrs; *Narmada Exp, 8233*, 1415, 1½ hrs; *Malwa Exp, 9367*, 1230, 1½ hrs.

**Ujjain** *p296, map p296*
Sights by taxi (Rs 500-700), auto-rickshaw (Rs 200-300), tempos and cycle-rickshaws. There are plenty of bicycles to hire.

**Air**
Nearest airport is at Indore (53 km), connected by regular flights with Delhi, Gwalior, Bhopal and Mumbai.

**Bus**
Hindi timetables only. Direct to **Bhopal**; regular to: **Dhar**, **Indore** (53 km, 1½ hrs), **Gwalior**, **Mandu** (149 km, 6 hrs), **Omkareshwar**.

**Train**
Pre-paid rickshaws. **Ahmadabad**: *Bhopal-Rajkot Exp, 1270*, 2315, 9 hrs; *Sabarmati Exp, 9166*, 2050, 10½ hrs. **Bhopal**: *Narmada Exp, 8233*, 1700, 5½ hrs; *Malwa Exp, 9367*, 1435, 4¾ hrs. **Indore**: *Narmada Exp, 8234*, 1130, 2¾ hrs; *Malwa Exp, 9368*, 1140, 1¾ hrs. **Mumbai (Central)**: *Avantika Exp, 2962*, 1735, 13¼ hrs. **New Delhi**: *Malwa Exp, 9367*, 1435, 17¼ hrs; *Indore-Nizamuddin Exp, 2415*, 1755, 12¼ hrs (HN).

**Mandu** *p297, map p298*
Just off NH3, Mandu is most accessible from Indore. Cycle-rickshaws (Rs 20 for 'sights') and bicycles are available. No taxis.

**Air**
Nearest airport is at **Indore** with Indian Airlines connections to Bhopal, Gwalior, Jaipur, Mumbai and Delhi.

**Bus**
Regular services to **Dhar** (35 km, 1½ hrs), first depart 0530; change there for **Indore** (99 km, 4-5 hrs) and **Ujjain**. There is one direct bus per day to Indore at 0720 (3½ hrs). Indore has better choice for other destinations. Also to **Bhopal** (286 km), **Ratlam** (124 km), **Ujjain** (152 km).

**Train**
Most convenient railheads are **Ratlam** (124 km) on Mumbai-Delhi line, and **Indore** (99 km) on branch route. Ratlam has connections from Vadodara, Bhopal, Kanpur.

**Maheshwar** *p300*
Regular bus services from Barwaha, Khandwa, Dhar and Dhamnod. The nearest railhead is Barwaha (39 km) on the Western Railway.

**Omkareshwar** *p300*
Omkareshwar is connected to Indore, Ujjain, Khandhwa and Omkareshwar Rd railway station (12 km) by regular bus services. The railhead is on the Ratlam-Khandwa section of the Western Railway.

## Directory

**Indore** *p294, map p294*
**Banks** State Bank of India, 13 Ranade Complex, Old Palasia. **Hospitals** Lifeline, Meghdoot Gdns, T0731 2575611. **Choithram Hospital**, Manikbagh Rd, T0731 2549090. Recommended. **Chemists**: on Maharani Rd. **Post** CTO: K Nehru Park, Fax, 0700-2000. GPO: AB Rd. **Tourist offices** MP, behind Ravindra Natyagrih, T0731 2528653. **Useful addresses** Ambulance: T102. Fire: T101. Police: T100.

**Ujjain** *p296, map p296*
**Banks** State Bank, Budhwariya off Udayan Marg, near Water Tower, changes cash (not TCs); after 1030. **Tourist offices** MP, railway station, T0734 2561544.

**Mandu** *p297, map p298*
**Bank** State Bank of India (no exchange), 1100-1500, closed Thu and Sun. **Tourist offices** Malwa Retreat, T07292 263221. Malwa Resort, T07292 263235 runs tours from Bhopal and Indore.

# Eastern Madhya Pradesh

## Jabalpur and around
→ *Phone code: 0761. Colour map 3, grid C2.*

*Population: 952,000.*

On the upper reaches of the River Narmada in the heart of India's forested tribal belt, Jabalpur is remarkably little visited. It serves as the main gateway to two of India's finest wildlife reserves, Kanha and Bandhavgarh. Jabalpur town was the capital and pleasure resort of the Gond kings during the 12th century. It was later the seat of the Kalchuri Dynasty until it fell to the Marathas. The British took it in 1817 and left their mark with the cantonment residences and barracks. » *For Sleeping, Eating and other listings, see pages 308-310.*

### Ins and outs

*Warning: rickshaws offer cheap fares to hotel and then charge a commission.*

**Getting there** Although there are long-distance buses to Jabalpur from the surrounding large cities, it is most comfortable to travel here by train. Under 8 hrs from Bhopal or Allahabad, there are also good connections to Nagpur and South India. The main station is on the edge of the Civil Lines, under 2 km from the town centre. The cheaper hotels are easily reached from the main bus stand. Hotel touts are very active round the station and bus stand so it is best to have a hotel in mind. » *See Transport, page 309, for further details.*

**Getting around** The town is too spread out to cover on foot easily but there are plenty of taxis, unmetered autos and cheap shared tempos for sights further afield.

### Sights

**Madan Mahal Fort** (1116) ⓘ *closed Mon and holidays, 1000-1700, free*, built by the Gond ruler Madan Shah on a hill just to the west of the city, has superb views. To get there take a tempo from stand near the Krishna Hotel to Sharda Chowk (Rs 5), then walk up the left-hand hill. **Rani Durgavati Museum** and Memorial houses a collection of sculptures and prehistoric relics, and the **Tilwara Ghat** where

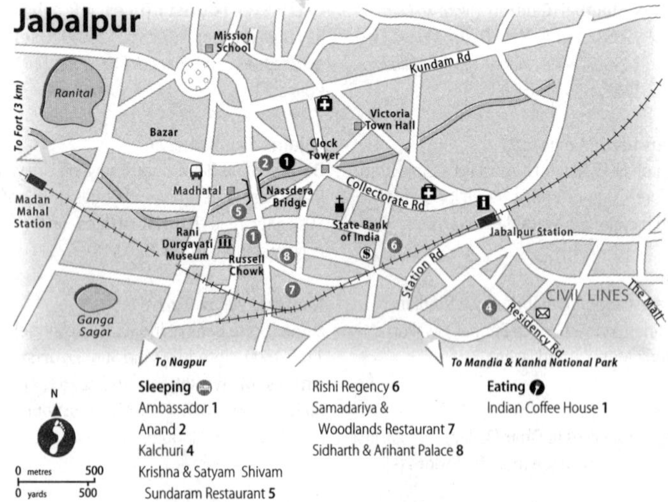

**Mahatma Gandhi's** ashes were immersed in the Narmada, are all places of interest. There are also Jain temples.

The **Marble Rocks** are 22 km west of Jabalpur. Captain J Forsyth wrote of them: "The eye never wearies of the effect produced by the broken and reflected sunlight, glancing from a pinnacle of snow-white marble reared against the deep blue of the sky and again losing itself in the soft bluish greys of their recesses". These white rocks, with views of black/dark green volcanic seams, rise to 30 m on either side of the Narmada River and in moonlight produce a magical effect; floodlights have been added, though boating may not be possible. Stalls sell cheap soap-stone carvings. There is accommodation if you need to stay, in Bhedaghat nearby. To get to the rocks take a tempo from the stand near Krishna Hotel to Bhedaghat, Rs 8, which takes you right to the Marble Rocks Car Park. A taxi from Jabalpur costs around Rs 500 return. Walk up to see the waterfalls, or go past the Mandir to the town and follow steps down for boat trips (30 mininutes, Rs 10, recommended, though if alone it costs Rs 200 to hire the whole boat).

Other sights nearby are the **Dhuandhar Falls** ('smoke cascade'), where the Narmada plunges through a narrow chasm, **Hathi-ka-paon** (Elephant's Foot Rock) and **Monkey's Leap** ledge. Nearby is the **Chausath Yogini Mandir**, a 10th-century temple with stone carvings. Legend suggests that it is connected to the Gond queen Durgavati's palace by an **underground passage**. Approached by a long flight of steps, there is an excellent view of the Narmada from the top. The British era **Pariyat tank**, 12 km from Jabalpur, is a popular picnic and fishing spot for locals, Rs 200 return by taxi.



## Mandla → *Colour map 3, grid C2.*

The capital of the ancient Gond Kingdom of Garha-Mandla early in the Christian era, Mandla is of great historical significance to the Gond tribal peoples. The Gond Queen Rani Durgavati took her life here when her army was cornered by Mughal forces under Asaf Khan in 1564. The **fort** was built in the 17th century and is surrounded on three sides by the Narmada River. It passed to the Marathas and then to the British in 1818. The jungle has since taken over the ruins (only a few towers remain), though there are some temples and ghats in the town. The Gond Raja Hirde Shah built a large **palace** in a commanding site nearby in **Ramnagar** (15 km), of which little remains.

## Kanha National Park → *Colour map 3, grid C2. Area: 1,945 sq km.*

ⓘ *Rs 200 (foreigners), Rs 20 (Indians). Movie cameras Rs 25-250. Visitor centres at Khatia and Mukki gates and at Kanha, the one at Kanha is the largest. 0700-1030, 1600-1800. Recommended: informative displays, short films, audio-visual shows and books for sale. Recommended minimum stay: two nights.*

This is the country about which Kipling wrote so vividly in his Jungle Books. The area was famed as a hunter's paradise but now the valley has been well developed as a national park. It is worth spending a couple of days here. Lying in the Maikal hills in the eastern part of the Satpura Range, 40 km from Mandla, the park has deciduous hardwoods, rolling grasslands and meandering streams of the Banjar River. The park forms the core of the Kanha Tiger Reserve. It was created in 1974 and also protects the rare hardground-adapted barasingha (swamp deer). George Schaller, the zoologist, conducted the first ever scientific study of the tiger here and research is also being done on deer and langur habitat. ▸▸ *For Sleeping, Eating and other listings, see pages 308-310.*

### Ins and outs

**Getting there** The journey by car takes about five hours from Jabalpur on a poor road. The main gates are at Kisli and Mukki. If arriving in the evening, stop overnight at

Khatia or Kisli as vehicles are not allowed into the park after dark. From Nagpur or Raipur enter via Mukki Gate. Diesel vehicles, motorcycles and bicycles are not allowed in the park. » *See Transport, page 309, for further details.*

**Getting around** Visitors may not walk around inside the park, you can walk in the peaceful forest between the gate at Kanha and the park itself.

**Climate** It can get very cold on winter nights. Summer: maximum 43°C, minimum 11°C; Winter: maximum 29°C, minimum 2°C. Annual rainfall: 1,250 mm; monsoon July-September. Best time to visit is January to June. Closed 1 July-31 October.

## Wildlife

Kanha has 22 species of mammal and the most easily spotted are the three-striped palm squirrel, common langur monkey, jackal, wild boar, cheetal, sambar, Branden barasingha and blackbuck. Less commonly seen are Indian hare, *dhole* (Indian wild dog) and gaur. Rarely seen are Indian fox, sloth bear, striped hyena, tiger (estimated at about 100), leopard, *nilgai* (blue bull), Indian porcupine, wolf (outside park proper) and the Indian pangolin (sometimes called a scaly anteater).

As for birds, Kanha has 230 species recorded. Good vantage points are in the hills where the mixed and bamboo forest harbours many species. Commonly seen species are: leaf warblers, minivets, black ibis, common peafowl, racket-tailed drongo, hawk eagle, red-wattled lapwing, various species of flycatcher, woodpecker, pigeon, dove, parakeet, babbler, mynah, Indian roller, white breasted kingfisher and grey hornbill.

## Viewing

Forest Department guides accompany visitors around the park on mapped-out circuits to see a cross-section of wildlife from a jeep (about Rs 400 or Rs 9 per km); tours start at Kisli 0600, 1800. Reserve seats on arrival and share with others for economy. However, a traveller comments: "vehicles chase each other round, their paths crossing and re-crossing and their noisy engines presumably driving the more timid wildlife way back from the tracks". It is better to stop the vehicle on the forest track and in front of the grasslands.

The *sal* forests do not normally allow good viewing. The best areas are the meadows around Kanha. **Bamni Dadar** (Sunset Point) affords a view of the dense jungle and animals typical of the mixed forest zone: sambar, barking deer and



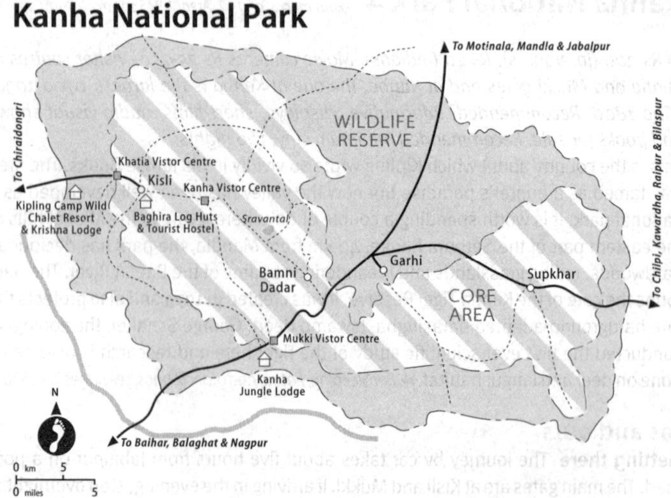

chausingha (four-horned antelope). Early morning and late afternoon are ideal times and binoculars are invaluable. *Machans* (viewing platforms/observation towers), are available for use during daylight; those above waterholes (eg *Sravantal*), are recommended.

Elephants, once used for tiger tracking, are now only available for 'joy rides' outside the park at Kisli, and can sometimes be ridden inside the park once a predator has been tracked. MP Tourism hires out Gypsy four-wheel-drives and jeeps from the **Baghira Log Huts**, Kisli in the park (for maximum six), Rs 9 per km. Petrol is often not available at Kisli; nearest pumps at Mandla. Book previous day.



## Bandhavgarh National Park → *Phone code: 07653. Altitude: 800 m.*

The park is set in extremely rugged terrain with many hills. The marshes which used to be perennial now support a vast grassland savanna. Though it involves quite a journey you may be rewarded with sighting one of the few tigers; a three-day stay gives you a 90% chance of seeing one! There are also interesting cave shrines scattered around the park, with Brahmi inscriptions dating from the first century BC. You can visit the remains of a fort believed to be 2,000 years old where you may spot crag martins and brown rock thrush.

Bandhavgarh (pronounced Bandogarh) is not very far from Rewa, famous as the original home of the white tiger, now only found in zoos. Before becoming a national park in 1968, it was the game reserve of the Maharajas of Rewa. The conservation programme helps to protect wildlife from disease, fire, grazing and poaching.

### Ins and outs

This compact park is in the Vindhya hills with a core area of 105 sq km and a buffer zone of 437 sq km. The main entrance and park office is at Tala to the north of the park. Rs 200 (foreigners), Rs 20 (Indians), still camera Rs 10, video Rs 100 per day, so retain receipt. See Viewing for Getting around information. Best time to visit: February-June. Closed 1 July-31 October. Temperature range: 42-2°C. Rainfall: 1,500 mm. » *See Transport, page 310, for further details.*

### Wildlife

The park has a wide variety of game and has a longer 'season' than Kanha. Its main wild beasts are tiger, leopard, sloth bear, gaur, sambar, chital, muntjac, *nilgai*, chinkara and wild pigs. There are over 60 tigers, but they remain very elusive. The flowering and fruit trees attract woodland birds which include green pigeon, Jerdon's leaf bird, crested serpent eagle and variable hawk eagle.

### Viewing

Jeeps are available from dawn to 1000 and 1600 until dusk when the animals are most active; compulsory Forest Department guide, Rs 50. The short way round is 18 km, the long, 37 km. The fort, 18 km away, requires a four-wheel drive vehicle; ask at the **White Tiger Forest Lodge** about MP Tourism Jeeps (Rs 9 per km). Jeep Tours (up to six passengers), Rs 550; private hire from Talu Rs 400 (each entry) after bargaining; vehicle entry Rs 25 per day.

Forest Department elephants (two-seater), Rs 200 plus Rs 50 per person per hour, are recommended. 'Tiger Show' (visitors are rushed by jeep to an elephant which has tracked a tiger) costs Rs 50 but this may be stopped. Some feel the constant traffic of elephants and jeeps is affecting wildlife – "a bit like a circus". Viewing *machans* are available during the day; Bhadrashila Watch Tower attracts gaur.

## Sleeping

**Jabalpur** *p304, map p304*

B **Samdariya**, off Russell Chowk, T0761 2316800, www.samdariya.com. Modern, quiet, with a/c rooms (some cheaper), good **Woodlands** South Indian restaurant.

B **Satya Ashoka**, Wright Town, T0761 2415111, www.hotelsatyaashoka.com. 45 rooms, central a/c, restaurant, bar, garden, tours. Recommended.

B-C **Krishna**, near Rani Durgavati Museum, Napier Town, T0761 5004023, krishnahotel @hotmail.com. 25 rooms, some a/c, restaurant, garden, pool.

C-D **Arihant Palace**, Russell Chowk, T0761 2327311. Modern, pleasant and quiet, poor restaurant.

C-D **Kalchuri** (MP Tourism), Wright Town, near railway, T0761 267 8491, www.mp tourism.com. 36 clean rooms (14 a/c), good restaurant, bar, good value but close to noisy temple.

C-D **Rishi Regency**, opposite **State Bank of India**, T0761 2621804, www.hotelrishi regency.com. 42 rooms, a/c or air-cooled, restaurant, bar, exchange.

D **Sidharth**, Russell Chowk, T0761 2409247. Some a/c rooms, modern.

F **Anand**, near Nassdera Bridge. Clean rooms with bath though noisy, helpful staff.

**Kanha National Park** *p305, map p306*

Some hotels will arrange pick-up from Jabalpur. Meals may be included. Reserve rooms in advance; most are open 1 Nov-30 Jun. Private lodges are outside the park and usually offer good discounts in May-Jun when the park is closed.

LL **Kanha Jungle Lodge**, Balaghat-Raipur Rd, just south of Mukki, T07637-216015, www.adventure-india.com. 12 km from Baihar and main road. 19 simple clean, comfortable rooms with hot shower, restaurant, bar, meals included (only Indian but excellent), surrounded by *sal* forest, good bird-watching, park tours with good guides.

LL-L **Royal Tiger Resort**, Mukki Gate, T07637 216028, www.royaltiger.com. 18 comfortable suites, good baths.

L **Kipling Camp**, near Khatia, T07649 277218, www.kiplingcamp.com. 18 Chalets, pleasant ambience and well run, all-inclusive package though breakfast boxes "on the stingy side", contact Bob Wright, **Tollygunge Club**, 120 Deshapran Sasmal Rd, Kolkata, T033 24733306, or **Sita Travels** in major cities.

A **Shergarh**, Bahmni Village, T07637 226215 Nov-May or T0044 (0)7969 804472 Jun-Oct. Beautiful new camp run by Anglo Indian couple, 6 tents surrounding picturesque lake, 2 safaris and all meals included, plus possibilities to birdwatch, visit local markets and even paint elephants, highly recommended.

A-B **Krishna Jungle Lodge**, near Kipling Camp, T07649 277207, krishnahotel @hotmail.com. 30 rooms, good food, pool, contact **Hotel Krishna**, Jabalpur, T0761-2310318, F2315153.

B **Wild Chalet Resort**, Mocha Village, T07649 277203. Cottages with shower overlooking river, good food and park tours, helpful and efficient manager, recomm-ended, contact **Asian Adventures**, T0120 2551963, www.indianwildlife.com.

**Inside the park**

D **Baghira Log Huts**, Kisli, T07649-277227, www.mptourism.com. 16 rooms, restaurant, cheaper canteen, restaurant. Reservations, MP Tourism, Bhopal, T0755 2554340.

F **Tourist Hostel**, Kisli, opposite bus stand, www.mptourism.com. 24 dorm beds (roof may leak), no nets (mosquito ridden), Rs 240 includes uninspiring veg meals in a grim canteen. Reservations, MP Tourism, Bhopal, T0755 2554340, F2552384.

**Bandhavgarh National Park** *p307*

AL **Bandhavgarh Jungle Lodge**, within walking distance of the Park gates, T07627 265317, www.welcomheritage.com. 10 comfy cottages and 2 4-room houses with modern facilities (hot and cold showers and toilets), resident naturalist, jeep and animal excursions, reserve through **Tiger Resorts**, T011-26853760, tigerresortstigersindia.com. The dhabas opposite the Jungle Lodge serve good snacks, breakfasts and thalis.

AL **Jungle Camp**, west of Tala gate, reservations: **Tiger Tops Mountain Travel**, 1/1 Rani Jhansi Rd, New Delhi, www.tiger mountainindia.com. Specializes in upmarket tours.

**B Tiger Trails**, east of Tala Gate, T07627 265325, iawr@vsnl.com. Brick cottages in large estate with a lake and stream, separate dining hall, library, experienced naturalist, jungle visits, contact **Indian Adventures**, T0222 6408742, F26432622.

**B-C White Tiger Forest Lodge** (MP Tourism), Tala, overlooking river, T07627 265308, www.mptourism.com. 26 rooms (8 a/c), restaurant (expensive, tiny portions, but good), bar, jeep hire (for residents), modest but good value, the best rooms are in detached cottages by the river, "in need of a good sweep". Reservations: **MP Tourism**, Bhopal, T0755 2554340, F2552384. Also Forest Rest House.

**C-D Patel Lodge**, near Natural Heritage Lodge. Rooms with bath, and 3 meals, pleasant location, good food.

**D V Patel Resort**, off Umaria Rd, T07653 265323. 4 clean rooms with bath (hot water), meals in garden; also complete packages.

**E Kum-kum**, opposite **White Tiger**, T07627 265324. 4 very basic, large, clean rooms with fan, hot water, excellent veg food (Rs 25 for 'all you can eat'), friendly, helpful, well-run, jeep driver Saleem is expert tiger spotter. Recommended.

## Eating

**Jabalpur** *p304, map p304*

**TT Samdariya**. International. Smart decor, meals or snacks.

**T Indian Coffee House**, near Clock Tower. South Indian, good breakfasts, snacks, coffee.

**T Satyam Shivam Sundaram**, 1st floor (air-cooled) near Jyoti Cinema. Vegetarian Indian. Very good value, tasty *thalis*.

**Kanha National Park** *p305, map p306*

Most lodges include meals.

**Baghira Log huts**, Kisli, have a restaurant and bar (see above). Ask for boiled water specifically; water served at the private lodges is generally filtered. Cold drinks are usually available but fresh fruit is not.

## Shopping

**Jabalpur** *p304, map p304*

**Universal Book Service**, opposite India Coffee House. Interesting stock. Recommended.

## Activities and tours

**Jabalpur** *p304, map p304*

**Chadha Travels**, Jackson's Hotel, T0761 2322178, F2322066. Reliable service. Recommended.

## Transport

**Jabalpur** *p304, map p304*

**Air**

Indian Airlines, T0761 2322178, www.indian-airlines.nic.in, flies 3 times a week to **Delhi** via **Gwalior** (though airport regularly closed, making Bhopal the nearest airport).

**Bus**

Services for Kanha via Mandla; MP Tourism bus from their railway station office at 0800 (6 hrs, Rs 100), is much faster than 1100, Rs 50 (see Kanha below). **Khajuraho**, 0900. Also to Allahabad, Bhopal, Nagpur, Varanasi and other main centres by private coach.

**Train**

Jabalpur is on the Mumbai-Allahabad-Kolkata railway line. **Allahabad**: *Mumbai Howrah Mail, 3004*, 1400, 6½ hrs. **Bhopal**: *Narmada Exp, 8234*, 2215, 8 hrs. **Delhi** (HN): *Mahakosal Exp, 1449*, 1500, 19¾ hrs; *Gondwana Exp, 2411*, 1540, 15¾ hrs (both stopping at **Agra Cantt** 4-4½ hrs earlier). **Lucknow**: *Chitrakoot Exp, 5009*, 1900, 15 hrs. **Kolkata**: *Shakipunj Exp, 1448*, 1900, 19½ hrs.

**Kanha National Park** *p305, map p306*

**Air**

Indian Airlines flies to Nagpur (226 km) from **Mumbai**, **Kolkata** and **Bhubaneswar**, **Hyderabad**, **Delhi** and **Bhopal**.

**Bus**

Kanha connected with **Jabalpur**, **Nagpur** and **Bilaspur** by motorable, but often poor roads. Buses daily, from Jabalpur to **Kisli** (0800, 1100) via Mandla and Chiraidongri; faster 0800 (MP Tourism, railway station) takes 6 hrs (Rs 100) arriving in time for park transport; 0900 goes to Mukki. To Jabalpur, 0800 (slow), 1200 (faster).

**Jeep**

Private hire to **Jabalpur** around US$55.

**Train**
**Jabalpur** (173 km) on the **Mumbai-Allahabad-Kolkata, Delhi-Jabalpur** and **Chennai-Varanasi** main lines; or via **Raipur**, 230 km. A wonderful narrow gauge (diesel) train runs between Mandla and Jabalpur.

**Bandhavgarh National Park** *p307*
**Air**
Khajuraho airport nearest, then by road.

**Bus**
From **Tala**, buses to **Rewa** and others; from **Satna**, 5 hrs, and Katni Rail Junction.

**Jeep**
From Tala possible to get a jeep seat (Rs 50) to Satna (insist on your full seat!); poor road, bumpy and dusty 3-hr ride. From **Umaria**: jeep to Tala for park, Rs 200, good for sharing, or rickshaw (Rs 10) from Umaria rly station to bus station and get a local bus to Tala. From **Jabalpur** drive to Shajpura (144 km) then take a country road (fairly hilly) to Umaria. From **Khajuraho** (237 km) 5 hrs. Taxis available from **Satna** (129 km) 3 hrs, Katni and Umaria.

**Train**
**Umaria** (35 km) is the nearest station on the Katni-Bilaspur sector (1 hr by road), where you can get a bus to Tala. Direct train from Umaria to **Delhi**: *Utkal Express, 8477*, 2010, 17¼ hrs. To **Bhubaneswar**, *Utkal Express, 8478*, 0641, 28¼ hrs. To **Jabalpur**, *Mahakosal Exp, 1450*, 0855, 1½ hrs. **Varanasi**, *Sarnath Exp, 4259*, 0700, 9 hrs (book well ahead for a berth). From Satna to **Katni**, 0815. From Katni to **Umaria**, 0955, 2 hrs, Rs 9.

## Directory

**Jabalpur** *p304, map p304*
**Banks** State Bank of India, Jackson's Hotel advise on getting cash against credit cards. **Tourist offices** MP Tourism, railway station, T0761 2677690, F2677590, car hire, runs daily bus to Kanha, dep 0800, return 1900.

**Kanha National Park** *p305, map p306*
**Banks** You can't cash TCs at Kanha, Kisli, Mukki or Mandla, nor at any of the lodges. The nearest bank for exchange is in Jabalpur. **Hospitals** Basic hospitals are Mandla Civil Hospital and Katra Mission Hospital. Only basic first aid at Mukki, Mocha and Baihar. **Post** At Mocha and Mukki. **Telephone** At Khatia (non-STD). Nearest STD at Mandla. **Tourist offices** MP, Jabalpur Railway Station, T0761 2677690. For car hire and and accommodation, contact Bhopal, T0755 2553006, F2553076.

# Chhattisgarh

→ *Population: under 21 mn. Area: 135,000 sq km.*

## Background

### The land

The hilly and forested region of Chhattisgarh ('36 forts'), one of the least densely populated and urbanized regions of peninsular India, retains a strongly rural character. The ancient granites, gneisses and sedimentaries which comprise the major geological formations of the state contain an abundance of minerals, from gold and diamonds to coal and iron ore, dolomite and bauxite. Chhattisgarh is estimated to have reserves of nearly 27 billion tonnes of coal and nearly 200 million tonnes of top quality iron ore. Yet there is also fertile agricultural land, and where the brown forest soils have been converted to agricultural land they yield good rice harvests, lending the state the reputation of being India's 'rice bowl'. Forest cover extends up to 40% of the state's area, with 70% of India's *tendu* leaf production, used for making *bidis*.

## Industry

Despite the poverty which still characterises much of Chhattisgarh, the new state already has a wide range of mineral based industries. It earns approximately US$400 mn a year from mining alone and the state has over 75 large or medium scale plants producing such goods as cement, steel, iron and rails. The new Chief Minister, Ajit Jogi, has been pushing for large scale multinational investment in the mining industry. Chhattisgarh is also a significant power surplus state, and is continuing to develop its thermal electricity capacity to export to other states.

## Modern Chhattisgarh

Chhattisgarh became an independent state on 1st November 2000, though the first demand for the creation of a state for the region can be traced back to 1925. It comprises the largely tribal districts of the southeast corner of Madhya Pradesh. Some suggested that the long-standing tribal demand for a separate state was finally ceded by Madhya Pradesh because of the difficulty of controlling the violent Naxalites, groups of revolutionary guerrillas. While that may be an exaggeration - the violent-death rate is far lower than in many American cities, for example – it was one of the least developed parts of Madhya Pradesh, and the political and economic challenge facing the new state government is huge.

The challenge is particularly obvious in terms of social and economic development. Literacy rates are among the lowest in India, with 43% literate across the state as a whole, 58% of men but only 28% of women, and Bastar District having over 80% still illiterate. Half the households have no drinking water, only one third have any electricity connection, over 40% of girls are married before they are 20 and infant mortality is still 84%.

# Exploring Chhattisgarh

## Raipur → *Phone code: 0771. Colour map 6, grid A3. Population: 605,000.*

Raipur is the rapidly growing new state capital of Chhattisgarh, and also the regional transport centre. Water tanks and a temple date from the 17th and 18th centuries. Jai Stambh Chowk (Chhattisgarh Circle) is generally regarded to be the centre of town with the Head Post Office, State Bank and several hotels close by.

## Durg

Durg, west of Raipur on the NH6, is now joined to the Hindustan steel works town at **Bhilainagar**. Durg is the only place with reasonable accommodation in the area.

## Kawardha

Kawardha is a small town in the Rajnandgaon region of Chhattisgarh. In this remote area Maharaja Vishwaraj Singh welcomes visitors to his late 1930s palace. It provides a delightfully quiet unspoiled contrast with India's big cities and with the much busier tourist route of Rajasthan's 'palace circuit'. The Radha Krishna family temple with underground rooms is nearby. You can visit the 11th-century Chandela style temples at nearby Bhoramdev with beautiful carvings, stepwells, enjoy excellent bird- watching or explore the area's natural beauty on foot with the Yuvraj. The Gonds and the gentle Baiga tribe continue to follow a primitive lifestyle in the surrounding forests; ecologically sensitive visits are arranged.

## Bilaspur

Unless you have a passionate interest in cement production, or have chosen a particularly circuitous train routing to reach a cricket match, there is little reason to stop here. However, if forced to stay overnight there are a number of reasonable hotels and an excellent restaurant (at **Shyama hotel**) about 2 km from the railway station.

## Kanker

Some 140 km south of Raipur, Kanker is a district headquarters town, with some fine century-old colonial buildings. It nestles by a tributary of the Mahanadi River, amidst unspoilt forests and hills, the home of several tribal groups who continue to practise age old crafts and traditions. Kanker's royal family, who trace their ancestors back to the 12th century, welcomes guests to their palace to share their region's culture and history.

## Bastar District

Lying in the southern tip of Chhattisgarh, Bastar district is home to several indigenous tribal groups in one of the state's more densely forested areas. There are two national parks within driving distance of Jagdalpur, the district headquarters, which also serves as a useful base for visiting the region's tribal areas. To visit the area, car hire costs around Rs 3000 per day from Kanker Palace

**Jagdalpur**, 160 km south of Kanker, is the centre of the tribal heartland of Bastar where you can see the Gond, Halba, Muriya, Madia, Dhurwa and Bhattra people. *Mrignayani* emporium collects and sells their arts and crafts. There is a small **tribal museum** maintained by the Anthropological Society of India.

Situated 35 km south west of Jagdalpur, in the transition zone marking the natural southern limit of *sal* and the northern limit of teak, **Kanger Valley National Park** is a narrow stretch of mixed virgin forest, playing host to tiger, panther, sambhar, wild pig, flying squirrel as well as a wide range of reptiles and birds. Within the park the **Kailash** and **Kutumsar Gupha** are attractive limestone caves which are popular with visitors. Forest guides are available. The 100-ft **Tirathgarh Falls**, 39 km south west of Jagdalpur, sees the Kanger River descend the valley in a series of steps. Overnight stay is possible in basic forest rest houses at Kutumsar, Netanar and Teerathgarh. Contact Director Kangerghati NP, Jagdalpur, T07782 222261.

## Indravati National Park

This park along the Indravati River was designated a Project Tiger reserve in 1982. The dense monsoon forest interspersed with grassy glades is known as ancient Dandakaranya, cited in the *Ramayana* as the place where Rama was exiled. Apart from increasing tiger protection, the park is seen as the best reserve for the wild buffalo (*Bubalus amee*) and an ideal alternative home for the endangered Branden barasingha (hardground swamp deer), which is only found in Kanha further north. The NH43 is a good, scenic road, ideal for seeing the Bastar tribal area. Following the Indravati west from Jagdalpur, the popular waterfalls at **Chitrakote** (38 km) drop some 30 m in a horseshoe curve and provide an attractive diversion.

## Barnawapara Sanctuary

ⓘ *Permission to enter from DFO, Wildlife Division, Old Chhattisgarh College Campus, Raipur, T0771 2425064.*

Occupying 245 sq km in the northern part of Mahasamund district, near Sirpur, this Sanctuary offers the chance to see several species of deer in the hilly *sal* forest as well as sloth bear and bison; tigers and panthers are present though rarely seen. Migratory birds are attracted by artificial waterholes in the winter. **Dev Travels** organize tours. The best time to visit is from November to April.

You can stay in forest rest houses on the outskirts of the sanctuary or inside at Barnawapara which has two basic rooms.

## Sleeping

### Raipur *p311*

**B Mayura**, GE Rd, near Raj Talkies, 2 km from stations, T0771 2536001, hotelmayura@rediffmail.com. 50 good rooms, central a/c, TV, excellent **Kapri** restaurant, airport pick up.

**B Piccadily**, Mohaba Bazar, 5 km from town towards Durg, T0771 2575210, www.hotelpiccadily.info. 54 comfortable rooms, a/c, attached bath with tubs, TV, airport/ station pick up, pool (roadside), friendly staff, well-run, out of town location only drawback.

**B-C Aditya**, KK Rd, T0771 2223281. 34 decent rooms, central a/c, TV.

**D-E Chhattisgarh**, Teli Bandha, 4 km from centre towards airport, T0771 2442769, visitcg@mantrafreenet.com. 30 rooms, some a/c, hot bath, TV, restaurant.

**D-E Radhika**, Jai Stambh Chowk, T0771 2233806. 26 rather scruffy rooms with TV and bath, some a/c, those at front suffer from road noise, good restaurant.

Several **E-F** hotels near railway station. Earplugs may be needed for a good sleep.

### Durg *p311*

**D-E Sagar**, opposite railway station, T0788-2321120, has 60 clean rooms with bath (some a/c), a/c restaurant, friendly. Recommended but often full.

**D-E Sheela**, Indira Market, with clean, well-furnished rooms (some a/c), good a/c restaurant, bar, friendly. Cycle-rickshaws offer free transfer from station (paid by hotel).

### Kawardha *p311*

**AL-A Palace Kawardha**, T07741-232085, www.pant.co.uk/travel/kawardha. 5 large suites with pleasant verandahs, western baths, imposing Durbar Hall, attractive gardens, a unique experience visiting tribal settlements, temples, wildlife Kanha, jeep excursions, short treks nearby into surrounding hills (5-8 km, 2½-5 hrs), longer treks into the jungle with advance notice, very warm hospitality. US$108 includes meals, reservations essential.

### Kanker *p312*

**AL-A The Royal Palace**, in a garden setting, T07868-222005, kankerpalace@rediffmail.com. Once residency of British Agent, has 3 modern suites but aims to retain "earthy flavour". Maharajkumar Surya Pratap Deo arranges interesting excursions to explore both the natural surroundings as well as the area's rich tribal heritage. Reserve a month ahead.

### Jagdalpur *p312*

**Bastar Village Farm**, in a nearby village, owned by the Kanker family, has 3 comfortable cottages for visitors who wish to experience rural living with a difference (advance notice needed).

**D-E Hotel Akansha Deluxe**, T07782 225336, has rooms, some a/c, and a restaurant. Cheaper options include **Akash**, **Anand** and **Athithi**.

## Activities and tours

### Raipur *p311*

**Dev Travels**, behind Netaji Subhash Stadium, Ahmedji Colony, T0771 2421303, devtravel@yahoo.com. Professional agency, can arrange cars for visiting tribal areas, wildlife sanctuaries etc.

**Oberoi Tours & Travels**, KK Rd, opposite **Aditya**, T0771 2539988, oberoitours@hotmail.com. Efficient air ticketing office.

## Transport

### Raipur *p311*

#### Air

Mana airport, 15 km southeast of town. Taxis take around 30 mins to the centre; the better hotels provide free pick up with advance notice. **Indian Airlines**, T0771 2583072, airport T2418201, www.indian-airlines.nic.in. Daily flights to **Delhi** via **Jabalpur** (Tue, Sat) or **Nagpur** (other days). Also 3 flights per week to **Mumbai** via **Bhubaneswar**.

#### Bus

New Bus Stand, 3 km from the railway station has services to all towns in Chhattisgarh and Madhya Pradesh.

#### Train

Enquiry, T0771 2528130/131. **Ahmedabad**: *Howrah Ahmedabad Exp, 8034*, 1155, 27½ hrs. **Allahabad**: *Sarnath Exp, 5159*, 2055, 16½ hrs (to **Varanasi**, 20½ hrs). **Kolkata (H)**: *Gitanjali Exp, 2859*, 0055, 14 hrs; *Mumbai Howrah Mail, 2809*, 1640, 15 hrs. **Mumbai (CST)**: *Gitanjali Exp, 2860*, 0200, 19½ hrs; *Howrah Mumbai Mail, 2810*, 0940, 21½ hrs. **New Delhi**: *Chhattisgarh Exp, 8237*, 1440, 30½ hrs (via **Bhopal**, 16 hrs).

**Kawardha** *p311*

**Bus**

Express buses run from Raipur and Bilaspur, where cars can also be hired, or ask for pick up from either city (4½ hrs) or **Kanha National Park** (5½ hrs; US$65 for 3).

**Jeep**

Ask at Palace Kawardha, Raipur US$40, Kanha US$50.

**Train**

From Raipur (140 km) and Bilaspur (124 km).

## Directory

**Raipur** *p311*

**Banks** ICICI, opposite Raj Kumar College, GE Rd. Exchanges cash and TCs, also ATM. State Bank of India, Jai Stambh Chowk. Cash and Tcs. **Hospitals** Government Medical College Hospital, T0771 2511101. Private MMI, T0771 2412310. **Internet** At Planet Café, opposite Old Bus Stand, has good connection. **Post** Head Post Office, Jai Stambh Chowk. **Tourist office** Chhattisgarh, Chhattisgarh Hotel, Teli Bandha (4 km), T0771 5066415, visitcg@rediffmail.com. Minimal information.

**Jagdalpur** *p312*

Tourist Office, Snajay Market, T07782 221686.

# Rajasthan

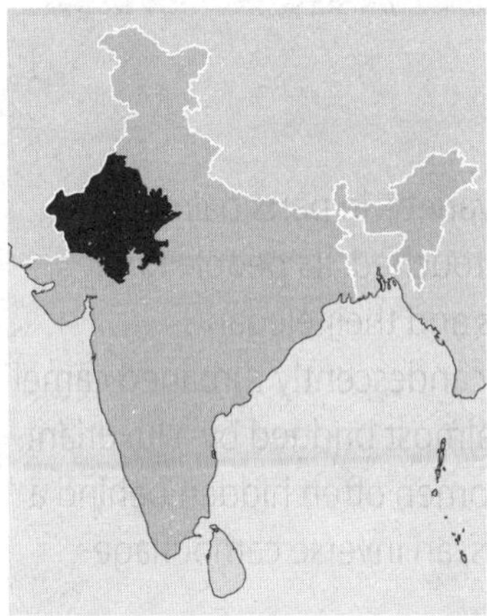



## Footprint features

# Introduction

Rajasthan is a land of unending variety, in parts painfully touristy, in others completely untouched. Its people range from suave, polo-playing Rajputs and their elegant, jewellery-draped wives to tall, incandescently turbaned camel drivers, a gold hoop in each ear almost bridged by a luxuriant moustache, the hard-working women often hidden behind a swathe of brilliantly bright fabrics, an inverse camouflage against the surrounding sand.

Its history is one of fierce pride, unflinching chivalry and unequivocal independence. This varied past has left behind unparalleled riches: a collection of forts, palaces, temples and treasures which no other area can begin to equal. Rajasthan's cities are still wonderfully atmospheric, their tight lanes a defence against the advance of modernity. The forts of Amber, Bikaner, Chittaurgarh and Bundi are all impressive, but it is those of Jaisalmer and Jodhpur which really stand out, as much for the sheer dominance of their positions as their architectural prowess. Of Rajasthan's magnificent palaces, Samode, Deogarh, Udaipur's City Palace and, perhaps the most authentic of them all, Dungapur's untouched Juna Mahal, are all well worth a visit.

As well as its people and places, Rajasthan's landscapes also leave a lasting impression, from the endless expanses of desert sand to forests of tiger-concealing trees and green, rolling hills. Pride of place amongst Rajasthan's wildlife must go to the tigers of Ranthambore, but don't get too caught up in the tiger hunt; all manner of monkeys, deer, leopards and hyenas also compete for attention, watched over by the imperious blue bull.

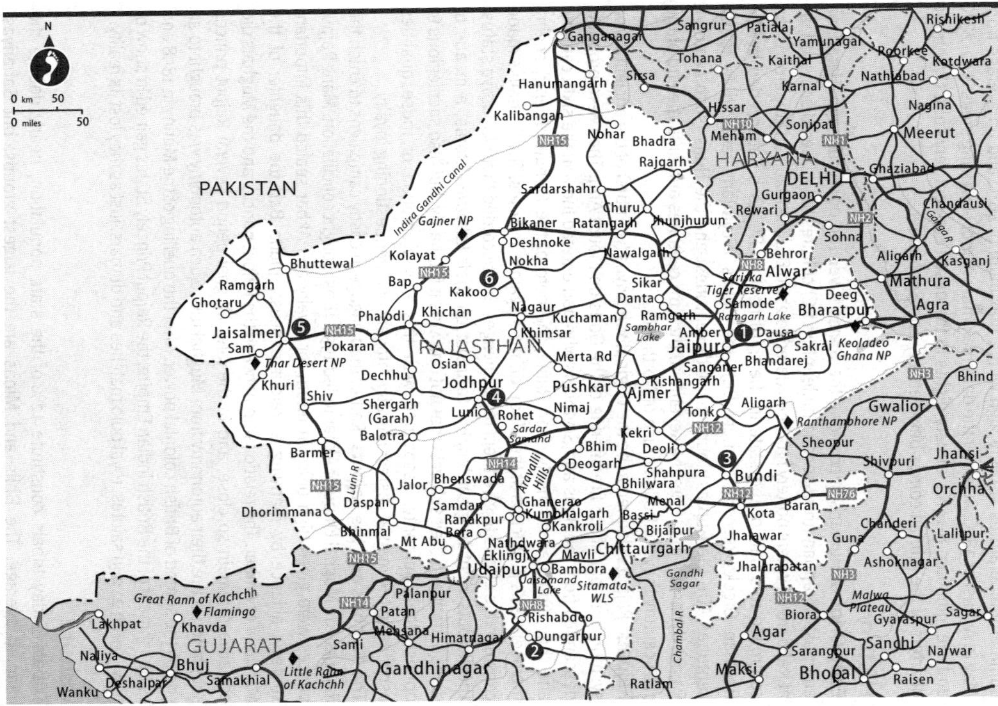

## ★Don't miss...

1 **Nahargarh Fort** A great place to watch the sun go down over the 'pink city', page 327.

2 **Juna Mahal** The most evocative palace in Rajasthan, seemingly untouched for centuries, page 354.

3 **Bundi** A stroll through the sleepy streets of this unspoilt town is like taking several steps back in time, page 374.

4 **Meherangarh Fort** A recently introduced audio guide has made an already magnificent building truly world class, page 383.

5 **Jaisalmer** You might have trouble believing your eyes on the approach, as the fairytale fort rises from the featureless desert around it, page 394.

6 **Kakoo** An easily accessible taste of life in the desert, and a great place for a camel safari, page 433.

# Background → *Population: 56.47 mn. Area: 342,000 sq km.*

## The land

**Geography** Running like a spine through Rajasthan the Aravalli Hills are some of the oldest mountains in the world. A series of jagged, heavily folded ranges, they stretch from Mount Abu in the southwest (1,720 m) to Kota and Bundi in the east. In the northwest is the forbidding Thar Desert, with its shifting sand dunes and crushingly high summer temperatures. In the south the average elevation is higher (330-1,150 m). In the northeast the landscape forms part of the nearly flat Yamuna drainage basin.

**Wildlife** The natural jungle is ideal territory for tigers, leopards, sloth bear, sambhar (large deer) and chital (smaller spotted deer) now normally restricted to game reserves. Nilgai (blue bulls), blackbuck and ravine deer are fairly numerous on the plains and a great variety of birds. Bharatpur and other low-lying swampy areas in the southeast are popular winter grounds for migratory birds from Siberia and Northern Europe.

**Climate** Rajasthan is one of the driest regions of India. Except in the hills the summer temperatures are very high with a maximum of 46°C and an average from May to August of 38°C. In winter the daily maximum in most low lying areas is 22-28°C and the minimum 8-14°C. January nights in the desert can feel very cold. Over three quarters of the rainfall comes between July and September.

## History

**Early Origins** Humans lived along the **Banas River** 100,000 years ago. **Harappan** and post-Harappan (third-second millennium BC) cultures have been discovered, as at Kalibangan where pottery has been dated to 2700 BC. The Mauryan Emperor Asoka controlled this part of the state in the third century BC, to be succeeded by the Bactrian Greeks (second century BC), the Sakas (Scythians, second to fourth centuries AD), the Guptas (fourth to sixth centuries) and the Huns (sixth century). Rajput dynasties rose from the seventh to the 11th centuries and until the end of the 12th century they controlled much of North India.

**Rajputs** Rajputs claimed to be the original *kshatriyas* (warriors) of the ancient *varna* system, born out of the fire offering of the Gods on Mount Abu. They were probably descended from the Huns and Scythians who had entered India in the sixth century, and they modelled themselves on Rama, the hero of the *Ramayana* epic, seeing themselves as protectors of the Hindu *dharma* against invaders. The Brahmins made considerable efforts to give them royal lineages and accorded them *kshatriya* status. The Rajputs went to great lengths to insist on their *kshatriya* status, a means of demonstrating to their subjects that not only was it foolhardy, but also sacrilegious to oppose their authority. Associated with this was promotion of those qualities ascribed to the martial castes: chivalry, bravery and unquestioning loyalty.

**The Mughals and the Rajputs** Rather than engage in costly campaigns to crush the Rajputs, the Mughal Emperor **Akbar** (ruled 1556-1605) sought conciliation. Many Rajput princes were given high office in return for loyalty and Akbar sealed this important strategic alliance by marrying a Rajput princess, **Jodha Bai**, the daughter of the Maharaja of Amber. The relationship between the Rajput princes and the Mughals did not always remain so close, and in the later Mughal period several Rajput princes sought to secure their autonomy from Mughal rule. Such autonomy was brought to an end by the spread of British colonial power. After the quelling of the Mutiny in 1858 and establishment of the British Indian Empire, the Rajput Princely States gained in show of power, with 21 gun salutes, royal polo matches and durbars, just as they lost its reality.

## Culture

**Tribals** Today tribals constitute 12% of the state population, nearly double the national average. The Bhils and Minas are the largest groups, but Sahariyas,

### Waiting for rain

Rajasthan has not had good monsoon rains for a number of years now, and while the situation has not yet reached the drought conditions seen in the 1980s, the lack of rain is beginning to have a significant impact. Udaipur's Lake Pichola, an artificial lake to begin with, has suffered particularly badly, its famous lake palace surrounded by dry land since 2003. A traveller who visited Tilwara fair in 2005 reported that instead of the usual 50,000 cattle, only 11,000 were present. One good monsoon however, would change all this.

Damariyas, Garasias and Gaduliya Lohars are all important. The tribes share many common traits but differences in their costumes and jewellery, their gods, fairs and festivals also set them apart from one another. The **Bhils** comprise nearly 40% of Rajasthan's tribal population with their stronghold in Baneshwar. *Bhil* (bow) describes their original skill at hunting. Physically short, stocky and dark with broad noses and thick lips, the Bhils once lived off roots, leaves and fruits of the forest and the increasingly scarce game. Most now farm land and keep cattle, goats and sheep, or as day labourers. Thousands congregate near the confluence of the Mahi and Som rivers for the Baneshwar fair in January and February. The **Minas** are Rajasthan's largest and most widely spread tribal group. Tall, with an athletic build, light brown complexion and sharp features, men wear a loincloth round the waist, a waistcoat and a brightly coloured turban while the women wear a long gathered skirt (*ghaghra*), a small blouse (*kurti-kanchali*) and a large scarf. Most Minas are cultivators who measure their wealth in cattle and other livestock. Like other tribal groups they have a tradition of giving grain, clothes, animals and jewellery to the needy.

**Language** The principal language is Rajasthani, a close relative of Hindi.

**Crafts** **Bandhani** is an ancient technique of tie-dyeing. The fabric is pinched together in selected places, tied round with twine or thread and then dyed. **Miniature paintings** using old paper or silk, using natural colours derived from minerals, rocks and vegetables following old techniques are produced in varying degrees of quality. The princely states were important patrons of medieval miniature painting and various schools developed in different areas drawing from local traditions and combining them with Mughal art. **'Jaipur Blue Pottery'** uses a coarse grey clay that is quite brittle even when fired. It is then decorated with floral and geometric patterns along Persian lines utilizing rich ultramarines, turquoise and lapis.

## Modern Rajasthan

After Independence the region's 18 princely states were ultimately absorbed into the new state of Rajasthan on 1 November 1956. The successors of royal families have lost power but retain considerable political influence. The palaces, many of them converted to hotels with varying degrees of success, maintain the memory of princely India.

**Economy** Rajasthan is one of the least densely populated and poorest states in India. Primarily an agricultural and pastoral economy, it does have good mineral resources. Tourism makes a large contribution to the regional economy. The main industries are textiles, the manufacture of rugs and woollen goods, vegetable oil and dyes. Heavy industry includes the construction of railway rolling stock, copper and zinc smelting. The chemical industry also produces caustic soda, calcium carbides and sulphuric acid, fertilizer, pesticides and insecticides. There is a rapidly expanding light industry which includes television assembly. Traditional handicrafts such as pottery, jewellery, marble work, embossed brass, block printing, embroidery and decorative painting are now very good foreign exchange earners.

# Jaipur and around

*The bustle of Jaipur, the capital of Rajasthan and the state's most visited city, is at stark contrast to the tranquillity of the area surrounding it. Jaipur has much to offer, but can be something of an assault on your defences. Having savoured its sights, you might therefore appreciate the opportunity to escape the city, and won't need to go far to find perfect places to unwind. There are hunting lodges, palaces and forts, many set in rural surroundings and perfectly equipped to refresh and revive the city's sated sightseers.*

## Jaipur

→ *Phone code: 0141. Colour map 2, grid B5. Population: 2,600,000.*

*Jaipur, the 'pink city' and gateway to Rajasthan for many visitors, is on the popular 'Golden Triangle' route of Delhi-Agra-Jaipur-Delhi ensuring a steady stream of tourists; meaning that the town has to do little to attract visitors. Its historical monuments, although impressive, have been poorly looked after of late and it's not as pink a city as it once was, but still merits a stopover en route to the numerous attractions which surround it. The Old City, with its bazars, palaces and* havelis, *as well as a couple of forts and the ancient city of Amber nearby, are well worth exploring.*
▸▸ *For Sleeping, Eating and other listings, see pages 328-335.*



### Ins and outs

**Getting there** Sanganer Airport, 15 km south of town, has flights from Ahmadabad, Aurangabad, Delhi, Jodhpur, Mumbai, Rajkot and Udaipur. Airport buses, taxis and auto-rickshaws take 30 minutes to the centre. The railway station has links with most major cities. The Main Bus Terminal is used by state and private buses. Buses from Delhi use the dramatically improved NH8; the journey now takes under four hours by car. The alternative Gurgaon-Alwar-Jaipur route is more interesting but much slower. Most hotels are a short auto-rickshaw ride away from the station and bus terminal.

**Getting around** The Old City, to the northeast of town, holds most of the sights and the bazar within its walls. It's best explored on foot, although you may want to hire a rickshaw to get there. The sprawling new town has spread out dramatically over recent years leaving its few attractions best explored by rickshaw, bus or taxi. ▸▸ *See Transport, page 334, for further details.*

**Tourist information** Government of India ⓘ *T0141 511 0591*, and Hotel Khasa Kothi. **Rajasthan**, Paryatan Bhavan, **Tourist Hotel**, MI Road, T0141 2365256. Counters at railway station and Central Bus Stand. Guides for four to eight hours, about Rs 250-400 (Rs 100 extra for French, German, Japanese, Spanish).

## History

Jaipur (City of Victory) was founded in 1727 by **Maharaja Jai Singh II**, a Kachhawaha Rajput, who ruled from 1699-1744. He had inherited a kingdom under threat not only from the last great Mughal Emperor Aurangzeb, but also from the Maratha armies of Gujarat and Maharashtra. Victories over the Marathas and diplomacy with Aurangzeb won back the favour of the ageing Mughal, so that the political stability that Maharaja Jai Singh was instrumental in creating was protected, allowing him to pursue his scientific and cultural interests. Jaipur is very much a product of his intellect and talent. A story relates an encounter between the **Emperor Aurangzeb** and the 10-year-old Rajput prince. When asked what punishment he deserved for his family's hostility

## Devotion across the seas

The present maharaja's grandfather was an extremely devout Hindu. Any physical contact with a non-Hindu was deemed to be ritually defiling, so contact with the British carried awkward ritual problems. Whenever required to meet a British official, including the Viceroy, the maharaja would wear white gloves, and after any meeting would ritually purify himself in a bath of Ganga water and have the clothes he wore burnt. When he went to England to celebrate Queen Victoria's Diamond Jubilee Sawai Madho Singh had a P&O liner refitted to include a Krishna temple and carried sufficient Ganga water with him in two 309 kg silver urns, the largest in the world and currently on display in Jaipur's City Palace, to last the trip.

and resistance to the Mughals, the boy answered "Your Majesty, when the groom takes the bride's hand, he confers lifelong protection. Now that the Emperor has taken my hand, what have I to fear?". Impressed by his tact and intelligence, Aurangzeb bestowed the title of *Sawai* (one and a quarter) on him, signifying that he would be a leader.

Jai Singh loved mathematics and science. A brilliant Brahmin scholar, Vidyadhar Bhattacharya from Bengal, helped him to design the city. Jai Singh also studied ancient texts on astronomy, had the works of Ptolemy and Euclid translated into Sanskrit. Work began in 1727 and it took four years to build the main palaces, central square and principal roads. The layout of streets was based on a mathematical grid of nine squares representing the ancient Hindu map of the universe, with the sacred Mount Meru, home of Siva, occupying the central square. In Jaipur the royal palace is at the centre. The three by three square grid was modified by relocating the northwest square in the southeast, allowing the hill fort of Nahargar (Tiger Fort) to overlook and protect the capital. At the southeast and southwest corners of the city were squares with pavilions and ornamental fountains. Water for these was provided by an underground aqueduct with outlets for public use along the streets. The main streets are 33-yards wide (33 is auspicious in Hinduism). The pavements were deliberately wide to promote the free flow of pedestrian traffic and the shops were also a standard size. Built with ancient Hindu rules of town planning in mind, Jaipur was advanced for its time. Yet many of its buildings suggest a decline in architectural power and originality. The architectural historian, Giles Tillotson, argues that the "traditional architectural details lack vigour and depth and are also flattened so that they become relief sculpture on the building's surface, and sometimes they are simply drawn on in white outline".

In addition to its original buildings, Jaipur has a number of examples of late 19th-century buildings which marked an attempt to revive Indian architectural skills. A key figure in this movement was Sir Samuel Swinton Jacob. A school of art was founded in 1866 by a group of English officers employed by Maharaja Sawai Madho Singh II to encourage an interest in Indian tradition and its development. In February 1876 the Prince of Wales visited Jaipur, and work on the Albert Hall, now the Central Museum, was begun to a design of Jacob. It was the first of a number of construction projects in which Indian craftsmen and designers were employed in both building and design. This ensured that the Albert Hall was an extremely striking building in its own right. The opportunities for training provided under Jacob's auspices encouraged a new school of Indian architects and builders. One of the best examples of their work is the Mubarak Mahal (1900), now Palace Museum, designed by Lala Chiman Lal.

# Jaipur

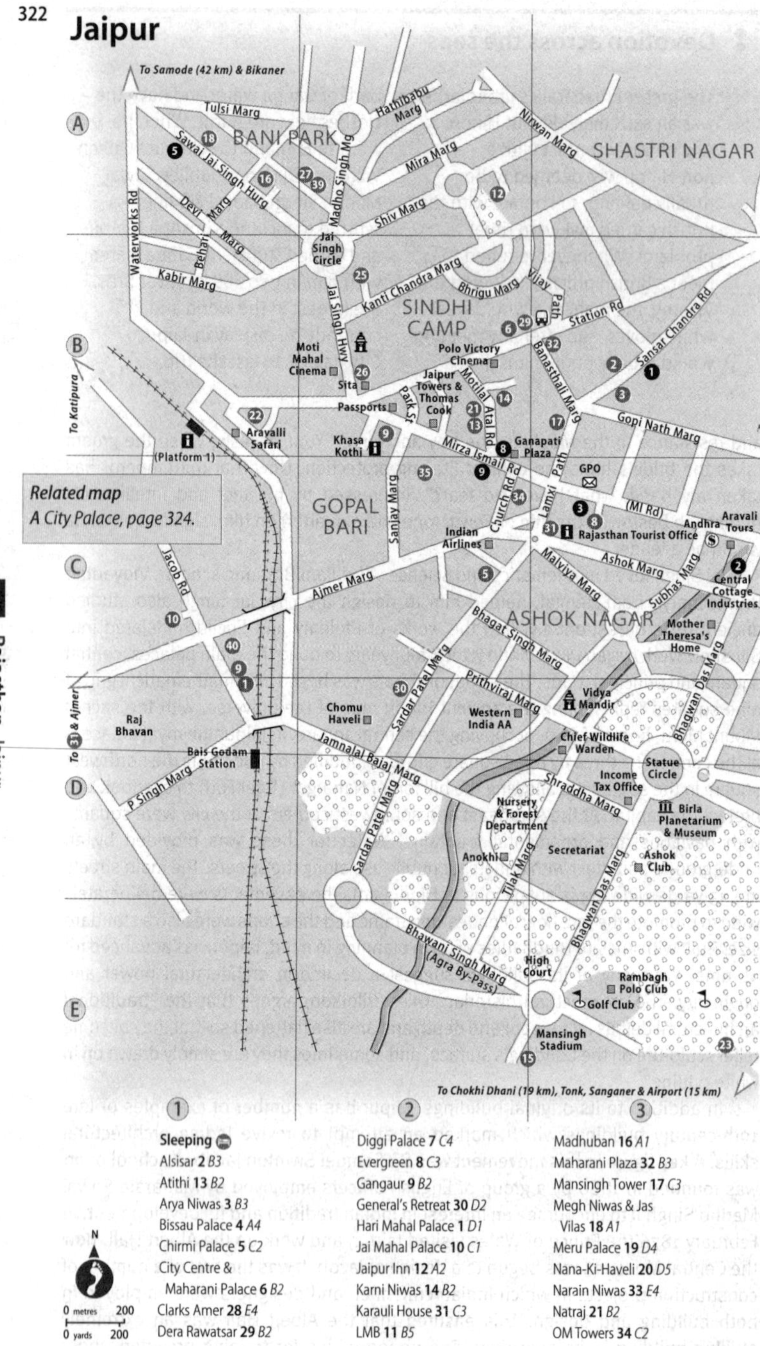


**Sleeping**

Alsisar **2** *B3*
Atithi **13** *B2*
Arya Niwas **3** *B3*
Bissau Palace **4** *A4*
Chirmi Palace **5** *C2*
City Centre & Maharani Palace **6** *B2*
Clarks Amer **28** *E4*
Dera Rawatsar **29** *B2*
Diggi Palace **7** *C4*
Evergreen **8** *C3*
Gangaur **9** *B2*
General's Retreat **30** *D2*
Hari Mahal Palace **1** *D1*
Jai Mahal Palace **10** *C1*
Jaipur Inn **12** *A2*
Karni Niwas **14** *B2*
Karauli House **31** *C3*
LMB **11** *B5*
Madhuban **16** *A1*
Maharani Plaza **32** *B3*
Mansingh Tower **17** *C3*
Megh Niwas & Jas Vilas **18** *A1*
Meru Palace **19** *D4*
Nana-Ki-Haveli **20** *D5*
Narain Niwas **33** *E4*
Natraj **21** *B2*
OM Towers **34** *C2*

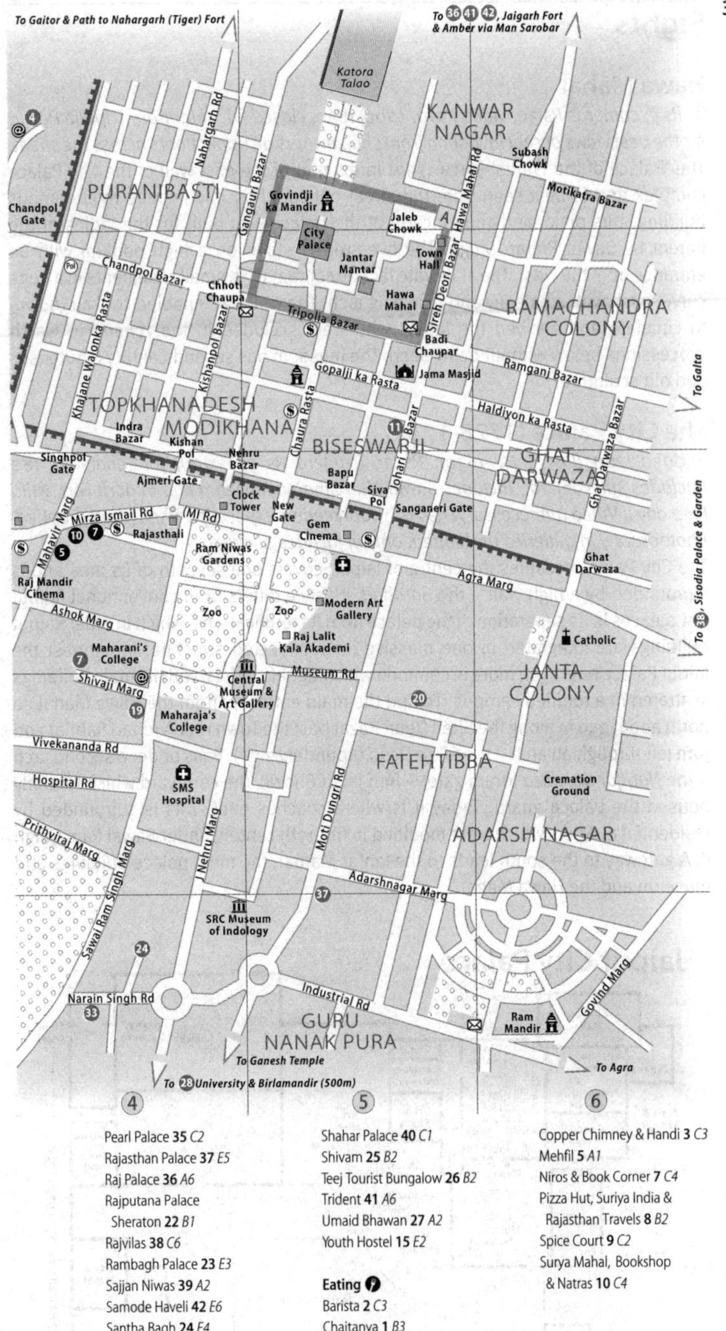


Pearl Palace **35** *C2*
Rajasthan Palace **37** *E5*
Raj Palace **36** *A6*
Rajputana Palace Sheraton **22** *B1*
Rajvilas **38** *C6*
Rambagh Palace **23** *E3*
Sajjan Niwas **39** *A2*
Samode Haveli **42** *E6*
Santha Bagh **24** *E4*
Shahar Palace **40** *C1*
Shivam **25** *B2*
Teej Tourist Bungalow **26** *B2*
Trident **41** *A6*
Umaid Bhawan **27** *A2*
Youth Hostel **15** *E2*

**Eating**
Barista **2** *C3*
Chaitanya **1** *B3*
Copper Chimney & Handi **3** *C3*
Mehfil **5** *A1*
Niros & Book Corner **7** *C4*
Pizza Hut, Suriya India & Rajasthan Travels **8** *B2*
Spice Court **9** *C2*
Surya Mahal, Bookshop & Natras **10** *C4*

# Sights

## Hawa Mahal

ⓘ *Rs 5; cameras Rs 30, video Rs70, 1000-1630, closed Fri, enter from Tripolia Bazar; for the best views accept invitation from shop owners on upper floors across the street.*
The 'Palace of the Winds' (circa 1799) forms part of the east wall of the City Palace complex and is best seen from the street outside. Possibly Jaipur's most famous building, this pink sandstone façade of the palace was built for the ladies of the harem by Sawai Pratap Singh. The five storeys stand on a high podium with an entrance from the west. The elaborate façade contains 953 small casements in a huge curve, each with a balcony and crowning arch. The windows enabled cool air (*hawa*) to circulate and allowed the ladies who were secluded in the *zenana* to watch processions below without being seen. The museum has second-century BC utensils and old sculpture.

## The City Palace (1728-1732)

ⓘ *0930-1700 (last entry 1630). Rs 35 (camera Rs 50 extra), foreigners Rs 180 (includes still camera), includes Sawai Man Singh II Museum and Jaigarh Fort, valid for 2 days. Video (unnecessary) Rs 200; doorkeepers expect tips when photographed. Photography in galleries prohibited, only of façades allowed.*
The City Palace occupies the centre of Jaipur, covers one seventh of its area and is surrounded by a high wall – the *Sarahad.* Its style differs from conventional Rajput fort palaces in its separation of the palace from its fortifications, which in other Rajput buildings are integrated in one massive interconnected structure. In contrast the Jaipur Palace has much more in common with Mughal models, with its main buildings scattered in a fortified campus. To find the main entrance, from the Hawa Mahal go north about 250 m along the Sireh Deori Bazar past the Town Hall (Vidhan Sabha) and turn left through an arch – the *Sireh Deori* (boundary gate). Pass under a second arch – the *Naqqar Darwaza* (drum gate) – into Jaleb Chowk, the courtyard which formerly housed the Palace guard. Today it is where coaches park. This is surrounded by residential quarters which were modified in the 19th century under Sawai Ram Singh II. A gateway to the south leads to the Jantar Mantar, the main palace buildings and museum and the Hawa Mahal.

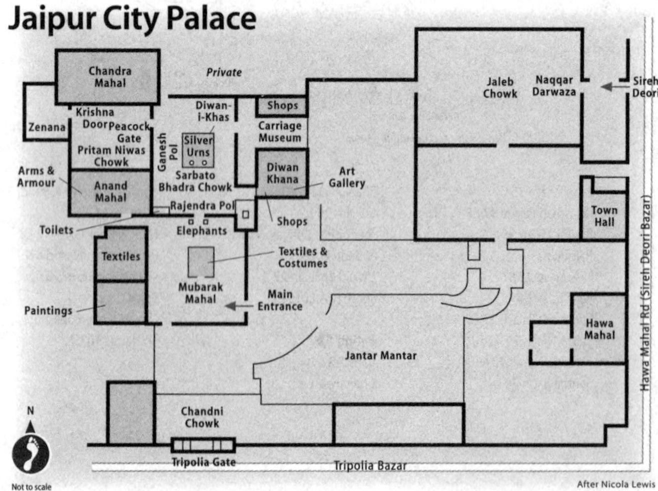

**Mubarak Mahal** The main entrance leads into a large courtyard at the centre of which is the Mubarak Mahal, faced in white marble. Built in 1890, originally as a guest house for the Maharaja, the Mubarak Mahal is a small but immaculately conceived two-storeyed building, designed on the same cosmological plan in miniature as the city itself – a square divided into a 3 x 3 square grid, see page 321.

The **Textile and Costume Museum** on the first floor has fine examples of fabrics and costumes from all over India, including some spectacular wedding outfits, as well as musical instruments and toys from the royal nursery. In the northwest corner of the courtyard is the **Armoury Museum** containing an impressive array of weaponry – pistols, blunderbusses, flintlocks, swords, rifles and daggers, as well as some fascinating paintings on the way in. This was originally the common room of the harem. From the north facing first floor windows you can get a view of the Chandra Mahal (see below). Just outside the Armoury Museum is **Rajendra Pol**, a gate flanked by two elephants, each carved from a single block of marble, which leads to the inner courtyard. There are beautifully carved alcoves with delicate arches and *jali* screens and a fine pair of patterned brass doors.

**Diwan-i-Khas (Sarbato Bhadra)** The gateway leads to the courtyard known variously as the Diwan-i-Am, the Sarbato Bhadra or the Diwan-i-Khas Chowk. Today, the building in its centre is known as the Diwan-i-Khas (circa 1730). Originally the Diwan-i-Am, it was reduced to the hall of private audience (Diwan-i-Khas) when the new Diwan-i-Am was built to its southeast at the end of the 18th century. The courtyard itself reflects the overwhelming influence of Mughal style, despite the presence of some Hindu designs, a result of the movement of Mughal-trained craftsmen from further north in search of opportunities to practise their skills. In the Diwan-i-Khas (now known by the Sanskrit name Sarbato Bhadra) are two huge silver urns, ratified by Guiness as being the largest pieces of silver in the world, used by Sawai Madho Singh for carrying Ganga water to England, see box.

**Diwan-i-Am (Diwan Khana) Art Gallery** Entered in the southeast corner of the Diwan-i-Am courtyard, the 'new' Hall of Public Audience built by Maharaja Sawai Pratap Singh (1778-1803) today houses a fine collection of Persian and Indian miniatures, some of the carpets the maharajas had made for them and an equally fine collection of manuscripts. To its north is the Carriage Museum, housed in a modern building. In the middle of the west wall of the Diwan-i-Am courtyard, opposite the art gallery, is the **Ganesh Pol**, which leads via a narrow passage and the Peacock Gate into **Pritam Niwas Chowk**. This courtyard has the original palace building 'Chandra Mahal' to its north, the *zenana* on its northwest, and the Anand Mahal to its south. Several extremely attractive doors, rich and vivid in their peacock blue, aquamarine and amber colours, have small marble Hindu gods watching over them.

**Chandra Mahal** Built between 1727 and 1734 the Moon Palace is the earliest building of the palace complex. Externally it appears to have seven storeys, though inside the first and second floors are actually one high-ceilinged hall. The two top floor storeys give superb views of the city and Tiger Fort. On the ground floor (north) a wide verandah – the **Pritam Niwas** (House of the beloved) – with Italian wall paintings, faces the formal Jai Niwas garden. The main section of the ground floor is an Audience Hall. The place is not always open to visitors.

The hall on the first (and second) floors, the **Sukh Niwas** (House of pleasure), underwent a Victorian reconstruction, above which are the **Rang Mandir** and the

*In Jai Singh's day, the buildings were painted in a variety of colours, including grey with white borders. Pink, a traditional colour of welcome, was used in 1853 in honour of the visit by Prince Albert, and the colour is still used.*

 Sobha Niwas, built to the same plan. The two top storeys are much smaller, with the mirror palace of the **Chavi Niwas** succeeded by the small open marble pavilion which crowns the structure, the **Mukat Niwas.**

In the northeast corner of the Pritam Niwas Chowk, leading into the *zenana*, is the **Krishna door**, its surface embossed with scenes of the deity's life. The door is sealed in the traditional way with a rope sealed with wax over the lock.

**Govind Deo Temple and beyond** North of the Chandra Mahal, the early 18th-century Govind Deo Temple, which was probably built as a residence, has been restored by an ancient technique using molasses, curd, coconut water, fenugreek, rope fibres and lime, but is again not always open to visitors. The furniture is European – Bohemian glass chandeliers – the decoration indian. Following the steps around you will see a *mandala* (circular diagram of the cosmos), made from rifles around the royal crest of Jaipur. The ceiling of this hall is in finely worked gold. Further on are the beautiful Mughal style fountains and the **Jai Niwas gardens** (1727), laid out as a *char bagh*, the **Badal Mahal** (circa 1750) and the **Tal Katora** tank. The view extends across to the maharaja's private Krishna temple and beyond the compound walls to the Nahargarh (Tiger Fort) on the hills beyond.

## Jantar Mantar (Observatory)

ⓘ *1000-1630, Rs 10 (Mon free), camera Rs 50, video Rs 100 (stills better).*

Literally 'Instruments for measuring the harmony of the heavens', the Jantar Mantar was built between 1728 and 1734. Jai Singh wanted things on a grand scale and chose stone with a marble facing on the important planes. Each instrument serves a particular function and each gives an accurate reading. Hindus believe that their fated souls move to the rhythms of the universe, and the matching of horoscopes is still an essential part in the selection of partners for marriage. Astrologers occupy an important place in daily life and are consulted for all important occasions and decision-making. The observatory is a fascinating. We recommend you hire a guide to explain the functions of the instruments. There is little shade so avoid the middle of the day.



Moving clockwise you will see the following instruments or **yantras**:

1 **Small 'Samrat'** is a large sundial (the triangular structure) with flanking quadrants marked off in hours and minutes. The arc on your left shows the time from sunrise to midday, the one on the right midday to sundown. Read the time where the shadow is sharpest. The dial gives solar time, so to adjust it to Indian Standard Timebetween one minute 15 seconds and 32 minutes must be added according to the time of year and solar position as shown on the board.

2 **'Dhruva'** locates the position of the Pole Star at night and those of the 12 zodiac signs. The graduation and lettering in Hindi follows the traditional unit of measurement based on the human breath calculated to last six seconds. Thus: four breaths = one *pala* (24 seconds), 60 palas = one *gati* (24 minutes), 60 gatis = one day (24 hours).

3 **'Narivalya'** has two dials: south facing for when the sun is in the southern hemisphere (21 September-21 March) and north facing for the rest of the year. At noon the sun falls on the north-south line.

4 **The Observer's Seat** was intended for Jai Singh.

5 **Small 'Kranti'** is used to measure the longitude and latitude of celestial bodies.

6 **'Raj'** (King of Instruments) is used once a year to calculate the Hindu calendar, which is based on the Jaipur Standard as it has been for 270 years. A telescope is attached over the central hole. The bar at the back is used for sighting, while the plain disk is used as a blackboard to record observations.

7 **'Unnathamsa'** is used for finding the altitudes of the celestial bodies. Round-the-clock observations can be made and the sunken steps allow any part of the dial to be read.

8 **'Disha'** points to the north.

**9 'Dakshina'**, a wall aligned north-south, is used for observing the position and movement of heavenly bodies when passing over the meridian.

**10 Large 'Samrat'** is similar to the small one (1) but ten times larger and thus accurate to two seconds instead of 20 seconds. The sundial is 27.4-m high. It is used on a particularly holy full moon in July/August, to predict the length and heaviness of the monsoon for the local area.

**11 'Rashivalayas'** has 12 sundials for the signs of the zodiac and is similar to the Samrat yantras. The five at the back (north to south), are Gemini, Taurus, Cancer, Virgo and Leo. In front of them are Aries and Libra, and then in the front, again (north-south), Aquarius, Pisces, Capricorn, Scorpio and Sagittarius. The instruments enable readings to be made at the instant each zodiacal sign crosses the meridian.

**12 'Jai Prakash'** acts as a double check on all the other instruments. It measures the rotation of the sun, and the two hemispheres together form a map of the heavens. The small iron plate strung between crosswires shows the sun's longitude and latitude and which zodiacal sign it is passing through.

**13 Small 'Ram'** is a smaller version of the Jai Prakash Yantra (12).

**14 Large 'Ram Yantra'** Similarly, this finds the altitude and the azimuth (arc of the celestial circle from Zenith to horizon).

**15** 'Diganta' also measures the azimuth of any celestial body.

**16 Large 'Kranti'** is similar to the smaller Kranti (5).

## Nahargarh (Tiger Fort)

ⓘ *1000-1630, Rs 5, camera Rs 30, video Rs70.*

The small fort with its immense walls and bastions stands on a sheer rock face. The city at its foot was designed to give access to the fort in case of attack. To get there on foot you have to first walk through some quiet and attractive streets at the base of the hill, then 2 km up a steep, rough winding path to reach the top. Alternatively, it can also be reached by road via Jaigarh Fort. Beautifully floodlit at night, it dominates the skyline by day. Much of the original fort (1734) is in ruins but the walls and 19th-century additions survive, including rooms furnished for maharajas. This is a 'real fort', quiet and unrushed, and well worth visiting for the breathtaking views, to look inside the buildings and to walk around the battlements. Women alone may feel vulnerable here. There are snacks and drinks for sale at **Durg Café. Padco Café**, on a terrace at the end of the ruins, has not much in the way of food and drink but is one of the best spot's in Jaipur for a beer at sunset. You can combine this visit with Jaigarh Fort, see page 338, 7 km away (part of the same defensive network), along the flat-topped hill.

## Central Museum and Modern Art Gallery

ⓘ *Museum 1000-1630, closed Fri, Rs 30 (Mon free); gallery 1000-1700, free, closed 2nd Sat of month and Sun; garden 0900-1700, Rs 100 foreigners, Rs 10 Indians.*

Within the Ram Niwas Gardens you can visit the museum, gallery and a zoological garden. Housed in the beautiful Albert Hall is the **Central Museum**, displaying mainly excellent decorative metalware, miniature portraits and other art pieces. It also features Rajasthani village life – including some gruesome torture techniques – displayed through costumes, pottery, woodwork, brassware etc. The first floor displays are covered in dust and poorly labelled. **Modern Art Gallery**, Ravindra Rang Manch, has an interesting collection of contemporary Rajasthani art. Finally, in the gardens is the **Zoological Garden** containing lions, tigers, panthers, bears, crocodiles and deer, plus a bird park opposite.

## SRC Museum of Indology

ⓘ *24 Gangwal Park, 0800-1800, Rs 35 (groups of 10, Rs 10 each).*

Further south, along J Nehru Marg, is the extraordinarily eclectic, and not a little quirky, SRC Museum of Indology. It houses a collection of folk and tantric art including all manner of manuscripts, textiles, paintings, Hindi written on a grain of rice, Sanskrit on a rabbit hair, fossils, medals, weapons and so on.

## Birla Mandir

Something of an architectural curiosity, the modern temple built by the Birla family in the southeast of the city is impressive in scale and in the eclecticism of its religious art. The quality of the marble used can be seen in its near transparency.

## Surya Mandir

ⓘ *Galta Pol can be reached by taking a bus, or by walking 2 km east from the Hawa Mahal. From there it is about 600 m uphill and then downhill.*

From Galta Pol take a walk to the 'Valley of the Monkeys' to get a view of the city from the Surya Mandir (Sun Temple), which is especially impressive at sunset. It is not on the tourist circuit and so you are less likely to get hassled here.There are plenty of monkeys on the way up to the temple and you can buy bags of nuts to feed them. Walk down the steps from the top of the ridge to the five old temples, with impressive wall paintings, dedicated to Rama-Sita and Radha-Krishna. You can watch hundreds of monkeys playing in the water tank below.

# Sleeping

**Jaipur** *p320, map p322*

The city's popularity has meant that foreigners are being targeted by hotel and shop touts, so you need to be on your guard. Auto-rickshaw drivers often get commission as hotel touts. MG Rd is Mahatma Gandhi Rd, MI Rd is Mirza Ismail Rd.

**LL Rajvilas** (Oberoi), slightly inconveniently situated 8 km from town on Goner Rd, T0141-268 0101, www.oberoihotels.com. This award-winning hotel is housed in a low-lying re-created fort-palace building situated within large, exquisitely landscaped gardens with orchards, pools and fountains. There are 71 rooms including 13 'tents' and 3 private villas with their own pools! Room interiors are not especially imaginative, the 'tents' however are delightful. Bathrooms are impressive. There is also an ayurvedic spa in a restored *haveli*. It's fantastically indulgence but slightly lacking in atmosphere.

**LL-L Jai Mahal Palace** (Taj), Jacob Rd, Civil Lines, T0141-222 3636, www.tajhotels.com. 100 rooms in 250-year-old palace which has managed to maintain a real sense of authenticity. Bathrooms not as good as some but rooms are tastefully decorated and set in very attractive, peaceful gardens. Attentive staff. Pool is lovely.

**LL-L Rambagh Palace** (Taj), Bhawani Singh Rd, T0141-238 1919, www.tajhotels.com. 90 luxuriously appointed rooms arranged around a central courtyard in a former maharaja's palace, still feels like the real thing. Set in 47 acres of beautifully maintained garden, larger groups are invited to participate in elephant polo on the back lawn! Stunning indoor pool, but the real piece de resistance is the spectacular dining hall, reminiscent of Buckingham Palace. Pleasant, relaxed atmosphere, good food and friendly staff. Recommended.

**L Rajputana Palace Sheraton** (Welcomgroup), Palace Rd, T0141-510 0100, www.welcomgroup.com. 216 rooms in low-rise, modern '*haveli*'-stylebuilding, starting to look a little worn. Rooms unexceptional, excellent bookshop, rather impersonal overall.

**L Trident** (Hilton), Amber Rd, opposite Jal Mahal, T0141-267 0101, www.trident-hilton.com. 138 modern, attractive rooms, overlooking lake or hills, fully equipped, excellent service. European feel to restaurant. Recommended.

**LA Raj Palace** (GKV Heritage), **Chomu Haveli**, Zorawar Singh Gate, Amer Rd, T0141-263 4077, www.rajpalace.com. 25 spacious suites with modern baths (extra bed US$15), 5-storeyed *haveli* (1728) with character carefully restored, traditional courtyard, Darbar Hall, garden, well managed, friendly service.

**LA Mansingh Tower** and **A Hotel Mansingh**, Sansar Chandra Rd, T0141-237 8771, www.mansinghhotels.com. Adjacent hotels owned by same group. Tower (45 rooms) modern, tastefully and imaginatively designed, **Hotel Mansingh** (95 rooms) older and less appealing. Reports of noise from top floor restaurant/nightclub.

A **Clarks Amer**, JL Nehru Marg, 8 km from centre, T0141-255 0616-19, www.hotelclarks.com. 197 rooms, friendly, good shops, garden, food occasionally inspired. Rooftop bar original and unexpected, a real treat.

A **Meru Palace**, Sawai Ram Singh Rd, T0141-237 1111, merupalace@hotmail.com. Business hotel, 48 rooms, good veg restaurant, bar, exchange, marble building, friendly staff, not a palace but pleasant.

A **Samode Haveli**, Gangapol, Old City, T0141- 263 2407, www.samode.com. 21 lovely rooms in charming, beautifully decorated 19th-century *haveli*. Magnificent dining room, great pool, friendly atmosphere, good rooftop views over city at dawn and sunset. Highly recommended, reservations essential.

B **Alsisar Haveli**, Sansar Chandra Rd, T0141-236 8290, www.alsisarhaveli.com. 36 intricately painted a/c rooms, modern frescoes, excellent conversion of 1890s character home, attractive courtyards, average food (try **Chaitanya** nearby, listed below), beautiful pool, village safaris, 'super-quiet', service variable.

B **Bissau Palace**, outside Chandpol Gate, T0141-230 4371, www.bissaupalace.com. 45 a/c rooms, some charming, in the home of the Rawal of Bissau (built 1919) with library and royal museum, interesting 'memorabilia' and antiques, bookshop, pleasant front garden, good views from terrace of city and nearby forts, tours, excellent camel safaris, exchange etc from **Karwan Tours**, but temple music may irritate.

B **Hari Mahal Palace**, Jacob Rd, Civil Lines, T0141-222 6920, www.harimahalpalace.com. 11 large, quirky rooms with big bath tubs, period furniture in old mansion, large lawn, old world feel.

B **Jas Vilas**, next to **Megh Niwas**, C-9 Sawai Jai Singh Highway, Bani Park, T0141-2204638, www.jasvilas.com. An excellent family-run hotel. 9 a/c rooms with bath (tub, power shower), internet, delicious home-cooked meals, pool surrounded by a lawn, friendly family. Recommended.

B **Karauli House**, New Sanganer Rd, Sodala (towards the airport), T0141-221 1532, www.karauli.com. 6 rooms in a family 'retreat', large garden, pool, personal attention, home-cooked meals.

B **LMB**, JohariBazar, Old City, T0141-256 5844, info@lmbhotel.com. 33 centrally a/c rooms, currently undergoing wholesale renovation. New rooms are equipped with all mod cons and very comfy beds. Location convenient but can be noisy.

B **Maharani Plaza**, opposite Sindhi Camp Bus Stand, T0141-237 1717, www.maharanihotels.com. Better bet than nearby **Maharani Palace**. 53 modern rooms, clean and quiet, friendly management, small pool.

B **Narain Niwas, Kanota Bagh**, Narain Singh Rd, T0141-256 1291, www.hotelnarainniwas.com. 36 well presented rooms in characterful old mansion, great dining room and lounge, clean pool in beautiful gardens, patchy reports on food and service.

B **Om Towers** (Best Western), Church Rd, off MI Rd, T0141-236 6683, ommljaipur@yahoo.com. 58 ultra modern, international style rooms. Main draw is the revolving restaurant.

C **Chirmi Palace**, Dhuleshwar Garden, Sardar Patel Marg, T0141-236 5063, www.chirmi.com. 23 spacious but variable a/c rooms in 150-year-old *haveli* conversion. Traditional Rajasthani decor, attractive dining room, lawns, pool (summer only), e-mail, gentle staff, slightly run down but pleasant overall.

C **Dera Rawatsar**, D-194/C, Vijay Path, behind Sindhi Camp Bus Station, T0141-236 0717, www.derarawatsar.com. 7 rooms (more planned) in smart new premises, all done to a high standard. Family run, has a homely feel and pleasant location.

C **General's Retreat**, 9 Sardar Patel Rd, T0141-237 7134. 8 rooms with bath, some with kitchenettes, attractive bungalow of a retired general, pleasant gardens, restaurant.

C **Madhuban**, D237 Behari Marg, Bani Park, T0141-220 0033, www.madhuban.net. Classy, characterful hotel, 25 beautifully furnished rooms, small pool, pleasant garden, helpful staff, good food. Recommended.

*For an explanation of sleeping and eating price codes used in this guide, see inside the front cover. Other relevant information is found in Essentials, see pages 56-61.*

**C Megh Niwas**, C-9 Jai Singh Highway, Bani Park, T0141-220 2034, www.meghniwas.com. 27 tastefully decorated,comfortable rooms, run by charming, knowledgeable family, good pool, excellent food, very soothing feel. Recommended.

**C Nana-ki-Haveli**, Fateh Tiba, Moti Dungri Rd, near Old City, T0141-261 5502, nanakihavelijaipur@yahoo.com. 12 spacious a/c rooms in a modernized 1918 garden house, very hospitable, friendly family, excellent home cooking. Recommended.

**C Natraj**, 20 Motilal Rd, T0141-236 1348, www.hotelnatraj.com. 20 large, clean, quirkily decorated rooms, good veg restaurant, piped muzak throughout.

**C Santha Bagh**, Kalyan Path, Narain Singh Rd, T0141-256 6790. 12 simple, comfortable rooms (a/c or air-cooled), very friendly, helpful and charming staff, excellent meals, lawn, quiet location. Recommended.

**C Shahar Palace**, Barwada Colony, Civil Lines, T0141-222 1861, www.shaharpalace.com. 6 rooms in a separate annexe of a residential home. Well maintained gardens, home-cooked food and friendly but discreet attention make this a soothing retreat. Recommended.

**C Umaid Bhawan**, D1-2A Bani Park, T0141-231 6184, www.umaidbhawan.com. 28 beautifully decorated and ornately furnished rooms, many with balconies, plus a lovely pool and friendly, knowledgeable owners. Recommended.

**C-D Diggi Palace**, SMS Hospital Rd, T0141-237 3091, www.hoteldiggipalace.com. 43 attractive rooms in charming 125-year-old building. Large range of rooms for every budget, Rs 500 category particularly good value. Lovely open restaurant, great homegrown food, peaceful garden, enthusiastic, helpful owners, calming atmosphere. Highly recommended.

**C-D Rajasthan Palace**, 3 Peelwa Gardens, 1 km from Sanganeri Gate, Moti Dungri Rd, T0141-261 1542, rajasthanmotel@yahoo.co.in. 40 rooms, some old-fashioned and wacky, others modern and clean plus budget rooms with shared WC, around pleasant gardens and small pool. Not a palace though.

**D Arya Niwas**, Sansar Chandra Rd (behind Amber Tower), T0141-237 2456, www.aryaniwas.com. 95 very clean, simple rooms but not always quiet, modernized and smart, good very cheap veg food, pleasant lounge, travel desk, tranquil lawn, friendly, helpful, impressivemanagement, book ahead (arrive by 1800), great value. Highly recommended.

**D Atithi**, 1 Park House Scheme,T0141-237 8679, atithijaipur@hotmail.com. 24 very clean rooms, wonderful hot showers, relaxing roof terrace, internet, good veg food, helpful, friendly staff. Recommended.

**D Gangaur** (RTDC), MI Rd, T0141-237 1641. 63 rooms, some a/c, restaurant, coffee shop, a little neglected, convenient for bus/railway.

**D Tiger Fort**, T0141-236 0238, for an atmospheric stay. Here, you'll find 2 simple rooms with bath. Enquire at **Durg Café**.

**D-E Jaipur Inn**, B17 Shiv Marg, Bani Park, T0141-220 1121, www.jaipurinn.net. 16 very clean rooms with attached WC, 6 basic rooms with shared facilities plus 12 dorm beds and camping space (**F**). Delightful owners will bend over backwards to help. Pleasant café plus a rooftop restaurant offering excellent views. 27 years experience and it shows. Highly recommended.

**D-E Karni Niwas**, C-5 Motilal Rd, T0141-236 5433, karniniwas@hotmail.com. 13 clean rooms (15 more planned) with hot shower, some large a/c, some with balconies, breakfast and snacks, internet, very friendly and helpful owners. Recommended.

**D-E Pearl Palace**, Hathroi Fort, Ajmer Rd, T0141-237 3700, www.hotelpearlpalace.com. 25 spotless, modern rooms, with or without a/c in quiet location. Run by enthusiastic, innovative owners, personal touches everywhere, stunning rooftop restaurant. Delicious food, remarkably good value. Highly recommended.

**E City Centre**, near Central Bus Stand, T368320. Good sized, clean rooms, western toilet, hot showers, good value, rickshaws reluctant (no commission).

**E Evergreen**, Keshav Path, Ashok Marg, C-Scheme, T0141-236 2415, evergreen34@hotmail.com. 97 rooms (but standard and prices vary, see first) long-established haunt of backpackers and long-termers, good restaurant and travel desk, peaceful garden, small pleasant pool, cyber café, often full.

**E Sajjan Niwas**, Via Bank Rd, Bani Park, T0141-231 1544, www.sajjanniwas.com. A pale imitation of **Umaid Bhawan** next door but 22 rooms are not bad value and owners are eager to please. Top floor rooms with balconies are the best. Food recommended.

**E Shakuntala**, D-157 Durga Marg, Bani Park, T0141-220 3225. 16 adequate rooms, family run, attentive service, meals available.
**E Tourist Hotel** (RTDC), MI Rd, same building as tourist office, T0141-2360238. 47 simple rooms with bath, dorm (Rs 50), little atmosphere, beer bar, tours, well located.
**F Shivam**, A26, C1, Bharatia Path, Kanti Chandra Rd, Bani Park (behind **Ashok**), T201008. 5 rooms, some with hot shower, dorm in converted garage (Rs 60), mosquito menace, hop over fence and use **Ashok's** pool for Rs 100! Nothing special but one of Jaipur's few cheap options.
**F Youth Hostel**, T0141-274 1130, near the SMS Stadium, out of town. 8 clean double rooms plus 3 dorms (Rs 40), renovated, good value. Discounts for YHA members.

**Paying guests**
Good home-cooked meals are a big bonus.
**E Mandap Homestays**, 1 Bhilwa Garden, Moti Dungri Rd, T0141-261 4389. 10 rooms, more under construction, in friendly home of former ruling family.
**E Shri Sai Nath**, 1233 Mali Colony, outside Chandpol Gate, T0141-230 4975, shreesainath@indya.com. 10 clean, quiet rooms, meals on request, very hospitable, helpful and warm.

## Eating

**Jaipur** *p320, map p322*
**TTT Jaimahal Palace**, see Sleeping, for international cuisine in beautiful surroundings, buffet breakfast and dinner recommended; but snack bar inadequate.
**TTT Rambagh Palace**, see Sleeping, for inter- national cuisine in a beautiful restaurant, attractive decor in coffee shop, popular for lunch, pricey but generous.
**TTT Spice Court**, Hari Bhawan, Achrol House, Jacob Rd, Civil Lines, T0141-222 0202. Newly opened multicuisine restaurant with distinctive, relaxed 'clubhouse' ambience, superb range of food and drink and outstanding management. Recommended.
**TT Chaitanya**, Sansar Ch Rd, 100 m from Alsisar, in shopping complex on opposite side of road. Excellent vegetarian in civilized surroundings. Extensive menu includes Rajasthani, Italian and Mexican specialities.
**TT Copper Chimney**, MI Rd. International. A/c, open for lunch and dinner only, quality food, large non-veg selection including seafood from Sep to Mar. Incessant muzak.
**TT Evergreen**, see Sleeping. Good Western. Full of backpackers. Watch bill.
**TT Handi**, back of Maya Mansion. Indian. Partly open-air, simple canteen style.
**TT LMB**, Johari Bazar. Rajasthani vegetarian in slightly confused contemporary interior matched by upbeat dance tunes. Tasty (if a little overpriced) *thalis*; (panchmela saag particularly good).
**TT Mehfil**, sweets and *kulfis* outside. New location in tower block basement. Good range of quality Indian, Chinese and Western dishes, friendly service, live music, beer.
**TT Natraj**, M1 Rd. Rajasthani, some Chinese, veg only. A/c, much smarter inside than out. Good range of *thalis* and sweets, western classical on stereo.
**TT Niros**, MI Rd, T374493. International. A/c, with its bland decor you could be anywhere but there's a good choice of Indian, Chinese and Continental dishes, all set to popzak.
**TT Shiv Sagar**, 2nd floor, Mall 21, opposite Raj Mandir Cinema. Strong South Indian selection in fun, modern surroundings.
**TT Suriya India**, B Ganpati Plaza, Motilal Atal Rd, T0141-360749. Good selection of pure veg North Indian, live music every evening.
**TT Surya Mahal**, MI Rd. East meets west in chaotic clash of interiors. Wide variety including Mexican and pizzas, food far superior to music.

## Entertainment

**Jaipur** *p320, map p322*
**Ayurvedic treatments**
Many of the top hotels offer Ayurvedic treatments to non-residents.

**Cinema**
**Raj Mandir Cinema**, 'experience' a Hindi film in shell pink interior.
**Ravindra Rang Manch**, Ram Niwas Garden. Hosts cultural programmes and music shows.

**Meditation**
**Vipasana Centre**, Dhammathali, Galta, T0141-268 0220 (3 km east of centre). Runs courses for new and experienced students.

## A prayer for a good husband

Ishar and Gangaur are the mythical man and wife who embody marital harmony. During the Gangaur Fair colourfully dressed young women carrying brass pitchers on their heads make their way through the streets to the temple of Gauri (another name for Parvati). Here they ceremonially bathe the deity who is then decked with flowers. Young women pray for good husbands, and the long life of their husbands (if they are already married). It ends with singing and rejoicing as it is believed that if a woman is unhappy while she sings she will be landed with an ill-tempered husband! The festivities end when Siva arrives, accompanied by elephants, to escort his bride Gauri home.

## Festivals and events

**Jaipur** *p320, map p322*
See also p61 for nationwide festivals.
**14 Jan** **Makar Sankranti** The kite flying festival is spectacular. Everything closes down in the afternoon and kites are flown from every rooftop, street and even from bicycles! The object is to bring down other kites to the deafening cheers of huge crowds.
**Mar** **Elephant Festival** (14 Mar 2006, 3 Mar 2007) at Chaugan Stadium, procession, elephant polo etc.
**Apr** **Gangaur Fair** (11-12 Apr 2006, 1-2 Apr 2007) about a fortnight after **Holi**, when a colourful procession of women start from the City Palace with the idol of Goddess Gauri. They travel from the Tripolia gate to Talkatora, and these areas of the city are closed to traffic during the festival. See box.
**Jul/Aug** **Teej** (28-29 Jul 2006, 15-16 Aug 2007). The special celebrations in Jaipur have elephants, camels and dancers joining in the processions.

## Shopping

**Jaipur** *p320, map p322*
Jaipur specializes in printed cotton, handicrafts, carpets and *durries* (thick handloomed rug); also embroidered leather footwear and blue pottery. You may find better bargains in other cities in Rajasthan.

### Antiques and art

**Art Palace**, in Chomu Haveli. Specializes in 'ageing' newly crafted items – alternatives to antiques. Also found around Hawa Mahal.
**Manglam Arts**, Amer Rd. Sells modern miniature paintings and silver.
**Mohan Yadav**, 9 Khandela House, behind Amber Gauer, SC Rd, T0141-378009. Visit the workshop to see high quality miniatures produced by the family.

### Bazaars

Traditional bazaars and small shops in the Old City are well worth a visit; cheaper than MI Rd shops but may not accept credit cards. Most open 1030-1930; closed on Sun.
**Bapu Bazar** specializes in printed cloth.
**Chaupar** and **Nehru Bazars** for textiles.
**Johari Bazar** for jewellery.
**Khajanewalon-ka-Rasta**, off Chandpol bazar, for marble and stoneware.
**Maniharon-ka-Rasta** for lac bangles which the city is famous for.
**Ramganj Bazar** has leather footwear while opposite Hawa Mahal you will find the famous featherweight Jaipuri *rezais* (quilts).
**Tripolia Bazar** (3 gates) for inexpensive jewellery.

### Blue pottery

**Blue Pottery Art Centre**, Amer Rd, near Jain Mandir. For unusual pots. Recommended.
**Kripal Kumbha**, B-18, Shiv Marg, Bani Park.

### Books

**Book Corner**, MI Rd by **Niro's Restaurant**. Good selection.
**Bookwise**, Rajputana Sheraton Hotel, also in Mall 21 opposite Rajmandir Cinema. Vast range, excellent service, fair price.

### Carpets

**Channi Carpets and Textiles**, Mount Rd opposite Ramgarh Rd. Factory shop, watch carpets being handknotted, then washed, cut and quality checked with a blow lamp!
**Kashmiri Carpet Museum**, 327 Old Amer Rd, near Zorawar Singh Gate. Excellent stock.
**Maharaja**, Chandpol (near **Samode Haveli**). Watch carpet weavers and craftsmen, good value carpets and printed cotton.
**The Reject Shop**, Bhawani Singh Rd. For 'Shyam Ahuja' durrie collections.

### Fabrics

**Chirag International**, 771 Khawasji ka Rasta, Hawa Mahal Rd. Wholesale warehouse, with a corresponding vast selection.
**Ridhi Sidhi Textiles**, 9 East Govind Nagar, Amber Rd.

### Handicrafts

**Anokhi**, 2 Yudhistra Marg, opposite Udyog Bhawan. Well-crafted, attractive block -printed clothing, linen etc. Recommended.
**Gems & Silver Palace**, G11 Amber Tower, Sansar Ch Rd. Good choice of 'old' textiles, reasonable prices, helpful owners.
**Handloom Haveli**, Lalpura House, Sansar Ch Rd.
**Handloom House**, Rituraj Building, MI Rd (near Tourist Hostel).
**Rajasthali**, Government Handicrafts, MI Rd, 500 m west of Ajmeri Gate.
**Rajasthan Fabrics & Arts**, near City Palace gate. Exquisite textiles.

### Jewellery

Jaipur is famous for gold, jewellery and gem stones (particularly emeralds, rubies, sapphires and diamonds, but the last requires special certification for export). Semi-precious stones set in silver is more affordable (but check for loose settings, catches and cracked stones); sterling silver items are rare in India and the content varies widely. Bargaining is easier on your own so avoid being taken by a 'guide'. For about Rs 40 you can have gems valued. Do not use credit cards to buy these goods and never agree to 'help to export' jewellery. Report of misuse of credit card accounts at **Monopoli Gems**, opposite Sarga Sooli, Kishore Niwas (1st floor) Tripolia Bazar, **Apache Indian Jewellers** (also operating as **Krishna Gems** or Ashirwad Gems & Art) opposite Samodia Complex, Loha Mandi, SC Rd.
**Bhuramal Rajmal Surana**, 1st floor, between nos 264 and 268, Haldiyon-ka-Rasta. Highly recommended.
**Beg Gems**, Mehdi-ka-Chowk, near Hawa Mahal.
**Dwarka's**, H20 Bhagat Singh Marg. Crafts high-quality gemstones in silver, gold and platinum in modern and traditional designs.
**Gem Testing Laboratory**, off MI Rd near New Gate (reputable jewellers should not object). Check for members of 'Gems and Jewellery Association of Rajasthan'.
**Johari Bazar**, you may be able to see craftsmen at work.
**NK Meghraj**, 239-240 Johari Bazar.
**Ornaments**, 32 Sudharma Arcade, Chameliwala Market, opposite GPO (turn left, first right and right again), T0141-365 051. Recommended for stones and silver (wholesale prices; made up in 24 hrs).

### Silverware

**Amrapali Silver Shop**, Chameliwala Market, opposite GPO, MI Rd.
**Arun's Emporium**, MI Rd.
**Balaji's**, Sireh Deori Bazar (off Johari Bazar).
**Mona Lisa**, Hawa Mahal Rd.
**Nawalgarh Haveli**, near Amber Fort Bus Stop.
**Silver and Art Palace**, Amer Rd.

## Activities and tours

**Jaipur** *p320, map p322*
Some hotels will arrange golf, tennis, squash.
**Ashok Club**, Bhagwandas Rd, T0141-381690. Has a squash court (mediocre); temporary membership, Rs 350 per month. Has interesting memorabilia.

### City tours

RTDC City Sightseeing, half day: 0800-1300, 1130-1630, 1330-1830, Rs 100; Central Museum, City Palace, Amber Fort and Palace, Gaitore, Nawab ki Haveli, Jantar Mantar, Jal Mahal, Hawa Mahal; City Sightseeing, full day: 0900-1800, Rs 150; including places above plus Nahargarh Fort, Indology Museum, Dolls Museum, Galta, Sisodia Rani Garden. Jaigarh Fort. Nahargarh evening tour, 1800-2200, includes non-veg meal, folk dances. Call T0141-237 5466 or book at

Railway station, the hotels, Gangaur or Tourist Hotel (see Sleeping for details). Other operators also offer city sightseeing: half/full day, Rs 100-150. The tours are worthwhile, but may miss out promised sights claiming they are closed. Some may find the guides' English difficult to follow and the obligatory trip to shops, tedious.

**Walking tour**
An excellent new initiative is the Heritage Walk of Jaipur, a guided walking tour of some of the lesser known parts of the old city. It leaves from Albert Hall at 0830 every Sat and lasts 2 hrs, covering a distance of 2½ km. There is no charge as such, but donations towards the upkeep of Jaipur's heritage buildings are appreciated. Call T0141-236 7678 for more information.

**General tours**
**Aravalli Safari**, opposite Rajputana Palace Hotel, Palace Rd, T0141-237 3124, aravalli2@datainfosys.net. Very professional.
**Chetan**, 17 Muktanand Nagar, Gopalpura Bypass, Tonk Rd, T0141-254 5302. Experienced, reliable, car tours.
**Forts & Palaces Tours**, S-1, Prabhakar Apartment, Vaishali Nagar, T0141-235 4508, www.palaces-tours.com. A very friendly, knowledgable outfit offering camel safaris, sightseeing tours and hotel reservations, etc.
**Karwan Tours**, Bissau Palace Hotel, Chandpol Gate, T0141-230 8103, karwantours@mailcity.com. For camel safaris, tours, taxis, ticketing, exchange, very helpful.
**Marudhar Tours**, H-20 Bhagat Singh Marg, C-scheme, T0141-237 1768, marudhar@datainfosys.net.in, car hire, air/train tickets.
**Rajasthan Travel**, 52 Ganpati Plaza, MI Rd, T0141-236 5408, rtsjaipur@bhaskarmail.com. Ticketing, reliable guides. Recommended.
**Sohan Singh Shekhawat** is a private guide (English and German speaking), T0141 4071525, 141 224 4032 (mob), www.sohans4@yahoo.com. Recommended.

## Transport

**Jaipur** *p320, map p322*
**Air**
Sanganer airport has good facilities. Transport to town: taxi, 30 mins, Rs 250; auto rickshaw Rs 120. **Indian Airlines**, Nehru Pl, Tonk Rd, T274 3500; airport, T272 1519, flies to **Aurangabad**, **Delhi**, **Jaisalmer**, **Jodhpur**, **Mumbai**, **Udaipur**, **Ahmedabad**, **Kolkata**, **Dubai**, **Bangkok** and **Singapore**. Jet Airways, T360763, airport T551352, flies to **Delhi**, **Mumbai** and **Udaipur**. Sahara Airlines, T237 7637, flies to **Delhi** and **Kolkata**.
**Airlines offices** Air India, Ganpati Plaza, MI Rd (opposite All India Rd), T236 8569. Lufthansa, T256 1360; others at Jaipur Tower, MI Rd, T237 7051.

**Auto rickshaw**
Avoid hotel touts and use the pre-paid auto-rickshaw counter to get to your hotel.
Station to city centre hotel, about Rs 25; sightseeing (3-4 hrs) Rs 200, 6-7 hrs, Rs 300. From railway and bus stations, drivers (who expect to take you to shops for commission) offer whole day hire including

Amber for Rs 150; have your list of sights planned and refuse to go to shops.

**Bus**

**Local** To get around the city, unless you have plenty of time or a very limited budget, an auto is recommended. To **Amber** buses originate from Ajmeri Gate, junction with MI Rd so get on there if you want a seat.

**Long distance** Central Bus Stand, Sindhi Camp, Station Rd. Enquiries: Deluxe, T511 6031, Express, T511 6044 (24 hrs), Narain Singh Circle, T256 4016. State and private 'Deluxe' buses are very popular so book 2 days in advance. Deluxe buses depart from Platform 3 which has the reservation counter. Journeys can be very bumpy and tiring. Left luggage, Rs 10 per item per day. To **Agra** about hourly from bus station 6½ hrs with 1 hr lunch stop, Rs 135/227a/c, pay when seat number is written on ticket; (230 km, 5 hrs, via Bharatpur) – you can get off at the 2nd (last) stop to avoid being hassled by rickshaw drivers; **Ajmer** (131 km, ½ hourly, 3 hrs, rs67/87a/c); **Bharatpur** Rs 90; **Delhi** (261 km, ½ hourly, 5½ hrs, Rs 240/375a/c/425a/c Volvo); **Jaisalmer** (654 km, 2145, 13 hrs via Jodhpur, Rs 235). **Jodhpur** (332 km, frequent, 7 hrs, Rs 154); **Udaipur** (374 km, 12 hrs, Rs 202/252a/c/282a/csleeper 282).

**Cycle rickshaw**

(Often rickety) station to central hotels, Rs 15; full day Rs 100.

**Taxi**

Unmetered taxis; 4 hrs Rs 350 (40 km), 8 hrs Rs 550 (city and Amber). Out of city Rs 5 per km; Marudhar Tours (see Activities and tours) recommended; or try RTDC, T315714. Also Pink City Taxis, T511 5100, excellent radio cab service.

**Train**

Enquiry, T131, T133, reservation T135. Computerized booking office in separate building to front and left of station; separate queue for foreigners. Persistent auto-rickshaw drivers, in addition to being hotel touts, may quote Rs 10 to anywhere in town, then overcharge for city tour. Use pre-paid rickshaw counter. **Abu Rd (for Mount Abu)** *Ahmadabad Mail, 9106*, 0455, 8½ hrs, *Aravali Exp (goes on to Mumbai), 9708*, 0840, 9½ hrs; **Agra Cantt**: *Marudhar Exp, 4854/4864*, 1310, 7 hrs. **Ahmadabad**: *Aravali Exp, 9708*, 0840, 14 hrs; *Ashram Exp, 2916*, 2050, 11½ hrs. *Rajdhani Exp, 2958*, Tue, Thu, Sat, 0045, 9 hrs. **Ajmer**: *Aravali Exp, 9708*, 0840, 2½ hrs; **Bikaner**: *Bikaner Exp, 4737*, 2100, 10 hrs; *Intercity Exp, 2468*, 1500, 7 hrs. **Chittaurgarh**: *Jaipur-Purna Exp, 9769*, 1220, 7½ hrs; *Chetak Exp, 9615*, 2050, 8½ hrs. **Delhi**: Shatabdi 2016, 1745, 4 hrs 25 mins, *Jodhpur Delhi Exp, 4860*, 0600, 5 hrs; *Jaipur Delhi Exp, 2414*, 1620, 5½ hrs; *Ahmadabad Mail, 9105*, 2340, 5½ hrs. **Indore**: *Jaipur-Purna Exp, 9769*, 1220, 16½ hrs. *Jaipur Indore Exp 9308*, 1545, 16 hrs; **Jodhpur**: *Jodhpur Delhi Exp, 4859*, 2330, 6 hrs. **Mumbai (C)**: *Jaipur Mumbai Exp 2956*, 1330, 18½ hrs; **Udaipur** *Chetak Exp, 9615*, 2220, 12 hrs. **Varanasi** via **Lucknow**: *Marudhar Exp, 4854/4864*, 1325, 20 hrs.

## Directory

**Jaipur** *p320, map p322*

**Banks** Several on MI Rd. Open 1030-1430, 1530-1630; most change money. Andhra Bank, MI Rd. For Visa: Indus Bank, C-Scheme; SBBJ, both recommended. Thomas Cook, Jaipur Towers, 1st floor, MI Rd (500 m from railway station, T236 0801, 0930-1730, open Sun). No commission on own TCs, Rs 20 for others. Recommended. Often easier to use hotels, eg Rambagh Palace (0700-2000). Karwan Tours, Bissau Palace (sunrise until late). Jewellery shops opposite Hawa Mahal often hold exchange licences but travellers report misuse of credit cards at some.

**Hospitals** Santokba Durlabhji, Bhawani Singh Rd, T256 6251. SMS, Sawai Ram Singh Marg, T256 0291.

**Internet** At Ganpati Plaza basement, Re 1 per min. Cyber Café, 15 Nandisha Inn, Sivaji Rd. Reliable. Interphase, C-Scheme, plus many others scattered around city. At hotels: Mewar, near Central Bus Stand, T206042. Jaipur Inn, Rs 3 per min. Also 34 Station Rd (behind Polo Victory Cinema).

**Post** GPO, MI Rd. Excellent parcel service.

**Useful numbers** Ambulance: T102. Fire: T101. Police: T100. Foreigners' Registration Office: Hazari Garden, behind Hawa Mahal.

# Around Jaipur

*Amber Fort is one of Jaipur's biggest draws, with an elephant ride to the top high on many people's 'to do' list. It's still an impressive building but has been poorly maintained in recent years. Sanganer and Bagru offer good opportunities to see handicrafts in production, while Samode is perhaps the last word in elegant living.*

▸▸ *For Sleeping, Eating and other listings, see pages 339-340.*

## Amber (Amer) → *Colour map 2, grid A5. 11 km north of Jaipur.*

Today there is no town to speak of in Amber, just the palace clinging to the side of the rocky hill, overlooked by the small fort above, with a small village at its base. In the high season this is one of India's most popular tourist sites, with a continuous train of colourfully decorated elephants walking up and down the ramp to the palace. One penalty of its popularity is the persistence of the vendors.

### History

Amber, which takes its name from Ambarisha, a king of the once famous royal city of Ayodhya, was the site of a Hindu temple built by the Mina tribes as early as the 10th century. Two centuries later the Kachhawaha Rajputs made it their capital, which it remained until Sawai Jai Singh II moved to his newly planned city of Jaipur in 1727. Its location made Amber strategically crucial for the Mughal emperors as they moved south, and the Maharajahs of Amber took care to establish close relations with successive Mughal rulers. The building of the fort palace was begun by Raja Man Singh, a noted Rajput General in Akbar's army, in 1600, and Mughal influence was strong in much of the subsequent building.

### The approach

ⓘ *Rs 400 per elephant carrying four, no need to tip, though the driver will probably ask, takes 10 mins. Jeeps Rs 100 each way, or Rs 10 per seat. It can be quite a long wait in a small garden with little shade and you will be at the mercy of the hawkers. If you do want to buy, wait until you reach the steps when the price will drop drammatically.*

From the start of the ramp you can either walk or ride by elephant; the walk is quite easy and mainly on a separate path. Elephants carry up to four persons on a

**Amber Palace**

Shila Mata **1**
Diwan-i-Am (Daftar Khana above) **2**
Jai Singh I Garden **3**
Jai Mandir (Jas Mandir, 1st floor) **4**
Sohag Mandir (1st floor) **5**
Palace of Man Singh I (1st floor) **6**
Zenana **7**

Not to scale

padded seat. The ride can be somewhat unnerving when the elephant comes close to the edge of the road, but it is generally perfectly safe. You have to buy a 'return ticket' even if you wish to walk down later. The elephants get bad tempered as the day wears on. If you are interested in finding out more about the welfare of Amber's elephants, or indeed any of Jaipur's street animals, you should contact an organization called **Help in Suffering** ⓘ *T0141-276 0803, www.his-india.com.*



## The Palace

ⓘ *0900-1630. Worth arriving at 0900. Tickets in the Chowk, below the steps up to Shila Mata. Rs 50, camera Rs 25, video Rs 100. Take the green bus from the Hawa Mahal, Rs 5. Auto-rickshaw Rs 50 (Rs 125 for return, including the wait). Guides are worth hiring, Rs 400 for a half day (group of 4), find one with a government guide licence.*

After passing through a series of five defensive gates, you reach the first courtyard of the **Raj Mahal** built by Man Singh I in 1600, entered through the **Suraj Pol** (Sun Gate). Here you can get a short ride around the courtyard on an elephant, but bargain very hard. There are some toilets near the dismounting platform. On the south side of this Jaleb Chowk with the flower beds, is a flight of steps leading up to the **Singh Pol** (Lion Gate) entrance to the upper courtyard of the palace.

A separate staircase to the right leads to the green marble-pillared **Shila Mata Temple** (to Kali as Goddess of War) ⓘ *opens at certain times of the day and then, only allows a limited number of visitors at a time so ask before joining the queue*, which contains a black marble image of the goddess that Man Singh I brought back from Jessore (now in Bangladesh; the chief priest has always been Bengali). The silver doors with images of Durga and Saraswati were added by his successor.

In the left-hand corner of the courtyard, the **Diwan-i-Am** (Hall of Public Audience) was built by Raja Jai Singh I in 1639. Originally, it was an open pavilion with cream marble pillars supporting an unusual striped canopy-shaped ceiling, with a portico with double red sandstone columns. The room on the east was added by Sawai Ram Singh II. **Ganesh Pol** (circa 1700-1725), south of the chowk, colourfully painted and with mosaic decoration, takes its name from the prominent figure of Ganesh above the door. It separates the private from the public areas.

This leads onto the **Jai Singh I** court with a formal garden. To the east is the two-storeyed cream coloured marble pavilion – **Jai Mandir** (Diwan-i-Khas or Hall of Private Audience) below and **Jas Mandir** (1635-1640) with a curved Bengali roof, on the terrace above. The former, with its marble columns and painted ceiling, has lovely views across the lake. The latter has colourful mosaics, mirrors and marble *jali* screens which let in cooling breezes. Both have **Shish Mahals** (Mirror Palaces) faced with mirrors, seen to full effect when lit by a match. To the west of the chowk is the **Sukh Niwas**, a pleasure palace with a marble water course to cool the air, and doors inlaid with ivory and sandalwood. The Mughal influence is quite apparent in this chowk.

Above the Ganesh Pol is the **Sohag Mandir**, a rectangular chamber with beautiful latticed windows and octagonal rooms to each side. From the rooftop there are stunning views over the palace across the town of Amber, the long curtain wall surrounding the town and further north, through the 'V' shaped entrance in the hills, to the plains beyond. Beyond this courtyard is the **Palace of Man Singh I**. A high wall separates it from the Jai Singh Palace. In the centre of the chowk which was once open is a **baradari** (12-arched pavilion), combining Mughal and Hindu influences. The surrounding palace, a complex warren of passages and staircases, was turned into *zenana* quarters when the newer palaces were built by Jai Singh. Children find it great fun to explore this part.

## Old Palace and nearby temples

Old Palace of Amber (1216) lies at the base of Jaigarh fort. A stone path (currently being restored) from the Chand Pol in the first courtyard of Amber Palace leads to the ruins. Though there is little interest today, nearby are several interesting temples. These include the **Jagatsiromani Temple** dedicated to Krishna, with carvings and paintings; it is associated with **Mira Bai**. Close by is the old temple to Narasinghji and *Panna Mian-ki-Baoli* (step well). Some of the *chhatris* on Delhi Road still retain evidence of paintings.

## Jaigarh Fort

*ⓘ 0900-1630. Rs 20 Indian, Rs 35 foreigners including still camera, video Rs150, vehicle entry Rs 50. To reach the fort, from Amber Palace turn right out of the Suraj Pol and follow a stone road past the old elephant quarters. This is the start of the ascent – a steady climb of about 25 minutes, or take a taxi. What appears at first to be two adjoining forts is in fact all part of the same structure. There is also a good road from the Jaipur-Amber road which goes straight to Jaigarh Fort and on to Nahargarh.*

Above the palace on the hill top stands the gigantic bulk of Jaigarh, impressively lit at night, its *parkotas* (walls), bastions, gateways and watchtowers a testimony of the power of the Jaipur rulers. It is well worth a visit. The forbidding medieval fort was never captured and so has survived virtually intact which makes it particularly interesting. In the 16th-century well-planned cannon foundry you can see the pit where the barrels were cast, the capstan-powered lathe which bored out the cannon and the iron-workers' drills, taps and dies. The armoury has a large collection of swords and small arms, their use in the many successful campaigns having been carefully logged. There is an interesting photograph collection and a small café outside the armoury. There are gardens, a granary, open and closed reservoirs; the ancient temples of Ram Harihar (10th-century) and Kal Bhairava (12th-century) are within the fort. You can explore a warren of complicated dark passageways among the palaces. Many of the apartments are open and you can see the collections of coins and puppets (shows on demand). The other part of the fort, at a slightly higher elevation, has a tall watch tower. From here there are tremendous views of the surrounding hills. The massive 50 tonne **Jai Ban cannon** stands on top of one tower. Allegedly the largest cannon on wheels in the world, with an 8 m barrel, it had a range of around 20 km, but it was never used. Some 7 km further along the top of the hill is the smaller Nahargarh Fort overlooking Jaipur itself. See page 327.

## Ramgarh Lake and Jamwa Sanctuary → *30 km northeast.*

This 15 sq km lake, of Jamwa Ramgarh, which attracts large flocks of waterfowl in winter, lies within a game sanctuary with good boating and bird watching. It was the venue for yachting and other sports in the 1982 Asian Games and is being developed as a water sports resort. Built to supply Jaipur with water it now provides less than one per cent of the city's needs and in years of severe drought it may dry up completely. In the summer of 2000, at the end of a particularly hot dry spell, the lake's crocodiles were reported to be searching the few remaining mud pools in the rapidly drying lake bed. The 300-sq km Jamwa Sanctuary which once provided the Jaipur royal family with game still has some panthers, nilgai and small game. Contact Jaipur Tourist Office for details of public buses. It is about a 45-minute drive.

## Madhogarh → *45 km southeast of Jaipur, off the Jaipur-Agra Rd.*

Madhogarh is a small but impressive fort, with a strong medieval flavour, and a pleasant place to break your journey between Jaipur and Ranthambore if you have your own transport. It is located on a hillock, and has huge walls, bastions, wells and turrets. The Rajput-Maratha battle of Tunga was fought at the nearby village, with the Jaipur army based at Madhogarh, during the mid-18th century.

## Samode

*→ Phone code: 01423. Colour map 2, grid A5. 42 km northwest of Jaipur.*

At the head of the enclosed valley in the dry rugged hills of the northern Aravallis, Samode stands on a former caravan route. Today, the sleepy village, with its local artisans producing printed cloth and glass bangles, nestles within its old walls. The old painted *havelis* are still full of character. Samode is well worth the visit from Jaipur or en route to the painted towns of Shekhawati, see page 437. Both the palace and the *bagh* are wonderful, peaceful places to spend a night.

The **palace**, which dominates the village, is fabulously decorated with 300-year old wall paintings (hunting scenes, floral motifs etc) which still look almost new. Around the first floor of the Darbar Hall are magnificent alcoves, decorated with mirrors like *shish mahal* and *jali* screens through which the royal ladies would have looked down into the grand jewel-like Darbar Hall.

Towering immediately above the palace is **Samode Fort**, the maharajah's former residence, reached in times of trouble by an underground passage. The old stone zigzag path has been replaced by 300 steps. Though dilapidated, there are excellent views from the ramparts; a caretaker has the keys. The main fort gate is the starting point of some enticing walks into the Aravallis. A paved path leads to a shrine about 3 km away. There are two other powerful forts you can walk to, forming a circular walk ending back in Samode. Allow three hours, wear good shoes, a hat and carry water.

**Samode Bagh**, a large 400-year-old Mughal-style formal garden with fountains and pavilions, has been beautifully restored. It is 3 km southeast of Samode, towards the main Jaipur-Agra road. Within the grounds are modest-sized, but elaborately decorated tents.

## Sleeping

**Ramgarh Lake and Jamwa Sanctuary** *p338*

**A-B Ramgarh Lodge** (Taj), overlooking the lake, T01426-252217, www.tajhotels.com. 18 elegant a/c rooms (2 enormous suites) in the former royal hunting lodge with a museum and library, furnished appropriately, hunting trophies, limited restaurant, delightful walks, fishing and boating plus ruins of old Kachhawaha fort nearby.

**D Jheel Tourist Village** (RTDC), Mandawa Choraha, T01426-252170. 10 not especially well-maintained rustic huts in pleasant surroundings.

**Madhogarh** *p338*

**B Madhogarh**, T0141 291409. A Rajput Special Hotels with 25 quaint rooms (some in the tower) with views of the countryside. Good (though rather spicy) food, interesting temples nearby, family run, recently converted so still finding its feet. Great atmosphere on the ramparts in the evening when the family and guests enjoy tea.

**Samode** *p339*

**L-A Samode Palace**, T01423-240014, www.samode.com. 43 a/c rooms, tastefully modernized without losing any of the charm (but short of hot water), courtyard and modern indoor restaurants (international menu). The dining room serves buffets to groups, gardens, beautiful, secluded pool with plenty of space to lounge, magnificent setting, shop with good textiles, camel rides around village and to Samode Bagh (but some animals are in poor condition), generally friendly, really remark- able for its setting and atmosphere but some- what impersonal, disappointing service (tip-seeking), Rs 100 entry for non-residents, well worth a visit even if not staying. Highly recommended. Half price 1 May to 30 Sep. Samode Haveli T0141 263 2407, reserve and arrange taxi (Rs 950) from Jaipur. Reservations essential.

**A Samode Bagh**, T01423-240235, 3 km away from palace, www.samode.com. 44 luxury a/c tents decorated in the Mughal style, each with a beautiful modern bath- room and its own verandah. *Darbar* tent, al fresco meals, pool with slide, tennis, volley-ball, badminton, lovely setting in peaceful walled Mughal gardens, plenty of bird-watching, safaris to sand dunes, amazing. Recommended. Reservations essential.

**B-C Maharaja Palace**, modern hotel. 18 rooms (some a/c) in mock *haveli*, restaurant, garden with village style huts.

## Shopping

**Amber** *p336*

At Amber near the *baoli* and temples, you can see demonstrations of block printing and other handicrafts, simple snacks, shops selling gems, jewellery, textiles, handicrafts and 'antiques' (objects up to 90 years old; genuine 100-year old antiques may not be exported). Amber is a tax holiday zone, and products manu- factured by industries here are 10-15% cheaper than at Jaipur (though the benefit may not be passed on to the customer). Travellers warn that the privately owned **Rajasthan Small Scale Cottage Industries**, on Jagat Shiromani Temple Rd, looks like a government fixed price shop but charges very high prices.

**Samode** *p339*

A small artists' colony in the village produces good quality miniature paintings on old paper. Contact Krishan Kumar Khari, often found at the hotel entrance.

## Activities and tours

**Ramgarh Lake and Jamwa Sanctuary** *p338*

Polo can be played at **Ramgarh Resort** (HRH), T0294-252 8016, www.hrhindia.com. An exclusive facility for polo enthusiasts with a full size polo field near the lake, occasional matches and polo training camps run by World Cup Indian captain Lokendra Singh. **A** deluxe tented accommodation for participants, restaurant, pool and riding stable.

**Samode** *p339*

See **Samode Bagh**, Sleeping, for activities around this Moghul garden/hotel. See also **Samode Palace** for camel safaris. Birdwatching around this area is good.

## Transport

**Samode** *p339*

Samode is a 1-hr drive from Jaipur. Buses from Chandpol Gate go to Chomu where you can pick a local bus to Samode. A taxi costs Rs 950.

# Southern Rajasthan

*Possibly the most varied region in Rajasthan, the main draw is incomparable Udaipur. The area around is equally appealing however, from time-warped, untouristy Bundi and Chittaurgarh in the east to the quirky charms of Mount Abu, Rajasthan's only hill station and a great escape from the heat of the summer, in the west. To the south lie delightful Dungarpur and a range of small heritage hotels dotted around the countryside, perfect places to unwind away from the tourist fray. To the north is the majestic Kumbhalgarh Fort, its mammoth walls so vast they're visible from space, and the exquisite Jain temples at Ranakpur, comparable to those in Mount Abu but in a far more tranquil setting. Fascinating drives through the surprisingly green Aravalli hills link one place to the other, passing through picturesque rural villages and agricultural areas unlike those anywhere else in Rajasthan along the way.*

# Udaipur

→ *Phone code: 0294. Colour map 2, grid B4. Population: 500,000.*

*Set in the Girwa valley amidst the Aravalli hills of south Rajasthan, Udaipur is a beautiful city, regarded by many as one of the most romantic in India. In contrast to some of its desert neighbours it presents an enchanting image of white marble palaces, placid blue lakes, attractive gardens and green hills that keep the wilderness at bay. High above the lake towers the massive palace of the maharanas. From its rooftop gardens and balconies, you can look over Lake Pichola, at the summer palace, 'adrift like a snowflake' in its centre. Sadly in the last few years the monsoon has bypassed the city which has led to the lake being dry for much of the year. Around the lake, the houses and temples of the old city stretch out in a pale honeycomb making Udaipur an oasis of colour in a stark and arid region.* ▸▸ *For Sleeping, Eating and other listings, see pages 347-353.*

*In April 2005, Lake Pichola was almost completely dry and has been for the last couple of years. No boat trips are possible. One good monsoon will put this right but check with a good travel agent on the current situation. Despite this, the view across to the Monsoon Palace and the surrounding hills is still wonderful.*

## Ins and outs

**Getting there** The airport, about 30-45 minutes by taxi or City Bus, is well connected. The main Bus Stand is east of Udai Pol, 2-3 km from most hotels, while Udaipur City Railway Station is another 1 km south. Both have auto-rickshaw stands outside as well as pushy hotel touts. Udaipur station to the north is inconvenient.

**Getting around** The touristy area around the Jagdish temple and the City Palace, the main focus of interest, is best explored on foot but there are several sights further afield. Buses, auto-rickshaws and taxis cover the city and surrounding area; some travellers prefer to hire a scooter or bike. ▸▸ *See Transport, page 352, for further details.*

**Tourist information** Be prepared for crowds, dirt and pollution and persistent hotel touts who descend on new arrivals. It is best to reserve a hotel ahead or ask for a particular street or area of town. Travellers risk being befriended by someone claiming to show you the city for free. If you accept, you run the risk of visiting one shop after another with your 'friend'. **Rajasthan** ⓘ *Tourist Reception Centre, Fath Memorial, Suraj Pol, T0294-241 1535, 1000-1700, guides 4-8 hrs, Rs 250-400.*

## History

The legendary **Ranas of Mewar** who traced their ancestry back to the Sun, first ruled the region from their seventh-century stronghold Chittaurgarh. The title 'Rana', peculiar to the rulers of **Mewar**, was supposedly first used by Hammir who reoccupied Mewar in 1326. In 1568, **Maharana Udai Singh** founded a new capital on the shores of Lake Pichola and named it Udaipur (the city of sunrise) having selected the spot in 1559. On the advice of an ascetic who interrupted his rabbit hunt, Udai Singh had a temple built above the lake and then his palace around it.

In contrast to the house of Jaipur, the rulers of Udaipur prided themselves on being independent from other more powerful regional neighbours, particularly the Mughals. In a piece of local princely one-upmanship, **Maharana Pratap Singh**, heir apparent to the throne of Udaipur, invited Raja Man Singh of Jaipur to a lakeside picnic. Afterwards he had the ground on which his guest had trodden washed with sacred Ganga water and insisted that his generals take purificatory baths. Man Singh reaped appropriate revenge by preventing Pratap Singh from acceding to his throne. Udaipur, for all its individuality, remained one of the poorer princely states in Rajasthan, a consequence of being almost constantly at war. In 1818, Mewar, the Kingdom of the Udaipur Maharanas, came under British political control but still managed to avoid almost all British cultural influence.

# Sights

## The Old City

Udaipur is a traditionally planned fortified city. Its bastioned rampart walls are pierced by massive gates, each studded with iron spikes as protection against enemy war elephants. The five remaining gates are: **Hathi Pol** (Elephant Gate – north), **Chand Pol** (Moon Gate – west), **Kishan Pol** (south), the main entrance **Suraj Pol** (Sun Gate – east) and **Delhi Gate** (northeast). On the west side, the City is bounded by the beautiful Pichola Lake and to the east and north, by moats. To the south is the fortified hill of Eklingigarh. The main street leads from the Hathi Pol to the massive City Palace on the lake side.

The walled city is a maze of narrow winding lanes flanked by tall whitewashed houses with doorways decorated with Mewar folk art, windows with stained glass or *jali* screens, majestic *havelis* with spacious inner courtyards and shops. Many of the houses here were given by the Maharana to retainers – barbers, priests, traders and artisans while many rural landholders (titled jagirdars), had a *haveli* conveniently located near the palace.

The **Jagdish Mandir**, 150 m north of the palace (1651), was built by Maharana Jagat Singh. The temple is a fine example of the Nagari style, and contrasts with the serenity of Udaipur's predominantly whitewashed buildings, surrounded as it often is by chanting Sadhus, gamboling monkeys and the smell of incense. A shrine with a brass Garuda stands outside and stone elephants flank the entrance steps; within is a black stone image of Vishnu as Jagannath, the Lord of the Universe.

The lovely 18th-century **Bagore ki Haveli** has 130 rooms and was built as a miniature of the city palace. There are cool shady courtyards containing some peacock mosaic and fretwork, carved pillars made from granite, marble and the local blueish grey stone and lime plastered walls. The museum has a beautiful collection of folk costumes, turbans, hookahs, local art and utensils.



## City Palace

ⓘ *From Ganesh Deori Gate: Rs 50 (more from near Lake Palace Ghat). Camera/video Rs 200. 0930-1730, last entry 1630. From 'Maharajah's gallery', you can get a pass for Fateh Prakash Palace, Shiv Niwas and Shambu Niwas, Rs 75. Guided tour, 1 hr, Rs 100 each. Guides hang around the entrance; standards vary wildly and they can cause a scene if you already have hired a guide. Ask at the ticket office.*

This impressive complex of several palaces is a blend of Rajput and Mughal influences. Half of it, with a great plaster façade, is still occupied by the royal family. Between the **Bari Pol** (Great Gate, 1608, men traditionally had to cover their heads with a turban from this point on) to the north, and the **Tripolia Gate** (1713), are eight *toranas* (arches), under which the rulers were weighed against gold and silver on their birthdays, which was then distributed to the poor. One of the two domes on top of the Tripolia originally housed a water clock; a glass sphere with a small hole at the base was filled with water and would take exactly one hour to empty, at which point a gong would be struck and the process repeated. The gate has three arches to allow the royal family their private entrance, through the middle, and then a public entry and exit gate to either side. Note the elephant to the far left (eastern) end of the gate structure; they were seen as bringers of good fortune and appear all over the palace complex. The Tripolia leads in to the **Manak Chowk**, originally a large courtyard which was converted in to a garden only in 1992. The row of lumps in the surface to the left are original, and demarcate elephant parking bays! Claiming descent from Rama, and therefore the sun, the Mewars always insured that there was an image of the sun available for worship even on a cloudy day, thus the beautiful example set in to the exterior wall of the palace. The large step in front of the main entrance was for

# Udaipur

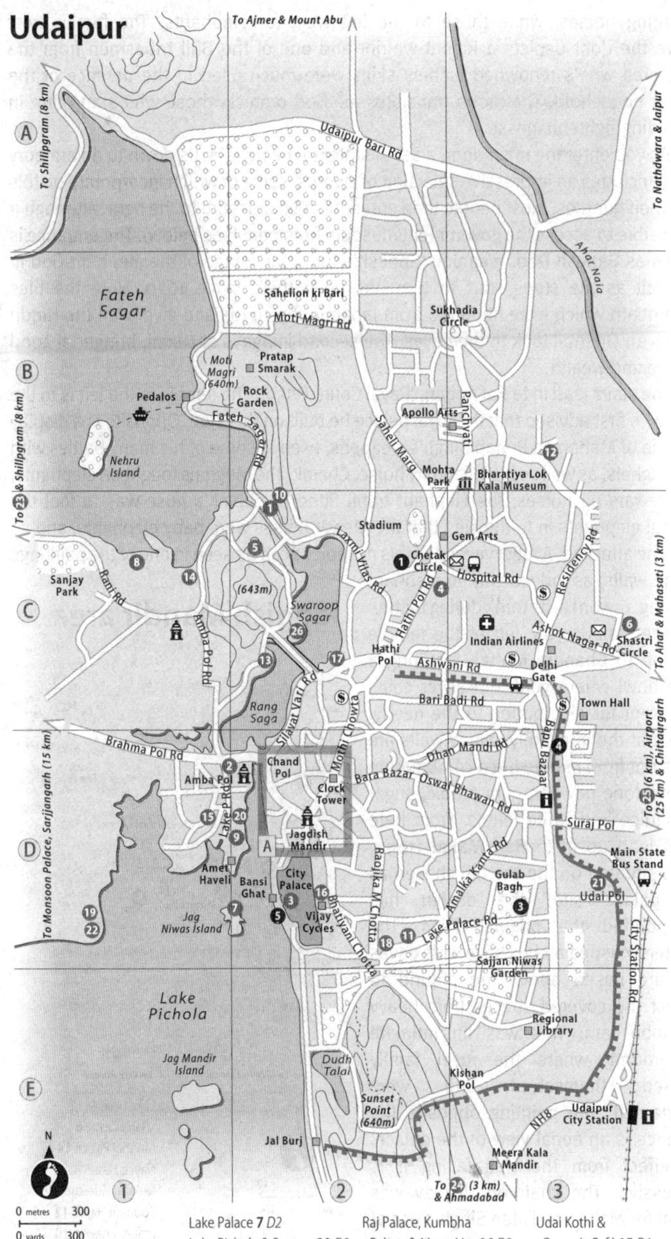


**Sleeping**
Anand Bhawan **1** *C2*
Ashish Palace **4** *C2*
Dream Heaven **2** *D2*
Fateh Prakash & Shiv Niwas **3** *D2*
Hilltop Palace **5** *C2*
Kajri **6** *C3*
Lakend **8** *C1*
Lake Palace **7** *D2*
Lake Pichola & Sarovar **20** *D2*
Lake Shore, Wonder View & Bharti Restaurant **9** *D2*
Laxmi Vilas Palace **10** *C2*
Mahendra Prakash **11** *D2*
Mewar Inn **12** *B3*
Natural **13** *C2*
Pratap Country Inn **25** *D3*
Rajdarshan & Delhi Darbar Restaurant **17** *C2*
Raj Palace, Kumbha Palace & Mona Lisa **16** *D2*
Rampratap Palace **14** *C1*
Rang Niwas Palace & Palace View Restaurant **18** *D2*
Rani Village **23** *C1*
Ranjit Niwas **19** *D2*
Shirkarbadi **24** *E3*
Swaroop Vilas **26** *C2*
Trident **19** *D1*
Udai Kothi & Queen's Café **15** *D1*
Udai Vilas **22** *D1*
Yatri Guesthouse **21** *D3*

**Eating**
Berrys **1** *C2*
Garden Hotel & Hariyali **3** *D3*
Park View & Natraj **4** *D3*
Sunset Terrace **5** *D2*

mounting horses, while those to the left were for elephants. The family crest above the door depicts a Rajput warrior and one of the Bhil tribesmen from the local area who's renowned archery skills were much used in the defence of the Mewar household. The motto translates as 'God protects those who stand firm in upholding righteousness'.

As you enter the main door, a set of stairs to the right leads down to an armoury which includes an impressive selection of swords, some of which incorporate pistols in to their handles. Most people then enter the main museum to the right, although it is possible to access the government museum from here (see below). The entrance is known as **Ganesh Dori**, meaning 'Ganesh's turn'; the image of the elephant God in the wall as the steps start to turn has been there since 1620. Note the tiles underneath which were imported from Japan in the 1930s and give even the Hindu deities an Oriental look to their eyes. The second image is of Laxmi, bringer of good fortune and wealth.

The stairs lead in to **Rai Angan**, 'Royal Court' (1559). The temple to the left is to the sage who first advised that the royal palace be built on this side. Opposite is a display of some of Maharana Pratap Singh's weapons, used in some of his many battles with the Mughals, as well as his legendary horse, Chetak. The Mughals fought on elephants, the Mewars on horses; the elephant trunk fitted to Chetak's nose was to fool the Mughal elephants in to thinking that the Mewar horses were baby elephants, and so not to be attacked. A fuller version of this nosepiece can be seen in one of the paintings on the walls, as indeed can an elephant wielding a sword in its trunk during battle.

The stairs to the left of the temple lead up to **Chandra Mahal**, featuring a large bowl where gold and silver coins were kept for distribution to the needy. Note that the intricately carved walls are made not from marble but a combination of limestone powder, gum Arabic, sugar cane juice and white lentils. From here steps lead up in to **Bari Mahal** (1699-1711), situated on top the hill chosen as the palace site; the design has incorporated the original trees. The cloisters' cusped arches have wide eaves and are raised above the ground to protect the covered spaces from heavy monsoon rain. This was an intimate 'playground' where the royal family amused themselves and were entertained. The painting opposite the entrance is an aerial view of the palace, the effect from the wall facing it is impressive. The chair on display was meant for Maharana Fateh Singh's use at the Delhi Darbar, an event which he famously refused to attend. The chair was sent on and has still never been used.

The picture on the wall of two elephants fighting shows the area that can be seen through the window to the left; there is a low wall running from the Tripolia gate to the main palace building.

## Jagdish Mandir area

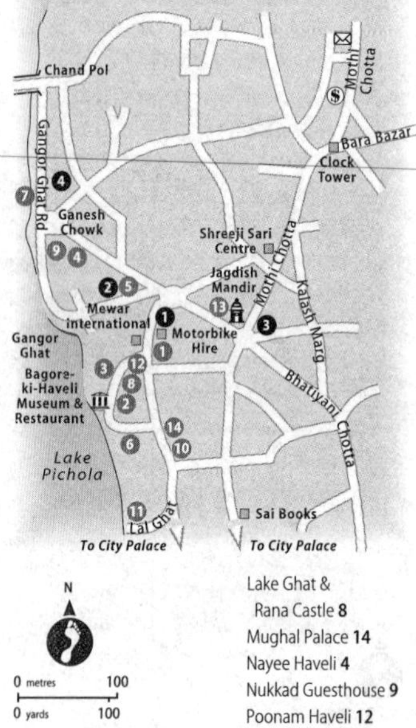

**Sleeping**
Badi Haveli & Lehar **1**
Caravanserai **2**
Evergreen & Lalghat Guest House **3**
Gangaur Palace **5**
Jagat Niwas & Kankarwa Haveli **6**
Jheel **7**
Lake Ghat & Rana Castle **8**
Mughal Palace **14**
Nayee Haveli **4**
Nukkad Guesthouse **9**
Poonam Haveli **12**
Pratap Bhawan **10**
Ratan Palace & Sai Niwas **11**
Udai Niwas **13**

**Eating**
Gokul **4**
Heaven **1**
King Roof Café **2**
Mayur **3**

An elephant was placed either side of the wall, and then each had to try to pull the other until their opponent's legs touched the wall, making them the victor.

The next room is known as **Dil Kushal Mahal**, 'love entertainment room', a kind of mirrored love nest. This leads on to a series of incredibly intricate paintings depicting the story of life in the palace, painted 1782-1828. The **Shiv Vilas Chini ki Chatar Sali** incorporates a large number of Chinese and Dutch tiles in to its decoration, as well as an early petrol-powered fan. Next is the Moti Mahal, the ladies' portion of the mens' palace, featuring a changing room lined with mirrors and two game boards incorporated in to the design of the floor.

**Pritam Niwas** was last lived in by Maharana Gopal Singh, who died in 1955 having been disabled by polio at a young age. His wheel armchair and even his commode are on display here. This leads on to **Surya Chopar**, which features a beautiful gold leaf image of the sun; note the 3D relief painting below. The attractive **Mor Chowk** court, intended for ceremonial darbars, was added in the mid-17th century, and features beautiful late 19th-century peacock mosaics. The throne room is to its south, the **Surya Chopar**, from which the Rana (who claimed descent from the Sun) paid homage to his divine ancestor. The **Manak Mahal** (Ruby Palace)was filled with figures of porcelain and glass in the mid-19th century. To the north, the **Bari Mahal** or Amar Vilas (1699-1711) was added on top of a low hill. It has a pleasant garden with full grown trees around a square water tank in the central court

A plain, narrow corridor leads in to the **Queen's Palace**, featuring a series of paintings, lithographs and photographs, and leading out in to **Laxmi Chowk**, featuring two cages meant for trapping tigers and leopards. The entrance to the **government museum** ⓘ *1000-1630, closed Fri, Rs 3*, is from this courtyard. The rather uncared for display includes second century BC inscriptions, fifth- to eighth-century sculpture and 9,000 miniature paintings of 17th- and 19th-century Mewar schools of art but also a stuffed kangaroo and Siamese twin deer.

On the west side of the Tripolia are the **Karan Vilas** (1620-1628) and **Khush Mahal**, a rather grotesque pleasure palace for European guests, whilst to the south lies the **Shambhu Niwas Palace** the present residence of the Maharana.

Maharana Fateh Singh added to this the opulent **Shiv Niwas** with a beautiful courtyard and public rooms, and the **Fateh Prakash Palace**. Here the Darbar Hall's royal portrait gallery displays swords still oiled and sharp. The Bohemian chandeliers (1880s) are reflected by Venetian mirrors, the larger ones made in India of lead crystal. Both, now exclusive hotels (see below), are worth visiting.

**Crystal Gallery** ⓘ *open to guests at lunch and dinner, Rs 300 for a guided tour with a talk on the history of Mewar, followed by a cup of tea (overpriced with a cold reception reported by some. Avoid the cream tea as the scones are so hard they will crack your teeth)*, on the first floor has an extensive collection of cut-crystal furniture, vases etc, made in Birmingham, England in the 1870s, supplemented by velvet, rich 'zardozi' brocade, objects in gold and silver and a precious stone-studded throne.

"The Legacy of honour", outlining the history of the Mewar dynasty, is a good **Son et Lumière**, the first privately funded one in India. There are two shows daily at 1930 and 2030, Rs 200, book at the City Palace ticket office.

## Lake Pichola

Fringed with hills, gardens, *havelis*, ghats and temples, Lake Pichola is the scenic focus of Udaipur though parts get covered periodically with vegetation, and the water level drops considerably during the summer. Set in it are the Jag Niwas (Lake Palace) and the Jag Mandir Palaces.

*The gold cupolas on top of the palace's many domes are the only ones of their kind. They are taken to denote the proud independence of the Mewar Dynasty, the world's second longest family lineage after the Japanese Samurai.*

**Jag Mandir**, built on an island in the south of the lake, is notable for the Gul Mahal, a domed pavilion started by Karan Singh (1620-1628) and completed by Jagat Singh (1628-1652). It is built of yellow sandstone inlaid with marble around an attractive courtyard. Maharajah Karan Singh gave the young Prince Khurram (later Shah Jahan), refuge here when he was in revolt against his father Jahangir in 1623, cementing a friendly relationship between the Mewar Maharaja and the future Mughal Emperor. Refugee European ladies and children were also given sanctuary here by Maharana Sarap Singh during the Mutiny. There is a lovely pavilion with four stone elephants on each side (some of the broken trunks have been replaced with polystyrene!). You get superb views from the balconies. An enjoyable **boat trip** ⓘ *Apr-Sep 0800-1100, 1500-1800, Oct-Mar 1000-1200, 1400-1700, the 1-hr boat trip, on the hour, Rs 150, landing on Jag Mandir, 30-min boat ride, Rs 75*, operates from Bansi Ghat (City Palace) Jetty. It's especially attractive in the late afternoon light.

**Jag Niwas** (Lake Palace) ⓘ *for non-residents boat ticket from Bansi Ghat jetty with buffet meal, Rs 500-625 (see Eating); tour operators make block bookings so book in advance or try your luck at the jetty*, island has the Dilaram and Bari Mahal Palaces. They were built by **Maharana Jagat Singh II** in 1746 and cover the whole island. Once the royal summer residences (now a hotel), they seem to float like a dream ship on the blue waters of the lake. The courtly atmosphere, elegance and opulence of princely times, the painted ceilings, antique furniture combined with the truly magical setting make it one of the most romantic in India. There are, of course, superb views.

**Jal Burj** is on the water's edge, south of the town. A pleasant two-hour walk to the south of the city takes you to the Sunset Point which has excellent views. The path past the café (good for breakfast) leads to the gardens on the wall; a pleasant place to relax. Although it looks steep it is only a 30-minute climb from the café.

From the small **Dudh Talai** (Milk Lake) ⓘ *Rs 5 day time, Rs 10 evening*, nearby, there is an attractive walk to the main lake (especially pleasant in the evening; large fruit bats can also often be seen). A left turn up a new road leads to Manikya Lal Verma Park which has a 'musical fountain' which is switched on in the evening.



## Fateh Sagar and around

This lake, north of Lake Pichola, was constructed in 1678 during the reign of Maharana Jai Singh and modified by Maharana Fateh Singh. There is a pleasant lakeside drive along the east bank but, overall, it lacks the charm of the Pichola. Nehru Park on an island (accessible by ferry) has a restaurant.

Overlooking the Fateh Sagar is the **Moti Magri** (Pearl Hill) ⓘ *Rs 10, camera free*. There are several statues of local heroes in the attractive rock gardens including one of Maharana Pratap on his horse Chetak, to which he owed his life. Local guides claim that Chetak jumped an abyss of extraordinary width in the heat of the battle of Haldighati (1576) even after losing one leg. To find out more look at *Hero of Haldighati*.

**Sahelion ki Bari** ('Garden of the Maids of Honour') ⓘ *0900-1800, Rs 2, plus Rs 2 for 'fountain show'*, a little northwest from Moti Magri, is an ornamental pleasure garden; a great spot, both attractive and restful. There are many fountains including trick ones along the edge of the path which are operated by the guide clapping his hands! In a pavilion in the first courtyard, opposite the entrance, a children's museum has curious exhibits including a pickled scorpion, a human skeleton and busts of Einstein and Archimedes! Beautiful black marble kiosks decorate the corners of a square pool. An elegant round lotus pond has four marble elephants spouting water. To the north is a rose garden with over 100 varieties.

At **Ahar** (3 km east) are the remains of the ancient city which has some Jain **chhatris** set on high plinths in the Mahasati (royal cremation ground). A small **museum** ⓘ *1000-1630, closed Fri and holidays, Rs 3*, contains pottery shards and terracotta toys from the first century BC and 10th-century sculptures. Nearby are the temples of Mira Bai (10th century), Adinatha (11th century) and Mahavira (15th century).

## Sleeping

**Udaipur** *p341, map p343 and p344*

Frenzied building work continues to provide more hotels while restaurants compete to offer the best views from the highest rooftop. The area around the lake is undeniably the most romantic place to stay, but also the most congested. The hotels on Lake Palace Rd and on the hilltop above Fateh Sagar Lake offer more peaceful surroundings, while Swaroop Sagar offers a good compromise between calmness and convenience. Paying guest accommodation list at Tourist Reception Centre, Fateh Memorial.

**LL Lake Palace** (Taj), Lake Pichola, T0294-252 8800, www.tajhotels.com. 84 rooms, most with lake view, in one of the world's most spectacularly located hotels. Standard rooms tasteful but unremarkable, suites outstanding, small pool, quite an experience, service can be slightly abrupt.

**LL Udai Vilas** (Oberoi), Lake Pichola, T0294-243 3300, www.oberoihotels.com. The elegant but monochrome exterior of this latter day palace does nothing to prepare you for the opulence within; the stunning entry courtyard sets the scene for the staggeringly beautiful interiors. The 87 rooms are the last word in indulgence; some have one of the hotel's 9 swimming pools running alongside their private balcony. The setting on the lake, overlooking both the lake and city palaces, is superb, as are the food and service. Outstanding.

**LL-L Fateh Prakash** (HRH), City Palace, T0294- 252 8017, www.hrhindia.com. 19 well-appointed, lake-facing rooms in modern 'Dovecote' wing and 7 superb suites in main palace building. Original period furniture, great views from Sunset Terrace restaurant, facilities of Shiv Niwas, good service (residents may ask for a 'Pass' at entrance of City Palace, for a short cut to hotel).

**LL-L Shiv Niwas** (HRH), City Palace (right after entrance), T0294-252 8018, www.hrhindia.com. 19 tasteful rooms, 17 luxurious suites including those stayed in by Queen Elizabeth II and Roger Moore, some with superb lake views, very comfortable, good restaurant, very pleasant outdoor seating for all meals around a lovely marble pool (non-residents pay Rs 300 to swim), tennis, squash, excellent service, beautiful surroundings, reserve ahead in season. Recommended.

**LL-L Trident** (Oberoi/Hilton), overlooking Lake Pichola, peaceful farside, T0294 243 2200, www.trident-hilton.com. 143 rooms, tastefully decorated, all facilities, good pool, varied restaurants, polite but friendly, lush gardens, unpretentious, relaxing, own ferry to City Palace. Recommended.

**LL-AL Laxmi Vilas Palace**, on hillock above Fateh Sagar, 5 km station, T0294-252 9711, www.thegrandhotels.net. 54 rooms are situated in the royal guesthouse (built in 1911), which are still atmospheric, and comfortable, but have less character. Good pool (non-residents, Rs 175), tennis. The suites are in the main palace.

**A-B Hilltop Palace**, 5 Ambavgarh near Fateh Sagar, T0294-243 2245, hilltop@datainfosys.net. 62 pleasant rooms (large rooms upstairs with balcony), restaurant (visit for a view from the roof!), bar, exchange, pool, good food, friendly and efficient service.

**B Jagat Niwas**, 24-25 Lal Ghat, T0294-242 0133, www.jagatniwaspalace. com. 30 individual, very clean rooms in beautifully restored 17th-century 'fairy tale' *haveli*, very good restaurant, helpful staff, good travel desk, excellent service. Recommended.

**B Lake Pichola**, Hanuman Ghat,overlooking lake, T0294-243 1197. 30 rooms, some a/c, poorly maintained, tired old baths, fantastic views from some rooms, boat rides, friendly, relatively cheap food.

**B Rajdarshan**, 18 Pannadhai Marg, inside Hathipol against the walls, by Swaroop Sagar lake edge, T0294-252 6601, rdarshan@sancharnet.in. 52 international standard, central a/c rooms, very good restaurant, bar, exchange, pool, good views from balconies though sacred peepul tree may block out your view! Pleasant service.

**B Rampratap Palace**, Fateh Sagar, T0294-243 1701, www.hotelrpp.com. A Rajput Special Hotel. Smart rooms, some a/c, most with lake views in new attr- active hotel, lawns, on busy road but friendly.

**B Shikarbadi** (HRH), Govardhan Vilas, Ahmedabad Rd, 5 km from centre, T0294-258 3201, www.hrhindia.com. 26 good, refurbished a/c rooms, pool, horse riding, attractive 100-year-old royal hunting lodge and stud farm with lake, lovely gardens, deer park, charming and peaceful.

B **Udai Kothi**, Hanuman Ghat, T0294-243 2810, www.udaikothi.com. 24 attractive rooms, real piece de resistance is Udaipur's only rooftop pool, a real treat. Management reported as uncaring. One guest was forced to sleep on the roof after her room caught fire!

B-C **Caravanserai**, Jaiwana Haveli, part mid-18th century, 14 Lal Ghat, T0294-252 1252, hotelcaravanserai@yahoo.com. 18 clean, modern rooms, some with great views, particularly good from rooftop restaurant.

B-C **Lakend**, Alkapuri, Fateh Sagar, T0294-243 1400, www.lakend.com. 78 average rooms, some a/c and private balconies, poorly maintained pool, large lakeside garden, very peaceful, excellent views.

B-C **Rang Niwas Palace**, Lake Palace Rd, T0294-252 3980, rangniwas75@hotmail.com. 20 beautifully renovated a/c rooms in 200-year-old building, some in newer annexe, old-world charm, restaurant, lovely pool, gardens, helpful staff, good location. Recommended.

C **Ashish Palace**, 125 Chetak Marg, T0294-252 5558, ashishpalace@rediffmail.com. 32 good rooms (most a/c) with bath, restaurant, friendly and helpful manager, crowded area but convenient for sightseeing, GPO, Tourist Office.

B-C **Sarovar**, Hanuman Ghat outside Chand-pol, T0294-243 2801, www.hotelsarovar.com. 21 slightly musty rooms on 3 floors in a new hotel, 13 with a/c overlook the lake, rooftop restaurant, sunbathing terrace, free use of good pool near Shilipgram (3 km away).

B-C **Swaroop Vilas**, 6 Ambavgarh, Swaroop Sagar Lake, T0294-243 0207, www.swaroopvilas.com. 28 a/c rooms in well-maintained, tastefully decorated hotel, okay views of lake, pleasant gardens and management.

C **Kankarwa Haveli**, 26 Lalghat, T0294-241 1457, khaveli@yahoo.com. 3 mins from bazar but quiet, impressive views from terrace, 14 clean, well-maintained rooms, some face lake, in renovated 250-year-old *haveli* on lake shore, breakfast and snacks on the roof terrace, meals on request, family run, lack of common sitting areas a problem in summer.

C **Sai Niwas**, 75 Navghat, T0294-242 1586. 6 slightly overpriced but characterful rooms in attractive old building, beautiful roof-terrace with good views of lake.

C-D **Anand Bhawan** (government run), Fateh Sagar Rd, T0294-252 3256. 22 rooms (lake-facing deluxe a/c rooms best), hilltop location with spectacular views, pleasant gardens, 1930s royal guesthouse, but getting increasingly rundown with unsatisfactory service, unhelpful management.

C-D **Kajri** (RTDC), Shastri Circle, T0294-241 0501. 53 rooms, some a/c, and dorm, deluxe overlooking garden best, restaurant (dull food), bar, travel, Tourist Reception Centre.

C-D **Poonam Haveli**, 39 Lal Ghat, T0294-241 0303, poonamhaveli@hotmail.com. 16 modern, attractive, clean rooms plus large roof terrace.

C-D **Raj Palace**, at 103, T0294-241 0364, rajpalaceudr@yahoo.com. 26 clean, comfortable rooms arranged around pleasant courtyard garden, rooftop restaurant, excellent service.

C-D **Wonder View**, 6 Panch Dewari Marg, near **Lake Pichola Hotel**, T0294-243 2494. 8 rooms (more coming) on 4 floors, fabulous views especially from rooftop restaurant (food arrives slowly from ground floor kitchen!), very friendly, excellent taxis, peaceful and relaxed part of town.

C-E **Mahendra Prakash**, Lake Palace Rd, T0294-241 9811, udai99@hotmail.com. 20 large, spotless, well furnished rooms, some a/c, pleasant patio garden, excellent pool, owner/manager of the Maharana's family, friendly, excellent service. Recommended.

D **Lake Ghat**, 4/13 Lalghat, 150 m behind Jagdish Mandir T0294-252 1636. 13 well-maintained rooms, clean, friendly, great views from terraces, good food.

D **Pratap Bhawan**, 12 Lal Ghat, T0294-256 0566, pratapbhawan@yahoo.co.in. 10 large, very clean rooms with baths in a lovely guest house, lake-facing terrace restaurant, excellent, home-cooked meals, warm welcome from retired army colonel and his wife. Recommended.

D **Pratap Country Inn**, Airport Rd, Titadhia Village, T0294-258 3138. 20 rooms, few a/c, restaurant, horse and camel safaris, riding, pool (sometimes empty), old royal country house in attractive grounds, 6 km centre (free transfer from railway station).

*For an explanation of sleeping and eating price codes used in this guide, see Inside the front cover. Other relevant information is found in Essentials, see pages 56-61.*

D-E **Jheel Guest House**, 56 Gangor Ghat (behind temple), T0294-421 352. 6 pleasant rooms in new extension with bath and hot water, 8 in older part, good rooftop restaurant, friendly owner, fantastic views.
**D-E Yatri Guest House**, 3/4 Panchkuin Rd, Udaipol, near the bus stand, T0294-241 7251. 13 simple rooms, helpful, knowledgeable owner, best option in area.
**E Dream Heaven**, just over Chandpol, on the edge of the lake, T0294-243 1038, deep_Rg@yahoo.co.uk. 6 clean, simple rooms with bath, family run, no frills but excellent rooftop restaurant.
**E Minerwa**, 5/13 Gadiya Devra, Chandpole, T0294-252 3471, minerwa66@hotmail.com. 16 plain, clean rooms in a modern, marble building, good restaurant (see Eating).
**E Udai Niwas**, near Jagdish Temple, Gangaur Marg, T0294-512 0789, hoteludainiwas@yahoo.co.in. 14 renovated rooms in friendly hotel with a pleasant rooftop and good views.
**E-F Badi Haveli**, near Jagdish Temple, T0294-241 2588, hotelbadahaveli@hotmail.com. 8 rooms with bath, some good, restaurant, travel services, terraces with lake view, pleasant atmosphere, very friendly owner.
**E-F Gangaur Palace**, 339 Ghadiya Devra Marg, T0294-242 2303. 17 rooms, some in old part of 250-year-old *haveli*, good standard, rooftop restaurant has 2 screens showing Octopussy plus one other film every night, friendly, if slightly slick, management.
**E-F Kumbha Palace**, 104 Bhatiyani Chotta, T0294-242 2702. 9 rooms, clean and quiet, good linen, very good rooftop restaurant (see below), atmospheric, views, attractive.
**E-F Lake Shore**, on Lake Pichola, near Lake Palace Rd, T0294-243 2480. Good views of ghats, 7 funkily decorated rooms, superb terrace, garden, very relaxing, friendly owner.
**E-F Lalghat Guest House**, 33 Lal Ghat, T0294-252 5301. 24 rooms, best with great lake views, best dorm in town (Rs 50), good clean beds with curtains (!), spotless baths, breakfast, snacks, drinks, good views from terraces, very relaxed, good travel desk. Recommended.
**E-F Mewar Inn**, 42 Residency Rd (pleasantly away from centre), T0294-252 2090, mewarinn@hotmail.com. 20 spotless rooms, some with (brief!) hot shower, street side very noisy, no commission to rickshaws (if they refuse to go; try a horse carriage!), **Osho** veg restaurant, good cheap bike hire, rickshaw to town Rs 10-20, very friendly, YHA discounts. Recommended.
**E-F Mughal Palace**, tucked away behind Lal Ghat, T0294-241 7954, mughalpalace2001@hotmail.com. 9 clean, smallish rooms, some with bath, Indian terrace restaurant, individually decorated home, solar power, internet, good value.
**E-F Natural**, 55 Rang Sagar (between New and Chandelle bridges), T0294-243 1979, hotelnatural@ hotmail.com. 16 clean, basic rooms with hot showers, sunny balconies facing lake, good restaurant (see below), peaceful, family-run, "a home from home".
**F Lehar**, T0294-241 7651. 5 rooms with bath, best with lake view. Run by charming lady.
**F Mona Lisa**, 104 Bhatiyani Chotta, T0294-256 1562. 8 rooms, some air-cooled, with bath, good breakfast, garden, newspaper, pleasant and quiet, family run, good value.
**F Nayee Haveli**, 55 Gangor Marg, T0294-512 0611, nayeehaveli@yahoo.co.uk. 5 clean, basic rooms in friendly family home, home-cooked food. Recommended.
**F Nukkad Guest House**, 56 Ganesh Ghat (signposted from Jagdish Temple). 10 small, simple rooms, some with bath, in typical family house, home-cooked meals, rooftop, very friendly and helpful, clean.
**F Rana Castle**, 4, Lal Ghat, T0294-241 3666, singh_bhagwat1@yahoo.com. 8 well-maintained rooms, particularly charming lower down. Pleasant rooftop restaurant.
**F Queens Café**, 14 Bajrang Marg (from Jagdish Temple, cross Chand Pol, then 1st left, continue for a few minutes to find the hotel on your right), T0294-243 0875. 2 decent rooms, shared bath, roof terrace with good views, home cooked meals (including continental Swiss), informal, welcoming family. Meenu teaches cooking and hindi. Highly recommended. See below.

## Eating

**Udaipur** *p341, map p343 and p344*
Try the local *daal, bhati, choorma*. The larger hotels have bars. Plush Heritage hotels (see Sleeping) have expensive menus. These are worth it just for the visit but the non-vegetarian buffet food can be kept warm for long periods and so can be risky. Below are a mix of restaurants within hotels and

just restaurants. Many of the budget places are in the Lal Ghat area. The usual fare includes pancakes, macaroni etc for the homesick westerner; some still show the locally shot Octopussy! Those near Jagdish Mandir do not serve alcohol.

**TTT Lake Palace**, see Sleeping, buffet lunch 1230-1430, dinner 1930-2030 often preceded by puppet show at 1800, expensive drinks (check bill), best way for non-residents to experience this unique palace Fateh Prakash's beautiful Gallery Restaurant. Superb views but pretty tasteless continental food, English cream teas. Tea also at Darbar Hall (see above).

**TTT Shiv Niwas**, see Sleeping, wonderful buffet followed by disappointing desserts, eat in the bar, or dine in luxury by the pool listening to live Indian classical music (Rs 1,000); bar expensive but the grand surroundings are worth a drink.

**TTT Sunset Terrace**, Bansi Ghat, Lake Pichola. Very pleasant, superb views of City Palace Complex and lake, good à la carte selection.

**TT Bagore-ki-Haveli**, Gangaur Ghat, T0294-309 0686. Multi-cuisine menu including some local specialities in fantastic setting by lake. Recommended.

**TT Berrys**, near Chetak Circle. International. Standard menu, comfortable, friendly, beer available, open 0900-2300.

**TT Jagat Niwas**, see Sleeping. Mainly Indian. Jarokha rooftop restaurant with fabulous lake views, excellent meals, breakfast, ices.

**TT Kumbha Palace**, see Sleeping, T0294-242 2702. Excellent Indian and western food. Rooftop, simple seating under awning (chocolate cake, baked potato, pizzas, milk shakes), friendly, helpful service, closed 1500-1800.

**TT Park View**, opposite Town Hall, City Station Rd. Good North Indian. Comfortable.

**TT Sai Niwas**, see Sleeping, 75 Nav Ghat. International. Excellent views from roof terrace, good evening meal, freshly cooked, attentive service.

**TT Sankalp**, outside Suraj Pol, City Station Rd, T0294-510 2686. Upmarket South Indian, modern, great range of chutneys.

**T Dream Haven**, 22 Bhim Parmeshver Marg, across Chandpol. Excellent, never ending *thalis* (Rs 25) on rooftop "watch the sun go down over the lake listening to the drums from the Jagdish Mandir".

**T Garden Hotel**, opposite Gulab Bagh, Gujarati/Rajasthani. The former royal garage of the Maharanas of Mewar. The original fuel pumps can still be seen in the forecourt where 19 cars from the ancestral fleet have been displayed. Air-cooled, excellent veg *thalis*, Rs 45 (try khadhi, khaman, makkhan buda), busy at lunch but not for dinner, interesting building, elderly waiters (will show you around kitchen). Recommended.

**T Gokul**, Gadiya Devra. Good range, great location, well-maintained. Recommended

**T Hariyali**, near Gulab Bagh. Has good North Indian in a pleasant garden setting.

**T Heaven**, street corner near Lal Ghat. International. A long climb up to rooftop, stunning uninterrupted lake views, usual fare (also cheap rooms).

**T King Roof Café**, Gangor Ghat. North Indian. Delicious spicy dishes, comfy chairs, usual rickety bamboo and matting for shade, most hospitable owner.

**T Mayur**, Mothi Chowtha, opposite Jagdish Temple. Mainly Indian. Pleasant for veg *thali* (Rs 45) snacks and Octopussy, but slow service, also exchange after hours (good rate if you walk away!), internet.

**T Natraj**, near Town Hall. Rajasthani. Excellent *thalis* in family run simple dining hall, very welcoming.

**T Purohit**, Anand Plaza. Good dosas.

**T 4 Seasons**, near City Palace, and **Green Rose Café**. Western and Indian (mild). Very good food (but irregular hours). Both recommended.

**T Queens Café**, 14 Bajrang Marg (see Sleeping). Fantastic unusual dishes including mango curries and irresistible chocolate balls. Highly recommended. Also cooking lessons, see below.

**T Samore Garden**, opposite Rang Niwas Hotel, Lake Palace Rd, has a wide international menu, open later than most, no beer.

## Entertainment

**Udaipur** *p341, map p343 and p344*

**Bagore-ki-Haveli**, T0294-242 3610 after 1700. Daily cultural shows 1900-2000, enjoyable music and dance performances, reservations unnecessary.

**Bharatiya Lok Kala Museum**, T0294-252 9296. The 20-min puppet demonstrations during the day are good fun. Evening

puppet show and folk dancing 1800-1900, Sep-Mar, Rs 30, camera Rs 50. Recommended.
**Meera Kala Mandir**, south of railway station, T0294-258 3176. Daily except Sun, 1900-2000, Rs 60; cultural programme, a bit touristy and amateurish. See Shilipgram in the sights section above.

## Festivals and events

**Udaipur** *p341, map p343 and p344*
Mewar Festival (1-2 Apr 2006, 21-22 Mar 2007). See also p61 for statewide festivals.

## Shopping

**Udaipur** *p341, map p343 and p344*
The local handicrafts are wooden toys, colourful portable temples (*kavad*), Bandhani tie-and-dye fabrics, embroidery and Pichchwai paintings. Paintings are of 3 types: miniatures in the classical style of courtly Mewar; phads or folk art; and pichchwais or religious art (see Nathdwara, p355). The more expensive ones are 'old' – 20-30 years – and are in beautiful dusky colours; the cheaper ones are brighter.

The main shopping centres are Chetak Circle, Bapu Bazar, Hathipol, Palace Rd, Clock Tower, Nehru Bazar, Shastri Circle, Delhi Gate, Sindhi Bazar, Bada Bazar.

### Books

**Mewar International**, 35 Lalghat. A wide selection of English books, exchange, films.
**Pustak Sadan** (Hindi sign), Bapu Bazar, near Town Hall. Good for Rajasthani history.
**Sai**, 168 City Palace Rd, 100 m from palace gate. Good English books (new and second-hand), internet, exchange, travel services.
**Suresh**, Hospital Rd, good fiction, non-fiction and academic books.

### Fabric

**Ashoka**, opposite entrance to Shiv Niwas. Good quality but very expensive.
**Monsoon Collection**, 55 Bhatiyani Chotta. Quick, quality, tailoring. Recommended.
**Shree Ji Saree Centre**, Mothi Chowtha, 200 m from Temple. Good value, very helpful owner. Recommended.
**Udaipur New Tailors**, inside Hathipol. Gents tailoring, reasonably priced, excellent service.

### Handicrafts and paintings

Some shops sell old pieces of embroidery turned into bags, cushion covers etc. Others may pass off recent work as antique.
**Ashoka Arts**, **Uday Arts**, Lake Palace Rd, **Apollo Arts**, 28 Panchwati. Paintings on marble paper and 'silk', bargain hard. Hathipol shop has good silk scarves (watch batik work in progress).
**Gallery Pristine**, T0294-242 3916, Kalapi House, Bhatiyani Chotta, Palace Rd. Good collection of contemporary art, including original 'white on brown' paintings, pleasant ambience. Recommended.
**Gangour**, Mothi Chowtha. Quality miniature paintings.
**Gem-arts**, near Chetak Circle.
**Jagdish Emporium**, City Palace Rd. For traditional Udaipur and Gujarati embroideries.
**KK Kasara**, opposite Nami Gali, 139 Mothi Chowtha. Good religious statues, jewellery.
**Shivam Ayurvedic**, Lake Palace Rd. Also art store, interesting, knowledgeable owner.
**Sisodia Handicrafts**, entrance of Shiv Niwas Palace. Miniature 'needle paintings' of high quality – see artist at work, no hard sell.

## Activities and tours

**Udaipur** *p341, map p343 and p344*

### Art, cooking and hindi classes

**Hare Krishna Arts**, City Palace Rd, T0294-242 0304. Rs 450 per 2-hrart lesson, miniature techniques a speciality. Cooking classes too.
**Queens Café**, 14 Bajrang Marg, T0294-243 0875. Rs900 for 5-hr introductory class in basics of Indian cooking. Also Hindi lesson. Both are highly recommended.

### Massage

**Bharti Guesthouse**, Lake Pichola Rd, T0294-243 3469. Indian, Swiss and Mexican styles at reasonable prices.

### Riding

On elephant, camel or horse: travel agencies (eg **Namaskar**, **Parul** in Lalghat) arrange elephant and camel rides, Rs 200 per hr but need sufficient notice. Horse riding through hotels (**Shikarbadi**, **Pratap Country Inn** and some castles around Udaipur).

**Sightseeing tours**

Offered by RTDC Fath Memorial, Suraj Pol. City sightseeing: half day (0800-1230) Rs 75(reported as poor). Excursion: half day (1400-1900), Haldighati, Nathdwara, Eklingji, Rs 105. Chittaurgarh (0800-1800), Rs 230 (with lunch); Ranakpur, Kumbhalgarh (0800-1900) Rs 230; Jagat-Jaisamand-Chavand-Rishabdeo (0800-1900) Rs 230 (with lunch).

Some of the following tour operators offer, as well as sightseeing tours, accommodation bookings and travel tickets.

**Aravalli Safari**, 1 Sheetla Marg, Lake Palace Rd, T0294-2420282, F2420121. Very professional. Recommended.

**Forts & Palaces**, 34-35 Shrimal Bhawan, Garden Rd, T0294-417359, jaipur@palaces-tours.com.

**Parul**, **Jagat Niwas Hotel**, Lalghat, T0294-242 1697, parul_tour@rediffmail.com. Air/train, palace hotels, car hire, exchange. Highly recommended.

**Rajasthan Travels**, excellent service.

**Srinath Travel**, T0294-252 9391. Direct buses to Mount Abu, Mumbai etc. Recommended.

**Tourist Assistance Centre**, 3 Paneri House, Bhatiyani Chotta, T0294-252 8169. Guides.

**Swimming**

Some hotel pools are open to non-residents: **Lakshmi Vilas** (Rs 175); **Rang Niwas** (Rs 100); **Shiv Niwas** (Rs 300). Also at Shilipgram Craft Village, Rs 100.

## Transport

**Udaipur** *p341, map p343 and p344*

**Air**

Dabok airport is 25 km east, T0294-265 5453. Security check is thorough; no batteries or knives allowed in hand luggage. Transport to town: taxis, Rs 190. **Indian Airlines**, Delhi Gate, T0294-241 0999, 1000-1315, 1400-1700. Airport, T0294-265 5453, enquiry T142. Reserve well ahead. **Indian Airlines** flights to **Aurangabad**; **Delhi**, US$90; **Jaipur**, **Jaisalmer**, **Jodhpur**, **Mumbai**. Jet Airways, T0294-256 5105, airport T0294-265 6288: **Delhi** via **Jaipur**, **Mumbai**. UP Air, daily to **Delhi**, **Jaipur**, **Mumbai**, **Rajkot**.

**Auto-rickshaw**

Rs 5, then Rs 3 per km; about Rs 50 per hr.

**Bicycle**

**Vijay Cycles**, half way down Bhatiyani Chotta, charge Rs 25 per day for hire, well-maintained and comfortable. Also shops near **Kajri Hotel**, Lalghat and Gangor Ghat area, which also have scooters (Rs 125 per day).

**Bus**

**Long distance** Main State Bus Stand, near railway line opposite Udai Pol, T0294-248 4191; reservations 0700-2100. State RTC buses to **Agra** 15 hrs; **Ahmadabad** 252 km, 7 hrs; **Bhopal** 765 km, 15 hrs; **Bikaner** 13 hrs; **Delhi** 635 km, 17 hrs; **Indore** 635 km; **Jaipur** 405 km, 10 hrs; **Jaisalmer** 14 hrs; **Jodhpur** 8 hrs (uncomfortable, poorly maintained road); **Mount Abu** 270 km, 0800, 1030 and 1500, 7 hrs), Rs 50 (Tourist bus, Rs 75, not much faster); **Mumbai** 802 km, very tiring, 16 hrs; **Pushkar** (Tourist bus, 7 hrs, Rs 90); **Ujjain** (7 hrs). Private buses and Luxury coaches run mostly at night. **Ahmadabad** with Bonney Travels, Paldi, Ahmedabad, has a/c coaches with reclining seats (contact Shobha Travels, City Station Rd), departs 1400 (6½ hrs), Rs 225, with drink/snack stops every 2 hrs. Highly recommended. Shrinath and Punjab Travels have non a/c buses to **Ahmedabad** and **Mount Abu**. **Jaipur**: several 'deluxe' buses (computerized booking) with reclining seats, Rs 200, more expensive but better. **Jaisalmer**: change at Jodhpur, Rs 160. **Jodhpur**: several options but best to book a good seat, a day ahead, RS90. Tour operators have taxis for **Kumbhalgarh** and **Ranakpur**.

**Motorbike**

Scooters and bikes can be hired from Heera Tours & Travels in a small courtyard behind Badi Haveli (Jagdish Temple area), Rs150-300 per day depending on size of machine.

**Taxi**

RTDC taxis from Fath Memorial, Suraj Pol. Private taxis from airport, railwayy station, bus stands and major hotels; negotiate rates. Taxi Stand, Chetak Circle, T0294-252 5112. Tourist Taxi Service, Lake Palace Rd, T0294-252 4169.

**Train**

Udaipur City station, 4 km southeast of centre, T0294-131. **Ahmadabad**:

*Ahmadabad Exp, 9943*, 2115, 9½ hrs. **Ajmer**: *Delhi SR Exp, 9944*, 0800, 13 hrs; *Chetak Exp, 9616*, 1810, 8½ hrs. **Delhi (SR)**: *Delhi SR Exp, 9944*, 0800, 23½ hrs; *Chetak Exp, 9616*, 1810, 17½ hrs (best to change at Jaipur at 0715 to faster Intercity for Delhi Junction station). **Jalgaon**: (day and night trains) to visit Ajanta, Aurangabad, Ellora. **Jaipur**: *Delhi SR Exp, 9944*, 0830, 15 hrs; *Chetak Exp, 9616*, 1810, 11½ hrs.

## Directory

**Udaipur** *p341, map p343 and p344*

**Banks** Foreign exchange at Andhra Bank, Shakti Nagar. Cash advance against Visa/ Mastercard, efficient. Bank of Baroda, Bapu Bazar. For Amex. Bank of Bikaner & Jaipur, Chetak Circle. Thomas Cook, inside City Palace. But poor rates. Trade Wings, Polo Ground Rd, Vijaya Bank, City Palace entrance. **Chemists** On Hospital Rd. **Hospitals** General Hospital, Chetak Circle. Aravali Hospital (private), 332 Ambamata Main Rd, opposite Charak Hostel, T0294-243 0222, very clean, professional. Recommended. **Internet** Mayur, Mothi Chowtha. Mewar, Raj Palace Hotel, Bhatiyani Chotta, One Stop Shop, near Lal Ghat Guest House. Sai, 168 City Palace Rd. Thomas Cook in City Palace Courtyard. Cyber Café near Jagat Niwas. **Post** The GPO is at Chetak Circle. Posting a parcel can be a nightmare. Poste Restante: Shastri Circle Post Office. **Useful addresses** Ambulance: T223 333. Fire: T227 111. Police: T100.

# Around Udaipur

*The area around Udaipur is dotted with a wide range of attractions, from some of the grandest of Rajasthan's heritage hotels to some of its cosiest castles, from secluded forest lakes, surrounded by wildlife, to one of the largest reservoirs in Asia. It's also home to some ancient temples and perhaps the most evocative of Rajasthan's plentiful palaces, the Juna Mahal near Dungarpur.*

## Ins and outs

Most of the sights in this area are a little isolated and so not well connected by train. However, the quality of the region's roads has greatly improved recently, making travel either by bus or taxi both quick and convenient. » *See Transport, page 357, for details.*

## Monsoon Palace

ⓘ *No formal fee but caretaker expects a tip (about Rs 20 per person). 15 km west. Taxis minimum Rs 300 (tourist taxis Rs 450 including road toll), auto-rickshaws Rs 200 return including road toll. Allow about 3 hrs for the round trip.*

There are good views from this deserted palace on a hilltop. The unfinished building on **Sajjangarh**, at an altitude of 335 m, which looks picturesque from the west facing battlements, was named after Sajjan Singh (1874-1884) and was planned to be high enough to see his ancestral home, Chittaurgarh. Normally, you need a permit from the police in town to enter though many find a tip to the gateman suffices. It offers panoramic views of Udaipur (though the highest roof is spoilt by radio antennas); the windows of the Lake Palace can be seen reflecting the setting sun. The palace itself is very rundown but the views from the hill top are just as good. A visit in the late afternoon is recommended; take binoculars.

## Jaisamand Lake → *Colour map 2, grid B4. 52 km southeast of Udaipur.*

Before the building of huge modern dams in India, Jaisamand was the second largest artificial lake in Asia, 15 km by 10 km. Dating from the late 17th century, it is surrounded by the summer palaces of the Ranis of Udaipur. The highest two of the surrounding hills are topped by the **Hawa Mahal** and **Ruti Rani palaces,** now empty but worth visiting for the architecture and the view. A small sanctuary nearby has deer, antelope and panther. Tribals still inhabit some islands on the lake. Crocodiles, keelback water snakes and turtles bask on other islands.

## Bambora → *45-minutes' drive southeast of Udaipur.*

The imposing 18th-century hilltop fortress of Bambora has been converted to a heritage hotel by the royal family of Sodawas at an enormous restoration cost yet retaining its ancient character. The impressive fort is in Mewari style with domes, turrets and arches. To get here from Udaipur, go 12 km east along the airport road and take the right turn towards Jaisamand Lake passing the 11th-century Jagat Temple (38 km) before reaching Bambora.

## Sitamata Wildlife Sanctuary → *117 km from Udaipur.*

The reserve of dense deciduous forests covers over 400 sq km and has extensive birdlife (woodpeckers, tree pies, blue jays, jungle fowl). It is one of the few sanctuaries between the Himalayas and the Nilgiris where giant brown flying squirrels have been reported. Visitors have seen hordes of langur monkey, nilgai in groups of six or seven, four-horned antelope, jackal and even panther and hyena, but the thick forests make sighting difficult. There are crocodiles in the reservoirs.

## Rishabdeo → *63 km south of Udaipur along the NH8.*

Rishabdeo, off the highway, has a remarkable 14th-century Jain temple with intricate white marble carving and black marble statuary, though these are not as fine as at Dilwara or Ranakpur. Dedicated to the first Jain Tirthankar, Adinath or Rishabdev, Hindus, Bhils as well as Jains worship there. An attractive bazar street leads to the temple which is rarely visited by tourists. Special worship is conducted several times daily when Adinath, regarded as the principal focus of worship, is bathed with saffron water or milk. The priests are friendly; a small donation (Rs 10-20) is appreciated.



## Dungarpur → *Phone code: 02964. Colour map 2, grid B5. Population 50,000.*

Dungarpur ('City of Hills') dates from the 13th century. The district is the main home of the Bhil tribal people, see page 318. It is also renowned for its stone masons, who in recent years have been employed to build Hindu temples as far afield as London. The attractive and friendly village has one of the most richly decorated and best preserved palaces in Rajasthan, the Juna Mahal. Surrounded on three sides by Lake Gaibsagar and backed by picturesque hills, the more recent **Udai Bilas Palace** (now a heritage hotel, see Sleeping) was built by Maharawal Udai Singhji in the 19th century and extended in 1943. The huge courtyard surrounds a 'pleasure pool' from the centre of which rises a four-storeyed pavilion with a beautifully carved wooden chamber.

*Dungarpur is a bird-watchers' paradise with lots of ducks, moorhens, waders, ibises at the lake, tropical green pigeons and grey hornbills in the woods.*

The **Juna Mahal**, above the village, dates from the 13th century when members of the Mewar clan at Chittaur moved south to found a new kingdom after a family split. It is open to guests staying at Udai Bilas and by ticket for non residents, obtainable at the hotel. The seven-storeyed fortress-like structure with turrets, narrow entrances and tiny windows has colourful and vibrant rooms profusely decorated over several centuries with miniature wall paintings (among the best in Rajasthan),and glass and mirror inlay work. There are some fine *jarokha* balconies and sculpted panels illustrating musicians and dancers in the local green-grey parava stone which are strikingly set against the plain white walls of the palace to great effect. The steep narrow staircases lead to a series of seven floors giving access to public halls, supported on decorated columns, and to intimate private chambers. There is a jewel of a Sheesh Mahal and a cupboard in the Maharawal's bedroom on the top floor covered in miniatures illustrating some 50 scenes from the Kama Sutra. Windows and balconies open to the breeze command lovely views over the town below. Perhaps nowhere else in Rajasthan gives as good an impression of how these palaces must have been hundreds of years ago; it is completely unspoilt and hugely impressive. 

Some interesting temples nearby include the 12th-century Siva temple at **Deo Somnath**, 12 km away, and the splendid complex of temple ruins profusely decorated with stone sculptures.

## Khempur

This small, attractive village is conveniently located midway between Udaipur and Chittaurgarh. To find it turn off the highway, 9 km south of Mavli and about 50 km from Udaipur. The main reason for visiting is to eat or stay in the charming heritage hotel here, see Sleeping.

## Eklingji and Nagda → *22 km from Udaipur.*

*ⓘ 0400-0700, 1000-1300 and 1700-1900. No photography.*

The white marble **Eklingji Temple** has a two-storey mandapa to Siva, the family deity of the Mewars. It dates from AD 734 but was rebuilt in the 15th century. There is a silver door and screen and a silver Nandi facing the black marble Siva. The evenings draw crowds of worshippers and few tourists. Many smaller temples surround the main one and are also worth seeing. Nearby is the large but simple **Lakulisa Temple** (972), and other ruined semi-submerged temples. The back-street shops sell miniature paintings, see page 318. It is a peaceful spot attracting many waterbirds. Occasional buses go from Udaipur to Eklingji and Nagda which are set in a deep ravine containing the Eklingji Lake. RTDC run tours from Udaipur, 1400-1900.

At Nagda, are three temples: the ruined 11th-century Jain temple of **Adbhutji** and the **Vaishnavite Sas-Bahu** ('Mother-in-law'/'Daughter-in-law') temples. The complex, though comparatively small, has some very intricate carving on pillars, ceiling and mandapa walls. You can hire bicycles in Eklingji to visit them. There are four 14th century Jain Temples at **Delwara** about 5 km from Eklingji which also boast the Devi Garh, one of India's most luxurious hotels.

## Nathdwara → *Colour map 2, grid B4. 48 km from Udaipur.*

This is a centre of the Krishna worshipping community of Gujarati merchants who are followers of Vallabhacharya (15th century). Non-Hindus are not allowed inside the temple which contains a black marble Krishna image, but the outside has interesting paintings. **Shrinathji temple** is one of the richest Hindu temples in India. At one time only high caste Hindus (Brahmins, Kshatriyas) were allowed inside, and the *pichhwais* (temple hangings) were placed outside, for those castes and communities who were not allowed into the sanctum sanctorum, to experience the events in the temple courtyard and learn about the life of lord Krishna. You can watch the 400-year-old tradition of *pichhwai* painting which originated here. The artists had accompanied the Maharana of Mewar, one of the few Rajput princes who still resisted the Mughals, who settled here when seeking refuge from Aurangzeb's attacks. Their carriage carrying the idol of Shrinathji was stuck at Nathdwara in Mewar, 60 km short of the capital Udaipur. Taking this as a sign that this was where God willed to have his home, they developed this into a pilgrim centre for the worship of lord Krishna's manifestation, Shrinathji. Their paintings, *pichhwais*, depict Lord Krishna as Shrinathji in different moods according to the season. The figures of lord Krishna and the gopis (milkmaids) are frozen on a backdrop of lush trees and deep skies. The Bazar sells pichchwais painted on homespun cloth with mineral and organic colour often fixed with starch.

## Rajsamand Lake → *Colour map 2, grid B4. 56 km north of Udaipur.*

At **Kankroli**, is the Rajsamand Lake. The **Nauchoki Bund**, the embankment which contains it, is over 335-m long and 13-m high, with ornamental pavilions and *toranas*, all of marble and exquisitely carved. Behind the masonry bund is an 11-m wide earthen embankment, erected in 1660 by Rana Raj Singh who had defeated Aurangzeb on several occasions. He also commissioned the longest inscription in the world, "Raj Prashasthi Maha Kavyam", which tells the story of Mewar on 24 granite slabs in skanskrit. Kankroli and its beautiful temple are on the southeast side of the lake.

## Deogarh → *Colour map 2, grid B4. 2 km off the NH8. Altitude: 700 m.*

Deogarh (Devgarh) is an excellent place to break journey between Jaipur or Pushkar, and Udaipur to visit sights nearby. It is a very pleasant, little frequented town with a dusty but interesting bazar (if you are interested in textiles, visit **Vastra Bhandar**, T02904 252187, for reasonably priced and good quality textiles). Its elevation makes it relatively cool and the countryside and surrounding hills are good for gentle treks. There is an old fort on a hill as well as a magnificent palace on a hillock in the centre with murals illustrating the fine local school of miniature painting. **Raghosagar Lake**, which is very pleasant to walk around, has an island with a romantic ruined temple and centotaphs (poor monsoons leave the lake dry). It attracts numerous migratory birds and is an attractive setting for the charming 200-year-old palace, **Gokal Vilas**, the home of the present Rawat Saheb Nahar Singhji and the Ranisahiba. Their two sons have opened the renovated 17th-century **Deogarh Mahal Palace** to guests, see Sleeping. The Rawat, a knowledgeable historian and art connoisseur, has a private collection of over 50 paintings which guests may view, advance notice required. The shop at the hotel has good modern examples to buy. There is plenty to do here including an excellent 45-minute train journey from Deogarh to Phulud which winds down through the Aravalli hills to the plain below through tunnels and bridges.



## Sleeping

### Jaisamand Lake *p353*

**B Jaisamand Island Resort**, Baba Island on Jaisamand Lake, T02906-234 723, www.lakend.com. 40 well equipped a/c rooms, restaurant (international menu), pool, garden, excellent location, great views, mixed reports on food and service.

### Bambora *p354*

**A Karni Fort** (Heritage Hotel), Bambora, T0291-251 2101, www.karnihotels.com. 30 beautifully decorated rooms (circular beds!) in large, imposing fort, marble bathrooms, mod- ern facilities, impressive interiors, enthusiastic and friendly manager, exceptional marble pool, folk concerts, great beer bar, delicious food, hugely enjoyable. Recommended.

### Sitamata Wildlife Sanctuary *p354*

**B-C Fort Dhariawad**, Sitamata Wildlife Sanctuary, T02950-220050. 14 rooms and 4 suites in restored and converted, mid-16th century fort (founded by one of Maharana Pratap's sons) and some in contemporary cottage cluster, meals (international menu), period decor, medieval flavour, great location by sanctuary (flying squirrels, langur monkeys in garden, crocodiles in reservoir), tribal village tours, jeeps to park, horse safaris, treks.

**D Forest Lodge**, Sitamata Wildlife Sanctuary, Dhariawad. Rather expensive considering lack of amenities, but fantastic location and views, a paradise for birders.

*For an explanation of sleeping and eating price codes used in this guide, see inside the front cover. Other relevant information is found in Essentials, see pages 56-61.*

**Dungarpur** *p354*

**A Udai Bilas Palace**, 2 km from town, Dungarpur, T02964-230 808, www. udaibilas palace.com. 20 unique a/c rooms (including 10 suites of which 3 are vast 'grand suites') mirror mosaics, some dated with art deco furniture, marble bathrooms some with modern furniture in old guest house, all with either a lake or garden view, good food (lunch Rs 380) a 'Country House' style hotel (guests dine together at one table) where Harshvardhan Singh is a charming host, beautiful new pool, boating, TCs and credit cards accepted, idyllic setting, very relaxing. Highly recommended.

**E-F Vaibhav**, Saghwara Rd, Dungarpur, T02964-230 244. Simple rooms, tea stall style restaurant, owner very friendly and helpful.

**Khempur** *p355*

**B Ravla Khempur**, Khempur, T02955-237 154, www.ravlakhempur.com. The former home of the village chieftain, this is a charming, small-scale heritage property. The rooms have been sensitively renovated with modern bathrooms, pleasant lawns, horse rides a speciality.

**Eklingji and Nagda** *p355*

**B Heritage Resort**, Eklingji, T0294-440382. Fabulously located by the lake and ringed by hills. 30 excellent a/c rooms, contemporary building in traditional design, good food, pool, jacuzzi, boating, riding, good walking and cycling. Recommended.

**LL Devi Garh**, at Delwara, 5 km from Eklingji, T02953-289211, www.deviresorts. com, for the ultimate in luxury. It specializes in letting all 30 individually decorated suites for fabulous weddings or parties!

**Nathdwara** *p355*

**D-E Gokul** (RTDC), near Lalbagh, 2 km from bus stand, Nathdwara, T02953-230 917. 6 rooms and dorm (Rs 50), restaurant.

**D-E Yatika** (RTDC), Nathdwara, T02953-231 119. 5 rooms and dorm (Rs 50).

**Deogarh** *p356*

**A-B Deogarh Mahal**, Deogarh, T02904-252 777, www.deogarhmahal.com. 50 rooms in superb old fort built in 1617, including atmospheric suites furnished in traditional style with good views, best have balconies with private Jacuzzis. Fabulous keyhole-shaped pool, Keralan massage Mewari meals, home grown produce (room service 50% extra), bar, good gift shop, log fires, folk entertainment, boating, bird watching, jeep safaris, talks on art history, hospitable and delightful hosts. Outstanding hotel. Reserve well ahead. Highly recommended. The family have also renovated the **Singh Sagar** fort, 5 km from Deograh, with 4 superbly decorated suites. It is in the middle of a small lake (sadly dry) and is an ideal hideaway. Prices start at US$350 per night.

## ❁ Festivals and events

**Dungarpur** *p354*

**Baneshwar Fair** (8-12 Feb 2006, 29 Jan-2 Feb 2007). The tribal festival at the Baneshwar Temple, 70 km from Dungarpur, is one of Rajasthan's largest tribal fairs when Bhils, see p, gather to the temple in large numbers for ritual bathing at the confluence of rivers. There are direct buses to Baneshwar during the fair. The temporary camp during the fair is best avoided. **Vagad Festival** in Dungarpur offers an insight into local tribal culture. Both are uncommercialized and authentic. Details from **Udai Bilas**, see Sleeping.

## Transport

**Around Udaipur** *p353*

For **Nathdwara**, several buses from Udaipur from early morning. Buses also go to **Nagda**, **Eklingji** and **Rajsamand**. Private transport only for Khempur and Deogarh.

From Dungarpur buses travel to/from **Udaipur** (110 km), 2 hrs, **Ahmadabad** (170 km), 4 hrs by car. You will need to hire a taxi to get to the other destinations.

# Kumbhalgarh, Ranakpur and around

*Little-known Kumbhalgarh is one of the finest examples of defensive fortification in Rajasthan. You can wander around the palace, the many temples and along the walls – 36-km long in all – to savour the great panoramic views. It is two hours north (63 km) of Udaipur through the attractive Rajasthani countryside. The small fields are well kept and Persian wheels and 'tanks' are dotted across the landscape. In winter, wheat and mustard grow in the fields, and the journey there and back is as magical as the fort.*

*The temples of Ranakpur are incredibly ornate and amazingly unspoilt by tourism, having preserved a dignified air which is enhanced by the thick green forests that surround them. There are a number of interesting villages and palaces in the nearby area; if time allows this is a great region to explore at leisure, soaking in the unrushed, rural way of life.* ➡ *For Sleeping, Eating and other listings, see pages 360-362.*

## Kumbhalgarh → *Phone code: 02954. Colour map 2, grid B4. 63 km from Udaipur.*

### Kumbhalgarh Fort → *Altitude: 1,087m.*

Kumbhalgarh Fort, off the beaten tourist track, was the second most important fort of the Mewar Kingdom after Chittaurgarh. Built mostly by Maharana Kumbha (circa 1485), it is situated on a west facing ridge of the Aravalli hills, commanding a great strategic position on the border between the Rajput kingdoms of Udaipur (Mewar) and Jodhpur (Marwar). It is accessible enough to make a visit practicable and getting there is half the fun. There are superb views over the lower land to the northwest, standing over 200 m above the pass leading via Ghanerao towards Udaipur.

**The approach** Passing though charming villages and hilly terrain, the route to the fort is very picturesque. The final dramatic approach is across deep ravines and through thick scrub jungle. Seven gates guarded the approaches while seven ramparts were reinforced by semicircular bastions and towers. The 36 km-long black walls with curious bulbous towers exude a feeling of power as they snake their way up and down impossibly steep terrain. They were built to defy scaling and their width enabled rapid deployment of forces – six horses could walk along them side by side. The walls enclose a large plateau containing the smaller Katargarh Fort with the decaying palace of Fateh Singh, a garrison, 365 temples and shrines, and a village. The occupants (reputedly 30,000) could be self-sufficient in food and water, with enough storage to last a year. The fort's dominant location enabled defenders to see aggressors approaching from a great distance. Kumbhalgarh is believed to have been taken only once and that was because the water in the ponds was poisoned by enemy Mughals during the reign of Rana Pratap.

**The gates** The first gate Arait Pol is some distance from the main fort; the area was once thick jungle harbouring tigers and wild boar. Signals would be flashed by mirror in times of emergency. Hulla Pol (Gate of Disturbance) is named after the point reached by invading Mughal armies in 1567. Hanuman Pol contains a shrine and temple. The Bhairava Pol records the 19th-century Chief Minister who was exiled. The fifth gate, the Paghra (Stirrup) Pol is where the cavalry assembled; the Star tower nearby has walls 8-m thick. The Top-Khana (Cannon Gate) is alleged to have a secret escape tunnel. The last, Nimbu (Lemon) Pol has the Chamundi temple beside it.

**The palace** ⓘ *Rs 5, Rs 100 foreigners.* It is a 30-minute walk (fairly steep in parts) from the car park to the roof of the Maharana's darbar hall. Tiers of inner ramparts rise to the summit like a fairytale castle, up to the appropriately named Badal Mahal (19th century) or Palace in the Clouds, with the interior painted in pastel colours. Most of the empty palace is usually unlocked (a chaukidar holds the keys). The views over the walls to the jungle-covered hillsides (now a wildlife reserve) and across the deserts of Marwar towards Jodhpur, are stunning. The palace rooms are decorated in a 19th-century style and some have attractive coloured friezes, but are unfurnished. After the maze-like palace at Udaipur, this is very compact. The Maharana's palace has a remarkable blue darbar hall with floral motifs on the ceiling. Polished chunar – lime – is used on walls and window sills, but the steel ceiling girders give away its late 19th-century age. A gap separated the mardana (men's) palace from the *zenana* (women's) palace. Some of the rooms in the *zenana* have an attractive painted frieze with elephants, crocodiles and camels. A circular Ganesh temple is in the corner of the *zenana* courtyard. A striking feature of the toilets was the ventilation system which allowed fresh air into the room while the toilet was in use.

## Kumbhalgarh Wildlife Sanctuary

ⓘ *Rs 10, Rs 100 foreigner, open sunrise to sunset.*

The sanctuary to the west of the fort covering about 600 sq km has a sizeable wildlife population but you have to be extremely lucky to spot any big game in the thick undergrowth. Some visitors have seen bear, panther, wolf and hyena but most have to be contented with seeing nilgai, sambhar deer, wild boar, jackal, jungle cat, and birds. Crocodiles and water fowl can be seen at **Thandi Beri Lake**. Jeep and horse safaris can be organized from hotels in the vicinity including **Aodhi**, **Ranakpur**, **Ghanerao**, **Narlai**. The rides can be quite demanding as the tracks are very rough. There is a four-wheel drive jeep track, and a trekking trail through the safari area can be arranged through **Shivika Lake Hotel**, Ranakpur (see below).

The tribal **Bhils** and **Garasias**, see page 318 – the latter found only in this belt – can be seen here, living in their traditional huts. The Forest Department may permit an overnight stay in their **Rest House** in **Kelwara**, the closest town, 6 km from sanctuary. With steep, narrow streets devoid of cars it is an attractive little place.

# Ghanerao and Rawla Narlai → *Colour map 2, grid B4.*

Ghanerao was founded in 1606 by Gopal Das Rathore of the Mertia clan, and has a number of red sandstone *havelis* as well as several old temples, *baolis* and marble *chhatris*, 5 km beyond the reserve. The village lay at the entrance to one of the few passes through the Aravallis between the territories held by the Rajput princes of Jodhpur and Udaipur. The beautiful 1606 castle has marble pavilions, courtyards, paintings, wells, elephant stables and walls marked with canon balls. The present Thakur Sajjan Singh has opened his castle to guests, see Sleeping, and organizes two- to three-day treks to Kumbhalgarh Fort, 50 km by jeepable road, and Ranakpur.

The **Mahavir Jain Temple**, 5 km away, is a beautiful little 10th-century temple. It is a delightful place to experience an unspoiled rural environment.

**Rawla Narlai**, 25 km from Kumbhalgarh Fort, and an hours drive from Ranakpur, is a Hindu and Jain religious centre. It has a 17th-century fort with interesting architecture, right in the heart of the village, which is ideal for a stop over.

# Ranakpur → *Phone code: 02934. Colour map 2, grid B4. 90 km Udaipur, 25 km Kumbhalgarh.*

ⓘ *Daily; non-Jains may visit the Adinatha 1200-1700. Photos (1200-1700) with permission from Kalyanji Anandji Trust office next to the temple, camera Rs 50, video Rs 150, photography of the principal Adinatha image is prohibited.*

One of five holy Jain sites and a popular pilgrimage centre, it has one of the best known Jain temple complexes in the country. Though not comparable to the Dilwara temples in Mount Abu, it has very fine ornamentation and is in a wonderful setting with peacocks, langurs and numerous birds. The semi-enclosed deer park with spotted deer, nilgai and good birdlife next to the temple, attracts the odd panther! You can approach Ranakpur from Kumbhalgarh through the wildlife reserve in 1½ hours although you will need to arrange transport from the Sanctuary entrance. A visit is highly recommended.

*Shoes and socks must be removed at the entrance. Black clothing is not permitted. No tips though unofficial 'guide' may ask for baksheesh.*

The **Adinatha** (1439), the most noteworthy of the three main temples here, is dedicated to the first Tirthankar. Of the 1,444 engraved pillars, in Jain tradition, no two are the same, each individually carved. The sanctuary is symmetrically planned around the central shrine and is within a 100-sq m raised terrace enclosed in a high wall with 66 subsidiary shrines lining it, each with a spire; the gateways consist of triple-storey porches. The sanctuary with a clustered centre tower contains a *chaumukha* (four-fold) marble image of Adinatha. The whole complex, including the extraordinary array of engraved pillars, carved ceilings and arches are intricately decorated, often with images of Jain saints, friezes of scenes from their lives and holy sites. The beautiful lace-like interiors of the corbelled domes are a superb example of western Indian temple style. The **Parsvanatha** and **Neminath** are two smaller Jain temples facing this, the former with a black image of Parsvanatha in the sanctuary and erotic carvings outside. The star-shaped **Surya Narayana Temple** (mid-15th century) is nearby.

There is a beautiful 3.7-km trek around the wildlife sanctuary, best attempted from November to March, contact sanctuary office next to temples for information.

## Sleeping

**Kumbhalgarh** *p358*

**A Aodhi** (HRH), 2 km from fort gate, T02954-242 341, www.hrhindia.com. Closest place to fort, great location set in to the rock face. 27 rooms in modern stone 'cottages' decorated in colonial style to good effect with attached modern bathrooms. Beautiful restaurant and coffee shop, pool, relaxing atmosphere, very helpful staff, fabulous views, very quiet, superb horse safaris (US$200 per night), trekking, tribal village tours. Highly recommended.

**B Kumbhalgarh Fort**, Kelwara-Kumbhalgarh Rd, T02954-242 057, hilltop@bppl.net.in. 21 a/c rooms in attractively designed stone building, superb location with hill, lake and valley views, garden, restaurant, bar, lovely pool, cycle hire, riding, friendly staff.

**B-C Kumbhal Castle**, Khelwara Kumbhalgarh Rd, T02954-242 171, hotelkumbhal castle@yahoo.co.in. 12 simply decorated rooms, some a/c, in new construction which feels a little unfinished. Basic restaurant, good views.

**C-D Ratnadeep**, Kelwara, in the middle of a bustling village, T02954-242 217, www.hotel sofrajasthan/kumhalgarh/ratnadeep.html. 14 reasonably clean rooms, some deluxe with cooler and marble floors, Western toilets, small lawn, restaurant, camel, horse and jeep safaris, friendly, well-run.

**D Forest Department Guest House**, near the Parsram Temple, about 3 km by road and 3 km off the road (access by 4WD jeep or trek) from Aodhi. Basic facilities but fantastic views over the Kumbalgarh sanctuary towards the drylands of Marwar.

**Ghanerao and Rawla Narlai** *p359*
**B Thakur Sajjan Singh castle**, see Sights, Ghanerao, call Mumbai for reservations, T022 5555 1101, www.nivalink.com/ghanerao, has suites, a restaurant (simple food), slightly run down but has nostalgic appeal of faded glory, charming hosts, expensive local guide (bargain hard if buying paintings), jeeps and camping arranged.
**B-C Fort Rawla Narlai**, Rawla Narlai, T02934-282 425, www.ajitbhawan.com. 21 rooms (11 a/c) individually decorated with antiques in the renovated fort, new showers, plus 5 luxurious, well-appointed 'tents', good simple meals under the stars, helpful, friendly staff, attractive garden setting, good riding, overlooked by huge boulder rock; temple on top can be reached via 700 steps.
**C Kotri Rawla**, Ghanerao, T0294-2560822. 8 rooms, 2 suites in 17th-century royal 'bungalow', excellent horse safaris run by thakur Mahendra Singh, an expert on Marwari horses and his son, a well known polo player.
**E Bagha-ka-Bagh** (Tiger's Den), Ghanerao. Spartan hunting lodge among tall grass jungle near wildlife sanctuary gate. 10 very basic rooms, 5 with bucket hot water, dorm, generator for electricity, breathtaking location, wildlife (including panther, nilgai), rich birdlife, 5-day treks including Kumbhalgarh, Ranakpur. Contact North West Safaris, T079-6560962, ssibal@ad1.vsnl.net.in.

**Ranakpur** *p360*
**B Fateh Bagh Palace** (HRH), on the highway near the temple, T02934-286 186, www.hrhindia.com. A 200-year-old fort was dismantled in to 65,000 pieces and transported here from it's original site 50 km away in order to make this palace. The result is a beautiful property, cleverly combining old and new. There are 20 tastefully decorated, well-appointed rooms, 6 more on the way, including 4 suites, best of which have attached Jacuzzis, good pool, friendly staff.
**B Maharani Bagh** (WelcomHeritage), Ranakpur Rd, T02934-285 105, balsamand_1@sify.com. 19 well-furnished modern bungalows with baths in lovely 19th-century walled orchard of Jodhpur royal family, full of bougainvillaea and mangos, outdoor Rajasthani restaurant (traditional Marwari meals Rs 300), pool, jeep safaris, horse riding.
**B-C Ranakpur Hill Resort**, Ranakpur Rd, T02934-286 411, www.ranakpurhiliresort.com. 9 good-sized, well-appointed rooms, 5 a/c, in new construction, pleasant dining room, clean pool, friendly owner.
**C Shivika Lake Hotel**, T02934-285078, www.indiaoverland.com/ranakpur, borders the lake in pleasant jungle setting. A Rajput Special Hotel, 9 simple but comfortable rooms (2 a/c) with baths, hot water, 2 tents with shared bath, delicious Rajasthani food, swimming pool overlooks lake and wooded hills. Thakur Devi Singh Ji Bhenswara organises treks, excellent jeep safaris with spotter guide in Kumbhalgarh sanctuary (he is the honorary warden), camping trips, personal attention, friendly hosts. Recommended.
**C-D Roopam**, Ranakpur Rd, T02934-285 321, roopaminn@hotmail.com. 12 well-maintained rooms, some a/c, pleasant restaurant, attractive lawns.
**D-E Shilpi** (RTDC), T02934-285 074. 12 cleanish rooms, best with hot water and a/c, dorm (dirty), veg meals.
**F Dharamshala** has some comfortable rooms, simple and extremely cheap veg meals.

## Eating

**Kumbhalgarh** *p358*
**TTT Aodhi** is a thatched restaurant with central barbecue area. Good Indian (try *laal maas*, a mutton dish), authentic 7-course Mewari meal but service can be very slow.
**TT Ratnadeep** has an à la carte veg menu.

**Ranakpur** *p360*
There are no eateries near the temple, only a tea stall, but the dharamshala serves very good food at lunchtime and sunset, Rs 20.
**TT Roopam**, Ranakpur-Maharani Bagh Rd, near Shivika. Good Rajasthani food. Pleasant village theme setting, modern, popular.
**TT Shivika Lake**, part open-air restaurant by lake with hill views. Delicious Rajasthani lunches, non-spicy curries possible, barbecued chicken, excellent breakfasts, tea by the lake, family run, clean.

## Transport

While most of the places in this section do have bus links, a private car is indispensable and makes the most of the scenic drives on offer. A round-trip from Udaipur could also take in Eklingji, Nagda and Nathdwara.

**Kumbhalgarh** *p358*
For the fort: buses (irregular times) from Chetak Circle, Udaipur go to **Kelwara**, Rs 20, 3 hrs (cars take 2 hrs); from there a local bus (Rs 2) can take you a further 4 km up to a car park; the final 2-km climb is on foot; the return is a pleasant downhill walk of 1 hr. Jeep taxis charge Rs 50-100 from Kelwara to the fort (and say there are no buses). Return buses to Jaipur from Kelwara until 1730.

From Udaipur, a taxi for 4, Rs 1,200, can cover the fort and Ranakpur in 11 hrs; very worthwhile.

**Ranakpur** *p360*
From Udaipur, there are 6 buses daily (0530-1600), slow, 4 hrs from **Jodhpur** (doesn't stop long enough to see the temples so break your journey here) and **Mount Abu**. The nearest railway line is Palna Junction on the Ajmer-Mount Abu line, 39 km away. For the taxi options see above.

# Mount Abu and around

*Mount Abu, Rajasthan's only hill resort, stretches along a 20-km plateau. Away from the congestion and traffic of the tourist centres on the plains, Mount Abu is surrounded by well-wooded countryside filled with flowering trees, numerous orchids during the monsoon and a good variety of bird and animal life. Many of the rulers from surrounding princely states had summer houses built here and today, it draws visitors from Rajasthan and neighbouring Gujarat who come to escape the searing heat of summer (and Gujarat's alcohol prohibition) and also to see the exquisite Dilwara Jain temples. There are also some fabulous heritage hotels in the area, well off the beaten track and unique experiences in themselves.* » *For Sleeping, Eating and other listings, see pages 367-370.*



## Ins and outs

**Getting there** The nearest railway station is at Abu Road, 27 km away. It is usually quicker to take a bus directly to Mount Abu, instead of going to Abu Road by train and then taking a bus up the hill. » *See Transport, page 370, for further details.*

**Getting around** The compact area by Nakki Lake, with hotels, restaurants and shops, is pedestrianized. Taxis are available at a stand nearby. A form of transport unique to Mount Abu is the *baba gari*, a small trolley generally used to pull small children up the steepest of Mount Abu's hills.

**Tourist information Rajasthan Tourism** ⓘ *opposite bus stand, T02974-235 151. 0800-1100, 1600-2000.* Guides available, four to eight hours, about Rs 250-400.

# Mount Abu → *Phone code: 02974. Colour map 2, grid B3. Population: 15,600. Altitude: 1,720 m.*

## Background

Mount Abu was the home of the legendary sage Vasishtha. One day Nandini, his precious wish-fulfilling cow, fell into a great lake. Vasishtha requested the gods in the Himalaya to save her so they sent Arbuda, a cobra, who carried a rock on his head and dropped it into the lake, displacing the water, and so saved Nandini. The place became known as Arbudachala, the 'Hill of Arbuda'. Vasishtha also created the four powerful 'fire-born' Rajput tribes, including the houses of Jaipur and Udaipur at a ritual fire ceremony on the mount. Nakki Talao (Lake), sacred to Hindus, was, in legend, scooped out by fingernails (*nakki*) of gods attempting to escape the wrath of a demon. Abu was leased by the British Government from the Maharao of Sirohi and was used as the HQ for the Resident of Rajputana until 1947, and as a sanatorium for troops.

## Dilwara Jain Temples

Set in beautiful surroundings of mango trees and wooded hills, 5 km from the town centre, the temples have superb marble carvings. The complex of five principal temples is surrounded by a high wall, dazzling white in the sunlight. There is a resthouse for pilgrims on the approach road, which is also lined with stalls selling a collection of tourist kitsch lending a carnival atmosphere to the sanctity of the temples.

**Chaumukha temple** The grey sandstone three-storey building is approached through the entrance on your left. Combining 13th- and 15th-century styles, it is generally regarded as inferior to the two main temples. The colonnaded hall (ground floor) contains four-faced images of the Tirthankar Parsvanatha (hence *chaumukha*), and figures of *dikpalas* and *yakshis*.

**Adinatha Temple** (Vimala Shah Temple) This temple lies directly ahead; the oldest and most famous of the Dilwara group. Immediately outside the entrance to the temple is a small portico known as the Hastishala (elephant hall), built by Prithvipal in 1147-1159 which contains a figure of the patron, Vimala Shah, the Chief Minister of the Solanki King,

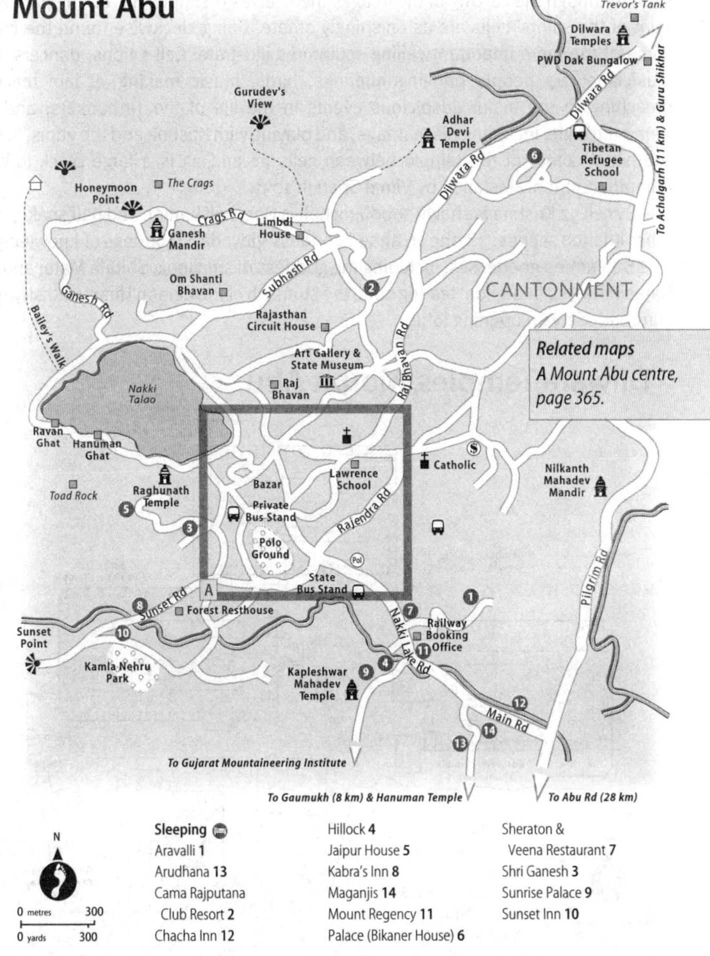

 on horseback. Vimala Shah commissioned the temple, dedicated to Adinatha, in 1031-1032. The riders on the 10 beautifully carved elephants that surround him were removed during Alauddin Khilji's reign. Dilwara belonged to Saivite Hindus who were unwilling to part with it until Vimala Shah could prove that it had once belonged to a Jain community. In a dream, the goddess Ambika (Ambadevi or Durga) instructed him to dig under a champak tree where he found a huge image of Adinatha and so won the land. To the southwest, behind the hall, is a small shrine to Ambika, once the premier deity. In common with many Jain temples the plain exterior conceals a wonderfully ornately carved interior, remarkably well preserved given its age. It is an early example of the Jain style in West India, set within a rectangular court lined with small shrines and a double colonnade. The white marble of which the entire temple is built was brought not from Makrana, as other guidebooks suggest, but from the relatively nearby marble quarries of Ambaji in Gujarat, 25 km south of Abu Road. Hardly a surface is left unadorned. Makaras guard the entrance, and below them are conches. The cusped arches and ornate capitals are beautifully designed and superbly made.

Lining the walls of the main hall are 57 shrines. Architecturally, it is suggested that these are related to the cells which surround the walls of Buddhist monasteries, but in the Jain temple are reduced in size to house simple images of a seated Jain saint. Although the carving of the images themselves is simple, the ceiling panels in front of the saints' cells are astonishingly ornate. Going clockwise round the cells, some of the more important ceiling sculptures illustrate: Cell 1 lions, dancers and musicians; 2-7 people bringing offerings, birds, music making; 8 Jain teacher preaching; 9 the major auspicious events in the life of the Tirthankars; and 10 Neminath's life, including his marriage, and playing with Krishna and the gopis. In the southeast corner of the temple between cells 22 and 23 is a large black idol of Adinath, reputedly installed by Vimal Shah in 1031.

By cell 32 Krishna is shown subduing Kaliya Nag, half human and half snake, and other Krishna scenes; 38, the 16 armed goddess Vidyadevi (goddess of knowledge); 46-48 16 armed goddesses, including the goddess of smallpox, Shitala Mata; and 49 Narasimha, the 'man-lion' tearing open the stomach of the demon Hiranya-Kashyapa, surrounded by an opening lotus.



## Dilwara Temples, Mount Abu

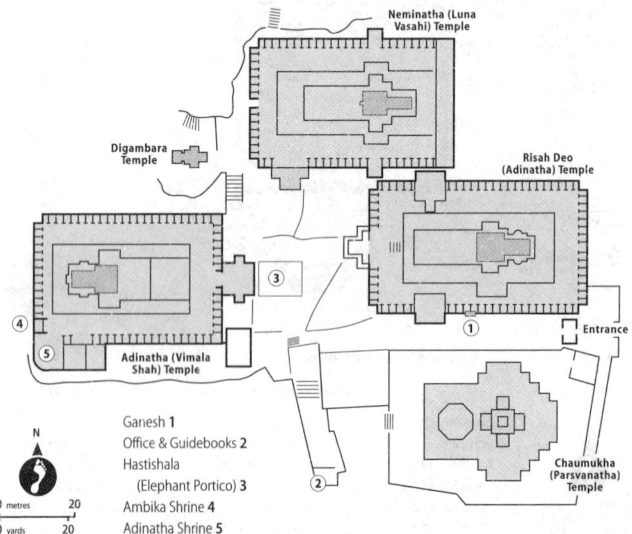

As in Gujarati Hindu temples, the main hall focuses on the sanctum which contains the 2½ m image of Adinatha, the first Tirthankar. The sanctum with a pyramidal roof has a vestibule with entrances on three sides. To its east is the Mandapa, a form of octagonal nave nearly 8 m in diameter. Its 6-m wide dome is supported by eight slender columns; the exquisite lotus ceiling carved from a single block of marble, rises in 11 concentric circles, carved with elaborately repeated figures. Superimposed across the lower rings are 16 brackets carved in the form of the goddesses of knowledge.

**Risah Deo Temple** Opposite the Vimala Visahi, this temple is unfinished. It encloses a huge brass Tirthankar image weighing 4.3 tonnes and made of panchadhatu (five metals) – gold, silver, copper, brass and zinc. The temple was commenced in the late 13th century by Brahma Shah, the Mewari Maharana Pratap's chief minister. Building activity was curtailed by war with Gujarat and never completed.

**Luna Vasihi or Neminatha Temple** (1231) ⓘ *free (no photography), shoes and cameras, mobile phones, leather items and backpacks (Rs 1 per item) are left outside, tip expected; 1200-1800 for non-Jains; some guides are excellent, it's a 1-hr uphill walk from town, or share a jeep, Rs 5 each.* To the north of the Adinatha Temple, this one was erected by two wealthy merchants Vastupala and Tejapala, and dedicated to the 22nd Tirthankar; they also built a similar temple at Girnar. The attractive niches on either side of the sanctum's entrance were for their wives. The craftsmanship in this temple is comparable to the Vimala Vasahi; the decorative carving and *jali* work are excellent. The small domes in front of the shrine containing the bejewelled Neminatha figure, the exquisitely carved lotus on the sabhamandapa ceiling and the sculptures on the colonnades are especially noteworthy.

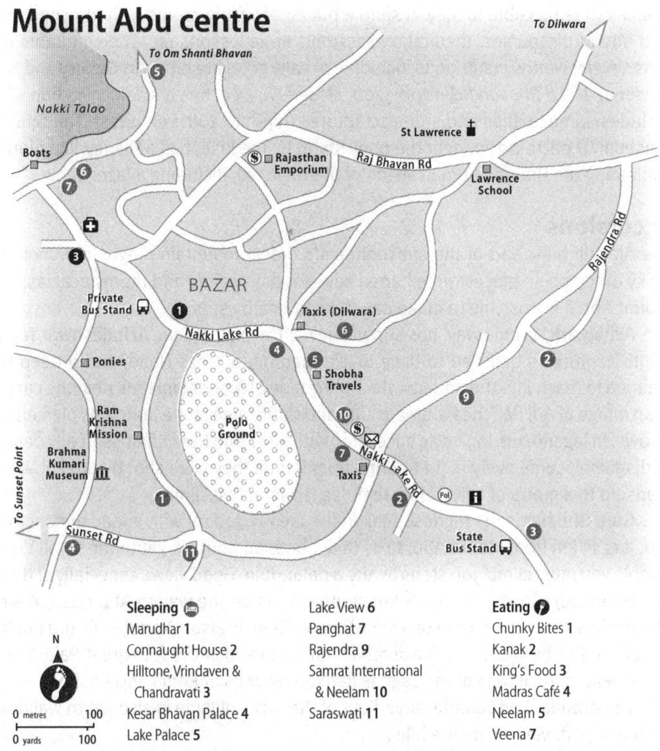

There is a fifth temple for the Digambar ('sky-clad') Jains which is far more austere.

## Walks

**Trevor's Tank** ⓘ *Rs 5, car/jeep taken up to the lake Rs 125*, 50 m beyond the Dilwara Jain temples, is the small wildlife sanctuary covering 289 sq km with the lake which acts as a watering hole for animals including sloth bear, sambhar, wild boar, panther. Most of these are nocturnal but on your walk you are quite likely to see a couple of crocodiles basking on the rocks. The birdlife is extensive with eagles, kites, grey jungle fowl, red spurfowl, francolin, flycatchers, bulbuls etc seen during walks on the trails in the sanctuary. There are superb views from the trails.

**Adhar Devi**, 3 km from town, is a 15th-century Durga temple carved out of a rock and approached by 220 steep steps. There are steep treks to Anandra point or to a Mahadev temple nearby for great views.

Around **Nakki Lake Honeymoon Point**, and **Sunset Point** to the west, give superb views across the plains. They can both be reached by a pleasant walk from the bus stand (about 2 km). You can continue from Honeymoon Point to **Limbdi House**. If you have another 1½ hours, walk up to **Jai Gurudev's meditation eyrie**. If you want to avoid the crowds at Sunset Point, take the **Bailey's Walk** from the **Hanuman Temple** near Honeymoon Point to **Valley View Point**,which joins up with the Sunset Point walk. You can also walk from the Ganesh temple to the Crags for some great views.

## Spiritual University movement, Art Gallery and State Museum and Spiritual Museum

The headquarters of the Spiritual University movement of the Brahma kumaris is **Om Shanti Bhavan** ⓘ *T02974-238 268*, with its ostentatious entrance on Subhash Road. You may notice many residents dressed in white taking a walk around the lake in the evening. It is possible to stay in simple but comfortable rooms with attached baths and attend discourses, meditation sessions, yoga lessons etc. The charitable trust runs several worthy institutions including a really good hospital. **Art Gallery and State Museum** ⓘ *Raj Bhavan Rd, 1000-1700, closed Fri, free*, has a small collection which includes some textiles and stone sculptures (ninth to 10th centuries). The **Spiritual Museum** ⓘ *0800-2000*, near the pony stand by the lake, has a Disney-like diorama explaining the Brahma Kumari vision of the universe, including a lazer show.

## Excursions

The Aravalli hills, part of the subcontinent's oldest mountain range, look more like rocky outcrops, in places quite barren save for date palms and thorny acacias. From Mount Abu it is possible to make day-treks to nearby spots.

**Achalgarh**, 11 km away, has superb views. The picturesque **Achaleshwar Temple** (ninth century) is believed to have Siva's toeprint, a brass Nandi and a deep hole claimed to reach into the underworld. On the side of **Mandakini tank** near the car park is an image of Adi Pal, the Paramara king and three large stone buffaloes pierced with arrows. In legend, the tank was once filled with ghee and the buffaloes (really demons in disguise), came every night to drink from it until they were shot by Adi Pal. A path leads up to a group of carved Jain temples (10-minutes' climb).

**Guru Shikhar** is the highest peak in the area (1,720 m) with a road almost to the top. It is 15 km from Mount Abu, taxis take about an hour. To get to the small Vishnu temple you must climb 300 steps or hire a palanquin. Good views especially at dawn.

**Gaumukh** (Cow's Mouth), 8 km southeast, is on the way to Abu Road. A small stream flows from the mouth of a marble cow. There is also a Nandi bull, and the tank is believed to be the site of Vasishtha's fire from which the four great Rajput clans were created. An image of the sage is flanked by ones of Rama and Krishna.

The **Arbuda Devi Temple** carved out of the rocky hillside is also worth walking to for the superb views over the hills.

# Around Mount Abu

## Bera → *34 km from Sirohi.*

The large panther population in the surrounding hills of Bera and the Jawai River area draws wildlife photographers. Antelopes and jackals also inhabit the area. Visit the **Jawai Dam**, 150 km from Mount Abu towards Jodhpur, to see historic embankments, numerous birds and basking marsh crocodiles. A bed for the night is provided by **Leopard's Lair** in a colourful Raika village near the lake and jungle, see Sleeping.

## Jalor → *160 km north of Mount Abu.*

Jalor is an historic citadel. In the early 14th century, during court intrigues, the Afghani Diwan of Marwar, Alauddin Khilji, took over the town and set up his own kingdom. Later, the Mughal emperor Akbar captured it and returned the principality to his allies, the Rathores of Marwar by means of a peaceful message to the Jalori Nawabs, who moved south to Palanpur in Gujarat.The medieval fort straddles a hill near the main bazaar and encloses Muslim, Hindu and Jain shrines. It is a steep climb up but the views from the fort are rewarding. The old Topkhana at the bottom of the fortified hill has a mosque built by Alauddin Khilji using sculptures from a Hindu temple. Of particular interest are the scores of domes in different shapes and sizes, the symmetry of the columns and the delicate arches. Jalor bazaar is good for handicrafts, silver jewellery and textiles, and is still relatively unaffected by tourist pricing.

## Bhenswara → *16 km east of Jalor.*

Bhenswara is a small, colourful village on the Jawai River. It has another Rajput country estate whose 'castle' has been converted into an attractive hotel. The jungles and the impressive granaite Esrana hills nearby have leopard, nilgai, chinkara, blackbuck, jungle cat, jackal, porcupines and spiny tailed lizards. It makes a good place to stay for a couple of nights.

## Bhinmal → *95 km northwest of Mount Abu.*

Bhinmal has some important archaeological ruins, notably one of the few shrines in the country to Varaha Vishnu. It is also noted for the quality of its leather embroided mojdis. Nearby at Vandhara is one of the few marble *baolis* (step wells) in India, while the historic **Soondha Mata Temple** is at a picturesque site where the green hills and barren sand dunes meet at a freshwater spring fed by a cascading stream.

## Daspan → *25 km north of Bhinmal.*

Daspan is a small village where the restored 19th-century castle built on the ruins of an old fort provides a break between Mount Abu and Jaisalmer.

# Sleeping

**Mount Abu** *p362, map p363 and p365*

Touts can be a nuisance to budget travellers at the bus stand. Prices shoot up during Diwali, Christmas week and summer (20 Apr-20 Jun) when many **D-F** hotels triple their rates; meals, and ponies and jeeps cost a lot more too. Off-season discounts of 30 and 50% are usual, sometimes 70% in mid-winter (when it can get very cold). For a list of familities receiving paying guests visit the tourist office.

**A Cama Rajputana Club Resort** (Heritage), Adhar Devi Rd, T02974-238 205, cama rajputana@rediffmail.com. Refurbished old club house (1895) for Mount Abu's royal and British residents, guests become temporary members, 42 rooms in split level cottages with views, 2 period suites, lounge with fireplaces and old club furniture, average restaurant, eco-friendly (recycled water, alternative energy, drip irrigation), beautifully landscaped gardens, billiards, tennis etc, efficient service, immaculate pool.

**A Hillock**, opposite petrol pump, T02974-238 463, www.hotelhillock.com. 41 a/c rooms, ostentatiously decorated, swanky restaurant, pleasant garden and pool (close to road), well presented if anonymous, some staff unhelpful.

**A The Jaipur House**, above Nakki Lake, T02974-235 176, www.royalfamilyjaipur.com. 9 elegant rooms in the Maharaja of Jaipur's former summer palace, unparalleled location, fantastic views, especially from terrace restaurant, friendly, professional staff. Recommended.

**A-B Hilltone**, set back from road near petrol pump, T02974-383 913, www.hilltone.com. 66 tastefully decorated rooms (most a/c), attractive Handi (a style of cooking using baking/steaming in covered pots) restaurant, pool, garden, quiet, most stylish of Mt Abu's modern hotels, helpful staff. Recommended.

**B Connaught House** (WelcomHeritage), Rajendra Marg, uphill from opposite bus stand, T02974-238 560, www.welcomheritage.com. British Resident of Jodhpur's colonial bungalow, 6 good, old fashioned rooms (royal memorabilia), good bathrooms, 8 modern rooms in quieter new cottage, comfortable, restaurant (average à la carte, good Rajasthani meals), trekking with guide (Rs 2000 plus), beautiful gardens filled with birds, interesting old retainer of the Jodhpur family, efficient management. Recommended.

**B Kesar Bhavan Palace**, Sunset Rd, facing polo ground, T02974-235 219, www.mountsabu.com. 19th-century residence of the Sirohi royal family, 16 renovated rooms in main palace and 10 attractive rooms with period furniture in stable wing, comfortable, modernized, balconies, western breakfast, family run, environment friendly.

**B Palace Hotel** (Heritage), Bikaner House, Dilwara Rd, 3 km from centre, T02974-235 121, bikhouse@sancharnet.in. 38 large renovated rooms with period and reproduction furniture in Swinton Jacob's imposing 1894 hunting lodge, also new annexe, atmospheric public rooms, grand dining hall (good English breakfast, Rajasthani meals, memorable à la carte, expensive set menu), tennis etc, civilized but average service, very quiet, set in sprawling grounds and backdrop of hills.

**B-C Maganjis**, Mount Rd, T02974-238 337, maganjis@datainfoysis.net. 25 well-maintained rooms in modern building, pleasant lawn, welcoming staff.

**B-C Sunrise Palace**, Bharatpur Kothi, T02974-235 573, www.sunrisepalace-mtabu.co.in. 16 large, sparsely furnished rooms, great bathrooms, in a grand, slightly unloved converted mansion, good small restaurant, open-air BBQ, elevated with excellent views.

**B-D Mount Regency**, near petrol pump, T02974-235 200, www.mountsabu.com. 20 a/c rooms in high quality modern construction with balconies, lawn, friendly and experienced management.

**C Chacha Inn**, Main Rd (2 km from centre), T02974-235 374, www.chacha-inn-hotel.com. Attractive though a bit brash, with lots of artefacts on display, 22 good a/c rooms with modern facilities, some with balconies offering hill views, restaurant, bar, garden really good fun; dining lawns with magic and puppet shows, dancing and music.

**C Lake Palace**, facing lake, T02974-237 154, savshanti@hotmail.com. 13 rooms (some a/c), garden restaurant, beautifully situated with great lake views from terrace, rear access to hill road for Dilwara, well run and maintained. Recommended.

**C Sunset Inn**, Sunset Rd, 1 km centre, T02974-235 194, thomasg1956@yahoo.com. 40 spacious rooms, some a/c, modern facilities, veg restaurant, outdoor dining, garden, pleasant atmosphere, popular.

**C-D Aravalli**, Main Rd, T02974-235 316. 40 rooms (12 in cottages, 10 in new wing) on different levels with hill views, good restaurant, very well maintained, landscaped terraced garden, pool, gym, good off-season discount, very helpful staff. Recommended.

**C-D Kabra's Inn**, Sunset Rd, T02974-238 095. 8 light, clean, modern rooms, small restaurant, relaxed management.

**C-D Marudhar**, opposite polo ground, T02974-238 620. Attractive, modern sandstone exterior conceals 32 standard rooms, lift, okay views.

**D Aradhana**, St Mary's Rd, T02974-237 227. 8 clean, modern rooms, some a/c, in family home, large terraces, pleasant atmosphere, 10 mins walk from town.

**D Samrat International**, near bus stand, T02974-235 173, hillock@sancharnet.in. 50 comfortable rooms, Takshila veg restaurant, travel, pleasant terraces, welcoming staff.

**D-E Sheraton**, near Bus Stand, T02974-238 366. 40 rooms,modern hotel, clean, characterless, but enthusiastic owner.

**E Panghat**, overlooking Nakki Lake, T02974-238 886. 10 small but adequate rooms in great location, friendly staff.

**E Saraswati**, west of Polo Ground, T02974-238 887. 36 rooms (some with balconies), better in annexe, good views from upstairs, simple, clean, large rooms with bath and hot water, smart restaurant (Gujarati *thalis* only), best of many options in area.

**E Vrindavan**, near bus stand, T02974-235 147. 30 standard rooms set back from busy road, indifferent management, good value.

**E-F Lake View**, beautiful location on a slope facing the Lake, T02974-238 659. 15 rather shabby rooms, Indian WC, helpful staff.

**E-F Neelam**, near Samrat, Main Rd, T02974-235 296. 10 well-maintained, modern rooms in annexe of family home, friendly hosts.

**E-F Shri Ganesh**, west of the polo ground, uphill behind Brahma Kumari, T02974-237 292, lalit_ganesh@yahoo.co.in. 23 clean, simple rooms, plenty of solar-heated hot water, very quiet, good rooftop café, one of the few places catering specifically for foreigners, 16 years' experience shows, recommended. Ring ahead for free pick up.

**F Chandravati Palace**, 9 Janta Colony, T02974-238 219. 4 clean rooms in slightly distant but friendly, quiet location.

**F Krishna**, Raj Bhawan Rd, T02974-238 045. 12 clean, simple rooms, quiet and homely.

**F Rajendra**, Rajendra Rd (from bus stand, turn right at post office), T02974-238 174. Well designed, clean rooms with bucket hot water, *thalis*, huge balcony, friendly management.

### Around Mount Abu *p367*

**A Leopard's Lair**, in a colourful Raika village, Bera, T02933-43478. 7 a/c rooms in well designed stone cottages, modern amenities, delicious meals included (fresh fish from lake), bar, pool, garden, riding, birdwatching, panther viewing 'safaris' with owner.

**C Rawla Bhenswara**, Bhenswara, T02978-22080. Reservations from **North West Safaris**, T079-6302019, ssibal@ad1.vsnl.net.in. A Rajput Special Hotel, 20 comfortable rooms with bath, painted exterior, inspired decor ('Badal Mahal' with cloud patterns, 'Hawa Mahal' with breezy terrace etc), breakfast treats of masala cheese toast or vegetarian parathas, delicious Marwari meals, parakeet-filled orchards, court-yard lawns. Walk to parakeet-filled orchards and pool at the nearby Madho Bagh. Shiv Pratap and his hospitable family are very knowledgeable and enterprising. They will organise great visits to Rabari herdsmen, Bhil tribal hamlets, night safaris for leopards as well as camping safaris including one at the Tilwara cattle fair or even treks to Mt Abu. Highly recommended.

**D Castle Durjan Niwas**, Daspan, T02969-73523. 11 rooms, pleasant open sitting areas, folk entertainment, knowledgeable owners, camel rides (Rs 200 per hr; Rs 800 per day).

## Eating

### Mount Abu *p362, map p363 and p365*

Small roadside stalls sell tasty local vegetarian food. You can also get good *thalis* (Rs 30-40) at simple restaurants.

TTT **Handi**, Hilltone Hotel. Gujarati, Punjabi, Western. Plenty of choice, very comfortable but pricey, 0900-2300. Has a bar.

TT **Neelam**, near bus stand. Indian meals (Rs 50-75), Chinese dishes, Western snacks.

TT **Shere-e-Punjab**, among best in town for veg/non veg Indian (some Chinese/ western).

T **Chunky Bites**, on main drag, good selection of Punjabi, pizza, pasta and chaat.

T **Kanak** and **Purohit**, near Bus Stand. Great Gujarati *thalis* and South Indian snacks (Rs 30-50). Quick service, popular.

T **King's Food**, near MK, Nakki Lake Rd. Very popular for North Indian veg meal (Rs 40); Chinese, South Indian and western snacks.

T **Madras Café**, Nakki Lake Rd. Indian. Veg 'hot dog', *thalis*, juices, real coffee and milk shakes in a garden, meals indoors.

T **Maharaja**, near bus stand. Gujarati. Simple, clean, produces excellent value *thalis*.

T **Veena**, near taxi stand. Brews real coffee, serves traditional Indian meals and a few western favourites, very clean, outdoors, loud music, best of many on same strip.

## Festivals and events

### Mount Abu *p362, map p363 and p365*

An annual **Summer Festival, 1-3 Jun** every year, features folk music, dancing, fireworks etc. **Diwali** is especially colourful.

**Around Mount Abu** *p367*
In Bhinmal the **Navratri Festival** is held in **Sep**. Despan also holds special Navratri celebrations.

## Shopping

**Mount Abu** *p362, map p363 and p365*
Shopping is less hassle here than in the tourist towns; most are open 0900-2100 daily. Ready-made Indian clothing and silver jewellery are particularly good value. For Garasia tribal jewellery try stalls near the GPO.
**Saurashtra** and **Rajasthan emporia**, Raj Bhavan Rd, opposite the bus stand, sell a good selection.
**Chacha Museum**, good metal, wood, stone crafts, paintings and odd curios (fixed price but may give a discount).
**Khadi Gramudyog**, opposite pony hire. Handloom fabric, carved agate boxes, marble figures.
**Roopali**, near Nakki Lake. Silver jewellery.

## Activities and tours

**Mount Abu** *p362, map p363 and p365*
**Mountain sports**
For rock climbing, rapelling, contact **Mountaineering Institute**, near Gujarat Bhawan Hostel. Equipment and guide/instructors are available. Swimming, tennis, billiards. Non-residents can pay to use facilities at the **Cama Rajputana** and **Bikaner House Palace hotels**.

### Tours

**Rajasthan Tourism**, and **Rajasthan SRTC**, run daily tours to Dilwara, Achalgarh, Guru Shikhar, Nakki Lake, Sunset Point, Adhar Devi and Om Shanti Bhavan, 0830-1300, 1330-1900, Rs 80. **Gujarat**, **Maharajah**, **Shobha** (T02974-238 302) and **Green Travels** also offer similar tours for Rs 40-60; Ambaji-Kumbhairyaji tours Rs 120.

A wildlife guide who comes very highly recommended is **Charles**, T0-94141 54854, mahendradan@ yahoo.com, also contactable through **Lake Palace Hotel**. He offers a wide range of treks from 3-4-hr excursions at Rs 150 per person to longer overnight camping trips, very knowledgeable and enthusiastic.

## Transport

**Mount Abu** *p362, map p363 and p365*
Toll on entering town, Rs 5 per head. Frequent rockfalls during the monsoon makes the road from Mount Abu hazardous; avoid night journeys. The nearest airport is at Udaipur.

### Bus

For **Dilwara** and/or **Achalgarh**; check time. State Bus Stand, Main Rd (opposite Tourist Office); Private Bus Stand, north of Polo Ground (towards lake). To **Abu Rd**: hourly bus (45 mins-1 hr) Rs 10. **Ahmadabad**: several (7 hrs, Rs 100) via Palanpur for Bhuj (3 hrs); **Delhi**: overnight. **Jaipur** (overnight, 9 hrs), **Jodhpur** am and pm (6 hrs). **Mumbai, Pune**: early morning (18 hrs). **Udaipur**: 0830, 1500, 2200 (5-6 hrs, Rs 80). **Vadodara**: 0930, 1930 (5 hrs). **Shobha** and **Gujarat Travels** run private buses.

### Taxi and jeep

Posted fares for sightseeing in a jeep; about Rs 700 per day; anywhere in town Rs 30; to Sunset Point Rs 50. Taxi (for sharing) Abu Rd Rs 250; Dilwara stand is near the bazar.

### Train

**Western Railway Out Agency** has a small reservation quota, 0900-1600, Sun 0900-1230. Book well in advance; you may have to wait 2-3 days even in the off-season. Abu Rd is the railhead with frequent buses to Mt Abu. To **Ahmadabad**: *Ashram Exp, 2916*, 0423, 3½ hrs; *Ahmadabad Mail, 9106*, 1305, 4½ hrs; *Aravali Exp, 69708*, 1615, 4½ hrs (continues to Mumbai, further 8½ hrs). **Jaipur**: *Aravalli Exp, 9707*, 1110, 9 hrs; *Ahmadabad-Delhi Mail, 9105*, 1430, 9 hrs. **Jodhpur**: *Ranakpur Exp, 4708*, 0440, 5½ hrs; *Surya Nagri Exp, 4846*, 0150, 5½ hrs. **Delhi**: *Ahmadabad Delhi Mail, 9105*, 1430, 15¾ hrs; *Ashram Exp, 2915*, 2123, 13¾ hrs.

**Around Mount Abu** *p367*
Trains to **Bera** from **Mumbai** and **Ajmer** via Abu Rd (*Aravalli* and *Ranakpur Exp*) stop at Jawai Dam and Mori Bera. For **Bhenswada**, trains and buses from Abu Rd. From **Bhinmal**, trains from **Jodhpur**, 1530, 2230 (4½ hrs); to **Jodhpur**, 0530, 2030. From **Ahmadabad**, 2130 (12 hrs); to **Ahmadabad**, 1940.

# Chittaurgarh and around

*This is a relatively undiscovered corner of Rajasthan but is home to some of the state's oldest and most interesting treasures. Chittaurgarh's 'Tower of Victory' has become well-known in recent years, but the whole of this ancient, historically important city is worth exploring. Kota and the area around Jalawar contain some of the oldest, and most impressive, temples and cave paintings in India, while nowhere takes you back in time as far as Bundi, seemingly untouched for centuries. Limited transport links mean that a visit to this region does require a little more time and effort than to other areas in Rajasthan, but also that the region has remained uncrowded, unspoilt and hugely hospitable.* » *For Sleeping, Eating and other listings, see pages 377-380.*

## Ins and outs

**Getting there** There are no flights in to this area. All of the region's major towns are served by the railway, but often by branch lines some way off the main routes. Buses starting from all the major cities surrounding the area give quick access to the main towns; Chittaurgarh is 2½ hours from Udaipur for example.

**Getting around** Most of the principal sights are fairly close together, making travel by road a convenient option. Frequent buses criss-cross the area, but a private taxi might be worth considering as some of the sights and most interesting places to stay, are somewhat off the beaten track. » *See Transport, page 380, for further details.*

## Chittaurgarh → *Phone code: 01472. Colour map 2, grid B5. Population: 100,000.*

The hugely imposing Chittaurgarh Fort stands on a 152 m high rocky hill, rising abruptly above the surrounding plain. The walls, 5-km long, enclose the fascinating ruins of an ancient civilization, while the slopes are covered with scrub jungle. The modern town lies at the foot of the hill with access across a limestone bridge of 10 arches over the Gambheri River.

*Visiting the fort on foot means a circuit of 7 km; allow four hours. The views from the battlements and towers are worth the effort.*

### History

One of the oldest cities in Rajasthan, Chittaurgarh was founded formally in 728 by Bappu Rawal, who according to legend was reared by the Bhil tribe. However, two sites near the River Berach have shown stone tools dating from half a million years ago and Buddhist relics from a few centuries BC. From the 12th century it became the centre of Mewar. Excavations in the Mahasati area of the fort have shown four shrines with ashes and charred bones, the earliest dating from about the 11th century AD. This is where the young Udai Singh was saved by his nurse Panna Dai; she sacrificed her own son by substituting him for the baby prince when, as heir to the throne, Udai Singh's life was threatened.

### Sights

The fort dominates the city. Until 1568 the town was situated within the walls. Today the lower town sprawls to the west of the fort. The winding 1½-km ascent is defended by seven impressive gates: the **Padal Pol** is where Rawat Bagh Singh, the Rajput leader, fell during the second siege; the Bhairon or **Tuta (broken) Pol** where Jaimal, one of the heroes of the third siege, was killed by Akbar in 1567 (*chhatris* to Jaimal and Patta); the Hanuman Pol and Ganesh Pol; the Jorla (or Joined) Gate whose upper arch is connected to the Lakshman Pol; finally the Ram Pol (1459) which is the main gate. Inside the walls is a village and ruined palaces, towers and temples, most of which are out in the open and so easy to explore.

**Rana Kumbha's Palace**, on the right immediately inside the fort, are the ruins of this palace (1433-1468), originally built of dressed stone with a stucco covering. It is approached by two gateways, the large Badi Pol and the three-bay deep Tripolia. Once there were elephant and horse stables, *zenanas* (recognized by the *jali* screen), and a Siva temple. The jauhar committed by Padmini and her followers is believed to have taken place beneath the courtyard. The north frontage of the palace contains an attractive combination of canopied balconies. Across from the palace is the Nau Lakha Bhandar (The Treasury; nau lakha – 900,000). The temple to Rana Kumbha's wife **Mira Bai** who was a renowned poetess is visible from the Palace and stands close to the Kumbha Shyama Temple (both circa 1440). The older 11th-century Jain **Sat Bis Deori** with its 27 shrines, is nearby. The **Shringara Chauri Temple** (circa 1456), near the fort entrance, has sculptured panels of musicians, warriors and Jain deities.

**Rana Ratan Singh's Palace** is to the north by the Ratneshwar Lake. Built in stone around 1530 it too had stucco covering. Originally rectangular in plan and enclosed within a high wall, it was subsequently much altered. The main gate to the south still stands as an example of the style employed.

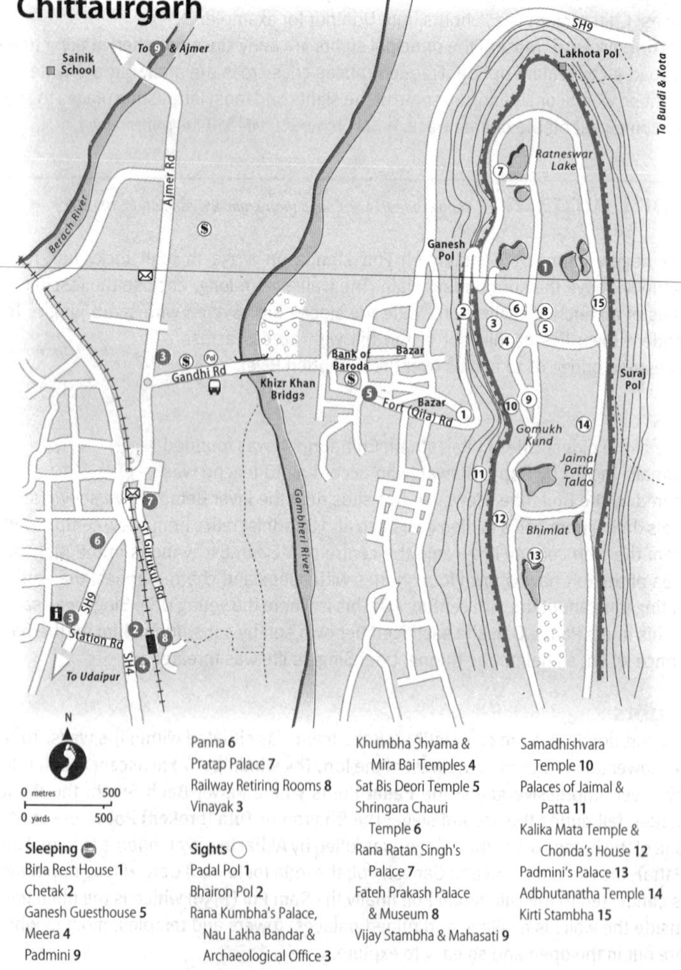


**Sleeping**
Birla Rest House **1**
Chetak **2**
Ganesh Guesthouse **5**
Meera **4**
Padmini **9**
Panna **6**
Pratap Palace **7**
Railway Retiring Rooms **8**
Vinayak **3**

**Sights**
Padal Pol **1**
Bhairon Pol **2**
Rana Kumbha's Palace, Nau Lakha Bandar & Archaeological Office **3**
Khumbha Shyama & Mira Bai Temples **4**
Sat Bis Deori Temple **5**
Shringara Chauri Temple **6**
Rana Ratan Singh's Palace **7**
Fateh Prakash Palace & Museum **8**
Vijay Stambha & Mahasati **9**
Samadhishvara Temple **10**
Palaces of Jaimal & Patta **11**
Kalika Mata Temple & Chonda's House **12**
Padmini's Palace **13**
Adbhutanatha Temple **14**
Kirti Stambha **15**

## The jauhar – Rajput chivalry

On three occasions during Chittaurgarh's history its inhabitants preferred death to surrender, the women marching en masse into the flames of a funeral pyre in a form of ritual suicide known as *jauhar* before the men threw open the gates and charged towards an overwhelming enemy and annihilation.

The first was in 1303 when Ala-ud-din Khalji, the King of Delhi, laid claim to the beautiful Padmini, wife of the Rana's uncle. When she refused, he laid siege to the fort. The women committed *jauhar*, Padmini entering last, and over 50,000 men were killed in battle. The fort was retaken in 1313.

In 1535 Bahadur Shah of Gujarat laid claim to Chittaurgarh. Every Rajput clan lost its leader in the battle in which over 32,000 lives were lost, and 13,000 women and children died in the sacred *jauhar* which preceded the final charge.

The third and final sack of Chittaurgarh occurred only 32 years later when Akbar stormed the fort. Again, the women and children committed themselves to the flames, and again all the clans lost their chiefs as 8,000 defenders burst out of the gates. When Akbar entered the city and saw that it had been transformed into a mass grave, he ordered the destruction of the buildings.

In 1567 after this bloody episode in Chittaurgarh's history, it was abandoned and the capital of Mewar was moved to Udaipur. In 1615 Jahangir restored the city to the Rajputs.



The early 20th-century **Fateh Prakash Palace** built by Maharana Fateh Singh (died 1930) houses an interesting museum (0800-1630; closed Friday, Rs 3). To the south is the **Vijay Stambha** (1458-1468), one of the most interesting buildings in the fort, built by Rana Kumbha to celebrate his victory over Mahmud Khilji of Malwa in 1440. Visible for miles around, it stands on a base 14 sq m and 3 m high, and rises 37 m. The nine-storeyed sandstone tower has been restored; the upper section retains some of the original sculpture. For Re 0.50 you can climb to the top. Nearby is the Mahasati terrace where the ranas were cremated when Chittaurgarh was the capital of Mewar. There are also numerous sati stones. Just to the south is the **Samdhishvara Temple** to Siva (11th and 15th centuries), which still attracts many worshippers and has some good sculptured friezes. Steps down lead to the deep Gomukh Kund, where the sacred spring water enters through a stone carved as a cow's mouth (hence its name).

Of the two palaces of **Jaimal and Patta**, renowned for their actions during the siege of 1567, the latter, based on the *zenana* building of Rana Kumbha's Palace, is more interesting. You then pass the Bhimtal before seeing the **Kalika Mata Temple** (originally an eighth century Surya temple, rebuilt mid-16th) with exterior carvings and the ruins of Chonda's House with its three-storey domed tower. Chonda did not claim the title when his father, Rana Lakha, died in 1421.

**Padmini's Palace** (late 13th century, rebuilt end of the 19th) is sited in the middle of the lake surrounded by pretty gardens. Ala-ud-din Khilji is said to have seen Padmini's beautiful reflection in the water through a mirror on the palace wall. This striking vision convinced him that she had to be his.

You pass the deer park on your way round to the **Suraj Pol** (Sun Gate) and pass the **Adbhutanatha Temple** to Siva before reaching the second tower, the **Kirti Stambha,** a Tower of Fame (13th and 15th centuries). Smaller than the Vijay Stambha (23 m) with only seven storeys, but just as elegant, it is dedicated to Adinath, the first Jain Tirthankar. Naked figures of Tirthankars are repeated several hundred times on the face of the tower. A narrow internal staircase goes to the top.

Of particular interest are the number of tanks and wells in the fort that have survived the centuries. Water, from both natural and artificial sources, was harnessed to provide an uninterrupted supply to the people.

## Chittaurgarh to Kota

**Bassi**, 28 km from Chittaurgarh, is famous for handicrafts and miniature wooden temples painted with scenes from the epics. The palace, a massive 16th-century fort, has been opened as a hotel, see Sleeping page 377.

**Bijaipur** is a feudal village about 50 km south of Chittaurgarh. The 16th-century **castle**, set among the Vindhya hills and now open as a hotel, see Sleeping page 377, has a splendid location near the **Bassi-Bijaipur wildlife sanctuary** which is home to panther, antelope and other wildlife. The forests are interspersed with lakes, reservoirs, streams and waterfalls with good birdlife in the winter months. The ruined **Pannagarh Fort** facing a lily covered lake is believed to be one of the oldest in Rajasthan.

## Kota

Kota's attractive riverside location and decent hotels make it a comfortable place to stay. The town itself is of no special appeal, but can be used as a base from which to visit nearby Bundi.

At the south end of the town, near the barrage, is the vast, strongly fortified **City Palace** (1625) which you enter by the south gate having driven through the bustling but quite charming old city. There are some striking buildings with delicate ornamental stonework on the balconies and façade, though parts are decaying. The best preserved murals and carved marble panels are in the chambers upstairs and in the Arjun Mahal. These murals feature motifs characteristic of the Kota School of art, including portraiture (especially profiles), hunting scenes, festivals and the Krishna Lila.

The 15th-century **Kishore Sagar** tank between the station and the palace occasionally has boats for hire. **Jag Mandir Island Palace**, closed to visitors, is in the centre of the lake. The **Chambal Gardens** by **Amar Niwas**, south of the fort, is a pleasant place for a view of the river, although therare fish-eating gharial crocodiles with which the pond was stocked are rarely seen these days. A variety of birds, occasionally including flamingos, can be seen at the river and in nearby ponds.

The **Umed Bhawan** (1904), 1 km north of town, was built for the Maharao Umaid Singh II and designed by Sir Samuel Swinton Jacob in collaboration with Indian designers. The buff-coloured stone exterior with a stucco finish has typical Rajput detail. The interior, however, is Edwardian with a fine drawing-room, banquet hall and garden. It has now been converted in to a heritage hotel, see below.

## Bundi → *Phone code: 0747. Colour map 2, grid B5. Population: 100,000.*

Bundi lies in a beautiful narrow valley with Taragarh Fort towering above. It can easily be visited on a day trip from Kota. The drive into the town is lovely as the road runs along the hillside overlooking the valley opposite the fort. Completely unspoilt and rarely visited, it is well worth spending a day or two here to soak in the atmosphere.

### History

Formerly a small state founded in 1342, Bundi's fortunes varied inversely with those of its more powerful neighbours. Neither wealthy nor powerful, it nevertheless ranked high in the Rajput hierarchy since the founding family belonged to the specially blessed

Hada Chauhan clan. After Prithviraj Chauhan was defeated by Muhammad Ghuri in 1193, the rulers sought refuge in Mewar. However, adventurous clan members overran the Bhils and Minas in the Chambal valley and established the kingdom of Hadavati or **Hadoti** which covers the area around Bundi, Kota and Jhalawar in southeastern Rajasthan. It prospered under the guidance of the able 19th-century ruler Zalim Singh, but then declined on his death. The British reunited the territory in 1894.

*Bundi is especially colourful and interesting during the festivals, see Festivals and events page 380.*

## Sights

**Taragarh Fort** ⓘ *0700-1700, foreigner Rs 50, Indian Rs 20, camera Rs 50, video Rs 100.* (1342) stands in sombre contrast to the beauty of the town and the lakes below. There are excellent views but it is a 20-minute difficult climb; good shoes help. The eastern wall is crenellated with high ramparts while the main gate to the west is flanked by octagonal towers. The **Bhim Burj** tower dominates the fort and provided the platform for the Garbh Ganjam, a huge cannon. A pit to the side once provided shelter for the artillery men, and there are several stepped water tanks inside. Cars can go as far as the TV tower then it is 600 m along a rough track.

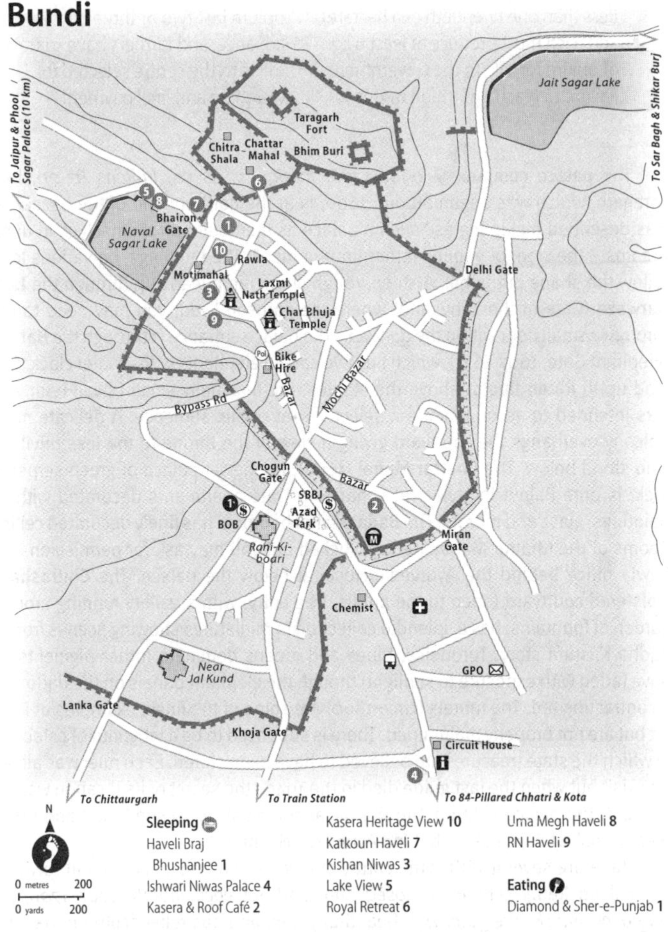

## Flower power

Crossing the high plateau between Bundi and Chittaurgarh the landscape is suddenly dotted with tiny patches of papery white flowers. These two Rajasthani districts, along with the neighbouring districts of Madhya Pradesh, are India's opium poppy growing belt, accounting for over 90% of production. As early as the fifteenth century this region produced opium for trade with China. Today the whole process is tightly monitored by the Government. Licences to grow are hard won and easily lost. No farmer can grow more than half a *bigha* of opium poppy (less than one twentieth of a hectare), and each must produce at least 6 kg of opium for sale to the Government. Failure to reach this tough target results in the loss of the licence to grow. Laying out the field, actual cultivation and sale are all government controlled. Between late February and early April the farmers harvest the crop by incising fine lines in one quarter of each poppy head in the evening, and collecting the sap first thing in the morning. The harvesting has to be so precise that each evening a different quarter of the seed head will be cut on a different face – north, south, east or west. Finally the Government announces the collection point for the harvested opium just two or three days in advance, and farmers have to travel miles to the centre selected for weighing and final payment.



The **palace complex** ⓘ *0900-1700, foreigners Rs 50, Indians Rs 20*, below Taragarh, which was begun around 1600, is at the northern end of the bazaar, and was described by Kipling as "such a palace as men build for themselves in uneasy dreams – the work of goblins rather than of men". The buildings, on various levels, follow the shape of the hill. A steep, rough stone ramp leads up through the **Hazari Darwaza** (Gate of the Thousand) where the garrison lived; you may need to enter through a small door within the *darwaza*. The palace entrance is through the **Hathi Pol** (Elephant Gate, 1607-1631), which has two carved elephants with a water clock. Steps lead up to **Ratan Daulat** above the stables, the unusually small Diwan-i-Am which was intended to accommodate a select few at public audience. A delicate marble balcony overhangs the courtyard giving a view of the throne to the less privileged, who stood below. The **Chattar Mahal** (1660), the newer palace of green serpentine rock, is pure Rajput in style and contains private apartments decorated with wall paintings, glass and mirrors. The **Badal Mahal** bedroom has finely decorated ceilings. Rooms of the Chattar Mahal are kept locked but you may ask for permission at the Rawla office behind the Ayurvedic Hospital below the palace. The **Chitrashali**, a cloistered courtyard (open to the public, free entry) with a gallery running around a garden of fountains, has a splendid collection of miniatures showing scenes from the Radha Krishna story. Turquoise, blues and greens dominate (other pigments may have faded with exposure to sunlight) though the elephant panels on the dado are in a contrasting red. The murals (circa 1800) are some of the finest examples of Rajput art but are not properly maintained. There is supposed to be a labyrinth of catacombs in which the state treasures are believed to have been stored. Each ruler was allowed one visit but when the last guide died in the 1940s the secret of its location was lost! At night, the palace is lit up and the bazar comes alive. To see Badal and Chattar Mahals, ask at Rawla office behind Ayurvedic Hospital.

There are several 16th-17th-century stepwells and 'tanks' (*kunds*) in town. The 46-m deep **Raniji-ki-baori** ⓘ *closed Sun, 2nd Sat each month, 1000-1700, free, caretaker unlocks the gate*, with beautiful pillars and bas relief sculpture panels of

Vishnu's 10 *avatars*, is the most impressive. No longer in use, the water is stagnant. 
**Sukh Niwas (Mahal)**, a summer pleasure palace, faces the **Jait Sagar** lake where Kipling spent a night in the original pavilion. Further out are the 66 royal memorials at the rarely visited **Sar Bagh**, some of which have beautiful carvings. The caretaker expects Rs 10 tip. The square artificial **Naval Sagar** lake has in its centre a half-submerged temple to Varuna, the god of water. The lake surface beautifully reflects the entire town and palace, but tends to dry up in the summer months. West of the Naval Sagar, 10 km away, is **Phool Sagar Palace**, which was started in 1945 but was left unfinished. Prior permission is needed to view.

## Excursions

On the road to Chittaurgarh, **Menal**, 96 km, has a cluster of Siva temples believed to date from the time of the Guptas. They are associated with the Chauhans and other Rajput dynasties. Though neglected the temples have some fine carvings and a panel of erotic sculptures somewhat similar to those at Khajuraho in Madhya Pradesh. Behind is a deep, wooded ravine with a seasonal waterfall.

**Jhalawar,** 85 km southeast of Kota, was the capital of the princely state of the Jhalas which was separated from Kota by the British in 1838. It lies in a thickly forested area on the edge of the Malwa plateau with some interesting local forts, temples and ancient cave sites nearby. The **Garh Palace** in the town centre, now housing government offices, has some fine wall paintings which can be seen with permission. The **museum** ⓘ *closed Fri, 1000-1630, Rs 3*, here, established in 1915, has a worthwhile collection of sculptures, paintings and manuscripts. **Bhawani Natyashala** (1921) was known for its performances ranging from Shakespearean plays to Shakuntala dramas. The stage with a subterranean driveway allowed horses and chariots to be brought on stage during performances.

The small walled town of **Jhalarapatan**, 7 km south of Jhalawar, has several fine 11th-century Hindu temples, the **Padmanath Sun Temple** on the main road being the best. The **Shantinath Jain temple** has an entrance flanked by marble elephants. There are some fine carvings on the rear façade and silver polished idols inside the shrines.

About 7 km away, **Chandrawati**, on the banks of the Chandrabhaga River, has the ruins of some seventh-century Hindu temples with fragments of fine sculpture.

## Sleeping

**Chittaurgarh** *p371, map p372*

**B-C Pratap Palace**, Sri Gurukul Rd, near Head Post Office, T01472-240 099, hpratapp@hotmail.com. A Rajput Special Hotel. Clean, well-maintained rooms, some a/c, 2 with ornately painted walls good fun, good food in restaurant or in the pleasant garden, jeep and horse safaris visiting villages. Recommended.

**C Padmini**, Chanderiya Rd, near Sainik School, T01472-241 718, hotel_padmini@rediffmail.com. 46 clean rooms, 30 a/c, Indian style furniture, gloomy restaurant, quiet, airport transfer from Udaipur.

**C-D Meera**, near railway station, Neemuch Rd, T01472-240934. Modern, 24 a/c and non a/c rooms with TV and phone, restaurant, bar, laundry, car rental, travel assistance, internet, characterless but efficient.

**C-D Vinayak**, Collectorate Circle, T01472-245 035. 13 clean rooms in convenient but noisily located modern block, good restaurant.

**D-E Chetak**, opposite railway station, T01472-241 679. Modern hotel, 23 clean, fairly pleasant rooms, only 'deluxe' have Western toilets and hot showers.

**D-E Panna** (RTDC), Udaipur Rd, near railway station, T01472-241 238. 31 simple rooms, some a/c, best with fort view, dorm (Rs 50), veg dining hall, bar, run down but attentive service. Indian business hotel, popular with those visiting quarries/mines.

**E-F Ganesh Guest House**, New Fort Rd, opposite Sukhadiya Park, T01472-248 240. 20 basic but well-maintained rooms, Indian toilets only, clean, friendly.

**F Birla**, near the Kirti Stambh in the fort has been opened by the dharamshala group,

T01472-246939. 17-room guest house, very basic but only Rs50 per double, great location, water a problem in the summer.

**Chittaurgarh to Kota** *p374*

**B Bassi Fort Palace**, Bassi, T01472-225 321, www.bassifortpalace.com. 18 unpretentious rooms in a family run 16th-century fort. Same family has an abandoned fort on top of the nearby hill (where dinners can be arranged) and a hunting lodge 6 km away accessible by boat or horse. Safaris to this lodge and local tribal villages can be arranged. Refreshingly informal. Recommended.

**B Castle Bijaipur** (Rajput Special Hotels), Bijaipur, T01472-240 099, www.castlebijaipur.com. 25 simple rooms decorated in traditional style with comfortable furniture and modern bathrooms in castle and a new wing, lawns and gardens, great hill views from breezy terrace, superb pool, delicious Rajasthani meals, also tea on medieval bastion, jeep/ horse safaris with camping, jungle trekking.

**Kota** *p374*

Kota has a good selection of mid-range hotels, but little to suit the budget traveller, There's a far better choice in nearby Bundi.

**A-B Brijraj Bhawan Palace**, Civil Lines, T0744-450 529, www.indianheritage hotels.com. 7 spacious a/c rooms with verandahs, fixed Indian meals, old British Residency with character, stately drawing and dining rooms (regal memorabilia), superb location overlooking river, immaculate gardens, croquet, tennis, very civilized.

**A-B Umed Bhawan** (WelcomHeritage), Palace Rd, T0744-232 5262, www.welcom heritage.com. 32 large, comfortable rooms, sympathetic conversion, interesting memor- abilia and state rooms, elegant dining room, great beer bar, sunny terraces, behind woods (langurs, deer, parakeets, peacocks), billiards, tennis, attentive staff. Recommended.

**C Palkiya Haveli**, Mokha Para (in walled city), near Suraj Pol, T0744-2327 375, www.alsisarhaveli.com. 6 traditionally furnished a/c rooms with bath (tubs), well restored, carved wood furniture, exquisite murals, very good fixed meals, very peaceful courtyard garden (full of birds), family run.

**C Sukhdham Kothi**, Civil Lines, T0744-232 0081, www.indianheritagehotels.com. 15 elegant rooms (size varies), 10 a/c, in a 19th-century British residence with sandstone balconies and screens, good fixed meals, large, private garden well set back from road, family run, friendly. Recommended.

**C-D Navrang**, Collectorate Circle, Civil Lines, T0744-232 3294. Much more ornate inside than out, 25 rooms, deluxe much better than standard, aircooled or a/c, TV, **C** suites, new a/c vegetarian restaurant, well managed. Superior to nearby 'Phul Plaza'.

**D Chambal** (RTDC), Nayapura, T0744-232 6527. 12 rooms, nothing special but clean, friendly staff, well located close to old city.

**C Surpin**, Jhalawar Rd, T0744-232 4710. 18 a/c rooms with hot showers, restaurant, popular, fairly modern, long way from old city but convenient if going on to Bundi.

**F** budget hotels near the bus stand and station can be noisy and dirty.

**Bundi** *p374, map p375*

**B-D Haveli Braj Bhushanjee**, below the fort, opposite Ayurvedic Hospital (entrance in alley), T0747-244 2509, www.kiplingsbundi.com. 16 quaint rooms (each different) with clean bath (hot showers), in 19th-century 4-storey *haveli* with plenty of atmosphere and interesting memorabilia, home-cooked Brahmin vegetarian meals (no alcohol), pleasant terrace, good fort views, pick-up from station on request, good craft shop below. Recommended.

**C-D Ishwari Niwas Palace**, 1 Civil Lines, T0747-244 2414, www.angelfire.com/amiga/inheritage. 20 simple air-cooled rooms (period furnishings) with bath, around a courtyard, tired looking old Rajput family home, traditional meals (Rs 250), friendly, peaceful, good local tours, "underwhelming".

**C-D Royal Retreat**, below Fort, T0747-244 4426, jpbundi@yahoo.com. Looks rundown but quite clean and well kept inside, open courts, 5 largish rooms most with bath, family run, good veg restaurant, café, rooftop dining with views, good craft shop, internet, a little overpriced but in a fabulous location.

*For an explanation of sleeping and eating price codes used in this guide, see inside the front cover. Other relevant information is found in Essentials, see pages 56-61.*

D **Purvaj**, centre of Jhalawar, a delightful old *haveli*, owned by an interesting family, delicious and simple homecooked meals.

D-E **Katkoun Haveli**, near Gopal Mandir, Balchand Para, T0747-244 4311, raghunandansingh@yahoo.com. 6 clean, newly built rooms with modern bathrooms in pleasant family home, some with small balconies.

D-E **Vrindavati** (RTDC), 300 m from Sukh Mahal, on Jait Sagar Lake, T0747-244 2473. 7 rooms in old bungalow in attractive garden with beautiful views, but poorly maintained and a long way from town.

E **Menal Motel**, Menal, has 1 simple room – handy for a cup of tea or a simple meal.

E-F **Kasera**, Haveli Dev Baxjiki, Nagadi Bazar (old part of town), T0747-244 6630. 8 simple, clean rooms, some with air-cooler and hot shower, good vegetarian meals in rooftop restaurant, special lassi, cane juice, atmospheric 350-year-old *haveli*, pleasant family.

E-F **Kasera Heritage View**, below palace, T0747-244 4679. 11 cute rooms all with attached bathrooms, rooftop restaurant with good views of the palace and a varied menu. Same family owns **Kasera** and is soon to open **B-D Kasera Paradise**, which should become Bundi's best hotel, with 10 a/c rooms, marble bathrooms and a rooftop restaurant 5 storeys up in an old *haveli*.

E-F **Kishan Niwas**, near Laxmi Nath Temple, Nahar ka Chohtta, by Moti Mahal, T0747-244 5807. 8 spartan, clean rooms with bath (hot water), good home cooking, Mr Singh is very friendly and helpful.

E-F **Lake View Paying Guest House**, Bohra Meghwan ji ki Haveli, Balchand Para, below the palace, by Nawal Sagar, T0747-244 2326, lakeviewbundi@yahoo.com. 7 simple clean rooms (3 in separate, basic garden annexe with shared bath) in 150-year-old *haveli* with wall paintings, private terrace shared with monkeys and peacocks, lovely views from rooftop, warm welcome, very friendly hosts.

E-F **R.N. Haveli**, behind Laxmi Nath Temple, T0-98293 39036, RNHaveli2004@yahoo.co.in. 5 rooms in a friendly family home run exclusively by women, excellent home cooking. Recommended.

E-F **Uma Megh Haveli**, Balchand Para, T0747- 244 2191. 11 unrestored but very atmospheric rooms, 7 with basic attached bathrooms, plus a pleasant garden and restaurant.

## Eating

### Chittaurgarh *p371, map p372*

For the best places to eat, visit the hotels.

TT **Pratap Palace**, tasty Indian in pleasant surroundings.

TT **Vinayak**, extensive menu including wide range of sweets.

T **Fort View Garden**, Rana Sanga Market, near Chandralok Cinema. Punjabi, Gujurati and Rajasthani, good *thalis*, pleasant lawn.

T **RTDC Café**, near the Vijay Stambha is handy for visitors to the fort.

### Kota *p374*

The best, and most expensive, places to eat are the hotels; those listed below offer more reasonable alternatives. Good kulfis and homemade ices in Sindhi shops.

TT **Payal**, Nayapura. Good Indian. Also some Chinese, and Indianized Continental.

TT **Venue**, Civil Lines. A/c, good ,but very spicy Indian, disappointing western.

T **Hariyali**, Bundi Rd. Good Punjabi, some Chinese/Continental. Pleasant garden restaurant, outdoors or under a small shelter, very popular but some way out of town.

T **Jodhpur Sweets**, Ghumanpura Market. Saffron *lassis* and flavoured milks.

T **Priya**, Nayapura. Popular for Indian veg.

T **Palace View**, outdoor meals/snacks. Handy for visitors to the City Palace.

### Bundi *p374, map p375*

Several of the hotels have pleasant rooftop restaurants, see Sleeping above.

T **Diamond**, Suryamahal Chowk, in hotel. Very popular locally for cheap vegetarian meals, handy when visiting stepwells.

T **Sathi Cold Drinks**, Palace Rd, in hotel. Excellent *lassis* (try saffron, spices, pistachio and fruit), pleasant seating.

T **Sher-e-Punjab**, in hotel, near **Diamond**, serves non-vegetarian.

## Festivals and events

### Chittaurgarh *p371, map p372*

Mira Utsav is held in **Oct/Nov** every year, 2 days of cultural evening programmes and religious songs in the fort's Mira temple.

**Kota** *p374*
Colourful **Gangaur** (1-2 Apr 2006, 21-22 Mar 2007) and **Teej** (28-29 Jul 2006, 15-16 Aug 2007). **Dasara Mela** (30 Sep-2 Oct 2006, 19-21 Oct 2007). Great atmosphere, with shows in lit up palace grounds.

**Bundi** *p374, map p375*
Bundi is especially colourful and interesting during the festivals; **Kajli Teej** (11-12 Aug 2006, 30-31 Aug 2007), and **Bundi Utsav**, which takes place 3 days after the Pushkar fair has finished, see box page 428. Jhalawar sees the **Chandrabhaga Fair**, a cattle and camel fair with all the colour and authenticity of Pushkar without its commercialization. Animals are traded in large numbers in the fields, pilgrims come to bathe in the river as the temples become the centre of religious activity and the town is abuzz with all manner of vendors.

## Transport

**Chittaurgarh** *p371, map p372*
**Bicycle**
Bike hire, opposite railway station, Rs 5 per hr.

**Bus**
Enquiries, T01472-241 177. Daily buses to **Bundi** (4 hrs), **Kota** (5 hrs), **Ajmer** (5 hrs) and **Udaipur** (2½ hrs along a picturesque route passing fields of pink and white poppies, grown legally for opium).

**Train**
Enquiries, T01472-240 131. A 117 km branch line runs from Chittaurgarh to **Udaipur**. At **Mavli Junction** (72 km) another branch runs down the Aravalli scarp to **Marwar Junction** (150 km). The views along this line are very picturesque indeed. By taking this route you can visit Udaipur, Ajmer and Jodhpur in a circular journey. **Ajmer**: *Purna-Jaipur Exp, 9770*, 0550, 4½ hrs. *Ahmadabad DSR Exp, 9944*, 1500, 6 hrs. **Indore**: *Jaipur-Purna Exp, 9769*, 2015, 7½ hrs; **Jaipur**: *Purna Jaipur Exp, 9770*, 0550, 8½ hrs; *Chetak Exp, 9616*, 2200, 8½ hrs; both continue to **Delhi** 15-16 hrs. **Udaipur**: *Chetak Exp, 9615*, 0650, 3½ hrs; *DSR Ahmadabad Exp, 9943*, 1345, 4½ hrs, (continues to **Ahmadabad**, 17 hrs).

**Kota**
**Bus**
At least hourly bus to **Bundi** (45 mins) and a few daily to **Ajmer**, **Chittaurgarh**, **Jhalarapatan** (2½ hrs); also to **Gwalior**, **Sawai Madhopur** and **Ujjain**.

**Train**
From Kota Junction: **Bharatpur**: *Golden Temple Mail, 2903*, 1130, 4 hrs (and Mathura, 5 hrs). **Mumbai** (Central): *Rajdhani Exp, 2952*, 2050, 11¾ hrs; *Paschim Exp, 2926*, 2355, 15½ hrs; *Golden Temple Mail, 2904*, 1455, 15¼ hrs. **New Delhi**: *Rajdhani Exp, 2951*, 0430, 5½ hrs; *Golden Temple Mail, 2903*, 1130, 7½ hrs; *Dehra Dun Exp, 9019*, 1955, 10½ hrs – all via **Sawai Madhopur**, 1½ hrs.

**Bundi** *p374, map p375*
**Bus**
Enquiries: T0747-224 5422. To **Ajmer** (165 km), 5 hrs; **Kota** (37 km), 45 mins; **Chittaurgarh** (157 km), 5 hrs; **Udaipur** (120 km), 3 hrs. For **Jhalarapatan** catch a bus from **Kota** to **Jhalawar**; then auto-rickshaw or local bus for sights. The Ujjain-Jhalawar road is appalling.

**Train**
Enquiries: T0747-224 3582. The station south of town has a train each way between **Kota** and **Neemuch** via **Chittaurgarh**.

## Directory

**Kota** *p374*
**Hospitals** MBS Hospital, T0744-245 0241. **Internet** Acme, 2nd floor, Kalawati Paliwal Market, Gumantpura. **Police** T0744-245 0066. **Tourist office** Rajasthan, Nayapura Bagh, T0744-232 7695.

**Bundi** *p374, map p375*
**Banks** Exchange can be a problem; try Bank of Baroda, T0747-244 3706. **Hospitals** T0747-244 2833, City, T0747-244 2333. SS Nursing Home, T0747-244 2627. **Internet** Dotted around town. **Tourist office** Circuit House, T0747-244 3697.

# Western Rajasthan

*The Rajasthan of most people's imagination is found in this part of the state; camels crossing windswept sand dunes, colourful tribes dancing against a stark desert landscape, and some imperious buildings surveying the scene from on high. Jaisalmer is perhaps the ultimate expression of these romantic desert images. However, perhaps no other fort in Rajasthan exudes the same authority as Jodhpur's Meherangarh, watching over the town with unmatched majesty. The area south of Jodhpur is dotted with some of the state's most secluded heritage hotels, while to the north lie the utterly authentic attractions of Nagaur and Osian.*

# Jodhpur and around

*→ Phone code: 0291. Colour map 2, grid B3.*

*Rajasthan's second largest city, Jodhpur is entirely dominated by its spectacular fort, towering over proceedings below with absolute authority. The fascinating old city is a hive of activity, the colourful bazaars and narrow lanes often frequented by equally colourful tribal people from the surrounding areas. South of the railway line things are altogether more serene, and nowhere more so than the massively impressive Umaid Bhawan Palace, its classic interior belying the art deco extravaganza within. There are also some remarkable sights around Jodhpur: the temples of Osian, Nagaur and some great heritage hotels set in quiet villages.* *» For Sleeping, Eating and other listings, see pages 388-393.*

## Ins and outs

**Getting there** Jodhpur has good air, rail and road links with the other major cities of Rajasthan as well as Delhi and Mumbai. Many visitors stop here either on the way to or from Jaisalmer, or on their way down to Udaipur.

**Getting around** The train and bus stations are conveniently located close to the old city, with most hotels a Rs 20-30 rickshaw ride away, while the airport is 5 km south of town. The old city is small enough to walk around, although many people find a rented bicycle the best way to get about. *» See Transport, page 393, for further details.*

**Tourist information** The government tourist office is on the grounds of the RTDC **Hotel Ghoomar** ⓘ *High Court Rd, T0291-254 5083*. As well as the usual supply of maps and pamphlets, it also organize half-day city tours and village safaris. Also, **International Tourist Bureau** ⓘ *Railway station, T0291-243 9052*.

## History

The **Rathore** Rajputs had moved to **Marwar** – the 'region of death' – in 1211, after their defeat at Kanauj by Muhammad Ghori. In 1459 Rao Jodha, forced to leave the Rathore capital at Mandore, 8 km to the north, chose this place as his capital because of its strategic location on the edge of the Thar Desert. The Rathores subsequently controlled wide areas of Rajasthan. Rao Udai Singh of Jodhpur (died 1581) received the title of Raja from Akbar, and his son, Sawai Raja Sur Singh (died 1595), conquered Gujarat and part of the Deccan for the Emperor. Maharaja Jaswant Singh (died 1678), having supported Shah Jahan in the Mughal struggle for succession in 1658, had a problematic relationship with the subsequent Mughal rule of Aurangzeb, and his son Ajit Singh was only able to succeed him after Aurangzeb's own death in 1707. In addition to driving the Mughals out of Ajmer he added substantially to the Meherangarh Fort in Jodhpur. His

### True blue

As you approach the fort you will notice the predominance of blue houses which are often inaccurately referred to as "Brahmin houses" – the colour being associated with the high caste. In fact they are blue due to termites (white ants). It appears that the white lime-wash used originally did not deter the pests which caused havoc, making unsightly cavities in local homes. The addition of chemicals (eg copper sulphate), which resulted in turning the white lime to a blue- wash, was found to be effective in limiting the pest damage and so was widely used in the area around the fort. This also happens to be a part of town where large numbers of the Brahmin community live.

successor, Maharaja Abhai Singh (died 1749) captured Ahmedabad, and the State came into treaty relations with the British in 1818.

Jodhpur lies on the once strategic Delhi-Gujarat trading route and the Marwaris managed and benefited from the traffic of opium, copper, silk, sandalwood, dates, coffee and much more besides.

# Jodhpur

## The Old City

The Old City is surrounded by a huge 9½-km long wall which has 101 bastions and seven gates, above which are inscribed the names of the places to which the roads underneath them lead. It comprises a labyrinthine maze of narrow streets and lively markets, a great place to wander round and get lost. Some of the houses and temples are of richly carved stone, in particular the red sandstone buildings of the Siré (Sardar) Bazar. Here the **Taleti Mahal** (early 17th century), one of three concubines' palaces in Jodhpur, has the unique feature of *jarokhas* decorated with temple columns.

## The new city

The new city beyond the walls is also of interest. Overlooking the Umaid Sagar is the **Umaid Bhawan Palace** on Chittar Hill. Building started in 1929 as a famine relief exercise when the monsoon failed for the third year running. Over 3,000 people worked for 14 years, building this vast 347 room palace of sandstone and marble. The hand hewn blocks are interlocked into position, and use no mortar. It was designed by HV Lanchester, with the most modern furnishing and facilities in mind, and completed in 1943. The interior decoration was left to the artist JS Norblin, a refugee from Poland; he painted the frescoes in the Throne Room (East Wing). For th architectural historian, Tillotson, it is "the finest example of Indo-Deco. The forms are crisp and precise, and the bland monochrome of the stone makes the eye concentrate on their carved shapes". The royal family still occupy part of the palace. Part is a museum and part a luxury hotel (see Sleeping), and the interior produces a remarkable sensation of separation from the Indian environment in which it is set. There is a subterranean swimming pool decorated with signs of the zodiac; the murals are Norblin's. **Umaid Bhawan Palace Museum** ⓘ *T0291-251 0101, 0900-1700, Rs 10, foreigners Rs 40*, includes the Darbar Hall with its elegantly flaking murals plus a good collection of miniatures, armour and quirky old clocks as well as a bizarre range of household paraphernalia; if it was fashionable in the 1930s, expensive and not available in India, it's in here. The plans and photographs of the rest of the palace are also worth seeing.

**Government Museum** ⓘ *Umaid Park, closed Fri, 1000-1630, Rs 3,* is a time-capsule from the British Raj, little added since Independence, with some moth-eaten stuffed animals and featherless birds, images of Jain Tirthankars, miniature portraits and antiquities. A small zoo in the gardens has a few rare exotic species.

Just southeast of Raikabagh Station are the **Raikabagh Palace** and the **Jubilee Buildings**, public offices designed by Sir Samuel Swinton Jacob in the Indo-Saracenic style. On the Mandore Road, 2 km to the north, is the large **Mahamandir** temple.

## Meherangarh

ⓘ *T0291-254 8790, 0900-1700, Rs 20, foreigners Rs 250 including excellent MP3 audio guide and camera fee, video Rs 200, allow at least 2 hrs, there is a pleasant restaurant on the terrace near the ticket office.*

The 'Majestic Fort' sprawls along the top of a steep escarpment with a sheer drop to the south. Originally started by Rao Jodha in 1459, it has walls up to 36 m high and 21 m wide, towering above the plains. Most of what stands today is from the period of Maharajah Jaswant Singh (1638-1678). On his death in 1678, Aurangzeb occupied the fort. However, after Aurangzeb's death Meherangarh returned to Jaswant Singh's son Ajit Singh and remained the royal residence until the Umaid Bhavan was completed in 1943. It is now perhaps the best preserved and presented palace in Rajasthan, an excellent example which the others will hopefully follow.

The summit has three areas: the palace (northwest), a wide terrace to the east of the palace, and the strongly fortified area to the south. There are extensive views from the top. One approach is by a winding path up the west side, possible by rickshaw, but the main approach and car park is from the east. The climb is quite stiff; the disabled may use the elevator.

**The gateways** There were originally seven gateways. The first, the **Fateh Gate**, is heavily fortified with spikes and a barbican that forces a 45° turn. The smaller **Gopal Gate** is followed by the **Bhairon Gate**, with large guardrooms. The fourth, **Toati Gate**, is now missing but the fifth, **Dodhkangra Gate**, marked with cannon shots, stands over a turn in the path and has loopholed battlements for easy defence. Next is the **Marti Gate**, a long passage flanked by guardrooms. The last, **Loha (Iron) Gate**, controls the final turn into the fort and has handprints (31 on one side and five on the other) of royal *satis*, the wives of maharajas, see page 1316. It is said that six queens and 58 concubines became *satis* on Ajit Singh's funeral pyre in 1724. *Satis* carried the Bhagavad Gita with them into the flames and legend has it that the holy book would never perish. The main entrance is through the **Jay (Victory) Pol**.

**The palaces** From the Loha Gate the ramp leads up to the Suraj (Sun) Pol, which opens onto the Singar Choki Chowk, the main entrance to the museum, see below. Used for royal ceremonies such as the anointing of rajas, the north, west and southwest sides of the Singar Choki Chowk date from the period immediately before the Mughal occupation in 1678. The upper storeys of the chowk were part of the *zenana*, and from the **Jhanki Mahal** ('glimpse palace') on the upper floor of the north wing the women could look down on the activities of the courtyard. Thus the chowk below has the features characteristic of much of the rest of the *zenana*, *jarokhas* surmounted by the distinctive Bengali style eaves, and beautifully ornate *jali* screens. These allowed cooling breezes to ventilate rooms and corridors in the often stiflingly hot desert summers.

*In 1886 the Jodhpur Railway first introduced camel drawn trains until steam engines were acquired. The maharaja's luxurious personal saloons which date from 1926 are beautifully finished with inlaid wood and silver fittings and are on display near the Umaid Bhawan Palace.*

Also typical of Mughal buildings was the use of material hung from rings below the eaves to provide roof covering, as in the columned halls of the **Daulat Khana** and the **Sileh Khana** (armoury), which date from Ajit Singh's reign. The collection of Indian weapons in the armoury is unequalled, with remarkable swords and daggers, often beautifully decorated with calligraphy. Shah Jahan's red silk and velvet tent, lavishly embroidered with gold thread and used in the Imperial Mughal campaign, is in the **Tent Room**. The **Jewel House** has a wonderful collection of jewellery, including diamond eyebrows held by hooks over the ears. There are also palanquins, howdahs and ornate royal cradles, all marvellously well preserved.

The **Phool Mahal** (Flower Palace), above the Sileh Khana, was built by Abhai Singh (1724-1749) as a hall of private audience. The stone *jali* screens are original and

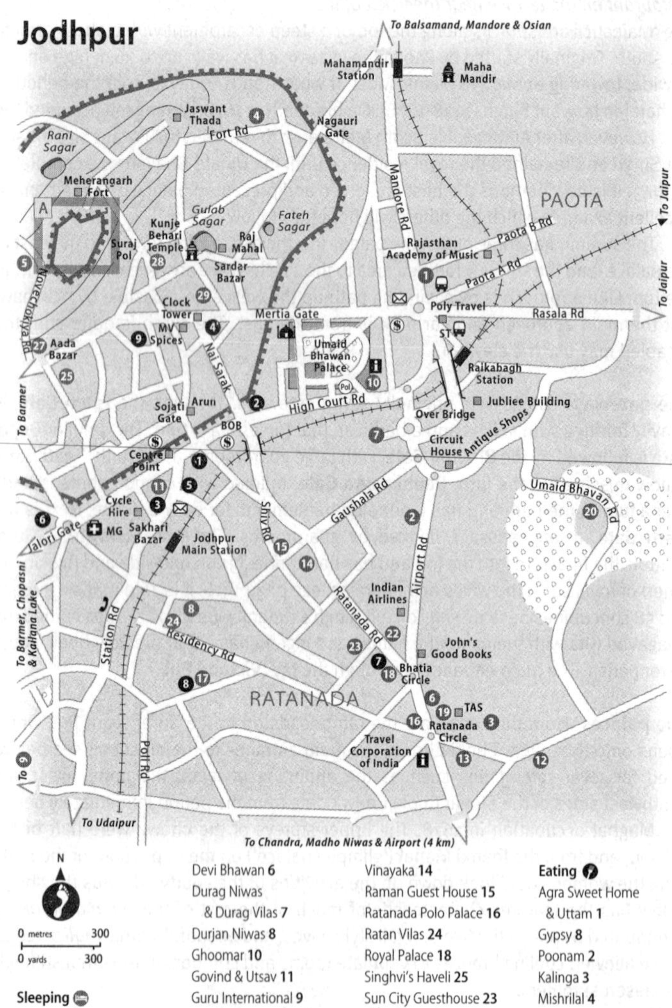


**Sleeping**

Abhay Days 1
Ajit Bhawan, Ranbanka & On the Rocks 2
Blue House 27
Chauhan's 4
Cosy Guest House & Yogis 5
Devi Bhawan 6
Durag Niwas & Durag Vilas 7
Durjan Niwas 8
Ghoomar 10
Govind & Utsav 11
Guru International 9
Haveli Guest House 28
Haveli Palace Inn 29
Inn Season 17
Karni Bhawan 12
Madho Niwas 3
Newton's Manor 13
Vinayaka 14
Raman Guest House 15
Ratanada Polo Palace 16
Ratan Vilas 24
Royal Palace 18
Singhvi's Haveli 25
Sun City Guesthouse 23
Taj Hari Mahal 19
Umaid Bhawan Palace 20
Youth Hostel 22

**Eating**

Agra Sweet Home & Uttam 1
Gypsy 8
Poonam 2
Kalinga 3
Mishrilal 4
New Jodphur Lodge 9
Rawat Mishtan Bhandar 5
Sankalp 7
Shandar 6

### The Bishnois

The Bishnois (Vishnois), follow '29' (bish-noi) principles of a non-violent Vaishnava sect, founded in the 15th century by Jambeswarji. They are known for their reverence for wildlife and their careful environmental management, protecting, especially, green vegetation and preserving the blackbuck antelope from extinction. They are a gentle community of potters, weavers, leather embroid-erers and camel herders. Some groups are being helped to over-come their addiction to opium.

there are striking portraits of former rulers, a lavishly gilded ceiling and the Jodhpur coat of arms displayed above the royal couch; the murals of the 36 musical modes are a late 19th-century addition.

The **Umaid Vilas**, which houses Rajput miniatures, is linked to the **Sheesh Mahal** (Mirror Palace), built by Ajit Singh between 1707 and 1724. The room has characteristic large and regularly sized mirror work, unlike Mughal 'mirror palaces'. Immediately to its south, and above the Sardar Vilas, is the **Takhat Vilas**. Added by Maharajah Takhat Singh (1843-1873), it has wall murals of dancing girls, love legends and Krishna Lila, while its ceiling has two unusual features: massive wooden beams to provide support and the curious use of colourful Belgian Christmas tree balls.

The **Ajit Vilas** has a fascinating collection of musical instruments and costumes. On the ground floor of the Takhat Vilas is **Sardar Vilas**, and to its south the **Khabka** and **Chandan Mahals** (sleeping quarters). The **Moti Vilas** wings to the north, east and south of the Moti Mahal Chowk, date from Jaswant Singh's reign. The women could watch proceedings in the courtyard below through the *jali* screens of the surrounding wings. Tillotson suggests that the **Moti Mahal** (Pearl Palace) ⓘ *15 mins for Rs 150*, to the west, although placed in the *zenana* of the fort, was such a magnificent building that it could only have served the purpose of a Diwan-i-Am (Hall of Public Audience). The Moti Mahal is fronted by excellently carved 19th-century woodwork, while inside waist-level niches housed oil lamps whose light would have shimmered from the mirrored ceiling. A palmist reads your fortune at Moti Mahal Chowk (museum area).

**Mehrangarh Fort Palace Museum** is in a series of palaces with beautifully designed and decorated windows and walls. It has a magnificent collection of the maharajas' memorabilia – superbly maintained and presented.

**Jaswant Thada** ⓘ *off the road leading up to the fort, 0900-1700, Rs 10*, is the cremation ground of the former rulers with distinctive memorials in white marble which commemorate Jaswant Singh II (1899) and successive rulers of Marwar. It is situated in pleasant and well-maintained gardens and is definitely worth visiting on the way back from the fort.

## Excursions

A village safari visiting a **Bishnoi village** is recommended, although they have naturally become more touristy over the years. Most tours include the hamlets of **Guda**, famous for wildlife, **Khejarali**, a well-known Bishnoi village, **Raika** cameleers' settlement and **Salawas**, see page 387.

The small, semi-rural village of **Jhalamand**, 12 km south of Jodhpur, is a good alternative to staying in the city, particularly if you have your own transport. It works especially well as a base from which to explore the Bishnoi and Raika communities.

**Marwar**, 8 km north of Jodhpur, is the old 14th-century capital of Mandore, situated on a plateau. Set around the old cremation ground with the red sandstone *chhatris* of the Rathore rulers, the gardens are usually crowded with Indian tourists at weekends. The **Shrine of the 33 Crore Gods** is a hall containing huge painted rock-cut figures of heroes and gods, although some of the workmanship is a little crude. The largest deval, a combination of temple and cenotaph, is Ajit Singh's (died 1724); worth a closer look but is unkempt. The remains of an eighth-century Hindu temple is on a hilltop nearby.

**Bal Samand Lake** is the oldest artificial lake in Rajasthan, 5 km north. Dating from 1159, it is surrounded by parkland laid out in 1936 where the 19th-century **Hawa Mahal** was turned into a royal summer palace. Although the interior is European in style, it has entirely traditional red sandstone filigree windows and beautifully carved balconies. The peaceful and well-maintained grounds exude calm and tranquillity, while the views over the lake are simply majestic.

# Around Jodhpur

The temples of Osian are remarkable as much for their location in the middle of the desert as their architecture, while Nagaur is one of Rajasthan's busiest but most unaffected cities. The area south of Jodhpur is refreshingly green and fertile compared to the desert landscapes of most of Western Rajasthan (although it canbe very dry from March until the monsoon). Leaving the city, the landscape soon becomes agricultural, punctuated by small, friendly villages, some housing stunning heritage hotels.

## Osian

Surrounded by sand dunes, this ancient town north of Jodhpur in the Thar desert contains the largest group of eighth- to 10th-century Hindu and Jain temples in Rajasthan. The typical Pratihara Dynasty **temple complex** is set on a terrace whose walls are finely decorated with mouldings and miniatures. The sanctuary walls have central projections with carved panels' and above these rise curved towers. The doorways are usually decorated with river goddesses, serpents and scrollwork. The 23 temples are grouped in several sites north, west and south of the town. The western group contains a mixture of Hindu temples, including the **Surya Temple** (early eighth century) with beautifully carved pillars. The Jain **Mahavira Temple** (eighth to 10th centuries) the best preserved, 200 m further on a hillock, rises above the town, and boasts a fantastically gaudy interior. The 11th- to 12th-century **Sachiya Mata Temple** is a living temple of the Golden Durga. Osian is well worth visiting.

## Khimsar

On the edge of the desert, 80 km northeast of Jodhpur, Khimsar was founded by the Jain saint Mahavir 2,500 years ago. The isolated, battle scarred, 16th-century moated castle of which a section remains, had a *zenana* added in the mid-18th century and a regal wing added in the 1940s. See Sleeping for one of the best hotels in the state.

## Nagaur

ⓘ *Rs 10, foreigners Rs 50, still camera Rs 25, video Rs 50.*

Nagaur, 137 km north of Jodhpur, was a centre of Chishti Sufis. It attracts interest as it preserves some fine examples of pre-Mughal and Mughal architecture. The dull stretch of desert is enlivened by Nagaur's fort palace, temples and *havelis*. The city walls are said to date from the 11th- to 12th-century Chauhan period. Akbar built the mosque here and there is a shrine of the disciple of Mu'inuddin Chishti of Ajmer, see page 420. **Ahhichatragarh Fort**, which dominates the city, is absolutely vast, contains palaces of the Mughal emperors and of the Marwars, and is being restored with help from the Paul Getty Foundation. The Akbar Mahal is really stunning, unspeakable elegant and perfectly proportioned. The fort also has excellent wall paintings and interesting ancient systems of rainwater conservation and storage, ably explained by a very knowledgeable curator. It was awarded a UNESCO Heritage Award in 2000.

## Khichan

Four kilometres from Phalodi, southwest of Bikaner, just off the NH15, is a lovely, picturesque village with superb red sandstone *havelis* of the Oswal Jains. Beyond the village are sand dunes and mustard fields, and a lake which attracts ducks and other waterfowl. The once small quiet village has grown into a bustling agricultural centre and a prominent bird feeding station. Jain villagers put out grain behind the village for winter visitors; up to 8,000 demoiselle cranes and occasionally Common eastern cranes can be seen in December and January on the feeding grounds.

## Pokaran

Pokaran, between Jaisalmer and Jodhpur, stands on the edge of the great desert with dunes stretching 100 km west to the Pakistan border. It provides a mid-way stopover between Bikaner/Jodhpur and Jaisalmer for tourists as it did for royal and merchant caravans in the past. The impressive 16th-century yellow sandstone Pokaran fort, overlooking a confusion of streets in the town below, has a small museum with an interesting collection of medieval weapons, costumes and paintings. There are good views from the ramparts. Pokaran is also well known for its potters who make red-and-white pottery and terracotta horses/elephants. **Ramdeora**, the Hindu and Jain pilgrim centre nearby, has Bishnoi hamlets and a preserve for blackbuck antelope, Indian gazelle, bustards and sand grouse. **Ramdeora Fair** is an important religious event (12-13 September 2005, 2-3 September 2006, 21-22 September 2007).

**Khetolai**, about 25 km northwest of Pokaran, is the site of India's first nuclear test explosion held underground on 18 March 1974, and of further tests in May 1998.

## Salawas

Salawas, about 30-minutes' drive south from Jodhpur, is well known for its pit loom weaving. The village produces *durries*, carpets, rugs, bed covers and tents using camel hair, goat hair, wool and cotton in colourful and interesting patterns. You can visit the weavers' co-operative **Roopraj Durrie Udyog**, where you can buy authentic village crafts, but watch out for high prices and pushy salesmen.

## Luni

The tiny bustling village of Luni, 40 km from Jodhpur, sits in the shadow of the 19th-century red sandstone Fort Chanwa which has been converted to a hotel. With its complex of courtyards, water wheels, and intricately carved façades, the fort and its village offer an attractive and peaceful alternative to the crowds of Jodhpur. The village of Sanchean, which you will pass through on the way, is worth exploring.

## Rohet and Sardar Samand

Rohet, 50 km north of Jodhpur, was once a picturesque hamlet settled by the Bishnoi community. It is now a busy highway village although it has a busy bazar and is pleasant to wander around. At the end of the village a lake attracts numerous winter migrants in addition to resident birds. Here also are the family cenotaphs. Rohetgarh, a small 'castle' beside the lake, which has been converted in to a hotel, has a collection of antique hunting weapons. The hotel will organise trips to the local bishnoi villages. It is quite usual to see blue bull, black buck and other antelopes in the fields. Village life is very hard at the moment but the Bishnoi are a dignified people who delight in explaining their customs. You can take part in the opium tea ceremony which is quite fun and somewhat akin to having a pint with the locals down at the pub.

The lake nearby is a beautiful setting for the royal 1933 art deco hunting lodge, **Sardar Samand Palace**, see page 391. The lake attracts pelicans, flamingos, cranes, egrets and kingfishers and the wildlife sanctuary has blackbuck, gazelle and nilgai, but the water level drops substantially during summer; the lake has actually dried up from April-June in recent years. Sardar Samand is 60 km southeast of Jodhpur.

## Nimaj

A small feudal town 110 km east of Jodhpur on the way to the Jaipur-Udaipur highway, the real attraction is the artificial lake, **Chhatra Sagar**, 4 km away. The ex- ruling family have recreated a 1920s style tented hunting lodge on the lake's dam, which offers amazing views over the water and a genuine family welcome. See Sleeping.

## Balotra and around

The small textile town, 100 km southwest of Jodhpur, is known for its traditional weaving using pit looms and block prints, although many are now mechanised causing pollution of the Luni River. Nearby is the beautiful Jain temple with elephant murals at **Nakoda**. **Kanana**, near Balotra, celebrates **Holi** with stage shows and other entertainment. There is a *dharamshala* at Nakoda and guesthouses at Balotra. At **Tilwara**, 127 km from Jodhpur, the Mallinathji **cattle fair** is a major event, which takes place on the the dry Luni riverbed. Held just after **Holi** every year, over 50,000 animals (although this has declined in recent years due to the drought), including Kapila (Krishna's) cows and Kathiawari horses, are brought making it Rajasthan's largest. Few tourists make it as far as this so it is much less commercial than Pushkar. Try and go with a Rajasthani-speaking guide as the farmers and traders are very happy to allow you in on the negotiations as well as describing the key things to look for when buying a camel (the front legs should not rub against its belly for instance). There are some interesting trade stalls including sword makers.



## Sleeping

**Jodhpur** *p381, map p384*

**LL-L Umaid Bhawan Palace**, T0291-251 0101, www.amanresorts.com. Under renovation at time of research.

**L Taj Hari Mahal**, 5 Residency Rd, T0291-243 9700, www.tajhotels.com. 93 plush rooms blending traditional and modern, imaginatively designed, good restaurants, excellent pool, the epitome of comfort.

**A Ajit Bhawan**, Airport Rd, near Circuit House, T0291-251 1410, www.ajitbhawan.com. 65 a/c rooms, 50 in cottages, best heritage rooms in main building plus 5 attractive tents. Great pool, good Indian buffets although poor coffee shop with inattentive staff, well-kept garden, 'village safari' (see Around Jodhpur p386), group-oriented, could do with a face-lift.

**A Bal Samand Palace** (WelcomHeritage), see Excursions p385, T02912-572 321, www.welcomheritage.com. In extensive grounds on the lake, 9 attractively furnished suites in the separate atmospheric palace and 26 rooms in the imaginatiively renovated stables, restaurant (mainly buffet), lovely pool, boating, pleasant orchards which attract nilgai, jackals, peacocks, has a calming, tranquil atmosphere.

**A Ranbanka**, Circuit House Rd, T0291-251 2801, www.ranbankahotels.com. 31 renovated rooms in period property, communal areas a little unloved but staff are charming, small pool, large garden.

**B Abhay Days**, Mandore Rd, off Paota Circle, T0291-254 2980, www.daysindia.com. 72 a/c rooms in modern hotel with western standards, excellent reasonably priced vegetarian restaurant, good pool and health club, good value.

**B Durjan Niwas**, Daspan Vihar, off Loco Shed Rd, Ratanada, T0291-264 9546, www.durjanniwas.com.16 comfortable, a/c rooms with balcony, pool, old house of Thakur family in a quiet location, friendly, helpful.

**B Jhalamand Garh**, Jhalamand, see Excursions p385, T0291-272 0481, www.heritagehotelsindia.com. 17 comfortable rooms in whitewashed, family-run period property. Good local dishes in atmospheric dining hall, jeep, horse and camel safaris arranged, perhaps not the most professional set up but all the more charming for it.

**B Karni Bhawan**, Palace Rd, T0291-251 2101, www.karnihotels.com. 30 clean, simple, classy rooms ( 20 a/c), each with a different theme and period furniture to match, in 1940s sandstone 'colonial bungalow' (on 3 floors!). Village theme restaurant, peaceful lawns, clean pool, unhurried helpful staff.

**B Royal Palace**, Bhatia Circle, Ratanada, T0291-515429, hrpalaceindia@yahoo.com. 24 a/c rooms, 2 suites, modern 4-storey building, restaurant, helpful family and staff.

**B-C Inn Season**, PWD Rd, T0291-261 6400, www.innseasonjodhpur.com. 11 classy a/c rooms in smart, well-run hotel, good pool in beautiful gardens, a definite cut above.

**B-C Ratan Vilas**, Loco Shed Rd, Ratanada, T0291-261 4418. 11 rooms (more on way), some a/c, arranged around beautiful courtyard in elegant period property. Peaceful as no TVs. Very well maintained, lovely gardens, friendly family. Recommended.

**C Guru International**, 26 Nai Sarak, T0291-263 7152, www.hotelguruinternational.com. The best of the many similar, Indian business class hotels on the same street. 22 a/c rooms, okay value, friendly, helpful staff.

**C Utsav**, Raibahadur Bazar, MG Rd, T0291-510 5100, hotelutsav@mailinfinity.com. 42 a/c rooms in modern, contemporary style, good views from top floors, discreet staff.

**C-D Devi Bhavan**, 1 Ratanada Circle, T0291-251 1067, www.devibhawan.com. 10 rooms (2 more on the way) with bath, most with a/c, delightful shady garden, excellent Indian dinner (set timings), Rajput family home. Popular with independent travellers.. Recommended.

**C-D Haveli Palace Inn**, behind clock tower in the middle of town, T0291-261 2519, haveliinn@rediffmail.com. 8 atmospheric, spotless rooms (more planned) in authentic 200-year-old *haveli* complete with elaborately decorated drawing room/mini-museum, charming owners, good views from roof bar restaurant. Recommended.

**C-D Hotel Ghoomar (RTDC)**, High Court Rd, T0291-254 4010. Most rooms not worth considering, but 'super-deluxe' a/c rooms have been renovated to a high standard and are good value at Rs 900.

**C-D Newton's Manor**, 86 Jawahar Colony, Central School Rd, T0291-243 0686, www.newtonsmanor.com. 5 quaintly kitsch a/c rooms, touches of Victoriana plus stuffed animals, breakfast and dinner on request, a break from the norm.

**C-E Haveli Guest House**, Makaran Mohalla, opposite Turji ka Jhalra, T0291-261 4615, www.haveliguesthouse.net. Attractive sandstone building with 7 balconies, 22 simple, clean rooms, cheerful decor, breezy roof terrace with veg restaurant and great views of fort. Reports of poorly prepared food and unscrupulous payments to rickshaw drivers.

**C-E Sun City Guest House**, 1/C High Court Colony, Ratanada, T0291-262 5880. 8 good-sized, clean, basic rooms run by very enthusiastic and friendly family.

**D Vinayaka Guest House**, Shiv Rd, Ratanada, T0291-251 4950, vinayaka_td@rediffmail.com. 6 clean, well looked after rooms in tasteful, spacious family home. Lawn, quiet location, charming hosts.

**D-E Blue House**, Sumer Bhawan, Moti Chowk, T0291-262 1396, bluehouse36@hotmail.com. 7 clean rooms, 5 with bath (hot water all day), home-cooked meals, great views from rooftop restaurant, mixed about food and service. Be wary of trips to cousin's overpriced handicrafts shop.

**D-E Govind**, Station Rd, opposite GPO, T0291-262 2758, www.govindhotel.com. 12 cleanish rooms, some a/c, good rooftop veg restaurant with fort views but slow service (breakfast from 0530!), camel safaris, bus and rail ticketing, internet, friendly, very helpful owner but noisy location.

**D-E Madho Niwas**, New Airport Rd, Ratanada, T0291-251 2486, madhoniwas@ satyam.net.in. A Rajput Special Hotel, 16 comfortable rooms in art deco1920s bungalow. Thakur Dalvir Singh oversees excellent Marwari meals in garden, small pool. His family atBhenswar and Ranakpur can organise excellent safaris, treks etc.

**D-E Singhvi's Haveli**, Navchokiya, Ramdevji ka Chowk, T0291-262 4293, singhvi15adhaveli@hotmail.com. 7 rooms in charming, 500-year-old *haveli*, tastefully decorated, friendly family. Recommended.

**D-F Chauhan's Guest House**, Fort Rd, T0291-254 1497. Quirky home-stay offering courses in Hindi, yoga, music, art, relaxing café, family run, shop, book exchange.

**D-F Cosy Guest House**, Novechokiya Rd, Brahm Puri, just west of the fort, T0291-261

2066, cosyguesthouse@yahoo.com. 6 simple clean rooms, good home-cooked meals (other restaurants 15-min walk), bus bookings, rooftop views of fort and old city, quiet, reports of unfriendly behaviour.

**D-F Yogi's Guest House**, Raj Purohit ji ki Haveli, Manak Chowk, old town, T0291-264 3436, yogiguesthouse@hotmail.com. 12 rooms, most in 500-year-old *haveli*, clean, modern bathrooms, camel/jeep safaris, friendly and experienced management.

**E Durag Vilas**, 1 Old Public Park, near Circuit House, T0291-251 2298. 10 very clean, quiet, air-cooled rooms with shower, travel bookings, desert safaris, family run, friendly, helpful, free lift from station/airport.

**E Hotel Shiva**, Station Rd, T0291-262 4774. 14 clean, well-maintained rooms, peaceful atmosphere, friendly staff.

**E-F Hare Krishna Guest House**, Killi Khana, Mehron Ka Chowk, old town, T0291-265 4367, panditart1500ad@yahoo.co.in. 7 small, clean, characterful and airy rooms in family home, very welcoming.

**E-F Raman Guest House**, opposite Keshar Bagh, Shiv Rd, T0291-251 3980. 20 clean though simply furnished rooms with bath (hot water), 3 with a/c, family atmosphere, traditional meals, quiet area, pleasant rooftop, friendly and efficient owner.

**F Youth Hostel**, Bhatia Circle, Ratanada, T0291-251 0160. 5 rooms and 6 dorms in attractive, well-located building. Friendly staff, camping.

**Osian** *p386*

**L Camel Camp**, on the highest sand dunes, T0291-243 7023, www.camelcamposian.com. A beautiful complex of 50 double bedded luxury tents with modern conveniences (attached baths, hot showers), superb restaurant and bar plus an amazing pool – quite a sight at the top of a sand dune! Tariff inclusive of meals and camel safaris, ask in advance for jeep/camel transfers to avoid a steep climb up the dunes. Recommended. Also some **E** and **F** guesthouses in town.

**Khimsar** *p386*

**A Khimsar Fort**, T01585-262 345, www.khimsarfort.com. 48 large, comfortable a/c rooms, good restaurant on breezy rooftop with lovely views, fabulous pool, yoga, gym, beautiful large gardens, fire dances at the illuminated medieval fort, award-winning heritage hotel, one of the best in Rajasthan. Highly recommended.

**A Khimsar Sand Dunes Village**, 6 km from the fort, contact fort as above. 16 ethnically styled luxury huts in the heart of the dunes around a small lake, unbeatable setting.

**Nagaur** *p386*

**A Royal Camp**, T0291-257 2321, www.welcomheritage.com. Operates during the camel fair (when the price rises **L**) and Oct-Mar. 20 delightful deluxe 2-bed furnished tents (hot water bottles, heaters etc), flush toilets, hot water in buckets, dining tent for buffets, all inside fort walls, an experience.

**C-E Mahaveer International**, Vijay Vallabh Chowk, near bus stand, T01582-243 158. 15 okay rooms, 7 a/c, huge dining hall, friendly knowledgeable manager.

**D Shree Aditya**, Ajmer Rd, near Vyas petrol pump, T01582-245 438. 24 modern rooms, 12 a/c, in brand new building.

**Pokaran** *p387*

**B-C Manwar Desert Camp**, 61 km from Pokaran in Manwar, has beautifully designed cottages with attractive interiors, some a/c, restaurant (a good lunch stop), handicrafts.

**C Fort Pokaran**, T02994-222 274. 14 quaint, quirky rooms with bath (some rundown), old 4-posters, some carved columns, good hot lunches Rs 200-250 (order ahead if passing through town), service a little detached.

**D Motel Pokaran** (RTDC), on NH15, T02994-222 275. 8 sparse rooms in a ramshackle building, plus 5 passable garden cottages.

**Tented Resort**, 61 km from Pokaran in Manwar, 2½ km on a sand dune, reservations T02928-66137. Good 2-bed tents with hot showers, flush toilets, meals, camel, jeep safaris and visits to Bishnoi villages.

**Luni** *p387*

**A-B Fort Chanwa**, T02931-284 216, www.fortchanwa.com. 31 good rooms in 200-year-old fort, not large but well furnished, individually designed (best in the keep), excellent Rajasthani meals in impressive dining room, pleasant lawn for drinks, excellent pool, well managed, a little impersonal.

**Rohet and Sardar Samand** *p387*

**A Rohetgarh**, Rohet, T0291243 1161, www.rohetgarh.com. 32 pleasant rooms, some cramped, attached baths (avoid rooms near outdoor restaurant), in 1622 fort. Fine Rajasthani food, ordinary architecture but in beautiful environment, pleasant lake view terraces, lovely pool, health club, riding and safaris to Bishnoi, Raika and artisans' villages, boating on the lake, a relaxing getaway.

**A Sardar Samand Palace**, Sardar Samand, T02960-245 001, www.welcomheritage.com. 19 colonial style rooms (11 a/c), in a slightly forbidding looking building. Built in 1933 as a hunting lodge, much of the furniture is original, and lends a very unIndian feel. Safaris and boating trips arranged in the season, Nov best time for birdspotting on the lake, good pool and tennis court, isolated but atmospheric.

**Nimaj** *p388*

**L Chhatra Sagar**, 4 km from Nimaj, T02939-230 118, www.chhatrasagar.com. 11 beautiful colonial-style tents on the banks of a very picturesque reservoir. The ex-rulers of Nimaj have recreated the hunting lodge of their forefathers to great effect, and still live on the lake themselves, so a very convivial family atmosphere. Safaris arranged, all meals included in the tariff, recommended. Open 1 Oct-31 Mar.

## Eating

**Jodhpur** *p381, map p384*

The best restaurants are in hotels; reserve ahead. The bars in **Umaid Palace, On the Rocks, Ashok** and **Kalinga Restaurant**, see Sleeping, are open to the public for drinks and snacks. For *Daal-bhatti, lassi* and *kachoris* head for Jalori and Sojati gates.

**TTT Ajit Bhawan**, T0291-251 1410. Evening buffet, excellent meal in garden on a warm evening with entertainment, but poor atmosphere if eating indoors in winter.

**TTT Umaid Bhavan**, T0291-251 0101. Fabulous setting and fine food make it a great place for dinner. **Pillars**, a tiny garden restaurant, can be hired for one couple for Rs 2000, the most romantic setting in town.

**TT Gypsy**, PWD Colony, T510 3888. 1130-1530 and 1900-2300. Good range of Indian, Continental and Mexican dishes, choice of indoor or outdoor seating, swanky place popular with well-off locals.

**TT Kalinga**, opposite station. Western and Indian. A/c, good food (try butter chicken and aubergine dishes), friendly service, music may not please, breakfast good value.

**TT On the Rocks**, near **Ajit Bhavan**, T0291-510 2701, good mix of Indian and Continental, plus a relaxing bar, patisserie, ice-cream parlour and lovely gardens.

**TT Sankalp**, Bhati Circle, Ratanada, T0291-510 9192, 1030-2300. Upmarket a/c South Indian, dosas come with a fantastic range of chutneys, good service. Recommended.

**T Hotel Priya**, 181 Nai Sarak. Fantastic special *thalis* for Rs 49 and extra quick service.

**T Jodhpur Coffee House**, Sojati Gate. Good South Indian snacks and *thalis*.

**T New Jodhpur Lodge**, a real challenge to find, ask for Golion ki Haveli in Tripoliya Bazar in the old city, 261 3340. A family home which offers good, basic *thalis* for Rs30 in a shaded courtyard, quite an experience.

**T Poonam**, High Court Rd. Pure veg Indian. "Gorgeous 4-foot masala dosas".

**T Shandar**, Jalori Gate. Indian vegetarian. Good food and sweets.

**T Uttam**, High Court Rd, near Sojati Gate. Good a/c *thali* restaurant friendly, fast service.

## Festivals and events

**Jodhpur** *p381, map p384*

Several are special to Rajasthan. See also p. **Jul/Aug**, **Nag Panchami**, when *Naga* (*naag*), the cobra, is worshipped. The day is dedicated to *Sesha*, the 1000-headed god or *Anant* ('infinite') *Vishnu*, who is often depicted reclining on a bed of serpents. In Jodhpur, snake charmers gather for a colourful fair in Mandore. **Marwar Festival** (**26-27 Oct 2004**, 16-17 Oct 2005, 6-7 Oct 2006), held at full moon, includes music, puppet shows, turban tying competitions, camel polo and ends with a fire dance on the dunes at Osian.

**Nagaur** *p386*

The popular **Cattle and Camel Fair** (**15-18 Feb 2005**, 4-7 Feb 2006, 25-28 Feb 2007) is held just outside the town during which there are camel races, cock fights, folk dancing and music. The fields become full of encampments of pastoral communities, tribal people and livestock dealers with their cattle, camels, sheep, goat and other animals.

## Shopping

**Jodhpur** *p381, map p384*
Jodhpur is famous for its once popular *jodhpurs* (riding breeches), tie-and-dye fabrics, lacquer work and leather shoes. Export of items over 100-years-old is prohibited. The main areas are: **Sojati Gate** for gifts; **Station Rd** for jewellery; **Tripolia Bazar** for handicrafts; **Khanda Falsa** for tie-and-dye; **Lakhara Bazar** for lac bangles. Shoes are made in **Mochi Bazar, Sardarpura** and **Clock Tower**, *bandhanas* in **Bambamola**, and around **Siwanchi** and **Jalori Gates**. *Durries* are woven at **Salawas**, 18 km away.

### Antiques

Shops on road between Umaid and Ajit Bhawans, flourishing trade though pricey.
**Kirti Art Collection**, T0291-512 136. Has a good selection. Recommended.

### Handloom and handicrafts

**Khadi Sangh**, Station Rd. Quality, fair prices.
**Marasthaly**, High Court Rd. Quality, fair prices.
**Marwar Heritage Art School**, 116 Kamal, T0291 5132187, are trying to keep the miniature painting traditionalive.
**Rajasthan Khadi Sangathan**, BK ka Bagh.
**Shriganesham**, 1st floor Pal-Haveli, behind clocktower. Wide selection, honest.

### Spices

**Mohanlal Verhomal Spices**, 209B, Kirana Merchant (from clock tower enter vegetable market, then turn right), T0291-5109347, www.mvspices.com. Sought after for hand-mixed spices, more expensive than competitors but quality assured and is simply the best spice oulet in the city. Usha, along with her 6 sisters and mother, runs the shop. Insist your guide takes you here as many have tried to pass themselves off as her shop.

**Pokaran** *p387*
**Kashida**, just outside town, Jaisalmer-Bikaner Rd, T02994-222 511. Excellent handwoven crafts from the desert region, clean, well laid out, reasonably priced, profits help local self-help projects, part of the URMUL trust, see box p433.

## Activities and tours

**Jodhpur** *p381, map p384*
Many of the hotels organize village safaris, as does the tourist office, which charges Rs 1,100 for 4 people including car, guide and tips given to villagers. City sightseeing, starts from Tourist Office at **Ghoomar Hotel**, T0291-254 5083: half day (0830-1300, 1400-1800). Fort and palaces, Jaswant Thada, Mandore Gardens, Government Museum, bazar around Old City clock tower.
Tour operators include:
**Aravali Safari**, 4 Kuchaman House Area, Airport Rd, T0291-2626799.
**Forts & Palaces**, 15 Old Public Park, T0294-251 1207, www.palaces-tours.com.
**Poly Travels**, 10D Bus Stand, Paota, T0291-254 5210, poly@nda.vsnl.net.in.
**Exclusive India**, Kishan Villas, Police Line Road, Ratanada, T0291-342 006, exclinjdh@datainfosys.net. Ask for Rajendra

Singh Rathore who is very knowledgeable and an excellent companion.
Ayurvedic massages are offered by **Ajit Bhawan**, **Balsamand Palace** and **Khimsar Fort**, see Sleeping.

## Transport

**Jodhpur** *p381, map p384*
**Air**
Transport to town: by taxi, Rs 200; auto-rickshaw, Rs 120. **Indian Airlines**, near Bhati Cross Roads, T510757. 1000-1300, 1400-1700; airport enquiries T0291-251 2617, reservations T0291-251 0757. **Indian** Airlines flies to **Delhi**, **Jaipur**, **Mumbai**, **Udaipur**. Jet Airways, T0291-230 2222, airport T0291-233 1331, **Delhi**.

**Bus**
**Local** Mini-buses cover most of the city except Fort and Umaid Bhavan Palace. For **Mandore**, frequent buss leave Jodhpur, 100 m from the station and Paota Bus Stand.
**Long distance** Earplugs are useful on video coaches. Allow time to find the correct bus; match number on ticket with bus plate.

A convenient bus route links Jodhpur with **Ghanerao** and **Ranakpur**, **Kumbhalgar** and **Udaipur**. RST Bus Stand, near Raikabagh railway station, T0291-254 4989. 1000-1700; bookings also at tourist office. **Ahmadabad**, 11 hrs; **Jaipur**, frequent, 8 hrs; **Mt Abu Rd**, 6½ hrs; **Ajmer**, 4½ hrs; **Jaisalmer**, 0630 (depart Jaisalmer, 1400), 5-6 hrs, Rs 90; faster than train but scenically tedious; **Pali**, 4 hrs, Rs 30; **Udaipur**, 8-9 hrs, best to book a good seat a day ahead. Private operators: **HR Travels, Sun City Tours**, and **Sethi Yatra**, opposite Main Railway Station. For private buses ask at **Govind Hotel**, opposite Railway Station. Deluxe video coaches and Express buses between Jodhpur and **Delhi, Ahmadabad, Bikaner, Bhilwara**: most depart 0600 and 2200. **Jaipur**: 5 hrs; **Jaisalmer**: about hourly from 0600 ('when full'), 4-5 hrs, Rs 100 (tickets from travel agents); comfortable buses on good road, but beware of touts on arrival at Jaisalmer; decide on hotel in advance.

**Car**
Car hire from tourist office, **Ghoomer Hotel**, whole day about Rs 550; half day Rs 300. For a taxi, T0291-262 0238.

**Rickshaw**
Railway station to fort should be about Rs 25 (may demand Rs 50; try walking away).

**Train**
Jodhpur Station enquiries: T131/132. Open 0800-2400. Reservations: T0291-263 6407. Open 0900-1300, 1330-1600. Advance reservations, next to GPO. Tourist Bureau, T0291-254 5083 (0500-2300). **International Tourist Waiting Room** for passengers in transit (ground floor), with big sofas and showers; clean Indian toilets in 2nd Class Waiting Room on the 1st floor of the Station Foyer. To **Abu Rd (Mount Abu)**: *Ranakpur Exp, 4707*, 1515, 5½ hrs. **Agra**: *Marudhar Exp, 4854/4864*, 0700, 14 hrs *Jodhpur-Howrah Exp, 2308*, 1715, 12¾ hrs. **Ahmadabad**: *Surya Nagri Exp, 4845*, 1855, 9½ hrs. **Barmer**: *Barmer Exp, 4807*, 0805, 4½ hrs. **Delhi** (no 1st class): *Mandore Exp, 2462*, 1930, 11 hrs (OD); *Jodhpur Delhi Exp, 4860*, 2300, 12½ hrs (OD) **Jaipur**: *Inter-City Exp, 2467*, 0545, 6 hrs; *Mandore Exp, 2462*, 1930, 5 hrs; *Marudhar Exp, 4854/4864*, 0700, 5 hrs. **Jaisalmer**: *Jodhpur Jaisalmer Exp,* and *4810 Exp*, 2315, 6½ hrs. **Varanasi** via Lucknow: *Marudhar Exp, 4854/4864*, 0700, 19 hrs (Lucknow), 26 hrs (Varanasi).
Buses from Jodhpur travel to **Salawas**. Trains and buses to **Luni** from Jodhpur (40 km). For **Rohet**, frequent buses leave from Jodhpur (50 km north). Jodhpur-Jaisalmer train stops at **Osian**, 4 daily buses from Jodhpur, 2 hrs.

## Directory

**Jodhpur** *p381, map p384*
**Banks** 1030-1400. For Visa. **Punjab National Bank**, Ratanada. For TCs. **State Bank of India**, High Court Rd (inside High Court complex). Currency and TCs.
**Hospital** **MG Hospital**, T636437. Dispensary: Paota, Residency. Open 0800-1200, 1700-1900, Sun 0800-1200.
**Internet** **Amardeep**, Sardarpura, 3 km southwest of railway station, above Marudhar Jewellers, Ghoomer Hotel. **Post** **GPO**, south of Jodhpur station, 1000-2000, Sat 1000-1600. **Useful addresses** **Ambulance**: T102. **Fire**: T101. **Police**: T100.

# Jaisalmer and around

→ *Phone code: 02992. Colour map 2, grid A2. Population: 80,000.*

*The approach to Jaisalmer is magical as the city rises out of the barren desert like an approaching ship. With its crenellated sandstone walls and narrow streets lined with exquisitely carved buildings, through which camel carts trundle leisurely, it has an extraordinarily medieval feel and an incredible atmosphere. The fort inside, perched on its hilltop, contains some gems of Jain temple building, while beautifully decorated merchants'* havelis *are scattered through the town. That said, some travellers find the town is overrated and people unfriendly. It is true, parts are decaying and wear an air of neglect, though efforts are being made; all new structures must now be built out of the local honey-coloured sandstone. Jaisalmer is also the gateway to the desert. Many of the settlements close to the city however have become well used to tourists, so it's worth venturing a little further out to get an idea of life in the desert. Highlights include the remarkable ghost city of Khuldera, and of course the chance to take it all in from on top of a camel.* ▸▸ *For Sleeping, Eating and other listings, see pages 399-404.*

## Ins and outs

**Getting there** The nearest airport is at Jodhpur, 275 km away. Trains from Jodhpur arrive at Jaisalmer railway station. Your hotel may offer a pick-up. Most long-distance buses arrive at the bus stand and then go to Amar Sagar Pol, 15-minute walk from the fort.

*The best light for photography is in the late afternoon.*

**Getting around** Unmetered jeeps and auto-rickshaws can be hired at the station but they are no help inside the fort so you may have to carry your luggage some distance uphill if you choose a fort hotel. You can hire a bike from Gopa Chowk (Rs 25) though the town is best explored on foot. Most hotels and restaurants are clustered around the two chowks and inside the fort. ▸▸ *See Transport, page 403, for further details.*

**Tourist offices** **Rajasthan** ⓘ *near TRC, Station Rd, Gadi Sagar Pol, T02992-252 406, 0800-1200, 1500-1800*. Counter at railway station.



## Background

Founded by Prince Jaisal in 1156, Jaisalmer grew to be a major staging post on the trade route across the forbidding Thar desert from India to the West. The merchants prospered and invested part of their wealth in building beautiful houses and temples with the local sandstone. The growth of maritime trade between India and the West caused a decline in trade across the desert which ceased altogether in 1947. However, the wars with Pakistan (1965 and 1971) resulted in the Indian government developing the transport facilities to the border to improve troop movement. This has also helped visitors to gain access. Today, the army and tourism are mainstays of the local economy; hotel touts and pushy shopkeepers have become a problem in recent years.

# Jaisalmer

## The fort

On the roughly triangular-shaped Trikuta Hill, the fort stands 76 m above the town, enclosed by a 9-km wall with 99 bastions (mostly 1633-1647). You enter the fort from the east from Gopa Chowk. The inner, higher fort wall and the old gates up the ramp (Suraj, Ganesh, Hawa and Rang Pols) provided further defences. The Suraj Pol (1594), once an outer gate, is flanked by heavy bastions and has bands of decoration which imitate local textile designs. Take a walk through the narrow streets within the fort, often blocked by the odd goat or cow, and see how even today about a 1,000 of the town's people live in tiny houses inside the fort often with beautiful carvings on doors and balconies. It is not difficult to get lost.

As with many other Rajput forts, within the massive defences are a series of palaces, the product of successive generations of rulers' flights of fancy. Often called the Golden Fort because of the colour of the sandstone, it dominates the town. The stone is relatively easy to carve and the dry climate has meant that the fineness of detail has been preserved through the centuries. The *jali* work and delicately ornamented balconies and windows with wide eaves break the solidity of the thick walls which gives protection from the heat, while the high plinths of the buildings keep off the sand. **'Sunset Point'**, just north of the fort, is popular at sundown for views over Jaisalmer.

**Fort Palace Museum and Heritage Centre** ⓘ *0800-1800 summer, 0900- 1800 winter, Rs 10, Rs 70 foreigners, camera Rs 50, video Rs 150.* The entire palace has been recently renovated and an interesting series of displays established, including sculpture, weapons, paint ings and well presented cultural information. The view from the roof, the highest point inside the fort, is second to none. The Juna Mahal (circa 1500) of the seven-storey palace with its *jali* screens is one of the oldest Rajasthani palaces. The rather plain *zenana* block to its west, facing the *chauhata* (square) is decorated with false *jalis*. Next to it is the *mardana* (men's quarters) including the Rang Mahal above the Hawa Pol, built during the reign of Mulraj II (1762-1820), which has highly detailed murals and mirror decoration. Sarvotam Vilas built by Akhai Singh (1722-1762) is ornamented with blue tiles and glass mosaics. The adjacent Gaj Vilas (1884) stands on a high plinth. Mulraj II's Moti Mahal has floral decoration and carved doors.

**Jain temples** (12th-16th centuries) ⓘ *0700-1200, Rs 10, camera Rs 50, video Rs 100, leather shoes not permitted.* The open square beyond the gates has a platform reached by climbing some steps; this is where court was held or royal visitors entertained. There are also fascinating Jain temples within the fort. Whilst the Rajputs were devout Hindus they permitted Jainism to be practised. The **Parsvanatha** (1417) has a fine gateway, an ornate porch and 52 subsidiary shrines surrounding the main structure. The brackets are elaborately carved as maidens and dancers. The exterior of the **Rishbhanatha** (1479) has more than 600 images as decoration whilst clusters of towers form the roof of the **Shantinatha** built at the same time. **Ashtapadi** (16th century) incorporates the Hindu deities of Vishnu, Kali and Lakshmi into its decoration. The **Mahavir Temple** ⓘ *view 1000-1100*, has an emerald statue. The **Sambhavanatha** (1431) ⓘ *1000-1100*, has vaults beneath it that were used for document storage. The **Gyan Bhandar** here is famous for its ancient manuscripts.

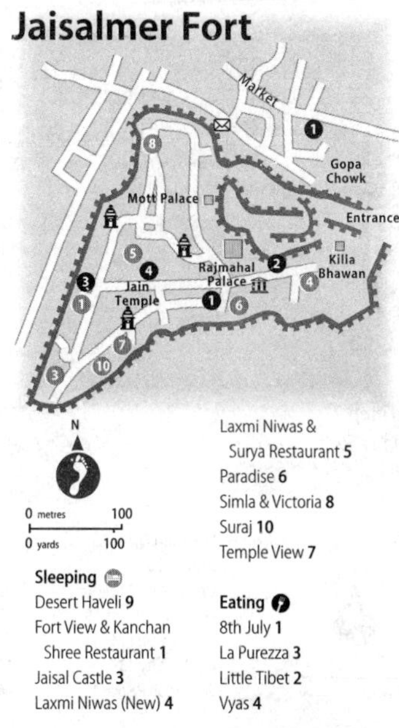

## Havelis

There are many exceptional *havelis* (mansions of rich merchants, see box page 440) both in the fort and the walled town. Many have beautifully carved façades, *jali* screens and oriel windows overhanging the streets below. The ground floor is raised above the dusty streets and each has an inner courtyard surrounded by richly decorated apartments. An unofficial 'guide' will usually show you the way for about Rs 20.

Inside Amar Sagar Pol, the former ruler's 20th-century palace **Badal Mahal** with a five-storeyed tower, has fine carvings. **Salim Singh-ki Haveli** (17th century) ⓘ *0800-1800, Rs 15, good carvings but being poorly restored, over-long guided tour*, near the fort entrance is especially attractive with peacock brackets and because of its distinctive and decorative upper portion is often referred to as the Ship Palace. **Nathumal-ki Haveli** (1885) ⓘ *when the havelis are occupied, you may be allowed in on a polite request, otherwise, your 'guide' will help you gain access for a small fee (though this may just get you as far as the shops in the courtyard!)*, nearer Gandhi Chowk, was built for the Prime Minister. Partly carved out of rock by two craftsmen, each undertaking one half of the house, it has a highly decorative façade with an attractive front door guarded by two elephants. Inside is a wealth of decoration; notice the tiny horse-drawn carriage and a locomotive showing European influence!

**Patwon-ki Haveli** (1805) ⓘ *best 1030-1700, Rs 2 to view the gold ceilings and enjoy the view from the rooftop, Rs 10 for the private museum*, further east, is a group of five built for five brothers. Possibly the finest in town, they have beautiful murals and carved pillars. A profusion of balconies cover the front wall and the inner courtyard is surrounded by richly decorated apartments; parts well-restored. The main courtyard and some roofs are now used as shops.



## Jaisalmer

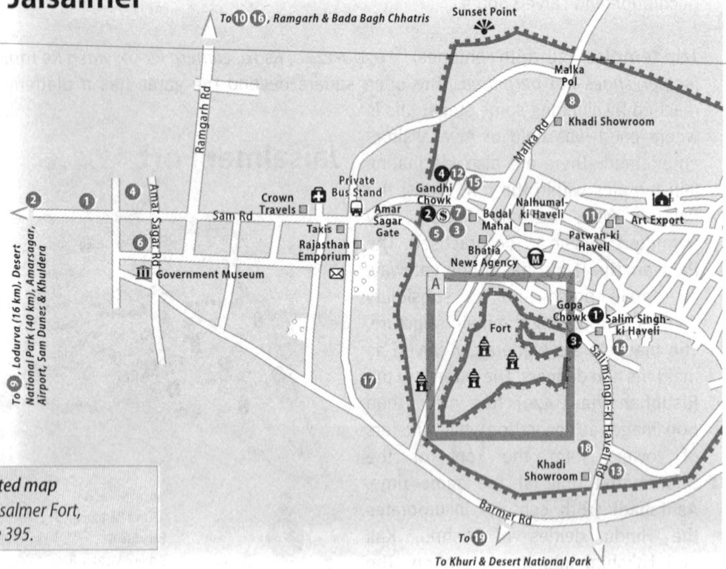

*Related map*
*A Jaisalmer Fort, page 395.*

**Sleeping**
Ashoka 23
Dhola Maru 21
Fifu Guest House 19
Fort Rajwada 25
Golden City 13
Gorbandh Palace 1
Heritage Inn 2
Himmatgarh Palace 10
Jaisal Palace & Kalpana Restaurant 3
Jawahar Niwas 4
Mahadev Palace 20
Mandir Palace 5
Moomal 6
Nachana Haveli 7
Narayan Niwas 8
Pleasure 12
Rajdhani & Residency Centre Point 11
Rajwada 22

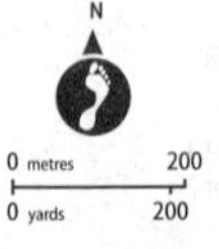

## Desert Cultural Centre

**Desert Cultural Centre** ⓘ *Gadisar Circle, T02992-252 188, 1000-1700, Rs 10*, was established in 1997 with the aim of preserving the culture of the desert. The museum contains a varied display of fossils, paintings, instruments, costumes and textiles which give an interesting glimpse in to life in the desert.

## Gadi Sagar tank

The Gadi Sagar (Gadisar or Gharisar) tank, southeast of the city walls, was the oasis which led Prince Jaisal to settle here. Now connected by a pipe to the Indira Gandhi Canal, it has water all year. It attracts migratory birds and has many small shrines around it and is well worth visiting, especially in the late afternoon. The delightful archway is said to have been built by a distinguished courtesan who built a temple on top to prevent the king destroying the gate. Boats are available for trips round the lake from Rs 50 for half an hour on a pedalo made for two.

# Around Jaisalmer

## Amar Sagar and Lodurva

The pleasant **Amar Sagar** ⓘ *free, Rs 10 foreigners, camera Rs 50, video Rs 100*, 5 km northwest, was once a formal garden with a pleasure palace of Amar Singh (1661-1703) on the bank of a lake which dries up during the hot season. The Jain temple there has been restored.

A further 10 km away is **Lodurva** ⓘ *0630-1930, free, Rs 10 foreigners, camera Rs 50, video Rs100*. It contains a number of Jain temples that are the only remains of a once flourishing Marwar capital. Rising honey-coloured out of the desert, they are beautifully carved with *jali* outside and are well maintained. Worth visiting. The road beyond Lodurva is unsealed.

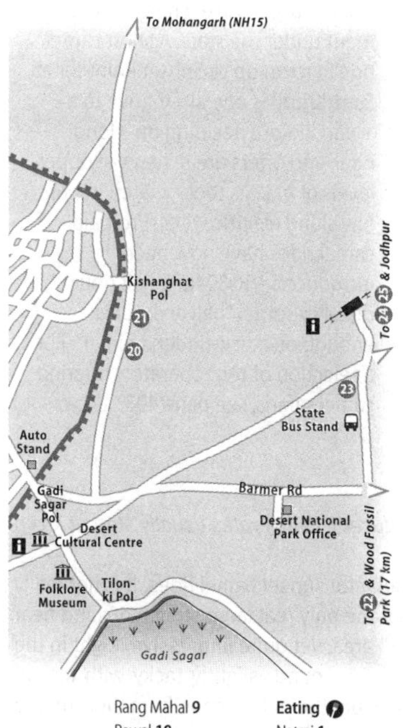


Rang Mahal **9**
Rawal **18**
Rawal-kot **24**
Samrat **14**
Shahi Palace **17**
Suman Motel **16**
Swastika **15**

**Eating**
Natraj **1**
Ringo Rooftop **4**
Sky, Trio, Top Deck & Thar Safari **2**
Treat **3**

## Khuldera

This is a fascinating ghost town, and well worth stopping at on the way to Sam. The story goes that 400 or so years ago, Salim Singh, the then prime minister of Jaisalmer, took a distinct shine to a Paliwal girl from this village. The rest of the Paliwal people did not want this beautiful girl taken away from them, and so after intense pressure from the PM decided to abandon the village one night, with everyone dispersing in different directions, never to return. It is remarkably well preserved, and best visited with a guide who can point out the most interesting buildings from the many still standing. **Khabha**, just south of here, is also recommended.

## On a camel's back

Camel safaris draw many to Jaisalmer. They give an insight into otherwise inaccessible desert interiors and a chance to see rural life, desert flora and wildlife. The 'safari' is not a major expedition in the middle of nowhere. Instead, it is often along tracks, stopping off for sightseeing at temples and villages along the way. The camel driver/owner usually drives the camel or rides alongside (avoid one sharing your camel), usually for two hours in the morning and three hours in the afternoon, with a long lunch stop in between. There is usually jeep or camel cart backup with tents and 'kitchen' close by, though thankfully out of sight. It can be fun, especially if you are with companions and have a knowledgeable camel driver.

They vary greatly in quality with prices ranging from around Rs 350 per night for the simplest (sleeping in the open, vegetarian meals) to those costing Rs 4,500 (deluxe double-bedded tents, attached western baths). Bear in mind that it is practically impossible for any safari organiser to cover his costs at anything less than Rs350 – if you're offered cheaper tours, assume they'll be planning to get their money back by other means, ie shopping/drug selling along the way. Safaris charging Rs 500-1,000 can be adequate (tents, mattresses, linen, cook, jeep support, but no toilets). It's important to ascertain what is included in the price and what are extras.

The popular 'Around Jaisalmer' route includes Bada Bagh, Ramkunda, Moolsagar, Sam dunes, Lodurva and Amar Sagar with three nights in the desert. Some routes now include Kuldhara's medieval ruins and the colourful Kahla village, as well as Deda, Jaseri lake (good birdlife) and Khaba ruins with a permit. Most visitors prefer to take a two days/one night or three days/two nights camel safari, with jeep transfer back to Jaisalmer. A more comfortable alternative is to be jeeped to a tented/hut camp in the desert as a base for a night and enjoy a camel trek during the day without losing out on the evening's entertainment under the stars. A short camel ride in town up to Sunset Point (or at Sam/Khuri) is one alternative to a 'safari' before deciding on a long haul, and offers great views of upper levels of havelis too! – watch out for low slung electric wires. Pre-paid camel rides have now been introduced – Rs80 for a half hour ride. For some, "half an hour is enough on a tick-ridden animal". For a selection of tour operators offering camel safaris, see page 403.



## Sam dunes (Sain)

*ⓘ Rs 2, car Rs 10 (camera fees may be introduced), camel rates usually start at Rs 50 per hr but can be bargained down.*

Sam dunes, 40 km west of Jaisalmer, is popular for sunset camel rides. It is not really a remote spot in the middle of the desert but the only real large stretch of sand near town; the dunes proper only covering a small area, yet quite impressive. Right in the middle of the dunes, **Sunset view** is like a fairground, slightly tacky with lots of day-trippers – as many as 500 in the high season; the only escape from this and the camel men is to walk quite a way away!

## Khuri

*ⓘ Rs 3 (may be increased in line with Desert National Park), car Rs 10, buses from Jaisalmer take 1½ hrs, jeep for 4, Rs 450 for sunset tour.*

Khuri, 40 km southwest of Jaisalmer, is a small picturesque desert village of decorated mud thatched buildings which was ruled by the Sodha clan for four centuries. Visitors are attracted by shifting sand dunes, some 80 m high, but the peace of the village has been spoilt by the growing number of huts, tents and guesthouses which have opened along the road and near the dunes. Persistent hotel and camel agents board all buses bound for Khuri. The best months to visit are from November to February.

## Thar Desert National Park

ⓘ *T02992-252 489, Rs 200 per person. Permission to enter the park is needed from the Collector as well as the Director.*

The Desert National Park is near Khuri, the core being about 60 km from Jaisalmer (the road between Sam and Khuri is motorable with a high clearance vehicle). The park was created to protect 3,000 sq km of the Thar Desert, the habitat for drought resistant, endangered and rare species which have adjusted to the unique and inhospitable conditions of extreme temperatures. The desert has undulating dunes and vast expanses of flat land where the trees are leafless, thorny and have long roots. Fascinating for birdwatching, it is one of the few places in India where the **Great Indian bustard** is proliferating (it can weigh up to 14 kg and reach a height of 40 cm). In winter it also attracts the migratory **houbara bustard**. You can see imperial black-bellied and common Indian sand grouse, five species of vultures, six of eagle, falcons, and flocks of larks at Sudasari, in the core of the park, 60 km from Jaisalmer. Chinkaras are a common sight, as are Desert and Indian foxes. Blackbuck and Desert cat can be seen at times. Closer to sunset, you can spot desert hare in the bushes.

While most hotels will try to sell you a tour by four-wheel drive vehicle, this is no longer necessary. You can hire any jeep or high clearance car (Ambassador, Sumo) for the trip to the park. Off-the-road journeys are by camel or camel cart (park tour Rs 50 and Rs 150 respectively).

## Barmer

This dusty desert town, 153 km south of Jaisalmer, is surrounded by sand dunes and scrublands. It is a major centre for wood carving, *durrie* rug weaving, embroidery and block printing (you can watch printers in Khatriyon ki galli). The 10th- to 11th-century Kiradu temples, though badly damaged, are interesting. **Someshvara** (1020), the most intact, has some intricate carving but the dome and the tower have collapsed. The town itself is surprisingly industrial and not especially charming; those interested in seeking out handicrafts are well advised to locate **Gulla**, the town's only guide. He can normally be contacted at the **KK Hotel**, see below, or emailed in advance on gulla_guide@yahoo.com. The small number of visitors to Barmer means that he doesn't get too many opportunities to practice his profession; be sure to explain exactly what you would like to see, and try to fix a price before starting the tour.

## Dhorimmana

The area further south of Barmer has some of the most colourful and traditional Bishnoi villages and a large population of *chinkaras* and desert fauna. The village women wear a lot of attractive jewellery but may be reluctant to be photographed so it is best to ask first. **PWD Rest house** has clean and comfortable rooms.

## Sleeping

**Jaisalmer** *p394, map p396 and p395*
Some hotels close in Apr-Jun. Very low room prices may be conditional on taking the hotel's camel safari – check; refusal may mean having to move out. Some budget places allow travellers to sleep on the roof for Rs 30-50. The tourist office has a Paying Guest list. Avoid Himalayan Guest House.

**A Fort Rajwada**, 1 Hotel Complex, Jodhpur Rd, T02992-253 533, www.fortrajwada.com. 65 top-class, central a/c rooms and 4 suites conceived by an opera set designer, in a modern luxury hotel, deceptively old-looking from the outside, built in strict accordance to the principles of vaastu, India's answer to feng shui. Architectural features have been recovered from crumbling local *havelis* and incorporated in to the stylish interior, which houses all the expected mod cons, of which the exquisite bar is particularly worthy of mention. Friendly management, eager staff.
**A Heritage Inn**, 4 Hotel Complex, Sam Rd, T02992-250 901, www.carnivalhotel.com. 15 uninspired rooms plus 40 far superior cottages, single-storey sandstone desert architecture, restaurant, bar, pleasant interior, garden, pool, well-managed.
**A Jawahar Niwas**, Bada Bagh Rd, T02992-252 208, www.jawaharniwas palace.com. 22 period furnished rooms in small but attractive carved *haveli*. Larger rooms in main palace, cheaper rooms in annexe, unimaginative dining hall but lovely pool, and superb views. Whole place could use a lick of paint, however, and staff slightly aloof.
**A Rawal-Kot** (Taj), Jodhpur Rd, T02992-252 638, www.tajhotels.com. 32 large, comfortable, a/c rooms, attractively furnished, good restaurants, modern yet medieval atmosphere, good views of fort from beautiful pool, friendly.
**A-B Rang Mahal**, Sam Rd, T02992-250 907, www.hotelrangmahal.com. 53 spacious but slightly sterile rooms, desert architecture, pleasant gardens, pool free to restaurant guests, book ahead for a 20% discount.
**A-C Mandir Palace**, T02992-252 788, mandir palace@hotmail.com. 27 well-maintained, a/c rooms in exclusive location inside royal palace. Not very well run but an experience.
**B Dhola Maru**, Jethwai Rd, T02992-252 863, www.hoteldholamaru.com. 42 a/c, 'ethnic style', slightly musty rooms in attractive sandstone building but standards slipping and mixed reports of unhelpful staff, informative lectures by owner though, okay pool and a wacky bar.
**B Gorbandh Palace** (HRH), Sam Rd, T02992-253 801, www.hrhindia. com. 67 unremarkable rooms around courtyard in plush hotel, traditional decor, a/c, luxury tents, good but pricey set meals, noisy entertainment, pool, book/crafts shop, airport/ station transfer.
**B Himmatgarh Palace**, 1 Ramgarh Rd, 2½ km from town, T02992-252 002, Himmat GH@sanchar.net.in. 40 a/c rooms and cottages in attractive, slightly quirky sandstone building, great views from garden and pool.
**B Jaisal Castle**, in fort, T02992-252 362, nnpjsm@sancharnet.in. 11 quirky rooms in rambling, characterful old *haveli*. Undergoing extensive renovation.
**B Killa Bhawan**, Kotri Para, T02992-251 204, www.killabhawan.com. 6 rooms, 2 a/c, in characterful old building, beautiful interiors, classiest place in fort by some margin.
**B Mahadev Palace**, Jethwai Rd, T02992-253 789, www.mahadevpalace.com. 31 a/c rooms in modern sandstone building, interiors uninspired but clean and friendly, pleasant gardens and pool, depressing restaurant.
**B Narayan Niwas Palace**, opposite Jain Temple, Malka Rd, T02992-252 408, www. narayanniwas.com. A converted caravanserai with 43 disappointing a/c rooms; rest of property is far more impressive and could be amazing if better maintained. Pillared indoor pool is remarkable, and views from rooftop restaurant exceptional. Good reports on entertainment provided.
**B-C Nachana Haveli**, Gandhi Chowk, T02992-251 910, nachana_haveli@yahoo. com. 9 rooms, 6 more coming, in converted 18th-century Rajput *haveli* with carved balconies and period artefacts. Extensive renovation underway. Rooms are stylishly done with great bathrooms, particularly upstairs suites. Rooftop restaurant in the season, has very authentic feel overall.
**C-D Jaisal Palace**, near Gandhi Chowk, behind SBI, T02992-252 717, www.hotel jaisalpalace.com. 14 clean, simple rooms with bath, 6 a/c, 8 air cooled, 1st floor balconies with views, Rajasthani food on roof terrace in season, train/bus bookings.
**C-D Moomal** (RTDC), Amar Sagar Rd, T02992-252 342. 60 rooms, 17 a/c, better than RTDC average but still has institutional air, rooms could be cleaner, mediocre restaurant, bar, tours, friendly and helpful.

*For an explanation of sleeping and eating price codes used in this guide, see inside the front cover. Other relevant information is found in Essentials, see pages 56-61.*

**C-E Desert Boy's Guest House**, Vyasa Para in fort, T02992-253 091, desert_p@yahoo.com. 14 jauntily furnished rooms in attractive property, good Italian rooftop restaurant.
**D-E Fifu Guest House**, opposite Nagarpalika (1 km out of town), T02992-254 317, www.rajasthan-desert-tour.com. 8 well-decorated rooms in modern building with excellent rooftop views. Location slightly inconvenient but hosts are charming and free bike hire for guests. Ring ahead for free pick up.
**D-E Rawal**, Salim Singh-ki Haveli Marg, Dibba Para, T02992-252 570. 20 clean, wallpapered rooms, all with attached bathrooms, Indian restaurant, good views from rooftop, pleasant, relaxed.
**D-E Shahi Palace**, near Government Bus Stand, T02992-255 920, shahipalace@yahoo.co.in. 9 tasteful rooms (7 more coming) in classy new establishment built almost entirely from sandstone. Outstanding bathrooms, likeable manager. Recommended.
**D-E Simla**, Kund Para, T02992-253 061, simlahaveli@yahoo.co.in. 5 clean rooms in thoughtfully renovated 550-year-old *haveli*, attractive wall hangings, 1 large with bath, others minute with bath downstairs, no safari pressure, friendly management, a cut above the norm.
**D-E Suraj**, behind Jain Temple, T02992-251 623, hotelsurajjaisalmer@hotmail.com. 5 basic but clean rooms with bath (some large, painted) in beautiful 530-year-old *haveli*, some with view, atmospheric. Also 7 more rooms in annexe opposite, standard equally high.
**D-F The Desert Haveli**, near Jain Temple, T02992-251 555, desert_haveli@yahoo.com. 7 characterful rooms in charming, 400-year-old *haveli*, honest, friendly owner. Recommended.
**D-F Paradise**, opposite Royal Palace, T02992-252674, hotelparadise_gsm2001@yahoo.co.in. 24 basic rooms, best **C** with hot showers, most with balcony and views, camping on roof terrace, safe lockers, limited room-service, long-established but some reports of being hassled.
**E Swastika**, Chainpura St, T02992-252483. 9 clean, well-kept rooms, all with bath, okay view, free tea and pick-ups, charming owner.
**E-F Golden City**, Dibba Para, T02992-251 664, hotelgoldencity@hotmail.com. Clean comfortable air cooled rooms with hot shower, 3 **D** a/c, rooftop restaurant with good views, free station transfer, exchange, internet, family atmosphere plus a lovely new swimming pool, outstanding value.
**E-F Laxmi Niwas**, T52758, in Fort (signposted). 6 simple but clean rooms with bath in newer section at east end of fort, better upstairs, with good views from terrace, good breakfast; also cheaper 5 basic, homely rooms with common bath in older section (west of fort), warm welcome.
**E-F Moti Palace**, Chogun Para, T02992-254 693, kailash_bissa@yahoo.co.uk. 5 clean, modern rooms, interesting location above main entrance to fort, great views from roof.
**E-F Temple View**, next to Jain Temple, T02992-252 832, jaisalmertempleview@hotmail.com. 7 well decorated rooms, 3 with attached bath, attention to detail, great view of temples from roof, entertaining owner.
**E-F Hotel Victoria**, Kund Para in fort, T02992-252 150, hotelvictoria@rediffmail.com. 6 quirky rooms in family home, owner amiably eccentric, good home-cooked veg meals, a little bit different.
**F Hotel Ashoka**, opposite Railway station, T02992-256 021. 20 cleanish rooms in quiet location, good option if you want to be close to the station.
**F Hotel Pleasure**, Gandhi Chowk, T02992-252 323, hotelpleasure@rediffmail.com. 5 clean rooms in homely establishment with innovative facilities including free washing machine and filtered drinking water.
**F Rajdhani**, near Patwon-ki Haveli, T02992-252746. 7 clean rooms with hot shower, great view from rooftop, friendly staff, calm atmosphere.
**F Residency Centre Point**, near Patwan ki Haveli, T02992-252 883. 5 basic but characterful rooms in quiet, family run hotel, good views from roof.
**F Samrat**, south of Salim Singh-ki-Haveli, T02992-251 498. 10 average rooms, some with bath and balcony, rooftop restaurant, helpful, family run, slightly downtrodden feel.

**Sam dunes** *p398*
**D Samdhani (RTDC)**, T02992-252 392. 8 huts facing the dunes, very busy in late afternoon and sunset but very pleasant at night and early morning.

**Khuri** *p398*
**D-E Khuri Guest House**, T03104-274 044. Simple rooms or huts, friendly management. Recommended.
**D-E Mama's**, T01304-274 023. Cool, thatched huts, tasty meals, recommended.

**Thar Desert National Park** *p399*
**E Rest Huts**, facing the park, are adequate, contact Park Director on T02992-252 489

**Barmer** *p399*
**D-E KK Hotel**, Station Rd, T02982-230 038. 24 okay rooms, some a/c, very similar to Krishna nearby.
**D-E Krishna**, Station Rd, a few mins' walk from station, T02982-220 785. The biggest and best in town with 32 decent rooms, some a/c, but no restaurant.

## Eating

**Jaisalmer** *p394, map p396 and p395*
**¥¥ 8th July**, just inside fort (another opposite Fort Gate). Vegetarian. Pleasant rooftop seating – popular for breakfast, pizzas, food average, pleasant for evening drink, mixed reports on service.
**¥¥ La Purezza**, Vyas Para. Excellent salads, Italian cheese veggies and other unusual offerings. Has another outlet in Manali.
**¥¥ Little Tibet**, beyond the palace chowk. Momos and much more of travellers' choice, generous, hygienic, enthusiastic staff, popular.
**¥¥ Natraj**, next to Salim Singh-ki-Haveli. Mixed. Spacious rooftop with good views and a/c room, beer bar, wide choice (meat dishes Rs 80-100), average Indian and Chinese, clean toilet, pleasant spot.
**¥¥ Sky**, Gandhi Chowk, mainly Indian, 'English' breakfasts and some Italian. On rooftop, Rajasthani dancers and musicians, colourful and noisy!
**¥¥ Surya**, near Laxmi Niwas. Mixed. Good food, colourful, atmospheric, sit on cushions overlooking the city, outstanding views. Recommended.
**¥¥ Top Deck**, Gandhi Chowk, good meat dishes (lamb steaks, southern fried chicken, Rs 60), staff very cool.
**¥¥ Trio**, Gandhi Chowk, partly open-air, tented restaurant with small terrace, choice of cushions or chairs, excellent 'proper' tea, good atmosphere and creative food (try safari soup), musicians at dinner expect tips, view of Mandir Palace and fort illuminated, usually crowded, mixed reports on food and service, perhaps becoming a victim of its own success.
**¥ Palace View Restaurant**, Gandhi Chowk, near Jain Temples. Varied selection but main attraction is the home made apple pie.
**¥ Ringo Rooftop** (separate from hotel), Gandhi Chowk, good north Indian including meat dishes. Superb views of fort.
**¥ Vyas**, Fort. Simple, good veg *thalis* (Rs 20-30), pleasant staff.

### Snacks and drinks
Chai stalls at **Gopa Chowk** make good 'Indian' tea before 1730. Hot and crisp kachoris and samosas opposite Jain temples near **Narayan Niwas**, are great for breakfast or high tea.
**Dhanraj Bhatia**, scrumptious Indian sweets including Jaisalmeri delights (try *godwa*).
**Doodh bhandars** in Hanuman Chauraya sell a delicious mix of creamy milk, cardamom and sugar, whipped up with a flourish, between sunset and mid-night.
**Kanchan Shree**, Gopa Chowk, 250 m from Salim Singh ki Haveli. Still among the best for drinks. *Lassis* (19 varieties) and ice cream floats, as well as cheap, tasty *thalis*.
**Mohan Juice Centre**, near **Sunil Bhatia Rest House**. Delicious lassis, good breakfasts.

## Entertainment

**Jaisalmer** *p394, map p396 and p395*
The more expensive hotels have bars.
**Desert Cultural Centre**, Gadisar Circle. Two puppet shows every evening, at 1830 and 1930, Rs 30 entry, Rs 20 camera, Rs 50 video.

## Festivals and events

**Jaisalmer** *p394, map p396 and p395*
**Feb/Mar Holi** is especially colourful but gets riotous.

**Sam dunes** *p398*
**Feb** 3-day **Desert Festival** (10-12 Feb 2006, 31 Jan-2 Feb) with *Son et Lumière* amid the sand dunes at Sam, folk dancing, puppet shows and camel races, camel polo and camel acrobatics, Mr Desert competition.

You can also watch craftsmen at work. Rail and hotel reservations can be difficult.

**Barmer** *p399*
Thar Festival in **Mar** highlights desert culture and handicrafts.

## Shopping

**Jaisalmer** *p394, map p396 and p395*
Shops open 1000-1330 and 1500-1900. Jaisalmer is famous for its handicrafts – stone-carved statues, leather ware, brass enamel engraving, shawls, tie-and-dye work, embroidered and block printed fabrics, but garments are often poorly finished. Look in **Siré Bazar**, **Sonaron-ka-Bas** and the narrow lanes of the old city including **Kamal Handicrafts**, **Ganpati Art Home**, and **Damodar** in the Fort. In Gandhi Chowk: **Rajasthali**, closed Tue; the good, fairly-priced selection at **Khadi Emporium** at the end of the courtyard just above Narayan Niwas Hotel. **Jaisalmer Art Export**, behind Patwon-ki Haveli has high-quality textiles.

For tailors try, **Mr Durga**, small shop near fort entrance (between New Tourist and Srilekha Hotels). Excellent western-style tailoring. Shirts made to measure, around Rs 200. Also **Nagpur**, Koba Chowk, and **Raju**, Kachari Rd, outside Amar Sagar Pol, for western-style tailoring.

## Activities and tours

**Jaisalmer** *p394, map p396 and p395*

**Camel safaris**
**Thar Safaris**, T02992 252722, charges Rs 950); **Safari Tours**, T02992 251058, has Rawla Kanoi with 10 'desert huts' with shared facilities and 10 tents with private bathrooms, about 8 km from Sam; **Royal Desert Safaris**, T02992 252538 has 85 Swiss-cottage tents with attached toilets near the dunes charges Rs 4500 per night. **Sahara Travels**, **Comfort Tours** (Gorbandh Palace), **Aravalli Safaris**, **Travel Plan**, also offer reliable safaris. Less upmarket, but still reliable options include those from **Shahi Palace**, **Fifu Guesthouse** and **Desert Haveli**.

**Cooking**
Learn Indian cookery with Karuna at Ishar palace, in the fort near the Laxminath Temple, T02992-253 062, karunaacharya@yahoo.com. Courses of any length can be arranged, and come highly recommended.

**Music**
Anyone interested in learning to play a Rajasthani musical instrument, or to hear a performance, should contact Kamru Deen on T02992-254 181, arbamusic@yahoo.co.in.

**Paragliding**
**SPSKaushik**, T94143 05121, offers paragliding in the desert, with participants being towed behind a jeep for Rs 750 a go. A unique way to see the desert!

**Sightseeing tours**
**Aravali Safari**, near Patwon-ki Gali, T02992-252 632. Professional. Recommended.
**Forts & Palaces**, Nachna Haveli, Gandhi Chowk, T02992-252 538, jaipur@palaces-tours.com. Experienced, efficient.
**Rajasthan Tourism**, T02992-252 406. City sightseeing: half day, 0900-1200. Fort, *havelis*, Gadisagar Lake. Sam sand dunes: half day, 1500-1900.
**Sahara Travels**, Gopa Chowk, right of the 1st Fort gate, T02992-252609. Mr (Desert) Bissa's reliable camel safaris with good food.
**Thar Safari**, Gandhi Chowk, near Trio, T02992-252722. Reliable tours.

**Swimming**
**Gorbandh Palace** (non-residents Rs 350); also **Heritage Inn** (meal plus swim deals) and **Fort Rajwada**.

## Transport

**Jaisalmer** *p394, map p396 and p395*
Jaisalmer is on NH15 (Pathankot-Samakhiali). Transport to town from train and bus station is by autorickshaws or jeeps; police are on duty so less harassment.

**Air**
No flights from the nearest airport at Jodhpur. **Alliance Air** from Delhi, 1030, via Jaipur; to Delhi, 1330. Check with **Crown Travels**, Sam Rd, T02992-252 632

**Bus**
Be aware that touts may board buses outside town to press you to take their jeep; it is

better to walk 10-15 mins from Amar Sagar Pol and choose a hotel.

State (Roadways) buses, from near the station, T02992-251 541, and near Amar Sagar Pol. Services to **Ajmer**, **Barmer**, **Bikaner** (330 km on good road, 7 hrs, Rs 104), **Jaipur** (638 km); Abu Rd for **Mount Abu**. **Jodhpur** (285 km) hourly service, 5 hrs, Rs 70, RTDC coach, depart Jaisalmer, 1400 (depart Jodhpur 0630). **Udaipur**: (663 km), tiring 14 hrs. Private deluxe coaches from outside Amar Sagar Pol, to Jodhpur and Bikaner. Operators: **Marudhara Travels**, Station Rd, T02992-252 351. **National Tours**, Hanuman Choraha, T02992-252 348.

### Train

Foreign Tourist Bureau with waiting room, T02992-252 354, booking office T02992-251 301. **Jodhpur**: *Jaisalmer Jodhpur Exp, 4609, 4809 Exp,* 2225, 7 hrs, sleeper, Rs 510. Can get very cold (and dusty) so take sleeping bag, or book bedding. (From Jodhpur, *4810,* depart 2315, 6½ hrs).

**Barmer** *p399*
From **Barmer**, the hot and dusty bus journey to Jaisalmer takes 4 hrs; Mt Abu, 6 hrs.

## Directory

**Jaisalmer** *p394, map p396 and p395*
**Banks** Open 1030-1430, Mon-Fri, 1030-1230, Sat, closed Sun. On Gandhi Chowk: **Bank of Baroda** and **SBBJ**, TCs and cash against credit cards; **State of Bank of India**, Nachna Haveli, currency only. There is also an ATM which accepts international cards close to Hanuman Chowk on the road which leads to Sam. **Hospital** **S J Hospital**, Gandhi Marg, T02992-252 343. **Internet** **Joshi Travel**, opposite PO, Central Market, Gopa Chowk, T02992-250455 joshitravel@hotmail.com. Cyber café, modern equipment, also STD, fax etc. **Desert Cyber Inn**, inside fort close to Little Tibet restaurant. Others may have problems connecting. **Post** The GPO is near Police Station, T02992-252 407. With Poste Restante. **Useful addresses** **Fire**: T02992-252 352. **Police**: T02992-252 668.



# Eastern Rajasthan

*This is one of the most visited regions of Rajasthan, lying as it does on the well-trodden 'Golden Triangle' route of Delhi-Agra-Jaipur, but retains some hidden treasures and surprisingly untouched towns. All within easy range of Delhi, there is an amazing variety of towns and villages from the busy pilgrimage centre of Ajmer in the south, and its laid-back neighbour Pushkar, to the utterly unspoilt towns of Alwar and Deeg in the north. They are also surrounded by a natural world in which wild animals and birds continue to find a protected home in sanctuaries and wildlife parks, including the magnificent Bharatpur-Keoladeo Ghana National Park, home to the rare Siberian Crane during its migratory season and a great place for a cycle, and the incomparable Ranthambhore National Park, one of the world's top venues for tiger spotting, but also a beautiful landscape to explore even when the tigers don't show.*

# Alwar, Sariska and around

*Alwar has fascinating monuments including the Bala Quilla fort, overlooking the town, and the Moti Doongri fort, in a garden. The former, which was never taken by direct assault, has relics of the early Rajput rulers who had their capital near Alwar, the founders of the fort. Over the centuries it was home to the Khanzadas, Mughals, Pathans, Jats and finally the Rajputs. There are also palaces and colonial period parks and gardens. The town itself is very untouristy and spread over a large area, making navigation difficult at times, but is generally very welcoming.*

*The 480-sq-km Sariska sanctuary is a dry deciduous forest set in a valley surrounded by the barren Aravalli hills. The princely shooting reserve of the Maharajah of Alwar in the Aravallis was declared a sanctuary in 1955 and is a tiger reserve under Project Tiger. Although the chances of spotting a tiger here are not as good as at Ranthambore, it still has a rugged appeal.* ▸▸ *For Sleeping, Eating and other listings, see pages 406-407.*

## Ins and outs

**Getting there and around** Alwar is well connected to both Delhi and Jaipur by bus and train, and is only a three-hour drive from Delhi, or 1½ hours from Jaipur. Sariska is an easy 35 km drive from Alwar. ▸▸ *See Transport, page 407, for further details.*

**Tourist information** **Rajasthan** ⓘ *Tourist Reception Centre, Nehru Marg, opposite railway station, Alwar, T0144-234 7348, closed weekends.*

## Background

As Mughal power crumbled Rao Pratap Singhji of Macheri founded Alwar as his capital in 1771. He shook off Jat power over the region and rebelled against Jaipur suzerainty making Alwar an independent state. His successors lent military assistance to the British in their battles against the Marathas in AD 1803, and in consequence gained the support of the colonial power. The Alwarroyals were flamboyant and kept a fleet of custom-made cars (including a throne car and a golden limousine), and collected solid silver furniture and attractive walking sticks.

# Alwar

→ *Phone code: 0144. Colour map 2, grid A6. Population: 211,000.*

Alwar is protected by the hilltop **Bala Quilla** which has the remains of palaces, temples and 10 tanks built by the first rulers of Alwar. It stands 308 m above the town, to the northwest, and is reached by a steep four-wheel drive track (with permission from the police station). There are splendid views.

The **Vinai Vilas Mahal**, the City Palace (1840) ⓘ *1000-1630, free, museum Rs 3*, with intricate *jali* work, ornate *jarokha* balconies and courtyards, houses government offices on the ground floor, and a fine museum upstairs. The palace is impressive but is poorly maintained, with dusty galleries (you may find children playing cricket in the courtyard). The Darbar Room is closed, and the throne, miniatures and gilt edged mirrors can only be viewed through the glass doors and windows or by prior permission of the royal family (not easily obtained). The museum is interesting, housing local miniature paintings, as well as some of the Mughal, Bundi and other schools, an array of swords, shields, daggers, guns and armour, sandalwood carvings, ivory objects, jade art, musical instruments and princely relics. Next to the city palace are the lake and royal cenotaphs. On the south side of the tank is the Cenotaph of Maharaja Bakhtawar Singh (1781-1815) which is of marble on a red sandstone base. The gardens are alive with peacocks and other birds. To the right of the main entrance to the palace is a two-storey processional elephant carriage designed to carry 50 people and be pulled by four elephants.

The **Yeshwant Niwas**, built by Maharaja Jai Singh in the Italianate style, is also worth seeing. Apparently on its completion he disliked it and never lived in it. Instead he built the **Vijay Mandir** in 1918, a 105-room palace beside Vijay Sagar, 10 km from Alwar. Part of it is open to the public with prior permission from the royal family or their secretary but is worth seeing it from the road, with its façade resembling an anchored ship. When not in Delhi, the royal family now live in Phool Bagh, a small 1960s mansion opposite the New Stadium.

# Alwar to Sariska

At **Siliserh**, 15 km to the west, runs an aqueduct which supplies the city with water. The lake, a local picnic spot, has boats for hire. **Kesroli**, 10 km northeast, has a seven-turreted 16th-century fort atop a rocky hillock, now sympathetically (though more modestly) restored into a hotel by the owners of Neemrana (see page 127). It is a three-hours' drive from Delhi and convenient for an overnight halt. Turn left off NH8 at Dharuhera for Alwar Road and you will find it. **Kushalgarh Fort** is en route to Sariska. Near Kushalgarh is the temple complex of **Talbraksha** (or Talvriksh) with a large population of rhesus macaque monkeys. Guides report panthers having been seen near the **Cafeteria Taal** here, probably on the prowl for monkeys near the canteen.

## Sariska Tiger Reserve → *Phone code: 0144. Colour map 2, grid A5.*

ⓘ *Rs 25, free on Sat, foreigners Rs 200 every day including still camera, video Rs 200; vehicle Rs 125 per trip. Early morning jeep trips from* Sariska Palace Hotel *or* Tiger Den *go into the park as far as the Monkey Temple, where you can get a cup of tea and watch monkeys and peacocks. Jeep-hire for non-standard trips in the reserve, Rs 700 for 3 hrs, excluding entry fees. Further information from Wildlife Warden, T0144-233 2348.*

*In the spring of 2005, a survey discovered that no tigers were left at Sariska prompting a major scandal in the wildlife service. It was presumed that they had been poached for the Chinese medicinal market.*

The main rhesus monkey population live at Talvriksh near Kushalgarh (see above), whilst at Bhartri-Hari you will see many langurs. The chowsingha, or **four-horned antelope**, is found at Sariska. Other deer include chital and sambar. You may see nilgai, wild boar, jackals, hyenas, hares and porcupines, though leopards are more rarely seen, since the reserve is closed at night to visitors. During the monsoons the place is alive with birds but many animals move to higher ground. There are ground birds such as peafowl, jungle fowl, spur fowl and the grey partridge. Babblers, bulbuls and tree pies are common round the lodges.

The **Kankwari Fort** (20 km), where Emperor Aurangzeb is believed to have imprisoned his brother **Dara Shikoh**, the rightful heir to the Mughal throne, is within the park. The old **Bhartrihari** temple (6 km) has a fair and six-hour dance-drama in September to October. **Neelkanth** (33 km) has a complex of sixth- to 10th-century carved temples. **Bhangarh** (55 km), on the outskirts of the reserve, is a deserted city of some 10,000 dwellings established in 1631. It was abandoned 300 years ago, supposedly after it was cursed by a magician. **Sariska**, the gateway for the Sariska National Park, is a pleasant, quiet place to stay and relax. Excursions by jeep are possible to forts and temples nearby.

The park is open all year round. During the monsoon travel through the forest may be difficult. The best season to visit is between November and April. In the dry season, when the streams disappear, the animals become dependant on man-made water holes at Kalighatti, Salopka and Pandhupol.

### Sleeping

**Alwar** *p405*

**B-C Alwar**, 26 Manu Marg, T0144-2700012, www.hotelalwar.com. Set off road in attractive garden, 16 rooms, 7 in new block, attached baths (hot showers), TV, fridge, phone, restaurant, use of pool and tennis courts at nearby club, efficient service, popular.

**B-C Kothi Rao**, 31 Moti Dungri, T0144-270 0741, kothirao@yahoo.com. 9 a/c rooms in extremely homely hotel, reminiscent of an English B&B, run by polite, welcoming family.

**B-E Aravali**, Nehru Marg, near the station, T0144-233 2883. 30 rooms of widely ranging styles and standards, from suites to dorms, plus a restaurant and bar. There's a pool, but even guests have to pay to use it! 50% discount to YHA members.

**C-E Ankur**, Manu Marg, T0144-2333025. Same hotel occupies two buildings on opposite sides of square. The 27 rooms (10 a/c) in the motel-style block closest to the 'Imperial' are significantly better than the 19 rooms opposite, pick of the nearby options.

**C-E New Tourist**, 2 Manu Marg, T0144-270 0897. 20 rooms of a higher standard than most here, keen and friendly management, beer bar, homely. Recommended.

**C-F Ashoka**, Manu Marg, T0144-234 6780. 30 rooms, clean and comfortable, deluxe rooms have TV, running hot water and western toilets, cheaper rooms have Indian toilets and hot water in buckets, restaurant (Rs 35 *thalis*), good value.

**D Meenal** (RTDC), near Circuit House, T0144-234 7352. 6 rooms with bath (2 a/c), restaurant, bar, quiet location.

**D-E Atlantic**, Manu Marg, T0144-234 3181. 15 rooms with attached baths, only **D** a/c and deluxe rooms have Western toilets.

**E Alka**, Mangal Marg, T332796. Basic rooms.

**E Saroop Vilas Palace**, near Moti Doongri, T0144-233 1218. Renovated royal mansion taken over by private entrepreneur, 4 rooms with attached baths (western toilets), vegetarian restaurant serving reasonable Chinese and South Indian fare.

**Alwar to Sariska** *p406*

**B Hill Fort Kesroli** (Heritage Hotel), Alwar Rd, Kesroli, T01468-289352, www.neemranahotels.com. Around a courtyard are 22 comfortable, if eccentric, airy rooms, reasonable restaurant and service, relaxing, and in a lovely isolated rural location.

**C-D Lake Palace** (RTDC), Siliserh, T0144-2886322. 10 rooms, 5 a/c, restaurant, modest but superb location.

**Sariska** *p406*

**A Sariska Palace**, 40 km from Alwar railway, T0144-284 1322, www.sariska.com. 72 refurbished a/c rooms, (annexe lacks the charm of the lodge), restaurant and bar (generally only open for residents), gym, pool, new ayurvedic and yoga centre, tours, enormous converted royal hunting lodge, built in 1898, full of photographs and stuffed tigers, set in expansive and well-maintained gardens. Rs 500 entry fee for non-residents, off set against restaurant bill.

**C Baba Resorts**, T0144-288 5231, next door to **Sariska Tiger Camp**, is similar to its neighbour. Both are good options for the price.

**C Sariska Tiger Camp**, 19 km towards Alwar on main road, T0144-288 5311. 8 mud-walled but classy rooms in pleasant surroundings, plus 20 luxury tents during the winter season. Looks better from inside than out.

**C-D Tiger Den** (RTDC), in the sanctuary, T0144-284 1342. Superbly located tourist bungalow with views of hill and park, 30 rooms with attached baths (hot showers) but shabby, dirty public areas, veg restaurant (Indian buffets Rs 130-150), bar (no snacks, carry your own to have with beer/drinks) shop sells cards and souvenirs, nice garden, friendly management.

**D Forest Rest House**, Main Rd, opposite turning to Kushalgarh. 3 simple rooms, only open during the winter season.

## Eating

**Alwar** *p405*

**ΨΨ Narulas**, Kashiram Circle, T0144-233 3966. Indian/Chinese/Continental. A/c restaurant, popular for Punjabi non veg and veg dishes.

**Ψ Baba**, Hope Circle. Popular for 'milk cake' (*kalakand*) and other Rajasthani sweets.

**Ψ Imperial Guest House**, 1 Manu Marg, T0144-270 1730. Rooms disappointing but South Indian restaurant is popular and good value.

**Ψ Moti Doongri Park** has a number of stalls selling cheap south Indian snacks in the evening. Some Chinese and north Indian.

## Transport

**Alwar** *p405*

**Bus** Regular buses to/from **Delhi** (4½-5 hrs) and **Jaipur**. Frequent service to **Bharatpur** (2½ hrs), **Deeg** (1½ hrs) and **Sariska** (1 hr).

**Train New Delhi**: *Shatabdi Exp, 2016*, not Sun, 1941, 2½ hrs. **Delhi**: *Jodhpur Delhi Exp, 4860*, 0835, 3 hrs; *Jaipur-Delhi Exp, 2414*, 1845, 3 hrs.

**Sariska** *p406*

**Air** Nearest airport at Jaipur (110 km).

**Train** Nearest at Alwar (36 km), with buses to the sanctuary.

# Deeg, Bharatpur and around

*For a typical dusty and hot north Indian market town, Deeg gained the somewhat surprising reputation as the summer resort of the Raja of Bharatpur. Located on the plains just northwest of Agra, the Raja decided to develop his palace to take full advantage of the monsoon rains. The fort and the 'Monsoon' pleasure palace have ingenious fountains and are of major architectural importance, their serenity in stark contrast to the barely controlled chaos of the rest of the town.*

*One of the most popular halting places on the 'Golden Triangle', Bharatpur, is best known for its Keoladeo Ghana Bird Sanctuary. Once the hunting estate of the Maharajas of Bharatpur, with daily shoots recorded of up to 4,000 birds, the 29-sq km piece of marshland, with over 360 species, is one of the finest bird sanctuaries in the world. Lesser visited are the sights off the road which connects Agra to Jaipur, NH11, which sees huge volumes of tourist traffic. The Balaji temple is particularly remarkable.* » *For Sleeping, Eating and other listings, see pages 412-414.*

## Ins and outs

There are regular bus services from both Mathura and Bharatpur to Deeg, with the road from Bharatpur being by far the smoother of the two. Bharatpur, 40 km south of Deeg, has good bus and train connections from Agra, Jaipur and Delhi. Keoladeo Ghana National Park is 4 km south of Bharatpur town.



## Deeg → *Phone code: 05641. Colour map 2, grid A6. Population: 38,000.*

The rubble and mud walls of the square **fort** are strengthened by 12 bastions and a wide, shallow moat. It has a run-down *haveli* within, but is otherwise largely abandoned. The entrance is over a narrow bridge across the moat, through a gate studded with anti-elephant spikes. Negotiating the thorny undergrowth, you can climb the ramparts which rise 20 m above the moat; some large cannons are still in place on their rusty carriages. You can walk right around along the wide path on top of the walls and climb the stairs to the roof of the citadel for good views all round.

The **palaces** ⓘ *0930-1730, closed Fri, Rs 5, foreigners Rs 100*, directly opposite the fort, are flanked by two reservoirs, Gopal (west) and Rup Sagar (east), and set around a beautifully proportioned central formal garden in the style of a Mughal *char bagh*. The main entrance is from the north, through the ornamental, though unfinished, Singh (Lion) Pol; the other gates are Suraj (Sun) Pol (southwest) and Nanga Pol (northeast). The impressive main palace **Gopal Bhavan** (1763), bordering Gopal Sagar, is flanked by Sawon and Bhadon pavilions (1760) named after the monsoon months (mid-July to mid-September). Water was directed over the roof lines to create the effect of sheets of monsoon rain. The palace still retains many of the original furnishings, including scent and cigarette cases made from elephant's feet and even a dartboard. There are two separate veg and non-veg dining rooms, the former particularly elegant, with floor seating around a low-slung horseshoe-shaped marble table. Outside, overlooking the formal garden, is a beautiful white marble *hindola* (swing) which was brought as booty with two marble thrones (black and white) after Suraj Mal attacked Delhi.

To the south, bordering the central garden, is the single-storey marble **Suraj Bhavan** (circa 1760), a temple and **Kishan Bhavan** with its decorated façade, five arches and fountains. The water reservoir to its west was built at a height to operate the fountains and cascades effectively; it held enough water to work all the fountains for a few hours though it took a week to fill from four wells with bullocks drawing water up in leather buckets. Now, the 500 or so fountains are turned on once a year for the **Monsoon festival** in August. All these are gravity fed from huge holding tanks on the palace roof, with each fountain jet having its own numbered pipe leading from the tank. Coloured dyes are inserted into individual pipes to create a spectacular effect. The (old) **Purana Mahal** beyond, with a curved roof and some fine architectural points was begun by Badan Singh in 1722. It now houses government offices but the simple wall paintings in the entrance chamber of the inner court are worth seeing.

**Keshav Bhavan,** a *baradari* or garden pavilion, stands between the central garden and Rup Sagar with the **Sheesh Mahal** (Mirror Palace, 1725) in the southeast corner. **Nand Bhavan** (circa 1760), north of the central garden, is a large hall 45 m long, 24 m wide and 6 m high, raised on a terrace and enclosed by an arcade of seven arches. There are frescoes inside but it has a deserted feel. The pavilion took the monsoon theme further; the double-roof was ingeniously used to create the effect of thunder above-water channelled through hollow pillars rotated heavy stone balls which made the sound! On a sunny day the fountains are believed to have produced a rainbow.

## Bhandarej to Bharatpur

**Bhandarej**, 62 km from Jaipur, south of NH11 after Dausa, is a relaxing place to stop for the night, see below. The NH11 then goes through a series of small towns and villages to **Sakrai** (77 km) where there is a good road side RTDC restaurant. Some 15 km after Sakrai is the turning for Balaji, home to the really extraordinary **Balaji Temple**. This is where people come who believe themselves to have been possessed by devils, and who want the evil spirits exorcised. The scenes on the first floor in particular are not for the faint-hearted; methods of restraining the worst afflicted include chaining them to the walls and placing them under large rocks. Most exorcisms take place on Tuesdays and Saturdays, when there are long queues to get in. From **Mahuwa** a road south leads through Hindaun to Karauli (64 km).

Noted for its pale red sandstone, widely used for building, **Karauli**, founded in 1348, was the seat of a small princely state which played a prominent part in support of the Mughal Emperors. The impressive **City Palace** has some fine wall paintings, stone carvings and a fine Darbar Hall. Fairs are held at nearby temples lasting a week to a fortnight, see below Mahavirji, associated with the 24th Tirthankar Mahavir, is an important Jain pilgrimage centre.

## Bharatpur → *Phone code: 05644. Colour map 2, grid A6. Population: 157,000.*

Built by Suraj Mal, the **Lohagarh Fort** appears impregnable. The British, initially repulsed in 1803, took it in 1825. There are double ramparts, a 46 m wide moat and an inner moat around the palace. Much of the wall has been demolished but there are the remains of some of the gateways. Inside the fort are three palaces (circa 1730) and Jewel House and Court to their north. The **museum** ⓘ *1000-1630, closed Fri, Rs 3,* in the Kachhari Kalan exhibits archaeological finds from villages nearby, dating from the first to 19th centuries as well as paintings and artefacts; the armoury is upstairs.

**Peharsar** ⓘ *Rs 30 to 'headman' secures a tour,* 23 km from centre, with a carpet weaving community, makes a very interesting excursion from Bharatpur.

## Keoladeo Ghana National Park

*ⓘ Rs 25, Rs 200 foreigners, payable each time you enter, professional video camera Rs 1,500, amateur video Rs 200, car Rs 50. Café provides good lunch stop.*

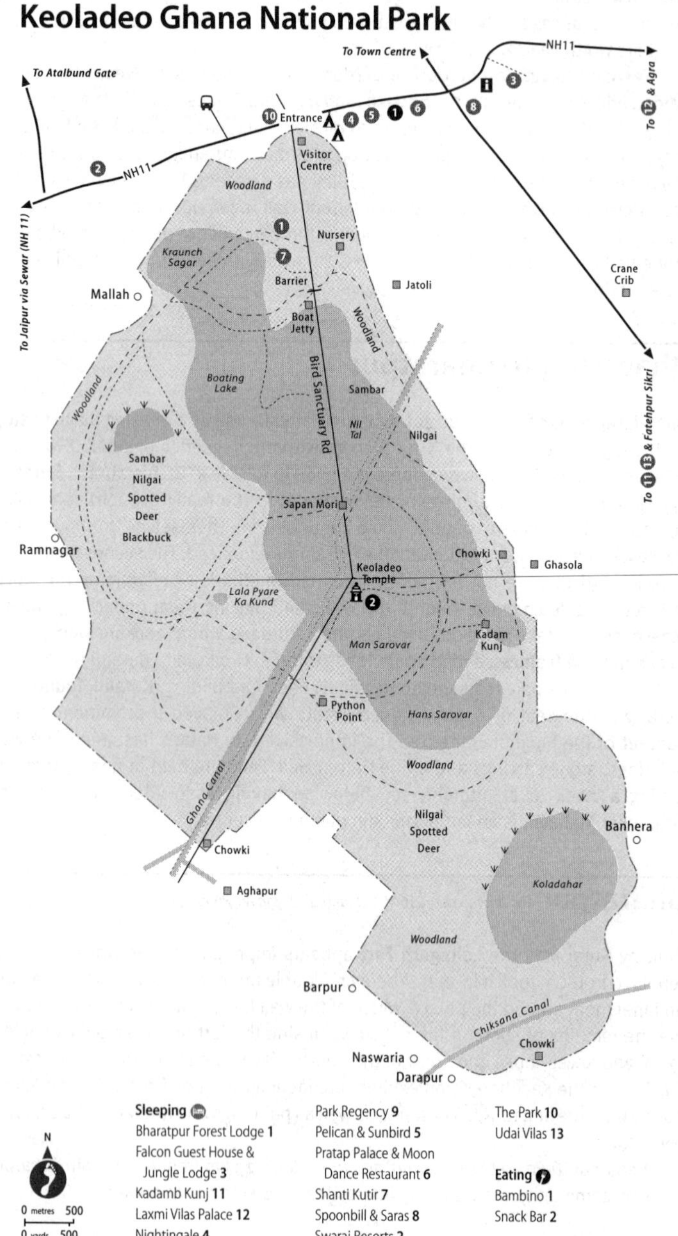

The late Maharaja Brajendra Singh converted his hunting estate into a bird sanctuary in 1956 and devoted many of his retired years to establishing it. He had inherited both his title and an interest in wildlife from his deposed father, Kishan Singh, who grossly overspent his budget – 30 Rolls Royces, private jazz band and extremely costly wild animals including "dozens of lions, elephants, leopards and tigers" – for Bharatpur's jungles. It has been designated a World Heritage site, and can only be entered by bicycle or cycle rickshaw, thus maintaining the peaceful calm of the park's interior.

*Allow a full day, though you can spot many species in just two hours. It is best to carry your own pair of binoculars.*

## Ins and outs

**Getting around** Good naturalist guides cost Rs 100 per hour per group or Rs 50 per hour per person at entrance, or contact Nature Bureau ⓘ *Haveli SVP Shastri, Neemda Gate, T/F05644-225498*. Official cycle-rickshaws at the entrance are numbered and work in rotation, Rs 50 per hour for two (but drivers may be reluctant to take more than one). Well worthwhile as some rickshaw-wallahs are very knowledgeable and can help identify birds (and know their location): a small tip is appropriate. The narrower paths are not recommended as the rough surface make them too noisy. It is equally feasible to just walk or hire a bike. A boat ride is highly recommended for viewing.

**Tourist information** **Rajasthan** ⓘ *Hotel Saras, T05644-22542*, and **Wildlife office** ⓘ *Forest Rest House, T05644-22777*. Guides available. For tours contact **GTA** ⓘ *near Tourist Lodge, Gol Bagh Rd, T05644-28188, vfauzdar@yahoo.com*. Knowledgeable English speaking guides, Rs 300 for two hours. It is worth buying the **Collins Handguide to the Birds of the Indian Sub-continent** (available at the Reserve and in booksellers in Delhi, Agra, Jaipur etc), well illustrated. **Bharatpur: Bird Paradise** by Martin Ewans, Lustre Press, Delhi, is also extremely good.

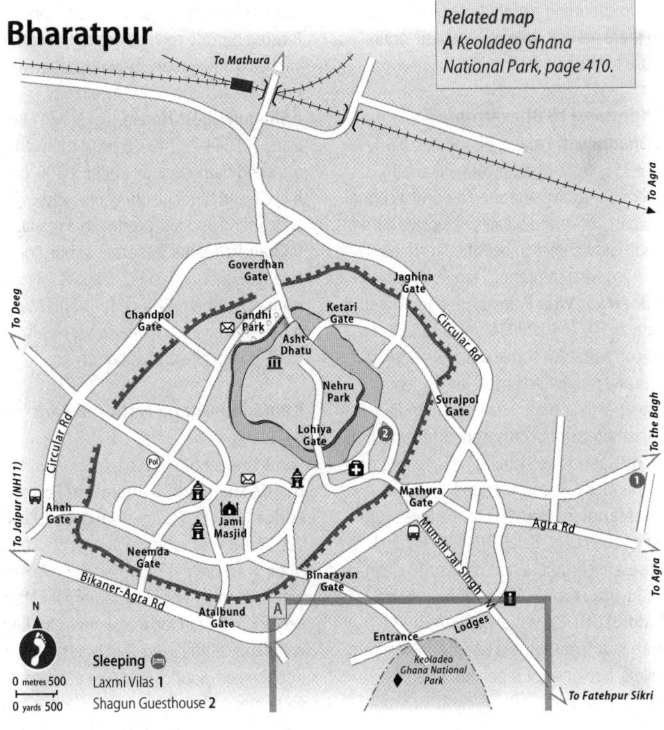

**Climate** Winters can be very cold and foggy, especially in the early morning. It is especially good November-February when it is frequented by Northern hemisphere migratory birds.

## Sights

A handful of rare Siberian Crane visit annually. The ancient migratory system, some 1,500 years old, is in danger of being lost since young cranes must learn the route from older birds (it is not instinctive). These cranes are disappearing – eaten by Afghans and sometimes employed as fashionable 'guards' to protect Pakistani homes (they call out when strangers approach). September to October is the breeding season but it's worth visiting any time of the year.

Among other birds to be seen are egrets, ducks, coots, storks, kingfishers, spoonbills, Sarus cranes, birds of prey including Laggar falcon, greater spotted eagle, marsh harrier, Scops owl and Pallas' eagle. Shortage of water may result in migrants failing to arrive. There are also chital deer, sambar, nilgai, feral cattle, wild cats, hyenas, wild boar and monitor lizards, whilst near Python Point, there are usually some very large rock pythons.

Birds can be watched from a short distance from the road between the boat jetty and Keoladeo temple, especially Sapan Mori crossing, since they have got accustomed to visitors. Dawn (which can be very cold) and dusk are the best times; trees around Keoladeo temple are favoured by birds for sleeping in, so are particularly rewarding at dawn. Midday may prove too hot so take a book and find a shady spot. Carry a sun hat, binoculars and plenty of drinking water.

## Sleeping

### Deeg *p408*

Avoid spending a night here but if you have to there are a couple of very basic options close to the bus station.

### Bhandarej to Bharatpur *p409*

**B Bhadrawati Palace**, Bhandarej, T01427-283 351, www.bhadrawatipalace.com. 35 adequate rooms arranged around a central lawn in converted palace, extensive gardens, pool, wide choice in beautiful restaurant; orchard with camping, 5 km from palace.

**B Bhanwar Vilas Palace** (Heritage Hotel), Karauli, T07464-220024, www.karauli.com. 29 comfortable rooms, including 4 a/c suites in converted palace, most air-cooled (cheaper in cottage), restaurant (Indian, Rajasthani), pool, tours, camping, amazingly ornate lounge and dining halls, real air of authenticity. Recommended.

**C-D Manglam Inn**, next to the Balaji turn off on the NH11, Balaji, T01420-247 393. The closest accommodation option, 10 clean, good-sized rooms, 3 a/c, friendly owners.

**E Motel** (RTDC), Mahuwa, T07461-33210. With 5 simple rooms, a fast food restaurant, toilets, basic motor repair facilities.

### Bharatpur *p409, map p411*

Most of Bharatpur's accommodation is located outside town, close to the entrance to the bird sanctuary. However, there is a great budget choice in the old city.

**F Shagun Guest House**, just inside Mathura Gate, T05644-232 455. 6 basic rooms, 1 with attached bathroom, all under Rs100, plus bicycle and binocular hire. Friendly, welcoming and knowledgeable manager.

**C Chandra Mahal**, Peharsar, Jaipur-Agra Rd, Nadbai, Peharsar, T05643-243238. 23 rooms in simply furnished, 19th-century Shia Muslim *haveli* with character, quality set meals (from Rs 250), jeep hire and good service.

### Keoladeo Ghana National Park *p410, map p410*

Some budget hotels have tents.

**Inside the park** **B Bharatpur Forest Lodge** (Ashok), 2½ km from gate, T05644-222 760, 8 km from railway and bus stand, book in advance. 17 comfortable a/c rooms with balconies, pricey restaurant and bar, very friendly staff, peaceful, boats for bird watching, animals (eg wild boar) wander into the compound. Entry fee each time you enter park.

**E Shanti Kutir Rest House**, near boat jetty. 5 clean rooms in old hunting lodge, mostly used by guests of the Park Director.

**Outside the park** **AL-A The Bagh**, Agra Rd, 4 km from town, T05644-228 333, www.thebagh.com. 14 classy, well decorated, centrally a/c rooms with outstanding bathrooms in upmarket garden retreat. Attractive dining room, pool and coffee shop planned, beautiful 200-year-old gardens, some may find facilities rather spread out.

**A Swaraj Resorts**, opposite park, T05644-233 250, swarajresorts@hotmail.com. 12 modern, well-equipped rooms plus many facilities: restaurant, gym, pool, billiards and table tennis. Not good value.

**A Udai Vilas**, Fatehpur Sikri Rd, 3 km from park, T05644-233 161, www.udaivilaspalace.com. 24 contemporary rooms in impressively run hotel, excellent restaurant, pleasant gardens, a cut above. Recommended.

**A-B Laxmi Vilas Palace** (Heritage Hotel), Kakaji ki Kothi, Agra Rd, 2½ km from town (auto-rickshaws outside), T05644-223 523, www.laxmivilas.com. 30 elegant, a/c rooms around a lovely central courtyard, good food and service, attractive 19th-century hunting lodge decorated in period style (jackals spotted), pleasantly old fashioned, welcoming friendly staff, exceptional pool and Jacuzzi. Recommended.

**B Kadamb Kunj**, Fatehpur Sikri Rd, 3 km from park, T05644-220 122, www.kadambkunj.com. 16 modern, a/c rooms plus well-kept lawns, a good gift shop and restaurant.

**B-C Park Regency**, opposite park, T05644-224 232, hotelparkregency@yahoo.co.uk. 8 large, modern, clean rooms, 24-hr room service, lawns, friendly, good value.

**B-E Crane Crib**, Fatehpur Sikri Rd, 3 km from park, T05644-222 224. Attractive sandstone building contains 25 rooms of wide-ranging standards and tariffs, but all reasonable value. Added attractions include a small cinema where wildlife shows are filmed nightly, bonfires on the lawn during winter and the welcoming staff. Recommended.

**C The Park**, opposite Park gate, T05644-233 192, bansal39@sancharnet.in. 10 large, clean rooms plus an atypically light restaurant and well maintained lawn.

**C Sunbird**, near Park gate, T05644-225 701, www.hotelsunbird.com. Clean rooms with hot shower, better on 1st floor, very pleasant restaurant, friendly staff, bike hire, good value, well maintained. Highly recommended.

**C-D Pratap Palace**, near Park Gate, T05644-224 245, www.hotelpratappalace.net. 30 rooms (10 a/c) with bath, whole place feels slightly rundown, mediocre restaurant but helpful management, good value.

**C-D Saras** (RTDC), Fatehpur Sikri Rd, T05644-223 722. 25 simple clean rooms, some a/c (limited hot water), dorm (Rs 50), restaurant (indifferent food), lawns, camping, dull.

**D-E Falcon Guest House**, near Saras, T05644-223 815. 10 clean, well-kept rooms, some a/c with bath, owned by naturalist, good information, bike hire, quiet, very helpful, warm welcome, off-season discount.

**D-F Nightingale** and **Tented Camp**, near Park gate, T05644-227 022. Deluxe 2-bed tents with bath, others with shared bath, good food, open during the winter.

**E Jungle Lodge**, Shankar Colony (next to Falcon), T05644-225 622. 8 basic but clean rooms, excellent meals for residents (huge portions, cheap), quiet, friendly family, 'no Indians' policy, motorbike hire.

**E-F Kiran Guest House**, 364 Rajendra Nagar, 300 m from park gate, T05644-223 845. 5 clean rooms, excellent meals in rooftop restaurant, peaceful, safe, homely, helpful and knowledgeable family, free station pick ups. Recommended.

**E-F Pelican**, near Park gate, T05644-224 221. 9 clean rooms with fan, best No 8 with hot (salty!) shower (ask for towel), quite modern with tiny balcony, restaurant, friendly, bike hire (Rs 40 per day), good information.

**E-F Spoonbill**, near Saras, T05644-223 571, hotelspoonbill@rediffmail.com. Good value rooms with shared facility (hot water in buckets), dorm (Rs 60), run by charming ex-Army officer, courteous and friendly service, good food, bike hire, also 4 more good-size rooms in 'New Spoonbill' down the road.

## Eating

**Keoladeo Ghana National Park**

*p410, map p410*

**Inside the park** **TTT Forest Lodge**, over-priced buffets feeding the many tour groups. **Snack Bar**, dirty, serving drinks and biscuits.

**Outside the park** All restaurants offer some Indian and Western dishes.

ΨΨΨ **Laxmi Vilas**, wide choice but some find it disappointing, standard fare for Westerners.
ΨΨ **Eagle's Nest**, new 100-seater restaurant with the promise of a/c to come.
ΨΨ **Moon Dance** tent, near **Pratap Palace**. Good food, lively atmosphere, beer.
Ψ **Bambino**, open-air dining in a garden.
Ψ **Pelican**, good choice, chicken, vegetarian, Israeli dishes, 'westernized'.
Ψ **Spoonbill**, good food obliging (beer and special *kheer* on request). Recommended.

## Festivals and events

**Bhandarej to Bharatpur** *p409*
In Karauli, **Sivaratri** (**26 Feb 2005**, 10 Feb 2006, 7 Feb 2007), **Kaila Devi** (**6 Apr 2005**, 26 Mar 2006,16 Mar 2007).

**Bharatpur** *p409, map p411*
**Brij Festival**, a few days before Holi, honours lord Krishna with folk dances and drama relating the love story of Radha-Krishna. **21-23 Mar 2005**, 10-12 Mar 2006, 27 Feb-1 Mar 2007.

## Transport

**Bhandarej to Bharatpur** *p409*
All trains except *Rajdhani Express* stop at Gangapur City, 30 km from Karauli.

**Bharatpur** *p409, map p411*
The nearest airport is at Agra (55 km).

The buses to Bharatpur tend to get very crowded but give an insight into Indian rural life. From **Agra** (55 km, 1½ hrs, Rs 12), **Deeg** Rs 15; **Delhi** (185 km, 6 hrs, Rs 70) and **Jaipur** (175 km, 5 hrs, Rs 60) arrive at Anah Gate just off NH11 (east of town).

Train from: **Delhi (ND)**: *Paschim Exp, 2925*, 0630, 4 hrs; *Golden Temple Mail, 2903*, 1540, 3½ hrs; *Mumbai-Firozepur Janata Exp, 9023*, 0800, 5½ hrs. **Sawai Madhopur**: *Paschim Exp, 2926*, 1955, 2½ hrs; *Golden Temple Mail, 2904*, 1055, 2½ hrs.

An auto-rickshaw from train station (6 km) to park Rs 50; from bus stand (4 km), Rs 20.

**Keoladeo Ghana National Park** *p410, map p410*
There are bikes for hire near Saras or ask your hotel; Rs 40 per day; hire on previous evening for an early start next day.

## Directory

**Bharatpur** *p409, map p411*
**Banks** SBBJ, near Binarayan Gate, may ask to see proof of purchase, or refuse to change TCs.



# Ranthambhore National Park

→ *Phone code: 07462. Colour map 2, grid B6.*

*The park is one of the finest tiger reserves in the country; most visitors spending a couple of nights here are likely to spot one of these wonderful animals, although there have been reports of their numbers dwindling due to poachers. Once the private tiger reserve of the Maharaja of Jaipur, in 1972 the sanctuary came under the Project Tiger scheme. It covers 410 sq km and runs from the easternmost spur of the Aravallis to the Vindhya range. It has both the old fort and the wildlife sanctuary, also known as Sawai Madhopur, after the nearby town, which has some Jain temples with gilded paintings. Set in dry deciduous forest, the area covers rocky hills and open valleys dotted with small pools and fruit trees. The fort dominates the landscape. The path to it zigzags up the steep outcrop in a series of ramps and through two impressive gateways.* » *For Sleeping, Eating and other listings, see pages 417-418.*

## Ins and outs

**Getting there and around** The national park is 10 km east of Sawai Madhopur, with the approach along a narrow valley; the main gate is 4 km from the boundary.

The park has good roads and tracks. Entry is by park jeep or open bus (Canter) on three-hour tours; 18 jeeps (or Gypsys) and 20 Canters are allowed in at any one time to minimize disturbance. Jeeps are better but can be difficult to get in the peak season so request one at the time of booking your lodge. Visitors are picked up from their hotels. The park is open 1 October-30 June. Tours: winter 0700-1000, 1500-1800; summer 0630-0930, 1430-1730. Jeep hire: Rs 750 for up to five passengers; jeep entry Rs 125; guide Rs 150; plus individual entry fee Rs 25 (Indians), Rs 200 (foreigners). Camera free, video Rs 200. Seat in a Canter, Rs 200. Bookings start at 0600 and 1330 for same day tours; advance bookings from 1000-1330.

**Climate** From November to April. The vegetation dies down in April exposing tigers. Temperatures from 49-28°C. It can be very cold at dawn in winter.

## Background

Much of the credit for Ranthambhore's present position as one of the world's leading wildlife resorts goes to India's most famous "tiger man", Mr Fateh Singh Rathore. His enthusiasm for all things wild has been passed on to his son, Dr Goverdhan Singh Rathore, who set up the Prakratik Society in 1994. This charitable foundation was formed in response to the increasing human encroachment on the tiger's natural forest habitat; in 1973 there were 70,000 people living around Ranthambhore Park, a figure which has now increased to 200,000.

The human population's rapidly rising firewood requirements were leading to ever-more damaging deforestation, and the founders of the Prakratik Society soon realized that something needed to be done. Their solution was as brilliant as it was simple; enter the "biogas digester". This intriguingly named device, of which 225



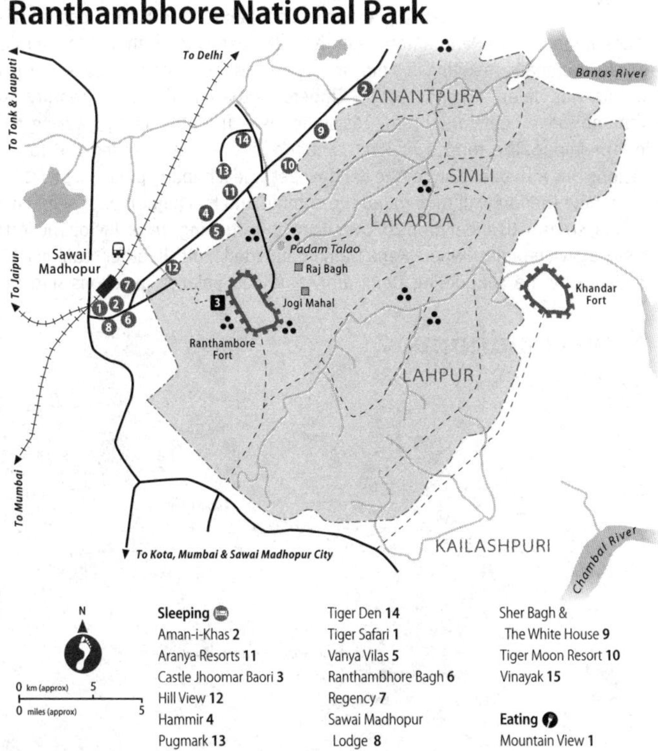

 have so far been installed, uses cow dung as a raw material, and produces both gas for cooking, negating the need for firewood, and organic fertilizer, which has seen crop yields increase by 25%. The overwhelming success of this venture was recognized in June 2004, when the Prakratik Society was presented with the prestigious Ashden Award for Sustainable Energy in London.

## Wildlife

Tiger sightings are reported almost daily, usually in the early morning, especially from November to April. Travellers see them "totally unconcerned, amble past only 30 ft (10 m) away"! Sadly, poaching is prevalent, and the tiger population has been depleted to around 30. The lakeside woods and grassland provide an ideal habitat for herds of chital and sambar deer and sounders of wild boar. Nilgai antelope and chinkara gazelles prefer the drier areas of the park. Langur monkeys, mongoose and hare are prolific. There are also sloth bear, a few leopards, and the occasional rare caracal. Crocodiles bask by the lakes, and some rocky ponds have fresh water turtles. Extensive birdlife includes spurfowl, jungle fowl, partridges, quails, crested serpent eagle, woodpeckers, flycatchers etc. There are also water birds like storks, ducks and geese at the lakes and waterholes. Padam Talao by the Jogi Mahal is the park's favourite water source; there are also water holes at Raj Bagh and Milak.

## Ranthambhore fort

ⓘ *Free. The entrance to the fort is before the gate to the park. Open dawn to dusk, though the Park Interpretation Centre near the small car park may not be open.*

*Avoid weekends when there are larger numbers of noisy visitors.*

There is believed to have been a settlement here in the eighth century. The earliest historic record is of it being wrested by the Chauhans in the 10th century. In the 11th century, after Ajmer was lost to Ghori, the Chauhans made it their capital. Hamir Chauhan, the ruler of Ranthambhore in the 14th century gave shelter to enemies of the Delhi sultanate, resulting in a massive siege and the Afghan conquest of the fort. The fort was later surrendered to Emperor Akbar in the 16th century when Ranthambhore's commander saw resistance was useless, finally passing to the rulers of Jaipur. The forests of Ranthambhore historically guarded the fort from invasions but with peace under the Raj they became a hunting preserve of the Jaipur royal family. The fort wall runs round the summit and has a number of semi-circular bastions, some with sheer drops of over 65 m and stunning views. Inside the fort you can see a Siva temple – where Rana Hamir beheaded himself rather than face being humiliated by the conquering Delhi army – ruined palaces, pavilions and tanks.

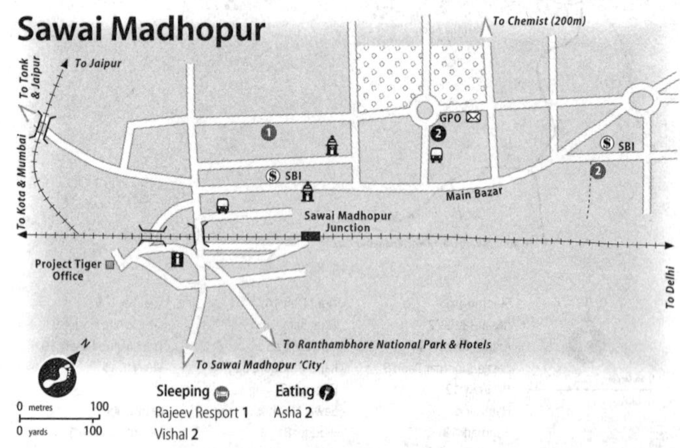

Mineral water, tea and soft drinks are sold at the foot of the climb to the fort and next to the Ganesh temple near the tanks.

## Sleeping

**Ranthambhore National Park**

*p414, maps p415 and p416*

Book well ahead. Hotels tend to be over-priced – rooms dusty and electricity erratic. Carry a torch. Most **B** category and above are geared for tour groups so may neglect independent travellers. In Sawai Madhopur, the hotels in the market areas are seedy.

**LL Aman-i-Khas**, close to park, T07462-252 052, www.amanresorts.com. 6 super luxury a/c tents in beautiful surroundings, minimum 3-night stay on all-inclusive basis (US$2,250).

**LL Vanyavilas** (Oberoi), T07462-223 999, www.oberoihotels.com. 20 acre, very upmarket garden resort set around a re-created *haveli* with fantastic frescoes. 25 unbelievably luxurious a/c tents (wood floor, TV, marble baths), pool, billiards, elephant rides, nightly wildlife lectures, dance shows in open-air auditorium, "fabulous spa", friendly and professional staff. Exceptional.

**LL-L The Pugmark**, Khilchipur, T07462-252 205, www.thepugmark.net. 22 luxury a/c cottages, including one with its own pool, in an entertainingly over the top resort. Defining feature is the "imaginatively landscaped" garden, replete with all manner of waterways, plastic rocks and illuminations.

**L Sawai Madhopur Lodge** (Taj), Ranthambhore Rd, T07462-220 541, www.tajhotels.com. 20-min drive from park, 32 a/c rooms (6 tents Oct-Mar), dated hunting lodge but comfortable, good buffet in stately wood-panelled dining hall watched over by tigers' heads, pool, tennis front desk lacks sparkle, park tour by jeep Rs 1420 each.

**L Sherbagh Tented Camp**, Sherpur-Khiljipur, T07462-252 120, www.sherbagh.com. 12 luxury tents with hot showers, award winning eco-camp, bar, dinner around fire, lake trips for birders, jungle ambience, well organized. Open 1 Oct-30 Mar, tariff includes all meals.

**AL-A The Whitehouse**, close to Sher Bagh, T07462-252 099. www.ranthambhore.co.uk. 3 very comfortable rooms in charming period property set in peaceful gardens. Common leopard sightings at nearby waterhole. All meals included. Owned by the Singh Rathore family.

**A Ranthambhore Regency**, T07462-223 456, www.ranthambhor.com. 39 a/c rooms in cottages in swanky modern surroundings. Very clean pool and huge, 100 cover dining hall, plus evening folk performances.

**A Tiger Den Resort**, Khilchipur, Ranthambhore Rd, T07462-252 070, www.tigerdenresort.com. 40 simple but pleasant a/c rooms in brick cottages around a well-kept lawn, evening meals (Indian buffet) seated around braziers, surrounded by farmland near guava groves, 6 km from park. All meals included.

**A Tiger Moon Resort**, near Sherpur on the edge of the park, 12 km from railway, T07462-252 042, www.indianadventures.com. 32 stone (25 a/c), and 5 simple bamboo cottages, all with modern fittings, hot water, some tents are added in the peak season, buffet meals, bar, library, pool, pleasant "jungle ambience". All meals and 2 safaris included.

**B-C Aranya Resorts**, Ranthambore Rd, T07462-221 121, aranyaresort@rediffmail.com. 10 clean, modern rooms in convenient location for park, reasonably priced veg food.

**B-C Hill View**, Ranthambhore Rd, T07462- 222 173, hillviewholidayresort@rediffmail.com. Attractive, large garden complex set in hills with great views, 17 cottage rooms (8 a/c), attached baths, fixed meals, great lawns.

**B-C Ranthambore Bagh**, Ranthambhore Rd, T07462-221 728, www.ranthambhore.com. 12 luxury tents and 12 simple but attractive rooms in this pleasantly laid back property. Family run, pride has been taken in every detail; the public areas and dining hall are particularly well done. Highly recommended.

**C Hammir**, T07462-220 562. One of the oldest hotels, undergoing much-needed renovation. 20 rooms, 8 a/c, plus a new pool and a friendly, cheerful manager.

**C Jhoomar Baori** (RTDC), Ranthombore Rd, T07462-220 495. Set high on a hillside, this former hunting lodge is an interesting building and offers fantastic views of the area. There are 12 rooms, some bigger than others, but all quirkily arranged, plus a small bar and okay restaurant. Good value.

**C-D Vinayak** (RTDC), Ranthambhore Rd, close to park, T07462-221 333. 14 adequate rooms, including 5 a/c, plus pleasant lawns in a good location, and a gloomy restaurant which serves fantastic veg *thalis*.

**D-E Tiger Safari**, T07462-221 137, www.tigersafariresort.com. 14 cosy rooms, plus 4 attractive a/c cottages, very clean baths (hot shower), quiet, arranges park jeep/bus, very helpful manager, good value. Recommended.

**E-F Rajeev Resort**, 16 Indira Colony, Civil Lines, Sawai Madhopur, T07462-221 413. 12 fairly decent rooms, 2 a/c (some with western toilets), and larger 4-bedded rooms, simple meals to order.

**F Vishal**, Main Bazar, opposite SBI, Sawai Madhopur, T07462-220 695. 7 passable rooms some with bath (hot water in buckets).

## Eating

**Ranthambhore National Park**

*p414, maps p415 and p416*

**Mountain View Restaurant**, Ranthambhore Rd. Standard menu but pleasant lawns to sit out on and a friendly welcome.

**Asha**, T07462-220 803. Don't be put off by uninviting exterior, this is a great little eatery, friendly, fast service, cheap and scrumptious.

## Transport

**Ranthambhore National Park**

*p414, maps p415 and p416*

**Bus** stand is 500 m from railway station. To **Sawai Madhopur** from Kota and Jaipur are slow (4 hrs); trains are better.

The **railway** station at Sawai Madhopur Junction, T07462-220 222, is on the main Delhi-Mumbai line. From **Jaipur**: *Jaipur-Mumbai, 2956*, 1350, 2 hrs. **Jaipur**: *Mumbai-Jaipur Exp, 2955*, 1035, 2 hrs. **Jodhpur**: *Sawai Madhopur-Jodhpur Intercity Exp, 2465*, 1710. **Kota**: *Golden Temple Mail, 2904*, 1320, 1¼ hrs; *Mumbai Exp, 2956*, 1550, 1½ hrs. **Mumbai**: *Jaipur Mumbai Exp, 2956*, 1550, 16 hrs; *Paschim Exp, 2926*, 2220, 17¼ hrs; *Golden Temple Mail, 2904*, 1320, 15 hrs. **New Delhi** (via Bharatpur and Mathura) *Golden Temple Mail, 2903*, 1300, 6 hrs; *Dehra Dun Exp, 9019*, 2140, 8 hrs.

## Directory

**Ranthambhore National Park**

*p414, maps p415 and p416*

**Internet** Cyber Café on Ranthambhore Rd near to Ankur Resort. **Useful numbers** Tiger Watch, T07463-220811.

# Ajmer and Pushkar

*Although geographically close, these towns could hardly be more different. Situated in a basin at the foot of Taragarh Hill (870 m), Ajmer is surrounded by a stone wall with five gateways. Renowned throughout the Muslim world as the burial place of Mu'inuddin Chishti, who claimed descent from the son-in-law of Mohammad, seven pilgrimages to Ajmer are believed to equal one to Mecca. Every year, especially at the annual Islamic festivals of Id and Muharram, thousands of pilgrims converge on this ancient town on the banks of Ana Sagar Lake. Many visitors are discouraged by the frantic hustle of Ajmer on first arrival, but it's worth taking time to explore this underrated city.*

*Pushkar lies in a narrow dry valley overshadowed by impressive rocky hills which offer spectacular views of the desert at sunset. The lake at its heart, almost magically beautiful at dawn and dusk, is one of India's most sacred. The village has been markedly changed in recent years by the year-round presence of large numbers of foreigners who were originally drawn by the Pushkar fair. There are now many hotels, restaurants, cafés and shops catering to Western tastes and many travellers find it hard to drag themselves away from such a feast of creature comforts. Note that it is not to everybodies taste as there is a high hassle factor. The village is transformed once again during the celebrated camel fair into a colourful week of heightened activity.*

▸▸ *For Sleeping, Eating and other listings, see pages 423-429.*

## Ins and outs

**Getting there** There are trains and buses to Ajmer from the surrounding main towns and cities. Ajmer is the main transport hub for Pushkar although there are some direct bus services. Buses for Pushkar from Ajmer use the stand nearby the railway station; the main State and Private Bus Stands are chaotic and dirty, 2 km away. Buses to Pushkar head for the Central (Marwar) Bus Stand, overrun by aggressive hotel touts. Ask to be dropped before hand on entering the town.

**Getting around** The main sights and congested bazaars of Ajmer, which can be seen in a day at a pinch, are within 15-20-minutes walk of the railway station but you'll need a rickshaw to get to Ana Sagar. Pushkar is small enough to explore on foot. Hire a bike to venture further. ▸▸ *See Transport, page 429, for further details.*

**Tourist information** In Ajmer, there is an office alongside **Khadim Hotel** ⓘ *T0145-52426, 0800-1800, closed Sun and second Sat of month*. Very helpful. Approved guide (four to eight hours, about Rs 250-400) and tourist taxi hire.

# From Jaipur to Ajmer

## Sambhar Lake

The salt lake, one of the largest of its kind in India, until recently attracted thousands of flamingoes and an abundance of cranes, pelicans, ducks and other waterfowl. About 120 species of birds have been checklisted. However, the poor monsoons of recent years have caused the lake to dry up leaving only a few marshy patches. Check the situation before visiting. Nilgai, fox and hare are spotted around the lake. The saline marshes are used for production of salt. **Sakambari Temple** nearby, dedicated to the ancestral deity of the Chauhans, is believed to date from the sixth century.

## Kuchaman

Kuchaman is a large village with temples and relics. Many visitors stop here for tea and snacks between Shekhawati and Ajmer. If you do stop, make time for a visit to the fort; it is a unique experience. Before the eighth century, Kuchaman lay on the highly profitable Central Asian caravan route. Here Gurjar Pratiharas built the massive **clifftop fort** with 10 gates leading up from the Meena bazaar in the village to the royal living quarters. The Chauhans drove the Pratiharas out of the area and for some time it was ruled by the Gaurs. From 1400, it has been in the hands of the Rathores who embellished it with mirrors, mural and gold work in superb palaces and pavilions such as the golden Sunheri Burj and the mirrored Sheesh Mahal, both in sharp contrast to the fort's exterior austerity. The Sariska Palace Group have restored and renovated the fort at enormous cost. You can also visit the **Krishna temple** with a 2,000-year-old image, and the **Kalimata ka Mandir** which has an eighth-century black stone deity, shop in the **Meena Bazar** or watch local village crafts people.

## Kishangarh → *Population: 22,000.*

Kishangarh was a small princely state, founded by Kishan Singh in 1603 as an independent state with a fort facing Lake Gundalao. Local artists – known for their depiction of the Krishna legend and other Hindu themes – were given refuge here by the royal family during the reign of the Mughal emperor, Aurangzeb, who, turning his back on the liberal views of earlier emperors, pursued an increasingly zealous Islamic purity. Under their patronage the artists reached a high standard of excellence and they continue the tradition of painting Kishangarh miniatures which are noted for sharp facial features and elongated almond-shaped eyes. Most of those available are cheap copies on old paper using water colours instead of the mineral pigments of the originals. The town has a bustly charm, and is an interesting place to wander around.

The fort palace stands on the shores of Lake Gundalao. Its Hathi Pol (Elephant Gate) has walls decorated with fine murals, and, though partly in ruins, you can see battlements, courtyards with gardens, shady balconies, brass doors and windows with coloured panes of glass. The temple has a fine collection of miniatures.

### Roopangarh

About 20 km from Kishangarh, Roopangarh was an important fort of the Kishangarh rulers founded in AD 1649 on the old caravan route along the Sambhar Lake. The fort stands above the centre of the village which is a centre for craft industries – leather embroidery, block printing, pottery and handloom weaving can all be seen. The Sunday market features at least 100 cobblers making and repairing *mojdi* footwear.

## Ajmer → *Phone code: 0145. Colour map 2, grid B5. Population: 490,000. Altitude: 486 m.*

The **Dargah of Khwaja Mu'inuddin Chishti** (1143-1235) is the tomb of the Sufi saint (also called 'The Sun of the Realm') which was begun by Iltutmish and completed by Humayun. Set in the heart of the old town, the entrance is through the bazar. Access to the main gate is on foot or by tonga or auto. The Emperor Akbar first made a pilgrimage to the shrine to give thanks for conquering Chittor in 1567, and the second for the birth of his son Prince Salim. From 1570 to 1580 Akbar made almost annual pilgrimages to Ajmer on foot from Agra, and the *kos minars* (brick marking pillars at about two-mile intervals) along the road from Agra are witness of the popularity of the pilgrimage route. It is considered the second holiest site after Mecca. On their first visit, rich Muslims pay for a feast of rice, ghee, sugar, almonds, raisins and spices to be cooked in one of the huge pots in the courtyard inside the high gateway. These are still in regular use. On the right is the Akbar Masjid (circa 1570), to the left, an assembly hall for the poor. In the inner courtyard is the white marble Shah Jahan Masjid (circa 1650), 33 m long with 11 arches and a carved balustrade on three sides. In the inner court is the Dargah (tomb), also white marble, square with a domed roof and two entrances. The ceiling is gold-embosse velvet, and silver rails and gates enclose the tomb. At festival times the tomb is packed with pilgrims, many coming from abroad, and the crush of people can be overpowering.

The whole complex has a unique atmosphere. The areas around the tomb have a real feeling of community; there is a hospital and a school on the grounds, as well as numerous shops. As you approach the tomb the feeling of religious fervour increases, often heightened by the music being played outside the tomb's ornate entrance. For many visitors, stepping in to the tomb itself is the culmination of a lifetime's ambition, reflected in the ardour of their offerings.

Nearby is the **Mazar** (tomb) of Bibi Hafiz Jamal, daughter of the saint, a small enclosure with marble latticework. Close by is that of Chimni Begum, daughter of Shah Jahan. She never married, refusing to leave her father during the seven years he was held captive by Aurangzeb in Agra Fort. She spent her last days in Ajmer, as did another daughter who probably died of tuberculosis. At the south end of the Dargah is the **Jhalra** (tank).

The **Arhai-din-ka Jhonpra Mosque** ('The Hut of two and a half days') lies beyond the Dargah in a narrow valley. Originally a Jain college built in 1153, it was partially destroyed by Muhammad of Ghori in 1192, and in 1210 turned into a mosque by **Qutb-ud-din-Aibak** who built a massive screen of seven arches in front of the pillared halls, allegedly in two and a half days (hence its name). The temple pillars which were incorporated in the building are all different. The mosque measures 79 x 17 m with 10 domes supported by 124 columns and incorporates older Hindu and Jain masonry. Much of it is in ruins though restoration work was undertaken at the turn of the century; only part of the 67 m screen and the Jain prayer hall remain.

**Akbar's Palace**, built in 1570 and restored in 1905, is in the city centre near the east wall. It is a large rectangular building with a fine gate. Today it houses the **Government Museum** ⓘ *1000-1630, closed Fri, Rs 3, no photography*, which has a dimly presented collection of fine sculpture from sixth to 17th centuries, paintings and old Rajput and Mughal armour and coins.

*From Station Road, a walk through the bazars, either to Dargah/Masjid area or to Akbar's Palace/Nasiyan Temple area, is interesting.*

The ornate **Nasiyan Jain Temple** (Red Temple) ⓘ *Prithviraj Marg, 0800-1700, Rs 5*, has a remarkable museum alongside the Jain shrine, which itself is open only to Jains. It is well worth visiting. Ajmer has a large Jain population (about 25% of the city's total). The Shri Siddhkut Chaityalaya was founded in 1864 in honour of the first Jain Tirthankar, Rishabdeo, by a Jain diamond merchant, Raj Bahadur Seth Moolchand Nemichand Soni (hence its alternative name, the Soni temple). The opening was celebrated in 1895. Behind a wholly unimposing exterior, on its first floor the Svarna Nagari Hall houses an astonishing reconstruction of the Jain conception of the Universe, with gold plated replicas of every Jain shrine in India. Over 1,000 kg of

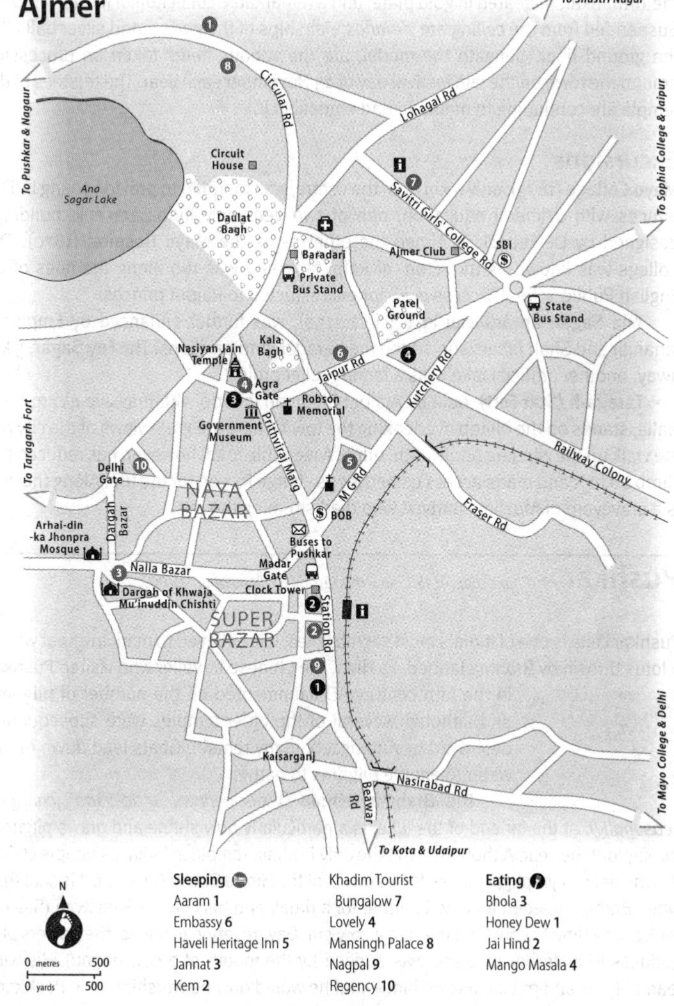

**“” As you approach the tomb the feeling of religious fervour increases, often heightened by the music being played. For many visitors, stepping in to the tomb itself is the culmination of a lifetime's ambition...**

gold is estimated to have been used, and at one end of the gallery diamonds have also been placed behind decorative coloured glass to give an appearance of backlighting. It took 20 people 30 years to build. The holy mountain, Sumeru, is at the centre of the continent, and around it are such holy sites as Ayodhya, the birthplace of the Tirthankar, recreated in gold plate, and a remarkable collection of model temples. Suspended from the ceiling are *vimanas* – airships of the gods – and silver balls. On the ground floor, beneath the model, are the various items taken on procession around the town on the Jain festival day of 23 November each year. The trustees of the temple are continuing to maintain and embellish it.



### Excursions

**Mayo College** (1873), only 4 km from the centre, was founded to provide young Indian princes with a liberal education, one of two genuinely Indo-Saracenic buildings designed by De Fabeck in Ajmer, the other being the **Mayo Hospital** (1870). The College was known as the 'Eton' of Rajputana and was run along the lines of an English Public School. Access is no longer restricted to Rajput princes.

**Ana Sagar**, an artificial lake (circa 1150), was further enhanced by Emperors Jahangir and Shah Jahan who added the baradari and pavilions. The **Foy Sagar**, 5 km away, another artificial lake, was a famine relief project.

**Taragarh (Star Fort)**, built by Ajaipal Chauhan in 1100 with massive 4½ m thick walls, stands on the hilltop overlooking the town. There are great views of the city but the walk up the winding bridle path, tiring. A jeepable road, however, has reduced the climb on foot and made access easier. Jeeps charge Rs 500 for the trip. Along the way is a graveyard of Muslim 'martyrs' who died storming the fort.

## Pushkar → *Phone code: 0145. Colour map 2, grid B5. Population: 15,000.*

*There are dozens of temples here, most of which are open 0500-1200, 1600-2200.*

Pushkar Lake is one of India's most sacred lakes. It is believed to mark the spot where a lotus thrown by Brahma landed. Fa Hien, the Chinese traveller who visited Pushkar in the fifth century AD, commented on the number of pilgrims and although several of the older temples were subsequently destroyed by Aurangzeb, many remain. Ghats lead down to the water to enable pilgrims to bathe.

The **Brahma temple** ⓘ *0600-1330, 1500-2100 (changes seasonally)*, at the far end of the lake, is a particularly holy shrine and draws pilgrims throughout the year. Although it isn't the only Brahma temple in India, as people claim, it is the only major pilgrim place for followers of the Hindu God of Creation. It is said that when Brahma needed a marital partner for a ritual, and his consort Saraswati (Savitri) took a long time to come, he married a cow-girl, Gayatri, after giving her the powers of a goddess (Gayatri because she was purified by the mouth of a cow or gau). His wife learnt of this and put a curse on him – that he would only be worshipped in Pushkar.

## A saint of the people

Khwaja Mu'inuddin Chishti probably came to India before the Turkish conquests which brought Islam sweeping across northern India. A sufi, unlike the Muslim invaders, he came in peace. He devoted his life to the poor people of Ajmer and its region. He was strongly influenced by the *Upanishads*; some reports claim that he married the daughter of a Hindu raja.

His influence during his lifetime was enormous, but continued through the establishment of the Chishti school or *silsila*, which flourished 'because it produced respected spiritualists and propounded catholic doctrines'. Hindus were attracted to the movement but did not have to renounce their faith, and *Sufi khanqah* (a form of hospice) were accessible to all.

Almost immediately after his death Khwaja Mu'innuddin Chishti's followers carried on his mission. The present structure was built by Ghiyasuddin Khalji of Malwa, but the embellishment of the shrine to its present ornate character is still seen as far less important than the spiritual nature of the Saint it commemorates.

There are 52 ghats around the lake, of which the Brahma Ghat, Gan Ghat and Varah Ghat are the most sacred. The medieval **Varah temple** is dedicated to the boar incarnation of Vishnu. It is said the idol was broken by Emperor Jahangir as it resembled a pig. The **Mahadev Temple** is said to date from 12th century while the **Julelal Temple** is modern and jazzy. Interestingly enough the two wives of Brahma have hilltop temples on either side of the lake, with the Brahma temple in the valley. A steep 3-km climb up the hill which leads to the **Savitri Temple** (dedicated to Brahma's first wife), offers excellent views of the town and surrounding desert.

The **Main (Sadar) Bazar** is full of shops selling typical tourist, as well as pilgrim knick-knacks and is usually very busy. At full moon, noisy religious celebrations last all night so you may need your ear plugs here.

## Sleeping

**Jaipur to Ajmer** *p419*

**AL Kuchaman Fort** (Heritage Hotel), Kuchaman, T01586-220 882, www.thekuchamanfort.com. 35 distinctive a/c rooms in a part of the fort, attractively furnished, restaurant, bar, jacuzzi, gym, luxurious pools (including a 200-year-old cavernous one underground), camel/horse riding, royal hospitality, superb views and interesting tour around the largely unrestored fort.

**B Phool Mahal Old City**, Kishangarh, T01463-247 405, www.royalkishangarh.com, superbly located at the base of Kishangarh Fort on the banks of Gundalao lake (dries up in summer). This 1870 garden palace has 16 well maintained a/c rooms, as well as an elegant lounge and dining room, all with period furnishings and marble floors.

**B Roopangarh Fort** (Heritage Hotel), Roopangarh, T01497-220 217, www.royal kishangarh.com. 20 large, high-ceilinged rooms, rich in character, in places the furnishing is basic. Marwar decor and cuisine, free village safaris plus excursions, good sunrise and sunset views, friendly staff.

**D Sambhar Lake Resorts**, Sambhar Lake, T01425-224 034. 6 cottage rooms, bath with hot showers, friendly staff, camel rides and jeep safaris across the saline marshes and dunes, also short rail journey on diesel locomotive driven trolleys that carry salt from the pans to the towns. Rs 1150 includes meals and safaris. Day visit (Rs 500) includes veg lunch, tea and a tour of the salt marshes.

**Ajmer** *p420, map p421*

Prices rise sharply, as much as 10 times, during the week of the mela. Many hotels are booked well in advance. The tourist office has a list of Paying Guest accommodation.

**A Mansingh Palace**, Ana Sagar Circular Rd, T0145-242 5702, www.mansinghhotels.com. 60 rooms in attractive sandstone modern building, most comfortable in town. Pleasant restaurant, comfortable bar and clean pool.

**B-C Hotel Embassy**, Jaipur Rd, T0145-262 3859, hotel embassy@hotmail.com. 31 smart a/c rooms in building undergoing renovation to 3-star standard. Enthusiastic, professional staff, elegant restaurant.

**C-D Aaram**, off Ana Sagar Circular Rd, opposite Mansingh, T0145-242 5250. 22 slightly grubby rooms, some a/c, restaurant, small garden, friendly manager.

**C-D Hotel Ajmeru**, Khailand Market, near Akbar Fort, T0145-243 1103, www.hotel ajmeru.com. 12 very clean, light, modern rooms, 8 a/c, in relatively quiet location.

**C-D Hotel Jannat**, very close to Durgah, T0145-243 2494, www.ajmerhoteljannat. 36 clean, modern rooms in great location, friendly staff, a/c restaurant, all mod cons.

**C-D Khadim** (RTDC), Savitri Girls' College Rd, near bus station, T0145-262 7490. 55 rooms, some a/c (**C** suites), best are the uncarpeted, recently renovated rooms, dorm (Rs 50), gloomy restaurant, bar, Tourist Information, car hire, pleasant setting, usual RTDC service.

**C-D Regency**, Delhi Gate, near Dargah, T0145-262 2439, www.bahubalugroup.com. 24 ordinary rooms, some a/c, off unloved corridors. Lobby has feel of unfilled pool, a/c restaurant, bar, travel, in very crowded area but set back from road, genial management.

**C-E Nagpal**, T0145-262 7427. 19 rooms, 3 a/c, sizes vary widely but all well maintained, rooms at rear less noisy.

**D Fort Khejarla**, Khejarla, T02930-58311, madhoniwas@satyam.net.in. A Rajput Special Hotels. Simple rooms in the old part, meals (Rs 180), excursions to Raika and Bishnoi tribal villages. Contact Curvet India, Delhi T011-2684 0037.

**D Haveli Heritage Inn**, Kutchery Rd, T0145-262 1607. 8 good-sized, clean, comfortable rooms in homely 125 year old building. Family run, good home cooking, located on busy main road but set back with a pleasant courtyard, very charming owner.

**D Raj Palace Motel**, Merta Rd, T1590-220 202, 25 clean rooms with bath, 6 a/c, friendly family. Recommended.

**E Hotel Lovely**, opposite Sabji Mandi, Agra Gate, T0145-262 2191. 8 okay rooms in modern building, friendly, hard-working owner.

**E-F KEM**, Station Rd, T0145-242 9936. 45 rooms in period building near the railway station, 1st class rooms are clean and acceptable, 2nd class less so. Service practically non-existant. Attached bath.

**Pushkar** *p422, map p425*

The town suffers from early morning temple bells. During the fair, hotel charges can be 10 times the normal rate. Booking in advance is essential for the better places. Some budget hotels offer views of the lake from communal rooftops; to escape the noise of the Main Bazar, choose one in a back street of Bari Basti or near Ajmer Bus Stand.

**L-A Pushkar Palace** (WelcomHeritage), on lakeside, T0145-277 2001, pushkarpalace. com. 52 overpriced rooms including 25 suites overlooking the lake, in beautifully renovated old palace, attractive gardens. It looks good but is rather uncomfortable. Dine on the atmospheric lakeside terrace, food is ordinary, staff are not very helpful.

**A Jagat Palace** (WelcomHeritage), Ajmer Rd, T0145-277 2001, www.pushkarpalace.com. 36 a/c rooms in new building made to resemble a Rajput fort, colourful, naturally lit interiors, attractive vegetarian restaurant, beautiful pool and gardens, room sizes vary.

**A Pushkar Resorts**, Ganhera Village, Motisar Rd, 5 km out of town, T0145-277 2944, www.pushkarresorts.com. Pushkar's most upmarket resort, 40 individual a/c cottages decorated in European style, extensive gardens, delicious meals (home-grown produce), beautiful pool, sports (putting green, golf practice tees), book/handicraft shop, unique camel kafila (caravan) tours, desert jeep safaris, quite an oasis.

**C Pushkar Villas Resort**, Panch Kund Rd, T0145-277 2689, arajoria@hotmail.com. Newish place which feels a little unfinished,

*For an explanation of sleeping and eating price codes used in this guide, see inside the front cover. Other relevant information is found in Essentials, see pages 56-61.*

very popular with tourist taxi drivers. 13 good-sized rooms (7 a/c) around pleasant gardens and a well-maintained pool.

**C-D New Park**, Panch Kund Rd, T0145-277 2464, www.newparkpushkar.com. Some distance from town but set in a peaceful location surrounded by fields. 24 adequate if pricey rooms (14 a/c), lovely gardens, pool.

**C-E JP's Tourist Village Resort**, Ganhera, 2 km from town, T0145-277 2067, www.pushkarhotelbooking.com. 30 very rustic, basic rooms built in traditional style, with mud walls, thatched roofs, hand painted decorations and too basic bathrooms. Whole place has a quirky feel, great gardens, dusty pool, terrific treehouses, definitely different.

**C-F Sarovar** (RTDC), on lakeside, T0145-277 2040. 38 clean rooms (best with lake view, in old part), some a/c with bath, cheap 6-bed dorm, set around courtyard in former lakeside palace, indifferent vegetarian restaurant, attractive gardens.

**D-E Bharatpur Palace**, lakeside, T0145-277 2320. 18 unusually decorated rooms, clean bathrooms, exceptional views of the ghats.

**D-E Chandra Lake**, on Chandra Ghat, T0145-277 2896. 6 to 8 very basic rooms and bathrooms but what a view! If you can do without your creature comforts, it's a hugely authentic experience.

**D-E Inn Seventh Heaven**, next to Mali ka Mandir, T0145-510 5455, www.inn-seventh-heaven.com. 8 beautiful rooms in a fantastically well-restored 100-year-old *haveli*. Very friendly, informal, excellent rooftop restaurant, charming owner. Highly recommended.

**D-E Navratan Palace**, near Brahma temple, T0145-277 2981. 33 clean rooms, some a/c with hot showers (Rs 300-600), comfortable though not particularly attractive, clean pool, small garden with views, well maintained, some have found management unfriendly.



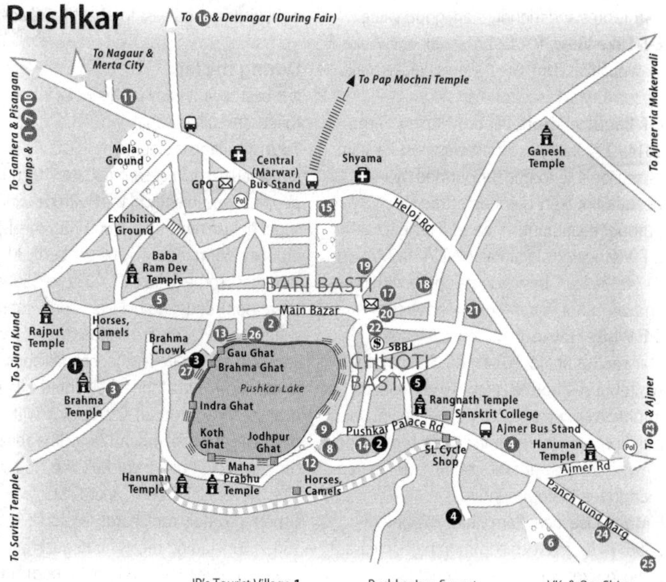

**Sleeping**

Bharatpur Palace **13**
Chandra Lake **26**
Colonel's Camp **10**
Inn Seventh Heaven **21**
Jagat Palace **23**
JP's Tourist Village **1**
Kanhaia **19**
Lake View **2**
Navratan Palace **3**
New Park **25**
Oasis **4**
Paramount **5**
Peacock Holiday Resort **6**
Peacock International Camp **16**
Purple Garden **18**
Pushkar Inn, Sunset & Bro-Sis Restaurant **8**
Pushkar Palace **9**
Pushkar Resorts **7**
Pushkar Villas Resort **24**
Rainbow **27**
RTDC Tourist Village **11**
Sarovar **12**
Shanti Palace **20**
Shiva Guest House & Sri Savitri **17**
Shyam Krishna **22**
VK & Om Shiva Restaurant **14**
White House & Raghav Resort **15**

**Eating**

Juice Centre **1**
Little Italy Pizzería **4**
Moondance **2**
Rainbow **3**
Venus **5**

Ghat (steps) ≡

**D-E Peacock Holiday Resort**, 1 km from centre, near Ajmer Bus Stand, T0145-277 2093, arajoria@hotmail.com. 30 rooms, some a/c, pleasant shady courtyard and small clean pool, rooms vary in size but are all a reasonable standard, laid-back staff.

**D-E Sunset**, on the lake, T0145-277 2382, hotelsunset@hotmail.com. 20 plain, clean rooms, 3 a/c, attractive garden. Well located close to lake, plus access to **Sunset Café**.

**D-F Oasis**, near Ajmer Bus Stand, T0145-277 2100, www.hoteloasispushkar.com. 34 clean rooms with bath, some a/c, in motel-style arrangement, garden, well maintained pool.

**D-F Paramount Palace**, Bari Basti, T0145-277 2428, hotelparamountpalace@hotmail.com. 16 clean, basic rooms, some with bath, best with balcony elevated site with splendid views from rooftop.

**E-F Kanhaia**, near Mali Mandir, T0145-277 2146. 14 rooms, best has sofa, with good bathrooms and friendly staff, good value.

**E-F Lake View**, T0145-277 2106, www.lakeviewpushkar.com. Great views of lake make up for very average rooms.

**E-F Raghav Resort**, Panday Nursery Farm, T0145-277 2207, www.lakeviewpushkar.com. 14 reasonable rooms surrounded by beautiful nursery gardens, attractive outdoor restaurant, a peaceful retreat.

**E-F VK**, near Pushkar Palace, T0145-277 2174. 13 clean, basic rooms, some with bath and 24-hr hot water (power shower!).

**E-F White House**, in narrow alley near Marwar Bus Stand, T0145-277 2147, hotelwhitehouse@hotmail.com. 10 very clean, impressively white rooms in well maintained building overlooking nursery gardens. Good views from pleasant rooftop restaurant, free mango tea. Recommended.

**F Mona Lisa**, near Ram Ghat, T0145-277 2356. 10 rooms with common bath, pleasant atmosphere, hot showers, friendly.

**F Purple Garden**, near Gautam Ashram, Choti Basti, T0145-277 2920, purplegardenhotel@yahoo.co.in. 7 well-maintained but basic rooms with attached bathrooms, 4 with common facilities. Some nice touches added by the owner's New Zealand wife. Main garden is indeed purple and looks lovely from the small rooftop café. Recommended.

**F Rainbow**, Mahadev Chowk, T0145-277 3309. 11 rooms with bath and hot water, rooftop restaurant with pool table and good views but noisy area.

**F Shanti Palace**, near Varah temple, T0145-277 2422, shantipalace@hotmail.com. 12 basic rooms in very peaceful surroundings, plus a friendly owner and good views of town.

**F Shiva Guest house**, near market post office, T0145-277 2120. Basic but clean rooms in calm environment enhanced by presence of 7 tortoises in central courtyard.

**F Shubham Palace**, near Sub Tahseal, T0145-277 3695, vandanagupta280@ yahoo.com. 10 basic rooms in very homely and relaxing homestay, plenty of shaded outdoor seating.

**F Shyam Krishna Guest House**, Chhoti Basti, T0145-277 2461. Part of 200-year old temple complex with 25 rooms around a courtyard, some with *jali* work on upper floor, run by friendly Brahmin family.

**F Sri Savitri**, near market post office, T0145-277 2327. 7 slightly ramshackle but characterful rooms, highly recommended by frequent visitors, not least for the friendly owner.

### During the fair

It is best to visit early in this week when toilets are still reasonably clean.

**Tourist Village** is erected by RTDC. A remarkable feat, it accommodates 100,000 people. Conveniently placed with deluxe/super deluxe tents (Rs 5-6,000 with meals), ordinary/dorm tents (Rs 200 per bed), 30 'cottages', some deluxe (Rs 4000; Rs 350-850 off-season). Beds and blankets, some running water, Indian toilets are standard. Meals are served in a separate tent (or eat delicious cheap, local food at the tribal tented villages near the show ground). Reservation with payment, essential (open 12 months ahead); contact RTDC, Chandralok Building, 36 Jan Path, New Delhi 110001, or at Jaipur.

Others, privately run charge about US$ 150-250 including meals for Regular and 'Swiss' double tent (US$15 extra bed). Some private camps are some distance from fair ground and may lack security:

**Colonel's Camp**, Motisar Rd, Ghanera, T0141-220 2034, www.meghniwas.com. 120 Deluxe tents with toilet and shower in attractive gardens.

**Peacock International Camp Resort**, T0145-277 2689. 25 tents with common facilities among orchards with pool at Devnagar (2 km from Mela Ground), free transport.

**Pushkar Palace** (see above). Sets up 50 'Swiss' tents and 50 Deluxe.
**Royal Tents Camp** (WelcomHeritage) comfortable tents with verandah, flush toilet, hot water in buckets or shower of sorts, Rajasthani cuisine, very well organized. Reserve through WelcomHeritage or T0291-251 0101.
**Wanderlust Desert Camp**, T011-2467 9059, www.wanderlustindia.cim. 120 Swiss tents with bath, electricity, varied meals.

## Eating

**Ajmer** *p420, map p421*
*Son halwa*, a local sweet speciality, is sold near the dargah and at the market.
**Mansingh Palace**, Ana Sagar Circular Rd. International. Pricey, unexciting food.
**Mango Masala**, Sandar Patel Marg, T0145-242 2100. American Diner-styled place with wide-ranging menu including pizzas, sizzlers, Indian and sundaes. Standard is high, portions large and service outstanding.
**Silver Leaf**, in **Embassy Hotel** (see above). Good range of multi-cuisine choices in sophisticated surroundings.
**Bhola**, Agra Gate, good vegetarian food, no nonsense service.
**Honey Dew**, Station Rd. Indian, Continental. Pleasant shady garden, good Indian snacks all day, disappointing Western.
**Jai Hind**, in alley by clock tower, opposite railway station. Best for Indian vegetarian. Delicious, cheap meals.
**Madeen**, opposite station. Simple but tasty.
**Tandoor**, Jaipur Rd, 1 km from bus station. Dinner in the garden with log fires, a/c section for lunch, good food (try paneer butter masala and tandoori chicken), cake shop, icecreams, takeaway snacks, cyber café. Recommended.

**Pushkar** *p422, map p425*
No meat, fish or eggs are served in this temple town. Alcohol and 'narcotics' are banned. Take special care during the fair: eat only freshly cooked food and drink bottled water. Long-stay budget travellers have encouraged western and Israeli favourites like falafel and apple pie, while Nepali and Tibetan immigrants have brought their own specialities. Roadside vendors offer cheap, filling *thalis* close to Ajmer bus stand.
**Honey & Spice Café**, in alleyway of Laxmi Market, old Rangji Temple Complex, fantastic coffee, cakes and light meals, superb.
**Little Italy Pizzeria**, Panch Kund Rd, high quality Italian dishes supervised by ex-pat Italian chef, plus Israeli and Indian specialities.
**Moondance**, just by the turning to Pushkar Palace. Western. Run by friendly Nepalese, service can be slow. Recommended.
**Pushkar Palace**, recommended for evening buffet in luxurious surroundings, great views and atmosphere, fine food.
**Halwai ki gali** and other sweet shops sell *malpura* (syrupy pancake), as well as usual Rajasthani/Bengali sweets.
**Karmima**, and other small places opposite shish-Manish Riding, offer home cooked *thalis* (Rs 15/20) and excellent fresh, pure orange/sweet lime juice.
**Om Shiva**, 20 m from **VK Hotel** in a garden. Good breakfasts (brown bread, garlic cheese, pancakes, fruit), buffets (Rs 45) or à la carte, well presented and hygienic. Another branch, opposite State Bank of Bikaner & Jaipur, is inferior.
**Rainbow** (above Krishna), Brahma Chowk. Wide choice (pizzas, jacket potatoes, enchiladas, humous, falafel, Indian dishes), fruit crumble with choc sauce and ice cream.
**RS**, near Brahma Temple. Good Indian, some Chinese and western (Rs 40-50).
**Sunset Café** by Pushkar Palace. Particularly atmospheric in the evening when crowds gather to listen to music and watch sunset, extensive menu. Recommended.
**Venus**, Ajmer Rd. Mixed menu. A la carte (good sizzlers) in the garden, also *thalis* (Rs 40), on the attractive rooftop.

## Festivals and events

**Ajmer** *p420, map p421*
**Urs Festival** commemorating Khwaja Mu'inuddin Chishti's death in 1235 is celebrated with 6 days of almost continuous music, and devotees from all over India and the Middle East make the pilgrimage. Qawwalis and other Urdu music developed in the courts of rulers can be heard. Roses cover the tomb. The festival starts on sighting the new moon in Rajab, the 7th month of the Islamic year. The peak is reached on the night between the 5th and 6th days when 10s of 1000s of pilgrims

## The pull of the cattle and camels

The huge *Mela* is Pushkar's biggest draw. Over 200,000 visitors and pilgrims and hordes of cattle and camels with their semi-nomadic tribal drivers, crowd into the town. Farmers, breeders and camel traders buy and sell. Sales in leather whips, shoes, embroidered animal covers soar while women bargain over clay pots, bangles, necklaces and printed cloth.

Events begin four to five days before the full moon in November. There are horse and camel races and betting is heavy. In the *Ladhu Umt* race teams of up to 10 men cling to camels, and one another, in a hilarious and often chaotic spectacle. The Tug-of-War between Rajasthanis and foreigners is usually won by the local favourites. There are also sideshows with jugglers, acrobats, magicians and folk dancers. At nightfall there is music and dancing outside the tents, around friendly fires – an unforgettable experience despite its increasingly touristy nature – the 2003 edition even featured a laser show! The cattle trading itself actually takes place during the week before the fair; some travellers have reported arriving during the fair and there being no animals left!

pack the shrine. At 1100 on the last morning, pilgrims and visitors are banned from the dargah, as the khadims, who are responsible through the year for the mainten ance of worship at the shrine, dressed in their best clothes, approach the shrine with flowers and sweets. On the final day, women wash the tomb with their hair, then squeeze the rose water into bottles as medicine for the sick.

**Pushkar** *p422, map p425*
Kartik Purnima is marked by a vast **cattle and camel fair** (12-15 Nov 2005, 2-5 Nov 2006, 21-24 Nov 2007'), see box. Pilgrims bathe in the lake, the night of the full moon being the most auspicious time, and float 'boats' of marigold and rose petals in the moonlight. Camel traders often arrive a few days early to engage in the serious business of buying and selling and most of the animals disappear before the official starting date. Arrive 3 days ahead if you don't want to miss this part of the fair. The all-night drumming and singing in the Tent City can get very tiring, but the fair is a unique spectacle. Travellers warn of pickpockets.

## Shopping

**Ajmer** *p420, map p421*
Fine local silver jewellery, tie-and-dye textiles and camel hide articles are best buys. The shopping areas are Madar Gate, Station Rd, Purani Mandi, Naya Bazar and Kaisarganj. Some of the alleys in the old town have good shopping.
**Arts and Art's**, Bhojan Shala, near Jain Temple.

**Pushkar** *p422, map p425*
There is plenty to attract the western eye; check quality and bargain hard. Miniatures on silk and old paper are everywhere.
**JP Dhabai's**, opposite Shiva Cloth Store near Payal Guest House, Main Bazar. Offers fine quality (painted with a single squirrel hair!) minatures at a price. Recommended.
**Essar**, shop 6, Sadar Bazar, opposite Narad Kunj. Excellent tailoring (jacket Rs 250-300 including fabric).
**Harish**, Brahma Temple Rd, for light weight razai quilts, bedsheets, cloth bags.

## Activities and tours

**Pushkar** *p422, map p425*
Horses Rs 150-200 per hr, camel Rs 30-50 per hr, at most hotels and near Brahma temple. Lessons: Rs 150 per hr (minimum 10 hr over 5 days) from **Ashish-Manish**, opposite Brahma Temple, or **Shannu's Riding School**, owned by a French Canadian, Panch Kund Rd, T0145-277 2043. For camel safaris that come well recommended contact **Purple Garden** hotel on T0145-277 2920.

For swimming pools: **Sarovar**, **Oasis**, **Peacock hotels**, non-residents pay Rs 40-50.
At Pushkar Palace Hotel, **Pushkar Travels**, offers tours, excellent service, good buses, ticketing Rs 50.

## Transport

**Jaipur to Ajmer** *p419*
For **Sambhar Lake** take the train to **Phulera**, 7 km from Sambhar village, 9 km from the lake. Jeeps charge Rs 50 for the transfer.

Kishangarh is an important railway junction between **Jaipur** and **Ajmer**, with regular trains from both places.

**Ajmer** *p420, map p421*
**Auto rickshaw**
To **Pushkar**, Rs 60 after bargaining.

**Bus**
Enquiries, T0145-242 9398. Buses every 30 mins to **Agra**, Rs 157, 9 hrs, **Delhi**, Rs 177, 9 hrs, **Jaipur**, Rs 56, 2½ hrs, **Jodhpur**, Rs 89, 5 hrs; **Bikaner**, Rs 116, 7 hrs; **Chittaurgarh** Rs 79, 5hrs **Udaipur** Rs 120, 7 hrs via Chittaurgarh, **Kota** via Bundi. Buses for **Pushkar** (Rs 10) which leave from near the station, are very crowded.

**Train**
Ajmer Station is seemingly overrun with rats and is not a great place to wait for a night train. Mansingh Palace Hotel allows short-stay rates, useful if you have a wait of several hours.

Reservations, T0145-243 1965, 0830-1330, 1400-1630, enquiries, T131/132. **Ahmadabad**: *Aravali Exp, 9708*, 1005, 11½ hrs; *Ahmadabad Mail, 9106*, 0735, 10 hrs; *Ashram Exp, 2916*, 2325, 8½ hrs, last 3 via **Beawar**, 1 hr; **Chittaurgarh**: *Ahmadabad Exp, 9943*, 0750, 5 hrs; *Chetak Exp, 9615*, 0150, 4½ hrs. **Jaipur**: *AjmerJaipur Exp, 9652*, 0640, 3 hrs. *Aravali Exp, 9707*, 1733, 2½ hrs; *Shatabdi Exp, 2016*, 1530, not Sun, 2 hrs. **Delhi**: *Ahmadabad Delhi Mail, 9105*, 2033, 9 hrs; *Shatabdi Exp, 2016* not Sun, 1530, 6½ hrs; (OD) *Ashram Exp, 2915*, 0215, 8 hrs; **Jaipur**: *Aravali Exp, 9707*, 1735, 2½ hrs. **Jodhpur**: *Jodhpur Mail, 4893*, 0545, 6 hrs. **Udaipur**: *Ahmadabad Exp, 9943*, 0750, 8½ hrs.

**Pushkar** *p422, map p425*
**Auto-rickshaw**
To **Ajmer** Rs 60 after bargaining.

**Bicycle/motorbike**
Rs 10 entry 'tax' per vehicle. Hire: **Michael Cycle SL Cycles**, Ajmer Bus Stand Rd, very helpful, Rs 3 per hr, Rs 25 per day; also from the market. **Hotel Oasis** has Vespa scooters, Rs 300 per day. Enfield Ashram, near **Hotel Oasis**, Rs 400 per day for an Enfield.

**Bus**
Frequent service to/from **Ajmer** Rs10. Direct buses to **Jodhpur** via Merta (8 hrs) but it is quicker to return to Ajmer and take an express bus (4-5 hrs) from there ('First class' passengers travel on the roof!). **Pushkar Travels**, good minibuses; avoid **Shrinath Travels**, overcrowded, often late, charges last minute premiums.

**Car**
Rs 10 entry 'tax' per vehicle. **Delhi**, 8 hrs; **Jaipur**, 3 hrs.

## Directory

**Ajmer** *p420, map p421*
**Banks** Bank of Baroda, opposite GPO, accepts Visa, Mastercard; **State Bank of India** near Bus Stand, changes cash, TCs. Government approved money changers in Kavandas Pura main market.

**Pushkar** *p422, map p425*
**Banks** SBBJ changes TCs; **Hotels Peacock** and **Oasis** offer exchange for a small commission. **Internet** Near **Oasis Hotel**, Ajmer Bus Stand, and now all over town. **Hospitals** Shyama, Heloj Rd, T72087. **Post** One at the Chowk with a very helpful Postmaster, east end of Main Bazar.

# Northern Rajasthan

*This is one of the less-visited regions of Rajasthan, but is well worth passing through on your way to the better-known areas. Bikaner, perhaps the least touristy big city in Rajasthan, has until now been somewhat overshadowed by the state's other cities, but is gaining popularity both as an interesting place in its own right, and as a place to go for a camel safari; as scenic as Jaisalmer but far less commercial. Even further off the beaten track, desert villages such as Kakoo offer an accessible insight into rural desert life, while wildlife enthusiasts will find plenty of interest in both Gajner National Park and Tal Chappar Wildlife Sanctuary.*

*Shekawati has its own quirky charm; still largely undeveloped, its outdoor treasures sit as silent testimony to an illustrious past, strangely at odds with the day to day bustle on their doorsteps. The region's boom days, when the indigenous Marwari businessmen were trading with the four corners of the globe, constantly vying to out do each other in the elaborateness of their* haveli *homes, are long gone. Marwari traders still enjoy a reputation as astute businessmen, but today operate in India's major business centres, many of their* havelis *having fallen in to disrepair but still intact enough to give a fascinating glimpse of a time gone by.*

# Bikaner and around



*Bikaner is an oasis town among scrub and sand dunes. The rocky outcrop in a barren landscape provides a dramatic setting for the Junagarh Fort, one of the finest in western Rajasthan. The old walled city retains a medieval air, and is home to over 300* havelis, *while outside the walls some stunning palaces survive. Well off the usual tourist route, Bikaner is en route to Jaisalmer from Jaipur or Shekhawati, and well worth a visit.* » *For Sleeping, Eating and other listings see pages 434-437.*

## Ins and outs

**Getting there** Bikaner is a full day's drive from Jaipur so it may be worth stopping a night in Samode or the Shekhawati region, see pages 339 and 437. The railway station is central and has services from Delhi (Sarai Rohilla), Jaipur and Jodhpur. The New Bus Stand is 3 km to the north but if coming from the south you can ask to be dropped in town. There are regular bus services to Desnok, but to get to Gajner, Kakoo or Tal Chappar you'll need to hire private transport. » *See Transport, page 436, for further details.*

**Getting around** The fort and the Old City are within easy walking distance from the station. Autos and cycle-rickshaws transfer passengers between the station and the New Bus Stand. Taxis can be difficult to get from the Lalgarh Palace area at night.

**Tourist information** Dhola-Maru Tourist Bungalow ⓘ *Poonam Singh Circle, T0151-527445, 0800-1800, Oct-Mar.* As well as information, car hire is available.

## Bikaner → *Phone code: 0151. Colour map 2, grid B3. Population: 530,000.*

### Sights

**Junagarh Fort** ⓘ *1000-1630 (last entry), Rs 50, Indians Rs 10; camera Rs 30, video Rs 100 (limited permission), guided tours in Hindi and English, private guides near the gate offer better 'in-depth' tours; Rs 100 for 4, 2 hrs,* is one of the finest examples in Rajasthan of the paradox between medieval military architecture and beautiful interior decoration. Started in 1588 by Raja Rai Singh (1571-1611), a strong ally of the

Mughal Empire, who led Akbar's army in numerous battles, it had palaces added for the next three centuries.

You enter the superbly preserved fort by the yellow sandstone **Suraj Prole** (Sun Gate, 1593) to the east. The pale red sandstone perimeter wall is surrounded by a moat (the lake no longer exists) while the Chowks have beautifully designed palaces with balconies, kiosks and fine *jali* screens. The interiors are beautifully decorated with shell-work, lime plaster, mirror-and-glass inlays, gold leaf, carving, carpets and lacquer work. The ramparts offer good views of the elephant and horse stables and temples, the old city with the desert beyond, and the relatively more recent city areas around the medieval walls. The walls of the **Lal Niwas**, which are the oldest, are elaborately decorated in red and gold. Karan Singh commemorated a victory over Aurangzeb by building the **Karan Mahal** (1631-1639) across the Chowk. Successive rulers added the **Gaj Mandir** (1745-1787) with its mirrored Shish Mahal, and the **Chattra Niwas** (1872-1887) with its pitched roof and English 'field sport' plates decorating the walls. The magnificent **Coronation Hall**, adorned with plaster work, lacquer, mirror and glass, is in Maharaja Surat Singh's **Anup Mahal** (1788-1828). The decorative façades around the Anup Mahal Chowk, though painted white, are in fact of stone. The fort also includes the **Chetar Mahal** and **Chini Burj** of Dungar Singh (1872-1887) and **Ganga Niwas** of Ganga Singh (1898-1943), who did much to modernize his state and also built the Lalgarh Palace to the north. Mirror work, carving and marble decorate the ornate **Chandra Mahal** (Moon Palace) and the **Phul**

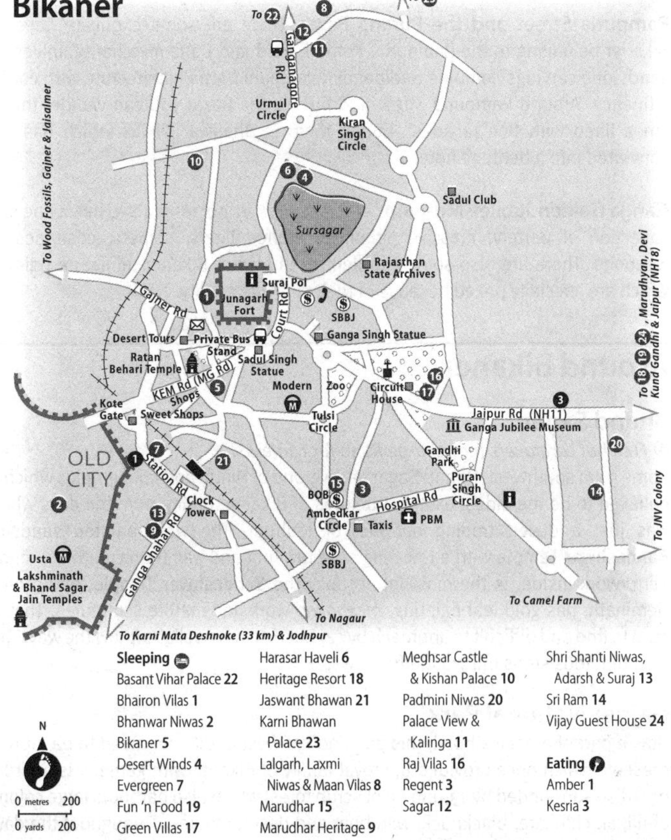

 Mahal (Flower Palace), built by Maharaja Gaj Singh. These last two are shown to foreigners at the end as a 'special tour' when the guide expects an extra tip! The royal chamber in the Chandra Mahal has strategically placed mirrors so that any intruder entering could be seen by the maharaja from his bed. The fort **museum** has Sanskrit and Persian manuscripts, miniature paintings, jewels, enamelware, silver, weapons, palanquins, howdahs, and war drums. **Har Mandir**, the royal temple where birth and wedding ceremonies were celebrated, is still used for Gangaur and other festivities. The well nearby is reputedly over 130 m deep. **Prachina Museum** ⓘ *0900-1800, Rs 25 (guided tour), Rs10 Indians, shop, small clean café outside is open air but shady*, in the grounds, exhibits beautifully crafted costumes, carpets and ornamental objects.

**Lalgarh Palace** ⓘ *palace closed Wed, museum closed Sun, 1000-1700, Rs 40 (museum extra Rs 20)*. The red sandstone palace stands in huge grounds to the north of the city, surrounded by rocks and sand dunes. Designed by Sir Swinton Jacob in 1902, the palace complex, with extensions over the next few decades, has attractive courtyards overlooked by intricate *zenana* screen windows and *jarokha* balconies, columned corridors and period furnishings. The banquet hall is full of hunting trophies and photographs. His Highness Doctor Karni Singh of Bikaner was well known for his shooting expertise – both with a camera and with a gun. The bougainvillaea, parakeets and peacocks add to the attraction of the gardens in which the Bikaner State Railway Carriage is preserved. The Lalgarh complex now has several hotels, see Sleeping page 434.

**Rampuria Street and the Purana Bazar** There are some exquisite *havelis* in Bikaner belonging to the Rampuria, Kothari, Vaid and Daga merchant families. The sandstone carvings combine traditional Rajasthani *haveli* architecture with colonial influence. Around Rampuria Street and the Purana Bazar you can wander through lanes lined with fine façades. Among them is **Bhanwar Niwas** which has been converted into a heritage hotel.

**Ganga Golden Jubilee Museum** ⓘ *Public Park, 1000-1630, Rs 3*, has a fine small collection of pottery, massive paintings, stuffed tigers, carpets, costumes and weapons. There are also some excellent examples of Bikaner miniature paintings which are specially prized because of their very fine quality.

## Around Bikaner

### Bhand Sagar

ⓘ *Free but caretakers may charge Rs 10 for cameras.*

Some 5 km southwest, Bhand Sagar has a group of Hindu and Jain temples which are believed to be the oldest extant structures of Bikaner, dating from the days when it was just a desert trading out-post of Jodhpur. The white-painted sandstone **Bandeshwar Temple** with a towering *shikhara* roof and painted sculptures, murals, mirrorwork inside, is the most interesting. The **Sandeshwar Temple**, dedicated to Neminath, has gold leaf painting, *meenakari* work and marble sculptures. They are hard to find and difficult to approach by car but rickshaw wallahs know the way. There are numerous steps but wonderful views.

### Gajner National Park

Now a part of a palace hotel, this park, 30 km west of Bikaner, used to ba a private preserve which once provided the royal family of Bikaner with game. It is a birder's paradise surrounded by 13,000 ha of scrub forest which also harbours large colonies of nilgai, chinkara, blackbuck, wild boar and desert reptiles. Throughout the day, a

## Life after the rains

When in Bikaner, try to spare the time to drop in at URMUL's showroom, Abhiviyakyi, opposite the new bus stand. A fair trade NGO, URMUL works with the marginalized tribes-people of the Thar desert. The droughts of the 1980s made farming, the traditional source of livelihood for the majority of these people, no longer a viable option. URMUL was formed in 1991 with the aim to teach these people new skills which could bring them the income that the absent rains had taken away. As the range of products on offer testifies, the project has been a huge success. All the items on sale, including clothing, tablecloths, bed linen, shoes and bags, have been made by the projects participants, and are of a quality previously unseen in the often all too amateur 'craft' sector.

train of antelope, gazelle and pigs can be seen arriving to drink at the lake. Winter migratory birds include the imperial black-bellied sand grouse, cranes and migratory ducks. Some visitors have spotted Great Indian bustard at the water's edge. It is worth stopping for an hour's mini-safari if you are in the vicinity.

### Kolayat

Some 50 km southwest via Gajner road, Kolayat is regarded as one of the 58 most Hindu important pilgrimage centres. It is situated around a sacred lake with 52 ghats and a group of five temples built by Ganga Singhji (none of which is architecturally significant). The oasis village comes alive at the November full moon when a three-day festival draws thousands of pilgrims who take part in ritual bathing.

### Karni Mata Mandir

ⓘ *Closed 1200-1600, free, camera Rs 40.*

This 17th-century temple, 33 km south of Bikaner at Deshnoke, has massive silver gates and beautiful white marble carvings on the façade. These were added by Ganga Singh (1898-1943) who dedicated the temple to a 15th-century female mystic Karniji, worshipped as an incarnation of Durga. A gallery describes her life. Mice and rats, revered and fed with sweets and milk in the belief that they are reincarnated saints, swarm over the temple around your feet; spotting the white rat is supposed to bring good luck. Take socks as the floor is dirty, but note that the rats are far less widespread than they are made out to be. Sensationalized accounts give the impression of a sea of rats through which the visitor is obliged to walk barefoot, whereas in reality, while there are a good number of rats, they generally scurry around the outskirts of the temple courtyard – you're very unlikely to tread on one! The temple itself is beautiful, and would be well worth visiting even without the novelty of the rats.

### Kakoo

This picturesque village, 75 km south of Bikaner, with attractive huts and surrounded by sand dunes, is the starting point for desert camel safaris costing Rs 1500 per day with tented facilities. Staying here makes a fantastic introduction to the practicalities of life in the desert; this is probably the most authentic desert settlement in this area that can be easily reached by road.

### Kalibangan and Harappan sites

One of North India's most important early settlement regions stretches from the Shimla hills down past the important Harappan sites of **Hanumangarh** and **Kalibangan**, north of Bikaner. Late Harappan sites have been explored by archaeologists, notably A

 Ghosh, since 1962. They were identified in the upper part of the valley, the easternmost region of the Indus Valley civilization. Across the border in Pakistan are the premier sites of Harappa (200 km) and Moenjo Daro (450 km). Here, the most impressive of the sites today is that of **Kalibangan** (west off the NH15 at Suratgarh). On the south bank of the Ghaggar River it was a heavily fortified citadel mound, rising about 10 m above the level of the plain. There were several pre-Harappan phases. Allchin and Allchin record that the bricks of the early phase were already standardized, though not to the same size as later Harappan bricks. The ramparts were made of mud brick and a range of pottery and ornaments have been found. The early pottery is especially interesting, predominantly red or pink with black painting.

## Sleeping

**Bikaner** *p430, map p431*
Budget hotel rooms usually have shared bath; often serve Indian veg food only. Tourist office has list of Paying Guest hotels.

**AL-A Laxmi Niwas**, Lalgarh Palace Complex, T0151-220 2777, www.laxminiwaspalace.com. 42 large, tastefully furnished rooms and suites with fabulous carvings and beautifully painted ceilings, all arranged around the stunningly ornate courtyard. Superb bar, restaurant and lounge, discreet but attentive service, absolutely unique. Recommended.

**A Heritage Resort**, along the Jaipur highway, '9 Km' post, T0151-752 393, www.carnival-hotels.com. 36 modern, well- appointed cottage rooms in a pleasant location. Attractive gardens, outdoor coffee shop, pool, 3-hole golf course, friendly management.

**A Lalgarh Palace**, 3 km from the railway, T0151-254 0201, lallgarhpalace@realbikaner.com. 38 large a/c rooms in beautiful and authentic surroundings (see Sights p430), magnificent indoor pool, atmospheric dining hall, mixed reports on food but quite an experience.

**A Raj Vilas**, Public Park, T0151-252 5901, www.rajvilaspalace.com. Large, modern hotel with 55 uninspired but functional central a/c rooms, 2 restaurants and a cramped pool.

**A-B Bhanwar Niwas**, Rampuria St, Old City (500 m from Kote Gate), ask for Rampuria Haveli, T0151-2 52 9323, www.bhanwarniwas.com. 26 beautifully decorated rooms (all different) around a fantastic courtyard in an exquisite early 20th-century *haveli*.Original decor has been painstakingly restored to stunning effect, the last word in style, great service. Highly recommended

**B Karni Bhawan Palace** (HRH), Gandhi Colony behind Lalgarh Palace, T0151-252 4701, www.hrhindia.com. 12 comfortable a/c rooms and spacious suites in completely original art deco mansion. Elegant furniture, modern fittings,good restaurant, large garden, peaceful, attentive service, feels like the original inhabitants have just stepped out for a while.

**C Basant Vihar Palace**, Ganganagar Rd, T0151-225 0675, www.basantviharpalace.com. Rooms in attractive early-20th century palatial sandstone mansion built by Maharajah Ganga Sinhji, magnificent darbar hall, pool, large gardens, old lily ponds.

**C Bhairon Vilas**, near fort, T0151-254 4751, www.hotelbaironvilas.tripod.com. Restored 1800s aristocratic *haveli*, great atmosphere, 18 eclectic rooms decorated with flair, excellent rooftop restaurant (musicians, dancers), good views, lawn, a carnival of kitsch but mixed reports about the service.

**C Fun 'n' Food**, NH11 8 km from town, T0151-752 589, www.realbikaner.com. Good option for families; reasonable rooms plus 2 pools, fairground rides and a boating lake.

**C Sagar**, next to Lalgarh Palace, T0151-520 677, www.sagarhotelbikaner.com. 42 reasonablerooms in modern building, half with a/c, plus 6 round huts, popular restaurant, expensive exchange, reports of poor service, strong commercial bias.

**C-D Padmini Niwas**, 148 Sadul Ganj, T0151-252 2794, padmini_hotel@rediffmail.com. 8 (4 more planned) clean, basic, comfy rooms (some a/c) in laid-back bungalow in quiet location. Pool under construction, pleasant lawn. Recommended.

**C-D Palace View**, near Lalgarh Palace, T0151-527 072. 15 clean, comfortable rooms (some a/c), good views of palace and gardens, food to order, small garden, courteous, hospitable family.

**C-E Marudhar Heritage**, Bhagwan Mahaveer Marg, near Station Rd, T0151-252 2524, hmheritage20000@yahoo.co.in. 27 variable rooms, aircooled or a/c, bath with hot showers (am), TV, clean and comfortable, generous *thalis* (Rs 50), friendly owner.

**C-E Meghsar Castle**, 9 Gajner Rd, T0151-527 315, www.hotelmeghsarcastle.com. 16 aircooled rooms in modern hotel built in traditional Rajput sandstone style, attractive garden, friendly manager.

**C-F Harasar Haveli**, opposite Karni Singh Stadium, T0151-220 9891, www.hotelharasar haveli.com. Notorious for paying hefty commissions to rickshaw drivers; often full when others empty. Otherwise a nice enough; 24 rooms (8 more plus pool planned) in converted mansion, some with verandahs and good views, dining room with period memorabilia, plus great rooftop restaurant, garden, internet, clean, friendly.

**D Hotel Bikaner**, off KEM Rd, T0151-252 6516, hotlbkn@yahoo.com. Classic modern Indian-style hotel, clean and friendly, a/c rooms not bad value, a/c bar and restaurant.

**D Jaswant Bhawan**, Alakh Sagar Rd, near railway station, T0151-548 848. A Rajput Special Hotels,15 rooms in a charming old building, quiet location, restaurant, lawn, good value. Recommended.

**D Marudhar**, Ambedkar Circle, T0151-204 853, hotelmarudhar@yahoo.com. 26 clean, well-maintained rooms, 9 a/c, friendly staff. Better than **Thar** and **Ashoka** next door.

**D-E Desert Winds**, opposite Karni Stadium, next to Harasar Haveli, T0151-254 2202. 6 clean, comfortable rooms, good food, pleasant balcony and garden, friendly family. Run by knowledgable ex-tourist officer.

**D-E Hotel Regent**, Sadul Colony, near PBM Hospital, T0151-254 1598, bituharisingh @yahoo.com. 11 modern, clean, comfortable rooms, 4 a/c, in quiet area. Excellent home-cooked meals, owner Hari is a most hospitable and knowledgeable host, good value, recommended. Camel safaris also arranged.

**D-E Sri Ram**, A-228, Sadul Ganj, T0151-252 2651, www.hotelsriram. A hotel, guest house and youth hostel in one! 20 rooms, all clean and well-maintained, some a/c, run by a knowledgable, entertaining ex-army man and family, free pick ups. Recommended.

**D-E Suraj Hotel**, near Railway Station, Rani Bazar, T0151-2521 902, surajhotel@vsnl.com. 20 rooms in modern building, well run, slightly shabby but good value. Attached veg restaurant recommended.

**D-F Shri Shanti Niwas**, GS Rd, near Railway Station, T0151-542 320, shrishanti@vsnl.com. Wide range of rooms incl. some a/c, well maintained, friendly staff.

**E Kalinga**, Lallgarh Palace Complex, T0151-209 751. 9 clean, adequate rooms, a/c particularly good value.

**E-F Evergreen**, Station Rd, T0151-254 2061. Clean, professionally run and maintained to a high standard. Easily the best of the budget options in this area; consider nearby **Delight** and **Deluxe** only if this is full.

**E-F Green Villas**, behind **Raj Vilas**, T0151-252 1877. 4 simple, clean rooms in a friendly homestay, home-cooked meals great value.

**E-F Vijay Guest House**, opposite Sophia School, Jaipur Rd, T0151-223 1244, www.camelman.com. 6 clean rooms with attached bathrooms, plus 2 with common bath. Slightly distant location compensated for by free use of bicycles or scooter, free pick-ups from bus/train, and even free rickshaw rides to town. Delicious home-cooked meals, pleasant garden, quiet, very hospitable (free tea and rum plus evening parties on lawn), knowledgeable host, great value. Good camel safaris. Recommended.

**E-F Vinayak Guest House**, near Mataji Temple, Old Ginani, T0151-220 2634. Friendly homestay run by manager of URMUL shop, single women and couples preferred.

**F Adarsh Guest House**, GS Road, near the train station, T0151-206 731. 8 basic rooms set back from road, not bad for the money.

**F Railway Retiring Rooms** and dorm are good value.

### Around Bikaner *p432*

**A Gajner Palace**, Gajner National Park, T01534-255 061, www.hrhindia.com. 44 a/c rooms in the elegantpalace and its wings, set by a beautiful lake. Rooms in main building full of character (Edwardian Raj nostalgia), those in wings well maintained but very middle England. Sumptious lounge bar and restaurant overlooking lake, magnificent gardens, boating, good walking, pleasantly unfrequented and atmospheric, friendly manager and staff, no pool. Visitors are welcome from 0800 to 1730, Rs 100.

**E Dr Karni Singh's Rest House**, adjoining the home of his forefathers, Kakoo, T01532-253 006. 6 simple rooms and 4 rustic huts with attached baths, hot water in buckets for overnight stay, only place in town but a great experience. Good camel safaris arranged, with the advantage of getting straight in to the desert rather than having to get out of town first as in Jaisalmer/Bikaner.
**F Yatri Niwas**, near Karni Mata Mandir, has simple rooms.

## Eating

**Bikaner** *p430, map p431*
You can dine in style at the first 4 hotels listed. Try the local specialities – *Bikaneri bhujia/ sev/namkeen* – savoury snacks made from dough. Purana Bazar for ice-cold lassis by day, hot milk, sugar and cream at night.
**TT Amber**, Indian, some western dishes. Most popular, and the veg *thali* is exceptional but some reports of falling standards.
**TT Bhairon Vilas**'s breezy rooftop for Rajasthani meals, atmospheric, order ahead.
**TT Bhanwar Niwas**, amazingly ornate dining hall, good way of having a look around if you're not staying there.
**TT Kesria**, Jaipur Rd. Pleasant countryside location, popular on breezy summer evenings but disappointing food.
**T Vijay Guest House**, delicious home-cooked veg *thalis*, non-veg set menu (Rs 60-100).

## Festivals and events

**Bikaner** *p430, map p431*
Camel Fair (**Jan** 24-25 in 2005, 13-14 2006, 2-3 2007) and **Diwali** (**Oct/Nov**) are especially spectacular in Junagarh Fort, in the Old City near Kote Gate and some smaller palaces.

**Around Bikaner** *p432*
In Kolayat, the **Cattle and Camel Fair** (12-21 Nov 2005, 1-9 Nov 2006) is very colourful and authentic but it can get quite riotous after dark. Since facilities are minimal, it is best to arrive before the festival to find a local family with space to spare, or ask a travel agent in Bikaner.

## Shopping

**Bikaner** *p430, map p431*
Bikaner is famous for *Usta* work which includes footwear, purses and cushions. You can also get local carpets and woodwork. The main shopping centres are on KEM (MG) Rd (from near the fort) and around Kote Gate in the Old City, Modern Market.
**Abhivyakti**, URMUL Desert Craft, Sri Ganganagar Rd, next to new bus stand, T0151-252 2139. Run by the URMUL trust, see box p433.
**Kalakar Arts**, Sardar Hall, Lalgarh Palace Rd, T0151-220 4477. Good selection of silver jewellery and other artefacts.

## Activities and tours

**Bikaner** *p430, map p431*
The main tour here is a camel safari. You have to arrange these through private operators; the 4 below are recommended.
**Aravalli Tours**, opposite Municipal Council Hall, Junagarh Rd, T571124. Rs 1600 per person (toilet tent between 5 2-person tents) for upmarket experience. Other tours too.
**Camel Man**, Vijay Guest House, Jaipur Rd, T0151-223 1244, www.camelman.com. Offers good value, reliable, friendly and professional safaris, jeep tours, cycling. Light weight 'igloo' tents, clean mattresses, sheets, good food and guidance. Safaris to see antelopes, colourful villages and potters at work; vary from 1-2-hr rides to those lasting 5 days; Rs 500-800 per person per day.
**Thar Desert Safari**, Ganganagar Rd, behind new bus stand, T0151-252 1661, www.thardesertsafari.com. Honest, unpretentious outfit offering simple, no frills camel tours.
**Vino Desert Safari**, Gangashahar, T0151-227 0445, www.vinodesertsafari.com. Runs good value, low-key safaris, including some longer distance 'inter-city' treks, eg Bikaner-Osian, 12 days.

## Transport

**Bikaner** *p430, map p431*
**Bus**
The New Bus Stand is 3 km north of town. Private buses leave from south of the Fort.

Rajasthan Roadways, enquiries, T0151-252 3800; daily deluxe buses to **Ajmer, Jodhpur, Jaisalmer** (8 hrs), **Udaipur**. 2 daily to **Delhi** via Hissar (12 hrs).

**Rickshaw/taxi**
Autos between station and Bus Stand or Lalgarh Palace, Rs 25. Taxis are unmetered. Found at train station, bus stand or hotels.

**Train**
Enquiries, T0151-220 0131, reservations, 0800-1400, 1415-2000, Sun 0800-1400. For tourist quota (when trains are full) apply to Manager's Office by Radio Tower near Jaswant Bhawan Hotel. **Delhi**: *Bikaner-DSR Exp, 4790*, 0830, 10 ½ hrs; *Bikaner-DSRi Mail, 4792*, 1945, 10 hrs. From Delhi (SR), the overnight train (*DSR Bikaner Mail, 4791*, 2125, best 2nd Class sleeper), gives very good sunrise views. **Jaipur**: *Intercity Exp, 2466*, 0540, 5 hrs. **Jodhpur**: *KJC Exp, 4667*, 1230, 5½ hrs; *Ranakpur Exp, 4707*, 0935, 5½ hrs (continues to Ahmadabad, further 10 hrs) and Mumbai (Bandra), another 10½ hrs.

**Around Bikaner** *p432*
For **Karni Mata Mandir** the train leaves Bikaner at 1000, returns 1230, buses from Bikaner New Bus Stand or Ganga Shahar Rd, hourly, Rs 7 (share auto-rickshaw from Station Rd to Bus, Rs 3), on return journey, for Station Rd, get off at Thar Hotel and walk or take auto-rickshaw, taxi about Rs 200 return.

For **Kalibangan** catch the bus from **Suratgarh**, which can be reached by bus from Bikaner, Hanumangarh, Sirsa (Haryana) or Mandi Dabwali (Punjab). Alternatively, the broad gauge train line connects Suratgarh with **Anupgarh**, about 15 km from the Pakistan border, where it terminates. Kali- bangan is about half way to Anupgarh. The nearest station is Raghunathgarh, but travel from there to Kalibangan is difficult (check at Suratgarh or Anupgarh). From Suratgarh to Anupgarh: Passenger, 0755, 2¼ hrs. Trains from **Suratgarh**: **Bikaner** (Lalgarh Junction): *Chandigarh Exp, 4887*, 0835, 3¼ hrs. **Bhatinda**: *Chandigarh Exp, 4888*, 1955, 3¼ hrs.

## Directory

**Bikaner** *p430, map p431*
**Banks** Bank of Baroda, Ambedkar Circle, cash against Visa; State Bank of Bikaner & Jaipur, Ambedkar Circle; also near fort's Suraj Pol. Changes TCs but may charge up to 10% commission! Harasar Haveli Hotel charges 1%. **Hospital** PBM Hospital, Hospital Rd, T0151-252 5312. **Internet** Meghsar Castle, Hotel Sagar and Harasar Haveli, Rs 2 per min; others at Sadulganj, Sagar Rd, Jaipur Rd and near the fort. **Post** GPO: behind Junagarh Fort. **Useful addresses** Police: T100/ T0151-252 2225.

# Shekhawati

*Covering an area of about 300 sq km on the often arid and rock-studded plains to the northwest of the Aravalli mountain range, Shekhawati is the homeland of the Marwari community. The area is particularly rich in painted* havelis*; Sikar district in the southwest and Jhunjhunun in the northeast form an 'open-air art gallery' of paintings dating from the mid-19th century. Although a day trip gives you an idea of its treasures, it is better to spend two or three nights in Shekhawati to see the temples, frescoed forts,* chhatris *and step-wells at leisure. There are other diversions laid on such as horse or camel safaris and treks into the hills. Shekhawati sees far fewer visitors than the better-known areas of Rajasthan, and as such retains something of a 'one pen/rupee' attitude to tourists. This is generally quite innocent and should not be a deterrent to potential visitors.* » *For Sleeping, Eating and other listings, see pages 442-444.*

## Ins and outs

**Getting there** You can get to the principal Shekhawati towns by train but road access is easier. A car comes in handy, though there are crowded buses from Delhi, Jaipur and Bikaner to some towns. Buses leave every 30 minutes from 0500-2000 from Jaipur's Main Bus Station and take three hours. » *See Transport, page 444, for further details.*

**Getting around** You can get from one Shekhawati town to another by local bus which run every 15 to 20 minutes, and take about an hour. Within each town it is best to enlist the help of a local person (possibly from the hotels listed below) to direct you to the best *havelis*, as it can be very difficult to find your way around.

**Tourist information** Recommended reading includes *The painted towns of Shekhawati* by Ilay Cooper, a great Shekhawati enthusiast, with photos and maps.

## History

The 'garden of Shekha' was named after Rao Shekhaji of Amarsar (1433-1488) who challenged the Kachhawahas, refusing to pay tribute to the rulers at Amber. These Rajput barons made inroads into Muslim territory even during Mughal rule, and declared Shekhawati independent from the Jaipur suzerainty until 1738. During this period the merchants lavishly decorated their houses with paintings on religious, folk and historical themes. As Mughal power collapsed Shekhawati became a region of lawless banditry. In the early 19th century the British East India Company brought it under their control, bringing peace but also imposing taxes and tolls on trade which the Marwaris resented. Many of the merchants migrated to other parts of the country to seek their fortune and those who flourished returned their wealth to their homeland and took over as patrons of the artists.



# Sights

Ramgarh has the highest concentration of painted *havelis*, though they are not as well maintained as those of Nawalgarh which has the second largest selection. It is easier to visit *havelis* in towns that have hotels, such as Nawalgarh, Mandawa, Dundlod, Mukundgarh, Mahansar, Fatehpur, Baggar and Jhunjunun, and where the caretakers are used to visitors. though towns like Bissau, Alsisar, Malsisar and Churu have attractive *havelis* as well.

The *havelis* are often occupied by the family or retainers who will happily show you around but many charge a fee of about Rs 20. Many *havelis* are in a poor state of repair with fading paintings which may appear monotonously alike to some.

## Sikar District

**Sikar** The late 17th-century fort was built when Sikar was an important trading centre and the wealthiest *thikana* (feudatory) under Jaipur. It now has a population of 148,000. You can visit the old quarter and see the Wedgwood blue 'Biyani' (1920) and 'Mahal' (1845), Murarka and Somani *havelis* and murals and carvings in Gopinath, Raghunath and Madan Mohan temples. From Jaipur take the NH11 to Ringas (63 km) and Sikar (48 km).

**Laksmangarh** Founded early 19th century, the town plan was based on Jaipur's model; this can be seen by climbing up to the imposing old fort which has now been renovated by the Jhunjhunwala family. The fine *havelis* include one of the area's grandest – Ganeriwala with char chowks (four courtyards) – the 'Rathi' *haveli* near the Clock Tower in the market, and others in the Chowkhani.

**Pachar** This is a little town west of Jaipur in the middle of the sand dunes with the golden sandstone castle scenically situated on a lakeshore. A road north from Bagru on the NH8, also gives access. The place is pleasantly free from 'give me pen, give me rupees' children.

**Ramgarh** Ramgarh was settled by the Poddars in the late 18th century. In addition to their many *havelis* and that of the Ruias, visit the *chhatris* with painted entrances near the bus stand, the temples to Shani (with mirror decoration) and to Ganga. Ramgarh has the highest concentration of painted *havelis*, though they are not as well maintained as those of Nawalgarh which has the second largest selection. Town has a pleasantly laid back feel.Look for handicrafts here.

**Danta** Danta, originally a part of Marwar, was given to Thakur Amar Singhji in the mid-17th century. It is well of the beaten track and as such is completely unspoilt. Two empty *kilas* (forts) and the residential wing (early 18th-century) combine Mughal and Rajput art and architectural styles.

## Jhunjhunun District

**Mukundgarh** Mukundgarh is the market for textiles and brass betel cutters. The town lies 10 km south of Jhunjhunun. The Ganeriwala *havelis* (1860s and 1870s) are worth visiting as well as the Jhunjhunwala (1859) haveli with Krishna stories and Sukhdev haveli (circa 1880).

**Nawalgarh** Nawalgarh, some 25 km southeast of Mandawa, was founded in 1737 by Thakur Nawal Singh. There are numerous fine *havelis* worth visiting here. The town has a colourful bazar – though lone tourists have been harassed in the bazar – and two forts (circa 1730). **Nawalgarh fort** has fine examples of maps and plans of Shekhawati and Jaipur. The **Bala Kila** which has a kiosk with beautiful ceiling paintings is approached via the fruit market in the town centre and entered through the **Hotel Radha**. It also has the **Roop Niwas Palace** (now a hotel) and some 18th-century temples with 19th- and early-20th-century paintings. There are other interesting temples in town including Ganga Mai near Nansa Gate.

The **Anandilal Poddar Haveli**, now converted to the **Poddar Haveli Museum** ⓘ *Rs 70 (foreigners) includes camera and guide*, is perhaps the best restored *haveli* of Shekhawati. The 1920s *haveli* has around 700 frescoes including a Gangaur procession, scenes from the Mahabharata, trains, cars, the avatars of Vishnu, bathing scenes and British characters, some of the best frame the doors leading from the courtyard to the rooms. The upper storey of the *haveli* is now a school but the ground floor has been opened as a museum. The photo-gallery records the life of Congressman and freedom fighter Anandilal Poddar, and the merchant-turned-industrialist Poddar family. There is a diorama of costumes of various Rajasthani tribes and communities, special bridal attires, a gallery of musical instruments, the frescoes in the courtyard, which have been remarkably restored, are worth seeing. Among the remarkable Murarka *havelis* are the 19th-century **Kesardev Murarka** which has a finely painted façade and the Radheshyam Murarka which was built in the early-20th century. The latter portrays processions, scenes from folk tales, Hindu and Christian religious paintings, sometimes interspersed with mirrorwork. Other fine *havelis* are those of the Bhagat, Chokhani, Goenka, Patodia, Kedwal, Sangerneria, Saraogi, Jhunujhunwala, Saha and Chhauchuria families. The paintings here depict anything from European women having a bath (Aath – 'eight' – Haveli complex) to Hindu religious themes and Jesus Christ. Some of the *havelis* are complexes of several buildings which include a temple, dharamshala, cenotaph and a well). ⓘ *Most charge Rs 15-20 for viewing.*

## Fit for a merchant

The *havelis* in Shekhawati were usually built around two courtyards – one for general use, and the other a *zenana* courtyard for the women. The latter was also used for laundry and so often had a well and occasionally a play area for children. Security was a prime concern so a haveli was typically entered by a solid gate with a smaller door in it for regular use by residents. Watchmen had rooms on either side of the entrance. The *baithak* (reception room) had mattresses and bolsters for sitting on the floor while others were set aside for sleeping or storage. The *havelis* were enlarged as the families grew larger or wealthier, and with the onset of peaceful times, they became more palatial and lavished with decoration.

The *haveli* was made from brick or local stone. It was plastered in two layers with decorations on the second layer – a polished lime plaster finish often set with agate and other semi-precious stones. Murals were either painted on dry surfaces or on wet plaster. Mineral colours were derived from indigo, ochre, lead, copper, lapis lazuli, lime and even gold. Synthetic blue was imported and only the wealthiest could afford strong blue tones on their *havelis*. Some of the finest frescoes were near the door separating the courtyard from the main chambers and these were often restored or repainted during weddings and festivals. The subject of the paintings varied. The 10 avatars of Vishnu were popular, especially scenes from *Krishna Lila* and the *Ramayana*. The *Mahabharata*, the *Ragamala* (depicting musical modes of different seasons), folk tales, historic events, daily life in Shekhawati and floral and faunal themes were also popular, together with a fascination for portraying the British and their curious ways.



**Parasarampura** About 12 km southeast of Nawalgarh, Parasarampura has a decorated *chhatri* to Sardul Singh (1750) and the adjacent Gopinath temple (1742); these are the earliest examples of Shekhawati frescoes painted with natural pigments (caretaker has keys, and will point things out with a peacock feather).

**Dundlod** West of Nawalgarh, the best murals are in the **castle** (1750) ⓘ *Darbar Hall Rs 20 for non-residents*, now a Heritage Hotel. You enter the moated castle by the Suraj Pol and proceed through the Bichla Darwaza and Uttar Pol (north) before arriving at the courtyard. Steps lead up to the majestic Diwan Khana furnished with period furniture, portraits and hangings; there is a library with a collection of rare books of Indian history and the *duchatta* above, which allowed the ladies in *purdah* to watch court ceremonies unobserved. Ask for the key to the painted family *chhatris* nearby. The Goenka haveli near the fort has three painted courtyards, and the Satyanarayan temple has religious paintings but both these may be closed in the low season. The interesting deep step well now has an electric pump. The Polo Centre provides an opportunity to see camel, horse and bicycle polo, tent pegging etc. Mukundgarh is the nearest station where you can get jeeps and taxis.

**Jhunjhunun** Jhunjhunun was a stronghold of the Kayamkhani Nawabs until defeated by the Hindu Sardul Singh in 1730. The Mohanlal Iswardas Modi (1896), Tibriwala (1883) and the Muslim Nuruddin Farooqi Haveli (which is devoid of figures) and the *maqbara* are all worth seeing. The *Chhe* (6) Haveli complex, Khetri Mahal (1760) and the Biharilal temple (1776), which has attractive frescoes (closed during lunch time), are also interesting. The Rani Sati temple commemorates Narayana Devi who is believed to have become a sati; her stone is venerated by many of the wealthy *bania* community and an annual Marwari fair is held (protesting women's groups feel it glorifies the practice of *sati*). Since 1947, 29 cases of *sati* have been recorded in the Sikar and its two neighbouring districts.

**Baggar** The grand *haveli* of the Makharias, 10 km north east of Jhunjhunun, has rooms along open corridors around grassy courtyards and wall paintings of gods and angels being transported in motor cars!

**Mahansar** Founded in the mid-18th century, the town, 30 km northeast of Jhunjhunun, has a distinctly medieval feel. It has the Poddar haveli of Son Chand, the Rama Temple (ask for the key to the Golden Room; expensive at Rs 100 but very well preserved and the large Raghunath Temple with some of the finest paintings of the region. The fort (1768) has palaces and a baradari which were added later.

**Churu** Set in semi-desert countryside, Churu, northwest of Baggar, was believed to have been a Jat stronghold in the 16th century. In the 18th century it was an important town of Bikaner state and has an 18th-century fort. The town thrived during the days of overland desert trade. The local Rajputs barons revolted only to be crushed by the royals of Bikaner. The town has some interesting 1870s Oswal Jain *havelis* like those of the Kotharis and the Suranas. **Banthia** (early-20th century), **Bagla** (1880), **Khemka** (1800s). There are also the Bajranglal mantri haveli and the Poddar haveli and numerous towers, temples, wells and reservoirs which are interesting. The main attraction, however, is the extraordinary **'Malji-ka-Kamra'**, a crumbling, colonnaded *haveli* which houses some amazing interior scenes, get there before it's too late.

**Tal Chappar** A possible day excursion from one of the castle hotels is a visit to **Tal Chappar Wildlife Sanctuary** near Sujjangarh covering 71 sq km of desert scrubland with ponds and salt flats. It has some of the largest herds of Blackbuck antelope in India (easily seen at the watering point near the park gate itself during the dry season), besides chinkara gazelle, desert cat, desert fox and other dryland wildlife. Huge flocks of demoiselle and common cranes can be seen at nearby lakes and wetlands during the winter months (Septemer-March) where they feed on tubers and ground vegetation. Some 175 different species of bird visit the park over the course of a year, including sandgrouse, quails, bar headed geese and cream coloured desert courser. The best time to visit is just after the rainy season, generally August and September The enthusiastic and charming forest guard, Brij Dansamor, is a good guide to the area. A local NGO, Krishna Mirg, is active in tree plantation and in fund-raising for the eco-development of Tal Chappar, providing support fodder during dry months to blackbuck and cranes. **Forest Department Rest House** has five basic but adequate rooms at Rs 300 per double. To book ahead call the head office in Churu on T01562 250938. Try **Hanuman** tea stall for delicious *chai* and the local sweet, malai laddoo. the drive to Tal Chappar can be long and tiring. If you are travelling between Bikaner and Shekhawati in a jeep, it is worth making a detour. **Riaskhan,** T01425-24391, has a fleet of open, convertible and hardtop (closed) jeeps for visiting Tal Chappar from Kuchaman, Sambhar or Roopangarh, at Rs 1200-1500.

## Sleeping

**Sikar District** *p438*

**B Castle Pachar**, Pachar, T01576-264 611. 16 very well-decorated rooms in a fascinating old property, good collection of portraits, paintings and weaponry, delicious if very rich food, charming hosts, swimming pool under construction. Recommended.

**C Ashirwad Palace**, Churu Bypass, NH11, 2 km from Fatehpur, T01571-222 635. 12 clean, modern, slightly overpriced rooms around a small lawn.

**C Dera**, off the high street, Danta, T01577-270 041. Open 1 Oct to 31 Mar. 14 large, characterful rooms in residential wing below the 2 old forts, good restaurant (meals Rs 160), peacocks at dawn, camel rides (Rs 250 per hr, Rs 550 per 3 hrs), horse safaris (see above), Jeep safaris (minimum 4 persons), Rs 1,200 each per day, unique.

**C-D Hotel Niros**, Station Rd, Sikar, T01572-255 815. 31 rooms in upmarket establishment including an a/c restaurant boasting some unusual water features.

**D Haveli** (RTDC), Sikar Rd, 500 m south of bus stand, Fatehpur, T01571-230 293. 8 clean rooms, some a/c with bath, pleasant building, dull restaurant, best bet in town.

**E Aravalli Resort** NH11, Sikar. Two air-cooled rooms with bath (simple, shabby), inexpensive Indian restaurant, gift shop, popular tourist stop to pick up mineral water.

**E Shekhaji Resort**, opposite Asirwad Palace, Fatehpur, T01571-222 078. 4 basic rooms plus an airy restaurant, pool planned.

**Jhunjhunun District** *p439*

**B Castle Mandawa** , Mandawa, T01592-223 124, www.mandawahotels.com. Huge castle with lots of character but parts rather run-down. 68 a/c rooms, some in tower, complete with swing, most with 4-posters and period trappings but rooms vary so select with care ("cheerless, cold, hard beds"), excellent views, atmospheric but a bit overpriced, mixed reports, some disappointed with meals (Rs 450-500).

**B Desert Resort**, Mandawa, T01592-223 151, 1 km south, www.mandawahotels.com. 60 rooms in 3 wings including a *haveli*, modern amenities, pricey restaurant (Rs 250-500 and only buffets for tour groups), pool, shady garden, good views of countryside, camel rides. Again lacks warmth, very business-like.

**B Dundlod Fort**, Heritage Hotel, in village centre, Dundlod, T01594-252519, www.dundlod.com. 42 rooms, but only 11 open at time of writing. Upgraded rooms particularly good, others mediocre with poor bathrooms, good state rooms with period furniture, **A** suites with terraces, good food (Rs 180-220), power cuts can be a problem but full of atmosphere and interesting murals, pool, library, tours, horse safaris a speciality, warm welcome, very hospitable and helpful. Recommended

**B Mukundgarh Fort** (Heritage Hotel), Mukun- dgarh, T11-3094 1192, pleasurehotels@rediff mail.com. 45 rooms in converted mid-18th- century fort ) with frescoes along wide corri- dors, slightly musty but authentic interiors, modern bathrooms, restaurant, bar and pool, friendly management, slightly rundown

**B Piramal Haveli**, Baggar, T0159-222 220, www.neemranahotels.com. 100-year-old home, restored sensitively, excellent vegetarian meals and attentive service, quirky original frescoes, simple but overpriced, not as much atmosphere as at castle hotels.

**B Roop Niwas Palace**, Nawalgarh, T01594-222 008, www.roopniwaspalace.com. 1 km north of town. 37 rooms (older ones are large, air-cooled and simply furnished with old fashioned Western bathrooms, the newer are a/c but smaller), most are in 3 storeys around courtyards and a few in garden-side annexe. Good food, large gardens (peacocks), pool, horse safaris a speciality, qualified guides, attractive, small 90-year old palacebut service disappointing.

**C Heritage Mandawa**, off Mukundgarh Rd, Mandawa, T01592-223 742, www.hotelheritagemandawa.com, 200 m from the main bazar street and the bus stand. 13 rooms with local 'ethnic' furnishings in an old *haveli*, attached baths, dining hall, clean and pleasant, manager and staff very friendly and accommodating (good discounts in the low-season), camel rides, guides, taxis. Camping possible in grounds.

**C Jamuna Resort**, Baggar Rd, Jhunjhunun, T0159-2232 871, www.shivshekawati.com. 4 a/c cottage rooms with attractive mirror work and murals, 'Golden Room' with painted ceiling "like a jewel box", frescos, open-air Rajasthani veg/non-vegetarian restaurant serves delicious food, gardens, pool (open to hotel/restaurant guests only), local guided tours. Recommended.

**C Mandawa Haveli**, near Sonthaliya Gate, Mandawa, T01592-223 088, http://hotel mandawa.free.fr. 7 rooms with modernized baths in a 3-storeyed, characterful *haveli* with original 19th-century frescoes in court-yard, Rajasthani meals, museum and library. Friendly staff, authentic feel. Recommended.

**C Narayan Niwas Castle**, near bus stand, Mahansar, T01562-264 322. 16 rooms open of a total of 500 in fort, no's 1 and 5 really exceptional, poor bathrooms, attractive wall paintings, pleasingly unspoilt, converted by Thakur Tejpal Singh, delicious meals (cooked by his wife), homemade liquers, charming owners, a "Fawlty Towers" experience.

**C-D Hotel Shekawati Heritage**, off Station Rd, Jhunjhunun, T01592-237 134, www. hotelshekhawatiheritage.com. 22 rooms, 10 a/c, certainly not heritage but clean and friendly, quiet location.

**C-D Natraj Hotel**, Churu, T01562-257 245. 28 clean, modern rooms, best bet in town.

**C-D Shiv Shekhawati**, Muni Ashram, Khemi Sati Rd, Jhunjhunun, T0159-2232 651, www.shivshekawati.com. 20 simple clean rooms, 8 a/c, all with bath and hot water, good veg restaurant, tourist office (guides). Same owner of both, LK Jangid, is friendly and very knowledgeable.

**D Apani Dhani**, Jhunjhunu Rd, 1 km from railway station, 500 m north of Bus Stand, Nawalgarh, T01594-222 239, www.apani dhani.com. 8 environmentally friendly huts on an ecological farm run by the charming and authoritative Ramesh Jangid. Attractive, comfortable, solar-lit thatched cottages traditionally built using mud and straw, modern bathrooms (some with "footprint" toilets), home-grown veg, immaculately presented, relaxing atmosphere. Accommodation and education in one enticing package. Recommended.

**D Hotel Shekawati**, off Mukandgarh Rd, Mandawa, T01592-223 036. Simple, basic rooms, only budget place in town, adequate.

**D-E Hotel Aman**, near railway station, Jhunjhunun, T01592-231 090. 10 rooms, 4 a/c, reasonable restaurant, 24 hour checkout.

**D-F Neelam**, opposite Khetan Hospital, Jhunjhunun, T0159-238415. 24 rooms, a/c and air-cooled, economical rooms with shared facilities, restaurant serving snacks, slightly shabby.

**E Shekawati Guest House**, near Roop Niwas, Nawalgarh, T01594-224 658, www.shekawatirestaurant.com. 6 clean, well presented rooms and an attractive thatched restaurant run by the friendly and refreshingly female Kalpana Singh. She is a qualified cook; the food here is exceptional and cooking classes can be arranged, as can local tours, recommended. The DS Bungalow next door is a poor imitation.

**E Tourist Pension**, behind Maur hospital, Nawalgarh, T01594-224 060, www.apani dhani.com. 8 rooms in modern house run by Ramesh's brother, Rajesh (see above). Lacks the charm of apani dhani but is clean, well priced and welcoming.

**E-F Sangam**, near bus stand, Jhunjhunun, T0159-232 544. Clean rooms, better with bath at rear, veg meals, best budget option.

## Eating

### Sikar District *p438*

ǂ **Natraj Restaurant**, Main Rd, Sikar. Does good meals and snacks, clean, reasonable.

ǂ **Paradise**, inexpensive Indian food.

### Jhunjhunun District *p439*

ǂǂ **Roop Niwas**, Nawalgarh, for heritage experience (and unreliable service).

ǂ **Shekawati Guest House**, Nawalgarh, for delicious, hygienically prepared fare.

## Activities and tours

### Camel safaris

Roop Niwas Palace, Apani Dhani (Nawalgarh), **Dundlod** and **Mandawa** offer these. On a 5-day safari, you might cover Nawalgarh-Mukundgarh-Mandawa-Mahans ar-Churu, crossing some of the finest sand dunes in Shekhawati; Nawalgarh to Fatehpur for 3-day safaris, and 1 week country safaris to Tal Chappar Wildlife Sanctuary. The cost depends on the number in the group and the facilities provided ranging from Rs 800-1,500 per day. 1-day safaris arranged by the heritage hotels cost about Rs 800 with packed lunch and mineral water.

### Horse safaris
Dundlod Fort and Roop Niwas at Nawalgarh offer 1-week safaris with nights in royal tents (occasionally in castles or heritage hotels) to cover the attractions of the region. The most popular take in the Pushkar or Tilwara fairs. You can expect folk music concerts, camp- fires, guest speakers, masseurs, and some- times even a barber, all with jeep support. You ride 3 hrs in the morning and 2 hrs in the afternoon, and spend time visiting eco- farms, rural communities and *havelis* en route.

### Trekking
There are some interesting treks in the Aravalli hills near Nawalgarh starting from Lohargal (34 km), a temple with sacred pools. Local people claim that this is the place recorded in the *Mahabharata* where Bhim's mace is said to have been crafted. A 4- to 5-day trek would take in the Bankhandi peak (1,052 m), Krishna temple in Kirori Valley, Kot Reservoir, Shakambari mata temple, Nag Kund (a natural spring) and Raghunathgarh fort. The cost depends on the size of the group and the facilities provided. **Apani Dhani** arranges highly recommended treks with stays at the temple guest houses and villages for US$ 50 per person per day for minimum of 2 persons.

## Transport

### Bicycle
Apani Dhani, **Nawalgarh**, arranges cycle tours in Shekhawati.

### Bus
To **Nawalgarh** from Delhi, best from ISBT daily at 0800, 2200 and 2300, 8 hrs. From **Jaipur** frequent buses from 0630-1830 (Express in the morning), 3½ hrs. Also to **Sikar** from Jaipur and Bikaner.

### Jeep
For hire in **Nawalgarh**, **Mandawa** and **Dundlod**, about Rs 1,200 per day.

### Taxi
From **Jaipur**, diesel Ambassador, Rs 1,200 for day tour of parts of Shekhawati; with detours (eg Samode), up to Rs 1,500; Rs 1,700 including 1 night. A/c cars can be twice as much. Local hire is possible in **Mandawa**, **Mukundgarh** and **Nawalgarh**.

### Train
From **Jaipur**, 3 trains run daily to stations to Shekhawati. *Shekhawati Exp* (Delhi-Jaipur): To **Mukundgarh** from Delhi, 2315, 7½ hrs; from Jaipur, 1015, 1330, 1805, 4 hrs. To **Nawalgarh** from Delhi, 2230, 8½ hrs. To **Jhunjhunun** from Delhi, departs 2315, 7½ hrs, arriving in Sikar after 2 hrs; from Jaipur, departs 1805, 5 hrs, continues to Delhi, 6 hrs. To **Sikar** from Bikaner, dep 2025, 7 hrs.

## Directory

**Jhunjhunun District** *p439*

**Banks** SBBJ and Bank of Baroda, Mandawa. In Nawalgarh, SBBJ changes currency and TCs, but poor rate. **Roop Niwas** can sometimes help get better rates. **UCO Bank** changes currency in Dundlod.

# Haryana and Punjab

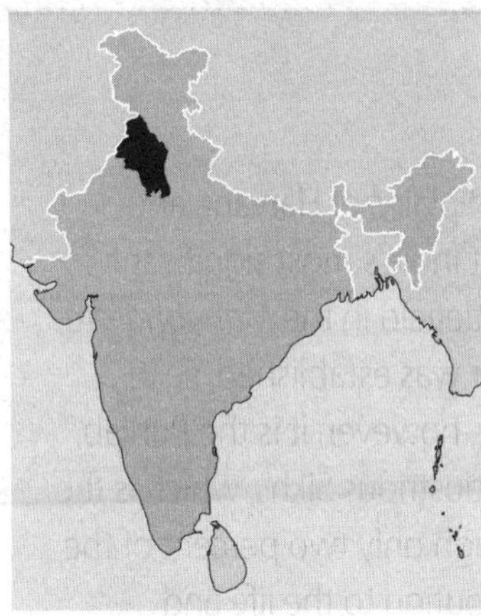



**Footprint features**

# Introduction

The flat, open and richly cultivated plains of Haryana and Punjab witnessed some of ancient India's most significant battles. Kurukshetra, Krishna's battlefield in the *Mahabharata*, and Panipat, where Muslim power was established, lie in Haryana just north of Delhi. Today, however, it is the Punjab, peopled by the gregarious and industrious Sikhs, which is the foremost of the two states. Although only two percent of the Indian population, the Sikh contribution to the life and character, not to mention cuisine, of Northern India, greatly outweighs their relatively meagre numbers. Amritsar's Golden Temple, one of the great treasures of North India and compared by many to the Taj Mahal, is the holiest centre of worship for the Sikhs, whose roots lie in the soil of the Punjab. Le Corbusier's specially designed capital, Chandigarh, modernist in conception and secular in spirit, could scarcely stand in greater contrast. Ironically many now seem to visit Chandigarh more for the quixotic delights of Nek Chand's 'Rock Garden' than for its European architect's alien buildings. Harayana has a less distinct identity, culturally subsumed by the capital city which it surrounds, and for most visitors will simply serve as a transit state on their way elsewhere.

Through extensive irrigation Haryana and Punjab have become the most productive states of India. Most of the major towns and cities of the region are close to the Grand Trunk Road, the great highway from Peshawar to Calcutta which Rudyard Kipling described as "the backbone of all Hind". These two states also hold the key to Delhi's water supply, giving them powerful political leverage which has been regularly applied in the past when things have not been going their way.

## ★ Don't miss...

1 **Chandigarh** After Le Corbusier's modernist buildings, Nek Chand's Rock Garden offers much light relief, page 449.

2 **Sobraon** The area around Ludhiana was fiercely fought over in the first Sikh War. The British finally broke the spirit of the magnificent Sikh army at Sobraon on the banks of the Sutlej River, page 455.

3 **Golden Temple** The stunning temple at Amritsar is a haven of peace and best seen at dawn, page 460.

4 **Wagha Border** Catch the ceremonial changing of the guards at the Wagha Border crossing between India and Pakistan, page 465.

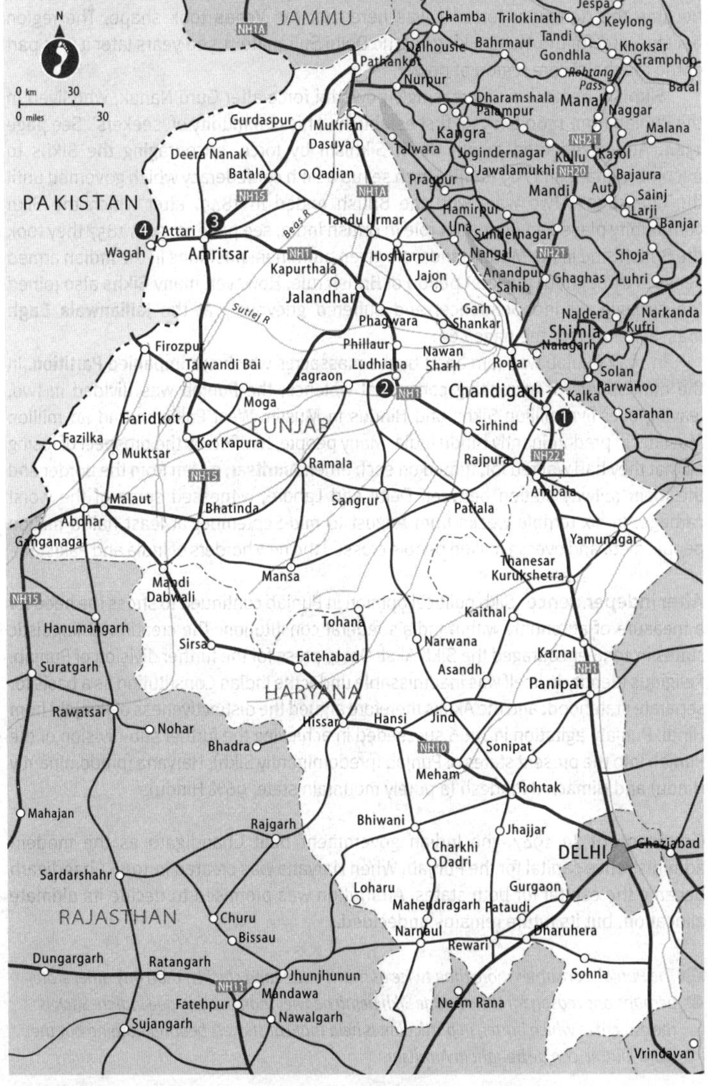

# Background → *Haryana Population: 21.1 mn. Area: 44,200 sq km.*

*Punjab Population: 24.29 mn. Area: 50,300 sq km.*

## The land

Punjab and Haryana occupy the strategic borderlands between the Indus and Yamuna-Ganga river systems. Well over 1000 km from the sea, their gently sloping plains are less than 275 m above sea level. In the southwest, on the arid borders of Rajasthan, sand dunes form gentle undulations in the plain.

## History

**Before independence** The **Ghaggar Valley**, running from the Shiwaliks down to the Rajasthan desert, was the home of fortified urban settlements before 3000 BC and the rise of the Harappan civilization. The rising tide of Aryan influence steadily became the dominant force. It was here that the **Vedas** took shape. The region became vital for the Muslim kings of the Delhi Sultanate; 1,500 years later it was part of the Mughals' core region of power.

**Sikhism** became an increasingly powerful force after Guru Nanak, who lived in the Punjab from 1469 to 1539, first established his community of 'seekers'. See page 1344. Aurangzeb tried to put down Sikhism by force, encouraging the Sikhs to become militant. In 1799 **Ranjit Singh** set up a Sikh confederacy which governed until the late 1830s. Two wars with the British ended in 1849, after which the Sikh community played an important role in British India, see page 1343. In 1857 they took the British side in the Mutiny, and were given prominent positions in the Indian armed services throughout the later period of British rule. However, many Sikhs also joined the struggle for Independence, and suffered grievously at the **Jallianwala Bagh** massacre in 1919, see page 464.

In 1947 Punjab was torn apart by the massacres which accompanied **Partition**. In the atmosphere of increasing communal violence, the Punjab was divided in two, leaving over five million Sikhs and Hindus in Muslim West Pakistan and 40 million Muslims in predominantly Hindu India. Many people, terrified by the prospect of losing all that they had worked for, turned on each other. **Amritsar**, 24 km from the border and the main railway station between Delhi and Lahore, witnessed some of the worst carnage. In six terrible weeks from August to mid-September at least half a million people died, and over 13 million people crossed the new borders of India and Pakistan.

**After independence** Sikh political opinion in Punjab continued to stress the need for a measure of autonomy within India's federal constitution. The creation of linguistic states in 1956 encouraged the Sikh Akali Dal to press for the further division of Punjab. Religious identity in itself was inadmissable under the Indian Constitution as a basis for separate statehood, and the Akalis therefore argued the distinctiveness of Punjabi from Hindi. Punjabi agitation in 1966 succeeded in achieving the further sub-division of the Punjab into the present states of Punjab (predominantly Sikh), Haryana (predominantly Hindu) and Himachal Pradesh (a purely mountain state, 96% Hindu).

**Government** In 1947, the Indian government built Chandigarh as the modern administrative capital for the Punjab. When Haryana was created in 1966 Chandigarh became the capital for both states. Arbitration was promised to decide its ultimate allocation, but its future remains undecided.

*The Punjab consumes more than twice as much butter and chicken than any other state, perhaps one reason for the average Sikh being heavier than the average Indian. Such is the esteem in which butter, in particular, is held that car stickers bearing nothing but the word 'butter' can be bought in Amritsar.*

**Recent political developments** **Punjab** has 13 seats in the Lok Sabha (Lower House) and seven seats in the Rajya Sabha (Upper House) in the national parliament in New Delhi. In recent years Punjab has had several periods of direct rule from New Delhi. After the decade of political turmoil in the 1980s, marked by widespread violence surrounding the emergence of an Independence movement in Punjab, normality has returned. In the February 2002 elections the Congress recaptured power from the Akali Dal and the BJP combine which had governed since 1997, and the Party President, Captain Amarinder Singh, became the State's 21st Chief Minister, and continues to be in charge in 2005. He recently described his time thus far in office as "A saga of new goals and bold initiatives', which gives a fair impression of his forthright zeal.

**Haryana** has five seats in the Rajya Sabha and 10 seats in the Lok Sabha in New Delhi. Following a trend seen in many states recent assembly elections have seen regional parties gain increasing strength at the expense of national parties like the Congress. In the February 2000 Assembly elections the Indian National Lok Dal ( a party which, despite its name, is almost entirely restricted to Haryana) won 47 of the 90 seats, Congress being the runner up with 21, a result which brought Mr Om Prakash Chautala to the office of Chief Minister for the fifth time, a position he still holds in early 2005.

## Culture

Despite the strong influence of Hinduism and to a much lesser extent Islam, Sikhism displays a distinctive character of its own. Its literature has strong connections with Sufism. Guru Nanak used the Punjabi language as a medium for poetry. Typically Hindu celebrations and festivals such as *Dasara* and *Diwali* are enthusiastically observed, as are the birth and death anniversaries of the gurus and saints. Sikh music, much of it like the Mughal *ghazal* and *qawwali* is immensely popular.

The long *kurta* (shirt) and baggy trousers drawn in at the ankle are traditional and popular forms of dress with Punjabi men. Women usually wear a similar *salwar kamiz* with a *dupatta* (long scarf). Sikh men are distinctive for their turbans and beards. See page 1343. The Sikhs are often thought of as enterprising and practical people, using machines from tractors to tubewells, threshing machines to grinders. They are now found driving buses, taxis, and hire cars. They were the drivers in the Indian army and have maintained this role ever since.

Two-thirds of the 21 million people in Punjab speak **Punjabi**, a close relative of Hindi, while the remainder speak **Hindi**.



# Chandigarh and around

➔ *Phone code: 0172. Colour map 1, grid B3. Population: 900,900.*

*In 1947 when Lahore, Punjab's former capital, was allocated to Pakistan, the Indian government decided to build a new capital for the Indian state of the Punjab. The result is Chandigarh, a planned city in the post-war modernist style, acting as the dual capital of Punjab and Haryana states. Some critics describe Chandigarh as soulless; anyone familiar with England may find themselves reminded of Milton Keynes. Not quite the garden city it was dreamt to be, it is nevertheless a convenient stop en route to Himachal Pradesh, or before flying to Leh.* *» For Sleeping, Eating and other listings, see pages 456-459.*

## Ins and outs

**Getting there** The airport and railway stations are some distance from the centre with pre-paid auto rickshaws to town. From the large bus terminus in the busy Sector 17, you can walk across to several budget hotels and restaurants.

**Getting around** Buses serve the different sectors but if you are only here for a few hours, it is best to hire transport as there are long distances to cover in this widely spread out city and it is not always easy to find a taxi or auto-rickshaws for single journeys. » *See Transport, page 458, for further details.*

**Climate** Temperature: summer, maximum 39°C, minimum 25°C; winter, maximum 20°C, minimum 7°C. Rainfall: over 250 mm from June-August. Best time to visit: November-March.

## Background

The initial plans for the creation of the city were drawn in New York by Mayer and Novicki. When the latter died in 1950 the work was entrusted to the internationally renowned architect **Le Corbusier** who supervised the layout and was responsible for the grand buildings. Fry and Drew designed the residential and commercial areas.

Jawaharlal Nehru said of Chandigarh "Let this be a new town symbolic of the freedom of India, unfettered by the traditions of the past, an expression of the nation's faith in the future". Its detractors describe it as a concrete prairie, the product of 'the ivory tower school of architecture' and despite its planning many regard Chandigarh as a characterless failure. Today there is a growing scarcity of land, despite the complete ban on industrial activity, a ban which has had the advantage of greatly limiting air pollution.

*Related map*
*A Sectors 17 & 22, page 451.*

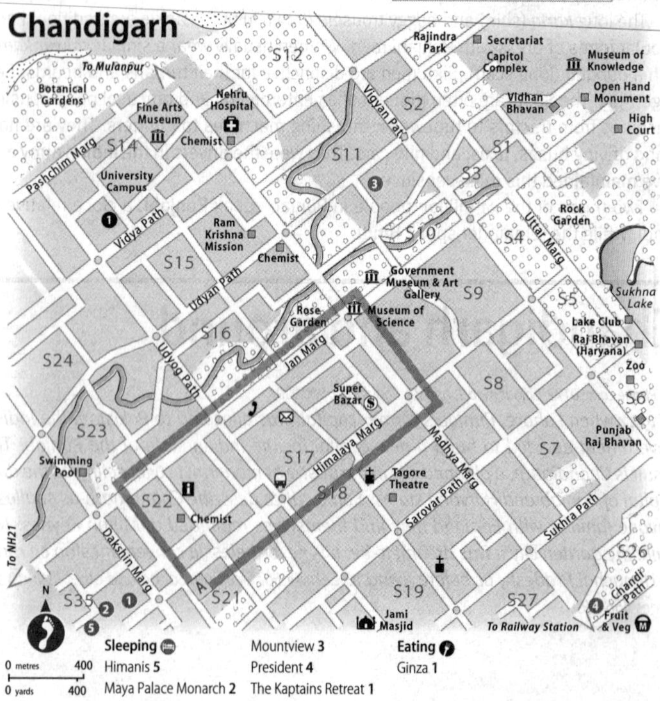

### Chandigarh

0 metres 400
0 yards 400

**Sleeping**
Himanis 5
Maya Palace Monarch 2
Mountview 3
President 4
The Kaptains Retreat 1

**Eating**
Ginza 1

## Sights

Chandigarh's major centres are: the **Capitol Complex** consisting of the Secretariat, Legislative Assembly and High Court in the northeast with the Shiwalik Hills as a backdrop; **Sector 17**, the central business district with administrative and state government offices, shopping areas and banks; a **Cultural Zone** in Sector 14, for education which includes a museum and a campus university with institutions for engineering, architecture, Asian studies and medicine. A vast new colonnaded **Shopping Mall** has opened in Sector 35, with hotels, restaurants, banks, a well-stocked supermarket, internet/international phones etc.

The multi-pillared **High Court** stands nearby with a reflective pool in front. Primary colour panels break up the vast expanses of grey concrete but this classic work of modernist architecture looks stark and bleak. The **Legislative Assembly** has a removable dome and a mural by Le Corbusier that symbolizes evolution. In the same sector is the **Open Hand Monument**. The insignia of the Chandigarh Administration, it symbolizes 'the hand to give and the hand to take; peace and prosperity, and the unity of humankind'. The metal monument rotates in the wind, 14 m high and weighing 50 tonnes, sometimes resembling a bird in flight. The geometrical hill nearby, known as the **Tower of Shadows** ⓘ *tours 1030-1230 and 1420-1630, ask at Secretariat reception desk (you may need special permission to enter)*, was designed to beautify the complex, breaking its symmetrical lines.

**Government Museum and Art Gallery** ⓘ *closed Mon, 1000-1630, S10*, has a collection of stone sculptures dating back to the Gandhara period, miniature paintings and modern art. Also prehistoric fossils and artefacts. **Museum of Evolution of Life** ⓘ *closed Mon, 1000-1630, S10*, has exhibits covering 5,000 years from the Indus Valley Civilization to the present day. **Fine Arts Museum**, Punjab University, S14. All the faculties of the university are in Gandhi Bhavan, S14; the university specializes in Gandhi studies.

**Rose Gardens** ⓘ *rose show in early March, till sunset, S16*, one of the largest in Asia (25 ha), contains over 1,500 varieties of roses; well worth visiting in spring.

This unique and imaginative place, the **Rock Garden** or **Garden of Nek Chand** ⓘ *Apr-Sep, 0900-1300, 1500-1900, (1400-1800, Oct-Mar), Rs 15, allow 3 hrs*, is the creation of Nek Chand, a road inspector in the Capitol City project. The 'garden' comprises an extraordinary collection of stones from the nearby Shiwaliks (carried on his bike) and domestic rubbish transformed into sculptures. Nek Chand dreamed of 'creating a temple to Gods and Goddesses' out of discarded items of everyday use, for

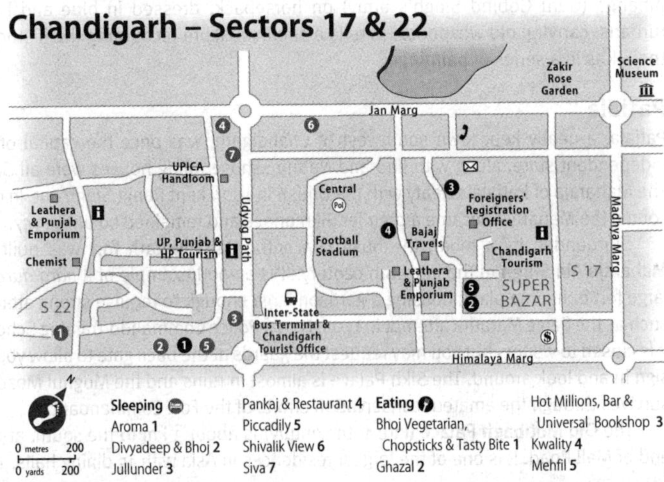

 example bottle tops, fluorescent lights, mud guards, tin cans, and by highly imaginative re-assembling made models of people and animals. These have been set out along a maze of paths, creating an often amusing and enjoyable park. First opened in 1976 the park is still being extended. The low archways make visitors bow to the gods who have blessed the park.

Just below the rock garden is **Sukhna Lake**, an artificial lake, the venue of the Asian rowing championships and circled by a walk. Crowded on holidays and Sunday. There are cafeterías, boating and fishing (permits).

**Zoological Park** ⓘ *Rs 100 per car, Rs 10 per person*, in Chaat Bir, a few kilometres out of the city centre, also has a lion and deer safari park.

## Chandigarh to Himachal Pradesh → *Colour map 1, grid B3.*

### Pinjore (Pinjaur)

The **Yadavindra Gardens**, at Pinjore, 20 km on Kalka Road, were laid out by Aurangzeb's foster brother Fidai Khan, who also designed the Badshahi Mosque in Lahore. Within the Mughal *charbagh* gardens are a number of palaces in a Mughal-Rajasthani style: Shish Mahal, which has mirror-encased ceiling and is cooled by water flowing underneath (remove a slab to see!); Rang Mahal, a highly decorated pavilion andJal Mahal, set among fountains, cool and delightful. There are also camel rides and fairground attractions to tempt city dwellers. Keep a close eye on your belongings at all times; thefts reported.

### Anandpur Sahib

Anandpur Sahib (City of Divine Bliss), in a picturesque setting at the foot of the Shiwaliks by the river Sutlej, was established by the ninth Guru, Tegh Bahadur, in 1664, when the Sikhs had been forced into the foothills of the Himalaya by increasing Mughal opposition. Guru Tegh Bahadur himself was executed in Delhi, and his severed head was brought to Anandpur Sahib to be cremated. The event added to the determination of his son, Guru Gobind Singh, to forge a new body to protect the Sikh Community. The Khalsa Panth was thus created on Baisakhi Day in 1699. Anandpur Sahib became both a fortress and a centre of Sikh learning. *Hola Mohalla* is celebrated the day after Holi when battles are re-enacted by nihangs (Guru Gobind Singh's army) on horseback, dressed in blue and huge turbans, carrying old weapons. There is a small museum recounting the history of the Sikhs in a series of paintings.

*Kalka, beyond Pinjore, is the starting point for the mountain railway to Shimla; see page 477. The quickest route to Dharamshala is via Ropar and Anandpur Sahib.*



### Patiala

Patiala, a neatly kept town southwest of Chandigarh, was once the capital of an independent state, along with Jind and Nabha, whose ruling houses were all Sikh. The Maharaja of Patiala's treaty with the British in 1809 kept Ranjit Singh out. In due course the Maharaja became a premier Sikh prince and remained so until 1947.

Surrounded by a moat, the huge concentric **Bahadurgarh fort** was built by **Maharaja Ala Singh** in the late 18th century. It is a good example of a *nara durg*, a large fort built on a plain, housing a garrison large enough to repulse strong attacks such as the fierce Maratha attempt in 1794. Now a Police Commando Training School, it is closed to visitors but you may request the guards at the back gate to allow you to sign in and look around. The Sikh Palace is almost in ruins and the Moghul Mosque survives through the amateur conservation efforts of the Fort Commandant.

The **Old Motibagh Palace** (late 19th century) is about 3 km to the south, at the end of Mall Road. It is one of the largest residences in Asia with 15 dining halls. The grotesquely oversized rambling central building is surrounded by lawns and trees. A combination of European, Rajput and Mughal styles, part of it is now the National Institute for Sports. The Sheesh Mahal has a **Museum and Art Gallery** housing ethnography, arms, natural history and miniature paintings. There is an unusual sunken lake and a curious 19th-century suspension bridge.



## Chandigarh to Delhi → *Colour map 1, grid B3 and C3.*

From December to March the fields are green with wheat, though towards Delhi many are now planted with vegetables for the Delhi market. If travelling by train through this area at harvest time, expect to find your nostrils, clothes and luggage filled with dust and chaff! The Grand Trunk Road through Haryana is one of the busiest in India. It has long stretches lined with magnificent trees, and villagers have to buy rights to the leaves and wood.

### Ambala

Ambala, now the district headquarters, became a large British cantonment, laid out from 1843 onwards in grid fashion. The famous Gupta iron pillar now at the Qutb Minar in Delhi was originally on the hill just outside town.

### Kurukshetra

The battlefield where Arjuna learned the meaning of *dharma* has left no trace. See page 1316. The flat plain around Kurukshetra is described in Sanskrit literature as '*Brahmavarta*' (Land of Brahma). Like many other sacred sites it becomes the special focus of pilgrimage at the time of exceptional astronomical events. In Kurukshetra, eclipses of the sun are marked by special pilgrimages, when over one million people come to the tank. It is believed that the waters of all India's sacred tanks meet together at the moment of eclipse, giving extra merit to anyone who can bathe in it at that moment.

**Brahmasar Lake**, 1 km west, a pilgrim site, is visited by a wide range of wildfowl, particularly from December to February. Temples and ghats surround the tank. The modern temple can best be described as kitsch, a reproduction of earlier temple styles. But the site is important for its influence on the development of Hindu ideas, not Hindu architecture. There are also the remains of a **Muslim Fort**, including the **Tomb of Shaikh Chilli Jalal** (died 1582) and **Lal Masjid**, a small red sandstone mosque. The carving on the domes is similar to that at Fatehpur Sikri.

### Karnal

Karnal was taken by the British in 1797 who established a cantonment here in 1811. At Uchana, 3 km north, Haryana Tourism has created an artificial lake.

### Panipat

Panipat is the site of three great battles which mark the rise and fall of the Mughal Empire. It stands on the higher ground made up of the debris of earlier settlements near the old bank of the River Yamuna. Today it is an important textile town with over 30,000 looms. A high proportion of the products, carpets, curtains and tablewear, is exported.

In the first battle of Panipat on 21 April 1526 Babur, the first Mughal Emperor, fought Ibrahim Lodi, the Sultan of Delhi, reputedly resulting in the death of 20,000 of the sultan's army, including Ibrahim Lodi. The second battle, on 5 November 1556, changed the course of India's history, as it secured Mughal power. **Akbar**, who had just succeeded his father Humayun, and his general, defeated Hemu, the nephew of the Afghan Sher Shah. There was a mass slaughter of the captives, and in the gruesome tradition of Genghis Khan, a victory pillar was built with their heads plastered in. The third battle took place on 13 January 1761. The once great Mughal Empire was threatened from the west by the resurgent **Rajputs** and from the northwest by the Afghans. The distracted Mughal minister called in the Marathas. Despite their numbers, the Marathas lost and their soldiers fled. However, the Afghan leader **Ahmad Shah Durrani** was unable to take advantage of his victory as his followers mutinied for the two-years' arrears of pay he owed them. North India was thus left in a political vacuum which adventurers tried to fill during the next 40 years. The main old building in Panipat is a shrine to the Muslim saint Abu Ali Kalandar.

## Southwestern Haryana → *Colour map 2, grid A5 and A6.*

Road and rail criss-cross the largely flat plain where irrigation sustains lushly cultivated fields. Further west dry land predominates, shading into the deserts of Rajasthan. The NH10 gives access to several remote archaeological sites and India's most important early settlement region but it is rarely visited.

### Rohtak → *77 km from Delhi.*

The archaeological sites at **Khokhra Kot** and **Ramala Ala** have revealed pottery from pre-Harappan and early historical times after 1500 BC. Coin moulds from the first century have thrown valuable light on the processes of minting coins. Today, it is well known for its turbans, interwoven with gold and silver thread.

### Hissar

Hissar was founded in 1354 by Firuz Shah Tughlaq who constructed a canal to bring water to his hunting ground. This was renovated in the 19th century and incorporated into the West Yamuna Canal. The Gujari Mahal in the old fort was built from the remains of a Jain temple. The citadel contains the Mosque of Firuz Shah (late 14th century) and the Jahaz (ship) east of the city, which takes its name from its shape (reminiscent of that at Mandu – see page 298). Hissar exports cattle all over India and is widely known for its twice yearly **cattle fairs.**

### Sirsa

Sirsa was settled from around 1500 BC with pottery known as Rang Mahal Ware. Thus it was clearly occupied long before the traditional date of its founding – the sixth century AD – when it was known as Sarasvati. Just north of **Sirsa** the road crosses the usually dry bed of the Ghaggar River, one of North India's most important early settlement regions. The **Kalibangan** Harappan site is just beyond Suratgarh to the west, see page 433. There is a large cattle fair here in August to September.

## Chandigarh to Amritsar → *Colour map 1, grid B2 and B3.*

Many of the small towns along this route show signs of Punjab's rapid industrialization; steel rolling, textiles, sugar mills, food processing and a whole range of small industrial services from computers to advertising.

### Sirhind

Mahmud of Ghazni extended his control to the town in the early 11th century when it became the border town for Muslim possessions in India, hence Sar-i-Hind ('Frontier of India'). Later it became Sher Shah Suri's capital, whose army was defeated by Humayun in 1555.

The town's period of greatest splendour was between 1556 and 1707. The stone-built Tomb of Mir Miran is an octagon topped by a dome. Another octagonal tomb, ornately decorated with painted flowers, is that of Pirbandi Nakshwala, with its pear shaped dome covered in glazed tiles. Salabat Beg Haveli is a large and well-preserved Mughal house whilst the Sarai of the Mughal emperors, in the southeast of the town, is now a public hall. For the Sikhs, Sirhind is associated with the brutal execution of the two younger sons of the 10th Guru, who were bricked up alive in the fort in 1705 for refusing to convert to Islam. 

## Ludhiana

A major textile (hosiery) and light engineering centre, Ludhiana's predominantly concrete grey hue bears testimony to both the rapid pace of its development and its somewhat unfinished feel.. Here you can get good quality fabric from the market and garments copied cheaply by expert tailors. The rich agricultural area around it supports a large grain market. Founded in 1480 by Lodi princes from Delhi (hence its name), Ludhiana subsequently passed through a number of hands. The surrounding area was fiercely fought over during the First Sikh War with the British in 1845-46. The three major battlefields at **Mudki**, **Firozshah** and **Sobraon** all have commemorative obelisks. The town is also the home of the **Christian Medical College Hospital**, which is in partnership with the CMC hospital in Vellore. The world famous **Punjab Agricultural University**, on the edge of town, has a good museum. In Februrary, a show of **Rural Games** of Punjab is organized at Kila Raipur nearby.

## Jalandhar

Jalandhar (Jullundur) is an ancient city of which very little survives, although it retains a more established, settled feel than nearby Ludhiana. It was sacked by Mahmud of Ghazni and under the Mughals it was an important administrative centre. Today, it is a major road and rail junction with a busy market, the Rainik Bazar, a network of narrow, atmospheric alleys which are worth exploring. The cantonment area to the southeast was established in 1846 to house army units after the treaties signed in Lahore in March and December 1846 which ended the First Sikh War.

## Kapurthala

Kapurthala is the capital of the former Sikh princely state and the home town of the **Ahluwalia** family who conquered it in 1747. Its army fought against the British at Aliwal in the First Sikh War but took the British side during the Second Sikh War (1848) and the Mutiny (1857). There are buses from Jalandhar and Amritsar.

Later governed as a model city-state, the French-educated ruler Jagajit Singh, who ascended the throne in 1890, tried to make his capital city a Parisian replica. His palace, the **Jalaukhana**, might have come straight out of the French Renaissance, except that the red sandstone with which it was started had to give way to pink stucco when funds ran out. The palace is now a boys' school. The Maharaja's international preferences changed when he married a Spanish dancer, however, and the **Villa Buena Vista** (1894) has an Iberian flavour.

## Firozpur

Firozpur, southwest of Jalandhar and close to the Pakistan border, was founded during the rule of Firoz Shah Tughluq in the mid-14th century, passed to the Sikhs, and then the British in 1835. There is a British cemetery on the GT Road link to Ludhiana. The extension of the Sirhind Canal in the 1880s transformed the previously poverty-stricken agricultural region into a prosperous canal colony and is intensively cultivated today.

## Goindwal and Tarn Taran

On the way from Jalandhar to Amritsar there are important *gurudwaras* where Sikhs on pilgrimage traditionally stop. There are separate bathing places for men and women at Goindwal, with a small market place outside the temple. The *gurudwara* at Taran Tarn is surrounded by a busy bazar. It is quite impressive, with a water tank all around and cloisters providing welcome shade.

## Sleeping

**Chandigarh** *p449, maps p450 and p451*
Rickshaw drivers act as hotel touts.
**A The Kaptain's Retreat**, 303 S35-B, T0172 2500 5599, www.kaptainsretreat.com. Owned by the legendary cricketer, Kapil Dev, this is Chandigarh's first boutique hotel. Each room is named after one of the great man's achievements, eg 'nine wickets', and is contemporary yet comfortable with excellent attention to detail. There's also an attractive bar and restaurant, recommended.
**A Mountview**, S10, T0172 274 0544, citco10@sanchar.net.in. 156 centrally a/c rooms, pool, government run business hotel boasting all 5-star amenities.
**A Piccadily**, Himalaya Marg, S 22-B, 500 m from ISBT, T0172 2707571, thepiccadily @rediffmail.com. 48 a/c, well-maintained rooms, smart restaurant, bar, friendly and enthusiastic staff.
**A Shivalik View**, S17, T0172 270 0001, shivalikview@citcochandigarh.com. 108 rooms with all mod cons in government run hotel, business centre, good Chinese restaurant, friendly, well located.
**B Aroma**,Himalaya Marg, S22, T0172 508 5001, www.hotelaroma.com. 30 clean, contemporary a/c rooms, plus a cavernous "water-featured" restaurant, a good location and friendly staff.
**B Maya Palace**, SCO 325-28, S35-B, T0172 260 0547, maya@chl-vsnl-net.in. 28 a/c rooms in modern, well-appointed hotel with a large restaurant and 24-hr coffee shop.
**B Monarch**, 351-352, S35-B, T0172 260 9991. Effciently run, modern hotel with popular, well-priced basement bar. Rates negotiatiable.
**B North Park**, out of town at Pachkula, near Ghaggar Bridge, T0172 256 1212. 43 comfortable rooms in business class hotel.
**C Classic**, S35-C, T0172 266 3275, www. hotelclassicchandigarh.com. Comfortable modern hotel (buffet breakfast included), bar, reasonable value, lively bar and disco.
**C Himani's**, 469-70, S35-C, T0172 266 1070. 17 adequate rooms in a good location close to bars and restaurants, friendly, good value.
**C Pankaj**, S22-A, T0172 270 9891, colhar sharam@hotmail.com. 14 comfortable rooms, some a/c rooms with bath, good restaurant, exchange, slightly out on a limb.
**C-D Jullunder**, S22, opposite ISBT, T0172 270 6777, www.jullunderhotel.com. 17 cleanish rooms, hot water, Indian restaurant.
**D Divyadeep**, S22-B, T0172 270 5191). 15 rooms, some a/c, neat and clean, good *Bhoj* restaurant.
**E Siva**, half way along Udyog Path, 1st floor, S22, few clean rooms, hot shower, meals.

**Patiala** *p452*
**C Green's**, Mall Rd, T0175-221 3071. 12 rooms, most a/c, restaurant, bar, pleasant. Cheaper hotels are near the bus station.

**Ambala** *p453*
**D Batra Palace**, Lawrence Rd, behind Bus Station, T0171-640159. Comfortable rooms with 'proper' bathroom (hot water), friendly room service with good food. Recommended.
**D Kingfisher** (Haryana Tourism), 5 km north of town (near junction of Amritsar-Chandigarh roads), T0171-443732. 13 rooms, 2 a/c, restaurant, attractive gardens and pool.

**Kurukshetra** *p453*
**D-E Neelkanthi Krishna Dham**, has simple rooms, dorm beds, Rs 75-100, restaurant, lockers and camping.

**Panipat** *p453*
**B-C Gold**, GT Rd, south of town, T0180 266 0012. 29 a/c rooms, restaurants, bar, pool.
**C-D Skylark**, GT Rd, T0180 264 1051. 16 a/c rooms and dorm (Rs 100), restaurant, fast food.
**C-D Midtown**, GT Rd, town centre, T0181 266 7901. 28 a/c rooms, restaurant.

**Rohtak** *p454*
**C-D Tilyar**, T01262-273119, has 12 a/c rooms and dorms (Rs 100), restaurant and boating.

**Hissar** *p454*
**C-D Flamingo**, T01662-225702, 6 a/c rooms, restaurant and bar.

**Sirhind** *p454*
**D Bougainvillea Tourist Complex**, GT Rd towards Mandi Gobindgarh, outside town, T01763 555 570. 8 rooms, 4 a/c, floating restaurant, camping and showers.
**D Mulsari Tourist Complex**, Aam Khas Bagh, in town centre, T01763 222 250. Old caravanserai conversion, 8 rooms (4 a/c), restaurant, beer bar, Mughal garden, archaeological ruins nearby.
**E Queens Flower Tourist Resort**, on Sirhind canal at Neelon, T0161 283 3832. 6 rooms, some a/c, restaurant, bar, garden.

**Ludhiana** *p455*
**A Majestic Park Plaza**, Ferozepur Rd, (0161) 277 3000, www.majesticparkplaza.com. 120 elegant rooms plus usual 5-star facilities including pool, part of nationwide chain.
**A-B Friends Regency**, Ferozepur Rd, T0161 277 1111, hotelfriendsregency@yahoo.com. 21 classy rooms in impressive building, good value.
**B Gulmor**, Ferozepur Rd, (0161) 277 1700. 28 rooms, central a/c, restaurant, exchange, pleasant gardens, relaxed atmosphere, well-maintained, recommended.
**B Nagpal Regency**, Bhaibala Chowk, Ferozepur Rd, T0161 277 2394. 30 well presented rooms in modern building plus friendly staff and a well-stocked bar.
D Numerous, much of a muchness, options close to railway station.

**Jalandhar** *p455*
**A Radisson**, Windsor Fountain, GT Rd, T0181 508 1234, www.radisson.com/jalandharin. 47 rooms to usual high Radisson standard, good facilities, reasonable value.
**B Kamal Palace**, EH-192, Civil Lines, T0181-245 8473, www.kamalpalace.com. 41 very comfortable rooms, central a/c, modern and well-presented.
**B Leo Fort**, GT Road, (0181) 224 4890, www.leoforthotel.com. 61 modern rooms, central a/c, health club, pool, great bar, outstanding value, recommended.
**C-D Plaza**, Old Court Rd, New Plaza Chowk, T0181-2225833, plaza@jla.vsnl.net.in. 23 rooms, some a/c rooms with bath, restaurant, bar.
**D-E Centrepoint**, BMC Chowk, T0181 223 8808. Low on atmos- phere but the best value a/c rooms in town.

**Kapurthala** *p455*
**D Magnolia Tourist Complex**, on western edge of town, T0181 278 2322. 4 rooms, restaurant, bar, garden, very pleasant for a break or an overnight stop.

## Eating

**Chandigarh** *p449, maps p450 and p451*
**TTT Curry's**,in Piccadily hotel, upmarket Indian in luxurious surroundings
**TTT Mehfil**, 183, S17-C, T0172 270 4224. International. Upmarket, a/c, comfortable seating, spicy meals.
**TTT Elevens**,in Kaptain's Retreat hotel, unusual combination of Pakistani, Indian and Thai cuisines in Mediterranean-styled interior, recommended.
**TT Bhoj**, Divyadeep Hotel, S22-B, Himalaya Marg. Indian Vegetarian. Good set *thalis*,only, pleasant, clean, busy at lunch, good value.
**TT Chopsticks**, Himalaya Marg. Chinese. Smart, cool, reasonable food.
**TT Ghazal**, 189, S17-C. International. Comfortable, good Indian, popular with families, separate bar.
**TT Khyber**, S35-B. Excellent Frontier style cuisine in pleasant ground floor restaurant plus 'Wild West' bar in basement, complete with cowboy waiters. Recommended.
**TT Kwality**, 20, S17. International. Usual fare, good ices. Others nearby do good spicy chicken dishes.
**TT Sagar Ratna**, S35-C. High quality South Indian. Well presented, nationwide chain, very professional.
**T Ginza**, 40, S14 (University Campus). Chinese.

**Fast food**
**Barista**, S35-C, nationwide coffee chain, plus good snacks in relaxing surroundings.
**Hot Millions**, S17, wide choice. 3 places.
**Tasty Bite**, Himalaya Marg. Good South Indian eats and burgers.
**Down Under** 183-4, S17, is a pleasant bar.



*For an explanation of the sleeping and eating price codes used in this guide, see inside the front cover. Other relevant information is found in Essentials pages 56-61.*

**Ludhiana** *p455*
**Cafe 33**, 33 SCF, Sarabha Nagar Market. Indian.
**Chicken Plaza**, Ghumar Mandi. Fantastic chicken with nan, try haryali chicken.
**City Heart Hotel**. International. Wide choice, well prepared, generous portions, chilled beer, genial, helpful and prompt service.
**Gazebo**, 15 Bhadaur House Market. International menu in a/c comfort.
**Hot Breads**, 32-C Sarabha Nagar.
**Kabab Corner**, 186 Rani Jhansi Rd, Civil Lines.
**Larks**, City Market. Punjabi. Typical *dhaba*, but clean, chicken dishes recommended.

**Jalandhar** *p455*
🍴🍴 **La Roma**, next to **Radisson Hotel**, "Italian by flavour, Indian by heart".
🍴 **Eat Well**, close to Clock Tower, quick and clean, also **DearNear** juice bar next door.
🍴 **Clock Tower**, Nehru Garden. Also has a bar.

## Festivals and events

**Chandigarh** *p449, maps p450 and p451*
All the Hindu festivals are celebrated especially **Baisakhi**, celebrated by both Hindus and Sikhs as **New Year's Day (13/14 Apr)**. Bhangra dancers perform.

## Shopping

**Chandigarh** *p449, maps p450 and p451*
Most shops open 1000-1330, 1530-1945; closed Sun. Small shops in S19 and S22 open on Sun. A large new Mall has been built in S35. S17 and 22 have **State Govt Emporia**.

**Patiala** *p452*
Lacquerware at 94 Bichittar Nagar.

## Activities and tours

**Chandigarh** *p449, maps p450 and p451*
**Swimming**
**Lake Pool Complex**, S23, temporary membership available.

**Tour companies**
**Chandigarh Tourism**, Chandigarh Emporium, S17-B, T0172 270 4356. Local tours and further afield to Pinjore Gardens, Bhakra dam, Shimla, Kullu and Manali and Amritsar (minimum 20 persons). Also from Chandigarh Tourism Office, ISBT. Local tour departs at 1130, Rs 50, 4 hrs; visit the Rock Garden independently for a leisurely visit.
**Cozy Tours**, SCF I Sector 10, T0172 2740850.

**Yoga**
**Yoga centre**, S23, near nursery.

## Transport

**Chandigarh** *p449, maps p450 and p451*
**Air**
Airport, 11 km. Taxis charge Rs 300 to centre. Indian Airlines: reservations, S17, T0172 270 4539, airport, T0172 265 6029 1000-1630. To **Amritsar, Delhi** Thu, Sat; **Leh** Wed (highly weather dependent), US$75. **Jet Airways**, 14 S 9D Madhya Marg, T0172 274 0550, airport T0172 265 8935, daily to **Delhi**.

**Bicycle**
Cycles hired free to CITCO hotel guests.

**Bus**
**Local** CTU run reasonably good city service.
**Long distance** It is easier to get a seat on the Shimla bus from Chandigarh than from Kalka. Many buses daily from ISBT, S17, with a post office and tourist office. Transport offices: ISBT, S17 (0900-1300, 1400-1600), Chandigarh, T0172 270 4005; Haryana, T0172 270 4014; Himachal, T0172 270 4015; Punjab, T0172 270 4023. Buy bus tickets from the designated booths next to platforms before boarding. Seat numbers (written on the back of tickets) are often assigned. Shimla buses (via Kalka) leave from platform 10. To **Amritsar**, 6 hrs (from *Aroma Hotel*, T0172 2700045); **Pathankot**, 7 hrs; **Dharamshala**, 10 hrs; **Kalka** (from Platform 10), Rs 11-28. Buses to Shimla also stop at Kalka; **Kullu** 12 hrs. Also Himachal Tourism coaches during the season, to **Delhi**, 5 hrs, Rs 180; **Manali**, 0800, 10 hrs, Rs 280; **Shimla**, 5 hrs, Rs 100.

**Rickshaw**
Auto-rickshaws are metered with a minimum fare, but you can bargain. Stands at Bus Station, Railway Station and the Rock Garden. Cycle rickshaws are unmetered.

**Taxi**
Private taxi stands in S22, S17, S35.
**Chandigarh Tourism** (CITCO), S17, T0172 270 3839. To Kalka, up to Rs 400.

**Train**

The station (8 km) has a clean waiting room but a poor bus service to the city. Prepaid auto-rickshaws, Rs 45 to S22; to bus stand Rs 34; to Kalka (for the brave) Rs 200. Enquiries/reservations, T0172 265 3131, 1000-1700; City Booking Office, 1st floor, Inter-State Bus Terminal (ISBT), S17, T0172 270 8573, Mon-Sat 0800-1345, 1445-2000, Sun 0800-1400. Tourist office, 0600-2030. **New Delhi**: *Shatabdi Exp, 2006*, 0650, 3¼ hrs; *Shatabdi Exp, 2012*, 1220, 3¼ hrs; *Himalayan Queen, 4096*, 1738, 4½ hrs. **Old Delhi**: *Kalka-Howrah Mail, 2312*, 0100, 5½ hrs. **Shimla**: *Amritsar Kalka Exp, 4536*, 0700, 1¼ hrs to **Kalka**, then 3 hr wait for *Exp 255* to Shimla (1105, 6 hrs).

**Anandpur Sahib** *p459*

Bus from Chandigarh and Ropar. Train to Ambala: Himachal Exp, 4544, 2210, 3½ hrs. To Nangal Dam Express, 4553, 0620, 30 mins.

**Patiala** *p452*

The railway and bus stations are at the north end of Mall Rd, 1 km from the centre.

Daily buses to Delhi, other towns in Punjab and neighbouring states.

Patiala is on the branch line to Bhatinda and Firozpur.

**Ambala** *p453*

New Delhi: *Shatabdi Exp, 2006*, 0723, 2½ hrs. *Shatabdi Exp, 2012*, 1302, 2½ hrs. Frequent trains to **Chandigarh**. Northern Railway connects **Shimla** trains with those from **Jammu Tawi** and **Lucknow**.

**Ludhiana** *p455*

Long distance daily bus services connect Ludhiana with Delhi and towns in Punjab and neighbouring states.

Trains include: **To Amritsar**: *Shatabdi Exp, 2013*, 2021, 1¾ hrs; *Katihar Amritsar Exp, 5705*, 1010, 2½ hrs; *Paschim Exp, 2925*, 1645, 2½ hrs; *New Delhi-Amritsar Exp, 4659*, 1930, 2½ hrs. **To Delhi**: *Shatabdi Exp, 2014*, 0703, 3¾ hrs; *Paschim Exp, 2926*, 1100, 5½ hrs; *Golden Temple Mail, 2904*, 0025, 7 hrs.

**Jalandhar** *p455*

A/c **coach** connects with **Air India** flights from Delhi airport to London, 1700 (9 hrs), return 0400; Rs 350.

The City and Cantt **train** stations are on the same line, though not all trains stop at both. There are many trains to Amritsar and Ludhiana. From City station: **Amritsar**: *Katihar Amritsar Exp, 5705*, 1110, 1½ hrs; *Shatabdi Exp, 2013*, 2105, 1 hr; *Dadar-Amritsar Exp, 1057*, 1515, 1½ hr; *Paschim Exp, 2925*, 1810, 1 hr. **Kolkata**: via Ludhiana and Varanasi, *Amritsar-Howrah Mail, 3006*, 1955, 34 hrs. **Delhi**: via Ludhiana and Meerut, *Shatabdi Exp, 2014*, 0614, 4½ hrs; *Paschim Exp, 2926*, 0908, 7 hrs; *Golden Temple Mail, 2904*, 2255, 8½ hrs.

**Firozpur** *p455*

Train from Firozpur Cantt: Jalandhar, Tawi Exp, 4806, 1010, 2¾ hrs. From Firozpur City: New Delhi, Punjab Mail, 2138, 2150, 7¼ hrs; Janata Exp, 9024, 0430, 9¼ hrs.

## Directory

**Chandigarh** *p449, maps p450 and p451*

**Banks** Exchange: **Paul's Merchants**, S22-A, T0172 270 4279, speedy, efficient, good rates, will send rep to hotel. Recommended. American Express TCs only. **Hospitals** (with 24-hr chemists): **General Hospital**, S16, T0172 278 0756; **PG Institute**, S12, T0172 274 7610. **Tourist offices** at ISBT, S17: Chandigarh, 1st floor, ISBT (Main Bus Terminal), T0172 270 4614, Mon-Fri 0900-1700, Sat 0900-1300. **Himachal**, 1st floor, ISBT, T0172 2708569. **Useful addresses** Ambulance: T102. Fire: T101. Police: T100. **Foreigners' Registration Office**: Town Hall Bldg, S17 (1000-1700), T0172 2741100.

**Patiala** *p452*

**State Bank of Patiala**, in the centre, changes money reasonably quickly.

**Jalandhar** *p455*

**Thomas Cook**, for exchange, 2 Alpha Estate, 39 GT Rd, T0181 223 8790.

*Sikhs are officially exempt from wearing motorcycle helmets, although strictly speaking the length of cloth used to form the turban should be not less than 5 metres as anything less is not deemed to give adequate protection.*

# Northern Punjab

*Northern Punjab is defined more than anything by its proximity to the Pakistan border, with a heavy military presence always in attendance. Pre-partition the Punjab extended well in to present day Pakistan, and many families still have members or property on both sides of the divide, many of whom have not seen each other for generations. Today the area is dominated by agriculture, with the efficiently farmed plains providing a stark contrast to the soaring peaks of neighbouring Kashmir, and by Amritsar's incomparable Golden Temple.* ▸▸ *For Sleeping, Eating and other listings, see pages 466-468.*

## Amritsar → *Phone code: 0183. Colour map 1, grid B2. Population: 976,000.*

Amritsar (Pool of the Nectar of Immortality) is named after the sacred pool in the Golden Temple, the holiest of Sikh sites. The temple itself, the city's singular attraction, is a haven of peace amidst an essentially congested city. The atmosphere is particularly powerful from before dawn to early light, when the surrounding glistening white marble pavement is still cold under foot and the gold begins to shimmer on the lightening water. You cannot help but be touched by the sanctity of the place. ▸▸ *For Sleeping, Eating and other listings, see pages 466-468.*

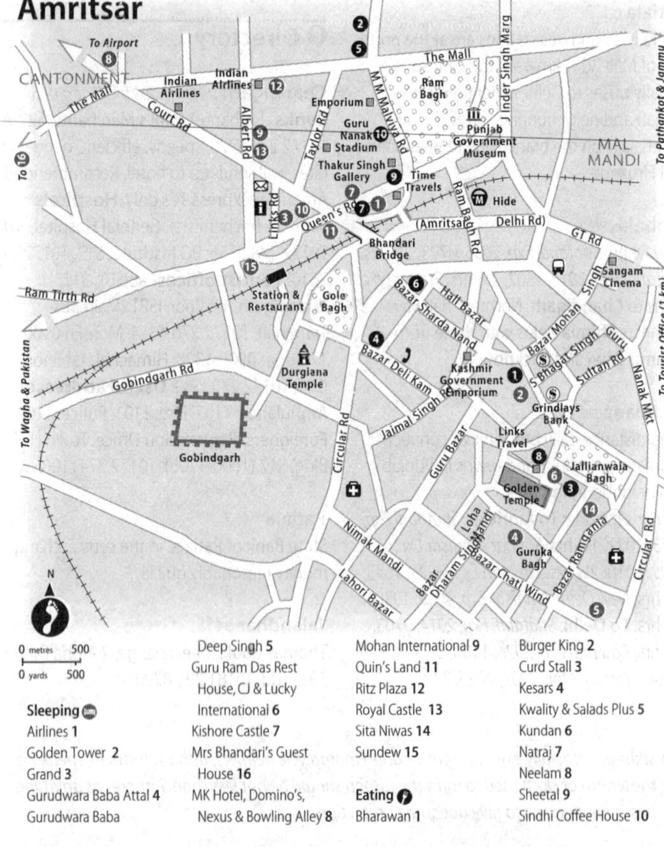

## Ins and outs

**Getting there** Rajasansi airport is 11 km away with taxi or auto-rickshaw transfers. The railway is central, the bus station 2 km east; both are a 15-min auto-rickshaw ride from the Golden Temple to the south. If you have a couple of hours to spare between connections, you can a fit in a visit. ▸▸ *See Transport, page 467, for further details.*

**Getting around** The city is quite spread out. Cycle-rickshaws squeeze through the crowded lanes. Auto-rickshaws are handy for longer journeys unless you get a bike.

## Background

The original site for the city was granted by the Mughal Emperor Akbar (ruled 1556-1605) who also visited the temple and it has been sacred to the Sikhs since the time of the fourth guru, Ram Das (Guru 1574-1581). He insisted on paying its value to the local Jats who owned it, thereby eliminating the possibility of future disputes on ownership. Ram Das then invited local merchants to live and trade in the immediate vicinity. In 1577 he heard that a cripple had been miraculously cured while bathing in the pool here. The pool was enlarged and named Amrit Sarovar ('Immortality'). Arjan Dev (Guru 1581-1601), Ram Das' son and successor, enlarged the tank further and built the original temple at its centre from 1589-1601. The Afghan Ahmad Shah Durrani, desecrated the Golden Temple in 1757. The Sikhs united and drove him out, but four years later he defeated the Sikh armies, sacking the town and blowing up the temple. Later, the Sikhs re-conquered the Punjab and restored the temple and tank. Under their greatest secular leader, Maharaja Ranjit Singh, the temple was rebuilt in 1764. In 1830 he donated 100 kg (220 lbs) of gold which was applied to the copper sheets on the roof and much of the exterior of the building, giving rise to the name 'The Golden Temple'. Now Punjab's second largest town, Amritsar was a traditional junction of trade routes. The different peoples, Yarkandis, Turkomans, Kashmiris, Tibetans and Iranians, indicate its connections with the Old Silk Road.

# The Golden Temple

The spiritual nerve centre of the Sikh faith, every Sikh tries to make a visit and bathe in the holy water. It is immensely powerful, spiritual and welcoming to all, with an all-pervasive air of strength and self-sufficiency.

**Visiting the temple** Shoes, socks, sticks and umbrellas are left outside at the cloakroom at no charge. Visitors should wash their feet outside the entrance. It is best to go early as for much of the year the marble gets too hot by noon. Dress appropriately and cover your head in the temple precincts. Head scarves are available during the day but not at night; a handkerchief suffices. Avoid sitting with back towards the temple. Tobacco, narcotics and intoxicants are not permitted. You may wish to visit the community kitchen for breakfast (dawn to 0900) before visiting the temple. The Information Office near the main entrance is very helpful.

**Worship** Singing is central to Sikh worship, and the 24 hour-chanting at the Golden Temple adds greatly to the reverential atmosphere. After building the temple, Arjan Dev compiled a collection of hymns of the great medieval saints and this became the *Adi Granth* (Original Holy book). It was installed in the temple as the focus of devotion and teaching. Gobind Singh, the 10th and last Guru (1675-1708) revised the book and also refused to name a successor saying that the book itself would be the Sikh guru. It thus became known as the *Granth Sahib* (The Holy Book as Guru).

**The temple compound** Entering the temple compound through the main entrance or Clock Tower you see the Harmandir (also spelt *Harimandir*, and known by Hindus as the Durbar Sahib), the Golden Temple itself, beautifully reflected in the stunning expanse of water which surrounds it. Each morning (0400 summer, 0500 winter) the

## 66 99 The third Guru, Amar Das (1552-1574), abolished the custom of eating only with others of the same caste. He even refused to bless the Mughal Emperor Akbar unless he was prepared to eat with everyone else who was present...

Guru Granth Sahib is brought in a vivid procession from the **Akal Takht** at the east end to the **Harmandir**, to be returned at night (2200 summer, 2100 winter). The former represents temporal power, the latter spiritual – and so they do not quite face each other. Some like to attend Palki Sahib (night ceremony).

All pilgrims walk clockwise round the tank, stopping at shrines and bathing in the tank on the way round to the Harmandir itself. The tank is surrounded by an 8-m wide white marble pavement, banded with black and brown Jaipur marble.

**East End** To the left of the entrance steps are the bathing ghats and an area screened off from public view for ladies. Also on this side are the **68 Holy Places** representing 68 Hindu pilgrimage sites. When the tank was built, Arjan Dev told his followers that rather than visit all the orthodox Hindu places of pilgrimage, they should just bathe here thus acquiring equivalent merit.

A shrine contains a copy of the **Granth Sahib**. Here and at other booths round the tank the Holy Book is read for devotees. Sikhs can arrange with the temple authorities to have the book read in their name in exchange for a donation. The *granthi* (reader) is a temple employee and a standard reading lasts for three hours, while a complete reading takes 48 hours. The tree in the centre at the east end of the tank is popularly associated with a healing miracle.

**Dining Hall, Kitchen, Assembly Hall and Guesthouses** The surrounding white arcade of buildings (*bunghas*), are hostels for visitors. Through the archway a path leads to the Guru Ram Das Langar (kitchen and dining hall) immediately on the left, while two tall octagonal minarets, the 18th-century Ramgarhia Minars, provide a vantage point over the temple and inner city. At the far end of the path are the Guru Ram Das Sarai and the Guru Nanak Niwas, where pilgrims can stay free for up to three nights. Sikhs have a community kitchen where all temple visitors, regardless of their religious belief, can eat together. The third Guru, **Amar Das** (1552-1574), abolished the custom of eating only with others of the same caste, and Amar Das. He even refused to bless the Mughal Emperor Akbar unless he was prepared to eat with everyone else who was present. Voluntary service, which continues to be a feature of modern Sikhism, extends to the kitchen staff and workers; visitors are also welcome to lend a hand. The Amritsar kitchen may feed up to 10,000 people a day, with 3,000 at a sitting. It is free of charge and vegetarian, though Sikhs are not banned from eating meat. Lunch is 1100-1500 and dinner 1900 onwards. Next to the Amar Das Langar is the residence of Baba **Kharak Singh** who is hailed by Sikhs as a saint. His followers are distinguished by their orange turbans while temple employees and members of the militant Akali sect wear blue or black turbans.

Returning to the temple tank, the shrine on the south side is to Baba **Deep Singh**. When Ahmad Shah Durrani attacked Amritsar in 1758, Baba Deep Singh was copying out the Granth Sahib. He went out to fight with his followers, vowing to defend the temple with his life. He was mortally wounded, 6 km from town; some say that his head was hacked from his body. Grimly determined and holding his head on with one hand he fought on. On his way back to the temple he died on this spot. The story is recounted in the picture behind glass.

**West end** The complex to the west has the Akal Takht, the flagstaffs, and the Shrine of Guru Gobind Singh. The **flagstaffs** symbolize religion and politics, in the Sikh case intertwined. They are joined in the middle by the emblem of the Sikh nation, the two swords of Hargobind, representing spiritual and temporal authority. The circle is inscribed with the Sikh rallying call *Ek Omkar* (God is One).

Started when Arjan Dev was Guru (1581-1605), and completed by Guru Hargobind in 1609, the **Akal Takht** is the seat of the Sikh's religious committee. It is largely a mixture of 18th- and early 19th-century building, the upper storeys being the work of Ranjit Singh. It has a first floor room with a low balcony which houses a gilt covered ark, central to the initiation of new members of the **Khalsa** brotherhood.

To the side of the flagstaffs is a **shrine** dedicated to the 10th and last guru, Gobind Singh (Guru 1675-1708). In front of the entrance to the temple causeway is a square, a gathering place for visitors.

Sometimes you may see Nihang (meaning 'crocodile') Sikhs, followers of the militant Gobind Singh, dressed in blue and armed with swords, lances and curved daggers.

At the centre of the tank stands the most holy of all Sikh shrines, the **Harmandir** (The Golden Temple). Worshippers obtain the sweet *prasad* after crossing the causeway to the temple where they make an offering. The 60-m long bridge, usually crowded with jostling worshippers, is built out of white marble like the lower floor of the temple. The rest of the temple is covered in copper gilt. On the doorways verses from the Guru Granth Sahib are inscribed in Gurumukhi script while rich floral paintings decorate the walls and excellent silver work marks the doors. The roof has the modified onion-shaped dome, or inverted lotus, characteristic of Sikh temples, but in this case it is covered in the gold that Ranjit Singh added for embellishment.

The ground floor of the three-storey temple contains the Holy Book placed on a platform under a jewel encrusted canopy. **Guru Granth Sahib** contains approximately 3,500 hymns. Professional singers and musicians sing verses from the book continuously from 0400-2200 in the summer and 0500-2200 in winter. An excited crowd of worshippers attempts to touch the serpent horn. Each evening the holy book is taken ceremoniously to the Akal Takht and brought back the next morning; visitors are welcome. The palanquin used for this, set with emeralds, rubies and diamonds with silver poles and a golden canopy, can be seen in the treasury on the first floor of the entrance to the temple. Through the day, pilgrims place offerings of flowers or



## Golden Temple

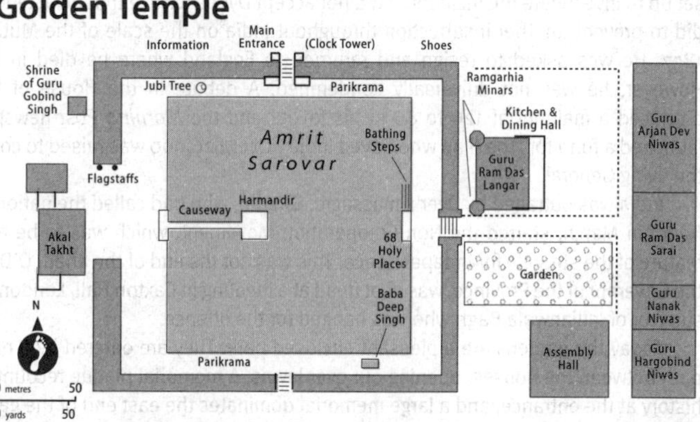

 money around the book. There is no ritual in the worship or pressure from temple officials to donate money. The marble walls are decorated with mirrorwork, gold leaf and designs of birds, animals and flowers in semiprecious stones in the Mughal style.

On the first floor is a balcony on which three respected Sikhs always perform the **Akhand Path** (Unbroken Reading). In order to preserve unity and maintain continuity, there must always be someone practising devotions. The top floor is where the gurus used to sit and here again someone performs the *Akhand Path*; this is the quietest part of the building and affords a good view over the rest of the complex.

On the edge of the tank just west of the entrance is the **Tree Shrine**, a gnarled, 450-years old *jubi* tree, reputed to have been the favourite resting place of the first chief priest of the temple. Women tie strings to the ingeniously supported branches, hoping to be blessed with a son by the primaeval fertility spirits that choose such places as their home. It is also a favourite spot to arrange and sanctify marriages, despite the protests of the temple authorities. **Sikh Museum** at the main entrance to the temple (just before steps leading down to the *parikrama*) is somewhat martial, reflecting the struggles against the Mughals, the British and the Indian Army. **Sikh Library** in the Guru Nanak Building has a good selection of books in English (as well as current national newspapers); closed on Sundays.

## The town

The old city is south of the railway station encircled by a ring road which traces the line of the city walls built during the reign of Ranjit Singh. **Jallianwala Bagh**, noted for the most notorious massacre under British rule, is 400 m north of the Golden Temple.

Relations with the British had soured in 1919. *Hartals* became a common form of demonstration. The Punjab, which had supplied 60% of Indian troops committed to the First World War, was one of the hardest hit economically in 1918 and tension was high. The Lieutenant Governor of the province decided on a 'fist force' to repulse the essentially non-violent but vigorous demonstrations. Some looting occurred in Amritsar and the British called in reinforcements. These arrived under the command of **General Dyer**.

Dyer banned all meetings but people were reported to be gathering on Sunday 13 April 1919 as pilgrims poured into Amritsar to celebrate *Baisakhi*, the Sikh New Year and the anniversary of the founding of the *khalsa* in 1699. That afternoon thousands were crammed into Jallianwala Bagh, a piece of waste ground popular with travellers, surrounded on all sides by high walls with only a narrow alley for access. Dyer personally led some troops to the place, gave the crowd no warning and ordered his men to open fire leaving 379 dead and 1,200 wounded. Other brutal acts followed.

The **Jallianwala Bagh massacre** was hushed up and the British Government in London was only aware of it six months later at which time the Hunter Committee was set up to investigate the incident. It did not accept Dyer's excuse that he acted as he did to prevent another insurrection throughout India on the scale of the Mutiny of 1857. He was asked to resign and returned to England where he died in 1927. However, he was not universally condemned. A debate in the House of Lords produced a majority of 126 to 86 in his favour and the *Morning Post* newspaper launched a fund for 'The Man who Saved India'. Over £26,000 was raised to comfort the dying General.

India was outraged by Dyer's massacre. **Gandhi,** who had called the nationwide *hartal* in March, started the Non Co-operation Movement, which was to be a vital feature of the struggle for Independence. This was not the end of the affair. O'Dwyer, the Governor of the Province, was shot dead at a meeting in Caxton Hall, London, by a survivor of Jallianwala Bagh who was hanged for the offence.

Today the gardens are a pleasant enclosed park. They are entered by a narrow path between the houses, opening out over lawns. A memorial plaque recounts the history at the entrance, and a large memorial dominates the east end of the garden.

There is an interesting museum. On the north side is a well in which many who tried to escape the bullets were drowned, and remnants of walls have been preserved to show the bullet holes.

The old town has a number of mosques and Hindu temples – the **Durgiana Temple** (16th century), and the new **Vaishnodevi Temple** which imitates the difficult access to the famous Himalayan original in requiring the worshipper to wade awkwardly through water. Northeast of the railway station are the **Ram Bagh** gardens, the Mall and Lawrence Road shopping areas.

## Border crossings

### To Pakistan → *Pakistan time is 30 mins behind IST.*

The road continues west to the Pakistan border. Despite the easing in the political situation in Punjab there are numerous police check posts so motor bikes and cars may be stopped several times. It is better to take Pakistani rupees into Pakistan to avoid being hassled. You can change money in Amritsar (Link Road/Albert Road) or just across the border. The **road** crossing for foreigners is currently through the Wagha check post, 35 km from Amritsar along the attractive and tree-lined GT Rd to **Attari,** the last town before the border, just 2 km from Wagha. From **Amritsar,** frequent minibuses take about one hour to Attari, where you get a rickshaw to Wagha; Taxis Rs 500 (Rs 550 return, to see flag ceremony) take 30 minutes; auto-rickshaw Rs 250 (Rs 350 return). The **train** goes from India (Amritsar) to Pakistan (Lahore) on Monday and Thursday (*Amritsar Lahore Exp, 4607)* at 0700, arrives at Atari (on the border) at 0740, and with four hours scheduled for the border crossing, it's not due to arrive in Lahore until 1615. The train (*Lahore Amritsar Exp, 4608*) returns on Tuesday and Friday at 0800. This train is seriously affected by the state of political relations between India and Pakistan. At the end of November when Sikhs visit shrines in Pakistan the train may be restricted to Sikh pilgrims.When running, it can be a very slow journey with sometimes protracted customs and immigration formalities. Crossing the border by road is more convenient than by train. We highly recommend Footprint's Pakistan Handbook.

### Wagha

The changing of the guards and the ceremonial lowering of the flags ceremony at sundown carried out with great pomp and rivalry, is quite a spectacle. There is much synchronized foot stamping, gate slamming and displays of scorn by colourful soldiers! New viewing galleries have been built but crowds still clamour to get the best view. Women are allowed to get to the front, and there is a VIP section (open to foreign visitors) next to the gate. It is best to get there near closing time though photography is difficult with the setting sun.

It is best to cross in the morning; allow an hour for formalities though it can take longer especially for a bus load (five different passport and customs checks on the Indian side; three on the Pakistan side taking nearly three hours to process 15 travellers). The border check post is nominally open from 1000-1500, Indian time, but is subject to change. Unless you have your own vehicle or are on the new through-coach from Delhi to Lahore, you have to walk from the Indian check post to the Pakistani check post. Indian porters can carry your luggage to the border line, where it is transferred to a Pakistani porter; expect to pay Rs 25-50 after bargaining (Indian side) and Rs 30-50 (Pakistani) respectively. There is a bank within the customs area with foreign currency exchange facilities. Beyond Pakistani immigration and customs, there is a taxi and minicab park; you can usually share one to Lahore (30 km). Amritsar to Lahore usually takes three to five hours though there can be unexpected delays.

A luxury coach runs between Delhi and Lahore, see page 123. At the border, **Niagra Falls Restaurant** has four air-cooled rooms, restaurant and a beer bar.

## Pathankot

Pathankot, a crossroads town and trading centre on the border with Himachal Pradesh, is the gateway to Jammu Kashmir and western Himachal. It is also the starting point for the Kangra Valley Railway but has little else to offer. **Shapur Kandi Fort** (16th century), 13 km to the north, is on the banks of the Ravi River, once the stronghold of the Rajas of Pathan and now no more than a ruin, has a hydro electricity power station at Ranjit Sagar Dam.

## Sleeping

**Amritsar** *p460, map p460*

**A MK**, Dist Shopping Centre, Ranjit Ave, T0183 250 4610, www.mkhotel.com. New hotel in quiet location with 75 good-sized rooms, restaurant, pool on 2nd floor.

**A Mohan International**, Albert Rd, T0183 222 7801, hotel@jla.vsnl.net.in. 65 Indian-style rooms, good restaurants (authentic Punjabi), big, clean pool (non-residents Rs 100), enthusiastic staff

**A Ritz Plaza**, 45, The Mall, T0183 256 2836, http://sarovarparkplaza.com. Well located, recently renovated, 35 classy rooms, stylish restaurant, bar, small pool, large grounds.

**C Mrs Bhandari's Guest House**, 10 Cantonment, northwest of town, T0183 222 8509, http://bhandari_guesthouse.tripod.com. 9 a/c rooms with bath in 1930s building, no TV, has character – Heath Robinson baths, fire places, hot water bottles, sepia prints, 'English' meals, pool (Mar-Nov), large grounds, quiet, attractive, camping (Rs 150), pricey car hire, no credit cards, attentive service. Recommended.

**C CJ International**, opposite the Golden Temple, T0183 254 3478, www.cjhotel.net. 22 clean, modern rooms in only upmarket option close to temple.

**C Golden Tower**, Chowk Fuwara, T0183 2534446, www.hotelgoldentower.com. 20 rooms (15 a/c) with hot showers.

**C Grand**, Queens Rd, opposite train station, T0183 256 2424, www.fhrai.com. 25 modern rooms, some a/c, popular restaurant/bar, good food, beer, nice garden for tea, very friendly management. Recommended.

**C Kishore Castle**, 10 Queens Rd, T0183 240 2818, kishorecastle_hotel@yahoo.com. 25 rooms, room service only, friendly staff.

**C Royal Castle**, 309 Albert Rd (corner of Court Rd), T0183 222 5562, royal_castle@hotmail.com. 28 modern a/c rooms, bathrooms a little tatty, very smart restaurant, bar, coffee shop.

**C Sun City Towers**, Queens Rd, T0183 222 9636, hotelsuncity@comeconnect.com. 24 modern, well-maintained a/c rooms, friendly management, kitchen available for groups.

**C-D Quin's Land**, 3 Queen's Rd, T0183 222 4052. 30 clean rooms with air cooler, 3 a/c, a little dark but reasonable and friendly.

**D-E Sundew**, off Queens Rd (left out of station, then 100 m left through an arch, down narrow lane). Range of rooms, spotless, breakfast by room service, very helpful.

**C-F Sita Niwas**, east of Golden Temple, T0183 254 3092. 100 rooms from very basic to all mod cons, fans or a/c, hot water in buckets, bit run down, room service (cheap Indian meals), can be noisy at dawn (pilgrims), very helpful, friendly manager. Recommended.

**E Lucky**, Mahna Singh Road, near Golden Temple, T0183 254 2175. 16 rooms, some a/c, friendly, one of better cheap options.

**F Rest houses** in /near the Golden Temple. Some free (up to 3 nights), very simple food; please leave a donation. Tobacco, alcohol and drugs are prohibited.

**Local Sikh families** welcome guests, Rs 1500 for two including meals. Contact Time Travels (see Activities and tours).

## Eating

**Amritsar** *p460, map p460*

Eating with pilgrims can be a great experience. The corner of the Mall and Malaviya Rd comes alive with ice cream and fast-food stalls in the evening. *Dhabas* near the station and temple sell local *daal, saag paneer* and mouth-watering *stuffed parathas*.

₹₹₹ **MK, Mohan, Royal Castle**, International. Smart, comfortable, good food.
₹₹₹ **Mrs Bhandari's**, see Sleeping. For unexpected Raj tones, ring ahead for a table.
₹₹ **Burger King**, near Salads Plus.
₹₹ **Crystal**, Queens Rd, T0183 222 5555. Good food, excellent service, pleasant ambience, huge portions.
₹₹ **Domino's Pizza**, 50 Dist Shopping Centre.
₹₹ **Kwality**, The Mall, T0183 222 4849. International. Dated interior, good Indian, pleasantly informal.
₹₹ **Salads Plus**, also South Indian snacks under canopy outside.
₹₹ **Sindhi Coffee House**, Malviya Rd, T0183 256 6039. Unprepossessing exterior conceals dark but super-funky 70s interior, and surprisingly good food.
₹ **Bharawan's**, near Town Hall (excellent breakfast and lunch *thalis*), for good veg.
₹ **Curd stall**, opposite **Ashar Guest House**, sells excellent, safe *lassis*.
₹ **Gagan**, 34 Sita Niwas Rd, near the Golden Temple. Simple, good Indian, not spicey.
₹ **Kesars**, Passian Darwaza, near Durgiana Temple (and elsewhere).
₹ **Neelam**, near Jallianwalla Bagh. Indian, Chinese. Cheap, plentiful and really tasty.

### Cakes

Newish patisseries on Link and Queens rds:
**Bakewell**, Cooper Rd. Good for cakes and fruit puddings.
**La Patisserie**, though not brilliant, offesr good choice.
**Popular Bakery**, Queen's Rd.

## Festivals and events

**Amritsar** *p460, map p460*
**Apr** Baisakhi, for Sikhs, the Hindu New Year marks the day in 1699 Guru Gobind Singh organized the Sikhs into the Khalsa, see page 1343. The vigorous *bhangra* dance is a common sight in the villages. The birth anniversaries of the 10 gurus are observed as holy days and those of Guru Nanak (**Oct/Nov**), and Guru Gobind Singh (**Dec/Jan**), are celebrated as festivals with *Akhand Path* and processions. **Oct/Nov** Diwali Illumination of the Golden Temple, fireworks.

## Activities and tours

**Amritsar** *p460, map p460*
**Time Travels**, 14 Kapoor Plaza, Crystal Sq, T0183 240 0131, www.travelamritsar.com. Organizes tours to Dharamshala, Manali, Shimla etc, local villages, as well s to important Gurudwaras in the state. Very efficient, helpful. Recommended.

## Transport

**Amritsar** *p460, map p460*

### Air

Rajsansi Airport, T0183 259 2166; taxi (Rs 250) or auto-rickshaw (Rs 70) to town. **Indian Airlines**, 39A Court Rd, T0183 221 3393, . **New Delhi**: Tue, Thu, Sat. Also weekly flights to/from London and Birmingham on **Uzbek and Turkmenistan Airways**. Contact in UK T0207-9354775. **Singapore Airlines**, T0183 250 1001

### Bicycle

A bicycle is worthwhile here; hire from Hide Market.

### Bus

Daily (from *OD Swarna Shatabdi, 2029*, 0630, 5½ hrs) services to **Delhi** (tiring 10 hrs); **Dharamshala** (change at Pathankot, 7 hrs); **Dalhousie** (8 hrs), **Jammu** (5 hrs); **Pathankot** (3 hrs); **Chandigarh** (5 hrs); **Shimla** 0530 and 0730, 10 hrs. *Link Travels* luxury coach to Delhi, Jammu (overnight); Jammu, Chandigarh 0600, 1400.

### Rickshaw

**Auto-rickshaw/tonga**: full day, Rs 500, half day Rs 300.

### Taxi

**Local** Non-a/c car from *Time Travels* and *Link Travels* (see Directory): full day, Rs 800, half day Rs 550, Wagha Rs 600. *Link Travels*, outside Golden Temple Clock Tower Car Parking.
**Long distance** To **Delhi** Rs 5,200, **Dharamshala** Rs 2,700.

*For an explanation of the sleeping and eating price codes used in this guide, see inside the front cover. Other relevant information is found in Essentials pages 56-61.*

**Train**

Some trains to and from Jammu don't stop at Pathankot Junction but at Chakki Bank. There is a tempo service between the two stations. T131. Computerized reservations in the Golden Temple Complex (far right of the office), open until 2000 on weekdays..

**Kolkata**: via Lucknow (16½ hrs) and Varanasi (22¼ hrs); *Amritsar-Howrah Mail, 3006*, 1745, 37¼ hrs. **Mumbai (Central)**: *Golden Temple Mail, 2904*, 2130, 32½ hrs; *Paschim Exp, 2926*, 0755, 31½ hrs. **New Delhi**: *Shatabdi Exp, 2014*, 0515, 5¾ hrs; *Flying Mail, 4648*, 1130, 9 hrs (OD); *Amritsar Shatabdi, 2032*, 1705, 5¾ hrs. **Pathankot**: *Ravi Exp, 4633*, 0915, 2¼ hrs ; *Muri Exp, 8101*, 0555, 2¾ hrs. See 'Border crossing' below for details of train to Lahore (Pakistan).

**Pathankot** *p466*

**Bus**

Bus and railway stations are 100 m apart. Buses to all important towns nearby.

**Taxi**

Shared taxis available at the railway station if the prospect of a hill bus journey fails to thrill.

**Train**

For main connections see page 467. A spectacular narrow gauge Kangra Valley Railway, built in 1928, runs to Jogindernagar, 56 km northwest of Mandi in HP. See page 523. **Baijnath Paprola**: *3PB Passenger*, 0835, 5½ hrs. **Baijnath and Jogindernagar**: *3PBJ Passenger*, 0920, 6½ and 8¾ hrs. **Amritsar**: *Hatia Exp* 8102, 1645, 2¾ hrs and to **Delhi**: 12 hrs.

## Directory

**Amritsar** *p460, map p460*

**Bank** Punjab Bank, next door to Golden Temple, quick.Tourist office, opposite the railway station, T0183 240 2452.

# Himachal Pradesh

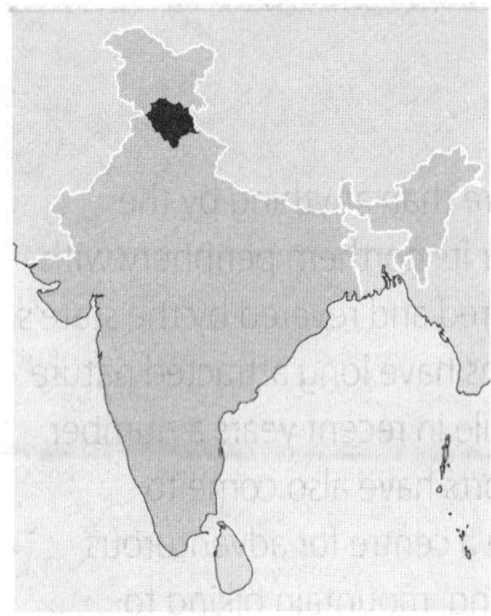



## Footprint features

# Introduction

Himachal Pradesh is defined more than anything by the mighty Himalayas, towering over its northern periphery with implacable dominance, both feared and revered by the state's sparse population. The mountains have long attracted nature lovers, climbers and trekkers, while in recent years a number of more adrenaline-inducing sports have also come to prominence; Manali has become a centre for adventurous activities; from heli-skiing to rafting, mountain biking to paragliding and horse riding there's a huge range on offer. The arrival of the Tibetans after the Chinese invasion of Tibet in 1959 has added attractions of an altogether more mellow manner. Dharamsala, home to his Holiness the Dalai Lama, has become a mecca for the more spiritual pursuits; many come to follow courses in yoga, meditation, Buddhism, or to learn about the Tibetan cause.



Some of the state's finest mountain views can be seen from Dalhousie, a popular hill station during the Raj and today a quaint if anachronistic reminder of how the British used to build their homes. Himachal's other Raj relic, and its capital city, Simla, is part quaint English village, part traffic, touts and mayhem. Arriving via the 'toy train' from Kangra is by far the best way and the scenery almost painfully picturesque. Although most people come to Himachal to see the mountains, the plains also have much to offer. Kangra Valley is especially pretty, with charming villages connected by quiet, windy roads. Those in search of more rugged adventures should head for Kinnaur, Spiti and Lahaul, accessible only in the summer when the snow melts on the higher passes, meaning they can be crossed by road, giving access to the barren but spectacular scenery beyond. This area also forms the start of the incomparable Manali-Leh road, the highway from Himachal to Ladakh and one of the world's best road trips.

# ★ Don't miss...

1 **Simla** Stroll around the faded streets of Simla, page 473.
2 **Bhimakali Temple** Climb behind Bhimakali Temple in Sarahan for a picturesque view, page 479.
3 **Chos Khor Gompa** For an immense sense of the spiritual, this monastery at Tabo is unsurpassed in this region, page 488.
4 **Kullu Valley and Naggar** Travel through the apple orchards in the Kullu Valley to reach Naggar with its interesting castle, page 500.
5 **Manali to Leh road** If you have a head for heights, take this road and stop at the Rohtang Pass for spectacular views of precipitous cliffs, page 513.
6 **Dharamshala** Many head here, for its numerous attractions: as home of the Dalai Lama, wonderful trekking or for the spectacular journey on the mountain railway, page 518.
7 **Pragpur** India's first 'heritage village', it gives an excellent idea of how traditional rural life has been lived by in this area for the last few hundred years, page 523.

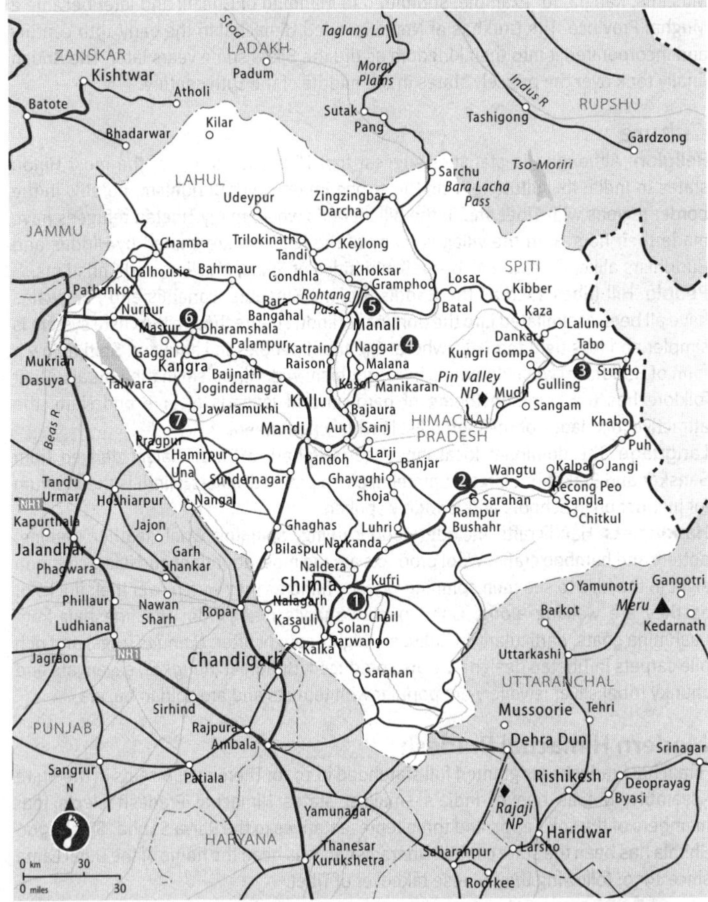

# Background → *Population: over 6 mn. Area: 55,673 sq km.*

## The land

**Geography** Himachal Pradesh (Himalayan Province) is wholly mountainous, with peaks rising to over 6,700 m. The **Dhaula Dhar** range runs from the northwest to the Kullu Valley. The **Pir Panjal** is farther north and parallel to it. High, remote, arid and starkly beautiful, Lahul and Spiti are sparsely populated. They contrast strongly with the well-wooded lushness of those areas to the south of the Himalayan axis.

**Climate** At lower altitudes the summers can be very hot and humid whereas the higher mountains are permanently under snow. In Shimla, the Kangra Valley, Chamba and the Kullu Valley, the monsoon arrives in mid-June and lasts until mid-September, giving periods of very heavy rain; in the Kullu Valley there can be sudden downpours in March and early April. To the north, Lahul and Spiti are beyond the influence of the monsoon. Consequently they share the high altitude desert climatic characteristics of Ladakh.

## History

Originally the region was inhabited by a tribe called the Dasas who were later assimilated by the Aryans. From the 10th-century parts were occupied by the Muslims. Kangra, for example, submitted to Mahmud of Ghazni and later became a Mughal Province. The Gurkhas of Nepal invaded Himachal in the early 19th century and incorporated it into their kingdom as did the Sikhs some years later. The British finally took over the princely states in the middle of the 19th century.

## Culture

**Religion** Although the statistics suggest that Himachal is one of the most Hindu states in India, its culture reflects the strong influence of Buddhism, notably in the border regions with Tibet and in the hill stations where many Tibetan refugees have made their homes. In the villages many of the festivals are shared by Hindus and Buddhists alike. There are also small minorities of Sikhs, Muslims and Christians.

**People** Hill tribes such as the Gaddis, Gujars, Kinnaurs, Lahaulis and Pangwalas have all been assimilated into the dominant Hindu culture though the caste system is simpler and less rigid than elsewhere. The tribal peoples in Lahul and Spiti follow a form of Buddhism while Kinnauris mix Buddhism with Hinduism in their rituals. Their folklore has the common theme of heroism and legends of love and Natti, the attractive folk dance of the high hills, is widely performed.

**Language** The dominant local language is Pahari, a Hindi dialect derived from Sanskrit and Prakrit but largely unintelligible to plains dwellers. Hindi is the medium for instruction in schools and is widely spoken.

**Handicrafts** Handicrafts include wood carving, spinning wool, leather tanning, pottery and bamboo crafts. Wool products are the most abundant and it is a common sight in the hills to see men spinning wool by hand as they watch over their flocks or as they are walking along. Good quality shawls made from the fine hair from pashmina goats, particularly in Kullu, are highly sought after. *Namdas* (rugs) and rich pile carpets in Tibetan designs are also produced. Buddhist *thangkas*, silverware and chunky tribal silver jewellery are popular with tourists and are sold in bazars.

## Modern Himachal Pradesh

Himachal Pradesh was granted full statehood in 1970. There are 68 seats in the State Assembly, but as one of India's smallest states Himachal Pradesh elects four members of the Lok Sabha and three representatives to the Rajya Sabha. Since 1966 Shimla has been the state capital. Dharamshala has been the home of the Dalai Lama since 1959, following the Chinese takeover of Tibet.

**Current political developments** Even though Himachal is quite close to Delhi, it still has the feel of a political backwater. News from the state rarely makes the national newspapers, and while the contest for representation in the Lok Sabha and in the Assembly is intense, the two-horse race between Congress and the BJP rarely attracts much attention. The Congress party gained power in March 2003 under Chief Minister Shri Virbhadra Singh, his third appointment to the post after earlier tenures covering much of the 1980s and 1990s.

# Southern Himachal

*Southern Himachal offers an intriguing mix of experiences. Shimla's colonial past, with its little England architecture and anachronistic air, seems to be fighting for survival amidst the modern day bustle of Himachal's capital city. The area around Shimla offers stunning views of the foothills of the Himalayas, and plenty of attractive places to stay nestled amongst the cool pine forests. This area is also the gateway to the altogether more rugged landscapes of Kinnaur, a world far less affected by the advance of time. For trekking information, see page 534.* » *For Sleeping, Eating and other listings, see pages 480-484.*

## Shimla

→ *Phone code: 0177. Colour map 1, grid B3. Population: approx 150,000. Altitude: 2,213 m.*

Once a charming hill station and the summer capital of the British, an air of decay hangs over many of Shimla's Raj buildings, strung out for about 3 km along the ridgeline. Below them a maze of narrow streets, bazars and shabby 'local' houses with corrugated iron roofs cling to the hillside. Some find it delightfully quaint and less spoilt than other Himalayan hill stations. There are still some lovely walks, lined with magnificent pines and cedars giving a beautifully fresh scent to the air.

### Ins and outs

**Getting there** Despite the romance of the narrow gauge railway from Kalka, see page 477, most people get to Shimla by bus or taxi as it is so much quicker. The bus stand and the station are on Cart Road, where porters and hotel touts jostle to take your luggage up the steep hill to a hotel. If you are staying on the western side of town it is worth getting off the bus at the railway station. Buses from the east, including Rampur and Kinnaur, stop at the Rivoli bus stand. Shimla (Jabbarhatti) airport has a coach (Rs 50) in season, and taxis (Rs 400-500) for transfer.

**Getting around** The Mall can only be seen on foot, it takes about half an hour to walk from the Viceroy's Lodge to Christ Church. The main traffic artery is Cart Road which continues past the station to the Main Bus Stand, taxi rank and the two-stage lift which goes to the Mall above (Rs 5). The Victory Tunnel cuts through from Cart Road to the north side of the hill. » *See Transport, page 483, for further details.*

**Climate** October-November are very pleasant, with warm days and cool nights. December-February is cold and there are snowfalls. March-April are changeable, storms are not infrequent and the air can feel very chilly. Avoid May-June, the height of the Indian tourist season prior to the monsoon.

### Sights

Shimla is strung out on a long crescent-shaped ridge which connects a number of hilltops from which there are good views of the snow-capped peaks to the north: Jakhu (2,453 m), Prospect Hill (2,176 m), Observatory Hill (2,148 m), Elysium Hill (2,255 m) and Summer Hill (2,103 m). For the British, the only way of beating the hot weather on the plains in May and June was to move to hill stations which they endowed with mock Tudor houses, churches, clubs, parks with bandstands of English county towns, and a main street invariably called the Mall.

**Christ Church** (1844), on the open area of The Ridge, dominates the eastern end of town. Consecrated in 1857, a clock and porch were added later. The original chancel window, designed by Lockwood Kipling, Rudyards father, is no longer there. The mock tudor **library** building (circa 1910) is next door. The Mall joins The Ridge at Kipling's **'Scandal Point'**, where today groups gather to exchange gossip. Originally the name referred to the stir caused by the supposed 'elopement' of a lady from the Viceregal Lodge and a dashing Patiala prince after they arranged a rendezvous here.

The **Gaiety Theatre** (1887) and the **Town Hall** (circa 1910) are reminiscent of the 'Arts and Crafts' style, as well as the timbered **General Post Office** (1886). Beyond, to the west, is the **Grand Hotel**. Further down you pass the sinister looking **Gorton Castle**, designed by Sir Samuel Swinton Jacob, which was once the Civil Secretariat. A road to the left leads to the railway station, while one to the right goes to Annandale, the racecourse and cricket ground. The Mall leads to the rebuilt **Cecil Hotel**. On Observatory Hill (the watershed), the **Viceregal Lodge** (1888) was built for Lord Dufferin in the Elizabethan style but with an indoor tennis court. Now the **Rashtrapati Niwas** ⓘ *1000-1630, Rs 10 including a very brief guided tour*, it houses the Indian Institute of Advanced Study (IIAS) and stands in large grounds with good views of the mountains. Reminders of its British origins include a gatehouse, a chapel and the meticulously polished brass fire hydrants imported from Manchester. Inside, you may only visit the main reception rooms and the library which are lined from floor to ceiling with impressive teak panelling. It is a long uphill walk from the gate.

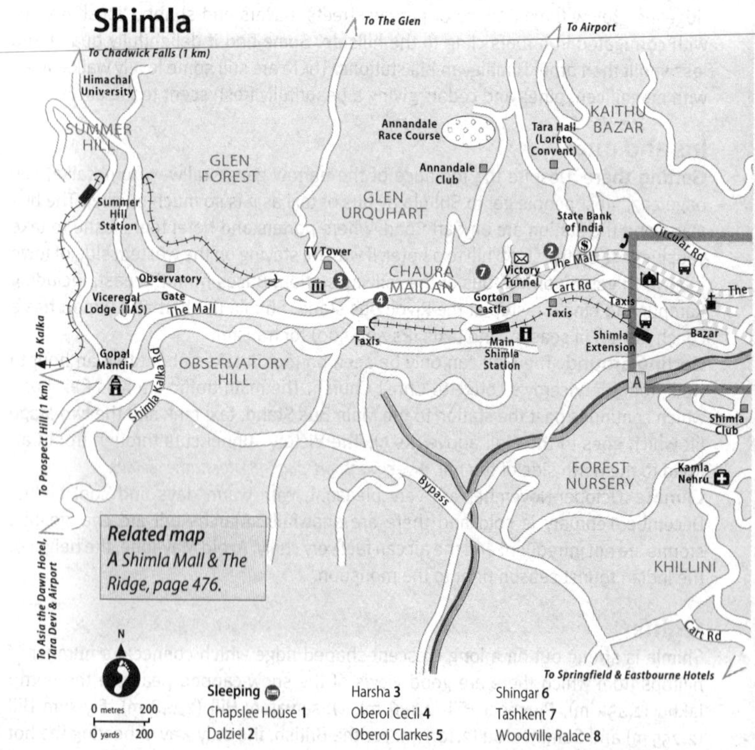


*Related map*
*A Shimla Mall & The Ridge, page 476.*

## The seasonal move of government

So beneficial were the effects of the cooler mountain air that Shimla, 'discovered' by the British in 1819, became the summer seat of government from 1865 to 1939. The capital was shifted there from Calcutta and later from Delhi (1912 onwards) and all business was transacted from this cool mountain retreat.

Huge baggage trains were needed to transport the mountains of files and the whole operation cost thousands of rupees. At the end of the season back they would all leave.

Women heavily outnumbered men, as wives of many British men who ran the empire escaped to the hills for long periods. Army officers spent their leave there. Social life in hill stations became a round of parties, balls, formal promenades along the Mall and brief flirtations.

**Himachal State Museum** ⓘ *closed Mon, 1000-1330, 1400-1700, free*, near Chaura Maidan, is a 30-minute walk west from the GPO along the Mall; then a short climb from the Harsha Hotel. Small, with a good sculpture collection and miniatures from the Kangra School; also contemporary art including work by Roerich, costumes, jewellery, bronzes and textiles. Well labelled.

### Walks

There are several pleasant walks in and around Shimla. **Jakhu Temple** on a hill with excellent views (2,455 m), dedicated to Hanuman the monkey god, is 2 km from Christ Church. Walking sticks (handy for warding off monkeys, which can be vicious – keep your distance and all food out of sight and reach) are available at *chai* shops at the start of the ascent.

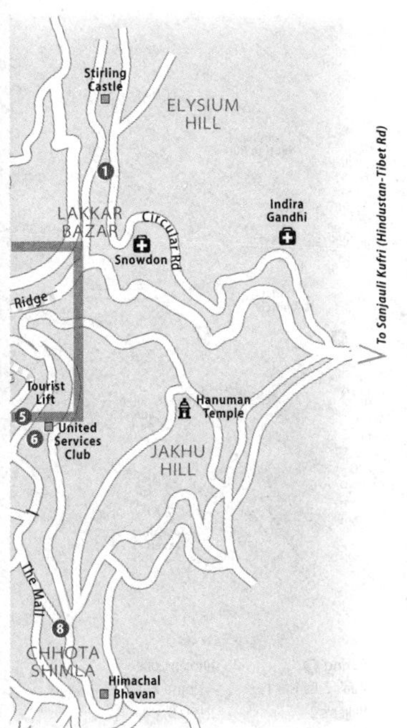


**The Glen** (1,830 m), to the northwest, is a 4-km walk from the centre past the **Cecil Hotel. Summer Hill** (1,983 m), a pleasant 'suburb' 5 km from town, is a stop on the Shimla-Kalka railway. **Chadwick Falls** (1,586 m), 3 km further, drops 67 m during the monsoons.

**Prospect Hill** (2,175 m) is 5 km from The Ridge and a 20-minute walk from Boileauganj to the west. **Tara Devi** (1,851 m), with a hilltop temple, 11 km southwest from the railway station, can also be reached by car or train.

## Around Shimla

### Kufri

About 16 km from Shimla, at 2,500 m, Kufri hosts a winter sports festival in January which includes the National Snow Statue Competition. Don't expect European or American resort standards though. There are some attractions around and about the town. At **Danes Folly** (2,550 m), 5 km away, is a government run orchard. A 10-minute walk uphill takes you to a mini zoo of Himalayan wildlife. **Mahasu peak** ⓘ *bus, Rs 15,* 20 minutes from a path behind the Kufri Resort cottages, offers fabulous mountain views on a clear day and there is a small but interesting temple at the start of the walk. The best time to visit is in January and February.

## Chharabra

Chharabra is an enjoyable 3-km forest walk down from Kufri. The Wildflower Hall which once stood here was the residence of **Lord Kitchener,** Commander-in-Chief of the Indian Army. The original building was replaced; its successor was converted into a hotel which burnt down in 1993. Oberoi has opened a new luxury hotel.

## Naldera

Off the Hindusthan-Tibet road, 26 km north of Shimla, Naldera has a nine-hole golf course, possibly the oldest in India, and one of the highest in the world and the beautiful Mahung temple. The colourful **Sipi Fair** in June attracts crowds from surrounding villages who sell handicrafts.

## Chail

In a superb forest setting with fine snow views, 45 km southeast of Shimla; off the NH22, Chail was once the Maharaja of Patiala's summer capital. Built on three adjacent hills, it is claimed to have the country's highest cricket ground at 2,444 m, a 2-km walk from the bus stand! The old palace on Rajgarh Hill has been converted to a hotel while the old residency, 'Snow View', and a Sikh temple stand on the other two hills. The **Chail Sanctuary,** once a private hunting reserve, is popular with birdwatchers. A cheer pheasant breeding programme was started here in 1988. It is

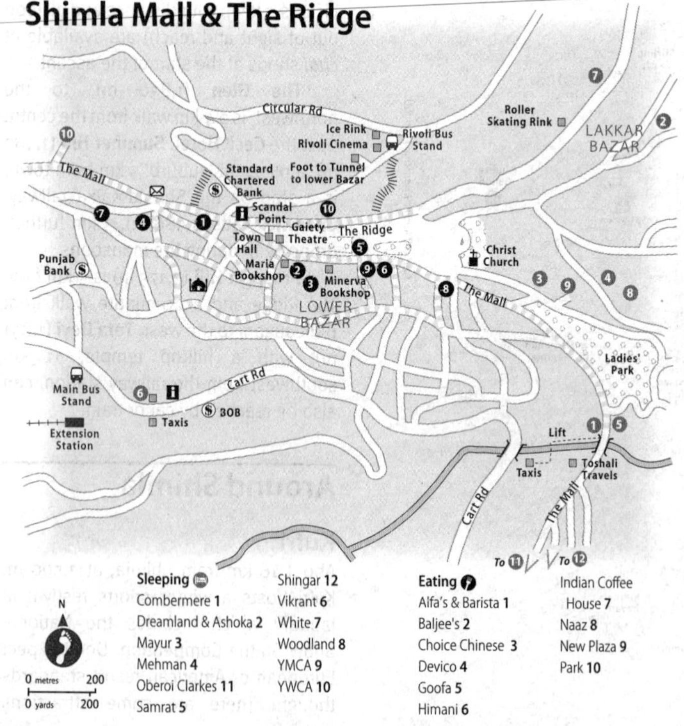

an idyllic spot but not when the weekend day-trippers descend on the tiny resort. You can take the bus from Shimla, taking 2½ hours.

## Kalka

Kalka is the terminus for the narrow gauge railway from Shimla. The Kalka-Shimla line (0.76 m), completed in 1903, runs 97 km from Kalka in the foothills to Shimla at over 2,000 m. The magnificent journey takes just over five hours. The steepest gradient is 1 in 33; there are 107 tunnels covering 8 km and 969 bridges over 3 km. Order a meal in advance at Kalka or Shimla station. See below.

## Nalagarh

The area around Nalagarh was once ruled by the Chandela Rajputs. The fort has wonderful views above an estate of forests and orchards and is built on five levels around manicured grassy courts. Originally built in the 15th century; the Diwan-i-Khas (1618) is now the Banquet Hall. The present Raja has opened his home to guests. You can request the Nalagarh Resort hotel pick-up from Ropar (20 km) or Kalka (40 km).

# Old Hindustan Tibet Road

→ *Colour map 1, grid B3 and 4.*

The Old Hindustan Tibet road runs east from Shimla to the Tibetan border through a landscape of lush tropical valleys, snow-clad peaks and precipitous gorges. Connecting a string of prosperous looking farms, villages and towns, it passes through terraced slopes covered with orchards before entering the high altitude deserts of Spiti. As the narrow road winds even deeper towards the Tibetan border its unprotected sides plunge hundreds of metres to the roaring monsoon-swollen River Sutlej below, grasping at huge boulders brought down by thundering landslides into the gloomy gorges. By bus or jeep, this road is not for the faint-hearted.

*The road may be severely damaged in the rains.*

## Ins and outs

Inner Line Permits are needed for travel close to the Tibetan border, essentially the area between Kaza and Jangi, but are easy to get to. Overnight stay is not permitted in Puh, Khabo and Sumdo. Rules may be further relaxed, so check with the tourist office. Permits are issued free to individuals, for seven days from the date (easily renewable for three days at Kaza or Recong Peo). Take three passport photos, valid passport, two copies of the back page of passport and Indian Visa and complete the form from Sub-Divisional Magistrate's office (SDM) in Shimla, T0177265 5988, Recong Peo T01786 222 452 or Kaza T01906 222 212 (difficult in the last). Permits also available (in theory) from: Resident Comissioner of Himachal Pradesh ⓘ *Himachal Bhavan, 27 Sikandra Rd, New Delhi T011 2371 6574*, and other magistrates officers. Permits say "no overnight halts and no photography" though rules have been relaxed considerably. In Shimla, travel agents charge Rs 150. In Kaza, you need the additional 'No Objection' certificate from the Chief of Police – a mere formality of a stamp and signature. In Recong Peo, the whole process takes about an hour (which may include 'chai' or breakfast with the SDM). Accommodation is limited to simple rest houses, lodges or tents. In some places enterprising local families are opening their modest homes to paying guests. Local village shops often stock canned food and bottled water. It is virtually impossible to get foreign exchange in this area.

## Narkanda

The small market town at 2,700 m occupies a superb position on the col. The town offers a base from which to ski however the skiing does not compare with that found in western resorts. Enquire at Marketing Office in Shimla for skiing excursions in winter and seven day beginners course (Rs 4,500-5,000).

## Nirath

The road drops sharply through woodland interspersed with apple orchards from Narkanda, down to Kingel from where it zig-zags down to Sainj. The seasonal route is best by 4WD though buses cover this route very carefully. Some 5 km beyond Sainj there are superb views both across the valley, and of a wall of eroded outwash deposits at least 50 m thick. The main road passes through Nirath where there is a **Surya Temple** believed to date from the eighth century which still has some fine carving preserved on the outer walls and has carved wooden panels within. At an altitude of between 800-900 m the Sutlej Valley towards Rampur has a subtropical summer climate, with mango trees and bananas replacing apples.

## Rampur Bushahr

This is one of Himachal's most important market towns. **Padam Palace** (1920s), opposite the bus stand, once the residence of the Raja, has interesting carved wooden panels and wall murals, but is difficult to enter. **Sat Narain Temple** in the main bazar (1926) has a beautiful but decaying façade. **Lavi Fair** (November) draws large crowds of colourful hill people who bring their produce – handicrafts, carpets, rugs, fruit and nuts and animals – to the special market. There are sporting competitions in the day, and dancing and making music around bonfires after dark.

## Rampur to Sarahan

From Rampur the highway enters one of the most exciting, and geologically active, stretches of road in the region. During the rains the Sutlej River is a surging torrent of muddy water, dropping over 450 m in under 30 km and passing through gorges and deeply incised valleys. Although an ancient trade route, the road is comparatively recent and is constantly being upgraded particularly in connection with the Nathpa-Jhakhri HEP scheme, with a 28-km long tunnel from **Nathpa**, near **Wangtu**, to **Jhakhri**, about 10 km beyond Rampur. When completed this will be one of the largest Hydel schemes in the world. The blasting both for the shafts and for road widening has further destabilized the already landslide-prone hillsides and during the rains the



## Around Shimla

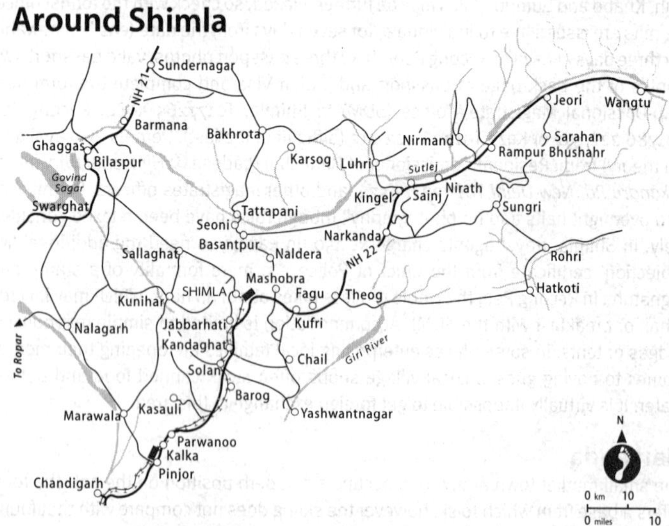

### Human sacrifice in the Himalaya

Human sacrifice was practised for centuries in the original Bhimakali temple in Sarahan. During the 16th and 17th centuries this was carried out with elaborate rituals. The sacrificial victim would be kept in the adjoining Narasimha Temple. After the ritual offering his blood would be placed on Bhimakali's tongue for her to 'drink' and would then be used to wash the feet of a second deity Ushadevi. The priest would also place a mark of blood on the forehead of each worshipper. The sacrificed head would finally be thrown into the Sutlej river and the body into the well in the courtyard which is now blocked.

road may be blocked. Blockages are usually cleared within hours, though travelling times are wholly unpredictable. You also need a strong stomach, both for the main road and for diversions, especially up the Baspa Valley to Sangla. Some 9 km west of Jeori the river passes through a dramatic gorge. On the north side of the river isolated tiny pockets of cultivated land cling to the hillside. **Jeori** is the junction for Sarahan, 21 km south, an hour away. There are several provisions stores to pick up the basics here since Sarahan has very limited supplies.

## Sarahan → *Phone code: 01782. Colour map 1, grid B3. Population: 1,200. Altitude: 2,165 m.*

An important market for traders of neighbouring regions. It is an attractive town, surrounded by high peaks, with a pheasant breeding centre nearby. The bazar is interesting: friendly villagers greet travellers, shops sell flowers, bright red and gold scarves and other offerings for worshippers among local produce, fancy goods, clothes and jewellery. It is also a stop on the trekkers' route.

Sarahan was the old capital of the local Rampur Bushahr rulers and has a palace complex containing the strikingly carved wood-bonded **Bhimakali Temple** (rebuilt circa 1927), in a mixture of Hindu and Buddhist styles. The two temples stand on a slope among apple and apricot orchards behind the bazar. The Bhimakali is dedicated to Durga as the destroyer of the *asuras* (demons) and has a Brahmin priest in attendance. Plan for an early morning visit to the temple to see morning prayers; evening prayers are around 1900. Leave shoes and leather objects with the attendant and wear the saffron cap offered to you before entering. You may only photograph the outside of the temples. It is worth climbing around the back of the complex for a picturesque view.

According to some sources the ancient temple on the right (closed for safety reasons) is many centuries old (see box). Built in traditional timber-bonded style it has white-washed dry stone and rubble masonry alternating with horizontal deodar or spruce beams to withstand earthquakes. The upper floors have balconies and windows with superb ornamental woodcarving; the silver repoussée work doors are also impressive. The first floor has a 200-year-old gold image of goddess Bhimkali which is actively worshipped only during the **Dasara festival** when animals and birds are sacrificed in the courtyard, while on the second floor daily early morning *puja* is carried out to a second image. The sacrificial altar and the old well are in the courtyard with three other shrines. The palace of the Rampur rajas behind the temple has a drawing room with ornate furniture and a painted ceiling; the caretaker may let you in.

**Pheasant Breeding Centre** ⓘ *summer 0830-1830, winter 0930-1630, free*, on a hill, a 1-km strenuous walk from the main road, on a wooded trail, has Monal, Khalij, Western Tragopan and other varities in cages.

A pilgrimage route encircles **Shrikhand Mahadev** peak (5,227 m), which takes pilgrims seven days to go round. On a clear day you get fantastic panoramic views of the snow-covered peaks.

## Sleeping

**Shimla** *p473, maps p474 and p476*
Prices soar in May and Jun when modest accommodation can be difficult to find especially if you arrive after midday, so book ahead. Some close off-season, whilst those that remain open may offer discounts of 30-50%. From the railway or bus station it is a stiff climb up to hotels on or near the Ridge. Porters available (agree about Rs 20 per heavy bag). Go to the hotel of your choice.

**LL-L Oberoi Cecil**, Chaura Maidan (quiet end of the Mall), T0177 280 4848, www.oberoihotels.com. 79 sumptious rooms, colonial grandeur on the edge of town, with superb views, beautifully renovated, stylishly furnished, good restaurant, special ultra modern pool, full-board. Recommended.

**AL Chapslee House** (Heritage), Lakkar Bazar, T0177 280 2542, www.chapslee.com. 6 suites only, charming, full of character, large grounds, exquisite interior, good views, excellent meals (disappointing *thali* though) and excellent service, if you can get in.

**AL Oberoi Clarkes**, The Mall, near Lift, T0177 265 1010, clarkes@sancharnet.com. 39 large, comfortable rooms, those with mountain views at rear may suffer from traffic noise at night, front rooms with town views quieter, impressive dining room (good buffets), pleasant bar, has character, well run but lacks some **A** facilities, no pool, front has had a facelift, full-board only.

**AL-B Combermere**, 2 entrances, next to the Lift at top and bottom, T0177 265 1246, www.hotelcombermere.com. 40 decent rooms (including penthouses) on 6 levels (partly served by lift), well located, friendly, efficient, very helpful, pleasant terrace café and bar, games room, central heating/a/c, super deluxe rooms worth the extra Rs 200.

**A Eastbourne**, Khillini, 5 km from bus stand, T0177 262 3664, www.eastbourneindia.com. 28 alpine style rooms (noisy near reception), good restaurant, flower-filled gardens in wooded setting, well furnished, friendly, long way from town but free daily shuttle.

**A Springfields** (Quality Inn), opposite Tibetan School, Chhota Shimla, T0177 262 1297, www.ushashriramhotels.com. 11 huge, light and airy rooms with modern bathrooms in old Maharaja's bungalow "where staff refused to be tipped"! Superb views, lawns, restaurant, very professionally run.

**A Woodville Palace** (Heritage), Raj Bhavan Rd, The Mall, T0177 262 4038 www.woodvillepalace.com. 14 rooms (variable), some good **A** suites with period furniture (freezing in winter), dining hall worth visiting for eclectic mixture of portraits, weapons and hunting trophies! (non-residents on advance notice), owned by Raja of Jubbal's family and featured in Jewel in the Crown, good views, spacious, large grounds, one of the quietest.

**A-B Peterhoff** (HPTDC), Chaura Maidan, near All India Radio, T0177 265 2538, www.hptdc.nic.in. 35 sombre but spacious rooms in very quiet location with beautiful lawn terrace and friendly, helpful staff.

**B Harsha**, The Mall, next to State Museum, T0177 265 8441, hotelharsha @hotmail.com. 21 rooms, restaurant, rather uninspired but friendly service, pleasant and quiet location.

**B Leela**, near Winter Field, Cart Rd, T0177 265 7187. 27 very modern rooms in new hotel in central location with car park.

**B Shingar**, The Mall, T0177 265 2881, stylco @sify.com. 30 clean rooms, restaurant, TV, car park and pleasant garden.

**C Dalziel**, The Mall, above Station, T0177 265 2394, hoteldalziel@hotmail.com. 15 clean enough, comfy, creaky rooms with bath (hot water) in heritage building, Indian meals, not bad value, prices depend on size of TV!

**C Mayur**, above Christ Church, T0177 265 2393, hotel_mayur@vsnl.com. 28 70s style rooms, some with mountain views, some with tub, good restaurant but check bill, modern and clean, lift, helpful staff.

**C Mehman**, above Christ Church, T0177 281 3692. 21 rooms (some with mirrored ceilings),

*For an explanation of the sleeping and eating price codes used in this guide, see inside the front cover. Other relevant information is found in Essentials pages 56-61.*

plumbing suspect, modern, very clean, great views from the front, very helpful staff.

**C Samrat Regency**, The Mall, T0177 265 8572, www.samrat regency.com. 20 small rooms, restaurant, helpful.

**C-D White**, Lakkar Bazar, T0177 265 5276, www.hotelwhiteshimla.com. 25 basic but clean, well-maintained rooms with bath, TV, some with good views and balcony.

**C-E Woodland**, Daisy Bank, The Ridge, T0177 281 1002, 21 rooms, some wood-panelled, downstairs with views, some with bath, avoid noisy downstairs rooms near Reception, friendly, good room service, safe luggage storage, off-season bargain.

**D Dreamland**, The Ridge, T0177 280 6897, www.hoteldreamlandshimla.com. 31 clean rooms that vary in size and quality of bathroom, check first, plus good views.

**D-E YMCA**, The Ridge, above Christ Church, T0177 265 0021. 40 rooms (**D** in annexe best with bath), clean linen, hot water in mornings, clean bathrooms on 2nd floor, avoid west side near noisy cinema, mediocre meals (breakfast included), quiet, relaxed, popular but very efficient/institutionalized, gym and billiards.

**E-F Vikrant**, near the bus terminal, T0177 265 5334. 23 clean rooms, shared bath (bucket hot water), some attached, TV, efficient.

**E-F YWCA**, Constantia, T0177 280 3081. 11 clean if musty rooms for both sexes, heavily booked May-Jun, off-season discounts, water at certain times of day, superb position, safe and very good value, but now starting to crumble slightly.

**Kufri** *p475*

**A Kufri Holiday Resort**, T0177 264 8300, www.kufriholidayresort.com. 30 rooms and 8 modern cottages (2 and 3 bedrooms), limited hot water, cold in winter, but attractive design and setting with flower-filled gardens, outstanding views from cottages above and good walks.

**C Himachal Holidays**, Zero Mile, T0177 264 8663, himachalholidays@rediffmail.com. 20 rooms plus 2 restaurants and a bar, also organizes local treks and tours.

**Chharabra** *p476*

**LL Wildflower Hall**, T0177 264 8585, www.oberoihotels.com. Former residence of Lord Kitchener, retains period exterior but has been completely refurbished inside. 87 sumptuous rooms, beautifully decorated, mountain views, good restaurants and lovely gardens surrounded by deodar forest with beautifully peaceful walks, plus usual five star facilities including an indoor heated pool.

**Naldehra** *p476*

**A The Chalets Naldehra**, Durgapur Village, T0177 274 7715, www.chaletsnaldehra.com. 14 alpine style pine chalets plus restaurant and a wide range of outdoor activities including world's highest golf course.

**B Koti Resort**, T0177 274 0177, www.koti resort.net. 40 modern if slightly spartan rooms in beautifully located hotel surrounded by deodar forest, friendly manager, very relaxing.

**C Golf Glade (HPTDC)**, T0177 274 7739, www.hptdc.nic.in. 5 rooms, 7 log huts, restaurant, bar and all golfing requirements including clubs and instructors.

**Chail** *p476*

**A Toshali Royal View Resort**, Shilon Bagh (5 km outside Chail), T0177 273 3470, www.toshaliroyal view.com. 77 modern rooms in this huge alpine style lodge, great views from dining terrace, friendly staff.

**A-B Chail Palace**, T01792 248 141, www.hptdc.nic.in. 19 rooms and 3 suites in old stone-built mansion; avoid basement rooms 21, 22, 23, dark, dingy wooden chalets but others OK, billiards, tennis, orchards, well maintained lawns and gardens, slightly institutional feel, interesting museum.

**B-C Rashi Resorts**, T01792 248 732, vashimap@bol.net.in. Modern hotel with nice enough rooms, good views from balconies, friendly, unassuming staff.

**D Himneel**, T01792 248 141, www.hptdc. nic.in 16 rooms, restaurant, modest but full of character. **Kailash** restaurant serves good value breakfasts and lunches.

**Kalka** *p477*

**F Retiring Rooms**, good for early morning departures, can be in demand in season so reserve ahead at Kalka or Shimla.

If using your own transport, there are many hotels, guesthouses and *dhabas* along the Kalka-Shimla road. Kasauli is an attractive hill resort with a distinctly English feel, 16 km

off the main road with a few hotels, notably:
**A Kasauli Resorts**, T01792 273 651, www.kasauliresort.net. 20 luxurious rooms in a modern, upmarket development in the hills.
**B Alasia**, T01792 272 008, www.hotzinc.com. 13 rooms in hugely atmospheric Raj era hotel, remarkably authentic English cuisine, impeccable staff.

**Nalagarh** *p477*
**A Nalagarh Resort** , T01795 223 179, www.nalagarh.com. 15 comfortable rooms (some suites), with modern baths, traditional furniture, good food but buffets only, small pool, tennis, rural surroundings, plenty of atmosphere. Recommended. Book ahead.

**Rampur Bushahr** *p478*
**B-D Bushehar Regency**, 2 km short of Rampur on NH22, T01782 234 103. 20 rooms, some a/c, well positioned, restaurant, huge lawn, bar nearby.
**E-F Bhagwati**, below bus stand near river, T01782 233 117. 24 clean rooms with bath (hot water), TV, restaurant, friendly.
**E-F Narendra**, Indira Market near bus stand on the river, T01782 233 155. 15 rooms with bath, TV, restaurant, bar. Others shared bath.
**F Bodh**, near bus stand, (01782)-233 302. 5 rooms, dorm, Tibetan/Chinese restaurant, friendly, helpful owner.

**Sarahan** *p479*
**C-D Srikhand** (HPTDC), T01782 274 234, www.hptdc.nic.in, on a superb hilltop site, overlooking the Sutlej valley, Srikhand peak and the range beyond. 19 rooms with bath and hot water (3 large with balcony, 8 smaller with views, 4 in annexe cheaper), dorm (Rs 75), 2-bedroom royal cottage, restaurant but limited menu.
**E Sangrika**, near Police Assistance, T01782 274 491, F278 243. 8 rooms with Indian toilets, 6 planned with western toilets on 1st floor, family run, home-cooked meals.
**E-F Temple rooms**, Rs 100-300, dorm Rs 25. New guesthouses opening. *Dhabas* in town have basic food (rice, daal and snacks).

## Eating

**Shimla** *p473, maps p474 and p476*
The first four options listied are situated in hotels.
TTT **Cecil**, atmospheric, plush, modernized.
TTT **Chapslee**, old-fashioned.
TTT **Clarke's**, good set lunch but painful classical music at dinner.
TTT **Woodville Palace**, intimate.
TT **Alfa's**, modern interior, range of continental dishes in addition to good *thalis*, courteous service.
TT **Guptajee's Vaishnav Bhojanalaya**, 62 Middle Bezar. Excellent vegetarian Indian.
TT **Himani**, The Mall. Indian. Restaurant above, tasty Mughlai, bar below, average food but informal atmosphere and excellent service compensates.
TT **Nalini**, The Mall, International. Pleasant, good service, 0830-2200; also ice creams and sweets counters.
T **Choice**, Middle Bazar. As the name reveals, there's a wide choice. Chinese.
T **Indian Coffee House**, The Mall. International. South Indian snacks, excellent coffee, some western dishes, old world feel, uniformed waiters, spartan and dim.
T **Malook's**, opposite Gaiety Theatre, down steps. Good Tibetan dishes (excellent *thukpas* and noodles).
T **New Plaza**, 60/61 Middle Bazar, down steps. Excellent value, friendly, simple but clean, serves a variety of western dishes.
Below the Mall, towards Lower Bazar, good cheap *dhabas* sell snacks (eg *tikki channa*).

### Cafés and fast food

**Baljees**, 26 The Mall, opposite Town Hall. Good snacks, justifiably packed, cakes and sweets from takeaway counter.
**Barista**, The Mall, part of national, Starbucks-styled chain, good coffee and snacks.
**Goofa** (below Ashiana), The Ridge. Veg, dull, dimly lit but decent pizzas and *thalis*.
**Park**, just above Mall, beyond Scandal Point. Indian, Continental. Very popular traveller hangout (great pizzas, excellent espresso coffee). Recommended.

## Festivals and events

**Shimla** *p473, maps p474 and p476*
In **May-Jun** the **Summer Festival** includes cultural programmes from Himachal and neighbouring states, and art and handicrafts exhibitions. There's also an ice skating carnival on Christmas Day.

## Shopping

**Shimla** *p473, maps p474 and p476*
The main shopping areas are The Mall, Lower Bazar and Lakkar Bazar
**Himachal Emporium**, The Mall, opposite Telegraph Office, for local woollen items at fixed prices.
**Maria Brothers**, 78 The Mall, good selection of antiquarian books, maps and prints, 1030-1300, 1700-2000.
**Minerva**, 46 The Mall, opposite Gaiety Theatre, for books and maps, good range.
**Tibetan Self-Help Handicrafts Centre**, near Kusumpti, 6 km, produces carpets and woven goods, keeping Tibetan traditions alive, sold through other outlets in town.

## Activities and tours

**Shimla** *p473, maps p474 and p476*
**Golf**
Naldera, 9-hole. Casual members: green fee and equipment, about Rs 100, see page 476.

**Ice skating**
Skating rink: below Rivoli, on ice in winter, day's membership Rs 50 to skate to loud Indian film hits.

**Skiing**
Early Jan to mid-Mar. Ski courses at Narkanda (64 km) organized by Himachal Tourism, 7 and 15-day courses, Jan-Mar, Rs 1,700-3,000; see page 477 and Manali, page 501.

**Tour companies**
**Band Box**, 9 The Mall, T0177 265 8157, bboxhv@satyam.net.in. Jeep safaris round Kinnaur & Spiti (around Rs 1600 per day), helpful advice, recommended
**Hi-Lander**, 62 The Mall, T0177 280 1565, www.hilandertravels.com, adventure tours and treks, hotel and transport bookings.
**HPTDC's** various tours during the season are well run, usually 1000-1700 (Rs 150). All start from Rivoli, enquire when booking for other pick up points. Return drop at Lift or Victory Tunnel. Two tours visit Kufri, Chini Bungalow and Nature Park; one returns to Shimla via Fagu, Naldehra and Mashobra, the other by Chail and Kairighat. A further tour visits Fagu, Theog, Matiana and Narkanda. Book in advance at the HPTDC marketing office on The Mall. Tour companies charge Rs 700-800 per car for 5.

## Transport

**Shimla** *p473, maps p474 and p476*
**Air**
Shimla (Jabbarhatti) airport (23 km from town) has daily flights from **Delhi** and **Kullu** all year round, as well as some extra flights during summer. **Jagsons**, 58 The Mall, T/F0177 262 5177 or **Indian Airlines**, T0177 265 8014. Flights can be badly disrupted by the weather especially during the monsoon. Taxis charge Rs 400-500 to town.

**Bus**
**Local** From Cart Rd. Lift: 2-stage lift from the Taxi Stand on Cart Rd and near **Hotel Samrat** on The Mall, takes passengers to and from The Mall, 0800-2200, Rs 5.
**Long distance** From **Main Bus Stand**, Cart Rd, T0177 265 8765. Buy tickets from counter before boarding bus (signs in Hindi so ask for help) some long-distance buses can be reserved in advance: HPTDC coaches during the season are good value and reliable: to **Chandigarh** 4 hrs, Rs 80, **Dehra Dun** 9 hrs, Rs 138**Delhi** 10-12 hrs, Rs 380, overnight to **Dharamshala** 10 hrs, Rs 159. **Manali** dep outside the 'Tunnel', 8-10 hrs, Rs 180, tickets from Main Bus Stand. HPRTC deluxe buses between Shimla and Delhi in the summer (9 hrs). From **Rivoli** (Lakkar Bazaar) T0177 281 1259: **Rampur** hourly from 0530, 8 hrs, and **Chitkul**, 2 daily; **Jeori** for Sarahan (8 hrs).

**Taxi**
**Local** Near lift on Cart Rd, T0177 265 7645; fixed fares.
**Long distance** Union Stands near the lift, T0177 280 5164, and by the Main Bus Stand on Cart Rd. **Chandigarh**, Rs 1,250; **Kalka** (90 km), Rs 920; **Mussoorie**, Rs 2,800, 8 hrs, incl-uding stops; **Rekong-Peo**, Rs 2,800 (11 hrs).

**Train**
Enquiry T131. The main station has computerized reservations (T0177 265 2915), 1000-1330, 1400-1700, Sun 1000-1400. The newer extension station,

where some trains start and terminate, is just below the Main bus stand. Travel to/from Shimla involves a change of gauge at Kalka (see Box and Kalka below). It is quicker by bus but requires a stronger stomach. **To Chandigarh** via Kalka: Shimla to Kalka on *Shimla-Kalka Exp, 256,* depart 1035, 5½ hrs, then Kalka to Chandrigarh on *Himalayan Queen, 4096,* 1640, 40 mins. **To New Delhi** via Kalka: Shimla to Kalka on *Shimla-Kalka Exp, 256,* 1035, 5½ hrs, then Kalka to New Delhi on *Himalayan Queen, 4096,* 1640, 5½ hrs. **To Old Delhi**: Shimla to Kalka on *Shimla-Kalka Mail, 252,* 1805, 5 hrs, then Kalka to Old Delhi on *Kalka-Howrah Mail, 2312,* 2345, 6¾ hrs. The day train to Delhi is recommended. **From Delhi to Kalka**: *Himalayan Queen, 4095,* ND, 0600, 5¼ hrs; *Howrah-Kalka Mail, 2311,* OD, 2250, 6¼ hrs, then change to narrow gauge to Shimla (see Kalka). **By narrow gauge**: **To Kalka**: *Exp 258* (Season), 0925, 6 hrs; *Exp 256,* 1035 (1000 from Shimla Ext), 3½ hrs; *Rail Car102* (Season, for minimum 6), 1130, 5 hrs; *2KS Passenger*, 1425 (1400 from Shimla Ext), 6 hrs; *Exp 254* (Season), 1550, 5¼ hrs; *Sivalik Deluxe Exp 242*, 1730, 4¾ hrs; *Mail 252*, 1745, 5½ hrs.

**Kalka** *p477*

Easily reached from **Shimla**, by bus or taxi (Rs 800), and from **Chandigarh** by taxi (Rs 400).

The train often arrives on the Kalka platform already full of locals who board it while it waits in the siding. Worth paying Rs 150-170 plus reservation fee of Rs 20 to guarantee a seat on 1st class. 1st class waiting room for ticket holders only. It is essential (especially during the 'season') to have an advance reservation for the narrow gauge train. The quicker 16-seater glass top *Rail Car* can only be booked at Kalka. Season (for *254/257*): 1 May-15 Jul (school holidays start at end- May); 15 Sep-30 Oct; 15 Dec-1 Jan. The daily *Sivalik Deluxe Express* (No *241/242*), boasts "Toilet fittings of latest variety" and "Curtains of latest design"! The pricier ticket (Rs 305) includes tea and breakfast/dinner at Barog. **To Chandigarh**: *Shatabdi Exp, 2006,* 0600, 45 mins (to New Delhi, 4 hrs); *Himalayan Queen, 4096,* 1650, 45 mins (to New Delhi, 5½ hrs). **To Old Delhi**: *Kalka-Howrah Mail,* 2312, 2345, 5½ hrs. **From Delhi to Kalka**: *Himalayan Queen, 4095,* ND, 0600, 5¼ hrs; *Howrah-Kalka Mail, 2311,* OD, 2250, 5¼ hrs. **By narrow gauge**: **To Shimla**: *1KS Passenger,* 0400, 5½ hrs; *Sivalik Exp Deluxe 241,* 0530, 4¾ hrs; *Exp 253* (Season), 0600, 5 hrs; *Mail 251,* 0630, 5½ hrs; *Rail Car 101* (Season), 1135, 4 hrs; *Exp 255, 1155, 5½ hrs; Exp 257 (Season), 1230, 6 hrs.*

**Rampur Bushahr** *p478*

Buses are often late and overcrowded. To **Chandigarh**, **Delhi**; **Mandi** (9 hrs); **Recong Peo** (5 hrs) and **Puh**; **Sarahan** (2-3 hrs), better to change at Jeori; **Shimla**, several (5-6 hrs); **Tapri** (and Kalpa) 0545 (3¾ hrs), change at Karchham for Sangla and Chitkul.

**Sarahan** *p479*

Daily buses between **Shimla** (Rivoli Bus Stand) and **Jeori** on the Highway (6 hrs), quicker by car. Local buses between Jeori and the army cantonment below Sarahan.

## Directory

**Shimla** *p473, maps p474 and p476*

**Banks** Changing foreign currency outside Shimla is not easy except in Manali or McLeodganj. Do not depend on credit cards for cash. Exchange procedure is awkward; photocopies of passport and visa needed. Grindlays, The Mall, and UCO quick and efficient. **Hospital** Tara Hospital, The Ridge, T0177 280 3785: Dr Puri, Mehghana Complex, The Mall, T0177 280 1936, speaks fluent English, is efficient, and very reasonable. **Internet** Tourist office, The Mall, 2 machines, Rs 50 per hr, also 2 at Telegraph Office and others springing up all over town. **Post** GPO, The Mall, T0177 265 2518. Open 1000-1600 Sun. Poste Restante: Counter 10 (separate entrance), chaotic, 0800-1700, Sun 1000-1600. CTO nearby. **Tourist offices** Himachal (HPTDC), The Mall, T0177 265 2561, www.hptdc.nic.in. 0900-1800, in season, 0900-1900, very helpful. Victory Tunnel, Cart Rd, T0177 265 4589, 1000-1700. Himachal Tourism has a/c and non-a/c cars. Corporate Office, Ritz Annexe, T0177 265 2704.

# Kinnaur and Spiti

→ For trekking information, see page 534.

*The regions of Kinnaur and Spiti lie in the rainshadow of the outer Himalayan ranges. The climate in Spiti is much drier than in the Kullu Valley and is similar to that of Ladakh. The temperatures are more extreme both in summer and winter and most of the landscape is barren and bleak. The wind can be bitingly cold even when the sun is hot. The annual rainfall is very low so cultivation is restricted to the ribbons of land that fringe rivers with irrigation potential. The crops include potatoes, wheat, barley and millet. The people are of Mongol origin and almost everyone follows a Tibetan form of Buddhism.*

*Kinnaur and Spiti can only be seen by following the circular route (the southern part of which is the Old Hindustan Tibet Road which follows the Sutlej River). The Baspa valley is a side route up a dead end valley via Sangla to Chitkul, recommended for its views and landscapes, villages, pagodas and culture. Kinnaur is the only route into Spiti, which has the evocative Tibetan Buddhist sites of Tabo and Kaza, set against the backdrop of a rugged landscape. The road then goes on round to the Rohtang Pass and Manali, or on up to Ladakh.* » For Sleeping, Eating and other listings, see pages 493-496.

*! Most Kinnauri Buddhist temples only accept visitors at around 0700 and 1900. You must wear a hat and a special belt available locally.*

## Kinnaur

### Along the Sutlej

An exciting mountain road runs through cliffside cuttings along the left bank of the Sutlej – frequently blocked by rockfalls and landslides during the monsoons. At **Choling** the Sutlej roars through a narrow gorge, and at **Wangtu** the road re-crosses the river where vehicle details are checked. Immediately after crossing the Wangtu bridge a narrow side road goes to **Kafnoo village** (2,427 m), in the Bhabha Valley (a camping site and the start for an attractive 10-day trek to the Pin Valley). From Wangtu the road route runs to **Tapri** (1,870 m) and **Karchham** (1,899 m) both of which have hot springs. Here the Baspa River joins the Sutlej from the south. A hair-raising excursion by a precipitous winding rough road leads 16 km up the Baspa Valley to Sangla; buses take approximately 1½ hours.

### Baspa Valley

→ Colour map 1, grid B4.

The valley carries the marks of a succession of glacial events which have shaped it, although the glaciers which formed the valley have now retreated to the high slopes above Chitkul at over 4,500 m. All villages in Baspa are characterized by exaggerated steeply sloping slate roofs, rich wood carving and elaborate pagoda temples. Although Kinner Kailash (sacred to Hindus and Buddhists) is not visible from here, the valley is on the circumambulating *Parikrama/Kora* route which encircles the massif. Fields of the pink coloured *ogla*, a small flower seed grown specifically in the Baspa Valley for grinding into grain, add a beautiful colouring in the season.

**Sangla** Sangla, at 2,680 m, is built on the massive buttress of a terminal moraine which marked one of the major glacial advances about 50,000 years ago. The Baspa River has cut a deep trench on its south flank. Immediately above is the flat valley floor, formed on the lake bed which was once dammed behind the moraine. Sangla village has excellent carving and is full of character. No foreign exchange is available but there are telephone facilities. There is a **saffron** farm just north of Sangla, claimed to be better than at Pampore in Kashmir, and it is famous for its apples.

The old seven-storey **Killa** (Fort) ⓘ *0800-0900, 1800-1900*, where the Kinnaur rajas were once crowned, is 1 km north of new Sangla just before the road enters the village. It was occupied by the local rulers for centuries. It now has a temple to Kamakshi where the idol is from Guwahati, Assam658.

**Barseri** Barseri, 8 km from Sangla, is situated on an outwash cone which has engulfed part of the Baspa's valley floor. This well-kept 'green village' is happy to show visitors its solar heaters, *chakkis* (water mills) and water driven prayer wheels. The Buddha Mandir with *Shakyamuni* and other images and a large prayer wheel is beautiful inside. Villagers weave shawls and do woodcarving.

The Rakcham pagoda-style temple with beautiful wood carving is to Shamshir Debta, Devi and Naga, combining Buddhist and Hindu deities. The ibex horns on the roof are ancient male fertility symbols. There is also a pre-Buddist, animist Bon cho shrine and a Siva temple.

**Chitkul** Some 18 km from Barseri, with an altitude of 3,450 m, it is the furthest point foreigners can travel without special permits. With its typical houses, Buddhist temple and a small tower, it is worth the trip. The Kagyupa (Oral Transmission School), has a highly valued, old image of the Shakyamuni Buddha. There are four directional kings on either side of the door as well as a Wheel of Life. You can walk along the Baspa River which has paths on both sides. The rough path along the

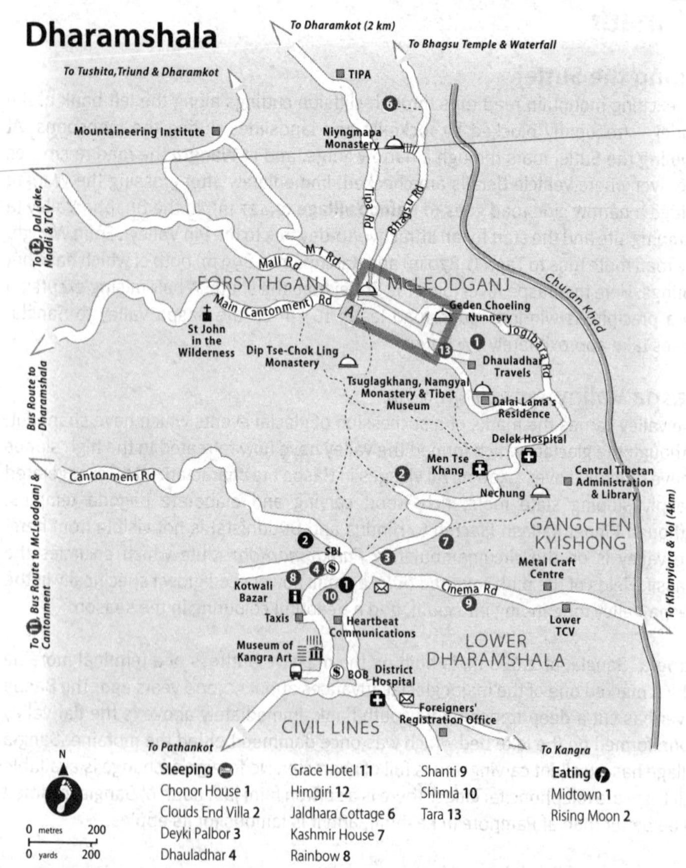

### The stuff of epics

The bhoj patra, found distinctively in the Sangla Valley, is a revered product. The extraordinarily fine waterproof layers just beneath the bark of the bhoj patra tree were used for writing centuries ago, particularly where palm leaves were not available. Renowned for its suppleness, strength and apparent indestructibility, bark from this valley was used for some of Hinduism's most ancient writings, including the epics, and it is still highly valued for copying sacred texts. Genealogies which trace the descent of some families in the Sangla Valley to the legendary Pandavas are still widely accepted, and connections between the residents of the valley and the early roots of Hinduism are treasured.

tributary starting at the bridge across the river, below the bus stand, is very steep in places with loose stones. Do not attempt alone. A shop sells a few provisions.

**Recong Peo** Also called 'Peo', at 2,290 m, the District HQ is a busy little market town. The Sub-Divisional Magistrate's office in a three-storey building below the bus stand deals with Inner Line Permits (see page 477). A short walk above the town takes you to the Kalachakra Temple with a large Buddha statue outside – good views of Kinner Kailash. A shop here sells provisions, medicines and has a telephone but there aren't any exchange facilities.

**Kothi** village, reached by a path from the Kalachakra Temple, has ancient Hindu temples associated with the Pandavas. One has a tank of sacred fish, 30 minutes' walk from the bazar.

**Kalpa** Kalpa (Chini), 12 km from Recong Peo at 2,960 m, is reached after a stiff climb. It has an interesting temple complex and Budh mandir and is surrounded by apple, *bemi* (wild apricot) and plum orchards and chilgoza pine forests.

**Pangi** A high road from Kalpa/Recong Peo with little traffic passes through Chilgoza pine forests, north to the hamlet of Pangi, 10 km away. Pangi is surrounded by apple orchards. The colourful Sheshri Nag temple at the top of the village has an inscription in a strange script above the entrance and standing stones in the courtyard. Apart from two Buddhist temples, the carved pagoda temple to Sheshri's mother encloses a huge boulder representing the Devi. The road then goes over bare and rugged hills beyond to **Morang** which has impressive monasteries with wood carvings and sculptures.

**Jangi** At Jangi there is a check post; from here the road goes to Puh, just south of Kah which is a steep climb with hairpin bends. The road follows the Spiti while the Sutlej valley disappears to the east towards the Tibet border.Spiti

"At last they entered a world within a world – a valley of leagues where the high hills were fashioned of the mere rubble and refuse from off the knees of the mountains .... Surely the gods live here."

*Rudyard Kipling*

## Khabo

Khabo (2,831 m), a morning's drive from Kalpa, is at the confluence of the Sutlej and Spiti rivers. The entry into the Spiti valley at Khabo is a rare example of crossing from the Himalaya to the Trans-Himalaya without going over a major pass. The 180 km State Highway 30, which joins Sumdo with Batal (Sumdo is the last village of Kinnaur

– has a Border Police check post and a tea shop), passes through an arid valley with small patches of cultivation of peas and barley near the snow melt streams. It is 31 km to Tabo from Sumdo.

## Tabo → *Colour map 1, grid B4. Altitude: 3,050 m.*

At the crossroads of two ancient trade routes, Tabo was one of the great centres of Buddhist learning and culture. Founded in 996, the Chos Khor Gompa is the oldest living Buddhist establishment in this part of the world. Today, the small town is rapidly being modernized with paved streets and electric lights. Government offices have appeared alongside traditional mud homes and the local shops stock basic provisions for trekkers. There is a post office.

**Chos Khor Gompa** Founded in 996 as a scholastic institution, the monastery's original layout was planned as a *mandala* centred around a **Du khang** (Assembly Hall). The deodar wood used was imported from Kullu, Kinnaur, Chamba and Kashmir while the lack of quality structural stone resulted in the extensive use of earth, strengthened with gypsum for the high walls. Today the gompa houses 60 lamas and has a good collection of scriptures, *thangkas* and art pieces. It is most important and has an immense sense of the spiritual. Carry a torch. No photography allowed.

Many of the **colourful murals** come close to the pure Indian style identified with Ajanta. The technique required the surface to be coated with several thin layers of lime and yak-skin glue and burnished vigorously to provide the 'ground' which was then smoothed and freshened with animal fat and butter. Natural vegetable dyes and powdered stone colours were mixed with *dzo* milk and yak urine for painting. The early Indian style murals used a profusion of reds and yellows with little stress on landscaping, the area around the principal figures being filled with small divinities. These images wear seraphic smiles and have half-shut dreamy eyes depicting introspective meditation. The later 17th-century paintings illustrate the Central Tibetan/ Chinese art form where ultramarine takes over from the earlier dominance of reds and yellows, and landscapes become lively and vivid with the appearance of cliffs, swirling clouds, stylized flames, flora and fauna. Here the twists and turns of the limbs and the flowing elaborate drapery show great fluency. This is one of the few gompas in the Tibetan Buddhist influenced areas of Ladakh, Lahaul and Spiti where the highly structured art of painting the complex Tibetan religious iconography is taught. What appears outwardly as a free art form is taught on lined grid paper where each shape and form is closely measured.



**Nine temples Tsuglhakhang** ('academy') The 'resplendent' central *Mahavairochana* – a composite of four figures, each facing a cardinal direction, represents the unity of all Buddhas. On the walls inside are stucco figures of different Buddhas and Bodhisattvas. The floral ceiling decorations are in the Ajanta style.

**Dri Tsang khang** (Inner Sanctum) and **Kora** (Circumambulatory Path) At the centre of the 'mandala', the five *Dhyani* Buddhas escorted here by four Bodhisattvas, emerge from the darkness lit by a shaft of sunlight.

Masks, weapons and ritual costumes are stored in the **Gon Khang** which is closed to visitors. **Zhalma** (Picture Hall) has a 17th-century entrance temple where the murals are recent and in pure Tibetan style.

**Dromton Lhakhang Chenpo** (17th century) Dominated by Medicine Buddhas. The ceiling, in high Tibetan style, is exceptional, depicting *nagas*, titans, peacocks and parrots amongst rainbows.

*A large Mala (sacrificial wood) tree at the northwest corner of the monastery, the only one of four to survive, is held sacred by the villagers.*

**Ser Khang** (Golden Temple) The walls were believed to have been coated with a layer of gold dust as thick as a yak's skin for painting the numerous larger-than-life figures. They were renewed in 16th and 17th centuries.

**Chamba Chenpo La Khang** Dedicated to the Maitreya (Future) Buddha, this temple has a 6-m high seated statue. The murals of the eight Buddhas may be some of the earliest in Tabo.

**Buddhist caves** To the north, the small natural caves above the road were an integral part of the monastic complex. Pho Gompa, the only surviving, with early murals showing pure Indian influence, has been restored. These post Ajantan paintings, however, are already fading. On open ground to the east, on both sides of a dyke, there are pre-Buddhist rock carvings on metamorphosed igneous rocks showing ibex, swastikas, *yonis*, horses, panthers and human figures.

## Dankar

Once the capital of Spiti, Dankar is a tiny village. The early 16th-century fort/monastery **Dankar Gompa** (3,890 m), which once served as a jail, stands on an impressive overhang, perched on crumbling towers. Today it has over 160 lamas in residence. The 'highest temple' has a collection of Bhotia Buddhist scriptures, a four-in-one *Dhyani Buddha* and interesting murals of Medicine Buddhas and protector deities. The gompa is a two-hour very steep climb from a point 2 km away, beyond Shichling on the main road. The jeepable road from the SH30, about 1 km west of Shichling, winds up 8 km to Dankar (a two-hour walk) and is easier. A beautiful large pond at just under 4,100 m is reached by a 2½ km track.

## Lalung Gompa

Lalung Gompa, known for its carved wood panelling, is off the SH30, 22 km from Kaza, reached by 8-km narrow, motorable track. From Dankar Gompa this is a two-hour trek. Carry plenty of water as there are no streams and it can get very hot.

## Pin Valley

*Although rugged, the summer brings more rain here than the rest of Spiti resulting in a profusion of wild flowers.*

About 5 km from Dankar is a sign for the Pin Valley National Park which is on the other side of the river. The Pin River joins the Spiti at Attargo. Above Attargo, 10 km along the Pin Valley, is the **Kungri Gompa** (circa1330), which though not old is in an established monastic site with old-carved wooden sculptures and is commonly understood to be a Bon monastery still practising elements of the pre Buddhist Bon religion. The trek from the Bhabha Valley ends at the road head at Kungri, see page 536. One bus a day departs from Kaza at 1200, goes along the Pin Valley as far as Mikkim and turns straight back at 1400, not allowing enough time to visit the Gompa. You therefore face a long walk unless you can hitch a lift on a passing tractor or truck.

At the confluence of the Pin River and one of its tributaries, 1 km from Mikkim, **Sangam** can be reached by one of two pulley systems. The one nearest the bus stop, across a bridge, requires your own rope harness. The other, 750 m west along the river has a person-size bucket. Both require a reasonable degree of fitness to negotiate, especially if crossing alone. The local greeting is *joolay, joolay*!

**Pin Valley National Park** is described as the 'land of ibex and snow leopard' and was created to conserve the flora and fauna of the cold desert. It adjoins the Great Himalayan National Park (southwest), and Rupi Bhabha Sanctuary (south) with the Bara Shigri Glacier forming its north boundary. The park covers 675 sq km with a buffer zone of 1,150 sq km mainly to its east where there are villages, and varies in altitude from 3,600 m to 6,630 m. The **wildlife** includes Siberian ibex, snow leopard, red fox, pika, weasels, lammergeier, Himalayan griffon, golden eagle, Chakor partridge, Himalayan snow cock and a variety of rose finches. The Siberian ibex can be sighted at high altitudes, beyond Hikim and Thango village. From July to September the young ibex kids need protection and so the females move up to the higher pastures near cliffs while the adult males concentrate on feeding lower down. The 60-km long Lingti Valley is famous for its fossils.

## Kaza

Kaza, at 3,600 m, is 13 km from Lingti village. Old Kaza has village homes while New Kaza sports government offices. It is a busy bus terminus with a small market, a basic health centre and jeeps for hire. Inner Line Permits are issued by the SDM's office. Tourist facilities are open May to October. No foreign exchange is available. If you are in need of supplies, Kibber, 19 km away, has a school, Post, a bank and several provisions stores for trekkers.

There is an attractive one-day circular trek from here to **Hikim** and **Komik** villages visiting the monastery midway. Hikim gompa (early 14th century), modelled on a Chinese castle, was built under Mongol patronage.

## Kibber-Gete Wildlife Sanctuary

One of the world's highest wildlife sanctuaries covering an area 98 sq km, it has **Mount Gya** (6,754 m) to the north and **Kamelong** (5,867 m) to the south. On the drive from Kibber to Tashigang, you may spot musk deer and bharal sheep but to see larger mammals (bear, wolf and the rare snow leopard) you would need to trek. Also to be seen are Himalayan birds of prey as well as snowcock and other high-altitude birds. Buses from Kaza takes about an hour.

## Tashigang

Tashigang, 18 km away, is one of the highest villages in the world connected by road. **Ki Monastery** on the way is the largest in Spiti and houses 300 lamas. Although it has suffered from wars, fires and earthquakes it still has a good collection of *thangkas* and *kangyurs* (scriptures). Although no permit is needed, the monks have instituted their private 'entrance fee' system which, by all accounts, appears quite flexible and linked to the visitors perceived ability to pay. There are a few cheap guest houses and camping is possible. If you cannot stay take a bus up and walk down via the Ki Monastery, 11 km from Kaza.

## To Lahul

**Losar**, at 4,079 m, is the last village in Spiti reached after driving through fields growing peas and cabbage among poplars, willows and apple orchards. There is a rest house and guesthouse and a couple of cafes serving Tibetan/Spitian food.

The road continues up for 18 km to the **Kunzum La** (Pass) at 4,551 m. It means 'meeting place for ibex' and gives access to Lahul and good views of some of the highest peaks of the Chandrabhaga (CB) group notably CB 14, 16 and 17 that lie immediately opposite the Kunzum La to the west. To the southeast is the Karcha Peak (6,271 m). The pass has an ancient chorten marker. The temple to **Gyephang**, the presiding deity, is circumambulated by those crossing the pass; the giver of any offering in cash which sticks to the stone image receives special blessing.

The road does 19 hairpin bends to descend down the rock strewn terrain to the valley of the river Chandra to **Batal** where the tea shop serves noodles and sells biscuits and bottled water, and on to **Chhota Dhara** and **Chhatru,** with rest houses and eateries, and then **Gramphoo** joining the Manali-Keylong-Leh highway (three hours journey from the pass). Gramphoo is 62 km from Manali.

# Shimla to the Kullu Valley

## Bilaspur and Bhakra-Nangal Dam

**Bilaspur** used to be the centre of a district in which the tribal Daora peoples panned in the silts of the Beas and Sutlej for gold. Their main source, the Seer Khud, has now been flooded by the Bhakra Nangal Lake and they have shifted their area of search upstream. For a bite to eat visit the **Lake View Café**.

The **dam** on the river Sutlej is one of the highest dams in the world at 225 m and was built as part of the Indus Waters Treaty between India and Pakistan (1960). The Treaty allocated the water of the rivers Sutlej, Beas and Ravi to India. The dam provides electricity for Punjab, Haryana and Delhi. It is also the source for the Rajasthan Canal project, which takes water over 1,500 km south to the Thar desert. There is accommodation should you wish to stay.

## Una to Mandi

Having passed through Una, along the main bus route, **Ghanahatti**, a further 18 km on, has the adequate **Monal Restaurant**. There are some magnificent views, sometimes across intensively cultivated land, sometimes through plantations of chilgoza, khir and other species. In **Shalaghat**, further on, accommodation is available. The road descends into a deep valley before climbing again to the small market town of **Bhararighat**. A jeep can take over two hours for this part of the journey. In **Brahmpukar** the road to Beri and Mandi is a very attractive country lane. The more heavily used though still quiet road to the main Bilaspur-Manali road joins it at **Ghaghas**. During the monsoons landslides on the NH21 may result in very long delays. Carry plenty of water and some food. The tree-lined and attractive approach to **Sundernagar** from the south gives some indication of the town's rapid growth and prosperity.

## Mandi (Sahor) → *Phone code: 01905. Colour map 1, grid B3. Population: 26,900. Altitude: 760 m.*

Founded by a Rajput prince in circa 1520, Mandi is held sacred by both Hindus and Buddhists. The old town with the main (Indira) bazar is huddled on the left bank of the Beas at the southern end of the Kullu Valley, just below its junction with the Uhl River. The Beas bridge – claimed to be the world's longest non-pillar bridge – is across Sukheti Khad at the east end of town. The main bus station is across the river, just above the open sports ground. It is worth stopping a night in this quaint town with 81 temples, a 17th-century palace and a colourful bazar.

**Triloknath Temple** (1520), on the river bank, built in the Nagari style with a tiled roof, has a life-size three-faced Siva image (Lord of three worlds), riding a bull with Parvati on his lap. It is at the centre of a group of 13th to 16th-century sculpted stone shrines. The Kali Devi statue which emphasizes the natural shape of the stone, illustrates the ancient Himalayan practice of stone worship.

**Panchavaktra Temple,** at the confluence of the Beas and a tributary with views of the Trilokinath, has a five-faced image (*Panchanana*) of Siva. The image is unusually conceived like a temple *shikhara* on an altar plinth. Note the interesting frieze of yogis on a small temple alongside.

**Bhutnath Temple** (circa 1520) by the river in the town centre is the focus at *Sivaratri* festival (see below). The modern shrines nearby are brightly painted.

In lower Sumkhetar, west of the main bazar, is the 16th-century **Ardhanarishvara Temple** where the Siva image is a composite male/female form combining the passive Siva (right) and the activating energy of Parvati (left). Although the *mandapa* is ruined, the carvings on the *shikhara* tower and above the inner sanctum door, are particularly fine.

From the old suspension bridge on the Dharamshala road, if you follow a narrow lane up into the main market, you will see the slate roof over a deep spring which is the **Mata Kuan Rani Temple**, dedicated to the 'Princess of the Well'. The story of this Princess of Sahor (Mandi) and her consort **Padmasambhava**, who introduced Mahayana Buddhism in Tibet, describes how the angry king condemned the two to die in a fire which raged for seven days and when the smoke cleared a lake appeared with a lotus – Rewalsar or *Tso Pema* (Tibetan 'Lotus Lake').

## Around Mandi

The small dark **Rewalsar Lake**, 24 km southeast, with its floating reed islands, is a popular pilgrimage centre. The colourful Tibetan Buddhist monastery was founded in the 14th century though the pagoda-like structure is late 19th century. The Gurudwara commemorates Guru Gobind Singh's stay here. Start early for the hilltop temples by the transmission tower as it is a steep and hot climb. The *Sisu* fair is held in February/March. There are many buses from Mandi, originating from bus stand with pick up from below the palace, Indira Bazar, to the lake taking an hour, Rs 14.

At **Prashar**, the three-tiered pagoda Rishi temple by a sacred lake is in a basin surrounded by high mountains with fantastic views of the Pir Panjal range. The rich woodcarvings here suggest a date earlier than the Manali Dhungri Temple (1553) which is not as fine. No smoking, alcohol or leather items are allowed near the temple or lake. There are basic Pilgrim Rest Houses. A forest rest house is 1 km west of temple. To reach the temple, follow a steep trail through the forest of rhododendron, oak, deodar and kail (three hours). After arriving at a group of large shepherd huts the trail to the left goes to the temple, the right to the Forest Rest House.

You can walk to **Aut**, see below, from Prashar in six to seven hours. A level trail east crosses a col in under a kilometre. Take the good path down to the right side of the *nullah* (valley) and cross the stream on a clear path. Climb a little and then follow a broad path on the left bank to the road. Turn right and down to **Peon village** in the Chir nullah and continue to Aut.

## Tirthan Valley and Jalori Pass

From Mandi the NH21 runs east then south along the left bank of the Beas, much diminished in size by the dam at **Pandoh**, 19 km from Mandi, from which water is channelled to the Sutlej. The dam site is on a spectacular meander of the Beas (photography strictly prohibited). The NH21 crosses over the dam to the right bank of the Beas then follows the superb **Larji Gorge**, in which the Beas now forms a lake for a large part of the way upstream to Aut. A large Hydro-Electric project is being constructed along this stretch. At **Aut**, pronounced 'out', there is trout fishing (season March to October, best in March and April). Permits issued by the Fishery Office in Largi, Rs 100 per day. The main bazar road has a few cheap hotels and eating places. It is also a good place to stop and stock up with trekking supplies such as dried apricots and nuts.

From Aut, a road branches off across the Beas into the **Tirthan Valley** climbing through beautiful wooded scenery with deodar and larch up to the Jalori Pass. Allow at least 1½ hours by jeep to **Shoja**, 42 km from Mandi, and another 30 minutes to Jalori. Contact tourist office in Kullu or **Doli Guest House** for trekking routes. One suggested trek is Banjar-Laisa-Paldi-Dhaugi/Banogi-Sainj, total 30 km, two days.

**Banjar**, with attractive wood fronted shops lining the narrow street, has the best examples in the area of timber bonded Himalayan architecture in the fort-like rectangular temple of **Murlidhar** (Krishna). Half way to Chaini, 3 km away, the large **Shring Rishi temple** to the deified local sage is very colourful with beautiful wooden balconies and an impressive 45-m tall tower which was damaged in the last earthquake. The entrance, 7 m above ground, is reached by climbing a notched tree trunk. Such free-standing temple towers found in eastern Tibet, were sometimes used for defence and incorporated into Thakur's castles in the western Himalaya. The fortified villages here even have farmhouses like towers.

From Banjar the road climbs increasingly steeply to **Jibhi**, 9 km away, where there is also accommodation and trekking. Contact Mr BS Rana at **Doli Guest House** or **Seraj Himalayan Tours** who also arrange safaris. Two kilometres beyond is **Ghayaghi**, also with some accommadation. A few kilometres on is **Shoja**, a Rajput village in the heart of the forest, offers a base for treks in the Great Himalayan National Park.

Finally you reach the **Jalori Pass**, open only in good weather from mid-April (altitude: 3,350 m), which links Inner and Outer Seraj and is 76 km from Kullu. You may wish to take the bus up to the Pass and walk down, or even camp a night at the Pass. Check road conditions before travelling. A ruined fort, **Raghupur Garh**, sits high to the west of the pass and from the meadows there are fantastic views, especially of the Pir Panjal range. Take the path straight from the first hairpin after the pass and head upwards, for about 30 to 40 minutes. The road is most suitable for four-wheel drive vehicles. There is a very pleasant, gradual walk, 5 km east, through woodland (one hour), starting at the path to the right of the temple. It is easy to follow. **Sereuil Sar** ('Pure Water') is where local women worship Burhi Nagini Devi, the snake goddess, and walk around the lake pouring a line of *ghee*. The lake is perpetually clean. It is claimed that leaves are cleared in the mornings by a pair of resident birds! *Dhabas* provide simple refreshments and one has two very basic cheap rooms at the Pass.

**Great Himalayan National Park and Tirthan Sanctuary** ⓘ *Rs 4, still camera Rs 4, video Rs 2000, filming Rs 20,000*, lies southeast of Kullu town in the Seraj Forest Division, an area bounded by mountain ridges (except to the west) and watered by the upper reaches of the rivers Jiwa, Sainj and Tirthan. The hills are covered in part by dense forest of blue pine, deciduous broadleaved and fir trees and also shrubs and grassland; thickets of bamboo make it impenetrable in places. Attractive species of iris, frittilaria, gagea and primula are found in the high altitude meadows. Wildlife include the panther, Himalayan black bear, brown bear, tahr, musk deer, red fox, goral and bharal. The rich birdlife includes six species of pheasant. The national park was created in 1948 and has its headquarters in Shamshi. The park is 60,561 ha with an altitude of 1,500-5,800 m and the sanctuary is 6,825 ha. Access is easiest from April to June and September to October. **Goshiani** is the base for treks into the park. The first 3 km is fairly gentle and runs along the river before rising to harder rocky terrain, allowing plenty of opportunity to see birds and butterflies. The trout farm here sells fresh fish at Rs 150 per kg. Fishing permits, Rs 100, are obtainable from the Fisheries Department.

## Sleeping

**Sangla** *p485*

**A Banjara Camps**, Barseri, 6 km beyond Sangla, T01786 242 536, www.banjaracamps.com. Superb riverside site with 18 twin bed and some 4-bed deluxe tents, separate (or attached) bath tents, varied meals included, friendly staff, excellent site, mountain biking, trekking, Lahul, Spiti, Ladakh tours. Highly recommended. Buses stop 2 km from the campsite, where road drops down to right, car park at foot of hill is 500-m walk from camp (horn will summon porters!).

D **Kinner Camp**, Barseri, T01786 242 382. Small tents with beds/sleeping bags, shared baths, bird watching, trekking, jeep safaris, meals, cafeteria, superb location.

**E-F Mount Kailash**, T01786 242 227. 8 clean, pleasant rooms (hot shower), 4-bed dorm too.

**F Sangla Guest House**, near shops. Clean rooms with bath (hot water), restaurant.

**F Trekker's Lodge**, leaving town, towards Chitkul. Run by a veteran mountaineer.

*For an explanation of the sleeping and eating price codes used in this guide, see inside the front cover. Other relevant information is found in Essentials pages 56-61.*

**Baspa Valley** *p485*

**C Kinner Villa**, 4 km outside Kalpa, T01786 226 006, circuits@vsnl.net.in. 11 rooms with bath, in new building, attractively located, seasonal tents.

**C-E Kinner Kailash Cottage** (HPTDC), open May-Nov, Kalpa, T01786 226 159, www.hptdc.nic.in. Commanding position, 5 rooms (bath tub Rs 1100), limited menu, camping.

**E Forest Rest House**, 2 km from Kalpa, caretaker can prepare meals, modern building, camping overnight (with permission) in school grounds from 1600-1000.

**E Sambala Guest House**, near bus stand, Recong Peo, T01786 222 852. 6 rooms and a restaurant.

**E Shivling Guest House**, near bus stand, Recong Peo, T01786 242 421. 7 rooms with bath, cable TV, restaurant and bar, good view of Shivling peak, very friendly.

**E-F Aucktong Guest House ("Aunties")**, near Circuit House, 1 km north on Pangi road, Kalpa, T01786 226 019. 6 clean spacious rooms, large windows, restaurant, pleasant, very friendly ("arrived for one night and stayed a week!").

**E-F Thakur Guest House**, Chitkul, 4 rooms with bath, 3 with shared bath, varied meals.

**F Amar Guest House**, Chitkul, clean double rooms (Rs 100), hot water, friendly family atmosphere. Recommended.

**F PWD Rest House**, Chitkul, 4 rooms, lawns, attractive.

**Tabo** *p488*

**C Banjara Retreat**, signposted on main road, overlooks monastery, T01906 233 381, www.banjaracamps.com. 8 double rooms and a family suite, meals in reataurant, beautiful location, well organized. Recommended.

**D-E Millennium Guest House**, run by monks in the complex, 13 colourful rooms (rats for company), shared dirty toilets, hot water on request, meals.

**Tanzin**, near monastery. Tibetan food, friendly, family run, best in village.

Also cheaper guesthouses in the village, many allowing camping.

**Dankar** *p489*

Sleeping is limited here. The Gompa has 2 rooms; only one has a bed.

**Pin Valley** *p489*

Norzang Guest House, rooms for Rs 100. PWD Rest House. Sub-Post but no provisions.

**Kaza** *p490*

Kaza is also ideal for camping.

**A Kaza Retreat**, T01906 222 236, www.banjaracamps.com. 11 clean, modern rooms with attached bathrooms.

**C-D Pomodoro Country**, Kaza-Rangrik Rd, 8 km northwest of town. 6 rooms (hot showers) in Italian family run farmhouse, excellent restaurant (homemade pasta and breads), 4 Teepee style tents, riding, treks.

**D-E Kunpen Gakyith**, near Post. Newish building, restaurant, lawn.

**E Kaycee Lodge**, simple rooms, good service.

**F Mahabhadra**, basic but large room, shared bath, very clean, meals. Recommended.

**Shalaghat** *p491*

**D Mehman**, and restaurant occupies an extraordinarily bold setting.

**Sundernagar** *p491*

**D-E Relax Inn**, on Mandi side of town, T01907 262 409. Modern, clean.

**Mandi** *p491*

**B-C Visco Resorts**, 2 km south of Mandi, T01905 225 057, www.viscoresorts.com. 18 large rooms (some for 4) in modern resort, spotlessly clean, lovely setting by river, good cheap veg restaurant, extremely well run, highly recommended.

**C-D Mayfair**, corner of Indira Bazar, T01905 222 777. 14 a/c rooms with bath, good restaurant (see eating below), clean, well-kept.

**D Mandav** (HPTDC), above Main Bus Stand, T01905 235 503, www.hptdc.nic.in. 13 cleanish rooms with bath (cheaper **E** in annexe), 2 **C** a/c, restaurant, beer, friendly but a little shabby.

**D Munish Resorts**, on hillside 2 km above New Beas Bridge, T01905 235 035, munishresorts@rediffmail.com. 15 clean rooms with bath, restaurant, lovely views, colourful garden with tempting fruit (Rs 100 fine for each fruit/flower picked!), friendly family.

**D-E Evening Plaza**, Indira Bazar, T01905 225 123. 14 reasonable rooms, some a/c, TV, changes cash and TCs at a good rate (1% commission).

**E Rawalsar Inn (HPTDC)**, above the lake, T01905 280 252, www.hptdc.nic.in. It has 12 reasonable rooms with bath, some with TV and balcony, dorm (Rs 75), good lake views.
**E-F Raj Mahal**, lane to right of Palace/District Court, Indira Bazar, T01905 222 401. 12 rooms, including atmospheric deluxe rooms with bath (sharpened sword in one might be mistaken for a towel rail!), 4 'special' rooms, period furniture and paintings, others **F**, former 'Palace' has character but in need of attention, restaurant, bar, garden temple, a fine example of Pahari art – run by the polite 'raja' and his efficient staff, recommended.
**F Vyas**, 5-min walk from bus stand, past sports ground (signs), T01905 235 556. 6 small rooms (more coming), 4-bedded dorm (Rs 40), clean enough, quiet location overlooking Beas, good value.

**Tirthan Valley and Jalori Pass** *p492*
**A Shoja Retreat**, Shoja, T01902 238 070, www.banjaracamps.com. 5 double rooms and two suites in wooden lodge with fantastic views, good food and trekking information.
**E Raju's Place**, Goshiani, is a family run river-facing guesthouse, 3 rooms with bath. They offer meals, treks and safaris.
**E-F Dev Ganga**, 9 km from Banjar in Jibhi, T01902 238 706, 4 double rooms.
**F Forest Rest House**, near Shoja, enjoys a spectacular and isolated position just below the Jalori Pass.
**F Meena**, beyond bus stand, Banjar, T01902 238 258, 4 double rooms.

## Eating

**Kaza** *p490*
**Layul**, a restaurant, does Chinese, Tibetan and Indian dishes, and cold beer. Also several bakeries and cafés.

**Mandi** *p491*
**Café Shiraz**, HPTDC, Gandhi Chowk, near Bhutnath Temple. Snacks only, dim, bus ticketing available.
**Gomush Tibetan Restaurant**, near Gompa at Rewalsar Lake, does excellent momos.
**Mayfair**, efficient and tasty North Indian, some continental and Chinese. Best in town.
**Raj Mahal**, quiet, peaceful (interesting photos and antiques), pleasant garden, good value but limited menu and surly waiters. Some *dhabas* are by the bus terminal.

## Festivals and events

**Mandi** *p491*
**Feb/Mar Sivaratri Fair**, a week of dance, music and drama as temple deities from surrounding hills are taken in procession with chariots and palanquins to visit the Madho Rai and Bhutnath Temples.

## Transport

**Sangla** *p485*
**Bus** to Chitkul (often 2-3 hrs late); **Shimla** via Tapri (9 hrs); **Recong Peo**, 0630; from Tapri, 0930. 4WD recommended between Karchham and Chitkul in bad weather.

**Chitkul** *p486*
Two **buses** a day to/from **Karchham** (0930) via Sangla (1100) and Rakcham; from **Tapri**, 0930; from **Recong Peo** 0600 (prompt).

**Recong Peo** *p487*
Reserve tickets from booth shortly before departure. Bus to **Chandigarh**; **Delhi** 1030; **Kalpa**, occasional; **Kaza** (9 hrs), gets very crowded so reserve seat before 0700; **Puh**; **Rampur**, frequent (5 hrs); **Sangla/Chitkul** (4 hrs); **Shimla**; **Tabo**, via Kaza (9-10 hrs), Rs 65.

**Kalpa** *p487*
**Bus** to **Shimla**, 0730; **Chitkul**, 1300. To get to Peo for Kaza bus at 0730, walk down (40 mins) or arrange taxi from Peo. Travellers may not be allowed beyond Jangi without an 'Inner Line' permit. Contact SDM in Recong Peo a day ahead, see page 477.

**Tabo** *p488*
Bus to **Chandigarh** via Kinnaur, 0900; **Kaza**, 1000.

**Kaza** *p490*
Reserve a seat at least 1 hr ahead or night before. The road via Kunzum-La and Rohtang Pass can be blocked well into Jul. New Bus Stand, bottom end of village. In summer: from **Manali** (201 km), 12 hrs via Rohtang Pass and Kunzum La; **Shimla** (412 km) on the route described, 2 days. Approx-imate times shown: daily to **Chango**, 1400;

**Kibber** 0900, **Losar** 0900; **Mikkim** (19 km from Attargo), in the Pin Valley, 1200 (2 hrs); returns 1400. Long-distance buses to **Kullu**, 0400; **Manali** (from Tabo), 0500; **Chandigarh** 0630. The last 3 are heavily used.

**Mandi** *p491*
**Bus**
Bus info T01905 235 538. **Chandigarh** 11.00(203 km, Rs138, 5 hrs). **Dharamshala** 1215, Rs 82, 6 hrs; **Kullu/Manali** every ½ hr, 3 hrs, Rs 52 (Kullu), 4 hrs, Rs 78 (Manali); **Shimla** (5½ hrs, Rs 120). Book private buses in town or opposite the bus stand at least **one day in advance**; they do not originate in Mandi. **Dharamshala**, 5 hrs, Rs 250. Kullu/Manali, 2 hrs (Kullu), 3½ hrs (Manali), Rs 150.

**Taxi**
Rs 600 to **Kullu**; Rs 1000 to **Manali**; Rs 1200 to **Dharamshala**.

**Train**
**Jogindernagar** (55 km), T01908 222 088, is on the narrow gauge from Pathankot.

**Tirthan Valley and Jalori Pass** *p492*
Taxis from **Banjar** to **Jalori Pass** cost Rs 600 (Rs 900 return), to **Jibhi/Ghayaghi** Rs 200, to **Kullu** Rs 600, to **Manali** Rs 1200, to **Mandi** Rs 700, to **Shimla**, Rs 3000, buses are rare.

From **Jibli** the bus to **Jalori** can take 1 hr (Rs 5). Some go via **Ghayaghi** (approximate times): **Kulla-Bagipul**, 0800; **Manali- Rampur**, 1000; **Kullu-Dalash**, 1100; **Manali-Ani**, 1100. If heading for Shimla or Kinnaur, change buses at Sainj on NH22.

Bus from **Ani** and **Khanag** to the south, runs to **Jalori Pass** and back. 4 buses daily traverse the pass in each direction when it is open (8-9 months). Bus to **Sainj**, 3½ hrs, and on to **Shimla**, 5 hrs.

## Directory

**Mandi** *p491*
**Banks** Bank of Baroda, Hospital Rd, in the old town centre, can take over an hour to change Visa; **Indian Overseas Bank** changes TCs. **Evening Plaza Hotel** is the only place to change cash (see above). Mandi has one of the few banks in Himachal able to give cash on Visa cards. Useful numbers Tourist info T01905 225 036, Police T01905 235 536, Hospital T01905 222 102.

# Kullu Valley

→ *Colour map 1, grid B3 and 4. For trekking, see page 534.*

*The Kullu Valley was the gateway to Lahul for the Central Asian trade in wool and borax. It is enclosed to the north by the Pir Panjal range, to the west by the Bara Bangahal and to the east by the Parvati range, with the Beas river running through its centre. The approach is through a narrow funnel or gorge but in the upper part it extends outwards. The name Kullu is derived from Kulantapith 'the end of the habitable world'. It is steeped in Hindu religious tradition; every stream, rock and blade of grass seemingly imbued with some religious significance. Today, the main tourist centre is Manali, a hive of adventurous activity in the summer months, a quiet and peaceful place to relax in the winter snow.* » *For Sleeping, Eating and other listings, see pages 504-512.*

## Kullu

→ *Phone code: 01902. Colour map 1, grid B3. Population: 18,300. Altitude: 1,219 m.*

Sprawling along the grassy west bank of the Beas, Kullu, the district headquarters, hosts the dramatically colourful Ḍasara festival. Less commercialized than its neighbour Manali, it is known across India as the home of apple growing and the locally woven woollen shawls. There is little to occupy you here as a tourist.

## Ins and outs

**Getting there** Kullu-Manali (Bhuntar) airport, 10 km south, has flights from Delhi, Shimla and Ludhiana; transfer by bus or taxi (Rs 150), to Manali (Rs 650), Manikaran (Rs 500). For buses from the south, get off at Dhalpur Bus Stand.

**Getting around** The Main Bus Stand and Dhalpur with ample hotels and restaurants are close enough for walking. Buses and taxis go to nearby sights. » *See Transport, page 511, for further details.*

**Climate** Mid-September to mid-November are the best seasons. May and June are hot but offer good trekking. March to mid-April can be cold with occasional heavy rain.

## Sights

The bulky curvilinear temples seem to resemble the huge boulders found in river beds and on hillsides. A peculiar feature of the Nagari temples is the umbrella-shaped covering made of wood or zinc sheets placed over and around the *amalaka* stone at the top of the spire.

The **Raghunathji Temple** is the temple of the principal god of the Dasara festival. The shrine houses an image of Shri Raghunath (brought here from Ayodhya in circa 1657), in his chariot. **Bhekhli**, a 3-km climb away, has excellent views from the **Jagannathi Temple**. The copper 16th-17th-century mask of the Devi inside has local

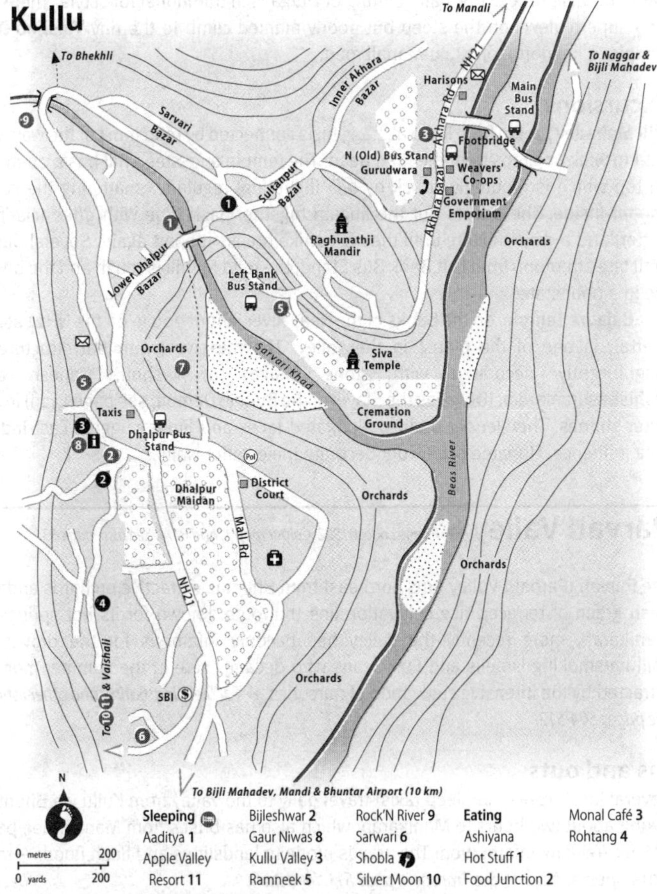

### Dasara in Kullu

Dasara celebrates Rama's victory over the demon Ravana. From their various high mountain homes about 360 gods come to Kullu, drawn in their raths (chariots) by villagers to pay homage to Raghunathji who is ceremoniously brought from his temple in Kullu.

The goddess Hadimba, patron deity of the Kullu Rajas has to come before any other lesser deities are allowed near. Her chariot is the fastest and her departure marks the end of the festivities. All converge on the maidan on the first evening of the festival in a long procession accompanied by shrill trumpeters. Thereafter there are dances, music and a market. During the high point of the fair a buffalo is sacrificed in front of a jostling crowd. Jamlu, the village God of Malana, high up in the hills, follows an old tradition. He watches the festivities from across the river, but refuses to take part! See page 538. On the last day Raghunathji's rath is taken to the river bank where a small bonfire is lit to symbolize the burning of Ravana, before Ragunathji is returned to his temple in a wooden palanquin.

Gaddi tribal features. The wall painting of Durga is in traditional folk style. There are also superb views on the steep but poorly marked climb to the tiny **Vaishno Devi Temple**, 4 km north, on Kullu-Manali road.

## Excursions

**Bijli Mahadev**, 11 km from Kullu at 2,435 m, is connected by road most of the way with a 2-km walk up steps from the road head. The temple on a steep hill has a 20-m rod on top which is reputedly struck by *bijli* (lightning) regularly, shattering the stone *lingam* inside. The priests put the lingam together each time with *ghee* (clarified butter) and a grain mixture until the next strike breaks it apart again. Several buses until late afternoon from Left Bank Bus Stand, the road to Bijli is rough and the buses are in a poor state.

**Bajaura Temple**, on the banks of the Beas River, about 200 m off the NH21 at **Hat** (Hatta), is one of the oldest in the valley. The massive pyramidal structure is magnificently decorated with stone images of Vishnu, Ganesh and Mahishasuramardini (Durga as the Slayer of the Buffalo Demon, see page 1329) in the outer shrines. The slender bodies, elongated faces and limbs suggest East Indian Pala influence. Floriated scrollwork decorate the exterior walls.



# Parvati Valley → *Phone code: 01902. Colour map 1, grid B3/4. See also page 536.*

The Parvati (Parbati) Valley runs northeast from Bhuntar. Attractive orchards and the fresh green of terraced rice cultivation line the route. Known for its hot springs at Manikaran, more recently the valley has become infamous for the droves of chillum-smoking Israelis and Europeans who decamp here in the summer months attracted by the intensive cultivation of narcotics. » *For Sleeping, Eating and other listings, see pages 504-512.*

## Ins and outs

Several local buses (and jeep taxis) travel daily to the valley from Kullu via Bhuntar, taking about two hours to Manikaran, which also has buses from Manali. See page 538 for trekking information. The area is prone to landslides and flash floods – take extra special care. » *See Transport, page 511, for details.*

## Disappearances in the valley

Cases of Western travellers going missing in the Kullu Valley in recent years continue to be reported. They seem to have occurred mostly when trekking alone or camping. Some suggest that there have beeen genuine accidents in the mountains or that some drug users have "opted out" and chosen to sever their ties and remain with sadhus in remote caves. On the other hand, in the summer of 2000 three trekkers were found dead, victims of two savage attacks. The threat to personal safety is very real so if you are trekking beyond Manikaran, or from Naggar across the Chandrakhani Pass to the Malana Valley, you should not walk alone. Only use registered guides through local trekking agents.

## Jari

Jari is the point where the deep Malana Nala joins the Parvati River. It is a popular resting place for trekkers but also for drug users. The guesthouses vary; a few away from the village centre have better views.

## Kasol

Kasol is the next village enroute to Manikaran. The rapidly expanding village has spread on both sides of the road bridge which crosses a tributary that flows into the Parvati, not far from the village itself. About half a kilometre beyond the village, a narrow side road leads to the river and the location of a fine hot spring on the river bank. Kasol is the main destination for long stay visitors, many of whom sit in a haze of charas smoke by day, repeating the process by night! **Chhalal** is a 20-minute walk from Kasol. It is a quiet village where families take in guests. A couple of guesthouses have also sprung up here.

## Manikaran

Manikaran, 45 km from Kullu, is at the bottom of a dark gorge with **hot sulphur springs** emerging from the rock strewn banks of the Parvati. The local legend describes how while Parvati bathed in the river, Naga, the serpent god stole her *manikaran* (earrings). At Siva's command Naga angrily blew them back from underground causing a spring to flow. Hindu and Sikh pilgrims come to the Rama temple and the gurdwara and gather to cook their food by the springs, purportedly the hottest in the world. There are separate baths for men and women. Manikaran, though not attractive in itself, provides a brief halt for trekkers. Short treks go to Pulga and Khirganga beyond while a footpath (affected by landslips in places), leads to the Pin Valley in Spiti. If trekking this route, go with a registered guide. Do not attempt alone. A road goes on for 15 km to **Barseni**. It has become a popular place with long-term travellers.

## Pulga and Khirganga

**Pulga**, a noisy village, seemingly overrun by giggling children, is in a beautiful location with some cheap guesthouses. It is a good four-hour walk east of Manikaran. Some longstay travellers prefer the basic airy guesthouses outside the village which offer meals.

**Khirganga** is along the trek which winds through the lush Parvati Valley, east of Pulga. It is known for its sacred ancient hot springs marking the place where Siva is thought to have meditated for 2,000 years. There is an open bathing pool for men and an enclosed pool for women, next to the humble shrine at the source. A few tents may be hired. *Dhabas* sell vegetarian food. This is the last village in this valley.

# Kullu to Manali → *Colour map 1, grid B3.*

The NH21 continues north along the west side of the Beas. The older road to the east of the river goes through terraced rice fields and endless apple orchards, and is rougher and more circuitous but more interesting. Sections of both roads can be washed away during the monsoon.

## Kullu to Katrain

As you wind out the centre of Kullu along the right bank you'll pass the **Sitaramata Temple** embedded in the conglomerate cliff and **Raison**, a grassy meadow favoured by trekkers. **Katrain**, in the widest part of the Kullu Valley, mid-way between Kullu and Manali, is overlooked by **Baragarh Peak** (3,325 m). There are plenty of options for an overnight stay. Across the bridge at **Patli Kuhl**, the road climbs through apple orchards to Naggar.

## Naggar → *Phone code: 01902. Colour map 1, grid B3.*

Naggar's (Nagar) interesting castle sits high above Katrain. Built in the early 16th century, it withstood the earthquake of 1905 and is a fine example of the timber-bonded building of West Himalaya. It was built around a courtyard with verandahs, from where there are enchanting views over the valley. With a pleasant, unhurried atmosphere, it is a good place to stop a while. It is also an entry for treks to Malana, see page 539.

The **castle**, probably built by Raja Sidh Singh, was used as a royal residence and state headquarters until the 17th century when the capital was transferred to Sultanpur (see Kullu). It continued as a summer palace until the British arrived in 1846, when it was sold to Major Hay, the first Assistant Commissioner, who Europeanized part of it, fitting staircases, fireplaces et cetera. Extensive renovations have produced fine results, especially in the intricately carved woodwork. In the first courtyard are several black *barselas* (sati stones) with primitive carvings. Beyond the courtyard and overlooking the valley the **Jagti Pat temple** houses a cracked stone slab measuring 2½ m by 1½ m by 2 m believed to be a piece of Deo Tibba which represents the deity in 'the celestial seat of all the gods'. A priest visits the slab every day.

The small **museum** ⓘ *Rs 10*, has some interesting exhibits, including examples of local women's dress and headdress (*pattu* and *thippu*) and folk dance costumes (*chola*). There are also local implements for butter and tea making, and musical instruments like the broad bell horn (*karnal*) and long curled horn (*singa*).

**Roerich Art Gallery** ⓘ *closed Mon, 0900-1300 (winter from 1000), 1400-1700, Rs 10*, a 2-km climb from the castle, is Nicholas Roerich's old home in a peaceful garden with excellent views. The small museum downstairs has a collection of photos and his distinctive stylized paintings of the Himalayas using striking colours.

**Uruswati Institute** ⓘ *Rs 15*, uphill from the main house, was set up in 1993. The Himalayan Folk and Tribal Art Museum is well presented, with contemporary art upstairs. One room upstairs is devoted to a charming collection of Russian traditional costumes, dolls, musical instruments.

There are a number of **temples** around the castle including the 11th-century Gauri Shankar Siva near the bazar, with some fine stone carving. Facing the castle is the Chaturbhuj to Vishnu. Higher up, the wooden Tripura Sundari with a multi-level pagoda roof in the Himachal style celebrates its fair around mid-May. Above that is the Murlidhar Krishna at Thawa, claimed as the oldest in the area which has a beautifully carved stone base. Damaged in the 1905 earthquake, it is now well restored. There are fine mountain views from here.

# Manali

→ *Phone code: 01902. Colour map 1, grid B3. Population: 6,300. Altitude: 1,926 m.*

Manali occupies the valley with the once unspoilt Old Village to the north and Vashisht, up on the opposite hillside across the river. Set amidst picturesque apple orchards, Manali is packed with Pahari-speaking Kullus, Lahaulis, Nepali labourers and enterprising Tibetan refugees who have opened guesthouses, restaurants and craft shops. The town has become increasingly built-up with dozens of new hotel blocks. It is also a major tourist destination for Indian holidaymakers. Others, together with adventure seeking foreigners, are attracted by the culturally different hill people and the scenic treks this part of the Himalaya offers. It is the start of the recommended two-day road route to Leh in the summer months. ▸▸ *For Sleeping, Eating and other listings, see pages 504-512.*

## Ins and outs

**Getting there** Kullu-Manali (Bhuntar) airport (near Kullu) is 50 km away with bus and taxi transfers. The bus and taxi stands are right in the centre (though many private buses stop short of the centre) within easy reach of some budget hotels – the upmarket ones are a taxi ride away. ▸▸ *See Transport, page 511, for further details.*

**Getting around** Manali and around, though hilly, is ideal for walking. For journeys outside taxi rates are high, so it is worth hiring a motorcycle to explore.

**Climate** Best season is March-April but occasional heavy rain and cold with snow in the villages. May-June and post monsoon mid-September to mid-November offer better trekking.

## Sights

The **Tibetan Monastery**, built by refugees, is not old but is attractive and is the centre of a small carpet making industry. Rugs and other handicrafts are for sale. The colourful **bazar** sells Kullu shawls, caps and Tibetan souvenirs.

**Old Manali** is 3 km away, across Manalsu Nala. Manali is named after Manu, the Law Giver, who legend tells arrived here by boat when fleeing from a great flood centuries ago. The road from newer Manali crosses Manalsu Nala and climbs uphill and through some unspoilt villages continuing to the modern Manu Mandir – visitors may have to abandon their aged rickshaws and walk up part of the hill. The last few years have seen continuing building work in the lower reaches of the village, where the buildings close to the bridge wear a look of fatigue. Higher up, newer guesthouses mingle with attractive old farmsteads with wooden balconies and thick stone tiled roofs. While out of season Old

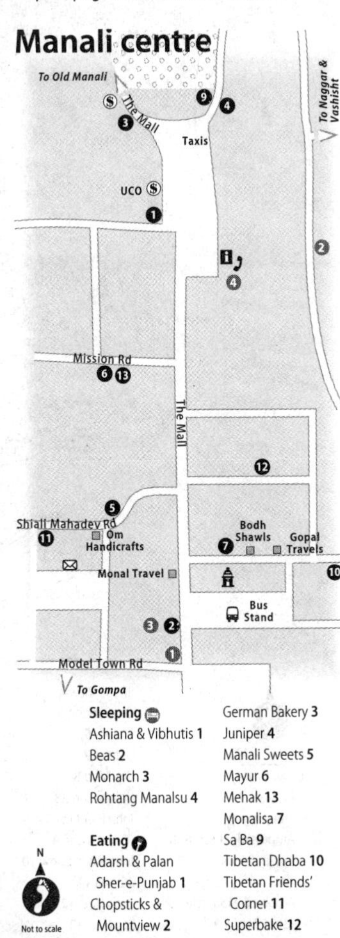

# Manali

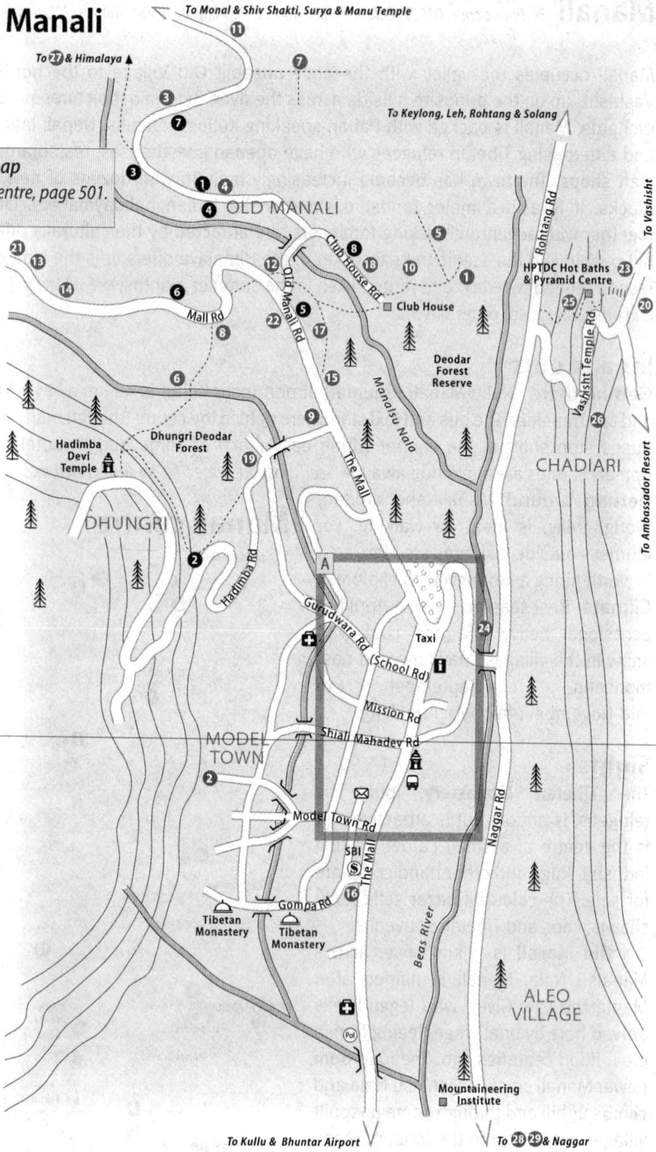

**Related map**
*A Manali centre, page 501.*

To 27 & Himalaya
To Monal & Shiv Shakti, Surya & Manu Temple
To Keylong, Leh, Rohtang & Solang
To Vashisht
To Ambassador Resort
OLD MANALI
Club House Rd
Old Manali Rd
Mall Rd
Club House
Rohtang Rd
HPTDC Hot Baths & Pyramid Centre
Vashisht Temple Rd
Deodar Forest Reserve
Manalsu Nala
The Mall
CHADIARI
Hadimba Devi Temple
Dhungri Deodar Forest
DHUNGRI
Hadimba Rd
Gurudwara Rd (School Rd)
Taxi
Mission Rd
Shiali Mahadev Rd
MODEL TOWN
Model Town Rd
Naggar Rd
SBI
Gompa Rd
Tibetan Monastery
Tibetan Monastery
Beas River
ALEO VILLAGE
Mountaineering Institute
To Kullu & Bhuntar Airport
To 28 29 & Naggar

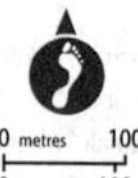


**Sleeping**
Ambassador Resorts **26**
Apple View & Upcountry Lodge **1**
Ambika & Mountview **2**
Ashok Mayur **3**
Bridge View **4**
Cairn Lodge **5**
Chetna **6**
Dragon **7**
Highland **8**
Holiday Inn **28**
John Banon's Guesthouse **9**
Jungal Bungalow **10**
Krishna **11**
Leela Huts **12**
Log Huts **13**
Manali Heights **14**
Manali Resort **29**
Mayflower **15**
Piccadily **16**
Pinewood **17**
Riverside Cottage **18**
Rockway **27**
Rohtang Manalsu **19**
Sita **20**
Snowcrest Manor **21**
Sunshine **22**
Surabhi **23**
Tourist Lodge **24**
Vishranti **25**

**Eating**
German Bakery **1**
Il Forno **2**
Ish **3**
Moondance **4**
Nirvana **5**
Rohtang Café **6**
Shiva **7**
Tibetan Kitchen **8**

## Freedom walking

Popular in Nepal, hiking independently is not feasible here; porters and/or horses are required to carry tents, food and so on. These are not always easily available and prices fluctuate considerably. A good arrangement is to go on an organized trek with a group. You can do it independently but it requires greater planning. Treks into or from Zanskar are recommended for the vigorously fit.

Manali retains a quiet charm, this can be diminished during the tourist season by the arrival of techno music and the drug scene.

**Vashisht** is a small hillside village that can be reached by road or a footpath, a 30-40-minute walk from tourist office. Note the carvings on the houses of the wealthy farmers. Below the village, there is a temple to Rama and Vashisht, with sulphur springs; remove shoes at the entrance (small fee). **Hot springs** at the top of the hill lead to free communal baths in the village centre.They can get dirty - best in the morning.Clean well-maintained baths are lower down but they were closed in 2001 and have yet to re-open. The village, with its messy jumble of old village houses and newer buildings, has cheap places to stay which attract a new generation of young travellers. A two-hour walk past the village up the hillside leads to a **waterfall**.

**Dhungri Village** is at the top of Hadimba Road. Follow the road uphill, past the gates leading to the temple and take the path 50 m further to arrive at the village centre. The village houses have cedar wood carving and balconies with superb views across the valley. Travellers are welcomed into family homes and traditional village life carries on around the guests, although several new developments, including a fun fair,are starting to change the flavour of the lower half of the village

**Hadimba Devi Temple**, the Dhungri temple (1553), in a clearing among ancient deodars, is an enjoyable 2-km walk from the tourist office. Built by Maharaja Bahadur Singh, the 27-m high pagoda temple has a three-tier roof and some fine naturalistic wood carving of animals and plants, especially around the doorway. The structure itself is relatively crude, and the pagoda is far from perfectly perpendicular. Massive deodar planks form the roof but in contrast to the scale of the structure the brass image of the goddess Hadimba inside, is tiny. A legend tells how the God Bhima fell in love with **Hadimba**, the sister of the demon Tandi. Bhima killed Tandi in battle and married Hadimba, whose spirituality, coupled with her marriage to a god, led to her being worshipped as a goddess. Today, she is seen as an incarnation of Kali. The small doorway, less than 1 m high, is surrounded by wood-carved panels of animals, mythical beasts, scrolls, a row of foot soldiers and deities, while inside against a natural rock is the small black image of the Devi. To the left is a natural rock shelter where legend has it that Hadimba took refuge and prayed before she was deified. The greatly enlarged footprints imprinted on a black rock are believed to be hers. Hadimba Devi plays a central part in the annual festival in May, at both Kullu and Manali. To prevent the master craftsman producing another temple to equal this elsewhere, the king ordered his right hand to be cut off. The artist is believed to have mastered the technique with his left hand and reproduced a similar work of excellence at Trilokinath in the Pattan Valley. Unfortunately, his new master became equally jealous and had his head cut off (see page 515)!

A **feast and sacrifice** is held in mid-July when the image from the new temple in Old Manali is carried to the Hadimba temple where 18 ritual blood sacrifices are performed. Sacrifices include a fish and a vegetable (!), but ends with the beheading of an ox in front of a frenzied crowd. This ceremony is not for the faint-hearted. Pickpockets are rife, and known to take advantage of awestruck tourists, so take care.

## Walks

Manali is the trail-head for a number of interesting and popular treks. There are also the following short hikes. Beyond Old Manali, the **shepherd trail**, which winds its way up and down the hillside, allows you to capture a picture of Himalayan life as well as see some superb birdlife. The path starts at some concrete steps (after *Ish* restaurant) on the first hairpin bend along the paved road to Old Manali (or you can pick it up where the road ends and taxis turn around at the top of the hill) and continues along the cemented path, which turns into a dirt trail. Return the same way four to five hours.

**1.** This walk takes you towards Solang. In Old Manali Village take the right fork and then turn left in front of the new temple. This trail is a classic, following the right bank of the Beas River up towards the Solang Valley passing the villages of **Goshal**, **Shanag**, **Buruwa** to **Solang** (2,480 m), a small ski resort with all of 2½ km of runs! Solang is 14 km (five hours). You can get tea, biscuits and nuts along the walk and even be tempted by steaming spicy noodles, there are also places to stay. See under Manali sleeping listings. To return to Manali it is a steady walk down the valley side to the main Rohtang Pass-Manali Highway where you can pick up a bus (Rs 5) or shared jeep (Rs 10).

**2.** Go prepared for cold for this walk as it takes you through woodland shading you from the sun. Keeping the **Hadimba Temple** on your right follow the contour of the hill and bear right to pick up a clear pack-horse trail which heads up the steep valley. This is a steady uphill climb through woodland giving superb views of the river below, abundant Himalayan birdlife and a chance to see all manner of activity in the woods, chopping, cutting and burning. An enjoyable 3 to 4 hour walk.

**3.** This walk takes you to the village of **Sethan** (12 km). Take a local bus to the *Holiday Inn* on the Naggar road. With the hotel behind you, cross the road and pass through the orchard and fields which have low mud walls all round which can be walked on. Bear east till you come to a disused track and then bear right and follow it to the once untouched village of **Prini** which now has several five-star hotels! If you are lucky the *chai* shop will be open. Further east, the trail to Sethan village becomes somewhat indistinct, though local people are at hand to point you in the right direction. It is a superb three-hour hike up a wooded valley to Sethan (3,000 m), which is well off the tourist trail.



## Sleeping

**Kullu** *p496, map p497*
The choice of hotels is widening, some good hotels in all ranges, though very full during Dasara. Large off-season discounts (30-50%).

**A Apple Valley Resorts**, Mohal, NH21, on the Beas River, 6 km from airport, T01902 260 001, aplvaley@nde.vsnl.net.in. 36 comfortable, very well-designed modern chalets in landscaped grounds, excellent food, friendly reception, rafting nearby.

**B Gaur Niwas**, Dhalpur, close to tourist office, T01902 226 675. 4 spacious, comfortable rooms in charming period property, beautiful balconies, easily most atmospheric place in town.

**B-C Shobla**, T01902 222 800, 25 rooms, flashy exterior, central, clean, pleasant atmosphere, airy restaurant, overlooking river.

**C Silver Moon** (HPTDC), perched on a hill, 2 km south of centre, T01902 222 488, www.hptdc.nic.in (taxis Rs 50 from Kullu centre, buses stop at gate if requested – ask for the last barrier south out of Kullu). 6 rooms with bath and heaters, each with small sitting room in traditional style, very clean, good food, has character (enhanced because Mahatma Gandhi stayed here).

**C Vaishali**, Gandhinagar, 1 km south of bus stand No 2, T01902 224 225, hnsingh2001 @yahoo.com. 33 rooms, excellent restaurant, immaculate kitchen, pleasant small garden running down to river, rafting 4 km south.

**C-D Sarwari**(HPTDC), 10-min walk south of Dhalpur Bus Stand, T01902 222 471. 16 simple but comfortable rooms (10 in more spacious new wing), 8-bed dorm (Rs 75), good value restaurant, beer, pleasant gardens, elevated with good views, peaceful.

**D Rock 'n' River**, near Sarwari Bridge, T01902 224 214. 16 clean rooms with good views of the river, pleasant location, friendly manager.

**D-E Aaditya**, Lower Dhalpur, T01902 224 263. Decently furnished rooms with bath (hot shower), some with river-facing balcony, others cheaper, smart, room service meals, bar.

**D-E Ramneek**, Dhalpur, T01902 222 558. 21 clean rooms with bath (hot water), TV, decently maintained.

**E Bijleshwar View**, T01902 222 677. 10 rooms with fireplace, TV, bath (hot water), new restaurant, peaceful garden, friendly.

**E Rohtang**, Dhalpur, T01902 222 303. 12 rooms with bath, restaurant (Indian, Chinese), simple, clean and good value.

**E-F Kullu Valley Hotel**, Akhara Bazar, T01902 222 223. Rooms with TV, phone, bath tub, restaurant.

**Jari** *p499*

**F** options are springing up along the main road, but the following is in the most peaceful setting:

**F Village Guest House**, TT01902 273 236, follow signs, a 10-minwalk up, through and beyond village. There are 5 simple rooms with clean, shared hot bath and a restaurant in an excellent location on the edge of a traditional farming village, very friendly, good value.

**Kasol** *p499*

**C-D Sandhya ( formerly Kasol Resorts)**, T01902 173 047. Good choice of 20 smart, modern rooms including 1 **B** family suite, hot water, TV, rooftop restaurant.

**F** There are now at least 30 guesthouses and family houses which take in paying guests in this expanding village, some of the best are:

**Holiday Home**, 15 okay rooms, closed off season.

**Yerpa's**, on the main drag, T01902 227 363. Large, fairly modern building which grows every year, offers reasonable rooms and a pleasant rooftop restaurant.

**Bhoj**, a family home close to Yerpa's, basic rooms in an interesting family environment.

**Manikaran** *p499*

**C-D Country Charm**, main bus stand, T01902 273 703. Not really in the country, but one of the smarter places in town, with 10 brand new rooms, good value off season.

**D Parvati**, near the temple, T01902 273 735. 10 simple rooms, sulphur baths, restaurant.

**D Shivalik**, T01902 273 817. 20 acceptable rooms with TV, restaurant with good choice of dishes.

There are a large number of **E** and **F** guesthouses in the lower part of the village, some with baths fed by the hot springs. However, prices in season rise to unbelievable rates given that most rooms are of the basic to very basic variety, at best. Some obviously cater for the drug-induced end of the market, so choose carefully. Local families also take paying guests.

**Katrain** *p500*

**A Span Resort**, T01902 240 138, spanres@del3.vsnl.net.in. 25 rooms in 8 attractive stone cottages with overlooking the river, sports, riding, good views, trout hatchery nearby ensures good river fishing, very comfortable, but some **C** category facilities.

**C River View (HPTDC)**, T01902 240 836, www.hptdc.nic.in. 2 family sized cottages, attractive décor, comfortable.

**C-D Orchard Resorts**, in Dobhi, 2 km south of Katrain, T01902 240 160.16 attractive wood-panelled 'cottages', with hot water, TV, heaters, good off season discount.

**E Anglers' Bungalow**, T01902 240 136, 6 spartan rooms with superb views.

**Naggar** *p500*

**B-C Castle**, T01902 247 816, www.hptdc.nic.in. Built in 1460, has been a hotel since 1978, 13 rooms, stylish but traditional decor and furniture, comfortable beds, fireplaces, modernized baths, best **B** overlook valley, some share bath (**E**), very basic dorm (Rs 75), restaurant, good service.

**D Ragini**, T01902 248 185, raginihotel@hotmail.com. 16 smart rooms with modernized baths (hot water), large windows, good views from rooftop restaurant, good value, friendly.

**D-E Poonam Mountain Lodge**, T01902 247 747. 6 spotless rooms, constant hot water, very good food, but avoid insistence on booking treks.

**D-E Sheetal**, T01902 248 250. 14 very pleasant rooms with bath, overlooking valley, clean and spacious, hot water (some tubs), TV, use of kitchen.

**E-F Snow View**, down steps past Tripura Sundari Temple, T01902 248 325, 7 rooms and restaurant plus weaving co-op outlet.

**F Alliance**, 200 m above castle, T01902 47763. 6 rooms, hot water, meals, clean, simple, homely, run by French ex-pat, very good value.

**F Chand Kulvi**, near Bus Stand, T01902 248 379. 8 rooms, some with bath, away from road, lovely garden.

**F Uttam**, near bus stand. Pleasant clean rooms with hot shower.

**Manali** *p501, maps p502 and p501*

Hotels are often full in May and Jun so better to visit off-season when most offer discounts. Winter heating is a definite bonus. There are many cheap hotels on School Rd. Model Town offer modest rooms, often shared baths. May only provide hot water in buckets. Families in Dhungri Village offer rooms with basic facilities (Rs 50-70). Several are in traditional houses, clean rooms, basic bedding, small stove (fuel can be bought), some have balconies with fantastic views. The village of Vashisht is another option. In Old Manali, generally the further you walk, the greater the reward. Those above the Club House are almost out of Old Manali and are in a great location overlooking the valley but close to town still. Those options listed below that are outside the centre of Manali are stated as being so in the address.

**L Highland Park**, 5 km from Solang towards Manali, T01902 256 501. New development consisting of well made Swiss chalets, each containing two bedrooms, with good riverside views in pleasant surroundings.

**AL Holiday Inn**, 2.5 km south of Manali on Naggar Rd, T01902 251 777, www.holidayinn-manali.com. 55 rooms in luxury hotel boasting usual five star facilities, better than unprepossessing exterior suggests.

**AL Manali Resorts**, 5 km south of Manali on Kullu Rd, T01902 252 274, www.manaliresorts.com. 37 rooms, a luxury base for winter sports, lovely position with landscaped gardens by Beas River.

**AL-A Ambassador Resorts**, Sunny Side, Chadiari, overlooking Old Manali, T01902 252 235, www.ambassadorresorts.com. 53 smart, imaginative rooms, most done in a contemporary design using wood and marble , good views and facilities, a definite cut above, recommended.

**A Leela Huts**, Sunshine Orchards, The Mall (N), T01902 252 464, www.leelahuts.com. Not really huts but small stone houses, 3 with 3 bedrooms and 2 with 2, plus drawing/dining room and kitchen, done to a good standard, not bad value for size, set in well tended gardens.

**A Log Huts** (HPTDC), top of Circuit House Rd high above Manalsu Nala, T01902 253 225. 2-bedroom cottages, 12 newer and modern, 6 spacious though dated and somewhat musty (built in 1965), kitchen, attractive views, cafeteria nearby and room service.

**A Piccadily**, The Mall, T01902 252 113, www.piccadilyhotel.com. 70 rooms, clean, modern though signs of wear, welcoming reception, good restaurant but very slow service, many facilities including pool and gym.

**A Snowcrest Manor** , beyond Log Huts, T01902 253 351, www.ushashriramhotels.com. 32 comfortable, Rohtang-facing rooms, modern hotel, on steep hillside, great views (especially from dining terrace), every conceivable facility including gym, bar, disco, kids particularly well looked after.

**A-B Banon Resorts**, T01902 253 026, banonresorts@vsnl.net. 32 well appointed rooms in modern hotel, good views from balconies, attractive garden.

**B Manali Heights**, near Log Huts, T01902 252 621, www.manaliheights.com. 31 centrally heated rooms, bath tubs, direct dialling, all comforts, discount packages available.

**B Orchard Greens**, Log Huts Area, T01902 252 444, www.togmanali.com. 29 modern

*For an explanation of the sleeping and eating price codes used in this guide, see inside the front cover. Other relevant information is found in Essentials pages 56-61.*

rooms, pleasant lawn and terrace, eager staff, reasonable value.

**B-C Highland**, near Log Huts, T01902 252 399. 36 predominantly pine rooms (22 new centrally heated), some with balcony, hot showers, restaurant (mainly Chinese), pleasant garden, starting to show its age.

**B-C John Banon's Guest House**, Manali Orchards, T01902 252335. 12 rooms with snow views (6 newer **B**), full board (good Continental), garden, peaceful, simple, rustic but pleasant.

**C Johnson's Lodge**, The Mall, T01902 253 023, jayajc@hotmail.com. 12 very elegant rooms (cottages also available), great bathrooms, outstanding restaurant (see eating listings), recommended.

**C Mayflower**, The Mall, opposite Circuit House, T01902 252 104, negismayflower @sancharnet.in. 18 rooms, spacious, tastefully decorated wood-panelled suites, TV, restaurant only in high season, great value, friendly, well-run, recommended.

**D Ashiana**, T01902 52232. Clean, comfortable rooms with hot shower, good restaurant.

**D Bhrigu**, just above HPTDC Baths, Vashisht, T01902 253 414. Comfortable, if dated rooms with bath, some with good views, restaurant.

**D Chetna**, near Log Huts, T52245. 13 comfortable rooms with balconies, hot water, good open-air restaurant, lawns, elevated, with beautiful views.

**D Pinewood**, The Mall, T01902 250 118. 10 old fashioned but atmospheric, heated roomsplus restaurant, gardens, good views and a quiet location.

**D Rohtang Manalsu (HPTDC)**, near Circuit House, The Mall, T01902 252 332, www.hptdc.nic.in. 27 large rooms, good restaurant, garden, superb views.

**D Sita**, near HPTDC Baths, Vashisht, T01902 252 164. Good rooms and restaurant.

**D Sunshine**, The Mall, T01902 252 320. 9 rooms in old traditional house, others in newer cottage, log fires, lot of character, restaurant, lovely garden, peaceful, family atmosphere, friendly, good value.

**D Surabhi** below Vashisht, T01902 252 796. Clean, attractive rooms, modern bath fittings (real tubs!), big windows facing mountains, cable TV, restaurant, exchange, exceptional value off-season.

**D-E Ashok Mayur**, about 300 m from bridge (opposite Shiva Café), Old Manali. The few comfortable rooms here benefit from a terrace and restaurant.

**D-E Beas (HPTDC)**, near bridge, T01902 252 832, www.hptdc.nic.in. 31 somewhat run down rooms with bath, TV, breakfast, room service meals, magnificent river views.

**D-E Dragon**, Old Manali, T01902 252 790, dragontours@hotmail.com. 16 comfortable rooms with bath, traditional construction, internet, fine mountain views, garden, apple orchard, café.

**E Ambika**, Model Town, T01902 252 203. 28 large and airy rooms with clean bath, mountain views, average meals, use of kitchen, excellent value, best of many.

**E Cairn Lodge**, above Club House, Old Manali, T01902 252 861. 3 pleasant, comfortable, wood-panelled rooms, attached hot bath, good café.

**E Monarch**, above Chopsticks restaurant, The Mall, T01902 252 539. Basic but well kept rooms in good location, friendly, honest manager.

**E Mountview**, end of Model Town Rd, T01902 252 465. 23 cozy rooms, shower and western toilet, some with great views, heater Rs 50, discounts off-season when restaurant is closed.

**E-F Bodh**, Vashisht, T01902 254 165, bunteee23@hotmail.com. 5 clean, tidy rooms, shared bath (hot shower), good views from terrace.

**E-F Monal**, above Old Manali, beyond Manu Temple, up steep cemented steps, T01902 253 848. 9 rooms, some with hot showers, others shared, café, pretty garden, superb views all round.

**E-F Shiv Shakti**, above Old Manali, beyond Manu Temple, T01902 254 170. 4 pleasant rooms and café attached hot bath, friendly farming family, fine views across valley and mountains beyond.

**E-F Upcountry Lodge**, above Club House, Old Manali, T01902 252 257. 9 clean rooms, attached hot bath, quiet location in orchards, pleasant garden.

**F Apple View**, above Club House in orchard, Old Manali, T01902 253 899. 4 clean rooms with shared hot bath in quiet location.

**F Freedom Café**, Dhungri Village, takes guests.

**F Himalaya Cottage**, above Old Manali, 8 simple rooms, restaurant, fine location by the river.

**F Jungal Bungalow**, above Club House, Old Manali, T01902 252 278. 7 clean rooms, common hot shower, good service, friendly, pleasant atmosphere.
**F Krishna**, Old Manali on the village outskirts, T01902 253 071. Well established, 8 basic rooms, common bath (hot water), verandah with great views of snowy peaks.
**F Rockway Cottage**, above Old Manali, the last one before the wilderness, a 10-min walk from the road, T01902 254 328.10 well crafted, but simple rooms, most with local heaters, clean common bath, very friendly, excellent location. Recommended.
**F Scenic Cottage**, Dhungri Village, some rooms with baths.
**F Surya Cottage**, above Old Manali, beyond Manu Temple, T01902 254 362. 6 rooms with shared hot bath, simple, friendly, good value.

## Eating

**Kullu** *p496, map p497*
**Ashiyana** in hotel, Sarvari Bazar. Clean, good south Indian.
**Hot Stuff Food Junction**, near tourist information. Good for snacks, light meals, outdoor seating.Planet Food, next door to above, similar but slightly more upmarket with beer bar as well, good value thalis.
**Monal Café**, simple meals.
**Shobla**, in hotel. Has pleasant restaurant. Vaishali's a/c restaurant is excellent.

**Kasol** *p499*
**Deep Forest**, at the back of the village, open 24 hrs in the season, usual travellers fare.
**Evergreen Restaurant** is the most popular with a wide choice of Indian and western food including all the travellers' favourites plus more. A major meeting place in season.
**Moondance**, in centre of village, pleasant building with good German Bakery.

**Manikaran** *p499*
**Sikh Gurudwara**, does excellent meals, steam cooked at the springs (donation only). Wayside stalls serve local food, while some near the springs cater for westerners; there are also a couple of okay *dhabas* by the bus stand. Others include: **Holy Palace**, in bazar, look for the finely carved doors. There is a classier sister concern of **Evergreen** in Kasol, similar menu.

**Pulga** *p499*
**Paradise Restaurant**, in the village, does great vegetarian dishes. Also has information on guides and equipment for treks up the valley and over the Pin-Parvati Pass (5,300 m). If you are lucky, you may be able to persuade the watchman of the old **Forest Rest House** to let you in. The 'visitors' registration book' contains entries that date back to the 1930's and include several well known mountaineers who have passed by.

**Naggar** *p500*
**Chandrakhani Himalayan Health Food**, Roerich Marg, above Tripura Sundari temple. Serves local food – millet, brown rice, tofu, fresh pasta and cheese.
**Nightingale**, 200 m above bus stand. Trout.
**Ristorante Italiano**, bus stand. Open in season, Fri-Sun.

**Manali** *p501, maps p502 and p501*
Hotels may need advance notice from non-residents. Some close in the off-season. In Dhungri Village, there is a bakery and restaurant opposite the temple. Stalls sell snacks, drinks and necessities. In Old Manali there are plenty of Israeli dishes and music which can range from techno to Tibetan.
𝚈𝚈𝚈 **Johnson's Café**, Circuit House Rd, T01902 253 023. Western (varied menu). Elegant restaurant in a large garden, specializes in trout, excellent home made pasta, good filter coffee, delicious icecreams. Recommended.
𝚈𝚈 **Adarsh**, The Mall (opposite Kunzam). One of many Punjabi places, but has more style and better menu than others.
𝚈𝚈 **Chopsticks**, The Mall, opposite Bus Stand. Tibetan, Chinese, Japanese. Very good food, large helpings, very good curd and pancakes, also good breakfast (porridge), friendly, warm (wood-burning stoves), welcoming.
𝚈𝚈 **Juniper**. Good Indian, Chinese.
𝚈𝚈 **Il Forno**, Hadimba Rd. Italian. Attractive pizzeria, half way up hill.
𝚈𝚈 **Italiano**, corner of Mall and Circuit House Rd, 1st floor. Well cooked selection of pizza, pasta and fish, good value.
𝚈𝚈 **Mayur**, Mission Rd. Vast international menu. Excellent food, smart, efficient service, subdued decor, very pleasant with linen table cloths and candles on tables, Indian classical music, great ambience, cosy with wood-burning stove and generator.

**ŸŸ Mehak**, next to **Mayur**, cheaper imitation but does very tasty Gujurati and Punjabi.
**ŸŸ Monalisa** in Bazar. International. Friendly, smallish, good choice, popular.
**ŸŸ Mountview**, The Mall, opposite Bus Stand. Good Tibetan, Japanese, some Chinese. Unpretentious, pleasant, warm (wood-burning stove), friendly amiable owner.
**ŸŸ Sa Ba**, Nehru Park. Mixed. Excellent Indian, snacks, pizzas, cakes, some outdoor seating to people-watch, recommended (no toilet).
**ŸŸ Vibhuti's**, The Mall, corner of Model Town Rd, up short flight of steps. South Indian vegetarian. Delicious *masala dosas*.
**Ÿ Green Forest**, Dhungri Village, on the forest path, past temple down towards Old Manali, just after leaving the forest. Vegetarian. Excellent breakfasts and meals.
**Ÿ Ish**, Old Manali, on left past shops going uphill (before road swings to right). Fruit muesli, pizzas.
**Ÿ Manali Sweets**, Shiali Mahadev Rd. Excellent Indian sweets (superb *gulab jamuns!*), also good *thalis* (Rs 40).
**Ÿ Moondance**, opposite **Pizza Olive**, Old Manali. Good choice of western favourites. Recommended.
**Ÿ Mountview**, end of Model Town Rd. Italian, Indian. Good pizzas, spaghetti, opens 0600 for breakfast.
**Ÿ Palan Sher-e-Punjab**, near Taxis, The Mall. Good Punjabi vegetarian.
**Ÿ Pizza Olive**, Old Manali, lives up to its name.
**Ÿ Rasta Café**, above Old Manali, near **Surya**. Popular, modern, with ubiquitous Bob Marley!
**Ÿ River Music**, by bridge. Popular hangout, travellers' staples plus Israeli.
**Ÿ Tibet Kitchen**, across Manalsu bridge, Club House Rd. Tasty momos, pleasant ambience, friendly service.
**Ÿ Tibetan Dhaba**, back of bus station. Very small and cosy, great *momos*.
**Ÿ Tibetan Friends' Corner**, behind the post office. Shop with café above. Excellent *momos* and Tibetan dishes, good value.
**Ÿ Yangkhor**, past **Moondance**. Tibetan and western favourites.

**Cafés and fast food**

**German Bakery**, opposite Nehru Park, good cakes, breads, real coffee, friendly, popular.
**Lhasa Café**, in Vashisht, above **Vashisht Video Hall** (which shows 2-3 films daily).
**Pyramid Centre**, path below HPTDC Baths, Vashisht. Western. Set in beautiful relaxing garden with wonderful views across valley, hot/cold drinks, cakes, 0700-2200; glassed-in section offers tasty and varied veg dishes (Italian manager), massage, London trained hairdresser in summer, local information on activities.
**Shiva Garden Café**, 100 m further uphill in Old Manali. Good food with an adventurous international flavour plus 'German bakery', delightful spot, pleasant ambience with open-air seating, restful music (Tibetan enterprise) good views over Manalsu Nala, very reasonable.
**Superbake**, Vashisht, has some good bread, cakes, biscuits and chilled drinks.
**Tibetan Kitchen, German Bakery**, over-the-counter branch, just beyond Manalsu bridge, and left, Old Manali. Reasonably priced cakes, breads, real coffee, trekkers' supplies.
**Zodiac Café**, Vashisht, for food, music and wonderful cinnamon *chai*, great for meeting other travellers.

## Festivals and events

**Kullu** *p496, map p497*

**End-Apr** Colourful 3-day **Cattle Fair** attracts villagers from the surrounding area. Numerous cultural events accompany. **Dasara** is sacred to the goddess Durga which, elsewhere in India, tends to be overshadowed by **Diwali** which follows a few weeks later. In this part of the Himalaya it is a great social event and a get-together of the Gods.

**Manali** *p501, maps p502 and p501*

**Mid-Feb** Week-long **Winter Sports** Carnival. **May** 3-day colourful **Dhungri Forest festival** at Hadimba Devi Temple, celebrated by hill women.

## Shopping

**Kullu** *p496, map p497*

Best buys are shawls, caps, *gadmas*. The state weaving co-operative, **Bhutti Weavers Colony**, 6 km south, has retail outlets, **Bhuttico**; 1 store 2 km south of **Apple Valley Resorts**.

Akhara Bazar has a **Govt Handicrafts Emporium, Himachal Khadi Emporium** and Khadi Gramudyog. **Charm Shilp** is good for sandals.

**Manali** *p501, maps p502 and p501*

**Books**

**Bookworm**, NAC Market, behind Bus Station. Huge stock of quality paperbacks, reasonably priced. Highly recommended. New branch near Manali Post, 1000-1800.

**Crafts and local curios**

**Bhutico Bodh**, along the Hindu Temple in bazaar, T52269, has a good range of shawls.
**Charitable Trust Tibetan Handicrafts**, the Mall, government shop.
**Manushi**, in the market, women's co-op producing good quality shawls, hats, socks.
**Om Collection**, good Tibetan T-shirts, dresses, jewellery, jumpers.
**Shree-la Crafts**, friendly owner, good value silver jewellery. Tibetan Bazar and Tibetan Carpet Centre.

**Tailors**

**Gulati Traders**, Gulati Complex, Sikh tailors, quick, good quality, copies and originals (caps to order, ready in hrs, Rs 75).

**Trekking equipment**

**Ram Lal and Sons**, E9 Manu Market, behind bus stand, good range of well-made products, friendly, highly recommended.

## ▲ Activities and tours

**Kullu** *p496, map p497*

**Look East**, c/o Bajaj Autos, Manikaran Chowk, Shamshi, T01902 065771. Operator recommended for river rafting and bike hire.

**Naggar** *p500*

For trekking to Malana, it is best to employ a local guide. Pawan, from the old *chai* shop in the main village, is recommended. Avoid **Poonam's**.

**Manali** *p501, maps p502 and p501*

**Skiing and mountaineering**

**Mountaineering and Allied Sports Institute**, 1.5 km out of town, T01902 252 342, organizes courses in mountaineering, skiing, watersports, high altitude trekking and mountain-rescue courses; 5 and 7-day ski courses, Rs 3,000 for the latter, Jan-Mar. There is a hostel, an exhibition of equipment and an auditorium.

**Tour companies**

**Himalayan Adventurers**, opposite Kunzam, T01902 252 750, www.himalayanadventurersindia.com. Wide range of itineraries and activities.
**Swagatam**, opposite Kunzam, The Mall, T01902 252 990. Long-distance buses, trekking, rafting, very efficient.
**HPTDC**, T01902 253 531 or 252 116. Daily, in season by luxury coach (or car for five): to Nehru Kund, Rahla Falls, Marhi, Rohtang Pass, 1000-1700, Rs 150 (car Rs 1,000); to Solang, Jagatsukh and Naggar; 1000-1600, Rs 170 (car Rs 1,100); to Manikaran, 0900-1800, Rs 175 (car Rs 900).
**Club House**, HPTDC, on river bank, has snooker, billiard, badminton, table tennis, well-appointed restaurant and bar, Rs 5 plus table/court fees. Also a small museum on Himachali culture. A gym and steam bath are planned. Primarily in place for domestic visitors.

**Trekking**

Clarify details and number of trekkers involved and shop around before making any decisions.
**Himalayan Journeys**, near German Bakery, T01902 252 365, www.himalayanjourneysindia.com. Good range, experienced guides.
**Magic Mountain**, no office as such, but call Raju on T98160 56934, www.magicmountainadventures.com. Manali's most experienced cycling guide, Raju also offers trekking and jeep safaris, and is honest, friendly and reliable, highly recommended.
**Shambala**, Shop no 24, New Shopping Complex Market, behind bus stand, T01902 252 690, www.shambhalatreks.com. Excellent guides, horses and food, knowledgable and friendly owner, eco friendly, highly recommended
**Shangri-la Adventures**, Tibetan Colony, Rohtang Rd, T01902 252 734, shang-adv@hotmail.com. Treks to Zanskar, Ladakh, Spiti, fishing, rafting, experienced Tibetan guides, competitive pricing for small groups, excellent service from Jigme, honest, friendly.
**WH Adventure Travel**, opposite Rambagh Taxi Stand, The Mall, T98170-69096, whadventure@yahoo.com. Mr Ghosh is very

knowledgeable, advises on routes; organizes treks, jeep safaris, mountaineering in Lahul, Spiti, Zanskar and Ladakh.

## Transport

**Kullu** *p496, map p497*

**Air**

Transport to town: buses and taxis at the airport. **Jagson**, Dhalpur Maidan, T01902 266 187, Apt T01902 265 303, to **Delhi, Shimla**, flights often cancelled, also **Indian Airlines**, T01902 265 037.

**Bus**

Most buses coming to Kullu continue to Manali. Main Bus Stand, Sarvari Khad with a booking office: for long distance and to **Manali**; Left Bank Bus Stand across the bridge: buses for **Naggar** (half hourly in summer) and **Bijli Mahadev**; some go to **Manali**; Dhalpur Bus Stand for buses to the south but board these at the Main Bus Stand to be sure of a seat. HPTDC deluxe bus to **Chandigarh** (270 km), 0800, 8 hrs, Rs 320; **Delhi** (512 km) 15 hrs (extra buses during season), government and *HPTDC buses* are better than some private ones, leaves Delhi 1600, Rs 400 (a/c Rs 600, plus new Volvo service, rs800); **Dharamshala**, 0800-0900, 8 hrs, Rs 250; **Shimla** (235 km), 0900, 8 hrs, Rs 250. Tickets from Tourist Office.

**Parvati Valley** *p498*

There are frequent buses from Bhuntar airport (which has buses to Kullu/Manali 1 hr 50 mins, Rs 20).

**Naggar** *p500*

The bus stop is in the Bazar, below the castle. Daily bus between **Kullu** and **Manali** via Naggar by the scenic east bank route; Kullu and Manali (1½ hrs each, Rs 5). Manali to **Patli Kuhl** (6 km from Naggar, 45 mins, Rs 10); where you can get a local bus (half hourly in summer), rickshaw (Rs 60).

**Manali** *p501, maps p502 and p501*

**Air**

Flights connect Bhuntar Airport near Kullu T01902 265 037, with Delhi, Shimla and Ludhiana. **Jagsons**, T01902 252 843. Transport to town: taxi to Manali, Rs 800 for 4 persons. Himachal Transport (green) bus, every 15 mins, Rs 25 (allow 2½ hrs travel time from Manali).

**Bus**

Bus Stand T01902 252 323

**Long distance** See page 123. HPTDC coaches in season (fewer in winter); Deluxe have 2 seats on either side: **Harisons** and **Swagatam** (see directory), run own buses. **Chandigarh** 0700, 10 hrs, Rs 225; **Delhi** a/c 1530, 15 hrs, Rs 585; non a/c 1700, Rs 350. **Dharamshala** 0530, 0810, Rs 191, **Keylong** 0600, 6 hrs, Rs 98. **Kullu** via **Naggar**: 2 daily, Rs 30, 1 hr; other Kullu buses via NH stop at **Patli Kuhl** (see Naggar above). **Mandi**, Rs 87. **Rohtang Pass** 0900, day trip with photo-stops, striking scenery (take sweater/jacket), 1½ hrs at pass, Rs 120. **Shimla** (280 km), 0900, 1900, 9 hrs, Rs 250. **To Leh** HPTDC and private coaches run ordinary and luxury buses during the season (mid-Jun to end-Sep), but not always daily; usually based on demand. Seats should be reserved ahead. Front seats are best though the cab gets filled by locals wanting a 'lift'. Those joining the bus in Keylong must reserve from Manali to be certain of a seat. Rs 400-850 (Rs 1,200 including tent and meals); usual overnight stop is at Sarchu where other cheaper tents may be available (some choose to sleep on the bus). The 530 km takes about 24-28 hrs on the road, 0600, arrive Leh next afternoon. Various State RTCs offer direct services to major towns. HRTC Bus Stand, The Mall, reservations, 1000-1200, 1400-1600. Reports of some drivers getting drunk, hence unsafe.

**Motorbike**

Enfields and Hondas for hire; reasonable charges at **Enfield Club**, Vashisht Rd, T01902 254 090, friendly, honest service.

**Nirvana**, Circuit House Rd, T01902 253 222. Choice of bikes in good condition (on-site mechanic), Enfield Rs 6,000 per month, others Rs 5,000, daily rate Rs 300, 3rd party insurance, helmets, professional service. Recommended. Passport or air ticket must be left as a deposit; reserve ahead in high season.

**Bony Sony Motors**, Old Manali, T01902 253 967, good service, knowledgable and experienced mechanics, recommended. The uncrowded Kullu-Manali road via Naggar is an ideal place for a test ride.

**Taxi**

**Local** The local union is very strong, office near tourist office, T01902 252 450. Fares tend to be high; from bus stand: Rs 50 for hotels (2-3 km). To Vashisht or top of Old Manali Rd, Rs 60; auto-rickshaws Rs 30. **Long distance** **Aut**, Rs 900, Rs 1,200 (return); **Darcha**, Rs 3,000; **Keylong**, Rs 2,400; **Kullu**, Rs 550 (Rs 800 return); **Mandi**, Rs 1,200 (Rs 1,500 return); **Naggar**, Rs 350 (Rs 400 return); **Rohtang Pass**, Rs 900, Rs 1,200.

**Train**

From Delhi, up to **Chandigarh** or **Shimla**, or via Pathankot to **Jogindernagar**, and then bus transfers, see page 123

## Directory

**Kullu** *p496, map p497*

**Banks** State Bank of Patiala, T01902 222 457 (1100-1400), Akhara Bazar (north of town) for foreign exchange (cash and TCs only); State Bank of India, off NH21, south of town, T01902 225 902. Nearest Visa exchange at Mandi. **Internet** Internet facilities are growing. **Tourist offices** Himachal, T01902 222 349, near Maidan, 1000-1700, local maps available, advises on exchange, trekking in the Tirthan Valley etc, very friendly and eager to please.

**Manali** *p501, maps p502 and p501*

**Banks** State Bank of India, The Mall, 100 m above Picadilly Hotel, T01902 252 405. Only changes AmEx TCs. UCO Bank, The Mall, opposite Nehru Park (1000-1430, closed Tue), T01902 252 330, changes TCs, quicker and more polite than the SBI. Signs indicate exchanges on The Mall; try Swagatam opposite Kunzam, changes major TCs, cash against Visa. **Hospitals** Mission Hospital, T01902 252 379. Men Tsee Khang, Gompa Rd, highly recommended for Tibetan herbal/mineral treatments. Chemists: opposite NAC Market. **Internet** Nirvana Café, Circuit House Rd, Old Manali, T01902 253 222. 9 machines, well run. Several others in town and Old Manali. **Post** GPO, off Model Town Rd, T01902 252 324. 0900-1700, Mon-Sat. Very efficient. **Telephone** Telecom office, south of Shiali Mahadev Rd. Gopal Travels, opposite temple in bazar. Friendly, ISD phone, receives faxes, photocopies. **Tourist offices** HPTDC, next to Kunzam Hotel, The Mall, T01902 252 175, helpful for bus and hotel bookings.



# Lahul and the Manali-Leh road

→ *Colour map 1, grid A3 and B3. For trekking information, see page 534.*

*Lying between the green alpine slopes of the Kullu and Chamba valleys to the south and the dry, arid plateau of Ladakh, the mountainous arid landscapes of Lahul manage to get enough rain during the monsoon months to allow extensive cultivation, particularly on terraces, of potatoes, green peas and hops (for beer making). Lahul potatoes are some of the best in the country and are used as seed for propagation. These and rare herbs have brought wealth to the area. Most people follow a curious blend of both Hindu and Buddhist customs though there are a few who belong wholly to one or the other religion.* » *For Sleeping, Eating and other listings, see pages 517.*

## Ins and outs

The whole region can be approached by road from three directions: Shimla via the Spiti Valley; Manali over the Rohtang Pass (3,985 m) into Upper Lahul; and from Zanskar and Ladakh over the Shingo La and Baralacha La (passes). The Shingo La gives access to Lahul from Zanskar (see page 569), while the Baralacha La (4,880 m) on the Leh-Manali road provides access from Ladakh. There is a trekking route from Manali to Zanskar. Streams cross the road at several places. These may be impassable during heavy rain, and those fed by snow-melt swell significantly during the day as meltwater increases, so travel in the late afternoon can be more difficult than in the early morning when the flow is at its lowest. Rockfalls are also a common hazard. »» *See Transport page 517 for details.*

## History

Historically there are similarities between this region and Ladakh since in the 10th century Lahul, Spiti and Zanskar were part of the Ladakh Kingdom. The Hindu Rajas in Kullu paid tribute to Ladakh. In the 17th century Ladakh was defeated by a combined Mongol-Tibetan force. Later Lahul was separated into Upper Lahul which fell under the control of Kullu, and Lower Lahul which came under the Chamba Rajas. The whole region came under the Sikhs as their empire expanded, whilst under the British Lahul and Kullu were part of the administrative area centred on Kangra.

# Manali to Leh

This stunningly beautiful road, one of the highest in the world, is currently the main route for foreigners into the region of Lahul and on to Leh. The 530-km highway is usually open from July to September, depending on snow fall; most buses stop in mid-September. The first 52 km runs up the Kullu valley, then climbs through the Rohtang Pass. The Pass itself normally opens at the end of May and is the only way into Lahul until the new tunnel is completed (2006). No permits are necessary.

## Leaving Manali

From Manali the NH21 goes through the village of Palchan and then begins a sharp climb to **Kothi**, at 2,530 m, set below towering cliffs. Beautiful views of coniferous hillsides and meadows unwind as the road climbs through 2,800 m, conifers giving way to poplars and then banks of flowers. The 70-m high **Rohalla Falls**, 19 km from Manali at an altitude of 3,500 m, are a spectacular sight.

The landscape, covered in snow for up to eight months of the year, becomes totally devoid of trees above Marrhi, a seasonal settlement and restaurant stop, as the road climbs through a series of tight hairpins to the Rohtang Pass.

## Rohtang Pass

From the pass you get spectacular views of precipitous cliffs, deep ravines, large glaciers and moraines. Buses stop for photos. From June until mid October, when Himachal Tourism runs a daily bus tour from Manali, the pass becomes the temporary home to a dozen or more noisy roadside 'cafes'.

The descent to **Gramphoo** (Gramphu), which is no more than a couple of houses at the junction of the road from Tabo and Kaza, offers superb views of the glaciated valley of the Chandra River, source of the

 Chenab. To the north and east rise the peaks of Lahul, averaging around 6,000 m and with the highest, Mulkila, reaching 6,520 m. As the road descends towards Khoksar there is an excellent view of the Lumphu Nala coming down from the Tempo La glacier. An earlier glacial maximum is indicated by the huge terminal moraine visible half way up the valley.

There is a police check post in **Khoksar**, at 3,140 m, where you may be required to show your passport and sign a register. This can take some time if more than one bus arrives at once. About 8 km west of Khoksar work has started on the proposed Rohtang tunnel to link the Solang Valley with the Chandra Valley. If you cross the bridge here you find an attractive waterfall.

### Gondhla to Keylong and the Pattan Valley

It is worth stopping here to see the 'castle' belonging to the local *thakur* (ruler), built around 1700. The seven-storey house with staircases made of wooden logs has a verandah running around the top and numerous apartments on the various floors. The fourth floor was for private prayer, while the Thakur held court from the verandah. There is much to see in this neglected, ramshackle house, particularly old weapons, statues, costumes and furniture. The 'sword of wisdom', believed to be a gift from the Dalai Lama some time ago, is of special interest. On close inspection you will notice thin wires have been hammered together to form the blade, a technique from Toledo, Spain! The huge rock near the Government School, which some claim to be of ancient origin, has larger-than-life figures of *Bodhisattvas* carved on it.

As the road turns north approaching **Tandi** the Chandra rushes through a gorge, giving a superb view of the massively contorted, folded and faulted rocks of the Himalaya. Tandi itself is at the confluence of the Chandra and Bhaga rivers, forming the Chandrabhaga or Chenab. Keylong is 8 km from here, see page 516. At Tandi you can take a left turn and visit the Pattan Valley before heading to Keylong to continue on the journey.



## Pattan Valley → *Colour map 1, grid A3 and B3.*

The Pattan Vally has a highly distinctive agricultural system which despite its isolated situation is closely tied in to the Indian market. Pollarded willows are crowded together all around the villages, offering roofing material for the flat-roofed houses and fodder for the cattle during the six-month winter. Introduced by a British missionary in the 19th century to try and help stabilize the deeply eroded slopes, willows have become a vital part of the valley's village life, with the additional benefit of offering shade from the hot summer sun. Equally important are the three commercial crops which dominate farming; hops, potatoes and peas, all exported, while wheat and barley are the most common subsistence grain crops.

### Tandi to Trilokinath

Just out of Tandi after crossing the Bhaga River on the Keylong road, the Udeypur road doubles back along the right bank of the Chenab running close to but high above the river. The road passes through Ruding, Shansha, 15 km from Tandi, Jahlma, 6 km and Thirot, another 11 km on (rest house here). A bridge at Jhooling crosses the Chenab. Some 6 km further on, the road enters a striking gorge where a bridge crosses the river before taking the road up to Trilokinath, 6 km away.

### Trilokinath

Trilokinath, at 2,760 m, is approached by a very attractive road which climbs up the left bank of the Chenab. The glitteringly white-painted Trilokinath temple stands at

## Motorcycling from Manali to Leh

Allow four days on the way up, to help acclimatize as the 500 km road will take you from 2,000 m to 5,420 m and down to 3,500 m (Leh). The last petrol station is in Tandi, 7 km before Keylong. A full tank plus five to 10 litres of spare petrol will take you to Leh. Above 3,500 m, you should open the air intake on your carb to compensate for the loss of power.

Apart from Keylong, there are no hotels, only a few tented camps, providing basic food and shelter from mid-June to mid-September. Some will be noisy and drafty. The lack of toilet facilities leads to pollution near the camps (don't forget your lighter for waste paper). A tent and mini stove plus pot, soups, tea, biscuits, muesli, will add extra comfort, allowing you to camp in the wild expanses of the Moray Plains (4,700 m).

Unless you plan to sleep in the camp there, you must reach Pang before 1300 on the way up, 1500 on the way down, as the police will not allow you to proceed beyond the checkpoint after these times. The army camp in Pang has helpful officers and some medical facilities.

the end of the village street on top of a cliff. The Siva **temple** has been restored by Tibetan Buddhists, whose influence is far stronger than the Hindu. Tibetan prayer-flags decorate the entrance to the temple which is in the ancient wooden pagoda style. In the courtyard is a tiny stone Nandi and a granite lingam, Saivite symbols which are dwarfed in significance by the Buddhist symbols of the sanctuary; typical prayer-wheels constantly being turned by pilgrims, and a 12th-century six-armed white marble Avalokiteshwara image (Bodhisattva) in the shrine along with other Buddhist images. The original columns date from Lalitaditya's reign in the eighth century, but there has been considerable modernization as well as restoration, with the installation of bright electric lights including a strikingly garish and flickering *chakra* on the ceiling. Hindus and Buddhists celebrate the three-day **Pauri Festival** in August.

## Udeypur

Ten kilometres from the junction with the Trilokinath road is Udeypur (Udaipur). Visited in the summer it is difficult to imagine that the area is completely isolated by sometimes over 2 m of snow during the six winter months. It is supplied by weekly helicopter flights (weather permitting). The helipad is at the entrance to the village. Trekking routes cross the valley here and further west, see page 535.

The unique **Mrikula** (Markula) **Devi temple** (AD 1028-1063) is above the bazar. The temple dedicated to Kali looks wholly unimposing from the outside with a battered looking wood-tiled 'conical' roof and crude outside walls. However, inside are some beautiful, intricate deodar-wood carvings belonging to two periods. The façade of the shrine, the *mandapa* (hall) ceiling and the pillars supporting it are earlier than those beside the window, the architraves and two western pillars. Scenes from the *Mahabharata* and the *Ramayana* epics decorate the architraves, while the two door guardians (*dvarapalas*), which are relatively crude, are stained with the blood of sacrificed goats and rams. The wood carvings here closely resemble those of the Hadimba Temple at Manali and some believe it was the work of the same 16th-century craftsman. See page 503. The silver image of Kali (*Mahisha- shurmardini*) 1570, inside, is a strange mixture of Rajasthani and Tibetan styles (note the Lama-like headcovering), with an oddly proportioned body.

# Keylong → *Phone code: 019002. Colour map 1, grid B3. Altitude: 3,350 m.*

The principal town of the district of Lahul, Keylong is set amidst fields of barley and buckwheat surrounded by brown hills and snowy peaks and was once the home of Moravian missionaries. Only traders and trekkers can negotiate the pass out of season. Keylong is an increasingly widely used stopping point for people en route to Leh or trekking in the Lahul/Spiti area. Landslides on the Leh-Manali road can cause quite long delays and the town can be an unintended rest halt for a couple of days. It has little to offer, though the views are very attractive and there are pleasant walks.

There is a pleasant circuit of the town by road which can be done comfortably in under two hours. Tracks run down into the town centre. The **local deity** 'Kelang Wazir' is kept in Shri Nawang Dorje's home which you are welcome to visit. There is a **Tibetan Centre for Performing Arts**. A statue in the centre of Keylong commemorates the Indian nationalist **Rash Behari Bose**, born 15 May 1886 near Kolkata.

**Khardong Monastery**, 3½ km away across the Chandra River up a steep tree-shaded path, is the most important in the area. It is believed to have been founded 900 years ago and was renovated in 1912. Nuns and monks enjoy equality; married lamas spend the summer months at home cultivating their fields and return to the monastery in winter. The monastery, with its four temples, contains a huge barrel drum, a valuable library and collections of *thangkas*, Buddha statues, musical instruments, costumes and ancient weapons.

**Sha-Shur Monastery**, a kilometre away, was in legend reputedly founded as early as 17 AD by a Buddhist missionary from Zanskar, Lama Deva Tyatsho who was sent by the Bhutanese king. It has ancient connections with Bhutan and contains numerous wall paintings and a 4½-m *thangka*. The annual festival is held in June/July.

**Tayul Monastery**, above Satingri village, has a 4-m high statue of Padma Sambhava, wall paintings and a library containing valuable scriptures and *thangkas*. The *mani* wheel here is supposed to turn on its own marking specially auspicious occasions, the last time having been in 1986.

# Keylong to Leh

From Keylong the road passes through very high altitude desert with extraordinary mountain views. **Jispa**, 21 km on at an altitude of 3,200 m, has a hotel, a campsite, a few tea stalls and a mountaineering institute. Himachal Tourism's concrete 'lodge' with three basic rooms with toilets, cheap camping in the yard. About 2 km beyond Jispa is **Teh** which has accommodation. There is a 300-year-old palace, built in the Tibetan style, comprised of 108 rooms over four storeys, and apparently the largest traditional structure in Lahaul, 3½km off the main highway (turn off at Ghemur, between Keylong and Jispa) in a village called **Kolong**, which has recently been converted in to a heritage hotel. A museum has also been opened there, with some interesting exhibits depicting the traditional and ceremonial life of the local rulers, who still own the property.

All vehicles must stop for passport checks at **Darcha** check post where the Bhaga River is bridged. Tents appear on the grassy river bank in the summer to provide a halt for trekkers to Zanskar. The road climbs to **Patseo** where you can get a view back of Darcha. A little further is **Zingzingbar**. Icy streams flow across the road while grey and red-brown scree reach down from the bare mountainside to the road edge. The road then goes over the **Baralacha La** (54 km; 4,880 m), 107 km from Keylong, at the crossroads of Lahul, Zanskar, Spiti and Ladakh regions before dropping to **Sarchu** (HP border). There are a dozen or so tented camps in Sarchu, among them **Tented Camp** (Himachal Tourism), mostly with two-bed tents (sometimes reported dirty), communal toilet tents, late night Indian meal and breakfast; private bus passengers without reservations are accommodated whenever possible (Rs 150 per person); open mid-June to mid-September.

The road runs beyond Brandy Nala by the Tsarap River before negotiating 22 spectacular hairpin bends, known as the 'Gata Loops', to climb up to the **Nakli La** (4,950 m) and **Lachalung La** (5,065 m). It then descends past tall earth and rock pillars to **Pang**, a summer settlement in a narrow valley where you can stop for an expensive 'breakfast' (usually roti, vegetables and omelettes to order). The camp remains open beyond 15 September; overnight stop is possible in communal tents. The 40 km wide Moray plains (4,400 m) provide a change from the slower mountain road. The road then climbs to **Taglang La** (5,370 m), the highest motorable pass along this route and the second highest in the world; the altitude is likely to affect many travellers at this point. You descend slowly towards the Indus valley, passing small villages, before entering a narrow gorge with purple coloured cliffs. The road turns left to continue along the Indus basin passing **Upshi** with a sheep farm and a check post, and then **Thikse**, before reaching **Leh.**



## Sleeping

**Udeypur** *p515*
**E Forest Rest House**, off the road in a pleasant raised position, 2 rooms with bath, very basic, bring your own sleeping bag. Camping is possible in an attractive site abut 4 km beyond the town (permission from Forest Officer) but since there is no water supply, nearby water has to be carried in from a spring about 300 m further up the road. Carry provisions as there is little in the bazar.

**Keylong** *p516*
**C-D Tashi Deleg**, on main road through town. Does well from being the first place you come to from Tandi, slightly overpriced as a result. Rooms are comfortable though, and the restaurant is one of the best in town. Also has a car park.
**D Dekyid**, below police station. 3-storey hotel, friendly, helpful reception, decent sized rooms with bath, quiet, excellent views over fields, good restaurant but service very slow.
**D Snowland**, above Circuit House, T01900 222 219. 15 rooms with bath, modest but adequate, friendly reception. Recommended.
**E Gyespa**, on main road, T01900 222 873. 11 basic but adequate rooms plus a good restaurant.
**E Tourist Bungalow** (HPTDC), (01900) 222 247. 3 rooms with bath, 2-bed tents, dorm (Rs 50), meals to order, solar heated pool, reserve ahead, open mid-Jun to mid-Oct.

**Keylong to Leh** *p516*
**B Khangsar Sarai**, Kolong, T01900 233 329. 4 deluxe rooms in a recently converted 300 year old palace, unique in the area and well worth a visit, highly recommended.

**Jispa** *p516*
**C Ibex Hotel**, T01900 233 204, nomad_adventures@yahoo.com. Glass and cement block, 27 comfortable rooms, although the whole place is in need of a lick of paint, ISD, reserve ahead.

## Transport

**Keylong** *p516*
State and private luxury **buses** are most comfortable but charge more than double the 'B' class fare (see below). To **Manali** (6-8 hrs); to **Leh** (18 hrs, Rs 400-475). To board deluxe buses to Leh in Keylong, reserve ahead and pay full fare from Manali (Rs 900, plus Rs 300 for tent and meals in Sarchu).

To **Manali** by **jeep**, 4 hrs, weather permitting; **Sarchu** 6 hrs, **Leh** 14 hrs.

## Directory

**Keylong** *p516*
**Banks** State Bank of India; no foreign exchange.

# Northern Himachal

→ For trekking, see page 534.

*Dominated by Dharamsala, this is a region replete with some of the most breathtaking mountain views imaginable. From Dalhousie eastwards there are tantalising glimpses of snow-capped peaks, while McLeod Ganj has been attracting Western travellers for decades, coming in search of peace, tranquillity, the Dalai Lama and sometimes even themselves. The Kangra Valley sees far less visitors, but has a unique, unhurried charm, epitomised by Pragpur, India's first heritage village.* » For Sleeping, Eating and other listings, see pages 526-534.

## Dharamshala

→ *Phone code: 01892. Colour map 1, grid B3. Population: 8,600.*

Dharamshala has a spectacular setting along a spur of the Dhauladhar range, varying in height from 1,250 m at the 'Lower Town' bazar to 1,768 m at the pleasanter McLeodganj. It is this 'Upper' and more attractive part of town that attracts the bulk of visitors. Although the centre of the town itself has now become somewhat overdeveloped, it is surrounded by forests of chir pine, rhododendron and Himalayan Oak, set against a backdrop of high peaks on three sides, with superb views over the Kangra Valley and Shiwaliks, and of the great granite mountains that almost overhang the town.

### Ins and outs

**Getting there** Flights to Gaggal Airport (13 km). Lower Dharamshala is well connected by bus with towns near and far. You can travel from Shimla to the southeast or from Hoshiarpur to the southwest along the fastest route from Delhi. The nearest station on the scenic mountain railway is at Kangra while Pathankot to the west is on the broad gauge.

**Getting around** From Dharamshala, it is almost 10 km by the bus route to McLeodganj but a shorter, steeper path (3 km), takes about 45 minutes on foot. Local jeeps use this bumpy, potholed shortcut. Compact McLeodganj itself, and its surroundings, are ideal for walking.

### Background

The hill station was established by the British between 1815 and 1847, but remained a minor town until the **Dalai Lama** settled here after Chinese invasion of Tibet in October 1959. There is an obvious Tibetan influence in McLeodganj. The Tibetan community has tended to take over the hospitality business, sometimes a cause of friction with the local population. Now many westerners come here because they are particularly interested in Buddhism, meditation or the Tibetan cause. A visitor's attempt to use a few phrases in Tibetan is always warmly responded to: *tashi delek* (hello, good luck), *thukje-chey* (thank you), *thukje-sik* (please), *gong-thag* (sorry), *shoo-den-jaa-go* (goodbye) and reply *chipgyu nang-go*! Foreign volunteers are often accepted at the hospital and other units here. Also ask at **Hotel Tibet, Green Shop** or **Khana Nirvana** or the free monthly *Contact*, T98161 55523, contactmag@hotmail.com, which carries news of opportunities. English language teachers are in high demand to teach newly-arrived refugees, for short or long term.

### Sights

**Church of St John-in-the-Wilderness** (1860) ⓘ *1000-1700*, with attractive stained glass windows, is a short distance below McLeodganj. Along with other buildings in the area, it was destroyed by the earthquake of 1905 but has been rebuilt. In April 1998 thieves tried to steal the old bell, cast in London, which was installed in 1915, but could only move it 300 m. The Eighth **Lord Elgin**, one of the few Viceroys to die in office, is buried here according to his wish as it reminded him of his native Scotland.

**Namgyal Monastery** at McLeodganj, with the Buddhist School of Dialectics, mostly attended by small groups of animated 'debating'monks, is known as Little Lhasa. This Tsuglagkhang ('cathedral') opposite the Dalai Lama's residence resembles the centre of the one in Lhasa and is five minutes' walk from the main bazar. It contains large gilded bronzes of the Buddha, Avalokitesvara and Padmasambhava. To the left of the Tsuglagkhang is the **Kalachakra Temple** with very good modern murals of *mandalas*, protectors of the Dharma, and Buddhist masters of different lineages of Tibetan Buddhism, with the central image of Shakyamuni. Sand mandalas (which can be viewed on completion), are constructed throughout the year, accompanied by ceremonies. The temple is very important as the practice of Kalachakra Tantra is instrumental in bringing about world peace and harmony.

The **Dalai Lama** usually leads the prayers on special occasions – 10 days for *Monlam Chenmo* following *Losar*, *Saga Dawa* (May) and his own birthday (6 July). If you wish to have an audience with him, you need to sign up in advance at the Security Office (go upstairs) by **Hotel Tibet**. On the day, arrive early with your passport. Cameras, bags and rucksacks are not permitted. His Holiness is a Head of State and the incarnation of Avalokitesvara, the Bodhisattva of Love and Great Compassion; show respect by dressing appropriately (no shorts, sleeveless tops, dirty or torn clothes); monks may 'monitor' visitors. See page 41. **Dip Tse-Chok Ling Monastery**,

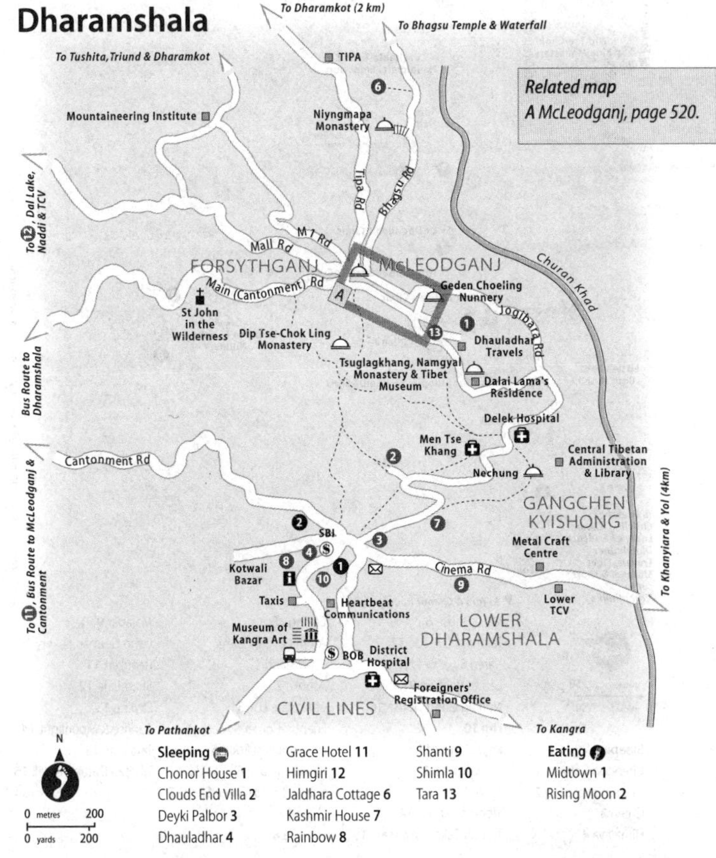

with its golden roof in a wooded valley, can be seen from above. See sleeping below. Further down the 3-km steep motorable road to Dharamshala is the Nechung Monastery in **Gangchen Kyishong** with the Central Tibetan Administration (CTA) which began work in 1988.

**Norbulingka Institute** ⓘ *T01892 246 402, www.norbulingka.org*, is becoming a major centre for Buddhist teaching and practical work. Named after the summer residence of the Seventh Dalai Lama built in 1754, it was set up to ensure the survival of Tibetan Buddhism's cultural heritage. Up to 100 students and 300 Tibetan employees are engaged in a variety of crafts in wood, metal, silk and metal, *thangka* painting (some excellent) and Tibetan Language. The temple has a 4.5-m high gilded

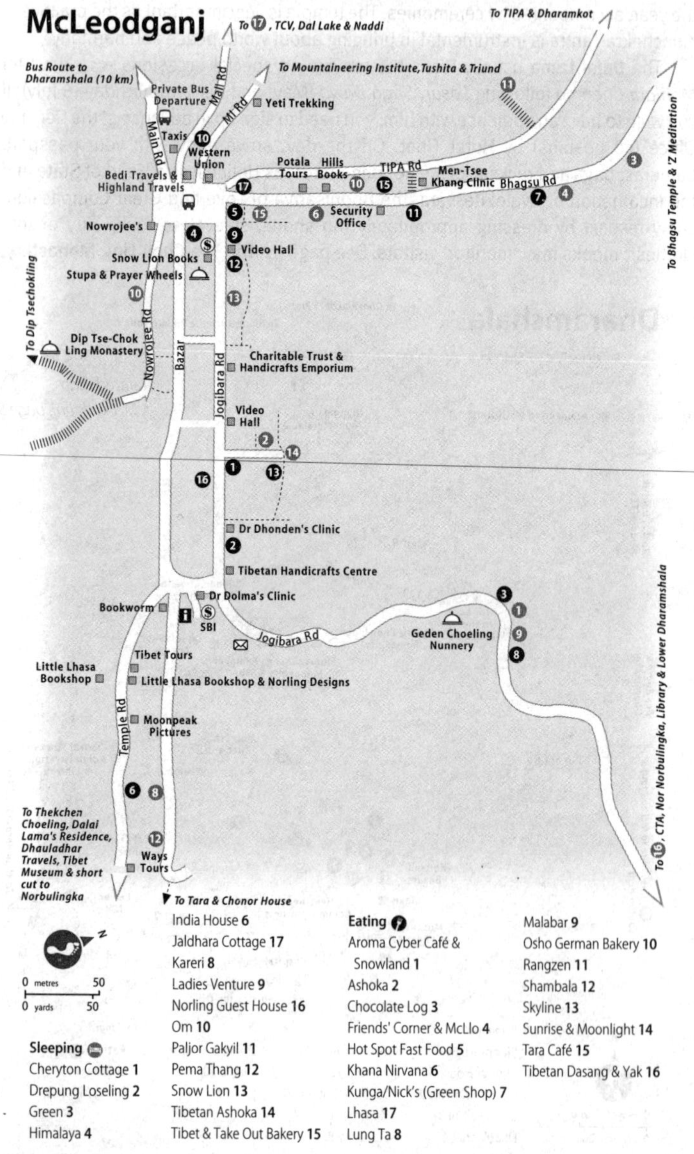

## Fight over the flight of the living Buddha

Rival claims by two boy-gods to the position of the 17th Karmapa, the head of the Kagyu Buddhist sect and the inheritor of the coveted black hat 'woven from the hair of 10,000 angels', has created a rift in high Buddhist clerical circles. The Indian headquarters of the powerful and affluent Kagyu sect is in Rumtek in Sikkim. On 5 January 2000, the dramatic appearance of the 14 year old Urgyen Thinley in Dharamshala after a strenuous mountain crossing after escaping from captivity in Tibet, has put the cat among the pigeons. The older claimant, Thaye Dorje now 19, who escaped from Tibet as the 17th incarnation of a 12th-century spiritual leader in 1994, is being groomed in the quiet backwaters of Kalimpong, away from the warring monks of Rumtek, for the third highest position (after the Dalai Lama and the Panchen Lama) in Tibetan Buddhism. Thaye Dorje's supporters are ready to oppose any move by the Karmapa to usurp the 'throne' they feel rightfully belongs to their earlier find.

statue of the Buddha and over 1,000 painted images. There is a small **museum** of traditional 'dolls' made by monks and a **Tibetan Library** with a good range of books and magazines. You can attend lectures and classes on Tibetan culture and language and Buddhism or attend two **meditation** classes, free but a donation is appreciated. Those attending regularly pay Rs 100 per meditation session.

**Museum of Kangra Art** ⓘ *Main Rd, closed Mon, 1000-1700 (closed 1330-1400), free, allow ½ hr*, near the bus stand in Lower Dharamshala, includes regional jewellery, paintings, carvings, a reminder of the rich local heritage contrasted with the celebrated Tibetan presence. Copies of Roerich paintings will be of interest to those not planning to visit Naggar.

Located near Namgyal Monastery in McLeodganj, the **Tibetan Museum** ⓘ *www.thetibetmuseum.org, Tue-Sun, 1000-1800, Rs 5*, has an interesting collection of documents and photographs detailing Tibetan history, the Chinese occupation of Tibet and visions of the future for the country. It is an essential visit for those interested in the Tibetan cause.

### Walks around McLeodganj

**Bhagsu**, an easy 2-km stroll east, or Rs 30-40 auto ride, has a temple to Bhagsunath (Siva). Outside the rainy season lovely walks are possible. The mountain stream here, feeds a small pool for pilgrims, while there is an attractive waterfall 1 km beyond. It is a relaxing place with great views, and so attracts some to stay here. Unfortunately this has resulted in it becoming very touristy, with increasing building activity up the valley towards Dharamkot and an influx of noisy day-trippers.

**Dharamkot**, 3 km away, has very fine views and you can continue on towards the snowline. In September, a fair is held at **Dal Lake** (1,837 m), 3 km from McLeodganj bus stand; it is a pleasant walk but the 'lake', no more than a small pond, is disappointing.

**Naddi Gaon** ⓘ *buses from Dharamshala, 0800-1900*, 1½ km further uphill from the bridge by Dal Lake, has really superb views of the Dhauladhar Range. **Kareri Lake** is further on. The TCV (Tibetan Childrens' Village) nearby educates and trains children in traditional handicrafts. Big hotels are rapidly appearing next to the traditional Naddi village. Most enjoy excellent views.

It is an 8-km trek to **Triund**, 2,827 m, at the foot of the Dhauladhar where there is a **Forest Lodge** on a hill top. Some trekkers pitch tents, whilst others make use of caves or shepherds' huts. Take provisions and warm sleeping gear if planning to stay overnight. Well worth the effort. A further 5 km, one-hour walk, brings you to **Ilaka**.

# Kangra Valley

The Kangra Valley, between the Dhaula Dhar and the Shiwalik foothills, starts near Mandi and runs northwest to Pathankot. It is named after the town of Kangra but now the largest and main centre is Dharamshala. Chamba State, to its north, occupies part of the Ravi River Valley and some of the Chenab Valley. » *For Sleeping, Eating and other listings, see pages 526-534.*

## History

In 1620 Shah Jahan captured Kangra fort for his father Jahangir, and Kangra became a Mughal province. Many of the court artists fled to neighbouring Chamba and Kullu as the Rajas submitted to Mughal rule. When Mughal power weakened, the 16-year-old **Sansar Chand Katoch II** (1775-1823) recaptured the fort and the Rajas reasserted their independence. Under his powerful leadership, Kangra sought to extend its boundaries into the Chamba and Kullu Valleys but this was forestalled by the powerful Gurkhas from Nepal. With the rise of the Sikh Empire, the valley was occupied until the Treaty of Amritsar. Then under the British, Dharamshala was made the administrative capital of the region which led to the decline of Kangra.

**Kangra School of Painting** originated by virtue of Raja Goverdhan Singh (1744-1773) of Guler who gave shelter to many artists who had fled from the Mughals, and during the mid-18th century a new style of miniature painting developed. Based on Mughal miniature style, the subject matter derived from Radha/Krishna legends, the rajas and gods being depicted in a local setting. Under Sansar Chand II the region prospered and the Kangra School flourished. Kangra fort, where he held court for nearly 25 years, was adorned with paintings and attracted art lovers from great distances. The 1905 earthquake damaged many of these buildings though you can still see some miniature wall paintings.



## Kangra → *Phone code: 01892. Colour map 1, grid B3. Altitude: 615 m.*

Kangra, 18 km south of Dharamshala, was once the second most important kingdom in the West Himalaya after Kashmir. Kangra town, the capital, was also known as Bhawan or Nagarkot, and overlooks the Banganga River. It claims to have existed since the Vedic period with historical reference in Alexander's war records.

**Kangra fort** ⓘ *US$2, Indians Rs 5, auto Rs 70 return, taxi Rs 100*, stands on a steep rock dominating the valley. A narrow path leads up to the fort which was once protected by several gates and had the palace of the Katoch kings at the top. The fort, 5 km from the road bridge, is worth the effort. At its foot is a large modern Jain temple which has pilgrim accommodation (worth considering for its peaceful location). There is also a British Cemetery nearby. Inside the fort itself is an old Jain temple which is still in use. At the very top, the remains of Sansar Chand's palace offer commanding views.

**Brajesvari Devi Temple**, in Kangra Town, achieved a reputation for gold, pearls and diamonds and attracted many Muslim invaders from the 11th century, including Mahmud of Ghazni, the Tughlaqs and the Lodis, who periodically plundered its treasures and destroyed the idols. In the intervening years the temple was rebuilt and refurbished several times but in the great earthquake of 1905 both the temple and the fort were badly damaged. The Devi received unusual offerings from devotees. According to Abul Fazal, the pilgrims "cut out their tongues which grew again in the course of two or three days and sometimes in a few hours"! The present temple in which the deity sits under a silver dome with silver *chhatras* (umbrellas) was built in 1920 and stands behind the crowded, colourful bazar. The State Government maintains the temple; the priests are expected to receive gifts in kind only. The area is busy and quite dirty, with mostly pilgrim-oriented stalls. Above these is **St Paul's**

## The little-known 'mountain' railway

A superb narrow gauge railway links Pathankot in the west with Jogindernagar via Kangra (near Dharamshala) and Baijnath. The views of the Kangra Valley are quite spectacular. This is very much a working service and not a 'relic' (this train can be packed with ordinary users). Sadly, it is often very late as it is incredibly slow, and very uncomfortable because of the hard seats. 'Tourists' would do better to sample short sections of the line, and allow for delays – any purposeful journey is better done by bus. See page 533 for an optimistic timetable.

**Church** and a Christian community. Along the river between Old Kangra and Kangra Mandir is a pleasant trail, mostly following long-disused roads past ruined houses and temples which evidence a once sizeable town.

## Masrur → *34 km southwest of Dharamshala. Altitude: 800 m.*

A sandstone ridge to the northeast of the village has 15, ninth-10th century *sikhara* temples excavated out of solid rock. They are badly eroded and partly ruined. Even in this state they have been compared with the larger rock cut temples at Ellora in Maharashtra and at Mamallapuram south of Chennai. Their ridge-top position commands a superb view over the surrounding fertile countryside, but few of the original *shikharas* stand, and some of the most beautifully carved panels are now in the State Museum, Shimla. There are buses from Kangra.

## Jawalamukhi

This is one of the most popular Hindu pilgrimage sites in Himachal and is recognized as one of 51 *Shakti pitha*. The **Devi temple**, tended by the followers of Gorakhnath, is set against a cliff and from a fissure comes a natural inflammable gas which accounts for the blue 'Eternal Flame'. Natural springs feed the two small pools of water; one appears to boil, the other with the flame flaring above the surface contains surprisingly cold water. Emperor Akbar's gift of gold leaf covers the dome. In March/April there are colourful celebrations during the **Shakti Festival**; another in mid-October. There is accommodation here, and there are buses from Kangra.

## Pragpur

Pragpur, across the river Beas, 20 km southwest of Jawalamukhi, is a medieval 'Heritage' village with cobbled streets and slate-roofed houses. The fine 'Judges Court' (1918) nearby has been carefully restored using traditional techniques. A three- to four-day stay is recommended here and it is advisable to reserve ahead.

## Stops along the Kangra Valley Railway → *Enquiry Kangra T01892 252 279.*

**Jogindernagar** is the terminus of the beautiful journey by narrow gauge rail from Pathankot via Kangra. The hydro power scheme here and at nearby Bassi channels water from the River Uhl. Paragliding and hang gliding is possible at Billing (33 km), reached via Bir (19 km).

**Baijnath**'s temples are old by hill standards, dating from at least 1204. Note the Lakshmi/Vishnu figure and the graceful balcony window on the north wall. The **Vaidyanatha Temple** (originally circa 800), which contains one of 12 *jyotirlingas*, stands by the roadside on the Mandi-Palampur road, within a vast rectangular enclosure. Originally known as **Kirangama**, its name was changed after the temple was dedicated to **Siva** in his form as the Lord of Physicians. It is a good example of the Nagari style; the walls have the characteristic niches enshrining images of

 Chamunda, Surya and Karttikeya and the *sikhara* tower is topped with an *amalaka* and pot. A life-size stone Nandi stands at the entrance. There is a bus to and from Mandi taking 3½ hours, Rs 50

**Palampur** is a pleasant little town for walking, 16 km from Baijnath, 40 km from Dharamshala (via Yol), with beautiful snow views, surrounded by old British tea plantations, thriving on horticulture. It is a popular stop with trekkers; see page 540. The Neugal Khad, a 300-m wide chasm through which the Bandla flows is very impressive when the river swells during the monsoons. It holds a record for rainfall in the area!

**Andretta** is an attractive village surrounded by orchards and tea gardens, 13 km from Palampur. It is associated with **Norah Richards**, a follower of Mahatma Gandhi, who popularized rural theatre, and with the artist **Sardar Sobha Singh** who revived the Kangra School of painting. His paintings are big, brightly coloured, ultra-realistic and often devotional incorporating Sikh, Christian and Hindu images. There is an art gallery dedicated to his work and memory; prints, books, soft drinks are sold in the shop. The Andretta Pottery (signposted from the main road), is charming. It is run by an artist couple (Indian/English), who combine village pottery with 'slipware'. The Sikh partner is the son of Gurcharan Singh (of Delhi Blue Pottery fame) and is furthering the tradition of studio pottery; works are for sale.

# Chamba Valley

## Dalhousie → *Phone code: 01899. Colour map 1, grid B2. Population: 7,400. Altitude: 2,030 m.*

Dalhousie, named after the Governor-General (1848-1856), was developed on land purchased by the British in 1853 from the Raja of Chamba. It sprawls out over five hills ranging from 1,600-2,400 m, just east of the Ravi River. By 1867 it was a sanatorium and reached its zenith in the 1920s and 1930s as a cheaper alternative to Shimla, and the most convenient hill station for residents of Lahore. Rabindranath Tagore wrote his first poem in Dalhousie as a boy and Subhash Chandra Bose came secretly to plan his strategies during the Second World War, see page 764. Its popularity declined after 1947 and it became a quiet hill station with old colonial bungalows, surrounded by thick pine forests interspersed with oak and rhododendron. Its spectacular mountain views mean that it remains a popular bolt hole for tourists from the plains, but its importance today is mainly due to the number of good schools and the presence of the army.

The three Malls laid out for level walks are around Moti Tibba, Potreyn Hill and Upper Bakrota. The last, the finest, is about 330 m above **Gandhi Chowk** around which the town centres. From there two rounds of the Mall lead to Subhash Chowk. Tibetans make and sell handicrafts, woollens, jackets, cardigans and rugs. Their paintings and rock carvings can be seen along Garam Sarak Mall.

Just over 2 km from Gandhi Chowk is **Martyr's Memorial** at Panchpulla (five bridges), which commemorates Ajit Singh, a supporter of Subhash Bose and the Indian National Army during the Second World War. On the way you can see the **Satdhara** (seven springs), said to contain mica and medicinal properties. **Subhash Baoli** (1½ km from the square), is another spring. It is an easy climb and offers good views of the snows. Half a kilometre away **Jhandri Ghat**, the old palace of Chamba rulers, is set among tall pine trees. For a longer walk try the Bakrota Round (5 km), which gives good views of the mountains and takes you through the Tibetan settlement.

## Kalatope and Khajjiar

**Kalatope**, 9 km from Dalhousie, with good mountain views, is a level walk through a forest sanctuary with accommodation. The road is jeepable. **Khajjiar**, 22 km further along the motorable road, is a long, wide glade ringed by cedars with a small lake.

You can explore the area in a pleasant three-day walk. Alternatively you can extend the day's walk to Khajjiar into a short trek to Dharamshala over two days. A 30-km path through dense deodar forest leads to Chamba. Buses to Khajjiar from Dalhousie leave at 0930 and return 1530. They take an hour and cost Rs 13.

## Chamba → *Phone code: 01899. Colour map 1, grid B2. Altitude: 996 m.*

Picturesque Chamba is on the south bank of the Iravati (Ravi), its stone houses clinging to the hillside. Some see the medieval town as having an almost Italian feel, surrounded by lush forests and with its Chaugan or grassy meadow in the centre, although recent developments have somewhat diminished its appeal. Most hotels, temples and palaces are within walking distance of the bus stand.

Founded in the 10th century, Chamba State was on an important trade route from Lahul to Kashmir and was known as 'The Middle Kingdom'. Though Mughal suzerainty was accepted by the local Rajas, the kingdom remained autonomous though it came under Sikh rule from 1810-1846. Its relative isolation led to the nurturing of the arts – painting, temple sculpture, handicrafts and unique 'rumal'. These pieces of silk/cotton with fine embroidery imitate miniature paintings; the reverse is as good as the front.

Chamba is the centre of the **Gaddis**, shepherds who move their flocks of sheep and goats, numbering from a couple of hundred to a thousand, from lower pastures at around 1,500 m during winter to higher slopes at over 3,500 m, after snowmelt. They are usually only found in the Dhaula Dhar range which separates Kangra from Chamba. Some believe that these herdsmen first arrived in this part of Himachal in the 10th century though some moved from the area around Lahore (Pakistan) in the 18th century, during the Mughal period. Their religious belief combines animism with the worship of Siva; Bahrmaur with its distinctive Manimahesh temple is their principal centre of worship (see below). In the winter the Gaddis can be seen round Kangra, Mandi and Bilaspur and in the small villages between Baijnath and Palampur. The men traditionally wear a *chola* (a loose white woollen garment), tied at the waist with a black wool rope and a white embroidered cap.

The **Chaugan**, almost a kilometre long, is the central hub of the town but sadly, over the last two decades, shops have encroached into the open space. There are



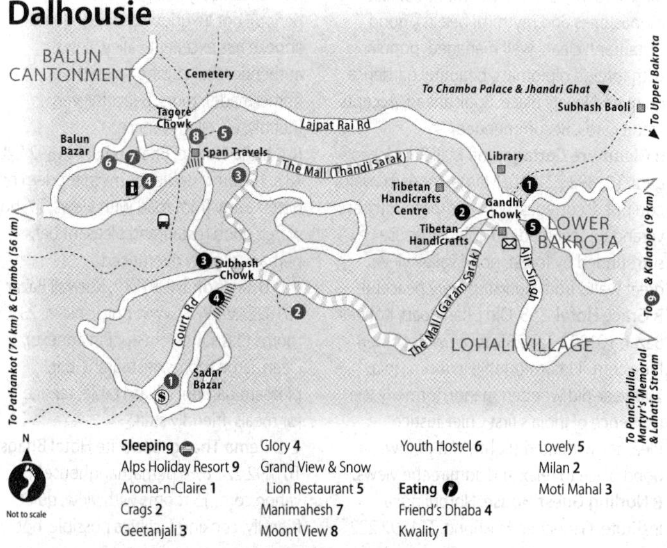

several ancient Pahari temples with attractive curvilinear stone towers. The **Lakshmi Narayana** Temple Complex (ninth to 11th centuries) contains six *sikhara* temples with deep wooden eaves, several smaller shrines and a tank. These are dedicated to Vishnu and Siva, with some of the brass images inlaid with copper and silver. The **Hari Rai Temple** (14th century) contains a fine 11th-century bronze Chaturmurti (four-armed Vishnu), rarely visible as it is usually 'dressed'. The 10th-century wooden **Chamunda Devi Temple**, 1 km north uphill from the bus stand, has some interesting wood carvings and stands over the river with commanding views. Others of note are the Bajreshwari, Bansigopal and Champavati.

The Akhand Chandi, the Chamba Maharajas' palace, beyond the Lakshmi Narayan complex, is now a college. The old **Rang Mahal** (Painted Palace) in the Surara Mohalla, was built by Raja Umed Singh in the mid 18th-century. A prisoner of the Mughals for 16 years, he was influenced by their architectural style. The wall paintings in one room are splendid. The theme is usually religious, Krishna stories being particularly popular. Some of these were removed to the Bhuri Singh Museum after a fire, together with wood carvings and manuscripts.

**Bhuri Singh Museum** ⓘ *daily except Sun, 1000-1700*, near the Chaugan, in a three-storey building houses a heritage collection, craft items including some excellent *rumals*, carvings and fine examples of Chamba, Kangra and Basholi schools of miniature paintings.

## Sleeping

**Dharamshala** *p518, maps p519 and p520*
Most visitors stay in McLeodganj. In Mar, May and early Jun accommodation may be hard to find. A 40% seasonal discount is usually given from mid-Jun to Aug. Check out time is mostly 1200. Check what time gate closes at night to avoid being locked out.

**B Chonor House**, Thekchen Choeling Rd, McLeodganj, T01892 221 077, www.norbulingka.org. 11 very comfortable, stylish rooms furnished in Tibetan style (murals of lost monasteries and mythical beasts), good restaurant, clean, well managed, popular with foreign diplomats, beautiful garden, a quiet and lovely place. Book ahead. Accepts credit cards. Recommended.

**B Glenmore Cottages**, off Mall Rd, McLeodganj, T01892 221010. 5 large, modern, well-equipped 'cottages' with bedroom, kitchen, verandah, secluded old colonial house surrounded by forest, good valley views, great walks from doorstep, very peaceful.

**B Grace Hotel**, 558, Old Chari Road, Kotwali Bazar, T01892 223 265, www.welcomheritage.com. 11 comfortable in rooms in a 200-year-old wooden manor, formerly the residence of India's first Chief Justice. Pleasantly situated slightly out of town, a good place to relax and admire the views.

**B Norling Guest House**, Norbulingka Institute, Gangchen Kyishong, T01892 222 664, norling@vsnl.com. Clean, comfortable rooms, in modern facilities in a Tibetan style house. Café accepts Master/Visa cards.

**B Surya**, T01892 221 418, www.suryaresorts.com. 53 large rooms, comfortable, quiet, good views, good restaurant with bar, exchange, friendly.

**B-C Clouds End Villa**, steep approach off Jogibara Rd, T01892 222 109, www.royalkangra.com. 7 rooms and 1 bungalow in Raja of Lambagraon's bungalow (Raj period), not luxurious but very clean, annexe has excellent valley views, authentic local cuisine (everything home-made), tours, peaceful, very friendly, excellent service.

**B-C India House**, Bhagsu Rd, T01892 220 431. 18 comfortable rooms in modern hotel, better away from road with views, TV, hot water, good restaurant, pleasant bar, perhaps slightly overpriced.

**C-D Dhauladhar**(HPTDC), Kotwali Bazar, T01892 224 926, www.hptdc.nic.in. 23 rooms (2 **B** suites, cheaper in annexe), clean, large rooms, restaurant, bar, pleasant garden, billiard table, terrace for meals, friendly staff.

**C-D Pema Thang**, opposite Hotel Bhagsu, T01892 221 871, pemathanghouse@yahoo.com. 15 rooms with view, quiet, friendly, cooking facilities possible, hot water, good pizza and pasta restaurant, recommended.

**C-D Tibet**, behind Bus Stand, T01892 221 587, htdshala@sancharnet.in. 20 well maintained rooms with bath and TV, not much difference between standard and deluxe, those on roadside can be noisy, good restaurant, cozy bar, accepts credit cards.

**D Kareri**, T01892 221 132, karerihl@hotmail.com. 5 recently renovated rooms with bath (tub), phone, TV, best with own balcony, good value, friendly

**D Kashmir House**(HPTDC), T01892 222 977, www.hptdc.nic.in. 10 large rooms (1 **C** suite) in beautiful period property, hot water, TV, good value.

**D-E Cheryton Cottage**, Jogibara Rd, enquire at Chocolate Log, T01892 221 237, 4 very smart rooms with bath, garden.

**E Dream**, Pathankot Rd (9 km from town). 3 very clean rooms with bath, quiet, idyllic spot beside river Gaj.

**E Ladies Venture**, Jogibara Rd, T01892 221 559. 13 clean rooms, some with bath, good dorm (Rs 50), peaceful, small restaurant (good Chinese and Western), terrace, very friendly.

**E Snow Lion**, near prayer wheels, T01892 221 289. 8 rooms with bath, good view from rear, good Tibetan restaurant (excellent cakes), friendly.

**E Tara**, near Bhagsu Hotel, T01892 221 189, tamdintara@hotmail.com. 12 large, clean rooms, comfortable and safe, bath and 24-hr hot water, lovely views, warm friendly family, home cooked snacks, internet.

**E-F Chamunda**, Khanyara Rd, T01892 225 608. 15 basic rooms including 2 singles, good views, hot water, slightly superior to next door Shanti.

**E-F Dip Tse-Chok Ling Monastery**, below McLeodganj, climb down 300 steps, TT01892 221 726. 20 clean rooms, 3 attached, some singles, hot showers, breakfast and dinner at set times, "wonderfully peaceful".

**E-F Drepung Loseling**, Jogibara Rd, T01892 221 087. 17 clean, well maintained rooms with bath (some with hot water), dorm (Rs 30), terrace, friendly.

**E-F Green Hotel**, T01892 221 200. 70 variable rooms from rs60 (avoid ones near the noisy courtyard), restaurant, popular with backpackers, good internet

**E-F Himalaya**, Bhagsu Rd, T01892 220 5237. 8 very basic but clean rooms, one with bath (hot shower), restaurant (good Tibetan brown bread, muesli, pancakes).

**E-F Om**, western edge of bazar, T01892 221 322. 18 spartan but clean rooms, excellent shower, very good restaurant, great views at sunset, friendly

**E-F Paljor Gakyil**, T01892 221 443, TIPA Rd, up steps. 14 clean rooms with bath (hot shower), dorm (Rs 25), excellent views, charming owners lived in Europe so speak French and German, prices unchanged since '96, best of nearby bunch, recommended.

**E-F Rainbow Lodge**, Old Charri Rd, Kotwali Bazar, T01892 222 647. 8 rooms, some with bath, TV, slightly quieter location than those on main drag

**E-F Tibetan Ashoka**, T01892 221 763. 41 very clean rooms, some with hot shower and good views (cheapest with shared shower, bucket hot water extra Rs 10, no views), strict on check-out time.

**F Danubemiami**, a block up from bus station. Rooms with bath (bucket), fan, simple meals (Rs 50), courteous and friendly staff, pleasant.

**Walks around McLeodganj** *p521*

**B Anand Palace** (Best Western), Bhagsu, T01892 220 506, hotel_anandpalace@sancharnet.in. 50 rooms in surprisingly Indian style by this American chain's standards, usual facilities, friendly manager, pool and lift planned.

**B Dev Cottages**, off McLeodganj to Dharamkot Rd (well signed), T01892 221 558. 12 comfortable, spacious rooms in 2-storey 'cottages', attached hot bath, TV, friendly but a little overpriced.

**B Jukaso Palace**, Naddi Gaon, T01892 221 336, jukaso@hotmail.com 8 slightly bare rooms in otherwise cozy surroundings, lovely dining terrace, 50% discount off season.

**B-C Udechee Huts**, Naddi Gaon, T01892 221 781. 8 pleasantly furnished circular huts with bath (hot water), blending in with local style, restaurant plus dining terrace, well kept, friendly hosts, recommended.

***For an explanation of the sleeping and eating price codes used in this guide, see inside the front cover. Other relevant information is found in Essentials pages 56-61.***

C **Nishaad Resorts**, Cantt area, Naddi Gaon, T01892 221 707. 10 rooms, 6 in cottages, some with great views, large gardens, good for kids, somewhat spartan overall.
D **Gaggan Resorts**, next to Dev Cottages, Dharamkot, T01892 220 324. 8 clean, modern rooms in brand new development, good views from balconies, feels a little unfinished but is good value for location.
D **Hill View**, Naddi Gaon, T01892 221 432. 6 rooms with good attached bathrooms plus great views from balconies, good value.
E **Bhagsu View**, next to car park, Bhagsu. 16 clean, modern rooms, and a remarkably good restaurant and German bakery.
E **Pink White**, Bhagsu, T01892 221 209. 18 rooms, some with bath, meals, friendly, clean, TV, ISD, good views from some rooms.
E-F **Omni**, above Bhagsu, T01892 221 594). 11 rooms, 6 newer with attached bath, restaurant, friendly owner, quiet location.
F **Shiv Shakti Rishi Bhawan**, off Dharamkot Rd, T01892 221 875. 18 basic rooms with attached bath plus a stand alone, well equipped cottage available on a daily or monthly (Rs 5,000) basis. Run by friendly father and son, new restaurant and internet.
F **ZKL Guesthouse**, above Bhagsu Rd 500 m before Bhagsu itself, T01892 220 581. 12 very basic but clean rooms in this charming monastery, Buddhist teachings and a café in the summer, outstanding value at Rs 80 double.

### Kangra *p522*

Most hotels on the busy main road are noisy – even at night.
E **Anand**, Nehru Bazar, above shops, T01892 225 243. 10 rooms, dining hall.
E **Jannai**, Chamunda Road, T01892 265 479. 5 rooms, restaurant, TV, hot water, closest to Kangra Mandir railway station.
E-F **Dilraj Guest House**, near Tehsil Chowk (taxi stand), T01892 265 362. 5 simple rooms in friendly family house, meals available. Recommended.
F **Gupt Ganga Dharamshala**, 30 rooms and 3 halls, donation expected.

### Stops along the Kangra Valley Railway *p523*

B-C **Taragarh Palace** (WelcomHeritage), in Al-hilal, 11 km southeast of Palampur, T01894-63034, taragarh@vsnl.com. 12 rooms in 1930s summer resort, period furniture, atmospheric, tastefully decorated, good restaurant, tennis, pool, lovely gardens and mango orchards, luxury Swiss tents in summer.
B-C **Silver Oaks**, Bandla Tea Estate, 2 km from Palampur, T01894-230747, www.silver-oaks-palampur.com. 18 large rooms, dorm for budget travellers, welcoming, quiet, scenic location with views of Dhaula Dhar peaks, friendly, knowledgable manager
C-D **T-Bud**, 1 km from bus stand, Palampur, T01894-231298. Beautiful setting, 31 rooms but only deluxe category are worth considering, hot water, restaurant, pleasant lawn, clean, quiet, good service.
C-E **Yamini**, Ghaggar Rd, Palampur, T01894 230 631. 25 rooms with bath, quality varies, 8-bed dorm.
D-E **Uhl**, on hill outside Jogindernagar, T01908-22002. 16 rooms with bath, best upstairs with balcony, simple, clean and peaceful, restaurant.
F **Standard**, Baijnath, behind bus station. 5 fairly clean and surprisingly tidy rooms with bath and hot water.

### Pragpur *p523*

B **Judge's Court** (Heritage), set in a large orchard, T01970 245 035, www.judgescourt.com. 7 tastefully decorated rooms in a fine mansion, one in annexe, 1 large private modernized suite with verandah overlooking the Dhauladhar in separate building. Family hospitality, home-grown vegetables and fruit, fresh river fish, traditional meals, tours of Kangra Fort and other sights included (a ride on a part of the narrow-gauge mountain railway is possible) friendly, efficient management.

### Dalhousie *p524, map p525*

Some hotels look neglected and run down, often because the cost of maintaining the Raj-built structures is prohibitive. Most have good mountain views and discounts off-season.
B **Alps Holiday Resort**, Khajjiar Rd, Bakrota Hills, T01899 240 775, www.alpsresortdalhousie.com. 19 smart rooms in modern hotel, with large lawns, fine views, 2 km climb.
B **Grand View**, near Bus Stand, T01899 240 760, www.grandviewdalhousie.com. 26 spacious, well equipped rooms in the best preserved of Dalhousie's many Raj era hotels. The views from the terrace are stunning,

while the restaurant and lounge bar are quintessentially British, recommended.

**B-C Manimahesh** (HPTDC), near bus stand, T01899 242 793, hptdcdlu@sancharnet.in. 18 well maintained, carpeted rooms, restaurant, bar, good mountain views.

**B-C Mount View**, next to bus stand, T01899 242 120, www.hotelmountainview.com. The elegant, period, oak-panelled reception flatters to deceive; all 24 rooms are in a modern block to the rear, only the cramped restaurant is in the older building.

**B-C Silverton**, near Circuit House, The Mall, T01899 242 329. Old colonial building in large grounds, rooms with phone, TV, closed off season

**C-D Aroma-n-Claire**, Court Rd, T01899 242 199. If the exterior looks quirky, wait until you get inside! Kitsch collectables adorn every available space in this utterly unique interior. The rooms are spartan, the bathrooms remarkable, worth a visit.

**D Geetanjali** (HPTDC), Thandi Sarak, near Bus Stand, T01899 242 155. 10 rooms with bath, simple restaurant in run down building.

**E-F Crags**, off The Mall, T01899 242 124. The 100 steps separating this place from the Mall are the only real disadvantage. The rooms are dated butclean with bath (hot water), meals, good views down valley, friendly, well used to catering to foreign travellers.

**F Glory**, near Bus Stand, T01899 242 533. 4 rooms with bath, good restaurant.

**F Youth Hostel**, behind Manimahesh, T01899 242 189. 2 double rooms (rs200) and 6 dorms (Rs 40 student/Rs 60 adult) in well maintained, modern building.

**Kalatope and Khajjiar** *p524*

All the below are in Khajjiar.

**C Devdar**, T01899 236 333. 12 clean rooms, dorm and beds in cottage, simple restaurant, horse riding, beautiful setting.

**B-C Mini Swiss**, T01899 236 365, www.mini swiss.com. 34 comfortable, very clean rooms, great views, good restaurant, boating lake.

**Chamba** *p525*

**B-D Aroma Palace**, near Pink Palace, Court Lane, T01899 225 577, www.aromaincham bahp.com. The best hotel here by some margin; range from dorm rooms to sumptious honeymoon suite, all spotless, plus there's a restaurant, internat facility and the friendly, hospitable manager even accepts credit cards.

**C-D Iravati** (HPTDC), Court Rd, near Bus Stand, T01899 222 671. 17, variable but mostly clean rooms with bath and hot water, restaurant, friendly management.

**E Akhand Chandi**, College Rd, Dogra Bazar. 6 rooms in attractive stone building.

**E The Orchard Hut**, 8 km out of town (book through **Mani Manesh Travels** next to Lakshmi Narayana Temple, T01899 222 607), prakashd@nde.vsnl.net.in. Idyllic location (20 mins from nearest road), 4 rooms in guesthouse set in delightful garden, clean shared shower and toilets, pitch a tent in garden for Rs 100, superb home cooking (great all-inclusive deal), very friendly family, book at office in town first. Recommended.

**E Rishi**, opposite Lakshmi Narayana Temple, T01899 224 343. Rooms with bath (hot water), TV, good value meals, friendly owner.

## Eating

**Dharamshala** *p518, maps p519 and p520*

Enterprising Tibetans in the upper town offer good traveller favourites for those tired of curries; some serve beer. Try Tibetan soups (*thukpa*), noodle dishes, steamed or fried *momos* and *shabakleb*. Consider refilling your bottles with safe filtered, boiled water at the eco-friendly **Green shop** on Bhagsu Rd, Rs 5 per litre, take used batteries here for recycling.

¥¥ **McLlo**, near Bus Stand, McLeodganj. Indian, Western. Glassed in, beer, good value.

¥¥ **Midtown**, Kotwali Bazar. Indian and Chinese, some continental, best in town.

¥¥ **Rising Moon**, Tibetan, Chinese.

¥ **Amdo Chachung**, Jogibara Rd. Good Tibetan. Nice terrace, cable TV.

¥ **Ashoka**, Jogibara Rd. Mainly North Indian,. pleasant atmosphere, very good curry.

¥ **Friends Corner**, near Bus Stand. Good breakfasts, dim but popular.

¥ **Hotel Tibet**, good Tibetan/Japanese restaurant and take-out bakery.

¥ **Khana Nirvana**, Temple Rd. Well-prepared Mexican/Italian dishes, juices, organic coffee, herb teas, American run, excellent ambience, good service, talks on Sun (1800) from Tibetan prisoners of conscience, music/poetry on Mon evening. Sun-Fri, orders taken between 0909-2047. Highly recommended.

¥ **Lhasa**, on 1st floor above **Tibet Tours**.

Tucked away, very mellow interior serving good Tibetan dishes, well worth a visit.
🍴 **Lung-Ta**, Jogibara Rd. Classy Japanese veg restaurant, non-profit making concern, daily set menu or à la carte, good breads and cakes. Mon-Sat 1200-2030. Highly recommended.
🍴 **Om**, west end of bazar. Indian. Very good meals from Rs 35.
🍴 **Pema Thang**. Good veg buffet brunch (Rs 150) on Sun 1000-1400, plus normal menu featuring great pasta, salads and pizza.
🍴 **Shambala**, excellent breakfasts, western cakes and pancakes, try apple pie and lemon curd, good portions, very good value, pleasant atmosphere (records on request), quick and friendly. Recommended.
🍴 **Shangrila**, near prayer-wheels. Meal (Rs 25), delicious cakes.
🍴 **Snow Lion** offers good Tibetan and western meals, excellent cakes.
🍴 **Snowland** Jogibara Rd. Tibetan. Highly recommended for cheese momos.
🍴 **Tibetan Dasang/Lhoka**, Jogibara Rd. Tibetan. Also excellent porridge, fruit muesli.
🍴 **Yak**, Jogibara Rd. Tibetan.

**Cafés and fast food**

**Chocolate Log**, Jogibara Rd. International. Log-shaped, pleasant surprise, excellent cakes and snacks, clean, terrace or indoor seating below (closed Mon). Recommended.
**German Bakery**, Ml Rd, steep road to Dharamkot, best bread, brown rice, open till 0100.
**Hot Spot**, near Bus Stand, for fast food.
**Kunga's/Nick's Italian Kitchen**, Bhagsu Rd. Good veg Italian including excellent gnocchi plus quiches, pies, cakes etc, but some small portions, now has a huge terrace, deservedly popular, recommended.
**Moonlight** and **Sunrise**, opposite Tibetan Welfare Office, Bhagsu Rd. Small chai shops adjacent to each other with basic food. Excellent for meeting other travellers, especially in the evenings when overspill occupies benches opposite.
**Rangzen** (Freedom), Bhagsu Rd. Good health food, cakes.
**Tara Café**, Bhagsu Rd. Huge pancakes, friendly. Recommended.

**Walks around McLeodganj** *p521*

**Sri Guru Kirpa Restaurant**, Bhagsu, good veg Indian and Chinese meals, or pizzas, though the spices can make you hit the roof.
**Pizza House**, on the east side of Dharamkot. Pizzas and cakes.
**Unity**, Dharamkot towards Bhagsu. English owner creates amazing food, well presented.

**Kangra** *p522*

**Chicken Corner**, Dharamshala Rd near the main bazar, an eccentric though fairly clean little hut does chicken dinners.

**Dalhousie** *p524, map p525*

**Friend's Dhaba**, Subhash Chowk, good, unpretentious Punjabi, *paneer burji* to die for.
**Kwality**, Gandhi Chowk. Good Indian and Chinese if a bit pricey. Nice place with TV.
**Lovely**, near Gandhi Chowk, funky mirrored interiors, tasty North Indian.
**Napoli**, near Gandhi Chowk. Similar to Kwality. Very friendly, serves large portions.
**Moti Mahal**, Subhash Chowk, north Indian.
**Snow Lion**, near **Grand View**, Tibetan dishes.

**Chamba** *p525*

There are a number of really atmospheric little *dhabas* in the alleys through Dogra Market.
Ravi View Café, okay food plus beer and a pleasant location.
**Park View and Jagaan**, both on the 1st floor above main drag, reasonable selection, relatively calm.

## Entertainment

**Dharamshala** *p518, maps p519 and p520*

See *Contact*, a monthly, free publication.
**TIPA** (Tibetan Institute of Performing Arts), www.tibetanarts.org, McLeodganj, stages occasional music and dance performances; details at Tourist Office.
Two video halls on Jogibara Rd showing western films; also documentaries on Tibet (look for posters/blackboards), new places springing up all the time.

## Festivals and events

**Chamba** *p525*

Gaddis and Gujjars take part in many cultural events to mark the start of harvesting.
**Apr**: Suhi Mela lasts 3 days. **Jul-Aug**: Minjar, 7-day harvest festival when people offer thanks to Varuna the rain god. Decorated

horses and banners are taken out in procession through the streets to mark its start. Sri Raghuvira is followed by other images of gods in palanquins and the festival ends at the river Irawati where people float *minjars* (tassels of corn and coconut).

## Shopping

**Dharamshala** *p518, maps p519 and p520*
It is pleasantly relaxed to shop here, although competition has increased in recent years. You are usually quoted a fair price from the start by the Tibetans. McLeodganj Bazar is good for Tibetan handicrafts (carpets, metalware, jewellery, jackets, handknitted cardigans, gloves); special Sunday market.
**Bookworm**, near **Surya Resort**, has a good selection of paperbacks, some second-hand.
**Charitable Trust Bookshop**, cards, books on Tibet and Buddhism.
**DIIR**, cards, books on Tibet and Buddhism.
**Green shop**, Bhagsu Rd, sells recycled and handmade goods including cards and paper.
**Little Lhasa Bookshop**, Temple Rd. Modern, computerized, same day service.
**Tibetan Children's Villages (TCVs)** outlets.
**Tibetan Handicrafts Centre**, ask at office for permission to watch artisans working on carpets, *thangkas* etc, reasonable prices.

**Chamba** *p525*
**Handicrafts Centre**, Rang Mahal. Rumal embroidery and leather goods.

## Activities and tours

**Dharamshala** *p518, maps p519 and p520*
**Meditation**
**Asho Spiritual Healing Institute**, Bhagsu, hardeshsood@hotmail.com. Offers 10-day course on healing, 2 hrs per day, US$100 in season, less off season, maximum 6 people per course. Also Hindi lessons, Rs 100 per hr.
**Himachal Vipassana Centre**, Dhamma Sikhara, next to Tushita, T01892 221 309, www.sikhara. dhamma.org. 10-day retreat, meditation in silence, donations only, reserve in advance, information and registration Mon-Sat 1600-1700. Interesting **"Z Meditation"** course including yoga and meditation. Retreats offered in silence with separate discussion sessions, 5 days (starting Mon 1600 until Sat 1100), Rs 3500 includes a 'humble' breakfast; highly recommended for beginners, run by friendly couple in peaceful location with beautiful views. Information and registration at 1230 only, past post office, down stairs of Yongling School, follow ZM signs.
**Himalayan Iyengar Yoga Centre**, Dharamkot. Offers 5-day course in Hatha yoga, starting every Thu at 0830. Information and registration Mon, 1330.
**Tushita Meditation Centre**, T01892 221 866, www.tushita.info, quietly located in Dharamkot village 2 km north of McLeodganj, offers individual and group meditation; 10-day 'Introduction to Buddishm' including lectures and meditation (residential courses get fully subscribed), enquiries Mon-Sat, 0930-1130, 1300-1630, simple accommodation on site. See also **Tibetan Library** above and **Tibet travel agent** below.

**Horse trekking**
**Highpoint Adventures** at **Sagar Book Shop**, Bhagsu Rd, also at **Kareri hotel**, T01892 221 132, karerihl@hotmail.com. Half or full day round trips, Rs 500-800, also offers treks and jeep safaris.

**Tour companies**
**Bedi Travels**, Mall Rd, McLeodganj, T01892 221 359, waystrvl@nde.vsnl. For bus tickets.
**Dhauladhar Travels**, Temple Rd, McLeodganj, T01892 221 158, dhauladhar @hotmail.com. Agents for **Indian Airlines**.
**HPTDC** luxury coach in season: Dharamshala to McLeodganj, Kangra Temple and Fort, Jawalamukhi, 1000-1900, Rs 200; Dharamshala to McLeodganj, Bhagsunath, Dal Lake, Talnu, Tapovan, Chamunda, 0900-1700, Rs 200. Tickets from HPTDC Marketing Office, near SBI, Kotwali Bazar in Dharamshala, T01892 223 107.
**Summit Adventures**, main square, Bhagsu Nag, McLeodganj, T01892 221 679, www.summit-adventures.net. Specialist in trekking and climbing, also cultural trips.
**Tibet Tours**, Temple Rd, T01892 221 539, www.tibettours.com. Comprehensive range of tours, very professional, include

pilgrimage tours, with lectures by eminent Buddhist lamas. Recommended.
**Trans Himalaya**, 4 Foxcote Gardens, Frome, Somerset, BA11 2DS, T01373 455518, www.trans-himalaya.com. This UK-based company specializes in touring the Himalayan region. With an indepth knowledge of Buddhist heritage, it offers cultural tours and eco-trekking.
**Ways Tours & Travels**, Temple Rd, T01892 221 910, waystour@vsnl.net. Most reliable, Mr Gupta is very experienced, professional service.

### Tibetan cookery

**Sangye**, at **Dreamland Hotel**, ssangye@hotmail.com. Runs 3 courses (soups, bread, momos), 1000-1200, 1700-1900, Rs 200 each. Friendly, fun, eat what you cook!

### Trekking

Best season Apr-Jun and Sep-Oct.
**Highland Trekkers**, opposite Taxi Union, T01892 221 740, hltrekkers@hotmail.com. Organize treks for smaller groups and a range of package tours.
**Himalayan Trekkers**, Dharamkot, T01892 221 260, anilsingh143@hotmail.com. Good range of treks and other mountain activities including climbing.
**Mountaineering Institute** on MI Rd, T01892 221 787. Invaluable advice on routes, equipment, accommodation and camp sites etc. Equipment and porters can be hired for groups of eight or more, reasonable charges. The Deputy Director (SR Saini) has described many routes in *Treks and Passes of Dhauladhar and Pir Pinjal*, (Rs 150) although the scale of maps can be misleading. Consult the author for detailed guidance. Mon-Sat, 1000-1700.

**Dalhousie** *p524, map p525*
**HPTDC** have daily tours during the tourist season to Khajjiar, 0900-1500, Rs 600 (car for 5) or Rs 85 by luxury coach; to Chamba, 1000-1900, Rs 120 by luxury coach; to Pathankot (one way) by luxury coach, Rs 120.

## Transport

**Dharamshala** *p518, maps p519 and p520*
It is dangerous to drive at night in the hills. The roads are not lit and the risks of running off the edge are great.

### Air

Nearest airport at Gaggal T01892 232 374, 13 km (taxi Rs 250-300). **Indian Airlines** T011 2331 0517 from Delhi (Mon, Wed, Fri), 1315, 1½ hrs (return to Delhi at 1500). **Jagson Airways** T011 2371 1069, similar services.

### Bus

**Local** Between Dharamshala and McLeodganj, 10 km, 30 mins' bus ride, Rs 10.
**Long distance** Most originate in Dharamshala,T01892 224 903, but some super and semi-deluxe buses leave from below the taxi stand in McLeodganj. HPTDC luxury coach (in season): to **Dalhousie** and **Chamba**: 1730, Rs150, 9 hrs; **Manali**: 2030, Rs 201, 8 hrs. HRTC buses to **Baijnath**: 2½ hrs, Rs 30; **Chandigarh**: (248 km), 9 hrs, Rs 160 via Una (overnight stop possible); **Delhi** (Kashmir Gate, 521 km), Deluxe coach departs McLeodganj 1630, 1815, 1930, 14 hrs, Rs 280; departs Delhi at same times.

1930, arrives Lower Dharamshala 1000, recommended for best morning views of the foothills (stops en route); Super Deluxe Coach to Connaught Place, 1900, Rs 400. Also deluxe buses to **Dehra Dun**: 2100, Rs 275 and **Shimla**, 1930, 2130 (from Dharamshala), Rs 190. **Kangra**: 50 mins, Rs 14; **Kullu** (214 km) 10 hrs; **Manali** (253 km) 11 hrs, Rs 130 (private Rs 250); best to travel by day (0800), fabulous views but bus gets overcrowded; avoid sitting by door where people start to sit on your lap! Always keep baggage with you; **Pathankot** (90 km) 4 hrs, connection for Amritsar, 3 hrs; **Shimla** (317 km, via Hamirpur/Bilaspur) 10 hrs. **Private buses** service **Dalhousie**: 0740, 6 hrs, Rs 125; **Delhi (Connaught Place)**: 1800, 1900, 11 hrs, Rs 400; **Dehra Dun**: 1900, 12 hrs, Rs 350; **Manali**: 0900, 2100, 8 hrs, Rs 250. Several private agents, although Bedi Travels have buses in the best condition (just!).

### Taxi

**Local** Shared by 4, pick up shuttle taxi at Kotwali Bazar on its way down before it turns around at the bus stand, as it is usually full when it passes the taxi stand.
**Long distance** Can be hired from near the bus stands, T01892 221 205. Full day (80 km), Rs 800; between Dharamshala and McLeodganj, Rs 100

### Train

Nearest broad gauge railhead is at Pathankot; booking office at bus stand, below tourist office, 1000-1100 (no computer). For narrow gauge, see page 523.

### Kangra *p522*

Gaggal airport T01892 232 374, 7 km away, has flights from Delhi (Mon, Wed, Fri).

**Buses** to **Dharamshala**: Rs 10, from bus stand about 1 km to temple; cross the railway track and follow the path all the way down to the road bridge, way below; stop the bus to Dharamshala on the opposite side of the bridge (under 1 hr). A taxi to **Dharamshala** Rs 400.

**Trains** include the narrow gauge to **Pathankot**: 0540, 0907, 1136, 1608, 1755, 1928, 4½ hrs; to **Baijnath**: 0807, 1038, 1817, 2027; to **Jogindernagar**: 0628, 1508; from **Pathankot:** 0435, 0835, 0921, 1300, 1600, 1800, 5 hrs (often 1 hr late!); continues to **Baijnath**, 2¼ hrs. The faster *Kangra Queen* from Pathankot, 0820, goes to Palampur. Kangra station serves Old Kangra with the fort, near the main road, while Kangra Mandir station is near the temple, bazar and most of the hotels. During the day there are regular rickshaw shuttles between Kangra Mandir station and Tehsil Chowk, Rs 3.

### Dalhousie *p524, map p525*

Dalhousie is on NH1A. From: **Delhi** (559 km); **Chandigarh** (336 km); **Shimla** (414 km).

Long-distance **buses** to **Chamba** (56 km via Khajjiar) 1½ hrs; **Dharamshala** (180 km, 7 hrs via Gaggal on the Shimla bus, change at Gaggal, 30 mins from Dharamshala); **Pathankot** 120 km, 3 hrs. **Jeeps** from bus stand, up to Gandhi Chowk, Rs 50, Bakrota Rs 90.

Nearest **train** station is at Pathankot, 2 hrs by taxi.

### Palampur *p524*

Chandigarh, 265 km (via Nangal, Una, Kangra), 5½ hrs; Delhi, 535 km, 10 hrs. The nearest airport is at Gaggal, T01892 232 374, 28 km with flights from Delhi (Mon, Wed, Fri). From **Delhi ISBT**, overnight deluxe **bus**. To **Andretta** (Private) from the bus station. **Dharamshala**, State buses from near the Nehru statue at the top of the main street. The town is 5 km from the **railway** station (taxi Rs 50). From Pathankot (narrow gauge) *Kangra Queen,* 0820, 4½ hrs, return departs Palampur 1345, via Kangra and Jawalamukhi, Rs 330 or Rs 190.

### Chamba *p525*

**Buses** arrive at the north end of the Chaugan. **Dalhousie** (2 hrs plus stop in Khajjiar); direct to **Amritsar**, 0745, 8 hrs. **Jeep** hire is relatively expensive. Special service during Manimahesh Yatra.

## ❶ Directory

### Dharamshala *p518, maps p519 and p520*

**Banks** Bank of Baroda, Kotwali Bazar. For Visa/Mastercard cash advances, T01892 223 175, collect on next working day (Rs 100, plus 1% commission). State Bank of India, T01892 222 996, and McLeodganj, changes TCs, 1000-1400. Western Union, near bus stand, McLeodganj, T01892 221 745. Money transfer and exchange, 1000-1930.

**Hospitals** Delek Hospital, T01892 221 626, often foreign volunteer doctors, good for dentistry. District Hospital, T01892 222 133. Men Tse Khang (Tibetan Medical Institute) T01892 222 484, Gangchen Kyishong, for Tibetan herbal medicine. Dr Dolma's and Dr Dhonden's clinics, near McLeodganj Bazar for Tibetan treatment. **Internet** Those with several machines are normally more reliable but power cuts not uncommon. **Post** GPO, 1 km below tourist office on Main Rd T01892 222 912, Mon-Sat, 1000-1630, another in Kotwali Bazar. In McLeodganj, the post office, Jogibara Rd, has poste restante. **Tourist offices** In McLeodganj: HPTDC Tourist Information, behind post office, T01892 221 205. Mon-Sat, 1000-1700. **Useful addresses** Foreigners' Registration Office: Civil Lines, beyond GPO, near petrol pump. Police: T01892 224 893.

**Dalhousie** *p524, map p525*
**Banks** Punjab Bank, Court Rd, changes TCs. **Hospital** Civil Hospital, T01899 242 125. **Post** GPO: Gandhi Chowk. **Tourist offices** HP, near Bus Stand, T01892 242 736, 1000-1700, helpful, but opening irregular especially out of season.

**Chamba** *p525*
**Banks** State Bank of India, Court Rd, Punjab Bank, Hospital Rd, change Amex TCs. **Tourist office** Hotel Iravati, T01899 224 002.

# Trekking in Himachal

*Himachal has something to offer every type of trekker. From short, leisurely walks through the pine forests that surround Shimla, with ample food and accommodation options meaning that nothing need be carried, to demanding treks over the high passes of Lahaul, Kinnaur and Spiti, the choice is almost as staggering as the views.*

## Trekking from Shimla

From Shimla on the Hindustan-Tibet Highway, there are opportunities for short and long treks. These include **Chharabra**, 13 km beyond Shimla at 2,593 m and **Naldera**, 23 km from Shimla, which was Curzon's summer retreat, see page 476.

Still further on at **Narkanda**, 64 km from Shimla, is another trek with very good walks, especially up Hattu Peak. From Narkanda the road runs down to the Sutlej valley and enters Kinnaur and Spiti. Foreigners are allowed into Spiti with permits.

From just beyond Narkanda you can trek northwest over the **Jalori Pass** (3,350 m) in the **Seraj** region. Starting from Ani village reached by bus/jeep from Luhri in the Sutlej Valley below Narkanda, you trek into the lower part of the Kullu Valley, joining the Kullu-Manali road at Aut. There is a jeepable road over much of this route. An alternative is to proceed 65 km from Narkanda to **Rampur** and then trek into the Kullu Valley via the **Bashleo Pass** (3,600 m). There are forest rest houses en route so a tent is not essential. The pass is crossed on the third day of this five-day trek. Both treks end at **Banjar** in the Tirthan Valley from where there are buses to Kullu.

## Trekking in Lahul, Kinnaur and Spiti

The border areas are being opened to trekkers with permits. At the same time the local tribal people are being exposed to outside influences which started with the introduction of television in these valleys. Now enterprising families open their homes to paying guests, youths offer their services as guides and muleteers and shops stock bottled drinks and canned food. However, anyone trekking in this region is advised to carry food, tents and all essentials.

## Lahul

Lahul (and Zanskar and Ladakh) are ideal trekking destinations during the monsoon as they are not nearly as wet as most other regions. The best time to go is from mid-June to mid-October but some passes, eg Shingo-La, Parvati Pass, may remain snow bound until mid-July or even later.

You can take a trek from **Darcha**, see page 516, up the valley over the **Shingo La** and on to **Padum**, the capital of the Zanskar region. Padum is linked with Leh. Shingo La is over 5,000 m so some acclimatization is desirable. The route is well marked.

An alternative route to Zanskar is up the Chandra valley and over **Baralacha La**. From here a trail leads over a high pass to Phuktal, where you join the main trail coming from Darcha. Most travellers drive into Darcha; however, a fine trek past the 'Lake of the Moon' or Chandratal makes a nice and less known addition for those with a little more time. The route taken from **Manali** is over the **Hamta Pass** with good views of Deo Tibba (6,001 m), weather permitting, to **Chhatru** village in the Chandra Valley where a rest house has camping in the grounds and local families accommodate visitors in very basic homes. It is four days' trek from Manali. Two days along the dirt road brings you to **Batal** (to save time you can take the bus from Manali over the Rohtang Pass). The next stage of both variations is to Chandratal.

**Chandratal** (4,270 m) is 18 km from Batal. The first section up to Kunzum Pass is on the bus route. The remaining 8½-km trail is open June-October and brings you to the beautiful clear blue water lake, about a kilometre long and half a kilometre wide which lies on a glacial bowl. Carry your own tent and provisions. The lake can also be reached on a lower 14-km trail that directly runs from Batal (no regular buses from Manali). From Chandratal the route crosses several fast flowing streams before reaching the Baralacha La (usually three days). You need to be very careful and take adequate safety precautions while negotiating these stream crossings. It then goes over another pass along the same ridge as the Shingo La, to join the main Darcha-Padum trail. From here you can continue on to **Padum** or return to Darcha in Lahul. This second option makes for a very good circular trek.

Another possibility is to trek down the Chenab Valley and either cross the Pir Panjal by one of a number of passes into the Ravi Valley via Bahrmaur, to Chamba or carry on to Kishtwar.

Around lower Lahul, you can trek from the district town of **Udeypur** at the base of the Miyar Nullah, the upper section of which is glaciated. To the east, high passes give access to the Bhaga valley and to the west to the Saichu Nala (Chenab tributary). The Trilokinath Temple nearby is well worth a visit, see page 514.

Trails run into the Miyar Nullah, renowned for flowers, then over the 5,100 m Kang La pass to Padum. Alternatively, you can follow the Chandrabhaga River to the scarcely visited Pangi valley with its rugged scenery and then over the 4,240 m Sach Pass leading to Chamba District.

In the Pangi Valley, the Chandrabhaga flows at over 2,400 m after the two rivers meet in this desolate and craggy region. The cheerful and good-looking Pangiwals keep their unique heritage alive through their singing and dancing. The Mindhal temple to Devi is their focus of worship. **Kilar** is the HQ which has a rest house and the Detnag Temple nearby. From Kilar a wide trail follows the steep slopes above the Chandrabhaga (Chenab) River to Dharwas on the Himachal/Kashmir border and then onwards to **Atholi** in the Paddar region of Kishtwar, known for its sapphire mines.

## Kinnaur

Close to the Tibetan border on its east, Kinnaur has the Sutlej flowing through it. Garhwal is to the south, Spiti Valley to the north and Kullu to the west. See page 485. The rugged mountains and sparse rainfall make Kinnaur resemble Lahul. The Kinners are Hindu but the Tibetan Buddhist influence is evident in the numerous gompas that can be seen alongside the temples. The **Phulaich** (Festival of Flowers) takes place in

 September when some villagers leave for the mountains for two days and nights to collect scented blossoms, then return on the third day to celebrate with singing and dancing. Kinnaur, including the lovely side valleys of **Sangla** and **Bhabha**, is now open with permits easily available from the District Magistrates in Shimla, Kullu or Keylong. These treks are immensely enjoyable; although there are stone huts and the occasional rest house, always carry a tent in this area.

**Baspa Valley** Starting from **Sangla** (2,680 m), you can take a fairly level forest walk up to Batrseri (5 km), then along the road up to Rakcham (8 km; 3,130 m) and climb gradually to reach **Chitkul** (18 km; 3,450 m), passing through Mastrang. Another option is to start at **Morang**, see page 487, which has a bus from Kalpa. The trail follows the Sutlej River bank for a short distance until the Tirung Gad meets it. Here it turns southeast and after going through a narrow valley reaches **Thangi**, a village connected to Morang by jeepable road where mules are available for hire. The track continues along barren hills to Rahtak (camping possible), before rising steeply to Charang Pass (5,266 m), then drops down following a mountain stream to Chitkul.

**Bhabha Valley** Another beautiful valley to trek, starting from **Kafnoo** (2,427 m), 22 km from Wangtu. Permit details have to be entered and stamped at the police post 1 km before Kafnoo reservoir. They are checked at Tabo.

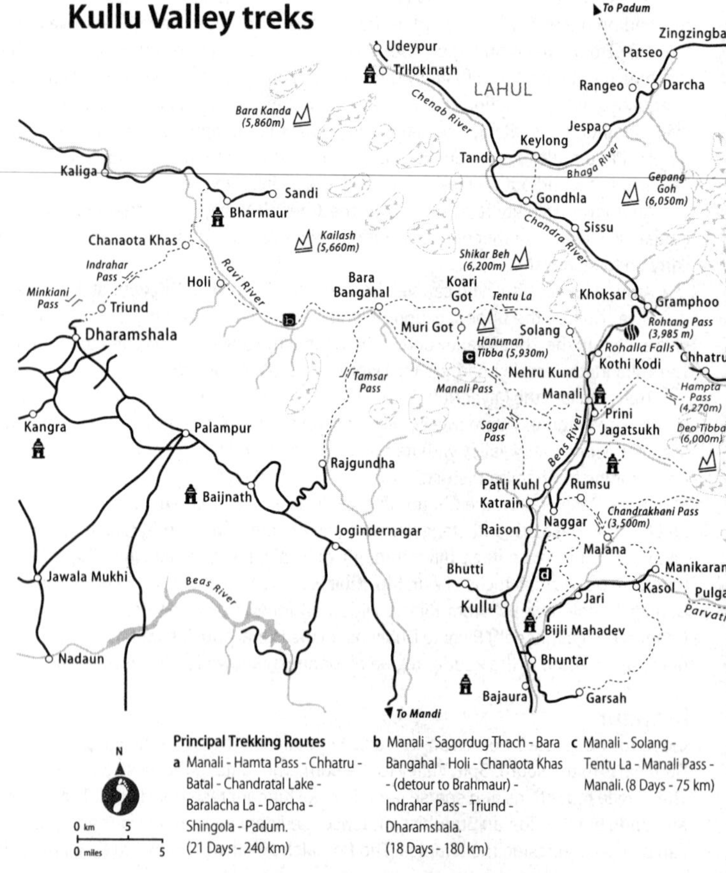


**Principal Trekking Routes**

**a** Manali - Hamta Pass - Chhatru - Batal - Chandratal Lake - Baralacha La - Darcha - Shingola - Padum. (21 Days - 240 km)

**b** Manali - Sagordug Thach - Bara Bangahal - Holi - Chanaota Khas - (detour to Brahmaur) - Indrahar Pass - Triund - Dharamshala. (18 Days - 180 km)

**c** Manali - Solang - Tentu La - Manali Pass - Manali. (8 Days - 75 km)

There is level ground at the end of the road by the reservoir suitable for camping, but it can get flooded. Local guides available. From Kafnoo, the trail follows the right bank of the river for about a kilometre before crossing over to the left bank over a new bridge. From here, the trail gradually ascends to **Chokhapani** (known locally as Sholti), about a five-hour walk away. The riverside trail is slippery and not recommended. The upper trail climbs past Yangpa II then through fields around Musrang hamlet. There is an adequate campsite at Chokhapani (10 km, 3,000 m).

From Chokhapani to **Upper Mulling** (3,470 m) is a beautiful 8 km, four hours' walk (including lunch stop), following the left bank of the Bhabha stream. Initially going through forests the track then crosses open meadows. At the far end of the meadows is an ideal camping site by the river. The trail from Mulling enters a forested section leading to a snow bridge across the stream. Cross the stream and follow the steeply rising trail to the **Kara** meadows where the Government Animal Husbandry Department has a Merino sheep breeding centre. Ford the Bhabha River with care (either on horseback or by wading across with support from a fixed line), to the campsite at Pasha. This section takes three hours, so you can continue to the **Kara-Taria Pass Base**. The 5-km walk up a steep trail along the right fork of the Bhabha stream takes another four hours. Taria Base Pass (4,290 m) camp is below the steep slope leading to the Pass. Camp well away from the slope as it is prone to rock falls.

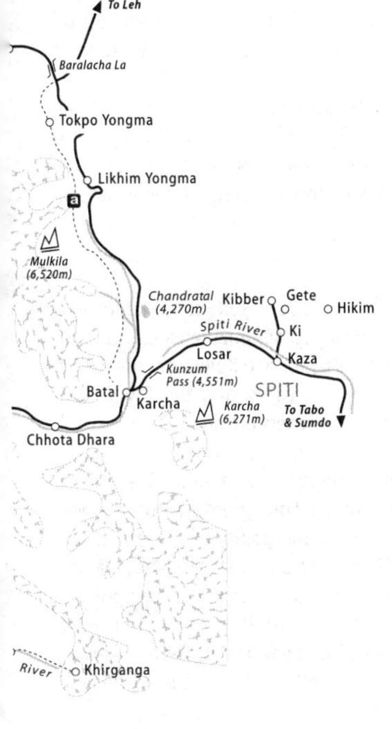


**d** Manali - Naggar - Malana - Manikaran - Kasol - Jari - Bijli Mahadev - Naggar - Manali. (9 Days - 140 km)

**Pin Valley** There is a steep descent over scree for the first kilometre from **Taria Pass**, followed by a five-hour 15-km walk along a narrow but clear trail to the first camp in the Pin Valley. None of the apparently promising campsites on the way has a good water source. The **Bara Boulder** site has a stream and good grazing for horses.

The 11-km stretch from Bara Boulder to **Mudh** (3,925 m) takes four hours. It is the highest permanently inhabited village in the Pin Valley and is surrounded by summer cultivation. Log bridges cross several streams feeding into the Pin River. There are places to stay and food is available but some villagers charge up to Rs 200-300 for a room. It is possible to camp outside the village. One campsite is on the flat plateau overlooking the river near the summer hut of the lay *lama* (before crossing the narrow foot bridge on the river), another is near the fields immediately below the village where a side stream runs below the old monastery into the Pin. It is worth visiting the old gompas in the village.

From Mudh to **Gulling** is a gentle five-hour trek (15 km) along the right bank of the Pin. A single log bridge takes the path into Tilling village, followed by a gentle climb to the big village of **Sangam**

### The valley of the Gods

No one knows the origin of the village of Malana. People believe that a band of renegade soldiers who deserted Alexander's army in the 4th century BC settled here (some wooden houses have soldiers carved on them); it is more probable that their antecedents were from the Indian plains. Their language, Kanashi, has no script but is linked to Tibetan. The villagers are directly involved in taking decisions on important matters affecting them, thus operating as an ancient democratic 'city state'. Language, customs and religious practices too differ from neighbouring hill tribes, polygamy being permitted.

A charming myth is associated with Jamlu, the principal deity in the valley. Jamlu, possibly of pre-Aryan origin, was carrying a casket containing all the important deities of Hinduism and while crossing the mountains through the Chandrakhani Pass into Kullu, a strong gust of wind blew open the box and spread the deities all over the valley. Since then Malana has been known as 'The Valley of the Gods'.

on the opposite bank, see page 489. The track crosses a rocky spur and descends steeply to some small fields beside the river. Descend to the sandy river bed and cross diagonally to the single wire rope strung across the river. A makeshift pulley and harness crossing has to be rigged up here unless a suitable shallow spot can be found further downstream. Camp can be set up in the fields just below the road immediately above the crossing point.

From this point arrange to be picked up to drive to Spiti. You can visit the small but locally important Nyingmapa Gompa of Kungri (Ghungri), just above the road, and if you have an extra day based here you can walk up the short stretch of dirt road towards Sangam, then turn right into the virtually unknown Parahio River valley, an important tributary of the Pin.

## Spiti

Meaning literally 'the place of Mani', Spiti is a high altitude desert, bare, rugged and inhospitable, with the Spiti River running from the slopes of Kunzum La (4,551 m) to Sumdo (3,230 m). Kunzum La offers seasonal access by road to Kullu from the valley, and it is also directly connected with Shimla via the NH22 and the SH30. Like neighbouring Lahul, Spiti is famous for its *gompas*. Foreigners are now allowed to trek in this region up to Kibber with permits.

At **Tabo**, the Buddhist monastery is one of the region's most famous, see page 488. There is a dispensary and two adequate teashops. Foreigners are now allowed to stay overnight in Tabo. There are other important gompas at Dankar, Ki, Kungri and Lalung. Trekkers interested in **fossils** choose a trail starting at **Kaza** and travel to **Langza** (8½ km), which has a narrow motorable track. The trek goes to Hikim, the Tangyut monastery, Komik (8 km) and returns to Kaza (6 km). From Kibber (4,205 m) there is a 6-km track through alpine meadows to **Gete** (4,520 m) which claims to be one of the highest permanent settlements in the world only reached on foot.

# Trekking in the Kullu and Parvati Valleys

Treks here vary in duration and degree of difficulty. There are pleasant walks up the subsidiary valleys from Aut and Katrain with the opportunity to camp in spectacular and high locations without having to spend very long getting there. An option is to take the bus up to the Rohtang Pass, 51 km from Manali, which is very spectacular and then walk down. There is a path, and it only takes a few hours.



The post-monsoon period (September to mid-November) is the most reliable **season**. Longer treks with crossings of high passes can be undertaken then, before the winter snows arrive. During the monsoon (June to September) it is wet but the rain is not continuous. It may rain all day or for only an hour or two. Visibility is affected and glimpses of mountains through the clouds are more likely than broad clear panoramic views. However, many flowering plants are at their best. There is trekking in the spring, that is April to May, but the weather is more unsettled and the higher passes may still have quite a lot of snow on them. There can be very good spells of fine weather during this period and it can get quite hot in May.

You will need to take your own **equipment** since that hired out by local agencies is often of an inferior quality. Kullu now has pony unions with fixed rates for guides, porters and horses. Ask at the Tourist Office and the Mountaineering Institute for information and assistance.

## Routes

From **Manali** you can go north into **Lahul** (Map trek **a**) and **Spiti** Valleys by crossing the Rohtang (3,985 m) or the Hampta Pass (4,270 m). Once over the great divide of the Pir Panjal the treks are as briefly described – see Trekking in Lahul, Kinnaur and Spiti above. West of Manali there are routes into the **Chamba** and **Kangra** Valleys (Map trek **b**).

The trek to Malana Valley offers an opportunity to see a relatively isolated and comparatively unspoilt hill community. From Manali you go to Naggar (28 km, which can also be reached by bus) and stay at **Rumsu** (2,377 m) which is higher. The Chandrakhani Pass (3,500 m) takes you into the Malana Valley at the head of which is the glacier. On the third day you can reach **Malana** (2,650 m, 20 km from Naggar), which has two guest houses. In the past you could only enter with permission from the villagers but this is no longer needed. On the fourth day you trek to **Jari** (1,500 m) where you can catch a bus to Kullu. The road from Jari to Malana may destroy the uniqueness of the community. The whole of the Malana Valley is dominated by **Deo Tibba** peak in the north.

## Parvati Valley

To extend the trek from Malana it is possible to continue to **Manikaran** and onwards to Pulga and beyond in the scenic Parvati Valley. You can also get to Manikaran by bus from Kullu, see page 498. Up to **Khirganga** the trail is fairly clear but take care since the area is prone to heavy rain and land slips. Beyond Khirganga, the trek follows the valley up-river passing the tree line to Pandav Bridge and eventually arriving at the sacred lake and shrine at **Mantalai**. Here it splits leading up and over the Pin-Parvati Pass, and down into the dry Pin Valley.

Alternatively, you can explore the lower Parvati Valley by walking to **Kasol**, and then to Jari and Naggar via the temple of Bijli Mahadev (Map trek **d**).

## Pin Valley

The difference between the Parvati and the Pin Valley is striking. Immense glaciers and bizarre moonscape rock formations here contrast with the verdant pastures and evergreen forests of the Parvati valley behind. The trek leads down to the traditional village of **Mudh**, see page 537. The road to Mudh is still incomplete so it takes about five hours to walk to Sangam and Chatral, leading to Kinnaur and Spiti. There are buses from Chatral to Kaza, see page 490. The trek from Manikaran to Kaza with passes over 5,300 m, can take 10-14 days. Guides and porters are necessary.

# Trekking in Kangra

**Baijnath, Palampur** and **Dharamshala** are popular starting points. See pages 518 and 522. From here you go over the **Dhaula Dhar** at passes such as the Indrahar and Minkiani (both from Dharamshala) and the Waru (from Palampur), then enter a feeder of the Upper Ravi Valley.

*There are very pleasant day walks throughout the Kangra Valley. Longer, more arduous treks are north over the Dhaula Dhar to Chamba or the Kullu Valley.*

Midway up the valley which lies between the Manimahesh Dhar and Dhaula Dhar ranges is Bara Bangahal. From there you can go downstream to **Chamba** or upstream which offers the choice of at least three passes for crossing into the Kullu Valley. The northernmost of these is the Solang Pass which passes Beas Kund beneath Hanuman Tibba. In the middle is the Manali Pass whilst the southernmost is Sagar Pass. A good trip which includes the upper part of this valley is the round trip trek from Manali, see page 539.

# Trekking from Chamba

The Chamba region receives less rain than the Kangra Valley to the south. A trek, particularly over the Pir Panjal into Lahul is possible during the monsoon months (June-September). The ideal season, though, is just after the monsoon. There are several short and longer treks from Chamba and Bahrmaur in the Upper Ravi Valley.

To the north there are three main passes over the **Pir Panjal** into Lahul: the Kalicho, Kugti and Chobia Passes. At least five days should be allowed for crossing them as their heights are around 5,000 m and acclimatization is highly desirable. All the first stages of the walks are along the Budhil River. After the first two days, the services of a guide or porters are recommended for picking the right trail. Views from the passes are very good both of the Himalaya to the north and the Chenab Valley to the south. The descent from the passes is very steep. On reaching the road you can take a bus from **Udeypur** or **Trilokinath** in the Pattan Valley, to the Kullu Valley over Rohtang Pass. Several trails cross the high passes over the Pir Panjal range to give access to the Pattan valley of Lahaul. The semi nomadic Gaddi shepherds regularly use these to take their flocks across to the summer grazing grounds located in the high side valleys of Lahaul.

**Bahrmaur** (1,981 m), also spelt Brahmaur or Bharmaur, is 65 km from Chamba and can be reached by bus. It was the original capital Brahmapura for four centuries and has 8th-10th-century *Pahari* style temples. The best known are the Lakshminarayan group which is the centre of worship for the semi-nomadic Gaddi tribe. From Bahrmaur a three-day trek is possible to **Manimahesh Lake** (3,950 m), 34 km, in the Manimahesh Kailash (5,575 m), a spur running off the Pir Panjal. The **Manimahesh Yatra** begins in Chamba and ends at the lake, revered by local people as a resting place of Siva. Pilgrims arrive at the Manimahesh temple here and take a holy bath a fortnight after *Janmashtami* (September/October). The temple has a brass *Mahisasuramardini* image. During the *yatra* period buses, minibuses and taxis are laid on from Chamba to Bahrmaur. Many pilgrims trek the next 12 km to Hadsar although jeeps are available. From here it is a two-day climb to the lake with a night halt at Dhanchho. Himachal Tourism tents available at Bahmaur and there is also a rest house, Hadsar, Dhanchho and Manimahesh; contact tourist office, Dalhousie, T01899 242 736. Ponies and porters can be hired at each place. The nine-day trek starting from Chamba includes **Rakh** (20 km) on Day 1, **Bahrmaur** on Day 2, a rest stop there, then continuing to **Hadsar** (12 km), **Dhanchho** (7 km) and **Manimahesh** (7½ km) with a brief halt at **Bhairon Ghati**. The return is by the same route.

# Jammu and Kashmir

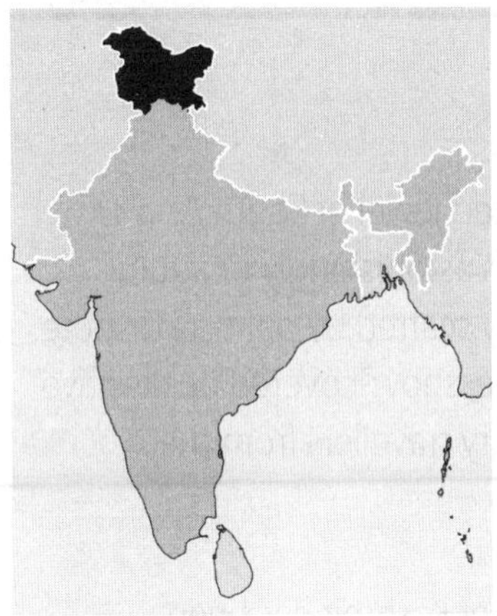



## Footprint features

# Introduction

Jammu and Kashmir, the contested jewel of South Asia's northernmost region, has seen its astonishingly beautiful valleys and mountains repeatedly scarred by political dispute. Its lakes, fertile valleys and remote, snow-covered peaks have drawn rulers, pilgrims and ordinary travellers from the Mughals onwards.

Tragically, the beauty of the Vale of Kashmir has been effectively out of bounds for over 15 years. However, the state has other fascinating and accessible regions, set in some of the world's most beautiful scenery. The spectacular high altitude deserts of Ladakh and Zanskar provide the setting for a hardy Buddhist culture, whose villages and monasteries retain strong links with Tibet. Alchi, Hemis and Thikse are just three of the most striking of the many monasteries clinging to mountainsides, and some of the highest altitude passes in the world allow entry to one of India's least known regions.

Sadly, although the major pilgrimage to Amarnath is massively guarded by the army, treks in the region cannot be regarded as safe. It is currently almost impossible to trek in Jammu and Kashmir, though it is still possible to get into Ladakh.

All foreigners entering the Vale of Kashmir and Ladakh are required to register their arrival. Despite the fact that visitors still go to the Vale of Kashmir there is a very obvious military presence and frequent acts of violence. Do not believe those touts and 'travel agents' in Delhi and elsewhere who will try to persuade you that everything is normal and perfectly safe in the Vale. It is not.

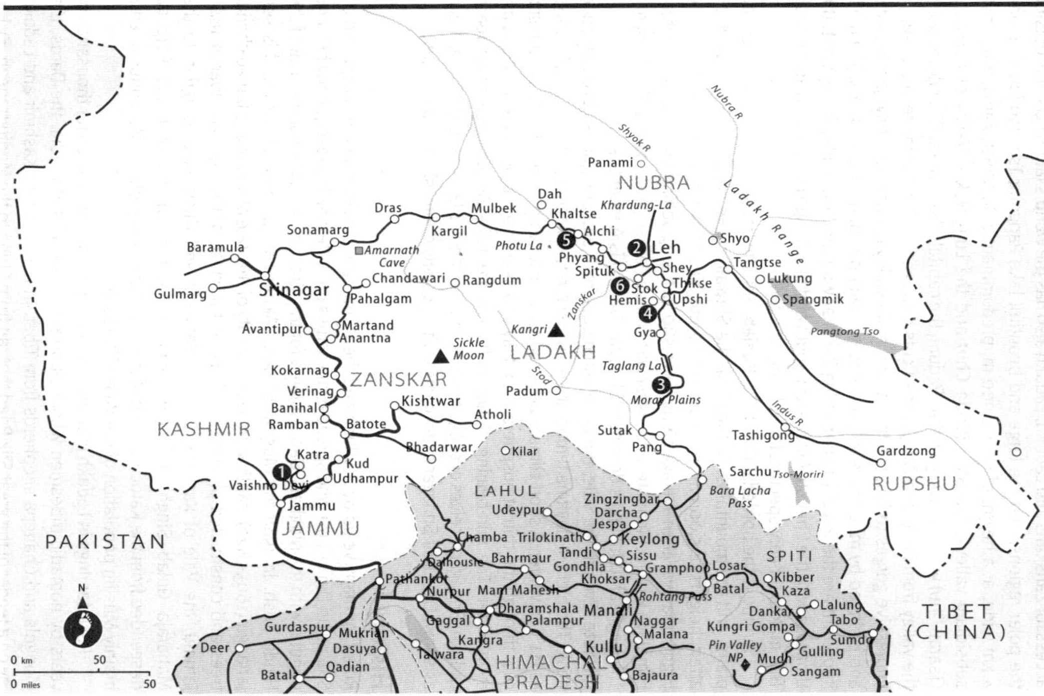

## ★ Don't miss...

1 **Vaishno Devi** If it's safe, witness the yatra, many find it very moving, page 551.

2 **Leh** Mysterious and dust-covered, Leh is fascinating; don't miss out on the bazar but remember to bargain hard, page 555.

3 **The Manali to Leh Road** A must for adrenalin junkies with some interesting monasteries to visit en route, page 559.

4 **Hemis** Stay overnight and attend morning prayers at this monastery, the largest of those in Ladakh, page 560.

5 **Alchi** Another important monastery that's well worth a visit, page 562.

6 **Spituk to Hemis** If you have the time and energy, walk this trek, page 567.

# Background → *Population: 10.1 mn. Area: 222,000 sq km.*

## The land

**Geography** The largest of India's Himalayan states comprises three regions: **Jammu**, the mainly Hindu foothills in the south, the borderland with the Punjab and the transitional zone between the plains and the mountains; the **Vale of Kashmir**, overwhelmingly Muslim in the centre, lying between the Pir Panjal and the High Himalaya, where the Nagin and Dal lakes dominate Srinagar; **Ladakh** and **Zanskar**, the predominantly Buddhist western highlands of the great Himalayan axis.

Four mountain ranges cross Ladakh – Gt Himalaya, Zanskar, Ladakh and Karakoram – as do the river Indus and its tributaries the Zanskar, Shingo and Shyok. The Zanskar runs its course of 120 km before joining the Indus at Nimmu near Leh, the capital of Ladakh. During the winter months the frozen Zanskar provides the only access for Zanskaris into Ladakh. Ladakh also has the world's largest glaciers outside the polar regions, and the large and beautiful lake Pangong Tso, 150 km long and 4 km wide, at a height of over 4,000 m, predominantly Buddhist. Zanskar has two subsidiary valleys, the Stod (Doda Chu) and the Lung-Nak – Valley of darkness (Tsarap Chu) which converge below Padum, the capital. The Zanskar River flows along the valley from Padum to Zangla, then cuts through the Zanskar range in a series of impressive gorges to join the Indus. The main valley is approximately 300 km long and is ringed by mountains so access to it is over one of the high passes. The most important are the Pensi La connecting Zanskar with the Suru Valley in the west, the Umasi La with the Chenab Valley in the south and the Shingo La with Lahul in the east. This makes for very spectacular trekking country.

Jammu is the borderland with the **Punjab**, and the transitional zone between the plains and the mountains. To the north the Shiwaliks give onto the Pir Panjal which attain heights of 5,000 m. The Vale of Kashmir, lies between the Pir Panjal and the High Himalaya, at an average altitude of 1,580 m. Rising behind the Vale are the Great Himalaya which culminate in the west with Nanga Parbat ('Naked Mount' – 8,125 m). The Nagin and Dal lakes dominate Srinagar. Nearby is Anchar Lake.

**Climate** Even in the Vale, the air in summer is fresh and at night can even be quite brisk. The highest daytime temperatures in July rarely exceed 35°C but may fall as low as -11°C in winter. A short climb quickly reduces these tempertures. In Ladakh the sun cuts through the thin atmosphere, and daily and seasonal temperature variations are even wider. The rain-bearing clouds drifting in from the Arabian Sea never reach Ladakh. Srinagar receives over 650 mm per annum whereas Leh has only 85 mm, much as snow. Over half Srinagar's rain comes with westerly depressions in the winter.

## History

Ruled for many years by Scythian and then Tartar princes, **Kashmir** was captured by Shams ud Din in 1341 who spread Islam across the Vale which subsequently became popular with the Mughals. Babur longed for the streams and cool mountain air of the Hindu Kush. In 1588 the Mughal Emperor Akbar conquered Kashmir and his son Jahangir (1605-1627), captivated by the beauty of the Vale of Kashmir, planted chenar trees and constructed pleasure gardens. At the close of the first Sikh War in 1846 Jammu, the Vale of Kashmir, Ladakh, Baltistan and Gilgit were assigned to the Maharaja Gulab Singh of Jammu, who founded a dynasty of Dogra Rajputs, descended from the Katoch branch of the lunar race of Rajputs. Thus, Hindus ruled a mainly Muslim population of the Vale of Kashmir.

Rock carvings in Ladakh indicate that the region has been used for thousands of years by nomadic tribesmen who include the Mons of North India, the Dards, the Mongols and Changpa shepherds from Tibet. In Roman times Kashmir and Ladakh lay on a feeder of the great Silk Road that ran from China to the Mediterranean. By the

## Warning

Visitors to India have been advised not to travel to the Kashmir Valley. Several of the splinter groups opposed to the Indian Government have taken hostages as a means of putting pressure on the government so the risks of travel to Kashmir are still real.

An increasing number of domestic tourists are visiting the valley – take advice from your own consulate.

end of the 10th century, Ladakh was controlled by the Thi Dynasty which founded a capital at Shey and built many forts. Tibetan Lamaistic Buddhism took hold at the same time and over 100 gompas were built. In 1533 Soyang Namgyal united the whole region up to the outskirts of Lhasa and made his capital at Leh. The Namgyal Dynasty still exists today and the Rani (Queen) of Stok was elected to the Indian Parliament. During the reigns of Senge Namgyal (circa 1570-1620) and Deldan Namgyal (circa 1620-1660) Ladakh was threatened from the south and west by the Baltis, who had enlisted the assistance of the Mughals. They were beaten back and the Namgyals extended Ladakhi power. The expansionist era came to an end when the fifth Dalai Lama of Tibet, Nawang Lobsang Gyatso (1617-1682) persuaded the Mongols, whom he had converted to Buddhism, to enter a military campaign against West Tibet and Ladakh. The Ladakhis were unable to repel the invading Mongol forces and in desperation Delegs Namgyal turned to Kashmir for help. The Mughal Governor of Kashmir sent troops to help the King of Leh regain his throne but in return he had to pay regular tribute and build a mosque. From then on the country became an extension of the Mughal Empire. In 1834 Zorwar Singh, an Army General, conquered Ladakh and brought the area under the control of the Dogra Maharajah of Kashmir. The dethroned royal family received the Stok Palace where they still live today.

Zanskar became an administrative part of Ladakh under Senge Namgyal whose three sons became the rulers of Ladakh, Guge and Zanskar/Spiti. This arrangement collapsed after Ladakh's war with Tibet and the Zanskar royal house divided, one part administering Padum, the other Zangla. Under the Dogras, the rulers were reduced to puppets as the marauding army wreaked havoc on the villages, monasteries and population.

Kashmir's future remained unresolved at Independence. Eighteen months of fighting in 1948-1949 left the state split by a UN monitored ceasefire line, much of which remains the de facto border between India and Pakistan. Of the total area of the pre-Independence State, over which India continues to claim the legitimate right to govern, 78,000 sq km are currently controlled by Pakistan and a further 42,600 sq km by China. Kashmir has remained the single most important cause of conflict between the two countries ever since 1949, while arguments for autonomy within the Kashmir Valley have periodically dominated the political agenda. Since 1989 the Indian army has struggled to keep control against a Pakistan-backed militia.

Following India's independence and partition in 1947 Ladakh, like Kashmir, was divided. Indian and Chinese troops have been stationed on the eastern border since the Chinese invasion of Tibet in 1950-1951. From the early 1950s Chinese troops were stationed in the Aksai Chin, which India also claimed, and without Indian knowledge built a road linking Tibet with Xinjiang. This was one of the two fronts in China's war with India in 1962, which confirmed China's de facto hold on the territory. India still disputes its legality. Since the 1962 war the Indian army has maintained a very strong presence in Ladakh. The strategic requirements of better links with the rest of India were primarily responsible for Ladakh being 'opened up' to some influences from outside.

## The current political situation

In May 2002 tension between India and Pakistan over Kashmir nearly boiled over into war. A terrorist attack on the Indian Parliament in December 2001 led India to move over half a million troops to the border, and many in India demanded military strikes in response to what they claimed was continuing Pakistan support for cross-border terrorism. A further attack on a bus and an army post in Jammu in May raised worldwide fears of a full-scale war, possibly escalating to nuclear conflict. Following huge diplomatic pressure, the tension was beginning to ease and there are encouraging signs following the 'cricket diplomacy' in the spring of 2004. Furthermore, after 14 months of improving Indo-Pakistan relations, the first tangible development came in the form of a fortnightly bus service between Srinagar and Muzaffarabad, in Pakistan's Azad Kashmir, launched on 8 April 2004. This route had been closed for almost 60 years, and its reopening was seen by many as an encouraging sign of progress between the two nations. However Jammu and and the Vale of Kashmir seem set to remain completely out of bounds for the foreseeable future.

## Culture

Culturally the people of Jammu, Kashmir and Ladakh could scarcely be more different from each other. The ten million people are unevenly scattered. The Vale of Kashmir has over half, whilst Ladakh is the most sparsely populated. Jammu was traditionally the seat of Dogra power and serves a largely Hindu population with its affinities more with the Punjab than the Vale. Kashmir marks the northernmost advance of Islam in the Himalaya while Ladakh is aptly named 'Little Tibet'. Ethnically the Ladakhis are of Tibetan stock. Indeed, it was once a province of Tibet and was governed in secular matters by an independent prince and in spiritual affairs by the Dalai Lama. Tibetan Changpas form the bulk of the population in central and eastern Ladakh. These nomadic herdsmen can be seen living in black yak-hair tents on the mountains with their yaks, goats and sheep. They still provide the fine pashm goat wool. The Mons, nomads of Aryan stock, introduced Buddhism and established settlements in the valleys. The Droks or Dards from the Gilgit area settled along the Indus valley and introduced irrigation; many converted to Islam 300 years ago. Most are cultivators speaking a language based on Sanskrit. The Baltis with Central Asian origins mostly live in the Kargil region. The Zanskaris are of the same stock as the Ladakhis and because of the sheer isolation of their homeland were able to preserve their Buddhist culture against the onslaughts of Islam. The majority of Zanskaris are Buddhist, though there are Muslim families in Padum, the capital, dating from the Dogra invasion.

**Kashmiri** is influenced by Sanskrit and belongs to the Dardic branch of the Indo-Aryan languages. Linguistically and physically Kashmiris are similar to the tribes around Gilgit in Pakistan. The Ladakhis physically reveal Tibetan- Mongolian and Indo-Aryan origins while their language belongs to the Tibetan-Burmese group.

## Religion

In the Vale of Kashmir, 95% of the people are **Muslim**, the majority being Sunnis, while in Jammu over 65% are **Hindu**. In Ladakh, 52% are Lamaistic **Buddhists**. Most follow Mahayana Buddhism of theVajrayana sect with a mixture of Bon animism and Tantric practices. The Red Hat Drukpa (or Kagyupa) sect of Tibetan monastic Buddhists enjoy royal patronage. The reformist Yellow Hat sect are Gelugpa Buddhists, and like the Dalai Lama, wear a yellow head-dress with their maroon robes. The more ancient Nyingmapa Buddhist have their seat in Tak-thok. Ladakhi lamas may also be physicians, teachers and astrologers; they also work in the fields, as do the *chomos* (nuns). Nearly every family has a member who chooses to become a lama (often the third son) or a chomo. The most important in the Tibetan tradition are recognized reincarnate *lamas* (Trulku), who are born to the position. The Buddhist *gompas* (monasteries) are places of worship, meditation and religious instruction

## Surviving in a harsh climate

An almost total lack of precipitation has meant that cultivation must rely on irrigation. The rivers have been harnessed but with difficulty as the deep gorges presented a problem. In Ladakh it is restricted to the areas immediately around streams and rivers, and altitude and topography determine the choice of crop. Barley forms the staple food while peas are the most common vegetable and apples and apricots the most popular fruits. Because of the harshness of the climate and lack of rain, the cropping season usually lasts from April to October. Apple and apricots grow well, with the latter being dried for the winter, the kernel yielding oil for burning in prayer-lamps. At lower altitudes, grape, mulberry and walnut are grown. Travellers venturing out of Leh are likely to see villagers using traditional methods of cultivation with the help of *dzos* and donkeys and implements that have not changed for centuries.

Livestock is precious, especially the yak which provides meat, milk for butter, hair and hide for tents, boots, ropes and dung for fuel. Goats, especially in the eastern region, produce fine *pashm* for export. The Zanskar pony is fast and strong and therefore used for transport – and for the special game of Ladakhi polo!

and the structures, often sited on spectacular mountain ridges, add to the attraction of the landscape while remaining a central part of Ladakhi life. Ladakh also has a large number of Shi'a Muslims, mainly in Kargil District, many being immigrant Kashmiris and Dards. Their mosques and imambaras, influenced by Persian architecture, can be found in Leh proper and villages nearby.

The foundation of Sani in the 11th century is recognized as the first monastery in Zanskar. Phugtal and Karsha date from the same period. The sects developed alongside those in Ladakh. The Gelugpa (Yellow Hat) order was established in the 15th century and monasteries at Karsha, Lingshet and Mune belong to this. The Drukpa sect set up monasteries at Bardan and Zangla and 'occupied' that at Sani. These have links with Stakna near Leh and the Gelugpa is associated with the Lekir monastery. Traditional Ladakhi and Zanskari life, even today, comes close to Gandhi's idealized vision of life in ancient India.

## Handicrafts

Kashmir is renowned for its distinctive and fine handicrafts. Many of these developed when Srinagar was an entrepôt on the ancient trans-Himalayan trade route. High quality craftsmanship in India initially owed much to the patronage of the court and Kashmir was no exception. From the 15th century onwards, carpet making, shawl weaving and embroidery and decorative techniques were actively encouraged and the tradition grew to demands made at home and abroad. Since tourism has been severely affected in the Vale since 1989, Kashmiri tradesmen have sought markets in other parts of India.

Kashmir **shawls** are world renowned for their softness and warmth. The best are pashmina and shahtush, the latter being the warmest, the rarest and, consequently, the most expensive. Prized by Moghuls and Maharajas they found their way to Europe and through Napoleon's Egyptian campaign became an item of fashion in France. The craft was possibly introduced from Persia in the 15th century. Originally a fine shawl would take months to complete especially if up to 100 colours were used. The soft fleece of the pashmina goat or the fine under hairs of the Tibetan antelope were used, the former for pashmina (cashmere) shawls, the latter for shahtush. The very best

## Ladakhi dress

Ladakhis dress in *gonchas,* loose woollen robes tied at the waist with a wide coloured band. Buddhists usually wear dark red while Muslims and nomadic tribes often use undyed material. The head dress varies from the simple Balti woollen cap with a rolled brim and the traditional *gonda* (a high embroidered hat) to the snake-shaped ornate black lambskin *perak* worn by some women. Studded with turquoise and lapis lazuli these are precious enough to be handed down as heirlooms.

were soft and warm and yet so fine that they could be drawn through a finger ring. The designs changed over the years from floral patterns in the 17th century to Paisley in the 19th century. The Mughals, especially Akbar, used them as gifts. However, with the introduction of the Jacquard loom, cheap imitations were mass produced at a fraction of the price but shawl weaving. The Kashmir shawls thus became luxury items, their manufacture remainsing an important source of employment in the Vale, but they ceased to be the major export.

*All trade in Shahtush and articles made from the wool of the Chiru is banned, hence buying and exporting an article is illegal.*

Hand knotted **carpets** are available in pure wool and mixed with cotton or silk. The patterns tend to the traditional, the Persian and Bukhara styles being common, though figurative designs such as The Tree of Life are becoming increasingly popular. Young boys work with a master and it is common to hear them calling out the colour changes in a chant. Child labour in carpet making across North India is increasingly widely criticized. Government attempts to insist on limiting hours of work and the provision of schooling often seem to be ignored. A large carpet will take months to complete, the price depending on the density of knots and the material used, silk being by far the most expensive. The salesmen usually claim that only vegetable dyes are used and whilst this is true in some instances, more readily available and cheaper chemical dyes are commonplace. After knotting, the pile is trimmed with scissors, loose threads burnt off and the carpet washed and dried. Look for the rug mark awarded when no child labour is used.

Papier mâché boxes, trays, coasters make ideal gifts. Paper is soaked, dried in a mould, then painted and lacquered. Traditionally, natural colouring was used (lapis lazuli for blue, gold leaf for gold, charcoal for black) but this is unlikely today. The patterns can be highly intricate and the finish exquisite.

Other crafts include crewel work (chain stitching) on fabric, fur coats and 'Kashmiri silver' jewellery, silk and fine woodcarving, particularly on walnut wood.



## Modern government

The state enjoys a special status within the union. As defined in Article 370 of the constitution, since 1956 Jammu and Kashmir has had its own constitution affirming its integrity. The central government has direct control over defence, external affairs and communications within the state and indirect influence over citizenship, Supreme Court jurisdiction and emergency powers. In normal times the state sends six representatives to the Lok Sabha and two members who are nominated by the governor to the Rajya Sabha.

In Ladakh, the local government body, the Ladakh Hill Council, has once again put forth a demand to the Indian Government to separate the district from the rest of the state of Jammu and Kashmir. Citing reasons of cultural uniqueness and the fact that they do not wish to be part of any separatist movement in Kashmir, the Ladakhis demand being made into an 'Union Territory' directly funded by the central government.

# Kashmir Valley

## Srinagar → *Colour map 1, grid A2. Population: 894,900. Altitude: 1,730 m.*

Founded by Raja Pravarasen in the sixth century and beautifully located around a number of lakes, Srinagar, 'the beautiful city', is divided in two by the river Jhelum which is crossed by a number of bridges (*kadal*). Despite the name, the beauty of Kashmir has never been reflected in that of its main town. The city's daily life revolves around the river and Dal and Nagin lakes but the lack of tourists has led to neglect. In view of the present political situation this edition of the Handbook does not carry details of places to visit outside Srinagar. » *For Sleeping, Eating and other listings see pages 552-554.*

### Ins and outs

**Security** A few travellers continue to visit Srinagar, some using the road to Leh to enter Ladakh. It is essential to be extremely careful. Moving around the town can be hazardous, especially after dark – only a few suitable hotels and houseboats are open; there are no bars, beer shops or cinemas and phone links with the rest of India, let alone overseas, are poor. Dusk-to-dawn curfews are not uncommon. It still may not be possible to visit some of the sites outlined below.

**Getting there** Srinagar has daily flights from Delhi via Jammu and weekly flights from Leh. The taxi transfer takes 45 minutes. Buses from Delhi and Jammu arrive after a tediously slow trip with army escorts. This journey must be undertaken in daylight.

**Getting around** Take care at all times, but especially after dark. Taxis are recommended. » *See Transport, page 554, for further details.*

### Sights

The **Jama Masjid** (1674) is notable for the wooden pillars supporting the roof, each made from a single *deodar* tree. To the southeast is the **Rozahbal mosque**, which has the 'tomb of Jesus' (Holger Kersten's *Jesus Lived in India* recounts the legend). Across the river is the **Pattar Masjid** (1623) built for the Empress Nur Jahan and renamed Shahi Mosque. **Shankaracharya Hill** is behind the Boulevard. The temple was built during Jahangir's reign but is said to be over a second-century BC temple built by Asoka's son. The hill was known as Takht-i-Sulaiman – The Throne of Solomon.

**Dal Lake** is 6.4 km long and 4 km wide and is divided into three parts by manmade causeways. The small islands are willow covered, while round the lake are groves of *chinar*, poplar and willow. The Mihrbahri people have lived around the lakes for centuries and are market gardeners, tending the floating beds of vegetables and flowers that they have made and cleverly shielded with weeds to make them unobtrusive. Set in front of a triangle of the lake created by the intersecting causeways with a slender bridge at the centre lies the famous **Nishat Bagh** (Garden of Gladness). Sandwiched between the hills and the lake, it was laid out by Asaf Khan, Nur Jahan's brother, in 1632, see page 158.

**Shalimar Bagh** is about 4 km away and set back from the lake. A channel extends up to their edge. Built by Jahangir for his wife, Nur Jahan, the gardens are distinguished by a series of terraces linked by a water channel. These are surrounded by decorative pools which can only be reached by stepping stones. The uppermost pavilion has elegant black marble pillars and niches in the walls for flowers during the day and candles or lamps at night. **Chashma Shahi** (Royal Spring, 1632) is a much smaller garden built around the course of a renowned spring and is attributed to Shah Jahan though it has been altered over the centuries.

## The most expensive spice in the world

Pampore, 16 km from Srinagar, is the centre of Kashmir's saffron industry. Saffron, a species of crocus (Crocus sativus), grows here in abundance, and in a few other places in the world, and is harvested by hand. Within each purple bloom, the three orange-red anthers yield pure saffron. Over 4,500 blooms make one ounce (28 g) of the spice, so the price of this delicate flavouring and colouring in cooking is high (once far more valuable than gold). Its value has led the Indian Government to set up a saffron research farm at Sangla in Himachal Pradesh.

The precious orange coloured dye was used by royalty and the colour saffron was chosen by monks for their robes after the Buddha's death.

**Hazratbal** (Majestic Place) is on the western shore of the lake and commands excellent views. The modern mosque has a special sanctity as a hair of the **prophet Mohammad** is preserved here. Just beyond is the **Nazim Bagh** (Garden of the Morning Breeze), one of the earliest Mughal Gardens and attributed to Akbar.

# Jammu → *Phone code: 0191. Colour map 1, grid A2. Population: 378,400.*

Jammu, the second largest city in the state, is the winter capital of government and main entry point for Kashmir by rail. Not an attractive city, with few open spaces and too much traffic, it is chaotic with little to recommend it.

## Ins and outs

**Getting there** There are flights from Delhi and Srinagar. The railway station is in the New Town, across the Tawi River, and a few kilometres from the old hilltop town where most of the budget hotels are located. The General Bus Stand where inter-state buses come in, is at the foot of the steps off the Srinagar Road in the Old Town. » *See Transport, page 554, for further details.*

**Getting around** The frequent, cheap city bus service or an auto-rickshaw comes in handy as the 2 parts of the town and some sights, are far apart. **Climate** Temperature: Summer, maximum 40°C, minimum 28°C. Rainfall: July-August 310 mm, other months average 40 mm. Best time to visit: November-March.

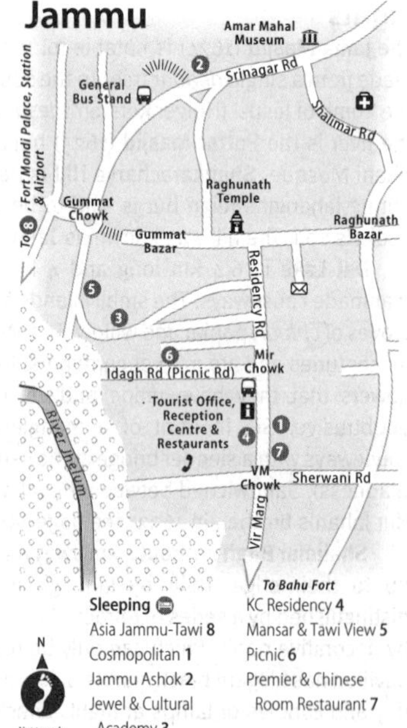


## Sights

**Raghunath Temple** (1857) in the old centre is one of the largest temple complexes in North India. The temple has seven shrines, with gold plated interiors. The most important houses the

Dogras' patron deity, Rama, Vishnu's eighth incarnation. The arches and architectural details show Mughal influence. Morning and evening *aartis* are ritually attended.

**Rambiresvar Temple** (1883), centrally located about 500 m from the Dogra Art Gallery on the Shalimar Road, is dedicated to Siva. It has a 75-m tower and extraordinary crystal lingams and is the largest Siva temple in North India.

**Bahu Fort** with its ruined ramparts stands on a rock face overlooking the river south of the city, the oldest remaining building in the region. The original structure was improved and rebuilt as the Mondi Palace (circa 1880) by the Dogra rulers. Bagh-e-Bahu gardens around the fort has a cafetería. The Old Palace is now the **High Court**.

**Amar Mahal Museum** ⓘ *winter 1000-1200, 1500-1700, summer 1700-1900, Sun 1000-1200, closed Mon, Rs 5, fine views of the river but no photography, Rs 25 by auto-rickshaw*, superbly sited on the bend of the Tawi, is just off Srinagar Road. There is a portrait gallery, Pahari paintings of *Mahabharata* scenes and royal memorabilia. The early 20th-century palace is a curiosity; its French designer gave it château-like sloping roofs and turrets. Four rooms are open but you can look into others through the windows.

## Vaishno Devi → *Colour map 1, grid A2. 61 km north of Jammu.*

The Vaishno Devi cave is one of the region's most important pilgrim sites. As the temple draws near you hear cries of 'Jai Matadi' (Victory to the Mother Goddess). Then at the shrine entrance, pilgrims walk in batches through cold ankle-deep water to the low and narrow cave entrance to get a glimpse of the deity. Visitors joining the yatra find it a very moving experience.

The main pilgrimage season is March to July. The arduous climb along the 13-km track to the cave temple has been re-laid, widened and tiled, and railings provided. Another road from Lower Sanjichat to the Darbar brings you 2 km closer with 300 m less to climb. Ponies, *dandies* and porters are available from Katra at fixed rates. Auto-rickshaws and taxis can go as far as the Banganga. Yatra slips issued by the Shrine Board in Katra must be presented at Banganga checkpoint within six hours. Tea, drinks and snacks are available on the route.

Visitors should leave all leather items in a cloakroom at Vaishno Devi before entering the cave; carry bottled water and waterproofs. If you are on your own or in a small group, to avoid a wait for a group allocation, present yourself at Gates 1 or 2, and smile. **Katra** is an attractive town at the foot of the Trikuta Hills where visitors to the Vaisho Devi cave can stay.

## Srinagar to Leh Road

The road to Leh from Srinagar must be one of the most fascinating journeys in the world as it negotiates high passes and fragile mountainsides. There are dramatic scenic and cultural changes as you go from Muslim, verdant Kashmir to Buddhist, ascetic Ladakh. Because of political unrest in Kashmir, the route, which runs very close to the Line of Control, may be closed to travellers. The alternative route to Leh from Manali is equally fascinating, see page 513.

**Sonamarg**, 'Path of Gold', 84 km from Srinagar at an altitude of 2,740 m, is the last major town in Kashmir before the Zoji La and Ladakh. From Zoji La the road descends to **Minamarg** meadow and Dras. The winter temperatures go down to -50°C, and heavy snow and strong winds cut off the town. The broad Kargil basin and its wide terraces are separated from the Mulbekh valley by the 12-km long **Wakha Gorge**.

On the bank of the River Suru, **Kargil**, at 2,740 m, was an important trading post on two routes, from Srinagar to Leh, and to Gilgit and the lower Indus Valley. Before

1990 it was the overnight stop on the Srinagar-Leh highway, and in 1999 the Pakistan army took control briefly of the heights surrounding the town before being forced to retreat.

From Kargil the road goes on 30 km to **Shergol**, the cultural boundary between Muslim and Buddhist areas and then passes **Mulbekh** after another 9 km and **Namika La**, at 3,720 m, known as the Pillar in the Sky. It climbs to **Photu La** at 4,093 m, the highest pass on the route. From here you can catch sight of the monastery at Lamayuru. The road does a series of loops to descend to **Khaltse** where it meets the milky green Indus River.

In **Lamayuru**, the monastery, 10 km from Khaltse, is perched on a crag overlooking the Indus in a striking setting between a drained lake and high mountains. The complex, which includes a library, thought to be the oldest in the region, was founded in the 11th century and belongs to the Tibetan Kagyupa sect. The present monastery dating from the 16th century was partly destroyed in the 19th. You can still see some of the murals, the 11-headed and 1,000-armed Avalokiteshvara image, along with the redecorated *Du-khang* (assembly hall). There are caves carved out of the mountain wall and some of the rooms are richly furnished with carpets, Tibetan tables and butter lamps. Festivals are in February/March and July. There are daily buses from Leh. Sleeping at **Monastery Hotel** or a few guesthouses. They do meals too. Camping near the stream in a willow grove.

**Rizong**, 53 km away, has a monastery and nunnery, which may accommodate visitors. **Saspul** village marks the wide valley from which you can reach **Alchi** by taking a branch road across the Indus after passing some caves. **Lekir** is off the main road, 8 km after Saspul. Further along the road you catch sight of the ruins of **Basgo** before it crosses the Chargyal Thang plain with chortens and *mani* walls and enters **Nimmu**. The road rejoins the Indus valley and rises to another bare plateau to give you the first glimpse of Leh, 30 km away. **Phyang** is on a hill and finally **Spituk** is reached, see page 559 for details of monasteries.

There are check points on some routes and foreigners will need to register at Upshi (Manali-Leh) or Khaltse (Srinagar-Leh). Visitors from Leh approach Lamayaru along this road.



## Sleeping

**Srinagar** *p549*
Since the clampdown in Kashmir many hotels are occupied by military personnel. It is impossible to give reliable information. Check www.jktourism.org for up to date list.

**LL Grand Palace**, Gupkar Rd, T0194 247 0101, www.intercontinental.com. 125 rooms in re-opened luxury palace.

**AL-A Hotel Broadway**, Malana Azad Rd, T0194 245 9001, www.hotelbroadway.com. 105 comfortable rooms in modern hotel offering all mod cons including pool.

**A-B Shah Abbas**, Boulevard Rd, T0194 247 9861, www.shahabbashotel.com. 84 rooms facing lake or mountains.

**C Ahdoos**, Residency Rd, T0194 247 2593, adhooshotel@yahoo.com. 24 rooms, convenient for airport.

**C-D Metro Hotel**, Dalgate, T0194 247 7126, metrokhaz@sancharnet.in. 50 rooms and 2 multi-cuisine restaurants.

**D Tourist Reception Centre**, Maulana Azad and Sherwani Rds, T0194 247 4060, F247 6107. Rooms and dorm in hostel.

**E Cathay**, Dal Gate, T0194 247 4014.

**E Shabnam**, Dal Gate, T0194 245 1813.

**Houseboats**
Houseboats are peculiar to Srinagar and are moored along the shores of the Dal Lake, the quieter and distant Nagin Lake and

*For an explanation of the sleeping and eating price codes used in this guide, see inside the front cover. Other relevant information is found in Essentials pages 56-61.*

along the busy Jhelum. In the valley's hey day the boats were well kept and delightfully cosy. Still mostly family run, they usually include all meals. It is best to see the boat and make sure what services are included before hiring.

**Bambri Palace**, Dal Lake, Gate 2, T0194 247 5774, immaculate, Md Yusuf Khankashi takes excellent care, well-furnished.

**Garden of Eden**, Dal Lake, T0194 247 5407, owned by a reliable family.

**Gurkha Houseboats**, Nagin Lake, T0194 242 1001, gurkhahb@ndf.vsnl.net.in. Very comfortable with 4 bedrooms, excursions.

**Jammu** *p550, map p550*

A-B **Asia Jammu-Tawi**, Nehru Market, north of town, T0191 243 5757, www.asiahotelsjammu.com. 44 rooms, good restaurant, exchange, pool, clean, comfortable.

B **Hari Niwas Palace**, 3.5 km from centre, T0191 254 3303, hariniwas@hotmail.com. 40 a/c rooms in heritage property with attractive garden.

B **Jammu Ashok**, opposite Amar Mahal, T0191 254 3571, www.theashokgroup.com. 48 rooms, restaurant, pool.

B **KC Residency**, Vir Marg, T0191 252 0770, www.kcresidency.com. 61 a/c rooms, excellent restaurant, exchange, pool.

C **Jewel**, Jewel Chowk, T0191 252 0801, jewels@vsnl.com. 18 centrally a/c rooms, restaurant (mainly fast food).

C-D **Cosmopolitan**, Vir Marg, T0191 254 7561. 28 rooms, some a/c, good restaurant, bar.

C-E **Tourist Reception Centre**, Vir Marg, T0191 2579554. 173 rooms with bath, a few air-cooled, good value with best in Blocks NA and A, poor dorm,m restaurant.

D **Premier**, Vir Marg, T0191 254 3234. 21 rooms, some a/c, restaurants, bar.

E **Tawi View**, below Gummat, T0191 254 3752. Few air-cooled rooms.

**Vaishno Devi** *p551*

This is a selection of over 50 places, in Katra unless stated.

A **Country Inn**, T01991 233214, amerihotel@vsnl.com. 77 centrally a/c rooms in modern hotel.

B **Asia Vaishnodevi**, T01991 232061, www.asiavaishnadevi.com. 37 rooms, some a/c, restaurant, transport to Banganga.

B-C **Ambica**, T01991-232062, www.hotelambica.com. 50 rooms, a/c, puja shop and health centre.

D **Durga**, 30 rooms, restaurant.

E **Prem**, Main Bazaar, T01991 232014. Rooms with hot water and a fire, adequate.

E **Tourist Bungalow**, T01991 232009. 42 rooms.

E-F **Retiring Centre**, T01991 232309. Rooms and dorm, near the bus stand.

F **Dormitories**, at the half-way point to Vaishno Devi. Simple rooms provide sheets and blankets.

## Eating

**Srinagar** *p549*

Kashmiris tend to eat at home, so the choice is limited.

ǂǂ **Mughal Darbar**, Residency Rd, specializes in Kashmiri wazwan.

ǂǂ **Tao Café**, Residency Rd, in attractive gardens.

ǂ **Hideout**, Lambert Lane, best place for a snack.

**Jammu** *p550, map p550*

ǂǂǂ **KC Residency**, in hotel. International. Bizarre revolving restaurant, trundles round with an occasional jolt but serves excellent food, good views.

ǂǂ **Cosmopolitan**, in hotel. Good Chinese and Kashmiri.

ǂ **Amritsarian**, in Raghunath Bazar. Veg.

ǂ **India Coffee House**, Exhibition Ground.

ǂ **Kailash**, in Raghunath Bazar. Veg.

**Vaishno Devi** *p551*

Excellent vegetarian food is available – curd and *panir* (curd cheese) dishes are especially good. For non-*dhaba* food try the two vegetarian fast food places on the main street. Both are clean and good. No alcohol.

## Shopping

**Jammu** *p550, map p550*

Wool tunics (*pherans*), fine pashmina shawls and woodcarvings are good, as well as dried fruit and nuts. Main shopping areas: Raghunath Bazar, Hari Bazar, Upper Gummat.

## Transport

**Srinagar** *p549*
Srinagar is on NH1A linked to the rest of India by 'all-weather roads' (closed for 2 weeks in Feb 2005 due to heavy snowfall!), some through superb scenery.

### Air
**Srinagar Airport**, 14 km, T0194 2430334. Taxi to town: Rs 300. Stringent security checks so arrive at least 2 hrs ahead for departure. **Indian Airlines** T0194 245 2358, airport T0194 243 0334, flies to **Delhi**, and **Jammu** daily (same flight); **Leh**, daily. **Jet Airways** T0194 248 0801, airport T0194 243 3007: **Delhi** via **Jammu** daily.

### Bus
To **Jammu** (293 km), by a narrow mountain road, often full of lorries and military convoys, takes 12 hrs; few stops for food and facilities. Long-distance State Roadways buses run to **Jammu** from Delhi, Chandigarh and Amritsar; some continue to **Srinagar**. J&KSRTC, TRC, Srinagar, T0194 245 5107. Summer 0600-1800, winter 0700-1700. Bus to **Kargil** (alternate days in summer, Rs 120-200), **Leh** (434 km, Rs 200-360).

### Ferry
Shikaras (boats): Rs 30 per hr but some ask for Rs 60.

### Train
The nearest railhead is Jammu Tawi with coach (12 hrs) and taxi transfer (9 hrs). Govt TRC, 0700-1900. T0191 243 1582 for reservation of 2nd-Class Sleeper and a/c only. Summer 0830-1900, winter 1000-1800.

**Jammu** *p550, map p550*

### Air
Rambagh Airport, 6 km. Transport to town: taxis (Rs 200) and auto-rickshaws. **Indian Airlines**, TRC, Vir Marg, T0191 254 2735, Apt T0191 243 0449, flies to **Delhi** and **Srinagar** daily; **Leh** (Mon, Fri). **Jet Airways, KC Residency Hotel**, T0191 257 4312, T0191 245 3999; to **Delhi** and **Srinagar** daily.

### Bus
Sumos run to Katra from the station. J&K SRTC, TRC, Vir Marg, T0191 257 9554 (1000-1700), General Bus Stand, T0191 257 7475 (0400-2000) direct buses to **Srinagar** (293 km), **Katra (for Vaishno Devi), Pathankot** and **Kishtwar**. Punjab Roadways T0191 254 2782. To **Delhi** (586 km), daily. **Srinagar** buses leave from the railway station, usually 0600- 0700.

### Taxi
Un-metered, T0191 253 3485. Tourist taxis, T0191 254 6266.

### Train
Station, T0191 245 3027. To **Delhi (OD)**: *Jammu Tawi Mail, 4034*, 1535, 14¼ hrs; *Jammu Tawi Delhi Exp, 2404*, 1800, 10½ hrs. **Delhi (ND)**: *Jammu Tawi Indore Malwa Exp, 9368*, 0815, 10½ hrs; *Jhelum Exp, 1078*, 2135, 12¼ hrs; *Shalimar Exp, 4646/6788*, 2050, 14¼ hrs; *Rajdhani Exp, 2426*, Sat, 2030, 9 hrs. **Kolkata (Sealdah)**: *Jammu Tawi Exp, 3152*, 1850, 45 hrs.

**Vaishno Devi** *p551*
Buses and taxis leave from General Bus Stand, Jammu (or the railway station at peak season) and go to Katra (48 km); Rs 25, a/c Rs 55; taxi Rs 500 for 4.

## Directory

**Srinagar** *p549*
**Travel agent** Sita, at Hotel Broadway, Maulana Azad Rd, T0194 247 7186, www.sitaindia.com. **Tourist office** J&K, TRC, T0194 2452690, Adventure Tourism T0194 247 2644. **Useful addresses** Ambulance: T0194 247 4591. Fire: T0194 247 2222. Police: T100.

**Jammu** *p550, map p550*
**Banks** State Bank of India, Hari Market, among several. **Post** GPO: Pacca Danga. Post Offices in Old Palaces, near Dogra Art Gallery and Raghunath Temple. **Tourist offices** J&K Tourism, Tourist Reception Centre, Vir Marg, T0191 254 6266. Jammu Tawi, Railway Station, T0191 254 4842. JKTDC, T0191 257 9554. **Useful addresses** Fire: T101. Hospital: T0191 254 7637. Police: T100. Foreigners' Registration Office: Supt of Police, Canal Rd, T0191 254 2676. Foreigners must register.

# Ladakh

→ Colour map 1, grid A3. Population: 175,000. Altitude: 2,500-4,500 m, passes 4,000-6,000 m, peaks up to 7,500 m.

*The mountains of Ladakh – literally 'many passes' – may not be as typically spectacular as some parts of the high Himalaya, for as even the valleys are at an altitude of 3,500 m the summits are only 3,000 m higher. Because it is desert there is little snow on them and they look like big brown hills, dry and dusty, with clusters ofwillows and desert roses along the streams. Yet for thousands of visitors Ladakh is acompletely magical place, remote, with delightful, gentle, ungrasping people.*

» For Sleeping, Eating and other listings see pages 569-576.

## Ins and outs

**Entry permits** For the recently opened areas of Nubra and Shyok Valleys and Drokhpa, Khardung La, Tso-moriri and Pangong Tso, the permit costs US$20, while trekkers in the Hemis High Altitude Park must pay Rs 25 (Indians Rs 10) per day. As a matter of course you should carry your passport with you since Ladakh is a sensitive border region.

*Given the darkness of many buildings even at midday it is well worth taking a torch wherever you go; a must at night.*

**Inner Line Permits** Areas which would normally be restricted but are open to tourists include Rizong, Likir, Phyang, Shey, Thikse, Chemrey and Tak-thok gompas. A permit is needed to visit the newly opened areas. Permits are available from the DC office in Leh. Almost all monasteries in Ladakh now charge foreigners Rs 25 entry fee. The area is virtually cut off for six months when roads become impassable; the only link with the outside world is by air. The frozen Zanskar River, the 'Tchadar', links Padum with Nimmu near Leh. Animal transport is provided by yaks, ponies, Bactrian camels and the broad backed *hunia* sheep.

**Climate** The temperature can go down to -30°C in Leh and Kargil and -50°C in Dras, remaining sub-zero from Dec to Feb. Yet on clear sunny days in the summer, it can be scorching hot and you can easily get sunburnt. Rainfall is only 50 mm annually and there are even occasional dust storms. Take plenty of sun cream.

## Background

Until very recently Ladakhi society has generally been very introverted and the economy surprisingly self-sufficient. Ladakh also developed a very distinct culture. Polyandry (where a woman has more than one husband) was common but many men became *lamas* (monks) and a few women *chomos* (nuns). Most people depended on subsistence agriculture but the harsh climate contributed to very high death rates and a stable population. That is rapidly changing. Imported goods are increasingly widely available and more and more people are taking part in the monetary economy. Ladakh and its capital Leh have only been open to tourists since 1974 but some argue that already there are too many.

# Leh

→ Phone code: 01982. Colour map 1, grid A3. Population: 27,500. Altitude: 3,500 m.

Mysterious dust-covered Leh sits in a fertile side valley of the Indus, about 10 km from the river. Encircled by stark awe-inspiring mountains with the cold desert beyond, it is the nearest experience of Tibet in India. The old Palace sits precariously on the hill to the north and looms over Leh. The wide Main Bazar Street (circa 1840s), which once accommodated caravans, has a colourful vegetable market where remarkably unpushy Ladakhi women sell local produce on the street side while they knit or chat.

### Conversation to construction

If you are interested in **voluntary work**, get in touch with the different organizations in Leh (SECMOL, LEDeG). There is a range of possibilities around Leh for potential volunteers – from teaching English to construction work. Alternatively, contact Ladakh Project, Apple Barn, Week, Dartington, Devon TQ9 6JP, UK, or 850 Talbot Ave, Albany, CA 94796, USA. Farm volunteers with the Ladakh Project are welcome from May-October, for a minimum of a one-month to stay and work with a Ladakh farming family. A contribution of about US$200 plus a nominal amount for daily lodging is expected.

Makeshift craft and jewellery stalls line parts of Fort Road to the east to attract summer visitors along with Kashmiri shopkeepers who have come in search of greener pastures. The Old Village, mainly to the east of the Main Street, with its maze of narrow lanes, sits on the hillside below the Palace and is worth exploring. ⏩ *For Sleeping, Eating and other listings see pages 569-576.*

## Ins and outs

**Getting there** For seven to eight months in the year Leh's sole link with the outside world is by air. Tickets are in heavy demand so it is essential to book well ahead (you can do this from home on the internet). From mid-Jun to end-Sep (weather permitting), in addition to air passengers and trekkers, the Manali-Leh Highway opens to traffic bringing travellers to the New Bus Stand, south of town. There are jeeps from here as well as from the airport.

**Getting around** Most hotels are within a few mins' walk of the Main Bazar St around which Leh's activities are concentrated. All the places of interest in Leh itself can also be tackled on foot by most visitors though those arriving by air are urged to acclimatize for 48 hrs before exerting themselves. For visiting monasteries and spots out-of-town arrange a jeep or taxi. ⏩ *See Transport, page 575, for further details.*

## History

The city developed as a trading post and market, attracting a wide variety of merchants – from Yarkand, Kashgar, Kashmir, Tibet and North India. Tea, salt, household articles, wool and semi-precious stones were all traded in the market. Buddhism travelled along the Silk Road and the Kashmir and Ladakh feeder, which has also seen the passage of soldiers, explorers and pilgrims, forerunners of the tourists who today contribute most to the urban economy.

## Sights

**Leh Palace** ⓘ *summer 0700-0930, and also sometimes 1500-1800, Rs 25*, has been described as a miniature version of Lhasa's Potala Palace. Built in the mid-16th century, the Palace was partly in ruins by the 19th century. It has nine storeys, sloping buttresses and projecting wooden balconies. From the town below it is dazzling in the morning sun and ghostly at night. Built by King Singe Namgyal and still owned by the royal family, it is now unoccupied – they live in the palace at Stok. Visible damage was caused during Zorawar Singh's invasion from Kashmir in the last century. Be careful of the hazardous holes in the floor. After a steep climb some find the Palace disappointing, but the views from the roof are exceptional. A part of the palace is a **museum**. Like the Lhasa Potala Palace it has numerous rooms, steps and narrow passages lined with old *thangkas*, paintings and arms. The central prayer room (not in use), usually locked but opened on request, has religious texts lining the walls. The

Archaeological Survey of India is responsible for restoration and you may be able to watch work in progress. There are many painted scrolls, murals and old manuscripts in the ruined palace.

The 15th-century **Tsemo Gompa** (*tsemo* – red) ⓘ *0700-0900, Rs 25*, is a strenuous walk north of the city and has a colossal two-storey high image of *Maitreya*, flanked by figures of *Avalokitesvara* (right) and *Manjusri* (left). It was founded by the Namgyal rulers and a portrait of Tashi Namgyal hangs on the left at the entrance. Of the monasteries, the **Soma Gompa** or the New Monastery (1957) in the main street of the Old Village was built to commemorate the 2,500th anniversary of the birth of Buddha. The remains of the **Leh Gompa** houses a large golden Buddha. **Sankar Gompa** (17th-18th centuries) ⓘ *0700-1000, 1700-1900, prayers at 1830 (before visiting, check at the Tourist Office) with chanting, drums and cymbals, Rs 25*, of the Yellow Hat Sect, is one of the few gompas built in the valley bottom. It is an enjoyable 3-km walk past the **Himalayan Hotel** through fields. It houses the chief lama of Spituk

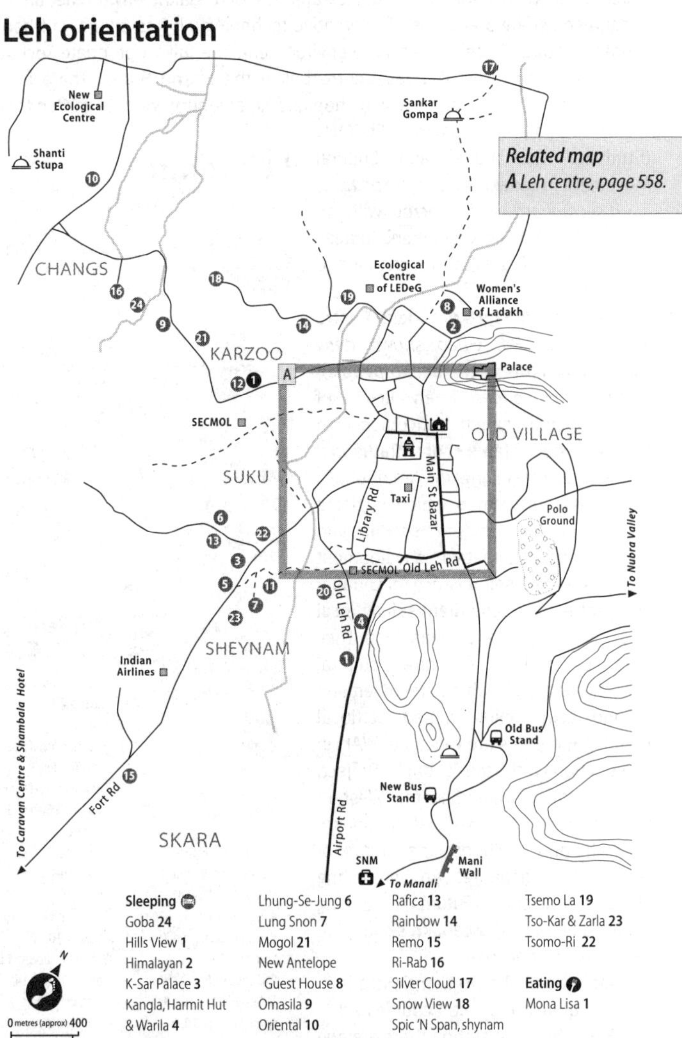

and 20 others. The newer monks' quarters are on three sides of the courtyard with steps leading up to the *Du-Khang* (Assembly Hall). There are a number of gold statues, numerous wall paintings and sculptures including a large one of the 11 headed, 1,000-armed *Avalokitesvara*.

On the Changspa Lane across the stream, you reach the start of the stiff climb up to the white Japanese **Shanti Stupa** (1989). This is one of a series of 'Peace Pagodas' built by the Japanese around the world. There are good views from the top where a tea room offers a welcome sight after the climb. There is also a jeepable road.

The architecturally striking **Leh Mosque** in the main bazar is worth visiting – the inner section is not open to woman visitors. The Sunni Muslim mosque is believed to stand on land granted by King Deldan Namgyal in the 1660s; his grandmother was the Muslim Queen of Ladakh.

Visit the **Ecological Centre of LEDeG** (Ladakh Ecological Development Group) and the Craft Shop ⓘ *T01982 252546, Mon-Sat, 1400-1800*, next to **Tsemo La Hotel**, which opened in 1984 to spread awareness of Ladakhi environmental issues, encourage self-help and use of alternative technology. It has a library of books on Ladakhi culture, Buddhism and the environment. The full 'Appropriate Technology' display is at the **New Ecology Centre** below the Shanti Stupa. There is also a handicrafts centre, a technical workshop and an organic vegetable garden there.

The non-profit making **SECMOL** (Students' Educational and Cultural Movement in Ladakh) ⓘ *T01982 252421, www.secmol.org*, is in Karzoo with an office in the Old Leh Road. It encourages the teaching of Ladakhi history, culture and crafts.

**Women's Alliance of Ladakh Centre** ⓘ *off Sankar Rd, video shown daily except Sun, 1500 (minimum 10 people), highly recommended*, is an alliance of 3,500 Ladakhi women, concerned with raising the status of traditional agriculture, preserving the traditionally high status of women which is being eroded in the modern sector, and creating an alternative development model based on self-reliance for Ladakh. The centre has a restaurant selling local and organic foods, and a craft shop. They hold spectacular festivals, cultural shows, dances etc which are advertised around Leh; mainly aimed at local people, but others are welcome. WAL, in conjunction with the Ladakh Project, runs a Farm Volunteer Scheme. Western volunteers live and work on a Ladakhi farm, helping to boost the status of traditional agriculture. An interesting video 'Ancient Futures' tracing ecologically sensitive Ladakh's changing face over two decades.

**Mahabodhi Meditation Centre** is in town. Enquire about short courses.

From the radio station there are two

## Leh centre

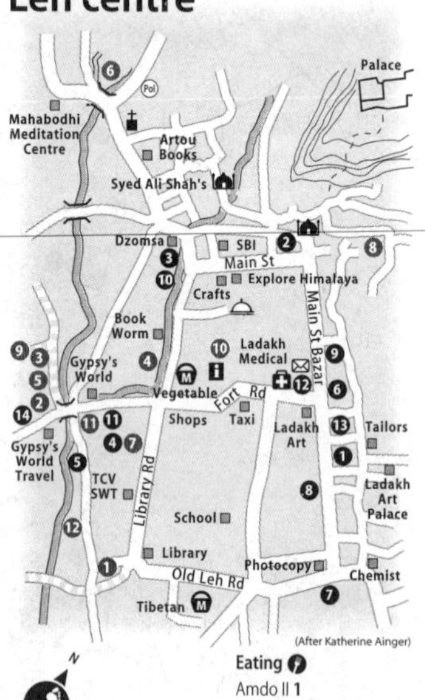

(After Katherine Ainger)

**Sleeping**
Bijoo 1
Bimla Guest House 2
Galdan Continental 4
Indus 5
Kang-lha Chen 6
Kangri & Exchange 7
Lasermo 12
Old Ladakh 8
Ti-Sei Guest House 9
Tourist Lodge 10
Yak Tail 11

**Eating**
Amdo II 1
Budshah Inn & Tailors 2
Devi Tibetan 3
Dreamland & Hilife 4
In-Style & Bakery 5
Kokonor 6
Kyishong 7
La Montessori 8
Nepali 9
Pumpernickel German Bakery 10
Summer Harvest 11
Tenzin Dichey 14
Tibetan Friend's Corner 12
Wok Tibetan Kitchen 13

long **mani walls**. *Rongo Tajng* is in the centre of the open plain and was built as a memorial to Queen Skalzang Dolma by her son Dalden Namgyal. It is about 500 m long and was built in 1635. The stones have been meticulously carved. The other, a 350-m wall down the hill, is believed to have been built by Tsetan Namgyal in 1785 as a memorial to his father the king.

## Leh Manali Highway → *Colour map 1, grid A3.*

This is an amazing stretch that also has the added advantage of having monasteries en route. If you are short of time, try to see Thikse and Hemis, at least. On all trips go with a local Ladakhi guide as the Lamas can refuse admission if unaccompanied. Camera flash is usually not allowed in monasteries to reduce damage to wall paintings and *thangkas*. If you hire a car or jeep, which is good value when shared by four, you can visit the places below in a day. Carry a torch. Most expect a donation of Rs 25. The same advice applies to the monasteries along the Srinagar Road.

### Choglamsar

Choglamsar, south of Leh on the east bank of the Indus, is a green oasis with poplars and willows where there are golf links and a polo ground as well as horticultural nurseries. Some village houses use solar energy. The Central Institute of Buddhist Studies is here with a specialist library. Past the Tibetan Refugee Camps, Children's Village and the Arts and Crafts Centre, the Choglamsar Bridge crosses the Indus. The Chochot Yugma Imambara, a few minutes' walk from the bridge, is worth a visit. Buses depart Leh hourly buses from 0800-1800.

### Stok

Across Choglamsar Bridge, 16 km south of Leh, is the royal palace dating from the 1840s when the King of Ladakh was deposed by the invading Dogra forces. The last king died in 1974 but his widow continues to live here. His son continues the royal line and ascended the throne in July 1993. The palace is a rambling building where only a dozen of the 80 rooms are used. The small **Palace Museum** ⓘ *May-Oct, 0800-1900, Rs 25*, with three rooms, is worth visiting. It is a showpiece for the royal *thangkas*, many 400 years old, crown jewels, dresses, coins, *peraks* (headdresses) encrusted with turquoise and lapis lazuli as well as religious objects.

There is an **archery** contest in July. The **gompa**, a short distance away, has some ritual dance masks. *Tsechu* is in February. A three-hour **walk** up the valley behind Stok takes you to some extraordinary mountain scenery dominated by the 6,121-m high Stok Kangri. Below the museum there is a clean hotel with good views.

Buses to Stok leave at 0730 and 1700. Taxis from the Leh central taxi stand are available at fixed rates at any time.

### Shey

ⓘ *All day; try to be there 0700-0900, 1700-1800 when prayers are chanted, Rs 15.*
Until the 16th century, Shey was the royal residence, located at an important vantage point in the Indus Valley. Kings of Leh were supposed to be born in the monastery. The royal family moved to Stok in order to escape advancing Dogra forces from Kashmir who came to exploit the trade in pashmina wool. Shey, along with Thikse, is also regarded as an auspicious place for cremation.

Much of the palace and the fort high above it have fallen into disrepair and is dirty though the soot covered wall paintings in the palace have now been restored. The palace gompa with its 17.5-m high blue-haired Maitreya Buddha, imitating the one at Tsemo Gompa, is attended by Drukpa monks from Hemis. It is made of copper and brass but splendidly gilded and studded with precious gem stones. The large victory *stupa* is topped with gold. There are extensive grounds to the east (which once was a lake) with a large number of *chortens* in which cremated ashes of important monks, members of the royal family and the devout were buried. A newer temple houses another old giant Buddha statue. There are several rock carvings; particularly noteworthy is that of five *dhyani* Buddhas (circa eighth century) at the bottom of the hill. The small hotel below the gompa has spartan but clean rooms. It is 15 km southeast of Leh on the Indus River or can be reached along a stone path from Thikse. Hourly buses depart Leh from 0800 until 1800.

## Thikse

ⓘ *Rs 15 (mostly for restoration and maintenance), hourly buses, 0800-1800.*
Situated 25 km south of Leh on a crag overlooking the flood plain on the east bank of the Indus, this is one of the most imposing monasteries in Ladakh and was part of the original Gelugpa order in the 15th century. The 12-storey monastery painted deep red, ochre and white, with typical tapering walls has 10 temples, a nunnery and 60 lamas in residence whose houses cling to the hillside below. The complex contains numerous stupas, statues, *thangkas*, wall paintings – note the fresco of the 84 *Mahasiddhas*, high above – swords and a large pillar engraved with the Buddha's teachings.

The new temple interior is dominated by a giant 15 m-high Buddha figure near the entrance. The principal *Dukhang* (assembly hall) right at the top of the building has holes in the wall for storing religious texts; good views from roof. The temple with the Guardian Deities, which in other monasteries may be closed to women, is open to all since parts of the offending figures are covered. The *Dukhang* lower down has Tibetan style wall paintings. Thikse is a good place to watch religious ceremonies, usually at 0630 or 1200. An early start by taxi makes even the first possible. They are preceded by the playing of large standing drums and long horns similar to *alpenstock*. Masked dances are performed during special festivals.

## Stakna

Across the valley on a hill is the earliest Drukpa monastery which was built before Hemis, though its decorations are not as ancient. It is also called 'Tiger's nose' because of the shape of the hill site. This small but well-kept monastery has a beautiful silver-gilt *chorten* in the Assembly Hall which was installed around 1955 and some interesting paintings in the dark temple at the back. No need for a local guide as the lamas are always willing to open the doors. There are excellent views of the Indus valley and the Zanskar range.

## Hemis

On the west bank of the Indus, 45 km south of Leh, the monastery, built on a green hillside surrounded by spectacular mountain scenery, is hidden in a gorge. It is the biggest and wealthiest in Ladakh and is a 'must' for visitors. You walk past *chortens* and sections of *mani* walls to enter the complex through the east gate which leads into a large 40 m x 20 m courtyard where sacred dances are performed during the *Hemis Tsechu*, end of June to early July. It commemorates the birth of Guru Padmasambhava who is believed to have fought local demons to protect the people. Young and old of both sexes, and lamas take part in masked dance-dramas while stalls sell handicrafts. The Drukpa monastery was founded by Stagsang Raspa during the reign of Senge Namgyal (circa 1630). Colourful flags flutter in the breeze from the four posts against the white walls of the buildings. On the north side are two assembly halls approached by a flight of steep stone steps. The large *Dukhang* to the right used for ceremonies is rather plain; the smaller *Tshogskhang* (the main temple) contains some silver gilt *chortens* and a Kashmiri lacquered-wood throne. The murals in the verandas depicting guardian deities, the *kalachakra* (wheel of life) and 'Lords of the four quarters' are well preserved. A staircase alongside the *Tshogskhang* leads to a roof terrace where there are a number of shrines including a bust of the founder. The *Lakhang* (chapel) has ancient Kashmiri bronzes and silver *chortens*, an important library of Tibetan style books and an impressive collection of *thangkas*, the largest of which is displayed every 12 years (next 2004). The heavy silk *thangka* is beautifully embroidered in bright coloured threads and pearls.

There is a pleasant 3-km walk uphill to another gompa. A stay in Hemis overnight enables you to attend early morning prayers, a moving experience and strongly recommended. Bus services have improved making a day trip possible.

## Along the Srinagar Road

→ *Colour map 1, grid A3.*

The Srinagar road out of Leh passes through a flat dusty basin mostly occupied by Army encampments with mile after mile of wire fencing. The scenery is stunning and as with the Leh Manali Highway, is punctuated with monasteries. See that section for advice when visiting them.

### Spituk

Some 8 km from Leh, Spituk, standing on a conical hill with three chapels, was founded in the 11th century but the buildings, in a series of tiers with courtyards and steps which date from the 15th century. The newest is electrified. The Yellow-Hat Gelugpa monks created the precedent in Ladakh of building on mountain tops rather than valley floors. You can get good views of the countryside around.

The long 16th- to 17th-century **Du-khang** is the largest building and has two rows of seats along the length of the walls to a throne at the far end. Sculptures and miniature *chortens* are displayed on the altar. Spituk has a collection of ancient Jelbagh masks, icons and arms including some rescued from the Potala Palace in Lhasa.

The 16th- to 17th-century **Mahakal Temple** ⓘ *Srinagar buses drop you on the highway, 4 daily, 20 mins*, higher up the hill contains a shrine of Vajrabhairava, often mistaken for the goddess Kali. The terrifying face is only unveiled in January, during the Gustor festival.

### Phyang

Phyang ⓘ *3 buses daily, 1 hr; the morning bus allows you to explore the valley and walk back to Leh, but the afternoon bus only allows 20 mins for visit (last return, around 1700)*, 16 km from Leh, dominates a side valley with a village close by. It belongs to the Red Hat Kagyupa sect, with its 16th-century Gouon monastery built by the founder of the Namgyal Dynasty which is marked by a flagstaff at the entrance. It houses hundreds of statues including some Kashmiri bronzes (circa 14th century), *thangkas* and manuscript copies of the Kangyur and Tengyur. The temple walls have colourful paintings centering on the eight emblems of happiness which have been restored. It is the setting for a spectacular July **Tseruk festival** with masked dancing.

### Phyang to Nimmu

About 2 km before Nimmu the Indus enters an impressive canyon before the Zanskar joins it, a good photo opportunity. As the road bends, a lush green oasis with lines of poplars comes into view. The mud brick houses of Nimmu have grass drying on the flat rooftops to provide fodder for the winter. A dry stone *mani* wall runs along the road; beyond Nimmu the walls become 2 m wide in places with innumerable *chortens* alongside. The rocky outcrops on the hills to the right appear like a natural fortress.

### Basgo

The road passes through Basgo Village with the ruins of a Buddhist citadel impressively sited on a spur overlooking the Indus Valley. See Alchi below on how to get there. It served as a royal residence for several periods between the 15th and 17th centuries. The Fort Palace was once considered almost impregnable having survived a three-year siege by Tibetan and Mongol armies in the 17th century.

Among the ruins only two temples have survived. The higher Maitreya Temple (mid-16th century) built by Tashi Namgyal's son contains a very fine Maitreya statue at the rear of the hall, flanked by *bodhisattvas*. Some murals from the early period illustrating the Tibetan Buddhist style have also survived on the walls and ceiling; among the Buddhas and *bodhisattvas* infilled with details of animals, birds and mermaids, appear images of Hindu divinities. The 17th-century Serzang (Gold and Copper) Temple, with a carved doorway, is the other and contains another large Maitreya image whose head rises through the ceiling into a windowed box-like structure which can be seen by climbing up to the gallery above. The murals look faded and have been damaged by water.

## Lekir (Likir)

Some 5½ km from Basgo, a road on the right leads to Lekir by a scenic route. The picturesque white-washed monastery buildings rise in different levels on the hillside across the Lekir River. A huge saffron coloured Maitreya Buddha towers over the fields below. Lekir was built during the reign of Lachen Gyalpo who installed 600 monks here, headed by Lhawang Chosje (circa 1088). The gompa was invested with a collection of fine images, *thangkas* and murals to vie with those at Alchi. The present buildings date mainly from the 18th century since the original were destroyed by fire. A rough path up leads to the courtyard where a board explains the origin of the name: Klu-Khyil (snake coil) refers to the *nagas* here, reflected in the shape of the hill. Lekir was converted to the Gelugpa sect in the 15th century. The head lama, the younger brother of the Dalai Lama, has his apartments here, which were extended in the mid 1990s.

The **Du-khang** ⓘ *bus from Leh each afternoon, return each morning; see Alchi*, contains huge clay images of the Buddhas (past, present and future) and Kangyur and Tengyur manuscripts, the Kangyur having been first compiled in Ladakh during Lachen Gyalpo's reign. The **Nyenes-Khang** contains beautiful murals of the 35 confessional Buddhas and 16 arahats. The **Gon-Khang** houses a statue of the guardian deity here. A small but very interesting **museum** ⓘ *Rs 15, opened on request (climb up to a hall above, up steep wooden stairs)*, displays *thangkas*, old religious and domestic implements, costumes et cetera which are labelled in English.

Village craftsmen produce *thangkas*, carved wooden folding seats and clay pottery. If you wish to overnight, *Norbu Spon Guest House*, 3 km off main road towards Lekir, also allows camping and the two-storeyed white-washed *Lhankay Guest House* stands in fields.

## Alchi

The road enters Saspul, 8 km from the Lekir turn-off. About 2 km beyond the village, a link road with a suspension bridge over the river leads to Alchi which is hidden from view as you approach. A patchwork of cultivated fields surround the complex. A narrow path from the car park winds past village houses, donkeys and apricot trees to lead to the Dharma Chakra monastery. You will be expected to buy a ticket from one of the lamas on duty. The whole complex, about 100 m long and 60 m wide, is enclosed by a white-washed mud and straw wall. Alchi's large temple complex is regarded as one of the most important Buddhist centres in Ladakh and a jewel of monastic skill. A path on the right past two large prayer wheels and a row of smaller ones leads to the river which attracts deer down to the opposite bank in the evenings. At the rear, small *chortens* with inscribed stones strewn around them, line the wall. From here, you get a beautiful view of the Indus River with mountains as a backdrop.

Founded in the 11th century by Rinchen Zangpo, the 'Great Translator', it was richly decorated by artists from Kashmir and Tibet. Paintings of the mandalas which have deep Tantric significance are particularly fine; some decorations are reminiscent of Byzantine art. The monastery is maintained by monks from Lekir and is no longer a place for active worship.

**The temple complex** The three entrance chortens are worth looking in to. Each has vividly coloured paintings within, both along the interior walls as well as in the small chorten-like openings on the ceilings. The first and largest of these has a portrait of the founder Rinchen Zangpo. Some of the paintings here are being restored by researchers.

The **Du-khang** is the oldest temple, which has a courtyard (partially open to the sky) with wooden pillars and painted walls; the left wall shows two rowing boats with fluttering flags, a reminder perhaps of the presence in ancient times of lakes in this desert. The brightly painted door to the Du-khang, about 1½ m high, and the entrance archway has some fine woodcarving; note the dozen or so blue pottery Buddhas stuck to the wall! The subsidiary shrines on either side of the doorway contain *Avalokitesvaras* and *bodhisattvas* including a giant four-armed Maitreya figure to the extreme right. This main Assembly Hall which was the principal place of worship suffers from having very little natural light so visitors need a good torch. The 'shrine' holds the principal gilded *Vairocana* (Resplendent) Buddha (traditionally white, accompanied by the lion) with ornate decorations behind, flanked by four important Buddha postures among others. The walls on either side are devoted to fine *Mandala* paintings illustrating the four principal manifestations of the *Sarvavid* (Omniscient) Buddha – *Vairocana*, *Sakyamuni* (the Preacher), *Manjusri* (Lord of Wisdom) and as *Prajna Paramita* (Perfection of Wisdom) described in detail by Snellgrove and Skorupski. There are interesting subsidiary panels, friezes and inscriptions. Note the terrifying figure of *Mahakala* the guardian deity above the door with miniature panels of royal and military scenes. The one portraying a drinking scene shows the royal pair sanctified with haloes with wine-cups in hand, accompanied by the prince and attendants – the detail of the clothing clearly shows Persian influence.

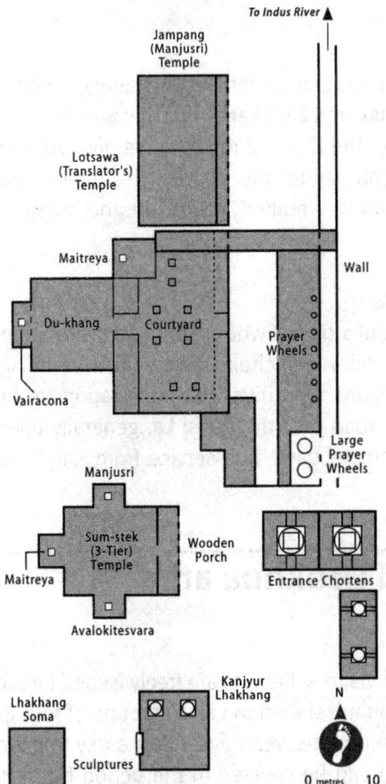


The **Lotsawa** (Translator's) and **Jampang** (Manjusri) Lhakhangs were built later and probably neglected for some time. The former contains a portrait of Rinchen Zangpo along with a seated Buddha while the latter has *Manjusri* where each directional face is painted in the colour associated with the cardinal directions of north (dark green), south (yellow), east (blue) and west (red). There are two small temples beyond.

**Sum-stek,** the three-tier temple with a carved wooden gallery on the façade, has triple arches. Inside are three giant four-armed, garlanded stucco figures of *bodhisattvas*: the white *Avalokitesvara* on the left, the principal terracotta-red *Maitreya* in the centre at the back, and the ochre-yellow *Manjusri* on the right; their heads project to the upper storey which is reached by a rustic ladder. The remarkable features here are the brightly painted and gilded decorations on the clothing of the figures which include historical incidents, musicians, palaces and places of pilgrimage. Quite incongruous court scenes and Persian features appear on *Avalokitesvara* while the figures on *Maitreya* have Tantric connotations illustrating the very different styles of ornamentation on the three figures. The walls have numerous *mandalas* and inscriptions.

**Lhakhang Soma** (New temple) is a square hall with a *chorten* within; its walls are totally covered with *mandalas* and paintings portraying incidents from the Buddha's life and historic figures; the main figure here is the preaching Buddha. There is an interesting panel of warriors on horseback near the door. **Kanjyur Lhakhang** in front of the Lhakhang Soma houses the scriptures.

## Zanskar → *Colour map 1, grid A2/3.*

Zanskar is a remote area of Ladakh contained by the Zanskar range to the north and the Himalaya to the south. It can be cut off by snow for as much as seven months each year when access is solely along the frozen Zanskar River. This isolation has helped Zanskar to preserve its cultural identity, though this is now being steadily eroded. Traditional values include a strong belief in Buddhism, frugal use of resources and population control. Values, which for centuries, have enabled Zanskaris to live in harmony with their hostile yet fragile environment. The long Zanskar Valley was 'opened' up for tourism even later than the rest of Ladakh and quickly became popular with trekkers. There is now river rafting on the Zanskar River. ⏩ *For Sleeping, Eating and other listings see pages 569-576.*



### History

Zanskar became an administrative part of Ladakh under Senge Namgyal whose three sons became the rulers of Ladakh, Guge and Zanskar/Spiti. This arrangement collapsed after Ladakh's war with Tibet and the Zanskar royal house divided, one part administering Padum, the other Zangla. Under the Dogras, the rulers were reduced to puppets as the marauding army wreaked havoc on the villages, monasteries and population.

### Padum → *Colour map 1, grid A3. No permit needed.*

Padum, the capital, has a population of about 1,000 of whom about 40% are Sunni Muslim. The present king of the Zanskar valley, Punchok Dawa who lives in his modest home in Padum, is held in high regard. On arrival you must report to the Tourist Officer. Access is either by the jeep road over the **Pensi La**, generally open from mid-June to mid-October with an alternate days' bus service from Kargil, 18 hours. The alternative method is to trek in.

## Nubra Valley, Nyoma and Drokhpa area

→ *Colour map 1, grid A4.*

These once restricted areas are now open to visitors. Permits are freely issued by the District Magistrate (District Development Commissioner) in Leh to groups of four or more travelling together by jeep, for a maximum of seven days. Allow a day to get a permit which costs Rs 250. A lot of ground can be covered in the period but it is necessary to consult a Leh-based trekking and travel agent. You need to go fully equipped with tents, food and sleeping bags although there are a few rest houses and temporary lakeside tented camps are occasionally set up by tour companies.

## Tso-Moriri

The Rupshu area, a dry, high altitude plateau to the east of the Leh-Manali Highway, is where the nomadic Changpas live, see page 546, in the bleak and windswept Chamathang highlands bordering Tibet. The route to the beautiful Tso-Moriri (*tso* – lake), the only nesting place of the bar-headed geese on the Indus is open to visitors. It is 220 km from Leh, jeeps make the journey. To the south of the 27-km long lake is the land of the Tibetan wild ass.

You can travel either via **Chhumathang**, 140 km, visiting the hot spring there or by crossing the high pass at Taglang La, leaving the Manali-Leh Highway at Debring. The route takes you past **Tsokar** basin, 154 km, where salt cakes the edges. A campsite along the lake with access to fresh water is opposite **Thukje** village which has a gompa and a 'wolf catching trap'! The road then reaches the hot sulphur springs at **Puga** before reaching the beautiful Tso-Moriri, about four hours drive from Tsokar. You can follow the lake bank and visit the solitary village of **Karzog**, at 4,500 m, north of the lake, which has a gompa. There are some rest houses and guest houses at Chhumathang and Karzog and camping at Tsokar and Karzog as well as a tent camp at Chhumathang.

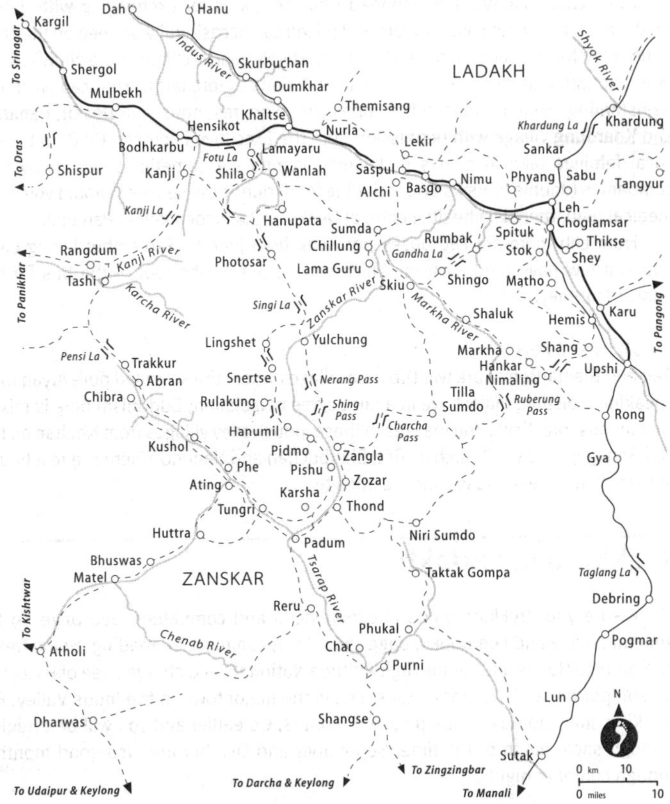

## Pangong-Tso

From Leh you can also get a permit to visit the narrow 130-km long Pangong-Tso, at 4,250 m, the greater part of which lies in Tibet. The road, which is only suitable with four-wheel drive in places, is via **Karu** on the Manali-Leh Highway, where the road east goes through **Zingral** and over the Chang La pass. Beyond are **Durbuk**, a small village with low-roofed houses, and **Tangste**, the 'abode of Chishul warriors' with a Lotswa Temple, which is also an army base with a small bank. The rough jeep track takes you through an impressive rocky gorge which opens out to a valley which has camping by a fresh water stream in the hamlet of **Mugleb** and then on to **Lukung**, the last check-point and finally **Spangmik**, 153 km from Leh. On the way you will be able to see some Himalayan birds including *chikhor* (quail) which may end up in the cooking pot.

An overnight stop on the lake shore allows you to see the lake in different lights. You can walk between Lukung and Spangmik, 7 km, on this second day, passing small settlements growing barley and peas along the lake shore. Both villages have yaks which you can experience a ride on! You return to Leh on the third day. Tented camps at Durbuk, Tangtse, Lukung and Spangmik. Jeeps make the journey from Leh.

## Nubra Valley

For an exhilarating high-altitude experience over possibly the highest motorable pass in the world travel across the Ladakh range over the 5,600 m **Khardung La**. North of Leh, this is along the old Silk Route to the lush green Nubra Valley up to **Panamik**, 140 km from Leh, which has reddish, sulphurous hot springs nearby. It is best to visit this region after mid-June.

Once camel caravans transported Chinese goods for exchanging with Indian produce. Camels which are now rare and prized can occasionally be seen on the sand dunes near Nubra, see also page 569. The relatively gentler climate here allows crops, fruit and nuts to grow, so some call it 'Ldumra' (orchard). You can visit the **Samstanling**, **Sumur** and **Deskit** gompas. There are rest houses at **Deskit**, **Panamik** and **Khardung** village with permission from the Executive Engineer, PWD, in Deskit. Local families take in guests and tented camps are sometimes set up by tour companies (double tents Rs 800 including food) during the season. Should you need medical help, there is a health centre at Deskit and a dispensary at Panamik.

From Leh there are two buses per week from June to September taking eight hours; a few have tried by bike, which can be put on the roof of the bus for the outward journey.

## Drokhpa area

**Dah** and **Biama**(Bema) are two Drokhpa villages where the so-called pure Aryan tribe speaking a distinct dialect live in a fair degree of isolation; Buddhism here is mixed with animist practices. You may reach these Indus valley villages from **Khaltse** on the Leh-Srinagar road via Dumkhar, Tirit, Skurbuchan and Hanudo. There is a rest house at Biama and guest houses and a campsite.

# Trekking in Ladakh

Make sure your trekking guide is experienced and competent. See page 69 for general advice and see Books, page 1364, for recommended reading. Some treks, eg Spituk to Hemis and Hemis High Altitude National Park, charge a fee of Rs 25 per person per day or Rs 10 for Indians. Leh is the major town in the Indus Valley. For trekking, July and August are pleasant months. Go earlier and you will be trudging through snow much of the time. September and October are also good months, though colder at night.

## Spituk to Hemis

Both places are in the Indus Valley, just 30 km apart. A very satisfying nine to 10 days can be undertaken by traversing the Stok range to the Markha Valley, walking up the valley and then back over the Zanskar range to Hemis. The daily walking time on this trek is five to six hours so you must be fit.

There is an interesting monastery at **Spituk**, a short drive from Leh, see page 561. From Spituk proceed southwest of the Indus along a trail passing through barren countryside. After about 7 km you reach the **Jinchan Valley** and in a further five hours, the beautiful Rumbak village. Camp below the settlement. You can also trek here from Stok which takes two days and a steep ascent of the **Namlung La** (4,570 m).

From Rumbak it is a five-hour walk to Utse village. The camp is two hours further on at the base of the bleak **Gandha La** (4,700 m), open, bare and windswept. To go over the pass takes about three hours, then the same time again to negotiate the wooded ravine to Skiu. Here the path meets the Markha Valley. You can make a half day round trip from Skiu to see the impressive gorges on the Zanskar River. The stage to Markha where there is an impressive fort, is a six-hour walk. The monastery, which is not particularly impressive from the outside, has some superb wall paintings and *thangkas*, some dating from the 13th century. You need to take a torch.

The next destination is **Hankar** village, whose ruined fort forms an astonishing extension of the natural rock face, an extremely impressive ruin. From here the path climbs quite steeply to a plateau. There are good views of Nimaling Peak (6,000 m) and a number of *mani* walls en route. From **Nimaling** it is a two-hour climb to **Gongmaru La** (5,030 m) with views of the Stok range and the Indus Valley. The descent is arduous and involves stream crossings. There is a lovely campsite at **Shogdu** and another at **Sumda** village, 3 km further on. The final stage is down the valley to Martselang from where you can walk down 5 km to **Karu** village on the Leh-Manali road or take a 2 km diversion to visit Hemis monastery.

## Hemis High Altitude National Park

Set up in 1981, the park adjoining the monastery covers 600 sq km, comprising the catchments of Markha, Rumbak and Sumda nalas, with plans to extend across another 1,670 sq km. The rugged terrain with valleys often littered with rocks and rimmed by high peaks (some over 6,000 m), supports limited vegetation but contains some rare species of flora and fauna. For example the ibex, Pallas's cat, *bharal* and *shapu* inhabit the area and a reserve to protect the endangered snow leopard is planned. It is hoped to restrict the activities of local villagers who graze livestock within the park, to a buffer zone so that their animals can be kept safe from attack by wolves and snow leopards.

There are camping sites which you can reserve through the Wildlife Warden, Leh. Since most of the park lies within 'Restricted' areas, you need a special Group Permit for entry, also issued in Leh. Contact a local travel agent for advice.

## Lamayaru to Alchi

This is a shorter trek of five to six days, however, the average daily walking time is 6½ hours so don't think that the shortness of the trek means less effort. Three passes, the **Printiki La** (3,500 m), **Konke La** (4,570 m) and **Stapski La** (5,200 m) are crossed rewarding the exertion of reaching them with excellent views.

The first stage involves walking from the usual campsite just below the monastery down the valley for 2 km then over the **Printiki La**. You then descend the Shillakong Valley and climb to **Phangi** village, passing huge boulders brought down by a landslide, and impressive irrigation in such a forbidding landscape. From Phangi you walk up the Ripchar Valley to **Khaltse**, crossing the river a number of times. There are a number of small settlements until you reach the summer grazing ground a few kilometres below the pass. The **Konke La** is a steep two-hour climb. From here you will see the Zanskar River and gorge and the Stok range.

The fourth stage should be with a guide since the trail splits, one leading to **Chillung** on the Zanskar River, the other to **Sumdahchenmo**, the latter being quite treacherous as it involves many river crossings (about three hours below Sumdahchenmo there is a path which climbs the ridge above the river; it is quite easy to miss this, hence the guide). There is a monastery here with an impressive statue of the Buddha and some attractive wall paintings. A camping site lies just beyond the village. The last stage of the trek is long, about eight hours walking, and takes you over the **Stapski La** to **Alchi**. The views from the top are superb. From Alchi you can get a bus to Leh.

## Trekking in Zanskar

Trekking in Zanskar is not easy. The paths are often rough and steep, the passes high and the climate extreme. Provisions, fuel and camping equipment should be taken along from Kishtwar, Manali or Leh. You may get necessities such as dried milk, biscuits and sugar from Padum, though probably not at the beginning of the season. In Padum the Tourism Officer and Govt Development Officer will be able to advise and maybe even assist in hiring horses. Porters can be hired at **Sani** village for the traverse of the **Umasi La** into Kishtwar. Horses cannot use this pass. In Padum you may be able to hire porters with whom you can cover rougher terrain. It is best to contact a trekking agent in advance. See page 70 and Activities and tours below.

**Pensi La to Padum** You can trek this three-day route before the road opens (June-October) when it is free of vehicles.

**Karsha to Lamayaru** This is a demanding nine-day trek which includes seven passes, five of which are over 4,500 m. The highest is the Singi La (5,060 m). It is essential to be very fit before starting the trek. Each day's walking should take under six hours, but with time for rests and lunch this adds up to a full day. An extra day allows for flexibility.

The 16th-century monastery of the Tibetan Gelugpa (Yellow Hat) sect at **Karsha** is the largest and wealthiest in the Zanskar Valley and is occupied by nearly 200 monks. Karsha has an inn with dormitory beds and a vegetarian canteen.

**Padum to Leh** This is another demanding trek which also takes about 10 days. Some are through the spectacular gorges between Markha and Zangla. A local guide is recommended as this is truly a wilderness area. The trek involves walking along stream beds and in July there is still too much snow melt to allow safe crossings. Recommended only for August/September.

It is seven hours walking from Padum to Zangla and this includes crossing the Zanskar River by a string and twig bridge that spans over 40 m. Ponies are not allowed on it and if it is windy sensible humans don't cross! At **Zangla** you can see the King's palace, which has a collection of *thangkas* painted by the king's son (who was once a monk). The third stage takes you over the **Charcha La** (5,200 m). On the next stage river crossings are again necessary. This is time consuming and if you are travelling in mid-summer, an extra day may be called for.

You then follow the **Khurna River** to a narrow gorge that marks the ancient border between Zanskar and Ladakh, and end up below the **Rubarung La**. When you cross this you get good views of the Stok range. You then descend into the Markha valley and from here you can reach Leh in six stages by heading west into the heart of the valley and then crossing the Ganda La to Spituk, or in three stages by crossing the Gongmaru La and descending to Martselang and nearby Hemis.

**Padum to Darcha** This is a week-long trek and starts with a walk along the Tsarap Chu to **Bardan**, which has stupas and interesting idols, and **Reru**.

After two stages you reach **Purni** (with a couple of shops and a popular campsite), where you can stay two nights and make a side trip to the impressive 11th-century **Phugtal monastery** (a two-hour walk). On a spectacular site, it has been carved out of the mountainside round a limestone cave. Usually there are about 50 monks in attendance. From Purni you continue on to Kargya, the last village before the **Shingo La**. It's another day's walk to the camp below this high pass (5,200 m).

The mountain scenery is stunning with 6,000 m plus peaks all around. Once over the pass you can stop at **Rumjack** where there is a campsite used by shepherds or you can go further to the confluence of the **Shingo River** and the **Barai River** where there is now a bridge. From here the trail passes through grazing land and it is about 15 km from the river to Darcha, the end of the trek. Keen trekkers can combine this with a trek from **Darcha** to **Manali**. The average daily walking time of the Padum-Darcha trek is six hours so you have to be very fit.

## Trekking in the Nubra and Shyok valleys

The gradual easing up of controls to visit the Nubra-Shyok valleys has now made possible treks that start from points in the Indus valley not far from Leh, cross the Ladakh Range to enter the Shyok River valley and then recross the Ladakh range further to the west to re-enter the Indus valley near Phyang monastery. Ask a good local trekking agent for advice on how to get required 'Restricted Area Permits'.

**Day 1** Drive from Leh south along the Manali road to Karu, near Hemis, where you turn left and drive about 10 km to the roadhead at the village of Sakti, just past **Takthak monastery**. Trek about 90 minutes to **Chumchar** and camp.
**Day 2** Cross the Ladakh range at the **Wari La** (4,400 m) and descend to Junlez on the northern flank.
**Day 3** Walk downhill to **Tangyar** (3,700 m) with a nice gompa.
**Days 4, 5, 6** A level walk along the **Shyok River** valley takes you to **Khalsar** from where you follow the military road west to the confluence of the Shyok and Nubra rivers at **Deskit**. On a hill above the village is a Gelugpa sect **monastery** (the largest in Nubra) built by the Ladakhi king Sohrab Zangpo in the early 1700's. There is large statue of Tsongkhapa and the Rimpoche of Thikse monastery south of Leh oversees this monastery also. The Rimpoche was nominated to the Rajya Sabha in 1998. The next biggest monastery in Nubra is near **Tiggur** halfway along the road north of Deskit to **Panamik** in the Nubra Valley. Called the **Samtanling** gompa, it was founded in 1842 and belongs to the Gelugpa sect. The Permit allows travel only up to the village of Panamik (see Nubra Valley above).
**Days 7, 8, 9** Three days to gradually ascend the northern flanks of the Ladakh Range passing the hamlets of **Hundar, Wachan** and **Hundar Dok** to the high pastures of **Thanglasgo** (4,700 m).
**Days 10, 11** Trek back over the Ladakh Range via the Lasermo La pass (5,150 m) to a campsite on the southern base of the pass.
**Day 12** Camp at Phyang village about 1 km above Phyang monastery before driving back to Leh.

## Sleeping

**Leh** *p555, maps p557 and p558*
Advance reservations in **B** and **C** grade hotels may not be honoured in the peak season (mid-Jul to end-Aug) since they cater for tour/trekking groups whose arrival and departure can be unpredictable. Hotel touts can be a nuisance during the 14-day Ladakh festival. Outside the peak period expect discounts though few places remain open in the winter, eg **Siachen**, and **Kangri**. Many

traditional Ladakhi homes offer rooms during the summer. Those in Karzoo and Changspa (some way from the bus stand) are quieter and preferable to those near the bazar. Top hotels often include meals in the room rate.

There is some budget accommodation along the Old Rd and in the Changspa area; some are very basic with cold water only. Fleas and bed bugs can be a problem; use your own sleeping bag if possible.

**A Lharimo**, T01982 252101, F253345. 30 simple but comfortable rooms with baths, good views from balconies, restaurant, attractive, central.

**A Shambala**, Skara, T01982 252607, www.hotelshambhala.com. 24 large airy rooms, good restaurant (often caters for German packages), meals included, very pleasant, friendly staff, peaceful away from crowds, attractive garden with hammocks, free transport to centre, recommended

**A-B Caravan Centre**, Skara, T01982 252282, . 25 comfortable rooms, including 3 suites, all with views, attractive gardens, "oasis in the desert", friendly staff, restaurant.

**A-B Galdan Continental**, off Fort Rd, T01982 252173, F252414. 46 comfortable but somewhat old-fashioned rooms, some with bath tub, around a grassy quad, suites not recommended.

**A-B K-Sar Palace**, T 01982 252348, kesarbadam@hotmail.com. 22 large rooms with pleasant views, exchange.

**A-B Omasila**, Changspa, T01982 252119. 34 luxurious rooms, ornate restaurant (fresh garden vegetables), garden, pleasant quiet location, own spring water.

**A-B Spic-n-Span**, Old Rd, T01982 252765, www.reachladakh.com/spicnspan. 29 rooms which actually live up to the name, good views from roof, attractive building.

**B Bijoo**, near Library, 100 m from Bazar, T01982 252131, hotel_bijoo@rediffmail.com. 2-storey white building hidden by wall, 18 good rooms with bath, good restaurant, pleasant flower-filled garden and shady seating, treks and tours.

**B Dragon**, T01982 252139, www.travel ladakh.com. 30 rooms with bath, improved, almost always filled with trekking parties (porters camp in garden!), higher standard than most in this price range.

**B Kang-lha Chen**, T01982 252144, klcleh@ sancharnet.in. 25 simple rooms, most with baths, good restaurant, pleasant shaded inner courtyard garden, own spring, quiet and peaceful, old fashioned but well maintained, open May-Oct.

**B Kangri**, Nehru Park, T01982 252311, F252051. 22 basic rooms with bath, restaurant, loud generator nearby a nuisance until 2300, indifferent service.

**B Lasermo**, Old Road Chulung, T01982 252313, www.lasermo.com. 19 rooms around pleasant courtyard, deluxe rooms very smart.

**B Mogol**, Ghangspa, T01982 253438, hotelmogol@rediffmail.com. 20 well-presented, comfortable rooms around a pleasant garden.

**B Pangong**, Chulung, T01982 254665, pangong@sancharnet.in. 18 clean, spacious rooms, covered parking, very well run.

**B Rafica**, off Fort Rd, T01982 252258. 16 okay (no TV), some large, pleasant outdoor restaurant recommended (worth 1 hr wait for fresh food), friendly, exceptional staff, quiet (except front rooms), among fields, treks and tours.

**B Shynam**, Old Rd, T01982 252345. 15 comfortable rooms, huge dining hall, beautiful gardens, very well run.

**B Tsomo-Ri**, Fort Rd, T01982 253611, www.ladakhtsomori.com. 15 surprisingly quiet rooms around central courtyard, very hospitable manager.

**B Yak Tail**, Fort Rd, T01982 252118. 30 rooms, some 'houseboat style' (newer have balconies), nice courtyard garden restaurant (good, reasonably priced Indian), exchange, open Apr-Sep, pleasant atmosphere.

**B-D Padma**, off Fort Rd at end of alley, T01982 252630, www.reachladakh.com/ padma.htm. 6 clean, charming rooms with common bath in guesthouse, upstairs has mountain views, plus 15 rooms in newer hotel, beautiful, peaceful garden, cheap meals to order, outstanding hospitality, highly recommended.

**C Ri-Rab**, Changspa, T01982 253108,

*For an explanation of the sleeping and eating price codes used in this guide, see inside the front cover. Other relevant information is found in Essentials pages 56-61.*

## Prepare for a different lifestyle in Leh

The whitewashed sun-dried brick walls of a typical two-storey, flat-roofed Ladakhi house, often with decorative woodwork around doors and windows and a carefully nurtured garden, look inviting to a traveller after a very long hard journey, whether by road or air. Local families are opening their homes to provide for the increasing demand for accommodation for a very short peak season and new hotels are springing up. These are listed by the Tourism Department as A-D class hotels or as guesthouses and must charge fixed rates. However, prices do not reflect the type of furniture, furnishings and plumbing you might expect elsewhere in India although on the whole the rooms are kept clean. There is usually a space for sitting out – a 'garden' with a tree or two, some flower beds and some grass struggling to establish itself.

Electricity is limited, so expect power cuts which are random and unpredictable. Some hotels have generators. Those without may run out of tap water but buckets are always at hand. Hot water is a luxury, available only during mornings and evenings. Plumbing allows for flush WCs in at least D category hotels but the water from the basin disappears down the plughole only to emerge around your feet as there is only one drain in a corner of the bathroom!

Guests are encouraged to economize on water and electricity – you will notice the low-power bulbs and scarcity of lights in rooms and public areas, so put away your reading until sunrise.

chhospel@hotmail.com. 18 clean simple rooms with baths, restaurant (own fresh garden vegetables), parking.

**C-D Himalayan**, Sankar Gompa Rd, T01982 252104. 26 rooms, most with bath, old building in a quiet, shady willow grove by a stream, restaurant, camping.

**C-D Lhung-Se-Jung**, Fort Rd, T01982 252193, modhalileh@yahoo.com. 14 charming, old-fsahioned rooms with bath, 2-storey old building and small annexe, upstairs better, restaurant, small garden, quiet location, student discount, good service, friendly manager, recommended.

**C-D Snow View**, Karzoo, past Ecological Centre, T01982 252336. 10 rooms (upstairs with good views), peaceful, far from bazar.

**D Padmaling**, Changspa, T01982 252933. 10 clean, well-maintained rooms with bath, hot water morning and evening, helpful manager, *Mona Lisa* restaurant next door, pleasant garden, good views over Stok Kangri.

**D Tso-Kar**, Fort Road, T01982 253071, afzalmitoo@hotmail.com. 14 rooms in charming cottage, small restaurant, cyber café next door.

**D-E Saser**, near Ecological Centre, T01982 250162, saser_15@rediffmail.com. 13 modern rooms, pleasant garden, friendly manager.

**D-E Silver Cloud**, on the road opposite Sankar Gompa, 15 mins walk from centre, T01982 253128. 15 very clean rooms, 9 with bath (1 **C**), in Ladakhi guesthouse, excellent food, large garden, friendly, helpful family.

**D-E Hills View**, T01982 252058, adventurehills@vsnl.net. 12 clean, charming rooms, 12 more coming, authentically rickety, some with good views, breakfast and snacks, pleasant staff, pretty garden, relaxing, safe, stores luggage.

**D-F Oriental**, below Shanti Stupa, T01982 253153, www.oriental-ladakh.com. 35 very clean rooms in traditional family home, good home cooking, great views across the valley, friendly, treks and travel arrangements reliable.

**E Bimla Guest House**, Suku, T01982 252754. 18 rooms, sitting area, welcoming.

**E Goba**, in Chongspa down side alley, T01982 253670. 15 simple byut attractive rooms, very peaceful garden, home-cooked food, lovely family, recommended.

## Unlucky in Leh

The supply of clean water and the sewage system can come under heavy pressure in the tourist season. Drink pressure boiled water from Dzomsa (see map) only or use water purification tablets. Bottled water can sometimes be more than a year old and doesn't always conform to safety standards. Meat is sometimes brought in unrefrigerated lorries having travelled two days, so is best avoided.

**E Indus**, Suku, T01982 252502, masters_adv@yahoo.co.in. 17 large rooms some with bath (hot water in buckets), better upstairs, food, simple but homely, peaceful garden.
**E New Antelope Guest House**, Main St, T01982 252086. 11 simple, clean rooms, some with bath, good food, quiet, shady garden.
**E Old Ladakh**, in the Old Town. 8 rooms, varying in comfort, has character, pleasant atmosphere, good place to meet others.
**E Rainbow**, Karzoo. Big, clean rooms with wonderful views of mountains and Shanti Stupa, hot water in buckets, great hospitality, good breakfasts. Recommended.
**E Shanti Guest House**, below Shanti Stupa, T01982 253084. 9 well-heated rooms, most with great views, very good food, summer/winter treks arranged with guide, friendly Ladakhi family.
**E Zarla**, Sheynam Old Rd, down dirty alley but worth the effort, T01982 252 672. 10 simple rooms in friendly family house.
**E-F Harmit Hut**, Old Road Chulung, T01982 251348. 9 cozy rooms with attached barthrooms, quiet and charming.
**E-F Kangla**, Airport Rd, T01982 252506. 14 slightly tatty rooms but very friendly, helpful, organize treks.
**F Lung Snon**, Sheynam Chulli Chan. 8 rooms, delightful guesthouse in peaceful countryside, clean and friendly, but simple, earth toilet.
**F Remo**, Fort Rd, T01982 253336. Clean, quiet, simple rooms, shared toilets, bucket hot water (no charge), very kind family.
**F Ti-Sei Guest House**, Suku. Good value rooms in peaceful location, 'glass room' (**E** ), meals, terrace.
**F Wari-La**, Old Road near **Hotel Horzey**, T01982 253302. 6 charming rooms, good views, home-cooked food on demand.

**Thikse** *p560*
**E Shalzang Chamba Hotel**, with outdoor restaurant.

**Hemis** *p560*
Many householders take in guests.
**F Tourist**, camp or sleep on the floor, own sleeping bag, Rs 25. The tented restaurant is basic and grubby.

**Alchi** *p562*
Near Alchi car/bus park there are tea stalls and a few guesthouses. A couple of kilometres away in Saspul are **Carefree Travels Camp** and **Worldroof Camping Resort and Restaurant**.
**E-F Lotsava**, on the path, simple.
**F Uley Tokpo Camp**, a few km before Alchi.
**F Zimskhang**, very basic rooms, walled-in open-air restaurant for light meals and snacks, camping.

**Padum** *p564*
Places to stay are limited, being mostly dormitory style. There is a Tourist complex with basic rooms, meals, you can camp.
**E Ibex** has the best rooms and a restaurant.

## Eating

**Leh** *p555, maps p557 and p558*
**TTT Mona Lisa**, Changspa, T01982 252687. International. Good atmosphere, quiet garden with shady trees, hanging lanterns, excellent food (try pizzas, momos, garlic cheese with bread), scrawny chickens, no desserts, service can be indifferent.
**TT Dreamland** (separate from hotel). International. Good atmosphere and food especially Chinese, excellent breakfasts.
**TT Hi Life**, exceptional range of high quality food, friendly owners, seating indoor and out, highly recommended.

## Gomptas and festivals

Buddhist festivals usually take place in the bleak winter months when villagers gather together, stalls spring up around the gompas and colourful dance dramas and masked dances are performed in the courtyards. Musical instruments, weapons and religious objects are brought out during these dance performances. The *Kushak* (high priest) is accompanied by monks in monotonous recitation while others play large cymbals, trumpets and drums. The serious theme of victory of Good over Evil is lightened by comic interludes. A few monasteries celebrate their festivals in the summer months for example Lamayuru, Hemis and Phyang.

**In-Style**, Fort Rd. International. Al fresco at back, popular for breakfast, takeaway snacks, also Chinese menu. Both have 'notice boards'.

**Kokonor**, entrance on alley off Main St, 2nd floor. "Chinese and Tibetan specialities and western encouragements served with generosity and flair", very popular.

**La Montessori**, Main St Bazar. Excellent Tibetan and Chinese. Filling soups, interesting local clientele.

**Summer Harvest**, Fort Rd, 1st floor, next to *Dreamland*. Mainly Indian, also Chinese, Tibetan. Extensive menu of local and 'tourist' dishes from mutton *thukpa* (Rs 30) to tandoori chicken (Rs 160).

**Amdo II**, Main Bazar. Tibetan. Good fried momos, Rs 25-35 per dish, friendly (better than **Amdo Café** opposite).

**Budshah Inn**, Lal Chowk, top floor. North Indian. Lacks ambience but excellent Kashmiri (Rs 45, dish).

**Devi Tibetan**. Traditional meals, refreshing spiced teas.

**Nepali**. Nepali, Tibetan. Excellent veg *momos*.

**Tenzin Dichey**, for good Tibetan, Rhoockosy recommended.

**Tibetan Friend's Corner**. Clean, simple, delicious *kothay* (fried *momos*) Rs 25, huge pancakes, friendly, locally popular.

### Confectionery

Four German bakeries sell good bread (trekking bread keeps for a week) and excellent cakes and muesli.

**In Style**, similar fare to **Pumpernickel**.

**Mona Lisa**, similar fare to **Pumpernickel**.

**Pumpernickel**, Main St Bazar, the original German bakery is the best and friendliest, indoor/outdoor seating, excellent apricot and apple crumble/pie, message board for trekkers.

## Entertainment

**Leh** *p555, maps p557 and p558*

The Ecological Centre shows occasional films, see page 558. Ladakhi dancing and singing, below entrance to Palace, 1800 (1 hr), Rs 50. Disappointing.

## Festivals and events

**Leh** *p555, maps p557 and p558*

Dates vary depending on the lunar calendar. **Losar** which originated in the 15th century to protect people before going to battle is celebrated in **Dec**. The main events of the **Ladakh Festival** (1-15 Sep) are held in the Leh Polo grounds with smaller events arranged in other districts. Arranged by the State Government usually during the 1st week in Sep, there are 4 days of dances, displays of traditional costumes, Ladakhi plays and polo matches. **Buddha Purnima** (**Apr-May** full moon) marks the Buddha's birth.

**Hemis** *p560*

Usually held in Jun, Hemis Festival is perhaps the biggest such event in Ladakh, a colourful display of Ladakhi Buddhist culture, it always attracts large numbers of foreign visitors.

## Shopping

**Leh** *p555, maps p557 and p558*

Please use your own bags. Plastic bags are not allowed in the bazar as they are not bio-degradable and were finding their way into streams when not piled on unsightly heaps.

Leh Bazar is full of shops selling curios, clothes and knick-knacks. Tea and *chang* (local barley brew) vessels, cups, butter churns, knitted carpets with Tibetan designs, Tibetan jewellery, prayer flags, musical bowls, are all available. Prices are high especially in Kashmiri shops so bargain vigorously. It is usually better to buy Ladakhi jewellery and souvenirs from Ladakhis who generally ask a fair price. There are tight restrictions on the export of anything over 100 years old. Baggage is checked at the airport partly for this reason. However, even though most items are antique looking, they are, in fact, fresh from the backstreet workshops. If you walk down the narrow lanes, you will probably find an artisan at work from whom you can buy direct.

**Books**

**Artou Books**, opposite Post Office, Zangsti and in Main Bazar has a good selection, especially on trekking in the region, also fax and international phone.

**Book Worm**, near Galdan Hotel, second-hand.

**Crafts**

A group of Ladakhis have stalls off the Fort Rd.

**Cottage Emporium**, opposite Dreamland Hotel, many carpets and pashminas.

**Chan Gali**, worth exploring for curios.

**Ladakh Arts & Craft House**, top of Fort Rd, opposite PO has a few interesting bric-a-brac.

**Ladakhi Village Curios**, selection of *thangkas*, inlaid bowls, baubles, bangles and beads.

**LEDeG Craft Shop**, at the Ecology Centre, and opposite State Bank in the Main Bazar.

**Sonam Bongo**, top of Main Bazar St, has local costumes.

**Tibetan Arts**, selection of *thangkas*, inlaid bowls, baubles, bangles and beads.

**Fruit and nuts**

Available in season. Dried apricots can be bought along any roadside in Aug-Sep. Bottled juice is sold by the *Dzomsa* Laundry.

**Photography**

**Syed Ali Shah's Postcard Shop**, Choterantag St, is worth a visit. An authentic photographer's studio; collection of old photocopies sold, postcards, camera films.

**Tailor**

Next to Budshah Inn near mosque, excellent shirt maker, made-to-measure. Also several in Nowshara Gali.

## Activities and tours

**Leh** *p555, maps p557 and p558*

**Archery**

The Archery Stadium is nearby where winter competitions attract large crowds; the target is a hanging white clay tablet.

**Mountaineering**

Local tour companies offer treks and mountain climbing.

**Polo**

Polo, the 'national' sport, is popular in the summer and is played in the polo ground beyond the main Bus Stand. The local version which is fast and rough appears to follow no rules! The Polo Club is the highest in the world and worth a visit.

**Tours**

Women on their own should take special care when arranging a tour with a driver/guide.

**Explore Himalayas**, PO Box 45, Main Bazar (opposite SBI), T/F01982 253354, wangchuks @hotmail.com. Highly recommended, excellent crew, friendly, good to animals, environment conscious.

**K2**, Main Bazar, T01982 253532, good rates for treks (Markha Valley), very friendly, environment conscious.

**Mountain Experience**, Hotel Saser, T01982 250162. 20 years of trekking experience.

**Rimo Expeditions**, Kang-lha Chen Hotel, T01982 253644, treks and rafting.

**White water rafting and kayaking**

Possible on the Tsarap Chu and Zanskar rivers from mid-Jun; the upper reaches of the former (grade 4 rapids) are suitable for professionals only, though the remaining stretch can be enjoyed by the inexperienced. Along the Indus: Hemis to Choglamsar (easy, very scenic); Phey-Nimmu (grade 3); Nimmu-Khaltse (professional). Ensure the trip is organized by a well-experienced rafter and that life jackets and wet suits are provided. Half to full day, including transport

## To fly or not to fly

Travel by road gives you an advantage over flying into Leh as it enables you to acclimatize to a high altitude plateau and if you are able to hire a jeep or car it will give you the flexibility of stopping to see the several sights on the way. However, some people find the bus journey from Manali (or Srinagar) terrifying and very uncomfortable, and most healthy people find that if they relax completely for two days after flying in, they acclimatize without difficulty. If you have a heart condition, consult your doctor on the advisability of your going to Leh.

and lunch, Rs 800-1,400. See also Tour s above.

**Zanskar** *p564*

**Ibex** and **NEI** in Delhi organize trekking and rafting in Zanskar. See page 121.

**Zanskar Tours and Travels**, T01983-245064, in Padum.

## Transport

**Leh** *p555, maps p557 and p558*

### Air

The small airport is 5 km away on Srinagar Rd. It is surrounded by hills on 3 sides and the flight over the mountain ranges is spectacular. Transport to town: buses, and jeep-taxis (Rs 150), for sharing. Weather conditions may deteriorate rapidly even in the summer resulting in flight cancellations (especially outside Jul and Aug) so always be prepared for a delay or to take alternative road transport out of Ladakh. Furthermore, the airlines fly quite full planes into Leh but can take fewer passengers out because of the high altitude take-off. This adds to the difficulty of getting a flight out. **Book your tickets as soon as possible** (several months ahead for Jul and Aug). You can book on the internet before you depart for India (eg www.welcometravel.com).

Flights are often cancelled. Tickets bought in Leh may not be 'confirmed'. The **Indian Airlines** office is near Shambala Hotel and is often chaotic. Avoid connecting with an onward flight or train immediately after your visit to Ladakh. If you fail to get on the outward flight, you do not get an immediate refund from the airline but have to reclaim it from the travel agent. It is therefore essential to have enough money to travel out by road if your return is imperative; remember, a taxi to Manali takes 2 days and to Delhi, up to 4 days. Despite the difficulties, even if you do not have a firm outward booking and have been 'wait-listed' you may sometimes get on a flight at short notice, if weather conditions improve. It is worth asking. Check-in early to stand a better chance. **Indian Airlines**, T01982 252076, airport T01982 252255, www.indianairlines.nic.in flies from **Delhi**, 0620, Mon, Wed, Fri, Sun in season (Jul-Sep), with an additional 7 flights per week offered through its subsidiary **Alliance Air**, returns 1110 same days (in winter, this is the only link between Ladakh and the outside world); to **Jammu**, Mon, Fri; **Chandigarh**, Wed; **Srinagar**, Sun. **Jet Airways**, T01982 250999, airport T250324, www.jetairways.com to **Delhi**.

### Bus

**Local** The New Bus Stand is near the cemetery. The vehicles are ramshackle but the fares are low. See under monasteries for details. Enquiries J&KSRTC, T01982 252285.

**Long distance** Himachal Tourism runs regular (not daily) Deluxe and Ordinary buses between Manali and Leh, usually mid-Jun to end-Sep, 2 days. To **Manali**, 530 km, 'Deluxe', booked at HPTDC, Fort Rd, or at travel agents, Rs 800 (Rs 1,100 includes camp bed and meals in Sarchu). Ordinary (Private) booked at bus stand, 'A' Rs 500, and 'B', Rs 350, stop overnight at Keylong. J&KSRTC bus **Kargil**, 230 km (alternate days in summer) Rs 110-180, **Srinagar** 434 km, Rs 200-360.

### Road

If you have travelled by road you may already be better acclimatized, but a mild headache is common and can be treated with aspirin or paracetamol. Drink non-alcoholic fluids on journeys.

Leh is connected to Manali via Keylong (closed Oct to mid-Jun or longer) and to Srinagar, via Kargil, by a State Highway. Both can be seriously affected by landslides, causing long delays. The Leh-Srinagar Road is also often blocked by army convoys. Information on road conditions from the Traffic Police HQ, Maulana Azad Rd, Srinagar.

The road to **Manali**, crossing some very high passes, is open mid-Jun or early Jul, until end-Sep (depending on the weather) and takes 2 days. Road conditions may be poor in places. Departure from Leh can be early (0400) with overnight stop in Keylong; next day to Manali. Alternatively, camp in Sarchu (10 hrs from Leh), or Jespa; next day 14 hrs to Manali (Rs 150 each in Sarchu, camp). Roadside tents provide food en route during the tourist season; carry snacks, water and a good sleeping bag when planning to camp. Many travellers find the mountain roads extremely frightening and they are comparatively dangerous. Some are cut out of extremely unstable hillsides, usually with nothing between the road's edge and the nearly vertical drop below; parts remain rough and pot-holed and during the monsoons, landslides and rivers can make it impassable for 2-3 days. It is also a long and uncomfortable journey, but there is some spectacular scenery.

### Taxi

4WD between Leh and Manali are expensive but recommended if you want to stop en route to visit monasteries. 2-day trip, about Rs 13,000. Taxis often return empty to Manali (some visitors choose to fly out of Leh) so may agree a much reduced fare for the return leg. Officially, Manali (or Srinagar) taxis are allowed to carry their passengers to and from Leh but are not permitted to do local tours, a rule fiercely monitored by the Leh Taxi Operators' Union.

Tourist taxi and jeep: **Ladakh Taxi Operators' Union**, Fort Rd. Fixed fares point-to-point. From the airport to Main Bazar, about Rs 80; from Bus Stand Rs 60. A day's taxi hire to visit nearby *gompas* costs about Rs 1,000-1,200; Nubra Rs 6,000.

### Alchi *p562*

Srinagar bound buses stop at Saspul; from there it is a 2½-km walk across the bridge. Buses depart for Leh for Alchi, around 0630, 1500, nearly 3 hrs.

## Directory

### Leh *p555, maps p557 and p558*

**Banks** It is not possible to get money on credit cards, and as yet there is no international ATM. **J&K Bank**, Main Bazar; **State Bank of India**, exchange only next to tourist office, but slow. Large hotels and **Amex** (1030-1430, Sat 1030-1230) in Kangri and **Yak Tail**, charge a steep commission. **Hospitals** **SNM Hospital**, T01982 252014, 0900-1700 (also for advice on mountain sickness), after hours, T01982 253629. During the day, doctors have little time; better at clinics in evenings. **Soway Clinic**, in Bazar; **Kunfan Octsnang Clinic**; **Ladakh Medicate**, behind post office (ask for Dr Norbu, Old Leh Rd). **Internet** Email very erratic. Phone connections with the rest of India are unpredictable. On Fort Rd. **Post** Head Post Office and Telegraph Office: Airport Rd, 3 km from Leh centre (1000-1500); parcels often disappear. Mail may be sent via **Gypsy's World**, Fort Rd, T01982 252935 (not fail safe); make sure addressed c/o Gypsy's World, PO Box 160, Leh, Ladakh 194101, India. **Telephone** Pick up faxes here for a small fee; **Tourist offices** J&K, 2 km south, on Airport Rd, T01982 253462. **Useful addresses** Ambulance: T102. Police: T01982 252018. **Foreigners' Registration Office**: T01982 252200.

# East India

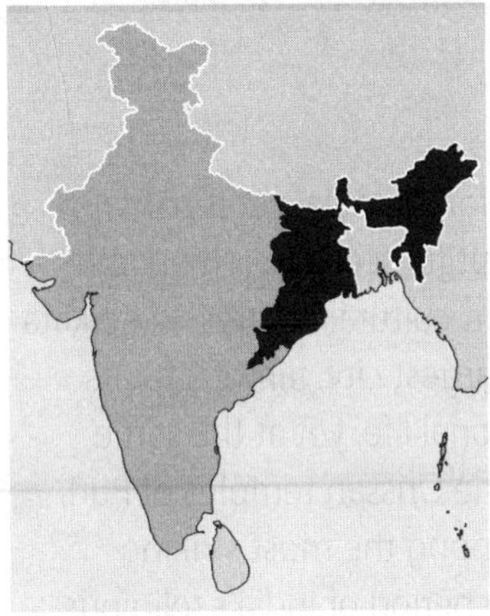

# Introduction

East India is the least visited region of India, yet it contains some of the country's most beautiful scenery, remarkable religious monuments and vibrant cultural centres. In Kolkata (Calcutta) it has India's second largest city, famous for its cultural contribution to the national life, yet at the same time notorious for its poverty. The Orissan temples of Puri, Bhubaneswar and Konark are among the most striking architectural monuments of any period of India's religious building, while in the interior of Orissa, Bihar and Jharkhand, as well as in the Northeastern Hill States and the Andaman and Nicobar Islands, some tribal societies are only just being brought into contact with the modern world. Forming the most impressive mountain frontier in the world, the Himalaya to the north have some of their most magnificent peaks in East India, with Kangchendzonga towering over Sikkim and the northern hill stations of West Bengal.

# West Bengal

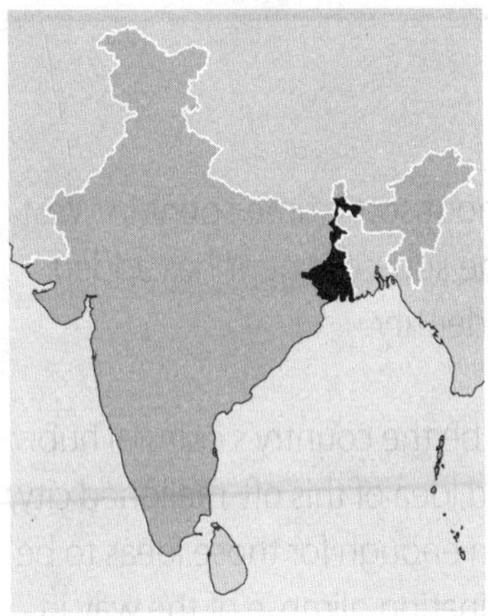



## Footprint features

# Introduction

No visit to India is complete without some time spent in West Bengal; this cultured corner of the sub-continent has added immeasurably to India's overall identity.

Kolkata is considered by many to be the country's cultural hub. Many visitors have a preconceived idea of this oft-maligned city, but a little time spent here is often enough for those ideas to be rapidly dispelled, and gives a fascinating glimpse of the way in which 13 plus million people live together. From rich to poor and educated to illiterate, Kolkatans melt together in a way that isn't seen in other cities.

Travelling north takes you through a land that has been left wonderfully fertile by both the ever shifting course of the great Ganga River and by run off from the Himalayas. Intensely populated and cultivated the area contains treasures such as the terracotta temples at Bishnupur and Shantiniketan, home of the great Bengali poet Rabindranath Tagore.



Darjeeling is synonymous with tea the world over. Made popular by the British, Darjeeling has always been a holiday destination, particularly during the summer months, when the cool mountain air provides relief from the heat of the plains. With large Tibetan and Nepali populations Darjeeling and the region around it have a very different feel to the India of the plains. The monasteries and prayer flags give a taste of the land and its peoples that lie deeper into the Himalayas.

If the mountains are too cold you can always head south from Kolkata to the Sunderbans. These mangrove forests contain a large Bengal tiger population. The area is protected and listed a World Heritage Site. Besides big cats, the park contains some fantastic wildlife, ranging from deer to crocodiles to monkeys.

## ★ Don't miss...

1 **Kolkata** Contrast Lord Curzon's Victorial Memorial with the South Park Street cemetery, the last resting place of many of the Raj's servants, and round off your day pampering your tastebuds with some king prawn cutlets followed by mishti (sweetmeats) at Kolkata's Bengali restaurants, page 584.

2 **Santiniketan** After the noise and bustle of Kolkata, spend a peaceful day at this university town, with its quiet, rural charm, page 608.

3 **Darjeeling** Visit a tea estate and trek through the flowering magnolias and rhododendron bushes in the spring, page 614.

4 **Kalimpong** There is a great Wednesday and Sunday market here with lots of unusual goods, page 621.

5 **Sunderban** If it is too cold in the hills, head down to the coast and see if you can spot a tiger swimming in the mangrove swamps, page 631.

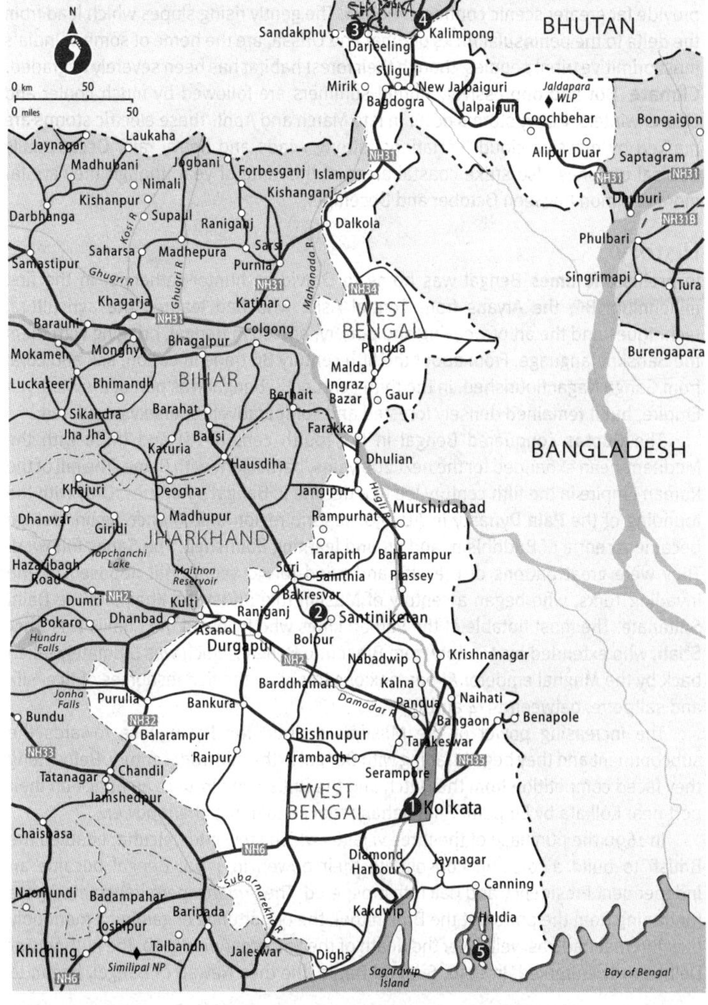

# Background → *Population: 80.2 mn. Area: 88,752 sq km.*

## The land

**Geography** Graphically described as being made up of "new mud, old mud and marsh", most of West Bengal lies on the western delta of the Ganga. Its limited higher ground, the basalt **Rajmahal Hills** just west of Murshidabad, are an extension of the ancient rocks of the peninsula. All that remains of the dense forests that once covered the state are the mangrove swamps of the **Sunderbans** in the far south and a narrow wooded belt along the southern slopes of the Himalaya. The apparently unchanging face of the Bengali countryside is highly misleading. Rivers have constantly changed their courses, and over the last 300 years the Ganga has shifted progressively east, leaving the Hugli as a relatively minor channel. Minor variations in height make enormous differences to the quality of land for farming. The chief variety in the landscape of the plains of Bengal however comes from the contrasting greens of the different varieties of rice, often producing startlingly attractive countryside. The dominating mountains to the north and the plateau and hills of the southwest provide far greater scenic contrasts though. The gently rising slopes which lead from the delta to the peninsular rocks of Bihar and Orissa, are the home of some of India's most primitive tribal peoples, though their forest habitat has been severely degraded.

**Climate** Hot and oppressively humid summers are followed by much cooler and clearer winters. Heavy storms occur in late March and April. These electric storms are marked by massive cloud formations, strong winds and heavy rain. Occasionally tropical cyclones also strike coastal areas at this time of year, though they are far more common between October and December.

## History

In **prehistoric times** Bengal was home to Dravidian hunter-gatherers. In the first millennium BC, the Aryans from Central Asia, who had learned the agricultural techniques and the art of weaving and pottery, arrived in Bengal, bringing with them the Sanskrit language. From about the fifth century BC trade in cotton, silk and coral from Ganga Nagar flourished. In the third century BC Bengal was part of the Mauryan Empire, but it remained densely forested and comparatively sparsely populated.

The **Guptas** conquered Bengal in the fourth century AD and trade with the Mediterranean expanded for the next 200 years, particularly with Rome. The fall of the Roman Empire in the fifth century led to a decline in Bengal's fortunes. Only with the founding of the **Pala Dynasty** in AD 750 was the region united once again. Bengal became a centre of Buddhism, and art and learning flourished. The **Senas** followed. They were great patrons of the arts and ruled for 50 years until deposed by the invading Turks, who began a century of Muslim rule under the Khaljis of the Delhi Sultanate. The most notable of the Pathan kings who followed the Khaljis was **Sher Shah**, who extended his territory from Bihar into Bengal, which was ultimately taken back by the Mughal emperor Akbar, anxious to obtain the rich resources of rice, silk and saltpetre, between 1574 and 1576.

The increasing power of the Muslims spurred the **Portuguese** towards the subcontinent and they began trading with Bengal in the mid-16th century. Before long they faced competition from the Dutch and the British and in 1632 an attack on their port near Kolkata by Emperor Shah Jahan reduced their merchant power.

In 1690 the purchase of the three villages which grew into Calcutta, enabled the British to build a fort and consolidate their power. In 1700, Bengal became an independent Presidency and Calcutta prospered. The *firmans* (permits) granted were for trading from the ports but the British took the opportunity of gaining a monopoly over internal trade as well. After the death of the Emperor Aurangzeb, the authority of Delhi slowly crumbled. In 1756, Siraj-ud-Daula, the then Nawab of Bengal, began to take note of Kolkata's growing wealth. Finding the British strengthening the fortifications he attacked Fort William, finding little difficulty in capturing the city. Within a year, however, Clive took the city back and then defeated the Nawab at Plassey – a turning point for the British in India. Through the 19th century West Bengal became the economic and political centre of **British India**.

Calcutta developed as the major centre of cultural and political activity in modern India. Bengali literature, drama, art and music flourished. Religious reform movements such as the **Brahmo Samaj**, under the leadership of **Raja Ram Mohan Roy** in the 1830s, grew out of the juxtaposition of traditional Hinduism with Christian missionary activity in the early 19th century. Later, one of India's greatest poets, Nobel Prize winner **Rabindranath Tagore** (1861-1941), dominated India's cultural world, breathing moral and spiritual life into the political movement for independence.

Until 1905 Bengal had included much of modern Bihar and Orissa, as well as the whole of Bengal. Lord Curzon's short-lived Partition of Bengal in 1905 roused fierce opposition, and also encouraged the split between Muslims and Hindus which finally resulted in Bengali Muslim support for the creation of Pakistan in 1947. The division into the two new states was accompanied by the migration of over five million people and appalling massacres as Hindus and Muslims fled. West Bengal was again directly affected by the struggle to create Bangladesh, when about 10 million refugees arrived from East Pakistan after 25 March 1971. Most returned after Bangladesh gained its independence in December 1971.

## Culture

The majority of the people are Bengalis. Tribal groups include Santals, Oraons and Mundas in the plains and the borders of Chota Nagpur, and Lepchas and Bhotias in the Himalaya. Over 85% of the population speak Bengali. Hindi, Urdu and tribal languages account for most of the remainder.

Bengalis are said to be obsessed about what they eat. The men often take a keen interest in buying the most important elements of the day's meal, namely fresh fish. Typically, it is river fish, the most popular being *hilsa* and *bekti* or the widely available shellfish, especially king prawns. *Bekti* is grilled or fried and is tastier than the 'fried fish' of the west as it has often been marinated in mild spices first. The prized smoked *hilsa*, although delicious, has thousands of fine bones. *Maachh* (fish) comes in many forms as *jhol* (in a thin gravy), *jhal* (spicy and hot), *malai curry* (in coconut milk, mildly spiced), chop (in a covering of mashed potato and crumbs) or *chingri maachher* cutlet (flattened king prawn 'fillets', crumbed and fried). 'Chop' and 'cutlet' are hangovers, in name only, from the days of the Raj! Bengali cooking uses mustard oil and mustard which grows in abundance, and a subtle mixture of spices. *Mishti* (sweetmeats) are another distinctive feature. Many are milk based and the famous *sandesh, roshogolla, roshomalai, pantua* and *Ladycaney* (named after Lady Canning, the wife of the first Viceroy of India!) are prepared with a kind of cottage cheese, in dozens of different textures, shapes, colours and tastes. Pale pinkish brown, *mishti doi*, is an excellent sweet yoghurt eaten as a dessert, typically sold in hand-thrown clay pots. You will only find the true flavour of Bengali cooking in someone's home, or at a couple of special Bengali restaurants.

## Crafts

**Silk** has been woven in India for more than 3,500 years. The tradition continues with the weaving of the natural coloured wild silk called *tassar*. Bengal silk, commonly found as block-printed saris, has had a revival in the exquisite brocade weaving of *baluchari*, produced in the past under royal patronage, and is carried out today in Bankura. The saris are woven in traditional style with untwisted silk and have beautiful borders and *pallu* (the end section), which often depict horses, peacocks, flowers and human figures. **Fine cotton** is woven also.

The Bankura horse has become a symbol of **pottery** in West Bengal which still flourishes in the districts of Bankura, Midnapore and Birbhum. Soft **soap-stone** is used for carving copies of temple images, while **shell** bangles are considered auspicious. **Ivory** carvers once produced superb decorative items, a skill developed in the Mughal period. Today, bone and plastic have largely replaced ivory in inlay work. **Metal** workers produce brass and bell-metal ware while the tribal *dhokra* casters still follow the ancient *cire perdue* or lost-wax method, see page 699. The Kalighat *pat* paintings are in a primitive style using bold colours and mythological themes. *Pats* go back to a time when travelling painter-storytellers went from village to village.

## Modern West Bengal

Since the mid-1960s political life has been dominated by the confrontation between the Communist Party of India Marxist (the CPM) and the Congress Party. The CPM has held power in the State Assembly continuously since June 1977. The Congress, the second largest party, has performed consistently better in the Lok Sabha parliamentary elections. Although the CPM retained power in the 1996 Assembly elections, its share of the urban vote, especially in Kolkata, dropped sharply, but Jyoti Basu, its octogenarian Chief Minister, remained one of India's most respected politicians. Jyoti Basu's retirement led some to expect an upset for the Communists. However, the Assembly elections continue to be won convincingly by the CPM-led Left Front under Chief Minister Buddhadeb Bhattacharjee.

# Kolkata (Calcutta)

→ *Phone code: 033. Colour map 4, grid C2. Population: 13.22 mn.*

*To Bengalis Kolkata is the proud intellectual capital of India, with an outstanding contribution to the arts, services, medicine and social reform in its past, and a rich contemporary cultural life. As the former Imperial capital, Kolkata retains some of the country's most striking colonial buildings, yet at the same time it is truly an Indian city. Unique in India in retaining trams and in its underground metro, you take your life in your hands each time you cross Kolkata's streets. Hugely crowded, Kolkata's maidan, the parkland, give lungs to a city packed with some of the most densely populated slums, or bustees, anywhere in the world.* » *For Sleeping, Eating and other listings, see pages 597-607.*



## Ins and outs

**Getting there** Subhas Chandra Bose airport at Dum Dum serves both international and domestic flights with a taxi or coach transfer to the city centre taking 30-45 minutes. Haora (Howrah) station, on the west bank of the Hugli, can be daunting and the taxi rank outside is often chaotic. Long-distance buses arrive at Esplanade, within 15-20 minutes' walk of most budget hotels. » *See Transport, page 604, for further details.*

*Sightseeing takes time, and Kolkata can be very hot and humid outside November to early March. Asthma sufferers find the traffic pollution very trying.*

**Getting around** You can cover much of Central Kolkata on foot. For the rest you need transport. You may not fancy using hand-pulled rickshaws (unique to Kolkata), but they become indispensable when the streets are flooded. Buses and minibuses are often jam-packed and best avoided. The electric trams can be slightly better outside peak periods. The Metro, though on a limited route, is one of the easiest ways of getting around the city. Taxis are relatively cheap but allow plenty of time to get through very congested traffic. Despite the footpath, it is not permitted to walk across the Vidyasagar Bridge. Taxi drivers expect passengers to pay the Rs 7 toll.

## Background

Calcutta, as it came to be named, was founded by the remarkable English merchant trader **Job Charnock** in 1690. He was in charge of the East India Company factory (ie warehouse) in Hugli, then the centre of British trade from eastern India. Attacks from the local Muslim ruler forced him to flee – first down river to Sutanuti and then 1,500 km south to Chennai. However, in 1690 he selected three villages – Kalikata, Sutanuti and Govindpur – where Armenian and Portuguese traders had already settled, leased them from Emperor Aurangzeb and returned to what was to become the capital of British India.

The first fort here, named after King William III (completed 1707), was on the site of the present BBD Bagh. A deep defensive moat was dug in 1742 to strengthen the fort – the Maratha ditch. The Maratha threat never materialized but the city was captured easily by the 20-year-old **Siraj-ud- Daula**, the new Nawab of Bengal, in 1756. The 146 British residents who failed to escape by the fort's river gate were imprisoned for a night in a small guard room about 6 m by 5 m with only one window – the infamous **'Black Hole of Calcutta'**. Some records suggest 64 were imprisoned and only 23 survived.

The following year **Robert Clive** re-took the city. The new Fort William was built and in 1772 Calcutta became the capital of British administration in India with Warren Hastings as the first Governor of Bengal, see page 1306. Some of Calcutta's most impressive colonial buildings were built in the years that followed, when it became the first city of British India. It was also a time of Hindu and Muslim resurgence.

Colonial Calcutta grew as new traders, soldiers, administrators and their wives arrived, establishing their exclusive social and sports clubs. Trade in cloth, silk, lac, indigo, rice, areca nut and tobacco had originally attracted the Portuguese and British to Bengal. Later Calcutta's hinterland producing jute, iron ore, tea and coal led to large British firms establishing their headquarters in the city. Calcutta prospered as the commercial and political capital of British India up to 1911, when the capital was transferred to Delhi.

Kolkata had to absorb huge numbers of migrants immediately after Partition in 1947. When Pakistan ceased trading with India in 1949, Kolkata's economy suffered a massive blow as it lost its supplies of raw jute, and its failure to attract new investment created critical economic problems. In the late 1960s the election of the Communist Party of India Marxist (**CPM**) led to a period of stability. As the party of Government the CPM has become committed to a mixed economy and has actively sought foreign private investment.

# Central Kolkata

## BBD Bagh (Dalhousie Square) and around

Many historic Raj buildings surround the square which is quietest before 0900. Re-named Benoy Badal Dinesh (BBD) Bagh after three Bengali martyrs, the square has a small artificial lake, fed by natural springs. On Strand Road North is the dilapidated **Silver Mint** (1824-1831). The **Writers' Building** (1780), designed by Thomas Lyon as the trading HQ of the East India Company, was refaced in 1880. It is now the state Government Secretariat. The classical block with 57 sets of identical windows was built like barracks inside. **Mission Row** (now RN Mukharji Road) is Kolkata's oldest street, and contains the **Old Mission Church** (consecrated 1770), built by the Swedish missionary Johann Kiernander.

South of BBD Bagh is the imposing **Raj Bhavan** (1799- 1802), the residence of the Governor of West Bengal, formerly Government House. It was modelled on Kedleston Hall in Derbyshire, England (later Lord Curzon's home), and designed by **Charles Wyatt**, one of many Bengal engineers who based their designs on famous British

# Kolkata

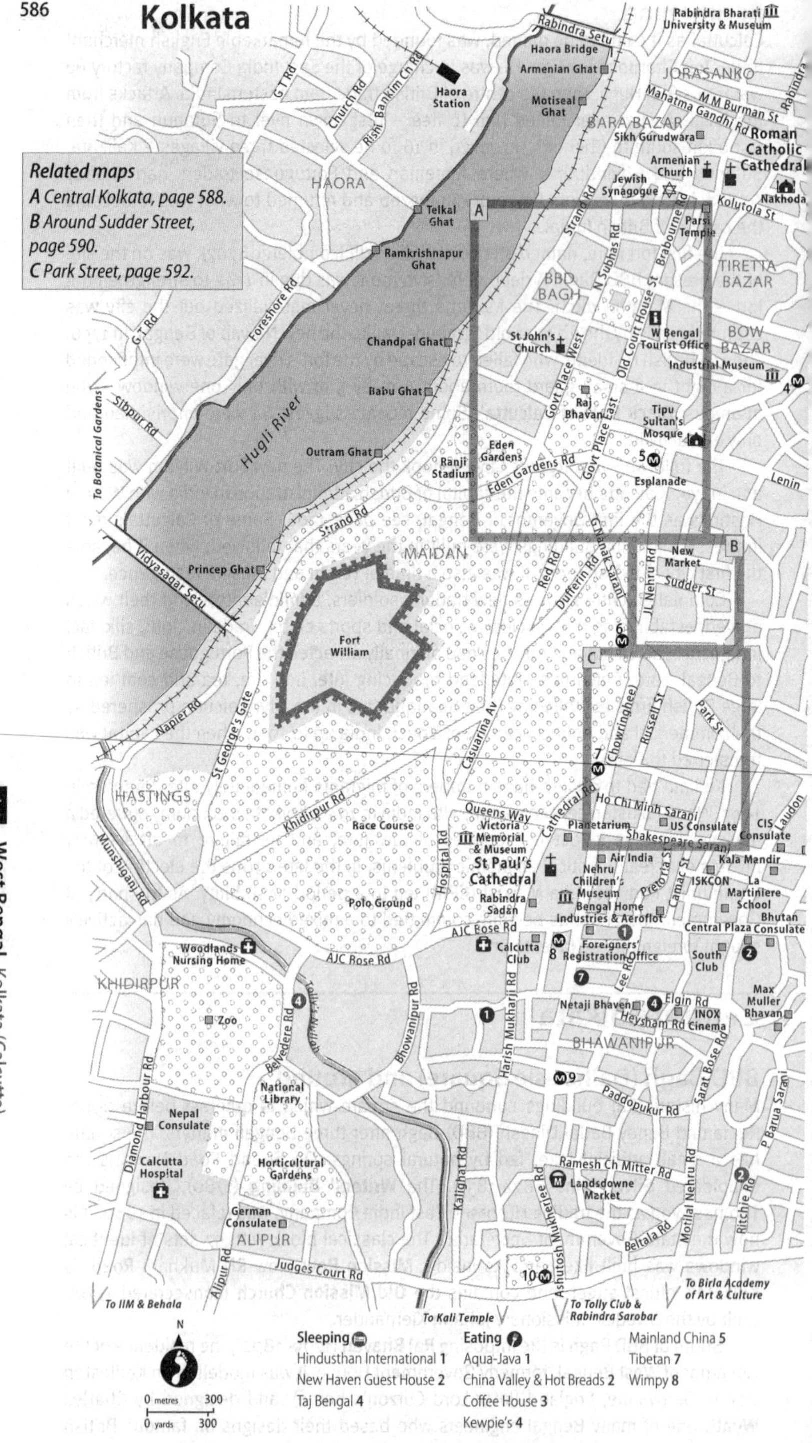
Related maps
A Central Kolkata, page 588.
B Around Sudder Street, page 590.
C Park Street, page 592.
Rabindra Setu
Haora Bridge
Armenian Ghat
Haora Station
Motiseal Ghat
Rabindra Bharati University & Museum
JORASANKO
M M Burman St
Mahatma Gandhi Rd
BARA BAZAR
Sikh Gurudwara
Roman Catholic Cathedral
Armenian Church
Jewish Synagogue
Nakhoda
Kolutola St
Parsi Temple
HAORA
Telkal Ghat
Ramkrishnapur Ghat
G T Rd
Church Rd
Rishi Bankim Ch Rd
Foreshore Rd
Strand Rd
N Subhas Rd
Brabourne Rd
TIRETTA BAZAR
BBD BAGH
Old Court House St
W Bengal Tourist Office
BOW BAZAR
St John's Church
Chandpal Ghat
Industrial Museum
Govt Place West
Govt Place East
Babu Ghat
Raj Bhavan
Tipu Sultan's Mosque
Sibpur Rd
To Botanical Gardens
Hugli River
Outram Ghat
Eden Gardens
Ranji Stadium
Eden Gardens Rd
Esplanade
Lenin
MAIDAN
New Market
Sudder St
JL Nehru Rd
Princep Ghat
Vidyasagar Setu
Red Rd
Dufferin Rd
G Nanak Sarani
Fort William
Chowringhee
Russell St
Park St
Napier Rd
St George's Gate
Casuarina Av
HASTINGS
Khidirpur Rd
Race Course
Queens Way
Victoria Memorial & Museum
Cathedral Rd
Planetarium
Ho Chi Minh Sarani
US Consulate
CIS Consulate
Laudon
Shakespeare Sarani
St Paul's Cathedral
Air India
Kala Mandir
Nehru Children's Museum
Pretoria St
Camac St
ISKCON
La Martiniere School
Munshiganj Rd
Hospital Rd
Polo Ground
Rabindra Sadan
Bengal Home Industries & Aeroflot
Bhutan Consulate
Central Plaza
AJC Bose Rd
Woodlands Nursing Home
Calcutta Club
Foreigners' Registration Office
South Club
KHIDIRPUR
Harish Mukharji Rd
Lee Rd
Max Muller Bhavan
Zoo
Tolly's Nullah
Belvedere Rd
Bhowanipur Rd
Netaji Bhaven
Elgin Rd
INOX Cinema
Heysham Rd
BHAWANIPUR
Sarat Bose Rd
Diamond Harbour Rd
National Library
Paddopukur Rd
P Barua Sarani
Nepal Consulate
Calcutta Hospital
Horticultural Gardens
Kalighat Rd
Ramesh Ch Mitter Rd
Landsdowne Market
Motilal Nehru Rd
Ritchie Rd
German Consulate
ALIPUR
Ashutosh Mukherjee Rd
Beltala Rd
Judges Court Rd
Alipur Rd
To IIM & Behala
To Kali Temple
To Tolly Club & Rabindra Sarobar
To Birla Academy of Art & Culture
N
0 metres 300
0 yards 300
Sleeping
Hindusthan International 1
New Haven Guest House 2
Taj Bengal 4
Eating
Aqua-Java 1
China Valley & Hot Breads 2
Coffee House 3
Kewpie's 4
Mainland China 5
Tibetan 7
Wimpy 8

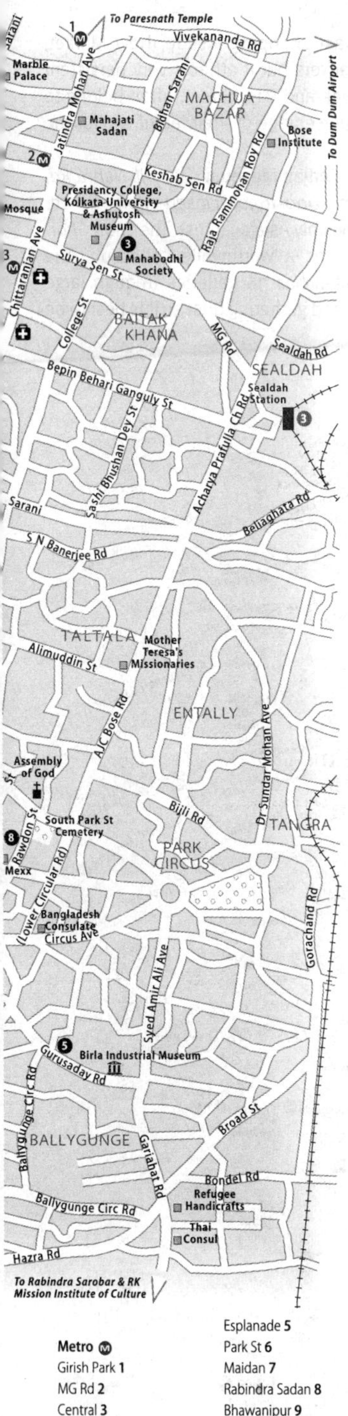


buildings. Entry is restricted. The **Town Hall** (1813) has been converted into a museum. The **High Court** (1872) was modelled on the medieval cloth merchants' hall at Ypres in Flanders.

**Ochterlony Monument** (1828), re-named Shahid Minar (Martyrs' Memorial) in 1969, was built as a memorial to **Sir David Ochterlony,** who led East India Company troops against the Nepalese in 1814-1816. The 46-m tall Greek Doric column has an Egyptian base and is topped by a Turkish cupola.

**St John's Church** (1787) ⓘ *0900-1200, 1700-1800*, like the later St Andrew's Kirk (1818), was modelled partially on St Martin-in-the-Fields, London. The soft sub-soil did not allow it to have a tall spire and architecturally it was thought to be 'full of blunders'. Verandahs were added to the north and south in 1811 to reduce the glare of the sun. Inside are Warren Hastings's desk and chair and the tomb of Bishop Middleton, first Bishop of Calcutta. 'The Last Supper', by **Johann Zoffany** in the south aisle, shows the city's residents dressed as the Apostles. Job Charnock is buried in the old cemetery. His octagonal mausoleum, the oldest piece of masonry in the city, is of Pallavaram granite (from Madras Presidency), which is named charnockite after him. The monument to the **Black Hole of Calcutta** was brought here from Dalhousie Square (BBD Bagh) in 1940.

## Eden Gardens

ⓘ *Usually open for matches only, a small tip at Gate 14 gains entry on other days.*
These gardens, which are situated in the northwest corner of the Maidan, were named after Lord Auckland's sisters Emily and Fanny Eden. There are pleasant walks, a lake and a small Burmese pagoda (typical of this type of Pyatthat). Laid out in 1834, part forms the Ranji Stadium where the first cricket match was played in 1864. Today, Test matches (November-February), international tennis championships and other sports fixtures attract crowds of 100,000.

## Around Sudder Street

Conveniently close to Chowringhee and the vast shopping arcade, New Market, Sudder Street is the focus for Kolkata's backpackers but it attracts very persistent touts and drug pushers. Beggars on Chowringhee and Park Street, often belong to organized syndicates who have to pay a large percentage of their 'earnings' for the privilege of working that area.

Around the corner from Sudder Street is the **Indian Museum** ⓘ *27 JL Nehru Rd, T033 2499902, Mar-Nov 1000-1700, Dec-Feb 1000-1630; closed Mon, Rs 10, foreigners Rs 150, cameras Rs 50, guidebook*, possibly Asia's largest. The *'Jadu Ghar'* (House of Magic) was founded in 1814 and has a worthwhile collection. The colonnaded Italianate building facing the Maidan has 36 galleries (though large sections are often closed off). Parts are poorly lit and gathering dust so it is best to be

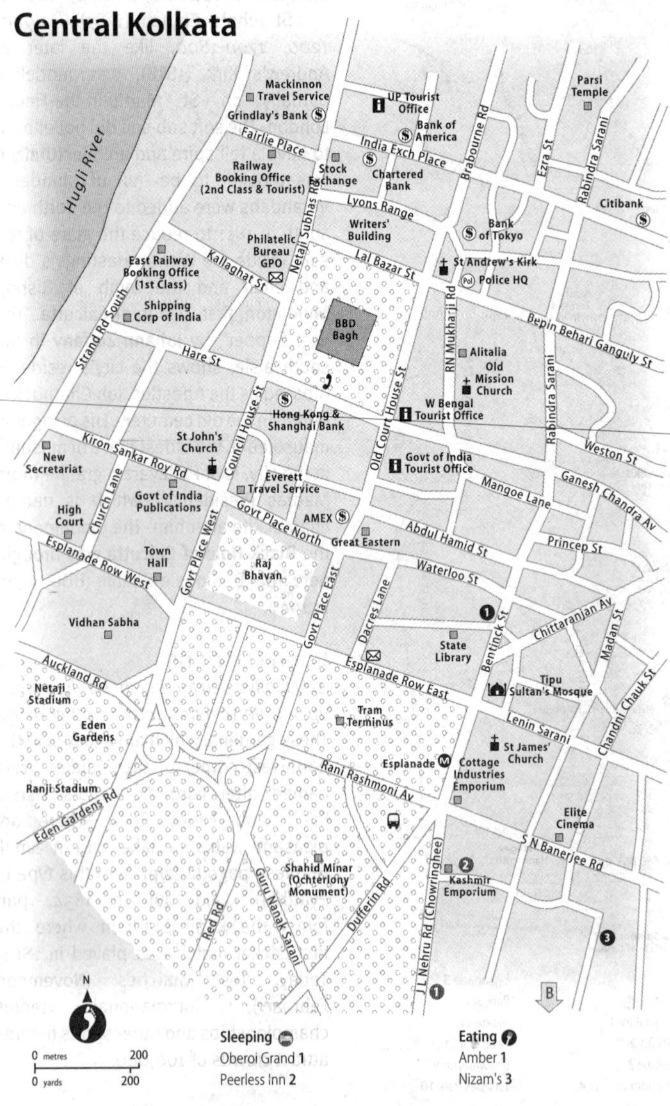

## Kolkata's place in the cosmic dance

Kolkata's site was particularly holy to Hindus. According to one myth, **King Daksa** was enraged when his daughter **Sati** married **Siva**. He organized a **Yajna** (grand sacrifice) to which he invited everyone in the kingdom – except his son-in-law. Distraught, **Kali** (Sati) threw herself on the sacrificial flames. Siva in turn arrived on the scene to find his wife's body already burnt. Tearing it from the flames, he started his dance of cosmic destruction. All the other gods, witnessing the devastation that Siva was causing in his anguish, pleaded with Vishnu to step in and end the chaos. **Vishnu** intercepted him with his *chakra* (discus-like weapon) and, in order to dislodge Kali's body from Siva's shoulder, chopped it into 51 pieces, which were flung far and wide. The place where each one fell became a place of pilgrimage – a *pithasthana*. Kali's little toe fell at Kali Ghat. The place, Kalikshetra or Kalikata, gave the city its name.

selective: geological collection including Siwalik fossils, good natural history and anthropology, outstanding exhibits from the Harappa and Moenjodaro periods, prized collection of Buddhist art, miniature paintings, 'Art and Textile' with ivory, glass and silverware, 'Theme Gallery' with rare paintings and 200-year-old hand-drawn maps, and many more. You need permission to see the exceptional collection of over 50,000 coins. Allow a couple of hours.

## Park Street

**South Park St Cemetery** was opened in 1767 to accommodate the large number of the British who died serving their country. The heavily inscribed, decaying headstones, obelisks, pyramids and urns have been somewhat restored. A good booklet is available. Allow about 30 minutes. If alone, avoid going when it is deserted. A security guard opens the gate for foreigners, and will expect you to sign the visitors' book.

The cemetery is a quiet space on the south side of one of Kolkata's busiest streets. Gardners are actively trying to beautify the grounds. Several of the inscriptions make interesting reading. Death, often untimely, came from tropical diseases or other hazards such as battles, childbirth and even melancholia. More uncommonly, it was an excess of alcohol, or as for Sir Thomas D'Oyly, through "an inordinate use of the hokkah". Rose Aylmer died after eating too many pineapples! Tombs include those of **Col Kyd**, founder of the Botanical Gardens, and the great oriental scholar **Sir William Jones**.

**Asiatic Society** ⓘ *1 Park St, weekdays 1000-2000 , weekends 1000-1700*, the oldest institution of Oriental studies in the world, was founded in 1784 by the great Orientalist, Sir William Jones. It is a treasure house of 150,000 books and 60,000 ancient manuscripts in most Asian languages. The museum includes an Asokan edict, rare coins and paintings.

## The Maidan

This area, 200 years ago, was covered in dense jungle. Often called the 'lungs' of the city, it is a unique 'green', covering over 400 ha along Chowringhee (JL Nehru Road). Larger than New York's Central Park, it is perhaps the largest urban park in the world! In it stands Fort William and several club houses providing tennis, football, rugby, cricket and even crown green bowls. Thousands each day pursue a hundred different interests – from early morning yogis, model plane enthusiasts, weekend cricketers and performers earning their living, to vast political gatherings.

## Chowringhee and around

You can still see some of the old imposing structures with pillared verandahs (designed by Italian architects as residences of prominent Englishmen) though modern high rise buildings have transformed the skyline of this ancient pilgrim route to Kalighat.

**St Paul's Cathedral** ⓘ *0900-1200, 1500-1800, 5 services on Sun*, is the original metropolitan church of British India. Completed in 1847, its Gothic tower (dedicated in 1938) was designed to replace the earlier steeples which were destroyed by earthquakes. The cathedral has a fine altar piece, three 'Gothic' stained glass windows, two Florentine frescoes and the great West window by **Burne-Jones**. The

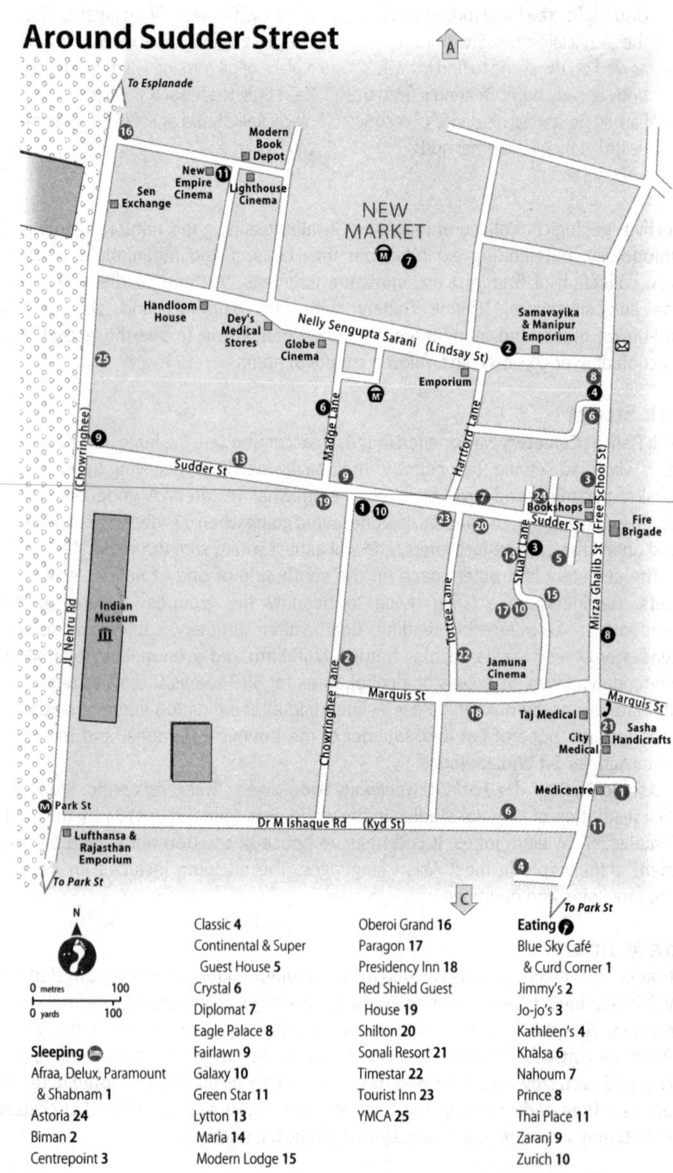

original stained-glass East window, intended for St George's Windsor, was destroyed by a cyclone in 1964 and was replaced by the present one four years later.

**Academy of Fine Arts** ⓘ *Cathedral Rd, closed Mon, 1500-1800*, was founded in 1933. The collection includes miniature paintings, textiles, works of Jamini Roy, Tagore and Desmond Doig and modern Indian sculpture in the gardens. Galleries exhibit works of local artists. Guide service and occasional films.

**Victoria Memorial** ⓘ *Mar-Oct 1000-1630, Nov-Feb 1000-1530; museum closed Mon (very crowded on Sun), 1000-1530, Rs 5 (foreigners Rs 150), guided tours at 1030 (allow at least 1 hr), cameras not permitted. Sound & Light show, summer 1945, winter 1915, 45 mins, Rs 20 front seats, Rs 10 elsewhere*, (1906-21) was designed by Lord Curzon. The white marble monument to Queen Victoria and the Raj designed in Italian Renaissance-Mughal style stands in large, well-kept grounds with ornamental pools. A seated bronze Queen Victoria dominates the approach, while a marble statue stands in the main hall where visitors sometimes leave flowers at her feet! The building is illuminated in the evening; the 'musical fountain' is a special draw. The statues over the entrance porches (including Motherhood, Prudence and Learning), and around the central dome (of Art, Architecture, Justice, Charity) came from Italy. The impressive weather vane, a 5-m tall bronze winged figure of Victory weighing three tons, looks tiny from below. The principal gallery, covering the history of the city, includes a wealth of Raj memorabilia. There are fine miniatures, a rare collection of Persian manuscripts, and paintings by **Zoffany**, the two **Daniells**, and Samuel **Davis**.

### Fort William

After the defeat in 1756, see page 582, the British built a new massive fort on the site of the village of Govindapur. Designed to be impregnable, it was roughly octagonal and large enough to house all the Europeans in the city in case of an attack. Water from the river Hugli was channelled to fill the wide moat and the jungle around it was cleared to give a clear field of fire, which later became the Maidan. The barracks, stables, arsenal, prison and St Peter's Church are still there. Today the fort is the Eastern Region's Military Headquarters so you need permission to enter.

## North Kolkata

### Dakshineshwar Kali temple

On the opposite side of the river from Belur Math, this temple built in 1847 by Rani Rashmoni. The 12 smaller temples in the courtyard are dedicated to Siva, Radha and Krishna. Because of the Rani's low caste, no priest would serve there until Ramakrishna's elder brother agreed and was succeeded by Ramakrishna himself. Here, **Ramakrishna** achieved his spiritual vision of the unity of all religions. The temple is often crowded, and is open to all faiths.

### Chitpur and Kumartuli

South of the temple is Chitpur and Kumartuli. Off Chitpur Road, the *kumars* or potters work all year, preparing clay images around cores of bamboo and straw. For generations they have been making life-size idols for the *pujas* or festivals, particularly of Goddess Durga on a lion, slaying the demon. The images are usually unbaked since they are immersed in the holy river at the end of the festival. As the time of the *pujas* approaches, you will see thousands of images, often very brightly painted and gaudily dressed, awaiting the final finishing touch by the master painter. There are also *shola* artists, who make decorations for festivals and weddings .

Just north of the Belgachia metro station is the ornate Digambar Jain **Paresnath Temple** ⓘ *0600-1200, 1500-1900, no leather*, dedicated to the 10th Tirthankara. Consecrated around 1867, it is richly decorated with mirrors and Venetian glass mosaics.

## College Street

This is the heart of intellectual Kolkata with the **university** and several academic institutions, including the old **Sanskrit College** and the élite **Presidency College**. Europeans and Indian benefactors established the Hindu College (1817) to provide a "liberal education". In 1855, this became the Presidency College. A centre for 19th-century Bengali writers, artists and reformers, it spawned the early 20th-century Swadeshi Movement. The famous **'Coffee House'** (opened in 1944), the smoke-filled, cavernous haunt of the city's intelligentsia, still sells a good cup of coffee. Along the pavements are interesting second-hand book stalls. **Asutosh Museum** ⓘ *University Centenary Building, closed Sun and University holidays, weekdays 1030-1630, Sat 1030-1500*, of eastern Indian art and antiquity includes textiles, terracotta figures and Bengali folk art, but is poorly maintained with large sections frequently closed off.

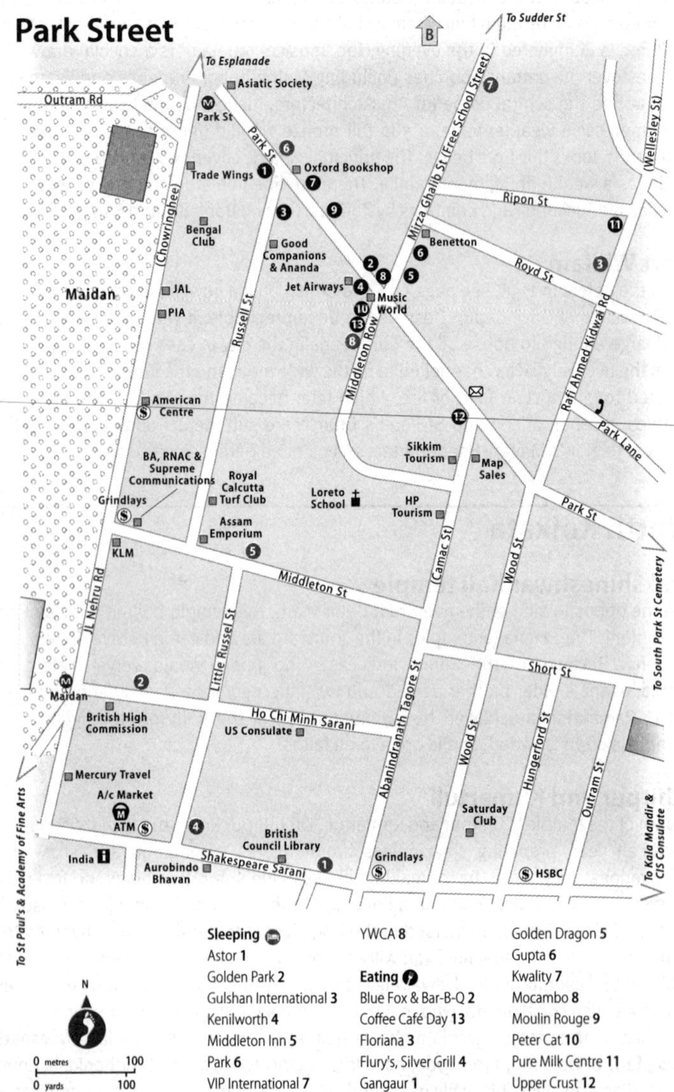

## Worship of the clay goddess

Durga Puja, the 17th-century festival in honour of the 'clay goddess', precedes the full moon in late September/early October, when all offices and institutions close down and the Metro only operates from the late afternoon.

Images of the 10-armed, three-eyed goddess, a form of Shakti or Kali (see page 1331) astride her 'vehicle' the lion, portray Durga slaying Mahisasura, the evil 'buffalo' demon. Durga, shown with her four children Lakshmi, Sarasvati, Ganesh and Kartik, is worshipped in hundreds of brightly illuminated and beautifully decorated pandals (marquees) made of bamboo and coloured cloth. The priests perform prayers at appointed times in the morning and evening. On the fourth and last day of festivities, huge and often emotionally charged processions follow devotees who carry the clay figures to be immersed in the river at many points along the banks. The potters return to collect clay from the river bank once again for the following year.

You can see the imagemakers in Kumartuli (see page 591) a few days earlier and visit the *pandals* early in the evening, before they become crowded. Local communities are immensely proud of their *pandals* and no effort is spared to put on the most impressive display. The images are decorated with intricate silver, golden or *shola* (white pith) ornaments, there are 'moving' electric light displays and huge structures are built (sometimes resembling a temple) in order to win competitions. The WB Tourist Bureau offers an all-night bus tour (Rs 50) as well as a two-hour launch trip on the Hugli to watch the immersion ceremony on the last night.

### Rabindra Bharati University Museum

ⓘ *6/4 Dwarakanath Tagore Lane (red walls visible down lane opposite 263 Rabindra Sarani), 1000-1700, Sat 1000-1330, Sun and holidays 1100-1400.*

This museum houses the life and works of Rabindranath Tagore, who won the Nobel prize for Literature in 1913, and the 19th-century Renaissance movement in Bengal, in his family home.

### Marble Palace

ⓘ *closed Mon and Thu, 1000-1600, free pass from WB Tourist Bureau, 3/2 BBD Bagh, 24 hrs ahead, shoes must be removed, photography restricted.*

The 'Palace' is in *Chor Bagan* (Thieves' Garden) at 46 Muktaram Babu Street. The one-man collection of Raja Rajendra Mullick is in his ornate home (1835) with an Italianate courtyard, classical columns, a large tank and Egyptian sphinxes. Six sleeping marble lions and statuary grace the lawns. The long galleries are crammed with statues, pottery, mirrors, chandeliers and English, Dutch and Italian paintings, disorganized and gathering dust. Allow 45 minutes. The rambling museum on two floors has curiosity appeal.

### Jorasanko and Haora Bridge area

Jorasanko, north of the Marble Palace, is the family home of Rabindranath Tagore, see page 609. This is also the **Rabindra Bharati** University (see also museums below). Further north on Baghbazar Street is the **Girish Mancha**, the Government theatre complex. The gorgeously well-kept **Armenian Church** of Holy Nazareth (1724) reminds us of the important trading role the small Armenian community who mostly came from Iran, played from the 17th century. Though the church is locked on weekdays you may ask to look around as the vestry is open during office hours. The 200 or so

 Armenians in the city still hold a service in Armenian in one of their two churches here every Sunday. Their college in Mirza Ghalib Street only has about half-a-dozen pupils since it admits only those of Armenian descent. On its east side is the **Roman Catholic Cathedral** (1797), built by the Portuguese. The **Jewish** community, mostly Sephardic, of Baghdadi origin, was also once very prominent in commerce. Their two cavernous synagogues, the grander in Canning Street, are well maintained and still used for services on alternate Saturdays. There are only around 50 Jews left in the city who continue to congregate at Nahoum's bakery in the New Market; the Jewish Girls School in Park Street has no pupils from the community.

**Haora Bridge** (pronounced How-ra), or 'Rabindra Setu', was opened in 1943. This single-span cantilever bridge, a prominent landmark, replaced the old pontoon bridge, which joined the city with Haora and the railway station. To avoid affecting river currents and silting, the two 80-m high piers rise from road level; the 450-m span expands by a metre on a hot day. Best avoided in rush hour, but enjoy the sight of wrestlers underneath the bridge. The 1993 **Vidyasagar Setu**, further south, has eased the burden (no pedestrians).

## South Kolkata

### Kali Temple

ⓘ *0500-2000.* This is the temple to Kali (1809), the patron goddess of Kolkata, usually seen in her blood-thirsty form garlanded with skulls. There was an older temple here, where the goddess's little toe is said to have fallen when **Siva** carried her charred corpse in a frenzied dance of mourning, and she was cut into pieces by Vishnu's *chakra*, see page 589. Non-Hindus have limited access to this important Hindu pilgrimage centre. Where once human sacrifices were made, only goats are offered daily on two wooden blocks to thesouth of the temple. When visiting the temple, priests will attempt to snare foreigners for the obligatory 'puja'. A barrage may start as for away as 500 m from the temple. Don't be fooled in to handing over your shoes and surcoming to any priests until you are clearly inside the temple, despite being shown 'priest i.d.' cards. Once settled with a priest the experience can be well worth the initial hassle. An acceptable minimum donation is Rs 50-60. Books showing previous donations of Rs 1000's are probably faked. Having done the puja, you'll probably be left alone to soak up the atmosphere.

### Mother Teresa's Homes

Mother Teresa, an Albanian by birth, came to India to teach as a Loreto nun in 1931. She started her Order of the Missionaries of Charity in Kalighat to serve the destitute and dying 19 years later. *Nirmal Hriday* ('Pure Heart'), near the Kali Temple, the first 'home' for the dying was opened in 1952. Mother Teresa died on 5 September 1997 but her work continues. You may see nuns in their white cotton saris with blue borders busy working in the many homes, clinics and orphanages in the city. Anyone interested in voluntary work should write in advance to the office at the Mother House ⓘ *54A AJC Bose (Lower Circular) Rd, T033 22497115*. There is also a **museum** ⓘ *T033 22449267, closed Thu, 0800-1200, 1500-1800.*

### National Library

ⓘ *Weekdays, 1000-1800.* The former winter residence of the Lieutenant Governors of Bengal is on Belvedere Road in Alipur. Warren Hastings was given the site on which he built an "ordinary Anglo-Indian building", which later additions made more impressive. Built in the Renaissance Italian style, it stands in large wooded grounds. There are 15 km of closed stacks while the reading room has 10,000 reference books. There is a Rare Books Section and the **Asutosh Mookerjee** collection.

## Birla Academy of Art and Culture and Birla Industrial Museum



The Academy ⓘ *108/109 Southern Ave, T033 24662843, closed Mon, 1600-2000*, housed in a modern high rise concentrates on medieval and contemporary paintings and sculpture. It is worth visiting. **Birla Industrial and Technological Museum** ⓘ *19A Gurusaday Rd, Tue-Sun, 1000-1700, Rs 7; Rs 2 for coal mine etc*, has some interesting models and displays. Try the mock coal mine tour; give the robots a miss.

# Haora (Howrah) and the West Bank

North of the city, some 16 km across the Ganga, is **Belur Math** ⓘ *winter, 0630-1100, 1600-1930; 1530-1900*, the international headquarters of the **Ramakrishna Mission**, founded in 1899 by **Swami Vivekananda**, a disciple of the 19th-century Hindu saint Ramakrishna (see page 887). He preached the unity of all religions and to symbolize this the *Math* ('monastery') synthesizes Hindu, Christian and Islamic architectural styles in a peaceful and meditative atmosphere.

**Botanical Gardens** ⓘ *0700-1700, avoid Sun and public holidays when it is very crowded*, on the west bank of the Hugli, 20 km south from BBD Bagh, were founded in 1787 by the East India Company. The flourishing 250-year-old **banyan tree**, with a circumference of over 300 m, is perhaps the largest in the world. The original trunk was destroyed by lightning in 1919 but over 1,500 offshoots form an impressive sight. The Orchid Houses and Palm House are closed on Sunday. **National Herbarium** ⓘ *closed Sun and 2nd Sat, 1015-1600*, has 1½ million specimens of dried plants, the largest collection in South and South East Asia. The gardens are sadly neglected (dirty, rubbish heaps, no waste bins, tree labels missing) but can still make a welcome change from the city. To reach the Botanical Gardens catch the white and orange CTC bus from Esplanade across the 'new' bridge which takes 15 minutes. Avoid the slower Bus 55 and minibuses which may take an hour negotiating the old bridge.

# Excursions

There are several interesting places within reach of a day's outing. Road travel is very slow so leave central Kolkata well before 0800 to avoid the worst traffic. For visiting the Sunderbans, see page 631.

## Barrackpur and Hugli District → *25 km away.*

The riverside Gandhi Ghat has a museum and there is a pleasant garden in memory of Jawaharlal Nehru. The bronze Raj statues which were removed from their pedestals in Central Kolkata after Independence have found their way to the gardens of the bungalow of the former Governor (now a hospital) in Barrackpur. The tower in the garden was part of the river signalling system.

Many European nations had outposts along the River Hugli. Hugli District has a rich history. When the Mughals lost power, several of the ancient seats of earlier rulers of Bengal became centres of foreign trade. The Portuguese and British settled at Hugli, the Dutch chose Chinsura, the French Chandernagore, the Danes Serampore, the Greeks had an outpost at Rishra and the Germans and Austrians one at Bhadreswar!

## Srirampur (Serampore) → *24 km north of Kolkata.*

Founded by the Danes in 1616 as Fredricnagore, 'Serampore', a garden city, became a Danish colony in 1755. From the early 19th century it was the centre of missionary activity, until sold to the East India Company in 1845. The Government House, two churches and a Danish cemetery remain. **College of Textile Technology** ⓘ *12 Carey Rd, 1000-1630 (Sat 1000-1300)*. The Baptist missionaries **Carey**, **Marshman** and **Ward** came to Serampore since they were not welcomed by the English administrators in Calcutta. They set up the Baptist Mission Press, which by 1805 was printing in seven Indian languages. **Serampore College** (1818) ⓘ *visit Mon-Fri 1000-1600, Sat 1000-1300, with permission from the Principal*, India's first Christian Theological college, was allowed to award degrees by the Danish king in 1829. The library has rare Sanskrit, Pali and Tibetan manuscripts and the Bible in over 40 Asian languages.

## Chandernagore

The former French colony, which dates back to 1673, was one of the tiny pockets of non-British India that did not gain independence in 1947, but was handed over to India after a referendum in 1950. The churches, convents and cemeteries of the French are still there, although the old French street names have been replaced by Bengali. The former Quai de Dupleix, with its riverfront benches, still has a somewhat Gallic air. The Bhubanesvari and Nandadulal **temples** are worth visiting, especially during *Jagaddhatri Puja*. **'Institute Chandernagar'** ⓘ *weekdays 1600-1830, Sun 1100-11700, closed Thu*, at the **Residency** has interesting documents and relics of the French in India. The orange-painted Italian missionary **church** (1726) also stands witness to Chandernagore's European past.

## Chinsura and Hugli

The Dutch acquired Chinsura from the Nawab of Murshidabad in 1628 and built the **Fort Gustavus**, but it was exchanged with Sumatra (Indonesia) and became British in 1825. The octagonal **Dutch church** (1678) with its cemetery nearby, a 17th-century Armenian church and three East India Company barracks remain. The Dutch are still remembered at the **Shandesvar Siva temple** on special occasions, when the lingam is bizarrely decked in Western clothes and a Dutch sword!

The Portuguese set up a 'factory' in Hugli in 1537 but Emperor Shah Jahan took the important trading post in 1632. The East India Company built their 'factory' in 1651, destroyed in skirmishes which marked the following six years, but Clive regained Hugli for the Company in 1757.

The Shi'a **Imambara** of Hazi Mohammed Mohasin (1836-1876) has fine marble inlay decoration, a silver pulpit and elaborate lanterns. In **Chota Pandua** nearby, interesting Muslim buildings include the ruins of the 14th-century Bari Masjid which has elements of Buddhist sculpture. **Amulya Pratnasala Museum** ⓘ *closed 2nd and 4th Tue, Wed, 1400-2100*, in Rajbalhat has sculpture, coins, terracottas and manuscripts.

**Kolkata excursions**

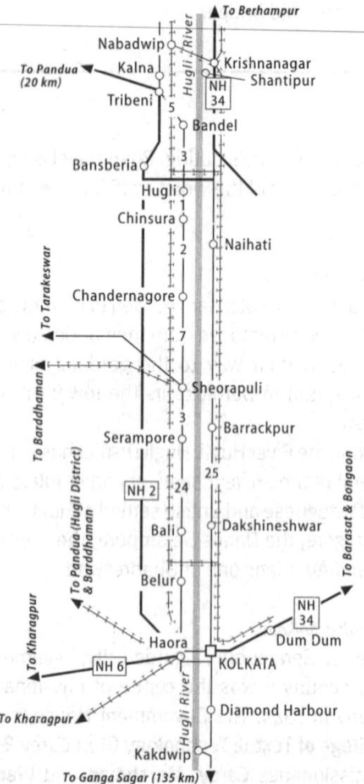


## Bandel

Bandel (Portuguese *bandar* – 'wharf') is now a railway junction town. The Portuguese built **Bandel Church** to Our Lady of the Rosary around 1660, on the site of an older Augustinian monastery. The keystone of the original church

(1599), perhaps the earliest in Bengal, is on the riverside gate. Destroyed in 1640 by Shah Jahan, the church was reinstated 20 years later. The seafaring Portuguese believed that the statue of Our Lady of Happy Voyages in the bell tower could work miracles. Lost in the river, while being carried to save it from Shah Jahan's soldiers, it miraculously 'reappeared' two centuries later. The 18th-century stone and terracotta **Hanseswari Temple** is 4 km away.

## Tribeni and Pandua

Originally '*Saptagram*' (seven villages), **Tribeni** (three rivers) is particularly holy, being at the confluence of the Ganga, Saraswati and Kunti. It has many Hindu temples and 11th to 12th-century Vaishnavite and Buddhist structures. The remains of the **Mazar of Zafarkhan Ghazi** (1313), the earliest mausoleum in eastern India, shows how black basalt sculpture and columns of earlier Hindu temples and palaces were incorporated into Muslim buildings. **Pandua** (Hugli District) has several remains of the Pala and Sena periods. Shah Sufi-ud-din is thought to have built the 39-m **Victory Tower** after defeating the local Hindu ruler in 1340. Its circular base had a court house. Outside, a staircase spirals up the fluted surface, while inside there is enamelled decoration. Hoards of Kushana and Gupta Dynasty gold coins have been found in nearby **Mahanad**.

## Kalna

The town north of Pandua, centred on the Maharaja of Burdwan's palace, has several fine 18th-century terracotta temples. Look for the Ramayana scenes on the large Lalji (1739), Krishna panels on the Krishnachandra (1752), assorted friezes on the Ananta Vasudeva (1754) and the later Pratapesvara (1849). Across the way is the unusual circular Siva temple (1809) with 108 small double-vaulted shrines. Kalna has trains from Kolkata and rickshaws at the station, 3 km from the temples.

## Nabadwip

The birthplace of Sri Chaitanya, see page 614, is a pilgrimage centre for his followers and the river ghats are lined with temples where devotees worship by singing *keertans* and *bhajans*. **ISKCON** (International Society for Krishna Consciousness) has its Chandrodaya Mandir at **Mayapur** ⓘ *until 1300*, across the river. Nabadwip has trains from Sealdah and Haora, and ferries across to Mayapur.

## Sleeping

Watch out for 10% luxury tax, 10% service charge and 20% expenditure tax. For usual facilities in different categories, see page 57. Medium price and budget hotels attracting foreigners are concentrated in the Sudder St area. Mid-priced hotels often have a few a/c rooms but may not have a generator and so have power cuts, especially in summer. For telephone number changes T1952 (dial old number to get new). 'Ask Me' T033 24746363, advises on local affairs/numbers/addresses etc.

**Central Kolkata** *p585, maps p588, p590, p592*

**LL Oberoi Grand**, 15 JL Nehru, T033 22492323, oberoi@giascl01.vsnl.net.in. 218 rooms and suites in an atmospheric Victorian building opposite the Maidan, exquisitely restored, suites have giant 4-posters, tea lounge, excellent restaurants including French, lovely pool for residents.

**LL Park**, 17 Park St, T033 22499000 , www.theparkhotels.com. 150 rooms in this trendy designer hotel, good Chinese restaurant, health club, service not always up to decor, entrance themed on underground car park.

**LL Taj Bengal**, 34B Belvedere Rd, Alipore, T033 22233939, www.tajhotels.com. 250 rooms, railway 10 km, opulent and modern, restaurants are plush, imaginative, intimate, with good food (ground floor Indian cheaper than 5th floor), leisurely service (unusual Bengali breakfast), *Khazana* shop for excellent textiles, *Baluchari* saris, *kantha* embroidery etc.

**AL Kenilworth**, 1 & 2 Little Russell St, T033 22823939, www.kenilworthhotels.com.

105 well appointed rooms with good buffet breakfast and coffee shop (excellent lunch buffet), English style pub (members and residents only), quiet. Recommended.

**AL-A Golden Park**, 13 Ho Chi Minh Sarani, T033 22883939. 78 rooms 'boutique hotel' with all facilities including pool and health club, restaurants, London-style pub (residents and members only).

**A Lytton**, 14 Sudder St, T033 22521872, www.lyttonhotelindia.com. 74 comfortable, tastefully furnished rooms, better in new block, good restaurants, bar, efficient, good value.

**B Astor**, 15 Shakespeare Sarani, T033 22829950, www.astorcalcutta.com. 35 comfortable a/c rooms with bath tubs (inferior annexe), open-air restaurant.

**B Fairlawn**, 13A Sudder St, T033 22521510, www.fairlawnhotel.com. 20 a/c old-fashioned rooms (US$50 full board), semi-formal meals at set times. The hotel and management provide a throwback to the Raj, bric-à-brac everywhere, quite a place.

**B Gulshan International**, 21B Royd St, T033 22290566, alambhai12@hotmail.com. 16 clean, comfortable rooms, complimentary breakfast, efficient staff.

**B Middleton Inn**, 10 Middleton St, T033 22160449, mchamber@vsnl.net. 19 pleasantly furnished a/c rooms with hot bath (fridge, TV), not particularly spacious though spotlessly clean, original art, quiet and convenient, breakfast included. Recommended.

**B Peerless Inn**, 12 JL Nehru Rd, T033 22280301, www.peerlesshotels.com. 123 decent rooms, modern business hotel but drab exterior, excellent **Aaheli** restaurant.

**B VIP International**, 51 Mirza Ghalib St, T033 22296428, hvipcal@hotmail.com. 33 a/c rooms, clean and comfortable, hot bath, friendly efficient staff make up for a fairly drab hotel.

**B-C Presidency Inn**, 2/1 Marquis St, T033 22520057, www.hotelpresidencyinn.com. 36 spotless a/c rooms in new hotel (2002), restaurant.

**C Astoria Hotel**, 6 Sudder St, near fire station, T 033 22522241, http://travel .vsnl.com/astoria. 41 rooms of various standards. Recommended.

**C Eagle Palace**, 12/2 Lindsay St, T033 2252 4259, taran_eagle@yahoo.com. 18 good-sized, clean rooms with hot bath and TV, OK but a bit pricey.

**C-D Crystal**, 11/1 Kyd St, T033 22266400, hcrystal@vsnl.net. 29 good, clean rooms (mostly a/c), phone and TV, those on top floor are light and airy (and cheaper), a bit pricey but OK.

**D Biman**, 8/1B Chowringhee Lane, 2nd floor, T033 2252 1379.www.hotelbiman.8k.com, clean rooms (10 a/c) with TV, bath, friendly.

**D Galaxy**, 3 Stuart Lane, T033 22524565. 4 good rooms with attached bath and TV, decent choice but often full. Try at around 10.30am just after check out.

**D Super Guest House**, 30A Mirza Ghalib St, T033 22520318, pub@yahoo.com. This super guesthouse has 4 very clean a/c rooms with hot bath. The only truly spotless rooms in the area! Also friendly management.

**D YMCA**, 25 Jl Nehru Rd, T 033 22492192. 17 rooms, including 2 a/c, with bath, in large, rambling colonial building run down but clean linen, check room first, some better than others. Helpful staff, maximum stay 7 days, dorms (3, 4 and 7-bedded, Rs 260 per head), rates include meals (tiny gym next door, Rs 25).

**D YWCA**, 1 Middleton Row, T033 2297033. 30 a nice old airy colonial building with good atmosphere. Some rooms with bath, dorm, everyone welcome, very friendly staff. Rates include breakfast and dinner, a pleasant oasis in the city. A recommended alternative to Sudder St.

**D-E Classic**, 6/1A Kyd St, T033 22297390. 18 clean rooms (some a/c), some with bathsingles with common bath.

**D-E Diplomat**, 10 Sudder St,T033 22538434. 18 rooms, some a/c with hot bath, others with common cold bucket bath, a bit run-down, air ticketing, exchange.

**D-E Green Star**, 33 Mirza Ghalib St, T033 22170616. 22 decent, clean rooms with bath, some a/c, some deluxe with TV, but staff pester for tips.

**D-E Sonali Resort**, 21A Mirza Ghalib St, T033 22521844, subir4uin@yahoo.co.in. 13 good, clean rooms with bath, good choice.

**E Afraa**, B/33/H/3 Mirza Ghalib St, 3rd flr, T033 22520087. 21 clean, small rooms, TV.

*For an explanation of the sleeping and eating price codes used in this guide, see inside the front cover. Other relevant information is found in Essentials pages 56-61.*

**E Capital Guest House** 11B, Chowringhee Lane. Not a bad place, tucked away from the road. Clean rooms, some with windows.
**E Centrepoint**, 20 Mirza Ghalib St, T033 22528184 ian_rashid@yahoo.com. 22 decent enough small rooms, some a/c, clean sheets and bath, grubby carpet, standard menu restaurant. Not a bad choice.
**E Continental Guest House**, 30A Mirza Ghalib St, T033 22450663, continental-cal@hotmail.com. 19 clean rooms with decent tiled baths, cheaper rooms with clean common bath.
**E Delux**, B/33/H/4 Mirza Ghalib St, 3rd floor, T033 22292703. 8 small but clean rooms with bath. Tucked away, friendly staff.
**E Maria**, 5/1 Sudder St, T033 22520860. 24 clean, basic rooms (hard beds), some with bath, dorm (Rs 70), internet, renovated early 2002. Popular budget place.
**E Paramount**, 33/4 Mirza Ghalib St, T033 22290066. 40 clean rooms with bath and TV, helpful staff.
**E Shabnam**, B/33/H/4 Mirza Ghalib St, T033 22296061. 20 small, clean rooms, bath and TV.
**E Shilton**, 5A Sudder St, T033 22521512, shiltoncal@hotmail.com. 27 decent- sized rooms with bath, some triples, clean.
**E Timestar**, 2 Tottee lane, T033 22528028. 30 reasonable airy rooms, some with proper windows attached bath. Singles to 4-bedded, TV optional.
**E Tourist Inn**, 4/1 Sudder St, T033 22529818. 9 small, clean rooms with common bath.
**E Udayachal Tourist Lodge** (WBTDC), DG Block Sector II, Salt Lake, T033 23378246. Centre 20 km, 19 simple rooms, 5 a/c, dorm (Rs 80), meal included.
**E-F Paragon**, 2 Stuart Lane, T033 22522445. 45 rooms and dorms,some tiny but clean. New water heater to fill buckets. Open communal spaces, friendly but indifferent management, popular with backpackers.
**E-F Red Shield Guest House**, 2 Sudder St, T033 22520599. 7 modest rooms, varying rates, some with bath, cramped bumper to bumper 6 and 10-bedded dorms (Rs 60/Rs 65), TV/sitting room, maximum stay 7 nights, lights out at 2200! A good place to stay and the building has character.
**F Modern Lodge**, 1 Stuart Lane, T033 22524960. 14 rooms, attached or common bath,brightly painted with pleasant lounge, very popular, almost permanently full, indifferent staff, no reservations so try at 1000.

**South Kolkata** *p594, map p586*
**L Hindusthan International**, 235/1 AJC Bose Rd, T033 22830505 www.hindusthan.com. 212 rooms on 8 floors, railway 10 km, good buffet lunches and coffee shop, slow service, pool (non-residents Rs 250).
**C-D New Haven Guest House**, 19B Ritchie Rd, T033 24754097. Simply furnished, cleanish rooms with bath, small front garden, only breakfast, residential area with good *dhaba* and Chinese restaurants within 10 mins' walk.

**Excursions** *p597*
The following are in Nabadwip.
**D-F ISKCON Guesthouse**, some with bath, a/c, inexpensive 4-6 bed dorm, cheap meals.
**E Indrajit**, rooms with bath and restaurant.
**E Trimurti**, rooms with bath and restaurant.
**F Akintak Kutir** is basic.
**F Baishakhi**, some rooms with bath.

## Eating

Thursdays are 'meatless' days but chicken and fish are available. Licensed restaurants serve alcohol (some are no longer pleasant places to eat in since the emphasis is on drink). Be prepared for a large surcharge for live (or even recorded) music. This, plus taxes, can double the price on the menu. Many restaurants, outside hotels, do not accept credit cards.

**Central Kolkata** *p584, maps p588, p590, p592*
**TTT Amber**, 11 Waterloo St, T033 22486746. North Indian. 3 floors of gourmet delights (try *tandoori*), generous helpings, fast service, bar, reservations essential. Highly recommended.
**TTT Ban Thai, Oberoi Grand**, T033 22492323. Excellent, imaginative décor (Rs 600 each), reserve ahead.
**TTT Bar-B-Q**, 43 Park St (closed Thu),T033 22299078 Adjacent restaurants serve Indian and Chinese; bar.
**TTT Blue Fox**, 55 Park St, T033 22297948. Bar, popular, excellent sizzlers (lobster, crab and chicken *tetrazzini*). Recommended.
**TTT Chinoiserie**, Taj Bengal, T033 22233939.

¥¥¥ **Ming Room**, Grand, T033 22492323. Chinese.

¥¥¥ **Zaranj**, 26 JL Nehru Rd. Tasteful, stylish, subdued decor, excellent food – try *pudina paratha, murgh makhani, tandoori* fish.

¥¥ **Badshah**, New Market. Well known for *kebab rolls*, bar (non a/c).

¥¥ **Blue Sky Café**, 3 Sudder St. Western, Chinese, Continental. Good choice, very popular budget travellers' meeting place, always full and cramped, good food.

¥¥ **Curd Corner**, Sudder St. Very small but popular, excellent snacks.

¥¥ **Don Giovannis**, 22 Park St. Pizza café, and other western.

¥¥ **Elfin**, near New Market. Cheap *thalis* and Chinese lunches.

¥¥ **Floriana**, 13-D Russell St. Pleasant, north Indian, Chinese, good portions.

¥¥ **Golden Dragon**, 40 Park Mansions, Park St. Standard Chinese (closed Wed).

¥¥ **Gupta**, 53C Mirza Ghalib St. Good Indian and Chinese. Small, intimate, softly lit, low ceilings (beware of fans!).

¥¥ **Jimmy's**, 14D Lindsay St. Chinese. Small, a/c, good *momos*, Szechuan dishes and ice cream.

¥¥ **Jo-jo's**, 30 Mirza Ghalib St (6 Sudder St), next to *Shilton*. Good Indian snacks and meals. 1st floor, a/c. Pleasant decor, run by friendly Sikh.

¥¥ **Kathleen's**, 12 Mirza Ghalib St (closed Thu). A good bakery, serving range of cakes and pastries etc. No seating.

¥¥ **Khalsa**, 4C Madge Lane. Punjabi (no smoking). Try *malai korma, veg tarka* and carrot trifle cake. Western breakfasts, excellent service, cheap, long-standing favourite.

¥¥ **Kwality**, 17 Park St (closed Thu) and 2 Gariahat Rd (closed Wed). Famous for ice creams but also for excellent Indian and continental, usually crowded.

¥¥ **Mocambo**, 25B Park St. International. A/c, pleasant, highly descriptive menu, outstanding grilled *hilsa* served on banana leaf.

¥¥ **Moulin Rouge**, 31 Park St. International. Comfortable, a/c, good menu, service slow.

¥¥ **Peter Cat**, T033 22298841 18A Park St (closed Thu). International. Good kebabs and sizzlers, cheap cocktails, pleasant ambience.

¥¥ **Prince**, 17 Mirza Ghalib St. Basic Indian. Limited menu but praiseworthy Bengali dishes (great *mishti doi*), clean.

¥¥ **Silver Grill**, 18E Park St. Chinese. Extensive menu, specialities *Limkai* chicken, Thai prawns.

¥¥ **Thai place** Downstairs in the New Empire Cinema is this simple Thai restaurant. New. Atmosphere more sterile than cosy.

¥¥ **Zurich**, 3 Sudder St. Snacks. Laid-back café atmosphere, excellent snacks, breakfasts, clean and friendly, often full. Recommended.

**South Kolkata** *p594, maps p586*

¥¥¥ **China Valley**, Ideal Plaza, Sarat Bose Rd. Chinese. Luxurious, with fountains.

¥¥¥ **Mainland China**, 3A Gurusaday Rd, T033 22872006. Excellent Chinese. Unusual offerings, especially fish and seafood, tastefully decorated with burnished ceiling and evocative wall mural, pleasant ambience, courteous.

**Bengali**

No alcohol will be served. See page 583.

¥¥ **Aaheli** at Peerless Inn, T033 22280301. Excellent, unusual menu, comfortable a/c, fairly pricey.

¥¥ **Kewpie's**, 2 Elgin Lane (between Elgin and Heysham Rds), T033 24759880, closed Mon. Authentic Bengali, home-cooking at its best, add on special dishes to basic *thali* (Rs 200), unusual fish and vegetarian. Few tables in rooms in a residence, a/c, open for lunch and dinner, sells recipe book and pickles. Highly recommended, reserve.

¥¥ **Radhu's**, Lake Market. Superb fish fry and chicken or prawn cutlet.

¥¥ **Suruchi**, T033 22291763 (All Bengal Women's Union), 89 Eliot Rd. Simple surroundings but carefully prepared by self-help women's group at lunchtime.

**Bengali snacks**

Fresh every afternoon at most sweet shops (1600-1730): try *shingaras, kochuris* and *nimkis*.

**Gangaur**, Russell St/ AJC Bose Rd corner.

**Krishna**, Camac St.

**Radhu's**, Lake Market. Superb snacks, rich *Mughlai paratha* and *aloor domm*.

**Bengali sweets**

**Bhim Chandra Nag**, 8 Vivekananda Rd.

**Chappan Bhog**, 28B Shakespeare Sarani. Recommended for *chandrakala*, almond

*pista barfi*, mango *roshogolla*, *kheer mohan (also savouries)*.
**KC Das**, 11 Esplanade, Gariahat Rd.
**Nepal Chandra**, Landsdowne Rd.
**Pure Milk Centre** near Rafi Ahmed Kidwai St/Ripon St corner. Good sweet 'curd' (*mishti doi*), usually sold out by lunchtime. Excellent hot *roshogollas*.

### Cafés and fast food

**Aqua-Java**, 79 Sambhunath Pandit St (south of the cathedral). Smart set coffee bar with innovative concoctions and snacks.
**Café Coffee Day**, 18K Park St. T033 39597985. Western style café chain serving the usual range of coffees and cakes/slices.
**Coffee House**, College St (see page 592).
**Garden Café**, Alipore Rd. For pizzas and *dosas*, burgers and Chinese fast food.
**Wimpy**, Rawdon St corner.

### Chinese

Connoisseurs of Chinese cuisine go to South Tangra Rd. Eateries are basic – Formica-top tables etc – but they serve excellent food (approach is unpleasant though past tanneries and open drains):
**Ka Fu Lok** and **Sin Fa**, do excellent soups, jumbo prawns and honey chicken, best to go early (noon for lunch, 2000 for dinner).
**Lily's Kitchen**, try garlic chicken, sweet and sour fish, chop suey, steamed fish (40 mins), very generous so order half-plates.

### Confectionery

**Flury's**, 18 Park St (closed Mon). Traditional English breakfasts, good afternoon teas, pastry counter, but slow service.
**Hot Breads**, Central Plaza, 2/6 Sarat Bose Rd. Excellent breads, pastries and cakes.
**Kathleen's**, several branches, including 12 Mirza Ghalib St, corner of Lord Sinha Rd.
**Kookie Jar**, Rawdon St. One of the best, though pricey.
**Nahoum**, F20, New Market. Good pastries, cakes, savouries.
**Upper Crust** 1/1 Camac St (and Judges Court Rd). A/c, clean, modern, delicious cakes, pastries (try strawberry tarts), brown bread and pizzas.

### Kathi-rolls

Kathi-rolls (tender kebabs wrapped in *parathas*) are hard to beat. Try mutton/chicken egg roll (if you don't want raw onions and green chillis, order "*no piaaz e mirchi*").
**Manjinder Singh's**, Ballygunge Phari, always busy; excellent Mughlai.
**Nizam's**, off SN Bannerjee Rd (opposite Elite Cinema), and 22/25 New Market.
**Rehmania**, Park St/AJC Bose Rd corner.

### Other nationalities

**Pemayangtse**, 1 Meher Ali Rd, Park Circus, serves Tibetan.
**Tibetan**, near Elgin Rd corner of JL Nehru Rd. Excellent dishes under Rs 50.

### Vegetarian

**Anand**, Chittaranjan Ave. Good South Indian.
**Gokul**, Lord Sinha Rd. Excellent Rajasthani meals and sweets.
**Gupta Brothers**, Mirza Ghalib St. *Thalis* and Indian sweets, stand-up vegetarian and Bengali confectionery, good value.

## Bars and clubs

### Bars

The larger hotels have pleasant bars and upmarket restaurants serve alcohol. The top hotels are well stocked, luxurious but pricey. In Sudder St, **Fairlawn**'s pleasant garden terrace is popular at dusk attracting anyone seeking a chilled beer, while **Lyttons** is also open to thirsty travellers from neighbouring hotels. Independent bars, open usually until 2230, lack atmosphere; some are positively men only. At the **New Empire Cinema**, between New Market and Chowringhee, is the **Lighthouse Bar and Restaurant**. Recommended.

### Clubs

Some are affiliated to a number of Indian and foreign clubs including Royal Overseas League, Travellers, St James's, National Liberal, Oxford and Cambridge Universities.
**Bengal Club**, 1/1 Russell St, T033 22499443, the former house of Lord Macaulay, has an excellent dining room.
**Tollygunge Club**, 120 DP Sasmal Rd, T033 24732316. Built on an old indigo plantation, 18-hole golf course, riding, tennis, pool, away from centre, atmosphere and location compensate for average rooms and restaurant.

## Entertainment

Contact www.tulleeho.com for nightlife in metro cities. *Calcutta: This Fortnight* is distributed free by West Bengal Tourist Office. The *Sunday Telegraph* magazine and English language dailies (*Statesman*, *Times of India*, *Asian Age*, *Hindustan Times*) carry a comprehensive list. **CalCalling** is a monthly listings booklet available from **Oxford Book Shop**, Park St. Rs 20.

### Cinema

A/c and comfortable cinemas showing English language films are mostly off JL Nehru Rd, near Esplanade. **Elite** T033 22441383, SN Banerjee Rd. **Globe** T033 22496665, Lindsay St. **Jumna**, Marquis St. **Lighthouse** T033 22491052, Humayun Place. **Metro**, JL Nehru Rd. **Minerva** T033 22280141, Chowringhee Place. **Nandan**, T033 22231210, has festivals and screens all-time greats. New multiplex **Inox**, Forum. Mall, 10 Elgin Rd, T033 23584499, www.inoxmovies.com. Showing Hollywood/Bollywood mix. 10-min walk from Rabindra Sadan station. Between New Market and Chowringhee is the **New Empire Cinema**. Convenient location. Shows a mixture of movies.

### Dance, music and theatre

Regular performances at **Rabindra Sadan**, Cathedral Rd. **Kala Mandir**, 48 Shakespeare Sarani. **Gorky Sadan**, Gorky Terrace, near Minto Park. **Sisir Mancha**, 1/1 AJC Bose Rd. Some of these also hold art exhibition as at **Academy of Fine Arts**, Cathedral Rd, and **Ramakrishna Mission**, Gol Park. You can see Bengali theatre of a high standard at **Biswaroopa**, 2A Raja Raj Kissen St and **Star Theatre**, 79/34 Bidhan Sarani.

### Discos and nightclubs

**At hotels**: **Anticlock** (Hindustan International). Good live band, young crowd, good sizzlers, pool tables, ocean-liner décor. **Incognito** (Taj Bengal). Understated, relaxed ambience, 30-plus crowd, good food, taped music, fussy dress codes. **Someplace Else** (Park). Pub, live bands favoured by the young. **Tantra** (Park). Live bands/taped music, large floor, young crowd, adjacent **Bodhi Bar** has good single malts and cigars; closed Mon.

### Performing arts

English-language productions staged by **British Council** and theatre clubs. **Sangeet Research Academy**, near Tollygunge Metro station, a national centre for training in Indian Classical music, stages free concert on Wed evenings. **Rabindra Bharati University**, 6/4 Dwarakanath Tagore Lane, holds performances, particularly during the winter, including singing, dancing and *jatras*. *Jatra* is community theatre, highly colourful and exaggerated both in delivery and make-up, drawing for its subject romantic favourites from mythology or more up to date social, political and religious themes.

## Festivals and events

**Jan** Ganga Sagar Mela at Sagar, 105 km south of Kolkata, where the River Hugli joins the sea, draws thousands of Hindu pilgrims. See page 631. **Mar/Apr** Holi (Dol Purnima) is the spring festival. **Jun-Jul** The Ratha Yatra (**Jun-Jul**) at Mahesh, nearby. **Sep-Oct** Durga Puja, Bengal's celebration of the goddess during Dasara. See box. **Oct-Nov** Diwali (*Kali Puja* in Bengal) is the festival of lights. **Dec** Christmas. Numerous churches hold special services, including Midnight Mass, and the New Market takes on a new look in Dec as Barra Din (Big Day) approaches with temporary stalls selling trees and baubles. Other religious festivals are observed as elsewhere in India.

## Shopping

Most shops open 1000-1730 or later (some break for lunch) weekdays, 1000-1300 on Sat.

### Art

**Centre Art Gallery**, 87C Park St. Mainly works by Bengali artists.
**Emerald Isle**, 40A Park Mansion, 57 Park St (1400-1900).
**Gallerie 88**, 28B Shakespeare Sarani. Contemporary art (1200-2000).
**Metropolitan**, 7 JL Nehru Rd (2nd Floor). Old prints and 'antiques', with maps.
**Saroj**, 3B Camac St. Old prints and 'antiques'.

### Books

**Kolkata Book Fair**, Maidan near Victoria Memorial. End of Jan for a fortnight, stalls sell

paperback fiction to antiquarian books.
**Modern Book Depot**, 15a JL Nehru Rd, opposite Lighthouse Cinema, T033 22490933. Long tradition, will search out titles.
**Oxford Book Shop**, Park St. New English titles, postcards, tiny café upstairs.
**College St**, a wealth of second-hand pavement bookstalls along this street mainly cater for students but may reveal an interesting 1st edition for a keen collector (see under Sights).

### Clothes and accessories

**Allen Solly**, Rawdon St/Shakespeare Sarani corner, for menswear.
**Ananda**, 13 Russell St.
**Anokhi**,6 Russell St. Cottage industry supplied textiles and clothes.
**Burlington**, 43 Park Mansions, 57 Park St. Sells foreign labels.
**Fabindia**, 16 Hindustan Park. Clothes textiles and household items from fair trade based company.
**Kali**, Judges Court Rd. Eastern and Western wear.
**Meera Basu**, 8 Sarat Bose Rd. *Kurtas* and saris.
**Metro**, outside Grand Hotel. For pricey leather goods.
**Mexx**, Rawdon St/Shakespeare Sarani corner. Western clothes and shoes.
**Monapali**, 15 Louden St, sells designer *salwar, kurtas*.
**Ogaan**, P545 Lake Rd Extn. High quality clothes including swimwear and lingerie.
**Ritu's Boutique**, 46A Rafi Ahmed Kidwai Rd. *Kurtas* and saris.
**Taj Bengal** arcade. For pricey leather goods.
**Zenon**, 111 Park St is more affordable.

### Government emporia

Government emporia are mainly in the town centre and are fixed price shops; **Assam**, 8 Russell St. **Bihar**, 145 Rashbehari Ave. **Cauvery** and **Central Cottage Industries**, 7 JL Nehru Rd. **Handloom House**, 2 Lindsay St. **Kashmir Art**, 12 JL Nehru Rd. **Khadi Gramodyog**, 28 Chittaranjan Ave. **Manipur**, 15L Lindsay St. **Manjusha**, 7/1D Lindsay St. **Meghalaya**, 9 Russell St. **Phulkari**, Punjab Emporium, 26B Camac St. **Rajasthali**, 30E JL Nehru Rd. **Refugee Handicrafts**, 2A Gariahat Rd. **Tripura**, 58 JL Nehru Rd. **UP**, 12B Lindsay St. Several at **Dakshinapan**, near Dhakuria Bridge, Mon-Fri 1030-1930, Sat 1030-1300, convenient, excellent selection of handloom and handicrafts.

### Handicrafts and handloom

Several in Park St and streets leading off it.
**Bengal Home Industries**, 11 Camac St. Good selection of printed cottons, relaxed.
**Jete**, 71 Park St.
**Manjusha**, 71 Park St.
**Priyadarshini**, 14C Lindsay St.

### Jewellery

Bepin Behari Ganguly St (Bow Bazar) is lined with mirrored jewellers' shops; **PC Chandra, BB Dutt, B Sirkar** are well known.

### Markets

The **New Market**, Lindsay St, behind the original Hogg Market (largely rebuilt since a fire in 1985), has over 2,500 shops. It used to be said that you could buy anything from a needle to an elephant (on order) in one of its stalls. Today it is still worth a visit, preferably early in the morning, to watch it come alive. You will find mundane everyday necessities to exotic luxuries, from fragrant florists to gory meat stalls. Be prepared to deal with pestering porters.

For conventional shopping try **a/c Market**, Shakespeare Sarani, **Park Centre**, Park St, **Vardaan Market**, Camac St. Opposite the New Market, **Shriram Arcade** is "like shopping in Singapore"! Kolkata has a number of **bazars**, each with a character of its own.

In **Bentinck St** are Muslim tailors, Chinese shoemakers interspersed with Indian sweetmeat shops and tea stalls. **Gariahat** market early in the morning attracts a very diverse clientele (business-men, academics, cooks) who come to select choice fresh fish. In **Shyambazar** the coconut market starts business at 0500 and you will miss it if you arrive 2 hrs later. The colourful flower market is on **Jagannath Ghat** on the river bank. The old **China Bazar** no longer exists although Tiretta Bazar area still retains its ethnic flavour; try an exceptional Chinese breakfast off street stall!

### Music

**Music World**, 18G Park St, T033 22170751, sells wide range of all genres.

### Tailors

Garments can be copied skilfully around New Market at **Mr Alibaba**, 13 Sudder St (opposite), **S. Charran Singh**, 7/1/c Lindsay St, T033 2443662, among many.

### Women's self-help centre

Shops where you can watch handloom weaving, batik printing, embroidery, handblock printing being practised are recommended.

**All Bengal Women's Union**, 89 Elliot Rd.
**Good Companions**, 13C Russell St.
**Karma Kutir**, 32 Ballygunge Place. Embroidery.
**Nari Seva Sangha** in Jodhpur Park.
**Sasha**, 27 Mirza Ghalib St (off the Rd). Tue-Sat 1000-1900, Sun, Mon 1000-1300, excellent handicrafts including cane, bamboo, *dokra*, *kantha*, leather and crafts.
**Women's Friendly Society**, 29 Park Lane. Good embroidery and linen.

## Activites and tours

### Cricket

Occasional Test matches and One Day Internationals at Eden Gardens, see page 587, 100,000 capacity; get tickets in advance.

### Football

The season starts in May and continues through the monsoons. The club grounds are on the Maidan (try **East Bengal Football Club**, T033 22484642).

### Golf

Several courses include the **Royal Calcutta Golf Club**, 18 Golf Club Rd, T033 24731352, founded in 1829, the oldest golf club in the world outside the UK; it moved to its present course in 1910 having taken the radical step of admitting women in 1886.
**The Tollygunge Club**, 120 Despran Sasmal Rd, T033 24735954, course is on land that was once an indigo plantation.

### Horse racing

**Royal Calcutta Turf Club**, T033 22291104. Racing takes place in the cool season (Nov to early Apr) and monsoon (Jun-Oct); tote, bookmakers available. The Derby is in the first week of Jan.

### Sightseeing tours

**WBTDC Tours** departure point is Tourism Centre, 3/2 BBD Bagh E, 1st Floor, T033 2248 8271, wbtc@cal2.vsnl.net.in (1000-1330, 1415-1530). Daily coach tours (except Mon). 0730-1140 and 1240-1700. A/c, full day, Rs 100.
**Morning tour**: 0730, Eden Gardens, High Court, Writers' Building, Botanical Gardens, Belur Math, Dakshineswar, Kali Temple, Jain Temple and Esplanade, Indian Museum, Nehru Children's Museum, Victoria Memorial, The Zoo. Entry fees not included. CRUTA, 67B Beadon Street, T033 2544497, offers 2-hr walking tours of North Kolkata, through the old streets. Private tour operators also offer city tours. Approved guides from WBTDC Tourist Office: about Rs 75 for half day; Rs 150 for full day.
**Long distance** Tourist coaches to Digha, daily, Rs 60; Santiniketan-Bakreswar; Malda-Murshidabad-Gaur-Pandua; Antpur-Bishnupur-Mukutmanipur-Jairambati-Kamarpukur- Tarakeswar, Rs 415; Mayapur (ISKCON)-Krishnanagar-Bethuadari Deer Park; Sunderbans- Tiger and Crocodile projects (not Jul to mid-Sep). Rs 750. Approved guides from WBTDC Tourist Office.

### Swimming

**Oberoi Grand** and **Hindustan International** hotel pools are open to non-residents (Rs 250).

### Tour operators

Best deals in air tickets to/from the East (through Bangkok) are offered by agents in the Sudder St area (about US$120).
**American Express**, 21 Old Court House St, T033 22486181. **Mercury**, 46c JL Nehru Rd, T033 22423535. **Thomas Cook**, Chitrakut (2nd floor), 230a AJC Bose Rd, T033 22475354. **TCI**, 46C JL Nehru Rd. **Travel Planners**, 7 Red Cross Place, T033 22488304,leisure@ giascl01.vsnl.net.in. Recommended.

## Transport

Kolkata is at the eastern end of the Grand Trunk Rd (NH2); AA (East India), 19 Ballygunge Circ Rd, T033 24755131. Many of the city centre roads become one-way between 1400 and 2100 so expect tortuous detours.

### Air

Enquiries T033 25118787. The spacious and fairly new terminal buildings are well organized and spotless. There is adequate seating in the departure lounge as well as a bookshop, drink dispenser and clean toilets. A Reservation counter for rail (same day travel only) and one for hotels are in the arrivals hall. At the **International terminal**: **State Bank of India** (24 hrs, changes rupees into US$ only).

For transport to town the pre-paid taxi service (closes at 2200) from Dum Dum to the city centre is excellent value, Rs 135, about 40 mins (but Deluxe cars, Rs 400-650). Return from the city centre costs more - Rs 150 if you bargain. A/c coach transfer to **Indian Airline's** city office, approximately 2 hourly from 0530, Rs 75. The public bus is a nightmare; strongly not recommended. The nearest Metro station is at Dum Dum (Rs 5 to city centre); auto-rickshaws to there, about Rs 60; total 40 mins. Transit passengers with onward flights may use the Airport Rest Rooms (some a/c, doubles, dorm, all good value).

Domestic flights include **Indian Airlines** flights to Agartala; Ahmadabad, Aizwal, Bangalore, Bagdogra, Bhubaneswar, Chennai, Delhi, Dibrugarh, Dimapur, Guwahati, Hyderabad, Imphal, Jaipur, Jorhat, Lucknow, Mumbai, Nagpur, Patna, Port Blair, Ranchi, Silchar, Tezpur, Visakhapatnam. **Jet Airways** flies to Bagdogra, Bangalore, Bhubaneswar, Chennai, Delhi, Guwahati, Hyderabad, Imphal, Jorhat, Mumbai. **Sahara** and **Deccan** fly to several destinations also. For international flights, see page 35.

### Airline offices

**International**: Aeroflot, 1stFl Lord's Building, 7/1 Lord Sinha Rd 033 T22823765, . **American Airlines**, 230A AJC Bose Rd T033 22801335. **Air France**,230A AJC Bose Rd T033 22408646 . **Bangladesh Biman**, 30C Chowringhee Rd T033 22292843, airport T033 25118787. **British Airways**, 41 Chowringhee Rd T033 9831377470, airport T033 25118262. **Cathay Pacific**, 1 Middleton St, T033 22403211. **Delta**, T033 22405182. **Druk Air**, 51 Tivoli Court, 1A Ballygunge Circular Rd T033 22402419, airport T033 25119976. **Gulf Air**, 230A AJC Bose Rd, T033 22477783. **Japan Airlines**, 35A Chowringhee Rd, T033 22468363. **KLM**, 1 Middleton St, T033 22830151, airport T033 25118329. **Kuwait Airways**, 230A AJC Bose Rd, T033 22801335. **Lufthansa**, 30A/B JL Nehru Rd, T033 22299365, airport T033 25118528. **Qantas**, 58 Chitrakoot Building, 230A AJC Bose Rd, T033 22470718. **Royal Brunei**, T033 22297112. **Royal Jordanian**, 2/7 Sarat Bose Rd, T033 24745094. **Royal Nepal**, 41 Chowringhee Rd, T033 2288534. **SAS**, 228A AJC Bose Rd T033 22405182. **Singapore Airlines**, 1 Lee Rd, 2nd Fl T033 22809898. **Sri Lankan**, 230A AJC Bose Rd, T033 22477783. **Tarom**, 2/7 Sarat Bose Rd, T033 22405178, airport T5119031. **Thai Airways**, 229 AJC Bose Rd, 8th floor, T033 22801630.

**National airlines**: Air India, 50 Chowringhee Rd T033 22822356, Airport T033 25119031. **Indian Airlines**, 39 Chittaranjan Ave, T033 22110810, Reservations T1401/033 22116869 and Hotel Hindusthan International, T033 22476606, airport T033 25119721, Tele check-in T033 25119633 (J class), T033 25118564 (Y class).

**Private airlines**: Jet Airways, Stephen Court, 18D Park St, T033 22292227, airport T033 25119894. **Sahara**, 2A Shakespeare Sarani, T033 22826118, airport T033 25119545.

### Bicycle

Bike hire is not easy; ask at your hotel if a staff bike is free. Spares are sold along Bentinck St, north of Chowringhee.

### Bus

**Local** State Transport services run throughout the city and suburbs from 0500-2030; usually overcrowded after 0830, but very cheap. Faster, private minibuses (little more expensive) cover major routes. South Bengal minibuses are bigger and will often stop on request.

**Long distance** An extensive hub and spoke bus operation from Kolkata allows cheap travel within West Bengal and beyond. The Tourist Office, 3/2 BBD Bagh, has timetables. Advance bookings at computerized office of Kolkata State Transport Corp (STC), Esplanade, T033 22481916. **Kolkata STC**: to Balurghat; Digha; Diamond Harbour; Farakka; Mayapur; Siliguri etc. **North Bengal STC**: T033 22430726; **Digha**; **Jalpaiguri**; **Cooch Behar**; **Malda**; **Siliguri**, 12 hrs. **South Bengal STC**, Bankura,

Bishnupur and Purulia. **Orissa & Bihar STC**, T033 25530340. **Puri**, 11 hrs. **Gaya**; Bokaro. **Sikkim Govt**, Gangtok via Siliguri. **Bhutan Govt**, Phuntsholing via Siliguri. **Bangladesh**, Syamoli Paribahan, 8 Marquis St, runs buses to Dhaka from **VIP Hotel**.

### Ferry

**Local** To cross the Hugli, eg from Haora station, except Sun.

**Long distance** Shipping Corp of India, 13 Strand Rd, T033 22484640 (recorded information T033 22485420), operates a steamer to **Port Blair** in the Andamans. Some 2 or 3 sailings a month (3-4 days) with tickets available from 1000, 7 days ahead (be there at 0830; huge queue for 'bunk class'). See page 772.

### Rickshaw

Hand-pulled rickshaws are used by the local people especially along the narrow congested lanes. Auto-rickshaws operate outside the city centre, especially as shuttle service to Metro stations.

### Taxi

Car hire with driver, from Rs 700-1,050 (a/c) for 8 hrs. **Gainwell**, 8 Ho Chi Minh Sarani, T033 22426667; **Mercury**, 46C JL Nehru Rd, T033 22423555; **Wenz**, at Oberoi Grand, at Airport T033 22492323; **Wheels**, 150 Lenin Sarani, T033 2273081. Tourist taxis from India and WB Tourist Offices. Local taxis are yellow. Old meters start at Rs 5; double the reading and add 20% (Rs 12 minimum). Drivers carry conversion charts. Computerized meters are being introduced. For taxi rides further afield, at **Sealdah** ignore touts who quote Rs 100 for Sudder St; instead, join the queue for licensed cabs. Fare to Sudder St Rs 60. At **Haora** there are prepaid taxis; or get the Ferry across the river to Chandpal/Babu Ghat and hire a taxi or walk from there. Buses and minibuses get very crowded.

### Tram

Kolkata is the only Indian city to run a network from 0400-2300, min Rs 2. Often crowded except on Sun.

### Train

The metro is usually clean, efficient and punctual. The 16½-km route from Dum Dum to Tollygunge runs from 0700-2145, Sun 1500-2145; fare Rs 3-5. Enquiries T033 22261054. Note that trains are not as long as the platforms!

Kolkata is served by 2 railway stations, **Haora** ('Howrah', still used on timetables) and **Sealdah**. Haora station has a separate complex for platforms 18-21. Enquiries, Haora, T033 26607410, 'New' Complex, T033 26602217, Sealdah, T033 23503535. Central Enquiry, T033 22203545. Reservation, T135 (computerized). Computerized Booking Office, Rabindra Sadan, 61 JL Nehru Rd, T033 22472143. Railway Reservations, 6 Fairlie Place, BBD Bagh, T135; 0900-1300, 1330-1600, Sun 0900-1400 (best to go early). At Fairlie Place, tourists are automatically told to go to the Foreign Tourist Counter, upstairs (very efficient). However, unless you have an Indrail Pass or are buying one, it is worth checking whether seats are available for the trains you want downstairs first, as this can often be much quicker.

**Foreign Tourist Quota** If the trains you want are listed as 'Full', try the Tourist Counter, upstairs. It usually takes at least 30 mins, though some reported a miracle in 5 mins! Check carefully which queue to join for the region you want to travel in, as there are separate queues for Northern and South Eastern Railways. You will need to show your passport and an encashment or ATM receipt as well as the filled out form.

Trains listed depart from Haora (Howrah), unless marked '**S**' for Sealdah (timings change every Apr and Oct). To **Allahabad**: see New Delhi. **Agra Fort**: *Bikaner Exp, 2307*, 2330, 20½ hrs. **Bhubaneswar**: *Dhauli Exp, 2821*, 0600, 7½ hrs; *Falaknuma Exp, 2703*, 0700, 7½ hrs; *Howrah Puri Exp, 8007*, 2105, 7½ hrs. **Chennai**: *Coromandel Exp, 2841*, 1425, 28½ hrs; *Howrah Chennai Mail, 6003*, 2105, 33½ hrs. **New Delhi** via **Patna** and **Allahabad**: *Rajdhani Exp, 2301*, 1615 (except Sun), 16½ hrs; *Rajdhani Exp, 2305*, 1300 (Sun), 20 hrs; (**S**) *Rajdhani Exp, 2313*, 1635 (Daily), 17½ hrs. **Mumbai (CST)** : *Gitanjali Exp, 2860*, 1330, 32½ hrs (via **Nagpur**, 18½ hrs); *Howrah Mumbai Mail, 2810*, 1930, 35½ hrs (via **Nagpur**, 19½ hrs); *Howrah Mumbai Mail, 2321*, 2200, 38 hrs. **Mumbai (Lokmanya Tilak)** : *Jnaneswari SD Exp, 2102*, 2315 (Mon, Wed, Thu, Sun), 32½ hrs (via **Nagpur**, 19 hrs). **Nagpur**: See Mumbai trains plus *Howrah Ahmedabad Exp, 8034*, 2050, 22½ hrs. **New Jalpaiguri (NJP)**: (**S**) *Kanchenjunga Exp, 5657*, 0625, 11½ hrs; (**S**) *Darjeeling Mail, 2343*, 2205, 13 hrs; *Kamrup Exp, 5959*, 1735, 14 hrs. **Puri**: *Jagannath Exp, 8409*, 1835, 11 hrs; *Howrah Puri Exp, 8007*, 2205, 11 hrs. **Ranchi**: *Howrah Shatabdi Exp, 2019*, 0605, 7hrs.

## Directory

### Banks

Mon-Fri 1030-1430, Sat 1030 1230. **Foreign Banks**: cash on Mastercard/Visa from **SC/ Grindlay's**, 19 Netaji Subhas Rd and 41 JL Nehru Rd, T033 22202546. ATM at **HKSB**, 8 Netaji Subhas Rd, T033 22201833, 3A Shakespeare Sarani, 31 BBD Bagh. **Thomas Cook**, 2nd floor, 230A AJC Bose Rd. **Travellers Express**, 20 Mirza Ghalib St.

### Chemists

**Angel**, 151 Park St (24-hr). **Dey's**, 6/2B Lindsay St. **Lawrence & Mayo**, 20F Park St. Opticians. **Moonlight**, 180 SP Mukherjee Rd (24-hr).

### Consulates and High Commissions

**Bangladesh**, 9 Bangabandhu, Sheikh Mujib Sarani T033 22475208. **Bhutan**, 48 Tivoli Court, P Barua Sarani (off AJC Bose Rd). **Denmark**, 3 Netaji Subhas Rd, T033 22487478. **France**, 4th Fl, 2 Clive Ghat St T033 22204571 **Germany**, 11 Hastings Park Rd, T033 24791141. **Italy**, 3 Raja Santosh Rd, T033 24792414. **Israel**,86 C Topsia Rd (south) T033 22800028. **Japan**, 55 M N Sen Lane, Tollygunge T033 224211970. **Nepal**, 1 National Library Avenue T033 24561224. **Netherlands**, 502 Mangalam A, 24 Hemant Basu Sarani T0333 22424979. **Norway**, 5B, Roudon St T033 22472052. **Spain**, 1 Taratolla Rd, T033 24695954. **Sri Lanka**, 2 Hare St, T033 22485102. **Sweden**, 9 Elgin Rd T033 22807136. **Switzerland** 113 Park St, T033 2295557. **Thailand**, 18B Mandeville Gardens, T033 24407836. **UK**, 1 Ho-Chi-Minh Sarani, T033 22885172. **USA**, 5/1 Ho-Chi-Minh Sarani, T033 22823611.

### Cultural centres and libraries

**Alliance Française**, 3 West Range T033 22815198, afcalcut@cal.vsnl.net. **British Council** Information Centre (relocated), Larsen & Tubro Building, 16 Camac St (near Shakespeare Sarani), T033 22825370. Good for UK newspapers and journals, reference books. Useful internet. Tue-Sat, 1100-1900. **Max Mueller Bhavan**, 8 Pramathesh Barua Sarani, T033 24759398.

### Hospitals

Government: **Medical College Hospital**, 88 College St, T033 22443213. **Private: Apollo**, 5B Canel Circular Rd, T033 23585211. **Belle Vue**, 9 Dr UN Brahmachari St, T033 22472321. 24-hr Ambulance and blood bank **Woodlands**, 8B Alipore Rd, T033 24567080. **Lifeline Centre ( 24-hr Ambulance)**, 4A Wood St, T033 22478083.

### Internet

Many across the city; several in Sudder/Park St area. Some charge as little as Rs 25 per hr.

### Post

Poste Restante, 0700-2230. Closed Sun and holidays. **Speed Post** At major post offices including Airport, Esplanade and Park St. **Central Telegraph Office** 8 Red Cross Place is open 24 hrs.BBD Bagh (W).

### Tourist offices

**Govt of India**, 4 Shakespeare Sarani, T033 22825813 (airport T033 25116026). **Govt of West Bengal**, 2 Brabourne Rd, T033 22254723; **WBTDC**, Netaji Indoor Stadium, T033 22487302, wbtdc@cal2.vsnl.net.in. **Tourism Centre**, 3/2 BBD Bagh (E), T033 22103199. Closed 1330-1415. **ITDC**, 46C, Chowringhee Rd, T033 22880901. **State Governments**: Andaman & Nicobar Islands, 2nd floor, 3a Auckland Place, T033 22475084. **Assam**, 8 Russell St, T033 22295094. **Bihar**, 26B Camac St, T033 22803304. **Manipur**, 26 Rowland Rd, T033 24758163. **Meghalaya**, 120 Shantipally, EM Bypass T033 24411932. **Mizoram**, 24 Old Ballygunge Rd, T033 24757887. **Nagaland**, 11 Shakespeare Sarani, T033 22825247. **Orissa**, 41 Lenin Sarani, T033 22260556. **Sikkim**, 4/1 Middleton St T033 22815328. **Tripura**, 1 Pretoria St, T033 22425703.

# Bishnupur and Santiniketan

## Bishnupur → *Phone code: 03244. Colour map 4, grid C1. Population: 61,900.*

The warrior Malla Kings of Bengal ruled this area from Bishnupur for nearly two centuries. The British subsequently sold it to the Maharajah of Burdwan. The Mallas were great patrons of the arts and built uniquely ornamental terracotta temples. It is also where the Dhrupad style of classical Indian singing originated. Local handicrafts include silk, tassar, conch-shell and bell-metal ware and the famous terracotta 'Bankura horse', Dokhra, and also slate statues and artefacts. Bengali sweetmeats and flavoured tobacco are local specialities.
▸▸ *For Sleeping, Eating and other listings, see pages 610-611.*

*The temples can be very difficult to find on foot in the maze of narrow streets. It is best to arrange a cycle-rickshaw for a tour, Rs 50 for 2½ hours.*

### Sights

There are more than two dozen temples in Bishnupur, mostly dedicated to Krishna and Radha. They are usually built of brick but sometimes of laterite and on a square plan with a gently curved roof imitating the Bengali thatched (*chala*) hut. The terracotta tiles depict episodes from the *Ramayana* and *Mahabharata*, and also scenes from daily life. Inside, there is a sanctuary (*thakurbari*) and a platform (*vedi*) for the image, on one side. The upper storey has a gallery topped by one, five or even nine towers.

Most of the temples are concentrated within the fort, which was built later by Muslim rulers. Distances given are from the **Tourist Lodge**. The **Rasmancha** (3 km) is a unique Vishnu shrine. The well-preserved cannons, in particular the 4-m long **Dalmadal** to the south of the Rasmancha, date back to the Mallas. The **Jor Mandir** (5 km), a pair of hut-shaped temples with a single *sikhara*, built in 1655 by Raghunath Singh, has attractively ornamented panels. He also built the **Shyam Rai Temple** (7 km), perhaps the earliest example of the *pancharatna* (five towers) and a fine *sikhara*. Each façade is triple arched and the terracotta panels show scenes from the *Ramayana* and Krishna's life. The large **Madan Mohan Temple** (5 km), with a white façade, was built of brick with terracotta panels in 1694 by King Durjan, while the 17th-century **Lalji** and **Madan Gopal** are built of laterite. The **Mrinmoyee Mandir** (3 km) has a clay idol of Durga dating from AD 997, and in the courtyard a curiosity of nine trees growing together. Little remains of the Malla Kings' **Fort** (3½ km). You can see the gate of laterite, with firing holes drilled in different directions and a 13th-century stone chariot. The water reservoirs are still there though the moat, once served by seven lakes, is partly dry.

## Santiniketan → *Phone code: 03463. Colour map 4, grid C1. Population: 65,700.*

Santiniketan, the 'Abode of Peace', is a welcome change from the hectic traffic, noise and dirt of Kolkata. Even a brief visit to the shady university campus with an imprint of its artistic heritage, and its quiet, rural charm makes a profound impression on most visitors. ▸▸ *For Sleeping, Eating and other listings, see pages 610-611.*

### Ins and outs

**Getting there** The nearest railway station is Bolpur, which has trains from Kolkata's Haora and Sealdah stations (booking essential). Cycle-rickshaws charge Rs 15-20 to Santiniketan, 3 km away. Local buses use a stand near the station. The road journey from Kolkata on the congested NH2 takes longer (213 km) as it can be very slow.

**Getting around** The Visva Bharati campus and Santiniketan's residential area around are ideal for exploring on foot. To get further afield you will need a cycle-rickshaw. ▸▸ *See Transport, page 611, for further details.*

## Sights

**Vishva Bharati University** ⓘ *closed Wed and Tue afternoon, sightseeing is permitted only after university hours – summer 1430-1700, winter 1415-1630 and during vacations 0700-1200, Rs 5, no photography, all compounds are sub-divided by wire fences – effectively it is 3 km from the hotels in Bolpur*, has an interesting history. The Maharishi Debendranath Tagore, father of Rabindranath Tagore, the Nobel Laureate, started an *ashram* which was later named 'Santiniketan'. In 1901 Rabindranath started an experimental place of learning with a 'classroom' under the trees, and a group of five pupils. It went on to become the Vishva Bharati University in 1921. It now attracts students from all over the world and aspires to be a spiritual meeting ground in a serene, culturally rich and artistic environment. Open-air classes are still a feature of this unique university. Among the many *Bhavans* are those concentrating on fine art (Kala Bhavan), and music and dance (Sangit Bhavan). The **Uttarayan Complex** where the poet lived consists of several buildings in distinctive architectural styles. **Sadhana** Prayer Hall, where Brahmo prayers are held on Wednesday, was founded in 1863, see page 1336. The unusual hall enclosed by stained glass panels has a polished marble floor which is usually decorated with fresh *alpana* designs. **Chhatimtala**, where Maharishi Debendranath sat and meditated, is the site of special prayers at Convocation time. In keeping with its simplicity, graduates are presented with a twig with five leaves from the locally widespread *Saptaparni* trees.

**Rabindra Bhavan** ⓘ *closed Tue afternoon, Wed, 1030-1300, 1400-1630, no photography, bags may not be permitted, shoes must be removed before entering each building*, is a museum and research centre in the Uttarayan complex, containing photographs, manuscripts and Tagore's personal belongings; the peripheral buildings contain photos too. Well documented and very informative so allow at least an hour to read the 'small print'. The garden is delightful, particularly when the roses

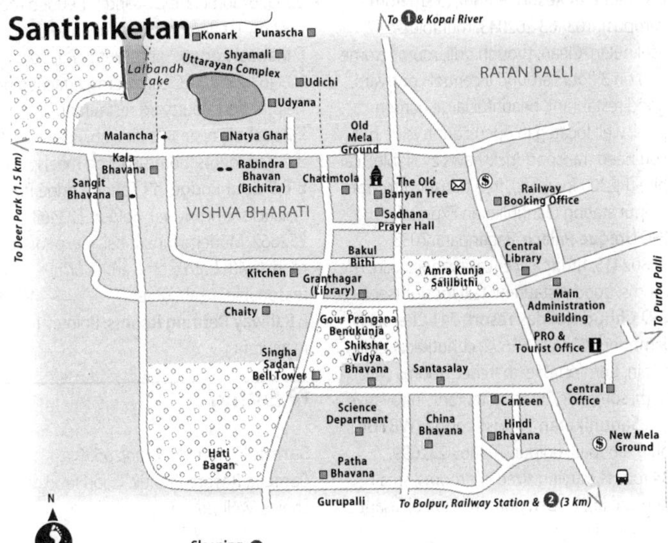

 are blooming. **Kala Bhavan Gallery** ⓘ *closed Wed, 1500-1700*, has a rich collection of 20th-century Indian art, particularly sculptures, murals and paintings by famous Bengali artists. **Nandan Museum** ⓘ *Bharati, closed Wed. 0730-1200, 1400-1600*, has a collection of terracotta, paintings and original tracings of Ajanta murals.

**Surul** (4 km), with its evocative village atmosphere and small terracotta temples with interesting panels on their façades, makes a pleasant trip. The *zamindari* 'Rajbari' with its durga shrine gives an impression of times past.

**Ballavpur Deer Park** (3 km) ⓘ *closed Wed, 1000-1600*, is an area of rapidly eroding laterite *khowai* which has been reclaimed and forms a wooded area with spotted deer and winter migratory birds.

## Excursions

**Bakresvar**, 58 km northwest of Santiniketan, is known for its medicinal sulphurous hot springs (separate bathing areas for men and women, though you may not fancy the tepid pools full of people doing laundry). There are seven important kunds (springs) where the temperature varies from 36°C to 67°C, the hottest being Agnikunda (fire spring). Temples to Siva, Sakti, Kali and Vishnu make it a Hindu pilgrimage centre. The temples are small, modern and white tiled though the Kali temple is old, painted red and set in a clean courtyard. Allow five hours for the trip.

## Sleeping

**Bishnupur** *p608*

**D-E Tourist Lodge**, T03244 252013, 10 rooms, 5 a/c, 4-bed dorm (Rs 80), restaurant, also serves beer.

**F Retiring Rooms. Guest 'n Rest**, near Tagore's statue, serves Bengali food only.

**Santiniketan** *p608, map p609*

There are no options within the campus.

**B-C Camelia Resort**, Prantik (3 km from campus), T03463 262043, multiple@cal2.vsnl.net.in. Clean, though dull, rooms (some a/c) on 3 floors around a central courtyard, good restaurant, beautiful large garden, pool, well located in open countryside but you need transport (rickshaws available), car hire (Rs 300 for 4 hrs), free transport to/from Bolpur station (Santiniketan Express).

**B-C Unique Palace**, Baganpara, T033 26802415, htunpalace_cal@yahoo.co.in. A/c rooms, good restaurant, taxi for sightseeing.

**C-D Chhuti Holiday resort**, 241 Charupalli, Jamboni, T03463 252692, chhuti@cal.vsnl.net.in. Comfortable 'thatched' rooms with bath, some a/c, good restaurant, innovative.

**C-E Santiniketan Tourist Lodge (WBTDC)**, off main road, Bolpur, T03463 252699. 34 rooms, varying sized a/c rooms, small non-a/c (**E**), 13 bed dorm (Rs 80), pleasant garden, poor food.

**D Mayurakshi**, Prantik, near station, T03463 252958. Some a/c rooms, unimaginative modern block but comfortable.

**D Rangamati**, Prabhat Sarani, Bhubandanga, Bolpur, T03463 252305. 22 decent rooms (6 a/c), dorm (Rs 75), restaurant (Indian and Chinese).

**D-E Sathi**, Bhubandanga Rd, Bolpur, T03463 256576. Some a/c, 3, 4 and 5-bedded rooms, best on 1st floor terrace (front and back).

**E Manasi Lodge**, Santiniketan Rd, Bolpur, T03463 254200. Clean rooms, attached bath, helpful staff, courtyard restaurant.

**E Poushali**, near Kala Bhavan, Pearsonpalli. 3-7 bed rooms, home-cooked meals .

**E-F Bolpur Lodge**, off Tourist Lodge Rd (ask rickshaw drivers), Bolpur, T03463 252662. Modern, functional, inexpensive rooms with bath (some a/c), dorm, reasonable meals, quiet.

**F Railway Retiring Rooms**, Bolpur, 1 a/c, restaurant.

## Eating

**Santiniketan** *p608, map p609*

**Camelia Resort**, Prantik. Good food, wide choice, well-priced.

*For an explanation of the sleeping and eating price codes used in this guide, see inside the front cover. Other relevant information is found in Essentials pages 56-61.*

**Chhuti** and **Poushali**, see Sleeping, have restaurants but may require advance notice. **Kalor Dokan**, an 'institution', open all hours. **Maduram**, this sweet shop in Bolpur on Santiniketan Rd, near the petrol station, next to NIIT computer centre, has been highly recommended.

## Festivals and events

**Bishnupur** *p608*
**Aug**: Jhapan, in honour of the serpent goddess *Manasa*, dates from the 17th century. This regional harvest festival is linked with the fertility cult and is unique. Venomous snakes (cobras, pythons, vipers, kraits, flying snakes) are brought in baskets by snake-charmers who display amazing tricks.

**Santiniketan** *p608, map p609*
Poush Mela (**23-25 Dec**), an important fair, coinciding with the village's Foundation Day. Folk performances include *Santals* dances and *baul* songs. Bauls are Bengal's wandering minstrels, who are worshippers of Vishnu. They travel from village to village singing their songs, accompanied by a single string instrument, *ektara*, and a tiny drum. Tribal silver and 'Dhokra' metal crafts make attractive buys. Magh Mela (**end of Jan**), an agricultural and rural crafts fair at Sriniketan, marks the anniversary of the founding of *Brahmo Samaj*. Vasanta Utsav coincides with *Holi*. Programmes of dance, music and singing are held throughout the year, particularly good during the various festivals.

## Shopping

**Bishnupur** *p608*
Cottage industries flourish in the different *paras* (quarters) each devoted to a specialized craft - pottery in Kamarpara, *sankha* (conch-shell) cutting in Sankharipara, and weaving, particularly Baluchari silk saris, in Tantipara. Silk Khadi Seva Mandal, Boltala, and Terracotta Crafts, 500 m from the Tourist Lodge, are recommended.

**Santiniketan** *p608, map p609*
The local embossed leather work is distinctive. **Suprabhat**, Prabhat Sarani, Bhuban Nagar, opposite Tourist Lodge, Bolpur, T03463 253963. Excellent, creative embroidery (including *kantha*), readymade or to order, crafted by local village women, interesting owner. Handicrafts at **Gramin** and **Sarvodaya Ashram** in Bolpur; also Vishva Bharati **Silpa Sadans** in Santiniketan and Sriniketan.

**Books**
**Manisha Granthalaya**, Sriniketan Rd, Bolpur and **Subarnarekha** in Santiniketan sell rare books.

## Transport

**Bishnupur** *p608*
For the area around car hire from Tourist Lodge; Kiron Homeo Hall, Matukgunge. Cycle rickshaws are widely available.

WBSTC buses from Esplanade, Kolkata. STC Super Express buses from Durgapur, 1115 (1 hr). Cars take up to 5 hrs on appalling roads. Train from Kolkata (H) to **Bankura**: *Howrah-Purulia Exp, 8017*,1645, 4 hrs.

**Santiniketan** *p608, map p609*
Mainly cycle rickshaws and taxis available.

Train from **Kolkata** (H): *Ganadevta Exp, 3017*, 0605, 2¾ hrs; *Shanti Niketan Exp, 3015*, 1005, 2½ hrs. From **Bolpur** to **Kolkata** (H): *Shanti Niketan Exp, 3016*, 1310, 2½ hrs; *Kanchenjunga Exp, 5658*, (**S**), 1633, 4 hrs, booking highly recommended (avoid station counter as the pleasanter University booking office, 1030-1530, has a daily quota of 50 reserved seats, Rs 60). Also trains to New Jalpaiguri (for Darjeeling) via Malda.

## Directory

**Bishnupur** *p608*
**Banks** State Bank of India changes foreign cash. **Hospital** Sub-Division Hospital, near the Court. Vishnu Pharmacy in Maruee Bazar.

**Santiniketan** *p608, map p609*
**Banks** State Bank of India, Bolpur and Santiniketan; foreign TCs cashed in Santiniketan only. **Hospital** Pearson Memorial Hospital, Santiniketan. **Tourist office** Tourist Lodge, Bolpur, T03463 252398. PRO, Vishva Bharati Office, T03463 252751. 1000-1700, closed Tue afternoon, Wed.

# North of Kolkata

*This area has the peaceful University town of Santiniketan, home of Tagore, the 300-year-old terracotta temples of Bishnupur and one of the Indian Rhino's last safe havens in the Jaldapara Wildlife Sanctuary. It also has West Bengal's principle destination, Darjeeling, the Queen of hills. The old colonial summer retreat is surrounded by wonderful walks and is the place to get a decent cuppa.* » *For Sleeping, Eating and other listings, see pages 623-631.*

## Murshidabad → *Phone code: 03482. Colour map 4, grid C1. Population: 36,900.*

Named after Nawab Murshid Kuli Khan, a Diwan under Emperor Aurangzeb, Murshidabad, 12 km from Baharampur, became the capital of Bengal in 1705 and remained so up to the time of the battle of Plassey.

**Nizamat Kila** on the river bank, near the town centre, encloses the Nawabs' old **Hazarduari** (1,000 doors) **Palace** ⓘ *closed Fri, 1000-1630, Rs 2, no photography*, built in the Italian style in 1837. It is now a splendid museum with a portrait gallery, a circular durbar hall and a library and contains a rare collection of old arms, curios, china and paintings. The large newer **Imambara** (1847), opposite the palace, is also Italianate in style. The domed, square pavilion (**Madina**) with a verandah nearby may be what remains of the original Imambara. There are numerous 18th-century monuments in the city. Mir Jafar and later his son Miran lived at **Jafaragunj Deorhi**, known as the traitor's gate. **Kat-gola**, the garden-house of a rich Jain merchant, has a collection of curios and an old Jain temple. The **Palace of Jagat Sett**, one of the richest financiers of the 18th century, is 2 km from the Jafargung Cemetery to the north of the palace. The **Katra Mosque** (1724), modelled on the great mosque at Mecca and an important centre of learning, is outside the city to the east. It was built by Murshid Kuli Khan who lies buried under the staircase. **Moti Jheel** (pearl lake) and the ruins of **Begum Ghaseti's palace** are 3 km south of the city. Only a mosque and a room remain. **Khosbagh** (Garden of Delight) across the river has three walled enclosures.



## Malda → *Phone code: 03512. Colour map 4, grid B1.*

Once the Dutch and French traded from Old Malda, which lies at the confluence of two rivers 4 km away. Around 1680, the English established a market town here when they bought the village from a local landlord, and then moved to nearby **Ingraz (English) Bazar** (Englezabad) in 1771 where they built a fort. Now it is famous only for its juicy large Fajli mangoes and gives access to Gaur and Pandua. The **Jami Masjid** in Old Malda was built in 1596 out of decorated brick and stone and displays some good carving on the entrance pillars. The 17-m **Nimasarai tower** across the river dating from the same period has strange stones embedded on the outer surface, which may have once been used to display beheaded criminals. **Malda Museum** (1937) has a collection of stone images, coins and inscriptions from Gaur and Pandua. The **market** behind the **Tourist Lodge** is fascinating. Malda has several banks, post offices and hospitals.

## Gaur and Pandua → *Colour map 4, grid B1.*

Gaur's situation on the banks of the River Ganga, yet within easy reach of the Rajmahal Hills with their fine black basalt, made it possible for gifted stonemasons to construct beautiful religious and secular buildings. Muslim monuments of the Sultanate period are strewn around the quiet, deserted city. Pandua alternated with Gaur as a capital of Bengal between 1338 and 1500, when it was abandoned. Some of the ruins here show clearly how the Muslims made free use of material from Hindu temples near Malda. 

## Gaur

On the ancient site of Lakshanavati, Gaur was the capital of King Sasanka in the seventh century, followed by the Buddhist Pala kings. The city became famous as a centre of education and culture during the reign of the Hindu Sena kings in the 12th century. At the beginning of the 13th century it was invaded by Bhaktiar Khalji and then captured by the Afghan Fakhr-ud-din Dynasty in the 14th century. They plundered the temples to construct their own mosques and tombs. Gaur was sacked by Sher Shah Suri in 1537 and the city's population was wiped out by plague in 1575.

The remains of the embankments of the fort are to the south on the bank of the Bhagirati. The great golden mosque, **Bari Sona Masjid** or Baroduari (12-door), was built in 1526 and is an enormous rectangular stone-faced brick structure with a large open square in front. Fine marble carving is still visible on the remains of the minarets. Note the small Kali temple at the entrance.

Bangladesh can be seen from the **Dakhil Darwaza** (early 15th century), the main fort gateway with its five-storeyed towers. It was built of small red bricks embossed with terracotta decorations. The turrets and circular bastions produce a striking contrast of light and shade with decorative motifs of suns, rosettes, lamps and fretted borders. During the 15th century, a number of mosques and mausoleums were built in the new architectural style.

The **Firuz Minar** (Victory Tower) built by Sultan Firuz Shah in 1486 has a spiral staircase. The lower storeys are 12 sided while the upper are circular, with striking blue and white glazed tiles, used in addition to the terracotta and brick. The builders of the **Chika Mosque** (Bat Mosque, early 15th century), near the Kadam Rasul, made free use of Hindu idols in its construction. The **Chamkati Mosque** (circa 1475) shows the vaulted ceiling of the verandah. Inside the southeast corner of the Fort is the massive **Baisgazi Wall** (height being '22 yard') which enclosed the Old Palace with its *darbar*, *harem* etc. **Kadam Rasul** (1513) is a domed building with a Bengali *chala* roof, which housed the relic of the Prophet, a footprint in stone. The two-storeyed **Lukochuri Darwaza** (Hide-and-Seek Gate, circa 1655) is in the later Mughal style.

The **Tantipara Mosque** (circa 1475; *tanti*, weaver) has superbly decorated red brick with five entrance arches and octagonal turrets, while the elegant **Lattan** (Painted) **Mosque** (1475), attributed to Yusuf Shah, was decorated with bands of blue, green, yellow and white glazed tiles. Some 2 km south, the ruined **Chhoti Sona Masjid**, has a carved gate. It is close to the border with Bangladesh.

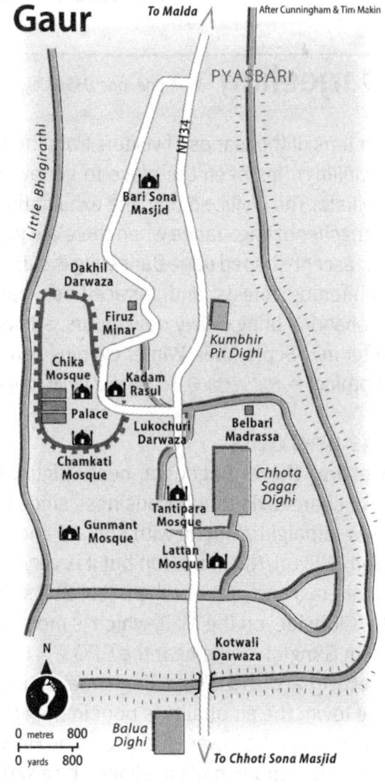

**Ramkeli**, not far from the Bari Sona Masjid, has the Madan Mohan Jiu Mandir and is of particular religious significance for the followers of **Sri Chaitanya**, the 14th-century Bengali religious reformer. **Tamaltola** marks the place where he meditated under a tree and pilgrims come here to see a footprint in stone.

To get to the site, from Malda get a bus for Mohodipur from near the Tourist Lodge and ask to be dropped at Pyasbari (tea and snacks available). Stay on the narrow tarmac road and you won't get lost. Turn right from the NH34 for the site in which you can wander around free. To return to Malda, stop a bus or share a taxi.

## Pandua

The old brick-paved road, nearly 4-m wide and about 10-km long, passes through the town and most of the monuments stand close to it. The **Adina Masjid** (1364-1374) ① *free*, exemplifies Muslim architecture in medieval Bengal. Built by Sultan Sikander Shah and once comparable to the great eighth-century mosque at Damascus, it is sadly in a poor state of repair. The vast space enclosed by pillared aisles has an 88-arch screen around a quadrangle with the mosque. Influence of 12th-century Sena architecture is evident in the tall, ornate, tiered *sikhara* and trefoil arches and the remarkable absence of a large entrance gateway. Most of the substructure, and some pillars, was of basalt plundered from existing Hindu temples and palaces. A small doorway in the western back wall of the mosque, clearly taken from an earlier Vishnu temple, exhibits the stonemasons' skill and the exceptional metalwork of the time. The **Eklakhi Mausoleum**, built of brick (circa 1412), has a Hindu idol carved on its front lintel. The **Qutb Shahi Mosque** (also *Sona* or Golden Mosque) was built in 1582. Further along are the ruins of the 17th-century **Chhoti** and **Bari Dargahs**.

To get to the site, from the **Tourist Lodge** in Malda get a Siliguri or Raiganj bus (Rs 5) and ask to be dropped at Pandua Bus Stand (tea and snacks are available). The narrow tarmac road to the site, off the NH34, is easy to follow and gives a fascinating 'behind-the-scenes' view of Bengali village life. Buses from Adina return to Malda.

# Darjeeling → *Phone code: 0354. Colour map 4, grid A1. Population: 107,500. Altitude: 2,134 m.*



For tens of thousands of visitors from the steamy summer heat of the plains Darjeeling (Darjiling) has been the place to get away from it all. It is the principal escape from Kolkata. The idyllic setting, the exhilarating air outside town and stunning views of the Kangchendzonga range when there are gaps in the clouds attract trekkers too. Built on a crescent-shaped ridge Darjeeling is surrounded by hills which are thickly covered with coniferous forests and terraced tea gardens. Between June and September the monsoons bring heavy downpours, sometimes causing landslides, but the air clears after mid-September. Winter evenings are cold enough to demand log fires and warm clothing. ▸▸ *For Sleeping, Eating and other listings, see pages 623-631.*

## Ins and outs

**Getting there** Bagdogra, near Siliguri, is Darjeeling's nearest airport where jeeps and share-taxis tout for business since buses only run from Siliguri. Trains connect New Jalpaiguri/Siliguri with Kolkata and other major cities. The diesel 'toy train' runs from Siliguri/NJP in season but it is very slow. Most people reach Darjeeling by bus or share-taxi and arrive at the Bazar Bus stand in the lower town, though some taxis go to 'Clubside' on the Mall, which is more convenient for most accommodation. Buses from Gangtok arrive near the GPO.

**Getting around** Darjeeling's roads slope quite gently so it is easy to walk around the town; the air quality is poor in the lower town due to exhaust fumes. The railway station is in the lower part of town on Hill Cart Road, with the taxi and bus stands. The lower and upper roads are linked by a series of connecting roads and steep steps. For

## A mini miracle

For many people the somewhat erratic narrow gauge Toy Train between New Jalpaiguri and Darjeeling, with its 0.6 m (2 ft) gauge track which used to be hauled by sparkling tank engines, is a rewarding experience. The brainchild of an East Bengal railway agent Franklyn Prestage, the train promised to open access to the hills from the sweltering humidity of the Kolkata plains in the summer. Following the line of an earlier steam tramway, the name was changed to the Darjeeling Himalayan Railway Company in 1881. It is a stunning achievement, winding its way up the hillside, often with brilliant views over the plains covering the 82 km with gradients of up to one in 19. At Ghoom, it reaches 2,438 m and then descends 305 m to Darjeeling. The DHR has been upgraded to a 'World Heritage Site' and has newly refurbished carriages with cushioned seats and window curtains for the steam 'Tourist trains'. It is a must for steam buffs – despite derailments which are "swiftly dealt with and you are lifted back on the tracks within 20 minutes".

sights away from the centre you need to hire a taxi. Clubside is the most convenient rank. Be prepared for seasonal water shortages and frequent power cuts. After dark a torch is essential. » *See Transport, page 628, for further details.*

*Roads can get washed away during the monsoons and may remain in poor condition even in October.*

## History

Darjeeling (official but rarely used spelling – Darjiling) means 'region of the *dorje* – thunderbolt'. The surrounding area once belonged to Sikkim, although parts were annexed from time to time by the Bhutanese and Nepalese. The East India Company returned the territory's sovereignty to the Rajas of Sikkim, which led to the British obtaining permission to gain the site of the hill-station called Darjeeling in 1835, in return for an annual payment. It was practically uninhabited and thickly forested but soon grew into a popular health resort after a road and several houses were built and tea-growing was introduced. The Bengal Government escaped from the Kolkata heat to take up its official summer residence here. The upper reaches were originally occupied by the Europeans, who built houses with commanding views. Down the hillside on terraces sprawled the humbler huts and bazars of the Indian town.

## Sights

**Observatory Hill**, sacred to Siva, is pleasant for walks though the views of the mountains are obscured by tall trees. Further north is **Himalayan Mountaineering Institute and Everest Museum** ⓘ *T0354 2252438, closed Tue in winter, 0900-1300, 1400-1600, Rs 15 (includes Zoo), still camera Rs 10, video Rs 20, entrance is through the zoo on Jawahar Rd West.* Previously headed by the late Tenzing Norgay who shared the first climb of Everest in 1953, it traces the history of attempted climbs from 1857 and displays old mountaineering equipment including that used on that historic Tenzing-Hillary climb. Recommended. The **zoo** ⓘ *1000-1600, Rs 15 (includes institute)*, is next to the Mountaineering Institute. High-altitude wildlife includes Himalayan black bear, Siberian tiger, red pandas, yaks and llama. There are large enclosures over a section of the hillside though at feeding time and wet weather they retreat into their small cement enclosures giving the impression that they are restricted to their cells. There is a reasonably successful snow leopard breeding programme.

*Visit the Shrubbery behind Raj Bhawan on Birch Hill for spectacular views of Kangchendzonga.*

Back into the centre of the town, the pedestrianized **Mall** to the east of Observatory Hill offers good views near the Chowrasta. Beware of the monkeys; they bite. The **Natural History Museum** ⓘ *off Mall Rd, closed Wed afternoons and Thu, 1000-1600, Rs 2*, has a large collection of fauna of the region. A visit is recommended. The **Tibetan Refugee. Self-help Centre** ⓘ *T0354 2253122, closed Sun, walk to viewpoint 500 m beyond Windamere hotel and then walk down for about 30 mins (ask around)*, with its temple, school and hospital is north of town. After the Chinese invasion, thousands of Tibetan refugees settled in Darjeeling (many having accompanied the Dalai Lama) and the rehabilitation centre was set up in 1959 to

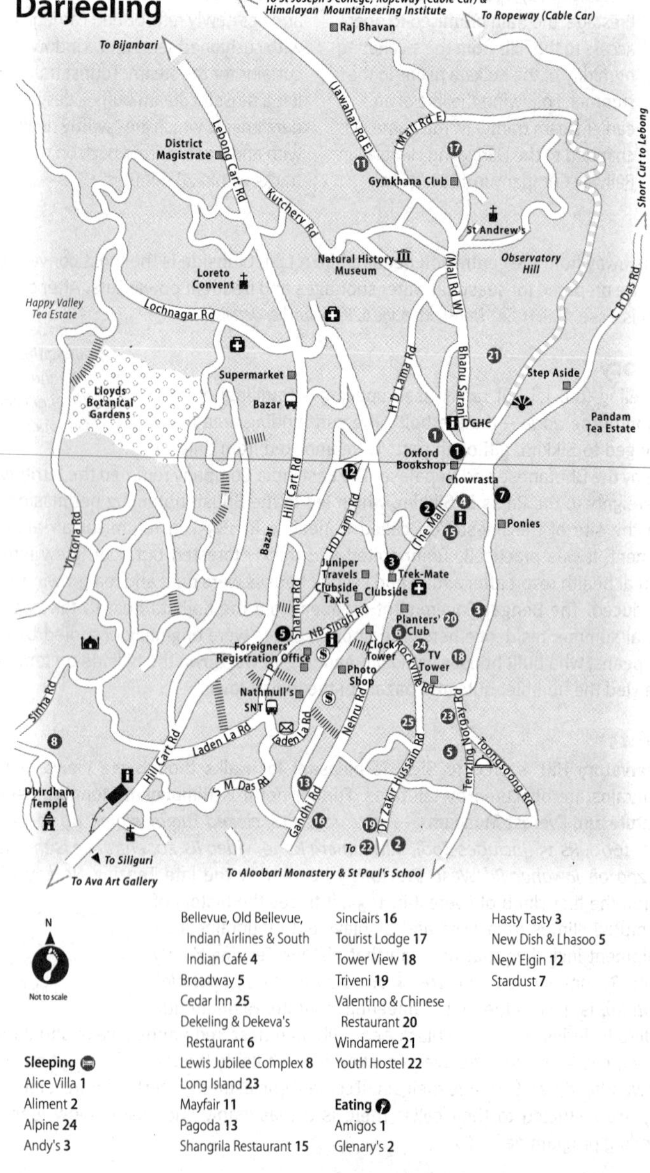

enable them to continue to practise their skills and provide a sales outlet. You can watch them at work (carpet weaving, spinning, dyeing, woodwork, etc) during the season, when it is well worth a visit (closes for lunch). The shop sells carpets (orders taken and posted), textiles, curios or jewellery, though not cheap to buy.

South of town, the **Aloobari Monastery**, on Tenzing Norgay Road, is open to visitors. Tibetan and Sikkimese handicrafts made by the monks are for sale. **Ava Art Gallery** ⓘ *Ghoom, T0354 2252469, 0800-1200, 1230-1800*, has exceptional embroidered portraits.

To the east of town are the **Lloyds Botanical Gardens** ⓘ *closed Sun and bank holidays, 0600-1700*, near the market. These were laid out in 1878 on land given by Mr W Lloyd, owner of the Lloyd's Bank. They have a modest collection of Himalayan and Alpine flora including banks of azaleas and rhododendrons, magnolias, a good orchid house and a herbarium. It is a pleasant and quiet spot. **Victoria Falls** which is only impressive in the monsoons provides added interest to a three-hour nature trail. The closest tea gardens to Darjeeling is the **Happy Valley Tea Estate** ⓘ *closed Sun, Mon, visitors 0800-1200, sometimes 1300-1630 (best in the morning), with good guide informative tours*, a 2-km walk from the market, which uses the 'orthodox' method, see box page 618.

## Excursions

**Ghoom Monastery**, at an altitude of 2,550 m, is the important Yiga-Choling Gompa, a Yellow-hat Buddhist Monastery. Built in 1875, it houses famous Buddhist scriptures. You can visit Ghoom 8 km away, on the steam 'Tourist Train' April-June, October-November. There is an interesting Darjeeling Himalayan Railway museum at the station. A few spruced up carriages do the 'tourists only' ride in summer with a photo stop at Batasia, departing at 1000, returning at 1230 (check). The fare is Rs 240 but limited to 40 persons so go early to join the queue; tickets go on sale at 0800. See also 'Toy Train' under Siliguri on page 630. Alternatively, go on the diesel train at 0900, Rs 25 (1st class); Rs 4 (2nd class) and return on foot or by bus.

**Batasia Loop**, 5 km away on the way to Ghoom, which allows the narrow-gauge rail to do a figure of eight loop, has a war memorial with a pleasant small park with good mountain views (Rs 3).

**Chunnu Falls**, 10 km down a steep switchback road, has turned an impressive waterfall into an artificial concrete park with flower beds, metal stairways and viewing platforms. Limited refreshments are served on a pleasant terrace.

The disused **Lebong Race Course**, 8 km away, was once the smallest and highest in the world and still pleasant for a walk.It was started as a parade ground in 1885.

It is worth rising as early as 0400 to make the one hour journey for a breathtaking view (weather permitting) of the sunrise on Kangchendzonga at **Tiger Hill** ⓘ *jeeps from Darjeeling, Rs 400 – you may wish to walk back from Tiger Hill (about 2 hrs, 11 km) or visit Ghoom on the way back (altitude: 2,590 m)*. Mount Everest (8,846 m), 225 km away, is visible on a clear day. The crowds at sunrise disappear by mid-morning.

# Trekking around Darjeeling

The trekking routes around Darjeeling are well established, having been popular for nearly 100 years. Walks lead in gentle stages along safe roads and through wooded hills up to altitudes of 3,660 m. Trails pass through untouched nature filled with rhododendrons, magnolias, orchids and wild flowers, together with forests, meadows and small villages. All this to a back drop of mountains stretching from Mount Everest to the hills of Bhutan, including the third highest mountain in the world, Kanchendzonga. The best trekking season is in April-May when the magnolias and rhododendrons are in full bloom, or October-November. In spring there may be

## Quali-tea brew

An ancient Chinese legend suggests that 'tay', tea, originated in India, although tea was known to have been grown in China around 2700 BC. It is a species of Camellia, Camellia thea. After 1833, when its monopoly on importing tea from China was abolished, the East India Company made attempts to grow tea in Assam using wild 'chai' plants found growing there and later introduced it in Darjeeling and in the Nilgiri hills in the South. Today India is the largest producer of tea in the world. Assam grows over half and Darjeeling about a quarter of the nation's output. Once drunk only by the tribal people, it has now become India's national drink.

The old 'orthodox' method of tea processing produces the aromatic lighter coloured liquor of the Golden Flowery Orange Pekoe in its most superior grade. The fresh leaves are dried by fans on 'withering troughs' to reduce the moisture content and then rolled and pressed to express the juices which coat the leaves. These are left to ferment in a controlled environment to produce the desired aroma. Finally the leaves are dried by passing them through a heated drying chamber and then graded – the unbroken being the best quality, down to the 'fannings' and 'dust'. The more common 'crushing, tearing, curling' (CTC) method produces tea which gives a much darker liquor.

Most of Darjeeling's tea is sold through auction houses, the largest centre being in Kolkata. Tea tasting and blending are skills which have developed over a long period of time and are highly prized. The industry provides vital employment in the hill areas and is an assured foreign exchange earner.

the occasional shower. In the autumn the air is dry and the visibility excellent. In winter the lower altitude trails that link Rimbick with Jhepi (18 km) can be very attractive for birdwatchers. Ask in Darjeeling for trekking routes as there is an extensive network of varied trails that link the hillside towns and villages. The agents in Darjeeling can organize four-seven day programmes. For trek agents, see Darjeeling above or see West Bengal Tourism wed-site:www.wbtourism.com.

The Tourist Bureau in Darjeeling will provide detailed information, plan the trek and book your accommodation and also obtain necessary equipment (sleeping bag, wind-jacket etc) and arrange a Sherpa guide. The Glenarys can arrange huts and some equipment, and put you in touch with guides. Trekking gear can also be hired from the Youth Hostel where there is a very useful book of suggestions from other trekkers. Himalayan Mountaineering Institute, see page 615, runs some courses for trekkers about Rs 250 for Indians, Rs 1,200 for foreigners.

## Sandakphu and Phalut

Most trekkers and visitors either walk or drive by jeep to **Sandakphu**, a small settlement located at 3,636 m on the Singalila Ridge, 57 km from Darjeeling. A good viewing point 100 m above Sandakphu offers fantastic views, including the famous northern face of Everest (8,846 m), Kangchendzonga (8,598 m), Chomolhari, the highest peak in Bhutan, and numerous peaks such as Pandim that lie in Sikkim. Everest is 140 km from Sandakphu as the crow flies. The entire area is a birdwatcher's paradise with over 600 species including orioles, minivets, flycatchers, finches, sunbirds, thrushes, piculets, falconets and Hoodson's Imperial pigeons. The mixed rhododendron, oak and conifer forests of the area are particularly well preserved.

**Phalut**, 22 km from Sandakphu, along an undulating, partly jeepable track, is at the junction of Nepal, Sikkim and West Bengal. It offers even closer views of

Kangchendzonga. It is best to avoid trekking here in May-June and mid-September to 25 October when large numbers of college trekking teams from West Bengal can descend on the area. March and November are highly recommended for clear mountain views.

## Sandakphu to Rimbick

Although Gorkhey, Phalut, Rammam and Rimbick lie just south of the border with Sikkim, entering Sikkim is not permitted on this route. To do a circular walk continue 21 km along the Singalila ridge to **Phalut** (3,600 m) where there is a Trekkers' Hut. Alternatively you can retrace your steps 4 km back towards **Bhikebhanjang** and then take a 16-km long trail through fine forests of the Singalila National Park down to **Rimbick** from where there is a daily bus to Darjeeling. From Phalut continue for 7 km down to the Trekkers' Hut at **Gorkhey** where you can stay the night, or walk 3 km to the village of **Samanden**, 'hidden' in a hanging valley and a further 6 km to **Rammam**. The clean, comfortable Sherpa Lodge, in a nice garden, recommended for friendly service (bus tickets and seats reserved) and good food. Alternatively, the Trekkers' Hut is about 1 km before Rammam village. From Rammam it is a two-hour walk down to the attractive Trekkers' Hut at **Siri Khola** and a further two hours to Rimbick. This entire area is particularly rich in birdlife.

## Sabarkum via Ramman to Molley or Bijanbari

An alternative quieter trail links Sabarkum (7 km before Phalut on the main Sandakphu-Phalut trail) with Rammam with a possible overnight halting place at the **Molley** Trekkers' Hut. Good *dahl bhat* and *rakshi/tongba:* share the kitchen fire with the family. Sherpas eat in a shack 200 m uphill from the Youth Hostel. Those with five days to spare can return by the **Rammam-Rimbick-Jhepi-Bijanbari** route (153 km). From Rammam you can cross by a suspension bridge over the Siri Khola River and follow the path up the valley, which leads to Dentam in Sikkim (entry into Sikkim is

## Darjeeling treks

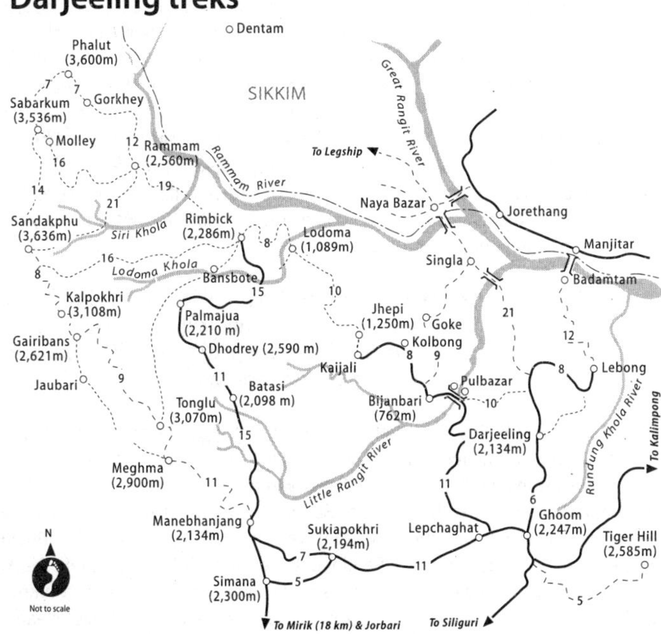

not permitted). This less well-trodden valley has rich birdlife (particularly kingfishers), and excellent views of undisturbed forest. From **Bijanbari** (762 m) it is possible to return to Darjeeling, 36 km away, in a jeep or climb a further 2 km to Pulbazar and then return to Darjeeling 16 km away. Those wishing only to go to Rimbick may return to Manebhanjang via Palmajua and Batasi (180 km), which takes one day.

## Singalila trek

The 160-km Singalila trek starts from the small border town of **Manebhanjang**, 26 km from Darjeeling. The journey to and from Darjeeling can be done by bus or you can hire a Land Rover or jeep and be driven there early in the morning in 1½ hours. There is a frontier check post at **Sukiapokhri**, 7 km short of Manebhanjang, where you need to enter your passport details in the register. If you have not arranged for transport to meet you at a particular point then it is entirely possible to travel back to Darjeeling from every roadhead by public bus with services at least once daily, often three to four times daily.

Sleeping at Trekkers' Huts, mostly with 15-25 beds and costing Rs 25-50/bed have been built or refurbished in Tonglu, Sandakphu, Phalut, Gorkhey, Molle, Rammam, Rimbick and Siri Khola. Although usually available, it is wise to book in advance from the Deputy Commissioner, Improvement Fund Trust, Darjeeling, during May/June and October when these trails can be very busy. Any trek agent in Darjeeling will arrange these bookings for a small fee. Private lodges such as Sherpa Lodge in Rimbick and Rammam, and other trailside lodges in Meghma, Jaubari and Kalpokhri, are usually friendly, flexible and provide a reasonable but basic accommodation.

**Day 1 To Tonglu (or Tumling)** 1 km beyond Manebhanjang town you reach a rough stone paved track leading sharply up to the left. Tonglu (3,030 m) is 11 km from this point if you follow the jeep track, slightly less if you take the frequent but very steep short cuts. Alternatively, head for Tumling, just the other side of the peak of the hill from Tonglu (you take the alternative road from Meghma and rejoin the main route, 1 km after Tumling). Sleeping at **Tonglu**. A Trekkers' Hut has 24 beds and a fine view of the Kangchendzonga range. From here you can also see the plains of North Bengal, some valleys of Nepal in the distance. Closer to hand are the snow fed rivers, the Testa in the East and Koshi in the West. Also in **Tumling** where Shikhar Lodge has simple basic and clean rooms, very pleasant, local teacher's friendly family, "fabulous supper and breakfast", lovely garden. There are tea shops at **Chitre** and **Meghma**. Meghma has an interesting monastery noted for its large collection of Buddhist sculptures – 108 statues, according to locals. Ask at the teahouse opposite, to get in. Hotel Indica, Meghma, is a simple Tibetan home with homemade cheese hanging from ceiling, but it is unfortunately dirty.

**Day 2 To Jaubari and Gairibans** A level walk along the ridge takes you past the long 'mani' wall to the Nepalese village of Jaubari where the trail turns sharply to the right back into Indian territory and down through bamboo and rhododendron forests to the village of Gairibans in a forest clearing. No visa necessary.

**Day 3 To Sandakphu** It is 14 km uphill to Sandakphu, with a lunch break in Kalpokhri with its attractive attractive 'black' lake surrounded by fir trees, about midway. The name kalpokhri means 'black lake'. Even in winter the lake never freezes. The last 3 km from Bhikebhanjang (tea shop) to Sandakphu are particularly steep, the walk takes more than an hour but the views from the Singalila Ridge make it all worthwhile. Another viewpoint is 100 m above Sandakphu (see above). There are three Trekkers' Huts each with its own dining area, toilets and cookhouse – caretakers can arrange simple meals on extra payment. Sherpa Chalet, Sandakphu, is basic, clean and comfortable and provides good food. The drive back to Manebhanjang by pre-arranged four-wheel drive can take four hours along a very rough track. 

## Mirik and Kurseong

**Mirik**, 49 km from Darjeeling, at an altitude of 1,730 m, has forests of japonica, orange orchards, tea gardens and cardamom plantations. It once held the promise of an attractive resort but is sadly neglected. **Sumendu Lake**, with its 3½-km cobbled promenade, offers boating. You can visit the carpet weaving centre at **Krishannagar**, south of the lake, or trek to **Kurseong** and **Sandakphu**.

The small, peaceful hill station of **Kurseong** ('Place of the White Orchid') (altitude: 1,458 m) to the east of Mirik, is surrounded by tea gardens and has some popular boarding schools. Travellers suggest stopping here overnight on the Toy Train between Siliguri and Darjeeling. You can visit the **Makaibari Tea Estate** 4 km way (closed Monday) and the **Forest Museum** on Dow Hill.

At **Tung** nearby, the St Alphonsus Social and Agricultural Centre, run by a Canadian Jesuit is working with the local community through education, housing, agricultural, forestry and marketing projects. They welcome volunteers, contact ⓘ *SASAC, Tung, Darjeeling, West Bengal, T0354 2242059.*

## Kalimpong → *Phone code: 03552. Colour map 4, grid B2. Population: 43,000. Altitude: 1,250 m.*

Set in beautiful wooded mountain scenery, Kalimpong, a remote hill station, has been a meeting point of the once 'three Closed Lands' on the trade route to Tibet, Bhutan and Nepal. It has a relaxed and unhurried air about it. Away from the crowded and rather scruffy centre near the Motor Stand with the sports ground to one side, the town becomes more spaced out as mountain roads wind up and down the hillsides leading up to the monasteries, mission schools and orchid nurseries nearby. The name is said by some to be derived from pong *(stronghold) of* kalon *(king's minister), or from* Kalibong, *a plant fibre.* ▸▸ *For Sleeping, Eating and other listings, see pages 623-631.*

### Ins and outs

**Getting there** Bagdogra is the nearest airport and New Jalpaiguri the nearest railhead. Buses and shared taxis from there arrive at the bazar Motor Stand in about three hours. From Darjeeling, the 51-km journey (2½ hours) is through beautiful scenery. The road winds down through the Lopchu former Peshok tea estates and then descends to 250 m at Tista where it crosses the river on a 'new' concrete bridge. 'Lovers' Meet' and 'View Point' give superb views of the Rangit and Tista rivers.
**Getting around** The centre is compact enough to be seen comfortably on foot. The surroundings are ideal for walking, though some may prefer transport to visit nearby sights. ▸▸ *See Transport, page 629, for further details.*

### Sights

The traditional market at the 10th Mile has great atmosphere. The *haat* here every Wednesday and Saturday draws colourful villagers who come to sell fruit, unfamiliar vegetables, traditional medicines, woollen cloth, yarn and much more. It is remarkably clean and laid back, a delight to explore and find unusual merchandise - curly young fern tops, bamboo shoots, dried mushrooms, fragrant spices, musk, *chaang* paraphernalia, large chunks of brown soap, and tiny chickens in baskets alongside gaudy posters. The oldest, the **Thongsa Gompa Bhutanese monastery**, 10th Mile (1692) has been renovated. Further north, the Tibetan monastery (Yellow Hat) at Tirpai, the **Tharpa Choling** (1922) has a library of

 Tibetan manuscripts and *thangkas*, see page 546. The **Pedong Bhutanese monastery** (1837) near the old Bhutanese Damsang Fort at Algara (15 km) holds ceremonial dances every February. At Durpin Dara, the highest point in Kalimpong with superb views, stands the **Ringkinpong monastery** of Zang Dog Palri Phodrang. Unique outside Tibet, it has a school of Tibetan Medicine and is particularly interesting when prayers are being chanted. **Doctor Graham's Homes**, 3 km, was started by the missionary Doctor John Anderson Graham in 1900 when he admitted six needy children. Now there are 1,200 pupils. Volunteers able to spend at least six months should write in advance. There are pleasant **hikes** through Tista Road and rice fields to **Chitray Falls**, 9 km, a three-hour walk to **Bhalu Khop** and a 1½ hours' downhill walk from the Motor Stand to the Relli River. You can **trek** from **Lava** (32 km; monastery and weekly market on Tuesday), or **Lolaygaon** (56 km), which has spectacular views of Kangchendzonga, or picnic on the river beaches at Tista Bazar and Kalijhora.

There are a few nurseries as Kalimpong excels in producing orchids, amaryllis, roses, cacti, dahlias and gladioli. Ganesh Mani Pradhan on 12th Mile, Universal on 8th Mile, Shanti Kunj on BL Dikshit Road, Himalayan on East Main Road, are among many. The Takdah Orchid Centre (44 km) sells 110 varieties. Some are disappointed.



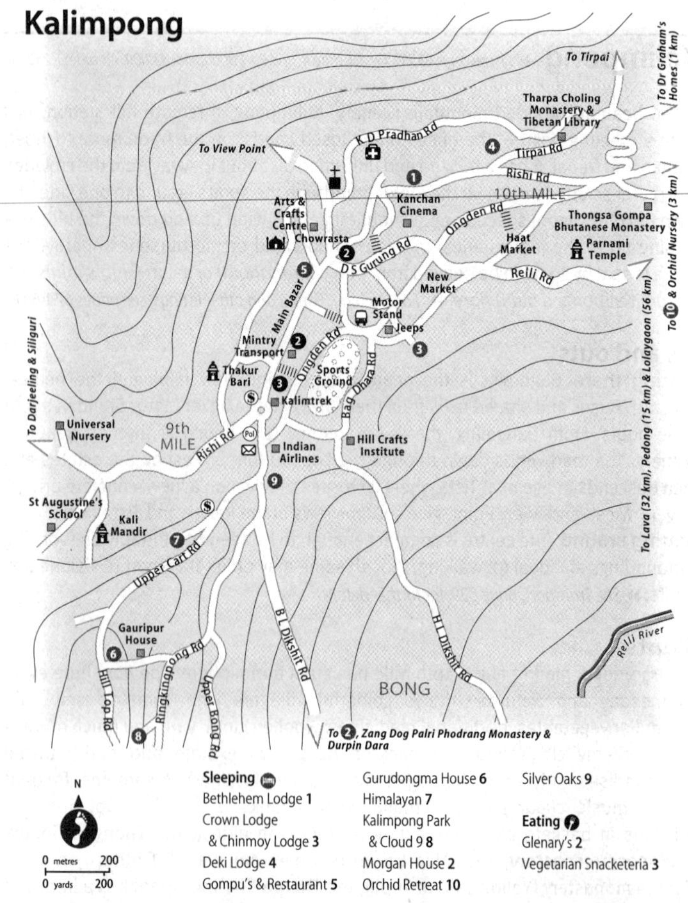

## Siliguri and Jaldapar → *Phone code: 0353. Colour map 4, grid A1.*

Surrounded by tea plantations, **Siliguri** is a largely unattractive transport junction with a vast truck park to the north and a busy main road lined with shops. The narrow-gauge steam 'Toy Train' to Darjeeling starts from here during the tourist season. It is also used as a base for travel into the hills and to the Jaldapara National Park.

The River Torsa flows through **Jaldapara Wildlife Sanctuary**. The riverine forests of sal, khair, sheeshu harbour the one-horned rhino, elephants, wild boar, bison, deer, leopard, gaur and the occasional tiger. It covers an area of 116 sq km and is situated close to Phuntsoling in Bhutan. Trained elephants are available to take visitors around, alternatively vehicle safaris are also possible. It is 160 km from Bagdogra airport, 224 km from Darjeeling. The best time to visit is from November to April when forest cover is thinner.

## Sleeping

**Murshidabad** *p612*
E **Whitehouse**, 30 KN Rd, near local bus stand, T03482 255443;
F **Youth Hostels** at Lalbagh and Murhsidabad, reserve through Youth Services, 32/1 BBD Bagh S, Kolkata, T03482280626.

**Malda** *p612*
D **Chanakya**, NH34, town centre, T03512 266620. 12 rooms, some a/c, restaurant, clean, modern.
D-F **Tourist Lodge**, Ingraz Bazar, just northeast of bridge over NH34, T03512 266123. 13 rooms around courtyard (4 a/c) some with bath, a/c bar, restaurant. Reservations: Kolkata, T033 22488271.
E **Purbanchal**, 500 m north of Chanakya, T03512 266183, or reservations on Kolkata, T033 2224278, 30 rooms, restaurant, bar, car hire.
E **Railway Retiring Rooms**. A/c rooms and dorm, modernized, helpful staff. (South Indian platform snacks recommended).
F **Continental Lodge**, 22 KJ Sanyal Rd, by State Bus Stand, T03512 252388. 42 rooms, restaurant, friendly, clean, recommended.

**Darjeeling** *p614, map p616*
Most hotels are within 1 km from the station. Several include all meals in season (Mar-Jun, Sep-Nov) and offer discounts off-season. Some charge extra for Christmas, New Year.
AL-A **Mayfair**, The Mall, opposite Raj Bhavan gate, T0354 2256376, www.mayfairhotels.com. Superb location, among terrace gardens, 21 rooms (5 attractive wooden attics), 11 cottages on hillside below Mall, good Tiffany's restaurant.
AL-A **Windamere**, Observatory Hill, T0354 2254041, www.windamerehotel.com. 27 spacious rooms (no phone or TV), dated bathrooms (limited hot water), enviable position with good views (when clear), sun terraces, charming, plenty of character, a 'Raj' experience – memorabilia, coal fires ("fill room with smoke"), 'hotties' in bed, pre-war piano favourites to accompany 'tea', US$132 includes meals.
A **Cedar Inn**, Dr Zakir Hussain Rd, T0354 2254446, www.cedar-inn.com. A little way out of town, but with great views. Free taxi service around town. Family friendly, sauna/gym, nice garden. Wood panelled rooms.
A **Fortune Resort Central**, Robertson Rd, just below Club side, T0354 2254480, centralresort@fortuneparkhotels.com. 52 rooms, re-opened after renovation.
A **Sinclairs**, 18/1 Gandhi Rd, T0354 22 56431, www.sinclairshotels.com. 54 rooms (central heating), restaurant, bar fairly central location.
A-B **Darjeeling Gymkhana Resort**, The Mall, T0354 2254391. 12 modern rooms, Indian veg restaurant, club on doorstep offering sports/activities, wooded location. Good spot.
A-B **Dekeling Resort at Hawk's Nest**, 2 AJC Bose Rd, 15-min walk from centre, T0354 2253347, www.dekeling.com. 4 spacious suites with fireplaces in restored old wooden Raj retreat, charming Tibetan hospitality, superb isolated position with mountain views, delicious food.
B **Shangrila**, 5 Nehru Rd, near Chowrasta, T0354 2254149, 10 rooms, some with good

views, good restaurant, large communal space, exchange.

**B-C Bellevue**, Chowrasta, T0354 2254075, www.darjeeling-belleviewhotel.com. 43 rooms with bath and hot water (mornings), some large, bright and airy (eg Rooms 35, 49), all rooms have loads of character with many old wooden fittings, good K'dzonga view from roof at sunrise,limited food. Ask for the owner, Lawang, for any tourist information. Friendly management. Very central.

**B-C Main Old Bellevue Hotel**, Chowrasta, T0354 2254178, www.darjeelinghotels.com (above the newer section). Rooms with character in the Heritage building in a pleasant garden.

**B-D Tourist Lodge**, Bhanu Sarani, behind Gymkhana Club, T0354 2254411. 15 rooms, some rather dilapidated, poor service.

**C Dekeling**, 51 Gandhi Rd (the Mall), on Club side, T0354 2254159, www.dekeling.com. 11 rooms with bath on upper floors, 4 attic front rooms with views (noisy when jeeps depart at 0400 for Tiger Hill with lots of hooting!), good restaurant, charming family, 'brilliant hosts', reserve ahead, 40% less in low-season.

**C Alice Villa**, 41 HD Lama Rd below DGHC Tourist Office, Chowrasta, T0354 2254181. 21 large clean rooms (fireplace in some, bucket of coal Rs 75), cosy bungalow, food by arrangement, good value.

**C Valentino**, 6 Rockville Rd, T0354 2252228. 17 clean rooms with mountain views, central heating, good Chinese restaurant, bar.

**C-E The Alpine Hotel**, 104 Rockvile Rd, T0354 2256355, alpinedarj@yahoo.com. Just down from TV tower, clean and bright rooms.

**E Andy's**, 102 Zakir Hussain Rd, 5 mins from Chowrasta past pony sheds towards TV tower, T0354 2253125, slg_mgurung@sancharnet.in, 10 very clean, airy rooms, some with Indian WC, upper floors with small hot shower, bird'seye views from rooftop, kitchenette, communal space, storage for trekkers, friendly family atmosphere. Recommended.

**E Lewis Jubilee Complex** (DGHC), Dr SK Pal Rd, T0354 2256395, 30 rooms, 6-bed dorm (Rs 30), indifferent service.

**E-F Pagoda**, 1 Upper Beechwood Rd, very friendly, clean but basic rooms, some with bath (limited bucket hot water), central yet quite peaceful, good value.

**F Hotel Long Island**, Rochville Dham, down backside of TV tower, near Tower View, T0354 2252043, pritaya19@yahoo.com. Communal hot shower, restaurant, quite location10mins from Chowrasta. Great views from rooftop and upper rooms. Clean basic rooms. Run by very friendly Nepali family. Well recommended!

**F Aliment**, 40 Zakir Hussain Rd, 100 m below Hostel, T 0354 2255068, alimentweb @sify.com. small, clean, bright rooms, hot shower, cheap food in bright restaurant, internet, packed with travellers, good atmosphere, 'library', quiet, friendly owner.

**F Broadway**, 3 Coochbehar Rd, 29 rooms, good location with rooftop views.

**F Tower View**, Rockville Dham, down back-side of TV Tower, pleasant, clean rooms with toilet, shared hot shower, dorm, good food.

**F Triveni**, 85 Dr Zakir Hussain Rd, T0354 2253114. Well-kept basic rooms, home-cooked meals.

**F Youth Hostel** (WB), Dr Zakir Hussain Rd, T0354 2252290, mainly dorm (Rs 25) being renovated, superb position, no restaurant, trekking info, out of town but popular.

### Trekking around Darjeeling *p617*

**C Karmi Farm**, Bijanbari, a haven of rural peace at Kolbong, which you may choose to use as a base, north of Bijanbari (access via Kaijali, four-wheel drives stop 20 mins walk away, or it is 2-3 hrs by pony from Pulbazar). 7 double rooms with bath, simple but spotless, superb food, run by Andrew Pulger-Frame, US$20 includes food, porters etc. Contact **Samsara Travel** in Darjeeling, T0354 2256370, samsara@dte.vsnl.net.in.

**F Teacher's Lodge**, Jaubari, excellent value. There is a large **Trekkers' Hut** at Gairibans with about 20 beds.

### Mirik and Kurseong *p621*

**A-C Orange County Retreat**, Mirik, T0354 2443612, www.glenarys.net. 12 stone cottages, plus a 'honeymoon suit'. Catering more to Indian tourists. Plenty of views and nature. Can arrange treks in the Singalila

*For an explanation of the sleeping and eating price codes used in this guide, see inside the front cover. Other relevant information is found in Essentials pages 56-61.*

range. Owned by **The Glenary**'s restaurant in Darjeeling.

**B-C Jagjeet**, Mirik, T0354 2443231, good rooms, restaurant, bar.

**C-D Tourist Lodge**, Hill Cart Rd, Kurseong, T0354 2344409, 16 rooms, fast food restaurant, bar, good views.

**D Tourist Lodge & Cottages** (DGHC), Mirik, T0354 2443237, modern rooms (Rs 350), dorm (Rs 40), pleasant cottages above lake (Rs 750), good restaurant.

**D-E Amarjeet**, 12Hill Cart Rd, Kurseong, T0354 2344240, 14 rooms, restaurant.

**F Lodge Panchasil**, Krishna Nagar, Mirik, T0354 2443282. Small bright rooms, hot water by the bucket

### Kalimpong *p621, map p622*

Hotels open all year may offer discounts from Nov to Mar; not all accept credit cards.

**A Silver Oaks**, Main Rd, T03552 255296, silveroaks@sify.com. 25 rooms, some with good views, good restaurant (own fruit and vegetables), pleasant garden.

**A-B Himalayan** (Heritage Hotel), Upper Cart Rd, 10-min walk town centre, T03552 255248, himhot@satyam.net.in. 20 rooms, 8 spacious suites in newer imaginatively designed 'cottages', rest in stone-built characterful family home of the MacDonalds (rooms better upstairs), lovely verandah, mountain views, attractive gardens, set menu meals at set times, helpful management.

**B Gurudongma House**, Hill Top Rd, T03552 255204, gurutt@satyam.net.in. Rooms in charming family house and cottage with meals, Alpine tents, gardens, personal service (collect from motor stand), book ahead. Also restored farmhouse at Samthar where you can enjoy country pleasures and wonderful food; contact **Gurudongma Tours and Treks**, gurutt@satyam.net.in.

**B Orchid Retreat**, Ganesh Villa, longish walk from town, T03552 2255389, thakro@cal2.vsnl.net.in. In interesting orchid nursery, 6 rooms in traditional thatched cottages (built with local materials), hot water (no TV or phone), home-cooked meals (Rs 100-150), lovely terrace garden with special palm collection, personal attention, peaceful.

**B-C Kalimpong Park**, Ringkingpong Rd, T03552 255304, parkotel@satyam.net.in. 19 simply furnished, good-sized, airy rooms, **B** suites (some in older 2-storeyed house), good restaurant, bar, exchange, garden, pleasant peaceful location, knowledgeable owner. WB Tourism lodges are clean and simple, breakfast and dinner usually included.

**B-C Morgan House**, Singamari, Durpin Dara Hill, T03552 255384, 3 km frin the centre. 7 rooms with bath (good views from upstairs), restaurant, bar, beautiful location, gardens.

**C Cloud 9**, Ringkingpong Rd, T03552 257304, cloud9kpg@yahoo.com. Clean attractive rooms, good restaurant.

**D Crown Lodge**, off Bag Dhara Rd, near Motor Stand, T03552 255846, slg_ramklg @sancharnet.in. 21 clean well- maintained rooms with bath, hot water, generator, very friendly and helpful, pleasant.

**D-E Bethlehem Lodge**, Rishi Rd (5-min walk from Motor Stand), T03552 255185. Decent rooms with bath, newish and quite clean.

**E-F Chinmoy Lodge**, near Motor Stand, T03552 256264. Newish rooms with bath.

**E-F Deki Lodge**, Tirpai Rd, uphill from Motor Stand, T03552 255095. Clean, basic rooms, good meals, very friendly Tibetan family, good value.

**E-F Gompu's**, off Main Rd, T03552 255818. Clean rooms, good restaurant, questionable reports.

### Siliguri *p623*

Hill Cart Rd is officially Tenzing Norgay Rd.

**B Cindrella**, Sevoke Rd, '3rd mile' (out of town), T0353 2544130, www.cindrella hotels.com. 50 comfortable rooms, some a/c, competent vegetarian restaurant, pool, internet, car hire, pick-up from airport, efficient.

**B Sinclairs**, Mallaguri (Airport Rd), T0353 2517647, pressman_india@hotmail.com. 54 comfortable rooms, good restaurants, pool, attentive service.

**B-D Hotel Conclave**,Hill Cart Rd, (opposite SNT bus stand), T0353 2516144, hotelcon clave@rediffmail.com. A brand new hotel in the centre of town. Good quality rooms, a/c, satelite TV, internet, parking, restaurant serving Indian/European food. Licensed bar.

**B-D Mainak** (WBTDC), Hill Cart Rd (near railway station; auto from NJP Rs 120), T 0353 2513989, maitd@dte.vsnl.net.in. 38 comfortable rooms, 14 a/c (rooms vary), well-kept gardens, restaurant and bar, helpful staff (can book **Tourist Lodge**, Madarihat , see page 626).

**C-D Rajdarbar**, Hill Cart Rd, next to **Hotel Conclave**, T0353 2514316, tapas_kg@hotmail.com. A friendly place, well situated with restaurant

**D-E Embassy**, Sevoke More, near Hill Cart Rd, T0353 2536548. Comfortable rooms with bath.

**D-E Ranjit**, Hill Cart Rd, T0353 2431680. 48 clean but variable rooms, few a/c, good restaurant, bar.

**D-E Vinayak**, Hill Cart Rd, T0353 2431130. 45clean rooms with bath, some a/c, good restaurant.

**D-F Yatri Hotel**, opposite the main bus stand, T0353 734403, yatrihotel@hotmail.com. Basic, cheap rooms with bath, reasonably priced, restaurant next door.

**E Mount View**, Hill Cart Rd, opposite main bus station, T0353 2515919. Basic rooms, good restaurant (wide choice),car parking.

**E Siliguri Lodge**, Hill Cart Rd (near SNS bus stand), T0353 2515290. 10 rooms with bath, dorm.

**E Tourist Services Agency**, a quiet street opposite, Central Bus Terminus, T0353 2531959. Some newer rooms upstairs, relaxed and popular.

**F Railway Retiring Rooms**, Siliguri Junction, and New Jalpaiguri. 4 rooms and 6 dorm beds in each, good vegetarian snacks.

**F Youth Hostel**, Kangchendzonga Stadium, 130 beds.

### Jaldapara Wildlife Sanctuary *p623*

**C Tourist Lodge**, Hollong, 6 km from Madarihat, T03563 262230, built of timber on stilts deep inside the sanctuary. 7 rooms (all meals), the lodge is very popular and is en route to Phuntsholing in Bhutan, book well in advance either through the Tourist Bureau, Siliguri T0353 734401, or DFO T03582 227185, or contact the lodge directly.

**F Nilpara Forest Bungalow**, Hasimara. 2 rooms, very basic, caretaker will prepare a simple meal if requested but take all provisions.

**F Youth Hostel and Lodge**, 4 km from Hasimara railway station, 18 km from Madarihat, at Baradabri. 3 rooms, 14 beds in 4 dorms, poor catering, reserve through DFO, Tourism Centre, Jalpaiguri, T03563 262239 or Kolkata, T 033 22488271.

## Eating

### Darjeeling *p614, map p616*

Hotels with restaurants will usually serve non-residents. Several have bars.

¥¥¥ **New Elgin**. Charming dining room with character, good meals, very pleasant service.

¥¥ **Dekeva's**, 52 Gandhi Rd, near club side. Nice little Tibetan place, cosy, local meals, also fast food.

¥¥ **Glenary's**, Nehru Rd (the Mall), T0354 2257554 glens_getaways@sancharnet.in . Modern tea-room with excellent confectionery, friendly, 1st class breakfast, Kalimpong cheese and wholemeal bread sold, licensed restaurant upstairs pricier, bar downstairs with a 1950's rock around the clock theme. Live music Thu-Sun from 6.30. Internet café (Rs 30 per hr). For trekking to Sandakphu and Rimbik and information about Mirik ask at the travel desk on the ground floor.

¥¥ **New Dish** JP Sharma Rd, below **Lhasoo**. Chinese. Adventurous menu, excellent chicken entrées, friendly staff.

¥¥ **Valentino**, Chinese and Continental.

¥ **Amigos**, good Chinese.

¥ **Fiesta**, Chowrasta. Café style restaurant serving a typical full range menu. Popular but without views.

¥ **Gol Ghar**, Main Bazar. Indian. Excellent meat dishes with *chapatis*, *naan* and *rotis*.

¥ **Lhasoo**, JP Sharma Rd. Tibetan. Friendly.

¥ **South Indian Café**, Chowrasta. Indian. Very good vegetarian meals.

¥ **Stardust**, Chowrasta. Basic range of North and South Indian dishes, pure veg, great views from the terrace.

### Cafés

**Hasty Tasty**, Laden La Rd. Very good Indian fast food, not the cheapest but worth it.

### Kalimpong *p621, map p622*

Most restaurants shut at 2000.

**Cloud**, very good food.

**Fresh bite restaurant**, DB Giri Rd, above Abacus clothes shop. This restaurant with bar offers good range of food including pizza. Friendly staff.

**Glenary's**, opposite Arts Centre and on Main Rd. Bakery sells good bread etc, with tables.

**Gompu's**, rear of hotel, informal, good views, friendly, very good food, including Chinese.

**Vegetarian Snacketeria**, Main Rd, opposite Main Bazar. Very good indian snacks.

## Festivals and events

**Darjeeling** *p614, map p616*
Buddha Jayanti in **Apr-May** celebrates the birth of the Buddha in the monasteries.

## Shopping

**Murshidabad** *p612*
Woven and handblock-printed silk saris and bell-metal ware are the main local industries. Murshidabad also produces excellent mangoes.

**Darjeeling** *p614, map p616*
The markets are colourful and worth visiting.

**Books**
**Greenland**, Laden La Rd, up some steps near entrance to **Prestige Hotel**. Book swap.
**Oxford Bookshop**, Chowrasta, good stock especially local interest, amiable staff.

**Photography**
**Das Studios**, on Nehru Rd, stationery, postcards, interesting black-and-white prints from Raj days; order from album (1-2 days).

**Handicrafts**
The local handicrafts sold widely including Buddhist *tankhas* which are hand painted scrolls surrounded by Chinese brocade, good wood carving, carpets, hand-woven cloth, jewellery, copper, brass and white metal religious curios such as prayer wheels, bowls and statues. The Chowrasta shops are closed on Sun and Chowk Bazar on Thu.
**Dorjee**, Laden La Rd.
**Eastern Arts**, Nehru Rd.
**Gram Shilpa**, for *khadi* cotton and silk, well stocked and very helpful.
**H Mullick**, curios from Chowrasta, a cut above the rest.
**Hayden Hall**, 42 Laden La Rd, colourful woollen goods made by local women's co-op.
**Nepal Curios**, Laden La Rd.
**Tibetan Refugee Self-Help Centre**, Gandhi Rd. See under Sights.

**Tea**
**Nathmull's**, Laden La Rd (above GPO), nathmulls@goldentipstea.com. An institution, vast selection (Rs 90-3,000 a kg), avoid fancy packs, knowledgeable owner.

**Kalimpong** *p621, map p622*
**Handicrafts**
Tibetan and Nepalese handicrafts and woven fabrics are particularly good
**Arts & Crafts Centre**, near Motor Stand, embroidered clothes, fire-screens.
**Gangjong**, Puritam Rd (near Sports ground). Interesting hand-made paper factory.
**Soni Emporium**, near Motor Stand, Mani Link Rd, specializes in Himalayan handicrafts.

## Activities and tours

**Darjeeling** *p614, map p616*
**Clubs**
The old **Gymkhana Club** has 3 good snooker tables, badminton, squash, tennis and roller skating. Temporary membership Rs 30 per day, up to Rs 55 for activities, staff excellent.
**Darjeeling Club**, Nehru Rd, T0354 2254348, the old Planters' Club, a relic of the Raj, membership (Rs 50 per day), allows use of pleasant colonial restaurant (Rs 200 buffet), bar, billiards, a bit run down, but log fires, warm and friendly.

**Riding**
Pony rides are popular on the Mall starting at Chowrasta; also possible to do a scenic half-day ride to Ghoom – agree price, in writing!

**River rafting**
On the Tista, a range of trips, from ½ day to 2-day all-inclusive tented trips covering11 -65 km, Rs 450-1200, contact DGHC Tourism.

**Tour operators**
**Clubside Tours & Travels**, T16 JP Sharma Rd, T0354 2254646, hotel, tours/treks, good jeep hire, air tickets.
**Juniper Tours**, behind police island, New Car Park, Laden La Rd, T0354 2252095, also **Indian Airlines**, Jet Airways agent.
**Pineridge Travels**, Chowrasta, T0354 2253912.
**DGHC**, from Tourist Office (minimum 8).
**Tour 1**: Tiger Hill, Senchal Lake, Ghoom Monastery, Batasia Loop. 0400-0730. Rs 60.
**Tour 2**: Local sightseeing. Ava Gallery, Manjusha Emporium, Dhirdham Temple, Himalayan Mountaineering Institute, Zoo,

Ropeway, Lebong Racecourse, Tibetan Refugee Self-help Centre. 0930-1230, 1330-1630. Rs 60.
**Tour 3**: Mirik. 0800-1730. Rs 95.
**Road tours**: Clubside Tours, JP Sharma Rd, T0354 2254646; **Darjeeling Transport Corp**, 30 Laden La Rd, T0354 2252074. Maruti vans, jeeps, Land Rovers and a few Sumos are available. Prices vary according to the season so negotiate rates.

### Trekking agents

**Himalayan Adventures**, Das Studios, Nehru Rd, T0354 2254090, dastrek@aussiemail.com.au.
**Glenarys**, T0354 2257554 glens_getaways@sancharnet.in. It has taken over some of the trekking operations from the WBTDC and now run trekking huts. It offers accommodation along a 5-night/6-day trek stopping at Tongu, Sandakphu, Phalut, Gorkhey, and Siri Khola. Beds are Rs 80-150 per person. Food and guide are extra.
**Himalayan Travels**, at Sinclairs, Gandhi Rd, T0354 2255405, long established.
**Himalayan Nature Foundation**, opposite Dirdham Temple, T52237, experienced trekking agent, for Singalila, Sikkim etc.
**Trek-Mate**, Singalila Arcade, Nehru Rd, T0354 2274092. Well-equipped.

### Kalimpong *p621, map p622*

**Kalimpong Tours & Travels**, T03552 255545.
**Kalimtrek**, Main Market, Himalayan Stores, T03552 255448, organizes treks, arranges paying-guest accommodation.
**Mintry Transport**, Main Rd, T03552 55741.

## Transport

### Murshidabad *p612*

Buses from Baharampur local bus stand to Lalbagh, 1 hr, Rs 3; or shared auto-rickshaw, 30 mins, Rs 6. Then cycle-rickshaw to Hazarduari gate, Rs 8. The train *Lalgola Passenger* from Kolkata (S).

### Malda *p612*

Buses are cheap and rickshaws are common. For **Gaur and Pandua**, buses and tongas; **Murshidabad** has a bus service. Long-distance services include: N Bengal STC: regular Express services to Kolkata, 8 hrs. Reservations: Esplanade Terminus, Kolkata or at KJ Sanyal Rd, Malda, T03512 252465. For **Gaur and Pandua**, a taxi costs about Rs 300. Train for **Kolkata (S)**: *Kanchenjunga, 5658* (AC/II), 1242, 8 hrs.

### Darjeeling *p614, map p616*

**Air**

Nearest airport, **Bagdogra** (90 km), see page 629. Transfer by car or coach is 3-3½ hrs. Pre-paid taxi counter to left of exit, Rs 750 (sharing possible); the W Bengal Tourism Coach costs Rs 80 each. **Indian Airlines**, Belle Vue Hotel, Chowrasta, T0354 2252355 Weekdays 1000-1700, Sun 1000-1300. Tourist Information counter.

**Bus**

NH31 connects Darjeeling with other parts of India. Local bus operators: **N Bengal STC**, T0354 223133; **Gurkha PAKU**, Chowk Bazar Bus Stand, T0354 2253487; **Darjeeling Siliguri Syndicate**, Motor Stand; **Singamari Syndicate**, Main Taxi Stand, T0354 2252820; *Sikkim SNT agent*, T0354 2252101.

Fast, long-distance services between **Kolkata and Siliguri** with connections to Darjeeling (see Siliguri, page 630). North Bengal STC, Darjeeling, T0354 2235133. Darjeeling to/from **Siliguri and Bagdogra** during the 'season', W Bengal STC bus from Bazar Bus Stand, or more comfortable Tourist Coach (minimum 6 passengers), leaving from Tourist Lodge and the traffic island near Keventers (3-3½ hrs) – tickets from tourist office, **Bellvue Hotel**. One visitor felt "for thrills and spills, no fairground attraction can rival the narrow hairpinned, switchback road that climbs the Himalayan foothills to Darjeeling".
**Gangtok**: SNT bus from near post office. **Darjeeling Motor Service**, Laden La Rd, T0354 2252101. Service to **Kalimpong** include jeeps and buses from the Bazar Motor stand: direct jeep (2 hrs) and DGHC minibus; buses are infrequent, slower and not much cheaper. In winter, Kalimpong Motor Syndicate, small office tucked away under the bazar, Rs 60. For **Nepal**, Land Rovers between 0600 and 0900 travel to the border (Panitanki-Kakarbhitta). Private buses have connections from Siliguri (see above), through ticket (Rs 450). Alternatively, Pashupati Fatak on the border (Mirik Rd) has buses to Kathmandu.

**Jeep**
Share jeep is the quickest and most convenient way of getting around the mountains. Jeeps leave regularly to most local destinations, and if you pick a jeep that is already over half full, you wont be waiting long before you set off. The price per person in a share jeep are: Rs 70 to **Siliguri** (2½ hrs via short cut); to **Gangtok** Rs 90-100, to **Kalimpong** Rs 40. Alternatively, you can hire the whole jeep and pay Rs 900 to**Kalimpong or Bagdogra**; **Siliguri**, Rs 600; **Gangtok**, Rs 1,500.

**Ropeway Cable Car**
Starts from North Point, 3 km from Chowk Bazar (share taxi Rs 5) connects Top Station with Takver in Singla Valley on the Little Rangit River. In season, 0930-1600 (15 mins each way) Rs 60 return.

**Taxi**
Private taxis charge approximately Rs 7 for Nehru Rd to Top Station. Stand, Robertson Rd/Laden La Rd.

**Train**
Darjeeling station has some old steam engines. Computerized Reservation allows nationwide booking; 0800-1400. Diesel service to **Siliguri** (narrow gauge), which is 80 km away, and **New Jalpaiguri Junction** (broad gauge), see page 630. At 0915 (7.5hrs). The narrow gauge steam 'Tourist' train to Ghoom departs 1000, stops at Batasia Loop, Rs 240 (see Ghoom above).

**Mirik** *p621*
Access from Bagdogra airport (55 km), Darjeeling (50 km) and Siliguri (52 km). To/from Darjeeling: buses, 0630 to 1500; Jeep, 1200, 1330.

**Kurseong** *p621*
51 km from Siliguri, off the main Darjeeling road, or via Pankhabari. Buses and taxis from Siliguri, 3 hrs, Darjeeling, 2 hrs.

The 'Toy Train' stops here; passenger service from 0645 to Darjeeling most of the year, Rs 10, 3½ hrs. The refurbished steam train runs a 'School' service between Darjeeling and Kurseong on weekdays in term time.

**Kalimpong** *p621, map p622*
**Air**
Nearest airport is at Bagdogra. A new airport is planned which will allow flights to Paro, Kathmandu and Dhaka, 80 km, 3-3½ hrs by car, Rs 700 (see Siliguri); also taxi seat or bus Rs 75. **Indian Airlines** information, T0354 2511495.

**Bus**
Kalimpong is off the NH31A to Gangtok. Taxis to Siliguri and Bagdogra, last depart 1500. State and private buses use the Motor Stand. Several to **Siliguri**, 3 hrs; **Darjeeling**, 3½ hrs; **Gangtok**: 3½ hrs (very scenic), Rs 37. N Bengal STC sells tickets, Motor Stand, T55719, SNT, Bus Stand, T0354 2255319. **Kolkata**: fast 'Rocket' buses. **Darjeeling**: DGHC minibus (contact **Kalimpong Tours & Travels**).

**Jeep**
Faster; every 30 mins, 2-3 hrs, Rs 600; ask for pick-up point in Darjeeling for return trip.

**Train**
The nearest railhead is New Jalpaiguri/ Siliguri station, 67 km. Tickets from **Rly Out Agency**, Kalimpong Motor Stand.

**Siliguri** *p623*
Try to arrive in Siliguri or New Jalpaiguri in daylight (before 1900).

**Air**
Nearest airport, **Bagdogra**, 14 km away, with tourist information counter and little else; security checks can be rigorous. Flights to **Kolkata**, Delhi and Guwahati. **Indian Airlines**, Mainak Tourist Lodge, T0353 2511495, airport T0353 2551192; **Jet Airways**, Vinayak Bldg, Hill Cart Rd, T0353 2538001, airport T0353 2551588, daily. **Helicopter** daily in fine weather to Sikkim (see page 644). Transfer: STC buses to Darjeeling and Gangtok. Taxis (for sharing) to Darjeeling (Rs 700), Gangtok (Rs 1,200), Kalimpong and Siliguri (Rs 160).

**Bus**
Siliguri is on NH31; Darjeeling (80 km), Gangtok (114 km) and Kalimpong (54 km) and served by State buses from WB, Bihar, Sikkim and Bhutan.

**Tenzing Norgay Central Bus Terminus** (CBT) next to the Junction Railway Station; **SNT Bus Station**, is across the Hill Cart Rd. Buses to N Bengal go from the **Dooars Bus Stand** at the junction of Sevoke and Bidhan Rds. The overnight North Bengal STC's 'Rocket' bus service between **Kolkata and Siliguri** depart 1845from Hill Cart Rd, 12 hrs, Rs 215, a/c Rs 350. Reserve seats in Kolkata, or in Burdwan Rd, Siliguri. They can be very full and noisy. There are also many private operators just outside the bus stand offering similar services. **Darjeeling** State buses (4 hrs, Rs 50) from CBT and Sevoke Rd, or more comfortable Tourist Bus (for minimum 6), Rs 80. **Kalimpong** 2-3 hrs Rs 35. N Bengal STC, Sevoke Rd. **Madarihat** (for Jaldapara) leave from bus station on Hill Cart Rd. **Gangtok** SNT buses, leave regularly thoughout the morning, Rs 70-90,5 hrs; reserve near Mahananda Bridge, Hill Cart Rd. Deluxe private buses from CBT, Junction Station (separate ticket window), Rs 100.
**Bhutan**: Bhutan Transport, Hill Cart Rd (0900-1130, 1330-1630). To **Phuntsholing**: few buses daily, Rs 100, 3-4 hrs. N Bengal STC from CBT run at 0700,1430, Rs 60.
**Nepal**: to **Kathmandu** buses (or more conveniently taxi or Land Rover), to Panitanki on the border (35 km, 1 hr); transfer to Kakarbhitta by cycle-rickshaw. **Kakarbhitta**, the Nepalese border town has only basic accommodation. **Visas** are $30 or Rs 1700 to be paid in cash and you'll also need 1 passport photo. Buses depart at 0400, 0500 to arrive at Kathmandu (or Pokhra) via W Nepal Highway (595 km), same evening (15-16 hrs); the journey can be very tiring. Tickets from Tourist Services Agency, Pradhan Nagar, Siliguri, T0353 2531959, bytours@cal2.vsnl.net.in; Siliguri to Kakarbhitta (Rs 120); Kakarbhitta to Kathmandu/Pokhra (Nep Rs 320); also through tickets. From Kakarbhitta it is also possible to **fly** (seasonal) from Bhadrapur (34 km, with free transfer to airstrip) to Kathmandu (1 hr) by RNAC or Everest Air (Nep Rs 1400); agent Sharma Travels. Alternatively, get a taxi to Biratnagar in Nepal (150 km) and fly from there to Kathmandu (US$99).

### Taxi

Opposite Air View Hotel, Hill Cart Rd and on Sevoke Rd, and railway stations to connect with most trains. To **Darjeeling**, share jeep (Rs 70) for 5-7 passengers, 3-3½ hrs.

### Train

**Siliguri Junction** (narrow gauge, T0353 2423333) and **New Jalpaiguri** ('NJP' broad gauge, T0353 2561555), 5 km away, both for **Toy Train**, with tourist information. There are buses, cycle-rickshaws (Rs 25), trains and taxis (Rs 80) between the two. NJP has good connections to other important centres in India. For long distance rail journeys from NJP, first buy tickets at Siliguri (Computerized Reservations, Bidhan Rd near Stadium), 1000-1300, 1330-1700 (to avoid the queue; go to Chief Reservations Officer at side of building), then to NJP station for train. Porters demand Rs 50 for 2 cases.
**Darjeeling**: from **Kolkata** to NJP by train, then bus or narrow-gauge '**Toy Train**' from **NJP** station (see page 615), also stops at **Siliguri Junc**. Steam 'Tourist' trains operate in the summer between Darjeeling and Ghoom but the daily service is diesel (Rs 42, Rs 247 1st class), depart 0900, 6½ hrs). Services are often disrupted by landslides during the rains, though the upper section from Kurseong (accessible by bus/jeep) continues to run; check beforehand. Take special care of luggage; thefts reported. From NJP to **Kolkata (S)**: *Darjeeling Mail, 2344* (AC/CC&AC/II), 1940, 12 ½ hrs. **Kolkata (H)**: *Kamrup Exp, 5960* (AC/II), 1645, 13½ hrs; *Kanchenjunga Exp, 5658* (AC/II), 0800, 12 hrs. **New Delhi**: *NE Exp, 5621*, 1720, 27 hrs; *Rajdhani Exp* (Mon, Wed, Thu, Fri), 2423, 1240, 21 hrs. From **Kolkata (S)**: *Darjeeling Mail, 2343*, 2205, 13 hrs, connects with the Toy Train from NJP.

### Jaldapara Wildlife Sanctuary *p623*

### Air

Indian Airlines has daily flights from Kolkata to Bagdogra (½ hr) and also from Guwahati and Delhi. From airport, bus to Siliguri; then 4 hrs' scenic drive through tea gardens to Jaldapara (155 km). There is an airfield at Hasimara.

### Bus

Express buses from Kolkata to Madarihat or Siliguri to Park (128 km). Forest Department transport to Hollong inside the sanctuary.

**Train**
Hasimara/ Madarihat Station (18 km from park) has trains from Siliguri Junction.

## Directory

**Darjeeling** *p614, map p616*
**Banks** (Limited hrs) **Grindlays** for Visa/Mastercard (£/$, 1130-1330), Rs 250 commission (less for next day collection). **Chemists** Frank Ross, Nehru Rd, Puri, Nehru Rd, above Keventer's. **Hospitals** **Planters' Hospital**, Nehru Rd, T0354 2254327. **Sadar Hospital**, T0354 2254218. **Mariam Nursing Home**, below Gymkhana Club, T0354 2254328, has been recommended for its medical facilities. **Tibetan Men Tse Khang**, 26 HD Lama Rd (Mon-Fri 0900-1200, 1400-1600). **Post** GPO, Laden La Rd. **Tourist offices** W Bengal, 'Belle Vue', 1st floor, 1 Nehru Rd, T0354 2254102. 0930-1730, off-season 1030-1630, not much info available. Also at railway station, and at New Car Park, Laden La Rd. **Darjeeling, Gorkha Hill Council (DGHC)**, Silver Fir (below Windamere), The Mall, T/F0354 2255351. **Sikkim**, T0354 2225277, issues permits free of charge. **Useful addresses** Foreigners' Registration Office: Laden La Rd, T0354 2254204; for **Sikkim** permits: go to District Magistrate, Lebong Cart Rd (north of centre), then get form stamped at FRO, and return to DM; 2 hrs.

**Kalimpong** *p621, map p622*
**Banks** Banks don't change money; Emporium, Mani Link Rd, accepts Visa and Mastercard. Most arrange car/jeep hire. **Useful addresses** There is a hospital and a post office near the police station.

**Siliguri** *p623*
**Banks** **State Bank of India**, Hill Cart Rd. Amex TCs. **Chemist** On College Rd. **Hospital** T0353 2521920; **North Bengal Clinic**, T0353 2420441. Recommended. **Internet** Moulik, behind Vinayak, Hill Cart Rd, T0353 2432312. **Tourist offices** **Bhutan**, near railway station. **Sikkim**, Hill Cart Rd; **W Bengal**, 1st floor, M4 Hill Cart Rd, T0353 2511974 sig_omntdc@sancharnet.in; also at Mainak, NJP Station and airport. **Travel agent** Help Tourism (Association of Conservation & Tourism), 143 Hill Cart Rd (1st floor), T0353 2535893, helptour@shiva net.com. Recommended for eastern Himalaya. **Useful addresses** Railway booking office, Road Station More T0353 2423333, Railway Enquiry at NJP T 0353 2561555.

# South of Kolkata

*To the south of Kolkata lie the tidal estuary of the Hugli and the mangrove forests of the Sundarbans. Famous for their population of Bengal tigers, the Sundarbans stretch across into Bangladesh, but it is possible to take a day trip right down to the mouth of the Hugli or boat trips into the Sundarbans themselves.* ▸▸ *For Sleeping, Eating and other listings, see page 632.*

## Sagardwip

**Ganga Sagar Mela** is held in mid-January, attracting over half a million pilgrims each year who come to bathe and then visit the **Kapil Muni Temple**. The island has been devastated many times by cyclones. To reach the island catch a bus or take a taxi to Harwood Point, Kakdwip and then take a ferry across to Kochuberia Ghat (Sagardwip). From there it is a 30-minute bus ride across island to where the Ganga meets the sea.

## Sunderbans Tiger Reserve → *Colour map 6, grid A6.*

Sunderbans (pronounced Soonder-buns) or 'beautiful forests', is named after the 'Sunderi' trees. The mangrove swamps are said to be the largest estuarine forests in the world. Improved management is battling to halt the loss of mangrove cover as it is exploited for fuel. Most villagers depend on fishing and forestry, while local honey gatherers who are active in April and May, are said to wear masks on the backs of their heads to frighten away tigers, which they believe only attack from the rear! You will notice large areas of *bheries* for aquaculture. Prawn fisheries are the most lucrative and co-operative efforts are being encouraged by the government.

The biosphere reserve, a World Heritage Site, still preserves the natural habitat of about 300 **Bengal tigers** (*Panthera tigris*). They are bigger and richer in colour than elsewhere in South Asia and are thought to survive on salt water; rainwater is the only source of fresh water in the park. Tigers here have become strong swimmers, and are known to attack fishermen. Methods of improved management include providing permanent sources of fresh water for tigers by digging deep, monsoon-fed ponds, and solar-powered lighting to scare them away from villages, and electrifying dummy woodcutters! Spotted deer, wild boar, monkeys, snakes, fishing cats, water monitors, Olive Ridley sea turtles and a few large estuarine crocodiles are the other wildlife here, particularly on Lothian Island and Chamta block. You may see deer, boar, macaque and some birds but are very unlikely to see a tiger. However, it is wonderfully peaceful.

The best season is from November to March. Heavy rains and occasional severe cyclones in April to May and November to December can make a visit impossible, so best in December-February. Carry bottled water, torch, mosquito repellent and be prepared for cool nights in winter. You must always be accompanied by armed Forest Rangers. Motor launches can be hired from Canning, Basanti, Namkhana and Raidighi but it is better to go down the narrow creeks in country boats. Occasionally you can go ashore on bamboo-and-palm jetties to walk in the fenced-in areas of the forest which have watch towers (open, dawn to dusk only). Contact the Field Director ⓘ *Sunderbans Tiger Reserve, Canning, 24 Parganas*.

You need a permit – valid four to five days – from Secretary ⓘ *Department of Forests, Writers Building, T033 22145600, or contact WB Tourist Office, BBD Bagh, Kolkata*, where you can book a package tour; take your passport.

**Sajnekhali** has a **sanctuary** for water birds which you get to from Canning or Basanti. There is a small Forest Department Visitor Centre with a turtle hatchery, a crocodile tank and a mangrove nursery.



## Digha → *185 km from Kolkata.*

Digha was described by Warren Hastings visiting over 200 years ago as the 'Brighton of the East', though there is not a pebble for at least 2,000 km! The casuarina-lined, firm wide beach is very popular with Bengalis. The small **Chandaneswar Temple,** 10 km away, actually in Orissa, is an important Siva temple which can be reached by bus.

## Sleeping

**Sagardwip** *p631*
WBTDC organizes 2-day boat trips with accommodation on board.
**F Youth Hostel**.
Dharamshala, free for 3 days.

**Sunderbans Tiger Reserve** *p631*
**D Tourist Lodge**, Sajnekhali, contact throught WBTDC, T033 22488271, raised on pillars and fenced from wildlife, solar power, 30 small, basic rooms with mosquito nets (ask for linen), 14 with Western toilets, hot water in buckets, 20-bed dorm (Rs 200), simple meals (poor choice but if you buy local fish, restaurant will cook it), no alcohol. Reserve in advance and carry your permit.

**Digha** *p632*
**C Sea Coast**, T03220-266305.
Some a/c rooms.
**C-E Tourist Lodge**, T03220-266255.
Rooms on 3 floors, 4 a/c, 5-bed dorm (Rs 80), meals, bar.
**D Sea Hawk**, T03220-266235.
Comfortable rooms, some a/c, cottages and cheaper dorm.

## Activities and tours

**Sunderbans Tiger Reserve** *p631*
**WBTDC Tours**: 2-day, 1-night (not during monsoons, ie Jul-Sep) by coach and launch (crowds of other visitors may scare wildlife away, though), staying at **Sajnekhali Lodge**. A 3-day cruise by launch – accommodation varies; 'Luxury' launch has decent facilities (fridge and TV), Rs 1,800 (4 person cubicle with comfortable beds), Rs 2,900, meals included. Acceptable food, helpful staff.
**Pugmarks**, 10 Meher Ali Rd, Kolkata, T033 22873307, www.pugmarks.org, specializes in adventure tours in the area and have their own launch. Will arrange permits.

## Transport

**Sunderbans Tiger Reserve** *p631*
**Road and boat**
By car from Kolkata or bus: from Babu Ghat, Strand Rd, to **Basanti** via Sonakhali (first depart 0600, Rs 20, 3 hrs; last return to Kolkata, 1600), then hire a **boat** to the Lodge (Rs 250-300, 3 hrs). Alternatively, from Basanti, take public ferry to **Gosaba**, then travel across the island by 'van (flat-bed) rickshaw' (5 km) which enables you to see interesting village life, and finally take a boat to Sajnekhali (3 hrs from Basanti); recommended for at least one way. Ask Lodge staff to arrange boat hire with park guide. Since these are tidal waterways, boats are not always able to moor near the ghats. Enquire about timing.

**Train and boat**
Kolkata (Sealdah) to **Canning** (105 km) and then **boat** to Docghat where you can get autos (shared) or a bus to Basanti where you get another boat. From Canning you can get a private boat direct to **Sajnekhali Lodge** (Rs 450-500 per day).

**Digha** *p632*
**Bus**
Express buses and WBTDC luxury buses from Kolkata take 6 hrs, the route having been shortened by the Norghat Bridge. Kolkata-Digha depart 0700 from Esplanade, Rs 35.

**Train**
The nearest railway halts are at Kharagpur (116 km) and Contai Rd (151 km) stations on the Southeast Railway.

**Footprint features**

# Introduction

Kangchendzonga, the third highest mountain in the world, dominates the skyline of Sikkim. The state is renowned as much for its wonderful wildlife and rich variety of plants and flowers as for its ethnically varied population. Sikkim's original inhabitants, the Lepchas, call the region Nye-mae-el, meaning 'Paradise'. To the later Bhutias it is Beymul Denjong, 'The Hidden Valley of Rice'. The name Sikkim itself is commonly attributed to the Tsong word Su-khim, meaning New or Happy House.



With 660 species of orchids, some found at altitudes as high as 3,000 m, Sikkim is an orchid-lovers' paradise. Tourism is still in its infancy, with the monasteries of Rumtek and Pemayangtse just two of the fascinating centres of Buddhism in the state, which is attracting growing numbers of visitors. Sikkim is beginning to attract ramblers and trekkers too.

You can stay a few days in Gangtok, making day trips to Rumtek and Phodong then move to Gezing or Pelling. From there you can walk up to Pemayangtse and perhaps visit Khechopari Lake before continuing to Kalimpong or Darjeeling in West Bengal. Numerous hairpin bends make road journeys extremely slow so expect to cover 30 to 40 km per hour. Conditions deteriorate considerably during the monsoon and can sometimes make travel impossible.

## ★ Don't miss...

1 **Tashi Viewpoint** Get up early, make your way to this spot and watch the sunrise over the Kangchendzonga range, page 642.

2 **Rumtek Monastery** This faithful reproduction of Chhofuk in Tibet is very impressive, page 645.

3 **Saramsa Gardens** If orchids are your things, head here where there are over 500 species, page 645.

4 **Pemayangtse Monastery** Stay overnight at this awe-inspiring place and take an early morning walk to see a breathtaking sunrise in perfect peace, page 646.

5 **Khechopari Lake** Trek to the lake and watch leaflamps float on the clear water during evening prayers, page 646.

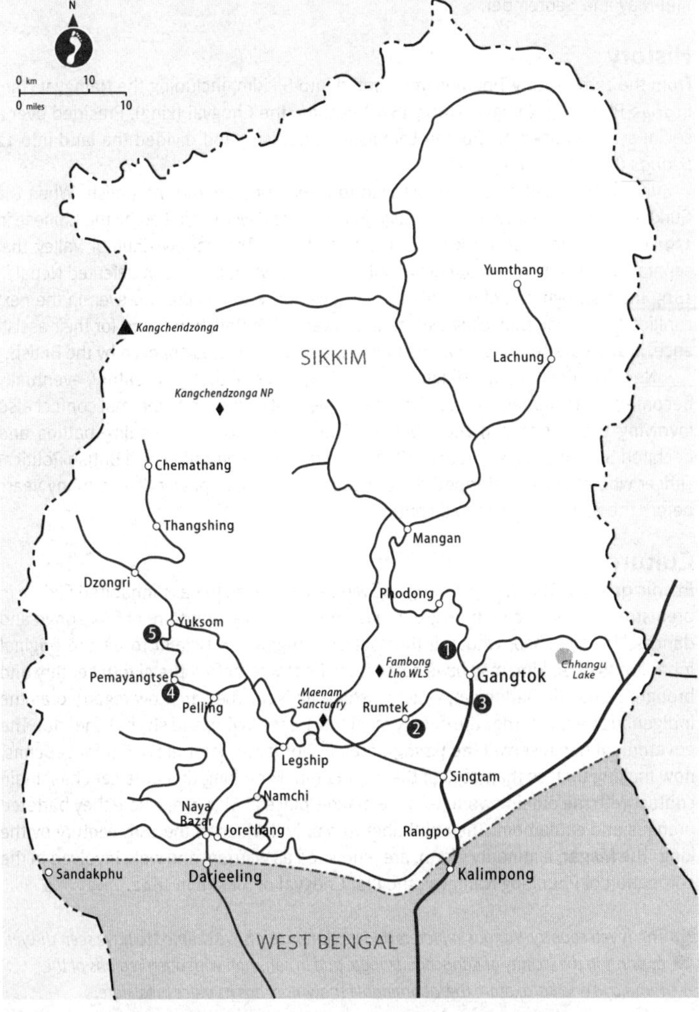

# Background → *Population: 540,500. Area: 7,298 sq km.*



## The land

**Geography** Sikkim nestles between the peaks of the eastern Himalaya, stretching only 112 km from south to north and 64 km from east to west. Flat land is a rarity and the state encompasses the upper valley of the Tista River, a tributary of the Brahmaputra, while the watershed forms the borders with Tibet and Nepal. In the east the Chumbi valley lies between Sikkim and Bhutan, a tongue of Tibetan land that gives Sikkim its strategic and political sensitivity. The Sikkimese believe Kangchendzonga (8,586 m, *Kanchenjunga*), the 'Five Treasures of the Great Snows', to be the repository of minerals, grains, salt, weapons and holy scriptures. On its west is the massive 31-km long Zemu glacier.

**Climate** In the lower valleys Sikkim's climate is sub-tropical. Above 1,000 m, it is temperate, while the tops of the higher mountains are permanently under snow. Sikkim is one of the wettest regions of the Himalaya, most rain falling between mid-May and September.

## History

From the 13th century Tibetans immigrated into Sikkim, including the Namgyal clan. In 1642 Phuntsog Namgyal (1604-1670) became the Chogyal (king). Presided over a social system based on Tibetan Lamaistic Buddhism, and divided the land into 12 *Dzongs* (fortified districts).

In the 18th century Sikkim lost land to Nepal, Bhutan and the British. When the Gurkhas of Nepal launched a campaign into Tibet and were defeated by the Chinese in 1791-1792, Sikkim won back its northern territories. The narrow Chumbi Valley that separates Sikkim from Bhutan remained with Tibet. When the British defeated Nepal in 1815, the southern part of the country was given back to Sikkim. However, in the next conflict with Nepal, Darjeeling was handed over to the British in return for their assistance. In 1848 the Terai region at the foot of the mountains was annexed by the British.

Nepalis migrated into Sikkim from the beginning of the 19th century, eventually becoming more numerous than the local inhabitants. This led to internal conflict also involving the British and the Tibetans. The British won the ensuing battles and declared Sikkim a Protectorate in 1890. The state was controlled by a British Political Officer who effectively stripped the *Gyalpos*, of executive power. It was many years before the Sikkimese regained control.

## Culture

**Ethnic groups** The Naong, Chang and Mon are believed to have inhabited Sikkim in prehistoric times. Each ethnic group has an impressive repertoire of folk songs and dances. The **Lepchas**, who call themselves Rongpas and claim to be the original inhabitants of Sikkim, may have come from Tibet well before the eighth century and brought Lamaistic Buddhism, which is still practised. They are now regarded as the indigenous peoples. They are deeply religious, peace loving and shy but cheerful. The government has reserved the **Dzongu** area in North and Central Sikkim for Lepchas, now making up less than 10% of the population. For a long time, the Lepchas' main contact with the outside world was the market-place at Mangan, where they bartered oranges and cardamom. Their alphabet was only devised in the 18th century by the king. The **Magar**, a minority group, are renowned as warriors and were involved in the coronation of Phuntsog Namgyal, the first Chogyal of Sikkim in 1642.

*This is yeti country. Various explorers and mountaineers have claimed to have seen the yeti or prints in the vicinity of Kangchendzonga, and in common with other regions of the Himalaya and Karakoram the 'abominable snowman' has its place in folklore.*

## Permits

Free Inter Line Permits (ILPs) are issued to foreigners to enter Sikkim for up to 15 days (renewable twice). These allow visits to Gangtok, Rumtek, Phodong, Mangan, Gezing, Pemayangtse, Namchi, Pakyong, Rabangla and Soreng. Contact an Indian mission abroad when applying for an Indian visa (enclosing two extra photos), or at any FRO (Foreigners' Registration Office) or the Sikkim Tourism Office in New Delhi, Kolkata or Siliguri. Rangpo can issue a 15-day permit extendable in Gangtok or any District headquarter or by the Superintendent of Police, namchi and Mangan. Certain areas in north and west Sikkim (Chumthang, Yumthang, Lachen, Chhangu, Dzongri) have been opened to groups of two to 20 trekkers and for mountain biking and water sports. Protected Areas Permits (PAP) can be arranged by some local travel agents; apply with a photocopies of passport (Indian visa, personal details), ILP and two photos.

To get your permit extended at the Foreigners' Registration Office at Gangtok, first visit the Magistrate's Office at the Secretariat on the ridge overlooking town to get a 'No Objection' endorsement.

The **Bhotias** (meaning 'of Bhot/Tibet') or Bhutias entered Sikkim in the 13th century from Kham in Tibet. Many adapted to sedentary farming from pastoral nomadism and displaced the Lepchas. Some, however, retained their older lifestyle, and combined animal husbandry with trading over the Trans-Himalayan passes: Nathula (4,392 m), Jelepla (4,388 m), Donkiala (5,520 m) and Kongrala (4,809 m). Over the years the Bhotia have come into increased contact with the Lepcha and intermarried with them. Nearly every Bhotia family has one member who becomes a monk. Monasteries remain the repositories of Bhotia culture and festivals there are the principle social events. However, those who have visited Ladakh or Zanskar may find them architecturally and artistically a little disappointing. The Bhotias are famous for their weaving and are also skilled wood carvers.

The **Newars** entered Sikkim in large numbers from Nepal in the 19th century. Skilled in metal and woodwork, they were granted the right by the Chogyal to mine copper and mint the Sikkimese coinage. Other Nepali groups followed. With high-altitude farming skills, they settled new lands and built houses directly on the ground unlike the Lepcha custom of building on stilts. The Newars were followed by the Chettris and other Nepali clans who introduced Hinduism, which became more popular as their numbers swelled.

**Religion** In Sikkim, as in Nepal, Hinduism and Buddhism have interacted and amalgamated so Himalayan Hinduism includes a pantheon of Buddhist *bodhisattvas* as well as Hindu deities. The animist tradition also retains a belief in evil spirits.

Buddhist **prayer flags** flutter in the breeze everywhere. The different types (wind, luck, victory etc) are printed with texts and symbols on coloured pieces of cloth and are tied to bamboo poles or trees. **Prayer wheels** carrying inscriptions (which should be turned clockwise) vary in size from small hand-held ones to vast drums which are installed by a monastery or stupa. Whitewashed masonry **chortens** (stupas) but usually commemorate the Buddha or Bodhisattva; the structure symbolizing the elements (earth, water, fire, air, ether). The eight **lucky signs** appear as parasol, pot or vase, conch shell, banner, two fishes, lotus, knot of eternity and the wheel of law (Dharma Chakra). Bowls of water (Thing Duen Tsar) are offered in prayer from left to right during Buddhist worship. The gift of water from one who is free from greed and meanness is offered to quench thirsty spirits and to wash the feet, and represents flower (or welcome), incense, lamp, perfume and food.

**Festivals** Since the 22 major festivals are dictated by the agricultural cycle and the Hindu-Buddhist calendar, it is best to check dates with the Tourist Office.

In **February**, **Losar** takes place, Tibetan New Year – preceded by Lama dances in Rumtek. **Bumche** at Tashiding. In **June** is **Saga Dawn**, a Buddhist festival with huge religious processions round Gangtok. **Rumtek Chaams Dance festival** is held in commemoration of the eight manifestations of Guru Padmasambhava, who established Buddhism in Tibet. In **August/September**, **Pang Lhabsol** commemorates the consecration of Kangchendzonga as Sikkim's guardian deity; the Lepchas believe that the mountain is their birthplace. The masked warrior dance is especially spectacular – Kangchendzonga appears in a red mask, her commander in a black one, while warriors wear traditional armour of helmets, swords and shields. Special celebrations are held in Pemayangtse. In **September/October**, **Dasain** is one of the most important Nepali festivals. It coincides with **Dasara** in North India, see page 63. On the first day barley seeds are planted in prayer rooms, invocations are made to Durga, and on the eighth day buffalo and goats are ritually sacrificed. **Diwali** (the Festival of Lights) follows **Dasain**. In **December**, **Kagyat Dances** performed by monks (especially at Enchey), accompanied by religious music and chanting, enact themes from Buddhist mythology and end with the burning of effigies made of flour, wood and paper. This symbolizes the exorcism of evil spirits and the ushering in of prosperity for the coming year. **Losoog** (**Namsoong** for Lepchas at Gangtok) is the Sikkimese New Year, also called **Sonam Losar**. Farmers celebrate their harvest and beginning of their new cropping calendar.

## Gangtok

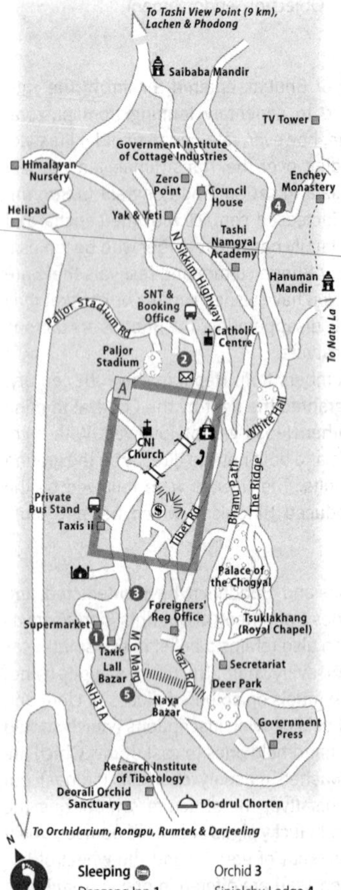


## Modern Sikkim

In 1950, Sikkim became a Protectorate of India. In 1973 demands for accession to India by the local population consisting mainly of Nepalis grew, and Sikkim was formally made an associate state. The Gyalpos lost their power as a result of the new democratic constitution and Sikkim became the 22nd state in the Union in 1975. Although there is no separatist movement, India's takeover and the abolition of the monarchy, supported by many of those of Nepali origin, is still resented by many Sikkimese who don't really regard themselves as 'Indians'. The state enjoys special tax and other privileges, partly because of its highly sensitive geopolitical location on the disputed border with China.

# Gangtok

→ *Phone code: 03592. Colour map 4, grid A2. Population: 55,200.*

*Gangtok or 'High Hill', the capital, sits on a ridge overlooking the Ranipul River at an altitude of 1,547 m. The setting is spectacular with fine views of the Kangchendzonga range but the town appears to have lost some of its quaint charm with the mushrooming of concrete buildings along the national highway and the main road. The crowded New Market (Naya Bazar) on Mahatma Gandhi Marg and the colourful Lall Bazar are where all the town's commercial activity is concentrated. Away from the bustle, there are many serene areas and quiet back alleys which remain virtually untouched.* ▸▸ *For Sleeping, Eating and other listings, see pages 642-644.*

## Ins and outs

**Getting there** There is an airport near Gangtok which is linked to Bagdogra airport, 124 km away, by a regular helicopter service. There are flights to Bagdogra from both Delhi and Kolkata. Most visitors arrive by the very attractive road from North Bengal (NH31A) which is motorable throughout the year except in very wet weather (mid-June to September), when there may be landslips. The old Teesta suspension bridge was taken down and a new bridge was built further down in 1996. Permits and passports are checked at Rangpo where 15-day permits (extendable in Gangtok or district headquarters for up to 45 days) are available. SNT buses terminate at the Paljor Stadium Road stand while private buses stop short of the main bazar. Ask to be dropped near the Tourist Office which has some hotels and restaurants within easy reach. If you hire a jeep to Gangtok ask to be taken to your hotel since the taxi/jeep stand is 2 km short of the centre. ▸▸ *See Transport, page 644, for further details.*

**Getting around** The busy hub around MG Marg is a 20-minute walk from end to end. Away from the bazars, the town is very pleasant for walking around (get map *Gangtok, an Artist's Impression*, Rs 50). For venturing further you will need to hire a jeep or taxi.

## Sights

At the north end of the town the **Government Institute of Cottage Industries** ⓘ *closed Sun and 2nd Sat of month, 0900-1230, 1330-1530*, produces a wide range of local handicrafts, eg woollen carpets, jackets, dolls, handmade paper, carved and painted wooden tables. Good quality and prices but no parcel service.

**Enchey Monastery** is 3 km northeast of the main bazar, a pleasant walk. Built by the eighth Chogyal in the 1840s the present building dates from 1909. Religious dances are held in August and December; see Festivals above.

The **Palace of the Chogyal** is only open once a year in the last week of December for the **Pang Lhabsol Festival**. Below this is the **Tsuklakhang** or Royal

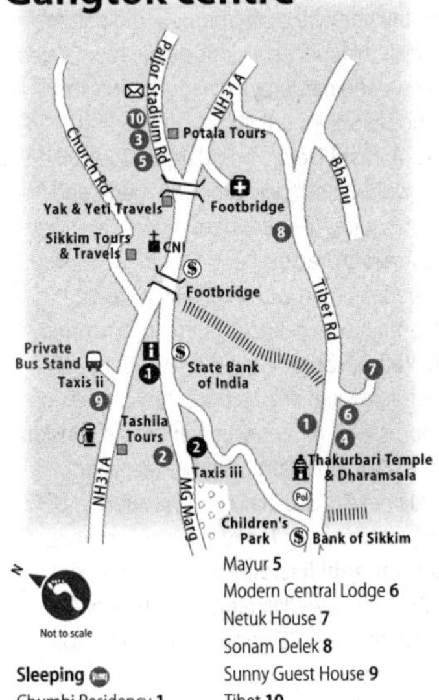


**Sleeping**
Chumbi Residency 1
Green 2
Jopuno & Mist Tree Mountain 3
Lhakpa 4
Mayur 5
Modern Central Lodge 6
Netuk House 7
Sonam Delek 8
Sunny Guest House 9
Tibet 10

**Eating**
Blue Sheep 1
House of Bamboo 2

 Chapel, standing on a high ridge where coronations and royal marriages took place. This is the major place of worship and has a large and impressive collection of scriptures. The interior is lavishly decorated with woodcarving and murals and houses a number of Buddha images. Visitors are welcome during Tibetan New Year but may not be permitted at other times; photography prohibited.

Moving south along the road you pass the **Secretariat** complex on your left. Beyond this is the **Deer Park**, loosely modelled on the famous one at Sarnath, see page 180, with a statue of the Buddha. To the south, the important **Do-drul Chorten** with a golden top, contains relics and a complete set of holy texts. The surrounding 108 prayer wheels should be turned clockwise only. Nearby is a monastery for young lamas with large statues of the Buddha and Guru Padmasambhava.

The unique **Research Institute of Tibetology** ⓘ *1000-1600, closed Sun*, on a hilltop was established in 1958 to promote research on Tibet and Mahayana Buddhism. The library maintains a large and important Buddhist collection with many fine *thangkas*, icons and art treasures on display. For orchid lovers the small Flower show near Whitehall has a good display, from mid-March.

**Deorali Orchid Sanctuary**, south of town, has 200 species. There are some lovely walks around the capital. **Tashi Viewpoint** via Enchey Monastery is 9 km away. Go early to watch the sun rise over the Kangchendzonga range. **Hanuman Tok**, a hill with a small temple, 8 km away, is another viewpoint.



## Sleeping

**Gangtok** *p641, maps p640 and p641*
Heating is essential in winter. Some budget hotels charge extra for heaters. Dogs bark at night so take some ear plugs. Discounts Jul-Aug, Dec-Jan.

**AL-A Norkhill**, T03592 225637, www.elginhotels.com. 30 clean rooms in old palace, meals included, spacious public rooms, good views and gardens, exchange, curio shop, once excellent but standards slipping.

**AL-A Tashi Delek**, MG Marg, T03592 202991, www.hoteltashidelek.com. 60 rooms and some suites (better on top floors), excellent restaurant, bar, exchange, airlines counter, terrace garden with enthralling views, friendly service. Pricey but recommended.

**A Netuk House**, Tibet Rd, T03592 222374, netuk@sikkim.org. 8 comfortable, clean rooms with modern shower in an extension to a traditional family home, excellent Sikkimese meals, bar, quiet location, mountain views, friendly, excellent service.

**B-C Chumbi Residency**, Tibet Rd, T03592 226618, www,sikkiminfo.net/chumbi. Tall modern hotel, 25 good rooms, suites too, clean and quiet, dynamic manager.

**B-C Golden Nest**, Nam Gang, below Assembly Building, T03592 227008, nest_golden@hotmail.com. Clean, well furnished, 'superior' rooms very comfortable, restaurant (limited menu, beer), good service, mainly groups.

**B-C Tibet** (Dalai Lama Trust), PS Rd, T03592 202523, www.sikkiminfo.net/hoteltibet. 30 rooms. Good views from rooms at rear, restaurant, bar, exchange, Tibetan books and crafts for sale, very pleasant, peaceful and charming (but some critical reports).

**C Denzong Inn**, near Lall Bazar, T03592 202692, www.hoteltashidelek.com. 24 rooms, good suites, restaurant.

**C-D Mist Tree Mountain**, PS Rd, Pradhan Towers, T03592 223827. Newish, good value rooms, 7-bed dorm (Rs 100), restaurant.

**C-D Sonam Delek**, Tibet Rd, T03592 202566, www.sikkiminfo.net/sonamdelek. 15 rooms with bath, best choice for views, pleasant restaurant (great local food), terrace garden.

**D Jopuno**, PS Rd, T03592 223502. 12 rooms (4 **C** deluxe), good restaurant and service, eager young staff (at Institute of Hotel Management).

**D Mayur** (Sikkim Tourism), PS Rd, T03592 202825. 27 rooms with bath (rooms vary), restaurant, bar.

**D Orchid**, NH31A, T03592 223151. 21 clean rooms, some with bath, front rooms better, restaurant (good Chinese), bar, good value.

**D Sunny Guest House**, T03592 202179. Some rooms with bath in pleasant hotel, super K'dzonga views from top floor.

**D-E Green**, MG Marg, T/F03592 223354, slg_greehot@sancharnet.in. 45 rooms, some with bath but no views (Rs 250-475), good restaurant (Indian/Chinese).

**D-E Siniolchu Lodge**, near Enchey Monastery, T03592 202074. 24 rooms on 3 floors up a hillside, some with bath and heating, good views, restaurant, bar, tours.

**E Lhakpa**, Tibet Rd, T03592 223002. 3 clean rooms in traditional house, some with bath, cheaper dorm, restaurant/ bar (very good Chinese), roof terrace, views, good value.

**E Modern Central Lodge**, Tibet Rd, T03592 223330. Clean rooms with toilets, some with bath, hot showers, best in front on upper floors, a bit noisy, basic but good restaurant, friendly bar, good-value jeep tours, very friendly and helpful, backpackers' choice.

**F Primula Lodge**, Church Rd, T03592 225496. Clean, basic with shared bath.

## Eating

**Gangtok** *p641, maps p640 and p641*

Lightly spiced Sikkimese meat and vegetable dishes are usually eaten with noodles or rice. 'Churpi' is a local yak milk curd cheese. For 'Chimney Soup' order a day ahead.

ΨΨΨ **Blue Poppy**, **Tashi Delek**. International. Good meals from Rs 300 (Sikkimese recommended, order in advance).

ΨΨΨ **Netuk House**, see Sleeping, T03592 202374. Excellent Sikkimese (order ahead). Unusual, delicately flavoured authentic home-cooking, charming service, try *chhang*.

ΨΨΨ **Snow Lion**, in **Hotel Tibet**, T0359 202523. Very good Sikkimese and Tibetan but some poor reports: "flat beer, noisy and crowded".

ΨΨ **Mayur**, see Sleeping. Good Tandoori.

ΨΨ **Tibet**, below High Court, MG Rd (also Kazi Rd). Westernized café menu, very clean.

Ψ **Blue Sheep**, Tourist Office Building. Indian, Continental, Sikkimese at lunchtime, fast food on ground floor. Traditional, clean, bar.

Ψ **China Pilot**, Star Cinema Building, MG Rd. Very good-value Chinese.

Ψ **House of Bamboo**, MG Rd. Indian veg.

Ψ **Porkey's**, Supermarket, MG Rd. Fast food, sausages etc, young crowd.

## Bars and clubs

**Gangtok** *p641, maps p640 and p641*

Bars in most restaurants serve local spirits distilled at Rangpo – brandy, rum, whiskey and liqueurs. *Chhang* is the unofficial national drink. A bamboo mug (*thungba*) is filled with fermented millet through which boiled water is allowed to percolate; the drink is sipped through a bamboo straw. You can enjoy this mildly intoxicating pleasant drink for over an hour simply by adding hot water.

## Shopping

**Gangtok** *p641, maps p640 and p641*

**Handicrafts**

Traditional crafts include carpets, *thangkas*, traditional jewellery, shirts, boots and fur caps and wood carving.

**Charitrust Handicrafts**, Tibet Hotel, modest collection, good quality; books on Tibet.

**Handcrafts Centre**, Zero Point, Mon-Sat 0930-1230, 1300-1530, where you can watch artisans.

**Rural Development Agency**, MG Marg and Naya Bazar.

**Markets**

The markets are interesting; **Lall Bazar** (Haat on Sun, closed Thu) sells some unusual local fruit and vegetables and yak's milk cheese fresh and dried (skewered on string).

## Activities and tours

**Gangtok** *p641, maps p640 and p641*

**Mountaineering**

Himalayan Mountaineering Institute based in Yuksom offers climbing courses in stunning surroundings. For trekking contact tourist offices or tour companies.

**River rafting**

On rivers Tista (from Dikchu or Singtam, 1 hr drive from Gangtok) and Rangit (from Melli Bazar, 4 km from Teesta Bridge, which has a **Wayside Inn** for refreshments, or **Rishi**) arranged by Tourism Department and private travel agents, eg Tashila, 1 day US$45, 2-day US$70, some Grade 2-3 rapids. A 2-hr ride en route to Pemayangtse is ideal for the beginner; wonderful scenery.

**Tour operators**

Members of *TAAS* Travel agents Association of Sikkim, can organize permits for trekkers. Contact them in advance by email or fax.

**Namgyal Treks and Tours**, 75 Tibet Rd, T03592 223701, trekking@sancharnet.in.

Experienced, well organized, expedition experience.

**Sikkim Tours**, PO Box 155, GPO, Church Rd, T03592 202188, slg_lukendra@sancharnet.in. For treks and birdwatching.

**Singalila**, NH31A opposite petrol pump, T03592 221556, singalila@hotmail.com. Arranges coach tours and river rafting.

**Yak & Yeti, Hotel Superview Himalchuli**, NH31A, Zero Point, T0353 202076, www.yaknyeti.com. Adventure tours and trekking (US$35-40 per day), efficient.

**Yuksom Tours and Treks**, above Telephone Exchange, T03592 226822, takapa@sancharnet.in. Professional, well- equipped treks, good food, all inclusive US$55 per day.

### Tours

**Gangtok** From Tourist Information Centre, T03592 221634. **Morning tour**: Government Institute of Cottage Industries, Deer Park, Chorten, Research Institute of Tibetology, Orchid Sanctuary and Enchey Monastery. In season daily 0930-1230. Rs 45. **Afternoon tour**: Orchidarium and Rumtek Monastery, 1400/1430-1700. Rs 55.

**Phodong** Rs 70 (more expensive by car).

**West Sikkim** Requires a minimum 16. Fri at 1030 returning Sun 1600 (2 nights), Rs 600.

## Transport

**Gangtok** *p641, maps p640 and p641*

### Air

Nearest airport is Bagdogra (124 km); see page 628. **Indian Airlines**, Green Hotel, MG Marg, T03592 223354, www.indian-airlines.nic.in. 1000-1300, 1400-1600; **Jet Airways**, RNC, MG Marg, T03592 223556, www.jetairways.com. To Gangtok: shared taxi, 4-5 hrs, Rs 250 each, or Snow-Lion mini-bus; or get an SNT bus to Siliguri where bus/taxi to Gangtok is available. A daily government 4-seater helicopter runs between Bagdogra and Gangtok; unreliable since heavy cloud or rain prevents flights – but is an excellent option (Rs 1,500 each way, 45 mins, 10 kg luggage) with mesmerizing views.

### Bus

SNT (Sikkim Nationalized Transport) Bus Stand, NH31A, 0900-1300, 1400-1600. Private buses from West Point Taxi Stand, NH31A, T03592 202858. Some only operate in the high season. Buy tickets 24 hrs in advance; hotels can help. Long distance journeys about Rs 60. To **Rumtek** 1600 (1500 holidays) 1 hr; **Namchi**, which has a Govt 80-bed **Youth Hostel**, 0800, 1500 (4½ hrs); **Namok, Phodong, Chungthang, Mangan**, 0800, 1300 (return 1500); **Gezing**, 0700, 1300 (5 hrs); **Jorethang (then Pelling)**, 0800. For North Bengal: **Bagdogra** (about 5 hrs); **Darjeeling**, 94 km, between 0700-1330; from Darjeeling 0730-1400 (6-7 hrs); to **Kalimpong**, 75 km, 0830-1930 (4-4½ hrs), from Kalimpong 0700-1315; to **NJP/Siliguri** (115 km), 0700-1415 (4½-5 hrs); from Siliguri 0630-1300, 5 hrs. To **Kolkata** 1300; from Kolkata 1700; a/c bus Rs 280.

### Taxi/jeep

Taxis charge exhorbitant rates to ferry passengers arriving at the taxi stand; from there it is a stiff 2-km climb to the centre.

For sharing: Stands (i) Lall Bazar (East Sikkim) (ii), Private Bus Stand (for North Bengal) and (iii) Children's Park (West Sikkim). Fixed rate charts within Gangtok, but negotiable for sightseeing. Rs 1,200 per day for travel outside Sikkim, Rs 1,000 within Sikkim; plus night halt Rs 200. **Chhangu**, Rs 400 return; **Rumtek**, shared, from 1030, Rs 25; **Yoksum**, Rs 800.

### Train

Nearest railway stations are at **Siliguri/New Jalpaiguri**, Computerized Bookings, SNT Compound, for tickets, 0800-1400.

## Directory

**Gangtok** *p641, maps p640 and p641*

**Banks** 1000-1400, Sat 1000-1200 (difficult to get exchange). **State Bank of India**, MG Marg. **State Bank of Sikkim**, Tibet Rd, UTI, New Market, has international ATM. **Hospitals** On Stadium Rd: **STNM Hospital**, opposite Hotel Mayur, T03592 202059. Also, **Unique Chemists**. **Internet** Green Hotel on request. **Post** GPO, Stadium Rd and PO in Gangtok Bazar. **Tourist offices** Sikkim, MG Marg, Gangtok Bazar, T03592 221634. In season Mon-Sat 0900-1900, off season 1000-1600. Apply for permits here. **Dept of Tourism**, T03592 223425. **Useful contacts** Ambulance: T03592 231137. Fire: T03592 222001. **Police**: T03592 202033.

# Around Gangtok

## Rumtek Monastery → *Phone code: 03592. Colour map 4, grid A2. 24 km southwest of Gangtok. Altitude: 1,550 m.*

Standing in one of the attractive lower valleys with fluttering prayer flags, the monastery is the headquarters of the Kagyu ('Black Hat') order of Tibetan Lamaistic Buddhism. The monks fled Tibet after the Chinese invasion, bringing with them whatever statues, *thangkas* and scriptures they could carry. At the invitation of the Chogyal they settled in Rumtek. The new monastery was built in the 1960s in the traditional style as a faithful copy of the Kagyu headquarters in Chhofuk, Tibet, with typical monastic paintings and intricate woodwork. The **Dharma Chakra Centre** with the unique **golden reliquary** of the 16th Gyalwa Karmapa, who died in 1981, is here.

Visitors are dropped at the gate at the bottom of a gentle uphill path; passports may be checked. A 20-minute walk past local houses and a couple of typical curio shops leads to the monastery. Outside, you may see pairs of monks chanting prayers in their quarters or catch some younger ones playing football in the field! The main hall is very impressive but lacks the atmosphere of Pemayangtse. Visitors are welcome are requested not to disturb the monks during prayers (usually 0400, 1800). In the adjacent building you can watch the wood-block printing of texts on handmade paper. The peace is broken when hordes of tourists arrive.

## Saramsa Gardens and Rangpo → *14 km south of Gangtok.*

The gardens contain over 500 indigenous species in what is more like a botanical garden with large orchidariums. Best season is March to early May, you may be disappointed at other times. The road to Saramsa forks east off the NH31a a few kilometres south of **Tadong** which has a couple of places with rooms and refreshments including the fairly modern **Tashi Tadong** and the **Daragaon**.

Further south, near the West Bengal border, Rangpo has a small bazar. Entry Permits are issued and checked here.

## Chhangu (Tsomgo) Lake → *36 km from Gangtok. Altitude: 3,774 m.*

The lake is on the Nathu La Highway, the old trade route to Lhasa which until 1962 saw regular mule trains leave and return to Gangtok. The precipitous road passes through the Kyongnosla Sanctuary and leads to the holy lake which is completely frozen in winter, up to mid-May. It is best to visit March to May, September to mid-December. There are excellent views of Kangchendzonga from the nearby ridge and superb sunsets. On the way there is the **Shiv Gufa**, a few minutes' walk from the road. You have to enter the tiny cave on your hands and knees to see a small Siva image and several tridents embedded in the soft floor. The drive there is scenic but the lake area is overcrowded and spoilt by snack kiosks and loud Hindi music. Allow an hour to walk around the 1-km long lake. There are organized tours and permits are needed (apply with photo and passport a day ahead). Allow six hours for the return trip. If you go independently, a jeep/minivan will cost around Rs 800.

## Kyongnosla Alpine Sanctuary → *Altitude: 3,200 m- 4,100 m.*

The sanctuary, 31 km from Gangtok, extends from the '15th Mile' check post to the ridges bordering Rongchu and Chhangu Lake. Among the junipers and silver firs the sanctuary harbours some rare ground orchids and rhododendrons and numerous medicinal plants including the *Panax pseudo-ginseng*. The best season is from April to August, October to November. The Himalayan marmot has been reintroduced here. Other mammals include goral, serow, red panda, Himalayan black bear, Tibetan fox and yellow-throated martens, together with very colourful pheasants.

Two easy treks lead to the Shiv Gufa (1 km away) and Kheding (4 km) while longer and more difficult ones to Simulakha, Namnang Lakha and Nakcho are very scenic. Trekkers with permits for Chhangu may return from Nakcho via the lake.

## Gezing → *105 km west of Gangtok.*

Gezing (Gyalshing) is at the crossroads of bus routes and has a busy market with food stalls and shops selling provisions. An early bus or jeep from Gangtok allows you to see Tashiding, then stop overnight at Gezing or Pelling.

## Pemayangtse → *112 km west of Gangtok. 72 km from Darjeeling. Altitude: 2,085 m.*

A full day trip by car from Gangtok, along a very scenic road, Pemayangste (Perfect Sublime Lotus) was built during the reign of the third Chogyal Chador Namgyal in 1705. It is about 7 km from Gezing, above the main road to Pelling.

The awe-inspiring **monastery** ⓘ *0700-1600, Rs 10, good guided tours, 0700-1000 and 1400-1600 (if closed, ask for key), no photography inside*, Sikkim's second oldest, is near the start of the Dzongri trek. For many, the monastery is the highlight of their visit to Sikkim – it has a certain aura about it. Take an early morning walk to the rear of the monastery to see a breathtaking sunrise in perfect peace. The walls and ceiling of the large *Dukhang* (prayer hall) have numerous *thangkas* and wall paintings, and there is an exceptional collection of religious artworks including an exquisite wooden sculpture on the top floor depicting the heavenly palace of Guru Rimpoche – the *Santhokpalri,* which was believed to have been revealed in a dream. The old stone and wood buildings to the side are the monks' quarters. According to tradition the monks have been recruited from the leading families in Sikkim as this is the headquarters of the Nyingmapa sect. Annual *chaam* dances are held at the end of February, and in September.

**Denjong Padma Choeling Academy** (DPCA), set up to educate needy children, has several ancillary projects – crafts, weaving, dairy – and welcomes volunteers who can at the same time learn about Buddhism and local culture. The Meditation Centre offers courses and can accommodate visitors for a small charge and volunteers for free at the new hostel (see below). It can be a very rewarding experience. Volunteers spend a maximum of six weeks, between March and December. Contact Jules Stewart, London, T0207-229 4774, jjulesstewart@aol.com.

**Rabdanste**, the ruined palace of the 17th- to 18th-century capital of Sikkim, is along the Gezing-bound track from the monastery, 3 km from Pelling. From the main road, turn left just before the white sign "Gezing 6 km", cross the archery field and turn right behind the hill (road branches off just below Pemanyangtse). Follow the narrow rocky track for 500 m to reach the palace.

## Pelling → *2 km from the monastery and 9 km by road from Gezing.*

Pelling sits on a ridge with good views of the mountains. The small town has three areas linked by a winding road: Upper and Middle with views and hotels, and Lower Pelling with banks and other services. Upper Pelling is expanding rapidly with new hotels springing up to accommodate honeymooners from Kolkata.

You can visit the **Sanga Choelling Monastery** (circa 1697), possibly the oldest in Sikkim, which has some colourful mural paintings. The hilltop monastery is about 3 km along a fairly steep track through thick woods (about 30 minutes). The area is excellent for walking.

## Khechopari Lake, Tashiding and Yuksom

A three-day gentle trek to this 'wishing' lake, Yuksom and back to Pelling is possible without a permit. A road west of the Pelling-Yuksom road leads to this tranquil lake where the clear waters reflect the surrounding densely wooded slopes of the hills with a monastery above – Lepchas believe that birds remove any leaf that floats down.

Prayer flags flutter around the lake and it is particularly moving when leaflamps are floated with special prayers at dusk. The sanctity of the lake may be attributed to its shape in the form of a foot (symbolizing the Buddha's footprint), which can be seen from the surrounding hills.

The gold-topped **monastery**, 40 km from Gezing, built in 1716, stands on a conical hill between the Rathong and Rangit rivers on a spot consecrated by Guru Rimpoche. The gompa has been refurbished and all the frescos repainted. The most sacred *chorten* in Sikkim is here so even the sight of Tashiding is thought to bring blessing. You will see numerous stones with high-class carvings of *mantras* around the monastery. Pilgrims attend the **Bumchu festival** in February/March to drink water from the sacred pot which has never run dry for over 300 years. Below the monastery is the small Tshchu Phur cave where Guru Rinpoche meditated; follow the trail on the left of the entrance to Tashiding until you see a small house opposite and the painting on the rocks. Carry a torch if you plan to crawl into the cave.

**Yuksom**, 42 km north from Pelling by jeepable road, is where the first Chogyal was crowned in 1641. The wooden altar and stone throne above the Kathok lake are below the Norbu Gang chorten in a beautifully peaceful pine forest. The simple Hermit's retreat at **Dhubdi** (circa 1700) is up on a hill, 45 minutes' walk away. Yuksom is quiet and relaxing.

## Phodong → *Colour map 4, grid B1.*

The renovated early 18th-century monastery is 1 km above the north Sikkim Highway, about 2 km before Phodong village. It is a pleasant walk up to the little-visited gompa where friendly monks show you around; the track is jeepable. A further hike of 2 km takes you to the **Labrang** monastery of the Nyingmapa sect. Below the track nearby is the ruined palace of **Tumlong**, which was the capital of Sikkim for most of the 19th century.

## Shingba Forest Reserve and Yumthang → *Colour map 4, grid A2. 135 km north of Gangtok. Altitude: 3,700 m.*

The road to Yumthang enters the Shingba Forest Reserve, which is lined with rhododendrons which harbouring civets and blood pheasants. The Rhododendron Sanctuary has 24 of the 40 species found in Sikkim and has attractive ground cover of aconites, gentians, poppies, saxifrages, potentillas and primulas.

The attractive high valley of **Yumthang** is surrounded by mountains. The alpine meadow near the tree-line is a seasonal grazing ground for yaks. A few minutes' walk from the main road beyond a log bridge over the river Lachung are some sulphur hot springs. There is also a **Log House** with two rooms (no electricity); contact Forest Department. Permit needed. You can hire a jeep hire from Gangtok or go on an organized by a travel agent. Yumesamdung above Yumthang is now accessible.

## Sleeping

**Rumtek Monastery** *p645*

**A Martam Village Resort**, Gangkha, Upper Martam, 5 km from the monastery, T03592 223314. 11 thatched cottages built in traditional style with large picture windows overlooking the valley, good meals, pleasant, recommended.

**B Shamhbala Mountain Resort**, T03592 252241, parekh.house@gems.net.in. In a large estate, 500 m before the monastery. 31 cottages in traditional tribal styles spread around grounds, or comfortable rooms in main building, most with good views from balconies, veg restaurant (wide choice), bar, exchange, pick-up from Siliguri arranged.

**D-E Jharna**, T03592 202714. Some rooms with hot water, restaurant, bar.

**F Sangay**, near monastery gate. Basic rooms in old guesthouse, fairly clean shared toilet, friendly.

### Kyongnosla Alpine Sanctuary *p645*

**F Log Huts**, with 2 rooms in each at Kyongnosla and Lamnang Lakha. You must apply for a permit (Rs 5) to Chief Wildlife Warden, Sikkim Forest Department, Deorali, Sikkim 737102, to enter the sanctuary.

### Gezing *p646*

Most accommodation is above the main square including **D-E Atri**, T03592 250602, and **E-F Kanchendzonga**, T03592 250789.

### Pemayangtse *p646*

**D Mount Pandim** (15-min walk, below monastery), T03593-250756. 25 large rooms with bath (barely OK), some with beautiful views, Indian and Chinese meals (non-residents order in advance), very slow service (get there early for breakfast), peaceful but run down, reservations, Tourist Office, Gangtok.
**F DPCA Hostel**, half-way to Pelling, 9 decent dorms, geysers and vegetarian meals.

### Pelling *p646*

Power and water cuts can last 4 hrs or more and dogs are prone to bark through the night! With over 30 places to choose from, the following are recommended.
**C Sikkim Tourist Centre**, Upper Pelling, near Jeep Stand, T03595 258556. Simple rooms, some with views, cheaper on roadside, rooftop restaurant (cooking excellent but service limited; only snacks after 1400), tours.
**C-D Touristo**, T03595 258206, nice rooms.
**D Norbu Gang**, Main Rd, T03595 250566. Rooms with bath, better views from those away from road, views from the terrace are superb. Restaurant.
**D Phamrong**, near Garuda, Upper Pelling, T03595 250660. Clean, reasonable rooms, good service, but poor breakfast, email.
**D-E Haven**, Khechopari Rd, Middle Pelling, T03595 258238. Clean doubles with running hot water.
**E Garuda**, Upper Pelling, near bus stop, T03595 250614. Rooms in basic lodge with bath, hot water (heaters Rs 35), dorm, restaurant (breakfast on rooftop with mountain views), backpackers favourite (interesting info).
**F Sisters Family Guest House**, near Garuda, T03595 250569. 8 simple clean rooms, shared bath (bucket hot water), great food, very friendly.

### Khechopari Lake *p646*

Families also offer to take in guests (further 25 mins' walk up the hill).
**F Pilgrims' Lodge**, on edge of lake. Renovated, transformed, cleaner (Rs 140), enterprising Mr Tenang provides Sikkimese porridge and millet bread (and much more), short hikes (circular) that bring guests back to the lodge for another night's stay!

### Tashiding *p646*

**F Blue Bird**, T03595 243248.
**F Laxmi**, cheap rooms OK, common bath not. **F Siniolchu**,T03595 243211 5 clean rooms (3 on upper floor are big and beautiful). Dorm beds, shared bath, hot water, meals, friendly.

### Yuksom *p646*

**C Tashigang**, Main Road, T03595 241202, tashigang2@yahoo.com. 21 good, clean rooms with lovely views, own vegetable garden, tennis, quiet, very welcoming.

### Phodong *p647*

**F Yak and Yeti**, T03595 260884. Quiet and clean. Some rooms with toilet, hot water in buckets, but meals are pricey and take ages. Recommended.

### Yuksom, Tsokhaand and Dzongri *p651*

**E Trekkers' Huts**, with rooms and dorm for overnight stops, are fairly clean although the toilets are basic. Bring sleeping bags; meals are cooked by a caretaker. The huts are in picturesque locations at Pemayangtse, Yuksom, Tsokha and Dzongri.

*For an explanation of the sleeping and eating price codes used in this guide, see inside the front cover. Other relevant information is found in Essentials pages 56-61.*

## Eating

**Pelling** *p646*
Don't miss local *chhang* brewed in the area. **Alpine**, Khechopari Rd (below Garuda). Chinese, Kashmiri especially good. Wooden cottage, painted yellow, run by friendly Ladakhi lady.

**Phodong** *p647*
**Northway** serves excellent Indian food, and is friendly, relaxed, efficient and good value.

## Festivals and events

**Rumtek Monastery** *p645*
**Feb** Special colourful **Losar** dances are held 2 days before the Tibetan New Year (check date). Arrive 3 days earlier to see rehearsals without masks, *pujas* and ceremonies are held during this period.
**Jun** The important Rumtek *chaam* is performed on the 10th day of the 5th month of the Tibetan calendar; masked dancers present eight manifestations of the Guru Rimpoche. Tours in Jul-Aug from Gangtok.

## Activities and tours

**Pelling** *p646*
**Help Tourism**, Sikkim Tourist Centre, T03595 250855, good information and tours.

## Transport

Buses can be crowded, especially during *Pujas* and *Diwali*; get ticket on bus if ticket counter is busy. There are SNT buses to Gangtok (0800, 1300), 5 hrs, Rs 50 (or go via Pelling and Jorethang); Yuksom via Tashiding (1300), 4 hrs; Siliguri (0630, 1300), 5 hrs. A shared jeep to Darjeeling, Rs 60.

**Rumtek Monastery** *p645*
Bus from **Gangtok** about 1600 (1 hr) along a steep narrow road, return depart about 0800. A shared jeep: Rs 25 each; last return to Gangtok 1300. **Rumtek** to **Pemayangtse**, 4 hrs. Taxi from Gangtok, Rs 300 (return Rs 500, 1½ hr wait).

**Pemayangtse** *p646*
From Gezing: bus to monastery, 1000-1430, Rs 15. Shared jeep, Rs 60.

**Pelling** *p646*
To **Gezing** bus or walk along steep downhill track, 1 hr. To **Khechopari Lake**: last bus dep 1400, or you can walk 5 hrs (part very steep; last 3 hrs follows road). Buses and share-jeeps to **Yuksom, Damthang, Gangtok** (4 hrs), **Darjeeling** via Jorethang, tickets from **Father Travels** opposite Hotel Garuda, Rs 180. **Siliguri**: SNT bus 0700; tickets sold at provision store next to **Hotel Pelling** where bus starts, and stops uphill at Garuda at the jeep stand.

**Khechopari Lake** *p646*
From **Pelling**: jeep share, 1½ hrs; **Tashiding** (3 options): 1. 0700 bus to Gezing, then jeep. 2. Bus to Yuksom 1500 (irregular) from 'junction', 10 km from lake; overnight in Yuksom, then bus at 0700 (or jeep) to Tashiding, 1 hr. 3. Hitching a lift on the Pelling to Tashiding jeep, which passes the 'junction' at about 1400; try sitting on top of jeep to enjoy the beautiful scenery!

**Tashiding** *p646*
From Yuksom or Gezing: bus or jeep via Legship; or climb 6 km (2 hrs). From Pemayangtse: a day's walk.

**Yuksom** *p646*
Bus: to **Gezing and Tashiding**, 0700. Shared jeep: to **Pelling**, 0600, 2 hrs, Rs 70 each, from market place; buy ticket a day ahead. **Gangtok**, Rs 120 each; sightseeing Rs 800; guide Rs 110.

**Phodong** *p647*
From Gangtok bus to start of jeep track, 0800 (2 hrs), Rs 35; return bus, 1500. Jeeps travel up to **Labrang**.

## Directory

**Pelling** *p646*
**Bank** State Bank of India, exchange rates unavailable daily so unable to help! **Tourist offices** Sikkim, Upper Pelling, near Garuda, T03595 250855. Helpful.

# Trekking in Sikkim

*Trekking is in its infancy and many of the routes are through areas that seldom see foreigners. Consequently, facilities are poorly developed though the paths are usually clear. You do not need previous experience since most treks are between 2,000-3,800 m. An added attraction is that dzos (cross between a cow and a yak) will carry your gear instead of porters but they are slower. The trekking routes also pass through villages that give an insight into the tribal people's lifestyle.*

## Ins and outs

*Best time to visit is March-late May, October-early December. April is best for flowers.*

Foreigners must be in a group of two at least before applying for a **permit** to trek (approved agents can assist). Lachung and Yumthang valleys in North Sikkim (five days) and Chhangu in East Sikkim (one day) are open to foreigners. **Trekking agents** are listed under Activities and tours in the Gangtok and Darjeeling sections. Tourist Information Centre, Gangtok has tents for Rs 25 per night. Yuksom can arrange guides Rs 300-400, cook Rs 250, porter Rs 100 and yak/pony Rs 150; book trekkers' huts (Rs 50 per head). **Leeches** can be a problem in the wet season, below 2,000 m. *A Guide to Sikkim, Darjeeling Area and Bhutan* by **Rajesh Verma**, 1995, introduces the state and has descriptions of treks, with trekking profiles. The U 502 sheets for Sikkim are NG 45-3 and NG 45-4. PP Karan published a



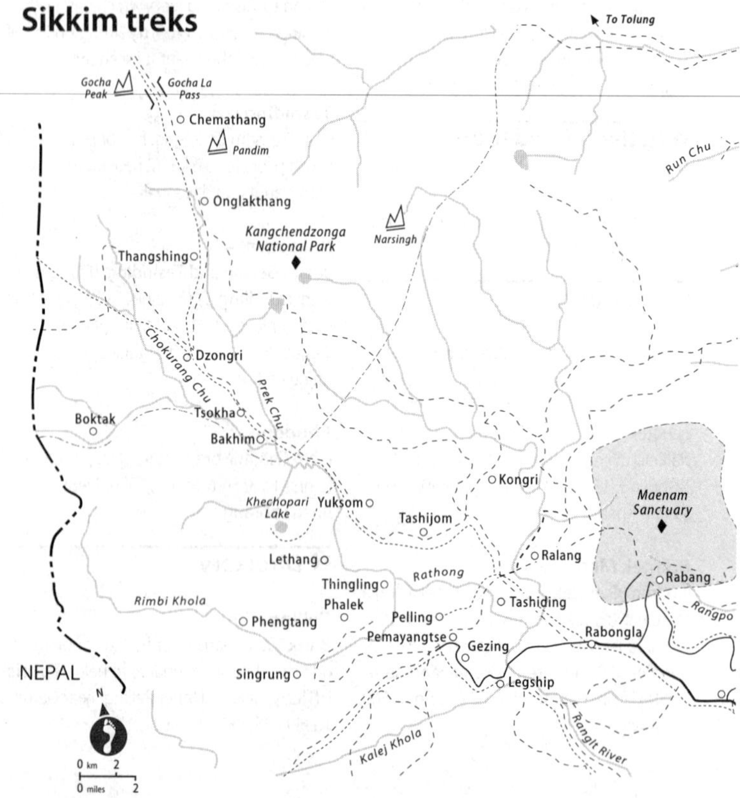

map at the scale of 1:150,000 in 1969. Price US$3, available from the Program Director of Geography, George Mason University, Fairfax, VA 22030, US. *Sikkim Himalaya* (Swiss Alpine Club) – Huber 1:50,000. Very detailed, £16.



## Maenam Sanctuary

**Rabongla**, at an altitude of 2,155 m, 24 km east of Legship, has **Hotel Maenam** with simple, clean rooms, and excellent food. **Mount Narsing Village Resort**, 15th Mile, 3 km from Rabongla, has bungalow rooms and safari tents. The trek from there through the sanctuary to **Maenam peak** (3,260 m) which dominates the town, takes about three hours. The sanctuary harbours red panda, civet, blood pheasant and black eagle and is most beautiful when the magnolia and rhododendron are in bloom in April-May. **Bhaledunga**, another 30-minute hike along the ridge, on the steep cliff edge above the Teesta, juts out in the shape of a cock's head.



## Kangchendzonga National Park

ⓘ *Rs 180 (5 days), Rs 50 for each extra day, camera Rs 10, porter Rs 5, pack animal Rs 5, camping Rs 25 per tent, trekkers' hut Rs 50 per person, Tsokha Hut Rs 75 per bed.* The park offers trekking routes through picturesque terraced fields of barley, past fruit orchards to lush green forests of pines, oak, chestnut, rhododendrons, giant magnolias, then to high passes crossing fast mountain streams and rugged terrain. Animals in the park include Himalayan brown bear, black bear, the endangered musk deer, flying squirrel, Tibetan antelope, wild asses and Himalayan wild goats. The red panda, found between 3,000-4,000 m, lives mostly on treetops. There are about 600 species of birds. The Kangchendzonga trek now falls wholly within the newly designated national park. The park office in **Yuksom**, about 100 m below the trekkers' huts, housed in a shiny new building has interesting exhibits – stuffed birds, posters about the local wildlife and a couple of locally found musk deer in an enclosure in the wooded yard. Helpful staff.

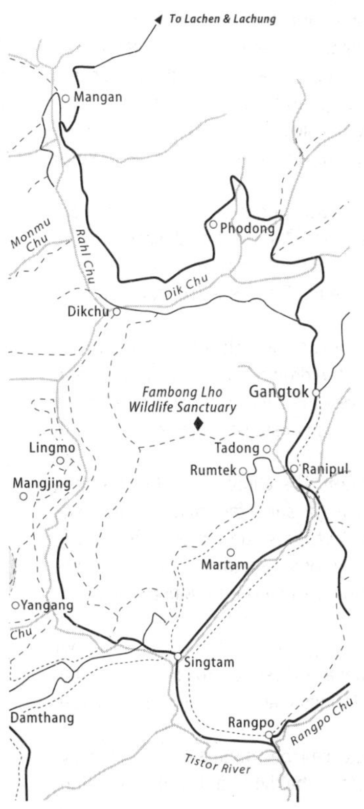


## Fambong Lho Wildlife Reserve

The reserve, a little beyond Rumtek, is 25 km from Gangtok across the Ranipool Valley. There are serene junglewalks in the hills, leading to waterfalls, mountain views, jungles with orchids, birds and wildlife (marten, fox, red panda, boar – even wolf and sloth bear). You are free to go on your own (though this is not advisable on some stretches) and can climb or walk for anything from one to six days. The entry fee is Rs 5 and there are log huts at Golitar and Tumin, Rs 50.

## Gangtok-Pemayangtse-Yuksom-Dzongri

It is possible to trek from **Pemayangtse** (eight to 15 days) or **Naya Bazar** (seven to eight days). From Darjeeling, a shorter trek goes to Singla and Pemayangtse. See also Darjeeling Treks, page 617. The route is from Gangtok to Pemayangtse via Rumtek, then on to Yuksom, Bakhim and Dzongri (described briefly below). Although it is not a long trek there are excellent views throughout as you travel up the Ratong Chu River to the amphitheatre of peaks at the head of the valley. These include Kokthang (6,150 m), Ratong (6,683 m), Kabru Dome (6,604 m), Forked Peak (6,116 m) and the pyramid of Pandim (6,720 m) past which the trail runs. From Pemayangtse the route passes through terraced fields of rice, barley and corn. After crossing the Rimbi Khola River on a narrow suspension bridge, the road gradually rises to Yuksom.

## Yuksom – Thangshing – Gocha La

Yuksom, 28 km from Pemayangtse – a two-hour drive, is the base for a trek to the Gocha La. This eight to nine day trek includes some magnificent scenery around Kangchendzonga.

**Day 1 Yuksom to Tsokha** An eight- hour climb to the growing village of Tsokha, settled by Lepcha yak herders and Tibetan refugees. The first half of the climb passes through dense semi-tropical forests and across the Prek Chu on a suspension bridge. A steep climb of six hours leads first to **Bakhim** (2,740 m) which has a tea stall and a Forest Bungalow. There are good views back down the trail. The track then goes on through silver fir and cypress to Tsokha (2,950 m), the last village (which is very Tibetan) on the trek. **Trekkers' hut**, camping ground and good **Mountain Hut** private lodge at Tsokha.

**Day 2 Tsokha to Dzongri** Mixed temperate forests gradually give way to rhododendron. **Phodang** is less than three hours up the track. Pandim, Narsingh and Joponu peaks are clearly visible, and a further one hour climb takes the track above the rhododendron to a ridge. A gentle descent leads to Dzongri (4,030 m, 8 km from Bakhim), where nomadic yak herders stay in huts. There is a **Trekkers' hut** and camping ground. Dzongri attracts occasional pilgrims to its *chortens* containing Buddhist relics. From the exposed and windswept hillsides nearby you can get a good panoramic view of the surrounding mountains and see a spectacular sunrise or sunset on Kangchendzonga.

**Day 3 Dzongri to Thangshing** A trail through dwarf rhododendron and juniper climbs the ridge for 5 km. Pandim is immediately ahead. A steep drop descends to the Prek Chu again, crossed by a bridge, followed by a gentle climb to Thangshing (3,900 m). The southern ridge of Kangchendzonga is ahead. There is a **Trekkers' hut** and camping ground.

**Day 4 Thangshing to Samity Lake** The track leads through juniper scrub to a steeper section up a lateral moraine, followed by the drop down to the glacial – and holy – Samity Lake. The surrounding moraines give superb views of Kangchendzonga and other major peaks. You can camp here at 4,250 m or stay at a **Trekkers' hut** with two rooms and a kitchen.

**Day 5 To Chemathang and Gocha La and return** The climb up to Chemathang (4,800 m) and Gocha La (4,900 m) gives views up to the sheer face of the eastern wall of Kangchendzonga itself. Tibetans collect sprigs of the scrub juniper that grow in abundance here to use in religious rites. It is a vigorous walk to reach the pass, but almost equally impressive views can be gained from nearby slopes. Much of the walk is on the rough moraine.

**Day 6 Samity Lake to Thangshing** Return to Thangshing. This is only a two-hour walk, so it is possible to take it gently and make a diversion to the yak grazing grounds of Lam Pokhari Lake (3,900 m) above Thangshing. You may see some rare high altitude birds and blue sheep.

**Day 7 Thangshing to Tsokha** The return route can be made by a lower track, avoiding Dzongri. Dense rhododendron forests flank the right bank of the Prek Chu, rich in birdlife. The day ends in Tsokha village.

# Northeastern Hill States

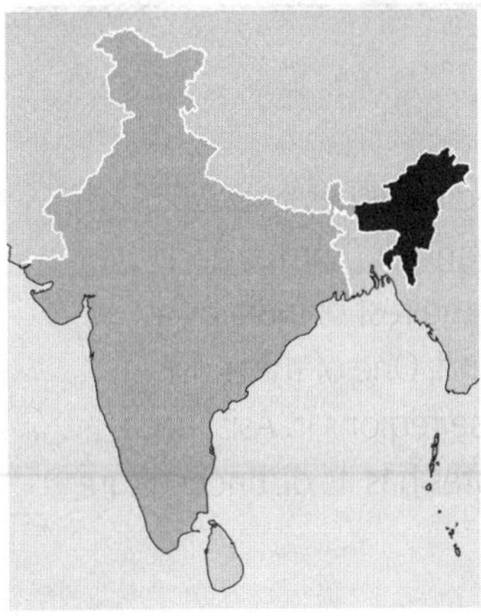



## Footprint features

# Introduction

The Northeast is a true frontier region. It has over 2,000 km of border with Bhutan, China, Myanmar (Burma) and Bangladesh, and is connected to the rest of India by a narrow 20-km wide corridor of land. One of the most ethnically and linguistically diverse regions in Asia, each of the seven Northeastern Hill states has its distinct culture and tradition.



Deep forests cover the sparsely populated foothills of the Himalaya, which comprise Arunachal Pradesh, only recently opened to visitors. To its south, Assam, which occupies the lush lowlands of the Brahmaputra Valley, is the most densely populated and largest of the states. Meghalaya's beautiful hills have the dubious distinction of being the wettest region in the world. The little-visited four southeastern states of the region, Nagaland, Manipur, Mizoram and Tripura, make up a fascinating area, hilly, remote, and a zone where the tribal cultures of South and Southeast Asia intertwine.

The Northeast has been a politically sensitive region since Independence. Insurgency in places continues to surface making travel in some areas unsafe. Arunachal Pradesh, most of Assam, Meghalaya and Mizoram are largely free of problems. Nevertheless, advice on travel to these and the other states should be taken locally. Permits are required for Arunachal Pradesh, Mizoram, Nagaland and Manipur.

## ★ Don't miss...

1 **Kaziranga National Park** The place to see the Indian greater one-horned rhino (from the back of an elephant), page 660.
2 **Nameri National Park** Stay at the eco camp and go rafting and fishing, page 662.
3 **Archery Stakes** Place a bet at this daily occurrence in Shillong, page 671.
4 **Mawsynram** Visit the wettest place in the world which has over 11 metres of rain every year, page 673.
5 **Tawang Monastery** Embark on the spectacular four-day journey to this remote place, page 678.
6 **Kohima** Stop at the cemetery where the British prevented the Japanese invasion of India in April 1944, page 681.

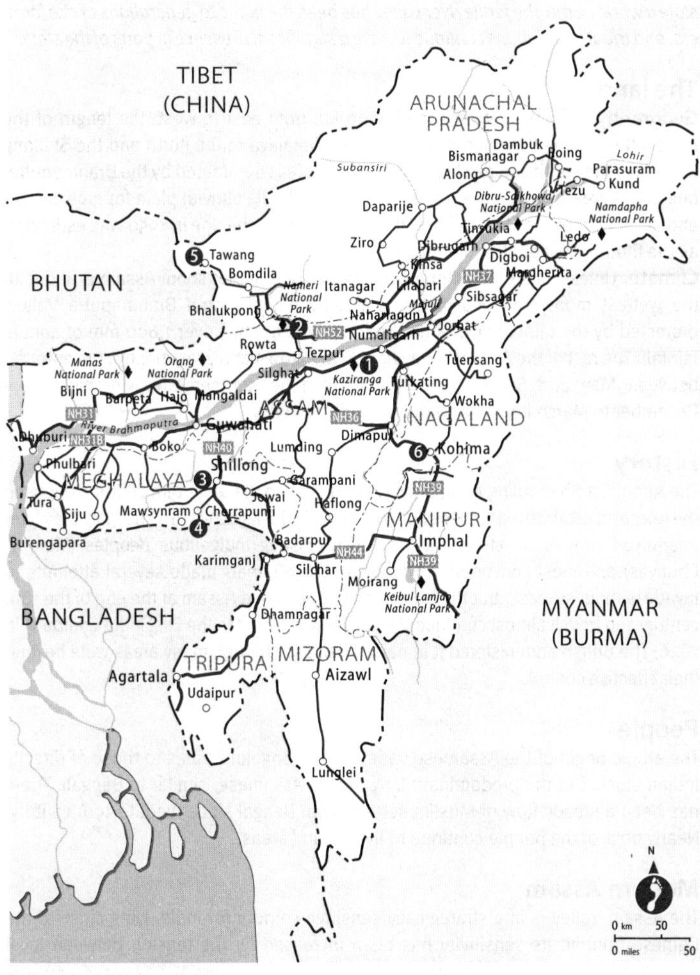

## Visiting the Northeast

Visitors to Assam, Meghalaya and Tripura do not need permits but may need to register on arrival and departure. Foreigners visiting Arunachal Pradesh, Nagaland, Manipur and Mizoram may obtain Restricted Area Permits from the Ministry of Home Affairs, Foreigners Division, Lok Nayak Bhavan, Khan Market, New Delhi 110003. Send two photos and allow up to six weeks. Indians require Inner Line Permits from the Ministry of Home Affairs. Groups of four should travel together to get a permit; the State Tourist Offices can usually help.



# Assam

→ *Population: 26.6 mn. Area: 78,438 sq km.*

*The lush valley of the Brahmaputra, one of the world's great rivers, provides the setting for Assam's culturally rich and diverse communities. Although it is tea that has given the state a world name, the fertile river valley has been the home to generations of rice farmers, and tribal populations continue to have a significant presence in parts of the state.*

## The land

**Geography** Assam stretches nearly 800 km from east to west, the length of the narrow floor of the Brahmaputra Valley. The Himalaya to the north and the Shillong Plateau to the south can be clearly seen. The state is dominated by the Brahmaputra, one of the great rivers of the world, which has a fertile alluvial plain for growing rice and is also famous for tea. Earthquakes are common, the one in 1950 was estimated as the fifth biggest earthquake ever recorded.

**Climate** Unless you really want to see rain, avoid the monsoon! Assam is in one of the wettest monsoon belts in the world. Even the central Brahmaputra Valley, protected by the rainshadow of the Shillong Plateau, has over 1,600 mm of annual rainfall. The rest of the Assam Valley has up to 3,200 mm a year, mostly concentrated between May and September. Although summer temperatures are high, from December to March it can be cold, especially at night.

## History

The Ahoms, a Shan ruling tribe, arrived in the area in the early 13th century, deposed the ruler and established the kingdom of 'Assam' with its capital in Sibsagar. They later intermixed with Aryan stock and also with existing indigenous peoples (Morans, Chutiyas) and most converted to Hinduism. The Mughals made several attempts to invade without success, but the Burmese finally invaded Assam at the end of the 18th century and held it almost continuously until it was ceded to the East India Company in 1826. The British administered it in name until 1947 though many areas were beyond their effective control.

## People

The ethnic origin of the Assamese varies from Mongoloid tribes to those of directly Indian stock, but the predominant language is Assamese, similar to Bengali. There has been a steady flow of Muslim settlers from Bengal since the late 19th century. Nearly 90% of the people continue to live in rural areas.

## Modern Assam

The Assam Valley is in a strategically sensitive corridor for India, lying close to the Chinese frontier. Its sensitivity has been increased by the tension between local

Assamese and immigrant groups. The failure of the AGP (Assam Gana Parishad) to hold its alliance together and to control the violence that has become endemic through Assam contributed to its downfall. Congress returned to power under Chief Minister Tarun Gogoi, a lawyer and long serving member of the Lok Sabha. 

# Guwahati → *Phone code: 0361. Colour map 4, grid B4. Population: 808,000.*

Despite its commanding position on the south bank of the mighty Brahmaputra, it is easy to forget that Guwahati is a riverside town, the waterside having little impact on people's lives. The main entrance point for visitors to the Northeastern states, the city retains a relaxed and friendly atmosphere. Paltan Bazar, where most visitors arrive, is very busy and crowded. North of the railway it is much quieter and has a rural feel.
» *For Sleeping, Eating and other listings, see pages 664-670.*

## Ins and outs

**Getting there** Borjhar airport (23 km) has flights to Kolkata, Delhi, Bagdogra and airports throughout the Northeast. Flights to Bangkok were inaugurated in 2002. Some 1,151 km from Kolkata, Guwuhati is at the junction of NH31, 37 and 40, and sowell connected by road to all major centres of the northeast region. It has occasional coaches, shared taxis and auto-rickshaws for transfer to town. The railway station is in the central Paltan Bazar, while most state and private buses arrive immediately to its south. » *See Transport, page 667, for further details.*

**Getting around** It is easy to walk around the two main commercial areas of Paltan and Pan (pronounced *Paan*) Bazars, which have most of the hotels and restaurants. Red minibuses or 'canters' are cheap and very efficient around the city (conductors call out the stops), whereas auto-rickshaws need hard bargaining. Political incidents in the city are rare so military presence usually remains discreet and low-key. Carry a torch when walking at night – large holes in pavements in places lead straight down into sewer channels.



## History

Guwahati, on the site of the ancient capital of a succession of local chieftains, was once known as *Pragjyotishpur* ('the city of astrology'). The **Navagrah** (nine planets) **Temple** on a hill here was the ancient centre of astronomy and astrology. It was also a centre of learning and a place of Hindu pilgrimage. In the seventh century, Hiuen Tsang described its beautiful mountains, forests and wildlife. Today it is the business capital while **Dispur**, the 'Capital Area', is just to the south.

## Sights

The 10th-century **Janardhan Temple**, in the heart of the city, was rebuilt in the 17th century. The Buddha image here uniquely blends Hindu and Buddhist features. The **Umananda** (Siva) **Temple**, on Peacock Island in the Brahmaputra, can be reached by ferry. An Ahom king built the temple in 1594, believing Uma, Siva's consort, had stayed there. Ask the priests about the few rare golden langurs here. **Assam State Museum** ⓘ *closed Mon and 2nd, 4th Sat, 1000-1615 (Nov-Mar), 1000-1700 (Apr-Oct), Rs 2, photography with permission*, covers epigraphy, sculpture, natural history et cetera; sections on village life, crafts and ethnography are particularly interesting. A small museum, well lit, thoughtfully displayed with notes in English and informative on neighbouring cultures. **Commercial Museum** ⓘ *Mon-Sat, closed Sun and University holidays, 1230-1830, no photography*, at Guwahati University, has collections of art and craft, commercial products, minerals and rocks, coins etc. **Srimata Sankaradeva Kalakshetra** ⓘ *Panjabari, on road to Narangi, closed Mon, 0800-2200, bus 8*, is a cultural complex set up to serve as a centre for Assamese dance, drama, music, fine arts and literature ("a theme park of Assamese life"). It features a museum, theatre, artists' village and heritage park.

## Excursions

**Kamakhya Temple** ⓘ *0830-1300, 1500-1600 (Sun 0830-1200)*, 8 km south- west, is believed to be an old Khasi sacrificial site on Nilachal Hill. It has been a centre for Tantric Hinduism and Sakti worship. Rebuilt in 1665 after the 10th-century temple was destroyed by a Brahmin convert to Islam, it typifies Assamese temple architecture with its distinctive beehive-shape *sikhara* (spire), the nymph motifs and the long turtleback hall. The dark sanctum contains the creative part of the goddess which is said to have fallen here, see page 594, and pilgrims enter to touch the wet *yoni* of Kamakhya (Sakti). Western visitors may be allowed into the sanctum but should be prepared for the charged atmosphere and to walk barefoot on a floor sprinkled with the sacrificial blood of a goat. Ask for Hemen Sarma, a knowledgeable resident Brahmin, on entering the complex. Further up the hill is a smaller temple and a Viewpoint with panoramic views of the Brahmaputra. See Festivals below. It can be visited by bus from MG Rd (towards Adabari Bus Stand) which can drop you near Kamakhya. From here take a 'canter' from AT Road to the temple or walk up the steep and slippery rocky path at the back of the hill.



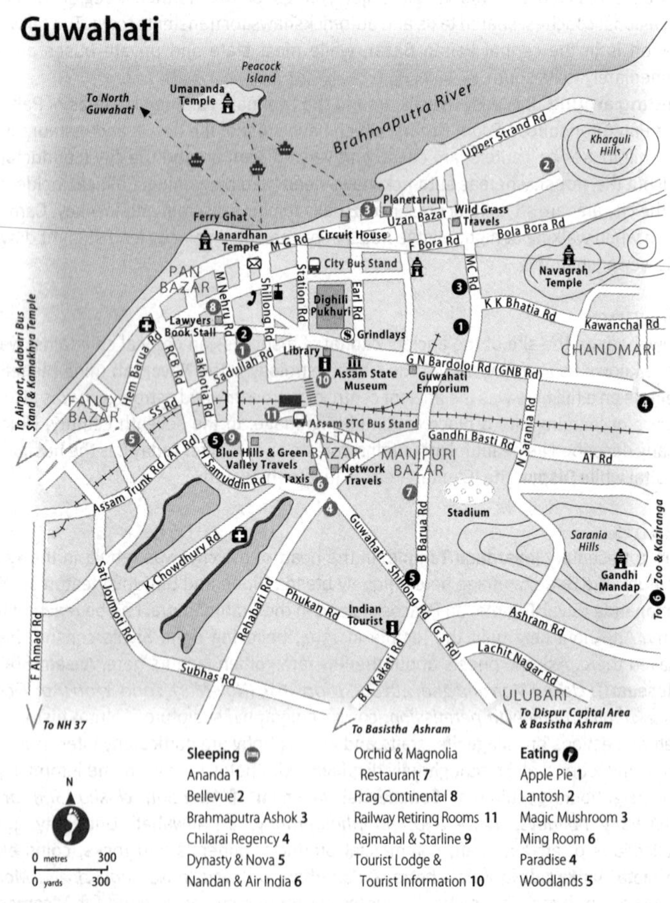

## Plantation labour

Today Assam produces most of India's tea. Old colonial tea planters' bungalows surrounded by neat rows of emerald green tea bushes dominate the landscape, particularly in Upper Assam. After an early experiment using imported Chinese labourers ended in near mutiny, the British began the mass recruitment of Adivasis from the Choto Nagpur plateau, Andhra Pradesh and Orissa. They have now been assimilated into Assamese society. One of the largest groups of organized labour in India today, they enjoy benefits undreamed of by other workers including free health care, education and subsidized food. The lifestyle of the plantation, hardly changed since the days of the Raj, has been tarnished lately by the rise of insurgency, with tea companies being targeted for extortion and kidnapping.

**Basistha Ashram**, 12 km away, is believed to be sage Basistha's (Vasistha) hermitage, it is a scenic spot with three mountain streams nearby. **North Guwahati** is a sleepy town across Saraighat Bridge, which can also be reached by any ferry from the ghat. The **Digheswari Temple** is worth a visit. Take a rickshaw from the other bank or an auto-rickshaw or shared four-wheeler.

# Around Guwahati

**Hajo**, a friendly and peaceful town, 34 km across the river, produces bell-metal work and is sacred to three religions. **Hayagriba Madhab** Hindu temple is said to contain a Buddhist relic. Some believe this is where the Buddha attained Nirvana. Its hilltop location is more spectacular than the temple itself. The 'main' street behind the tank stocked with fish leads to an old Ganesh temple after 2 km; a friendly priest might allow you in. Hajo is also sacred to Muslims since the **Pao Mecca Mosque** built by Pir Ghiasuddin Aulia is supposed to have 'quarter' (*pao*) of the sanctity of Mecca. Take a bus from Adabari Bus Stand. They take one hour, the last return bus departs around 1600 but may be very crowded – you may have to travel on the roof.

The small village of **Sualkuchi**, on the north bank of the Brahmaputra, is famous for silk production from non mulberry leaf-fed worms, hence its unique natural colour. Every household is involved with weaving of *muga*, *endi* or *pat* silk; prices are 30% cheaper than in Guwahati. Take the ferry from Guwahati or a bus from Hajo taking 20 minutes.

**Pabitora** is a small wildlife sanctuary a two-hour drive from Guwahati (60 km), on the border of Nagaon and Kamrup districts, has rhinos. **Madan Kamdev**, 45 km north of Guwahati, has been called Assam's Khajuraho. The temples which may date from the 11th-12th century, possibly reconstructed in the 18th, are believed to be associated with tantric practices. The principle shrine to Uma-Mahesvara or Siva-Parvati is still in use. Buses from Guwahati go to Baihata on NH31, 5 km from the site; rickshaws take over.

# Manas National Park → *Phone code: 03666. Colour map 4, grid A3.*

A World Heritage Site, and one of India's most beautiful sanctuaries, Manas lies in the Himalayan foothills, southeast of the river Manas, on the Assam-Bhutan border. Over half the area is covered with tall grass and scattered patches of woodland. This changes to dense semi-evergreen forest in the upper reaches and even to conifer on hills towards Bhutan. ›› *For Sleeping, Eating and other listings, see pages 664-670.*

## Ins and outs

It is essential to enter via Barpeta Road by car or taxi. Permits are issued by the Field Director, Manas Project Tiger, Barpeta Road, after he obtains confirmation of a police escort to accompany you. Pick up provisions. Use the Bansbari gate with a Forest Range Office (20 km, 30 minutes) to get to Mathanguri inside the park (20 km, 30 minutes). Do book a car/taxi for the return journey. If you travel during dawn (0500) and before sunset (0400) you may see some wildlife. Travel is not permitted after sunset. Summer maximum 35°C, minimum 18°C; winter maximum 24°C, minimum 7°C. Annual rainfall: 4,100 mm. Season: November-March. Take something warm for evenings, a hat and shoes for wading through slippery streams essential.

*The town has medical facilities, a Tourist Information Office, banks and a post office.*

## Background

The Manas, with a buffer zone 2,800 sq km (including two other far flung sanctuaries), and a core area of 391 sq km, was demarcated in 1977-1978 when the preservation programme 'Project Tiger' was launched. At the last count there were over 80 tigers. UNESCO has released funds to help the national park recover from damage caused by Bodo rebels. Political troubles can lead to sudden closure of the park so get local advice before visiting; contact **Wild Grass Tours**, Guwahati, above.

## Sights

The forests are home to most of the larger animals found in Kaziranga, most common being wild buffalo, swamp deer, hog deer, sambar and elephant. Some 22 of the animal and bird species are on the endangered list of the IUCN including the rare capped and golden langur which can be seen among the flowering trees, mostly on the Bhutan side. There are also pigmy hog, hispid hare, slow lorris, clouded leopard, rhino and tiger. The sanctuary is rich in birdlife (over 400 species), and attracts migratory flocks of redstarts, forktails, mergansers and ruddy shelduck. Otters are frequently seen in the Manas River.

Occasionally boats, for two to eight, are for hire from the Forest Beat Officer, Mathanguri. To see the animals from close range, an elephant ride is best. These start from Mathanguri for one hour (0900-1200, 1400-1700, Rs 525 for foreigners). Charges for entry and camera are similar to Kaziranga.



# Kaziranga National Park

→ *Phone code: 03776. Colour map 4, grid B4.*

Kaziranga Reserve Forest was declared a game sanctuary in 1916 to save the Indian greater one-horned rhino and became a national park in 1974. It is now a World

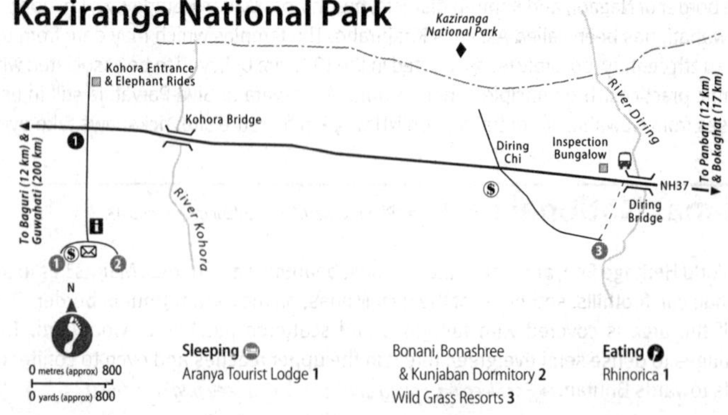

Heritage site. In a beautiful setting on the banks of the Brahmaputra, and with the Karbi Anglong Hills to the south, the 430 sq km park combines elephant grass mixed with thorny rattan cane, areas of semi-evergreen forest and shallow swamps. ▸▸ *For Sleeping, Eating and other listings, see pages 664-670.*

## Ins and outs

Guwahati is 215 km from Kohora, the entry point to Kaziranga on the NH37. Park roads open 0800-1100, 1400-1630. Foreigners, Rs 175. Cameras (for each trip during any day): still, Rs 175, telephoto lens, Rs 210, video, Rs 525 (professional, Rs 7,000). 25% discount on fees after three consecutive days. Summer maximum 35°C, minimum 18°C; Winter maximum 24°C, minimum 7°C. Annual rainfall 2,300 mm, heavy in summer. Best season: mid-November to end-April (December and January are the best for birds); closed mid April-mid October during monsoons. Wear cottons but take a jacket. ▸▸ *See Transport, page 668, for details.*

## Sights

The **rhino** population is about 1,200 here (1,500 in the country) but you can still easily see them in the marshes and grasslands. Poachers still kill the animal for its horn for its use in Chinese and Tibetan medicine. The park also has over 1,000 wild buffalo, sambar, swamp deer (over 500), hog deer, wild pig, hoolock gibbon, elephants (about 1,000) pythons and tiger (80 in 1997), the only predator of the docile rhino. There is a rich variety of shallow-water fowl including egrets, pond herons, river terns, black-necked stork, fishing eagles and adjutant storks, pelicans and the rare Bengal florican. There are otters and dolphins in the river.

There are three road routes for visiting the park: **The Kaziranga Range** – Kohora, Daflang, Foliomari which is full of big mammals; the **Western Range** – Baguri, Monabeel, Bimoli, Kanchanjuri with tall elephant grass so visibility not great; and the **Eastern Range** – Agortoli, Sohola, Rangamatia, where you may see a lot of wildlife but at a distance. Keep receipts as fees are valid for several trips during one day.

**Entry** into the park is by own vehicle, hired jeep or trained elephants. Although elephants cover less ground than motor vehicles, they can get a lot closer to the wildlife, particularly rhinos and buffalo.However, the elephant rides get mixed reports; the general consensus seems to be that they are less enjoyable when demand is heavy. They carry four and a seat may be booked through the Forest Range Officer, the night before the visit (0530-0630 or 0630-0730, Rs 525 foreigners (Indians Rs 120), plus jeep transfer between town and elephant pick-up, Rs 120). The viewing posts just inside the park may offer quieter viewing.

The Department of Tourism, Kaziranga and private agents hire out **jeeps** for five to six people. Government: Rs 400 for three hours; private: Rs 550 for 50 km or 2½ hours; Wild Grass Resorts charge Rs 10 per km, for example Eastern Range, Rs 700. A car or jeep must be accompanied by a Forest Department guide (free), who can give directions as well as spot wildlife. Cars and jeeps pay a road toll, Rs 150.

**Panbari Forest Reserve**, 12 km from Kaziranga, has hoolock gibbons and a good variety of birdlife. Contact the Forest Office, Guwahati, for permission to visit.

# Tezpur and around

→ *Phone code: 03712. Colour map 4, grid A4.*

Tezpur, on the north bank of the Brahmaputra, 180 km northeast of Guwahati, is the site of Assam's first tea plantations. Its ancient origins can be seen at Da Parbatia, west of town, which has the entrance gate of an early Gupta style temple.

An interesting excursion is to take a Guwahati-bound bus, get off at the bridge over the Brahmaputra, then negotiate with a boatman to take you to the river's confluence with the Bhoreli for some river dolphin watching. Some hotels, **Luit** for example, offer such trips. It involves a 30-minute rickshaw ride, Rs 150, followed by boat hire, Rs 800.

**Nameri National Park**, a 210 sq km park on the Arunachal border, is on the river Jia Bhoreli, about 40 km north of Tezpur. There are tigers and elephants – 29 and 225 counted in 1997 – Indian bison, barking and hog deer. It is home to about 20 endangered white-winged wood ducks among 300 bird species, with evergreens, bamboo and some open grassland. The best time to visit is from October to April. Viewing is on elephant back as there are no roads; you can trek within the park with a forest guide. Entry and camera fees are similar to Kaziranga.

**Bhalukpong**, 20 km west of Nameri, just beyond the Arunachal Pradesh border, en route to Tawang, has a hot spring an orchid garden and good fishing. You can camp (own tent) on the picturesque bank of the River Jia Bhoreli. A taxi to Tezpur, taking one hour, costs around Rs 250. Or catch a bus from Balipura, change for Bhalukpong.

**Orang National Park** is often called a miniature Kaziranga. The 76 sq km park, 66 km northwest of Tezpur, has similar flora and fauna, though viewing is not as rewarding. This is compensated by its peaceful and intimate atmosphere, especially if staying inside the park. Arriving by car is best from Tezpur. From Orang, it is a 15-km bumpy, dust track to the park.



## Northeast Assam

### Jorhat
→ *Colour map 4, grid A5.*

Jorhat is one of Assam's major tea centres and is convenient for visiting Majuli Island to the north. The **Tea Festival** is held in November.

### Majuli Island
→ *Colour map 4, grid A5.*

Majuli Island is possibly the largest river island in the world, though constantly changing, and now reduced to around 700 sq km. The flooding of the Brahmaputra River means that at times Majuli is reduced to a cluster of islands, some as small as a hut top. Roads keep shifting but villagers adapt to rerouting by building cost effective bamboo bridges. Cut off from the mainland to the south about 400 years ago, it is served by ferries from Jorhat and North Lakhimpur, but it can still be accessed from the north by road during summer. Majuli is also a birdwatchers' paradise. Foreigners must register on arrival and departure at the nearest police station.

At the forefront of Assamese Vaishnava culture, the island is an important centre for arts, crafts and science. Work is in progress to declare it a World Heritage Site. The *satras* (monasteries) here, inspired by the 15th-century saint Sankardeva and his disciple Madhavdeva, are worth visiting. They are essentially small, self-contained, self-sufficient villages where Vishnu is worshipped through regular performances of dance-dramas at the temples.

Some *satras* can be visited on foot in and around **Kamalabari** and **Garmur** but for others a rickshaw is handy. **Auniati**, a few kilometres west of Kamalabari, has an Angami tribal museum with old manuscripts, utensils, jewellery and handicrafts. **Bengenatti**, east of Uttar Kamalabari, is a centre for performing arts and tribal dance forms. Others worth visiting are at Nauten Kamalabari and Dekhinpat.

### Hollong Park Gibbon Sanctuary

The sanctuary at **Bhalowguri**, 16 km from Majuli Island, was designated in 1998, but is scarcely visited by tourists. Few leave disappointed; part of the appeal being the low-key nature of the operation. Viewing the wild elephants requires an overnight stay in the specially constructed hut on stilts. The current fee is a meagre Rs 20 per person (four hours' viewing), which includes an armed escort/guide, though the dense forest growth makes the gibbons hard to spot. Contact District Forest Officer in

Jorhat, then Forest Range Officer at Mariani. To reach the park catch a bus from the top of MG Road in Jorhat and go via Mariani, 18 km southeast.



## Sibsagar and around

District headquarters of the largest tea and oil producing area in the Northeast, **Sibsagar** was the Ahom capital for two centuries. There are several royal tanks. Daupadi (the Ahom King's wife) built the huge tank here in 1734. On the east bank there is birdwatching tower and a library. The tower of the Siva Dol on its bank is one of the tallest Siva temples in India. **Sivaratri** is celebrated in March.

The **Joysagar** at **Rangpur**, 5 km away, and the three temples on its bank date from 1697. **Talatal Ghar**, 6 km away, is a seven-storeyed palace with three underground floors, built between 1696-1714. Take a bus from BG Rd Bali Ghat in Sibsagar (Rs 5, 20 minutes); then cycle-rickshaw (Rs 15).

## Digboi

The oil fields of upper Assam were first exploited in 1879, the first wells came on stream here in 1892 and a refinery opened in 1900. Although Digboi's own resources are drying up, the region has considerable potential. The surrounding forest is also a haven for birdlife. You may visit at your own risk with permission of OIL. There is an 18-hole golf course and a British Second World War cemetery nearby. For those wishing to visit Arunachal for Miao, Deban Valley, Namdapha Forest Reserve, be aware facilities are limited.

## Dibrugarh, Tinsukia and Borajan Reserve Forest

Much of the old town of Dibrugarh was destroyed during the 1950 earthquake. The new town on the Brahmaputra is surrounded by tea estates. Tinsukia, a major transport junction in the Northeast, is convenient for visiting the nearby Dibru-Saikhowa National Park and the small Borajan Reserve Forest.

**Borajan Reserve Forest**, 5 km from Tinsukia, is a small (½ sq km) patch of forest which is home to five species of primate (Hoolock gibbon, capped langur, slow loris, stump tailed macaque and common macaque) but are not easy to spot.

## Dibru-Saikhowa National Park

A national park since March 1999, on the southern flood plain of the Brahmaputra near Tinsukia, this is largely a semi-wet evergreen forest. The 340 sq km core area within a large bio-sphere reserve is a refuge for some endangered species – tiger, leopard, leopard cat, clouded leopard, elephant. The rich birdlife includes the very rare white-winged wood duck. The best time to visit is November to March. Temperature ranges from 6 to 36°C. Average annual rainfall ranges from 2,300 to 3,600 mm.

Entry points are at **Guijan** on the southern boundary and **Dhola** (near Saikhowa Ghat) at the northern edge, both accessible by bus from Tinsukia. From Guijan, a boat across the river takes you to the Range Office at the park entrance. If you cross from Dhola, the Range Office is 5 km into the park at Narbarmora; it is better to notify your arrival beforehand. See Kaziranga above for usual park fees. The Forest Department has one double-bedded room at Guijan, carry provisions. Contact DFO, Rangagora Rd, Tinsukia, T0374 2331472. The retired DFO, Mr Eunush Ali, knowledgeable about wildlife and the Northeast, T0374 2333079.

## Margherita → *Colour map 4, grid A6.*

Margherita, the constituency of the present Chief Minister, is on Dihing river at the foot of the Patkoi Range, and was named by Italian railway engineers in the late 19th century after the Queen of Italy. The town is surrounded by tea estates and is the Northeast headquarters of Coal India Ltd. The last of the steam railway engines in Assam is still operating.

## Ledo → *Colour map 4, grid A6.*

The small coal mining town of Ledo, 6 km northwest of Margherita, was the headquarters of Northern Combat Area Command during the Second World War and is the start of the 470-km Stilwell Road.

Named after General Joseph Stilwell, the road was the most ambitious and costliest engineering project of the war, US$137,000,000 at the time. Once a two lane, all-weather bitumen highway linking Ledo with Myitkyina in North Burma through the Pangso Pass and with Kunming in China (1,029 miles) it is now closed beyond Nampong in Arunachal Pradesh. A sign, 6 km west of Ledo, commemorates the Road to Mandalay but there is little else that remains of the massive Allied presence here.

## Sleeping

**Guwahati** *p657, map p658*
Hotel staff often speak little English. There are some budget hotels at Sadullah and M Nehru Rd crossing; those in Paltan Bazar are often full by the afternoon. Most medium priced hotels have some a/c rooms and tend to serve Indian meals only. You may need to complete 4 copies of the hotel registration slip and then register with the police (fairly quick). Most hotels outside Guwahati require photocopies of passport identification and the visa page.

**A Brahmaputra Ashok**, MG Rd, T0361 2602281, www.theashokgroup.com. 40 rooms (on riverside best), central a/c, TV, bamboo and cane furniture, good restaurant, credit cards, good travel agency.

**A Dynasty**, SS Rd, T0361 2516021, dynasty_hotel@sify.com. 68 comfortable rooms, good restaurants.

**B Nandan**, GS Rd, opposite **Indian Airlines**, T0361 2540855, www.hotelnandan.com. 55 rooms, some a/c, expensive suites, restaurants, **Upavan** for snacks, bar.

**B Rajmahal**, Paltan Bazar (near bus stand), T0361 2522478, www.rajmahalhotel.com. 80 rooms (good value), excellent restaurant, all services, pool in summer (non-residents Rs 75, 45 mins).

**B-C Prag Continental**, M Nehru Rd, Pan Bazar, T0361 2540850, F2540217. 62 rooms, some a/c, terrace restaurants, **Continental Café**.

**C Bellevue**, MG Rd, on river front opposite Raj Bhawan, T0361 2545750. 45 rooms, restaurant (Continental recommended), elevated woodland setting, quiet.

**C-D Chilarai Regency**, HP Brahmachari Rd, Paltan Bazar, T0361 2541530, F2547917. 44 large rooms (some a/c), bar, exchange.

**C-D Nova**, SS Rd, T0361 2523464, F2633629. Clean rooms (some **C** a/c) in 4-storey block, reasonable restaurant (Indian, Chinese) but slow service (room service quicker), pleasant, friendly and helpful.

**D-E Starline**, Md Shah Rd, Paltan Bazar, T0361 2518541, F2542450. 74 clean rooms, 12 a/c with hot water 24 hrs, Indian/Chinese restaurant, polite and helpful staff.

**E-F Ananda**, M Nehru Rd, T0361 2544832. Small dark rooms but pleasant, vegetarian dining hall.

**E-F Orchid**, B Barua Rd, opposite stadium, T0361 2544471. 23 clean rooms, 5 a/c, hot water in buckets, set back from road in own compound with excellent **Magnolia** restaurant.

**F Railway Retiring Rooms**, rooms (some a/c), small dorm, book at Enquiry Counter.

**F Tourist Lodge** (Assam Tourism), opposite railway station, T0361 2544475. 21 fairly clean simple rooms with nets, toilets and balcony, canteen, staff speak little English but are friendly, tourist information, good value.

**Manas National Park** *p659*

**E Doli**, 200 m from station, 18 rooms with fan, net, bath, abundant food, helpful staff.

**F Mathanguri Forest Lodge**, built on hill overlooking Manas River, is in a poor state but has the advantage of being within the park.

*For an explanation of the sleeping and eating price codes used in this guide, see inside the front cover. Other relevant information is found in Essentials pages 56-61.*

Forest Deparment's **Forest Lodge**, and **Bhutan Tourist Lodge**, Mathanguri, are very simple but clean and well maintained, cook available but bring provisions (from Barpeta Rd), camping possible, book well in advance. Prefabricated **Rest House** provides linen but no electricity, open Nov-Apr. Contact Field Director, Manas Tiger Reserve, PO Barpeta Rd, T03666 233413. If you arrive late at Barpeta Rd you will need to spend the night there.

**Kaziranga National Park** *p660, map p660*
B-C **Wild Grass Resorts**, lovely location, 1.5 km from NH37, 5.5 km from Kohora, ask for Kaziranga IB Bus Stop, 400 m north of resort, T03776 2262011, www.nivalink.com/wild grass. 19 rooms, wood floors, cane furniture, deluxe camping (4 tents, common bath), can get very cold in winter, very good buffet lunch (Rs 50/65), huge pool, excellent service, spotless, relaxing, beautiful walks through forests and tea plantations, tours, pick up from Guwahati for groups, occasional cultural shows.
D **Aranya Tourist Lodge**, 1 km south of Kohora, T03776 2262429. 24 rooms with bath and balcony, some a/c, simple garden, restaurant and bar (slow service, order ahead), friendly.
D-E **Bonani**, near Aranya Tourist Lodge, T03776 2262423. 5 a/c rooms, limited menu.
F **Bonashree**, still cheaper, 9 rooms, a large verandah, pleasant garden, but often full.
**Kunjaban Dormitory**, linen optional, 5 or 12-bed (Rs 30-50), no cupboards.
Reservations: Deputy Director, Tourism, Bonani, Kaziranga, T03776 2662423.
**Dhansri** and **Green Reed**, off the main road.
**Rhinorica Restaurant** is at the bus stop on the main road.

**Tezpur and around** *p661*
C-D **Eco Camp**, Nameri National Park, T03714 244246. Swiss cottage tents with thatched cover, some with bath, 6-bed dorm (Rs 125), wash block, meals. Contact **Wild Grass Tours**, T0361-2546827.
C-D **Luit**, Ranu Singh Rd, 100 m bus stand, Tezpur, T03712 222083. 38 clean rooms, some a/c, best in new wing, restaurant, bar.
E **Basanth**, Main Rd, Tezpur, T03712 230831. Good, clean, well-maintained rooms (Rs 250).
E **Durba**, KK Rd, Tezpur, T03712 224276. Clean rooms with TV, **Appayam** restaurant.

F **Bungalows**, Orang National Park. Two at the entrance, two 1½ km inside the park, overlooking river. Bring own provisions – the cook/guide will prepare your food. Reservations, Divisional Forest Officer, Mangal Doi, T03713-222065.
F **Forest Lodge**, Nameri National Park, contact Range Officer.
F **Tourist Lodge**, opposite Chitralekha Udyan, Tezpur, T03712 221016. 6 large rooms with bath and dorm, very quiet and peaceful, tourist information.

**Jorhat and Majuli Island** *p662*
D **Dilip**, near **Paradise Hotel**, Jorhat, T0376-23321610. Clean, friendly, one of few places to accept foreigners.
D **Paradise**, Solicitor's Rd (off AT Rd), Jorhat, T0376-3321521, F23323512. 31 rooms, 9 a/c, hot water, restaurant, bar, exchange.
F **Circuit House**, Kamalabari, Majuli Island, Garmur (Rs 100), contact SDO, Majuli, T03775-274424, ahead but often booked.
F **Guest House**, at Nauten Kamalabari (8 km from Garmur), Majuli Island, spartan, no hot water (Rs 30).
F **Uttar Kamalabari Satra**, Kamalabari, Majuli Island, very basic, bring own bedding and leave a donation, usually booked through **Wild Grass** but you may try to reserve on T03775-273392, ask to call Dulal Saikia (the head priest) to the phone, then ring back after 10 mins.

**Sibsagar** *p663*
E **Siddhartha**, BG Rd, T0376-2223276. 29 rooms, restaurant, bar, modern.
E-F **Brahmaputra**, BG Rd, T0376-2222000. 48 rooms, restaurant, helpful, clean.
F **Tourist Lodge**, near Siva Dol, T0376-2222394. 6 rooms (often full), very helpful Tourist Office.

**Digboi** *p663*
C **Guest House**, Indian Oil Corporation, 22 large, spacious rooms, hot water, TV, excellent location. Reservations, Mr SR Koneru, T03751-2264715.

**Dibrugarh, Tinsukia and Borajan Reserve Forest** *p663*
B **Chang Bungalow**, near Dibrugarh. A 'Heritage' Planter's bungalow, sparkling clean, fabulous food, excellent staff, car and

guide included. Contact **Purvi Discovery**, T0373 2301166, csn@purvidiscovery.com.
C-E **Mona Lisa**, Mancotta Rd, Chowkidinghee, Dibrugarh, T0373-2320416. 19 rooms, some large and a/c, best in new wing, good restaurant, bar.
D-E **Goswami**, few doors from **Mona Lisa**, Dibrugarh, T0373-2321250. 12 rooms, some a/c, dining hall, **Green Valley Tours** and bus pick-up.
D-E **Highway**, AT Rd, Tinsukia, T0374-2336383, 500 m from New Tinsukia station. 20 rooms, some a/c, veg restaurant, modern.
D-E **Jyoti**, Rangagora Rd, Tinsukia, T0374-2339573. 20 rather grubby rooms, some a/c, hot water, restaurant.
F **President**, Station Rd, Tinsukia, T0374-2320789. 32 rooms, veg restaurant, TV, basic, noisy.
F **Retiring Rooms**, Tinsukia, very basic veg refreshments.
F paying guest accommodation in Dibrugarh in an Assamese home, about Rs 200 including breakfast, contact Binoy Dowerah, T0373-2322289.

## Eating

**Guwahati** *p657, map p658*
Assamese *thalis* including rice, fish and vegetable curry, often cooked with mustard. You might try vegetarian *Kharoli*, Omita *Khar* (papaya cooked with burnt 'bark' of the banana plant). Only larger hotels serve Continental food and have bars.
TTT **Bellevue** for Continental. Recommended.
TTT **Dynasty** for Chinese. Recommended.
TTT **Rajmahal**, recommended.
TT **Ming Room**, Rajgarh Rd, near Chandmari Flyover. Very good Chinese.
T **Apple Pie**, MC Rd. Pastries, ice creams.
T **Hits Cafeteria**, near Central School, Khanapara, T0361 2300090. Out in the suburbs, offers great lunch and dinner.
T **Lantosh**. Assamese. Takeaway and ice cream, clean.
T **Magic Mushroom**, MC Rd. International. Clean, good quality, varied menu, psychedelic decor, very friendly and helpful owner.
T **Magnolia**, **Orchid Hotel**, B Barua Rd.
T **Paradise**, GNB Rd, Chandmari, T0361 2546904. Assamese. Great *thalis* (Rs 55), very clean and friendly, closes 1530-1800 (cycle rickshaw from station, Rs 10).
T **Station restaurant**, good omelettes.
T **Woodlands**, AT Rd (older branch on GS Rd). Indian vegetarian. Clean, a/c, specializes in lunch and dinner thalis (Rs 40).

**Jorhat and Majuli Island** *p662*
On Majuli Island, food is available at simple eateries. Carry drinking water. Those listed below are situated in Jorhat.
**Belle Amies Food & Fun Junction**, Gar-Ali. Indian/Chinese. Colour-coded menu to indicate hotness!
**Canteen** at State Bus Stand. Cheap, does good *roti* breakfasts (toilets).
**Rajhans**, AT Rd. Indian snacks.
**Woodlands**, BG Rd (between MG Rd and Gar Ali). Indian. Good thalis.

## Festivals and events

**Guwahati** *p657, map p658*
Magh Bihu in **Jan** and **Rongali Bihu** in **mid-Apr**, the week-long festivities are celebrated with singing and dancing. **Jun**: **Ambubachi** marks the end of Mother Earth's menstrual cycle with a fair at Kamakhya Temple. In **Sep** the **Manasa Festival** honours the Snake goddess. You can watch devotees dancing and entering into trances from galleries on the hillside. **Assam Tea Festival** is celebrated on **26-28 Dec** with events in various places.

## Shopping

**Guwahati** *p657, map p658*
**Silk and handicrafts**
*Muga, pat* and *endi* silks, hats, bamboo and cane baskets, flutes, drums and pipes are typical of the area. Guide prices: silk per metre: *muga* Rs 400+ (saris Rs 4,000+), *pat* Rs 250 (saris Rs 2,000+), *endi* Rs 150-300. *Pat mikhala* and *shador*, Rs 1,500, *endi* shawls Rs 300+. Bargain in Pan Bazar and Fancy Bazar.
**Assam** at Ambari, sells silks, bamboo, wood, brass and ceramics.
**Assam Co-op Silk House**, HB Rd, Pan Bazar, for pure silk items.
**Khadi Gramudyog**, near Guwahati Emporium.
**Manipur**, Paltan Bazar.
**Purbashree**, GNB Rd, has traditional crafts.
**Tantuja**, Ulubari, has Bengal handloom.

## Activities and tours

**Guwahati** *p657, map p658*
**Assam Tourism**, **Tourist Lodge**, Station Rd, T0361 2547102. **City**: Basistha Ashram, Zoo, Museum, Kamakhya Temple, Govt Sales Emporium. 0900-1500. Rs 90. Tue, Sun (minimum 10). **River cruises**: from near Janardhan Temple, winter 1500, 1600; summer 1600, 1700, 1 hr, Rs 50. **Kaziranga**: Nov-Apr, departs 0900, arrives 1600, return 1600 on following day, Rs 600, foreigners Rs 1,250 (inclusive) allows only from 1500 to 1000 (on next day) in the park. Separate morning buses, departs 0700, 5½ hrs. **Shillong**: departs 0700, Rs 255 (tiring, since the windy hill roads take 3½ hrs each way). Private companies (see below) may be more reliable.
**Hemanta Doley**, Sankardeva Udyan, Machkhowa, T0361 512121, for river trips.
**Network Travels**, GS Rd, T0361 2512700. Imaginative tours, **Indian Airlines** agent, efficient and reliable.
**Purvi Discovery**, T0373 2301166, csn@purvidiscovery.com, varied tours. Excellent service.
**Rhino**, M Nehru Rd, T0361 2540061. For visiting game reserves and Shillong.
**Traveland**, 1st floor, **Brahmaputra Ashok**, MG Rd, T0361 2541064, rchaliha@hotmail.com. Knowledgeable and helpful.
**Wild Grass**, Barua Bhavan, 107 MC Rd, Uzan Bazar, T0361 2546827, wildgrss@sancharnet.in. Very helpful, knowledgeable, efficient. Highly recommended for good value wildlife, tribal tours and Arunachal (can get a permit in 5 days), free travel advice on phone (Nov-Apr).

**Manas National Park** *p659*
**Assam Bengal Naviagation**, 10 Barley Mow Passages, London, W4 4PH, T020 8995 3642, assambengal@aol.com. In addition to having a lodge in the park, this outfit conducts long-distance cruises along the Brahmaputra aboard RV *Charaldew*, with 12 ensuite cabins.

**Kaziranga National Park** *p660, map p660*
**Assam Tourism** offers a 2-day tour (see under Guwahati above).
**Wildgrass**, wildgrss@sancharnet.in.

**Tezpur and around** *p661*
**Eco camp**, Potasali, T03714 244246, organizes white-water rafting and mahseer fishing on the Bhoreli.
**Assam Anglers' Association**, T02712-220004, assamangling@yahoo.com, operates a strict 'catch-record-release' system to conserve the golden mahseer.
Rafting, for fishing or nature watching, for two people on rubber rafts, Rs 650 per day, Rs 300 transport to/from raft.

## Transport

**Guwahati** *p657, map p658*
**Air**
Information T0361 284235. Transport to town: **Indian Airlines** and **Rhino Travels** coaches connect with Kolkata flights, Rs 40, 1 hr. Taxi, Rs 300, share taxi, Rs 100, 45 mins. Auto-rickshaw, Rs 150. **Indian Airlines**, Ganeshguri, near Dispur, T0361 2264420, airport, T0361 2840279, www.indian-airlines.nic.in; 0900-1600. **Kolkata**, 2 daily; some weekly to **Agartala**, **Delhi**, **Imphal**, **Lilabari**.

Jet Airways, Panchvati, GNB Rd, T0361 2662396, airport T0361 2840130, www.jetairways.com: to **Bagdogra**, **Delhi**, **Imphal**, **Kolkata**; Sahara, GS Rd, T0361 2548676, airport T0361 2840128, www.airshara.net: to **Delhi**, **Dibrugarh**. **Helicopter**: Meghalaya Transport Corp, T0361 2840300, to **Shillong**, Mon-Sat, Rs 1,000, on to **Tura**; tickets at airport. **Airlines** Air India, GS Rd, T0361 2561881; BA, Pelican Travels, Hotel Brahmaputra Ashok, T0361 2630123, **Jet**, T0361 2662396 (airport T2840130), www.jetairways.com; Sahara, T0361 2548676, www.airshara.net, or try agents at Rajmahal Hotel.

### Bus

Between midnight and 0500 buses are not allowed to enter the city, but taxis are. **Local** Red minibus 'canters' or 'Omni taxis' cover main roads. Prone to accidents. **Long distance** Private coaches (and taxis) operate from Paltan Bazar, with waiting rooms, left-luggage, snack bars. Operators: Assam Valley, T0361 2546133, **Blue Hills**, T0361 2540061, **Green Valley**, T0361 2543646, and others have buses to all the Hill States. **Assam STC Stand**, Paltan Bazar, T0361 2544709. Left-luggage, Rs 3 per day. Reservations 0630-1230, 1330-1700. Meghalaya STC, T0361 2547668. Buses to: **Aizawl** (11 hrs); **Imphal** (579 km); **Itanagar** (11 hrs); **Jorhat via Kohora (for Kaziranga)** (6 hrs); **Kaziranga and Upper Assam**: bus for Tinsukia and Digboi (0700 a/c; 0730), halt at Wild Grass Resorts after 4 hrs. **Kohima** 2000, 2015, 2030 (13 hrs); **Shillong** (103 km) hourly, 0600-1700, Rs 40 (3½ hrs); **Silchar** 1730; **Siliguri**; **Tezpur** every 30 mins (3½ hrs). **City Bus Stand**, Station Rd (north end): to **Hajo**,(1½ hr). **Adabari Bus Stand**, AT Rd (4 km west of centre) reached by 'canters' from MG Rd, has buses to Hajo, Orang and Nalbari.

### Ferry

To **North Guwahati** from MG Rd Ferry Ghat. To **Peacock Island**: Rs 6 each way. 0700-1700.

### Rickshaw

From Paltan Bazar to Fancy Bazar Rs 25, Fancy Bazar to Navagraha Temple Rs 30.

### Taxi

**Local** Sightseeing Rs 100 per hr (excluding petrol); **Guwahati Taxis**, Paltan Bazar, near Police Station; **Green Valley**, Silpukhuri, T0361 2543646, cars/jeeps Rs 700 per day plus overnight Rs 150. **Traveland**, 1st floor, Brahmaputra Ashok, MG Rd, T0361 2541064, F2520762. Reliable and efficient. **Chandana**, Goswami Villa, Zoo Narengi Rd, T0361 255 7870, has Tata Sumo (a/c), Rs 1500 per day. **Long distance** From Paltan Bazar: **Shillong**, Rs 625 (5 sharing, Rs 125 each, they fill up quickly when trains arrive).

### Train

Station has snack bars, chemists, tourist information, left-luggage (trunks and suitcases only), on showing ticket. Enquiries: T0361 2540330. Reservations: 100 m north of the station on Station Rd, T0361 2541799, 0800-1330,1400-2000; Foreign Tourists, Counter 3, where great patience is needed! The new line from Guwahati, along the south bank of the Brahmaputra to Jogighopa, should cut delays and speed up journey times when fully operational. To **Kolkata (H)**: *Kanchenjunga Exp, 5658* (AC/II), 2200, 22½ hrs (via **New Jalpaiguri**, 10 hrs); *Kamrup Exp, 5960* (AC/II), 0700, 23½; *Saraighat Exp, 3026*, Mon, Thu, Fri, 1000, 18 hrs (via **New Jalpaiguri**, 8 hrs). To **Delhi (ND)**: *Rajdhani Exp, 2423*, via Patna and Kanpur, Mon, Thu, Fri, 0600, 28 hrs; *Rajdhani Exp, 2435*, via Lucknow, Wed, Sun, 32½ hrs. To **Dibrugarh** Via Dimapur: *Brahmaputra Mail, 4056*, 1430, 16 hrs; *Kamrup Exp, 5959*, 1630, 14½ hrs.

### Manas National Park *p659*

Buses travel on a good fair weather road between Guwahati and Barpeta Rd but no buses beyond; taxis charge, Rs 450-600 per journey. The nearest train station is at Barpeta Rd (40 km) with trains to **Guwahati** and **Kolkata**.

### Kaziranga National Park *p660, map p660*

### Air

Nearest airport is at Jorhat (88 km). See page 668. Foreign tourists must use Guwahati's Borjhar airport, see page 657.

### Road

Best to ask **Wild Grass**, if they have a vehicle going from Guwahati, or confirm timings of private buses. **ASTC** buses between Guwahati and Jorhat via **Kohora** stopping at

**Nagaon** (30 mins, where you can stop overnight ); departs 0900, 1000, 1100, 1230, Rs 85, 5-6 hrs. **Private: Green Valley** (office behind bus station) coaches dep Guwahati for Tinsukia and Digboi, 0700 (non a/c, Rs 95), 0730 (a/c, Rs 135); lunch stop at **Wild Grass Resorts**, after 4 hrs. **Guwahati**: a/c bus from Dibrugarh stops at resort for lunch; leaves at 1330. **Kaziranga Forest Lodge** has 10 seats reserved on the Express coach between Golaghat and Guwahati. Assam Tourism bus, depart 0930 from **Bonashree Lodge**, arrive Guwahati 1600, Rs 85 (lunch Rs 40). It is a very bumpy ride. From **Shillong** get a Jorhat bus and switch at **Jorabat** for Kaziranga.

**Train**
Furkating (75 km) has the nearest station with trains from Guwahati; buses via Golaghat.

**Tezpur and around** *p661*
Saloni **airport** is to the north of Tezpur: Indian Airlines, T03712 2231657, www.indian-airlines.nic.in. Flies to/from **Kolkata** via **Imphal** twice weekly, and also to **Dimapur** twice weekly. Frequent **buses** to/from **Guwahati**; **Kaziranga** until 1400. Daily to **Itanagar** (4 hrs); **Tawang** (12 hrs). **Taxi** to **Orang/Nameri**, Rs 550 plus petrol.

**Jorhat** *p662*
**Air**
Jorhat has the main airport 7 km from town with airlines coach or autos for transfer. Private taxis Rs 100 to town or Rs 600 to Kaziranga. **Indian Airlines**, T0376 2321521, Airport, T0376 2340294, www.indian-airlines.nic.in, to **Kolkata** via **Dimapur**; **Jet Airways**, Hotel Paradise, T0376 3325652, Airport, T0376 2340881, ww.jetairways.com: **Kolkata**, Wed, Thu, Fri, Sun. **Imphal**, Wed, Thu, Fri, Sun.

**Bus**
ASTC Stand on AT Rd has a good canteen. Private buses leave from outside ASTC: to **Guwahati**, 0600-0730 and 2000-2130, 7 hrs; **Sibsagar** (55 km); **Dibrugarh** (131 km). Ticket booths are nearby.

**Train**
The station (3 km southeast of bus stand) has no toilets. To **Guwahati**: *Intercity Exp, 5606*, 2005, 10½ hrs, via Lumding with narrow gauge to **Haflong**: 0715, 4½ hrs (beautiful route but tourists are discouraged; Haflong Tourist Lodge is occupied by the military).

**Majuli Island** *p662*
**Bus**
Buses from Jorhat (at junction of MG and AT Roads) to **Neemati** (13 km north); allow 1 hr.

**Ferry**
Government ferry from **Neemati**, 1000, 1600, return 1330 (confirm timings); crossing time varies seasonally as boats have to circumna- vigate sand bars. Buses run from the ghat to **Kamalabari** (about 5 km) and **Garmur** (8.5 km). You can also arrange private boats at the jetty for transporting a car.

**Sibsagar** *p663*
Nearest airport: Jorhat (60 km). Nearest railway station: Simaluguri (20 km). Regular buses to Guwahati, Kaziranga, Simaluguri.

**Dibrugarh** *p663*
**Air**
The airport is 16 km from town. **Indian Airlines**, T0373 2300114, Airport, T2382777, www.indian-airlines.nic.in, to **Kolkata**, Tue, Wed, Thu, Sun. **Sahara**, T0373 2327493, airport 3282573, www.airsahara.net. Delhi via **Guwahati**, daily.

**Bus**
Private stand on AT Rd. **Green Valley** bus to Guwahati (Rs 190), Kaziranga (Rs 150) pick up from Goswami Guest House at 0715.

**Train**
To **Guwahati**: *Brahamaputra Mail, 4055*, 2015, 15½ hrs; *Rajdhani Exp, 2423A*, Thu, 1615, 12 hrs (continues to **New Delhi** in further 28 hrs); *Kamrup Exp, 5660* (AC/II), 1415, 16½ hrs (continues to **NJP** and **Kolkata (H)** in further 24 hrs). Local *BG Pass* to Ledo (via Tinsukia), 0700, 1600 (not Sat).

**Tinsukia** *p663*
ASTC bus stand on AT Rd; private buses from top end of Rangagora Rd. To Jorhat, Rs 80.
The 2 train stations are 3 km apart. New Tinsukia has most of the long-distance trains.

## Directory

**Guwahati** *p657, map p658*
**Banks** United Bank of India, HB Rd, Pan Bazar. TCs, min Rs 50 commission. **Grindlays** Bank, Dighali Pukhari, GNB/Earl Rds, Mon-Fri 1000-1500, Sat 1000-1230. TC Commission 1% or Rs 100, but quick and efficient. **Hospitals** Christian Hospital, Chatribari, T0361 2540193. Good Health, GS Rd, T0361 2566911. Medical College, Bhangagarh, T0361 2561477. With 24-hr chemists outside. MM Choudhury Hospital, Pan Bazar, T0361 2543998. **Internet** Sangita Communications, Anuradha Cinema Complex, GNB Rd, 0830-2000. **Post** GPO (entrance on Shillong Rd) with Speed Post (7 days). Counter 1 for evaluation and 14 for stamps, then basement for franking. CTO: in Pan Bazar. **Tourist offices** Assam, Directorate, Station Rd, T0361 2547102, www.assamtourism.org. Tourism, B Barua Rd, T0361 2454421, astdcorpn@sancharnet.in. Counters at airport and railway station. Arunachal Pradesh, RC Barua Rd, Bhaskar Nagar, T0361 2562859, F2566720. India, BK Kakati Rd, Ulubari, T0361 2547407. Mon-Fri 0930-1730, Sat 1000-1300, airport counter, helpful for planning trips to other parts of India. Manipur, Rajgarh Rd, T0361 2540707. Meghalaya, Ulubari, GS Rd, T0361 2527276. 1000-1700 except Sun; Rehabari, AK Azad Rd, T0361 2544343. Tripura, GS Rd, Ulubari, T0361 2528761. **Useful numbers** Ambulance: T0361 2561477. Fire: T0361 2540222. Police: T100.

**Kaziranga National Park** *p660, map p660*
**Post** Near the Tourist Lodge and at the park. **Useful addresses** The Wildlife Society has a library of books and magazines and may show wildlife films to groups. Range Officer, T03776 2262423. Divisional Forest Officer, Bokakhat, T03776 262429. Kaziranga Safari, T03776 2325468, F2325782, can book accommodation.

**Jorhat** *p662, map p*
**Banks** State Bank of India, AT Rd. Exchanges TCs (show proof of purchase). **Internet** Sigma, AT Rd (near Gar-Ali). **Tourist office** Station Rd.

**Tinsukia** *p663*
**Internet** Sygma Systems, near Railway Overbridge, AT Rd. **Travel agent** Classic Travels AT Rd, T0374 2786125.

# Meghalaya

→ *Entry permits, see page 656. Population: 2.3 mn. Area: 22,500 sq km.*

*Meghalaya, the 'abode of the clouds', with its pine-clad hills, beautiful lakes, high waterfalls and huge caverns, has been called 'the Scotland of the East' because of the similarity of climate, terrain and scenery. The wettest region in the world, between May and September the rain comes down like waterfalls as the warm monsoon air is forced up over the hills. Home to the Garo, Khasi and Jaintia tribes, the hill state retains an untouched feel. There are traditional Khasi villages near Shillong with views into Bangladesh.* » *For Sleeping, Eating and other listings, see pages 674-676.*

## The land

Much of the plateau is made up of the same ancient granites as are found in peninsular India; its south facing slope, overlooking Bangladesh, is very steep. The hills rise to heights just under 2,000 m which makes it pleasantly cool but it is also one of the wettest places on the earth (Mawsynram has received more than 20 m of rainfall in one year). Much is still densely forested. Shillong is the only important town; 80% of the people live in villages. Compact and isolated, Meghalaya's rolling plateau lies in a severe earthquake belt. In 1897, Shillong was entirely destroyed in an earthquake.

### The Archery Stakes

The Archery Stakes, unique to Shillong, take place every day except Sunday. Members of different clubs shoot 1,500 arrows at a cylindrical bamboo target for four minutes. The punters count the number that stick and anyone who has guessed the last two digits of the number of arrows that stick is rewarded with an 80:1 win. A second shoot takes place an hour later when the odds are 6:1 but if you correctly forecast both results the odds are as high as 4,500:1. Naturally, the bookies are the best-dressed men in town!

Start times of the event vary so ask locally in the morning, and to find the exact field, go to the Polo Ground and mime! There are bookies' shops all over town and elsewhere in the state; bets are even placed as far off as Kolkata and Mumbai! The Stakes were legalized only in 1983 when the state government realized that it could raise a hefty 40% tax on the daily money spinner.

## History

The Khasi, Jaintia and Garo tribes each had their own small kingdoms until the 19th century when the British annexed them. The Garos, originally from Tibet, were animists. The Khasis are believed to be Austro-Asiatic. Jaintias are Mongolian and similar to the Shans of Burma. They believed in the universal presence of god and so built no temples. The dead were commemorated by erecting **monoliths** and groups of these can be seen in Khasi villages in central Meghalaya between Shillong and Cherrapunji. In the 19th century many Jaintias were converted to Christianity by missionaries, although they continued many of their old traditions.

## People

Meghalaya is divided into three distinct areas, the Garo, Khasi and Jaintia Hills, each with its own language, culture and particular customs. All three tribes are matrilineal, passing down wealth and property through the female line, with the youngest daughter taking the responsibility of caring for the parents.

## Government

The hill-state was created on 21 January 1972. Since 1980 the Congress Party has dominated Lok Sabha elections, but it has never won more than 25 of the 60 State Assembly seats. The Hill Peoples Union, though a minority, has claimed the largest number of seats, but once again the Congress won both Lok Sabha seats in the 2003 elections.

# Shillong → *Phone code: 0364. Colour map 4, grid B4. Population: 132,900. Altitude: 1,496 m.*

Shillong, among pine-clad hills and lakes, retains a measure of its colonial past especially around the Ward Lake. Unattractive newer buildings have encroached open spaces and an air of decay is beginning to set in.

The horseshoe shaped **Ward Lake** set in a landscaped botanical garden and popular for boating is near Raj Bhavan, a two-minute walk from Police Bazar. The **Botanical Garden** ⓘ *0900-1700*, is behind it. **Butterfly Museum** ⓘ *1000-1600*, is in a private house between Police Bazar and Wahingdoh, where butterflies are bred for conservation and sale. The golf course, amidst pines, is ideal for an early morning walk. **Tee & Putt** provides good freshly brewed coffee. **Bara Bazar** is well worth a visit to see authentic local colour. It attracts tribal people, mainly women, who come to buy and sell produce – vegetables, spices, pots, baskets, chickens and even bows and arrows. Small stalls sell real Khasi food. Just over a kilometre away is **Lady Hydari Park** ① *0830-1630, Rs 2, cameras: still, Rs 10, video/movie, Rs 1,000*, designed like a Japanese garden, where you will see the pine native to the area – *Pinus khasiana*. It is well laid out with its **Forest Museum** and **Mini Zoo**. The nearby **Crinoline Waterfalls** has a swimming pool surrounded by orchids, potted bonsais and a rock pool with reeds and water lilies. At Lumparing, Laban, the Buddhist **Lamasery** near the Assam Club is interesting but be prepared for a steep climb.

*Due to simmering ethnic tension it is unsafe to walk around in unfamiliar parts of town after dark, although it is all right to travel by car.*

**Shillong Peak** (10 km, 1,960 m) is 3 km from the Cherrapunji Road, commanding spectacular views, **Laitkor Peak** on the same ridge, 3 km from the Shillong-Jowai Road, is under Air Force control; visitors have to report at the barrier. Buses drop you at the appropriate junction. **Elephant Falls** (12 km), off the Cherrapunji Road, is a scenic spot with two high falls. You can walk down to the lowest pool and get a good view, though the falls themselves are less impressive between November and May. The attractive **Umiam Lake** (Barapani), 16 km, offers fishing and boating.

**Rhino Memorial Museum**, Hospital Road, in a striking building, has a good tribal collection with a bizarre mix of military paraphernalia!



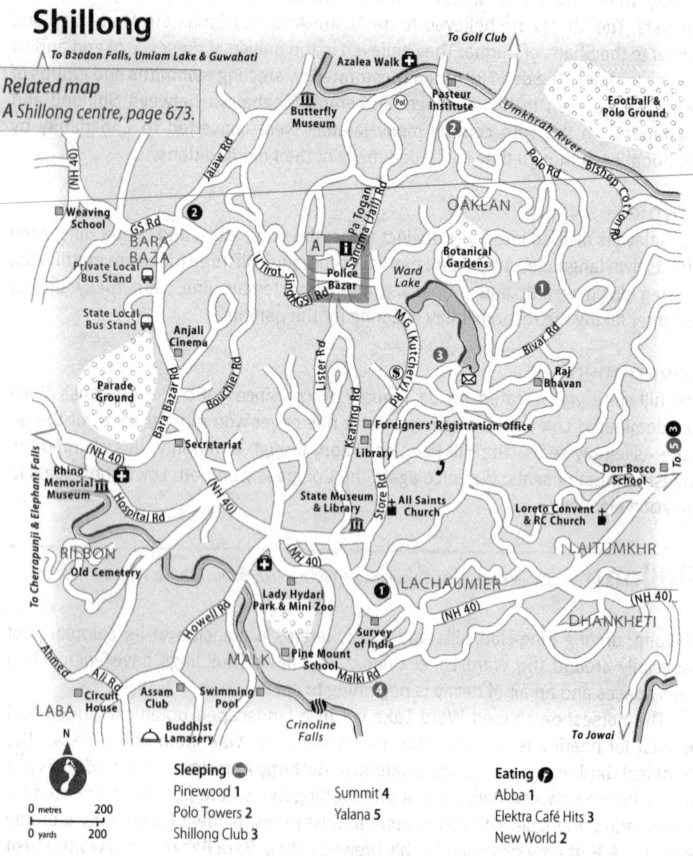

# Around Shillong

## Mawsynram → *55 km from Shillong.*

**Mawjymbuin Cave** has water dripping from a breast-shaped stone on to what looks like a Siva lingam. The rainfall record in Mawsynram has beaten that of Cherrapunji with over 20 m in one year. Take a bus from Shillong from Bara Bazar at 1400. It takes three hours (Rs 20). **Jakrem**, 64km away, has hot springs. Buses leave Shillong at 1400, taking three hours.

## Cherrapunji → *Colour map 4, grid B4. Altitude: 1,300 m.*

The old administrative headquarters of the Khasis, picturesque Cherrapunji is a pleasant, quiet town spread out along a ridge with gravestones dotting the surrounding hillocks. Best time to visit for spectacular views is October-January, the drier months. The heat and humidity can be oppressive much of the year. By March it is hazy most days and the odd torrential shower is not unusual. It once held the record as the wettest place on earth, but nearby **Mawsynram** has surpassed this. On average it still gets 11,500 mm annually.

The colourful weekly **Ka Iewbah Sohrarim market** is held every eight days. The local orange flower honey is sold from a house (clearly signed) just below Cherra Bazar (about 100 m on the road; avoid plastic bottles). Surprisingly, a variety of banana here actually contains seeds.

**Nohkalikai Falls**, reputedly the world's fourth highest, is 5 km away, near Sohrarim. A vendor sells good orange flower honey. Montana Tourism, Cherra Bazar, arranges group tours (US$10). Limestone caves nearby include Krem Mawmluh (4,503 m) with a five river passage and Krem Phyllut (1,003 m) at **Mawsmai**, with a large fossil passage and two stream ways. Mawsmai also has high waterfalls in the wet season.

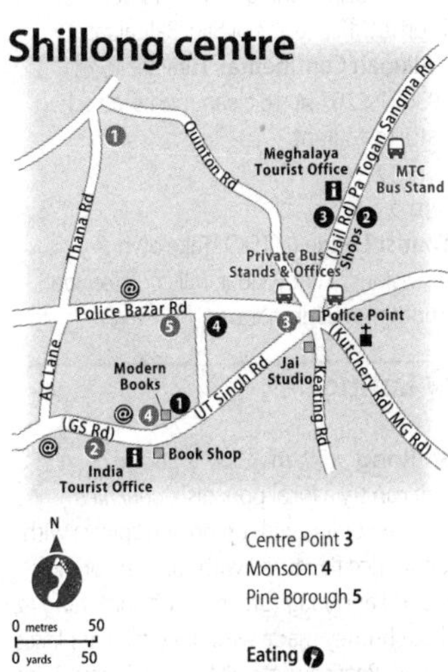


Sleeping
Alpine Continental 1
Baba Tourist Lodge 2
Centre Point 3
Monsoon 4
Pine Borough 5

Eating
Abba 1
Bakery 2
Eecee 3
Jadoh Stall 4

## Jowai

**Jowai**, 64 km southeast of Shillong on NH44, is the headquarters of the **Jaintia Hills**, circled by the Myntdu River. The market, full of tribal women, is particularly colourful. From Shillong cars take 2½ hours, buses a little longer.

**Syndai**, 40 km further south, has many caves used by ancient warriors as hide-outs including 'Krem Sweep' which has a vast chamber. India's longest (6,381 m) and deepest (106.8 m) Eocene Age cave with several cataracts and waterfalls is **Krem Um-Lawan**, 60 km southeast of Jowai near **Lumshnong**.

## Tura

The headquarters of the West Garo Hills District, Tura, 220 km southwest of Guwahati, sits at the foot of the jungle-clad 1,457 m Nokrek Peak. It is a spread-out town with a slow pace of life. Tura Bazar is dominated by the new supermarket, a three-storey red-and-white, mini shopping mall and underground car park. The small fruit and vegetable market in the basement is well organized. A Museum-cum-Cultural Complex is planned 200 m west of **Orchid Lodge**. Weekly tribal markets are held in surrounding villages.

Nokrek Peak can be reached by a 5-km trek, but involves rock climbing, so is best not attempted alone. **Nokrek National Park** is 55 km away. Jeeps from Tura Bazar cost Rs 1,150-1,500 for the round trip (daily rate). Ask the tourist office for a guide. **Naphak Lake**, 112 km, near the Simsang River is good for fishing and birdwatching.

## Siju → *Colour map 4, grid B3.*

Southeast of Tura just below the town, with others nearby, is one of India's longest caves (4.8 km) with a fine river passage. Groups of at least four are needed for going caving so look out on noticeboards. It is more enjoyable and cheaper to travel this way. Bus to Baghmara, 45 km, 1½ hours; from there to Tura, leaves at 0900.



## Sleeping

**Shillong** *p671, maps p672 and p673*

**B Polo Towers**, Polo Grounds, Oakland Rd, T0364 2222341, www.hotelpolotowers.com. 50 well-appointed rooms, exchange (cash), modern and efficient.

**C Alpine Continental**, Thana-Quinton Rd, T0364 2220991, alpine@sancharnet.in. 41 comfortable rooms and suites, hot water (0730-1030), reasonable restaurant, small cosy bar, exchange (cash, TCs), terrace garden, prompt room service.

**C Centre Point**, GS Rd, Police Bazar, T0364 2225210, centrept@dte.vsnl.net.in. 24 comfortable modern rooms with views, good restaurant (Indian, Chinese).

**C Pinewood**, Rita Rd, near Raj Bhavan, T0364 2223146, F2224176. 40 old-fashioned rooms (crying out for a coat of paint), **B** suites, a Raj relic, best in nostalgic old bungalow, spacious grounds, restaurants, bar, exchange, golf, well located, otherwise disappointing.

**C-D Shillong Club**, MG Rd (near Ward Lake), T0364 2225533, resi@hotmail.com. 18 rooms in 'colonial' club, Indian restaurant, bar, tennis, billiards.

**C-D Summit**, Sikandra, 23 Lachaumiere (south of NH between Dhankheti and Malki), T0364 2226216, fmh_sikandra@hotmail.com. Well-furnished, comfortable rooms, good food, family atmosphere. Recommended.

**D-E Monsoon**, GS Rd, T0364 2223316, hotelmonsoon@hotmail.com. 25 a/c rooms with bath, hot water (noisy on road side), Indian meals.

**E Baba Tourist Lodge**, GS Rd, T0364 2211285. 27 rooms, restaurant, basic, friendly, clean.

**E Pine Borough**, Police Bazar Rd, T0364 2220698. 20 rooms with bath, restaurant, bar.

**E Yalana**, Main Rd, Laitumkrah (near Don Bosco), T0364 2211240. 17 rooms in comfortable hotel, good restaurant, very friendly.

**Tura** *p673*

**E Orchid Lodge** (MTDC), New Tura (4 km from Tura Bazar), city bus to Dakopgre stops outside, or auto-rickshaw (Rs 50; Rs 70 at night), T03651-222568. 7 rooms, dorm (Rs 70), TV (variable reception despite a giant satellite dish), dining hall meals at set times, Tourist Office (tours of Siju, Balpakram).

**E Rikman Continental**, Tura Bazar, T03651-220744. 16 clean rooms, attached bath, restaurant.

**Siju** *p674*

**Tourist Lodge** (MTDC). Take own provisions, a chowkidar will cook for you. Another at Baghmara.

## Eating

**Shillong** *p671, maps p672 and p673*

You can try a local pork dish, *dohkhleh* (minced brains with onion and spices) with *jadoh* (rice flavoured with turmeric or pig's blood!) and *saag* (greens) with spicy *tung tap* (hot chutney made with dried fish) at places in Bara Bazar and a stall behind Centre Point.

¶¶ **Abba**, Malki Point and GS Rd. Delicious Chinese, closed Sun.

¶¶ **Bakery** with pizzas and fast food. Recommended.

**Eecee**, near Bus Stand, Police Bazar. Western. Good restaurant and great cakes.
**Elektra Café Hits**, Nazareth Hospital, Laitumkhra. International. Excellent for breakfast and lunch, delicious chocolate cake.
**New World**, GS Rd. Good Chinese.

**Cherrapunji** *p673*
**Orchid Restaurant**, opposite the falls, serves good food. **Cherra Bazar** has a few eateries.

## Bars and clubs

**Shillong** *p671, maps p672 and p673*
Better bars at **Pinewood, Polo Towers** and **Shillong Club** for more atmosphere. *Kiad*, the local rice wine, is popular in roadside bars.

## Shopping

**Shillong** *p671, maps p672 and p673*
You can get handwoven shawls, canework, Khasi jewellery, handicrafts, orange flower honey. Govt Emporia are on Jail Rd and GS Rd. In Bara Bazar, tribal women sell attractive Khasi silver, gold and amber jewellery.

## Activities and tours

**Shillong** *p671, maps p672 and p673*
**Golf**
19-hole course at the Golf Club; clubs for hire; the wettest, and also one of the most beautiful 'natural' courses in the world.

**Swimming**
Club near Crinoline Waterfalls, 0600-1630 (ladies 1100-1200, 1400-1500).

**Tour operators**
**Blue Hill Travels**, Police Bazar. Very helpful.
**Cultural Pursuits**, Mawlai, Nongpdeng, T0364 2229016. Organizes 'eco-adventure' tours of Assam, Meghalaya, and promise an unusual adventure.
**Meghalaya Adventures**, Hotel Centre Point, T0364 2225210. Offers cave tours. Visitors may contact Patricia Mukkim, a local teacher-cum-journalist, T0364 2230593, patria@technologist.com. She is well informed about local culture, history etc.
**Meghalaya Tourism**, T0364 2226220, departs from MTDC, Jail Rd, local tours stopping a few mins at most sights, 2½ hrs at Umiam Lake). 0830-1530. Rs 85. Cherrapunji, Nohkalikai Falls, Mawsmai cave (torch essential!) and Falls: 0800-1600 (15-20 mins at each place). Rs 100. Recommended.

**Watersports**
Umiam Lake (16 km) for water-skiing, boating and fishing.

## Transport

**Shillong** *p671, maps p672 and p673*
**Air**
**Meghalaya Helicopter** at Meghalaya Transport Corporation (MTC), T0364 2223200, flies from Guwahati (Mon-Sat) and Tura. Tickets from MTC Bus Stand, Jail Rd. Transport to **Guwahati airport** (127 km): taxi, Rs 850 (3 hrs), nearly double for depart after 1100, or hourly bus, Rs 50.
**Airlines** Sheba Travels, Police Bazar, T0364 2227222. Indian Airlines agent, and airport coach.

**Bus**
Meghalaya TC, Jail Rd. To **Guwahati**, frequent, 0600-1700, 3½ hrs; **Silchar**, 2100, 11½ hrs. Also from stands near Anjali Cinema, Bara Bazar to towns in Meghalaya. Private bus companies have offices/booths around Police Bazar for long-distance connections in the Northeast.

**Taxi**
**Local** Metered, yellow-top taxis cruise the town picking up passengers to share rides. Flag one down and hop in if he is going your way; short hops, eg Police Bazar to Laitumkhrah, Rs 10. MTDC taxis at Pinewood Ashok or the Tourist Office. Sightseeing, Rs 1,400 (8 hrs, 100 km).
**Long distance** Tourist Taxi Association, Police Bazar, share taxi to Guwahati, Rs 150 each, 3 hrs.

**Train**
Guwahati (103 km) the nearest railhead. Tickets from MTC Bus Stand, T0364 2223200. 0600-1100, 1300-1600.

**Cherrapunji** *p673*
**Bus**
From Shillong (Bara Bazar), to Cherrapunji, 1½ hrs; Mawmluh, 2 hrs.

**Taxi**
From Cherra Bazar for Nohkalikai Falls, Krem Mawmluh and a view over the plains of Bangladesh (on a clear day), Rs 300 with bargaining; also share taxis to both. Meghalaya Tourism, Shillong, runs tours which visits several sights nearby.

**Tura** *p673*
**Air**
Helicopter services to/from **Shillong** and **Guwahati**.

**Bus**
To **Baghmara** 106 km (for Siju, none direct), 1300, 4-5 hrs, along the Bangladesh border. Buy a ticket a day ahead from the booth near the MTC Bus Stand, Tura Bazar; to avoid a rugby scrum, ask your hotel to buy your ticket for a small fee. Private buses to **Guwahati** (8 hrs), **Shillong** (12 hrs, night bus arrives at 0400), **Siliguri** from Tura Bazar. Booking offices are easy to find.

## Directory

**Shillong** *p671, maps p672 and p673*
**Banks** State Bank of India, MG (Kutchery Rd), 1st Floor. Mon-Fri 1130-1400. Indian Overseas Bank, GS Rd (Police Bazar end). Both change currency and Tcs. **Hospitals** Civil Hospital, GS Rd, T0364 2226381. Nazareth Hospital, Laitumukhrah, T0364 2224052. Ambulance, T0364 2224100. Chemists in Police Bazar. **Internet** On GS Rd and Police Bazar Rd. **Post** GPO GS Rd, Police Bazar. **Tourist offices** India, GS Rd, Police Bazar, T0364 2225632. 1000-1700, free Shillong map. Meghalaya, opposite Meghalaya Bus Stand, Jail Rd, T0364 2226220. Directorate of Tourism, Nokrek Building, 3rd Meghalaya Secretariat, Lower Lachaumiere, T0364 2226054, www.meghalayatourism.com. 0700-1800. Very helpful. MTDC, Orchid Hotel, T0364 2224933, mtdc@meghalaya.ren.nic.in. 1030-1630. **Useful addresses** Foreigners' Registration Office, Lachumiere near State Museum.



# Arunachal Pradesh

*Population: 1.1 mn. Area: 84,000 sq km.*

*This is Northeast India's largest and most remote state with a population of just over one million. The Tawang Monastery, birthplace of the sixth Dalai Lama and home to countless Buddhist treasures, is a major attraction, along with the state's rich tribal heritage and its wonderful variety of orchids.* *For Sleeping, Eating and other listings, see pages 679-680.*

## The land

On the Northeast frontier of India, Arunachal Pradesh is India's least densely populated state with just 13 people per sq km. It stretches from the foothills of the eastern Himalaya to their permanently snow-capped peaks to the north. The Brahmaputra, known here as the Siang River, enters the state from China and flows through a deeply cut valley. Stretching from the Himalaya to the steamy plains of the Brahmaputra valley, Arunachal Pradesh has an extraordinary range of forests from the Alpine to the subtropical – from rhododendrons to orchids, reeds and bamboo. It is an orchid lover's paradise with over 550 species identified. The wildlife includes elephants, clouded leopard, snow leopard, tiger, sloth bear, Himalayan black bear, red panda and musk deer. The Namdapha National Park is near Miao.

## History

The entire region had remained isolated since 1873 when the British stopped free movement. After 1947 Arunachal became part of the North East Frontier Agency (NEFA). Its strategic significance was demonstrated by the Chinese invasion in 1962, and the Indian government subsequently broke up the Agency giving statehood to all the territories surrounding Assam. Arunachal became the 24th state in 1987, though China continues to argue that until the international border between it and India are

### Entering Arunachal

Permits may be given by the Resident Commissioner, Govt of Arunachal Pradesh, Nyaya Marg, Delhi, T3013956 or Liaison Officer, Roxi Cinema, JL Nehru Road, Kolkata, or Arunachal State Government (ask Wild Grass, Guwahati). Foreigners must book a group tour through an approved Indian travel agent. Independent travel is not encouraged. Itanagar, Ziro, Along, Pasighat, Miao, Namdapha, Tipi and Bhalukpong are open to tourists. The daily tariff requirement is US$150 (US$50 to the state government and US$100 to cover the costs of the travel agent). See page 656.

agreed some of the territory remains disputed. At the same time the state is disputing its southern border with Assam, and in April 2001 the state government lodged a petition with India's Supreme Court against the government of Assam for "large scale encroachment" on its territory. Having long borders with China and Myanmar, it is a truly Frontier State. The state was opened to tourists in 1995 with the first foreigners being given permission to trek only as recently as 1998.

### Culture

The Arunachali people are the state's greatest attraction. In the capital Itanagar you may even see Nishi warriors wearing hornbill feathers in their caps, carrying bearskin bags and their knives in monkey-skin scabbards.

A great diversity of the tribal people speak over 60 different dialects. Most have an oral tradition of recording their historic and cultural past by memorizing verses handed down through generations. Some Buddhist tribes have, however, maintained written records, largely recording their religious history. Some tribes worship Donyi and Polo, the Sun and Moon gods.

## Itanagar-Naharlagun

→ *Phone code: 0360. Colour map 4, grid A5. Population: 61,900.*

Itanagar, the new capital and Naharlagun, the old town 10 km away, together provide the capital's administrative offices. Itanagar, sited between two hills, has the Governor's Residence on one and a new Buddhist temple on the other, with shops, bazar, traditional huts and more recent earthquake-proof wooden-framed buildings in between. The capital has been identified as Mayapur, the 11th-century capital of the Jitari Dynasty.

### Ins and outs

**Getting there** Visitors arriving at Lilabari or North Lakhimpur in Assam take two hours by bus (or a little less by taxi) to Itanagar, calling at Naharalagun Bus Station before climbing up along a scenic road to the new capital. Regular buses from Guwahati and Shillong. ▸▸ *See Transport, page 680, for further details.*

**Getting around** Frequent buses run between Itanagar and Naharalagun from 0600-2000. Cycle-rickshaws only available in Naharlagun.

### Sights

The yellow-roofed **Buddhist Temple** stands in well-kept gardens on a hilltop with good views. The **Gyaker Sinyi** (Ganga Sekhi Lake), 6 km, is reached by a rough road through forests of bamboo and tree ferns. On reaching the foot of the hill, walk across a bamboo bridge, up steps cut on the hillside to reach a ridge overlooking the forest lake. The brick fort (14th-15th century) is believed to have been built by King Ramachandra. In Naharlagun, the **Polo Park** is on top of a ridge with interesting botanical specimens including the cane thicket, which looks like palm, as well as a small **zoo**.

**Jawaharlal Nehru Museum** ⓘ *closed Mon*, has good coverage of tribal people – collection of art, wood carvings, musical instruments and religious objects. The first floor has archaeological finds from Malinthan, Itafort, Noksaparbat and others.

## Bomdila and Tawang Monastery → *Colour map 4, grid A4.*

The whole journey, to reach Tawang from Tezpur in Assam – the nearest airport – is spectacular, passing waterfalls, terraced paddy fields, alpine forests and mountain streams. The road north crosses the border at **Bhalukpong**, see page 662, and continues towards Bomdila passing through low wooded slopes for about 60 km. On the bank of the Bhoreli River in the upper plains is **Tipi**, with the Orchid Research Centre and a glasshouse with 500 species of orchids. From there the road rises sharply to reach Bomdila.

### Bomdila → *Altitude: 2,530 m.*

Bomdila has marvellous views of the snow-capped mountains. It has a craft centre, apple and cherry orchards and Buddhist *gompas*. Buses from the main bus stand. Lower Town Tezpur and Tawang take eight hours. Private buses from Himalayan Holidays to Tezpur, take seven hours.

### To Tawang

For the next 180 km the route passes through the pretty Dirang Valley shrouded in pine woods, then climbs to the **Sela Pass** at 4,215 m which presents a far starker view. The successor to Lama Guru Rimpoche has been found in a village nearby. Stop a while here, along one of the highest motorable roads in the world. **Jaswantpur**, 4 km from the pass, has the *samadhi* to the brave Jawan (soldier) Jaswant Singh which commemorates how he, his fiancée and her friend valiantly held up the advancing Chinese army in 1962 for three days before laying down their lives. Drivers along this road, many of them ex-army personnel, stop to pay their respects at the poignant memorial. You see a high-altitude lake and the trout hatchery at Nuranang just below the pass before reaching Tawang.

### Tawang Monastery → *Phone code: 03794. Population: 4,600.*

Set in breathtakingly beautiful scenery at over 3,000 m, the monastery, one of the largest in India, is the birthplace of the sixth Dalai Lama. Dating originally from 1642, it is the second oldest Buddhist monastery in the world (after Lhasa), and houses over 500 *lamas* belonging to the Gelugpa (Reformed) Sect of Mahayana Buddhist monks. Buddhism arrived in the area with Padmasambhava in the eighth century but the local Monpas were converted to the Tantric Buddhist cult only after the establishment of the monastery here in the 17th century. During renovations, the main building was completely rebuilt. Treasures include a 5½-m high Buddha, numerous sculptures, *thangkas* and priceless manuscripts. Tawang also has the 350-year old Tawang Gompa among dense forest which is the only Lady Lamasery (Buddhist Monastery for nuns) in Asia. The three-day annual **Losar festival** is usually in early January. Prayers are held every morning and afternoon. A craft centre produces woollen carpets.

To reach the monastery take one of the regular buses or Tata Sumo services from Bomdila and Tezpur. Cars take nearly two days from Guwahati (400 km) through rough terrain. Foreigners should to travel in a small group in a hired vehicle from Tezpur (12 hrs). Check feasibility locally and don't travel after dark – visibility on the narrow mountain roads can be very poor at night.

## Lake District

Just above Tawang, beyond the monastery is the **Lake District**, an exceptionally beautiful area with about 30 high altitude lakes. After a fork and an army outpost, the road continues towards **Klemta**, just a few kilometres from the Indian border. There are a few scattered monasteries and a shrine to all faiths at the spot where Guru Nanak rested as he trekked into Tibet, 500 years ago. It is all worth it for the breathtaking mountain scenery. **Ptso**, 25 km from Tawang, has a small cabin by a lake. To explore this area hire a jeep and guide, carry snacks and drinks, and be prepared for steep, treacherous mountain roads.

## Ziro → *150 km north of Itanagar. Altitude: 1,475 m.*

Ziro lies in a very picturesque level valley of the Apatani plateau, surrounded by pine-covered mountains. The **Apatani tribals** who live in small, densely populated villages, have evolved a sophisticated system of irrigated paddy cultivation. You can also visit Nisi tribal settlements. There are daily buses from Itanagar (200 km) and Lilabari (100 km).

## Parasuram Kund

This lake, in Eastern Arunachal, attracts thousands of pilgrims at **Makar Sankranti** (mid-January) who come to the fair and to take a holy bath. Spartan Government **Tourist Lodge**; contact Dy Commissioner, Tezu, well in advance. From Tinsukia, launch along the Brahmaputra (1½ hrs) to Sadiya Ghat, there are buses to Parasuram Kund.

## Namdapha National Park

This park, at an altitude of 200-4,500 m, is close to the Myanmar border and can be approached from Deban. It is unique as it is home to four particular members of the cat family – tiger, leopard, snow leopard and clouded leopard. There are also elephants, sambhar, deer, gaur, goral and wild hogs, and rich birdlife. Best season is from October to April. The variety of vegetation is fascinating.

Entry Permit from Field Director, Miao; also accommodation at Deban 25 km away. Dibrugarh (140 km) has the nearest airport. State buses from there go to Miao, the entry point, via Margherita (64 km), the nearest railhead where you can also hire taxis.

## Sleeping

**Itanagar-Naharlagun** *p677*
Reserve hotels at least a month in advance.
B **Donyi-Polo Ashok**, Sector C, Itanagar, T0360 2212626. 20 rooms, 2 a/c suites, restaurant.
D **Arun Subansiri**, Itanagar, T0360 2212806. 30 rooms, restaurant.
E **Arunachal**, Naharlagun, T0360 2244960. 15 a/c rooms (some deluxe).
E **Bomdila**, Itanagar, T0360 2203537.
E **Hornbill**, Naharlagun, T0360 2244419. 14 rooms, some deluxe.
F **Lakshmi**, Naharlagun, 19 rooms (1st floor better).

*For an explanation of the sleeping and eating price codes used in this guide, see inside the front cover. Other relevant information is found in Essentials pages 56-61.*

F **Youth Hostel**, Naharlagun. Baisc affair with 60 beds.

**Bomdila** *p678*
C-F **Siphiyang Phong**, **Tourist Lodge** and **La**, are a few of the options in town.

**Tawang Monastery** *p678*
D-E **Paradise**, Old Bazar, T03794 222063, F222307. A private lodge with pleasant, clean, spacious rooms with bath, some deluxe, small dining room serving simple, freshly cooked meals. The manager also arranges jeep hire and takes guided tours.
D-E **Tourist Lodge**, T03794 222359. 20 well-furnished but poorly maintained rooms, contact Deputy Commissioner.

**Ziro** *p679*
E **Blue Pine** and other guest houses.
F **Inspection Bungalow** and **Circuit House**, 8 rooms. Reservations Dy Comm, Lower Subansiri District.

**Namdapha National Park** *p679*
E **Camp Namdapha**, bamboo huts, log cabins and tented accommodation.
F **Deban Forest Bungalow**, overlooking the Noa Dihing River.

## Shopping

**Itanagar-Naharlagun** *p677*
The cotton textiles are colourful and are beautifully patterned. You can also get wooden masks and figures, cane belts and caps. **Handicrafts Centres** have shawls, *thangkas*, handloom, wood carvings, cane and bamboo work and carpets; you can watch tribal craftsmen trimming, cutting and weaving cane.

## Activities and tours

**Itanagar-Naharlagun** *p677*
**Arunachal Travels**, Itanagar, agents for Indian Airlines.
**Himalayan Holidays**, Naharlagun, T0360 2246232, www.himalayan-holidays.com.
**Nature Expeditions India**, Gurgaon, T0124-2368601, www.himalaya-india.com.

**Bomdila** *p678*
**Himalayan Holidays**, ABC Buildings, Main Market, T03782 222017, www.himalayan-holidays.com.

**Tawang Monastery** *p678*
**Himalayan Holidays**, T03794 223151, www.himalayan-holidays.com, organizes tours and jeep hire.

## Transport

**Itanagar-Naharlagun** *p677*

**Air**
Nearest airport is **Lilabari** in Assam, 57 km from Naharlagun, 67 km from Itanagar, which has twice weekly flights from Guwahati. Transfer by bus. **Indian Airlines**; T03752 223725, www.indian-airlines.nic.in. From Kolkata access is best through **Dibrugarh** (1½ hrs) by **Indian Airlines**, Mon, Wed, Fri, Sun.

**Bus**
APST from Naharlagun Bus Station. **Guwahati**, 381 km, 8 hrs, Rs 135; **Shillong**, 481 km, Rs 170. **Ziro**, 6 hrs, **North Lakhimpur**; **Bomdila**, Mon, Thu, 12 hrs. Blue Hills overnight coach to Guwahati, 11½ hrs. Enquiries: T0360 2244221.

**Taxi**
Naharlagun/Itanagar, Rs 170 plus fuel; Rs 25 (shared taxi).

**Train**
The nearest railhead is North Lakhimpur in Assam, 50 km from Naharlagun and 60 km from Itanagar; Harmoti station is 23 km from Naharlagun. **Railway Out Agency**, Naharlagun bus station, T0360 2244209. Nearest railheads for the bigger towns: **Along**: Silapathar; **Tezu**: Tinsukia; **Namdapha**: Margherita.

## Directory

**Itanagar-Naharlagun** *p677*
There are banks and post offices.
**Hospitals** Itanagar, Naharlagun. **Tourist offices** India, Sector 'C', Naharlagun, T0360 2212949, www.arunachaltourism.com. Arunachal Pradesh, Naharlagun.

# Nagaland → *Entry permits, see page 656. Population: 2 mn. Area: 16,579 sq km.*

*Nagaland, the narrow strip of mountain territory, has a long border with Myanmar (Burma) to the east. There are green valleys with meandering streams, high mountains with deep gorges and a rich variety of wildlife and flora.* *» For Sleeping, Eating and other listings, see pages 682-683.*

## History

The British reached peace with the Nagas at the end of the 19th century and found them useful allies in the war against the Japanese, who advanced as far as Kohima before finally retreating from the region. After Indian independence, Nagaland became a separate state on 1 December 1963. A separatist movement for full independence continues, as the 1975 Shillong Accord was rejected. A series of month- to-month cease fires have been in effect during the 1990s with a year-long extension (the longest yet) being agreed since the present BJP government came to power.

## Culture

**Tribal groups** Nagaland is almost entirely inhabited by 15 groups of the Tibeto-Burmese tribes – among them are the Angamis, Aos, Konyaks, Kukis, Lothas, Semas and Wanchus, collectively known as the **Nagas**. There are many tribal languages spoken: Angami, Ao, Chang are a few. The Nagas were once head hunters and have been known for their fierceness and the regular raids they made on Assam and Burma. The warring tribes believed that since the enemy's animated soul (*yaha* in Wanchu dialect) was to be found at the nape of the neck, it could only be set free once beheaded. However, since the spiritual soul, *mio*, resided in the head and brought good fortune, enemy heads (and those of dead comrades) were prized as they could add to a community's own store of dead ancestors. The hilltop villages are protected by stone walls. The *morung*, a meeting house, acts as a boys' dormitory, and is used for storing weapons and once displayed the prizes of war (enemy heads). The huge sacred drum stands by each *morung* is a hollowed-out tree trunk carved to resemble a buffalo head. Some believe that the Nagas' ancestors came from the seafaring nation of Sumatra and retain their link with their island past in their legends, village drums and ceremonial jewellery, which uses shells.

**Religion** Today 90% of the Nagas are Christians. Originally, although they revered natural 'spirits', the Nagas believed in a single overseeing but unknown superforce, and hence accepted the Christian Gospel quite readily. The Bible was translated into many of the Naga dialects (nearly every village has a church), yet the people have retained many of their old customs. There are also remains of the Hindu Kingdom of the Kacharis at Dimapur near the present capital Kohima, which was destroyed by the Assamese Ahoms in the 16th century.

**Crafts** The ancient craft of weaving on portable looms is still practised by the women. The strips of colourful cloth are stitched together to produce shawls in different patterns which distinguish each tribe. Ao warriors wear the red and black striped shawl with a central white band embroidered with symbols.

## Kohima → *Phone code: 0370. Colour map 4, grid B5. Population: 78,600. Altitude: 1,500 m.*

The British-built town of Kohima lies in the valley between higher hills, alongside the immaculately kept war cemetery. Kohima attracted world attention during the Second World War because it was here that the Japanese advance was halted by the British and Indian forces. The original Angami Kohima Village is set on a hill above overlooking the Main Bazar. There may be a strong military presence in town.

The **Second World War Cemetery** is in a beautiful setting, with well maintained lawns where rose bushes bloom in season. Two tall crosses stand out at the lowest and highest points. The stone markers each have a polished bronze plaque with epitaphs commemorating the men who fell here, to halt "the invasion of India by the forces of Japan in April 1944" by the British 14th Army under General William Slim. The flowering cherry tree which was used by Japanese soldiers as a snipers' post was destroyed; what grew from the old stump marks the limit of the enemy advance. At the base of the 2nd Division lower cross, near the main entrance, are the lines:

*When you go home*
*Tell them of us and say*
*For your tomorrow*
*We gave our today.*

The striking red-roofed **Cathedral of Reconciliation** (1995) on a hill overlooks the cemetery. Part funded by the Japanese government, representatives from both sides of the conflict attended the inauguration.

The **Main Bazar** attracts colourful tribal women who come to buy and sell their produce. The vast **Kohima Village** (Bara Basti) has a traditional Naga ceremonial gateway carved with motifs of guns, warriors and symbols of prosperity, though the 20th century has had its impact. The traditional Naga house here has crossed 'horns' on the gables, carved heads to signify the status of the family, huge baskets to hold the grain in front of the house and a trough where rice beer is made for the community.

**Nagaland State Museum** ⓘ *Bayavu Hill Colony, 1.5 km from centre, 0930-1430, closed Sun and 2nd Sat,* has a collection of anthropological exhibits of the different Naga tribes. The basement has birds and animals of the Northeastern Hill states.

## Around Kohima

**Khonoma** is an authentic tribal village, 20 km southwest, with a proud past surrounded by extensive terraces for rice cultivation. Another 20 km along the same road takes you to **Dzulekie,** at 2,134 m,with attractive waterfalls and trout streams in a deep rocky gorge. There is a Tourist Rest House and Cottages.

Trek to **Jopfu Peak**, at 3,043 m, 15 km south, between November and March for clear mountain views. **Dzukou Valley**, at 2,438 m, 15 km further south, is best from June to September, for its colourful rhododendrons, lilies and meadow flowers. A new campsite should be ready on the Jakhama route.

## Dimapur

Dimapur, on the edge of the plains northwest of Kohima, is the railhead and has Nagaland's only airport. Busy and crowded, it is the state's main trading and commercial centre.

This was the old capital of the Kacharis (13th-16th century) and the **Kachari relics**, including a huge brick-built arch, are 1 km from the NST Bus Station. Nearby are 30 huge mushroom-shaped carved megaliths believed to represent the fertility cult. Visit **Chumukedima** old village on a hill above town, or trek to the **Triple Falls** at Seithekima.

## Sleeping

**Kohima** *p681*
**B-C Japfü** (ITDC), PR Hill, T0370 2240211, hoteljapfu@yahoo.co.in. 27 large heated rooms, restaurants.
**E Ambassador**, D Block, T0370 2222444. 12 rooms.
**E Pine**, Phool Bazar, T0370 2222234. 7 rooms with bath, 7 rooms.

**E Valley View**, Old Bus Station, T0370 2222738. 16 rooms.
**F Tourist Lodge**, New Minister's Hill, T0370 22431247. 17 rooms.

**Dimapur** *p682*
**C-E Tragopan**, Circular Rd near Overbridge, T03862-221416, F225537. 22 rooms, some a/c, restaurant.
**D Tourist Lodge**, near Nagaland Bus Station, T03862-226335. Double rooms, tourist office.

## Eating

**Kohima** *p681*
Local dishes are simple but may include the unusual: zongtak beans, water snails, eels and fermented fish! Most places offer Indian and Chinese dishes.
ǂ **Dimori Cove**, 6 km along NH39 towards Manipur. The eatery has a small swimming pool, good views.
ǂ **Naga**, Secretariat, also offers Japanese. Pleasant, lively.

## Festivals and events

**Kohima** *p681*
The different tribes celebrate their special festivals when priests perform ceremonies followed by dancing, singing and drinking.
**Feb**: Sekrenyi is celebrated by Angamis for 10 days when all work in the fields ceases.
**Apr**: Konyak Aoling, a 6-day 'New Year' festival marking the beginning of spring.
**May**: Ao Moatsu, 6-day festival marking the beginning of the growing season. Tourism Cultural Festivals in **May** and **Oct**.

## Shopping

**Kohima** *p681*
Warm and colourful Naga shawls are excellent. You can also get beads, shoulder bags, decorative spears, table mats, wood carvings and bamboo baskets.
**Gürttel** is recommended.

## Activities and tours

**Kohima** *p681*
**Nagaland Tourism**, offers 4-5-day group cultural, adventure (trekking, tribal) tours.

## Transport

**Kohima** *p681*
**Air and train**
Dimapur has the nearest airport and railhead; buses (Rs 50) and taxis take about 3 hrs to Kohima centre. See the section below for details.

**Bus**
**Blue Hills** luxury coaches go to other capitals in the Northeast; **Green Hills**, Taxi Stand, for coaches and flight bookings.

**Taxi**
Taxis from Dimapur, Rs 500, shared, Rs 100. Nagaland State Transport (NST), T0360 2222265.

**Dimapur** *p682*
**Air**
The airport is 5 km from town. **Indian Airlines**, T03862 229366. Airport, T038622 242441. www.indian-airlines.nic.in. To **Kolkata** via **Guwahati**, Tue, Thu, Sat, Sun.

**Bus**
From Golaghat Rd to **Guwahati** 292 km (10-11 hrs), **Imphal** 142 km (5-6 hrs); from Nagaland Bus Stand to **Kohima**, 3 hrs.

**Train**
Enquiries T03862 131To **Delhi (OD)**: *Brahmaputra Mail, 4055*, 0510, 48 hrs. **Dibrugarh**: *Kamrup Exp, 5959*, 2225, 8½ hrs. *Brahmaputra Mail, 4056*, 2005, 9½ hrs. **Guwahati**: *Rajdhani, 2423A*, Thu, 2315, 5½ hrs; *Kamrup Exp, 5960*, 2235, 8 hrs.

## Directory

**Kohima** *p681*
There are banks, a post office and hospital, T0360 2222916. Tourist offices, T0360 2270107.

*For an explanation of the sleeping and eating price codes used in this guide, see inside the front cover. Other relevant information is found in Essentials pages 56-61.*

# Manipur

→ *Population: 2.4 mn. Area: 22,327 sq km.*

*The former princely state of Manipur, the 'land of jewels' bordering Myanmar, has a low-lying basin in its centre surrounded by hills that rise to over 2,000 m. The reedy Lake Loktak, the largest freshwater lake in the Northeast, and the flat-bottomed basin and river valleys that drain into it, add to the beauty of the land. It is the land of graceful Rasa dances, of the famous Women's market in Imphal, of rare orchids, and the endangered thamin, the brow-antlered deer.* » *For Sleeping, Eating and other listings, see pages 687-687.*

## History

Manipur has always been quite independent of its neighbouring tribal areas. It was often invaded from Burma but also enjoyed long periods of relatively stable government. At the end of the Indo-Burmese War in 1826 it was brought into India by the Treaty of Yandabo, British sovereignty being recognized in 1891. In 1939 a remarkable women's social revolt ('Nupilan' from '*nupi*' – women and '*lan*' – war) led to government action against monopolistic traders. The contemporary party *Nisha Bandh* consists of an all-women patrol that seeks to keep the streets safe at night. The role of women traders can be seen most colourfully in the women's market. During the Second World War Imphal was occupied by the Japanese. After Indian independence Manipur became a Union Territory and achieved statehood in 1972.

*Entry permits, see page 656. Five-day permits can be issued by all missions abroad, all FRROs, Home Commissioner, Imphal.*



## People

The majority of the population are Vaishnavite Hindus. They belong to the *Meithe* tribe and are related to the *Shans* of Burma, who live in the valleys. The 20 or so hill-tribes who constitute about a third of the population are Christian. Like the Nagas, the Manipuris have a reputation for being great warriors, still practising their skills of wrestling, sword fighting and martial arts. Most of wars were fought across the border in Burma. They are also keen on sport, and polo, which is said to have originated in Manipur, is the principal sport.

## Dance, drama and music

The ancient musical forms of the valley dwellers are closely connected to the worship of Vishnu, expressed in Manipuri dancing. The *Rasa* dances performed at every ceremony are characterized by graceful and restrained movements and delicate hand gestures. The ornate costumes worn by the veiled women are glittering and colourful; the stiff, heavy skirts barely move. The *Sankirtana* dance often precedes the *Rasa*. It is usually performed by men and is vigorous, rhythmic and athletic, and they play on the *pung* (drums) and cymbals while they dance. The tribal ritual dances, some of which are performed by priests and priestesses before deities, may end in a trance. Others can last several days, observing a strict form and accompanied by the drone of a bowed instrument, *pana*. *Thang-ta* is a skilful martial art performed to beating drums, and is practised by both sexes dressed in black.

## Political developments

Troubled by a variety of internal conflicts since the late 1980s and with separatist movements voicing open dissent with rule from New Delhi, Manipur's State Assembly has had an unsettled recent history. Although democracy is highly popular, with over 90% of the 1.3 million electorate turning out to vote in the

> “” **The tribal ritual dances, some of which are performed by priests and priestesses before deities, may end in a trance. Others can last several days, observing a strict form and accompanied by the drone of a bowed instrument...**

election held in February 2000, instability has continued. While the Congress party won the largest number of seats in the 60-strong Assembly the government was formed by an alliance of minority parties, led by the Samata Party, which was a partner of the BJP in India's central government. In May 2001 the coalition broke down. In the face of continuing political violence, on 2 June 2001 the Central Government imposed President's Rule, despite the pleas of a new five party alliance, the People's Democratic Alliance, to try and form a government including the BJP at its core. There were significant riots during 2004 in response to the alleged killing by security forces of a woman from one of the rebel factions. The situation in early 2005 was still unclear, with peace talks between the United Committee of Manipur (UCM) and the central government leading the former to describe the latter as, “just like the monkey who distributes chapatti”. Be sure to find out about the current situation before travelling to Manipur.

## Imphal → *Phone code: 0385. Colour map 4, grid B5. Population: 217,300.*

The capital Imphal (from *yumpham*, homestead) lies in the heart of an oval-shaped valley cut through by narrow rivers and surrounded by forested hills. The city has the large open space of the Polo Ground but is otherwise not particularly attractive. Because of its location it has become a principal export route for Myanmar's illegal drugs.

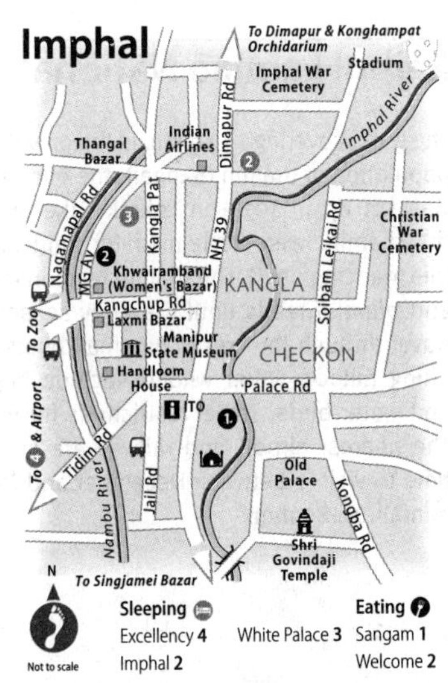


### Ins and outs

**Getting there** The airport is 8 km south of the city with taxis and autos for transfer. Bus travel is tiring because of the long distances involved. ▸▸ *See Transport, page 687, for further details.*

**Getting around** The dusty centre and the 'Ima Market' are easy to cover on foot. Auto and cycle-rickshaws can take you to places beyond the centre.

### Sights

The **Shri Govindaji Temple** to Krishna with two golden domes adjoins the royal palace. This Vaishnavite centre with shrines to Vishnu, Balaram,

Krishna and Jagannath has regular performances of ceremonial dancing (Manipuri dancing originated here). Overlooking the University (8 km), the historic palace of **Langthaband**, with its ceremonial houses and temples, stands on the hills among formally planted pine and jackfruit trees, 8 km along the Indo-Burma road.

**Khwairamband Bazar** ('Ima Market') ⓘ *0700-1900*, in the town centre is the largest women's bazar perhaps anywhere in the country. It is an excellent place for handicrafts and handloom goods, as well as vegetables, fish and other foodstuffs, jewellery and cosmetics. As many as 3,000 women gather here every day. It represents a form of family work-sharing, for while younger mothers stay at home to look after children, the older women and grandmothers come to market. The women do not bargain and will be offended if you try to pick through fruit or vegetables, as they take great pride in serving only the best quality at a fair price. Their own union helps to maintain the bazar and is a potent political force.

The **War Cemeteries** are managed by the Commonwealth War Graves Commission, one on the Imphal-Dimapur NH39 and the other on the Imphal-Ukhrul Road. They are beautifully maintained and serenely peaceful sites.

The **Konghampat Orchidarium** ⓘ *best season is Apr-May*, 12 km along the NH39, set up by the Forest Department, has over 120 species of orchids including some rare ones.

**Manipur State Museum** ⓘ *near Polo Ground, T0385 2220709, closed Mon, 1000-1630*, has a collection of art, archaeology, natural history, geology and textiles, and also costumes, portraits and old arms. **Matua Museum** is a private collection of art, textiles and manuscripts to preserve the identity of Manipuri culture.



### Excursions

**Moirang**, 45 km from Imphal, on Loktak Lake, is noted for its early Manipuri folk-culture and the traditional folk dance form. The temple to the forest god, *Thankgjing*, has robes of the 12th-century Moirang kings and holds a ritual dance festival each summer. During the Second World War Moirang was the HQ of the Indian National Army (INA) for a short time, and their flag was raised in the palace grounds as a symbol of national independence for the first time on 12 April 1944. There is an INA memorial and a war museum. You can stay on **Sendra Island** in Loktak Lake, see page 687.

## Keibul Lamjao National Park

The park, covering 25 sq km, is the only floating sanctuary of its kind. It has a small population of thamin (Sangai), the endangered brow-antlered deer. The Sanctuary was set up in 1977 on Loktak Lake when the swamps, the natural habitat of the thamin, were reclaimed for cultivation resulting in the near extinction of this 'dancing deer'. The thamin feed on mats of floating humus covered with grass and *phumdi* reeds until the rainy season when they move to the hills. You can travel through the creeks on small boats. There is also a viewing tower on Babet Ching hillock. Other wildlife include hog deer, wild boar, panther, fishing cat and water birds. Travel restrictions for foreigners as elsewhere in the Northeast. The nearest airport and railway are at Dimapur, 32 km from Imphal. The best time to visit is between December and May. Temperature range: 41°C to 0°C and rainfall: 1,280 mm.

## Sleeping

**Imphal** *p685, map p685*
**D Anand Continental**, Khoyathong Rd, T0385 2223422. Good rooms with bath, TV.
**D Imphal**, Dimapur Rd, T0385 2220459, manipur@x400.nicgw.nic.in. 60 large rooms, some a/c, modern facilities, restaurant.
**D White Palace**, 113 MG Ave, T0385 2220599. 26 rooms.
**D-E Excellency**, Airport Rd, T0385 2225401. Varied rooms, some a/c, restaurant.
**F Sendra Tourist Home**, on Sendra Island, cheap beds, small restaurant, contact Department of Tourism, T0385 2220802 (Imphal). A very peaceful spot with lovely views of the lake where fishermen, who live on islands of floating weeds, use nets to farm fish and water chestnut (*singhara*).
**F Youth Hostel**, Khuman Lampak, dorm (Rs 30), T0385 2223423. Govindaji Temple prepares local dishes with advance notice.

**Keibul Lamjao National Park** *p686*
**Forest Lodges** at Phubala and Sendra.

## Eating

**Imphal** *p685, map p685*
Manipur is a 'dry' state. In hotel restaurants, try *iromba*, the Manipuri savoury dish of fish, vegetables and bamboo shoots and the sweet *Kabok* made with molasses and rice. **Sangam** and **Welcome** are inexpensive.

## Entertainment

**Imphal** *p685, map p685*
Cultural shows with Manipuri dancing at **Rupmahal**, BT Rd, and at **Kala Academy**.

## Festivals and events

**Imphal** *p685, map p685*
**Feb-Mar**: Yaosang on full-moon night, boys and girls dance the Thabal Chongba and sing in a circle in the moonlight. A festival in **May-Jun** is held in honour of forest gods. **Sep**: **Heikru Hitongba** is mainly non-religious, when there are boat races along a 16-m wide moat in narrow boats with large numbers of rowers.

## Activities and tours

**Imphal** *p685, map p685*
**India**, Old Lambulane, Jail Rd, T0385 2221131. Closed Sat, Sun, airport desk opens for flights.
**Manipur**, **Hotel Imphal**, T0385 2220802, manipur@x400.nicgw.nic.in. 0900-1630, closed Sun, 2nd Sat.
**Manipur Tourism** tours to Sri Govindaji Temple, Bishnupur, INA Memorial, Moirang, KL National Park and the Loktak Lake, depart **Hotel Imphal**, Sun 0800.
**Meghalaya**, Hotel Imphal, T0385 2220459.
**Seven Sisters**, North AOC, T0385 2228778. For touring the region.

## Transport

**Imphal** *p685, map p685*

**Air**
Taxi to town, Rs 150. **Indian Airlines**, MG Ave, T0385 2221999, airport T2220888, www.indian-airlines.nic.in: **Kolkata**, daily (some via **Aizwal**); **Delhi**, **Guwahati**, **Jorhat**, **Silchar**, 2-3 weekly**Jet Airways**, Hotel Nirmala, MG Ave, T0385 24415461, airport T2455054: **Guwahati**, Tue, Wed; **Kolkata** (via Guwahati), Tue, Wed (via Jorhat), Thu, Sun.

**Bus**
Buses connect Dimapur (215 km) the nearest railhead, with **Imphal** (8 hrs), Rs 45; share taxi Rs 100. Daily private buses (some a/c) for **Guwahati** (579 km), 24 hrs, via Silchar (198 km) to Shillong, through: **Blue Hills**, MG Ave, T0385 2226443. **Manipur Golden Travels**, MG Ave, T0385 2221332. **Kangleipak**, T0385 2222131.

**Taxi**
Tourist taxis from Tourist Information Centre. Rest unmetered.

## Directory

**Imphal** *p685, map p685*
**Banks** Banks in Bazar, Thangal Bazar and MG Ave. **Hospital** Hospitals at Porompat and Lamphalpat. **Post** There is a GPO.

# Mizoram

→ *Population: 891,100. Area: 21,000 sq km.*

*The southernmost of the Northeastern Hill States, Mizoram lies between Myanmar (Burma) and Bangladesh. Until 1972 it was known as the 'Lushai Hills', a district of Assam. The half a dozen or so parallel north-south ranges of hills rising to over 2,000 m are covered in dense forests of bamboo and wild banana. At the bottom of the deep gorges the rivers run in narrow ribbons.* ▸▸ *For Sleeping, Eating and other listings, see pages 689-689.*

## Culture

**Tribal groups** **Mizo** is derived from *mi* (man) and *zo* (highland), a collective name given by their neighbours to a number of tribes that settled in the area. The different groups of tribal people are thought to have originally come from Northwest China in the seventh century, gradually travelled southwards and reached this area less than 300 years ago. The Mizos were animists, believing in good and evil spirits of the woodland. Mizo villages perch on top of the ridges with the chief's house and the *zawlbuk* (bachelors' dormitory) in the centre. Built on steep slopes, houses often have front doors at street level while the backs stand precariously on stilts. Every home proudly displays orchids and pots of geranium, begonia and balsam. Over a thousand varieties of medicinal plants grow wild.

*Entry permits, see page 656. The state government can also issue permits.*

**Religion** The raiding of British tea plantations up until the end of the 19th century led to the introduction of Inner Line permits which restricted movement of people but gave free access to missionaries, who carried out their religious duties and introduced literacy, which is exceptionally high in this state, the language having adopted the Roman script. Most Mizos are Christian converts and have a strong tradition of Western choral singing. The mainly nomadic Chakmas along the western border practise a religion which combines Hinduism, Buddhism and animism. Some even claim descent from one of the lost tribes of Israel. A few **Kukis** who were once headhunters, and **Chins**, have converted to Judaism.



## Economy

Rice and maize, supplemented by shifting cultivation, supports 75% of the population. There are no mineral resources exploited yet and no large-scale industries though the government has sponsored some light industrial development in Aizawl. Handicrafts and handwoven textiles predominate.

## Aizawl

→ *Phone code: 0389. Colour map 4, grid B5/C5. Population: 229,700. Altitude: 1,132 m.*

The road from Silchar comes upon the isolated capital Aizawl (pronounced Eye-jull), built along a central ridge and several surrounding spurs. White-painted churches stand out above the residential buildings that cling precariously to the hillsides.

**Bara Bazar**, the main shopping centre, is on the other side of the central ridge. The steep Zion Street is lined with stalls selling garments and Mizo music cassettes. In the main market people gather in their traditional costumes to sell produce from farms and homesteads including river crab in little wicker baskets.

At the **Weaving Centre** you can watch women at their looms weaving traditional shawls which are for sale. **Luangmual Handicrafts Centre**, 7 km away, has a *khumbeu* ceremonial bamboo hat made using waterproof wild *hnahthial* leaves.

**Mizoram State Museum** ⓘ *McDonald's Hill, Tue-Fri 0930-1600, Mon 1200-1600*, is small but has an interesting collection of historical relics, ancient costumes and traditional implements.

> “” The Mizos were animists, believing in good and evil spirits of the woodland... Every home proudly displays orchids and pots of geranium, begonia and balsam. Over a thousand varieties of medicinal plants grow wild...

## Champhai

Champhai, on the Indo-Myanmar border and known as the fruit bowl of the North East, is worth a visit for its stunning location and sense of history.

### Sleeping

D **Ahimsa**, Zarkawt, T0389 2341133. Comfortable rooms, restaurant.
D-E **Ritz**, Bara Bazar, Chaltlang, T0389 2323358. Comfortable rooms, some with bath, good restaurant.
E **Tourist Lodge**, Chaltlang, T0389 2341083. 14 large but tired rooms, good restaurant, good views.

### Eating

**Labyrinth**, Chandmari. Serves cheap Chinese and Indian food.
You can also find cheap local Mizo food around Bara Bazar.

### Festivals and events

**Early Mar**: **Chapchar Kut**, a traditional spring festival marking the end of *Jhumming* is celebrated with singing dancing and feasting. **Cheraw** is performed by nimble-footed girls who dance in and out of bamboo poles, clapped together by teams of young men. Similar dances are performed in Myanmar, Thailand and the Philippines.

### Transport

**Air**
Flights connect Aizawl with Kolkata, Guwahati and Imphal. Travellers from the rest of the Northeast usually arrive by bus via Silchar to the north.

**New Langpui Airport** (37 km north); for tickets and bus transfer **Quality Travels**, Chandmari, T0389 2341265.

**Indian Airlines**, T0389 2341265, airport T0389 2344733, www.indian-airlines.nic.in, flies to **Kolkata** and **Guwahati**, Mon, Wed, Fri, with some flights via Imphal.

**Bus**
The major operator in the state is Mizoram State Transport. It runs buses to **Silchar**, 180 km (9 hrs), Rs 150, which is the nearest railhead; the four-wheel-drive Sumos however are quicker and not too pricey. Private buses to **Guwahati** via Silchar and Shillong, Rs 280.

**Taxi**
It costs around Rs 200 for 2 hrs' sightseeing in town.

### Directory

**Bank** State Bank of India. **Post** GPO, Treasury Square. **Hospital** Civil Hospital, T0389 2322318, Presbyterian Hospital, Durtland (7 km), T0389 2361222. **Tourist office** Mizoram, Treasury Square, T0389 2333475; for permits elsewhere you need to apply to Mizoram House.

# Tripura

→ *Population: 3.19 mn. Area: 10,492 sq km.*

*Still extensively forested, the tiny former Hindu Princely State of Tripura managed to retain a large degree of independence through much of the last millennium. Extensively forested, its predominantly tribal people retain centuries-old practices, though Agartala begins to show signs of modern development.* ▸▸ *For Sleeping, Eating and other listings, see pages 692-692.*

## The land

Covering just under 10,500 sq km, Tripura is almost surrounded on the north, west and south by Bangladesh. The north falls into four valleys, separated by hills rising to just under 1,000 m. The more open land of the south is still forested. Indian hardwoods include sal. Parts of the state get over 4,000 mm of annual rainfall.

## History

Tripura is believed to have existed in the times of the epic *Mahabharata*. Historically, it was ruled by the **Manikyas** of Indo-Mongolian origin from the 14th century. Since Tripura was constantly feuding with her neighbours, particularly the Nawabs of Bengal, the British offered help to the Maharaja and established a protectorate, separating the princely state from tribal lands outside the control of the Hindu rajas. The Manikyas ruled continuously right up to 15 October 1949 when Tripura acceded to India. It became a full state in 1972. In the 1930s, Maharaja Bir Bikram made his kingdom more accessible by opening an airport. **Rabindranath Tagore** based his play *Visarjan* and novel *Rajasri* on the legends of the Manikyas.



## Culture

Tripura remains predominantly tribal, with distinctive customs. A typical tribal welcome involves building a bamboo arch, garlanding the honoured guest while wafting incense. An egg, believed to absorb evil spirits, is rubbed in paddy, dipped in water and then symbolically thrown away. You may notice brightly coloured parasols in the village pond which are put there in honour of dead ancestors.

## Modern Tripura

Rice is the main crop while rubber has gained importance (now second only to Kerala in production). Jute, cotton, tea and fruit are important cash crops. Sugarcane, mustard and potatoes are also grown. In the last 10 years the Indian Government has encouraged small industries. Weaving, carpentry, pottery and basket making are common. Tripura suffers from the continuing failure of Bangladesh and India to agree a trade and travel treaty, which would allow goods to be taken in transit across Bangladesh. This adds hugely to the time and cost of transport to Kolkata, still a major market for Tripura goods, and lorries can take two weeks to make a journey that could take two days by the direct route.

The **democratic process** in the state operates under severe constraints. Politically motivated killings and kidnaps are common. The Disturbed Areas Act operates in the majority of the 45 police station areas. Reang refugees continue to flood in from Mizoram and the temporary camps in the north are full. Election to the Tripura Hill Areas Autonomous District Council held on 3 May 2000 were won by the newly formed Indigenous Peoples Front of Tripura who defeated the Left Front, but there were widespread threats and intimidation.

There is a high degree of **literacy** in the state, in 2001 total literacy reaching nearly 75%, and despite its small size it has has no less than 17 daily newspapers (two in English and 15 in Bengali)!

# Agartala
→ *Phone code: 0381. Colour map 4, grid C4. Population: 189,300. Altitude: 1,280 m.*

Once a pleasant city, Agartala has mushroomed unchecked and the growth in population has far outstripped essential services. The city's redbrick official buildings contrast with the British preference for white paint, still obvious on some important structures, notably the Maharaja's palace. While there are some pleasant suburbs, the centre's open drains with wooden covers are prone to flooding in the monsoons.

## Ins and outs

**Getting there** The most convenient way to get to Agartala is by air but tickets are in short supply. Travellers must register their arrival and departure. Transfer from the airport is by taxi or bus which arrive at the Motor stand to the southeast of the palace.
**Getting around** The centre can be covered on foot; otherwise you can get a rickshaw. There may be a strong military presence in town. ▸▸ *See Transport, page 692, for further details.*
**Climate** Summer maximum 35°C, minimum 24°C. Winter maximum 27°C, minimum 13°C. Annual rainfall: 2,240 mm, June-August. Best season: September-March.

## Sights

The airport road from the north of town leads to the **Ujjayanta Palace**. Built by Maharaja Radha Kishore Manikya in 1901, it stands amidst large well-kept 'Mughal' gardens with pools and floodlit musical fountains. The vast palace has magnificent tiled floors, a carved wooden ceiling in the Chinese room, and beautifully crafted front doors. Now the State Legislature, it is normally closed to visitors, but you may ask to look around when the Assembly is not in session. The late 19th-century **Jagannath temple** across an artificial lake in front of the palace, rises to a striking orange four-storeyed *sikhara*.

The **Temple of Chaturdasa Devata**, 8 km east, near Old Agartala, is dedicated to 14 gods and goddesses, represented by their heads only. It combines the Bengali Bankura style with a Buddhist *stupa* type structure. In July, *Kharchi Puja*, which has evolved from a tribal festival, attracts worshippers from all over Tripura.

**Tripura Government Museum** ⓘ *HG Basak Rd, weekdays 1000-1700*, has a small but well-displayed collection of rare stone images, old coins, Bengal *kantha* embroidery and archaeological finds from the region including 8th- to 10th-century Buddhist sculptures from Pilak.

## Excursions

Travelling outside Agartala is hazardous because of tribal insurgents who have taken to kidnapping for ransom. Some sections of the Agartala-Assam Highway are closed except to vehicles travelling in convoy; there are usually three or four daily. Seek advice before travelling around the state.

**Sipahijala** The **botanical garden** ⓘ *0700-1600*, with a small zoo and a boating lake, is well worth a visit. It is 33 km away. The zoo is beautifully kept (Mr Bhowmik, in charge, was trained in London) and new enclosures provide a more natural habitat. There are tigers, lions, cheetahs, bears and a rhino; the spectacle monkeys live in the trees above while the lake attracts migrating birds. Elephant rides are offered too. It may be possible to visit a rubber plantation and watch the processing on a trip. There are hourly buses from Agartala.

**Neermahal** Some 53 km south, this water-palace, in the middle of **Rudrasagar Lake**, was built in 1930 by the late Maharaja. The striking white and red fairytale castle with towers, kiosks, pavilions and bridges is fun to explore. Now being restored, it is particularly beautiful illuminated at night. The lake itself attracts migratory birds. Tourist coaches leave from Agartala, and once there, singing boatmen row you across the lake!

 **Tripura Sundari Temple** This temple, 57 km away, in the ancient capital Udaipur, was built on Dhanisagar hill in the mid-16th century. The 'Matabari' is believed to be one of the 51 holy *pithasthans* mentioned in the *Tantras*, where the Mother Goddess is served by red-robed priests. The pond behind has huge turtles which are delighted to be fed. A large fair is held during **Diwali** in October/November. There is a good lodge. Buses and jeeps from Agartala.

## Sleeping

**Agartala** *p691*
Most **D-E** have some a/c rooms.
**C-D Welcome Palace**, HG Basak Rd, T0381 2384940, welcome_palace@usa.net. The newest and most comfortable hotel with some very clean a/c rooms, good restaurant.
**D Rajdhani**, BK Rd, near Indian Airlines (northeast of Palace), T0381 2223387. 27 clean rooms with bath, car hire, 'first lift in Tripura!'.
**D Royal Guest House**, Palace Compound, West Gate, T0381 2225652. Rooms with bath, restaurant.
**D-E Brideway**, Palace Ground, T0381 2207298. 12 rooms (some a/c with bath), room service (Indian, Chinese).
**D-E Meenakshi**, Hawkers Corner, Khushbagan (near Museum), T0381 2225810. Indian meals.
**D-F Ambar**, Sakuntala Rd (south of Palace), T0381 2228439. Rooms with bath (some a/c), restaurant.
**E-F New Sonali**, GB Hospital Rd, Kunjaban, T0381 2225322. 12 rooms, Indian and Chinese food.

**Sipahijala** *p691*
**F Forest Bungalow**, in well-kept gardens above the lake, meals provided. Contact Chief Conservator of Forests, Agartala, T0381 2223779.

**Neermahal** *p691*
**E-F Sagarmahal Tourist Lodge**, on the lake, with 44 comfortable rooms, restaurant.

## Eating

**Agartala** *p691*
**Abhishek**, LNB Rd, has seating outside and in. Decent Indian.
**Kurry Klub**, at Welcome Palace, offers comfortable a/c, and serves good Indian and Chinese.

**Neermahal** *p691*
Superb Bengali snacks and sweets are sold along the road and simple clean restaurants serve good meals (Rs 25-40).

## Transport

**Agartala** *p691*
**Air**
Airport transfer, 13 km: taxi, Rs 135; auto-rickshaw, Rs 70. **Indian Airlines**, Palace Compound, T0381 2325470, Airport, T0381 2342020, to **Kolkata**, daily; **Guwahati**, Wed, Sat, Sun.

**Bus**
Travelling around Agartala is difficult. Tripura STC Bus Stand is on LN Bari Rd. To/from **Dharmanagar**, 8 hrs. There are private buses to **Silchar** (317 km). Bangladesh border crossing, just 2 km from the centre, is convenient for anyone with a visa to get to Dhaka which is 4 hrs by road and 3 hrs by train. The Bangladesh Visa Office is by **Brideway Hotel**; the fee for UK nationals is about US$46 for 6 months; It is about US$23 for nationals of USA and Australia.

**Taxi**
Tourist taxi from Directorate of Information, about Rs 500 per day. Rickshaws, Rs 70.

**Train**
Kumarghat, 140 km, is the nearest railhead. Bookings at State Bus Stand.

## Directory

**Agartala** *p691*
**Bank** State Bank of India, HG Basak Rd. **Hospital** GB Hospital, Kunjaban. **Post** GPO: Chowmohani. **Tourist office** Ujjayant Palace, East Wing, T0381 2225930.

# Orissa

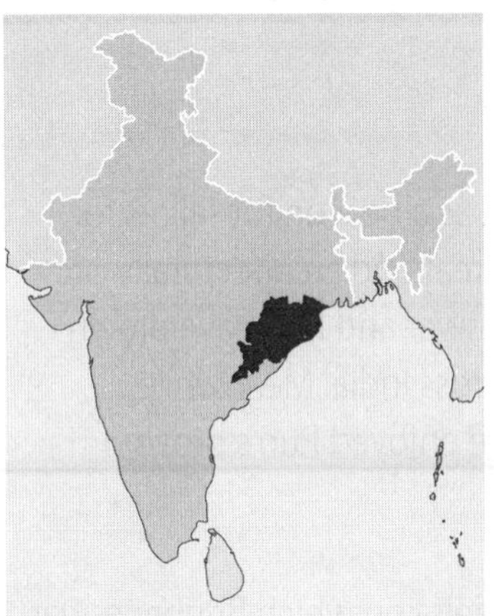



## Footprint features

# Introduction

The Sun Temple at Konark acted as a beacon for sailors for nearly a millennium, while the great and architecturally astonishing temples of Bhubaneswar and Puri have drawn pilgrims in their millions from across India. Meanwhile, holidaymakers from Kolkata have enjoyed Puri's broad and sandy beaches.

Over 2,000 years ago the fertile delta on which Bhubaneswar, the modern capital, stands witnessed one of the most significant battles of India's history when the Emperor Asoka, having massacred his Kalingan opponents, converted to Buddhism and laid the foundations for one of the great empires of world history.

Inland, Orissa's beautiful hills, home to the tribal peoples, are among the least densely populated and most densely forested regions of India. Beneath them lie rich resources of iron ore, coal, bauxite and other minerals, but despite some mining activity much of the interior retains its remote charm.

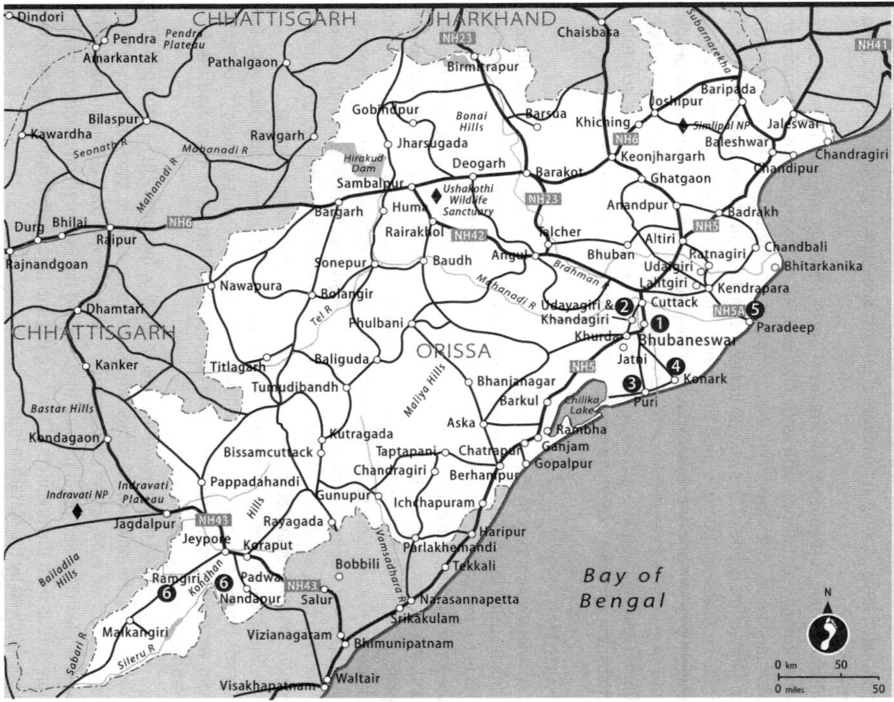

## ★ Don't miss...

1 **Bhubaneswar** Visit a few of the 500 or so temples surrounding Bindusagar Tank and then see a performance of the classical Odissi dance or some folk dancing, page 701.

2 **Rani Gumpha** Visit the Jain Caves at Udayagiri, this one is particularly fine, page 706.

3 **Puri** Watch the Kolkata crowd enjoying themselves here especially at the end of June during the car festival (Rath Yatra) when 500,000 celebrate in a riot of colour and noise, page 709.

4 **Konark** Check out the temple porch at this World Heritage site, which has some of the best sculptures in India, page 711.

5 **Paradeep** If you can cope with the pollution and lack of accommodation, Paradeep, at the mouth of the Mahanadi River, is the place to watch the giant Pacific Ridley turtles lay their eggs, page 722.

6 **Nandapur and Ramgiri** Visit the interesting and picturesque markets, page 731.

# Background → *Population: 36.7 mn. Area: 156,000 sq km.*



## The land

**Geography** Near the coast it is easy to get the impression that Orissa is nothing but a flat alluvial plain with mile after mile of paddy fields along the coastal plains. Chilika Lake, in the south, only a few metres deep, covers up to 1,100 sq km. The coastline has shifted significantly in the last 2,000 years as the land has risen relative to sea level along long stretches. Chilika Lake itself had become cut off from the sea until a newly opened channel reconnected it, allowing sea water to replenish the declining salinity levels.

Inland it is a different story. Ninety per cent of Orissa is made up not of alluvium but of the ancient rocks of peninsular India, some with huge iron ore resources. Until recently the densely forested hills were made inhospitable both by the difficulty of clearing the forest and by the devastating prevalence of malaria. Dense deciduous *sal* forest, peopled only by tribal groups living in isolation with a 'stone age' culture, dominated the landscape, and shifting cultivation was widely practised. There are still rarely travelled roads and the scenic rewards for the slowness of parts of the journey are great. The lakes to the south of Koraput in the 3,000 million year old hills are particularly striking. Much of the forest has now been severely thinned and cultivation has spread up many of the valleys but there remain remote and sparsely populated areas, and an atmosphere of quiet stillness unimaginable when you are on the plains.

**Climate** Lying just south of the Tropic of Cancer, Orissa is very warm throughout the year, though the hills are sufficiently high to bring a welcome coolness. January and February are dry, but showers increase through the spring and the monsoon from June to September is one of the wettest in India. Coastal districts are particularly at risk from cyclones in October and November. The most recent of these was the catastrophic cyclone of October 1999 which caused the death of over 8,000 people, and an estimated three million cattle, as well as inflicting massive damage to villages, forests and agricultural land. It is best to avoid the monsoon season. Even in October-November cyclones may strike the coastal districts with devastating force.

## History

Coastal Orissa, a part of the ancient kingdom of Kalinga, grew prosperous through trading, using its port of Kalinganagar as early as the fourth century BC. Their colonial influence extended as far as modern Indonesia. The Mauryan Emperor Asoka crushed the Kalingan Kingdom at Dhauligiri in 262 BC, but after experiencing the horrors of war and the accompanying bloodshed he converted to Buddhism. He preached the philosophy of peace, and while Buddhism flowered, his tolerance allowed Jainism and Hinduism to continue. After Asoka, the first century BC King Kharavela, a fervent Jain, built up a vast empire, recorded in the remarkable Udayagiri caves near Bhubaneswar. After Kharavela, separate political territories emerged in the north and centre of the region. Maritime trade flourished and Buddhism became a popular again.

The greatest period of temple building in Bhubaneswar coincided with the **Kesaris** (sixth-11th century), to be followed by the Ganga Dynasty (11th-15th century), who were responsible for the Jagannath Temple in Puri (circa 1100) and the Sun Temple at Konark (circa 1250).

Orissa resisted the annexation of her territory by **Muslims**. After a short period of Afghan rule, the powerful Mughals arrived as conquerors in 1592 and during their reign destroyed many of the Bhubaneswar temples. It was their violent disruption of temple life in Puri and Bhubaneswar that later led the Brahmin community to ban all non-Hindus from the precincts of the Lingaraj and Jagannath temples. The Mughals were followed by the Marathas in 1751.

In 1765 after Clive's win at Plassey, parts of Orissa, Bihar and Bengal were acquired by the **East India Company** with further gains in Cuttack and Puri at the beginning of the following century. Thus, by 1803, British rule extended over the whole region.

## Culture

**Tribal groups** Orissa has the third highest concentration of tribals in India. The tribal population, nearly 25% of the total, live mainly in the Koraput, Kandhamal, Sundargarh and Mayurbhanj districts. Some 62 *Adivasi* ('ancient inhabitants') or tribal groups live in remote hill regions of the state, some virtually untouched by modern civilization, and so have kept their tribal traditions alive. Each has a distinct language and pattern of social and religious customs. They are not economically advanced and literacy is low. However, the tribal groups have highly developed artistic ability, as seen in their body paintings, ornaments, weaving and wall paintings. Music and dance also form an integral part of life-cycle ceremonies and seasonal festivals. They are remarkable in having maintained their distinct identities in a hostile and exploitative environment. There has been a new interest in their rich heritage and the Tourism Department is keen to promote visits to tribal areas, see page 731.

*Suggested reading, Norman Lewis 'A Goddess in the Stones'.*

The **Khonds**, the most numerous (about 100,000), live mainly in the west and speak Kuvi, a Dravidian language, and Kui. They used to practise human 'Meriah' sacrifice (now replaced by animal sacrifice), offering the blood to their supreme goddess represented by a piece of wood or stone, to ensure fertility of the soil. They use bows and arrows to protect themselves against wild animals.

The **Santals**, the second most numerous group, come from the northern districts of Mayurbhanj and Balasore. In the northwestern industrial belt, they have abandoned their aboriginal lifestyle to go and work in the steel mills. They belong to 12 patrilineal clans (*paris* or *sibs*) and speak Santali, one of the oldest languages in India. Santals believe that evil spirits in trees, forests and rivers have to be appeased by magic. The women carry out witchcraft while the *ojhas* are the medicine men. Music and dance are an integral part of their daily life, particularly during festivals in October-November and March-April.

In the southern districts, especially in Koraput, there are about 6,000 of the **Bondos** ('naked people') of Tibeto-Burmese origin. They live isolated on high hills, growing rice by shifting cultivation and keeping domesticated cows and goats, and can only be seen when they come to trade in local markets. Bondo women are noticeable for their striking bead, brass and silver necklaces, and their shaved heads, decorated with plaits of palmyra leaves.

The **Saoras**, another major tribe, mostly live in hilly areas of Parlakhemundi (Gajapati district) and Gunupur (Rayagada district). Saoras live in extended families (*birindas*), descended from a common ancestor, under a headman who is helped by a religious leader. The *shamans* are able to communicate with watchful deified ancestors. Village houses of mud and stone walls are raised on plinths with high wooden platforms inside to store grain. The walls are decorated with remarkable paintings; traditional designs now incorporate hunters on aeroplanes and bicycles!

The **Koya** who live in villages in clearings in the middle of dense forest are distinguished by their headgear made of bison horn.

**Dance, drama and music** The region's magnificent temple sculpture gave rise to a classical dance form, **Odissi**, which shadows the postures, expressions and lyrical qualities of the carved figures. The dance was a ritual offering performed in the *nata mandirs* by the *maharis* (temple dancers) resplendent in their costume and jewellery. The subject is often Jayadev's *Gita Govinda* (12th century), which explores the depths of Krishna's love for Radha, the dancer expressing the sensual and the devotional.

## Orissan temples

Orissan temples are graced by a tall, curvilinear tower, the *deul* (pronounced *day-ool*) or *rekha deul*, and a much lower, more open structure or porch in front of the entrance to the tower, the *jagamohana*. The dark interior of the sanctuary is designed to allow only a glimpse of the presiding deity and to enable priests to conduct ritual worship. A dancing hall (*nata mandir*) and a hall of offering (*bhoga mandir*) were often added in later temples.

The square plan of the sanctuary tower and the porch are broken vertically by the inward curving form of the main tower. Each exterior face of the sanctuary tower is divided by vertical, flat-faced projections (*rathas*).

Some Orissan architects likened the structure of the temple to that of the human body, and the names given to the vertical sections correspond to main parts of the body.

**1** The platform (*pishta*) Early temples had no platform. In contrast, in highly developed temples (eg Surya temple at Konark), the platform may be more than 3 m high.

**2** The lower storey (*bada*) corresponds to the lower limbs. In early temples this was divided into three parts, the base (the foot), above which was a perpendicular section corresponding to the shin. This was topped by a set of mouldings. In some mature temples the scale of this section was greatly elongated and was itself then divided into five layers.

**3** The upper storey (*gandi*, or human trunk) is a curvilinear spire in the case of the sanctuary, or a pyramidal roof in the case of the porch.

**4** The head (*mastaka*) with crowning features. Divided into a series of elements, the 'head' or mastaka of the sanctuary developed over time. The 'neck' (*beki*) – a recessed cylindrical portion, is surmounted by the skull, amla. This is represented by a symbolic fruit, the amalaka. On the *amla* rests a 'water pot', an auspicious symbol, then on top of all comes the sacred weapon of the deity.



The **folk dances** usually performed during festivals take various forms – day-long *Danda Nata*, the traditional fishermen's dance, *Chaitighoda* which requires a horse dummy, the battle dance called *Paika Nritya*, and *Chhau*, the dance-drama reminiscent of Orissa's martial past. There are also tribal dances performed in colourful costumes with distinctive headgear made of animal horns and shells, to the accompaniment of string instruments, flutes and drums.

**Food and drink** Rice forms the staple food, wheat taking second place. Meals include lightly spiced side dishes of vegetables and pulses, chutneys and pickles. Fresh seafood, especially prawns and the flat *pomfret* fish, are common in coastal areas. Try *mahura* or *saga bhaja* (fried mustard or spinach leaves), *dahi baigono* (aubergines cooked with yoghurt) or the festive *besara* (vegetables cooked with mustard seed paste).

Orissa is particularly noted for its milk sweets – *rasamalai, khiramohan, rajbhoga, rabidi, chhenapodapitha* and *kalakanda. Khiri* is prepared with milk and rice, semolina or vermicelli while special *pithas* are often filled with sweetened coconut.

## Art and architecture

The temples of Bhubaneswar, along with those of Puri and Konark, represent a remarkably full record of the development of Orissan architecture from the seventh to the 13th century AD. Although some of the temples have suffered structural damage many are virtually intact and some are still in everyday use – centres of active pilgrimage, worship and faith.

## Crafts

**Stone carving** has been highly developed in Orissa for over 2,000 years. The artistry that produced the early sculptures and the superb carvings on Orissan temples in Bhubaneswar, Puri and Konark is still kept alive by modern craftsmen. They produce beautiful figures, bowls or plates carved out of soft soapstone, hard *kochila* or multicoloured serpentine from Khiching. Orissa also has a tradition of **hornwork** in Parlakhemundi and Cuttack, buffalo horn being carved into the typical small flat figures of animals and birds.

**Silver filigree** is perhaps one of the most distinctive and exquisite works of the Cuttack jewellers who turn fine silver wire into beautiful, fragile objects with floral patterns. The metal used is close to sterling silver which is drawn through finer and finer holes to make the wire.

**Metal work** is popular. Craftsmen use brass (alloy of copper and zinc) and bell-metal (alloy of copper and tin) to produce small figurines, vases and plates. The tribal metal casting in the *dhokra* style by the lost-wax (*cire perdue*) process is found in Dhenkanal and Mayurbhanj districts. A clay core of the basic shape is covered by fine wax 'threads' before the whole is enclosed in a shell of straw and clay and then baked in a tiny charcoal fire. At the firing, molten metal is poured in, to displace the melting wax. Similar casting is done by tribal peoples in Bihar, Madhya Pradesh, Manipur and West Bengal.

Brightly coloured **wood carvings** of the deities in the Jagannath temple, and figures of animals and birds make attractive gifts. **Ivory** inlay (now replaced by plastic) was traditionally carried out for rich patrons of the Puri temple, and also for making illustrated wooden covers for palm leaf manuscripts. The tradition of using **papier-mâché** masks of deities and animal characters to tell stories from the epics also comes from Orissa.



## Orissan temple

After Brown

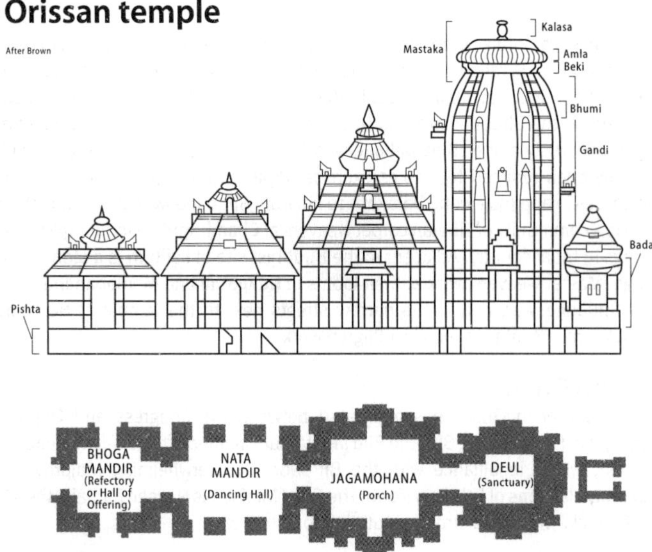

The *chitrakars* (picture makers), particularly from the village of Raghurajpur, 12 km from Puri, **paint** the *pattachitras* on specially prepared cloth, coated with earth to stiffen it and finally finished with lacquer after painting, producing pictures and attractive playing cards. Old sets of *ganjapa* cards consisted of 96 discs. The vibrant colours traditionally came from earth, stone, leaves and flowers. The best *chitrakars* are those allowed the honour to paint the Puri temple deities and their 'cars' each year. They are also commissioned by the rich to produce fine temple murals and manuscripts on paper and palmleaf. However, what are usually available in the bazars are cruder examples for pilgrims to take home.

Finds of the 16th century reveal how illustrated manuscripts were produced by holding an iron stylus stationary while moving a **palm leaf** underneath. It was a technique that helped to give the Oriya script its rounded form. The leaves were first prepared by drying, boiling, drying again, and then flattening them before coating with powdered shell. After inscribing, the grooves were rubbed with soot or powdered charcoal, while colour was added with a brush. The leaves were then stacked and strung together and placed between decorative wooden covers. The *pattachitra* artists in Raghurajpur have also revived this art form.

Pipli, a small town about 20 km southwest of Bhubaneswar, is famous for its **appliqué** work using brightly coloured embroidered cloth, probably originally designed for use in the Jagannath temple. The roadside stalls sell items for the house and garden – parasols, cushion covers, wall-hangings – using striking animal, bird and flower patterns on a backcloth. Unfortunately, mass production has resulted in the loss of attention to detail of the original fine 'Pipli work' which picked out the motifs by cleverly stuffing sections of the pattern. The best pieces now tend to be sent away to the government emporia in Bhubaneswar, Delhi and Kolkata.



**Textile weaving** has been a traditional craft throughout Orissa for generations and thousands are still employed in this cottage industry. It is one of the few regions in India producing **ikat** – see also page 1035 – the technique of 'resist-dyeing' the warp or weft thread, or both, before weaving, so that the fabric that emerges from the loom has a delicate enmeshed pattern. The favourite designs include rows of flowers, birds and animals, using either tussar or cotton yarn. **Berhampur**, **Sambalpur**, **Mayurbhanj** and **Nuapatna** all produce silk and cotton ikat saris. Some also produce tapestry, bedspreads and embroidered fabric.

**Crafts villages** While some (for example Raghurajpur and Pipli) are used to passing tourists, others are rarely visited by foreigners. It is worth visiting to see craftsmen at work and perhaps buy their goods. In **Raghurajpur** (reached via Chandapur, 10 km from Puri on the Bhubaneswar road), you can watch artists painting *pattachitras* in bright folk-art style or etching palm leaves (see *chitrakars* above). Sadly, the village has now been reduced to a sales exercise. **Pipli**, on the Bhubaneswar-Puri Road, specializes in appliqué work, **Balakati**, 10 km from Bhubaneswar, in bell-metal, while there is a community of Tibetan carpet weavers at **Chandragiri** near the Taptapani Hot Springs in tribal country. Adjacent to the Buddhist site of **Lalitgiri** is a stone-carvers' village. Master-weavers work at their looms in **Nuapatna** and **Maniabandha**, 100 km from Bhubaneswar, and in the narrow streets next to the temple at **Berhampur**. **Cuttack** remains famous for silver filigree work.

## Modern Orissa

Political power in Orissa has alternated between the Congress and Opposition parties, most recently the BJD (the Biju Janata Dal – named after its former leader Biju Patnaik), which in alliance with the BJP won an overwhelming majority in the Assembly elections of February 2000. The Chief Minister is Naveen Patnaik, the son of Biju Patnaik, who has a strong reputation for integrity.

# Mahanadi Delta

## Bhubaneswar

→ *Phone code: 0674. Colour map 6, grid A6. Population: 647,300.*

Set on the edge of the lush green rice fields of the Mahanadi Delta, the pleasantly broad streets of the planned town of Bhubaneswar offer a striking contrast to the architectural legacy of its period of greatness over one thousand years ago. Named after 'The Lord of the Universe', Bhubaneswar still has some 500 of the original '7,000' temples that once surrounded Bindusagar Tank. The graceful towers of those early temples, complemented by the extraordinary fineness of the stone carving, make Bhubaneswar one of the most rewarding destinations in East India. ›› *For Sleeping, Eating and other listings, see pages 714-719.*

### Ins and outs

**Getting there** The airport is 4 km from the centre and several hotels are within 1 km of the railway station on the main Kolkata-Chennai line. Although the new bus stand is 6 km out of town long-distance buses stop at the Old Bus Stand in the centre first. Buses for Konark and Puri can be boarded by the State Museum.

**Getting around** The temples are quite spread out so it is best to hire a rickshaw, though you can get round on foot if you have plenty of time. ›› *See Transport, page 718, for further details.*

### History

Several sites testify to the importance of the Bhubaneswar region far earlier than the seventh to 11th centuries, when the Kalinga kings ruled over the area. Both Jain and Buddhist shrines give clear evidence of important settlements around Bhubaneswar in the first two centuries BC. The remains of a ruined moated city, Sisupalgarh (opposite the Dhauligiri battlefield and Asokan edicts), show that it was occupied from the beginning of the third century BC to the middle of the fourth century AD and the pottery shows Roman influence. Bhubaneswar is the capital of Orissa, chosen in 1948 in place of Cuttack partly because it was the ancient capital of the Kalinga Empire.

### Sights

**Parsuramesvara Temple** The seventh-century temple, though small, is highly decorated, and is the best preserved of the early Bhubaneswar temples. The rectangular porch and the stepped roof indicate an early date. Even so, the porch was probably built after the sanctuary itself, as suggested by the rather crude junction between the two. In the early period the masonry was kept in place by weight and balance alone. Other features include the carving of a goddess and two sea-monsters on the lintel over the sanctuary door.

The temple marks an important stage in the development of Hindu power at the expense of Buddhism in seventh-century Orissa, illustrated by the frequent representation of **Lakulisa**, the seventh-century priest responsible for Hindu proselytism. He is sculpted in Buddha-like form, and often surrounded by disciples. Note also, the distinctive *chaitya* windows developed earlier in Buddhist *chaitya* halls, as at Ajanta. There are two on the front of the sanctuary tower.

> *Temple priests may approach you for donations; these are not compulsory.*

The sanctuary is divided horizontally and vertically into three sections. The carvings show motifs and styles that were to reach their full flowering in later temples. The base, for example, has a top moulding (close to the ground) decorated with scrolls, birds, humans and floral motifs. At about eye level, the mouldings are distinctive. The recessed frieze (discarded in later designs) is embossed with early examples of the amorous couples which were to become such a prominent feature of the Konark temple, interspersed with *vyalas* (rampant lions) astride crouching elephants. In addition to the main entrance to the porch there is a door on the south side and four latticed windows. The vigorous and graceful sculptures of musicians and dancers he carvings on each side of the western doorway are outstanding.

The main accessory deities are placed in niches on each side of the sanctuary housing the principal deity. The Parsuramesvara Temple was dedicated to Siva; only

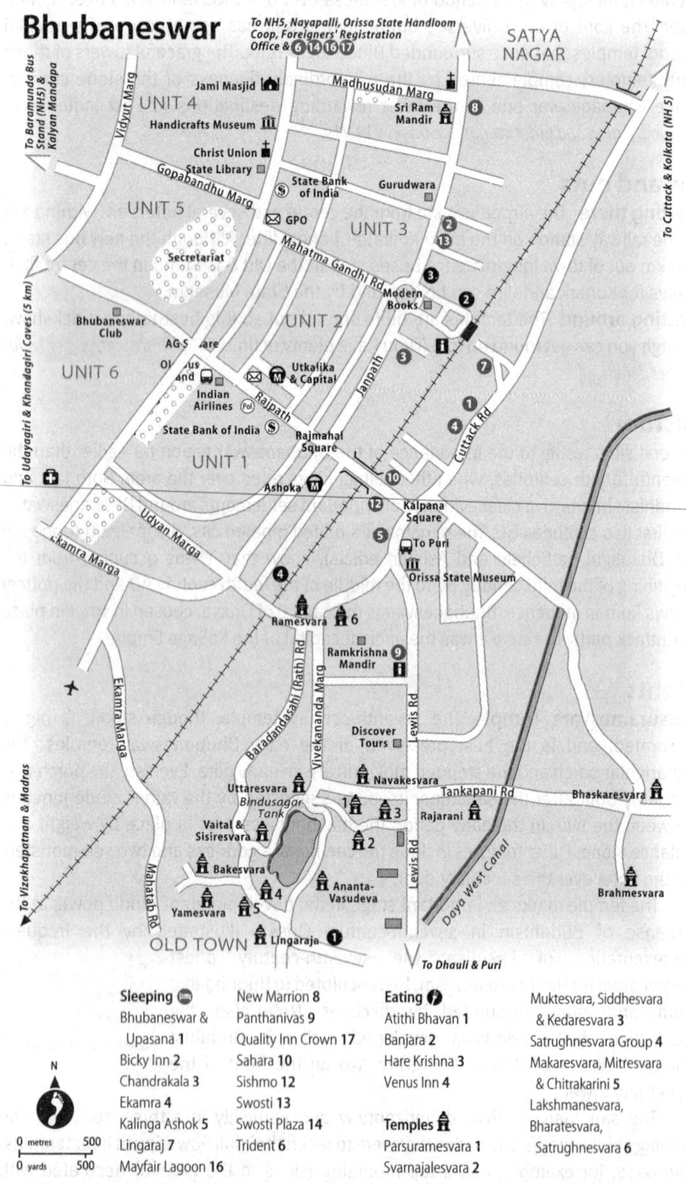

two of the three original deities survive. On the south of the sanctuary, at eye level in the middle of the tower, is the four-armed elephant-headed Ganesh, his trunk curled towards a bowl of *laddus,* his favourite sweet. In the southern niche is Karttikeya (Subrahmanya) with a peacock, carrying a fruit in his right hand and a spear in his left. The lintel above Karttikeya illustrates the marriage of Siva and Parvati; to their right are Agni (Fire), the kneeling Brahma, and Surya (Sun).

**Muktesvara Temple** Beautifully decorated with outstanding carvings, this late 10th-century temple belongs to the end of the first phase of temple building. Although it still has the three-fold horizontal division of the lower storey, a feature of the early period, the plan of the sanctuary is now divided into the five-sectioned form. Also, the platform here consists of five mouldings, as in later temples.

New designs include graceful female figures and pilasters carved with *nagas* and *naginis* (snakes). Most strikingly, the porch has a new and more dramatic layered form. Ketu, too, is introduced as the ninth planet and Ganesh is joined by his mount, the mouse.

The Muktesvara displays the unique gateway arch (*torana*) dated at about AD 900; although the upper portion is restored, the original skill can still be seen in the graceful female figures. The rectangular tank at its east end, used by priests and devotees, and the well to the south, into which women still toss coins in the hope of curing infertility, symbolize the continued holiness of the site. On the door frame of the well is the figure of Lakulisa (see Parsuramesvara above).

The *chaitya* windows carved on the sanctuary tower show the finest examples of the *bho* motif – the grinning face of a lion with beaded tassels emerging from its mouth, flanked by two dwarves. Notice the monkey scenes on the outer frame of the diamond-shaped lattice windows on the north and south walls.

**Siddhesvara Temple** Immediately to the northwest of the Muktesvara is the later Siddhesvara Temple. It shows the mature Orissan temple form almost complete. The vertical lower section is divided into five parts and the *amla* on top of the sanctuary is supported by four squatting figures. However, the overall effect is comparatively plain, as sculptures marked out on the rock were never executed.

**Gauri Temple** The Gauri Temple to the south is probably of the late 10th century but it is built in the *khakhara* form (see Vaital Deul below), and has been substantially repaired. The porch was rebuilt in the early 20th century but still has a few original sculptures of real merit. Note the girl shown leaning against a post with a bird perched on it, on the south face of the eastern projection of the sanctuary. On the western projection is an equally beautiful sculpture of a girl removing her anklets.

**Rajarani Temple** ⓘ *0600-1800, foreigners US$2, Indians Rs 5, video camera Rs 25.* The entrance to the temple (early 11th century) is about 300 m east of the main road, set back 200 m from the road. It no longer has an image of the deity in the sanctuary and is therefore out of use. The main tower is surrounded by four miniature copies, giving the sanctuary an almost circular appearance.

The porch (*jagmohana*) is comparatively plain even though it has the mature style of a pyramidal roof. Many of the carvings remain unfinished but give an insight into the method of cutting the stone into sections ('blocking out') followed by rough shaping ('boasted'), to be finished later by the master sculptor. The finished work in the main sanctuary is extremely fine.

Perhaps the best-preserved features of the temple are the *Dikpalas* (Guardians of the eight cardinal directions) who protect the central shrine from every quarter. They are placed in pairs about 3 m above ground level, in the lower section of the main sanctuary tower.

Starting from the left (south) of the porch they appear in the following order:

**1** Facing east, **Indra**, the guardian of the east, holds a thunderbolt and an elephant goad, and his vehicle is the elephant.

**2** At right angles to Indra, facing south, is the pot-bellied and bearded **Agni**, god of fire, riding a ram, guarding the southeast.

**3** Moving a few metres along the wall, on the far side of the projection, is the south-facing **Yama**, holding a staff and a noose, with his vehicle the buffalo. The skull on his staff is a Tantric symbol.

**Dikpalas: the Directional Guardians**

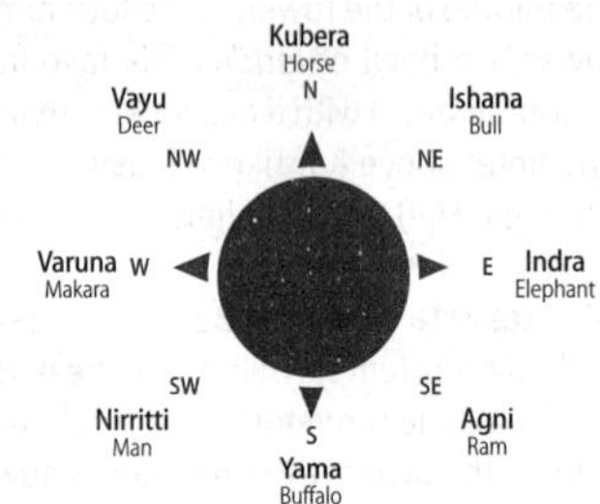


**4** Again at right angles to Yama is the west-facing **Nirritti**, guardian of the southwest. Nirritti, the god of misery, holds a severed head and a sword over the lying figure of a man.

**5** Again facing west, but on the north side of the sanctuary's central projection, is the guardian of the west, **Varuna**. He holds the noose symbolizing fate in his left hand. His vehicle is the sea creature *makara*.

**6** At right angles to Varuna, facing north, is **Vayu** (meaning 'wind'), guardian of the northwest. He holds a fluttering banner, and his vehicle is the deer.

**7** The last pair of guardians are on the further side of the central projection, on the north and east facing sides respectively. First is **Kubera**, guardian of the north (pot-bellied to symbolize prosperity), placed above seven jars of precious stones. He has a horse.

**8** **Ishana**, guardian of the northeast, symbolizing fecundity, is shown as was customary, with an erect phallus and accompanied by an emaciated figure.

**Brahmesvara Temple** The temple (built in 1060) is still in use today. As you enter from the north you pass through the two enclosure walls, the inner forming a compact surround for the temple complex, which is raised on a platform. Facing you is a well-oiled image of Lakshmi, covered in cloth, with incense sticks burning in front. The sanctuary itself houses a Siva *linga*. There are minor shrines in each corner of the compound.

The sanctuary tower has a five-fold vertical division, typical of the later temples. The base (*pabhaga*) and the top of the wall (*varanda*) have rich carvings. The lower section of the wall is decorated alternately by miniature *khakhara* style 'temples', sculptures of rampant lions, while the central niches of the miniature temple carvings at the corners of the lower section have *Dikpalas*. In the corresponding spaces of the upper section are miniatures of the normal temple sanctuary towers, and graceful secular figures, including erotic couples.

**Satrughnesvara Group Lakshmanesvara**, **Bharatesvara** and **Satrughnesvara** temples are almost certainly the oldest in Bhubaneswar, dating from the late sixth century. The southernmost temple in the group has been rebuilt by the Archaeological Department of Orissa. Only the cores of these three temple are now visible.

**Vaital Temple** A significant feature of this small, late eighth-century temple is its form. Seen from the road the semi-cylindrical shape in section of the *deul* is distinct immediately. Its *khakhara* style derives, as Percy Brown says, from the shape of the *gopurams* of Dravida temples in South India, taken originally from the Buddhist *chaitya* halls. Another striking feature is the temple's tantric associations, marked by its presiding deity, Chamunda (a terrible form of Durga). Durga herself appears on the north face of the *bada* as the eight-armed *Mahishasuramardini* (slayer of the buffalo demon) holding a snake, bow, shield, sword, trident, thunderbolt and an arrow, and she is piercing the neck of the demon.

Outside, on the east face of the *deul*, the lower of the two *chaitya* windows has a beautifully carved figure of the sun god Surya, with Usha (Dawn) and Pratyusha shooting arrows on either side of him while Aruna (also Dawn) drives a chariot in front. It has a certain incongruity in view of the image within the sanctum itself. The upper *chaitya*window has a 10-armed Nataraja, or dancing Siva.

Further evidence of the tantric basis of the temple comes from the stone post to which sacrifices were tethered, just in front of the *jagamohana*. The figure of Chamunda in the central niche is extremely difficult to see without artificial light, though very early morning sun penetrates the gloom of the interior. The most chilling of the other figures is that of a male on the north wall "rising from the ground after filling his skull-cup with the blood of a person whose severed head lies on the right; on the pedestal is an offering of two more heads".

**Lingaraja Temple** Along with the Jagannatha Temple at Puri the Lingaraja Temple (AD 1000), built 100 years earlier, represents the peak of achievement of the Orissan middle period. Non-Hindus are not allowed inside but you may get a view from a special platform outside the north perimeter wall; early morning and late afternoon are best for photography.

Even from a distance the sanctuary's 54-m high tower (the *Sri Mandir*) dominates the landscape. It is one of the four main buildings in the temple compound, with several subsidiary shrines. To the left of the tower is the *Jagamohana* (pillared porch), then the *Nata Mandir* (dancing hall) and finally the *Bhoga Mandir* (Hall of Offering). The latter two were added a century after the sanctuary and the porch.

The monumental tower which rises in a distinctive curve, is 17 m sq in plan with projecting faces. The *amla* head with a pot-shaped pinnacle carrying the trident of Siva is supported by four mythical gryphons. The middle section has vertical lines of miniature towers sculpted in sharp relief on a background of horizontal mouldings. The massive protruding sculpture of a lion crushing an elephant on each side is a common symbol in Orissan architecture.

**Ekamra Kanan** The Government Regional Plant Resource Centre in Nayapally (north of town) has a large rose garden (Flower Show, December/January), woods, flowerbeds and a large lake which attracts migratory birds. It also boasts a Cactus Garden with over 550 species of cacti and succulents, one of the largest collections in India.

**Nandan Kanan** ⓘ *0730-1730 (summer), 0800-1700 except Mon, Rs 5 (foreigners, Rs 40), camera Rs 5, video Rs 500, guide Rs 45 but unnecessary. Cable car across the lake, Rs 22, last return 1600. Safari Rs 12, closed 1130-1400.* The subsidiary road from Bhubaneswar to Cuttack, the medieval regional capital, passes Nandan Kanan after 20 km where the zoo and botanical garden are surrounded by dense forest. There are tigers, including rare white ones, lion and white tiger safaris, rhinos, panthers, leopards and a variety of wildfowl and reptiles, in their natural surroundings. It has also succeeded in breeding black panthers and *gharials* in captivity. The botanical gardens with its cactus house and rosarium are across the lake; much of it is derelict. The **Shradhanjali Restaurant**, near the entrance serves good *thalis* and snacks.

**Orissa State Museum** ⓘ *Gautam Nagar, closed Mon and Govt holidays, 1000-1300, 1400-1700 (last entry 1600), Re 1.* The collection includes archaeological exhibits, copper plates, coins, sculptures, musical instruments and rare palm leaf manuscripts; good anthropological section. Allow an hour or two.

**Tribal Museum of Man** ⓘ *CRP Square, 1000-1700 except Sun, northwest of town, off NH5 on bus route.* The Tribal Research Institute's museum has a collection of tribal dress, weapons and jewellery.

**Kalanagar** ⓘ *1000-1700 except Sun, on the Khandagiri Rd.* Display of traditional art and crafts, stone sculptures, *pattachitras*, brass casting, horn ware, terracotta and silver filigree.

## Udayagiri and Khandagiri caves

→ *Colour map 6, grid A5.*

The caves, 6 km from Bhubaneswar, on the two low hills of Udayagiri and Khandagiri, date from the time of Jain occupation of the region, at least the second century BC. A narrow valley winds between the hills, the route of an early Buddhist pilgrim track leading to a stupa which probably stood on the present site of Bhubaneswar. The coarse-grained sandstone which forms Khandagiri ('broken hill') and Udayagiri ('hill of the sunrise') rises nearly 40 m above the surrounding lateritic and infertile plain. The crumbling nature of the sandstone into which the caves were dug has exposed them to severe damage, moderately repaired by the Archaeological Survey of India.

▸▸ *For Sleeping, Eating and other listings, see pages 714-719.*

### Ins and outs

**Getting there** The caves are very easy to visit by car, bus, rickshaw (Rs 120 return, includes waiting) or bicycle from Bhubaneswar, but the area can get very crowded.
**Getting around** You can take the path up towards Udayagiri to the right of the hills as you face them, and follow the route indicated to visit the caves in order. Some with sculptures are protected by wire-meshed gates. The most significant are described



## Around Bhubaneswar & Cuttack

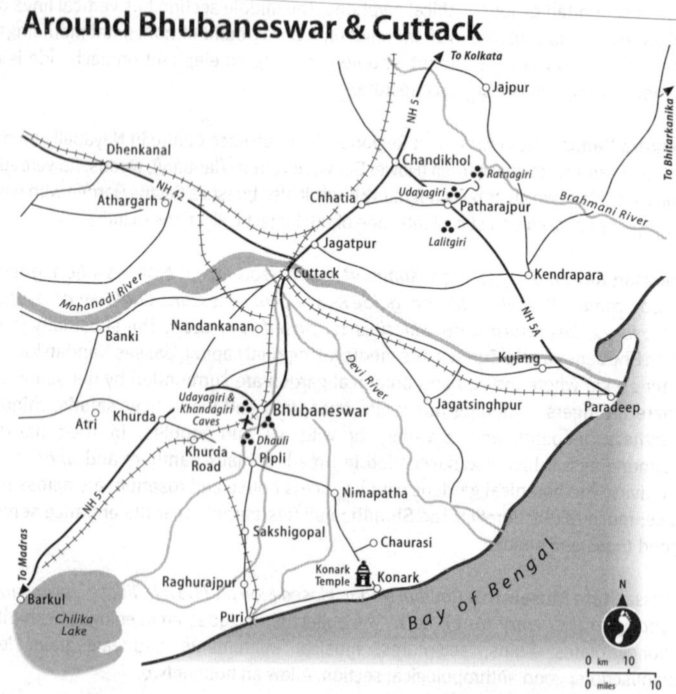

below. ⓘ *Foreigners US$2, video Rs 25 for Udayagiri. Khandagiri is free. 0800-1800.* Allow two to three hours.

## History

The **Jain caves** are among the earliest in India. Furthermore, some of the rock inscriptions found above the *Hati Gumpha* (Elephant Cave, No 14) and elsewhere, speak of the Chedi Dynasty who ruled over Kalinga from their capital, probably at Sisupalgarh, 9 km southeast of Khandagiri.

**Kharavela**, according to his own record, extended his rule across a large part of North, Central and South India. At home he made great efforts to improve canals, rebuild his capital city of Kalinganagara, and also to excavate some of the caves at Udayagiri-Khandagiri. Probably all the caves now visible were constructed during the 150 years before Christ. Designed for the ascetic life of Jain monks, they simply provided dry shelter, with no concessions to any form of comfort. Too low to stand in, the cells are no more than cramped sleeping compartments.

Although the Jains did not enjoy royal patronage after the fall of Kharavela's Dynasty, Jain occupation was continuous throughout successive Buddhist and Hindu periods in the region. The Parsvanatha temple on top of Khandagiri was built in the early 19th century, while the Hindu temple dates from the 1970s.



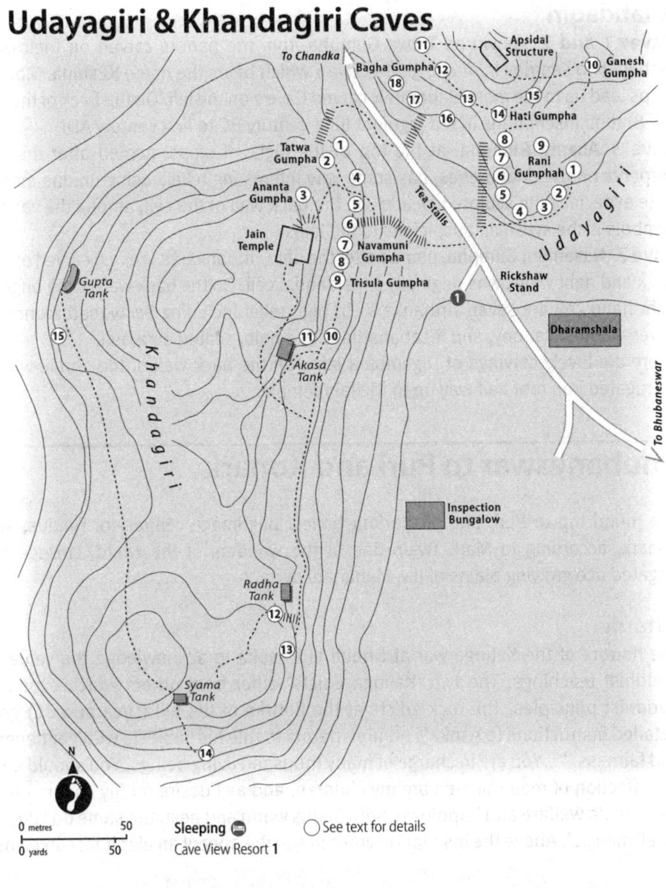

## Udayagiri

**Cave 1** The **Rani Gumpha**, on the path to the right, is the largest and most impressive of the caves. It is a double-storeyed monastery cut on three sides of a quadrangle with fine wall friezes and some pillars that have been restored. The right wing of the lower storey is guarded by two sentries. The pilasters at the entrance to the cell and the arches are beautifully carved with religious and royal scenes while the main central wing celebrates the king's victory march. There are two small guard rooms with decorative outer walls. In the upper storey, the doorway arches to the cells are ornately carved; auspicious Jain symbols (snake and lotus) appear among vivid secular friezes of a woman's abduction, an elopement, and a duel between a man and a woman.

**Cave 10 Ganesh Gumpha** About 50 m from the top of the steps. Friezes illustrate the Sanskrit love story of Udayan and Bassavadatta. From Cave 10 go up the path to the right, where an **apsidal structure** was unearthed in 1958. Very similar to a Buddhist *chaitya* hall in plan, it was almost certainly a place of worship for Jain monks.

**Cave 12 Bagha Gumpha** is carved bizarrely into the shape of a tiger's open mouth, an inscription showing it to have been the cave of the town judge.

**Cave 14** The last important cave on Udayagiri, the **Hati Gumpha** (Elephant Cave), has the most important inscription, that of King Kharavela. Protected by a masonry shelter since 1902, it is in the Magadhi script.

## Khandagiri

**Caves 1 and 2** Known as **Tatwa Gumpha** from the parrots carved on their door arches. Two sentries in *dhotis* guard Cave 1 which bears the name **Kusuma**. Modern steps lead up to the more elaborately carved Cave 2 on the left. On the back of the cell are Brahmi inscriptions in red pigment (first century BC to first century AD).

**Cave 3 Ananta Gumpha**, at the top of the flight of steps, named after the two serpents on the door arches, has some very interesting reliefs using unique motifs; note especially the sculpted façade. On the back wall of the cell, among the various symbols is the *svastika*, auspicious to the Jains.

**Cave 7 Navamuni Gumpha**, named after the nine Tirthankaras (*munis*) carved on the back and right walls, was originally a residential cell. On the back wall of the original right hand cell are seven Tirthankaras in high relief including Parsvanatha under a seven-hooded canopy, and Risabanatha with a halo, seated on a bull.

There are lovely carvings of Digambara Jains on the back wall of the shrine with a corrugated iron roof half way up to the Jain temple.

# Bhubaneswar to Puri and Konark

The round trip to Puri, one of the four holiest pilgrimage centres for Hindus, and Konark, according to Mark Twain one of the wonders of the world, crosses the irrigated rice growing plains of the Mahanadi delta.

## Dhauli

The horrors of the Kalinga war at Dhauli led Asoka to acknowledge the value of Buddhist teachings. The two 'Kalinga Edicts' differ from others which expound Buddhist principles. The rock edicts at the bottom of the hill (circa 260 BC) give detailed instructions to Asoka's administrators to rule his subjects with gentleness and fairness. "...You are in charge of many thousand living beings. You should gain the affection of men. All men are my children, and as I desire for my children that they obtain welfare and happiness both in this world and next, the same do I desire for all men ...". Above the inscription you can see the front of an elephant carved out of an enormous rock. Unfortunately, the edict is difficult to see clearly behind its protective cage.

Now the rock edicts are almost ignored by the bus loads of tourists who are taken on up the hill to the Buddhist **Peace Pagoda**. Known as the **ShantiStupa**, the Pagoda was built in the early 1970s by the Japan Buddha Sangha and Kalinga Nippon Buddha Sangha. The old Hindu temple of Lord Dhavaleswar which was reconstructed in 1972 is also on the hilltop here.

## Puri → *Phone code: 06752. Colour map 6, grid A5. Population: 157,600.*

Puri's tourist guesthouses cater to the flocks of Kolkata holidaymakers who take advantage of the highly revered Jagannath Temple and the good sandy beach to combine pilgrimage with relaxation. The massive curvilinear temple tower dominates the skyline, and the otherwise sleepy town seethes with life during the car festival (*Rath Yatra*). Yet for most of the year Puri feels like an out of season backwater with quiet shady lanes with prettily painted houses. » *For Sleeping, Eating and other listings, see pages 714-719.*

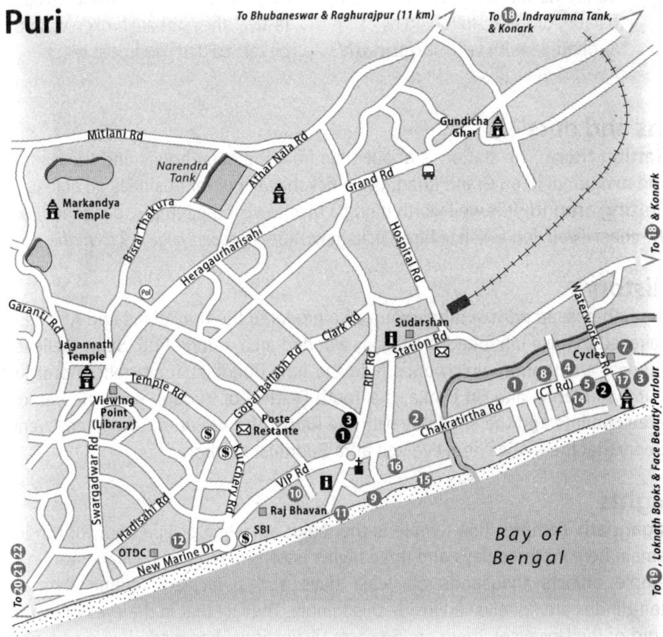


Sleeping
Arya Palace 1
BNR 2
Derby 3
Gandhara & Sun Row Cottage 4
Hans Coco Palms 21
Holiday House & Kasi's Castle 5
Lotus & Harry's Café 7
Love & Life 8
Mayfair Beach Resort 9
Nilachal Ashok 10
Panthanivas & OTDC Tourist Office 11
Pearl Beach Club 20
Pink House 19
Puri 12
Shankar International 14
Sterling Resorts 22
Toshali Sands 18
Vijoya International 15
Youth Hostel 16
Z 17

Eating
Chung Wah 1
Peace 2
Wild Grass 3

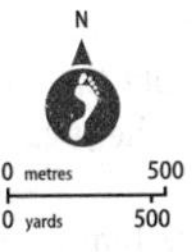

## Rath Yatra

Lord Jagannath's 'car' festival commemorates Krishna's journey from Gokul to Mathura in an extraordinary riot of colour and noise. Shaped like a temple sanctuary and brightly decorated, Lord Jagannath's 13-m tall 'car', the largest, has 16 wheels each 2 m in diameter. Loud gongs announce the boarding of the deities onto the chariots with the arrival of the Raja of Puri accompanied by bedecked elephants. With a golden broom and sprinkling holy water, the Raja fulfils his role as the 'sweeper of the gods', symbolizing that all castes are equal before God. The procession is led by Balabhadra's car, followed by Subhadra's with Lord **Jagannath**'s bringing up the rear, about 4,000 people being needed to draw each chariot.

During the week away, the deities are daily dressed in new garments and treated to special rice cakes (*podapitha*), before they return with a similar procession. Jagannath has to implore Lakshmi (his consort) who had to remain behind and now bars his way, to allow him in! The ceremonies and the fairs attract more than 500,000 devotees to Puri each year. In the past some were said to have thrown themselves under a massive wheel to die a blessed death. The short journey may take as much as 24 hours. After the festival, the raths are broken up and bits are sold to pilgrims as relics.



## Ins and outs

**Getting there** The station is about 1 km from the main hotels and the bus stand, 500 m north of it, on Grand Road. Cycle-rickshaws tout for business all across town. **Getting around** It is well worth hiring a bike to visit the temple, bazar and explore the coast if you don't wish to hire a rickshaw. ▸▸ *See Transport, page 719, for further details.*

## History

The Sabaras, an *adivasi* tribal group who predated the Dravidians and Aryans, were believed to have inhabited the thickly wooded area around Puri. Some believe that this was **Dantapura**, which once held the holy Buddhist Tooth relic. According to Murray, in Japan and Sri Lanka, the **Tooth Festival** of Buddha was celebrated with three chariots and the similarity with the **Rath Yatra** at Puri further strengthens the theory that the deities here evolved from Buddhist symbols.

## Sights

**Jagannath Temple** This temple is the major attraction of Puri and, for Hindus, to remain here for three days and three nights is considered particularly rewarding. The temple attracts thousands on feast days and particularly during **Rath Yatra**. Non-Hindus are not allowed inside this temple. The fact that in the eyes of Jagannath (Lord of the Universe), there are no caste distinctions, has made Puri a very popular destination with the devout. The wooden figures of the three deities, **Jagannath, Balabhadra** and **Subhadra** stand in the sanctuary garlanded and decorated by the priests. The extraordinary form that Jagannath takes is believed to be the unfinished work of the craftsman god Viswakarma, who in anger left this portrayal of Lord Vishnu incomplete. Small wooden replicas of the three images are available around the temple. There are vantage points for viewing the temple, for example the roof of Raghunandan Library opposite the main entrance to the east or from the **Jaga Balia Lodge** nearby; a small donation is expected in return.

The temple is referred to by some as the 'white pagoda' (the Konark Temple being the 'black pagoda') and was completed at the end of the 12th century. The original temple built in the Kalinga style consisted of the **deul** (sanctuary) and the **jagamohan** (audience hall) in front of it. It was only in the 14th or 15th century that the **'nata mandir'** (dance hall) and the '*bhoga mandir*' (hall of offerings) were added in alignment in the style of other Orissan temples. The **nata mandir** is unusual in that it has 16 pillars in four rows to support the large ceiling. The site is a virtual 200 m sq enclosed within an outer wall 6-m high. Within is another concentric wall which may have acted as fortification, inside which stands the tallest temple in Orissa, 65 m high, crowned by the wheel of Vishnu and a flag. On the higher ground in the enclosure are 30 small shrines, much in the Buddhist stupa tradition. Pilgrims are expected to visit at least three of these smaller temples before proceeding to the main temple. The outer wall has the main **Lion entrance**. On this east side there is an intricately carved 10-m high free-standing stone pillar with a small figure of *Aruna*, the charioteer of the Sun. This once stood in front of the *Nata Mandir* at Konark, see page 712. To the left of the main entrance is the temple kitchen which daily prepares 56 varieties of food making up the *Bhogas* which are offered to the deities five times a day; the *mahaprasada* is then distributed from the Ananda Bazar to thousands. At festival times as many as 250,000 are served daily. The temple is supposed to be a self-sufficient community, served by 6,000 priests and over 10,000 others who depend on it for their livelihood. The four sacred *tanks* in Puri provide thousands of pilgrims with the opportunity to take a holy dip. The **Narendra Tank** is particularly famous since the deities are taken there during the Snana Yatra.

**Gundicha Ghar** The terminus of the **Rath Yatra**, where the deities from the Jagannath Temple spend a week, is open to Hindus only. It shows the unique and ingenious way wrought-iron framework supported the laterite lintels of the massive temples.

**The beach** The long stretch of Puri's golden beach is shallow enough to walk out a long distance. Sunrise is particularly striking. The currents can be treacherous at times. Take great care and avoid swimming out too far. The best hotels have a stretch of fairly clean sand. The customary *nolia*, fisherman turned life-saver in a distinctive conical hat, may be hired for either half or a full day, at a small price. The fishing villages along the coast are worth visiting, but be prepared to pick your way carefully!

# Konark → *Phone code: 06758 .Colour map 6, grid A6.*

Konark (Konarak) is one of the most vivid architectural treasures of Hindu India and is a World Heritage Site. It no longer stands as a landmark on the sea shore since the land has risen and the sea is now 2 km away. Though much of it now lies in ruins, the porch is still magnificent. » *For Sleeping, Eating and other listings, see pages 714-719.*

## Ins and outs

**Getting there** The 35-km drive from Puri (small toll charged) through attractive scenery passes a Turtle Research Centre off the Marine Drive after 10 km, and through coastal villages with beautifully decorated houses including Chaitan, a stone carvers' hamlet. The energetic can cycle to Konark and bring the bike back on the bus.
**Getting around** The site is very compact and can only be seen on foot. » *See Transport, page 719, for further details.*

## History

The Sun Temple was built by King Langula Narasimha Deva in the 13th century, although there may have been an older ninth-century temple on the same site. Built of *khondalite*, it is said to have taken 1,200 masons 16 years to complete. It was only in 1901 that the first tentative steps were taken to reclaim the ruins of the temple from the encroaching sand. By that stage not only had the sanctuary or *deul* collapsed but a number of the statues had been removed, many in the 1830s by the Hindu Raja of Khurda, who wanted them to decorate temples he was building in his own fort, 100 km away, and at Puri. There has been substantial renovation, some of it protective and some replacing fallen stonework and sculptures.

## The site

The **Surya Temple** is set back 180 m from the road and is reached by a wide laterite path. The sanctuary has no deity for worship, so shoes may be worn. The exception is the small structure in the northeast corner of the site which houses the old *Navagraha* (nine planets) doorway arch, removed from the temple. The path to the temple is lined with beggars, as in major centres of Hindu pilgrimage.

Archaeological Survey and Government approved **guides** conduct tours of under an hour. Unofficial guides will press their services, but can be unreliable.



## The temple compound

At the eastern entrance is the *bhoga mandira* (refectory), an isolated hall with pillars raised on a richly decorated platform; some believe this may have been a *nata mandira* (dancing hall). To its west is an open space leading to the porch (*jagamohana*) which rises magnificently to its original height of 39 m. To its east is the massive lower section of the original sanctuary (*deul*), once over 60 m tall.

From the south wall you can see that the temple was built in the form of a war chariot. Twelve pairs of great wheels were sculpted on either side of the temple platform. In front of the eastern entrance a team of seven horses were shown straining to pull the chariot towards the dawn. In Hindu mythology the Sun god traverses the sky in a chariot drawn by seven horses, each representing a day of the week. The 12 pairs of wheels may have symbolized the 12 months (24 fortnights) of the year, and the eight spokes in each wheel, the divisions of the day into eight *prahars*. Each wheel also functions as a working sundial!

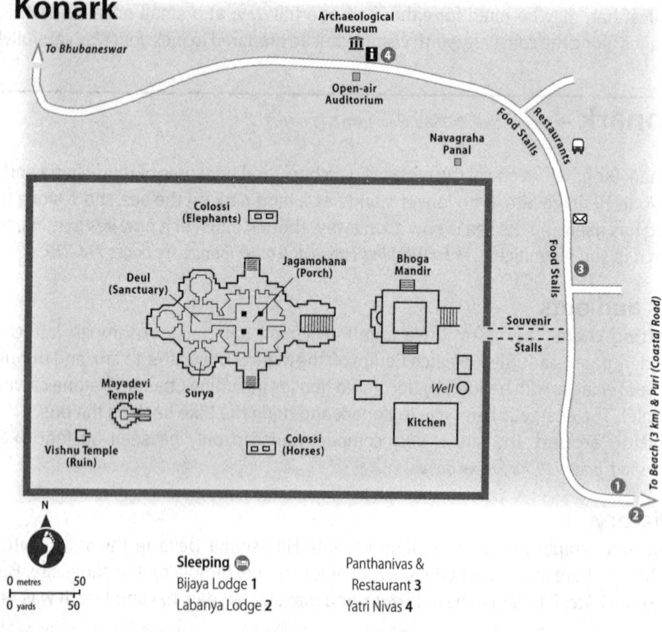

## The sculptures

The walls of the *bhoga mandir* are covered by carvings, but as Debala Mitra writes, there are of "mediocre quality". The platform gives an excellent view of the whole east front of the main temple with its porch doorway, and the large, remarkably vivid carvings on the terraces of its pyramidal roof, unique in Orissan architecture, see page 698.

The sculptures draw for their subject from every aspect of life – dancers, musicians, figures from mythology, scenes of love and war, of court life, hunting, elephant fights. Since the temple was conceived to reflect a rounded picture of life and since *mithuna* or union in love is a part of that, a significant section of the sculpture is erotic art. Konark is unusual in that the carvings are found both on the outer and inner surfaces.

The porch roof is divided into three tiers, separated by terraces. Above the bottom and middle tiers is a series of musicians vividly captured in a variety of rhythmic poses playing drums, cymbals and *vinas*. On the bottom tier at either end of the central segments are dramatic sculptures of Siva as the awe-inspiring Bhairava. The top of the porch is crowned with the flattened spheres typical of Orissan temples.

**The plinth** (*upana*), a few centimetres high, runs right round the base of the temple, and is decorated with a variety of friezes – elephants (estimated at over 1,700, and each different!), including wild elephants being trapped, military marches, hunting, journeys, and a variety of other animals including crocodiles and a giraffe.

**The platform** is divided into the same five horizontal layers that characterize the temple itself. These are richly decorated with creepers and scrolls, and end with tiny motifs of *chaitya* windows. Along the lower mouldings are spaced miniature temple-like façades – *khakhara-mundis* – which contain niches. Set into these are figures, often of young women – caressing a bird, washing hair, playing the *vina*. The slabs between have a variety of carvings – some are erotic, some are *nagas* or *naginis*, each with a human head but with the tail of a snake.

The middle of the platform has three horizontal mouldings at about eye level. Above this, the *upper jangha* is richly sculpted, sometimes with religious scenes such as *Mahishasuramardini* (Durga as the Goddess of destruction) and *Jagannatha*, enshrined in a temple. Other sculptures show royal courts or simple family scenes. Along the top of the platform is the verandah, consisting of two mouldings separated by a narrow recess. Though severely damaged, these are decorated with friezes.

From the platform you will see the intricately carved eight-spoked wheels, each shown with its axle, a decorated hub and an axle pin. Floral motifs, creepers and the widely shown *chaitya* windows cover the stonework. Medallions with gods such as Surya and Vishnu, erotic figures, noblemen and animals – all add immense life to the structure.

## The sanctum sanctorum

Although the *jagmohana* is now the dominant building of the complex, the scale of the sanctuary is still evident. The climb up the outer walls and then down into the sanctuary itself, which is possible for the reasonably agile, allows you to see at close quarters the remarkable chlorite statues of Surya on the outer south wall and offers an almost unique opportunity to see the inside of a temple sanctuary in full light.

It is best to climb up the main eastern steps of the porch and to walk round it to the left (south) side. The east door of the porch is the best preserved. Each door jamb is divided into eight facets, all carved with a variety of reliefs. The larger than life-sized grey-green chlorite statue of Surya is in sharp contrast with the surrounding yellowish-orange *khondalite* stone. He stands on a chariot drawn by his seven horses, lashed by Aruna, the charioteer, surrounded by two four-armed gods, a pot-bellied Brahma on the right and possibly Vishnu on the left. Below them are possibly four wives of Surya.

The original approach was through the porch. Now, a flight of steps from the west end of the temple leads down into the inner sanctum. The main feature inside is the chlorite platform at the western end of the 10 m sq room intended for the presiding deity. This image from the pedestal was moved to the Jagannath Temple complex in Puri. The platform that remains is nonetheless outstanding; some carvings almost certainly show the King, the donor of the temple, accompanied by priests. The hollows on top of the platform's eastern edge resulted from the placing of pots over a long period.

## The temple grounds: the colossi

ⓘ *0600-1800, foreigners, US$ 5, video Rs 25. Official guides, Rs 75-100 per hr.* Originally each of the three staircases to the porch was guarded by a pair of colossi – rampant lions on top of a crouching elephant to the east, decorated elephants to the north, and war horses to the south. The last two pairs have been remounted a short distance from their original sites. The lions have been put in front of the eastern steps up to the *Bhoga mandira* near the entrance.

## Archaeological Museum

ⓘ *Closed Fri, 0900-1700, Rs 5, near Travellers' Lodge.* This museum has a small collection including many important pieces from the Sun Temple complex. Occasional lectures and film shows. Archaeological Survey publications for sale.

## Sleeping

**Bhubaneswar** *p701, map p702*

**AL Trident. Bhubaneswar**, CBI, Nayapalli, off NH5, T0674 2301010, www.trident-hilton.com. 70 well-furnished, recently renovated a/c rooms in hotel recently taken over by the Hilton group.

**AL-A Mayfair Lagoon**, 8B Jaydev Vihar, Nayapalli, 5 km from centre, T0674 2360101, mayfairlagoon@hotmail.com. Modern, low-level 'palace' style hotel with 63 attractive cottages set around lagoon, all facilities, very stylish, friendly efficient staff. Best of the 5-stars. Recommended.

**A Kalinga Ashok**, Gautam Nagar, T0674 2431055, www.theashokgroup.com. 32 clean rooms (4 **A** suites), all a/c, TV, hot bath, restaurant, coffee shop, bar, exchange.

**A Quality Inn Crown**, IRC Village, Nayapalli on NH5, 5 km from town, T0674 2555500, thecrown@vsnl.net. 68 comfortable a/c rooms with hot bath (tubs), double-glazed, so quiet, good pool, bar, efficient, friendly.

**A Sishmo**, 86/A1 Gautam Nagar, T0674 2433600, www.hotelsishmo.com. 72 comfortable a/c rooms, all facilities including health club and pool, good restaurant, well-run hotel, best in town centre.

**A Swosti**, 103 Janpath, T0674 2535771, www.swosti.com. 60 a/c rooms, restaurant, bar, overpriced compared to those out of town, good discounts when quiet.

**A Swosti Plaza**, P-1 Jaydev Vihar, 5 km from centre, T0674 2300008, www.swosti.com. 106 a/c rooms in distinctive hotel based on Orissan temple design, fair-sized rooms though some road noise, 3 restaurants, Scottish theme bar.

**A The New Marrion**, 6 Janpath, opposite Sri Ram Mandir, T0674 2502328, marrion@sancharnet.in. 60 a/c rooms, very spongy carpets in standard class (like moon-walking!), restaurant, bar, pool exposed to dust from road, pleasant garden being sacrificed for larger bar.

**C-D Bicky Inn**, 61 Janpath, T0674 2536435. Range of 26 small, but well-kept rooms, mostly a/c, Indian-style hotel, roof-top restaurant.

**C-E Sahara**, 76 Buddha Nagar, T0674 2313631. 25 decent, good-sized rooms with hot bath, some a/c, quiet, reasonable restaurant, friendly helpful staff. Recommended, although some reports of not being given the room you're first shown.

**D Upasana**, Cuttack Rd, behind Bhubaneswar, T0674 2314144, upanasa_bbsr@yahoo.co.in. 20 good clean rooms, some a/c, with hot bath, TV, away from main road so quieter, friendly. Recommended.

**D-E Bhubaneswar**, Cuttack Rd, T0674 2313245, www.orissaindia.com/bhubaneswarhotel. 42 rooms with bath,

some a/c, clean, good value though staff could be more helpful.
**D-E Chandrakala**, 74 Ashok Nagar, T0674 2532411. 31 small, clean rooms with bath, TV, room service (veg), handy for station.
**D-E Panthanivas**, Jaydev Marg, T0674 2432314, www.panthanivas.com. Clean, spacious rooms, hot bath, some a/c, restaurant, 0800 check out, tourist office.
**E Ekamra**, Kalpana Square, T0674 2311732. Simple, grubby rooms, though clean linen, cheap singles, restaurant, good internet café below.
**E-F Lingaraj**, Old Station Bazar, T0674 2313565. Basic clean rooms, dorm.

### Udayagiri and Khandagiri caves

*p706, map p707*

**D-E Cave View Resort**, T0674 2472288. 5 rooms.

### Puri *p709, map p709*

Avoid arriving at your hotel by rickshaw as commission will be added to the room rate. Instead, get down nearby and walk. Most backpackers stay in hotels on CT Rd towards the fishing village at the eastern end. Domestic visitors prefer the seaside resorts along Marine Drive. Most check out at 0800 and several have a 2200 curfew. Check before staying out late. Top hotels will arrange pick-up from the station.
**A Hans Coco Palms**, Swargdwar, off New Marine Dr, T06752 230038, www.hanshotels.com. 40 good sea-facing a/c rooms with balconies/terraces, palm-filled restaurant, pleasant garden, good pool, friendly staff, knowledgeable manager, book ahead in season. Recommended.
**A Mayfair Beach Resort**, CT Rd, T06752 227800, mayfair1@sancharnet.in. 34 well-furnished a/c cottages and rooms, some with sea view, rampant tropical garden, good pool (residents only), clean section of beach, good restaurants, very well run, friendly staff. Recommended.
**A-B Toshali Sands**, Konark Marine Drive (8 km), T06752 250271, www.toshalisands.com. 104 rooms (mostly suites) in cottages and villas set in attractive and extensive gardens (butterflies' paradise!), all very comfortable, 2-km walk to beach, sports facilities though pool could be cleaner, pricey restaurant with little choice nearby.
**B Nilachal Ashok** (ITDC), next to Raj Bhavan, VIP Rd, T06752 223639, www.theashokgroup.com. 34 clean, good-sized a/c rooms, TV, some with sea view, beach access via scrubby back garden.
**B Pearl Beach Club**, Sipasurabali, next to Sterling Resorts (5 km), T06752 230109. Large new resort, first of several destined to appear in this area. 224 comfortable a/c rooms with all facilities, boat service to cross river to beach.
**B-C Asian Inn Beach Resort**, New Marine Dr, T06752 231307. New hotel with 31 rooms, some a/c and suites, smallish but clean and comfortable, TV, good restaurant, well run.
**B-D Sterling Resorts**, Sipasurabali Village, 5 km west of Marine Parade by rough, sandy track, T06752 230391, www.sterlingresorts.org. 350 comfortable rooms with kitchenettes in the sprawling complex, refurbished in 2002, all facilities including decent pool, boat to beach, for domestic holidaymakers.
**C Vijoya International**, CT Rd, T06752 222702, hotelvijoya@rediffmail.com. 44 clean but dark rooms, half a/c, large garden, quiet, friendly staff, pool and health club.
**C-D Arya Palace**, CT Rd, T06752 232688, bksteels@onlysmart.com. 32 rooms (some a/c) in new hotel clean and airy, hot bath, TV, generous discounts when quiet.
**C-D Samudra**, CT Rd, T06752 222705, hsamudra@yahoo.co.in. 52 decent clean rooms, all with breezy sea facing balconies, better at front on higher floors with sea view, TV, restaurant, friendly staff.
**C-E Panthanivas** (OTDC), CT Rd, T06752 222740, www.panthanivas.com. 48 rooms including 3 **B** suites, a few a/c, rooms in old block run down, better in newer block, tour booking, pleasant garden with beach access.
**D BNR**, CT Rd, T06752 222063, bnrhotel@hotmail.com. Revamped, 34 large, clean rooms, some a/c, 1st floor better with wide verandahs overlooking sea, siestas encouraged (quiet hours 1400-1600!), an old-world curiosity, claim to serve the best continental food here, billiards, croquet, a unique choice.
**D-E Holiday House**, CT Rd, T06752 223782, F224363. 45 reasonable, good-sized clean rooms, better sea facing (prices rise with altitude!), restaurant.
**D-E Puri**, Marine Parade, T06752 222114, www.purihotelindia.com. Huge hotel on seafront with 127 rooms, including 9 and

10-bedded rooms! Popular Indian family hotel so quieter during the week, wide choice, clean, some a/c, veg restaurant.

D-E **Shankar International**, CT Rd, T06752 222696. 30 rooms with beach views, plus 6 cottages, in Indian-style hotel set around lawn, small but clean, restaurant.

D-F **Gandhara**, CT Rd, T06752 224117, F225909. Clean, comfortable rooms, some a/c, friendly, good value, cheap dorms, restaurant, popular.

E-F **Kasi's Castle**, CT Rd, T06752 224522. 9 spotless rooms with attached bath in friendly family house, good choice but avoid arriving by rickshaw (commission demanded).

E-F **Lotus**, CT Rd, T06752 223852. 9 simple rooms (mostly **F**), quite clean, good restaurant (**Harry's Cafe**, see Eating).

E-F **Love & Life**, CT Rd, T06752 224433, love&life@satyam.net.in. Good value rooms in 3-storeyed, airy building with cottages at rear, theoretical hot water, nets, dorm, very clean, good choice.

E-F **Sun Row Cottage**, CT Rd, T06752 223259. 10 simple rooms in double cottages set around small, colourful garden, restaurant, long-stay discounts.

E-F **Z**, CT Rd, T06752 222554, www.zhotelindia.com. 12 spacious rooms plus dorm in old mansion, best sea facing, terrace, some wirh clean shared bath, good food, friendly, solar-powered, pleasant garden, TV/games room, popular. Recommended, book ahead.

F **Derby**, CT Rd, T06752 223961. 10 sea facing rooms with bath, garden, popular.

F **Pink House**, CT Rd, T06752 222253. 15 rooms, some 3-5 bedded, directly on beach, friendly, popular with backpackers, beach shack restaurant (suspect hygiene).

F **Santana**, CT Rd (at end of fishing village), T06752 2226641. Simple rooms in friendly, secure hotel, popular with Japanese.

F **Youth Hostel**, CT Rd, T06752 222424. Separate, though somewhat dishevelled male and female dorms, some 2-3 bedded, camping, good Indian meals.

**Konark** *p711, map p712*

D-E **Panthanivas** (OTDC), opposite temple, T06758 236831. 11 clean rooms with nets, 2 a/c with hot bath, smaller rooms a bit dark, separate **Geetanjali** restaurant.

E-F **Yatri Nivas**, T06758 236820, F236821. 28 good value, clean rooms with nets, some 4-bedded, 8 a/c with geyser and TV, pleasant gardens, restaurant, dorm beds (Rs 30) in open-air auditorium except during festival, free cultural programme on weekend evenings during season.

F **Bijaya Lodge**, T06758 236478. Basic rooms with attached bath.

F **Labanya Lodge**, away from temple, T06758 236430. Best of the budget lodges. 13 clean rooms, mostly with attached bath, breakfast available, cycle hire, travel.

## Eating

**Bhubaneswar** *p701, map p702*

TTT **Mayfair Lagoon**, very pleasant restaurants include outdoor truck-stop style. Great Western fast food and sweets.

TTT **Quality Crown Inn**, 1970's Bollywood theme restaurant.

TTT **Sishmo**. International. Excellent food, pleasant decor.

TTT **Swosti**. Varied menu. Dimly lit, generous portions, local specialities to advance order.

TT **Banjara**, Station Square. Good Indian for lunch and dinner.

TT **Hare Krishna**, Lalchand Complex, Janpath, T0674 2503188. Strict vegetarian. Upstairs, a/c, smart, tasty food.

TT **Panthanivas**, local specialities with advance notice.

T **Atithi Bhavan**, near Lingaraj Temple.

T **Green Park**, 74 Buddha Nagar. Excellent fresh food, popular with local people.

T **New Ganguram Sweets**, Brit Market, Station Square. Delicious Indian sweets and snacks.

T **Venus Inn**, 217 Bapuji Nagar (2nd Floor). Good South Indian vegetarian.

**Puri** *p709, map p709*

There is an abundance of fresh fish; ensure all is fresh and thoroughly cooked. Hotels expect advance notice from non-residents.

TT **Chung Wah**, Hotel Lee Garden, VIP Rd, has good Chinese.

TT **Wild Grass**, VIP Rd. Pleasant open-air restaurant with rustic theme. Good North Indian veg and non-veg, some Orissan specialities, friendly. Recommended.

T **Harry's café**, CT Rd. Pure veg (no onion or garlic) South Indian. Good *thalis* and snacks.

T **Peace**, CT Rd. Friendly, good food.

**Konark** *p711, map p712*
There are plenty of cheap eating places and stalls lining the road opposite the temple entrance, serving *thalis* and snacks.

## Entertainment

**Bhubaneswar** *p701, map p702*
Programmes of Odissi and folk dances and folk drama are staged regularly and worth seeking out. **Rabindra Mandap**, near GPO and **Suchana Bhavan** near Bus Stand.

**Puri** *p709, map p709*
Top hotels and resorts have bars. Classical *Odissi* dance, folk dances and drama which are always performed for festivals are also staged from time to time and are worth seeking out.

## Festivals and events

**Bhubaneswar** *p701, map p702*
**End-Jan**: **Tribal Fair** attended by groups from different regions – excellent performances and crafts exhibitions.
**Mar/Apr**: **Asokashtami**, the **Lingaraja Car Festival**. The image of Siva is drawn on a chariot from the Lingaraja Temple to visit the Ramesvara Temple for 4 days.

**Puri** *p709, map p709*
**Feb/Mar**: **Beach Festival**, 1 week of cultural shows, crafts and food stalls.
**Mid-Apr**: 21-day **Chandan Yatra** coincides with the Hindu New Year when images of Jagannath, his brother and sister are taken out in boats on the Narendra Tank. *Chandan* is the sandal paste used to anoint the deities. **Snana Yatra**, which follows, marks the ritual bathing of the deities on a special barge. For 15 days the gods are kept out of sight, when worshippers may only pray before *pattachitras* (paintings). Every few years new images of the deities are carved from specially selected trees and the old ones are secretly buried by the temple priests.
**Jun/Jul**: **Rath Yatra**, see box on page 710.

**Konark** *p711, map p712*
**Feb**: Honouring the Sun god; pilgrims flock here from evening to sunrise.
**1-5 Dec**: **Classical dance festival** at the open-air auditorium opposite *Yatri Nivas*.

## Shopping

**Bhubaneswar** *p701, map p702*
Many shops close on Thu and take a long lunch break. Market Building shops have fixed prices.
**Khadi Gramodoyag Bhavan**, Kalpana Sq. Hand-spun cotton garments.
**Orissa State Handloom** (West Market) is recommended for saris and handloom fabrics.
**Utkalika** (East Tower) sells Orissa handloom and handicrafts.

**Puri** *p709, map p709*
Visit the vast **bazar** around the Jagannath Temple, along Bada Danda and Swargadwara, but you have to bargain. Pathuria Sahi is the stone carvers' quarter and Raghurajpur (12 km) produces *pattachitras* and etchings on palm leaf, see page 699. See also page 700.

### Books
**Loknath**, CT Rd. Second-hand, sale/exchange, library (Rs 7 per day), postcards.

### Hairdresser
**Face Beauty Parlour**, CT Rd, towards fishing village. Excellent service, including expert massage by woman owner.

### Handicrafts
Stone carvings, papier-mâché masks, painted wood figures, paintings, appliqué, hornwork make good buys.
**Akbar**, CT Rd. Cheap painted cards.
**Odissi**, Dolamandap Sahi. Handlooms.
**Sudarshan**, Station Rd. Stone carving, where you can also watch masons at work carving out images of deities.
**Sun Crafts**, Tinikonia Bagicha.
**Utkalika** and **Crafts Complex**, Mochi Sahi Sq.
**Weavers' Co-op Society**, Grand Rd. Handlooms.

## Activities and tours

**Bhubaneswar** *p701, map p702*
**OTDC**: by 'luxury' coach from Transport Unit, behind *Panthanivas*, T0674 2431299. Ask about special tours to **Chilika Lake**. Will pick up/drop from hotels. Daily tours to

Nandankanan, Khandagiri, **Udaigiri, Dhauli** and **museum** with good guide. 0900-1730 (except Mon), Rs 140. **Pipli, Konark** and **Puri.** 0900-1800, Rs 170. **Puri** and **Satpada.** 0830-1800, Rs 175. **Barkul** and **Narayani.** 0830-1800, Rs 160. **OTDC** and private operators have a/c and non a/c cars for full and half day sightseeing. A round trip by car visiting Konark and Puri from Bhubaneswar takes 6-8 hrs. Allow at least 1 hr for Konark.

**Discover Tours**, 463 Lewis Rd, T0674 2430477, www.orissadiscover.com. For special interest tours (treks, wildlife parks, tribal and textile villages), US$250 for 5-day tour. Sarat Acharya and Bijaya Pattnaik are excellent guides, very knowledgeable, US$20 per day. Can organize tours even at a day's notice, though ask ahead for full service. Highly recommended.

**Swosti Travels**, 103 Janpath, T0674 2535773, www.swosti.com. Good, but expensive, specialist tours (tribal, architectural, wildlife), though not the most welcoming.

**Puri** *p709, map p709*

Tourist Office has a list of government approved tour companies. Almost every hotel on CT Rd has a travel office.

**Heritage Tours**, Mayfair Beach Resort, T06752 227800, is reliable and offers a good benchmark for comparing prices.

**OTDC**, T06752 223526, to Konark, Dhauli, Bhubaneswar, Khandagiri, Udayagiri and Nandankanan Zoo. It is a long day. 0630-1900, Rs 130 non a/c, Rs 160 a/c. Chilika Lake (Satpada), 0630-1930, Rs 110. Private operators offer similar tours at cheaper rates, including more leisurely Konark only tours and specialized cultural trips.

## Transport

**Bhubaneswar** *p701, map p702*

**Air**

Airport 4 km. Taxi transfer, Rs 100 through OTDC. From airport Rs 100-150. **Indian Airlines**, Rajpath, T0674 2530380, airport, T2534472, www.indian-airlines.nic.in. Daily to **Delhi** and **Kolkata. Chennai** and **Visakhapatnam**, Mon, Wed, Fri, Sun. **Mumbai** and **Hyderabad**, Tue, Thu, Sat. **Air Sahara**, T0674 2535007, airport T0674 2535729, www.airsahara.net. Daily flights to **Kolkata**, 3 flights weekly to **Kolkata** and **Mumbai**.

**Bus**

**Local** City buses are cheap and cover major routes but avoid evening rush hour.

**Long distance** New Bus Stand is at Baramunda on the NH5 (6 km from centre) where there are auto rickshaws for transfer. Enquiries T0674 2354695. Some long-distance buses go through the city first, stopping at the Old Bus Stand, off Rajpath. Regular buses to **Puri** and **Konark** (both 1½-2 hrs) pick up passengers from outside the museum on Lewis Rd. Most are quite full though local people will often offer their seats to foreigners. If you choose to be noble and stand, these buses usually thin out at Pipli. Buses to **Cuttack** (1 hr) stop on the opposite side of the road.

### Taxi

Tourist taxis, unmetered, Rs 50 minimum. OTDC (Transport), T0674 2431515, cars, Rs 440, a/c, Rs 600, for 8 hrs or 80 km. Out-of-town rates are higher.

### Train

Reservations, T0674 2532350, enquiries, T0674 2532233. Computerized booking hall is in separate building opposite the station. Auto and cycle-rickshaws for transfer. **Chennai**: *Coromandal Exp, 2841*, 2040, 21 hrs; *Howrah Chennai Mail, 6003*, 0320, 25½ hrs. **Kolkata (H)**: *Dhauli Exp, 2822*, 1355, 8 hrs; *Coromandal Exp, 2842*, 0520, 8½ hrs; *Falaknuma Exp, 2704*, 1110, 8½ hrs; *Chennai Howrah Mail, 6004*, 2215, 9 hrs; *Puri Howrah Exp, 8008*, 2100, 9½ hrs; *Jagannath Exp, 8410*, 2300, 9½ hrs; *East Coast Exp, 7046*, 0505, 10½ hrs; *Tirupati Howrah Exp, 7480*, 1510, 13 hrs. **Mumbai (CST)**: *Konark Exp, 1020*, 1350, 38½ hrs. **Secunderabad**: *Falaknuma Exp, 2703*, 1540, 20½ hrs; *Konark Exp, 1020*, 1350, 21 hrs; *East Coast Exp, 7045*, 1910, 24 hrs; *Visakha Exp, 7615*, 0725, 25 hrs.

### Puri *p709, map p709*

### Air

Bhubaneswar 60 km, is the nearest airport (see page 718). Taxi to Puri around Rs 450, 1-1½ hrs.

### Bus

The huge, open bus stand on Grand Road runs regular buses to **Bhubaneswar** and **Konark**. Minibuses are faster. Also services to **Cuttack, Visakhapatnam** and **Kolkata**. OSRTC, T06752 223786.

### Bicycle and motorcycle

Either hiring a bike or a motorbike is a good option for exploring the coast. Several outlets on CT Rd. Cycles Rs 15-25 per day. Motorbikes Rs 150-250 per day.

### Cycle rickshaw

Available all over town. Bus Stand to CT Rd, Rs 15; railway station Rs 10. To prevent commission being added to room price, get dropped off at BNR and walk along CT Rd to desired hotel.

### Taxi

Tourist taxis from larger hotels and Taxi Stand, T06752 222161; Rs 550 per 8 hrs or 80 km.

### Train

Enquiry, T131. **Kolkata (H)**: *Puri Howrah Exp, 8008*, 1900, 11½ hrs; *Jagannath Exp, 8410*, 2115, 11½ hrs. **New Delhi**: *Purushottam Exp, 2801*, 2015, 32½ hrs.

### Konark *p711, map p712*

OTDC by 'luxury' coach from Puri and Bhubaneswar (65 km), or you can hire a car.

## Directory

### Bhubaneswar *p701, map p702*

**Banks** State Bank of India, Rajpath, by Police Station. Exchange on 1st floor, £ and US$ cash and TCs (closed Sun). Also at IDCO Towers, Janpath on the way to NH5. ICICI, near Shree Raj Talkies, Janpath for over the counter exchange. Separate ICICI Centre on Janpath has an ATM which can be used by Visa card holders. **Hospital** Capital Hospital, Unit 6, T0674 2401983. **Internet** At Ekamra Hotel and next to Sahara. **Post** GPO, Sachivalaya Marg. **Tourist offices** Orissa, Jayadev Marg, behind Panthanivas, T0674 2431299. 1030-1700, closed Sun. Airport counter, T0674 2534006. Rly station counter, T0674 2530715. Govt of India, B-21, BJB Nagar, T0674 2432203. **Useful addresses** Foreigners' Registration Office, Sahid Nagar, T0674 2540555.

### Puri *p709, map p709*

**Banks** Allahabad Bank, Temple Rd is best for changing cash. Andhra Bank, near GPO gives cash on Visa cards. Other exchanges on CT Rd. **Hospital** District HQ Hospital, T06752 222062. ID Hospital, Red Cross Rd, T06752 222094. **Post** GPO on Kutchery Rd. PCOs and internet on CT Rd. **Tourist office** Orissa, Station Rd, T06752 222664, 1000-1700, closed Sun) with a museum above. Tourist counter, railway station, T06752 223536.

### Konark *p711, map p712*

**Post** Sub Post Office, near Panthanivas. **Tourist office** Yatri Nivas, T/F06758 236821.

# The Northeast

*It is possible to visit several places of historic and religious interest in the north of Orissa in three to seven days, as well as to see outstandingly beautiful scenery and the Similipal National Park. Some of the accommodation is excellent value (particularly at Chandipur), though in places it is very basic.* » *For Sleeping, Eating and other listings, see pages 724-727.*

## Cuttack → *Phone code: 0671. Colour map 6, grid A6. Population: 535,100.*

Cuttack occupies an important strategic position in relation to the network of canals in the region. Situated at the head of the Mahanadi delta and surrounded by the great river and its tributary the Kathjuri, the town is almost an island, its crowded streets and bazars clustered up towards its western end.

Cuttack is one of Orissa's oldest cities and its medieval capital. It was founded by Nrupat Kesari (ruled 920-935). It remained the administrative centre until the end of the British Raj and was the state capital until 1956. The ancient **stone embankment** to the south was built in the 11th century by the Kesari ruler to protect the town from flooding by the Kathjuri River. It still stands as a reminder of the engineering skills

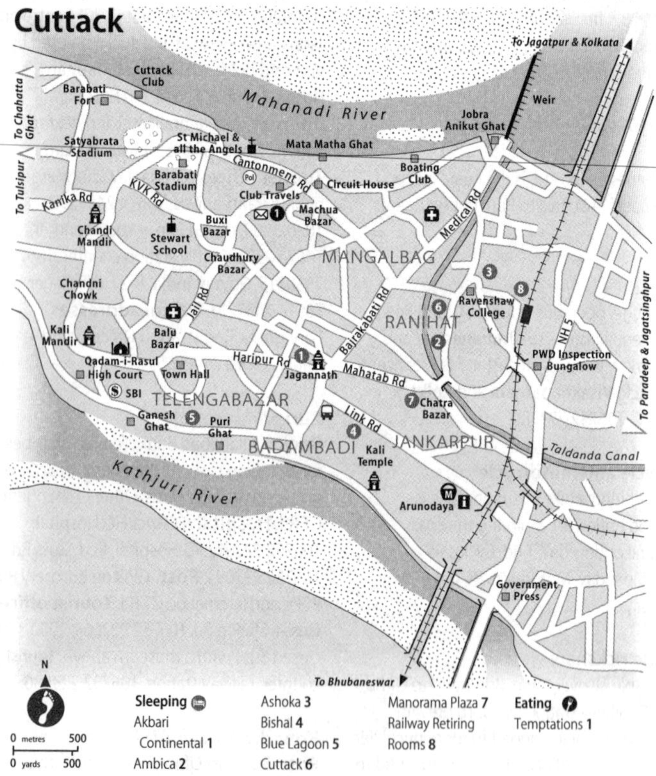

practised 900 years ago. The **Qadam-i-Rasul** (Kadam Rasul) in the centre of the old city, visited as a shrine by both Muslims and Hindus, has three 18th-century mosques with beautiful domes and a music gallery. The shrines contain relics of the Prophet Mohammad; the Prophet's footprint is carved on a circular stone. The famous silver filigree shops are nearby in Balu Bazar.

The blue granite 13th-century **Barabati Fort** to the northwest is being excavated by the Archaeological Survey. Its wide moat and a gateway are still there but the nine-storeyed palace has disappeared. Probably built by one of the Ganga rulers in the early 13th century, it was in Marhatta hands when it was taken by the British in 1803. Close to the fort is the vast **Barabati Stadium** where major sporting and cultural events are held. The **Church of St Michael and all the Angels** (CNI) by the river, typical of Raj-style church buildings, is worth a visit.

## Ratnagiri, Udayagiri and Lalitgiri → *Colour map 6, grid A6.*

The beautiful hills and rice growing lands are home to remarkable Buddhist remains of the Vajrayana sect, set in an idyllic situation surrounded by green fields. The excavations at the three sites have revealed Buddhist structures, both stupas and monasteries, as well as sculptures and Buddha images.

### Ins and outs

**Getting there** The sites can all be visited in a day from Cuttack or Bhubaneswar by car. If you go by bus you will need to stay overnight. » *See Transport, page 726, for further details.*

**Getting around** Rickshaws can be hired at Patharajpur.

### Ratnagiri → *70 km from Cuttack, 115 km from Bhubaneswar.*

ⓘ *Museums, Sat-Thu, 1000-1700, foreigners US$2.*

Ratnagiri, the site of the 'Jewel Hill', on the bank of River Keluo, has produced the best finds. The extensive remains show excellent sculptural skill combining different coloured stones, from blue-green chlorite to the purple-red garnets encrusted in brownish silver khondalite. The finds include three monasteries (two quadrangular), eight temples and several stupas believed to date from the seventh-century. The largest monastery (No 1) is 55 m sq with a surrounding verandah with 60 pillars built around a courtyard entered through a carved gateway. At one end a shrine has a khondalite Buddha image and remnants of about two dozen cells for monks which were built of brick but had stone door frames. Look for the intricate carving on the doorway of the back porch wall: a dancer stamping her feet; a royal lady with her arm around a maid; a woman meditating. The seventh-century University of *Pushpagiri* may have flourished here; Hiuen Tsang, the Chinese traveller, after his visit in AD 639 described it as one of Orissa's two Buddhist centres of learning. Four galleries display fine sculptural figures dating from the ninth-10th centuries, terracotta and ivory objects, inscribed copper plates and miniature bronzes produced by the lost-wax process.

### Udayagiri → *10 km south of Ratnagiri.*

ⓘ *Foreigners US$2.*

Excavations by the Archaeological Department (in progress in mid-2001) have unearthed better preserved carvings including the door jambs to the sanctum. The monastery, within a large compound, has 18 cells with a verandah arranged around a courtyard. The 3-m Lokesvar Buddha image here has an eighth-century inscription on it. Further up the hill, fragments of sculpture have been excavated among the ruins.

### Lalitgiri

ⓘ *Foreigners US$2.*

The site about 3 km south of Bandareswar village was first excavated by the ASI in 1985. Large architectural remains including a 20-m high apsidal temple have been found together with sculptures and decorated door jambs. A stone platform with inscriptions dates this site closer to the second century although Kushana Brahmi inscriptions on an underlying brick stupa suggest Buddhist occupation around the first century BC. Three caskets were also found, two of which contained stone, silver and gold caskets with preserved relics inside. The caretaker will open the small museum. There is a stone-carvers' village at the base of Lalitgiri which traces its connections back to ancient times and produces excellent pieces of sculpture.

## The coastal towns

### Paradeep → *94 km from Cuttack on the NH5A.*

Paradeep is a port at the mouth of the Mahanadi River. Some 2,500 years ago Orissan sailors regularly set sail for Indonesia and mainland Southeast Asia from this point. Thousands of giant Pacific Ridley turtles migrate from as far afield as South America yearly to lay their eggs but now many face their death as they approach the shore, see box page 723. Visitors today find they can't escape industrial pollution even here – "a layer of black dust settles on every surface in no time". There are a few overnight options. Regular buses arrive from Cuttack and Bhubaneswar.

### Baleshwar

Northeast from Bhubaneswar, this medieval maritime trading port was first established by the British in 1642 with subsequent competition from the French who called it *Farasidinga* and the Dutch *Dinamardinga*. Ruins of **Dutch tombs** can still be seen and traces of **canals**, up which ocean-going ships were hauled inland. The Khirachora Gopinath Temple is at Remuna (9 km) and Panchalingesvar Temple, 30 km away.

### Chandipur

Chandipur, 16 km from Balashwar, on the coast has one of Orissa's finest beaches. The tide recedes 5 km daily and the dunes and casuarina groves make it particularly attractive and a pleasant, quiet stopping place. When the tide is in, scores of fisherfolk trawl for small fish along the coast. About 3 km north of *Panthanivas* is the fishing harbour at Balarama Gadi where fresh fish can be bought daily. The occasional explosions that can be heard come from the missile testing site nearby, on the road to Baleshwar.

## Mayurbhanj District

The district is thickly forested with hills, waterfalls and streams and is the home of much of India's wildlife which can now be seen at Similipal. There are prehistoric sites at Kuchai and Kuliana. The historic sites are Khiching, Baripada and Haripur, where the Bhanja rulers have left their mark.

The area produces excellent tussar silk, carvings in multi-coloured translucent serpentine stone (from Khiching) and tribal metal casting of toys and cult images. The tribal people have enriched the culture of the district particularly with their traditional dances. Accommodation throughout the district is very basic.

## Turtles in peril

Virtually every species of mangrove is found in the mangrove forests in the Bhitarkanika Wildlife Sanctuary, north of Paradeep, but their swamps are better known for their estuarine crocodiles, water monitors, cobras and above all Olive Ridley turtles (*Lepidochelys olivacea*), which have mysteriously arrived each year in vast numbers to lay eggs on a 10 km stretch of Gahirmatha beach.

Sea turtles are believed to return to nest where they hatched so the cycle continues. They arrive at night, for a fortnight around the full moon from October to May, with a spectacular *arribadas* (Portuguese 'the coming') in February, when record numbers find their way from the Indian Ocean or from Australia, via the Pacific. They lay their eggs in nests excavated in the sand, a safe distance above the waterline and shed a salty 'tear' afterwards. The eggs hatch about two months later, the incubation temperature deciding the sex; clutches are male around 24-26°C and female around 30-32°C, mixed when temperatures are in between.

The turtles compete for food with the fishermen and already thousands have met their death when trapped by their nets.

### Haripur → *16 km southeast of Baripada.*

Haripur was founded by Maharaja Harihar in 1400 as the capital of the Bhanja Dynasty. A later king built the magnificent **Rasikaraya Temple** which, though now in ruins, is a unique example of a brick-built Orissan temple. The area is still fascinating as it has several other historic buildings nearby. The ruins of Ranihamsapur, the inner apartment of the queen, is to the north of the courtyard while the remains of the Durbar Hall with its beautiful sculptured stone columns and arches is to the east. The brick-built **Radhamohan Temple** and 14th-century **Jagannath Temple** are architecturally interesting although the deities were moved and are now worshipped in **Pratapapur** nearby.

### Baripada

The district headquarters has a **museum** to the east of town with a small collection of stone sculpture, coins, seals, terracottas and inscriptions (summer 0700-1200, winter 1000-1700, closed Monday and holidays). **Chhau dance festival,** known as **Chaitra Parba,** in mid-April; the **Rath Yatra** in July is unique because the chariot carrying *Subhadra* is drawn by women.

### Similipal National Park → *Colour map 3, grid A6.*

*ⓘ Rs 100 (foreigners); vehicle charge, Rs 100; camera fee, Rs 50. Video cameras are only allowed with prior written permission from Chief Wildlife Warden, Bhubaneswar. Malaria prophylaxis is strongly recommended. Entry is from Pithabata, near Baripada (NH5), or Jashipur (NH6). Entry permits from the Range Officer, Pithabata Check Gate or the Assistant Conservator of Forests, Khairi, Jashipur, T06797-232474. Some tour operators in Bhubaneswar can make all the arrangements (eg Discover Tours) but need 4 weeks notice – otherwise try for a permit on the day with a local agent (try Ambika in Baripada, see Sleeping). Day visitors 0600-1200, those with reservations 0600-1400. All must leave before sunset. Best time to visit: Nov to Feb (park open 1 Nov-15 Jun); May to Jun can be very hot. Temperature, 45-5°C. Rainfall, 2,000 mm.*

 Similipal is Orissa's principal wildlife sanctuary covering 2,750 sq km at the heart of which is one of the country's earliest tiger reserves. The area has majestic sal forests interspersed with rosewood and flowering trees, expanses of grassland, waterfalls, gorges and river valleys. Spend two to three days to make the visit worthwhile.

The 42 species of animals include tiger (99), elephant (449), leopard (119), wolf, chital, sambar, deer, gaur and flying squirrel. There are over 230 species of birds including mynahs, parakeet and peacocks. To view the park's inhabitants, open jeeps or Tata Sumos (more comfortable, though enclosed), are the usual choice of vehicle inside the park (Rs 1,200-1,500 for up to five). Jeep hire can be arranged through the Forest Office, Jashipur, Baripada Tourist Office or **Ambika** (see Sleeping in Baripada) which can also help to arrange accommodation. However, logging disturbance and dense vegetation make viewing difficult and is further hindered by noisy visitors (who ignore the 'Silence' signs). and there is an increasing problem of littering in the park. Visitors are allowed to go to the waterfalls, the **Chahala woodland** and **Nawana valley**, in the core area, on the dedicated forest road. The **Barehipani waterfall** with a drop of 400 m, and the **Joranda Falls**, 150 m, are both very impressive as are the **Bachhurichara grassland** where you might see a herd of elephants and the 1,158 m peak of Meghasani. However, most of the larger wildlife prefer to remain further inside the core area which does not allow visitors.



## Khiching → *20 km west of Joshipur along the NH6.*

The capital of the **Bhanja** rulers in the 10th-11th century, a visit to Khiching can be combined with an excursion to Similipal from Chandipur (see above). The local deity **Kichakesvari**, once the family goddess of the Mayurbhanj royal family, has a unique temple built entirely of chlorite slabs. The reconstructed 20th-century temple, which has fine carvings, is believed to have used the traditional temple building skills which date back to the eighth century. Nearby there are a number of other temples built in the Kalinga style, some of which are still in use.

## Sleeping

**Cuttack** *p720, map p720*

B **Akbari Continental**, Haripur Rd, Dolmundai, T0671 2423251. 60 rooms, central a/c, hot bath with tubs, balconies view of garden obscured by ugly extension, inefficient reception, all a bit tatty.

B-C **Blue Lagoon**, Ring Rd, near Puri Ghat, T0671 2631884, F2611936. Central a/c, cramped singles, river views, overpowering blue decor, decent restaurant and fast food corner, overly helpful staff, newish but showing signs of wear, plush in design though not in execution.

D **Manorama Plaza**, Mahatab Rd, T0671 233 1681. 54 clean, reasonable though small rooms, most a/c, restaurant, quiet area, travel desk, bizarre 'birdsong' door bells.

D-E **Ashoka**, Ice Factory Rd, College Square, T0671 2647509, ashok@dte.vsnl.net.in. 50 clean rooms, half a/c with hot bath, chaotic reception but rooms OK once allocated! Restaurant, taxi service, handy for trains.

D-F **Ambica**, Pilgrim Rd, College Sq, T0671 2610137, hotelambica@yahoo.com. Range of rooms from a/c to cheap singles with shared bath, clean and simple, friendly manager, veg restaurant, close to railway.

E **Bishal**, Link Rd, Badambadi, T0671 231 0993. 15 rooms (4a/c), quite comfortable and clean, hot bath, TV, handy for bus station but suffers from road noise.

E-F **Railway Retiring Rooms**. 4 rooms (1 a/c), cheap dorm (Rs 25).

F **Cuttack**, College Rd, T0671 2610766. Basic, but serviceable, some with bath.

*For an explanation of the sleeping and eating price codes used in this guide, see inside the front cover. Other relevant information is found in Essentials pages 56-61.*

**Ratnagiri, Udayagiri and Lalitgiri** *p721*
**F Panthasala**, Patharajpur, Cuttack T0671 2312225. Simple rooms, caretaker may provide a meal with advance notice.

**Baleshwar** *p722*
**B Torrento**, Januganj, 4 km from centre near NH5, T06782 263481. 28 comfortable rooms, some a/c, recently renovated, good restaurant, exchange, pool and health club.
**C-F Sahadevkhunta**, close to bus stand (turn left), T06782 262657. Wide range of rooms with bath, some a/c, restaurant/bar.
**E-F Railway Retiring Rooms**. A/c and non a/c rooms, dorm (Rs 30).

**Chandipur** *p722*
Other hotels on the main road are reluctant to accept foreigners.
**D-E Panthanivas** (OTDC), on the beach, T06782 270051, www.pathanivas.com. 33 rooms, a few a/c, dorm (Rs 70), nets, ISD/internet facility, decent food, helpful staff, better in newer block, ample mosquitoes and cockroaches in old block closer to beach. Conducted tours including Similipal (minimum 10 people).
**D-E Shubnam**, T06782 270025. 29 rooms (6 a/c), clean, friendly, nets, better maintained than Panthanivas.
**E Chandipur**, T06782 270030. Small, simple rooms with attached bath, clean linen, nets.

**Baripada** *p723*
**D-E Ambika**, Roxy Rd, T06792-252557. 20 reasonably clean rooms, some a/c, friendly and helpful staff, decent restaurant, tour of Similipal arranged, good value.
**D-E Mohapatra**, opposite Bus Stand, T06792-255226. 8 simple rooms, some a/c, bit grubby, balconies overlook the bus stand.
**D-E Sibapriya**, Traffic Square, T06792 255138. 20 rooms, 'best in town' but non a/c rooms grubby, a/c better, restaurant.
**E-F Ganesh Bhavan**, Main Market, T06792-252784. 32 basic rooms, some with bath.

**Similipal National Park** *p723*
**D Camp Polpola Retreat**, inside the park, www.pugmarks.org, can be booked through Pugmarks, 10 Meher Ali Rd, Kolkata, T033-2873307, who organizes tours to Simlipal.
**E Forest Rest Houses**, though the booking process is complicated and all food provisions should be taken with you. The caretaker at each will help you to cook a meal. Most rooms have several beds and average out at around Rs 200-400 per head for foreigners if full, otherwise it can work out quite expensive. Maximum stay is 3 nights. Those at **Chahala** (an old hunting lodge, 35 km from Jashipur), **Nawana** (60 km), **Joranda** (72 km) and **Barehpani** (with view of waterfall, 52 km) must be booked through Field Director, Similipal Tiger Reserve Office, PO Bhanjpur, Baripada, 757002 Orissa. Write enclosing a self- addressed envelope (minimum 30 days and maximum 60 days before proposed date of stay) and include names of group members, sex, age, nationality, visa/passport details. You will hear about method of advance payment. Rest Houses at **Badampahar** (16 km from Jashipur), **Gudgudia** (25 km), and **Jamuani** (25 km), though not in the core area, are easier to reserve, in person, up to 10 days in advance from DFO, Karanjia, Jashipur, T06796-220226. Reservation counter open 1000-1330 every day.
**E-F Aranyanivas** (OTDC), at Lulung (3 km from Pithabata Gate). 8 double rooms, two 12-bed dorms, restaurant (only one inside park), completely run on solar power.
**Panthasala**, outside the park area, 35 km from Baripada towards Jashipur, has 4 double rooms. Reserve both through Tourist Officer, Baripada or www.panthanivas.com.

**Khiching** *p724*
**Inspection Bungalow**, contact Executive Engineer, PO Baripada.
**Revenue Rest Shed**, PO Khiching, contact Dist Magistrate, PO Baripada.

## Eating

**Cuttack** *p720, map p720*
Outside the better hotels there is little to attract the gourmet. In the evenings street stalls set up around Buxi Bazar for cheap bites.
**Temptations**, near Buxi Bazar, has the best and safest ice creams in town, also reasonable pizzas and snacks.

## Entertainment

**Cuttack** *p720, map p720*
You can try a makeshift pedalo on the Mahanadi River. **Mahanadi Boating Club**

(2 men, a few chairs and an umbrella), on Ring Rd, charge Rs 15 per person per half hr. Also power boat at Rs 550 per hr.

## Shopping

**Cuttack** *p720, map p720*
**Utkalika**, Jail Rd, has a very good selection of textiles and handicrafts including horn and brass objects and jewellery. The famous silver filigree shops are in Nayasarak and Balu Bazar.

## Activities and tours

**Cuttack** *p720, map p720*
**Club Travels**, Mani Sahu Chowk, Buxi Bazar, T0671 2304999.

## Transport

**Cuttack** *p720, map p720*
**Bus**
Long-distance buses stop at the Bus Stand in Link Rd. Services to all points in Orissa from the main bus stand in Badambari. Regular services to **Bhubaneswar**. Also state transport to major towns in **Andhra Pradesh**, **Chhattisgarh**, **Madhya Pradesh** and **West Bengal** (including Kolkata).

**Taxi**
At railway station and some hotels. Full day trip to **Lalitgiri**, **Ratnagiri** and **Udayagiri** (excluding entrance fees), Rs 600-800, depending on bargaining skills.

**Train**
East of town. **Bhubaneswar** and **Puri**: Several express and passenger trains, but timings can be unreliable, so quicker to take bus. **Chennai**: *Coromandal Exp, 2841*, 2000, 21½ hrs; *Howrah Chennai Mail, 1935*, 0230, 26½ hrs. **Kolkata (H)**: *Dhauli Exp, 2822*, 1425, 7½ hrs; *Coromandal Exp, 2842*, 0600, 7½ hrs; *Falaknuma Exp, 2704*, 1150, 8 hrs; *Jagannath Exp, 8410*, 2345, 9 hrs; *East Coast Exp, 7046*, 0550, 10 hrs. **New Delhi**: *Purushottam Exp, 2801*, 2225, 30½ hrs. **Secunderabad**: *Falaknuma Exp, 2703*, 1500, 21½ hrs; *East Coast Exp, 7045*, 1830, 24 hrs.

**Ratnagiri, Udayagiri and Lalitgiri** *p721*
It is possible to do a day excursion from Cuttack or Bhubaneswar by car (Rs 800). Get to Chandikhol on NH5 (43 km), with some roadside eating places and turn right on NH5A (towards Paradeep) and then take the first turn left (at '12 km', before Patharajpur). Udayagiri is 1.5 km west of the road (8 km from NH5A) and Ratnagiri, 10 km further north. Return to the NH5A and continue towards Paradeep passing the Patharajpur **Panthasala** (Rest House) on the right. Turn right (south) at '20 km' for Lalitgiri which is 5 km away. Alternatively, buses from Cuttack stop at Chandikhol where you can hire a car for a 85 km return journey. Or take another bus towards Patharajpur hire a rickshaw and visit the first 2 sites.

**Baleshwar** *p722*
**Bus**
Bus Stand is on Sahadevkhunta Rd with services to all major towns, though few to **Chandipur**.

**Train**
Railway station is 500 m from Bus Stand, on the main Chennai-Kolkata line.
**Bhubaneswar** (spelt **Balasore** in timetables): best is *Dhauli Exp, 2821*, 0946, 3½ hrs. **Chennai**: *Coromandel Exp, 2841*, 1707, 24½ hrs; *Howrah Chennai Mail, 6003*, 2325, 29½ hrs. **Kolkata (H)**: *Coromandel Exp, 2842*, 0907, 4½ hrs; *Falaknuma Exp, 2704*, 1457, 4½ hrs; *East Coast Exp, 7046*, 1025, 5½ hrs. **New Delhi**: *Rajdhani Exp, 2421*, 1232 (Wed, Sun), 21½ hrs; *Purushottam Exp, 2801*, 0145, 27 hrs. **Puri**: *Jagannath Exp, 8409*, 2240, 6½ hrs. **Secunderabad**: *Falaknuma Exp, 2703*, 1202, 24½ hrs.

**Chandipur** *p722*
There are only 4 or 5 **buses** per day to/from **Baleshwar**. Ask at Panthanivas for approximate timings. Ask for Rs 170 for a **taxi** to/from **Baleshwar**.

**Baripada** *p723*
Private and government **buses** serve all major towns in the region. **Jeeps** are available for hire to visit Similipal. Ask at

**Ambika** (see Sleeping) or the tourist office. The nearest train stations are at Baleshwar (Balasore) and Tata Nagar.

**Similipal National Park** *p723*
The road from Baripada is via Lulung, 30 km west, which has a regular bus service. The nearest train stations on the Southeastern Railways are at Tatanagar and Balasore.

**Khiching** *p724*
Regular buses from Baripada, 150 km. Nearest train station is 96 km away, but it is better to get down at Balasore, 210 km, which has a fast service on the Southeast Railway.

## Directory

**Cuttack** *p720, map p720*
**Banks** State Bank of India, near High Court, exchanges £ and US$ TCs and cash. Forex on first floor. **Hospital** Christian Mission Hospital, recommended. Private clinics on Medical Rd. **Internet** 3 on Jail Rd next to Rajtarangiri Cinema. Decent connections, Rs 25 per hr. **Tourist office** Orissa, Arunodaya Market Building, Link Rd, T0671 2312225. Railway Station Counter, T0671 2610507. Both have helpful staff.

**Baleshwar** *p722*
**Banks** State Bank of India, Branch, near ITT, 3 km from the railway station; the only bank authorized to deal in foreign exchange between Cuttack and Kolkata, so come prepared! **Tourist offices** Orissa, SPA Marketing Complex, Block B, Station Square (at end of Station Rd, immediately opposite to the left, 1st floor), T06782 262048. Railway Station Counter, platform 1. T263123.

**Baripada** *p723*
**Banks** Nearest foreign exchange is at Baleshwar. The Central Co-op Bank paints a list of its top ten defaulters on the wall outside! **Tourist office** Baghra Rd, near Bus Stand, T06792 252710. **Tiger Reserve Office**, Bhanjpur (2 km), T06792 252593, simitig@dte.vsnl.net.in. **Useful services** There is a District Hospital, post office and shops selling local handicrafts and handloom.



# Western Orissa

*Settled in ancient times, Ptolemy's text of the second century refers to this area as a diamond trading centre. In the eighth century King Indrabhuti became a Buddhist and a preacher of the Vajrayana sect.* » *For Sleeping, Eating and other listings, see page 729.*

## Sambalpur and around → *Phone code: 0663. Colour map 6, grid A5.*

Sambalpur is a pleasant, small town with a number of decent hotels and a few restaurants grouped in the centre. The presiding deity Samalesvari to whom a temple was built here by the Chauhans in the mid-16th century probably accounts for the town's name. The district is famous for its textiles, particularly its tie-and-dye *ikat* work.

The villages and the countryside are pleasant in themselves and you might consider visiting **Baragarh**, 1½ hours, and **Barpali**, three hours' drive, with a guide, if you are interested in weaving. **Sonepur**, a lively small town with a colourful market square and temple, is particularly rewarding. A scenic road from Sambalpur along the Mahanadi River ends in a footpath down across the wide sandbank over half the river in the dry season. Small boats ferry passengers across the remainder.

**Debjharan Sanctuary** has been recently created and developed as a picnic spot in forest situated 35 km south of Sambalpur, 5 km east of the NH6. There is a small waterfall and a dam with waterhole at Chaura Asi Mal and a Forest Rest House. Taxis from Sambalpur cost Rs 300-400 for a return day trip.

## Ushakothi → *48 km east of Sambalpur on the NH6.*

Ushakothi Wildlife Sanctuary is densely forested and covers 130 sq km. The sanctuary has wild elephant, leopard, tiger, bison, wild boar and *chital* (barking deer). The best time to visit is from November to June, at night. Take a guide with search lights and see the wildlife from the watch-towers sited near watering points to which the animals come. Open hooded jeeps are recommended. Permits to visit, and guides, from the Forest Range Officer, PO Badrama. **Forest Rest House,** Badrama, 3 km away, is very basic with no electricity; on site ask for Choudhary Babu, Dealing Clerk, between 1000-1600.

## Hirakud Dam

The Mahanadi created enormous problems every year through devastating floods of the delta region and in order to combat these the Hirakud Dam was built about 20 km northwest of Sambalpur. The key section is a 1,100 m long masonry dam, with a further earth dam of over 3,500 m. One of the longest mainstream dams in the world, it is over 60 m high and drains an area twice the size of Sri Lanka. Since its completion in 1957 there have been no serious floods in the Mahanadi delta and allows the irrigation of vast areas of high quality land. You get an excellent view from the revolving tower, Gandhi Minar at one end of the dam. Contact the Deputy Superintendent of Police, Security Force, Hirakud before visiting. There are regular buses from Sambalpur.



## Debrigarh Wildlife Sanctuary

This sanctuary adjoins Hirakud Lake, around 50 km from Sambalpur. With an area of 347 sq km, the dry deciduous forest is home to tiger, leopard, sloth bear, chital, sambar, nilgai and a number of resident and migratory birds. Muggar crocodiles and freshwater turtles are amongst the reptiles present. Entry to the sanctuary is at Dhodrokusum, with a watchtower at Pathedurga. There are basic **Forest Rest Houses** at Dhodrokusum and Dechua, or a **Tourist Cottage** at Chaurasimal. The best season to visit is from October to May. For permission and guides, contact DFO (Wildlife), Motijharan, T0663-2402741. For information contact Chief Wildlife Warden (Orissa), Bhubaneswar, cwlwob@hotmail.com.

## Huma → *About 32 km south of Sambalpur.*

Huma has a famous **Leaning Temple**, on the bank of the Mahanadi, dedicated to Lord Siva. The temple leans southwards but the pinnacle is vertical. The colourful Kudo fish, easily seen from January to June, are believed to belong to Siva so are never caught by fishermen; visitors may feed them grain. Country boats are available for hire. There are regular buses from Sambalpur to Huma Chowk, then walk 2 km to the temple.

## Sundargarh District

To the north of Sambalpur is Sundargarh District. In the tribal heartland, it is an area of undulating hills with the richest deposits of mineral wealth in the state. Cave paintings are evidence of the existence of early man. Once relatively untouched by modern civilization, the district was chosen for the siting of the first public sector steel plant at Rourkela. The route from Sambalpur to Rourkela runs north, 192 km, passing through some glorious scenery. The Brahmani flows along a wide rocky and sandy bed, a torrent in the monsoon, with forested hills on either side. A large industrial town girdled by a range of hills and encircled by rivers, **Rourkela** was selected for its prime position as a steel plant in 1955 which has a Fertilizer Complex attached to it. The power for the steel plant comes from Hirakud. Both may be visited with permission from the PRO. There are banks, post offices, shops and hospitals.

## Sleeping

**Sambalpur** *p727*

**C-D Saket**, T0663 2402345. 30 decent, clean rooms with hot bath, TV, some a/c, restaurant.

**C-D Sheela Towers**, VSS Marg, T0663 2403111, F2403456. 41 clean, comfortable though smallish rooms, TV, 2 restaurants.

**D-E Panthanivas** (OTDC), Brook's Hill, end of VSS Marg, T0663 2411282, www.panthanivas.com. 24 rooms (half a/c with TV), restaurant, bar, clean linen, all rooms with balconies but few with decent views.

**D-E Uphar**, T0663 2403078. Slightly cheaper sister concern of **Uphar Palace**.

**D-E Uphar Palace**, T0663 2400519. 29 good clean rooms with attached bath, some a/c, TV, 2 restaurants (good South Indian).

**D-F Li-n-ja**, near Ashoka Talkies, T0663 2521301. Clean rooms, grubby building.

**F Rani Lodge**, next to **Uphar Palace**, T0663 2522173. Clean, simple rooms with bath, nets.

**Hirakud Dam** *p728*

**E Ashok Nivas**, good guesthouse at one end of the dam.

**Sundagarh District** *p728*

**B Mayfair Garden**, Panposh Rd, 3 km from Rourkela, T0661 2520001, rkl_mayfair@sancharnet.inl. Touted as a 'farm resort', 18 comfortable rooms, decent restaurant, pool.

**D Radhika**, Bisra Rd, opposite railway station, Rourkela, T0661 2510300, F2523196. 60 large rooms, reasonably clean, helpful staff.

**D-E Panthanivas** (OTDC), Sector 5, 2 km from Rourkela, T0661 2643280, www.panthanivas.com. 17 rooms, mostly a/c, restaurant/bar.

## Activities and tours

**Sambalpur** *p727*

Providing jeeps and taxis for sight-seeing: **Nalini Travels**, Buddharaja, near flyover, and **Swati Travels**, near Ashoka Talkies.

## Transport

**Sambalpur** *p727*

**Bus**

Sambalpur has 2 bus stands, one for government buses, the other for private buses near Laxmi Talkies. Both are within a short cycle-rickshaw ride from VSS Marg, though the latter has more regular services to major towns in the area.

**Jeep/taxi**

Jeep/taxi hire is the easiest way to visit wildlife sanctuaries. See Directory for travel agents or contact tourist office. Return jeeps to **Debjharan**, Rs 300-400; to **Ushakothi** (1600-0400), Rs 500.

**Train**

Sambalpur has 2 stations, Khetrajpur and Sambalpur Rd. Both are between 2-3 km from the hotels on VSS Marg. **Kolkata (H)**: *Koraput Howrah Exp, 8006*, 1640, 13 hrs. **Puri** (via **Bhubaneswar**): *Tapaswini Exp, 8451*, 2220, 9½ hrs (6½ hrs).

**Sundagarh District** *p728*

**Bus**

Rourkela's New Bus Stand is within walking distance of hotels on Bisra Rd. Turn right and right again. Government and private buses to all major destinations in the region.

**Train**

Rourkela's station is 1-min walk from Bisra Rd and hotels. **Kolkata (H)**: *Shatabdi Exp, 2022*, 1405, 7 hrs; *Ispat Exp, 8112*, 1240, 8 hrs. **Mumbai (CST)** : *Gitanjali Exp, 2860*, 1930, 26 hrs. **Patna**: *South Bihar Link Exp, 3287*, 1425, 18 hrs. **Puri** via **Bhubaneswar**: *Tapaswini Exp, 8451*, 1910, 12½ hrs (10 hrs); *Utkal Exp, 8478*, 1800, 16 hrs (12½ hrs).

## Directory

**Sambalpur** *p727*

**Bank** State Bank of India, near Collectorate, for foreign exchange.

**Post** Main post office, near Collectorate. Several internet cafes on VSS Marg (Rs 20-25 per hour). **Tourist offices** Orissa, at Panthanivas, T0663 2411118. Very helpful staff, worth a visit to plan excursions. Railway counter at **Khetrajpur**, T2521661. Tours are often cancelled due to lack of passengers.

# Southern Orissa

## Chilika Lake → *Colour map 6, grid A5 and B5.*

ⓘ *Boats, 1½ hrs, Rs 20. Nalabana bird watching trip, Rs 120, 4 hrs. Book 2000 night before, pay 0730 on day and wait until the boat is full.*

Chilika is the largest brackish water lake in Asia (1,100 sq km) stretching across the Khurdha, Puri and Ganjam districts, and forms an enormous lagoon as it is joined to the Bay of Bengal with a narrow mouth, a sandy ridge separating it from the sea. The lake is the winter home of migratory birds, some flying great distances from Iran, Central Asia and Siberia. During the winter months, from November to February, you can watch white bellied sea eagles, ospreys, golden plovers, sandpipers, flamingos, pelicans, shovellers and gulls. The lake attracts fishermen who come in search of prawn, mackerel and crab. Some ornithologists blame the growth in prawn farming, as well as the increasing discharge from rivers, silting and salinity for reduced bird numbers. The large Nalabana Island (Reed Island) sanctuary is often under water.

*Mosquitoes can be a problem here.*

The **Kalijai Temple** stands on one of the tiny rock islands. Weekends get very crowded. **Satpada**, on the other side of the lake, has a Tourism Complex.



## Ganjam District → *Colour map 6, grid B5.*

Ganjam District, south of Chilika Lake, takes its name from the Persian '*Ganj – Am*', meaning granary of the world, a testimony to its agricultural fertility. Still largely covered in dense forest, it was settled in prehistoric times and came under the influence of Emperor Asoka's rule. The handicrafts of the region include brass and bell-metal ware, hornwork, wood carvings, silks and carpets. » *For Sleeping, Eating and other listings, see pages 732-734.*

### Ganjam

Ganjam was the District Headquarters, but the administration was moved to Chatrapur because of its unhealthy location. Its chief interest is the small East India Company fort and a Christian cemetery at the north end of town, near a large factory between the main road and the sea. An interesting excursion inland takes you to Aska (52 km) and Bhanjanagar (85 km).

### Berhampur

A trading centre for silk fabric, Berhampur is the major commercial town of the District. The **Thakurani, Jagannath** and **Nilakanthesvar Siva temples** ⓘ *near DIG Residence, summer 0700-1400, winter 1000-1700, closed Mon and Government holidays*, are worth visiting. It is also a good place to shop for silks. The museum has a collection of sculpture, anthropological and natural history specimens; no photos.

### Gopalpur → *Phone code: 0680.*

Gopalpur was an ancient sea port from which early settlers from Kalinga sailed as far as Java, Bali and Sumatra. Then it was a port for the export of Aska sugar and 'coolie' labour to the Assam tea gardens. Later still it became a popular seaside resort for the British offering a beautiful sandy beach. Today, however, it has a rather faded feeling and appearance. Sand dunes, groves of coconut and casuarinas separate the small town from the beach, while the backwaters, creeks and lagoons give some variety.

A red and white lighthouse opens to visitors briefly each afternoon; there are good views but photography is not allowed. 

### Taptapani

Water from the very hot sulphur springs discovered at Taptapani in a forest setting, 50 km from Berhampur, is channelled to a pool for bathing. There is a shrine to goddess Kandhi inside the original *kund* (pool) as it is believed to cure infertility – tribal women come to the hot water pool near the **Panthanivas hotel** (D-E) to try to pick up a seed pod from the mud at the bottom. Direct buses leave from Berhampur, 50 km away, and Bhubaneswar, 240 km away.

### Chandragiri

In the tribal hills, 32 km south of Taptapani, Tibetan carpet weavers have settled in a refugee colony at Chandragiri. The temple and Buddhist prayer flags lend a distinctive atmosphere. You can watch weavers and craftsmen at work; good prices.

### Jaugada → *35 km north of Berhampur.*

Jaugada in the Malati Hills is famous for one of **Asoka's 'Kalinga Edicts'** (see Dhauli above) which was discovered in the early 19th century, but the shelter was built only in 1975. Emperor Asoka's doctrine of conquest through love instead of the sword and his declaration "All men are my children" appear here. Sadly, some parts of the inscriptions have disappeared. The old fort (circa sixth century) contains stone images of the five *Pandavas* which are worshipped in the Guptesvar Temple. Jaugada is reached by a jeep road from Purusottampur which has buses from Berhampur.

**Buguda**, a few kilometres away, has the Viranchinarayan Temple with its beautifully carved wooden *Jagamohan* and murals depicting stories from the epic Ramayana. Also, close by, **Buddhakhol** has Buddhist sculptures and shrines to Siva.



## Tribal areas → *Colour map 6, grid B3.*

Orissa's rich tribal heritage has survived among the hills and forests across the districts of Koraput, Kandhamal, Kalahandi, Ganjam, Keonjhar, Dhenkanal and Mayurbhanj. The state government is actively promoting tourism in some of these areas, see page 697. It is best to book a tour at least a month ahead to allow time to get permits to visit tribal territories. Without permits, tours are restricted to roadside villages where development programmes are already changing traditional values and in some cases the influx of tourism has created a disappointing 'circus' effect, with demands of money for photos, dances and sweets for the children. With permits and a guide, it is possible to visit the more isolated villages. Individual visitors face difficulties from the local police, so it is best to take a guide in any instance. Always seek out the village chief for permission to enter a village. Photography is prohibited in Bondo and Dongariya territories. Permission should always be asked before taking photographs of tribal people. Respect their privacy should they decline. Walking around settlements with a video camera glued to the eye is not appreciated. Away from the main towns accommodation is very basic and some camping is necessary when trekking. Transport is usually by non-a/c car, jeep or minibus. Foreign exchange is only available in Sunubeda so it is best to change money in advance.

### Tribal markets

Typical 'Social Interest' tours offered by travel agents include a number of tribal villages with a chance to attend interesting festivals and markets. Some of the tribes seen in these areas may include Dongariya Kondhs, Dhurubas, Parajas, Koyas,

 Bondos and Gadabas. In Koraput District, **Ramgiri**, 70 km southwest of Jeypore, has a very picturesque Tuesday market where Kondh people come to sell fresh vegetables and baskets and to buy salt. **Nandapur**, 44 km south of Koraput. Brings tribal ladies to the colourful Wednesday market where they sell beedi leaves and large almond-flavoured seeds. **Ankadeli**, 90 km southwest of Koraput, has a Thursday market where Bondo women, clad entirely in bead, come to sell handloom fabric, beads and exquisite woven grass headbands. **Rayagada** has some good accommodation. Sleeping and eating also available at **Laxmipur** and **Baliguda** (see page 732).

## Jeypore → *Phone code: 06854.*

Jeypore itself is unspoilt by tourism and the scenery around is very beautiful. There are several monuments including a fort and palace. It is quite possible to organize your own tour from Jeypore and reportedly easier to get permits to visit tribal areas in Koraput rather than in Bhubaneswar.

## Koraput

Koraput is a useful base for visiting the tribal areas. There is a small tribal **museum** ⓘ *closed Wed, 1500-1700, Sun 1000-1600*, although you may need a guide to understand the exhibits. There are large modern Jagannath Temples (Hindus only) where large galleries of images are reproduced from shrines. The Orissa Coffee Planters' Association, located around 20 km from Koraput, are happy to show visitors around the plantation which has fruits and spices as well as coffee.

## Kotapad → *46 km northwest of Jeypore on N43.*

The clean area of weavers' houses in Kotapad has large pots of cotton and tussore silk soaking in natural dyes, while keins hang drying. Weavers are happy to show you work in progress. The Co-op ensures even pricing – Rs 350-600 buys a 3-m shawl. It is worth seeking out award winner Jagabandhu Samarth. As the word gets around, weavers will find you to show their pieces but there is no pressure to buy.

## Sleeping

**Chilika Lake** *p730*

**D-E Panthanivas** (OTDC), 1 km from road end, Barkul, T06756- 220488, www.panthanivas.com. 20 small rooms, some a/c, bar, restaurant, tourist office, boating complex, 0800 check out, busy at weekends/holidays.

**D-E Panthanivas** (OTDC), Rambha, T06810-278346, www.panthanivas.com. 11 rooms, some a/c, half-rate for day visitors 0900-1700.

**E-F Yatri Nivas**, Satpada, north side of the lake, closest to Puri, T06752-262077. Attractive location, decent rooms. Best 1st floor for views and balconies.

**F Shree Khrishna Lodge**, Barkul (500 m from Panthanivas), T06756-221195. Simple, clean rooms, some with bath.

**Berhampur** *p730*

Few visitors stay overnight, preferring to head on to Gopalpur. However, if arriving late, the following are adequate:

**C-E Hotel Radha**, near the Old Bus Stand, T0680 2222341. 45 rooms, some a/c.

**C-E Radha Hotel**, close to railway station on Station Road, T0680 2211283, radhahotelbam@rediffmail.com. 28 rooms, 7 a/c.

**D-F Udipi**, near the Old Bus Stand, T0680 222 2196.

**F Gitanjali**, close to railway station, T0680 2204822.

**F Puspa**, Gatekeeper's Square, 1½ km from the New Bus Stand. Basic.

**F Railway Retiring Rooms** and dorm.

**F Ranjan**, Gatekeeper's Square, 1½ km from the New Bus Stand. Basic.

**Gopalpur** *p730*

**AL Oberoi Palm Beach**, T0680 222021, pbeach@sancharnet.in. Renovated with 18 rooms around gardens, good restaurants, bar, private beach, sports facilities, run like a British country house, relaxing.

**C-D Sea Pearl**, T0680 2242556. Decent, albeit pricey rooms with bath and TV, all with balcony though some face the building next door.
**D Song of the Sea**, next to lighthouse, T0680 2242347. Clean, light and airy rooms in family run hotel, peaceful location, simple restaurant, best at front on first floor with sea view, pleasant though pricey.
**D-E Green Park**, T0680 2242016, greenpark 016@yahoo.com. 17 clean rooms (some a/c), simple Indian-style hotel, best with sea view, 24-hr check out.
**D-E Holiday Home**, T0680 2242049. Simple rooms, some with TV, clean bath and linen, small singles, restaurant, large terrace overlooking sea.
**D-E Panthanivas** (OTDC), T0680 2242088, www.panthanivas.com. 15 stuffy rooms in run-down building, 2 a/c with TV, mosquito-infested dorm, restaurant.
**D-E Sea Side Breeze**, T0680 2242075. Only hotel right on the beach, 14 clean rooms, food on order, ideal for backpackers.
**E Mermaid**, T0680 2242050. Good, clean breezy rooms, better on 1st floor with sea-facing balconies, one of best, food not so.
**F Heaven Spot**, Rewu St, T0680 2243274. 5 small, basic but clean rooms with attached bath, away from beach, serves as a base.
**F Nataraj**, T0680 2242340. 10 simple rooms, away from beach, attached bath, food sold.
**F Rosalin**, T0680 2242710. 9 very basic rooms, some with attached bath, small garden, food on order, friendly but prepare for mosquitoes.
**F Sai Tourist Lodge**, T0680 2242041. 6 basic rooms in family house with attached or shared bath.

**Rayagada** *p732*
**C-D Sai International**, JK Rd, T06856 2225555, has 40 good, comfortable rooms, several a/c, TV, hot bath, restaurant, bar, staff not used to foreigners but excellent value.
**E-F Jyoti Mahal**, Convent Rd, T06856 2223015, 25 reasonably sized rooms with bath, bit grubby but friendly, good restaurant.
**E-F Swagath**, New Colony, T06856 2222208, 44 clean rooms, good local style restaurant.

**Laxmipur** *p732*
**Hotel Konark**, green building by Ambedkar Chowk. Good *thalis*, friendly young English speaking owner. Good lunch stop.

**Baliguda** *p732*
Baliguda is basically a one-street town, a quiet, friendly place with a slow pace of life.
**F Santosh**, off Main Road, with 16 rooms, best on the 1st floor with attached bath.

**Jeypore** *p732*
**C Hello Jeypore**, East Octroi Check Post, NH43, 2 km centre, T06854 2231127, hellojeypore@yours.com. Best in town though noisy area, 30 comfortable, well-furnished a/c rooms overlooking lovely garden, hot power shower in mornings, TV, efficient service, excellent restaurant (try *alu raita*). Recommended.
**D-E Princess**, near Bus Stand, NH43 (corner of Main Rd), T06854 2230027, princessco@ vsnl.com. 40 reasonable rooms, some a/c, hot bath, TV, cheaper singles, good restaurant, accommodating staff, well run.
**D-F Madhumati**, NKT Rd, T06854 2240307. 30 large rooms, some a/c, TV, mosquitos, restaurant, bar, very helpful manager.
**F Roseland Lodge**, T06854 2230639. Very cheap rooms (all under Rs 75), common bath, basic but friendly.

**Koraput** *p732*
**E-F Ambica Heavens**, T06852 2251136. Decent rooms with bath, TV, quiet at back.
**E-F Athithi Bhavan**, T06852 2250610. Managed by the Jagannath Temple Trust, simple rooms with bath, TV, temple food, can be noisy.

## Eating

**Jeypore** *p732*
**Girija**, Main Rd. Good chicken and Chinese.
**Hello Jeypore**, see Sleeping, excellent food.
**Kasturi**, *thalis*.
**Princess**, see Sleeping, reasonable but dark.

**Koraput** *p732*
**Dolphin's Plaza**, below Ambica Heavens, is worth a try for meals.

## Activities and tours

**Jeypore** *p732*
**Discover Tours**, see Bhubaneswar. Highly recommended.
**Perfect Travels**, Rajmahal Chowk, T06854 2421856. Car and driver, Rs 850 per day.

**Travel Care**, Sardar Patel Marg, T06854 2422291, F2423286. For tours write to Mr Pujari 4-6 weeks in advance with a photocopy of the relevant passport pages.

## Transport

### Chilika Lake *p730*

Chilika Lake is easiest to reach by road (NH5) from Barkul, 6 km south of Balugaon or Rambha at the south end of the lake.

#### Bus

Buses from **Bhubaneswar** and **Berhampur**. Satpada at the northern end can only be reached via **Puri** from where there are plenty of day trips offering 'dolphin safaris'.

#### Ferry

OTDC motor launches are available from Barkul, Rambha and Satpada although during the week it may not be cost effective. Dolphin watching is the main focus of boats from Satpada. Private country boats are also available at Barkul and Rambha.

#### Train

Slow passenger trains on the Chennai-Kolkata line stop at **Balugaon**, **Chilika**, **Khallikote** and **Rambha**.

### Berhampur *p730*

#### Bus

The Old and New Bus Stands are about 3 km from the railway station, 2 km from each other. Government buses use the Old Bus Stand, private buses (which are more regular and reliable) the New Bus Stand and cover major towns in Orissa and neighbouring states. Several buses to Bhubaneswar a day, Rs80, 4 hrs on good road.

#### Train

On the main Chennai-Kolkata line. Berhampur is referred to as **Brahmapur** in timetables. **Chennai**: *Coromandel Exp, 2841*, 2340, 18 hrs; *Howrah Chennai Mail, 6003*, 0645, 22½ hrs. **Kolkata (H)** via **Bhubane- swar**: *Coromandel Exp, 2842*, 0230, 11½ hrs; *Falaknuma Exp, 2704*, 0805, 11½ hrs; *Chennai Howrah Mail, 6004*, 1855, 12½ hrs; *East Coast Exp, 7046*, 0140, 14½ hrs; *Tirupati Howrah Exp, 7480*, 1115, 16½ hrs. **Secunderabad**: *Falaknuma Exp, 2703*, 1850, 17½ hrs; *Konark Exp, 1020*, 1645, 18 hrs; *East Coast Exp, 7045*, 2240, 20 hrs; *Visakha Exp, 7615*, 1025, 21½ hrs.

### Gopalpur *p730*

Regular private buses from New Bus Stand, Berhampur (Rs 6, 30 min).

### Jeypore *p732*

#### Bus

Night buses from Berhampur.

#### Car

If travelling by car from the coast, make sure the car can manage the hill roads and the driver is not worried about entering tribal areas.

#### Train

The station is 7 km away. A daily train connects with Vishakhapatnam. From Vizag, *Kirandol Exp*, 0745, 8 hrs. Superb views for first 3 hrs uphill then down to Araku Valley; 2nd class is full of firewood and farm produce and so best avoided. From the north, travel to Vizianagaram station, and from there by bus (or taxi).

### Koraput *p732*

Trains to **Bhubaneswar**: *Hirakhand Exp, 8447*, 1130, 10 hrs. From Bhubaneswar, *Hirakhand Exp, 8447*, 2120, 14½ hrs. **Kolkata (H)**: *Koraput Howrah Exp, 8006*, 0415, 25 hrs.

## Directory

### Chilika Lake *p730*

A post office, a Govt dispensary and a tourist office at Barkul, T06756 2220855.

### Berhampur *p730*

**Bank** State Bank of India, Main Branch, State Bank Rd, changes foreign cash and TCs. **Tourist office** New Bus Stand, 1st floor, T0680 2280226. Railway station counter, T2203870. **Useful services** Christian Mission Hospital, post offices and shops.

### Koraput *p732*

**Bank** Sunabeda, 18 km away. State Bank of India, the only one in the area. **Tourist office** Orissa, Koraput Club, T06852-2240318.

# Bihar and Jharkhand

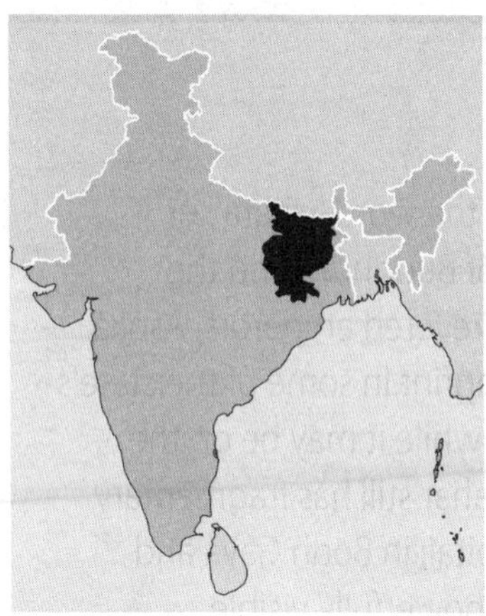



## Footprint features

# Introduction

Bihar, which takes its name from the word 'vihara', or monastery, was the early home of Buddhism and the birthplace of one of India's most revered emperors, Asoka. His Buddhist legacy has left its imprint in some of the state's most visited pilgrimage sites, for while it may be on the outskirts of modern Patna, Kumrahar still has fragmentary remains of the early Mauryan capital; in Bodh Gaya and Nalanda, Buddhism's tradition is powerfully visible.

After the creation of the new state of Jharkhand modern Bihar is confined to the densely populated, and desperately poor, Ganges plains. The state has a chequered recent political history. Separated from Bengal in 1912, in 1936 another partition led to the creation of Orissa. After Independence the reorganization of Indian states saw the transfer of territory from Bihar to West Bengal, while the tribal groups had already begun to campaign for a separate state for the tribal areas of the Chota Nagpur plateau in South Bihar. On 15 November 2000 this dream was finally achieved with the division of Bihar into two, the Chota Nagpur plateau becoming the new state of Jharkhand.

## ★Don't miss...

1 **Sonepur Fair** One of Asia's most remarkable cattle fairs, which takes place in November, page 743.

2 **Kolhua Asoka Pillar** Take the very pleasant 5-km walk at Vaishali to one of the only two Asoka pillars that remain in situ, page 743.

3 **Nalanda** Visit the impressive ruins here, possibly the site of the world's oldest university, page 746.

4 **Bodh Gaya** This place can resemble a medieval encampment as pilgrims from all over the world visit one of the holiest Buddhist pilgrimage centres, page 751.

5 **Sher Shah's mausoleum** The tomb, at Sasaram, appears to float in an artificial tank; the area around is a great place for relaxing, page 753.

6 **Parsnath Hill** Join pilgrims at 0400 and climb the hill to catch superb views of the sunrise and surrounding countryside, page 758.

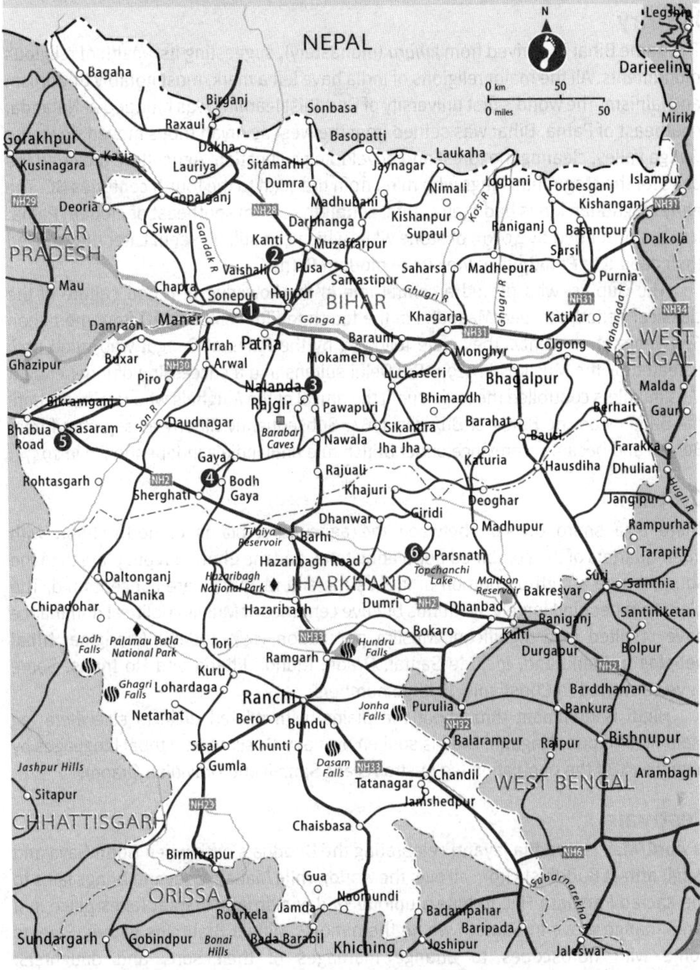

# Background → *Population: Bihar 82.88 mn, Jharkhand 26.9 mn. Area: Bihar 174,000 sq km, Jharkhand 65,000 sq km.*

## The land

Bihar and Jharkhand form a region of transition. The wet lowlands to the east give way to the much drier and now more prosperous alluvial plains to the west. From north to south, the two states stretch 600 km from the foothills of the Himalaya across the flat plains to the forested and mineral-rich hills of Chota Nagpur (now in Jharkhand). The River Ganga runs through the heart of the plains, joined by its tributaries from the Nepal Himalaya to the north and from the Vindhyan Hills of the Peninsula to the south. To the north of the Ganga are the scars of old river beds which often form chains of lakes during the monsoon and provide a vital source of fish. North Bihar is India's biggest producer of freshwater fish, over half of which is sold to Kolkata. Torrential rain in the Himalayan foothills and the flatness of the Ganga valley floor cause some of the rivers, like the Kosi, to flood catastrophically. Over a period of 130 years the Kosi has moved over 110 km westwards.

## History

The name Bihar is derived from *vihara* (monastery), suggesting its wealth of religious monuments. All the major religions of India have left a mark, most notably Buddhism and Jainism. The world's first university of Buddhist learning was founded at Nalanda, southeast of Patna. Bihar was settled from the west as Aryan tribes moved down the Ganga valley, clearing the forest and developing cultivation. Agriculture provided the base for the Magadhan kings who ruled from the sixth to the fourth centuries BC. The early Magadhan kings had their capital at **Rajgir**, 100 km southeast of modern Patna. It was surrounded by 40 km of stone walls which can still be seen. Later they moved their capital to **Pataliputra**, the site of modern Patna.

The Guptas, who played a central role in the flowering of Hindu culture of the classical period, rescued Magadha in the fourth to fifth centuries AD from more than 600 years of obscurity. They were followed by the Palas of Bengal who ruled until defeated by the Muslims in 1197. The Delhi sultans and a succession of independent Muslim rulers controlled the region until the arrival of the Mughals who retained it until the British won the Battle of Buxar in 1764. Subsequently Bihar was separated from Bengal and became a province under British rule until India's independence in 1947.

## Culture

There is a sharp division between the agricultural plains of north Bihar, with three-quarters of the combined population total, and the Chota Nagpur plateau to the south, where a high proportion of India's mineral resources are concentrated. The plains are peopled largely by Hindus but five centuries of Muslim political dominance have resulted in a significant Muslim population (14% today). Aboriginal **tribal peoples** in Jharkhand, include Santal, Oraon, Munda Kharia and Ho tribes. Some have converted to Christianity in large numbers.

Hindi is dominant throughout the plains, with related dialects elsewhere (eg Maithili, Bhojpuri, Magahi). Urdu is spoken by many Muslims, and tribal languages by nearly 10% of the population (eg Austro-Asiatic Santali and Dravidian Oraon).

## Festivals

In **April/May** is **Buddha Jayanti** celebrating the Buddha's birth when Bodh Gaya and Rajgir attract Buddhists from all over the world, while **Mahavira Jayanti** brings Jains to the sacred Parsnath Hill. In **June** a unique 14-day **marriage market** takes place in a large mango grove in Saurath where the nation's Mithila Brahmins gather. Parents come with horoscopes to arrange marriages of their sons and daughters.

### Bihar's plains: gift of the Himalaya?

Severe flooding of Bihar's rivers has prompted some environmentalists to blame deforestation in Nepal. Rising population, commercial logging and bad agricultural practices have been held responsible for widespread damage on Bihar's plains. But recent research sheds doubt on this apparently simple cause and effect. For one thing, the River Kosi has been shifting its course for decades, and floods have washed down silt from the Himalaya for centuries. Without them the plains would not exist. To limit damage from the Kosi, a protective embankment along the southern flank of the Himalaya was built in 1960 to limit the flooding and westward movement of the river, and to protect agricultural land. Attempts to control the Kosi by building dams in Nepal are still under consideration, but the very large amounts of silt, plus the fact that the Himalayan foothills are a zone of major earthquakes, makes projects extremely difficult to implement effectively. To the south of the Ganga is another stretch of alluvium, much shallower than that to the north of the river and about 150 km wide. When the Ganga is in full flow it is higher than the tributaries which join it from the south, so it is also subject to severe floods between July and October. The alluvium barely covers the ancient rocks of peninsular India which form the Chota Nagpur plateau, emerging in broken hills to the south. There is beautiful open parkland scenery in Chota Nagpur itself, much of the original forest having been cleared.

**October/November** has **Pataliputra Festival** starting with **Dasara** in October and ends with the Sonepur Fair. **Durga puja, Dasara** and **Diwali** are celebrated. **Chhath** or **Surya Puja** takes place six days after **Diwali.** To mark the harvest, fresh paddy, sweets and fruit are offered by devotees in procession; women, waist deep in the Ganga, offer homage at sunrise and sunset. **Sonepur Fair** is the scene of one of Asia's most remarkable cattle fairs in November.

## Food and drink

The typical Bihari meal consists of boiled rice, unleavened bread, lentils and vegetables cooked with hot spices. *Sattoo*, a combination of grains, is made into a dough and eaten either as a savoury, or a sweet when mixed with sugar or jaggery. The mixture can also be taken as a drink when mixed with milk or water and flavoured with cardamoms and cloves. *Puri-aloo*, deep fried Indian bread with potatoes cooked with onions and garlic, and *kachoris* made with wheat and lentil flour and served with *kala chana* (black gram), are tasty snacks.

## Modern Bihar

From its pre-eminent position in the culture and politics of early and classical India, Bihar has declined today to one of India's poorest and most badly administered states. There are periodic outbreaks of caste-based violence in the countryside, notably in Jharkhand. Many of the tribal peoples have been under pressure from agricultural settlers from the plains. Often in desperation the poor have moved to cities like Kolkata and Mumbai, or to work on tea estates.

Bihar is one of the most troubled political administrations of modern India. Successive governments have been charged with corruption and maladministration, and it is widely regarded across India as the most lawless state in the country. Since the mid 1990s the state government has been run by Laloo Prasad Yadav and his wife Rabri Devi, currently at the head of the Rabri Janata Dal (RJD).

Laloo Prasad had been forced out of office in 1997 as a result of corruption charges, to be replaced as Chief Minister by his wife Rabri Devi, who served three terms as Chief Minister. Elections held in February 2005 produced no clear results; at the time of writing the state is under presidential rule until some sort of ruling coalition can be formed, a situation which should be resolved by mid-2005.

# Patna

→ *Phone code: 0612. Colour map 3, grid B5. Population: 1.4 mn.*

*Despite its size, Patna, Bihar's straggling capital, in its more attractive areas has the air more of a semi-rural provincial town. However, it is one of India's poorest cities, stretching along the south bank of the Ganga for about 15 km. Divided in two by the large open Maidan, the central city is crowded, dusty and has little of architectural interest. Scant evidence remains of its earlier wealth and political supremacy. Thousands sleep on the streets and there are few street lights at night. However, around the station food stalls are neatly set out and illuminated, and it can be interesting to take a cycle-rickshaw round by day or night. Many tribal people come into the town, often working on roads or building sites.* » *For Sleeping, Eating and other listings, see pages 744-746.*

## Ins and outs

**Getting there** Patna airport, 7 km from town, has coaches and taxis for transfer. Long-distance State buses arrive at the Gandhi Square Bus Stand, which is between 15-25 minutes' walk from most budget hotels. These are strung out down Fraser Road towards Patna Junction railway station and Vir Kunwar Singh (Hardinge) Bus Stand (serving Gaya, Varanasi and Nepal). » *See Transport, page 745, for further details.*

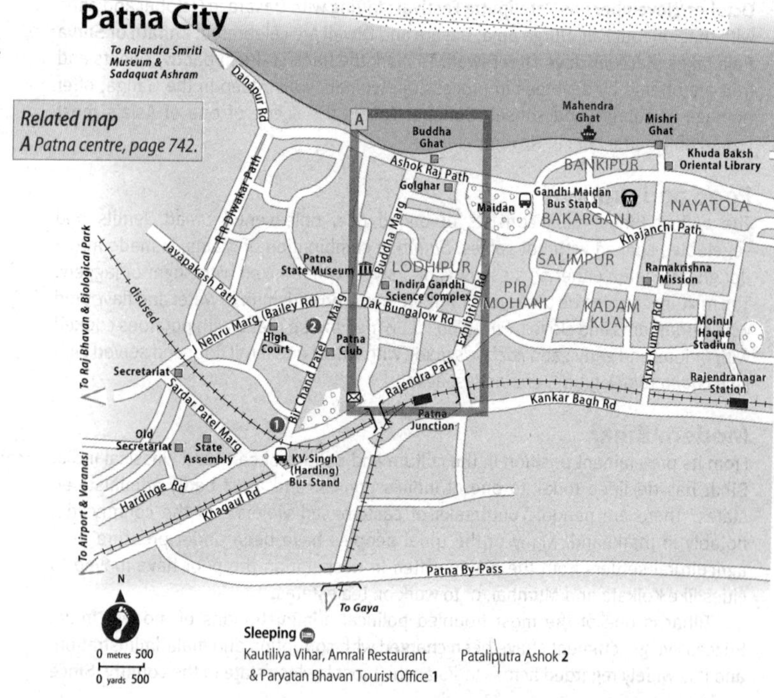

**Getting around** The centre of Patna is compact enough to walk around, though autos and cycle rickshaws are easily available. For longer distance trips you can hire unmetered taxis from major hotels.

## History

At the confluence of the rivers Son, Punpun, Gandak and Ganga, Patna's history can be traced back 2,500 years. Ajatasatru, the second Magadha king who ruled from Rajgir, built a small fort at Pataligrama. Later Chandragupta Maurya founded the Mauryan Empire with Pataliputra as its capital. Buddhist histories suggest that it was here that Asoka usurped the throne of his father, Bindusara, murdering all his rivals and starting a reign of terror, before a conversion eight years later. It marked the beginning of perhaps the greatest reforming kingship the world has known. The Greek ambassador Megasthenes was deeply impressed y the efficiency of the Chandragupta administration and the splendour of the city. Ruins can be seen at Kumrahar, Bhiknapahari and Bulandhi Bagh with its 75 m wooden passage. Excavations date the site back to the pre-Mauryan times of 600 BC. In the 16th century the Pathan Sher Shah Suri established the foundations of a new Patna, building a majestic mosque in 1540 which dominates the skyline.

# Sights

Patna's buildings reflect its administrative and educational functions. The Collectorate, Court and educational institutions are all close to the river bank in the western part of the city as are the Raj Bhavan, the High Court and the better residential quarters. To the east is Old Patna with its bazars, old mosques, Har Mandir and St Mary's Church.

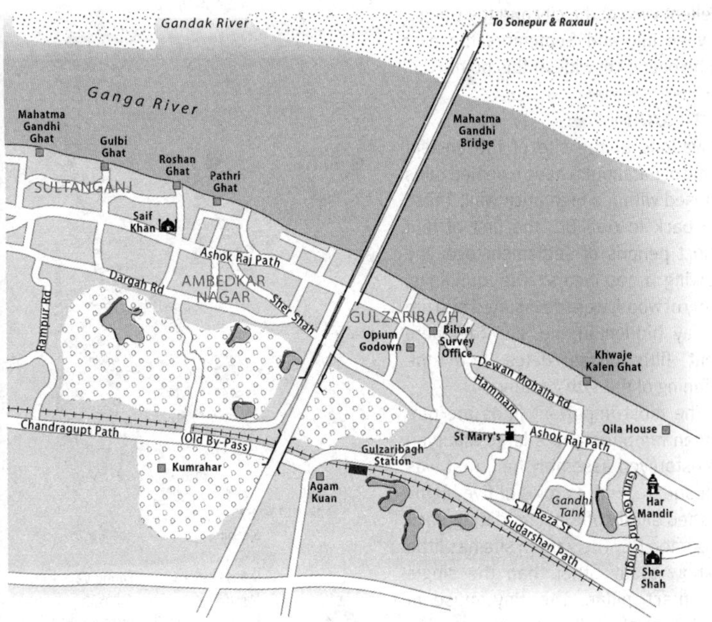

## The central area

**State Museum** ⓘ *closed Mon, 1030-1630, Buddha Marg*, has a collection of coins, paintings, terracotta, bronze and stone sculptures including the famous Mauryan Didarganji Yakshi (circa 200 BC), Jain sculptures (second, third centuries) and finds from Bodh Gaya, Nalanda etc. The presentation is uneven, with scarcely any labels and some moth-eaten exhibits. However, the first floor gallery is well lit with a collection of terracotta heads from the third century BC; the mezzanine floor has an interesting collection of Tibetan *thangkas*. **Indira Gandhi Science Complex**, corner of Buddha Marg and Bailey Road, includes a planetarium. Just to the east of the centre is **Khuda Baksh Oriental Public Library** (1900), which has one of the largest private collections of books and rare Persian and Arabic manuscripts, Rajput paintings and the only books rescued from the Moorish University of Cordoba, Spain. It is now a national library.

## Golghar

The *Gola* (round house), an extraordinary ovoid dome between the Maidan and the Ganga, was built of stone slabs in 1786 by Captain John Garstin of the Bengal Engineers, who planned this grain store for the army in case of a repeat of the 1770 famine. It has a base 125 m wide, where the wall is 3.6 m thick, with two brick staircases that spiral up the outside; the workforce were to carry the grain upatone and descend by the other. It was never completed so the last line of the inscription "First filled and publicly closed by ..." remains unfinished. Sometimes, it is possible to go inside and listen to the remarkable echo. It is well worth climbing the steps for an excellent view of the city and the Ganga. Between July and September the river can be over 5 km wide at this point.

## Kumrahar

Excavations at the site of the ancient capital of Pataliputra have revealed ruins enclosed within a high brick wall. These date back to 600 BC, the first of four distinct periods of settlement over the following 1,200 years. The buildings, mainly of wood, were devastated by a fire and lay hidden in the silt. The more recent fifth phase dates from the beginning of the 17th century.

The most important finds are rare wooden ramparts and a large Mauryan three-storeyed assembly hall, that was 77 m square, with 15 rows of five highly polished sandstone pillars dating back to 400-300 BC. The garden site has little to show today other than the single 6-m intact pillar. The tiny museum has its small collection of valuable finds almost invisibly shut away in a dark room.

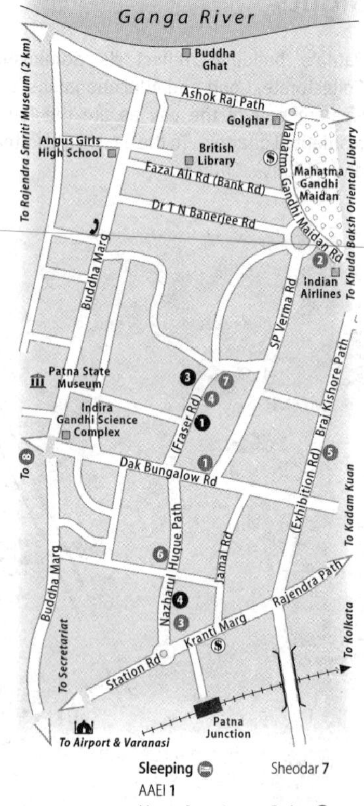

## Gulzaribagh

About 8 km east of the Golghar near Kumrahar, at Gulzaribagh, are the former East India Company's principal opium *godowns* (warehouses), now a Government printing press. The three long buildings with porticoes on each side were strategically placed by the river for boats to carry the opium down to Kolkata. The old *godowns*, ballroom and hall are open to visitors.

## St Mary's Church

St Mary's or Padri-ki-Haveli (Priest's House, circa 1775) is the oldest Christian church in Bihar. The fine 'Raj' cemetery alongside has gravestones dating back to 1760; some were connected with the opium trade. Now overgrown, it can still be worth exploring.

## Har Mandir and around

Har Mandir is in the Chowk area of old Patna. The *gurudwara* built by Maharaja Ranjit Singh is the second of the four great *takhts* (thrones) of the Sikhs and consecrates the birthplace of the 10th Guru, Gobind Singh, in 1660. The shrine of white marble with kiosks on the terrace above has a museum on the third floor.

**Jalan Museum** ⓘ *get prior permission from the owner, Mr BM Jalan, Hira Pl, Dak Bungalow Rd, Patna 1, T0612 2225070, quilahouse@hotmail.com*, in in Quila House , is across the road from Har Mandir. The private house was built over the ruins of Sher Shah's fort and is a museum containing Chinese paintings and a valuable collection of jade and silver filigree work of the Mughal period.

**Saif Khan's Mosque** (Pathar-ki- Masjid), on the river bank, was built in 1621 by Parwez Shah, the son of the Mughal Emperor Jahangir.

# Excursions

## Sonepur → *Colour map 6, grid A4.*

Near its confluence with the Gandak, 22 km across the Ganga, Sonepur has a station on the Northeast Railway. Sonepur witnesses Asia's biggest cattle market which begins on the full moon of the Hindu month of **Kartik Purnima** (October/November). The two-week fair draws thousands to the magic shows, folk dances, contests of skill and stalls selling handicrafts and handlooms. Mark Shand's *Travels on my Elephant* gives a colourful account of the fair. Elephants – as well as camels, horses and birds – are still bought and sold at this fair but numbers are dwindling. Bihar Tourism sets up a Tourist Village a week before the Fair and Swiss Cottage Tents are furnished and have attached baths.

*Sonepur and Vaishali can both be visited comfortably in a day. You can hire a taxi or take a tour.*

## Vaishali → *Colour map 3, grid B5.*

Vaishali – derived from King Visala, from the *Ramayana* – dates back to the sixth century BC when it was a flourishing city of the Lichchavis, reputedly one of the first cities in the world to adopt a republican form of government. This is where the Buddha preached his last sermon and announced his approaching Nirvana. A century later, in 383 BC, it was the venue of the second Buddhist Council, when two stupas were erected. Jains of the Svetambara sect believe that Mahavir was born in Vaishali in 599 BC. Today, the district is part of the Mithila region famous for Madhubani paintings on the walls of village houses.

The **Asoka Pillar** at **Kolhua**, also known as Bhimsen-ki-Lathi (stick), is a single 18 m piece of very highly polished red sandstone with a bell-shaped inverted lotus capital and a life-sized lion carved on top. Asoka pillars (*stambhas*) were unornamented, with a circular section that tapered like the trunk of a palm tree. They may have been forerunners of temples developed from the ancient form of worshipping in the forest. This is one of two Asoka pillars that remain in situ. The 'Wheel of Law' which tops many of the pillars – and appears on the Indian flag – is the mark of the social and political order laid down by the Emperor.

**Ramkund** is also known as Monkey Tank since it was thought to have been dug by monkeys who offered the Buddha a bowl of honey. The two Buddhist **stupas** are said to hold urns containing the Buddha's ashes; the second was only excavated in 1958. The ancient **Coronation Tank** (*Kharauna Pokhar*) contains holy water which was used for anointing the ruler of Vaisali at his coronation. The **Lotus Tank** nearby is thought to be a picnic spot of the sixth century BC.

A very pleasant, easy 5-km walk from the **Tourist Bungalow** to the Asoka Pillar takes you through picturesque villages, passing the Japanese stupa, the museum and an old small stupa.

## Sleeping

**Patna** *p740, maps p740 and p742*

Some streets have been renamed – Bir Chand Patel Path (or Marg) has replaced Gardiner Rd. Some old names continue to be used, eg Bailey Rd (J Nehru Marg), Fraser Rd (Nazharul Huque Path), Exhibition Rd (Braj Kishore Path).

**A Maurya Patna**, Fraser Rd, S Gandhi Maidan, T0612 2203040, maurya@sanchar net.im. 80 centrally a/c rooms and suites, modern, best in town. Pool (Rs 150 per day non-residents).

**B Pataliputra Ashok** (ITDC), Bir Chand Patel Path, T0612 2226270, patashok@bih.nic.in. 45 rooms (half-day rates), good restaurant, travel, tourist office.

**C Rajasthan**, Fraser Rd, T0612 2225102. 20 rooms some a/c, good veg meals, very welcoming.

**C Republic**, Lauriya Bagh, Exhibition Rd, T0612 2320021, lawlysen@sancharnet.in. 35 a/c rooms, dining hall (very good veg meals), exchange, roof garden.

**C-D Satkar International**, Fraser Rd, T0612 2220551, F2220556. 50 rooms, minimal maintenance, good restaurant.

**D-E Kautiliya Vihar** (Bihar Tourism), Bir Chand Patel Path, T0612 2225411, F2210242. 44 rooms, some a/c, dorm beds (Rs 50), restaurant, exchange, travel.

**E Mayur**, Fraser Rd, T0612 2224149. Basic and clean rooms, some with bath, good restaurant.

**E Sheodar**, Fraser Rd, T0612 2227210. 15 fairly clean rooms, some a/c.

**F AAEI**, Dak Bungalow Rd. 1 room with bath, good value, worth trying even if you are not a member.

Avoid Railway Retiring Rooms.

## Eating

**Patna** *p740, maps p740 and p742*

Hotels on Fraser Rd and Ashok Rajpath usually have a restaurant.

TTT **Pataliputra Ashok**. International. Good food, excellent kebabs, poolside barbecue, but slow service.

TT **Amrali**, Bir Chand Patel Path (Kautilya Vihar building). Indian vegetarian. Excellent dishes, quick service. Dimly lit but recommended.

TT **Ashok** (1st floor). Rather dark but good Indian. Good Chinese.

TT **Nalanda**, at Satkar International. Indian. Pleasant atmosphere, good food.

T **Marwari Awas Griha**. Small, busy dining hall serving excellent vegetarian thalis.

T **Mayfair**, inexpensive snacks and ice creams.

## Shopping

**Patna** *p740, maps p740 and p742*

Patna and its surrounding villages are known for wooden toys, inlay work, silver jewellery in beaten rustic style, *tussar* silk, lacquerware, leather shoes and *Madhubani* paintings. Govt emporia at **Bihar** on E Gandhi Maidan, **Khadi Gramudyog** and shops at Patna Market, New Market, Maurya Lok Complex and Boring Canal Rd. Govt **Lacquerware**, Maghalpura for lacquer on wood.

## Activities and tours

**Patna** *p740, maps p740 and p742*

**Ashok**, Hotel Pataliputra Ashok, T0612 2223238.

**TCI**, Maurya Hotel, T0612 2221699.

**Bihar Tourism (BSTDC)**, **Ashok Travels & Tours** and **Patna Tours**. All run City sightseeing Oct-Mar, Rajgir, Nalanda and Pawapuri, usually 0800-2200, Rs 80-100. Also to Vaishali, Bodh Gaya, Buxar and Sasaram. Buses can be slow and uncomfortable.

## Transport

### Patna *p740, maps p740 and p742*

**Air**

Transport to town, taxis, or **Indian Airlines**. Coach to City Office via some hotels, Rs 30; Tourist taxi transfers, about Rs 120 (Rs 350 deluxe). Airport enquiry, T0612 2223199. **Indian Airlines**, Gandhi Maidan, T0612 2226433, Airport T2223199, www.indian-airlines.nic.in. Daily to **Kolkata**, **Delhi**, **Lucknow**, **Mumbai** and **Ranchi**. **Sahara**, Mona Complex, East Gandhi Maidan,, T0612 2232722, airport 2211988, www.sahara.net, to**Delhi** and **Mumbai**.

**Bus**

Luxury and Express bus services between Patna and regional centres including **Kolkata**, **Siliguri**, **Bhagalpur**, **Ranchi**, **Hazaribagh**, **Monghyr** and **Gumra**. Bihar SRTC, Gandhi Maidan, opposite GPO, T2671682; Reservations: 1030-1800; at Junction railway Station, T2221093. Private bus stand opposite Vir Kunwar Singh (Harding) Park.

**To Nepal** STRCs and private buses run daily from Harding Park Bus Stand to Raxaul (5-7 hrs, Rs 60). However, timings are difficult and the buses extremely crowded and uncomfortable. Night buses reach the border early in the morning. Morning buses from Patna connect with the night bus to Kathmandu. Either way you have an overnight bus journey, unless you stay at Birganj – an unenviable option, though there are two modest hotels. Raxaul has little to offer; **Ajanta**, Ashram Rd, has rooms with bath. In **Raxaul** the tempo stand is south of the railway line and the Immigration and Customs office. You can cross the border to **Birganj** by rickshaw/tempo (15-20 mins). In Birganj the tempo stand and Bus Park are in Adarsh Nagar, to the south of town. In the morning, buses depart from the Bus Stand east of the Clock Tower. To **Tandi Bazar** (4 hrs, for Chitwan, Rs 60), **Pokhara** (11-12 hrs, Rs 90) and **Kathmandu** (11-12 hrs, Rs 95). Even Express buses are slow and packed. 'Tourist' minibuses are the only moderately comfortable option. You need an Exit stamp in **Raxaul** from the Indian Immigration office (round the corner, and across the road from the Customs office) - a great hassle. You may need Customs clearance first. After crossing the border you need to get an Entry stamp from the Nepalese Immigration counter (usually open early morning to late evening). Occasionally an unjustified additional fee is demanded for 'extras', eg Registration card, or a 'Visa' fee in US$.

**From Nepal** When travelling to India via Patna it is best to stay overnight in **Hetauda** and catch the 0530 bus to Birganj (3 hrs); go to the Bus Stand at 0500 to get a seat. At **Birganj**, walk or get a (pricey) horse-drawn rickshaw to the auto-tempo stand at the second crossroads. From there travel to Raxaul. Remember to get an Exit stamp from Nepalese Immigration before crossing the border and an Entry stamp from Indian Immigration in Raxaul.

**Car**

Tourist taxis, **TCI**, competitive rates, including longer tours; also **Ashok Travels and Tours**, about Rs 500 per 4 hrs to Rs 1,000 per 8 hrs for a/c. Out-of-town touring (600 km), eg Vaishali, Rs 1,200-1,700; Bodh Gaya, Rajgir, Nalanda, Rs 4,500 (a/c).

**Taxi**

Private unmetered taxis available from the airport, railway station, some hotels and important tourist sites. Fix rates beforehand. The same applies to rickshaws and tongas.

**Train**

Reservations on Northeast Railways, ie to Gorakpur, Raxaul, must be made at Sonepur station, not Patna.

Patna Junction railway Station, enquiries, T131/2427812, reservations, T2222197. **Delhi (ND)**: *Vikramshila/Magadh Exp, 3467/2391*, 1900, 16½ hrs; *Rajdhani Exp, 2423/2309*, 2115, not Wed or Sun, 13 hrs. **Delhi (OD)**: *Brahmaputra Mail, 4055*, 1323, 15½ hrs.

*For an explanation of the sleeping and eating price codes used in this guide, see inside the front cover. Other relevant information is found in Essentials pages 56-61.*

Dhanbad: *Damodar Exp, 3330*, 2245, 6½ hrs. **Gaya**: *Patna Hatia Exp, 8625*, 0950, 2½ hrs; *Palamau Exp, 3348*, 2000, 2½ hrs. **Guwahati**: *NE Exp, 5622*, 2220, 20½ hrs; *Rajdhani Exp, 2424*, 0555, Tue, Wed, Sat, 16 hrs. **Kolkata**: *Toofan Exp, 3008*, 0542, 12½ hrs; *Rajdhani Exp, 2306*, 0555, Mon, Fri, 7½ hrs; *Poorva Exp, 2304*, 0800, Wed, Thu, Sat, Sun, 8½ hrs. **Mumbai (Dadar)**: *Guwahati Dadar Exp, 5646/5648*, 1515, Tue, Wed, Sun, 32 hrs. **Varanasi**: *Farraka Exp, 3413/3483*, 0610, 6 hrs; *Sharmjevvi Exp, 2401*, 1105, 4 hrs.

## Directory

**Patna** *p740, maps p740 and p742*
**Banks** State Bank of India, Gandhi Maidan, may refuse to cash Amex TCs. Trade Wings, Hotel Maurya complex. Efficient, good rate. **Hospitals** Patna Medical College Hospital, Ashok Rajpath E, T0612 2670132. Nalanda Medical College Hospital, T0612 2631159, By-Pass Rd. **Post** GPO: Station Rd. Central Telegraph Office, Buddha Marg. **Library** British Library, Bank Rd, near Gandhi Maidan. 1030-1830 Tue-Sat. Very good collection and helpful staff. **Tourist offices** India, Sudama Bhawan near Overbridge, Kankarbagh, T0612 2345776. 1000-1700, excellent service, arranges local tours and excursions. Bihar, Paryatan Bhawan, Beer Chand Patel Marg, T0612 2225411, F2236218. Counters at Pataliputra Ashok, T2232238, Airport and Patna Junction Railway Station T0612 2221093. ITDC, Pataliputra Ashok, T0612 2226270. Tourism Department, Government of Bihar, 9D Hutment, Secretariat, T/F0612 2224531.



# Patna to Bodh Gaya

→ *Colour map 3, grid B5/6.*

*The area to the south of Patna has many major Buddhist sites, and also some Muslim and Hindu places of pilgrimage. This circular route to the southwest of Patna visits the ruins of Nalanda, one of the world's oldest universities, Rajgir, royal capital of the Magadh Empire, the Barabar Caves and Bodh Gaya. On the return journey to Patna, you can take a longer route via the immense tombs of Sher Shah at Sasaram. It is preferable to take at least two days even for the shorter trip. Once out of Patna the countryside is often very attractive, the early morning being particularly crisp and inviting. From March through to the monsoon it gets extremely hot during the day.*

» *For Sleeping, Eating and other listings, see pages 753-755.*

## Biharsharif and Pawapuri

On the NH31, these two towns can be visited prior to arriving at Nalanda. **Biharsharif**, 13 km from Nalanda, remained an Islamic cultural centre up to the 16th century. The *dargahs* (tombs) of Mukhdoom Shah, a 13th-century saint and Malik Ibrahim Baya, draw large numbers of Muslims, particularly during the annual **Urs fair**.

**Pawapuri**, also Apapuri – 'sinless town', is particularly sacred to the Jains since Mahavir, the founder of Jainism, gained enlightenment here. The lotus pond where he bathed and on whose bank he was cremated has a white marble temple, the *Jalamandir*, in its centre and Samosharan Temple.

## Nalanda

→ *Colour map 3, grid B6.*

Nalanda has the ruins of one of the world's oldest universities, founded in the fifth century AD on an ancient site of pilgrimage and teaching which had been visited by the Buddha and Mahavir (who spent '14 rainy seasons' in the area). According to Ghosh, Hiuen Tsang ascribed its name, which means 'charity without intermission', to the Buddha's liberality in an earlier birth.

## History

Nalanda was hidden under a vast mound for centuries. Its archaeological importance was only established in the 1860s with most of the excavation taking place over about 20 years from 1916. The monasteries went through varying periods of occupation, and in one case nine different levels of building have been discovered. The Buddhist monastic movement resulted in large communities withdrawing into retreats. Even in the seventh century, according to Hiuen-Tsang, Buddhism was declining except in Bihar and Bengal where it enjoyed royal patronage and the support of the laity. The sanctuaries were often vast, as is the one here (500 m x 250 m).

## The site

ⓘ *0900-1750.*

The remains of 11 monasteries and several *chaityas* (temples) built mainly in red brick, have been found as well as a large stairway, a library, lecture halls, dormitories, cells, ovens and wells. The buildings are in several storeys and tiers on massive terraces of solid brick, with stucco decorations of the Buddha as well as Hindu deities, and secular figures. Several of the monasteries have a guarded entrance on the western wall; the monks' cells are around a central courtyard with a wide verandah (or a high wall in some cases). Opposite the entrance, the centre of the eastern wall has a shrine which must have contained an impressive image. Remains of drains which carried sewage to the east, and staircases giving access to the different storeys can be seen.

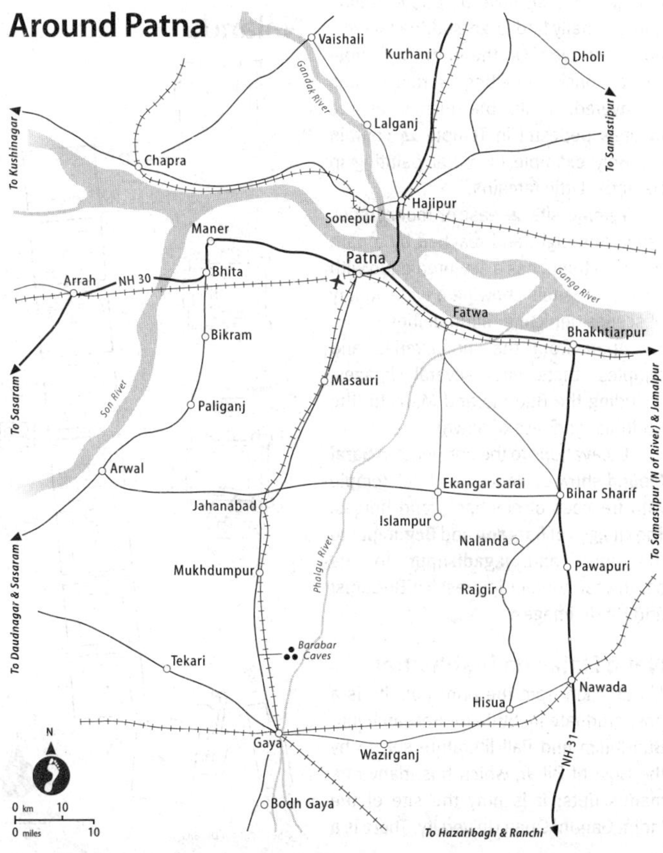

The monasteries are numbered one to 11, from south to north. The path from the gate enters the complex between one and four and goes across an open space to **Temple No 3**, the largest here. Almost certainly this was originally built by Asoka. The earliest temples were small structures, completely incorporated into the successively larger mounds. The north facing shrine chamber on top may have once contained an enormous Buddha image. The highest point gives a commanding view over the site as a whole, particularly impressive in the evening light.

*Nalanda by A Ghosh, 6th ed, 1986, gives excellent detailed descriptions of the site and the Museum.*

Returning east, **Monasteries 1, 1A** and **1B** are the most important of the monastery group. Ghosh suggests that the lower monastery was built by a Sumatran king in the reign of the third Pala king, Devapala, between AD 810-850. There was an earlier monastery underneath, which had been substantially damaged. It is possible to walk around all three of these southern monasteries.

There are several interesting features in the other monasteries: double rows of cells in **Monastery 5**, brick courtyards and two sets of double ovens in the upper courtyard of **6**, and evidence of three successive monasteries built on the same site at **7**. There is an imposing shrine and unique doorway in **8**, striking drains in **9** and arched doorways in **10**. The fragments of 25 stone pillars were recovered from the ruins of **11**, which stood 1 m apart and 2 m high. Ghosh suggests that fire was a recurrent hazard, and that every monastery was deserted and reoccupied.

In addition to the monasteries and the main temple, four other temples have been excavated. **Temples 12, 13** and **14** are in a line stretching north from the main temple. They all have a square outline and originally had large Buddha images, now destroyed. On the north of Temple **13** a brick smelting furnace was discovered, while the niches of the image's pedestal in Temple **14** contain the only example of mural painting in Nalanda. Little remains.

**Temple site 2**, east of monasteries seven and eight and reached by a path between them, has a sculpted dado with over 200 panels showing a wide variety of scenes depicting Hindu deities.

Apart from the monasteries and temples there are several images, including the Buddha and Marachi (the Buddhist goddess of dawn).

Excavations to the northeast in **Sarai Mound** show evidence of a brick temple with frescoes of elephants and horses. The villages of **Bargaon** and **Begampur** to the north and **Jagadishpur** to the southwest contain impressive Buddhist and Hindu images.

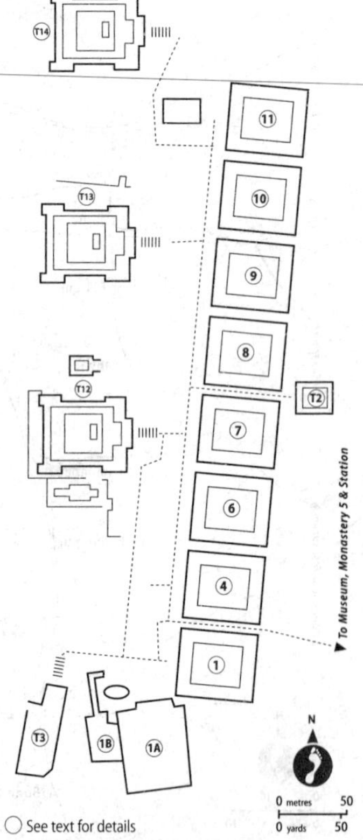


## Nava Nalanda Mahavihar

About 2 km from the principal site is a post-graduate Institute for Research into Buddhism and Pali literature set up by the Govt of Bihar, which has many rare manuscripts; it is now the site of the Indira Gandhi Open University. There is a

## Monastic University for the Buddhist world

It is assumed that the Gupta emperors were responsible for Nalanda's first monasteries. In the seventh century Hiuen-Tsang spent 12 years, both as a student and a teacher, at Nalanda which once had over 3,000 teachers and philosophers. The monks were supported by 200 villages, and a library of nine million manuscripts attracted men from countries as far flung as Java, Sumatra, Korea, Japan and China. Great honour was attached to a Nalanda student and admission was restricted with seven or eight out of 10 applicants failing to gain a place.

I-Tsing, another Chinese scholar, arrived here in AD 673 and also kept detailed records, describing the severe lifestyle of the monks. The divisions of the day were measured by a water-clock, and the syllabus involved the study of Buddhist and Brahmanical scriptures, logic, metaphysics, medicine and Sanskrit grammar.

The University flourished until 1199 when the Afghan Bhaktiar Khalji sacked it, burning, pillaging and driving the surviving residents into hiding. It was the end of living Buddhism in India until the modern revival.

colourful **Thai Temple** built in the 1980s. **Kundalpur**, 1.6 km north of Nalanda, is believed by the Digambara sect of Jains to be the birthplace of Mahavir.

# Rajgir → *Phone code: 6119. Colour map 3, grid B6. Population: 33,700.*

Encircled by rugged forested hills, Rajgir is held sacred by both Buddhists and Jains for its association with Mahavir, who taught here for many years, and the Buddha. You can still see parts of the 40-km cyclopean drystone wall that once enclosed the ancient city and fort. Today, the *kund* (hot springs) with large open-air baths are a special attraction. Non-Hindus are not allowed into the Surya Temple. The Kund Market nearby, where buses stop, has shops, stalls and local eating places with basic rooms.

## The site

**Gridhrakuta**, the 'Hill of Vultures', was one of the Buddha's favourite places where he delivered many important sermons, and was where he is believed to have converted the Magadhan King **Bimbisara**, who had built the old stone road leading up the hill. It was used by Hiuen-Tsang in the seventh century and still provides the best access. Rock-cut steps lead to the two natural caves; plaques and Buddhist shrines were found in the area (now in Nalanda Museum). The first Buddhist Council was held in the **Saptaparni Cave** on Vaibhara Hill, six months after the Buddha's death, and his teachings were written down for the first time. On the way to the cave is the large, 7-m high **Pippala stone house**, an extraordinary 'watchtower' built of blocks of stone. On all sides there are small cells for guards which were later used by monks.

*Rajgir by Md Hamid Kuraishi, 5th ed, 1987, describes the site with maps.*

Little survives of the fifth-century BC **Ajatasatru Fort**. The outer wall was built with blocks of stone up to 1½ m long, with smaller boulders in its core. In places it was 4 m high and over 5 m wide. Of the 32 large gates (and 64 small ones) mentioned in ancient texts, only one to the north has survived. Of the inner city wall, which was about 5 km long and roughly pentagonal, only a section to the south remains, with three gaps through which the old roads ran. A part of the deep moat which was cut into the rock can also be seen. In the valley, a 6-m high circular brick structure, decorated with stucco figures, had an old Jain shrine called **Maniyar Math**.

Nearby **Venuvana**, the bamboo grove where the Buddha spent some time, where excavations revealed a room, some stupas and the Karanda Tank, is now a deer park with a small zoo. To the south of Venuvana there are Jain and Hindu temples. Ruins of Buddha's favourite retreat within the valley, the **Jivakamarvana Monastery** (fourth to third century BC), have been found with four halls and several rooms.

The **Visva Santi Stupa** ⓘ *cable car (600 m) for access, usually 0900-1300, 1500-1700, (good for the views)*, built by the Japanese on top of Ratnagiri is dedicated to world peace. The large white Nipponzan Myohoji stupa has four golden statues of the Buddha representing his birth, enlightenment, preaching and death.

**Mahavir** spent "14 rainy seasons" in Rajgir and the 20th Tirthankara was born here so it is a major Jain pilgrimage centre, with temples on most of the hilltops.

# Gaya → *Phone code: 0631. Colour map 3, grid B5. Population: 383,200.*

Gaya, on slightly raised ground in the valley between two hills, was blessed by Vishnu with the power to absolve all temporal sins. Its many sacred shrines attract Hindus at Pitrapaksh Tarpan (September-October), when prayers are offered for the dead before pilgrims take a dip in the seasonal holy River Phalgu. Cremations take place on funeral pyres in the burning ghats along the river.

## Sights

There are several old Buddhist temples and monastery remains around Gaya. In the centre of the town is the **Vishnupad Temple**, supposed to have been built over Vishnu's footprint, which is imprinted on a rock set in a silver basin. The 30-m high temple has eight rows of beautifully carved pillars supporting the *mandapa* (pavilion), which were refurbished in 1787. Only Hindus are permitted into the sanctum and temple grounds which has the *Akshayabat* (the immortal banyan tree under which the Buddha is believed to have meditated for six years), where the final puja for the dead takes place. Brahmayoni Hill, 1 km southwest, with its 1,000 stone steps, which lead to a vantage point for viewing both Gaya and Bodh Gaya.

The **Surya Temple** at **Deo**, 20 km away, dedicated to the Sun God, attracts large crowds in November when **Chhatt Puja** is celebrated.

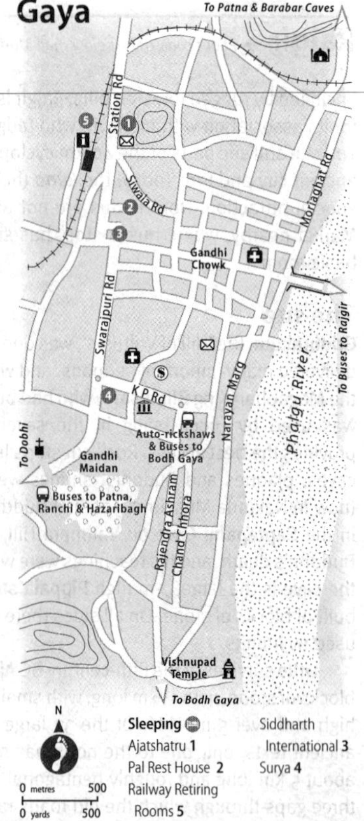


## Excursions

**Barabar Caves** is 35 km north. The 22-km rough track leading to the caves in the impressive granite hill turns east off the main road to Patna at **Belagunj** (30 minutes from Gaya, two hours from

Patna) where buses stop. From here allow four hours to walk up (45 km by four-wheel drive, "a real challenge"). It is only safe to go in daylight and not alone; a solitary sadhu is inclined to jump out at you from nowhere! Enquire about safety at Belagunj Police Station.

The whale-backed quartzite gneiss hill stands in wild and rugged country. Inscriptions reveal that, on instructions from Asoka, four chambers were excavated, cut and chiselled to a high polish by the stonemasons, as retreats for ascetics who belonged to a sect related to Jainism. Percy Brown pointed out that the extraordinary caves, particularly the *Lomas Rishi* and the *Sudama*, are exact copies of ordinary beehive shaped huts built with bamboo, wood and thatch. The barrel-vaulted chamber inside the *Sudama* is 10 m long, 6 m wide and 3½ m high which through a doorway leads to a circular cell of 6 m diameter. The most impressive craftsmanship is seen on the façade of the *Lomas Rishi* which replicates the horseshoe shaped gable end of a wooden structure with two lunettes which have very fine carvings of lattice-work and rows of elephants paying homage to Buddhist stupas. Excavation is incomplete as there was a possibility of the cave collapsing. There is also a Siva temple on the Siddheshwar peak.

*The caves inspired the setting of* EM Forster's A Passage to India. *They date from the third century BC and are the earliest examples of rock-cut sanctuaries.*

At **Nagarjuna Hill** there are three further rock-cut sanctuaries, 1 km northeast from Barabar. The *Gopi* (Milkmaid's) cave having the largest chamber. Inscriptions date these to about 50 years after the excavations at Barabar.

# Bodh Gaya → *Phone code: 0631. Colour map 3, grid B5. Population: 30,900.*

Bodh Gaya, a quiet village near the river Niranjana (Phalgu), is one of the holiest Buddhist pilgrimage centres. It was under the Bo tree here that Gautama, the prince, attained enlightenment to become the Buddha. *For Sleeping, Eating and other listings, see pages 753-755.*

## Ins and outs

**Getting there** Travel in daylight only, for your own safety. Buses run from Gaya, Patna, Nalanda and Rajgir. *See Transport, page 755, for further details.*

**Getting around** Hotels, temple and monasteries are a few mins' walk from the bus stand.

## The site

Bodh Gaya was 'lost' for centuries until rediscovered by Burmese Buddhists in 1877 which led to restoration work by the British. UNESCO has recently given its preliminary approval to declare Bodh Gaya as a World Heritage site, with the event to be marked by the arrival of a 152 m high bronze statue (made in the UK).

Lamas, Rimpoches and Buddhists from all over the world assemble here during the *monlam* when the area north of the bus station resembles a medieval encampment with tents serving as informal restaurants and accommodation. The food is smoky and there are long waits, but it is atmospheric and full of colour. The 'tourist season' draws to a close at the end of February when many restaurants close and meditation courses stop running. Unfortunately the air can get heavily polluted, partly due to badly serviced buses, making a walk along the road rather unpleasant.

## Mahabodhi Temple

ⓘ *Temple Office T0631 2200620, cameras, Rs 5, access is by a road alongside the Birla Dharamshala and Tibetan Guest House.*

Asoka's original shrine near the Bodhi tree was replaced by this temple in the second century, which in turn went through several alterations. The temple on a high and broad plinth, with a soaring 54-m high pyramidal spire with a square cross-section and four smaller spires, houses a gilded image of the Enlightened Buddha. The smaller spires may have been added when Burmese Buddhists attempted extensive rebuilding in the 14th century. An ornately carved stone railing in bas relief surrounds the temple on three sides and several carved Buddhist stupas depict tales from the Buddha's early life. Unlike earlier circular railings this had to conform to the quadrangle of the temple structure. Its height of 2 m, its lighter proportions and the quality of the carving dates it to the Sunga period (early first century BC). The *entrancetorana* (ornamental archway) is on the east side. The lotus pond where the Buddha may have bathed is to the south. To the north is the *Chankramana*, a raised platform (first century) with lotus flowers carved on it, which marks the consecrated promenade used by the Buddha while meditating. Numerous attempts to restore the temple have obscured the original. The candle-lit evening ceremony is worth attending.

The original Bodhi tree (pipal or *Ficus religiosa*) was supposedly destroyed by Asoka before he was converted, and others which replaced it also died. The present tree behind the temple is believed to come from the original stock – Prince Mahinda carried a sapling from the sacred Bo tree to Sri Lanka when he went to spread Buddhism there. This in turn produced a sapling which was brought back to Bodh Gaya. The red sandstone slab, the **Vajrasila**, under the tree marks the place where Gautama sat in meditation. Today, pilgrims tie pieces of coloured cloth on its branches when they come to pray.

**Animeshlochana** is another sacred spot where the Buddha stood to gaze in gratitude at the Bodhi tree for a week, after his Enlightenment. The temple also attracts Hindu pilgrims since the Buddha is considered to be one of the *avatars* or incarnations of Vishnu.

## Other temples

Pilgrims from many lands have built their own temples. You can start at the giant 20-m stone **Buddha statue** which was installed at the end of the road in 1989. The modern two-storey, spotless **Japanese Temple** ⓘ *0700-1200, 1400-1800*, next door with beautiful polished marble floors has gold images of the Buddha. The **Tibetan**



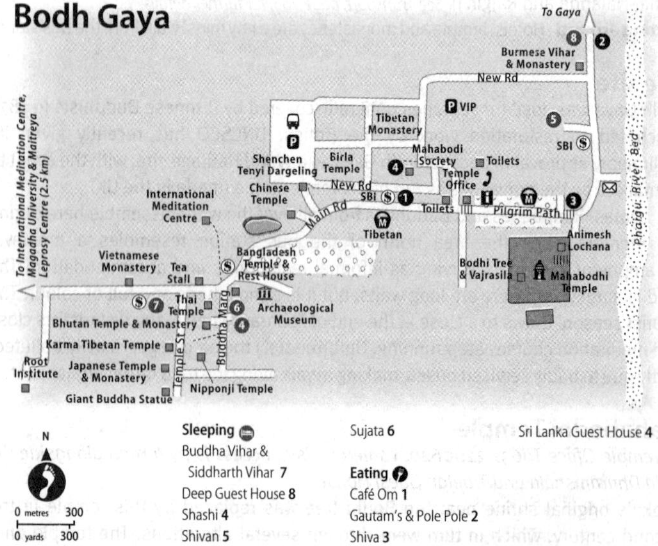

Temple and **Monastery** next to this (1938) is ornately painted and has a *Dharma Chakra* (Wheel of Law) which must be turned three times when praying for forgiveness of sins. A large 2-m metal ceremonial drum in red and gold is also on display. Opposite is the **Nipponji Temple** complex with a free clinic, monastery and a Peace Bell (rung from 0600-1200 and at 1700). Returning to the Mahabodhi Temple you will pass the colourful **Bhutan Temple** protected by carved Himalayan deities, a glittering pagoda-style **Thai Temple** and a **Bangladesh Temple**. The **Chinese Temple** houses an enormous, revolving ceremonial prayer drum.

## Teaching centres

**Magadha University**, an international centre for studies in history, culture and philosophy, is about 3 km from the Mahabodhi Temple. The **Tibetan Medical and Astro Institute** carries out research and gives advice. **Meditation courses** varying from a week to a month during the winter, follow both the Mahayana and Hinanyana traditions; enquire at the Burmese, Tibetan and Thai monasteries. The **International Meditation Centre** ⓘ *enquiries to Woodland Rd, Denbury, Devon, England, TQ12 6DY, opposite the Thai monastery, T0631 2200707*, also holds courses. The **Root Institute**, off the Magadha University Road which is involved in community self-help schemes, also runs popular short introductory courses.

## Sasaram

→ *Colour map 3, grid B5.*

**Sher Shah Suri**, who was responsible for the tombs, asked the master-builder Aliwal Khan to build a tomb for his father **Hasan Khan** around 1535. This later inspired the building of the impressive second tomb for Sher Shah himself. The first imitated the octagonal structure and walled enclosure of the earlier Lodi tombs but was rather plain. What followed, however, was extraordinary not only in scale, but also in its conception. **Sher Shah's mausoleum** ⓘ *Mar-Jul 0700-1800, Aug-Feb 0800-1700, Rs 2*, 500 m away, was set in a large artificial lake so it appears to float. A modern redbrick gateway opposite the Dak Bungalow leads down to the tombs. You enter it by a causeway after going through a guard room on the north bank (originally visitors approached by barge from the ghat on the east side). The pleasant grounds and the lake provide a relaxing break.

*This Muslim site, between Gaya and Varanasi, is well worth a visit. The tombs are a short rickshaw ride from the railway station.*

## Sleeping

**Nalanda** *p746*

E **Tathaghat Vihar**. Modest rooms.

F **Ajatashatru Vihar**. Very basic affair offering dorm rooms only.

F **Burmese Rest House**, beyond museum.

F **Inspection Bungalow**, meals to order, contact Supt, Archaeological Survey of India, Patna.

F **Youth Hostel**.

**Rajgir** *p749*

There are several Jain Dharamshalas near the station.

A **Centaur Hokke**, 2 km from Kund Market, T06112 255245, www.theroyalresidency.net. 24 comfortable rooms (few Western style), primarily for Japanese pilgrims, excellent Japanese restaurant (fresh ingredients daily), open Nov-Mar, reserve well ahead (guaran- tees 'beds' not 'rooms' in high season).

A **The Rajgir Residency**, T06112 255404, rajgirresidency@hotmail.com. 28 a/c rooms plus authentic Korean, Japanese, Thai food.

D **Gautam Vihar**, T06112 225273, 15 rooms (some a/c) with bath and verandah.

D-E **Siddharth**, near Kund Market, T06112 255616, has good rooms with bath, and decent food.

D-E **Tathagat Vihar**, T06112 225176. 32 simple rooms (some a/c), dorm, Indian restaurant, open Nov-Mar.

**Gaya** *p750, map p750*
Mostly very basic with non a/c rooms.
**B-C Siddharth International**, off Station Rd, T0631 2436243. Some a/c rooms, modern, great food, but noisy and overpriced.
**D-E Ajatshatru**, opposite railway station, T0631 2434584. Range of rooms with bath (hot water), some gloomy and noisy, but popular ground floor restaurant has large menu, cheap but good basic food.
**D-E Surya**, Swarajpuri Rd, between **Samrat Hotel** and bus stand, T0631 2224004. Some rooms with bath and hot water, cleanest of the cheap hotels, and quieter being away from extremely noisy railway station.
**F Pal Rest House**, off Station Rd, T0612 2229042. Some rooms with bath, quieter at rear.
**Railway Retiring Rooms**, at Gaya Junction. 6 rooms, 2 a/c.

**Bodh Gaya** *p751, map p752*
Simple budget hotels often quote higher rates so bargain.
**AL-A The Royal Residency**, Dumahan Rd, T0631 2200124, www.theroyal residency. net. 67 rooms, central a/c, most luxurious in town.
**A Lotus Nikko Hotel**, T0631 2200700, www.lotustranstravels.com. 34 renovated rooms, most a/c.
**B-C Siddhartha International**, Station Rd, T0631 2436243, siddharth@ndf.vsnl. net.in. 68 rooms, 26 a/c, very convenient for train station.
**B-C Sujata**, Buddha Marg, past the Bangladesh Temple, T0631 2200761, hotel_sujata@yahoo.com. 27 rooms, some Japanese baths, restaurant, exchange.
**C Shashi**, next door, T0631 2200459. Small, clean rooms, restaurant.
**D-E Deep Guest House**, next to Burmese Monastery, near Sujata Bridge, T0631 2200463. Clean rooms, friendly staff, roof terrace, peaceful atmosphere.
**D-E New Mahayana**, Main Rd. Good value clean rooms.
**E Root Institute**, Magadha University Rd, T0631 2200714. Rooms in traditional local huts in a peaceful, shared bath, rural setting (Rs 360 double including breakfast), excellent food.
**F Buddha Vihar**, next door to **Siddharth Vihar**, T0631 2200445, 3 to 6 bed dorms (Rs 75), very basic.
**F Shivan**, near temple. Clean rooms, some with bath, hot water, friendly.

**Monasteries**
Some monasteries provide spartan accommodation primarily for pilgrims; contact the monk in charge. They expect guests to conform to certain rules of conduct.
**D Japanese Monastery**, near Buddha Statue, T0631 2200747. Comfortable spotless rooms sometimes available, good Japanese meals.
**E-F Mahabodhi Soc**. 6 rooms, 3 dorms, vegetarian canteen.
**F Bhutan Monastery** (Druk Do Nagcholing). 18 rooms in guesthouses, shared facilities.
**F Burmese Vihar**, Gaya Rd. Simple rooms (some newer) with nets, dorm, no fan, garden (eat at **Pole Pole** opposite).

**Sasaram** *p753*
It is advisable to avoid staying overnight here.
**F Shilpa Deluxe**, GT Rd, T06184-2223305. 15 rooms, dirty, staff have TV on loud non-stop.
**F Youth Hostel**. Station Refreshment Room for breakfast and simple thalis, fairly clean, "nice waiters at least try to chase the rats"!

## Eating

**Rajgir** *p749*
**Green**, Kund market near Bus Stop. Basic, cheap, simple Indian – tables in verandah.

**Bodh Gaya** *p751, map p752*
Most of the tent restaurants operate in winter only.
**Café Om**, best Tibetan *thukpa*. Also excellent fresh cakes, cheesecakes and a stall with cheap attractive items.

*For an explanation of the sleeping and eating price codes used in this guide, see inside the front cover. Other relevant information is found in Essentials pages 56-61.*

**Gautam's**, tent nearby for apple strudel and cinnamon rolls.
**The Lotus Nikko** has a good a/c restaurant serving tasty food.
**Pole Pole**, tent opposite Burmese Vihar. Clean, excellent management, good though not exceptional food.
**Shiva**, diagonally opposite entrance to temple. Japanese food and simple Western.
**Sri Lanka Guest House** does Chinese.

## Activities and tours

**Gaya** *p750, map p750*
**Sakun**, Shyam Bazar, Ramna Rd.

**Bodh Gaya** *p751, map p752*
**Insight Meditation**, www.insightmeditation.org, runs a silent, residential retreat with Western teachers at the Thai Monastery in January every year.

## Transport

**Nalanda** *p746*
Regular buses from **Patna** (90 km north), **Rajgir** (15 km) with the nearest railway station. Cycle-rickshaw and tonga: outside the Tourist Information Centre.

**Rajgir** *p749*
Bus to **Patna** (105 km), 4 hrs; and **Gaya** 3 hrs. Auto-rickshaw or share-taxi to visit the sites, and Nalanda.

**Gaya** *p750, map p750*
**Bus**
**Local** To **Bodh Gaya**: buses from the station; from Zila School Bus Stand, mini-buses and autos, but always very crowded; rickshaws (6-seater), Rs 8 per seat, better value. Try to persuade a cycle-rickshaw driver to take you; worth it for the relative peace and comfort. None after 1800.
**Long distance** From Stand across the river: to **Rajgir**; from Gandhi Maidan Bus Stand: Patna, Ranchi and Hazaribagh.

**Rickshaw**
Auto and cycle-rickshaws: easily available.

**Train**
Gaya is on the Grand Chord line of the Delhi-Kolkata section of Eastern Railway. Gaya Junction railway Station, enquiries and reservations: T0631 2432031, 0900-1600. **Delhi (ND)**: *Rajdhani Exp, 2301/2421*, 2211, 12 hrs; *Purushottam Exp, 2801*, 1338, 15 hrs;. **Kolkata (H)**: *Howrah Exp, 2308*, 2043, 8 hrs; *Kalka-Howrah Mail, 2312*, 2320, 7½ hrs; *Rajdhani Exp, 2302/2422*, 0433, 6½ hrs; plus others. **Patna**: *Palamau Exp, 3347*, 0217, 2½ hrs; *Hatia Patna Exp, 8626*, 1415, 2½ hrs. **Varanasi**: *Doon Exp, 3009*, 0547, 5½ hrs; *AC Exp, 2381*, Wed, Thu, Sun, 1600, 3½ hrs. *Poorva Exp, 2381*, 1600, Wed, Thu, Sun, 3½ hrs; plus lots that arrive/ depart in middle of night.

**Bodh Gaya** *p751, map p752*
Patna has the nearest airport, while Gaya (16 km) has the nearest railway station. The main bus stand is opposite the Mahabodhi Temple. Auto-rickshaws and overcrowded buses take about 30 mins from Gaya.

**Sasaram** *p753*
Train to **Gaya**, *Doon Exp, 3009*, 1908, 2 hrs. From **Gaya**, 0607, 1½ hrs; to **Varanasi**, 0755, 3½ hrs; from **Varanasi**: 1620, 2½ hrs.

## Directory

**Gaya** *p750, map p750*
**Post** Station Rd. Warning from travellers whose mail/parcels were pilfered here.
**Tourist office** Bihar, Gaya Junction railway Station Main Hall, T0631 2420155, 0600-2100.

**Bodh Gaya** *p751, map p752*
**Banks** Bank of India in Embassy Hotel changes cash (up to US$100), **State Bank of India** in New Mahayana Hotel. Changes cash, TCs, Mon-Fri 1030-1430, Sat 1030-1230.
**Post** T0631 2400742. Mon-Sat 1000-1700.
**Tourist office** Bihar, 34-35 Mahabodhi Temple Market Complex, T0631 220 0672. 1000-1700.

# Jharkhand

## Background

**The land** Jharkhand lies on the once densely forested northern edge of the Indian Peninsula. The rolling plateau, lying at an altitude of between 300-400 m, with occasional outcrops rising to nearly 1,000 m, is largely comprised of the granites and gneisses of ancient Gondwanaland. On the north it drops quite sharply to the plains of the Ganges, while a great fault has created the valley of the mineral rich Damodar. The plateau still has an open feel, forest being interspersed by agricultural land, except where coal and iron ore mining have created a scarred industrial landscape of mines and soil tips. To the south of the Damodar valley are the Ranchi plateaus, broken up by remarkable looking flat-topped hillocks or *mesas*. Up to 20% is still under forest, though exploitation of the forest continues apace. The soils are often poor, sometimes lateritic, and easily eroded if proper conservation measures are not adopted.

**Politics** The inauguration of the state in the early hours of 15 November 2000 was set symbolically on the birth anniversary of Birsa Munda, leader of the Santhal rebellion in 1831-1832. The origins of the present state can be traced to the formation of the Chota Nagpur Unnati Samaj in 1921, which proposed the creation of a separate Jharkhand state in 1928. The State Assembly (81 seats) had until recently been dominated by the National Democratic Alliance (NDA), but elections in February 2005 failed to produce a clear majority. While the JMM leader, Shibu Soren, was initially sworn in as Chief Minister, he was then replaced on 12 March 2005 by the BJP's Arjun Munda. Jharkhand's future is heavily dependent upon the exploitation of its mineral wealth, targeted to contribute annually Rs 1,500 crore to the state's coffers.



## Ranchi → *Phone code: 0651. Colour map 3, grid C6. Population: 846,500.*

Once the summer capital of Bihar state, Ranchi still attracts holidaymakers for its location on higher ground in the heart of the Chota Nagpur tribal country. An industrial town and a major educational centre, Ranchi is also known for its mental asylum at Kanke, 9 km north. The town is surrounded by rolling forested land with waterfalls and lakes and is in the heart of one of India's great tribal belts. The Ranchi district has been the recent scene of violently suppressed demonstrations, opposed to Koel-Karo dam project. ▸▸ *For Sleeping, Eating and other listings, see pages 758-760.*

### Sights

**Ranchi Lake** is popular for local people to relax, while the adjacent **Ranchi Hill** offers good views of the town and surrounding countryside. **Tagore Hill**, 3 km away, is named after Rabindranath Tagore who wrote several books and poems here. **Ranchi University** ⓘ *1100-1700*, has ethnographic collections of central Indian states and Andaman and Nicobar Islands. **Ranchi Museum** ⓘ *Tribal Research Institute Building, Morabadi Rd, closed Sun, 1030-1700, free*, 4 km away, has a collection of stone sculpture, terracottas and arms as well as ethnological objects at the Institute itself.

The 17th-century **Jagannath Temple** on a hillock at Jagannathpur, 10 km southwest, is in the style of the great temple in Puri (annual **Ratha Yatra** in June/July).

### Excursions

The Subhanarekha River, which rises southeast of the town, is interrupted by several impressive waterfalls, within easy range of Ranchi. **Hundru Falls**, 45 km east, are formed by the 100 m drop of the river, particularly impressive just after the monsoons. You can picnic and bathe in the pools at the bottom. Others in the area include **Johna**, 40 km east on the Purulia Road, and **Dassamghagh Falls** (34 km) which has a tea house. It is dangerous to bathe at Dassamghagh; several people have drowned. Mundas believe that the god of the Falls demands sacrifices.

## Chota Nagpur plateau → *Colour map 3, grid B5 and C5.*

There are game reserves set in often stunningly beautiful and remote scenery on the Chota Nagpur plateau, which can be easily reached from Ranchi. This is one of the poorest areas of India, with extensive missionary activity.

### Palamau (Betla) National Park

Palamau's vegetation is mainly *sal* and bamboo, though it is now considerably degraded. Once the home of the extinct Indian cheetah, the world's first tiger census was taken in this Project Tiger Reserve in 1932. The wildlife also includes leopard, gaur, sambar, muntjac and nilgai, Indian wolf and many species of birds. The North Koel River and its tributary run through the park but in the summer animals become dependent on waterholes. The Flame of the Forest (*Butea monosperma*) and *mahua* flowers also attract wildlife. The **Hathibajwa** wooden tower and **Madhuchuhan** hide, 'Tree Top' and 'hides' at **Kamaladah** are good vantage points. Elephants can be seen after the monsoons and until the waterholes begin to dry up in March. Over 200 species of water and woodland birds, the remains of two 16th-century **forts** of Chero kings who once ruled from here, and hot springs add to the interest. Jeeps for viewing the animals can be hired from the Forest Department.

*The park is open throughout the year, though the best time to visit is from October to April.*

### Hazaribagh Wildlife Sanctuary

ⓘ *Evening park tour from Divisional Forest Office, Hazaribagh, 1700-2200, Rs 50.*

Hazaribagh ('thousand gardens') town is close to the wildlife sanctuary, waterfalls, Tilaiya Dam (55 km) and Konar Dam (51 km). Set in hilly terrain but slightly lower than the town at 550 m, the park, a Project Tiger Reserve, is a part of the Chota Nagpur plateau in forested tribal territory, interspersed with grass meadows and some deep waterways. The park supports sambar, nilgai, deer, chital, leopard, tiger, wild boar and wild cat. There are 10 watchtowers and hides for viewing. Roads allow easy access; the NH33 takes you to the Pokharia gate, 16 km from Hazaribagh. The best time to visit is from February to April.

## Eastern Jharkhand

### Jamshedpur → *Phone code: 0657. Population: 570,300.*

This flourishing steel town lies 130 km southeast of Ranchi, established as a planned township by the Parsi industrialist Jamshedji Tata in 1908. Located close to rich iron and coal deposits, there are also limestone quarries and some magnesite. The town has retained much of its natural attraction, with its lakes and rivers enclosed by the Dolma hills, in spite of the pollution from its heavy plants. The town is split in two by the steel plant and rail sidings. **Keenan Stadium** in Bistupur, north of town, is the venue for international cricket matches. **Dalma Wildlife Sanctuary**, a few kilometres out of Jamshedpur, on the Ranchi Road is noted for its elephant population.

## Damodar Valley

Other centres have emerged along the Damodar Valley which cuts through the Chota Nagpur plateau through rocky, thickly wooded areas which are the home of the many aboriginal tribal people of Jharkhand. The Santals, Bedia, Khond, Munda and Oraon were the original inhabitants and though a few still live in isolated villages, most have joined the workforce in the industrial townships. The river valley has a number of hydro-electric power stations and with them large dams. The activities in this valley are coal in Dhanbad, locomotives in Chittaranjan and in Bokaro.

## Parsnath Hill → *Colour map 3, grid B6. Altitude: 1,366 m.*

About 150 km along the Kolkata Road from Bodh Gaya, near Dumri and Madhuban, is the holy hill of Parsnath. Particularly sacred to the Jains, a track winds up through Parsnath's forested slopes to the 24 shrines which crown the hilly northern outcrops of the Indian Peninsula. The shrines are rarely visited by foreigners but are a regular pilgrimage site for thousands of devout Jains and Hindus. The highest shrine is dedicated to the last forerunner of Mahavir himself, Lord Parsvanatha, see page 1344, who is believed to have achieved enlightenment while meditating in the cave, now enshrined in the temple. Leather items are not allowed on the hill.

*Madhuban's dharamshalas and lodges may be full during holidays and festivals.*

Most pilgrims start climbing at 0400, the best time to catch superb views of sunrise and the surrounding countryside. It is a three-hour climb but *dhoolis* are available; allow eight hours in all. The super-fit can manage a climb in just over two hours and run down much faster. A visit is highly recommended.



## Sleeping

**Ranchi** *p756*
Finding accommodation in Ranchi can be difficult, most hotels are generally full. Book in advance if possible.
**A Ranchi Ashok**, Doranda, T0651 2480759, www.theashokgroup.com. 30 rooms, central a/c, multi-cuisine restaurant.
**A Yuvraj Palace**, Doranda, T0651 2480326, www.hotelyuvrajpalace.com. Best in town, 25 central a/c rooms, multi-cuisine restaurant, bar; sister hotel **Yuvraj**.
**B-C Kwality Inns**, T0651 2460128. 36 rooms, mostly a/c, reasonable, clean, restaurant, though lack-lustre staff.
**B-D BNR**, Station Rd, T0651 2208048. 22 rooms in cottages in old station building, some a/c, restaurant, lawns, tennis, old-world feel.
**C Hindustan**, Main Rd, T0651 2206032, F2205565. 32 reasonable rooms with TV, some a/c, decent restaurant, overpriced but likely to have vacancies.
**C Yuvraj**, Doranda, T0651 2482423. 35 rooms, some a/c, restaurant/bar.
**E-F Birsa Vihar**, Main Rd, T0651 2314826. 30 simple rooms, dorm, tourist office.

**Palamau National Park** *p757*
**D-F Van Vihar**, inside Reserve, Betla, T06562-256513. 25 rooms, fairly comfortable a/c, good deer viewing, Tourist Information, but reports of no electricity or food.
**E Debjani**, food available.
**E Forest Rest Houses**, inside Reserve. 20 basic rooms.
**E Forest Rest Houses**, Kehr and Kechki. Reservations: Field Director, Project Tiger, Palamau, Daltonganj,T06562.222650
**E Rest Houses** at Mundu, Garu, Chhipadohar and Baresand, contact Div Forest Officer, S Forest Div, Daltonganj, T06562 222427.
**E Tourist Lodge**, near Reserve. 10 rooms.

**Hazaribagh Wildlife Sanctuary** *p757*
**D-E Tourist Lodge**, T06546-224337. 9 rooms, some a/c, Tourist information.
**Govt Guest House**, 12 rooms, near Bus Stand.

*For an explanation of the sleeping and eating price codes used in this guide, see inside the front cover. Other relevant information is found in Essentials pages 56-61.*

**Forest Rest Houses** at Rajdewra and Harhad within the sanctuary area are very spartan.

**Jamshedpur** *p757*
Budget hotels are close to Tata Nagar railway station. Mid-range hotels are 2-3 km from bus and train stations in Bistupur.
**B Fortune Hotel Centrepoint**, 2, Inner Circle Road, Bistupur, T0657 2224200, www.centrepointhotel.com. 42 rooms, central a/c, modern health club, good business facilities.
**B-C Darshan**, opposite Ram Mandir, Main Rd, T0657 2424317, F2430973. 26 decent, clean a/c rooms, restaurant.
**C Boulevard**, Main Rd, Bistupur, T0657 2425321, ronald_d@vsnl.com. 36 large, sparse rooms, TV, hot bath, clean, friendly. Recommended.
**C-D South Park**, Q Rd, Bistupur, T0657 2425001. Comfortable rooms, some a/c, clean hot bath, good restaurant, helpful staff. Recommended.

## Activities and tours

**Jamshedpur** *p757*
**Eastern Travel**, Bistupur, T0657 2424910.
**Skyways**, Jugsalai, T0657 2426502.

## Transport

**Ranchi** *p756*
**Air**
The airport is 13 km away. **Indian Airlines**, Main Rd, T0651 2206160, airport, T141, T2501554, www.indian-airlines.nic.in. Daily to **Delhi**, **Mumbai** and **Patna**. Four flights a week to **Kolkata** and **Lucknow**.

**Bus**
Private bus stand at Kantatoli, 2 km from Main Rd, T0651 2308907; serves major towns in Jharkhand and surrounding states. Government bus stand, Station Rd, T0651 2304328. Also Ratu Rd bus stand (4 km) for buses towards Madhya Pradesh (eg Daltonganj).

**Train**
Enquiries, T131. Reservations, T135. Computerized Reservation Centre, G-41 Sainak Market, Main Rd, T0651 2301097. **Dhanbad**: *Maurya Exp, 5027*, 1700, 4½ hrs. **Gaya**: *Hatia Patna Exp, 8626*, 0625, 7½ hrs; *Hatia Patna Exp, 8624*, 1840, 8½ hrs. Both continue to **Patna**, 10 hrs and 11½ hrs. **Kolkata (H)**: *Hatia Howrah Exp, 8616*, 2005, 12½ hrs. **New Delhi**: *Rajdhani Exp, 2439*, 1640 (Wed), 18 hrs.

**Palamau National Park** *p757*
The nearest airport is at Ranchi, 140 km away. If in a car, take the road west north west out of Ranchi for **Kuru** (57 km), in Kuru fork right to Tori, then towards Daltonganj. The train from **Daltonganj** (25 km), or **Chhipadohar** (80 km).

**Hazaribagh Wildlife Sanctuary** *p757*
If in a car, go north from Ranchi on the NH33 through Ramgarh to Hazaribagh (91 km) and to the main gate at Pokharia. The nearest train station is Hazaribagh Rd Station, 66 km away.

**Jamshedpur** *p757*
**Bus**
Jamshedpur Bus Stand is situated at Mango, 4 km from Bistupur, with regular services to the main centres in the region.

**Rickshaw**
Auto-rickshaws (unmetered) run on a shared basis along the main routes. Otherwise you are at the mercy of a 'reserved rickshaw', expect to bargain. Tata Nagar to Bistupur should be no more than Rs 30.

**Train**
**Tata Nagar** station is on the SE railway on the Kolkata (Howrah)-Mumbai line. Enquiries, T131. To **New Delhi**: *Purushottam Exp, 2801*, 0625, 22½ hrs. **Kolkata (H)**: *Shatabdi Exp, 2022*, 1650 (not Sat), 4½ hrs; *Steel Exp, 8014*, 0600, 4½ hrs; *Gitanjali Exp, 2859*, 1030, 4½ hrs. **Puri** via **Bhubaneswar**: *Purushottam, 2802*, 2025, 10½ hrs; *Utkal Exp, 8478*, 2130, 12½ hrs. **Ranchi**: *Howrah Hatia Exp, 8615*, 0220, 5½ hrs.

**Parsnath Hill** *p758*
From Dhanbad, the nearest large town with hotels (see Damodar Valley): Train *Asansol-Varanasi Pass, 129*, 0805, then minibus from Parsnath station to Madhuban, Rs 15, 40 minutes, or taxi, Rs 200. Buses also from Dhanbad, 0545, to Isri; then taxi (if you

want to return that day) or another bus to Madhu- ban at 1000, and stay overnight in a dharam- shala. Return bus from Madhuban at 1530.

## Directory

**Ranchi** *p756*
Tourist Office, Birsa Vihar Tourist Complex, T0651 2310230/2300646, rch_tourismj@sancharnet.in, Railway Station T0651 2208815.

**Jamshedpur** *p757*
**Banks** Bank of Baroda, Main Rd, Bistupur; for cash on credit cards. ICICI, K Rd, Bistupur; ATM for Visa withdrawals. **Tourist office Jharkhand**, near Air India office, Bistupur, T0657 2431002.

# Andaman and Nicobar Islands

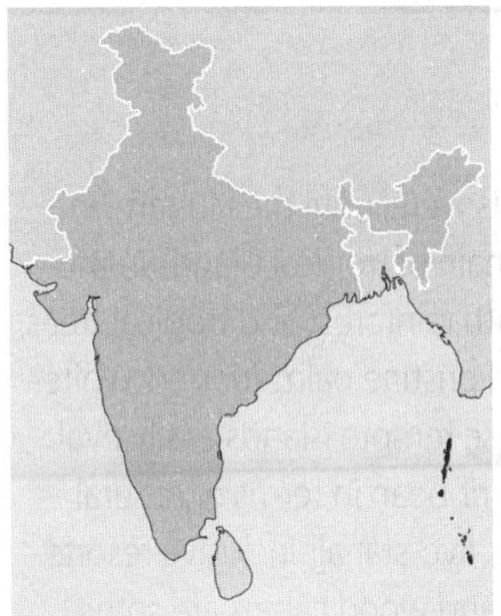



## Footprint features

# Introduction

The Andaman and Nicobar Islands were, until the tsunami in December 2004, a little-known chain of tropical islands in the Bay of Bengal. Thickly forested with rainforest and tropical trees, edged by mangrove swamps and pristine palm-fringed, white-sand beaches and coral reefs, these remote islands easily rival the likes of the Maldives or the Caribbean in terms of natural beauty. The only thing they lack is five-star all-inclusive resorts. However, joining the hammocks and wood cabins are some small resorts with all the creature comforts.

The sparkling clear water and pristine corals make it one of the best places in the world to explore the seabed with rare species – dugong, grey teal, Estuarine crocodile and marine turtles – as well as tropical fish and coral. Birdwatchers are also in paradise with 242 species recorded. The canopied rainforests harbour 3,000 species of plants including mangroves, ferns, orchids, palms, climbers and tropical fruits. Of the 58 species of mammals and 83 reptiles, many are endemic, as the islands are isolated.

The islands' aboriginal tribal people are of special interest to anthropologists. Some, like the Jarawas and Sentinalese in the Andamans, have remained isolated and hostile to outsiders even up to the end of the 20th century. Others, the Great Andamanese for example, have interacted with non-tribal settlers for decades and now there are very few left. The Government of India keeps the Primitive Tribal Reserve Areas out of bounds.

The tsunami devasted parts of this paradise; the southern chain of islands, the Nicobars, was badly hit resulting in many deaths. Only the southernmost island in the Andamans – Little Andaman – was substantially affected. Parts of the Andaman are accessible to foreigners, the Nicobars are off-limits.

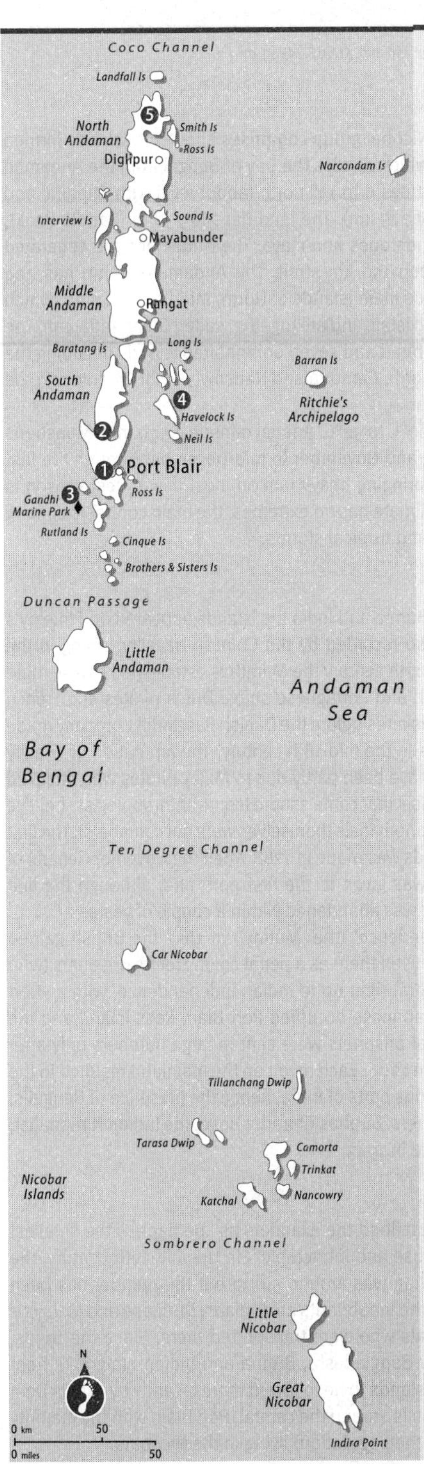


## ★ Don't miss...

1 **Port Blair** Learn about the area's penal past with a visit to the eerie, abandoned Viper Island and then take a trip to Cellular Jail, pages 768 and 769.

2 **South Andaman** Hire a scooter and explore the island along its quiet roads, page 774.

3 **Marine National Park and the Off Islands** When access is allowed, here you can experience some of the world's finest coral reefs, page 775.

4 **Havelock Island** The most developed of all the islands, this is home to an award-winning beach and some great places to stay, page 777.

5 **Saddle Peak National Park** Get active and explore this beautiful area, page 781.

# Background → *Population: 356,300. Area: 8,249 sq km.*

## The land

**Geography** The Andaman and Nicobar group comprises about 300 islands formed by a submarine mountain range which divides the Bay of Bengal from the Andaman Sea. The islands lie between latitudes 6 to 14° north (about level with Chennai and longitudes 92-94° east, a span of 725 km). The land rises to 730 m (Saddle Peak), formed mainly of limestones, sandstones and clays. The Andamans are separated from the Nicobars by a 90-m deep 150 km strait. The Andamans group has 204 islands (26 inhabited) with its three main islands of North, Middle and South, which are separated by mangrove-fringed islets and are together called Great Andaman. The Nicobar Islands comprise 12 inhabited and seven uninhabited islands including the three groups, Car Nicobar in the north, Camorta and Nancowry in the middle and the largest, Great Nicobar in the south.

**Climate** Tropical. Temperature: 20°C to 32°C. Annual rainfall: 2,540 mm. Monsoons – usually May to mid-September, and November to mid-December (though the first may arrive as early as mid-April, bringing heavy rain on most days). Best season is end-November to mid-April. The climate has no extremes, the main contrasts coming with the arrival of the monsoons and tropical storms.

## History

Lying on the trade route between Burma and India the islands appeared on Ptolemy's second century map and were also recorded by the Chinese traveller I-Tsing in the seventh century. At the end of the 17th century the Marathas established a base there to attack the trading British, Dutch and Portuguese ships. Dutch pirates and French Jesuits had made contact with the islands before the Danish East India Company made attempts to evangelize the islands in the mid-18th century. The reputation of ferocity attributed to the Nicobarese may have been partly due to Malay pirates who attacked and killed sailors of any trading vessel that came ashore (some anthropologists believe that in spite of common belief, the aboriginals themselves were not cannibals). The first British attempt to occupy the islands was made in 1788 when the Governor General of India sent Lt Blair (whose name was given to the first port) and, although the first convicts were sent there in 1794, it was abandoned within a couple of years.

After the 'First War of Independence' (the 'Mutiny') in 1857 the British gained control of most of the islands and used them as a penal colony for its prisoners (who until then had been sent to Sumatra) right up to Indian Independence, with a short break from 1942-1945 when the Japanese occupied Port Blair, Ross Island and the Nicobar Islands. However, political prisoners were sent in large numbers only after the completion of the Cellular Jail in 1906. Each revolt on the mainland resulted in the transportation of people from various parts of India, hence the presence of Bengalis, Malayans and Burmese among others. Subhas Chandra Bose, the Indian Nationalist, first raised the Indian tricolour here in 1943.

## Culture

Sir Arthur Conan Doyle in 1890 described the islanders as "perhaps ... the smallest race upon this earth... fierce, morose and intractable". In the mid-19th century, the British guessed the tribal population was around 5,000 but the number has been steadily dwindling. Today most of the inhabitants are Indians, Burmese and Malays – some, descendants of the criminals who were transported there. Since the 1950s, refugees from East Pakistan (now Bangladesh), Burma and Indian emigrants from Guyana have settled on the main islands to be followed more recently by Tamils from Sri Lanka. The largest concentration is around the capital, Port Blair, with the majority of the tribal people (about 15% of the population) living in the Nicobars.

## Tribals of Andaman and Nicobar

One story goes that the monkey god Hanuman stopped in the Andamans on his way to Lanka in search of Sita (see page 1319), giving the islands his name. They have been inhabited by Aboriginal tribes (some Negrito) for thousands of years but remained unexplored because anyone attempting to land would be attacked. Today there are only a few **Andamanese**, who once inhabited the Great Andamans, some **Onges** in Little Andaman who traditionally painted their naked bodies, the fierce **Jarawas** on South Andaman and the **Sentinelese** on North Sentinel. Car Nicobar (Carnic) is inhabited by the mongoloid **Nicobarese**, the most numerous groups, and **Shompens** who may have been of pre-Dravidian stock, live in Great Nicobar.

Hunting wild pigs, fishing with nets and catching turtles with harpoons from dug-out canoes, the islanders used iron for arrowheads and metal from wrecks for harpoons. Some tribes made pottery but the **Andamanese** particularly were exceptional since they had not discovered fire-making.

The Anthropological Survey of India and the Andaman Administration have been jointly trying to establish friendly contact with the Jarawas and Sentinelese since the 1960s. They consistently repelled groups of explorers with poisoned arrows. More recently, some **Sentinelese** have picked up coconuts (which do not grow on their island) that were left on the beach as a gesture of friendship by anthropologists. In January 1991, Indian anthropologists succeeded in landing on North Sentinel and in February, a few Sentinelese boarded a lifeboat to accept gifts of coconuts. Study groups have made regular visits, removing most of their clothes in order to be accepted. The 400 or so Sentinelese do not appear to have a hierarchical social structure; they are naked, painting their bodies with chalk and ochre and wearing bead and bone ornaments. The **Jarawas** remain in the Tribal Reserve set aside to the west of the Andaman Trunk Road, all along the South and Middle Andamans.

Hindi, Bengali, Tamil, Malayalam and English are spoken. The Andamanese language, which bears no resemblance to any other language, uses prefixes and suffixes to indicate the function of a word and is extraordinary in using simply two concepts of number, 'one' and 'greater than one'.

## Modern Andaman and Nicobar

**Economy** Tourism before the tsunami was rapidly becoming the Andamans' most important industry and the runway at the airport was extended in 2003. Forests represent an important resource. The government has divided 40% of the forests into Primitive Tribal Reserve areas which are only open to Indian visitors with permits, and the remaining 60% as Protected Areas set aside for timber for export as plywoods, hardwoods and matchwoods (a Swedish multinational owns extensive logging rights). Rubber and mahogany have been planted in addition to teak and rosewood which are commercially in demand. Fishing – lobsters, prawns and sea fish – and agriculture are also important, with rice a staple food crop.

**Government** As a Union Territory the Andamans and Nicobar Islands have a Lieutenant Governor, Shri Nagendra Nath Jha, a retired member of the Indian Foreign Service and member of the BJP's National Executive since 1994. The islands also have one MP, Shri Bishnu Pada Ray (BJP).

## Tsunami

In December 2004, following the powerful earthquake off the coast of Indonesia, devastating tidal waves hit many countries. In this region, the aboriginal tribals living on the Nicobar Islands bore the brunt of the casualties. The official human fatalities are daunting: 8,000 died in the Nicobars alone, and 80 died on Little Andaman. But this published death toll is contested by aid agencies, who say it is likely that more than half the archipelago's population of 35,000 were lost to the waves. As with all the countries affected, tourism is being encouraged as a direct way of spurring the economic revival that is needed to fund the relief effort and visitor permits are being issued to the Andamans, but the Nicobars, long closed to tourism to protect their tribal cultures, remain so. Of the 572 islands, Car Nicobar was the worst affected. Elsewhere, Little Andaman's two resorts were razed, and many of the other businesses on the islands have let go of staff, but hotels are open and operating. Port Blair, the Andaman's capital, was unscathed. Havelock Island, the government's prime focus for tourism, was not badly damaged, and the corals around Ritchie's Archipelago are all mostly intact and marine life abundant – so there's still good reason, besides those humanitarian, to visit.



# Ins and outs

## Getting there

Foreigners with tourist visas for India are allowed a maximum stay of 30 days on arrival at Port Blair, the capital, by air or sea, but may not visit tribal areas or restricted islands including Nicobar. It is no longer necessary to get a permit in advance. CID will extend your permit up to a maximum stay of 15 days without difficulty, but only when your initial period of approval is about to expire. Any extension is only valid for staying in Port Blair. Foreign tourists may now apply and get a Restricted Area Permit after Registration at Immigration at a cost of US$30 (payable in dollars or rupees, but must be cash). Officially, permits allow foreigners to visit and stay overnight in Port Blair, Havelock, Long Island, Neil Island, entire islands of South and Middle Andaman (excluding tribal reserve), Baratang, Rangat, Mayabunder, Diglipur, North Passage Island, Little Andaman Island (excluding tribal reserve), and all islands in Mahatma Gandhi Marine National Park except Boat, Hobay, Twin Island, Tarmugli, Malay and Pluto Island. You can also visit Jolly Buoy, Red Skin, South Cinque, Mount Harriet and Madhuban, Ross Island, Narcondam, Interview, Brother, Sister and Barren Island during the daytime. In practice, requests to visit remote islands such as Barren, North Passage and Narcondam, which have recently been opened to tourists, are often refused even though ships sail to them. Some dive companies arrange overnight stays on courses. Foreigners working in the Andamans can get a four-month visa but to extend the stay, the person must leave India and re-enter with a new visa and permit. Indians may visit the Andamans and Nicobars without a permit but must obtain a permit for restricted areas. ▸▸ *For Transport details, see page 771.*

## Getting around

Hiring a scooter can be handy for visiting place around Port Blair. Recommended particulalry for trips to Wandoor, Chiriya Tapu, Mt Harriet and Corbyn's Cove. Buses cover sights and towns on the limited road network. Inter-island ferries sail to coastal towns and islands which are far more relaxing than the capital.

# Port Blair

→ *Phone code: 03192. Colour map 6. Population: 100,200.*

*Port Blair, the capital, about 1,200 km from Kolkata and Chennai, has only a handful of sights. The small town has changed in the last three decades from one which saw a ship from the mainland once a month if the weather permitted, to a place connected by flights from Chennai and Kolkata several times a week. It now has a hospital, shops, schools and colleges and a few museums, in addition to resort hotels and watersports facilities.* ▸▸ For Sleeping, Eating and other listings, see pages 769-773.

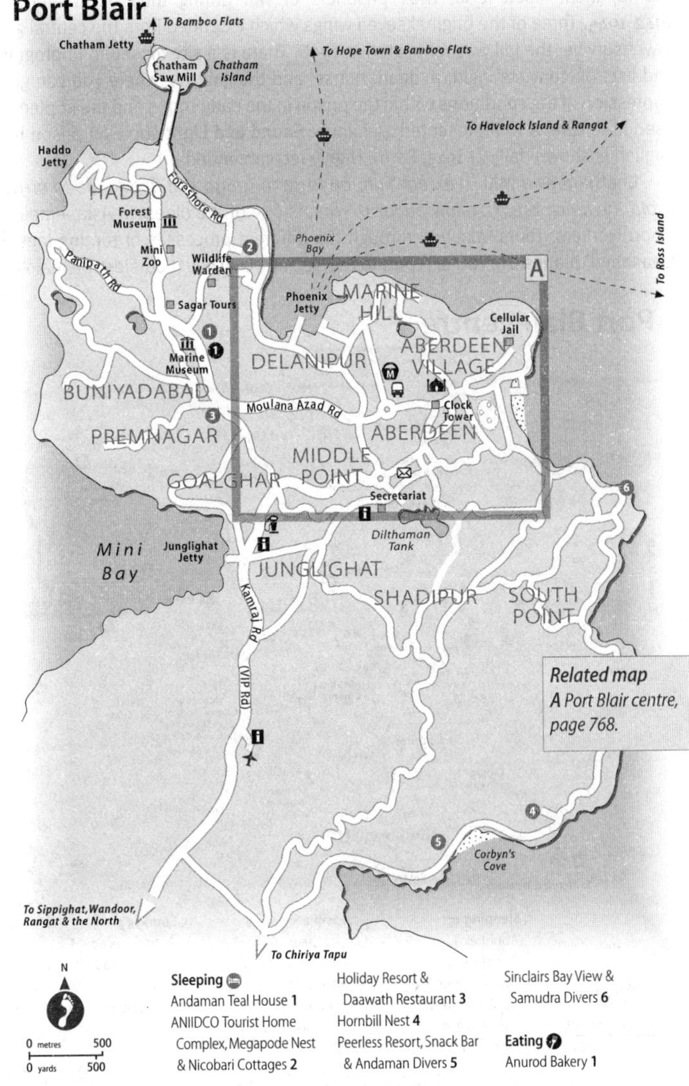

## Ins and outs

**Getting there** Lamba Line airport, 3 km south of Port Blair, has flights from Kolkata and Chennai. You can get a bus or taxi to town. Ships from the mainland dock at Haddo jetty where you can get taxis but they invariably overcharge.

**Getting around** As Port Blair is very small, you can easily see the sights in a couple of days. Aberdeen Village with the bazar in the town centre has most of the budget hotels, the bus station, shops and offices.

## Sights

The **Cellular Jail** (north of Aberdeen Jetty, 1886-1906) ⓘ *closed Mon, 0900-1200, 1400-1700, Rs 5, camera, Rs 10, video camera, Rs 50, allow 1 hr,* was originally built by the British to house dangerous criminals. Subsequently it was used to place Indian freedom fighters until 1938; it could hold 698 solitary prisoners in small narrow cells. The Japanese used it for their prisoners of war during their occupation from 1942-1945. Three of the original seven wings which extended from the central guard tower survive; the jail was renovated in 1998. There is a site **museum**, photographs and lists of 'convicts' held, a 'death house' and the gallows, where you can get an impression of the conditions within the prison in the early 1900s and the implements used in torture. A well-presented 45-minute **Sound and Light** show on prison life in English is shown daily at 1915, Rs 10. Highly recommended.

**Chatham Saw Mill** ⓘ *except Sun, 0630-1430 (0830 is a good time to arrive to avoid the lunch break), allow about 1½ hrs,* is one of the oldest in Asia, employing 1,000 workers. Tours take you through the different processes of turning logs into 'seasoned' planks. For tours, report to the Security Office just outside the main gate.



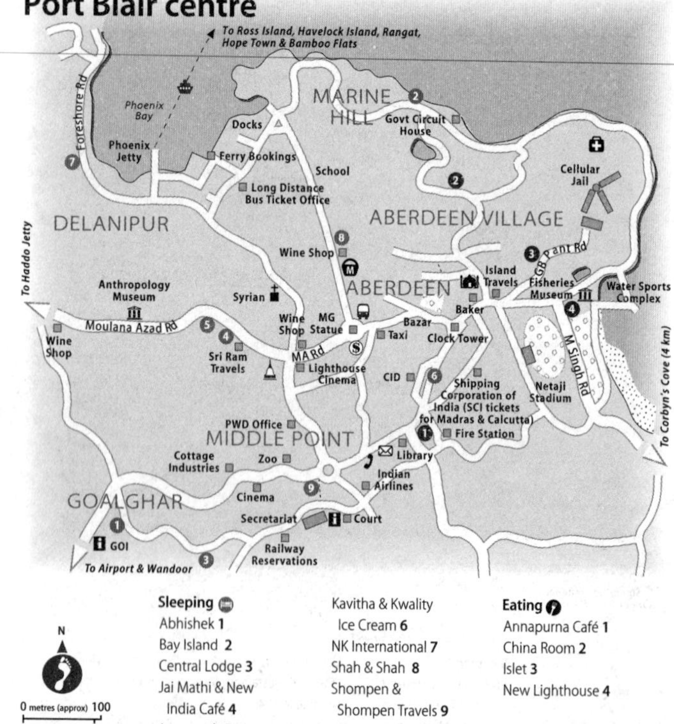

Photography is not allowed. The **Forest Museum** ⓘ *0800-1200, 1430-1700*, here has unusual local woods including red paduk, satin and marble woods and shows the use of different woods in the timber industry and methods of lumbering and finishing.

The **Mini Zoo** ⓘ *closed Mon, 0800-1700*, has a small, uninspiring collection in some very old wooden cages with a few specimens of unusual island fauna including a sea crocodile farm. **Marine Museum** ⓘ *opposite Andaman Teal House, closed Mon, 0830-1200, 1400-1700, Rs 10, camera, Rs 20, video camera, Rs 40, allow 30 mins*, has a collection of corals and shells and a display of 350 species of marine life. **Anthropological Museum** ⓘ *closed Mon, 1000-1230, 1400-1600*, has a small but interesting collection of photographs and artefacts, and records of exploratory expeditions. Worth a visit.

At **Sippighat Farm** ⓘ *closed Mon, 0600-1100, 1200-1600*, 14 km away, you can see cash crops such as spices and other plants being propagated. A watersports complex has been developed nearby (see Entertainment below).

**Viper Island**, near Haddo Wharf, is at the mouth of Port Blair harbour where convicts were interned before the Cellular Jail was built.

Although the only beach close to Port Blair, **Corbyn's Cove**, 5 km from Port Blair, is only busy at weekends. The water is warm with gentle surf and the white-sand beach is clean and palm fringed. A government Eco-friendly Tourist Village is under way 1½ km north of the Cove.

## Sleeping

**Port Blair** *p767, maps p767 and p768*
Many hotels offer discounts Apr-Sep.

**A Bay Island**, Marine Hill, 2 km, T03192 234101, www.welcomegroup.com. 48 a/c rooms, some small, imitating local huts (not all have sea view), cool open lounge and restaurant, good gardens but poor tennis court, sea water pool, keen on conservation , far from beach but excellent view across harbour entrance.

**A-B Peerless Resort**, Corbyn's Cove (4 km), set back from beach, T03192 233461, ppbeachin@sancharnet.in. 48 rooms, 4 cottages, good Snack Bar (see eating below), pleasant and airy, well-kept mature gardens, tennis, beach nearby (take own snorkelling equipment), dive centre, excellent service, warm atmosphere, free airport transfer but need taxis to town (in daytime, best to wait on beach for one passing).

**B Megapode Nest**, Haddo Hill. 25 good a/c rooms off central lounge area (no view), short walk from restaurant, large terrace, very peaceful, very good but no food or drink outside mealtimes.

**B Sinclairs Bay View**, South Pt, T03192 233236, sinclairsbayview@nivalink.com. Refurbished resort hotel in elevated location overlooking Ross Island, no beach, 24 rooms, some a/c, restaurant, excellent and popular bar, pool, dive centre.

**B-D Shompen**, 2 Middle Pt, T03192 233236, hotelshompen@hotmail.com. 40 rooms (noisy in front, windowless and very hot in centre), 15 a/c overpriced, rooftop restaurant, free airport transfer, tours, popular with backpackers, friendly, helpful staff, off-season/long stay discounts.

**B-E Hornbill Nest**, 10 mins' walk from Corbyn's Cove, T03192 246042, hornbillresort @rediffmail.com. Clean rooms, some on hillside overlooking sea, central open-air lounge and restaurant, transport difficult (stop a 'returning empty' taxi), best for those wanting cheapish shared room near beach.

**C Nicobari Cottages**, Haddo Hill, T03192 232207. 2 a/c rondavels, mainly for officials.

**C-E Holiday Resort**, Prem Nagar, T03192 230516, holidayresort88@hotmail.com. Large clean rooms with bath, bucket hot water, good restaurant, TV in lounge, helpful manager, stores luggage, internet.

**D NK International**, Fore Shore Rd, T03192 233066. 31 very simple rooms, some a/c with bath, few with good view across Phoenix Jetty, functional grey concrete block.

*For an explanation of the sleeping and eating price codes used in this guide, see inside the front cover. Other relevant information is found in Essentials pages 56-61.*

## Into the deep

There are many excellent locations for snorkelling. The most popular site for a day trip was MG National Marine Park (Wandoor) though this is currently off-limits to the vast majority of visitors. Another site, Chiriya Tapu, is very easy to reach from Port Blair. It is best to bring your own mask and snorkel. You may need to pay up to Rs 5,000 as deposit when hiring equipment. Most close from early May during the monsoons.

Scuba diving is a boom business in the Andamans and the number of diving schools is growing. It is difficult to find a cheaper and more beautiful location to learn to dive in the world. For fanatics, longer dive trips can be organized to unexplored sites around the Andamans providing enough people are interested. The best dive sites for a day trip are in the vicinity of Cinque Island though the Government tax of Rs 1,000 for dives makes it pricey.

Please do not remove dead coral even if you find pieces on the beach.



**D Tourist Home**, Haddo Hill, 18 refurbished rooms attached to the reception area, restaurant, very good value. Reservations: New Marine Dry Docks, T03192 32376.

**D-E Abhishek**, Goalghar, T03192 233565, hotelabhishek@hotmail.com. Inconvenient location. Friendly, helpful management, good restaurant and bar, snorkel equipment for hire, free transfer (usually meets flights).

**E Andaman Teal House**, Delanipur, T03192 232642. 27 cleanish rooms with bath, some a/c, comfortable wicker furniture, good views, spacious lounge-restaurant.

**E Jagannath**, Moulana Azad Rd, 7 mins from bazar, T03192 232148. 15 clean rooms, some with bath and balcony in newer block but no hot water, filtered water, helpful staff.

**F Central Lodge** Middle Point, Goalghar, T03192 33634. One of the cheapest, some rooms with bath but often full, camping. Set back off road.

**F Jai Mathi**, 78 Moulana Azad Rd, T03192 33457. Large rooms, generally clean but variable standard, bucket hot water, very good cheap food (try ginger fish, prawn *biriyani*), bar, helpful staff.

**F Kavitha**, Aberdeen Bazar, opposite CID, T03192 233762. 24 rooms, often has room when all others full (at time of ship arrive/depart), 1 night only.

**F Shah and Shah**, near Aberdeen Bazar, T03192 233696, shahnshahrediff@mail.com. 23 excellent large clean rooms, huge first floor balcony. Recommended.

**ANIIDCO Tourist Home Complex**, Haddo Hill, T03192 32380. Has a central restaurant, bar and gardens with superb views to the port and Phoenix Bay.

## Eating

Good seafood is now widely available and even the cheapest hotels offer prawn and crab curries. Larger hotels have a wider selection, but meals (most ingredients imported from the mainland) and drinks can be expensive. There are several juice bars between the bus stand and clock tower. Government Guest Houses are open to non-residents. All Indian restaurants have excellent fish fry (spiced tuna or mackerel chunks) for under Rs 15. Highly recommended, especially for trips out of Port Blair.

**TTT Bay Island**, Marine Hill. International. Luxurious surroundings, seafood recommended, lunch buffet Rs 350.

**TT China Room**, Aberdeen Village. Chinese. Owned by Burmese/Punjabi couple. Eat in pleasant shady outdoor yard, dinner by candlelight (but mosquito problem), freshly prepared with home-grown veg, not drenched in oil, soya or tomato sauce, order your own seafood 'specials' the day before, beer.

**TT Islet**, 1st floor, GB Pant Rd (takeaway downstairs). Indian, Chinese. Relax with a cool beer on the narrow balcony with views across stadium, generous portions but quality overrated.

**New India Café**, next to Hotel Jaimathi. Good Indian, some Western dishes. Great food and prices, Continental breakfast, lobster and other specials on request, but very slow service (wait an hour for dinner).

**New Lighthouse**, opposite Municipal Guest House, Indian, Chinese. Wide choice in small open-air café, evening BBQ, closes 2145.

**Shompen Rooftop**. Indian, Continental. Limited menu (try *aloo jeera* and *daal*), fish dishes a bit hit-and-miss.

**Annapurna Café**, Aberdeen Bazar. International. Wide selection, try their different *dosas* and Indian sweets, best place for European style breakfast, a/c rooms, very popular. Recommended.

**Anurod Bakery**, towards Teal House. Sell good cakes, snacks and cornflakes.

**Daawath**, below Holiday Resort. Mainly Indian. Good breakfasts and curries, avoid Western.

**Kwality** ice cream next door to Kavita.

**Snack Bar** at Peerless Beach Resort serves reasonable food (fish and chips), open all day, friendly staff, quick service, good toilets at resort with lockers and changing rooms.

**Teal Bakery** behind bus stand. Good fruit cakes.

**Tourist Home Complex**, Haddo. Indian. Excellent *thali* lunches, try the chicken dishes in the evening.

## Bars and clubs

**Peerless Beach Resort**, **Sinclairs Bay View**, **Tourist Home Complex**, **Abishek** and **Shompen** have bars. Beers and spirits from bar below **Shalimar Hotel**, Delanipur.

## Festivals and events

**End-Feb**: **Island Tourism Festival** for 10 days, with music and dancing from all over India and focusing on local crafts, culture and food.

## Shopping

Local curio shops are by the clocktower and opposite the post office. Tailors sell hammocks.

**Andaman Teal House**, hires out tents, good condition (deposit, Rs 2,500, Rs 50-70 per day).

**Sagarika Cottage Emporium**, next to tourist office, open 0900-1800, closed Sun. Selection of souvenirs in wood and shell (the government limits for collection of shells).

## Activities and tours

### Diving

Havelock also has dive centres.

**Andaman Divers**, Peerless Resort, see Sleeping. Run PADI courses and trips.

**Samudra**, Sinclair Bay View Hotel, see Sleeping. Again PADI courses and trips.

### Swimming

Swimming is excellent. The best spot is the crescent shaped Corbyn's Cove or 1 of the uninhabited islands which tourists may visit for the day.

### Tour operators

**A&N Islands Tours and Travels**, 20/4 Air Rd, Delanipur, T01392 245068, anislands@rediffmail.com. Offers a wild range of sightseeing and tour packages. Efficient and professional.

**Island Travel**, Aberdeen Bazar, T03192 233358. **Indian Airlines/Alliance Air**, **Jet Airways** agents, good for excursions, car hire, postcards and exchange.

**Sagar Tours**, 7 Krishna Building, Haddo, T03192 233703.

**Shompen Travels**, 2 Middle Pt, T03192 232644. Local tours, Wandoor to Jolly Buoy/Red Skin ferry.

### Watersports

Resort hotels have limited equipment.

**Andaman Adventure**, near **Holiday Inn**, has good snorkelling equipment for hire, Rs 60/day, US$100 deposit.

**Andaman Water Sports Complex**, next to Fisheries Museum, Sippighat, T03192 230769. 0700-1100, 1500-2000. Sailing, paddle boats, wind surfing, paragliding.

## Transport

Make sure you confirm reservations. Problems can occur from mid-Apr to mid-May and during the Tourism Festival.

### Air

Alliance Air flights from Kolkata and Chennai, 5 times a week and **Jet Airways** daily from Chennai. The new extended runway may permit flights to/from Delhi. Transport to town: most buses pass the airport entrance. Taxis should charge Rs 30 per person; fix fare first. Some hotels send taxis. Flights are always fully booked at least a month ahead (earlier for Apr-May). However, because of the strict enforcement of the 30-day stay regulations, officials may find you a seat to fly out even at the last moment. If stuck, try for tickets from **Island Travels** or from **Jet Airways**, or **Indian Airlines/Alliance Air**, and ask the office manager to be placed on the priority waiting list. Book well ahead. You may request your international carrier to get Andaman's tickets, preferably 6 months ahead. Reconfirm on arrival in India, and after you get to Port Blair. Avoid mid-Apr when the summer holiday rush starts. **Indian Airlines**, G55 Middle Pt, behind PO, T03192 234744. Airport T03192 32983. **Jet Airways**, 189 Main Rd, Junglighat, T03192 236922, airport T03192 235911.

### Bicycle

Hire from shop between Aberdeen Bazar and the Bus Stop (about Rs 5 per hr) but you need to be very fit to manage the hilly island.

### Bus

Central Bus Station near Aberdeen Bazar serves state and private buses, T03192 232278. Regular service to villages and districts. Bus stops at **Shompen Hotel** and near the airport. A few private buses run between Chatham jetty and the Cellular Jail. To **Rangat**, 2 private buses daily (6-7 hrs), 1 via Mayabunder at 0420. **Mayabunder** daily departs 0530-0630, Rs 70 (deluxe, Rs 120); often noisy video bus. Buy tickets a day ahead from agents around the bus stand. For state buses go to the transport office opposite entrance to Phoenix jetty; numbered tickets go on sale at 1400. Long queues, plenty of touts. *Diglipur Express* is the quickest to the far north, and the only way of reaching Diglipur (which involves crossing 3 creeks) the same night. Depart 0530, arrive 1930 (Rs 90). Others to Mayabunder miss the last ferry to Kalighat (1630) which connects to Diglipur.

### Ferry

There are a bewildering range of **inter-island and harbour ferries** operating from Port Blair. Most operate from Phoenix Bay Jetty. Details from Directorate of Shipping Services, Port Blair, T03192 232426. Passengers may feel sea-sick! Regular sailings to **Havelock, Neil** and **Long Islands, Rangat Bay, Mayabunder** and **Aerial Bay** appear in the *Daily Telegrams* newspaper (or ring Shipping Corp of India for times, T03192 233347). There are 2 decks and hawkers sell snacks on board. **Diglipur** via Aerial Bay Jetty, Tue evening and Fri morning, Rs 90, 14 hrs. **Havelock,** Rs 25, 4 hrs, direct. **Neil**, Wed and Fri, 4 hrs. **Rangat**, 4 a week, 7 hrs. There are also less frequent services to the 2 volcanic islands of Narcondam and Barren. **Little Andaman** (Hut Bay), once a week, Rs 25-70, 8 hrs. Fares are often doubled if tickets are not bought in advance. A Harbour ferry operates from Phoenix Jetty (vehicular only) to Hope Town, Bamboo Flats, Ross Island daily except Wed, 0830, 1000,1230, Rs 20; Cholunga Wharf, Phoenix Bay: Harbour Cruise, Rs 25, 1500-1700, including Viper Island. From Chatham Jetty to Bamboo Flats and Dundas Pt, about hourly, 0600-2025 (2 hrs).

**Mainland ferries** sail between **Haddo Jetty**, Port Blair and Kolkata (66 hrs) and Chennai (60 hrs) run to a schedule of sorts 3 to 4 times a month. Also **Vishakapatnam** (56 hrs) once a month. For immigration formalities, see page 766. Tentative schedules for the month are usually available at the end of the previous month; times of departure and arrival appear about a week before in the local papers. Last minute changes are made depending on weather conditions and tides. Tickets are issued 7 days ahead but are not sold on the day of sailing. They can be difficult to get. Apply with 3 photos to **Shipping Corporation of India**, 2 Supply Rd, near Mosque, T03192 233347, for tickets. Sailing schedules are also available opposite **Lakshmi Narayan Hotel**, Aberdeen Bazar. The Directorate of Tourism (see above) has a tourist quota of 12 bunk class berths for each sailing from Port Blair to Kolkata and Chennai. Put your name down well in advance. A few days before sailing, collect a form which entitles you to claim a berth from the Shipping Corporation of India a day or 2 before tickets go on public sale. Ships vary but prices are approximately: Deluxe Cabin (2 beds, shower), Rs 3,900 each; 1st/A Class (4 bunks, shower), Rs 2,400; B Class (4/8 berth), Rs 2,800; 2nd Class (for 6), Rs 2,700; a/c dormitory, Rs 1,800 (on MV *Akbar* only); Bunk Class, Rs 1,150. The ships are 25 to 65 years old! Meals cost Rs 120 (cabin), Rs 60 (bunk) per day but some may not find them suitable. Carry some snacks. A kiosk sells biscuits, cigarettes, mineral water, soft drinks. Disembarkation can be chaotic and a free-for-all. Taxis demand Rs 50 to go anywhere.

### Motorbike

Hire from **Prashant Travels**, Phoenix Bay, and next to **Jagannath Hotel**. Newish fleet of motorbikes, Rs 150 per day (Rs 1,000 deposit) return by 1900; scooters, Rs 120; **TSG** (TS Guruswamy), Moulana Azad Rd, near Anthropology Museum, T03192 232894. **GDM**, further up the same road, has good Kinetic Hondas, Rs 200 per day (very good condition, start first time!). Check insurance papers.

### Rickshaw and taxi

Please use pre-paid **Traffic Complaint Cards** to report taxi and rickshaw drivers who refuse to use a meter to take you to your destination etc. In time, this may lead to positive action. Available from the Inspector, Traffic Branch, Police Station, Aberdeen (opposite Bus Stand), T03192 234472, ext 309. **Central Taxi Stand**, opposite bus station and by clocktower, Aberdeen Bazar, charge Rs 20 about town, Rs 50 for Corbyn's Bay and Haddo Jetty. They generally refuse to use meters and are overpriced.

### Train

**Railway Reservations Office**, near Secretariat, T03192 233042, 0800-1230, 1300-1400. Supposedly separate queues for Kolkata and Chennai, but a total free-for-all in a small building – a sad sight of a crowd behaving badly. Best avoided. Buy tickets in advance on the mainland if possible.

## Directory

**Banks** Credit cards are not accepted anywhere in the Andamans. TCs are only changed at **Island Travels**, Aberdeen Bazar, Port Blair. **Island Travels** change currency and TCs. Hotels **Shompen** and **Bay Island** will change TCs if you spend foreign currency there. **State Bank of India** opposite bus station. Open 0900-1300, Sat 0900-1100. **Laundry** Near Bazar Taxi stand recommended. **Libraries** State Library, near **Annapoorna Café**, has a small collection of reference books on the Andamans, useful for identification of corals and fish. Open 1230-1945. **Post** GPO, near centre, by Indian Airlines office. 0700-2200 weekdays, 0800-1800 weekends. **CTO**, for international calls and fax service. Also several private STD and ISD booths. Make your important international calls in Port Blair since links from elsewhere on the islands are unreliable. **Tourist offices** **Govt of India**, 2nd floor (above Super Shoppe), 189 Junglighat Main Rd (VIP Rd), T03192 233006. Enthusiastic, knowledgeable officer (printout of local information). **Director of Tourism**, opposite Indian Airlines, T03192 232694. Register on the Tourist Quota for boats to Kolkata and Chennai. Unhelpful reception desk (notice "Your time is precious, do not waste it here" sums it up!). Poor postcards. Airport counter open at flight times, T03192 232414. **ANIIDCO** (Andaman and Nicobar Islands Integrated Dev Corp), New Marine Dry Docks (first gate after entrance to Phoenix jetty), T03192 32098/33695. Airport counter T03192 232414. Runs **Tourist Home Complex**, Haddo. Screens occasional films about the islands. **Useful addresses** Fire, T03192 232101. **Hospital**, T03192 232102. **Police**, T03192 233077. **Chief Conservator of Forests**, T03192 233321; Deputy, T03192 232816. Helpful. **PWD Office**, between **Shompen** and **Lighthouse Cinema**, T03192 233050.

# South Andaman and the Marine National Park

## Chiriya Tapu

Chiriya Tapu, 28 km from Port Blair, at the southern tip of South Andaman, is only an hour by road. Popular for birdwatching, it has excellent beaches with good snorkelling. From the bus stop, which has some tea shops, a track past the **Forest Guest House** (not possible to stay here), leads to the first beach. Continue along the trail through the forest for 20 minutes (several smaller trails are ideal for birdwatching), until you reach a second beach with very good corals 50 m out; at low tide you can walk a long way. The corals are not so spectacular along the coastline, but there is a large range of fish. » *For Sleeping, Eating and other listings, see page 776.*

## Mount Harriet

The hill is good for either a morning or a whole day trip but make an early start to avoid the heat. A path through the forest starts by the derelict water viaduct in Hope Town, which joins the surfaced road near the top (excellent vines for would-be-Tarzans

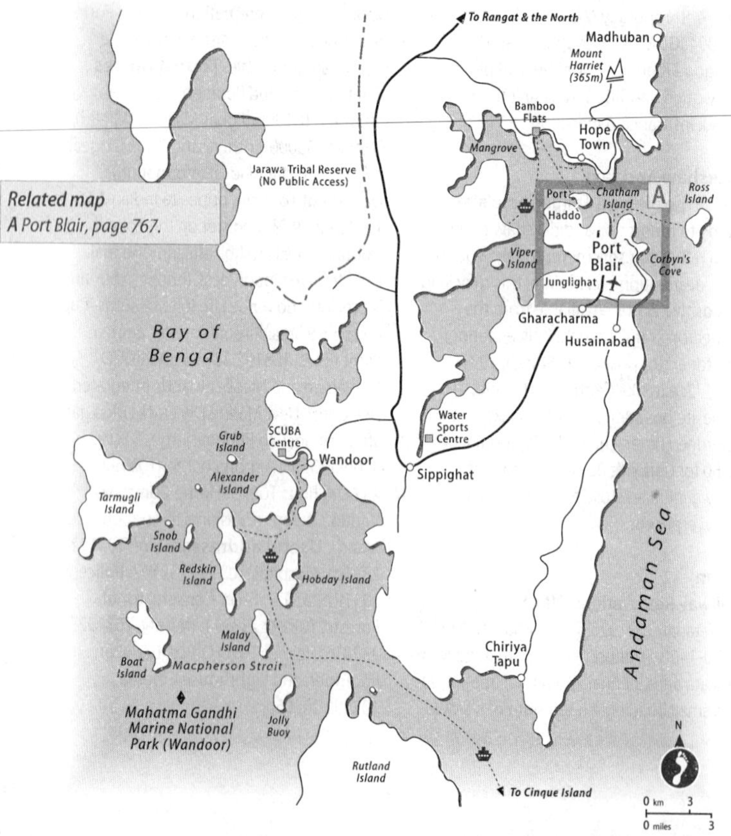

**The rest of the buildings on Ross Island are ruins with spotted deer living peacefully among them. In many cases the walls are only still standing because of the climbing trees...**

here!). Allow 1½ hours to the top. Alternatively, the bus from the jetty stops in Hope Town near the viaduct, or will drop you at the start of the road up the hill with a 4-km walk from here. Near the top of the road lie the ruins of the Chief Commissioner's bungalow, abandoned in 1942. Signs show where the rooms were.

It is also possible to ride a scooter to the top but you will pass the **Forest Check Post** ⓘ *Rs 10, scooter Rs 10, camera Rs 25, video camera Rs 1,500,* where national park fees are charged. Taking the forest path on foot avoids the check post and fees.

## Black Rocks

Black Rocks (Kalapathar) is 2 km from Mount Harriet and **Madhuban** via Mount Carpenter, 16 km. A signpost marks the start of the nature trail from Mount Harriet which is easy to follow as far as the Black Rocks, the spot where prisoners were pushed to their death. After Black Rocks, the trail is unclear; it is easy to get lost so take a guide if you plan to walk the whole route. The walk back along the rocky coast is uninteresting; you can get a bus 5 km after the lighthouse. **Madhuban Beach** is on the east side where young elephants are trained for forestry; at **Burma Nalla**, 3 km away, they are used for lumbering.

## Ross Island

Ross Island was originally developed under the British as the Residence of the Chief Commissioner, and the administrative headquarters. During the Second World War, it was occupied by the Japanese whose legacy is an ugly complex of concrete bunkers which are still intact. The rest of the buildings on the island are ruins with spotted deer living peacefully among them. In many cases the walls are only still standing because of the climbing trees. However, the church in the centre and the Subalterns' club are impressive. The small **museum** ⓘ *open dawn to dusk, except Wed, Rs 10 on arrival; foreigners must sign a registration book, allow 2 hrs, boat charter Rs 1,000 (no tourist boat),* by the cafeteria has interesting old photos. The island is officially still under the jurisdiction of the Indian Navy and swimming is not allowed despite the clear enticing waters by the jetty.

## Mahatma Gandhi Marine National Park

ⓘ *Entry is currently closed to tourists, except those on foreign registered yachts who can receive prior permission at the time of application. Private boat operators (local) are currently not allowed to conduct trips/tours to Jolly Buoy or Red Skin for the time being. The situation remains fluid, though as there is intense lobbying to get the decision reversed. Cinque Island is technically accessible on a tour, but at present there are no local tour operators conducting tours. Snorkelling around Wandoor is still allowed.*

About 30 km southwest of Port Blair, the Mahatma Gandhi Marine National Park protects some exceptional coral beds and underwater life off some of these uninhabited islands. Covering an area of 280 sq km, the park is a group of 15 islands with blue waters separating them. It includes Grub, Redskin, Jolly Buoy, Pluto, Boat

Island, with Tarmugli to the west, Kalapahar or Rutland to the east and the Twins to the south. It is very rich, not only in marine life, but also in the variety of tropical flowers and birds. The dense forests come down to the beach where the mangrove thrives on the water's edge. There are angelfish, green parrot, yellow butterfly, black surgeon, blue damsel fish, silver jacks, squirrel, clown fish and sweetlips as well as sea cucumbers, sea anemones, starfish and a variety of shells – cowries, turbots, conches and the rarer giant clam, up to a metre wide (coral and shell collecting is strictly forbidden). There are turtles, sharks and barracudas on the outer reefs and many beautiful corals including brain, finger, mushroom and antler, the colours derived from the algae that thrive in the living coral.

## Sleeping

**Chiriya Tapu** *p774*
There are excellent camping spots here, with fresh water, in the village set back from the Munda Pahar Beach. The trail continues through the forest to a couple of smaller beaches.

**Mount Harriet** *p774*
**Forest Guest House** (with permission). You can get water and tea from the caretaker. There is an octagonal viewing platform at the top with good views of Ross Island, and a small garden for picnics.

## Eating

**Ross Island** *p775*
A small cafeteria sells cold drinks and biscuits. Take a picnic if you plan to spend the day, and if the cafeteria is shut, try cracking open a fallen coconut.

## Transport

**Chiriya Tapu** *p774*
Buses leave from Port Blair stand at 0500, 0730, 1030, 1200 (1 hr) but often late; returns 10 mins after arrivals; last at 1900. It is an easy journey by hired scooter but beware of oncoming traffic; the single-track road has many blind bends. Taxi Rs 120 one way.

**Mount Harriet** *p774*
Tours are operated by the Directorate of Shipping from Phoenix Bay Jetty, T03192 232725. Vehicles must take a ferry from Phoenix Bay to Bamboo Flats. Chatham to Hope Town or Bamboo Flats carry foot passengers only; from Bamboo Flats it is a 20-min walk along the coast to Hope Town. A bus (0600, 0800) runs along this road. For return from Hope Town jetty: 1315, 1415 to Bamboo Flats and 1500 to Phoenix Bay; Bamboo Flats to Chatham Jetty: 1520, 1615, 1735, 1830. Taxis charge Rs 350 return to the top from Bamboo Flats jetty. By road alone it is 45 km instead of 15 km.

**Ross Island** *p775*
Boats (daily except Wed) from Phoenix Jetty, 0830, 1030, 1230, 1400, 1500. Take early boat as later ones get crowded, especially at weekends. Return boat at 0840, 1040, 1240, 1410, 1640.

## Activities and tours

**Mahatma Gandhi National Park** *p775*
Tours depend on demand, minimum 10 people; ask your hotel to enquire. The cost, around Rs 1,000, covers transport to/from any hotel in Port Blair, park entry fee, simple packed lunch, soft drinks and bottled water. You will be picked up around 0530 and taken to Wandoor Village by boat (3½-4 hrs, depending on the tide) allowing a maximum of four hours on the island since boats must return before dark.

## Transport

**Mahatma Gandhi National Park** *p775*
From Port Blair there are frequent public buses to Wandoor, where from the wooden jetty by the Park Reception Centre, tour boats leave daily at 1000 and return about 1430. Bus, Rs 8 (tour operators charge Rs 100 return!); 0830 bus connects with the 1000 tour.

# Ritchie's Archipelago

*The archipelago lies between 20 and 40 km off the east coast of south Andaman and Baratang Islands. Most are inhabited, but only three are open to foreign visitors: Havelock, Neil and Long Island. They are the focus of the government's tourist effort and can be reached by the regular ferry service between Port Blair (Phoenix Jetty) and Rangat Bay (Nimbutala Jetty).* ▸▸ *For Sleeping, Eating and other listings, see pages 778-779.*

## Havelock Island

This beautiful island with pristine white beaches is the government's principal centre for tourist development outside Port Blair. It is the island chosen by most visitors as an escape from Port Blair. Despite its popularity, you can – as anywhere in the Andamans – escape from other visitors and find your private bit of beach for the day.

**South Andaman & Ritchie's Archipelago**

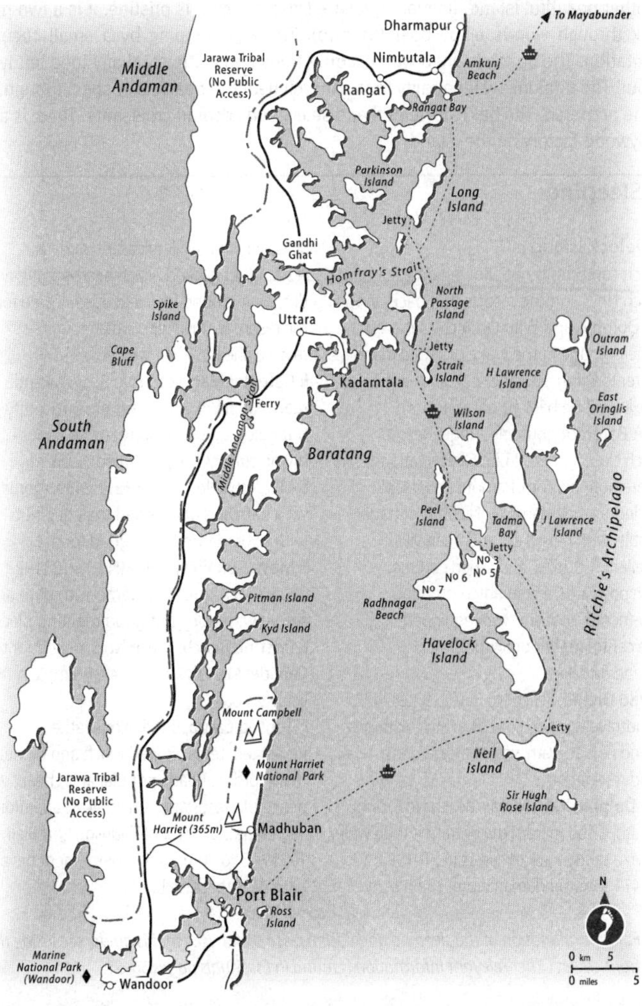

In November 2004, *Time* magazine (Asia) voted beach No 7 on Havelock Island the best beach in Asia. You can cycle along the road to Radhnagar beach (No 7), 11 km to the southwest of the Jetty (No 1), and one of the best in the Andamans. Beach No 3 is 3 km from the jetty, while No 5 is further south. A week-long **Mela** marking the birth of Subhas Chandra Bose is held in January with special Bengali cultural programmes. On arrival passports and permits are checked at the jetty where guesthouse touts pester new arrivals. There is a rather confusing system of referring to beaches and settlements on the island by numbers. Sand flies can be a real nuisance.

## Neil Island

Neil is the smallest island in the Andamans you can stay on. Lushly forested with good snorkelling, it is very relaxed and attracts fewer visitors than Havelock. The best beach is close to the jetty and you will find shops sell provisions and basic camping gear but not tents or hammocks. Camping is allowed. Beach No 1 is unspoilt and peaceful though visitors often leave litter behind. Ask to get water from a farm well.

## Long Island

Another beautiful island, its main beach – Lalaji beach – is pristine. It is a two-hour walk through woods or by boat (Rs 200). There is camping by a small coconut plantation. The beach is lined with coconut trees and cattle steal any food left lying about! The drinking water quality from the well near the beach is suspect though, so come prepared. The baker is helpful and sells good coconut croissants. There is also a plywood factory on the island.

## Sleeping

**Havelock Island** *p777*
Beach camping is not allowed on the island. Beach No 5 and the resorts that back on to it – **Dolphin** and **Wild Orchid** – suffered some damage in the wake of the tsunami (water logging, subsidence). It is expected that all will be back to normal soon.

**AL-A Barefoot** (formerly **Jungle Resort**), Beach No 7, T03192 237656, reservations @barefootindia.com. Remote and deeply shaded, 9 small, bamboo, Nicobari cottages on stilts with nets, 8 a/c andaman villas, excellent, 1 duplex and 4-bed cottage. Beer, postcards, restaurant, promoting 'eco-friendly tourism', well-equipped dive centre (**Barefoot Scuba**). Price includes breakfast.

**B Wild Orchid**, Beach No 3, T03192 282472, islandtravel@yahoo.com. Thai-style cottages, ac and non ac, bath, verandah, gardens, good restaurant.

**B-D Dolphin Yatri Niwas**, Beach No 5, public bus stops 100 m from the entrance, then walk down a sandy track to campsite, T01392 282411, www.andaman.nic.in. 18 huts on stilts, very thin walls, pleasant gardens, restaurant, no good beach nearby as it is a dumping ground for felled trees cleared for the resort, popular with Indian tourists so reserve ahead.

**E Café del Mar**, Beach No 3, www.andamanscubaclub.com. 6 simple but comfy bungalows, good restaurant, spacious, diving run by 2 experienced Swiss.

**E MS**, Jetty (No 1), T01392 282439, rooms with bath and open-sided thatched huts with floor mattress, net, good food.

**E Maya Sea View**, Jetty (No 1), T03192 282367, 8 rooms vary, some with bath and sea view, shabby but good meeting place.

**E Pristine Beach**, Beach No 3, next door to Café del Mar, T03192 82344. 6 simple huts, licensed bar.

**F Tented Camp**, Beach No 5, rather neglected, tents, limited lunch and dinner thalis (order ahead), popular and cheap, very peaceful, closes at first rainfall. Reservation Secretariat, Director of Tourism, Port Blair, T03192 32694. There is a permanent naval base near this beach.

*For an explanation of the sleeping and eating price codes used in this guide, see inside the front cover. Other relevant information is found in Essentials pages 56-61.*

**Neil Island** *p778*
D-E **Hawabill Nest**, T03192 82630, simple, clean rooms (Rs 400-800 if a/c works) with hot shower, dorm (Rs 75), cook (buy provisions in the market and ask him to prepare meal), snorkel hire. Reservation, Secretariat, Director of Tourism, Port Blair, T03192 82694.

**Long Island** *p778*
F **Forest Dept Guest House**, on path uphill to the left from jetty, simple but only Rs 20. Must book ahead in Port Blair or Rangat.

## Eating

**Havelock Island** *p777*
Near Jetty, No 1, there are several basic places serving reasonable fish, vegetable and rice dishes: **Das** is the friendliest and best; **MS**, wonderful garlic fish (pick your own!); **Women's Co-op Café** does good *thalis*.
At Beach No 7, aside from the resorts: **Harmony**, near the beach, serves excellent lunch/dinner, Rs 60 (delicately spiced huge fish steak, spicy vegetables, chips, dessert) but order before owner's market visit, pots of tea all day (books, cassettes to accompany), great atmosphere, packed in the evening, may have to wait 2 hrs in season so friendly and enterprising Ashok has set up chess, backgammon and *carom*.

**Neil Island** *p778*
**Chand**, in the village, does great chick pea *daal*, egg rolls and *vadai*s.
**Shanti**, next door, is good too. Bottled water is in short supply.

## Shopping

**Havelock Island** *p777*
Village No 3 has a good market.
**General Stores**, varied camping equipment.

## Activities and tours

**Havelock Island** *p777*
**Andaman Scuba Club**, Beach No 3 at Café del Mar, www.andamanscubaclub.com (better areas and prices than from Port Blair), Swiss run, professional and friendly, digital equipment, PADI course, 2-dive trip with dive master.
**Barefoot Scuba**, Beach No 7 at **Barefoot**. Recently set up so equipment brand new. Offer good trips.

## Transport

**Havelock Island** *p777*
Two taxis and a jeep drive from the jetty to Beach Nos 3, 5 and 7, Rs 10-30.

**Bikes**
Bikes and scooters: for hire at Jetty (ask at hotel) or at the *paan* shop under **Susmita Electronics**. Also outside **Dolphin Yatris Niwas**. Bikes, Rs 35; scooters, Rs 125.

**Bus**
Regular service from Jetty (No 1) all the way to Radhnagar Beach (No 7), via Village No 3 and **Dolphin Resort** (No 5); 2 hourly, 0700-1100, 1500-1900; from No 7, 0600-1000, 1400-1800. Avoid being swamped by school children at 0800 and 1500.

**Ferry**
Inter-island, from Phoenix Jetty to Havelock, daily, 0600, 4-6 hrs depending on boat; new faster service on Rangat 0600, 1200 (not daily, usually weekends), 2 hrs (buy ticket at Phoenix Jetty the day before 0900-1100).

**Neil Island** *p778*
Neil Island to Port Blair takes 4 hrs, Rs 9; Neil Island to Havelock, 2½ hrs, Rs 6.

**Long Island** *p778*
There are usually 3 boats a week from Port Blair, Phoenix Bay Jetty, via Havelock.

## Directory

**Havelock Island** *p777*
**Bank** for exchange. **Internet** at No 7.
**Medical centre** at No 3.

# Middle and North Andamans

*The Andaman Trunk Road is the only road to the north from Port Blair. Since it passes through the restricted Jarawa tribal reserve, it is not possible to drive along this yourself. There are daily buses to Rangat and Mayabunder. Occasionally the more adventurous Jarawas hitch a lift on the bus to the edge of the reserve. The route runs through some spectacular forest but sadly, despite controls, there has already been a lot of selective clearance of hardwoods. Accommodation options are limited.* » *For Sleeping, Eating and other listings, see pages 782-784.*

## Middle Andaman

### Rangat

It is the only place with a choice of private accommodation for at least 20 visitors. **Amkunj Beach**, 8 km away, has little shade left but there is good snorkelling off the rocks at the top end of the beach: from Rangat, take any bus heading for Nimbutala or Mayabunder up to the fork for Rangat Bay, then walk 1 km along track to right just after the heli-pad.

There is a good sandy beach across the road from **Hawksbill Nest**. Ideal for swimming but it is a Wildlife Sanctuary where turtles nest between November to April. In order to step onto the beach permission is needed from the Forest Department at Rangat, Mayabunder or the Beat Officer at Betapur, 4 km north of Hawksbill Nest; entrance fee Rs 10 per day. Those caught on the beach without permission are promised "an unpleasant experience".

### Mayabunder → *157 km by sea from Port Blair.*

Mayabunder is the administrative centre for Middle and North Andaman. All amenities are situated along a single road which runs along the brow of a ridge sticking out into the bay; the port is at the north end.

You can visit **Karmateng Beach**, 25 minutes away by bus. A shallow sandy slope over 1 km long, with a few rocks at the north end, it is not so good for snorkelling or swimming, as it is exposed and the sea is choppy. A short distance from Karmateng is another idyllic beach popular with foreign tourists at **Gujinala**. You need permission from DFO in Mayabunder or from Beat Officer at Karmateng.

There are several islands in the bay opposite the jetty which can be reached by *dunghy*; ask fishermen and expect to pay Rs 120 for a boat charter for several hours. All offer safe beaches for swimming but there is no good coral.

### Avis Island and around

This tiny island is just east of Mayabunder but its ownership is disputed between the Forestry Department and The Coconut Society of Mayabunder. To visit, get permission from DCF, Mayabunder, and charter a *dunghy*. Foreign tourists are also permitted to visit (with permission from DCF, Mayabunder) **Curlew Island, Rayhill Island, Sound Island, Interview Island** and **Mohanpur** on the eastern coast of North Andaman. Tourists are encouraged to destroy illegal deer traps they find.

### Interview Island

The island which has wild elephants now has a Protected Forest. Day visits can in theory be organized from Mayabunder, 20 km away. You may be able to stay overnight at the **Forest Department Guest House** with three rooms; contact DCF, Mayabunder. It can only be visited in a private boat.

## Barren Islands

Across to the east from Middle Andaman, Barren has India's only active volcano which erupted in 1991 causing widespread destruction of the island's ecosystem. Smoky fire belches from the side of the crater. It is only possible to visit on a day trip with no landings permitted. Sailings are infrequent and it is essential to get a permit from the tourist office in Port Blair.

# North Andaman

## Kalighat

It is a small settlement at the point where the creek becomes too shallow for the ferry to go any further. Of no particular interest, it still makes a very pleasant and peaceful stopover between Port Blair and the north. You can cross the river by the mangrove footbridge and follow the path up into the forest which is good for birdwatching. Sadly you also get a good impression of how many hardwoods are being logged.

You can (with some effort; little English spoken) take a bus to the beach at Ramnagar (11 km). Better still, hire a cycle for Rs 5 per hour and enjoy a very pleasant push, ride, free-wheel, with a refreshing swim at the end as a reward.

## Diglipur

Previously known as Port Cornwallis, Diglipur is the most northerly commercial centre which foreigners can visit. There is a good market and shops; a special **Mela** is held during January/ February which attracts traders.

## Aerial Bay

The small fishing village is the last peaceful location before returning to Port Blair. Most of the fish is taken to the market in Diglipur.

## Smith and Ross Islands

From Aerial Bay, you can visit the islands just north where it is possible to camp on pleasant forested beaches (though there are plans to build bungalows here, in which case free camping may be banned). You need permission from the Range Officer, opposite Jetty entrance. The ferry leaves at 0600 and 1400 (Rs 5), or hire a dunghy.

## Saddle Peak National Park

Theoretically 'Lamia Bay Permits' for Saddle Peak and Lamia Bay are available from the Beat Officer in Lamia Bay. However, the path from Lamia Bay to Saddle Peak is very overgrown. **Kalipur** is a small group of farm houses on both

 sides of the road with a shop and a **Yatri Niwas** a few kilometres south of Aerial Bay. There is a very interesting beach at Kalipur with Saddle Peak as an impressive backdrop, accessible via a small path almost opposite the **Turtle Resort**.

**Lamia Bay** has a pebble beach south of Kalipur which you can walk to. From the bus stop the road leads straight ahead onto a path which is easy to follow (30 minutes). It is possible to camp under a small, round palm-leaf shelter. To the north, there are small bays strewn with large eroded boulders, whilst the beaches to the south lead towards Saddle Peak (730 m), 4½ km away.

Despite the relatively short distance to **Saddle Peak**, the rocky beach, the steep climb, the thick forest and the heat, mean that you need a whole day for the trek, starting early in the morning after camping in Lamia Bay. Don't attempt the whole trip in a day from Aerial Bay.

## Narcondam Island

East of North Andaman, this is the most remote island in the group. An extinct craterless volcano, it is covered in luxuriant forest that is the home of the unique Narcondam hornbill was declared a sanctuary in 1977. It is a birdwatchers' paradise though permission to visit is very hard to get and only 24-hour stops are allowed. There are occasional sailings from Aerial Bay.



## Sleeping

### Rangat *p780*

E **Hawksbill Nest**, Cuthbert Bay, 18 km from Rangat (buses to Mayabunder go past all day, ask for 'Yatri Niwas'). 8 clean sea-facing rooms (Rs 250, better views on 1st floor), 2 a/c (Rs 400) 4-bed dorms (Rs 75). Book ahead at Secretariat, Director of Tourism, Port Blair, T03192 282630.

F **Chandra Mohan Lodge**, blue wooden building on outskirts of town, rundown, but friendly staff.

### Mayabunder *p780*

E **Swiftlet Nest**, 10 km from Mayabunder, away from the beach, contact Directorate of Tourism, T03192 273495, overlooking paddy fields (forest not cleared at the beach). 10 good rooms (Rs 250), 4 a/c (Rs 400), dorm (Rs 75), 'manager absent' but good food, helpful staff.

F **Dhanalakshmi** and **Lakshmi Narayan** have small, dirty rooms.

As a last resort, **Jetty Waiting Rooms** provide some shelter and canteen food.

### Kalighat *p781*

There are a few hotels near the jetty.

F PWD **Rest House**, on a hill, 2 mins' walk from jetty (book ahed in Port Blair). 3 rooms (1 for VIPs only), friendly house-keeper, excellent vegetable *thalis*, generous portions.

### Diglipur *p781*

E **Drua**, 15 rooms (Rs 200), unhelpful manager.

F **Laxmi**, 4 clean rooms with common bath (Rs 120), friendly, helpful. Recommended.

**Sports Stadium**, with clean, spacious, guarded area for travellers with immaculate toilets and showers. Recommended.

### Aerial Bay *p781*

F PWD **Rest House** high up on a hill (book ahead in Port Blair). 2 rooms, often full. Also an unmarked wooden hotel on the left, coming into town from Diglipur.

### Saddle Peak National Park *p781*

E-F **Turtle Resort Yatri Niwas**, 8 rooms, Rs 250 (4 a/c, Rs 400), dorm (Rs 75), poor food, dirty public areas, unhelpful staff. Very peaceful, on a hillock overlooking paddy fields with thick forests leading up to the Saddle Peak National Park to the south. Though called 'Turtle Resort', the rooms are named after birds like Ostrich and Penguin! Contact T03192 2747.

## Eating

### Rangat *p780*

**Annapurna**, on corner of vegetable market (from bus stand, turn left opposite **Krishna Lodge**, then right and left again). Good food.

**Darbar Bakery**, near bus stand (on right, at

start of road leading to PWD Rest House). Good selection.

**Kalighat** *p781*
**Viji** has okay food, with a**bakery**, next door.

**Diglipur** *p781*
Plenty of snack bars, tea houses and fresh fruit in the market.

**Aerial Bay** *p781*
Excellent fish is sold near harbour gates; larger fish (tuna and barracuda) in the afternoon (Rs 20-30 per kg). A few shops sell basic provisions and there is a small market by the bus stand.
**Mohan**, owner speaks some English and is helpful, will prepare excellent fish dishes for you, good thalis, selection of drinks.

## Transport

**Rangat** *p780*
**Bus**
To **Mayabunder** 0600, connects with ferry to Kalighat at 0930, later bus at 1145; to **Port Blair** *Exp* (B), daily, 0800, 0900 (Rs 33). From **Port Blair** by bus to Rangat there are 2 ferry crossings (Nilambur and Gandhi Ghat). Takes up to 8 hrs to Rangat town, depending on bus connections, ie whether your bus goes on this ferry and/or if bus is waiting on other side at Nilambur.

**Ferry**
The jetty is at Rangat Bay (Nimbutala), 7 km from town. To **Port Blair** 0600, 7 hrs, buy tickets (Rs 30) on board. There is an 'Inner' (Creek) and an 'Outer' route, the latter via Strait, Havelock (30-min stop) and Neil islands (see Transport under Port Blair). Lumber boats from Mangrove Jetty go to **Long Island**; **Mayabunder**, 3 per week, 3 hrs.

**Mayabunder** *p780*
**Bus**
**Port Blair** *Exp* (A) and (C), depart 0600, tickets sold from 1500 the day before, at bus station (2 km from jetty). **Rangat** local bus, 0830-1700. Also some private buses. **Karmateng** many for beach, 0715-1700 (return bus approximately 35 mins after these times). **Diglipur** the road is still under construction.

**Ferry**
For **Diglipur** take local ferry to Kalighat, or wait for the inter-island ferry from Port Blair which calls here en route to Aerial Bay every 11-12 days. **Kalighat** small sea ferry daily, 0930, 1445, 2½ hrs (Rs 3), is very crowded, with little shade. Private *dunghies* leave at dawn; they can carry 20 people (Rs 25 each) and the occasional scooter; a charter costs Rs 400. **Port Blair** Check outside Asst Commissioner's office near police station for schedules.

**Kalighat** *p781*
**Bus**
To **Diglipur** Regular local service (45 mins), 0630, 0800, 1030, 1130, 1400, connect with ferry from Mayabunder.

**Ferry**
To **Mayabunder** daily, 0500, 1230, 2 hrs (Rs 3), can get very crowded and virtually no shade; also *Dunghy*, 0600, 2 hrs (Rs 15); or charter a *dunghy* at any time for about Rs 300 (the rate for a full boat).

**Diglipur** *p781*
Buses to all the surrounding villages and beaches. Regular service to Kalighat, 45 mins (last at 1900) and Aerial Bay (30 mins) which has the occasional boat to Port Blair.

**Aerial Bay** *p781*
**Bus**
It is not possible to reach Port Blair by bus in 1 day, the furthest you can hope to get is Rangat. Private and public buses to **Diglipur** and **Kalipur**, approximately every hour.

**Ferry**
To **Mayabunder** and **Port Blair** (2 sailings a month). The jetty ticket office is not always sure when the next boat is due; better to contact the coastguard tower who have radio contact with Port Blair (no telephone connection with South Andaman). Fare: bunk Rs 47, deck Rs 27 (cabins for Govt officials only); Indian canteen meals. Tickets go on sale the day before departure at the Tehsildar's office, next to Diglipur *Rest House*; to avoid a long wait there, buy on the boat, though you may sometimes have to pay more, and only get a deck ticket.

**Saddle Peak National Park** *p781*

**Bus**

Buses between Diglipur and Kalipur, via Aerial Bay. From Kalipur: departs 1230, 1330, 1530, 1740, 2015; to Aerial Bay, 25 mins, Rs 2.

## Directory

**Rangat** *p780*

**Banks** State Bank of India, by the bus stand.

**Post** opposite the Police Station.

# Little Andaman Island

This large island lies 120 km south of Port Blair across the Duncan Passage. It takes about eight hours to get here. The main village, **Hut Bay** to the southeast, is 2 km away from the jetty. Heavily deforested during the 1960s and 1970s, much of the island has become virtually treeless. Betel, red palm and banana plantations dominate the scenery. There were two resorts, both were razed during the tsunami. Prior to the arrival of the resorts, it was possible to camp on the large beach in the north of the island, around 22 km from the jetty. If you do make the trip take food and water. Be aware that the area is notorious for malaria.

# Nicobar Islands

The names given by travellers and sailors from the east and the west all referred to these islands as the Land of the Naked – Nicobar is derived from the Tamil word *nakkavaram*. The islands which lay on the trade route to the Far East were visited in the 11th century by the seafaring Cholas during the rule of King Rajendra I who attempted to extend his rule here. Before the British used the Nicobars as a penal territory in the late 19th century, European missionaries (particularly the Danish) made converts during the 17th and 18th centuries but few survived the difficulties of the climate and most died of fever within a year.

The islands, including **Katchal** with a large rubber plantation, **Nancowry** harbour, **Indira Point**, India's southernmost tip and **Campbell Bay** (Great Nicobar), are closed to foreign visitors; Car Nicobar to the north can be visited by Indians with a permit. The significant tribal population live in distinctive huts, which look like large thatched domes that are raised on stilts about 2 m high and are entered through the floor. The Nicobarese enjoy wrestling, fishing, swimming and canoeing but are best known for their love of music. Villages still participate in competitions of traditional unaccompanied singing and dancing which mark every festivity.

# South India

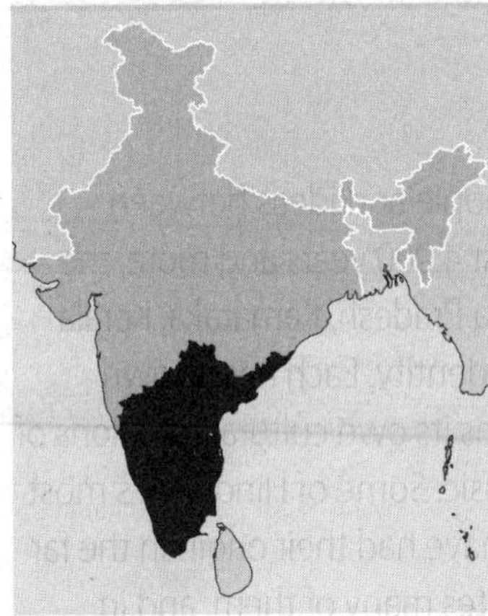

# Introduction

Despite the continuous flow of people and ideas between North and South India over the last 4,000 years and more, the four states of South India – Andhra Pradesh, Karnataka, Kerala and Tamil Nadu – have a distinct identity. Each has its own major language, and the region has its own cultural traditions of literature, art, architecture and music. Some of Hinduism's most important schools of philosophy have had their origin in the far south, yet here Christianity pre-dates many of them, and in Kerala and Tamil Nadu makes a far more visible contribution to life than in most other parts of India.

As a backdrop to this cultural diversity is a great range of often beautiful scenery. The Nilgiris ('blue hills') may be thought of as only hills in comparison with the Himalaya, but soaring to over 2,500 metres they often present a dramatic wall overlooking the plains of Tamil Nadu to the east or the narrow coastal strip of Kerala and Karnataka to the west. Delightful hill stations – Kodaikkanal, Coonoor, Munnar and the more popular Ooty – enjoy the best of a low latitude, high altitude climate. On the plains below are some of India's greatest cultural treasures, including the distinctive southern temples at Madurai, Thanjavur and Mamallapuram among many, while forts and palaces add another dimension to the visitor's choices.

# Tamil Nadu

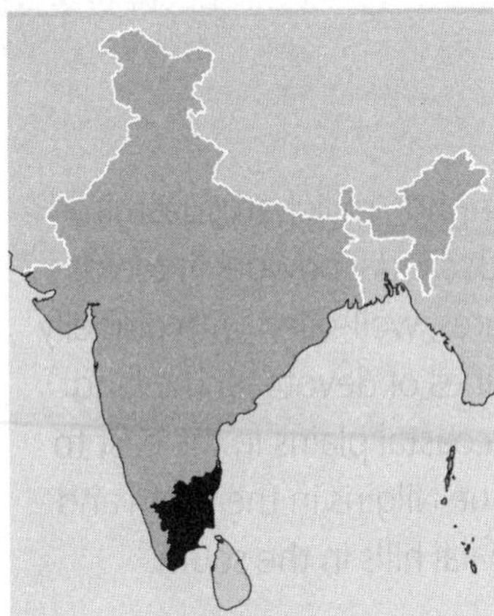



## Footprint features

# Introduction

Tamil Nadu smells of burning camphor, milk baths, jasmine garlands and has gods awash with sandal powder; it teems with beautiful carved granite figures, well-oiled with gingelly smeared from the palms of centuries of devotees. The land rises from the hot, dry and dusty coastal plains in the east to the magnificent Western Ghats: the Nilgiris in the north and the Palani, Cardamom and Anamalai hills in the south.

About 90 per cent of the 60-million strong Tamil population is Hindu and religious ritual here is lived and breathed: men's whole foreheads are given over to great daubs of potash, huge horizontal sweeps or fingernail-thin red edges drawn from the hair's centre-parting sideways, and women sprinkle 'kolam' of ground rice powder on the freshly water-packed earth outside their homes in a routine as mundane as brushing their teeth. It's rare to find a temple that has outlived its religious purpose – hardly any shrine is merely a monument. But nor is worship confined to the feats of architecture that dot Tamil Nadu. Any banyan tree you pass will be dangling with sacks from cow births; tridents are slammed into the ground to create makeshift mounds of worship; village gods in life-size stucco renderings bare their teeth and brandish knives at every roadside.

Here, for the tourist, is the heady temple trail: Kancheepuram, Mahabalipuram, Chidambaram, Tanjore, Madurai, the second Varanasi of Rameswaram, and the holy toe-tip of India in Kanniyakumari; or the very different ashram atmospheres of Tiruvannamalai and Auroville. Welcome antidotes to temple fatigue come in the form of domestic architecture in French Pondicherry and the palatial homes in Chettinad, or in big breaths of nature in the Nilgiri blue mountains around Ooty and Kodai.

## ★ Don't miss...

1 **Bharat Natyam dancing in Mylapore** Chennai's cultural quarter, page 804.
2 **The food in Pondicherry** Rejoice that the French were more concerned with bequeathing edible culture than the British, page 826.
3 **Thanjavur** The beautiful Big Temple's *Nandhi* is washed with milk and gingelly each fortnight before a spellbound audience of devotees, page 842.
4 **Chidambaram** Explore the unique temple society of the Brahmins, page 846.
5 **Nilgiri Blue Mountain railway** The rack-and-pinion climb up the ghats to the summer bolt-hole of the Madras Presidency, page 853.
6 **Madurai** The crowds at the Minakshi Temple can be overpowering but the experience is unforgettable, page 871.
7 **Chettinad** Architectural salvage and antique shopping in ramshackle stores where the dealers from Cochi and Bombay come to stock up, page 879.

# Background → *Population: 62.1 mn. Area: 130,000 sq km.*

## The land

**Geography** Tamil Nadu rises from the flat coastal plains in the east to the Western Ghats – the Nilgiris in the north and the Palani, Cardamom and Anamalai hills in the south. The Nilgiris – 'blue mountains' – rise like a wall above the haze of the plains to heights of over 2,500 m. The plains are hot, often dry and dusty, with isolated blocks of granite forming often bizarre shapes on the ancient eroded surface. The coast itself is a flat alluvial plain, with deltas at the mouths of major rivers. The medieval rulers in Tamil Nadu often created tanks which now add a beautiful touch to the landscape.

**Climate** Most rain falls between October and December and is the worst time to travel. The best time to visit is from mid-December to early March when the dry sunny weather sets in and before the heat gets too crushing. The hills can then be really cold, especially at night. In the rain shadow of the Western Ghats, temperatures never fall much below 21°C except in the hills, but although humidity is often high maximum temperatures rarely exceed 42°C.

## History

Tamil Nadu's cultural identity has been shaped by the Dravidians, who have inhabited the south since at least the fourth millennium BC. Tamil, India's oldest living language, developed from the earlier languages of people who were probably displaced from the north by Aryan-based culture from 2000 BC to 1500 BC.

By the fourth century BC Tamil Nadu was under the rule of three dynasties. The **Cholas**, the **Pandiyas** and the **Cheras**. The **Pallavas** of Kanchi came to power in the fourth century AD and were dominant between AD 550-869. Possibly of northern origin, under their control Mahabalipuram (Mamallapuram) became an important port in the seventh century. The **Cholas** returned to power in 850 and were a dominant political force until 1173 before the resumption of Pandiya power for a further century. The defeat of the great Vijayanagar Empire by a confederacy of Muslim states in 1565 forced their leaders south. As the Nayaka kings they continued to rule from as far south as Madurai well into the 17th century. Ultimately when Muslim political control finally reached Tamil Nadu it was as brief as it was tenuous.

It was more than 150 years after their founding of Fort St George at Madras in 1639 before the **East India Company** could claim political supremacy in South India. Haidar Ali, who mounted the throne of Mysore in 1761, and his son Tipu Sultan, allied with the French, won many battles against the English. The Treaty of Versailles in 1783 brought the French and English together and Tipu was forced to make peace. The English took Malabar in 1792, and in 1801 Lord Wellesley brought together most of the south under the Madras Presidency, see page 991. **The French** acquired land at Pondicherry in 1673. In 1742, Dupleix was named Governor of the French India Company and took up residence at Pondicherry. He seized Madras within a few years but in 1751 Clive attacked Arcot. His victory was the beginning of the end of French ambitions in India. The Treaty of Paris brought their Empire to a close in 1763 although they retained five counting houses.

## Culture

The great majority of Tamilians are Dravidians with Mediterranean ethnic origins. They have been settled in Tamil Nadu for several thousand years. Tamil is spoken by over 85% of the population. Hindus make up nearly 90% of the population, and over five per cent are Christian, a group especially strong in the south where Roman Catholic and Protestant missions have been active for over 500 years. There are a small but significant minorities of Muslims, Jains and Parsis. There are isolated

## The effect of the tsunami

Official reports record that the tsunami waves triggered by the Bay of Bengal earthquakes on 26 December 2004 struck over 2,000 km of India's coastline, penetrating as far as 3 km inland with waves of up to 10 metres. Twelve tremors were over six on the Richter scale, a further 103 measured over five. It was a natural disaster of huge humanitarian scale throughout the Indian Ocean: on the Indian mainland alone, according to a UN, World Bank and Asian Development Bank joint assessment, nearly 11,000 people died, nearly 8,000 of these in the south Indian state of Tamil Nadu. The situation worsens the further south you go: over 6,000 people died in the southern district of Nagapattinam alone. India wide, almost 6,000 more were missing, and nearly 7,000 injured. The livelihoods of 645,000 families (that's 3.2 million people), chiefly fisherfolk, already at risk of poverty, continue to be jeopardized. The waves have touched all areas of Tamil life: 150,000 homes were hit, 68,000 boats destroyed, 252 schools wiped out. Where seawater washed inland over farmland it has left 30 cm thick saline deposits. Agricultural observers say it will take three monsoons before the land can be used again. The last thing the affected states need during this period of reconstruction, is for tourists, with their potential income to the State purse, to stay away. There is plenty your rupees can bankroll: sanitation, psycho-social support and AIDS prevention measures are of urgent use in relief camps which house, in Tamil Nadu alone, 44,207 displaced people. Many of these are expected to remain in temporary housing for three years. It is a reconstruction effort on a huge scale (the total cost to India is put at $1.2 bn) that involves the rebuilding of homes, schools, health centres, roads, power lines. The death toll was highest in Nagapattinam, but tourist centres of Chennai, Mahabalipuram, Kanyukumari and Pondicherry were all hit. Although key sites such as Mahabalipuram's Shore Temple are in tact, some seaside tourist cottages and hotels were damaged, but the government has been swift to rebuild to allow tourism to support towns' businesses and people. Of the natural attractions, while the Point Calimere Sanctuary is saltier than before, and the flamingoes have flown inland, ecologists believe the tsunami's effects to be glancing. The Gulf of Mannar Marine National Park was sheltered by Sri Lanka. Only two per cent of India's coral reef appears to have been damaged.

groups of as many as 18 different types of **tribal people** who live in the Nilgiri Hills. Some of them are of aboriginal stock although local archaeological discoveries suggest that an extinct race preceded them. The **Todas'** life and religion revolve around their long-horned buffalo which are a measure of their wealth. Their small villages are called *munds* with half a dozen or so igloo-like, windowless bamboo and dried grass huts. Their chief goddess 'Tiekirzi', the creator of the indispensable buffalo, and her brother 'On', rule the world of the dead and the living. There are only about 1,000 Todas left. The **Badagas** are the main tribal group and probably came from Karnataka. They speak a mixture of Kannada and Tamil and their oral tradition is rich in folktales, poetry, songs and chants. Agriculturalists, their villages are mainly in the upper plateau, with rows of three-roomed houses. They worship Siva and observe special tribal festivals. Progressive and adaptable, they are being absorbed into the local community faster than the others.

## All's fair in love, film and politics

Tamil Nadu's lively temple society also keeps aflame sculpture and the arts, and makes for a people singularly receptive to iconography: Tamil film-making is every bit as prolific and profitable as its closest rival, Hindi-language Bollywood. The state's industry is famous for its dancing and choreography and the super-saturated colour of its film stock. Film stars too, are massive here: heroes worshipped like demigods, their careers have all too often offered them a fast lane into politics. Both the cherished MGR (MG Ramachandran, the film star and charismatic Chief Minister during the 1980s) and Jayalalitha, his one-time girlfriend and enormously contentious successor (denigrated as 'thunder thighs', is still in office despite her party failing to win a majority), hopped from the screen into the state's political driving seat as chief ministers.

**Cuisine** Many Tamilians are vegetarian and the strict Brahmins among them avoid the use of garlic and onion and in some cases even tomatoes. Favourites for breakfast or '*tiffin*' (snack) include *dosai* (thin crisp pancakes, plain or *masala* when stuffed with mildly spiced potato and onion), *idli* (steamed, fermented rice cakes), delicious rice-based *pongal* (worth searching out) and *vadai* (savoury lentil doughnuts), all served with a coconut chutney and *sambar* (a spicy lentil and vegetable broth). A *thali* here centres around boiled rice with a selection of vegetable preparations served in small steel containers, as well as pickles, *papadum*, *rasam* (a clear, peppery lentil 'soup'), plain curd. The food from Chettinad tends to be particularly hot and spicy. The dessert is usually *payasam* (similar to creamy rice pudding) to round off the meal. South Indian coffee is a treat. It is freshly ground and filtered, mixed with hot milk and sugar, and traditionally served frothed up in small stainless steel tumblers.

**Literature** Tamil is the oldest of India's living languages, with a literature stretching back to the early centuries before Christ. From around the second century AD a poets' academy known as the **Sangam** was established in Madurai. Sangam literature suggests that life in Tamil society had a social hierarchy with the sages at the top, followed by peasants, hunters, artisans, soldiers, fishermen and scavengers – quite different from the caste system that existed in the rest of the subcontinent. From the beginning of the Christian era Tamil religious thinkers began to transform the image of Krishna from the remote and heroic figure of the epics into the focus of a new and passionate devotional worship – *bhakti*. From the seventh to the 10th century there was a surge of writing new hymns of praise, sometimes referred to as 'the Tamil *Veda*'.

**Music** Changes constantly occurred in different schools of music within the basic framework of **raga-tala-prabandha** which was well established by the seventh century. From the 13th century the division between the *Hindustani* or the northern system (which included the western and eastern regions as well) and the *Carnatic* or the southern system, became pronounced. The southern school has a more scale-based structure of *raga* whereas the northern school has greater flexibility and thus continued to develop through the centuries. The *tala* too is much more precise. It is also nearly always devotional or didactic whereas the northern system also includes non-religious, everyday themes which are sometimes sensuous. The language that lends itself naturally to the southern system is Telugu and the only bowed instrument that is used to accompany vocal music is the violin, imported from the West but played rather differently.

**Dance and drama** **Bharata Natyam** is thought to be the oldest form of classical dance in India. Originating in Tamil Nadu, it is essentially a highly stylized solo

### Tamil stats in words

Wealth and literacy rates, sadly for a state with such a deep history of civilization, are far lower here than they are in neighbouring Kerala (Tamil Nadu's per capita income is US$36 per month). Tamil is deeply agricultural: Keralites, whose educations have made them tire of tending fields, import most of their vegetables from here. The bullock cart continues to square up against the goods truck on the state's roads and while people aspire to, and in many places can and do build square box bungalows as their homes, mudhuts with thatched woven banana roofs lower than head height are routine. Migrant workforces in steel, cotton, or road-building, zig-zag across the countryside. At the higher end of society, the metro lifestyles of Chennai and preferably Bangalore beckon.

feminine dance which combines movement, music and mime with *nritta* (pure dance) and *nritya* (expression), usually on the theme of spiritual love.

## Modern Tamil Nadu

Tamil Nadu took its present form as a result of the States Reorganization Act of 1956. Until 1967 the Assembly was dominated by the Indian National Congress, but after an attempt by the central government to impose Hindi as the national language the Congress Party was routed in 1967 by a regional party, the Dravida Munnetra Kazhagam (the DMK) under its leader CN Annadurai. After his death the party split and since then either the DMK, or the splinter party, the All India Anna DMK, has been in power in the State. Neither party has any constituency beyond Tamil Nadu and thus at the all India level each has been forced to seek alliances with national parties. From the late 1960s the AIADMK, which controlled the State Assembly for most of the time, has been led by two film stars. The first, MG Ramachandran remained the Chief Minister until his death even after suffering a stroke which left him paralysed. The record of Jayalalitha, his successor, one-time lover and fellow film star, has been less consistent, and her rule dogged by scandal. She and her party were ousted by the DMK in the May 1996 elections and she was temporarily jailed until, cleared of a wide range of criminal charges, she re-entered the Legislative Assembly in March 2002, taking over once more as Chief Minister after winning the state elections with an 80% margin (her administration then arrested the previous chief minister, 77-year-old Karunanidhi, in a corruption case that some say was motivated by revenge). In the May 2004 national elections, though, the party, allied to the BJP and vocal in its opposition to Sonia Gandhi's foreign origin, failed to win a single seat. A coalition of opposition parties, arguing that she had lost her political mandate, demanded Jayalalitha's resignation, but she hung on to office, albeit swiftly reversing a raft of controversial policies – these had included scrapping free electricity schemes, reducing rice rations, banning animal sacrifices – introduced during the earlier years of power. State elections are due again before May 2006.

**Economy** Since Independence in 1947 Tamil Nadu has become one of India's leading industrial states. With a quarter of India's spinning capacity textiles are tremendously important and the state is famous both for handloom cottons and silks and for factory-made textiles. Leather and fabrics have also long been a vital export industry, but in recent years a range of new industries have developed using locally available raw materials like iron ore, bauxite and magnesite. Chennai has become home to the Ford car factory and the city also makes lorries, buses and trains.

# Chennai and the Pallava country

*Chennai (Madras), as South India's sprawling chief metropolis, is the headquarters for NGOs, foreign high commissions, call centres and software businesses, and the city has long been a gateway for westerners bound for any of Tamil Nadu's many world-famous ashrams. For all that, and although Chennai has grown dramatically from its old core between Fort St George and the harbour, the city with its low-slung skyline remains slower, more traditional, less cosmopolitan and dynamic than Bangalore, just a few hours up the road. It is India's fourth largest city and an estimated 40% of Chennaians now live in slums. Squatter settlements and informal housing are still scattered throughout the city, a reminder that alongside growing*

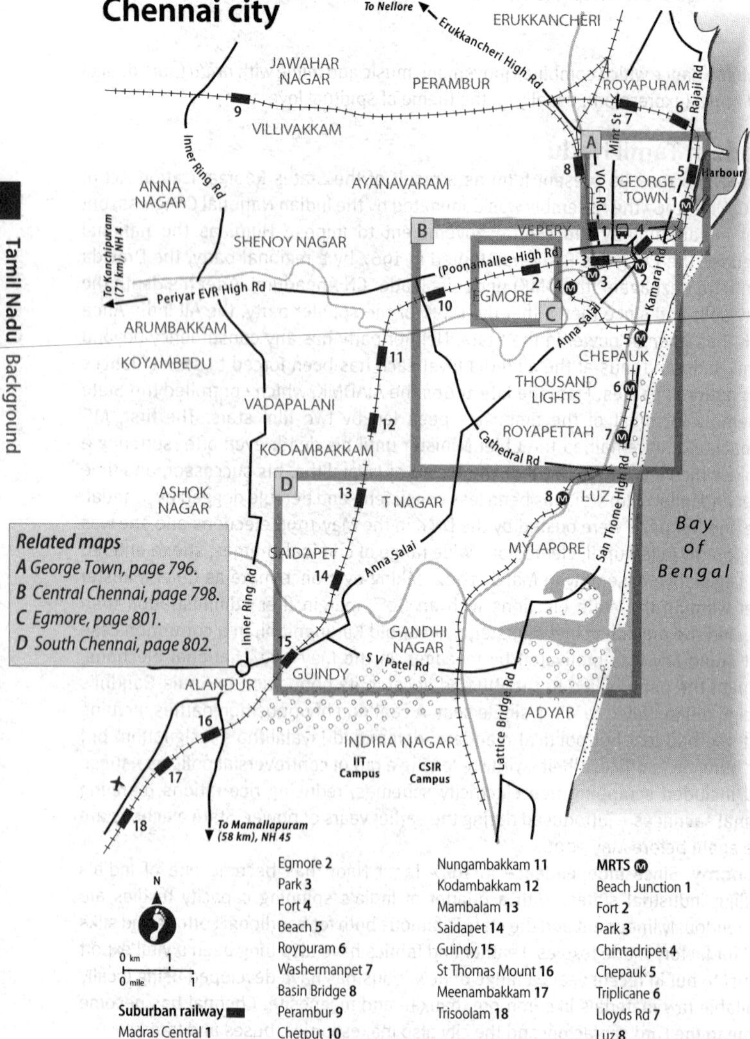

*modernization and prosperity poverty is still widespread. Not everyone is a fan of the city, but it's got stunning Indo-Saracenic architecture, some of the oldest buildings from the British Raj, and unrivalled high culture.*

*Kancheepuram, the historic capital of the Pallavas until the eighth century and one of India's seven sacred cities, is amazingly quiet by comparison. Here you can wander about scores of temples and buy beautiful silk straight from the town's famous looms – three-quarters of the town's population is dependent on the trade. Within the same radius of Chennai, but on the coast, is Mahabalipuram, a town that echoes with the sound of sculptors' chisels tapping on granite and where everywhere you look there are workshop yards stacked full of fantastical, beautifully carved deities.* ▸▸ *For Sleeping, Eating and other listings, see pages 813-825.*

# Chennai (Madras)

→ *Phone code: 044. Colour map 7, grid A6. Population: 5.36 mn.*

Apart from anomalous little ex-pat pockets, like Chetbet's Jamaican and South African communities, life in Chennai is led much as it always was: there are brahminical neighbourhoods that still demand strict vegetarianism of all tenants and flat-sharing, a commonly accepted practice among the young in Bangalore, is taboo. Superstition is big here too: rents are decided according to vasthu, India's equivalent of feng shui, and a wrong-facing front door can slash your payments. You have to squint hard today to picture the half-empty grandeur that was the Madras of the East India Presidency. Triplicane, often mistaken for a slum, is dubbed the bachelors' neighbourhood thanks to the high density of ambitious, urbanized young Indian men living here in hotels and as paying guests. It is also home to some of the city's finest examples of Indo-Saracenic buildings, the architectural legacy of the British. Marina beach, the second widest in the world, is a cushion of gold sand opposite some of these imposing buildings. The Bay of Bengal here is hardly enticing: it's used as a toilet, a lovers' lane, a shaving zone, a place to carry out last rites for the dead, a jogging track, a makeshift bed and a cow-wash. Amongst all this, the city's high-tech credentials make for a strange bedfellow. At traffic junctions next to roadside slums, light-emitting diodes count down to the traffic-light change.

## Ins and outs

**Getting there** Chennai 's international and domestic air terminals are about 15 km from the city: allow 50 minutes, although it may take as little as half an hour. Airport buses run the circuit of the main hotels, and include Egmore station; otherwise it's best to get a pre-paid taxi. You can either choose the Government Taxis (black with yellow tops) or the private cabs (more comfortable and more expensive). Have some small change ready to pay the counter staff. Note the taxi number written on your charge slip (one copy is for the passenger and the other is for the driver to collect the fare from the counter). Trains from the north and west come into the Central Station behind the port. Lines from the south terminate at Egmore, which has hotels nearby. There are several buses that ply in and out of Madras from nearby cities like Bangalore. All state-owned buses terminate at the Koyembedu Moffusil Bus Terminus while the private buses terminate at the Omni bus terminus at Koyembedu. Both these termini are close to each other but its better to know where exactly you want the taxi/autorickshaw to take you, especially if you are travelling with luggage. Buses usually drop passengers at various points in the city before reaching the terminus. So feel free to ask the driver or fellow passengers the closest drop-off point to your destination.

**Getting around** Chennai is very spread out and walking is usually uncomfortably hot so it's best to find an auto. Most, however, refuse to run their meter, so ask your hotel for an approximate rate to your destination. Taxis are comparatively rare and expensive. The bus service is extensive and frequent, but often very crowded. ▸▸ *See Transport, page 820, for further details.*

**Orientation and information** Chennai is not an 'organized city' like Bangalore. The main harbour near the old British military zone of **George Town** is strewn with cranes for the import/export cargo business. Just near the port is the **Fort**, the old British headquarters and now the Tamil government offices, and the brilliant High Court buildings. The **Burma bazaar**, a long line of pokey shops with corrugated-iron blinds that sell white goods, runs between the two near Parry's Corner. The **Pondy bazaar** is the 'common man' bazaar, **T Nagar** is the main shopping district (Anna Salai is best for clothes). South of **Adya** are the headquarters of automotive companies like Hyundai and Ford. **Mylapore**, older than Chennai itself and the cultural heart of the city, is just south of the city centre.

**Tourist information Tamil Nadu Tourism** ⓘ *Tourism Complex, Wallaja Rd, T044-25388785, www.tamilnadutourism.org*. See also www.chennaionline.com.

## History

Armenian and Portuguese traders had settled in the San Thome area before the arrival of the British. In 1639, **Francis Day**, a trader with the East India Company, negotiated the grant of a tiny plot of sandy land to the north of the Cooum River as the base for a warehouse or 'factory'. It was completed on 23 April 1640, St George's Day. The choice was dictated partly by local politics – Francis Day's friendship with

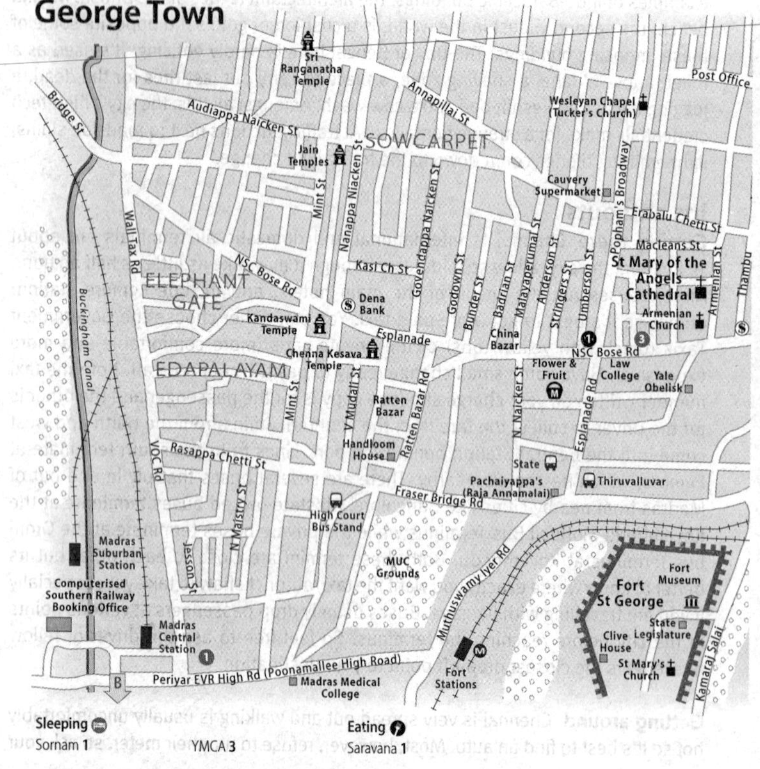

Ayyappa Nayak, brother of the local ruler of the coast country from Pulicat to the Portuguese settlement of San Thome – but more importantly by the favourable local price of cotton goods.

By 1654 Fort St George had a church and English residences – the 'White Town'. To its north was 'Black Town', referred to locally as Chennaipatnam, after Chennappa Nayak, Dharmala Ayyappa Nayak's father. The two towns merged and Madraspatnam grew with the acquisition of neighbouring villages of Tiru-alli-keni (Lily Tank) now Triplicane, in 1676. In 1693, Governor Yale (founder of Yale University in the USA) acquired Egmore, Purasawalkam and Tondiarpet from Emperor Aurangzeb, who had by that time extended Mughal power to the far south. In 1746 Madras was captured by the French, to be returned to British control as a result of the Treaty of Aix-la-Chapelle in 1748. By the middle of the 18th century many other villages such as Nungambakkam, Ennore, Perambur, San Thome and Mylapore (the 'city of the peacock') were added with the help of friendly Nawabs. In 1793 Calcutta became the chief centre of British administration in India, though Madras continued to be the centre of the East India Company's expanding power in South India.

It was more than 150 years after their founding of Fort St George at Madras in 1639 before the East India Company could claim political supremacy in South India. Haidar Ali, who mounted the throne of Mysore in 1761, and his son Tipu Sultan, allied with the French, won many battles against the English. The Treaty of Versailles in 1783 brought the French and English together and Tipu was forced to make peace. The English took Malabar in 1792, and in 1801 Lord Wellesley brought together most of the south under the Madras Presidency, see page 991.

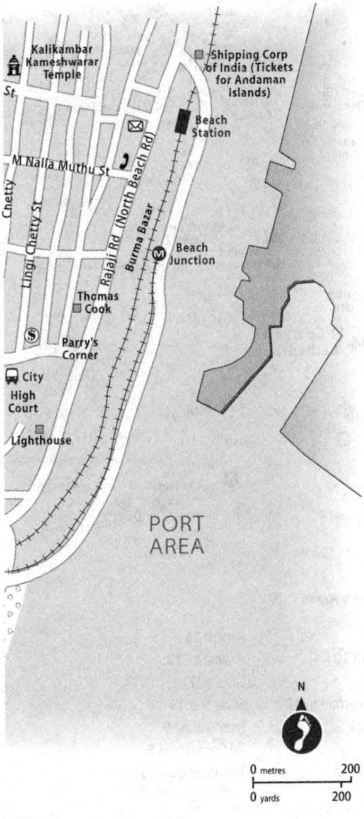

The city is still growing, although many services, including water supply and housing, are stretched beyond breaking point. Since Independence an increasing range of heavy and light goods industries have been added to the long established cotton textiles and leather industries. The opening of a new Ford Motor Company plant in Sriperumbudur, between Chennai and Kanchipuram, has led some in the city to claim it as "the Detroit of India".

## The fort and port: St George and George Town

Madras began as nothing more than a huddle of fishing villages on the Bay of Bengal, rechristened Madras by British 17th-century traders after they built the 'Factory House' fortifications on the beach. It was completed by the British in 1654 but was rebuilt several times. The present structure of Fort St George, a fine example of 17th-century British military architecture, was mostly built in 1666. The country's tallest flagstaff, thought to be over 300 years old, stood here. The 24 black **Charnockite** pillars, see page 1348, were reclaimed by the British in 1762 after the French had carried them off to Pondicherry in 1746. Today the fort

# Central Chennai

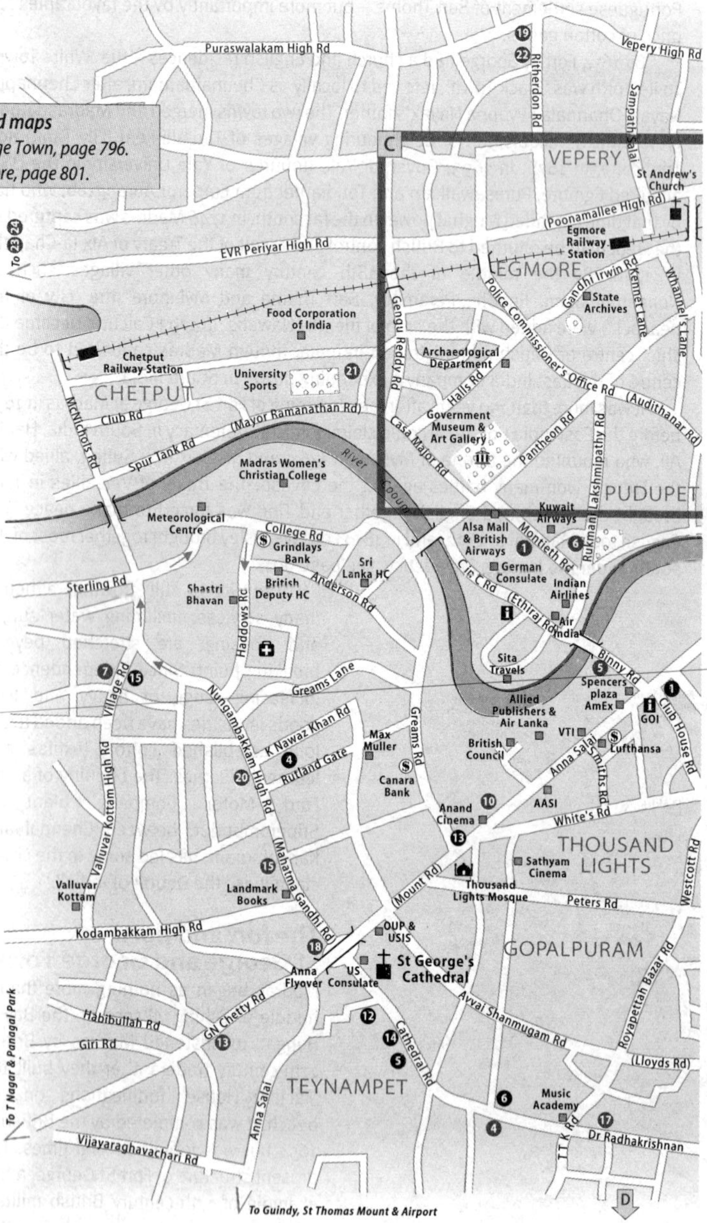

Related maps
*A George Town, page 796.*
*B Egmore, page 801.*

Puraswalakam High Rd
Vepery High Rd
Ritherdon Rd
Sampath Salai
VEPERY
St Andrew's Church
(Poonamallee High Rd)
Egmore Railway Station
EVR Periyar High Rd
EGMORE
Gandhi Irwin Rd
State Archives
Kennet Lane
Whannel's Lane
Food Corporation of India
Gengu Reddy Rd
Police Commissioner's Office Rd
(Audithanar Rd)
Archaeological Department
Halls Rd
Chetput Railway Station
University Sports
CHETPUT
McNichols Rd
Club Rd
(Mayor Ramanathan Rd)
Government Museum & Art Gallery
Casa Major Rd
Pantheon Rd
Lakshmipathy Rd
Spur Tank Rd
Madras Women's Christian College
River Cooum
PUDUPET
Kuwait Airways
Rukmani Rd
Meteorological Centre
College Rd
Grindlays Bank
Alsa Mall & British Airways
Montieth Rd
German Consulate
Sri Lanka HC
British Deputy HC
Anderson Rd
Cir C Rd
(Ethiraj Rd)
Indian Airlines
Air India
Sterling Rd
Shastri Bhavan
Haddows Rd
Sita Travels
Binny Rd
Spencers plaza
AmEx
GOI
Club House Rd
Greams Lane
Allied Publishers & Air Lanka
Village Rd
Nungambakkam High Rd
K Nawaz Khan Rd
Max Muller
Greams Rd
British Council
VTI
Lufthansa
Anna Salai
Smiths Rd
Valluvar Kottam High Rd
Rutland Gate
Canara Bank
AASI
Anand Cinema
White's Rd
THOUSAND LIGHTS
(Mahatma Gandhi Rd)
Sathyam Cinema
Westcott Rd
Valluvar Kottam
Landmark Books
(Mount Rd)
Thousand Lights Mosque
Peters Rd
Kodambakkam High Rd
OUP & USIS
GOPALPURAM
Anna Flyover
US Consulate
St George's Cathedral
Royapettah Bazar Rd
Habibullah Rd
GN Chetty Rd
Avvai Shanmugam Rd
Giri Rd
Cathedral Rd
(Lloyds Rd)
TEYNAMPET
Music Academy
Anna Salai
To T Nagar & Panagal Park
T T K Rd
Dr Radhakrishnan
Vijayaraghavachari Rd
To Guindy, St Thomas Mount & Airport

0 metres 300
0 yards 300

**Sleeping**
Ambassador Pallava **1**
Breeze **24**
Broadlands **2**
Chola Sheraton **4**
Comfort **2**
Cristal **3**
Guru **6**
Grand Orient **10**
Harrisons **7**
Himalaya International **8**
Merryland **23**
Paradise **2**
Park Chennai **18**
Ranjith **15**
Residency **13**
Savera **17**
Silver Star **19**
Sree Krishna **9**
Taj Connemara **5**
Taj Coromandel **20**

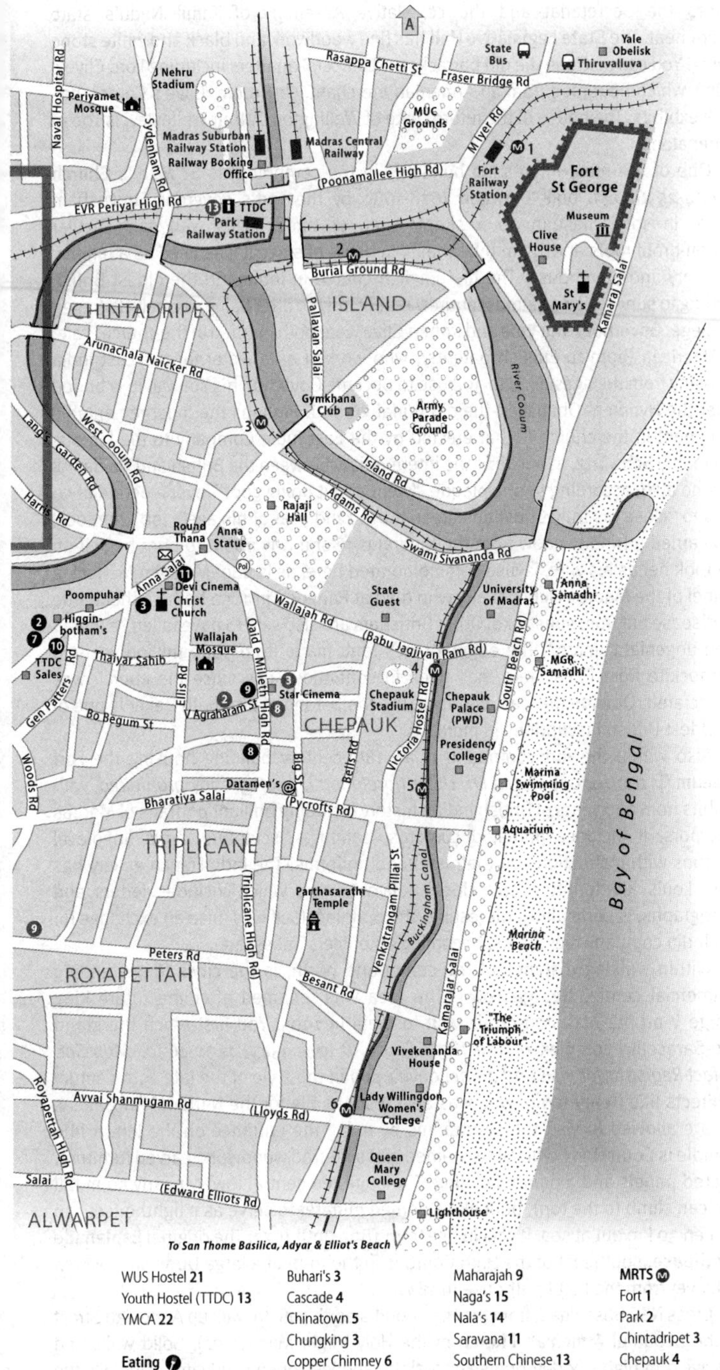


WUS Hostel **21**
Youth Hostel (TTDC) **13**
YMCA **22**

**Eating**
Aavin **1**
Annalakshmi **2**
Buhari's **3**
Cascade **4**
Chinatown **5**
Chungking **3**
Copper Chimney **6**
Dasaprakash **7**
Gem **8**
Maharajah **9**
Naga's **15**
Nala's **14**
Saravana **11**
Southern Chinese **13**
Udipi **10**
Woodlands Drive-in **12**

**MRTS**
Fort **1**
Park **2**
Chintadripet **3**
Chepauk **4**
Triplicane **5**
Lloyd's Rd **6**

houses the Secretariat and the Legislative Assembly of Tamil Nadu's state government. The **State Legislative Hall** has fine woodwork and black and white stone paving. You can also see the old barracks and officers' quarters including Lord Clive's house, which he rented from an Armenian merchant. One room, Clive's Corner, has small exhibits. The house of the future Duke of Wellington, Arthur Wellesley, is 100 m further along.

One of the most interesting buildings in the compound is **St Mary's Church** ① *T044-25382023*, built between 1678-1680 by the Fort's governor Streynsham Master in solid masonry to a simple plan of three aisles with semi-circular cannon-proof roofs and 1.3-m thick walls. In times of siege it was used as a military dormitory and storehouse. The first English church in India and the oldest British building to survive, it was almost entirely rebuilt in 1759 after being severely damaged in a siege. **Governor Elihu Yale** and Robert Clive were both married in the church. Yale, an American (born to English parents), who worked as a writer for the East India Company from the ages of 24 to 39, rose to become Governor: his son David is buried under the Hynmers Obelisk in the old burial ground. Perhaps the most remarkable monument in the church is that erected by the East India Company to the famous missionary **Schwartz**, at one time the intermediary between the British and Haidar Ali but who also, according to one plaque, "went about doing good" over a period of 50 years to "close his truly Christian career in the 72nd year of his age". Job Charnock, who carried a Hindu widow from the funeral pyre she was about to burn herself on and took her as his wife, is also commemorated here, as is poor Malcolm McNeill, a colonel of the Madras Light Cavalry who died at Rangoon in 1852 from neither battle nor disease but from sunstroke. Other Britishers are also said to have fallen "a martyr to an ungenial climate." The original black font, made from 3000 million year-old Charnockite from Pallavaram, has been in continuous use since the church was consecrated. Outside the west entrance, the tombstone of Elizabeth Baker is one of the oldest British inscriptions in India.

Also within the fort compound is an 18th-century building housing the **Fort Museum** ① *1000-1700, closed Fri, US$2 (foreigners), photography prohibited*, with exhibits from 300 years of British Indian history including brilliant portraits of Madras Governors. It includes prints, documents, paintings, sculpture, arms (medieval weapons with instructions on their use) and uniforms. The Indo-French gallery has some Louis XIV furniture and clocks. Clive Corner, which includes letters and photographs, is particularly interesting. The building itself was once an exchange for East India company merchants, becoming an officers' mess later.

Within walking distance of the compound north, is the city's long-standing commercial centre, **George Town**. The area was renamed after the future King George V on the occasion of his visit to India in 1905. You first reach the grand Indo-Saracenic complex of the **High Court** ① *1045-1345, 1430-1630, Mon-Sat, contact Registrar for visit and guide*, developed in the style of the late 19th-century architects like **Henry Irwin**, who was also responsible for the National Art Gallery. You are allowed to visit the courtrooms by using the entrance on the left. A fine example is Court No 13 which has stained glass, fretted woodwork, carved furniture, silvered panels and a painted ceiling. The huge red central tower, nearly 50 m tall (you can climb to the top), built like a domed minaret to serve as a lighthouse, can be seen 30 km out at sea. It was in use from 1894 until 1977. The original **Esplanade Lighthouse**, southeast of the High Court, is in the form of a large Doric pillar which took over from the Fort lighthouse in 1841.

Cross NSC Bose Road, from the High Court's north gate to walk up Armenian Street for the beautiful **Armenian Church** of the Holy Virgin Mary (1772). Solid walls and massive 3 m high wooden doors conceal the spotless open courtyard inside. On the site of an ancient cemetery, the oldest Armenian tombstone in the courtyard dates from 1663. The East India Company valued the Armenian community for their 'sober, frugal and wise' style of life and they were given the same rights as English settlers in 1688. Immediately north again is the Roman Catholic Cathedral, **St Mary of the Angels** (1675). The date 1642, inscribed at the entrance to the Church, is when the Capuchin monks built their first church in Madras. The lawyer Stephen Popham, who was in Madras from 1778-1795, was particularly enthusiastic about improving the city's sanitation and laid out what was to become Madras's main commercial street, still known as **Popham's Broadway,** which is west from St Mary's Cathedral. Just off Popham's Broadway in Prakasham Road is the **Wesleyan Church** (1820).

In the 18th century major commercial expansion took place between what is now First Line Beach (North Beach Road) and **Mint Street** to the west of George Town. The Mint was first opened in 1640, and from the end of the 17th century minted gold coins under licence for the Mughals, though it did not move to Mint Street until 1841-1842.

The 19th-century growth of Madras can be traced north from **Parry's Corner. First Line Beach**, built on reclaimed land in 1814 fronted the beach itself. The **GPO** (1844-1884) was designed by Chisholm. The completion of the harbour (1896), transformed the economy of the city.

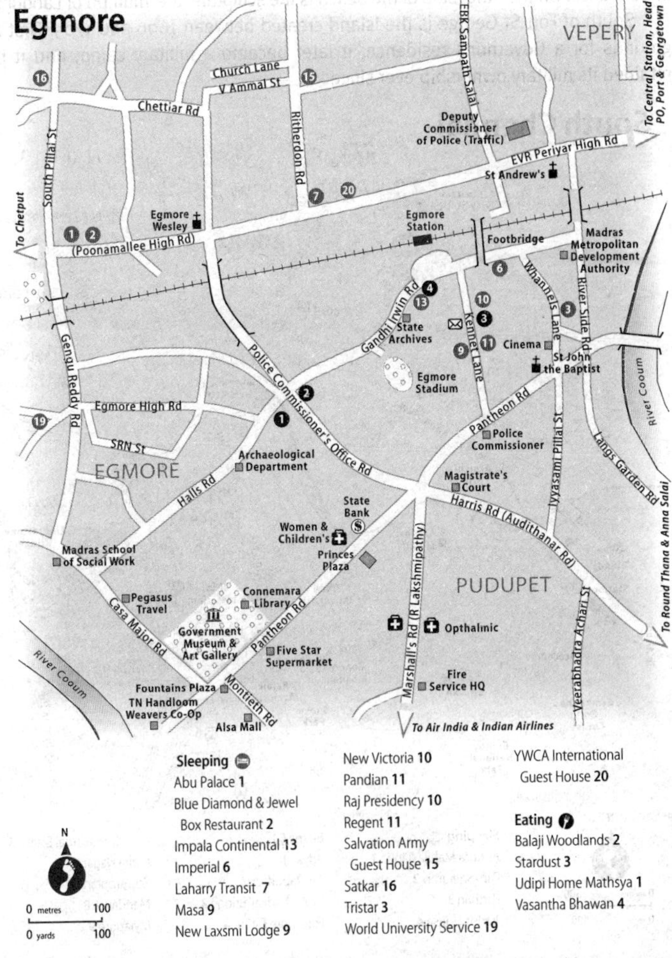

## Central Chennai and the Marina

**Triplicane** and **Chepauk** contain some of the finest examples of late 19th-century Indo-Saracenic architecture in India, focused on the University of Madras. The Governor of Madras, Mountstuart Elphinstone Grant-Duff (1881-1886), decided to develop the Marina, especially as a promenade. Ever since, it has been a favourite place for thousands of city dwellers to walk on Sunday evenings.

Until the harbour was built at the end of the 19th century the sea washed up close to the present road, but the north-drifting current has progressively widened the Marina beach. **Anna Park** is named after the founder of the DMK, CN Annadurai. The **MGR Samadhi**, commemorating **MG Ramachandran**, the film star and charismatic Chief Minister during the 1980s, has become a focus of pilgrimage. **Chepauk Palace,** 400 m away on South Beach Road, was the former residence of the Nawab of the Carnatica. The original four-domed Khalsa Mahal and the Humayun Mahal with a grand *durbar* hall, had a tower added between them in 1855. The original building is now hidden from the road by the modern Public Works Department (PWD) building, Ezhilagam. Immediately behind is the Chepauk **cricket ground** where test matches are played. Lining the Kamaraj Salai (South Beach Road) is a succession of university buildings. Despite its unlikely appearance, **Vivekenanda House** was Madras' first 'ice house' for storing imported ice. On the other side of the beach is the sculpture 'the Triumph of Labour'.

South of Fort St George is the Island created between 1696 and 1705. First the grounds for a Governor's residence, it later became a military camp, and it has retained its military ownership ever since.



## South Chennai

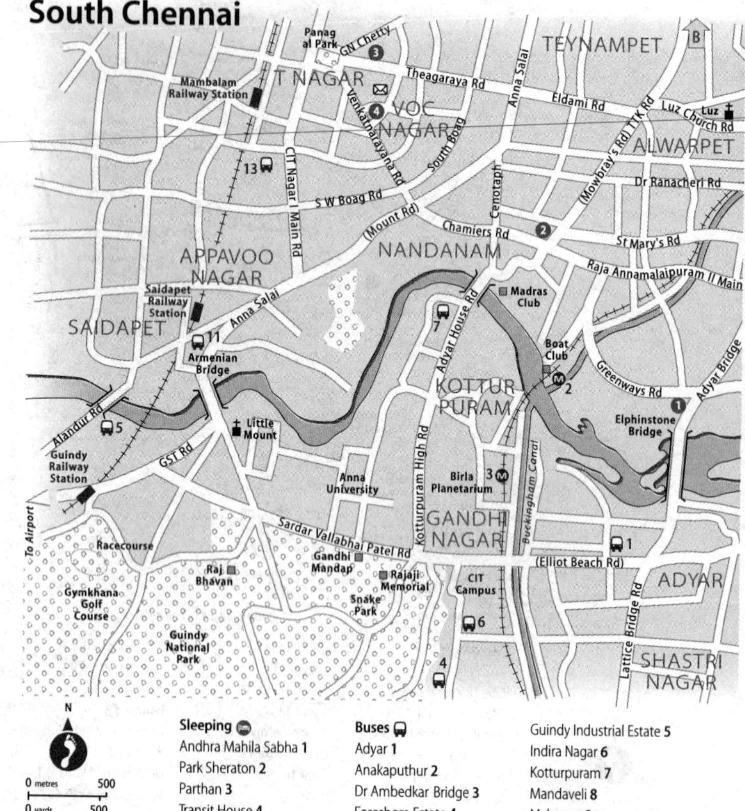

Near the Round Thana is the Banqueting Hall of the old Government House, now known as **Rajaji Hall** (1802). Built to mark the British victory over Tipu Sultan, it is in an attractive setting, designed in the Greek temple style.

**Wallajah Mosque** ⓘ *0600-1200, 1600-2200*, the 'Big Mosque', was built in 1795 by the Nawab of the Carnatic. There are two slender minarets with golden domes on either side. **Parthasarathi Temple**, near the tank, is the oldest temple structure in Chennai and was built by eighth-century Pallava kings, and later renovated in the 16th by Vijayanagara rulers. Dedicated to Krishna as the royal charioteer, it shows five of Vishnu's 10 incarnations and is the only one dedicated to Parthasarathi.

A bridge across the Cooum at Egmore was opened in 1700. In the late 18th century, the area around Pantheon Road, between the Poonamallee High Road and the Cooum, became the centre of Madras's social and cultural life, a 'place of public entertainment and balls'. Egmore's development, which continued for a century, started with the building of Horden's 'garden house' in 1715. The original 'pantheon' (public assembly rooms) which stood here, on **Pantheon Road** was completely replaced by one of India's National Libraries. The origins of the **Connemara Library** (built 1896) go back to 1662, "when a bale of calico from Madras was exchanged for books in London". At the southwest corner of the site stands Irwin's Victoria Memorial Hall, now the **Government Museum and Art Gallery** ⓘ *486 Pantheon Rd, T044-28193238, 0930-1700, closed Fri and Bank holidays, US$5, US$2.50 children, US$1.50 students/ teachers*. The red brick rotunda surrounded by an Italianate arcade was described by Tillotson as one of "the proudest expressions of the Indo-Saracenic movement". Look for the excellent bronzes and locally-excavated Stone and Iron Age implements. Although poorly maintained, the Art Gallery has striking bronzes including a 11th-century Nataraja from Tiruvengadu, seated images of Siva and Parvati from Kilaiyur, and large standing figures of Rama, Lakshmana and Sita from Vadakkuppanaiyur. Buddhist bronzes from Nagapattinam have been assigned to Chola and later periods. There's also a good collection of old paintings and sculptures including Tanjore paintings on glass, Rajput and Mughal miniatures and 17th-century Deccan paintings. On the first floor, the **Gallery of Modern Art** ⓘ *T044-28193035*, has a permanent collection of contemporary art with temporary exhibitions.

**Egmore** has a number of other reminders of the Indo-Saracenic period of the 19th and early 20th centuries, the station itself, built in the 1930s, being one of the last. To the northeast of the station is the splendid **St Andrew's Church** ⓘ *Poonamalle High Rd, T044-25383508*, standing in a spacious compound. Consecrated in 1821, the church still has an active congregation. Apart from the façade which resembles St Martin-in-the-Fields in London, it is

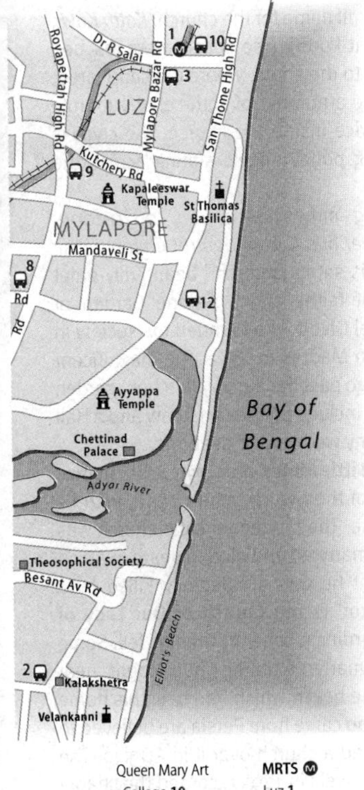


Queen Mary Art College **10**
Saidapet **11**
Taramani **12**
T Nagar **13**

**MRTS**
Luz **1**
Mandavalli (Planned) **2**
Greenways Rd **3**

 essentially circular, 25 m in diameter, and has a magnificent shallow-domed ceiling. You may ask to go up the tower.

## Mylapore and South Chennai

Mylapore is technically older than Chennai and is the seat of city's urban elite. The present **Basilica of San Thomas** ⓘ *24 San Thome High Rd, T044-28545444*, built in 1898, surrounded now by the tenement rehousing scheme of a fishermen's colony, is claimed as one of the very few churches to be built over an apostle's tomb. St Thomas Didymus (Doubting Thomas) is believed to have come to India in AD 52. According to one legend, he travelled across the peninsula from his landing point on the west coast to reach Mylapore – 'town of peacocks' – where he lived and preached. To escape persecution he took shelter in Little Mount (see below). An alternative story recalls how he was invited to visit the King Gondophernes in Taxila, where he converted the king and his court before moving to South India. Some claim that his body was ultimately buried in the Italian town of Ortona. The basilica is now subject to an ambitious, Rs 6,700,000 restoration project. To stop the Mangalore tile roof leaking, concrete reparations are being peeled back and replaced with original lime mortar.

**Kapaleeswarar Temple** ⓘ *0600-1200, 1600-2200*, nearby to the west, is a 16th-century Siva temple with a 40-m *gopuram* (gateway), built after the original was destroyed by the Portuguese in 1566. Sacred to Tamil Shaivites, non-Hindus are only allowed in the outer courtyard where there are several bronze statues.

The diminutive **Luz Church**, 1547-1582 (the date of 1516 in the inscription is probably wrong), is possibly the oldest church in Chennai. It was built by the Portuguese in honour of Our Lady of Light. The Tamil name for the church, *Kattu Kovil*, means 'jungle temple', and a story suggests that Portuguese sailors were rescued from a storm by following a light. They trakced it to the shore, where it disappeared, and on this spot they built the church. There are a number of 19th-century marble plaques to dead wives of the Madras civil service inside the church, the crypt is extremely ornate and has slightly bored-looking podgy angels staring across the imperious Virgin and Jesus.

The **Theosophical Society** ⓘ *Sat morning only, closed Sun, 0830-1000, 1400-1600, entrance south of Elphinstone Bridge, bus 5 from Central Chennai, ask taxi for Ayappa Temple on San Thome High Rd*, is set in large and beautifully quiet gardens. There are several shrines of different faiths and a Serene Garden of Remembrance for Madame Blavatsky and Colonel Olcott who founded the society in New York in 1875 and moved its headquarters to Madras in 1882. The magnificent 400-year-old banyan tree is of particular interest; go past the nursery (kitchen) garden and look on the left at the central circle. Buildings include the Adyar Library and a Hall of Meditation.The brackish river here attracts many waders and seabirds.

A small hill tucked away near Saidapet is the **Little Mount** area, where **St Thomas** is believed to have spent some time. The older of the two churches (1551), with its small vaulted chapel, was built by the Portuguese. The modern circular church was built in 1971. St Thomas is believed to have been martyred and bled to death in AD 52 on the **Great Mount**, though others believe that he was accidentally killed by a hunter's arrow. On top of the 90 m high 'mount' is the **Church of Our Lady of Expectation**. The altar marks the spot where, according to legend, Thomas fell. Some legends suggest that after St Thomas had been martyred on the Little Mount, near Saidapet Bridge, his body was brought back to the beach which had been his home and was buried there. The **Armenian Christians** who came from Persia are believed to have found St Thomas' grave and built a tomb and a church over it in AD 530. The village was called San Thome. Marco Polo in his travels in 1293 recorded the chapel on the seashore and a Nestorian monastery on a hill to the west where the apostle was put to death. In 1523, when the Portuguese started to rebuild the church they discovered the tomb containing the relics consisting of a few bones, a lance head and

### The new organ grinders

While neighbouring Karnataka pitches itself as a new health tourism destination, with much crowing about its glut of world-class cardiac surgeons, Tamil Nadu has drummed up its own slightly less enviable reputation on the operating table. The state is at the centre of the Indian organs racket: its poor have taken to harvesting the most readily available cash crop of all – their own kidneys. A paper published in the Journal of the American Medical Association revealed that 96% of donors had gone under the knife to pay off debts. The fee? Not steep, by international standards, Indian donors typically get something in the region of £620, or US$1,070. Still, not bad for a state where the poverty line is $538 a year per family. Transplant tourism, according to the British national newspaper *The Guardian*, began in the 1980s when wealthy Asians took to jetting in to the sub-continent to snap up organs from living donors. It estimated that half of those kidneys bought abroad failed and a third of patients die, but with 30% of the 40,000 awaiting transplant in Europe dying in the queue for a legal donor, the odds seem worth it.

The racket was made illegal in India in 1995, but carries on unabated, the trade driven underground or the law sidestepped – six transplant centres have sprung up in southern India alone over the past 10 years. The law demands that donors go up before Medical Authorization Committees to confirm they are the relative or spouse of the recipient – to prove the altruism, rather than financial gains, of such a donation – but this has been circumvented by speedy weddings between Gulf men and Indian women, the latter finding themselves quickly divorced after their kidney has been removed. Sadly, medical research shows that most of those who have donated kidneys to pay off debts are swiftly back at the same levels of indebtedness, only now in ailing health because they are one kidney down.

an earthen pot containing bloodstained earth. The church was replaced by the neo-Gothic structure which has two spires and was granted the status of a basilica in 1956. The relics are kept in the sacristy and can be seen on request. There are 13th-century wall plaques, a modern stained glass window, a 450-year-old Madonna brought from Portugal and a 16th-century stone sundial.

## The coastal road to Mahabalipuram

There are two strong reasons to break your journey from Chennai to Mahabalipuram. The first is 19 km outside Chennai at **Cholamandal Artists' Village** ⓘ *East Coast Rd, Enjampakkam, T044-24490092, 0900-1900, free*. The artists' community, started in 1969, provides living, working and exhibition space for artists creating graphics, sculptures, pottery and batik. They sometimes hold dance performances in a small open-air theatre. Try and stop for a short visit. The second reason to stop is the Madras Craft Foundation's well-regarded model village of **Dakshinchitra** ⓘ *East Coast Rd, T044-24918943, Rs 50, 1000-1800, closed Tue*. It presents the arts and crafts of the four southern states and performance of folk arts (eg puppet shows) in a setting of traditional 19th- and early 20th-century architecture. This living museum has a crafts shop and restaurant. Recommended.

# Mahabalipuram (Mamallapuram) → *Phone code: 04114. Colour map 7, grid B6. Population: 12,050.*

Mahabalipuram echoes with the industrious sound of chisels tapping on stone and everywhere you look are workshops' yards crowded with fantastic and ambitious sculptures of deities. Now one of South India's most visited historic sights, Mahabalipuram occupies a stunning position on a rocky outcrop between the beach and a lagoon. The expanding village alongside, with its inviting sandy beach, is a popular haunt of foreign backpackers and there are now plenty of budget hotels and breezy beachside cafés. However, Mahabalipuram's real claim to fame rests on its ancient history and magnificent rock temples and carvings. » *For Sleeping, Eating and other listings, see pages 815-825.*

## Ins and outs

**Getting there** Several daily buses from Chennai take about 1½ hours to the bus stand in the centre of the small village. They may stop at hotels north of Mahabalipuram, on the way, otherwise autos from anywhere in the village will ferry you there for Rs 50.

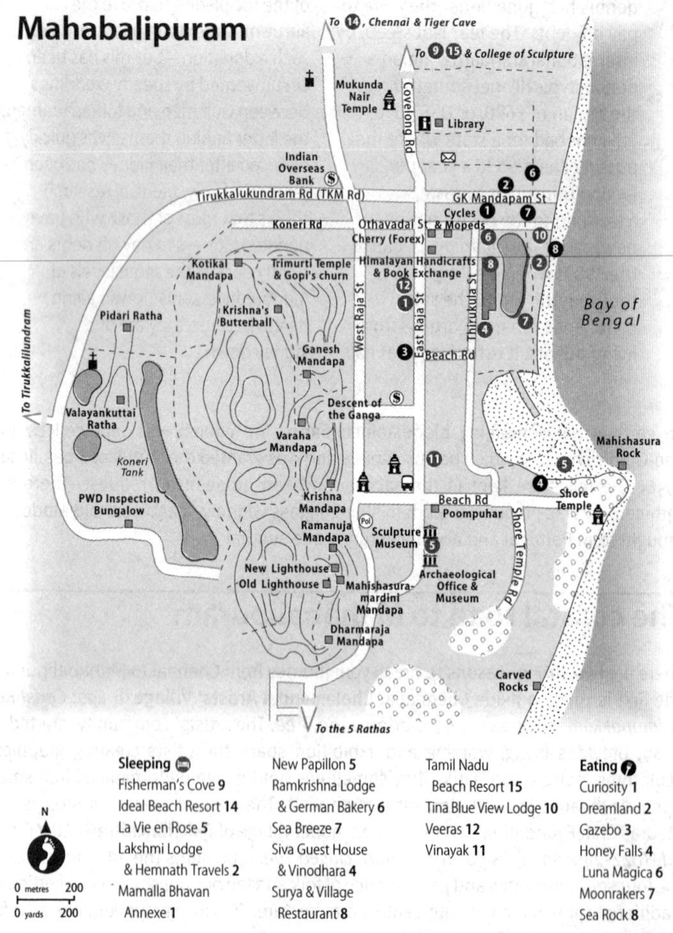

Arriving by car, you may have to pay a Rs 20 toll at the booth near the post office on Covelong Rd. 

**Getting around** Hiring a bike to get further afield can be fun. Beware of con men.

▸▸ *See Transport, page 823, for further details.*

## Background

The coastal temple town Mahabalipuram is officially known as Mamallapuram after 'Mamalla' (great wrestler), the name given to Narasimhavarman I Pallavamalla (ruled 630-668). The Pallava ruler made the port famous in the seventh century and was largely responsible for the temples. There are 14 cave temples and nine monolithic *rathas* (shrines in the shape of temple chariots), three stone temples and four relief sculptured rock panels.

The **Dravida** or Dravidian style underwent several changes over the course of the different dynasties that ruled for about 1,000 years from the time of the Pallavas who laid its foundations. In Mahabalipuram, rock-cut cave temples, *mandapas* (small excavated columned halls), and *rathas* were carved out by the early Pallavas. These were followed by structural temples and bas relief sculptures on giant rocks. The Ekambaresvara Temple in Kanchipuram (see page 812) shows the evolution of the Dravidian style – the shrine with its pyramidal tower and the separate *mandapa* (pillared portico) all within the courtyard with its high enclosure wall made up of cells. Six centuries later the two separate structures were joined by the covered hall (*antarala*). A large subsidiary shrine there, which took the place of an entrance gateway, also hinted at the later *gopuram*.

A characteristic feature of the temples here was the system of water channels and tanks, drawn from the **Palar River,** which made it particularly suitable as a site of religious worship. The *naga*, or serpent cult associated with water worship, can be seen to be given prominence at Bhagiratha's Penance.

Carving in stone is still a living art; stone masons can be heard chipping away from dawn to dusk along the dusty roadsides, while students at the **Government School of Sculpture** ⓘ *closed Tue, 0900-1300, 1400-1830,* near the Bus Stand, continue to practise the skills which flourished centuries ago.

## Sights

**Bhagiratha's Penance** *Descent of the Ganga*, sometimes referred to as **Arjuna's Penance,** is a bas relief sculpted on the face of two enormous adjacent rocks, 29-m long and 7-m high. It shows realistic life-size figures of animals, gods and saints watching the descent of the river from the Himalaya. Bhagiratha, Rama's ancestor, is seen praying to Ganga. A contrived waterfall fed from a collecting chamber above, issues from the natural crack between the two rocks. Some see the figure of an ascetic (on the upper register of the left hand side rock, near the cleft) as representing Arjuna's penance when praying for powers from Siva, though other authorities dispute this. The two large elephants are remarkable and there are also scenes from the fables in the *Panchatantra* and a small shrine to Vishnu. The characteristic system of water channels and tanks, drawn from the Palar River made this a particularly suitable site of religious worship associated with the *naga* (serpent) cult. Look for the group of three monkeys to the right of the panel.

*The best time to walk round is early morning, especially for the best light on Bhagiratha's Penance. Allow two hours for a circuit. The paths on the top of the rock are not always clear, but it is difficult to get really lost.*

A path north from here goes to the double-storeyed rectangular **Ganesh** *ratha* with a highly decorative roof, and two pillars with lions at their base – an architectural feature which was to become significant. The Ganesh image inside is mid-20th century. To the west are the **Valayankuttai** and twin **Pidari** *rathas*. The path continues past the extraordinary, curiously poised, isolated rock, **'Krishna's Butterball'**, through some huge boulders at the north end of the hillock to the **Trimurti Temple** caves which have three shrines to Brahma, Vishnu and Siva, the last with a lingam.

## Stephen Cox

When the British Council first sponsored the Bristol-born artist Stephen Cox to scout India for a place to make his huge-scale stone works for the national art prize the Indian Triennale, he trailed about the subcontinent's very best art schools – Baroda, Varanasi, Delhi – before he plumped for a little fishing village on the Coromandel coast of Tamil Nadu. It may sound bloody-minded, until you arrive in Mahabalipuram, where the whole air clatters with the sound of chisel on rock. It must be the most industrious seat of Hindu idol-making the world over; everywhere you look masons sit on their haunches hammering away at the local dolerite rock. As Cox explains: "I didn't go to India to work with like-minded contemporary artists, I wanted people who could work with great big blocks of stone without fear. Mahabalipuram is totally unique in having this unbroken, living tradition of making idols for people to pray to, and that means that they are also used to working with huge monolithic stone so no-one's daunted by making my 14-tonne sculptures." Although he has kept a studio there from that first year, 1986, you won't find any of his sculpture in the town itself – these are mainly kept for cities: the British High Commission at Delhi, the British Council's office in Chennai and dotted about London's Square Mile. Indeed his work, too minimalist for Hindu temple carving purists, has been received with something less than gusto by some of the local craftsman. Ganapathi Stapati, a local master, denounced his visiting guest at one leaving party Cox had thrown, saying: "He is carrying nothing from Mahabalipuram except a few pieces of stone." Journalist Mark Tully, meanwhile, devoted a whole chapter to what he took to be the 'neo-colonialism' inherent in Cox's use of Indian labour – one sculpture alone can take up to a year to make and will have passed through, on average, 20 pairs of Indian hands before being shipped for exhibition. Cox is defiant: "we have a good working relationship" he says of his craftsmen and is also very alive to the fact that some stonemasons in the village have cottoned on to his work's value on the open market (some of the many wayside workshops offer to knock you off imitations of his pieces for a fraction of the genuine articles' cost). And he's not the only one profiting from India's workforce: whole temples are carved here for export to the US and UK, often for less than the price of uncarved rock from Europe. "At the end of the day, though, of course, I wouldn't be working in India over Carrara in Italy if it wasn't economically viable," he says. The town has changed dramatically since 1986, but what really riles Cox is not the mushrooming restaurants, hotels, and Kashmiri enterprises, but the maintenance of the monuments themselves. "Since it was declared a World Heritage Site, they've buggered the Shore Temple up: it's not a shore temple anymore, instead it sits in a bijou plot of grassland, while the five *rathas* are fenced off, destroying the whole beauty of these wonderful monuments in a natural environment. The temple is still amazing: its beauty only enhanced by the way it has weathered." And his favourite piece of sculpture in a town teeming with them? It's the Pallava's flair for observation that still gets him: "the naturalism that Giotto was supposed to have invented you find in a ninth-century relief carving here. It is amazing. I hope fewer and fewer people come here."

There will be shows to commemorate Cox's 20th year in India in 2006/2007.

**Mandapas** ⓘ *US$5*. The 10 *mandapas* are fairly shallow pillared halls or porticos excavated out of the rocky hillside. They provide space for superbly executed sculptures to illustrate tales from mythology, and illustrate the development of the Dravidian (South Indian) temple style.

On the south is a **Durga niche** (AD 630-660), while next door is the **'Gopi's Churn'**, a Pallava cistern. Walk back along the ridge, passing 'Krishna's Butterball' on your left and some boulders with evidence of incomplete work. The **Varaha Mandapa** (AD 640-674) on the left of the ridge, shows two incarnations of Vishnu – Varaha (boar) and Vamana (dwarf) among scenes with kings and queens. The base forms a narrow receptacle for water for pilgrims to use before entering the temple. From here you can walk to the top of 'Bhagiratha's Penance'.

**Krishna Mandapa** (mid-seventh century) has a bas relief scene of Krishna lifting Mount Govardhana to protect a crowd of his kinsmen from the anger of the Rain God, Indra. The portrayal of a cow licking its calf while being milked is remarkably realistic.

**Kotikal Mandapa** (early seventh century) may be the earliest of the *mandapas*, roughly carved with a small shrine with no image inside. **Ramanuja Mandapa** was originally a triple-cell Siva temple, converted later into a Vaishnava temple.

South of the new lighthouse the simple **Dharmaraja cave** (early seventh century) contains three empty shrines. To its west is **Isvara Temple** (or Old Lighthouse), a truncated Siva temple still standing like a beacon on the highest summit, with a view for miles around. (To the south, across the 'Five Rathas', is the nuclear power station of Kalpakkam; to the west is the flat lagoon and the original port of Mahabalipuram.)

**Mahishasuramardini Mandapa** (mid-seventh century) is immediately below. It has fine bas relief and carved columns with lion bases. The main sculpture shows the goddess Durga slaying the buffalo demon Mahishasura while another relief shows Vishnu lying under Adishesha, the seven-hooded serpent.

**Rathas** These mid-seventh-century monolithic temples, 1½ km south of the Old Lighthouse were influenced by Buddhist architecture as they resemble the *vihara* (monastery) and *chaitya* (temple hall). They imitate in granite temple structures that were originally built of wood and are among the oldest examples of their type.

The five *rathas* to the south of the hill are named after the Pancha Pandava (five Pandava brothers) in the epic *Mahabharata* and their wife Draupadi. The largest is the domed **Dharmaraja** with numerous images including an interesting Ardhanarishvara (Siva-Parvati) at the rear. The barrel-vaulted **Bhima** nearby has a roof suggestive of a thatched hut, while next to it the dome-shaped ratha **Arjuna** imitates the Dharmaraja. **Draupadi ratha**, is the smallest and simplest and is again in the form of a thatched hut. The base, now covered by sand, conceals a lion in front which appears to carry it, which suggests that it may be a replica of a portable shrine. Immediately east is a large unfinished *Nandi*. To its west is the apsidal **Nakula-Sahadeva ratha** with a free-standing elephant nearby. The Bhima and Nakula-Sahadeva follow the oblong plan of the Buddhist *chaitya* hall and are built to two or more storeys, a precursor to the *gopuram*, the elaborate entrance gateway of the Dravidian temple.

**Shore Temple** ⓘ *US$5, includes Five Rathas*. The temple by the sea is surrounded by gardens designed according to descriptions of the original layout from ancient texts. The World Heritage Site is immensely popular with day-trippers and school groups. Built at the end of the seventh century by King Rajasimha, it is unusual for its shrines to both Siva and Vishnu. The sandstone temple has a granite base and a

*'Temple cars' or 'rathas' are tall and often elaborately carved and painted chariots, shaped liked temples themselves, which are used at times of festival to bear deities through the streets in celebratory procession. You will often see them parked under corrugated iron canopies at the side of temples between festivals.*

## The terrifying guardian deities

Many Hindu villagers in Tamil Nadu believe in guardian deities of the village – Ayyanar, Muneeswaram, Kaliamman, Mariamman and many more. Groups of larger-than-life images built of brick, wood or stone and covered in brightly painted lime plaster (*chunam*) guard the outskirts of several villages. They are deliberately terrifying, designed to frighten away evil spirits from village homes, but villagers themselves are also very frightened of these gods and try to keep away from them.

The deities are supposed to prevent epidemics, but if an epidemic does strike special sacrifices are offered, mainly of rice. Firewalking, often undertaken in fulfilment of a vow, is a feature of the special festivals at these shrines. Disease is also believed to be held at bay by other ceremonies, including piercing the cheeks and tongue with wire and the carrying of *kavadis* (special carriages or boxes, sometimes designed like a coffin).

basalt *kalasha* at the very top. Its position on the water's edge, with an east-facing altar designed to catch the rising sun and a stone pillar to hold the beacon for sailors at night, meant that there was no space for a forecourt or entrance gateway. Two additional shrines were built to the west asymmetrically. The second smaller spire adds to the temple's unusual structure. The outer parapet wall has lines of *Nandi* (Siva's sacred bull) and lion pilasters.

**Saluvankuppam** Five kilometres north of Mahabalipuram, on the coast, is the excavated temple at Saluvankuppam which has the **Tiger Cave** *mandapa* with carvings of tigers' heads. The cave, not signposted from the beach, is secluded and very peaceful – a lovely place for a picnic. On the way you will see the **Mukunda Nayar Temple.**

**Beaches** Check about safety of swimming in the sea. To avoid hassle and have an undisturbed day by the beach, pay Rs 100 to use the small pool at **Crystal Shore Palace** or **Sea Breeze**, or the bigger pool, 1 km north at **Tamil Nadu Beach Resort**. Be warned: the beach north of the temples towards the **Ashok** and the rocky area behind the Descent of the Ganga are open latrines for the village.

## Excursions

**Tirukkalukundram** is a small Siva temple dedicated to Vedagirishvara on top of the 3,000 million year-old rock 14 km west of Mahabalipuram. About 400 steps take you to the top of the 160 m hill which has good views and also some very materialistically-conscious priests and 'guides'. Be prepared for a hot barefoot climb, 'donations' at several shrines and Rs 10 for shoe custodian! At midday it is said that you will see two Neophran vultures (Pharaoh's chickens) fly down to be fed by the priests – but you may be disappointed. The Bhaktavatsleesvara in town with its *gopuram* (gateway) stands out like a beacon. The tank is considered holy and believed to produce a conch every 12 years. Small shops in the village sell cold drinks. Buses from Mahabalipuram take 30 mins or you can hire a bike.

**Sriperumbudur,** 44km from Chennai on National Highway 4, is the birthplace of the 11th-century Hindu philosopher Ramanuja, is the town where Rajiv Gandhi was assassinated on 21 May 1991. There is a memorial at the site with sculpted columns in a well-kept garden.

# Kanchipuram → *Phone code: 04112. Colour map 7, grid A5. Population: 153,000.*

What Darjeeling is to tea, and Cheddar is to cheese, so Kanchipuram is to silk. One of Hinduism's seven most sacred cities (see page 1324), 'the Golden City of a Thousand Temples', dates from the early Cholas in the second century. The main temple complexes are very spacious and only a few of the scattered 70 or so can be seen in a day's visit. The town itself relatively quiet except for crowds of pilgrims.

## History

The **Pallavas** of Kanchi came to power in the fourth century AD and were dominant between AD 550-869. Possibly of northern origin, under their control Mahabalipuram (Mamallapuram) became an important port in the seventh century. Buddhism is believed to have reached the Kanchipuram area in the third century BC. Successive dynasties made it their capital and built over 100 temples, the first as early as the fourth century. In addition to being a pilgrimage centre, it was a centre of learning, culture and philosophy. Sankaracharya and the Buddhist monk Bodhidharma lived and worked here.

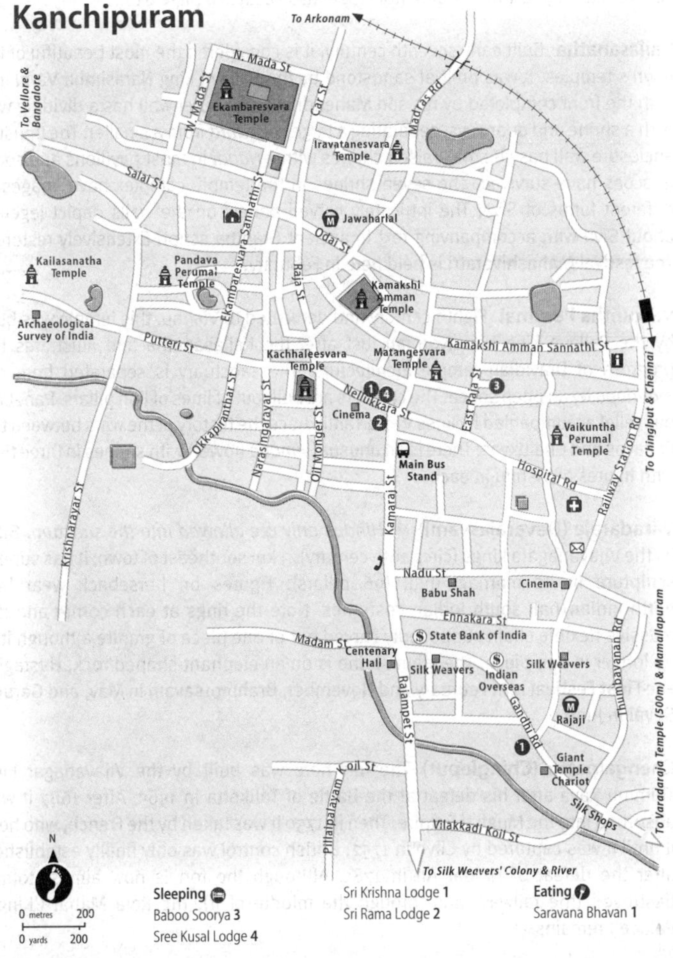

**Ekambaresvara Temple** ⓘ *Small entry fee, cameras Rs 3, only Hindus are allowed into the inner sanctuary.* The temple has five enclosures and a 'Thousand-pillared Hall' (for the pedantic, the number is actually 'only' 540). Dedicated to **Siva** in his ascetic form it was begun by the Pallavas and developed by the Cholas. At the beginning of the 16th century the Vijayanagara king Krishna Deva Raya built the high stone wall which surrounds the temple and the 59-m tall *rajagopuram* (main tower) on which are sculpted several figures of him and his consort.

*Have change ready for 'donations' to each temple you visit. Temples are generally open from 0700 and closed from 1200-1600.*

The main sanctuary has a *lingam* made of earth (Siva as one of the elements) and the story of its origin is told on a carved panel. The teasing Parvati is believed to have unthinkingly covered her husband Siva's eyes for a moment with her hands which resulted in the earth being enveloped in darkness for years. The enraged Siva ordered Parvati to do severe penance during which time she worshipped her husband in the form of an earth *lingam* which she created. When Siva sent a flood to test her, she clung to the *lingam* with her hands until the waters subsided. Some believe they can see her fingerprints on the *lingam* here. On 18 April each year the sun's rays enter the sanctum though a small square hole. See also Festivals, page 818.

**Kailasanatha** Built early seventh century, it is considered the most beautiful of the town's temples. It was built of sandstone by the Pallava king Narasimha Varman II with the front completed by his son Mahendra III. The outer wall has a dividing wall with a shrine and doorways, separating a large courtyard from a smaller. The unusual enclosure wall has 58 small raised shrines with a *Nandi* in most pavilions and some frescoes have survived. The seven shrines in the temple complex have images of different forms of Siva. The intricately carved panels on the walls depict legends about Siva with accompanying text in ancient Grantha script. Extensively restored. The festival **Mahashivaratri** is held here in February.

**Vaikuntha Perumal** Eighth century and dedicated to Vishnu, this temple was built by the Pallava king Nandivarman just after the Kailasanatha and illustrates the progress of Dravidian temple architecture. The sanctuary is separated from the *mandapa* by an open space. The cloisters are built out of lines of lion pillars. Panels of bas relief accompanied by lines in old Tamil, trace the history of the wars between the Pallavas and Chalukyas. There is an unusual *vimana* (tower) with shrines in three tiers with figures of Vishnu in each.

**Varadaraja (Devarajasvami)** ⓘ *Hindus only are allowed into the sanctum.* Built by the Vijayanagara kings (circa 16th century), 3 km southeast of town, it has superb sculpture in its marriage hall (96 pillars). Figures on horseback wear half north Indian/half south Indian costumes. Note the rings at each corner and the massive flexible chain supposedly carved out of one piece of granite although it is no longer in one piece. The main shrine is on an elephant-shaped rock, Hastagiri. The **Float Festival** is in February and November, **Brahmotsavam** in May, and **Garuda Sevai** in June.

**Chengalpattu (Chingleput)** The fort here was built by the Vijayanagar king Thimmu Raya after his defeat at the Battle of Talikotta in 1565. After 1687 it was absorbed into the Mughal Empire. Then in 1750 it was taken by the French, who held it until it was captured by Clive in 1752; British control was only finally established after the defeat of Haidar Ali in 1781. Although the fort is now almost totally destroyed (the railway runs through the middle of it), the Raja Mahal ('King's Palace') remains.

## Excursions

On the Trichy Road, 87 km from Chennai and 60 km from Mahabalipuram, **Vedanthangal Bird Sanctuary** and Karikili Tank are thought to have existed as a protected area for about 250 years. The marshy site attracts numerous water fowl and provides their main nesting place. Visitors and residents include crested cormorants, night herons, grey pelicans, sand pipers, grey wagtails, open-billed storks, white ibis, egrets, little grebe and purple moorhens. Best time to visit: November to February, dawn and 1500-1800; avoid weekends and holidays.

**Marakkanam**, mentioned in Roman records as an important port in the first century AD, has an ancient Siva temple with many inscriptions. Immediately inland is the Kaliveli Tank, an extremely important staging post and wintering area for about 40,000 migratory water fowl, including over 200 pelicans.

## Sleeping

**Chennai** *p795*
Chennai has a wealth of accommodation options; however, at the top end, excluding the Taj offerings, these are very much pitched at the city's growing business market lack character. At the budget end, cheaper options are strung within 1 km of Anna Salai (Mount Rd) in Central Chennai.

**Airport** *p795*
These hotels offer free airport transfers. Other hotels are 12-15 km from the airport.
L **Trident**, 1/24 GST Rd, T044-2234 4747. 166 rooms in characterless but functional hotel. Nice pool in the garden.
AL **Le Royal Meridien**, T044-2231 4343, www.royalmeridien-chennai.com. Plush new hotel with all facilities including good restaurants and bars.
B-C **Mount Heera**, 287 MKN, Alandur, T044- 22335656, hotelmountheera@yahoo.com. New hotel with modern facilities and free airport transfers.

**George Town** *p797, map p796*
Good location for Central Station and State Bus Stands. Many cheap hotels are along VOC (Walltax) Rd.
E **Great Hotel**, 149 VOC Rd, T044-25331706. 44 rooms, 3 a/c, all with TV, spacious. Recommended.
E **Railway Retiring Rooms**, Central Station, T044-25353337, some a/c rooms, dorms too.
E **Sornam International**, 7 Stringer St, T044-25353060. 50 rooms with TV, balcony, hot water, rooftop vegetarian restaurant, pleasant.
E **Youth Hostel (TTDC)**, EVR Park (near Central Railway Station), T044-25389132. Reasonably quiet.
F **YMCA**, NSC Bose Rd, T044-25383941, opposite City bus stand.

**Central Chennai** *p802, map p798*
Many hotels are strung out within 1 km either side of Anna Salai (Mount Rd).
A-E hotels collect an extra 20-30% tax.
L **Chola Sheraton**, 10 Cathedral Rd, T044-2811 0101. 80 rooms 'boutique hotel', good restaurants (including *Peshawari*), airport transfer.
L **The Park Chennai**, 601 Anna Salai T044-5214 4000, www.theparkhotels.com. Converted from the site of the Gemini Film Studios, this is a quintessentially 'filmi' hotel. Very Conran interiors with original film posters lining the walls, world-class business facilities and lovely rooftop pool with excellent views over the city.
L **Taj Connemara**, Binny Rd (off Anna Salai), T044-5500 0000, connemara.chennai@tajhotels.com. Extremely comfortable hotel with 148 renovated rooms which retain splendid art deco features. Excellent restaurants, bar and good **Giggles** bookshop. Heavily booked Dec-Mar.
L **Taj Coromandel**, 37 Mahatma Gandhi Rd, Nungambakkam, T044-5500 2827, coromandel.chennai@tajhotels.com. 201 rooms, fine restaurants, good pool. Recommended but Western tours dominate.
AL **Ambassador Pallava**, 53 Montieth Rd, T044-2855 4476, pallava.sales@wipro.net.in.

*For an explanation of the sleeping and eating price codes used in this guide, see inside the front cover. Other relevant information is found in Essentials pages 56-61.*

120 rooms in rather run-down hotel, good restaurants (especially Chinese), pool (open to non-residents), health club.

**A-B Grand Orient**, 693 Anna Salai, T044-28523411, F28523412. 66 rooms, half have been renovated but others are very worn, clean (usual hazard of cockroaches), helpful staff, good location.

**B Residency**, 49 GN Chetty Rd (convenient for airport), T044-2825 3434, www.theresidency.com. 112 very comfortable spacious rooms, 4th floor upwards have good views (9th floor, plush **A** suites). Excellent **Ahaar** restaurant (good buffet lunches), exchange, good car hire with knowledgeable drivers. Better rooms and service than some higher priced hotels. Highly recommended, reserve ahead.

**B Savera**, 69 Dr Radhakrishnan Rd, T044-2811 4700, hotsave@md2.vsnl.net.in. 260 comfortable rooms, good pool (non-residents, Rs 150), older hotel but smart and clean (standard rooms identical to superior!), disaster prone travel desk.

**D Broadlands**, 16 Vallabha Agraharam St, T044-2854 8131. 50 rooms, a few with shower, dorm (Rs 50), set around lovely shady courtyards, clean with good service, reasonably quiet and extremely popular though some find it overrated and over-priced, helpful management but they operate "no-Indians" policy.

**D Comfort**, 22 Vallabha Agraharam St, T044-2858 7661. 40 rooms, some a/c, clean friendly Indian hotel 5 mins from Marina Beach.

**D Guru**, 69 Marshall's Rd, reasonably near Egmore railway station, T/F044-2855 4067. Large hotel, fairly clean rooms, some a/c, good vegetarian restaurant, no credit cards.

**D Harrisons**, 154/5 Village Rd, T044-2827 5271. Some a/c rooms, restaurant (South Indian/Chinese), bar.

**D Himalaya International**, 54 Triplicane High Rd, T044-2854 7522. 45 rooms with nice bath, some a/c, modern, welcoming, clean, bright, no food but available from *Hotel Gandhi* next door.

**D Paradise**, 17/1 Vallabha Agraharam St, T044-2854 7542, F8530052. Spacious clean rooms with fans (some with 2!), shower, good value, very friendly and helpful owners.

**D Ranjith**, 9 Nungambakkam High Rd, T044-2827 0521, F8277688. 51 rooms, some a/c, restaurant (good non-vegetarian continental), excellent and reasonable bar, cool, pleasant and relaxing, travel desk.

**E Sree Krishna**, 159 Peters Rd, T044-2852 2897. 15 rooms, some a/c with bath.

**E YMCA**, 14 Westcott Rd, Royapettah, T044-2853 2158.

**Egmore** *p803, map p801*

Many hotels (including several good budget options) are clustered around the station and the EVR Periyar (Poonamallee) High Rd, an auto-rickshaw ride away to the north of the railway line. Kennet Lane budget hotels are often full.

**A-B New Victoria**, 3 Kennet Lane (200 m from station), T044-2819 3638, F28190070, www.hotelnewvictoria.com. 51 a/c rooms, restaurant (excellent *Lido* breakfast), bar, spacious, quiet, ideal business hotel. Recommended.

**B Tristar**, 29 Whannels Rd, T044-2855 0006, F8550561. New hotel with good a/c rooms, all facilities.

**C Abu Palace**, 926 EVR Periyar High Rd, T044-2643 1010, F26428091. Plush, well insulated rooms, restaurant, bar, smart business hotel, concrete fortress-like exterior, huge enclosed lobby.

**C Breeze**, 850 EVR Periyar High Rd, T044-2641 3334, F26413301. 94 rooms, modern, popular: fridges, satellite TV, internet facilities.

**C-D Raj Residency**, 2 Kennet Lane, T044-2821 2214, www.rajresidency.net. 72 rooms with balcony, veg restaurant, bar, recently opened, spacious.

**D Blue Diamond**, 934 EVR Periyar High Rd, T044-2641 2244, F6428903. 33 rooms, some a/c, quieter at rear, good a/c restaurant (crowded at peak times), exchange.

**D Pandian**, 15 Kennet Lane, T044-2819 2727, www.hotelpandian.com. 90 rooms, some a/c, a/c restaurant, bar, clean but spartan, helpful staff, expensive room service. Branch of *i-way* internet.

**D YWCA International Guest House**, 1086 EVR Periyar High Rd, T044-2532 4234. Restaurant (rate includes breakfast), 60 rooms, with bath, few a/c, for men and women, popular so book early, excellent value, also camping ground.

**D-E Imperial**, 6 Gandhi Irwin Rd, T044-2825 0376, F2825 2030. 80 good size, average

rooms, some a/c, best at rear, 4 restaurants, good food, reasonable price, bar, friendly.
**E Impala Continental**, opposite station, T044-2825 0564. 50 very nice, clean rooms with TV, near *Vasanta Bhavan* restaurant, good service.
**E Masa**, 15/1 Kennet Lane, T044-2825 2966, F8251261. 88 clean functional a/c rooms, hot water.
**E New Laxmi Lodge**, 16 Kennet Lane, T044-2825 4576. 50 rooms around courtyard in old building, set back in garden.
**E Regent**, 8 Kennet Lane, T044-2825 3347. 45 renovated clean rooms set around courtyard, friendly. Recommended.
**E Satkar**, 65 Ormes Rd (Flowers and Millers Rd junction), T044-2642 6304. Spotless rooms with bath, some a/c, good vegetarian *Suryaprakash* restaurant, helpful staff, good value but very noisy.
**E Silver Star**, 5 Purasawalkam High Rd, T044-2642 4414. 38 simple clean rooms back from road, open air restaurant in courtyard, helpful and friendly staff.
**E YMCA (1)**, 14 Westcott Rd, Royapettah and **(2)** at 17 Ritherdon Rd, Vepery, T044-2532 2831, where there are D rooms with bath.
**F Cristal**, 34 CNK Rd, Triplicane, T044-2857 2721. Clean basic rooms with [illegible] bath, very helpful service, better and cheaper than some others in the area.
**F Laharry Transit Hostel**, for women under 30 only, very cheap and good value.
**F Railway Retiring Rooms**, T044-[illegible]5 2527.
**F World University Service**, East Spur Tank Rd, T044-2826 3991. Some rooms with bath, dorm, International Student cards needed, couples not allowed to share a room, cheap canteen for Indian snacks, good value, well located for Egmore and south central Chennai.

### South Chennai *p804, map p802*

**L-AL Park Sheraton**, 132 TTK Rd, T044-2499 4101, F4997201. 160 rooms, Dakshin Chettinad restaurant, good pool.
**C Parthan**, 75 GN Chetty Rd (near Panagal Park), T044-2815 8792, www.parthan.com. 29 clean, large, comfortable and quiet rooms, restaurant (Chinese), exchange. Recommended.
**D Transit House**, 26 Venkataraman St, T Nagar, T044-2434 1346. Some a/c rooms, dorm (Rs 60), snack bar and pleasant garden, no credit cards.
**E Andhra Mahila Sabha**, 12 D Deshmukh Rd, T044-2493 8311. Some **D** a/c rooms, vegetarian restaurant.

### Mahabalipuram *p806, map p806*

Even modest hotels charge 20% luxury tax. There are several new places in the Othavadai Street area. Places get booked up at the time of the January dance festival.
**L-AL Fisherman's Cove** (Taj), Covelong Rd, 8 km north, T04114-272304. 80 rooms, some a/c cottages with sea view, excellent seafood at restaurant right on the beach ("very special"), beautiful site, very good facilities, ask reception about seasonal turtle walks.
**B-C Ideal Beach Resort**, Covelong Rd (3½ km north), T04114-242240, www.idealresort.com. 30 rooms in cottages, some a/c (limited hours), good restaurant, exchange, pool and gardens, clean, comfortable. Poor service reported though.
**C-D Seabreeze**, T04114-243035, seabreezehotel@hotmail.com. Clean, spacious, well-furnished rooms (some a/c, Rs 700), pleasant position, direct beach access (dubious swimming), pool (non- residents Rs 100), good food, Chennai airport pick-up Rs 600. The annexe next door, see below, is cheaper.
**D Mamalla Bhavan Annexe**, 104 East Raja St, T04114-242260. 43 clean, pleasant rooms, 17 a/c, nice balconies, excellent vegetarian restaurant, exchange, travel, spotless, friendly, very good value. Highly recommended.
**D Sea Breeze Annexe**, see above, clean double bedrooms with fan and deck. Tariff includes access to the hotel swimming pool.
**D Tamil Nadu Beach Resort**, T04114-242361, F42268. 48 cottages, some a/c but neglected, damp, restaurants, bar (limited hours), exchange, good pool (gets deep suddenly!) (non-residents Rs 75), beautiful setting.
**D-E Surya**, 1 Thirukula St, T04114-242292, F42992. 12 cottages overlooking small lake (1st floor with balcony dearer), very clean, some a/c, in quiet shaded gardens, a/c restaurant, camping, very knowledgeable, friendly manager.
**D-E Veeras**, East Raja St, T04114-242288. 16 rooms (10 a/c), clean, well kept, good restaurant, bar.
**D-E Vinayak**, 68 East Raja St, next to bus stand, T04114-242445. 14 rooms with

balcony overlooking garden in new hotel, TV, phone, comfortable.

**E Lakshmi Lodge**, Othavadai St, T04114-242463. 26 clean rooms, upstairs small but light, downstairs dark and poor, restaurant with beach view, friendly, popular with backpackers, notice "prohibits drugs but staff try to sell you hemp'.

**E-F Siva Guest House**, 2 Othavadai Cross St, T04114-243234, F243334, sivaguesthouse@hotmail.com. 11 very clean rooms in new hotel, taxi hire, internet, friendly. Highly recommended.

**E-F Tina Blue View Lodge**, [illegible]avadai St, T04114-242319, F242511. [illegible]ms with bath and balcony (Room 9), cottages for long term rent, garden, friendly. Recommended.

**F La Vie en Rose**, 9 Old Colle[illegible] near bus stand, T04114-242522, la[illegible]ose 45@hotmail.com. 7 rooms over[illegible]ng garden, friendly, internet, inter[illegible] 'backpacker restaurant' with balc[illegible] French spoken.

**F New Papillon**, off Beach Rd, towa[illegible] Sunrise. Clean but simple rooms, shower (Rs 70), good restaurant upstairs (try muesli).

**F Ramakrishna Lodge**, 8A Othavadai St, T04114-242431. 31 well-kept, clean rooms with fan, shower, western toilets, no nets (Rs 125), courtyard, good rooftop restaurant with travellers' menu and music, friendly, good value (contact Vijay for informal yoga classes). Recommended.

**Kanchipuram** *p811, map p811*

**C-D Baboo Soorya**, 85 East Raja St, T04112-222555, set back off main road down palm fringed lane. 38 clean, spacious rooms, some a/c, restaurant, snack bar, glass 'bubble' lift, friendly staff, quiet.

**E Sri Rama Lodge**, 20 Nellukkara St, near Bus Stand, T04112-222435. Fairly basic rooms, some a/c and TV, a/c restaurant, quite quiet, helpful staff.

**F Sree Kusal Lodge**, 68C Nellukkara St, T04112-223356. 25 clean and good value rooms, TV, veg restaurant.

**F Sri Krishna Lodge**, 68A Nellukkara St, T04112-222831. 28 good, clean rooms, some with bath, helpful, friendly manager.

## Eating

**Chennai** *p795*

**Central Chennai** *p802, map p798*

Most restaurants are in Central Chennai and are open 1200-1500, 1900-2400. Those serving non-vegetarian dishes are often more expensive.

**TTT Chola Sheraton**, see Sleeping. Chinese in the hotel (chef from Beijing) and good rooftop restaurant, superb views.

**TT Copper Chimney**, opposite Chola Sheraton. International, a/c, good tandoori, very clean, pleasant seating.

**TT Patio**, at the Taj Coromandel, see Sleeping, is exquisite Continental but pricey. Also at the **Golden Dragon** does excellent Chinese; **Southern Spice** offers very good South Indian, along with evening dance recitals and freezing a/c.

**TT Raintree**, at Taj Connemara, see Sleeping, is a romantic outdoor restaurant with good food, atmosphere and ethnic entertainment but cavalier service. Very good buffet dinner on Sat night.

**TT [illegible]vera**, see Sleeping, has an excellent [illegible] very friendly, helpful service, live music in the evenings.

**T Lakshmi**, Anna Salai (near Higginbotham's bookshop). Wholesome, health-restoring offerings, Southeast Asian spe[illegible]s (profits to charity, run by vol[illegible]s). Recommended.

**TT Bu[illegible]s**, 83 Anna Salai. Good Indian. Has a terraced dimly lit a/c restaurant, with unusu[illegible]cor, try crab curry, egg rotis and Muslim [illegible]es; branch in Park Town near Central [illegible]on.

**TT Cascad[illegible]**, 5 Khaderi Nawaz Khan Rd. Chinese, T[illegible] Japanese and Malay.

**TT Chinato[illegible]**, 74 Cathedral Rd (a/c). Chinese.

**TT Chungkin[illegible]**, 67 Anna Salai (opposite PO) (1030-2200). Chinese, where lack of atmosphere (dim lighting) is compensated for by good food.

**TT Dasaprakash**, Anna Salai (next to Higginbotham's bookshop). 1200-1445, 1900-2345. South Indian (buffets Rs 120), also excellent milk shakes.

**TT Dynasty**, at Harrison, see Sleeping, is a recommended Chinese restaurant.

**Gem**, Triplicane High Rd (200 m south of Broadlands). Non-vegetarian. Tiny Muslim restaurant.
**Jewel Box**, at Blue Diamond, see Sleeping. Cool a/c, good for breakfasts, snacks and main courses (also Chinese).
**Southern Chinese**, 683 Anna Salai, Thousand Lights (next to Anand Theatre). Recommended.
**Maharaja**, Triplicane High Rd, 100 m from Broadlands hotel. Indian vegetarian.
**Saravana**, 209 NSC Bose Rd, 2 floors. Extremely clean, excellent snacks, fruit juices (try pomegranate!), sweetmeats, all freshly made.
**Udipi**, 8/9 Anna Salai (near Higginbotham's), good range of snacks.
**Woodlands Drive-In Restaurant**, 30 Cathedral Rd. 0600-2100. Rows of tables, simple, busy, go for breakfast.

**Egmore** *p803, map p801*
**Stardust**, 5 Kennet Lane. Multi-cuisine and pizzas, dimly lit.
**Balaji Woodlands**, Vee Yes Hotel, Egmore. Indian vegetarian.
**Udipi Home Mathsya**, 1 Hall's Rd (corner of Police Commissioner's Rd), Egmore. A/c, excellent, wide range of food. Recommended.
**Vasanta Bhavan**, 10 Gandhi Irwin Rd, opposite Egmore station, 1st floor. Very clean, excellent food, friendly staff, downstairs bakery does delicious sweets.

**Mahabalipuram** *p806, map p806*
Beachside cafés are pleasant for a drink: Sea Rock and Luna Magica in particular. In top hotels waterfront cafés are especially attractive in the evening.
**Curiosity**, Othavadai St. Wide range, excellent food, very willing to please.
**Gazebo**, East Raja St. Charcoal-grilled fish, pleasant seating.
**German Bakery**, selling good bread, great cakes, tasty pastas (try yak cheese lasagne) and Chinese dishes, very friendly, relaxed atmosphere, Nepali-run, open Dec-Apr. Recommended.
**Honey Falls**, Shore Temple Rd. Few tables, served with delicious fish.
**La Vie en Rose** hotel, upstairs near the Archaeological Office. French. Very good food, 'special teas' (in absence of licence), friendly French manager.
**Moonrakers**, Othavadai St, www.moonrakersrestaurant.com. Pleasant and friendly. Recommended.
**Temple View**, GRT Temple Bay Kovalam Rd, T4114-242251. Multi-cuisine restaurant overlooking shore temple, open for breakfast lunch and dinner, plus less formal, open air 'Beach Comber' and 'High Tide' bars (1000-2200).
**Tina Blue View Lodge**, breezy restaurant, mixed reports (sometimes slow, unfriendly service).
**Village**, near Surya. Some outdoor seating in pleasant lakeside position, rustic design, average food, chilled beers.
**Dreamland**, Othavadai St. Western favourites, very friendly, relaxed.
**Mamalla Bhavan Annexe** hotel. Good South Indian vegetarian restaurant. Try paper *dosa* and outstanding *palak* dishes. Indoors a/c, or outdoors evenings.

**Kanchipuram** *p811, map p811*
**Baboo Soorya** hotel, a/c, cheap Indian vegetarian restaurant, good *thalis*.
**Bakery Park Place**, Odai St, cakes and sweets.
**Saravana Bhavan**, next to Jaybala International 504 Gandhi Rd (50 m off the road). "Best in town".
**Sri Rama Lodge**, a/c, and **Sri Vela**, Station Rd, good breakfasts.

## Bars and clubs

**Chennai** *p795*
You can buy booze without difficulty despite local restrictions. Regulations change periodically, however, and All India Liquor Permits are available from either an Indian mission or a Govt of India Tourist office abroad or in one of the regional capitals.
**Bikes and Barrels**, Sri Thyagaraya Rd, T Nagar, T044-2815 6363. Restaurant and bar, playing rock, trance and house.
**Dublin**, Park Sheraton hotel, TTK Rd, T044-2499 4101. Irish pub-cum-nightclub.
**The Leather Bar**, The Park, 601 Anna Salai, T044-5214 4100. A dark womb of a bar with black leather floors and olive suede walls.
**Oakshott Bar**, Taj Connemara Hotel, Binny Rd, is a large, bright bar, offering huge tankards of beer, "exceptional 'side-snacks', huge TV; casual clothes accepted".

## Entertainment

### Chennai *p795*

Although Chennai is revered for its strong cultural roots, much of it is difficult for the common tourist to access. Events are often publicized only after they have passed.

### Cinemas

Those which show foreign (usually English language) films are mostly in the centre of town on Anna Salai.

### Music, dance and art galleries

**Chennai Music Academy**, TTK Rd, is the scene of numerous performances of Indian music, dance and theatre, not only during the prestigious 3-week Music Festival from mid-Dec but right through the year; **Sabhas** are membership societies that offer cultural programmes 4 times a month to its members, but occasionally tickets are available at the door.

**Kalakshetra**, Tiruvanmiyur, T044-24461943. 1000-1800 daily. A temple of arts founded by Rukmani Devi Arundale in 1936 to train young artists to revive Bharat Natyam.

**Shree Bharatalaya**, in Mylapore. One of the key dance fine arts institutes run by respected guru Sudharani Raghupathy, Sura Siddha, 119 Luz Church Rd, T044-2499 4460.

## Festivals and events

### Chennai *p795*

On **Jan 14 Pongal Makara Sankranti**, the harvest thanksgiving, is celebrated all over Tamil Nadu for 3 days (public holiday). After ritually discarding old clothes and clay pots, festivities begin with cooking the first harvest rice in a special way symbolizing good fortune, and offering it to the Sun god. The second day is devoted to honouring the valuable cattle; cows and bulls are offered special new-rice dishes prepared with jaggery or nuts and green lentils. You will see them decorated with garlands, bells and balloons, their long horns painted in bright colours, before being taken out in procession around villages. Often they will pull carts decorated with foliage and flowers and carrying children, accompanied by noisy bands of musicians. On the final day of feasting, it is the turn of the 'workers' to receive thanks (and bonuses) from their employers.

### Mahabalipuram *p806, map p806*

**Dec-early Feb**: 6-week Dance Festival starting on 25 Dec; at Bhagiratha's (Arjuna's) Penance, Classical 1800-2030, Folk 2030-2100, every Sat, Sun and holidays. Long speeches in Tamil on opening (full moon) night. **Mar**: Masi Magam attracts large crowds of pilgrims. **Apr-May**: Brahmotsava lasts for 10 days. **Oct-Nov**: the **Palanquin Festival** is held at the Stalasayana Perumal Temple.

### Kanchipuram *p811, map p811*

The **Panguni Uthiram Festival** in **Mar-Apr**, is the largest and possibly the most atmospheric of Kanchipuram's festivals, celebrated all over Tamil Nadu though.

## Shopping

### Chennai *p795*

**Parry's Corner** and **Anna Salai** are principal centres. Most shops open Mon-Sat 0900- 2000, some close for lunch 1300-1500. Weekly holidays may differ for shops in the same locality. Bear in mind that drivers – even those from reputable agents and companies – see little wrong in collecting a sweetening kickback from Kashmiris staffing huge shopping emporia, in exchange for dumping you on their doorstep. These are expert salesmen, and do have some absolutely beautiful things, but will ask at least double price for most of them. The commission is creamed from whatever you buy, so exercise restraint. There are often discount sales during the festival seasons of Pongal, Diwali and Christmas. The weekly *Free Ads* (Rs 5, Thu) has listings for second-hand cameras, binoculars etc which travellers might want to buy or sell.

### Books

Most bookshops open 0900-1900. Also in hotels.

**Higginbotham's**, 814 Anna Salai and F39 Anna Nagar East, near Chintamani Market.

**Side Effects**, G17 Eldorado, 112 NH Rd, closes 1430-1600.

### Clothes and crafts

**Poompuhar**, 818 Anna Salai, specializes in 1st class bronzes.
**Victoria Technical Institute**, Anna Salai near Taj Connemara and opposite the Life Insurance Corporation of India. This fixed-rate, Government-backed operation is the best for South Indian handicrafts (wood carving, inlaid work, sandalwood).
Other Govt Emporia are along Anna Salai,
**Atmosphere**, K Nawaz Khan Rd. Beautiful modern furniture fabrics and curtains – mostly silks – which can be shipped anywhere within India within 72 hrs.
**Cane & Bamboo**, 26 C-in-C Rd.
**Central Cottage Industries**, opposite Taj Coromandel, is recommended.
**Cinnamon**, 27 Shafee Mohammed Rd. Designer clothes and modern design items by Indian designers.
**Habitat**, K Nawaz Khan Rd nearby, good for special, unusual gifts.
**Jamal's**, 44 Devraja Mudali St.
**Kalakshetra** at Thiruvanmiyur excels in *kalamkari* and traditional weaving, also good household linen.
**Kalpa Druma**, 61 Cathedral Rd (opposite Chola Sheraton), has attractive selection of wooden toys and panels.
**Khazana** at Taj Coromandel, good for special, unusual gifts.
**New Kashmir Arts**, 111 Anna Salai, for good carpets.
**Tiffany's**, 2nd floor, Spencer's Plaza (antiques, bric-à-brac).
**Vatika**, 5 Spur Tank Rd, good for special, unusual gifts.

### Department stores

Most open 0900-2000.
**Burma Bazar**, Rajaji Salai, for imports, especially electronic goods, bargain hard.
**Five Stars**, 60 Pantheon Rd, Egmore.
**Harringtons**, 99 Harrington Rd, Chetput.
**Isapahani Centre**, 123/4 Nungambakkam High Rd. This is where the hip Madrasis hang out and has some very snazzy designer 'ethnic' clothes shops.
**Spencer's Plaza**, Anna Salai near Taj Connemara, is a dizzyingly huge mall that offers excellent choice for shopping in comfort.
**Supermarket**, 112 Davidson St and TNHB Building, Annanagar (closed Fri).

### Fabrics

Chennai was founded because of the excellence and cheap prices of the local cotton.
**Co-optex** (Government run) shops stock handloom silks and cottons.
**Khadi** stores specialize in handspun and handwoven cotton.
**Shilpi**; **Urvashi**, TTK Rd, good for cottons.

### Jewellery

**Sri Sukra Jewels**, 42 North Mada St Mylapore, T044-2464 0699, www.sukra.com. Brilliant temple – ie costume – jewellery. Fixed price. Next door, at 43 is
**Radha Gold Jewellers**, T044-2491923. You can also get 'antique' finished things and dance jewels 0930-1300 1600-2100.

### Silk and saris

Look out for excellent Kanchipuram silk and saris. Recommended for quality and value:
**Handloom House**, 7 Rattan Bazar.
**Nalli** (opposite Panagal Park) with excellent selection, both in T Nagar.
**Rupkala**, 191 Anna Salai, good prices, helpful staff.

### Mahabalipuram *p806, map p806*

Handicrafts shops sell small figures in soapstone and metal.
**Hidesign**, 138 East Raja St. Excellent Western-style leather goods, very reasonable. Recommended.
**Himalayan Handicrafts**, 21 East Raja St, also has 900 books for exchange.
**JK Books**, off the beach on Othavadai St. Books and newspapers.
**Silver Star**, 51 East Raja St, good tailor.

### Kanchipuram *p811, map p811*

Silk and cotton fabrics with designs of birds, animals and temples or in plain beautiful colours, sometimes 'shot', are sold by the metre in addition to saris. It is best to buy from Government shops or Co-operative Society stores.
**AS Babu Shah**, along Gandhi Rd, has high quality silks.
**BM Silks**, 23G Yadothagari, Sannathi St. Worth a look.
**Sreenivas**, 135 Thirukatchi Nambi St (Gandhi Rd).

## Activities and tours

**Chennai** *p795*

**Sports clubs**

Temporary membership is available at most clubs, sometimes for sports only.

**Chennai Cricket Club**, Chepauk. Tennis, swimming, cricket, billiards, bar.

**Chennai Gymkhana Club**, Anna Salai. Tennis, swimming, cricket, billiards, library, bar.

**Chennai Riders' Club**, Race View, Race Course, Velachery Rd. Riding (including lessons) throughout the year except Jun. Facilities in clubs are for members only, but you may be allowed in on being recommended by a member. Some hotel facilities may be used on payment of a fee.

**Cosmopolitan Club**, Anna Salai. Tennis, billiards, golf, library, bar.

**Golf**

At Guindy Race Course.

**Swimming**

Hotel pools open to non-residents: **Ambassador Pallava, Savera**.

**Chennai Cricket Club** has an excellent pool (less crowded before noon); you need an introduction. Others open to the public are at Marina Beach and the YMCA pool at Saidapet. Sea bathing is safe at Elliot's Beach, though no longer attractive.

**Tennis**

Clubs allowing members' guests and temporary members to use courts are: **Chennai Club, Gymkhana Club, Cricket Club, Cosmopolitan Club, Presidency Club** and **Lady Willingdon Club**. YMCA at Saidapet also has courts.

**Tours**

The following are on deluxe coaches and accompanied by a guide:

**Tamil Nadu Tourism (TTDC)**. Departure points and reservations: Sales Counters at 4 EVR Periyar High Rd (opposite Central Station), T044-2536 0294; Express Bus Stand near High Ct compound, T044-2534 1982 (0600-2100).

Sales agents: **Welcome Tours**, 150 Anna Sali (Agarchand Mansions), T044-2852 0908.

**City sightseeing half-day** daily 0800-1300, 1330-1830. Fort St George, Government Museum (closed on Fri), Valluvar Kottam, Snake Park, Kapaleeswarar Temple, Elliot's Beach, Marina Beach. Rs 105, a/c Rs 150.

**Full-day** daily 0800-1900. Drive along Marina Beach, Kapaleeswarar Temple, Snake Park, Vallavur Kottam, Museum, Fort St George (US$2 entry), St Mary's Church, Birla Planetarium, Muttukadu Boat House and VGP Golden Beach. Rs 160 (a/c Rs 240). Visitors have found the tours disappointing.

**Excursions** Mahabalipuram and Kanchipuram, 0730-1900, Rs 200 (a/c Rs 350) and Tirupati, 0630-2200, Rs 375 (a/c Rs 600).

**Tour operators**

**Cox & Kings**, A15 Eldorado Building, NH Rd.

**Mercury**, 191 Anna Salai, T044-28522993.

**STIC**, 142 NH Rd, T044-28271195

**Sita**, 26 C-in-C Rd, T044-28278861.

**Southern Holidays**, 19, Nageswara Rd, T044-28236029, www.southernholidays.com.

**Surya**, 1st fl, Spencer's Plaza, Anna Salai. Very efficient, friendly, personal service.

**Thomas Cook**, 45 Montieth Rd, opposite Ambassador Pallava hotel.

**Welcome**, 150 Anna Salai, near India Tourist Office, T044-2852 0908. Open 24 hrs.

**Mahabalipuram** *p806, map p806*

**Hi Tours**, 123 East Raja St, T04114-243260, travexs@vsnl.com. Train/air tickets, tours, foreign exchange, Kerala house boats.

**Tamil Nadu Tourism (TTDC)**: to Kanchipuram and Mahabalipuram. 0500-1900. Tiring, but good value if you don't mind being rushed. It also includes a stop at the appallingly garish Indian kitsch, VGP Beach Resort.

**Kanchipuram** *p811, map p811*

Tourist information at Hotel Tamil Nadu, T04112-222461, 1000-1700.

## Transport

**Chennai** *p795*

**Air**

The **Aringar Anna International airport** (named after CN Annadurai) with 2 terminals and the **Kamaraj Domestic airport** are on one site at Trisoolam in

Meenambakkam, 12 km from the centre. Enquiries, T140, arrivals and departures, T142. **Pre-paid taxis** from both; to Chennai Central or Egmore, Rs 150-180 (yellow taxis are cheaper than private), 30 mins; Rs 450 to Mahabalipuram. Buses to centre Rs 75 (day), Rs 100 (night). Airport, T044-2234 6013. **Auto-rickshaws** to Chennai Central, Rs 100. **Suburban Railway** the cheapest way into town, from Trisoolam suburban line station to Egmore and Fort, but trains are often packed. **Free Fone** in the main concourse, after collecting baggage in the international airport, you can use this phone to ring hotels. Railway Bookings 1000-1700. Watch out for International prices for food and drink. **Indian Airlines**, 19 Marshalls Rd, T044-2855 5200 (daily, 0800-2000). Reservations, all 24 hrs: T044-2855 5209. Mini Booking Offices: 57 Dr Radhakrishnan Rd, T044-2827 9799; Umpherson St (near Broadway); 9 South Bagh Rd, T Nagar, T044-2434 7555; Airport T044-2234 3131. Check-in T044-2234 8483. To **Bangalore, Bhubaneswar, Coimbatore, Delhi, Goa, Hyderabad, Kochi, Kolkata, Madurai**, via Tiruchirappalli; **Mumbai, Port Blair** and **Pune, Puttaparthy, Thiruvananthapuram, Visakhapatnam**. International flights include: **New York, Kuwait, London, Paris, Bangkok, Kuala Lumpur** and **Singapore**.

**Airlines** Jet Airways, 43 Montieth Rd, Egmore, T044-28414141, airport T044-2256 1818. **Air India**, 19 Marshalls Rd, T044-2855 4477 (0930-1730, avoid 1300-1400), airport T044-2234 4927. **Air France**, 43 Montieth Rd, T044-2855 4916. **Sri Lankan**, 73 Cathedral Rd, T044-2826 1535. **British Airways**, Khalili Centre, Montieth Rd, T044-2855 4680, Airport T044-2234 8282. **Cathay Pacific**, Spencer's Plaza, 769 Anna Salai, T044-2852 2418. **Gulf Air**, 52 Montieth Rd, T044-2855 3091. **KLM**, Taj Connemara, T044-2852 4437. **Kuwait Airways**, 43 Montieth Rd, T044-2855 3797. **Lufthansa**, 167 Anna Salai, T044-2852 5095. **Malaysian Airlines**, 498 Anna Salai, T044-2434 9651. **Qantas**, 112 NH Rd, T044-2827 8680. T044-2852 2871. **Sabena**, 47 White's Rd, T044-2851 4337. **Saudia**, 560 Anna Salai, T044-2434 9666. **Singapore Airlines**, 108 Dr Radhakrishna Rd, T044-2852 2871. **Swissair**, 47 Whites Rd, T044-2852 6560. General Sales Agents (GSA): **Air Kenya, Garuda Airways, Japan Airlines**, Global Travels, 703 Anna Salai, T044-285 23957. **Alitalia**, 548 Anna Salai, T044-2434 9822. **American Airways, Air Canada, Bangladesh Biman, Royal Jordanian** and **TWA**, Thapar House, 43 Montieth Rd, T044-2856 9232. **Delta**, at Aviation Travels, 47 Whites Rd, T044-2825 9655. **Iberian** and **Royal Nepal Airlines**, at STIC Travels, 142 NH Rd, T044-2827 1195. **Egypt Air** and **Yemen Air**, at BAP Travels, 135 Anna Salai, T044-284 9913. **Maldive Airways**, at Crossworld Tours, 7 Rosy Tower, NH Rd. **Thai International**, at Inter Globe, 144 Kodambakkam High Rd, T044-2826 2294. **Sahara**, T044-2826 3661.

### Auto-rickshaw

Three-wheeler scooter taxis, taking 2 adults and a child or more for a negotiable fee will hike charges by 25% between 2100-0500. In theory: Rs 7 should be the minimum charge for 1st km, after which it should be metered. You can insist on using the meter, but these can be rigged and will often result in your driving around in circles to rack up the rate. Locally, most people agree a fare to a fixed destination: Rs 30 gets you between most neighbourhoods. As always, drivers get kickbacks from emporium owners to encourage detours via shops. Cycle- rickshaws are often no cheaper.

### Bus

**Local** The cheap and convenient local bus service is not overcrowded and offers a realistic alternative to auto-rickshaws and taxis outside the rush hour (0800-1000, 1700- 1900). Make sure you know route numbers as most bus signs are in Tamil (timetables from major bookshops). **Pallavan Transport Corp (PTC)**, Anna Salai, runs an excellent network of buses from 0500-2300 and a skeleton service through the night. 'M' service on mini-buses are good for the route between Central and Egmore stations and journeys to the suburban railway stations. The 'V' service operates fast buses with fewer stops and have a yellow board with the route number and LSS (Limited Stop Service). PTC has a ½ hourly 'luxury' mini-bus service between **Egmore Station, Indian Airlines**, Marshall's Rd office and the airports at **Meenambakkam** picking up passengers from certain hotels (inform time keeper at Egmore in advance, T044-2536 1284). The fare is about Rs 20.

**Long-distance** For long-distance journeys, the state highways are reasonably well maintained but the condition of other roads varies. The new East Coast Rd (ECR) for Express buses and cars only has helped to cut some journey times. Fast long-distance Korean air buses now run on some routes, giving a comfortable ride on air-cushioned suspension.

Chennai is amazingly proud of its new bus station, **Mofussil Bus Terminus** on Jawaharlal Nehru Rd, near Coimbedu Market T044-2479 4705: Asia's biggest, it has 30 arrival and 150 departure terminals.

**Tamil Nadu Govt Express Parry's**, T044-2534 1835, offers good connections within the whole region and the service is efficient and inexpensive. Best to take a/c coaches or super deluxe a/c. Bookings 0700-2100. Other state and private companies cover the region but you may wish to avoid their video coaches which make listening, if not viewing, compulsory as there are no headphones! **Interstate Bus Depot**, Broadway Bus Stand, handles enquiries and reservations. Computer reservations are now made on long distance routes.

Beware of children who 'help' you to find your bus in the expectation of a tip; they may not have a clue! There have also been reports of men in company uniforms selling tickets which turn out to be invalid; it is best to buy on the bus. The listings given are for route number, distance. **Coimbatore** *No 460*, 500 km; **Chidambaram** and **Nagapattinam** *326*; **Kanchipuram** *76B*; **Kanniyakumari** *282 and 284*, 700 km; **Kumbakonum** *303F*, 289 km, 6½ hrs; **Madurai** *137*, 447 km, 10 hrs; **Mahabalipuram** *109*, Rs 19, 1½ hrs (*108B* goes via Meenambakkam airport, 2½ hrs) can be very crowded; **Nagercoil** *198*, 682 km, 14 hrs; **Ooty** *468*, 565 km, 13 hrs; **Pondicherry** *803*, 106 km, 3 hrs; **Thanjavur** *323*, 320 km, 8 hrs; Tiruchirappalli *123*, 320 km and Route *124*, 7 hrs; **Tiruvannamalai** 180 km, 5 hrs; **Yercaud** *434*, 360 km, 8 hrs; **Bangalore (via Vellore and Krishnagiri)** *831*, 360 km, 8 hrs; **Bangalore (via Kolar)** 350 km, 7½ hrs; **Mysore via Bangalore** *863*, 497 km, 11 hrs; **Tirupati via Kalahasti** *802*, 150 km, 3½ hrs. Also several **Andhra Pradesh STC** buses to Tirupati daily. APSTC runs daily buses to many other towns in the state, as does **Karnataka State Express Bus Service** to Karnataka.

**Car**

A/c or ordinary cars with drivers are good value and convenient for sightseeing, especially for short journeys out of the city when shared between 3 and 5 people. Large hotels can arrange, eg Regency (Rs 600 per 8 hrs; Rs 750 for Mahabalipuram). **Ganesh Travels**, 36 PCO Rd, T8250066; **Window to the World** (Trichy), T0431-2436052, faithpandian@sify.com, for tours from Chennai (and other towns); **Hertz**, 426 Anna Salai, T044-24330684; **TTDC**, 4 EVR Periyar Rd, T044-25360294.

**Ferry**

Visas are now also issued on arrival at Port Blair. Regular passenger ships to the Andaman and Nicobar Islands take 3 days. The **Shipping Corporation of India**, Jawahar Building, Rajaji Saiai, T044-2523 1401. Also, **Deputy Directorate of Shipping Services**, A & N, 6 Rajaji Salai, T044-2522 6873. **Tickets to the Andaman Islands** At 0900 pick a 'letter of intent' to visit the Andamans, and collect details of sailings from the Shipping Corporation of India office. Go to the Foreigners' Registration Office at Shastri Bhavan, 26 Haddows Rd, and complete an application form for a **permit** and submit it with 2 photos before 1230; pick up at 1700 on the same day (or a day later if the application is submitted after 1230). Next day, take photocopies of your passport identification/Indian Visa pages and also of the Andamans permit, to the SCI office. Pick up a **Ticket "Order Form"**, fill it in and queue for a ticket, 1000-1300. Women have an advantage when queuing!

**Motorbike hire or purchase**

Southern Motors, 282 TTH Rd, T044-2499 0784, is a good modern garage with efficient service. The YWCA, EVR Periyar Rd, is a good hotel for bikers and has a big shaded garden to park bikes securely.

### MRTS

The Mass Rapid Transit System (raised, above-ground railway) covers the Beach-Chepauk and Chepauk-Mylapore sections.

### Taxi

Bharati Call Taxi, T044-28142233. Chennai Call Taxi, T044-25384455. Fast Tack, T044-24732020. Tourist cabs are the best choice in case you want to tour the city all day or visit nearby places like Mahabalipuram etc. It costs about Rs 4 per km and Rs 30 per hour as hire charges. The minimum hire is for 5 hrs or 50 km. Tiruvalluvar Travels, T044-24745807.

### Train

**Suburban railway** Inexpensive and handy, but very crowded at peak times. Stops between Beach Railway Station and Tambaram (every 5 mins in rush hour) include Fort, Park, Egmore, Chetpet, Nungambakkam, Kodambakkam, Mambalam, Saidapet, Guindy, St Thomas Mt. Also serves suburbs of Perambur and Villivakkam. Convenient stop at Trisoolam for the airports, 500 m walk from the terminals.

**Long distance** Smoking is banned on trains, stations and in railway offices. There is a penalty of Rs 100. Chennai has 2 main stations, Chennai Central (MC) for broad gauge trains to all parts of India and Egmore (ME) for metre gauge (and some sections converted to broad gauge). The 2 have a mini-bus link; taxis take 5 mins. Beach Station is for suburban services. Chennai Central enquiry, T131, reservations, T132, arrivals and departures, T133, then dial train no. Advance Reservations Centre, Southern Railway, is in a separate building in front of suburban station, open 0800-1400, 1415-2000, Sun 0800-1400. You can also order bedding. Indrail Passes and booking facilities for foreigners and NRIs on the 1st floor. Egmore enquiry, T135, arrivals and departures, T134. There are also Southern Railway Booking Offices in Mambalam, T044-2483 3755, Tambaram and Chennai Beach. Meenambakkam Airport has a Rail Booking Counter. You may reserve 30 days in advance. From **Chennai Central** **Bangalore** *Shatabdi Exp, 2007*, 0600, not Tue, 7 hrs; *Lalbagh Exp, 2607*, 1545, 5¾ hrs; *Brindavan Exp, 2639*, 0715, 6 hrs. **Coimbatore** *Kovai Exp, 2675*, 0615, 7¾ hrs; *West Coast Exp, 6627*, 1100, 8¾ hrs; *Cheran Exp, 2673*, 2145, 8½ hrs. **Delhi (ND)** *Tamil Nadu Exp, 2621*, 2200, 33½ hrs; *G.T. Exp, 2615*, 1630, 37½ hrs. **Delhi (HN)** *Rajdhani Exp, 2431*, 1915, Tue, Thu, 29½ hrs. **Guntakal** (for Hospet): *Chennai Dadar Exp, 1064*, 0650, 8 hrs; *Chennai-Mumbai Mail, 6010*, 2220, 10 hrs. **Hyderabad** *Charminar Exp, 2759*, 1810, 14½ hrs; *Chennai-Hyderabad Exp, 7053*, 1600, 15 hrs. **Kochi (Cochin)** *Chennai-Aleppey Exp, 6041*, 1945, 13¾ hrs; *Guwahati Cochin Exp, 5624*, 1210, Fri, 14¾ hrs. **Kolkata (H)** *Coromandel Exp, 2842*, 0905, 29 hrs; *Howrah Mail, 6004*, 2230, 32½ hrs. **Mettupalayam** *Nilgiri Exp, 6605*, 2015, 10 hrs. **Mumbai (CST)** *Chennai-Mumbai Mail, 6010*, 2155, 30 hrs; *Chennai-Mumbai Exp, 6012*, 1145, 27 hrs. **Mysore** *Shatabdi Exp, 2007*, 0600, daily not Tue, 7 hrs; *Chennai Mysore Exp, 6222*, 2245, 9¼ hrs. **Thiruvananthapuram** *Guwahati Trivandrum Exp, 5628*, 1210, Wed, 19¼ hrs; *Howrah Trivandrum Exp, 6324*, 0440, Tue, Sun, 18½ hrs. From **Egmore** **Kanniyakumari** *Chennai- Kanniyakumari Exp, 6121*, 1900, 15 hrs. **Madurai** *Chennai-Kanniyakumari Exp, 6121*, 1815, 10 hrs; *Vaigai Exp, 2635*, 1225, 8 hrs; *Pandyan Exp, 6717*, 2100, 9½ hrs via Kodai Rd (this connects with the bus service at **Kodaikkanal** arriving at midday). **Tiruchirappalli** *Vaigai Exp, 2635*, 1225, 5½ hrs; *Pallavan Exp, 2606*, 1530, 5½ hrs.

**Mahabalipuram** *p806, map p806*

Bicycle hire from tourist office and shops in East Raja St and hotels, Rs 25 per day. Recommended for **Tirukkalukundram** – from Dec-Feb a comfortable and very attractive ride. VM Hire, Othavadai St (opposite Uma Lodge). Bicycle Rs 25, moped Rs 100. Mopeds also at **Bala Lodge** and **Vinodhara**, Rs 125.Car hire from the tourist office. Buses from Chennai also go to **Tirukkalukundram** and **Pondicherry**. *Nos 19C, 68, 119A*. Taxis charge Rs 700-1000 for 1-day excursion from Chennai; Rs 450 to airport. To **Pondicherry**, Rs 700 (bargain hard).

The nearest train station is Chengalpattu, 29 km away with buses taking an hour.

**Kanchipuram** *p811, map p811*
The town is flat and easy to negotiate so the best and cheapest way to get about is by hiring a bike from near the bus stand or off East Raja St. **Cycle** and **auto-rickshaws** are available for visiting temples.

The bus station in the middle of town with direct Govt Express to **Chennai** (*No 828*) 2½ hrs, **Bangalore** (*No 828*), **Kaniyakumari** (*No 193*), **Pondicherry** (*No 804*, 109 km) 3½ hrs, and **Tiruchirappalli** (*No 122*). For **Mahabalipuram** (65 km) 2 hrs, direct bus or take a bus to Chengalpattu (35 km) and catch one from there. Very frequent buses to **Vellore**, other buses go to **Tirupati** and **Tiruttani**.

The train station, on a branch line, is under 1 km to the northeast of the bus stand. There is 1 direct train to **Chennai Egmore** and **Chennai Beach**: *Kanchipuram-Chennai Beach Pass, 172 (S)*, 0705, 2 hrs **Egmore**; 2½ hrs **Chennai Beach**. Also trains to Arakkonam on the Chennai-Bangalore line.

**Vedanthangal Sanctuary** *p813*
From Chennai by car or bus from the Broadway Bus Stand, Chennai (only weekends) or one from Mahabalipuram. It is also included in some coach tours.

The train to **Chengalpattu** (28 km) and then bus or taxi, 30 km to sanctuary.

## Directory

### Chennai *p795*

**Banks**
Most open either 0830-1230 or 1000-1400 on weekdays; morning only on Sat. Closed Sun, national holidays and 30 Jun and 31 Dec (foreign exchange dealing may close an hr early). A few big hotels have 24-hr banks. **State Bank of India, Thomas Cook, TT Travels** at International Airport, 24 hrs. **American Express**, G17, Spencer Plaza, Anna Salai, T044-285 23628, 0930-1930, offers all foreign exchange and TC services. **Thomas Cook** branches at: 45 Montieth Rd, Egmore. 20 Rajaji Salai. 112 NH Rd, T044-282 74941, Mon-Fri 0930-1830 (closed 1300-1400), Sat 0930-1200. Both recommended. **Madura Travels**, Kennet Lane (near corner of Gandhi Irwin Rd), Egmore, change TCs, good rate. Many banks have branches on Anna Salai, Cathedral, Dr Radhakrishnan and EVR Periyar Rds. Visa ATMs at **CitiBank**, Anna Salai (24 hrs). Alsa Promenade, Door 149, AA Block, 3rd Ave, Anna Nagar. Pushpa Shoppe, Adyar. **HSBC**, 30 Rajaji Salai. Pushpa Shoppe No 1, Adyar. **Standard Chartered Bank**, 37 Royapettah High Rd.

**Embassies and consulates**
Most open 0830-1330, Mon-Fri.
**Austria** 115 NH Rd, T044-2827 6036.
**Belgium** 97 Anna Salai, T044-2235 2336.
**Denmark** 8 Cathedral Rd, T044-2827 3399.
**Finland** 742 Anna Salai, T044-2852 4141.
**France** 16 Haddows Rd, T044-2826 6561.
**Germany** 22 C-in-C Rd, T044-2827 1747.
**Greece** 72 Harrington Rd, T044-2826 9194.
**Italy** 19 Rajaji Salai, T044-2534 2141.
**Japan** 60 Spur Tank Rd, T044-2826 5594.
**Malaysia** 6 Sri Ram Nagar, T044-2434 3048.
**Mauritius** 145 Starling Rd, T044-2827 1841.
**Netherlands** 64 Armenian St, T044-2538 4894.
**Norway** 44-45 Rajaji Salai, T044-251 7950.
**Singapore** 109 Habibulla Rd, T044-2827 6393.
**Spain** 8 Nimmo Rd, San Thome. **Sri Lanka** 9D Nawab Habibulla Av, off Anderson Rd, T044-2827 6751. **Sweden** 6 Cathedral Rd, T044-2827 5792. **UK** **Deputy High Commission**, 24 Anderson Rd, Nungambakkam, T044-2827 5130.
**USA** 220 Anna Salai, T044-2827 3040.

**Internet**
**Cybervision**, off Anna Salai, 64 k ISDN; **Datamen's**, 273 Pycrofts Rd, good access, Rs 90 per hr; serves soft drinks. **SRIS**, 1st floor, F22-A, Spencer Plaza, 769 Anna Salai.

**Language schools**
**Bharatiya Vidya Bhavan**, 38/39 R E Mada St, T044-2494 3450, for Sanskrit. **Hindi Prachar Sabha**, T Nagar, T044-244 1824. **International Inst of Tamil Studies**, Central Polytechnic, T044-241 2992. Some of the foreign cultural centres have libraries and arrange film shows. **Alliance Française**, 3/4A College Rd, Nungambakkam, T044-2827 2650. **American Center**, 561 Anna Salai, library 0930-1800, closed Sun, T044-2827 7825. **British Library**, 737 Anna Salai, 1000-1900, closed Mon, T044-2285 2002. **Russian**, 27 Kasturi Rangan Rd, T044-2499 0050. **Max Müeller Bhawan**,

0900-1900, closed Sun, 13 Khadar Nawaz Rd, T044-2826 1314.

**Medical services**

**Ambulance services** Ambulance (Government), T102; St John's Ambulance, T044-2826 4630, 24-hr. Dental hospital (Government), T044-2534 0411; All-in-One, 34 Nowroji Rd, T044-2641 1911, 0400-2000, 0900-1200 Sun. **Chemists** SS Day & Night Chemists, 106D, 1st Main Rd, Anna Nagar. **Hospitals** Apollo Hospital, 21 Greams Rd, T044-2827 7447. CSI Rainey, GA Rd, T044-2595 1204. Deviki Hospital, 148 Luz Church Rd, Mylapore, T044-2499 2607. National Hospital, 2nd Line Beach Rd, T044-2251 1405.

**Post**

Poste restante at the GPO, Rajaji Salai, George Town; other major post offices which accept Speed Post Mail are in Anna Salai, Pondy Bazar, T Nagar, Meenambakkam, NH Rd, Flower Bazar and Adyar. CTO, Rajaji Salai (near Parry's Corner). Opening times vary, 1st 3 open 0800-2030. Computerized ISTD booths all over town, some open 24 hrs.

**Telephone**

Directory enquiry (national) T183, only from Chennai city itself.

**Tourist offices**

Govt of India (GITO), 154 Anna Salai, T044-2852 4785, Mon-Fri 0915-1745, Sat until 1300. Domestic Airport Counter, 24 hrs; International Airport Counter, at flight times.
India Tourism Development Corporation (ITDC), 29 Victoria Crescent, C-in-C Rd, T044-2827 8884, 0600-2000, Sun 0600-1400.
Tamil Nadu (TTDC), 4 EVR Periyar Rd (opposite Central Station), T044-2538 2916, www.tamilnadutourism.com, includes booking of TTDC hotels and tours; Express Bus Stand, T044-2534 1982.
TTDC, 25 Radhakrishnan Rd, T044-2854 7335; Information centres at Central Railway, Gate 2 (Sales Counter on Sun), Egmore stations, and domestic airport terminal, T044-2234 0569, 0700-2300.
Govt of Tamil Nadu, Pangal Building, Saidapet. State tourist offices usually open from 1030-1700 on weekdays (closed Sun and 2nd Sat).
Andaman and Nicobar Islands, Andaman House, North Main Rd Ext, Anna Nagar West Ext, Padi Village, T044-2625 9295.

**Useful addresses**

Foreigners' Registration Office, ground floor, Shastri Bhavan Annexe, 26 Haddows Rd. T044-2827 8210, for visa extensions, Mon-Fri 0930-1800. Govt of Tamil Nadu, Pangal Building, Saidapet. State tourist offices usually open from 1030-1700 on weekdays (closed Sun and 2nd Sat). Andaman and Nicobar Islands, Andaman House, North Main Rd Ext, Anna Nagar West Ext, Padi Village, T044-2625 9295.

**Mahabalipuram** *p806, map p806*

**Banks** Cherry, Beach St, for exchange. LKP, 130 East Raja St. Good rate, speedy. Prithvi Securities, opposite Mamalla Bhavan Annexe, no commission, transfers money. **Libraries** Has English language dailies. Book exchange at Himalayan Handicrafts. **Post** Post office on a back street off Covelong Rd. **Tourist offices** Tamil Nadu, Covelong Rd (300 m north of Othavadai St), T04114-242232, 0945-1745, closed Sat, Sun. 2 guides available here; others from Chennai. Car and cycle hire possible.

**Kanchipuram** *p811, map p811*

**Banks** State Bank of India, Gandhi Rd. Amex TCs not accepted; Indian Overseas Bank, Gandhi Rd. **Post** Head Post Office, 27 Gandhi Rd.

# Pondicherry and Auroville

*Pondy doesn't exactly have the outright lazy charm of some former French colonies; its tax status guarantees it is a bustling commercial marketplace for booze and white goods, while the many pale grey-painted buildings housing offshoots of the Sri Aurobindo Ashram – whose devotees are encouraged to support the ashram's coffers with entrepreneurial endeavours – add an extra layer of ethnic, health-conscious businesses to the mix. But the union territory is still evidence of the wonder that is town planning: the Dutch, who also once held the port, laid down a grid system that is found throughout the city except the Muslim area whose streets are at a slight angle to adhere to Mecca's directional pull. French colonial architecture is particularly obviously found clustered around the southern end of town where big whitewashed buildings froth with bright pink bougainvillea. The food here, too, smacks gloriously of Gaul: excellent French breads, ratatouilles that run with olive oil, hard cheese and real French wines (for a price).*

*Up the road is the westernized branch of Aurobindo's legacy, Auroville, the 'City Of Dawn'. Its founding credo in 1968 was that it become a city 'that no nation could claim as its sole property, a place where human beings could live freely as citizens obeying one single authority, that of the supreme Truth.' This is the industrious fulcrum of people seeking an alternative lifestyle – this is where spirulina is harvested, incense pressed, and white cotton pyjama suits are de rigeur.* » For Sleeping, Eating and other listings, see pages 830-833.



## Ins and outs

**Getting there** Buses take under four hours from Chennai on the East Coast Road. Both the State and private bus stands are just west of the town, within walking distance, or a short auto-ride from the centre, but hassle from rickshaw drivers can make arrival a chaotic experience. The train station on a branch line from Villupuram, with trains to major destinations, is a few minutes' walk south of the centre.

**Getting around** Pondicherry is pleasant to explore on foot, but hiring a bike or moped gives you the freedom to venture further along the coast independently. » See Transport, page 832, for further details.

**Tourist information** **Pondicherry Tourism** ⓘ *40 Goubert Salai, T0413-2339497, www.tourismpondicherry.com, 0845-1300, 1400-1700*. Town maps, brochures, tours, sea cruises, fishing, car/bicycle hire, well run. The **Indian National Trust for Art and Cultural Heritage** is particularly active in Pondicherry and runs heritage walks from its offices ⓘ *14 Rue Labourdonnais, T0413-222 5991*.

## Pondicherry (Puducherry) → *Phone code: 0413. Colour map 7, grid B5.*

*Population: 220,700.*

Today, many travel to Pondicherry for the Ashram founded by Sri Aurobindo Ghosh and his chief disciple Mirra Alfassa, 'The Mother'. With over 2,000 permanent residents, it pervades much of the town's life with portraits of Sri Aurobindo and The Mother very much in evidence. Sri Aurobindo Ghosh was an early 20th-century Bengali nationalist and philosopher who struggled for freedom from British colonial power (see page 1335). He started the Ashram here to put into practice his ideals of a peaceful community. In this aim he found a lifelong French companion in Mirra

*Many's the company that's set up in Pondy to take advantage of its tax breaks. These include Whirlpool, Vipro, Infosys, Unilever and Hush Puppies.*

**“” This is the industrious fulcrum of people seeking an alternative lifestyle – where spirulina is harvested, incense pressed, and white cotton pyjama suits are de rigeur...**

Alfassa, who became universally known as the Mother. After his death in 1950, she continued as the spiritual successor and charismatic figure of Pondicherry until her own death in 1973 at the age of 93.

## History

The site of the town has been identified as ancient Vedapuri where the sage **Agastya Muni** had his hermitage in 1500 BC. In the first century AD Romans traded from nearby Arikamedu. The **French** acquired land at Pondicherry in 1673 and renamed it Puducherry. In 1742, Dupleix was named Governor of the French India Company and took up residence at here. In 1746 British lost Fort St George in Madras to Dupleix but in 1751 Clive returned by attacking Arcot and by capturing Pondy in 1761 and razing it to the ground. Puducherry was voluntarily handed over to the Indian Government in 1954 and became the Union Territory of Pondicherry.

## Sights

Pondicherry is a town made for ambling about in on foot. The town is cleaved into two: the **French quarter** along the beach with its pretty high-ceilinged wood-slatted residential houses with their walled gardens and bougainvillea frills, and the **Tamil** ('black') town of 'talking streets' with long front verandas for talking with passers-by, markets, mess and business, to its west. While the French area, 300 heritage buildings, is well maintained (80% are owned by the ashram), the Tamil area, despite holding 1,000 homes now classified as heritage, is now under threat from neglect. However, the European commission has stumped up cash to fund the restoration of an entire street, Calve Subraya Chetty (Vysial) street (between Mission and Gandhi Streets). Muslim domestic architecture is well-represented in the rues Kazy, Mulla and Tippu Sultan, in the South side of the Tamil quarter.

**Sri Aurobindo Ashram** ① *0800- 1200, 1400-1800, free, meditation: Mon, Tue, Wed, Fri, 1925-1950; in the Playground: Thu, Sun, 1940-2015,* has its main centre in rue de la Marine. The Ashram buildings can be recognized by the pale grey highlighted with white. The focus of reverence in the Main Building is the stone Samadhi (memorial) of the founders which is under a tree within the complex. It is a very peaceful spot. The Bureau Central on Ambur Salai is the Information Centre which has occasional films, lectures and other performances. There is a **library** ① *0730-1130, 1400-1645.*

**The French Institute**, rue St Louis, was set up in 1955 for the study of Indian culture; the Scientific and Technical Section for ecological studies. There's a superb library overlooking the sea, with many books in French and English and the colonial building itself is worth seeing.

**Pondicherry Museum** ① *next to the library, rue St Louis, 1000-1700, except Mon and public holidays, free,* has a good sculpture gallery and a section of archaeological finds from the Roman settlement at Arikamedu. The French gallery charts the history of the colony and includes the four-poster bed in which Dupleix is believed to have slept. Another place worth seeking out is the grand white-washed **Lycée Français**, rue Victor

# Pondicherry

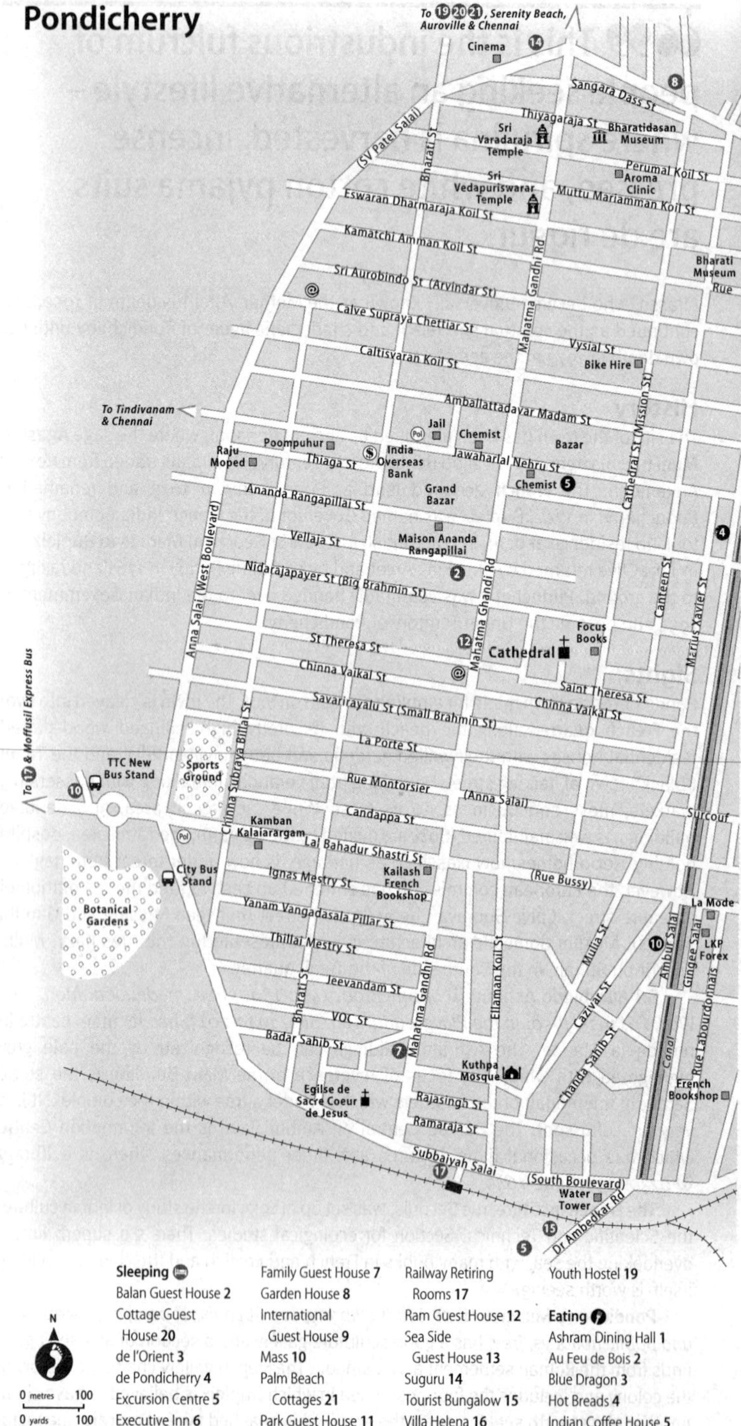

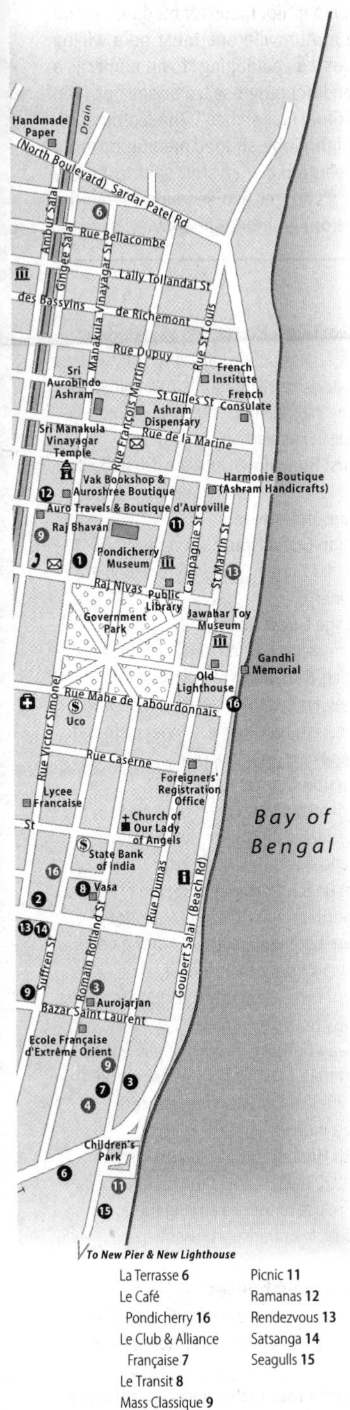


Simonel, with its shady courtyard, columns and balconies, which is interesting and well preserved.

The French Catholic influence is evident in a number of churches, notably the **Jesuit Cathedral** (Notre Dame de la Conception; 1691-1765). The lovely amber and pink **Church of Our Lady of Angels** (1855) is worth stepping into for an oil painting of Our Lady of Assumption given to the Church by King Louis Napoleon III.

The **Botanical Gardens**, south of City Bus Stand, opened in 1826, are pleasant after some renovation. The **Government (Pondicherry) Park**, laid out with lawns, flower beds and fountains (one at the centre is of Napoleon III period), is in front of the Raj Niwas, the residence of the Lieutenant Governor. The park was originally the site of the first French garrison, Fort Louis, destroyed in 1761 by the British.

## Auroville

→ *Phone code: 0413. Colour map 7, grid B5.* *Population 1,700.*

ⓘ *Visitors' centre, T0413-2623449, mm access@auroville.org.in, 0945-1200 and 1345-1600 Mon-Sat, 0945-1230 Sun. All visitors must come here first to park their cars. Passes for visits to Matrimandir Gardens and Amphitheatre will be issued only from here for same-day visits. Visits are 1000-1230 and 1400-1630 Mon-Sat, 1000-1300 Sun. It is only possible to visit the Inner Chamber of the Matrimandir if you have already visited the Gardens and Amphitheatre, Sun 1430-1730. Bookings should be made in advance.*

Auroville, 'City of Dawn', was set up in 1968 as a tribute to Sri Aurobindo, and draws more Europeans and Americans than the Pondicherry Ashram. Futuristically designed, the layout of Auroville and its major buildings were to reflect the principles of Sri Aurobindo's philosophy. Far from fully complete (development since 1968 has been very slow), it is nonetheless a striking living experiment and the community welcomes visitors who have a genuine interest in its philosophical basis.

The Mother had hoped that Auroville would be a major focus for meditation and spiritual regeneration. The Charter says "To live in Auroville one must be a willing servitor of the Divine Consciousness" and describes it as belonging "to humanity as a whole... the place of an unending education, of constant progress... a bridge between the past and the future... a site of material and spiritual researches". The Matrimandir (started 1968) at the centre of Auroville is a 30-m high globe-shaped meditation room with a lotus bud shaped foundation urn and a centrepiece crystal, said to be the largest in the world. Open to visitors 1600-1700 ("you get five seconds to see the crystal"), but to spend time in meditation (1700-1800) go independently.

## Sleeping

**Pondicherry** *p826, map p828*

**A Hotel de l'Orient**, 17 Romain Rolland St, T0413-2343067, orient1804@satyam.net.in. Beautifully renovated old school now a small exclusive hotel, with 10 tastefully decorated rooms in colonial style with objets d'art. Excellent restaurant (French/Creole) and service, very smart, spotlessly clean, book ahead. Highly recommended.

**B Hotel de Pondicherry**, 38 rue Dumas, T0413-2227409, www.hoteldepondichery.com. 10 rooms in the same colonial-style building as the popular French bistro Le Club (so can get noisy). Simple, clean, tastefully decorated (some with no windows but private courtyard), very friendly and efficient staff. A/c. Babysitting available.

**B Villa Helena**, 14 Suffren St, T0413-2226789, galleryhotels@hotelstamilnadu.com. 5 comfortable rooms with antique furniture around large shady courtyard (1 first floor suite), includes breakfast.

**C Executive Inn**, 1a Perumal Koil St, T0413-2330929, sumer@satyam.net.in. 11 a/c suites, TV, restaurant, internet, no smoking, no alcohol, quiet yet short walk from beach front and bazaar, good value. Recommended.

**C Mass**, Maraimalai Adigal Salai, T0413-2337221, just off the NH45A, near Bus Stand. 111 clean a/c rooms, restaurants, pastry shop, bar, exchange, internet, helpful staff.

**C-D Suguru**, 104 Sardar Patel Rd, T0413-2339022. Good, clean rooms, some a/c, excellent South Indian restaurant, bit noisy.

**D-E Family Guest House**, 526 MG Rd, T0413-2340346, familyguesthouse@pondicherry.everyone.net. 4 rooms, TV, hot water, bit cramped but very clean, roof terrace, hall, dining area, friendly.

**D-E Ram Guest House**, 546 MG Rd, T0413-2220072, ramguest@hotmail.com. Recently opened, 20 excellent rooms, maintained to European standards, spotless, good breakfast from clean kitchen. Recommended.

**E Tourist Bungalow**, Uppalam (Dr Ambedkar) Rd, T0413-2226376. 12 rooms, some a/c, and VIP suites, in a garden.

**E-F Balan Guest House**, 20 Vellaja St, T0413-2330634. 17 immaculate rooms with bath, clean linen.

**F Cottage Guest House**, Periarmudaliarchavadi, T0413 2338434, on beach, 6 km north of town. Rooms in cottages, French food, bike and motorcycle hire, peaceful, good beach under palm and casuarina trees, very popular.

**F Excursion Centre**, Uppalam (Dr Ambedkar) Rd. Very cheap bunk-beds in dorm, suitable for groups, south of town, clean and quiet, very good value.

**F Palm Beach Cottages**, by Serenity Beach, 5 km north of town. Clean huts (Rs 150), concrete beds with mattress, small garden, 5-min walk from beach, friendly staff, excellent food, especially fish, good for bikers but noisy from the highway.

**F Railway Retiring Rooms** for passengers. Quieter than most stations! These are all about 20-30 mins' walk from the centre, so hire a bicycle.

**F Youth Hostel**, Solaithandavan Kuppam, T0413-2223495, north of town. Dorm beds (Rs 30); close to the sea among fishermen's huts. Bicycle or transport essential.

**Ashram guesthouses**

Though these are mainly for official visitors, they are open to others (but 'not to hippies');

*For an explanation of the sleeping and eating price codes used in this guide, see inside the front cover. Other relevant information is found in Essentials pages 56-61.*

no alcohol or smoking. They close by 2230 (latecomers may be locked out). Book well in advance, with a day's rate.

**D Park Guest House**, near Children's Park, T0413-2237495, parkgh@auroville.org.in. 93 excellent sea-facing rooms (Rs 400), breakfasts, clean, quiet, great garden, reading room, ideal for long stay. Recommended.

**D Sea Side Guest House**, 14 Goubert Salai, T0413-2331713, seaside@sriaurobindo society.org.in. 25 excellent, large rooms, hot showers, breakfast, spotless, sea views. Recommended.

**E-F International Guest House**, Gingee Salai, T0413-2336699. 57 very clean and airy rooms, some a/c, huge for the price, very popular so often full.

**F Garden House**, 136 Akkasamy Madam St (north of town). Decent, clean rooms with bath (major bed bug problem and sewer nearby), quiet, gates locked at 2230.

**Auroville** *p829*

Food is available at most guesthouses and there are a number of restaurants and bakeries in Auroville. *Experience! Auroville* guide, e-india@webstudio6.com, available from Pondicherry Tourism, has an excellent breakdown of the accommodation options. Guests are accommodated in 5 settings (Central; Exurban; Beach; Farm and Forest; Pukka), each of which has its own characteristics (location, quietness, family-orientated, interaction with Aurovilians, language, etc). There are 39 guesthouses and 412 beds Costs vary from **C-F**, though some operate a 'kibbutz'-type arrangement.

**D-E Centre Guest House**, T0413-2622155. Most short-stay visitors are accommodated here ("welcomes those who wish to see and be in Auroville, but not to work there"), lovely setting, famous weekly pizza.

**E-F New Creation**, T0413-2622125.

**F Coco Beach Cottage**, East Coast Main Rd, Kottakuppam, opposite turning for Auroville. 4 rooms, a very friendly, clean guesthouse with a popular restaurant.

## Eating

**Pondicherry** *p826, map p828*

**TTT Le Club**, 38 rue Dumas, T0413- 2339745. French and Continental. Smart, excellent cuisine (Rs 400 for a splurge), French wine (Rs 1000), opinions differ, "we could have been in a French Bistro!" to "dearest but not the best", (0830-1830, closed Mon).

**TT Blue Dragon**, 30 rue Dumas near the New Pier (south end of Goubert Salai). Chinese. Excellent food, surrounded by antique furniture.

**TT La Terrasse**, 5 Subbaiyah Salai. Excellent Continental. Good value, huge salads, no alcohol (0830-2000, closed Wed).

**TT Paris**, 104 Ambur Salai. Vietnamese (closed Fri).

**TT Rendezvous**, 30 Suffren St. French and Continental. Attractive, modern, reasonable food (dish Rs 100) but overpriced wine, nice roof terrace, pleasant atmosphere: the owner worked for a wealthy American family for 20 years and so his continental grub is first-rate.

**TT Satsanga**, 30 rue Mahe de Labourdonnais, T0413-2225867. Closed Thu. Continental (quite expensive wine Rs 200), friendly, French atmosphere with art 'gallery', pleasant outdoor setting. Mixed reports on food.

**TT Seagulls**, near Children's Park. Continental and others. Large 1st floor terrace overlooking sea, bit overpriced, bar.

**T Ashram Dining Hall**, north of Govt Pl. Indian vegetarian. Simple, filling, meals (Rs 20 per day) in an unusual setting, seating on cushions at low tables, farm grown produce, non-spicy and non-greasy. 'Ticket' from Ashram guesthouses or Central Bureau; then turn up at 0640, 1115, 1745 or 2000. Recommended though staff can be off-hand.

**T Au Feu de Bois**, rue Bussy. Pizzas, salads, crêpes at lunchtime.

**T Hot Breads**, Ambur Salai. Good burgers, chicken puffs (Rs 35) pizzas, pastries, great sandwiches, shakes (Rs 18), 0700-2100.

**T Indian Coffee House**, 41 Nehru St. Real local vegetarian fare from 0700.

**T Le Café Pondicherry**, Goubert Salai, by Gandhi statue. Pleasant spot, but ordinary snack fare (daytime).

**T Mass Classique**, Bazar St Laurent, bakery.

**T Picnic**, Kamaraj Salai. Very good vegetarian.

**T Ramanas**, 25 Nehru St, excellent Indian, tasty fast food, a/c section.

## Festivals and events

**Pondicherry** *p826, map p828*

**4th-7th Jan**: International Yoga Festival held at Kamban Kalairangam, contact

Pondicherry Tourism for full details. **Jan**: **Pongal** is a 3-day harvest, earth and sun festival, popular in rural areas. **Feb/Mar**: **Masi Magam** on the full moon day of the Tamil month of Masi, pilgrims bathe in the sea when deities from about 40 temples from the surrounding area are taken in colourful procession for a ceremonial immersion. 'Fire walking' sometimes accompanies festivals here. **14th Jul**: **Bastille Day**. **Aug**: **Fete de Pondicherry** is a cultural programme.

## Shopping

**Pondicherry** *p826, map p828*

The shopping areas are along Nehru St and Mahatma Gandhi Rd. *Experience! Pondicherry* booklet has a good shopping guide.

Dolls of papier-mâché, terracotta and plaster are made and sold at Kosapalayam. Local grass is woven into *Korai* mats. Craftsmen at the Ashram produce marbled silk, hand dyed cloths, rugs, perfumes and incense sticks.

**Antiques** **Heritage Art Gallery**, rue Romain Rolland.

**Books** **Focus**, 204 Cathedral St, good selection of Indian writing in English, cards, stationery, CDs, very helpful.

**Kailash French Bookshop**, 87 Lal Bahadur Shastri St, large stock.

**Clothes and crafts** Several Ashram outlets on Nehru St.

**Aurosarjan**, rue Bussy. Auroville clothes and crafts.

**Cluny Centre**, 46 Romain Rolland St, T/F0413-2335668. Run by a French order in a lovely colonial house where nuns design and oversee high quality embroidery.

**Curio Centre**, 40 Romain Rolland St, has some fine antiques and good reproduction colonial furniture.

**Kalki**, 134 Cathedral St, T0413-239166. Produces exceptional printed and painted silk scarves, hangings etc.

**Sri Aurobindo Handmade paper 'factory'**, 44 Sardar Patel Rd. Shop sells attractive products.

**Vasa**, rue Mahe de Labourdonnais, next to Hotel Qualité, Smart ladies' clothes.

## Activities and tours

**Pondicherry** *p826, map p828*

**Fishing** Deep-sea fishing trips booked through **Pondicherry Tourism (PTDC)** (see below), 6/12 hrs, Rs 1,500/2,500.

**Swimming** Pools in **Hotel Blue Star** and **Calva Bungalow**, Kamaraj Salai open to non-residents for a fee.

**Tours and tour operators**

**Auro Travels**, Karikar Building, Nehru St. Efficient, quick service.

**PTDC** Sightseeing, Rs 45, Ashram, 0815-1300: Ashram and related departments. Auroville (Matrimandir), 1430.

**Sita**, 124 Cathedral St, T0413-2336860.

**Yoga** **Ananda Ashram**, on Yoga Sadhana Beach, 16 Mettu St, Chinamudaliarchavadi, Kottakuppam. It runs 1-, 3- and 6-month courses starting in Jan, Apr, Jul and Oct; or book through Pondicherry Tourism, Rs 1,500 for 10 lecture modules.

**Auroville** *p829*

**Tours** 0830-1100 from Ashram in Pondicherry, autocare@auroville.org.in. 1430-1745 from Cottage Complex, Ambur Salai, includes Auroville Visitors' Centre and Matrimandir. Visitors recommend going independently. A 5-day residential introduction to Auroville is available through the Centre Guest House, T0413-2622155 (Rs 1,000).

## Transport

**Pondicherry** *p826, map p828*

**Bicycle/scooter hire**

Super Snack, Nehru St opposite Information Centre. **Jaypal**, Gingee Salai. Also a hire shop just off Subbaiyah Salai (South Blvd). **Vijay Arya**, 9 Aurobindo St. Daily: cycle, Rs 25, scooter, Rs 120. Well worthwhile as the streets are broad, flat and quiet.

Motorbikes for travelling round South India, Rs 250 per day. **Pondicherry Tourism** (PTDC) and **Le Café Pondicherry**, Beach Rd, hire bicycles, Rs 5 per hr, Rs 40/400 per day/month.

**Bus**

**Local** Negotiate fare first; bus stands to centre, Rs 20. Also cycle-rickshaws and auto-rickshaws found here. **Local Bus Stand**: T0413-2336919. 0430-1230, 1330-2130.

**Long distance** State Express Bus Stand, NH45A, just west of the traffic circle. T0413-2337464. Computerized Reservations:

0700-2100 (helpful staff). **Mofussil (New) Bus Stand**, further west, serves all other bus companies. **Pondicherry Tourism Corporation (PTC)**, T0413-2337008, 0600-2200, also runs long distance services. Check times.

**Bangalore**: 7½ hrs; **Chennai**: frequent Express buses, under 3 hrs; **Chidambaram**: frequent buses by all companies, 1½ hrs; **Coimbatore** via **Salem** and **Erode**: 8½-9½ hrs; **Gingee**, infrequent, 2 hrs; **Kanniyakumari**: overnight service; **Kannur** and **Mahé**: 15 hrs; **Karaikal**: 4 hrs; **Madurai** via **Tiruchirappalli**: 6½-8 hrs overnight; **Mahabalipuram**: several, about 4 hrs; **Tirupati**: 6½-7 hrs; **Tiruvannamalai** (via **Villupuram**): 3-3½ hrs; **Kottakarai**, frequent service from Town Bus Stand.

### Car hire
Round trips to many destinations can be arranged at reasonable rates, eg return to **Bangalore** (310 km) Rs 2,000; **Chidambaram** (74 km), Rs 550; **Chennai** (166 km), Rs 1000; **Mahabalipuram** (130 km), Rs 800.

### Taxi
Particularly along the canal; 4 hrs (50 km) Rs 250, 8 hrs (100 km) Rs 500. **Jupiter Travels**, 170A Anna Salai, has luxury taxis.

### Train
Reservations, T0413-2336684, 0800-1400, 1500-1900, Mon-Sat; 0800-1400, Sun. 4-m gauge trains (1 hr) daily to **Villupuram** which offer prompt main line connections to **Chennai**, **Madurai**, **Tiruchirappalli**. No *652*, 0745 for Chennai and Madurai; *654*, 1920 for Chennai; *646*, 1655 for Chennai and Tiruchirappalli; *656*, 0500 for *Pandyan Exp 6717* to Tiruchirappalli, Kodai Rd and Madurai; *Quilon Mail 6105* to Tiruchirappalli and Kollam. From **Villupuram**: 4 trains daily for Pondy departs 0610, 0900, 1745, 2025. The half hourly bus to Villupuram stops 100 m from station and connects with trains. Railway station, enquiries: 0900-1200, 1500-1800. It is possible to make computerized reservations from Pondy station to any other station, and has a quota on major trains leaving from Chennai Central.

### Auroville *p829*
### Bicycle
Rent a bicycle (Rs 15 per day, though at some guesthouses they are free) and take advantage of the many cycle paths. **Centre Guest House** is one of several places renting bikes/mopeds.

### Rickshaw/taxi
Mopeds and taxis cost Rs 60/100 per day. Either of the 2 roads north from Pondicherry towards Chennai leads to Auroville. A rickshaw from Pondicherry will cost around Rs 100, a taxi not much more (or Rs 300 for a 3-hr wait-and-return).

## Directory

### Pondicherry *p826, map p828*
**Banks** Andhra Bank, Cathedral St, cash against Visa. **State Bank of India**, 5 Suffren St, changes cash and TCs (Amex, Thomas Cook), 24-hr ATM. **UCO Bank**, rue Mahé de Labour- donnais, opposite Government Park, quick and efficient. **LKP**, rue Mahé de Labour- donnais. No commission. **Cultural centres** **French Institute**, rue St Louis, close to the north end of Goubert Salai, and **Alliance Française** at the southern end of Goubert Salai for cultural programmes, 0800-1230, 1500-1900, Mon- Fri, 0830-1200, Sat. **Embassies and consulates** French Consulate, 2 Marine St. **Hospitals** **General Hospital**, rue Victor Simone, T0413-2336389; **Jipmer**, T0413-2372381. **Ashram Dispensary**, Depuis St, near seaside. **Internet** Café.com, Dolphin House, 236 Mission St, plays DVDs, serves great coffee and real Italian pasta besides. **Ohm Infotech**, 11 Nehru St. High speed. There are also several other options. **Post** **Head Post Office**, northwest corner of Govt Place. **CTO**, Rangapillai St. **Useful addresses** Foreigners' Regional **Registration Office**, Goubert Salai.

# Palar Valley

*The broad flat bed of the River Palar runs between the steep-sided northern Tamilnad hill ranges, an intensively irrigated, fertile and densely populated valley cutting through the much poorer and sometimes wooded high land on either side. The whole valley became the scene of an Anglo-French-Indian contest at the end of the 18th century. Today it is the centre of South India's vitally important leather industry and of intensive agricultural development.* ▸▸ *For Sleeping, Eating and other listings, see pages 837-838.*

## Vellore → *Phone code: 0416. Colour map 3, grid A5. Population: 177,400.*

The once strategically important centre of Vellore, pleasantly ringed by hills, is now a dusty, though busy, market town; its fort and temple are reminders of its historic importance. The fort is a major attraction, but Vellore is now world famous for its **Christian Medical College Hospital**, founded by the American missionary Ida Scudder in 1900. Started as a one-room dispensary, it extended to a small hospital through American support. Today it is one of the country's largest hospitals with over 1,200 beds and large out-patients' department which caters for over 2,000 patients daily. The college has built a reputation for research in a wide range of tropical diseases.

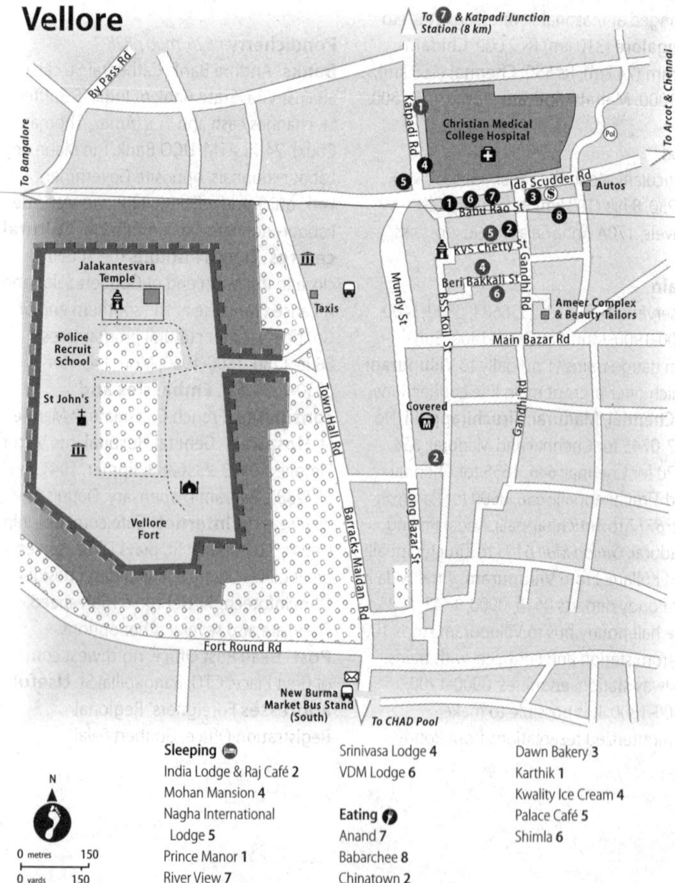


**Sleeping**
India Lodge & Raj Café 2
Mohan Mansion 4
Nagha International Lodge 5
Prince Manor 1
River View 7
Srinivasa Lodge 4
VDM Lodge 6

**Eating**
Anand 7
Babarchee 8
Chinatown 2
Dawn Bakery 3
Karthik 1
Kwality Ice Cream 4
Palace Café 5
Shimla 6

One of its earliest and most lasting programmes has been concerned with leprosy and there is a rehabilitation centre attached. In recent years it has undertaken a wide-ranging programme of social and development work in villages outside the town to back up its medical programmes.

Vijayanagar architecture is beautifully illustrated in the temple at **Vellore Fort**, a perfect example of military architecture and a *jala durga* or water fort. Believed to have been built by the Vijayanagara kings and dating from the 14th century, the fort has round towers and huge gateways along its double wall. The moat, still filled with water by a subterranean drain, followed ancient principles of defence: a colony of crocodiles. A wooden drawbridge crosses the moat to the southeast. In 1768 Vellore came under the control of the British, who defended it against Haidar Ali. After the victory in Seringapatnam in 1799, Tipu Sultan's family was imprisoned here and a mutiny of 1806, in which many British and Indian mutineers were killed, left many scars. In the fort is a parade ground, the CSI church, the Temple and two-storeyed mahals which are used as Government offices.

**Jalakantesvara Temple** ⓘ *bathing Rs 2*, with a 30-m high seven-storeyed granite *gopuram*, has undergone considerable restoration. Enter from the south and inside on the left, the *kalyana mandapa* (wedding hall), one of the most beautiful structures of its kind, has vivid sculptures of dragons and 'hippogryphs' on its pillars. The temple consists of a shrine to Nataraja in the north and a lingam shrine in the west.

## Gingee → *Phone code: 04145. Colour map 3, grid B5.*

*It is best to climb the fort in the morning when it is cooler and less hazy. And it's really only an option for the fit and healthy.*

Gingee (pronounced *Senjee*), just off the NH45, between Chennai and Tiruvannamalai, has a remarkable 15th-century Vijayanagar fort with much to explore. It is well off the beaten track, very peaceful and in beautiful surroundings. Spend the night here if you can. Lovers come here at the weekends; it's on the domestic tourist map because it is often used as a film location. The landscape is made up of man-sized boulders, like Hampi, piled on top of each other to make mounds the texture of cottage cheese.

**The fort** ⓘ *0900-1700, allow 2½ hrs for Rajagiri, and 2 hrs for Krishnagiri (if you have time), Rs 100 includes both forts*, was intensely contested by successive powers before being captured by an East India Company force in 1762, by the end of the century however, it had lost its importance. Although it had Chola foundations, the 'most famous fort in the Carnatic' was almost entirely rebuilt in 1442. It is set on three Charnockite hills, Krishnagiri, Chakklidrug and Rajagiri, all strongly fortified. In places the hills on which the fort stands are sheer cliffs over 150 m high. The highest, Rajagiri ('King's Hill'), has a south-facing overhanging cliff face, on top of which is the citadel. The inner fort contains two temples and the Kalyana Mahal, a square court with a 27-m breezy tower topped by pyramidal roof, surrounded by apartments for the women of the Governor's household. On top of the citadel is a huge cannon and a smooth granite slab known as the Raja's bathing stone. An extraordinary stone about 7-m high and balanced precariously on a rock, surrounded by a low circular brick wall, is referred to as the Prisoner's Well. There are fine Vijaynagara temples, granary, barracks and stables and an 'elephant tank'. A caretaker may unlock a temple and then expect a tip.

The Archaeological Survey of India Office is just off the main road towards the fort. They may have guides to accompany you to the fort. Carry provisions, especially plenty of drinks, a few refreshments are sold, but only at the bottom of the hill.

## Tiruvannamalai → *Phone code: 04175. Colour map 3, grid B5. Population: 130,300.*

In a striking setting at the foot of the rocky Arunachala Hill, Tiruvannamalai is one of the holiest towns of Tamil Nadu, and locally considered the home of Siva and his consort Parvati. It is a major pilgrimage centre.

One of the largest temples in South India, **Arunachala Temple** ⓘ *may close 1230-1530*, (16th and 17th centuries) was built mainly under the patronage of the Vijayanagar kings: its massive *gopurams* the tallest of which is 66 m high, dominate the centre of the town. It is dedicated to Siva as God incarnate of Fire. The temple has three sets of walls forming nested rectangles. Built at different periods they illustrate the way in which many Dravidian temples grew by accretion. The east end of each is extended to make a court, and the main entrance is at the east end of the temple. The lower parts of the *gopurams*, built of granite, date from the late Vijayanagar period but have been added to subsequently. The upper 10 storeys and the decoration are of brick and plaster. There are some remarkable carvings on the *gopurams*. On the outer wall of the east *gopuram*, for example, Siva is shown in the south corner dancing, with an elephant's skin. Inside the east doorway of the first courtyard is the 1,000-pillared *mandapa* (hall, portico) built late in the Vijayanagar period. To the south of the court is a small shrine dedicated to Subrahmanya. To the south again is a large tank. The pillars in the *mandapa* are typically carved vigorous horses, riders and lion-like yalis. The middle court has four much earlier *gopurams* (mid-14th century), a large columned mandapa and a tank. The innermost court may date from as early as the 11th century and the main sanctuary with carvings of deities is certainly of Chola origin. In the south is Dakshinamurti, the west shows Siva appearing out of a lingam, and the north has Brahma. The outer porch has small shrines to Ganesh and Subrahmanya. In front of the main shrine are a brass column lamp and the *Nandi* bull.

*Priests insist on guiding visitors (and expect payment).*

**Sri Ramana Maharishi Ashram** ⓘ *T04175-237 491, www.ramana-maharishi.org*, founded by Sri Ramana Maharishi, the Sage of Arunachala, born in 1879 and died in 1950, apparently spoke little and wrote less: not for him the life of a globetrotting guru. Age 16 he set out to seek enlightenment at the sacred mountain in Tiruvannamalai, which is revered as Siva in mountain form. He spent 20 years in caves, until his mother died at the base of the mountain in 1922, and he formed an ashram there. He was, albeit quietly, accessible to everyone 24-seven, unlike the choreographed darshans held at the ashrams of Amma and Satya Sai Baba. There is a library (with 40,000 spiritual books), whose president is Maharishi's nephew's son, and which is frequented by a fairly sizeable community of westerners (who, come April, have mostly left the south for ashrams in Rishikesh, Dharamsala and the cooler mountains of North India). There are huge numbers of photographs of Maharishi, the last of which were taken by the late, great Henri Cartier-Bresson, who photographed him when he was alive and also the morning after his death in April 1950. Foreigners wishing to stay at the ashram need to write to the President of the ashram with proposed dates of stay.

**Tiruvannamalai**



**Sleeping**
Aakash 1
Arunachala 2
Aruna Lodge 3
Ramakrishna 4

**Eating**
Brindavan 1

## Sleeping

**Vellore** *p834, map p834*
**D Prince Manor**, 41 Katpadi Rd, T0416-227106, central. Comfortable rooms, very good restaurant.
**D River View**, New Katpadi Rd, T0416-225251, 1 km north of town. 31 rooms, some a/c (best on tank side), modern hotel, pleasant inner courtyard with mature palms, 3 good restaurants.
**F India Lodge**, inexpensive rooms and **Raj** Café, good vegetarian restaurant downstairs.
**F Mohan Mansion**, 12 Beri Bakkali St, T0416-227083, 15 mins' walk from bus stand. Small hotel, basic and clean, quieter than others near hospital.
**F Nagha International Lodge**, 13/A KVS Chetty St, T0416-2226731. Some **E** a/c deluxe rooms.
**F Srinivasa Lodge**, Beri Bakkali St, T0416-226389. Simple and clean.
**F VDM Lodge**, T0416-2224008. Very cheap, pleasant, helpful staff.

**Gingee** *p835*
**E Shivasand**, M Gandhi Rd, opposite bus stand, T04145-222218. 21 clean, adequate rooms with bath, 1 dearer a/c, vegetarian restaurant, a/c bar and non-vegetarian meals, good views of fort from roof, helpful manager.
Avoid **Aruna Lodge**, near bus stand.

**Tiruvannamalai** *p835, map p836*
At full moon pilgrims arrive to walk around Arunachala Hill and hotels are over-booked.
**D-E Arunachala**, 5 Vadasannathi St, T04175-228300. Fairly new hotel with 32 clean, rooms, 16 a/c, TV, hot water, best away from temple end, can get noisy during festivals, veg meals.
**D-E Ramakrishna**, 34F Polur Rd, T04175-225004, info@hotelramakrishna.com. Recently opened, 42 rooms, 21 a/c, TV, hot water, excellent vegetarian tandoori restaurant, parking, modern, helpful and friendly staff. Recommended.
**F Aakash**, 9 Polur Rd, T04175-222151. 22 rooms, friendly but rather noisy.
**F Aruna Lodge**, 82 Kosamadam St, T04175-223291. 24 clean, adequate rooms with bath.

## Eating

**Vellore** *p834, map p834*
**Anand**, Ida Scudder Rd, for excellent breakfasts.
**Babarchee**, Babu Rao St, Good fast food and pizzas.
**Best**, Ida Scudder Rd, some meals very spicy, nice parathas, 0600 for excellent breakfast.
**Chinatown**, Gandhi Rd, a/c, small, friendly – good food and service.
**Dawn Bakery**, Gandhi Rd, fresh bread and biscuits, cakes, also sardines, fruit juices.
**Geetha** and **Susil**, Ida Scudder Rd, rooftop or inside, good service and food.
**Hotel Karthik's**, has a good veg restaurant.
**Shimla**, Ida Scudder Rd, tandoori, naan very good.

**Tiruvannamalai** *p835, map p836*
**Brindavan**, 57 A Car St. This town is a *thali* lover's paradise with plenty of 'meals' restaurants including this one, Rs 15.
**Auro Usha**, varied menu, **Manna**, salads and snacks, and **German Bakery**.

## Festivals and events

**Tiruvannamalai** *p835, map p836*
Karthikai Deepam Full moon day in **Nov-Dec**. A huge beacon is lit on top of the hill behind the temple. The flames, which can be seen for miles around, are thought of as Siva's lingam of fire, joining the immeasurable depths to the limitless skies. A cattle market is held.

## Shopping

**Vellore** *p834, map p834*
Most shops are along Main Bazar Rd and Long Bazar St. Vellore specializes in making 'Karigari' glazed pottery in a range of traditional and modern designs. Vases, water jugs, ashtrays and dishes are usually coloured blue, green and yellow.
**Beauty**, Ameer Complex, Gandhi Rd. Cheapest good quality tailoring.
**Mr Kanappan**, Gandhi Rd. Very friendly, good quality tailors, a little more expensive.

## Activities and tours

**Vellore** *p834, map p834*
**Hillside Resort**, CHAD (Community Health and Development), south of town. Excellent private pool, Rs 250 per day. Popular with CMC medical students. Open early morning to late evening, closed Mon and from 1200-1500. Good snack bar.

## Transport

**Vellore** *p834, map p834*
**Bus**
The Bus Station is off Long Bazar St, east of the Fort. Buses to **Tiruchirappalli**, **Tiruvannamalai** (from Burma Market Bus Stand), **Bangalore**, **Chennai**, **Ooty**, **Thanjavur** and **Tirupathi**. The regional state bus company PATC runs frequent services to **Kanchipuram** and **Bangalore** from 0500 (2½ hrs) and **Chennai**.

**Train**
Katpadi Junction, the main station, 8 km north of town is on the broad gauge line between **Chennai** and **Bangalore**. Buses and rickshaws (Rs 35) into Vellore. **Chennai (C)**: *Cheran Exp, 2674,* 0505, 2¼ hrs; *West Coast Exp, 6628,* 1303, 2½ hrs; *Kovai Exp, 2676,* 1915, 2 hrs. **Bangalore** (C): *Brindavan Exp, 2639,* 0903, 4¼ hrs; *Chennai-Bangalore Exp, 6023,* 1515, 4½ hrs; it is also on the metre gauge line to **Villupuram** to the south, with daily passenger trains to **Tirupathi**, **Tiruvannamalai** and **Pondicherry**. The Cantonment Station is about 1 km south of the GPO, and has a daily train to **Tiruchchirappalli**, *Tirupati Tiruchchi Exp, 6801,* 1910, 10¾ hrs.

**Gingee** *p835*
**Bus**
Buses to/from **Pondicherry**, infrequent direct buses (2 hrs); better via Tindivanam (45 mins). To/from **Tiruvannamalai**, 39 km: several buses (1 hr), Rs 13; Express buses will not stop at the fort. TPTC bus 122 to/from **Chennai**.

**Cycle-rickshaw**
To visit the fort take a cycle-rickshaw from the bus stand to the hills; about Rs 30 for the round trip, including 2-hr wait. There are bicycles for hire by the bus station.

**Tiruvannamalai** *p835, map p836*
**Bicycle**
Bicycle hire near the Bus Stand is not recommended; cycling can be hazardous in this very busy small town.

**Bus**
Buses to major cities in **Tamil Nadu**, **Kerala** and **Karnataka**. Local people will point out your bus at the bus stand; you can usually get a seat although they do get crowded. To **Gingee**, frequent, 1 hr; **Chennai**, 5 hrs, Rs 30; **Pondicherry**, 3-3½ hrs.

**Train**
Train to **Tirupati** via Vellore Cantt, Katpadi and Chittor: *Tiruchchi Tirupati Exp, 6802,* 2300, 6½ hrs. **Pondicherry**: *Tirupati-Pondicherry Fast Pass, 641 (S),* 0640, 3½ hrs.

## Directory

**Vellore** *p834, map p834*
**Banks** Central Bank, Ida Scudder Rd, east of hospital exit, is at least 10 mins faster at changing TCs than the State Bank. **Hospital** CMC, Ida Scudder Rd, T0416-232102. **Internet** Net Paradise, north of bus stand. **Post** CMC Hospital has PO, stamps, takes parcels.

**Tiruvannamalai** *p835, map p836*
**Bank** Vysya Bank, Sannathi St. Quick for cash and TCs. **Internet** TICS, 4 Kosamadam St. Also Western Union. **Post** A Car St.

# Chola Heartland and the Kaveri Delta

*This region is something like the South's answer to the golden triangle circuit of the Taj, Jaipur and Delhi. The Big Temple in the charming agricultural town of Tanjore, for three centuries the capital of the Cholas; Trichy's 21-gopuram, seven-walled island city of Sri Rangam, a patchwork quilt of a temple tanks to input from successive waves of dynasties from the Cholas, the Cheras, the Pandyas, Hoysalas, Vijayanagar Kings up to the Nayaks of Madurai; and the beautiful Nataraja Temple at Chidambaram, with its two towers given over to bas reliefs of the 108 mudras, or dance postures, of classical dance. You will be drunk on temples by the time you leave this district.*

*» For Sleeping, Eating and other listings, see pages 849-853.*

## Tiruchirappalli

→ *Phone code: 0431. Colour map 3, grid B5.*

Trichy, at the head of the fertile Kaveri delta, is an industrial city that is more spread out than Madurai although its population is smaller. Land prices are high here, and houses, as you'll see if you climb up to its 84-m high rock fort, are incredibly densely packed, outside of the elegant doctors' suburbs. If you are taking public transport you will want to break here to visit the sacred Srirangam temple but if you have your own wheels you may prefer to bypass the city, which has little else to offer by way of easily accessed charms: allow at least half a day to tour Srirangam, then stay in the more laid-back agricultural centre of Tanjore to the north or the more atmospheric temple madness of Madurai further south.

### Ins and outs

**Getting there** Trichy airport, 8 km from the centre, has flights to Madurai and Chennai. Well connected by train to major towns, the Junction Railway Station and the two bus stations are in the centre of the main hotel area, all within walking distance.

**Getting around** Much of Trichy is quite easy to see on foot, but plenty of autos and local buses run to the Rock Fort and Srirangam. *» See Transport, page 851, for further details.*

### Background

Trichy was mentioned by Ptolemy in the second century BC. A Chola fortification from the second century, it came to prominence under the Nayakas from Madurai who built the fort and the town, capitalizing on its strategic position. In legend its name is traced to a three-headed demon, Trisiras, who terrorized both men and the gods until Siva overpowered him in the place called Tiruchi. Cigar-making became important between the two World Wars, while the indigenous *bidis* continue to be made, following a tradition started in the 18th century. Trichy is the country's largest artificial diamond manufacturing centre. Jaffersha Street is commonly known as 'Diamond Bazaar'. The town is also noted for its high quality string instruments, particularly veenas and violins.

*Temple cars can weigh 300 tonnes and have now very much entered the 21st century: some have hyrdraulic brakes, iron wheels and are propelled by bulldozers.*

# Sights

**Rock Fort**, 1660, stands on an 84-m high rock. **Vinayaka Temple** (or Ucchi Pillayar Koil) ⓘ *0800-1300 then 1400-2000, camera Rs 10, video Rs 50, closed Mon,* approached from Chinna Bazar, is at the highest point, from which you get marvellous views. It is a fairly easy climb up 437 rock cut steps to reach it. The temple itself is disappointing. On your way up you come to the main 11th-century defence line and the remains of a thousand-pillared hall, destroyed in 1772, at the top of the first flight of steps. Further up is a hundred-pillared hall where civic receptions are held. At the

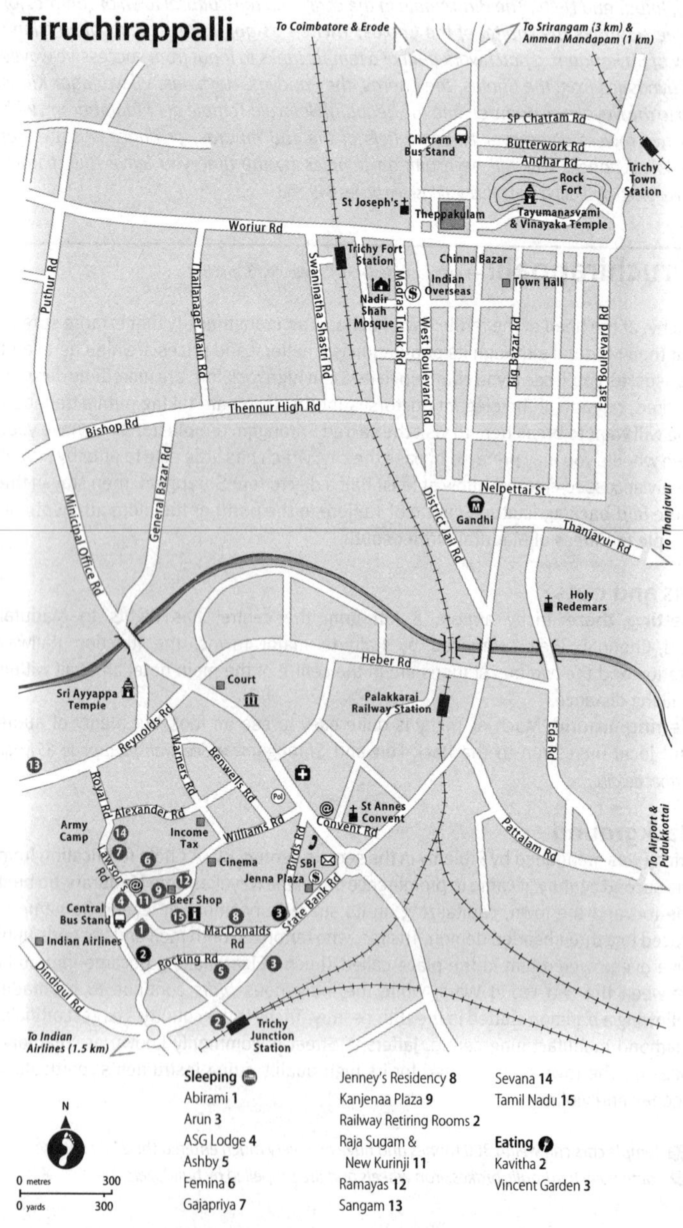

end of the last flight is the **Tayumanasvami Temple**, dedicated to Siva, which has a golden *vimana* and a lingam which is carved out of the rock itself. There are also other seventh-century Pallava cave temples which have beautiful carved pillars and panels.

It is worthwhile discovering the old city on foot, particularly **Big Bazar Street** and **Chinna Bazar**. The Gandhi Market is a colourful vegetable and fruit market.

Among the dozen or so mosques in the town, the **Nadir Shah Mosque** near the city railway station stands out with its white dome and metal steeple, said to have been built with material taken from a Hindu temple. **St Joseph's College Church** (Church of our Lady of Lourdes), one of several Catholic churches here, designed as a smaller version of the Basilica at Lourdes in France has an unusual sandalwood altar but is rather garish inside. The grounds are a peaceful spot. The 18th-century **Christ Church**, the first English church, is north of the Teppakulam, while the early 19th-century **St John's Church** has a memorial plaque to Bishop Heber, one of India's best known missionary bishops, who died in Trichy in 1826.

# Around Trichy

## Srirangam

The temple town on the Kaveri, just north of Trichy, is surrounded by seven concentric walled courtyards, with magnificent gateways and several shrines. On the way to Srirangam, is an interesting river *ghat* where pilgrims take their ritual bath before entering the temple. The countryside to the west of the temple is an excellent place to sample rural Indian life; a good way to spend a couple of hours.

**Sri Ranganathasvami Temple** ⓘ *0615-1300, 1515-2045, camera, Rs 20, video Rs 70 (Rs 10 for the rooftop viewing tower), allow about 2 hrs, guides will greet you on arrival – their abilities are highly variable, some tell you that the staircase to the viewpoint will close shortly – usually a scam to encourage you to use their services*, is one of the largest in India and dedicated to Vishnu. It has some fine carvings and a good atmosphere. The fact that it faces south, unlike most other Hindu temples, is explained by the legend that Rama intended to present the image of Ranganatha to a temple in Sri Lanka but this was impossible since the deity became fixed here, but it still honours the original destination. The temple, where the Vaishnava reformer **Ramanuja** settled and worshipped, is famous for its superb sculpture, the 21 impressive *gopurams* and its rich collection of temple jewellery. The 'thousand' pillared hall (904 columns) stands beyond the fourth wall, and in the fifth enclosure there is the unusual shrine to Tulukka Nachiyar, the God's Muslim consort. Non-Hindus are not allowed into the sanctuary but can enter the fourth courtyard where the famous sculptures of *gopis* (*Radha's* milk maids) in the Venugopala shrine can be seen.

Nearby, on the north bank of the Kaveri, **Amma Mandapam** is a hive of activity. The *ghats*, where devotees wash, bathe, commit cremated ashes and pray, are interesting to visit, although some may find the dirt and smell overpowering.

So named because a legendary elephant worshipped the lingam, **Tiruvanaikkaval** is 3 km east of Srirangam. It has the architecturally finer **Jambukesvara Temple** ⓘ *0600-1300, 1600-2130 officially, camera Rs 10, non-Hindus are not allowed into the sanctuary*, with its five walls and seven splendid *gopurams*, is one of the oldest and largest Siva temples in Tamil Nadu. The unusual lingam under a *jambu* tree always remains under water. It is 200 m east off the main Tiruchi-Chennai road, a short stroll from Srirangam or easily reached by bus.

## Pudukkottai and around

Pudukkottai, 50 km south of Trichy, was the capital of the former princely state ruled by the Tondaiman Rajas, founded by Raghunatha Raya Tondaiman in 1686. At one entrance to the town is a ceremonial arch raised by the Raja in honour of Queen Victoria's jubilee celebrations. The town's broad streets suggest a planned history – the temple is at the centre, with the old palace and a tank. The new palace is now the District Collector's office.

The rock-cut **Sri Kokarnesvarar Temple** ⓘ *at Thirukokarnam, 5 km north of the railway station, closed 1200-1600,* dates from the Pallava period. The natural rock shelters, caves, stone circles, dolmens and Neolithic burial sites show that there was very early human occupation.

The **museum** ⓘ *Big St, Thirukokarnam 5 km away, except Fri, 2nd Sat, public holidays, 0930-1700, free, allow 40 mins, recommended,* has a wide range of exhibits including sections on geology, zoology and the economy as well as sculptures and the arts. The archaeology section has some excellent sculptures from nearby temples. There is a notable carving of Siva as *Dakshinamurti* and some fine bronzes from Pudukkottai itself.

**Sittannavasal**, 13 km away, has a Jain cave temple (circa eighth century) with sculptures, where monks took shelter when they fled from persecution in North India. In a shrine and verandah there are some fine frescoes in the Ajanta style and bas-relief carvings. You can also see rock-hewn beds of the monks. The *Brahmi* inscriptions date from the second century BC.

# Thanjavur (Tanjore) → *Phone code: 04362. Colour map 3, grid B5. Population: 215,700.*

Thanjavur's mathematically perfect Brihadisvara Temple, a World Heritage Site, is one of the great monuments of South India, its huge Nandi bull washed each fortnight with water, milk, turmeric and gingelly in front of a rapt audience that literally packs out the whole temple compound. In the heart of the lush, rice growing delta of the Kaveri, the upper echelons of Tanjore life are landowners, rather than industrialists, and the city itself is mellow in comparison with Trichy. ▸▸ *For Sleeping, Eating and other listings, see pages 849-853.*

## Ins and outs

**Getting there** Most long-distance buses stop at the New bus stand 4 km southwest of the centre, but there are frequent buses and autos (Rs 25) to town and train station. **Getting around** It is less than a 15-minute walk from the hotels to the Brihadisvara Temple. ▸▸ *See Transport, page 852 for further details.*

## Sights

**Brihadisvara Temple** ⓘ *0600-2030; inner sanctum closed 1230-1600,* known as the 'Big Temple', was the achievement of the Chola king Rajaraja I (ruled AD 985-1012). The magnificent main temple has a 62-m high *vimana* (the tallest in India), topped by a dome carved from an 80-ton block of granite, which needed a 6.5 km-ramp to raise it to the top. The attractive gardens, the clean surroundings and well-lit sanctuaries make a visit doubly rewarding, especially in the evening. The entrance is from the east. After crossing the moat you enter through two *gopurams*, the second guarded by two *dvarapalas* typical of the early Chola period, when the gopurams on the outer enclosure walls were dwarfed by the scale of the *vimana* over the main shrine. An enormous Nandi, carved out of a single block of granite 6 m long, guards the entrance to the sanctuary. According to one of the many myths that revolve around the image of a wounded Nandi, the Thanjavur Nandi was growing larger and larger, threatening the temple, until a nail was driven into its back. The temple, built mainly with large granite blocks, has superb inscriptions and sculptures of Siva, Vishnu and Durga on three sides of the massive plinth. Siva appears in three forms, the dancer with 10 arms, the seated figure with a sword and trident, and Siva bearing a spear. The carvings of dancers showing the 81 different Bharat Natyam poses are the first to record classical dance form in this manner. The main shrine has a large lingam. In the inner courtyard are Chola frescoes on walls prepared with lime plaster, smoothed and polished, then painted while the surface was wet. These were hidden under later Nayaka paintings. Since music and dance were a vital part of temple life and dancing in the temple would accompany the chanting of the holy scriptures which the community attended, Rajaraja also built two housing colonies nearby to accommodate 400 *devadasis* (temple dancers). Subsidiary shrines were added to the main temple at different periods. The Vijayanagara kings built the Amman shrine, the Nayakas the Subrahmanya shrine and the Marathas the Ganesh shrine.

**The Palace** ⓘ *closed Wed, 0900-1300, 1400-1700*, built by the Nayakas in the mid-16th century and later completed by the Marathas, is now partly in ruins, its walls used as makeshift hoardings for the latest Tamil movie release or political campaign. Still, there's evidence of its original splendour in the ornate Durbar Hall. The towers are worth climbing for a good view; one tower has a whale skeleton which was washed up in Chennai. The **art gallery** ⓘ *0900-1300, 1500-1800*, with bronze and granite sculptures, **Sangeeta Mahal** with excellent acoustics, and the **Tamil University Museum** are here, together with some Government offices. The pokey **Saraswati Mahal Library** ⓘ *1000-1300, 1330-1730 closed Wed*, is brilliant: among its

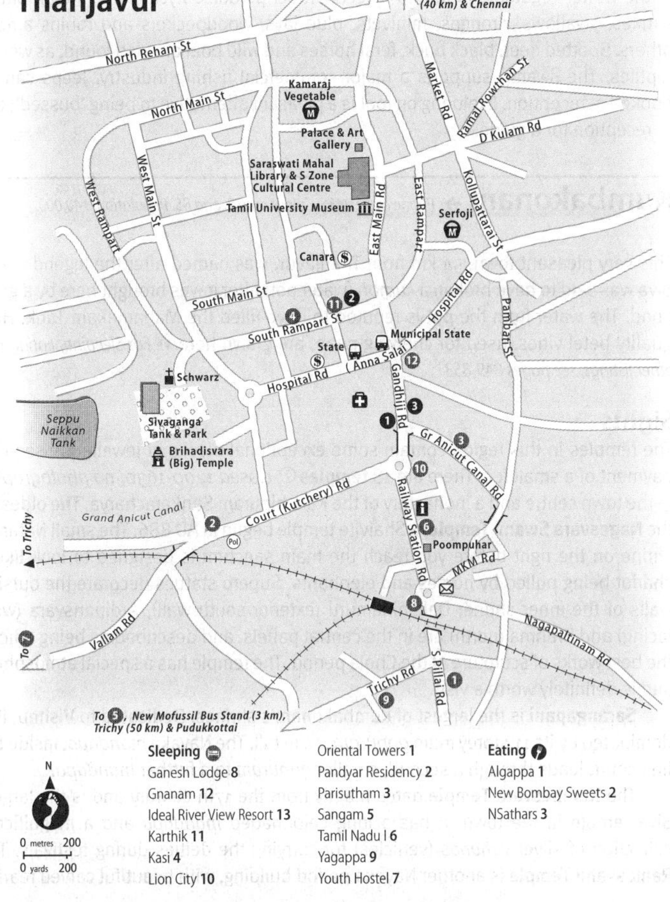

 40,000 rare books are texts from the medieval period, beautiful botanical pictures from the 18th century, palm leaf manuscripts of the Ramayana, intricate 250-year old miniatures, and splendid examples of the gaudy Tanjore style of painting. It also has old samples of dhoti cloth design, and 22 engravings illustrating methods of torture from other oriental cultures in the 'Punishments of China'.

## Excursions

A visit to **Thiruvaiyaru**, 13 km away, with the Panchanatheswara Siva temple, known for its **Thyagaraja Music Festival**, gives a glimpse of South Indian rural life. Hardly visited by tourists, music connoisseurs arrive in large numbers in January. Performances vary and the often subtle music is marred by loud amplification. The Car Festival is in March. Catch one of the frequent, crowded buses from the old bus station in Thanjavur, taking 30 minutes.

**Point Calimere (Kodikkarai) Wildlife and Bird Sanctuary** ⓘ *open throughout the year, best season – mid-Dec to Feb, Rs 5, camera Rs 5, video Rs 50*, is 90 km southeast of Thanjavur. The coastal sanctuary, half of which is tidal swamp, is famous for its migratory water birds. The Great Vedaranayam Salt Swamp (or 'Great Swamp') attracts one of the largest colonies of flamingos in Asia (5-10,000) especially in December and January. Some 243 different bird species have been spotted here. In the spring the green pigeons, rosy pastors, koels, mynahs and barbets can be seen. In the winter vegetable food and insects attract paradise flycatchers, Indian pittas, shrikes, swallows, drongos, minivets, blue jays, woodpeckers and robins among others. Spotted deer, black buck, feral horses and wild boar are also found, as well as reptiles. The swamp supports a major commercial fishing industry. Jeeps can be booked at reception. Exploring on foot is a pleasant alternative to being 'bussed'; ask at reception for a guide.



# Kumbakonam → *Phone code: 0435. Colour map 3, grid B5. Population: 140,000.*

This very pleasant town, 54 km from Thanjavur, was named after the legend where Siva was said to have broken a *kumbh* (water pot) after it was brought here by a great flood. The water from the pot is reputed to have filled the Mahamakam Tank. High quality betel vines, used for chewing paan, are grown here. » *For Sleeping, Eating and other listings, see pages 849-853.*

## Sights

The temples in this region contain some exceptional pieces of jewellery – seen on payment of a small fee. There are 18 **temples** ⓘ *closed 1200-1630, no photography*, in the town centre and a monastery of the Kanchipuram Sankaracharya. The oldest is the **Nagesvara Swami Temple**, a Shaivite temple begun in AD 886. The small Nataraja shrine on the right before you reach the main sanctum is designed to look like a chariot being pulled by horses and elephants. Superb statues decorate the outside walls of the inner shrine; Dakshinamurti (exterior south wall), Ardinarisvara (west facing) and Brahma (north) are in the central panels, and described as being among the best works of sculpture of the Chola period. The temple has a special atmosphere and is definitely worth a visit.

**Sarangapani** is the largest of Kumbakonam's shrines. Dedicated to Vishnu, it is dominated by its 11-storey main *gopuram*, 44 m tall. The Nayaka *mandapa*, inside the first court, leads through a second, smaller *gopuram* to a further *mandapa*.

The **Kumbesvara Temple** dates mainly from the 17th century and is the largest Siva temple in the town. It has a long colonnaded *mandapa* and a magnificent collection of silver *vahanas* (vehicles) for carrying the deities during festivals. The **Ramasvami Temple** is another Nayaka period building, with beautiful carved rearing horses in its pillared *mandapa*. The frescoes on the walls depict events from the *Ramayana*. The Navaratri Festival is observed with great colour.

The **Mahamakam Tank** is visited for a bathe by huge numbers of pilgrims every 12 years, when 'Jupiter passes over the sign of Leo'. It is believed that on the day of the festival nine of India's holiest rivers manifest themselves in the tank, including the Ganga, Yamuna and Narmada.

## Darasuram

About 5 km south of Kumbakonam, is Darasuram with the **Airavatesvara Temple** ⓘ *open sunrise to sunset*, after Thanjavur and Gangaikondacholapuram, the third of the great Chola temples, built during the reign of **Rajaraja II** between 1146-1172. The entrance is through two gateways. A small inner gateway leads to a court where the mainly granite temple stands in the centre. The *gopuram* is supported by beautifully carved *apsaras*. Inside, there are friezes of dancing figures and musicians. The *mandapa* is best entered from the south. Note the elephant, ridden by dwarfs, whose trunk is lost down the jaws of a crocodile. The pillars illustrate mythological stories for example 'the penance of Parvati'. The five gods Agni, Indra, Brahma, Vishnu and Vayu in the niches are all shown paying homage to Siva. The **main mandapa**, completely enclosed and joined to the central shrine, has figures carved in black basalt on the outside. The ceilings are also richly decorated and the pillars have the same flower emblems as in the outer *mandapa*. The main shrine has some outstanding sculptures; the guardians on the north are particularly fine. Sculpted door-keepers with massive clubs guard the entrance to the main shrine which has a *Nandi* at the entrance. Some of the niches inside contain superb early Chola sculptures of polished black basalt, including a unique sculpture of Ardhanarisvara with three faces and eight arms, a four-armed Nagaraja and a very unusual sculpture of Siva

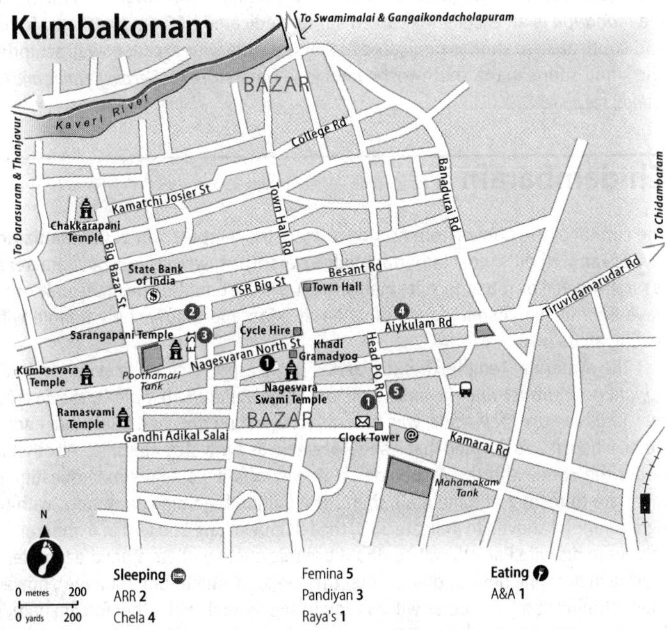

 destroying Narasimha. The **outer walls** are also highly decorative. Siva as Dakshinamurti on the south wall, Brahma on the north wall and Siva appearing out of the lingam on the west wall. The inner wall of the encircling walkway (*prakara*) is divided into cells, each originally to house a deity. The corners of the courtyard have been enlarged to make four mandapas, again with beautiful decoration.

## Gangaikondacholapuram

Once the capital of the Chola king Rajendra (1012-1044), the town of Gangaikondacholapuram (meaning 'The city of the Chola who conquered the Ganga') has now all but disappeared. The temple and the 5-km long 11th-century reservoir embankment survive.

The **temple** which Rajendra built was designed to rival the Brihadisvara temple built by Rajendra's father Rajaraja in Thanjavur. Unlike the *Nandi* in Thanjavur, the huge *Nandi* facing the *mandapa* and sanctuary inside the compound by the ruined east *gopuram* is not carved out of one block of stone. As in Thanjavur, the *mandapa* and sanctuary are raised on a high platform, orientated from west to east and climbed by steps. The whole building is over 100 m long and over 40 m wide. Two massive doorkeepers (*dvarapalas*) stand guard at the entrance to the long closed *mandapa* (the first of the many subsequent *mandapas* which expanded to 'halls of 1,000 pillars'); the plinth is original. A narrow colonnaded hall (*mukha-mandapa*) links this hall to the shrine. On the east side of this hall are various carvings of Siva for example bestowing grace on Vishnu, who worships him with his lotus-eye. On the northeast Is a large panel, a masterpiece of Chola art, showing Siva blessing Chandikesvara, the steward. At the centre of the shrine is a huge *lingam* on a round stand. As in Thanjavur there is a magnificent eighth-tiered, pyramidal *vimana* (tower) above the sanctuary, nearly 55 m high. Unlike the austere straight line of the Thanjavur temple, however, here gentle curves are introduced. Ask the custodian to allow you to look inside (best for light in the morning). Immediately to the north of the *mandapa* is an excellently carved shrine dedicated to Chandikesvara. To north and south are two shrines dedicated to Kailasanatha with excellent wall sculptures. The small shrine in the southwest corner is to Ganesh. » *For Sleeping, Eating and other listings, see pages 849-853.*

## Chidambaram → *Phone code: 04144. Colour map 3, grid B5. Population: 59,000.*

The capital of the Cholas from AD 907 to 1310, the temple town of Chidambaram is one of Tamil Nadu's most important holy towns. The town has lots of character and is rarely visited by foreigners. Its main attractin is the temple, one of the only ones to have Siva in the cosmic dance position. It is an enormously holy temple with a feeling all its own.

The **Nataraja Temple** ⓘ *0400-1200, 1630-2100, visitors may be asked for donations, entrance into the inner sanctum Rs 50, enter the temple by the East Gate, men must remove their shirts*, was the subject of a supreme court battle that ended in Delhi, where it was decided that it should remain as a private enterprise. All others fall under the state, with the Archeological Survey of India's sometimes questionable mandate to restore and maintain them. The unique brahmin community, with their right forehead shaved to indicate Siva, the left grown long and tied in a front top knot to denote his wife Parvati, will no doubt trot this out to you. As a private temple, it is unique in allowing non-Hindus to enter the sanctum sanctorum (for a fee), however, the brahmins at other shrines will ask you to sign a book with other foreign names in it, supposedly having donated Rs 400. The lack of state support does make this temple poorer than its neighbours, but if you want to give a token rupee coinage instead then do so. The atmosphere of this temple more than compensates for any money-grabbing tactics, however. Temple lamps still hang from the hallways, the temple music is rousing and the *puja* has the statues coming alive in sudden illumination. The brahmins themselves have a unique, stately presence too. One legend surrounding its construction suggests that it was built by 'the golden-coloured Emperor', Hiranya Varna Chakravarti, who suffered from leprosy. He came to Chidambaram on a pilgrimage from Kashmir in about AD 500. After bathing in the temple tank he was reputed to have recovered from the disease, and as a thanks-offering rebuilt and enlarged the temple. The evening puja at 1800 is particularly interesting. At each shrine the visitor will be daubed with *vibhuti* (sacred ash) and paste. It is not easy to see some of the sculptures in the interior gloom. You may need patience and persuasive powers if you want to take your own time but it is worth the effort.

There are records of the temple's existence before the 10th century and inscriptions from the 11th century. On each side are four enormous *gopurams*, those on the north and south being about 45 m high. The east *gopuram* (AD 1250), through which you enter the temple, is the oldest. The north *gopuram* was built by the great Vijayanagar king **Krishna Deva Raya** (1509-1530). Immediately on entering the East Gate is the large **Sivaganga** tank, and the **Raja Sabha**, a 1,000 columned *mandapa* (1595-1685). In the northwest of the compound are temples dedicated to Subrahmanya (late 13th century), and to its south the 12th century shrine to Sivakumasundari or Parvati (circa 14th century). The ceiling paintings are 17th century. At the southern end of this outer compound is what is said to be the largest shrine to **Ganesh** in India. The next inner compound has been filled with colonnades and passageways. In the innermost shrine are two images of Siva, the Nataraja and

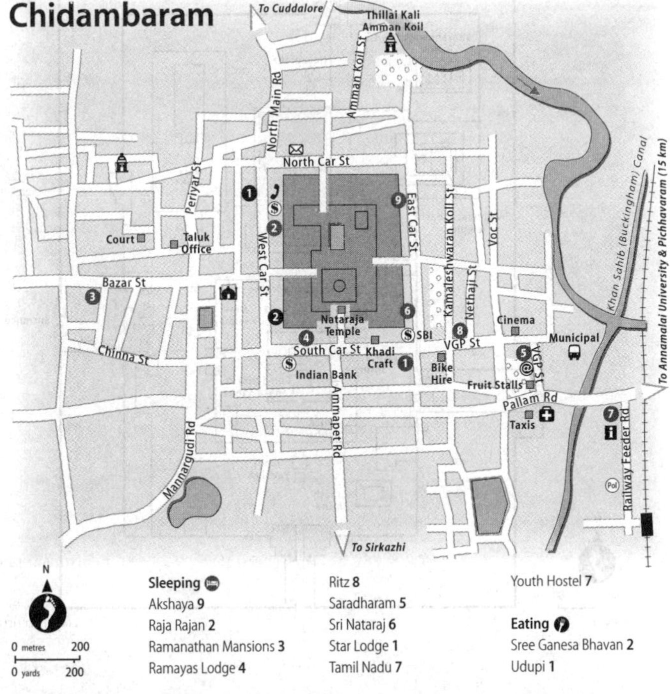

the lingam. A later Vishnu shrine to Govindaraja was added by the Vijayanagar kings. The **inner enclosure**, the most sacred, contains four important *Sabhas* (halls), the **deva sabha**, where the temple managers hold their meetings; the **chit sabha** or *chit ambalam* (from which the temple and the town get their names), meaning the hall of wisdom; the **kanakha sabha**, or golden hall; and the **nritta sabha**, or hall of dancing. Siva is worshipped in the *chit ambalam*, a plain wooden building standing on a stone base, in his form as Lord of the Dance, Nataraja. The area immediately over the deity's head is gold plated. Immediately behind the idol is the focus of the temple's power, the 'Akasa Lingam', representing the invisible element, 'space', and hence is itself invisible. It is known as the 'Chidambaram secret'.

## Excursions

The Danish king Christian IV received permission from Raghunath Nayak of Thanjavur to build a fort here at **Tranquebar** (Tharangampadi) in 1620. The Danish Tranquebar Mission was founded in 1706 and the Danesborg **fort** and the old **church** still survive. The Danes set up the first Tamil printing press, altering the script to make the casting of type easier and the Danish connection resulted in the National Museum of Copenhagen today possessing a remarkable collection of 17th-century Thanjavur paintings and Chola bronzes. There is a **museum** and a good beach. From Chidambaram most transport requires a change at Sirkazhi. From Thanjavur, some direct buses; others involve change at Mayiladuthurai (24 km)



## Nataraja Temple, Chidambaram

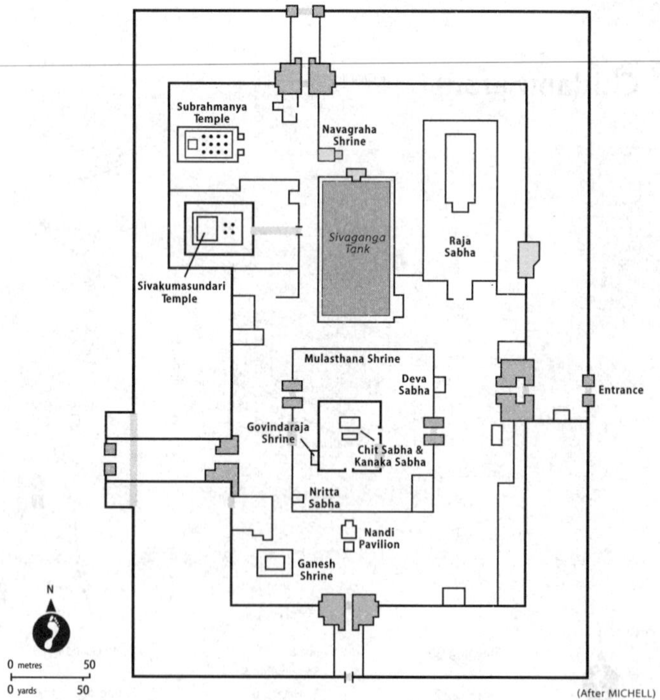

## Sleeping

**Tiruchirappalli** *p839, map p840*
**A Jenney's Residency**, 3/14 Macdonalds Rd, T0431-2414414, www.Jenneysresidency.com. 93 top quality a/c rooms, good restaurants, pool (non-residents Rs 100), excellent travel desk, exchange, hair/beauty salon.
**B-D Femina**, 14C Williams Rd, T0431-2414501, try_femina@sancharnet.in. 157 clean rooms, 140 a/c, vegetarian restaurants, bar, pool in new block, good value, modern, comfortable 4-storey hotel.
**C Sangam**, Collector's Office Rd, T0431-2464480. 58 comfortable a/c rooms and restaurants (great tandoori), good breakfast in coffee shop, pleasant bar, exchange, OK pool, spacious lawns, very friendly.
**C-D Kanjenaa Plaza**, 50 Williams Rd (2-min walk from bus stand), T0431-2401501, kanjenaaplaza@rediffmail.com. 90 spacious, comfortable rooms with bath, 26 a/c, restaurant, bar, travel agent, very quiet, new and clean.
**C-D Ramyas**, 13D/2 Williams Rd, T0431-2415128, vatnaa@eth.net. 78 spotless rooms, 24 a/c, restaurants, bar.
**D Abirami**, 10 Macdonalds Rd, T0431-2415001. 55 rooms, some a/c with bath, good busy a/c restaurant (vegetarian), exchange, old fashioned, noisy location.
**D-E Ashby**, 17A Junction Rd, T0431-2460652. 20 large a/c rooms with bath set around courtyard, good restaurants, bar, oldest hotel in town, with Raj character, a bit noisy but excellent friendly staff, good value.
**D-E Gajapriya**, 5 Royal Rd, T0431-2414411. 66 good value rooms, 28 a/c (no twin-bedded), non-veg restaurant, bar, library, car parking, spacious hotel, quieter than most.
**D-E Tamil Nadu** (TTDC), Macdonalds Rd, Cantt, T0431-2414346. 36 rooms (run down), some a/c with bath, restaurant, bar and tourist office.
**E-F Sevana**, 5 Royal Rd, Cantt, T0431-2415201. 44 rooms, some a/c with bath, a/c restaurant (Indian), bar, quiet, friendly.
**F Arun**, 24 State Bank, Rd T0431-2415021. 40 rooms in garden setting, restaurant, bar, TV, excellent value. Recommended.
**F ASG Lodge** opposite. Very noisy but quite clean (from Rs 75).
**F Raja Sugam**, 13b Royal Rd, T0431- 2460636.

**Thanjavur** *p842, map p843*
Even modest hotels charge 20% Luxury Tax. The last three listings are for Point Calimere (Kodikkarai) Wildlife Sanctuary. There, Nov and Dec are busy; advance reservation is recommended from: Wildlife Warden, 3 Main St, Thanjavur.
**A Parisutham**, 55 GA Canal Rd, T04362-231801, www.hotelparisutham.com. 52 clean a/c rooms in 1980s designed, double-decker quality hotel, good restaurants (live local music from 1945), lovely pool, exchange, friendly, helpful, good atmosphere (avoid smaller, noisy a/c ground floor rooms).
**B Ideal River View Resort**, Vennar Bank, Palli Agraharam, 6 km north of centre, T04326-250533, www.idealresort.com ideal@md2.vsnl.net.in. Clean, comfortable cottages (some a/c) in large grounds, restaurant, boating, peaceful, big swimming pool, shuttle to town. Recommended.
**C-D Hotel Gnanam**, Anna Salai (Market Rd), T04362-278501, www.hotelgnanam.com. 30 rooms (some A/C) with hot water, vegetarian multi-culisine restaurant, safety deposit lockers and travel desk. Mid-range sister hotel to Parasutham.
**D Pandyar Residency**, Kutchery Rd, near Big Temple, T04362-230574. 63 rooms, some a/c, some overlook temple, restaurant, bar.
**D-E Lion City**, 130 Gandhiji Rd, T04362-275650, hotellioncity@hotmail.com. 25 well-appointed rooms in recently opened hotel, TV, hot water, clean, spacious, good service. Recommended.
**D-E Tamil Nadu I** (TTDC), Gandhiji Rd, 5-min walk from railway, T04362-231421. 32 small rooms with bath, rather dark, some a/c, in pleasant setting around a cool inner court-yard, simple restaurant, bar, Tourist Office.
**D-E Yagappa**, off Trichy Rd, south of station, T04362-230421. Good size, comfortable rooms with bath, restaurant, bar, good value.

*For an explanation of the sleeping and eating price codes used in this guide, see inside the front cover. Other relevant information is found in Essentials pages 56-61.*

**E-F Karthik**, 73 S Rampart St, T04362-278662. 43 adequate rooms, 3 a/c, popular vegetarian restaurant (eat off a banana leaf at lunch time), friendly.
**E-F Kasi**, 1494 S Rampart St, T04362-231908. 42 nice, clean rooms (from Rs 115), some with TV, hot showers, 3 a/c. Recommended.
**F Calimere Rest House**, Point Calimere (Kodikkarai) Sanctuary, 4 derelict rooms.
**F Ganesh Lodge**, next to railway station, T04362-231113. 25 basic but clean rooms (de luxe over-priced), good veg restaurant.
**F Poonarai Ilam**, Point Calimere (Kodikkarai) Sanctuary, 14 simple rooms with bath and balcony (Rs 15 per person), caretaker may be able to arrange a meal with advance notice, intended for foreign visitors, rooms often available.
**F PV Thevar Lodge**, 40 North Main St, Vedaranyam, 50 m from bus station (English sign high up only visible in daylight), T250330. 37 basic rooms with bath and fan, can be mosquito-proofed, fairly clean, very friendly owners, good value. Indian vegetarian meals are available in the bazaar near the bus stand.
**F Youth Hostel**, Medical College Rd, T04362-223597. Dorm (Rs 40).

**Kumbakonam** *p844, map p845*
20% Luxury Tax is always added.
**D Chela**, 9 Ayekulam Rd, T0435-2430336. 30 rooms, 8 a/c, clean, restaurant, spacious. Recommended.
**D Raya's**, 18 Head PO Rd, near tank, T0435-2432170. 43 clean rooms, some a/c with bath, TV, safes, mirrored VIP suite, good restaurant, bar, 24-hr check-out, exchanges cash.
**E ARR**, 21 TSR Big St, T0435-2421234. 50 good size, clean rooms, some a/c, with bath, TV, bar, room service meals.
**E Femina**, Head PO Rd (towards tank), T0435-2420369. Clean and quiet rooms.
**F Pandiyan**, 52 Sarangapani East Sannadi St, T0435-2430397. 20 clean rooms with bath (some dark), good restaurant, good value.

**Chidambaram** *p846, map p847*
**C-D Saradharam**, 19 VGP St, T04144-221336. 46 basic, tired, grubby overpriced rooms, noisy, but very good restaurants.
**D Ritz**, 2 VGP (Venugopal Pillai) St, T04144-223312.18 excellent a/c rooms very clean, modern hotel, rooftop restaurant. Highly recommended.
**D-E Akshaya**, 17-18 East Car St, T04144-220192. 24 rooms, mostly non a/c, rooftop overlooks temple grounds, comfortable small hotel right in the centre (can be noisy).
**F Raja Rajan**, 162 West Car St, T04144-222690. 14 pleasant rooms, 1 good a/c, friendly.
**F Ramanathan Mansions**, 127 Bazar St, T04144-222411. 28 rooms with bath, spacious and airy (no power sockets), quieter than most, away from busy temple area, friendly.
**F Ramayas Lodge**, 120 South Car St, T04144-223011. 24 clean rooms with bath in newish hotel, 2 a/c, TV, phone, good value.
**F Star Lodge**, 101 South Car St, T04144-222743. 37 basic rooms set around open central landings, friendly.

## Eating

**Tiruchirappalli** *p839, map p840*
**TT Abirami's**, T0431-2460001. A/c Vasantha Bhawan at the back, serves excellent vegetarian; front section is a 'meals' type eatery.
**TT Jenney's Residency**, T0431-2461301. Good Chinese, extensive menu, attentive service but freezing a/c. Also Wild West bar.
**TT Kavitha**, Lawson's Rd. A/c. Excellent breakfasts and generous vegetarian *thalis*.
**TT Sangam's**, T0431-2464480. Indian, Continental.
**TT Vincent Garden**, Dindigul Rd. Very pleasant garden restaurant and pastry shop, lots of coloured lights but on a busy road.

Some good Indian vegetarian restaurants in Chinna Bazar include:
**T New Kurinji**, below **Hotel Guru**, Lawson's Rd. A/c vegetarian.
**T Vasantha Bhawan** and **Ragunath**, for *thalis*, good service.

**Thanjavur** *p842, map p843*
**TT Oriental Towers**, for quality food.
**TT Parisutham**, good North Indian meat dishes, excellent vegetarian *thalis* ("best of 72 curries"!), service can be slow.
**T Algappa**, Gandhiji Rd. A/c, non-vegetarian.
**T New Bombay Sweets**, tasty Indian snacks.
**T Sathars**, Tandoori. Recommended.
**T Vasantha Vihar** on west side of Railway Station Rd between station and *Tamil Nadu hotel*. Good *thalis* and snacks.

**Kumbakonam** *p844, map p845*
**A&A**, Ayekulam Rd. Excellent veg restaurant. Good, clean, north and south Indian meals.

**Chidambaram** *p846, map p847*
**Hotel Saradharam**, 10 VGP St. A/c. Excellent range of meals, pizzas and European dishes. Good variety and value, popular.
**Sree Ganesa Bhavan**, West Car St. South Indian vegetarian. Friendly, helpful staff.
**Udupi**, West Car St. Good veg, nice and clean.

## Entertainment

**Thanjavur** *p842, map p843*
**Bharat Natyam**, performances by Guru Herambanathan from a family of dancers, 1/2378 Krishanayar Lane, Ellaiyamman Koil St, T04362-233759.
**South Zone Cultural Centre Palace**, T04362-231272, organizes programmes in the Big Temple, 2nd and 4th Sat; free.

## Festivals and events

**Tiruchirappalli** *p839, map p840*
**Mar**: Festival of Floats on the Teppakulam when the temple deities are taken out onto the sacred lake on rafts.

**Around Trichy** *p841*
In **Srirangam** Vaikunta Ekadasi (bus No 1 (C or D) from Trichy or hire a rickshaw), and associated temple car festival, in **Dec/Jan** draws thousands of pilgrims who witness the transfer of the image of the deity from the inner sanctum under the golden *vimana* to the *mandapa*.

In **Tiruvanaikkaval**, there are special festivals in **Jan** and the **spring**. In **Aug** Pancha Piraharam is celebrated and in the month of **Panguni** the images of Siva and his consort Akhilandesvari exchange their dress.

In **Pudukkottai**, in **Jan** and **Feb** bullock races (*manju virattu*) are held in the area.

**Chidambaram** *p846, map p847*
**Feb/Mar**: Natyanjali dance festival for 5 days starting with Maha Sivaratri. **Jun/Jul**: Ani Tirumanjanam Festival. **Dec/Jan**: Markazhi Tiruvathirai Festival.

## Shopping

**Thanjavur** *p842, map p843*
You may not export any object over 100 years old. Thanjavur is known for its decorative copper plates with silver and brass relief (*repoussé*) work, raised 'glass' painting, wood carving and bronze and brass casting. Granite carving is being revived by the Government through centres which produce superbly sculpted images. Crafts shops abound in Gandhiji Rd Bazar.
**Govindarajan's**, 31 Kuthirai Katti St, Karandhai (a few kilometres from town), T04362-230282, is a treasure house of pricey old, and affordable new pieces; artists and craftsmen at work.

## Activities and tours

**Tiruchirappalli** *p839, map p840*
**Galaxy**, Williams Rd (Kanjenaa Plaza). For air and train tickets.
**Window to the World**, 33 Chandra Nagar, Srirangam, T0431-2435219, www.tourism-southindia.com. Tours from Chennai, Bangalore, Kochi, Madurai and Thiruvananthapuram. Recommended for tours (good cars with drivers), ticketing, general advice.

**Thanjavur** *p842, map p843*
**TTDC** Temple tour of Thanjavur and surroundings by a/c coach; enquire at Tourist Office. Mon-Fri, 1000-1745.

## Transport

**Tiruchirappalli** *p839, map p840*
**Air**
The airport is 8 km from the centre (taxi Rs 75). **Indian Airlines**, Dindigul Rd, 2 km from Express Bus Stand, T0431-2481433, airport T0431-2420563; flies to **Chennai** daily except Mon and Fri. **Sri Lankan**, 14 Williams Rd, T0431-2414076 (0900-1730) to **Colombo**.

**Bus**
**Local** Good City Bus service. From airport Nos 7, 63, 122, 128, take 30 mins. The Central State Bus Stand is across from the tourist office (No 1 Bus passes all the sights); 20 mins to Chatram Bus Stand.

**Long distance** The bus stands are 1 km from the railway station and are chaotic; TN Govt Express, T0431-2460992, Central, T0431-2460425. Frequent buses to **Coimbatore** 205 km (5½ hrs), **Kumbakonam** 92 km, **Chennai** (6 hrs), **Madurai** 161 km (3 hrs), **Palani** 152 km (3½ hrs), **Thanjavur** (1½ hrs). Also 2 to **Kanniyakumari** (9 hrs), **Kodai** (5½ hrs) and **Tirupati** (9½ hrs).

### Taxi
Unmetered taxis, and tourist taxis from Kavria Travels, Hotel Sangam, Collector's Office Rd, T0431-2464480. **NB Cycle-rickshaws** and **auto-rickshaws** are best avoided.

### Train
Enquiries, T131. **Bangalore**: *Thanjavur Mysore Exp, 6231*, 2040, 9½ hrs, continues to **Mysore**, 3¼ hrs. **Chennai**: *Pallavan Exp, 2606*, 0630, 5½ hrs; *Vaigai Exp, 2636*, 0910, 5¼ hrs. **Kollam**: *Nagore-Quilon Exp, 6361*, 1615, 12½ hrs. **Madurai**: *Vaigai Exp, 2635*, 1745, 2¾ hrs. **Villupuram (for Pondicherry)**: *Tiruchi Tirupati Exp, 6802*, 1400, 7 hrs; *Cholan Exp, 6854*, 0800, 6½ hrs, plus frequent bus to Pondicherry (1 hr) or another train (4 daily).

## Pudukkottai *p841*
### Bus
To **Tiruchirappalli**, **Thanjavur**, **Madurai**, **Ramnad**, **Ramesvaram**, and to **Sittanavasal** (see above).

### Train
The station is 2 km southwest of the bus stand. Trains for Egmore, change at Tambaram. **Trichy** 1¼ hrs. **Ramesvaram** *Tambaram Ramesvaram Exp, 6701*, 0833, 5¼ hrs.

## Thanjavur *p842, map p843*
### Air
Tiruchirappalli airport is about 1 hr by car.

### Bus
Old State and Municipal Bus Stand, south of the fort, for local services. Buses from Kumbakonam stop at the corner before going out to the New Bus Stand, T04362-233455. CRC (Cholan), T04362-232455. New (Mofussil) Bus Stand is on Trichy Rd. Daily service to **Chidambaram** (4 hrs), **Kumbakonam** (1 hr), **Chennai** (8 hrs), **Madurai** (3½ hrs), **Pondicherry** (6 hrs), **Tirupathi**, **Tiruchirappalli** (1½ hrs). Also to **Vedaranyam** (100 km) for Point Calimere, about hourly, 4-4½ hrs.

### Train
Reservations, T04362- 231131, 0800-1400, 1500-1700 Mon-Sat; 0800-1400 Sun. **Bangalore**: *Thanjavur Mysore Exp, 6231*, 1845, 11½ hrs, continues to **Mysore**, 3¼ hrs. **Chennai (ME)**: *Rockfort Exp, 6878*, 2000, 9 hrs. **Tiruchirappalli**: *Tambaram Rameswaram Exp, 6701*, 0520, 2 hrs; *Fast Passenger Exp, 6761*, 1300, 3 hrs; *Cholan Exp, 6853*, 1700, 1¾ hrs.

## Kumbakonam *p844, map p845*
Car hire for half day for excursions, Rs 400. TN Govt Express buses to **Chennai**, No 305, several daily (7½ hrs); half hourly to Thanjavur. The railway station is 2 km from town centre. Trains to **Chennai** (Egmore), 1010- 2110, change at Tambaram (8½-9 hrs), **Chidambaram** (2 hrs), **Thanjavur** (50 mins) and **Tiruchirappalli**, 0600-1555 (2½ hrs).

## Chidambaram *p846, map p847*
The **bus** station is chaotic with daily services to **Chennai**, **Madurai**, **Thanjavur**, and to **Karaikal** (2 hrs), **Nagapattinam** and **Pondicherry** (2 hrs).

**Train** reservations T04144-222298, 0800-1200, 1400-1700; Sun 0800-1400. **Chennai (E)** (change at Tambaram): *Rameswaram Tambaram Exp, 6702*, 2307, 6¾ hrs; *Cholan Exp, 6854*, 1153, 6 hrs. **Kumbakonam**: *Sethu Exp, 6713*, 1832, 2 hrs, continues to **Thanjavur**, 3 hrs and **Tiruchirappalli**, 5 hrs; *Cholan Exp, 6853*, 1410, 2 hrs, continues to **Thanjavur**, 3 hrs, and **Tiruchirappalli**, 4¾ hrs.

## Point Calimere (Kodikkarai)
**Buses** via Vedaranyam which has services to/from **Thanjavur**, **Tiruchirappalli**, **Nagapattinam**, **Chennai** etc. From Thanjavur buses leave the New Bus Stand for **Vedaranyam** (100 km) about hourly (4-4½ hrs); buses and vans from there to **Kodikkarai** (11 km) which take about 30 mins. Avoid being dropped at 'Sri Rama's Feet' on the way, near a shrine which is of no special interest.

## Directory

**Tiruchirappalli** *p839, map p840*
**Banks** Exchange is available at Western Union money transfer in Jenne Plaza, Cantonment. 0900-1730 Mon-Sat. Quick, good rates. **Internet** Mas Media, Main Rd, 6 terminals; Central Telegraph Office, Permanent Rd.

**Pudukkottai** *p841*
**Banks** State Bank of India, East Main St.

**Thanjavur** *p842, map p843*
**Banks** Canara Bank, South Main St, changes TCs. **Hospitals** Govt Hospital, Hospital Rd, south of the old town. **Post** Head Post and Telegraph Office are off the Railway Station Rd. **Useful addresses** Police, south of the Big Temple between the canal and the railway, T04362-232200.

**Kumbakonam** *p844, map p845*
**Banks** Changing money is difficult. State Bank of India, TSR Big St. **Internet** End of Kamaraj Rd, close to clock tower. **Post** Near Mahamakam Tank.

**Chidambaram** *p846, map p847*
**Banks** Changing money can be difficult. City Union Bank, West Car St has exchange facilities. Indian Bank, 64 South Car St, changes cash. **Post** Head Post Office, North Car St.

# Tamil's hill stations

*The Tamil ghats were once shared between shola forest and tribal peoples. Then the British, limp from the heat of the plains, invested in expeditions up the mountains and before long had planted eucalyptus, established elite members' clubs and substituted jackals for foxes in their pursuit of the hunt. Don't expect to find the sheer awe-inspiring grandeur of the Himalaya, but there is a charm to these hills where neatly pleated, green tea plantations run like contour lines about the ghats' girth, bringing the promise of a restorative chill and walking tracks where the air comes cut with the smell of eucalyptus.* *►► For Sleeping, Eating and other listings, see pages 861-870.*

## Ins and outs

The northern Nilgiris or the more southerly Palani hills offer rival opportunities for high altitude stop-overs on the route between Tamil Nadu, Karnataka and Kerala. The most visited towns of Ooty and Kodai both have their staunch fan-bases: Ooty tends to attract nostalgic British and rail enthusiasts, while Kody gets the American vote, thanks in part to its international schools. Both are well-connected by road: Kody is best approached from Madurai, while Ooty makes a good bridge to Kerala from Mysore or Tamil's more Northern temple towns: the famous narrow gauge rack-and-pinion railway is most dramatic between Mettupalayam and Coonoor, which in turn has trains from Coimbatore and Chennai. *►► See Transport, page 868, for further details.*

*The roads worsen dramatically when you cross the Tamil border from Kerala, in line with the different levels of affluence between the two states.*

## Udhagamandalam (Ooty) → *Phone code: 0423. Colour map 3, grid B3.*

*Population 93,900. Altitude: 2,286 m.*

Ooty has been celebrated for rolling hills covered in pine and eucalyptus forests and coffee and tea plantations since the first British planters arrived in 1818. A Government House was built, and the British lifestyle developed with cottages and clubs – tennis, golf, riding – and teas on the lawn. But the town is no longer the haven it once was; the centre is heavily built up and can be downright unpleasant in the holiday months of April to June, and again around October. Either stay in the grand ruins of colonial quarters on the quiet outskirts where it's still possible to steal some serenity or opt instead for the far smaller tea garden town of Coonoor, see page 856, just 19 km down mountain.

## Sights

The **Botanical Gardens** ⓘ *0800-1800, Rs 25, camera, Rs 50, video Rs 500, 3 km northeast of railway station,* holds over 1,000 varieties of plant, shrub and tree including orchids, ferns, alpines and medicinal plants, but is most fun for watching giant family groups picnicking and gambolling together among beautiful lawns and glass houses. To the east of the garden in a Toda *mund* is the Wood House made of logs. The Annual Flower Show is held in the third week of May. The **Rose Garden** ⓘ *0800-1800, 750 m from Charing Cross,* has over 1,500 varieties of roses.

**Ooty Lake** ⓘ *0800-1800, Rs 3, camera Rs 10, video Rs 100,* 2½-km long, built in 1825 as a vast irrigation tank, is now more than half overgrown with water hyacinth though it is still used enthusiastically for boating and pedallo hire.

**Kandal Cross** ⓘ *3 km west of the railway station,* is a Roman Catholic shrine considered the 'Jerusalem of the East'. During the clearing of the area to make way for a graveyard in 1927, an enormous 4-m-high boulder was found and a cross was

## Udhagamandalam (Ooty)

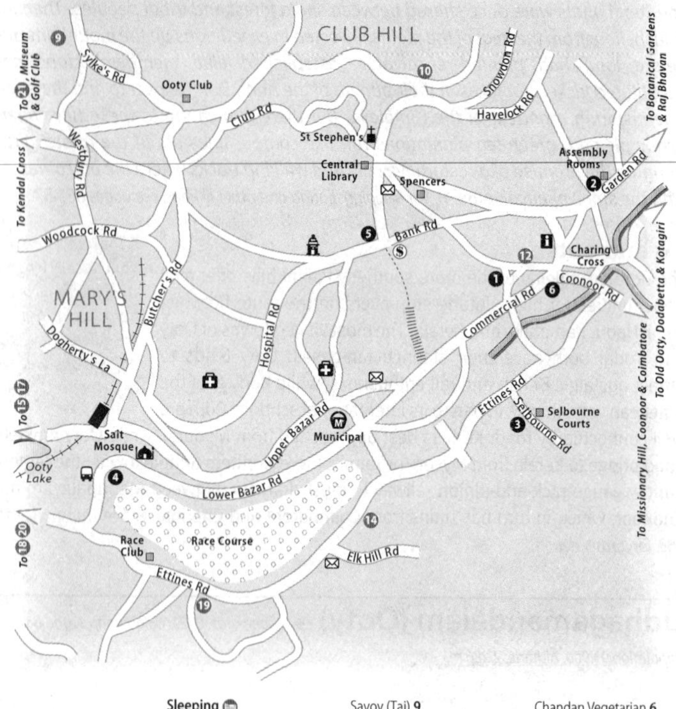


**Sleeping**
Fernhills Palace 20
Glyngarth Heritage 21
Lakeview 17
Nilgiri Woodlands 19
Reflections Guest House 15
Regency Villa 18
Savoy (Taj) 9
Southern Star 10
Tamil Nadu 12
YWCA Anandagiri 14

**Eating**
Blue Hills 1
Chandan Vegetarian 6
Garden Café 6
Hot Breads 2
Sharma Bhojanalaya 4
Shinkow's 5
Pavilion 3

## The Blue Mountain Railway

The delightful narrow gauge steam Mountain Railway, in its blue and cream livery, goes from Mettupalayam to Ooty via Coonoor, negotiating 16 tunnels and 31 major bridges and climbing from 326 m to 2,193 m. It was opened on 15 June 1899. The railway scenes of the 'Marabar Express' in the film of *A Passage to India* were shot here. The whole 4½-hour (46 km) journey through tea plantations and lush forests is highly recommended for the scenery (First Class front coach for best views).

Hillgrove (17 km) a 'watering stop' in the past, and Coonoor (27 km) with its loco shed, have refreshments and clean toilets.

The train has limited First Class seating and can get very crowded in season, though some trains have a new, more spacious, First Class carriage. See Mettupalayam, page 856 .

For enthusiasts, the more expensive Heritage Steam Chariot with special spacious carriages runs between Ooty and Runneymede picnic area, 23 km away, at weekends (more often in season). The drawback is that you can be stranded for hours when the engine breaks down; some decide to scramble to the nearest road to flag down a bus.

erected. Now a relic of the True Cross brought to India by an Apostolic delegate is shown to pilgrims every day. The annual feast is in May.

**St Stephen's Church** was Ooty's first church, built in the 1820s. Much of the wood is said to be from Tipu Sultan's Lal Bagh Palace in Srirangapatnam. The inside of the church and the graveyard at the rear are worth seeing.

**Dodabetta**ⓘ *buses from Ooty, 1000-1500, autos and taxis (Rs 200 round trip) go to the summit,* is 10 km east of the railway station off the Kotagiri road. The 'big mountain' reaches 2,638 m and is the second highest in the Western Ghats sheltering Coonoor from the southwest monsoons when Ooty gets heavy rains. The top is often shrouded in mist. There is a viewing platform at the summit. The telescope really isn't worth the even nominal Rs 2 fee.

## Walks and hikes around Ooty

Hiking or simply walking is excellent in the Nilgiris. It is undisturbed, quiet and interesting. Climbing Dodabetta or Mukurti is hardly a challenge but the longer walks through the *sholas* are best undertaken with a guide. It is possible to see characteristic features of Toda settlements such as *munds* and *boas*, see page 790.

*There are isolated groups of as many as 18 different types of tribal people who live in the Nilgiri Hills, see page 790.*

**Dodabetta-Snowdon-Ooty walk** starts at 'Dodabetta Junction' directly opposite the 3-km road to the summit. It is a pleasant path which curves gently downhill through a variety of woodland (eucalyptus and conifer mainly) back to Ooty and need take no more than a couple of hours. For longer treks, contact **Nilgiris Trekking Association** ⓘ *Kavitha Nilayam, 31-D Bank Road, or R Seniappan, 137 Upper Bazar, T0423-2444449, sehiappan@yahoo.com.*

**Mukurti Peak**ⓘ *buses from Ooty every 30 mins from 0630 or you can take a tour (see page 867), book early as they are popular,* is 36 km away, off the Gudalur road. After 26 km you reach the 6-km-long Mukurti Lake. Mukurti Peak (the name suggests that someone thought it resembled a severed nose), not an easy climb, is to the west. The Todas believe that the souls of the dead and the sacrificed buffaloes leap to the next world from this sacred peak. It is an excellent place to escape for walking, to view the occasional wildlife, to fish from the lake or go boating.

**Avalanche** ⓘ *buses from Ooty, 1110*, a valley, is a beautiful part of the *shola*, 24 km from town, with plenty of rhododendrons, magnolias and orchids and a trout stream running through it, and is excellent for walking. The Forestry Department Guest House is clean and has good food.

The **River Pykara** ⓘ *several buses from 0630-2030, or take a car or bicycle*, 19 km from Ooty, has a dam and power plant. There is breathtaking scenery. The Falls, about 6 km from the bridge on the main road, are best in July though it is very wet then, but they are also worth visiting from August to December.

## Coonoor → *Phone code: 0423. Colour map 3, grid B3. Population: 50,100. Altitude: 1,800 m.*

Coonoor, smaller and much less developed than Ooty, is an ideal point from where to walk into nature and ramble past villages. There's no pollution, no noise, and very few people. The gentle covered market, as with many towns or cities in South India, is almost medieval: cobblers, jewellers, tailors, pawn brokers and merchants selling everything from jasmine to beetroot. The picturesque hills around the town are covered in coffee and tea plantations.

*When you arrive by train, or by bus, which doesn't always visit the main bus-stand if continuing to Ooty, the main town of Lower Coonoor will be to the east, across the river. Upper Coonoor, with the better hotels 2-3 km away, is further east.*

The real attraction here is the walking, though there are a couple of sights in town. The large **Sim's Park** ⓘ *0800-1830, Rs 5*, named after a secretary to the Madras Club, is a well maintained botanical garden on the slopes of a ravine with over 330 varieties of rose but only really worth the journey for passionate botanists. Contact the United Planters' Association of South India (UPASI), Glenview, to visit tea and coffee plantations. The **Wellington Barracks**, 3 km northeast of Lower Coonoor, which are the raison d'être for the town, were built in 1852. They are now the Headquarters of the Indian Defence Services Staff College and also of the Madras Regiment, which is over 250 years old, the oldest in the Indian Army.

**Lamb's Rock**, on a high precipice, 9 km away, has good views over the Coimbatore plains and coffee and tea estates on the slopes. At **Dolphin's Nose** ⓘ *several buses 0700-1615*, 12 km away, you can see Catherine Falls, a further 10 km away. Best in the early morning. **Droog** ⓘ *buses 0900, 1345*, 13 km away, has ruins of a 16th-century fort used by Tipu Sultan, and requires a 3-km walk. **Kotagiri** ⓘ *frequent services from Coonoor, Mettupalayam Railway Station and Ooty*, has an altitude of 1,980 m and is 29 km from Ooty. It sits on the northeast crest of the plateau overlooking the plains. It has a milder climate than Ooty. The name comes from Kotar-Keri, the street of the *Kotas* who were one of the original hill tribes and who have a village to the west of the town. You can visit some scenic spots from here: **St Catherine Falls** (8 km) and **Elk Falls** (7 km), or one of the peaks – **Kodanad Viewpoint** (16 km) which you reach through the tea estates or one of the several buses running from 0610 – or **Rangaswamy Pillar**, an isolated rock, and the conical Rangaswamy Peak.

## Mettupalayam and the Nilgiri Ghat Road

The journey up to Coonoor from Mettupalayam is one of the most scenic in South India, giving superb views over the plains below. Between Mettupalayam and the start of the Ghat road, there are magnificent groves of tall, slender areca nut palms. Mettupalayam has become the centre for the areca nut trade as well as producing synthetic gems. The palms are immensely valuable trees: the nut is used across India wrapped in betel vine leaves – two of the essential ingredients of India's universal after-meal digestive, *paan*. The town is the starting point of the ghat railway line up to

Ooty, see Blue Mountain Railway box. If you take the early morning train you can continue to Mysore by bus from Ooty on the same day, making a very pleasant trip.

## Mudumalai Wildlife Sanctuary → *Colour map 3, grid B3.*

*0630-0900, 1600-1800, Rs 150; still camera Rs 10. There is a Ranger Office at Kargudi and a Reception Centre, 0630-1800, at Theppakadu where buses between Mysore anld Ooty stop.*

*Best time to visit is September-October and March-May when the undergrowth dies down and it is easier to see the animals, particularly when they are on the move at dawn.*

The sanctuary adjoins Bandipur National Park (see page 993) beyond the Moyar River, its hills (885-1,000 m), ravines, flats and valleys being an extension of the same environment. The park is one of the more popular and is now trying to limit numbers of visitors to reduce disturbance to the elephants.

There are large herds of elephant, gaur, sambar, barking deer, wild dog, Nilgiri langur, bonnet monkey, wild boar, four-horned antelope and the rarer tiger and leopard, as well as smaller mammals and many birds and reptiles. Elephant Camp, south of Theppakadu, tames wild elephants. Some are bred in captivity and trained to work for the timber industry. You can watch the elephants being fed in the late afternoon, learn about each individual elephant's diet and the specially prepared 'cakes' of food.

You can hire a jeep for about Rs 6 per km but must be accompanied by a guide. Most 'Night Safaris' are best avoided. Elephant rides at 0630 (Rs 100 per elephant for four for 45 minutes); check timing and book in advance at the Wildlife Office, Mahalingam Building, Coonoor Road, Ooty. They can be fun even though you may not see much wildlife. The 46-seater coach, first come, first served, Rs 25 each, can be noisy with shrieking children. There are *machans* near water holes and salt licks and along the Moyar River. With patience you can see a lot, especially rare and beautiful birds. Trekking in the remoter parts of the forest with guides can be arranged from some lodges. You can spend a day climbing the hill and bathe at the impressive waterfalls. The core area is not open to visitors.

## Coimbatore and the Nilgiri Hills

### Coimbatore → *Phone code: 0422. Colour map 3, grid B3. Population: 923,000.*

Coimbatore, as one of South India's most important industrial cities since the 1930s development of hydro-electricity from the Pykara Falls, holds scant charm to warrant more than a pit-stop. It was once the fulcrum of tussles between Tamilian, Mysorean and Keralite coastal rulers (the word palayam crops up tellingly often in Coimbatore – its translation being 'encampment'), and sadly violence continues today. You are likely to stay here only if fascinated by the cotton trade or stuck for an onward bus or train.

### Salem → *Phone code: 0427. Colour map 3, grid B4. Population: 693,200.*

Salem, an important transport junction, is surrounded by hills, the Shevaroy and Nagaramalai Hills to the north and the Jarugumalai Hills to the southeast. It is a busy, rapidly growing industrial town – particularly for textiles and metal-based industries – with modern shopping centres.

The old town is on the east bank of the River Manimutheru. Each evening around Bazar Street you can see cotton carpets being made. The **cemetery**, next to the Collector's office, has some interesting tombstones. To the southeast of the town on a

*They say Coimbatore is 'India's Manchester', and certainly its capital of cotton weaving – you'll see skyscrapers named 'Viscose Towers'.*

ridge of the Jarugumalai Hills is a highly visible *Naman* painted in *chunam* and ochre. The temple on the nearby hill (1919) is particularly sacred to the weavers' community. Some 600 steps lead up to excellent views over the town.

### Yercaud and the Shevaroy Hills → *Phone code: 04281. Altitude: 1,515 m.*

The beautiful drive up the steep and sharply winding ghat road from Salem quickly brings a sharp freshness to the air as it climbs to over 1500 m. The minor 'resort' has a small artificial **lake** and Anna Park nearby. Some attractive though unsignposted walks start here. In May there is a special festival focused on the **Shevaroyan Temple**, on top of the third highest peak in the hill range. Many tribal people take part, but access is only possible on foot. Ask for details in the Tamil Nadu Tourist Office in Chennai, see page 820. There's also a tourist information office in the Tamil Nadu hotel in town, see page 864.

Just outside the town is **Lady's Seat**, which overlooks the ghat road and gives wonderful views across the Salem plains. Near the old Norton Bungalow on the Shevaroyan Temple Road, is another well known local spot, **Bear's Cave**. Formed by two huge boulders, it is occupied by huge colonies of bats. The whole area is full of botanical interest. There is an **orchidarium-cum-nursery** and a **horticultural research station**.

## Kodaikkanal (Kodai) and the Palani Hills → *Phone code: 04542. Colour map 3, grid C4. Population: 32,900. Altitude: 2,343 m.*



The climb up the Palanis starts 47 km before Kodaikkanal (Kodai) and is one of the most rapid ascents anywhere across the ghats. The views are stunning. In the lower reaches of the climb you look down over the Kambam Valley, the Vaigai Lake and across to the Varushanad Hills beyond. Set high in the Palani Hills around a small artificial lake, the town has crisply fresh air, even at the height of summer, and the beautiful scent of pine and eucalyptus make it a popular retreat from the southern plains. Today Kodai is a fast growing resort centre and many believe it superior to Ooty. The lake, created in 1910 by the building of a dam just below the International School (established in 1901), acts as a focus for the town. The 5-km walk around its perimeter gives beautiful and contrasting views across the water and into the surrounding woods. ▸▸ *For Sleeping, Eating and other listings, see pages 861-870.*

### Ins and outs

Buses make the long climb from Madurai and other cities to the central bus stand, which is within easy walking distance from most hotels. The nearest train station is Kodai Rd. Kodai is small enough to walk around, though for some of the sights it is worth getting an un-metered taxi. ▸▸ *See Transport, page 870, for further details.*

### Background

The **Palani Hills** were first surveyed by British administrators in 1821, but the surveyor's report was not published until 1837 – 10 years after Ooty had become the official 'sanitorium' for the British in South India. A proposal to build a sanitorium was made in 1861-1862 by Colonel Hamilton, who noted the extremely healthy climate and the lack of disease. Despite the warmth of that recommendation the sanitorium was never built because the site was so difficult to get to. It was the freedom from malaria that was the greatest incentive to opening a hill station there. The American Mission in Madurai, established in 1834, had lost six of their early missionaries within a decade. It looked as if the Sirumalai Hills, at around 1,300 m, might provide a respite from the plains, but it was soon discovered that they were not high enough to eliminate malaria. The first two bungalows were built by June 1845.

The major transformation came at the turn of the 20th century with the arrival of the car and the bus. In 1905 it was possible to do the whole journey from Kodai Road station to Kodai within the hours of daylight. The present road, up 'Law's Ghat' was opened to traffic in 1916.

## Sights

**Kodaikkanal Lake** ⓘ *Rs 5, toilets at south entrance*, covers 24 ha in a 'star' shape surrounded by wooded slopes. The walk around the lake takes about one hour, boating is popular and you can fish (with permission), although the water is polluted. The view over the plains from **Coaker's Walk**, built by Lieutenant Coaker in the 1870s, can be magnificent; on a clear day you can see Madurai. It is reached from a sign-posted path just above the bazaar, 1 km from the Bus Stand.

**Kurinji Andavar Temple**, northeast of the town, past Chettiar Park, is dedicated to Murugan associated with the *kurinji* flower that blossoms once in 12 years. There are excellent views of the north and southern plains, including Palani and Vagai Dams. **St Peter's Church** (Church of South India) built in 1884, has a stained glass window dedicated to Bishop Caldwell. **The International School** has a commanding position on the lakeside, and provides education for children from India and abroad between the ages of 5 and 18. There is also the Highclere School for Girls and the Bhavan's Gandhi Vidyasram School, founded in 1983, on the way to Pillar Rocks.

**Bear Shola Falls**, named because it once attracted bears, is a favourite picnic spot about 2 km from the Bus Stand. These falls and others around Kodai have been

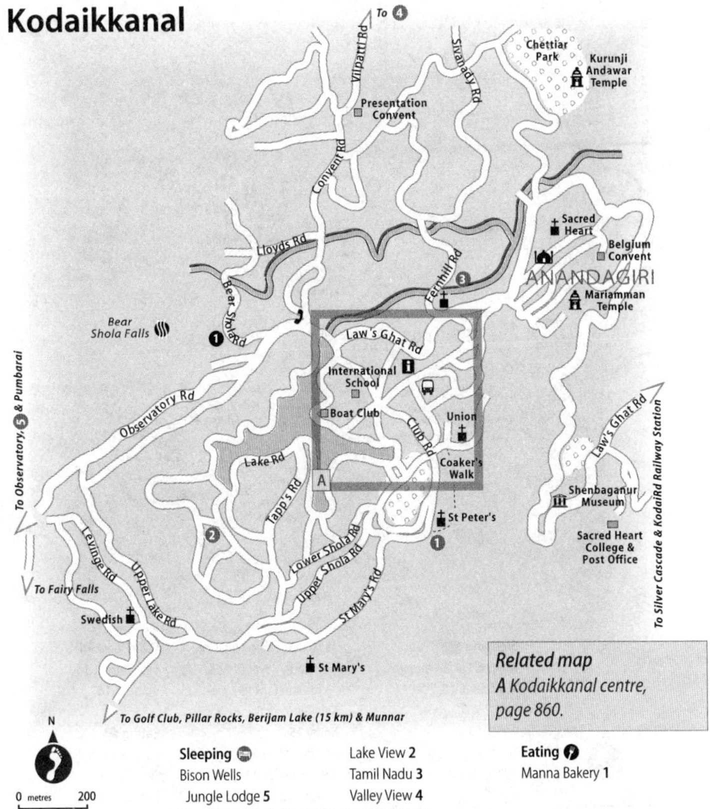

reduced to a trickle. **Solar Physical Observatory** ⓘ *during the season, Fri, 1000-1230, 1900-2100; 1000-1200, T04542-240588, 4 km to the west from the Bus Stand*, was established in 1899 at a height of 2,347 m. **Pillar Rocks**, 7 km from the lake, is another striking viewpoint. There are three granite formations over 120 m high. There have been over 100 dolmens and other megalithic remains discovered in the Palanis, all datable to around the second century AD.

The small but interesting **Shenbaganur Museum** ⓘ *1000-1130, 1500-1700*, is the local flora and fauna museum including 300 orchid species at the Sacred Heart College, a theological seminary founded in 1895. It also has some archaeological remains. There is an attractive walk downhill from the town passing waterfalls.

## Around Kodaikkanal

A road runs west past the golf course and Pillar Rocks to **Berijam Lake**, 15 km away, which has beautiful views over the lake before running down to it. Apart from timber lorries the road is little used. You can walk to Berijam in about four hours and stay at the adequate **Forest Rest House**, Rs 50. There is a restaurant but no store here.

You can continue the next day, by a short cut to **Top Station** in Kerala in five to six hours, where there is Forest Hut and shops and tea stalls selling snacks. There are then buses to **Munnar** 41 km away.

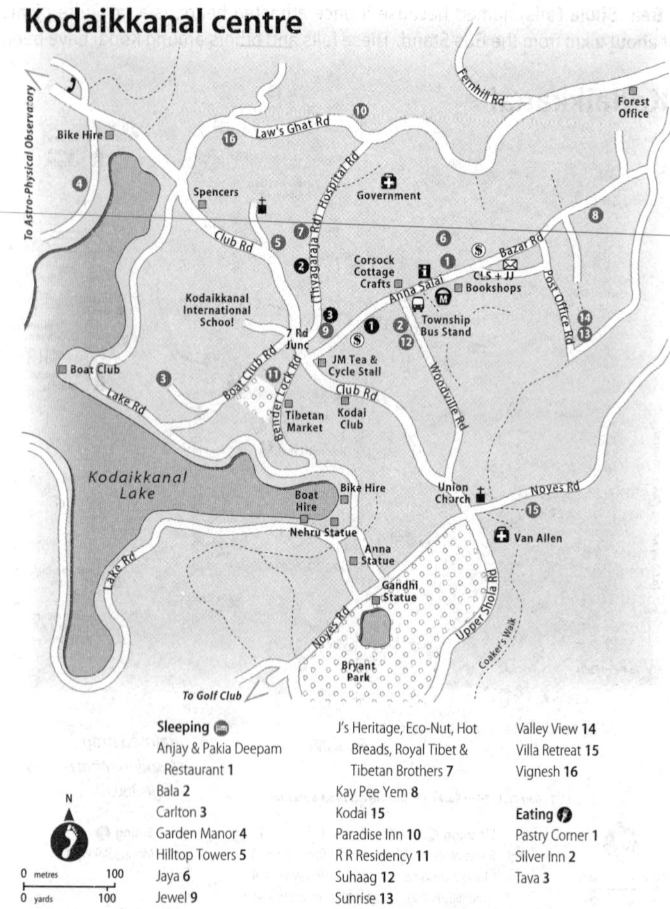

The ghat road to **Palani** passes through coffee, orange and banana smallholdings. Interplanting of crops such as pepper is further increasing the yields from what can be highly productive land, even on steep slopes. The hilltop shrine to **Murugan** (Subrahmanya) is a very important site of pilgrimage. At full moon in January to February pilgrims walk from up to 80 km around and climb the 659 steps up to the shrine. Many carry shoulder-poles with elaborate bamboo or wooden structures on each end, living out the myth which surrounds the origin of the shrine. There are buses to Kodai and Madurai (three hours).

**Pollachi** has a population of 88,300 and is 61 km from Madurai. It has been an important trading centre for over 2,000 years, as is witnessed by the finds of Roman silver coins bearing the heads of the Emperors Augustus and Tiberias. Today it still occupies an important position on the route from east to west through the Palakkad Gap. It is also the gateway to the small but very attractive sanctuary.

**Anamalai (Indira Gandhi) National Park** ⓘ *best time to visit Dec-Jun, avoid Sun, 0630-1830, Reception and Information Centre is at Top Slip, written permission is needed from District Forest Officer, Pollachi, T04259-225356 (1½ km out of town on road towards Top Slip)*, near Pollachi, covers an area of 960 sq km in the western ghats. It is a beautiful, unspoilt forest, rarely visited, except by Indian day-trippers. Wildlife includes Nilgiri langur, lion-tailed macaque, elephant, *gaur*, tiger, panther, sloth, wild boar, birds – including pied hornbill, drongo, red whiskered bulbul, black-headed oriole – and a large number of crocodiles in the Amaravathi reservoir. There is an elephant camp reached by a minibus ride through the forest, but rides can be disappointing. To view there are Forest Department vans (for eight), Rs 80. Restricted zone viewing, 0630-1900, 1700-1830. Birdwatching from Kariam Shola watch tower, 2 km from Topslip.

There are some **trekking** routes that vary from easy treks to Pandaravara (8 km), Kozhikamuthi (12 km) to Perunkundru peak (32 km) which is demanding. Permits from Range Officer, Topslip. Private guides charge Rs 50 for two.



## Dindigul

Now a large market town, Dindigul, north of Madurai, commands a strategic gap between the **Sirumalai Hills** to its east and the **Palani Hills** to the west. The market handles the produce of the Sirumalai Hills, including a renowned local variety of banana. Dindigul is particularly known for its cheroots.

The massive granite rock and **fort** ⓘ *0730-1730, Rs 5, foreigners Rs 100, 2 km west of the bus stand, autos Rs 20*, towers over 90 m above the plain. The Mysore army captured it in 1745 and Haidar Ali was appointed Governor in 1755. It was ceded to the British under the Treaty of Seringapatam. There are magnificent views of the town, the valley and the hills on either side from the top of the rock fort. **Our Lady of Dolours Church**, one of several churches in the town, is over 250 years old and was rebuilt in 1970. The Old City is interesting to walk around; you can walk up to the fort from there. The station is 2 km south of the bus stand which has cheap lodges nearby.

## Sleeping

**Ooty** *p853, map p854*
Rates quoted are for the 'Season'. Good discounts Jul-Mar except during Puja and Christmas. Add 30% tax in upper categories. Winter nights can be bitterly cold and hotel fireplaces are often inadequate. Avoid the budget accommodation round Commercial Rd and Ettines Rd, particularly if you are a woman travelling alone.

**LL-L Fernhills Palace**, Fernhill Post, T0423-2443910-15. After years of stop-start renovation, Wodeyar, the current Mysore Maharajah is poised to open his ancestral palace as a luxury heritage hotel. It promises teak furniture, wooden panelling on walls and ceilings, fireplaces and jacuzzis in each of the 28 rooms, plus correspondingly high price tags.

**AL Savoy** (Taj), 77 Sylkes Rd, T0423-2444142. 40 well maintained rooms with huge wood doors and separate dressing areas. (**A** off-season.) Worth visiting for its interesting history and lovely gardens.

**B-C Hotel Regency Villa**, Fernhill Post, T0423-2442555, regency@sancharnet.in. The Maharajah of Mysore's staff had some of the best sunset views of the blue hills from their bungalows: today carpets are mismatched, paint is peeling, and the cheaper rooms are small and musty, but for all that the Regency, with its rows of colonial photographs, reeks of character too. Log fire fuel costs extra.

**C Glyngarth Heritage**, Golf Club Rd, Fingerpost (2 km from centre), T0423-2445754, glyngarth@sify.com. Just 5 huge double rooms with period furniture plus original fittings including all-teak floors and fireplaces in a 2-story Raj building – complete with metal roof – dating from 1853. Modern bathrooms, varied meals made from fresh garden produce, large grounds, clean, excellent service, tremendously characterful, good value. Walking distance to golf course.

**C-D Hotel Lakeview**, West Lake Rd, T0423-2443580, lakeview@md3.vsnl.net.in. A little bit of an Indian hillstation Butlins: 115 big rooms in rows of pinkish bungalows with fireplaces, TVs, and matching furniture. Lawns to sit out on with bus loads of domestic tourists.

**C-D The Nilgiri Woodlands**, Race Course Rd, T0423-2442551, nilgiris_woodlands@yahoo.com. 22 rooms ranging from paint-peeling doubles to spacious cottages. Shared veranda outside racecourse-facing rooms that give onto a garden and the pink/green/blue bungalows of Ooty central. Quiet and spacious rooms tucked round the back (without views) are best value.

**D Tamil Nadu** (TTDC), Charing Cross, up steps by Tourist Office, T0423-2444378. Rooms and penthouse with good views, restaurant, bar, exchange, pleasant hotel.

**D YWCA Anandagiri**, Ettines Rd, T0423-2442218. 32 rooms spread around large complex screened from town by pine trees, basic, a little institutional, with nice sitting rooms and dining hall, potted geraniums littered around. Pleasant, large cottages, dorm beds Rs 99.

**D-E Reflections Guest House**, North Lake Rd, T0423-2443834. 9 rooms (cheaper dorm beds), clean, homely, quiet with good views of the lake, pleasant dining and sitting room serving good food, friendly owners. Rs 50 for wood for the fire or to use the stove for your own cooking, restricted hot water.

**Coonoor** *p856*

Most hotels are 3-5 km from the station and bus stand.

**AL-A Taj Garden Retreat**, Church Rd, Upper Coonoor, T0423-2230021, www.tajhotels.com. 32 rooms, spacious cottage style and homely (**A** off-season), many with open fires, very well kept, good dining room though service can be slow, beautiful gardens, yoga studio, treadmill, table tennis, tennis, ayurvedic centre, although no pool. Wood-panelled high ceilinged bar, **The Hampton**, 1130-1500, 1830-2200. Lunch 1230-1500, dinner 1930-2230.

**A The Tryst**, Carolina Tea Estate, Coonoor, T0423-2207057, www.trystindia.com. The shelves at this homestay groan under years of hoarding, the playlist strictly jazz or Country and Western. 5 double rooms in this deceptively large house with well-stocked library, snooker table, games galore and gym. Unexpected and in an outstanding location away from all other accommodation cradled in the nape of a rolling tea estates. Excellent walking. Book in advance.

**E Tamil Nadu** (TTDC), Ooty Rd, Mt Pleasant (1 km north of station), T0423-2232813. Simple rooms, TV, restaurant, bar and Youth Hostel dorm.

**E 'Wyoming' Holiday Home** (YWCA), near Hospital, Upper Coonoor (auto from bus stand Rs 25), T0423-2234426. 8 large rooms and 2 dorms (8-bedded), in 2-storey house with both character and idyllic views, excellent food (no alcohol) but some warn

*For an explanation of the sleeping and eating price codes used in this guide, see inside the front cover. Other relevant information is found in Essentials pages 56-61.*

you should check bill and watch out for the neurotic Labrador who is known to bark through the night. Garden, friendly, helpful, popular. Manager qualified in alternative therapies (runs clinic and courses). Book ahead.

E **Top Hill Lodge**, near police station, Kotagiri. With rooms, restaurant and bar.

F **Blue Star**, Kotagiri, next to bus station. Rooms with shower and toilet in modern building.

### Mettupalayam *p856*

D **Saravana Bhavan**, out of town on Ooty road near gates to Black Thunder Water theme park. New and finding its feet.

E-F **Bharath Bharan**, 200 m from railway station. Very basic, some with bath and a/c, could be cleaner, quiet surroundings.

F **Surya International**, town centre, fairly clean rooms (Rs 150), rooftop restaurant, often empty, quiet, but characterless.

**Karna Hotel** in the bus station is good for *dosas*.

### Mudumalai Wildlife Sanctuary *p857*

Advance booking is essential especially during season and at weekends. Accommodation is better near Masinagudi which also has restaurants and shops but there is some in Bokkapuram, 3 km further south. Ask private lodges for pick-up if arriving by bus at Theppakadu.

B **Bamboo Banks Farm Guest House**, Masinagudi, T0423-2526222, bambanks@hotmail.com. 6 clean rooms, 4 in cottages in a fine setting, attractive garden, good food, birdwatching, riding, jeep.

C **Jungle Retreat**, Bokkapuram, T0423-2526469, www.jungleretreat.com. 5 large rooms and 7 cottages with modern baths, private terrace, superb views, "wonderful quiet place", friendly relaxed owners (Mr and Mrs Mathias), high standards, good treks with local guides, elephant rides, TCs accepted. Highly recommended.

C **Monarch Safari Park**, Bokkapuram, on a hill side, T0423-2526326. 14 rooms in twin *machan* huts on stilts with bath (sadly rats enter at night), open-sided restaurant, cycles, birdwatching, good riding (Rs 150 per hr), some sporting facilities, meditation centre, large grounds, "lovely spot", management a bit slack but friendly, if slow, service.

C-D **Blue Valley Resorts**, Bokkapuram, T0423-2526244. 8 comfortable huts (**C** suites), restaurants, scenic location, wildlife tours.

C-D **Jungle Hut**, near Bokkapuram, T0423-2526240. 12 clean, simple rooms with bath in 3 stone cottages in valley, good food – "lovely home cooking", pool, jeep hire, game viewing and treks, very friendly welcome. Recommended.

D **Forest Hills Farm**, 300 m from Jungle Hut, T0423-2526216. 6 modern rooms with bath and views, good food, friendly, game viewing. Recommended.

D **Jungle Trails**, 2 km off Sighur Ghat Rd (23 km from Ooty, ask bus to stop; flat walk, well marked), T0423-2526256. 3 clean rooms in a bungalow, rustic ("bamboo shutters propped open with poles"), dorm beds (Rs 100), and *machan* hut good for viewing the moving tapestry (4 trails and a water hole are visible). Meals Rs 200. The place is dedicated to animal watching: be quiet after dark, no candles on verandah, and no sitting in the garden by moonlight. Read *Cheetal Walk*, 1997, by A Davidas, the owner's father. Recommended.

D-E **Mountania**, Masinagudi (500 m from bus stand), T0423-2526337. Rooms in cottages (prices vary), "nice but a bit overpriced", restaurant, jeep tour to waterfalls, easy animal spotting (evening better than morning).

E **Tamil Nadu** (TTDC Youth Hostel), Theppakadu, T0423- 2526249. 3 rooms, 24 beds in dorm (Rs 45), restaurant, van for viewing. Several Government Forest Department huts charge Rs 80 for double rooms; reserve in advance through the Wildlife Warden, Mudumalai WLS, 1st floor, Mahalingam Building, Coonoor Rd, Ooty, T0423-244098 or Wildlife Warden, Kargudi.

F **Peacock**, Kargudi, dormitory, 50 beds, food excellent.

**Abhayaranyam Rest House**, Kargudi, 2 rooms.

**Annexe**, Kargudi, 2 rooms. Recommended.

**Minivet** and **Morgan**, Kargudi, dormitory, 8 and 12 beds. All Rs 5 per bed.

**Rest House** and **Annexe**, Kargudi, ask for deluxe rooms.

**Log House**, Masinagudi, 5 rooms.

**Rest House**, Masinagudi, 3 rooms.

**Coimbatore** *p857*

**B Heritage Inn**, 38 Sivaswamy Rd, T0422-2231451, www.hotelheritageinn.com. 63 modern, a/c rooms ('standard' good value), good restaurants, internet, excellent service.

**B Nilgiris Nest**, 739-A Avanashi Rd, T0422-2217247, nilgiris@md3.vsnl.net.in, 2 km railway. 38 a/c rooms, some small, restaurant, bar, amazing supermarket downstairs (for Western snacks and last stop for supplies like tampons), business facilities, roof garden. Recommended.

**B-C City Tower**, Sivaswamy Rd (just off Dr Nanjappa Rd), Gandhipuram, near bus stand, T0422-2230641, hotelcitytower@sify.com. 91 very good, redecorated rooms, some a/c, small balconies, 2 restaurants (ground floor; rooftop tandoori), no alcohol, very good service. Recommended.

**D-F Channma International**, 18/109 Big Bazar St, T0422-2396631. 36 spacious clean rooms, tiny windows, in oldish hotel with art deco styling, restaurant, internet, health club and pool next door.

**E-F KK Residency**, 7 Shastri Rd, by Central Bus Stand, Ramnagar, T0422-2232433. 42 smallish but clean rooms, 6 a/c, good condition, restaurant, friendly service. Recommended.

**E-F Meena**, 109 Kalingarayar St, T0422-2235420. 30 clean and pleasant rooms in small family-hotel, veg restaurant.

**Salem** *p857*

It is advisable to choose rooms away from the side of the road.

**C Salem Castle**, A-4 Bharati St, Swarnapuri, 4 km railway, T0427-2448702. Rather brash modern hotel with 64 comfortable, very clean a/c rooms. Restaurants (good Chinese but expensive, the rest are Indian-style), coffee shop, bar, exchange, pool.

**D-E City View**, Omalur Main Rd, T0427-2449715. Rooms with bath, some clean, strong a/c, meals, travel. **Shree Saravanabhavan** in the same block does good south Indian vegetarian.

**D-E Ganesh Mahal**, 323 Omalur Rd, T0427-2332820. 45 pleasant rooms, TV, good restaurant, bar. Modern and comfortable.

**D-E Raj Castle**, 320 Omalur Rd, T0427-2333532. 21 nicely fitted rooms, 4 a/c, some with balcony, TV, hot water mornings, tourist car.

**D-E Selvam**, T0427-2449331. Clean rooms with bath, some a/c, good restaurant.

**F Railway Retiring Rooms**, battered but with olde-worlde feel.

**Yercaud** *p858*

Most hotels offer off-season discounts Jan-Mar, Aug-Dec.

**C Sterling Resort**, near Lady's Seat, T04281-222700. 59 rooms (few **B** suites), modern, excellent views.

**D Shevaroys**, Main (Hospital) Rd, near lake, T04281-222288. 32 rooms, 11 **C** cottages with baths, restaurant, bar, good views.

**D Tamil Nadu** (TTDC), Salem-Yercaud Ghat Rd, near lake, behind Panchayat Office, T04281-222273. 12 rooms, restaurant, garden.

**E Kapilaksa**, Arthur Seat Rd (10-min walk from bus stand). Clean rooms, good views from balcony and roof, quiet, no discount.

**F Youth Hostel**, dorm bed (Rs 125), simple, reservations: Manager at Chennai, T04281- 2830390.

**Kodaikkanal** *p858, map p859 and p860*

More expensive hotels are some distance from the centre. Off-season rates are given. From Apr-Jun prices rise by 30-50%; 20% tax and service charges apply. On Anna Salai cheap basic lodges, mostly with shared bathroom, can charge Rs 400 in season.

**A Carlton**, Boat Club Rd, T04542-240056, carlton@krahejahospitality.com. 91 excellent rooms, fully modernized but colonial-style hotel. Excellent restaurant, billiards, tennis, golf and boating, superb position on lake, often full in season. Recommended.

**A-B Lake View** (Sterling), 44 Gymkhana Rd, T04542-240313. Cottages, modern hotel/apartment complex.

**B Valley View** (Sterling), Pallangi Rd, Vilpatti, T04542-240635. 39 modern rooms but most without valley view, half-board in season, a bit overpriced.

**C Green Acres**, 11/213 Lake Rd, T04542-242384. Well appointed, clean rooms in pleasant colonial-style home, quiet, peaceful.

**C RR Residency**, Boathouse Rd, T04542-244300, rrresidency@rediffmail.com. 7 well furnished, top quality rooms in new hotel though no views, veg restaurant next door.

**C-D Bala**, 11/49 Woodville Rd, opposite the bus station (entrance tucked away in private courtyard), T04542-241214, www.

balacares.com. Classy hotel, 57 rooms, good vegetarian restaurant, friendly staff.

**C-D Bison Wells Jungle Lodge**, Camp George Observatory, T04542-2240566, www.wilderness-explorer.com. This is truly for the nature purist: there's not even electricity, there's only space for a maximum of three in this cottage, a whole mountain range away from the rest of the hill station. Jeep transport from Kody arranged on request at extra cost.

**C-D Garden Manor**, Lake Rd (10-min walk from bus), T04542-240461. 7 rooms (including a 4-bed), restaurant with tables outdoors, good location in pleasant gardens overlooking lake.

**C-D J's Heritage**, PT Rd, T04542-241323, jaherit@md5.vsnl.net.in. 14 clean, comfortably furnished rooms, quiet, friendly and helpful management but perhaps expensive for what it is.

**C-D Tamil Nadu** (TTDC), 47 Fernhill Rd, T04542-241336. 15 mins' walk from Bus Station (away from most interesting walks), restaurant and bar.

**C-D Villa Retreat**, Coaker's Walk, T04542-240940, www.villaretreat.com. 8 deluxe rooms in an old house, 3 cottages (open fireplace), rustic, good service. Garden setting, excellent views, clean but overpriced.

**D Hilltop Towers**, Club Rd, T04542-240413, httowers@md3.vsnl.net in. 26 modern comfortable rooms, can be noisy but very friendly management, good restaurant, bakery. Recommended.

**D Kodai**, north end of Coaker's Walk, T04542-240632, krh@pronet.net.in. 50 well-furnished 'cottages' with balcony, great views, restaurant. Clean, spacious, quiet setting.

**D-E Suhaag**, opposite bus stand, T04542-241143. 20 comfortable rooms, TV, hot water; buses silent at night. Good value.

**E Jewel**, 7 Rd Junction, T04542-240518. 9 clean, adequate rooms, 24-hr hot water, friendly, good value.

**E Kay Pee Yem Lodge**, Anna Salai, T04542-240555. With 16 rooms.

**E Paradise Inn**, Laws Ghat Rd, T04542-241075. 40 comfortable spacious rooms now rather faded, but good views, restaurant.

**E Vignesh**, Laws Ghat Rd, near lake, T04542-244348. 6 spacious rooms (can interconnect) in old period-style house, good views, garden setting. Recommended.

**E-F Anjay**, Anna Salai, T04542-241080. 24 adequate rooms with balcony, popular.

**E-F Sunrise**, PO Rd. Basic, but clean, rooms with bath, front rooms best with excellent views, good value.

**F Railway Station**, cheap rooms and dorm.

### Youth hostels

**F Greenlands**, St Mary's Rd, Coaker's Walk end, T04542-240899. 15 very basic, clean rooms (jug and bucket of hot water 0700-0900), overpriced at Rs 225 but amazing views. There are a few new rooms which are less atmospheric but have hot water on tap. Pleasant gardens, 62-bed dorm (Rs 55-65). Clean, but food poor and student groups can be noisy.

**F Youth Hostel** (TTDC), Fernhill Rd, T04542-241336. **D** rooms, dorm beds (Rs 60-1255).

### Around Kodaikkanal *p860*

**E Sakti**, Pollachi. Newish, large and smart, rooms, vegetarian restaurant.

**F Forest Rest Houses**, Top Slip, Mt Stuart, Varagaliar, Sethumadai and Amaravathi-nagar. May only allow 1 night stay. Reservations: District Forest Officer, Coimbatore S Div, Mahalingam Nagar, Pollachi, T04259-22508. The friendly canteen serves good *dosa* and *thalis* for lunch.

### Dindigul *p861*

**B Cardamom House**, Athoor village, Kamarajar Lakeside, T0451-2624710. 7 rooms spread across three buildings all with lake views tucked out of the way at the foothills of the Palani hills overlooking the birdlife-rich lake. The pretty home of a retired British doctor from Southsea introduces you to Tamil village life in Athoor: it is a good bridge for journeys between either Kerala and Tamil Nadu or Trichy and Madurai.

**C-D Maha Jyothi**, Spencer Compound, T0451- 2434313, hotelmahajyothi@rediff mail.com. Range of rooms, a/c, clean, modern.

**D Sukanya Lodge**, by bus stand. Small, rather dark a/c rooms, but very clean, friendly staff, good value.

**F Prakash**, 9 Thiruvalluvar Salai, T0451-2423577. 42 clean, spacious rooms. Recommended.

**F Venkateshwar Lodge**, near bus stand, T0451-2425881. 50 rooms, basic, clean, very cheap; vegetarian restaurant next door.

## Eating

### Ooty *p853, map p854*

There are usually bars in larger hotels. Southern Star is recommended, though pricey.

**Savoy**, olde-worlde wood-panelled dining hall serving up and good food. Also has bar, café, snooker and table tennis halls.

**Chandan Vegetarian**, Nahar Nilgiris, Charing Cross, T0423-2442173. 1230-1530, 1900-2230. Roomy restaurant inside the Nahar hotel complex serving up vegetarian north Indian and Chinese food.

**The Pavilion**, Fortune Hotel, Sullivan Court, 123 Shelbourne Rd, T0423- 2441415. Half a kilometre from town in the modern hotel: good multi-cuisine plus separate bar.

**Blue Hills**, Charing Cross. Good value Indian and Continental, non-vegetarian.

**Garden Café**, Nahar Nilgiris, Charing Cross. 0730-2130. Lawn-side coffee shop and snack bar with South Indian menu: *iddli*, *dosa* and *chats* from Rs 30.

**Hot Breads**, Charing Cross. Tasty hot dogs, pizzas etc.

**Hotel Ooty Saravanaa's**, 302 Commercial Rd. 0730-1000, 1130-2230. The place for super-cheap south Indian breakfast: large mint green place that does a fast trade in *iddli*, *dosa* and meals.

**Sharma Bhojanalaya** 12C Lower Bazar Rd. Gujarati and North Indian food served upstairs in comfortable (padded banquettes) but not aesthetically pleasing venue, overlooks race course, good vegetarian lunch *thali* (Rs 40).

**Shinkow's**, 38/83 Commissioner's Rd (near Collector's Office) T0423-2442811. Authentic Chinese, popular, especially late evening. Chicken chilli Rs 120. Tartan tablecloths and fishtank. Highly recommended. 1200-1545, 1830-2145.

#### Cafés

Try the local institutions **Sugar Daddy** and **King Star** (established in 1942) for brilliant homemade chocolates like fruit'n'nut and fudges 1130-2030.

**Nilgiri Dairy Farms** outlets sell quality milk products.

### Coonoor *p856*

**Velan Hotel Ritz**, Bedford, T0423-2230632. 0730-1030, 1230-1530, 1930-2230. Good multi-cusine restaurant overlooking the Ritz's lawns – don't expect speedy service though.

**The Only Place**, Sim's Park Rd. Simple, homely, good food.

**Sri Lakshmi**, next to bus station. Freshly cooked, quality veg; try *paneer* butter masala and *Kashmiri naan*.

### Coimbatore *p857*

**Cloud Nine**, City Tower Hotel. Excellent views from rooftop of one of city's tallest buildings, good international food (try asparagus soup), buzzy atmosphere especially when it's full of families on Sun evening, and pleasant service but slightly puzzling menu.

**Dakshin** in Shree Annapoorna Hotel Complex, 47 East Arokiasamy Rd, RS Puram. International. Very smart serving good food.

**Dasa**, vegetarian. A/c, good ice creams.

**Solai Drive-in**, Nehru Stadium, near VOC Park. Chinese, Indian food and good ice creams.

**Indian Coffee House**, Ramar Koil St. South Indian snacks.

**Royal Hindu**, opposite Junction station. Indian vegetarian.

### Kodaikkanal *p858, map p859*

**Carlton Hotel**, set in very pleasant grounds overlooking lake and Garden Manor, good for tea and snacks.

**Tava**, Hospital Rd, very good Indian.

**Royal Tibet Hotel**, J's Heritage Complex, "try noodle soup and beef momos".

**Silver Inn**, Hospital Rd. Travellers' breakfasts and Indian choices. Popular but slow service.

**Tibetan Brothers Hotel**, J's Heritage Complex. 1200-2200 (closed 1600-1730) serves excellent Tibetan, homely atmosphere, good value. Highly recommended.

**Apna Punjab** in 7 Rd (Indian).

#### Bakery and fast food

**Eco-Nut**, J's Heritage Complex, good whole foods, brown bread, jams, peanut butter etc (cheese, yoghurts, better and cheaper in **Dairy** across the road).

**Hot Breads**, J's Heritage Complex. For very good pastries.

**Jacob**, Main Bazar. Vasu, Lake Rd near Telephone Exchange.

**Pastry Corner Anna Salai Bazar**, has brown bread and some pastries.
**Philco's Cold Storage**, opposite Kodai International School, J's Heritage Complex. For homemade choc, cakes, frozen foods, delicatessen. Also Internet.
**Spencer's Supermarket**, Club Rd. Has a wide range of local and foreign products (cheeses).
**Manna Bakery** on Bear Shola Rd. Also serves pizzas and western vegetarian.

**Dindigul** *p861*
**Cascade Roof Garden**, at Sree Arya Bhavan, 19 KHF Building, near the bus stand, which serves very good vegetarian. West of the bus stand, Main Road is the shopping area.
**Janakikarm**, near new Roman Catholic Church. Don't miss their pizzas, sweets and snacks, surprisingly good value – "*channa samosa* to die for".

## Festivals and events

**Ooty** *p853, map p854*
**Jan**: Pongal. **May**: the **Annual Flower and** Dog Shows in the Botanical Gardens. Summer Festival of cultural programmes with stars from all over India.

**Kodaikkanal** *p858, map p859*
**May**: Summer Tourist Festival: Boat race, flower show, dog show etc.

## Shopping

**Ooty** *p853, map p854*
Most shops open 0900-1200, 1500-2000. The smaller shops keep longer hours.
**Higginbotham's**, Commercial Rd, Ooty, T0423-2443736. 0930-1300, 1550-1930, closed Wed. Bookseller.
**Toda Showroom**, Charing Cross, sells silver and tribal shawls.
**Variety Hall**, Silver Market, old family firm (1890s) for good range of silk, helpful, accepts credit cards.

**Kodaikkanal** *p858, map p859*
**Belgian Convent** shop, east of town. Has hand embroidered linen.
**Cottage Crafts Shop**, Anna Salai (Council for Social Concerns in Kodai). Volunteer-run, 0900-1230, 1400-1830, Mon-Sat.
**Govt Sales Emporium** near Township Bus Stand. Only open in season.
**Kashmir Handicrafts Centre**, 2 North Shopping Complex, Anna Salai. For shawls, jewellery, brass, walnut wood crafts and 'Numdah' rugs.
**Khadi Emporium, Handloom Co-op, Travancore Craft Works**, Post Office Rd.

## Activities and tours

**Ooty** *p853, map p854*
**Horse riding**
**Gymkhana Club**, T0423- 2442254. Big bar open 1130-1530 or 1830-2300. temporary membership; beautifully situated amidst superbly maintained 18-hole golf course. Riding from Regency Villa: Rs 500 for 2 hrs with 'guide'; good fun but no helmets.

**Tours**
Reservations, **TTDC**, Hotel Tamil Nadu, T0423-2444370. Ooty and Mudumalai: Ooty Lake, Dodabetta Peak, Botanical Gardens, Mudumalai Wildlife Sanctuary. 0830-2000. Rs 150. Kotagiri and Coonoor: Kotagiri, Kodanad View Point, Lamb's Rock, Dolphin's Nose, Sim's Park. 0830-1830. Rs 130.
**Woodlands Tourism**, Race Course Rd, T0423-2442551. Offers Ooty and Coonoor: 0930-1730. Rs 130. Stunning views.

**Tour operators**
**Blue Mountain**, Nahar Complex, Charing Cross, T0423-2443650. Luxury coach bookings to neighbouring states.
**George Hawkes**, 52C Nahar Complex, T0423-2442756. For tourist taxis.
**Sangeetha Travels**, 13 Bharathiyar Complex, Charing Cross, T0432-2444782. Steam train.

**Yoga**
**Rajayoga Meditation Centre**, 88 Victoria Hall, Ettines Rd.

**Coonoor** *p856*
**TTDC** from Ooty (reserve in Ooty Tourist Office). Coonoor-Kotagiri Rs 120, 6 hrs; visiting Valley View, Sim's Park, Lamb's Rock, Dolphin's Nose, Kodadu view point.

**Yercaud** *p858*
Tourist information at **Hotel Tamil Nadu**, T04281-22273.

**Kodaikkanal** *p858, map p859*

**Boating**

**Boat Club**, T04542-241315. Allows daily membership with club facilities. 0900-1730.
**TTDC Boathouse**, next door. 0900-1730.

**Golf**

**Club**, T04542-240323.

**Riding**

Ponies near the Boat House; officially Rs 100 per hr, doubled to include 'guide' (bargaining essential).

**Tour operators**

**Sugam**, PO Rd, Upper Coonoor, Railway Out Agency.
**Vijay Tours**, near Tourist Information Centre, Anna Salai, T04542-241137. Local sights, Rs 70-80 per person.

## Transport

**Ooty** *p853, map p854*

Arrive early for buses to ensure a seat. They often leave early if full. Ghat roads have numerous hairpin bends which can have fairly heavy traffic and very bad surfaces at times. The Gudalur road passes through Mudumalai and Bandipur sanctuaries (see page 857). You might see an elephant herd and other wildlife – especially at night.

**Air**

Nearest airport, Coimbatore, 105 km. Taxis available.

**Bus**

Cheran, T04223-2443970. Frequent buses to **Coonoor** (every 10 mins, 0530-2045), **Coimbatore** (every 20 mins, 0530-2000, 3½ hrs) and **Mettupalayam** (0530-2100, 2 hrs). Also to **Bangalore** (0630-2000), **Mysore** (0800-1530, 3½-5 hrs) and **Kozhikode** (0630-1515), **Chennai** (1630-1830), **Palakkad** (0715-1515), **Palani** (0800-1800). Daily buses to **Kannur** (0915, 2000), **Hassan** (1130, 1500), **Kanniyakumari** (1745), **Kodaikkanal** (0630, 9½ hrs via magnificent route through Palani, Madikere (0700, 1100), **Pondicherry** (1700), **Salem** (1300). Check timings. Several on the short route (36 km) to **Masinagudi/Mudumalai**, Rs 7, 1½ hrs; a steep and windy but interesting road.

**Train**

Railway station, T0423-2442246. From **Mettupalayam** *Blue Mountain* (steam to **Coonoor**; then diesel to Ooty), 2 return-trains daily, see Mettupalayam transport, below. The *Heritage Steam Chariot* to **Runneymede** runs at weekends (more frequent in season). It departs Ooty 1000, returns 1600 (delayed when engine runs out of steam!). Highly recommended. Tickets include Indian packed lunch: Rs 280, or Rs 550 in Maharaja coach, from *Sangeetha* (listed above) or Ooty railway station.

**Coonoor** *p856*

**Bus**

Frequent buses to **Ooty** (every 10 mins from 0530) some via Sim's Park and many via Wellington. Also regular services to **Kotagiri** and **Coimbatore** (every 30 mins) through **Mettupalayam**. Direct bus to **Mysore** (or change at Ooty).

**Train**

The *Blue Mountain Railway* runs from **Mettupalayam** to Coonoor (steam), 3 hrs; continues to **Ooty** (diesel), 1½ hrs. See Mettupalayam transport, below. The *Heritage Steam Chariot* runs from Ooty to **Runneymede** beyond Coonoor. See Ooty transport, above.

**Mettupalayam** *p856*

The *Nilgiri Exp* from Chennai via Coimbatore, connects with the *Blue Mountain Railway*. (This line is subject to landslides and washouts that can close the route for some months. Check before travelling.) From **Chennai** *6605*, 2015, 10 hrs; to Chennai, *6606*, 1925, 10½ hrs. For those coming from Coimbatore, it is better to arrive in advance at Mettupalayam by bus; this avoids a mad dash at the station from Platform 2 to 1 to catch the connecting train.

The first part of the *Blue Mountain Railway* from Mettupalayam to Coonoor is by steam when not disrupted by landslides (great to look around the engine sheds!); from there to Ooty by diesel. To **Coonoor** and **Ooty** 2 return trains daily; *562(S)*, 0710, arrive Coonoor, 1030, Ooty, 1200 (5½ hrs); return from Ooty, *561(S)*, 1500, arrive Coonoor, 1605, Mettupalayam 1835, 3½ hrs. Also *564(S)*, 1315, arrive Coonoor, 1610,

Ooty, 1745; return from Ooty next day *567(S)*, 0915, arrive Coonoor, 1025, Mettupalayam 1245. The *Heritage Steam Chariot* runs from Ooty to Runneymede. See Ooty above.

**Mudumalai Wildlife Sanctuary** *p857*
Theppakadu is on the Mysore-Ooty bus route. From **Mysore**, services from 0615 (1½-2 hrs); last bus to Mysore around 2000. From **Ooty** via **Gudalur** on a very winding road (about 2½ hrs); direct 20 km steep road used by buses, under 1 hr. Few buses between Theppakadu and Masinagudi.

Jeeps are available at bus stands and from lodges.

**Coimbatore** *p857*
**Air**
Peelamedu Airport, 12 km centre, runs airport coach into town, Rs 25; taxis Rs 150-200; auto-rickshaw Rs 85. On Trichy Rd: **Indian Airlines**, T0422-2399833, airport T0422-2574623, 1000-1300, 1345-1730. To **Bangalore**, **Chennai**, **Delhi**, **Kochi**, **Kozhikode**, **Mumbai**. Jet Airways: 1055/1 Gowtham Centre, Avinashi Rd, T0422-2212034, airport T0422-2575375 to **Bangalore**, **Chennai**, **Mumbai**.

**Bus**
City buses run a good service: several connect the bus stations in Gandhipuram with the Junction Railway Station 2 km south. No 20 goes to the airport (Rs 20).

There are 4 long-distance bus stations, off Dr Nanjappa Rd. **City or 'Town' Bus Stand** in Gandhipuram. **Thiruvallur Bus Stand**, Cross Cut Rd. Computerized reservations 0700-2100, T0422-226700. Frequent Government Express buses to **Madurai** (5 hrs), **Chennai** (12 hrs), **Mysore** (6 hrs), **Ooty** (3 hrs), **Tiruchirappalli** (5½ hrs). **'Central' Bus Stand** is further south, on corner of Shastri Rd. State buses to **Bangalore** and **Mysore**; **Ooty** via **Mettupalayam** (see below for train connection) and **Coonoor** every 20 mins, 0400-2400, 5 hrs. **Ukkadam Bus Stand**, south of the city, serves towns within the state (**Pollachi**, **Madurai**) and in northern Kerala (**Pallakad**, **Thrissur**, **Munnar**).

**Taxi**
Tourist taxis and yellow top taxis are available at the bus stations, railway station and taxi stands. Rs 2.50 per km; for out-station hill journeys, Rs 3 per km; minimum Rs 30.

**Train**
Junction Station, enquiries, T132, reservations, T131, 0700-1300, 1400-2030. **Bangalore**: *Tilak Exp, 1014*, 0515, 7¼ hrs; *Intercity Exp, 2678*, 1425, 7 hrs; *Kanniyakumari Bangalore Exp, 6525*, 1955, 9 hrs. **Chennai**: *West Coast Exp, 6628*, 0630, 9 hrs; *Kovai Exp, 2676*, 1340, 7½ hrs; *Nilgiri Exp, 6606*, 2040, 9¼ hrs. **Kochi (HT)**: *Tiruchirappalli-Kochi Exp, 6865*, 0045, 5½ hrs; *Hyderabad-Kochi Exp, 7030*, 0935, daily, 5½ hrs. Other trains: *W Coast Exp (Chennai – Coimbatore – Kozhikode – Bangalore)*, daily to Kozhikode (4½ hrs) and Bangalore (9 hrs). For **Ooty**, train departing 0625 connects with narrow gauge steam train from Mettupalayam. Line to Coonoor is subject to landslides. Narrow gauge diesel from Coonoor to Ooty. There are two connecting trains daily: *Nilgiri Exp, 6605*, 0525, change to train *562 (S)*, 0710, arrive Ooty 1200; *Trichur-Mettypalayam Pass, 534 (S)*, 1100, change to train *564 (S)*, 1315 arrive Ooty 1745.

**Salem** *p857*
**Bus**
The new bus stand (T0427-2265917), north of the Hospital, off Omalur Rd, has buses to **Namakkal**, 1¼ hrs. Salem is well connected by bus with all major towns in Tamil Nadu, Kerala and South Karnataka. TN Government Express buses, to **Dindigul**, 4 hrs.

**Train**
Junction is the main station. Enquiries, T132. Reservations, T131, 0700- 1300, 1400-2030. **Bangalore**: *Tilak Exp, 1014*, 0750, 4½ hrs; *Intercity Exp, 2678*, 1705, 4 hrs. **Chennai (C)**: *Coimbatore-Chennai Exp, 2680*, 0835, 5 hrs. **Kochi (HT) (Cochin)**: *Hyder-abad Cochin Exp, 7030*, 0615, not Tue, 9 hrs; *Raptisagar Exp, 5012/5222*, 0830, Mon, Thu, Fri, Sun, 9¾ hrs. **Madurai**: *Mumbai-Nagercoil Exp, 6339*, not Tue, Wed, Sun, 1735, 6 hrs. **Ramesvaram**: no direct trains, change at Dindigul. For **Ooty**, *Nilgiri Exp, 6605*, 0135, connects with narrow gauge steam train from Mettupalayam; departs from **Mettupalayam** at 0745, arrives Ooty at 1200.

**Yercaud** *p858*
There are no local buses but some from Salem (1 hr) continue through town and connect with nearby villages.

**Kodaikkanal** *p858, map p859*
**Bicycle**
Bikes can be hired at the top of the bazaar. JM Tea shop and cycle hire, at Junction of Club Rd and Anna Salai, good bikes Rs 5 per hr, Rs 50 per day.

**Bus**
Check timings; reservations possible. To **Bangalore**, overnight, 12 hrs; **Chennai** (497 km) 12 hrs, **Coimbatore** (171 km) 6 hrs; **Dindigul** (90 km) 3½ hrs, Kodai Rd, **Madurai** (120 km), 0730-1830, 4 hrs, about Rs 25; **Kumily** (Periyar), 1415, 5½ hrs, Rs 35 (very busy) change buses at Vatigundu; **Palani** (65 km) 3 hrs; **Tiruchirappalli** (197 km) 5 hrs, during the season.

**Taxi**
Unmetered taxis available. Tourist taxis only from Madurai.

**Train**
Reservations, Jayaraj Hall, Coaker's Walk Rd. **Kodai Road**, 80 km away, is the nearest station.

**Around Kodaikkanal** *p860*
From chaotic bus station at Pollachi (for Parambikulam) 0600, 1130, 1500 (check timings); ask for Top Slip, from Perambikulam, 0700, 1300.

**Dindigul** *p861*
Good and frequent bus service to **Tiruchirappalli**, **Chennai**, **Salem** and **Coimbatore** as well as longer distance connections.

Train to **Chennai (ME)** *Vaigai Exp, 2636* (AC/CC), 0745, 6¾ hrs via **Tiruchirappalli** 1½ hrs. **Madurai** *Vaigai Exp, 2635* (AC/CC), 1905, 1¼ hrs. Broad gauge to **Karur** 2240, 1½ hrs.

## Directory

**Ooty** *p853, map p854*
**Banks** State Bank of India, on Bank Rd, deals in foreign exchange. **Internet** Gateways, 8/9 Moosa Sait Complex, Commercial Rd. Excellent, fast, ISDN lines, Rs 30 per hr. **Hospital** Govt Hospital, Hospital Rd, T0423-2442212. **Post** Head Post Office, Collectorate and Telegraph Office, Town W Circle. **Tourist offices** Tamil Nadu, 7/72 Commercial Rd, Super Market, Charing Cross, T0423-2443977, lacks efficiency. **Useful addresses** Police, T100. Wildlife Warden, 1st floor, Mahalingam Building, T0423-244098, 1000-1300, 1400-1730.

**Coonoor** *p856*
**Banks** Travancore Bank, Upper Coonoor, (Bedford Circle) changes cash. South Indian Bank, Mount Rd, 1000-1400 changes cash and TCs. **Hospital** Lawley Hospital, Mt Rd, T0423-2231050.

**Yercaud** *p858*
**Banks** Banks with foreign exchange are on Main Rd. **Hospitals** Govt Hospital, 1 km from Bus Stand; Providence Hospital, on road to Lady's Seat. **Post** On the Main Rd.

**Coimbatore** *p857*
**Banks** Several on Oppankara St. State Bank of India (exchange upstairs), and Bank of Baroda are on Bank Rd. **Hospital** Government Hospital, Trichy Rd. **Post** Near flyover, Railway Feeder Rd, fax. **Travel agents** Alooha, corner near Heritage Inn, helpful. **Useful addresses** Automobile Association, 42 Trichy Rd, T0422-2222994.

**Kodaikkanal** *p858, map p859*
**Banks** Several on Anna Salai, 1000-1400 Mon to Fri, 1000-1200 Sat. Indian Bank, for 15-min service. Hotel Tamil Nadu, has an exchange counter. **Hospitals** Van Allan Hospital, T04542-241273, is recommended. Consultations (non- emergency): 0930-1200, 1530-1630 Mon-Fri. 1000-1200 Sat. Clean and efficient, good doctors (not inclined to prescribe antibiotics unnecessarily). Government Hospital, T04542-241292. **Post** Head Post Office on Post Office Rd. Others in Main Bazar, Observatory, Lake View, Anantha Giri, Pambapuram and Shenbaganur. **Tourist offices** Tamil Nadu, Rest House, near bus stand, T04542-241675. 1000-1745, except holidays. Helpful staff, maps available.

# Madurai and around

→ *Phone code: 0452. Colour map 3, grid C4. Population: 922,900.*

*Madurai is a maddening whirl of a temple town: on any single day 10,000 pilgrims arrive to tour the sanctuary of the 'fish-eyed goddess'. A whole host of small-scale businesses unfurls along the streets radiating out like bicycle spokes from the temple. With beggars, Brahmins and babies all vying for your buck, it can feel overwhelming to the Westerner, no matter how hardened. There is the usual combination of messy crumbling buildings harking back to times of greater architectural aspirations, modern glass-and-chrome palaces, internet cafés and Kashmiri antique and shawl dealers. The centre seems all dust and cycle-rickshaws, but Madurai, as the second biggest city in Tamil Nadu, is also a modern industrial place that never sleeps. Around the city the area of fertile agricultural land is dotted with exotically shaped granite mountain ranges such as Nagamalai ("snake hills") and Yanaimalai ("elephant hills").* » *For Sleeping, Eating and other listings, see pages 880-884.*

## Ins and outs

**Getting there** The airport is 12 km from town and is linked by buses to the city centre, but there are also taxis and autos. The railway station is within easy walking distance of many budget hotels (predatory rickshaw drivers/hotel touts may tell you otherwise). Hire an auto to reach the few north of the river. The main express bus stand is next to the station though there are two others 3-6 km away, with bus links between them. » *See Transport, page 883, for further details.*

**Getting around** The city centre is compact and the temple is within easy walking distance of most budget hotels. Prepare for hordes of touts. To visit the sights around the city, buses and taxis are available.

**Tourist information** ⓘ *W Veli St, T0452-2337471, 1000-1745, Mon-Fri,* has useful maps, tours arranged through agents, guides for hire. Also at Madurai Junction Railway Station ⓘ *Main Hall, 0630-2030,* and airport counter, during flight times.

# Madurai

## History

According to legend, drops of nectar fell from Siva's locks on this site, so it was named 'Madhuram' or Madurai, the nectar city. The city's history goes back to the sixth century BC. Ancient Madurai, which traded with Greece and Rome, was a centre of Tamil culture, famous for its writers and poets during the last period of the three *'Sangam'* (Tamil 'Academies') nearly 2,000 years ago. The Pandiyans, a major power from the sixth to the beginning of the 10th century, made Madurai their capital. For the following 300 years, they remained here, although they were subservient to the Cholas who gained control over the area, after which the Pandiyans returned to power. For a short period it became a Sultanate after Malik Kafur completely destroyed the city in 1310. In 1364 it was captured by Hindu Vijayanagar kings, who remained until 1565, after which the local governors the Nayakas asserted their independence.

*William Dalrymple explains in* The Age of Kali *that the Vaigai River, along whose banks Madurai is laid out, "was created by Lord Sundareshvara, the husband of Minakshi, to quench the thirst of one of his wedding guests, a dwarf named Pot Belly who had developed an unbearable thirst after eating three hundred pounds of rice."*

After the defeat of Vijayanagar by the Muslim sultans of the Deccan, the Hindu rulers were pushed further south. The **Nayakas** emerged in the 17th century with their capital at Madurai and continued to build temple complexes with tall *gopurams*. These increased in height to become dominating structures covered profusely with plaster decorations. The tall *gopurams*of Vijayanagar and Nayaka periods may have served a strategic purpose, but they moved away from the earlier *Chola* practice of giving the central shrine the tallest tower. The *kalyana mandapa* or marriage hall with a 'hundred' or 'thousand' pillars, and the temple tank with steps on all four sides, were introduced in some southern temples, along with the *Nandi* bull, Siva's 'vehicle', which occupies a prominent position at the entrance to the main Shaivite shrine.

By the fourth century, Madurai, Tirunelveli and a part of southern Kerala were under the **Pandiyas**. Their power rose after the decline of the Cholas and they ruled from 1175 to 1300. In the 13th century, international trade flourished under their control and was only superseded by the rise of Vijayanagar (see Hampi, page 1011).

The defeat of the great Vijayanagar Empire by a confederacy of Muslim states in 1565 forced their leaders south. As the Nayaka kings they continued to rule from as far south as Madurai well into the 17th century. Ultimately when Muslim political control finally reached Tamil Nadu it was as brief as it was tenuous.

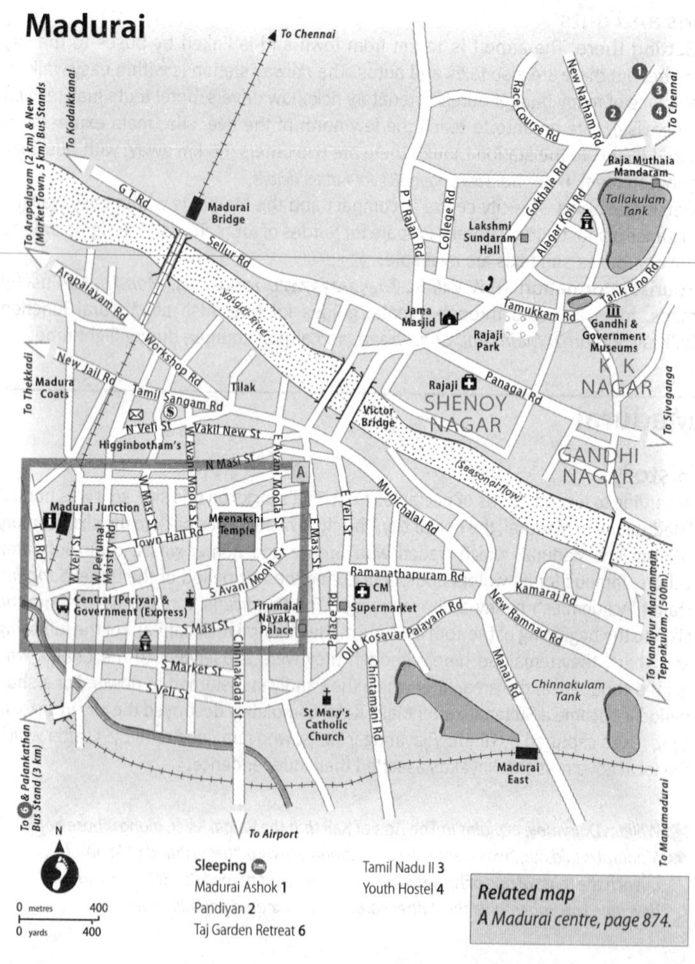


*Related map*
*A Madurai centre, page 874.*

The Nayakas have been seen essentially as warriors, given an official position by the Vijayanagar rulers; though in Sanskrit, the term applied to someone of prominence and leadership. Burton Stein comments, "the history of the Vijayanagara is essentially the history of the great Telugu Nayakas" from Madurai.

The Vijayanagar kings were great builders and preserved and enriched the architectural heritage of the town. The Nayakas laid out the old town in the pattern of a lotus with narrow streets surrounding the Minakshi Temple at the centre. The streets on the four sides of the central temple are named after the festivals which take place in them and give their relative direction, for example South 'Masi' Street, East 'Avanimoola' Street and East 'Chitrai' Street. The greatest of the Nayaka rulers, Thirumalai (ruled 1623-1655), built the *gopurams* of the temple. In 1840, after the Carnatic Wars, the British destroyed the fort, filling in the surrounding moat (its original site now followed by the four Veli streets).

## Sights

**Meenakshi Temple** ⓘ *Inner Temple 0500-1230, 1600-2130, camera fee Rs 30, video not allowed, tickets at South Entrance (valid for multiple entry), the sanctuary is open only to Hindus, art museum 0600-2000, Rs 2, camera fee Rs 30 at the temple office near the South Tower – good views from the top of the South Gate when open*. This is an outstanding example of Vijayanagar temple architecture, exactly contemporary with the Taj Mahal in Agra. Meenakshi, the 'fish-eyed goddess' and the consort of Siva, has a temple to the south, and Sundareswarar (Siva), a temple to the west. Since she is the presiding deity the daily ceremonies are first performed in her shrine and, unlike the practice at other temples, Sundareswarar plays a

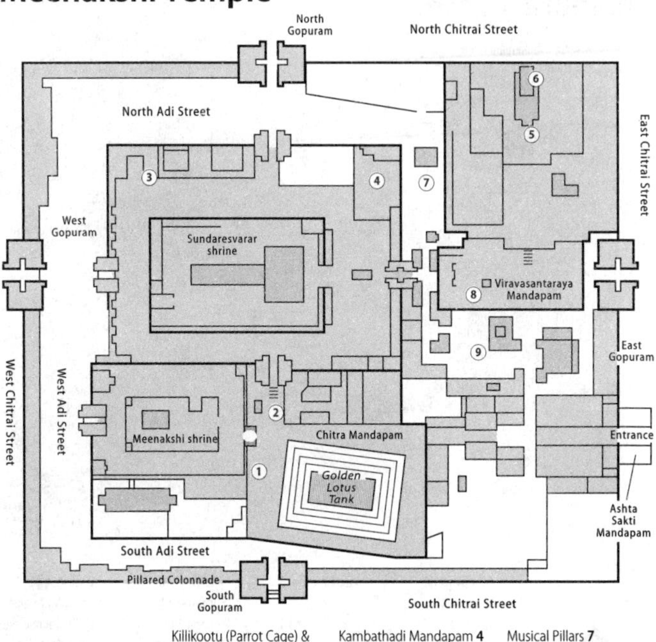

Killikootu (Parrot Cage) & Oonjal (Swing) Mandapams **1**
Subrahmanya Shrine **2**
Tamil Sangam College **3**
Kambathadi Mandapam **4**
Ayirakkal Mandapam, 'Thousand Pillared Hall' & Museum **5**
Sabhapati Shrine **6**
Musical Pillars **7**
Nandi Pavillion **8**
Kalyan Mandapam **9**

secondary role. The temple's nine towering *gopurams* stand out with their colourful stucco images of gods, goddesses and animals which are renewed and painted every 12 years. There are about 4,000 granite sculptures on the lower levels. In addition to the Golden Lotus tank and various pillared halls there are five *vimanas* over the sanctuaries.

The temple is a hive of activity, with a colourful temple elephant, flower sellers and performances by **musicians** ⓘ *1800-1930, 2100-2200*. At 2110 an image of Sundareswarar is carried in procession (worth attending) from the shrine near the east *gopuram* to Meenakshi, to 'sleep' by her side, and is returned the next morning. The procession around the temple is occasionally led by the elephant and a cow. During the day the elephant is on continual duty, 'blessing' visitors with its trunk and then collecting a small offering. A banana pleases him enormously, but not his keeper! The flower and vegetable market, north end of East Chitrai Street, is colourful but watch out for the holes in the floor. You may be troubled by touts who suggest good vantage points for viewing which invariably turn out to be roofs of nearby shops.

The **main entrance** is through a small door of the *Ashta Sakthi Mandapa* (Porch of the Eight Goddesses) which projects from the wall, south of the eastern *gopuram*. Inside, to the left is the sacred Tank of the Golden Lotus, with a lamp in the centre, surrounded by pillared cloisters and steps down to the waters. The Sangam legend speaks of the test that ancient manuscripts had to undergo – they were thrown into the sacred tank, if they sank they were worthless, if they floated they were considered worthy! The north gallery has 17th-century murals, relating 64 miracles said to have been performed by Siva, and the southern has marble inscriptions of the 1,330 couplets of the *Tamil Book of Ethics*. To the west of the tank is the *Oonjal Mandapa*,



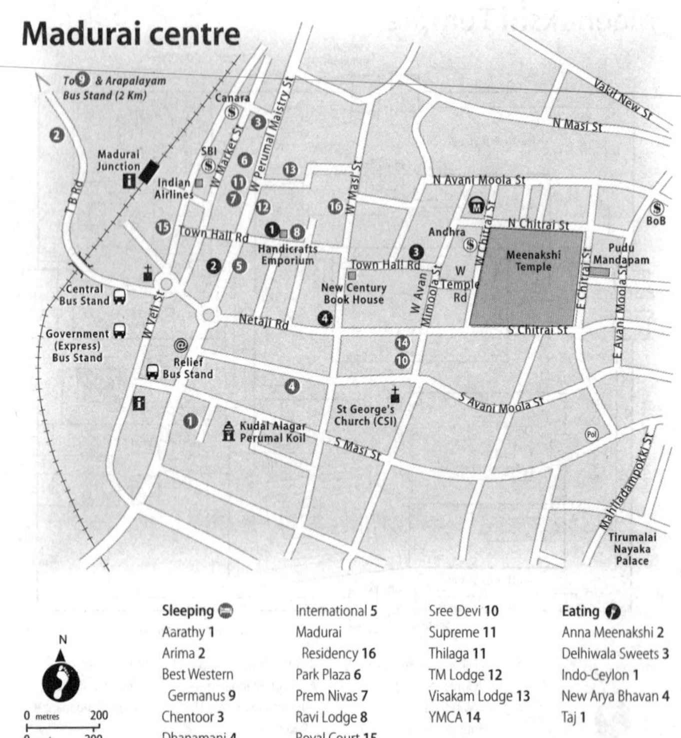

the pavilion leading to the Meenakshi shrine. Here the pillars are carved in the form of the mythical beast *yali* which recurs in temples throughout the region. Golden images of Meenakshi and Sundareswarar are brought to the *oonjal* or swing each Friday evening where they are worshipped. Cages with parrots, Meenakshi's green bird which brings luck, hung from the ceiling of the neighbouring *Kilikootu Mandapam* which is flanked by finely carved columns. The *Meenakshi shrine* with the principal image of the goddess, stands in its own enclosure with smaller shrines around it.

To the north of the tank is another enclosure with smaller *gopurams* on four sides within which is the **Sundareswarar shrine** guarded by two tall *dwarapalas*. In the northeast corner, the superb sculptures of the divine marriage of Meenakshi and Sundareswarar being blessed by Vishnu and Brahma, and Siva in his 24 forms are in the 19th-century *Kambathadi Mandapa*, around the golden flagstaff.

The thousand-pillared hall, mid-16th century, is in the northeast corner of the complex. The 985 exquisitely carved columns include a lady playing the *vina*, a dancing Ganesh, and a gypsy leading a monkey. The **art museum** here exhibits temple art and architecture, fine brass and stone images, friezes and photos (the labelling could be improved). Just inside the museum to the right is a cluster of five musical pillars carved out of a single stone. Each pillar produces a different note which vibrates when tapped. Nayaka musicians could play these as an instrument.

The **Nandi pavilion** is to the east and is often occupied by flower sellers. The long *Pudu Mandapa* (New Mandapa), with its beautiful sculptures of *yalis* and Nayaka rulers and their ministers, is outside the enclosure wall, between the east tower and the base of the unfinished *Raya Gopuram* which was planned to be the tallest in the country.

Northeast of the Meenakshi Temple, off N Avani Moola Street, is the **flower market**, at its best from 0500-0730. It is a two-storey hall with piles of jasmine of all colours, lotuses, and huge jumbles of heaped floral prettiness in a sea of decomposing mulch of flowers trampled underfoot.

**Thirumalai Nayaka Palace** ⓘ *0900-1300, 1400-1700, bus 17, 17A, 11, 11A*. Built in 1636 in the Indo-Mughal style, its 15 domes and arches are adorned with stucco work while some of its 240 columns rise to 12 m. Its *Swarga Vilasam* (Celestial Pavilion), an arcaded octagonal structure, is curiously constructed in brick and mortar without any supporting rafters. Special artisans skilled in the use of traditional lime plaster and powdered seashell and quartz have renovated parts. The original complex had a shrine, an armoury, a theatre, royal quarters, a royal bandstand, a harem, a pond and a garden but only about a quarter survives since Thirumalai's grandson removed sections to build another palace in Tiruchirappalli, and the original *Ranga* Vilasam was destroyed by Muslim invaders. It is a bit run down.

**Vandiyur Mariammam Teppakulam** ⓘ *Buses 4 and 4A take 10 mins from the Bus Stand and Railway Station*. To the southeast of town, this has a small shrine in its centre where the annual *Float Festival* takes place in January/February.

**Gandhi Museum** ⓘ *1000-1300, 1400-1730, free, excellent bookshop*. This is Madurai's best museum, situate in the 300-year old Rani Mangammal Palace. It contains an art gallery, memorabilia (Gandhi's *dhoti* when he was shot), traces history of the Independence struggle from 1800, and the 'Quit India' movement. Informative, interesting and well laid out. Also has sections for Khadi and Village Industries and South Indian handicrafts. Yoga classes, offered daily (but only in Tamil), 0630.

**Thirumalai Nayaka Palace Museum** This museum concentrates on the history of Madurai with galleries on the famous Nayaka king and the art and architecture of Tamil Nadu. Sound and Light show, see Entertainment, page 882.

# Ramesvaram and around → *Phone code: 04573. Colour map 3, grid C5.*

*Population: 38,000.*

The conch-shaped island of Ramesvaram is normally lapped by Gulf of Mannar waters that are limpid blue, but which can be whipped by cyclones into ferocious storm waves. This is where Rama is believed to have worshipped Siva, making it sacred to both Shaivites and Vaishnavites, and so a pilgrim to Varanasi is expected to visit Ramesvaram next, if he is to reach salvation. » *For Sleeping, Eating and other listings, see pages 880-884*.

## Ins and outs

**Getting there** Ramesvaram is connected to Madurai and other centres by regular bus and train services. The bus stand is 2 km from the centre, the railway station 1 km further in and about 1 km southwest of the great temple.

**Getting around** Local buses go to the temple where there are a few places to stay. Avoid visiting on Mon; too crowded with pilgrims. » *See Transport, page 884, for further details.*

**Tourist information** Offices ⓘ *14 East Car St, T04573-221371, 1000-1700*. Railway Station ⓘ *T04573-221373, open (with breaks) 0700-2030*. Temple Information, east side of the temple.

## Background

The *Ramayana* tells how the monkey king Hanuman built the bridges linking Ramnad to Pamban and Danushkodi (a spot where Rama is believed to have bathed) in order to help rescue Sita from the demon king Ravana. When he returned he was told by the *rishis* that he must purify himself after committing the sin of murdering a Brahmin, for *Ravana* was the son of a Brahmin. To do this he was advised to set up a *lingam* and worship Siva. The red image of Hanuman north of the main East Gate illustrates this story.

The original shrine long predates the present great Ramesvaram temple. It is one of India's most sacred shrines and is visited by pilgrims from all over India. The temple benefited from enormous donations from the 17th-century *Setupatis* ('guardians of the causeway'), who derived their wealth from the right to levy taxes on crossings to the island. The temple stands on slightly higher ground, surrounded by a freshwater lake.

## To Ramesvaram and Adam's Bridge

Seen from the air the plains of the Vaigai River form one of the most remarkable landscapes in India, for there are over 5,000 tanks, and irrigation has been so

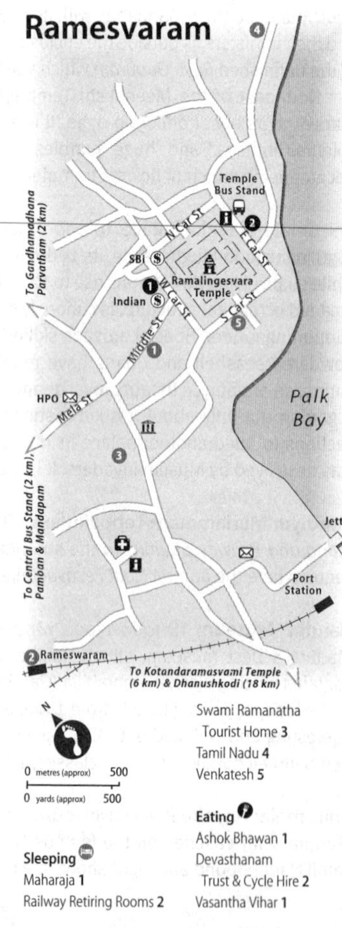

## Holy dips

Pilgrims, once they've travelled the two days from North India and Varanasi will part with any money to attain the sanctity they came for. It's a seller's market for the priests at the temple here: unlike Madurai where the Meenakshi temple has clear tariffs for *pujas*, the brahmins here (there are supposed to be 420 employees of the temple) make an assessment from your clothes, your talk, your skin. If you want to experience the *theertham* (dunking) – the emptying of 22 buckets drawn from holy wells, ponds, and the sea, you shouldn't really pay more than 100 rupees for the whole process, but it seems somehow churlish to bargain with holy men, and most pilgrims don't. Also, take care: despite the best efforts of the *natrajs* (the temple guardians) local guides will of course do the decent thing and hold on to your belongings when you are being doused. Thefts do occur. Leave valuables outside the temple if you are bathing, and it's wise to bring a change of clothes (there are changing rooms inside the temple).

widely developed that scarcely a drop of water is wasted. The coastal districts of Ramnad have their own highly distinct economy and society. For the Hindus the sand banks barely concealed in the Palk Strait are like giant stepping stones linking India and Sri Lanka – Adam's Bridge. Both Hindu and Muslim communities have long established trading links across the Bay of Bengal – to Malaysia and Southeast Asia and to Sri Lanka. Small towns and villages along the coast such as Kilakkarai have long been associated with smuggling. The civil war in Sri Lanka has made it a sensitive region.



### Ramesvaram

The **Ramalingesvara (or Ramanathasvami) Temple** was founded by the Cholas but most of the temple was built in the Nayaka period (16th-17th centuries). It is a massive structure, enclosed by a huge rectangular wall with *gopurams* in the middle of three sides. Entrances through the east wall are approached through columned *mandapas* and the east *gopuram* is on the wall of the inner enclosure rather than the outer wall. Over 45 m high, it was begun in 1640 but left incomplete until recently. The west *gopuram* is comparatively new. In contrast the north and south *gopurams* were built by Keerana Rayar of the Deccan in about AD 1420. The most remarkable feature of the temple is its pillared *mandapas*. The longest corridor is over 200 m long. The pillars, nearly 4 m tall, are raised on moulded bases and the shafts decorated with scrollwork and lotus motifs. They give an impression of almost unending perspective, those on the north and south being particularly striking. There are two gateways on the east side which give access to the Parvati and Ramalinga shrines at the centre. The masonry shrine is probably the oldest building on the site, going back to 1173. On entering the East Gate you see the statue of Hanuman, then the *Nandi* flanked by statues of the Nayaka kings of Madurai, Visvanatha and Krishnama. The *Sphatikalinga Puja* is performed daily at 0500. Worshippers take a holy bath in the sea in a very calm bay 25 km away, where the waters are believed to wash away their sins. Fishermen occasionally offer to take visitors for a boat ride. The fishing village offers good views, but is extremely pungent.

### Gandhamadana Parvatam

Gandhamadana Parvatam, just over 2 km north of Ramesvaram takes, its name from the Sanskrit words *gandha* (fragrance) and *mad* (intoxicate), 'highly fragrant hill'.

### Spice of life

Chettinad food is famous as South India's spiciest: its hallmarks are fresh ground ginger and garlic pastes plus heaps of pepper, cloves, saffron and cinnamon. Chettinad's pepper chickens are recommended anywhere, but while in Chettinad itself go looking for *nandu* (crab) and *yerra* (prawn) in *varuvals* (fries), *puttus* (minces) or curries. *Paal Paniharam* is a special *kheer* (milk and rice pudding).

Dedicated to Rama's feet, this is the spot from which Hanuman is believed to have surveyed the area before taking his leap across the narrow Palk strait to Sri Lanka. You can get an excellent view from the top of the *mandapa*.

### Dhanuskodi

Dhanuskodi, – 'the end of the bow' – is the island's toe-tip where the Bay of Bengal meets the Indian Ocean, so named because Rama, at the request of Vibishana, his friend, destroyed the bridge to Sri Lanka with the end of his bow. Some 20 km to the east of Ramesvaram island, it is considered particularly holy. There is a good beach, on which pilgrims will be making *puja*, and beautiful flat turquoise waters in which they take their holy bath, not to mention excellent views. A trip across the scrappy sand dunes is only recommended for the really hardy – get a local person to go with you. Travel by bus, and then join a pilgrim group on a jeep or lorry for the last desolate few miles (this should cost Rs 50 round trip but establish the price up front). Alternatively, take an auto to Adam's Bridge; insist on going as far as the radio mast for beach and fishing shack photos.



## The Cardamom Hills → *Colour map 3, grid C3/4.*

To the south of Madurai is a series of modest towns in the lee of the southern ranges of the Western Ghats. It is a comfortable day's drive from Madurai to Thiruvanathapuram, either via Tirunelveli or over the ghats, but there are several interesting places on the way if you wish to take your time. » *For Sleeping, Eating and other listings, see pages 880-884.*

### Rajapalayam

ⓘ *To Sankaracoil, Rs 5, 30 mins; from there to Kalugumalai, Rs 3, 30 mins, buses to and from Tenkasi, Rs 10, 2 hrs.*

The town originated on the dispersal of the Vijayanagar families after 1565, see page 966. The Sankarankovil temple is worth visiting. The Western Ghats rise to heights of over 1,200 m immediately behind the town. Wild elephants still come down through the forests, devastating farmland.

### Tenkasi

ⓘ *To Courtallam Falls frequent buses, Rs 3, to Courtallam Bus Stand, then walk through the grey arch to the 'Main Falls'. See Rajapalayam for transport to Tenkasi.*

Literally the Kashi (Varanasi) of the South, Tenkasi is the nearest town to the Kuttalam (Courtallam) Falls, 6 km away. The impressive 16th-century Visvanatha Temple dedicated to Siva, has some fine carvings inside. The temple flagstaff is believed to be 400 years old. From Tenkasi the road goes through a low pass into the densely forested hills of Kerala.

## Courtallam (Kuttalam)

Courtallam, with average temperatures of 22-23°C, is a very popular health resort, especially during the monsoon. The most impressive, and busiest, 'Main Falls' is in town where the river Chittar cascades over 92 m. The approach is lined with spice, banana chips and knick-knacks stalls, then at the Falls you'll find pilgrims washing themselves and their clothes. There is massage, toilets, special postal and other facilities available there. The waters, widely believed to have great curative powers, draw big crowds at the **Saral Festival** in July. The **Thirukutralanathar Temple** contains old inscriptions while the small **Chitra Sabha Temple** nearby contains religious murals.

## Virudhunagar

The name Virudhupatti (Hamlet of Banners) was changed to Virudhunagar (City of Banners) in 1915, and was upgraded to a full municipality in 1957, reflecting the upwardly mobile social status of the town's dominant local caste, the Nadars. Originally low caste toddy tappers, they have established a wide reputation as a dynamic and enterprising group. The powerful Congress leader, Kamaraj Nadar, was chiefly responsible for Mrs Gandhi's selection as Prime Minister.

## Kalugumalai

Some 6 km south of Kovilpatti, Kalugumalai (Kazhugumalai) has a profusion of magnificent fifth-century bas-relief Jain figures on a huge rock which are well worth the detour. The Jain temple is to the north of the rock and is easily missed. There is also an unfinished monolithic cave temple to Siva (circa AD 950).

# Chettinad

→ *Colour map 3, grid B5 and C5.*

Occupying the hot and often dusty coastal plain to the east of Madurai is Chettinad, home to some of South India's wealthiest merchant families, the Nattukottai Chettiars. The fortress houses the Chettinad people built are great big wedding cake-like structures that make a thoroughly welcome change from the relentless temple trail. They are built on a grid pattern and walking through the villages is to experience an endless succession of monumental entrances. Sadly, the some 75 Chettinad villages across 600 km, often feel like ghost towns. The antique merchants and architectural salvage traders that thrive here are drawn by the reduced circumstances of many of the house-owners, who surrender family portraits and granite pillars to stave off financial hardship. In the better days of the 19th century, the mercantile men would set off on the seas to Burma, shipping back teak, or satinwood from Lanka, from which they built their mansions, leaving their wives to handle home affairs, breeding an highly independent group of women. They are renowned as much for their success in trading as their philanthropy: a tenth of their salaries would traditionally go towards charitable or community works.

**Karaikkudi** is in the heart of Chettinad, and has several typical mansions, as well as antique and textile shops. You can visit the local *santhat* (market), see craftsmen working in wood and metal, and gold and silversmiths in their workshops. At **Avudayarkoil**, 30 km northeast of Karaikkudi, the **Athmanathar temple** has one of the most renowned sites in Tamil cultural history. A legend tells that Manickavaskar, a Pandyan Prime Minister, redirected money intended for the purchase of horses to build the temple. However, his real fame lies as author of the *Thiruvasakam* ('Holy Outpourings'), one of the most revered Tamil poetic texts. Completely off the beaten track, the temple has superb sculptures, and is noted for the absence of any images

*Even the roofs of Chettiar buildings are symbols of their wealth: look up to see the wanton use of tiles, layered many times over on top of each other.*

of Siva or Parvati, the main deities, whose empty pedestals are worshipped. The wood carvings on the temple car are notable too.

**Kanadukathan,** 5 km north of Karaikkudi, has a number of formerly magnificent mansions, some of them empty except for bats, monkeys – and antique dealers. You can visit the **Raja of Chettinad's Palace,** an amazing place overlooking the town's pond and full of sepia, larger than life-size portraits of stern family members, the frames garlanded with heavy yellow flowers. Next door is **Visalakshi Ramaswamy's house,** with a museum of local crafts, artifacts and handlooms upstairs. The Raja's waiting room at the railway statio is also pretty special.

It has been estimated that the Burma teak and satinwood pillars in just one of the village's Chettiar houses weighed 300 tonnes, often superbly carved. The plaster on the walls is made from a mixture of lime, eggwhite, powdered shells and myrobalan fruit (the astringent fruit of the tree *Phyllantles emblica*), mixed into a paste which, when dried, gave a gleaming finish. Most houses have the goddess of wealth, Lakshmi, made of stucco over the main arch.

**Devakottai,** 18 km away, is Chettinad's second largest town and offers similarly rich pickings in the way of old mansions and palaces: look out for the particularly grand Periya Minor's *veedu*. **Athangudi,** 8 km from Kairakudi, has factories making the town's famous eponymous hand-made terracotta tiles.

## Sleeping

**Madurai** *p871, maps p872 and p874*
20% tax is added by even modest hotels. Although there are slick hotels across the Vaigai these have neither character, easy access to the town's atmosphere, nor are they good value. Either visit Madurai from the charming remove of the Taj, on its hilltop, or abandon yourself to the throng and take a room near the temple.

**AL Taj Garden Retreat**, Pasumalai Hills, 7 TPK Rd, 5 km southwest of centre on NH7, T0452-2601020. 30 rooms (some in old colonial house) sheltered by the shade of trees, gardens full of peacocks, outdoor dining, good bookshop, lovely pool, great views over surrounding country: a real oasis.

**B Best Western Germanus**, 28 By-Pass Rd, T0452-2382001, www.bestwesterngermanus.com. Quiet, bright rooms, functional, fridge, bath, take rooms at the rear to save you from the busy roundabout in front, excellent food and service: standards assured through the chain's quarterly inspections. Rooftop restaurant 1900-2300 for Chettinad specials.

**B Royal Court**, 4 West Veli St, T0452-5356666, www.royalcourtindia.com. 70 extremely clean a/c rooms with bath, satellite TV and great views from rooftop (open 1900-2300) good value.

**B-C Park Plaza**, 114 W Perumal Maistry St, T0452-2342112, www.hotelparkplaza.com. 55 smart, 60s-print, stylish a/c rooms, some with temple views, all facilities, comp breakfast, excellent rooftop restaurant (1800-2300), bar. Free pick up airport/railway station. Recommended.

**B-C Supreme**, 110 W Perumal Maistry St, T0452-2343151, www.supremehotels.com. 69 modern clean rooms with marble and plastic furniture, 31 a/c on 7 floors, good rooftop restaurant (temple views Surya 1600-0000), bar, 24-hr travel, exchange, internet, a bit noisy, bit overpriced.

**C-E The Madurai Residency**, 14, 15 West Marret St, T0452-2343140, www.madurairesidency.com. Rather grand for Madurai – 75 rooms across 7 floors with glass elevator. Economy rooms are better than a/c because of musty smell.

**D Aarathy**, 9 Perumalkoil, west of Kundalalagar Temple, T0452-2731571. Decently appointed rooms if a bit dingy, some a/c with balcony, vegetarian restaurant, quiet, very friendly.

**D Tamil Nadu II (Star)**, Alagar Koil Rd, T0452-2537462. 51 rooms, some a/c, good restaurant, bar, exchange, quiet.

**D YMCA International Guest House**, Main Guard Sq, near temple, T0452-2746649, ymca@maduraionline.com. Simple a/c double rooms, profits to worthwhile projects.

**D-E International**, 46 W Perumal Maistry St, T0452-2341552, www.hotelinternational

ind.com. 34 clean and tidy rooms with views from upper floors, TV. Friendly.
**D-E Prem Nivas**, 102 W Perumal Maistry St, T0452-2342532, premnivas@eth.net. Shabby rooms with bath, 15 **D** a/c, 25 non a/c, a/c veg restaurant (ultra hot), basic but good value. Single rooms too small for comfort.
**E Arima**, 4 TB Rd, T0452-2603261. 37 rooms, some a/c, modern, simple, clean.
**E Hotel Tamil Nadu**, West Veli St, T0452-2337471. A very friendly tourist office, mint-coloured guesthouse dating from 1968 set around courtyard. In bad need of a new lick of paint – it's pretty grubby -- but there are TVs, huge rooms and the staff are charming.
**E Sree Devi**, W Avani Moola St, T0452-2747431. Rooms with bath, some **D** a/c, (avoid noisy ground floor), good value, cleanish, modern towerblock with views of temple gateway from rooftop, changes TCs, friendly staff.
**E TM Lodge**, 50 W Perumal Maistry St, T0452-2341651. 57 rooms (hot water), some a/c, some with TV, balcony, very clean, bookings for rail/bus journeys.
**E-F Dhanamani**, 20-22 Sunnamukara St, T0452-2342703. Nice rooms (some with bath, fan, TV), good roof terrace with temple views, sitting area (8th floor).
**E-F Ravi Lodge**, 12 Mandayan Asari Lane, Town Hall Rd, T0452-2343493. 30 clean rooms with shower, fan, very quiet, good value.
**F Thilaga**, 111 W Perumal Maistry St, T0452-2749762. 15 double clean rooms with TV, hot water, friendly. Recommended.
**F Tower View Lodge**, nice clean rooms with toilet, shared clean hot shower, excellent food, friendly and helpful family, internet.
**F Visakam Lodge**, 9 Kakathope St, T0452-2741241. 18 very clean rooms. Excellent value. Recommended.
**F Youth Hostel**, MGR Stadium, Race Course, dorm (Rs 40-50).

**Ramesvaram** *p876, map p876*
**D-E Hotel Tamil Nadu** (TTDC), 14 East Car St, T04573-221066. 53 rooms (2-6 beds), some a/c, clean with sea-facing balconies, grubby restaurant (breakfasts from 0700), bar, sea bathing possible nearby (when calm), exchange; very popular, book both well in advance.
**D-E Maharaja**, 7 Middle St, west of the Temple, T04573-221271. 30 rooms, some a/c with bath, exchange, temple music broadcast on loudspeakers, otherwise recommended.
**D-E Venkatesh**, West Car St, T04573-221296. Some a/c rooms, modern.
**F Swami Ramanatha Tourist Home**, between station and temple, opposite museum, T04573-221217. Good clean rooms with bath, best budget option.
**F Railway Retiring Rooms**, T04573-221226, 9 rooms and dorm.

**Chettinad** *p879*
There are very few suitable places to stay in the area. The below are in Karaikkudi unless stated otherwise.
**AL The Bangala**, Senjai, T04565-220221, bangala@vsnl.com. 8 bright and spacious a/c rooms with period colonial furniture, in restored 1916 bungalow, a heritage guest house of character amidst orchards and palms, authentic Chettinad meals (or Continental), serves full-on feasts for a fair whack at Rs 800 per meal and must be booked in advance, rest stop facilities for day visitors (lunch US$15-20), full-board option. Family, quite literally, wrote the (coffee table) book on Chettinad architecture.
**A-B Chettinadu Mansion**, Kanadukathan – book through Deshadan Tours and Travels 4th Floor South Sq, Ave Rd, Cochin, T0484-2317052, www.deshadan.com. A 105-year old house with 7 guestrooms – bright coloured hand-painted tiles and old phones. Meals cost Rs 300 each and must be booked in advance.
**C Hotel Subalakshmi**, T04565-235202, and **C-D Hotel Udayam**, T04565-233142. Both cheap options, but they do not have the guides on hand to gain access to the old private homes (without whose help the Chettinad Palace may be the only house you look inside).
**F Nivaas**, in Devakottai, 1st left from bus station coming from the north, (no sign in English), is basic (no electric sockets), no English spoken.

## Eating

**Madurai** *p871, maps p872 and p874*
**TTT Temple View**, at Park Plaza Hotel. Excellent rooftop venue.
**TT Surya**, Hotel Supreme, open 1700-2400. Seventh-floor rooftop restaurant with

international as well as Indian menu. Excellent Andhra *thalis*, very busy on Sun evenings.

**Anna Meenakshi**, W Perumal Maistry St. Popular South Indian.

**Delhiwala Sweets**, W Tower St. Delicious Indian sweets and snacks.

**Muniyandi Vilas**, at **Indo-Ceylon Restaurant**, and other outlets. Non-vegetarian. Try *paratha* and mutton curry.

**New Arya Bhavan**, North and South Indian choices, ice cream.

**Taj**, Town Hall Rd. Good value *thalis* (Rs 35), friendly.

**Tamil Nadu II** hotel restaurant. Good Indian/Chinese.

**Ramesvaram** *p876, map p876*
Don't expect anything other than *thalis* here. **Ashok Bhawan** and **Vasantha Vihar** on West Car St and also at the Central Bus Stand, Indian vegetarian including Gujarati, but even poorer than Hotel Tamil Nadu. **Devasthanam Trust**, has a canteen opposite the east gate of the temple.

## Entertainment

**Madurai** *p871, maps p872 and p874*
**Meenakshi Temple**: 'Bed time of the God' 2110, is not to be missed (see 'Sights' above). **Thirumalai Nayaka Palace**: Sound and Light show: English 1845-1930; Rs 5 (take mosquito repellent), sadly, "poor, faded tape". During the day, dance drama and concerts are held in the courtyard.

## Festivals and events

**Madurai** *p871, maps p872 and p874*
In **Jan/Feb** the annual **Float Festival** marks the birth anniversary of Thirumalai Nayaka. Many temple deities in silks and jewels, including Meenakshi and Sundareswarar, are taken out on a full moon night on floats colourfully decorated with hundreds of oil lamps and flowers. The floats carry them to the central shrine to the accompaniment of music and chanting. **Jallikattu Festival** (Taming the Bull) is held in **Jan. Chitrai Festival** in **Apr/May** is the most important at the Meenakshi Temple is the 10-day festival which celebrates the marriage of Siva and Meenakshi. In **Aug/Sep** the Avanimoolam is the Coronation Festival of Siva when the image of Lord Sundareswarar is taken out to the riverbank dressed as a worker.

## Shopping

**Madurai** *p871, maps p872 and p874*
Kashmiri 'emporia' pay 40-50% commission to touts. Best buys are textiles, carvings in wood and stone, brass images, jewellery and appliqué work for temple chariots. Most shops are on South Avani Moola St (for jewellery), Town Hall Rd, Masi St and around the Temple.

**Books**
**Higginbotham's Book Exchange**, near the temple.
**New Century Book House**, Town Hall Rd. Recommended.

**Handicrafts**
**Handicrafts Emporium**, 39-41 Town Hall Rd.
**Khadi Gramodyog Bhandar** and **Surabhi** on W Veli St.

**Textiles and tailors**
**Femina**, 10 W Chitrai St. Similar to market (you can take photos of the Meenakshi Temple from their rooftop).
**Hajee Moosa**, 18 E Chitrai St. Tailoring in 8 hrs; 'ready-mades' at **Shabnam**, at No 17.
**Market** near Pudu Mandapam, next to Meenakshi East Gate. Sells fabric and is a brilliant place to get clothes made.

**Chettinad** *p879*
Muneesvaran Kovil St in Karaikkudi is lined with antiques shops selling old sepia photographs, temple lamps, old advertising posters, scrap book matter, religious paintings and Czech pewter jars (from Rs 50).
**Kattu Raja's**, Palaniappa Chettiar St.
**Old Chettinad Crafters**, Murugen Complex, 37/6 Muneesvaran Kovil St, Karaikkudi, T098428-223060, chettinaduantiques@yahoo.co.in. One of the best.
**VJ Murugesan**, sells old wooden furniture, household articles, main doors, wooden pillars, glass.
**Venkateswara Furniture and Timber Merchant**, No 8 Keela Oorani West, Karaikkudi, T098424-232112. If you're in

the market for bigger objects and weight is no object, this architectural salvage yard is a good starting point. Bargain hard: a granite pillar shouldn't set you back more than Rs 1,500.

MM Street and The Weavers' Lane beside the Bangala have Chettinad cotton for sale straight off the loom. Ask locally for information on the next sandais, the colourful local weekly markets.

## Activities and tours

**Madurai** *p871, maps p872 and p874*

**Swimming**

Rs 300 gets you unlimited use of the Taj Garden Retreat swimming pool, a brilliant antidote to the craziness of the temple.

**Tours**

**TTDC**, book at Hotel Tamil Nadu, West Veli St, T0452-2337471. **Temple tour** of Madurai and attractive surroundings by a/c coach; half day, 0700-1200, 1500-2000. Rs 125. Recommended for an overview. Apr-Jun: **Courtallam** Rs 300. **Kodaikkanal** 0700-2100, Rs 250. **Rameswaram** Rs 275.

**Ex-Serviceman Travels**, 1 Koodalalagar, Perumal Kovil St, T0452-2730571, **City** half day, 0700, 1500, Rs 140; **Kodaikkanal** or Ramesvaram 0700-1900, Rs 2750; overnight to **Kanniyakumari** 2200-1900, Rs 350.

**Tour operators**

**Meraj**, 46B Perumal Koil South Mada St. Pleasant Tours and Travels, Mr. Ian Fernandez, Plot No. 6, St Joseph Street, (opposite Ellis Nagar Telephone Exchange T0452-2610614, ptt@sancharnet.in.

**Siraj**, 19A TPK Rd (opposite Malai Murasu), T0452-2739666, mshersha@md4.vsnl.net.in. Ticketing, good multilingual guides, cars, internet.

**Trade Wings**, 279 North Masi St, T0452-2730271.

**Window to the World** (Trichy), T0431-436052, faithpandian@sify.com. Tours from Madurai (and other towns). The Pandians are very helpful, efficient, South India tours, car with excellent driver. Highly recommended.

**Yoga**

Classes at Gandhi Museum, T0452-2481060. 0630, daily.

## Transport

**Madurai** *p871, maps p872 and p874*

**Air**

Airport to city centre (12 km) by Pandiyan coach (calls at top hotels); taxi (Rs 375) or auto-rickshaw (Rs 80). **Indian Airlines**, 7A W Veli St, T0452-2741234. 1000-1300, 1400-1700; Airport, T0452-2670433. Flights to **Chennai** and **Mumbai**. **Air India**, opposite railway station, W Veli St. **Jet Airways**, T0452-2526969; airport T0452-2690771. To **Chennai**.

**Bus**

**Local** There is a good network within the city and the suburbs.

**Long distance** Approaching on a long-distance bus from the south, to get to the centre, change to a city bus at Tirumangalam (15 km south). State and private companies (**MPTC**, **PRC**, but check bus details carefully) run services to other cities. Most intercity buses use the **New Central Bus Stand** (or Muttuthavani Bus Terminal), 6 km northeast of town, in open countryside, continuation of Alagar Koil Rd, on the toll Ring road (25 mins, Rs 40 by rickshaw, or city bus from town centre). Buses for **Bangalore** (11 hrs), **Ernakulam** (**Kochi**), **Chennai** (10 hrs), **Pondicherry** (9 hrs), **Thiruvananthapuram** (8 hrs), **Kumbakonum**, **Ramesvaram** (under 4 hrs, every 15 mins), **Thanjavur** (4 hrs), **Tiruchirappalli** (2½ hrs), **Tirunelveli** (4 hrs, Rs 40). **Arapalayam Bus Stand**, 3 km northwest of centre (Bus route No 7A, auto-rickshaws Rs 20), T0452-2603740, for destinations to the north and northwest, including **Kodaikkanal**, buses (crowded in peak season, Apr-Jul); 3½ hrs (longer via Palani), Rs 150. Also buses to **Coimbatore** (5 hrs, change there for Mysore or Ooty), **Periyar/ Kumili** (4 hrs), **Salem** (5½ hrs), **Dindigul**. Central (Periyar) Bus Stands, near W Veli St, are now used for buses around town and destinations in the immediate vicinity.

**Car**

To **Kodaikkanal** Rs 950 (Rs 1600 a/c), see local transport above.

**Rickshaw**

Autos Rs 25, cycle Rs 20 for trips around town. Bargain hard first.

**Taxi/car hire**
Unmetered; 10 hrs/225 km, Rs 450, Rs 675 (a/c); 6 hrs sightseeing, Rs 490 (Rs 750 a/c); 1 hr/10 km, Rs 65, Rs 100 (a/c). **Janakiraman**, 184 North Veli St; **Supreme**, 110 Perumal Maistry St, T0452-2743151.

**Train**
**Madurai Junction** is the main station: enquiries, T0452-237597, reservations: 1st Class T0452-223535, 2nd Class T0452-233535. 0700-1300, 1330-2000. New Computer Reservation Centre to south of main entrance. Left luggage facilities. Pre-paid auto-rickshaw kiosk outside.
**Chennai (ME)** via Villupuram for **Pondicherry**: *Vaigai Exp, 2636*, 0645, 8 hrs; *Pandiyan Exp, 6718*, 2020, 10 hrs.
**Coimbatore**: *Fast Pass Exp, 6716*, 2135, 7 hrs; *Quillon Coimbatore Exp, 6782*, 0640, 5 hrs. **Kollam**: connect with trains from Virudhunagar (see page 879).
**Kanniyakumari**: *Chennai Egmore Kanniyakumari Exp, 6121*, 0415, 5¾ hrs.
**Ramesvaram**: *Coimbatore- Ramesvaram Exp, 6715*, 0600, 4¾ hrs.
**Thiruvananthapuram**: see Virudhunagar on page 879. **Tiruchirappalli**: several, *Vaigai Exp, 2636*, 0645, 2½ hrs (beautiful countryside); *Pandiyan Exp, 6718*, 1925, 3½hrs.

**Ramesvaram** *p876, map p876*
**Bicycle**
You can hire a bicycle by the hour from West Car or East Car St.

**Bus**
**Local** Marudhu Pandiyan Transport Corporation (MPTC) covers the town and the area around. The bus station is 2 km west of the town. You can get a bus from the Railway Station to the Ramalingesvara Temple, to Pamban or to Dhanuskodi (both via the temple). From the temple's east gate to Dhanuskodi roadhead and to Gandha- madana Parvatam, both about every 2 hrs.
**Long distance** State, MPTC and private bus companies run regular services via **Mandapam** to several towns nearby. The central bus stand is 2 km from the main temple gate. **Govt Express Bus Reservations**, North Car St. 0700-2100. Frequent buses to **Madurai**, 173 km (4½ hrs); Tourist coach (hotel-to-hotel) is better.

**Taxi**
A few cars and jeeps are available from the Railway Station and hotels.

**Train**
Ramesvaram Railway Station, Enquiries and Reservations, T226. Open 0800-1300, 1330-1730. **Chennai**: *Sethu Exp, 6714*, 1510, 17¾ hrs via **Chengalpattu**, 16½ hrs.
**Coimbatore**: *Coimbatore Fast Pass, 6716*, 1610, 12¼ hrs. **Madurai**: *Coimbatore Fast Pass, 6716*, 1610, 5 hrs. **Tiruchirappalli**: *Ramesvaram Tambaram Exp, 6702*, 1200, 5½ hrs; *Sethu Exp, 6714*, 1510, 6¼ hrs.

**Virudhunagar** *p879*
**Bus**
Leave Madurai early morning for Kollam train; get off at police station and go to the end of the road opposite and turn left; the railway station is about 1 km on the right (take a rickshaw if carrying heavy luggage).

**Train**
To **Kollam** and **Thiruvananthapuram**, Platform 3 across the bridge. **Kollam**: *Fast Pass Exp, 6761*, 2150, 7 hrs.

**Chettinad** *p879*
Bus routes link Karaikkudi with every part of the state. The trains *The Ramesvaram* and *Sethu Exp* connect Tambaram and Ramesvaram with Karaikkudi.

## Directory

**Madurai** *p871, maps p872 and p874*
**Banks** Several on East Avani Moola St. **Andhra Bank**, W Chitrai St, accepts credit cards; **Canara Bank**, W Veli St, cashes Amex and sterling TCs. **Alagendran Finance**, 182D N Veli St, good rate for cash US$ but not for TCs. **Internet Dolphin**, Madurai Junction station. Many west of the temple and in the budget hotel area charge Rs 20 per hr.
**Hospitals Christian Mission Hospital**, East Veli St; **Grace Kennet Hospital**, 34 Kennet Rd.
**Post** The town GPO is at the north end of W Veli St (Scott Rd). In Tallakulam: Head Post Office and Central Telegraph Office, on Gokhale Rd.

# The far south

*The southernmost tip of mainland India is a focus of pilgrimage that captures the imagination of millions of Hindus on a daily basis. Kanniyakamari occupies a beautiful rocky headland site, where the Bay of Bengal, the Indian Ocean and the Arabian Sea meet to give spectacular sunrise, sunset and moonrise. An hour further towards Kerala is Padmanabhapuram Palace, the painstakingly maintained ancient seat of the Travancore rulers. Tirunelveli, one-time capital of the Pandyas, is now a market and educational centre that is often passed over on the trail towards Madurai.*

▸▸ *For Sleeping, Eating and other listings, see pages 888-890.*

## Tirunelveli and Palayamkottai → *Phone code: 0462. Colour map 3, grid C4. Population: 411,300.*

On the banks of the Tamraparni, the only perennial river of the south, Tirunelveli is an attractive town surrounded by a belt of rice fields ('nelveli' means 'paddy-hedge') irrigated from the river's waters. Rising only 60 km to the east at an altitude of over 1,700 m, the river benefits from both the southwest and southeast monsoons. It tumbles down to the plains where it is bordered by a narrow strip of rich paddy land.

Tirunelveli is now joined with the twin settlement of Palayamkottai. It is a market town and one of the oldest Christian centres in Tamil Nadu. St Francis Xavier settled here to begin his ministry in India in the early 16th century, but it has also been a centre of Protestant missionary activity. In 1896 it became the head of an Anglican diocese, now Church of South India.

**Kanthimathi Nellaiyappar Temple** ⓘ *closed 1230-1600, no photography*, is a twin temple, with the north dedicated to Siva (Nellaiyappar) and the south to Parvati (Kanthi). It's worth visiting. Each section has an enclosure over 150 m by 120 m. The temples have sculptures, musical pillars, valuable jewels, a golden lily tank and a 1,000-pillared *mandapa*. There is a large white Nandi at the entrance. **Car festival** in June/July. The old town area around the temple is well worth a couple of hours of anyone's time, with the blue-painted houses reminiscent of Jodhpur (but without the tourist crowds). **Palayamkottai** has **St John's Church** (Church Missionary Society) with a spire 35 m high, a landmark for miles around. The town produces palm-leaf articles.

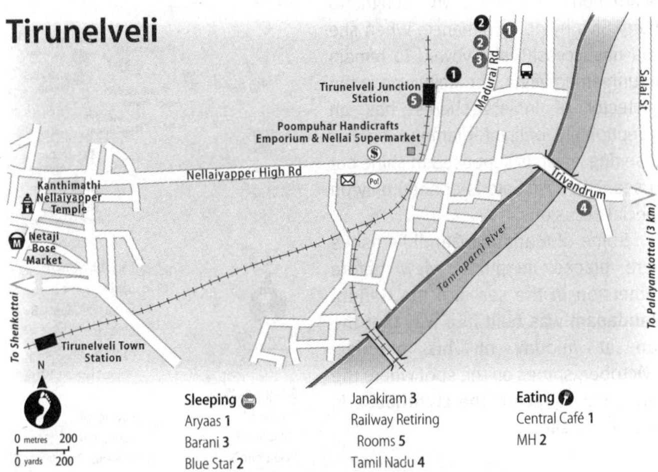

**Tiruchendur**, 50 km east of Tirunelveli, has a famous shore temple ⓘ *Rs 50 for 'fast darshan', men must remove shirts*, dedicated to Subrahmanya, see page 1005. It is considered to be one of his six 'abodes'. It is a hive of activity during festivals. There are caves with rock-cut sculptures along the shore.

**Manapad**, the predominantly Roman Catholic coastal village 18 km south of Tiruchendur, is where St Francis Xavier is said to have landed and lived in a cave near the headland. The Holy Cross Church (1581) close to the sea is believed to house a fragment of the True Cross from Jerusalem.

# Kanniyakumari → *Phone code: 04652. Colour map 3, grid C4. Population: 19,700.*

The southernmost point of mainland India and a site that captures the imagination of millions of Hindus, Kanniyakumari revolves largely around the pilgrim market that sells tacky plastic knick-knacks associated with the Goddess Kumari, the virgin, Kanniyakumari (Cape Comorin). The memorial to Swami Vivekananda, on a rocky promontory just over 400 m offshore, now dominates the view and the town heaves with pilgrims who assemble in the pre-dawn light to see the day break over it. The Bay of Bengal, the Indian Ocean and the Arabian Sea meet here, giving specta- cular sunrise, sunset and moonrise. In April the sun and the moon appear on the same horizon. The beach sands here are of different colours (black monazite and red garnet), having been deposited from different directions.

## Sights

The **Kanniyakumari Temple** ⓘ *0400-1200, 1700-2000, non-Hindus are not allowed into the sanctuary, shoes must be left outside and men must wear a dhoti to enter*, overlooks the shoreline. The legend tells of the Devi Kanya, one of the incarnations of Parvati, who sought to marry Siva by doing penance. When she was unsuccessful she vowed to remain an unmarried virgin. The deity who is the 'protector of India's shores' has an exceptionally brilliant diamond on her nose ring which is supposed to shine out to sea. The East Gate is opened only on special occasions.

Some of Mahatma Gandhi's ashes were placed in public view before immersion in the sea and the **Gandhi Mandapam** was built in a way that the sun at midday on his birthday, 2 October, shines on the spot where the ashes were placed. The **Lighthouse** is closed to visitors.

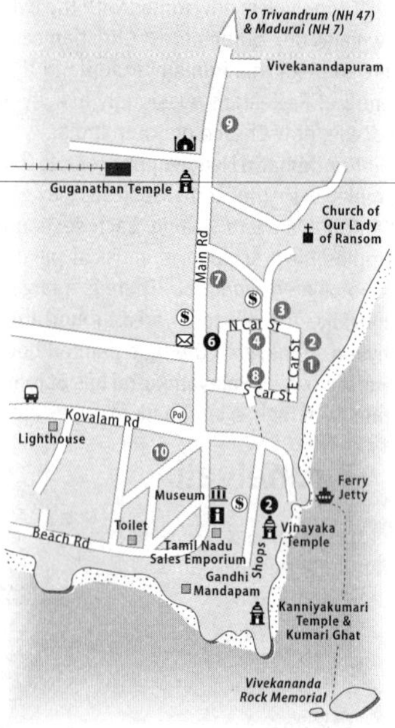


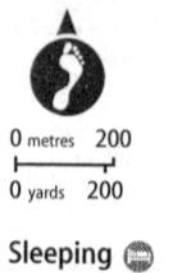


Sleeping
Lakshmi 1
Maadhini 2
Manickam 3
Parvathi Nivas 4
Sankar Guest House 7
Shivas Residency 8
Singaar 9
Tamil Nadu Guest House 10

Eating
Sangam 6
Sravanas 2

**Vivekananda Memorial** ⓘ *closed Tue, 0700-1100, 1400-1700, Rs 10, ferry Rs 20, 15 mins (see transport below), allow 1 hr for the visit, smoking and eating prohibited, take off shoes before entering, can be hot underfoot,* stands on one of two rocks separated by about 70 m, about 500 m from the mainland. The Bengali religious leader and philosopher Swami Vivekananda who came here as a simple monk and devotee of the Devi, swam out and sat in long and deep meditation on one of the rocks in 1892. He left inspired to speak on Hinduism at the Parliament of Religions in Chicago, preaching that "the Lord is one, but the sages describe Him differently". He looked on religion as the most powerful instrument of social re-generation and individual development. On his return, he founded the Ramakrishna Mission in Chennai, which now has spread across the world. The rock was renamed Vivekananda Rock and a memorial was built in 1970. The design of the *mandapa* incorporates different styles of temple architecture from all over India and now also houses a statue of Vivekananda. People also come to see Sri Pada Parai, the 'footprint' of the Devi where she did her penance on the rock – divine footprints are believed to be raised when enshrined on rock. A giant 40-m statue of the poet Thiruvalluvar is now installed on the rock nearby and work is progressing to allow visitors to land.

An informative photo exhibition, in **Vivekanandapuram**, 1 km north, can be reached by an easy walk along the beach though there is no access from the north side. The Yoga Kendra there runs courses from June to December. Further north there is a pleasant sandy beach, 3½ km along Kovalam Road.

## Around Kanniyakumari

**Suchindram temple** ⓘ *open to non-Hindus, priests acting as guides may expect donations,* was founded during the Pandiyan period but was expanded under Thirumalai Nayaka in the 17th century. It was also used later as a sanctuary for the rulers of Travancore to the west and so contains treasures from many kingdoms. One of the few temples dedicated to the Hindu Trinity, Brahma, Vishnu and Siva, it is in a rectangular enclosure which you enter through the massive ornate seven-storeyed *gopuram*. North of the temple is a large tank with a small shelter in the middle while round the walls is the typically broad street used for car festivals. Leading to the entrance is a long colonnade with musical pillars and sculptures of Siva, Parvati, Ganesh and Subrahmanya on the front and a huge Hanuman statue inside. The main sanctuary, with a *lingam*, dates from the ninth century but many of the other structures and sculptures date from the 13th century and after. There are special temple ceremonies at sunset on Friday.

**Nagercoil** is 19 km from Kanniyakumari and is set with a stunning backcloth of the Western Ghats, reflected from place to place in the broad tanks dotted with lotuses. The landscape begins to feel more like Kerala than Tamil Nadu. It is an important railway junction and bus terminal. It is often a bottleneck filled with lorries so be prepared for delays. The old town of **Kottar**, now a suburb, was a centre of art, culture and pilgrimage. The **temple** ⓘ *0630-0900, 1730-2000,* to Nagaraja, after which the town is named, is unique in that although the presiding deity is the Serpent God *Naga*, there are also shrines to Siva and Vishnu as well as images of Jain *Tirthankaras*, Mahavira and Parsvanatha on the pillars. The temple is alive with snakes during some festivals. Christian missionaries played an important part in the town's development and have left their mark in schools, colleges, hospitals and of course churches of different denominations. There is also a prominent Muslim community in Kottar which is reflected in the shops closing on Fridays and remaining open on Sunday.

## Padmanabhapuram

ⓘ *Closed Mon, 0900-1700 (last tickets 1630), Rs 5 (accredited guide is included, but expects a 'donation' after the tour), still camera Rs 5, video Rs 500. Best at 0900 before coach parties arrive.*

Padmanabhapuram, the old palace of the Rajas of Travancore, contains some fascinating architecture and paintings but some of the methods employed during its restoration have been criticized. Although decaying somewhat, the Kuthiramalika Palace in Trivandrum – if you are venturing into Kerala – might be better worth looking round. Padmanabhapuram's name (*Padma*, lotus; *nabha*, navel; *puram*, town) refers to the lotus emerging from the navel of Vishnu. From the ninth century this part of Tamil Nadu and neighbouring Kerala were governed by the Ay Dynasty, patrons both of Jainism and Hinduism. However, the land was always contested by the Cholas, the Pandiyas and the Cheras. By the late 11th century the new Venadu Dynasty emerged from the Chera rulers of Kerala and took control of Kanniyakumari District in AD 1125 under Raja Kodai Kerala Varman. Never a stable kingdom and with varying degrees of territorial control, Travancore State was governed from Padmanabhapuram between 1590-1790, when the capital was shifted to Thiruvananthapuram. Although the Rajas of Travancore were Vaishnavite kings, they did not neglect Siva, as can be seen from various sculptures and paintings in the palace. The King never officially married and the heir to the throne was his eldest sister's oldest son. This form of 'matrilineal descent' was characteristic of the earlier Chera Empire (who ruled for 200 years from the early 12th century). The palace shows the nice craftsmanship, especially in woodworking, that has been characteristic of Kerala's art and architecture. There are also some superb frescoes and excellent stone-sculpted figures. The outer cyclopean stone wall is fitted together without mortar. It encloses a total area of 75 ha, and the buildings of the palace cover 2 ha.

*Open courtyards, trefoil arches and chariot forms are the hallmarks of Rameswarem's distinctive style of temple architecture.*



## Sleeping

**Tirunelveli** *p885, map p885*

Hotels are often full during the wedding season (Apr-Jun). Book ahead or arrive early.

**B-D Janakiram**, 30 Madurai Rd, near Bus Stand, T0462-2331941. 70 clean, redecorated rooms, with hot shower, some a/c, lift, smart, brightly lit, outstanding vegetarian rooftop restaurant. Highly recommended.

**C-E Aryaas**, 67 Madurai Rd, T0462-2339001, www.hotelaryaas.net. 69 rooms, 25 a/c, in dark bordello style, non a/c better value, restaurants (separate vegetarian one, but it's also a mosquito's heaven), bar. Excellent internet café opposite. Several budget hotels are clustered near Junction Railway Station. Rooms usually with western toilet and shower.

**C-E Barani**, 29 Madurai Rd, T0462-2333234. 43 rooms, with hot shower, 10 a/c, clean, well maintained, vegetarian restaurant, in large, 4-storey modern block, lift, ample parking.

**E Tamil Nadu**, T0462-2324268. Some dull rooms, bath and restaurant, poorly maintained.

**F Blue Star**, 36 Madurai Rd, T0462-2334495. 50 rooms with cold shower, 10 a/c, good vegetarian restaurant, Indian style, modern. Good value.

**F Railway Retiring Rooms**. Clean, secure rooms and dorm. Excellent value.

**Kanniyakumari** *p886, map p886*

Hotels are in heavy demand; book well in advance. Better hotels have rooms with attached facilities (cold showers, hot tap and Western toilets)

**B Hotel Singaar**, 2 km from attractions, T04652-247992. Smart and popular large hotel

*For an explanation of the sleeping and eating price codes used in this guide, see inside the front cover. Other relevant information is found in Essentials pages 56-61.*

with nice pool, large rooms, many with balcony and decent restaurant. Tariff includes breakfast.

**B-C Maadhini**, East Car St, T04652- 2346787. Comfortable rooms with bath and fan (mosquito-proof), best with sea views (tell reception if you don't want be woken early to watch the sunrise!). 'Garden' restaurant in courtyard (evenings). Recommended.

**B-C Seaview**, East Car St, T04652-2347841. 61 excellent, large rooms, 30 a/c, in new hotel, all facilities, roof terrace. Highly recommended.

**B-C Singaar**, 5 Main Rd, T04652-2347992, singaar@sancharnet.in. 76 spacious, clean rooms, most a/c with balconies in modern hotel with well-maintained pool (non-residents Rs 100, 2 hrs), restaurant, extensive grounds, away from temple noise and crowds. Bit overpriced.

**C-D Tamil Nadu Guest House**, Beach Rd, T04652-2346257. 45 rooms, some with bath, 15 a/c, **B** twin cottages, good location, beautiful sunset views, but very slow service.

**D Lakshmi**, East Car St, T04652-2346333. 40 very clean rooms, some a/c with views, Indian WC, restaurant, 24-hr coffee shop, friendly and helpful staff, but noisy because guests arrive at 0400-0500 to see sunrise from the roof. Otherwise excellent value.

**D Shivas Residency**, South Car St, T04652-2346150. 18 rooms, 3 a/c, in new hotel. Spacious, quiet, very clean. Recommended.

**D-E Manickam**, North Car St, T04652- 2346387. 55 pleasant rooms, some with seaview and balcony, restaurant. Recommended.

**E Sankar Guest House**, Main Rd, T04652-2346260. 36 large rooms, some de luxe with TV, seaview.

**F Arunagiri**, 59 Madurai Rd, T04652-2334553. 62 rooms with TV, some balconies, spacious, shady courtyard. very good value.

**F Parvathi Nivas**, West Car St, T04652-2346352. 22 basic, cool rooms with character in old-style lodge. Interesting.

**Around Kanniyakumari** *p887*

**D Parvathi**, Nagarcoil, T04652-233020. Similar to Rajam.

**D Rajam**, MS Rd, Vadasery, Nagarcoil, T04652-232581. 32 rooms, some a/c, restaurant, roof garden, exchange, good value.

## Eating

**Tirunelveli** *p885, map p885*

**Central Café**, near station, good vegetarian.

**MH Restaurant**, opposite Aryaas. Western fast food, pizzas. Modern.

**Kanniyakumari** *p886, map p886*

**Sangam**, good *thalis*.

**Sravanas**, 2 near Jetty and on Sannathi St. Vegetarian. Recommended.

**TTDC Restaurant**, looks like a barracks, but excellent non-vegetarian Indian meals.

## Festivals and events

**Kanniyakumari** *p886, map p886*

Chitra Purnima is a special full moon celebration at the temple usually held in the 2nd week of **Apr**. Sunset and moonrise can be seen together. In 1st week of **Oct** Special Navarathri celebrations.

## Transport

**Tirunelveli** *p885, map p885*

Good bus connections to **Kanniyakumari**, **Thiruvananthapuram**, and to **Madurai** (faster to change buses at Tirumangalam), **Tiruchirappalli** and **Chennai**. For **Courtallam**, go to Tenkasi (Rs 12, 1½ hrs) and take bus to Courtallam (Rs 2, 20 mins).

Train to **Chennai (ME)**: *Nellai Exp, 6120* (AC/CC), 1900, 13¾ hrs. Broad gauge to **Chennai (MC)**: *Kanniyakumari Exp, 6020*, 1740, 15 hrs. Also to Madurai and Kanniyakumari.

**Kanniyakumari** *p886, map p886*

Central **bus** station, west of town, about 15 mins walk from centre, T04652- 271285. It has a restaurant, waiting room and **Retiring Rooms** upstairs. There are frequent services to **Nagercoil** (½ hr), **Kovalam** and **Thiruvananthapuram** (2½ hrs) but the journey can be tiring and uncomfortable. Govt Express buses go to other major towns including **Chennai** (16 hrs), **Madurai** (6 hrs), **Ramesvaram** (8½ hrs).

The **ferry** to **Vivekananda Rock**, at least every 30 mins, 0700-1100, 1400-1700; sometimes 2 run simultaneously. Rs 10. Expect long queues during festivals.

The **train** station to the north, off the Trivandrum Rd, is large and well organized, T71247. **Chennai (ME)** (via Madurai): *Kanniyakumari Chennai Egmore Exp, 6122,* 1550, 15¾ hrs. **Delhi (ND)**: *Him Sagar Exp, 6317/6787*, Fri, 1245 (it does not stop in Chennai; it stops at **Katpadi** and then **Gudur**. If you take this train to its ultimate destination of **Jammu** the journey lasts 3 days 1½ hrs, the longest in India!). **Madurai**: *Kanniyakumari Chennai Egmore Exp, 6122,* 1550, 5¼ hrs. **Mumbai (CST)**: *Kanniyakumari Mumbai Exp, 1082* (AC/II), 0445, 48 hrs. **Thiruvananthapuram**: *Kanniyakumari Mumbai Exp, 1082* (AC/II), 0445, 2¼ hrs.

**Around Kanniyakumari** *p887*
At **Nagarcoil**, the railway station is 3 km from the bus station. Mumbai (CST): Nagercoil-Mumbai Exp, 6340, Mon, Tue, Wed, Sat, 0545, 39½ hrs; Kanniyakumari Mumbai Exp, 1082, 0520, 47 hrs. Frequent bus connections to Thiruvananthapuram, Kanniyakumari and Madurai

**Padmanabhapuram** *p888*
Regular **buses** to **Thiruvananthapuram** and **Kanniyakumari**. Less frequent buses to and from **Kovalam**. From Kovalam, depart approximately 0940 to **Thuckalai**. Return buses from Thuckalai depart 1445, 1530.

A taxi from Kovalam and Thiruvananthapuram including Padmanabhapuram, Suchindram and Kanniyakumari costs approximately Rs 800.

## Directory

**Tirunelveli** *p885, map p885*
**Banks** Can be found on Trivandrum High Rd. **Hosptials** In High Ground, Palayamkottai. **Post** GPO, Trivandrum High Rd.

**Kanniyakumari** *p886, map p886*
**Banks** Branches of Canara Bank, Main Rd; State Bank of India; State Bank of Travancore, Beach Rd. **Post** Head Post Office, Main Rd. Branches at Vivekandandapuram. 1100-1600 and in Sannathi St, 1000-1400.

# Kerala

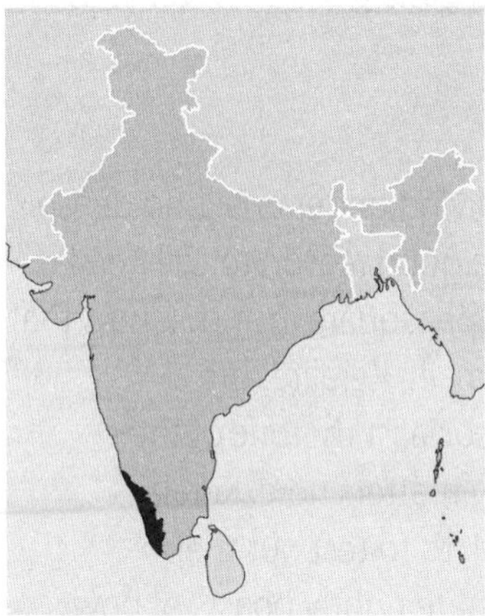



## Footprint features

# Introduction

Although you'll get the sense of living under one long dense coconut palm thicket, locals have good reason to call Kerala the city state: the ratio of people per square inch outstrips that of anywhere else in India. In the main, Keralites are a prosperous bunch: don't let the socialist rhetoric of their political parties fool you – money matters here. Kerala is where the marketing people flock to to test out their advertising campaigns, and the state rightly boasts of how highly it scores in all the quality of life indicators. But relative affluence brings with it social problems: Kerala also has both the highest suicide rate and one of the highest rates of alcohol consumption per capita on the subcontinent, and huge swathes of agricultural land goes uncultivated as high literacy creates a class with loftier ambitions than tilling the soil.

Paddling down the backwaters so lyrically brought alive by Arundhati Roy in *The God of Small Things* is one of the treats of a spell in Kerala: but it is a huge money-spinner and as a result sleepy Alappuzha (Alleppey) has grown into a dirty waterbus depot. Fort Kochi, with its old spice markets, blue-tiled synagogue, mural-covered palace and Chinese fishing-net studded shoreline, is one of India's most charming, slow-paced cities. Southwards are lakes, lagoons and a couple of beautiful beaches, Kovalam or the less visited Varkala. From Ponmudi in the south to Sulthan Bathery in the north, Kerala's hill stations support vast tea plantations and forests to walk through. The lesser-visited northern district of Malabar has a wholly different character from the south. This is the home to Kerala's ritual dance, Theyyam, and the martial art Kalarippayattu, as well the capital of the Muslim Moplah community with their strong Middle Eastern cultural and trading links.

## ★ Don't miss...

1 **Keraleeyamm** Kerala is the centre for ayurvedic medicine. Take part in a rejuvenation programme in this centre in Varkala, page 911.

2 **Backwaters** Watch waterside activities like coir making, toddy tapping and fishing from the quiet of a traditional dugout canoe or an exclusive kettuvallam-style houseboat, page 914.

3 **Alappuzha** This is the place to watch spectacular Snake Boat Races which are usually held in August, page 918.

4 **Fort Kochi** Wander around this charming town and then buy fresh fish from the Chinese fishing nets and have it fried in one of the pans nearby, page 925.

5 **Munnar** Surrounded by tea estates, this hill station has some lovely bike rides in the surrounding area, page 939.

6 **Thrissur** The Pooram, held at the end of April, is an unmissable grand festival with elephants, parasols, drums and fireworks, page 945.

7 **Theyyam** The dance of the possessed that takes place in the state's northern villages – the religious sister to the *Kathakali* dance form, page 957.

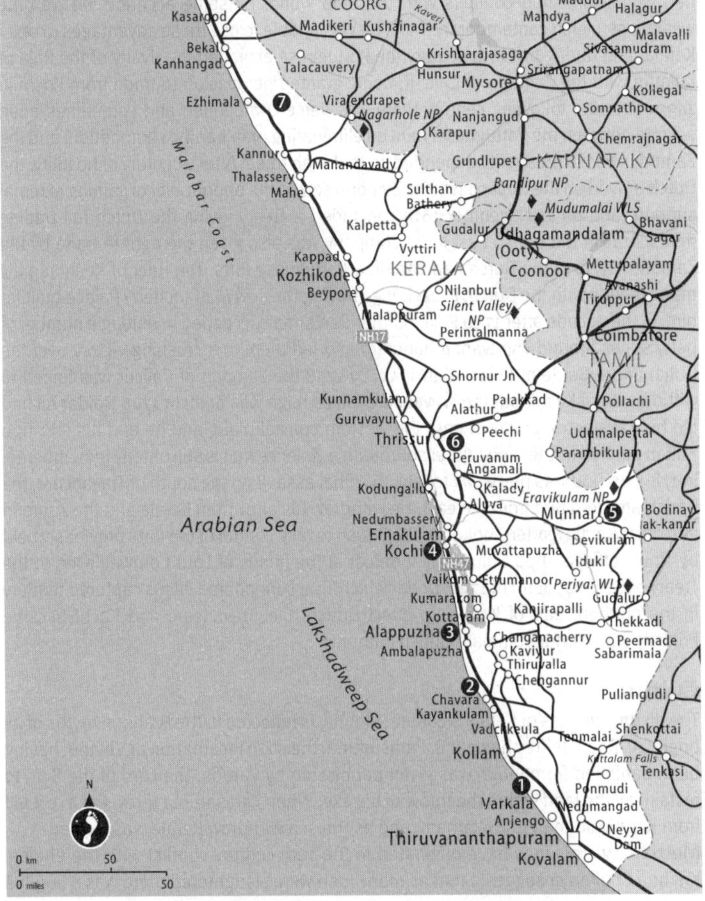

# Background → *Population: 32 mn. Area: 39,000 sq km.*

## The land

**Geography** Stretching from some of the highest mountains of the Western Ghats to the lush coastal plain, Kerala encapsulates the rich diversity of western India's coastal landscapes. Its narrow coastal fringe has been raised from the sea in the last one million years. Immediately inland are low, rolling hills of laterite, succeeded by the ancient rocks which form the backbone of the Western Ghats.

**Climate** Kerala does not have an extended totally dry season characteristic of the rest of India, but is particularly wet from June to September. Maximum temperatures rarely rise above 32°C while minimum temperatures at sea level are never below 20°C.

## History

The **Cheras**, who established themselves in the Kuttanad region around Alappuzha as the first Kerala power, developed a wide network of trade links in which both the long-established Christian community and the Jewish community participated fully. However, the neighbouring Cholas launched several successful attacks against Chera power from AD 985. When Chola power disintegrated at the end of the 11th century, Calicut gradually became dominant under the **Zamorin** (literally *Lord of the Sea*), who had well-established contacts with the Arab world. By some accounts he was the wealthiest ruler in contemporary India. He was unable to use these advantages to unite Kerala, and during the 16th century the Portuguese exploited the rivalry of the Raja of Kolattiri with the Zamorin of Calicut, being granted permission to trade from Kochi in 1499. Over the following century there was fierce competition and sometimes open warfare between the Portuguese, bent on eliminating Arab trading competition, and the Zamorin, whose prosperity depended on that Arab trade. After a century of hostility, the **Dutch** arrived on the west coast. The Zamorin seized the opportunity of gaining external support, and on 11 November 1614 concluded a Treaty giving the Dutch full trading rights. In 1615 the British East India Company was also given the right to trade by the Zamorin. By 1633 the Dutch had captured Portuguese forts. The ruler of Kochi rapidly made friends with the Dutch, in exchange having the new Mattancherry Palace built for him. In the decade after 1740 Raja Marthanda Varma succeeded in uniting a number of petty states around Thiruvananthapuram and led them to a crushing victory over the Dutch in the Battle of Kolachel in 1741. By 1758 the Zamorin of Calicut was forced to withdraw from Kochi, but the **Travancore** ruler's reign was brief. In 1766 Haidar Ali had led his cavalry troops down onto the western coastal plain, and he and his son Tipu Sultan pushed further and further south with a violence that is still bitterly remembered. In 1789, as Tipu was preparing to launch a final assault on the south of Travancore, the British attacked him from the east. He withdrew his army from Kerala and the Zamorin and other Kerala leaders looked to the British to take control of the forts previously held by Tipu's officers. Tipu Sultan's first defeat at the hands of Lord Cornwallis led to the Treaty of Seringapatam in 1792, under which Tipu surrendered all his captured territory in the northern part of Kerala, to direct British rule. Travancore and Kochi became Princely states under ultimate British authority.

## Culture

The distinctiveness of Kerala's cultural identity is reflected in the Brahmin myths of its origin. As Robin Jeffrey has put it, Parasurama, the sixth incarnation of Vishnu, having been banished from India, was given permission by Varuna, the Lord of the Sea, to reclaim all the land within the throw of his axe. When Parasaruma threw the axe it fell from Kanniyakumari to Gokarnam, and as the sea withdrew Kerala was formed.

**Matriarchy** This may have originated in the 10th-century conflict with the Cholas. Krishna Chaitanya suggests that as many men were slaughtered there was a surplus of women, encouraging the development of a matrilineal system in which women controlled family property. Kerala is the first state in India to claim 100% **literacy** in some districts and women enjoy a high social status. The 2001 Census shows that overall literacy has reached 91%, and uniquely in India there are more women than men in the population.

**Religion** The majority of the population is Hindu, but as much as a quarter of the population is Christian and there is also a large Muslim population. Religious communities have often lived amicably together. There is no conflict between the varying Hindu sects, and most temples have shrines to each of the major Hindu divinities. Christianity, which is thought to have been brought by St Thomas the Apostle to the coast of Kerala at Kodungallur in AD 52, has its own very long tradition. The equally large Muslim community traces its origins back to the spread of Islam across the Indian Ocean with Arab traders from the seventh century.

**Cuisine** Kerala's cuisine reflects its diverse religious traditions, its seaboard location and the ubiquitous presence of the coconut. Uniquely in India, for example, beef is widely eaten, although seafood is far more common. *Fish Moilee* is prepared with coconut milk and spices while for *pollichathu* the fish is baked with chilli paste, curry leaves and spices. Coconut based dishes such as *thoran*, a dry dish of mixed vegetables chopped very small, herbs and curry leaves, with *avial*, similar to *thoran* but cooked in a sauce, are widely eaten. *Erisseri* is a thick curry of banana or yam and *kichadi* is beetroot or cucumber in coconut-curd paste. You can try these with the soft centred, lacy pancake *appam* or the soft noodle rice cakes *iddiappam*. Jack fruit, pineapples, custard apples and a endless variety of bananas – also play a vital part in many dishes. For dessert, you might get milk *payasam,* made with rice or vermicelli.

**Language** Malayalam, the state language, is the most recent of the Dravidian languages, developing from the 13th century with its origin in Sanskrit.

**Dance** The special dance form of Kerala, **Kathakali**, has its origins in the *Theyyam*, a ritual tribal dance of North Kerala, and *kalaripayattu*, the martial arts practised by the high-caste Nayars, going back 1,000 years. In its present form of dance-drama, Kathakali has evolved over the last 400 years. The performance is usually outdoors, the stage bare but for a large bronze oil-lamp, with the drummers on one side and the singers with cymbal and gong, who act as narrators, on the other. The art of mime reaches its peak in these highly stylized performances which used to last through the night; now they often take just three to four hours. The costume consists of a large, billowing skirt, a padded jacket, heavy ornaments and headgear. The make-up is all-important: *Pacha* (green) characterizing the Good and *Kathi* (knife, shape of a painted 'moustache'), the Villain; *Thadi* (bearded) – white for superhuman *hanumans*, black for the hunter and red for evil and fierce demons; *Kari* (black) signifying demonesses; *Minukku* (shining) 'simple' make-up representing the Gentle and Spiritual. The paints are natural pigments while the stiff 'mask' is created with rice paste and lime. The final application of a flower seed in the lower eyelid results in the red eyes you will see on stage. This classical dance requires lengthy, hard training to make the body supple, the eyes expressive. The 24 *mudras* express the nine emotions of serenity, wonder, kindness, love, valour, fear, contempt, loathing and anger. The gods and mortals play out their roles amid the chaos brought about by human ambition, but the dance ends in peace and harmony restored by the gods.

## Modern Kerala

**Government** Government Kerala politics have often been unstable – even turbulent – since the first elections were held, after the reorganization of the Indian States, in March 1957, when Kerala became the first state in the world to democratically elect a Communist government. Between then and the mid-80s, President's Rule was imposed seven times. The debate has always been dominated by the struggle between the Marxist Communist Party, the Congress, and various minor parties: and the State government has often been formed by coalitions. Although some say their support has grown slightly, the Hindu nationalist BJP does not sit at the top table of politics in the left-leaning state – politics here are resolutely secular. The incumbent Congress party in the state though, whose term was defined by internecine fighting, fared little better, and failed to win a single seat for the Lok Sabha for the first time since Independence. The state in 2004, spurred on by the ruling Congress government's poor handling of one of the worst droughts in the state's history in the run-up to the elections, voted instead to be represented at the Center by the Communist Party of India (Marxist) and the Left Democratic Front.

**Economy** Traditionally Kerala's economy has depended heavily on agriculture. Estate crops, especially tea and rubber, make a major contribution to exports, while coconut and coconut products like coir, the coarse fibre used for matting and string and rope production, or copra, the oil-rich flesh of the coconut, continue to be vital to the state. Newer cash crops like pineapples have also begun to establish a national and international market. Rice production has been in long-term decline, and between 1990 and 2000 production fell by 25% as farmers converted paddy land to other more profitable uses, stimulated by the rise of Kerala as a remittance economy, with large flows of money being repatriated by Malayali workers in the Gulf to invest in land, housing and small-scale industries. Business leaders bemoan the leftist culture of the state and the stranglehold the trade unions have on its workforce, which makes for a working week dominated by strikes, thus barring the way for the high levels of foreign investment that characterize Bangalore, Hyderbad and Chennai's urban economies.



# Thiruvananthapuram and the far south

*The state capital, a pleasant city built over gently rolling coastal land, is very much a village as soon as you step away from the crowded centre: there's none of the throb, bustle and boom-time of Ernakulam, its northern sister city, and cosmopolitan it ain't: you'll be pushed to find a club or bar or even any traffic on the roads after midnight. It is, however, a stone's throw from here to the white sands of Kovalam, still a working fishing village, albeit one that survives under the lengthening shadow cast by unchecked tourist development. The backpackers who first populated Kovalam are now leaving it to the charter holidaymakers and mostly heading north to set up camp in Varkala, a beach defined by its sheer red rock face. Inland are the less visited forests of Ponmudi and just over the southern border lies Kanniyakumari: the sacred toe-tip of India where three seas converge.* ▸▸ *For Sleeping, Eating and other listings, see pages 903-914.*

## Ins and outs

**Getting there** Outside rush hour, the international airport is 15 minutes' drive from the centre, half an hour to Kovalam. You can hire a pre-paid taxi or auto into town or wait for a local bus. The railway and central bus stations are at the southern end of town; short-distance buses, including those bound for Kovalam, leave from the City stand, opposite the fort entrance. Buses to Kovalam stop at Waller Junction, before Kovalam, five minutes' walk from the Samudra beach hotels. A further 1.5 km on they turn off for the main bus stand at Ashok Hotel gate, five minutes from most southern hotels and cafés. Autos and taxis can get to the steep, narrow, Lighthouse Road. ▸▸ *See Transport, page 912, for further details.*

*Thiruvananthapuram is derived from Tiru Ananta Puram, the abode of the sacred serpent Ananta upon whose coils Vishnu lies in the main temple.*

# Thiruvananthapuram (Trivandrum)

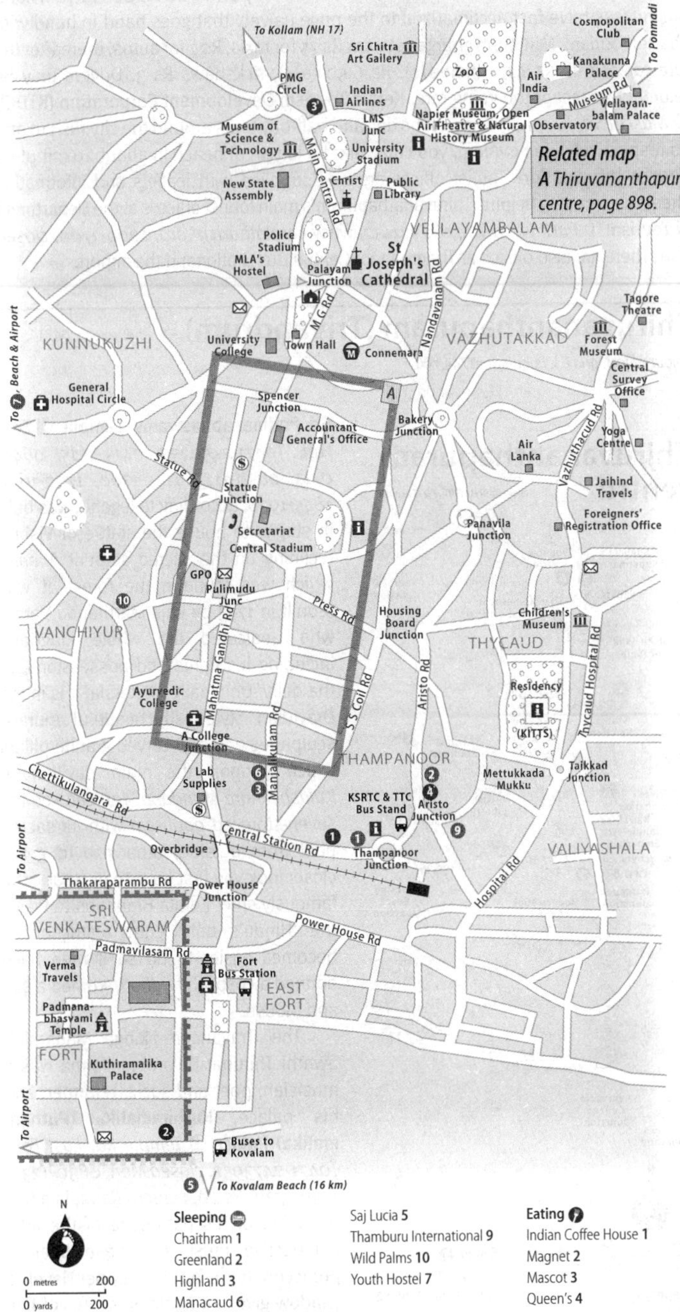


**Sleeping**
Chaithram 1
Greenland 2
Highland 3
Manacaud 6
Saj Lucia 5
Thamburu International 9
Wild Palms 10
Youth Hostel 7

**Eating**
Indian Coffee House 1
Magnet 2
Mascot 3
Queen's 4

**Getting around** Thiruvanathapuram is quite strung out, though the centre is compact. Autos or taxis are more convenient than the packed buses but bargain hard: businesses have fast acclimatized to the price naïvety that goes hand in hand with charter tourism. Minimum charges start at Rs 75 for taxis, Rs 7 for autos, thereafter the rate for cars is Rs 4.50 (non-a/c), Rs 6.50 (a/c), rickshaws Rs 3. Drivers may be reluctant to accept the going rate. **Kerala Tourism Development Corporation (KTDC)**, ⓘ *Mascot Sq, T0471-2330031*, runs day and half-day tours around the city (Rs 110 and 70 respectively). In Kovalam, you can walk the length of beach in about 20 minutes.

**Tourist information** Tourist offices are well supplied with leaflets and information sheets and are very helpful. Thiruvanathapuram's main tourist office is at the **Department of Tourism** ⓘ *Park View, T0471-2321132, www.keralatourism.org, 1000-1700, closed Sun*. There are also offices at Thampanoor Central Bus Stationand the airport.

# Thiruvananthapuram (Trivandrum) → *Phone code: 0471.*

*Colour map 3, grid C3. Population: 744,700.*

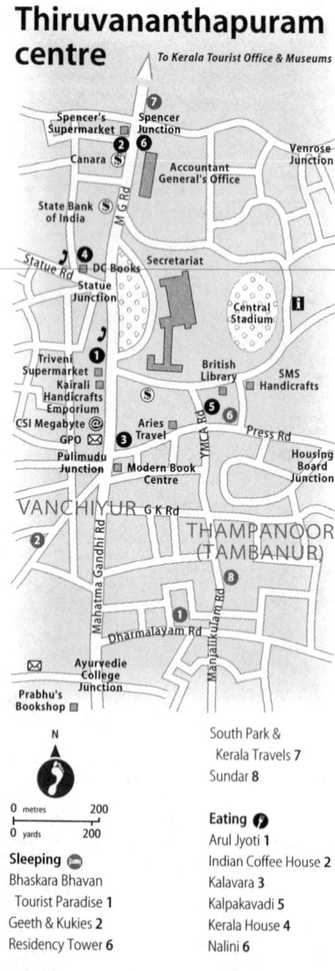


**Sri Padmanabhaswamy Temple** ⓘ *East Fort, T0471-2450233, 0415-0515, 0645-0715, 0830-1115, 1145-1200, 1700-1615, 1845-1930*, according to legend, was built in stages to house the statue of Vishnu reclining on the sacred serpent *Ananta*, which was found n the forest. It was rebuilt in 1733 by Raja Marthanda Varma who dedicated the whole kingdom, including his rights and possessions, to the deity. Unusually for Kerala, it is in the Dravidian style with beautiful murals, sculptures and 368 carved granite pillars which support the main pavilion or *Kulashekhara Mandapa*. You can see the seven-storeyed *gopuram* with its sacred pool from outside; otherwise to get a closer look you first have to persuade the famously strict Kerala Brahmins to waive the 'Hindu's only' entry restriction. It becomes easier to do so if men have donned a crisp white *dhoti*, women a sari and blouse.

The Travancore king, Maharajah Swathi Thirunal Balarama Varma was a musician, poet and social reformer, and his palace, **Kuthiramalika (Puthenmalika) Palace** ⓘ *Temple Rd, East Fort, T0471-2473952, closed Mon, 0830-1230, 1530-1730, Rs 20, camera Rs 15*, is a fine reflection of his patronage of the arts. Perspective must also have been a preoccupation: on the upper level a window gives an angle on scores of fine wood-carved horses to look like a huge cavalry charge, and among the portraits painted in the slightly unsettling

### Age old ayurveda

Ayurvedic massage, using aromatic and medicinal oils to tone up the nervous system, has been practised in Kerala for centuries. But recently, interest has been revived in this most ancient of medicine and there are several centres which include a 'rejuvenation programme'.

Ayurveda (science of life/health) is the ancient Hindu system of medicine – a naturalistic system depending on diagnosis of the body's 'humours' (wind, mucus, gall, and sometimes blood) to achieve a balance. In its early form, gods and demons were associated with cures and ailments; treatment was carried out by using herbs, minerals, formic acid (from ant hills) and water. Ayurveda classified substances and chemical compounds according to the theory of *panchabhutas* or five 'elements'. It also noted the action of food and drugs on the human body.

There are ayurvedic hospitals in the larger towns in Kerala, see 'Activities and tours' in each listings section.

Indian/European classical hybrid style is one from an artist who trumped his rivals by painting not just eyes that follow you around the room, but also feet. Sadly, it is ill maintained, but a gem nonetheless.

**Napier Museum** ⓘ *North Park Grounds, city north, T0471-2318294, closed Mon and public holidays, 1000-1645, Wed morning only*, is a spectacular landmark. The structure designed by RF Chisholm in traditional-Kerala-meets-Indo-Saracenic style, was completed in 1872. Today it houses a famous collection of eighth to 18th-century South Indian bronzes, mostly from Chola, Vijayanagar and Nayaka periods, a few Jain and Buddhist sculptures and excellent wood carvings. **Sri Chitra Art Gallery** ⓘ *just north, closed Mon and Wed mornings, 1000-1645, Rs 5*, has a fine catalogue of Indian art from early to modern schools: works by Raja Ravi Varma, 20th-century pioneer of the radical post-colonial school of painting. Sit by paintings from Java, Bali, China and Japan, Mughal and Rajput miniatures. The Tanjore paintings are studded with semi-precious stones. The **Zoological Park** ⓘ *closed Mon, 0900-1845, Rs 5, cameras Rs 15, entrance at southwest corner of park*, is a frangipani- and jacaranda-dotted hilly woodland with a wide collection of animals and a well-labelled botanical garden.

## Kovalam and surrounding resorts

➔ *Phone code: 0471. Colour map 3, grid C3. Population: 25,400.*

The small village that once lay quietly inland from a series of deserted sandy bays separated by rocky promontories jutting out into the Lakshadweep Sea has now been almost wholly swallowed up and spat out by the quick spinning wheel of tourist development. Although Kovalam, as the focus of one of the Government's main tourist drives, is choking under the weight of package tours from Europe, it is still a far cry from Calangute in Goa. But the narrow walkways that zigzag behind the town's beachside shop-fronts still link endless businesses in ayurveda, catering, accommodation and silverware. Sand is used up, if not in the drying and tending of fishing nets, then with the feet of foreign tourists' deck chairs.

North and south of Kovalam are four main stretches of beach, about 400 m long. A rocky promontory with the Charles Correa-designed **Le Meridien Hotel** divides them into north and south sections. The area to the north of the promontory – known as **Samudra and Pozhikara beaches** – 5 km away, offers the most sheltered bathing and the clearest water. The southern beaches (**Lighthouse and Eve's beach**) are more

# Kovalam

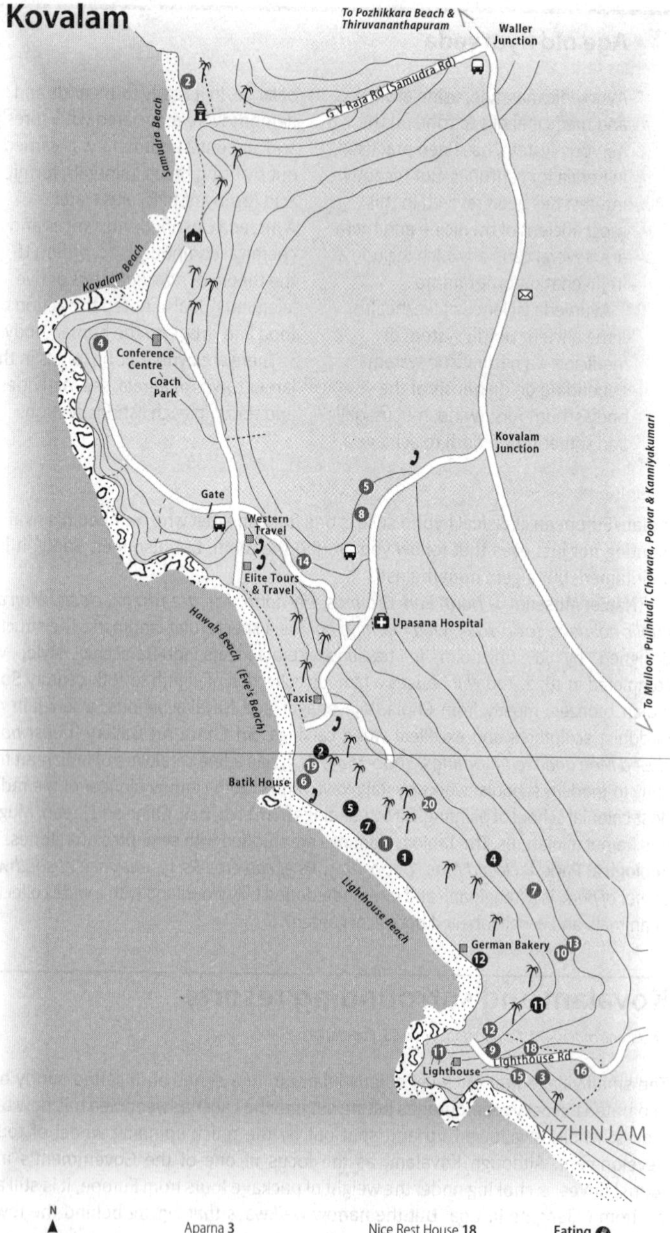

To Pozhikkara Beach & Thiruvananthapuram
Waller Junction
G V Raja Rd (Samudra Rd)
Samudra Beach
Kovalam Beach
Conference Centre
Coach Park
Kovalam Junction
Gate
Western Travel
Elite Tours & Travel
Upasana Hospital
Hawah Beach (Eve's Beach)
Taxis
Batik House
Lighthouse Beach
German Bakery
Lighthouse
Lighthouse Rd
VIZHINJAM
To Mulloor, Pulinkudi, Chowara, Poovar & Kanniyakumari

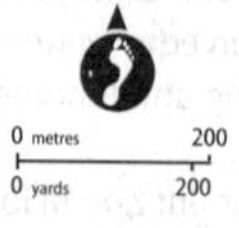


**Sleeping**
Abad Palm Shore 16
Achutha 1
Al Italia Beach Resort 2
Aparna 3
Beach Castle 14
Blue Sea 5
Dwaraka Lodge & Seashore Restaurant 6
Green Valley Cottages 7
Holiday Home Resort 8
Le Meridian Kovalam Beach Resort & Spa 4
Maharaju Palace 10
Nice Rest House 18
Paradise Rock 12
Pink Flowers 13
Raja 14
Rockholm 15
Sea Flower Beach Resort 11
Seaweed 9
Surya Nivas 13
Swami Tourist Home 19
Wilson Tourist Home 20

**Eating**
Flamingo 1
Lonely Planet 4
Neelkantha 5
Santana 7
Sea Face 2
Shell's Bar 11
Siva 12

crowded and buzzy. Lighthouse Beach is far and away the most happening and has a long line of bars screening pirated Hollywood films, cafés selling muesli and pastries and hawkers peddling crafts or drugs; but it is still low-key compared to some European holiday beaches. Further south still is where the classy resorts are clustered. **Pulinkudi** and **Chowara**, respectively 8 km and 10 km to the south, is where to go for hand-and-foot attentiveness, isolation, heritage-style villas and ayurveda in luxurious surrounds. Chowara beach has security staff but some sunbathers still feel plagued by hawkers. **Poovar Island**, 20 km south, approachable only by boat (Rs 200). There are now lifeguard patrols but you still need to be careful when swimming. The sea can get rough, particularly between April and October with swells of up to 6 m. From May the sea level rises, removing the beach completely in places, and swimming becomes very dangerous.

Within easy walking distance of Kovalam – sandwiched in between the Lighthouse and Poovar beaches – but scarcely visited by tourists is **Vizhinjam**, the capital of the later Ay rulers who dominated South Travancore in the ninth century AD. In the seventh century they had faced constant pressure from the Pandiyans who kept the Ay chieftains under firm control for long periods. There are rock-cut sculptures in the 18th-century cave temple here: there is a loose sculpture of Vinandhara Dakshinamurthi inside the shrine. The outer wall has unfinished reliefs of Shiva and Parvati. Today Vizhinjam is the centre of the fishing industry and is being developed as a major container port. The traditional boats are rapidly being modernized and the catch is sold all over India, but you can still see the keen interest in the sale of fish, and women taking headloads off to local markets.

## Around Kovalam

South of Kovalam, in Tamil Nadu, is **Padmanabhapuram**, the old wooden palace of the Rajas of Travancore. It is a beautiful example of the Kerala school of architecture and has murals, floral carvings and black granite floors. It makes an excellent day trip from town or from Kovalam, and is a neat stopover on the route to **Kanniyakumari** see page 886.

At the foot of the Western Ghats, 30 km east of Thiruvananthapuram, the **Neyyar Wildlife Sanctuary** ⓘ *free, speed boat, for 2 Rs 100/150, larger boats to view the forests enclosing the lake, Rs 20 each, mini bus safari Rs 10*, occupies a beautiful, wooded and hilly landscape, dominated by the peak of Agasthya Malai (1,868 m). The vegetation ranges from grassland to tropical, wet evergreen. Wildlife includes gaur, sloth bear, Nilgiri tahr, jungle cat, sambar deer, elephants and Nilgiri langur, but the most commonly seen animals are lion-tailed macaques and other monkeys. Tigers and leopards have also been reported. **Neyyar Dam** supports a large population of crocodiles and otters; a crocodile farm was set up in 1977 near the administrative complex.

Immediately to the northeast of the Neyyar Wildlife sanctuary a section of dense forest, **Agasthya Vanam**, was set aside as a biological park in 1992 to recreate biodiversity on a wide scale. Nearby, the **Sivananda Yoga Vedanta Dhanwantari Ashram** ⓘ *T0471-2290493, www.sivananda.org/neyyardam*, runs yoga and meditation courses. It is quite an intensive schedule though, with classes that start just after dawn, and a strict timetable including karma yoga (ie cleaning the site). As such it is only really suitable for the hardy; others may find it heavy on Hinduism and Indian diet (minimum stay three days).

Further north sits **Ponmudi** ⓘ *buses from central bus stand 0530-1630; return from between 0615 and 1905 (2½ hrs)*, the nearest hill station to Thiruvananthapuram, 65 km away. In a spectacular and peaceful setting, the tourist complex, though basic, serves as a good base for trekking, birdwatching and visiting the nearby minimalist deer park.

# Varkala → *Phone code: 0472. Colour map 3, grid C3. Population: 42,300.*

Physical obstacles may just help save Varkala from changing too fast: the sea is far from calm; the grey-gold beach less easily accessible than most, thanks to the sharp

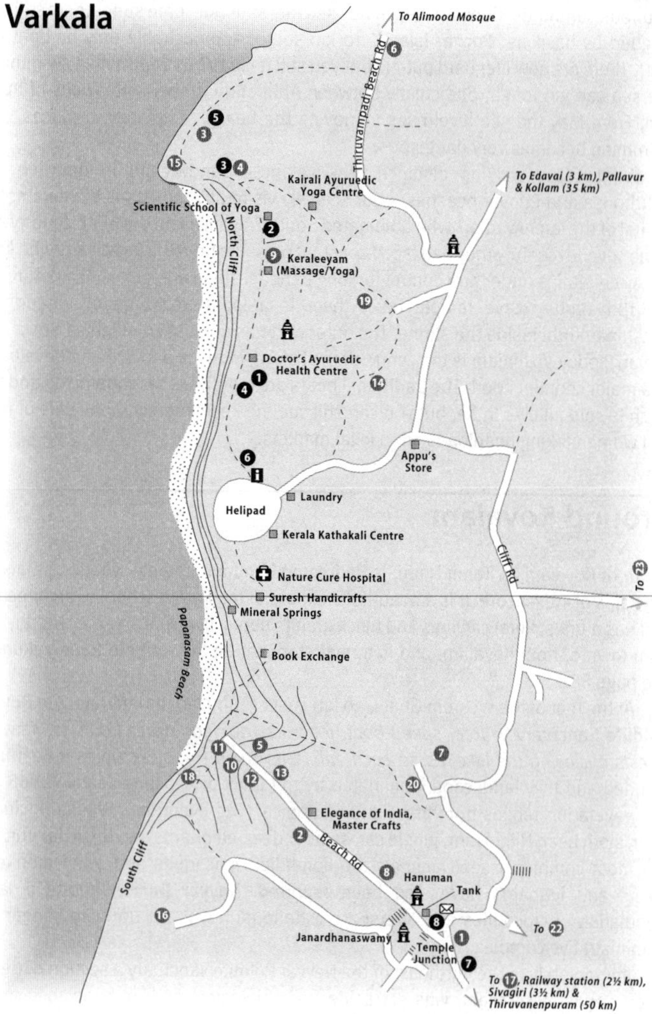

## Varkala

To Alimood Mosque
Thiruvampadi Beach Rd
To Edavai (3 km), Pallavur & Kollam (35 km)
Kairali Ayuruedic Yoga Centre
Scientific School of Yoga
North Cliff
Keraleeyam (Massage/Yoga)
Doctor's Ayuruedic Health Centre
Appu's Store
Helipad
Laundry
Kerala Kathakali Centre
Cliff Rd
To 23
Nature Cure Hospital
Suresh Handicrafts
Mineral Springs
Papanasam Beach
Book Exchange
Elegance of India, Master Crafts
Beach Rd
South Cliff
Hanuman
Tank
To 22
Janardhanaswamy
Temple Junction
To 17, Railway station (2½ km), Sivagiri (3½ km) & Thiruvanenpuram (50 km)

**Sleeping**
Ajantha Tourist Home **1**
Akshay **2**
Anandan Tourist Home **17**
Bamboo Village **3**
Blue Marine Beach Resort **15**
Chinnus Home **12**
Clafouti **4**
Eden Garden **5**
Evergreen Beach Palace **6**
Govt Rest House **7**
Gratitude Inn **8**
Hill Top Beach Resort **9**
Jacaranda **16**
Kera Village Resort **23**
Mamma Chompos & Pizzeria **10**
Nikhil Beach Resort **11**
Panchvadi **13**
Prasanth Garden **14**
Sea Pearl Chalets **18**
Summer Land **3**
Sunny Lodge **22**
Suvarna Sangeetha Bhavanum **19**
Taj Garden Retreat **20**
Thiruvambadi Beach Resort **6**

**Eating**
Café Italiano **1**
Chinnos **2**
Clafouti **3**
Kadaloram No 1 **4**
Kerala Coffee House **5**
Oottupura **6**
Sathram **7**
Sri Padman **8**

drop of the red-rock cliff wall, and drownings are more than possible. Fishermen haul in their catch at the south end of the beach, while backpackers – young and old – lie sunning themselves to the north in between classes in yoga or reiki. Three sets of steep steps hacked into the cliffs form the link from accommodation and restaurants making the beach uniquely free from commercial activity. On the high ground, is the tourist village's high street: sizeable concrete hotels are interspersed with travel agents, internet cafés, tailors stitching out endless pairs of fisherman's trousers and a huge preponderance of Kashmiri and Tibetan salespeople pushing their usual turquoise, silverware and carpets.

The North Cliff is where much of the action is, but the middle belt here can feel like you're running the gauntlet of one long, aggressive sales pitch. Further north and the tourist shacks bleed into fishing village life. The south is a relaxed place of traditional houses, temples, a big temple pond and a few sadhus, but the beach here reeks of fish from the daily catch. The main beach, Papanasam (Pavanacham) Beach is a little more conservative than Kovalam and is popular with Indian families at weekends, especially the southerly end. The beach has lifeguards, and it is essential to swim in the designated flagged area.

If shopping, bear in mind that prices are relatively high here: traders refuse to honour the standard rates for 92.5 silver, charging above value by the piece rather than by weight and steadfastly refusing to bargain. Shops around Temple Junction are more reasonable than those along the cliff. Watch your step around the cliff, particularly at night. Local authorities have not yet seen fit to install anything approaching a safety rail, and although a few local businesses have strung out bamboo poles, it's haphazard to say the least. Carry torches.

For more deserted beaches and interesting fishing settlements, either head north along the north cliff towards the **Alimood Mosque** in the middle distance, or scramble over the rocks at the bottom of Beach Road. Beachwear is not appropriate when visiting these predominantly Muslim fishing villages, but if you dress conservatively you will generally get a warm reception.

In the village, a short distance inland, is the south Kerala style **Janardhanaswamy Temple**, a centre for pilgrimage. Largely rebuilt in the 13th century, the minor shrines are older. The temple is primarily dedicated to Vishnu with subsidiary Shaivite shrines outside the main precinct. **Arattu festival** in March-April draws thousands of pilgrims. Non-Hindus are not permitted to enter. Opposite is the **Sri Rama Hanuman Temple**, with its busy temple tank. The main 'town' area (including the train station) is a further 2 km inland from Temple Junction.

On the cliff top to the north of the temple are the palace buildings of the Maharajah of Travancore, now a Government Guest House and branch of the Taj hotel chain. Behind this were buildings which housed the harems of the Maharajah, but these were sold off at Independence.

A two-hour excursion takes you to **Golden Island** for a glimpse of local backwaters: there's a small temple here but it's the type of visit you'd make for the atmosphere more than anything else. A boat round the island should cost Rs 50 for the hour.

## Sleeping

**Thiruvananthapuram** *p898, map p898*

**L-B Saj Lucia**, East Fort, T0471-2463443, www.sajlucia.com. 104 rooms, some a/c, large 'fantasy suites', others very small, good restaurant, exchange, pool.

**A-B Residency Tower**, Press Rd, T0471-2331661, www.residencytower.com. 80 top quality rooms in predominantly business hotel, 60 a/c with full facilities, highly efficient, good restaurants, bar, rooftop pool.

**C Wild Palms Guesthouse**, Mathrubhoomi Rd, Vanchiyoor, 10-min walk Statue Junction or ask for pick-up, T0471-2471175, www.wildpalmsguesthouse.com. 6 rooms in modern guesthouse in the subs (traditional design), some a/c, spacious, cool, welcoming.

**C-D Chaithram** (Kerala Tourism), Station Rd, T0471-2330977, www.ktdc.com. 80 rooms, 24 a/c, good a/c restaurant, bar, exchange, modern, very clean, next to railway and bus stand, noisy area but good value, often full.
**C-D Geeth**, off MG Rd, near GPO, Pulimudu, T0471-2471987. 50 rooms, some a/c, rooftop restaurant recommended.
**C-D Thampuru International**, Aristo Junction, opposite railway station, T0471-2321987. Pleasant interior, comfortable rooms (some a/c), excellent value, sometimes full.
**C-E Highland**, Manjalikulam Rd, T0471-2333200. 85 clean, comfortable rooms, some a/c in a tall block, satellite TV.
**E Asha**, 200 m from airport, T0471-2501050. Very handy for early departures, decent rooms with bath.
**F Bhaskara Bhavan Tourist Paradise**, near Ayurvedic College, T0471-2330662. 40 rooms, sombre but clean, good value.
**F Greenland**, near Aristo Junction, T0471-2323485, short walk from station and bus. Rooms with bath, very safe, good value.
**F Kukies Holiday Inn**, Luke's Lane, T0471-2478530. Small, quiet, with a pleasant flower-filled courtyard, good value.
**F Manacaud**, Manjalikulam Rd, T0471-2330360. 46 basic rooms, some with bath, very friendly.
**F Sundar**, Manjalikulam Rd, T0471-2330532. 45 very basic rooms in old-style lodge, very cheap.
**F Youth Hostel** (KTDC), Veli (10 km from centre). Rooms and dorm (Rs 10), very cheap vegetarian lunches, pretty lagoon separated from the sea by a sandbar, surrounded by coconut groves, clean beach, boating, some watersports, good views.

### Kovalam and surrounding resorts

*p899, map p900*

Long power cuts are common here, so a/c often doesn't work. Look for rooms with windows on two walls to get a good through-breeze. The area behind the Lighthouse Beach is full of hotels with a range of rooms from Rs 100-1,000. There are numerous budget cottages and rooms to let. Scouts greet arrivals at bus stand but you may pay considerably more if you use their services. You will find rooms to let, behind bars and restaurants, by walking from the Sea Rock hotel towards the lighthouse, and on the Samudra Beach and GV Raja Rd (Samudra Rd). Rates shown here are for the high season. Prices skyrocket in all hotels for the 2-week peak period (20 Dec-10 Jan), though it still pays to bargain. High season: 1-19 Dec, 11 Jan-28 Feb; in low season especially May-Jul: expect 40-75% discounts.
**L Le Meridien Kovalam Beach Resort and Spa**, T0471-2480101, www.lemeridien.com. 106 moderate size a/c rooms with sea view within peaceful grounds, 3 freshwater pools, tennis, badminton, catamaran and boat trips, tiny fenced beach and ayurvedic centre.
**L-AL Surya Samudra**, Mulloor PO, T0471-2480413, www.suryasamudra.com. Can book via *Toptour GMBH*, Piusallee 108, GD-48147 Münster, T251-235559. 15 large rooms in old Kerala houses reassembled and modernized, open-air bathrooms among banana plants no TV, 4 a/c (no sea view and no mosquitos), very good food, exclusive, secluded beach, stunning setting, popular with Germans. Recommended but overpriced and a bit pompous.
**L-A Karikkathi Beach House**, near Nagar Bhagavathy Temple at Mulloor Thottam, Pulinkudi, T0471-2400956, www.pulinkudi.com. 2 doubles with linked lounge, palm thatch roof, no AC or TV, perfect for honeymooners or those used to being kept: the house comes with private beach, private chef, waiter and servants. There's a cottage should families or groups need extra beds. Full board an extra US$18 per day.
**AL Poovar Island Resort**, Poovar Island, T0471-2212068, www.poovarislandresort.com. Award- winning boutique hotel with 'floating' cottages where the backwaters meet the sea.
**AL-A Isola Di Cocco**, Poovar Island, T0471-2210008, www.isoladicocco.com. Surrounded by water and with its own private beach, complex offers rooms in condominiums or villas within traditional-style houses. Ayurveda, internet café, doctor on call, and backwaters all offered.

*For an explanation of the sleeping and eating price codes used in this guide, see inside the front cover. Other relevant information is found in Essentials pages 56-61.*

**AL-A Lagoona Davina**, Pozhikkara beach, 2 mins' swim across the lagoon, T0471-2380049, www.lagoonadavina.com. 11 hand-painted rooms, each with butler service and mostly with sea views, yoga, meditation, reiki, low-fat Kerala cooking, in health and eco-retreat run by English woman – you can even phone ahead and they'll provide you with clothes and ayurvedic toiletries on your arrival.
**AL-A Somatheeram**, T0471-2268101 www.somatheeram.com. Ayurvedic health resort, 46 rooms, most in reassembled Kerala houses with original antique wooden panels, carved doors etc, huge windows with sea views, slow service in the restaurant, some modern cottages, yoga by the beach. Low voltage (slow fans, dim lights), gloomy at night. Little too far from beach. The cheaper sister concern,
**B Manatheeram**, T0471-2481610, is next door with 30 clean, breezy beach-facing circular huts, grass screen windows, fans, good showers, good seafood on beach. Specialist ayurvedic treatments at both, massage (US$15 per hr).
**A Travancore Heritage**, Chowara, T0471-2267828, www.thetravancoreheritage.com. 65 a/c rooms – bedrooms in Kerala-style cottages. Popular with package tourists, service can be surly, otherwise good. Ayurveda packages include 7-day programme (food, accommodation and treatment from €1,272.
**A-B Abad Palm Shore**, T0471-2481481, www.abadhotels.com. 35 a/c rooms, popular with groups, holiday camp atmosphere but lovely pool and beach access. Money change and ayurvedic health centre.
**A-B Dr Franklin's Panchakarma Institute**, Chowara, T0471-2480870, www.dr-franklin.com. Dr Franklin is a pukka ayurveda expert of world repute, and the institute here offers packages including *Born To Win*. Treatment packages include food, therapies and accommodation (yoga costs US$5 per class), but tend to have minimum stays of 7 days. 10 mins from the beach. See also page 911.
**B Beach Castle**, T0471-2480252, www.beachcastle.biz. 20 lovely sea-facing rooms in new hotel, some with tub, choose a/c or excellent suite, open-plan restaurant, great terrace views.
**B Bethsaida Hermitage**, Pulinkudi, T0471-2267554. 33 rooms in eco-friendly stone and bamboo beach *cabanas* in coconut groves built for single or double occupancy. Profits support 2,600 children at the orphanage next door. Family-friendly, informal and unpretentious.
**B Coconut Bay Beach Resort**, Mulloor, T0471-2480566, www.coconutbay.com. 13 spacious brick/stone cottages on beach, good restaurant, friendly, secluded location in traditional fishing village, next to Siddharth Ayurvedic and Yoga Centre. Recommended.
**B Raja**, T0471-2480355, www.rajahotel.net. 19 spacious, cool and calm rooms, 8 a/c, full facilities, bar, pool (non-residents Rs 150), fish pond containing your dinner!
**B-C Blue Sea**, near Telegraph office, T0471-2481401, www.hotelbluesea.com. A most unusual and relaxing hotel, 15 a/c rooms, in converted Kerala-style mansion with curious circular towers, large garden with good pool (non-residents Rs 150), great restaurant area.
**B-C Rockholm**, Lighthouse Rd, T0471-2480406, www.rockholm.com. 22 very good rooms and penthouse, wonderful position just above lighthouse, good terrace restaurant, clean and spacious, very pleasant hotel owned by an Anglo-Indian family with immaculately mannered staff: charmingly old-fashioned.
**B-D Hotel Seaweed**, Lighthouse Rd, Kovalam, T0471-480391. Green and white complex with huge sea-facing sit-outs from 12 of the 38 rooms. Money change, airport pick-up.
**C Wilson Tourist Home**, up path behind Neelkantha, T0471-2480051, wilson@md3.vsnl.net.in. 24 pleasant and quiet rooms with bath, 14 a/c, open-air restaurant, balconies with fan, exchange, garden, clean, safe, friendly and helpful service. Recommended.
**C-D Al Italia Beach Resort**, Samudra Beach, T0471-2480042. 4 simple but modern rooms, secluded beach front (fishermen, early morning), quiet, breezy, shady restaurant, delicious food.
**C-D Aparna**, Lighthouse Rd, uphill from beach, T0471-2480950. 8 excellent but small rooms in well-designed hotel, very pleasant.
**C-D Backwater House**, Pozhikkara beach, T0471-2590155, bwhouse2001@hotmail.com. Simple but comfortable rooms.

**C-D Maharaju Palace**, near the lighthouse, T0471-2485320, www.maharajupalace.com. 6 lovely rooms with balconies in beautiful, shady garden setting, very peaceful. Recommended.

**C-D Sea Flower Beach Resort**, Lighthouse Beach, T0471-2480554, visitindia@eth.net. Right on the beach with 9 rooms across 3 storeys and own rooftop restaurant. Nice doubles with basins built inside the rooms themselves and clean bathrooms.

**D Nice Rest House**, Lighthouse, T0471-2480684. 10 clean rooms across 2 wings, 1st floor has amazing views of the beach.

**D-E Holiday Home Resort**, Beach Rd (10 mins' walk from sea), T0471-2480497, www.holidayhomeresort.com. Clean, pleasant rooms and cottages, some a/c, dorm (Rs 150), good food, beautiful flower garden, internet, quiet, friendly, excellent service. Recommended.

**E Achutha**, Lighthouse Beach. Restaurant, good clean rooms and good food.

**E Dwaraka Lodge**, Lighthouse Beach, T0471-2480411, marytambini@hotmail.com. 8 basic but clean rooms, some with bath, restaurant, quiet beachfront location, art gallery, boat trips.

**E Green Valley Cottages**, T0471-2480636, indira_ravi@hotmail.com. 21 clean, fresh and quiet rooms with bath in lovely surroundings, restaurant. Recommended.

**E Paradise Rock**, Lighthouse Rd, T0471-2480658. 4 large rooms, hot showers, close to beach, good views and breeze.

**E White House**, Lighthouse Beach, T0471-2483388, whitehouse@vsnl.com. 12 clean and airy rooms, nets, use of common fridge and kitchen, close to beach, very good value. Recommended.

**F Pink Flowers**, Lighthouse Beach, behind Neptune hotel. 4 immaculate rooms with bath, good location, friendly.

**F Surya Nivas**, Lighthouse Beach. 4 very clean rooms with bath, quiet, friendly.

**F Swami Tourist Home**, with good clean rooms, good food and friendly service.

### Around Kovalam *p901*

**L Duke's Forest Lodge**, Anappara, near Ponmudi, T0471-2268822, www.dukesforest.com. 5 luxury villas on organic estate: each of which has its own personal plunge pool: great trekking.

**E Agasthya House** (Kerala Tourism), opposite viewing tower, near Forest Information Centre, Kattakada, T0471- 2272160. 6 rooms, on the edge of the reservoir, built like a concrete bunker, disappointing restaurant, lunch Rs 20-50, beer, views, very helpful staff.

**F Ponmudi Tourist Resort**, T0471-2890230. 24 rooms and 10 cottages, in attractive gardens surrounded by wooded hills, spartan facilities but spacious rooms, restaurant serves limited but reasonable vegetarian meals, beer available; also a post office and general stores.

### Varkala *p902, map p902*

There are at least 50 guesthouses, plus rooms in private houses. The North Cliff area is fairly compact, so look around until you find what you want: the northernmost area is where the most laid-back, budget options are and have the most character, while the far south side has a few fancier places. None, however, is actually on the beach. Outside the high season of Nov-Mar, prices drop by up to 50%, During the monsoon (Jun-Jul) many close.

**AL Taj Garden Retreat**, 500 m from the beach, T0470-2603978, retreat.varkala@tajhotels.com. 30 rooms, central a/c, partially obscured sea views, beautifully landscaped, pool, good but expensive restaurant. Lovely.

**B Villa Jacaranda**, Temple Rd West, South Cliff, T0470-2610296, www.villa-jacaranda.biz. 5 huge rooms stuffed with eclectic furniture and done up with photography (contemporary and old Indian family portraits) in new but classical- style guesthouse with lotus-filled pond and tropical garden. Guests have their own keys and entrance: set up by Londoners.

**B-C Hill Top Beach Resort**, north end, T0470-2601237, hill-top@rediffmail.com. 25 rooms, 3 cottages set amongst palms, internet, Ayurvedic treatments. Clean, pleasant and friendly.

**B-D Akshay Beach Resort**, Beach Rd (about 200 m from beach), T0470-2602668. 17 rooms, 4 spacious double a/c with bathtub and TV but singles very small, standard good value, bright, clean and smart, TV lounge, good restaurant.

**B-D Preeth Beach Resort**, T0470-2600942, www.preethbeachresort.com. Cottages and rooms (some a/c) with balconies, swimming pool and restaurant. New building.

**B-E Nikhil Beach Resort**, Beach Rd, T0470-2605191, www.nikhil-resort.com. 11 rooms, 4 a/c, exchange and money transfer. Clean, pleasant, good value.

**C Hill View Beach Resort**, North Cliff, T0470-2600566, www.hillviewbeachresort.com. 20 rooms (self-contained cottages, budget rooms with bathroom attached and de luxe room with bathtub), very quick on-site internet, pick-up from airport, hot and cold water. Efficient.

**C-D Blue Marine Beach Resort**, North Cliff, T0470-2606085. 3 sea view private cottages and 12 rooms in the main 3-storey building, restaurant on stilts, travel, internet. Design theme is the colour of strawberry Angel Delight. Full-moon parties feature fires and live tabla, flute and violin.

**C-D Eden Garden**, Beach Rd, T0470-2603910, edengarden.wheelofindia.com. 11 smallish but pleasant ethnic rooms, 1 suite, traditional-style buildings in beautiful garden-setting around a pond. Ayurvedic diets available, massage, quiet, family-run.

**C-D Thiruvambadi Beach Resort**, Thiruvambadi Beach Rd, Kurakkani, T0470-2601028, thiruvambadi@hotmail.com. 10 rooms, 7 with private balcony, hot water, rooftop restaurant, very quiet location, good value.

**D Panchvadi**, Beach Rd, T0470-2600200. 8 clean rooms (2 luxury) with bath (excellent showers), 24-hr check-in, laundry, Kerala-style restaurant, good security, friendly helpful staff, close to beach. Recommended.

**D Sea Pearl Chalets**, Beach Rd, T0470-2605875 seapearlvarkala@hotmail.com. 10 circular thatched huts in breezy location on south cliff, great views, breakfasts.

**D-E Clafouti**, T0470-2601414. 8 lovely rooms in new house (Rs 500), old house (Rs 200), all tiled baths, very clean, French-run bakery for excellent pastries.

**D-E Evergreen Beach Palace**, Thiruvambadi Beach Rd, Kurakkanni, T0470- 2603257. Large clean rooms with bath, a/c available, quite smart.

**D-E Marine Palace**, Papanasam Beach, on path down from cliff, T0470-2603204. 12 rooms, some a/c in small bungalows (not a palace), good Tandoori restaurant very close to beach (but very slow service), simple, comfortable, friendly, popular with the older people.

**D-E Prasanth Garden**, near North Cliff. 3 very nice thatched cottages with verandas in large, peaceful garden. Recommended.

**D-E Summer Land**, North Cliff. 4 very nice tiled-roof cottages, veranda, quiet and breezy location.

**D-E Suvarna Sangeetha Bhavanum**, near North Cliff. Rooms in large family house, popular with the "travellers".

**E Bamboo Village**, T0470-2610732, north cliff. 4 small very basic but charming thatched bamboo huts (painted neon yellow) with wash-basin and toilet, private verandas, among palms, very quiet with very great sea views.

**E Gratitude Inn**, Beach Rd (near Temple tank), T0470-2607841. 11 clean, spacious rooms with spring water in every tap, quiet, friendly manager offers ayurvedic guidance, bookshop, good value.

**E Mamma Chompos**, 100 m beyond Akshay hotel, T0470-2603995. 7 large rooms in traditional Kerala-style farmhouse above top quality pizza restaurant. Garden setting, friendly. Recommended.

**F Ajantha Tourist Home**, Temple Junction, T0470-2603684. 16 very clean rooms with bath, very friendly and helpful staff, good restaurant next door.

**F Anandan Tourist Home**, opposite train station, T0470-2602135. 32 very cheap rooms, some a/c, restaurant, clean modern building, noisy in early mornings (temple next door), good value.

**F Chinnus Home**, nearby. Spacious rooms, clean baths, hammocks among palms.

**F Govt Guest House**, towards Taj Garden Retreat, T0470-2602227. 8 rooms in the former summer residence of Maharaja, charming appearance, huge high ceilings, but not scrupulously clean (and snoring caretaker!), meals overpriced, no receipt, individual buildings are better, idyllic and quiet, wooden ceilings, marble floors, big baths, shaded porches, book in advance.

**F JA Tourist Home**, Temple Junction, T0470-2602453. 11 rooms, modern Indian hotel, good value, also excellent roof restaurant, delicious food, friendly but slow service.

**F Sea Shore**, a pretty basic (but clean) budget place run by Shine, with 5 rooms with en suite bathroom. Run by very nice people who pride themselves on keeping the place and rooms clean and the garden well tended.

**F Sea Splendour**, North Cliff end, Odayam Beach. Rooms with bath in retired teacher's guesthouse, excellent home cooking (unlimited and spoilt for choice), very quiet.

## Eating

**Thiruvananthapuram** *p898, map p898*
The first 4 options are in hotels, see Sleeping.
**TTT-TT Mascot**, excellent lunchtime buffet, pleasant, 24-hr coffee shop for all types of snacks, good value, a cool haven at midday.
**TTT-TT Orion**, for pepper steaks and cocktails recommended.
**TTT-TT Saj Lucia**, good buffet (outdoor barbecue) and southern dishes, poor service.
**TTT-TT South Park**, good tandoori and buffet lunches.
**TT Café Magnet**, Thycaud, T0471-2323301. Mixed menu. Boring decor but good food, which runs out because of popularity, not yet spotted by many Westerners (no beer).
**TT Kalavara**, Press Rd, T0471-2322195, Indian, Continental, Chinese fast food (burgers, shakes) takeaway. Food average, slow service but good value buffets in upstairs thatched section with a patch of garden – good ambience, limited views.
**TT Kalpakavadi**, Press Rd. Mixed menu. Modern and smart. Recommended.
**TT Kerala House**, near Statue Junction, T0471-2476144. Kerala cuisine in the basement of shopping complex. Clean, slow for breakfast but newspapers available, outside seating in the evening in roadside car park area is cheaper. Colourful and fun place to pass some time, even if the food arrives cold. Try *neem, kappa* and rice (delicious fish with tapioca), or inexpensive chicken dishes with coconut; bakery in the complex does excellent samosas and puffs.
**TT Queen's**, Aristo Junction. Indian non-veg. Chilli chicken and chicken fry recommended.
**T Arul Jyoti**, MG Rd, opposite Secretariat. South Indian vegetarian. With a/c family room, clean, wide choice of good value dishes, try jumbo *dosas*.
**T Indian Coffee House**, 2 on MG Rd (1 near YWCA, north of the Secretariat and another near KSRTC bus stand (the latter designed by the English architect Laurie Baker). Worth seeing, excellent value coffee and snacks.
**T Nalini**, near Spencer's supermarket. Excellent Indian sweets.

**Kovalam and surrounding resorts**
*p899, map p900*
Although there are hundreds of restaurants here, only a handful of places serve anything truly nice. Towards the lighthouse, a few seafood places display the day's catch (some 1-m long) on metal-top tables for you to select from. Tiger prawns and lobsters are pricey; avoid fish on Sun evenings, it is unlikely to be very fresh. The order of the day is not to rush, service is often slow as tiny kitchens are unable to cope with large numbers. Only a few hotels have licences; **Ashok** and **Samudra** are open to non-residents. Beach restaurants often sell beer; occasionally some spirits.
**TT The German Bakery**, has a justly evangelical following: cinnamon danish pastries, apple crumbles but also delicious fresh herbal teas and fish dishes.
**TT Fusion**, near sunset view rocks, fusion_in_kovalam@yahoo.co.in. Swish restaurant and coffee bar offering from the owner of the German Bakery. Stone banquets, varied menu (left side is Indian food, the right is continental, the middle panel is reserved for the food 'where east meets west') plus juices, herbal teas.
**TT Rockholm Hotel**. Very good international food served on a pleasant terrace with beautiful views, especially early morning.
**TT Santana**. Good atmosphere, music, backgammon, chess and good food (but very slow service), open until late.
**TT Sea Face**. Breezy raised terrace on the beach by pleasant pool (coconuts above netted for safety!). Varied choice of excellent food, including versatile fish and seafood. Friendly and attentive. Recommended.
**TT Suisse**, stylish venue, very clean, generous portions, personal attention, open kitchen and super pure juices and European food like pizza and crostini.
**T Beatles**, which also has an excellent branch in Varkala, serves fab fresh Western-style soups and salads.
**T Lonely Planet**. Wholesome, mildly spiced ayurvedic vegetarian food. Set inland around a pond babbling with ducks. Sells recipe books, and the walls are covered with 'conscious' slogan boards.
**T Roy's**, up from Sea Rock. Excellent local Kerala food, very clean, popular with locals.

### Video restaurants

Bootlegged videos of new Hollywood releases are shown free at some restaurants, but which often serve poorer food. The following are some of the better places to eat and watch at the same time:

**Flamingo** does good tandoori, especially barracuda.

**Neelkantha**, with comfortable seats and a generator to overcome regular power cuts.

**Shell's Bar**, excellent barbecue fish.

**Siva**, good tandoori, especially barracuda.

**Varkala** *p902, map p902*

Many restaurants close out of season. Take extra care with drinking water. There are numerous restaurants along North Cliff, most with very similar menus, excruciatingly slow service and questionable kitchens but try: **Chinnos**, **Kadaloram 1**, **Sunrise**, **Number One Beach Restaurant**. "Catch of the day" usually costs Rs 100-150 depending upon the type/size of fish, but make sure you don't get "catch of yesterday" (fresh fish keep their glassy eyes and bright silvery scales).

**TTT Taj Garden Retreat** hotel, (Rs 300, includes pool use), on Sun (1230-1530), good eat-all-you-want buffet, delicious rich vegetarian Indian.

**TT Beatles**, 0730-2300. Proper tables and chairs, hanging baskets and ice cubes made with purified water, safe, and delicious, salads plus yummy fish in banana leaves.

**TT Café Italiano**. Good Italian food, but quite pricey.

**TT Clafouti**. Offers fresh pastries and cakes, but standards seem to drop when the French-Keralan owners are away.

**TT Kerala Coffee House**. Popular drop in drop out place: usual fare, porridge banana, muesli and so on, but nicely done.

**TT Oottupura**, near helipad. Excellent vegetarian (*masala dosa* Rs 20, dishes Rs 30-40).

**TT Sathram**, Temple Junction. Excellent (daily changing *thalis* Rs 20), delicious small fish (Rs 10), popular with auto/bus drivers.

**TT Sri Padman**, offers good food, Western breakfasts, and overlooks the temple tank.

## Entertainment

**Thiruvananthapuram** *p898, map p898*

Performances of Kalarippayattu, Kerala's martial art, can be seen through:

**CVN Kalari**, East Fort, T0471-2474182 (0400-0700, 1700-2000); and **Balachandran Nair Kalari Martial Arts Gymnasium**, Cotton Hill (0600-0800 and 1800-1930).

**Kovalam and surrounding resorts**

*p899, map p900*

**Kalakeli Kathakali Troupe**, T0471-2481818. Daily at hotels **Ashok** and **Neptune**, Rs 100.

**Varkala** *p902, map p902*

Varkala is a good place to hang out, chill and do yoga but there's no organized nightlife to speak of, only impromptu campfire parties.

**Kerala Kathakali Centre**, by the helipad, holds a daily *Kathakali* demonstration (Rs 150, make-up 1700-1800, performance 1830-2000). The participants are generally students of the art rather than masters.

## Festivals and events

**Thiruvananthapuram** *p898, map p898*

**Mar**: Chandanakuda at Beemapalli, a shrine on Beach Rd 5 km southwest of the railway station, when local Muslims process to the mosque, holding incense sticks and pots. Marked by sword play, singing, dancing, elephant procession and fireworks. 10-day festival.

**Mar-Apr** (Meenam) and **Oct-Nov** (Thulam): Arattu is the closing festival of the 10-day celebrations of the Padmanabhaswamy Temple, in which the deity is processed around the temple inside the fort and then down to the sea (see also page 903).

**Sep/Oct**: Navaratri at the special *mandapa* in Padmanabhaswamy Temple. Several concerts are held which draw famous musicians. Thiruvonam week in **Sep**.

**Nov-Mar**: Nishangandhi Dance Festival, at weekends when all important classical Indian dance forms are performed by leading artistes at Nishagandhi open-air auditorium, Kanakakkunnu Palace.

**Oct**: A similar Soorya Dance Festival takes place from 1st-10th.

## Shopping

**Thiruvananthapuram** *p898, map p898*

Shopping areas include the Chalai Bazar, the Connemara market and the Main Rd from

Palayam to the East Fort. Usually open 0900-2000 (some take a long lunch break). Although ivory goods have now been banned, inlay on wood carving and marquetry using other materials (bone, plastic) continue to flourish. *Kathakali* masks and traditional fabrics can be bought at a number of shops.

The shopping centre opposite East Fort bus stand has a large a/c shop with good selection of silks and saris but not cheap. *Khadi* recommended from shops on both sides of MG Rd, south of Pulimudu Junction. **Co-optex**, Temple Rd, good for fabrics and *lungis*; **Handloom House**, diagonally across from Partha's has an excellent range of fabrics, clothes and export quality *dhurries*; **Partha's**, towards East Fort. Recommended; **Premier Stationers**, MG Rd, opposite Post Office Rd, are best in town; **Raymonds**, Karal Kada, East Fort has good men's clothing.

For handicrafts: **Gram Sree**, excellent village crafts; **Kairali**, has items of banana fibre, coconut, screw pine, mainly utilitarian, also excellent sandalwood carvings and bell-metal lamps, utensils; **Kalanjali**, Palace Garden, across from the museum, is recommended; **Natesan Antique Arts** and **Gift Corner**, MG Rd. Have high quality goods including old dowry boxes, carved wooden panels from old temple 'cars', miniature paintings and bronzes; **SMSM Handicrafts Emporium**, behind the Secretariat. Government-run, literally heaps of items reasonably priced.

#### Kovalam and surrounding resorts

*p899, map p900*

Numerous craft shops, including Kashmiri and Tibetan shops, sell a wide range of goods. The majority are clustered around the bus stand at the gate of the **Ashok** with another group to the south around the lighthouse. Possible to get good quality paintings, metalwork, woodwork and carpets at reasonable prices. Gems and jewellery are widely available but it is notoriously difficult to be sure of quality. Tailoring is available at short notice and is very good value with the fabrics available. Charges vary, about Rs 50-80 per piece.
**Brother Tailors**, 2nd Beach Rd;
**Raja**, near hotel Surya;
**Suresh**, next to restaurant Garzia.
**Zangsty Gems**, Lighthouse Rd, has a good reputation for helpfulness and reliability.

#### Varkala *p902, map p902*

Most of the handicraft shops are run by Kashmiris, who will tell you that everything (including the tie-dye t-shirts) is an antique from Ladakh.
**Elegance of India** and **Mushtaq**, Beach Rd. Sell Kashmiri handicrafts, carpets, jewellery etc, reported as honest, will safely air-freight carpets etc.
**Suresh**, on path south from helipad to Marine Palace, has handicrafts from Karnataka.

## Activities and tours

#### Thiruvananthapuram *p898, map p898*

#### Swimming

**Mascot Hotel**, small rooftop pool at the Residency Tower (0700-1900, Rs 250) with great views.
**Waterworks**, pool near museum, T0471-2318990. Entry Rs 2, 0830-1200, 1400-1530, 1815-2000, closed Mon.

#### Tours

**Kerala Tourism**, from Hotel Chaithram, T0471-2330031/695033, www.keralatourism.org.
**1 City tour**: 0800-1900, including Kovalam (125 km), Rs 130 including lunch, boating; half day, 1400-1900 including boating Rs 90.
**2 Kanniyakumari**: 0730-2100, including Kovalam, Padmanabhapuram and Kanniyakumari (200 km), Rs 250 daily (Padmanabhapuram closed Mon);
**3 Ponmudi**: 0830-1900, daily, Golden Valley and Ponmudi (125 km), Rs 210. Long tours can be very exhausting, the stops at sites of interest are often very brief.
**Great India Tour Co**, Mullassery Towers, Vanross Square, T0471-2331516, offers afternoon city tours, among others.

#### Tour operators

IATA approved agencies include:
**Aries Travel**, Press Rd, T0471-2330964, ariestravel@satyam.net.in.
**Gt India Tour Co**, Mullassery Towers, Vanross Junction, T0471-2331516, gitctrv@vsnl.net.in. Reliable but pricey.
**Jayasree**, PO Box 5236 Pettah, T0471-2476603, www.jayasreetravels.com. One-stop travel service, good coaches.

**TourIndia**, MG Rd, T0471-2330437, tourindia @vsnl.com. Runs unique tours, eco-friendly tree house, backwater cruises, Periyar trek, sport fishing off Kochi.

### Trekking and birdwatching

If you prefer to trek, this is best done in Dec-Apr. Get permission first from the Chief Conservator of Forests (Wildlife), Forest HQ, Thiruvananthapuram, T0471-2322217, or the Assistant Wildlife Warden at Neyyar Dam, T0471-2272182.

### Yoga

**Institute of Yogic Culture**, Vazhuthacaud.
**Sivananda Ashram**, T0471-2290493, Neyyar Dam, see page 901.

## Kovalam and surrounding resorts

*p899, map p900*

### Fishing

Can readily be arranged through the hotels, as can excursions on traditional catamarans or motor boats. Some near Ashok hotel beach promise corals and beautiful fish just offshore (do not expect to see very much).

### Tour operators

**East India Premier Tours**, behind Neelkantha Hotel, T0471-2483246. Can suggest unusual hotels.
**Great Indian Travel**, Lighthouse Rd, T0471-2481110, www.keralatours.com. Wide range, exchange, eco-friendly beach resort.
**Visit India**, Lighthouse Rd, T0471-2481069. Friendly and helpful, exchange, short country-boat backwater tours from Thiruvallam.

### Yoga, meditation and ayurveda

**Dr Franklin's Panchakarma Institute and Research Centre**, Chowara, T0471-480870, www.dr-franklin.com drfranklin@eth.net. The good doctor's family have been in ayurveda for 4 centuries, and he himself is the former district medical officer of Kerala Government. Specific treatment programmes for ailments include treatment for infertility, sluggishness, paralysis, obesity. Body purification therapy (*panchakarma* and *swetakarma*) lasts for 15 days and costs US$465. *Born To Win* programme 21 days US$630. Other programmes include *You and your spine*, *Body Mind Soul*, and there are age-reducing treatments including body immunization and longevity treatments (28 days at US$840). Straight slimming takes 28 days US$784. 51-day *panchakarma* US$1,650. Cheaper treatments are carried out too: the application of medicated fumes to ears lasts 5-10 mins and costs US$1, cleaning eyes US$4, face pack US$4, massages from US$14. Also runs training courses in massage, ayurvedic principles and *panchakarma*.
Ayurvedic treatment are also offered by most upmarket resorts (massage about Rs 700).
**Medicus**, Lighthouse Rd, T0471-2480596, where Dr Babu and his wife have clients returning year after year.
**Vasudeva**, T0471-2222510, behind Neptune Hotel, is simple but with experienced professionals.

## Varkala *p902, map p902*

### Tour companies

Most hotels offer tours, air tickets, backwater trips, houseboats etc, as do the many agents along North Cliff.
**JK Tours & Travels**, Temple Junction Varkala, T0802-6683334. Money change, 0900-2100, 7 days.

### Yoga and massage

**Keraleeyamm**, North Cliff. One of the best of the many yoga/ayurvedic massage centres.
**Lakshmi Herbal Beauty Parlour**, Clafouti Beach Resort North End Cliff, 0900-1800, T0470- 2606833. Individual attention, amazing massages plus waxing, henna etc.
**The Nature Cure Hospital**, opened in 1983, treats patients entirely by diet and natural cures including hydrotherapy, chromotherapy (natural sunbath with different filters) and mud therapy, each treatment normally lasting 30 mins.
**Naturomission Yoga Ashram**, near the Helipad. Runs 1-, 2- and 7-day courses in yoga, massage, meditation, and healing techniques. Payment by donation.
**Scientific School of Yoga and Massage**, Altharamoodu, Janardhana Temple. 10-day yoga and massage course (2 classes daily), Rs 500, professionally run by English- speaking doctor, T0470-2695141. Also shop selling ayurvedic oils, soaps, shampoo etc.

## Transport

**Thiruvananthapuram** *p898, map p898*

**Air**

The airport is closed at night so you can't wait there overnight, see Sleeping page 904. The airport is 6 km away from the beach. International flights via the Gulf states are very good value. **Transport to town**: by local bus No 14, pre-paid taxi (Rs 85) or auto (about Rs 30, 20 mins). Enquiry, T0471-2502323. Confirm international bookings and arrive in good time. Inflated prices at refreshments counter though cheap tea/coffee in the final lounge after 'Security' check. The banks at the airport are outside arrivals. **Johnson & Co** (travel agent) opposite Domestic Terminal, T0471-2503555.

**Airlines** Maldive Airways, Sri Lankan, Spencer Building, MG Rd, T0471-2322309, and T0471-2475541. **Gulf Air**, T0471-2501205, and **Kuwait Airways**, National Travel Service, Panavila Junction, T0471-2321295 (airport T0471-2500437). **Saudi Airways**, Arafath Travels, Pattom. **Indian Airlines**, Mascot Sq, T0471-2318288 (and **Sri Lanka**, T0471-2501140). **Air India**, Museum Rd, Velayambalam, T0471-2310310, A501426.

Indian Airlines flies to **Bangalore, Chennai, Delhi, Mumbai**. Air India flies to **Mumbai**. Jet Airways flies to **Chennai, Mumbai**. Indian Airlines fly to **Colombo** and **Male**. Air India flies to **London, New York, Frankfurt, Paris** and **the Gulf**.

**Auto-rickshaw**

Tell drivers which Kovalam beach you want to get to in advance, otherwise they will charge much more when you get there. Minimum Rs 6.50 (will use meter if pressed); you may need to bargain for Kovalam, especially in the evening (Rs 70 is fair).

**Bus**

City Bus Station, T0471-2463029. To **Kovalam** from East Fort, No 888, 30 mins, Rs 7. Long-distance journeys through heavy traffic can be very uncomfortable and tiring. Central Bus Station, near railway station, Thampanoor, T0471-2323886. Buses to **Kanniyakumari via Nagercoil** or direct, frequent depart, 2½ hrs; **Kozhikode**, 10 hrs (Exp); **Madurai**, 1230, 6½ hrs; **Thrissur**, 7 hrs (Exp). Buses to **Ernakulam/Kochi** via Alappuzha and Kollam, start early, 5 hrs (Exp) or 6½ hrs. You can include a section of the backwaters on the way to Kochi by getting a boat from Kollam (shared taxis there cost Rs 60 each, see below). **TNSTC** to **Chennai, Coimbatore, Cuddalore, Erode, Kanniyakumari, Madurai** from opposite the Central Railway station.

**Motorcycle**

Asian Trailblazers, MG Rd, T0471-2478211, asiantrailblazers@ yahoo.com, for Enfields.

**Taxi**

From outside **Mascot Hotel** charge about Rs 7 per km; to **Kovalam**, Rs 175, return Rs 225 (waiting: extra Rs 50 per hr).

**Train**

**Central Station**, after 1800. Reservations in building adjoining station, T132. Advance, upstairs, open 0700-1300, 1330-1930, Sun 0900-1700; ask to see Chief Reservations Supervisor, Counter 8; surprisingly no "Foreigners' quota". To **Alappuzha**: *Intercity 6342*, 1630, 3 hrs. **Bangalore**: *Kanniyakumari-Bangalore Exp, 6525*, 0920, 19½ hrs; *Trivandrum Bangalore Exp, 6322*, 1505, Wed, 18¾ hrs. **Chennai**: *Trivandrum-Guwahati Exp, 6321* (AC/II), Thu, 1245, 18¼ hrs; *Trivandrum Chennai Mail, 6320* (AC/II), 1400, 18 hrs. **Delhi (HN)**, *Rajdhani Exp, 2431*, 1915, Tue, Thu, 31 hrs. **Ernakulam (Kochi)**: 10 trains daily between 0500-2145. *Trivandrum Ernakulam Exp, 6342*, 1630, 4¼ hrs; *Kerala Exp, 2625* (AC/II), 1110, 4¼ hrs, are two. **Kolkata (H)**: *Trivandrum-Guwahati Exp, 5627* (AC/II), 1245, Sun, 49 hrs; *Trivandrum-Howrah Exp, 6323*, 1245, Thu, Sat, 49 hrs. **Kanniyakumari**: *Bangalore Kanniyakumari Exp, 6526*, 1515, 2¼ hrs. **Kollam via Varkala**: 12 trains 0725-2035, 1¼ hrs.

**Kovalam and surrounding resorts**
*p899, map p900*

There are 3 main points of access to Kovalam's beaches. Remember to specify which when hiring an auto or taxi.

**Auto-rickshaw**

To **Thiruvananthapuram**, Rs 70-80, but need to bargain hard.

### Bus

**Local** Frequent buses (0540-2100) into East Fort, **Thiruvananthapuram**, from bus stand outside Ashok Hotel gate (Kovalam beach), fast Rs 4.50, slow 3.30 (30 mins), also picks up from Waller Junction (Main Rd/Samudra beach). From East Fort bus station, auto-rickshaw to town centre, Rs 6, or walk. Green buses have limited stops; yellow/red buses continue through town up to museum.

**Long distance** To **Kanniyakumari**, **Kochi** via **Kollam (Quilon)** and via **Kottayam**, **Nagercoil**, **Padmanabhapuram**, **Varkala**, **Thodopuzha** via **Kottayam**.

### Taxi

From taxi stand or through Ashok or Samudra hotels. One-way to Thiruvananthapuram or airport, Rs 200; station Rs 175; city sights Rs 600; Kanniyakumari, Padmanabhapuram Rs 1,750 (8 hrs); Kochi Rs 2,250 (5 hrs); Kollam Rs 1100; Thekkady Rs 2,650 (6 hrs).

## Varkala *p902, map p902*

### Bus

To/from Temple Junction (not beach) for **Alappuzha** and **Kollam**, but often quicker to go to Paripally on NH47 and catch onward buses from there.

### Motorcycle

**Kovalam Motorcycle hire**, Voyager Travels, Eye's Beach Rd, T0471-2481993. Next door to **JA Tourist Home**, Temple Junction; and **Mamma Chompo**, Beach Rd.

### Rickshaw/Taxi

Catch them from Beach Rd and Helipad. Both charge Rs 25 to train station. A taxi to **Thiruvananthapuram**, Rs 350 (1¼ hrs).

### Train

Several daily to coastal towns including **Thiruvananthapuram**, 0435, 0810, 0940, 1752 and 2103 (50 mins). Also to **Kanniyakumari**: 1107, 1400 (3½ hrs); **Kollam**: 0550, 0640, 1710, 1834, 2150, 2232 (35 mins); **Mangalore**, 0640, 1834 (14 hrs).

# Directory

## Thiruvananthapuram *p898, map p898*

**Banks** Open 1000-1400, Mon to Fri, and 1000-1200, Sat. **State Bank of India**, near Secretariat, with 24-hr ATM; **Canara Bank**, near Spencer Junction, no hassle cash against Visa, friendly staff. **Andhra Bank**, near Canara Bank, on opposite side of road; cash against Visa. The airport has banks, including Thomas Cook, T0471-2502470. **Chemists** Many chemists, near hospitals; a few near Statue Junction. **Opticians: Lens & Frames**, Pulimudu Junc, T0471-2471354.

**Hospitals** General Hospital, Vanchiyoor, T0471- 2443874. **Ramakrishna Ashrama Hospital**, Sasthamangalam, T0471-2322123. **Ayurveda Hospital**, T0471-2340938. **Homeopathy Hospital**, T0471-2322125.

**Internet** **Megabyte**, CSI Building, 3rd and 4th floors, MG Rd, email: send Rs 15, receive Rs 10, friendly. **Tandem Communications**, Statue Rd (MG Rd end), good telephone and fax centre; colour photocopying, laser printing. **Central Telegraph office**: Statue Rd, 200 m to its north; open 24 hrs, best value internet. **Post** Poste Restante, Pulimudu Junction, T0471-2473071, 0830-1800, efficient. **PO**: north of Secretariat, off MG Rd, is better; Speed Post (computerized; affected by power failures); also PO at Thampanoor, opposite Manjalikulam Rd. **Useful address** Foreigners' Regional Registration **Office**, City Police Commissioner, Residency Rd, Thycaud, T0471-2320486; allow up to a week for visas, though it can take less. Open 1000-1700, Mon-Sat. **Wildlife Warden**, PTP Nagar, Vattiyoorkavu, T0471-2360762.

## Kovalam and surrounding resorts *p899, map p900*

**Banks** 3 ATMs: **Canara Bank**, T0471-2481950; **ICICI Bank**, both at Kovalam Junction; and **HDFC Bank**, Vazhuthakadu T0471-2337615. **Central Bank**, branch in Kovalam Hotel (around the corner near the bookshop) changes money and TCs for non-residents after 1045, T0471-2480101. Exchange at **Pournami Handicrafts**; **Wilson's**, T0471-2481647, changes money, any time, no hassle. Best rates (up to 3%

higher), however, are at the airport. Or try Phroze Framroze & Co near Kovalam Bus Station T0471-2487450. **Hospitals** Emergency assistance either through your hotel or from the Govt Hospital in Thiruvananthapuram. Upasana Hospital, near *Le Meridien* gate, has experienced English-speaking doctor; prompt, personal attention. T0471-2480632. **Internet** Several on Lighthouse Beach. **Post** Inside Le Meridien gate. **Telephone** Check printed prices before paying for calls. Some ISD booths near the bus stand. Western Travel, opposite Bus Stand, until 2200. Elite Tours, T0471- 2481405, 2nd Beach Rd (30 m below bus stand), 24-hr ISD from the Batik House, Lighthouse Beach.

**Varkala** *p902, map p902*
**Banks** State Bank of Travancore changes TCs, but will not change cash or accept Visa – Bank of Baroda, next door, does. Canara, near train station, gives advances on Visa cards (1% commission). There are several **moneychangers**: along the north cliff and around Temple Junction (lower than US$/£ rate at Trivandrum airport), and most will give cash advances on credit cards (at 5% commission!). **Internet** at several places along north cliff, helipad and Temple Junction (Rs 60 per hr). **Post** Next to Sree Padman, Temple Junction, Mon-Sat 1000-1400; ISD phones opposite; also at Maithalam and along North Cliff.

# The Backwaters

*To many travellers, Kerala quite simply is the Backwaters: the cat's cradle of endlessly intersecting rivers, streams, lagoons and tanks that flood the alluvial plain between the Indian Ocean and Western Ghats. They run all the way from Kollam via Alleppey and Kottayam to Kochi to give you a breathtaking, snail's pace window onto Keralite life lived out right on the waterfront. This is very much Arundhati Roy country and Kerala's most keenly Christian belt. Kottayam is the noisy, polluted headquarters of the Christian community but just to its west lie the idyllic backwater villages and bird sanctuaries of Vembanad Lake, where* The God of Small Things *was set, and the fertile fields of Kuttanad, where huge paddy ponds grow bright green beneath sea level.*

*A few languid hours on a boat let you in on the mundane tasks of the Kerala everyday domestic scene: clothes are pounded and smashed clean, teeth brushed, boys and girls cool off up to their necks, men clamber up coconut palms to fetch an evening cup of fresh toddy, and travelling salesmen pedal door-to-door in their dugouts. There are ways of seeing life on the Backwaters on any budget and attention span, but bear in mind that the houseboat industry has sadly contributed to the pollution of the natural environment.* » *For Sleeping, Eating and other listings, see pages 919-924.*

## Ins and outs

**Getting there and around** An important railhead, Kollam is 70 km north of Trivandrum and connected to Allapuzha, Kottayam and Kochi by road. Allapuzha is 64 km south of Kochi. The largest backwater body is the Vembanad Lake, which flows through Alappuzha and Kottayam districts to open into the sea at Kochi Port. This has made Allapuzha the main departure point for houseboat operators. Kollam sits on Ashtamudi Lake, the second largest after Vembanad. Starting here gives you the longest ride (eight hours). » *See Transport, page 923, for further details.*

**Tourist information** Kollam ⓘ *DTPC, Govt Guest House Complex, T0474-2742558, dtpcqln@md3.vsnl.net.in*, offers cruises and coach tours, details of Kathakali performances; ⓘ *KSRTC bus station, T0474-2745625*; and at the railway station and ferry jetty; ⓘ *KTDC, Yatri Nivas, Ashramam, T0474-2748638*. Alapuzha ⓘ *KTDC, Motel Araam, T0477-2244460*; ⓘ *ATDC, Komala Rd, T0477-2243462, info@atdcaalleppey.com*; DTPC ⓘ *KSRTC Bus Station near jetty, T0477-2253308, 0830-2000*, helpful, good backwaters trips. Kottayam ⓘ *Kerala Tourist office, Govt Guest House, Nattakom, T0481-2562219*.

# Kollam (Quilon) → *Phone code: 0474. Colour map 3, grid C3. Population: 361,400.*

Kollam is a busy shaded market town on the side of the Ashtamudi Lake and the headquarters of India's cashew nut trading and processing industry. At the south end of Kerala's backwaters, it is one of the main centres for boat trips up the canals. For details see page 923.

Known to Marco Polo (as *Koilum*), its port traded with Phoenicians, Persians, Greeks, Romans and Arabs as well as the Chinese. Kollam became the capital of the Venad Kingdom in the ninth century. The educated and accomplished king Raja Udaya Marthanda Varma convened a special council at Kollam to introduce a new era. After extensive astronomical calculations the new era was established to start on 15 August AD 825. The town was associated with the early history of Christianity.

Roughly 30% of the town is covered in the waters of the **Ashtamudi Lake** ⓘ *boats for hire from the Kollam Boat Club or DTPC, for 2 or 4, Rs 20 per hr each.* The lake, with coconut palms on its banks and picturesque promontories, extends north from the town. You might see some 'Chinese' fishing nets and in wider sections large-sailed dugouts carrying the local coir, copra and cashew.

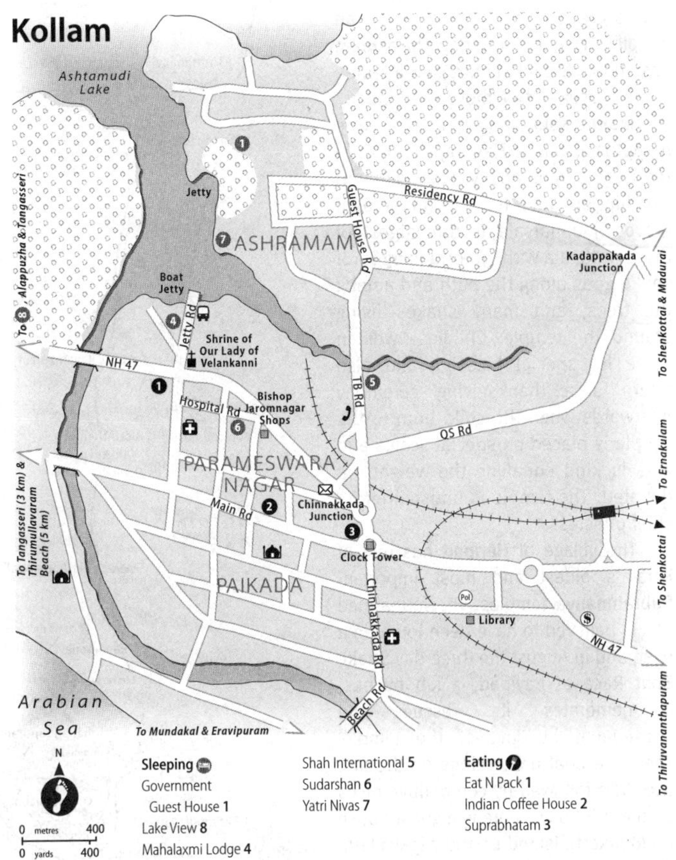

# Kollam to Alappuzha

**Mata Amritanandamayi Ashram** ⓘ *Vallikkavu, 10 km north of Kollam, accessible by boat or road (through Kayambkulam or Karungappally)*, a giant, pink skyscraper sandwiched on the backwaters between the sea and the river, is the ashram of Mata (the hugging 'Mother'). *Darshan* is attended by large numbers of villagers and western visitors who come to receive a hug from 'Mother'. She now spends increasing lengths of time on worldwide tours, and at this time the ashram takes on quite a different, more empty and lacklustre atmosphere. Amma has hugged three million people so far. In the early days, these used to last for minutes; now she averages one hug every 1.5 seconds, so she can happily hug 30,000 in a day. The ashram has shops, a bank, library and internet. Smoking, sex and alcohol are forbidden.

**Mannarsala**, 32 km before Alappuzha, has a **Nagaraja temple** in the forest. Traditionally *naga* (serpent) worshippers had temples in serpent groves. Mannarsala is the largest of these in Kerala with '30,000 images' of snake gods along the path and among the trees, and many snakes living around the temple. Childless women come for special blessing and also return for a 'thanksgiving' ceremony afterwards when the child born to the couple is placed on special scales and gifts in kind equalling the weight are donated. The temple is unusual for its chief priestess.

The village of **Haripad** has one of Kerala's oldest and most important **Subrahmanya temples**. The four-armed idol is believed to have been found in a river, and in August the three-day **Snake Boat Race** at Payipad, 3 km by bus, commemorates its rescue and subsequent building of the temple. There are boat processions on the first two days followed by competitive races on the third day. There is a guest house on **Mankotta Island** on the backwaters; the large comfortable rooms with bath are well kept.

## Kollam to Alappuzha backwaters

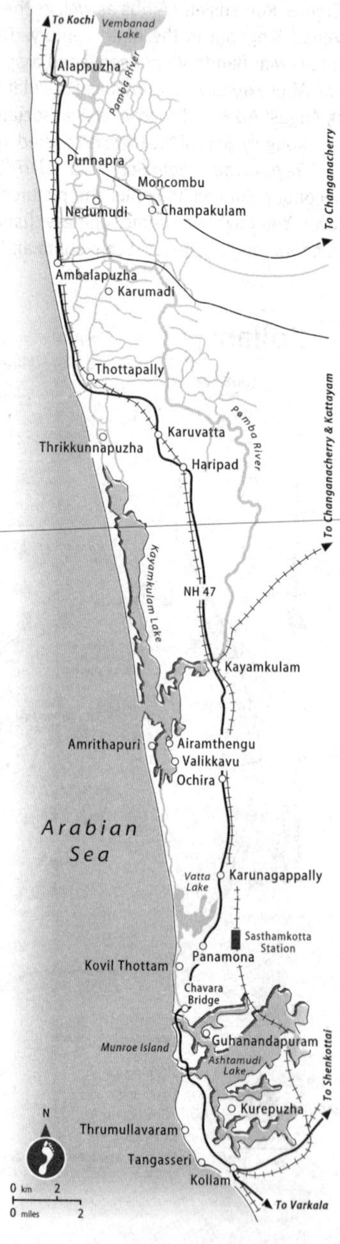


Kerala The Backwaters

## The backwaters

With only two permanent outlets to the sea, one at Kodungallur in the north and the other at Kochi, and a third opening during the southwest monsoon at Thottappally, the lagoons are fed by a network of perennial rivers. These flush out the salts between May and September, but seawater rushes in at the end of the monsoon reaching up to 20 km inland and the waters become increasingly brackish through the dry season. This alternation between fresh and saltwater has been essential to the backwaters' aquatic life. But reclamation for agriculture has reduced the surface water area, and the building of a barrier across the Vembanad Lake, north of Kumarakom, and other changes have altered the backwaters' ecology. Most of the original mangrove swamps have now been destroyed; a small residual patch at Kumarakom has limited protection. Many reclaimed areas (plots known as *pokkali*), are now used alternately for paddy, and for fish and shrimp farming.

On a backwaters trip you can see how *bunds* (embankments) have been built, enclosing areas from the main lake. These *bunds* (often granite and cement) are strengthened by planting coconuts, while electric pumps are used to dry out the normally flooded land. Below the *bund* the lake is suffering excessive saline flooding, and the reduced exchange between the lakes and the sea has severely worsened pollution. Mass fish kills are reported, and water weed infestation has increased with the excessive use of fertilizers on agricultural land. The dramatic increase in the land value across Kerala has resulted in pressure to put every square centimetre to economic use.

Few of these problems are immediately visible and the backwaters can be an idyllic experience. Waterside activities of coir making, toddy tapping, fishing, rice growing along the palm-lined banks and narrow strips of land that separate the waterways, and the constant quiet traffic of *vallam* (traditional dugouts) are typical. Advantage is taken of the comparatively long rainy season, so while coconuts provide a vital economic resource, the land underneath is often intensively cultivated. From the boat you will see papaya, mangoes, jack fruit and cassava (tapioca) growing. Tapioca, only introduced to Kerala in 1920, is very popular since it gives remarkably high yields from lateritic soils that are 'about as fertile as railway ballast'.

Traditional punted boats or motorized ferries provide one of the most delightful tours in India. The typical journey on a motor boat between Kollam and Alappuzha lasts over eight hours but some people find this too long. A shorter trip is possible, either by doing a round trip from Kollam, or by picking up or getting off the boat closer to Alappuzha (eg Changanacherry or Kottayam). Nearer Kochi too, a quiet half-day can be spent on a traditional dugout or you can have an exclusive upmarket overnight trip in a *kettuvallam*-style houseboat.

Squeezed between the backwaters and the sea, and 12 km from Haripad station, **Thottapally** makes a good stop on a backwaters trip, two hours from Alappuzha.

About 10 km from Chengannur, **Aranmula** has the **Parthasarathi Temple** and is known for its unique metal mirrors. The **Vallamkali (or Utthrittathi) festival** on the last day of Onam (August-September) is celebrated with the Boat Race. The festival celebrates the crossing of the river by Krishna, who is believed to be in all the boats simultaneously, so they are expected to arrive at the same time, not to race each other!

# Alappuzha (Alleppey) and around

→ *Phone code: 0477. Colour map 3, grid C3. Population: 177,100.*

Alappuzha (pronounced *Alappoorra*) has a large network of canals passing through the town and is probably the biggest transport depot for backwater cruises and the venue for the spectacular snake boat races, see pages 922 and 923 for details. There is little else of tourist interest, though St Thomas's Church is worth a look.

**Mararikulam,** 15 km north of Alappuzha on the coast, is a quiet, secluded beach which, until recently, was only known to the adjoining fishing village. The main village has a thriving cottage industry of coir and jute weaving.

Some 16 km southeast of Alappuzha, in the Backwaters village of **Champakulam** is **St Mary's Forane Church** (Syrian). It dates only from 1870 but is on the site of a previous church originally built in AD 427. The English-speaking priest is happy to show visitors round. Nearby the **St Thomas Statuary** makes wooden statues of Christ for export round the world. A 2-m statue of Jesus costs approximately US$450. The village is particularly charming because there is no traffic other than the occasional cycle, and the odd canoe. To get there take the Alappuzha-Changanacherry bus (every 30 minutes) to Moncombu (Rs 4), then rickshaw to Champakulam (4 km, Rs 12). Alternatively the Alappuzha-Edathna ferry leaves at 0615 and 1715 and stops at Champakulam. In the Backwaters village of **Edathna** you can visit the early Syrian **St George's Church.**

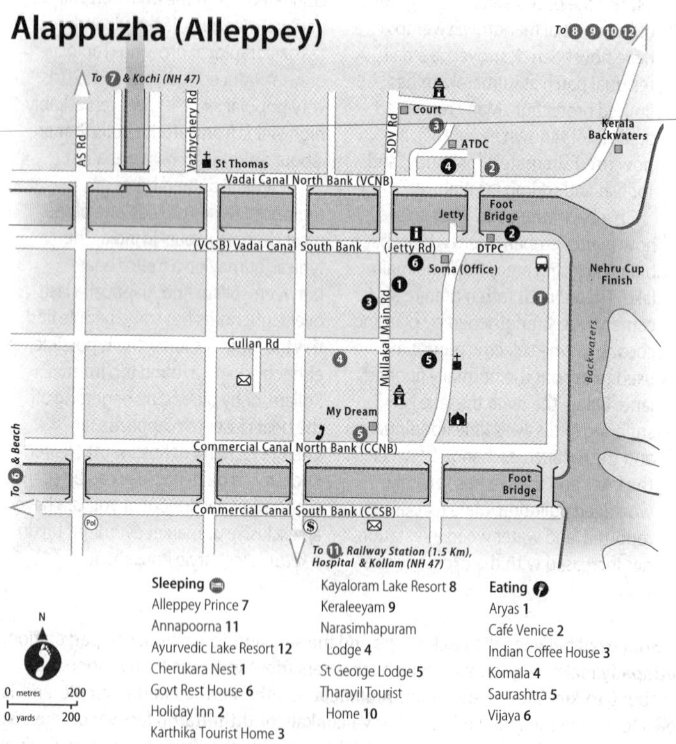


**Sleeping**
Alleppey Prince 7
Annapoorna 11
Ayurvedic Lake Resort 12
Cherukara Nest 1
Govt Rest House 6
Holiday Inn 2
Karthika Tourist Home 3
Kayaloram Lake Resort 8
Keraleeyam 9
Narasimhapuram Lodge 4
St George Lodge 5
Tharayil Tourist Home 10

**Eating**
Aryas 1
Café Venice 2
Indian Coffee House 3
Komala 4
Saurashtra 5
Vijaya 6

# Kottayam and Kumarakom

➔ *Phone code: 0481. Colour map 3, grid C3. Population: 60,700.*

Kottayam is surrounded by some of the most fertile and beautiful scenery in the state, with hills to its east and backwaters to its west. The compact town centre is noisy, busy and increasingly polluted, but things are better on the outskirts.

Kottayam is the main Christian centre in Kerala. The Christians in the state owed largely owed their allegiance to the Orthodox Syrian tradition until the arrival of the Portugese. Two Syrian Orthodox churches, 50 m apart, are on a hillock about 2 km north of town. The 450-year-old **Cheria Palli** ('Small' St Mary's Church) has beautiful vegetable dye mural paintings over the altar. The **Valia Palli** ('Big' St Mary's Church) was built in 1550. Here, two Nestorian crosses are carved on plaques inserted behind two side altars. One has a Pallavi inscription on it, the other a Syriac. The cross on the left of the altar is the original and may be the oldest Christian artefact in India; the one to the right is a copy. By the altar there is an unusual small triptych of an Indian St George slaying a dragon. Note the interesting Visitors' Book 1898-1935 – a paper cutting reports that "the church has attracted many European and native gentlemen of high position". Mass at Valia Palli at 0900 on Sunday, and Cheria Palli at 0730 on Sunday and Wednesday. The Malankara Syrian Church has its headquarters at Devalokam.

Tucked among the waterways of Vembanad Lake, in mangrove, paddy and coconut groves with lily-studded shores, is **Kumarakom**, 16 km from Kottayam. Here are stacks of exclusive hotels from where you can be buffed, ayurvedically preened, bend yourself into yoga postures, sunbathe in peace or take to the water to people- and/or birdwatch. The Tourism Department has developed an old rubber plantation set around the Vembanad Lake into a bird sanctuary ⓘ *1000-1800*. A path goes through the swamp to the main bird nesting area, while the island in the middle of the lake (**Pathiramanal** – 'midnight sands') can be reached by boat. It is worth hiring a guide for an early morning walk through the sanctuary. Ask at the entrance or at the hotels. The best season for birdlife is June to August.

## Around Kottayam

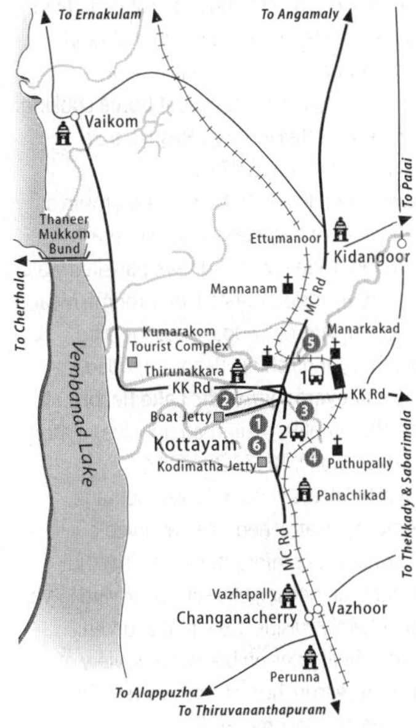


## Sleeping

**Kollam** *p915, map p915*

**A Aquaserene**, Paravoor, 15 mins from town by road or boat, T0474-2512410, aqserene@md3.vsnl.net.in. Splendid backwaters location, well-furnished chalets (some reassembled Kerala houses) with TV, restaurant, ayurvedic massage/treatment, boat rides.

**B Ashtamudi Resorts**, Chavara South (north of town), T0474-2882288, www.ashtamudiresorts.com. 30 mins by car, 10 mins speed boat, 20 rooms in 5 traditional chalets, more expensive 'Queen's Cottages' and 'King's Palace', all a/c with good views, catamaran trips, an ayurvedic resort.

**C Palm Lagoon**, Vellimon West, T0474-2547214, www.palmlagoon.com. Delightful setting 18 km from town centre on north side of Ashtamudi Lake, can be reached from backwater cruise, attractive thatched cottages, including full board.
**C-E Sudarsan**, Hospital Rd, Parameswar Nagar, 5 mins from jetty, T0474-2744322, www.hotelsudarsan.com. 35 rooms, some a/c with bath, rear quieter, dim a/c restaurant, bar, exchange, backwater trips.
**E Lake View**, Thoppikadavu, T0474-2794669, www.kollamlakeviewresort.com. Near Thevally Bridge (5 km from station; 10-min walk from small post office northwest of town). Beautiful position along lakeside. 4 clean, renovated rooms (2 have large balcony) (Rs 275+), lovely garden, good waterside restaurant, bar (occasionally noisy), friendly staff. Recommended.
**E Shah International**, TB Rd, Chinnakkada, T0474-2724362. 72 rooms, some **D** a/c, adequate restaurant, quiet, good value.
**E-F Yatri Nivas**, Guest House Compound by Ashtamudi Lake, Ashramam, T0474-2745538. 15 rooms and 2 6-bed dorms, great views from balconies, restaurant, beer (pricey), boating and free boat service from town jetty, ugly block building but clean and good value, cycles for hire, reservations at tourist office in Alappuzha, see page 918.
**F Govt Guest House**, Ashramam, T0474-2743620. 8 large rooms, simple meals, fine 200 year-old building with garden on edge of lagoon, former British Residency, boating, small pool and park by the lake, loads of character but therefore often full.
**F Mahalaxmi Lodge**, opposite bus station near Ashtamudi Lake, T0474-749440. 7 very small rooms (Rs 90), shared outside toilet, adequate.

**Kollam to Alappuzha** *p916, map p916*
**C-D Coconut Palms**, Pandavapuram Heritage Village, Thottapally, T0474- 2836251. Idyllic traditional house in shaded compound, on backwaters and 100 m from sea, package deals available including transport from **Aries Travel**, Trivandrum T0471-330964.
**E Ashram**, Vallikkavu. Spartan but spacious accommodation is offered in a multi-storey block here; Rs 150 includes very basic South Indian food. Western canteen (at extra cost) has a range of American-choice meals.

**Alappuzha and around** *p918, map p918*
Book ahead to avoid the scramble off the ferry. Hotels north of Vadai Canal are quieter.
**L The Marari Beach**, Mararikulam Alleppey T0478-2863801, www.casinogroup.com. 40 well-furnished, comfortable, a/c, local style cottages among palm groves – some with private pool, good sea food, pool, ayurvedic treatment, yoga, bikes, very friendly staff, discounts Apr-Sep. Recommended.
**A Kayaloram Lake Resort**, Punmamada, on Vembanad Lake, 4 km; 15 mins by boat from jetty then 300 m walk or at 'Punchiri', Jetty Rd, T0477-2232040, www.kayaloram.com. 12 Kerala-style wood and tile cottages around small inner 'courtyard' with 'open-to-sky' showers, pool, backwaters or lake trips, comfortable, very quiet and peaceful, restaurant (typical Kerala cuisine, Continental), ayurveda. Recommended.
**A Motty's Cottage**, Mararikulam Cherthala, T0477-2243535, motty1@satyam.net.in. 4 self-catering cottages right on Marari Beach in converted fisherman's shacks.
**A Motty's Homestay**, Kidangamparambu Rd, T0477-2260573, motty1@satyam.net.in. Just 2 double rooms -- old furniture and 4-poster beds – in private house on Alleppey's outskirts. Excellent home cooking.
**B Emerald Isle Heritage Resort**, on a backwater island, T0477-2703899, www.emeraldislekerala.com. 4 rooms in a 150-year-old traditional Kerala homestead with red oxide floors and teak-panelled walls (best with 'inside-outside' bathroom). Meals included. Internet, yoga, massage, bird watching and fishing. Recommended.
**B Keraleeyam Ayurvedic Lake Resort**, off the Thotampally main road (involves a short wooded walk), T0477-2231468, www.keraleeyam.com. 1930s 'Heritage home', now attached to an ayurvedic pharmacy, 5 comfortable a/c rooms (hut better than house), pleasant courtyard lawn, great Kerala cuisine, excellent ayurvedic centre, boat rides on backwaters, view of races in season, homely atmosphere but uneven a/c. Recommended.
**C-D Alleppey Prince**, AS Rd (NH47), 2 km north of centre, T0477-2243752. 30 good, clean rooms, central a/c, very dark bar, pool, luxury boats for backwaters.
**D Cherukara Nest**, just round the corner from bus station, T0477-2251509, zachs@

md4.vsnl.net.in. Pleasant traditional home, clean rooms with bath, very helpful staff, Kerala meals on request.
**D Green Palace**, Champakulam, T0477-2736262, www.greenpalacekerala.com. With Kerala meals and ayurvedic massage.
**D The Nest Home Inn**, Lal Bagh Factory Ward (West of Convent Sq), T0477-2245825. 5 rooms, each with balcony and attached bathroom in a family house with home-made, lightly spiced Kerala food, in Christian neighbourhood 3 mins from town centre. Johnson Gilbert, your host, is also a DJ.
**E Holiday Inn**, Vadai Canal North Bank, T0477-242955. Clean, spacious rooms, good value. Recommended.
**E Tharayil Tourist Home**, 750 m from boat jetty near lake, Thotampally, T0477-2236475, tharayiltouristhome@yahoo.co.in. Some a/c rooms, clean, local furniture in a family home.
**F Govt Rest House**, Beach Rd, 4 km bus stand, T0477-2254275. Excellent value, reasonable food (order in advance) but indifferent service. Reservations: Dist Collector, Collectorate, Dist HQ, Alappuzha.
**F Karthika Tourist Home**, near Zilla Court, SDV Rd, north of canal, opposite Jetty, T0477-2245524. 39 clean, pleasant rooms, some large with baths (cockroaches), best No 31, helpful and friendly staff, good value.
**F Narasimhapuram Lodge**, Cullen Rd, T0477-2262662. Some a/c rooms, occasional weight-lifting competition with live commentary over loudspeakers!
**F St George Lodge**, CCNB Rd, A-5, T0477-2251620. 80 basic rooms, some with bath, good value, popular with backpackers, exchange, book ahead.

### Kottayam and Kumarakom

*p919, map p919*

In Kumarakom, 26% taxes are added to bills.
**L Privacy at Sanctuary Bay**, Kannamkara, Chertala, opposite Kumarakom, T0484-2216666, www.malabarhouse.com. 2-bedroom bungalow for beautiful lakeside isolation owned by Malabar House designers and with same mixture of modern interiors and old Keralite building.
**AL Houseboat** (KTDC), Kumarakom. Unique, idyllic experience on the backwaters at a price. Kerala meals included, Rs 7,500 (day only), Rs 8,750 (1 night, 2 days). Contact Kumarakom Tourist Village, T0481-22524258. Highly recommended.
**AL-A Coconut Lagoon** Vembanad Lake Kumarakom (CGH Earth), T0481-2525843, www.casinogroup.com. 37 comfortable (some century-old) *tharavads* (traditional Kerala wooden cottages), some a/c, outdoor restaurant facing lagoon, good dinner buffet, good pool, yoga, very friendly, ayurvedic treatments, attractive waterside location, spectacular approach by boat (10 mins from road). Vechoor cows mow the lawns. Highly recommended. Discounts Apr-Sep.
**AL-A Kumarakom Lake Resort**, Kumarakom, T0481- 2524900, www.klresort.com. Villas with open-roofed showers set in delightful landscaped grounds. Recommended.
**AL-A Taj Garden Retreat**, 1/404, 14 km west of Kottayam, T0481-2524377, www.tajhotels.com. 19 a/c rooms, in attractive 120-year-old 'Bakers' House', sympathetically renovated, newer cottages and a moored houseboat, good meals, an intimate hotel but packed (perhaps boosted by the Prime Minister's stay in early 2001).
**A Golden Waters** (Tulip), Kumarakom, T0481-2525826, www.goldenwaters.com. Among paddy fields and coconut groves, accessed by boat or paths and bridges, 28 well-furnished, Kerala ethnic cottages on the water, pool, specialist ayurvedic centre.
**A Lake Village Heritage Resort**, near Kodimatha Jetty (next to **Vembanad Resort**), 3 km south Kottayam, T0481-2363739, wcastle@satyam.net.in. Comfortable bungalows with 'inside-outside' baths, excellent huge open-sided restaurant, very friendly.
**B Vallikappen Home Stay**, XIII/179B Manganam, T0481-2572530, simtom@satyam.net.in. A special alternative just outside Kottayam, 2 comfortable, clean rooms, interesting, cultured hosts, good Kerala/Western meals included, boats, heritage and wildlife visits.
**C Anjali**, KK Rd, 4 km from railway, Kottayam, T0481-2563661. 27 rooms with bath, central a/c, good restaurants, exchange (limited).
**C Vembanad Lake Resort**, near Kodimatha Jetty, 5 km from centre, 2 km from bus stand, T0481-2360866, www.vembanadlakeresort.

*For an explanation of the sleeping and eating price codes used in this guide, see inside the front cover. Other relevant information is found in Essentials pages 56-61.*

com. Simple rooms in 10 cottages (5 a/c), waterside garden, good houseboat restaurant.

**D Aida**, MC Rd, 2 km railway in Kottayam, T0481- 2568391, aida@sancharnet.in. 40 rooms with bath, some a/c, back quieter, restaurant, bar, clean and pleasant.

**D Green Park**, Kurian Uthup Rd, Nagampadam, T0481-2563331, greenparkhotel@yahoo.co.in. 33 rooms with bath, 11 with noisy a/c, non-a/c at back too hot, restaurant.

**D-E Aiswarya** (KTDC), near Thirunakkara Temple, 500 m from jetty, 2 km bus stand, Kottayam, T0481-2581440, aiswarya_int@yahoo.com. 30 rooms, some a/c, food, beer.

**E Ambassador**, KK Rd (set back), T0481-2563293. www.fhrai.com. 18 rooms, some a/c, pleasant Indian-style hotel and good restaurant, bar, exchange, friendly and helpful staff, very good value.

**F Govt Rest House**, on hill 2 km south of Kottayam, overlooking flat paddy land. Remarkable late 19th-century building with superb furniture and some original cutlery and tableware. Reservations: District Collector, Kottayam or Executive Engineer, PWD Kottayam.

**F Kaycees Lodge**, off YMCA Rd, Kottayam, T0481- 2563440. Good value, clean.

**F Venad Tourist Complex**, Ancheril Bldg, near State bus stand, Kottayam, T0481-2561383. Modern building, clean, restaurant. Recommended.

## Eating

### Kollam *p915, map p915*

**Eat N Pack**, near Taluk Office, Main St. Excellent value, clean, good choice of dishes, friendly. Recommended.

**Indian Coffee House**, Main Rd. For good coffee and non-vegetarian snacks, 0800-2030.

**Suprabhatam**, opposite Clock Tower, Main St. Adequate, vegetarian.

### Alappuzha and around *p918, map p918*

**TT Vemanad**, Alleppey Prince Hotel, International, comfortable a/c restaurant, reasonable food, alcohol in bar only.

**T Annapoorna**, does excellent vegetarian food – served by waitresses!

**T Aryas**, south of Jetty. Good for *iddli, dosa, vadai* etc.

**T Café Venice**, just by the DTPC office.

**T Indian Coffee House**, does good value, tasty non-vegetarian snacks.

**T Komala**, excellent South Indian *thalis* and some Chinese (poor rooms).

**T Saurashtra**, vegetarian, ample helpings on banana leaf, locally popular.

**T Vijaya**, good South Indian vegetarian and Chinese.

### Kottayam and Kumarakom

*p919, map p919*

The below are situated in Kottayam. For options in Kumarakom, see Sleeping.

**TT Aida**, large, uninspired menu, pleasantly cool ('chilled' drinks may arrive warm).

**TT Green Park**, international. Reasonable but slow service. Serves beers, dinner in mosquito-ridden garden (or in own room for guests).

On TB Rd near the State bus station:

**T Black Stone**, good vegetarian.

**T Milkshake Bar**, opposite Blackstone Hotel. Do 20 flavours, with or without ice cream.

## Festivals and events

### Kollam *p915, map p915*

**Jan**: Kerala Tourism **boat race** on 19 Jan. **Apr**: colourful 10-day **Vishnu festival** in Asram Temple with procession and fireworks. **Aug-Sep**: Avadayattukotta Temple celebrates a 5-day **Ashtami Rohani** festival. **Muharram** too is observed with processions at the town mosque.

### Alappuzha and around *p918, map p918*

For more details: www.keralatourism.org.

**9-12 Jan**: **Cheruppu** is celebrated in the Mullakkal Devi Temple with procession of elephants, music and fireworks. **17-19 Jan**: **Tourism Boat Race**. **Jul/Aug**: **DTPC Boat Race** (third Sat) in the backwaters. **Champakulam Boat Race**, Kerala's oldest, takes place 16-km ferry ride away on 'Moolam' day. The Nehru Trophy, inaugurated in 1952, is the largest **Snake Boat Race** in the state. As many as 40 'snake boats', with highly decorated and carved prows, are rowed by several dozen oarsmen before huge crowds. Naval helicopters do mock rescue operations and stunt flying. Entry by ticket; Rs 125 (Rs 60/75 tickets allow access in to overcrowded and dangerous areas). There are other snake boat races held throughout the year.

## Activities and tours

**Kollam** *p915, map p915*
You will be spoilt for choice where backwater trips are concerned. There are trips for groups of 10, or a 'cruise' for 20 to Alappuzha with a guide. Be aware that timings do alter. The gentle pace and quiet make this very worthwhile, but the heat and humidity may sometimes make overnight stays on houseboats uncomfortable (no fans).
**DTPC (District Tourism Promotion Council)**, Ashramam, T0474-2742558 dtpcqln@md3.vsnl.net, daily, 1030-1830, Rs 300 (ISIC Rs 250), half way to Alumkadavu, Rs 150, runs an 8-hr 'Luxury' cruise from the jetty near slaughter house in season. En route, stops may include the longest snake boat in the world, Champakulam, an 11th-century black granite Buddha statue at Karumadi, and a coir processing village at Thrikkunnapuzha. However, some travellers say that the only stops are for meals, so check in advance. Some find the trip a little too long and 'samey'. DTPC canal trip to Munroe Island village, 0900-1300, Rs 300, is an alternative. DTPC also has a more expensive alternative, the luxury *kettuvallam*, with between 1 and 3 bedrooms, a bath and a kitchen hired out for Rs 3,500-5,000 (full day or from afternoon till early the following morning), including traditional Kerala meals. The 24-hr, overnight trips start at Rs 8,200, or there are packages to combine day houseboat cruises with overnight stays at backwater resorts from Rs 5,500. The 25-hp outboard engine does about 10 km per hour. You can also hire motor boats for a 'safari cruise' for 8 people, Rs 400-500 per hr. Contact **DTPC, Soma**, T0471-2268101, or **TourIndia** T0471-2331507. Further details on www.dtpc-quilontourism.com.
Independent operators include:
**Visit Kerala**, opposite KRSTC Bus Station, Jetty Rd, Kollam, T0474-2740416. 8-hr cruise between Kollam and Alleppey, departs 1030, arrives 1830. Also offers houseboats between 1 and 2 nights. Backwater village tours: 1-hr motor boat, 2 hrs on small cruise, departs 0900-1300 or 1400-1800.
**Southern Backwaters Tour Operators**, Quilon Alleppey cruise, T0474-746037, www.southernbackwater.com. 8-hr cruises depart 1030-1830, report half hour before at Jetty Rd/Boat Jetty near KSRTC bus stand. Ferry Rs 300 one way. Lunch break. Village tours in country boat Rs 300.
**Tourindia** pioneered these houseboat trips; contact at Karukapparambil, near Nehru Trophy Finishing Point, T0474-2264961.

**Alappuzha** *p918, map p918*
Alappuzha is a starting point of backwater boat trips to Kollam, Changanacherry, Kottayam and Kochi. For information ask at **DTPC**, KSRTC Bus Station, Alappuzha, T0477-2253308.
**Alleppey Tourism Development Cooperative Society**, A837 Komala Rd, Alleppey, T0477-2243462, www.atdcalleppey.com. From Aug-May, 8-hr cruises depart at 1030, Mon, Wed, Fri, Rs 150, with stops for lunch and tea. Half-way cruise to Alamkadavu, Rs 100 (ISIC gets reduction) on a local ferry, one-way (29 km) costs Rs 10, from 0500-2100, 2½ hrs. Some visitors feel that this trip is so different from the Kollam-Alappuzha trip that it is worth doing both. Ferry to Kottayam, 1130, takes 2½ hrs, Rs 8. Towards Kochi on a large canal is less interesting. The journeys in the daytime are more interesting for watching unspoilt village life of Kerala.
Private operators offer similar trips, sometimes shorter (sometimes only stopping for a swim and lunch):
**Casino Group**,T0477-2668221, Kochi, casino@vsnl.com. US$325, runs a Spice Boat Cruise in modified *kettuvallams*, which are idyllic if not luxurious: shaded sit-outs, modern facilities including solar panels for electricity, two double rooms, limited menu.
**Rainbow Cruises**, VCNB Rd, opposite Boat Jetty, Alleppey, T0477-2241375, www.backwaterkerala.com, www.rainbowindia.com, has 10 boats a/c, non-a/c, solar powered with high safety standards and speed boat support for emergency (houseboats have been known to sink).
**Soma**, opposite the boat jetty, 212 Raiban Annex, T0477-261017, soma@md2.vsnl.net.in.

## Transport

**Kollam** *p915, map p915*
Local auto-rickshaws are plentiful and bikes are available for hire.

### Bus

Local buses are plentiful. Long distance from KSRTC, T0474-2752008. Buses every 30 mins to **Alappuzha** (85 km, 2 hrs) and **Kochi** (140 km, 3½ hrs) and other towns on the coast. Daily bus to **Kumily** village for **Periyar National Park** (change at Kottayam), 1000, 7 hrs. Also buses to **Kanniyakumari**. Frequent services to **Kochi**, 3 hrs; **Thiruvananthapuram**, 2 hrs. For **Varkala** difficult by bus; take one to Kollambalam and change. All southbound trains stop at Varkala.

### Train

The Junction railway station, T131, is about 3 km east of the boat jetty and bus station. **Chennai (MC)**: *Trivandrum Chennai Mail, 6320* (AC/II), 1520, 16¾ hrs. **Mumbai (CST)**: *Kanniyakumari Mumbai Exp, 1082*, 0845, 44 hrs. **Thiruvananthapuram**: *Vanchinad Exp, 6303*, 0853, 1½ hrs; *Parasuram Exp, 6350*, 1725, 1½ hrs; *Bangalore Kanniyakumari Exp, 6526*, 1335, 1¾ hrs, continues to **Kanniyakumari**, 2¼ hrs.

### Alappuzha and around *p918, map p918*

Rickshaw drivers board incoming ferries and help you with luggage and offer to transport you to the Kochi/Ernakulam bus stand, but it is only a 5-min walk away.

The bus station, T0477-2252501. Frequent buses to **Champakulam**; **Kochi**, 0630-2330, 1½ hrs; **Kollam** 2½ hrs; **Kottayam** 1½ hrs; **Thiruvananthapuram** 3½ hrs. Also to **Coimbatore**, 0615, 7 hrs.

For ferries, T0477-2252015. They sails to **Champakulam** 9 trips from 0430-2300, 1½ hrs; **Changanacherry**, 3½ hrs; **Chengannur**, 5 hrs; **Kollam**, 8 hrs etc.

The train station, T0477-2253965, is 3 km from the jetty with occasional buses from there. Trains to **Ernakulam (Junction)** depart 0600 to 1925. To **Chennai**: *Alleppey Chennai Exp, 6042*, 1500, 15¾ hrs. **Thiruvananthapuram**: *Ernakulam Trivandrum Exp, 6341*, 0615, 3½ hrs.

### Kottayam and Kumarakom
*p919, map p919*

### Bus

The New Private Bus Station is near the railway station. Buses from Kottayam, 30 mins, goes to the **Kumarakom** Tourist Village. There are fast and frequent buses to **Thiruvananthapuram**, **Kochi**, **Thekkadi**; also 4 daily to **Madurai**, 7 hrs; 5 to **Munnar**, 5 hrs. State Bus Station, 2 km south, is chaotic with often a mad scramble to get on the **Thekkadi/Periyar** bus. Direct bus departs 0900, 4 hrs; otherwise buses every 2 hrs to **Kumily** between 0900-2250, change at Kumily. The route from Thekkadi to Kottayam takes 7 hrs over the Thekkadi pass.

### Car

Car with driver to **Thekkadi**, Rs 850, 4 hrs.

### Ferry

All year (in summer, backwater boats leave from Kodimatha Jetty; during the monsoons, use the Town Jetty, 3 km southwest of the railway station). Ferries to **Alappuzha**, 0715-1730, 3 hrs; interesting trip but very busy in peak season. **Champakulam**, 1530, 4 hrs; **Mannar**, 1430, 3 hrs (attractive backwaters up to Nedumudi Jetty). To **Champakulam**, 1600, 4 hrs. Alternatively, take ferry fr[illegible] Kumarakom to **Muhama** village (½-[illegible]rly from 0630-2100), 40 mins, and then go to **Alappuzha** by bus.

### Train

**Kollam**: *Chennai Trivandrum Mail, 6319*, 0805, 2 hrs; *Bangalore Kanniyakumari Exp, 6526*, 1110, 2¼ hrs; *Vanchinad Exp, 6303*, 0655, 2 hrs (and on to **Thiruvananthapuram**, 3¼ hrs); also *Venad Exp, 6301* (AC/II), 1825, 3½ hrs.

## Directory

**Kollam** *p915, map p915*
**Hospitals** District Hospital, T0474-2793409. **Post** Head Post Office, Parameswara Nagar. Mon-Sat to 2000, Sun to 1800.

**Alappuzha and around** *p918, map p918*
**Bank** Bank of Baroda, Mullakal Rd, Visa/Mastercard advances. Canara, opposite DTPC, changes most TCs but not cash. **Hospitals** District Hospital, T0477-2253324. **Internet** Several on Mullakal Rd. **Post** Office off Mullakal Rd.

**Kottayam and Kumarakom**
*p919, map p919*
In Kottayam: Bank of India and Hotel Anjali only change currency and Amex TCs. **Post** MC Rd, 0800-2000, 1400-1730 on holidays.

# Fort Kochi and Ernakulam

→ *Phone code: 0484. Colour map 3, grid C2. Population: 1.15 mn (Kochi 596,500, Ernakulam 558,000).*

*Charming Fort Kochi (Cochin) and its twin town Mattancherry is an island of slowly disintegrating stone walls, crumbling shopfronts and well-tended churches. The Fort is where the chief tourist infrastructure is but you're never more than a few paces from a picturesque, narrow winding street. New building was banned in 1976 – too late to stop a few ugly concrete bungalows from cropping up – but the rest remains frozen in the 15th and 16th centuries. The city was created through flood, opening the estuary to make it one of the world's finest natural harbours. Narrow spits of land and coconut-covered islands jut out into the wide enclosed bay, whose neck is lined with the famous Chinese fishing nets of teakwood and bamboo poles first erected in 14th century. Mattancherry has row upon row of wood-fronted doors, behind which rice merchants and commission agents sit sifting their produce into small 'tasting' bowls. A ferry journey east across the Vembanad Lake lands you in Ernakulam, a dynamic city with soaring land prices, textile shops, air-conditioned bars and rapidly industrializing suburbs.* ►► *For Sleeping, Eating and other listings, see pages 930-935.*

## Ins and outs

**Getting there** The new Kochi International Airport is at Nedumbassery, 36 km away. Ernakulam Junction is the principal railway station, with the main long-distance bus station close by. Both are within easy walking distance of some hotels, though pleasanter Fort Kochi is a bus or ferry ride away. ►► *See Transport, page 934, for further details.*

**Getting around** During the day, a good, quick ferry service stops at major points around the bay. Once in Fort Kochi, the palace and the synagogue in 'Jew Town' are close enough to a jetty but some distance from the other sights eg St Francis' Church. Autos and bikes can be hired. There are three main parts. Fort Kochi occupies the southern promontory on the seaward side of the bay. Willingdon Island, with naval airport, Kochi harbour station, and very little in the way of charm, is awkwardly placed unless you have your own transport. Across the causeway from Willingdon Island is Ernakulam. Immediately opposite the jetty at Ernakulam is Bolghatty Island, and beyond it Vypeen Island.

**Tourist information** KTDC ⓘ *Shanmugham Rd, Ernakulam, T0484-2353234, 0800-1800*, helpful accommodation officer, where you can get a small booklet *Kerala Travel Facts* with useful listings. **Tourist Desk** ⓘ *Main Boat Jetty, Ernakulam, T0484-2371761, touristdesk@satyam.net.in, 0900-1800*. PJ Verghese helps tourists plan itineraries round Kerala on a voluntary basis, very helpful; maps, backwaters (country boat) tour, 0900, 1400, three hours, Rs 300, tickets for Alappuzha- Kollam boat trip.

## Background

A trading port since at least Roman times, Kochi was on the main trade route between Europe and China. Italian traveller Nicolas Conti remarked in the Middle Ages that "If China is where you make your money, then Kochi surely is the place to spend it." From 1795 until India's Independence the long outer sand spit, with its narrow beach leading to the wide bay inland, was under British political control. The inner harbour was in Kochi State, while most of the hinterland was in the separate state of Travancore. The division of political authority delayed development of the harbour facilities until 1920-1923, when the approach channel was dredged to allow any ship that could pass through the Suez Canal to dock safely, opening the harbour to modern shipping.

## Sights

A plaque in Vasco da Gama Square near the Customs Jetty commemorates the landing of Vasco da Gama in 1500. Next to it is the **Stromberg Bastion**, "one of the seven bastions of Fort Emanuel built in 1767", named after the Portuguese King. Little remains of the old Portuguese fort (founded 1503) except some ruins. Along the seafront are the Chinese fishing nets. Not unique to Kochi, but uniquely accessible to the short-stay visitor, the cantilevered fishing nets line the entrance to the harbour mouth. Chinese traders are believed to have originally introduced them in the late

## Kochi (Cochin) & Ernakulam

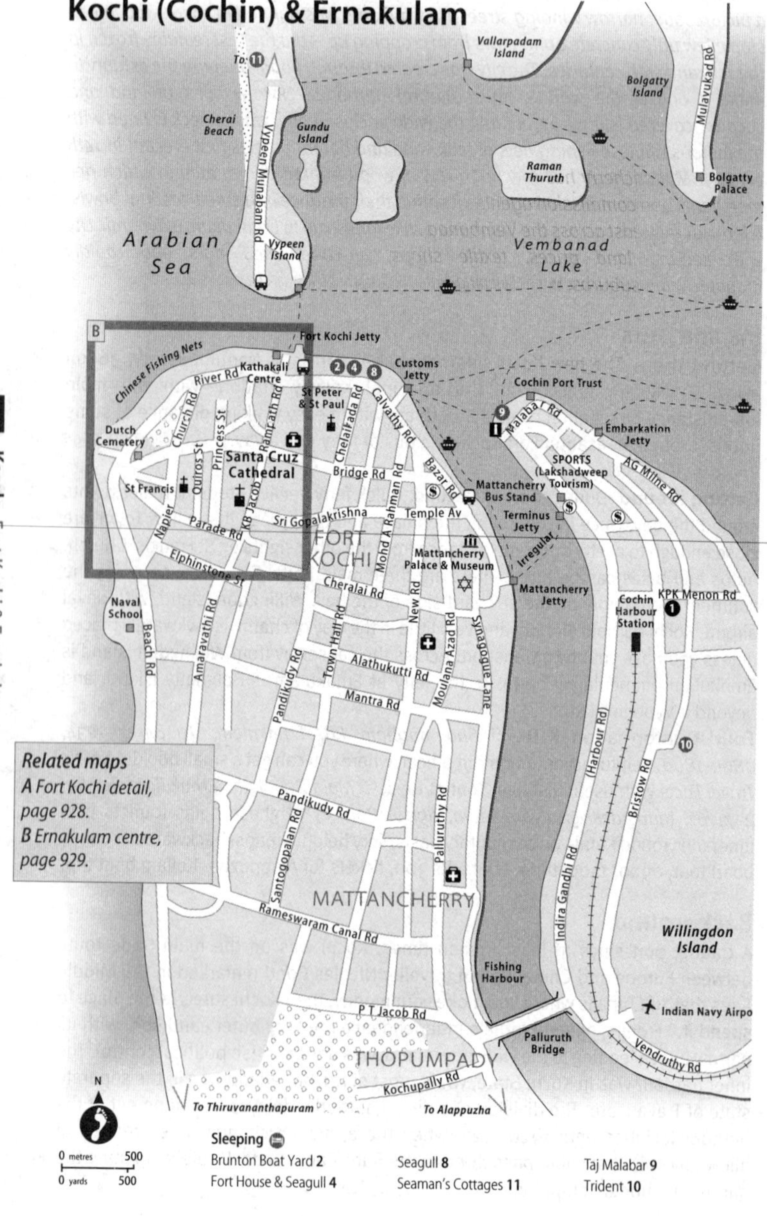

14th century although, today, parts of the nets are known by Portuguese names. They can best be seen either on the north end of the fort promontory, close to the Fort Kochi bus stand, or from a boat tour of the harbour.

**Mattancherry Palace** ⓘ *closed Fri and National holidays, 1000-1700, Rs 2, photo- graphy not allowed*, was built by the Portuguese (circa 1557) as a gift for the Raja Veera Kerala Varma of Kochi in exchange for trading rights. In 1663, it was largely rebuilt by the new occupants, the Dutch. Built on two floors round a quadrangle with a temple, the plan follows the traditional Kerala pattern known as *nalukettus* ('four buildings'). Although the palace has exhibits of the Rajas of Kochi (clothes, palanquins, etc) the main highlight is the series of murals painted on the wooden walls. These are remarkable, matched only by those in the Padmanabhapuram Palace, see page 888. The 'royal bedroom' has low wooden ceilings and walls covered in about 45 late 16th-century paintings illustrating the *Ramayana*, from the beginning to the point of Sita's return from captivity. Every available space is covered with rich red, yellow, black and white; blue and green are used sparingly. To the south of the Coronation Hall, the *kovinithilam* (staircase room) has six 18th-century, large murals including the coronation of Rama. The room to the north has a painting of Vishnu. Other rooms upstairs have more exhibits of the royal house. Two of the women's bedrooms downstairs have 19th-century murals with greater detail. They relate Kalidasa's *Kumarasambava* and themes from the *Puranas*.

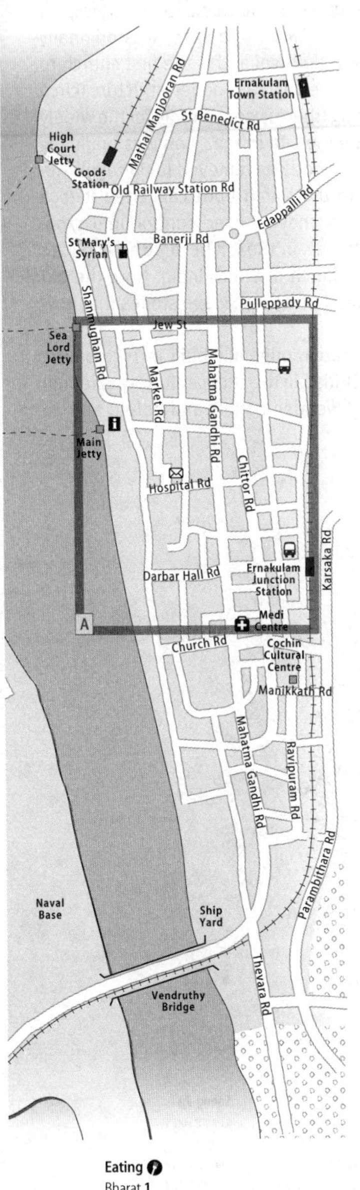


Eating
Bharat 1

The **synagogue** ⓘ *1000-1200, 1500-1700, closed Fri night, Sat and Jewish holi- days (when a giant oil candelabra lights up the courtyard), no video cameras, shoes must be removed*, dating from 1568 (rebuilt in 1662) near Mattancherry Palace, at the heart of what is known as Jew Town, is now a fascinating mixture of shops (some selling antiques), warehouses and spice auction rooms. Stepping inside is an extraordinary experience of light and airiness, given partly by the flooring of 18th-century blue Cantonese ceramic tiles, hand painted and each one different. There are original glass oil lamps. For several centuries there were two Jewish communities. The earlier group (often referred to as 'black' Jews), according to one source, settled here as early as 587 BC. The earliest evidence of their presence is a copper inscription dated AD 388 by the Prince of Malabar. Those referred to as 'white' Jews came much later, when, with Dutch and subsequently British patronage, they played a pivotal role as trading agents. Speaking fluent Malayalam, they made excellent go-betweens for foreigners seeking to establish contacts. The community has shrunk to half a dozen families, with many now settled at Moshav Nevatim in Israel's Negev desert. The second Jewish synagogue (in Ernakulam) is deserted.

**St Francis' Church** ⓘ *Fort Kochi, Mon-Sat, Sun afternoon, Sun services in English 0800 (except third Sun each month), visiting 0930-1730*, was originally dedicated to Santo Antonio, the patron saint of Portugal and is the first church to reflect the new, European-influenced tradition. The original wooden structure (circa 1510) was replaced by the present stone building (there is no authority for the widely quoted date of 1546). Vasco da Gama died on the site in 1524 and was originally buried in the cemetery. Fourteen years later his body was removed to Portugal. The church was renamed St Francis in 1663, and the Dutch both converted it to a Protestant church and substantially modified it. They retained control until 1795, adding the impressive gable façade at the entrance. In 1804, it became an Anglican church. In 1949 the congregation joined the Church of South India. Note the old string-pulled *punkahs* (fans) and the Dutch and Portuguese grave stones that now line the walls.

**Santa Cruz Cathedral**, near St Francis' Church, originally built in 1557 by the Portuguese, and used as a warehouse by the British in the 18th century, was rebuilt in the early 20th century. It has lovely carved wooden panels and pulpit, and an interesting graveyard.



## Fort Kochi detail

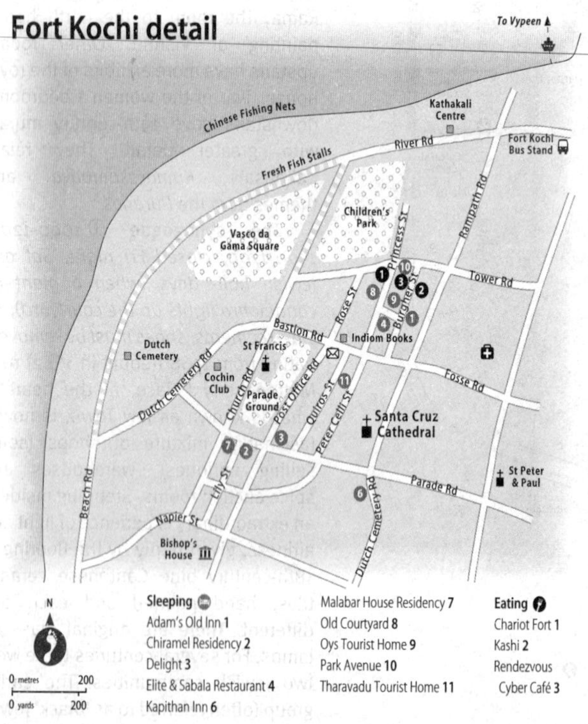

**Museum of Kerala History** ⓘ *Edappally, Kochi, closed Mon and national holidays, 1000-1200, 1400-1600*, starts with Neolithic man through St Thomas and Vasco da Gama. Historical personalities of Kerala are represented with sound and light.

## Excursions

**Bolghatty Island** has the 'palace' (circa 1745), set in large gardens and converted into a hotel. It was originally built by the Dutch and then became the home of the British Resident at the court of the Raja of Kochi after 1799. There is still some atmosphere of colonial decay which haunted the old building in its premodernized form and gave it much of its charm.

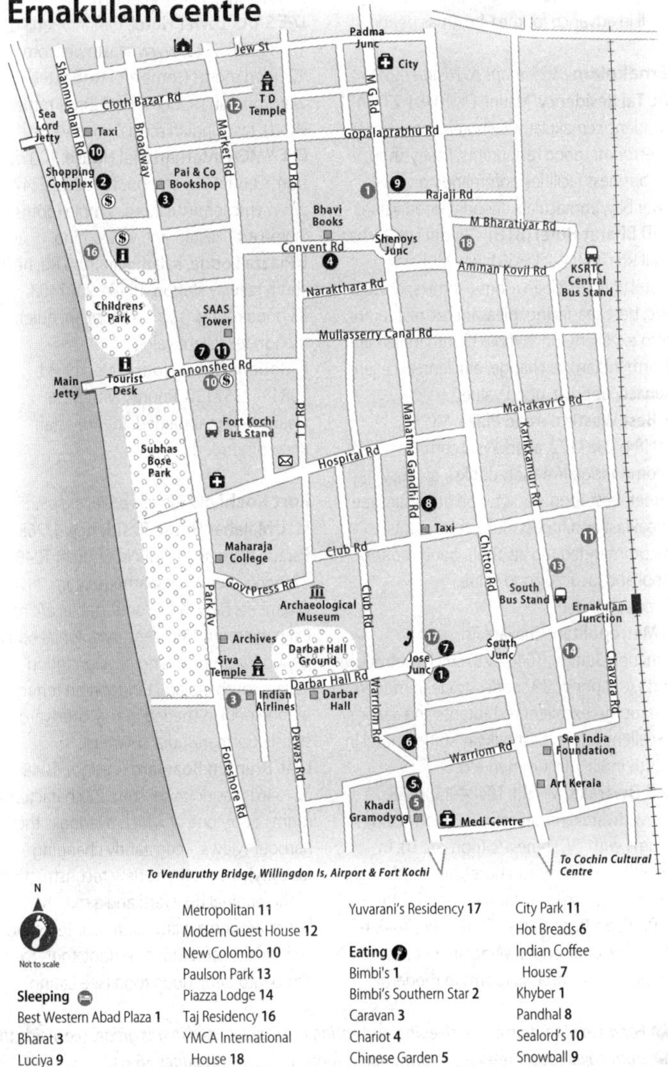

**Vypeen Island,** with the Portuguese Azhikotta Fort, built around 1503, stands by the police station. You can see cannon holes on the walls of the octagonal fort which was garrisoned by 20 soldiers when it guarded the entrance to the backwaters.

**Our Lady's Convent** ⓘ *Palluruthy, Thoppampady, 14 km south, by appointment, T0484-2230508*, specializes in high quality needlework lace and embroidery. The sisters are very welcoming and it is an interesting tour with items for sale.

**Raksha** ⓘ *Yasmin Manzil, VII/370 Darragh-es-Salaam Rd, Kochangadi, T0484-2227707*, works with children with physical and mental disabilities. Interested volunteers should contact the Principal.

## Sleeping

Fort Kochi has bags more character than the busy commercial centre of Ernakulam: book well in advance for the Christmas period.

**Ernakulam** *p925, maps p926 and p929*

**AL Taj Residency**, Marine Dr, T0484-2371471, residency.ernakulam@tajhotels.com. 109 rooms, good restaurants, pastry shop, all business facilities, commanding views over bay, immaculate, friendly, good value.

**B-D Bharat Hotel (BTH)**, Gandhi Sq, Durbar Hall Rd, T0484–2353501, www.bharathotel.com. 91 clean rooms, some spacious, a/c, best sea-facing, pleasant a/c restaurant, also excellent lunch *thalis* (South Indian and North Indian), exchange, efficient, excellent service, popular, good value.

**C Best Western Abad Plaza**, MG Rd, T0484- 2381122, abad@vsnl.com. 80 a/c rooms, fridge (free soft drinks), on busy street, best rooms quieter on 5th floor (free breakfast and fitness club), restaurants recommended (no alcohol), good rooftop pool and jacuzzi, good value. Recommended.

**C Metropolitan**, Chavara Rd, near Junction Station, T0484-2376931, metropol@md3.vsnl.net.in. 39 spotlessly clean modern a/c rooms, excellent restaurants and service, excellent value. "Best railway station hotel in South India". Recommended.

**C-D Dwaraka**, MG Rd, T0484-2383238, www.dwaraka-hotel.com. 39 good-sized rooms with TV, some a/c (non-a/c **D**), in established family-run hotel, fab South Indian vegetarian restaurant, good value.

**D Paulson Park**, Carrier Station Rd, T0484-2382179, paulsonpark@satyam.net.in. 55 clean, comfortable rooms in modern building, some good value a/c, restaurant, friendly staff. Recommended.

**D-E SAAS Tower Hotel**, Canon Shed Rd, T0484-236 5319, www.saastower.com. 72 good rooms (some a/c) with fitted wardrobes in modern hotel (beds rather short), tasty Indian meals, good value.

**D-E YMCA International House**, 100 m from Central Bus Station, T0484-2353479, www.ymcaernakular.org. Simple rooms (some a/c), restaurant, welcoming.

**E Piazza Lodge**, Kalathiparambu Rd, near south railway station, T0484-2367408. 33 good rooms (some a/c), clean, quiet, friendly, excellent value.

**F Modern Guest House**, Market Rd, T0848- 2352130. Rooms with bath, clean, well-maintained, friendly staff. Recommended.

**Fort Kochi** *p925, maps p926 and p928*

**LL-L Malabar House Residency**, 1/268 Parade Rd, near St Francis' Church, T0484-2216666, www.malabarhouse.com. Old meets new in 17 comfortable, a/c rooms in characterful 18th-century colonial house, period furniture, dining pavilion (good Italian, south Indian), tandoori on terrace, plunge pool in shaded grassy courtyard, stylish, German/Indian owners.

**L-AL Brunton Boatyard** (Casino), T0484-2215461, casino@vsnl.com. 22 characterful rooms every one of which overlooks the harbour (views – constantly changing tapestry), sympathetic new reconstruction of the original boatyard and a merchant's house around a giant raintree, interesting architecture and furniture (footstools to climb into bed), good food (see Eating),

*For an explanation of the sleeping and eating price codes used in this guide, see inside the front cover. Other relevant information is found in Essentials pages 56-61.*

discounts Apr-Sep. Air that's perfumed with lemongrass, and jasmine on your pillows, generous swimming pool: easily the best place to stay in Fort Kochi.

**A-B Old Courtyard**, 1/371, Princess St, T0484-2226302, www.oldcourtyard.com. 8 beautiful, comfortable rooms, superbly styled with old wooden furniture, overlooking sheltered courtyard, some with shared balconies, modern baths, no a/c or TV, attentive staff, breakfast included, average food but nice relaxed atmosphere. Recommended.

**B Caza Maria Hotel**, 6/125 Jew Town Rd, Mattancherry, T0484–2225678, cazamaria@rediffmail.com. Just 2 huge rooms in beautiful converted house, with tiled floors, huge wooden furniture and antiques: isolated (the only hotel in Jew Town), romantic and shabbily elegant. Fan only. Tariff includes breakfast.

**B-D Kapithan Inn**, Bernard Rd, 100 m south of Cruz Cathedral, T0484-2216560, www.kapithan@eth.net. 7 rooms, clean and pleasant, family run.

**D Delight**, Post Office Rd, opposite 'village green', T0484-2217658. 8 large rooms, spotless and stylish, breakfast served, very friendly, family run, in private house complete with lawn and white picket fence. Highly recommended.

**D Fort House**, 2/6A Calvathy Rd, T0484-2226103. A few simple rooms within a walled courtyard with its own little jetty, lovely outlook, excellent food.

**D Vintage Inn**, Ridsdale Branch Rd, near Jaliparambu Junction, T0484-2215064, vintageinn@hotmail.com. New in 2003, this small, homely and well-run place has maid service to clean rooms, washing line, TV, a/c, hot water on request all for very reasonable rates. Owners arrange 6-hr waterway cruise for Rs 400.

**D-E Park Avenue**, Princess St , T0484-2222671, hotel_parkavenue@bplnet.com. Marble-faced hotel with 25 spotless rooms with bath, some a/c, pleasant and airy, roof restaurant, quiet location. Good value.

**D-E Seagull**, Calvathy Rd, between the ferry stops, T0484-2228128. 8 rooms, some a/c (some damp and dark), good restaurant, exchange, converted old warehouses on the waterside.

**E Chiramel Residency**, 1/296 Lily St opposite Parade Ground, T0484-2217310. Characterful house, 5 clean rooms, some with bath, friendly family.

**E Elite**, Princess St, T0484-2225733. Cheaper rooms long way from toilets, rooms at rear quieter, cheap restaurant.

**E Oys Tourist Home**, Burgher St, T0484-2215475. 6 peasant rooms in lamp-lit old building, lots of plants, good value.

**E-F Adam's Old Inn**, CC1/430 Burgher St, T0484-2217595. 10 rooms with bath (1 a/c), in restored old building, dorm beds, meals, helpful hosts.

## Eating

**Ernakulam** *p925, maps p926 and p929*

**Avenue Regent**, excellent buffet lunch Rs 200.

**Bimbi's Southern Star**, Shanmugam Rd. Excellent food, generous portions.

**Canopy**, coffee shop for snacks, good food, buffet breakfast and service but no alcohol.

**Chinese Garden**, off MG Rd. A/c, authentic Chinese cuisine.

**Khyber**, serves North Indian meals upstairs.

**Pandhal**, MG Rd. Keralan, Chinese, Continental, a/c, clean, serving tasty meals, excellent value. Recommended.

**Sealord's**, rooftop for good fish dishes and Chinese.

**Bharat**, for very good vegetarian *thalis* and Indian specialities in clean surroundings.

**City Park**, opposite *New Colombo*, for excellent Keralan meals.

**Malabar**, Market Rd. Excellent South Indian but rather gloomy.

**New Colombo**, Canon Shed Rd (next to Maple). Good snacks, fruit juices.

### Cafés

**Bimbi's**, near Durbar Hall/MG Rd corner. Good fast food.

**Caravan**, Broadway (south). For ice creams and shakes.

**Chariot**, Convent Rd. Good café style meals.

**Coffee Beanz**, Shanmugan Rd. 0900-2300 daily, cold coffees, *appam*, *dosa*, popular poky a/c coffee bar with just 6 tables.

**Indian Coffee Houses**, opposite **Bimbi's**; also Park Av and Canon Shed Rd corner. Good coffee and snacks but tediously slow.

**Oven**, Shanmugham Rd. Good pizzas and snacks (savoury and sweet).
**Snow Ball**, Rajaji Rd, near Muthoot Towers. Ice creams and shakes.

**Fort Kochi** *p925, maps p926 and p928*
TTT **Brunton Boatyard**, History Restaurant revives old recipes of Dutch, Portuguese, Gujarati, British and Malabari merchants (interesting menu), Terrace Grill prepares freshly caught fish.
TTT **Malabar House Residency**, excellent seafood platter (Rs 180) and the chef's salad is excellent and a thing of huge dimensions, authentic Mediterranean and local dishes.
TT **Bhojana Shala**, Peter Celli St, T0484-2212494. Excellent lunch and evening eatery run by owners of **Kashi**.
TT **Chariot Fort**, Children's Park/Princess Rd corner. Upmarket outdoor café feel, delicious cold coffees and cheese omelettes, expensive but popular.
TT **Fort House** hotel. German/Indian run, in walled courtyard, "the best food ever".
TT **Kashi**, Burgher St, T0484-2221769. Healthy salads, good lunches, delicious cakes, herbal teas at 'Art café'. Limited menu but changes daily, small, good atmosphere, 0830-1430, run by expats. Recommended.
TT **Rendezvous Cyber Café**, Burgher St. Also serves traditional Kerala and continental.
T **Caza Maria**, Jew Town Rd (opposite the hotel). 1200-2130. 2 large rooms with wooden chairs, frescoes and old framed prints on the wall. Small menu includes fish *moilee* and lime rice, *palak paneer* and *chapatti* and apple pie and ice cream. Lovely atmosphere.
T **Rahmatulla Hotel**, Bazar Rd. This is famous among locals for its expert *biriyani*, chicken *kayees* and divine *parathas*. It's just a small shack open for lunch only that sells its melt- in-the-mouth rice dish hand over fist from noon. By 1245 the mutton's invariably sold out of all 400 portions, but it's worth checking if there's any chicken left.
T **Sabala**, at Elite hotel. Popular, pleasant atmosphere (good ice creams opposite).
T **Seagull**, Calvathy Rd. Good value (Rs 80 buffet lunch), pleasant verandah for drinks and dining overlooking harbour. For really original fast food buy your own fresh fish when brought in by boat or from the nets, take it over to **Europa**, 'you buy, we cook' stalls on the sea front where they will be grilled or masala-fried with chips (Rs 120). Delicious!

## Entertainment

**Kochi-Ernakulam** *p925, map p926*
There are daily Kathakali performances. Arrive early to watch the extraordinary make-up being applied.
**Cochin Cultural Centre**, Manikath Rd, off Ravipuram Rd, Ernakulam, T0484-2368153. A/c 'theatre', authentic, English explanations; 1830-1930, make-up 1630, Rs 125.
**ENS Kalari**, Nettoor, Fort Kochi, T0484-2809810. Kalarippayattu performances, 0400-0700 and 1700-2000.
**Kerala Kathakali Centre**, River Rd, New BusStand, Fort Kochi, T0484-2221827. Rustic surroundings but lively performance, enjoyable; 1830-1930 (make-up 1700) but check timing, Rs 100.
**See India Foundation**, Kalathil Parampil Lane (enter Chittoor Rd south) near Junction station, Ernakulam, T0484-2369471. Dr Devan's 'interpreted' taste of Kathakali with esoteric English commentary; 1845-2000 (make-up from 1800), Rs 125.

## Festivals and events

**Kochi-Ernakulam** *p925, map p926*
**Jan/Feb**: Ulsavam at the Siva Temple in Ernakulam for 8 days and at Tripunithura Temple in **Nov/Dec**. There are elephant processions each day and folk dance and music performances. **Aug/Sep**: Onam.

## Shopping

**Kochi-Ernakulam** *p925, map p926*
Coir products (eg mats), carvings on rose-wood and buffalo horn and some antiques may catch your eye here. Several of the narrow streets in Jew Town, towards the Synagogue, have become popular for 'anti-que' hunters in the last 25 years. 25 shops have a similar range of old and new curios. There are several Government Emporia on MG Rd, Ernakulam, including **National**

**Textiles** (another in Banerji Rd). Other shopping areas are in Broadway, Super Bazar, Anand Bazar, Prince St and New Rd.
**Bhavi Books**, Convent Rd. Recommended.
**Idiom Books**, VI/183 Synagogue Lane, Jew Town, T224028. Very good range on India, travel, fiction, religion, philosophy etc.
**Cinnamon**, Stuba Hall, 1/658 Ridsdale Rd, Parade Ground, Fort Kochi, T0484-2217124. Has lovely clothing, expensive fabrics and interiors.
**Dhamdhere**, Pandithan Temple Rd, Mattanchery, T0484-2224481. Interesting perfume manufacturers who confess many are synthetic (Rs 12), but the sandalwood oil is the real McCoy (Rs 100).

## Activities and tours

**Kochi-Ernakulam** *p925, map p926*
**Backwater tours**
**KTDC Backwater Village tours**, T0484-2371761. Daily from Kuthiathode, 0830- 1300, afternoon 1430- 1900 (40-min road transfer), country boat for 8-10, Rs 275. Special moonlight cruise on full moon nights.

An alternative 'backwater' trip is to get a boat from High Court jetty to Mulavukadu Jetty, then ask for the Varapuzha boat. Get off at the last stop, Chetty Bhagam. Boat every 30 mins, 2-hr journey, Rs 5.
**Tourindia**, T0477-264961, www.richsoft.com/tourindia. Also has *kettuvallams*; Ernakulam to Kuttanad backwaters and return. Rs 3,000 per head.
**Tourist Desk**, www.indiatouristdesk.com. One of the best budget tour operators. Tours include overnight houseboat, Rs 4,000 for 2. 7-hr backwater cruise from Kochi starts main boat jetty 0830-0700: 4 hrs is on a houesboat through wide canals then 3 hrs village cruise on country boat with *thali* meals: Rs 425.
**Visit India**, Mr A Edassery, Island Club House, 1st Main Rd, Willingdon Island, T0484- 2668819, www.visitindiatravel.com. Organizes a delightful boat tour along Kochi's back- waters in a dugout, punted and engineless, through very peaceful shady waterways passing unspoilt villages with toddy tappers, coir making, fishing etc; led by an excellent guide. Rs 350 for 4 hrs, depart 0830, 1430, 40-min drive to jetty. Highly recommended. They also have traditional *kettuvallams*; Rs 5000 (for couple) or Rs 8000 (2 bedroom); for 24 hrs, includes all meals.

**Massage**
**Be Beautiful**, Princess St, Fort Kochi, T0484-2215398. Beauty salon, 0900-2030, good, cheap beauty salon with massage, hairdressing, pedi/manicure.
**Sree Narayana Holistic Clinic**, Vypeen Island, Fort Kochi, T0484-2502362, ayurdara@sancharnet.in. Ayurveda, 1-hr massage plus a Keralan *thali* on a rooftop with harbour views, Rs 500.

**Sightseeing tours**
**KTDC** (see above), boat tours daily visiting Dutch Palace, Jewish Synagogue, St Francis' Church, Chinese Fishing Nets, Bolghatty Island. Depart from Sea Lord Jetty, Ernakulam. 0900-1230, 1400-1730; mornings cooler. Rs 70. Highly recommended.
**Visit India**, 35/871 North Janatha Rd, Palarivattom, T0484-2336483, tours@visitindiatravel.com. Also now has fleet of 10 houseboats and transport division with excellent drivers of standard, premium and luxury cars.

**Tour operators**
**CGH Earth**, Casino Building, Willingdon Island, T0484-2668221, 2666821.
**Clipper**, 40/6531 Convent Rd, T0484-2364443, clipcol@md2.vsnl.net.in.
**Olympus**, south end of MG Rd, near Little Kingdom shop, T0484-2373630. Very competent and helpful.
**Pioneer Travels**, Bristow Rd, Willingdon Island, T0484-666148, www.pner.com. Fleets of cars with tailor-made tour packages from a well established and highly competent tour company. Efficient and knowledgable, they can suggest unusual homestays and guesthouses.
**Sundale Vacations**, 39/5955 Atlantis Junction, MG Rd, T0484-2380127, www.sundale.com. Surface and hotel arrangements in Kerala, specializes in homestays catering to 'foreign independent tourists', thereby promoting insight into Kerala's customs. Programmes from US$467.
**Unusual Places**, 639 1st floor, Santo Complex, RS Rd, Aluva, Ernakulam,

www.unusualplaces.info. Will matchmake you with properties in Kerala (generally rooms without a/c and TV – old bedrooms but new bathrooms) divided into city, wildlife or beach categories.
**Weeks Tour**, T0484-2220168, w.e.e.k.s@usnl.com. Offer good value tours in Goa, Karnataka, Kerala and Tamil Nadu.

## Transport

### Kochi-Ernakulam *p925, map p926*

#### Air

New international airport, 36 km north-east, T0484-2610113. Pre-paid taxis to Fort Kochi, Rs 350-400. **Indian Airlines**, T0484-2360796, airport T0484- 2610041 (domestic), T0484-2610101 (international): **Bangalore**, **Chennai**, **Mumbai**, **Delhi** via Goa, **Thiruvananthapuram**: daily; **Coimbatore**, **Hyderabad**, **Kozhikode** and **Tiruchirapalli**, all several flights per week. Flights to **Doha**, **Kuwait**, **Muscat**, **Sharjah**. Jet Airways, T0484- 2369212, airport T0484-2610037: **Mumbai**, **Chennai**, **Bangalore**, daily.
**Airline offices** On MG Rd unless stated otherwise. International: **Air India**: T0484-2351260/2380700. **British Airways**, T0484-2364867. **Cathay Pacific** and **KLM**, T0484-2362064. **Lufthansa**, T0484-2370776. **Japan Airlines**, T0484-2350544. **Maldive Airlines**, T0484-2351051. **Singapore Airlines** and **Swissair**, T0484-2367911. Domestic: **Indian Airlines** and **Alliance Air**, Durbar Hall Rd, near Bharat Hotel, T0484-2370242. **Jet Airways**, Elmar Sq Bldg, MG Rd, T0484- 2369212.

#### Auto-rickshaw

Rickshaw drivers have a reasonably good reputation here. But, if you are likely to arrive late at night, insist on being taken directly to your hotel. Fares within Fort Kochi: Rs 20.

#### Bus

**Local** Journeys between Ernakulam, Willingdon and Fort Kochi are useful and fairly frequent after ferries stop running.
**Long distance** KSRTC, T0484-2360531, run 'Express' and 'Fast' services from Ernakulam Terminus near Junction Railway station to major cities in the south; computerized reservations not always available. To **Alappuzha**, every 20 mins, 1½ hrs, Rs 30; **Devikulam**, 6 hrs, Rs 42; **Kannur**, 7 hrs (Exp), 8½ hrs, Rs 85; **Kottayam**, 2½ hrs, Rs 38; **Kozhikode**, 5 hrs (Exp), Rs 72, 6½ hrs, Rs 65; **Munnar**, via **Aluva**, 4 hr, 0630; **Thekkadi** (Kumily) for **Periyar**, 0630, 6¾ hrs, Rs 80, or take later bus to Kottayam (frequent) which has several daily to Thekkadi; **Thiruvananthapuram**, 5 hrs (Exp), Rs 75, 6½ hrs, Rs 60; **Thrissur**, 1½ hrs (Exp), Rs 25. Interstate buses to: **Bangalore** via **Kozhikode**, **Sulthan Bathery** and **Mysore**, 0600-2100, night 12 hrs, day 15 hrs, Rs 175-210. **Mysore**, 2000, 10 hrs, Rs 190. TNSTC, T0484-2372616. To **Coimbatore** via **Thrissur** and **Palakkad**, 4¾ hrs (Exp), Rs 75; Kanniyakumari Exp, 8 hrs, Rs 110; **Chennai** via **Coimbatore**, **Erode**, **Salem**, 1530, 15 hrs, Rs 185; **Madurai**, via **Kottayam**, **Kumly**, **Thekkadi** 9 hrs (Exp), Rs 115; **Mysore**, 11 hrs, Rs 145. Private operators from Kalloor and Ernakulam South bus stands including **Indira Travels**, DH Rd, T0484-2360693 and **SB Travels**, MG Rd, opposite Jos Annexe, T0484- 2353080, **Princey Tours**, opposite Sealord Hotel, T0484-2354712. Overnight coaches to **Bangalore**, 12 hrs, and **Mysore** 10 hrs. To **Kottayam**, every 30 mins, 2 hrs, **Munnar**, 4 hrs. Also to Chennai and Coimbatore.

#### Ferry

Ferries are the best way of getting about as they are faster, cheaper and much more comfortable than buses or autos.
**Ernakulam** Main Boat Jetty is 200 m from Junction railway station; High Court Jetty for ferries to Bolghatty.
**Fort Kochi** 'Customs' (main stop) with a separate one for Vypeen Island.
**Willingdon Island** 'Embarkation' (north) and 'Terminus' (west). From Ernakulam, to **Bolghatty** public ferry every 20 min, from High Court Jetty, 0600-2200. Ferries do not operate on Sun. Some take bikes/motor bikes. To **Fort Kochi** Customs 0600-2110 (30 mins). To **Willingdon**: ½-hourly from 0630 to 2110. To **Vypeen Island** via Willingdon Embarkation: ½-hourly, from 0530-2230, 30 mins. To **Mattancherry**: 6 from 0710-1740, 30 mins. From Bolghatty to Ernakulam and Fort Kochi, 1745-2000, Rs 50; speed boat hire from Bolghatty Palace,

Rs 200 to Fort Kochi. From **Fort Kochi**: customers to Malabar Hotel, ½-hourly to Vypeen Island, about 2 car ferries per hr. To **Varapusha**, 6 boats, 0740-1500, 2 hrs. **Ferry hire**: motor boat for up to 20, from Sea Lord jetty, book at KTDC office, Rs 200 per hr. You can do a harbour tour and visit Fort Kochi sights in 3 hrs; allow longer for a leisurely visit. KTDC Fort Kochi tour, 0900, 1400, 3½ hrs, Rs 60. **Taxi boats** are faster and more convenient – jetty closer to Bolghatty Palace, Rs 20 per head.

### Taxi

Ernakulam Junction to Fort Kochi, Rs 150. On MG Rd, Ernakulam: Corp Taxi Stand, T0484-2361444.

### Train

Ernakulam/Kochi is on the broad gauge line joining Thiruvananthapuram to Mangalore, Bangalore and Chennai. Most trains from major cities stop at Ernakulam Junction (the main station) although a few stop at Ernakulam town, T0484-2390920. Enquiries: Ernakulam Junction, T131. From **Ernakulam Junction** to: **Alappuzha**: several including *Ernakulam Trivandrum Exp, 6341*, 0615, 1 hr; *Cannanore Ernakulam Alleppey Exp, 6308*, 1130, not Thu or Sat, 1¼ hrs; *Guruvayur Madurai Exp, 6726*, 2350, 1 hr. **Chennai (MC)**: *Alleppey Chennai Exp, 6042* (AC/II), 1500, 15¾ hrs; *Trivandrum Chennai Mail, 6320*, 1900, 13 hrs. **Delhi (HN)**: *Ernakulam Nizamuddin Mangala Lakshadweep Exp, 2617*, 1155, 40 hrs. **Thiruvananthapuram**: *Vanchinad Exp, 6303*, 0550, 4½ hrs; *Venad Exp, 6301* (AC/CC), 1715, 5 hrs. From **Ernakulam Town** to: **Mangalore**: *Parasuram Exp, 6349* (AC/CC), 1055, 10 hrs; *Malabar Exp, 6329*, 2305, 11¾ hrs. **Mumbai (CST)**: *Kanniyakumari Mumbai Exp, 1082* (AC/II), 1230, 40½ hrs. **Thiruvananthapuram**: *Parasuram Exp, 6350*, 1355, 5 hrs; *Cannanore Trivandrum Exp, 6348*, 0040, 5¼ hrs.



## Directory

**Kochi-Ernakulam** *p925, map p926*
**Banks** Thomas Cook, Palal Towers, 1st floor, Right Wing, MG Rd, T0484-2369729, Mon-Sat, 0930-1800, exchange, TCs, very quick service. **Union Bank**, Panampilly Nagar, opens Sun. Most banks open till 1500. Several on MG Rd, Shanmugham Rd and on Broadway, Ernakulam, and on Mattancherry Palace Rd, Fort Kochi. Ernakulam Head PO does Western Union money transfer. **Dentist** City Dental Clinic, T0484-2368164. **Internet** Net Point, near Junction Station. Fast connection Rs 30 per hr. **Café De Net**, Princess St, Fort Kochi, 0930-2230. Very fast internet plus coffee shop, film processing. **Hospitals** General Hospital, Hospital Rd, Ernakulam, T0484-2360002. **Govt Hospital**, Fort Kochi, T0484- 2224444. On MG Rd: **City**, T0484-2361809, and **Medical Trust Hospital**, T0484-2371852, have 24-hr pharmacies. **Post** Ernakulam Head PO, Hospital Rd, 0830-2000, Sat 0930-1430, Sun 1000-1600, other holidays 1400-1700. Kochi Main PO, Mattancherry (for **Poste Restante**), 0800- 2000, Sun 0930-1700; often empty. North End PO, Willingdon Island. **CTO**: (24 hrs) Jos Junction Building, 2nd floor, MG Rd, Ernakulam. **Useful addresses** AA: South India, MG Rd (opposite Hotel Dwaraka), T0484-2351369. **Tourist Police**: T0484- 2666076, help with information of all kinds. **Visa extension: City Police Commissioner**, High Court Ferry Station, Ernakulam, T0484-2360700. **Foreigners' Regional Registration Office**, T0484-2352454.

# Munnar and Idukki's high ranges

*Inland from the plains around Kottayam and Kochi lie first tropical evergreen forests, rubber and spice plantations. These give way to pepper then cardamom, till your climb up the ghats takes you to high hills rolling with tea and the thin clean air of the well-kept estates of Munnar in the north of landlocked Idukki district. To the south sit the evergreen forests and jungles of Periyar and Thekkadi. These make perfect high-mountain pauses before crossing the border into Tamil Nadu. Thekkadi comes covered in rubber and fruits and is chiefly peopled by tribals converted to Christianity: long lines of crucifixes litter some of the most beautiful mountain ridges here, while, at 1,600 m, Munnar is much higher and, once one of the summer bolthole for the British Government of South India, is now almost wholly owned by Tata's tea company. Three mountain streams meet at Munnar: Mudrapuzha, Nallathanni and Kundala, and it has one of the highest populations worldwide of the endangered ibex, or 'Nilgiri tahr'.*

▸▸ *For Sleeping, Eating and other listings, see pages 941-944.*

## Ins and outs

**Getting there and around** Munnar is closest to Kochi-Ernakulam while Thekkadi is best accessed from Kottayam: there are no train links to the high ranges, buses take a minimum of four hours to climb the hills to both hill stations, and roads linking the two take the same length of time. ▸▸ *See Transport page 944, for further details.*

**Tourist information** District tourism offices are at Kumily ⓘ *T0486-2322620*, and Old Munnar ⓘ *T04865-2531516*.

# Kottayam to Thekkadi

An interesting drive to the hills, this route follows the Ghat road which has superb views down the east side of the Ghats onto the Tamil Nadu plains. You may meet herds of Zebu cattle, buffalo and donkeys being driven from Tamil Nadu to market in Kerala. Above 1,000 m the air freshens and it can be cold. Be prepared for a rapid change in temperature.

**Pelai**, off the Kottayam-Thekkadi road, is a town famous for its learned citizens – graduates of the European-style gothic university built, with the gothic church, by one of its affluent sons. Nehru visited in the 1950s and said that Pelai was full of "people of vision". The town was the most literate place in India long before Kerala achieved 100% literacy, and Meenachil *Taluka* has the maximum number of educated women in the country. It is also famous for its tamarind and pepper and known for rubber estates belonging to the Dominic family whose beautiful 100-year-old traditional Kerala plantation bungalow and a 50-year old estate mansion is where hot Syrian-Catholic lunches are served. Plantation tours to watch latex collection and packing can be arranged through **CGH Earth**, see page 933. Further east lies **Erattupetta**, whose grey St George's Church holds naïve wood-painted doves, disembodied cherubims and hosts the **High Range Festival** every April. Carry on for **Vagamon**, a village set on a chain of three hills: Thangal, Murugal and Kurisumala, in a mark of religious harmony. A dairy farm here is managed by Kurisumala monks.

*The first rubber plantation was cultivated in 1902. India is now within the top three rubber producers worldwide, and most of that comes from Kerala.*

### A modern mass pilgrimage

Sabarimala pilgrims are readily visible in many parts of South India as they wear black *dhotis* as a symbol of the penance they must undergo for 41 days before they make the pilgrimage. In addition to the black dress, pilgrims must take two baths daily and only eat food at home during this period. The pilgrimage, which begins at Deepavali, is only for males and prepubescent and post-menstrual females, in order to avoid the defilement believed to be associated with menstruation.

The pilgrimage in January is deliberately hard, writes Vaidyanathan, because "the pilgrimage to the shrine symbolizes the struggle of the individual soul in its onward journey to the abode of bliss and beautitude. The path of the spiritual aspirant is always long, arduous and hazardous. And so is the pilgrimage to Sabarimala, what with the observance of severe austerities and trekking up forested mountains, risking attacks from wild animals". See below.

Some 25 km south from Vagamon is **Peermade** (regular buses between Kottayam and Kumily, three hours, Rs 45, several per day to/from Ernakulam) considerably lower than Thekkadi. It is surrounded by tea, rubber and cardamom plantations and there are a number of picturesque spots around the town, which was named after Peer Mohammed, a Sufi saint and crony of the royal family of Travancore. **Abraham's Spice Garden** ⓘ *Kottayam-Kumily Rd (bus route), Rs 50 expected,* offers excellent tours with a family member.

Many Hindu pilgrims make the journey to the forest shrine dedicated to Sri Aiyappan at **Sabarimala,** 191 km north of Thiruvananthapuram. Aiyappan is a particularly favoured deity in Kerala and there are growing numbers of devotees. It is only open on specific occasions: *Mandalam*, mid-November to end-December; *Makaravilakku*, mid-January; *Vishu*, mid-April; *Prathistha* one day in May-June; and during the *Onam* festival in August-September.

## Thekkadi (Periyar National Park)

➔ *Phone code: 0486. Colour map 3, grid C3.*

ⓘ *Rs 50 (foreigners) for 5 days. Video camera fees Rs 100.*

Set on an attractive Periyar lake side, significant wildlife sightings in this national park are uncommon, but the beautiful setting attracts over 300,000 visitors a year. In 1895 the lake was created by building a dam which covered 55 sq km of rich forest. A 180-m long tunnel led the water which had flowed into the Arabian Sea east into the Suruli and Vaigai rivers, irrigating extensive areas of Ramanathapuram and Madurai districts. The 780 sq km sanctuary was created by the old Travancore State government in 1934. The small Kumily village with most of the guest houses and eating places is 3 km above the lake.

### Ins and outs

**Getting there** Long-distance buses reach Thekkadi lakeside via Kumily. » *See Transport, page 944, for further details.*

**Getting around** Buses run between Kumily and the lake jetty, or you can hire a bike, share a jeep or take the pleasant walk. 'Cruises' at 0700, 0930, 1130, 1400, 1600.

**Tourist information** District Tourism Information Office ⓘ *T0486-2322620*, runs plantation tours to Murikkady (5 km); Vandiperiyer (18 km); and Vandanmedu (25 km).

## Sights

Some visitors are disappointed, due to the small number of wildlife sightings, but for others the beautiful setting compensates. It was designated a part of Project Tiger in 1973 though **tigers** are very rarely seen and it is better known for its **elephants**, which you are very likely to see until March/April. Most bull elephants here are tuskless (*makhnas*). **Bison, sambar, wild boar** and **barking deer** are also fairly common. In addition to 246 species of **bird**, there are 112 species of **butterfly**. Smaller animals include black Nilgiri **langur**, **bonnet** and **lion-tailed macaque**, **giant** and **flying squirrels** and **otter**; look out for a flight of flying foxes (fruit bats) over the Spice Village each evening at about 1830.

*Ideal times are dawn and dusk so stay overnight (winter nights can get quite cold). Avoid weekends and holidays.*

The forests have special viewing platforms which you can use if you prefer to walk with a Game Ranger who can act as guide. The three-hour **'trek'** is for five people only, 0700, Rs 60, and you need to queue for about an hour outside the office. Much depends on your guide and your luck but not everybody comes face to face with a herd of elephants; some return very disappointed. Carry water and beware of leeches. An overnight stay in a watch tower (24-hour trek) for two, Rs 100, gives you more chance of seeing deer, bears, bisons and elephants. Guides arrange unofficial walking tours privately in the park periphery in the afternoon (not the best time for spotting wildlife); try to assess the guide before signing up. A motor launch trip on the lake is recommended. Ask the Wildlife Preservation Officer.

There are a number of attractions that are within easy reach of Thekkadi. These include the traditional Keralan-style **Mangaladevi Temple**, situated amongst dense woodland on the peak of a 1,337 m hill, 15 km northeast of Thekkadi. Permission to visit the area must be obtained from the Wildlife Warden, Thekkadi, though the temple itself is only open during the *Chithra Pounami* holiday. Other picturesque spots around Thekkadi include **Pandikuzhi** (5 km) and **Chellarkovil** (15 km).



## Periyar Wildlife Sanctuary

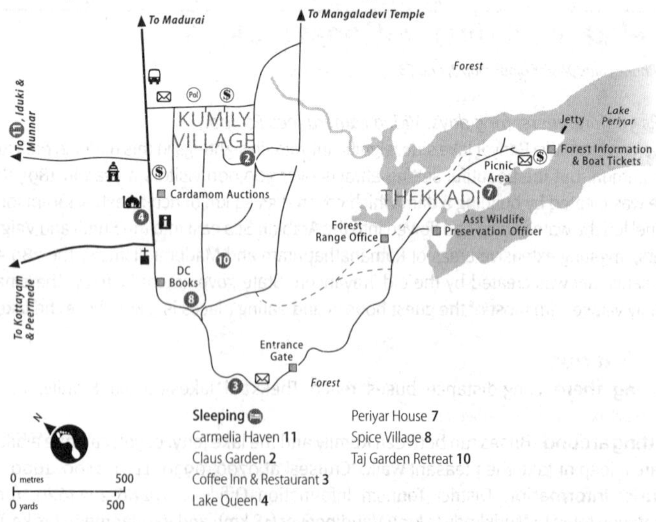

# The road to Munnar and the Palanis

There is a short drive from Kochi across the undulating and richly cultivated, densely populated lowlands before climbing rapidly up one of South India's most attractive ghat roads. **Ettumanoor**, to the south, has possibly the wealthiest temple in Kerala. The present Mahadeva Temple was reconstructed in 1542, and is famous for its murals depicting scenes from the *Ramayana* and the Krishna legends, both inside and outside the *gopuram*. The typical circular shrine with a copper covered conical roof encloses a square sanctuary. The **Arattu festival** in March draws thousands of pilgrims when gold elephant statues are displayed. They weigh 13 kg. The Kochi-Munnar Road leads from Kothamangalam, to the 25 sq km **Thattekkad Bird Sanctuary** ⓘ *20 km, contact the wildlife warden in charge of Idukki Wildlife Division at Vellappara 13 km northeast of Kothamangalam along the Pooyamkutti Rd.* A tropical evergreen and semi-evergreen forest with teak and rosewood plantations, the sanctuary is surrounded by the Periyar River which remains shallow most of the year. It attracts water birds and the indigenous Malabar grey hornbill, rose and blue-winged parakeet, egret, heron and mynah, while rarer birds like the Ceylon frog-mouth and rose-billed rollers are also sometimes seen here.

# Munnar → *Phone code: 04865. Colour map 3, grid C3. Altitude: 1,520 m.*

A major centre of Kerala's tea industry, and close to Anaimudi, at 2,695 m the highest peak in South India, Munnar is the nearest Kerala comes to a genuine hill station. The landscape is European Alpine – minus the snow. It is surrounded by about 30 tea estates, among the highest in the world, and forest that is still rich in wildlife, including the reclusive Nilgiri tahr, despite the increasingly commercial use of the hills. The workers on the tea estates are mostly Tamilians who moved here eight or nine generations ago. The surrounding hills are also home to the rare Neelakurunji orchid (*Strobilanthes*), which covers the hills in colour for a month once every 12 years (next due 2006).

## Ins and outs

**Getting there** The easiest access is by bus or taxi from Kochi, but there are daily buses to major towns in Kerala and Tamil Nadu. » *See Transport, page 944, for further details.*

**Getting around** The town is small and pleasant for walking around, though there are autos. It is worth hiring a bike or a jeep for trips out of town.

**Tourist information** DTPC ⓘ *T04865-231516, www.munnartourism.com*, runs plantation tours and rents cycles. Try also the free Tourist Information Service, Main Bazar, opposite bus stop. Joseph Iype is a mine of invaluable information.

## Sights

The **Tata Tea Museum** ⓘ *Nullatanni Estate, T04865-230561, www.keralatourism.org, 1000-1600, Rs 50*, has a heap of artifacts, curios and photographs to help conjure something of the lives of the men who opened up the High Ranges to tea. The crop has grown here for over a century so relics include a rudimentary tea roller from 1905 and a wheel from the Kundale Valley Light Railway that used to transport men and materials between Munnar and Top Station. The museum has descriptions of the fully automated technology of today from the tea factory at Madupatty. The museum can also arrange a visit to this factory, watching tea pickers at work and processing.

*Crops are determined by height: tea grows above 5,000 ft, cardamom, coffee and other spices between 5,000 and 2,000 ft, coconut and rubber below 2,000 ft.*

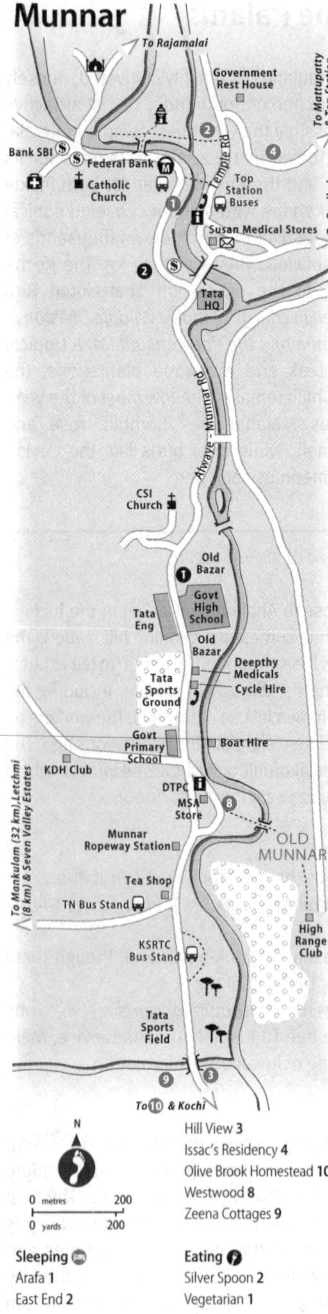


In the centre of Old Munnar, set on a hill immediately above the road in the centre of town, is **Christ Church**. Rather squat and now blackened by weathering, its exterior is unprepossessing, but inside it is a charming small church: ask to see the diminutive record of births and deaths of the town's founders, the British planters. Consecrated in 1910 it still contains its original 14 rows of wooden pews. A zig-zag path up the hill immediately behind the church leads to the small Pioneer cemetery which was actually established long before the church itself as the chosen burial ground of Mrs Eleanor Knight, General Manager Knight's 24-year-old bride who caught cholera just after arriving in the High Range in 1894. Originally built to serve the tea estate managers and workers of the High Ranges, the last English language service was held in 1981. Its origins are suggested in several of the memorial plaques on the wall and it is now shared between protestant Tamil and Malayalam worshippers. Sunday services today are in Tamil (0800, when the church is always full) and Malayalam (1000).

**Mount Carmel Roman Catholic church**, the first Catholic Church in the High Ranges, is in Old Munnar on the road up to the Tata General Hospital. The first chapel on the site was founded in 1898 by Fr Alphonse who arrived in Munnar from Spain in 1854. The present church was built by the then Bishop of Vijayapuram in 1938.

**High Range Club** ⓣ *T04865-230253*, is a private members' club more relaxed than the famously 'Snooty' Ooty Club (see page 853). A tradition allowed members to hang their hats on the wall of the bar after 30 years of belonging to the club – the last was hung in 1989 to make 51 hats in all. Saturday is strictly jacket and tie only: and backpackers will need to scrub up well to get in any day of the week: "we like scholars and researchers, professionals and club people," says the club secretary. "They know how to move in a club." It's a wonderful place with teak floors, squash courts, library and fascinating planters to chat to if you're interested in the planters' social history.

## Excursions

**Mattupatty Lake** ⓘ *T04865-230389, visits between 0900-1100, 1400-1530, Rs 5*, 13 km from Munnar and at an altitude of 1,700 m, is flanked by steep hills and woods. It was created by the small hydro-electricity dam. To its south is the Kerala Livestock Development Board's research and cattle breeding centre – formerly the Indo-Swiss dairy project. In a beautiful semi-Alpine setting surrounded for much of the year by lush green fields, the centre offers interesting insights into the practical realities and achievements of cattle breeding in India today.

**Top Station**, on the border with Tamil Nadu, 41 km from Munnar and at an altitude of 2,200 m, has some of the highest tea estates in India. It is an idyllic spot, with superb views over the Tamil Nadu plains and the edge of the Western Ghats. There are tea and soft drinks stalls in the hamlet. Top Station took its name from a ropeway that connected it via Middle Station to Lower Station at the valley bottom. The small town of **Bodinayakkanur**, which can be reached on the Devikulam road, lies in the valley. Buses leave from the shelter north of Munnar post office at 0715, 0915, 1115, to Kovilor, passes Mattupetty Lake and Kundala Dam. Get off at Top Station, return bus after about one hour.

**Eravikulam/Rajamalai National Park** ⓘ *closed during the monsoons, Rs 50, plus Rs 10 for vehicles taken into the park, visitors are allowed in the Rajamala section of the park only*, 14 km northeast of Munnar, was set up in 1978 to preserve the endangered Nilgiri tahr (Nilgiri ibex). The conservation programme has resulted in the park now supporting the largest population of the species in the world, of nearly 2,000. The sure-footed wild goats live in herds on the steep black rocky slopes of the Anaimudi mountains. They are brownish, have short, flat horns with the male carrying a thick mane, and can be easily seen around the park entrance. There are also elephants, sambars, gaurs, macaques and the occasional leopard and tiger. The scenery is magnificent, though the walks into the forest are steep and strenuous. There is an easier well-made, paved path from the park entrance following the road immediately below the bare granite outcrop of the Naikundi Hill to the Rajamalai Gap.

There are some excellent **cycle rides** around Munnar, not all of them steep. One ride goes up a gentle slope through a beautiful valley 8 km to the Letchmi Estate. There is a *chai* stall at the estate and the road continues to the head of the valley for views down to the forest beyond. A second ride (or walk) leaves Munnar by the south road for 3 km, turning left at the Head Works Dam, then takes a right turn past Copper Castle, then left to a tea-stall, sunset viewpoint, tea and cardamom plantations, again with spectacular views. Continue to the next tea-pickers' village for a further tea-stall. A shorter alternative to this route is to cross the dam and turn left, taking the quiet road north to the High Range Club and Munnar.

## Sleeping

### Kottayam to Thekkadi *p936*

AL **Paradisa Plantation Retreat**, Murinjapuzha, Kottayam-Kumily Rd, T0469-2701311, www.paradisaretreat.com. 10 traditional new-built cottages with beautiful antique granite pillars, Kerala door frames and walls from old rice *godowns* inside an organic plantation estate with stunning valley views, swimming pool. Yoga recommended but booking essential, the Swarmy jets in from Chennai.

A **Ann's Homestay**, Kurumannu, Pelai, T04822-221287, www.annshomestay.com. 4 doubles with amazing traditional Keralan cusine in large modern house on coffee, vanilla, rubber, coconut, pepper, pineapple and rubber plantation. Fresh milk from their own dairy. Advance booking essential.

A **Kottukapally Nazarani Tharawad**, Pelai, T0482-212348, www.nazarani tharawad.com. An opportunity to stay with the Kottukapally family, Kerala political royalty. There are grand Byzantine icons, Persian carpets and Travancore brass lamps. The roomy Kerala/Dutch/ Spanish-style house of teak, rosewood and Basel tiles, has 3 spacious doubles. Advance booking essential.

**A Velukunnel Villa**, Kondoor, Aruvithura, T04822-272460, vellytom@yahoo.com. 1 room in 100-year old house in 15 acres of rubber, vanilla and pepper, still home to large family including 7 children. A touch remote. Advance booking essential.

**A-B Vanilla County**, Mavady Estate, Teekoy, Vagamon, T0482-281225, www.vanillacounty.com. At the source of the Meenachil river. A charming, family-friendly place with 3 rooms within 60-year old house that you share with your hosts. Coffee is from the plantation around you and you can walk to swim in natural ponds. Internet access.

**B Grandma's Mansion**, Plassnal, near Pala, T04822-272080. 3 rooms in a charming homestay built in the traditional Christian style with a genteel, elderly hostess, Thankamma Joseph. An immaculately maintained house with fans, narrow beds and swinging daybeds and set in a garden with pond. Advance booking essential.

**Thekkadi** *p937*

**L Lake Palace**, T0486-2322024, www.ktdc.com. 6 rooms in interesting building (US$ 198, meals included), restaurant (adequate, uninspired) access by free ferry (20 mins) from jetty (last trip 1600), idyllic island setting, superb views, wildlife spotting from lawn, relaxed and informal.

**L Serenity**, Kanam Estate. 5 bedrooms in a 2-storey 1920s rubber estate in tropical spice gardens on a small hilltop on the way to Periyar: activities include plantation walk, cycling tours and day with the elephants.

**AL Spice Village** (CGH Earth), Thekkadi-Kumily Rd, T0484-2668221, www.cghearth.com. 52 rooms in cottages with elephant grass thatch (cool and dark with wide eaves), spice garden, good pool, very good restaurant though breakfast menu limited, buffet at lunch and dinner (Rs 350), chilled beer, pool, yoga centre, excellent ayurvedic massage, forest walks to see smaller wildlife, luxurious, quiet, restful, friendly, excellent service, discounts Apr-Sep.

**AL-A Taj Garden Retreat**, Amalambika Rd, T0486-2222403, www.tajhotels.com. 32 well-appointed rooms in thatched, a/c cottages, large windows with good views, attractive pool, excellent facilities, attentive.

**A-B Carmelia Haven**, Vandanmedu (20 km north on Puliyanmala Rd), on a tea, spice and coconut plantation, T0486-2870272, www.carmeliakerala.com. Exclusive and private, with a real tree house 6 m above ground, a cave house 3 m below, and a few discreetly spaced cottages in a local style using lots of thatch, excellent open-air restaurant serves delicious Malabari food. Tours of tea factory, cardamon plantations, treks and boating. Tea/cardamon for sale.

**B Cardamom Country**, between Kumily and Thekkadi, T0484-2381038, cardamom@hotelskerala.com. Spacious, comfortable cottages, good restaurant, nice pool, friendly (request off-season discount). Recommended.

**C Periyar House (KTDC)**, 5-min walk from lake, T0486-2322026, periyar@sancharnet.in. 48 rooms, some with bath (Rs 700 includes meals), simple, very pleasant, clean and comfortable, dorm is reasonable if slightly dingy, buffet meals, strong Goan beer available, pleasant place, good service.

**E Manakala Forest Rest House**, 7 km in the forest, T095486-322027 (book ahead). 3 rooms (sleep on wooden floor, bring sleeping bag, soft mat, net, mosquito repellant, food and plenty of water), cook/ guide accompanies, well placed for walks and watching animals close by at night, Rs 300 including boat transfer. Recommended.

**E Mickey Cottage**, Kumily, T0486-222 3696. Pleasant rooms, best with balcony, friendly family, excellent value. Highly recommended.

**E-F Coffee Inn**, 5-min walk from entrance gate and 3 km from information centre, coffeeinn@satyam.net.in. 12 rooms in basic cottages, fan, nets (Rs 150-400), clean shared baths, lockers, lovely garden with hammocks, popular budget traveller hang-out (no reservations; first come first served).

**E-F Hill Park**, Main St, T0486-2685509. 17 rooms with bath, fan, net, friendly, helpful.

**E-F Lake Queen**, T0486-2222084, www.chancellorresort.com. Basic rooms, fan, nets, small bath, pleasanter upper floors (Rs 150-300),

*For an explanation of the sleeping and eating price codes used in this guide, see inside the front cover. Other relevant information is found in Essentials pages 56-61.*

fairly clean, functional, run by Catholic Diocese (profits to charity).

**F Claus Garden**, Rosapukandam, 10 mins uphill from bus stand behind PO, 3rd turn right. Clean, simple rooms, shared toilet/shower, kitchenette, quiet, friendly.

**Road to Munnar and the Palanis** *p939*

**AL Plantation Homestay**, Mundackal Estate, Pindimana, Kothamangalam Junction, T0485- 570717, nestholidays@hotmail.com. 3 rooms in George and Daisy Jose's homestay that lies deep inside their rubber, pepper and coconut plantations. Daisy is a mean cook and offers lessons (US$20), while George arranges boat trips to the bird sanctuary.

**Munnar** *p939, map p940*

**AL Windermere Estate Plantation and Retreat**, Pothamedu, T04865-230512, www.windermeremunnar.com. 2 stand-alone cottages, an alpine farmhouse with 5 rooms and the planters' bungalow with 3 rooms. Off-season discounts 25%. Absolutely charming with amazing sweeping views on same range of hill as Tall Trees.

**B Copper Castle**, Kannan Devan Hills (out of town), T04865-230633, copper@md4.vsnl.net.in. Perched on hillside with beautiful views, good-sized comfortable rooms with baths (hot showers), restaurant (good sizzlers), friendly staff but slow service.

**B East End**, Temple Rd, T04865-230452. 18 pleasant rooms and some cottages (solar heated water), good but pricey restaurant, attractively designed, quiet garden location.

**B Olive Brook Homestead**, Pothamedu, 3 km south of Munnar, T04865-230588, www.olivebrookhomestead.com. 5 well-appointed double rooms in beautiful lush location, excellent al fresco bbqs on request.

**B Tall Trees**, PO Box 40, Bison Valley Rd, (out of town), www.thetalltreesmunnar.com. Very clean new cottages in beautiful location (many honeymooners!), excellent food, charming staff.

**B Tea Country** (KTDC), out of town, T04865-230460, www.ktdc.com. 43 rooms, good facilities, beautiful views, great walking, own transport essential.

**B Westwood**, T04865-230884. 40 spacious, clean rooms in modern wood-panelled hotel, lovely design, restaurant, quiet, friendly.

**B-C Isaac's Residency**, Top Station Rd, T04865-230501. 32 very nice rooms with ultra-modern furnishings, 'Executive' rooms with great views, 2 restaurants, bar, excellent quality, Recommended.

**C Homestay Kochery**, T04865-231147, kocheryhomestay@vsnl.net. Some of the best rooms in town are to be had from Kochery, chez Babu Peter and wife Mary. Rooms have balconies, there's a charming garden, 24-hr hot water, 2 mins from town.

**E Arafa Tourist Home**, Upper Bazar, T04865- 230302. 14 rooms with TV, phone in newly renovated lodge. Clean and excellent value.

**E Zeena Cottages**, near **Hill View Hotel** in Tata tea plantation, T04865-230560. Rooms in colonial house, good views, friendly people, ask at Tourist Information Service.

## Eating

**Thekkadi** *p937*

**Edassery's Farm Yard**, NH 49 Chattupara Adimali Idukki T04864-224210. 0600-2200, makes a good break on the Kottayam-Kumily road with tasty soups and meals, *dosa* and vegetable stews.

**TTT Spice Village**, international, excellent food and service, 'rustic' decor, fresh garden vegetables, "chef gives demonstration of a dish each night!"

**TT Coffee Inn**, international (0700-2200), tables outside under the palms, bonfire in the evening, relaxed and peaceful, friendly, but very slow.

**TT German Bakery**, Lake Rd. Delicious food, pleasant atmosphere, big set breakfast Rs 40.

**Munnar** *p939, map p940*

**TT East End's**, The Greens. Very pleasant with glassed-in verandah serving good food, smart. Alternative: very cheap simple meals, if you join the drivers in the eatery 'below stairs' entered from the lower car park!

**TT Royal Retreat**, international. Very pleasant, wide choice.

**T Silver Spoon**, near Munnar Inn, for good breakfast choices.

**T Vegetarian Restaurant** (next to Misha) Old Bazar, serves very good meals.

## Bars and clubs

**Munnar** *p939, map p940*
**High Range Club**, T04865-230253. Charming colonial-style planters' club, members only (or with reciprocal arrangements), visit by asking a planter to introduce you.
**KDH Club**, for Tata staff, also old-world, visit with permission, excellent pool table.

## Shopping

**Munnar** *p939, map p940*
**Munnar Supply Assoc** (MSA), next to tourist information. Established 1900, a bit of the old world, where you can get everything. Tailors in the bazaar can copy your garments in 24 hrs. The newer Main Bazar is to the north.

## Activities and tours

**Thekkadi** *p937*
**Periyar Tiger Trails**, trekking and camping programme IX/1007, Kumily, Thekkadi Rd, near Kerala Spices Centre, Kumily, T0486-2323208, www.tourindiakerala.com. Tropical rainforest guides are former bark collectors. 500,000 tourists go to Thekkady each year. This programme aims to reduce their impact and limits numbers to just 20 trekkers per week. Treks, for ages between 15 and 65 can last from overnight to 2 nights 3 days. Forest Park arranges jeep safaris and treks.

**Munnar** *p939, map p940*
**DTPC**, Old Munnar Bazar, run tours. Tea Valley, 1000-1800, Rs 250; Sandal Valley and Wildlife, 0900-1900, Rs 300. Idukki will escort you on excellent mountain walks.
**Sibi Thomas** at Toby's Trails, PB No 49 Kannan Devan Hills. For teks.

## Transport

**Thekkadi** *p937*
**Bus**
**Local** Minibuses hourly from Kumily go down to **Aranya Nivas** on the lakeside, Rs 2. At Kumily jeep drivers tell you there is no bus to Thekkadi and charge Rs 50 for the trip; autos charge Rs 25+.
**Long distance** Regular state and private buses run between from Kumily: to **Alappuzha** 1115, 1345; **Kochi/Ernakulam** (6 hrs), 6 per day; **Kodaikkanal** (cancelled occasionally), 0630 (5½ hrs), or go to **Vathalakundu** and change; **Thiruvananthapuram**, 285 km (8 hrs), 3 per day. Buses also go from Thekkadi itself (behind *Aranya Nivas*): to **Kottayam** (0600, 1430); several per hr to **Madurai**; late afternoon **Kollam** (4½ hrs). KTDC 2-day tours from Ernakulam, Sat depart 0730, return 2000, Rs 120.

**Motor launches**
On the lake 2-hr motor launch trips are inexpensive, scheduled every 2 hrs from 0700-1500; tickets sell out in peak season, Rs 50 (top deck Rs 90).

**Munnar** *p939, map p940*
**Bike hire** Raja, Rs 40 per day, Rs 20 per half day; from tourist information, Rs 50 per day. Joy Automobiles, GH Rd, recommended car mechanics.

**Bus**
Frequent services to **Mattupetty** (30 mins), **Devikulam** (30 mins), **Adimali** (1 hr) and **Top Station** (1 hr). Daily to **Coimbatore** (6 hrs); **Ernakulam/ Kochi** (4½ hrs); **Kodaikkanal** 0700 via Udumalpettai, change for Palani and Kodai. If the Palani-Kodai Rd is closed a further bus goes to Vatalakundu and then Kodai; **Kottayam** (5 hrs); **Madurai** via Theni (5 hrs); **Palani** (4½ hrs); **Thekkadi** (4½ hrs); **Thiruvanantha puram** (9 hrs), **Thrissur via Perumbavoor** (5 hrs).

**Jeeps/taxis**
Go to the Eravikulam National Park.

## Directory

**Munnar** *p939, map p940*
**Banks** Federal Bank, near Tata Hospital Rd, very helpful; State Bank of India, 1000-1400, Sat 1000-1200. **Internet** Next to Misha Hotel, Rs 40 per hr. Phone connections from Munnar are unreliable; alternative nearest ISD phone is in Kothamangalam. **Hospital** Excellent Tata General Hospital, T530270, on the north edge of town on the Rajamalai Rd. **Post**: New Town centre.

# Thrissur and Palakkad

*Busy Thrissur is the state's cultural capital: it is known chiefly for its annual fireworks display on Pooram (April/May) which attracts millions and never fails to make the national news – if in Kerala it's worth adjusting your schedule to take in the festival but be prepared to be packed sardine-style with unruly crowds. Coastal Guruvayur, meanwhile, is among Kerala's most sacred Hindu pilgrimage spots, has one of India's wealthiest temples as well as an elephant yard filled with huge tuskers and their mah- outs relaxing before they hit the road on the way to the next festival. Inland, the rich agricultural yields of nearby Palakkad make it Kerala's granary, and a good stopover point on the route to or from Tamil Nadu.* ▸▸ *For Sleeping, Eating and other listings, see pages 948-950.*

## To Thrissur and Palakkad via Kalady

One of South India's most important historically strategic routes, the road rises gently to the lowest pass through the Western Ghats along their entire length. **Kalady** ⓘ *0530-1230, 1530-2000*, on the bank of the Periyar River, 45 km from Kochi, is the birthplace of one of India's most influential philosophers, **Sankaracharya**. Living in the eighth century, Sankaracharya founded the school of *advaita* philosophy, see page 1323, which spread widely across South India. There are now two shrines in his memory, one as Dakshinamurti and the other to the Goddess Sarada. The management of the shrines is in the hands of the Math at Sringeri in Karnataka, see page 1005. The **Adi Sankara Kirti Stambha Mandapam** ⓘ *0700-1900, small entry fee, Kalady can easily be visited in an afternoon from Kochi or from Aluva by bus (40 mins)*, is a nine-storeyed octagonal tower, 46-m high, and details Sri Sankara's life and works and the Shan Maths, or six ways to worship. There are a couple of basic places to stay.

## Thrissur (Trichur) and around → *Phone code: 0487. Colour map 3, grid B2. Population: 317,500.*

Thrissur is on the west end of the Palakkad gap which runs through the low pass between the Nilgiri and the Palani Hills. The route through the Ghats is not scenic but it has been the most important link to the peninsula interior since Roman times. Thrissur is built round a hill on which stand the Vadakkunnathan Temple and an open green. The town's bearings are given in cardinal directions from this raised 'Round'.

The **Vadakkunnathan Temple** ⓘ *0400-1030, 1700-2030, non-Hindus are not permitted inside except during the Pooram festival*, a predominantly Siva temple, is also known as the Rishabhadri or Thenkailasam ('Kailash of the South'). At the shrine to the Jain Tirthankara Vrishabha, worshippers offer a thread from their clothing, symbolically to cover the saint's nakedness. The shrine to Sankara Narayana has superb murals depicting stories from the *Mahabharata*. It is a classic example of the Kerala style of architecture with its special pagoda-like roof richly decorated with fine wood carving. The temple plays a pivotal role in the *Pooram* celebrations, see Festivals page 949. In September/October, there are live performances of Chakyarkothu, a classical art form. There is a small elephant compound attached to the temple. The **Town Hall** is a striking building housing an art gallery with murals from other parts of the state. In the **Archaeological Museum** ⓘ *Town Hall Rd, 0900-1500, closed Mon*, ask to see the royal chariot. Next door, the **Art Museum**, has wood carvings, sculptures, an excellent collection of traditional lamps and old jewellery. Nearby, **Thrissur Zoo** ⓘ *closed Mon, 1000-1700, small fee*, is known for its snake collection. The impressive **Lourdes Church** has an interesting underground shrine.

*Pala is a type of tree and Kadu means forest: the area was once thickly covered in forests of this tree.*

The **Kerala Kalamandalam Vallathol Nagar** ⓘ *29 km north of Thrissur near Shornur Junction, T04884-262305, www.kalamandalam.com, closed Sat, Sun, public holidays and in Apr and May*, is Kerala's answer to Fame's hallowed campus. On the banks of the Nila river it is dedicated to preserving the state's unique forms of performance art and the college's foundation led to a revival of *Kathakali* dancing. It is a centre for teaching music, drama, *Mohiniyattam* and *Ottam Thullal* in addition to *Kathakali*. The school and the state tourism department runs a tour, *A Day With the Masters* (US$25), which is a three-hour programme with in-depth explanations of the significance and background of the art forms, the academy and its architecture, but you can still just walk in to look around the campus at the open air *kalaris* (classrooms) where classes start at 0400 and watch training sessions. There are all-night Kathakali performances: 26 January, 15 August, and 9 November. The college was built in 1930 after patronage for the arts from provincial rulers and rajas dwindled in line with their own plummeting wealth and influence. *Koodiyattam*, the oldest surviving form of Sanskrit theatre, is enshrined by UNESCO as an 'oral and intangible heritage of humanity'. Frequent private buses from Thrissur northern bus stand (Vadakkechira bus stand) go straight to Kalamandalam, about one hour.

## Palakkad (Palghat)

→ *Phone code: 0491. Colour map 3, grid B3. Population: 130,700.*

Kerala's 'rice cellar,' prosperous Palakkad is one of only a handful of districts in Kerala to come without a coast. Instead, it has a 'gap' – the only break in the mountain ranges that otherwise block the state from Tamil Nadu and Karnataka and through which great big sand squalls race in April. The gap has made the area one of strategic importance as the historical gateway for the state to mainland India. Whereas once this brought military incursions, today the gap bears tourist buses from Chennai and tracktors for the rich agricultural fields that few educated modern Keralites care to plough using the old bullock carts (although memories of the tradition are kept alive in January when yoked oxes are raced in 'kaalapoottu' through deep mud-churned paddy fields). The annual festival of **Chinakathoor Pooram** (end February to early March) held at the Sri Chinakathoor Bhagavathy Temple, Palappuram, features a 33-tusker procession, plus remarkable evening puppet shows. Bejewelled tuskers can also be seen at the 20-day **Nenmara-Vallangi Vela**, held at the Sri Nellikulangara Bhagavathy temple, Kodakara (early April): an amazing festival with grander firework displays than Trichur's Pooram but set in fields rather than across the city.

The region is filled with old architecture of *illams* and *tharavadus* belonging to wealthy landowners making a visit worthwhile in itself – but chief among the actual sights is **Palakkad Fort**, a granite structure in Palakkad town itself, built by Haider Ali in 1766, and taken over by the British in 1790. It now has a Hanuman temple inside. Also, ask directions locally to the 500-year-old Jain temple of **Jainimedu** in the town's western suburbs, a 32-ft-long granite temple with Jain *Thirthankaras* and *Yakshinis* built for the Jain sage Chandranathaswami. Only one Jain family is left in the region, but the area around this temple is one of the only places in Kerala where remnants of the religion have survived. Also well worth visiting in the region are the many traditional **Brahmin villages: Kalpathy,** 10 km outside Palakkad, holds the oldest Siva temple in Malabar, dating from 1425 AD and built by Kombi Achan, then Raja of Palakkad. But the village itself, an 800 year-old settlement by a self-contained Tamil community, is full of beautiful houses with wooden shutters and metal grills and is now a World Heritage Site that gives you a glimpse of village life that has been held half-frozen in time for nearly a thousand years. The temple here is called **Kasiyil Pakuthi Kalpathy** meaning 'Half Banares' because its situation on the river is reminiscent of the Banares temple on the Ganges. A **car festival** centred on this temple runs for 10 days in November and features teak chariots tugged by people and pushed by elephants.

Another unique feature of Palakkad is the **Ramassery Iddli** made at the **Sarswathy tea stall** ⓘ *0500-1830, 7 days a week, iddli Rs 1.50, chai Rs 2.50*. If you spend any time on the street in South India, your morning meal will inevitably feature many of these tasty steamed fermented rice cakes. Palakkad is home to a peculiar take on the dumpling: one that has been developed to last for days rather than having to be cooked from fresh. The four families in this poky teashop churn out 5,000 *iddlis* a day. Originally settlers from somewhere near Coimbatore, in Tamil Nadu, over 100 years ago, they turned to making this variety of *iddli* when there wasn't enough weaving work to sustain their families. They started out selling them door-to-door, but pretty soon started to get orders for weddings. The furthest the *iddlis* have travelled so far is to Delhi by plane in a shipment of 300. Manufacturers have lately been arriving to buy the secret recipe of the longlife *iddli*.

**Nelliyampathy**, 56 k from Palakkad town, is a hill station with a tiny community of planters. It is famous for its oranges, but there are also orchids, bison, elephant and butterflies in abundance. You get an amazing bird's eye view across the Keralite plains from Seethakundu – a third of the district lies spread out under you. Good trekking too.

## Kodungallur

At one time Kodungallur, just over the border into Trichur from Ernakulam district, was the west coast's major port, and the capital of the Chera king Cheraman Perumal. **Kottapuram**, nearby, is where St Thomas is believed to have landed in AD 52. The commemorative shrine was built in 1952. Kodungallur is also associated by tradition with the arrival of the first Muslims to reach India by sea. Malik-ibn-Dinar is reputed to have built India's first **Juma Masjid**, 2 km from town. It is worth visiting the **Tiruvanchikulam Temple** and the **Portuguese fort**. The Syrian orthodox church in **Azikode** blends early Christian architecture in Kerala with surrounding Hindu traditions. Thus the images of Peter and Paul are placed where the *dvarapalas* (door-keepers) of Hindu temples would be found, and the portico in front of the church is for pilgrims.

## Guruvayur

As one of the holiest sites in Kerala, Guruvayur, 29 km west of Trichur, is a heaving pilgrimage centre, filled with stalls and thronged from 0300 to 2200 with people wanting to take *darshan* of Guruvayurappan.

It is one of the richest temples in India: there is a waiting list for the auspicious duty of lighting its oil lamps that stretches to 2025. On well-augured marriage days there is a scrum in which couples are literally shunted from the podium by new pairs urgently pressing behind them in the queue, and the whole town is geared towards the wedding industry: most hotels here have huge marriage halls and expect guests to stay a maximum of two nights. The ceremony of children's first rice feed falls on the first of every *Malayali* month. The **Sri Krishna Temple** which probably dates from at least the 16th century has an outer enclosure where there is a tall gold-plated flagpost and a pillar of lamps. The sanctum sanctorum is in the two-storeyed *srikoil*, with the image of the four-armed Krishna garlanded with pearls and marigolds. Photography of the tank is not allowed. Non-Hindus are not allowed inside and are not made to feel welcome.

*There are some pleasant beaches nearby which you can get to by rickshaw but they haven't any facilities.*

On the left as you walk towards the temple is the **Guruvayur Devaswom Institute of Mural Painting** ⓘ *1000-1600 Mon-Fri*, a tiny educational institute where you can see the training of, and buy finished works from, the next generation of mural painters. In a similar vein to *Kathakali*, with the weakening structure of feudalism and opposition to the caste system, the age-old decorative arts of temple culture steadily declined during the 20th century. When Guruvayur lost three walls to a fire in 1970

*Guruvayur's Sri Krishna temple, in December 2003, collected no less than Rs 109,44,347 along with just short of 4 kg of gold and almost 14 kg of silver.*

there were hardly any artists left to carry out renovation, prompting authorities to build the school in 1989. Today the small institute runs a five-year course on a scholarship basis for just 10 students. Paintings sell from Rs 500-15,000 depending on size, canvas, wood, etc. Humans are stylized – facial expressions and gestures can be traced back to *Kathakali* and *Koodiyattom* – and have wide-open eyes, elongated lips, over-ornamentation and exaggerated eyebrows and hand gestures.

**Punnathur Kotta Elephant Yard** ⓘ *0900-1700, bathing 0900-0930, Rs 25, take care: elephants can be dangerous, buses from Thrissur (45 mins)*, is situated within a fort 4 km out of town. Temple elephants (68 at the last count) are looked after here and wild ones are trained. There are some interesting insights into traditional animal training but this is not everyone's cup of tea. Though captive, the elephants are dedicated to Krishna and appear to be well cared for by their attendants. The elephants are donated by pious Hindus but religious virtue doesn't come cheap: elephants go for Rs 500,000 a pop.

## Megalith trail: Guruvayur to Kunnamkulam

The Palakkad gap has been one of the few relatively easy routes through the Ghats for 3,000 years and this area is noted for its wide range of megalithic monuments. Megalithic cultures spread from the Tamil Nadu plains down into Kerala, but developed their own local forms. The small villages of Eyyal, Chovvanur, Kakkad, Porkalam, Kattakampala and Kadamsseri, between Guruvayur and Kunnamkulam have hoodstones, hatstones, dolmens, burial urns and menhirs.

## Sleeping

**Thrissur** *p945*
Reserve ahead during Pooram, prices rocket.

**A Kadappuram Beach Resort**, Nattika Beach, T0487-2394988, www.kadappurambeach resorts.com. 13 double rooms in eco- friendly bamboo and coconut cottages off the NH17. Ayurveda, yoga, meditation come first here. The beach is across a river over a rickety wooden bridge. Tariff includes 3 meals, drinks and snacks. Packages include 2 weeks *pancha -karma* plus yoga for US$520 per person.

**B River Retreat**, 1.5 km from train station, Cheruthuruthy, T04884-262244. The summer palace to the maharajas of Cochin with splendid views of Bharatpuza river, has been modernized to make 24 spacious a/c rooms with TVs, traditional furniture and modern baths. **The Riviera Restaurant** is good for a chilled beer and snacks.

**B-D Luciya Palace**, Marar Rd, T0487-2424731, luciyapalace@hotmail.com. 35 rooms, 15 a/c, 2 suites, Large, clean and quiet rooms, TV, garden restaurant, internet next door, good service, very pleasant hotel.

**C-D Surya**, 15 km from town, 8 km from beach, T0487-2331347, sureshpr@md3.vsnl.net.in. 10 rooms (some a/c) in impressive old buildings, vegetarian meals, ayurvedic treatments, yoga, exchange, lawn.

**D-E Bini Tourist Home**, Round North, T0487-2335703. 24 rooms, TV, shower, 10 a/c, rather spartan but clean and spacious rooms, restaurant, bar.

**F Railway Retiring Rooms**, well looked after and very good value.

**Palakkad** *p946*

**LL Kalari Kovilakom** or **The Palace of Ayurveda**, book through CGH Earth, Willingdon Island, Kochi, T0484- 2668221, 2666821, www.cghearth.com. Ayurveda for purists: far from the routine tourist-traps the Maharani of Palakkad's old palace has been restored at huge expense to cater to those who are very serious about their *veda*. Lessons include yoga, meditation, ayurvedic cookery. €300 per day all-inclusive with a 10-day minimum stay. Strictly no exertion: that means no sunbathing, no swimming.

**AL Kandath Tharavad**, Thenkurussi, T04922-284124, www.tharavad.com. A magical place tucked away in Palakkad's agricultural land, you stay inside a 200-year-old mud and teak ancestral home with natural-dyed floor tiles of ochre, terracotta and blue. Nadumuttams open out onto the stars and doors are thick wedges of teak wood and brass: its owner, your host

Bhagwaldas is very knowledgable. While the house is undoubtedly beautiful, and food delicious, one of the biggest benefits of staying here is his company; he takes guests around villages to show them culture and traditions. Strongly recommended.

**B-C Indraprastha**, English Church Rd, Palakkad, T0491-2534641, www.hotelindraprastha.com. Kitsch and cool: 30 rooms in 2-storey 1960s block, dark wood, leather banquettes and bronze lettering. Dark bar permanently packed, lawn service, 24-hr vegetarian coffee shop, foreign exchange, internet, bookshop. Multi-cuisine restaurant.

**B-D Fort Palace**, West Fort Rd, Palakkad, T0491-2534621. 19 rooms, groovy old-style hotel some good a/c, restaurant, brash mock turrets. Satellite TV and hot and cold water. Indian/continental food restaurant, and bar, both gloomy and packed (lawn service). Nice shared sit-out on 1st floor, spotless, large double beds. Chandeliers, wood panelling.

**D Garden House** (KTDC), Malampuzha, T0491-2815217. 17 somewhat chintzy rooms in a 1-star government-restaurant on hilltop overlooking popular domestic picnic spot (Malampuzha gardens with lotus pond). Mostly non a/c rooms, pleasant.

**F Green Land Farmhouses**, Palagapandy, Nelliyampathy, T04923-246 266. A complex of farmhouses perched on top of the hillside of Nelliyampathy set in large lawns and with lovely views from the 'Vantage' cottage.

**Guruvayur** *p947*

**A-C Mayura Residency**, West Nada, T0487-2557174, www.mayuraresidency.com. 65 value for money, well appointed rooms in high-rise hotel with excellent views from its rooftop. 24-hr coffee shop, **Amrutham** pure veg (continental, south or north Indian) restaurant, 2 function rooms for weddings.

**B Kairali Ayurvedic Health Resort**, Kodumbu, T04923-222553, www.kairali.com. Excellent resort, beautifully landscaped grounds, own dairy and farm, extensive choice of treatments, competent and helpful staff, pool, tennis etc. Recommended.

**B-D Hotel Vanamala**, Kusumam South Nada, T0487-2555504, www.vanamalakusumam.com. 2-star hotel (popular with domestic tourists), very clean rooms with big beds and TV, telephone and hot and cold water. A/c, vegetarian restaurant, laundry and credit (Keralan food 35 for meals 0600-2300).

**C Krishna Inn**, East Nada, T0487-2550777, www.krishnainn.com. Another glossy hotel: white marble floors and spacious. 2 function rooms again, 24-hr coffee shop, pure veg, multi-cuisine Thulasi restaurant.

**C-D Sree Hari Guest House**, Samuham Rd, West Nada, T0487-2556837. 8 big rooms some a/c, with hot water, draped with purple crushed velvet in guesthouse stuffed with Krishnas and 1960s-style curtains.

**D Vanamala Kusumam**, South Nada, T0487-2556702. 30 rooms, some comfortable a/c, vegetarian restaurant.

## Eating

**Thrissur** *p945*

Most **D** hotels have good restaurants, particularly **Siddhartha Regency's Golden Fork**. In general, though, eating out is still somewhat frowned on by the traditional Brahmin families of Kerala, so most eating options are down-at-heel *dhabas*.

**City Centre**, next to Priya Tourist Home. Western snacks, bakery and good supermarket.

**Navaratna**, Naduvilal, Round West, T0487-2421994. Pure vegetarian North Indian restaurant divided into booths, diner-style. 1000-2300.

**Elite Bharat**, Chembottil Lane. For good South Indian breakfast and lunch.

**Sapphire**, "for best chicken biriyani". Excellent lime green and stone eatery dishing up *thalis* (with chappati Rs 50) 0630-2200.

**Palakkad** *p946*

**Ashok Bhavan**. Modest vegetarian South Indian snacks.

**Hotel Noor Jehan**, GB Rd, Palakkad, T0491-2522717, www.hotelnoorjehan.com. Non vegetarian a/c restaurant that specializes in *moplah biryani* and *pathiri*, chappatis made from rice.

**KR Bakes**, a castle to cake: puffs, ice creams, *halva* plus juice bar and savoury meals after 1600. Open 0900-2300

## Festivals and events

**Thrissur** *p945*

**Jan-Feb**: Several temple festivals involving elephants are held in the surrounding villages which can be as rewarding as *Pooram* (eg **Koorkancherry Thaippoya Mahotsavam**, or **Thaipooya Kavadiyattam**, held at Sri Maheswara Temple, Koorkancherry, 2 km from Thrissur). Also held at the end of Feb is the **Uthralikavu Pooram**, at its most colourful at the Sri Ruthura Mahakalikavu Temple, Parithipra, Vodakancherry, on the route to Shornur Junction. **End-Mar**: 7-day **Arratupuzha Festival** at the Ayappa temple, 14 km from Thrissur. On the 5th day the deity processes with nine decorated elephants, while on the 6th day **Pooram** is celebrated on a grand scale with 61 elephants in the temple grounds. **Apr-May**: the magnificent 8-day **Pooram**, a grand festival with elephants, parasols, drums and fireworks, should not be missed. Several temples in town participate but particularly the Thiruvambady and Paramekkavu. It is marked by very noisy, colourful processions, joined by people from all religious communities, irrespective of caste. The festivities are held from around 1300-1700 and again at night from around 2000. Elaborately bedecked elephants (each temple allowed up to 15) specially decorated with lamps and palm leaves, process to the Vadakkunnathan Temple carrying priests and deities to the accompaniment of extraordinary drumming. On the final day temple teams meet on the Tekkinkadu *maidan* for the drumming and *Kudumattam* competition; the festival terminates with a huge display of fireworks. **Aug/Sep**: the district also celebrates **Kamdassamkadavu** Boat Races at *Onam*. Also performances of **Pulikali**, unique to Thrissur, when mimers dressed as tigers dance to drumbeats.

**Punnathur Kotta** *p948*
**Feb/Mar**: Utsavam, 10 days of festivities start with an elephant race and continue with colourful elephant processions and performances of *Krishnanattom* dances. Details from Kerala Tourist offices. **Nov-Dec**: 5-day Ekadasi with performances of *Krishnanattom*, a forerunner of *Kathakali* – an 8-day drama cycle.

## Transport

**Thrissur** *p945*
**Auto-rickshaw**
Yellow top local auto-rickshaws available.

**Bus**
There are yellow top local buses available. For long distance, there are 3 bus stands. KSRTC, near railway station, southwest of 'Round' including several to **Allapuzha** (3½ hrs), **Bangalore** (10 hrs), **Coimbatore** (3 hrs), **Guruvayur** (1 hr), **Kochi** (2 hrs), **Kozhikode**, **Chennai** (13 hrs), **Palakkad**, **Thiruvananthapuram** (7 hrs). North (Priyadarshini), just north of 'Round', buses to **Cheruthuruthy**, **Ottapalam**, **Palakkad**. Sakthan Thampuran, 2 km south of 'Round', for frequent private buses to **Guruvayur**, **Kannur**, **Kozhikode**.

**Train**
**Kochi (Cochin)**: *Tiruchchirappalli Cochin Exp, 6865*, 0335, 2¾ hrs; *Hyderabad Cochin Exp, 7030*, 1245, not Tue, 2¼ hrs; *Raptisagar Exp, 5012/5222*, 1530, Mon, Thu, Fri, Sun, 2¾ hrs. **Chennai (MC)**: *Alleppey-Chennai Exp, 6042* (AC/II), 1810, 12½ hrs; *Trivandrum Chennai Mail, 6320*, 2045, 11¼ hrs; *Raptisagar Exp, 5011* (AC/II), 1110, Tue, Wed, Fri, Sat, 12¼ hrs.

**Palakkad** *p946*
**Bus**
KSRTC, for long distance from Municipal Bus Stand: **Kozhikode**, **Mannarghat** (Silent Valley), **Pollachi**.

**Train**
The main Junction station is 5 km northeast of town. Also Town Station. **Coimbatore**: *West Coast Exp, 6628*, 0500, 1½ hrs; *Cochin Hyderabad Exp, 7029*, 1405, 1¼ hrs; *Kerala Exp, 2625*, 1905, 1¼ hrs. **Chennai**: *West Coast Exp, 6628*, 0500, 10½ hrs; *Alleppey Chennai Exp, 6042*, 2025, 10¼ hrs. **Ernakulam Junction**: *Kerala Exp, 2626* (AC/II), 0720, 3 hrs; *Hyderabad Cochin Exp, 7030*, 1045, not Tue, 3½ hrs. **Kochi** (Cochin): *Hyderabad Cochin Exp, 7030*, 1045, not Tue, 4¼ hrs.

## Directory

**Thrissur** *p945*
**Banks** State Bank of India, Town Hall Rd, Round East, near Paramekkavu Temple; State Bank of Travancore (upstairs), opposite. **Internet** Sruthy, north of temple ring. Good connections, Rs 30 per hr. **Hospital** Amala Cancer Hospital, Amalanagar (9 km, along the Guruvayur Rd), T0487-2211950. Recommended for medicine, surgery.

# The Malabar Coast

*The Malabar region is the unsung jewel of Kerala: the combination of the state's political administration down south plus the pious Muslim community and orthodoxy of the Hindu population have made it more resistant to tourist development than the more easy-going, Catholic-influenced stretch south from Kochi. Any cohesion between north and south Kerala is political, not cultural: Malabar was under the Madras Presidency before Independence, lumped together with the Travancore south only in 1956. The atmosphere couldn't be more different. Here then, friendly people are still intrigued by foreigners, it hasn't yet occurred to rickshaw-wallahs to hike their fares, and beaches are empty. The coastal towns of Calicut, Telicherry and Cannur are the strongholds of the Muslim Moplah community, whose long-standing trading links with the Middle East have also bred a deep cultural affinity. Arabic flavours are present in Malabari food, you'll find hubbly bubblies being enjoyed and plenty of gold being flashed about. In the Waynad district inland from Kozhikode experiences some of the heaviest levels of rainfall in the world and is covered in the familiar stubble of tea plantations. This region is also one of the best places to see Kerala's unique religious and cultural traditions in their proper context: Theyyam, the Hindu ritual temple dance that spawned kathakali and Kalari, the stunning martial art, are both practised here whether tourists are looking or not.* ▸▸ *For Sleeping, Eating and other listings, see pages 955-958.*

*Not catering to the tourist rupee means that beaches are often strewn with litter. Also, swimming togs can cause alarming levels of attention even outright hostility.*

## Kozhikode (Calicut) → *Phone code: 0495. Colour map 3, grid B2.*

*Population: 436,500.*

Kozhikode is a major commercial centre for northern Kerala and the centre for Kerala's timber industry; there is also a huge dependance on the petro-dollar, as testified by the scores of direct flights to the Gulf each day. The city itself is engaged in mostly small-scale retail. Off the ugly brash main boulevard, tiny roads thread through high laterite walls with everything happening on the street. Remnants of the spice trade remain and the markets are great – Court Road is home to pepper, the black gold that lured Vasco, as well as copra and coconut oil. There are beautiful wooden mosques built like temples, and in nearby Beypore, where the Chaliyar river meets the Arabian sea, you can see the engineering of *urus*: massive deep-sea hauler-sized wooden boats built by Khalasis in much the same way as they've done since Cheraman Perumal first ordered one for a visit to Arabia in the sixth century.

### Ins and outs

**Getting there and around** Karipur airport, 25 km south, has connections with several major Indian cities. The station and main bus stand are near the town centre within easy reach of several hotels. Autos are widely available and surprisingly cheap. **Tourist information** **Kerala Tourism**, Govt Guest House and Railway Station.

### Sights

The Sunni Muslim quarter of **Kuttichira**, behind the railway station towards the sea, to the west of town, holds several fascinating multi-tiered mosques made of wood that date from the 15th century. Women should cover head, shoulders and limbs in this area particularly. They bear a puzzlingly close resemblance to Hindu temple structures, complete with pillars, ventilation and huge green pond around which flocks of white-capped elders range up in the late afternoon (legend has it that a ghost within the pond seizes a human sacrifice each year: the body surfaces after three days). **Mishkal Masjid** is one of the oldest, and was named for the wealthy trader who built it, but also look for **Jami Mosque** and **Munchunthi Palli**. Muchunthi Palli has a 13th-century *vattezhuthu* (inscribed slab of stone) which proclaims the donation of the land to the mosque by a Zamorin.

Look too at the size of the houses around here: known to accommodate over 150 family members each because the *puyappala* tradition (literally translates as 'fresh husband') means that each marrying daughter takes the husband back into her parents' house. One house is supposed to have 300 people living under the same roof: each building has an average of three kitchens. ⓘ *For further details see www.calicut.net.* From here you can walk along the Beach Road: the old buildings here that were trading centres are now being busily demolished. The beach itself is more of a town latrine than a place for swimming.

**Pazhassiraja Museum** ⓘ *closed Mon, 1000-1230, 1430-1700, 5 km on East Hill,* has copies of original murals plus bronzes, old coins and models of the some of the area's megalithic monuments. The **Art Gallery** and **Krishna Menon Museum** ⓘ *Mon, Wed afternoon only, 1000-1230, 1430-1700, free,* named after the Kerala politician who became a leading left-wing figure in India's post-Independence Congress Government, is next door. There's an excellent collection of paintings by Indian artists; as well as wood and ivory carvings. A section of the museum is dedicated to VK Krishna Menon.



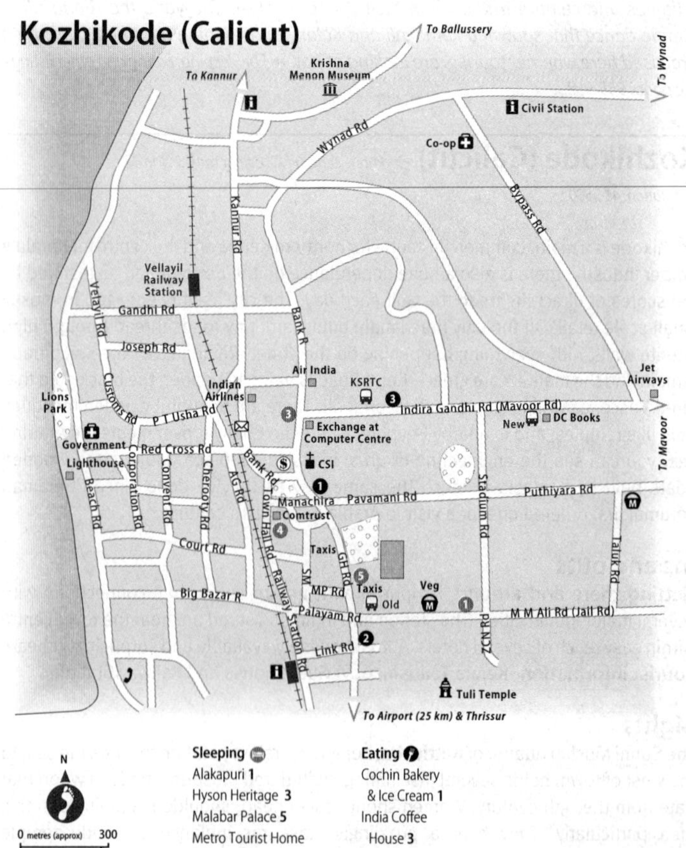

## Excursions

**Kappad**, 16 km north, and now the site of a small, poor, mainly Muslim fishing village, is where Vasco da Gama landed on 27th May 1498 with 170 men and has an old plaque by the approach road to the beach commemorating the event. Though it is a pleasant spot, the sea is unsuitable for swimming since pollution from Kozhikode filters down this far and the beach itself is used as a toilet by the fishermen.

**Beypore**, half an hour south of Calicut, was once a significant port, but is now famous only for its shipbuilding trade. You can visit the boatyard here, where families of Khalasis have used traditional methods to make *urus* – huge wooden vessels – for 1,500 years. These men craft the ships using ancient techniques (there are no engineers and no computers), but their popularity is dwindling. They used to work 365 days a year, now they'll have two or three months without work in between commissions from Arab clients.

# Mahé → *Colour map 7, grid B2.*

The borders of the 9 sq km that make up French Kerala are marked, not by baguette bakeries or pavement cafés, but by shops screaming 'Foreign Liquor'. By night, Mahé, the 35,000 members of the union territory of Pondicherry colony disappear to make way for the truckers who scream through to stock up on half price whiskies and brandies, taking advantage of the colony's special tax status. By day, Mahé is pretty enough: there are French hats on the policemen and the town is beautifully positioned on a slight hill overlooking the river; it was named after M Mahé de Labourdonnais, when he captured it for the French in 1725. Many still speak French and the very French **Church of St Theresa** celebrates her feast day on 14-15 October. The beaches to the south and north of town are dirty and not safe for swimming because of undercurrents.

# Thalassery (Tellicherry) → *Phone code: 0490. Colour map 7, grid B2.*

Thalassery, like everywhere along the Malabar's increasingly 'gold' coast, banks have queues for 'gold loans' where your branch manager doubles as pawn broker. Despite an obsession with wealth, at the wide, tree-covered street level you'll find a town that's friendly, brilliantly walkable and lined with 19th-century shops complete with their original wooden cupboards and cobwebs. It was here that the author Herman Hesse's mother was born.

Thalassery was set up by the British East India Company in 1683 to export pepper and cardamom. In 1708 they obtained permission to build a **fort** which, having survived a siege laid by Haidar Ali, is still standing today on a rocky promontory about 15 m above sea level. Its proud little gateway, raised on a flight of steps, is flanked by colourful mustachioed figures. There are some attractive old buildings. The **Armenian church** is rather shabby now but the Catholic church still thrives though the population is largely *Moplah* (Kerala Muslims). The **Odathil Mosque**, believed to be 400 years old, is in the traditional Kerala style with a gabled roof and copper sheeting.

**Mambally's Royal Biscuit Factory** ⓘ *near Old Police Station, T0490-2321207, 0900-2030,* established in 1880, claims to be where cake was first baked in Kerala. Nowadays you'll find jam rolls, ketchup, Nestlé milky bars and lime pickle along with the fresh bakes. The downstairs of double-decker shops is crowded with hessian sacks full of cinnamon from China, cloves from Madagascar, Ceylon and Hyderabad,

*The Calicut passport office is for six districts: the Waynad, Kannur, Kozhikode, Mallapuram and Pallakad. It processes 1,300 fresh passport applications daily. 1,200,000 Keralites work in the Gulf region and the revenue which Kerala gets from them is about US$12 bn.*

raisins from Afghanistan and star of anise from China and Vietnam. Some of the owners are third generation traders. The **fish market** ⓘ *0600-1800*, is one of the liveliest in Kerala. Men with cleavers stand tall over barracudas and manta, stacks of clams, mussels, shrimps and mackerel are constantly replenished with new loads. Fish are then sped along the state highway to reach markets in Cochin or even Mangalore.

Thalassery is also a centre for training in gymnastics and circus acts, so street performers and acrobats are not uncommon: 90% of India's circus companies originate here. You can see martial arts in local *kalaris*: one of the best being the tricky to find *kalari* of **K Viswanathan Gurukkal** ⓘ *MKG Kalari Sangham, Kuzhippangad, PO Chirakkara, T0490-237110, www.mkgkalari.tripod.com, call in advance.*

**Muzhapilangad Beach**, 8 km from Telicherry, nicknamed 'Drive In Beach', is an unspoilt, beautifully picturesque 4 km stretch of golden sand edged by palm trees at the northern end. Amazingly empty most of the time, it earnt its nickname from the local custom of ragging trucks or ambassadors up and down its firm sands.

## Kannur (Cannanore) → *Phone code: 0497. Colour map 3, grid B2.*

Kannur (Cannanore) stands on raised ground with cliffs at the sea face. The coconut-fringed coastline has some attractive beaches. Weavers' co-operatives and *beedi* factories provide employment but this is also the place to watch *Theyyam* dances.

Kannur, the centre of the Mopplah community, a group of Arab descent, was also the capital of the North Kolathiri Rajas for several hundred years. **Fort St Angelo** was built out of laterite blocks by the Portuguese in 1505 and taken over by the British in 1790 as their most important military base in the south. The highly picturesque **Moplah town** is round the bay to the south of the fort. The attractive **Payyambalam Beach** is just 2 km away. Handloom weavers produce silk and cotton saris, shirts, *lungis* and soft furnishings sold through local cooperatives. **Kanhirode Weavers' Cooperative Society** ⓘ *Koodali Kannur, T0497-2857259, www.weaveco.com, 0900-1700, free.* It was founded in 1952 on Gandhian principle, has a yearly turnover of Rs 150,000,000 (US$3.3 million) and exports 95% of its pure handloom fabric to the UK for the Futon Bed Company. Spun cotton is shipped in from Coimbatore, and dyed in huge vats after which the cooperative's 450 staff are expected to feed bobbins through the high wooden looms fast enough to make 42 m within 3½ days for ladies, or three for men. While some weave, others feed the raw heaps of cotton from wire frames onto wheels to make thread – in the silk section they use bicycle wheels. The rooms, chock-full with the Chettiar caste for whom this is hereditary occupation, clatter with activity. The daily wage is Rs 100 (US$2.2), and apparently the coop is having trouble recruiting more of the caste, who, as caste rules relax, are going for higher paid jobs elsewhere. Well worth the journey.

## Bekal and Kasaragod → *Phone code: 0499.*

Bekal, 16 km south of Kasaragod, has an ancient fort on the sea, the largest and best preserved in Kerala, which gives superb views of the coastline. Originally built by the Kadamba kings, the fort passed under the control of Vijayanagar and of Tipu Sultan before being brought into the hands of the East India Company. Excavations have exposed some interesting structures. Just outside the fort is the **Sri Mukhyaprana Temple.** Bekal also has a beautiful and undeveloped beachwhich Kerala Tourism talk of turning into a major resort. For *Theyyam* and *Yakshagana* performances contact the

*There is strong pro-Arab sentiment in Malabar. An advertisement for a cigarette brand in 2004 read: Indians have diwali. Americans have Baghdad. Not made in America. Thankfully.*

**Bekal Tourist Office** ⓘ *T0499-2736937.* En route to Bekal the road passes **Ezhimala**, with a beach and a hill famous for its ayurvedic herbs.

Kasaragod is the northernmost town in Kerala. From the bus stand, the walk to the sea through a sprawling residential area – mainly Mopplah – takes about 30 minutes. The beach is magnificent and deserted. You can walk a long way before scrambling back to the main road, crossing paddy fields, backwaters, and the Konkan railway line.

## The Waynad → *Phone code: 0493. Colour map 3, grid B2.*

The Waynad occupies some of Kerala's untouched, forest clad hills and is in part pure virgin rainforest and part cardamom, coffee, pepper tree and vanilla covered. The route from Kozhikode on the coast, across the Western Ghats to Mysore (214 km, 5½ hours) or Ooty, is one of Kerala's most picturesque journeys. Many of the tea and coffee plantations now take in paying guests, and a number of imaginative accommodation options have recently opened. The road to Mysore passes through **Vyittiri** (65 km), and **Kalpetta** (9 km) before dividing. The more northerly route passes through Mananthavady (30 km), whilst the more southerly route to Mysore is via Sulthan Bathery (25 km) and Waynad Wildlife Sanctuary. The route to Ooty via Gudalur is marginally less scenic than the road to Mysore.

**Kalpetta** lies at the heart of one of Kerala's most scenic regions, and provides a good base from which to explore the area. The rugged, wild **Chembra Peak** (2,100 m), 14 km west, the highest point in Waynad, is ideal for trekking. The hike south to **Pookot Lake** (10 km) is particularly rewarding. It is a popular destination for domestic tourists, making accommodation hard to come by during holiday periods. (The State Bank of Travancore offers foreign exchange.)

**Sulthan Bathery** (Sultan's Battery) ⓘ *the road from Sulthan's Bathery to Gudalur (Tamil Nadu) is very rough, especially across the border and can take 2½ hrs by bus,* to the east of Kalpetta was formerly known as Ganapathivattom, 'the fields of Ganapathi'. In the 18th century, Tipu Sultan built a fort here in the heart of the Waynad coffee and cardamom growing region, but not much of it remains. Some 6 km east of the fort is a natural deep crack in the rock on which four inscriptions have been carved and there are some rough drawings.

**Waynad Wildlife Sanctuary** is contiguous with Karnataka's Bandipur National Park and Tamil Nadu's Mudumalai National Park, although the latter two are far more developed in terms of accommodation and tours on offer. If you wish to visit the sanctuary, noted for its elephants, from the Kerala side, contact the Chief Conservator of Forests, Thiruvananthapuram, T0471-322217.

## Sleeping

**Kozhikode** *p951, map p952*

**A Harivihar Ayurvedic Heritage Home**, Bilathikulam, T0495-2765865, www.harivihar.com. 8 rooms in one-time home to Calicut royalty in wealthy walled old suburbs now painstakingly and elegantly restored to stand in manicured lawn with lily pond, jasmine trees and pool. Ayurvedic, pure vegetarian menu. Book in advance and arrange pick up. You can also take workshops on sanskrit or the *vedas*, or stay on a casual basis. The 10-day treatment programme starts at US$300 excluding food and room.

**B Malabar Palace**, GH Rd, Manuelsons' Junction, T0495-2721511, www.malabarpalacecalicut.com. 52 a/c rooms (Koran in every room), excellent a/c restaurant, bar, very helpful reception. Recommended.

**C Tasara**, North Beypore, T0495-2414233, www.tasaraindia.com. 6 rooms in homestay-cum-textile-weaving factory. Weaving courses available: 5-day 4-night package – tie-dyeing, batik printing, and weaving on silk, cotton, or wool, costs US$240.

**C-D Alakapuri Guest Houses**, Moulana Mohammed Ali Rd, T0495-2723451, www.alakapurihotels.com. 40 rooms set around a charming garden brimming with plants and trees and lotus pond. Simple, spacious, with old furniture, phone, tubs and TV. Dates from 1958, and is easily Calicut's most characterful mid-range option. Bar 1000-2200, dining hall 0700-2200.

**C-D Hyson Heritage**, 114 Bank Rd, T0495-2766423, www.hysonheritagekerala.com. 89 spotless, smallish rooms with phone, TV, bath, 47 a/c, set around a large courtyard. A breezy business hotel, peaceful, efficient. Well-maintained. Benhur restaurant. Cable TV.

**C-E Hotel Asma Tower**, Mavoor Rd, T0495- 2723560, www.asmatower.com. 44 a/c and non a/c rooms in gleaming new tower: inside expect two-tone mint green decor, frosty a/c system, perfumed air, muzak and TV and telephone in every room. Good value. Rs 400-800.

**E Gayathri Internationali**, T0495-2355367. 10 small cottage-like rooms with modern facilities, bar, restaurant.

**E-F Metro Tourist Home**, Mavoor Rd Junction, T0495-2766029. 42 rather pleasing rooms in bustling hotel, some with TV, a bit noisy, south Indian restaurant. Gloomy with grubby paintwork but clean sheets, big mirrors and good fans plus TVs and blaring Hindi film music.

**F Railway Retiring Rooms**, very spacious, clean, good service.

### Thalassery *p953*

**LL Ayisha Manzil**, Court Rd, T0490-234 1590, cpmoosa@rediffmail.com. A delightful mid-19th century, colonial style heritage home overlooking the sea. 6 massive a/c rooms with carved teak/ rosewood furniture, huge baths, lots of British and Malabari memorabilia, amazing fresh sea food and cookery courses, temple pond pool, superb panoramic views, excursions.

**C-E Pranam Tourist Home**, AVK Nair Rd, Narangapuram, T0490-232634. 14 cleanish rooms with bath – 4 with a/c, a little grubby. A/c De luxe has an extraordinary green carpeted sitting room attached.

**D-C Paris Presidency**, New Paris Complex, Logan's Rd, T0490-2342666, www.parispres idency.com. 24 clean and comfortable rooms with baths, TV, phone, restaurant, wood furniture, bright white walls in busy shopping area. Multi-cuisine restaurant.

### Kannur *p954*,

**B Costa Malabari Beach**, near Adykadalaya Temple, 6 km south of town (so on buses ask to get out at Thazhe Chowwa), T0497-2836174, www.costamalabari.com. An unpretentious guest house converted from a warehouse with 5 rooms off a main hall. The two-man partnership also authored a book on Kerala's festivals which gives them encyclopedic knowledge of the local *Theyyam* scene. There are 5 idyllic, wholly empty, beaches, within walking distance. Difficult to get to and far from the centre. Tariff includes meals.

**B Mascot Beach Resort**, near Baby Beach, Burnassery, 2 km from centre, T0497-2708445, mascot_beach_resort@vsnl.com. Good rooms in high-rise business hotel overlooking the sea, residents-only pool, located in the quiet cantonment area (ayurvedic centre attached).

**C-D Royal Omars Thavakkara Kannur**, T0497-2769091. Spanking new, very close to the railway station and colourful market area, has spacious standard non a/c doubles at bargain rates. 65 rooms, TVs, credit cards.

**D-E Hotel Savoy**, Beach Rd, T0497-2760074. Bags of character in this super-clean, old-fashioned complex of bungalow cottages set around a lawn. A/c cottages are wonderfully spacious and cool. Bar attached.

### The Waynad *p955*

**L Green Magic Nature Resort**, T0471-331507, www.richsoft.com/tourindia. Tree-house in the rainforest canopy, 26 m above ground open plan accessible only by a hand-winched wicker cage, has showers and flush toilets. Solar energy from Kozhikode by 4-wheel drive.

**B-C Green Gates**, 2 km north of Kalpetta, T04936-202001, www.greengateshotel.com. Scenically located on a hillside amid woods within walking distance from town. Modern rooms with a/c, TV and baths (hot showers), disappointing restaurant, sit-outs with views, ayurvedic spa, helpful travel desk arranges trips to caves, wildlife sanctuaries and tribal colonies of Waynad, and fishing.

**D-E Haritagiri**, Padmaprabha Rd, T04936-202673. A modern building in the heart of Kalpetta just off the highway, some a/c rooms, clean and comfortable, restaurant 'reasonable', good value but rather noisy.

**D-E Pankaj**, just off highway at south end of Kalpetta. Has a range of reasonable rooms, good cheap restaurant.

In Sulthan Bathery there are **E-F** guesthouses.

## Eating

**Kozhikode** *p951, map p952*

**Malabar Palace**, International, a/c, excellent food, efficient service.

**Dakshin**, 17/43 Mavoor Rd, Calicut, T0495-2722648. 0630-2230. Dead cheap place for dosa, pizza, cutlet and curd rice (meals from Rs 15).

**Hotel Sagar**, 5/3305 IG Rd, Calicut, T0495-2720152, abdul@sagarhotels.com. 0530 onwards, so popular they've launched their own hotel, and a second restaurant (the original is already multi-storey). Sagar is famous for its biriyanis. Here it's split into upstairs for families, and a/c rooms, downstairs is the cheaper scrum of cattle class.

**Woodlands**, GH Rd (near Old Bus Stand). South Indian vegetarian.

**Zain's Hotel**, Convent Cross Rd, T0495-2761482. A simple place run by a Muslim husband and wife: mussels, biriyanis for Rs 30 and fish curries for Rs 15.

**Thalassery** *p953*

**Ayisha Manzil**, Court Rd, T0490-2341590. Phone well in advance for a meal at this peerless homestay; the food is unlike anything you'll get anywhere else outside a home.

**Royal Visitors' Family Restaurant**, Pranam Tourist Home, T0490-2344292. 0630-2300. Grilled mussels etc.

**Kannur** *p954,*

**Chakara Drive in Restaurant**, Cliff Exotel International, Payyabalam Kannur, T0497-2712197. Specials are sizzlers plus spicy fried Kallumakais mussels and Malabar biriyani.

**Indian Coffee House**, Fort Rd. For snacks.

**Mascot Beach Resort's Restaurants**, near Baby Beach Burnasseri Cannanore, T0497-2708445, www.mascotresort.net. Some of the best top-end eating in town.

**MVK Restaurant**, SM Rd, T0497-2767192. A local institution with a green stripe down its walls and green stools has been packed from its opening 50 years back from 1000-2200 thanks to its commitment to fresh, home-ground spice mixes for its biriyanis, their rice grains steeped in ghee. Serves beautiful, potent lime tea too.

**Regency Snacks and Fast Food**, opposite Sangeetha Theatre, SN Park Rd, T0497-276 8676. Popular café with locals.

**Your Choice Restaurant**, Fort Rd. Authentic Malabari food.

## Activities and tours

**Kannur (Cannanore)** *p954,*

**Ayurveda**

**PVA Ayurvedic Multi Speciality Nursing Home**, Onden Rd, T0497-2760609, www.pvaayurvedic.com. The down at heel PVA provides training courses in ayurveda as well as rejuvenation, purification packages and direct treatments for ailments like disc prolapse, psoriasis and obesity. The 3 doctors here are highly regarded.

**Houseboats**

**Malabar floatels and cruises**, House Boats Kannur, T0497-3115551, www.holidayinmalabar.com. Tourism-starved North wants a piece of the action. Happily it has amazingly pristine mangrove. In 2004 there were 4 houseboats on the river north of Kannur.

**Theyyam dance**

At Parssinikadavu temple, 20 km north of Kannur, reached by bus. Performances (Dec-Mar) of ritual dance theatre at dawn (taxi essential) and often late afternoon continuing to dusk. Pilgrims sometimes seek blessing from the principal dancer who may go into a trance after taking on the role of Mutthapan, a manifestation of Siva as Hunter.

## Transport

**Kozhikode (Calicut)** *p951, map p952*

**Air**

Airport, T712762. Transport to town: pre-paid taxi Rs 250; but from town Rs 35. **Indian Airlines**, Eroth Centre, Bank Rd, T766243, Airport T766056, flies to Mumbai, Coimbatore, Goa (Mon, Fri), Chennai, Tiruchirapalli (Wed, Sun) and Bahrain, Doha, Fujairah, Kuwait, Ras-Al-Khaimah and Sharjah. **Air India**, Bank Rd. Mumbai and Middle East (Abu Dhabi, Dubai, Muscat). **Jet Airways**, 29 Mavoor Rd, T740518, Airport T712375, to Mumbai.

**Bus**
KSRTC, T722771, from Mavoor Rd (near Bank Rd junction) to **Bangalore**, **Thiruvanantha puram** (via Thrissur, Ernakulam, Alappuzha, Kollam), 0630-2200 (10 hrs), **Ooty** (see Waynad below), etc. The **New Bus Stand** is further east on Mavoor Rd for private buses to the north including **Kannur**. Buses to the south go from the **Old Bus Stand** (Palayam).

**Train**
Trains to **Mangalore** (5 hrs), **Ernakulam** (4½ hrs), **Thiruvananthapuram** (9½-10 hrs). Also to **Chennai** and **Coimbatore**, and **Goa** and **Mumbai** up the Konkan Railway line.

**Kannur (Cannanore)** *p954*
**Bus**
T707777. To **Kozhikode** (2½ hrs), **Mangalore** (4½ hrs), **Mercara** (6 hrs), **Mysore** (6 hrs).

**Train**
T705555. To **Mangalore**: *Chennai Mangalore Mail, 6601* (AC/II), 1045, 3¼ hrs; *Parasuram Exp, 6349* (AC/CC), 1820, 3¾ hrs. **Palakkad**: *Mangalore Tiruchchirappalli Exp, 6684*, 0920, 5½ hrs (continues to **Coimbatore**, add 1¼ hrs); *West Coast Exp, 6628*, 2315, 5¾ hrs (continues to **Chennai (MC)**, add 10½ hrs); *Mangalore Chennai Mail, 6602*, 1420, 5 hrs (continues to **Chennai (MC)**, add 10 hrs).

## Directory

**Kozhikode (Calicut)** *p951, map p952*
**Banks** Exchange at SBI, Bank Rd. Good rates, no commission, friendly. Also Thomas Cook. **Internet** Nidhi, near New Bus Stand or behind *Malabar Mansion*, SM St. Fast, Rs 30 per hr. **Sreeram Travels**, shop 3, opposite district hospital. T0495-2534807. **Hospitals** Govt Hospital, T0495-2365367. Medical College Hospital, T0495-2421050. **Post** Near Mananchira.

**Thalassery** *p953*
**Banks** The Federal Bank, MM Rd, 1000-1530 (Sat 1000-1230 Sun closed) for speedy transactions. **Internet** Telynet Internet Café, Masjid Building Near Municipal Office, MG Rd, T0490–2344390, telynet@rediffmail.com. 0900-2100.

**Kannur** *p954*,
**Internet** **Search World**, near Railway Station, MA Rd, T0497-2704 735. Very fast connection, Rs 30 per hr.

# Lakshadweep, Minicoy and Amindivi Islands

*→ Population: 60,600. 225-450 km west of Kerala. Area: 39,000 sq km. Total land area: 32 sq km.*

*The islands, which make up the Lakshadweep ('100,000 islands'), have superb beaches and beautiful lagoons. There are, despite the name, only 11 inhabited and 11 uninhabited islands making up the group. Minicoy, the southernmost island, is 183 km from Kalpeni, its nearest neighbour. Geologically they are the northernmost extensions of the chain of coral islands that extends from the far south of the Maldives. The atolls are formed of belts of coral rocks almost surrounding semi-circular lagoons, with none more than 4 m above sea level. They are rich in guano, deposits of centuries of bird droppings.The wealth of coral formations (including black coral) attracts a variety of tropical fish – angel, clown, butterfly, surgeon, sweetlip, snappers and groupers. There are also manta and sting rays, harmless sharks and green and hawksbill turtles. At the right time of the year you may be able to watch them laying eggs, arriving on the beach at night, each laying 100 to 200 eggs in the holes they make in the sand.* ▸▸ *For Sleeping, Eating and other listings, see pages 960-961.*

## Ins and outs

**Getting there** You can only visit the islands on a package tour – individuals may not book independently. Lakshadweep Tourism's Society for Promotion of Recreational Tourism and Sports (SPORTS) and other tour operators organize package tours.
▸▸ *See Tour operators and Transport, page 960, for further details.*

**Tourist information** Everyone needs a permit, for which you need to provide details of the place and date of birth, passport number, date and place of issue, expiry date, four photos; apply two months ahead. If you plan to dive, get a doctor's certificate. Foreign tourists may only visit Bangaram and Kadmat Islands; Indians, Kadmat, Kavaratti, Kalpeni and Minicoy. Thinakkara and Cheriyam are being developed.

## The islands

**Kavaratti**, the administrative capital, is in the centre of the archipelago. The Ajjara and Jamath mosques (of the 52 on the island) have the best woodcarvings and the former has a particularly good ceiling carved out of driftwood; a well inside is believed to have medicinal water. The aquarium with tropical fish and corals, the lake nearby and the tombs are the other sights. The woodcarving in the Ajjara is by superb local craftsmen and masons. *Dak Bungalow*, basic, with two rooms and a *Rest House* with four rooms may be reserved through the Administrator, Union Territory of Lakshadweep, Kozhikode 1. Local food from *dhabas*. There is a **bank** here.

Some of the other islands in the group are **Andratti**, one of the largest which was first to be converted to Islam, and **Agatt** (the only one with an airport which neighbours Bangaram) and also has a beautiful lagoon and 20-bed *Tourist Complex*.

Barren, desolate and tiny, **Pitti** Island comprises a square reef and sand bank at its south end. It is a crucially important nesting place for terns and has now been listed as a wildlife sanctuary. Conservation groups are pressing for a ban on the planting of trees and the mining of coral, but the main risk to the birds is from local fishermen who collect shells and the terns' eggs for food. Nearby **Cheriam** and **Kalpeni** have suffered most from storm damage.

**Bangaram** is an uninhabited island where the Casino Group runs the **Island Resort** (see Sleeping below).

**Kalpeni**, with its group of three smaller uninhabited satellite islands, is surrounded by a lagoon rich in corals, which offers excellent snorkelling and diving. The raised coral banks on the southeast and eastern shores are remains of a violent storm in 1847; the Moidin Mosque to the south has walls made of coral. The islands are reputedly free from crime – the women dress in wrap-around *lungis* (sarongs), wearing heavy gold ornaments here without any fear. Villagers entertain tourists with traditional dances, *Kolkali* and *Parichakkali*, illustrating themes drawn from folk and religious legends and accompanied by music and singing. On Koomel Bay overlooking Pitti and Tilakam islands, the *Dak Bungalow* and Tourist Huts provide accommodation.

**Minicoy** (Maliku), the southernmost and largest, is interesting because of its unique Maldivian character, having become a part of the archipelago more recently. The people speak *Mahl* similar to *Dhivehi* (the script is written right to left) and follow many of their customs; a few speak Hindi. The ancient seafaring people have been sailing long distances for centuries and the consequential dominance by women may have led Marco Polo to call this a 'female island'. Each of the nine closely-knit matrilineal communities lives in an *athir* (village) and is headed by a *Moopan*. The village houses are colourfully furnished with carved wooden furniture. Tuna fishing is a major activity and the island has a cannery and ice storage. The superb lagoon of the palm-fringed crescent-shaped island is enclosed by coral reefs. Good views from the top of the 50-m lighthouse built by the British. You can stay at the Tourist Huts.

The **Amindivi** group consists of the northern islands of **Chetlat, Bitra** – the smallest (heavily populated by birds, for a long time a rich source of birds' eggs), **Kiltan** where ships from Aden called en route to Colombo, **Kadmat** and the densely populated **Amini,** rich in coconut palms, which was occupied by the Portuguese. **Kadmat,** an inhabited island 9 km long and only 200 m wide, has a beach and lagoon to the east and west, ideal for swimming and diving. The tourist huts shaded by palms are away from the local village. The Water Sports Institute has experienced, qualified instructors. There are 10 executive and tourist cottages and a **Youth Hostel** with dorm for 40.

## Sleeping

Accommodation varies on the islands. Bangaram has special facilities. Kavaratti and Kadmat have basic tourist cottages resembling local huts. Each hut has 1 or 2 bedrooms, mosquito nets, fans and attached baths; electricity is wind or diesel. Meals are served on the beach and are similar to Keralan cuisine, with plenty of coconut. Breakfast might be iddlis or puris with vegetables. Lunch and dinner might be rice and vegetable curry, sambhar, meat or fish curry. Vegetarian meals available on request. Bangaram offers international cuisine.

Alcohol is available on board ship and on Bangaram Island (tourists requested not to carry it though).

## Activites and tours

### Watersports

Windsurfing, scuba diving (Poseidon Neptune School), parasailing, waterskiing and snorkelling. Deep sea fishing (barracuda, sailfish, yellow-fin, travelly) is possible on local boats with crew; serious anglers bring their own equipment; no diving or deep sea fishing Apr-Sep. The satellite islands of Tamakara, Parali I and II can be visited for the day. Package Rs 3,500-9,500 per head, ordinary and de luxe and depending on season. Reservation: **TCI**, MG Rd, Ernakulam, Kochi (opposite Kavitha Theatre), or in Mumbai office Chander Mukhi, Nariman Point, or **Casino Hotel**, Willingdon Island, Kochi, T0484-666821, F668001, casino@vsnl.com.

### Tours

Tourism is still in its infancy and facilities are limited on the islands you will be allowed to visit. The relatively expensive package tours (the only way to visit) operate from Oct-May. Schedules may change, so allow for extra days when booking onward travel. Most tours are monthly from end-Jan to mid-May. **SPORTS (Lakshadweep Tourism)** 3 packages costing Rs 6,000-10,000 per person (student discounts), including transport from Kochi. **Kadmat Water Sports**: 6 days (including 2-day sailing, stay in *Kadmat Cottages* or *hostel*). **Coral Reef**: 5 days to Kavaratti, Kalpeni and Minicoy Islands. **Paradise Island Huts**: 6 days to Kavaratti. **CGH Earth** For the resort only, US$250-350 (for 2), US$500-700 for 4, US$70 extra person (discounts Apr-Sep). **Bangaram** Kayaks, catamarans and sailing boats are free. For an extra charge each time: scuba diving for beginners and the experienced (equipment for hire); deep sea big game fishing from 1 Oct-15 May – only minimal fishing equipment and boat crew; excursion to 3 neighbouring islands or snorkelling at shipwreck (for 8); glass-bottomed boat. Snorkelling in the lagoon can be disappointing due to poor visibility and dead corals. **Katmad Island Scuba Diving**: US$800, 1 Star CMAS Certificate US$30, Certified diver US$25 per dive; accompanying adult US$350, child (under 10) US$165. Travel by ship from Kochi (deck class) included; return air from Kochi or Goa to Agatti, US$300; return helicopter (Agatti-Kadmat), 15 mins, US$60, or local *pablo* boat.

### Tour operators

Book at least 2 months ahead (see Ins and outs above).

**Ashok Travels**, Everest Bldg, 46 JL Nehru Rd, Kolkata, T033-22423254.

**Clipper Holidays**, 4 Magrath Rd, Bangalore, T080- 25599032, clipper@bangalore.wipro.net.in.

**CGH Earth**, Kochi, see page 933.

**ITDC**, Kanishka Plaza, 19 Ashok Rd, New Delhi, T011-23325035.

**Mercury**, Everest Bldg, 46 JL Nehru Rd, Kolkata, T033-22423555, and 191 Mount Rd, Chennai, T044-28522993.
**Lakshadweep Travels**, 1 Gandhi Rd, Kozhikode, T0495-2767596.
**Lakshadweep Foundation**, KSRM Bldg, Lighthouse Hill, Mangalore, T0824-221969.
**Lakshadweep Travelinks**, Jermahal 1st floor, Dhobitalo, Mangalore, T022-22054231.
**SITA**, F-12 Connaught Pl, New Delhi, T011-23311133.
**SPORTS** (Lakshadweep Tourism), Indira Gandhi Rd, Willingdon Island, Kochi T0484-2868387, T0484-2668141.

## Transport

### Air

Agatti has a basic airport. **Indian Airlines** by 15-seater Dorniers (baggage allowance, 10 kg), unreliable service, "plane broke down": to/from **Kochi**, daily except Tue and Sun; to/from **Goa**: Tue, Sat. 1¼ hrs, US$300 return; transfer by *pablo* boat; helicopter May-Sep. **Casino/Taneja** by 5-seater P68C, 2 a week.

### Ferry

MV *Tipu Sultan* sails from Kochi. 26 passengers in 1st and executive class have 2 and 4-berth a/c cabins with washbasins, shared toilets, Rs 5,000; 120 passengers in 2nd class in reclining seats in a/c halls, Rs 3,500. Ship anchors 30-45 mins away from each island; passengers are ferried from there. Total travel time from Kochi can take up to 30 hrs. **Inter-island transfers** are by helicopter (when available) during monsoons, 15 May-15 Sep (return US$60), or by *pablo* boats for 8.

## Directory

Agatti has a medical centre; emergencies on the islands have helicopter back-up.

# Karnataka

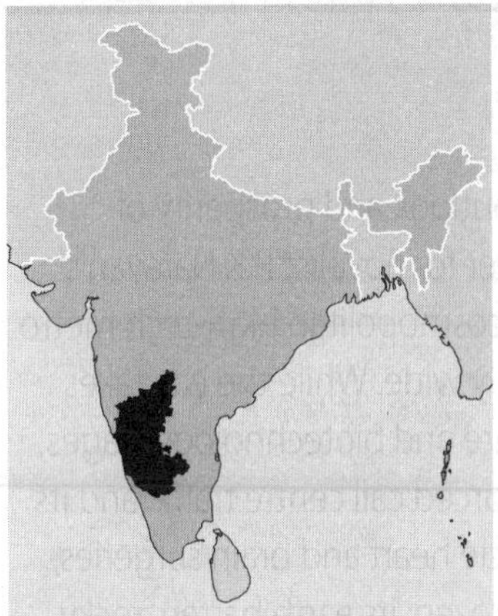



## Footprint features

# Introduction

The chasm between the values, outlook and prosperity of rural Karnataka – the source matter for novelist R K Narayan's *Malgudi Tales* – and the elegant, cosmopolitan high-tech metro of Bangalore, is at times shockingly wide. While the city takes huge strides on the global software and biotechnology stages, its switchboards hum with outsourced call centre traffic and its world-class medics perform miracle heart and brain surgeries, much of Karnataka remains as if frozen: its earth barren, rocky and covered with scrub, its villagers' concerns wholly agrarian.

Wealth has always come and gone here: the state's interior, home to some of the earliest settlements in peninsular India, bears chastening witness to the ravages of time. The state has been seat to a roll-call of dynasties, both alien and homegrown, Hindu, Muslim, Jain, British, whose once-great cities and civilizations now stand largely in dusty ruins. This all means that it is brimming with architectural and archaelogical riches: the still-emerging Vijayanagara kingdom capital Hampi in the north; Chalukyan and Hoysala temples throughout Pattadakal, Belur and Halebid; the Islamic palaces of Tipu Sultan in the south; the onion-dome tombs of his Turkish and Persian antecedents in the far northeast; the British boulevards of Bangalore and the wondrous palaces of the Maharajas of Mysore.

Karnataka's three great rivers, the Kaveri, Tungabhadra and Krishna, originate in the beautiful, forested hill country of the Western Ghats – the state's natural and hugely biodiverse border – making for awesome waterfalls, Jog Falls being one of the highest in the world, to stud the Malnad's wildlife parks. The little-visited coastline, from Coondapur to Karwar, is emerald lush with short fast-running river estuaries that empty down the sides of the Ghats to feed unique mangrove swamps that rival Kerala's famous backwaters.

## ★ Don't miss…

1 **Bangalore by night** Whether you want hip-hop or Bryan Adams gigs, the state capital's shady boulevards have plenty of small-scale, mellow venues – from the slick to the seedy – in which to sink a pint, page 968.

2 **Mysore** Sunday night sees the Maharaja's Mysore palace kitschly aglow with 97,000 light bulbs; and you can experience sensory hypnosis in a private performance with a silk pedallar, page 986.

3 **Coorg** Low-key, solitary rambling in lush, virgin rainforest balancing on the cusp of Kerala, page 993.

4 **Hampi** Hear every sound for miles bounce off giant boulders and visit Hanuman's birthplace for a 360-degree dusk: cross the river in a coracle, then cycle through paddy to climb the whitewashed steps to the temple where monkeys hiss over the prone bodies of stoned saddhus, page 1011.

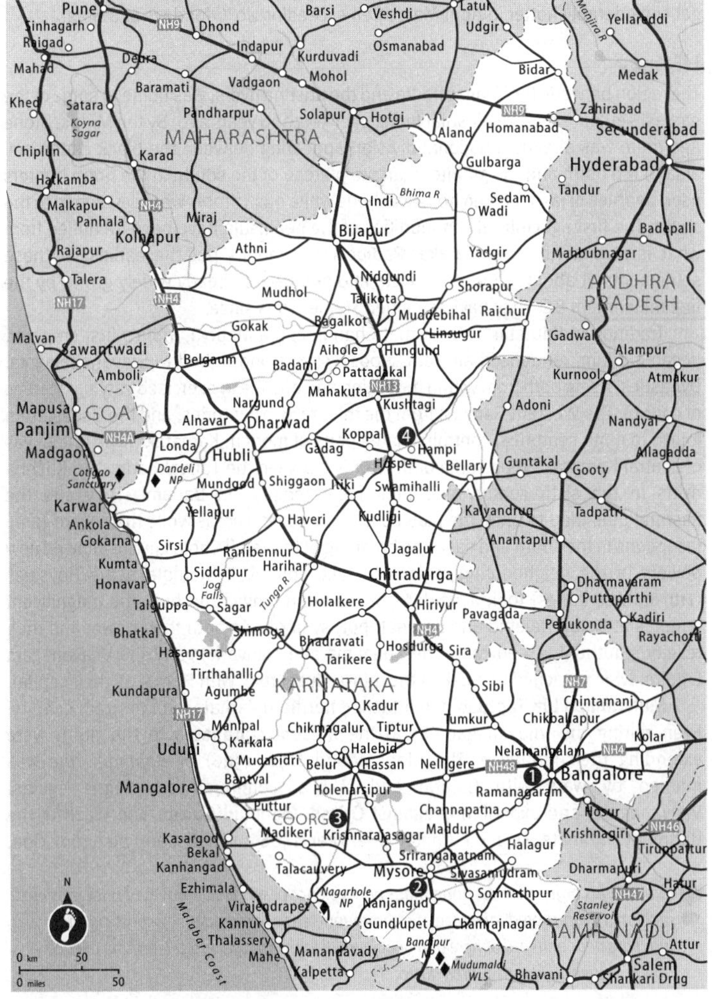

# Background → *Population: 52.7 mn. Area: 192,000 sq km.*

## The land

**Geography** The Western Ghats, called the Malnad or hill country, have beautiful forests with waterfalls and wildlife parks. To the east stretches the Mysore Plateau. Parts of northern Karnataka are barren, rocky and covered with scrub, but the state has a lush coastline. From Coondapur to Karwar, the estuaries of the short fast-running rivers flowing west from the Ghats still have mangroves, some in uniquely good condition, although commercial exploitation seriously threatens their survival.

**Climate** The whole of the west coast is extremely wet from June to September, receiving about 1,500 mm in June and July alone. However, immediately to the east of the Western Ghats rainfall decreases dramatically. Temperatures rise to the low 30°C between February and June but fall slightly during and after the monsoon. On the plateaus of the south, especially around Bangalore and Mysore, temperatures are moderated by the altitude (generally around 1,000 m), and night temperatures are pleasantly cool through most of the year. The central and northern parts of the state get considerably hotter in April-May, often exceeding 40°C for days at a time.

## History

The region between the Tungabhadra and the Krishna rivers, was home to some of the earliest settlements in peninsular India, over 500,000 years ago. By the Middle Stone Age there was already a regional division appearing between the black cotton soil area of the north and the granite-quartzite plateau of the south. In the north hunters used pebbles of jasper taken from river beds while quartz tools were developed to the south. The first agricultural communities of the peninsula have been identified from what is now northern Karnataka. Radiocarbon datings put the earliest of these settlements at about 3,000 BC; millets and gram were already widely grown by the first millennium BC. They have remained staple crops since.

Tradition in Karnataka states that Chandragupta Maurya, India's first emperor, became a Jain, renounced all worldly possessions and retired to Sravanabelagola. Dynasties, rising both from within the region and outside it, exercised varying degrees of control. The Western Gangas, from the third to 11th centuries, and the Banas, from fourth to ninth centuries, controlled large parts of modern Karnataka. The Chalukyas of central Karnataka took some of the lands between the Tungabhadra and Krishna rivers in the sixth century and built great temples in Badami. They and the Rashtrakutas tried to unite the plateau and the coastal areas while there were Tamil incursions in the south and east. The break-up of the Tamil Chola Empire allowed new powers in the neighbouring regions to take control. In Karnataka the Hoysalas (11th-14th centuries) took advantage of the opportunity, and built the magnificent temples at Belur, Halebid and Somnathpur, symbolizing both their power and their religious authority. Then came the Sangama and Tuluva kings of the Vijayanagara Empire, which reached its peak in the mid-16th century, with Hampi as their capital.

**Muhammad bin Tughlaq** had attacked northern Karnataka in the 13th century. Even during the Vijayanagar period the **Muslim sultanates** to the north were extending their influence. The Bidar period (1422-1526) of *Bahmani rule* was marked by wars with Gujarat and Malwa, continued campaigns against Vijayanagara, and expeditions against Orissa. **Mahmud Gawan**, the Wazir of the Bahmani sultanate, seized Karnataka between 1466 and 1481, and also took Goa,

*Kannadigas argue that the unanimous benevolence of successive waves of rulers has bred in them a deep-rooted tolerance: the communal tensions so endemic in post-partition India are near unheard of here and people of all faiths charge into celebration of each others' festive days with shared gusto.*

formerly guarded by Vijayanagar kings. By 1530 the kingdom had split into five independent sultanates. At times they came together to defend common interests, and in 1565 they co-operated to oust the Vijayanagar Raja, but two of the sultanates, Bijapur and Golconda, gathered the lion's share of the spoils and were rapidly succeeded by the Mughals and then the British. The south experienced a different succession of powers. While the Mughals were preoccupied fighting off the Marathas, the **Wodeyar** rulers of Mysore took Srirangapatnam and then Bangalore. They lost control to **Haidar Ali** in 1761, the opportunist commander- in-chief who with French help extended control and made Srirangapatnam his capital. The Mysore Wars followed and with Haidar Ali's, and then his son Tipu Sultan's death, the **British** re-established rule of the Wodeyars in 1799. The Hindu royal family was still administering Mysore up to the reorganization of the states in the 1950s when the Maharaja was appointed State Governor.

## Culture

While the **Lingayats** are the dominant caste group in northern Karnataka, a peasant caste, the **Vokkaligas**, is dominant in the south. Their rivalry still runs through Karnataka politics. Karnataka has its share of tribal people. The nomadic *Lambanis* in the north and west, are among several tribal peoples in the hill regions.

**Cuisine** Try a typical Udupi meal which follows the pattern of a south Indian vegetarian *thali*, and is traditionally served on a plantain leaf or stainless steel plate.

**Language** Most people speak the Dravidian language *Kannada* (Kanarese) although in the north there has been a lot of intermixture with speakers of Indo-Aryan languages. Kannada has the second oldest Dravidian literary tradition. The earliest classic known is *Kavirajamarga* which dates from the ninth century. A treatise on the writing of poetry, it refers to several earlier works which suggests that the language had been in existence for some centuries. Kannada inscriptions dating from fifth and sixth centuries support this view. Early writings in both Telugu and Kannada owe a lot to Jain influence.

**Art and architecture** Karnataka's role as a border territory was illustrated in the magnificent architecture of the Chalukyan Dynasty from AD 450 to 650. Here, notably in Aihole, were the first stirrings of *Brahman* temple design. A mixture of Jain temples illustrates the contact with the north of India which continued to influence the development of the Dravidian temples which grew alongside them. In Pattadakal alone it is possible to see examples of four temples built on North Indian '*Nagari*' principles and six built on South Indian '*Dravida*' lines.In Belur, Halebid and Somnathpur, the star-shaped plan of the base and the shrine, with the bell-shaped tower above and exquisitely crafted exterior and interior surfaces became a hallmark of their temples, a distinctive combination of the two traditions. The Vijayanagara kings advanced temple architecture to blend in with the rocky, boulder-ridden landscape at Hampi. Bijapur has some of the finest Muslim monuments on the Deccan from the austere style of the Turkish rulers to the refinement in some of the pavilions and the world's second largest dome at the Gol Gumbaz.

**Dance, drama and music** Open-air folk theatre or *Bayalata* of Karnataka has developed from religious ritual and is performed in honour of the local deity. The plays evolve and are improvised by the actors on an informal stage. The performances usually start at night and often last into the early hours. The famous *Yakshagana* or *Parijata* usually has a single narrator while the other forms have four or five, assisted by a jester. The plots of the *Dasarata* which enacts several stories and *Sannata* which elaborates one theme, are taken loosely from mythology but sometimes highlight real-life incidents. The *Doddata* is less refined than the *Yakshagana* but both have much in common, beginning with a prayer to the god Ganesh, using verse and drawing from the stories of the epics *Ramayana* and *Mahabharata*. The costumes are elaborate with fantastic stage effects, loud noises and war cries and vigorous dances.

## Modern Karnataka

**Government** The 19 districts are grouped into four divisions – Bangalore, Mysore, Belgaum and Gulbarga. Assembly elections on 5 October 1999 saw the Congress return to power, under the leadership of S M Krishna, at the expense of the Janata Dal. Caste rivalry between Vokkaligas and Lingayats remains a powerful factor in the state's politics, and faction fighting within the parties was a recurrent theme. In 2004, Congress suffered a swingeing backlash against its liberal economic policies that had fuelled Bangalore's rise to become the darling of the IT and biotechnology industries at the perceived cost of the common, rural man, and Chief Minister Krishna resigned in the city on 13 May. The BJP profited from the people's anti-incumbency mood.

**Economy** Karnataka is now widely known as one of India's most rapidly modernising states. Along with Hyderabad in Andhra Pradesh, Bangalore is an undisputed leader in IT skills and industrial activity. Based on its early development of aeronautics and high precision machine tools, Bangalore has become a world centre for the computer industry, receiving a much-quoted seal of approval from Bill Gates. Outside the cities agriculture and forestry remain important. Demand for irrigation is growing rapidly, causing tension with neighbouring states like Tamil Nadu and Andhra Pradesh. The state suffered drought in three out of the past five years.

# Bangalore

→ *Phone code: 080. Colour map 7, grid A4. Population: 6.2 mn.*

*Bangalore is one of the newest of India's cities to gain 'metro' status. Joining the ranks of the other megacities (Delhi, Kolkata, Mumbai and Chennai), it is contributing towards tugging India towards its 21st-century economic and intellectual resurgence, often leaving anachronistic agricultural regions in its wake. The city, despite its financial muscle and many millionaires, has a relaxed pace – people still move here from Mumbai to slow their heart rate and you never feel as hemmed in by a seething mass of humanity as you do in the capital. With its cosmopolitan café culture, great green lungs of Lal Bagh Gardens and Cubbon Park, and its dynamic, liberal-minded population, central Bangalore has more in common with San Francisco than the red baked earth of its surrounding states.*

*Millionaires need playgrounds, and their demand has nurtured Bangalore's nightlife into arguably India's coolest party destination: Mumbaikars and Goans often hop downstate to take in a gig or club night. The moneyed also like to dress sharply and Bangalore is a great place to pick up everything from Levi's to traditional fabrics. Alongside giant shopping malls are boutiques stocking the beautifully crafted 'ethnic' design clothes that Indian high society favours. In spite of all the outward-looking globalism of the city, walk into the ramshackle old area – Gandhi Bazar's chicken centres, wood shops, tailors and temples – to see the familiar response to any Indian town's everyday demands.* ▸▸ *For Sleeping, Eating and other listings, see pages 973-979.*

## Ins and outs

**Getting there** Bangalore's airport, with direct flights from Frankfurt, the Middle and Far East, Sri Lanka and Nepal is 9 km east of the Mahatma Gandhi (MG)/Brigade Rd area (which has the bigger hotels). There are airport buses, autos and pre-paid taxis into town. Only use rickshaws on the meter; they charge 50% extra after 2200. About 5 km west of MG Rd, the main City Station and bus stations are in Gandhi Nagar (along with most of the budget accommodation). For hotels in Sivaji Nagar and the MG Road area, get off at the Cantonment Station. ▸▸ *See Transport, page 977, for further details.*

**Getting around** Bangalore is very spread out and you need transport to get around. City buses run a frequent and inexpensive service throughout the city.

**Tourist Information** **Karnataka State Tourism Development Corporation** head office at ⓘ *No 49, Khanija Bhavan, West Gate, Race Course Rd, T080-22352901*; Booking Counter ⓘ *Badami House, NR Square, T080-22275869, www.karnatakatourism.com.* Pick up fortnightly listings magazine *City Info* (www.explocity.com) for events and clubs.

## History

The 16th-century Magadi chieftain Kempe Gowda built a mud fort and four watch towers in 1537 and named it Bengalaru (you can see his statue in front of the City Corporation buildings). Muslim king Haidar Ali strengthened those fortifications before his death at the hands of the British, leaving his son Tipu Sultan to pick up where he left off. When the British gained control after 1799 they installed the Wodeyar of Mysore as the ruler and the Rajas developed it into a major city. In 1831 the British took over the administration for a period of 50 years, making it a spacious garrison town, planting impressive avenues and creating parks, building comfortable bungalows surrounded by beautiful lawns with tennis courts, as well as churches and museums.

## Sights

The 3,000 acres of **Cubbon Park** in the Cantonment area was named after the 19th-century British representative in Bangalore: the leafy grounds, with bandstand, fountains and statues, are also home to the Greco-Colonial High Court, State Library and museums: now stared down upon by the post-Independence granite of Vidhana Soudha, the state's legislature and secretariat buildings across the street. A **musical fountain** – the water level rising to match crescendoing music – is at T Chodaiah Road, 1900 and 2000, Rs 10 Closed Mon.

**Government Museum** ⓘ *Kasturba Rd, Cubbon Park, T080-22864563, closed Mon, 1000-1800, Rs 4*, is idiosyncratic and slightly dog-eared; opened in 1886, it is one of the oldest in the country. There are 18 galleries: downstairs teems with sculptures, huge-breasted Durga and a 12th-century figure of Ganesh from Halebid sit alongside intricate relief carvings of Rama giving his ring to Hanuman, and there are even Buddhas from Bihar. An upstairs gallery holds beautiful miniatures in both Mysore and Deccan styles: including a painting of Krishnaraj Wodeyar looking wonderfully surly. Captions are brilliantly candid about archaelogical uncertainty: labels often carry question marks. There are also neolithic finds from the Chandravalli excavations, and from the Indus Valley, especially Mohenjo Daro antiquities.

**K Venkatappa Art Gallery** ⓘ *Kasturba Rd, Cubbon Park, T080-22864483, 1000-1700 closed Mon,* shows a small cross-section of work by the late painter Venkatappa (born 1887) – his paintings of the southern hill stations of Ooty and Kodai give an insight into the Indian fetishization of all things pastoral, woody and above all cool. There is also the story and blueprints of his truncated design for the Amba Vilas Durbar Hall in Mysore and miniatures of revered painter Abanindranath Tajore (1871-1951) alongside a second portrait of Krishnaraj Wodeyar. Upstairs galleries include Henry Moore-ish wooden sculptures from Rajaram.

**Visveswaraya Industrial and Technological Museum** ⓘ *Kasturba Rd, next to Museum, closed Mon, 1000- 1800, Rs 15,* will please engineering enthusiasts especially the basement which includes a 1917 steam wagon and India's oldest compact aircraft. Others might be left cold by exhibits on the 'hydrostatic paradox' or 'the invention of the hook and eye and zip fastener technology'. Upstairs is a wing devoted to educating Bangaloreans on genetic engineering. You might find the debate a little one-sided: "agricultural biotechnology is a process... for the benefit of mankind," it states in upper case. A small corner (next to the placard thanking AstraZeneca, Novo Nordisk Education Foundation, Novozymes and Glaxosmithkline), is dubbed 'Concerns' – but you can see how cloning and genetically strengthened, 'golden' rice might seem more attractive when put in the context of the huge, growling Indian belly.

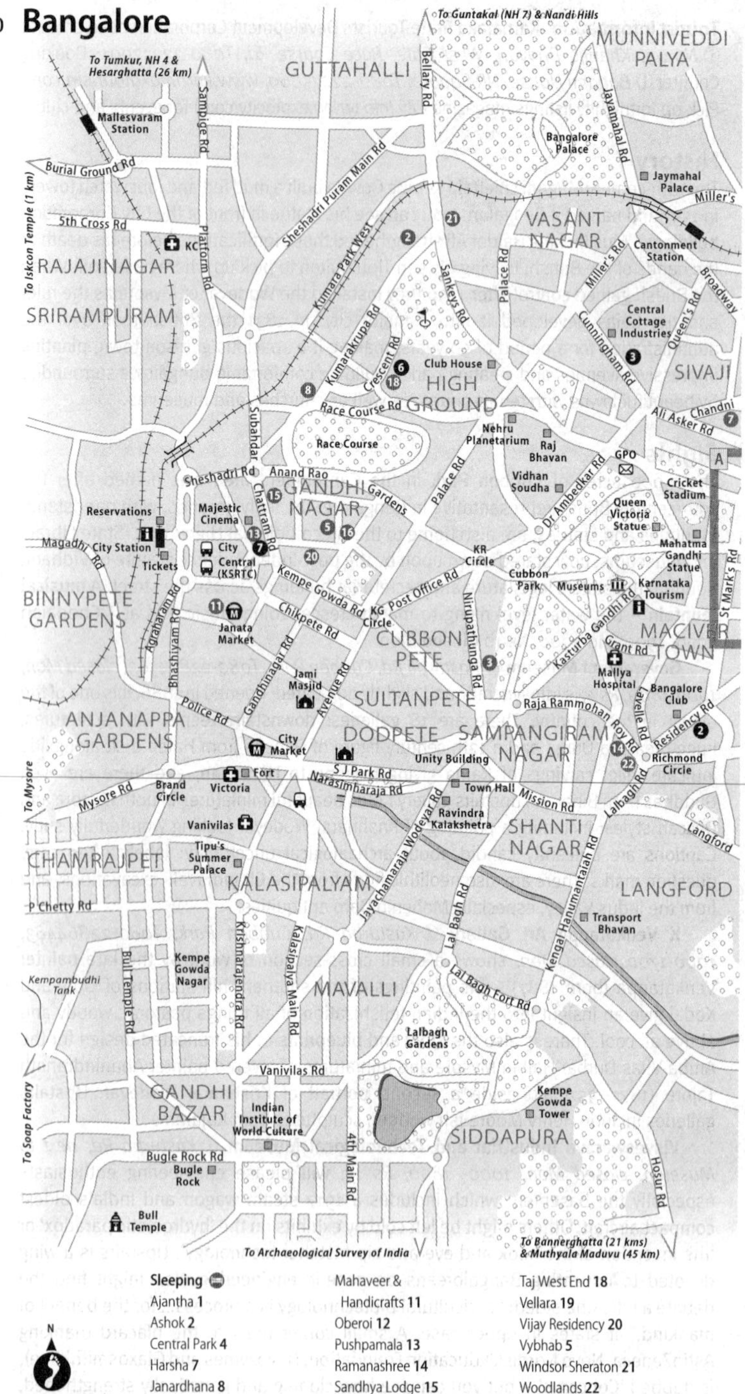


**Sleeping**

Ajantha 1
Ashok 2
Central Park 4
Harsha 7
Janardhana 8
Leela Palace 9
Mahaveer & Handicrafts 11
Oberoi 12
Pushpamala 13
Ramanashree 14
Sandhya Lodge 15
Shoba Lodge 16
Taj Residency 17
Taj West End 18
Vellara 19
Vijay Residency 20
Vybhab 5
Windsor Sheraton 21
Woodlands 22
YMCA 3

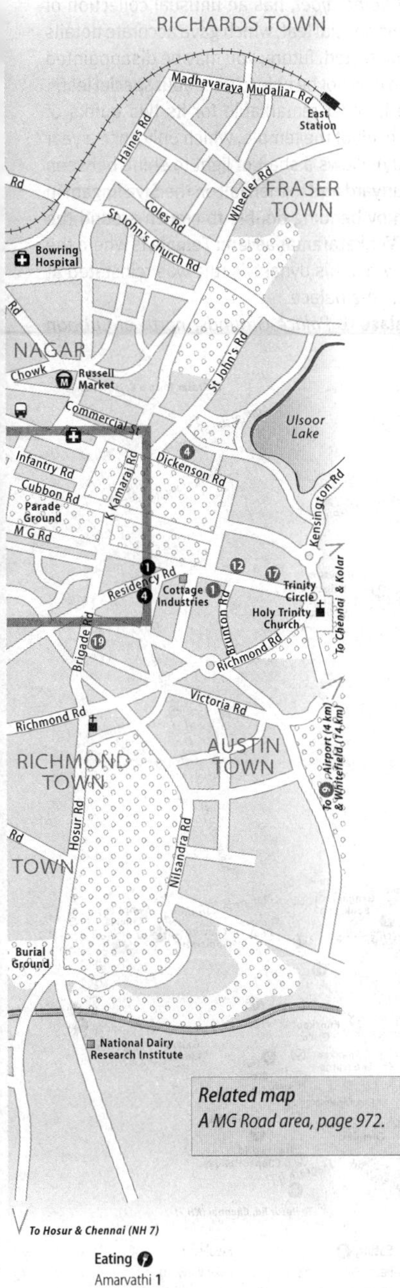


*Related map*
*A MG Road area, page 972.*

**Eating**
Amarvathi **1**
Casa Piccola **2**
Chalukma **6**
Pizza Hut **3**
Sapna **4**
Sukh Sagar **7**

To the southwest lies the summer palace that Tipu Sultan, the perennial thorn in the side of the British, boasted was 'the envy of heaven'. **Tipu's Summer Palace** ⓘ *City Fort, 0830-15300, US$2, video camera Rs 25*, was begun by his father Haidar Ali and completed by Tipu in 1789. Based on the Daria Daulat Bagh in Srirangapatnam, the splendidly simple two-storeyed structure is largely made of teak with walls and ceilings painted in brilliant colours with beautiful carvings. A room downstairs is given over to documenting Haidar and Tipu's reigns and struggles against the British.

**Lal Bagh Gardens** ⓘ *0800-1830, Rs 10, southeast of the Summer Palace*, the gardens laid out across 240 acres by Haidar Ali in 1760, are second only to Calcutta's in size. Tipu added a wealth of plants and trees from many countries (there are over 1,800 species of tropical, subtropical and medicinal plants) – and the British provided a bandstand. Sadly, the Indian affection for botanical beauty means that the rose gardens are kept behind bars. At dusk, Lal Bagh is popular with businessmen speedwalking off their paunches as well as courting couples and newlyweds who sit on the banks of the lotus pond eating ice cream. Climb the rocky knoll of the gardens for views over Bangalore. The Glass House, which echoes London's Crystal Palace and Kew Gardens, holds flower shows in January and August and there is a Kempe Gowda Tower (1537) here. Flower Shows are held on Republic Day (26 January) and Independence Day (15 August) weeks.

The hefty **Nandi Bull at Bull Temple** ⓘ *Bull Temple Rd, Basavanagudi*, further south, was carved at the behest of Kempe Gowda, making it one of the city's oldest temples. The monolithic Nandi is believed to have grown in size: he now towers near to 5 m in height and spans 6 m in length. His huge proportions, draped imperiously in jasmine garlands, are made of grey granite polished with a mixture of groundnut oil and charcoal. Nearby is one of Kempe Gowda's four towers.

**Palm Leaf Library** ⓘ *33, V Main Rd, Chamarajpet*, has an unusual collection of old leaves which one traveller found held his special leaf, which gave accurate details of his character, past, present and, yet to be tested, future; you may be disappointed if you come for the same since the custodian may not be able to trace your special leaf.

**Sri Gavi Gangadhareshwara Temple** is most remarkable for its two quirks of architecture. First, the 'open window' to the left of the temple, which only once a year (on Makara Sankrati day, 14th/15th January) allows a shaft of light to shine between the horns of the stone Nandi bull in the courtyard and to then fall on the Siva lingam in the inner sanctum. The second you reach by bending double to crouch around the back of the cave shrine. The Dravida-style **Venkataramanasvami Temple** is where the Wodeyar Maharaja chose to worship first, when his dynasty's rule was reinstated at the end of the 18th century, before entering the palace.

The grand, Tudor-style **Bangalore Palace** ⓘ *Palace Grounds, north of Cubbon*

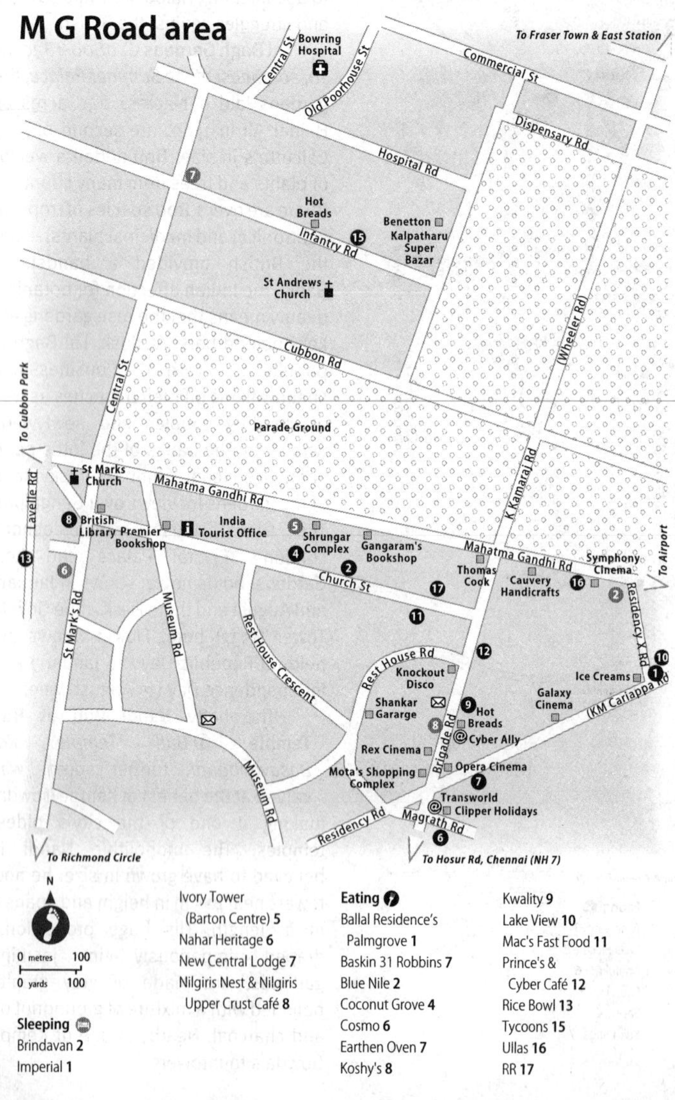

### Health tourism

For several decades, Western travel to India was synonymous with emaciated hippies, and backpackers' conversations invariably veered towards the scatological as everyone, at some stage, was sure to catch the dread 'Delhi belly'. The times, however, they are a-changing. Although the British National Health Service failed to award India its whole back-up project in 2004, the country has become a very real alternative to private health care, representing huge cost reductions on surgery. The centrepiece for this emerging industry is arguably Bangalore, which has the largest number of systems of medicine approved by the World Health Organization in a single city: cardiac, neurology, cancer care and dentistry are just a few of the areas of specialization, and clients include the NHS and America's largest insurance company. For the sake of comparison then, open-heart surgery will set you back US$4,500 in Bangalore, as opposed to US$18,000 abroad. And, afterards of course, there's ayurveda resorts to recuperate at.

*Park, T080-23341778, 0700-1300, 1600-2030, free, frequent buses from the City Station and Sivaji Nagar*, of the Mysore Maharajahs was incongruously inspired by Windsor Castle. It is only open to the public for a week around 1 November.

The sprawling **International Society for Krishna Conscious temple complex (ISKCON)** ⓘ *Hare Krishna Hill, 1R Block, Chord Rd, Rajaji Nagar, northwest of the centre, 0700-1300, 1615-2030*, holds five shrines, a multimedia cinema showing films on the Hare Krishna movement, lofty *gopurams* and the world's tallest *kalash shikara*, all surrounded by lush gardens and fountains. Around 9,000 visitors make the pilgrimage every day: *bhajans* – religious songs – are sung daily.

## Excursions

**Whitefield**, 16 km east of Bangalore on the airport road, is known for the **Sai Baba Ashram** at Brindavan. It also has the International Technical Park, a modern self-contained community of high tech workers.

**Nandidurg**, a fortified summer retreat for Tipu with sheer cliffs on three sides, lies on top of granite hills 10 km from Chikballapur to the north of Bangalore. Literally 'the fort of Nandi', the place, today a minor hill resort with great views from the 60-m 'Tipu's drop', was named after Siva's bull in the Nandi Hills. The ninth-century **Bhoganandisvara Temple** at the foot of the hill is a good example of the Nolamba style: its walls are quite plain but the stone windows feature carvings of Nataraja and Durga. The 16th century brought typical Vijayanagar period extensions such as the *gopuram* at the entrance. At the Central Bus Stand ask for Nandi Hill bus (not Nandidurga). They leave at 0730, 0830, 0930; return 1400, 1630, 1830.

**Nrityagram**, 30 km from Bangalor, is a dance village where young dancers are trained in all disciplines of traditional Indian dance. It was founded by the late Odissi dancer Protima Gauri. Guided tours include lunch, dance demonstrations and a short lecture.

## Sleeping

**Bangalore** *p968, maps p970 and p972*
Luxury hotels can add 25% in taxes. Power cuts are still routine so carry a torch.

**LL Oberoi**, 39 MG Rd, T080-25585858, www.oberoihotels.com. 160 superb rooms and suites with private sit-outs, attractively landscaped Japanese gardens but disappointing food in garden restaurant.

**LL-L Leela Palace**, No 23 Kodihalli, Airport Rd, T080-25211234, www.theleela.com. Impressive 254-room hotel, with pool, health club, ayurvedic centre.

**LL-L The Taj West End**, No 23 Race Course Rd, near railway, T080-22255055, www.tajhotels.com. 135 rooms, rooms around lawn better than in newer block, Old World rooms near entrance "dismal" so view first, superb lawns, excellent outdoor restaurants, pool (non-residents, Rs 500).

**LL-AL Windsor Sheraton and Towers**, Windsor Sq, no 25, Golf Course Rd, T080-22269898. 240 rooms, 100 in new Sheraton Tower, excellent restaurants (delicious Indian buffet, good Chinese, superb atmosphere, faultless service). Highly recommended.

**L-AL Taj Residency**, 41/3 MG Rd (Trinity Circle), T080-25584444, www.tajhotels.com. 162 rooms, balconies with bougainvillea, good Indian restaurant, excellent Chinese lunch buffets, bookshop sells foreign newspapers.

**AL Grand Ashok** (ITDC), Kumara Krupa High Grounds (get off at Cantt station if travelling by train), T080-22250202, www.bharathhotels.com. 187 comfortable rooms (baths could be better), spacious grounds, good pool (non-residents Rs 300).

**AL-A Central Park**, A7 Manipal Centre 47 Dickenson Rd, off MG Rd, T080-25584242, www.centralparkindia.com. 130 rooms, 'American style', very plush, Creole and continental food, live jazz Wed-Sat.

**A Villa Pottipati**, 142 8th Cross, 4th Main Rd, Mallesaram, T080-23360777, www.neemranahotels.com. 8 rooms in a grand 2-storey villa packed with original furniture like rosewood 4-poster beds and hung with sepia photographs of its owners. Set amongst jacaranda, mango and jackfruit trees in the quiet tree-lined avenues of Bangalore's Brahminical suburbs. A/c and internet facilities. Prices includes breakfast.

**A-B Ivory Tower**, Penthouse (12th) floor of Barton Centre, 84 MG Rd, T080-25589333, ivoryhor@satyam.net.in. 22 comfortable, spacious rooms (huge beds), Parsi cuisine, stunning views over city, spotless, excellent value if you like heights, friendly.

**A-B Ramanashree Comfort**, 16 Raja Rammohan Roy Rd, near Richmond Circle, T080-22235250. 68 rooms (a/c not always effective), Chinese restaurant, friendly service (may give discounts).

**A-B Vijay Residency** (Comfort Inn), 18, III Main Rd, near railway and City Bus Station, T080-22203024. 47 very comfortable rooms, good restaurant (no alcohol), very friendly.

**B Harsha Park Inn International**, 11 Venkataswamy Naidu Rd (Park Rd), Shivajinagar, T080-22865566, harshahotel@yahoo.com. 80 clean rooms, 40 a/c, restaurants, bar, exchange, pool.

**B Nahar Heritage**, 14 St Mark's Rd, T080-22278731, nahar@blr.vsnl.net.in. 48 rooms, friendly service, good restaurant, good value, popular with domestic business travellers.

**B Nilgiris Nest**, 171 Brigade Rd, T080-25588401, nilgirisnest@vsnl.net. 24 rooms, 5 a/c on upper floor, very central, restaurant, exchange, supermarket below, busy location, clean, comfortable, good value.

**B-D Woodlands**, 5 Raja Ram Mohan Roy Rd, T080-22225111. 240 rooms, some a/c and cottages, with attached baths and fridge, good a/c restaurant, bar, coffee shop, exchange, large but pleasant hotel, good value.

**D Brindavan**, 40 MG Rd, T080-25584000. 112 spacious rooms with shower, some C a/c, superb *thali* restaurant, fairly quiet, non a/c good value. Recommended.

**D Casa Piccola**, Devatha Plaza, 131 Residency Rd, T080-22270754, casapiccola@vsnl.com. 4 guest rooms with bath, breakfast, common living room and kitchen, excellent café (see Eating), Italian/ Indian owners.

**D Pulikeshi**, 168/29 5th Cross, Gandhinagar, T080-22269727. 22 very clean rooms, some a/c, very quiet, friendly. Recommended.

**D Vellara**, 283 Brigade Rd, T080-25369116. 36 immaculate and spacious rooms with TV (top floor best), excellent value and location. Recommended.

**D-E Ajantha**, 22A MG Rd (7 km, City railway), T080-25584321. 62 spacious rooms some a/c and cottages with WC (no showers), restaurant (South Indian vegetarian), very helpful, good information.

*For an explanation of the sleeping and eating price codes used in this guide, see inside the front cover. Other relevant information is found in Essentials pages 56-61.*

**E Imperial**, 93-94 Residency Rd, T080-25588391. 20 clean rooms with bath, good location, good value.

**E Janardhana**, Kumara Krupa High Grounds, T080-22254444. 58 good size rooms, spartan but clean, restaurant (South Indian), popular Indian business hotel.

**E Mahaveer**, 8/9 Tank Bund Rd, opposite bus station, near City railway station, T080-22873670. Modern 5-storey hotel with 44 smallish rooms, 5 a/c. Clean and basic, front rooms can be very noisy, larger (**D**) de luxe rooms at back quieter.

**E New Central Lodge**, 56 Infantry Rd, at the Central St end, T080-25592395. 35 simple, clean enough rooms, some with bath, hot water (0500-1000).

**E Pushpamala**, 9, 2nd Cross, SC Rd (neon sign stands out above others), T080-22874010, opposite Bus Station, travel agent. Clean, good value and surprisingly quiet, cheap and cheerful.

**E Railway Retiring Rooms**, 23 rooms cheaper dorm for passengers in transit.

**E Sandhya Lodge**, 70 SC Rd, T080-22874065. 100 good, rooms with bath, train reservations.

**E Vybhab**, 60 SC Rd, T080-22873997. 29 clean rooms with bath (cold water), TV, down a passage, opposite cinema, great value.

### Hostels

**E YWCA**, 40 Mission Rd, T080-22277334. Basic rooms with bath, open to both sexes.

**E-F YMCA** (City), Nrupathunga Rd, near Cubbon Park, T2211848. None too clean, but great atmosphere, excellent café.

**F YHA Guest House and Programme Centre**. Contact Mr Sridhara, KFC Bldg, 48 Church St, T080-25585417.

## Eating

**Bangalore** *p968, maps p970 and p972*

Try the local Kannada chicken and Maddur *vada*.

**TTT Ashok's**, Windsor Sheraton. Buffet lunches.

**TTT Cosmo**, Magrath Rd. Good 'fusion' food, anything from *burritos* to lamb bourgignon to *Pad Thai*.

**TTT Mandarin Room** (for Chinese) and the BBQ at the Taj West End are recommended.

**TTT Rice Bowl**, Lavelle Rd, T080-25587417, and Residency Rd. Chinese, Tibetan. Well cooked, large portions.

**TTT Tycoons**, 83 Infantry Rd, T080- 25591356. International, good steaks, garden seating.

**TT Amarvathi**, 45/3 Residency Rd. Spicy South Indian.

**TT Angan**, Lady Curzon Rd. North Indian in a re-created Punjabi *dhaba* setting.

**TT Coconut Grove**, Church St. Varied and good southern menu (Chettinad, Keralan and Kodagan), beers, sit out under shade.

**TT Earthen Oven**, 76, Residency Rd. Chicken tikka etc. Minimalist decor – room looks upside down – but the food's good.

**TT Koshy's**, 39 St Mark's Rd, T080- 22213793. Pleasant, old-fashioned, atmospheric, licensed. Good grills and roasts, Syrian Christian fish curries and Sunday South Indian brunch.

**TT Prince's**, 9 Brigade Rd, 1st Flr, with **Knock Out Disco** next door.

**T Ballal Residence Hotel**, 74/4 III Cross, Residency Rd, T080-25597277. Indian, a/c **Palmgrove** serves excellent giant lunch *thalis* Rs 75, "super atmosphere, surrounded by Indian families and businessmen".

**T Blue Nile**, Church St. Tasty North Indian and tandoori.

**T Rock Garden**, Infantry Rd. Small range of lunches between 1230-1500 for next to nothing.

**T RR Restaurant and Bar**, 55 Church St, T080-25112 323. A/c 1st floor restaurant dishing up excellent, spicy Andhra food like *biryani* on big banana leafs. Packed with busy Bangalorean office workers. 1100-1500, 1900-2300.

**T Sukh Sagar**, near Majestic Cinema, 6 SM Rd, 3 floors. Each serving different style of food, fresh fruit juice, excellent South Indian *thalis* and Chinese snacks, very clean, modern, a/c.

### Vegetarian

**T Chalukma**, Race Course Rd, by West End Hotel. Excellent vegetarian.

**T Darshini**, many outlets for fresh, cheap south Indian snacks.

**T Gautam**, 17 Museum Rd. Excellent South Indian vegetarian restaurant and juice bar. Spacious and comfortable.

**T Indraprastha**, 47 SC Rd, in Hotel Adora. Superb Indian, cheap, packed all day.

**T Ullas**, MG Rd, 1st floor verandah restaurant. Very good Indian and Chinese vegetarian, snacks, sweets. Tasty, excellent service, inexpensive and very popular.

### Cafés, bakeries and ice cream

**Casa Piccola**. Pizzas, burgers, steaks, ice cream desserts, "excellent food, very good hygiene, European coffee house atmosphere". Highly recommended '*Raga*' (good gift shop) next door.
**Hot Breads**, Infantry Rd, Residency Rd and 44 Brigade Rd. Good for pastries.
**Nilgiri's Upper Crust Café**, Brigade Rd. Sells snacks, breads, pastries and cheeses, slightly expensive, but good, clean toilets.
The city's best ice cream is found on Residency Rd, opposite **Gateway Hotel**.

## Bars and clubs

**Bangalore** *p968, maps p970 and p972*
Bangalore has a very cool laid-back party scene, with all sorts of musical genres represented – from hiphop and house to rock. Venues are mostly open from 1900-2300.
**13th Floor**, Hotel Ivory Tower, 84 MG Rd, T080-25589333. Includes open-air seating with grand views over Bangalore night skyline from 13th floor and Thai food to boot.
**F-Bar and Lounge**, at Le Meridien Fashion TV lounge. Occasional free drinks for women. See also **Insomnia** below.
**Geoffrey's**, The Royal Orchid, 1 Golf Av, Airport Rd, T080-25205566. Done up like a British pub with woodwork, stained glass and period artifacts – less overpowering music than your other options listed here.
**i-Bar**, at **The Park Hotel**, 14/7 MG Rd, T080-25594666, www.theparkhotels.com. One of the most stylish options, the DJs sometimes step outside to play around the pool.
**Insomnia**, at **Le Meridien Bangalore**, 28 Sankey Rd. If you want to party past midnight come here: it's the city's only nightclub. Owned by Fashion TV, there are huge screens of models on the catwalk!
**Nineteen Twelve**, 40 St Marks Rd, T080-22997290. Trendy bar and dance floor, with food and occasional live music.
**Spinn**, 80 3rd Cross, Residency Rd, T080-25581555. An old colonial house turned funk and house club, ranked Bangalore's Best Pub in the Times Food Guide (food and cocktails served).

## Shopping

**Bangalore** *p968, maps p970 and p972*
**Commercial Street, MG** and **Brigade Roads** were once the favourite hangout of the city's youth, drawn to the new phenomenon of shopping malls with elevators. Now, this old commercial centre is being given a serious run for its money by 21st-century Americana in the form of shopping malls like **The Forum**, Hosur Road, Kaoramangala. With boutiques for brands like Barbie, Tommy Hillfiger and Bose, it's the type of place that will jar with those who travel for the antediluvian India, but if you want a good slice of the subcontinent's wealthy modern society, a tremendous 50,000 Bangaloreans pass through the Forum's electric doors every weekend. The food court here has international food like *burritos* too, if you have a hankering for things un-Indian. It's unlikely you'll want to shop for Barbies, though, so for tourists the best place remains the **City Market** in Chickpet for silver, gold and silk saris; it's supposed to be the country's biggest silk wholesale/retail district. **Russel Market**, meanwhile, in Shivajinagar is stuffed with vegetable, meats and antiques.

Shops and markets open early and close late (about 2000) though they remain closed from 1300-1600.

### Local specialities

Most gold and jewellery is, logically enough, on Jewellers' St, but also look along MG Rd, Brigade Rd, Residency Rd, Commercial St. Bargains to be had from KG Rd, Melleshwaram and Shivajinagar include brass, copper, soapstone statues, sandalwood and rosewood carvings and coloured wood inlay work. Also sandalwood oils and soaps, incense sticks, lacquer work, ceramics, carpets, fabrics (silk, cotton, georgette), watches and silver jewellery.
**Cauvery**, MG Rd. **Khadi Gramudyog**, Silver Jubilee Park Rd, near City Market. **Manjusha**, MG Rd. **Mota Shopping Complex**, Brigade Rd. **Raga**, A-13, Devatha Plaza, 131 Residency Rd. For very attractive gifts. **Shrungar**, MG Rd. **UP Handlooms**, 8 Mahaveer Shopping Complex, Kempe Gowda Rd.

### Books

**Gangarams**, 72 MG Rd. Has a wid- ranging and expanding collection.
**Higginbotham's**, No. 68, MG Rd.
**Premier**, 46/1 Church St (and Museum Rd). Small, with a good selection of specialist and academic books (as well as an impressive PG Wodehouse collection), helpful owner.

### Silk and saris

**Deepam**, MG Rd. Reasonable prices, helpful assistants.
**Janardhana**, Unity Building, JC Rd.
**Karnataka Silks Industries**, Gupta Market, Kempe Gowda Rd.
**Mysore Silk Showroom**, Leo Complex, MG Rd.
**Vijayalakshmi**, Kempe Gowda Rd. Will also make shirts.

## Activities and tours

### Bangalore *p968, maps p970 and p972*

### Golf

**Bangalore Golf Club**, Sankey Rd. Foreign visitors pay US$35. New International Championship Golf Course, near the airport. 0600-1800, closed Mon.
**KGA Golf Club**, charges Rs 200 weekdays, Rs 400 weekends.

### Horse racing

Bangalore is famous for racing and stud farms. **Bangalore Turf Club**, Race Course Rd. Season May-Jul and Nov-Mar. The favourite always wins!

### Swimming

Expect to pay Rs 500 for pools in hotels (eg Ashok, West End, Windsor Manor). Pools at Corp Office, near Square, Kensington Park Rd, near Ulsoor Lake, Sankey Tank, Sadhiv Nagar, Jayanagar 3rd Block.

### Tours

**Karnataka State Tourism**, tours from Badami House, opposite Corporation Office NR Square, T080-22275883: **Bangalore City Sightseeing**: Tipu's Palace, Bull Temple, Lal Bagh, Ulsoor Lake, Vidhan Soudha, Museums, also stops at Government Emporia. Half-day, 0700-1330 and 1400-1930. Rs 90. Recommended. **India Tourism tour**, departing from Swiss Complex, No 33 Race Course Rd, T080-22560001, same schedule but lasts whole day and includes ISKCON. 0900-1700 Rs 130. **1-day Sravanabelagola, Belur and Halebid**, Fri, Sun (except monsoons), 0715-2200, Rs 340; **Mysore** daily, 0715-2300, Rs 240-300 including meals.

### Tour operators

**Clipper Holidays**, 4 Magrath Rd, T080-25599032, www.clipperholidays.com. Tours, treks (everything provided), Kerala backwaters etc. Very helpful and efficient.
**Greenwood Adventures**, 2080, 12th B Main, MIG 3rd Phase, Newtown, Yelhalanka, T080-28462354, greenwood_adventures@hotmail.com. Specializes in treks in Karnataka and Kerala.
**Regal Holidays**, 105/17 8th Cross, RMV Extn, T080-23314566, regal@giasbg01.vsnl.net.in. Royal connections, culture, wildlife, horse safaris (Rs 4000 a day).
**Sita**, St Mark's Rd, T080-2212826.
**Thomas Cook**, 55 MG Rd, T080-25594168 (foreign exchange and TCs), and 70 MG Rd (all services), T080-25586439.

## Transport

### Bangalore *p968, maps p970 and p972*

### Air

Transport to town: (9-14 km) taxi takes 20 mins but leave an extra ½ hr in case of roadworks, Rs 150-200; auto-rickshaw, Rs 80. KSRTC coach from airport to major hotels, MG Rd and bus station, Rs 40. To airport: special bus leaves from Sivajinagar Stop (near **Hotel Harsha**). **Indian Airlines** and **Alliance Air**, Cauvery Bhavan, Kempe Gowda Rd, T080-22211914, airport T080-25266233, Reservations T141: **Chennai, Coimbatore, Delhi, Goa, Hyderabad, Kochi, Kolkata, Mangalore, Mumbai, Pune, Thiruvananthapuram**. **Jet Airways**, 1-4 M Block, Unity Bldg, JC Rd, T080-22276617, airport T080-25220688: **Chennai, Coimbatore, Delhi, Goa, Hyderabad, Kochi, Kolkata, Mumbai**. **Sahara**: Church St, T080-25586976, airport T080-25262531. Twice daily to **Delhi** and **Mumbai**. **Air India** flies weekly to **Jakarta**.
**Airline offices** Air India, Unity Building, JC Rd, T080-22277747. **Alltalia**, G17 Gem Plaza, 66 Infantry Rd, T080-25591936. **Nippon/Virgin Atlantic/Iberia/Thai/**

Emirates/Royal Nepal, all at G 5, Imperial Court, Cunningham Rd, T080-22256194. At Sunrise Chambers, 22 Ulsoor Rd: **Air France**, T080-25589397, **Gulf Air**, T080-25584702. **Indian Airlines**, (City Office) T141 or T080-25226233. **Kuwait**, T080-25594243, **Royal Jordanian, American Airlines, TWA, Austrian, Bangladesh, Air Seychelles**, all on: T080-25594240, **British Airways**, 7 Sophia's Choice, St Marks Rd, T080-22271205. **Cathay Pacific**, Taj West End, Race Course Rd, T080-22255055. **El Al**, 131/132 1st Fl Devatha Plaza Residency Rd T080-22272575. **KLM**, Taj West End, T080-22265562. **Lufthansa**, 44/42 Dickenson Rd, T080-25588791. **Qantas**, Westminster Cunningham Rd, T080-22264719. **Royal Nepal Airlines**, 205 Barton Center, MG Rd, T080-25597878. **Singapore**, Park View, 17 Curve Rd, Tasker, T080-22867868. **South African Airways/Air New Zealand/Anset Australia/Varig/Canadian Pacific**, 17-20 Richmond Towers, 12 Richmond Rd, T080-22244625. **Sri Lankan Airlines**, CS Plaza Residency Rd, T080-22075020. **SwissAir/Sabena/Delta**, Park View, 17 Curve Rd, Tasker, T080- 22867873. **United Airlines**, 17-20 Richmond Towers, 12 Richmond Rd, T080-22244620.



### Bus

Long-distance video coaches can be noisy and very tiring. **City Bus Station**, opposite the City Railway Station, is extremely busy but well organized. **Central (KSRTC) Bus Station** is just to the south, T080-22871261. **Karnataka (KSRTC), Andhra (APSRTC)** and **Tamil Nadu (TTC)** run efficient, frequent and inexpensive services to all major cities in South and Central India. Frequent service to **Mysore** (3 hrs); several to **Hassan** (4 hrs), **Hyderabad**, **Madikeri** (6 hrs), **Madurai** (9 hrs), **Mangalore** (9 hrs), **Ooty** (7 hrs), **Puttaparthi** (4-5 hrs, Rs 65), **Tirupati** (6½ hrs). Private operators' De luxe or Ordinary coaches are usually more comfortable though a bit more expensive. They operate from the City and Kalasipalyam Bus Stations.

### Car

Firms for city and out-of- town sightseeing include **Cab Service**, Sabari Complex, Residency Rd, T080-5586121. **City Taxi**, T080-25539999. Use meters (min charge Rs 30), or Rs 400 for 4 hrs (40 km free then Rs 8 per km), call out service, reliable. **Europcar**, T080-22219502. **Hertz**, T080- 25599408. **Karnataka STDC** (see page 969). About Rs 600-800 for 8 hrs or 80 km; extra km Rs 4-7. Out-of-town, Rs 1,200 (Rs 2,000 a/c).

### Taxi

Taxis at railway stations.

### Train

Pre-paid taxi service available at City Station. Pre-paid auto-rickshaw to MG Rd, Rs 25-30. Enquiries and reservations, T132; arrival and departure, T133. City Railway Station, computerized advance reservations in newer building on right of entrance; No 14 is Foreigners' Counter (also for disabled); the Chief Reservations Officer is on the ground floor. For Tourist Quota you need your passport and a "wait-listed" ticket number (Ticket Office is to the left of the station). If you are booking a ticket for a journey out of the Southern Region go to 1st floor booking office and join the queue for your region; no special queue for foreigners on the 1st floor. Buying tickets here can be a complicated business. Cantt Station, T135. Disembark at Cantt Station for some hotels. **Bhopal**: *Rajdhani Exp, 2429*, Mon, Wed, Thu, Sun, 1835, 27 hrs (reaches **Delhi (HN)** in 35 hrs). **Chennai**: *Shatabdi Exp, 2008*, daily except Tue, 1625, 5 hrs; *Lalbagh Exp, 2608*, 0630, 5½ hrs; *Brindavan Exp, 2640*, 1430, 5¼ hrs; *Bangalore-Chennai Exp, 6024* (AC/II), 0800, 6 hrs. **Delhi (ND)**: see Bhopal. **Goa** (Londa): *Chalukya Exp, 1018*, Mon, Tue, Fri, 0600, 10½ hrs; *Ranichennamma Express, 6589*, 2030, 11 hrs. **Hospet**: *Hampi Exp, 6592*, 2200, 10 hrs. **Kolkata (H)**: *Bangalore Guwahati Exp, 5625*, Wed, Fri, 2330, 38¼ hrs. **Mumbai (CST)**: *Udyan Exp, 6530*, 2030, 24 hrs; *Chalukya Exp, 1018*, Mon, Tue, Fri, 0600, 26 hrs. **Maddur** and **Mysore**: *Chamundi Exp, 6216*,1815, 2½ hrs; *Tipu Express, 6206*, 1415, 2½ hrs; or **Mysore**: *Tipu Express 6206*, 1415, 2½ hrs; *Shatabdi Exp, 2007*,daily except Tue, 1100, 2 hrs (for a/c, Rs 280). **Secunderabad**: *Bangalore Secunderabad Exp, 7086* (AC/II), 1705, 13½ hrs. **Thiruvananthapuram**: *Kanniyakumari Exp*, 6526 (AC/II), 2100, 18¼ hrs.

## Directory

**Bangalore** *p968, maps p970 and p972*
**Banks** Usually open 1000-1400, Mon-Fri. There are hundreds of 24-hr ATMs that are compatible with cards bearing the Mastercard, Visa, Maestro, Cirrus or Plus logos. Citibank, Hongkong and Shanghai Banks, HDFC are reliable. In the MG Rd area try HSBC, 7 MG Rd, Citibank Nilgiris Complex, Brigade Rd. For counter services: Bank of Nova Scotia, MG Rd, T080-25581415, Citibank, MG Rd, T080- 25599855, HDFC, Kasturba Rd, T080-22223223, State Bank of India, St Mark's Rd, T080-22274701, Standard Chartered MG Rd, T080-25597777. **Chemists** At hospitals and Cure, 137 GF2, Business Point, Brigade Rd T080-22274246. **Cultural centres** Alliance Française, Millers Tank Bund Rd, off Thimmaiah Rd, opposite station. British Library, St Mark's Rd/Church St corner (Koshy's Bldg), 1030-1830, Tue-Sat. Max Mueller Bhavan, 3 Lavalle Rd. **Dentist** Grace, 1 Dinnur Main Rd, RT Nagar, T080-23334638. Excellent. **Hospitals** Bowring and Lady Curzon Hospital, Hospital Rd, T080- 25591362, north of Cubbon Park. Mallya Hospital, Vittal Mallya Rd, south of Cubbon Park, T080-22277979/7991, one of the best. **Internet** Computer Planet, 1st Floor 5th Avenue shopping plaza, Brigade Rd, T080- 25597116 superfast with USB ports and software/hardware retailer. Cyber Café on Brigade Rd (near Church St); very good, safe cold coffee. Cyber Q, Brigade Rd, near Vellara, with pool tables; St Mark's Business Centre, 8 St Mark's Plaza, 14 St Mark's Rd T080-51121032. 0830-1930 Closed Sun. Internet plus facilities for scanning, lamination, colour zerox and CD writing Trans World 2 Magrath Rd, with coffee shop. **Mobiles** Ericsson, T080-22994088, Siemens, T080-25263312, Philips, T080-23312184, Nokia, T080-25582439. **Post** GPO, Cubbon Rd near Raj Bhawan, open 1000-1800. Poste Restante, Mon-Sat, 1030-1600. UPS, 4 1st Cross 10th Main Indiranagar, T080-25253445. DHL, Jubilee Building, 43 Museum Rd, T080-25588855. **Useful addresses** Ambulance: T102. Visa extensions: Commissioner of Police, Infantry Rd. Police 100 Fire 101 Chief Wildlife Warden, Aranya Bhavan, 18th Cross, Malleswaram, T080-23341993.



# West of Bangalore

*The NH4 runs northwest from Bangalore to Hubli-Dharwad, Pune and Mumbai across the high open country of the Central Maiden, following one of the main routes for trade and military movement over centuries.*

*The road west from Bangalore crosses the intensively cultivated open plains of the Western Plateau, watered from tanks or the odd well by the Vokkaliga caste, South Karnataka's dominant agricultural community and longstanding rivals of the reformist Lingayats of the northern districts. Their land encircles the dwarfing 'sky-clad' (ie nude) Jain statue of Gommateshwara, standing lost in meditation on top of a lotus in Sravanabelagola and the intricate architecture commissioned to adorn the Hoysalas' temples in Belur and Halebid, the capitals of those great warriors' kingdom.* ▸▸ *For Sleeping, Eating and other listings, see pages 983-985.*

## The Central Maidan → *Colour map 7, grid A3.*

### Chitradurga → *Colour map 7, grid A3.*

Chitradurga, 202 km northwest of Bangalore, is at the foot of a group of granite hills, rising to 1,175 m in the south. The **Fort of Seven Rounds** ⓘ *closed public holidays, open sunrise to sunset, Rs 100, allow 2 hrs, 2 km from bus stand, 4 km from railway station,* was built in the 17th century by Nayak Poligars, semi-independent landlords who fled south after the collapse of the Vijayanagar Empire in 1565. They were crushed by Haidar Ali in 1779 who replaced the Nayaka's mud fort with stone and

 Tipu Sultan built a palace, mosque, granaries and oil pits in it. There are four secret entrances in addition to the 19 gateways, and ingenious water tanks which collected rainwater. There are also 14 temples, including a cave temple to the west of the wall. They are placed in an extraordinary jumble of granite outcrops, a similar setting to that of Hampi 300 km to the north. The Hidimbeshwara temple is the oldest temple on the site.

### Belgaum → *Phone code: 0831. Colour map 5, grid C4. Population: 399,600.*

An important border town, Belgaum makes an interesting stop on the Mumbai-Bangalore road or as a trip from Goa. The crowded market in the centre gives a glimpse of India untouched by tourism. With its strategic position in the Deccan plateau, the town had been ruled by many dynasties including the Chalukyas, Rattas, Vijaynagaras, Bahmanis and the Marathas. Most of the monuments date from the early 13th century. The **fort**, immediately east of the town centre, though originally pre-Muslim, was rebuilt by Yusuf Adil Shah, the Sultan of Bijapur, in 1481. Inside the **Masjid-i-Sata** (1519), the best of the numerous mosques in Belgaum was built by a captain in the Bijapur army, Azad Khan. Belgaum is also noted for its Jain architecture and sculpture. The late Chalukyan **Kamala Basti** with typical beautifully lathe-turned pillars and a black stone Neminatha sculpture, stands within the fort walls. To the south of the fort and about 800 m north of the **Hotel Sanman** on the Mumbai-Bangalore bypass, is a beautifully sculpted Jain temple, which according to an inscription, was built by Malikaryuna.

## Western Plateau Temples

Sravanabelagola, Belur and Halebid can all be seen in a very long day from Bangalore, but it is better to allow longer if you can and to stay in Hassan overnight. There are direct buses from Mysore and Bangalore. » *See Transport, page 985, for further details.*

### Sravanabelagola (Shravanabelgola) → *Phone code: 08176*

The ancient Jain statue of Gommateshwara stands on Vindhyagiri hill (sometimes known as Indrabetta or Indragiri) which is 150 m above the plain giving great views to its many visitors: Chandragiri to the north (also known as Chikka Betta) is just under half that height. The 17 m Gommateshwara statue, erected somewhere between AD 980 and 983, is of the englightened prince Bahubali, son of the first Tirthankara (or holy Jain teacher). The prince won a fierce war of succession over his brother, Bharata, only to surrender his rights to the kingdom to take up a life of meditation.

You'll have to clamber barefoot up over 700 hot steep granite steps that carve up the hill to reach the statue from the village tank (socks offer good insulation from the boiling stone; carry your own water), alternatively charter a *dhooli* to do the work for you. The small, intricately-carved shrines you pass on the way up are the **Odeagal Basti**, the **Brahmadeva Mandapa**, the **Akhanda Bagilu** and the **Siddhara Basti**, all 12th-century except the Brahmadeva Mandapa which is 200 years older.

The carved statue (see History above) is nude (possibly as he is a *Digambara* or 'sky clad' Jain) and captures the tranquillity typical of much Buddhist and Jain art. The depth of the saint's meditation and withdrawal from the world is suggested by the spiralling creepers shown growing up his legs and arms, and by the ant-hills and snakes at his feet. Although the features are finely carved, the overall proportions are odd: he has huge shoulders and elongated arms but stumpy legs.

The 'magnificent anointment' – or *Mastakabhisheka* – falls every 12th year when Jain pilgrims flock from across India to bid for 1,008 pots – or *kalashas* – of holy water that are left overnight at the saint's feet. The next morning their contents, followed

## Small is beautiful: the temples of Belur and Halebid

The Hoysalas, whose kingdom stretched between the Krishna and Kaveri rivers, encouraged competition among their artisans – their works even bear 12th-century autographs. Steatite gave the sculptors the opportunity to fashion doily-like detail from solid rock since it is comparatively soft when fresh from the quarry but hardens with exposure to air. The temples, built as prayers for victory in battle, are small but superbly conceived.

with ghee, milk, coconut water, turmeric paste, honey, vermilion powder and even a dusting of gold, are poured over the saint's head from specially erected scaffolding. Unusually for India, the event is watched by the thousands of devotees in complete silence. The next celebration will be between 2006-2008.

## Belur → *Phone code: 08177. Colour map 7, grid A2.*

Belur, on the banks of the Yagachi River, was the dynasty's first capital. The Krishna Chennakesavara, built over a century from 1116 to celebrate victory over the Cholas at Talakad, stands at the centre of a courtyard of temples. It is surrounded by a rectangular wall, built on a star-shaped platform with an ambulatory, its entrance guarded by the winged figure of Garuda, Vishnu's carrier, who faces the temple with joined palms.

**The temples** ⓘ *close at 2030, search light for interiors Rs 10; carry a torch, ASI trained guides on site (often excellent), Rs 60-75 for 4 visitors (though official rate is higher.*

At first glance the **Chennakesava Temple**, see also Somnathpur page 992, is unimpressive because the superstructure has been lost. However, exquisite sculptures cover the exterior with friezes. A line of 644 elephants (each different) surrounds the base, with rows of figures and foliage above. The detail of the 38 female figures is perfect. Look at the young musicians and dancers on either side of the main door and the unusual perforated screens between the columns. Ten have typical bold geometrical patterns while the other 10 depict scenes from the *Puranas* in its tracery. Inside superb carving decorates the hand lathe-turned pillars and the bracket-figures on the ceiling. Each round filigree pillar is different and bears witness to individual sculptors producing masterpieces in competition with each other. The **Narasimha pillar** at the centre of the hall is particularly fine and originally could be rotated. The detail is astounding. The jewellery on the figures is hollow and movable and the droplets of water seem to hang at the ends of the dancer's wet hair on a bracket above you. On the platform in front of the shrine is the figure of Santalesvara dancing in homage to Lord Krishna. The shrine containing a 3-m high black polished deity is occasionally opened for *darshan*. The annual **Car Festival** is held in March-April. To the west is the **Viranarayana Temple** which has some fine sculpture and smaller shrines around it.

## Halebid

The ancient capital of the Hoysala Empire was founded in the early 11th century as *Dvarasamudra*. It was destroyed by the armies of the Delhi Sultanate in 1311 and 1327, after which it was deserted and later renamed Halebidu or Halebid (Old Capital). Fortunately the great Hoysalesvara Temple, although incomplete after the best part of a century of toil, survived.

 **The temples** ⓘ *close at 2030,ASI trained guides on site, Rs 60-75 for 4 visitors (though official rate is higher).*
First detour 1 km south to walk around the Basthalli garden filled with remarkably simple 12th-century Jain Bastis.These have lathe-turned and multi-faceted columns, dark interiors and carved ceilings. The smaller **Kedaresvara Temple** with some highly polished columns is on a road going south. There are cycles for hourly hire so you can visit these quieter sites, untroubled by the crowds besieging the Hoysalesvara.

The **Hoysalesvara Temple** set in lawns, has two shrines dedicated to *Siva* with a *Nandi* bull facing each. The largest of the Hoysala temples, it was started in 1121 but remains unfinished. In structure it is similar to the one at Belur, but its superstructure was never completed. There are extraordinary half life-size statues of Hindu deities with minute details all around the temple. These, and the six bands of sculpture below, show the excellence of the artisans' craft. The lines of elephants at the base are followed by lions and then horsemen, a floral scroll and then most impressive of all, at eye level, stories from the epics and the *Bhagavata Purana*. This frieze relates incidents from the *Ramayana* and *Mahabharata*; among them Krishna lifting Mount Govardhana and Rama defeating the demon god Ravana. The friezes above show *yalis* and *hamsa* or geese. Of the original 84 female figures (like the ones at Belur) only 14 remain; over the years, 70 were stolen.

**Archaeological Museum** ⓘ *closed Fri 1000-1700, Rs 2, no photography*, is on the lawn near the south entrance where the Archaeological Survey of India maintains a gallery of 12th-13th-century sculptures, wood carvings, idols, coins and inscriptions. Some sculptures are displayed outside. To the west is a small lake.

## Chikmagalur

Chikmagalur, northeast of Belur, means 'younger daughter's town', and according to legend it was the dowry for the younger daughter of a local chieftain. In addition to the Hoysala style **Kodandarama Temple** there are mosques, the moated fort and the St Joseph's Roman Catholic Cathedral. The town is at the centre of one of India's major **coffee** growing areas. Coffee was first grown in the Baba Budan Hills, just to the north, in 1670. The Central Coffee Research Institute was set up in 1925.



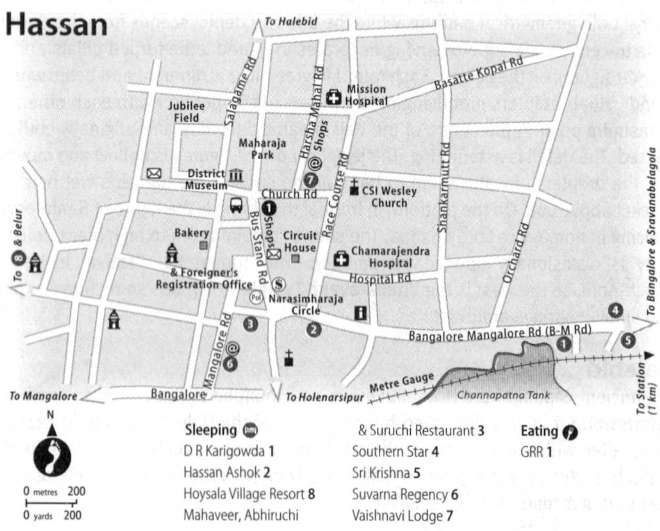

## Hassan → *Phone code: 08172. Colour map 7, grid A2. Population: 117,400.*

This pleasant, busy little town, is the best base for seeing Belur and Halebid. Buses pull in at the centre, most hotels are within a short walking distance. The railway station is 2 km to the east.

In the town itself is the **Bhandari basti** (1159 and added to later), about 200 m to the left from the path leading up to the Gommateshwara statue. Inside are 24 images of Tirthankaras in a spacious sanctuary. There are 500 rock-cut steps to the top of the hill that take half an hour to climb. It is safe to leave luggage at the tourist office branch at the entrance, which closes 1300-1415. The tourist office ⓘ *Vartha Bhavan, BM Rd, T08172-268862*, is very helpful.

There are 14 shrines on **Chandragiri** and the Mauryan emperor **Chandragupta**, who is believed by some to have become a Jain and left his empire to fast and meditate, is buried here. The temples are all in the Dravidian style, the Chamundaraya Basti, built in AD 982 being one of the most remarkable. There is a good example of a free-standing pillar or *mana-stambha* in front of the *Parsvanathasvami Basti*. These pillars, sometimes as high as 15 m, were placed at the temple entrance. Here, the stepped base with a square cross-section transforms to a circular section and the column is then topped by a capital.

## Jog Falls → *Colour map 7, grid A2.*

The falls are a magnificently spectacular sight in the wet season and the best time to visit is late November to early January. The 50-km long **Hirebhasgar Reservoir** now regulates the flow of the Sharavati River in order to generate hydro-electricity. The Mysore Power Corporation releases water to the falls every second Sunday from 1000-1800. Often during the monsoon the falls are shrouded in mist. Leeches are a hazard if you walk down to the base of the falls. In the dry season the water is often reduced to a trickle.

There are four falls. The highest is the **Raja**, with a fall of 250 m and a pool below 40 m deep. Next is the **Roarer,** while a short distance to the south is the **Rocket**, which spurts great shafts of water out into the air. In contrast the **Rani** (once called the White Lady) cascades over the rocks. The walk to the bottom of the falls is well worthwhile for the fit. A walk to the top (not in the monsoons) offering breathtaking views of the cascading river and the valley, is highly recommended. The Inspection Bungalow has excellent views.

## Sleeping

### Chitradurga *p979*

**C-D Amogha International**, Santhe Honda Rd, T08194-220762. Clean, spacious, modern rooms, some a/c suites, 2 restaurants, good vegetarian but service slow. Best in town.

**F Maurya**, Santhe Bagilu (within city walls), T08194-224448. 12 acceptable rooms, bit noisy.

### Belgaum *p980*

**C-D Adarsha Palace**, College Rd, T0831-2435777. Small, modern and 'personal', some a/c rooms, excellent **Angaan** veg restaurant (non-veg on rooftop), pleasant atmosphere, friendly staff, good value. Recommended.

**C-D Sanman Deluxe**, College St, T0831-2430777. Similar to **Adarsha Palace**, in a new building (much cheaper in old Sanman), 2 restaurants.

**D Milan**, Club Rd (4 km railway), T0831-2470555. 45 rooms with bath (hot shower), some a/c, vegetarian restaurant, good value.

**D-E Keerthi**, Poona-Bangalore Rd, short walk from Central Bus Stand, T0831-246699. Large modern hotel, some a/c rooms, restaurant.

**E-F Sheetal**, Khade Bazar near bus station, T0831-2470222. Cleanish rooms with bath (prices vary), vegetarian restaurant, Indian style, noisy hotel in busy and quite entertaining bazaar street.

**F Mayura Malaprabha** (KSTDC), Ashok Nagar, T0831-2470781. 6 simple clean rooms in modern cottages, dorm (Rs 40), restaurant, bar, tourist office.

**Sravanabelagola** *p980*

All facilities are very basic but it is worth staying overnight to see the statue early.

**E Karnataka Bhavan**, reserve at Karnataka Tourism, 9 St Mark's Rd, Bangalore, T08176-2579139. 50 rooms.

**F Vidyananda Nilaya Dharamshala**, closest to the bus stand, reserve through SDJMI Committee. Rooms with toilet and fan, "bucket shower", blanket but no sheets, courtyard, good value at Rs 60.

**F Yatri Niwas** (SDJMI), large rooms, good attached baths, clean (Rs 160).

**Belur** *p981*

**E Mayura Velapuri** (KSTDC), Temple Rd, T08177-222209. 2 old rooms, 10 newer, clean, spacious with bath (Rs 200), 20-bed dorms, reasonable restaurant (South Indian meals and egg curry quick service; non-veg slow), friendly and obliging staff make up for what it lacks in comfort.

**E-F Vishnu Lodge**, Main Rd, T08177-222263. 27 rooms with bath, some with TV (Rs 50-200), vegetarian restaurant.

**F Sri Raghavendra**, right by temple. Cosy rooms (Rs 75-100), homely and friendly.

**Halebid** *p981*

**F Mayura Shantala** (KSTDC), T08172-273224. Inspection Bungalow compound in nice garden overlooking temple. 4 rooms with fan, nets and bath (Rs 220, 2 better furnished), limited kitchen. Others, plainer but adequate (Rs 150).

**Chikmagalur** *p982*

**AL Taj Garden Retreat**, outside town, on a hill side, T08262-30217. 29 luxury a/c rooms lined along the pool, good for visiting Belur and Halebid (40 km).

**Hassan** *p983, map p982*

**B Hassan Ashok** (ITDC), BM Rd, 500 m from bus stand, T08172-268731, hsnashok@bgl.vsnl.net.in. 46 faded rooms, half a/c, good restaurant, bar, pleasant grounds, bad value.

**B Hoysala Village Resort**, Belur Rd, 6 km from town, T08172-256065. 33 cottage rooms, restaurant, bar, attractive resort with gardens and pool.

**B-C Southern Star**, BM Rd, T08172-251816, sshassan@vsnl.com. 48 very nice clean a/c rooms in modern hotel, TV, limited restaurant (good Indian across the road), bar, good views of countryside, excellent service.

**D-E Cauvery Comforts**, BM Rd, T08172-263117. 35 simple non a/c rooms with TV, bath (hot water mornings).

**D-E Sri Krishna**, BM Rd, T08172-263240. 40 a/c rooms with modern facilities, south Indian food, car hire, good value.

**D-E Suvarna Regency**, 97 BM Rd (500 m south of bus stand) T08172-264006, www.htoelsuvarna.com. 70 brilliant rooms, clean and cool, some with tub, modern, swish, good vegetarian restaurant, car hire. Very helpful, efficient, excellent value.

**E DR Karigowda**, BM Rd (1 km railway), T08172-264506. 30 modern, clean comfortable rooms, 2 a/c, quieter at back, restaurant (good choice), hospitable. Good value.

**E-F Mahaveer**, BM Rd, 250 m south of bus stand, T08172-268885. 22 rooms, good restaurant, very clean, quiet, friendly.

**F Vaishnavi Lodge**, Harsha Mahal/Church Rd, T08172-267413. 44 clean, spacious rooms, excellent value, friendly. Recommended.

**Jog Falls** *p983*

Hotels are very basic and there are no eating facilities available at night.

**E-F Mayura Gerusoppa** (KSTDC), T08186-44732. 10 rooms.

**F Youth Hostel**, Shimoga Rd. Empty rooms (no beds), some dorm beds with dirty bedding. Local families take in guests. Stalls near the falls serve reasonable breakfast and meals during the day.

## Eating

**Hassan** *p983, map p982*

**ƛƛ Hassan Ashok** hotel. International. Good food, prompt service.

**ƛƛ Suvarna Regency** hotel. Very good South Indian vegetarian, excellent breakfasts, popular **Golden Gate** bar and restaurant downstairs, T08172-260316.

**ƛ Abhiruchi**, Mahaveer's (North Indian, Chinese), scruffy surroundings, pleasant staff.

*For an explanation of the sleeping and eating price codes used in this guide, see inside the front cover. Other relevant information is found in Essentials pages 56-61.*

🍴 **GRR**, opposite bus stand. For non-vegetarian food and friendly staff.
🍴 **Suruchi**, below, for vegetarians.

## Transport

**Chitradurga** *p979*
Buses to/from **Bangalore, Davangere, Hospet, Hubli** and **Mysore**. Train from **Arsikere, Bangalore, Guntakal, Hubli**.

**Belgaum** *p980*
The airport is 10 km from the centre (no flights at present). Central Bus Stand for long distance services. **Panaji** (0600-1715), **Margao** (0545-1500), **Mapusa** (0715-1715) take 5 hrs, Rs 45. The train station is near the bus stand, 4 km south of the centre; autos available. **Bangalore**: *Ranichennamma Exp, 6590*, 1810, 13 hrs. **Mumbai (CST) and Pune**: change at Pune for Mumbai *Chalukya/ Sharavathi Exp, 1018/1036*, Mon, Tue, Fri, Sat, 1805, 14 hrs. **Goa via Londa** 8 trains daily, 0135-2030, 1 hr.

**Sravanabelagola** *p980*
Direct buses to/from **Mysore** and **Bangalore** run in the morning; in the afternoon, change at Channarayapatna. The morning express buses to/from Mysore serve small villages travelling over dusty, though interesting, roads up to Krishnarajapet, then very few stops between there and Mysore. There are also tours from Bangalore.

**Belur** *p981*
The **bus** stand is about 1 km from the temples. Half-hourly to **Hassan** (1 hr; last at 2030); to **Halebid** (30 mins). To **Shimoga** for **Hampi** and **Jog Falls** (4 hrs), 0800, 0845 (check at bus stand); to **Mysore** (1½ hrs).

**Halebid** *p981*
The **bus** stand, where you can get good meals, is near the temples. KSRTC buses, half-hourly to Hassan (45 mins) and from there to **Bangalore, Mangalore, Mysore**. Also direct to **Belur** (12 km, 1 hr) and from there to Hassan.

**Hassan** *p983, map p982*
**Bus**
For local buses, T08172-268418. Long distance buses at least hourly to **Belur** from about 0700 (35 km, 1 hr) and **Halebid** from about 0800 (31 km, 1 hr); all very crowded. Few direct to **Sravanabelagola** in the morning (1 hr); alternatively travel to Channarayapatna and change to bus for Sravanabelagola. Also to **Bangalore** about every 30 mins (4½ hrs), **Goa** (14 hrs), **Hampi, Mangalore** (5 hrs), **Mysore** hourly (3 hrs). You can reserve seats for the 0730 depart to **Hospet** (9 hrs).

**Taxi**
Private Tourist Taxis can be hired from Cauvery Tourist Centre, Race Course Rd, T08172-268026. Tongas are also available.

**Train**
Railway Station is 2 km east of centre. New broad gauge line is now running. **Arsikere**: 1050, 2100, 1 hr. **Mysore**: 0605, 1830, 3 hrs.

**Jog Falls** *p983*
**Buses** to/from **Karwar** daily, arriving evening, and leaving Jog in the morning. Other destinations include **Sagar, Shimoga** for **Belur** or **Hassan** (4 hrs), **Sirsi** (2 hrs). A new road connects Honavar with Jog. **Goa**: (8 hrs) bus to **Colva** at 1100 is very crowded, 2300 is easier to get a seat on.

**Taxi**
To **Panaji**, Rs 1,500 (6 hrs).

**Train**
Jog is 16 km from the railway at **Talguppa**. Trains from **Bangalore** involve a change in **Shimoga** town.

## Directory

**Hassan** *p983, map p982*
**Banks** State Bank of Mysore and State Bank of India, Narasimharaja Circle, change US$, £ and TCs. **Internet** next to Suvarna and Vaishnavi hotels. **Hospitals** General Hospital, Hospital Rd, Mission Hospital, Race Course Rd. **Post** 100 m from bus stand.

# Mysore and Southern Maidan

*The unruly city of Mysore, the former capital of the princely state, does a brisk trade in its eponymous shimmering silks, sandalwood and jasmine against a backdrop of its amazingly gaudy Indo-Saracenic palace. Americans flock here for the city's world-famous Mysore-style yoga. Nearby is Srirangapatna, the fascinating island fortress of Tipu Sultan, nemesis of the British, and the bird-crammed Ranganathittu Sanctuary. Further on is the Chennakesava Temple of Somnathpur, a spellbinding example of Hoysala architecture. Leopards and tigers stalk the two parklands, Bandipur and Nagarhole, that spill over Karnataka's borders with neighbouring Tamil Nadu and Kerala, and closer to the coast you can climb the Ghats to the tiny Kodagu district, with forests of wild elephants and coffee plantations nursed by its warrior people. Sera, in Kodagu, is the university at the centre of one of India's biggest Tibetan Buddhist refugee settlements.* ▸▸ *For Sleeping, Eating and other listings, see pages 996-1002.*

## Mysore → *Phone code: 0821. Colour map 7, grid B3. Population: 742,300.*

Mysore centre is a crowded jumble presided over by the gaudy, wondrous kitsch of the Maharajah's Palace, a profusion of turquoise pink and layered with mirrors. But today Mysore's world renown is centred less on the palace, or its silk production, sandalwood, or the deathplace of Haider Ali; above all Mysore is now the home to Sri



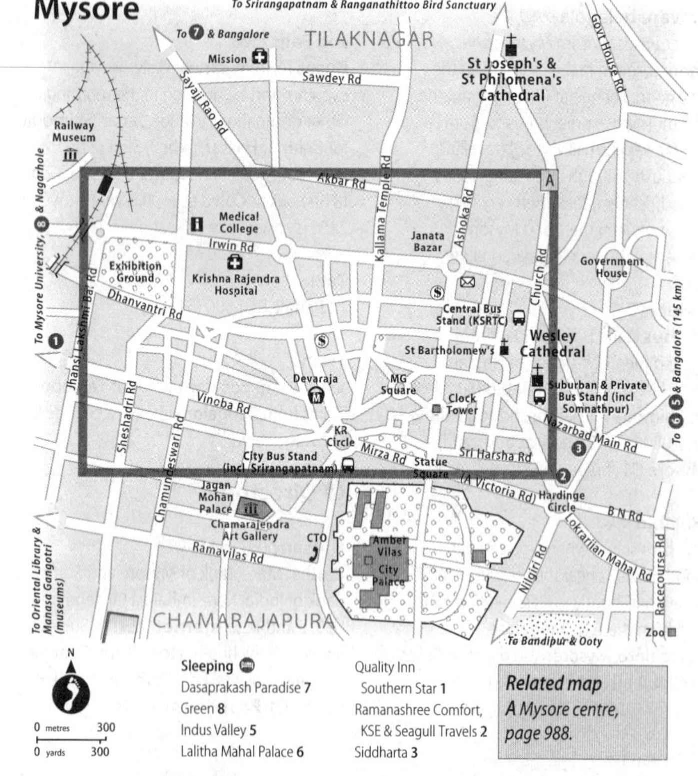

## Passage to Mysore

The southern route to Mysore through Kanakapura and Malvalli is longer than the more northerly rail and road route. This way crosses the open parkland of the Maidan, rising to over 1,200 m. The ancient rocks of some of the oldest granites in India which give reddish or brown soils, often with extraordinary hilly outcrops and boulders, provided David Lean and Richard Goodwin with the ideal filming location to capture the atmosphere of E M Forster's Barabar Cave for their film of *A Passage to India* without the hazards of working in Bihar. The lower cave sequences were filmed at **Savandurga**. Get BTS bus from Bangalore City bus stand 0700, 0900, or to Magadi, then auto-rickshaw, Rs 50, ask at the Lakshmi store for directions or a guide. It's a spectacular climb up Kempi Gowda hill.

There is also a small Forest Park and the upper caves at **Rama Dhavara**, 2 km from Ramanagaram. The caves are visible from the road and easy to find, though only false entrances were made for the film, with interior shots filmed in a studio.

Pattabhi Jois and his 'Mysore-style' ashtanga yoga practice. This all happens outside the chaotic centre, in the city's beautiful Brahmin suburbs – all wide boulevard-like streets overhung with bougainvillea.

## Ins and outs

**Getting there** The railway station is about 1 km to the northwest of the town centre while the three bus stands are all central within easy reach of hotels. ▸▸ *See Transport, page 1001, for further details.*

**Getting around** Karnataka's second-biggest town, Mysore is still comfortably compact enough to walk around, though there are plenty of autos and buses as well.

**Tourist information** Department of Tourism ⓘ *Old Exhibition Building, Irwin Rd, T0821-2422096, www.karnataka.com/tourism/mysore, 1000-1730*. Counters at train station and bus stand. **KSTDC** ⓘ *Yatri Nivas, 2 JLB Rd, T0821-2423652*, efficient.

## Sights

**Maharaja's Palace** ⓘ *T0821-2434425, enter by south gate, 1030-1730, Rs 15, cameras must be left in lockers (free, you take the key), allow 1 hr, 2 if you wish to see everything (worth taking a guide), guidebook, Rs 10. Go early to avoid the crowds. Downstairs is fairly accessible to the disabled. On Sun nights, public holidays and during festivals, the palace is lit by 50,000 light bulbs; well worth seeing after 1900.*

The City Palace (Amba Vilas), was designed by Henry Irwin and built in 1897 after a fire which burnt down the old wooden palace. It is in the Indo-Saracenic style in grand proportions, with domes, arches and colonnades of carved pillars and shiny marble floors – 'wondrous kitsch'. One of the largest palaces in the country with some art treasures, it is beautifully restored and maintained. The stained glass, wall paintings, ivory inlaid doors and the ornate golden throne (now displayed during *Dasara*) are all remarkable. The fabulous collection of jewels, 'amazing in its extravagance', is only rarely on display.

**Ground Floor** Visitors are led through the 'Car Passage' with cannons and carriages to the *Gombe thotti* (Dolls' pavilion). This originally displayed dolls during *dasara* and today houses, in addition, a model of the old palace, European marble statues and the golden *howdah* (the Maharaja used the battery-operated red and green bulbs on top of the canopy as 'Stop' and 'Go' signals to the *mahout*!). The last is still used during *dasara* but goddess Chamundeshwari rides on the elephant. The octagonal *Kalyana Mandap* (marriage hall), or Peacock Pavilion, south of the courtyard, has a beautiful stained glass ceiling and excellent paintings of scenes from the *dasara* and other festivities on 26 canvas panels. Note the exquisite details, especially of No 19. The Portrait Gallery and the Period Furniture Room lead off this pavilion.

**First Floor** A marble staircase leads to the magnificent *Durbar Hall* (47 m x 13 m), a grand colonnaded hall with lavishly framed paintings by famous Indian artists. The asbestos-lined ceiling has paintings of Vishnu incarnations. A passage takes you past the beautifully ivory-on-wood inlaid door of the Ganesh Temple, to the *Amba* (Amber) *Vilas* where private audiences (*Diwan-i-Khas*) were held. This exquisitely decorated hall has three doors. The central silver door depicts Vishnu's 10 incarnations and the eight *dikpalas* (directional guardians), with Krishna figures on the reverse (see the tiny Krishna on a leaf, kissing his toes!), all done in *repoussé* on teak and rosewood. The stained glass (possibly Belgian, in Art Nouveau style), cast iron pillars from Glasgow, carved wood ceiling, chandeliers, etched glass windows, the *pietra dura* on the floors and the elegant colour scheme all add to its grandeur.

The jewel-encrusted Golden Throne with its ornate steps, which some like to attribute to ancient Vedic times, was originally made of figwood decorated with ivory before it was embellished with gold, silver and jewels. Others trace its history to 1336 when the Vijaynagar kings 'found' it and, they say, passed it on to the Wodeyars who continue to use it during *dasara*.

**Maharaja's Residence** ⓘ *1000-1830, Rs 15.* Now a museum, the ground floor, with an enclosed courtyard, displays costumes, musical instruments, children's toys and numerous portraits. The upper floor has a small collection of weapons. Some find it disappointing.



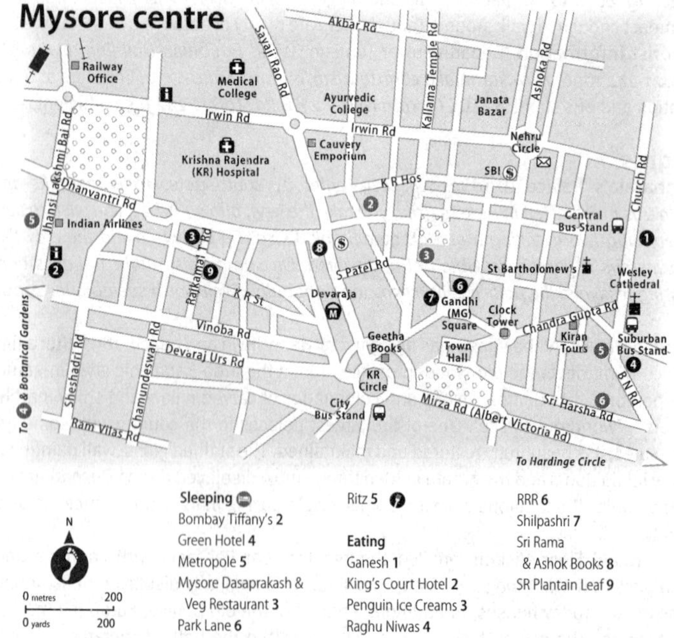

## Power yoga

Sri Krishna Pattabhi Jois, the octogenarian granddaddy of ashtanga – 'dynamic' or 'power' – yoga, divides opinion in the international yoga fraternity quite neatly in two. The lithe-limbed Americans who shell out US$500 a month for an hour of practice in his presence in the pre-dawn Mysore morning light fall, quite literally, at his feet in reverence. Others scoff at the cult of the 'Guru-ji', point out that he only teaches wealthy Westerners, is barely known in his homeland, and mock his money-making obsession.

One long-term student admits he's not without fault: "Gold is one thing he loves. He doesn't claim to be cheap. He doesn't claim to be doing karma (selfless) yoga. He's reassuringly human, greedy, wonderfully imperfect and honest about it... He used to be poor as a church mouse, but now others are making their fortune from it; why should the guy who developed the system earn less than his cannier Western students?" The yogic academic year kicks off with 30-odd students filing in from October to his *shala* (classroom) in the wealthy brahminical suburbs of Mysore, then swells to over 250 in Manhattan high season from February on.

Detractors say it's a waste of money, that the 89-year-old nods off in the squidgy red, cushion-strewn sofa students bought him – "It's too comfortable a chair for an old man," laughs a devoted student – meanwhile his grandson Shirat saunters out mid-class, and his daughter, a burly Indian matron, Saraswati, will apparently pause sessions to discuss nail polish.

Nor are the students themselves beyond reproach. One young English couple quietly confess that it's no ascetic life that they've opted for in the tree-lined streets of the university town's outskirts. "We live in India's version of Beverley Hills," they shrug happily. It's a pretty vapid life, where 'yoga plus one' is the mantra – yogis aim to get one thing done each day past practice. For the ambitious that 'one' can be going to an internet café, brunch at the Green Hotel, but more often than not it just involves swapping your Lycra for swimmers to lounge by the hotel pool at Southern Star. Hardly gruelling then, but if bed by 2100 and up at 0400 doesn't deter you, and you want to see Jois's teaching for yourself, you should write to his Ashtanga Yoga Research Institute in advance to advise your arrival dates and proposed length of stay.

**Market in Devaraja** This place is a treat: after 12 noon it's injected with fresh pickings of marigolds and jasmines. The bigger flowers – orange, white, yellow, are stitched onto a thread and wrapped into rolls. They come heaped in hessian sacks stacked on the heads of farmers.

**Chamundi Hill** ⓘ *vehicle toll Rs 10, City Bus No 185.* Immediately to the southeast of the town, the hill has a temple to Durga (Chamundeswari) celebrating her victory over the buffalo god. She became the guardian deity of the Wodeyars. Other than beautiful views on a clear day, there is little else to see but it's a pleasant trip all the same. The giant Nandi, carved in 1659, is on the motorable road down so it is possible to walk to it along the trail from the top and be picked up by a car later or catch a return bus from the road. If you continue along the trail you will end up having to get a rickshaw back, instead of a bus.

**Sandalwood Oil Factory** ⓘ *T0821-2483651, Mon-Sat, 0900-1100, 1400-1600 (prior permission required), no photography inside*. This is where oil is extracted and where incense is made. The shop sells soap, incense sticks etc.

**Silk Factory** ⓘ *Manathavadi Rd, T0821-481803, Mon-Sat, 0930-1630, no photography*. Here weavers produce Mysore silk saris, often with gold *zari* work. Staff will often show you the process from thread winding to jacquard weaving, but speak little English. The shop sells saris from Rs 3,000. Good walks are possible in the Government House if the guard at the gate allows you in.

**Jayachamarajendra Art Gallery** ⓘ *0830-1730, Rs 10, no photography*, at Jaganmohan Palace (1861). On view here are the priceless collections of Mysore's erstwhile rulers, including Indian miniature paintings and others, such as Ravi Varma and Nicholas Roerich. There's also an exhibition of ceramics, stone, ivory, sandalwood, antique furniture and old musical instruments. Unfortunately there are no descriptions or guidebooks and many items are randomly displayed but this makes for a relaxed atmosphere all the same.

**Sri Mahalingeshwara Temple** ⓘ *12 km from Mysore, 1 km off the Bhogadi road (right turn after K Hemmanahalli, beyond Mysore University Campus), taxi or auto-rickshaw*. The 800-year old Hoysala Temple has been carefully restored by local villagers under the supervision of the Archaeological Survey of India. The structure is an authentic replica of the old temple – here, too, the low ceiling encourages humility

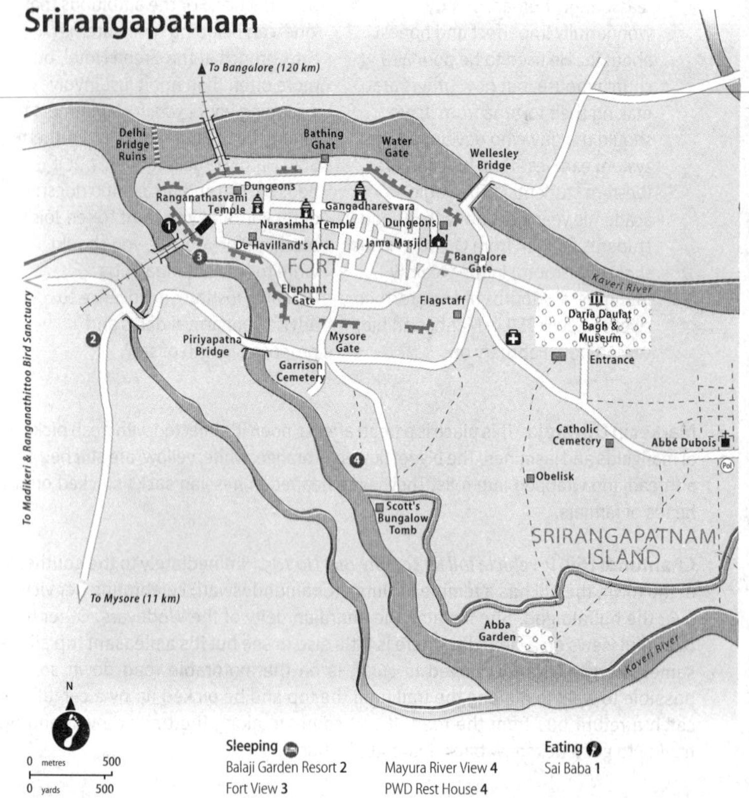

by forcing the worshipper to bow before the shrine. The surrounding garden has been planted with herbs and saplings, including some rare medicinal trees, and provides a tranquil spot away from the city. 

# Around Mysore

## Srirangapatnam → *Phone code: 08236. Colour map 7, grid B3. Population: 21,900.*

Srirangapatnam has played a crucial role in the region since its origins in the 10th century. Occupying an easily fortified island site in the Kaveri River, it has been home to religious reformers and military conquerors, and makes a fascinating day trip from Mysore, 12 km away. Daria Daulat Bagh and the Gumbaz are wonderful.

The name comes from the temple of Vishnu Sri Ranganathasvami, which is far older than the fort or the town. The site was frequently a focal point in South India's political development. The fort was built under the Vijayanagar kings in 1454. Some 150 years later the last Vijayanagar king handed over authority to the Hindu Wodeyars of Mysore, who made it their capital. In the second half of the 18th century it became the capital of Haidar Ali, who defended it against the Marathas in 1759, laying the foundations of his expanding power. He was succeeded by his son Tipu Sultan, who also used the town as his headquarters. Colonel Wellesley, the future Duke of Wellington, established his military reputation in the battle in which Tipu Sultan was finally killed on 4 May 1799, see page 1306, though victory should be more correctly attributed to his brother, the Governor General. Tipu died in exceptionally fierce fighting near the north gate of the fort; the place is marked by a very simple monument.

*! The island is over 3 km long and 1 km wide so it is best to hire a cycle from a shop on the main road to get around.*

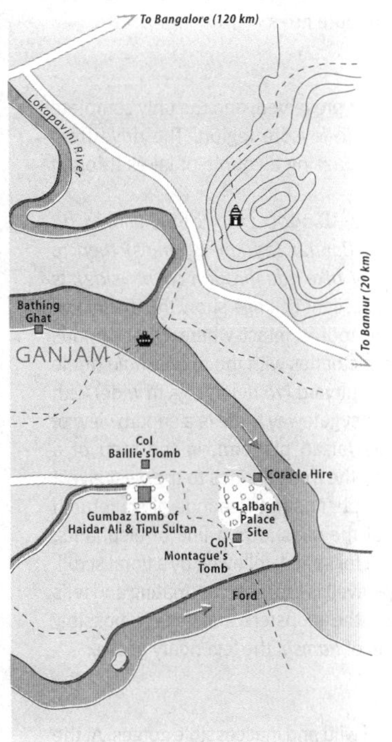


The fort had triple fortifications, but the British destroyed most of it. The **Jama Masjid** ⓘ *0800-1300, 1600-2000*, built by Tipu Sultan, has delicate minarets, and there are two Hindu **temples**, Narasimha (17th century) and Gangadharesvara (16th century). **Daria Daulat Bagh** (Splendour of the Sea) ⓘ *closed Fri, 0900-1700, US$2, 1 km to the east of the fort*, is Tipu's beautiful summer palace, built in 1784 and set in a lovely garden. This social historical jewel has colourful frescoes of battle scenes between the French, British and Mysore armies, ornamental arches and gilded paintings on the teak walls and ceilings crammed with interesting detail. The west wall shows Haidar Ali and Tipu Sultan leading their elephant forces at the battle of Polilur (1780), inflicting a massive defeat on the British. As a result of the battle Colonel Baillie, the defeated British commander, was a prisoner in Srirangapatnam for many years. The murals on the east walls show Tipu offering hospitality to neighbouring princes at various palace durbars. The small museum upstairs has 19th-century European paintings and Tipu's belongings all excellently maintained by the Archaeological Survey of India though the green sun screens make it look unpromising. **The Gumbaz** ⓘ *closed Fri, 0900-1700, donation collected*, the family mausoleum 3 km away, was built by Tipu in remembrance of his father. Approached through an avenue of cypresses, the ornate white-domed Gumbaz contains beautiful ivory-on-wood inlay and Tipu's tiger-stripe emblem. Some of his swords and shields are kept here. The tranquil atmosphere is a perfect setting for the elegant and quiet mausoleum which houses the tomb of Haider Ali in the centre, that of his wife on the east and of Tipu Sultan on the west. See Sleeping. On the banks of the Cauvery, just north of the Lal Bagh Palace (Rs 2), is a jetty where six seater **coracles** are available for river rides. Great fun.

## Ranganathittu Bird Sanctuary

ⓘ *0600-0900, 1600-1800, Rs 150, camera Rs 10. Boats (0830-1330, 1430-1830), Rs 10 each, minimum Rs 20. Jun-Oct best. Mysore City Bus 126, or auto from Srirangapatnam.* The riverine site of this sanctuary, 5 km upstream of Srirangapatnam, was established in 1975. Several rocky islands, some bare while the larger are well wooded, provide excellent habitat for waterbirds, including the black-crowned night heron, Eurasian spoonbill and cormorants. Fourteen species of waterbirds use the sanctuary as a breeding ground, most of which begin to breed in June. There is a large colony of fruit bats in trees on the edge of the river and a number of marsh crocodiles between the small islands. It is a popular tourist site, receiving hundreds of visitors every day. It is possible to go round some of the islands on the river by boat, but not to land. Boat and guide can be hired from the jetty for 15-20 minute rides.

## Somnathpur → *Phone code: 08227.*

This tiny village, east of Mysore, has one of the best preserved, and the only complete one, of approximately 80 Hoysala temples, in the Mysore region. The drive from Srirangapatnam via Bannur is particularly lovely, passing a couple of lakes through beautiful country and pretty, clean villages.

The small but exquisite **Kesava Temple** (1268) ⓘ *0900-1700, US$2, allow 1 hr, canteen, buses from Mysore take 1-1½ hrs; via Bannur (25 km, 45 mins) then to Somnathpur (3 km, 15 min by bus or lovely walk or bike ride through countryside)*, is maintained by the Archaeological Department. Excellent ceilings show the distinctive features of the late Hoysala style, and here the roof is intact where other famous temples have lost theirs. The temple has three sanctuaries with the *trikutachala* (triple roof) and stands in the middle of its rectangular courtyard (70 m long, 55 m wide) with cloisters containing 64 cells around it. From the east gateway there is a superb view of the temple with an ambulatory standing on its raised platform, in the form of a 16-pointed star. The pillared hall in the centre with the three shrines to the west give it the form of a cross in plan. Walk around the temple to see the bands of sculptured figures which are particularly fine. The lowest of the six shows a line of elephants, symbolizing strength and stability, then horsemen for speed, followed by a floral scroll. The next band of beautifully carved figures (at eye level) is the most fascinating and tells stories from the epics. Above is the *yali* frieze, the monsters and foliage possibly depicting the river Ganga and uppermost is a line of *hamsa*, the legendary geese.

## Sivasamudram → *Best in July and August.*

Here, the Kaveri plunges over 100 m into a series of wild and inaccessible gorges. At the top of the falls the river divides around the island of Sivasamudram, the Barachukki channel on the east and the Gaganchukki on the west. The hydro-electricity project was completed in 1902, the first HEP scheme of any size in India. During the wet season the falls are an impressive sight, as water cascades over a wide area in a series of leaps.

### Biligiri Rangaswamy Wildlife Sanctuary → *Altitude: 1,000-1,600 m.*

ⓘ *From Mysore, via Nanjangud (23 km) and Chamrajnagar, Nagavalli and Nellore villages. The Ghat Rd starts at the Forest Check Post after passing 2 lakes. The camp (90 km from Mysore) is beyond the second check post.*

This hilly area with moist deciduous and semi-evergreen forests interspersed with grassland, is southeast of Mysore. The best time for wildlife sighting is November to May. Soliga tribals pay special respect to an ancient champak tree (*Dodda sampige mara*) believed to be 1,000 years old. Wildlife includes panther, sloth bear (better sightings here than at other southern sanctuaries), elephant, deer, gaur and tiger (infrequent) as well as 270 species of birds.

### Bandipur National Park → *Colour map 7, grid B3. Altitude: 780-1,455 m. Area: 874 sq km.*

ⓘ *0600-0900, 1600-1800, Rs 150, still camera Rs 10, best time: Nov-Feb avoiding the hot, dry months, buses stop at the main entrance.*

Bandipur was set up by the Mysore Maharajah in 1931. It has a mixture of subtropical moist and dry deciduous forests (predominantly teak and anogeissus) and scrubland in the Nilgiri foothills. The wetter areas support rosewood, sandalwood, silk cotton and *jamun*. You should easily spot gaur, chital (spotted deer), elephant, sambar, flying squirrel and four-horned antelope, but tigers and leopards are rare. Also good variety of birdlife including crested hawk, serpent eagles and tiny-eared owls.

Private cars are not allowed. Jeeps and vans are available through Forestry Department; one-hour coach rides (morning and afternoon, 0630-1630), Rs 10 each but other noisy visitors scare away wildlife. Viewing is best from *machans* (raised platforms) near watering places; ask to reserve ahead. Dull coloured clothes are recommended. No extended elephant rides in the park now; only 30-minute 'joy rides' at 0930.

## Coorg (Kodagu)

Coorg, once a proud warrior kingdom, then a state, has now shrunk to become the smallest district in Karnataka. It is a beautiful anomaly in South India in that it has, so far, retained its original forests. Ancient rosewoods jut out of the Western Ghat hills to shade the squat coffee shrubs which the British introduced as the region's chief commodity. Like clockwork, 10 days after the rains come, these trees across whole valleys burst as one into white blossom drenching the moist air with their thick perfume, a hybrid of honeysuckle and jasmine. Although the climate is not as cool as other hill-stations, Coorg's proximity by road to the rest of Karnataka makes it a popular weekend bolt-hole for Bangaloreans. The capital of Coorg District, Madikeri, is an attractive small town in a beautiful hilly setting surrounded by the forested slopes of the Western Ghats and has become an attractive trekking destination. ➤ *For Sleeping, Eating and other listings, see pages 996-1002.*

### Ins and outs

**Getting there** Coorg is only accessible by road at present although an airport and railway station are planned. Frequent local and express buses arrive at Madikeri's bus stand from the west coast after a journey through beautiful wooded hills passing small towns and a wildlife sanctuary. From Mysore and Coimbatore an equally pleasant route traverses the Maidan. In winter there is often hill fog at night, making driving after dark dangerous.

**Getting around** Madikeri is ideal for walking though you may need to hire an auto on arrival to reach the better hotels. ➤ *See Transport, page 1002, for further details.*

## “” Like clockwork, 10 days after the rains come, rosewood trees across whole valleys burst as one into white blossom, drenching the moist air with their thick perfume, a hybrid of honeysuckle and jasmine...

### Background

Although there were references to the Kodaga people in the Tamil Sangam literature of the second century AD, the earliest Kodaga inscriptions date from the eighth century. After the Vjiayanagar Empire was defeated in 1565, many of their courtiers moved south, establishing regional kingdoms. One of these groups were the Haleri Rajas, members of the Lingayat caste whose leader Virarajendra set up the first Kodaga dynasty at Haleri, 10 km from the present district capital of Madikeri.

The later Kodagu Rajas were noted for some bizarre behaviour. Dodda Vira (1780-1809) was reputed to have put most of his relatives to death, a pattern followed by the last king, Vira Raja, before he was forced to abdicate by the British in 1834. In 1852 the last Lingayat ruler of Kodagu, Chikkavirarajendra Wodeyar, became the first Indian prince to sail to England, and the economic character of the State was quickly transformed. Coffee was introduced, becoming the staple crop of the region.

The forests of Kodagu are still home to wild elephants, who often crash into plantations on jackfruit raids, and other wildlife. The Kodaga, a tall, fair and proud landowning people who flourished under the British, are renowned for their martial prowess: almost every family has one member in the military. They also make incredibly warm and generous hosts, a characteristic you can discover thanks to the number of plantation homestays in inaccessible estates of dramatic beauty pioneered here following the crash in coffee prices. Kodagu also has a highly distinctive cuisine, in which pork curry *(pandi curry)* and rice dumplings *(kadumbuttu)* are particular favourites.

### Madikeri (Mercara)

➔ *Phone code: 08272. Colour map 7, grid B2. Population: 32,300. Altitude: 1,150 m.*

The **Omkareshwara Temple**, dedicated to both Vishnu and Siva, was built in 1820. The tiled roofs are typical of Kerala Hindu architecture, while the domes show Muslim influence. The **fort** with its three stone gateways, built between 1812-1814 by Lingarajendra Wodeyar II, is on high ground dominating the town. It has a small **museum** ⓘ *closed Mon and holidays, 0900-1700*, in St Mark's Church as well as the town prison, a temple and a chapel while the palace houses government offices. The **Rajas' Tombs** (*Gaddige*), built in 1820 to the north of the town, are the memorials of Virarajendra and his wife and of Lingarajendra. Although the rajas were Hindu, their commemorative monuments are Muslim in style; Kodagas both bury and cremate their dead. The Friday **Market** near the bus stand, is very colourful as all the local tribal people come to town to sell their produce. It is known locally as 'shandy', a British bastardization of the Coorg word *shante*, meaning simply 'market'. On Mahadevped Road, which leads to the Rajas' tombs, is a 250-year-old **Siva temple** with an interesting stone façade. Madikeri also has an attractive nine-hole golf course.

### Around Madikeri

Madikeri and the surrounding area makes for beautiful walking but if you want to venture further you'll need to take a guide as paths can soon become indistinct and confusing. **Abbi Falls** is a 30-minute rickshaw ride (9 km, Rs 150 round trip) through forests and coffee plantations. It is also an enjoyable walk along a fairly quiet road. The falls themselves are beautiful and well worth the visit. You can do a beautiful short **trek** down the valley and then up and around above the falls before rejoining the main road. Do not attempt it alone since there are no trails and you must depend on your sense of direction along forest paths. Honey Valley Estate (see page 998) has a book of walks around the guest house.

At **Bhagamandala** ⓘ *half-hourly service from Madikeri's private bus stand from 0630-2000, Rama Motors tour bus departs 0830, with 30-min stop*, 36 km southwest, the Triveni bathing ghat can be visited at the confluence of the three rivers, Kaveri, Kanike and Suiyothi. Among many small shrines the **Bhandeshwara temple**, standing in a large stone courtyard surrounded by Keralan-style buildings on all four sides, is particularly striking. You can stay at the temple for a very small charge.

**Kakkabe** ⓘ *from Madikeri to Kakkabe, bus at 0630; jeep 1 hr*, is a small town, 35 km from Madikeri, giving access to the highest peak in Coorg, **Thandiandamole** (1,800 m). Padi Iggutappa nearby is the most important temple in Coorg.

**Nisargadhama** ⓘ *0900-1800, Rs 150, still camera Rs 10*, is a small island reserve in the Kaveri River, 2 km from Kushalnagar, accessed over a hanging bridge. Completely untouched by tourism, it consists mostly of bamboo thickets and trees, including sandalwood, and is very good for seeing parakeets, bee eaters, woodpeckers and a variety of butterflies. There is a deer park, pedalo boating, a resident elephant and tall bamboo tree houses for wildlife viewing.

## Nagarhole (Rajiv Gandhi) National Park → *Colour map 7, grid B2.*

ⓘ *Main entrance is near Hunsur on the northern side of the Park. Buses run between Hunsur and Kote-Hand Post (35 km). Indians Rs 15, foreigners Rs 150, camera Rs 10. The southern entrance is 5 km from Kabini River Lodge at Karapur.*

Nagarhole – meaning snake-streams – was once the Maharajas' reserved forest and became a national park in 1955. Covering gentle hills bordering Kerala, it includes swampland, streams, moist deciduous forest, stands of bamboo and valuable timber in teak and rosewood trees. The Kabini River, which is a tributary of the Kaveri, flows

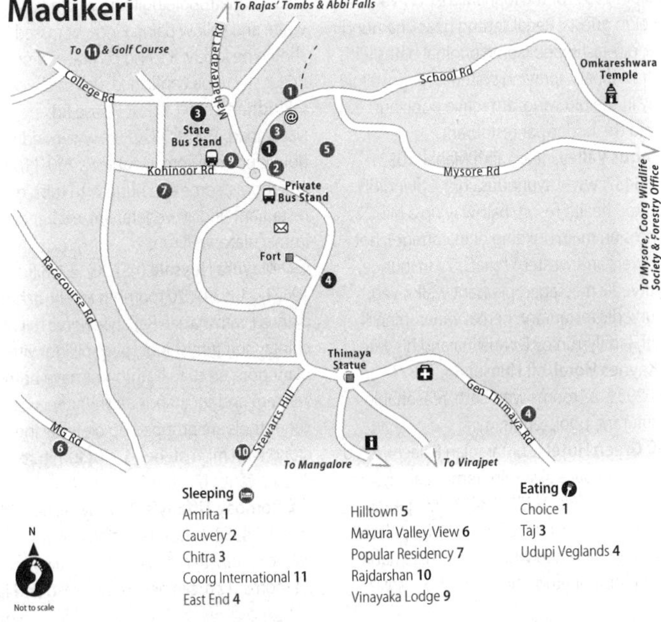

through the forest where the upper canopy reaches 30 m. The park is accessible both by road and river. A number of tribesmen, particularly Kurumbas (honey-gatherers) who still practise ancient skills, live amongst, and care for, the elephants.

In addition to elephants, the park also has gaur (Indian bison), dhole (Indian wild dogs), wild cats, four-horned antelopes, flying squirrels, sloth bears, monkeys and sambar deer ("better sightings than at Mudumalai"). Tigers and leopards are sighted very rarely. Many varieties of birds include the rare Malabar trogon, great black woodpecker, Indian pitta, pied hornbill, whistling thrush and green imperial pigeon, also waterfowl and reptiles.

The edge of the dam between March to June during the dry period, makes viewing easier. Jeeps, vans and guides are available through the Forest Department; one-hour tour at 1715 with viewing from *machans* near waterholes. Trekking is possible with permission (enquire at Hunsur office, T08222-252041 well in advance). You can also visit the Government's Elephant Training Camp at Haballa. Organized one-hour tours are available on 15 and 26 seater coaches – not very suitable for the purpose. Four-seater jeeps are far quieter.

## Sleeping

**Mysore** *p986, maps p986 and p988*

May is the most important wedding month and so hotels get booked in advance. In the expensive hotels sales tax on food, luxury tax on rooms and a service charge can increase the bill significantly. The Gandhi Square area has some Indian-style hotels which are clean and good value. JLB Rd is Jhansi Lakshmi Bai Rd, B-N Rd is Bangalore-Nilgiri Rd.

**LL-A Lalith Mahal Palace** (ITDC), Narasipur Rd, Siddartha Nagar T0821-2247047. 54 rooms (**A**), suites (US$230-740) in the palace built in 1931 for the Maharaja's non-veg, foreign guests. Regal setting near Chamundi Hill, old-fashioned (some original baths with extraordinary spraying system), for nostalgia stay in the old wing, attractive pool, but avoid the under-par restaurant.

**B Indus Valley**, near Lalith Mahal, T0821-2473437, www.ayurindus.com. Splendidly located health resort, half-way up a hill, 22 rooms (in main building or in cottage), hot showers and western toilets, TV in lounge, ayurvedic massages, pleasant walks, veg, ayurvedic restaurant, herbal wines, friendly staff, family-run by Dr Krishna and his wife.

**B Kaynes Hotel**, off Hunsur Rd, T0821-2402931. 22 rooms with bath, reasonable restaurant, pool, tennis, gym.

**B-C Green Hotel** (Chittaranjan Palace), 2270 Vinoba Rd, Jayalakshmipuram (near Mysore University), T0821-2512536, www.greenhotelindia.com. Princess's beautiful palace lovingly converted with strong sustainable development ethos: hot water from solar panels, profits going to charity and staff recruited from less advantaged groups. The best of the 31 rooms are in the palace but if you stay in the cheaper, newer block you can still loll about in the huge upper lounges: excellent library, chess tables and day beds. Unique, but beyond walking distance from Mysore centre.

**B-C Metropole**, 5 JLB Rd, T0821-2520681 www.junglelodges.com. After languishing in disrepair for years, the Karnataka government has resuscitated the glorious colonial Metropole building with a lick of white and yellow paint. Fingers crossed it should be lovely: it's also central and pristine. Prices still to be confirmed. Call to check.

**C Siddharta**, 73/1 Guest House Rd, Nazarabad, T0821-2522888, www.siddhartahotel@hotmail.com. Double Rs 760-1160. 105 rooms, some a/c, huge with tubs, good restaurant (Indian vegetarian), exchange, immaculate, well run.

**C-D Mayura Hoysala** (KSTDC), 2 JLB Rd, T0821-2425349. 20 rooms in lovely, ochre-painted, ramshackle Raj-style hotel: full of chintzy soft furnishings, overspilling with plant pots, en suite bathrooms have both western and squat loos, tiny whitewashed cane stools are propped up on terracing along with mismatched 1970s furniture. 3 restaurants, bar, tourist desk.

**C-E Bombay Tiffany's**, 313 Sayyaji Rao Rd, T0821-2435255, bombaytiffanys@yahoo.co.in. Affable owner in hotel with 54 rooms, 12 a/c in new hotel, clean and in

mint condition, if a little plasticky and gilt. The regular rooms are spartan, but the de luxe and a/c ones are very good value.
**D Hotel Ritz**, Bangalore-Nilgiri Rd near Central Bus Station, T0821-2422668, hotelritz@rediff mail.com. Bags of character in this 60-year-old house and garden set back from the busy road: 4 rooms with wood furniture off cool communal area with TV, dining table and chairs. Pleasant open shaded courtyard: a legendary budget options of backpacker folklore so book ahead.
**D-E Mysore Dasaprakash**, Gandhi Sq, T0821-2443456, www.hoteldasaprakash@ sancharnet.in. Holds 144 rooms in its labyrinthine blue-white complex set around an attractive, large courtyard. Milk coffee-coloured rooms are stocked with wood furniture and scrupulously clean white sheets. Peaceful and quiet despite being slap bang in the centre.
**F Greens' Boarding and Lodging**, 2722/2 Curzon Park Rd, T0821-2422415. Dark hallways give onto these green gloss-painted rooms with dark wood furniture. Cool, spacious, central and darn cheap, but bathrooms are not the best.
**F Park Lane**, 2720 Sri Harsha Rd, T0821-2430400, parklanemysore@ yahoo.com. 8 quirky, higgledy-piggledy rooms packed with shelving units, shared corridor/terrace area with wicker chairs. The noise, including nightly classical Indian performances, from popular downstairs restaurant does travel – chucking out is not till 2330. Restaurant 1030-2330.

**Srirangapatnam** *p991, map p990*
**C Fort View Resort**, T08236-252777. 12 upmarket rooms (4 with corner tub!), Rajasthani architecture, huge beds, shady landscaped gardens, gloomy restaurant (pricey), organic kitchen garden, pool, boating, fishing, efficient.
**D Mayura River View**, Mysore Rd, T08236-252114. Beautifully situated on the river (has crocs!), 8 comfortable rooms with sit-outs, 2 a/c, good vegetarian restaurant (Indian, Chinese), most relaxing, really quiet.
**D-E Balaji Garden Resort**, Mysore Rd (1 km from Piriyapatna Bridge), T08236-253297. 12 good value cottages and 28 smallish rooms built with some style around a central courtyard, well furnished, tiled and comfy, cottages are good value, pool, restaurant.
**F PWD Rest House**, charming former residence of George Harris. Basic rooms (Rs 50), but clean and quiet. Book ahead at PWD office near Ranganathaswami Temple, T08236-252051.

**Biligiri Rangaswamy Wildlife Sanctuary** *p993*
**B K Gudi Camp**, Kyathadevara. 8 twin-bedded quality tents with modern toilets, simple meals in the open air or 4 4-bedded rooms at the royal hunting lodge, elephant ride, birding, trekking, comfortable experience despite remoteness, contact **Jungle Lodges**, T080-25597025, www.junglelodges.com.

**Bandipur National Park** *p993*
Reserve rooms in advance; avoid weekends.
**L Bush Betta Wildlife Resort**, 5 km from entrance. 2 dirty jungle huts, lack staff, highly overpriced (foreigners pay double, US$200).
**B-C Tusker Trails**, Mangla Village, 3 km from Bandipur campus. 6 rustic cottages with verandahs around pool with good views, bamboo hut on stilts, nearby 'dam' attracts wildlife, includes meals, entry and park rides. Foreigners pay double.
**D Jungle Trails**, outside the park. A small guest house owned by wildlife enthusiast, simple meals, wildlife viewing from netted porch and *machans* on riverside.
**E Mayura Prakruti** (KSTDC), at Melkamanahalli nearby, T08229-233001. Simple rooms in cottages (Rs 400) and restaurant under shady trees.
**F Venuvihar Lodge**, in beautiful Gopalaswamy Hills (20 km). Meals available but take provisions. Book in advance through Forest Department, Woodyard, Mysore, T0821-2480110.

**Madikeri** *p994, map p995*
Power cuts are common. Carry a torch, keep candles handy. Book early during holidays.
**B Coorg International**, Convent Rd, T08272-228071. 27 large, comfortable rooms, poor restaurant, pool, tours, trekking, overpriced.

*For an explanation of the sleeping and eating price codes used in this guide, see inside the front cover. Other relevant information is found in Essentials pages 56-61.*

**C Capitol Village**, 5 km from town. 13 large, airy rooms, dorm (Rs 150), traditional Keralan building (tiled roof, wooden beams) set in a coffee, cardamom and pepper estate, very quiet, outdoor eating under shady trees (Rs 75-150), rickshaw from centre Rs 40. Book 10 days in advance through **Hotel Cauvery**.

**C-D Rajdarshan**,116/2 MG Rd, T08272-229142, hrdij@vsnl.net. 25 well laid-out, clean rooms (need renovating), excellent restaurant, friendly staff, modern, with views over town.

**D-E Cauvery**, School Rd, T08272-225492. 26 clean, pleasant but basic rooms with fans, Indian meals, bar, away from main road. Helpful management, information on trekking (stores luggage).

**D-E Hilltown**, Daswal Rd, T08272-223801, hilltown@rediffmail.com. 38 modern, pleasant and airy rooms with TV in new hotel, marble-floored throughout, restaurant, great value. Highly recommended.

**D-E Popular Residency**, Kohinoor Rd. 10 clean and pleasant rooms in new hotel, well fitted out, North Indian vegetarian restaurant, good value.

**E Amrita**, T08272-223607. Resembling something out of a Spanish soap opera, clean rooms with bath, restaurant and eager to please staff.

**E Chitra**, School Rd, near bus stand, T08272-225372. 31 non descript rooms with western toilets, hot shower, simple but clean, North Indian vegetarian restaurant, bar, helpful and knowledgeable English-speaking trekking guide (Mr Muktar).

**E East End**, Gen Thimaya Rd, T08272-229996. Darkish rooms but good restaurant, serves excellent *dosas*.

**E Mayura Valley View** (KSTDC), Raja's Seat, T08272-228387. Perched on clifftop, outstanding views over town particularly at sunset and across rolling forests, 25 rooms but sadly very run down and semi-deserted, book direct or at Karnataka Tourism, Bangalore, T080-22212901.

**E-F Vinayaka Lodge**, 25 m from bus stand, T08272-229830. 50 rooms with bath, hot water buckets, friendly staff, clean and quiet (bus stand can be noisy early morning), good value.

### Around Madikeri *p994*

**D-E Cauvery Nisargadhama**, Nisargadhama, contact Forestry Office, Madikeri, T08272-26308. 8 simple cottages, built largely of bamboo/teak, some with balconies on stilts over the water, electricity (no fan), hot water, peaceful (despite nocturnal rats), but poor food.

**D-E Palace Estate**, 2 km south of Kakkabe along Palace Rd, T08272-238446 (rickshaw from Kakkabe Rs 35). A small, traditional farm growing coffee, pepper, cardamom and bananas lying just above the late 18th-century Nalnad Palace, a summer hunting lodge of the kings of Coorg. It is isolated: 6, basic rooms with shared veranda looking across 180 degrees of forested hills all the way to Madikeri, an excellent base for walking – Coorg's highest peak is 6 km from the homestay. Home-cooked local food, English-speaking guide Rs 150.

**D-F Honey Valley Estate**, Yavakapadi, Kakkabe, 3 km up a track only a jeep can manage, T08272- 38339, honeyvalley_2001@yahoo.com. Has less stunning views than the Palace Estate (the house is blocked in by tall trees) but equally good access by foot to trekking trails. Facilities are mostly better and it can fit over 30 guests, charming host family too. Also has a hut 2 km into the forest for those wanting more isolation.

### Nagarhole *p995*

From Sep-Jun:

**AL-A Kabini River Lodges** (Karnataka Tourism), at Karapur on reservoir bank. 14 rooms in Mysore Maharajas' 18th-century hunting lodge and bungalow, 6 newer cabins overlooking lake, 5 tents, simple but acceptable, good restaurant, bar, exchange, package includes meals, sailing, rides in buffalo-hide coracles on the Kaveri, jeep/minibus at Nagarhole and Murkal complex, park tour with naturalist, very friendly and well run. Foreigners pay double. Reservations: **Jungle Lodges**, T080-25597025, www.junglelodges.com, or **Clipper Holidays**, T080-25592043, clipper@bangalore.wipro.net.in.

**AL-A Waterwoods**, 500 m away, surrounded by the Kabini river, T08228-244421. 6 luxury rooms with sit-outs in a ranch-style house, exquisitely furnished, beautiful gardens on water's edge, delicious home-cooking, environmentally conscious (solar power), friendly staff, boating, jeep, ayurvedic massage, gym, swimming, walking, charming, informal atmosphere, peaceful, secluded. Highly recommended.

**A Jungle Inn**, Veeranahosahalli, T08222-246022. 7 well-appointed rooms and 3 dorms, in colonial-style lodges, varied meals, boating, elephant rides. Contact through **Hammock Leisure Holidays**, Bangalore, T080-25307963. Forest Dept Rest Houses in the Park:

**B Gangotri**, book at least 15 days in advance on T0821-2480901. 3 rooms with bath, simple but comfortable, dorm beds (Rs 40), services of cook.

## Eating

**Mysore** *p986, maps p986 and p988*

**TTT Green**, excellent food served in the palace itself, under a veranda, or, best of all, under the stars at tables spaced far apart in the hotel's immaculate garden. One of the finest eateries in Mysore.

**TTT Ramanashree Comfort's Om Shanti**, in hotel. Pure vegetarian either with/without a/c, thronged with domestic tourists a fair reflection of its culinary prowess.

**TT King's Court** hotel, MG Sq, Mysore Memories and outdoor Raintree BBQ restaurants are popular.

**TT Park Lane** hotel. Red lights hang from the creeper-covered trellis over this courtyard restaurant: turn them on for service. Excellent classical music played every evening 1900-2130, good food, including BBQ nights. Popular, lively, and totally idiosyncratic.

**TT Shanghai**, Vinoba Rd. Superb Chinese despite shabby interior. 1100-1500, 1830-2300.

**TT Shilpashri**, Gandhi Sq. Comfortable rooftop, reasonably priced, tourist orientated, chilled beers, friendly but service can be slow.

**TT Siddharta** hotel, great South Indian but in crowded non-a/c room facing parking lot.

**T Amaravathi** (Roopa's), Hardinge Circle. Excellent, spicy hot Andhra meals on banana leaves.

**T Dasaprakash Hotel**, good breakfast, huge southern *thali* (Rs 25).

**T Ganesh** opposite central bus stand. Great *dosas*, sweets.

**T Jewel Rock**, Maurya Palace, Sri Harsha Rd. Dark interior, great chicken tikka, spicy cashew nut chicken, go early to avoid queueing.

**T Mylari**, Hotel Mahadeshwara, Nazarbad Main Rd (ask rickshaw driver). The best *dosas* in town served on a palm leaf, mornings until 1100, basic surroundings, may have to queue. Biriyanis also legendary.

**T RRR**, Gandhi Sq. Part a/c, tasty non-vegetarian on plantain leaves, good for lunch.

**T SR Plantain Leaf** (Chalukya's), Rajkamal Talkies Rd. Decent vegetarian *thalis* on banana leaf; also tandoori chicken.

**T Samrat**, next to Indra Bhavan, Dhanvantri Rd. Range of tasty North Indian vegetarian.

**T Santosh**, near bus station. Excellent value *thalis* (Rs 16).

### Cafés and fast food

**Bombay Tiffany's**, Devraja Market Building. Try the *Mysore Pak*, a ghee-laden sweet.

**Indra Café**, Sayaji Rd, on the fringes of the market. Excellent *bhel puri, sev puri, channa puri.*

**Penguin Ice-cream Parlour**, comfortable sofas shared with local teens listening to Hindi pop.

**Raghu Niwas**, B-N Rd, opposite **Ritz**. Does very good breakfasts.

**Sri Rama Veg**, 397 Dhanvantri Rd. Serves fast food, good juices.

**Madikeri** *p994, map p995*

**Capitol**, near private bus stand. Despite its exterior, serves excellent veg meals and snacks.

**Choice**, School Rd. Wide menu, very good food, choice of ground floor or rooftop.

**Taj**, College Rd. 'Cheap and best', clean and friendly.

**Udupi Veglands**, opposite fort. Lovely, clean, spacious wooden eatery, delicious and cheap vegetarian *thalis*.

## Bars and clubs

**Mysore** *p986, maps p986 and p988*

The best bars are in hotels: **Lalitha Mahal Palace** and **Lokranjan Mahal Palace**.

## Festivals and events

**Mysore** *p986, maps p986 and p988*

**Mar-Apr**: **Temple car festival** with a 15-day fair, at the picturesque town of Nanjangud, 23 km south (Erode road); **Vairamudi** festival which lasts 6 days when deities are adorned with 3 diamond crowns, at Melkote Temple, 52 km. **11 Aug**: **Feast of St Philomena**, 0800-1800, the statue of the saint is taken out in procession through the city streets ending with a service at the gothic, stained glass-laden cathedral. **End Sep-early-Oct**: **Dasara**, see box overpage.

## Medieval pageantry at Mysore

**Dasara** is celebrated with medieval pageantry for 10 days. Although the Dasara festival can be traced back to the Puranas and is widely observed across India, in the South it achieved its special prominence under the Vijayanagar kings. As the Mahanavami festival it has been celebrated every year since it was sponsored by Raja Wodeyar in September 1610 at Srirangapatnam. It symbolizes the victory of goddess Chamundeswari (Durga) over the demon Mahishasura. Today the festival is still enormously colourful. On the last day a colourfully bedecked elephant with a golden howdah carrying the statue of the goddess, processes from the palace through the city to Banni Mantap, about 5 km away, where the Banni tree is worshipped. The temple float festival takes place at a tank at the foot of Chamundi Hill and a car festival on top. In the evening there is a torchlight parade by the mounted guards who provide an exciting display of horse-manship and the night ends with a display of fireworks. A good time for cultural programmes particularly at the Palace Durbar Hall and Exhibition Grounds which along with other public buildings, are ablaze with illuminations.

## Shopping

**Mysore** *p986, maps p986 and p988*

**Books**

**Ashok**, Dhanvantri Rd, T0821-2435533. Excellent selection.

**Clothing**

**Badshah's**, 20 Devraj Urs Rd, T0821- 2429799. Beautifully finished salwar kameez, Mr Yasin speaks good English.

**Craft Emporium**, and cloth shops in the middle part of Vinoba Rd are recommended for good selection and good quality but beware those pretending to be government emporia. Competent tailors will make up and deliver within a couple of hours.

For silks at reasonable prices, try Sayaji Rao Rd. You can watch machine weaving at **Karnataka Silk Industry's** factory shop on Mananthody Rd, T0821-2481803. 1030-1200, 1500-1630, Mon-Sat.

**Handicrafts**

Superb carved figures, sandalwood and rosewood items, silks, incense sticks, handicrafts. The main shopping area is Sayaji Rao Rd.

**Cauvery Arts & Crafts Emporium**, for sandalwood and rosewood items, 1000-1330, 1500-1930, closed Thu (non-receipt of parcel reported by traveller).

**Devaraja Market**, lanes of stalls selling spices, perfumes and much more; good "antique" shop (fixed price) has excellent sandalwood and rosewood items. Worth visiting.

**Ganesh**, 532 Dhanvantri Rd.

**Shankar**, 12 Dhanvantri Rd.

**Sri Lakshmi Fine Arts & Crafts** (opposite the zoo) also has a factory shop at 2226 Sawday Rd, Mandi Mohalla.

## Activities and tours

**Mysore** *p986, maps p986 and p988*

**Horse racing**

A opportunity for lots of local fun.

**Swimming**

**Mysore University**, Olympic-sized swimming pool, hourly sessions 0630 until 0830 then 1500-1600, ladies only 1600-1700.

**Southern Star Mysore**, 13-14 Vinoba Rd, T0821-2421689, ushashriramhotels.com. More of a sunbathing swimming pool.

**Tours**

**KSTDC**, Yatri Nivas, 2 JLB Rd, T0821-2423492. Mysore, daily 0715-2030, Rs115, local sights and Chamundi Hill, Kukkara Halli Lake, Somanathapura, Srirangapatnam and Brindavan Gardens. **Belur, Halebid, Sravanabelagola**: Tue, Wed, Fri, Sun, 0715-2200, Rs 210 (long and tiring but worth it if you are not travelling to Hassan).

### Tour operators

**Seagull Travels**, 8 Hotel Ramanashree Complex, BN Rd, T0821-2529732, Seagulltravels@yahoo.com. Good for cars/drivers, flights, wildlife tours etc, helpful.
**Skyway International Travels**, No. 370/4, Jansi Laxmibai Rd, T0821-2444444, www.skywaytour.com.
**TCI**, Gandhi Sq, T0821-2443023. Very pleasant and helpful.

### Yoga

**Jois' Ashtanga Yoga Research Institute**, is not for dilettante yogis: it costs Rs 8,000 a month and you can't sign up for lesser stints. Go to www.ayri.org for more information.
**Sri Patanjala Yogashala**, Parakala Mutt, next to Jaganmohan Palace. Ashtanga Vinyasa yoga; daily instruction in English from BNS Iyengar, 0600-0900, 1600-1900, US$100 per month: some say the conditions here are slapdash, although teaching is good.

### Madikeri *p994, map p995*

### Fishing

**Coorg Wildlife Society**, see page 1002, can arrange a licence for fishing on the Kaveri river (Rs 500 per day, Rs 1000 weekend). The highlight is the prospect of pulling in a mahseer which can grow up to 45 kg in weight; all fish must be returned to the river. This is at Trust Land Estate, Valnoor, near Kushalnagar, where there is a lodge but you'll need to carry food. Mr Ponappa has the keys to the lodge and can also issue the licence. Contact Professor MB Madaiah, T0827-6 76443.

### Trekking

**Friends' Tours and Travel**, below Bank of India, College Rd. Recommended for their knowledge and enthusiasm.They do tailor-made treks at about Rs 275 per person per day including guide, food and accomm-odation in temples, schools, huts etc. They have a 'base camp' at Thalathmane, 4 km from Madikeri, which people can also stay at even if not trekking. Has basic huts and blankets for Rs 50 each, home cooking from nearby at little extra cost. Contact Mr Raja Shekar on T08272-29974, T08272-29102 (1000-1930) or T08272-25672 (2100-0900).
**Hotel Cauvery**, see page 998, will also arrange treks.

## Transport

### Mysore *p986, maps p986 and p988*

### Bus

**Local** City bus station, southeast of KR Circle, T0821-2425819. To Silk Weaving Centre, Nos 1, 2, 4 and 8; Brindavan Gardens, No 303; Chamundi Hill, No 201; Srirangapatnam, No 313. Central Bus Station, T0821-2529853. Bandipur, Platform 9, Ooty etc, Platform 11.
**Long distance** There are 3 bus stations: **Central**, mainly for long distance SRTC, T0821-2520853, City for local buses, and B3 Suburban and Private including Somnathpur. SRTC buses of Karnataka, Tamil Nadu and Kerala run regular daily services between Mysore and other major cities. Check timings. Many private companies near Gandhi Sq operate overnight sleepers and interstate buses which may be faster and marginally less uncomfortable. Book ahead for busy routes (eg Hassan). The bus station has a list of buses with reserved places.
**Somnathpur**: few from Surburban station, 1 hr direct, or longer via Bannur or via Narasipur. Several buses daily to many towns from Central bus station. **Bangalore**: every ¼ hr, from non-stop platform. Semi-de luxe, every ¼ hr. **Coimbatore**: 0845; **Hospet**: 1930 (10 hrs), very tiring; **Salem**: 1030 (7 hrs); **Thiruvananthapuram**: Super-de luxe, 14 hrs. Several to **Satyamangalam** where you can connect with buses to Tamil Nadu. The journey is through wilderness and forests with spectacular scenery as the road finally plunges from the plateau down to the plains.

### Car

Travel companies and KSTDC, about Rs 500 (4 hrs/40 km) for city sightseeing; Rs 850 to include Srirangapatnam and Brindavan. KSE charges Rs 700 for Somnathpur, Srirangapatnam and Bird Sanctuary.

### Train

Advance Computerized Reservations in separate section; ask for foreigners' counter. T131. Enquiries T0821-2520103, 0800-2000 (closed 1330-1400); Sun 0800-1400. Left luggage 0600-2200, Rs 3-Rs 6 per day. Tourist Information, telephone and toilets on Platform 1. Taxi counter at entrance. To **Bangalore** (non-stop): *Tipu Exp, 6205*, 1120,

2½ hrs; *Shatabdi Exp, 2008*, daily except Tue, 1410, 2 hrs (continues to **Chennai** another 5 hrs). **Bangalore** via **Srirangapatnam**, **Mandya** and **Maddur**: *Chamundi Exp 6215*, 0645, 3 hrs; *Kaveri Chennai Exp 6221*, 1805, 2¾ hrs. **Chennai**: *Chennai Exp 6221*, 1805, 10½ hrs; *Shatabdi Exp, 2008*, not Tue, 1410, 7 hrs. **Madurai**: change at Bangalore. **Mumbai**: *Sharavathi Exp, 1036*, Sat only, 0600, 26 hrs.

**Srirangapatnam** *p991, map p990*
Trains and buses between **Bangalore** and **Mysore** stop here but arrival can be tiresome with hassle from rickshaw drivers, traders and beggars. Buses 313 and 316 from Mysore City Bus Stand (half-hourly) take 50 mins.

**Bandipur National Park** *p993*
**Bus**
Bandipur is in Karnataka while the neighbouring park, Mudumalai, is in Tamil Nadu, but they are extensions of the same forest reserve which also stretches west to include the undeveloped Kerala reserve of Waynad. They are on the Mysore to Ooty bus route, about 2½ hrs south from Mysore and 2½ hrs from Ooty. Buses go to and from **Mysore** (80 km) between 0615-1530.

**Madikeri** *p994, map p995*
**Auto-rickshaw**
From **Hotel Chitra** to **Abbi Falls**, Rs 150 including 1 hr wait there.

**Bus**
Frequent express buses to **Bangalore** Plat 4, from 0615 (6 hrs); **Chikmagalur**; **Hassan** (3½ hrs); **Kannur**; **Mangalore**, Plat 2, 0530-2400 (3½ hrs); **Mysore** Plat 3, half-hourly 0600-2300 (3 hrs) via **Kushalnagar** (for Tibetan settlements) are very crowded during the rush hour; **Thalassery**. Daily to **Coimbatore**, **Kannur**, **Madurai** 1900, **Mumbai** 0930, **Ooty** 0730, 2030, **Virajpet**. **Private Bus Stand**: Kamadenu Travels above Bus Stand, T27024, for Purnima Travels bus to **Bangalore**. Shakti Motor Service to **Nagarhole** (4½ hrs); **Virajpet** .

**Nisargadhama** *p995*
The bus from Madikeri passes park gates 2 km before Kushalnagar. A rickshaw from Kushalnagar Rs 10.

**Nagarhole** *p995*
**Bus**
From **Mysore**, *Exp*, 3 hrs, Rs 35; **Madikeri**, 4½ hrs. **Bangalore**, 6 hrs. For **Kabini River Lodge** and **Waterworlds**, be sure to get the Karapur (not the Nagarhole) bus; Jungle lodges bus leaves Bangalore at 0730, stops in Mysore (around 0930), reaching Kabini around 1230; return bus departs 1315. State bus from Mysore to Karapur.

**Train**
Nearest, Mysore (96 km). See **Bandipur**, page 993.

## Directory

**Mysore** *p986, maps p986 and p988*
**Banks** State Bank of Mysore, corner of Sayaji Rao Rd and Sardar Patel Rd. and opposite GPO in city centre. LKP Forex, near Clock Tower. **Internet** Mysore I-Way, has a branch near Green Hotel and the Jois' yoga shala at 2996/1A ist Floor Kalidasa Road VV Mohalla T0821-2510467. Coca Cola Cyber Space, 2 Madvesha Complex, Nazarabad, near Sri Harsha Rd. Cyber Net Corner, 2/3B Indira Bhavan, Dhanvantri Rd. Pal Net, Nehru Circle. Avoid Internet World near Ritz. **Hospitals** Hospitals: Medical College, corner of Irwin and Sayaji Rao Rd. KR Hospital, T0821-2443300; Mission Hospital (Mary Holdsworth), Tilaknagar, in a striking building dating from 1906. **Post** GPO, on corner of Ashoka and Irwin rds; Poste Restante here. **Useful addresses** Forest Office, and Project Tiger, Forest Department, Woodyard, Ashokpuram, T0821-480110 (City Bus No 61).

**Madikeri** *p994, map p995*
**Banks** Canara Bank, Main Rd, accepts some TCs and Visa. **Internet** Cyber Zone, next to Chitra Hotel. Rs 30 per hr, excellent. **Post** Behind Private Bus Stand. **Useful addresses** Community Centre, south of Fort, Main Rd, holds occasional shows. Coorg Wildlife Society, 2 km from GT Circle along Mysore Rd, then 1 km to left, T08272-223505. Forestry Office, Aranya Bhavan, Mysore Rd, 3 km from town, T08272-225708.

# The west coast

*Poor transport made the route up the Karnataka's 'sapphire coast' to Goa one of the least travelled scenic routes in India. This is now changing and the state government is busily trying to draw tourists to their sands. The Western Ghats are never far away, while the road and the Konkan railway frequently skirt the Arabian Sea in the north passing some magnificent beaches. The hilly port town of Mangalore makes a pleasant, relaxing stop between Goa and Kerala; but the jewel in the Sapphire Coast's crown, thus far, is undoubtedly Gokarna – literally 'cow's ear' – a hippy stronghold, mass pilgrimage site and tremendously sacred Hindu centre. It's little more than one narrow street, lined with traditional wooden houses and temples, but it is packed with pilgrims and has been adopted, along with Hampi, by the Goa overspill – people lured by spirituality and the beautiful, auspicious-shaped Om beach. Days, however, are very much numbered for those still drawn to no-frills beachfront huts and hammocks costing 20 rupees a night: the snazzy, eco-conscious Keralite hotel group CGH Earth have just bought up 50 acres of the beach to turn it into a boutique yoga hotel.* » *For Sleeping, Eating and other listings, see pages 1008-1010.*

## Mangalore → *Phone code: 0824. Colour map 7, grid A2. Population: 328,700.*

Capital of South Kanara District, and rarely visited by Western tourists, Mangalore does in fact offer some interesting churches and decent accommodation and so is worth bearing in mind, if only as as a stopping point. Once a ship building centre (during Hyder Ali's time) it is now a major port for export of coffee spices and cashew nuts.

### Ins and outs

**Getting there** Bajpe airport is 22 km from town. The Konkan railway has trains from Goa and Mumbai while the old broad gauge goes down the coast to Kozhikode and then inland to Coimbatore. The new Kankanadi station is 6 km northeast of the City station which is just south of the centre at Hampankatta. The KSRTC Bus Station is 3 km north of the private bus stand in the busy town centre.

**Getting around** Although the centre is compact enough to be covered on foot, autos are handy but may refuse to use their meters. » *See Transport, page 1009, for further details.*

**Tourist information** Office at ⓘ *Hotel Nalapauds, Lighthouse Rd, Hampankatta, T0824-2442926*. Helpful, friendly, if limited, tourist information.

### Sights

**St Aloysius College Chapel** ⓘ *Lighthouse Hill, 0830-1000, 1200-1430, 1530-1800*, has remarkable 19th-century frescoes painted by the Italian-trained Jesuit priest Moscheni, which cover the walls and ceilings in a profusion of scenes. The town has a sizeable Roman Catholic population (about 20%).

The tile-roofed low structure of the 10th-century **Mangaladevi Temple** is named after a Malabar Princess, Mangala Devi, who may have given her name to Mangalore. The 11th-century **Sri Manjunatha Temple** (with the Kadri Caves), 3 km from the centre – a cycle rickshaw ride away – has a rough lingam; its central image is a bronze Lokeshwara (968 AD). **Shremmanti Bai Memorial Museum** ⓘ *0900-1700, free*, has a collection including archaeology, ethnology, porcelain and wood carvings. **Mahatma Gandhi Museum** ⓘ *Canara High School, closed Sun and holidays, 0930-1230, 1400-1730, free*, includes zoology, anthropology, sculpture, art and manuscripts.

There are also lakes which have water with medicinal properties, and the Old Lighthouse dating from the 18th century. It is generally believed to have been built by

 Haider Ali, who built a naval dockyard in Mangalore. You can take a trip out to the sand bar at the river mouth to watch fascinating boat building and river traffic on the Netravathi River.

## Excursions

The forested hills of the Western Ghats are home to some wonderful examples of Jain and Hindu sculpture and architecture. The temples are often centres of

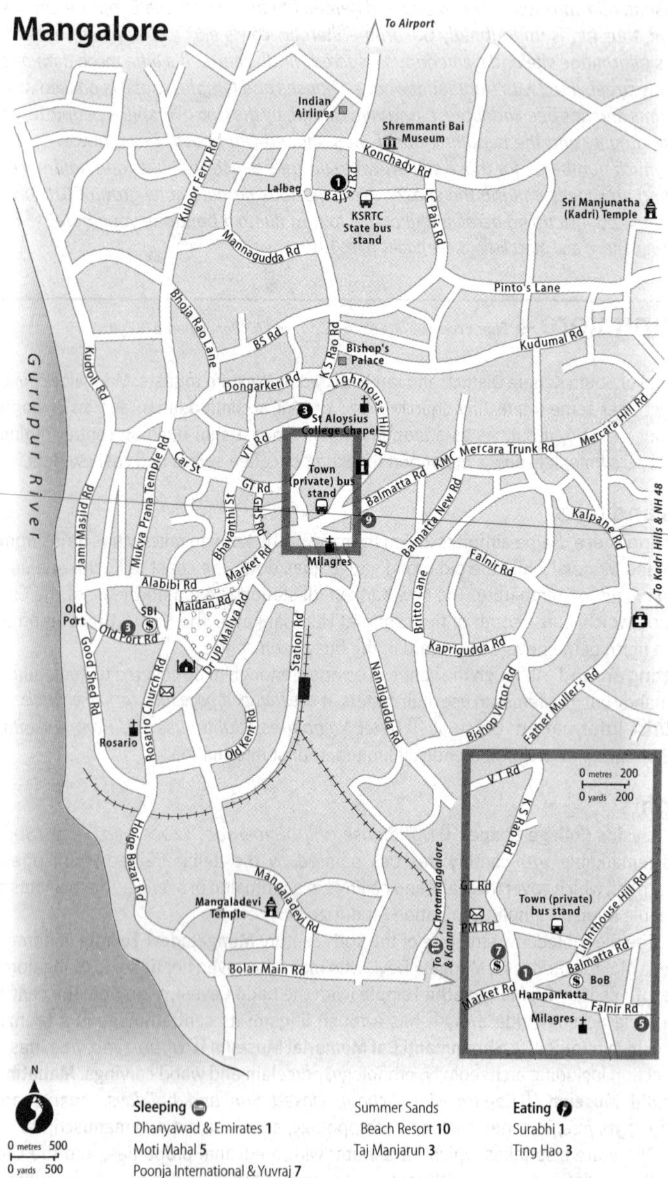

### Udupi – home of 'Brahmin meals ready'

The name of Udupi is associated across South India with authentic Brahmin cooking – which means vegetarian food at its best. But what is authentic Udupi cuisine? Pamela Philipose, writing in the *Indian Express*, suggests that strictly it is food prepared for temple use by Shivali Brahmins at the Krishna temple. It is therefore not only wholly vegetarian, but it also never uses onions or garlic.

Pumpkins and gourds are the essential ingredients, while sambar, which must also contain ground coconut and coconut oil, is its base. *Rasam*, the spicy pepper water, is compulsory, as are the ingredients jackfruit, heart-shaped colocasia leaves, raw green bananas, mango pickle, red chilli and salt. *Adyes* (dumplings) *ajadinas* (dry curries) and chutneys, including one made of the skin of the ridge gourd, are specialities. Favourite dishes are *kosambiri* with pickle, coconut chutney and *appalam*. At least two vegetables will be served, including runner beans, and rice. Sweets include *payasa* and *holige*.

pilgrimage, such as the **Subrahmanya Temple** at Sullia or the **Shaivite Temple** at Dharamashala. **Mudabidri**, the 'Jain Varanasi', has superbly carved *basti*. In Jain tradition, no two columns are alike, and many are elaborately carved with graceful figures and floral and knot patterns. **Karkala** has a giant monolithic Jain statue. The Hindu philosopher Sankaracharya was associated with the small town of **Sringeri**, near the source of the Tunga River.

## Karnataka's Sapphire Coast

→ *Colour map 7, grid A2.*

### Udupi (Udipi) and around

→ *Phone code: 0820. Population: 113,000.*

Udupi, one of Karnataka's most important pilgrimage sites, is the birthplace of the 12th-century saint Madhva, who set up eight sannyasi *maths* (monasteries) in the town, see page 1324. It is a pleasant place rarely visited by foreigners.

According to one legend the statue of Krishna once turned to give a low caste devotee *darshan*. The **Sri Krishna Math** (Car Street) in the heart of the town is set around a large tank, the *Madhva Sarovar*, into which devotees believe that the Ganga flows every 10 years. There are some attractive *math* buildings with colonnades and arches fronting the temple square, as well as huge wooden temple chariots. This Hindu temple, like many others, is of far greater religious than architectural importance, and receives a succession of highly placed political leaders. Visitors are 'blessed' by the temple elephant. In the biennial **Paraya Mahotsava,** on 17/18 January of even-numbered years, the temple management changes hands (the priest-in-charge heads each of the eight *maths* in turn). **Seven Day Festival,** 9-15 January, is marked by an extravagant opening ceremony complete with firecrackers, dancing elephants, brass band and "eccentric re-enactments of mythical scenes while towering wooden temple cars, illuminated by strip lights followed by noisy portable generators, totter around the square, pulled by dozens of pilgrims". **Sri Ananthasana Temple,** where Madhva is believed to have dematerialized while teaching his followers, is in the centre of the temple square. The eight important *maths* are around Car Street: Sode, Puthige and Adamar (south); Pejawar and Palamar (west); Krishna and Shirur (north); and Kaniyur (east). Udupi is almost as well known today as the home of a family of Kanarese Brahmins who have established a chain of coffee houses/hotels across South India.

Some 5 km inland from Udupi, **Manipal** is famous throughout Karnataka as the centre of **Yakshagana** dance drama, which like *Kathakali* in Kerala is an all night spectacle. **Rashtrakavi Govind Pai Museum** ⓘ *MGM College*, has a collection of sculpture, bronze, inscriptions and coins.

**Malpe**, 5 km west of Udupi, is one of the best port sites in southern Karnataka. Across the bay is the island of Darya Bahadurgarh and 5 km to the southwest is **St Mary's Isle**, composed of dramatic hexagonal basalt, where **Vasco da Gama** landed in 1498 and set up a cross. The fishing village at one end of the beach, and the fish market on the docks are very smelly; the beach too is used as a public toilet in places. If you are prepared for an unpleasant walk or cycle ride, you can reach a deserted sandy beach but there are no facilities so take your own food and water.

## Bhatkal → *Colour map 7, grid A1.*

One of the many bullock cart tracks that used to be the chief means of access over the Western Ghats started from Bhatkal. Now only a small town with a predominantly Muslim population, in the 16th century it was the main port of the *Vijayanagar* Empire. It also has two interesting small temples. From the north the 17th-century Jain *Chandranatha Basti* with two buildings linked by a porch, is approached first. The use of stone tiling is a particularly striking reflection of local climatic conditions, and is a feature of the Hindu temple to its south, a 17th-century Vijayanagar temple with typical animal carvings. In the old cemetery of the church is possibly the oldest British memorial in India, inscribed: "Here lyeth the body of George Wye merchant dec. XXXI March Anno Dom NRT Christi Sal Mundi MDCXXXVII, 1637".

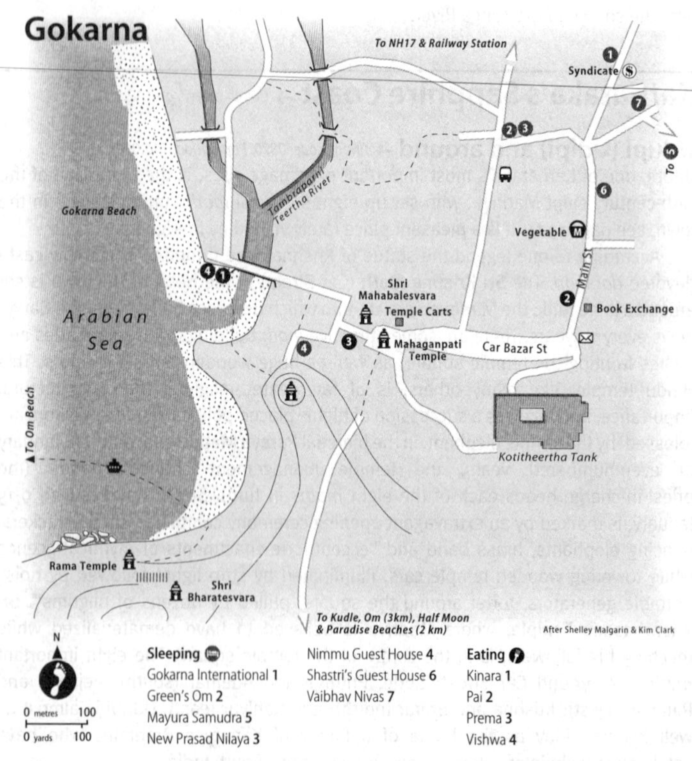

## Gokarna → *Phone code: 08386. Colour map 7, grid A1.*

The narrow streets, traditional houses and temples together with its long wide expanse of beach, have long lured backpackers moving on from Goa who search for an alternative hideaway on the five unspoilt beaches (besides Om these are Gokarna, Kudle, Half Moon and Paradise) to the south. There is a somewhat curious mix of Hindu pilgrims and castaways from the hippie era here who are tolerated rather than welcome. Visitors should respect local sensibilities and dress suitably in town. Gokarna means cow's ear and the name is possibly derived from the legend in which Shiva emerged from the ear of a cow – but also perhaps from the ear-shaped confluence of the two rivers here. Today Gokarna is also a centre of Sanskrit learning.

**Ganesh** is believed to have tricked **Ravana** into putting down the famous Atmalinga on the spot now sanctified in the **Mahabalesvara temple**. As Ravana was unable to lift the lingam up again, it is called *Mahabala* (the strong one). **Tambraparni Teertha** stream is considered a particularly sacred spot for casting the ashes of the dead.

Most travellers head for the beaches to the south. The path from town passing **Kudle** (pronounced *Koodlee*) **Beach** is well sign posted but quite rugged, especially south of the **Om Beach** (about 3 km), and should not be attempted with a full back pack during the middle of the day. Also, though parts are lit at night, stretches are isolated; single women especially should take a companion. Boats from Gokarna to Om charge around Rs 200 one-way. Om Beach can now also be reached by a motorable track which can be accessed from near Mayura Samudra hotel. It is no longer quite the secluded paradise it once was. As with Kudle, in season it can get extremely busy and the combination of too many people, shortage of fresh water and poor hygiene results in dirty beaches. **Half Moon** and **Paradise Beaches**, popular with long-stayers, can be reached by continuing to walk over the headlands and are another 2 km or so apart.

## Project Seabird, Karwar and Anjedives → *Colour map 7, grid A1.*

Karwar, on the banks of the Kalinadi River, is the administrative headquarters of North Kanara District. **Devbagh beach**, off the coast, has a deep-water naval port protected by five islands. One of these was 'Anjedive' of old, known to seafarers centuries before Vasco da Gama called at the island in 1498, and the Portuguese built a fort there. It was later used as a Goan penal colony. Since it is now under the control of the Navy it is off-limits to all foreigners. From 1638 to 1752 there was an English settlement here, surviving on the pepper trade. The Portuguese held it for the next 50 years until the old town was destroyed in 1801. Today Karwar, strung out between the port and the estuary, has an unpleasant beach. However, the beaches a little to the south rival those of Goa but are still deserted. Of interest is the hill fort, an octagonal church, and a 300-year old temple.

India's Western Naval Command, which controls the 'sword arm' of the subcontinent's powerful western fleet, has since the 1960s planned to move here from Mumbai – a principally commercial port and one that is worryingly close to Pakistani missiles – but work on the immense Project Seabird only began in October 1999. When complete (which could be as early as 2005) it will become the largest naval base this side of the Suez Canal and will hold 140 plus warships, aircraft and repair dockyards, while the hillsides will be put to use concealing submarines. Karwar, crucially, is 900 nautical miles from Karachi versus Mumbai's 580. Since the area is under the control of the Navy it is off limits to foreigners but driving past it gives a striking portrait of the subcontinent's military might and ambition.

## Sleeping

**Mangalore** *p1003, map p1004*
**A-B Taj Manjarun**, Old Port Rd, T0824-2420420, www.tajhotels.com. 101 excellent rooms with tubs ('budget' rooms perfectly adequate), some with sea/river view, restaurant, all facilities, pool (non-residents half-day Rs 200), friendly service.
**B-C Moti Mahal**, Falnir Rd, T0824-2441411, motimahal.vasnet.com. 90 a/c rooms, restaurant and bar, coffee shop, pool and poolside BBQ.
**C-D Hotel Mangalore International**, KS Rao Rd, T0824-2444860. 45 clean, well appointed rooms, 30 a/c, modern and airy, vegetarian restaurant (no alcohol), excellent service.
**C-D Poonja International**, KS Rao Rd, T0824-2440171, www.hotelpoonja international. com. 154 rooms, central a/c, wide range of facilities including exchange, spotlessly clean, excellent complimentary buffet breakfast, excellent value.
**C-D Summer Sands Beach Resort**, Ullal Beach, 10 km south, T0824-2467690, summer@ satyam.net.in. 85 rooms, 30 a/c, in simple but comfortable bungalows in the local style, superb Konkani meals, bar, good pool, ayurvedic treatments, yoga lessons, local trips arranged.
**D-E Dhanyawad**, Hampankatta Circle, T0824-2440066. 44 spacious rooms, good value, convenient (open late).
**F Adarsh Lodge**, Market Rd, T0824-2440878. 60 basic rooms, some with TV, well kept and friendly, excellent service, good value.
**F Surya**, Greens Compound, Balmatta Rd, T0824-2425736. 18 rooms with bath, excellent vegetarian restaurant, internet (Rs 30) with good connection, set back from road, uninspiring exterior but worth considering for tranquility.

**Udupi and around** *p1005*
**B-C Valley View International**, on campus, Manipal. Has 70 good a/c rooms with upmarket facilities, pool. Recommended.
**C-D Srirama Residency**, opposite Post Office, Udupi, T0820-2530761. 30 very nice rooms in top-quality new hotel, bar and 2 restaurants, travel desk, good service.
**C-E Swadesh Heritage**, MV Rd, Udupi, T0820- 2529605, www.hotelswadesh.com. 34 spotlessly clean rooms, 14 a/c, in newish hotel (even basic rooms very good value), bar, 2 restaurants. Highly recommended.
**D Green Park**, Manipal, has 38 rooms, some a/c, has a restaurant.
**D-E Udupi Residency**, near Service Bus Stand, Udupi, T0820-2530005. 33 excellent rooms, 11 a/c, clean, very well maintained, restaurant. Highly recommended new hotel.
**E Silver Sands**, T0820-222223, Thotham Beach, 1 km north of Malpe, hard to find. 8 pleasant cottages, limited menu restaurant, friendly. Recommended.
**E Tourist Home**, half way to Thotham Beach, Malpe. 4 pleasant, seaside rooms. Indian breakfast at the top of the road.

**Gokarna** *p1007, map p1006*
Mud and palm leaf huts with shared facilites charge Rs 30-60 (extra for a mattress). The lack of security in beach huts has prompted the guesthouses in town to offer to store luggage for a small charge. The 3 beach options mentioned below are secure.
**D-E Gokarna International**, Main Rd, Kumta Taluk, T08386-2656848, www.geocities.com/ hotelgokarna. 43 modern rooms (3 a/c) with bath and tubs, back quieter and have balconies, restaurant, bar, friendly staff, and the first lift in Gokarna! Recommended.
**E-F Green's Om**, Ganjigadde, 2-min walk from bus stand, T08386-2656445. 20 clean, airy, well-maintained rooms with bath, 2 a/c, restaurant (Nepali, Indian, Western) and bar operates in peak season. Very good value.
**E-F New Prasad Nilaya**, near New Bus Stand, Gangigadde T08386-2657135. Spacious but very run down rooms with shower, some balconies, upstairs slightly better, friendly staff.
**E-F Shri Laxmi**, Bus Stand Rd, T08386-2560365. Clean, spacious rooms in newly-converted family house. Small scale but friendly and good value.
**F Mayura Samudra** (KSTDC), 2 km north on hilltop facing the sea, T08386-256236. 3

rooms, dining room, garden, helpful staff but quite a trek.

**F Nimmu Guest House**, near Temple, Mani Bhadra Rd, T08386-2656730. 15 clean rooms with shared Indian toilets, 5 newest are better value as they are big, bright and catch the breeze, limited roof space for overspill, garden, laid-back and friendly, safe luggage storage. Recommended.

**F Shastri's Guest House**, Dasanamath, T08386-256220. 24 rooms with bath, some 3-4 bedded, set back from road, quiet.

**F Vaibhav Nivas**, Ganjigadde off Main St (5 mins walk from bazaar), T08386-256714. Family guest house, small rooms, annexe with 10 rooms, some with bath (Indian and western WC), meals, luggage store.

**On beaches F Shiva Prasad**, Kudle Beach, with decent brick-built rooms with fan.

**F Namaste**, Om Beach, acceptable rooms, though far from the best swimming areas.

**F Nirvana**, Om Beach, (Rs 40) for no bed. Hammock or inflatable mattress recommended, shower, restaurant.

## Eating

**Mangalore** *p1003, map p1004*

**TTT Embers**, for open-air dinners by the pool at Taj Manjarun Hotel.

**T Hao Hao** and **T Hao Ming**, in Balmatta, good Chinese, a/c.

**T Lalith**, Balmatta Rd, T0824-2426793. Basement restaurant with excellent food, cold beer and friendly service.

**T Surabhi**, Tandoori and cold beer, handy if waiting for a night bus.

**T Ting Hao** at Hotel Sujatha, KS Rao Rd. Dark, a/c, does large portions of Chinese/Indian (opens 1800).

**Udupi and around** *p1005*

**Dwarike**, Car St, facing Temple Sq, Udupi. Immaculately clean, modern, good service, comfortable, western and South Indian food, excellent snacks, ice creams.

**Gokul**, opposite Swadeshi Heritage hotel, Udupi. Excellent vegetarian, good value.

**JJ's Fast Food**, Hotel Bhavani, Parkala Rd, Manipal. For western snacks.

**Karwar** *p1007*

**Fish Restaurant**, in the Sidvha Hotel. Excellent bistro-type place.

**Gokarna** *p1007, map p1006*

Soft drinks can be wildly overpriced; check before ordering. Cheap vegetarian *thalis* are available near the bus stand and along Main St while shacks at the entrance to the town beach serve up the usual disarray of travellers' favourites. Standards are improving on the southern beaches with traveller food, drinks and internet access becoming available, though often only in the peak season. **Spanish Chai** shop, Kudle, and **Hotel Look Sea** are popular.

**T Kinara**, near Gokarna Beach. Ice creams, Indian and some western food. Basic but clean and well-run.

**T Pai**, near Vegetable Market, does good *masala dosa*.

**T Prema**, opposite Mahabalesvar temple. With a large room upstairs, does great fruit salads, ices, *gudbad* and its own delicious soft garlic cheese. Popularity has resulted in slow and surly service. Ice cream parlours abound; try *gudbad* with nuts and fruit.

**T Vishwa**, on the beach. Nepali-run, varied menu including Tibetan, large helpings.

## Transport

**Mangalore** *p1003, map p1004*

**Air**

**Bajpe airport** is 22 km out of town. Transport from town: taxi, Rs 200; shared Rs 50 each; coach from **Indian Airlines**, Hathill Complex, Lalbag, T0824-2455259. Airport, T0824-2752433. **Chennai** via Bangalore, **Mumbai**. **Jet Airways**: Ram Bhavan Complex, Kodaibail, T0824-2441181, airport, T0824-2752709. **Bangalore** and **Mumbai**.

**Auto-rickshaw**

Minimum charge Rs 8; Rs 35 to the Kankanadi station from the centre, and Rs 25 from KSRTC Lalbag, Bus Station (higher than the meter charge because of the 'locality').

**Bus**

Numerous private long-distance bus companies around the **Taj Mahal**

Restaurant, Falnir Rd (and a few opposite KSRTC) serve **Bangalore, Bijapur, Goa, Ernakulam, Hampi, Gokarna, Kochi, Mumbai, Udupi** etc. KSRTC State bus stand, Bajjai Rd, is well-organized. Booking hall at entrance has a computer printout of timetable in English; main indicator board shows different bus categories: red – ordinary; blue – semi-de luxe; green – super-de luxe. (*Exp* buses may be reserved 7 days ahead). For town centre and railway, leave bus stand, turn left 50 m to private bus shelter for bus 19 or 33. **Mysore** and **Bangalore**: 296 km, 7 hrs and 405 km, 9 hrs, ½ hrly from 0600 (route through Madikeri is the most pleasant); trains take 20 hrs. **Chennai** 717 km; **Madurai** 691 km, 16 hrs. **Mumbai**; **Panaji**, 10 hrs.

**Car**
Hire for Rs 4 per km, Rs 7 for a/c.

**Train**
Central Station has a computerized booking office. **Chennai**: *Mangalore Mail, 6602* (AC/II), 1115, 19 hrs; *West Coast Exp, 6628*, 2010, 19 hrs. **Kollam**: *Malabar Express, 6330*, dep 1630, 15 hrs, and to **Thiruvananthapuram**, 17 hrs: also *Parasuram Exp 6350*, 0345. **Madgaon (Margao)**: *Matsyagandha Exp, 2620*, 1450, 4½ hrs (on to Thane and LT for Mumbai). **Pala- kkad**: *Mangalore-Tiruchirappalli Exp, 6684*, 0600, 8 hrs; *W Coast Exp. 6628*, 2010, 8½ hrs. From **Kankanadi Station**: **Mumbai** (Lokman- ya Tilak) via Madgaon: *Nethravati Exp, 6346*, 1450, 17½ hrs. **Madgaon**: *Lakshadeep Exp, 2617*, 2310, 4 hrs.

**Udupi and around** *p1005*
**Bicycle**
Bicycles are available for hire in Udupi.

**Bus**
From Udupi, frequent service to **Mangalore** (1½ hrs). Mornings and evenings to **Bangalore** and **Mysore** from 0600; **Hubli** from 0900; **Dharmashala**, from 0600-0945, 1400-1830; **Mumbai** at 1120, 1520, 1700, 1920.

**Train**
The station is 5 km from the town centre; auto, Rs 35. **Madgaon**: *Netravati Exp, 6636*, 1608, 4 hrs, and on to **Mumbai** (LT).

**Gokarna** *p1007, map p1006*
**Bus**
KSRTC buses provide a good service: **Chaudi** 2 hrs; **Karwar** (via Ankola) frequent (1 hr); **Hospet** 0700, 1425 (10 hrs); **Jog Falls** 0700, 1130 (6 hrs); **Margao**, 0814 (4 hrs); **Mangalore** via **Udipi** 0645 (7 hrs); **Panaji** 0800 (5 hrs).

**Train**
Gokarna Road station is 10 km from the town, 2 km from the NH17; most trains are met by auto-rickshaws and a private bus. Rs 10 to Gokarna bus stand. State buses can be flagged down on the NH17. **Madgaon (Margao)**: *Mangalore-Madgaon Pass, KR2 (K)*, 1110, 2¼ hrs; **Mangalore**: *Madgaon-Mangalore Pass, KR1 (K)*, 1532, 5 hrs.

**Karwar** *p1007*
**Bus**
To **Jog Falls**, 0730 and 1500 (6 hrs). Frequent buses to **Palolem**, **Margao** (Madgaon) and **Panaji**, also direct buses to Colva. Buses often full – may have to fight to get on. The road crosses the Kali River (car toll, Rs 5) then reaches the Goa border and check post (8 km north).

## Directory

**Mangalore** *p1003, map p1004*
**Bank** Bank of Baroda, Balmatta Rd, exchange on credit cards. **Internet** Frontline, Ayesha Towers, KS Rao Rd, T0824-2441537, Rs 40 per hr. **Internet** World, City Light Building, Falnir Rd. Cheap, helpful. **Post** Panje Mangesh Rd (1st left after Poon- ja Arcade, by petrol station) has Speed Post.

**Gokarna** *p1007, map p1006*
**Exchange** Pai STD, opposite Ramdev Lodge, and Kiran's Internet, change money. **Internet** Several in town and on Kudle and Om beaches. **Sriram**, near post office, is best.

# Northern Karnataka

*After Goa's Dudhsagar falls, the train between Margao and Hospet climbs over jungle-covered mountains before reaching Karnataka's arable land stretching flatly, endlessly ahead. Sugar cane production dominates the workaday lives of most North Eastern Karnatakans: these arid pockets are among the state's most traditionally lived. Some come to visit at Hampi alone – attracted by the combination of an extraordinary boulder strewn landscape and the ruins of the great Vijayanagar Empire – but Aihole, Badami and Pattadakal are also worth seeing. The Islamic relics at Bijapur and Bidar are all the more striking for being lesser visited.* » *For Sleeping, Eating and other listings, see pages 1026-1030.*

## Hampi-Vijayanagara

→ *Phone code: 08394. Colour map 5, grid C5.*

Climb any boulder-toppled mountain around the ruins of the Vijayanagar Empire and you can see the dizzying scale of the Hindu conquerors' glory – Hampi was the capital of a kingdom that covered the whole of Southern India. Little of the kingdom's riches remain for future generations: now gypsies mud huts squat under the boulders where noblemen once stood, and the double decker shopfronts of the bazaar where diamonds were once traded by the kilo is now geared solely towards profiting from Western tourists and domestic pilgrims. Away from the bazaar, there is a unique romantic desolation. You'll need at least a full day to do it justice. » *For Sleeping, Eating and other listings, see pages 1026-1030.*

### Ins and outs

**Getting there and around** Apart from the hugely expensive five-seater aircraft, buses and trains arrive in Hospet, from there it is a 30-minute rickshaw (around Rs 200) or bus ride away. The site is spread out, hiring a bicycle is a good idea though some paths are too rough to ride on. » *See Transport, page 1028, for further details.*

**Tourist information** You enter the area from the west at Hampi Bazar or from the south at Kamalapuram. The tourist office is on the approach to Virupaksha Temple. US$5 to enter the Vitthala temple, with its amazing stone pillars. This includes the Lotus Mahal, same day only. The rest is free. A four-hour guided tour of the site (without going into the temples) costs around Rs 250. 0800-1230, 1500-1830. Before entering the precinct, foreigners are expected to register at the police office on the left.

### Background

Hampi was founded on the banks of the Tungabhadra river by two brothers, Harihara and Bukka, in 1336 and rose to become the seat of the mighty Vijayanagara Empire and a major centre of Hindu rule and civilization for two centuries. The city, which held a monopoly on the trade of spices and cotton, was enormously wealthy – some say greater than Rome– and the now-sorry bazaar was packed with diamonds and pearls, the crumbled palaces were plated with gold. Although it was well- fortified and defended by a large army, the city fell to a coalition of Northern Muslim rulers, the Deccan Sultans, at Talikota in 1565. The invading armies didn't crave the city for themselves, and instead sacked it, smiting symbolic blows to Hindu deities and taking huge chunks out of many of the remaining white granite carvings. Today, the craggy 26 sq km site holds the ghost of a capital with aquaducts, elephant stables and baths as big as palaces. The dry arable land is slowly being peeled back by the archaeologists to expose more and more of the kingdom's ruins – 80 have been found so far.

*Today Hampi has a population of 3,000 across its 62 sq km. Once that figure was closer to 1.5 million.*

The site for the capital was chosen for strategic reasons but the craftsmen adopted an ingenious style to blend in their architectural masterpieces with the barren and rocky landscape. Most of the site is early 16th-century, built during the 20-year reign of Krishna Deva Raya (1509-1529) with the citadel standing on the bank of the river. Excavations undertaken by the Archaeological Survey of India are still in progress.

## Sacred Centre

The road from the west comes over Hemakuta Hill, overlooking the sacred centre of Vijayanagara (the 'Town of Victory', 13 km northeast of Hospet town), the Virupaksha Temple and the Tungabhadra River to its north. On the hill are two large monolithic Ganesh sculptures: and some small temples. The road runs down to the village and the once world-famous market place. You can now only see the wide pathway running east from the towering **Virupaksha** (*Pampapati*) **Temple** with its nine-storey *gopuram*, to where the bazaar once hummed with activity.The temple is still in use; note the interesting paintings on the *mandapam* ceiling.

## The Riverside

You can walk along the river bank (1,500 m) to the famous Vitthala Temple. The path is easy and passes several interesting ruins including small 'cave' temples – worthwhile with a guide. Alternatively, a motorable road skirts the Royal Enclosure to the south, and goes all the way to the Vitthala Temple. On the way back (especially if it's at sunset) it's worth stopping to see the **Raghunatha Temple,** on a hill top, with its Dravidian style, quiet atmosphere and excellent view of the countryside from the rocks above.

After passing **Achyuta Bazar**, which leads to the Tiruvengalanatha Temple 400 m to the south, the riverside path goes near **Sugriva's Cave**, where it is said that Sita's jewels, dropped as she was abducted by the demon Ravana, were hidden by Sugriva. There are good views of the ancient ruined bridge to the east, and nearby the path continues past the only early period Vaishnavite shrine, the 14th-century **Narasimha Temple**. The **King's Balance** is at the end of the path as it approaches the Vitthala Temple. It is said that the rulers were weighed against gold, jewels and food, which were then distributed to Brahmins.

The **Vitthala Temple** ⓘ *US$5 (allows entry to Lotus Mahal on the same day 0800-1600)*, a World Heritage Monument, is dedicated to Vishnu. It stands in a rectangular courtyard, enclosed within high walls. Probably built in the mid-15th century, it is one of the oldest and most intricately carved temples, with its *gopurams* and *mandapas*. The *Dolotsava mandapa* has 56 superbly sculpted slender pillars which can be struck to produce different musical notes. It has elephants on the balustrades and horses at the entrance. The other two ceremonial *mandapas*, though less finely carved, neverthess depict some interesting scenes, eg Krishna hiding in a tree from the *gopis* and a woman using a serpent twisted around a stick to churn a pot of buttermilk. In the courtyard is a superb chariot carved out of granite, the wheels raised off the ground so that they could be revolved!

## Krishnapura

On the road between the Virupaksha Bazar and the Citadel, you pass Krishnapura, Hampi's earliest Vaishnava township with a Chariot Street 50 m wide and 600 m long, which is now a cultivated field. The **Krishna temple** has a very impressive gateway to the east. Just southwest of the Krishna temple is the colossal monolithic **statue of Lakshmi Narasimha** in the form of a four-armed man-lion with fearsome bulging eyes sheltered under a seven-headed serpent, Ananta. It is over 6 m high but sadly damaged.

The road south, from the Sacred Centre towards the Royal Enclosure, passes the excavated **Prasanna Virupaksha** (misleadingly named 'underground') **Temple** and interesting watchtowers.

## Royal Enclosure

At the heart of the Metropolis is the small **Hazara Rama Temple**, the Vaishanava 'chapel royal'. The outer enclosure wall to the north has five rows of carved friezes while the outer walls of the *mandapa* has three. The episodes from the epic *Ramayana* are told in great detail, starting with the bottom row of the north end of the west *mandapa* wall. The two-storeyed **Lotus Mahal** ⓘ *0600-1800, US$5 (allows entry to Vitthala Temple on the same day)*, is in the **Zenana** or ladies' quarter, screened off by its high walls. The watchtower is in ruins but you can see the domed **stables** for 10 elephants with a pavilion in the centre and the guardhouse. Each stable had a wooden beamed ceiling from which chains were attached to the elephants' backs and necks. In the **Durbar Enclosure** is the specially built decorated platform of the **Mahanavami Dibba**, from which the royal family watched the pageants and tournaments during the nine nights of *navaratri* festivities. The 8 m-high square platform originally had a covering of bricks, timber and metal but what remains still shows superb carvings of hunting and battle scenes, as well as dancers and musicians.

Karnataka Northern Karnataka

The exceptional skill of water engineering is displayed in the excavated system of aqueducts, tanks, sluices and canals, which could function today. The 22-m square **Pushkarini** is the attractive stepped tank at the centre of the enclosure. The road towards Kamalapuram passes the **Queen's Bath**, in the open air, surrounded by a narrow moat, where scented water filled the bath from lotus-shaped fountains. It measures about 15 m x 2 m and has interesting stucco work around it.

## Hospet → *Phone code: 08394. Colour map 5, grid C5. Population: 163,300.*

Hospet is famous for its sugar cane: the town exports sugar across India, villagers boil the milk to make jaggery, and a frothing fresh-wrung cup costs you just Rs 4. Other industries include iron ore, biscuit making and the brewing of Royal Standard rum. The main bazaar, with its characterful old houses, is interesting to walk around.

Muharram, the Muslim festival that marks the death of Mohammed's grandson Imam Hussein, is celebrated with a violent vigour both here and in the surrounding villages and with equal enthusiasm by both the area's significant Muslim population and Hindus. Ten days of fasting is broken with fierce drum-pounding, drink, and frequent arguments – sometimes accompanied by physical violence – each village clusters around icons of Hussein, whose decapitation is represented by a golden crown on top of a face covered with long strings of jasmine flowers held aloft on wooden sticks. Come evening, fires are lit. When the embers are dying villagers race through the ashes, a custom which may predate Islam's arrival. The beginnings or ends of livestock migrations to seasonal feeding grounds are marked with huge bonfires. Cattle are driven through the fires to protect them from disease. Some archaeologists suggest that Neolithic ash mounds around Hospet were the results of similar celebrations over 5,000 years ago.

The **Tungabhadra Dam** ⓘ *Rs 5, local bus takes 15 mins,* 6 km away, is 49 m high and offers panoramic views. One of the largest masonry dams in the country it was completed in 1953 to provide electricity for irrigation in the surrounding districts.

## Bijapur → *Phone code: 08352. Colour map 5, grid C5. Population: 245,900.*

Mohammed Adil Shah was not a man to be ignored: the tomb he built from the first day of his rule in anticipation of his own death hovers with dark magnificence over Bijapur and is so large it can be seen from over 20 km away. His brooding macabre legacy threw down the gauntlet to his immediate successor: Ali Adil Shah II, who took over from Mohammed in 1656, began his own tomb, which would surely have been double in size and architectural wonder had he not died too soon, 26 years into his reign, with only archways complete. His Bara Kamaan is nearby, while to the north of the city lies Begum's equally thwarted attempt to match Mohammed's strength in death. Bijapur has the air of a northern Muslim city with its mausolea, mosques and palaces. It has some of the finest mosques in the Deccan and retains real character. The chowk between the bus station and MG Rd is quite atmospheric in the evening. Overall it is a provincial, grubby but unhurried town. ⏩ *For Sleeping, Eating and other listings, see pages 1026-1030.*

### Ins and outs

**Getting there** The railway station is just outside the east wall of the fort under 1 km from the Gol Gumbaz while long-distance buses draw in just west of the citadel. Both arrival points are close enough to several hotels.

**Getting around** It is easy to walk or cycle round the town. There are also autos and tongas; negotiate for '8-sight tour price'. ⏩ *See Transport, page 1029, for further details.*

**Tourist information** Office opposite stadium ⓘ *T08352-2503592, 1030-1330, 1415-1730, Mon-Sat*, next to useless.

## History

The Chalukyas who ruled over Bijapur were overthrown at the end of the 12th century. In the early years of the 14th century the Delhi Sultans took it for a time until the Bahmanis, with their capital in Gulbarga, ruled through a governor in Bijapur who declared independence in 1489 and founded the Adil Shahi Dynasty. Of Turkish origin, they held power until 1686.

The canon, which weighs 55 tons, was employed against Vijayanagar. Ali Adil Shah I, whose war it was, was at least somewhat chastened at all the destruction his marauding Muslim armies had wreaked on the Hindu empire at Hampi. So, by way of atonement, and in a show of the inordinate riches that had fallen in to his lap by supplanting Vijayanagar, he went about his communal civic duty and built the exquisite Jama Masjid. It was his nephew Mohammed, he of the giant Gol Gumbaz, who later commissioned the rich Quaramic calligraphy which so sumptuously gilds the Western wall.

## Sights

The **Jama Masjid**, one of the finest in the Deccan, has a large shallow, onion-shaped dome and arcaded court. Built by Ali Adil Shah I (ruled 1557-1579) during Bijapur's rise to power it displays a classic restraint. The Emperor Aurangzeb added a grand entrance to the Masjid and also had a square painted for each of the 2,250 worshippers that it can accommodate. The **Citadel** with its own wall has few of its grand buildings intact. One is the Durbar Hall, **Gagan Mahal** (Sky Palace), open to the

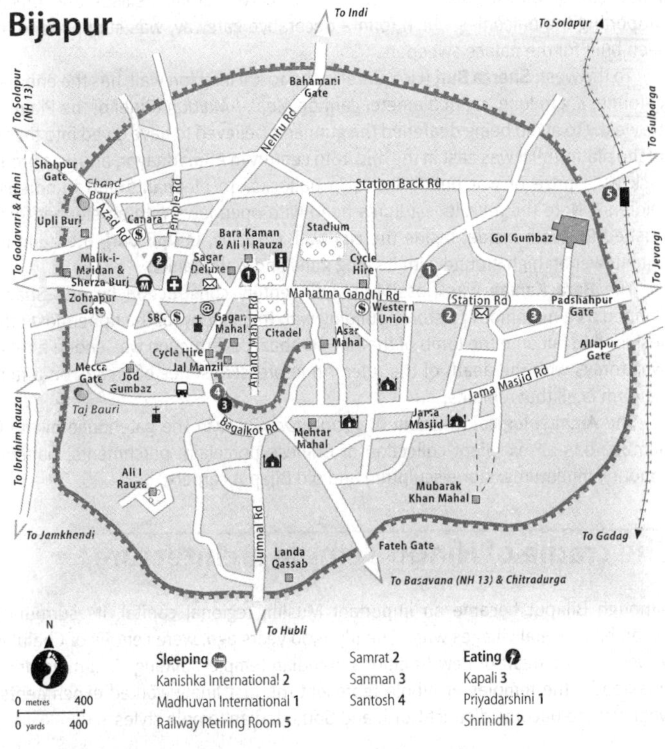

north so that the citizens outside were not excluded. It had royal residential quarters on either side with screened balconies for the women to remain unseen while they watched the court below. Another worth visiting is the **Jal Manzil,** or the water pavilion, a cool sanctuary.

**Ibrahim Rauza** ⓘ *0600-1800, US$2, video camera Rs 25, early morning best to avoid crowds*, the palatial 17th-century tomb west of the city wall, is beautifully proportioned. It has slender minarets and carved decorative panels with lotus, wheel and cross patterns as well as bold Arabic calligraphy, bearing witness to the tolerance of the Adil Shahi Dynasty towards other religions. Built during the dynasty's most prosperous period (after the sacking of Vijayanagara) when the arts and culture flourished, it also contains the tomb of Ibrahim Adil Shah II (ruled 1580-1626) who had it built for his wife but died first. Near the Rauza is a huge tank, the Taj Bauri, built by Ibrahim II in memory of his wife. The approach is through a giant gateway flanked by two octagonal towers.

**Gol Gumbaz** ⓘ *0630-1730, US$2, video camera Rs 25, some choose to just view it from the gate*, the vast whitewashed tomb of Mohammad Adil Shah buried here with his wife, daughter and favourite court dancer, has the world's second largest dome (unsupported by pillars), and one of its least attractive. Its extraordinary **whispering gallery** carries a message across 38 m which is repeated 11 times. However, noisy crowds make hearing a whisper quite impossible; it's quietest in the early morning. Numerous narrow steps in one of the corner towers, lead to the 3 m wide gallery. The plaster here was made out of eggs, cow dung, grass and jaggery. There is an excellent view of the city with its walls from the base of the dome.

The **Nakkar Khana**, the gate house, is now a museum. The **Asar Mahal** (circa 1646) was built with a tank watered by the old conduit system. It was used as a court house and has teak pillars and interesting frescoes in the upper floor. The **Mehtar Mahal** (1620) with its delicate minarets and carved stone trellises and brackets supporting the balconies which form a decorative gateway, was supposed to have been built for the palace sweepers.

To the west, **Sherza Burj** (Lion Gate) in the 10 km long fort wall, has the enormous 55 tonne, 4.3 m long, 1.5 m diameter cannon *Malik-i-Maidan* (Ruler of the Plains) on the west. (To avoid being deafened the gunner is believed to have dived into the tank off the platform!) It was cast in the mid-16th century in Ahmadnagar, and was brought back as a prize of war pulled by "400 bullocks, 10 elephants and hundreds of soldiers". Note the muzzle – a lion's head with open jaws with an elephant being crushed to death inside. Inside the city wall, close by, is **Upli Burj**, the 24-m high watchtower on high ground with its long guns and water tanks.

The **Bara Kaman** was possibly a 17th-century construction by Adil Shah III. Planned as a mammoth 12-storey building with the shadow of the uppermost storey designed to fall onto the tomb of the Gol Gumbaz, construction was ended after just two storeys with the death of the ruler. An impressive series of arches on a raised platform is all that remains.

The **Archaeological Museum** ⓘ *1000-1700, Rs 2*, in the gatehouse of the Gol Gumbaz has an excellent collection of Chinese porcelain, parchments, paintings, armoury, miniatures, stone sculpture and old Bijapur carpets.



## The cradle of Hindu Temple architecture

Although Bijapur became an important Muslim regional capital, its surrounding region has several villages which, nearly 1500 years ago, were centres of Chalukyan power and the heart of new traditions in Indian temple building. At a major Indian crossroads, the temples at Aihole represent the first finely worked experiments in what were to become distinct North and South Indian temple styles.

## Ins and outs



Since it takes a half day to see Badami, visiting the sites by bus doesn't allow time for Mahakuta. It is well worth hiring a car in Bijapur which allows you to see all the sites quite comfortably in a day. If travelling by bus it is best to visit Badami first, followed by Pattadakal and Aihole. By car it is best to start at Aihole and end at Badami. » *See Transport, page 1029, for further details.*

## Aihole → *Phone code: 0831. Colour map 5, grid C5.*

ⓘ *The main temples are now enclosed in a park, open sunrise to sunset, US$2, flash photography prohibited.*

Aihole was the first Chalukyan capital, but the site was developed over a period of more than 600 years from the sixth century AD and includes important Rashtrakuta and late Chalukyan temples, some dedicated to Jain divinities. It is regarded as the birthplace of Indian temple architectural styles, and the site of the first built temples, as distinct from those carved out of solid rock. Most of the temples were dedicated to Vishnu, though a number were subsequently converted into Shaivite shrines.

There are about 140 temples – half within the fort walls – illustrating a range of developing styles from Hoysala, Dravida, Jain, Buddhist, Nagara and Rekhanagara. There is little else. All the roads entering Aihole pass numerous temple ruins, but the road into the village from Pattadakal and Bagalkot passes the most important group of temples which would be the normal starting point for a visit. Some prefer to wander around the dozens of deserted (free) temples around town instead of joining the crowds in the park.

**Durgigudi Temple** is named not after the Goddess Durga but because it is close to the *durga* (fort). Dating from the late seventh century, it has an early *gopuram* structure and semi-circular apse which imitates early Buddhist *chaitya* halls. It has numerous superb sculptures, a series contained in niches around the ambulatory: walking clockwise they represent Siva and *Nandi*, Narasimha, Vishnu with *Garuda*, Varaha, Durga and Harihara.

**Lad Khan Temple** has been dated, according to recent research, from approximately AD 700, not from AD 450 as suggested by the first Archaeological Survey of India reports in 1907. This is indicated by the similarity of some of its sculptures to those of the Jambulinga temple at Badami, which has been dated precisely at AD 699. Originally an assembly hall and *kalyana mandapa* (marriage hall) it was named after Lad Khan, a pious Muslim who stayed in the temple at the end of the 19th century. A stone ladder through the roof leads to a shrine with damaged images of Surya, Vishnu and Siva carved on its walls. It bears a striking resemblance to the megalithic caves which were still being excavated in this part of the Deccan at the beginning of the period. The roof gives an excellent view of the village.

**Gaudar Gudi Temple**, near the Lad Khan temple, is a small, rectangular Hindu temple, probably dating from the seventh century. It has a rectangular columned *mandapa*, surrounded on three sides by a corridor for circumambulation. Its roof of stone slabs is an excellent example of North Indian architecture. Beyond the Gaudar Gudi Temple is a small temple decorated with a frieze of pots, followed by a deep well. There are others in various states of repair. To see the most important of the remaining temples you leave the main park. Excavations are in progress, and the boundaries of the park may sometimes be fenced. Turning right out of the main park, the Bagalkot road leads to the **Chikki Temple**. Similar in plan to the Gaudar Gudi, this temple has particularly fine carved pillars. The beams which support the platform are also well worth seeing.

**Ravan Phadi Cave Temple** is reached from the main park entrance on the left, about 300 m from the village. The cave (formerly known as the Brahman) itself is artificial, and the sixth century temple has a variety of carvings of Siva both outside and inside. One is in the *Ardhanarisvara* form (half Siva, half Parvati), another depicts

 Parvati and Ganesh dancing. There is a huge lotus carved in the centre of the hall platform; and two small eighth century temples at the entrance, the one to the northwest dedicated to Vishnu and that to the south, badly weathered, may have been based on an older Dravidian-style temple.

**The Buddhist Temple** is a plain two-storeyed Buddhist temple on a hill beyond the end of the village on the way to the Meguti Temple. It has a serene smiling Buddha with the Bodhi Tree emerging from his head, on the ceiling of the upper floor. Further uphill is the **Jain temple**, a plain structure lacking the decorations on the plinth, columns and *gopuram* of many Hindu temples. It has a statue of Mahavira in the shrine within. Climb up through the roof for a good view of Aihole.

The **Meguti Temple** (AD 634) is reached from the Buddhist Temple down a path leading to a terrace. A left hand route takes you to the foot of some stairs leading to the top of a hill which overlooks the town. This is the site of what is almost certainly the oldest building in Aihole and one of the oldest dated temples in India. Its 634 date is indicated by an inscription by the court poet to the king Ravikirtti. A Dravidian-style temple, it is richly decorated on the outside, and although it has elements which suggest Shaivite origins, it has an extremely impressive seated Jain figure, possibly Neminath, in the sanctuary which comprises a hall of 16 pillars.

**The Kunti Group** is a group of four Hindu temples (dating from seventh to ninth centuries). To find them you have to return down to the village. The oldest is in the southeast. The external columns of its *mandapa* are decorated with *mithuna*, or erotic couples. The temple to the northwest has beautifully carved ceiling panels of Siva and Parvati, Vishnu and Brahma. The other two date from the Rashtrakuta period.

Beyond these temples is the **Hucchappayya Math**, dating from the seventh century, which has sculptures of amorous couples and their servants, while the beams inside are beautifully decorated. There is a tourist rest house close to the temples should you wish to stay.



## Pattadakal

On the banks of the Malaprabha River, Pattadakal, a World Heritage Site, was the second capital of the Chalukyan kings between the seventh and eighth centuries and the city where the kings were crowned. Ptolemy referred to it as 'Petrigal' in the first century AD. Two of their queens imported sculptors from Kanchipuram. Most of the temples ① *sunrise to sunset, US$2*, cluster at the foot of a hill, built out of the pink-tinged gold sandstone, and display a succession of styles of the southern Dravida temple architecture of the Pallavas (even miniature scaled-down models) as well as the North Indian Nagara style, vividly illustrating the region's position at the crossroads of North and South Indian traditions. With one exception the temples are dedicated to Siva. Most of the site is included in the archaeological park. Megalithic monuments dating from the third-fourth centuries BC have also been found in the area.

*❢ There is no suitable accommodation though a new restaurant is opening. Stay either in Badami or at Bagalkot, see Sleeping.*

Immediately inside the entrance are the very small **Jambulinga** and **Kadasiddheshvara Temples** (eighth century). Now partly ruined, the curved towers survive and the shrine of the Jambulinga Temple houses a figure of the dancing Siva next to Parvati. The gateways are guarded by *dvarapalas*.

Just to the east is the eighth-century **Galaganatha Temple**, again partly damaged, though its curved tower characteristic of North Indian temples is well preserved, including its *amalaka* on top. A relief of Siva killing the demon Andhaka is on the south wall in one of three original porches.

The **Sangamesvara Temple** dating from the reign of Vijayaditya (696-733) is the earliest temple. Although it was never completed it has all the hallmarks of a purely Dravidian style. Beautifully proportioned, the mouldings on the basement and pilasters divide the wall. The main shrine, into which barely any light is allowed to pass, has a corridor for circumambulation, and a *lingam* inside. Above the sanctuary is a superbly proportioned tower of several storeys.

To the southwest is the late eighth-century North Indian-style **Kashi Vishveshvara Temple**, readily distinguishable by the *Nandi* in front of the porch. The interior of the pillared hall is richly sculpted, particularly with scenes of Krishna.

The largest temples, the **Virupaksha** (740-744) with its three-storeyed *vimana* and the **Mallikarjuna** (745), typify the Dravida style, and were built in celebration of the victory of the Chalukyan king Vikramaditya II over the Pallavas at Kanchipuram by his wife, Queen Trailokyamahadevi. The king's death probably accounted for the fact that the Mallikarjuna temple was unfinished, and you can only mark out some of the sculptures. However, the king's victory over the Pallavas enabled him to express his admiration for Pallava architecture by bringing back to Pattadakal one of the chief Pallava architects. The Virupaksha, a Shaivite temple, has a sanctuary surrounded by passageways and houses a black polished stone Siva *lingam*. A further Shaivite symbol is the huge 2.6-m high chlorite stone *Nandi* at the entrance, contrasting with the pinkish sandstone surrounding it. The three-storeyed tower rises strikingly above the shrine, the outside walls of which, particularly those on the south side, are richly carved. Many show different forms of Vishnu and Siva, including some particularly striking panels which show Siva appearing out of a *lingam*. Note also the beautifully carved columns inside. They are very delicate, depicting episodes from the *Ramayana*, *Mahabharata* and the *Puranas*, as well as giving an insight into the social life of the Chalukyas. Note the ingenuity of the sculptor in making an elephant appear as a buffalo when viewed from a different side.

In the ninth century the Rashtrakutas arrived and built a Jain temple with its two stone elephants a short distance from the centre. The carvings on the temples, particularly on the **Papanatha** near the village which has interesting sculpture on the ceiling and pillars, synthesizes Northern and Southern Indian architectural styles.

## Mahakuta

Mahakuta, which was reached by early pilgrims over rocky hills from Badami 5 km away, is a beautiful complex of Chalukyan temples dating from the late seventh century; worth a detour. The superstructures reflect both Northern and Southern influence and one has an Orissan *deul*.

The restored temple complex of two dozen shrines dedicated to Siva is built around a large spring-fed tank within an enclosure wall. The old gateway to the southeast has fasting figures of Bhairava and Chamunda. On entering the complex, you pass the *Nandi* in front of the older **Mahakutesvara Temple** which has fine scrollwork and figures from the epics carved on the base. Larger Siva figures appear in wall niches, including an *Ardhanarisvara*. The temple is significant in tracing the development of the superstructure which began to externally identify the position of the shrine in Dravidian temples. Here the tower is dome-like and octagonal, the tiers supported by tiny 'shrines'. The **Mallikarjuna Temple** on the other side of the tank is similar in structure with fine carvings at the entrance and on the ceiling of the columned *mandapa* inside, depicting Hindu deities and *mithuna* couples. The enclosure has many smaller shrines, some carrying fine wall carvings. Also worth visiting is the **Naganatha** Temple 2 km away.

## Badami → *Phone code: 08357. Colour map 5, grid C5. Population: 25,900.*

Badami occupies a dramatic site squeezed in a gorge between two high red sandstone hills. Once called Vatapi, after a demon, Badami was the Chalukyan capital from AD 543-757. The ancient city has several Hindu and Jain temples and a Buddhist cave and remains peaceful and charming. The transcendent beauty of the Hindu cave temples in their spectacular setting warrants a visit. The village with its busy bazaar and a large lake has white-washed houses clustered together along narrow winding lanes up the hillside. There are also scattered remains of 18 stone inscriptions (sixth-16th century). The sites are best visited early in the morning. They are very popular with monkeys, which can be aggressive, especially if they see food. End the day by watching the sun set from the eastern end of the tank.

The **South Fort** ⓘ *US$2*, is famous for its cave temples, four of which were cut out of the hillside in the second half of the sixth century. There are 40 steps to **Cave 1**, the oldest. There are several sculpted figures, including Harihara, Siva and Parvati, and Siva as Nataraja with 18 arms seen in 81 dancing poses. **Cave 2**, a little higher than Cave 1, is guarded by *dvarapalas* (door-keepers). Reliefs of Varaha and Vamana decorate the porch. **Cave 3**, higher still, is dedicated to Vishnu. According to a Kannada inscription (unique in Badami) it was excavated in AD 578. It has numerous sculptures including Narasimha (man-lion), Hari-Hara (Siva-Vishnu), a huge seated Vishnu and interesting friezes. Frescoes, executed in the tempera technique are similar to that used in the Ajanta paintings, and so are the carved ceilings and brackets. **Cave 4**, probably about 100 years later than the three earlier caves, is the only Jain cave. It has a statue of the seated Parsvanatha with two *dvarapalas* at the entrance. The fort itself above the caves is closed to the public.

*The area is well worth exploring by bicycle.*

The **Buddhist Temple** is in the natural cave near the ancient artificial Bhutanatha Lake (Agasthya Lake), where the mossy green water is considered to cure illnesses. The Yellamma Temple has a female deity, while one of the two Shaivite temples is to Bhutanatha (God of souls); in this form, Siva appears angry in the dark inner sanctuary.

The seventh-century **Mallegitti Sivalaya Temple**, one of the finest examples of the early Southern style, has a small porch, a *mandapa* (hall) and a narrower *vimana*

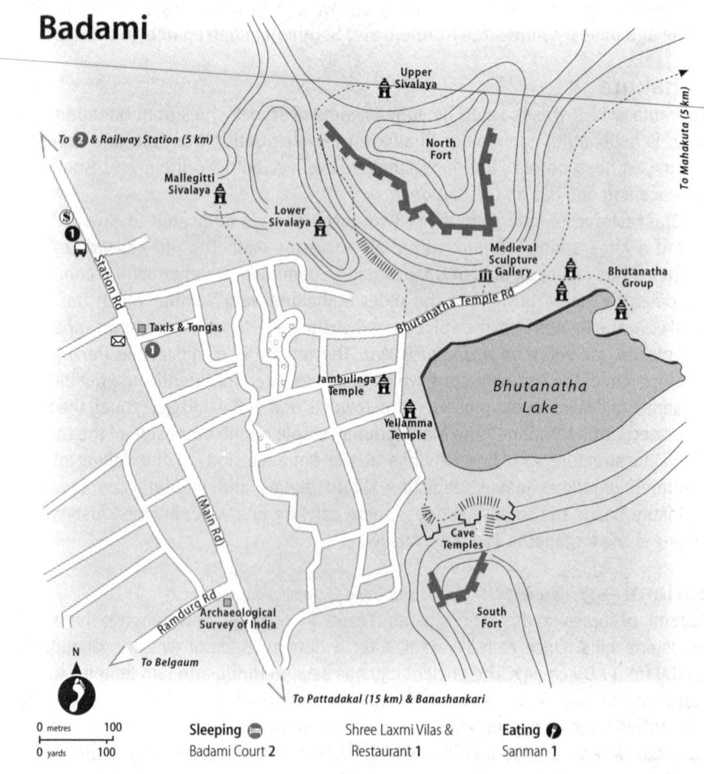

(shrine), which Harle points out is typical of all early Western Chalukya temples. The slim pilasters on the outer walls are reminders of the period when wooden pillars were essential features of the construction. Statues of Vishnu and Siva decorate the outer walls, while animal friezes appear along the plinth and above the eaves. These are marked by a moulding with a series of purely ornamental small solid pavilions.

**Jambulinga Temple** is an early temple in the centre of the town near the rickshaw stand. Dating from 699, as attested by an inscription, and now almost hidden by houses, the visible brick tower is a late addition from the Vijayanagar period. Its three chapels, dedicated to Brahma, Vishnu and Siva, contain some fine carving, although the deities are missing and according to Harle the ceiling decoration already shows signs of deteriorating style. The carvings here, especially that of the Nagaraja in the outside porch, have helped to date the Lad Khan temple in Aihole accurately (see above). Opposite the Jambulinga temple is the 10th-century Virupaksha Temple.

The **North Fort** temples ⓘ *Rs 2, carry water*, mainly seventh-century, give an insight into Badami's history. Steep steps, almost 1 m high, take you to 'gun point' at the top of the fort which has remains of large granaries, a treasury and a watchtower. The **Upper Sivalaya Temple**, though damaged, still has some friezes and sculptures depicting Krishna legends. (The North Fort was taken in a day by Col Munro in 1918, when he broke in through the east side.)

An ancient **dolmen** site can be reached by an easy hike through interesting countryside; allow 3½ hours. A local English-speaking guide, Dilawar Badesha at Tipu Nagar, charges about Rs 2.

Archaeological Survey's **Medieval Sculpture Gallery** ⓘ *closed Fri, 1000-1700, free*, north of the tank, has fine specimens from Badami, Aihole and Pattadakal and a model of the natural bridge at Sidilinapadi, 5 km away.

## Gulbarga → *Phone code: 08472. Colour map 5, grid B5. Population: 427,900.*

The dry and undulating plains from Hospet to Bidar are broken by rocky outcrops giving superb sites for commanding fortresses such as Gulbarga (and Bidar, see below). Gulbarga was the first capital of the Bahmanis (from 1347-1525). It is also widely known among South Indian Muslims as the home of Saiyid Muhammad Gesu Daraz Chisti (1320-1422) who was instrumental in spreading pious Islamic faith in the Deccan. The annual Urs festival in his memory attracts up to 100,000 people. ⏩ *For Sleeping, Eating and other listings, see pages 1026-1030.*

### Sights

The town sights and hotels are quite spread out so it is worth hiring an auto for half a day. The most striking remains in the town are the fort, with its citadel and mosque, the Jami Masjid, and the great tombs in its eastern quarter – massive, fortress-like buildings with their distinctive domes over 30 m high.

The **fort** is just 1 km west of the centre of the present town. Originally built by Ala-ud-din Bahmani, in the 14th century, most of the outer structures and many of the buildings are in ruins although the outer door of the west gate and the *Bala Hissar* (citadel), a massive structure, remain almost intact though the whole is very overgrown. A flight of ruined steps leads up to the entrance in the north wall. Beware of dogs. It's easy to see why the Bahamis were so keen to upgrade their fortress. The fat fort walls at Gulbarga – romantically named as the 'bouquet of lovers' – may sit proud above the more modern artificial lake, and the Bala Hissar (citadel) itself stands high with its plump rotund columns, but the whole is all too pregnable and too modest. And there's no commanding hilltop to provide the natural impenetrability which the plateaux around Bidar bequeathed the dynasty's subsequent rulers here. All that remains of the palace structures are solitary walls stamped with arches, but the **Jami Masjid**, with its incongruous, uncanny likeness to the mosque at Cordoba in Spain, is both active and well maintained (similarities with the mosque at Cordoba have contributed to the legend that it was designed by a North African architect from the Moorish court). Beautiful geometrical angles of archways form as you walk under the 75 small roof domes zagging between the four corner domes. The whole area of 3,500 sq m is covered by a dome over the *mihrab*, four corner domes and 75 minor domes, making it unique among Indian mosques. It was built by Firoz Shah Bahmani (1397-1432).

The **tombs** of the Bahmani sultans are in two groups. One lies 600 m to the west of the fort, the other on the east of the town. The latter have no remaining exterior decoration though the interiors show some evidence of ornamentation. The Dargah of the Chisti saint, **Hazrat Gesu Nawaz** – also known as Khwaja Bande Nawaz – who came to Gulbarga in 1413 during the reign of Firoz Shah Tughlaq, is open to visitors, see page 1303. The two-storey tomb with a highly decorated painted dome had a mother-of-pearl canopy added over the grave. Please note that women are not allowed to enter the tombs. The **Dargah library**, which has 10,000 books in Urdu, Persian and Arabic, is open to visitors.

The most striking of all the tombs near **Haft Gumbaz**, the eastern group, is that of **Taj-ud-Din Firuz** (1422). Unlike the other tombs it is highly ornamented, with geometrical patterns developed in the masonry.

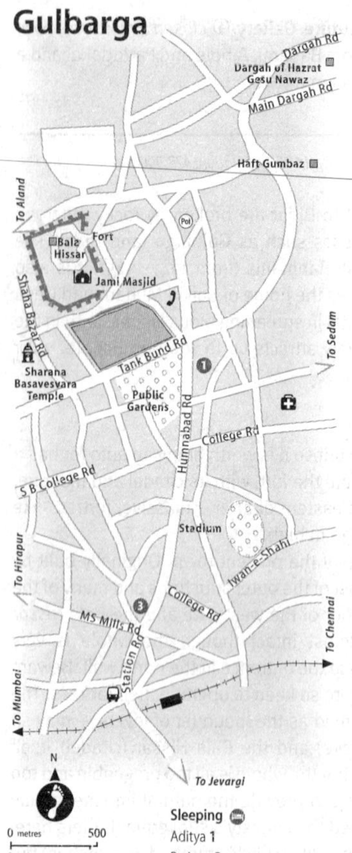


## Bidar

→ *Phone code: 08357. Colour map 5, grid C4. Population: 172,300.*

The scruffy bungalow town that is modern-day Bidar spreads out in a thin layer of buildings both within and without the imposing rust red walls of the 15th-century fort that once played capital to two Deccan-ruling Muslim dynasties. The buildings may be new but there's still something of a medieval undercurrent to life here. Islam still grows sturdily: apart from the store houses of government-subsidized industries to counter 'backwardness', the towns' outskirts are littered with long white prayer walls to mop up the human overflow from overburdened mosques during Id. A few lone tiles, tucked into high corners, still cling to the laterite brick structures that stand in for the succession of immaculately made palaces which must once have glowed incandescent with bright blue, green and yellow designs. Elsewhere you can only see the outline of the designs. The old fort commands grand vistas across the empty cultivated land below. Each successive palace was ruined by invasions then built anew a little further east. » *For Sleeping, Eating and other listings, see pages 1026-1030.*

## History

The walled fort town, on a red laterite plateau in North Karnataka, once the capital of the **Bahmanis** and the **Barid Shahis**, remained an important centre until it fell to Aurangzeb in 1656. The Bahmani Empire fragmented into four kingdoms, and the ninth Bahmani ruler, **Ahmad Shah I**, shifted his capital from Gulbarga to Bidar in 1424, rebuilding the old Hindu fort to withstand cannon attacks, and enriching the town with beautiful palaces and gardens. With the decline of the Bahmanis, the Barid Shahi Dynasty founded here ruled from 1487 until Bidar was annexed to Bijapur in 1619.

## Sights

The intermingling of Hindu and Islamic architectural styles in the town has been ascribed to the use of Hindu craftsmen, skilled in temple carving in stone (particularly hornblende), who would have been employed by the succeeding Muslim rulers. They transferred their skill to Muslim monuments, no longer carving human figures, forbidden by Islam, but using the same technique to decorate with geometric

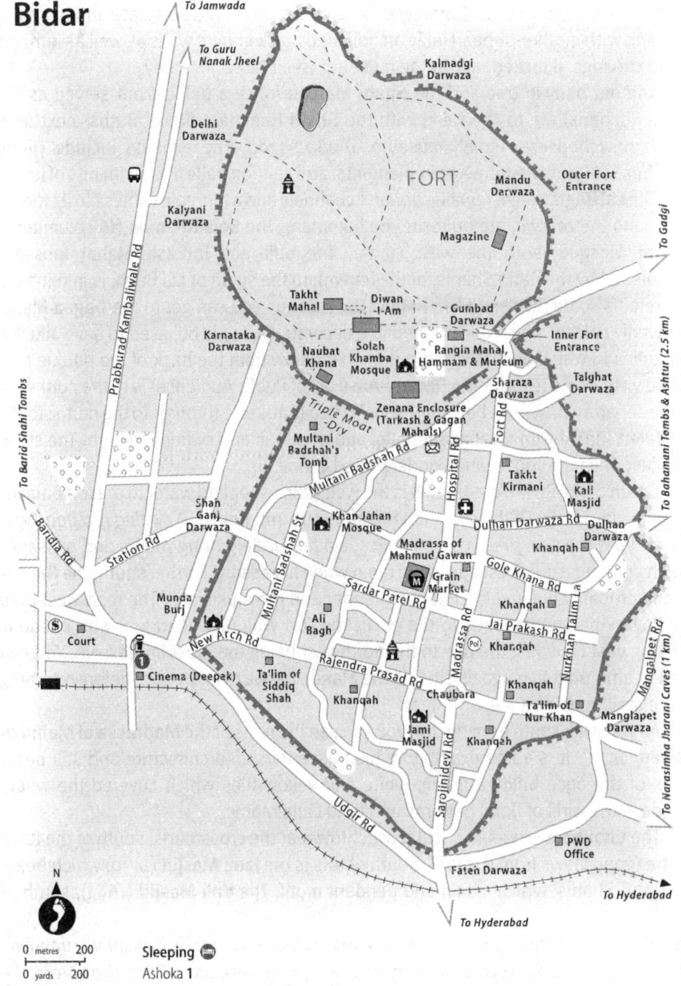

patterns, arabesques and calligraphy, wall friezes, niches and borders. The pillars, often of wood, were intricately carved and then painted and burnished with gold to harmonize with the encaustic tiles.

The **Inner Fort** built by Muhammad Shah out of the red laterite and dark trapstone was later embellished by Ali Barid. The steep hill to the north and east provided natural defence. It was protected to the south and west by a triple moat (now filled in). A series of gates and a drawbridge over the moat to the south formed the main entrance from the town. The second gate, the **Sharaza Darwaza** (1503) has tigers carved in bas relief on either side (Shia symbols of Ali as protector), the tile decorations on the walls and the *Nakkar Khana* (Drum gallery) above. Beyond this is a large fortified area which brings you to the third gate, the huge **Gumbad Darwaza**, probably built by Ahmad Shah Wali in the 1420s, which shows Persian influence. Note the decorated *gumbad* (dome).

You will see the triple moat to the right and after passing through the gateway, to your left are steps leading to the **Rangin Mahal** (Coloured Palace) where Muhammad Shah moved to, after finding the nearby Shah Burj a safe refuge in 1487 when the Abyssinians attacked. This small palace (an indication of the Bahmanis' declining years) was built by him, elaborately decorated with coloured tiles, later enhanced by Ali Barid with mother-of-pearl inlay on polished black granite walls as well as intricate wood carvings. If locked, ask at the museum (see below) for a key.

The old banyan tree and the **Shahi Matbak** (once a palace, but served as the Royal Kitchens) are to the west, with the **Shahi Hammam** (Royal Baths) next to it, which now houses a small **museum** ⓘ *0800-1700*. The exhibits include Hindu religious sculptures, Stone Age implements, and cannon balls filled with bits of iron.

The **Lal Bagh**, where remains of water channels and a fountain witness to its former glory, and the *zenana*, are opposite the hammam. The **Sola Khamba** (16 columns) or **Zanani Mosque** is to the west (1423). The adjacent **Tarkash Mahal** (possibly refurbished by the Barid Shahis for the harem), to the south of Lal Bagh, is in ruins but still retains some tilework. From behind the mosque you can get to the **Gagan Mahal** (Heavenly Palace) which once carried fine decorations and is believed to have allowed the ladies to watch animal fights in the moat below from the back of the double hall. (Good view from the roof.) The **Diwan-i-Am** (Hall of Public Audience) is to the northwest of the Zenana which once held the *Takht-i-Firoza* (turquoise throne). To the north stands the **Takht Mahal** with royal apartments, audience hall and swimming bath. The steep staircase will take you down to underground chambers.

South of the Royal Apartments is the well which supplied water to the fort palaces through clay pipes. Of the so-called **Hazar** (thousand) **Kothri** ⓘ *cycling is a good way of exploring the site, free*, you can only see a few underground rooms and passages which enabled a quick escape to the moat when necessary. Further south, the **Naubat Khana** probably housed the fort commander and the musicians. The road west from the Royal Apartments leads to the encircling Fort Wall (about 10 km) with bastions carrying vast canyons, the one to the northwest being the most impressive. You can see the ammunition magazine inside the **Mandu Darwaza** to the east before returning to the main fort entrance.

As you walk south from the fort you can see the ruins of the **Madrassa of Mahmud Gawan** (1472). It is a fine example of his native Persian architecture and still bears signs of the once brilliant green, white and yellow tiles which covered the whole façade with swirls of floral patterns and bold calligraphy.

The **Chaubara** is a 23-m circular watchtower at the crossroads, south of the town centre (good views from the top). South of this is the **Jami Masjid** (1430) which bears the Barid Shahis' typical chain and pendant motif. The **Kali Masjid** (1694), south of

*Bidar has a nearby Indian airforce base to which childless couples will voluntarily transfer in the hope that the legendarily virility-enhancing waters of Bidar will help them breed.*

the Talghat Darwaza, is made of black trapstone. It has fine plaster decorations on the vaulted ceiling. There are also a number of **khanqahs** (monasteries).

The road east from the Dulhan Darwaza, opposite the General Hospital, leads to the eight **Bahmani tombs** at **Ashtur** ⓘ *0800-1700, free, carry your own torch.* These are best seen in the morning when the light is better for viewing the interiors.

The square tombs, with arched arcades all round have bulbous domes. The exteriors have stone carvings and superb coloured tile decoration showing strong Persian influence, while the interiors have coloured paintings with gilding. The tomb of **Ahmad Shah I**, the ninth Bahmani ruler, is impressive with a dome rising to nearly 35 m, and has a particularly fine interior with coloured decorations and calligraphy in the Persian style, highlighted with white borders. To the east and south are minor tombs of his wife and son. The tomb of **Alauddin Shah II** (1458) is possibly the finest. Similar in size to his father's, this has lost its fine painting inside but enough remains of the outer tilework to give an impression of its original magnificence.

On the way back, is the **Chaukhandi of Hazrat Khalil-Ullah** which is approached by a flight of steps. Most of the tilework has disappeared but you can see the fine carvings at the entrance and on the granite pillars.

The **Barid Shahi tombs** each of which once stood in its own garden, are on the Nanded Road to the west of the old town. That of **Ali Barid** is the most impressive, with the dome rising to over 25 m, with granite carvings, decorative plasterwork and calligraphy and floral patterns on the coloured tiles, which sadly can no longer be seen on the exterior. Here, abandoning the customary *mihrab* on the west wall, Ali Barid chose to have his tomb left open to the elements. It includes a prayer hall, music rooms, a combined tomb for his concubines and a pool fed by an aqueduct are nearby. There are fine carvings on the incomplete tomb to his son **Ibrahim Barid**, to the west. You can also see two sets of granite *ranakhambas* (lit battleposts) which may have been boundary markers. Other tombs show the typical arched niches employed to lighten the heavy walls which have decorative parapets.

The road north from Ali Barid's tomb descends to **Nanak Jhera**, where a *gurdwara* marks the holy place where Sikhs believe a miracle was performed by Guru Nanak (see page 1344) and the *jhera* (spring) rose.



## Raichur → *Phone code: 08532. Colour map 5, grid C6. Population: 205,600.*

The main road from Hospet to Hyderabad passes through the important medieval centre of Raichur, once dominant in the Tungabhadra-Krishna *doab*, now an important but dusty market town, in the middle of a cotton-growing area.

The site of the **fort's citadel** at Raichur gives magnificent views over the vast open spaces of the Deccan plateau nearly 100 m below. Built in the mid-14th century Raichur became the first capital of the Bijapur Kingdom when it broke away from the Bahmani Sultans in 1489. Much of the fort itself is now in ruins, but there are some interesting remains. The north gate is flanked by towers, a carved elephant standing about 40 m away. On the inner walls are some carvings, and a tunnel reputedly built to enable soldiers access to barricade the gate in emergency. Near the west gate is the old palace. The climb to the citadel begins from near the north gate. In the citadel is a shrine with a row of cells with the Jami Masjid in the east. Its eastern gateway has three domes. The top of the citadel is barely 20 sq m.

There are some other interesting buildings in the fort below the hill, including the **Daftar ki Masjid** (Office Mosque), built around 1510 out of masonry removed from Hindu temples. It is one of the earliest mosques in the Deccan to be built in this way, with the bizarre result of producing flat ceilings with pillars carved for Chalukyan temples. The **Ek Minar ki Masjid** ('one-minaret mosque') is in the southeast corner of the courtyard. It has a distinctively *Bahmani*-style dome.

## Sleeping

**Hampi** *p1011, map p1013*
Some use Hospet as a base for visiting Hampi: it has plusher accommodation and the nearest railway station. However, it means a commute to Hampi. Hampi is quieter and more atmospheric. Across the river (by coracle, Rs 15) you can reach the hamlet of Anegundi, a beautiful paddy planted village with budget guesthouses, coco-huts and cottages to stay in. Power cuts are common so a supply of candles and a torch are essential. Mosquitos can be a real problem. A small selection from scores of guest houses are listed here. All are fairly similar. All are **E** or **F** category; prices rise 30% at the height of the season, Nov-Jan.

**D Ranjana Guest House**, behind Govt school, T08394-2441696. A friendly guest house with 5 rooms, plus hot water, cheaper rooms have a cooler, rather than a/c.

**D-E Mayura Bhuvaneswari**, 2 km from site, Kamalapuram, T08394-241574. 32 rooms (8 a/c, Rs 450), fairly clean, decent food, chilled beer, poor cycle hire.

**E Archana**, T08394-2441547. 8 rooms, very clean, quiet, with nets and roof area, attached shop.

**E Aum Guest House**, T08394-2441431. 4 rooms.

**E Gopi**, T08394-2441695. 10 rooms with bath, nets, board games.

**E Padma Guest House**, T08394-2441331. Family guesthouse 4 doubles, exchange.

**E Rahul**, south of the bus stand but quite quiet. Basic sleeping under nets, clean. Good simple vegetarian food, views from rooftop.

**E Raju**, T08394-2441349. 2 old buildings on either side of river, with 2 and 14 rooms respectively. Has character, is clean, and has a rooftop restaurant.

**E Shakti Guest House**, T08394-2441953. 1 double bedroom in quiet family house.

**E Shambhu**, T08394-2441383. 5 rooms with bath and nets, plenty of plants, rooftop restaurants (egg dishes), friendly.

**E Shanti Guest House**, down path to the right of the temple (signed), T08394-241568. 23 rooms with fans around pleasant courtyard with plenty of plants, common shower, roof for overspill, very clean, well run and friendly, cycle hire, good cakes (see Eating).

**E Vicky**, 200 m north of main road (turn off at tourist office), T08394-2441694, vickyhampi@yahoo.co.in. 7 rooms (4 with bath), bucket hot water, Indian toilet, good rooftop restaurant, internet Rs 60 per hr.

**Hospet** *p1014*
Station Rd has been renamed Mahatma Gandhi Rd (MG Rd).

**B-D Shanbhag Towers**, College Rd, T08394-2425910, shanbhagtowers@ yahoo.com. 64 spacious rooms, 32 a/c with tub, TV, fridge, in brand new hotel, breathtaking Hampi theme, restaurants (one rooftop with great views), bar.

**B-F Malligi**, 6/143 Jambunatha Rd, T08394-2428101. 140 rooms, 65 a/c, newer **D** are large with bath (4 **B** suites), always inspect first as standard varies enormously, restaurant and bar by pool (economy guests and non-residents pay Rs 25 per hr for pool), health club, exchange, travel (good Hampi tour Rs 80), creakingly slow internet and overpriced STD/ISD service.

**C-E Priyadarshini**, V/45 Station Rd, T08394-2428838. 82 fairly good rooms, 25 a/c, rather bare and bit overpriced, though friendly service, good restaurants, internet, parking.

**D-E Karthik**, 252 Sardar Patel Rd, T08394-2426643. 40 good sized, clean rooms, 10 a/c in quiet, modern hotel, garden dining, friendly and good value.

**D-E Nagarjuna Residency**, Sardar Patel Rd, opposite Karthik, T08394-2429009. Spotless, modern, excellent value rooms, some a/c, extra bed Rs 30-50, very helpful. Recommended.

**E SLV Yatri Nivas**, Station Rd, T08394-2421525. 15 bright, airy rooms in clean, well run hotel. Good vegetarian restaurant and bar. Recommended.

**E Shivananda**, next to bus stand, T08394-2420700. 23 rooms, 4 a/c, simple but clean, and complete with resident astrologer!

**F Viswa**, MG Rd, opposite bus station, away from the road, T08394-2427171. 42 clean rooms (some 4-bed) with bath, adjacent Shanthi restaurant. No frills but good value.

*For an explanation of the sleeping and eating price codes used in this guide, see inside the front cover. Other relevant information is found in Essentials pages 56-61.*

**Bijapur** *p1014, map p1015*

There has been a sudden spurt in decent hotels and restaurants.

**B Madhuvan International**, off Station Rd, T08352-255571. 35 rooms, 10 a/c, very pleasant, good vegetarian garden restaurant and rooftop terrace, beer in rooms only, travel desk, but a bit overpriced.

**B-D Hotel Kanishka International**, Station Rd, T08352-223788, www.kanishka bijapur.com. 24 rooms (10 a/c) with decidedly garish decor – giant mirrors – also has cable TV, telephone, en suite, laundry, plus the excellent Kamat Restaurant downstairs.

**C-D Hotel Pearl**, Opposite Gol Gumbaz, Station Rd, T08352-256002. 32 rooms (17 a/c) in a modern, 3-storey, scrupulously clean, modest, mint pastel-coloured hotel set round a central courtyard with vegetarian basement restaurant (booze and non- vegetarian food through room service). Telephones, cable TV in all rooms, laundry and parking.

**D-E Hotel Navaratna International**, Station Rd, T08352-222771. The grand colonnaded drive belies the modest price tag of the 34 rooms here (12 a/c). Communal areas scream with huge modernist paintings and rooms are done up with colour-coded care. TV, phone, etc and smaller rooms have sit-outs. Very popular non-vegetarian courtyard restaurant, bar and pure vegetarian restaurant. They also have rooms and baths for drivers – a giant leap in the humane direction for an Indian hotel.

**D-F Godavari**, Athni Rd, T08352-253105. 48 good rooms, friendly staff, good vegetarian and non-vegetarian food.

**D-F Samrat**, Station Rd, T08352-251620. Has 30 basic rooms, 6 with a/c are passable, but the rest are battered. Good vegetarian garden restaurant but mosquitos like to dine here as well.

**D-F Sanman**, opposite Gol Gumbaz, Station Rd, T08352-251866. 24 clean, pleasant rooms with shower, nets, 6 a/c. Very good value. Separate vegetarian restaurant and a non-vegetarian restaurant with bar. Recommended.

**E-F Santosh**, T52179. 70 good, clean rooms including some **D** a/c, quieter at back, convenient, good value.

**F Railway Retiring Room** and dorm, exceptionally clean, contact ticket collector on duty. Recommended.

**Badami** *p1019, map p1020*

There is no formal money exchange but the hotel Mukambika may be persuaded to change small value TCs.

**B Badami Court**, Station Rd, T08357-220230, www.hotelbadamicourt.com. 2 km from town (pleasant stroll or frequent buses). 26 clean, modern, though cramped rooms (bath tub), some a/c, good restaurant, pool (but small and only knee-deep, non-residents Rs 80 per hr) gym, garden. Friendly, well-managed, rates sometimes negotiable, only accepts rupees, tour of all nearby sites Rs 800.

**F Shree Laxmi Vilas**, simple rooms, 3 with balconies with great views back to the temples. Right in the thick of it, so it's interesting but noisy.

**Gulbarga** *p1021, map p1022*

**D Pariwar**, Humnabad Rd, near station, T08472-221522. Some a/c rooms (Rs 450), some good-value (**E**). Old but clean and tidy, it has friendly staff and tasty vegetarian meals (no beer).

**D Santosh**, University Rd (east of town), T08472-222661. Some a/c rooms, good non-vegetarian restaurant (beer). Best in town.

**D-E Aditya**, Humnabad Rd, T08472-202040. Reasonable rooms, some a/c with bath, clean vegetarian restaurant, very good value.

**Bidar** *p1022, map p1023*

**E Ashoka**, off Udgir Rd, near Deepak Cinema, T08482-226249. 21 clean, good-sized rooms, hot water, some a/c, restaurant ("bit of a drinking den but good tandoori"), friendly, only decent hotel in town. Recommended.

**F Mayura Barid Shahi** (KSTDC), Udgir Rd. Several very basic hotels near Old Bus Station. A roadside Punjabi *dhaba* near the junction of NH9 and the Bidar Rd serves very good meals, clean (including toilet at back).

**Raichur** *p1025*

**F Laxmi Lodge** at Koppal.

**F Railway Retiring Rooms** and dorm.

## Eating

**Hampi** *p1011, map p1013*

All restaurants are vegetarian, eggs are sometimes available.

🍴 **Boomshankar**, on path to Vittahla temple. Well-prepared, fresh river fish.

🍴 **Gopi**, for good simple, cheap *thalis*.

🍴 **Mango Tree**, river bank, 500 m west of Temple. Relaxed and pleasant.

🍴 **Manju** family-run, simple but enticing food (apple *parathas*), takeaways for tiffin boxes (will even lend boxes).

🍴 **Mayura Bhuvaneswari**, Kamalapuram, does cheap adequate meals.

🍴 **New Shanti**, does good carrot/apple/banana/chocolate cakes to order.

🍴 **Om Shiva**, excellent Western and Middle Eastern dishes, good hygiene.

🍴 **Shambhu**, opposite Shanti. For fresh pasta/noodles and espresso plus all the usual; also bus/train tickets for small commission.

🍴 **Suresh**, 30 m from Shanti, down a small alley. Very friendly family, made to order so takes a while, but worth the wait.

**Hospet** *p1014*
The hotels serve chilled beer.

🍴🍴 **Waves**, Malligi hotel, by pool. Multi-cuisine. Good food, bar.

🍴 **Iceland**, Station Rd, behind the bus station, good South Indian meals.

🍴 **Shanbhag**, near the bus station, good South Indian meals.

**Bijapur** *p1014, map p1015*

🍴 **Kapali**, opposite bus stand. Decent South Indian food.

🍴 **Priyadarshini**. Vegetarian snacks.

🍴 **Shrinidhi**. Quality vegetarian meals.

**Badami** *p1019*

🍴 **Dhabas** near the Tonga Stand sell snacks.

🍴 **Laxmi Vilas**, near taxi stand. Veg meals.

🍴 **Parimala** and **Geeta Darshini**, South Indian breakfasts.

🍴 **Sanman**, near bus stand. Non-veg food.

## Festivals and events

**Hampi** *p1011, map p1013*
**Jan-Feb**: Virupaksha Temple Car festival.
**3-5 Nov**: Hampi Music festival at Vitthala Temple when hotels get packed.

**Bijapur** *p1014, map p1015*
**Jan**: Siddhesvara Temple festival. Music festival accompanied by Craft Mela.

**Bagalkot** *p1018*
In **Jan Nrutytsava** draws many famous dancers and is accompanied by a Craft Mela. In **Mar-Apr Temple car** festivals at Virupaksha and Mallikarjuna temples.

## Shopping

**Bidar** *p1022, map p1023*
Excellent *bidriwork* (see page 1035) here, where it is said to have originated, particularly shops near the Ta'lim of Siddiq Shah. You can see craftsmen at work in the narrow lanes.

## Activities and tours

**Hospet** *p1014*
Tours from **KSTDC**, T21008, and **SRK Tours and Travels** at Malligi hotel, to Hampi, Rs 75 (lunch extra); 0930-1630. Daytrips to Aihole, Badami, Pattadakal 0830-1930 Rs 275 per person with trip. Long drive. Local sightseeing Rs 700 per day. Bijapur 1 day trip by public bus Rs 175, taxi Rs 2,100. English-speaking guide but rather rushed.

## Transport

**Hampi** *p1011*
**Bicycle hire** from Hampi Bazar (try stall behind the temple, Rs 30 per day), and Kamalapuram. **Coracles** take passengers across the river from the jetty west of the Virupaksha Temple, Rs 5 (Rs 10 with luggage). KSTDC has just introduced an air-route into Hampi from **Bangalore** – at US$1,700 for a 5-seater fixed-wing aircraft or US$3,990 for a 6-seater helicopter it's hardly for backpackers. If it's within your price range, contact the state tourism office, Badami House Opposite City Corporation Office, NR Square T080-22275869.

**Gadag**
Train to **Bijapur**: *Golgumbaz Exp, 7842*, 0715, 4½ hrs. **Guntakal** via **Hospet** (2 hrs): at 0037, 1412, 1802 and 2101, 4 hrs; **Hubli**: 8 daily 0322-2030, 1¾ hrs.

**Hospet** *p1014*
From Hospet to/from **Hampi**, travel via Kamalapuram, especially in the rainy season when the slower road to Hampi Bazar which

winds through villages, is barely passable. Auto-rickshaw to Hampi, Rs 200.

**Bus**
Frequent buses to **Hampi**'s 2 entry points (via Kamalapuram and museum, Rs 4 and via Hampi Bazar, 30 mins, Rs 3.50), from 0530; last return around 2000. Express bus to/from **Bangalore** (road now upgraded), several from 0700, 10 hrs; **Mysore**, 1830, 10½ hrs (Express buses to Belur/Halebid from both). Services to other sites, eg **Badami** (6 hrs), **Bijapur** (6 hrs), **Chitradurga** 0530 (3 hrs). Overnight Karnataka Tourism luxury coaches to various towns. Direct buses to **Panaji** (Goa); the road is being improved – *Luxury*, 0630 (10½ hrs), State bus, 0830 (reserve a seat in advance); others involve a change in Hubli (4½ hrs). Paulo Travels Luxury Sleeper coach from Hotel Priyadarshini, at 1845, Rs 350, daily; West Coast Sleeper, from Hotel Shanbhag, 1830, Rs 350; daily (Oct-Mar only); strangers may be expected to share a bunk. It is better to take a train to Londa (under 5 hrs) and get a bus to Madgaon or Panaji (3 hrs).

**Cycle-rickshaw**
From railway station to bus stand about Rs 20.

**Taxi**
KSTDC, T08394-21008, T08394-28537 or from Malligi Hotel; about Rs 700 per day.

**Train**
**Bangalore**, *Hampi Exp, 6591*, 2010 (via Guntakal, 2½ hrs) 10½ hrs. **Guntakal**: *Amaravati Exp, 7226*, 1610, 2½ hrs. For **Belur/ Halebid**: *Amaravati Exp, 7225,* 1050 to **Hubli**; then *Hubli-Arsikere Pass, 884 (S)*, 1440, arrive 2120. To **Badami**: via **Gadag**, 4 hrs. **Hyderabad** (via **Guntakal**): *Hampi/ Rayalaseema Exp, 6591/7430,* 2010, 14 hrs. **Madgaon**, *7227*, Tue, Fri, depart Hospet 1050, 9 hrs.

**Bijapur** *p1014, map p1015*
**Bus**
A service runs between the station (2 km east) to west end of town. Horse drawn carriages ply up and down MG Rd; a fine change from autos but bargain hard.

Buses are frequent between Bijapur and **Bidar**, **Hubli**, **Belgaum** and **Solapur** (2-2½ hrs). Buses to **Badami** 3½ hrs. For **Hospet**, travel via Gadag or Ikal. Reservations can be made on the following daily services to **Aurangabad**: 0600, 1830 (Rs 180), **Hospet**, **Bangalore**: 1700, 1800, 1930, 2130 (Rs 193, 12 hrs); Ultra fast at 1900, 2000 (Rs 252), **Belgaum**: 0630 (Rs 71), **Hubli**: 0900, 1400, 1600 (Rs 84), **Hyderabad**: 0600, 1800 (Rs 141); Deluxe at 2130 (Rs 203), **Mumbai (CT)** : 0800, 1600, 1700, 2030 (Rs 215), **Mumbai (Kurla)**: 1900, 2000, 2100 (Rs 210), **Mysore**: 1700 (Rs 230), **Panaji**: 1900 (Rs 126) and **Vasco de Gama**: 0715 (Rs 131). Several private agents also run services to **Bangalore** (Rs 220, 12 hrs), **Mumbai** (Rs 250, 11 hrs) and **Pune** (Rs 200, 7 hrs).

**Train**
Computerized Reservation Office open 0800-2000, Sun 0800-1400. **Solapur**: 0945, 1635 (2½ hrs). **Gadag**: 5 trains daily for long distance connections. Otherwise, buses are more convenient.

**Badami** *p1019, map p1020*
**Bicycle**
Bike hire from stalls along the main road, Rs 4 per hr; pleasant to visit Banashankari, Mahakuta and Pattadakal.

**Bus**
Few daily to **Hospet** (6 hrs), very slow and crowded but quite a pleasant journey with lots of stops; **Belgaum** via **Bagalkot**, 4 hrs; **Bijapur**, 0645-0930 (4 hrs). Several to **Pattadakal** and **Aihole** from 0730. **Aihole** (2 hrs), from there to **Pattadakal** (1600). Last return bus from Aihole 1715, via Pattadakal.

**Car**
Hire from Badami with driver for Mahakuta, Aihole and Pattadakal, about Rs 650.

**Train**
The station is 5 km north on the **Bijapur-Gadag** line, with 6 trains daily in each direction (enquire about schedules); frequent buses to town.

**Gulbarga** *p1021, map p1022*
**Bus**
There are bus connections to **Hyderabad** (190 km) and **Solapur**.

**Train**

**Mumbai (CST)**: 8 trains daily, 13 hrs. **Bangalore**: *Udayan Exp, 6529,* 1900, 13½ hrs; *Lokmanya Tilak, 1013,* 0905, 13 hrs. **Chennai (MC)**: *Chennai Exp, 6011* (AC/II), 0130, 15 hrs; *Mumbai Chennai Mail, 6009,* 1140, 18 hrs; *Dadar Chennai Exp, 1063,* 0605, 14 hrs. **Hyderabad**: *Mumbai-Hyderabad Exp, 7031* (AC/II), 0020, 5¾ hrs; *Hussainsagar Exp, 7001,* 0740, 5 hrs.

**Bidar** *p1022, map p1023*

**Auto-rickshaw**

Easily available, Rs 15 being the going rate for most short hops across town.

**Bicycle**

Cycling is the best way to get around and see the sights. 'Cycle taxis' can be hired for around Rs 20 per day from several outlets all over town and near the New Bus Station. You may have to ask 2 or 3 before you find a shop that will rent to you, but persevere. Don't waste time with Ganesh Cycle Taxi, near New Bus Station.

**Bus**

Services from New Bus Station, 1 km west of centre, to most regional destinations, but check timings since the last bus is often quite early. From **Hyderabad** or **Gulbarga** (under 4 hrs), or **Bijapur** (8 hrs). Private buses to **Mumbai**: 1700, 5 hrs, Rs 260. **Pune**: 1530, 3½ hrs, Rs 220. Taxi to **Gulbarga** Rs 800.

**Train**

Bidar is on a branch line from Vikarabad to Parbhani Junction. Too slow to be of much use. **Aurangabad**: *Kacheguda- Manmad Exp, 7664,* 2140, 8½ hrs. **Bangalore**: *Hampi Link Exp, 6593,* 1237, 18 hrs. **Secunderabad**: *Manmad-Kacheguda Exp, 7663,* 0352, 5 hrs.

## Directory

**Hampi** *p1011, map p1013*

**Exchange** Several agents on main street. Modi Enterprises, Main road, near Tourist Office, changes TCs and cash. Also Neha Travels. **Internet, money change and tour agent** On main street and some lodges (eg *Shanti, Sree Rama*), Rs 60 per hr; but frequent power cuts.

**Hospet** *p1014*

**Banks** State Bank of India, next to Tourist Office, only changes cash (US $ and UK £). Monica Travel, near Bus Station, changes TCs (3% charge). **Internet** Cybernet, College Rd, next to Shivananda. **Post** Opposite vegetable market.

**Bijapur** *p1014, map p1015*

**Banks** State Bank of India in the citadel, Canara Bank, north of market, best for exchange. **Internet** Cyber Park, first floor, Royal Complex, opposite GPO, 0930-2300 fast connections.

# Andhra Pradesh

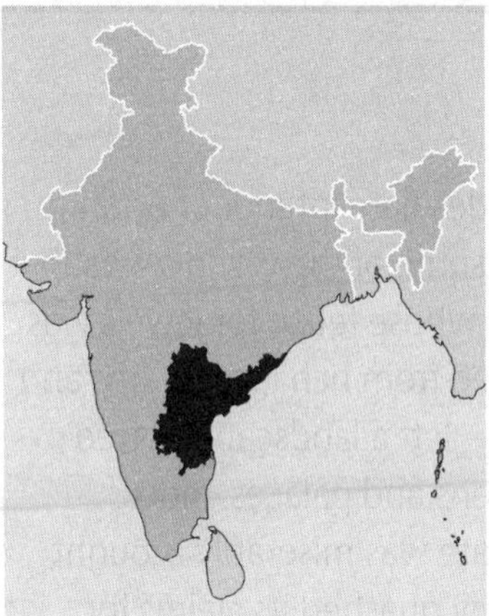



**Footprint features**

# Introduction

The thin red soil of the hot and desolate interior of Andhra Pradesh was once the stage for some of the world's wealthiest men. The Deccani Sultans – whose fetish for jewels was sated with the diamonds quarried from rich local seams and whose ears dripped with pearls – left a landscape dotted with their courtly pleasure gardens and palaces. India's largest Muslim-ruled princely state was miserably brought to its knees when the Indian army quashed its claims for independence, but much of the splendour of their architecture remains, particularly in Hyderabad and its nearby fortress city of Golconda and the city's fortunes are rising again with the rocketing software industries headquartered on its suburban hillsides at the glass-and-chrome satellite town of Cyberabad.

The watersheds of Andhra Pradesh's rivers, the Krishna and Godaveri, are second only to the Ganga and are vital in supporting the meager agricultural subsistence of the bullock-and-cart paddy economy. Rural Andhra also holds the ancient Buddhist centres of Nagarjunakonda and Amaravati, and one of India's most important modern Hindu pilgrimage centres, Tirumalai. Large areas of the northwest also hide the secretive Maoist Naxalite movement, a rebel army whose often violent opposition to aid and development has lead to the blocking of road-building efforts and the high-security that surrounds the state's chief minister.

## ★ Don't miss...

1 **Hyderabad** View the riches that once belonged to the Nizams at the Salar Jung Museum and visit the Mecca Masjid, especially during the quaranic call to prayer on Sunday afternoons when 40 people from ages 12 to 60 act as muezzin for the *adhan*, page 1036.

2 **Warangal** Walk through the ruins of the medieval city, page 1047.

3 **Nagarjunakonda Island** Take a boat ride across the lake to reach one of India's oldest Buddhist sites, page 1048.

4 **Tirupati temple** Attend at Darshan (special viewing) along with 10,000 other pilgrims, page 1062.

5 **Vijayanagar Gooty Fort** Climb to the top for spectacular views over the plains, page 1067.

# Background → *Population: 75.7 million. Area: 275,000 sq km.*

## The land

**Geography** For much of the year the interior looks dry and desolate although the great delta of the Krishna and Godavari rivers retains its lush greenness by virtue of their irrigation water. Water is the state's lifeblood, and the great peninsular rivers have a sanctity which reflects their importance. The Godavari, rising less than 200 km north of Mumbai, is the largest of the peninsular rivers. The Krishna rises near Mahabaleshwar at an altitude of 1,360 m. After the Ganga these two rivers have the largest watersheds in India, and between them irrigate nearly 6,000,000 ha of farmland.

**Climate** Andhra Pradesh is hot throughout the year. The interior is in the rain shadow of the Western Ghats and receives less rainfall than much of the coast. All regions have most of rain between June and October, although the south gets the benefit of the retreating monsoon between October and December. Cyclones sweeping across the Bay of Bengal can wreak havoc in the flat coastal districts in November-December.

## History

The first historical evidence of a people called the 'Andhras' came from Emperor Asoka. The first known Andhra power, the **Satavahanas** encouraged various religious groups including Buddhists. Their capital at Amaravati shows evidence of the great skill of early Andhra artists and builders. Around AD 150 there was also a fine university at Nagarjunakonda. In 1323 Warangal, just to the northeast of the present city of Hyderabad, was captured by the armies of Muhammad bin Tughlaq. Muslim expansion further south was prevented for two centuries by the rise of the **Vijayanagar Empire**, itself crushed at the Battle of Talikota in 1565 by a short-lived federation of Muslim States, and the cultural life it supported had to seek fresh soil.

From then on **Muslim rulers** dominated the politics of central Andhra, Telangana. The Bahmani Kingdoms in the region around modern Hyderabad controlled central Telangana in the 16th century. They were even able to keep the Mughals at bay until Aurangzeb finally forced them into submission at the end of the 17th century. **Hyderabad** was the most important centre of Muslim power in central and South India from the 17th to the 19th centuries. It was founded by the fifth in line of an earlier Muslim Dynasty, **Mohammad Quli Qutb Shah**, in 1591. Through his successors Hyderabad became the capital of a Princely State the size of France, ruled by a succession of Muslim Nizams from 1724 till after India's Independence in 1947.

Through the 18th century **British and French traders** were spreading their influence up the coast. Increasingly they came into conflict and looked for alliances with regional powers. At the end of the 18th century the British reached an agreement with the **Nizam of Hyderabad** whereby he accepted British support in exchange for recognition of British rights to trade and political control of the coastal districts. Thus Hyderabad retained a measure of independence until 1947 while accepting British suzerainty.

There was doubt as to whether the Princely State would accede to india after Partition. The Nizam of Hyderabad would have liked to join fellow Muslims in the newly created Muslim State of Pakistan. However, political disturbances in 1949 gave the Indian Government the excuse to take direct control, and the state was incorporated into the Indian Union.

## Culture

Most of Andhra Pradesh's 78 million people are Dravidians. Over 85% of the **population** speak Telugu. However, there are important minorities. Tamil is widely spoken in the extreme south, and on the border of Karnataka there are pockets of Kanarese speakers. In Hyderabad there are large numbers of Urdu speakers who make up seven per cent of the state's population.

Hyderabad, the capital of modern Andhra Pradesh, was the seat of government of the Muslim Nizams. Under their rule many Muslims came to work in the court, from North India and abroad. The Nizam's capital was a highly cosmopolitan centre, drawing extensively on Islamic contacts in North India and in west Asia – notably Persia.

Andhra **food** stands out as distinct because of its northern influence and larger number of non-vegetarians. The rule of the Muslim Nawabs for centuries is reflected in the rich, spicy local dishes, especially in the area around the capital. Try *haleem* (spiced pounded wheat with mutton), *paya* (soup) or *baghara baigan* (stuffed aubergines). Rice and meat *biryani, nahari, kulcha,* egg *paratha,* and *kababs* have a lot in common with the northern Mughlai cuisine. The growing of hot chillies has led to its liberal use in the food prepared. Good quality locally-grown grapes (especially *anab-e-shahi*) or *khobani* (puréed apricots) provide a welcome neutralizing effect.

## Craft industries

Andhra's **bidriware** uses dark matt gunmetal (a zinc and copper alloy) with silver damascening in beautiful flowing floral and arabesque patterns and illustrates the Persian influence on Indian motifs. The articles vary from large vases and boxes, jewellery and plates to tiny buttons and cuff links. The name is derived from Bidar in Karnataka and dates back to the Bahmani rulers.

Miniature wooden figures, animals, fruit, vegetables and birds are common subjects of *Kondapalli* **toys** which are known for their bright colours. *Nirmal* toys look more natural and are finished with a herbal extract which gives them a golden sheen, *Tirupati* toys are in a red wood while *Ethikoppaka* toys are finished in coloured lacquer. Andhra also produces fine figurines of deities in sandalwood.

Hyderabadi **jewellers** work in gold and precious stones which are often uncut. The craftsmen can often be seen working in the lanes around the Char Minar with shops selling the typical local bangles set with glass to the west. Hyderabadi cultured pearls and silver filigree ware from Karimnagar are another speciality.

The state is famous for **himru shawls** and **fabrics** produced in cotton/silk mixes with rich woven patterns on a special handloom. Silver or gold threads produce even richer 'brocade' cloth. A boy often sits with the weavers 'calling out' the intricate pattern. The art of weaving special **ikat** fabrics has been revived through the efforts of the All India Handicrafts Board. The practice of dyeing the warp and weft threads before weaving in to produce a pattern, additionally used oil in the process when it was woven into pieces of cloth *teli rumal* (literally oil kerchief) to be used as garments.

**Kalamkari paintings** (*kalam* refers to the pen used) produced in Kalahasti in the extreme south of Andhra, have a distinctive style using indigo and vegetable dyes extracted from turmeric, pomegranate skin et cetera, on cloth. The blues stand out markedly from the otherwise dullish ochre colours. Originally designed to tell stories from mythology (*Mahabharata* and *Ramayana*), they make good wall hangings.

## Modern Andhra Pradesh

**Government** In 1953 Andhra Pradesh was created on the basis of the Telugu-speaking districts of Madras Presidency. This was not enough for those who were demanding statehood for a united Telugu-speaking region. One political leader, Potti Sreeramulu, starved himself to death in protest at the government's refusal to grant the demand. In 1956, Andhra Pradesh took its present form; all Telugu-speaking areas were grouped together in the new State of Andhra Pradesh.

Andhra Pradesh was regarded as a stronghold of the Congress Party until 1983 when a regional party, the Telugu Desam, won a crushing victory in the State Assembly elections. The Assembly elections on 5 October 1999 saw a repeat performance, with the highly regarded modernising Chief Minister N Chandrababu Naidu, being swept back to power in the State Assembly with nearly a two thirds majority. Allied with the BJP in the governing coalition in New Delhi, the Telugu Desam had a reputation for pushing ahead with rapid economic modernisation, particularly visible in Hyderabad, but Naidu, who borrowed heavily from the World Bank and took China, Singapore and Malaysia as his business models, was forced from office before he could take up a third term in 2004. The Congress candidate YS Rajasekhara Reddy took charge of a state with high debts to the World Bank and where poverty remains endemic in many rural areas and where farmers had been routinely committing suicide in response to drought conditions. Hopes are high that his government will also strike a more conciliatory tone towards the extremist Naxalite movement and the Peoples' War Group (PWG) which have plagued some remote districts for over 30 years.

**Economy** The last decade has seen a great surge in Hyderabad's focus on IT and computing, but the city already had a significant industrial base from pharmaceuticals to aerospace electronics, and fertilizers to glass and watches. However, apart from coal mining in northern Andhra and the extraction of some copper, manganese and mica, the state's economy continues to depend heavily on agriculture which still employs nearly 70% of the population. Rice is by far the most important crop, especially in the fertile coastal districts where good soils also benefit from intensive irrigation. The much drier interior has a quite different range of crops, jowar and millets being dominant. Sugarcane, cotton and tobacco are particularly important cash crops, and forest products also contribute significantly to the state's income.

# North central Andhra Pradesh

## Hyderabad and Secunderabad

*→ Phone code: 040. Colour map 6, grid B1. Population: 5.5 mn.*



The Twin Cities, founded by the rulers of two separate Muslim dynasties, used to square off across the Hussain Sagar lake but have long since bled into one conglomerate metropolis. It is the southern (Hyderabadi) half that holds most allure for the outsider: the dusty and congested old city past the Musi River with its endless up-croppings of Islamic architecture. Nowhere else can you see in such close proximity the jumble of atavistic India, the elegant precision of Muslim mathematical architecture and the new rubric of the hyper-evolved high tech and biotech capitals. The success of the latter has spawned a new breed of millionaires to keep the old pearl peddlers' turnovers high since trade from their previous best customers, the jewel-draped Nizams, dried up. N Chandrababu Naidu, Andhra's chief minister from the late 1990s until 2004, had development dreams as lofty as the legendarily eccentric Nizam. The result is a city with town planning unequalled in India, huge theme resorts where you can stand at minus temperatures, a tribute to the famous heat of Andhra, and a Hi-Tech City to rival Silicon Valley, the brilliantly named Cyberabad, home to Microsoft's first overseas base. The wide streets of the modern city are spotlessly clean (in the Nizam's time they were washed twice a day), while the narrow lanes around Char Minaar throb with a very Muslim mania.

### Ins and outs

**Getting there** Begumpet airport is just 6 km from Secunderabad station and 15 km from Hyderabad Old City (which has most of the sights). Secunderabad station, with trains to major cities, is in the Cantonment area, while the Hyderabad City station at Nampally is close to the Abids district, with the majority of budget accommodation. The large Imbli-Ban Bus terminal for long-distance buses is on an island in the Musi River, south of Abids. The Jubilee Bus Terminal is in Secunderabad.

**Getting around** Autos (or taxis) are the best means of getting about the city north of the Musi and in Secunderabad, but in the congested old quarter you are best off walking, though there are cycle-rickshaws. *See Transport, page 1053, for further details.*

**Tourist offices** Govt of AP ⓘ *A Block, 3rd floor, Secretariat, T040-23456717; Tank Bund Rd, near Secretariat, T040-23453036.* APTDC ⓘ *3rd floor, FDC Complex, AC Guards, T040-23399416, apttdc@satyam.net.in, 0630-1830.*

## History

In 1323 Warangal, just to the northeast of the present city of Hyderabad, was captured by the armies of Muhammad bin Tughlaq. Muslim expansion further south was prevented for two centuries by the rise of the **Vijayanagar Empire**, itself crushed at the Battle of Talikota in 1565 by a short-lived federation of Muslim States, and the cultural life it supported had to seek fresh soil.

From then on **Muslim rulers** dominated the politics of central Andhra, Telangana. The Shiite Bahmani Kingdoms in the region around modern Hyderabad controlled central Telangana in the 16th century. They were even able to keep the Sunni rivals, the Mughals, at bay until Aurangzeb finally forced them into submission at the end of the 17th century. Hyderabad was the most important centre of Muslim power in central and South India from the 17th to the 19th centuries. It was founded by the fifth in line of an earlier Muslim Dynasty, **Mohammad Quli Qutb Shah**, under the original name of Bhagnagar, in 1591. Through his successors Hyderabad became the capital of a Princely State the size of France, ruled by a succession of Muslim Nizams from 1724 till after India's Independence in 1947, founding a dynasty that included some of the richest men in the world, famous for their beautiful 'monuments, mosques and mistresses' and also for their diamond markets.

Through the 18th century **British and French traders** were scrambling to win allies with regional rulers as their influence spread up the coast and the fight for supremacy in India became more embittered. At the end of the 18th century the British reached an agreement with the **Nizam of Hyderabad** whereby he would accept British support in exchange for recognition of British rights to trade and political control of the coastal districts. Thus Hyderabad retained a measure of independence until 1947 while accepting British suzerainty.

There was doubt as to whether the Princely State would accede to India after Partition. The Nizam of Hyderabad would have liked to join fellow Muslims in the newly created Muslim State of Pakistan. However, political disturbances in 1949 gave the Indian Government the excuse to take direct control, and the state was incorporated into the Indian Union.

Hyderabad has a large Muslim minority, even though the population was always predominantly composed of Telugu-speaking Hindus. Occasionally the political situation can become tense and parts of the city put under curfew.

## Old City and Char Minar

Facing the river is the **High Court**, on the new roads laid out along the Musi's embankments after the great flood, a splendid Mughal-style building in the old Qutb Shahi gardens, **Amin Bagh**, near the Afzal Ganj Bridge (New Bridge). Vincent Esch's most striking work, it was built in 1916 of local pink granite, with red sandstone carved panels and columns, a large archway and domes, now painted pink. A further recent change is the enclosure of the verandahs. The detail is Mughal, but some argue that the structure and internal form are Western.

*Devastating floods and outbreaks of plague at the beginning of the 19th century were followed by programmes of urban renewal initiated by Nizam Osman Ali Khan. A series of new public buildings date from this period including those from 1914-1921, under the supervision of British architect Vincent Esch, who attempted to build in an Indian style.*

# Hyderabad-Secunderabad

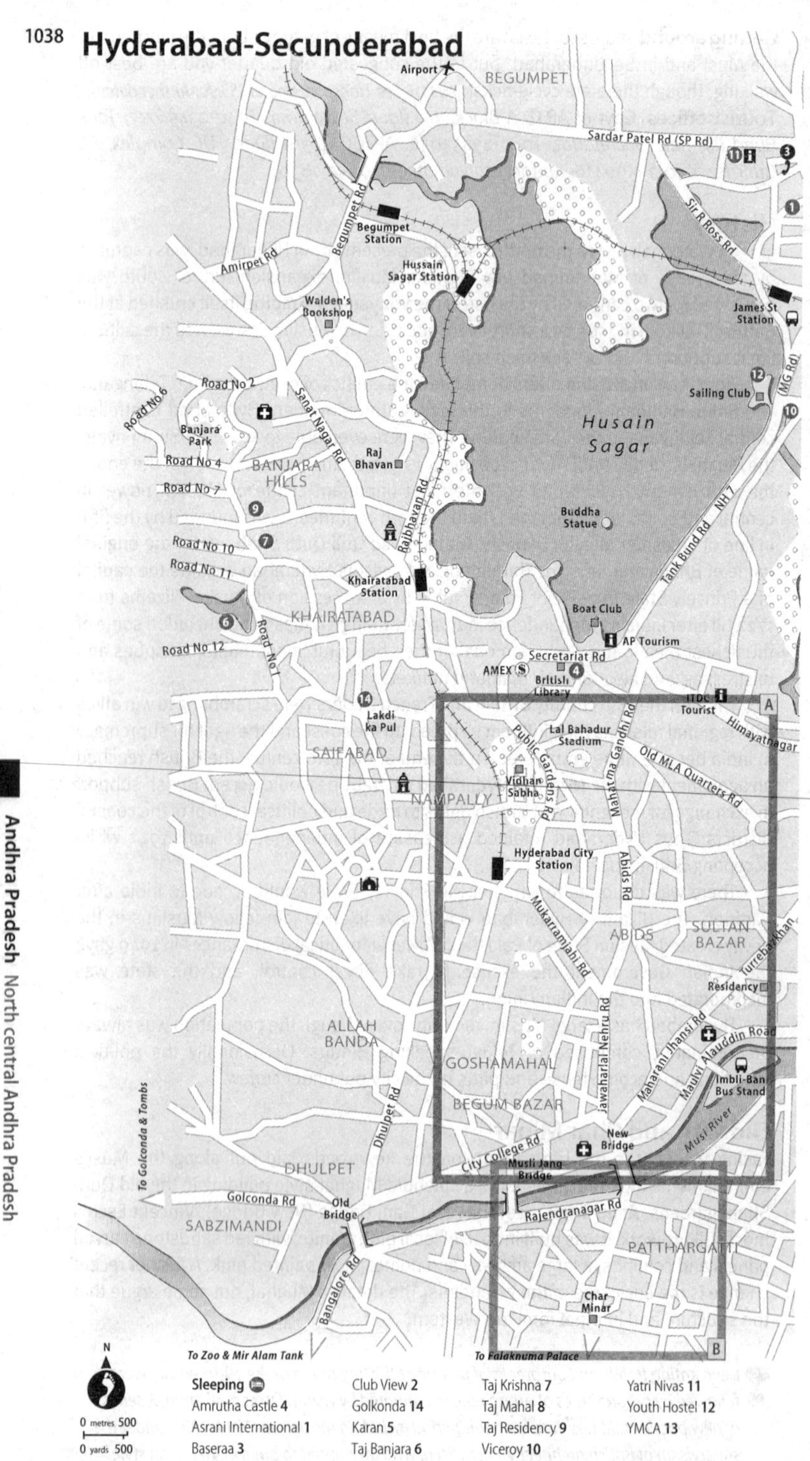

Eating 
Paradise 3

*Related maps*
*A Hyderabad centre, page 1042.*
*B The old city Char Minar, page 1040.*

Next door to the High Court is Esch's **City College** (1917-1920), originally built as the City High School for boys. Built largely of undressed granite, there are some distinctive Indian decorative features including some marble *jalis*. Esch deliberately incorporated Gothic features, calling his style 'Perpendicular Mogul Saracenic'.

Over the river is the **Osmania Women's College**, formerly the British residency to James Achilles Kirkpatrick at the centre of William Dalrymple's history, *White Mughals*, a colonial structure that has lately found its way on to the World Monuments Fund's list of One Hundred Most Endangered Buildings (Dalrymple's book was launched from the stately, ochre-painted building's Durbar Hall – a room of giant chandeliers, French windows and tatty fans and glorious floral tracings on its ceiling). Sadly it has earned its place on the list: windows are smashed in and the model of the Residency that Kirkpatrick commissioned for his Muslim bride so she could see the house without breaking her purda (go out Kings Gate then head left down a pathway towards the pigeon rook) has been almost entirely razed.

To the south of the river again, one of the oldest *imambaras* in the country, the **Badshahi** (Royal) **Ashurkhana**, or house of mourning, built in the Qutb Shahi style at the end of the 16th century, has excellent tile mosaics and wooden columns in the outer chamber, both of which were later additions.

South from the bridge down Sadar Patel Road is **Charkaman** with its four arches. The eastern Black Arch was for the drums, the western led to the palaces, the northern was the Fish Arch and the southern led to the Char Minar.

**Salar Jung Museum** ⓘ *Salar Jung Marg, closed Fri and public holidays, 1030-1700, Rs 150, cameras and bags must be left at counter, tape recorded guides at ticket office, allow 1½ hrs.*
Sir Yusuf Ali Salar Jung III was the Wazir (Prime Minister) to the Nizam between 1899-1949, and his collection forms the basis of the modern museum, one of the

 three national museums in India. Originally housed on the edge of the city in one of the palaces, it was rehoused in a purpose-built, if singularly dull and unattractive, building in 1968. There are informative descriptions of the exhibits in English, Urdu, Hindi and Telugu. The museum is designed to a semi-circular plan with the entrance off the reception area. Along the verandah, 19th-century copies of European statuary overlook a small open space. The collection includes Indian textiles, bronzes, paintings and fine ivory art pieces, armoury, Far Eastern porcelain and entertaining curiosities.

**Char Minar** ⓘ *Illuminations, 1900-2100. The site is closed to visitors but you can walk under the arches. Best to visit in the morning before the surrounding roads become almost impassable.* This was built between 1591 and 1612 by **Sultan Mohammad Quli Qutb Shah** as a showpiece at the centre of his beautiful city; it has become the city's symbol but it's crumbling. With its 56 m tall slender minarets with spiral staircases and huge arches on each side (the whole plastered with lime mortar) it stood at the entrance to the palace complex. Now, standing at the centre of a crossroads, it guards the entry to the main bazaar. There is a beautiful mosque on the second floor and a large water tank in the middle. There is a special market on Thursday.

**Mecca Masjid** Immediately to the southwest of Char Minar, this grand mosque was started in 1614 by the sixth **Sultan Abdulla Qutb Shah** and completed by Aurangzeb when he annexed Golconda in 1692. Built of enormous black granite slabs quarried nearby, it has tall pillars, stucco decorations and red bricks on its entrance arches believed to have been made from clay from Mecca mixed with red colouring. The vast mosque can accommodate 10,000 at prayers. The tombs of the Asaf Jahi rulers, the Nizams of Hyderabad, are in a roofed enclosure to the left of the courtyard. The **Jama Masjid** was the second mosque built in the old city at the end of the 16th century.



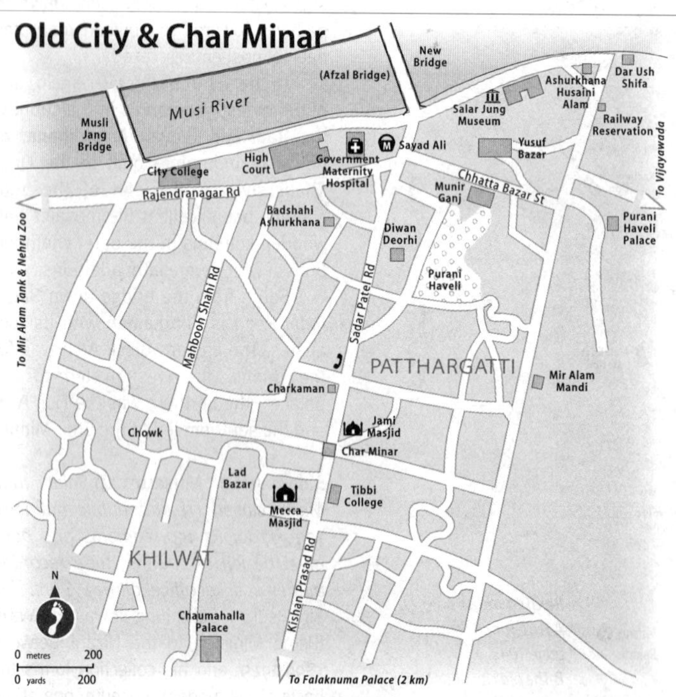

**Lad Bazar area** This area has interesting buildings with wood and stone carvings and pink elephant gates. It is at the heart of the Muslim part of the city, and so densely packed with people it can be very difficult even to look at the buildings (some women visitors have found it a bit daunting). You arrive at the **Chowk** which has a mosque and a Victorian Clock Tower. Southeast of the Lad Bazar is the huge complex of the palaces which were built by the different Nizams, including the grand **Chaumahalla Palace** around a quadrangle.

**Falaknuma Palace (1873)** Originally a rich nobleman's house, the palace was built in a mixture of classical and Mughal styles. Bought by the Nizam in 1897, it has a superb interior (particularly the state reception room) with marble, chandeliers and paintings. The palace houses Eastern and European treasures, including a collection of jade, crystal and precious stones and a superb library. The spectacular building is being converted into a hotel by the Taj Group.

## Hyderabad Centre: The New City

The **Osmania General Hospital** (1918-1921) is the third of Vincent Esch's impressive buildings in Hyderabad. It stands across the river, opposite the High Court. The 200 m long building was one of the largest – and best equipped – hospitals in the world when it was opened. Its Indian context is indicated by decorative detail rather than structural plan. To its east, also on the river, is the imposing **Asafia State Central Library** (1929-1934) with its priceless collection of Arabic, Persian and Urdu books and manuscripts. The Library was designed by anonymous architects of the PWD.

The **Public Gardens** ⓘ *closed on public holidays,* in Nampally, north of Hyderabad Station, contain some important buildings including the Archaeological Museum and Art Galleries and the State Legislative Assembly (Vidhan Sabha).

**Andhra Pradesh State Museum** ⓘ *1030-1700, closed public holidays, nominal entrance fee, photography Rs 10, guide book, Rs 15, near the Lal Bahadur Shastri Stadium, 10 minutes by car from Banjara Hills area,* is a small museum with sections on prehistoric implements, sculptures, paintings, inscriptions, illuminated manuscripts, coins, arms, bidri ware, china, textiles and a crowd-drawing 4,000-year-old Egyptian mummy. Behind the museum, in the Ajanta Pavilion are life-size copies of Ajanta frescoes while the Nizam's collection of rare artefacts are housed in the Jubilee Hall.

The **City Railway Station** (1914) was intended by Esch to be pure Mughal in style but built entirely of the most modern material then available – pre-cast, reinforced concrete. It has a wide range of distinctively Indian features – the *chhattris* of royalty, wide eaves (*chajjas*), and onion domes.

**Naubat Pahad** (Kala Pahad or Neeladri) are two hills to the north of the Public Gardens. The Qutb Shahis are believed to have had their proclamations read from the hill tops accompanied by drums. In 1940 pavilions were built and then a hanging garden was laid out on top of one (now occupy the Birla Planetarium and Science Centre).

**Venkatesvara Temple** ⓘ *summer 0900-1200, 1600-2000, Sun 2030; winter 0700-1200, 1330-2030, photography of inner sanctum prohibited, reached by a stall-lined path opposite Thomas Cook on Secretariat Rd,* is a modern, stunning white marble temple with an intricately carved ceiling which overlooks Husain Sagar. It was built by the Birlas, the Marwari business family who have been responsible for building important new Hindu temples in several major cities, including the Laxmi Narayan Temple in New Delhi. Completed in 1976, the images of the deities are South Indian, although the building itself drew craftsmen from the north as well, among them some who claimed to have ancestors who built the Taj Mahal.

*Hyderabad's face is changing. It's fast overtaking Bangalore as India's foremost garden city: 0.2 million sq ft of carpet lawn was sold in 1999, now that figure is 2 million sq ft. There's also been a huge jump in plant nurseries – and an increase in private pet care companies!*

## Hyderabad centre

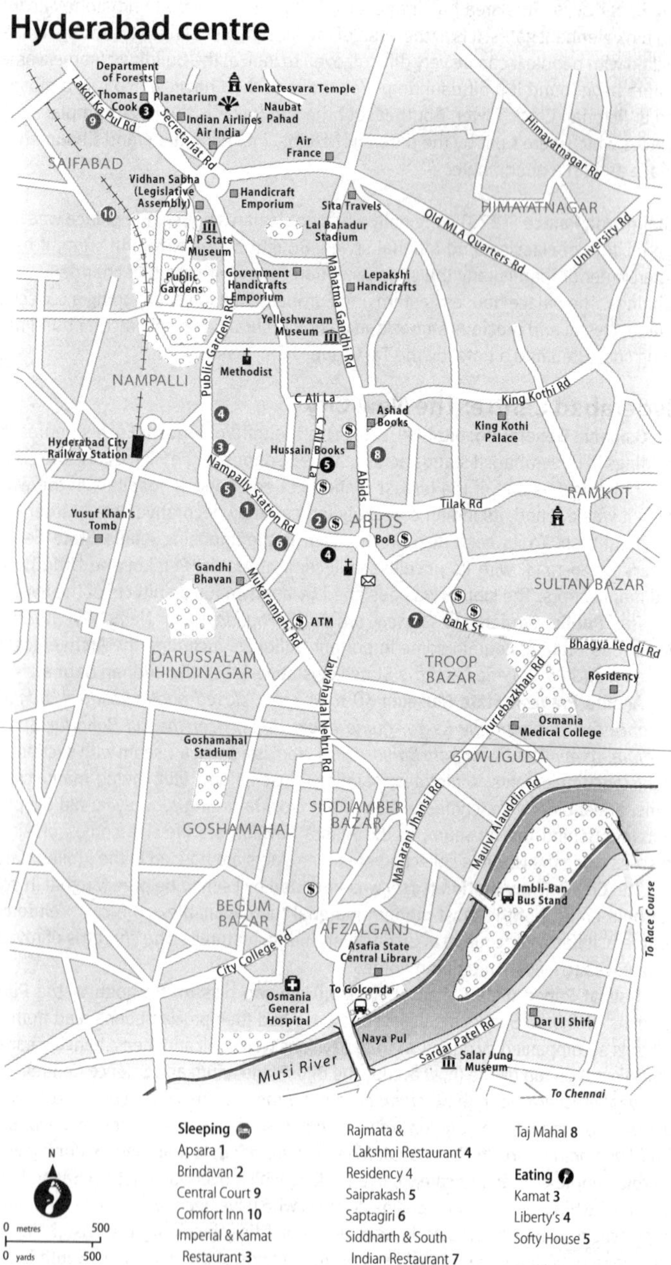


The massive State Legislative Assembly building, **Vidhan Sabha**, originally the Town Hall, was built by the PWD in 1922. Although Esch had nothing to do with its design, he reportedly admired it for its lightness and coolness, even on the hottest day. **Jubilee Hall** (1936), behind the Vidhan Sabha, is another remarkable PWD building, with clear simple lines.

**Husain Sagar** ⓘ *boat trips organized by APTDC leave from Lumbini Park, near the APTDC office on Secretariat Rd*, is 16-m deep and was created in the mid-16th century by building a bund linking Hyderabad and Secunderabad, and was named to mark the gratitude of Ibrahim Quli Qutb Shah to Hussain Shah Wali who helped him recover from his illness. The *bund* is a favourite promenade for the city dwellers. At the far end of the lake is the **Nizamia Observatory**. The 17.5 m high, 350 tonne granite **statue of the Buddha** was erected in the lake after years of successive disasters and finally inaugurated by the Dalai Lama in 1993. The tank, fed by streams originating from the Musi River, supplies drinking water to Hyderabad. Although it supports a rich birdlife and is used for fish culturing it also receives huge amounts of industrial effluent, agricultural waste and town sewage.

## Outside the city centre

**Osmania University**, built by the Nizam in 1939, is just outside the city, towards the east. Inaugurated in 1917 in temporary buildings, its sprawling campus with its black granite Arts College combines Moorish and Hindu Kakatiya architectural styles. There is a botanical garden and the **State Archives**.

The **tomb of Michel Raymond**, is off the Vijayawada Road, about 3 km from the Oliphant Bridge. The Frenchman joined the second Nizam's army in 1786 as a common soldier and rose to command 15,000 troops. His popularity with the people earned him the combined Muslim-Hindu name 'Moosa Ram', and even today they remember him by holding a commemorative *Urs* fair at his grey granite tomb which is 7 m high and bears the initials 'JR'.

**Mir Alam Tank**, to the southwest of the old city, is a large artificial lake. It was built by French engineers under instructions of the grandfather of Salar Jung III and is a popular picnic spot. It is now part of the Nehru Zoological Park which is to its north.

**Nehru Zoological Park** ⓘ *0900-1700, closed Mon, Rs 50, camera Rs 10, video Rs 75, bus 7Z from Secunderabad Station and Public Garden Rd*, occupies 13 ha of a low hilly area with remarkable boulders. The extensive grounds offer a welcome relief from the bustle of the city, and birdwatching here provides a good introduction to Indian avifauna – this is one of the best zoos in India (the animals are kept in natural surroundings) and well worth a visit. There's also a lion safari park and a nocturnal house. The Natural History Museum, Ancient Life Museum and Prehistoric Animals Park are here as well.

**Ramoji Film City** ⓘ *T08415 246201, 0900-1800, Rs 150 weekdays (children under 12, Rs 100), Rs 200 (children, Rs 150) weekends and public holidays*, 25 km from Hyderabad on the Vijayawada Road, is a sherbet-dipped shrine to the many uses of plaster of Paris. Bus tours take visitors around the 'city'. Conducted mainly in Hindi, you'll still gather that everywhere from Mumbai's Chor Bazar to Mysore's Brindavan Gardens have been re-created since media baron Ramoji Rao founded his film lot in 1991. Over 3,000 films have been shot here since then. Oddly compelling though it is to see an audience sit in rapt thrall to a show of aspiring film dancers gyrating in spandex hot pants, while their male opposite numbers inexplicably morris dance, this excursion is only for the committed Indian film buff. It doesn't have the diversionary value of Universal Studios, but there is a theme park **Fundustan** for kids. There are regular bus services from Hyderabad.

# Golconda

ⓘ *0700-2000. US$2. Official guides wait at the entrance (Rs 250), unofficial ones greet you with a hand-clap under the Fateh Darwaza. Allow 2-3 hours. Both the fort and the tombs are popular sites and can get crowded and very noisy after 1000; if you arrive early it is worth asking to be allowed in. Excellent Sound and Light show, 1 hr, English Nov-Feb 1830; Mar-Oct 1900. Tickets at Golconda 1 hr before start, Rs 25, or at*

*Yatri Nivas, 1000-1200. A coach trip from there (minimum number needed) departs at 1615 and returns 2115; Rs 100 includes show ticket and a couple of other sites. Some buy Sound and Light ticket as soon as the office opens and take a quick tour (45 mins) of the fort before sunset in time for the show. 11km west of Hyderabad. See Qutb Shahi Tombs for information on how to get there.*

Golconda, one of the most accessible of great medieval fortresses in India, was the capital of the Qutb Shahi kings who ruled over the area from 1507 to 1687. Nizam-ul-Mulk repossessed it in 1724 and restored it to its former glory for a time. Modern day restorations are being carried out by the Archaeological Survey of India.

## The fort

Originally built of mud in the 12th century by the **Hindu Kakatiyas**, the fort was reinforced by masonry by the Bahmanis who occupied it from 1363. The massive fort, built on a granite hill, was surrounded by three walls. One encircled the town, another the hill on which the citadel stood and the last joined huge boulders on the high ridge with parts of masonry wall. The citadel's 5-km double wall had 87 bastions with cannons and eight huge gates with outer and inner doors and guardrooms between. Some of the guns of the Qutb Shahis are still there with fortifications at various levels on the way up. Another of India's supposed underground tunnels is believed by some to run from a corner of the summit, about 8 km to Gosha Mahal. The fort had an ingenious system of laminated clay pipes and huge 'Persian Wheels' to carry water to cool the palace chambers up to the height of 61 m where there were hanging gardens. The famous diamond vault once held the *Koh-i-noor* and *Hope* diamonds. The fort fell to Emperor Aurangzeb after two attempts, an eight month siege and the help of a Qutb General who turned traitor. The English traveller Walter Hamilton described it as being almost completely deserted in



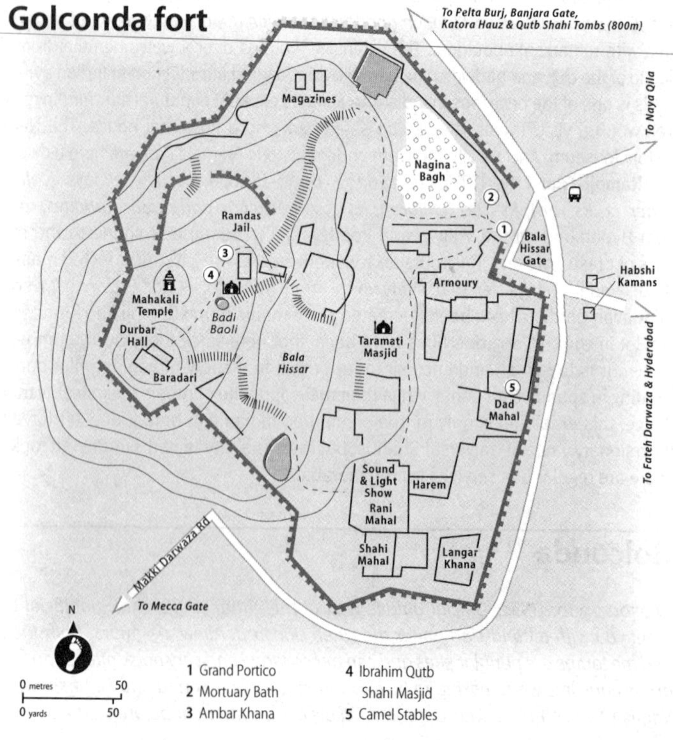

1820: "the dungeons being used by the Nizam of Hyderabad as a prison for his worst enemies, among whom were several of his sons and two of his wives".

The **Fateh Darwaza** or Victory Gate at the entrance, made of teak, with a Hindu deity engraved, is studded with iron spikes as a defence against war elephants. The superb acoustics enabled a drum beat or bugle call or even a clap under the canopy of this gate, to be heard by someone at the very top of the palace; it is put to the test by the visiting crowds today. A couple of glass cases display a map and some excavated finds.

Beyond the gate the **Mortuary Bath** on the right has beautiful arches and a crypt-like ceiling; you see the remains of the three-storeyed **armoury** and the women's palaces on the left. About half way up is a large water tank or well and to the north is what was once the most densely populated part of the city. Nearby, the domed store house turned into the **Ramdas Jail** has steps inside that lead up to a platform where there are relief sculptures of deities on the wall, dominated by Hanuman. The **Ambar Khana** (granary) has a Persian inscription on black basalt stating that it was built between 1626-1672. The steps turn around an enormous boulder with a bastion and lead to the top passing the Hindu **Mahakali Temple** on the way. The breezy **Durbar Hall** is on the summit. It is well worth climbing the stairs to the roof here for good views. The path down is clearly signed to take you on a circular route through the **harem** and **Rani Mahal** with its royal baths, back to the main gate. A welcome chilled drink and snack is available at several cafés opposite the gate.

## Qutb Shahi tombs

*ⓘ 0900-1630 except Fri, Rs 5, camera fee Rs 10, car Rs 10, bicycle Re 1. Allow 2 hrs, or half a day for a leisurely exploration. Inexpensive guidebook available. Getting there: bus (Nos 119 or 142M from Nampally or 66G from Charminar) takes 1 hr to the fort. Nos 123 and 142S go direct from Charminar to the Qutb Shahi Tombs, Rs 5. Autos about Rs 150 take 30 mins. Cycling in the early morning is a good option; it is an easy journey.*

About 800 m north-northwest of the fort on a low plateau (a road leaves Golconda Fort through the Banjara Gate) are the Qutb Shahi Tombs. Each tomb of black granite or greenstone with plaster decoration is built on a square or octagonal base with a large

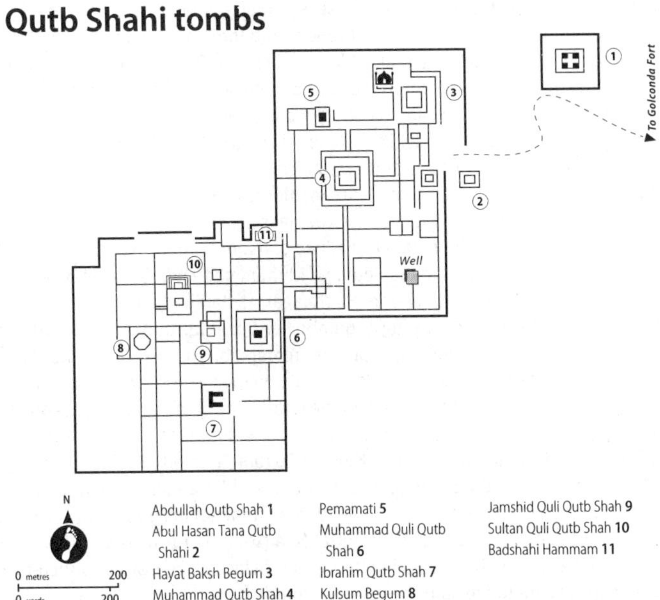

## Toddy tappers

In many villages of South India palm toddy is a common drink. Known locally as *karloo* this white, fizzy alcoholic drink is made by collecting sap from the palmyra palm. The tapper climbs the tree and cuts the main fronds of the palm, from which the sap is collected in small earthenware pots. This is poured into a larger pot carried by the toddy tapper on his waist band. If left the juice ferments, but it may also be drunk fresh. It is drunk by holding a folded palm leaf to your mouth in both hands while the juice is poured into it as you drink. Nod vigorously when you have had enough!

onion dome and arches with fine sculptures, inscriptions and remains of glazed decoration. The larger tombs have their own mosque attached which usually comprises an eastward opening hall with a *mihrab* to the west. The sides have inscriptions in beautiful Naksh script, and remnants of the glazed tiles which used to cover them can still be seen in places. The tombs of the rulers were built under their own supervision but fell into disrepair and the gardens ran wild until the end of the 19th century when Sir Salar Jang restored them and replanted the gardens. It is now managed and kept in an excellent state of repair by the Archaeological Survey of India. The gardens are being further improved.

The road north from Golconda Fort passes the tomb of **Abdullah Qutb Shah (1)** (1626-1672) as it approaches the entrance to the tombs, which is at the east gate of the compound. On the left side of the road just outside the compound is the tomb of **Abul Hasan Tana Qutb Shahi (2)** (ruled 1672-1687). He was the last of the kings to be buried here as the final king in the line of the Qutb Shahi Dynasty, Abul Hasan, died in the fort at **Daulatabad** in 1704. To the right of the entrance are the tomb of Princess **Hayat Baksh Begum (3)** (died 1677), the daughter of Ibrahim Qutb Shah, and a smaller mosque, while about 100 m directly ahead is the granite tomb of **Muhammad Qutb Shah (4)** (ruled 1612-1626). Tucked away due north of this tomb is that of **Pemamati (5)**, one of the mistresses of Muhammad Qutb Shah, dating from 1663. The path turns south and west around the tomb of Muhammad Qutb Shah. About 100 m to the south is a tank which is still open. The **Badshahi Hammam (11)**, the oldest structure in the compound, is the 'bath' where the body of the king was washed before burial. You can still see the channels for the water and the special platforms for washing the body. The Badshahi kings were Shi'a Muslims, and the 12 small baths in the Hammam stand symbolically for the two *imams* revered by the Shi'a community. Next door, a small **Archaeological Museum** ⓘ *1000-1630 (closed 1300-1400)*, has interesting items in a few glass cases.

To the south of the hammam is a series of major tombs. The most striking lies due south, the 54-m high mausoleum of **Muhammad Quli Qutb Shah (6)** (ruled 1581-1612), the poet king founder of Baghnagar (Hyderabad). It is appropriate that the man responsible for creating a number of beautiful buildings in Hyderabad should be commemorated by such a remarkable tomb. The underground excavations here have been turned into a Summer House. You can walk right through the tomb and on to the tomb of the fourth king of the dynasty, **Ibrahim Qutb Shah (7)** (ruled 1550-1580), another 100 m to the south. At the west edge of the compound is the octagonal tomb of **Kulsum Begum (8)** (died 1608), granddaughter of Mohammad Quli Qutb Shah. To its east is the tomb of **Jamshid Quli Qutb Shah (9)** (ruled 1543-1550), who was responsible for the murder of his 90 year old father and founder of the dynasty, **Sultan Quli Qutb Shah (10)** (ruled 1518-1543). This has the appearance of a two-storey building though it is in fact a single storey structure with no inscription. There are some other small tombs here.

# Warangal → *Phone code: 08712. Colour map 6, grid B1. Population: 528,600.*

The capital of the Kakatiya Empire in the 12th and 13th centuries, Warangal's name is derived from the Orugallu (one stone) Hill, a massive boulder with ancient religious significance which stands where the modern town is situated.

## Ins and outs

Warangal is 156 km northeast of Hyderabad and most express trains running between Chennai and Delhi stop here. Warangal Tourist Office ⓘ *1st Floor, Talwar Hyndai Show Room, Chaitanyapuri, opposite REC Petrol Pump, Kazipet, T0870-2446606.*

## History

The city was probably laid out during the reigns of King Ganapatideva (1199-1262) and his daughter Rudrammadevi (until 1294). Warangal was captured by armies from Delhi in 1323, enforcing the payment of tribute. Control of Warangal fluctuated between Hindus and Muslims but between the 14th and 15th centuries it remained in Bahmani hands. Thereafter it repeatedly changed hands, and Michell argues that although the military fortifications were repeatedly strengthened, the religious buildings were largely destroyed, including the great Siva temple in the middle of the city. Marco Polo was highly impressed by Warangal's riches, and it is still famous for the remains of its temples, its lakes and wildlife, and for its three circuits of fortifications though the modern town is not very interesting.

## Sights

At the centre of the **'fort'** ⓘ *US$2*, is a circular area about 1.2 km in diameter. Most of it is now farmland with houses along the road. Near the centre are the ruins of the original **Siva temple**. Remains include the large, beautifully carved stone entrance gateways to the almost square enclosure, aligned along the cardinal directions and beyond are overturned slabs, smashed columns, brackets and ceiling panels.

Nearby Siva temples are still in use, and to the west is the **Khush Mahal**, a massive royal hall used by the Muslim Shitab Khan at the beginning of the 16th century for state functions. It may well have been built on the site of earlier palaces, near its geometric centre while some structures in the central area may have been granaries.

From the centre, four routes radiate along the cardinal directions, passing through gateways in the three successive rings of fortification. The innermost ring is made of massive granite blocks, and is up to 6 m high with bastions regularly spaced along the wall. The middle wall is of unfaced packed earth, now eroded, while the outermost circuit, up to 5 m high, is also of earth. The four main roads pass through massive gateways in the inner wall, and there are also incomplete gateways in the second ring of fortifications. Some of the original roads that crossed the city have disappeared.

Some have suggested that the plan of Warangal conforms to early Hindu principles of town planning. **'Swastika towns'**, especially suited to royalty, were achieved following the pattern of concentric circles and swastika of the *yantras* and *mandalas*. They were a miniature representation of the universe, the power of god and king recognized symbolically, and in reality, at the centre.

The Chalukya style '1,000-pillar' **Siva Rudresvar temple** on the slopes of the Hanamakonda Hill, 4 km to the north, has beautiful carvings. It is a low, compact temple, built on several stepped platforms with subsidiary shrines to Vishnu and Surya, rock-cut elephants, a large superbly carved *Nandi* in the courtyard and an ancient well where villagers have drawn water for 800 years.

# Pakhal, Ethurnagaram and Lakhnavaram

ⓘ *Warangal Bus Station to Narsampet. Regular bus service from Narsampet to Pakhal Lake or take a taxi.*

The great artificial lakes 40 km northeast of Warangal – from the south, Pakhal, Lakhnavaram, Ramappa and Ghanpur – were created as part of the Kakatiya rulers' water management and irrigation schemes in the 12th and 13th centuries and are still in use. The lakes are fringed with an emerging marsh vegetation and surrounded by extensive grasslands, tropical deciduous forests and some evergreens. The park was set up in 1952, and although it is well established, some of the significant management problems include grazing by domestic livestock and illegal burning.

This is the richest area for wildlife in the state with tiger, panther, hyena, wild dogs, wild boars, gaur, foxes, spotted deer, jackals, muntjacks, sloth bears and pythons. There is also a large variety of waterbirds and fish, otters and alligators in the lakes. Pakhal Lake is particularly important as an undisturbed site well within the sanctuary, while the Laknavaram Lake is 20 km to the north. They are superb for birdwatching (numerous migratory birds in winter) and occasional crocodile spottings. Tigers and panthers live deep in the forest but are rarely seen. Forest rangers might show you plaster casts of tiger pug marks.

# Palampet → *Colour map 6, grid B2.*

Palampet lies close to the Ramappa Lake. The **Ramappa Temple**, dedicated to Siva as Rudreswara, was built in 1234 and is one of the finest medieval Deccan temples. The black basalt sculpture is excellent (even richer than that at the 1,000-pillar temple) with famous Mandakini figures of female dancers which appear on brackets at the four entrances. The base of the temple has the typical bands of sculpture, the lowest of elephants, the second, a lotus scroll, the third which is the most interesting depicting figures opening a window on the life of the times and finally another floral scroll. There are more fine sculptures inside, some displaying a subtle sense of humour in common with some of the figures outside, and paintings of scenes from the epics on the ceiling. Note that no bottled water is available.

# Nagarjunakonda → *Phone code: 08680. Colour map 6, grid C1.*

One of India's richest Buddhist sites, Nagarjunakonda, 150 km southeast of Hyderabad, now lies almost entirely under the lake created by the Nagarjunasagar Dam, completed in 1960. The remains of a highly cultured Buddhist civilization had remained almost undisturbed for 1,600 years until their discovery by AR Saraswati in March 1926. The reconstructed buildings are on a comparatively small scale, in a peaceful setting on top of the hilltop fort, now an island planted with low trees.

## Ins and outs

The island is 11 km from Vijayapuri. There are two ferries daily from the jetty, 0930 and 1330, other ferries serve APTDC tours organized locally or from Hyderabad. AP State Tourist Office ⓘ *Project House, Hill Colony, T08680-276333*. A guide is available through this office; others from the Hyderabad Tourist Office.

*The Nagarjunasagar Dam project, completed in 1966, is one of the largest in India. The 124 m high, 1 km long dam is constructed across the Krishna River out of stone masonry. Two of the irrigation tunnels are said to be among the longest in the world.*

## History

Rising from the middle of the artificial lake is the Nagarjuna Hill which was once nearly 200 m above the floor of the secluded valley in the northern ranges of the **Nallamalais** ('black hills') which surround the lake on three sides. On the fourth side was the great river **Krishna**, superimposed on the hills as it flows towards the Bay of Bengal.

Early archaeological work showed the remnants of Buddhist monasteries, many limestone sculptures and other remains. The Archaeological Survey carried out a full excavation of the sites for six years before they were covered by the rising waters of the lake. More than 100 distinct sites ranging from the prehistoric early Stone Age period to the late medieval were discovered. Some of the most important remains have been moved and reconstructed on the hilltop fort. These include nine monuments, rebuilt in their original form, and 14 large replicas of the ruins.

The **Ikshvakus** made Nagarjunakonda the centre of extraordinary artistic activity from the third century AD. In the mid-fourth century AD the Pallavas pushed north from Tamil Nadu and eclipsed the Ikshvaku Kingdom, reducing Nagarjunakonda to a deserted village. However, during the Chalukya period between the seventh and 12th centuries a Saiva centre was built at Yellaswaram, on the other bank of the Krishna. In the 15th and 16th centuries the hill became a fortress in the contest for supremacy between the Vijayanagar, Bahmani and Gajapati kings. After the fall of the Vijayanagar Empire both the hill and the valley below lost all importance.

## Sights

The Ikshvaku's capital was a planned city on the right bank of the Krishna – **Vijayapuri** ('city of victory'). The citadel had rampart walls on three sides with the river on the fourth. The buildings inside including houses, barracks, baths and wells were probably destroyed by a great fire. The nine temples show the earliest developments of Brahmanical temple architecture in South India. The Vishnu temple (AD 278) had two beautifully carved pillars which were recovered from its site. Five temples were dedicated to Siva or Karttikeya. The river bank was dotted with **Brahmanical shrines**.

Nagarjunakonda excavations also revealed some of India's finest early **sculptures** and **memorial pillars**. Over 20 pillars were raised in the memory not just of rulers and nobles but also of artisans and religious leaders. The sculptures represent the final phase of artistic development begun at Amaravati in the second century BC.

The **hill fort** (early 14th-century) has remnants of the Vijayanagar culture though the present layout of the fort probably dates from as recently as 1565. The main entrance was from the northeast, near where the ferry now lands on the island. In places the walls are still over 6 m high, with regular bastions and six gateways. There are two temples in the east, where the museum now stands.

**Museum** ⓘ *closed Fri, 0900-1600*, has a collection of beads, coins, relic caskets and a variety of ornaments, but most importantly sculptures (including a 3-m-high standing Buddha). Also prehistoric and protohistoric remains and several panels and friezes depicting Buddhist scenes.

# Srisailam Wildlife Sanctuary → *Colour map 6, grid C1. Altitude: 200-900 m.*

ⓘ *Worth visiting AP Dept of Forests (see Useful Addresses, page 1055). Cars are not permitted in the Tiger Reserve from 2100-0600. Temperature: 12-42°C. Rainfall: 1,500 mm.*

The largest of the State's wildlife sanctuaries is at Srisailam (201 km from Hyderabad) near Nagarjunasagar. The park, named after the reservoir, is India's largest tiger reserve covering 3,560 sq km in five neighbouring districts. At times the sanctuary is disturbed by political activists and can be very difficult to get permission to visit. Check latest position with Forest Officer.

The sanctuary, in an area deeply incised by gorges of the Nallamalai hills, has deciduous and bamboo forest as well as semi-desert scrubland. Besides tigers, there are leopards, Indian pangolins, panthers, wild dogs, civets, hyenas, jackals, wolves, giant squirrels, crocodiles, lizards, pythons, vipers, kraits and over 150 species of birds. Project Tiger was started here in 1973. Srisailam also attracts visitors to its **fort** and **temple** (originally, circa second century AD) with one of 12 *jyotirlingas* in the country. It is a small pilgrimage town in the heart of the vast reserve of hilly dry forest. The ancient **Mahakali Temple** on a hill rising from the Nallamalai forest contains a rare *lingam* which draws large crowds of pilgrims daily and especially at *Sivaratri*, see page 1067. There is a nature trail signposted 1 km short of Srisailam. Otherwise, you can walk the access road and explore from there. Guide available. The best time to visit is from October to March.

## Sleeping

The city suffers frequent electric power cuts. Larger hotels have enough power from their own generators, but a/c and lifts in smaller hotels often do not work. Street lighting is also affected: carry a torch. The city website, www.fullhyderabad.com, has pictures of some of the city's hotels.

**Hyderabad** *p1036, maps p1038 and p1042*
**AL Taj Banjara**, T040-55669999, tbhresv.hyd@tajhotels.com. 121 refurbished rooms, pleasant restaurant overlooking private lake, excellent local cuisine and barbecues, pool, tennis, boating.
**AL Taj Krishna**, T040-55662323, trn.hyderabad@tajhotels.com. 260 rooms, Presidential suite with private pool, 3 restaurants, large pool and beautiful gardens, immaculately kept, good bookshop.
**AL Taj Residency** 1 Banjara Hills, T040-55663939, residency.hyderabad@tajhotels.com. 140 rooms in a cream puff of a building, typical Taj facilities, restaurant (superb local cuisine, faultless service, affordable) attractive 'Gaudi-style' atrium coffee shop, good pool and gardens, quiet.
**A-B Amrutha Castle** (Best Western), opposite Secretariat, T040-23243095, amruthacastle@pol.net.in. 97 comfortable rooms furnished in individual style, attractive mock medieval public areas, themed restaurant and coffee shop, health club, roof-top pool, helpful staff. Recommended for imagination.
**A-B Central Court Hotel**, Lakdi Ka Pul, T040-23232323, www.thecentralcourt.com. 77 rooms, bath, phone, a/c, cable TV, travel desk, money change, business center: internet, scanner, coffee shop, multicuisine restaurant and bar, High Spirits.
**B Hotel Golkonda**, Masab Tank, Mahavir Marg, T040-23320303. 150 rooms across 6 floors each has direct dial and a/c. Complimentary airport transfers.
**B Residency** (Quality Inn), Public Garden Rd, T040-23204060, reservations@theresidency-hyd.com. 95 a/c rooms on 4 floors, polite service, popular with Indians, good vegetarian restaurant, popular basement pub (see bars), efficient business hotel.
**B-C Comfort Inn**, Woodbridge Mahavir Marg, Lakdi Ka Pul, T40-55666111. 55 comfortable rooms with phone, en suite and writing tables, car park, internet. Rooftop multicuisine restaurant **Degh** has panoramic views over city.
**C-D Saiprakash**, Nampally Station Rd, T040-24611726. 102 clean, comfortable rooms, some a/c, good **Woodlands** restaurant, efficient business hotel.
**D Rajmata**, Public Garden Road, opposite Hyderabad Station, T040-23201000. 48 reasonably clean rooms, TV, attached bath, quiet for the area, good **Lakshmi** restaurant (see Eating below).
**D Taj Mahal**, H-1-999 Abids Rd, corner of King Kothi Rd, set back from junction, T040-24758221. 65 good-sized simple rooms, bright, devoid of insects, some a/c, busy restaurant (South Indian vegetarian), room service meals, good value. Recommended.
**D-E Brindavan**, Nampally Station Rd, near the Circle, T040-23203970. 70 good, clean rooms, reasonable value, good restaurants, popular.

*For an explanation of the sleeping and eating price codes used in this guide, see inside the front cover. Other relevant information is found in Essentials pages 56-61.*

**D-E Saptagiri**, off Nampally Station Rd, T040-24603601. 40 clean enough rooms, some big with balcony, some a/c, quiet.
**D-E Siddharth**, Bank St, T040-24740222. 90 good rooms, some a/c, quiet location, good South Indian food in coffee shop, separate Chinese restaurant.
**E-F Apsara**, Nampally Station Rd, T040-24602663. 48 small, basic rooms, clean, room service, friendly, good budget choice.
**F Imperial**, corner of Nampally Station and Public Gardens Rds (5 mins from Hyderabad station), T040-23202220. 48 clean rooms, some with bath, avoid roadside rooms, bucket hot water, large Indian hotel, helpful, excellent service.

**Secunderabad** *p1036, maps p1038*
SD Rd is Sarojinidevi Rd.
**A-B Ramada Manohar**, by Airport Exit Rd, T040-2819917, manohar@hd1.vsnl.net.in. 135 well-designed, sound-proofed rooms, smart, modern business hotel, good value (a meal included) and service.
**A-B Viceroy**, Tank Bund Rd (taxi Rs 120 from airport), T040-27538383, viceroy@hd1.vsnl.net.in. 305 a/c rooms, most with fine views of lake, pool, sophisticated restaurant, excellent buffets, good but expensive travel desk, well located, excellent service. Highly recommended.
**B Green Park** (Quality Inn), Begumpet, Greenlands Arch, 2½ km airport, T040-2291919. 148 rooms, typical modern hotel.
**C Asrani International**, 1-7-179 MG Rd, T040-2842267. 65 rooms, good restaurants, bar, exchange.
**C Baseraa**, 9-1, 167/168 SD Rd, T040-27703200. 75 comfortable a/c rooms, restaurants recommended, bar, exchange.
**C-D Karan**, 1-2-261/1 SD Rd, T040-2840191, F848343. 44 rooms, central a/c, restaurants, coffee shop, exchange, roof-garden, pleasant position.
**D Club View**, 30 Wellington Rd, behind Secunderabad Club, T040-27845965. 30 quiet, clean rooms (some a/c), simply appointed, light and airy, pleasant management, meals on room service. Recommended.
**D Yatri Nivas** (AP Tourism), SP Rd, T040-27816881. 32 rooms, mostly a/c, 3 restaurants, bar, clean, airy, well-kept.
**E Taj Mahal**, 88 SD Rd, T040-2812105. Adequate, clean rooms, vegetarian restaurant.
**F Retiring Rooms**, at Railway Station.
**F YMCA**, SD Rd, T040-27806049. 15 rooms (mostly singles, but big enough to take an extra bed), shared bath, clean, roomy, friendly, 'treated as family', Rs 75 plus Rs 50 temporary membership.
**F Youth Hostel**, near Sailing Club, T040-27540763. 90 beds in dorms (Rs 20, plus Rs 20 temporary membership).

**Warangal** *p1047*
**D-E Ashoka**, T0870-278491. 55 clean rooms, good restaurant, bar, friendly service.
**E Ratna**, Ponchamma Maidan, T0870-223647. 50 rooms, some a/c.
**E-F Punnami Hotel**, Kazipet Rd opposite Regional Engineering College, 4 km away, T0870-2432312. 20 rooms – half a/c – 3 5-bed dorms, bar/restaurant and tourist information.
**F** hotels near Warangal station are often 'full' to backpackers.

**Palampet** *p1048*
The area is mosquito infested, so a net is essential.
**F Vanavihar Tourist Rest House**, nearby, also overlooking the lake. 4 simple and clean rooms, cook available but bring own provisions.

**Nagarjunakonda** *p1048*
There are no hotels in Nagarjunakonda, only at Nagarjunasagar. Nor is there western style accommodation; guest houses are for officials.
**E Soundarya Tourist Annexe** (APTDC), Hill Colony. 8 decent rooms, a/c or air-cooled.
**F Project House** (APTDC), T08680-276240. 25 rooms on ground floor, 18 rooms upstairs cheaper.
**F Vijaya Vihar Complex**, T08680-276325. 8 a/c rooms, restaurant, reservations: Assistant Manager.
**F Youth Hostel**. 12 rooms, contact Executive Engineer, B & R Hill Colony, T08680-272672, Reservations, T08680-272635.

**Srisailam Wildlife Sanctuary** *p1049*
**F Rest Houses**, contact Project Tiger HQ, Field Director at Sunnipanta (7 km from Srisailam). 3 rest houses.
**F Saila Vihar** (AP Tourism).
**F Temple cottages**, cook will prepare meals.

## Eating

**Hyderabad** *p1036, maps p1038 and p1042*
For a rundown of the cuisine in these parts, see page 1035.
**Taj Banjara**, top hotel. Recommended.
**Diwan**, near High Court.
**Liberty's**, Nampally Station Rd (Abids). Continental and Chinese.
**Residency**, hotel's *Madhubani* vegetarian. Lunch buffets popular so à la carte may be slow, try North Indian *thali*.
**Lakshmi**, by *Rajmata Hotel*, Nampally, across from railway station. Light meals.
**Palace Heights** (8th floor), Triveni Complex, Abids.
**Shan Bagh**, Basheerbagh Rd. Good value. Recommended.

**Vegetarian**
**Kamat**, Nampally Station Rd and 60/1 Saifabad, Secretariat Rd. Simple, quality food, good value.
**Softy House**, Chirag Ali Lane. Pizzas, burgers and good choice of safe ice cream, a welcome break from the heat of the day.

**Secunderabad** *p1036, maps p1038*
**Ramada Manohar**, in hotel. International. Recommended for service, surroundings and food.
**Viceroy**, in hotel. International, pleasant atmosphere, excellent preparations, seafood treats at *Gaiety*.
**Akbar**, 1-7-190 MG Rd. Hyderabadi.
**Asrani International**, hotel does good Mughlai.
**Baseraa**, hotel's Indian vegetarian restaurant is simple.
**Hyderabad House**, opposite Jntu College, Masab Tank, T040-23327861, and opposite Mosque Rd, no 3, Banjara Hills, T23554747. Serves up good fast-food biryanis.
**Kamat**, Sarojini Devi Rd. Vegetarian. Simple surroundings, clean, thalis.
**Kwality's**, 103 Park Lane. Mixed menu.
**Paradise**, 38 Sarojini Devi Rd/MG Rd. Hyderabadi cuisine in brightly lit complex.

## Bars and clubs

**Hyderabad-Secunderabad**
*p1036, maps p1038 and p1042*
Larger hotels have pleasant, well-stocked bars.
**One Flight Down**, below The Residency, opposite Hyderabad Railway Station, Public Garden Rd. Modern, British style pub (with same opening hours, 1100-2300!), snooker tables and TVs. Dark but popular. 1100-2300.

## Entertainment

**Hyderabad-Secunderabad**
*p1036, maps p1038 and p1042*
*Sound and Light*, at Golconda Fort; spectacular (see details below). Some cinemas show English language films.
**Lalit Kala Thoranam**, Public Gardens. Hosts art exhibitions and free film shows daily.
**Ravindra Bharati**, regularly stages dance, theatre and music programmes, a/c.

## Festivals and events

**Hyderabad-Secunderabad**
*p1036, maps p1038 and p1042*
**Jan**: Makara Sankranti (13-15) when houses bring out all their collections of dolls.
**Mar-Apr**: Ugadi, New Year in Andhra Pradesh – Chaitra Sudda Padyami.
Muharram and Ramzan are celebrated distinctively in Hyderabad.

## Shopping

**Hyderabad-Secunderabad**
*p1036, maps p1038 and p1042*
For more on Andhra Pradesh's craft tradition, see page . Most shops open 1000-1900 and some close on Fri, shopping for pearls you should look for shape, smoothness and shine first to determine quality. Size is the last criteria in deciding a pearl's price. Bargain for at least a 10% discount off asking prices. Also look for Bidri ware, crochet work, Kalamkari paintings, himroo and silk saris.
The **Lad bazar** around the Char Minar with colourful stalls is a fascinating glimpse into the past. Down the alleys, silver craftsmen work in their tiny rooms.

**Antiques**
**Govind Mukandas**, Bank St.
**Humayana** at *Taj Banjara*.

**Books**
**Akshara**, 8-2-273 Pavani Estates, Road No 2, Banjara Hills, T040-2213906. Excellent collection on all aspects of India in English.

**Haziq and Mohi**, Lal Chowk. Interesting antiquarian bookshop, especially for Arabic and Persian.
**Walden**, 6-3-871 Greenlands Rd, Begumpet, opposite Blue Moon hotel. Wide choice, open Sun.

### Handicrafts
Govt Emporia: **Nirmal Industries**, Raj Bhavan Rd; **Lepakshi**, and **Coircraft**, Mayur Complex, Gun Foundry.
**Co-optex**, and several others in Abids.
**Fancy Cloth Store**, the silk people, 21-2-28 Pathergatti, Hyderabad, T040-24523983. Exports cloth to British department store Selfridges.
**Khadi**, shops in Sultan Bazar and in Municipal Complex, Rashtrapati Rd, Secunderabad.
Others may charge a bit more but may have more attractive items.
**Bidri Crafts**, Abids.
**Kalanjali**, Hill Fort Rd, opposite Public Gardens. Has a large selection of regional crafts of high quality on 3 floors.
In **Secunderabad**:
**Baba Handicrafts**, MG Rd.
**Jewelbox**, SD Rd.

### Jewellery
**Mangatrai Pearl and Jewellers**, 6-3-883 Punjagutta, T040-23411816, www.mangatrai.com. Packed jewellers to Indian nobility (their guest book is like a photographic 'Who's Who' to Indian politics and movies). Especially pearls, stocks everything from Basra pearls to black Tahitian pearls.
**Sri Jangadamba Pearls**, MG Rd, Secunderabad.

## Activities and tours

### Hyderabad-Secunderabad
*p1036, maps p1038 and p1042*
**Swimming**
**BV Gurumoorthy Pool**, Sardar Patel Rd. Some hotel pools are open to non-residents.

### Tours
**APTTDC City sightseeing**: full day, 0800-1745 from offices at Yatri Nivas and Secretariat Rd, Rs 150; unsatisfactory as it allows only an hour at the Fort and includes unimportant sights.
**Golconda**: Shilparamam craft village, Hi-Tec city, Golconda (Sound & Light). 1600-2100, Rs 120.
**Nagarjunasagar**: daily to Dam, Nagarjunakonda Museum, Right Canal and Ethipothala Falls. 0700-2130, Rs 250.
**Ramoji Film City**: 0745-1800, Rs 400 including entrance fee. Allows 4-5 hrs at the studios, plus Sanghi Temple and time for shopping!

### Tour operators
**Mercury**, Public Gardens Rd, T040-2234441, SD Rd, Secunderabad, T040-2830670.
**Sita**, 3-5-874 Hyderguda, T040-2233628, and 1-2-281 Tirumala, SD Rd, Secunderabad, T040-2849155.
**TCI**, 680 Somajiguda, Greenlands Rd, T040-2212722.
**Thomas Cook**, Saifabad, T040-222689.

### Nagarjunakonda *p1048*
**AP Tourism's** day trip from Hyderabad can be very tiring with 4 hrs on a coach each way, but is convenient and cheap. 0645-2145, Rs 225 including lunch. Nagarjunasagar is the village beside the dam from which boats ferry visitors to the temples and museum on the island (at 0800, 1200, 1500, trip takes 1 hr). If you take the second boat you still have time to visit the sights and return on the next boat. You can leave your luggage for a few hours at this pier provided someone is on duty.

## Transport

### Hyderabad-Secunderabad
*p1036, maps p1038 and p1042*
**Air**
Transport to town: pre-paid taxi Rs 120-150; metered auto-rickshaw, Rs 65 to Banjara Hills, 30 mins. Airport, T140. **Bangalore**: 2 daily except Sun; **Kolkata**: some via Bhubaneswar and Nagpur; **Chennai**: 2 or 3 daily; **Delhi**: 2 daily; **Mumbai**: 3 daily; **Visakhapatnam**. **Bangalore, Chennai, Delhi, Kolkata, Mumbai, Tirupati, Visakhapatnam**, all daily. **Sahara**, opposite Secretariat, Secretariat Rd, T040-23212767: **Mumbai**.
**Airline offices** Air India, Samrat Complex, Secretariat Rd, T040-2237243. **Air France**, Nasir Arcade, Secretariat Rd, T040-2236947. British Airways, Chapel Rd, T040-2234927. Cathay Pacific, 89 SD Rd, Secunderabad,

T040-2840234. **Egypt Air**, Safina International, Public Garden Rd, T040-2230778. **Indian Airlines**: opposite Ravindra Bharati, Saifabad, T040-23299333. **Jet Airways**, 6-3-1109 Nav Bharat Chambers, Raj Bhavan Rd, T3401222; 201 Gupta Estates, Basheerbagh; airport T040-27900118. **KLM**, *Gemini Travels*, Chapel Rd, T040-2236042. **Lufthansa**, 86 Shantinagar, T040-2220352. **Saudia**, *Arafath Travels*, Basheerbagh, T040-2238175. **Singapore Airlines** and **Swissair**, Regency Building, Begumpet. **Thai**, Chapel Rd, T040-2236042.

### Auto-rickshaw

(Rs 6 for 2 km), will use meter after mild insistence and cheaper cycle rickshaws.Local taxis are expensive.

### Bicycle

Hire is easily available (ask for 'bicycle taxi' shop), Rs 20 per day but may ask for a large deposit; good for visiting Golconda, but the city is only for cyclists who are experienced with heavy, fast-flowing traffic.

### Bus

**Local** City buses are very crowded in rush hours. Nos 119, 142M: Nampally to Golconda Fort.

**Long distance** APSRTC, T040-24613955. The vast **Imbli-Ban Bus Station**, T040-24613955, is for long distance buses including Srisailam and Nagarjunasagar Dam. Private coaches run services to Aurangabad, Bangalore, Mumbai, Chennai and Tirupati. Reservations: *Royal Lodge*, entrance to Hyderabad Railway Station. Secunderabad has the **Jubilee** Bus Station, T040-27802203. **Nampally**: buses to Golconda. **Venus Travel**, opposite Residency Hotel, runs a bus to **Gulbarga**, 0730, 5 hrs.

### Car

Tourist taxis and luxury cars from AP Tourism, Tank Bund Rd, T040-23453036, **Ashok Travels**, Lal Bahadur Stadium, T040-2230766, **Travel Express**, Saifabad, T040-2234035. About Rs 550 per 8 hrs or 80 km, Rs 300 per 4 hrs.

### Train

Hyderabad (H); Secunderabad (S). South-Central Enquiries: T131. Reservations: T135. Bus No 20 links Hyderabad (Nampally) and Secunderabad stations, Rs 5. From **Hyderabad/Secunderabad** To: **Aurangabad**: *Manmad Exp, 7664* (AC/II), 1800 (S), 12½ hrs. **Bangalore**: *Secunderabad Bangalore Exp, 7085* (AC/II), 1740 (S), 13½ hrs; *Rajdhani Exp, 2430*, 1910 (Tue, Wed, Thu, Sun) (S), 12 hrs. **Chennai (MC)**: *Charminar Exp, 2760* (AC/II), 1900 (H), 1930 (S), 14½ hrs; *Hyderabad Chennai Exp, 7054*, 1550, 1625 (S), 14½ hrs. **Delhi (HN)**: *Rajdhani Exp, 2429*, 0645 (Mon, Tue, Thu, Fri) (S), 22½ hrs; *Dakshin Exp, 7021*, 2130 (H), 2200 (S), 32 hrs. **Delhi (ND)**: *New Delhi AP Exp, 2723*, 0640 (H), 0700 (S), 26 hrs. All Delhi trains go via **Nagpur** and **Bhopal**. **Guntakal**: (for Hospet and Hampi), *Secunderabad Bangalore Exp, 7085*, 1740, 6 hrs. **Kolkata (Howrah)**: *E Coast Exp, 7046*, 32½ hrs. **Mumbai (CST)**: *Hyderabad-Mumbai Exp, 7032*, 2040, 17 hrs; *Hussainsagar Exp, 7002*, 1430 (H), 15¾ hrs; *Konark Exp, 1020*, 1050 (S), 17½ hrs. **Tirupati**: *Krishna Exp, 7406*, 0530 (H), 0600 (S), 16 hrs; *Rayalaseema Exp, 7429* (AC/II), 1730 (H), 15½ hrs; *Narayanadri Exp, 7424*, 1800 (S), 13½ hrs.

### Warangal *p1047*

Many Express trains stop here. **Nagpur**: Several, 7½-8½ hrs. **Delhi (ND)**: *Tamil Nadu Exp, 2621*, 0724, 24 hrs; *Kerala Exp, 2625*, 1417, 25½ hrs. **Vijayawada**: *Kerala Exp, 2626*, 1140, 3¼ hrs; *GT Exp, 2616*, 1951, 3½ hrs. **Chennai (MC)**: *Tamil Nadu Exp, 2622*, 2101, 10 hrs; *GT Exp, 2616*, 1951, 10½ hrs. **Secunderabad**: *Vijaywada Secunderabad Intercity Exp, 2713*, 0902, 2½ hrs; *Konark Exp, 1020*, 0735, 3½ hrs; *Golconda Exp, 7201*, 1012, 3½ hrs; *Krishna Exp, 7405*, 1704, 3½ hrs.

### Srisailam Wildlife Sanctuary *p1049*

Buses from Imbli-Ban Bus Station, Hyderabad, about 6 hrs. The nearest train station is Marchelna (13 km). Hire jeep beforehand.

## Directory

### Hyderabad-Secunderabad

*p1036, maps p1038 and p1042*

**Banks** 1000-1400, Mon-Fri,1000-1200, Sat. In Hyderabad, several banks on Bank St, Mahipatram Rd and Mukaramjahi Market and in Secunderabad on Rashtrapati Rd. **Amex**, Samrat Complex, 5-9-12, Saifabad,

T040-23234591. **Thomas Cook**, Nasir Arcade, 6-1-57, Saifabad, T040-2596521. **Travel Club Forex**, next door, carries Western Union transfers. **Cultural centres and libraries** Alliance Française, near Planetrium, Naubat Pahad, T040-2220296. **British Library**, Secretariat Rd. 1100-1900 Tue-Sat. **Max Müller Bhavan**, Eden Bagh, Ramkote. **Bharatiya Vidya Bhavan**, King Kothi Rd, T040-2237825.
**Hospitals** Out-patients usually from 0900-1400. Casualty 24 hrs. **General Hospital** in Nampally, T040-2234344. **Newcity** (Secunderabad), T040-27805961.
**Internet** Several in Abids and Charag Ali Lane (Rs 30-40 per hr). Good coverage throughout the twin cities. **Post** In Hyderabad: **GPO** (with Poste Restante) and **CTO**, Abids. In Secunderabad: **Head PO** in RP Rd and **CTO** on MG Rd. **Useful addresses** AP Dept of Forests, Public Garden Rd, near Secretariat (opposite Reserve Bank), T040-24067551. Provides excellent advice, may help with arrangements to visit wildlife reserves – Assistant Conservator of Forests, is very helpful. **Foreigners' Regional Registration Office**: Commissioner of Police, Purani Haveli, Hyderabad, T040-2230191.

**Nagarjunakonda** *p1048*
Banks and post offices at Hill Colony and Pylon (4 km).

# Krishna-Godavari Delta

*The rice growing delta of the Krishna and Godavari rivers is one of Andhra Pradesh's most prosperous and densely populated regions, and the core region of Andhra culture. The flat coastal plains are fringed with palmyra palms and occasional coconut palms, rice and tobacco. Inland, barely 40 per cent of the land is cultivated. About 120 km to the west of the road south to Chennai run the Vellikonda Ranges, only visible in very clear weather. To the north the ranges of the Eastern Ghats can often be clearly seen.* » *For Sleeping, Eating and other listings, see pages 1056-1057.*

## Vijayawada → *Phone code: 0866. Colour map 6, grid C2. Population: 825,400.*

At the head of the Krishna delta, 70 km from the sea, the city is surrounded by bare granite hills. During the hot dry season these radiate heat, and temperatures of over 45°C are not uncommon in April and May. In winter they can be as low as 20°C. The Krishna delta canal scheme, one of the earliest major irrigation developments of the British period in South India completed in 1855, now irrigates nearly 1,000,000 ha, banishing famine from the delta and converting it into one of the richest granaries of the country. The Prakasam Barrage, over 1,000 m long, carries the road and railways. The name of this city, over 2,000 years old, is derived from the goddess Kanakdurga or Vijaya, the presiding deity. There is a temple to her on a hill along the river.

There are several sites with caves and temples with inscriptions from the first century AD. The **Mogalarajapuram Temple** has an Ardhanarisvara statue which is thought to be the earliest in South India. There are two 1,000-year-old **Jain temples** and the **Hazratbal Mosque** which has a relic of the Prophet Mohammed. The **Qutb Shahi** rulers made Vijayawada an important inland port. It has retained its importance as a commercial town, and has capitalized on its position as the link between the interior and the main north-south route between Chennai and Calcutta. A colossal granite Buddha statue (now in Guntur) shows that the site was an important Buddhist religious centre even before the seventh century AD, when it was visited by Hiuen Tsang. **Victoria Jubilee Museum** ⓘ *Bundar Rd, except Fri, 1030-1700, free, camera Rs 5*, collection includes sculpture and paintings. AP Tourist Office ⓘ *Hotel Ilapuram Complex, Gandhi Nagar, T0886-2570255. 0600- 2000*. AP Tourism counter at RTC Bus Stand, Machilipatnam Road and railway station.

## Amaravati

Amaravati is 30 km west of Vijaywada was the capital of the medieval Reddi kings of Andhra. Some 1,500 years before they wielded power Amaravati was a great Mahayana Buddhist centre (see page 1340). Initially the shrine was dedicated to the Hinayana sect but under Nagarjuna was changed into a Mahayana sanctuary where the Buddha was revered as Amareswara. Its origins go back to the 3rd-2nd centuries BC, though it was enlarged between the first-fourth centuries AD. Very little remains. Excavations were begun by Colonel Colin Mackenzie in 1797. Subsequently most of the magnificent sculpted friezes, medallions and railings were removed, the majority to the museums at Chennai and Kolkata. The remainder went to the British Museum in London. The **Archaeological Museum** ⓘ *0900-1700, closed Fri, free, buses via Guntur or by ferry from Krishneveni Hotel*, on site contains panels, mainly broken, railings and sculptures of the Bodhi Tree (some exquisitely carved), *chakras* and caskets containing relics. There are also pottery, coins, bangles and terracotta. Apart from items excavated since 1905, some exhibits relate to other sites in the Krishna and Visakhapatnam districts.

## Guntur → *Colour map 6, grid C2.*

From Vijayawada the NH5 southwest crosses the barrage – giving magnificent views over the Krishna at sunset – to Guntur, a major commercial town dealing in rice, cotton and tobacco where the ancient charnockite rocks of the Peninsula meet the alluvium of the coastal plain. In the 18th century it was important as the capital of the region known as the Northern Circars, and was under Muslim rule from 1766 under the Nizam of Hyderabad. The Archaeological Museum exhibits local finds including fourth-century Buddhist stone sculptures and 16th-century bronzes.

## Rajahmundry → *Phone code: 0883. Colour map 6, grid C3. Population: 313,300.*

The capital of the Eastern Chalukyas, Rajahmundry was captured by the Muslims from the Vengi kings in 1471, then returned to the Orissan Kingdom in 1512. The Deccan Muslims retook it in 1571 and it was repeatedly the scene of bitter hostilities until being granted to the French in 1753. It is remembered for the poet Nannayya who wrote the first Telugu classic *Andhra Mahabharathamu*. Every 12 years the Pushkaram celebration (last held in 2003) is held by the river bank. The **Markandaya** and **Kotilingeswara Temples** draw pilgrims. Rajahmundry is noted for its carpets and sandalwood products and as a convenient base from which to visit the coastal districts. There are simple economy hotels in the town. Rajahmundry is one of two places where you can divert towards the hills of the Eastern Ghats. The Godavari, 80 km northwest of the town, cuts through a gorge and there is a succession of stunningly beautiful lakes, reminiscent of Scottish lochs, where you can take boat trips.



## Sleeping

**Vijayawada** *p1055*
Bundar Rd is now MG Rd.
**D Ilapuram**, Besant Rd, T0866-2571282. 81 large clean rooms, some a/c, **C** suites, restaurants, travel.
**D Kandhari International**, Bundar Rd, Labbipet, T0866-2471311. 73 rooms, some a/c, a/c restaurants.
**D-E Mamata**, Eluru Rd (1 km centre), T0866-2571251. 59 rooms, most a/c with bath, good a/c restaurants (1 rooftop), bar.
**E Krishnaveni** (AP Tourism), Gopal Reddy Rd (opposite Old Bus Stand), T0866-2426382. Clean rooms, restaurant, tourist office, car hire.
**E Santhi**, Eluru Rd, T0866-2577355. Clean rooms with bath (hot water), good vegetarian restaurant.
There are some **F** hotels near the bus stand on Bundar Rd and near the railway station.
**F Railway Retiring Rooms**, the reasonable restaurant opens at 0600.

**Guntar** *p1056*
**D Vijayakrinshna International**, Collectorate Rd, Nagarampalem, T0863- 2222221. 42 rooms, some a/c, restaurant.

**D-E Annapurna Lodge**, opposite the APSRTC bus stand. A/c and non-a/c rooms, quality meals for Rs 22, helpful and obliging.
**D-E Sudarsan**, Kothapet, Main Rd, T0863-2222681. 28 rooms, some a/c, Indian vegetarian restaurant.

## Eating

**Vijayawada** *p1055*
The restaurants in the Kandhari and Mamata hotel are recommended.
**Greenlands**, Bhavani Gardens, Labbipet. Food served in 7 huts on the garden lawns.

## Shopping

**Vijayawada** *p1055*
Some shops are closed 1300-1600.
Local Kondapalli toys and Machilipatnam Kalamkari paintings are popular. The emporia are in MG Rd, Governorpet and Eluru Rd. **Apco**, Besant Rd, **Handicrafts Shop**, Krishnaveni Motel, **Lepakshi**, Gandhi Nagar are recommended. **Ashok**, opposite Maris Stella College, T0866-2476966.

## Activities and tours

**Vijayawada** *p1055*
**KL Rao Vihara Kendram**, Bhavani Island on Prakasham Barrage Lake, offers rowing, canoeing, water scooters, pedal boats.

## Transport

**Vijayawada** *p1055*
**Bus**
Good local network in city but overcrowded. SRTC buses to neighbouring states including **Chennai** (9 hrs). New Bus Stand, Bundar Rd, near Krishna River, T0866-2473333. Reservations 24 hrs.

**Car hire**
From AP Tourism.

**Ferry**
To **Bhavani Islands**, 0930-1730.
Also services between Krishnaveni Hotel and **Amaravati**. Daily 0800. Rs 50 return. Book at hotel or at RTC Bus Station.

**Rickshaw and taxi**
Very few metered yellow-top taxis. Tongas, auto- and cycle-rickshaws are available.

**Train**
Vijayawada is an important junction. Reservations, 0800-1300, 1300-2000; tokens issued 30 mins earlier. **Bhubaneswar**: *Coromandel Exp, 2842* (AC/II), 1600, 11½ hrs; *Konark Exp, 1019* (AC/II), 1440, 16 hrs. **Kolkata (H)**: *Coromandel Exp, 2842* (AC/II), 1600, 22 hrs. **Chennai (MC)**: *Pinakini Exp, 2711*, ), 0600, 7 hrs; *Coromandel Exp, 2841* (AC/II), 1045, 6¾ hrs. **Delhi (ND)**: *GT Exp, 2615*, 2315, 30 hrs; *Kerala Exp, 2625*, 1125, 28½ hrs. **Hospet**: *Amaravati Exp, 7225*, 2200, 13 hrs. **Secunderabad**: *Satavahana Exp, 2713*, 0610, 5½ hrs. **Hyderabad**: *Godavari Exp, 7007*, 2355, 7 hrs; *Krishna Exp, 7405*, 1330, 8¼ hrs (7 hrs to Secunderabad).

**Guntar** *p1056*
**Bus**
APSRTC bus stand is well organized and clean.

**Train**
**Kolkata**: *Faluknama Exp, 7201*, 2255, 23½ hrs. **Chennai**: *Hyderabad Chennai Exp, 7054*, 2200, 8 hrs. **Hospet**: *Amravati Exp, 7225*, 2310, 12 hrs. **Secunderabad**: *Palnad Exp, 2747*, 0525, 5 hrs; *Nagarjuna Exp, 7005*, 3, 6¼ hrs; *Golconda Exp, 7201*, 0530, 8 hrs.

**Rajahmundry** *p1056*
Trains to **Kolkata (H)**: *Coromandel Exp, 2842 (AC/II), 1830, 19½ hrs. Vijayawada: Coromandel Exp 2841, 0747, 2¾ hrs; Chennai Mail, 6003, 1635, 3½ hrs; Ratnachal Exp, 2717, 1550, 3 hrs. Visakhapatnam: Coromandel Exp 2842, 1830, 3¾ hrs; Chennai Howrah Mail, 6004, 0931, 4 hrs; Ratnachal Exp, 2718, 0829, 3½ hrs.*

## Directory

**Vijayawada** *p1055*
**Banks** State Bank of India and others on Babu Rajendra Prasad Rd. **Post** Kaleswara Rao Rd. **Useful addresses** Foreigners' Regional Registration Office, Super-intendent of Police, Bundar Rd.

# Northeastern Andhra Pradesh

*From Vijayawada the NH5 crosses the lush and fertile delta of the Krishna and Godavari to Rajahmundry and then across the narrowing coastal plain, the beautiful hills of the Eastern Ghats rising sharply inland. (Check weather forecasts before travelling.) The whole pattern of life here contrasts sharply with that further the south. Higher rainfall and a longer wet season, alongside the greater fertility of the alluvial soils, contribute to an air of prosperity. Village houses, with their thatched roofed cottages and white painted walls, are quite different and distinctive, as are the bullock carts.* ▸▸ *For Sleeping, Eating and other listings, see pages 1060-1061.*

## Background

The area was brought under Muslim rule by the Golconda kings of the Bahmani Dynasty in 1575 and ceded to the French in 1753. In 1765 the Mughal Emperor granted the whole area to the East India Company, its first major territorial acquisition in India. The region is also the most urbanized part of AP, with a dozen towns with more than 100,000 people. Most are commercial and administrative

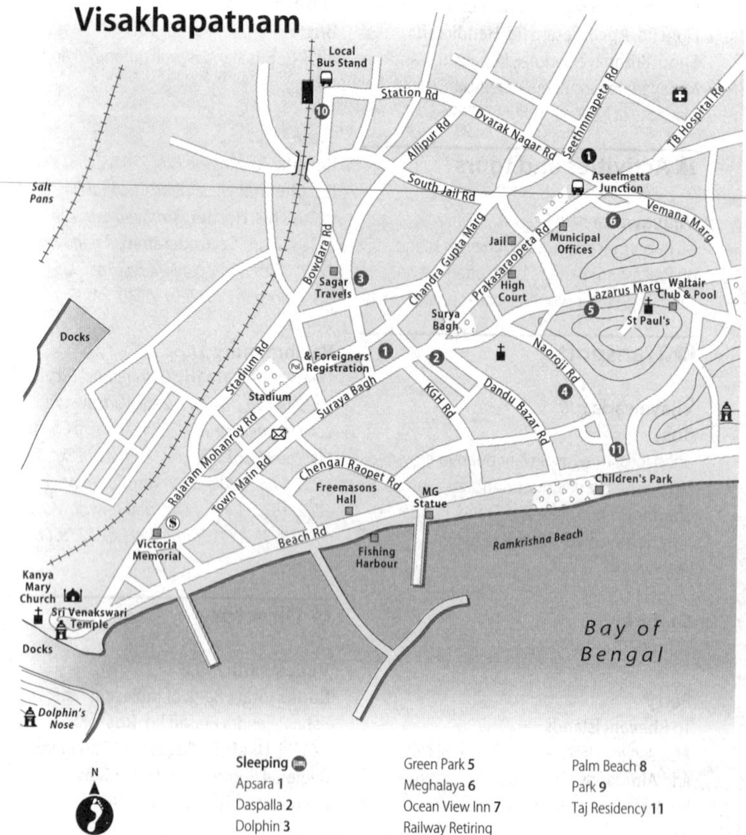

centres with neither the functions nor the appearance of industrial cities, but they serve as important regional centres for trade, especially in agricultural commodities, and they are the homes of some of the wealthiest and most powerful families in Andhra.

Although the building of dams on both the Krishna and the Godavari rivers has eliminated the catastrophic flooding common until the mid-19th century, the area is still prone to cyclones: in 1864 one claimed over 34,000 lives. The totally flat delta, lying virtually at sea level, was completely engulfed by a tidal wave in 1883 when the volcano of Mount Krakatoa blew up 5,000 km away. Further catastrophic cyclones in 1977 and 1996 caused massive damage and loss of life. You may notice the increasing number of small concrete buildings on raised platforms along the roadside designed to provide temporary shelter to villagers during cyclones.

## Visakhapatnam → *Phone code: 0891. Colour map 6, grid B4. Population: 969,600.*

Set in a bay with rocky promontories, Visakhapatnam (Vizag) commands a spectacular position between the thickly wooded Eastern Ghats and the sea. It has become one of India's most rapidly growing cities. Already India's fourth largest port it has developed ship building, oil refining, fertilizer, petro-chemical, sugar refinery and jute industries as well as one of India's newest and largest steel mills. This is also the Navy's Eastern Fleet's home base. On the Dolphin's Nose, a cliff rising 174 m from the sea, is a lighthouse whose beam can be seen 64 km out to sea.

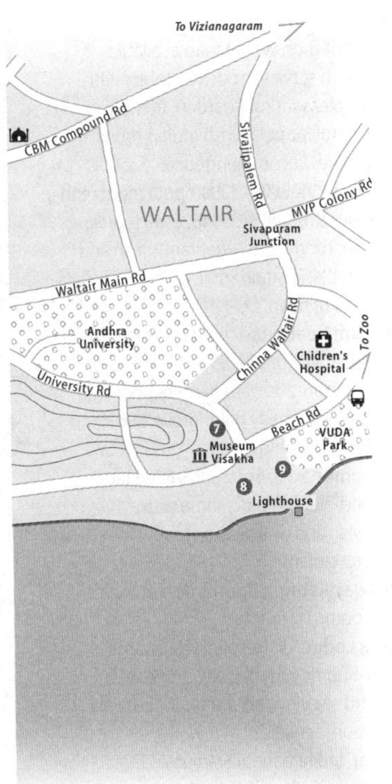


Eating
Blue Diamond 1

Its twin town of **Waltair** to the north used to be thought of as a health resort with fine beaches, though increasing atmospheric pollution is a problem. **Ramakrishna Beach**, along the 8 km Lawson's Bay and below the 300 m Mount Kailasa, 6 km away, is best. Don't swim at the harbour end of the beach.

### Ins and outs

AP Tourism ⓘ *LIC Building, Daba Garden, T0891-2713135, 1000-1700, closed Sun and 2nd Sat.* Also at Railway Station. Transport Unit ⓘ *8 RTC Complex, Dwarka Nagar, T0891-254646.*

### Sights

The **Andhra University** founded in 1926 is in the Uplands area of Waltair. The red stone buildings are built like a fortress and are well laid out on a large campus. The country's major **Ship Building Yard** at Gandhigram makes all types of ocean-going vessels – passenger liners, cargo vessels as well as naval ships. The

 **zoo** to the northeast is large and attempts to avoid cages, keeping its animals in enclosures which are close to their natural habitat.

Each of the three hills here is sacred to a different religion. The Hindu **Venkateswara Temple** on the Venkateswa Konda was built in 1866 by the European Captain Blackmoor. The Muslims have a **mausoleum of the saint Baba Ishaq Madina** on the Darga Konda, while the highest Ross Hill has a **Roman Catholic Church**. A Buddhist relic was discovered at **Dhanipura** nearby.

**Simhachalam**, 16 km northwest, is noted for its 13th-century Varaha Narasimha Temple, set in the Kailasa Hills, which are also noted for their hot springs.

## Sleeping

**Visakhapatnam** *p1059, map p1058*
Late night arrivals are quoted high prices by auto-rickshaws to go to the beach. Stay overnight at a simple hotel near the bus station (walk right from railway station) and move next morning.

**AL-A Taj Residency**, Beach Rd (2 km from centre), T0891-2567756. 95 narrow sea-facing rooms, spacious, light restaurant (pricey but generous), best in town, at centre of bay, with access to an unremarkable public beach across road.

**A Grand Bay Ravi** (Welcomgroup), 15-1-44 Naoroji Rd, Maharanipeta, T0891-2566550. 104 rooms, all business facilities.

**B Park**, Beach Rd, T0891-2554488. 64 rooms, expensive suites, bookshop, clean pool, well kept gardens, slick management, best for direct beach access (beware of rocks when swimming), popular with German and Czech expatriates.

**B-C Dolphin**, Daba Gardens, T0891-2567027. Family-run hotel with 147 rooms, popular restaurants, rooftop has good views, live band, also exchange and pool (but quite a distance from the beach). Excellent service. Highly recommended but reserve ahead.

**C Green Park**, Waltair Main Rd, T0891-256444. Modern business hotel, rooms vary.

**D Apsara**, 12-1-17 Waltair Main Rd, T0891-2564861. 130 rooms, central a/c, restaurants, bar, exchange, very helpful and friendly staff.

**D Daspalla**, Surya Bagh, T0891-2564825. 102 rooms, **C** suites, central a/c, 2 good restaurants (continental and *thalis*, bar, exchange, set back from road, no late-night check-in.

**D Punnai Punnami Beach Resort** (AP Tourism), Bhimili Beach Rd, Rushikonda beach (15 km away), T0891-2790734. New resort up steps from clean beach, rooms with sea views, good food.

**D-E Meghalaya**, Asilametta Junction (5-min walk from bus, short rickshaw ride from station), T0891-2555141. 65 rooms, some a/c, dull vegetarian restaurant (non- vegetarian available from room service), spacious lobby with murals, pleasant roof garden, friendly and helpful, popular with Indian tourists, good value. Recommended.

**D-E Ocean View Inn**, Kirlampudi (north end of the beach), T0891-2554828. 48 rooms, some a/c rooms, a/c restaurant, clean and comfortable, location spoilt by high-rise flats, quiet end of town.

**D-E Palm Beach**, Beach Rd (next to Park), Waltair, T0891-2554026. 34 rooms, 30 a/c, restaurant, beer garden, pool, pleasant with shady palm grove but run-down building.

**E Lakshmi**, next to St Joseph's Hospital, Maryland. 10 rooms a/c, some with bath, clean and welcoming, good Indian restaurant.

**E Railway Retiring Rooms** decent rooms, men's dorm.

**E Saga Lodge**, off Hospital Rd towards beach. Rooms with balcony, some with bath and sea view, no restaurant but very good room service

**E Viraat**, Indira Gandhi Stadium Rd, Old Bus Stand, T0891-2564821. 42 rooms with bath, some a/c, a/c restaurant and bar, exchange.

*For an explanation of the sleeping and eating price codes used in this guide, see inside the front cover. Other relevant information is found in Essentials pages 56-61.*

## Eating

**Visakhapatnam** *p1059, map p1058*
Most serve alcohol. Outside hotels there are restaurants on Station Rd.
**Black Dog**, Surya Bagh, near Jagdamba Theatre.
**Blue Diamond**, opposite RTC, Dabagardens.
**Delight**, 7-1-43 Kirlampudi, Beach Rd.

## Festivals and events

**Visakhapatnam** *p1059, map p1058*
**Dec**: **Navy Mela** and **Navy Day Parade** along Beach Rd.

## Activities and tours

**Visakhapatnam** *p1059, map p1058*
**Swimming**
Hotels Park and Palm Beach are open to non-residents.
Waltair Club has a pool.

**Tours**
**AP Tourism**, RTC Complex. Full day local sightseeing, 0830, Rs 75, Araku Valley, 0700, Rs 80.
**Taj Travels**, Meghalaya Hotel, T0891-2555141, ext 222.

## Transport

**Visakhapatnam** *p1059, map p1058*
**Air**
Airport is 16 km from city centre; taxi (Rs 180) or auto-rickshaw. **Indian Airlines**, T0891- 2565018, Airport, T0891-2558221 and Air India agent, **Sagar Travel**, 1000-1300, 1345-1700. Daily except Sun to **Hyderabad**; some to **Bhubaneswar**, **Kolkata**, **Chennai Mumbai**. Jet Airways, VIP Rd, T0891- 2762180, airport T0891-2622795, to **Hyderabad**.

**Bus**
Aseelmetta Junction Bus Station is well organized. APSRTC run services to main towns in the state. Enquiries, T0891-2565038, reservations 0600-2000. **Araku Valley**, **Guntur** (0930, 1545, 2045), **Hyderabad** (638 km, 1630), **Kakinda**, **Puri** (0700), **Rajahmundry**, **Srikakulam**, **Vijayawada** (1945, 2015), **Vizianagram** (57 km, 0610-2130).

**Ferry**
Operates from 0800-1700 between the Harbour and **Yarada Hills**. You can take one to visit the Dolphin Lighthouse. Also occasional service to **Port Blair** in the Andaman Islands, sometimes at short notice. Enquiries: M/s AV Banojirow & Co, PO Box 17, opposite Port Main Gate.

**Rickshaw**
Auto-rickshaws common (offer Rs 2 over meter-charge to make them use a meter); night fares exorbitant. Only cycle rickshaws in the centre.

**Taxi**
At the airport, railway station or from hotels: 5 hrs per 50 km, Rs 300; 10 hrs per 100 km, Rs 50 (higher for a/c).

**Train**
Enquiries, T0891-2569421. Reservations T0891-2546234. 0900-1700. Advance Reservations, left of building (facing it). Computer reservations close 2100, Sun 1400. Counter system avoids crush at ticket window. City Railway Extension Counter at Turner's Chowltry for Reservations. Taxi from centre, Rs 50. **Chennai**: *Howrah-Chennai Mail, 6003*, 1305, 16 hrs. **Kolkata (H)**: *Coromandel Exp: 2842*, 2235, 15 hrs; *Chennai Howrah Mail, 6004*, 1405, 17¼ hrs; **Secunderabad**: *Godavari Exp, 7007*, 1700, 13¾ hrs; *Palasa Kacheguda Visakha Exp, 7615*, 1635, 15½ hrs; *East Coast Exp, 7045*, 0525, 14 hrs; *Faluknama Exp 7027*, 0045, Tue, 12 hrs. **Tirupati**: *Tirumala Exp, 7488*, 1430, 16 hrs.

## Directory

**Visakhapatnam** *p1059, map p1058*
**Banks** Several on Surya Bagh. **State Bank of India** is at Old Post Office. **Medical services** Hospitals: **Seven Hills**, Rockdale Layout; **King George**, Hospital Rd, Maharani Peta, T0891-2564891. **Post office** Head Post Office, Vellum Peta; also at Waltair Railway Station. **Useful addresses** Foreigners' Regional Registration Office, SP Police, T0891-1562709.

# The Tamil borders

## Tirupati and Tirumalai → *Phone code: 08574 (Tirupati), 08577 (Tirumalai).*

*Colour map 7, grid A5. Population: 245,500.*

The Tirumalai Hills provide a picture-book setting for the famous Sri Venkatesvara temple, at the top of the Ghat road, which receives around 10,000 pilgrims daily. The main town of Tirupati lies at the bottom of the hill where there are several other temples, some also centres of pilgrimage in their own right. The seven hills are compared to the seven-headed Serpent God Adisesha who protects the sleeping Vishnu under his hood. » *For Sleeping, Eating and other listings, see pages 1065-1067.*

### Ins and outs

**Getting there** Flights from Chennai and Hyderabad arrive at the airport 15 km from Tirupati. The railway station in the town centre has several fast trains from Chennai and other southern towns while the main (central) bus stand is 500 m east of it with express buses from the region. To save time and hassle, buy a through 'Link' ticket to Tirumalai. » *See Transport, page 1066, for further details.*

**Getting around** Buses for Tirumalai leave from stands near the station, but there are also share taxis available. Some choose to join pilgrims for a four- to five-hour walk uphill, starting before dawn to avoid the heat though the path is covered most of the way. Luggage is transported free from the toll gate at the start of the 15 km path and may be collected from the reception office at in Tirumalai.

**Tourist information** **AP Regional tourist office** ⓘ *139 TP Area, near 3rd Choultry, T08574-255386.* **AP State tourist office** ⓘ *Govindraja Car St, T08574-124818.* **APTDC** ⓘ *Transport Unit, 12 APSRTC Complex, T08574-225602.* **Karnataka Tourism** ⓘ *Hotel Mayura Saptagiri* (see Sleeping). **TTD Information** ⓘ *1 New Choultry, T08574-222777* and at railway station and airport.

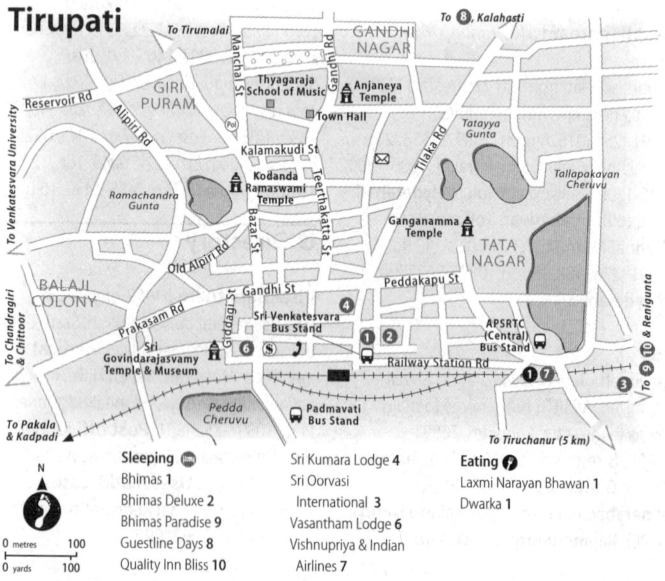

## Sights



**Sri Venkatesvara Temple** Dating from the 10th century, this temple is believed to have been dedicated by the Vaishnava saint Ramanuja and is known as *Balaji* in the north and *Srinivasa Perumalai* in the south. Of all India's temples, this draws the largest number of pilgrims. The town of Tirupati, at the base of the hill, was established in approximately AD 1131 under the orders of Ramanuja that the temple functionaries who served in the sacred shrines must live nearby. Although a road runs all the way up the hill to a bus stand at the top, most pilgrims choose to walk up the wooded slope through mango groves and sandalwood forest chanting "*Om namo Venkatesaya*" or "*Govinda, Govinda*". Order is maintained by providing 'Q sheds' under which pilgrims assemble.

The atmosphere inside is unlike any other temple in India. Turnstiles control the flow of pilgrims into the **main temple complex**, which is through an intricately carved *gopuram*, much of which is rebuilt, on the east wall. There are three enclosures. The first, where there are portrait sculptures of the Vijayanagar patrons, include Krishnadeva Raya and his queen and a gold covered pillar. The outer colonnades are in the Vijayanagar style; the gateway leading to the inner enclosure may be of Chola origin. The second enclosure has more shrines, a sacred well and the kitchen. The inner enclosure is opened only once every year. The main temple and shrine is on the west side of the inner enclosure. The **sanctuary** (ninth-10th centuries), known as *Ananda Nilayam*, has a domed *vimana* entirely covered with gold plate, and gold covered gates. The image in the shrine is a standing Vishnu, richly ornamented with gold and jewels. The 2-m high image stands on a lotus, two of his four arms carry a conch shell and a *chakra* or discus and he wears a diamond crown which is said to be the most precious single ornament in the world. It is flanked by *Sridevi* and *Bhudevi*, Vishnu's consorts. There is a small **museum** ⓘ *0800-2000*, of temple art in the temple compound, with a collection of stone, metal and wooden images.

There are two types of queues for *darshan* or special viewing: 'Sarvadarsan' is open to all, while those who pay for 'Special darshan' (Rs 30) enter by a separate entrance and join a short queue. The actual *darshan* (from 0600-1100) itself lasts a precious second and a half even though the 'day' at the temple may last 21 hours.



## Sri Venkatesvara temple

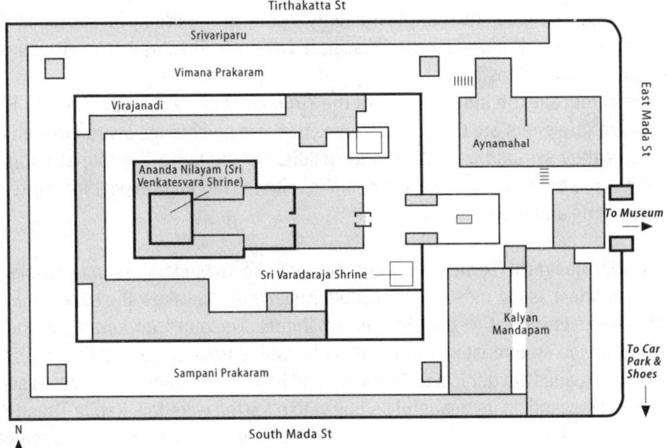

## Tirupati haircuts

Architecturally Sri Venkatesvara Temple is unremarkable, but in other respects is extraordinary. It is probably the wealthiest in India, and the *devasthanam* (or temple trust) now sponsor a huge range of activities, from the Sri Venkatesvara University at Tirupati to hospitals, orphanages and schools. Its wealth comes largely from its pilgrims, on average over 10,000 a day but at major festivals many times that number. All pilgrims make gifts, and the *hundi* (offering) box in front of the shrine is stuffed full with notes, gold ornaments and other offerings.

Another important source of income is the **haircutting service**. Many pilgrims come to Tirupati to seek a special favour – to seek a suitable wife or husband, to have a child, to recover from illness – and it is regarded as auspicious to grow the hair long and then to offer the hair as a sacrifice. You may see many pilgrims fully shaven at the temple when appearing before the deity. Lines of barbers wait the arriving pilgrims. Once, when coaches unloaded their pilgrims, one barber would line up customers and shave one strip of hair off as many heads as possible in order to maximize the number of customers committed to him before he returned and finished off the job! Now, a free numbered ticket and a razor blade can be collected from the public bath hall which pilgrims take to the barber with the same number to claim a free haircut. The hair is collected, washed and softened before being exported to the American and Japanese markets for wig making.

Suprabhatam 0300-0330 (awakening the deity) costs Rs 100; Tomala Seva 0330-0415 (flower-offering), Rs 200. Mornings are particularly busy. Monday and Tuesday are less crowded. The temple is 18 km up the Ghat road, see Transport page 1066, for more details.

Every day is festival day with shops remaining open 24 hours. The image of Sri Venkatesvara (a form of Vishnu) is widely seen across South India, in private homes, cars and taxis and in public places, and is instantly recognizable from his black face and covered eyes, shielded so that the deity's piercing gaze may not blind any who look directly at him. In the temple the deity's body is anointed with camphor, saffron and musk. The holy *prasadam* or consecrated sweet is distributed to well over 50,000 pilgrims at special festivals.

Theoretically the inner shrines of the Tirumalai temple are open only to Hindus. However, foreigners are usually welcome. They are sometimes invited to sign a form to show they sympathize with Hindu beliefs. According to the tourist information leaflet: "The only criterion for admission is faith in God and respect for the temple's conventions and rituals".

**Govindarajasvami Temple** In Tirupati itself the Govindarajasvami Temple (16th-17th centuries), is the most widely visited. Built by the Nayakas, the successors to the Vijayanagar Empire, the temple has an impressive outer *gopuram*. Of the three *gopurams* the innermost is also the earliest, dating from the 14th-15th centuries. The main sanctuaries are dedicated to Vishnu and Krishna. Another temple wroth seeing is **Kapilesvarasvami**, in its beautiful setting with a sacred waterfall, **Kapila Theertham**.

About 1 km away are strange **rock formations** in a natural arch, resembling a hood of a serpent, a conch and a discus, thought to have been the source of the idol in the temple. There is a sacred waterfall **Akasa Ganga**, 3 km south of the temple. The **Papa Vinasanam Dam** is 5 km north.

## Around Tirupati

**Chandragiri**, 11 km southwest, became the capital of the Vijayanagaras in 1600, after their defeat at the battle of Talikota 35 years earlier. The Palace of Sri Ranga Raya, built in 1639 witnessed the signing by Sri Ranga Raya of the original land grant to the East India Company of **Fort St George** ⓘ *state bus or taxi from Tirupati*, but seven years later the fort was captured by Qutb Shahi from Golconda. The fort was built on a 180 m high rock where earlier fortifications may date from several hundred years before the Vijayanagar kings took over. You can still see the well preserved defences and some of the palaces and temples. Visit the Rani Mahal and Raja Mahal with its pretty lily pond. The museum in Raja Mahal, contains Chola and Vijayanagar bronzes.

**Sri Kalahasti** or **Kalahasti** ⓘ *state buses run from Tirupati*, 36 km northeast of Tirupati, is very attractively sited on the banks of the Svarnamukhi River at the foot of the extreme southern end of the Vellikonda Ranges, known locally as the Kailasa Hills. The town and temple, built in the 16th and 17th centuries, developed largely as a result of the patronage of the Vijayanagar kings. The **Kalahastisvara Temple** dominates the town with its *gopuram* facing the river. It is built in the Dravida style like the famous temple of Tirumalai. The magnificent detached *gopuram* was built by the Vijayanagar Emperor Krishnadeva Raya. Set within high walls with a single entrance to the south, the temple is particularly revered for the white stone Siva *lingam* in the western shrine, believed to be worshipped by *sri* (spider), *kala* (king cobra) and *hasti* (elephant). The Nayaka style is typified by the columns carved into the shape of rearing animals and the riders. The temple to the Wind God *Vayudeva* is the only one of its kind in India. The bathing ghats of the Swarnamukhi (golden) River and the temple attract a steady flow of pilgrims. In addition to its function as a pilgrim centre, the town is known for its *kalamkaris*, the brightly coloured **hand-painted textiles** used as temple decoration. There are fine examples in the Salar Jung Museum in Hyderabad, see page 1039.

**Pulicat Lake**, on the coast, 50 km north of Chennai, is the second largest saltwater lagoon in India and one of the most important wetlands for migratory shorebirds on the eastern seaboard of India. The northern area has large concentrations of greater flamingos near the islands of Vendadu and Irukkam. There are also many birds of prey. The shallow brackish waters are rich in crustaceans and **Sriharikotta Island** has patches of residual dry evergreen forest, although it is perhaps noted more today for its rocket launching site. About 20 km north of Suluru is the **Neelapattu Lake**, which was given protected status in 1976 to conserve a large breeding colony of spotbilled pelicans.

## Sleeping

**Tirupati and Tirumalai** *p1062, map p1062*
Pilgrims are usually housed in well-maintained Temple Trust's *choultries* in Tirumalai which can accommodate about 20,000. They vary from luxury suites and well-furnished cottages to dormitories and unfurnished rooms (some free). Contact PRO, TT Devasthanams, T08577-22753 or Reception Officer 1, T08577-22571. The options listed below are in Tirupati.
**C Guestline Days**, 14-37 Karakambadi Rd, 3 km from town, T08574-228366. 140 rooms, central a/c, restaurants (including non-vegetarian), bar, pool.
**C Quality Inn Bliss**, Renigunta Rd near Overbridge, T08574-225793. 72 modern clean a/c rooms, restaurants.
**D Bhimas**, 42 Govindaraja Car St, T08574-220766. 59 clean rooms with bath, some a/c, near railway, restaurant (South Indian vegetarian), roof-garden.
**D Bhimas Deluxe**, 38 Govindaraja Car St (near railway), T08574-225521. 60 rooms, 40 a/c, a/c restaurant (Indian), exchange.

*For an explanation of the sleeping and eating price codes used in this guide, see inside the front cover. Other relevant information is found in Essentials pages 56-61.*

**D Bhimas Paradise**, 33-37 Renigunta Rd, T08574-225747. 73 clean rooms, some a/c, pool, garden, good restaurant.
**D Mayura**, 209 TP Area, T08574-225925. 65 rooms, half a/c, vegetarian restaurant, exchange. A bit more expensive than others in this price category.
**D Sri Oorvasi International**, Renigunta Rd, T08574-220202. 78 rooms, some a/c, 1 km railway, restaurant (vegetarian).
**D Vishnupriya**, T08574-225060. 134 rooms, some a/c, restaurants, exchange, **Indian Airlines** office.
**F Sri Kumara Lodge**, near railway station. Decent rooms.
**F Vasantham Lodge** 141 G Car St, T08574-220460. Reasonable rooms with bath.

## Eating

**Tirupati and Tirumalai** *p1062, map p1062*
In Tirumalai particularly, the Trust prohibits non-vegetarian food, alcohol and smoking. Outside hotels, vegetarian restaurants include: **Laxmi Narayan Bhawan** and **Dwarka**, opposite APSRTC Bus Stand; **Konark** Railway Station Rd; **New Triveni**, 139 TP Area; **Woodlands**, TP Area.
**Tirupathi-Tirumalai Devasthanam Trust (TTD)** provides free vegetarian meals at its guest houses.
**Indian Coffee House** and **Tea Board Restaurant** and both near the TTD Canteen and the APSRTC Bus Stand.

## Festivals and events

**Tirupati and Tirumalai** *p1062, map p1062*
**May/Jun**: Govind Brahmotsavam. **Sep-Oct**: Brahmotsavam is the most important, especially grand every 3rd year when it is called Navarathri Brahmotsavam. On the 3rd day the Temple Car Festival Rathotsavam is particularly popular. Rayalseema Food and Dance follows later in the month.

## Shopping

**Tirupati and Tirumalai** *p1062, map p1062*
Copper and brass idols, produced at Perumallapalli village, 8 km away, and wooden toys are sold locally. Try **Poompuhar** on Gandhi Rd and **Lepakshi** in the TP Area.

## Activities and tours

**Tirupati and Tirumalai** *p1062, map p1062*
**AP Tourism**, Room 15, Srinivasa Choultry, T08574-220602. Local tour starts at the APSRTC Central Bus Stand, 1000-1730. Rs 150. Tirupati (not Venkatesvara), Kalahasti, Tiruchanur, Chandragiri and Srinivasamangapuram. From Chennai to Tirumalai, Rs 300.

## Transport

**Tirupati and Tirumalai** *p1062, map p1062*

**Air**
Transport to town by APSRTC coach to Tirupati (Rs 20) and Tirumalai (Rs 30); taxis Rs 150. **Indian Airlines**, Hotel Vishnupriya, opposite central bus stand, T08574-222349. 1000-1730. To **Chennai**: Tue, Thu, Sun and **Hyderabad**: Tue, Thu, Sat. **Jet Airways**, T08574-256916, airport T08574-271471, to **Hyderabad**.

**Bus**
**Local** Service between Tirupati and Tirumalai every 3 mins, 0330-2200. In **Tirupati**: **Sri Venkatesvara** bus stand, opposite railway station for passengers with through tickets to Tirumalai; Enquiries: 3rd Choultry, T08574-220132. **Padmavati** bus stand in TP Area, T08574-220203; long queues for buses but buying a return ticket from Tirupati (past the railway footbridge) saves time at the ticket queue. The journey up the slow winding hill road – which some find worrying – takes about 45 mins. In **Tirumalai**, arrive at **Kesavanagar** bus stand, near central reception area, ½ km southeast of temple; walk past canteen and shop. Depart from **Rose Garden** bus stand, east of the temple.
**Long distance** Good service through SRTCs from the neighbouring southern states. **Chennai** 4 hrs, **Kanchipuram** 3 hrs, **Vellore** 2½ hrs. Central bus stand enquiries, T08574-222333. 24-hr left luggage.

**Rickshaw**
Auto-rickshaws: fixed point-to-point fares; cycle rickshaws: negotiable.

**Taxi**

Tourist taxis through AP Tourism from the Bus Stand and Railway Station to Tirumalai, Rs 600 return, for 5½ hrs. Share taxi between Tirupati and Tirumalai, about Rs 65 per person. **Balaji Travels**, 149 TP Area, T08574-224894.

**Train**

Trains are often delayed. Phone the station in advance if catching a night train as it could be delayed until next morning.
**Chennai (C)**: *Intercity Exp, 6204*, 0645, 3¼ hrs; *Saptagiri Exp, 6058*, 1720, 3¼ hrs. **Mumbai (CST)**: bus to Renigunta (10 km) for *Chennai-Mumbai Exp, 6012*, 1445, 24 hrs; or direct: *Tirupati-Mumbai CST Bi-Weekly Exp, 6354*, Thu, Sun, 2140, 24 hrs. **Guntakal**: *Kacheguda Venkatadri Exp, 7498*, 1750, 6¼ hrs; *Rayalaseema Exp 7430* (AC/II), 1850, 6½ hrs. **Mysore (via Chennai)**: *Saptagiri Exp, 6058*, 1720, 3¼ hrs, wait 2¼ hrs, then *Chennai Mysore Exp, 6222*, 2245, 11¼ hrs (total 16¾ hrs). **Hyderabad**: *Narayanadri Exp, 7423*, 1830, 13¾ hrs (for Secunderabad).

## Directory

**Tirupati and Tirumalai** *p1062, map p1062*
**Banks** Most are on Gandhi St. State Bank of India, opposite APSRTC. **Useful addresses** Foreigners' Regional Registration Office: 499 Reddy Colony, T08574-220503.

# The arid western borders

*For much of the way between Hyderabad and Bangalore the NH7 crosses the boulder covered plateau of the ancient peninsular granites and gneisses. On either side reddish or light brown soils are cultivated with millets or rice on the patches of irrigated land.* *» For Sleeping, Eating and other listings, see pages 1069-1070.*

## Kurnool → *Colour map 5, grid C6.*

Between 1950-1956 Kurnool, 214 km southwest of Hyderabad, was capital of the state of Andhra Desa before Hyderabad was chosen as the capital of the new state of Andhra Pradesh in 1956. At the junction of the Hindri and Tungabhadra rivers, it was an administrative centre for the Nawabs of Kurnool. Muslim influence is still evident in the ruined palace of the Nawabs on the steep bank of the Tungabhadra.

## Srisailam → *Colour map 6, grid C1.*

A longer excursion, 170 km east of Kurnool on the route through Doranala, takes you to this popular site of Saivite pilgrimage on the banks of the Krishna, see page 1050. The wooded Nallamalai Hills are home to the *Chenchu* tribes. The township has been built for workers on a massive dam construction project.

Srisailam's origins are obscure, and the **Mallikarjuna Temple** (14th-century) on a hill, containing one of 12 *jyotirlingas*, has often been attacked and damaged. Some 300 m long (dated to 1456), the outer face is richly decorated with carved figures. These include a portrait of Krishna Deva Raya, the Vijayanagar Emperor who visited the site in 1514. The walls and gates have carvings depicting stories from the epics. Non-Hindus are allowed into the inner sanctuary to witness the daily puja ceremony. To avoid the long queue in the middle of the day, it is best to arrive early – first prayers at 0545. **Mahasivaratri Festival** draws large crowds. Srisailam can also be reached straight from Hyderabad (200 km) across the wide open Telangana Plateau.

## Gooty → *Phone code: 08553. Colour map 5, grid C6.*

Gooty, south of Kurnool, has a dramatic **Vijayanagara Fort** with excellent views on an isolated granite outcrop 300 m high. In the 18th century the fort fell into the hands of a Maratha chief but was captured in 1776 by Haidar Ali after a siege of nine months. Sir Thomas Munro (Governor of Madras), who died nearby in 1827, has his grave in the cemetery by the path leading up to the Fort though his body was moved to Fort St George in Madras.

The town, 4 km from the railway station, is a major crossroads and truck stop. A bypass has taken many of the hundreds of lorries that used to pass through it every day, round its outskirts, leaving it once more as a typically pedestrian-dominated Indian market town.

## Guntakal → *Colour map 5, grid C6.*

Guntakal, 95 km west of Gooty, is an important railway junction with little to attract a tourist. It is en route to Bellary to visit Hampi and Hospet, see page 1014.

## Bellary → *Colour map 7, grid A3.*

The first agricultural communities of the peninsula lived around Bellary. The black cotton soils are pierced by islands of granite hills, and the **Neolithic communities** here lived at roughly the same time as the early Indus Valley civilizations. Radiocarbon datings put the earliest of these settlements at about 3,000 BC. **Ash mounds** have been discovered at four places in this area, close to the confluence of the **Krishna** and **Tungabhadra**, and to the south of Bellary. The mounds are where cattle were herded together. Evidence from later sites in Karnataka shows that millets and grain were already widely grown by the first millennium BC. The unusual fort on a single 'pebble' dominates the town (402 steps to the top from the southeast corner of the hill). The 1902 South African POW camp is 150 m north of the Cantonment Railway station, while the British cemetery is east of the rock.

## Anantapur

**Rural Development Trust** ⓘ *FVF Bangalore Highway, T08554-31503, fvfatp@hd2.dot.net.in*, is an NGO working with outcastes in over 1,500 villages. The Director, a former Spanish Jesuit, Vincente Ferrer, started the project, which covers health, education, housing etc, over 30 years ago. If you are interested in seeing the work visitors can be accommodated (for up to four days).

## Puttaparthi

Puttaparthi ⓘ *Bangalore bus takes 4-5 hrs*, just southeast of Dharmavaram, has the principle Sai Baba Ashram, **Prasanthi Nilayam** ⓘ *0400-2100*, attracting followers from all over India and some from abroad. The present Sai Baba is widely believed to be a reincarnation of the Maharashtrian Sai Baba of Shirdi. The Ashram accommodation is good and open 0800-1900 but it is only open to over-25s and to families. Flights from Chennai and Mumbai were introduced by the former Prime Minister Narasimha Rao, a Sai Baba follower.

## Penukonda

The second capital of the Vijaynagara Empire, the city grew in importance between the 14th and 17th century. It is possible to climb Penukonda (literally 'big hill') by a steep path that goes to the top. At the base, east of the hill, are huge walls and gateways of the old fortifications. The **Jain Parsvanatha Temple** has an 11th-century sculpture of Parshvanatha, naked in front of an undulating serpent in late Chalukyan style. There are also two granite Hindu temples from the early Vijayanagar period dedicated to Rama and Siva, the mosque of Sher Ali (circa 1600), the Jama Masjid with a near spherical dome, and the **Gagan Mahal** palace. The last has Islamic style arches, plaster decoration and features that are derived from temple architecture.

Penukonda became the headquarters of the districts ceded to the East India Company by the Nizam of Hyderabad in 1800. There is a well carved 10 m high column in the compound of the sub-collector's office.

## Lepakshi



Approaching Lepakshi, 35 km south of Penukonda, from Chilamattur you see a massive sculpture of Siva's bull (*Nandi*), carved out of a granite boulder, 5 m high and 8 m long. This tiny village has a temple of outstanding interest for its murals. The **Virabhadra Temple,** built in 1538 under the Vijayanagar Emperor Achutyadeva Raya, has well-preserved sculptures, but the mural paintings are particularly striking, depicting popular legends from the *Puranas*, see page 1317, and epics. On an outcrop of *gneiss*, the main temple is entered through two *gopurams* with unfinished brick towers. There are pyramidal brick towers over the main shrine.

Inside are large sculptures of Nataraja on a column while narrative reliefs on the south walls illustrate Siva legends, including Arjuna's penance. The principal sanctuary has a life-size Virabhadra, decked with skulls and carrying weapons, appropriate to this form of Siva, bent on revenge.

## Sleeping

**Kurnool** *p1067*
**D Raja Vihar Deluxe**, Bellary Rd, T0851-2820702. 48 rooms, half a/c, a/c Indian restaurants.
**D Raviprakash**, Railway Station Rd (500 m from railway), T0851-2821116. 46 rooms and bungalows, some a/c with baths, restaurants (Indian), lawns.

**Gooty** *p1067*
A very basic hotel (with restaurant) is next to the bus stand.

**Guntakal** *p1068*
An excellant value **F** hotel has a South Indian restaurant next door. Local rickshaw drivers will take you there if you have to spend the night.

**Bellary** *p1068*
**C Hotel Pola Paradise**, with comfortable a/c rooms, **B** suites, restaurant and pool.
**D Ashoka**, which is more modest.

**Penukonda** *p1068*
**F Sabina Lodge**, near the bus stand has simple clean rooms.

**Lepakshi** *p1069*
**F Rest House**, opposite temple. 2 very basic rooms, and a simple restaurant nearby. Alternatively stay in **Hindupur**, where there are several hotels by the state bus stand, near some good 'meals' restaurants.

## Activities and tours

**Penukonda** *p1068p*
Stree Sangsheema Trust, on the main street north of the centre, organizes tours, promotes women's co-operative efforts and sells the guide book, *Penukonda* by Torsten Otto, 2001, Rs 25.

## Transport

**Kurnool** *p1067*
**Train**
**Kurnool Town** to **Chennai (MC)** via **Tirupati**: *Venkatadri/Tirupati- Chennai Exp, 7497/6054*, 2237, 14 hrs. **Guntakal**: *Secunderabad-Bangalore Exp, 7085*, 2125, 2 hrs. **Secunderabad**: *Tungabhadra Exp, 7608*, 1510, 4½ hrs; *Bangalore Secunderabad Exp, 7086*, 0230, 4 hrs.

**Gooty** *p1067*
**Train**
**Bangalore**: *Udyan Exp, 6529*, 0120, 7¼ hrs. **Guntakal**: 14 Express/Mail trains daily including at 0005, 0210, 0700, 0910, 1805, 1950 and 2310, ½ hr. **Chennai (MC)**: *Mumbai Chennai Exp, 6011*, 0745, 9 hrs; *Mumbai Chennai Mail, 6009*, 1935, 10 hrs. **Mumbai (CST)** : *Kanniyakumari Mumbai Exp, 1082*, 0910, 29¾ hrs.

**Guntakal** *p1068*
**Train**
**Chennai (MC)**: *Mumbai Chennai Exp, 6011*, 0710, 8½ hrs; *Dadar Chennai Exp, 1063*, 1130, 8½ hrs; *Mumbai Chennai Mail, 6009*, 1835,

*For an explanation of the sleeping and eating price codes used in this guide, see inside the front cover. Other relevant information is found in Essentials pages 56-61.*

11 hrs. **Bangalore**: *Karnataka Exp, 2628*, 0745, 6 hrs; *Hampi Exp/Nanded Bangalore Link Exp, 6591*, 2300, 7½ hrs. **Kochi/ Ernakulam**: *Mumbai CST-Trivandrum Exp, 6331*, Tue, 0540, 20 hrs. **Hospet**: *Hampi Exp, 6592*, 0510, 3 hrs; *Guntakal Hubli Pass, 303*, 2120, 3¾ hrs; *Amaravati Exp, 7225*, 0815, 2½ hrs; *Haripriya Exp, 7315*, 0245, 2½ hrs. **Secunderabad**: *Bangalore Secunderabad Exp, 7086*, 2345, 6¾ hrs. **Hyderabad**: *Rayalaseema Exp 7430*, 0130, 8½ hrs. **Mumbai (CST)**: *Udyan Exp, 6530*, 0250, 17½ hrs; *Chennai Mumbai Mail, 6010*, 0750, 20½ hrs. **Londa** (for Goa via Hubli): *Haripriya Exp, 7315*, 0245, 7 hrs; *Amaravati Exp, 7225*, 0815, 5½ hrs.

**Bellary** *p1068*

**Train**

To **Gadag**: *Amravathi Exp, 7225*, 0905 3 hrs. To **Guntakal**: *Amravathi Exp, 7226*, 1730, 1¼ hrs.

# West India

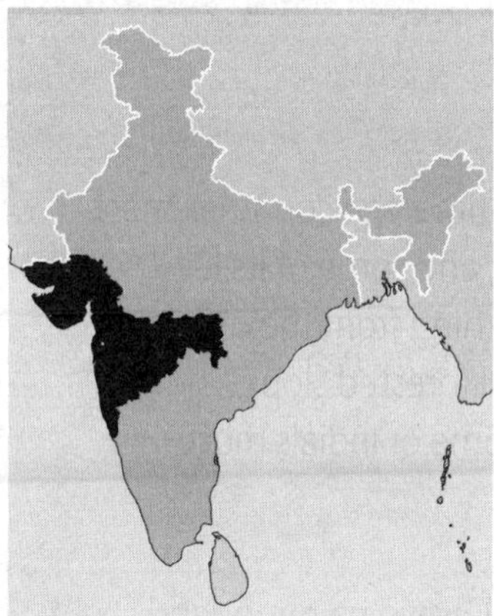

# Introduction

West India contains, at the same time, the countries most dynamic city, Mumbai (Bombay), and some of its least disturbed rural landscapes. Stretching from the deserts bordering Pakistan to the tropical forested slopes of the Western Ghats, it also includes some of India's most important historical sites.

Maharashtra's Buddhist and Hindu cave paintings and sculptures in Ajanta and Ellora caves are world famous, but many of its outstanding forts are virtually unknown, while the new Konkan railway to Goa and the south is opening up the undiscovered west coast.

Gujarat has both undisturbed beaches and magnificent Jain and Hindu temples, while Ahmadabad has some superb examples of Islamic architecture. But the history of Gujarat's people goes back to long before the arrival of Islam. The port of Lothal on the Gulf of Khambhat served traders from the Mohenjo Daro civilization over 2,000 years before the birth of Christ.

Goa itself is one of India's major tourist attractions, yet although its beaches draw hordes of tourists, it too contains many fascinating places completely off the beaten track.

# Maharashtra

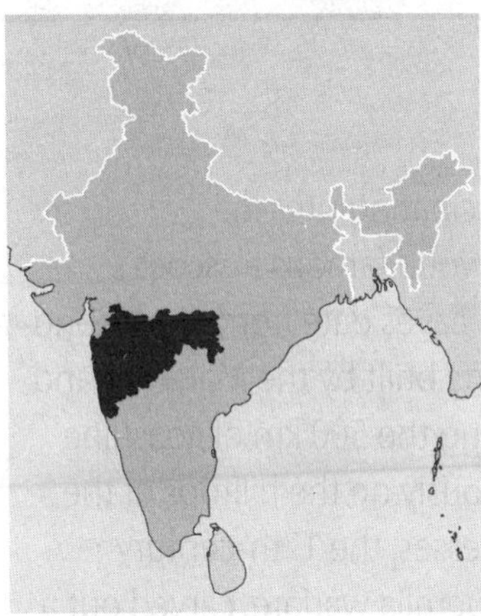



## Footprint features

# Introduction

There are some beautiful and fascinating sites in Maharashtra. The earliest of the world famous frescoes and carvings at Ajanta and Ellora caves date from the second century BC. Wonderful ruined forts built by the Marathas and the Portuguese are scattered along the 500 km of coastline while others are perched precariously on the hilltops of the Western Ghats. From these fastnesses, the 17th-century Marathas, masters in the art of guerrilla warfare, carved out a territory that stretched the width of India. Today Maharashtra boasts not only India's most vibrant city, Mumbai, and a diverse and rapidly growing industrial economy, but also a rich agricultural hinterland.

Small beaches offer an escape from the busy city while train buffs can enjoy a ride up the scenic narrow gauge railway to Matheran in the hills. The thriving 'modern' city of Pune across the Ghats attracts the visitors to the lavish Osho Commune which has drawn large numbers of Westerners in search of an alternative spiritual answer.

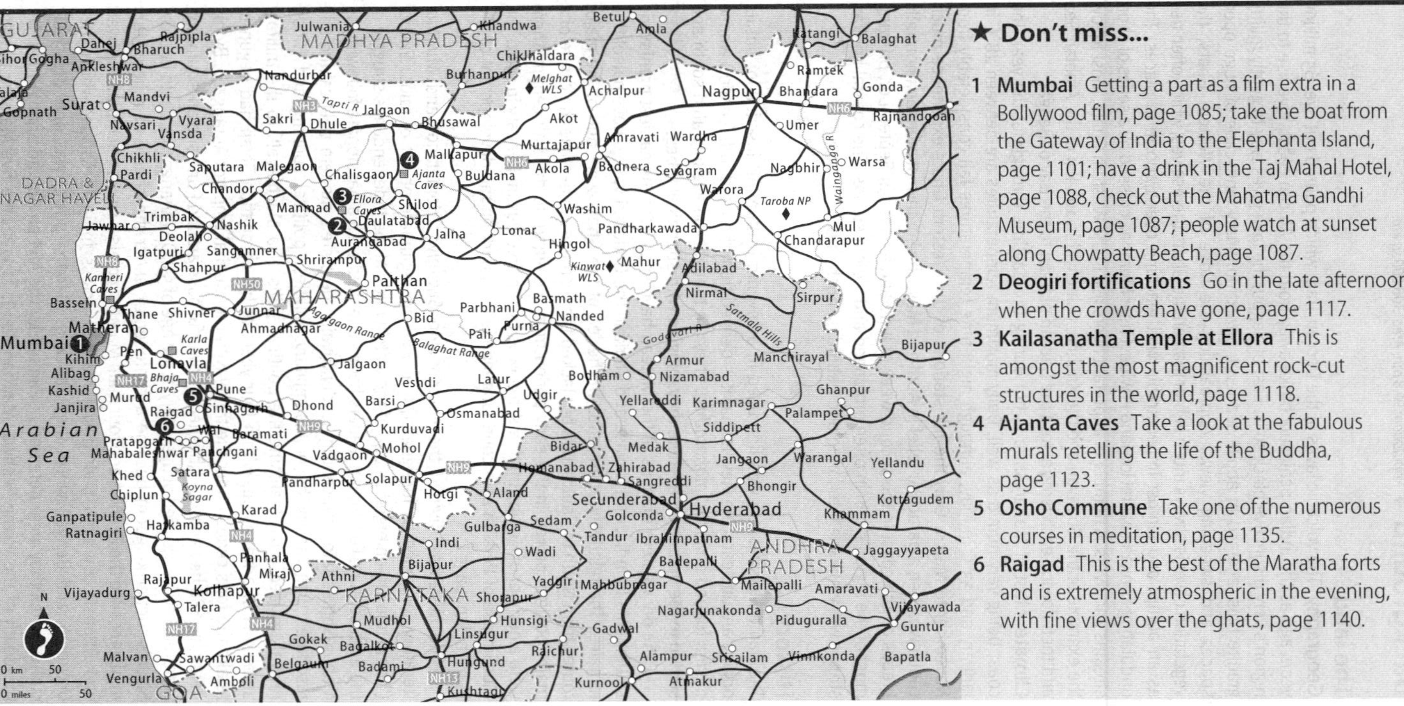


## ★ Don't miss...

1 **Mumbai** Getting a part as a film extra in a Bollywood film, page 1085; take the boat from the Gateway of India to the Elephanta Island, page 1101; have a drink in the Taj Mahal Hotel, page 1088, check out the Mahatma Gandhi Museum, page 1087; people watch at sunset along Chowpatty Beach, page 1087.

2 **Deogiri fortifications** Go in the late afternoon when the crowds have gone, page 1117.

3 **Kailasanatha Temple at Ellora** This is amongst the most magnificent rock-cut structures in the world, page 1118.

4 **Ajanta Caves** Take a look at the fabulous murals retelling the life of the Buddha, page 1123.

5 **Osho Commune** Take one of the numerous courses in meditation, page 1135.

6 **Raigad** This is the best of the Maratha forts and is extremely atmospheric in the evening, with fine views over the ghats, page 1140.

# Background → *Population: 96.8 mn. Area: 308,000 sq km.*

## The land

**Geography** The volcanic lavas of the Deccan Trap, which poured out over 65 million years ago as the Indian peninsula broke away from the African coast, give rise to the region's very distinctive black soils. East of Nagpur the lava gives way to gently rolling granite hills, 250-350 m above sea level, an extraordinary landscape of huge open spaces and sweeping views. Approaching the ridge of the Western Ghats, the vegetation cover is always much lighter than on the Ghats themselves, which often rise as an abrupt and almost impenetrable wall reaching over 1,400 m in places. The undulating Konkan coastal lowland is widest near Mumbai, crossed by a series of short streams and rivers. A number of important rivers rise in the Western Ghats. Most follow the example of the Godavari and the Krishna, rising within 100 km of the Arabian Sea and then flowing eastwards across the Deccan plateau to the Bay of Bengal.

**Climate** Most of Maharashtra is hot during the daytime throughout the year, the coast being very humid as well. Daily maximum temperatures are between 28°C in January and 33°C in May, although night-time temperatures fall considerably from November to March. Only the hill stations of the Western Ghats experience much cooler weather, a particular relief in April and May. The southwest monsoon normally breaks on the coast in the second week of June and finishes in September, bringing most of the region's rain in often prolonged and violent storms. The coastal Konkan strip is wet while the interior upland behind is much drier.

## History

The name Maharashtra was first used in a seventh century AD inscription, but its origins are unclear. One view is that it is derived from the word *rath* (chariot) whose drivers formed an army (*maharathis*). They are thought to have migrated south and settled in the upland area where they mingled with aboriginal tribes.

The dry western margins of the plateau have sites from the earliest **prehistoric** settlements in India, and Nevasa and Chirki in the Godavari valley, have paleolithic remains. The relatively open lands in the lee of the Ghats were one of the major routes from North to South India but lacked the resources to become the centre of a major political power. In the early period from the eighth to the 14th century there were a number of Hindu kingdoms, followed by the first Muslim Dynasty in 1307. The Muslim use of Persian as a court language left its mark on the development of the Marathi language.

The Marathas divided the country into *Swarajya* (Homeland) and *Mughlai* (territory controlled by foreigners), that was the legitimate object of raids. *Swaraj* ('home rule') re-emerged as one of the watchwords of the Independence struggle in the 20th century. Few Indian leaders have generated such a passionate following as Maharashtra's late 17th-century leader **Sivaji**. The state's modern political life still resonates with the myths of his military abilities, political cunning and Hindu revivalism (see box). Matching the political skills of a Machiavelli to the military ambitions of a Napoleon, within four years of his coronation Sivaji had begun to retake the forts ceded under the treaty with the Mughal Emperor Aurangzeb. By his death in 1680 he had re-established a powerful base around Pune and an expanding Maratha Empire. He died of dysentery at the age of 53. On Aurangzeb's death in 1707, Sivaji's former kingdom became a confederacy under the charge of a hereditary minister called the Peshwa and four main Maratha chiefs – Holkar, Scindia, Gaekwad and Bhonsla. By 1750 their power reached across India to Orissa, which they occupied, and Bengal, which they attacked. Maratha power was only decisively curbed when they were defeated at Panipat by the Afghan Ahmad Shah Abdali. On the death of the young Peshwa, Madhao Rao I, in 1772, the five Maratha powers became increasingly independent of one another. Weakened and divided, they were unable to resist the advance of British power.

## Culture

Ethnically, Maharashtra contains a variety of **peoples**. The Bhil, Warli, Gond, Korku and Gowari tribal groups living in the Satpura and Sahyadri ranges in the north are Australoid aboriginals. The Kunbi Marathas found all over the state are believed to be the descendants of immigrants from the north at the beginning of the Christian era. Parsis first arrived in the region in the eighth century from Persia. Just over 80% of the people are Hindus with Islam and Buddhism the most numerous minority religions. The Buddhists are recent converts from among formerly outcaste Hindus.

Marathi is the main regional **language** (spoken by 90% of the population), although both Hindi and English are widely understood, especially in the major cities. Konkani on the west coast and Gondi in the north are important regional languages.

The main regional **dishes** reflect Maharashtra's transition position between the wheat growing regions of the north and the rice growing coastal lands, while millets are grown in the interior. Lightly spiced vegetables and sweet and sour dishes are popular, with a distinctive emphasis on dried and salted fish such as Bombay Duck cooked with lentils. There are also recipes that use sprouting beans. Mumbai has the heaviest concentration of Parsis in the country, so try their cuisine here - *Dhansak*, a special lentil curry with lamb or chicken cooked with five varieties of spice, or *Patrani machli*, fish (often pomfret) stuffed with coconut chutney and coriander, steamed in banana leaves.

## Festivals

The majority of Hindu festivals are observed in the state. The highly colourful *Ranga Panchami* and *Holi*, marking the beginning of spring, are very popular. *Janmashtami* (July/August) celebrates the birth of Lord Krishna. Men and boys form human pyramids to break pots of curds that have been hung from high places. On *Ganesh Chaturthi* in Mumbai (August/September) massive figures of the ever popular elephant god Ganesh are immersed in the sea; Pune has special celebrations. *Dasara* is significant because it was the day on which the Marathas usually began their military campaigns. The Muslim festival of *Mohurram* which commemorates the martyrs of Islam, is often observed by Hindus as well.

## Modern Maharashtra

The old British administrative region of the Bombay Presidency had never coincided with the area in which Marathi was the dominant language. In 1948 the former princely state of Vadodara and some others were merged into Bombay. The present state did not take shape until 1960, when Gujarati areas in the north and Kannada speaking areas in the south were allocated to Gujarat and Karnataka respectively.

Maharashtra's **legislature** has two houses; the Vidhan Parishad (legislative council) and Vidhan Sabha (legislative assembly). Except for an annual meeting at Nagpur, the old Maratha capital, these meet in Mumbai. The state is represented by 48 members in the Lok Sabha (Lower House) and 19 members in Rajya Sabha (Upper House) of the national parliament in New Delhi. The Hindu -Maratha chauvinist party, the Shiv Sena, under the leadership of the former satirical cartoonist Bal Thackeray, has been a force in Maharastra's politics for over twenty years. However, the Shiv Sena-BJP combination suffered a severe setback in the 1998 Lok Sabha elections when the Congress took 37 of the 48 seats. In the State Assembly elections of October 1999, the Shiv Sena-BJP alliance suffered a further blow when it lost control of the State Assembly to a Congress-led coalition, although it remains in power within Mumbai. The Congress itself had split at the national level, one of Maharashtra's most powerful Congress politicians, Sharad Pawar, leaving to form the National Congress Party, or NCP. However his party remained allied to the Congress state level government under the Chief Ministership of Vilasrao Deshmukh, giving it sufficient support to hold on to power.

Maharashtra has been described as India's **industrial** and **commercial** backbone. The centre of India's stock market, the headquarters of a large number of Indian and multinational companies' operations in India and a major manufacturing state in its own right, Maharashtra has not only India's largest city, Mumbai, but a large number of rapidly industrialising smaller towns. These have been encouraged to develop through Government policies aimed at stimulating decentralised industrial growth. With only 10% of India's population Maharashtra acounts for nearly a quarter of India's total industrial output, with textiles, petro-chemicals, pharmaceuticals, electronics and a wide range of other products. However, agriculture remains important, cash crops like sugar cane accounting for 30% of the country's total sugar production. Alongside sugar, rice, sorghum, millets and gram are all important, while horticultural crops and fruit like mango, banana, oranges and grapes have rapidly grown in importance.

# Mumbai (Bombay)

→ *Phone code: 022. Colour map 5, grid B3.*

*You are always in a crowd in this city. Stand at Churchgate station or VT terminus any time after 0600 on a weekday and be overwhelmed with the tidal waves of humanity. Mumbai, India's economic capital for over 150 years, is the subcontinent's outward-looking commercial face and its melting pot. From the cluster of fishing villages first linked by the British East India Company, it has swelled to sprawl across seven islands joined into an artificial isthmus. Its problems – a population of 20 million, over two-thirds of whom live in slums – are only matched by the enormous drive which makes it the centre of business, fashion and film-making in modern India and the great repository for the country's hopes. Its skyline is a combination of gothic towers, skyscrapers, mill chimneys and shanties. The streets are giddying, aswarm with panel-beaten English double-decker buses, waspish yellow and black taxis, long wooden carts stacked with hessian-stitched blocks of cargo and mangoes carried in pyramids on plates.* ⏩ *For Sleeping, Eating and other listings, see page 1088-1100.*

## Ins and outs

**Getting there** Chhatrapati Sivaji International air terminal is 30 km from Nariman Point, the business heart of the city. The domestic terminals at Santa Cruz are 5 km closer. Pre-paid taxis to the city centre are good value and take between 40 minutes and 1½ hours, but there are also cheaper but slower buses. If you arrive late at night without a hotel booking it is best to stay at one of the hotels near the domestic terminal before going into town early in the morning. ⏩ *See Transport, page 1097, for further details.*

**Getting around** The sights are spread out and you need transport. Taxis are metered and generally good value. There are frequent buses on major routes, and the two suburban railway lines are useful out of peak hours on some routes, but get horrendously crowded. Auto-rickshaws are only allowed in the suburbs.

**Tourist information** **Government of India** ⓘ *123 M Karve Rd, opposite Churchgate, T022-2093229, Mon-Sat 0830-1730 (closed 2nd Sat of month from 1230); counters open 24 hrs at both airports; Taj Mahal Hotel, Mon-Sat 0830-1530 (closed 2nd Sat from 1230).* Helpful staff who can also issue liquor permits (essential for Gujarat). **Maharashtra Tourist Development Corporation** ⓘ *www.mtdcindia.com, CDO Hutments, Express Towers, 9th flr, Nariman Pt, T022-2024482; Madam Cama Rd, T022-2026713; Koh-i-Noor Rd, near Pritam Hotel, Dadar T022-4143200; CST Railway Station, T022-2622859; Gateway of India, T022-2841877.* Information and booking counters at international and domestic terminals.

# Mumbai

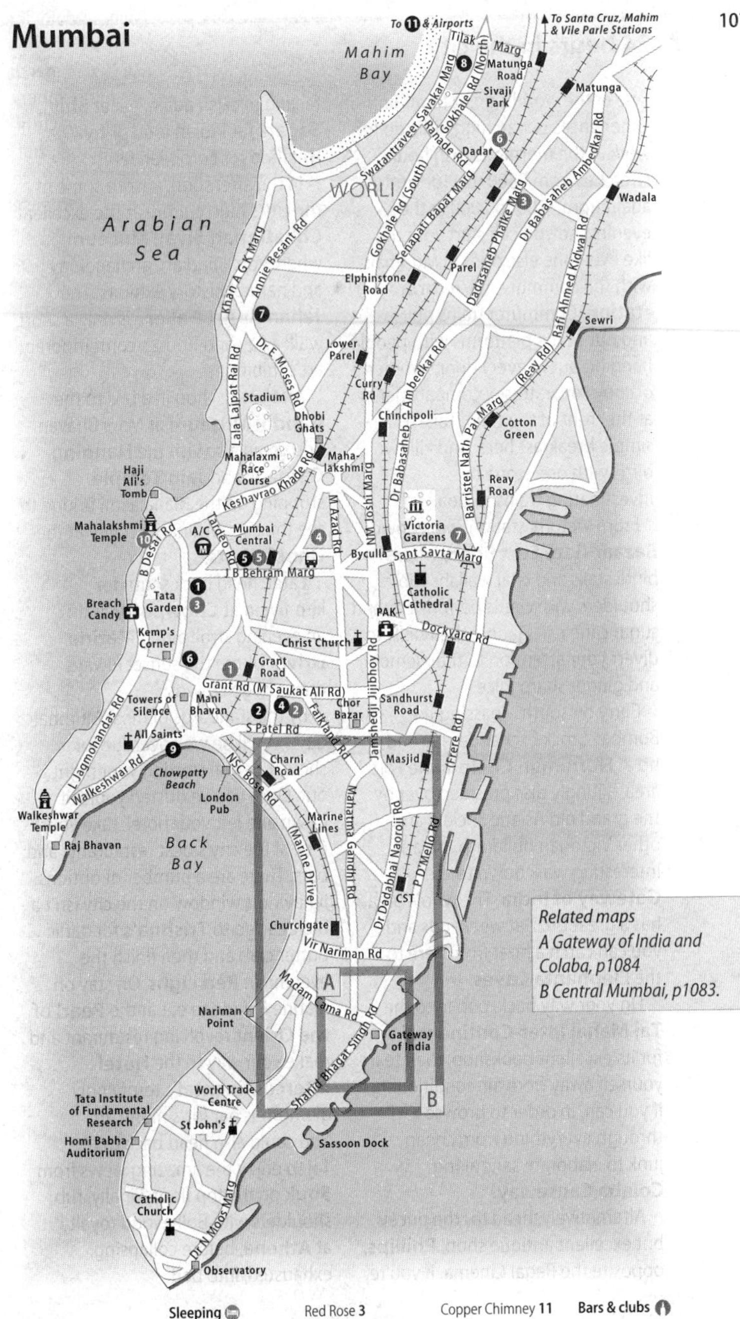


Related maps
A Gateway of India and Colaba, p1084
B Central Mumbai, p1083.

N

0 km 1
0 miles 1

**Sleeping**
Anukool **1**
Heritage **7**
Kalpana Palace **2**
Midtown Pritam **6**
Railway Retiring Rooms **5**
Red Rose **3**
YMCA International House **4**

**Eating**
Biscotti **1**
Bombay A1 **2**
Copper Chimney **11**
Goa Portuguesa **8**
Heaven **4**
Kamat **5**
Revival **9**
Under the Over **6**
Viva Paschim **7**

**Bars & clubs**
Café Olé **3**
Ghetto **10**

## 24 hours in the city

One of the world's great humbling experiences is watching India go to work in the morning. Rush hour stretches from 0800 to 1100 and again from 1700 to 2000 in the evening, so you can start your day like everyone else does in Mumbai: with the commute at **Victoria station**. Commuter trains pull in and out of the platforms with people hanging out of every door; women occupy separate-sex compartments at the front of the train. Take a simple breakfast here, and kill two birds with one stone by investigating trains to Goa.

From Victoria station, walk down **Bazaar Gate Fort Road**, where bindi stalls and chai wallahs rub shoulders with circus performers, and sugar cane carts jangle their bells to divert your attention to their lemon and ginger sharp juice.

Carry on south – passing the Bombay Stock Exchange – to end up at **Horniman Circle** in the Fort area, a jungly disc presided over by the grand old Asiatic Society and other Victorian buildings. It's an interesting walk down to the **Gateway of India**. The whole area has a great buzz at weekends and you can catch a boat from here to the **Elephanta Caves**.

On your way back, pop in to the **Taj Mahal Inter-Continental** for its excellent bookshop, then tear yourself away from air-conditioning, if you can, in order to browse through everything from cheap junk to elaborate saris along **Colaba Causeway**.

Alternatively, head for the pricey but excellent antique shop, **Phillips**, opposite the Regal Cinema. If you're feeling peckish again, eat at **Shiv Sagars** for Indian food or try **Basilico** for European fare.

In the afternoon, absorb some of the city's high culture at the excellent **Chhatrapati Sivaji Museum**, where you'll find art, archaeology and natural history exhibits. The **Jehangir Art Gallery** is only a short walk away and houses contemporary art exhibitions.

Afterwards, hop in a taxi to the **Gandhi Museum** at Mani Bhavan. You could also visit the **Hanging Gardens** and **Jain Temple**, stopping on the Mahalaxmi Bridge to see the extraordinary activity at the **Dhobi Ghats**.

Later, head back south for kite-flying at **Chowpatty** and an evening stroll along **Marine Drive**, where the sunset always draws huge crowds.

By the standards of most Mumbai days, you'll be well overdue for a shower before starting your night out. Once you've dusted yourself down and left your hotel, take your pick of the city's best restaurants and bars. There are a number of options. If having a window on the city isn't a big deal, go to **Trishna's** for garlic butter crab and then finish the evening at **Red Light**. Or, stay on Marine Parade to eat at the **Pearl of the Orient** revolving restaurant and make your way to the **Hotel Intercontinental**'s terrifyingly glamorous bar for a nightcap. You could also head back to the Taj to enjoy the amazing views from **Souk** on the top floor. Finally, rub shoulders with Bollywood royalty at **Athena**, before collapsing, exhausted, into bed.



*Bombay was called after the Portuguese for good harbour, 'bom bahia', but was renamed Mumbai after Mumba Devi, a Kali goddess, following fierce lobbying by Shiv Sena.*

## Background

Hinduism made its mark on Mumbai long before the Portuguese and then the British transformed it into one of India's great cities. The caves on the island of Elephanta were excavated under the Kalachuris (AD 500-600). Yet, only 350 years ago, the area occupied by this great metropolis comprised seven islands inhabited by Koli fishermen. The British acquired these marshy and malarial islands as part of the marriage dowry paid by the Portuguese when Catherine of Braganza married Charles II in 1661. Four years later, the British took possession of the remaining islands and neighbouring mainland area and in 1668 the East India Company leased the whole area from the crown for £10 a year, which was paid for nearly 50 years. The East India Company shifted its headquarters to Mumbai in 1672. Until the early 19th century, Mumbai's fortunes rested on the shipbuilding yards established by progressive Parsis.

Mumbai remained isolated by the sharp face of the Western Ghats and the constantly hostile Marathas. However, it thrived on trade and, in the cosmopolitan city this created, Parsis, Sephardic Jews and the British shared common interests and responded to the same incentives.

After a devastating fire on 17 February 1803, a new town with wider streets was built. Then, with the abolition of the Company's trade monopoly, the doors to rapid expansion were flung open and Mumbai flourished. Trade with England boomed. After the opening of the Suez Canal in 1870, Mumbai's greater proximity to European markets gave it an advantage over Kolkata. The port became the commercial centre of the Arabian Sea. Mumbai rapidly became the centre of an entrepreneurial as well as a commercial class. Mumbai has become the home of India's stock exchange (BSE) and headquarters for many national and international companies and is also a major industrial centre. With the sponsorship of the Tata family, Mumbai has also become the primary home of India's nuclear research programme, with its first plutonium extraction plant at Trombay in 1961 and the establishment of the Tata Institute for Fundamental Research, the most prestigious science research institute in the country.

Mumbai is still growing fast. One third of the population live in the desperately squalid *chawls* of cramped, makeshift hovels. There are also many thousands of pavement dwellers. Due to heavy demand for building space, property values are exceedingly high. New Mumbai across the Thane Creek has been developed to ease the pressure on the isthmus, but Great Mumbai remains a magnet to people from across India.

# Gateway of India and Colaba

The Indo-Saracenic-style Gateway of India (1927), designed by George Wittet to commemorate the visit of George V and Queen Mary in 1911, is modelled in honey-coloured basalt on 16th-century Gujarati work. The great gateway is an archway with halls on each side capable of seating 600 at important receptions. The arch was the point from which the last British regiment serving in India signalled the end of the empire when it left on 28 February 1948. The whole area has a huge buzz at weekends. Scores of boats depart from here for **Elephanta Island,** creating a sea-swell which young boys delight in diving into. Hawkers, beggars and the general throng of people all add to the atmosphere. A short distance behind the Gateway is an impressive statue of **Sivaji**. The original red-domed **Taj Mahal Hotel** has been adjoined by a modern skyscraper, the **Taj Mahal Inter-Continental**. It is worth popping into the **Taj** for a bite to eat or a drink, or to go to the disco with its clientele of well-heeled young Indians. Unfortunately, drug addicts, drunks and prostitutes frequent the area behind the hotel.

❢ *Bollywood churns out 860 films each year; of those 854 fail.*

South of the Gateway of India is the crowded southern section of Shahid (literally 'martyr') Bhagat Singh Marg, or Colaba Causeway. The Afghan Memorial **Church of St John the Baptist** (1847-1858) is at the northern edge of Colaba itself. Early English in style, with a 58-m spire, it was built to commemorate the soldiers who died in the First Afghan War. Fishermen still unload their catch early in the morning at **Sassoon Dock**, the first wet dock in India; photography prohibited. Beyond the church near the tip of the Colaba promontory lie the **Observatory** and **Old European cemetery** in the naval colony (permission needed to enter). Frequent buses ply this route.

## Central Mumbai

The area stretching north from Colaba Causeway to CST (Victoria Terminus) dates from after 1862, when Sir Bartle Frere became Governor (1862-1867). Under his enthusiastic guidance Mumbai became a great civic centre and an extravaganza of Victorian Gothic architecture, modified by Indo-Saracenic influences.

**Chhatrapati Sivaji (Prince of Wales) Museum** ⓘ *Oct-Feb Tue-Sun 1015-1730, Jul-Sep Tue-Sun 1015-1800, Mar-Jun Tue-Sun 1015-1830; foreigners Rs 350 (includes taped guide), Indians Rs 15, camera Rs 15 (no flash or tripods)*, is housed in an impressive building designed by George Wittet to commemorate the visit of the Prince of Wales to India in 1905. The dome of glazed tiles has a very Persian and Central Asian flavour. The archaeological section has three main groups: Brahminical; Buddhist and Jain; Prehistoric and Foreign. The art section includes an excellent collection of Indian miniatures and well displayed *tankhas*. There are also works by Gainsborough, Poussin and Titian as well as Indian silver, jade and tapestries. The Natural History section is based on the collection of the **Bombay Natural History Society**, founded in 1833. Good guidebooks, cards and reproductions on sale. **Jehangir Art Gallery** ⓘ *in the Chhatrapati Sivaji Museum complex*, holds small short term exhibitions of contemporary art, available to buy. The **Samovar café** is good for a snack and a drink including chilled beer in a pleasant garden-side setting. There are phones and toilets. Temporary members may use the library and attend lectures.

**National Gallery of Modern Art** ⓘ *Sir Cowasji Jehangir Hall, opposite the Chhatrapati Sivaji Museum, T022-852457*, is a three-tiered gallery converted from an old public hall which gives a good introduction to India's contemporary art scene.

**St Andrew's Kirk**, (1819), just behind the Chhatrapati Sivaji Museum, is a simple neo-classical church. At the south end of Mahatma Gandhi (MG) Road is the renaissance-style **Institute of Science** (1911) designed by George Wittet. The Institute, which includes a scientific library, a public hall and examination halls, was built with gifts from the Parsi and Jewish communities.

The **Oval garden** has been restored to a pleasant public garden and acts as the lungs of the southern business district. On the east side of the **Pope Paul (Oval) Maidan** is the Venetian Gothic-style **old Secretariat** (1874), with a façade of arcaded verandas and porticos faced in buff-coloured porbander stone from Gujarat. Decorated with red and blue basalt, the carvings are in white *hemnagar* stone. The **University Convocation Hall** (1874) to its north was designed by Sir George Gilbert Scott in a 15th-century French decorated style. Scott also designed the adjacent **University Library** and the **Rajabai Clocktower** (1870s) next door, based on Giotto's campanile in Florence. The sculpted figures in niches on the exterior walls of the tower were designed to represent the castes of India. Originally the clock could chime 12 tunes including *Rule Britannia*. The **High Court** (1871-1879), in early English gothic

*The acquisition of wealth is nothing new to Mumbai. The city has always worshipped money in the shape of Mahalaxmi, the temple to the goddess of wealth.*

# Central Mumbai

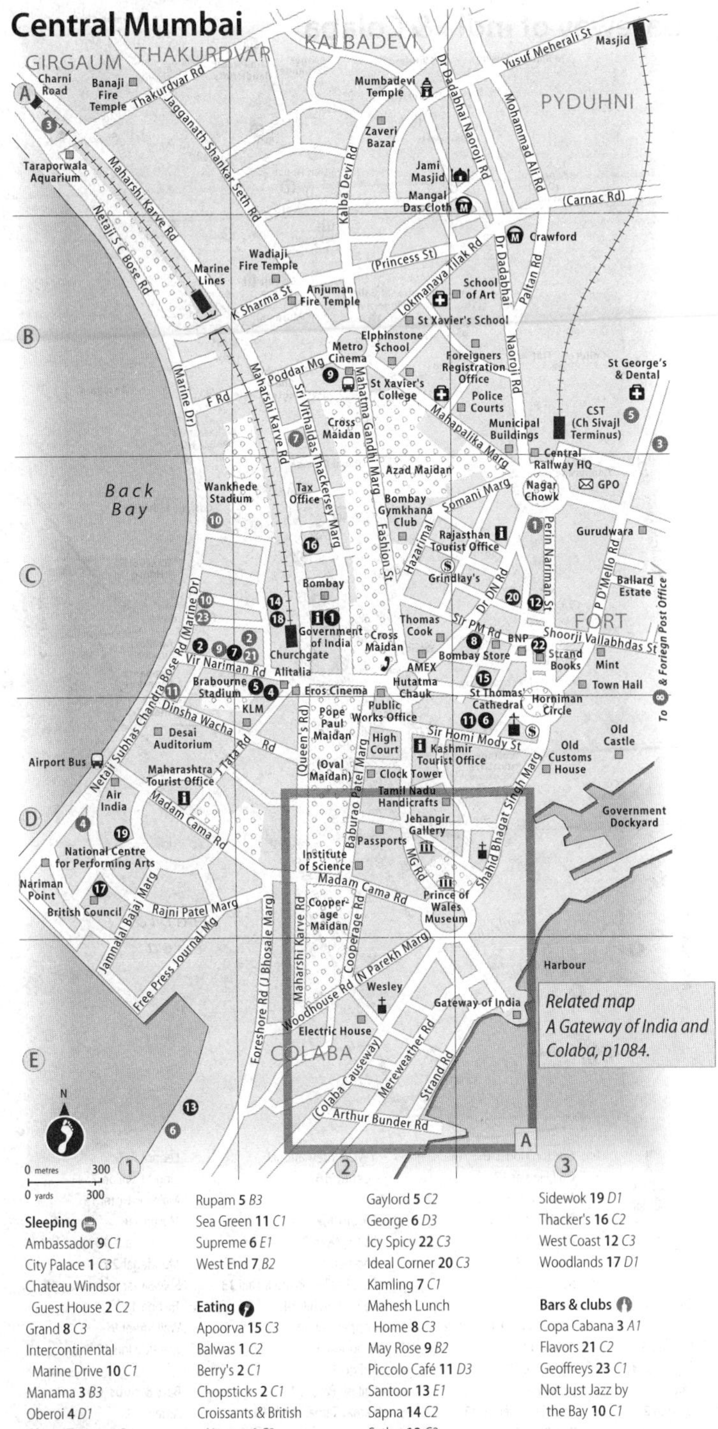


*Related map*
*A Gateway of India and Colaba, p1084.*

**Sleeping**
Ambassador **9** *C1*
City Palace **1** *C3*
Chateau Windsor Guest House **2** *C2*
Grand **8** *C3*
Intercontinental Marine Drive **10** *C1*
Manama **3** *B3*
Oberoi **4** *D1*
Oberoi Towers **4** *D1*
Rupam **5** *B3*
Sea Green **11** *C1*
Supreme **6** *E1*
West End **7** *B2*

**Eating**
Apoorva **15** *C3*
Balwas **1** *C2*
Berry's **2** *C1*
Chopsticks **2** *C1*
Croissants & British Airways **4** *C2*
Gaylord **5** *C2*
George **6** *D3*
Icy Spicy **22** *C3*
Ideal Corner **20** *C3*
Kamling **7** *C1*
Mahesh Lunch Home **8** *C3*
May Rose **9** *B2*
Piccolo Café **11** *D3*
Santoor **13** *E1*
Sapna **14** *C2*
Satkar **18** *C2*
Sidewok **19** *D1*
Thacker's **16** *C2*
West Coast **12** *C3*
Woodlands **17** *D1*

**Bars & clubs**
Copa Cabana **3** *A1*
Flavors **21** *C2*
Geoffreys **23** *C1*
Not Just Jazz by the Bay **10** *C1*

# Gateway of India & Colaba

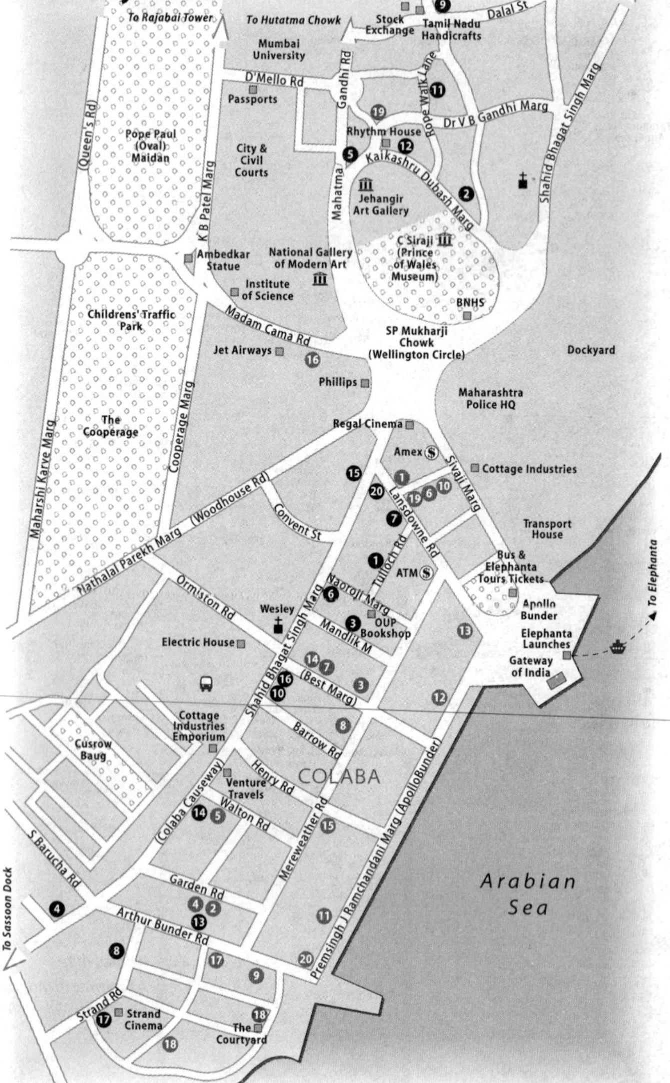

To Horniman Circle
To Rajabai Tower
To Hutatma Chowk
Stock Exchange
Tamil Nadu Handicrafts
Dalal St
Mumbai University
D'Mello Rd
Passports
Gandhi Rd
Rope Walk Lane
Dr V B Gandhi Marg
Shahid Bhagat Singh Marg
(Queen's Rd)
Pope Paul (Oval) Maidan
City & Civil Courts
Rhythm House
Kaikashru Dubash Marg
K B Patel Marg
Mahatma
Jehangir Art Gallery
C Siraji (Prince of Wales Museum)
Ambedkar Statue
National Gallery of Modern Art
Institute of Science
BNHS
Childrens' Traffic Park
Madam Cama Rd
SP Mukharji Chowk (Wellington Circle)
Dockyard
Jet Airways
Phillips
Maharashtra Police HQ
Maharshi Karve Marg
The Cooperage
Cooperage Marg
Regal Cinema
Amex
Cottage Industries
Sivaji Marg
Nathalal Parekh Marg (Woodhouse Rd)
Convent St
Lansdowne Rd
Transport House
Tulloch Rd
ATM
Bus & Elephanta Tours Tickets
To Elephanta
Ormiston Rd
Naoroji Marg
Wesley
OUP Bookshop
Apollo Bunder
Mandlik M
Elephanta Launches
Electric House
Gateway of India
(Best Marg)
Shahid Bhagat Singh Marg
Cottage Industries Emporium
Cusrow Baug
Barrow Rd
Henry Rd
Venture Travels
COLABA
(Colaba Causeway)
Walton Rd
Mereweather Rd
Premsingh J Ramchandani Marg (ApolloBunder)
S Barucha Rd
Garden Rd
Arabian Sea
To Sassoon Dock
Arthur Bunder Rd
Strand Rd
Strand Cinema
The Courtyard

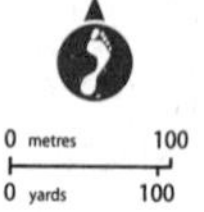


**Sleeping**
Apollo **1**
Cowie's **5**
Diplomat **3**
Fariyas **18**
Garden **2**
Godwin **4**
Gordon House **6**
Gulf Flower **17**
Moti **14**
Regency Inn **19**
Regent **7**
Salvation Army **8**
Sea Shore **9**
Shelley's **20**
Suba Palace **10**
Strand **11**
Taj Mahal **12**
Taj Mahal Intercontinental **13**
Whalley's **15**
YWCA International Centre **16**

**Eating**
Bade Miyan **7**
Bagdadi **1**
Café Basilico Bistro & Deli **13**
Café Churchill **14**
Copper Chimney **2**
Food-Inn **6**
Indigo **3**
Kailash Parbat **4**
Kamat Samarambh **10**
Khyber **5**
Leopold's **6**
Ling's Pavilion **7**
Majestic Hotel **15**
Martin's **8**
Ming Palace **16**
Mondegar **20**
Shiv Sagar Vegetarian **17**
Trishna **11**
Wall Street **9**
Wayside Inn **12**

**Bars & clubs**
Athena **18**
Red Light **19**

## Bright lights of Bollywood

Mumbai produces around 860 films a year, making Bollywood the world's second largest film-maker after Hong Kong. The stars live in sumptuous dwellings, many of which are on Malabar Hill, Mumbai's Beverley Hills, and despite the spread of foreign videos, their popularity seems to be undiminished.

It is difficult to get permission to visit a studio during filming but you might try **Film City**, Goregaon East, T022-8401533 or **Mehboob Studios**, Hill Road, Bandra West, T022-6428045. Alternatively, the staff at the **Salvation Army Hostel** (see Sleeping) may be able to help foreigners get on as 'extras' (blonde and tall preferred!); Rs 500 per day.

style, has a 57-m high central tower flanked by lower octagonal towers topped by the figures of Justice and Mercy. The **Venetian Gothic Public Works Office** (1869-1872) is to its north. Opposite, and with its main façade to Vir Nariman Road, is the former **General Post Office** (1869-1872). Now called the Telegraph Office, it stands next to the original Telegraph Office adding romanesque to the extraordinary mixture of European architectural styles.

The fort area is worth visiting after 1900, when the old buildings are floodlit. **Horniman Circle** was laid out in 1860. On the west edge are the Venetian Gothic **Elphinstone Buildings** (1870) in brown sandstone. **Cathedral Church of St Thomas** was begun in 1672, opened in 1718, and subject to a number of later additions. Inside are a number of monuments forming a heroic 'Who's Who of India'. The **Custom House** is believed to incorporate a Portuguese barrack block of 1665. Over the entrance is the crest of the East India Company. Parts of the old Portuguese fort's walls can be seen and many Malabar teak 'East Indiamen' ships were built here. **The Mint** (1824-1829), built on the Fort rubbish dump, has ionic columns and a water tank in front of it. The **Town Hall** (1820-1823) has been widely admired as one of the best neo-classical buildings in India. The original idea of paired columns was abandoned as being too monumental, and half the columns – imported from Britain – were used at Christ Church, Byculla. The Corinthian interior houses the **Assembly Rooms** and the **Bombay Asiatic Society.** From the imposing Horniman Circle, Vir Nariman Road leads to Flora (or Frere) Fountain (1869), now known as **Hutatma Chowk**.

## Around the CST or VT

*Join the crowds at sunset for an entertaining walk: hawkers and sand sculptors mingle with joggers and Mumbai's high society walking their dogs.*

**Chhatrapati Sivaji Terminus,** formerly Victoria Terminus or VT (1878-1887), the most remarkable example of Victorian Gothic architecture in India, was opened during Queen Victoria's Golden Jubilee year. The first train in India left from this terminus for Thane in April 1853. Now known as CST, over half a million commuters use the station daily.

The station was built at a time when fierce debate was taking place among British architects working in India as to the most appropriate style to develop to meet the demands of the late 19th-century boom. One view held that the British should restrict themselves to models derived from the best in western tradition. Others argued that architects should draw on Indian models, trying to bring out the best of Indian tradition and encourage its development. By and large, the former were dominant, but the introduction of gothic allowed a blending of western traditions with Indian (often Islamic Indian) motifs, which became known as the

### Dabbawallahs

If you go inside Churchgate station at mid-morning or after lunch, you will see the *dabbawallahs*, members of the Bombay Union of Tiffin Box Carriers. Each morning, the 2,500 *dabbawallahs* call on suburban housewives who pack freshly cooked lunch into small circular stainless steel containers – *dabbas*. Three or four are stacked one on the other and held together by a clip with a handle. Typically the *dabbawallah* will collect 30-40 tiffin boxes, range them out on a long pole and cycle to the nearest station. Here he will hand them over to a fellow *dabbawallah* who will transport them into the city for delivery to the consumer.

Over 100,000 lunches of maybe sabze (vegetable curry), chappattis, dal and pickle make their way daily across town to the breadwinner. The service, which costs a few rupees a day, is a good example of the fine division of labour in India, reliable and efficient, for the dabbawallahs pride themselves on never losing a lunch. He makes sure that the carefully prepared pukka (proper) food has not in any way been defiled.

Indo-Saracenic style. The giant caterpillar-like walkway with perspex awnings looks incongruous against the gothic structure of 'VT'. The frontage is symmetrical with a large central dome flanked by two wings, capped by a 4-m high statue of Progress. The booking hall with its arcades, stained glass and glazed tiles was inspired by London's St Pancras station.

Opposite the CST station are the grand **Municipal Buildings** (1893), built by Stevens. In Mahapalika Marg (Cruickshank Road) are the **Police Courts** (1888), **Cama Albless Hospital**, which has interesting gothic windows with conical iron hoods to provide shade, **St Xavier's College** founded in 1867, and **Elphinstone High School** (1872). On the opposite side of the road is the **Azad Maidan**.

**St Xavier's School** and **Gokuldas Tejpal Hospital** (1877), built by Parsi benefactors, are in Lokmanya Tilak Marg (Camac Road). On the southeast and southwest faces are medallions by Rudyard Kipling's father Lockwood Kipling. **Crawford Market**, Mumbai (1865-1871), now **Jyotiba Phule Market**, was designed by Emerson in the 12th-century French gothic style. Over the entrance is more of Lockwood Kipling's work; the paving stones are from Caithness. The market is divided into sections for fruit, vegetables, fish, mutton and poultry.

Between Crawford Market and Mumbai Central Railway Station is **Falkland Road**, the centre of Mumbai's red-light district. Prostitutes stand behind barred windows, giving the area its other name 'The Cages' – many of the girls are sold or abducted from various parts of India and Nepal. Medical reports suggest that AIDS is very widespread.



## Marine Drive, Malabar Hill and around

You can do an interesting half-day trip from Churchgate Station, along Marine Drive to the **Taraporewala Aquarium, Mani Bhavan** (Gandhi Museum), the **Babulnath Temple**, past the **Parsi Towers of Silence** to **Kamla Nehru Park**, the **Hanging Gardens** and the **Jain Temple**. If you wish, you can go further towards Malabar Point to get a glimpse of **Raj Bhavan** and the **Walkeshwar Temple**, before returning via the **Mahalaxmi Temple** and **Haji Ali's tomb**.

**Churchgate Station** (1894-1896) was designed by FW Stevens for the Mumbai, Baroda and Central India Railway. Stevens was a great protagonist of the indo-saracenic style. With its domes and façades, Churchgate Station is byzantine in flavour. The statue on the western gable shows a figure holding a locomotive and wheel, symbols of technological progress.



**Chowpatty Beach**, a long stretch of white sand, looks attractive from a distance, but is polluted. Swimming here is not recommended but there is a lot of interesting beach activity in the evening. Chowpatty was the scene of a number of important 'Quit India' rallies during the Independence Movement. At important festivals like **Ganesh Chaturthi** and **Dasara** (see Festivals), it is thronged with jubilant Hindu devotees. Netaji Subhash Road, better known as Marine Drive, runs round Back Bay along Chowpatty from just below the Hanging Gardens on Malabar Hill to **Nariman Point.** At night, lined with lights, it is a very attractive sight from Malabar Hill.

**Mahatma Gandhi Museum (Mani Bhavan)** ⓘ *west of Grant Rd, 19 Laburnum Rd, 0930-1800, Rs 3, allow 1 hr*, is further north towards Nana Chowk, at Mani Bhavan. This private house, where Mahatma Gandhi used to stay on visits to Mumbai, is now a memorial museum and research library with 20,000 volumes. There is a diorama depicting important scenes from Gandhi's life; slides without a mount are available, Rs 100. The display of photos and letters on the first floor is more interesting, and includes letters Gandhi wrote to Hitler in 1939 asking him not to go to war, and those to Roosevelt and Tolstoy; there are also letters from Einstein and Tolstoy.

In the heart of the Muslim quarter where agate minarets mingle with the upper storeys of 1960s residential towers lies **Chor Bazaar**. The atmosphere here is totally different from the crumbling colonial architectural glory of the Colaba and Fort area, and at sunset the ramshackle roads hum with yellow and black taxis, adolescent boys wielding wooden carts through traffic at a run, and Muslim women at a stroll. The jumble of the bazaar is a brilliant place to poke around in, there are tonnes of dealers in old watches, film posters, Belgian- or Indian-made temple lamps, enamel tiles and door-knobs. The area around Mutton Street is popular with film prop-buyers and foreign and domestic bric-a-brac hunters. Further out the produce is more local: tarpaulins and tools, Mecca paintings, and burqas with gold geometric embroidery. Balconies come bedecked with fairy lights on faded apartment blocks and wooden shutters lie over grilling, pollution stains streaked over the pastel buildings.

The **Towers of Silence**, Mumbai (Parsi 'temple') are in secluded gardens 500 m west of Mani Bhavan. This very private place is not accessible to tourists but it can be glimpsed from the road. Sir Jamshetji Jeejeebhoy gave a large area of land around the towers, thus affording them privacy and allowing the creation of a tranquil garden. Parsis believe that the elements of water, fire and earth must not be polluted by the dead, so they lay their 'vestments of flesh and bone' out on the top of the towers to be picked clean by vultures. The apparent depletion in the number of vultures is a cause for concern.

The **Hanging Gardens (Pherozeshah Mehta Gardens)** immediately south of the Towers of Silence, on top of a low hill, are so named since they are located on top of a series of tanks that supply water to Mumbai. The gardens are well kept with lots of topiary animals and there are good views over the city from the children's park across the road. Snake charmers operate from the roadside. Worth a visit.

Nearby is the Church of North India **All Saints' Church** (1882). Across the road from the Hanging Gardens is the **Kamla Nehru Park**, laid out in 1952 and named after the wife of India's first Prime Minister. The **Jain Temple** (1904) was built of marble and dedicated to the first Jain Tirthankar. Much of the decoration depicts the lives of the Tirthankars. Visitors can watch various rituals being performed. Jains play a prominent part in Mumbai's banking and commerce and are one of the city's wealthiest communities.

One of the oldest buildings in Mumbai, the **Walkeshwar Temple** ('Lord of Sand') was built about AD 1000. In legend this was a resting point for Rama on his journey from Ayodhya to Lanka to free Sita from the demon king Ravana. One day Rama's brother Lakshman failed to return from Varanasi at the usual time with a *lingam* which he fetched daily for Rama's worship. Rama then made a *lingam* from the beach sand to worship Siva.

On Bhulabhai Desai Road, Cumballa Hill are the **Mahalakshmi temples**, the oldest in Mumbai and dedicated to three goddesses whose images were found in the sea. **Haji Ali's Tomb** and the mosque here are devoted to a Muslim saint who drowned here. They are reached by a long causeway usable only at low tide. The moneychangers are willing to exchange 1 rupee coins into smaller coins, enabling pilgrims to make several individual gifts to beggars rather than one larger one, thereby reputedly increasing the merit of the gift.

From Haji Ali's Tomb go along Keshavrao Khade Road to **SG Maharaj Chowk (Jacob's Circle).** From the Mahalakshmi Bridge there is a view of the astonishing Municipal dhobi ghats. Go down Maulana Azad Road then turn left into Clare Road. On your right is **Christ Church**, Byculla (1835), which incorporated half the pillars originally intended for the Town Hall. Clare Road leads down the side of the **Victoria Gardens**.They are very attractive – marked as Jijamata Udyan on some maps.

North of Byculla Station is the **Victoria and Albert Museum (Bhav Daji Laud Museum)** ⓘ *Mon and Tue, Thu-Sat 1030-1700, Sun 0830-1645*. Inspired by the V&A in London and financed by public subscription, it was built in 1872 in a palladian style. The collection covers the history of Mumbai and contains prints, maps and models.

## Juhu Beach and Bandra

Juhu Beach, 20 km from the centre, used to be quite an attractivie and relaxed seaside area but the sea is now polluted. Having said that, a primarily residential area, it does make a more relaxing alternative to staying in the centre of the city. Bandra is a lively suburb, popular with the young wealthy set. There are some exciting places to eat and some of the coolest bars and clubs in town. If you really want to get under the skin of the city, a jaunt into the suburbs is essential.

## Sleeping

There's no low-season when it comes to accommodation in Mumbai: whenever possible make reservations in advance. If you have not, arrive as early in the day as you can. Most hotels are concentrated in the central area (Marine Drive, Nariman Point, Apollo Bunder and Colaba).

There are stacks of moderately priced hotels immediately behind the Taj Mahal Hotel. Backpackers usually head for the Colaba area to the south. The alternative is to look around CST and Dadar railway stations. On Arthur Bunder Rd, Colaba, there are several, often on upper floors, usually shared facilities, cold water only, some windowless rooms; arrive early and inspect room first. There are several 5-star hotels on Juhu beach and close to the airports. For paying guest accommodation contact India Tourist Office, 123 M Karve Rd, T022-2032932.

### Gateway of India and Colaba

*p1081, map p1084*

Rooms with sea view are more expensive. There are few budget hotels left in the area charging under Rs 400 though you may get a dormitory bed for Rs 250.

**LL Taj Mahal** Apollo Bunder, T022-56653366, www.tajhotels.com. The grand-dame of Mumbai lodging, over a century old, with 294 rooms on the Gateway to India and 306 in the **Taj Mahal Intercontinental**, its newer wing. So good, even the corridors look like art galleries. 9 restaurants and bars, plus fitness centre and even a yacht on call.

**L-AL Fariyas**, off Arthur Bunder Rd, Colaba, T022-2042911. 80 upgraded rooms, good restaurants, 'pub', roof garden, pool (open to non-residents), obliging service.

**L-AL Gordon House Hotel**, 5 Battery St, Apollo Bunder, Colaba, T022-2871122, www.ghhotel.com. Amazingly, a spiffingly spruce boutique hotel in the rundown Colaba district, on 3 themed floors that really do leave India outside: yellow Med-style walls in some, quilts in the country cottage rooms and all blonde wood on the Scandinavian floor.

**A Strand**, 25 PJ Ramchandani Marg, T022-2882222. Friendly, clean, decent rooms, some with bath and sea view.

**A-B Garden Hotel**, 42 Garden Rd, T022-2841476, gardenhotel@mail.com. Efficient sister hotel to the Godwin next door, with similar facilities. All rooms have bath tubs.

**A-C Godwin**, 41 Garden Rd, T022-2872050. 48 large, clean, renovated, a/c rooms (upper floors have better views), good rooftop restaurant (full of wealthy Mumbaiites on Fri and Sat night), very helpful management. Recommended.

**B Apollo**, 22 Lansdowne Rd, Colaba, behind Taj, T022-2020223. 39 rooms, some a/c, some with amazing sea views. Tatty linen and walls, but helpful, friendly service.

**B Diplomat**, 24-26 BK Boman Behram Marg (behind Taj), T022-2021661, diplomat@vsnl.com, 52 a/c rooms, restaurant, quiet, friendly, relaxed atmosphere, good value. Very simple furnishings, small beds. Recommended.

**B Gulf Flower**, Kamal Mansions, Arthur Bunder Rd, T022-2833742. Off-putting exterior but modern and clean rooms inside.

**B Regency Inn**, 18 Landsdowne Rd behind Regal Cinema, Colaba, T022-2020292. Spacious a/c rooms, fridge, good value.

**B Regent**, 8 Ormiston Rd (Best Marg), T022-2871854. 50 rooms in modern hotel that's popular with sheiks, hence the camels and pastels theme. Well-furnished a/c rooms, no restaurant but good room service.

**B Suba Palace**, Apollo Bunder, T022-2020636. Clean, modern, well run. Recommended.

**B-C Hotel Cowie's**, 15 Walton Rd, near Electric House, Colaba T022-2840232. 20 rooms, all with central a/c, bathroom en suite, television and phone, in old-world hotel on one of the tree-lined residential streets off Colaba Causeway. Excellent value.

**B-C Shelley's**, 30 PJ Ramchandani Marg, Colaba, T022-2840229, shelleyhotel@vsnl.com. Large comfortable, bright airy a/c rooms, some sea-facing with TV and fridge (more expensive), a 'heritage' building with character, breakfasts only, helpful and friendly owners. Recommended.

**C Moti Hotel**, 10 Best Marg, opposite Electric House, Colaba, T022-025714. 8 a/c rooms with slatted wood doors in ground floor of a mansion block, yellow walls made of ply, original mosaic flooring. Extremely narrow bathrooms with plastic mirrors, 24-hr hot water, TV.

**C-D Sea Lord**, 1/49 Kamal Mansion, Arthur Bunder Rd. 15 bright gloss-pink rooms and purple corridors, shower in room but no sink, 7 with window and TV and fan, 8 without. Sea view room has 4 beds. 2 rooms come with toilet, TV and hot water.

**C-D Whalley's**, 41 Mereweather Rd, T022-2834206. 25 rooms (inspect first), some good, a/c with balcony and bath, includes breakfast, accepts TCs, old-fashioned.

**C-D YWCA International Centre**, 2nd Fl, 18 Madam Cama Rd (entrance on side), Fort, T022-2020122. For both sexes, 34 clean, pleasant rooms with bath, breakfast and dinner included, essential to write in advance with Rs 1,300 deposit. Recommended.

**C-F The Salvation Army**, Red Shield House, 30 Mereweather Rd, T022-2841824, red-shield @vsnl.net. A/c (more expensive), includes all meals. Dormitory **F** rate includes breakfast only. Mostly dorm about Rs 130 including breakfast, Rs 200 including meals), some double rooms (Rs 450, all meals), lockers Rs 30 per item 0800-2200, showers, check out 0900, book in advance or arrive early when others check out, bus ticketing (eg Goa) at reception. Recommended as convenient, friendly, best value but could be cleaner. See box, page 1085.

*For an explanation of the sleeping and eating price codes used in this guide, see inside the front cover. Other relevant information is found in Essentials pages 56-61.*

**D India Guest House**, 1/49 Kamal Mansion, Arthur Bunder Rd. 20 rooms along long corridor, white partitions that you could, at a push, jump over. Fan, no toilet or shower. The corner room has a neat panorama over the bay. Sound will travel.

**D Sea Shore**, top floor, 1/49 Kamal Mansion, Arthur Bunder Rd. Kitsch as you like, pink and white moulding clad ceiling, desks and mirrors, TV, plastic flowers down the corridor.

### Around the CST or VT *p1085, map p1083*

**B Grand**, 17 Sprott Rd, Ballard Estate, T022-2618211. 73 a/c rooms, exchange, book counter, old-fashioned, built around a central courtyard, helpful service, very relaxing.

**B-C City Palace**, 121 City Terr (Nagar Chowk), opposite CST Main Gate, T022-2615515. Tiny though clean, functional rooms (some without windows), with bath (Indian WC), some a/c, helpful staff, convenient location. Recommended.

**D Popular Place**, 104-106 Mint Rd, near GPO, Fort Market, T022-2695506. Clean rooms with bath (hot water), some a/c, helpful staff good value.

**D-E Manama** , 221 P D'Mello Rd, T022-2613412. Reasonable rooms, few with bath and a/c, popular.

**D-E Rupam** , 239 P D'Mello Rd, T022-2618298. 37 rooms, some a/c with phone, clean, friendly, comfortable beds.

### Marine Drive, Malabar Hill and around *p1086, map p1083*

**LL Intercontinental Marine Drive**, 135 Marine Dr, T022-56399999, www.intercontinental.com. 59 rooms in boutique hotel overlooking Marine Drive. Bose stereo, plasma TV screens, Bulgari toiletries, personal butler service and beautiful rooftop pool.

**LL-AL The Oberoi**, Nariman Pt, T022-2325757. 350 large rooms, the newer Oberoi combining modern technology with period furniture, excellent restaurants.

**LL-AL Oberoi Towers**, Nariman Pt, T022-2324343. 650 rooms, superb views from the higher floors, good buffets, garden and swimming pool, excellent shopping complex. Recommended.

**LL-AL President**, 90 Cuffe Pde, T022-2150808. 317 rooms, most business facilities, good service but poor value, informal but lacks character.

**L-AL Ambassador**, Churchgate Extn, Vir Nariman Rd, T022-2041131. 127 rooms, all facilities, revolving restaurant and pastry shop, slightly run-down feel.

**AL Nataraj**, 135 Marine Dr, T022-2044161. 83 rooms, some with views over bay, food and live music in restaurant, good but a bit noisy and overpriced.

**A-B West End**, 45 New Marine Lines, T022- 2039121, westhotel@vsnl.com. The 80 small, suites are pleasant but need refurbishing. Good restaurant, excellent service, very efficient front desk, well located, good value Recommended.

**B-C Chateau Windsor Guest House**, 86 Vir Nariman Rd, T022-2043376, info@chateauwindsor.com. 36 rooms (some a/c) vary, some very small and dark, room service for light snacks and drinks, friendly, clean, good value. Recommended. Cash only.

**C Sea Green**, 145 Marine Dr, T/F022-2822294. 34 rooms, 22 a/c, pleasant breezy informal sitting area.

**C-D Astoria**, 4 J Tata Rd, Churchgate, T022-2852626. 75 a/c rooms, restaurant, bar.

**C-D Supreme**, 4 Pandey Rd, near President, T022-2185623. Clean rooms with bath, good service but can be a little noisy.

### Dadar, Mumbai Central Station and Grant Rd area *map p1083*

Dadar can be a good option to stay – plenty of restaurants and good trains to Churchgate and CST.

**A-B Midtown Pritam**, 20-B Pritam Estates, Senapati Bapat Marg, 2 mins to Dadar station, T022-4145555. 63 rooms, terrace garden.

**C Sagar**, Nagpada Junction (Bellasin Rd/JB Behram Marg corner), Byculla, T022-3092727. Very clean rooms, good restaurant, friendly. Recommended.

**C-D Red Rose**, Gokuldas Pasta Rd, Dadar East, T022-4137843. 31 rooms, some a/c, mostly shared but clean baths. Flexible checkout, friendly . Recommended.

**D Anukool**, 292-8 Maulana Saukat Ali Rd, T022-30814013, hotelanukool@hotmail.com. 23 rooms, some a/c, friendly, helpful, good value, but inspect room first.

**D Heritage**, Sant Savta Marg, Byculla, T022-3714891. 84 a/c rooms, restaurant (good Parsi), bar.

**D Kalpana Palace**, 181 P Bapurao Marg, opposite Daulat Cinema, Grant Rd, T022-3000846. 30 decent rooms, some a/c.
**D Railway Retiring Rooms**, Mumbai Central, T022-3077292. Some a/c with bath.
**D-E YMCA International House**, 18 YMCA Rd, near Mumbai Central, T022-3091191. Decent rooms, shared bath, meals included, temp membership Rs 60, deposit Rs 1,300, good value, book 3 months ahead.

**Juhu Beach and Bandra** *p1088*
The listings below are in Juhu Beach.
**L-AL Holiday Inn**, Balraj Sahani Marg, T022-6204444. 190 rooms, 2 pools, courtesy coach to town, reliable.
**AL Sun-n-Sand,** 39 Juhu Beach, T022-6201811. 118 rooms, best refurbished, comfortable, though cramped poolside, good restaurant.
**A Citizen**, 960 Juhu Tara Rd, T022-6117273, citizen@bom2.vsnl.net.in. Despite unexciting appearance, 45 smallish but very well appointed rooms, suites, efficient airport transfer. Recommended.
**B Juhu Hotel**, Juhu Tara Rd, T022-6184014. Spacious comfortable cottage-style rooms, sea-facing lawns, good restaurant (try seafood and *Mughlai*), soundproofed disco.
**B Sands**, 39/2 Juhu Beach, T022-6204511. 40 rooms, excellent restaurant. Recommended.

**Airport**
Most airport hotels offer free transfer. Tourist information at the airport will help to book.
**LL-L Leela Palace**, near International Terminal, T022-56911234, www.theleela.com. 460 modern rooms, excellent restaurants, pricey but excellent, bar (closed to non-residents after 2300).
**L Renaissance**, near Chinmayanand Ashram, Powai, 9 km from international airport, T022-6928888, www.renaissance hotels.com. 286 stylish rooms, excellent restaurants, pleasant green surroundings, large pool, relaxing.
**L-AL Orchid**, 70C Nehru Rd, Vile Parle (east), T022-6100707, 5 mins' walk from domestic terminal. Totally refurbished, attractive rooms, eco-friendly. Boulevard restaurant boasts a '15 min lightening menu' and good midnight buffet. Recommended.
**B Metro Palace**, Hill Rd, near Bandra station (W), T022-6427311. Convenient, close to domestic airport and shops, good restaurant.
**B Pali Hills**, 14 Union Park, Pali Hill, Bandra, T022-6492995. Quiet location, near market, continental restaurant (see below).
**B-C Atithi**, 77A Nehru Rd, 7 mins' walk from domestic terminal, T022- 6116124. 47 rooms, functional, clean, set meals included, good value, efficient desk, popular.
**B-C Residency**, Suren Rd, T022-6923000, residency@hotmail.com. New hotel 3 km from the airport, request free pickup. 72 a/c smallish rooms, good restaurant, quiet back street, friendly staff. Recommended.
**B-C Transit**, off Nehru Rd, Vile Parle (east), T022-6105812. 54 rooms, modern, reasonable overnight halt for airport, excellent restaurant (draught beer), airport transfer.
**D Airport Rest Rooms**, old Domestic Terminal, Santa Cruz. For passengers with connecting flights within 24 hrs of arrival, comfortable, clean, but often full.

## Eating

**Gateway of India and Colaba**
*p1081, map p1084*
**ᵀᵀᵀ All Stir Fry**, Gordon House Hotel, oriental nosh served up in *Wagamama*-style at long shared benches. DIY food too.
**ᵀᵀᵀ Copper Chimney**, 18 K Dubash Marg, T022-2041661. Indian. Subdued lighting and quietly tasteful, excellent North Indian dishes, must reserve.
**ᵀᵀᵀ Indigo**, 4 Mandlik Rd, behind Taj Hotel, T022-2856316. Excellent Mediterranean in smart new restaurant, good atmosphere, additional seating on rooftop.
**ᵀᵀᵀ Khyber**, 145 MG Rd, Kala Ghoda, Fort, T022-2632174. North Indian. For an enjoyable evening in beautiful surroundings, outstanding food, especially lobster and *reshmi* chicken kebabs, try *paya* soup (goats' trotters).
**ᵀᵀᵀ Ling's Pavilion**, 19/21 KC College Hostel Building, off Colaba Causeway (behind Taj and Regal Cinema), T022-2850023. Stylish decor, good atmosphere and delightful service, colourful menu, seafood specials, generous helpings. Recommended.
**ᵀᵀᵀ Souk**, Taj Mahal Apollo Bunder, T022-56653366, www.tajhotels.com. Taj's top floor is now home to a North African themed restaurant. Open from 1900, great views. You can just have a drink but a glass of imported red wine, excellent though it may be, costs Rs 500 before tax.

¥¥¥ **Tides**, Gordon House Hotel, seafood restaurant, bar, wines and coffee shop with submarine theme.

¥¥¥ **Trishna**, Sai Baba Marg, next to Commerce House, Fort T022-22614991, behind Kala Ghoda, by Old Synagogue. Indian. Good coastline cuisine, seafood, excellent butter garlic crab. Recommended.

¥¥ **Bagdadi**, Tullock Rd (behind **Taj Hotel**), T022-2028027. *Mughlai*. One of the cheapest, first-class food, fragrant biryani, delicious chicken, crowded but clean. Recommended.

¥¥ **Café Basilico Bistro & Deli**, Sentinel House, Arthur Bunder Rd, T022-56345670, www.cafebasilico.com. Very chi-chi, European-style café with waffles from Rs 85, soups, salads, pastas and smoothies.

¥¥ **Ming Place**, Apsara Building, Colaba Causeway, T022-2872820. Chinese. Big a/c place with cosmic murals and heavy wooden chairs. Try 'Shanghai potatoes'.

¥ **Bade Miyan**, behind Ling's Pavilion. Streetside Kebab corner but very clean. Try *baida roti*, *shammi* and *boti* kebabs

¥ **Café Churchill**, T022-22844689, 1000-2400. A tiny little caff with 7 tables crammed with people basking in a/c, towered over by a cake counter and a Winston Churchill portrait. Great breakfasts, club sandwiches, whoppers, seafood, fish and chips, lasagne, irish stew and so on.

¥ **Kamat Samarambh**, opposite Electric House, SB Singh Marg. Indian vegetarian. Very good *thalis* and snacks, try *chola battura* (*puri* topped with spiced chickpeas).

¥ **Majestic Hotel.** Bustling, cheap columned and boothed canteen doing a fast business in *thalis* and the old South Indian favourites like *iddly/sambar*.

¥ **Martin's**, near Strand Cinema. Goan. Simple, authentic Goan food, excellent seafood and pork *sorpotel*.

¥ **Paradise**, Sindh Chambers, Colaba Causeway, Tue-Sun. Parsi and others. Spotless, excellent dhansak; try *sali boti* (mutton and 'chips'), not a/c.

¥ **Shiv Sagar Vegetarian Restaurant**, mouth of Colaba Market, Mistry Chambers, opposite Telephone Bhawan, Colaba, T022-2811550. Excellent very simple veg restaurant, hygienic and clean that does South Indian snacks outside normal restaurant mealtimes.

**Cafés and fast food**

Many serve chilled beer and waiters care too much for large tips from tourist groups:

**Food-Inn**, 50 m from **Leopold's**. Mainly Indian (some western) snacks. Pleasant (a/c upstairs), reasonably priced, friendly. Recommended.

**Kailash Parbat**, 1st Pasta La, Colaba. Excellent snacks and chats. In an old-style eatery serving Punjabi *thalis*, tooth-rotting sweets from the counter.

**Leopold's**, Colaba, T022-2830585. An institution among Colaba backpackers and Mumbai shoppers, good western food and drink (limited Indian veg), but it's pricey too. Similar cafés nearby are far better value.

**Mondegar**, near Regal Cinema, T022-2812549. Similar, but a little cheaper and with a loud rock soundtrack.

**Wayside Inn**, 38 K Dubash Marg, T022-2844324. Quaint country inn-style place, good breakfast menu, average continental but perfect for an afternoon beer in heart of the city. Breezy, laid back and leisurely, moderately priced.

**Around the CST or VT** *p1085, map p1083*

¥¥ **Apoorva**, near Horniman Circle, Fort, T022-2881457. Very good seafood, especially crabs and prawns (menu is cheaper downstairs).

¥¥ **Bharat**, 317 SB Singh Marg, opposite Fort Market, T022-2618991. Excellent seafood and crab as well as naans and rotis: or try fried, stuffed Bombay Duck.

¥¥ **George**, 20 Apollo St, near Horniman Circle. Pleasant quiet atmosphere, colonial feel, good service, lunchtime biriyanis and *thalis*.

¥¥ **Sadanand**, opposite Crawford Market. Excellent *thalis* and veg food, popular with Indian families.

¥¥ **Wall Street**, 68 Hamam St, behind Stock Exchange. Coastal cuisine, excellent seafood, try spicy Malabari prawns, squid green garlic, fish *patta*.

¥ **Icy Spicy**, off PM Rd, next to Fort Central Restaurant. Veg snack bar. Great light meals.

¥ **Ideal Corner**, Hornby View, Gunbow St, Fort, CST. Lunchtime Parsi food and snacks in café.

¥ **Mahesh Lunch Home**, Sir PM Rd, Fort. Excellent for Mangalorean, Goan and tandoori seafood, a/c, bar, very popular.

¥ **West Coast**, Rustom Sidhwa Rd, off Sir Perin Nariman Rd. Very good meals. On MG

Rd (north end), you can have a traditional breakfast, often served as early as 0600.

**Marine Drive, Malabar Hill and around** *p1086, map p1083*

TTT **Gaylord**, Vir Nariman Rd, T022-2821231. Indian. Good food (huge portions) and service, tables inside and out, barbecue, pleasant, good bar, tempting pastry counter.

TTT **Indian Summer**, 80 Vir Nariman Rd, T022-2835445. Indian. Excellent food, tasty kebabs, interesting modern glass decor, smart dress, reserve.

TTT **Pearl of the Orient**, Ambassador Hotel, T022-2041131. Excellent Chinese, Japanese and Thai. The revolving restaurant offers stunning views especially at night. For a less expensive stationary view try the bar on the floor above which does simple meals.

TTT **RG's Kitchen**, Intercontinental, Marine Dr, T022-56399999. 3 open kitchens, one Indian, one Oriental and one Western. Where Mumbai's posh socialites eat.

TTT **Santoor**, Maker Arcade, Cuffe Parade, near **President Hotel**, T022-2182262. North Indian. Small place, *Mughlai* and Kashmiri specialities: creamy chicken *malai* chop, *chana*, Peshawari (*puri* with chickpeas), Kashmiri soda made with salt and pepper.

TTT **Sidewok**, next to NCPA theatre, T022-2818132. Interesting southeast Asian/ fusion cuisine. Innovative menu, imaginative cocktails (try non-alcoholic too), surprise entertainment by staff, a special, fun dining experience. Reserve.

TT **Berry's**, Vir Nariman Rd, near Churchgate Station, T022-2875691. North Indian. Tandoori specialities, good *kulfi*.

TT **Chopsticks**, 90A Vir Nariman Rd, Churchgate, T022-2832308. Chinese, good, hot and spicy. Offering unusual dishes (*taro* nest, date pancakes, toffee bananas).

TT **Kamling**, 82 Vir Nariman Rd, T022-2042618. Genuine Cantonese. Simple surroundings, but excellent preparations, try seafood, often busy.

TT **May Rose**, Cinema Rd (next to Metro), T022-2081104. Chinese. Clean a/c, very good food.

TT **Sapna**, Vir Nariman Rd. Indian, very traditional Mughlai delicacies, bar, some tables outside, attentive service, good value.

TT **Satkar**, Indian Express Building, opposite Churchgate station, T022-2043259. Indian. Delicious vegetarian, fruit juices and shakes; a/c section more expensive.

T **Balwas**, Maker Bhavan, 3 Sir V Thackersey Marg. Inexpensive, well-prepared food.

T **Piccolo Café**, 11A Sir Homi Mody St. Parsi. 0900-1800, closed Sat pm and Sun, profits to charity, homely, clean, good *dhansak*.

T **Purohit's**, Vir Nariman Rd. Indian. Excellent veg *thalis*, also Parsi.

T **Thacker's**, corner Maharshi Karve Rd and 1st Marine St. Indian. Good *thalis*.

T **Woodlands**, Mittal Chambers, Nariman Pt, Mon-Sat. South Indian. Excellent *iddli* and *dosai* and good *thalis*, busy at lunchtime.

**Cafés and fast food**

**Croissants**, Vir Nariman Rd, opposite Eros Cinema. Burgers, sandwiches, hot croissants with fillings, ice cream, lively atmosphere.

**Fountain**, MG Rd. For sizzlers and apple pie in a café atmosphere.

**Dadar, Mumbai Central Station and Grant Rd area** *map p1083*

TTT **Biscotti**, Crossroads, Haji Ali, T022-4955055. Excellent Italian. Wholesome, leisurely dining, try batter-fried calamari, giant prawns in liqueur, flavoured sugar-free soda, zabaglioni, bistro-style complete with fiddler.

TTT **Goa Portuguesa**, THK Rd, Mahim. Goan. Authentic dishes, taverna-style with guitarist, try *sungto* (prawn) served between *papads*, *kalwa* (oyster), *teesryo* (shell) and clams, lobsters cooked with tomatoes, onions and spices and *bebinca* to end the meal.

TTT **Revival**, Chowpatty Sea Face, near footbridge. Classy, good Indian/Continental buffets and desserts.

TT **Bombay A1**, 7 Vadilal A Patel Marg (Grant Rd Junction). Parsi. Cheerful, varied menu, try Patrani *machli*.

TT **Copper Chimney**, Dr AB Rd, Worli, T022-4924488. Indian. Window into kitchen, excellent food from extensive menu, reasonable prices, undiscovered by tourists.

TT **Under the Over**, 36 Altamount Rd (by flyover). Bistro-like, for Mexican, Creole dishes, sizzlers and rich desserts, reasonably priced, no alcohol.

TT **The Village**, Poonam Intercontinental, near Mahalaxmi racecourse. Gujarati. 'Village' setting, sea views, good authentic food.

ΨΨ **Viva Paschim**, City View, Dr AB Rd, Worli, T022-4983636. Quality coastal Maharashtrian. Sunday lunch buffet great value (Rs 225), folk dances at dinner often.
Ψ **Heaven**, corner of Grant Rd/P Bapurao Marg. Very cheap, friendly (*egaloo matar* Rs 10).
Ψ **Kamat**, Navrose Mansion, Tardeo Rd. Indian. Very inexpensive *thalis* and veg snacks.

**Juhu Beach and Bandra** *p1088*
ΨΨ **Gazalee**, Kadambari Complex, Hanuman Rd, Vile Parle (E), T022-8388093. Finest coastal cuisine, try stuffed Bombay Duck and shellfish.
ΨΨ **Just around the Corner**, 24th-30th road junction, TPS III, Bandra (W). Bright casual American-style diner. Extensive breakfast menu (0800-1100). Pay by the plateful, lots of combination options, excellent salads, low-calorie.
ΨΨ **Olive Bar & Kitchen**, Pali Hill Tourist Hotel, 14 Union Park Khar (W), T022-26058228, www.olivebarandkitchen.com. Olive caters to a very chic Bollywood Bombay crowd. This also means that they do not encourage male gawpers, so men need to be escorted by women to get in.
ΨΨ **Out of the Blue**, at Pali Hills. Steak and fondue, great sizzlers, unusual combinations, flavoured ice teas, flambéed desserts, UV lit inside or outside smoke-free.
ΨΨ **Trim with Taste**, 500 Sant Kutir, Linking Rd, Bandra (lane behind KBN store). Small, spotless, serving unusual health food. Try stuffed iddlis, peach and yoghurt smoothies.
Ψ **Crunchy Munchy**, Agarwal Market, next to Vile Parle (E) station. Open-air café serving veg Indian and Mexican mini-meals. Very clean, good service and portions.
Ψ **Kanchi**, Mittal Industrial Estate, Andheri-Kurla Rd, Marol, Andheri (E). Excellent South Indian vegetarian, unusual daily specials. Recommended.
Ψ **Lucky**, 9 SV Rd (Hill Rd junction), Bandra (W). Good *mughlai* especially chicken biriyani and tandooris.

## Bars and clubs

All major hotels and restaurants have bars, others may only serve beer. Many pubs expect couples Fri-Sun. Most pubs charge Rs 175-250 for a 'pitcher' (bottle); cocktails Rs 75-150. Pick up *Mumbai This Fortnight*, an informative free booklet on everything that is hot in the city, free from larger bookshops and stores.

**Gateway of India and Colaba**
*p1081, map p1084*
**Athena**, 41/44 Minoo Desai Marg, Colaba, T022-2028699, www.athenaontheweb.com, 1930-0130, food till 2345. At Chateau Indage, champagne cigar lounge and restaurant. A slick celeb-festooned hangout, 300 capacity joint. Rs1,000 per couple (Rs 300 entry then Rs 700 redeemed against drinks). Slick lounge with drapes and white leatherette and pearly pink lounge beds. Lounge music.
**Insomnia**, Taj. Snazzy.
**Polly Esther**, Gordon House Hotel. A reggae, pop, rock disco, retro-themed club.
**Provogue Lounge**, Phoenix Mills, Lower Parel. By day a boutique for natty fashion brand, by night they clad the clothes rails with white wood and the sales tills turn to ringing out tequilas. Very in-crowd Mumbai.
**Red Light**, Khala Gowda, sleazy as they come, see behaviour from Mumbaikars that would shock the hell out of you if you saw it on your local high-street disco, but brilliant all the same – proper *bhangra* and Hindi pop plus western dance music.

**Marine Drive, Malabar Hill and around** *p1086, map p1083*
**Intercontinental**, 135 Marine Drive, T022-56399999, www.intercontinental.com. Extremely expensive, and trendy, nightclub that comes alive with house music on Fri and Sat night. For beautiful people.
**Not Just Jazz by the Bay**, 143 Marine Dr, T022-2851876. Modern chrome and glass, live music (varied), karaoke, good food menu (great starters, desserts), generous portions, wide selection of drinks, very lively, a fun place.

**Central Mumbai** *p1082, map p1083*
**Flavors**, a bright 24-hr coffee shop-resto-bar. Chic, interesting cocktails and starters (PSP prawns, corn and spinach toast), barbecue buffet lunch (Rs 300-800), happy hour (1800-2000), try Graveyard (huge) or Flavothon (a shooter race), big screen, DJ (weekends). Fun at a price.
**Café Olé**, Ground floor, Cross Rds, Haji Ali, T022-4955123. Classic sports bar, chrome

and glass, interesting menu (some Indianized), try Cactus Passion or Red Ginger (non-alcoholic), mini dance floor, DJ at weekends, fun place, affordable drinks.
**Copa Cabana**, Dariya Vihar, 39/D Girgaum, Chowpatty, T022-3680274. Small, playing 70s hits and Latino music, packed at weekends so little space for dancing.
**Geoffreys**, **Hotel Marine Plaza**, Marine Dr, T022-2851212. Soft music, relaxing for a drink and a bite, no dancing.
**Ghetto**, B Desai Rd (100 m from Mahalakshmi Temple). Western pop from 60s, 70s, 80s, free entry (couples only), neon graffiti.
**Juhu Paparazzi**, opposite Juhu Bus Depot, Juhu Beach Rd, T022-6602199, Tue-Sun. Small, cosy disco bar, packed after 2300, drinks and snacks.
**Razzberry Rhinoceros**, **Juhu Hotel**, Juhu Tara Rd, T022-6184012. Disco, nightclub. Lots of space for dancing, pool tables, live acts.

## Entertainment

### Cinema

Bollywood films are screened in dozens of cinemas: try **Eros** opposite Churchgate station or **Metro**, on MG Rd, northwest corner of Azad Maidan.
English language films are shown at many, including **Regal**, Colaba Causeway, **New Empire** and **Sterling**, Marzaban Rd, southwest of CST station. It is best for women to get seats in the circle.

### Theatres

Plays are performed in English, Hindi, Marathi and Gujarati, usually beginning at 1815-1900. Check *Mumbai This Fortnight* for details. See a modern Hindi play at **Privthi Theatre** to sample local culture; cool café for drinks and snacks outside.

## Festivals and events

In addition to the national Hindu and Muslim festivals there are the following:
**First weekend in Jan** **Banganga Classical Music Festival** at Walkeshwar Temple. Magical atmosphere around temple tank with fine musicians taking part; tickets Rs 50-150 (much in demand).
**Feb** **Elephanta Cultural Festival** at the caves. Great ambience. Contact MTDC, T022-2026713, for tickets Rs 150-200 including launch at 1800. **Kala Ghoda Arts Festival.** New annual showcase of all forms of fine arts. T022-2842520; also weekend festival, mid-Dec to mid-Jan includes food and handicrafts at Rampart Row, Fort.
**Mar** **Jamshed Navroz**. This is New Year's Day for the Parsi followers of the Fasli calendar. The celebrations which include offering prayers at temples, exchanging greetings, alms-giving and feasting at home, date back to Jamshed, the legendary King of Persia.
**Jul-Aug** **Janmashtami** celebrates the birth of Lord Krishna. Boys and young men form human pyramids and break pots of curd hung up high between buildings
**Aug** **Coconut Day**. The angry monsoon seas are propitiated by devotees throwing coconuts into the ocean.
**Aug-Sep** **Ganesh Chaturthi**. Massive figures of Ganesh are worshipped and immersed in the sea on several days following the festival.
**Sep** **Mount Mary's Feast**, celebrated at St Mary's Church, Bandra. A fair is also held.
**Sep-Oct** **Dasara**. During this nationwide festival, in Mumbai there are group dances by Gujarati women in all the auditoria. There are also Ramlila celebrations at Chowpatty Beach. **Diwali** (The Festival of Lights) is particularly popular in mercantile Mumbai when the business community celebrate their New Year and open new account books.
**25 Dec** **Christmas**. Christians across Mumbai celebrate the birth of Christ. A pontifical High Mass is held at midnight in the open air at the Cooperage Grounds.

## Shopping

Most shops are open 1000-1900 (closed Sun), the bazaars sometimes staying open as late as 2100. Mumbai prices are often higher than in other Indian cities, and hotel arcades tend to be very pricey but carry good quality select items. Best buys are textiles, particularly tie-and-dye from Gujarat, hand-block printed cottons, Aurangabad and 'Patola' silks, gold bordered saris from Surat and Khambat, handicrafts, jewellery and leather goods.
**Crossroads** and **Pyramid**, Haji Ali, are modern shopping centres.

### Antiques

It is illegal to take anything over 100 years old out of the country.

**Natesan** in Jehangir Gallery basement and in **Taj Hotel**. For fine antiques and copies.

**Phillips**, Madame Cama Rd. An Aladdin's cave of bric-a-brac and curios.

### Bazaars

**Crawford Market**, Ambedkar Rd (fun for bargain hunting) and **Mangaldas Market**. Other shopping streets are South Bhagat Singh Marg, M Karve Rd and Linking Rd, Bandra. For a different experience try **Chor (Thieves') Bazaar**, on Maulana Shaukat Ali Rd in central Mumbai, full of finds from Raj left-overs to precious jewellery. Make time to stop at the **Mini Market**, 33-31 Mutton St, T022-34724257 (closed Fri), minimarket@rediffmail.com and nose through the Bollywood posters, lobby cards, and photo-stills. On Fri, 'junk' carts sell less expensive 'antiques' and fakes.

### Books

There are lines of 2nd hand stalls along Churchgate St and near the University. An annual book fair takes place at the Cross Maidan near Churchgate each Dec.

**Crossword**, 22 B Desai Rd, near Mahalakshmi Temple, smart, spacious, good selection.

**Danai**, 14th Khar Danda Rd. Books and music.

**Dial-a-book**, T022-6495618, for quick delivery.

**Nalanda**, Taj Mahal Hotel, excellent art books, western newspapers/magazines.

**Strand Books**, off Sir PM Rd near HMV, T022-2061994. Excellent selection, best deals, shipping (reliable).

### Clothes

**Benzer**, B Desai Rd, Breach Candy (open Sun), good saris and Indian garments.

**The Courtyard**, 41/44 Minoo Desai Marg, Colaba. Very new, very elite and fashionable mini-mall includes boutiques full of stunning heavy deluxe designs (Swarovski crystal- studded saris, anyone?) by **Rohit Bal**, www.balance.ws. **Rabani & Rakha** (Rs 17,000 for a sari) but probably most suitable to western eye is textile designer Neeru Kumar's **Tulsi** label, a cotton textiles designer from Delhi. Beautiful linen/silk stoles and fine *kantha* thread work. There's also a store from Indian designer **Pratap**, spelt à la Prada.

**Ensemble**, 130-132 South Bhagat Singh Marg, T022-2872882. Superb craftsmanship and service for women's clothes – Indian and 'east meets west'.

**Fabindia**, 66 Pali Hill, Bandra (W), handloom *kurtas* etc, Bamboo earthenware and jute home furnishings, *khadi* and *mulmul* cloth.

**Melange**, 33 Altamount Rd, T022-23854492. Western-tailored, Indian embroidery clothes. Stocks designs from great labels.

**Michele Boutique**, shop no 21, Shah House, Mandlik Rd, T022-22885312. 25 tailors, 24-hr turnaround, fabric on site includes linen, raw silk and cashmere.

### Crafts and textiles

Government emporia from many states sell good handicrafts and textiles; several at **World Trade Centre**, Cuffe Parade. In Colaba, a street **Craft Market** is held on Sun (Nov-Jan) in K Dubash Marg.

**Anokhi**, 4B August Kranti Marg, opposite Kumbala Hill Hospital. Good gifts.

**Bombay Store**, Western India House, 1st floor, PM Rd, Fort. Spacious, ethnic lifestyle, gifts (open Sun), value for money.

**Contemporary Arts and Crafts**, 19 Napeansea Rd, T022-23631979. Handicrafts, weaves and crockery, ethnic, traditional or modern.

**Cottage Industries Emporium**, Apollo Bunder. Represents a nationwide selection, especially Kashmiri embroidery, South Indian handicrafts and Rajasthani textiles. Shop at Colaba Causeway, next to BEST, with fabrics, ethnic ware, handicrafts.

**Curio Cottage**, 19 Mahakavi Bhushan Rd, near the Regal Cinema, T022-22022607. Silver jewellery and antiques.

**Good Earth**, 104 Kemp's Corner. Smart, trendy, pottery, glass and handmade paper stationery.

**Sadak Ali**, behind **Taj Hotel**. Good range of carpets, but bargain hard.

**Yamini**, President House, Wodehouse Rd, Colaba, especially for vibrant textiles.

### Jewellery

**Popli Suleman Chambers**, Battery St, Apollo Bunder, T022-2854757. Semi-precious stones, gems, garnets and pearls.

**Le Bijou Mahavir Bhuvansh**, 37 Hill Rd, Bandra, T022-26443473. Trinkets, junk jewels.

### Music

**Groove**, West Wing, 1st fl, Eros Cinema, Churchgate. Has café.
**Hiro**, SP Mehta St. Good Indian classical CDs.
**Planet M**, opposite CST station. Also has book/poetry readings, gigs.
**Rhythm House**, north of Jehangir Gallery. Excellent selection of jazz and classical CDs.
Musical instruments on VB Patel Rd, **RS Mayeka** at No 386, **Haribhai Vishwanath** at No 419 and **Ram Singh** at Bharati Sadan.

### Photography

**Kodak Express**,1B East and West Court, Colaba Causeway (near Churchill café).
**Mazda** at 231, T022-3004001. Hasselblad, Metz, Nikon, offers free pick up/delivery.
**Remedios**, opposite Khadi Bhandar, between CST and Flora Fountain, reliable repairs. Best buy cameras from DN Rd.
**Heera Panna Shopping Arcade**, Haji Ali, T022- 24946318. All things electrical: minidisc gadgets, camera, phone accessories etc.

### Silks and saris

Many including **Kala Niketan**, MG Rd and Juhu Reclamation.
**Sheetal**, Tirupati Apartments, B Desai Rd, saris from all over India; fair prices.
**Vama**, in Kanchenjunga (next to Kemp's Corner), tailoring possible.

## Activities and tours

### Adventure tourism

**Maharashtra Tourism** has been active in encouraging adventure tourism (including jungle safaris and watersports) by introducing 'rent-a-tent' and hiring out trekking gear. Prices range from US$35-150 per day/weekend depending upon season and activity. Some sites provide electricity, linen, bathrooms and authentic cuisine in rustic restaurants. It has also set up 27 'holiday resorts' providing cheap accommodation at hill stations, beaches, archaeological sites and scenic spots. Details from tourist offices.

### Horse racing

**Mahalaxmi Race Course**, opposite Haji Ali. Season Nov-Mar, Sun and holidays, 1400-1700. Many of India's top races are held at the delightful course (1878), including the Derby in Feb/Mar.

### Swimming

**Breech Candy Club**, B Desai Rd, T022-3612543. For the select set, 2 clean pools including a large one; non-members Rs 250.

### Tours

If you wish to sightsee independently with a guide, ask at the tourist office. See page 1078.
**City sightseeing** Approved guides from the India tourist office, T022-2036854.
City tour usually includes visits to The Gateway of India, the Chhatrapati Sivaji (Prince of Wales) Museum, Jain temple, Hanging Gardens, Kamla Nehru Park and Mani Bhavan (Gandhi Museum). Suburban tour includes Juhu Beach, Kanheri Caves and Lion Safari Park.
**MTDC**, Madam Cama Rd, opposite LIC Building, T022-2026713. City tour daily except Mon, 0900-1300 and 1400-1800, Rs 100. Suburban tour 0915 (from Dadar 1015-1815. Fort walk is a heritage walk around CST and Fort area with the Kala Ghoda Association, Army & Navy Building, T022-2852520, www.artindia.co.in.
Elephanta tours from Gateway of India. Boat, 0900-1415, Rs 70 return; reserve at Apollo Bunder, T022-2026364.
**Ajanta and Ellora MTDC** 4-day tour to the famous caves at Ajanta and Ellora.

### Yoga

**Iyengar Yogashraya Mumbai**, Elmac House, 126 Senapati Bapat Marg, Lower Parel 91, T022-24948416, info@bksiyengar.com. Iyengar drop-in centre.
**Kaivalyadahama**, next to Taraporewala Aquarium, Marine Dr.
**The Yoga Institute**, Praghat Colony, Santa Cruz (E).
**Yoga Training Centre**, 51 Jai Hind Club, Juhu Scheme.
**Yoga Vidhya Niketan**, Sane Guruji Marg, Dadar, T022-4306258.

## Transport

### Air

International Departure Tax, Rs 500 (Rs 250 within south Asia) is often included in the price of your ticket. Look for 'FT' in the tax column.
**Chhatrapati Sivaji International airport**, T022-6329090. Left luggage counter, across

the drive from end of departure terminal, Rs 35-45 per item per day. The tourist office counter helps to book rooms in upmarket hotels. There is an Indian Railways reservations and car hire counters inside, and domestic airlines' counters just outside the exit. The new domestic terminal (1A), exclusively for Indian Airlines, is about 400 m from the old terminal (1B), used by others. Enquiries: T140, 143.

Touts are very pushy at both terminals but the hotels they recommend are often appalling. It is worth making your own telephone call to hotels of your choice from the airport. The rest rooms in the old domestic terminal are clean, comfortable (rooms Rs 500, dorm Rs 200); available for those flying within 24 hrs, but are often full; apply to the Airport Manager.

**Transport to and from the airport**
Pre-paid taxis into town, from counter at the exit at the Chhatrapati Sivaji International terminal (ignore taxi touts near the baggage hall). Give the exact area or hotel, and the number of pieces of luggage. Hand the receipt to the driver at the end of the journey. There is no need to tip. To **Nariman Point** or **Gateway of India**, about Rs 260, 1 hr. During 'rush hour' it can take 2 hrs. Late at night, taxis take about ½ hr – hair-raising! To **Juhu Beach** Rs 150. From Santa Cruz: metered taxis should charge around the same. Dispatchers at the airport claim that each taxi can take only 3 passengers. Stand firm as this law is totally disregarded elsewhere. The red BEST buses connect both terminals with the city. No buses at present to New Mumbai.

### Airline offices

**Domestic** Air India to **Chennai**, **Delhi**, **Hyderabad**, **Kolkata**, **Thiruvananthapuram**. Indian Airlines, Nariman Pt, T022-2023031, to all major cities. Jet Airways, B1 Amarchand Mansions, Madam Cama Rd, T022-2855788, airport, T022-6156666, www.jetairways.com. To 23 destinations. Sahara, Tulsani Chambers, Nariman Pt, T022-2882718, airport T022- 6134159. **Bangalore**, **Bhopal**, **Delhi**, **Goa**, **Indore**, **Jaipur**, **Kolkata**, **Lucknow**, **Patna**, **Varanasi**.

**International** Air India, 1st flr, Nariman Pt (Counters also at Taj Mahal Hotel, Centaur Hotel and Santa Cruz), T022-2024142, Airport T022-8366767. **Aeroflot**, Tulsani Chambers, Nariman Pt, T022-2871942. **Alitalia**, Industrial Assur Bldg, Vir Nariman Rd, Churchgate, T022-2045023, airport T022-8379657. **Air Canada**, Amarchand Mansions, Madam Cama Rd, T022-2027632, Airport T022-6045653. **Air France**, Maker Chamber VI, Nariman Pt, T022-2025021, Airport T022-8328070. **Biman**, 199 J Tata Rd, Churchgate, T022-2824659. **British Airways**, 202-B Vulcan Ins Bldg, Vir Nariman Rd, T022-2820888, weekdays, 0800-1300, 1345-1800. Sat, 0900-1300, airport T022-8329061. **Canadian**, Taj Intercontinental, T022-2029112, Airport T022-8366205. **Japan**, Raheja Centre, Nariman Pt, T022-2874940. **Delta**, Taj Mahal Hotel, T022-2885660, Airport T022-8349890. **Emirates**, Mittal Chamber, Nariman Pt, T022-2871649. **Gulf Air**, Maker Chambers, 5 Nariman Pt, T022-2021626. **KLM**, 198 J Tata Rd, T022-2886973. **Kuwait**, 2A Stadium House, 86 Vir Nariman Rd, Churchgate, T022-2045351. **Lufthansa**, Express Towers, Nariman Pt, T022-2023430. **PIA**, Mittal Towers, Nariman Pt, T022 2021455. **Qantas**, 42 Sakhar Bhavan, Nariman Pt, T022-2020343. **Royal Jordanian**, 199 J Tata Rd, T022-2823065. **Saudia**, Express Tower, Nariman Pt, T022-2020199. **Singapore Airlines**, Taj Intercontinental, T022-2022747. **Sri Lanka**, Raheja Centre, Nariman Pt, T022-2844148, Airport T022-8327050. **Thai Airways**, 15 World Trade Centre, Cuffe Parade, T022-2186502.

### Auto-rickshaw

Not available in central Mumbai (south of Mahim). Metered; about Rs 8 per km, revised tariff card held by the driver (x8, in suburbs) 25% extra at night (2400-0500). Some rickshaw drivers show the revised tariff card for taxis! It's worth buying a card for a couple of rupees from hawkers at traffic junctions.

Victorias (horse-drawn carriages), available at Mumbai Central, Chowpatty and Gateway of India. Rates negotiable.

### Bus

Red BEST (Bombay Electrical Supply Co) buses are available in most parts of Greater Mumbai, T022-4128725. Within the Central Business District, buses are marked 'CBD'.

Maharashtra RTC operates bus services to all the major centres and District HQs in the state as well as to **Ahmadabad**, **Bangalore**,

**Goa**, **Mangalore**, **Indore**, **Vadodara** and **Hyderabad** in other states. Information on services from **MSRTC**, central bus stand, Mumbai Central, T022-3076622.

Private buses also travel long distance routes. Some long distance buses also leave from Dadar where there are many travel agents. Information and tickets from **Dadar Tourist Centre**, just outside Dadar station, T022-4113398.

### Car

For 8 hrs or 80 km: Luxury cars cost a/c Rs 1,500; Maruti/Ambassador, a/c Rs 1,000, non a/c Rs 800.
**Auto Hirers**, 7 Commerce Centre, Tardeo, T022-4942006. **Blaze**, Colaba, T022-2020073. **Budget**, T022-4942644, and **Sai**, Phoenix Mill Compound, Senapati Bapat Marg, Lower Parel, T022-4942644. Recommended. **Wheels**, T022-2822874. Holiday caravans with driver, T022-2024627.

### Taxi

Metered yellow-top or blue a/c: easily available. Rs 12 for first km and Rs 12 for each Re 1 on meter. Revised tariff card held by drivers. Taxis called by hotel doormen often arrive with meter registering Rs 12. Always get a prepaid taxi at the airport.

### Train

Suburban electric trains are economical. They start from Churchgate for the west suburbs and CST (VT) for the east suburbs but are often desperately crowded (stay near the door or you may miss your stop!); there are 'Ladies' cars. Trains leaving Mumbai Central often have seats at the terminus but soon fill up. Avoid peak hours (southbound 0700-1100, northbound 1700-2000), and keep a tight hold on valuables. The difference between 1st and 2nd class is not always obvious although 1st class is 10 times as expensive. Inspectors fine people for travelling in the wrong class or without a ticket.

Times for trains are published each Sat in the Indian Express newspaper. To book trains foreign tourists must have either foreign currency or an encashment certificate and passport.

Mumbai is the HQ of the **Central and Western Railways**, enquiries, T134/135; reservations, T022-2659512, 0800-1230, 1300-1630 (Foreigners' Counter opens 0900; best time to go). **Western Railway**, Churchgate, and Mumbai Central, 0800-1345, 1445-2000. All for 1st class bookings and Indrail Passes.
**Foreign tourists**: Tourist Quota counter on mezzanine floor above tourist office opposite Churchgate Station for Northern Railways. Otherwise, queue downstairs at reservations. For **Southern Railways**, at CST, the tourist counter is on the ground floor (towards the left), credit cards upstairs. **Railway Tourist Guides** at CST and Churchgate, bus 138 goes between them.

The following depart from CST unless specified by these abbreviations: Bandra (B), Central (C), Dadar (D), Lokmanya Tilak (LT):
**Ahmadabad** (all from Mumbai Central): *Shatabdi Exp 2009*, 0625, except Fri, 7 hrs; *Karnavati Exp 2933*,1340, except Wed, 7¾ hrs; *Saurashtra Mail 9005*, 2025, 9 hrs; *Gujarat Mail 2901*, 2150, 9 hrs. **Allahabad**: *Howrah Mail 3004*, 2110, 23½ hrs; *Mahanagari Exp 1093*, 2355, 24¼ hrs. **Agra Cantonment**: *Punjab Mail 2137*, 1910, 21½ hrs. **Aurangabad** (for **Ajanta** and **Ellora**): *Tapovan Exp 7617*, 0610, 7½ hrs; *Devgiri Exp 1003*, 2120, 7½ hrs. **Bangalore**: *Udyan Exp 6529*, 0755, 24¾ hrs; *Coimbatore Exp 1013*, 2220 (LT), 23¾ hrs. **Bhopal**: *Pushpak Exp 2133*, 0810, 14 hrs; *Punjab Mail, 2137*, 1910, 14 hrs. **Chennai**: *Dadar Chennai Exp 1063*, 2020 (D), 23¾ hrs; *Chennai Exp 6011*, 1400, 26¾ hrs.

**Ernakulam** (for **Kochi**): *Netravati Exp 6345*, 2300 (LT), 29½ hrs. **Guntakal** (for **Hospet/ Hampi**): *Dadar Chennai Exp 1063*, 2020 (D), 15 hrs; *Udyan Exp 6529*, 0755, 16¾ hrs; *Coimbatore Exp 1013*, 2220 (LT), 16¼ hrs; *Kanniyakumari Exp 1081*, 1535, 17¾ hrs. **Gwalior**: *Punjab Mail 2137*, 1910, 19¾ hrs. **Hyderabad**: *Hussainsagar Exp 7001*, 2155, 15¼ hrs; *Hyderabad Exp 7031*, 1235, 17½ hrs. **Kolkata** (**Howrah**): *Gitanjali Exp 2859*, 0600, 33 hrs; *Howrah Mail 8001*, 2015, 35½ hrs. **Lucknow**: *Pushpak Exp 2133*, 0810, 25½ hrs.

**Madgaon** (for **Goa**): The day train is a good option, the night service is heavily booked. Special trains during the winter. *Mandavi Exp 0103*, 0515, 11 hrs; *Konkan Kanya Exp 0111*, 2240, 12 hrs; *Netravati Exp 6635*, 1640, 13½ hrs (LT). **New Delhi**: *Rajdhani Exp 2951*, 1655 (C), 17 hrs; *Golden Temple Mail 2903*, 2130 (C), 21½ hrs; *August Kranti Rajdhani Exp 2953*, 1740 (C), 17¼ hrs (to Hazrat Nizamuddin). **Pune**: deluxe trains *Shatabdi Exp 2027*, 0640, 3½ hrs; *Deccan Queen Exp 2123*, 1710, 3½ hrs, among many. **Thiruvananthapuram**: *Netravati Exp 6345*, 2300 (LT), 35 hrs. **Ujjain**: *Avantika Exp 2961*, 1925 (C), 12½ hrs. **Varanasi**: *Lokmanya Tilak Varanasi Exp 2165*, 0520 (LT), Mon, Thu, Sat, 26 hrs; *Muzaffarpur/ Darbanga Exp 5217/5219*, 1125 (LT), 27¼ hrs.

## Directory

**Ambulance** T102. **Banks** Most are open 1000-1400, Mon-Fri, 1000-1200, Sat. Closed on Sun, holidays, 30 Jun, 31 Dec. Best to change money at the airport, or at Bureau de Change (upstairs) in Air India Building, Nariman Pt or at **Thomas Cook**, 324 Dr DN Rd, T022-2048556; also at 102B Maker Tower, 10th flr, F Block, Cuffe Pde;TCI, Chander Mukhi, Nariman Pt; A/2 Silver Arch, JB Nagar, Andheri; and at International Airport. **American Express**, Regal Cinema Building, Colaba. ATMs for Visa card holders using their usual PIN at **British Bank of the Middle East**, 16 Vir Nariman Rd; **Citibank**, Air India Building, Nariman Pt, 293 Dr DN Rd; **Hongkong Bank**, 52/60 MG Rd, Fort; Standard Chartered, 81 Ismaili Building, Dr DN Rd, 264 Annie Besant Rd and elsewhere. **Credit cards** American **Express**, Lawrence and Mayo Bldg, Dr DN Rd; **Diners Club**, Raheja Chambers, 213 Nariman Pt; **Mastercard**, C Wing, Mittal Tower, Nariman Pt; **Visa**, Standard Chartered Grindlays Bank, 90 MG Rd. Usually open 1000-1700. Sahar Airport 24 hrs. Post offices all over the city and most 5 star hotels. **Embassies and consulates** **Australia**, Maker Tower East, 16th flr, Cuffe Pde, T022-2181071. **Austria**, Maker Chambers VI, Nariman Pt, T022-2851066. **France**, Datta Prasad, NG Cross Rd, T022-4950918. **Germany**, 10th Flr, Hoechst House, Nariman Pt, T022-2832422. **Indonesia**, 19 Altamount Rd, T022-3868678. **Israel**, 50 Deshmukh Marg, Kailas, T022-3862794. **Italy**, Kanchenjunga, 72G Deshmukh Marg, T022-3804071. **Japan**, 1 ML Dahanukar Marg, T022-4934310. **Malaysia**, Rahimtoola House, Homji St, T022-2660056. **Netherlands**, 1 Marine Lines Cross Rd, Churchgate, T022-2016750. **Philippines** , Sekhar Bhavan, Nariman Pt, T022-2814103. **Spain**, 6 K Dubash Marg, T022-2874797. **Sri Lanka**, 34 Homi Modi St, T022-2045861. **Sweden**, 85 Sayani Rd, Prabhadevi, T022-4212681. **Thailand**, 43 B Desai Rd, T022-3631404. **UK**, Maker Chamber IV, Nariman Pt, T022-2830517. **USA**, Lincoln House, B Desai Rd, T022-3685483. **Fire** T101. **Internet** Among many: **British Council**, 'A Wing' 1st flr, Mittal Tower, Nariman Pt, T022-2823560, 1000-1745, Tue-Sat; **Cybercafé**, Waterfield, Bandra; **Infotek** , Express Towers, ground flr, Nariman Pt, I-way, Barrow Rd junction with Colaba Causeway and branches across Mumbai. Easily the fastest access, in this 2nd flr shop with heaps of terminals. You must first register as a member but it's well worth it. **Medical services** The larger hotels usually have a house doctor, the others invariably have a doctor on call. Ask hotel staff for prompt action. The telephone directory lists hospitals and GPs. Admission to private hospitals may not be allowed without a large cash advance (eg Rs 50,000). Guarantees from insurers may not be sufficient. **Prince Aly Khan Hospital**, Nesbit Rd near the harbour, T022-3754343, has been recommended. **Chemists** several open day/night especially opposite Bombay Hospital. **Wordell**, Stadium House, Churchgate; **New Royal Chemist**, New Marine Lines. **Police** Emergency T100. **Post** Nagar Chowk, Mon-Sat, 0900-2000 (**Poste Restante** facilities 0900-1800) and Sun 1000-1730; parcels from 1st flr, rear of building, 1000-1700 (Mon-Sat); cheap 'parcelling' service on pavement outside; **Central telegraph office** Hutatma Chowk, Churchgate PO, 'A' Rd, Colaba PO, Colaba Bus Station and also at Mandlik Rd, behind Taj Mahal Hotel. Foreign PO, Ballard Pier. Counter at Santa Cruz. **Travel agents** Cox and **Kings**, 270-271 Dr DN Rd, T022-2073066; **Everett**, 1 Regent Chambers, Nariman Pt, T022-2845339; **Mercury**, 70VB Gandhi Rd, T022-2024785; **Space Travels**, 4th flr, Sir PM Rd, T022-2864773, for discounted flights and special student offers, Mon-Fri, 1000-1700, Sat 1030-1500; **TCI**, Chandermukhi, Nariman Pt, T022-2021881; **Thomas Cook**, Cooks Building, Dr DN Rd, T022-2813454; **Venture**, Ground flr, Abubakar Mansion, South Bhagat Singh Marg, T022-2021304, efficient, helpful and friendly. **Useful addresses** **Foreigners' Regional Registration Office** Annexe 2, Police Commissioner's Office, Dr DN Rd, near Phule Market. **Passport office** T022-4931731.

# Excursions from Mumbai

*The Hindu caves of Elephanta and the Buddhist caves of Kanheri are within easy reach. You can also cross the bay to Chaul to the south, or head for the clean sandy beaches at Kihim. The old Portuguese fort of Bassein is to the north or go further afield to Mumbai's hill station of Matheran.* ▸▸ *For Sleeping, Eating and other listings, see pages 1109-1112.*

## Chaul, Kihim and Alibag beaches

A group of Moorish and Portuguese forts lie to the south at the mouth of Mumbai harbour. Chaul was taken in 1522 by the Portuguese. Similar to Bassein with a very attractive fort, it never equalled it in importance. The Marathas took it in 1739 and in 1818 it passed into British hands. Little remains of the settlement apart from ruined churches and broken walls. If you look across the creek you will see the hilltop Muslim fort of Korlai. The clean beach, safe waters and very pleasant surroundings make Kihim very attractive but the summer sun can be killingly hot. The beach is muddy at Alibag and it is possible to walk across to the fort at low tide but it is not worth the US$2 entrance. If you decide to stay, there are a few places on Kihim Beach.

## Elephanta Caves

The heavily forested Elephanta Island, often barely visible in the mist from Mumbai only 10 km away, rises out of the bay like a giant whale. The setting is symbolically significant; the sea is the ocean of life, a world of change (Samsara) in which is set an island of spiritual and physical refuge. The 'caves' excavated in the volcanic lava high up the slope of the hill saw Hindu craftsmen over 1,000 years ago, express their view of spiritual truths in massive carvings of extraordinary grace. Sadly a large proportion have been severely damaged, but enough remains to illustrate something of their skill. ▸▸ *For tours, see page 1111.*

### History

The vast majority of India's 1,200 **cave sites** were created as temples and monasteries between the third century BC and the 10th century AD. Jain, Buddhist and Hindu caves often stand side by side. The temple cave on Elephanta island, dedicated to Siva, was probably excavated during the eighth century by the Rashtrakuta Dynasty which ruled the Deccan from 757 to 973 AD, though the caves may have had earlier Buddhist origins. An earlier name for the island was Garhapuri – city of forts – but the Portuguese renamed it after the colossal sculpted elephants when they captured Mumbai from the Sultan of Gujarat in 1535, and stationed a batallion there. They reportedly used the main pillared cave as a shooting gallery causing some of the damage you see. Muslim and British rulers were not blameless either.

### The site

**The Entrance** Originally there were three entrances and 28 pillars at the site. The entrances on the east and west have subsidiary shrines which may have been excavated and used for different ceremonies. The main entrance is now from the north. At dawn, the rising sun casts its rays on the approach to the main shrine (*garbagriha*), housed in a square structure at the west end of the main hall. On your right is a carving of Siva as Nataraj, see page 1328. On the left he appears as Lakulisa in a much damaged carving. Seated on a lotus, the Buddha-like figure is a symbol of the unconscious mind and enlightenment, found also in Orissan temples where Lakulisa played a prominent role in attempting to attract Buddhists back into Hinduism, see page 701. From the steps at the entrance you can see the *yoni-lingam*, the symbol of the creative power of the deity.

**The Main Hall** The ribbed columns in the main hall, between 5 m and 6 m high and in a cruciform layout, are topped by a capital. At the corner of each pillar is a dwarf signifying the earth spirit (*gana*), and sometimes the figure of Ganesh (Ganapati). To the right, the main **Linga Shrine** has four entrances, each corresponding to a cardinal point guarded by a *dvarpala*. The sanctum is bare, drawing attention to the *yoni-lingam* which the devotee must walk around clockwise.

**The wall panels** To the north of the main shrine is **Bhairava killing the demon Andhakasura**. This extraordinarily vivid carving shows Siva at his most fearsome, with a necklace of skulls, crushing the power of Andhaka, the Chief of Darkness. It was held that if he was wounded each drop of his blood would create a new demon. So Siva impaled him with his sword and collected his blood with a cup which he then offered to his wife Shakti. In winter this panel is best seen in the early afternoon.

Opposite, on the south side of the main shrine is the damaged panel of **Kalyan Sundari**, in which Siva stands with Parvati on his right, just before their wedding (normally a Hindu wife stands on her husband's left). She looks down shyly, but her body is drawn to him. Behind Parvati is her father Himalaya and to his left Chandramas, the moon god carrying a gift – *soma*, the food of the gods. On Siva's left is Vishnu and below him Brahma.

At the extreme west end of the temple are **Nataraja** (left) and **Yogisvara Siva** (right). The former shows a beautiful figure of Ganesh above and Parvati on his left. All the other gods watch him. Above his right shoulder is the four-headed God of Creation, Brahma. Below Brahma is the elephant-headed Ganesh.

On the south wall, opposite the entrance are three panels. **Gangadhara** is on the west. The holy River Ganga (Bhagirathi) flowed only in heaven but was brought to earth by her father King Bhagiratha (kneeling at Siva's right foot) (see page 219). Here, Ganga is shown in the centre, flanked by her two tributaries, Yamuna and Saraswati. These three rivers are believed to meet at Allahabad (see page 184).

To the left of these is the centre piece of the whole temple, the remarkable **Mahesvara**, the Lord of the Universe. Here Siva is five-headed, for the usual triple-headed figure has one face looking into the rock and another on top of his head. Nearly 6 m high, he unites all the functions of creation, preservation and destruction. Some see the head on the left (your right) as representing Vishnu, the Creator, while others suggest that it shows a more feminine aspect of Siva. To his right is Rudra or Bhairava, with snakes in his hair, a skull to represent ageing from which only Siva is free, and he has a look of anger. The central face is Siva as his true self, Siva Swarupa, balancing out creation and destruction. In this mode he is passive and serene, radiating peace and wisdom like the Buddha. His right hand is held up in a calming gesture and in his left hand is a lotus bud.

The panel to the left has the **Ardhanarisvara**. This depicts Siva as the embodiment of male and female, representing wholeness and the harmony of opposites. The female half is relaxed and gentle, the mirror in the hand symbolizing the woman reflecting the man. Siva has his 'vehicle', Nandi on the right.

To the east, opposite the *garbha-griha*, was probably the original entrance. On the south is Siva and Parvati **Playing chaupar on Mount Kailash**. Siva is the faceless figure. Parvati has lost and is sulking but her playful husband persuades her to return to the game. They are surrounded by Nandi, Siva's bull, celestial figures and an ascetic with his begging bowl.

On the north is **Ravana Shaking Mount Kailash** on which Siva is seated. Siva is calm and unperturbed by Ravana's show of brute strength and reassures the frightened Parvati. He pins down Ravana with his toe, who fails to move the mountain and begs Siva's forgiveness which is granted.

## Kanheri Caves

Sanjay Gandhi National Park at Goregaon is worth a visit in itself for its dense deciduous and semi-evergreen forest providing a beautiful habitat for several varieties of deer, antelope, butterflies and birds. However, the main reason for visiting is for the Kanheri Caves situated in the heart of the national park.

Also known as the Mahakali Caves, the caves, 42 km north of Mumbai, are on a low hill midway between Borivli and Thane. The hills used to form the central part of Salsette Island, but the surrounding land has long since been extensively built on. Further up the ravine from the caves there are some fine views across the Bassein Fort and out to sea. Still shaded by trees, the entrance is from the south. There are 109 Buddhist caves, dating from the end of the second to the ninth century AD with flights of steps joining them. The most significant is the **Chaitya cave (3)** circa sixth century. The last Hinayana chaitya hall to be excavated is entered through a forecourt and verandah. The pillared entrance has well carved illustrations of the donors, and the cave itself comprises a 28 m x 13 m colonnaded hall of 34 pillars. At one end these encircle the 5 m-high dagoba. Some of the pillars have carvings of elephants and trees. Fifty metres up the ravine is **Darbar of the Maharajah cave (10)**. This was a *dharamshala* (resthouse) (22 m x 10 m), which has two stone benches running down the sides and some cells leading off the left and back walls. Above Cave 10 is **Cave 35** which was a *vihara* (monastery) (12 m x 14 m), which has reliefs of a Buddha seated on a lotus and of a disciple spreading his cloak for him to walk on. All the caves have an elaborate drainage and water storage system, fresh rainwater being led into underground storage tanks. Patrons endowed the monasteries so that they could be decorated with carvings.

Above the cave complex is *Ashok Van*, a sacred grove of ancient trees, streams and springs. From there, a three-hour trek leads to 'View Point', the highest in Mumbai. There are breathtaking views. Photography is prohibited from the radar station on top of the hill; there are excellent opportunities just below it.

The park is also home to hyena and panther, though they are rarely seen, while three lakes have ducks, herons and crocodiles. Nature trails lead from Film City (reached by bus from Goregaon station). A lion safari leaves from **Hotel Sanjay** near Borivli station. » *For tours, see page 1111.*

## North Konkan → *Colour map 5, grid B2/3.*

The undulating lowland of the North Konkan coast forms a narrow strip between the Arabian Sea and the often daunting west facing slopes of the Ghats. There are occasional good beaches, scattered mangrove swamps, and rice growing valleys, interspersed with poor laterite covered hills. The beaches to the north, a two-hour journey away, make them a popular getaway from Mumbai, although foreign tourists are virtually unheard of. They aren't comparable to the beaches of Goa or Kerala with litter and other debris present. For beaches to the south, see page 1107. » *For Sleeping, Eating and other listings, see pages 1109-1112.*

### Bassein (Vasai)

Bassein, at the mouth of the Ulhas River on the mainland, is 60 km north of central Mumbai. Due to silting, the fort on the Bassein Creek is now some distance from the sea. The structure is in ruins, but it is well worth walking round the sea face.

## India's first railway line

The opening of India's first railway line from Mumbai to Thane in 1853 prepared the route through the Ghats to the Deccan Plateau. Mumbai became the hub of regional and international trade. Victoria Terminus (CST now) was the product of a magnificent era of railway building at the end of the 19th century when the British Raj was striding confidently towards the 20th century.

With the disappearance of the East India Company after the Mutiny, the Government of India took over the responsibility for running the railways. On 16 April 1853 the first train made its run from Mumbai along 32 km of line to Thane. Subsequent advances were rapid but often incredible natural obstacles presented great challenges to the railway builders. The 263-km line to Surat encountered 18 rivers and some of the foundations for the bridges had to be driven 45 m in to the ground to cope with the monsoon floodwaters.

Originally built by Bahadur Shah, Sultan of Gujarat, it was one of a chain of forts against the Portuguese. However, the chain was breached, and the Portuguese remodelled the city along their own lines, renaming it **Vasai**. From 1534 to 1739 it became so prosperous as a centre of shipbuilding and the export of Bassein stone that it was called the Court of the North. As a walled city it contained a cathedral, five convents, 13 churches and the splendid houses and palaces of the aristocracy, or Hidalgos, who with members of the religious orders, alone were allowed to live within the walls. The Marathas took Vasai in February 1739 after a long and desperate siege. Almost the whole Portuguese garrison, 800 strong, was killed in the battle; the Marathas are thought to have lost 5,000 men. In 1780 the British evicted the Marathas, only to return it to them three years later under the Treaty of Salbai.

Approached from the north, the fort in the town contains the ruins of St Joseph's Cathedral (1536), St Anthony's, the Jesuit church and the convents, all belonging to Franciscans, Dominicans, Jesuits or Augustinians. **Nalasopara**, 10 km northwest, is the ancient Konkan capital where Buddhist relics have been found.



# The Ghats

→ *Colour map 5, grid B3.*

*Road travel is often disrupted in the rains.*

The Ghats represent an historic divide between the outward looking coastal lowlands with the trading centre of Mumbai at their hub, and the much drier interior, a battle ground of successive Indian dynasties. Today the hilltops are littered with fortified sites, while hill stations offer weekend breaks to Mumbai's élite. The routes through the Western Ghats from Mumbai climb to nearly 1,600 m through the forested slopes, particularly beautiful before the end of the rains in September when wild flowers are everywhere, and rivers and waterfalls are full. The railways through the ghats are spectacular. On the Nashik route alone the line passes through 10 tunnels, over five viaducts and 11 bridges. Between Neral and Lonavla, passing through stunning ravined countryside, the line has gradients of one in 37 to overcome the problems posed by 'the big step' the hills presented. » *For Sleeping, Eating and other listings, see pages 1109-1112.*

## Thane (Thana)

Thane, northeast of Mumbai, was the terminus of the first railway in India, built from Mumbai in 1853. As early as 1298, however, Marco Polo had written of Thane as "a great kingdom... there is much traffic here and many ships and merchants frequent the place".

It was an important Portuguese centre until the Marathas captured it in 1739. The English church in the town dates from 1825 but there is little in the way of tourist attractions. 

## Akloli and Ganeshpuri

Northeast of Thane, 913 km from Mumbai, at the start of the Ghats in Bhiwandi, a road leads up to the hot springs of Akloli, and to Ganeshpuri, 6 km from Shirshad, where the Vajreshwari Temple with hot springs is widely visited. There are a few sleeping options.

## Matheran → *Phone code: 02148. Colour map 5, grid B3. Population: 5,100. Altitude: 785 m.*

Mumbai's nearest hill station, in an extension of the Sahyadri range, Matheran, meaning 'Mother Forest' or 'Wooded Head', has stunning views, refreshingly cool air and pleasant walks. It maintains its quiet by banning all forms of motor vehicles within the town. It is very much geared towards the Mumbai weekender. A visit is recommended, but stay a night as it is too strenuous to do in a day from Mumbai.

The town sprawls out along a north-south ridge and from rocky promontories such as The Hart, Panorama Point, Chouk, Duke's Nose and Garbat there are splendid views down the almost sheer hillsides to the valleys below. The best views are from Little Chouk, Louisa and Porcupine, which is also known as Sunset Point. Allow one hour to walk and see the stunning sunsets. From the northernmost vantage points you can see the lights of Mumbai on a clear night. The layout of the town conforms with standard British Hill Station planning with central civic buildings and widely dispersed bungalows. You can sightsee on horseback here.

The most scenic route for this diversion is by the spectacular light railway through the ghats from Neral which may be closed during the monsoon. You will appreciate the problems facing the early railway engineers here, see box. The steam engines are no longer used after working the route for 77 years but you will see one proudly displayed at the station.

## Mahabaleshwar → *Phone code: 02168. Colour map 5, grid B3. Population 5,100. Altitude: 1370 m.*

In one of the wettest parts of the Western Ghats during the monsoon, Mahabaleshwar is in a pleasantly wooded setting at the head of the Krishna River. It is the main hill station for Mumbai and Pune. Cool and relaxed with some good walking trails and excellent views from the ghats, it's a good place to have an overnight stop. The altitude makes the climate very pleasant especially during the dry season. It is, however, becoming increasingly touristy with crowds of Mumbai holiday makers.

'Discovered' by General Lodwick in 1824, to whom there is still a monument on the Elephant's Head Point, Mahabaleshwar was declared an official British sanatorium in 1828 and was once the summer capital of the Bombay Presidency. These days there are pleasant walks and waterfalls to visit. **Arthur's Seat** (12 km) looks out over a 600 m precipice to the Konkan. The nine-hole Golf Course is built on a cliff side. **Venna Lake** has boating and fishing. From **Mumbai Point** and the hills around the town you can see the sea on a clear day.

There are several typical British hill station buildings: **Christchurch** (1842, enlarged 1867); the cemetery; **Frere Hall** (1864) with its mullioned windows and the Club, founded in 1882; **Government House** (1829) on Mount Malcolm; The **Lodwick Monument** (1874) in honour of the town's founder, and the **Beckwith Monument**.

The old town contains three temples (Krishnabai, Ram and Hanuman) which you can walk to from a turn off Elphinstone Road. **Krishnabai** or Panchganga with a self-formed *linga* resembling a piece of volcanic lava, is said to have five streams, including the Krishna, flowing from it. The 13th-century Yadav King Singhan built a small tank at the Krishna's source which starts its 1,400 km journey across the Deccan to the sea. This part of the 'Deccan Trap' has underground caverns which hold water and give rise to springs. There is a Rs 5 tax to enter town.

## Panchgani

Panchgani is set among casuarinas and silver oak, in spectacular scenery. At an altitude of 1,334 m, it is surrounded by the five hills from which it takes its name. It has a very compact centre with lovely walks, stunning views and very friendly people, which makes it well worth a visit.

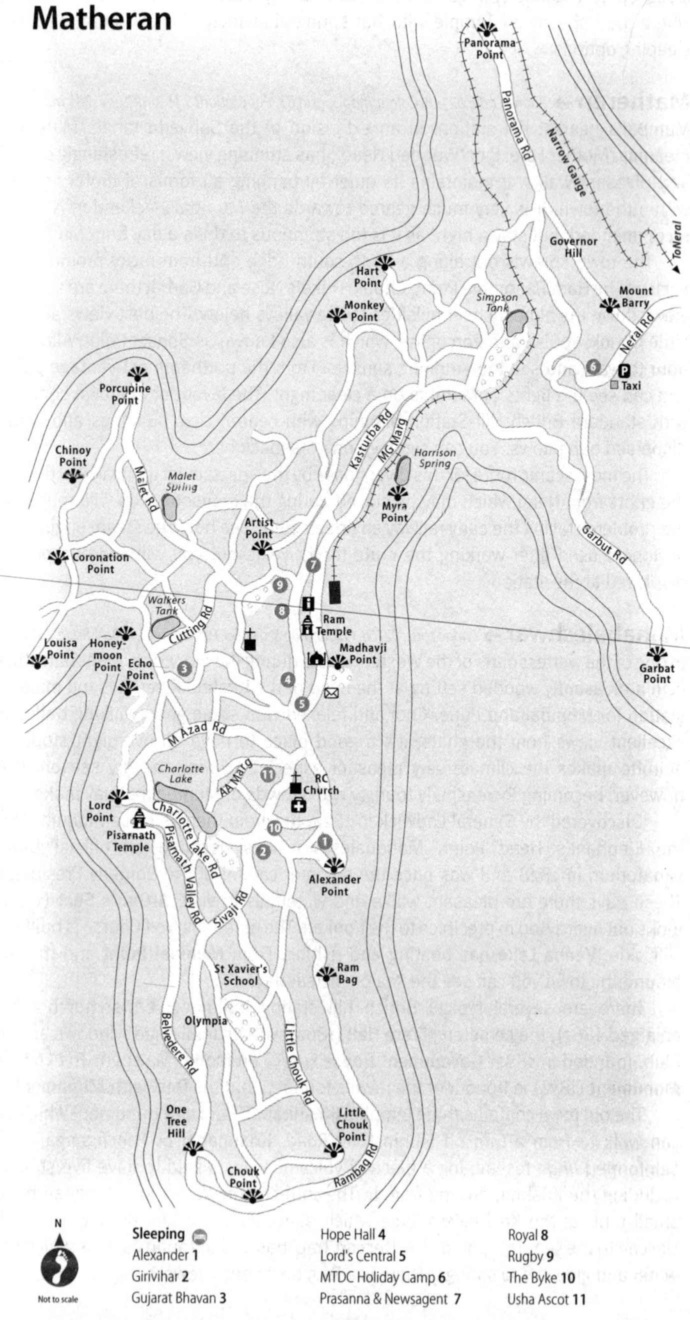

Settled as a hill station before Mahabaleshwar, it is known for its schools. MTDC is happy to arrange for you to visit some of the British and Parsi bungalows. There is a small art gallery on the State Highway, close to the bus stand. The drive to Mahabaleshwar offers beautiful views; sit on the left travelling from Panchgani.

### Pratapgarh

To the west of Mahabaleshwar, the setting for this Maratha fort is spectacular. From the summit (1,080 m) on which it is sited there is a splendid view down the forested hillside. A road leads to the foot of the hill, then 500 steps run up to the top.

The fort comprises a double wall with corner bastions. The gates are studded with iron spikes. Inside, the Bhavani temple in the lower fort has two *dipmal* (lantern towers); their exteriors are covered with regularly placed projections like giant coat hooks. Presumably lanterns were placed on these or hung from them, the towers then acting as beacons. The upper fort has a Siva temple. Its ramparts can be seen nearly all of the way down the very scenic (but slow) road to Poladpur.

### Chiplun

The NH17 runs south through Khed to Chiplun on the banks of the Vashishti River, fed from the **Koyna Lake**, one of the largest artificial lakes in the Western Ghats. There are spectacular views across the flat valley bottom, criss-crossed by the several courses of the meandering river. After Khed and 10 km before Chiplun, near an attractive small village and temple (difficult to find when travelling north) there is accommodation.

---

## South Konkan Coast → *Colour map 5, B3, C3 and C4.*

The 593 km coast route from Mumbai to Goa, now followed by the Konkan Railway and the NH17, runs through the South Konkan region. It passes a string of small towns which developed at the heads of estuaries. These were transshipment points for cargo brought by sea, then hauled by pack animals over the Ghats. Although lowland, it is far from flat. Many of the densely wooded slopes have been cleared, leaving the laterites bare and unproductive, alternating with patches of intensive rice cultivation and coconut groves. The coastal estuaries support mangrove swamps. Economically a backward region, it is scenically very attractive. » *For Sleeping, Eating and other listings, see pages 1109-1112.*

### Kashid Beach

Kashid has an excellent, unspoilt, 3-km silver sand beach near the town of Alibag, which is a popular weekend resort but deserted on weekdays. Unfortunately the sea is polluted and swimming is not advised. A good beach, 2 km away, is suitable for camping and nearby hills are good for walking.

### Murud-Janjira

Murud is 16 km south of Kashid and is worth a half day excursion. It is a good idea to hire a bike to explore the town. One kilometre north from Murud centre is the temple to the triple-headed **Dattatraya** representing Brahma, Vishnu and Siva. It is worth climbing up 250 steps, not least for the commanding views.

**Janjira Fort** is reputedly one of the strongest coastal forts in India and was uniquely successful in resisting attempts to capture it. According to legend one such attempt included the digging of a tunnel under the sea. The fort had been built by the Sidis from Abyssinia. Across the bay to the north can be seen Sambhaji's fort, built to combat Janjira, but Janjira was unique in holding out against Maratha attacks. The fort retains a number of remarkable buildings, including mosques, the *topkhana* guarded by canons and a five-storeyed **palace**, which is crumbling. An empty palace of the old nawab, 1 km north of Janjira-Rajpuri, is clearly visitble from the Murud Road. Signs warn tresspassers away, but a the caretaker may allow you to look at the ghost of the once opulent lifestyle of the nawabs, Rs 50 tip expected. Some decaying Muslim tombs stand among baobab trees, 1 km south of Rajpuri jetty. Boats take you from this jetty to the fort for either Rs 10 or Rs 150 on the Tourist boat.

## Ratnagiri

Now a rapidly growing unprepossessing port town with a lot of road works, Ratnagiri ('Jewel hill'), 13 km west off the NH17 at Hathkamba, was the birthplace of two leaders of the Independence movement, Gangadhar Tilak and GK Gokhale. It was also the internment home for the last king of Burma, King Thibaw, who was held here from 1886 until his death in 1916. His 'palace' is now part of the polytechnic. Sleeping at **Land-mark** as you approach the town.

## Ganpatipule

Revered and much visited by Hindus for its swayambhu ('naturally occurring' or 'self-created') Ganesh, Ganpatipule, north of Ratnagiri, has a beautifully white deserted beach to rival those of Goa which gets busy at weekends. The sea is clean but beware of strong currents. Jaigad Fort, 35 km, makes a pleasant excursion.

## Vijayadurg (Viziadurg)

A minor road west off the NH17 at Talera leads to the formidable fort guarding the river which was built on an ancient site. The Sultans of Bijapur enlarged it and Sivaji further strengthened it by adding the three outer walls. It has 27 bastions, an inner moat, good water supply and carried 278 guns in 1682. The Maratha pirate Kanhoji Angria made it his base in 1698, plundered European shipping and withstood assaults by the Portuguese and the British.

## Malvan

A coastal road south from Vijayadurg leads to Malvan. The old town straggles along a crowded little street down to its port. There is an unconventional statue of Sivaji and two well-known temples to Sri Devi Sateri and Rameshwar. It is being developed as a beach resort by MTDC. Sivaji's coastal fort of **Sindhudurg**, just south of Malvan, now deserted, is on a low-lying island just off the coast. Rowing boats ferry passengers from the tiny port. There are still several shrines – to Maruti, Bhavani, Mahadeo and uniquely to Sivaji.

## Vengurla

The former trading settlement on an island is now joined to the land. On the NH17, close to the Goa border, the coast here is lined with beautiful white sand beaches. Salt pans provide an important product for export from the region.

## Sawantwadi

Sawantwadi was the capital of the Bhonsle kings of southern Maharashtra who were constantly trying to extend their territory into Goa. Today it is a large market town, centred on the big tank and palace buildings with an out-of-town station on the Konkan railway. It was once noted for the production of fine hand-painted *gangifa* (playing cards) but this is a dying tradition. The Sawantwadi royal family is actively keeping this ancient art and other local crafts alive, allowing a few artists/craftsmen to work in the once impressive palace darbar hall. They also produce painted lacquered furniture, chessmen, board games and candle sticks.

The brightly coloured *gangifa* were originally produced by pasting layers of cloth together, using tamarind seed gum then coating the 'card' with chalk before polishing it with a stone to provide a smooth white base for decorating the face with natural pigments while the back was stiffened with lacquer. The packs of circular cards come in various sizes and suits. The ten suits of the *Dasavatara* (featuring Vishnu's 10 incarnations), for example, forms a pack of 120 cards while the *Navagraha* (nine planets) has nine suits. The miniature paintings with patterns drawn from mythology, history and nature, often reflect folk traditions. A few towns in Bengal and Orissa continue to produce *gangifa*. Prices range from Rs 800 to 3,000.

## Amboli

From Sawantwadi, a state road goes up the ghats to the minor hill station of Amboli, at an altitude of 690 m. The road contines on to Belgaum. Set on the flat-topped heights of the Western Ghats overlooking the coastal plain below, Amboli is a quiet and little-visited resort. There are attractive walks and several waterfalls. Bauxite mines, 10 km away, can also be visited.

## Redi Beach

Just 3 km north of the Goa border and Tiracol, a turn off from NH17, south of Shiroda, leads to Redi Village and beach. An old Maratha Fort, now in ruins but interesting to wander round, dominates the view over a stunning and almost unvisited bay. An idyllic picnic spot, for example for a day trip from Tiracol, but no facilities or shops so carry water and food.

## Sleeping

**Matheran** *p1105, map p1106*

Budget hotels near the station can be very noisy. Prices often include meals and rise considerably during holidays (eg Diwali) but most offer good off-season discounts.

**A-B Rugby**, Vithalrao Kotwal Rd, T02148 230291. 52 rooms (including large, family rooms), some a/c, gardens, restaurant, professionally run.

**A-B Usha Ascot**, MG Rd, T02148 230360. 64 rooms, most a/c, a resort hotel.

**B The Byke**, T02148 230365. 46 comfortable rooms, 5 a/c, excellent restaurants, good pool.

**B-C Lord's Central**, MG Marg, T02148 230228. 23 colonial style rooms ('Valley' room best), restaurant (meals included), bar, pool, park, riding, not plush but clean, friendly, with best views in Matheran, perched on the edge of the main ridge. Recommended.

**C-D Alexander**, Alexander Pt, T02148 230151. 24 rooms, 3 a/c, good restaurant, in unspoilt woodland.

**C-D Holiday Camp** (MTDC), 30 mins up hill from centre 1 km before Matheran (train stops at camp), T02148 230277, F30566. 39 rooms and cottages for 2 or 4, and dorm, limited catering.

**C-D Royal**, Kasturba Bhavan, T02148 230247. 61 rooms, 5 a/c, restaurant (Indian veg), bar, health club.

**D Gujarat Bhavan**, Maulana Azad Rd, T02148 230378. 22 clean rooms (some a/c), restaurant (Indian veg), garden.

**E Girivihar**, Sivaji Rd, T02148 230231. Peaceful, spacious gardens, some rooms with balconies.

**E Hope Hall**, MG Marg (opposite Lord's Central), T02148 230253. Good size, clean rooms with bath (bucket hot water), friendly family, pleasant location.

**E Prasanna**, opposite railway station, T02148 230258. 10 small, clean rooms, restaurant.

Several restaurants have 'Permit' rooms.

**Mahabaleshwar** *p1105*

Many hotels to choose from; several family run. The bazar sells local honey which is justly famous, as are jams from fruit grown in area.

**A Valley View Resort**, Valley View Rd, off James Murray Peth Rd, T02168 260066. 80 very clean rooms, 40 a/c, real grass to balconies(!), pure veg restaurant (no beer), fabulous views from garden. Recommended.

*For an explanation of the sleeping and eating price codes used in this guide, see inside the front cover. Other relevant information is found in Essentials pages 56-61.*

**B-C Brightland**, Nakhinda Village (4 km centre), Kates Pt Rd, T02168 260707. 30 rooms, restaurants, bar, pool, gardens.
**C Fountain**, opposite Koyna Valley, T02168 260227. 98 rooms, some air-cooled with TV, veg restaurant with a good choice.
**C Fredrick**, NH71 near Satara Rd junction, T02168 260240. 32 rooms, restaurant, bungalow hotel.
**C-D Dinas**, Pune Rd. Comfortable rooms, food.
**C-D Dreamland**, off MG Rd, behind ST Stand, T02168 260228. 80 rooms, old cottages and newer a/c suites by the pool, restaurant (Indian veg) in large garden.
**C-D Holiday Resort** (MTDC), T02168 260318. 100 cottages, rooms and garden suites in large complex, dorm (no beds) Rs 100, restaurant, permit room, pleasant setting and atmosphere, Tourist Office near gate, popular. 2 km from centre (taxi Rs 40).
**D Mahabaleshwar Club**, off SH71 towards Golf Links. Library attached, quiet, with character, temp membership to stay.
**D-E Grand**, Woodlawn Rd, away from centre, T02168 260322. Modest rooms with verandah, gardens.
**E Sai Niwas**, 338 Koli Alley, T02168 260549. Good value, clean rooms.

**Panchgani** *p1106*
**B-D Five Hills**, opposite Dr Ambedkar Nagar, Rajpuri Rd, T40301. 64 doubles and suites, good restaurant, all rooms only Rs 150 on weekdays.
**D Summer Palace** has clean, modern though characterless rooms.
**D-E Amer**, 188 Chesson Rd, T02168 240211. Some a/c rooms with bath.

**Chiplun** *p1107*
**A Gateway Riverview Lodge**, T02356 272233, www.chiplunhotels.com. With 37 comfortable rooms, most a/c, very good restaurant, pool to indulge in, helipad, attractive garden setting, peaceful. There are several very cheap lodges around the town centre.

**Kashid Beach** *p1107*
**B Kashid Beach Resort**, T02144 2785010. 500 m from beach across main road, has 25 split level rooms, some with good seaviews, bathrooms a bit run-down but rooms clean, restaurant (beer appears as 'snacks' on the bill), in large grounds, bike hire.

**Murud-Janjira** *p1107*
**A-B Holiday Resort** (MTDC/private), T02144 274078. 140 cottages (for 2 or 4) and rooms, basic, restaurant (monotonous menu).
**B Golden Swan**, Darbar Rd, T02144 274078, www.goldenswan.com. Comfortable rooms in cottages near the beach, adequate restaurant.
**E Seashore Resort** (no sign), 3 rooms, bath, friendly family, lovely garden on beach.
**E Anan**, Darbar Rd, T02144 274297. Simple rooms with bath, hammocks in garden.

**Ganpatipule** *p1108*
**B-C Abishek**, T022 2437 0801 (Mumbai), 500 m down dirt track opposite **Landmark**. Typical Indian hotel, restaurant with sea views from patio.
**B-C Landmark**, T02357 235284, on hill side going down to village. Good rooms, excellent Chinese/ Indian restaurant, beer.
**B-D Resort**, T02357 235348, on the beach, among palm trees. 68 clean, comfortable a/c suites to 4-bed rooms (11 and 12 best), poor and grubby restaurant (beer), **Bank of Maharashtra** on site changes TCs, poor service, demands advance payment, but great location, relaxing.

**Amboli** *p1109*
**D JRD International**, Vengurla-Belgaon Rd, 1 km from bus stand, T02363-276222. 30 pleasant, clean rooms, better in 'cottages', reasonable Indian restaurant, bar.
**D-E Resort** (MTDC/private), T02363-276239, offers a reasonably comfortable base with a choice of 21 rooms including some suites.

## Eating

**Matheran** *p1105, map p1106*
**Ỳ Kwality Fruit Juice House**, MG Rd, south of the train station among many. Excellent honey and *chikki* (a sweet peanut brittle).
**Ỳ Woodlands**, Chinoy Rd. Indian.

**Mahabaleshwar** *p1105*
**ỲỲỲ-ỲỲ Grapevine Restaurant**, Masjid Rd. Small eclectic restaurant with Thai, Italian and other non-Indian specials. Try lobster,

fresh strawberries washed down with Indian 'Chardonnay'. Excellent though pricey.

**Murud-Janjira** *p1107*
¥ **Nest**, Darbar Rd. Indian including *thalis*.
¥ **Vinayak**, try Chicken Manchurian Soup.

**Ganpatipule** *p1108*
Cheap *thalis* are served in 2 eateries outside the Ganesh Temple on the shopping street.

## Activities and tours

**Elephanta Caves** *p1101*
Maharashtra Tourism launches with good guides leave the Gateway of India every 30 mins from 0900 (last one leaves Elephanta at 1730) except during the monsoon from Jun-Sep. The very pleasant journey takes 1-1½ hrs (Rs 65-85 return).The higher fare is for 'deluxe' boats with an open upper deck. However, the boat boys demand extra payment to sit on top! Reservations, T022-2026364. Small private boats without guides continue during the monsoon when the seas can be very rough. From the landing place, a 300 m unshaded path along the quayside and then about 110 rough steps lead to the caves at a height of 75 m. The walk along the quay can be avoided when the small train functions (Rs 6 return). The climb can be trying for some, especially if it is hot, though *Doolies* (chairs carried by porters) are available for Rs 300 return, Rs 200 1-way (unnecessary for the reasonably fit). The monkeys can be aggressive. Elephanta is very popular with local day-trippers so avoid the weekend rush. At the start of the climb there are places selling refreshments, as well as lines of stalls with knick-knacks and curios along the way (including models of the Eiffel Tower!). Maharashtra Tourism normally organizes a festival of classical music and dance on the island in the third week of Feb. US$5 for foreigners, Rs 10 Indians. MTDC, has 2 rooms. Early morning is the best time for light and also for avoiding large groups with guides which arrive from around 1000. The caves tend to be quite dark so carry a powerful torch.

**Kaheri Caves** *p1103*
**MTDC** tours from Mumbai; or by train to Borivli station (from Mumbai Central, 30 mins). From there, by taxi or auto-rickshaw (10 km), or by bus on Sun and public holidays.

**Mahabaleshwar** *p1105*
**MTDC** deluxe buses for sightseeing, 1400, Pratapgarh, 0930, 1000, and Panchgani, 1100. Reservations at **Holiday Resort**, T02168 260318.

## Transport

**Chaul, Kihim and Alibag beaches** *p1101*
From the New Ferry Wharf, Gateway of India, it is a 90-min trip to Rewas. Then, a 6-km bus or auto ride to Kihim; or 30-km bus ride to Chaul. **MTDC** tours to Kihim include transport.

**Bassein (Vasai)** *p1103*
Trains go from Mumbai Central to Bassein (Vasai) Road station. From there hire a taxi for 11 km.

**Matheran** *p1105, map p1106*
From Neral, south of Kalyan, the atmospheric narrow gauge train takes 2 hrs to cover 21 km to reach Matheran. The station is in the town centre. A Capitation Tax (Rs 20) is charged on arrival – pay before leaving the station. It's necessary to book in advance for weekends. From Neral 1st Class window seats are Nos 1, 4, 5, 8; some 2nd Class are glazed for better viewing: sit on the right on the way up, for best views. From **Neral**, depart daily at 0840, 1100, 1700 (also 1015, mid Mar-mid-Jun). To connect in the morning: from **Mumbai (CST)**: *Deccan Exp* 1007 at 0640; *Local* 0721; *Koyna Exp* 7307 at 0845; From **Pune** *Sahayadri Exp* at 0730. There are trains from **Karjat Junction** to Neral. From **Matheran**: depart 0545, 1310, 1435, 1620.

**Mahabaleshwar** *p1105*
For the best views, sit on the right of the bus travelling from Pune to Mahabaleshhwar. Regular services to/from Pune, Rs 30 (4 hrs). MTDC several deluxe buses daily (except monsoons) to Mumbai 1500 (6½ hrs) and from Mumbai (7 hrs), Rs 145. The semi-luxury and luxury buses to Pune stop at Swargate, a Rs 15 auto ride away from

the railway station. Pune is the most convenient railhead.

**Panchgani** *p1106*
Buses run from Mumbai (via Mahad) and Pune ('Luxury' to Swargate stand only). The nearest railway station is Satara (28 km).

**Pratapgarh**
Buses to Pratapgarh from Mahabaleshwar (22 km), taking 50 mins.

**Kashid Beach** *p1107*
From Mumbai 4 hrs by car, 21 km south. Also daily 2 'Asiad' coaches from Central Bus Terminal (0545, 1200), Rs 45. Or, Mumbai-Rewas ferry runs hourly in daylight from the Ferry Wharf (Bhaucha Dhakka), 1½ hrs then frequent buses to Kashid, 55 km away, or rickshaws, known locally as 'Vikrams'.

**Murud-Janjira** *p1107*
From Mumbai, buses cover the 165 km in under 6 hrs but it may be quicker to get a bus to Alibag and pick up a local connection there. Mumbai-Rewas ferry runs hourly in daylight from the Ferry Wharf (Bhaucha Dhakka), 1½ hrs; local buses from there to Murud, though there can be a long wait.

**Ganpatipule** *p1108*
Direct State Transport buses run from **Mumbai**, **Pune** and **Ratnagiri**.

**Amboli** *p1109*
From the coastal towns of **Ratnagiri** (210 km) and **Vengurla** (50 km) there are buses. Or you can get the train to **Kolhapur** or **Belgaum**, then by local bus.

## Directory

**Matheran** *p1105, map p1106*
**Union Bank of India**, MG Rd, changes TCs and cash but poor rate; newsagents in Hotel Prasanna, Post Office and Tourist Information Bureau opposite railway station.

**Mahabaleshwar** *p1105*
Banks are on Dr Sabbana Rd. Tourist office at Holiday Resort, T60318, F60300, helpful; information near bus stand.

# Northwest Maharashtra

## Nashik (Nasik)

→ *Phone code: 0253. Colour map 5, grid A3. Population: 1.08 mn.*

**Nashik, an unprepossessing mixture of featureless market town, pilgrim centre and sprawling modern industrial estates, nonetheless has an old city area near the ghats with characteristic traditional buildings. It is one of Hinduism's most holy sites, taking its sanctity from its position on the headwaters of the Godavari River. It commands the strategic route from northwestern India to the southern Deccan.** » *For Sleeping, Eating and other listings, see pages 1114-1114.*

### Ins and outs

**Getting there** Trains arrive at Nasik Rd Station, 7 km south of town. City buses run to town (Rs 5), stopping at Shalimar Circle, 3 mins' walk from the Central Bus Stand (CBS) at the town centre; otherwise auto-rickshaws and taxis are around. Buses arrive from Aurangabad at the CBS, close to plenty of budget hotels. Mumbai buses use the Mahamarga Bus Stand, a few kilometres from the centre, where you can get an auto; trains from Mumbai are a faster and better option.
**Getting around** Buses to local places of interest use the CBS but few people speak English in case you need to ask the way. » *See Transport, page 1114, for further details.*

### Sights

Nashik shares the triennial **Kumbh Mela** with Ujjain, Haridwar and Allahabad (see page 185) and every 12 years millions of pilgrims converge on the river Godavari, sometimes referred to as the Ganga of the Deccan, to bathe. The Godavari, which rises 30 km away at Trimbak, is believed to have a common underground source with the Ganga itself. In the last 10 years Nashik has been one of India's fastest growing cities, but the town itself is undoubtedly ancient, and Ghose suggests that it has an unbroken history of over 2,500 years. At Pandu Lena (see below), within a few kilometres of the town centre, palaeolithic settlements have been discovered. Chalcolithic pottery has been found at Gangawadi, 15 km northwest of Nashik. Other finds date from the fifth century BC up to the first century AD and Roman pottery has been found in the third period level. However, none of Nashik's temples are very old. The Vaishnavite **Sundar Narayana Temple** (1756) on the west bank has three black Vishnu images. The **Ramesvara Temple** (18th century) is where Rama is believed to have carried out the funeral rites for his father and to have bathed in the **Rama Kund** nearby. It is a popular place to throw ashes of the dead into the river. The banyan-shaded **Sita Gupha** cave on the east side of town is where Rama's wife hid from Ravana the demon. Nearby is the **Kala** (black) **Rama Temple** (1782) which has a 25-m high *shikhara*. 

## Around Nashik

### Pandu Lena

Some 8 km southwest of Nashik there is a group of 24 rock cut Buddhist monuments on a hillock, the earliest dating from the first century BC. They include over 20 caves. Some have excellent carving, particularly on the exterior doorways. **Cave 3** has 19 monastic cells, a carved Buddha decorates the rear of **Cave 10**, while the exterior of the early **Cave 18**, a chapel (*chaitya*), is finely decorated.

### Deolali

Deolali, 7 km southeast, was the transfer camp for British soldiers going home during the two World Wars. To go 'Doolally Tap' was to go crazy with boredom waiting there. A mental hospital accommodated these casualties.

### Trimbak

The town of Trimbak, 30 km west of Nashik, is centred around the beautiful **Gangasagar Tank**. About 690 steps lead up the hill behind Trimbak to the source of the Godavari itself where you get good views. The town is partly surrounded by a fantastic semi-circle of hills, topped by a near vertical scarp. **Trimbakeshwar Temple**, an 18th-century Siva sanctuary with a *jyotirlinga*, is a pilgrimage site. In February/ March a large fair is held; the important **Sinhastha Fair** takes place every 12 years. There is a simple hotel here. **Prayag Tirth**, on the road to Trimbak, has a beautiful stone-lined tank with two temples. Further on near **Anjaneri**, two 300-m high conical hills are on either side of the road, sweeping round in a broad arc behind the town of Trimbak. Hourly buses from Nashik take about 45 minutes.

### Igatpuri

The 'Town of Difficulties' is on the plateau top at the end of the ghat section of railway. **Kalsubai** (1,540 m), the highest mountain in Maharashtra, is visible to the south. About 1 km beyond the town the road passes the end of the beautiful **Beale Lake**.

### Jawhar

The former capital of a tribal kingdom, Jawhar is noted for its *warli* paintings. Rice paste or poster colours are used to decorate the hut walls. **Jai Vilas**, the palace (ask locally to visit) and **Bhupatgad**, the fort, still show evidence of the tribal kingdom, while there are attractive waterfalls at Dadar Kopra.

## Sleeping

**Nashik** *p1112*

Cheap rooms are hard to come by.

A **Residency** (Taj), P-17 MIDC Ambad, Mumbai-Agra Rd (14 km from Nasik Rd station, 6 km from city), T0253 2384499, tajnsk@bom2.vsnl.net.in. 64 rooms, large grounds.

A-B **Regency** (Quality Inn), Pune Rd, Sivaji Nagar, T0253 2562442. 40 rooms, modern, pool, health club.

C **Holiday Cottages**, Mumbai-Agra Rd, Vilhouli (8 km from centre), T0253 2522376. 40 rooms, 30 a/c, comfortable, restaurant, pool.

C-D **Panchavati Elite**, Trimbak Rd, near Vinod Auto, T0253 2579031. 26 rooms, some a/c, restaurants (**Kwality**, **Coffee House**) and a cheaper guesthouse.

C-D **Panchavati Yatri**, 430 Vakil Wadi, T575771, F571823. 41 rooms, 30 a/c rooms (but cold showers), good restaurants, bar, coffee shop recommended, well run and efficient.

D **Green View**, 1363 Trimbak Rd, T572231, F579754. 24 rooms, 14 a/c, restaurant, garden, quiet.

E **Siddhartha**, Nashik Pune Rd, 2 km towards airport, T0253 2573288. 32 rooms, some D a/c, pleasant garden.

E-F **Basera**, Shivaji Rd, T0253 2575616. 60 clean rooms, hot water.

E-F **Pushkraj**, near Shalimar City Bus Stop, T0253 274838. 30 rooms, restaurant, helpful.

E-F **Rajmahal**, opposite the bus stand, T0253 2580501. 28 rooms, friendly, clean.

F **Mazda**, Old Agra Rd, 5-min walk from CBS, T0253 2579720. Basic rooms with bath, café.

## Eating

**Nashik** *p1112*

ꟾꟾ **Panchavati**, hotels, mostly Indian vegetarian, wide choice.

On MG Rd:

ꟾ **Anand**, for fast food.

ꟾ **Annapoorna Lunch House** for breakfast and South Indian dishes.

ꟾ **Dairy Don** for ice creams.

ꟾ **Shilpa Hotel**, does excellent Gujarati thalis.

ꟾ **Woodlands**, Nashik Pune Rd (opposite Siddhartha), recommended for South Indian vegetarian and coffee.

## Activities and tours

**Nashik** *p1112*

Best to book tours in advance by the evening before at CBS.

Nashik Darshan start from the Central Bus Stand (CBS) 0730-1700, Rs 71 (includes Hindi guide). Visits Pandu Lena, Bhaktidham, Kala Ram Mandir/Sita Gupha, Tapovan, Muktidham (lunch), Ved Mandir, Somneshwar, Trimbak; good value, well-timed, although the hour's stop at Trimbak allows a visit to the temple but is too short to see the source of the Godavari. Possible to leave the tour at this point and return to Nashik by bus or share taxis (Rs 20) which are available; it is a 30-min walk to the centre.

## Transport

**Nashik** *p1112*

From Mumbai airport, take taxi to Thane and then a shared taxi (Rs 80) to Nashik (total 4 hrs); also buses from Thane long-distance bus stand. For Aurangabad, buses depart 30 mins past the hour, 5 hrs, Rs 85; no share taxis.

**Train**

**Mumbai (CST)**: *Tapovan Exp, 7618*, 1822, 4½ hrs; *Panchavati Exp, 1402*, 0702, 4¼ hrs; several others scheduled throughout the day. **Bhopal**: *Punjab Mail, 2137*, 2310, 10 hrs; *Kushinagar Exp,1015*, 0227, 12 hrs.

## Directory

**Nashik** *p1112*

**Tourist offices** Maharashtra, T/1 Golf Club, Old Agra Rd, T0253 2570059. Sightseeing 0730-1500, Rs 80. **Goa**, Kirti Tours, 5 Maru Shopping Centre, Trimbak Rd, opposite Zilla Parishad, T0253 2576697.

**Useful services** State Bank of India, Vivekananda Rd.

# Central Maharashtra

## Aurangabad → *Phone code: 0240 .Colour map 5, grid A5. Population: 872,700.*

A pleasantly spacious town, Aurangabad is the most common starting point for visiting the superb caves at Ellora and Ajanta. The gates are all that is left of the old city walls. There is a university, medical and engineering colleges and an airport to complement the town's industrial and commercial activities. ▸▸ *For Sleeping, Eating and other listings, see pages 1129-1133.*

### Ins and outs

**Getting there** Chikalthana airport is 10 km east of the town with taxis, Rs 100 (a/c Rs 300) or hotel transport into the town centre. The railway station is on the southern edge of town, within walking distance of most hotels and the central bus stand just under 2 km north on Dr Ambedkar Road. ▸▸ *See Transport, page 1132, for further details.*
**Getting around** It is easy to navigate. There are plenty of autos to see the sights, most of which are too scattered to see on foot.

### History

Originally known as Khadke, the town was founded in 1610 by Malik Ambar, an Abyssinian slave who became the 'Wazir' (Prime Minister) to the King of Ahmadnagar. It was later changed to Aurangabad in honour of the last great Mughal, Aurangzeb, who built a new citadel. His wife is buried in the Bibi ka Maqbara and he is buried in a simple grave at Rauza. It acted as the centre of operations for his Deccan campaign which occupied him for the second half of his 49-year reign.

### Sights

The British **cantonment** area is in the southwest quadrant, along the Kham River and can be seen on the way to Ellora. The old Holy Trinity church is in very poor condition. To the northwest is the **Begampura** district in which there is the attractive Pan Chakki water mill and the Bibi ka Maqbara, both worth visiting.

Aurangzeb built the 4½-m high, crenellated city walls in 1682 as defence against the Marathas. **Killa Arrak** (1692), his citadel, lay between the Delhi and Mecca Gates. Little remains, though when it was Aurangzeb's capital over 50 Maharajahs and Princes attended the court. With Aurangzeb gone, the city's significance faded. At the centre in a grove of trees lies the **Jama Masjid**, a low building with minarets and a broad band carved with Koranic inscriptions running the length of the façade.

Other monuments in the old city are **Kali Masjid** (1600), a six-pillared stone mosque built by Malik Ambar. In the market square is the **Shahganj Masjid** (circa 1720) which has shops on three sides. The **Chauk Masjid** (1665) was built by Shayista Khan, Aurangzeb's uncle, and has five domes. The **Lal Masjid** (1655) is in red-painted basalt. The **City Chowk**, the market in the Old City, is worth visiting.

**Bibi ka Maqbara** ⓘ *sunrise to 2000, US$2 foreigners, Rs 5 Indians, floodlit at night*, beyond the Mecca Gate, is the mausoleum of Aurangzeb's wife, Rabia Daurani (1678). The classic lines of a garden tomb give it an impressive setting. However, closer is less impressive. Modelled on the Taj Mahal which was completed 25 years earlier, it is about half its size. Far less money was spent – one three-hundredth, by some estimates – and the comparative poverty of the finish is immediately obvious. It uses marble on the bottom 2 m of the mausoleum and four of the jali screens, but plaster elsewhere. The proportions are cramped and the minarets are too heavy in relation to the main mausoleum. Despite its failings it is one of the finest buildings of its period. The brass door carries an inscription which says Ata Ullah was the chief architect and Haibat Rai the maker of the door. On the tomb itself, in place of a marble slab, there is bare earth covered with a decorated cloth, a sign of humility. Light enters through a precisely angled shaft, allowing the early morning sun's rays to light the tomb for three minutes. The second tomb in the corner is said to be that of Rabia Daurani's nurse.

On the same side of the Kham River is the **Pan Chakki** (1696, Water Mill) ⓘ *sunrise to 2000, US$2 foreigners, Rs 5 Indians, refreshments*, which has a white

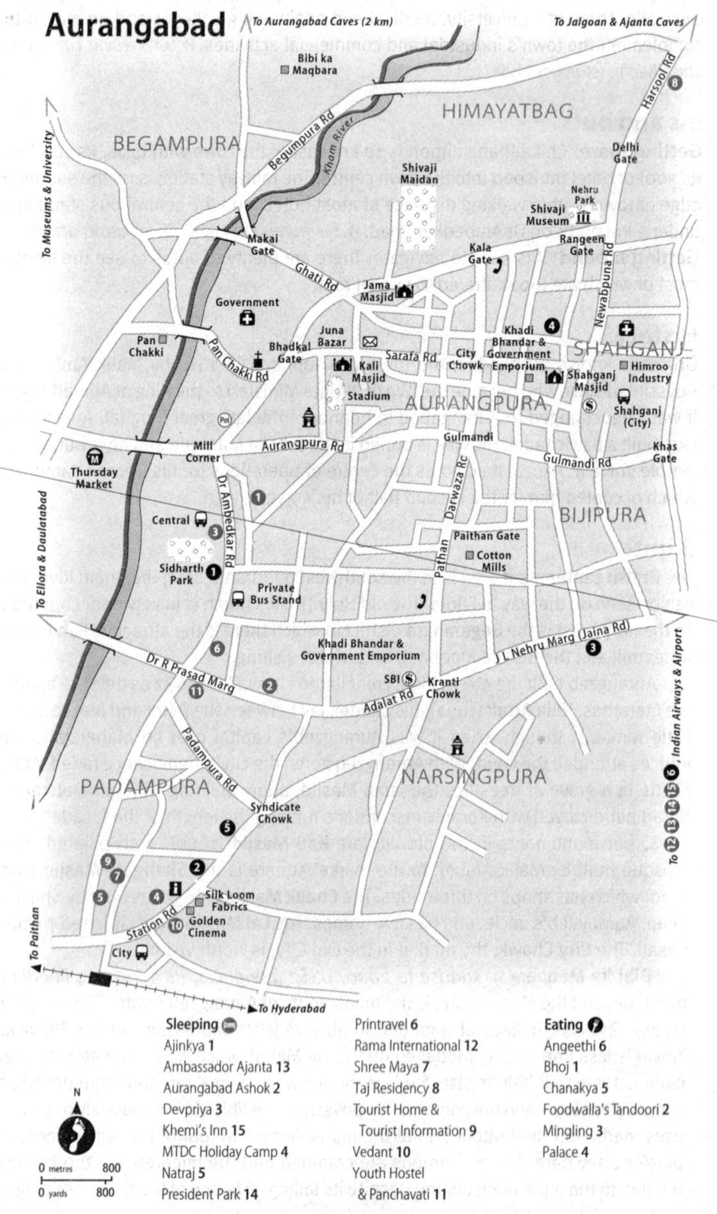

marble shrine to Baba Shah Muzaffar, the devout Aurangzeb's spiritual adviser. The pre-Mughal 17th-century mill for turning large grinding stones was powered by water channelled from a spring some distance away and released through a dam. 

## Aurangabad Caves

ⓘ *US$2 foreigners, Rs 5 Indians.*

Three kilometres north of Aurangabad, the Aurangabad Caves are very interesting though not a substitute for Ajanta and Ellora. Overlooking the town they fall into two groups of five each, about 1½ km apart. They date from the Vakataka (fourth and fifth centuries AD) and Kalachuri dynasties (sixth to eighth centuries), though the older Hinayana Cave 4 is believed to be at least first century, if not earlier. Waiting charges for auto-rickshaws can be high – bargain. Or, if it is cool and you are fit, you can walk back to the edge of town and get an auto-rickshaw back.

**The Western Group** are all viharas except for the earlier Cave 4 which is a chaitya. Cave 1 (incomplete) has finely carved pillars with figures on brackets and ornamentation around doorways and walls. Good views of the country around. Cave 2 has a shrine and columned hallways, a large Buddha and intricately carved panels. The larger Cave 3 has a plain exterior but superb carvings on 12 pillars of the hallway; the sanctuary has panels illustrating jataka stories and a fine large Buddha figure on his throne with attendant devotees illustrating contemporary dress and style. Cave 4, the chaitya has a rib-vaulted ceiling with a stupa containing relics and a Buddha figure outside. Cave 5 is damaged and retains little of its original carvings.

**The Eastern Group** has more sculptures of women and Bodhisattvas. Cave 6 has a large Buddha supporting Ganesh, indicating a later period when Hinduism was gaining in importance over Buddhism. Note the paintings on the ceiling of the balcony. Cave 7 is regarded as the most interesting of both groups. Columned shrines at each end of the verandah house images of Hariti (right) and six goddesses, including Padmini (left). The central shrine has an ambulatory passage around it and a large preaching Buddha at the back. The wall carvings depict deliverance and numerous female dancers and musicians. The importance of Tara and of Tantric Buddhism is evident here. There is little to see in the unfinished Cave 9; the carvings of pre-Nirvana figures suggest Buddhism was waning. The incomplete Cave 10 illustrates the first stages of cave excavation.



# Daulatabad → *Colour map 5, grid A4. 13 km from Aurangabad.*

On a volcanic lava rock towering 250 m above the surrounding countryside is the fort of Deogiri which dates from the Yadava period of the 11th-14th centuries although the first fort had probably been built in the ninth century. Before that it had been a Buddhist monastery. It is an extraordinary site, particularly attractive in the late afternoon when the crowds have gone. If you are lucky you may get the resident guide who takes visitors through the dark tunnels with a flaming torch.

## Deogiri fort

ⓘ *0600-1800, US$2 foreigners, Rs 5 Indians, allow 3 hrs.*

From Ala-ud-din Khalji's capture of Deogiri in 1296 until Independence in 1947, by which time it was under the control of the Nizam of Hyderabad, the fort remained in Muslim hands. Muhammad Tughluq - see page 108 - determined to extend his power south, seized Daulatabad, deciding to make it his capital and populate it with the residents from Delhi. Thousands died as a result of his misconceived experiment. The outermost of the three main ring walls and the bastion gates were probably built by the Muslims. For snacks there are numerous dhabas opposite the entrance.

## Deogiri fortifications

The hillside around Deogiri was made steeper to make scaling the fort extremely difficult. The three concentric walls had strong gates, surrounded by a deep moat and the path climbed through the gates then up the steep slope towards the citadel. Today a new path has been cut to avoid the obstacles that were designed to prevent attackers from gaining entry. There is an L-shaped keep, a long, tortuous tunnel which could be sealed by an iron cover at the top after firing with hot coals, and a chamber which could be filled with noxious fumes. At one point the tunnel divides and meets, to fool attackers to kill each other in the dark. The only genuine access was narrowed so that an invader would have to crawl through the last few metres, making it possible for defenders to kill them on sight. The bodies were disposed of by chutes down into the crocodile infested moat 75 m below. A guide will take you through. Take a torch and allow up to two hours to get the most out of the extraordinary fort and its setting.

The Persian style **Chand Minar** (1435) stands at the bottom of the fort, towering as a celebration of victory like the Qutb Minar in Delhi. Its original covering of Persian blue tiles must have made it even more striking. Opposite is the **Jama Masjid** (1318), with 106 pillars taken from a Hindu temple, and a large tank. The 31 m high victory tower built by Ala-ud-din Bahmani to celebrate his capture of the fort has at its base 24 chambers and a small mosque. The path passes bastions, studded gates, a drawbridge and the **Chini Mahal** where Abdul Hasan Tana Shah, the last King of Golconda, was imprisoned in 1687 for 13 years. The 6.6-m long Kila Shikan (Fort Breaker) iron cannon is on the bastion nearby. At the end of the tunnel (see box) inside the citadel is a flight of steps leading up to the **Baradari** (Pavilion), said to be the palace of the Yadavi Queen and later Shah Jahan. The **citadel** is reached by climbing 100 further steps and passing through two more gateways. At the top is another cannon with a ram's head on the butt; the Persian inscription around the muzzle reads 'Creator of Storms'. A 'Sound and Light' show is planned.



## Rauza

Rauza (or **Khuldabad**) ('Heavenly Abode') is 22 km from Aurangabad and was once an important town around which Aurangzeb built a wall with seven gates. He died at the age of 89 on Friday (the day of his choice), 20 February 1707. There is a simple tomb to him and over 20 others of Muslim rulers of the Deccan. Since Aurangzeb wanted a simple grave as a sign of humility, open to the sky, his grave has no canopy. The marble screen around it was erected later by Lord Curzon and the Nizam of Hyderabad. Close to Aurangzeb's tomb are those of various saints, going back to the 14th century. Some are decorated with silver. There are several relics – hairs of the Prophet's beard said to multiply every year, the Prophet's robe, and the supposed remnants of trees miraculously converted to silver by the saint Saiyed Burhan-ud-Din (died 1344).

## Ellora → *Phone code: 02437. Colour map 5, grid A4.*

The Hindu, Jain and Buddhist caves carved in the volcanic rocks at Ellora are among the finest in India. Lying near an important ancient trade route between Ujjain in Madhya

Pradesh and the west coast, the caves are thought to be the work of priests and pilgrims who used the route. » *For Sleeping, Eating and other listings, see pages 1129-1133.* 

## Ins and outs

Ellora, 26 km from Aurangabad, takes about 45 minutes. Hiring a taxi (Rs 650-1050) gives you flexibility to stop at other sites on the way, auto rickshaws around Rs 350. Alternatively, join a tour group (Rs 150 per person). Car and driver hired through a travel agent will cost around Rs 1,800 return (non a/c). Tour buses usually arrive at the car park, directly in front of the Kailasnatha temple itself. Arrive early and see the Kailasnatha first to avoid the very large crowds.

*For visiting Ellora and Ajanta, take lunch and drinks as decent optons are limited. Also wear a hat and comfy shoes and take a strong torch.*

## The site

ⓘ *Closed Tue, 0900-1730, Kailashnatha entry US$5 foreigners (other caves remain free), Rs 10 Indians. Cameras may be used outside, flash photography and tripods are not allowed inside. Guides available (some European languages and Japanese spoken). 'Light passes' for groups wishing to see darker caves illuminated are available (best to join a group if on your own). Painted caves open at 1000, others at 0900 – light is better in the afternoon. For the elderly and infirm, dhoolies (chairs carried by men) are available.*

Like the caves at Ajanta, Ellora's caves were also abandoned and forgotten. Twelve of the 34 caves are Buddhist (created from circa 600-800 AD), 17 Hindu (600-900 AD) and five Jain (800-1100 AD). Most have courtyards in front. They face west and are best seen in the afternoon. To see the caves in chronological order, start at the east end and visit the Buddhist Viharas first. In this way the magnificent Hindu Kailasnatha temple is seen towards the end.

**The Buddhist Caves: Nos 1-10 (7th-C) 11-12 (8th-C)** These belong to the **Vajrayana** sect of the Mahayana (Greater Vehicle) School. The caves include viharas (monasteries) and chaityas (chapels) where the monks worshipped. It has been suggested that the stone-cut structures were ideally suited to the climate which experienced monsoons, and rapidly became the preferred medium over more flimsy and less durable wood.

**Cave 1** A simple *vihara*.

**Cave 2** Adjoining is reached by a flight of steps. At the door of the cave are *dwarapala* (guardians) flanked by windows. The interior (14.5 sq m) comprises a hall supported by 12 pillars, some decorated with the pot and foliage motif. In the centre of the back wall is a 3 m high seated Buddha and two standing Buddhas while along each of the side walls are five Buddhas accompanied by Bodhisattvas and *apsaras* (celestial nymphs).

**Cave 3** Similar to cave 2, having a square central chamber with a Buddha image, this time seated on a lotus. Around the walls are 12 meditation cells.

**Cave 4** Two-storeyed and contains a Buddha sitting under the Bo (pipal) tree.

**Cave 5** The **Maharwada**, is the largest of the single storeyed caves in this group (17.6 m by 36 m). Two rows of 10 columns each run the length of the cave, as do two raised platforms which were probably tables, suggesting that this cave was a dining hall. There are attractive carvings on the first pillar on the left. The Buddha at the back is guarded on the left by *Padmapani*, a symbol of purity. On the right is *Vajrapani* holding a thunderbolt, the symbol of esoteric knowledge and the popular deity of the sect responsible for creating the caves. The Buddha is seated, not cross-legged on the floor as is usual, but on a chair or stool. He demonstrates some of the 32 distinctive marks: three folds in the neck, long ear lobes and the third eye. The *mudra* here signifies the Buddha's first sermon at the Deer Park, see page 180, and is a teaching pose.

The next four caves can be bypassed as they contain nothing new.

**Cave 10 Viswakarma**, or Carpenter's Cave, is the only *chaitya* (chapel) cave in the group. It was a monastery. This is on the ground floor and above are what are presumed to have been the living quarters of the monks. In front is a large courtyard approached by a flight of steps. The galleries around it have square-based pillars at the foot of which was a lion facing outwards. At the back of these galleries are two elaborately carved chapels. The exterior decoration gives the impression that instead of stone, wood was the building material, hence *Viswakarma*. The façade has a trefoil window with *apsara* groups for ornamentation. The main hall is large (26 m by 13 m, 10 m high). The curved fluted 'beams' suggest to some the upturned hull of a ship. The chamber has 28 columns, each with a vase and foliage capital, dividing it up into a nave and aisles. The aisle runs round the decorated stupa (*dagoba*) with a colossal 4.5 m 'Preaching Buddha' carved in front of it. The upper gallery, reached by an internal flight of steps, was supposed to have subsidiary shrines at either end but the left hand one was not finished. Decorating the walls are loving couples, indicating how much Buddhism had changed from its early ascetic days. You can get a view of the friezes above the pillars which show Naga queens, symbolic precursors of the monsoon, and dwarfs as entertainers, dancing and playing musical instruments.

*The circular window at the entrance enables sunlight to be cast on it giving the cave a truly ethereal quality.*

**Cave 11** (*Do Thal* – two-storeyed) was found to have a third storey in 1876 when the basement was discovered. The lowest level is a verandah with a shrine and two cells at the back of it. The middle level has eight front pillars and five rear cells of which only the central three are completed and decorated. The upper level has a porch opening into a long colonnaded hall with a Buddha shrine at the rear. Images of Durga and Ganesh suggest that the cave was later used by Hindus. Cave 11 and 12 illustrate the use of the upper levels of these caves as a residence for monks and pilgrim hostels.

**Cave 12** (*Tin Thal* – three-storeyed) has cells for sleeping (note stone benches) on the lower floors but it is the figures of the Buddha which are of particular interest. The rows of seven Buddhas are symbolic of the belief that he appears on earth every 5,000 years and has already visited it seven times.

**The Hindu Caves: (Nos 13-29)** These caves lie in the centre of the group and are the most numerous. **Cave 13** is a plain room while **Cave 14** (**Ravana ki khai**, seventh century), is single storeyed and the last of the collection from the early period. River goddesses and guardians stand at the doorway while inside is a broken image of Durga and figurative panels on the walls of the principle deities, Vishnu, Siva, Lakshmi and Parvati. **Cave 15** (*Das Avatara*, mid-eighth century), reached by a flight of steps, has a large courtyard and is two-storeyed.

**Kailasanatha Temple** (mid-eighth century onwards) This the most magnificent of all the rock-cut structures at Ellora, and is completely open to the elements. It is the only building that was begun from the top. Carved out of 85,000 cubic metres of rock, the design and execution of the full temple plan is an extraordinary triumph of imagination and craftsmanship. Excavating three deep trenches into the rock, carving started from the top of the cliff and worked down to the base. Enormous blocks were left intact from which the porch, the free standing pillars and other shrines were subsequently carved. The main shrine was carved on what became the upper storey, as the lower floor was cut out below. It is attributed to the Rashtrakuta king Dantidurga (725-755 AD) and must have taken years to complete. **Mount Kailasa** (6,700 m), the home of Siva, is a real mountain on the Tibetan plateau beyond the Himalaya. Its distinctive pyramidal shape, its isolation from other mountains, and the appearance to the discerning eye of a swastika etched by snow and ice on its rock face, imbued the mountain with great religious significance to Hindus and Buddhists alike. Kailasa was seen as the centre of the universe, and Siva is Lord of Kailasa, Kailasanatha. To imitate the real snow-covered peaks, the *sikharas* here were once covered with white plaster.

**The Entrance** The temple is 50 m long and 33 m wide and the tower rises 29 m above the level of the court. At the entrance gate, the threshold between the profane and sacred worlds, the goddesses **Ganga** and **Yamuna** form the door jambs. Just inside are two seated sages: **Vyasa**, the legendary author of the *Mahabharata*, and **Valmiki** to whom the *Ramayana* has been ascribed. In the porch four columns carry the North Indian vase and foliage motif, a symbol of fertility and well-being. On each side of the doorway there are images of **Kubera**, the god of wealth, with other symbols of well-being such as the conch shell and the lotus. Two more figures complete the welcoming party. They are **Ganesh** (left), the elephant headed son of Siva, bringer of good fortune, and **Durga** (right), Siva's wife who fought the demons.

In the antechamber opposite is **Lakshmi**, the goddess of wealth. In the courtyard, to your right and left are free-standing elephants. On the left round the corner is a panel depicting **Kama**, the god of desire, carrying his bow and five arrows, one for each of the senses. On the far wall to your left of the entrance, behind the pillars, is the shrine of the **Three River Goddesses** - Ganga (centre), Yamuna (left) and Sarasvati (right). Symbolically they stand for purity, devotion and wisdom respectively. This is a good place to photograph the central shrine. The two carved monolithic pillars are probably stylized flagstaffs indicating royal patronage – a practice that Asoka popularized in the third century BC.

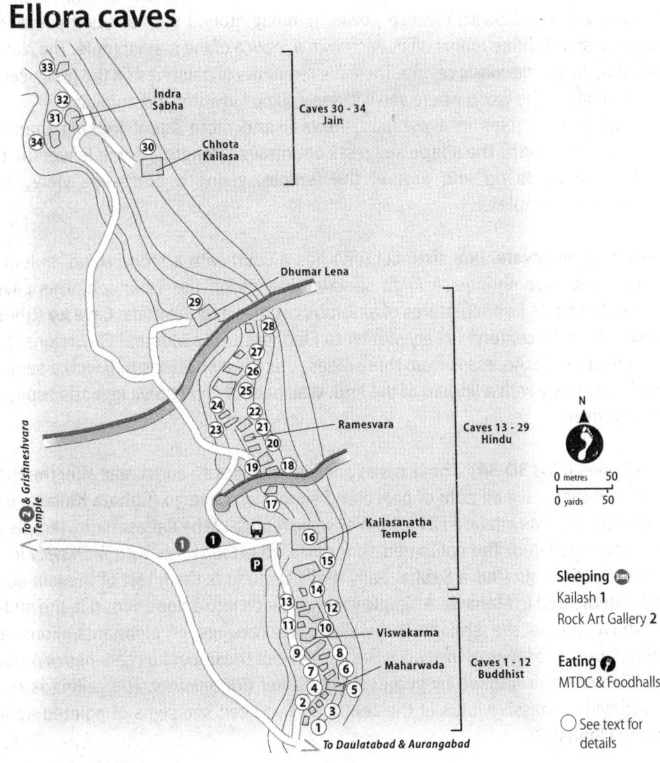

There are two distinct levels taking the worshipper from the courtyard by two staircases flanking the central hall, to the lower level with its processional path and then rising even higher to the upper level of the *mandapa*.

**The Central Assembly Hall** Around the central shrine is a colonnaded hall gouged from the rock, which in places overhangs menacingly. Inside this cloister is a series of panels portraying Siva and Vishnu myths. The whole can be viewed as a sort of instructional picture gallery, a purpose it served for worshippers from ancient times who could not read.

The south facing wall has *Ramayana* stories – **Ravana** offering his heads; Siva and Parvati with Nandi the bull and the lingam (creative power); Siva playing the vina; Siva and Parvati playing dice in a spirit of harmony; the marriage of Siva and Parvati; the origin of the lingam, the symbol of Siva and creative (male) energy; Siva dancing and Siva tricking Parvati. The panel on the south of the mandapa of Ravana shaking Mount Kailasa, attempting to carry it off, disturbing Parvati and her attendants, one of whom is seen frightened and fleeing, and Siva restoring order with the movement of his toe.

Along the north facing wall are stories from the *Mahabharata* above and **Krishna** legends below. The panels include **Krishna** stealing buttermilk; Vishnu as **Narasimha**, half man, half lion; Vishnu reclining on **Ananda** the serpent inbetween incarnations; Vishnu the **Preserver**. Finally there is **Annapurna**, Goddess of Plenty.

The inner porch contains two panels, Siva as **Lord of Knowledge** and Siva as **Bhairava** killing the Elephant Demon.

**The Main Shrine** Steps lead to the upper floor which contains a *mandapa* (central hall, 17 m by 16 m) of 16 stout pillars arranged in groups of four, with aisles corresponding to the cardinal points leading to an open central area. At the far end is the *garbhagriha* (shrine) with **Ganga** and **Yamuna** as door guardians. Inside is the *yoni lingam*, symbol of Siva's creative power. Running around the back is a passageway with five small shrine rooms off it, each with a replica of the main temple. The Nataraja painting on the *mandapa* ceiling. There are remnants of paintings on the porch ceilings (particularly to the west) where you will see *apsaras*, dwarfs and animals.

The temple rises in a pyramid, heavier and more squat looking than later towers in the north. The shape suggests enormous strength. As you leave, the path to the left leads up and around the temple, giving a bird's-eye view of the magnificent complex.

**Cave 21** (**Ramesvara**, late sixth century) has a court with a stone Nandi bull in the middle and side shrines. A *linga* sanctuary leads off the verandah. This cave is celebrated for its fine sculptures of amorous couples and the gods. **Cave 29** (**Dhumar Lena**, late sixth century) is very similar to Elephanta (see Mumbai Excursions, page 1101) in concept. Access is from three sides, there is a spacious hall with a separate small sanctuary with a *lingam* at the end. Wall panels depict Siva legends especially as Destroyer.

**Jain Caves (Nos 30-34)** These caves are something of an anticlimax after the Hindu ones, but they have an aura of peace and simplicity. **Cave 30** (**Chhota Kailasa**, early ninth century) was intended as a smaller scale replica of the Kailasanatha temple but was not completed. The columned shrine has 22 *tirthankaras* with *Mahavira* in the sanctuary. **Cave 32** (**Indra Sabha**, early ninth century) is the finest of the Jain series and is dedicated to **Mahavir**. A simple gateway leads into an open court in the middle of which stands the shrine. The walls have carvings of elephants, lions and *tirthankaras*. The lower of the two is incomplete but the upper has carvings of Ambika and also Mahavir flanked by guardians of earlier *tirthankaras*. The ceiling is richly carved with a massive lotus at the centre and you can see signs of painted figures among clouds.

# Ajanta → *Phone code: 02438. Colour map 5, grid A5.*

Older than those at Ellora, the caves date from about 200 BC to 650 AD. They are cut from the volcanic lavas of the Deccan Trap in a steep crescent-shaped hillside in a forested ravine of the Sahyadri hills. After the late seventh century, the jungle took over and they lay unnoticed for centuries. ▸▸ *For Sleeping, Eating and other listings, see pages 1129-1133.*

## Ins and outs

**Getting there** The bus or taxi drive from Aurangabad (106 km) takes 2½-three hours. Good tours are available from Aurangabad for Rs 200 per person (though a hired non a/c car and driver will cost around Rs 3,000). Taxis Rs 800-1000. Shilod (Silod) is a popular halting place and has a number of restaurants. About 10 km from Ajanta, the road descends from the plateau; then there are dramatic views of the Waghora valley, where the caves are located. ▸▸ *See Transport, page 1132, for further details.*

**Getting around** There is a small settlement with a restaurant, curio market and aggressive salesmen at the foot of the approach to the caves. It is a short uphill walk along a stepped concrete path to the entrance. There are *dhoolis* available for hire if you wish to be carried. You can approach the caves from the river bed in the bottom of the valley, where the bus stops; the View Point, is worth getting to. You have to buy your ticket from the kiosk first, and if there is water in the stream at the bottom you have to wade through, but it is much shadier than the path cut out of the cliff.

## History

In 1819, a party of British army officers from Madras noticed the top of the façade of Cave 10 while tiger hunting. They investigated and discovered some of the caves, describing seeing 'figures with curled wigs'. Others made exploratory trips to the fascinating caves. In 1843, James Fergusson, horrified by the ravages of the elements, requested that the East India Company do something to preserve and protect the deteriorating caves.

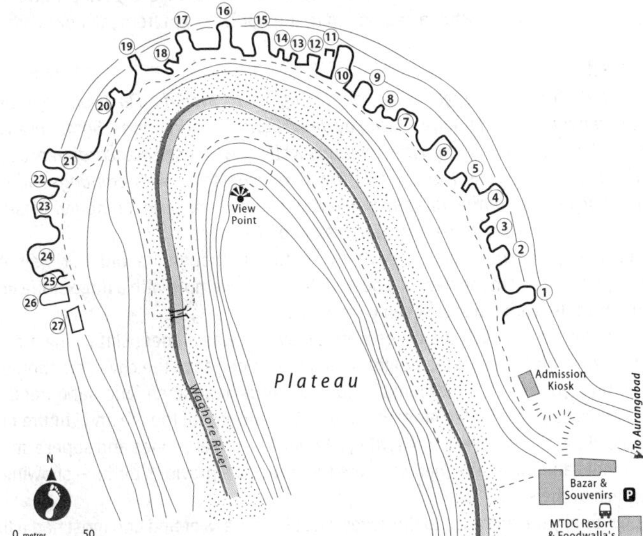

## The challenge of preservation

Preservation of the murals poses enormous challenges. Repeated attempts to reproduce and to restore them have faced major problems. After all but five of Robert Gill's paintings were destroyed by fire, the Bombay School of Arts sent out a team to copy the wall paintings under the guidance of the principal John Griffiths in the 1870s. The copies were stored in the Victoria and Albert Museum in London but this also had a fire in 1885, when 87 were destroyed.

In 1918 a team from Kyoto University Oriental Arts Faculty arrived at Ajanta to copy the sculptures. This they did by pressing wet rice paper against the surface to make casts which were then shipped back to Japan. In the early 1920s they were all destroyed by an earthquake.

In 1920 the Ajanta paintings were cleaned by the former Hyderabad Government under whose jurisdiction the caves lay. Two Italian restorers were commissioned, whose first priority was to fix the peeling paintings to the walls of the caves. They first injected casein between the paintings and the plastered wall, then applied shellac as a fixative. The Griffiths team from Bombay had also applied a coat of varnish to bring out the colours of the paintings.

However, these varnishes darkened over the years, rendering the murals less, not more visible. They also cracked, aiding the peeling process and the accumulation of moisture between the wall and the outer membrane. The Archaeological Survey of India is now responsible for all restoration at the site.

In 1844 **Captain Robert Gill**, an artist, was sent to copy the paintings on the cave walls. He spent 27 years living in a small encampment outside, sending each new batch of paintings to Bombay and London. After nearly 20 years his work was almost complete and displayed in the Crystal Palace in London. In December 1866 all but a few of the paintings were destroyed in a fire. Gill soldiered on for another five years before giving up, and died from illness soon afterwards. He is buried in the small European cemetery at **Bhusawal**, 60 km to the north, 27 km from Jalgaon.



## The site

ⓘ *Closed Mon, 0900-1730, US$5 foreigners, Rs 10 Indians. Flash photography is forbidden due to the damage caused by direct light to the paintings. Some caves have electric lights for illuminating the paintings while hawkers sell postcards very cheaply and slides for about Rs 100 a set. In the Mahayana caves with paintings there is a restriction on the number of visitors allowed in at any one time. Computer kiosks are planned, designed to show a 'virtual' history of the caves.*

Hiuen-Tsang, recorded in the seventh century (although he did not visit it), a description of the "monastery in a deep defile... large temple with a huge stone image of the Buddha with a tier of seven canopies".

The terrain in which the caves were excavated was a sheer cliff facing a deeply incised river meander. At the height of Ajanta's importance the caves are thought to have housed about 200 monks and numerous craftsmen and labourers. The masterpieces retell the life story of the Buddha and reveal the life and culture of the people of the times, royal court settings, family life, street scenes and superb studies of animals and birds. The *Jatakas* relate the Buddha's previous births – showing the progress of the soul.

Originally the entrance to the caves was along the river bed and most had a flight of stairs leading up to them. The first to be excavated was Cave 10, followed by the first Hinayana caves (in which the Buddha is not depicted in human form), on either side. Later Mahayana caves were discovered, completing the spectrum of Buddhist development in India.

There is a round trip walk, up the side of the valley where all the caves are located then down to the river to cross to the other side. An attractive low level walk through forest brings you back to the roadhead. **Caves 1, 2, 10, 16** and **17** have lights. **11, 19** and **26** are also particularly worth visiting.

**Mahayana group Cave 1** (late fifth century) is one of the finest *viharas* (monasteries), remarkable for the number and quality of its murals. A verandah with cells and porches either side has three entrances leading into a pillared hall. Above the verandah are friezes depicting the sick man, old man, corpse and saint encountered by the Buddha, who is shown above the left porch. The hall has 20 ornamented pillars, a feature of the late period caves. Five small monks' cells lead off three sides, and in the centre of the back wall is a large shrine of the Buddha supported by Indra, the rain god. At the entrance are the river goddesses Yamuna and Ganga and two snake-hooded guardians at the base.

The **murals** are among the finest at Ajanta. In the four corners are panels representing groups of foreigners. The Mahajanaka jataka (where the Buddha took the form of an able and just ruler) covers much of the left hand wall including Renunciation, and the scenes where he is enticed by beautiful dancing girls.

On either side of the entrance to the antechamber of the shrine room are two of the best known murals at Ajanta. On the left is the **Bodhisattva Padmapani** (here holding a blue lotus), in a pose of spiritual detachment, whilst on the right is the **Bodhisattva Avalokitesvara**. Together compassion and knowledge, the basis of Mahayana Buddhism, complement one another. Their size dwarfs the attendants to enhance the godlike stature of the bodhisattva. The Buddha inside the shrine is seated in the teaching position, flanked by the two carved bodhisattvas. Under the throne appears the **Wheel of Life**, with deer representing Sarnath where he preached his first sermon, see page 180.

One of the sculptural tricks that a guide will display is that when the statue is lit from the left side (as you face it), the facial expression is solemn, suggesting contemplation. Yet from the other side, there is a smile of joy, while from below it suggests tranquillity and peace. Note the paintings on the ceiling, particularly the elephant scattering the lotus as it rushes out of the pond, and the charging bull. Also look for the 'black princess' and the row of the dancer with musicians. On the way out is a pillar that has four deer sculpted skilfully, sharing the same head.

**Cave 2** (sixth century) is also a *vihara* hall, 14.6 sq m with 12 pillars, with five cells on each side of the left and right hand walls and two chapels on each side of the antechamber and shrine room. The verandah in front has a side chapel at each end. The doorway is richly carved. On the left hand wall is the mural depicting **The Birth of The Buddha**. Next to this is **The 'Thousand' Buddhas**, which illustrates the miracle when the Buddha multiplied himself to confuse a heretic. On the right are dancing girls before the king, shown with striking three-dimensional effect.

The cave is remarkable for its painted ceiling, giving the effect of the draped cloth canopy of a tent. The *mandala* (circular diagram of the cosmos) is supported by demon-like figures. The Greek key designs on the border are possibly influenced by Gandharan art, 1st-3rd centuries AD. The ceiling decorations portray a number of figures of Persian appearance apparent from the style of beard and whiskers and their clothing.

The Yaksha (nature spirits) Shrine in the left chapel is associated with fertility and wealth. The main shrine is that of Buddha in the teaching position, again flanked by the two bodhisattvas, both holding the royal fly whisk. The **Hariti** Shrine on the right is to the ogress who liked eating children! The panel on your left as you leave the hall is a *jataka* telling the story of the Bodhisattva's life as the Pandit Vidhura.

## Tempera techniques in cave painting

To prepare the rock for painting it was chiselled to leave a rough surface. Two layers of mud-plaster containing fibrous material (grain-husk, vegetable fibres and rock grit) was applied, the first coarse, the second fine. Metal mirrors must have been used by the artists, to reflect sunlight into the dark caves. It is thought that the tempera technique was used. On a dry surface, a red cinnabar outline defined the picture, filled in, possibly initially with grey and then numerous colour pigments usually mixed with glue; the completed painting was burnished to give a lustrous finish. The pigments were mainly taken from the land around, the principal ones being red and yellow ochre, white from lime and kaoline, green from glauconite, black from lamp-black and blue from imported lapis lazuli. The shellac used in restoration after 1819 was found to be cracking. Since 1951 this has been removed by the Archaeological Survey of India, with UNESCO's help. PVA is now used.

**Caves 3-7** are late fifth century. **Cave 3** has no verandah and **Cave 4** is the largest *vihara* at Ajanta, planned on an ambitious scale and not completed. The hall is 27 sq m and supported on 28 pillars. Along the walls are cells whilst at the rear is a large shrine. **Cave 5** is also unfinished.

**Hinayana group** A Hinayana group comes next (**Caves 6-10** and **12, 13** and **15**) dating from the second century BC. **Cave 6** is on two levels with only seven of the 16 octagonal pillars standing. A shrine contains a seated Buddha. **Cave 7** has no hall. The verandah has two porches each supported by heavy octagonal Elephanta-type columns. These lead to four cells. These and the antechamber are profusely carved. The shrine is that of Buddha, his hand raised in blessing. **Cave 8** (first century BC) is a small vihara. **Cave 9** (circa 100 BC), a *chaitya*, is 14 m long, 14 columns run the length of each side and 11 continue round the stupa. The vaulted roof was once wooden ribbed and leads back from a huge arched *chaitya sun* window which throws light on the *stupa* at the rear. Two phases of wall painting have been identified. The earlier ones dating from the construction of the cave can be seen at the far left side and consist of a procession to a stupa as well as a thin band above the left colonnade. Above this are later Buddha figures from the Mahayana period when the figures of the Buddha on either side of the entrance were painted.

**Cave 10** (circa 150 BC) is much larger. Like the previous cave the roof was once fitted with wooden ribs which subsequently collapsed. The long hall with an apse housing the *stupa* was one of the first excavated and also the first rediscovered by army officers. An inscription above the façade, now destroyed, dated the excavation to the second century BC through a generous donation by the king. The *dagoba* or *stupa* resembles that of Cave 9 and is a double storey drum. There are also paintings dating from the Hinayana and Mahayana periods. The early ones depict figures in costumes resembling those seen at Sanchi, see page 262. Traces of later paintings survive on the pillars and aisle ceilings and later Buddha figures are often superimposed on earlier works. The main subjects of the Hinayana paintings are *jataka* stories. On the rear wall are the King (in a ceremonial head-dress) and Queen approaching the Sacred Bodhi Tree, one of the earliest Ajanta paintings.

**Cave 11** (originally second century BC, with sixth century alterations), has a verandah and roof painted with birds and flowers, a hall supported by four heavy pillars and a stone bench running along the right side. There are five cells and a shrine of a seated Buddha. **Caves 12** (with glauconite rock wall) and **13** (second century BC) are small *viharas*. **Cave 14** (fifth century AD) was planned on a grand scale but not completed and can be missed along with **Cave 15** (fifth century) which is a long hall with a Buddha carved out of the rock.

**Later Mahayana period** The remaining caves all belong to the Later Mahayana period and date from the fifth century. **Cave 16**, with kneeling elephants at the entrance and the Cobra King, has a 20 m long and 3.5 m deep verandah that carries six plain octagonal pillars. There is a good view of the ravine from here. The magnificent columned hall inside has six cells on each side and a beamed ceiling. The Teaching Buddha is seated on a lion throne. On the left the 'Dying Princess' portrays Nanda's new bride being told that he has been ordained a monk and renounced the world. Her misery is shared by all and everything around her. On the right wall are the remains of a picture of Prince Siddhartha, later the Buddha, using a bow.

**Cave 17** (late fifth century) is similar to No. 16 in layout and has the greatest number of murals. On the left of the verandah is a painted Wheel of Life. Over the entrance door is a row of seven Past Buddhas and the eighth, the Maitreya or Future Buddha, above a row of amorous Yaksha couples. Sculpted deities are carved on either side.

Murals show scenes from 17 *jatakas*: the worship of the Buddha, the Buddha preaching; Hansa *jataka*, with paintings of geese; Vessantara *jataka*, where the greedy Brahmin is portrayed, grinning; the miraculous 'Subjugation of the rogue elephant', sent to kill the Buddha; and the ogress who turns into a beautiful maiden by day! There are also panels showing royal processions, warriors, an assembled congregation from which you can get an accurate and detailed picture of the times. **Cave 18** (late fifth century) has little of merit and can be missed.

**Cave 19** (late fifth century) is a Mahayana *chaitya* hall and was painted throughout. The façade is considered to be one of the most elegant in terms of execution and elaborate ornamentation, and has the arched *chaitya* window set into it. The interior is in the layout seen before, two rows of richly decorated columns leading up to and around the back of the standing Buddha, which here is in front of the slender stupa. This tall shrine has a triple stone umbrella above it. Note the seated Nagaraja with attendants.

**Cave 20** is comparatively small and has imitation beams carved into the ceiling.

**Later caves** The final few caves belong to the seventh century and are a separate and distinct group at the farthest end of the horseshoe near the waterfall. Only one, **Cave 26**, need be visited. **Cave 21** (early seventh century) has a fallen verandah with flanking chapels. **Cave 24** was intended to be the largest *vihara* but was not completed.

**Cave 26** is a large *chaitya hall*. A partly damaged columned façade stretches across the front with the customary side chambers at each end. The 3 m high window is flanked by sculptured Buddha reliefs. Inside, 26 pillars run in an elongated semi circle around the cylindrical *stupa* which is decorated with Buddhas. The walls are decorated with sculpture, including the temptations by Mara's daughters, but the most striking being a 9 m reclining image of the Parinirvana Buddha, about to enter Nirvana, his death mourned by his followers.

The walk back along the promenade connecting the shrines is pleasant enough but the return via the river, waterfall and forest walkway is delightful. Steps lead down from Cave 16 (with the carved elephants). The hilltop opposite the caves offers a fine view of the horseshoe shaped gorge.

## Jalgaon

Jalgaon, 64 km from Ajanta on the NH6, is the rail junction for the Ajanta Caves. It was once at the centre of a savannah forest region, the habitat of tigers, leopards and other game. Now it has become an important cotton growing area and is quite interesting to walk around.

# Eastern Deccan → *Colour map 5, grid A5, B4 and B5.*

To the east of Aurangabad the road and railway go down the gentle slope of the great basin of the Godavari. Ancient erosion surfaces covered in some of India's richest black lava soils dominate the landscape. Rainfall gradually increases eastwards, and on the lower land the soils are some of the best in the peninsula – rich black soils derived from the lava, though on the higher land the much poorer red soils surface. Given the relative dryness an extraordinarily high percentage is cultivated. Sorghum (*jowar*) and short stapled cotton dominate. In the west, pearl millet. ▸▸ *For Sleeping, Eating and other listings, see pages 1129-1133.*

## Jalna

Jalna is the town to which **Abul Fazl**, who wrote the *Ain i Akbari*, was exiled and ultimately murdered by Bir Singh Deo of Orchha, see page 274, at the instigation of Jahangir. The area is dotted with forts. There is a Dak Bungalow and a Rest House in the town.

## Lonar

Lonar is famous for its remarkable 2-km wide meteor crater, believed to have formed 50,000 years ago, which has temple ruins at the base. The pool of green water at the bottom, which you can walk down to, has its unique eco-system.

## Nanded

Guru Gobind Singh, the 10th Sikh guru, was assassinated here in 1708, see page 1343. There is an important *gurudwara* 1,500 m from the station, which is rumoured to be covered in gold in the near future. Today Nanded (Nander), which stands on the river Godavari, is an important administrative and commercial town. It is also on the main railway line between Hyderabad/Secunderabad and Aurangabad/Nashik.

## Paithan

One of the oldest cities of the Deccan, Paithan is on the north bank of the Godavari River as it leaves the Nath Sagar reservoir. The **Jayakwadi Project** at Nath Sagar is a large earthen dam and reservoir. The Left Bank scheme is already providing irrigation all the way down the Godavari to Nanded 140 km to the east, and the equivalent Right Bank scheme is in progress.

Paithan is famous for a special kind of silk sari with brocaded gold borders and *pallu* (end-piece). Motifs of geese, parrots, peacocks and stylized leaves, flowers and creepers in dark greens, red and blue are brocaded against the golden background.

## Ahmadnagar → *Phone code: 0241. Colour map 5, grid B4. Population: 307,500.*

Ahmadnagar, an historic Muslim town, has several Islamic monuments to visit. The town was founded in 1490 by Ahmad Nizam Shah Bahri, the son of a Brahmin from Vijayanagar who converted to Islam. His dynasty ruled the territory stretching from Aurangabad to Bassein until 1636. Its Islamic history reflects strong Persian influence, both architecturally in the Persian style Husaini Mosque, and theologically in the presence of Shi'a Muslims from Persia in the court.

**Alamgir's Dargah** is a small enclosure near the cantonment. **Aurangzeb**, who had begun his long Deccan campaign 24 years earlier, died here on 3 March 1707 and the dargah marks his temporary resting place before his body was moved to Aurangabad. To the east is a white marble **Darbar Hall**, well worth visiting for the view from the roof. **The fort** (1599) is 1 km to the east of the city, 4 km northeast of the railway station. Circular, it has an 18 m high wall reinforced with 22 bastions. The fort is now occupied by the army, but entry is possible (sign in at gate), to see the 'Leaders' Room' where Nehru and 11 colleagues spent 1942-45, now a small museum. No photography. Among the numerous **mosques** in the city are the small but attractive Qasim (1500-1508), the Husaini, with its Persian style dome, and the Damadi (1567) with its splendid carved stonework. The Malik-i-Maidan cannon now standing on the Lion Bastion at Bijapur (see page 1014), was cast here. The well-preserved **Tomb** of Nizam Shah is in a large garden on the left bank of the Sina River. 

## Junnar

The birthplace of **Sivaji** in 1627, Junnar is another rock-cut cave temple site. The hill fort contains a monument commemorating Sivaji and a temple. On the east side of the hill there are more than 50 **Buddhist caves**. Most are *viharas* (monasteries) and date from the second century BC to the third century AD. They comprise the **Tulja Lena Group**, 2 km west of the town, which includes an unusual circular *chaitya* (chapel, Cave 3) with a dome ceiling. The **Bhuta Lena Group** is on the side of Manmodi Hill, 1,500 m south of the town. The unfinished *chaitya* hall (Cave 40) has a well preserved façade containing reliefs of Laxmi. The **Ganesh Lena Group** is 4 km south of Junnar on the Lenyadri Hill. Cave 7 is a *vihara* with 19 cells leading off the main congregational hall and a colonnaded verandah. The octagonal columns are repeated in the *chaitya* hall next door (Cave 6).

**Shivner Fort** rises over 300 m above the plain and is approached from the south by a track that passes over the moat, through four gates, then dog-legs up the final stretch to the plateau. Sivaji's birthplace is to the north and not far from it is a ruined mosque. There are four tanks running down the centre. In the third century the site was a Buddhist *vihara* and on the east face there are about 50 rock cells. Maloji Bhonsla, Sivaji's grandfather, was granted the fort in 1599. Sivaji did not remain in it long as it was captured by the Mughals from the early 1630s. Several attempts to win it back failed.

## Bhimashankar

Completely off the beaten track, the pilgrim site of Bhimashankar can be reached by road from Shivner or from the NH50 at Narayangaon. However, even buses are infrequent. The site is important to Hindus for the Siva temple built by the Peshwa Nana Phadnavis to house one of Maharashtra's five *jyotirlingas*.

## Sleeping

**Aurangabad** *p1115, map p1116*
Some hotels offer discounts between Apr and Sep. Most will provide packed lunch for trip to the caves. Most are 24-hr check out.

**AL-A Residency** (Taj), 8N-12 CIDCO, 8 km railway, 9 km airport, T0240 2381106, trhgm.aug@tajgroup.sprintrpg.ems.vsnl.in. 40 large rooms, quiet swimming, excellent service, imposing building in lovely gardens, on outskirts, beautiful gardens, difficult for the disabled (no lift, some rooms on 1st floor, reception and restaurant on ground floor).

**A Ambassador Ajanta**, Airport Rd, Chikalthana, 4 km centre, T0240 2485211, amauabad@bom4.vsnl.net.in. 92 rooms, excellent food (can watch chef preparing meal), excellent pool in pleasant gardens (non-residents, Rs 300), squash, tennis, quiet, good service, generous discount for single occupancy. Recommended.

**A Rama International** (Welcomgroup), Airport Rd, R 3 Chikalthana, 4 km centre, T0240 2485411, ramaintl@bom4.vsnl.net.in. 90 rooms, central a/c, restaurant (variable), quiet, large gardens, pool.

**A-B President Park**, Airport Rd, T0240 2486201, hpp@bom4.vsnl.net.in. Impressive newer hotel, large grounds, environment friendly, 60 a/c rooms focusing around attractive large pool (non-residents, Rs 150), excellent vegetarian food, tennis.

**B Aurangabad Ashok** (ITDC), Dr Rajendra Prasad Marg, T0240 2332491, aubaashok@agd2.dot.net.in. 66 a/c rooms, pleasant restaurant, bar, good shops, small pool, reliable car hire and travel desk.

**B Khemi's Inn**, 11 Town Centre, CIDCO (4 km from town, first left after **Ambassador Ajanta**, then first right), T0240 2484868, khemis@vsnl.com. 10 spotless a/c rooms with hot bath, good home cooking, quiet, pleasant garden, has the feel of an English B&B, very hospitable.

**C-D Holiday Camp** (MTDC), Station Rd, T0240 2331513. 48 rooms (22 a/c) with bath and mosquito net, pleasant, busy, but poor restaurant, bar, Tourist office, checkout 0900.

**D-E Ajinkya**, east of Central Bus Stand, T0240 2335601. Ok rooms, some a/c.

**D-E Printravel**, Dr Ambedkar Rd, T0240 2352448, burzin1@vsnl.com. Old-fashioned but large clean rooms with bath, good *Patang* restaurant, very well run. Recommended.

**E Devpriya**, Circular building near Central Bus Stand Rd, Dr Ambedkar Rd, T339032. 62 OK rooms in family hotel (hot water in morning), restaurant, bar, travel desk, good value.

**E Shree Maya**, Bharuka Complex, behind Tourist Office, Padampura Rd, T0240 2333093, shrimaya@bom4.vsnl.net.in. 23 modern, clean, rooms with hot shower, 8 a/c, restaurant, will arrange bus tickets, 24-hr check out, mixed reports about management.

**E-F Railway Retiring Rooms**, T0240 2331015. 3 rooms (1 a/c), 4-bedded dorm.

**F Panchavati**, off Station Rd, Padampura, T0240 2328755. 25 clean simple rooms with bath, good restaurant/bar, friendly, good value.

**F Tourist Home**, Station Rd, T0240 2337212. 26 rooms with bath (Rs 150), friendly, meals.

**F Youth Hostel**, Station Rd, Padampura, T0240 2334892. 3 rooms, 40 beds in good segregated dorms (Rs 45), clean, well run, breakfast/evening meals (gates locked early so you may need to climb over!), very good value, recommended, reservations: a week's notice Aug-Feb with a day's payment.

**Ellora** *p1118*

**C-E Kailas**, near the bus stand, T02437 241043, www.kailas.com. 25 decent rooms in group of 'cottages', best a/c face the caves, dorm in annexe, restaurant, very pleasant garden, good service.

**E-F Rock Art Gallery**, T02437 244552. 9 very simple, rooms, 'art' including copies of murals.

**Ajanta** *p1123*

**C-F Holiday Resort** (MTDC), in Fardapur, 5 km from Ajanta caves, T/F02438 24230. 12 basic rooms with bath (mosquito net vital, not provided), 16 a/c rooms in gardens are better value, dorm (mattress only, Rs 100), restaurant.

**D Travellers' Lodge** (MTDC), T02438 24226. Has 4 clean rooms , chilled beer.

**D-E Resort Extension**, in Fardapur, T02438 24289. 12 rooms and dorm.

**Jalgaon** *p1127*

**D-E Tourist Resort**, Nehru Chowk, Station Rd, T0257 2225192. 26 clean spacious rooms with bath, 4 a/c, some have TV.

**E Plaza**, 241 Navi Peth, Station Rd, T0257 2227354. 10 air-cooled rooms with bath and TV, very clean, hot water in bucket, very helpful and friendly manager. Highly recommended.

**Lonar** *p1128*

**E-F** simple, clean places to stay.

**Nanded** *p1128*

**D-E Ashiana Park**, opposite Kala Mandir, off Doctor's Lane, near bus stand, T02462-236412. 21 good rooms, young enthusiastic manager, friendly, good value for a night halt.

**Paithan** *p1128*

**C-D Goradia**, off Pimpalwadi Rd, T02766-255257. 80 a/c rooms, Indian restaurant.

**D Sai Leela**, 9/5 Pimpalwadi Rd, near Temple, T02766-255139. 72 rooms, some a/c, restaurant, pool.

**D-E Pilgrim's Inn** (MTDC), near Sai Baba Shrine, T02766-255194. 50 rooms (10 a/c), Indian restaurant.

**E Lakeview Resort**, at Jayakwadi, by the dam, has 13 rooms, restaurant, beer.

**Ahmadnagar** *p1128*

**D Sanket**, Tilak Path, Station Rd, T/F358701. 30 rooms, some a/c, restaurant.

**E-F Swastik**, Station Rd, 1 km from station, T357575. 25 rooms.

*For an explanation of the sleeping and eating price codes used in this guide, see inside the front cover. Other relevant information is found in Essentials pages 56-61.*

## Eating

**Aurangabad** *p1115, map p1116*
ŸŸŸ **Ambassador**, ITDC, in hotel. Good Indian and Western.
ŸŸŸ **Ashok**, ITDC, in hotel.
ŸŸŸ **President Park**. International. Restaurant and coffee shop offer a varied choice of vegetarian dishes.
ŸŸ **Angeethi**, next to *Jet Airways*, Jalna Rd, T0240 2441988. Excellent Marathi specialities, book ahead.
ŸŸ **Chanakya**, Station Rd. North Indian. Fashionable, a/c, well-prepared, part outdoors, bar.
ŸŸ **Foodwalla's Tandoori**, 500 m from Holiday Camp. Indian. A/c, tender chicken preparations, popular, good value, bar.
ŸŸ **Mastercook**, at **Hotel Mayur**, Jalna Rd, is popular locally.
ŸŸ **Mingling**, at **Hotel Rajdoot**, JL Nehru Marg. Chinese.
ŸŸ **Palace**, Shahgunj, Indian (Mughlai).
Ÿ **Bhoj**, Ambedkar Marg (above **Manas Hotel**) near Central Bus Stand. Excellent vegetarian food. Friendly (arrive at 1845 to listen to *puja* in the kitchen with chanting and cymbals).
Ÿ **Guru**, Station Rd. Punjabi.
Ÿ **Youth Hostel**, best value *thalis*.

**Jalgaon** *p1127*
**Anjali** by the station, great spicy *thalis*.
**Bombay**, opposite, excellent food, well-stocked bar.
**Shreyas**, 201 Navi Peth. Inexpensive South Indian vegetarian. Good bakery and ice cream shop on Station Rd.

**Nanded** *p1128*
**Gujarati Bhoj Nalya** (sign in Hindi – look for *High Class Veg Lunch Home*), near bus stand. Excellent food in unlikely looking *dhaba*.

**Ahmadnagar** *p1128*
**Panchratna**, Shivaji Chowk, T02438 2359202. Cheap Indian and Continental cuisine.

## Festivals and events

**Aurangabad** *p1115, map p1116*
**Feb/Mar**: Mahashivratri, large fair at Ghrishneshwara Temple, near Ellora and Ellora Yatra.

## Shopping

**Aurangabad** *p1115, map p1116*
Shops usually open 1000-2000, closed Sun. The city is known for its handwoven Himroo shawls (brocades occasionally with Ajanta motifs), and special textile weaves - *Mashru*, *Patihani silk* and *Kinkhab* as well as artificial silk. You can also get good decorative lacquer work, Bidriware and agate articles. Main shopping areas are City Chowk, Gulmandi, Nawabpura, Station Rd, Shahganj, Sarafa, Mondha.
In Shahganj, **Cottage Industries**.
On Station Rd, **Silk Loom Fabrics** and **Govt. Emporium**, opposite Holiday Resort.
At Zaffar Gate, Mondha Rd is **Aurangabad Himroo Industry**, a factory showroom producing beautiful Ajanta patterns in silk, the young English speaking owner is very informative, recommended.

## Activities and tours

**Aurangabad** *p1115, map p1116*
**Tours**
**Ashoka Travels**, Station Rd, T0240 2320816, Mr Karolkar arranges hotels, cars and excursions, charges fairly and is dependable.
**Classic**, TRC Building, Station Rd, T0240 2337788, classictours@vsnl.com, and at **Ambassador Ajanta**. Helpful and efficient; car hire, ticketing, hotels, Ajanta/Ellora and city tour, Rs 200/150 per person.
**MTDC** (and others) operate good sightseeing to Ajanta, Ellora and the City. Ajanta tour highly recommended. Daulatabad and Ellora visits too many places. From MTDC **Holiday Camp** (pick-up from major hotels) and then **Central Bus Stand** (about 45 mins later): Ellora (closed Tue) and City, 0800-1700, Rs 150; Ajanta (closed Mon) 0800-1700, Rs 200; book at Window 1 (behind book stall) at Bus Stand – check timing. From **MTDC**. See also Directory.

**Swimming**
Some top hotels open their pools to non-residents for a fee, eg **Ambassador Ajanta**, Rs 250 (includes other sporting facilities), **Aurangabad Ashok**, Rs 125; **President Park**, Rs 125; and **Vedant** (Quality Inn), Station Rd, T350701, Rs 150.

## Transport

**Aurangabad** *p1115, map p1116*

**Air**

The airport is 10 km from city centre. Transport to town: Taxi, Rs 150 (Rs 300 through travel agents); **Indian Airlines**, near Rama International, Airport Rd, T485421, 1000-1700, Sun closed. Airport, T482111; daily flights to **Delhi** and **Mumbai.** Jet Airways, 4 Vidya Nagar, Jalna Rd, T441770. 0900-1800. Airport T484269. 1830-2130. Daily flight to **Mumbai.**

**Bicycle**

Bicycle hire: ('cycle taxi') from shops near railway station and Central Bus Stand (CBS). Rs 20 per day.

**Bus**

**Local** Services to **Daulatabad**, and **Ellora** (45 mins) from platform 7; **Ajanta** from platform 8 (3 hrs), **Jalgaon** (4½ hrs, **Fardapur** etc) from CBS. Also services to **Bangalore**, **Hubli**, **Hyderabad**, **Indore**, **Nashik** and **Pune**.

**Long distance** MRTC operates a/c luxury coaches to **Mumbai** (388 km) 10 hrs from CBS (Central Bus Stand), Dr Ambedkar Rd, Rs 200. To **Pune**, **Whilfood Tours** (T477844) bus depart 0730, Rs 100. Others, to **Bidar**, **Bijapur**, **Hyderabad**, **Indore**, **Nagpur** and **Nashik** (3 hrs), **Solapur** (8-9 hrs).

**Car**

Car hire: Rs 850 per day (Rs 1050, a/c) from Aurangabad Transport Syndicate, Hotel Rama International, T0240 2486766.

**Rickshaw**

Auto-rickshaw: Insist on using meter, about Rs 5 per km. Day hire to visit Daulatabad and Ellora Rs 350 from bus station.

**Taxi**

Rates Rs 350 for 4 hrs, 40 km. Rs 650 for 8 hrs, 80 km.

**Train**

Beware of touts at the station offering package tours to Ellora and Ajanta. Easier by local bus. **Mumbai**: *Devgiri Exp, 1004*, 2320, 8½ hrs; *Tapovan Exp, 7618*, 1440, 8¼ hrs. **Secunderabad (Hyderabad)**: *Kacheguda Exp 7663*, 1930, 13½ hrs. For **Delhi**: change at **Manmad**. From Aurangabad: 0627, 1010, 1440, 2105, 2-2½ hrs; from Manmad: *Punjab Mail, 2137*, 0020, 20 hrs; *Goa Exp, 2779*, 1010, 20½ hrs (HN); *Karnataka Exp, 2627*, 1550, 20¼ hrs; *Lakshadweep Exp, 2617*, 1900, 21 hrs (HN); *Jhelum Exp, 1077*, 2355, 21½ hrs;

**Ajanta** *p1123*

**Bus**

Regular buses from Fardapur (5 km from Ajanta Caves) to **Ellora** and **Aurangabad** (3 hrs), and **Jalgaon** (1½ hrs). Some buses also go direct from the caves to Aurangabad.

**Taxi/rickshaw**

Taxis and auto-rickshaws can be hired for the day for visiting the sights.

**Train**

The caves can also be visited from Jalgaon 59 km, which has the nearest railway station. *Gitanjali Exp* (convenient from Kolkata) does not stop at Jalgaon so best to get off at Bhusawal.

**Daulatabad** *p1117*

Buses from Aurangabad's Central bus stand (platform 8), not all Ellora buses stop here.

**Jalgaon** *p1127*

**Bus**

**Local** The bus stand is about 1 km from the railway; auto-rickshaws Rs 8-10 for transfer.

**Long distance** Direct buses to **Ajanta** from Bus Stand, 0815, 1030. Private buses from Station Rd for **Aurangabad**, **Indore**, **Hyderabad**, **Nagpur**, **Pune**, most between 2100-2200. Some via **Fardapur** (1½ hrs), go to Ajanta before continuing to Aurangabad (1st dep 0700, 4 hrs, Rs 50); pleasant, interesting journey.

**Train**

**Mumbai (CST)**: *Punjab Mail*, 2138, 2350, 7¾ hrs; *Kushinagar Vidarbha Exp*, 1016, 2205, 7¾ hrs. **Delhi** via **Bhopal** and **Agra**: *Punjab Mail*, 2137, 0215, 18 hrs.

**Jalna** *p1128*

Regular buses from Lonar (2 hrs), Aurangabad (2 hrs) and Nanded (5 hrs), Aurangabad trains daily at 0510, 0828, 1259 and 2010, 1-1½ hrs, Mumbai trains *Devgiri*

*Exp*, 1004, 2010, 9½ hrs; *Tapovan Exp 7618*, 1259, 10 hrs, Secunderabad *Kacheguda Exp 7663*, 2020, 11¾ hrs,

**Lonar** *p1128*
By bus from **Jalna** (75 km, 2 hrs), **Jintur** (50 km, 1½ hrs); **Ajanta/Fardapur** (137 km) via **Buldana** and **Mehkar** (total 5 hrs).

**Nanded** *p1128*
**Bus**
Connections to many destinations. Several agents by bus stand for private buses.

**Train**
**Aurangabad**: Mumbai trains and *Mudkhed Manmad Exp, 7688*, 0510, 5 hrs. **Bangalore**: *Link Exp, 6591A*, 0600, 24½ hrs. **Mumbai (CST)**: *Tapovan Exp, 7618*, 1015, 12½ hrs; *Devgiri Exp, 1004*, 1715, 12½ hrs. **New Delhi**: *Sachkhand Exp, 2715*, 0830 (not Mon, Thu), 29 hrs (onto **Amritsar**, 37¼ hrs).

**Ahmadnagar** *p1128*
**Bus**
Regular buses to **Mumbai**, **Pune** and other towns in the state.

**Train**
**Bangalore**: *Karnataka Exp 2628*, 1820, 19½ hrs. **Bhopal**: *Goa Exp 2779*, 0703, 12 ½ hrs; *Jhelum Exp 1077*, 2040, 12½ hrs (on to **New Delhi**, 24¾ hrs). **Pune**: *Jhelum Exp 1078*, 1200, 4 hrs; *Goa Exp 2480*, 1300, 4½ hrs (on to **Vasco de Gama (Goa)**, 18¾ hrs).

## Directory

**Aurangabad** *p1115, map p1116*
**Banks** State Bank of India, Kranti Chowk, Rajendra Prasad Marg (Adalat Rd), junction of Paithan Darwaza Rd, set back from Rd, deals in foreign currency.
**Hospitals** Medical College Hospital, T0240 224411, northwest of town; Govt Hospital, Shahganj. **Post** GPO: Juna Bazar Chowk. Cantt Post Office. **Tourist** offices Govt of India, Krishna Vilas, Station Rd, T0240 2331217. Open 0830-1830 weekdays, 0830-1330 Sat. Airport Counter open at flight times; MTDC, Holiday Resort, Station Rd, T0240 2331513. 0700-2100. Very helpful with practical information. Also more helpful officer at railway station, 0430-0830, 1100-1600, Tue-Sun 0900-1600.

# Southern Maharashtra

## Pune

→ *Phone code: 020. Colour map 5, grid B3. Population: 2.54 mn.*

After the small towns and seemingly endless spaces of the Deccan plateau, Pune comes as a vibrant surprise. Touched by the élan of Mumbai, within commuting distance down the ghat, the town comes to life in the early evening with open-air cafés and pavements crowded with young people out to enjoy themselves in a modern, cosmopolitan atmosphere, a place to see and be seen. It is an important and respected university town and one of the fastest growing IT centres of India, whilst the Osho Commune continues to attract large numbers of westerners seeking spiritual growth. ▸▸ *For Sleeping, Eating and other listings, see pages 1142-1148.*

*The climatic contrast between Pune and the ghats just 70 km away is astonishing. The monsoon winds of Jun-Sep drop most of their rain on the ghats, over 3,500 mm a year to Pune's 715 mm.*

### Ins and outs

**Getting there** The airport, 10 km to the northeast, has flights from major cities. There are airport buses, taxis and rickshaws to the centre. Pune is on the main railway line south from Mumbai and is served by frequent buses. Buses from the north terminate largely at Sivaji Nagar Bus Stand to the northwest of town, and those from the south at Swargate, 3 km to the south. Railway Bus Stand, north of the centre, serving the city and Mumbai, is within walking distance of hotels, restaurants and the MG Rd shops. Another cluster of hotels and popular restaurants are in the Deccan Gymkhana area to the west.

**Getting around** Pune is very spread out so it is best to hire an auto-rickshaw to get around. The museums and the Osho Commune are a long walk from the hotel areas.

▸▸ *See Transport, page 1146, for further details.*

## Background

The early home of Sivaji, Pune became the Maratha capital in 1750. After a period under the **Nizam of Hyderabad**'s rule it came under British control in 1817, who then developed it as a summer capital for Mumbai and as a military cantonment. It is now a major growth centre with a booming computer software industry.

For all its connections with the Marathas there are few physical reminders of their power. The Campsite has wide streets with a British colonial feel while old Pune still has narrow streets, old shops and brick and mud houses. The town is renowned for its military cantonment and educational and scientific institutions.

## Sights

The city stands on the right bank of the Mutha River before its confluence with the Mula and was divided up into 19 peths (wards). Some were named after the days of their weekly market, others after well-known people.

Near the railway station is the English Gothic style **Sassoon Hospital** (1867). Nearby is the Collectorate and the old Treasury. To the southwest is the **Oleh David Synagogue** (1867), sometimes known locally as the 'Red Mandir', and Sir David Sassoon's Tomb. **St Mary's Church** (1825) to the south was consecrated by Bishop Heber, who toured the country extensively in the 1830s. St Patrick's Cathedral is beyond the Racecourse. Immediately north are the **Empress Gardens**.

Moving back to the west by the river are **Visram Bagh**, a very attractive Maratha Palace. Now used to house Govt offices and a post office, the entrance and balcony have beautifully carved woodwork. Opposite is **Raja Kelkar Museum** ⓘ *1378 Shukrawar Peth, closed 26 Jan and 15 Aug, 0830-1800, foreigners Rs 120, Indians Rs 10, worth a visit*, with a private collection focusing on traditional Indian arts including carved temple doors, musical instruments, pottery, miniature paintings, nutcrackers, brass padlocks and lamps. The vast collection can only be displayed in rotation. **Shaniwar Wada Palace** (1736) ⓘ *0830-1800, US$2 foreigners, Rs 5 Indians*, built by Baji Rao, the last Peshwa's grandfather, was burnt down in 1827. Only the massive outer walls remain. The main entrance is by the iron-spiked Delhi Gate. Elephants were used for crushing people to death in the nearby street. The gardens were irrigated and contained the **Hazari Karanje** (thousand jet fountain) – in fact there were only 197 jets.

## Deccan Gymkhana area

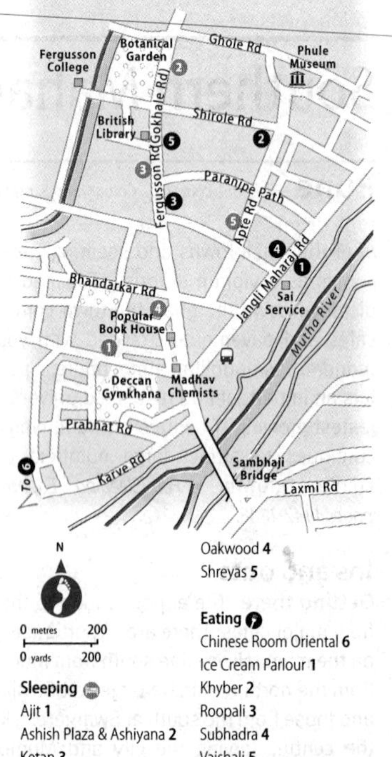


**Sleeping**
Ajit 1
Ashish Plaza & Ashiyana 2
Ketan 3
Oakwood 4
Shreyas 5

**Eating**
Chinese Room Oriental 6
Ice Cream Parlour 1
Khyber 2
Roopali 3
Subhadra 4
Vaishali 5

Cross the river by **Sivaji** (Lloyd) **Bridge** into Sivaji Road. Along this are the Pataleshwar Temple and the Military College (1922) – a 9-m high statue of Sivaji (sculpted by VP Karkomar), stands in front. **Sangam** (Wellesley) **Bridge** (1875) is near the confluence of the rivers. **Garden Reach** (1862-1864), 300 m beyond, is the family house of the influential Sassoon family. The main road then passes the **Institute of Tropical Meteorology** and the white domed Observatory.

**Raj Bhavan** (Government House, 1866) designed by James Trubshawe is in Ganeshkhind. Nearby is the impressive main building of the **University** of Poona in a sprawling campus. Three kilometres north, in Aundha Road, are the **Botanical Gardens**. From here on the way to Holkar's Bridge is **All Saints Church** (1841), which contains the regimental colours of the 23rd Bombay Light Infantry. One kilometre to the southeast is the Roman Catholic **Chapel of St Ignatius**. Cross the river by the Holkar's Bridge to the **Tomb of Vithoji Holkar**, trampled by an elephant in 1802, and the adjacent Mahadeo Temple built in his memory. Sir Henry St Clair Wilkins designed the **Deccan College** (1864).

To the east, on Ahmednagar Road, is the former **Palace of the Aga Khan** (1860) who was attracted to Pune by the horse racing. Mahatma Gandhi was placed under house arrest here and his wife Kasturba died here. The small **Gandhi National Memorial** ⓘ *0900-1745, Rs 2*, museum with personal memorabilia is worth a visit. Kasturba Gandhi's memorial tomb (*samadhi*) is on the estate. South of the Bund Garden (Fitzgerald) Bridge are the riverside **Bund Gardens**, a popular place for an evening stroll. Further south still is the **Tribal Museum** ⓘ *1000-1700, free*, an excellent, small museum of items relating to Maharashtra's tribal heritage, research encouraged. The 12 sections include domestic life (utensils, ornaments, musical instruments and house patterns), agriculture, weapons and wood carving.

Pune is home to the **Osho Commune International** (formerly 'Rajneesh Ashram') ⓘ *www.osho.com, tours Rs 10 (1-hr part tour, part video; 1030, 1430; booking 0930-1300, 1400-1600), other visitors are screened for HIV (recent certificate or blood test Rs 150-300); day pass, US$3.25, including meditation, entertainment, discussions, courses cost from US$1,000 per month*, in Koregaon Park, originally set

## Pune centre

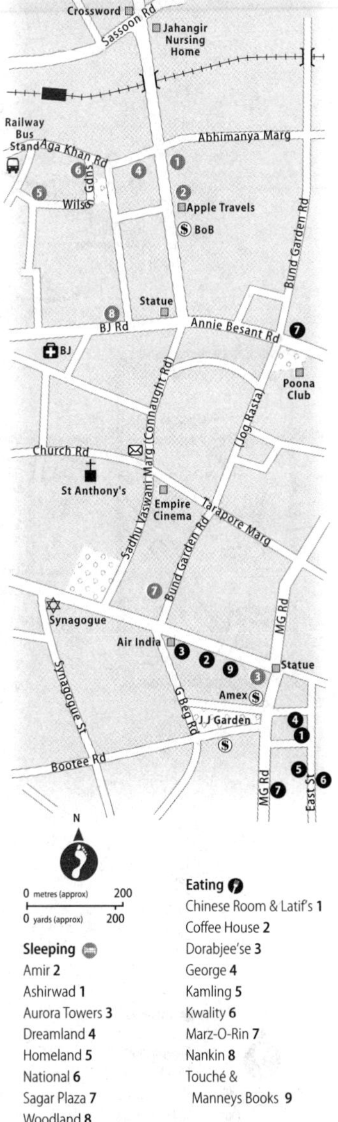

up by the controversial Bhagwan Rajneesh (Osho). Rajneesh died in 1990. The lushly landscaped 24-acre commune offers numerous programmes with an emphasis on meditation. The commune has gone to great lengths to convert a former rubbish tip in

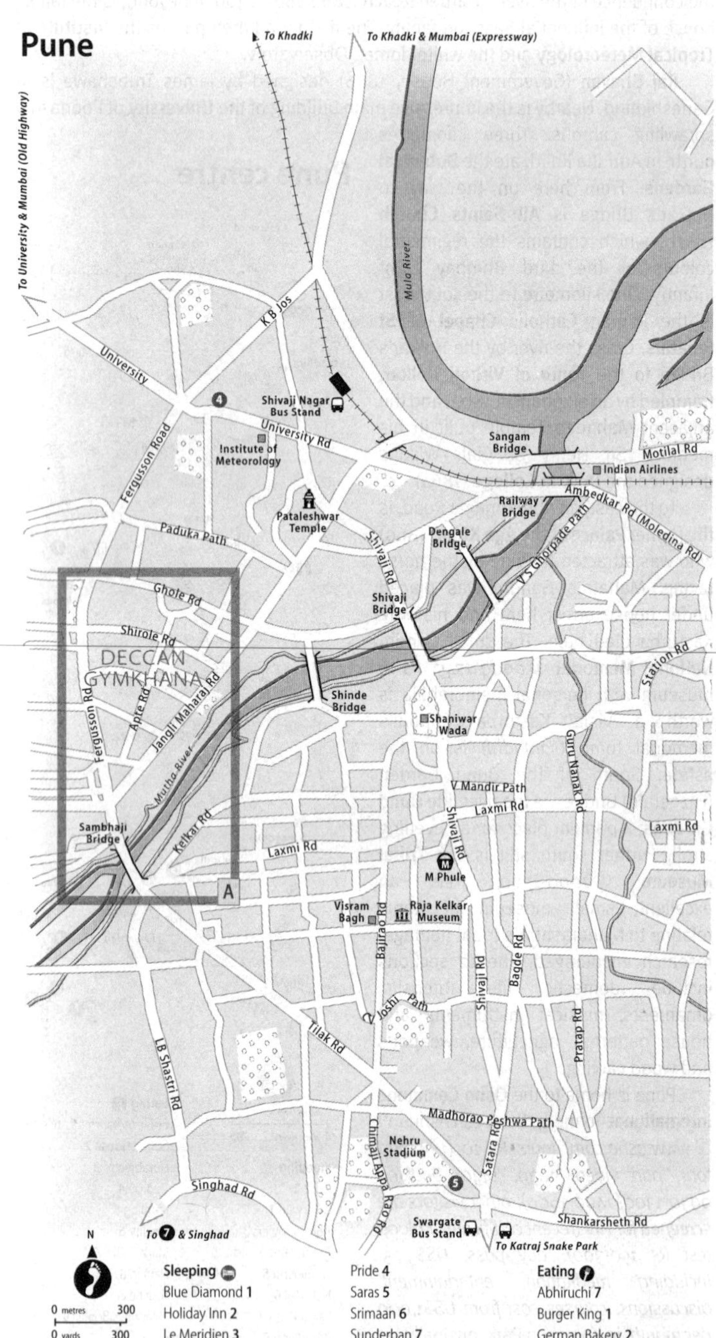

next door Koregaon Park into a beautifully maintained and landscaped garden, the Shunyo Park. Critics point out that "the inmates claim they follow no God, have no temple nor ritual, and are all individuals, yet, they worship the Bhagwan, meet in the

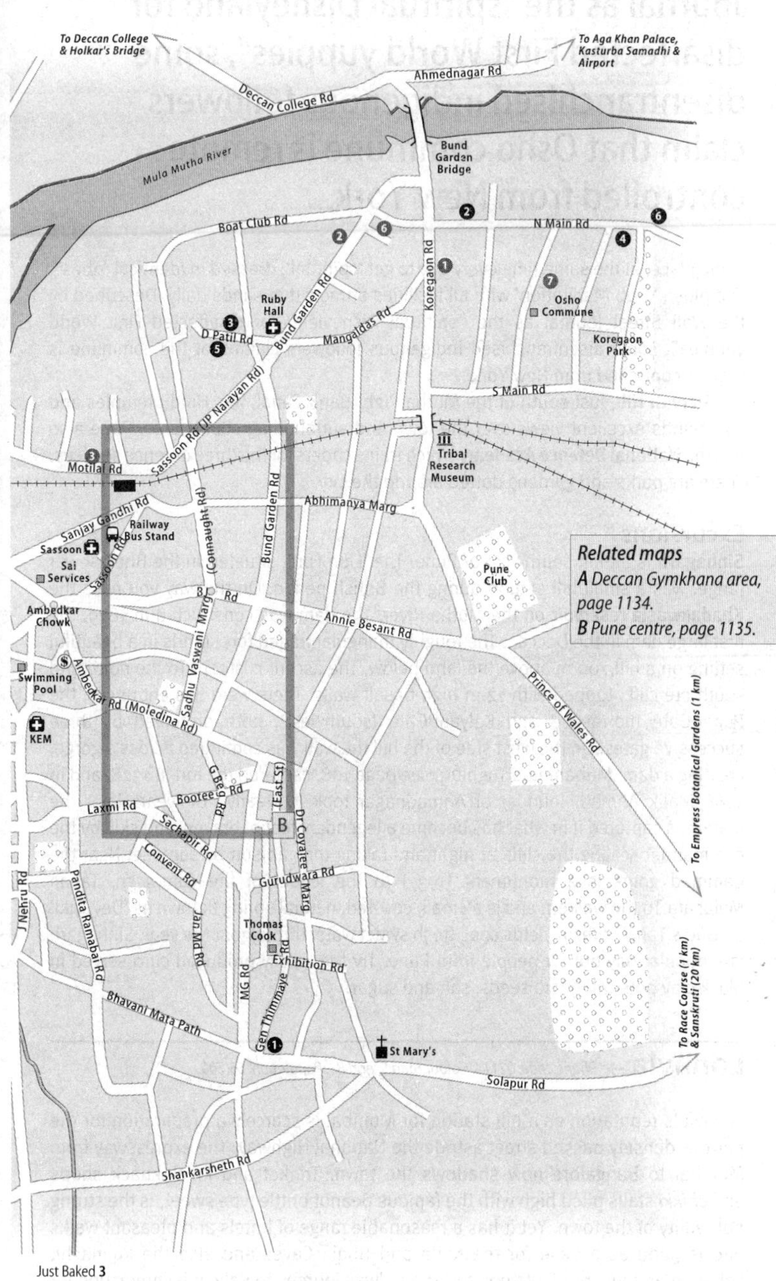


Just Baked **3**
Sangamitra **4**
Tamarind Court **6**
Zamu's Place **5**

“” Described by the Wall Street Journal as the “spiritual Disneyland for disaffected First World yuppies”, some disenfranchised indigenous followers claim that Osho commune is remote-controlled from New York...

same place, at the same time every day to get ‘spiritual’, dressed in identical robes”. The plush ‘Club Meditation’ with all facilities attracts thousands daily. Described by the Wall Street Journal as the “spiritual Disneyland for disaffected First World yuppies”, some disenfranchised indigenous followers claim that the commune is remote-controlled from New York!

**Parvati Hill**, just south of the Mutha Right Bank Canal, has Hindu temples and commands excellent views over the town and surrounding countryside. Pune also has the **National Defence Academy** which trains cadets for the three defence services. There are parks and gardens dotted around the city.

### Excursions

**Sinhagarh** is 24 km southwest of Pune. The ‘Lion Fort’, situated in the Bhuleshwar range, was a small hill station during the British period. On the way you pass the **Khadakwasla reservoir** on the Mutha River. The dam was constructed in 1879, the first large dam in the Deccan. The roughly triangular ruined **fort** stands in a beautiful setting on a hill 700 m above the land below. The ascent is steep. To the north and south are cliffs topped with 12-m high basalt walls. There were two entrances, the Pune Gate (northeast) and Kalyan Gate (southwest), both protected by three successive gates. On the west side of the hill the wall was continued across a gorge, creating a dam. Muhammad Tughluq, see page 108, captured the fort in 1328, and in 1486 Malik Ahmad, founder of Ahmadnagar took it. Nearly 200 years later the Marathas captured it in what has become a legendary feat of bravery and skill by the commander scaling the cliffs at night and taking the garrison by surprise. Near the dammed gorge is a monument (1937) to the leader of the campaign, Tanaji Malusara.To the western end is a small, covered, natural spring (known as ‘Dev Taki’ or ‘God’s Tank’), which yields cool, fresh sweet water throughout the year. Sinhagarh is a popular day out for people from Pune. Try the locally produced curd served in black clay pots with jeera seeds, salt and sugar.



## Lonavla → *Phone code: 02114. Colour map 5, grid B3. Population: 55,700.*

Lonavla’s reputation as a hill station for Mumbai is scarcely a preparation for the narrow, densely packed street astride the National Highway. The expressway from Mumbai to Bangalore now shadows the town. Trinket and knick-knack shops and *chikki* stalls piled high with the famous peanut brittle type sweet, is the strung out reality of the town. Yet it has a reasonable range of hotels and pleasant walks and is good as a base for the Karla and Bhaja Caves and also the Rajmachi, Lohagon and Visapur Forts nearby. The railway journey to Kalyan is interesting for rail enthusiasts.

## Sights

The town has some lovely walks around and about. **Ryewood Park** is within a few minutes' reach along Ryewood Road. Further along the same road, 1½ km from the Bazar, the scenic **Monsoon Lake** with a small island and its temple has a kilometre long dam which gives a good bird's eye view. A further 2 km along INS Shivaji Road leads to **Bushy Dam** which attracts crowds who come to soak themselves on monsoon weekends. **Old Khandala Road** which joins the highway near **Fariyas Hotel** was once the main approach to Lonavla. Now it is pleasantly quiet, lined with stately bungalows and is good for an evening stroll. **Tungarli Dam**, a disused water reservoir on a hill, is near **Lion's Den Hotel** and can be reached by taking the left turn from the highway petrol pump near **Jewel Resort**. Clean public toilets are at the start of Ryewood Road (market end). Pleasant circuits around town start at Lonavla Bazar.

## Excursions

**Ambavane Lake** ⓘ *ST buses to Ambavane village (depart 0915, 1200, 1630, 1815) take 90 mins then walk 1 km beyond 'Sahara', cars, about Rs 500 for half day trip*, is a quiet, small lake ideal for swimming and camping by. It lies at the end of a mud track beyond the Sahara Housing Project; best Nov-Feb but nights can be chilly. The drive there during the monsoon is scenic (but the lake is empty!). You will need to carry all provisions and equipment. **Khandala**, a quiet village overlooking a great ravine from which the Konkan region south of Mumbai can be seen.

# Karla and Bhaja caves → *Phone code: 02114.*

## Karla caves

ⓘ *US$2 foreigners, Rs 5 Indians.*

This is the largest and best preserved Buddhist *chaitya* (chapel) cave in India, dating from the second to first century BC. Here, as at Bhaja, the stone mason imitated the earlier wooden structures; the main *chaitya* shows evidence of stone supporting a wooden gallery. Unlike Ajanta and Ellora it is off the beaten tourist track for foreigners, though it can be crowded with local tourists at weekends.

The approach is across an excavated court. At the massive entrance stands a stone column topped with four lions (*sinha stambha*). The Hindu temple just outside the entrance may have been built over the remains of a second pillar. The façade contains a large horseshoe shaped window above the three doorways (one for the priest and the other two for pilgrims). In front of the side doors were shallow water-filled troughs through which the pilgrims walked to cleanse their feet. The remarkable sun window diffused the light into the hall, falling gently onto the stupa at the end. Buddha images (circa fifth century) partly decorate the exterior. There are also panels between the doorways depicting six pairs of donors.

The main chamber (38 m by 14 m), entered through a large outer porch, is supported by 37 pillars. It is 8 m from floor to ceiling which is barrel vaulted and ribbed with teak beams. There are 15 octagonal columns along either side, each capital having kneeling elephants carrying an embracing couple carved on it. The stupa is similar to that in Cave No 10 at Ellora but here is topped by a wooden umbrella which is carved with delicate patterns. The other caves to the right of the entrance are of little interest.

## Bhaja caves

There are 18 caves dating from the second century BC. You will need to climb about 170 steps. **Cave No 12** is the best and possibly the first apsidal *chaitya* (a long hall with a semi-circular end) in India. The apse contains a *dagoba*. The vaulted roof of the chapel is supported by 27 columns. The exterior was once covered in a bas-relief, much of this has now been defaced. On either side of the main cave are others which were probably nuns' cells and working quarters. The inner sanctum of the last cave to the south has very fine sculptures, including the 'Dancing Couple'; you will need to tip the caretaker to open the door (surprisingly only the central cell echoes). To the south are 14 *stupas*, five of which are inside the cave.

The ruined **Lohagen Fort** is about 4 km beyond Bhaja and was twice taken and lost by Sivaji. **Visapur Fort**, which stands 600 m from the foot of the hill, is nearby. You can see them from the Bhaja caves.

## South of Pune

### Raigad (Raigarh) → *Colour map 5, grid B3.*

ⓘ *Rs 5, foreigners US$ 2, cable car (Rs 100) avoids the 6-km walk up but power failures can cause delays, look for signs for 'Ropeway' leading to a right turn before reaching the end of the paved road and be prepared for a scary ride in a 'cage'.*

The views from the three-pronged hilltop fort are magnificent, especially the stunningly beautiful panorama across the lakes to the north. Difficult to reach, the fort is rarely visited by foreigners though there are plenty of Indian tourists since Sivaji is perhaps the greatest Maratha hero. Raigad dates from around the 12th century. Known as 'Rairi' it was the seat of a Maratha chief. Later it passed in turn to the Vijayanagaras, the Nizam of Ahmadnagar, the Bijapuri Adil Shahis until Sivaji regained it in 1648 and made it the home of his much-revered mother, Jiji Bai. In 1674 he chose it for his coronation at the hands of Brahmin priests but died here in 1680. Aurangzeb acquired it in 1690 but it soon reverted back to the Marathas who surrendered it to the British in 1818. The single path climbs 1,400 steps from its start at **Wadi**. The flat hilltop is about 2,500 m long and 1,500 m across at the widest. A bastioned wall encloses it while two outer curtain walls contour round the hillsides. Heavily fortified in each corner of the irregular triangle, in Sivaji's day the fort was one of the strongest in India. The main gate (Maha Darwaza) is flanked by two large bastions, both 21 m high, one concave, the other convex. Inside the fort, the extensive **Palace** and **Queen's Chamber** are placed between two tanks. In the courtyard is a low platform where the throne stood and after the coronation the title *Chhatrapati* – Lord of the Umbrella was bestowed on Sivaji. In the centre of the town was a market which had more than 40 shops in two parallel rows for the 2,000 people housed in the fort. To the northeast is Sivaji's **Samadhi** (memorial), as well as a *chhattri* for his dog. If you go up in the evening when the heat has died down, it is extremely atmospheric; a *dhoolie* can be hired.

*These Maratha forts south from Pune are best visited by hiring a car since bus journeys can be slow and tiring. The town was Sivaji's headquarters during the latter part of his reign.*

### Purandhar Fort

At an altitude of 1,220 m this fort commands a high point on the Western Ghats, 13 km diversion from the NH9. It is a double fort, the lower one, **Vajragad** to the east and **Purandhar** itself. Together they command a narrow passage through the hills. Like other hill forts, Purandhar was defended by curtain walls, in this case 42 km in extent, relieved by three gateways and six bastions. The earliest fortifications date from 1350.

### Wai

Wai stands on the left bank of the Krishna River where the riverside, lined with shady temples, is very attractive, particularly the finely carved *mandapam* in front of the Mahadev temple. Hills rise sharply around the town. On a hilltop is the fort of **Pandavgad**, which according to local tradition was visited by the Pandava brothers of the *Mahabharata*. The town's sanctity is enhanced by its proximity to the source of the Krishna.

## Satara

Satara lies in a hollow near the confluence of the Krishna and Venna rivers. It is considered a place of great sanctity and there are several temples on the banks at **Mahuli**. The cantonment contains Sir Bartle Frere's **Residency** (1820). A 'New Palace' (1838-44) was built by the engineer responsible for the bridges over the two rivers.

The ruling house of Satara was descended from Sahu, Sivaji's grandson, who was brought up at the Mughal court. Their **mansion**, 200 m from the New Palace, contains a number of Sivaji's weapons. These include the notorious 'tigers' claws (*waghnakh*) with which Sivaji is reputed to have disembowelled Afzal Khan. Other weapons include *Jai Bhavani*, his favourite sword (made in Genoa), and his rhinoceros hide shield. There is an **Historical Museum** (1930) which contains a fine collection of archival material on the Marathas. Satara Road railway station is 6 km from the city and bus stand.

**Wasota Fort** on the south side of the town can be reached by both road and footpath. Reputedly built by the Raja of Panhala in the 12th century, it's 14-m high walls (which remain only at the gateway) and buttresses contain the remains of the Rajah's Palace, a small temple and a bungalow. It passed to the Mughals under Aurangzeb, for a time, after he besieged the fort in 1699, but returned to the Marathas in 1705 with the help of a Brahmin agent who tricked the Mughals. Sleeping at *Monark*, Pune-Bangalore Rd, Powai Naka, T02162-2789, good restaurant, clean, though traffic noise.

## Kolhapur → *Phone code: 0231. Colour map 5, grid C4. Population: 485,200.*

Set in the wide open plains of the southern Deccan, Kolhapur, founded under the 10th-century Yadavas, was once one of the most important Maratha states. Sivaji's younger son inherited the southern regions of his father's kingdom, but after a history of bitter factional dispute it became an important Princely State under the British. Today it has the unlikely distinction of being at the heart of India's small wine producing region, and is also witnessing a flow of foreign investment, making it one of the major industrial centres of Maharashtra. The area has rich bauxite deposits and the damming of the Koyna, a tributary of the Krishna, is providing electricity for aluminium smelting.

The sacred **Panchganga River** skirts the north of the city, and ghats and temples, including the **Amba Bai** or Mahalaxmi Temple to the mother goddess, stand on its banks. It has 10th-century foundations, a tall pyramidal tower added in the 18th and an impressive carved ceiling to the pillared hall. **Note** Vishnu with the eight *Dikpalas*, see page 703. **Brahmapuri Hill** the Brahmin cremation ground, is in the west.

Much of Kolhapur's architecture can be attributed to the British army engineer Major Charles Mant. His **New Palace** (1881) belongs to the period when all the succession disputes had been resolved and Kolhapur was being governed as a model state. Built out of grey stone around a central courtyard dominated by a clocktower it contains elements from Jain temples and Deeg Palace. In 1871 he had also designed the **cenotaph** on the banks of the Arno River for Maharajah Rajaram, who died in Florence. Among his other buildings in the town are the **Town Hall** (1873), **General Library** (1875), **Albert Edward Hospital** (1878) and **High School** (1879).

Remnants of the pre-British period are found near the town centre. The **Rajwada** (Old Palace), which was badly damaged by fire in 1810, is entered through a traditional drum gallery or music hall (*nakkar khana*). Upstairs in the palace is the Durbar Hall and armoury which contains one of Aurangzeb's swords and other interesting memorabilia. The **Irwin Museum** has a bell taken from the Portuguese at Bassein in 1739. Near Brahmapuri Hill is the **Rani's Garden** where the royal family have memorial *chhattris*.

## Panhala

Panhala (977 m), 19 km northwest of Kolhapur, is where Rajah Bhoj II, whose territory extended to the Mahadeo Hills north of Satara, had his **fort**. However, it is particularly associated with Sivaji, who often stayed here. The Marathas and Mughals occupied it in turn until the British took it in 1844. The fort is triangular with a 7 km wall with three gates around it, in places rising to 9 m. The Tin Darwaza (three gates) leads to a central courtyard or 'killing chamber'; the inner gate leads to the Guard Room. The Wagh Gate (partly ruined) adopts similar principles of defence. Inside are vast granaries, the largest of which covers 950 sq m, has 11 m high walls and enabled Sivaji to withstand a five-month siege. By the ruins is a temple to Maruti, the Wind god. To the north is the two-storey Palace. See Sleeping for an overnight stop.

# Solapur and around

→ *Phone code: 0217. Colour map 5, grid B5.*

In the heart of the cotton growing area **Solapur** (Sholapur) has been a focus of the cotton trade for over a century. Almost entirely an industrial city it still has an atmospheric area with traditional old buildings along Navee Peth and Rajvadee Chowk.

From Solapur the main road to Pune follows the Bhima River northwest across the vast open fields and scattered settlements of the plateau. It is a region rich in archaeological sites, as it was a major centre of prehistoric settlement.

**Pandharpur**, on the south bank of the Bhima River, is regarded by many as the spiritual capital of Maharashtra. It has a shrine to Vithoba, an incarnation of Vishnu, dating from 1228. Although some tourist literature puts its origins as early as AD 83 there is no evidence for this early date. There are 12 bathing ghats on the river bank, and during the main pilgrimage season of July (Kartik Ekadashi Fair), tens of thousands of pilgrims converge on the town. *Rath Yatra*, or temple car procession, dates back to 1810.

## Sleeping

**Pune** *p1133, maps p1136, p1135 and p1134*
Cheap rooms are hard to find on arrival.
**AL Blue Diamond** (Taj), 11 Koregaon Rd, T020 26125555, www.tajhotels.com. 110 rooms, modern, comfortable, special discounts for business clients with partners.
**AL Holiday Inn**, 262 Bund Garden, T020 26137777, hip@holidayinnpune.com. 115 very comfortable rooms, good shops.
**AL Le Meridien**, RB Mill Rd, T020 26050505, meridien@pn2.vsnl.net.in. 176 rooms in Pune's latest luxury hotel, "feels like being inside a giant wedding cake".
**AL Pride**, 5 University Rd, Sivajinagar, T020 255345567, www.pridegroup.com. 111 rooms, clean, comfortable, good service, not the best pool but open to non-residents.
**A Sagar Plaza**, 1 Bund Garden Rd, T020 26122622, sparkplaza@wmi.co.in. 76 smallish but comfortable rooms, deluxe better, modern concrete and glass tower block, restaurants, exchange, small pool.
**A-B Aurora Towers**, 9 Moledina Rd, T020 26131818, hotelaurora@usa.net. 68 large rooms with views, good restaurants, friendly service, 24-hr exchange, terraced pool (non-residents Rs 100), good value.
**B Ashish Plaza**, 1198 Shivajinagar, FC Rd, T020 25336541, www.hotelashishplaza. com. 35 good rooms, some a/c, impressive reception though not efficient, overpriced.
**B Oakwood**, Good Luck Square, off FC Rd, T020 25670011, tghotels@hotmail.com. 41 comfortable rooms in plush business hotel, good service, airport transfer, internet.
**B-C Ashirwad**, 16 Connaught Rd, T020 26128585, F6126121. 44 good rooms, modern, neat, restaurant (good *thali*), exchange, helpful.
**B-C Srimaan**, 361/5 Bund Garden Rd, T020 26133535, www.littleitalyindia.com. 30 pleasant rooms, clean, Italian restaurant.
**B-C Woodland**, BJ Rd, T020 26126161, tghotels@hotmail.com. 102 well-kept pleasant rooms, most a/c, restaurant (Indian veg), airport transfer, busy, helpful.

**B-D Dreamland**, 2/14 Connaught Rd, T020 26122121. 43 rooms, some a/c, good veg *thalis*, well kept.
**B-D Sunderban**, 19 Koregaon Park, next to Osho Commune, T020 26124949 tghotels@hotmail.com. 58 rooms (rooms vary, wide range), restaurant planned (veg), exchange, gardens, everything spotless, serenaded by Osho meditations next door.
**C Ketan**, 917/19A Sivajinagar, FC Rd, T020 25655081. 28 rooms with bath, some spacious a/c, very clean, helpful.
**C-D Ashiyana**, FC Rd, T020 25332828, www.hotelashishplaza.com. Large, slightly dated, reasonable value.
**D Ajit**, 766/3 Deccan Gymkhana, T020 25671212. 16 rooms, some a/c (deposit requested), restaurant, small, dark but functional, peaceful location opposite Club.
**D Madhav**, 6a Tadiwala Rd, T020 26134219. Simple but friendly.
**D-E Homeland**, 18 Wilson Garden, T020 26127158, www.hotelhomeland.com. 22 rooms, clean but falling standards.
**E National**, 14 Sassoon Rd, T020 26125054. 27 rooms some with bath (quieter in 10 cottages), rooms in old building could be cleaner.
**E Saras**, Nehru Stadium, Swargate, T020 24430499, near bus station. 20 pleasant rooms, 1 a/c, restaurant, good value.

**Lonavla** *p1138*
Bombay-Pune Rd is NH4.
**L-AL Fariyas Holiday Resort**, Tungarli, Frichley Hills, T02114 273852. 103 luxurious rooms, some newer, solar heated pool, health club.
**A Duke's Retreat**, Mumbai-Pune Rd, 4 km Lonavla Railway in Khandala, T02114 273817. 62 rooms, restaurant, bar, lawns, pool, superb views.
**B Holiday Resort** (MTDC/private), Ryewood Park, T02114 273524. 22 rooms and cottages.
**B Lakeview Resort**, 4 Ryewood, T02114 272141. 22 airy, breezy rooms, very clean, excellent location overlooking lake.
**B Rainbow Retreat**, on NH4, opposite Valvan Dam (away from town), T02114 272128. 46 rooms, pricey bar, poolside disco at weekends, pleasant garden, modern.
**C Biji's Hill Retreat**, New Tungarli Rd, T02114 273025. 32 spacious rooms (round glass house with round bed!), restaurant, bar, pool.
**C Jewel Resort**, 80 Tungarli Dam Rd, T02114 270736. 32 rooms, 4 a/c, quiet, clean comfy, acceptable Indian restaurant, nice garden.
**C Rama Krishna**, NH4, near Bus Stand, T02114 273600. 45 very clean, comfortable rooms, new well-appointed, suites with tubs.
**C-D Chandralok**, Shivaji Rd, opposite Bus Stand entrance, T/F02114 272921. Large, clean, comfortable airy rooms, some a/c, excellent unlimited thalis (Rs 80-100).
**C-D Kadamba Sahyadri**, NH4 next to Valvan Dam turning, T02114 273234. Variety of clean rooms, best with a/c, geyser, others spartan, reasonable restaurant.
**C-D Lonavla Hotel**, NH4, near Bus Stand Lane, T02114 272914. 15 compact, very clean, refurbished rooms with good baths, some a/c, good non-veg restaurant.
**D-E Ahuja**, Victoria Cottage, off Ryewood Rd, T02114 272123. 18 very clean, comfortable rooms with bath (some 3-4 bedded), optional a/c, dining room, quiet area, modern guest house, very good value.
**E DT Shahani Health Home**, DT Shahani Rd, behind Bus Stand, T02114 272784. Very clean triples in quiet locality, varied menu in canteen.
**E Shamiana**, 66 Mumbai Pune Rd, opposite Bajrang Baug, T02114 272356. 7 cottage suites (2-4 beds) set in charming unkempt garden off the highway, nice but noisy, simple but comfortable (no mosquito nets), no food.

**Karla Caves** *p1139*
**C-E Holiday Camp** (MTDC), off Mumbai-Pune Rd (NH4), T02114 282230. 64 clean rooms in cottages for 2-4 (some comfortable a/c), canteen, bar, vast sylvan surroundings.
**E Peshwas Holiday Resort**, near Karla Caves. 15 rooms, restaurant.

**Kolhapur** *p1141*
**B-C Shalini Palace**, Rankala, A Ward, T0231 2620401. 41 rooms, some a/c, good value **D** rooms in extension at back, average food but good wine cellar, attractive gardens, built for Maharaja of Kohlapur in 1931 on the

*For an explanation of the sleeping and eating price codes used in this guide, see inside the front cover. Other relevant information is found in Essentials pages 56-61.*

lakeside (lots of mosquitors), real character, old furnishings but comfortable, out of town, very peaceful, sometimes have it to yourself, no exchange, tours arranged, auto-rickshaws at entrance.

**C Victor Palace**, Rukmini Nagar, Old Pune-Bangalore Rd, T0231 2662627. Modern a/c rooms, good restaurants, full facilities, excellent pool and gym, efficient and helpful, good value, central. Recommended.

**D Pearl**, New Sahupuri, T0231 2650451. 28 rooms, 20 a/c, restaurant, bar, garden.

**D Woodlands**, 204E Tarabai Park, T0231 2650941. 25 rooms, 8 a/c, restaurant, bar, garden, quiet.

**E Opal**, Pune-Bangalore Rd, T0231 2653622. 9 rooms with TV, restaurant (Maharashtrian).

**E-F Maharaja**, 514E Station Rd, opposite Bus Station, T0231 2650829. 26 rooms, some with bath, veg restaurant.

**Panhala** *p1142*

**D Mahalaxmi Resort** (MTDC/Private). 7 good rooms and an outdoor restaurant.

**D Valley View Grand**, has fabulous views from rooms and open air restaurant (very good food), and pretty gardens.

**Solapur** *p1142*

**D Pratham**, 560/61 South Sadar Bazar, T0231 2729581. 30 clean, modern, pleasant rooms, half a/c with bath, very good open-air restaurant, friendly and helpful staff.

**D Surya Executive**, 3/3/2 Murarji Peth, T0231 2729880, hotelsurya1@vsnl.com. Next door to **Surya International**. Good, clean excellent value, air-cooled rooms, restaurant.

**D Surya International**, 3/2/2 Murarji Peth, 200 m from bus stand, T0231 2729501. 32 rooms, 8 a/c, restaurant, ice cream parlour.

**E Srikamal**, 77 Rly Lines, T0231 722964. Newish clean rooms, hot shower, good terrace restaurant, run by very helpful, friendly family.

**F Railway Retiring Rooms** and dorm.

## Eating

**Pune** *p1133, maps p1136, p1135 and p1134*

**TTT Blue Diamond**, in hotel. China Town.

**TTT The Coffee Shop Plush**, in hotel. Good food, relaxing lunch stop, discourages informal dress (men in shorts).

**TTT Sangamitra**, North Main Rd, east of Osho. In hotel, Western. Attractive garden, candlelit in evenings, incredible lemon cheesecake, paté, tofu, homemade pasta.

**TT Abhiruchi**, Singhad Rd, 8 km outside of Pun. Rustic village style restaurant in 40 acres. Unlimited Maharashtrian *thali* (Rs 100) including 6 types of bread! More a day out than a lunch break. Recommended.

**TT Chinese Room**, Gen Thimmaya Rd. Chinese plus bar and ice creams.

**TT Chinese Room Oriental**, Continental Chambers, Karve Rd. Chinese, bar, ice cream.

**TT Garden Court**, NDA Rd, 5 km from Gymkhana. Excellent food and ambience overlooking the city. Recommended.

**TT Khyber**, 1258/2 JM Rd. Indian, some continental, beer bar and ice creams.

**TT Kwality's**, Gen Thimmaya Rd (East St). With bar.

**TT Latif's**, Gen Thimmaya Rd. Good for North Indian, chicken dishes recommended.

**TT Nanking**, opposite Pune Club, Bund Garden Rd.

**TT The Place, Touché the Sizzler**, Clover Centre, 7 Moledina Rd. 1130-1530, 1900-2100. Best sizzlers in town (the sizzler reputedly was invented by the present owner's father!). Also chicken platters, super ice creams (spotless toilets). Recommended.

**TT Sanskruti**, Solapur Highway (20 km). Similar to **Abhiruchi**. Palm reading, *mehndi*, *ghazal* singing, dancing, 16 item *thali* (Rs 120).

**TT Shriman**, near Osho Commune, North Main Rd. Italian. Recommended for tomato and mozzarella salad, great pizza, pasta, fresh bread, pleasant candlelit atmosphere.

**TT Tamarind Court**, 28/2 Koregaon Park, North Main Rd. Western, some Indian. Outdoor, set among huge shady trees.

**TT Zamu's Place**, Dhole Patil Rd. Western. Good sizzlers and Parsi dishes.

**T Kamling**, Gen Thimmaya Rd. Chinese.

**T Pune Coffee House**, 1256/2 Deccan Gymkhana. Large, live music.

**T Roopali**, FC Rd. Good for *thalis*, *dosas*.

**T Shabree**, Hotel Parichay, FC Rd. Unlimited Maharashtrian *thalis* (Rs 60), traditional.

**T Shri Krishna Palace**, Wilson Gardens, near railway station. Good value South Indian veg.

**T Vaishali**, FC Rd. South Indian. Starts early for breakfast, mainly snacks, their special SPDP (Shev Potato Dahi Puri) is a Pune institution, no one should leave town without trying it, very popular meeting place (queues in evenings for lovely rear garden), spotless. Highly recommended.

**Fast food**

**Coffee House**, 2 Moledina Rd. Good coffee and South Indian snacks.
**George**, 2436 Gen Thimmaya Rd. Part a/c, snacks and ice creams.
**Jaws**, 9 Castelhino Rd. Popular local hangout, pool, chess, in open-air setting. Locals prefer a Jaws burger over the McRival options.

**Bakeries**

**ABC Farms**, Koregaon Park. Specialist cheese producers, organic veg and rice, restaurant.
**German Bakery**, North Main Rd. Great coffee, cakes and snacks, suitably in tune with Osho.
**Just Baked**, Dhole Patil Road. Eat in/take out, baking can be watched through glass screen.
**Kayani**, East St. Irani bakery specializing in Mawa cakes and Shrewsbury biscuits!
**Marz-o-rin**, MG Rd. Good sandwiches, cakes, a Pune landmark, "reading and writing not allowed"!
**Spicers Health Foods**, MG Rd. Brown bread, peanut butter and tofu.

**Lonavla** *p1138*

ΨΨ **Lonavla Hotel**, 1st floor, a/c. Excellent Indian, pleasant ambience (try chicken kebabs), generous helpings, bar (affordable drinks), very clean (about Rs 150 each).
ΨΨ **Shivam Garden Restaurant** is cheaper but equally good and strictly pure veg.
Ψ **Hasty Tasty**, in bazar, for good snacks.
Ψ **Zeus Bakery** MG Rd, near National Chikki. Burger, sandwiches, snacks etc from Rs 25.

## Bars and clubs

**Pune** *p1133, maps p1136, p1135 and p1134*

Check daily *Pune Times* supplement in *The Times of India* for listings. Pune has quite an active night life. FC Rd and MG Rd are popular with students in the evenings.
**1000 Oats** is more of a family orientated place.
**Club Polaris**, club at Hotel Blue Diamond.
**Crystal Bar**, MG Rd, bar come club.
**Cyclone**, Hotel Mayur, club.
**Kaplia Hotel** (opposite Regency), has rooftop dancing, once a week (2200-0100).
**Nomads**, disco at Banjara Hills.
**Scream**, Le Meridien, club within the hotel.
**TDS (10 Downing Street)**, Boat Club Rd.

## Festivals and events

**Pune** *p1133, maps p1136, p1135 and p1134*

**Aug/Sep**: **Ganesh Chaturthi** 11 day MTDC festival with concerts, food fairs, bullock-cart races, folk shows. **Dec/Jan**: **Pune Marathon**.

**Lonavla** *p1138*

**Feb/Mar**: **Sivaratri** is celebrated at Mahadev Temple with great ceremony and a fair.

## Shopping

**Pune** *p1133, maps p1136, p1135 and p1134*

The main shopping centres in Pune are in MG Rd (Camp area), Deccan Gymkhana, Karve Rd, Laxmi Rd (for clothing and textiles) and Hanuman Mandir (for silver jewellery and leather *chappals*).

**Books**

**Crossword**, JPN Rd. Very modern, wide range of books and mags. Recommended.
**Manney's**, Clover Centre, Moledina Rd, comfortable a/c, excellent stock, bargains.
**Modern Book Store**, Gen Thimmaya Rd, good selection. Recommended.

**Mall**

**Nirman Shopping Complex**, opposite Shivaji Market, Convent St, is a modern mall.

**Textiles**

Look out for Pune saris (cotton-silk weave).
**Kalaniketan**, opposite Sancheti Hospital, JM Rd, for premium silkwear.
Wholesale sari market at **Raviwarpeth** ("Sunday Lane").

**Lonavla** *p1138*

Chikki, the candy mix of jaggery and dried fruit and nuts, is the local favourite, with endless variety in the shops in the market along MG Rd. About Rs 40 per kilo; dried fruit chikki, Rs 200 or more.
**Cooper's** famous for fudges; try coconut or choco walnut.
**Shakti**, Shivaji Rd/ Flyover junction. Excellent, unusual concoctions for health seekers; vitamin C rich Indian gooseberry

(*awala*), black sesame (*til*), sugar-free cashew and dried fruit is delicious.

## Activities and tours

**Pune** *p1133, maps p1136, p1135 and p1134*
**Apple Travels**, Amir Hotel Building, Connaught Rd, T020 26128185. Agent for **Indian Airlines**, efficient service.
**Sundar**, 19 MG Rd, T020 26131848.
**TCI**, Dhole Patil Rd, T020 26122126.
**Thomas Cook**, Gen Thimmaya Rd.

**Karla Caves** *p1139*
**Atmasantulana**, by MTDC Holiday Resort gate, is a holistic treatment centre combining ayurvedic, natural and yogic methods with medications and special dietary preparations produced at the complex; meditation, music therapy and spirituality are also practised. Patients should register a month ahead, about Rs 1000 per day. Visitors 1700-1900.

**Lonavla** *p1138*
**Kaivalyadhama Yogic Health Care Centre**, Valvan Dam approach road, T02114 273039, www.kdham.com. The 76-year old institute tries to demystify yoga and offers courses (1-yr diploma), cures, research and accommodation.
**Vedanta Academy**, Malavali Station Rd, T02114 282278, satva@vsnl.com). A lush haven off the Mumbai Pune Highway offers a free 3-year (or shorter) course for 50 students from around the world. Phone to visit.

## Transport

**Pune** *p1133, maps p1136, p1135 and p1134*
**Bangalore** (840 km); **Belgaum** (336 km); **Mumbai** (184 km); **Delhi** (1,424 km); **Mahabaleshwar** (120 km); **Nashik** (184 km).

### Air
Transport to town: Ex-Servicemen's coach for 8 km city transfer or airlines bus; taxi Rs 220. **Indian Airlines**, T020 24260932, enquiries T140, Airport T020 26689433. To **Bangalore** and **Delhi**, daily. **Jet Airways**, 243 Century Arcade, B/2 Narangi Bagh Rd, T020 2613 7181, Airport, T020 26685591. To **Mumbai**, 3 flights per day; **Bangalore** and **Delhi**, daily.

### Bus
**Local** City buses: in the city and suburbs (irregular).
**Long distance** **MSRTC** buses connect Pune with all major towns within the state. The new Mumbai to Bangalore expressway connects Pune. Travelling times on these routes will be cut considerably by those willing to pay the toll; Enquiry T020 2665516. Bright Star, 13 Connaught Rd, operates luxury coaches to **Ahmadabad**, **Bangalore**, **Panaji** (Goa), **Mangalore** etc. MTDC bus, Rs 125. Kadamba Transport Corporation (KTC, Goa) operates the **Panaji** route at 0630, 1800 and 1900, via Mapusa; buses poor and often dirty; Booking office open 0900-1200, 1500-1800. *Asiad* and *Express* buses run regular services. **City (Railway) Bus Stand**, T020 26126218, for the city and the South: **Belgaum**; **Chiplun**; **Ganpatipule**; **Hubli**; **Kolhapur**; **Mahabaleshwar**; **Panaji**; **Ratnagiri**; **Shirdi**; **Solapur**. Sivaji Nagar Bus Stand, T020 25536970, for the east/northeast: **Ahmadabad**; **Alibag (Kihim)**; **Amravati**; **Aurangabad**; **Hyderabad**; **Indore**; **Jalgaon**; **Nagpur**; **Nashik**; **Shirdi**; **Vadodara**. Swargate Bus Stand, T020 24441591, for the south and southeast. An auto from Swargate to Railway Station bus stand costs Rs 40. **Belgaum**; **Kolhapur**; **Mahabaleshwar**; **Mangalore** (starting from Mumbai); **Ratnagiri**; **Solapur**; **Thane**. Also private agents run deluxe a/c services direct to **Sahar International Airport**, 4 hrs, Rs 450, 0600, 0900, 1200, 1500, 1800, 2100. From the airport at 0030, 0230, 0430, 0630, 1800.

### Car
Car hire about Rs 800-1250 per day, or from Rs 9,000 per week with driver from **Sai Services**, Ashoka Pavillion, Dr Ambedkar Rd, T020 26055603. **Budget** cars, T020 25444118. **Wheels**, Pride Executive Hotel, T020 23255345; Airport T020 26683615.

### Rickshaw
Auto-rickshaws: best mode for town; driver carries a rate card, extra charges out-of-town and between 2400-0500.

### Taxi
Local taxis are not metered. To/from Mumbai Dadar station, Rs 900-1000.

**Train**

Bookings: City, Raviwar Peth, and Deccan, Karve Rd. Mon-Sat 0900-1200, 1300-1700, computerized. Enquiries T131, T020 2312 6575. **Bangalore via Guntakal**: *Udyan Exp, 6529*, 1200, 20½ hrs; *Coimbatore Exp, 1013*, 0215, 20 hrs. **Mumbai (CST)**: 17 trains daily, best are *Deccan Queen, 2124*, 0715, 3½ hrs; *Shatabdi Exp, 2028*, 1735, 3½ hrs; *Indrayani Exp, 1022*, 1820, 3¾ hrs; *Pragati Exp, 1026*, 0745, 3¾ hrs; *Sinhagad Exp, 1010*, 0605, 4 hrs; *Deccan Exp, 1008*, 1515, 4½ hrs. **Delhi (ND)**: *Jhelum Exp, 1077*, 1735, 27¾ hrs; (Hazrat Nizamuddin) *Goa Exp, 2779*, 0405, 26½ hrs. **Hyderabad**: *Mumbai-Hyderabad Exp, 7031*, 1650, 13¼ hrs; *Hussainsagar Exp, 7001*, 0150, 11½ hrs. **Secunderabad**: *Konark Exp, 1019*, 1925, 12¼ hrs. **Jammu Tawi**: *Jhelum Exp, 1077*, 1735, 42½ hrs. **Chennai via Solapur and Guntakal**: *Dadar Chennai Exp, 1063*, 0010, 20 hrs; *Chennai Exp, 6011*, 1815, 22½ hrs. **Vasco** de Gama (Goa): *Goa Exp, 2780*, 1730, 14½ hrs.

**Lonavla** *p1138*

**Bus**

ST buses to the **Caves**: couple of buses to Karla in the morning from 0600, last return about 1900. To **Rajmachi Fort** (north of Lonavla): buses are unpredictable; **Pune** (62 km) and **Mumbai** (101 km); special a/c every 30 mins, last dep 1630, Rs 81. **Lucky Travels**, Hotel Gulistan, Bombay Pune Rd, near Flyover, T02114 270332, runs a/c bus to Mumbai, Rs 170 (non-video preferable).

**Rickshaw**

Auto-rickshaw from Lonavla to the Karla and Bhaja Caves including waiting, about Rs 250, more for Bhedsa.

**Taxi**

Tourist taxis from near ST Bus Stand, **Ankush Stores**, T02114 274458; **Parekh**, in line with Adarsh Hotel, T02114 273886. Return hire to **Ambavane** Rs 500; **Karla**, Bhaja Rs 350 (the caves are some distance from the car park). One way to **Mumbai** Rs 750-1,000 (under 4 hrs), **Pune** Rs 500.

**Train**

Railway Station Enquiry, T02114 272215. Lonavla is on the **Mumbai (CST)** - **Pune** line with at least 16 trains daily in each direction. To **Mumbai**, 2½-3 hrs; **Pune**, 1-1½ hrs.

**Karla Caves** *p1139*

Tourist taxis charge Rs 350 from Lonavla to visit both caves. From the Karla/Bhaja crossroads on the NH4 at Karla village, turn left (north). The car park is at the bottom of the ridge with a steps up to the caves (20 mins). Buses from Lonavla: a couple from 0600; last return 1900.

**Bhaja Caves** *p1139*

From Karla village on the NH4, a road to the south goes to Bhaja after crossing the railway at Malavli. Vehicles stop at the car park in new Bhaja 'town', from there follow a path and then climb uphill for about 20 mins to the caves. Heavy rain can close part of the Bhaja Rd to vehicles. Alternatively, take a train to Malavli.

**Raigad** *p1140*

Buses go from both **Mumbai** (via Mahad, 210 km) and **Pune** (126 km). Pune is the nearest railhead.

**Kolhapur** *p1141*

Trains to Kolhapur arrive via Miraj. Enquiry, T131. Reservation: T654389. **Mumbai (CST)**: *Mahalaxmi Exp, 1012*, 1905, 11¾ hrs; *Koyna Express 7308*, 0750, 13½ hrs; *Mahalaxmi Sahyadri Exp, 7304*, 2230, 14¼ hrs. **Pune**: *Maharashtra Exp, 7383*, 1405, 8 hrs.

**Solapur** *p1142*

Excellent bus connections to **Mumbai**, **Hyderabad**, **Aurangabad** to the north and **Bijapur** (3 hrs) to the south.

Trains include: **Bangalore**: *Udyan Exp, 6529*, 1630, 16 hrs. **Bijapur**, *Golgumbaz Exp, 6541*, 2135, 2½ hrs; *Solapur Bijapur Pass, 245*, 1720, 3½ hrs. **Mumbai (Dadar)**: *Chennai Dadar Exp, 1064*, 2115, 9 hrs. **Mumbai (CST)**: *Chennai-Mumbai Mail, 6010*, 1720, 10¾ hrs; *Chennai Mumbai Exp, 6012*, 0425, 10½ hrs; *Siddheswar Exp, 1024*, 2030, 10 hrs. **Hyderabad**: *Mumbai Hyderabad Exp, 7031*, 2200, 8 hrs; *Hussainsagar Exp, 7001*, 0610, 7 hrs. **Chennai**: *Dadar Chennai Exp, 1063*, 0420, 15¾ hrs; *Mumbai Chennai Exp, 6011*, 2340, 17 hrs.

## ❻ Directory

**Pune** *p1133, maps p1136, p1135 and p1134*

**Banks** Amex, 19 MG Rd. **Central Bank**, MG Rd, accepts Mastercard and Visa. **Thomas**

Cook, 13 Thakers House, Gen Thimmaya Rd, T020 2648188 (1000-1700, closed Sun) is best for TCs. Many ATMs across the city, Citibank for Mastercard, ICICI for Visa, HDFC for both. **Internet** Numerous outlets across the city, Rs 20-30 per hr. **Hospital** Ruby Hall Clinic, T020 26123391. Sassoon (Govt), JP Narayan Rd, T020 26128000. **Post** Head Post Office (city): Laxmi Rd. **Tourist offices** Maharashtra, I Block, Central Building, T020 26126867. Information Counter, Pune Railway Station. Lohagaon Airport. Goa, Sam Travels, Karve Rd, T020 2333538. **Useful addresses** Ambulance: T102. Fire: T101. Police: T100. Foreigners' Registration Office, Ground Floor, Main Building, Police Commissioner's Office, Sadhu Waswani Rd, T020 26128977.

**Lonavla** *p1138*
**Banks** Bank of Maharashtra and State Bank of India, Tilak Rd. **Internet** Cybercafé Basement of *Kumar Resort*, Flyover, 1000-2300, Rs 30 for 30 mins. **Hospital** Dahanukar Hospital, T02114 272673; Favourite Medical, Tilak Rd. **Post** Shivaji Rd. **Tourist office** Maharashtra, near Lonavla Railway Station. **Useful services** Fire: T02114 272286. Police: T02114 272233.

**Kolhapur** *p1141*
**Bank** Only State Bank of India, Main Branch, Dasara Chowk Bridge (near railway station), changes cash, TCs from 1130. **Tourist offices** Maharashtra, Kedar Complex, Station Rd, T02114 2652935. Goa, Mohan Travels, 517E Pune-Bangalore Rd, T02114 2650911.

# Vidharba

## Nagpur → *Phone code: 0712. Colour map 6, grid A1. Population: 2 mn.*

Nagpur, the former capital of the Central Provinces, is one of the older towns of Central India. Today, although an important commercial centre attracting new businesses and multinationals, most of the industrial units are thankfully located on the outskirts so Nagpur retains a pleasant relaxed feel with friendly inhabitants and signs of fast growing affluence. Sometimes known as the winter capital of Maharashtra, the area is famous for its oranges, giving it the nickname 'The Orange City'. More recently strawberry farms have grown in importance while the surrounding countryside is a major cotton producing area.

The city stands on the Nag River and centres on the **Sitabuldi Fort** which is surrounded by cliffs and a moat. At the highest point there is a memorial to those who fell in the Battle of Sitabuldi between the Marathas and the British. The fort, now headquarters of the Territorial Army, is only open to the public on 26 January and 15 August. Among the British buildings scattered around the western half of the city are the red brick Council Hall (1912-1913); the Anglican Cathedral of All Saints (1851), and the High Court (1937-1942), suggestive of Rashtrapati Bhavan in New Delhi. On the other high hill in the town is the **Raj Bhavan** (Government House). The **Bhonsla Chhattris** are in the Sukrawari area south of the old city. Around the town there are also a number of 'tanks' (lakes) and parks; **Maharaj Bagh**, west of the Flyover is an attractive park/zoo.

## Ramtek

About 40 km northeast of Nagpur, Ramtek has a **fort** with several Hindu **temples** at its western end, some dating back to the fifth century AD. The fort walls on the well-wooded 'Hill of Rama' were built in 1740 by Raghoji I, the first Bhonsla of Nagpur. The citadel is older and the principal temples are those to Rama and Sita. The fort is approached by a flight of steps from the village of Ambala. The poet Kalidasa wrote his epic *Meghdoot* here. Nearby is Khindsey Lake, 8 km, a popular picnic spot with boating facilities. Ramsagar is another lake closer to town. The 15-day *Ramnavami* fair is held in November.

## Wardha and around → *Phone code: 07152. Colour map 6, grid A1. 62 km southwest.*

After vowing not to return to Sabarmati Ashram in Ahmedabad until India gained its independence, Mahatma Gandhi established his **Sevagram Ashram** (Gandhian Village of Service) in 1933. Jamnalal Bajaj, a dedicated follower of Gandhi, provided the land, 8 km outside of Wardha, and the resources to set up the ashram in which Gandhi remained until 1942 and visited regularly until his death in 1948. It is now a national institution where you can visit the residences *Nivases* and *Kutirs*, see the Mahatma's personal belongings, watch hand-spinning (*khadi* cloth is sold through shops) and attend prayers at the open-air multi-faith Prayer Ground (0430 and 1800). **Mahatma Gandhi Research Institute of Medical Sciences** and **Kasturba Hospital** with 325 beds to provide affordable health care for local villagers, is on the bus route. A path from here leads to the Ashram.

The **Magan Sanghralaya** (Centre of Science for Villages) is an alternative technology museum, on the Nagpur Road at **Duttapur**. Visitors are welcome to see papermaking, pottery, latrine making and other crafts. The **Chetna Organic Farm**, nearby, develops sustainable farming techniques. The **Laxmi Narayan Temple** claims to have been the first in India to have allowed *Harijans* to enter in 1928. The **Viswa Shanti Stupa** (1993), for 'World Peace', with 4 golden statues of Buddha, is a more recent attraction. Prayers are held each evening in the small prayer hall.

At **Paunar**, 10 km north of Wardha, **Vinoba Bhave**, one of Gandhi's keenest disciples, set up his Ashram. He championed the 'land gift' or **Bhoodan Movement**, seeking with remarkable success to persuade large landowners to give away land to the poor. The self-help concept is kept alive by his followers (mostly women) dressed in blue, unlike other ashramites elsewhere in India who conventionally adopt white or saffron. It is possible to hike across from the Sevagram hospital along a village track for about 45 minutes to get there.

## Taroba National Park

Approximately 100 km south of Nagpur, the area around Taroba was once in the possession of the Gond tribals. The compact 120 sq km park has rich deciduous forest – mainly teak with bamboo, gardenia and satinwood. There are several troops of langur monkeys, palm civets, gaur, jackal, wild boar, chital, bison, sambar and a few tigers (although you are more likely to see a leopard in the evening). Waterbirds attracted by the perennial circular lake include cattle egrets, purple moorhens and jacanas. It also has quite a number of marsh crocodiles with a breeding farm for the *palustris* species. There are minibuses for viewing, which is best in the evening around lake in the dry season. A road runs around the lake, while other roads radiate to the park perimeter. Best season to visit is between November and June. There are no official guides, but a forest guide will accompany you if you hire a searchlight. The nearest transport connections are at Chandrapur, 45 km away.

## Achalpur

Until 1853 this important market town was the capital of Berar Kingdom, established in 1484 by Imad Shah. The old cantonment, which had been occupied by a regiment of the Hyderabad infantry, was abandoned in 1903.

To the north, and just before reaching Chikhaldara, is the fort of **Gawilgarh** (Gavilgarh). An important fortress of the 15th-century Shahi Dynasty, it was taken over when the kingdom of Ahmednagar expanded in 1574. Arthur Wellesley, subsequently the Duke of Wellington, who had defeated Tipu Sultan of Mysore at Srirangapatnam just four years previously, captured the fort in 1803 during the second Maratha War. The defences were destroyed after the 'Indian Mutiny' in 1858. Today it is a deserted ruin.

## Chikhaldara

Known as the only hill station in the Vidharba region and as the northernmost coffee growing region in India, Chikhaldara is high in the Gavilgarh Hills, at an altitude of 1,200 m, a branch of the Satpura mountains. Established as a hill station by the British in 1839, historically the hills marked the southern limits of the core region within which the epics of Hinduism were played out. It remains a tribal region, peopled largely by the Korkus, an Austric tribal group. The settlement is reputed to have taken its name from Kichaka, a prince who was killed by Bhima, one of the Pandava brothers, for having insulted Draupadi. Today, the Satpura Range in which Chikhaldara lies mark the southern boundary of Hindi speech.

The **Melghat Sanctuary** surrounding Chikaldara was one of the earliest to be designated a Project Tiger reserve. Its altitude makes it pleasantly cool during January-June, the best months to visit. The latest count suggests it has 45 tigers, occasionally seen in the dense and dry deciduous teak forest which also supports panther, gaur, chital, sambar and nilgai.

## Sleeping

**Nagpur** *p1148*

**C** and **D** hotels don't have all usual facilities of the grade but all have restaurants, bars and free transfer for airport

**A-B Tuli International**, Residency Rd, Sadar, T0712 2534784, www.tuligroup.com. 107 well-appointed rooms and suites, central a/c, executive 'Business' floor, 3 restaurants and bar, excellent pool and health club (residents only), weekend disco. Best in town.

**B Pride** (was *Jagson's Regency*), Wardha Rd, 500 m from airport, T0712 2261102, www.pridegroup.com. 70 tired rooms, 30 new better, decent restaurant but inefficient reception, unappealing pool next to busy NH7.

**B-C Darshan Towers**, 60 Central Ave, T0712 2726845, h_darshantowers@ yahoo.com. Well-furnished rooms, central a/c, hot baths (some tubs), double-glazed so quieter than others, good restaurant/bar, friendly and efficient, recommended.

**B-C Radhika**, Panchsheel Sq, Wardha Rd, T0712 2522011, radhika@nagpur.dot.net.in. 60 clean rooms, some larger a/c with hot bath, dark corridors, unreliable TV, restaurant, bar.

**D Jagsons**, 30 Back Central Ave, T0712 2728611. 28 clean carpetted rooms, some a/c, TV, bar/restaurant.

**D Skylark** (*Tuli* group), 119 Central Ave, T0712 2724654. 48 decent, clean rooms, most a/c, efficient and friendly service, restaurant/bar, good value but suffers from road noise.

**D-E Blue Moon**, Central Ave, T0712 2726061, micron@bom3.vsnl.net.in. 30 clean rooms, some a/c, TV, room service, quieter rooms at rear.

**E Super Deluxe Guest House**, Back Central Ave. 32 clean rooms with bath and TV, friendly, away from main road so quieter.

**Ramtek** *p1148*

**D Resort**, (MTDC/private), Ramtek, T07114 255620. 17 rooms and a dorm.

**E Resort**, Khindsey Lake. Smaller with 4 simple rooms and camping.

**Wardha** *p1149*

**E Holiday Resort** (MTDC/private), near Bus Stand, T07152 243872. 18 rooms with bath, cheap singles, restaurant. Also some cheap hotels near railway station.

**F Ashram Guest House** and **Yatri Niwas**, at Sevagram, T07152 22172. Some doubles and dorm, serves cheap veg meals, check-out 0800, friendly, small bookshop of Gandhi's works. Highly recommended (donations welcome), reserve on arrival (or ahead if possible). Alcohol, smoking and non-vegetarian food are prohibited.

**Yatri Niwas**, at Paunar, similar to Sevagram but more female oriented.

**Taroba National Park** *p1149*

**E Mayur**, Mul Rd. 27 rooms, 1 km railway, restaurant, bar, and three forest rest houses, around the lake. Reserve through the Divisional Forest Officer, Mul Road, Chandrapur. Needs a day's notice.

**Chikhaldara** *p1150*
**B-D Green Vallies Resort** (MTDC), T07220 220215. 20 suites, wide choice, some a/c.
**C-D Convention Complex** (MTDC), T07220 2202234. 10 4 four-bed rooms, simple though adequate, and dorm with mattresses but no beds (Rs 50), restaurant nearby. Improved accommodation is planned.

## Eating

**Nagpur** *p1148*
Hotel restaurants at **Darshan Towers** and **Tuli International** are recommended. Several others are along Residency Rd and Wardha Rd near the junction with Central Bazar Rd.

**Wardha** *p1149*
**Annapurnat**, Wardha near station, Paunar; couple in Saraf Lines.

## Festivals and events

**Nagpur** *p1148*
**Apr/May**: Ram Naumi, colourful procession in various parts of the city. **Aug/Sep**: Janmashtami, Krishna's birthday is celebrated with the distinctive tradition of stringing clay pots full of curd high above the streets. Young men try to pull them down by forming human pyramids. **Pola**, the cattle and monsoon harvest festival. **Ganesh Chaturthi**, when idols of Ganesh are immersed in streams and tanks.

## Shopping

**Nagpur** *p1148*
Main areas are Sitabuldi, Dharampeth, Sadar and Itwari, Mahatma Phule Market.
**Gangotri UP Handicrafts**, in Sadar.
**Khadi Gramudyog**, in Mahal.

## Transport

**Nagpur** *p1148*
**Air**
The airport is 10 km south of the city centre with taxis for transfer. **Indian Airlines**, Amravati Rd, T0712 2523069, airport T0712 2260348, flight information T140/141: to **Delhi**, **Mumbai**, **Hyderabad** and **Kolkata**. **Jet Airways**, Shree Mohini Complex, 345 Kingsway, Sitabuldi, T0712 2559875, airport T0712 2273384: to **Mumbai**.

**Bus**
New Maharashtra ST Bus Stand, Ganesh Peth, southeast of the railway station, T0712 2726221, to towns in Maharashtra plus **Hyderabad**, **Allahabad** and **Varanasi**. MP Bus Stand, T0712 2533695, buses to **Bhopal**, **Indore** and **Raipur**. Madhya Pradesh buses use the stand just south of the train station.

**Car**
Car hire **Pigale**, Dharampeth, T0712 2522291. **Saibaba**, near Pancsheel Cinema, T0712 2522416; Rs 600 per 5 hrs.

**Train**
Nagpur is an important railway junction. The station is in the centre of town. Enquiry T131, Reservations T135. **Chennai**: *Tamil Nadu Exp, 2622*, 1410, 16½ hrs; *Grand Trunk Exp, 2616*, 1220, 18 hrs. **New Delhi**: *Andhra Pradesh Exp, 2723*, 1555, 16½ hrs; *Tamil Nadu Exp, 2621*, 1415, 17½ hrs; *Grand Trunk Exp, 2615*, 1015, 18½ hrs. **Kolkata (H)**: *Gitanjali Exp, 2859*, 2015, 18½ hrs; *Mumbai Howrah Mail, 2809*, 1130, 20½ hrs. **Mumbai (CST)**: *Vidarbha Exp, 2106*, 1500, 14¾ hrs; *Howrah Mumbai Mail, 2810*, 1555, 15½ hrs. **Mumbai (Dadar)**: *Sewagram Exp, 1440*, 2020, 16 hrs. **Pune**: *Maharashtra Exp, 7384*, 1100, 19½ hrs. **Secunderabad**: *Andhra Pradesh Exp, 2724*, 1010, 10½ hrs; *Dakshin Exp, 7022*, 1745, 13½ hrs.

**Wardha** *p1149*
**Bus**
Several to/from Wardha from **Nagpur**, 77 km, Express 2½ hrs; ask to be dropped off at **Paunar**. Local bus to **Sevagram** (8 km).

**Train**
Share auto-rickshaws from the station to Sevagram (25 mins). **Ahmedabad**: *Navjivan Exp, 6046*, 0250, 17½ hrs; *Howrah Ahmedabad Exp, 8034*, 2030, 19½ hrs. **Chennai**: *Navjivan Exp, 6045*, 2325, 18 hrs. **Kolkata (H)** via **Nagpur** and **Raipur**: *Mumbai Howrah Mail, 2809*, 0935, 22½ hrs; *Ahmedabad Howrah Exp, 8033*, 0425, 24½ hrs. **Mumbai (CST)**: *Vidarbha Exp, 2106*, 1615, 13½ hrs; *Howrah Mumbai Mail, 2810*, 1715 (1700 from Sevagram), 14½ hrs.

**Mumbai (Dadar)**: *Sewagram Exp, 1440*, 2150, 14½ hrs. **Nagpur**: Several fast trains daily; slow passenger trains stop at Sevagram, though the bus is quicker and more convenient. **Pune**: *Maharashtra Exp, 7384*, 1220, 18 hrs.

**Ramtek** *p1148*
Buses from ST Bus Stand, Nagpur, 70 mins. Buses run from Ramtek to **Khindsey Lake**. **Ramsagar** can be reached by auto-rickshaw.

**Chikhaldara** *p1150*
State buses from Amaravati, Nagpur, Wardha and Akola. Also, taxis from Amravati (100 km). **Badnera** is on the Mumbai-Kolkata train line, so is a convenient station. Amaravati is on a short spur (10 km) from Badnera.

## Directory

**Nagpur** *p1148*
**Banks** Kingsway; Sitabuldi and Central Ave. **Hospitals** Private. CIIMS, T0712 2236441, Jasleen, T0712 2523779, Orange City, T0712 2238431. **Internet** Rs 20 per hr. **Post** GPO, Palm Rd. **Tourist offices** Maharashtra, Sanskruti Bachat Bhavan, opposite Hardeo Hotel, near Lakshmie Theatre, Sitabuldi, T0712 2533325. Mainly for booking MTDC accommodation.

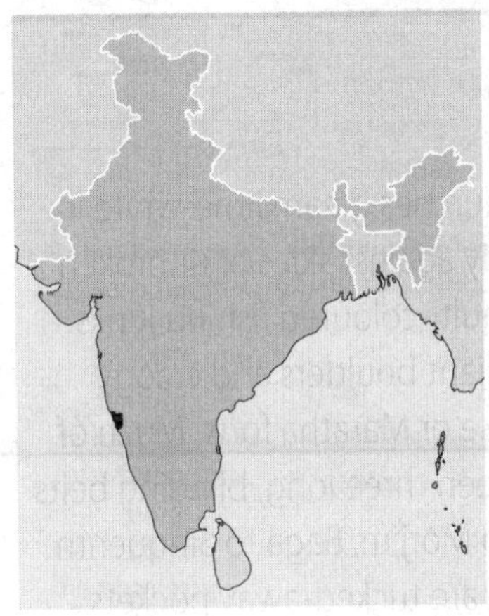



## Footprint features

# Introduction



Goa is awash with colour. The churches gleam lime-white in seas of lush parakeet green paddy against skies of unbroken bright blue. The seas bob with multi-coloured fishing junks. Rocky headlands, small bays of giant boulders and craggy cliffs are topped off by Portuguese or Maratha forts. Much of Goa's gold coast is divided between three long, blinding belts of sand that run from Arambol to Morjim, Baga to Sinquerim and Velsao to Mobor. Then there are tucked-away pockets and coves like tiny casuarina-backed Qeri beach, lorded over by Tiracol Fort.

Most people have heard high tales of the American and European Freak scene that swarmed down from Kathmandu to descend on Baga, Calangute and, latterly, Anjuna in the 60s. There's still the odd old-timer weaving their customized Enfield motorbike through the sand-tracks behind south Anjuna, and there's plenty of neon waistcoats stitched with day-glo *om* embroidery, ample acid trance parties throbbing through the coconut thickets and plenty of new shipments of youngsters to build a throng. These days, though, they are more likely to be Israelis fresh out of their military service uniform, English gap year lovelies, upper middle-class Russians and Mumbai and Delhi high society than drop-out hippies. The flea market reflects the shift in tourist demographic too: here they have both high-performance Goa Trance freak-wares and Burberry-check bucket hats.

## ★ Don't miss...

1 **San Thome and Fontainhas** Spend an afternoon zigzagging through the charming streets of these districts in Panjim, page 1162.

2 **Old Goa** A city of sprawling convents, churches and chapels, page 1163.

3 **Tito's** Have a night to remember at this nightclub in Baga, page 1193.

4 **Cabo da Rama** One of Goa's most dilapidated and ancient forts, page 1205.

5 **Palolem** Charter a fishing boat and escape the mainland for a peaceful afternoon, page 1206.

6 **Inland Goa** Explore atop a bicycle or a motorbike and experience the unmanufactured life of the state, page 1216.

7 **Spice plantations** A crash course in the medicinal values of plants, herbal viagra and a slap-up Goan meal while you're at it, page 1219.

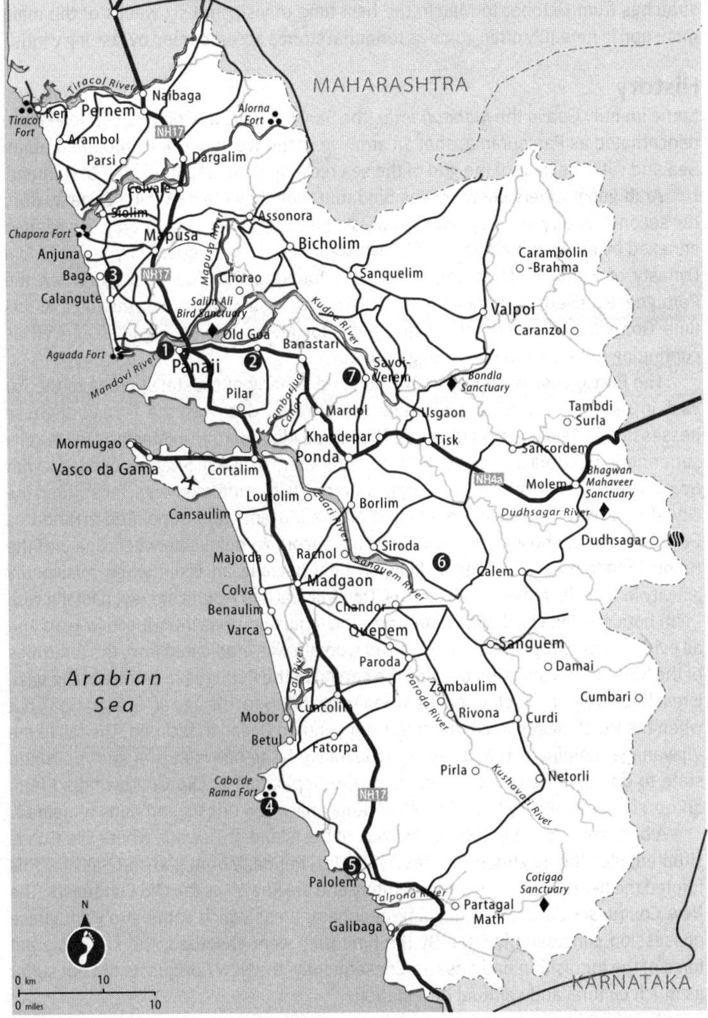

# Background → *Population: 1.3 mn. Area: 3,800 sq km.*

## The land

**Geography** By Indian standards Goa is a tiny state. The coastline on which much of its fame depends is only 97 km long. The north and south of the state are separated by the broad estuaries of the Zuari and Mandovi rivers. Joined at high tide to create an island on which Panaji stands, these short rivers emerge from the high ranges of the Western Ghats less than 50 km from the coast. Alfonso de Albuquerque grasped the advantages of this island site, large enough to give a secure food-producing base but with a defensible moat, at the same time well placed with respect to the important northwestern sector of the Arabian Sea.

**Climate** Throughout the year Goa is warm, but its position on the coast means that it never suffers unbearable heat. However, from mid-April until the beginning of the monsoon in mid-June, both the temperature and the humidity rise sharply, making the middle of the day steamy hot. The warm clear and dry weather of its tropical winter stretches from October to March, the best time to visit. The six weeks of the main monsoon in June-July often come as torrential storms accompanied by lashing winds.



## History

Some identify Goa in the *Mahabharata* (the Sanskrit epic) as Gomant, where Vishnu, reincarnated as Parasurama, shot an arrow from the Western Ghats into the Arabian Sea and with the help of the god of the sea reclaimed the beautiful land of Gomant.

**Arab** geographers knew Goa as Sindabur. Ruled by the Kadamba Dynasty from the second century AD to 1312 and by Muslim invaders from 1312 to 1367, it was then annexed by the Hindu Kingdom of Vijayanagar and later conquered by the Bahmani Dynasty of Bidar in North Karnataka, who founded Old Goa in 1440. When the Portuguese arrived, Yusuf Adil Shah, the Muslim King of Bijapur, was the ruler. At this time Goa was an important starting point for Mecca-bound pilgrims, as well as continuing to be a centre importing Arab horses.

**The Portuguese** were intent on setting up a string of coastal stations to the Far East in order to control the lucrative spice trade. Goa was the first Portuguese possession in Asia and was taken by **Alfonso de Albuquerque** in March 1510, the city surrendering without a struggle. Three months later Yusuf Adil Shah blockaded it with 60,000 men. In November Albuquerque returned with reinforcements, recaptured the city after a bloody struggle, massacred all the Muslims and appointed a Hindu as Governor. Mutual hostility towards Muslims encouraged links between Goa and the Hindu Kingdom of Vijayanagar. Religion only became an issue when missionary activity in India increased. Franciscans, Dominicans and Jesuits arrived, carrying with them both religious zeal and intolerance. The Inquisition was introduced in 1540 and all evidence of earlier Hindu temples and worship was eradicated from the territories of the 'Old Conquests'. Goa became the capital of the Portuguese Empire in the east. It reached its greatest splendour between 1575 and 1600, the age of 'Golden Goa', but when the Dutch began to control trade in the Indian Ocean it declined. The fall of the Vijayanagar Empire in 1565 caused the lucrative trade between Goa and the Hindu state to dry up. Between 1695 and 1775 the population of Old Goa dwindled from 20,000 to 1,600 and by the mid-19th century only a few priests and nuns remained.

Albuquerque's original conquest was of the island of Tiswadi, where Old Goa is situated, plus the neighbouring areas – Bardez, Ponda, Mormugao and Salcete. This formed the heart of the Portuguese territory and are known as the **Old Conquests**. The **New Conquests** cover the remaining peripheral areas which came into Portuguese possession considerably later. By the time they were absorbed, the full intolerant force of the Inquisition had passed. Consequently, the New Conquests did not suffer as much cultural and spiritual devastation.

The Portuguese came under increasing pressure in 1948 and 1949 to cede Goa, Daman and Diu to India. The problem festered until 1961 when the Indian Army, supported by a naval blockade, marched in and brought to an end 450 years of Portuguese rule. Goa became a Union Territory together with the enclaves of Daman and Diu, but on 30 May 1987 it became a full state of the Indian Union.

## Culture

**Religion** While in the area of the Old Conquests tens of thousands of people were converted to Christianity, the Zuari River represents a great divide between Christian and predominantly Hindu Goa. Today about 70% of the state's population is Hindu, and there is also a small but significant Muslim minority.

**Language** Portuguese used to be much more widely spoken in Goa than was English in most of the rest of India, but local languages remained important. The two most significant were Marathi, the language of the politically dominant majority of the neighbouring state to the north, and Konkani, the language commonly spoken on the coastal districts further south. Goa's official language now. English and Hindi are understood in the parts visited by travellers but in rural areas, Konkani predominates.

**Cuisine** The food in this region is hot, making full use of the small bird's-eye chillies grown locally. Common ingredients include rice, coconut, cashew nuts, pork, beef and a wide variety of seafood. Spicy pork or beef *vindalho*, marinated in garlic, vinegar and chillies is very popular (elsewhere 'vindaloo' refers to a hot, spicy curry). *Chourisso* is Goan sausage made of pork pieces stuffed in tripe, boiled or fried with onions and chillies. It is often eaten stuffed into bread. *Sorpotel*, a highly spiced dish of pickled pig's liver and heart, seasoned with vinegar and tamarind, is perhaps the most famous of Goan meat dishes. *Xacutti* is a hot chicken or meat dish prepared with coconut, pepper and star anise. For *Chicken Cafrial*, the meat is marinated in pepper and garlic and braised over a slow fire. 'Fish curry and rice', the common Goan meal, has become a catch phrase. Most beach shacks offer a good choice depending on the day's catch. *Apa de camarao* is a spicy prawn pie and *reichado* is usually a whole fish, cut in half, and served with a hot *masala* sauce. *Bangra* is Goa mackerel and *pomfret* a flat fish; fish *balchao* is a preparation of red masala and onions used as a sauce for prawns or kingfish. *Seet corri* (fish curry) uses the ubiquitous coconut. Spicy pickles and chutneys add to the rich variety of flavours.

Goan bread is good. *Undo* is a hard crust round bread, while *kankonn*, hard and crispy and shaped like a bangle is often dunked in tea. *Pole* is like chapatti, often stuffed with vegetables, and Goans prepare their own version of the South Indian *idli*, the *sanaan*. The favourite dessert is *bebinca*, a layered coconut and jaggery delicacy made with egg yolks and nutmeg. Other sweets include *dodol*, a mix of jaggery and coconut with rice flour and nuts, *doce*, looks like the North Indian *barfi*, *mangada*, a mango jam, and *bolinhas*, small round semolina cakes. There are also delicious fruits: *alfonso* mangos in season, the rich *jackfruit*, papaya, watermelons and cashew nuts.

Drinks in Goa remain relatively cheap compared to elsewhere in India. The fermented juice of cashew apples is distilled for the local brew *caju feni* (*fen*, froth) which is strong and potent. Coconut or *palm feni* is made from the sap of the coconut palm. *Feni* is an acquired taste; it is often mixed with soda, salt and lime juice.

## Modern Goa

The Goa Legislative Assembly has 40 elected members while the state elects three members to the Lok Sabha. Although the Congress has been the largest single party, political life is strongly influenced by the regional issue of the relationship with neighbouring Maharashtra. Regional issues remain important, but there is now also a strong environmental lobby, in which the Catholic Church plays a prominent part.

In common with much of the west coast of India, Goa's rural economy depends on rice as the main food crop, cash crops being dominated by coconut, cashewnut and areca nut. Mangos, pineapples and bananas are also important, and forests still give some produce. Seasonal water shortages have prompted the development of irrigation projects, the latest of which was the interstate Tillari Project in Pernem Taluka, completed with the Government of Maharashtra. Iron ore and bauxite have been two of the state's major exports but heavy industrial development has remained relatively limited. Tourism remains one of the state's biggest earners.



## Ins and outs → *For arrivals by train, see Panjim opposite.*

Vasco da Gama is the passenger railway terminus of the Central Goa branch line, and is the capital of the industrial heart of modern Goa. Dabolim airport is 3 km away, which was developed by the Navy and is now uncomfortably shared between the military's needs and the escalating demands of tourism. Vasco is 30 km from Panjim. Trains via Londa can now bring visitors from the north (Delhi, Agra) or the south (Hospet, Bangalore).

There are several flights daily from various cities in India to Goa with Air India, Indian Airways, and Jet Airways: Mumbai, Thiruvananthapuram, Bangalore, Delhi (some via Agra), Chennai. Package tour companies and luxury hotels usually arrange courtesy buses for hotel transfer. The pre-paid taxi counter immediately outside the arrivals hall has rates clearly displayed (eg Panjim Rs 340, 40 minutes; north Goa beaches from Rs 450; Tiracol Rs 750; south Goa beaches from Rs 240; Palolem Rs 700). State your destination at the counter, pay and get a receipt which will give the registration number of your taxi. Keep hold of this receipt until you reach your destination. The public bus stop on the far side of the roundabout outside the airport gates has buses to Vasco da Gama, from where there are connections to all major places in Goa (rail reservations T0832-2512833).

# Panjim (Panaji) and Old Goa

→ *Colour map 5a, grid B1.*

*This small city tucked into the narrow strip of land between the Altinho (meaning 'hill') and the coastal banks of Goa's most important river, the Mandovi, has to be a contender for most laid-back state capital in India. It's all the more surprising considering the fact that, on paper, Goa is the subcontinent's wealthiest state per capita, but the population has stayed small and there's been no rush of urban migration. In Panjim's relaxed commercial hub, the biggest business seems to be in the sale of kaju (cashews), gentlemen-shaves in the barbieris and feni-quaffing in the booths of pokey bars. It's a tiny, clean city that's great to walk around. If all goes to plan, from November 2004 it will host an international film festival which will make it India's answer to Cannes.* » *For Sleeping, Eating and other listings, see pages 1168-1173.*

*Panaji is the official spelling of the capital city, replacing the older Portuguese spelling Panjim. It is still most commonly referred to as Panjim, so we have followed usage.*

## Ins and outs

**Getting there** Prepaid taxis or buses run the short distance from Dabolim airport across Mormugao Bay. The Konkan Railway's main terminus is at the headquarters of South Goa district, Margao, for trains from Mumbai and the north or from coastal Karnataka and Kerala to the south. Taxis and buses run to Panjim from there. Karmali station in Old Goa is the closest to Panjim, where taxis wait to transfer you. The state Kadamba buses and private coach terminals are in Patto to the east of town. From there it is a 10-minute walk across the footbridge over the Ourem Creek to reach the city's guesthouses. ▸▸ *See Transport, page 1172 for further details.*

**Getting around** Panjim is very easy to negotiate on foot, but auto-rickshaws are handy and readily available. Motorcycle rickshaws are cheaper and more risky. Local buses run along the waterfront from the city bus stand past the market to Miramar.

**Tourist information** Panjim holds the archbishop's palace, a modern port, and government buildings and shops set around a number of plazas. It is laid out on a grid and the main roads run parallel with the seafront. Department of Tourism Office of the Government of Goa ⓘ *north bank of the Ourem Creek, beside the bus stand at Patto, T0832-2438750, Mon-Sat 0900-1130, 1330-1700, Sun 0930-1400.*

## History

The Portuguese first settled Panjim as a suburb of Old Goa, the original Indian capital of the sea-faring conquistadores, but its position on the left bank of the Mandovi River had already attracted Bijapur's Muslim king Yusuf Adil Shah in 1500, shortly before the Europeans arrived. He built and fortified what the Portuguese later renamed the Idalcao Palace, now the oldest and most impressive of downtown Panjim's official buildings. The palace's service to the Sultan was short-lived: Alfonso de Albuquerque seized it, and Old Goa upstream – which the Islamic rulers had been using as both a trading port and their main starting point for pilgrimages to Mecca – in March 1510. Albuquerque, like his Muslim predecessors, built his headquarters in Old Goa, stationed a garrison at Panjim and made it the customs clearing point for all traffic entering the Mandovi.

The town remained little more than a military outpost and a staging post for incoming and outgoing viceroys on their way to Old Goa. The first Portuguese buildings, after the construction of a church on the site of the present Church of Our Lady of Immaculate Conception in 1541, were noblemen's houses built on the flat land bordering the sea. Panjim had to wait over two centuries – when the Portuguese Viceroy decided to move from Old Goa in 1759 – for settlement to begin in earnest. It then took the best part of a century for enough numbers to relocate from Old Goa to make Panjim the biggest settlement in the colony and to warrant its status as official capital in 1833.

# The waterfront

Devanand Bandodkar (DB) Marg runs along the Mandovi from near the New Patto Bridge on the east of town to the once open fields of the Campal to the southwest. When Panjim's transport and communication system depended on boats this was the town's busiest highway and it still holds the city's main administrative buildings.

Walking from the east, you first hit **Idalcao Palace** ⓘ *behind the main boat terminal, DB Marg*. Once the castle of the Adil Shahs, the palace was seized by the Portuguese when they first toppled the Muslim kings in 1510 and was rebuilt in 1615 to serve as the Europeans' Viceregal Palace. It was the official residence to Viceroys from 1759 right up until 1918 when the Governor-General (the viceroy's 20th century title) decided to move to the Cabo headland to the southwest – today's Cabo Raj Niwas – leaving the old palace to become government offices. After independence it became Goa's secretariat building (the seat of the then Union Territory's parliament) until that in turn shifted across the river to Porvorim. It now houses the bureaucracy of the state passport office. Next to it is a striking dark statue of the **Abbé Faria** (1756-1819) looming over the prone figure of a woman. José Custodio de Faria, who went on to become a celebrated worldwide authority on hypnotism, was born into a Colvale Brahmin family in Candolim. The character in Dumas' Count of Monte Cristo may have been based on this AbbéFaria.

Further west, on Malacca Road, almost opposite the wharf are the **central library** and public rooms of the **Braganza Institute** ⓘ *Mon-Fri 0930-1300, 1400- 1745*. It was established as the **Instituto Vasco da Gama** in 1871, on the anniversary of the date that the Portuguese explorer da Gama sailed round the Cape of Good Hope, to stimulate an interest in culture, science and the arts. It was renamed for Luis Menezes de Braganza (1878-1938), an outstanding figure of social and political reform in early 20th century Goa. The blue tile frieze in the entrance, hand-painted by Jorge Colaco in 1935, is a mythical representation of the Portuguese colonization of Goa. An art gallery upstairs has paintings by European artists of the late 19th and early 20th centuries and Goan artists of the 20th century. The central libraryⓘ *0930-1300, 1200-1700*, dating from 1832, has a rare collection of religious and other texts.



## City centre

The giant white-washed 16th century **Church of the Immaculate Conception** ⓘ *Church Sq, Emidio Gracia Rd, Mon-Sat 0900-1300, 1530-1800, Sun 1030-1300, 1715-1900, free*, looms pristine and large over the main square, Largo Da Igreja. Its dimensions were unwarranted for the population of what was then, in Panjim, little

### Panjim

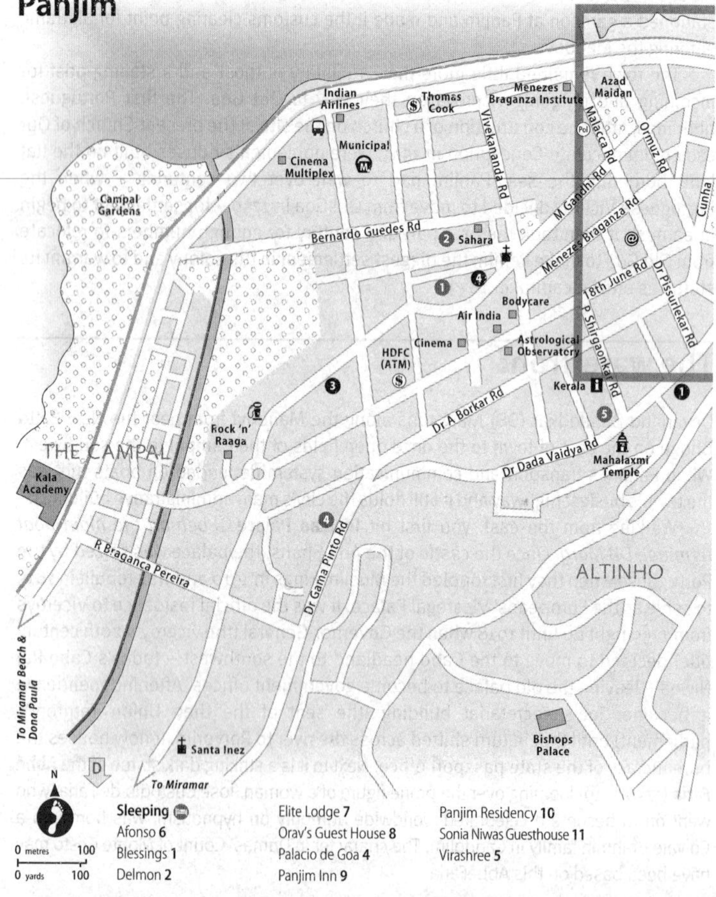

more than a marshy fishing village; its tall, Portuguese baroque twin towers were instead built both to act as a landmark for and to tend to the spiritual needs of arriving Portuguese sailors, for whom the customs post just below the hill at Panjim marked their first step on Indian soil. The church was built in 1541 then enlarged in 1600 to reflect its standing as the parish church of the capital; in 1619 it was completely rebuilt to its present design. Inside the church the main altar *reredos* (screens) and the altars on either side to Jesus the Crucified and to Our Lady of the Rosary, are typically ornate gilded baroque, in turn flanked by marble statues of St Peter and St Paul. The panels in the Chapel of St Francis, in the south transept, came from the chapel in the Idalcao Palace in 1918. The Feast Day is on 8 December. In 1945, the statue of Our Lady of Fatima was installed for whom parishioners gifted a crown of gold and diamonds five years later. This statue is carried in a candlelight procession each year on 13 October.

The Hindu **Mahalaxmi Temple** ⓘ *Dr Dada Vaidya Rd, free*, (originally 1818, but rebuilt and enlarged in 1983) is now hidden behind a newer building. It was the first Hindu place of worship to be allowed in the Old Conquests after the close of the Inquisition. The **Boca de Vaca** ('Cow's Mouth') spring, is near by.

***Related map***
*A Panjim centre, p1162.*

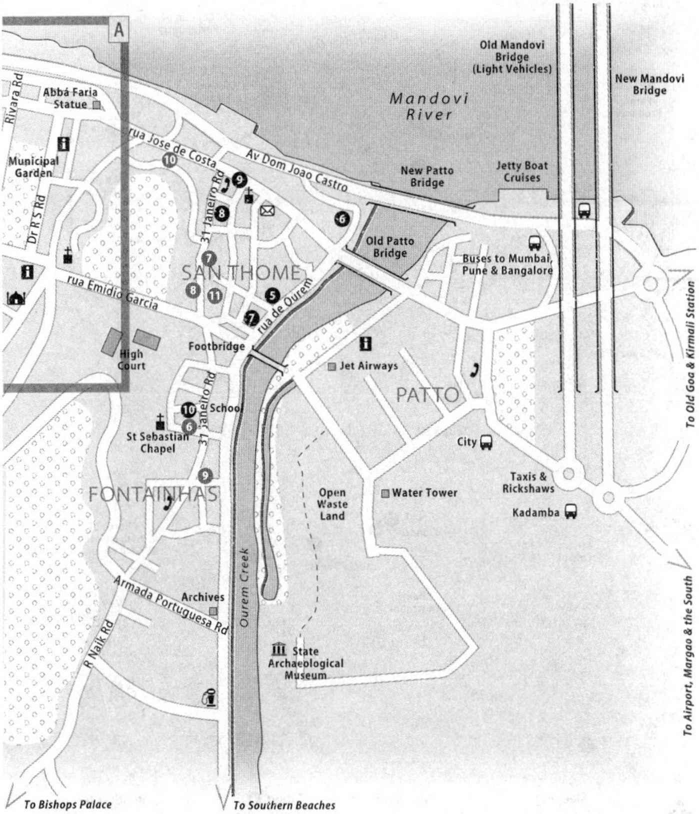

**Eating**
A Pastelaria **1**
Avanti Hotel **5**
Coriana **6**
Horseshoe **7**
Perry & Cookie **3**
Shiv Sagar **4**
Venite **8**
Vihar **9**
Viva Panjim **10**

## San Thome and Fontainhas

On Panjim's eastern promontory, at the foot of the Altinho and on the left bank of the Ourem Creek, sit first the San Thome and then, further south, Fontainhas districts filled with modest 18th- and 19th-century houses. The cumulative prettiness of the well-preserved buildings' colour-washed walls, trimmed with white borders, sloping tiled roofs and decorative wrought-iron balconies make it an ideal area to explore at walking pace. You can reach the area via any of the narrow lanes that riddle San Thome or take the footbridge across the Ourem Creek from the new bus stand and tourist office that feeds you straight into the heart of the district. A narrow road that runs east past the Church of the Immaculate Conception and main town square also ends up here. But probably the best way in is over the Altinho from the Mahalaxmi Temple: this route gives great views over the estuary from the steep eastern flank of



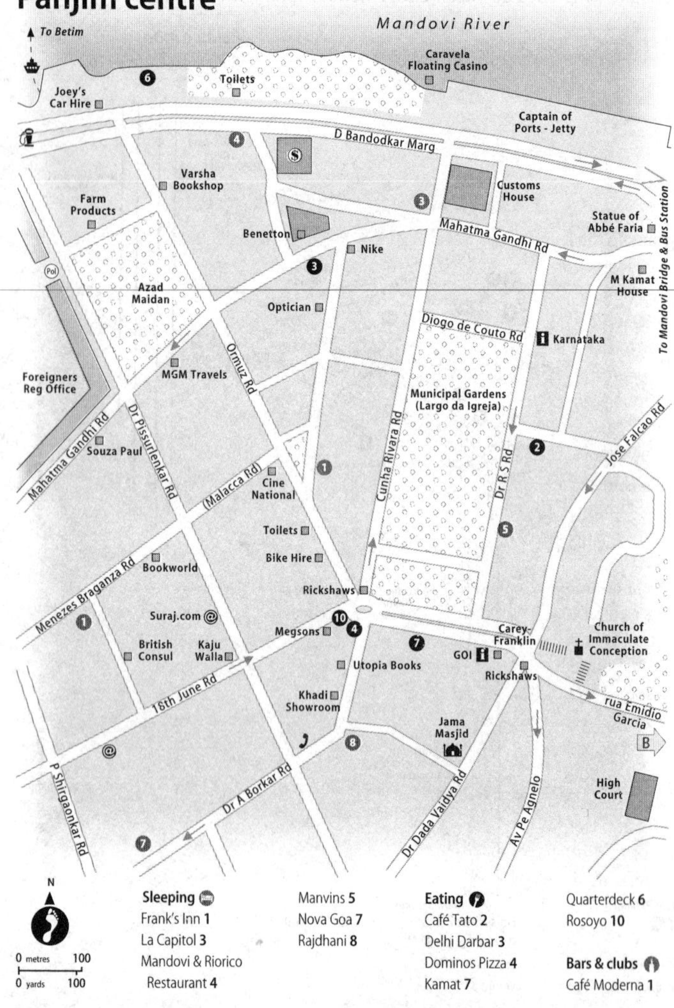

the hill, a vantage point once used for defensive purposes. A footpath drops down between the Altinho's 19th and 20th century buildings just south of San Sebastian Chapel to leave you slap bang in middle of Fontainhas.

The chief landmark here is the small **San Sebastian Chapel** ⓘ *St Sebastian Rd, open only during mass which is held in Konkani Mon and Tue, Thu-Sat 0715-0800, Wed 1800-1900, Sun 0645-0730, English mass Sun 0830-0930, free*, (built in 1818, rebuilt in 1888) which houses the large wooden crucifix that until 1812 stood in the Palace of the Inquisition in Old Goa where the eyes of Christ watched over the proceedings of the tribunal. For 100 years it rested in the chapel in the Idalcao Palace in Panjim before being moved here.

The **Goa State Museum** ⓘ *Patto, 0930-1730, free, head south of Kadamba Bus Stand, across the Ourem Creek footbridge, right across the waste ground and past the State Bank staff training building,* is an impressive building that contains a disappointingly small collection of religious art and antiquities. Most interesting are the original Provedoria lottery machines built in Lisbon that are on the first floor landing. A few old photos show how the machines were used.

# Old Goa and around

When the British explorer Richard Burton arrived in Goa on sick leave from his Indian army unit in 1850, he described Old Goa, once the oriental capital of Portuguese empire-building ambition and rival to Lisbon in grandeur, as a place of 'utter desolation'; its people 'as sepulchral-looking as the spectacle around them'. Today, Old Goa has a flagging melancholy beauty, revived by a steady flow of tourists and pilgrims to the remains of St Francis Xavier housed in the giddying baroque of Basilica of Bom Jesus, the only church you'll find in Goa to have escaped bright whitewashing.

## Ins and outs

**Getting there** Old Goa lies on the south bank of the Mandovi on the crest of a low hill 8 km from Panjim. The frequent bus service takes 15-20 minutes. Buses drop you off opposite the Basilica of Bom Jesus (Rs 5); pick up the return bus near the police station. Auto-rickshaws charge Rs 25, taxis, Rs 150 return. Karmali station on the Konkan Railway, just east of the centre, has taxis for transfer.

**Getting around** The major monuments are within easy walking distance of the bus stop. All the monuments are open daily, throughout the year, from 0830-1730.

## History

Old Goa is to Christians the spiritual heart of the territory. It owes its origin as a Portuguese capital to Afonso de Albuquerque and some of its early ecclesiastical development to St Francis Xavier who was here, albeit for only five months, in the mid-16th century. Before the Portuguese arrived it was the second capital of the Muslim Bijapur Kingdom. Today, all the mosques and fortifications of that period have disappeared and only a fragment of the Sultan's palace walls remain (see also Goa Velha below).

Old, or 'Velha', Goa – one time 'Rome of the East' – was a flourishing port with an enviable trade even before the Portuguese arrived. The bustling walled city was peopled by merchants of many nationalities who came to buy and sell horses from Arabia and Hormuz, to trade silk, muslin, calico, rice, spices and areca nuts from the interior and other ports along the west coast. It was a centre of ship-building and boasted fine residences and public buildings.

*Portuguese law decreed that owners colour-wash the outsides of their homes after each year's monsoon: the only buildings painted all white were churches, while secular buildings came in ochre with windows and door frames picked out in other colours.*

After the arrival of the Portuguese Old Goa swelled still further in size and significance. In the west lay barracks, mint, foundry and arsenal, hospital and prison. The banks of the Mandovi held the shipyards of Ribeira des Gales and next door lay the administrative and commercial centre. Streets and areas of the city were set aside for different activities and merchandise, each with its own character. The most important, Rua Direita ou dos Leiloes ('Straight Street') was lined with jewellers, bankers and artisans. It was also the venue for auctions of all manner of precious goods, held each morning except on Sundays. To the east was the market and the old fortress of Adil Shah, while the true centre of the town was filled with magnificent churches built by the Franciscans, themselves joined by waves of successive religious orders: first the Dominicans in 1548, the Augustinians from 1572, the Carmelites from 1612 and finally the Theatines from 1655. By the middle of the 17th century the city, plagued by cholera and malaria and crippled economically, it was abandoned for Panjim.



## The Basilica of Bom Jesus

The renaissance façade of Goa's most famous church, the **Basilica of Bom (the Good) Jesus**, a World Heritage Site, reflects the architectural transition to baroque taking place in Europe. Apart from the elaborate gilded altars, wooden pulpit and the candy-twist Bernini columns the interior is very simple.

The church contains the treasured remains of **St Francis Xavier**, a former pupil of soldier-turned-saint Ignatius Loyola, the founder of the Order of Jesuits. In 1613 St Francis' body was brought to the adjoining Professed House (see below) from the College of St Paul. It was moved into the church in 1624, and its present chapel in 1655 where it has remained ever since. St Francis was canonized in 1622.

The tomb, which lies to the right of the main chancel, (1698) was the gift of one of the last of the Medicis, Cosimo III, Grand Duke of Tuscany, and was carved by the Florentine sculptor Giovanni Batista Foggini. It took 10 years to complete. It consists of three tiers of marble and jasper: the upper tier has panels depicting scenes from the saint's life. The casket is silver and has three locks, the keys held by the Governor, the Archbishop and the Convent Administrator. You can look down on to the tomb from a small window in the art gallery next to the church.

After his canonization, St Francis' body was exposed for viewing on each anniversary of his death, but this ceased in 1707. Thereafter a few special private expositions were held until 1752, when the body was again put on public view, to quash rumours that the Jesuits had removed it. Since 1859, the exposition has taken place on the saint's death anniversary every 10 to 12 years: the next is scheduled for November 2004-January 2005. The relics are taken to the Sé Cathedral during this period to allow easier viewing for the vast numbers who attend. Feast Day is 3 December.

There is a **modern art gallery** ⓘ *only sporadically open*, next to the church with rather amazing surrealistic paintings by Goan painter Dom Martin alongside wooden statues of Christian saints. Next to the church, and connected with it, is the **Professed House for Jesuit fathers**, a handsome two-storey building with a typically Mediterranean open courtyard garden.

## Sé Cathedral

Across the square sits the **Sé Cathedral**, dedicated to St Catherine on whose day (25 November) Goa was recaptured by Alfonso de Albuquerque. Certainly the largest church in Old Goa, it could even be the biggest in Asia and was built on the ruins of a mosque by the Dominicans between 1562 and 1623. It is Tuscan on the exterior and

*The Basilica of Bom Jesus is on the list of the 100 most endangered sites according to the world momuments fund.*

Corinthian inside, with a barrel-vaulted ceiling and east-facing main façade. One of the characteristic twin towers collapsed in 1776 when it was struck by lightning. The remaining tower holds five bells including the Golden Bell (cast in Cuncolim in 1652). The vast interior, divided into the barrel-vaulted nave with clerestory and two side aisles, has a granite baptismal font. On each side of the church are four chapels along the aisles: on the right these are dedicated to St Anthony, St Bernard, The Cross of Miracles and the Holy Spirit, and on the left, starting at the entrance, to Our Lady of Virtues, St Sebastian, The Blessed Sacrament and Our Lady of Life. The clerestory windows are protected by a shield crowned by a balustrade to keep out the sun. The main altar is superbly gilded and painted, with six further altars in the transept. The marble-top table in front of the main altar is where, since 1955, St Francis Xavier's remains have been held during the exposition of the saint's relics. The main *reredos* has four panels illustrating the life of St Catherine. There is also an **art gallery** ⓘ *Mon-Thu, Sat 0900-1230, Sun 0900-1030, closed during services, Rs 5.*

*The ASI booklet on the monuments, 'Old Goa', by S Rajagopalan, is available from the Archaeological Museum here, Rs 10.*

## Around the cathedral

Southwest of the cathedral's front door are the ruins of the **Palace of the Inquisition**, where over 16,000 cases were heard between 1561 and 1774. The Inquisition was finally suppressed in 1814. Beneath the hall were dungeons. In Old Goa's heyday this was the town centre.

There are two churches and a museum in the same complex as the Cathedral. The **Church** (and Convent) **of St Francis of Assisi** is a broad vault of a church with two octagonal towers. The floor is paved with tombstones and on either side of the baroque high altar are paintings on wood depicting scenes from St Francis' life while the walls above have frescoes with floral designs. The original **Holy Spirit Church** in the Portuguese gothic (manueline) style was begun by Franciscan friars in 1517: everything except the old doorway was replaced by the larger present structure in the 1660s (itself restored in 1762-65). The convent now houses the **Archaeological Museum and Portrait Gallery** ⓘ *T0832-2286133, 1000-1230, 1500-1830, Rs 5,* whose collection of sculptures covers the period from before the arrival of the Portuguese. Many date from the 12th-13th centuries when Goa came under the rule of the

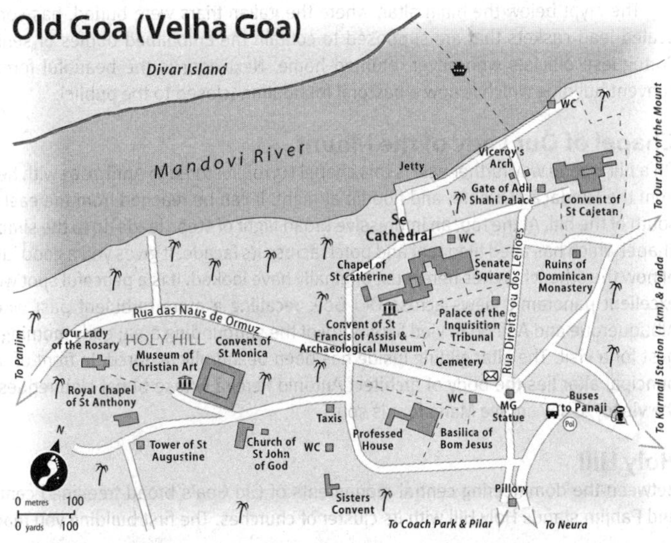

 Kadamba Dynasty. There are 'hero stones', commemorating naval battles, and 'sati stones' marking the practice of widow burning. There is also a rather fine collection of portraits of Portuguese Governors upstairs that is particularly revealing both for its charting of the evolution of court dress as well as the physical robustness of the governors inside that dress. Some governors were remarkable for their sickly pallor, others for the sheer brevity of their tenure of office, which must have set the portrait painters something of a challenge.

To the west is **St Catherine's Chapel**. It was built at the gate of the old city on the orders of Albuquerque as an act of gratitude after the Portuguese defeat of the forces of Bijapur in 1510. The original mud and thatch church was soon replaced by a stone chapel which in 1534 became the cathedral (considerably renovated in 1952), remaining so until Sé Cathedral was built.

On the road towards the Mandovi, northeast from the cathedral compound, lies the **Arch of the Viceroys (Ribeira dos Viceroys)**, commemorating the centenary of Vasco da Gama's discovery of the sea route to India. It was built at the end of the 16th century by his great-grandson, Francisco da Gama, Goa's Viceroy from 1597 to 1600. Its laterite block structure is faced with green granite on the side approached from the river. This was the main gateway to the seat of power: on arrival by ship each new Viceroy would be handed the keys and enter through this ceremonial archway before taking office. The statue of Vasco da Gama above the arch was originally surmounted by a gilded statue of St Catherine, the patron saint of the city. Walking east towards the convent from the arch you pass **the Gate of the Fortress of the Adil Shahs**, probably built by Sabaji, the Maratha ruler of Goa before the Muslim conquest of 1471. The now-ruined palace was home to the Adil Shahi sultans of Bijapur who occupied Goa before the arrival of the Portuguese. It was the Palace of the Viceroys until 1554 after which it served as both the hall of trials for the Inquisition and to house prisoners.



## Convent and Church of St Cajetan (Caetano)

A little further still stands the splendid, domed baroque **Convent and Church of St Cajetan (Caetano).** Pope Urban III dispatched a band of Italian friars of the Theatine order to spread the Gospel to the Deccani Muslim city of Golconda near Hyderabad but got a frosty reception so headed back west to settle in Goa. They acquired land around 1661 to build this church, which is shaped like a Greek cross and is partly modelled on St Peter's in Rome. It is the last remaining domed church in Goa.

The crypt below the main altar, where the Italian friars were buried, has some sealed lead caskets that are supposed to contain the embalmed bodies of senior Portuguese officials who never returned home. Next door is the beautiful former convent building which is now a pastoral foundation (closed to the public).

## Chapel of Our Lady of the Mount

On a hill a good way further east is this chapel (1510), restored in April 2001 with help from the **Fundação Oriente**, and floodlit at night. It can be reached from the east or south of the hill. At the top, an impressive broad flight of steps leads up to the simple chapel which has a red tiled roof and porch across its façade. It gives you a good idea of how the other churches here must originally have looked. It is a peaceful spot with excellent panoramic views across Old Goa, recalling a more turbulent past when Albuquerque and Adil Shah vied for control of the surrounding area; early morning is best for a visit. The altar gilding inside has been beautifully restored. In front of the principal altar lies the body of architect Antonio Pereira whose burial slab requests the visitor to say an Ave Maria for his soul.

## Holy Hill

Between the domineering central monuments of Old Goa's broad tree-lined centre and Panjim stands Holy Hill with its cluster of churches. The first building you reach (on your left) as you leave the central plaza is the **Church and Convent of St John of God**, built in 1685 and abandoned in 1835. To the right is the **Museum of Christian Art** ⓘ *Sun-Thu 1000-1700, Rs 5*, with 150 items gathered from Goa's churches, convents and Christian homes to show a rich cross-section of Indo-Portuguese sacred art workmanship in wood, ivory, silver and gold.

Next door sits **The Convent of St Monica** (1607-27), the first nunnery in India and the largest in Asia. A huge three-storey square building, with the church in the southern part, it was built around a sunken central courtyard containing a formal garden. At one time it was a Royal Monastery, but in 1964 became a theological institute, the Mater Dei Institute for Nuns. It was here in 1936 that Bishop Dom Frei Miguel Rangel is believed to have had a vision of the Christ figure on the Miraculous Cross opening his eyes, his stigmata bleeding and his lips quivering as if to speak. The vision was repeated later that year in the presence of the Bishop, the Viceroy Dom Pedro de Silva and a large congregation.

Take the left fork of the road to reach **The Royal Chapel of St Anthony** (1543) – dedicated to Portugal's national saint and restored by its government in 1961 – and, opposite, **the tower of St Augustine**. Although it is an uphill hike, it is very atmospheric and well worth the effort. The Augustinians came to Goa in 1572; the church they immediately began, bar the belfry, lies now in ruins. It once boasted eight chapels, a convent and an excellent library and was enlarged to become one of the finest in the kingdom. It was finally abandoned in 1835 because of religious persecution. The vault collapsed in 1842 burying the image; the façade and main tower followed in 1931 and 1938. Only one of the original four towers survives. The large bell now hangs in Panjim's Church of the Immaculate Conception. The Archaeological Survey of India is spearheading extensive repairs.

Behind is the **Chapel of Our Lady of the Rosary** (1526). Belonging to the earliest period of church building, it is called Manueline after Manuel I, the Portuguese king who oversaw a period of great prosperity that coincided with the country's conquest of Goa. The use of Hindu and Muslim craftsmen in building the chapel led to an architectural style that borrowed from Iberian decoration but also absorbed both local naturalistic motifs and Islamic elements (seen on the marble cenotaph). The church here has a two-storey entrance, a single tower and low flanking turrets. It was from here that Albuquerque directed the battle against the Adil Shahi forces in 1510.

# Around Panjim

## Miramar and Gaspar Dias

**Miramar** is 3 km along the Mandovi from the centre of Panjim, not far enough to stop the place soaking in a great deal of the feeling of the city. The water is dirty and the beach holds little allure, so it's hardly the ideal spot for a beach holiday. Even so, it's a pleasant drive with good views over the sea and, if you've got a little time to kill, offers the best quick escape from the city, as used by many locals at sunset.

**Gaspar Dias Fortress** was finished around 1606. The Panjim-Ribandar causeway, built in 1634, gave it direct land access to the capital at Old Goa and its significance grew accordingly. The walls, likely laterite blocks 1½ m thick and 5 m high, made space for 16 cannons. These saw repeated action against the Dutch until the middle of the 17th century, but the fortress' importance waned after the Maratha onslaught and it fell into disrepair under 15 years of occupation by a British garrison in the early 19th century. It was made new but the Portuguese army finally abandoned it in 1870 as a result of further damage sustained during the mutiny against the Prefect of 1835. For a while the military still stationed soldiers here to convalesce but by the 20th century it had crumbled beyond recognition. All that is left is one cannon at the Miramar circle that marks the possible site of the fort.

## Cabo Raj Niwas

From the roundabout by the **National Oceanography Institute** at the southern foot of Miramar beach, the road runs 600 m up to **Cabo Raj Niwas**, now Raj Bhavan, the **State Governor's House** ⓘ *closed to visitors but passes are given at the gate for mass, Sun 0930*. Inside the private grounds, six cannons and some sections of wall are all that is left of the Portuguese Cabo fort which stood on top of the cliffs of this rocky promontory. The first small **Our Lady of Cabo** shrine was built in 1541 before the fort was built. Documents of 1633 refer to both the chapel and various buildings of an incomplete fort with only four guns. During the Napoleonic Wars British troops garrisoned in the fort from 1799-1813 constructed more buildings for themselves (subsequently demolished by the Portuguese). A fair number of overgrown graves stand in the nearby **British Cemetery**, which still has a gate and four walls, to serve as a stark reminder. Around 1844, after the religious orders were abolished, the Archbishop of Goa was given the convent. He converted it into an impressive residence. Later, the Governor-General of Goa acquired the building and, after further upgrades, it became his official residence in 1918. Its grand interior was left intact after the Portuguese left in 1961. The splendid glassed-in veranda on the seaward side is a special feature. If you don't make it inside the residence for mass, it's still worth a detour up here for the viewing platform near the entrance that gives superb views over the sweep of the coastline across the Mandovi estuary to Fort Aguada. This is where some local Goans come to canoodle at dusk.



## Dona Paula

Dona Paula has a small palm-fringed beach with casuarina groves. The low laterite cliff forms a headland joined to the mainland by a short causeway. There's a platform that gives good views across the bay to Vasco da Gama and the busy shipping lanes that lead to the port of Mormugao. Fisherfolk turned local vendors sell cheap seaside knick-knacks and give speedy boat rides. It's a popular local picnic spot.

As is often the case in India, there is more than one story of who the Dona of the village's name could have been. Some say she was Paula de Menezes (the wife of a nobleman, Antonio de Souto Maior, and reputedly a mistress of the Viceroy), who died a young woman, in 1682: a black granite memorial stone is on a wall in the Chapel of Our Lady of Cabo and the family summerhouse still survives. Others link the village's name to a Paula who jumped from the cliffs when refused permission by her father to marry Gaspar Dias, a fisherman.

## Sleeping

Panjim has a wide choice of accommodation. There are upmarket options south of town in Miramar and Dona Paula, but for most character it's best to book into one of the guesthouses in the atmospheric Fontainhas district. If you don't wish to stay you can see most of the sights in a day. Guesthouses have 0800-0930 checkout to accommodate new arrivals on trains and buses.

**Panjim** *p1158, maps p1160 and p1162*

**A-B Mandovi**, D B Marg, T0832- 2426270, www.hotelmandovigoa.com. Old building with hints of art deco, relaxing but lacks great character. 66 large a/c rooms (more expensive river-facing), rates include breakfast. 1st floor **Riorico** restaurant, popular pastry shop, terrace bar, exchange.

**B Nova Goa**, Dr Atmaram Borkar Rd, T0832-2226231, www.hotelnovagoa.com. 85 good a/c rooms with bath, some have fridge, best with pool views, dull and dirty generally.

**B-C Delmon**, C de Albuquerque Rd, T0832-2226846, www.alcongoa.com. 50 clean rooms with TV and desk, some a/c, breakfast included. Modern, comfortable hotel with popular restaurant.

**C La Capitol**, MG Rd, next to Custom House, T0832-2231050, lsons@goatelecom.com. 12 renovated rooms (some smallish), TV, neat, clean, restaurant, friendly and willing staff, but noisy during the day, check out 0900.

**D Manvins**, 4th floor, Souza Towers, T0832-2224412, www.goamanvins.com. 40 good-size, clean rooms, compact bathroom, TV, stunning views over Municipal Gardens and Mandovi river. Terrace at the rear has a good view of Panjim Church and is a relatively private place to relax. Access via colourful passageway and lift to 4th floor.
**D Palacio de Goa**, Gama Pinto Rd, T0832-2221785. Modern 6-storey building, 55 decent rooms with phone, TV, (good value 4 or 5-bedded) a/c extra Rs 100, top floor best views, restaurant, far from bus stand.
**D Rajdhani**, Dr Atmaram Borkar Rd, T0832-2225362. 35 smallish clean rooms with bath, some a/c (Rs 100 extra), in modern Indian business hotel, a/c, pure veg restaurant.
**D-E Blessings**, MG Rd, behind Bhatkar House, T0832-2224770, hotelblessings@ yahoo.com. 18 ordinary rooms, TV (extra Rs 50), 2 have huge terraces instead of balconies, restaurant, quiet back yard full of trees.
**D-E Panjim Residency** (GTDC), overlooking the river, T0832- 2227103. 40 good-size rooms with balcony, some a/c (overpriced at Rs 950), best views from top floor, good open-air restaurant, often full.
**D-E Virashree**, opposite Mahalaxmi Temple, Dr Dada Vaidya Rd, T0832-2226656, vira shree@hotmail.com. 12 large, comfortable rooms with TV but lacking quality finish.
**E Orav's Guest House**, 31 Janeiro Rd, T0832-2426128. 16 good rooms with shower, some with pleasant balcony, clean modern block in old part of town.
**F Frank's Inn**, 83 Menezes Braganza Rd, T0832-2226716. 10 clean rooms, shared bath.

**San Thome and Fontainhas** *p1162*
**A The Panjim Peoples**, opposite the **Panjim Inn**, www.panjiminn.com. The 3rd heritage project from the Sukhija family behind the Panjim Inn, this one is properly top end with just 4 rooms, antique 4-poster beds and bathtubs, plus internet access.
**C Panjim Inn**, E212, 31 January Rd, T0832-2226523, www.panjiminn.com. Goa's first heritage hotel is idiosyncratic, even in the context of the historic Fontainhas district. 14 rooms of varying size all fitted with 4-poster beds, a/c comes for an extra Rs 250.
**C Panjim Pousada**, up the road from **Panjim Inn**. Slightly cheaper sister hotel to the **Panjim Inn** with double rooms set around a permanent art gallery in a courtyard. It is an evocative, attractive renovation. Best rooms at the back overlook another courtyard. Recommended.
**E Afonso**, near San Sebastian Chapel, Fontainhas, T0832-2222359. 8 clean rooms with bath, shaded roof terrace for breakfast, a family-run guesthouse, obliging and friendly, reserve ahead. Recommended.

**Around Panjim** *p1167*
All the below are in Miramar.
**AL-A Goa Marriott Resort**, Mandovi River, T0832-2463333, reservation@goamarriott resort.com. 153 large rooms, good facilities, pool (close to public beach), best hotel in area. Weekend buffet lunches popular with Panjim residents.
**B Swimsea Beach Resort**, T0832-2464481, swimsea@satyam.net.in. 28 a/c rooms with small balconies (in need of a makeover), sea facing best, pool, close to black sandy beach.
**C Blue Bay**, Caranzalem beach, T0832-2464881, bluebay@sancharnet.in. 12 simple modern rooms, some a/c, well kept grounds, friendly owner, quiet and isolated.
**D Miramar Beach Resort**, close to the beach, T0832-2227754. 60 clean rooms, some a/c, there are better (and cheaper) rooms in newer wing by shaded groves, good restaurant.

## Eating

**Panjim** *p1158, maps p1160 and p1162*
**TTT Rioricoi**, at the **Mandovi**, D Bandodkar Marg. Good seafood (tiger prawns Rs 600), Portuguese and Goan dishes, great buffet breakfast Rs 150.
**TT Avanti Hotel**, Rua de Ourem, T0832-2427179, near Old Patto Bridge, Mon-Sat. Popular local Goan food and chilled beers, a/c, outdoor balcony. Recommended.
**TT Delhi Durbar Restaurant and Bar**, MG Rd, T0832-2222544. Mughlai delicacies in plush environment. Kebabs, mutton rogan gosh, *paneer shashlik* etc. Panjim's finest North Indian food.

*For an explanation of the sleeping and eating price codes used in this guide, see inside the front cover. Other relevant information is found in Essentials pages 56-61.*

¥¥ **Goenchin**, off Dr Dada Vaidya Rd. Tasty Chinese with spicy seafood (Rs 80-140).

¥¥ **Horseshoe**, Rua de Ourem, T0832-2431788, Mon-Sat 1200-1430, 1900-1030. Low key Portuguese/Goan restaurant set across 2 orange and white high-ceiling rooms with exceptionally good service. Most meals are excellent value (Rs 60-80) but daily fish specials like red snapper are far more costly (from Rs 300). The cashew cake, Bolo San Rival (Rs 50), trumps all the great main courses; unique to the Horseshoe, it is worth a pilgrimage in itself. Highly recommended.

¥¥ **Quarterdeck**, next to Betim ferry jetty, T0832-2432905. Goan, Indian, Chinese. Riverside location is the best in Panjim, very pleasant in the evening when brightly lit cruise boats glide gaudily by. Live music.

¥¥ **Venite**, 31 Janeiro Rd, T0832-2225537, Mon-Sat 0800-2200, closes in the afternoon. The most charming of Panjim's eateries has 1st floor balconies overlooking the Sao Thome streetlife and good music. Simple breakfasts and good Goan food, Rs 80+ for main dishes, pricier lobsters. Beer.

¥¥ **Viva Panjim**, house no 178, signposted from 31 Janeiro Rd, T0832-2422405. This family-run place dishes up specials of Goan food along with seafood plus take-away parcels of Indian, Chinese and continental.

¥ **Annapurna**, Ormuz Rd. South Indian. Good *thalis* and *dosa* in large, clean eatery upstairs with families relaxing over *chai*.

¥ **Café Tato**, off east side of Church Sq, closed evenings. Something of a local institution, Tato is always busy at lunchtime when office workers descend for favourite genuine Goan grub. Upstairs is a/c.

¥ **Coriana**, in the lea of New Patto bridge, Mon-Sat, Goan. Dark purple decor and high backed booths give a slightly seedy feel, but the food is genuine, pleasant owner, excellent fresh fish, chilli fry, *sorpotel*, roast tongue.

¥ **Kamat**, south end of Municipal Gardens. Very popular dining hall (quiet a/c upstairs), excellent *masala dosa* (Rs 18) and *thalis* (Rs 28), no alcohol.

¥ **Rosoyo**, 18th June Rd. Serves a choice of excellent Gujarati *thalis*, Rs 40-50, generous refills (1130-1530), plus evening special, Rs 80. Recommended.

¥ **Shiv Sagar**, MG Rd. South Indian vegetarian. No *thalis*, tasty Mysore *masala dosa* (Rs 20), clean, popular, a/c upstairs.

¥ **Vihar**, R José de Costa. South Indian vegetarian. Well-prepared tasty *thalis* (Rs 50) and good choice of snacks, clean smart a/c upstairs.

### Bakeries, cafés and fast food

**A Pastelaria**, Dr Dada Vaidya Rd. Good variety of cakes, pastries and breads behind clean glass cases. **Mandovi Hotel** has a branch too (side entrance).

**Chicky Chocky** near Church of the Immaculate Conception. Good fast foods. '*Sizzle Point*' for speciality sizzlers.

**Perry & Cookie**, MG Rd, west end of town. Take-away kebab house and roast chicken.

### Around Panjim *p1167*

¥¥ **Beach Boogie**, Caranzalem beach, towards Miramar bus stand. Garden restaurant, varied menu, live music.

¥ **Foodland**, Miramar Beach Resort. Fast food.

¥ **Goa Marriott's pastry shop,** Mandovi River, Miramar, T0832-2463333. Has real continental delights (truffle torte, tiramisu).

¥ **Goan Delicacy**, Hawaii Beach, Dona Paula, T0832- 2224356. Look for the sign by the rickshaw stand on NIO Circle, follow track to left of Dona Paula road, turn left at the bottom and follow sandy path. Seafood, good local dishes, Tandoori oven, bar, family-run, very friendly. Relaxing atmosphere.

¥ **White House**, near NIO Post Office, Dona Paula, T0832-2221239. Goan and seafood with great views over the shoreline.

## Bars and clubs

### Panjim *p1158, maps p1160 and p1162*

You can't go 20 paces in Panjim without finding a bar: pokey little rooms with tables and chairs and some snacks being fried up in the corner. Many are clustered around Fontainhas. The *feni* (Goa's cashew- or coconut-extracted moonshine) comes delivered in jerry cans, making it cheaper than restaurants. Solitary women are rare.

**Café Moderna** near Cine National, food none too good, claustrophobic upstairs dining area, quality atmosphere.

## Entertainment

**Panjim** *p1158, maps p1160 and p1162*
Read the today's events columns in the local papers: it often happens that some great concerts and performances are underpromoted.

**Astronomical Observatory**, 7th floor, Junta House, 18th June Rd (entrance in Vivekananda Rd), open 14 Nov-31 May, 1900-2100, in clear weather. Rooftop 6 inch Newtonian reflector telescope and binoculars. Worth a visit on a moonless night, and for views over Panjim at sunset.

**Kala Academy**, D B Marg, Campal, T0832-2223288. This modern and architecturally impressive centre designed by Charles Correa was set up to preserve and promote the cultural heritage of Goa. There are exhibition galleries, a library and comfortable indoor and outdoor auditoria. Art exhibitions, theatre, and music programmes (from contemporary pop and jazz to Indian classical) are held, mostly during the winter months. There are also courses on music and dance.

**MV Caravela**, Fisheries dept building, D B Marg, Panjim www.casinocity.com/in/panjim/caravela. India's first floating casino is docked on the Mandovi, 215 ft of high-rupee-rolling catamaran casino, all plush wall-to-wall carpets, chandeliers and sari-wearing croupiers. The boat accommodates 300 people, has a sun deck, swimming pool and restaurant and the Rs 1,200 entrance includes short eats and dinner and booze from 1730 till the morning.

## Festivals and events

**Panjim** *p1158, maps p1160 and p1162*

**Jan** Fontainhas Festival of Arts. 30 old homes around Panjim are converted into galleries.

**Feb/Mar** In addition to the major festivals in Feb, the **Mardi Gras Carnival** (3 days preceding Lent in Feb/Mar) is a Mediterranean-style riot of merrymaking, marked by feasting, colourful processions and floats down streets: it kicks off near the Secretariat at midday. One of the best bits is the red-and-black dance held in the cordoned off square outside the old world Clube Nacional on the evening of the last day: everyone dresses up (some cross-dressing), almost everyone knows each other, and there's lots of old-fashioned slow-dancing to curiously country and western infused live music. The red and black theme is strictly enforced.

**Mar-Apr** Shigmotsav is a spring festival held at full moon (celebrated as Holi elsewhere in India); colourful float processions through the streets often display mythological scenes accompanied with plenty of music on drums and cymbals.

**First Sun after Easter** Feast of Jesus of Nazareth. Procession of all Saints in Goa Velha, on the Monday of Holy Week.

**Nov/Dec** Food and Culture Festival at Miramar beach.

**Dec 8** Feast of Our Lady of the Immaculate Conception. A big fair is held in the streets around Church Sq and a firework display is put on in front of the church each night of the week before the feast (at 1930). After morning Mass on the Sun, the Virgin is carried in a procession through the town centre.

## Shopping

**Panjim** *p1158, maps p1160 and p1162*

**Books**

**Mandovi Hotel** bookshop has a good range including American news magazines.

**Utopia**, Dr A Borkar Rd, near Dominos Pizza, 1000-2000. Goa tourism booklets and maps, and books on Goan and Indian cuisine, helpful staff.

**Varsha**, near Azad Maidan, carries a wide stock in tiny premises, and is especially good for books on Goa. Obscure titles are not displayed but ask knowledgeable staff.

**Clothes and textiles**

**Madame Butterfly**, opposite Azad Maidan. For carefully-crafted designer wear for women plus accessories.

**Sosa's**, E 245 Rue De Ourem Panjim, T0832-2228063. Clothes as well as jewellery in papier mâché and silver.

**Velha Goa Galeria**, 4/191 Rua De Ourem, Fountainhas, T0832-2426628. Hand-painted ceramics, tiles used as wall hangings to tabletops.

**Wendell Rodricks Design Space**, B5 Suryadarshan Colony, T0832-2238177.

Rodricks is probably Goa's most famous fashion designer who built his name making minimalist clothing. Here you'll find his luxury clothes and footwear.

**Carey Franklin**, Church Sq, next to GOI Tourist Office. Smart a/c shops near Delhi Durbar restaurant have genuine stock of international brands Adidas, Benetton, Jordache, Lacoste, Lee, Levi's (jeans Rs 1200-1600), Nike, Wrangler.

**Government Emporia** on RS Rd. Good value for fixed-rate clothes, fabric and handicrafts.

**Khadi Showroom**, Municipal (Communidade) Building, Church Sq, good value for fixed-rate clothes, fabric and handicrafts. Nehru jackets, Rs 250, plus perishable items such as honey and pickles.

### Handicrafts

Goa Government handicrafts shops are at the tourist hotels and the Interstate Terminus. There are other emporia on RS Rd.

**Kohinoor**, 14 Patto Plaza, Shiv Towers. For high class pieces, beautifully displayed.

## Transport

**Panjim** *p1158, maps p1160 and p1162*

### Air

The airport is at Dabolim. From Dabolim airport, 29 km via the Zuari Bridge from Panjim, internal flights can be taken through Air India to Mumbai and Thiruvananthapuram. For pre-paid taxis, see Ins and outs, page 1158.

**Airline offices** Air India, 18th June Rd, T0832-2431101. Indian Airlines and Alliance Air, Dempo House, D B Marg, T0832-2237821, reservations 1000-1300, 1400-1600, airport T0832- 2540788, flights to **Bangalore**, **Delhi** and **Mumbai** daily (US$95), and **Chennai**. British Airways, 2 Excelsior Chambers, opposite Mangaldeep, MG Rd, T0832-2224573. Jet Airways, Sesa Ghor, 7-9 Patto Plaza, T0832- 2431472, airport T0832-2510354. Flights to **Mumbai** (US$103), and **Bangalore**. Kuwait Airways, 2 Jesuit House, Dr DR de Souza Rd, Municipal Garden Sq, T0832-2224612. Sahara, Live-In Appt, Gen Bernard Guedes Rd, airport office, T0832-2540043. To **Mumbai**, US$95, daily, and **Delhi**.

### Auto-rickshaw

Easily available but agree a price beforehand (Rs 20-35), more after dark. Motorcycle taxis and private taxis are a little cheaper.

### Bus

**Local** Crowded Kadamba (KTC) buses and private buses operate from the bus stand in Patto to the east of town, across the Ourem Creek, T0832-2222634. Booking 0800- 1100, 1400-1630. The timetable is not strictly observed: buses leave when full. Frequent service to **Calangute** 35 mins, Rs 7; **Mapusa** 25 mins, Rs 5. Via Cortalim (Zuari bridge) to **Margao** 1 hr, Rs 8; **Vasco** 1 hr, Rs 8. To **Old Goa** (every 10 mins) 20 mins, Rs 5, continues to **Ponda** 1 hr, Rs 8.

**Long distance** 'Luxury' buses and 'Sleepers' (bunks are shared). **Private operators**: Laxmi Motors, near Customs House, T0832-2225745; company at Cardozo Building near KTC bus stand; Paulo Tours, Hotel Fidalgo, T0832-2226291. **State buses** are run by Kadamba TC, Karnataka RTC, Maharashtra RTC. Check times and book in advance at Kadamba Bus Stand. Unlicensed operators use poorly maintained, overcrowded buses; check out beforehand.

Buses to **Bangalore**: 1530-1800 (13 hrs), Rs 300; **Belgaum**: 0630-1300 (5 hrs); **Gokarna** and **Hospet (Hampi)**: 0915-1030 (10 hrs), Rs 150 (Rs 350 sleeper); **Hubli**: many; **Londa**: 4 hrs, Rs 60; **Mangalore**: 0615-2030 (10 hrs), Rs 180; **Miraj**: 1030 (10 hrs); **Mumbai**: 1530-1700 (15 hrs+), Rs 550 (sleeper), others (some a/c) Rs 300-450; **Pune**: 0615-1900 (12 hrs), Rs 200, sleeper Rs 400.

### Car hire

Sai Service, 36/1 Alto Porvorim, north of the Mandovi Bridge, T0832-2417063, or at airport. Hertz, T0832-2223998; Joey's, town centre opposite the Mandovi Hotel, T0832- 2422050, Rs 700 per day (80 km) with driver. Wheels, T0832-2224304, airport, T0832-2512138.

### Ferry

Flat-bottomed ferries charge a nominal fee to take passengers (and usually vehicles) when rivers are not bridged. **Panjim-Betim** (the Nehru bridge over the Mandovi supplements the ferry); **Old Goa-Diwar Island**; **Ribandar-Chorao** for Salim Ali Bird Sanctuary.

### Taxi

Tourist one are white. Can be hired from Goa Tourism, Trionora Apts, T0832-2223396, about Rs 700 per day (80 km). Share-taxis run on certain routes; available near the the ferry wharves, main hotels and market places (max 5). **Mapusa** from Panjim, around Rs 10 each. **Airport** about 40 mins; Rs 380.

### Train

Some Konkan Railway trains stop at **Karmali**, T0832-2286398, near Old Goa (20 mins taxi). **Rail Bookings**, Kadamba Bus Station, 1st flr, T0832-2435054, 0930-1300; 1430-1700. South Central Railway serves the Vasco-Londa/Belgaum line; for details see page 1158, and Margao (Madgaon), page 1213.

## Directory

**Panjim** *p1158, maps p1160 and p1162*
**Banks** Many private agencies change TCs and cash. **Sita** transfers money worldwide (see activities and tours); **Thomas Cook**, 8 Alcon Chambers, D B Marg, T0832-2431732, Mon-Sat. Also for Thomas Cook drafts, money transfers; **Amex**, at Menezes Air Travel, Rua de Ourem, but does not cash TCs. Cash against certain credit cards from **Central Bank**, Nizari Bhavan; **Andhra Bank**, Dr Atmaram Borkar Rd, opposite EDC House, T0832-2223513; **Bank of Baroda**, Azad Maidan; **HDFC**, 18 June Rd, T0832-2421922, 24 hr ATM, most convienient way to obtain cash in Panjim. **High commissions and consulates** Germany, Hon Consul, c/o Cosme Matias Menezes Group, Rua de Ourem, T0832- 2223261; **Portugal**, LIC Bldg, Patto, T0832- 2224233; **UK**, room 302, 3rd floor, Manguirish Bldg, 18th June Rd, T0832-2228571, bcagoa@goa1.dot.net. **Hospital Goa Medical College**, Av PC Lopez, west end of town, T0832-2223026, is very busy; newer College at Bambolim; **CMM Poly Clinic**, Altinho, T0832-2225918.
**Internet** Among many charging Rs 35-40 per hr: **little.dot.com cyber cafe**, 1st floor, Padmavati Towers, 18th June Rd, 0930-2300. Best in town: **Suraj Business Centre**, 5 terminals upstairs, excellent fast connection (128 Kbps ISDN line), 0900-2300. **Post** Old Tobacco Exchange, St Thome, towards Old Patto Bridge, with Poste Restante on left as you enter, Mon-Sat 0930-1730, closed 1300-1400.

# North Goa

*North Goa packs a mean punch when it comes to diversity of scenery, landscapes and social scenes, and its coastline comes littered with watchful war-torn forts. These stretch from the royal fort Reis Magos right up to the beautiful boutiquey hotel built into the ramparts of Goa's northernmost outpost Tiracol, whose church still serves the 350 Catholics living on this patch of Goa over the Maharashtra border. All are interspliced by some of Goa's most beautiful beaches, offering everything from outright yours-the-only-footprints-in-the-sand isolation to full-on blow-your-whistle hedonism, all within easy reach of the state's key cultural sites.* ▸▸ *For Sleeping, Eating and other listings, see pages 1185-1198.*

## Mapusa and the Bardez beaches

The faultless fawn sands of coastal Bardez, particularly Calangute, that until 40 years ago lay at the feet of a string of fishing villages, now act as sandpit to the head-quarters of Goa's travel trade. Chock full of accommodation, eateries, travel agents, money changers, beggars and tourists, the roads quickly become snarled up with tourist minivans and unchecked development has made for a largely concrete conurbation that is home to the majority of Goa's 20,081 charter tourists come peak season. Where the strip south of Baga is more about the bottle, Anjuna and up is inevitably fuelled on drugs. For all that, if you squint hard, or come in monsoon, you can see what once attracted the visitors: wonderful coconut-fringed sandy beaches backed by dunes that are only occasionally punctuated by rocky headlands and coves; you can walk ankle-deep in the Arabian sea almost uninterrupted all the way from fort to fort between Aguada and Vagator.

## Ins and outs

**Getting there** The NH17 acts as the main arterial road between all of Goa's coastal belt. From Panjim, the highway crosses the Mandovi Bridge to the area's main hub, Calangute (16 km from Panjim, 10 km from Mapusa). Cheap, slow buses run frequently to all points along the highway. Those from Mapusa (20 minutes) and Panjim (35 minutes), arrive at Calangute bus stand near the market; a few continue to Baga to the north, from the crossroads. You can charter tourist minivans from Panjim, Dabolim, etc. The closest stop on the Konkan railway route between Mumbai and Mangalore is Tivim near Mapusa. On market days there are boats from Baga to Anjuna. There are buses from Mapusa and Panjim to Calangute, Anjuna, Chopora and Arambol but many prefer to hire a motorbike or bike to find their stretch of sand.



**Getting around** The roads in this area are pretty free from potholes so night riding on bicycles, scooters and motorcycles is okay – but beware the sudden unflagged speed-breaker. Despite the hazards, two-wheelers offer unparalleled independence in zipping from one pocket of sand to the next, and perhaps packing a bag for a night and leaving the rest of your luggage in a cheap hotel. Taxis and motorcycle taxis are ubiquitous. Tourist vans and old ambassador cabs are also available; both cost Rs 8 per kilometre. Public buses run up and down the coast road, but for short distances it is often easier to charter motorcycle taxis or head for the sand and walk.

**Orientation and information** There are 9 km of uninterrupted starched sand between Fort Aguada and the tunnel-bridge over Baga river in the north. These are split into four beaches: Sinquerim, Candolim, Calangute and Baga, all of their sands doused with the Arabian Sea. Running parallel to the water on dry land there is one main thoroughfare that acts as an unofficial high street: of these, Calangute's is by far the most built up.

## Background

The name Bardez may have come from the term *bara desh* (12 'divisions of land') – a reference to the 12 Brahmin villages that once dominated the region. Another explanation is that it refers to 12 *zagors*, celebrated to ward off evil. Or it could be *Bahir des*, meaning 'outside land' – ie, the land beyond the Mandovi river. It was occupied by the Portuguese as part of their original conquest, and so bears the greatest direct imprint of their Christianizing influence.

## Mapusa → *Colour map 5a, grid A1.*

There's no beauty in Bardez's administrative headquarters: a buzzy, unruly market town filled with 60s low-rise buildings. The banks of the Mapusa river, once a transport artery, have been reclaimed for building and its waters now come sadly clogged by urban waste. It's a friendly town though and, however small and messy, manages to also stock pretty much everything under the sun in its shops. The town is an important junction both for interstate buses and local bus routes including those to the northern beaches.

The **municipal market** ⓘ *Mon-Sat, opens from early morning; peters out between noon and three, then gathers steam again till night*, has giant rings of chourica sausage, tumbles of spices and rows of squatting fruit and veg hawkers.

Walk east for the small 16th century **St Jerome's Church**, or 'Milagres', Our Lady of Miracles (1594), rebuilt first in 1674 then again in 1839 after a candle sparked a devastating fire. In 1961 the roof was badly damaged when the Portuguese blew up a nearby bridge in their struggle with the liberating Indian army. The church has a scrolled gable, balconied windows in the façade, a belfry at the rear and an interesting slatted wood ceiling. The main altar is to Our Lady, and on either side are St John and St Jerome: the *retables* (shelves behind the altar) were brought from Daugim. The church is sacred to Hindus as well as Catholics: not only because it stands near the site of the Shanteri Temple but also because 'Our Lady of Miracles' was one of seven Hindu sisters converted to Christianity. Her lotus pattern gold necklace (now kept under lock and key) may also have been taken from a Hindu deity who preceded her.

The **Maruti temple** ⓘ *west of the market opposite the taxi stand*, was built on the site of a firecracker shop where Rama followers in the 1840s would gather in clandestine worship of first a picture, then a silver image, of monkey god Hanuman after the Portuguese destroyed their Hindu temples.

Barely 5 km east of Mapusa finds you in **Moira**, deep in the belly of a rich agricultural district that was once the scene of Portuguese mass baptisms. The town is ancient – some say it was the site of a sixth or seventh century AD Mauryan settlement – and until the arrival of the Portuguese it must have been a Brahmin village. There were once seven important temples, but all were destroyed during the Inquisition and six idols moved to Mulgaon in Bicholim district (immediately east). Today the village is dominated by the unusual **Church of Our Lady of the Immaculate Conception**. Originally built of mud and thatch in 1619, it was rebuilt during the 19th century with square towers close to the false dome. The balustrades at the top of the first and second floors run the length of the building and the central doorways of the ground and first floors have Islamic-looking trefoil arches that contrast with the romanesque flanking arches. There is an interesting outside pulpit. Inside, the image of the crucifixion is unusual in having its feet nailed separately instead of together. A Siva *lingam* recycled here as the base of the font after its temple was razed is now in the Archaeological Museum at Old Goa. Moira's famous long red bananas (grown

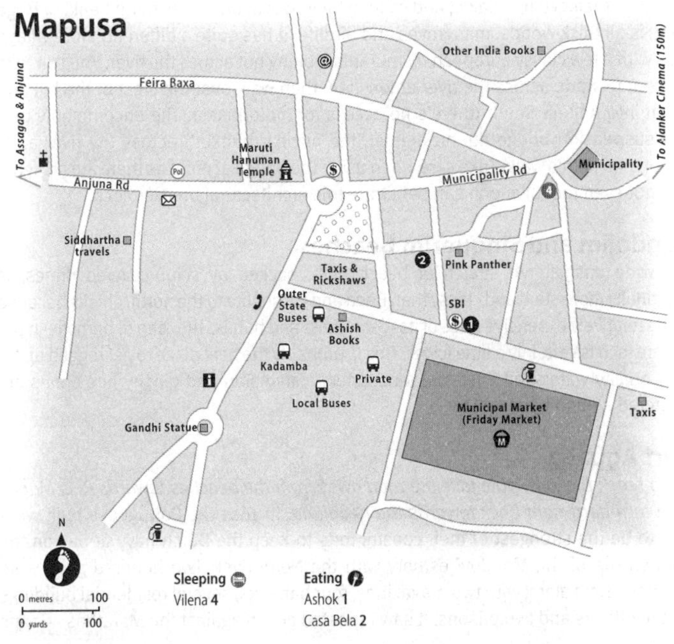

 nearby) are not eaten raw but come cooked with sugar and coconuts as the cavity-speeding sweet *figada*.

## Calangute

→ *Colour map 5a, grid A1.*

Bar the brilliantly quirky hexagonal *barbeiria* (barber's shop) at the northern roundabout, there is little to attract the aesthete's eye in Calangute. The main distinguishing feature of the streets is their commercialism: shops peddle everything from cheap ethnic tat to extravagant precious gemstones with varying degrees of aggression. Licensed shacks line the beach, some of which have great nosh and make cool places to hang out in the evening. Behind the busy beach front coconut trees still give shade to village houses; some offer private rooms to let. Any open space left over is being covered with concrete and steel for new buildings.

Away from the town centre, the striking gold and white **Church of St Alex** (rebuilt in 1741) gives a great taste of rococo decoration in Goa, while the false dome of the central façade is an excellent example of 18th-century architectural development. The delicate decoration of the pulpit and the *reredos* are particularly fine. The **Kerkar Art Complex** ⓘ *Gaurawaddo, T0832-2276017, www.subodhkerkar.com*, is also worth visiting. Medic-turned-contemporary artist Subodh Kerkar is on a one-man crusade to reverse Calangute's full-tilt slide into a cultural vacuum. His relaxed complex is an exhibition space for the work of many artists passing through Goa, while next door sits a gallery reserved for his own paintings and installation work, some of which are like lovely Indian interpretations of nature artist Andy Goldsworthy.

## Baga

The very distinct identity for which Baga was once a byword has been almost wholly engulfed to make it little more than Calangute north. Here too, away from the paddy marshes, water tanks and salt pans, it's very much the same story of congestion, shacks, fishing boats and sun loungers (prices doubling to Rs 100 a day during high season). However, the beach is still clean, there's good live music and the river that divides this commercial strip of sand from Anjuna in the north also brings fishermen pulling in their catch at dawn, and casting their nets at dusk. The north bank, or **Baga river**, is all thick woods, mangroves and birdlife: it has quite a different, more village feel, with a few classy European restaurants looking out across the river. You can take an hour to wade across the river at low tide, then walk over the crest of the hill and down into Anjuna South (there's no access for motorbikes). The uncommonly ugly box suspension bridge (its nickname: 'the nuclear bunker') across the river adds about 1 km to this walk. Take care when using the bridge at night as there are no lights and not even the full moon can penetrate this architectural breeze-block.

## Candolim and Sinquerim beaches

The wide unsheltered stretch of beach here, backed by scrub-covered dunes, is marginally more staid and classy than Baga and Calangute to the north, chiefly because of the relatively expensive price of its restaurants and hotels. The ratio of burnt flesh per square inch is certainly a little lower. This is probably the best place to get togged up for your quality watersports: jetskis, windsurfers, catamaran and dinghy hire shops are clustered around here.

## Fort Aguada

ⓘ *To reach the jail's gate take the road away from the beaches towards Reis Magos then turn hard right back towards the headland.* In 1612 the Portuguese built what was to be the strongest of their coastal forts to keep the Dutch navy at bay on the northern tip of the Mandovi estuary with the Nerul river. Two hundred guns were stationed here along with two magazines, four barracks, several residential buildings for the officers and two prisons. It saw repeated action against the Marathas - Goans

# Calangute

**Sleeping**
Coco Banana **4**
Estrela do Mar **8**
Goan Heritage **9**
Golden Eye **10**
Johnny's **12**
Kerkar Retreat & Waves **3**
Martin's Guest Rooms **13**
Paradise Village **16**
Pousada Tauma **17**
Santiago Resorts **18**
Villa Goesa **20**

**Eating**
A Reverie **3**
Infanteria **2**
Le Restaurant Français **4**
Plantain Leaf **7**
Souza Lobo **8**
Sublime Bistro Bar Panchayat **1**
Tibetan Kitchen **5**

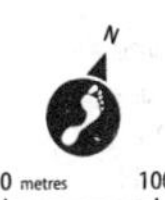

# Baga

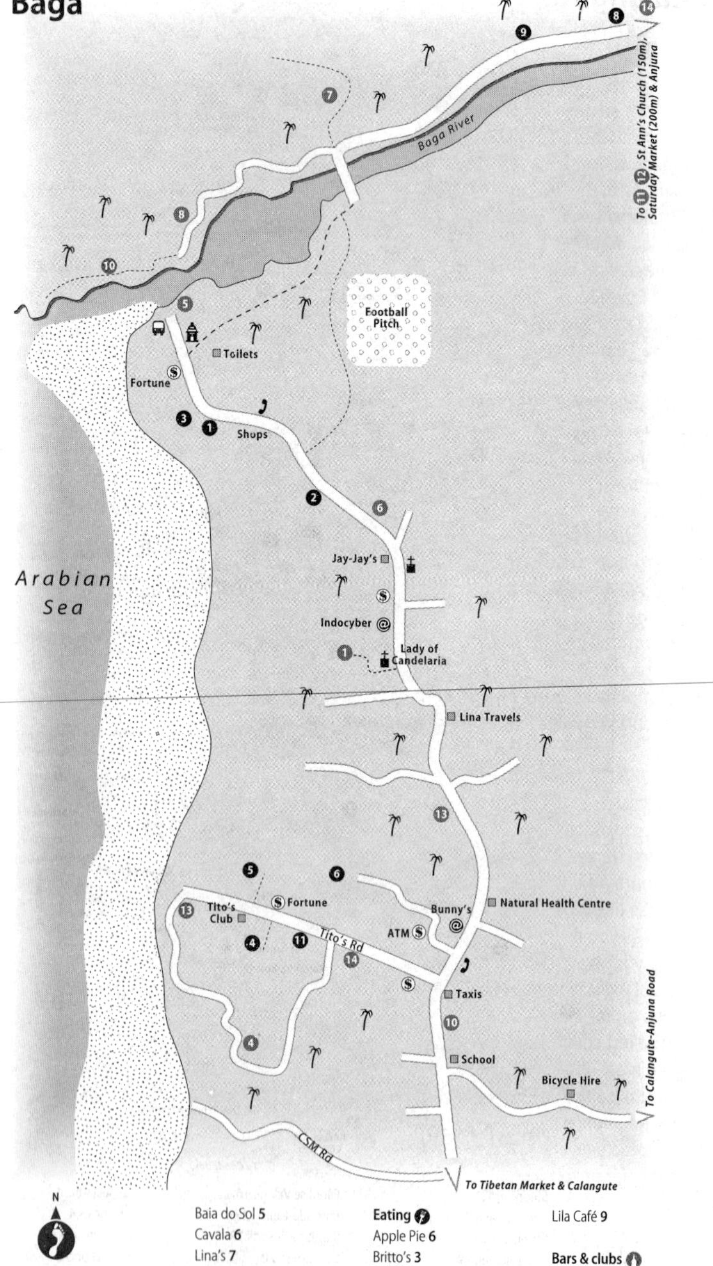


**Sleeping**
Alidia Beach Cottages **1**
Baga Queen Beach Resort **4**
Baia do Sol **5**
Cavala **6**
Lina's **7**
Nani's & Rani's **8**
Ronil Beach Resort **10**
Sun Village **11**
Villa Fatima Beach Resort **13**
Villa Melnisha **14**

**Eating**
Apple Pie **6**
Britto's **3**
Casa Portuguesa **2**
Citrus **11**
Domingo's **4**
Fiesta **5**
J&A's Italiano House **8**
Joe's Café & Health Food Shop **1**
Lila Café **9**

**Bars & clubs**
Club Cubana **12**
Kamaki **14**
Mambo's **13**
Sunset **10**

fleeing the onslaught at Bardez took refuge here, but its ramparts proved time and again impregnable. The main fortifications (laterite walls nearly 5 m high and 1.3 m thick ) are still intact: the buildings lower down where the waves crash formed what must be a contender for most beautifully positioned jail in the world. 

## Anjuna → *Colour map 5a, grid A1.*

Against all the odds, and in spite of the thousands who descend here every Wednesday in season for its flea market, many corners of Anjuna still cling to something of the alternative life. People, mostly European, often English, who've had it with home continue to come here, rent a house, buy a bike, meet a girl, start some small scale business to keep them in spliffs and booze, flipflops and motorbike fuel and proceed to pay less attention to hours and days than to seasons and sunsets. Decide for yourself whether it's idyllic or deluded, but it's likely you'll find it outright insular. It is a strong community, no doubt, but a judgmental one.

**The Flea Market** ⓘ *Dandovaddo, south Anjuna, Oct-Apr Wed 0800 till sunset, water taxis or shared taxis from anywhere in Goa*, is tourist India in overdrive: over 2,000 stalls descend on Anjuna every week during the season, coughing up Rs 200 rent apiece to hawk everything from Gujarati wooden printing blocks to Bhutanese silver and even Burberry-check pashminas. The trade is so lucrative that for six months several thousand Rajasthani, Gujaratis, Karnatakans and Tibetans, chiefly women, up sticks, leaving their families behind, to make their livings off the tourist dollar. The flea had very different origins, though, and was once an intra-community car boot-style bric-a-brac sale for the sixties freaks.

Few of Anjuna's visitors know anything of its pre-hippy past, yet it has a history of which the local population is very proud. Anjuna was an important Arab trading post in the 10th and 12th centuries. As was common with many such ports on the west coast of India, Arab Muslim traders represented only a small minority of the population, and Hindu influences were also important, as both the lineage of some of the important Hindu castes and the existence of ancient temples illustrates.

## South Anjuna to Chapora Fort

If this stretch of land were in the UK it's a safe bet that it would have picked up a stamped certificate of outstanding natural beauty by now. Once you've had enough of dunking yourself in the sea, pick your way along the coastal path for a sunset stroll from South Anjuna all the way to **Chapora Fort**, which has one of the grandest sunset vantages in Goa. There's a footpath just inland of the bungee jump in north Anjuna that takes you over the headland to Spaghetti Beach in Vagator where you'll have to thread your way down the gravelly terracing, climbing again to get onto the wide sands of Big Vagator beach: either stop here for an ear-rinsing sundowner at Nine Bar or keep on for the romantic desolation around the Fort.

The fort commands the hilltop at the north end of the bay, a short but steep walk immediately above the timeshare Sterling Resorts. Now in ruins, the fort stands on the south bank of the Chapora river and dominates the estuary. It was first built by Adil Shah, hence its original name *Shahpura*, or Chapora. Don't miss the views from the sea-facing walls – they're spectacular.

The flat arc of the estuary inland from the fort is both a docking point for fishing boats and a boat building and repair workshop. It's ideal for exploring by bicycle: the rim-side road will take you all the way out to the bridge at **Siolim** where you can loop back to take a look at the **Church of St Anthony** that dominates Siolim Square close to the village market. Built in 1606, it replaced an earlier Franciscan church (1568). St Anthony, the patron saint of Portugal, is widely venerated throughout the villages of Goa (prayed to both by Hindus and Catholics in the hope of good fishing catches). The high, flat-ceilinged church has a narrow balustraded gallery and Belgian glass chandeliers. The attractive and typically gabled west end has statues of Jesus and St

## The trance dance experience

When the freaks – not hippies but beatniks with super nomadic genes, giant drug habits and names like Eight Finger Eddie -- first kicked their scuffed shoes into Goan sand shortly after the departure of the Portuguese, some of them had guitars, that they'd strummed across their overland pilgrimages through Asia, slung over their shoulders. Once they'd absorbed a bit of Hindu spirituality on the route down, they were charged with picking out devotional songs by the beach campfire.

By the end of the 60s, thousands of freaks were swarming into Goa, often spilling down from Freak HQ in Kathmandu, and word had got back to proper paid-up acid rock musicians about the scene. Some more substantial entertainment was called for. People started playing records after the Flea Market.

The first music to run through the speakers was rock and reggae. Led Zeppelin, The Who and George Harrison rocked up and played live, but the freaks' entertainment was mostly recorded: Santana, Stones and Marley. Kraftwerk and synth had filtered in by the late 70s but the shift to electronica only really came in the early 80s when musicians got bored of the lyrics and blanked out all the words on albums of industrial noise, rock and disco, using the fully lo-fi production method of taping between two cassette decks. Depeche Mode and New Order albums were stripped down for their drum and synth layers. Some of the rock faithful were angry with the change in the soundtrack to their lives: at those early 80s parties, when the psychedelic-meets-machine-drum sound that still defines Goa trance was first being pumped out, legend has it that the decks had to be flanked by bouncers.

The music, developing in tandem to German nosebleed techno and UK acid house, locked into a worldwide tapestry of druggy drumscapes, but the Goan climate created its own sound. Because records would warp in India's high temperatures, music had to be put down on DATS rather than vinyl which in turn meant tracks were played out in full, ie unmixed. A track had to be interesting enough then, self-contained, so it could be played uninterrupted in full: producers had to pay more attention to intros, middles and outros – in short, the music had to have a story. It also meant there was less art to a Goan trance DJ's set than his opposite numbers in Manchester, Detroit and Paris, who could splice records together to make their own new hybrid sounds.

Many of the original makers of this music had absorbed a fair whack of psychedelia and had added the inevitable layer of sadhu thinking to this – superficially measured in incense, *oms*, dreads and the swirling dayglo mandalas that so unmistakeably mark out a Goa trance party. The music reflected this: sitars noodled alongside sequencer music to make the Goan signature sound.

By the 90s, though, ecstasy had arrived in Goa. The whole party scene opened right up, peopled by Spiral Tribe crusties as well as middle-class gap year lovelies and global party scenesters who came looking for an alternative to the more mainstream fare in Ibiza. Paul Oakenfold's Perfecto was a key label in fuelling the sound's popularity but there were more: Dragonfly, The Infinity Project, Return to the Source. Today the music comes from labels like Electrojump, Hux Flux, Errorhead, Color Drop, Wizzy Noise, Psycho+Trolls, Droidsect, Parasense, Peace Data, In-R-Voice. Although much of it hails from studios in Europe or Japan, there's the odd label that's more homegrown, like the resolutely Goan label 'Made In Chapora'.

Anthony. Some extremely fine Portuguese houses are scattered about the village's shadows in varying degrees of disrepair: it's worth walking around to take in some of the facades (you can stay in peerless boutique luxury inside Siolim House, one which has been happily refurbished, see Sleeping.

## Vagator

The gravelly windswept red earth on the approach to Vagator makes the village feel somewhat apocalyptic. The black tarmac approach road snakes through a desolate rusty headland whose chief landmark is the up-juttings of a half-built hotel and the concrete shells of other developments abandoned midway. The beaches here, muddied sand bays upset by slabs of gray rock, quite different from the bubblings of porous laterite in Anjuna, fall at the bottom of terraced red cliffs planted with coconut trees that lean out towards the crashing waves, some of their bellies painted neon. The main access road ends at a car park. To your right in the foreground is the long sweep of **Big Vagator beach**, behind it the profile of the wide outer rim of the ruined **Chapora Fort** against a stunning backdrop of India's western coastline, running well past Goa's northern-most state line and up into Maharashtra. Look for the silhouette of the hilltop factory that lies parallel to Tiracol fort for a visual signpost of the Goan border.



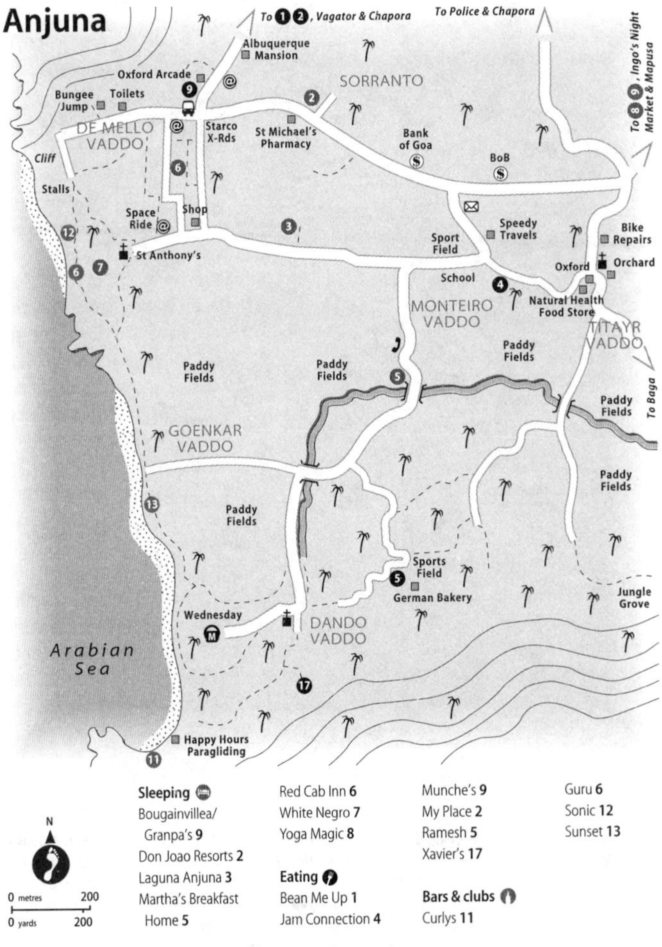

To your left, running inland, is the sometime free party venue **'disco valley'**, threaded through with a creek that opens onto the central **Little Vagator beach,** its terracing lorded over by Nine Bar, a giant venue with an unswerving musical loyalty to trance. Just out of sight is **Ozran** or **'spaghetti beach'** a scrappy, atmospheric bay with great swimming that ends with rocks and jungle. Most people turn right to Big Vagator. Spaghetti, christened by Anjuna's British residents after all the Italians settled here, though dogged by very persistent sarong sellers, is both more sheltered, more scenic and more remote. One of the shacks here has rooms but otherwise it's strictly a daytime hang out.

## Coastal Pernem → *Colour map 5a, grid A1.*



The long bridge that spans the Chapora River and joins Bardez to the last, and so most heavily Hindu, of the new conquests, Pernem, also acts as the gateway to a series of serene, largely empty beaches that hug the coastal road in an almost

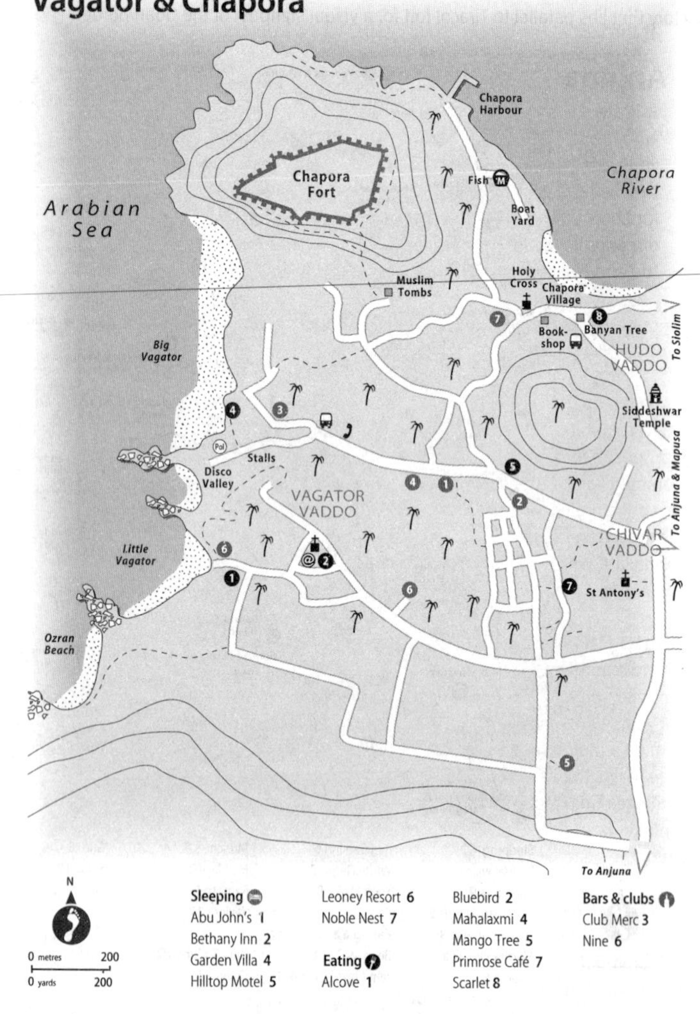

## Sun salutations and downward dog

Yoga, once seen as a politicized act of rebellion against British imperial rule, is not particularly popular among contemporary Indians. "For them, it's the equivalent of having hoards of middle-class Indians rocking up in Yorkshire to study something we consider as outmoded as morris dancing," admits Phil Dane, who runs a yoga-centric hotel near to Goa's foremost western-style yoga school, Purple Valley.

While some Indians look askance at the vast numbers of firangi yogis, others are making good coin from the trade. Devotees of Sri Pattabhi Jois, the venerated octogenarian who developed the 'ashtanga vinyasa' (dynamic) practice, joke that he has a new-found fondness for Louis Vuitton luggage sets. His disciples have been quick to cash in too and everywhere yoga, once the physical strand in the eight paths towards a Hindu spirituality, is fast becoming commercial. Danny Paradise, one of the first generation of western yoga teachers, today includes Goa on a year-round, global, and no doubt lucrative, yoga-teaching tour and has his own merchandising range that includes an 'asana CD' featuring cameos from students like Sting.

India remains, nevertheless, one of the best places to study the ancient art. If you want to include some informal, and inexpensive, practice in Goa, you'll find that teachers are as ubiquitous as fish curry. Like Goa's staple dish though, quality is far from assured. Arambol in Goa is a good starting point. If you are travelling to India specifically to practice it's worth doing your homework first. You need to book far in advance, both for courses and flights. See under Activities and tours in the listings sections of each individual town for further information.

unbroken strip right up to the border with Maharashtra. No sand in Goa is quite far enough to put it quite beyond the reach of busloads of daytrippers, and the impact the proposed airport in the northeast corner of Pernem would have on these gently uncommercialized beaches cannot be overstated, but so far, if you stay overnight up here, you're pretty sure of snaring yourself at the very least a secluded dawn. Arambol is the most developed of the district's five beaches but it has grown up in too much of a haphazard way for that development to have stopped it being resolutely relaxed.
⏩ *For Sleeping, Eating and other listings, see pages 1185-1198.*

### Ins and outs

The whole northern district of Pernem can easily be covered in one day's excursion from as far south as Panjim, but it's far better to give yourself a full day in each bay or plant yourself on one beach then go explore the rest. If you are crossing the bridge at Siolim on a motor- or push-bike turn left off the new main road immediately after the bridge to use the smaller, more scenic coastal roads. There are also regular buses to the villages from Mapusa and from Chopdem. Travelling here, particularly if you are on a bike, is as much fun as arriving: there is truly stunning agricultural landscape. Each of the beaches is within a 20-minute hop of the next.

### Background

Sandwiched between the Tiracol and Chapora rivers and their estuaries, Pernem was incorporated into Goa in 1788 as the final part of the New Conquests. Before this it was alternately under Hindu and Muslim rule. The Bhonsles of Sawantwadi in modern

 Maharashtra were the last rulers of this hilly district on the north fringes of Goa before being ousted by the Portuguese, and Maratha influences remain strong here.

## Arambol (Harmal) → *Colour map 5a, grid A1.*

Arambol, which you reach when the plateau road noses down through paddy fields and cashew trees, is one of the beaches people used to whisper of in hushed tones when damning the deterioration of Anjuna. It's a beautiful long stretch of sand at the bottom of a bumpy dirt track (signposted from the village crossroads beside the bus stop) now fringed with stalls selling brightly coloured, heavily embroidered clothes – halternecks and pretty *lungis* flutter in the breeze – and has attracted longstayers wanting somewhere more *shanti* than Goa's central beaches. Because people have put down roots here, the village is abuzz with industriousness. Bits of A4 paper advertise *satsang* with smiling western gurus: there's also *tabla* teaching, yoga teacher training, reiki, belly-dancing even.

Skirt the beach's northern cliff and tiny basalt rocky bays by foot to reach the real lure: a second bay cut off from the roads and **a natural 'sweet water' lake** that collects at the base of a jungle spring. The lagoon collects just metres from the high tide line where the lush forest crawls down to the water's edge. You can walk up the spring's path to reach a belt of natural mineral clay: an idyllic spot for self-service **mud baths**. Further into the jungle is the famous **banyan tree**, its branches straddling 50 m, which has long been a point of Hindu and hippy pilgrimage.



## Morjim (Morji) to Asvem

The most southern of Pernem's beaches, Morjim has two wide sweeping beaches that both sit at the bottom of separate dead end streets. This inaccessibility means that, development-wise, they've got away relatively unscathed. The southern, protected, turtle beach appears at the end of the narrow track that winds along the north bank of the Chapora river mouth. Loungers, mostly empty, are strewn haphazardly north of the official-looking **Turtle Nesting Control Room**. The wide shoreline with its gentle incline (the water is hip height for about 100 m) washed by easy rolling breakers makes it one of North Goa's best swimming beaches. The northern beach, or **little Morjim**, a left turn off the main coast road, is by comparison an established tourist hamlet with guesthouses and beach huts. Plans for an upmarket hotel complex here with a 'private' beach, which would deny local people free access to a section of the waterfront, have been dropped so this fine stretch of beach should be safe for some time to come.

The road from Morjim cuts inland over the low wooded hills running parallel to the coast. After a few kilometres the road drops down to the coast and runs along the edge of northeast tilting **Asvem beach**. (Morjim faces Chapora to the south and west.) The northern end of this peaceful palm fringed beach is divided by a small river.

## Mandrem

Mandrem creek forces the road to feed inland where it passes through a small commercial centre with a few shops and a bank. Mandrem village has the **Shri Bhumika Temple** housing an ancient image. In the **Shri Purchevo Ravalnatha Temple** there is a particularly striking medieval image of the half-eagle, half-human Garuda, who acts as the *vahana* (carrier) of Vishnu.

A little further on, a lane off to the left leads down towards the main beach and a secluded hamlet in a beautifully shaded setting. The **beach** is one of the least developed along this stretch of coast: for the moment it is managing to tread that fine line between having enough facilities for comfort and enough isolation to guarantee idyllic peace. Further north there is a lagoon fringed by palm trees and some simple rooms, virtually all with sea view. The beach has mercifully yet to draw hawkers, trinket sellers and tourist operators.

## Keri (Querim) and Tiracol Fort → *Colour map 5a, grid A1.*



Goa's northernmost beach is uniquely untouched. The drive towards Keri (Querim) along the banks of the Tiracol river from Pernem passes through some stunning rural areas that have been untouched by any tourist developments.

Walk across deep dunes to a casuarina thicket and out onto empty sand that stretches all the way from the mouth of the Tiracol river to the highland that splits it from Arambol. There's just one solitary shack at either end of the beach, both of which can arrange rooms with villagers from Rs 100. Querim is a popular weekend destination for bus-loads of domestic tourists but is not yet riddled with plastic bags and discarded water bottles. You can reach the beach from the north on foot from the Tiracol ferry terminal, or from the south by walking round the headland from Arambol. The Tiracol ferry runs half hourly from 0600 to 2130 taking 15 minutes. If you arrive outside these times you can charter a fishing boat for Rs 55.

Tiracol (Terekhol), at the northernmost tip of Goa, is an enclave of 350 Catholics on the Maharashtra border just 3½ km across where *feni* production is the biggest business. Its name probably comes from *tir-khol* (meaning steep river bank) and it's a jungly little patch of land full of cashew trees, banyans, orange blossoms, black-faced monkeys and squirrels.

The small but strategic **fort** ⓘ *0900-1800, cross Tiracol river by ferry (half-hourly, 0600-2130) and walk the remaining 2 km. Ferries take cars and motorbikes*, stands above the village on the north side of the Tiracol river estuary on a rugged promontory with amazing views across the water. Its high battlemented walls are clearly visible from the Arambol headland. Built by the Maharaja Khem Sawant Bhonsle in the 17th century, it is protected from attacks from the sea, while the walls on the land side rise from a dry moat. It was captured by the Portuguese Viceroy Dom Pedro Miguel de Almeida (Marques de Alorna) in 1746, who renamed it Holy Trinity and had a chapel built inside (now St Anthony's). Tiracol was only fully and legally incorporated into Goa in 1788. You can explore the fort's battlements and tiny circular turrets which scarcely seem to have been intended for the real business of shooting the enemy. The views from the fort looking south to Arambol, Chapora and Fort Aguada are magnificent. Steps lead down to a terrace on the south side while the north has an open plateau.

**St Anthony's Church** ⓘ *open on Wed and Sun for Mass at 1730*, inside the tiny fort, was built in the early 1750s soon after the Portuguese takeover. It has a classic Goan façade and is just large enough to cater for the small village. In the small courtyard, paved with laterite blocks, stands a modern statue of Christ. Inside, the church has several charming features. The Festival of St Anthony is held here at the beginning of May (usually on the second Tuesday) instead of on the conventional festival day of 13 June.

## Sleeping

**Mapusa** *p1174, map p1175*

None of the hotels here hold any special charm for the tourist: they are firmly geared towards the domestic business traveller.

**D-E Mandarin**, near Alankar Cinema, T0832-2262579. 21 basic rooms with bath (few a/c), clean rooftop restaurant.

**E Vilena**, opposite the Municipality, T0832-2263115, ticlotel@satyam.net.in. 16 neat, clean rooms, some a/c, good restaurants, bar, very friendly.

**Calangute** *p1176, map p1177*

**LL Pousada Tauma**, Porbavaddo, T0832-2279061, www.pousada-tauma.com. 12 unique rooms set in a lush garden around a pool, a luxurious setting where the management and staff are used to dealing with people who value their privacy. Easily the best accommodation in Calangute; some would argue, in the whole of Goa.

**B Goan Heritage**, Gauravaddo, towards Candolim, T0832-2276253, www.goanheritage.com. 70 large, pleasant rooms but can get stiflingly hot, a/c and fridge (Rs 400 extra when used), some have sea view, expensive restaurant (more nearby), good pool, beautiful garden, close to beach.

**B Kerkar Retreat**, Gauravaddo, T0832-2276017, www.subodhkerkar.com. 5 double bedrooms with an overspilling library set above local artist Subodh Kerkar's art gallery. Sedate for Calangute but creative with it.

**B Villa Goesa**, Cobravaddo, off Baga Rd, T0832-2277535, alobo@sancharnet.in. 57 clean rooms, some a/c, some very shaded, excellent restaurant,lovely gardens, pool, quiet, relaxing,very friendly owners, 300 m walk from beach. Recommended.

**B-C Paradise Village**, Tivai Vaddo, South Calangute, near the beach, T0832-2276351, www.paradisevillage.org. 64 comfortable rooms in 2-storey chalets, pleasant restaurant, large pool, excellent service and management.

**C Estrela do Mar**, Calangute-Baga Rd, T0832-2276014. 10 clean, well-kept rooms with nets (rare in these parts), size varies, restaurant, pool, pleasant garden, peaceful location with no buildings near by, close to beach. Good value. Highly recommended.

**D Coco Banana**, 5/139A Umtavaddo, back from Calangute beach, T/F0832-2276478, cocobanana@rediffmail.com. 6 spotless en-suite bungalows with nets, airy, light and comfortable, the Goan/Swiss owners have lived through all the changes in Goa and are caring and helpful. One of the best local guest houses. Highly recommended.

**D Golden Eye**, Philip's Cottages, Gauravaddo, T0832-2277308, www.hotelgoldeneye.com. 10 clean, comfortable rooms, half price singles, right on the beach (built before restrictions) with genuine sea views.

**D Martin's Guest Rooms**, Baga Rd, T0832-2277306, martins@goatelecom.com. 5 rooms in family house, clean, attractive verandas, use of kitchen but on the busy main road.

**D Souza Lobo**, on the beach, T0832-2276463, www.souzalobo.com. 8 rooms in well-known restaurant that has managed to retain a good reputation for years.

**E Johnny's**, Cobravaddo, T0832-2277458, johnnys_hotel@rediffmail.com. 12 rooms (1 a/c) with bath, rooftop terrace, good restaurant, interesting garden (fruit and spices), yoga, peaceful location, short walk to beach, call for collection from bus stand. Recommended. Also, 2-bed furnished apartments, Rs 8,000-10,000 per month.

**Baga** *p1176, map p1178*

Of the family guest houses on the northern side of Baga river, up towards Arpora, those to the left of the bridge (west or seaward) are quieter. Rooms in houses/cottages are available for about Rs 300 but good discounts are possible for weekly or monthly rental. Standards vary so check room and security first. Try Wilson Fernandes at **Nani's & Rani's** or ask at **Four Seasons Restaurant** at Jack's Corner.

**B Ronil Beach Resort**, T0832-2276099, ronil@sancharnet.in. 58 a/c rooms, pool, well run with a good local reputation, ideal for all Baga and Calangute nightlife, small grounds. Recommended.

**B-C Santiago Resorts**, close to Le Restaurant, T0832-2276491, desouza@goatelecom.com. Spacious rooms with TV, bar, fridge, balcony. Continental restaurant and bar by the pool, Chinese restaurant. Convenient for beach. Excellent attentive service, good-value resort hotel.

**C Baia Do Sol**, by bus stand, top end of Baga, T0832-2276084, www.ndnaik.com. 23 very clean rooms, a/c cottages, good restaurant with views (excellent seafood), riverside location.

**C-D Cavala**, Sauntavaddo, top end of Baga village, T0832-2276090, www.cavala.com. 30 clean rooms with bath (some a/c), best at rear, overlooking fields, pool across road. Banana Republic restaurant, relaxed bar, popular live music evenings, friendly and attentive management, short walk to beach, good all-round value. Recommended.

**D Alidia Beach Cottages**, behind the church, Sauntavaddo, T0832-2276835, alidia@goaworld.com. 16 good clean rooms with attached bath, restaurant, secure, friendly owners, beach 2-min walk, excellent value off-season. One of the best of its kind, book ahead for Christmas. Highly recommended.

**D Villa Fatima Beach Resort**, Main Rd, Baga-Calangute, Sauntavaddo, Calangute, T0832-2277418, villa.fatima@sympatico.ca. A pretty ramshackle three storey affair plonked at the bottom of Antonio Mascarenhas' elegant old house with a nice atmosphere, national flags fluttering and books piled high from former guests.

25 clean, attached bathrooms, separate balconies, deals for long-stayers.

**E Baga Queen Beach Resort**, T0832-2276880. 15 good-sized, clean rooms with bath, close to beach, better value than others near by.

**E Lina's**, north of Baga River, T0832-2281142. 4 good-value rooms in a secluded guest house. Recommended.

**E Villa Melnisha**, T0832-2277805. 4 simple, clean rooms with bath, kitchenette, good cheap *thalis*, owners live upstairs.

**E-F Nani's & Rani's**, T0832-2277014. 8 spartan rooms (shared or own bath), budget meals served in pleasant garden, bar, email, STD/ISD. One of the few local budget options with a sea view and a relaxing quiet location. Short walk across Baga Bridge for nightlife.

### Candolim and Sinquerim beaches

*p1176*

**L Fort Aguada Beach Resort**, Sinquerim, T0832- 2479123-36, www.tajhotels.com. The self-confessed sprawling Taj complex, divided into 3, spills across 88 acres of Sinquerim. In descending order of cost these consist of the 17 hilltop family villas that make up the Aguada Hermitage, the 130 rooms with sea views at the Fort Aguada Beach Resort, actually built in the fort's ruins, and the scores of cottages for up to 8 people on the beach in the Taj Holiday Village. The complex has all sorts of 5-star facilities including 2 freshwater pools, 9 restaurants, ayurvedic and other spa treatments, plus golf, tennis and a crèche.

**B-C Kamal Retreat**, Dando, towards Aguada, T0832-2476320, kmehra@goatelecom.com. 23 large, quality rooms (half a/c) on a spacious site with immaculate grounds, large pool, direct beach access, one of the few hotels in Candolim not to be hemmed in, nor will it be, charming owner ensures high standards. Recommended.

**C Aldeia Santa Rita**, towards Aguada, T0832-2479356, www.desouzahotels.com, 32 rooms with balcony (better upstairs) in colourful 'street' of villas in attractive setting, some a/c, good restaurant, bar, small pool, well-maintained grounds, good value. Recommended.

**C-D Costa Nicola**, near the health centre, 500 m from beach, Candolim, T0832-2276343, costanicola@yahoo.com. 7 rooms of varying size in old Goan house, full of character, 13 rooms in a functional new block, some with kitchenette, plus 9 rooms in Sandy Villa next door. Well kept-grounds, pool, friendly owners. Old house rooms excellent value in off season.

**D Ludovici Tourist Home**, Dando, Sinquerim, T0832-2379684. Just inland of the road leading to the fort sits this family home with 4 double rooms, all with fan and en suite and including breakfast. There's also a bar and restaurant and a lovely porch scattered with chairs that gives onto a spacious garden.

**D Marfran**, Sinquerim, T0832-2279274, private house with a few simple rooms. Good peaceful budget option.

**D Par Avel**, 100 m from beach towards Aguada, Candolim, T0832-2479074, www.paravel/ hotel/goacom.com. 6 simple rooms (Rs 650, a/c Rs 200 extra), courtyard garden for breakfast, friendly.

**D Village Belle**, near the main road by Taj Holiday Village, Sinquerim, T0832-2276151, vbelle@vsnl.com, 8 rooms (some a/c), good, cheap restaurant, among palms, 500 m from the beach, friendly owners, good value for the area. Recommended.

**D Xavier**, down a lane and round the corner from the State Bank of India, Candolim, T/F0832-2479911, www.goacom.com/ hotels/xavier. 10 spacious, well-furnished rooms, fan, balcony, sensible peak rates, excellent restaurant, close to beach, friendly, call in advance during monsoon season. Recommended.

**E D'Mello's Sea View**, Escrivaovaddo, turn at Monteiro Rd, Candolim, T0832-2275050. 15 rooms, good food (tandoori specials), pleasant area. Recommended.

### Anjuna *p1179, map p1181*

At the budget end, the best options in Anjuna, Vagator and Chapora tend to be unofficial, privately owned residences.

**AL-A Laguna Anjuna**, Sorantovaddo, T0832-2274305, www.lagunaanjuna.com. Looking a little dog-eared, but still a relaxed series of bungalows under 1 km from the hullabaloo of the beach. Not grandiose but happening: it has both a snooker table and a frangipani-fringed pool.

**B Hotel Bougainvillea/Granpa's**, Gaumwadi, T0832-2273270, www.goacom.com/hotels/granpas. A billiard table stands off an airy reception hall and all rooms are set around a garden of some sort. TVs, fridges and phones are in most rooms. Stays open over monsoon. More likely to attract TV crews and yogis than the party crowd. Recommended.

**C The Tamarind**, Kumar Vaddo, T0832-2274319 www.thetamarind.com. 22 rooms with flagstone floors and balconies in stone-built Portuguese-style house set in landscaped gardens with swimming pool 3 km inland from Anjuna. Courtesy bus service to beaches.

**C Yoga Magic**, Chinvar, T0832-3565717, www.yogamagic.net. A walk along from the Purple Valley drop-in centre at **Hotel Bougainvillea** gets you to just 7 tents under an awning of coconut trees. Its British owner has meticulously planned a system of solar lighting, heating and even composting to minimize environmental harm. A strong, but not evangelical, yogic philosophy prevails.

**C-D Don Joao Resorts**, Sorranto, T0832-2274325, luzco@sancharnet.in. 48 large rooms with balcony and fridge, some a/c, restaurant, exchange, small pool, friendly, away from beach.

**D Palacete Rodrigues**, Mazal Vaddo, T0832-2273358, www.palaceterodrigues.com. Another chance to sleep in a little bit of history: the Palacete is a lovely living relic to the Portuguese era. Many rooms have wooden 4-poster beds inside and give onto verandas. A family house away from the beach.

**D White Negro**, near St Anthony's Church, T0832-2273326, mjanets@goatelecom.com. 14 rooms with nets, good restaurant and bar, very clean.

**D-E Martha's Breakfast Home**, Monteiro Vaddo, T0832-2273365, mpd8650@hotmail.com. 8 clean, spacious rooms in separate block plus a couple of 2-bedroomed cottages, good brunch, waffles, crêpes. Small garden, quiet (except on Wed), friendly, well run.

**D-E Red Cab Inn**, De Mello Vaddo, T0832-2274427, redcabinn@rediffmail.com. 5-min walk from Starco crossroads. 4 newly decorated rooms in old house, high ceilings, nice and cool, plus a room on the roof, good for long stay, plus a bright red cottage in the garden. Very clean and neat, own fresh water well, good evening restaurant. 15 mins walk from the beach.

### South Anjuna to Chapora Fort *p1179*

**A Siolim House**, Vaddy, opposite Vaddy Chapel, T0832-2272138, www.siolimhouse.com. This beautiful restoration of a 2-storey 300-year-old house once owned by the governor of Macau has 7 large, simply furnished suites, some with giant bathrooms. Good Goan food, pool, gardens, video library: evocative of a past era. Recommended.

### Vagator *p1181, map p1182*

**B Leoney Resort**, T0832-2273634, www.leoneyresort.com. 13 rooms, 3 cottages, a/c extra Rs 400. Clean, modern, family run, low-key, quiet, pool, 10-min walk from beach.

**D Bethany Inn**, opposite **Mango Tree**, T0832-2273973, bethany@goatelecom.com. 7 clean, comfortable modern rooms with bath (some 4-bedded), central village location.

**E Abu John's**, 6 small rooms with bath, good restaurant, garden, pleasant, quiet.

**E Hilltop Motel**, away from the beach, T0832-2273665. 14 small rooms, those with bath reasonable, popular late night venue.

**E-F Garden Villa**, T0832-2273571. 8 clean rooms, some with bath, restaurant with a decent choice.

### Chapora *p1179, map p1182*

Caters mainly for long-term budget travellers.

**F Noble Nest**, opposite the Holy Cross Chapel, T0832-2274335. 21 rooms, 2 with bath but ample facilities for sharing, basic, but popular, exchange and internet.

### Arambol *p1184*

Arambol is a budget place: you'll likely need your own sleepsheet, rooms are exposed and lack the security of a hotel compound but often have small metal lockers for valuables. Guest houses higher up on the rocky hills charge more but are poorly maintained and, what's more, there's a whiff of sewage.

**D Famafa Beach Resort**, Beach Rd, Khalchawada, T0832-2292516, famafa_in@hotmail.com. You don't head for Arambol for its swanky accommodation: **Famafa**, 25 rooms in an unimaginative development on the right

*For an explanation of the sleeping and eating price codes used in this guide, see inside the front cover. Other relevant information is found in Essentials pages 56-61.*

of the stall-studded track down to the beach, is top of the range here. No a/c, but as pukka a hotel as it gets, just Rs 500 in high season.
**E Ave Maria**, inland, down track opposite police post, Modhlowado, T0832-2297674. One of the originals, offering some of the best accommodation. Simple but nevertheless recommended.
**E Luciano Guest Rooms**, Cliffside. Family house with toilet and shower: rooms on the cliffside get heavily booked up.
**E Oceanic**, inland at south end, T0832-2292296. Secluded guest house with simple rooms, all hidden behind wall in mature gardens, no drugs, popular. Recommended.
**E Residensea Beach Huts**, Arambol Beach, T0832-2292413, pkresidensea_37@hotmail.com. Basic bamboo shacks set around restaurant all have fans and secure locker facilities (outside toilets). German shepherd keeps watch.
**E Welcome,** at end of road on seafront, T0832-2297733. Clean rooms, bath with hot water, serves the best muesli, taxi hire.
**F Blue Fin**, north end of beach. 3 rooms (Rs 150), tucked behind a shop, small courtyard, limited views but more privacy than others nearby.
**F Lakes Paradise**. Tiny place that also serves Goan curry and rice.
**F Sky Blue**. 4 small rooms in a cottage, shared veranda, great beach view, usually taken by long-term visitors.

### Morjim to Asvem *p1184*

You really need your own motorbike to make the most of staying here.
**B The Olive Ridley**, Morjim, has a rather lovely two-bedroom house just over the coast road from their restaurant which you can rent out for a pretty hefty Rs 4,000 per night: double beds are set on concrete bases.
**C-D Montego Bay Beach Village**, Vithaldas Wado, Morjim, T0832-2982753. Rajasthani-style tents pitched in the shade past beach shrubs at the southern end of the beach.
**D Palm Grove**, Asvem towards Morjim. 6 cottages, fan, in a discreet low-lying stone building with communal veranda (Rs 250), 5 well-built tree houses (Rs 450) close to the beach among casuarinas, plus 2 very basic huts. Communal wash facilities. Recommended for long stays.
**E Arabian Sea**, Marddivaddo, T0832-2297432. 2 brick cottages and 3 rickety bamboo huts on stilts (overpriced at Rs 300), all set back from the beach, limited sea views, communal wash block, beach restaurant.
**E Silent Cottages**, Marddivaddo. Huts on stilts with much better views.

### Mandrem *p1184*

**B Elsewhere Beach House**, T0832-3738757, www.aseascape.com. 3 lovely-looking bedrooms in the understated luxury of a redecorated 19th century house on a sandy spit with the sea on one side and a salt water creek the other. Living, dining room and kitchen are sea-facing, facilities include maid service, day and nightwatchman, stereo: extra for cook. Minimum rent period 1 week at £670. Another of the family's ancestral homes is currently under conversion.
**B Elsewhere Otter Creek Tents**. Under same ownership, 3 luxury Rajasthani tents each with 4-poster beds, hot showers en suite and private jetties and sit outs.
**B-C Villa River Cat**, Junasvaddo, T0832-2247928, www.villarivercat.com. 13 rooms in a 3-tiered round-house overlooking the river and a wade over deep sand dunes from the beach. The whole place is ringed with a belt of shared balconies and comes with big central courtyards that are stuffed with swings, sofas, plantation chairs and daybeds. There's a mosaic spiral staircase and a cavalier approach to colour: it's downbeat creative and popular with musicians and actors – in the best possible way, the poor man's Nilaya. Strongly recommended: booking essential.
**C Mandrem Beach Resort**, Junasvaddo, far end of village from junction with main road, T0832-2297115, http://ashextourism.com/hotelsresorts/Goa/MandremBeachResort.htm. 24 rooms in cottages (fan, lockers), river or sea view, good off-season discounts, al fresco restaurant, tranquil setting, friendly team, many repeat guests. Beach to yourself beyond the dunes. Recommended.
**E Merrylands Paradise**, T0832-2297446, merrylandsparadise@hotmail.com. Cottages and fragile-looking bamboo tree houses. Right on the lagoon behind the beach.
**F Sea Paradise**, simple bamboo huts on stilts, great location by the lagoon. Along the quiet lane leading off the main road.

**Keri (Querim) and Tiracol fort** *p1185*
Around the Christmas, New Year period 3-4 shacks appear at the south end of the beach. Simple snacks are available from kiosks by the ferry at the north end of the beach, or buy mineral water and provisions back in the village.

**L Fort Tiracol Heritage Hotel**, Tiracol, T0832-66227631, nilaya@sancharnet.in. In 2003 the owners of Nilaya took over Fort Tiracol to create isolated, personalised luxury with unbroken views of the Arabian sea. Just 7 exquisite rooms, all with giant en suite, set in the fort walls that surround the Catholic Church which is still used by the 350 villagers of wholly Christian Tiracol for their mass. Goa's most romantic hotel.

## Eating

**Mapusa** *p1174, map p1175*
Food is also unlikely to be the highlight of a trip to Mapusa.

**ƚƚ Ashok**, opposite the market's entrance. Serves genuine South Indian breakfasts like *uttapam* and *dosa*.

**ƚƚ Casa Bela**, near Coscar Corner, specializes in Goan food.

**ƚƚ Hotel Vilena** has 2 restaurants, 1 on the rooftop and 1 a/c indoors. They serve some of the best food in town.

**ƚƚ Mahalaxmi**, Anjuna Rd. A/c, South Indian vegetarian.

**Calangute** *p1176, map p1177*

**ƚƚƚ A Reverie**, next to **Hotel Goan Heritage**, Holiday St, T0832-3174927, areverie@rediffmail.com. All white tablecloths and quiet garden, this is a splash-out venue. Pricey and out of the way, it is popular with the ex-pat crowd. Great chocolate mousse.

**ƚƚƚ Le Restaurant Français**, Baga Rd, T0832-2121712. Extremely pragmatically, the day-time dairy curd café the Milky Way gets a wave of a magic wand to become **Le Restaurant** by night. Sofas are wheeled in, huge paintings of French street scenes are erected to serve as backdrop to the Gallic menu: all winning a thumbs up from the French community themselves.

**ƚƚƚ Oceanic**, Gauravaddo. Well planned setting in neat gardens, varied seafood, pasta, good fun when busy.

**ƚƚƚ Souza Lobo**, on the beach, excellent fresh seafood, lobster (Rs 550) and sizzlers served on a shaded terrace, well-known restaurant that has managed to retain a good reputation for years. Recommended.

**ƚƚƚ Sublime Bistro Bar Panchayat**, 3/22 Tivaivaddo, behind the Falcon Beach Resort, T0832-2484051. This hidden gem is designed very Zen and has a dogged following.

**ƚ Infanteria**, 'the breakfast place' to locals, has Rs 125 set breakfast, eggs, coffee, juice, toast. Bakery and confectionery includes butterscotch swiss rolls.

**ƚ Plantain Leaf,** near petrol pump, Almita III. T0832-2276861. Mean *dosas*, jumbo *thalis*, sizzlers and a full range of curries: near unbeatable for your pukka pure veg Indian.

**ƚ The Tibetan Kitchen**, 0900–1500, 1800-22.30. This airy garden restaurant at the bottom of a track leading off Calangute Beach Rd is part tent, part wicker awning, part open to the skies. Tibet's answer to the ravioli – *momos* – are good here, but more adventurous starters like prawns, mushrooms and tomatoes seeping onto wilting lettuce leaves are exceptional.

**Baga** *p1176, map p1178*

**ƚƚƚ Fiesta**, Tito's Lane, T0832-2279894. Only open for dinner, closed Tue. One of Baga's destination eateries serving mediterranean nosh in stylish surroundings, unusual Portuguese and Italian dishes (Rs 200), and great desserts. Tends to attract the wealthy crowd before they move on to Tito's.

**ƚƚƚ J&A's Ristorante Italiano House**, 560 Baga river, T0832-2282364, www.littleitalygoa.com. Jamshed and Ayesha Madon's operation – along with their pizzas and pastas – has earned them an evangelical following in Goa. Next door is Bisque, their new foray into Spanish tapas. Both are open only for dinner between Oct-Apr.

**ƚƚ Apple Pie**, opposite **Tito's**, Tito's Lane, Sauntavaddo, T0832-2638898. 1200-2400. French-managed Apple Pie isn't short of repeat customers prepared to pick their way across the sandy wasteland running to it from Tito's Lane. Chicken dijonnaise and lemon cheesecake are first rate.

**ƚƚ Britto's Bar and Restaurant**, Baga beach, T0832-2277331. Cajie Britto's puddings are an institution and his staff (of 50) boast that in high season you'll be pushed to find an inch of table space from the restaurant's inside right out to the seashore. Seafood platters come for Rs 170, or plump for a breakfast of Heinz beans on toast for Rs 60. Good fish curry and rice too.

ΨΨ **Casa Portuguesa**, Baga Rd, a real institution of a restaurant run by German/ Goan couple with live music in the gloriously overgrown jungle of a garden. Strongly recommended.

ΨΨ **Citrus**, Tito's Rd, www.citrusvegetarian .com. Impeccable vegetarian med-style food in simple surround: prides itself on hygiene, European-run.

ΨΨ **Domingo's**, Tito's Rd, just off the road next to Zinho's Guesthouse. International. Well cooked and tasty food, safe, one of few not to play background music of any kind. A friendly, family-run concern. Strongly recommended.

Ψ **Joe's Café and Health Food Shop**, Baga beach, T0832-2276838. Joe has been here on the road to Baga for 10 years and has come over all new age and started to focus solely on health food. 72-year old Yoga Baba, who hangs here during the season before going back to Rishikesh for monsoon, promises to teach *asanas* and the other 7 limbs of the life science of yoga on the upstairs veranda if he's still alive.

Ψ **Lila's Café**, north bank of Baga River T0832-2279843, lilacafe@sify.com. Slick German-run restaurant, good selection of European dishes, check blackboard for specials, smoked kingfish Rs 110. Homemade cheeses and jams, muesli and orange juice Rs 60, fresh bread, good coffee. Also serves beers. Shaded terrace overlooking the river. Closed evenings. Recommended.

### Candolim and Sinquerim beaches *p1176*

ΨΨ **Casa Manolita**, behind Dona Alcina resort. European bistro run by Anglo-Indian couple, meals served on balustraded veranda of restored 19th-century Portuguese villa. Recommended.

ΨΨ **Fisherman's Cove**, opposite Alexandra Tourist Centre, excellent tandooris cooked to order.

ΨΨ **Mermaid**, opposite Whispering Palms Hotel, run by a Swedish-Goan couple, superb international and Goan cuisine at reasonable prices. Highly recommended.

ΨΨ **Oriental Royal Thai Cuisine**, Candolim Holiday Beach Rd, next to **Holiday Beach Resort**. T0832-2121549. Live music played in this relatively sedate restaurant for the neighbourhood, but has impeccable service and authentic Thai, buffet every Sun from 1900. Cooking classes held 1400-1700 on Mon (Rs 1,100 including a 5-course dinner).

ΨΨ **Palms 'n Sand**, near the beach. Has to merit a mention on the basis of its signature dish alone - roast piglet – which you need to order the day before.

ΨΨ **Titus Roma Pisa**, Candolim Beach Rd. More than just pizzas. Well-prepared food, very friendly staff (good place to ask about fishing trips, flea market etc), soccer bar for live football, but not rowdy at all, so not just for the younger crowd. Also has internet access. Highly recommended.

ΨΨ **Xavier**. Western. Excellent meals (owner/chef spent 30 years in England), very attentive service, roast dinner on Sun. Cocktail bar with a happy hour, 1800-1900. Recommended.

### Fort Aguada *p1176*

ΨΨΨ **Banyan Tree**, Taj Holiday Village. Exotic backdrop to delicious Thai food: a wide veranda, water garden and a great banyan tree; expensive though almost reasonable if you think in foreign tender.

### Anjuna *p1179, map p1181*

ΨΨΨ **Xavier's**, Praias de San Miguel (follow signs from behind small chapel near flea market site; bring a torch at night), T0832-2273402. One of the very first restaurants for foreigners has grown into a smart restaurant with 3 separate kitchens (Indian/Chinese/continental), excellent fresh seafood, tucked away under palm trees.

ΨΨ **Ramesh**. Traditional family restaurant that's been running as long as Xavier's; particularly good for fish.

Ψ **Bean Me Up**, 875 2 Soranto, T0832-2273977, www.travelingoa.com/ beanmeup. Open Sun-Fri 1200-1600, 1900-2300. Brilliant, world-standard soya station and salad bar with queues round the block as testimony to its tastiness. Vegetables come from its organic Osho Garden. Also does take away.

Ψ **The Jam Connection**, opposite Tin Tin in Tibet, nice garden for treats and cakes.

¥ **Munche's**, De Mello Vaddo, 24-hr cafe next to Oxford Arcade on Vagator Rd. In peak season, an informal assembly point before heading off to parties, an 'in' place.

¥ **Yoga Magic** Chinvar, T0832-3565717, www.yogamagic.net. Extraordinarily good home-cooked, health-conscious South Indian vegetarian supper served at this immaculately kept, eco-aware Rajasthani tent village. Meals are eaten communally in the middle of paddy fields and are prepared fresh chiefly for residents so visitors need to book before 1300 for the same evening.

**Vagator** *p1181, map p1182*

Several restaurants line the streets to the beach. Some serve good fresh fish including **Mahalaxmi**. **Primrose Café** serves tasty health foods and also hosts spontaneous parties.

¥¥ **The Alcove**, on the cliff above Little Vagator. Smartish, ideal position, excellent food, pleasant ambience in the evening, sometimes live music.

¥¥ **Bluebird**, T0832-2273695, quietly placed, en route to Ozran, does real French food (inventive menu), to be washed down with pricey French wines; one of the best here.

¥¥ **Mango Tree**, in the village, offers a wide choice of continental favourites.

¥¥ **My Place**. Father-son act knocking out fresh gnocchi and ravioli. The kitchen is world class and it's unlikely its owners will baulk at any number of covers in the fairy-lit garden; they used to cook caterer style for the Osho camp in Pune.

**Chapora** *p1179, map p1182*

**Scarlet**, beside the Banyan in Chapora village, Huddovaddo. Good muesli, ice creams and chilled fruitshakes, the place for a morning 'pick-me-up' after a night on the dance floor.

**Arambol** *p1184*

There are beach cafés all along the main beach and around the headland to the north. A basic eatery in the village serves delicious authentic Goan fish curry and rice for Rs 20. Also doubles up as the village bar.

¥ **Double Dutch**, from the beach turn left off the main beach road before Ganesh Stores. Arambol's best coffee shop – its cakes get distributed throughout the village – and is home to the 'bullshit info message board' where you can find information on the *bhajan* and *mantra* singing session group you'd always dreamed of. Excellent tea, coffee, good snacks through the day, imported journals.

¥ **Eyes Of Buddha**, Cliffside, Arambol Beach. Long on Arambol's catering scene, Eyes Of Buddha has you well looked after with scrupulously clean avocado salads and an enviable cliffside position looking onto the Arabian sea.

¥ **Full Moon**, secluded beach shack at south end. Seafood, drinks throughout the day. Recommended.

¥ **German Bakery**, Beach Rd and beachfront, T0832-2292510. Nothing very obviously Teutonic in the management of either of these so-called German bakeries, but they do offer the sweet cakes the German Bakery pseudo-franchise is famous for among travellers the length of India. The beachfront shack is maybe more 'scene', but both are good places to take the pulse of the beach.

¥ **Loekie Café** on the main beach approach road. Good varied menu, music in the eve.

¥ **Outback**, on the path to second beach. Popular bar on spacious terrace perched above the rocks.

¥ **Pirates Cabin**, Indian. Succulent tandoori grills, popular daytime hang-out.

¥ **Sunset Dream**, around headland on 2nd beach. Great setting above the beach and rocks. Fruit juices, seafood. All 'fresh' ingredients have to be carried by hand along the path but there's no sign of cool boxes.

**Morjim to Asvem** *p1184*

You're not spoiled for gastronomic choice in Morjim yet: **Hard Rock**, **Planet Hollywood** and, hilariously enough, **Harry Ramsden's**, are popular shacks on turtle beach and do decent, although average, fresh fish dishes.

¥¥ **Le Plage**, Asvem, T0832-2121712. Gives the impression of being rather a fancy French restaurant what with its Tibetan waiters in their natty black uniforms, plus **Le Plage** serves lovely things like brochetta. Recommended: also has a range of beautifully designed clothes on sale.

¥¥ **Olive Ridley**, Vithaldas Vaddo, Morjim, oliveturtle@rediffmail.com. Catch of the day is one of the specials in this leafy restaurant: a seafood platter including chips and salad will set you back Rs 250. Organic salads too. The best on this beach.

🍴 **The Other Side**, Morjim. Oddly enough, The Other Side is probably Goa's coolest bar, set in a neat pill box of a house surrounded by banana trees. It wouldn't look out of place in Ibiza but apparently has been slow to get a following here: the bar's well-stocked but it's a case of BYO when it comes to the crowd.

## Bars and clubs

**Baga** *p1176, map p1178*

**Cavala**, Sauntavaddo, top end of Baga village. One of the few genuine bars, with friendly atmosphere, attentive staff, great cocktails, and occasional live music evenings.

**Kamaki**, Tito's Lane. 'You've survived Kamaki's', reads the sign on this bar. Most do, but it's at your liver's peril that you enter here. Gets busy from 3am when the bigger venues down Tito's Lane start chucking out.

**Mambo's**, Tito's Lane. The slow crawl of the Tito's empire towards the beach continues with Mambo's, a touch more laid back than the original, no entrance fee.

**Sunset**, north of Baga river, a great place to watch the goings-on of Baga beach as dusk falls. Prime location but less hectic as it's north of the river bridge.

**Tito's**, Tito's Lane, www.titosgoa.com. So good, it got its own lane. From 2005, Tito's, one of Goa's first nightspots, will become the first venue to build itself a proper, international standard club. After a legal hiccup in 2004, it means that the club, famous among hip young things the length of India, should be back to full house music strength – the venue also serves excellent food through the night including reasonably priced wood-fired pizzas.

**Candolim and Sinquerim beaches** *p1176*

**Congo Lounge**, 242 Souzavaddo (Fort Aguada Rd), T0832-5644226. Snazzy super-modern venue serving breakfast, lunch and dinner. It's popular with the Mumbai/MTV crowd.

**Rock Your Blues**, south end of Candolim near Taj complex, open 2030. Playing retro music and selling sensibly priced drinks, this new venture is aimed not just at the Taj clientele.

**Anjuna** *p1179, map p1181*

Wed and Fri nights tend to be the main evenings, but there is usually something going on each night during Christmas-New Year period – just ask around (taxi drivers invariably know where). Venues are often recognizable by illuminated trees and luminous wall hangings. It is best to walk there and back in a large group. Politicians have tried to impose a ban or a curb on loud music after 2200. A purpose-built set, 'Jungle Grove', has been created inland, south of Anjuna.

**Curlys**, at the very far south of Anjuna, a kind of unofficial headquarters of the scene, playing techno and ambient music.

**Guru**, along the beach, popular, mops up after the flea market.

**Paradiso** The biggest, looks like a wild Fred Flintstone flight of fancy. Although it advertises itself as a performance art space, it's dyed in the wool techno.

**Sonic**, by the beach, under the palms on a raised terrace.

**Sunset**, close to Shore Bar, good raised platform with comfortable sunbeds.

**Vagator** *p1181, map p1182*

Locals know which way their bread is buttered, and in this neighbourhood, it's beer up. Many bars here have a happy hour from 1700-1930 and show live Premier League football, in a bit of a home-from-home for many visitors. Along the beach, shacks also serve a wide range of drinks and cocktails to sip while watching the sunset.

**Club Merc**, close to Vagator beach, turns into a party venue.

**Nine Bar**, Ozran beach. A booming mud-packed bar with huge gargoyle adornments and a manic neon man carved out of the fountain. Great sound system and majestic sunset views.

**Arambol** *p1184*

The southern end of Arambol's main beach is the only place to offer any real nightlife.

**Butterfly**, plays house and techno and charges an entrance fee (itself something of a shock here).

**Surfclub**, T0832-2292484, which is run by an English guy and has rock and live jamming sessions. Both wind down by 2300 to meet Goan laws curbing music played outdoors.

## Entertainment

**Calangute** *p1176, map p1177*
**Heritage Kathakali Theatre**, at the Hotel Sunflower, opposite the football ground, Calangute Beach Rd, T0832-2588059, daily in season, 1800-2000. The breathtakingly elaborate mimes of 17th-century Keralan mime dance drama take over 12 hrs to perform in the southern state. Here, however, it comes abbreviated for tourist attention spans: you watch the players apply their make-up, are spoon-fed a brief background of the dance, then performed a snatch of a classic dance-drama.

**Candolim and Sinquerim beaches** *p1176*
**Satya's Garden**, behind **Oceanic Shack**. An intimate living room screening room with Hollywood or Indian (mostly arthouse) films starting at 2130.

## Festivals and events

**Mapusa** *p1174, map p1175*
**Mon of the 3rd week after Easter** Feast of **Our Lady of Miracles** The *Nossa Senhora de Milagres* image is venerated by Christians as well as Hindus who join together to celebrate the feast day of the Saibin. Holy oil is carried from the church to Shanteri temple and a huge fair and a market is held.

**Calangute** *p1176, map p1177*
**Mar** Carnival is best celebrated in villages or in the main district towns but Calangute has brought the party to the tourists.
**May** (2nd week). **The Youth Fête** attracts Goa's leading musicians and dancers.

## Shopping

**Mapusa** *p1174, map p1175*
**Other India Bookstore**, 1st floor, St Britto's Apartment, above Mapusa clinic, T0832-2263306, is unconventional and excellent. It is heavily eco-conscious, has a large catalogue and will post worldwide.
The **municipal Mapusa Bazaar**, on the south edge of the fruit and vegetable market, has fixed-price basic food supplies like rice, spice, lentils and cereals: useful if you're here for the long term.

**Calangute** *p1176, map p1177*
**Book Palace**, Beach Rd, near the bus stand, is a relic from the old days when long-term residents spent their weeks reading.
**Casa Goa**, Cobravado, Baga Rd, T0832-2281048, cezarpinto@hotmail.com. Cezar Pinto's shop is quite a razzy lifestyle store: beautifully restored reclining plantation chairs next to plates brought over by the Portuguese from Macau plus modern-day dress from local fashion designer Wendell Rodricks. Cool modern twists on old Goan shoes by local Edwin Pinto too.
**Malini Ramini**, 156, opposite St Anthony's Chapel, T0832-2275305, www.maliniramini.com. Threads for the eccentrically ethnic – much here is for the hip Mumbai crowd but there's good bikinis, bags and beaded dresses. International price tags.
**Menezes supermarket**, near petrol pump, T0832-2279993. A real treasure trove of a supermarket: all the usual plus adaptor plugs, water heating filaments, quince jam, wine, cashew *feni* in plastic bottles to take home, full range of sun lotion factors and brands, tampons etc and money change.
**Tibetan Handicrafts Market**, Calangute Association. During the season the Tibetan community in exile gently sell silver from 2 markets in Calangute.

**Candolim and Sinquerim beaches** *p1176*
**Camelot**, 139 Fondvem, Ribandar, T0832-2234255. Classic countryside furniture.
**Rust**, 409A Fort, Aguada Rd, Candolim, T0832-2479340. Everything from wrought-iron furniture to clothes.
**Sangolda**, Chogm Rd, opposite Mac de Deus Chapel, Sangolda T0832-2409309, sangolda@sancharnet.in, Mon-Sat 1000-1930. Lifestyle gallery and café run by the owners of **Nilaya Hermitage** selling handcrafted metalware, glass, ethnic furniture, bed and table linen, lacquerware, wooden objects.
**Sankar's**, Acron Arcade, Fort Aguada Rd, Candolim, T0832-5643674, www.sankarsbooks.com. Probably North Goa's best bookshop: Indian fiction and history, spirituality and yoga, management and general fiction, both highbrow and pulp.
**Yamini**, Acron Arcade, Fort Aguada Rd, Candolim. Next door to **Sankar's**, selling some great, reasonably priced silk cushions, throws and beach mats.

**Anjuna** *p1179, map p1181*
**Flea Market**, Wed, attracts hordes of tourists from all over Goa. By mid-morning all approach roads are blocked with taxis, so arrive early.
**Natural Health Food Store**, Monteirovaddo.
**Orchard Stores**, Monteirovaddo. Amazing selection catering for western cravings. Olive oil, pasta, fresh cheese, frozen meats etc.
**Oxford Arcade**, De Mellovaddo, next to Munche's. Good general store close to the beach.
**Oxford Stores**, for groceries, foreign exchange and photo processing.

**Chapora** *p1179, map p1182*
**Narayan**, bookstall, sells local newspapers.
Do your homework before you buy: prices in tourist shops are massively inflated, and goods are often worth less than a third of the asking. 92.5 silver should be sold by weight: prices are quoted on the international market and in 2004 a biscuit would go for Rs 11 per g; pay a little more for elaborate workmanship.
The bigger Kashmiri shops, particularly, are notorious both for refusing to sell by weight, instead quoting by the 'piece'; taxi and rickshaw drivers routinely get Rs 100 per tourist delivered to shops plus 10% commission on anything sold.

## Activities and tours

**Calangute** *p1176, map p1177*
**River cruises**
**Floating Palace**. If your trip begins and ends in Goa then try a backwater cruise, Keralan-style, by staying overnight in this 4-cabin wooden houseboat. The bamboo, straw and coir structure was laboriously built in Kerala then shipped up the coast.
You depart from Mandovi in the late afternoon, are fed a high tea then a feast of a continental dinner passing the Chorao Island bird sanctuary. International standards of safety. Bookings can be arranged through **Amazing Images Tour Operators**, opposite Milky Way, Khobravaddo.

**Tour operators**
Many double as money changers.
**Day Tripper**, Gauravaddo, T0832-2276726, daytrip@ goatelecom.com. Offers tours all over Goa, best deals in the region, Palolem beach Rs 350; spice plantations Rs 700; backwaters Rs 1010, with pick-ups from your hotel. Recommended.

**Yoga**
**Holystamina Yoga Ashram**, Naikavaddo, T0832-2497400, www.cyril yoga.com. 3 classes held each day, first class costs Rs 150, then price rises to Rs 300 per class thereafter. Various courses for all abilities, beginners to advanced. Inner healing yoga meditation, juice bar, yoga camps and good karma-promoting volunteer activities also on offer.

**Baga** *p1176, map p1178*
**Boat trips and wildlife cruises**
**Fiesta Yacht**, **Fiesta Restaurant**, opposite Tito's, Tito's Lane. 36 ft, morning and sunset cruises for dolphin watching, Rs 400-800. Contact Maneck Contractor.
Mikes Marine, **Fortune Travels**, Sauntavaddo by the bus stand at the top end of Baga, T0832-2279782. Covered boat, dolphin trips, river cruises and bird watching.

**Diving and snorkelling**
**Goa Dive Center**, Tito's Rd, T0832-2157094. Goa isn't really on the diving map, chiefly because it has only 2 dive sites, both of which have what's known as 'variable', ie less than great, visibility. However, the Dive Center offers inexpensive PADI courses. Options range from half day Discover Scuba programme (from 10 years and up) for Rs 2,700 to the 4-day Open Water Diver programme, Rs 14,500. The centre also runs snorkelling tours.

**Ayurveda and yoga**
**Natural Health Centre**, opposite Tito's Rd, offers alternative therapies including ayurvedic massage and yoga lessons.
**The Ayurvedic Natural Health Centre**, Baga-Calangute Rd, Villa 2, Beira Mar Complex, www.healthandayurveda.com. Also in Saligao. The ANHC is not for the faint-hearted: the centre was originally built for the local community that it continues to serve and hasn't made many concessions to western sensibilities. Those checking into the 2-week *panchakarma* can expect almost every cavity to be flushed. They do offer smaller,

less daunting packages, like 2½ hr rejuvenations (Rs 300), and have a herb garden where you can taste first-hand leaves that tingle your tongue (used to stop stuttering) or others that eliminate your sense of sweet taste.

### Candolim and Sinquerim beaches

*p1176*

#### Ayurveda and massage

**Amrita Kerala Ayurvedic**, next to Lawande supermarket, Annavaddo, T0832-3125668/9, www.vedamassage.com, 0730-2000. This massage centre, set inside an old Goan villa, is neatly geared towards the foreign tourist. Westerners are on hand to explain the philosophy behind the Indian life science. As well as treatments the centre teaches massage. A basic course, scheduled for the morning to give you more time on the sand, takes 7 days. Panchakarma courses last 6 months (Rs 7,500). Rs 750 for 75-min massage.

#### Dolphin watching

**John's Boats**, T0832-2277780, promises 'guaranteed' dolphin watching, morning trips start around 0900, Rs 550 (includes meal and hotel pick-up). Also crocodile-spotting river trips with lunch.

#### Parasailing

Occasionally offered independently on Candolim beach, costing around Rs 600-850 for a 5-min flight.

#### Fort Aguada

**Taj Sports Complex**, Fort Aguada Beach Resort. Has excellent facilities that are open to non-residents at the Taj Holiday Village, and a separate access between Aguada Beach Resort and the Holiday Village. Rs 450 per day for the complex, Rs 350 for the pool. Tennis (Rs 450 per hr); squash and badmin- ton (Rs 150 for 30 mins); mini golf (Rs 200). Yoga classes. Scuba diving, sailing/ water skiing/windsurfing/rod fishing Rs 450-500 per hr; parasailing/jet ski Rs 900-950 per hr.

### Anjuna *p1179, map p1181*

#### Ayurveda, massage and yoga

As in Calangute, there are a number of yoga teachers who flood in to teach in Goa during the season: look around for signs. You'll also stumble on practitioners of all sorts of alternative therapies: reiki healers, acupuncturists, chakra and even vortex cleansing can all be bought.

**Healing Here And Now**, The Health Center, St Michael's Vaddo, T0832-2273487, www.healinghereandnow.com. If you want an 'ultimate cleanse' sign up for a 5-day detox: fasting, detoxifying drinks and twice daily enemas. Also offers parasite cleansing, kidney cleanse and wheat grass therapy. Yikes.

**Purple Valley**, either drop-in at the Hotel Bougainvillea in Anjuna T0832-2981341 or book a residential at the Hillside Retreat Assagao, www.yogagoa.com. Purple Valley attracts the heavy-weight superstars of the ashtanga vinyasa yoga circuit such as the respected John Scott, Madonna's teacher Danny Paradise and there's even talk in hushed deferential tones of 'guruji', Sri Patabhi Jois, jetting in from his *shala* in Mysore. You need to book courses (which include accommodation) at the Hillside Retreat Center in Assagao well in advance but can drop in to the classes (ashtanga/ hatha and meditation/pranayama all offered) in Anjuna at the Hotel Bougainvillea on an ad hoc basis: single classes cost Rs 3,000 for 10 or Rs 400 per session.

**Shri Dhanwantari's Ayur Sampada**, church grounds, near Tamarind T0832-2268361, mayura_goa@sancharnet.in. Dr Laxmi Bharne has 4 years of experience in treating specific ailments, gives treatment only after check up, dietary advice, pure herbal treatments. Also offers full body massage, *shirodhara*, etc.

#### Bungee jumping

Offered by a Mumbai-based firm with US trained staff, at Rs 500 a go. Safety is a priority with harnesses, carabinas and air bags employed. There are pool tables, a bar, an auditorium for slide/film shows and also beach volleyball. Open 1000-1230 and 1730 until late.

#### Paragliding

**Happy Hours Café**, south Anjuna beach, from 1230-1400; Rs 500 (children welcome), or at the hilltop between Anjuna and Baga, (and Arambol).

#### Windsurfing

Boards are sometimes available for hire at the south end of the beach for about Rs 100 per hr.

#### Tour operators

**Speedy** near post office Mazalvaddo, T0832-2273208, 0900-1830. Very helpful for all your onward travel arrangements, also a money changer. Very helpful, comprehensive service.

#### Arambol *p1184*

**21 Coconuts Inn**, 2nd restaurant on the left after stepping on to the beach. For dolphin watching trips or boats to Anjuna, Rs 150 for each.

**Himalaya Iyengar Yoga Centre**, T01892-221312, www.hiyogacentre.com. Classes conducted on a hard floor shaded by a parachute with breezes from the sea. *Tipis* are provided for long-term students.

**Paragliding** can also be arranged from beach shacks.

## Transport

### Mapusa *p1174, map p1175*

#### Bus

To **Calangute** (every 20-30 mins), some continue on to **Aguada** and **Baga**, some go towards **Candolim**; check before boarding or change at Calangute. Non-stop mini-buses to **Panjim**; buy tickets from booth at market entrance. Buses also go to **Vagator** and **Chapora** via **Anjuna** and towns near by. Buses to **Tivim** for Konkan Railway and trains to Mumbai, Rs 8 (allow 25 mins).

Long-distance buses, line up opposite the taxi stand, offering near-identical routes and rates. To **Bangalore**: 1830, 12 hrs, Rs 250 (Luxury), Rs 450 (Sleeper). **Hospet** (for Hampi): 1800, 10 hrs, Rs 350 (Sleeper). **Mumbai** 1600, 14 hrs, Rs 300 (Luxury), Rs 500 (Sleeper).

#### Car hire

Pink Panther, T0832-2263180.

#### Motorcycle hire

**Peter & Friends Classic Adventures**, Casa Tres Amigos, Socol Vado 425, Parra, Assagao, 5 km east (off the Anjuna Rd), T0832-2254467, www.classic-bike-india.de, recommended for reliable bikes and tours of Southern India, Himachal and Nepal. Also has some quality rooms.

#### Taxis

(often shared by up to 5); to **Panjim** Rs 70; **Calangute/Baga**, Rs 100; **Chapora/Siolim**, Rs 80. Auto to **Calangute**, Rs 50. Motorcycle taxi to **Anjuna** or **Calangute**, about Rs 40, but open to bargaining.

#### Train

Tivim train station on the Konkan railway is convenient if you want to head straight to the **northern beaches** (Calangute, Baga, Anjuna and Vagator), avoiding Panjim and Margao. A local bus meets each train and usually runs as far as the Kadamba bus stand in Mapusa. From here you either continue on a local bus to the beach or share a tourist taxi (rates above). Enquiries and computerized tickets: T0832-2298682.

To **Ernakulam** (for junction): *Mangalore Exp 2618*, 1952 (arr 1345), 18 hrs. To **Jaipur** (from Ernakulam): *Exp 2977*, 1138, Mon. To **Margao**: *Mandovi Exp 0103*, 1650, 90 mins; *Konkan Kanya Exp 0111*, 0924, 90 mins. To **Mumbai (CST)**: *Mandovi Exp 0104*, 1113, 10 hrs; *Konkan Kanya Exp 0112*, 1846, 11 hrs (via Pernem). To **Mumbai Kurla (Tilak)** (from Trivandrum): *Netravati Exp 6346*, 0747, 11 hrs. To **Thiruvananthapuram (Trivandrum)**: *Netravati Exp 6345*, 2152, 19 hrs (via Margao and Canacona for Palolem beach).

### Baga *p1176, map p1178*

The only place in Baga to hire bikes is 200 m down a small lane past the Hacienda, on the left. Rs 40 per day, a little extra to keep it overnight. As for scooters, almost every guesthouse owner or hotelier can rustle up a scooter at short notice – expect to pay Rs150 for one day or Rs100 per day for longer periods. Recycled water bottles of lurid orange liquid balanced in glass display boxes at roadsides denote your local gas station. Petrol is Rs 40 per litre.

### Arambol *p1184*

There are regular buses from **Mapusa** and a frequent service from **Chopdem**, 12 km along the main road (about 40 mins); the attractive coastal detour via Morjim being slightly longer. It's a 2-hr-walk north through Morjim and Mandrem by the coast. **Delight** and **Tara**, in the village, exchange cash and TCs, good for train tickets (Rs 100 service charge); also sells bus tickets.

**Mandrem** *p1184*
**Buses** towards **Siolem** pass along the main road at about 0930 and 1345. Direct services also to **Mapusa** and **Panjim**.

**Keri (Querim) and Tiracol fort** *p1185*
From **Panjim** direct bus at 1700, arrives 1930, returns to Panjim 0700 next morning.

## Directory

**Mapusa** *p1174, map p1175*
**Ambulance** T0832-2262372. **Banks** **Bank of India**, opposite Municipal Gardens, changes TCs, cash against Visa and Master-card. Mon-Fri 1000-1400, Sat 1000-1200. **State Bank of India**, exchanges cash and TCs, 15-20 mins. Foreign exchange on 1st floor, Mon-Fri 1000-1600, Sat 1000-1200. **Pink Panther Agency** changes Visa and Master- card, Mon-Fri 0900-1700, Sat 0900-1300. **Hospitals and medical services** Asilo Hospital, T0832-2262211. Pharmacies: including **Drogaria**, near the Swiss Chapel, open 24 hrs; **Mapusa Clinic**, T0832-2262350; **Bardez Bazar**. **Internet** several across town, well signed. Most charge Rs 90 per hr. Best at **LCC** 3rd Flr, Bhavani Apartments, Rs 15 per 15 mins; 6 terminals, 0700-2130, 7 days a week. **Police** T0832-2262231. **Post** Opposite the police station.

**Calangute** *p1176, map p1177*
**Banks** State Bank of India, Baga; Bank of Baroda, Baga. **Internet** I way, NetXcess Cyber Café, Shop No 1, Sunshine Complex, Baga Rd, T0832-2281516, netxcess@mail.com. Broadband internet chain I way's branch is faster than most. **Nikki's Internet Café**, Calangute Tourist Resort Annexe, T0832-2281950, 8 terminals, forex, pool table, café, 0900 to midnight, Rs 40 per hr. Useful during periods of frequent power cuts. **Police** T0832-2278284. **Telephone** Look for the yellow STD ISD signs.

**Candolim and Sinquerim beaches** *p1176*
**Health Centre**, Main Rd; **Bosto Hospital**, Panjim Rd.

**Anjuna** *p1179, map p1181*
**Banks** Bank of Baroda, Sorranto Vaddo, Mon-Wed, Fri 0930-1330, Sat 0930-1130, accepts most TCs, Visa/Mastercard, 1% commission (min Rs 50); also provide 'Safe Custody Packets'. There is no bank in Vagator or Chapora. Thomas Cook agent at **Oxford Stores**, central, quicker and more efficient. **Internet** Space Ride Internet, opposite St Anthony's Church, has high speed connections. In Chapora, **Sonya Travels** near Holy Cross, offers foreign exchange, money transfers, ticketing and internet. **Pharmacy** St Michael's Pharmacy, Main Rd, Sorranto, open 24 hrs. **Police** T0832-2273233. Poste Restante at post office, open 1000-1600, Mon-Sat; efficient, parcels are also accepted without a fuss.

**Arambol** *p1184*
**Pharmacy** On the main road; **Health centre** T0832-2291249. **Police** T0832-2297614. **Post** The small village post office is at the T junction, 1,500 m from the beach.

**Mandrem** *p1184*
**Banks** Canara Bank, on the main road accepts TCs. **Hospital** T0832-2230081.

# South Goa

*The Southern districts have a wholly different character to those of the north, both in culture and in sand. The Zuari river has long acted not only as a great political and cultural divide between Christian Salcete and Hindu Ponda but also as a much wider economic and cultural marker. Here the landscape is greener: the coconut thickets that stretch along the coast are topped up with broad swathes of iridescent paddy, broken only by the whitewash towers of some of Goa's finest churches. Beneath the coconut fronds sit the wealthy villages of fishermen and agriculturalists. Some of the deepest imprints of Portuguese culture were embedded in the landscape and minds of Salcete and in the district's interior are the centuries-old mansion estates of some of those that prospered most under European colonial rule.* » *For Sleeping, Eating and other listings, see pages 1208-1215.*



## Margao and coastal Salcete → *Colour map 5a, grid B2.*

The lazy sweep of Salcete's tremendously long, wide belt of sand is less distinctive than the north's pockets of coves, embayments, and red cliff-backed beaches. But government regulations have kept almost all the rather snazzy hotels here at arm's length from the sea, and the character of the unbroken wide sand nonetheless varies. The road runs slightly inland for miles along the coast with the occasional spur leading down to the different sections of beach. Some, like Varca and Cavelossim, are little more than an empty stretch of dune-edged sand and an isolated fishing hamlet. In contrast, Colva's tall coconut palms spill over the beach, shading restaurants and a cluster of hotels and shops. Goa's most luxurious beach resorts are spread along this coastal zone. The elite landowners from the villages of south Goa are known for their high culture, the grace of their lifestyles and their Europeanization: if you can tear yourself from the beaches for long enough you can visit some of their quite literally palatial ancestral homes in the interior.

### Ins and outs

The Konkan Railway connects Margao directly with Mumbai, Mangalore and Kerala. Madgaon/Margao station is 1.5 km southeast of the bus stands, municipal gardens and market area (where you'll find most of the hotels and restaurants). Rickshaws charge Rs 15 to transfer while locals walk the 800 m along the railway line. Interstate buses and those running between here and North Goa use the New Kadamba (State) bus stand 2 km north of town. City buses take you to the town bus stands for destinations south of Margao. Colva and Benaulim buses leave from the local stand east of the gardens. There are plenty of auto-rickshaws and eight-seater van taxis for hire in addition to city buses. » *See Transport, page 1213, for futher details.*

### Margao (Madgaon) → *Colour map 5a, grid B2.*

If you're travelling to Goa on the Konkan Railway, Margao may well be your first taste of Goa, but most people hotfoot it for the beaches, using Margao for an overnight stop only if they have to. This means that tourism has had little impact on what is Goa's largest commercial centre after Panjim and the capital of the state's richest and most fertile *taluka*, Salcete. You can still see examples of old Portuguese domestic architecture and fine churches against the backdrop of a fetching, bustling market town going about its everyday business. Pleasantly provincial, it was given the status of a *vila* (town) by royal decree in 1778.

The impressive Baroque **Church of the Holy Spirit** with its classic Goan façade dominates the Old Market square, the Largo de Igreja. Originally built in 1564, it was sacked by Muslims in 1589 and rebuilt in 1675. A remarkable pulpit on the north wall has carvings of the Apostles. There are also some glass cabinets in the north aisle containing statues of St Anthony and of the Blessed Joseph Vaz. Vaz was Goa's homegrown Catholic missionary who smuggled himself to Sri Lanka dressed as a coolie when the Dutch occupation threatened the faith of the Ceylonese. In the square there is a monumental cross with a mango tree beside it. The church's feast day is in June.

The real gem of Margao is the glut of run-down 18th-century houses particularly in and around Abade Faria Road. The **da Silva House** ⓘ *Da Silva's descendants continue to live in a small wing of the house and rarely give permission to enter: requests are fielded by the local tourist office at the GTDC Residency*, is a fine example of this regal type of town house. It was built around 1790, when Inacio da Silva stepped up to become Secretary to the Viceroy, and has a long façade whose roof was once divided into seven separate cropped 'towers' – hence its other name, **Seven Shoulders** – only three of these have survived. The house's grandeur is borne through in its interiors



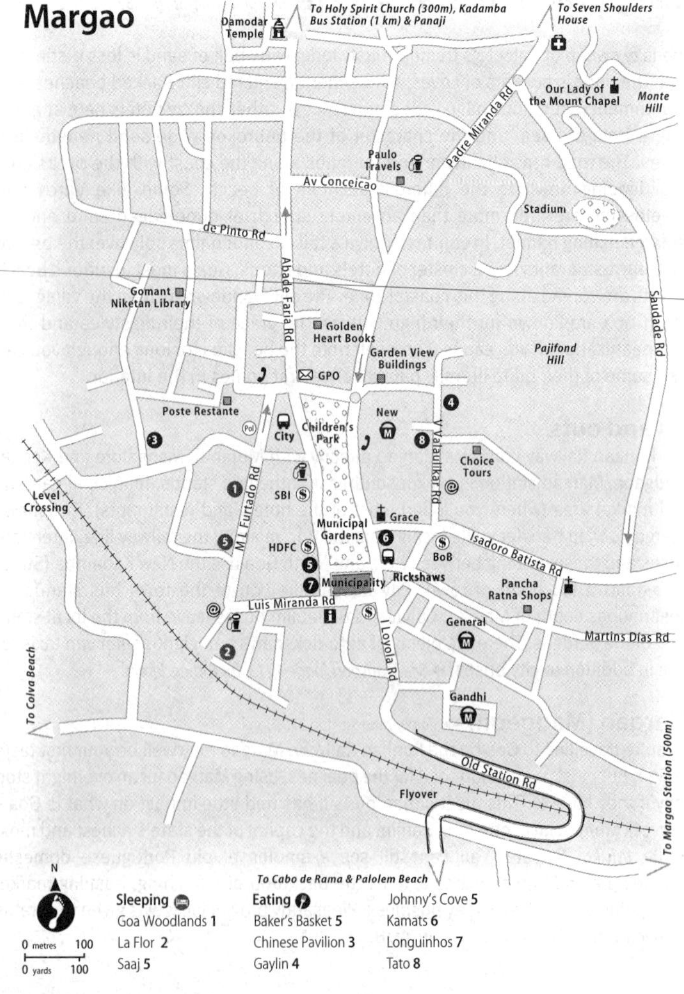

too: lavishly carved dark rosewood furniture, gilded mirrors and fine chandeliers. The first floor reception rooms that face the street are lit by large windows made of wood and oystershell that are themselves protected by wrought iron balconies.

## Colva (Colwa) → *Colour map 5a, grid B2.*

Colva, the tourist hub of the southern beaches just 6 km from the city, has nothing on the development of its overgrown opposite number in the north, Calangute, which makes it pretty pleasant. The beach was once used as a summer retreat before the monsoon by Margao's elite, who rented the houses of local fishermen, as they moved out to live in their shacks. The village itself is a bit scruffy, but the beach ticks all the right boxes: the requisite beautiful sands, gentle-swaying palms and blue waters. Entertainment-wise, everything in Colva winds down by 2300 and it's hard to get a cab past midnight so it attracts a more mellow tourist.

On the road into Colva from Margao you pass the large **Church of Our Lady of Mercy** (Nossa Senhora das Merces, 1630, re-built in the 18th century). The church has a relatively simple façade and a single tower on the south side that it is so short as to be scarcely noticeable, and the strong horizontal lines normally given to Goan churches by three of four full storeys is broken by a narrow band of shallow semi-circular arches above the second floor. However, the church is much less famous for its architecture than for its association with the miraculous **Menino Jesus**. Jesuit Father Bento Ferreira found the original image in the river Sena, Mozambique, en route to Goa, and brought it to Colva where he took up his position as rector in 1648. The image was found to have miraculous healing powers and became an object of special veneration. The story is celebrated today in the special annual festival, the **Fama of Menino Jesus** (Monday of 12-18 October), when thousands of pilgrims flock to see the statue in the hope of witnessing a miracle. Near the church, specially blessed lengths of string are sold, as well as replicas of limbs, offered to the image in thanks for cures. ⏩ *For Sleeping, Eating and other listings, see pages 1208-1215.*

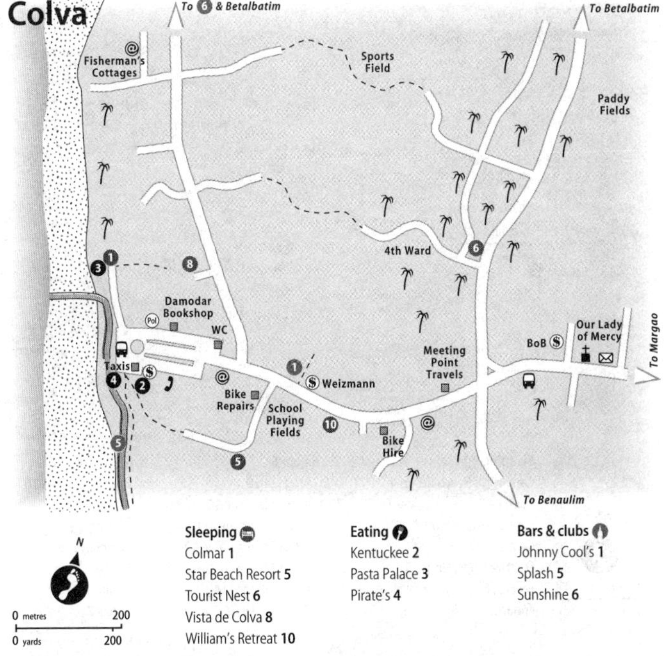

## Betalbatim to Velsao

Betalbatim, named after the main temple to Betall which stood here before the deity was moved to Queula in Ponda for safety, is a pleasant stretch with a mix of coconut palms and casuarinas on the low dunes that separate the seaside from the resort development. It still retains a rural feel: trinket sellers and taxi ranks do not yet loiter outside every hotel. Colva, and a more upbeat pace of life, is only a short walk to the south along the beach. At low tide, when the firm sand is exposed, it is possible to cycle for miles along the beach in either direction.

The four beaches north, **Velsao, Arossim, Utorda** and **Majorda** – broad, flat and open – are among the least heavily used of these beaches. Around the resort hotels there are small clusters of beach shack restaurants, and occasional fishing villages scattered under the coconut palms. Northwards up the beach you can see the Mormugao headland when it is not concealed by haze. The only blot on the landscape is the large industrial complex.

**Bogmalo**, the nearest beach to the airport (4 km, and a 10 minute drive away) is small, palm fringed and attractive, yet seldom visited. The road from the airport forks about 2½ km before reaching Bogmalo. The right fork leads to Bogmalo while the left goes to **Hollant Beach**, 2 km away, a small rocky cove that is fringed with coconut palms. **Santra Beach**, further south, can be reached by going through the village behind the **Bogmalo Beach Resort**. Local fishermen can ferry passengers to two small islands for about Rs 350 per boat.



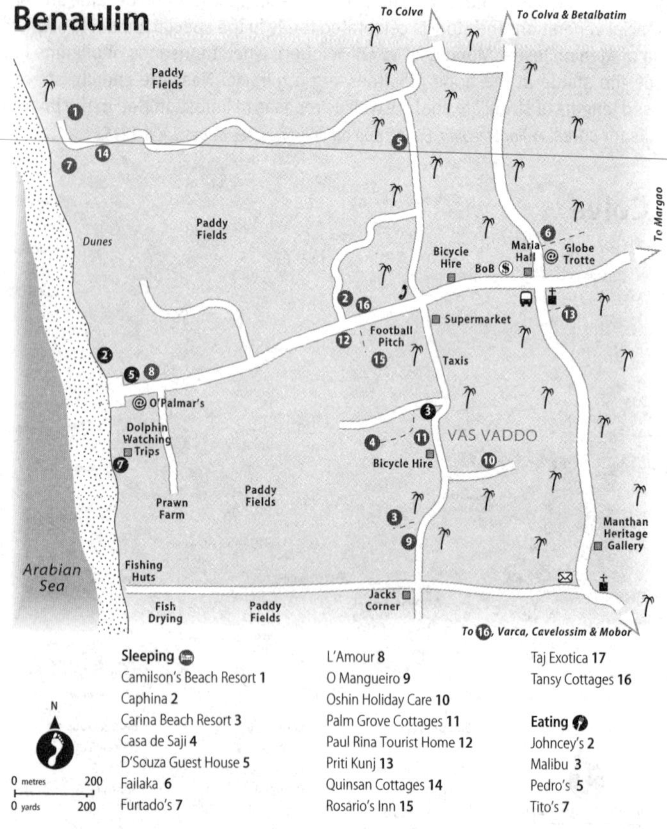


**Sleeping**
Camilson's Beach Resort 1
Caphina 2
Carina Beach Resort 3
Casa de Saji 4
D'Souza Guest House 5
Failaka 6
Furtado's 7
L'Amour 8
O Mangueiro 9
Oshin Holiday Care 10
Palm Grove Cottages 11
Paul Rina Tourist Home 12
Priti Kunj 13
Quinsan Cottages 14
Rosario's Inn 15
Taj Exotica 17
Tansy Cottages 16

**Eating**
Johncey's 2
Malibu 3
Pedro's 5
Tito's 7

One of the distinctive features of this section of coast is the strip of land that lies between the main series of villages and the dunes which actually front the sea, used for intensive rice cultivation. The road runs through these villages, set back 1-2 km from the sea. Old mansions of wealthy families still standing in the villages include **Utorda House**. There are also fine examples dotted about Velsao, in various states of repair. An afternoon exploring these quiet back lanes by bicycle gives a good window on village life. The villages from here southwards are noted for their high levels of emigration to the Gulf. Some have returned and invested money in the many new hotels.

## Verna

Verna (the 'place of fresh air') is inland from the northern Salcete beaches on the NH17. The **church** here was initially built on the site of the Mahalsa Temple before being transferred. According to old Portuguese records the original Mahalsa Temple which housed the deity now in Mardol (see page 1218) had some exquisite carvings. It was destroyed and marked by the cross to prevent it being re-used for Hindu worship. Serving as a sanctuary for widows who did not commit *sati*, it became known as the 'Temple of Nuns'. Verna is also the place chosen in 1988 for re-siting the ancient 2.5 m **Mother Goddess figure** (fifth century BC) from Curdi (Kurdi) in Sanguem, which was under threat of being submerged by the Selaulim Dam project. Two megalithic sites were found in the area. It is surrounded by seven springs with special healing properties.

Immediately north towards Cortalim are the **Kersarval springs**, which have medicinal properties but are no longer a 'natural' remote watering place. They are very popular with Goans as a picnic spot. From the large car park, paths lead past several enclosures through the gently sloping wooded hillside. The covered resting areas for picnics are near the entrance. The path to the springs leads down a short but steep slope into a vertical walled grotto where bathers can stand under the trickling spring water.

## Varca to Betul

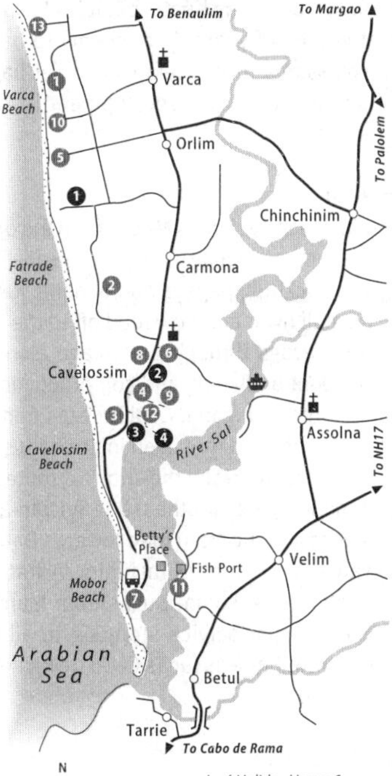

**Sleeping**
Club Mahindra 1
Dona Sa Maria 2
Dona Sylvia Resort 3
Gaffino's & Hippo Cool 4
Goa Renaissance Resort 5
José Holiday Home 6
Leela Palace 7
Mobor Beach Resort 8
Octima 9
Resorte de Goa 10
River Sal 11
Sao Domingos 12
Taj Exotica 13

**Eating**
Grill Room 1
Jazz Inn 2
Mike's Place 3
River View 4

## Benaulim to Mobor

→ *Colour map 5a, grid B2.*

Benaulim, according to the myth of Parasurama on the creation of Goa, is 'where the arrow fell'. Today it is the more tranquil and pleasant southern end of Colva beach, but during the season its approach road gets very busy and some complain of plagues of fruit and jewellery hawkers. It's easy to escape their advances by hiring a bike and peddling a little way south along the beach. Take the inland route for a walk or bike ride through the 4 km of idyllic countryside to Colva. Buses from all directions arrive at the hub of all the village activity at Maria Hall crossing, just over a kilometre from the beach. Autos and taxis wait at the crossing and at the end of the beach road.

The small **Church of St John the Baptist**, on a hill beyond the village, rebuilt 1596, is a superb example of Goan Christian architecture. The twin towers are surmounted by shallow domes while the typical scrolls are flanked by crosses. Although the gable façade is striking, the chief beauties of the church are inside. The magnificent altar *reredos* is uniquely decorated, and there is a wonderful rococo pulpit surmounted by a representation of the Lamb of the Apocalypse from the Book of Revelation.

The narrow and attractive road south from Benaulim runs about 1 km inland from the sea through small villages, some with superb white-painted churches. Paddy fields and palm groves alternate, and periodically roads run down to the sea, sometimes to small settlements, sometimes to deserted beaches. Benaulim beach runs into **Varca**, and then Fatrade. To reach **Cavelossim beach** involves a short walk through scrub vegetation and dunes.



Farthest south, **Mobor**, about 8 km from Varca, lies on the narrow peninsula where the river Sal joins the sea. Access to the beach near the river is somewhat restricted by the sprawling **Leela Palace** hotel complex. The Sal is a busy river and harbour for fishing boats, but it is also a very pleasant place for boat rides. Over the last couple of years there seems to have been a non-stop building campaign in Cavelossim and this relatively quiet backwater has lost some of its charm to the boom. However, the development is still nothing like what has occurred on the north coast.

## Betul

Betul, which overlooks Mobor from the opposite bank of the Sal in Quepem taluka, is an important fishing village in an idyllic setting, delightfully shaded by coconut palms, jackfruit, papaya and banana. Just after the bridge, which crosses the mouth of a small river, a narrow road off to the right by the shops (some buses turn around here), zigzags through the village along the south side of the Sal. The village is dependent on fishing and coir production. A sand bar traps the estuary into a wide and protected lagoon. Cool breezes from the sea moderate the temperatures of the plateau above so that even in the hottest season it is perfectly bearable.

From Cavelossim the shortest route to Betul is by taking the ferry across the Sal (signposted, just southeast) to Assolna; turn left off the ferry, then turn right in the village to join the main road towards Betul. From Margao, the NH17 forks right (6 km) towards Assolna at Chinchinim. A further 6 km on, there is a second turning in Cuncolim for Assolna. Buses from Margao to Betul can be very slow, but there is a fairly regular service stopping in all the settlements along the way (a couple of them continue as far as Cabo de Rama). Confirm the route when boarding the bus in Margao.

## Cuncolim

Cuncolim saw the destruction of its three principal Hindu temples (including the Shantadurga), when the Jesuits were christianizing the area and later building churches and chapels on the sites.

It was also the scene of the massacre of five Jesuits and several converts by local Hindu 'rebels' who had been incensed by the repeated destruction of temples and defilement of temple tanks. Most of them were subsequently captured by the captain of Rachol fort and 15 were killed by his soldiers. The Christian 'martyrs of Cuncolim' were initially buried in Rachol but were transferred to Old Goa where their relics are lodged in the Sé Cathedral. The golden bell, which is the largest in Goa, and which hangs in the remaining single tower of the Sé Cathedral, was cast here in 1652.

# Cabo de Rama and further south → *Colour map 5a, grid C2.*

Palolem is the closest you come to the picture postcard perfect beach ideal in Goa and naturally its beautiful curve of palm-fringed golden sand has not gone unnoticed. It's far from a deserted bay but remains lovely nonetheless: the narrow beach is top and tailed with rocky outcrops dubbed 'Pandava's drums' or 'footprints' by locals, there's a freshwater stream to the north and you can fetch up on the deserted jungle of the tiny Canacona Island with just a short swim or by wading across at low tide.

Palolem's popularity has led to tourism spilling out onto its neighbouring beaches. By and large there has been a southward drift to Calomb, Patnem and on to Galgibaga, skipping the beautiful Rajbag, whose charms are ringfenced by the new five-star development. Patnem, hemmed in by crags and river at either end, doesn't have the same rash of coconut trees that made Palolem so shadily alluring but the encroachment is already underway. Less visited, to the north, is the casuarina-backed bay of Agonda, a strung-out fishing village that pretty much ignores the few tourists lolling around in the sun. The sparsely visited but dramatic fort at Cabo de Rama lies midway between Agonda and Mobor to the north. » *For Sleeping, Eating and other listings, see pages 1208-1215.*



## Ins and outs

**Getting there** The nearest major transport junction for all these beaches is Canacona, also known as Chaudi, on the NH17 between Panjim and Karwar in Karnataka with direct transport links, but there are also less frequent direct buses between the beaches and Margao (37 km north) that take roughly an hour. From here buses shuttle fairly continuously down to Palolem and less frequently to Agonda. Canacona Junction on the Konkan railroad between Mumbai and Trivandrum is only 2 km from Palolem. Canacona's main square has the bus and auto stands: rickshaws cost between Rs 50-150 to any of these bays.

**Getting around** The area between the beaches is small and wandering between them becomes a leisure pursuit in itself. A motorbike is good for those with short beach attention spans. The drive to Cabo de Rama, although riddled with hair-pin bends, is particularly lovely and going under your own steam means you can look for the deserted beaches nearby and stop over at the fishing dock at the estuary north of Agonda. Buses run along this route between the bays on a roughly hourly basis.

## Cabo de Rama (Cape Rama) → *Colour map 5a, grid C2.*

Capo de Rama is named after the hero of the Hindu epic Ramayana, who is said to have lived there with his wife Sita during their period of exile. It was obvious that the cape was the perfect site for a fort to any power whose interests might be threatened from the sea. Its origins pre-date the arrival of the Portuguese who captured it in 1763 and used it as a prison too.

The gatehouse, which was restored less than five years ago now looks more rundown than most of the original fortifications. Sadly, it is a grubby mess of broken timbers and walls covered with graffiti. The main entrance seems far from impregnable, but the outer ramparts are excellently preserved, with several cannons still scattered along their length. Despite the absence of buildings, other than the church, the magnificence of the site gives it an extraordinary atmosphere. There are stunning views from several of its major bastions, and you can walk virtually the entire outer length of the fort.

The gatehouse is at the lowest point of the whole fort, the ground rising to its highest in the southwest and the wall then dropping down to the north. At its lowest it is only 20 m or so above the sea. At this point of the compound is the source of the fort's water supply. A huge tank was excavated to a depth of about 10 m, and even today it contains water right through the dry season. If the local herdsman is about, ask for directions to the two springs, one of which gives out water through two spouts at different temperatures. This tranquil place is well worth a visit.

## Agonda

Snake through forests and bright paddy south from Cabo De Rama towards Palolem to uncover artless Agonda, a windswept village backed by mountains of forestry full of acrobatic black-faced monkeys. Local political agitators thwarted plans for a five-star hotel and so have, temporarily at least, arrested the speed of their home's development as a tourist destination. Their success makes for a primitive holiday scene: a handful of internet points, less than a dozen restaurants and a small number of hotels and coco-huts are strewn out over the beach village's length. There's no house music, little throttling of Enfield engines and you need to be happy to make your own entertainment to stay here for any serious length of time. Less photogenic than Palolem, Agonda bay has pine-like casuarina trees lining the beach instead of coconuts and palms. The swimming is safe and the beach wonderfully calm. The northern end of the beach, close to the school and bus stop, has a small block of shops including the brilliantly chaotic original **Fatima stores & restaurant** (Fatima Rodrigues, not one to be a jack of all trades, has limited her menu to just spaghetti and *thali*) and **St Annes bookstore**, a video library. ▸▸ *For Sleeping, Eating and other listings, see pages 1208-1215.*



## Palolem → *Colour map 5a, grid C2.*

For a short spell, when the police cracked down most severely on parties up north, Palolem looked like it might act as the Anjuna overflow. Today **Neptune's Point** has permission to hold parties once a fortnight, but so far, Palolem's villagers are resisting the move to make the beach a mini-party destination and authorities are even stumping up the cash to pay for litter-pickers. The demographic here is chiefly late-twenties and thirty-something couples, travellers and students. Canacona is the nearest settlement of any significant size to Palolem and has shops and direct transport links – it is the southernmost stop on the Konkan Railway in Goa and is the crossroads on the NH17 between Panjim and the Karnataka port city of Karwar. The large church and high school of **St Tereza of Jesus** (1962) are on the northern edge of town.

## Beaches further south

Over the rocky outcrops to the south you come to the sandy cove of **Calomb**. Wholly uncommercial, its trees are pocked with longstayers' little picket fences and stabs at growing banana plants, their earthy homesteads cheek by jowl with fishermen's huts. The sound here is the rattle of coconut fronds and bird song. Little puppies lie panting corpse-like in the bush. You can hear every voice and every flip-flop flap. You could almost be on a different planet to Palolem.

At the end of the track through Calomb a collection of huts marks the start of the fine sweep of **Patnem beach**, which some reckon to be the new Palolem. Here, the 500 villagers have both put a limit on the number of shacks and stopped outsiders from trading, and as a result the beach has conserved much of its unhurried charm. The deep banks of sand are whipped up by winds to catch kite-flyers' fancy and cushion the falls of volleyball-players: but fishing boats still far outnumber sun loungers. The place is something of a hit with old rockers, Israelis and long-stayers: so far there are no parties, no nightlife and, no coincidence, a healthy relationship between villagers and tourism.

> *Hindu temples in Patnem have music most Fri and Sat with tabla, symbols and harmonica.*

*Patnem is developing fast. In 1996 there were just two cafés. By 2001 there were 22. During Christmas 2003, demand for accommodation was so high that people were sleeping outdoors in hammocks, while huts were rented out at an amazing Rs 5,000 a day.*

Further south, wade across a stream (possible before the monsoon) to reach the dune and casuarina-fringed **Rajbag Beach**, its southern waters a-bob with fishing boats. Although it's virtually unvisited and has perfect swimming, the luxury five-star that opened here in 2004 has provoked a storm of protest and prevented anyone else from moving in. Local criticism of the development centres on the whittling away of fisherfolk's access to the beach, the rebuilding of the ancient Shree Vita Rukmayee temple that villagers say is tantamount to the hotel 'swallowing our God' and the alleged flouting of the proviso that half the jobs created should go to local people. The isolated **Kindlebaga beach** is east of Rajbag, 2 km from Canacona.

## Galgibaga

South of the Talpona river, which has a ferry crossing, a short strip of land juts out to sea. Galgibaga is a change from the fishing villages across the river as it has well-built houses among lucrative casuarina plantations belonging to the townspeople. Galgibaga beach, like Morjim in the north, is a favourite stop-over for Olive Ridley turtles which travel vast distances to lay their eggs here each November. Shacks are mushrooming here, much to environmentalists' concern.

## Partagali and Cotigao Wildlife Sanctuary

→ *Colour map 5a, grid C3.*

Some 7 km south of Canacona is a left turn off the NH17 to Partagali. The massive concrete gateway here is to the Partagali temple. If you go a little further, your reach a 2-km road that leads to the Cotigao wildlife sanctuary. Partagali's **Shri Sausthan Gokarn Partagali Jeevotam Math** is on the banks of the river Kushavati. The *math* (religious establishment) was set up in AD 1475 at Margao when the followers, originally Saivites, were converted and became a Vaishnav sect. However, during the period of Portuguese Christianization (1560-68), the foundation was moved to Bhatkal (northern Karnataka). After a time, the sixth Swami (who was also responsible for the temple to Rama, Lakshman, Sita and Hanuman here), re-established the *math* at Partagali, where it has continued uninterrupted. The symbol representing the spiritual movement which is over 500 years old, is an ancient *Vatavriksha* (banyan tree) which spreads over an area of about 65 m x 70 m. Known as *Bramhasthan,* it has been a place for meditation, and the sacred tree with the *Ishwarlinga* (the *lingam* of the Lord, ie Siva) in front of it is believed to have drawn worshippers from the surrounding area for over 1,000 years. Partagali has been developed into a centre of culture and learning, while continuing with its ancient traditions. The temple, which also has a typical tall Garuda pillar, celebrates its festival in March/April.

**Cotigao Wildlife Sanctuary** ⓘ *60 km south of Panjim, Rs 5, 2-wheelers Rs 10, cars Rs 50; still camera Rs 25; video Rs 100, 0730-1730 throughout the year (but may not be worthwhile during the monsoon)*, is Goa's second largest and was established in 1969. In one of the most densely forested areas of the state, the 105 sq km sanctuary is hilly to the south and east and has the Talpona river flowing through it. There is a nature interpretation centre with a small reference library at the entrance. The vegetation is mostly moist deciduous with some semi-evergreen and evergreen forest cover. The sanctuary claims to have a wide range of mammals including panther, sloth bear and hyena, and several reptiles, but you are only likely to see wild boar, the odd deer and gaur and many monkeys; birdspotting is more rewarding. Birds not easily seen elsewhere in Goa include rufous woodpecker, Malabar crested lark and white-eyed eagle. You need your own vehicle to reach the treetop watch towers and water holes which are signposted, 3 km and 7 km off the main metalled road on a variable rough track. There are no guides but the forest office by the Interpretation Centre at the entrance has a map of the park roads on the wall. The forest paths are easy to follow but make sure you have drinking water and petrol. The chances of seeing much wildlife, apart from monkeys, however are slim, since by the opening time of 0730 it can be warm enough to reduce animal activity to a minimum. However, it can be rewarding to take a short walk through the forest and immerse yourself in the sounds of the jungle.

The first tower by a water hole is known as **Machan Vhutpal**, 400 m off the road. Unfortunately only if you are fit and have a good head for heights are you likely to venture up the steep wrought-iron ladder to the raised platform which offers a great view of the forest canopy. The second tower is far more substantial and the best place to spend a night if permission is granted (this should not be a problem).

Most visitors usually come for a day trip, but if you are keen on walking in the forest this is a great place to spend a day or two. You can either stay near the sanctuary office or spend a night in a watch tower deep in the forest. A short way beyond the sanctuary entrance the metalled road passes through a small hamlet where there is a kiosk for the villagers living within the reserve, which sells the usual array of basic provisions. If you are planning to spend a few days in the park it is best to bring your own fresh provisions and then let the staff prepare meals.

The cheapest way to visit the park is for a group to hire a taxi for a half-day in Palolem. If you leave the beach just before 0700 you will be at the park gates when they open. Motorbikes are also allowed in the sanctuary.



## Sleeping

**Margao** *p1199 and map p1200*
**D-E Goa Woodlands**, ML Furtado Rd, opposite City Bus Stand, T0832-2715521, woodland_goa@sancharnet.in. 35 rooms, 18 a/c, clean and spacious with bath, restaurant, bar, good value.
**D-E Saaj**, ML Furtado Rd (near the telephone exchange), T0832-2711757. 29 rooms, TV, basic singles, good 4-person rooms, restaurant, bar, near City bus stand, 24 hr check-out.
**E La Flor**, E Carvalho St, T0832-2731402, laflor@sancharnet.in. 35 rooms with bath, half a/c, restaurant, clean, on a side street away from the bustle of town.

**Colva** *p1201, map p1201*
Most hotels are 6-8 km from Margao railway station. Prices rise on 1 Dec. Discounts are possible for stays of a week or more.
**B Vista de Colva**, 4th Ward, T0832-2788144, colmar@satyam.net.in. 25 large a/c studio rooms, restaurant/bar with Goan specialities, small fish-shaped pool in an exposed paved area (non-residents pay Rs 50), live entertainment, very comfortable.
**B-C William's Retreat**, 500 m from beach, T0832-2788153, www.goagetaway.com. 36 clean rooms, some a/c, restaurant, large pool (non-residents Rs 50), tennis, friendly, good value but tired.
**C-D Star Beach Resort**, just off Colva Beach Rd, T0832-2734921, www.starbeachresortgoa.com. 41 large rooms, TV, some a/c, good value from mid-Jan (Rs 600), clean pool, children's pool, best rooms 1st floor poolside currently have uninterrupted views across paddy fields, restaurant.
**D Colmar**, on the beach (just beyond Colva Residency), T0832-2788043, atsfernandes@colmarbeachresort.com. 127 rooms, dearer than similar in area but popular, restaurant (see below), travel desk, motorbike hire, bus to Anjuna flea market (Rs 95), exchange. Long-term fixture in Colva.
**E Tourist Nest**, 2 km from the sea, T0832-2788624, touristnest@indiatimes.com. Old Portuguese house, 12 rooms in secure new block, fan, Rs 200 with bathroom, 2 small self-contained cottages, good restaurant. Old part of house recommended for atmospheric long stay (Rs 8,000 per month for 2 bedrooms), spacious dining area, large lounge with antique furniture, private balcony, bathroom and cooking facilities.
**F Maria Guest House**, 4th Ward, near beach cafés. 7 rooms, some with bath, very friendly, helpful, car hire, popular with backpackers, good value. Recommended.

**Betalbatim** *p1202*
**B Nanu Resort**, near the beach and paddy fields, T0832-2880111, www.nanuindia.com. 72 comfortable and spacious a/c rooms in 3-star, 2-storey 'chalet' complex, refurbished restaurant arranged in a neat terrace with sea views. Imaginatively planned, good pool

with great beach views, garden, beach beyond a narrow stream, tennis, badminton, secluded and peaceful. Very good value from 1 May-30 Sep. Recommended.

**D-E Manuelina Tourist House**, behind Ray's. 5 spacious, clean rooms with bath, TV lounge, some food available, pleasant, secure, quiet. Recommended.

**E Baptista**, Beach Rd. 2 simple rooms with fan, 2 self catering flats with gas stove, use of fridge and utensils (Rs 350), good for long stays, short walk from beach.

**Benaulim to Mobor** *p1203*

Budget hotels can be found along Benaulim Beach Rd, and in the coconut groves on either side. Rooms in private houses and 'garden cottages' go for Rs 80-150; south along the beach from **Johncy's**, rooms just off the beach with bath, are Rs 80-100.

**LL Taj Exotica**, Calvaddo, towards Varca, T0832-2771234, exoticabc.goa@tajhotels.com. 56 acres of greenery and views of virgin beaches from each of its 138 luxurious rooms. Good choice of restaurants, including Mediterranean, plus coffee shop, nightclub, excellent pool, golf course, floodlit tennis, kids' activities, jacuzzi, watersports, gym and jogging track, library and bike hire. The Taamra Spa offers treatments like acupuncture, aromatherapy and Balinese massage.

**L Club Mahindra**, Varca Village, Varca, T0832- 2744555, www.clubmahindra.com. 51 spotless rooms with tubs, 5 suites, spacious public areas, excellent pool, gym etc, direct access to quiet beach, bit isolated. Top class.

**C-D L'Amour**, end of Beach Rd, Benaulim, T0832-2770404. 20 rooms in a 2-storey block close to the sea, good terrace restaurant, handy for exchange and booking rail and bus tickets. Well-established hotel run by same team as Johncy's beach shack.

**D Failaka**, Adsulim Nagar, near Maria Hall crossing, Benaulim, T0832-2771270, hotelfailaka @hotmail.com. 16 spotless, comfortable rooms (Rs 400), 4 with TV, quieter at rear, excellent restaurant, friendly family set up. Recommended.

**D Gaffino's**, opposite Dona Sylvia, Mobor, 5 mins' walk from beach, T0832-2871441, briangaffino@yahoo.com. 16 clean, simple rooms with bath on 4 flrs, 2 a/c, balconies overlook river or sea (far away), b&b, personal service, package oriented, in the centre of all the action.

**D Hippo Cool**, next to Gaffino's, Mobor, T0832-2871201. 6 clean, very comfortable rooms with fan (a/c on request) and shower, restaurant, 5-min walk from the beach. Recommended.

**D-E Palm Grove Cottages**, Vas Vaddo, Benaulim, T0832-2770059, palmgrovecottages@yahoo.com. 14 clean spacious rooms. The newer block at rear with showers and balconies is better. Pleasant palm-shaded garden, good food, not on the beach but plenty of places to hire a bicycle just outside. Recommended.

**E D'Souza Guest House**, north of Beach Rd in Benaulim, T0832-2770583. 5 very clean rooms, good food (see below), garden, friendly family. Recommended.

**E Oshin Holiday Care**, House no. 126, Vas Vaddo, Benaulim, T0832-2770069. 14 good large rooms with bath on 3 floors (room 11 best, Rs 400), breakfast, evening meals on request, friendly manager, excellent well kept grounds, you will need a bicycle to get to the beach but the peaceful location overlooking ponds is well worth it. Highly recommended.

**E Tansy Cottages**, Beach Rd, Benaulim, T0832-2770574. 7 very clean, large rooms with bath, 2 cottages, good restaurant (super breakfast), friendly, good value. Recommended.

**F Furtado's**, T0832-2745474. 6 basic rooms arranged around small garden with palms, in the dunes just above the beach. Popular budget option. Shacks for meals nearby.

**Agonda** *p1206*

**E Casa Maria**, T0832-2647237. 4 rooms with clean tiled bathroom, fan, veranda, sea views, but overlooks the back of Eldfra.

**E-F Dercy Beach Resort**, T0832-2647503. 50-year-old family house developed to fit 12 clean rooms with bathrooms. Over the road on the beach are 12 basic bamboo huts with spotless shared wash block. Dynamic owner.

**F Sun Set Bar**, T0832-2647381. 7 simple cottages (more planned) with great views, shared facilities. The restaurant perched high

*For an explanation of the sleeping and eating price codes used in this guide, see inside the front cover. Other relevant information is found in Essentials pages 56-61.*

on the rocks has the prime location in Agonda. Recommended.

**Palolem** *p1206*

Palolem's popularity has soared inordinately. Off-season, bargain hard and ask around for rooms inside family houses. These can have very basic facilities (eg 'pig' toilets, raised on a platform where pigs do the necessary 'cleaning out' below), some are lovely though and let you use their kitchen and fridge, **F** price bracket.

**B Ciaran's Camp**, beach, T0832-2643 477, johnciaran@hotmail.com. Huts are spaced wide apart in palm-covered landscaped gardens. A library, lovely shop, table tennis and great restaurant plus promises of live jazz all make it the leader in Palolem cool.

**B-C Bhakti Kutir**, over the hill at the southern end, T0832-2643472, bhaktikutir@yahoo.com. A beautiful grove of trees hanging over 22 huts with bucket baths and compost toilets. Its German/Goan owners are steeped in ecology and spirituallty. More than a place to stay, it's a place to engage both brain and body. Away from the beach and very quiet. Children welcome. Highly recommended.

**B-C Café Del Mar**, Palolem Beach, T0832-3276520. The only a/c bungalows on the beach. Excellent restaurant and bar makes this an uptempo place to stay.

**C Sevas Eco-Friendly Huts and Cabanas**, opposite Bhaki Kutir, T0832-2311767, sevasmicho@yahoo.com. Close to Bhakti Kutir in distance as well as in spirit: but only some of these huts have fan.

**E Cozy Nook**, at northern end, T0832-2643550. Plastered bamboo huts, fans, nets, shared toilets, in a good location between the sea and river, ayurvedic centre, art and crafts, friendly. Recommended.

**F Palolem Beach Resort** and south of Cocohuts, camping and parking for campers and travellers (Rs 15-20 per day).

**Beaches further south** *p1206*

**LL InterContinenta**, Rajbaga, T0832-2644777, goa@interconti.com. 85 acres of 5 star hotel between the Talpone river and the Sahayadri mountain range. 255 sea-facing rooms, 9-hole golf course, 5 restaurants, health spa, watersports, even a luxury yacht.

**C–D Home Guesthouse**, Patnem, T0832-2643916, homeispatnem@yahoo.com. Just 8 rooms with fan and French linen close to the beach. Aims to become a forum for local artists and has occasional live music.

**D Solitude Dream Woods**, Patnem, T0832-2711186, ashper2002@yahoo.com. All-wood beach camp with pine and bamboo structures, one of the most advanced developments in Patnem.

## Eating

**Margao** *p1199 and map p1200*

**₸₸ Chinese Pavilion**, M Menezes Rd (400 m west of Municipal Gardens). Chinese. Smart, a/c, good choice.

**₸₸ Gaylin**, 1 V Valaulikar Rd. Chinese. Tasty hot Szechuan, comfortable a/c.

**₸₸ Longuinhos**, near the Municipality. Goan, North Indian. Open all day for meals and snacks, bar drinks and baked goodies.

**₸₸ Tato**, G-5 Apna Bazaar, Complex, V Valaulikar Rd. Excellent vegetarian, a/c upstairs.

**₸₸ Utsav**, Nanutel Hotel. Pleasant, serving a large range of Goan dishes.

**₸ Café Margao**. Good South Indian snacks.

**Colva** *p1201, map p1201*

**₸ Joe Con's**, 4th Ward. Excellent fresh fish and Goan dishes, good value.

**₸ Kentuckee**, good seafood, select from fresh fish brought to table.

**₸ Pasta Palace**, overlooking the beach at the Colmar. Good Italian with bar.

**₸ Pirate's**, near the beach. Recommended for seafood.

**Betalbatim** *p1202*

**₸₸₸ Martin's Corner**, T0832-2131 676, www.martinscorner.com. Coming from the south, look for sign on left after village, 500 m down lane on right, opposite open ground. Accommodates over 200 under cover in front of an old house. Extensive menu, excellent lobster Rs 1500, tiger prawns Rs 500-700, crab Rs 300-500. Recommended.

**₸₸ Roytanzil Garden Pub**, set back from the beach at end of Majorda beach road past Martin's Corner (no sea views). Neat grounds, al fresco and small covered area. Seafood and Indian. Large set-up with seating for 200+ under cover in front of an old house. One of the best restaurants on the south coast.

**Benaulim to Mobor** *p1203*
Beach shacks offer Goan dishes and seafood at reasonable prices. Around **Dona Sylvia**, several come alive in the evening.
🍴🍴🍴 **Taj Exotica's**, Benaulim, restaurants are faultless; spread of the Mediterranean, gourmet Goan or authentic Chinese.
🍴🍴 **Grill Room**, Fatrade Beach Rd, open 1830-2230. Pleasant steak house with a simple menu. Tiger prawns Rs 400, steaks Rs 150.
🍴🍴 **La Afra**, Tamborin, Fatrade. Excellent steaks and fresh fish, sensibly priced. Boatmen ferry holidaymakers to **River Sal**, Betul.
🍴🍴 **Pedro's**, by the car park above the beach, Benaulim. Good seafood and tandoori. Imaginative menu, friendly.
🍴🍴 **River View**, Cavelossim. Tranquil, open air location, overlooking the river. Wide choice, international menu, good ambience despite being surrounded by ugly hotel developments. Cocktails Rs 100, sizzlers Rs 150-200, Tiger prawns Rs 500.
🍴🍴 **Tito's**, Benaulim, on beach. English breakfasts, Rs 80.
🍴 **D'Souza's**, Benaulim, good juices, *lassis* and fast food.
🍴 **Goan Village**, lane opposite Dona Sylvia, Tamborim, south of Cavelossim. The best here for all cuisines.
🍴 **Johncy's**, Benaulim, varied menu, good seafood, big portions, tandoori recommended (after 1830) but service can be erratic, pleasant atmosphere though (backgammon, scrabble).
🍴 **Malibu**, Benaulim, nice lush garden setting for spicy fish/meat kebabs.

**Cabo de Rama** *p1205*
🍴 **Pinto's Bar**, near the fort entrance. Offers meals and cool drinks on a sandy shaded terrace, may also have rooms available. If there are few visitors about (most likely) ask here for a meal before exploring the fort to save time waiting later.

**Palolem** *p1206*
🍴🍴 **Bhakti Kutir** serves excellent fresh fish dishes, homegrown organic produce and fresh juices. Name any number of obscure nutritious grains; they'll be here.
🍴🍴 **Cool Breeze**, Main Rd, T9422060 564, coolbreezegoa@hotmail.com. One of the perennial favourites like Dropadi that's probably got the best steaks in town.
🍴🍴 **Dropadi Beach Restaurant and Bar**. Routinely packed out. Lobster and lasagne and North Indian food are the specials.
🍴🍴 **Mamoo's**, on the corner where the road turns to meet the beach, T0832-2644261, mamoosplace@rediffmail.com. A 3rd long-standing favourite, famous for its grilled fish. Only comes alive in the evening.
🍴🍴 **Oceanic Hotel**, up on the hill north of the beach. Fresh soup on the menu every day and their chef spent last season moving through the Delia Smith recipe books. Excellent seafood and cocktails: popular in the evening.
🍴 **Brown Bread and Health Food**, near Syndicate Bank, T0832-2643604. Quite probably the best breakfast in Palolem.
🍴 **Tibet Bar and Restaurant** , Main Rd, T9822142775. Super fresh ingredients in these excellent Himalayan dishes. Small restaurant that's worth stepping back from the beach for.

## Bars and clubs

**Colva** *p1201, map p1201*
**Johnny Cool's**, half way up busy Beach Rd. Scruffy surroundings but popular for chilled beer and late night drinks.
**Splash** is 'the' place for music, dancing and late drinking, open all night, trendy, very busy on Sat (full after 2300 on weekdays in season), good cocktails, poor bar snacks – may not appeal to all especially unaccompanied girls.
**Sunshine**, bar and restaurant, north end of beach, popular evenings, hammocks overlooking beach, pool table, 60s music, small dance floor, gardens. Relaxed atmosphere.

**Benaulim to Mobor** *p1203*
**Aqua**, Leela Palace, Mobor, is a gaming room and cigar lounge which turns into a late night disco after 2000.

## Festivals and events

**Colva** *p1201, map p1201*
**Oct 12-18** (Mon that falls between these dates) Fama of Menino Jesus when thousands of pilgrims flock to see the statue in the Church of our Lady of Mercy in the hope of witnessing a miracle.

**Benaulim to Mobor** *p1203*
In Benaulim, **Jun 24** Feast of St John the Baptist (*Sao Joao*) gives thanks for the arrival of the monsoon. Young men wearing crowns of leaves and fruits tour the area singing for gifts. They jump into wells (which are usually full) to commemorate the movement of St John in his mother's womb when she was visited by Mary, the mother of Jesus!

**Palolem** *p1206*
**Feb** Rathasaptami The Shri Malikarjuna Temple 'car' festival attracts large crowds.
**Apr** Shigmo, also at the Shri Malikarjuna Temple, also very popular.

## Shopping

**Margao** *p1199 and map p1200*
The Old Market was rehoused in the 'New' (Municipal) Market in town. The covered **market** (Mon-Sat, 0800-1300, 1600-2000) is fun to wander around. It is not at all touristy but holidaymakers come on their shopping trip to avoid paying inflated prices in the beach resorts. To catch a glimpse of the early morning arrivals at the **Fish Market** head south from the Municipal Building.

### Books and CDs

**Golden Heart**, off Abbé Faria Rd, behind the GPO, closed 1300-1500. Bookshop.
**Nanutel Hotel**. Small bookshop.
**Trevor's**, 5 Luis Miranda Rd. Sells CDs.

### Clothes

**MS Caro**, Caro Corner, has an extensive range including 'suiting', and will advise on tailors.
**J Vaz**, Martires Dias Rd, near Hari Mandir, T0832-2720086. Good quality men's tailor.

**Benaulim to Mobor** *p1203*
**Khazana**, Taj Exotica, Benaulim, a veritable treasure chest (books, crafts, clothes) culled from across India. Pricey.
**Manthan Heritage Gallery**, main road. Quality collection of art items.

## Activities and tours

**Colva** *p1201, map p1201*
**Meeting Point**, T0832-2723338, for very efficient, reliable travel service, Mon-Sat, 0830-1900 (sometimes open even later, if busy).

**Betalbatim to Velsao** *p1202*
**Goa Diving**, Bogmalo, have a morning office at Joet's, and are based at Chapel Bhat, Chicalim, T0832-2555117, goadiving@goatelecom.com. PADI certification from Open Water to Assistant Instructor.
**Splash Watersports**, Bogmalo, T0832-2409886. Run by Derek, a famous Indian champion windsurfer. Operate from a shack on the beach just below Joets, providing para-sailing, windsurfing, water skiing, trips to nearby islands; during the high season only.

**Benaulim to Mobor** *p1203*
**Dolphin watching** The trips are scenic and chances of seeing dolphin are high, but it gets very hot (take hat, water and something comfy to sit on). Groups of dolphins here are usually seen swimming near the surface. Boats from **Café Dominick**, Benaulim, (signs on the beach) and several others charge about Rs 300. Most hotels arrange river trips and dolphin viewing, or call T0832- 2871455. River trips last from 1600-1730, dolphin trips 0800-1000 and sunset cruises depart at 1700. Expect to pay Rs 250. **Betty's Place**, in a road opposite Holiday Inn, Mobor, arranges boat trips for fishing, dolphin viewing as well as trips up river Sal from 1030-1630 (food included). Recommended.
**Yoga** At Taj Exotica, Benaulim, indoors or on the lawn. Also aromatherapy, reflexology.

**Palolem** *p1206*
**Bridge and Tunnel Pub Living Huts**, in the rocks towards Calomb, T0832-2633237, sera_goa@rediffmail.com. Pool for Rs 100 per hr and a laid-back beach pub-lounge area filled with rugs and cushions.
**Cuba Beach Cafe**, behind Syndicate Bank, Palolem, T0832-2643449. Cool, upbeat bar for a sundowner, **Café Del Mar** next door does excellent fresh nosh too.
**Neptune's Point Bar and Restaurant**, T9822584968. Wide dance-floor for a mellow daily chill-out from 1700-2200 with a proper party on a weekly basis.
**Rock It Café**, north end of the beach, Palolem. Coffee from Bodum filters, backgammon, and Sade often on the playlist, it's a stoner's paradise shack.

**Boat hire and trips**

You can hire boats to spend a night under the stars on the secluded Butterfly or Honeymoon beaches, and many offer dolphin watching and fishing trips. You can see the dolphins from dry land around Neptune's Point, or ask for rowboats instead of outboard motor boats if you want to reduce pollution. Mornings between 0830-1230 are best. Arrange through **Palolem Beach Resort**, travel agents or a fisherman. 4 people for about Rs 600 for 1-hr trip, Rs 1500 for 3 hrs (take sun-screen, shirt, hat and drinking water).

**Ciaran's Camp**, T0832-2643477, runs 2-hr mountain bike tours and you can charter a yacht overnight through Ciaran's bar for Rs 8,000.

**Tour operators**

**Rainbow Travels**, T0832-2643912. Efficient flight and train bookings, exchange, Western Union money transfer, safe deposit lockers (Rs 10 per day), good internet connection.

**Bliss Travels** 118/1 near main gate, Palolem beach, T0832-2643456, bliss_travels@rediffmail.com. Air tickets (domestic and international), money change, bus services, speedy internet, ISD, plus package tours to nature reserves and retreat farm.

## Transport

**Margao** *p1199 and map p1200*

**Auto-rickshaw**

To **Colva**, Rs 30; beach, Rs 50.

**Bus**

The **local bus stand** is by the municipal gardens. You can usually board buses near the Kamat Hotel, southeast of the gardens.

The **Kadamba (new) bus stand** is 2 km north of town (city buses to the centre, or motorcycle taxi Rs 8); buses arriving before 1000 and after 1900, proceed to the centre. To **Benaulim, Cabo da Rama** 0730 (2 hrs); **Canacona and Palolem**, several; **Colva**: hourly; **Gokarna**, 1300 daily.

**Non-stop KTC buses** to **Panjim**: 1 hr. Buy tickets from booth at stand number 1.

**Private buses** (eg Paulo, Metropole Hotel, T0832-2721516), Padre Miranda Rd: to **Bangalore** (15 hrs); **Mangalore** 1800, 2130 (8-10 hrs), Rs 140; **Mumbai (Dadar/CST)** 1400, 1700 (16 hrs), Rs 600 (sleeper); **Pune** 1700 (13 hrs), Rs 450 (sleeper).

**Car hire**

Sai Service, T0832-2735772. Rs 700-900 per day with driver.

**Train**

Enquiries T0832-2732255. The new station on the broad gauge network is 500 m south of the old station. The reservation office on the 1st flr of the new station is usually quick and efficient, with short queues. Mon-Sat 0800-1400, 1415-2000, Sun 0800-1400. Tickets for **Mumbai** and **Delhi** should be booked well ahead. Confirm Indrail Pass reservations in Vasco, Mumbai or Mangalore.

Konkan Kanya Express (night train) and Mandovi Express (day train) from **Mumbai** also stop at **Tivim** (for northern beaches; take the local bus into Mapusa and from there catch another bus or take a taxi) and **Karmali** (for Panjim and Dabolim airport) before terminating at **Margao**. Both are very slow and take nearly 12 hrs. From **Mumbai (CST)**: Mandovi Exp **0103**, 0515 (arr 1815), (13 hrs, 2nd class 3-tier Rs 670), doesn't stop at Pernem; Konkan Kanya Exp **0111**, 2250 (arr 1045).

**Delhi (Nizamuddin)**: *Rajdhani Exp 2431*, 1145, Wed, Fri; *Goa Exp 2779*, 1427, 35 hrs. **Ernakulam (Jn)**: *Mangalore Exp 2618*, 2055, 17 hrs. **Hospet (for Hampi)**: *Vasco-da-Gama Vijayawada Exp 7228*, 0720, Wed, Sat, 8½ hrs. **Mumbai (CST)**: *Mandovi Exp 0104*, 1030, 11½ hrs (via Karmali, Tivim); *Konkan Kanya Exp 0112*, 1800, 12 hrs (via Karmali, Tivim, Pernem). **Mumbai Kurla (Tilak)**: *Netravati Exp 6346*, 0640, 12 hrs (via Karmali, Tivim). **Thiruvananthapuram (Trivandrum)**: *Rajdhani Exp 2432*, 1300, Mon, Wed, 18 hrs. *Netravati Exp 6345*, 2255, 18 hrs (via Canacona for Palolem beach).

The broad gauge line between **Vasco** and **Londa** in Karnataka runs through Margao and Dudhsagar Falls and connects stations on the line with **Belgaum**. There are services to **Bangalore** *Vasco Bangalore Exp 7310*, 2059, Mon, Thu.

The **pre-paid taxi stand** is to the right of the exit (charges are for 1 person with 1 piece of luggage); to **Margao centre** Rs 50, **Panjim** Rs 480 (45 mins), **Anjuna** Rs 670; **Calangute** Rs 600; **Colva** Rs 130, **Palolem**

Rs 480; rates are clearly displayed outside the office. **Autos** to **Colva** Rs 100, to **Panjim** Rs 320. Avoid tourist taxis, they can be 5 times the price.

**Colva** *p1201, map p1201*
From the airport, taxis charge about Rs 280. Those arriving by train at Margao, 6 km away, can choose between buses, auto-rickshaws and taxis for transfer. Buses pull in at the main crossroads and then proceed down to the beach about a kilometre away before turning around. Auto-rickshaws claim to have a Rs 30 'minimum charge' around Colva itself.

Bicycles mostly through hotels, Rs 20-25 per day (discounts for long term). Motorbikes for hire through most hotels (see also Panjim), Rs 200 per day (less for long term rental), more for Enfields, bargain hard.

**Bus** to **Anjuna** Wed for the Flea Market, tickets through travel agents, depart 0930, return 1730, Rs 90-100; to **Margao** half-hourly, take 30 mins, Rs 3 (last bus 1915, last return, 2000). Also to **Margao**, **motorcycle taxi**, Rs 20-25 (bargain hard); **auto-rickshaw**, Rs 30-40.

**Betalbatim to Velsao** *p1202*
**Bus**
Buses from Margao (12 km), **motorcycle taxis** charge Rs 35. The **Margao-Vasco** bus service passes through the centre of Cansaulim.

**Taxi**
**Taxis** to/from **airport**, 20 mins (Rs 300); **Margao** 15 mins (Rs 200). From **Nanu Resort** Panjim Rs 500, Anjuna Rs 750, or Rs 700 for 8 hrs, 80 km.

**Train**
**Cansaulim station** on the Vasco-Margao line is handy for **Velsao** and **Arossim** beaches and **Majorda station** for **Utorda** and **Majorda** beaches. Auto-rickshaws meet trains.

From **Cansaulim** there are 3 trains a day to **Vasco** (Rs 6) via **Dabolim** for the airport; 0746, 1411, 1818. For **Kulem** (Dudhsagar Falls) (Rs 12) via Margao (Rs 6), 0730, 1330, 1750.

From **Majorda** there are 3 trains a day to **Vasco** (Rs 5) 0741, 1406, 1813. For **Kulem** (Dudhsagar Falls) (Rs 10) via Margao (Rs 5), 0737, 1337, 1757.

**Benaulim to Mobor** *p1203*
Buses from all directions arrive at Maria Hall crossing, Benaulim. Taxis and autos from the beach esplanade near Pedro's and at Maria Hall crossing. To/from **Margao**: taxis Rs 100; autos Rs 80; bus Rs 5. **Anjuna** Wed flea market bus 0930, return 1530, about Rs 95, 2 hrs.

From Margao to **Cavelossim**, the bus is uncomfortably slow (18 km); autos transfer from bus stand to resorts. From **Margao** taxis charge around Rs 200, and from **Dabolim airport**, takes under 1 hr. It crosses the river Sal, southeast of Cavelossim and **Assolna**, which sells petrol, and the lane from the river joins the main road, NH17.

Rocks, outside Dona Sylvia, cycles Rs 10 per hr, Rs 150 a day; scooters Rs 300 a day without petrol, Rs 500 with 7 litres of fuel. In Benaulim, bikes and scooters for hire, Rs 35 and Rs 150 per day.

**Agonda** *p1206*
From Palolem/Chaudi Junc, auto-rickshaws charge Rs 120-150; turn off the road by the Niki bar and restaurant. **Dunhills Hotel**, Agonda, hire out scooters, motorbikes and cars.

**Bus**
First direct bus for **Margao** leaves between 0600-0630, last at 1000, takes about 1 hr. Alternatively, arrange a lift to the main road and flag down the next bus (last bus for Margao passes by at around 2000, but it is advisable to complete your journey before dark). Hourly buses between **Betul** and **Palolem** call at Agonda (and Cabo de Rama). Easy to visit for the day by taxi, motorbike or bicycle from Palolem beach.

**Palolem** *p1206*
**Bus**
There are 6 daily direct buses run between Margao and **Canacona** (40 km via Cuncolim), Rs 9, on their way to **Karwar**. From Canacona, taxis and auto-rickshaws charge Rs 40-60 to **Palolem** beach only 2 km away. From Palolem, direct buses for

**Margao** leave at around 0615, 0730, 0930, 1415, 1515, 1630 and take 1 hr. At other times of the day take a taxi or rickshaw to the main road, and flag down the next private bus. Frequent private services run to Palolem and Margao as well as south into Karnataka.

**Train**
From Canacona Junction station, 2 km away from Palolem beach. The booking office opens 1 hr before trains depart. Inside the station there is a phone booth and a small chai stall. A few auto-rickshaws and taxis meet all trains. If none is available walk down the approach road and turn left under the railway bridge. At the next corner, known locally as Chaurasta, you will find an auto-rickshaw to take you to **Palolem** beach (Rs 50) or **Agonda** beach; expect to pay double for a taxi.

To **Ernakulam Junction**, *Netravati Exp 6345*, 2325, 15 hrs, sleeper Rs 280, 3 tier a/c Rs 790, and on to **Thiruvananthapuram** (20 hrs); **Mangalore**, *Matsyagandha Exp 2619*, 0105, 6 hrs, Rs 49; **Margao**, 2 passenger trains a day, *KAM 2up*, 0630, *KAR 2up*, 1237, 45 mins, Rs 11; **Mumbai (Tilak)**, *Netravati Exp 6346*, 0548, 13 hrs, 2nd Cl sleeper Rs 300, 3 tier a/c Rs 800; via Margao 45 mins; **Mumbai (Thane)**, *Matsyagandha Exp 2620*, 1910, 12 hrs; via Margao 45 mins.

**Beaches further south** *p1206*
For **Canacona**, buses run to Palolem and Margao and also to Karnataka. You can hire a bicycle for Rs 4 per hr or Rs 35 per day. Direct buses for Margao leave at around 0615, 0730, 0930, 1415, 1515, 1630 and take an hour. Alternatively, take a taxi or rickshaw to the main road and flag down the next private bus. Palolem is 3 km from Canacona Junction station, which is now on the Konkan line (*Netravati Express*).

## Directory

**Margao** *p1199 and map p1200*
**Banks** Bank of Baroda, behind Grace Church; also in Market, Station Rd; Bank of India, exchanges cash, TCs, Visa and Mastercard; State Bank of India, west of the Municipal Gardens; HDFC, 24 hr ATM for MasterCard. Get exchange before visiting beaches to the south where it is more difficult. International money transfer is possible through Weizmann, 650 Costa Dias Building, NH 17 (Mon-Sat 1000-1800). There is also a branch in Colva. **Fire** T0832-2720168. **Hospital** Ambulance T0832-2722722; JJ Costa Hospital, Fatorda, T0832-2722586; Hospicio, T0832-2722164; Holy Spirit Pharmacy, 24 hrs. **Internet** Cyber Link, Shop 9, Rangavi Complex; Cyber Inn, 105 Karnika Chambers, V Valauliker Rd, 0900-2000, Rs 30 per hr. **Police** T0832-2722175. **Post office** North of children's park; Poste Restante, near the telegraph office, down lane west of park, 0830-1030 and 1500-1700 Mon-Sat.

**Benaulim to Mobor** *p1203*
In Benaulim: **Bank** Bank of Baroda, near Maria Hall, best rates (better than at travel agents and STD booths).Bank of Baroda, near the church in Cavelossim, accepts Visa, MasterCard, TCs; help- ful staff, open Mon-Wed, Fri, Sat 0930-1330. **Internet** GK Communications, Beach Rd. 24 hr phone, money exchange and internet with 4 terminals, book ahead when very busy, Rs 100 per hr. **Pharmacy** Late night near the main crossroads.

**Palolem** *p1206*
**Banks** Several exchanges along the beach approach road issue cash against credit cards, usual commission, 3-5%. **Internet** Widely available throughout the village, rates approximately Rs 60 per hr. Post Nearest in Canacona. **Useful services** Petrol Aryadurga HP station 1 km north of the Palolem turning, towards Margao.

# Ponda and interior Salcete

*There is enough spirituality and architecture in the neighbouring districts of Ponda and Salcete to reverse even the most cynical notions of Goa as a state rich in beach but weak on culture. Once you've had your fill of basking on the sand you'll find that delving into this geographically small area will open a window on a whole new, and richly rewarding, Goa.*

*Just over the water lies Salcete and the villages of Goa's most sophisticated and urbane elite, steeped in the very staunchest Catholicism. Here you can see the most eloquent symbols of the graceful living enjoyed by this aristocracy in the shape of palatial private homes, the fruits of their collusion with the colonizers in faith. Ironically, one of the finest – Braganza House in Chandor – is also the ancestral home of one of the state's most vaunted freedom fighters, Luis de Menezes-Braganza.*
▸▸ *For Sleeping, Eating and other listings, see pages 1223-1224.*



## Ponda and around → *Colour map 5a, grid B2.*

Ponda, once a centre of culture, music, drama and poetry, is Goa's smallest *taluka*. It is also the richest in Goan Hindu religious architecture. A stone's throw from the Portuguese capital of Old Goa and within 5 km of the district's traffic-snarled and fume-filled town centre are some of Goa's most important temples including the Shri Shantadurga at Queula and the Nagesh Temple near Bandora. Ponda is also a pastoral haven full of spice gardens and wonderfully scenic views from low hills over sweeping rivers. The Bondla Sanctuary in the east of the taluka, though small and underwhelming in terms of wildlife, is a vestige of the forest-rich environment that once cloaked the entire foothills of the Western Ghats.

### Ins and outs

**Getting there** Ponda town is an important transport intersection where the main road from Margao via Borlim meets the east-west National Highway, NH4A. Buses to Panjim and Bondla via Tisk run along the NH4A, which passes through the centre of town. ▸▸ *See Transport details, page 1224, for further details.*

**Getting around** The temples are spread out so it's best to have your own transport: take a bike or charter an auto-rickshaw or taxi: you'll find these around the bus stand.

### Background

The Zuari river represented the stormy boundary between the Christianized Old Conquests and the Hindu east for two centuries. St Francis Xavier found a dissolute band of European degenerates in the first settlers when he arrived in the headquarters of Luso-India and recommended the formation of an Inquisition. Although founded – in 1560 – to redress the failings within their own community, the Portuguese panel's remit quickly broadened as they found that their earliest Goan converts were also clinging clandestinely to their former faith. So the inquisitors set about weeding out these 'furtive Hindus', too, seeking to impose a Catholic orthodoxy and holding great show trials every few years with the public executions of infidels. Outside those dates set aside for putting people to death, intimidation was slightly more subtle: shrines were desecrated, temple tanks polluted and landowners threatened with confiscation of their holdings to encourage defection. Those unwilling to switch religion instead had to look for places to flee, carrying their idols in their hands.

When the Conquistadores – or *descubridores* – took to sacking shrines and desecrating temple images, building churches in their place, the keepers of the Hindu faith fled for the broad river's banks and the Cumbarjua creek to its west, crossing it to build new homes for their gods. 

## Ponda

Ponda wasn't always the poster-boy for Goa's Hindu identity that it is today. The **Safa Mosque** (Shahouri Masjid), the largest of 26 mosques in Goa, was built by Ibrahim 'Ali' Adil Shah in 1560. It has a simple rectangular chamber on a low plinth, with a pointed pitched roof, very much in the local architectural style, but the arches are distinctly Bijapuri. Because it was built of laterite the lower tier has been quite badly eroded. On the south side is a tank with *meherab* designs for ritual cleansing. Large gardens and fountains here were destroyed under the Portuguese, today the mosque's backdrop is all natural instead – it's set off by low rising forest-covered hills.

## Khandepar

Meanwhile, for a picture of Goa's Buddhist history, travel 4 km east from Ponda on the NH4A to Khandepar to visit Goa's best-preserved cave site. Believed to be Buddhist, it dates from the 10th or 11th century. The first three of the four laterite caves have an outer and an inner cell, possibly used as monks' living quarters. Much more refined than others discovered in Goa, they show clear evidence of schist frames for doors to the inner cells, sockets on which wooden doors would have been hung, pegs carved out of the walls for hanging clothing, and niches for storage and for placing lamps. The site is hidden on the edge of a wooded area near a tributary of the Mandovi: turn left off the main road from Ponda, look for green and red archaeological survey sign, just before the bridge over the river. Right after the football pitch then walk down the track off to the right by the electric substation.

## Farmagudi

On the left as you approach Farmagudi from Ponda is a **Ganesh temple** built by Goa's first Chief Minister, Shri D Bandodkar, back in the 1960s. It is an amalgam of ancient and modern styles. Opposite is a statue of Sivaji commemorating the Maratha leader's association with **Ponda's fort** The fort was built by the Adil Shahis of Bijapur and destroyed by the Portuguese in 1549. It lay in ruins for over a century before Sivaji conquered the town in 1675 and rebuilt it. The Portuguese Viceroy attempted to re-take it in October 1683 but quickly withdrew, afraid to take on the Maratha King Sambhaji, who suddenly appeared with his vast army.

## Velinga

**Lakshmi-Narasimha Temple** ① *from the north take a right immediately after crossing a small river bridge*, Goa's only temple to Vishnu's fourth avatar, the Lakshmi-Narasimha or Lakshmi-Narayana, is just north of Farmagudi at Velinga. The small half-man, half-lion image at this 18th century temple was whisked away from the torches of Captain Diogo Rodrigues in 1567 Salcete. Its tower and dome over the sanctuary are markedly Islamic. Inside there are well-carved wooden pillars in the *mandapa* and elaborate silver work on the screen and shrine.

## Priol

**The Shri Mangesh Temple** ① *to the northwest of Ponda set on a wooded hill at Priol on the NH4A leading to Old Goa*, is an 18th-century temple to Siva's incarnation as the benevolent Mangesh is one of the most important Hindu temples in Goa. Its Mangesh *lingam* originally belonged to an ancient temple in Kushatali (modern day Cortalim) across the river. The complex is typical of Goan Hindu temple architecture and the surrounding estate on which the temple depends provides a beautiful setting. Note the attractive tank on the left as you approach which is one of the oldest parts of the site. The complex, with its *agrashalas* (pilgrims' hostel), administrative offices and other rooms set aside for religious ceremonies, is a good representative of Goan Hindu temple worship: the temple is supported by a large resident community who serve its various functions. February 25 is *Jatra*.

## Mardol

Two kilometres on from Shri Mangesh, the early 16th century **Mahalsa Narayani Temple** is dedicated to Mahalsa, a Goan form of Vishnu's consort Lakshmi or, according to some, the god himself in female form *Mohini* (from the story of the battle between the *devas* and *asuras*). The deity was rescued from what was once a fabulous temple in Verna at around the same time as the Mangesh Sivalinga was brought to Priol. The entrance to the temple complex is through the arch under the *nagarkhana* (drum room). There is a seven-storeyed *deepstambha* and a tall brass Garuda pillar which rests on the back of a turtle, acting as an impressive second lamp tower. The half human-half eagle *Garuda*, Vishnu's vehicle, sits on top. A stone 'cosmic pillar' with rings, next to it, signifies the axis along which the temple is aligned. The new *mandapa* (columned assembly hall) is made of concrete, but is hidden somewhat under the red tiling, finely-carved columns and a series of brightly painted carvings of the 10 *avatars*, or incarnations, of Vishnu. The unusual dome above the sanctuary is particularly elegant. A decorative arched gate at the back leads to the peace and cool of the palm-fringed temple tank. A palanquin procession with the deity marks the February Mardol Jatra, Mahasivaratri is observed in February-March and Kojagiri Purnima celebrated at the August-September full moon.

## Bandora

A narrow winding lane dips down to this tiny hamlet and its **temple** ⓘ *head 4 km west from Ponda towards Farmagudi on the NH4A, looking for a fork signposted to Bandora*, to Siva as Nagesh (God of Serpents). The temple's origin is put at 1413 by an inscribed tablet here, though the temple was refurbished in the 18th century. The temple tank, which is well stocked with carp, is enclosed by a white-outlined laterite block wall and surrounded by shady palms. The five-storey lamp tower near the temple has brightly coloured deities painted in niches just above the base, the main *mandapa* (assembly hall) has interesting painted woodcarvings illustrating stories from the epics *Ramayana* and *Mahabharata* below the ceiling line, as well as the *Ashtadikpalas*, the eight Directional Guardians (Indra, Agni, Yama, Nirritti, Varuna, Vayu, Kubera and Ishana). The principal deity has the usual *Nandi* and in addition there are shrines to Ganesh and Lakshmi-Narayan and subsidiary shrines with *lingams*, in the courtyard. The Nagesh Jatra, normally in November, is celebrated at full moon to commemorate Siva's victory.

In a valley south of the Nagesh Temple lies the **Mahalakshmi Temple**, thought to be the original form of the deity of the Shakti cult. Mahalakshmi was worshipped by the Silaharas (chieftains of the Rashtrakutas, AD 750-1030) and the early Kadamba kings. The sanctuary has an octagonal tower and dome, the side entrances have shallow domes. The stone slab with the Marathi inscription dating from 1413 on the front of the Nagesh Temple refers to a temple to Mahalakshmi at Bandora. The *sabhamandap* has an impressive gallery of 18 wooden images of Vishnu. Mahalakshmi is special in that she wears a *lingam* in her head-dress and is considered a peaceful, 'Satvik', form of Devi: the first temple the Portuguese allowed at Panjim is also dedicated to her.

## Queula (Kavale)

Just 3 km southwest from Ponda's town centre bus stand is one of the largest and most famous of Goa's temples; dedicated to **Shantadurga** (1738), the wife of Siva as the Goddess of Peace. She earns the Shanti (Sanskrit for peace) prefix here because, at the request of Brahma, she mediated in a great quarrel between her husband and Vishnu, and restored peace in the universe. In the sanctuary here she stands symbolically between the two bickering gods. The temple, which stands in a forest clearing, was built by Shahu, the grandson of the mighty Maratha ruler Sivaji, but the deity was taken from Quelossim well before then, back in the 16th century. It is neo-classical in design: its two-storey octagonal drum, topped by a dome with a lantern, is a classic example of the strong impact church architecture made on Goan temple design. The interior of polished marble is lit by several chandeliers. Steps lead up to the temple complex which has a very large tank cut into the hillside and a spacious courtyard surrounded by the usual pilgrim hostels and administration offices.

**Shri Sausthan Goud Padacharya Kavale Math**, named after the historic seer and exponent of the Advaita system of Vedanta, was founded between Cortalim and Quelossim. This Hindu seminary was destroyed during the Inquisition in the 1560s and temporarily transferred to Golvan and Chinar outside Goa. After 77 years, in the early 17th century, the Math regrouped here in Queula, the village where the Shantadurga deity (which had also originated in Quelossim) had been reinstalled. There is a temple to Vittala at the Math. The foundation has another Math at Sanquelim.



## North of Ponda → *Colour map 5a, grid B2.*

### The Spice Hills

There are a number of spice plantations in the foothills around northeast Ponda that have thrown open their gates to offer in-depth tours that detail plants' medicinal and food uses during a walk through these cultivated forests. These are surprisingly informative and fun. Of these, Savoi Spice Plantation is probably the most popular and the guide is excellent.

*Taxis from the coastal resorts cost around Rs 700 return from Candolim, but it's better value to ask a travel agent as many offer competitive rates including entrance fees.*

**Savoi Spice Plantation** ⓘ *T0832-2340243, www.savoiplantation.com, 0800-1800, guided tour Rs 300, 1 hr, awkward to reach by public transport, ask buses from Ponda or Banastari heading for Volvoi for the plantation*, 6 km from Savoi, now over 200 years old, covers 40 ha focused around a large irrigation tank. Half the area is wetland and the other half on a hillside, making it possible for a large variety of plants and trees to grow. The plantation was founded by Mr Shetye and is now in the hands of the fourth generation of his family, who regularly donate funds to local community projects such as the school and temple. All plants are grown according to traditional Goan methods of organic farming. The tour includes drinks and snacks on arrival, and concludes with the chance to buy packets of spices (good gifts to take home) and a tot of *feni* to 'give strength' for the return journey to your resort. You will even be offered several cheap, natural alternatives to Viagra, whether you need them or not!

**Pascoal Spice Plantation** ⓘ *T0832-2344268, 0800-1800, tours Rs 300, signposted 1.5 km off the NH4A, near Khandepar between Ponda and Tisk*, grows a wide variety of spices and exotic fruit and is pleasantly located by a river. A guided tour takes you through a beautiful and fascinating setting. Spices are sold.

**Sahakari Spice Farm** ⓘ *on the Ponda-Khandepar road, Curti, T0832-2311394*, is also open to the public. The spice tour includes an authentic banana-leaf lunch.

**Tropical Spice Plantation** ⓘ *Keri, T0832-2340329, tours Rs 300, boats for hire Rs 100, clearly signposted off the NH4A (just south of the Sri Mangesh temple)*, is a very pleasant plantation situated in a picturesque valley in Keri. It has well-informed guides and friendly staff. It specialises in medicinal uses for the spices, the majority of which seem to be good for the skin. At the end of the tour an areca nut picker will demonstrate the art of harvesting by shinning up a tall palm with his feet tied together in a circle of rope. The demonstration ends with the equally impressive art of descent, a rapid slide down the trunk like a fireman. After the tour a delicious lunch is served in the shade overlooking a lake where there are a couple of boats for hire. Visitors arriving in the early morning will find the boats an excellent opportunity for viewing the varied birdlife around the lake. ➤➤ *For Sleeping, Eating and other listings, see pages 1223-1224.*

## Bondla Wildlife Sanctuary

ⓘ *Mid-Sep to mid-Jun, Fri-Wed 0930-1730; Rs 5, camera Rs 25, video Rs 100, 2-wheelers Rs 10, cars Rs 50, buses from Ponda via Tisk and Usgaon stop near the sanctuary where you can get taxis and motorcycle taxis. KTC buses sometimes run at weekends from Panjim. During the season the Forest Department minibus is supposed to do 2 daily trips (except Thu) between Bondla and Tisk: from Bondla, 0815, 1745; from Tisk, 1100 (Sun 1030) and 1900. Check at the tourist office first. If you are on a motorbike make sure you fill up with petrol – the nearest pumps are at Ponda and Tisk. Bondla is well signposted from the NH4A east of Ponda (5 km beyond Usgaon, a fork to the right leads to the park up a winding steep road).*

Bondla, 20 km northeast of Ponda, is the most popular of Goa's three sanctuaries because it is relatively easily accessible. The small, 8-sq km sanctuary is situated in the foothills of the Western Ghats; sambar, wild boar, gaur (Indian bison) and monkeys live alongside a few migratory elephants that wander in from Karnataka during the summer. The mini-zoo here guarantees sightings of 'Goa's wildlife in natural surroundings', although whether the porcupine and African lion are examples of indigenous species is another matter. Thankfully, the number of animals in the zoo has decreased in recent years and those that remain seem to have adequate space compared to other zoos in India. The small and basic Nature Education Centre has the facility to show wildlife videos, but is rarely used. You can take five-minute elephant rides between 1100-1200 and between 1600-1700. A deer safari (minimum eight people), between 1600-1730 costs Rs 10. The park also has an attractive picnic area in a botanical garden setting and a 2.4 km nature trail with waterholes, a lake and a tree-top observation tower.



# Chandor

→ *Colour map 5a, grid B2.*

By the late 18th century, an educated middle-class elite had emerged in the villages of the Old Conquests. With newly established rights to property, well-to-do Goans began to invest in large homes and very fine living. West of the Zuari River, the villages of Lutolim and Chandor are two of a number that saw the distinct development of estates and houses built on this grand scale. Their houses were stuffed with tokens of their Europeanization and affluence, mixed with traditions appropriated from their native ancestry, installing personal chapels instead of *devachem kuds*, or Hindu prayer rooms.

## Ins and outs

Chandor is closest to Margao but can also easily be visited from Panjim or the beaches in central Goa. It would be an arduous day trip from the northern beaches. Buses from Margao Kadamba bus stand (45 minutes) take you within walking distance of the sights but it is worth considering a taxi. Madgaon railway station with connections to Mumbai and the Konkan coastal route as well as direct trains to Hospet is close by.

## Sights

Although something of a backwater today, the once-grand village of Chandor nonetheless boasts several fine Portuguese mansions. Foremost among them the enormous **Menezes Braganza family house** ⓘ *13 km east of Margao, both wings are usually open 1000-1730 but best to confirm by telephone. West Wing:*

*To832-2784201, between 1300-1400 or early evening after 1830. East Wing: To832-2784227. A donation of Rs 100 at the end of the tour will be greatly appreciated.* Luis de Menezes Braganza was an influential journalist and politician (1878-1938) who not only campaigned for freedom from colonial rule but also became a champion of the less privileged sections of Goan society. The late 16th-century two-storey mansion he inherited (extended in the 18th and 19th centuries), still complete with much of the family furniture and effects, shows the sheer opulence of the life enjoyed by the old Goan families who established great plantation estates. The two wings are occupied separately by members of the Braganza family who have inherited the property.

The **West Wing**, which is better maintained and has finer antiques, is owned by Aida de Menezes Braganza. The guided tour by this elderly member of the family – when she resides here – is fascinating. She has managed to restore the teak ceiling of the 250-year-old library gallery to return it to its original state; the old *mareta* wood floor survived better since this native Goan timber can withstand water. There is much carved and inlaid antique furniture and very fine imported china and porcelain, some specially ordered, and bearing the family crest.

The faded **East Wing**, occupied by Sr Alvaro de Perreira-Braganza, partly mirrors the West Wing. It also has some excellent carved and inlaid furniture and a similar large salon with fine chandeliers. The baroque family chapel at the back now has a prized relic added to its collection, the bejewelled nail of St Francis Xavier, which had, until recently, been kept guarded away from public view. The guide from the East Wing of the Braganza House can also show you the **Fernandes House** ⓘ *open daily, phone ahead To832-2784245, suggested donation Rs 100*, if he's not too busy. It's another example of a once-fine mansion just to the southeast of the village, on the Quepem road. This too has an impressive grand salon occupying the front of the house and a hidden inner courtyard. Recent excavations have unearthed an underground hiding place for occasions when Christian families were under attack from Hindu raiders.

Back in Chandor village itself, the **Church of Our Lady of Bethlehem**, built in 1645, replaced the principal *Sapta Matrika* (Seven Mothers) temple, which was demolished in the previous century.

## Central and southern interior → *Colour map 5a, grid B2.*

Sanguem, Goa's largest taluka, covers the state's eastern hill borderland with the south Indian state of Karnataka. The still-forested hills, populated until recently by tribal peoples practising shifting cultivation, rise to Goa's highest points. Just on the Goan side of the border with Karnataka are the Dudhsagar falls, some of India's highest waterfalls, where the river, which ultimately flows into the Mandovi, cascades dramatically down the hillside. Both the Bhagwan Mahaveer Sanctuary and the beautiful, small Tambdi Surla Temple can be reached in a day from the coast (about two hours from Panaji). » *For Sleeping, Eating and other listings, see pages 1223-1224.*

### Ins and outs

**Getting there** Buses running along the NH4A between Panjim, Ponda or Margao and Belgaum or Bangalore in Karnataka stop at Molem, in the north of the taluka. Much of the southeastern part of Sanguem remains inaccessible. Trains towards Karnataka stop at Kulem (Colem) and Dudhsagar stations. Jeeps wait at Kulem to transfer tourists to the waterfalls. If you are traveling to Tambdi Surla or the falls from north or central Goa, then the best and most direct route is the NH4A via Ponda. By going to or from the southern beaches of Salcete or Canacona you can travel through an interesting cluster of villages, only really accessible if you have your own transport, to see the sites of rock-cut caves and prehistoric cave art. » *See Transport page 1224.*

**Getting around** There is no direct public transport between Molem and the sites, but the town is the start of hikes and treks in December and January.

## Bhagwan Mahaveer Sanctuary → *Colour map 5a, grid B3.*

ⓘ *To8324-2600231, 0830-1730 except public holidays, Rs 5, 2-wheelers Rs 10, cars Rs 500. Tickets at the Nature Interpretation Centre, 100 m from the police check post, Molem. Entrance to the Molem National Park, within the sanctuary, 100 m east of the Tourist Complex, is clearly signed but the 14 km of tracks within the park are not mapped.*

Goa's largest wildlife sanctuary holds 240 sq km of lush moist deciduous to evergreen forest types and a herd of gaur (*bos gaurus*, aka 'Indian bison'). The **Molem National Park**, in the central section of the sanctuary, occupies about half the area with the **Dudhsagar falls** located in its southeast corner; the remote **Tambdi Surla Temple** is hidden in the dense forest at the northern end of the sanctuary. Forest department jeeps are available for viewing within the sanctuary; contact the Range Forest Officer (Wildlife), Molem. Motorbikes can manage the rough track outside the monsoon period but not scooters. In theory it is possible to reach Devil's Canyon and Dudhsagar Falls via the road next to the Nature Interpretation Centre (from where entrance tickets are sold), although the road is very rough and it may require a guide. Make sure you have a full tank of petrol if attempting a long journey into the forest.

Sambar, barking deer, monkeys and rich birdlife are occasionally joined by elephants that wander in from neighbouring Karnataka during the summer months, but these are rarely spotted. Birds include the striking golden oriole, emerald dove, paradise flycatcher, malabar hornbill and trogon and crested serpent eagle.

## Dudhsagar Falls

The spectacular Dudhsagar Falls on the border between Goa and Karnataka, are the highest in India and measure a total drop of about 600 m. The name, meaning 'the sea of milk', is derived from the white foam that the force of the water creates as it drops in stages, forming pools along the way. They are best seen just after the monsoon, between October and December, but right up to April there is enough water to make a visit worthwhile. You need to be fit and athletic to visit the falls.

Until quite recently it was possible to visit Dudhsagar by rail as the line runs across about the mid-point of the vertical drop of the cascades, and the small Dudhsagar railway station ⓘ *at present the trains run twice a week (Tue and Sat from Margao), but there are no return trains on these days*, allowed you to step down and then walk back to the opening between the two train tunnels, offering a route to the beautiful pools. As the road route described below is in some ways tougher and less attractive than visiting by train we have retained the following description in case the station re-opens in the near future. When arriving by train, a rough, steep path takes you down to a viewing area which allows you a better appreciation of the falls' grandeur, and to a beautifully fresh pool which is lovely for a swim (take your costume and towel). There are further pools below but you need to be sure-footed. The final section of the journey is a scramble on foot across stream beds with boulders; it is a difficult task for anyone but the most athletic. For the really fit and adventurous the arduous climb up to the head of the falls with a guide, is well worth the effort. Allow three hours, plus some time to rest at the top.

By road, motorbikes, but not scooters, can get to the start of the trail to the falls from Molem crossroads by taking the road south towards Kulem. From there it is 17 km of rough track with at least two river crossings, so is not recommended after a long period of heavy rain. The ride through the forest is very attractive and the reward at the end spectacular, even in the dry season. A swim in the pool at the falls is particularly refreshing after a hot and dusty ride. Guides are available but the track is easy to follow even without one.

## Tambdi Surla

*ⓘ A taxi from Panjim takes about 2½ hrs for the 69 km. There is no public transport to Tambdi Surla but it is possible to hike from Molem. From the crossroads at Molem on the NH4A, the road north goes through dense forest to Tambdi Surla. 4 km from the crossroads you reach a fork. Take the right fork and after a further 3 km take a right turn at Barabhumi village (there is a sign). The temple is a further 8 km, just after Shanti Nature Resort. Make sure you have enough petrol before leaving Molem. It is also possible to reach the site along minor roads from Valpoi. The entrance to the temple is a short walk from the car park.*

This Mahadeva (Siva) Temple is a beautifully preserved miniature example of early Hindu temple architecture from the Kadamba-Yadava period. Tucked into the forested foothills, the place is often deserted, although the compound is well maintained by the Archaeology Department. The temple is the only major remaining example of pre-Portuguese Hindu architecture in Goa; it may well have been saved from destruction by its very remoteness.

## Sleeping

### Ponda *p1216*

Ponda is within easy reach of any of Goa's beach resorts and Panjim.

**C-D Menino**, 100 m east of Bus Stand junction, 1st flr, T0832-2313148. 20 rooms, some a/c, pleasant, comfortable, good restaurant serves generous main courses, impressive modern hotel, good value.

**E Padmavi**, Gaunekar House, 100 m north of bus stand on NH4A, T0832-2312144. 20 large clean rooms, some with bath and TV.

**E President**, 1 km east of bus stand, supermarket complex, T0832-2312287. 11 rooms, basic but clean and reasonable.

### Farmagudi *p1217*

**C-D Atish**, just below Ganesh Temple on NH4A, T0832-2335124, www.hotelatish.com. 40 comfortable rooms, some a/c, restaurant, large pool in open surrounds, gym, modern hotel, many pilgrim groups, friendly staff.

**E Farmagudi Resort**, attractively located though too close to NH4A, T0832-2335122. 39 clean rooms, some a/c, dorm (Rs 80), adequate restaurant (eat at Atish).

### The Spice Hills *p1219*

**B Savoi Farmhouse**, T0832-2340243, is an idyllic traditional Goan-style farmhouse built from mud with 2 adjoining en suite double rooms each with private veranda. There is electricity and hot water and rates are for full board and include the plantation tour. A night in the forest is memorable, highly recommended. Ideally, stay 2 nights exploring deep into the forested hills, good bird watchers.

### Bondla Wildlife Sanctuary *p1220*

**F Eco-Cottages**. 8 basic rooms with attached bath, newer ones better. Also 1 km inside park entrance (which may be better for seeing wildlife at night) are 2 12-bed dorms (Rs 30). Reserve ahead at Deputy Conservator of Forests, Wildlife Division, 4th Flr, Junta House, 18th June Rd, Panjim, T0832-2229701, although a room or bed is often available to anyone turning up.

### Chandor *p1220*

There was no accommodation in the village itself in 2004, but John at Ciaran's Camp in Palolem and Claudeo Braganza at the West Wing of Menezes Braganza House are both planning to set some up.

### Bhagwan Mahaveer Sanctuary *p1222*

There is no accommodation inside the sanctuary; carry provisions. The nearest GTDC accommodation is the Tourist Complex in Molem, east along the NH4A from the Molem National Park entrance.

**E Tourist Resort** (GTDC), 300 m east of police check post, about 500 m from the temple, Molem, T0832-2600238. 23 simple but well-maintained, clean rooms, some a/c, dorm, check-out 1200, giving time for a morning visit to Tambdi Surla, uninspired restaurant with limited menu serving north Indian food and beer.

**F Molem Forest Resthouse**, can be booked through the Conservator's Office, 3rd flr, Junta House, 18th June Rd, Panjim, T0832-2224747.

**Tambdi Surla** *p1223*

C **Shanti Nature Resort**, 500 m from the temple. Contact ahead **Passive Active Tourism** (Freedom Holidays), Hotel Four Pillars, Panjim, T0832-2222986. 9 large mud huts with palm-thatched roofs, electricity and running water in natural forest setting, emphasis on rest, ayurvedic treatment and meditation. Restaurant for all tastes, visits to spice gardens, bird-watching, hikes, trips to Dudhsagar, etc, arranged (2 nights, US$120). Highly recommended for location and eco-friendly approach.

## Eating

**Ponda** *p1216*

Ɏ **Amigos**, 2 km east of centre on the Belgaum road.

Ɏ **Spoon Age**, Upper Bazaar, T0832-2316191. Garden restaurant, serving Goan meals for local folk, friendly new set up. Occasional live music at weekend.

**The Spice Hills** *p1219*

ƔƔ **Glade Bar and Restaurant**, Pascoal Spice Plantation, 1130-1800, is good but pricey. **Tropical Spice Plantation** also serves delicious lunches.

**Bondla Wildlife Sanctuary** *p1220*

Ɏ **The Den Bar and Restaurant** near the entrance, serves chicken, vegetables or fish with rice. A small cafeteria, inside the park near the mini-zoo, sells snacks and cold drinks.

## Festivals and events

**Chandor** *p1220*

**Jan 6** Three Kings Festival Crowds gather on each year at Epiphany for the Three Kings Festival, which is similarly celebrated at Reis Magos, with a big fair, and at Cansaulim (Quelim) in southern Goa. The three villages of Chandor (Cavorim, Guirdolim and Chandor) come together to put on a grand show. Boys chosen from the villages dress up as the three kings and appear on horseback carrying gifts of gold, frankincense and myrrh. They process through the village before arriving at the church where a large congregation gathers.

## Activities and tours

**Bhagwan Mahaveer Sanctuary** *p1222*

Popular hiking routes lead to **Dudhsagar** (17 km), the sanctuary and Atoll Gad (12 km), Matkonda Hill (10 km) and Tambdi Surla (12 km). Contact the **Hiking Association**, 6 Anand Niwas, Swami Vivekananda Rd, Panjim.

## Transport

**Ponda** *p1216*

**Buses** to **Panjim** and **Bondla** via Tisk, but it is best to have your own transport.

**Bhagwan Mahaveer Sanctuary** *p1222*

**Road**

If coming from the south, travel via Sanguem. The road from Sanvordem to the NH17 passes through mining country and is therefore badly pot-holed and has heavy lorry traffic. From Kulem, **jeeps** do the rough trip to **Dudhsagar** (Rs 300 per head, Rs 1800 per jeep). This is a very tough and tiring journey at the best of times. From Molem, a road to the south off the NH4A leads through the forested hills of Sanguem taluka to **Kulem** and **Calem** railway stations and then south to **Sanguem**. From there, a minor road northwest goes to **Sanvordem** and then turns west to **Chandor**.

**Buses** between **Panjim**, **Ponda** or **Margao**, and **Belgaum/Bangalore**, stop at Molem for visiting the Bhagwan Mahaveer Sanctuary and Dudhsagar Falls.

**Train**

From the southern beaches, you can get the Vasco-Colem Passenger from Vasco at 0710, or more conveniently Margao (Madgaon) at 0800, arriving at **Kulem** (Colem) at 0930. Return trains at 1640, arriving **Margao** at 1810; leave plenty of time to enjoy the falls. Jeep hire is available from Kulem Station.

## Directory

**Ponda** *p1216*

**Internet** Fun World.Com, Viradh Building, T0832-2316717. **Useful contacts** Deputy Conservator of Forests (North) T0832-2312095. **Community Health Centre**, T0832-2312115.

# Gujarat

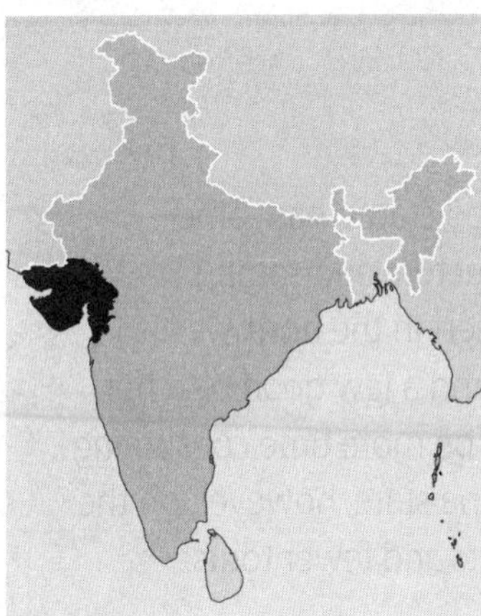



**Footprint features**

# Introduction

Gujarat, one of India's lesser visited states, has some fascinating and distinctive architecture and some picturesque landscapes from desert in the northwest to irrigated fields in the southeast, and a few good beaches. Due to the lack of tourism, it can be more time consuming to travel independently around the state, however, on the upside, there will be fewer tourists and fewer touts.



The major industrial, commercial and cultural city, Ahmadabad, retains excellent examples of Gujarati provincial architecture. The state also has a rich treasury of Jain and Hindu buildings, including the superb temples at Palitana and Modhera. Gujarat's ports have been important centres of trade and embarkation points for Muslim pilgrims bound for Mecca, while European colonial nations established factories and trading bases around the coast from the late 15th century onwards. Gujarat also has some vivid historical associations. Mahatma Gandhi was born at Porbandar and had his ashram at Sabarmati near Ahmadabad. There is an increasing interest in the unexplored delights to be found in the state which is prompting a number of the old princely mansions to open their doors to guests, as Heritage Hotels. In addition to abundant birdlife in the state, the Rann of Kachchh has the only surviving wild asses in India and the Velavadhar conserves the rare, swift-footed black buck. The last Asiatic lions are found in Gir National Park.

Kachchh is returning to normal after the devastation of the January 2001 earthquake. Despite the harsh environment, Kachchh people have developed an astonishingly vibrant identity, and tourism is an increasingly important source of earnings.

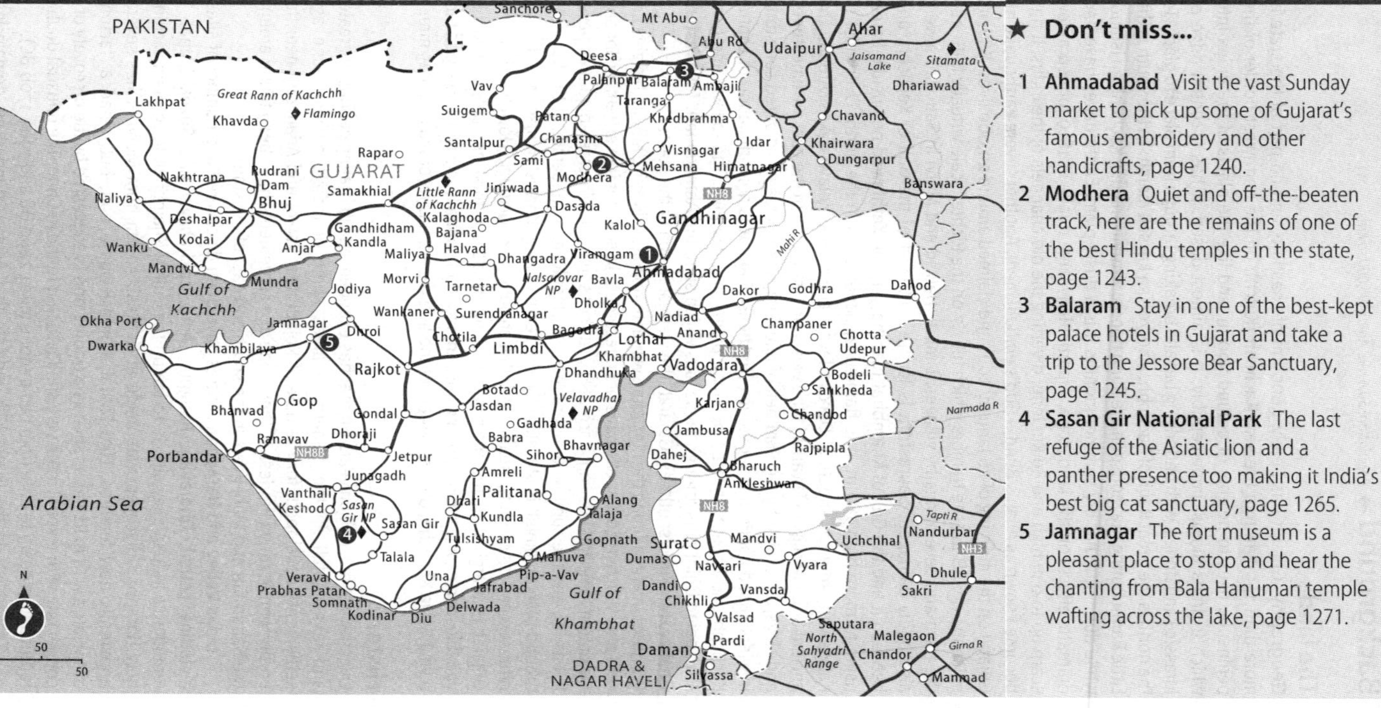


## ★ Don't miss...

1 **Ahmadabad** Visit the vast Sunday market to pick up some of Gujarat's famous embroidery and other handicrafts, page 1240.

2 **Modhera** Quiet and off-the-beaten track, here are the remains of one of the best Hindu temples in the state, page 1243.

3 **Balaram** Stay in one of the best-kept palace hotels in Gujarat and take a trip to the Jessore Bear Sanctuary, page 1245.

4 **Sasan Gir National Park** The last refuge of the Asiatic lion and a panther presence too making it India's best big cat sanctuary, page 1265.

5 **Jamnagar** The fort museum is a pleasant place to stop and hear the chanting from Bala Hanuman temple wafting across the lake, page 1271.

# Background → *Population: 50.6 mn. Area: 196,000 sq km.*



## The land

**Geography** Gujarat has nearly 1,600 km of coastline, and no part of the state is more than 160 km from the sea. **Kachchh** (Kutch), on the northwest border of the peninsula, rises to heights of around 300 m, and like the plains of the Indus into which it drops almost imperceptibly, it is almost desert. It has a central ridge of Jurassic sandstones, with underlying basalts breaking through from place to place. To the north is the Great Rann of Kachchh, a 20,700 sq km salt marsh. To the south is the Little Rann. During the monsoon the Rann floods, virtually making Kachchh an island, while during the hot dry summer months it is a dusty plain. Earthquakes have had dramatic effects on the landscape. A particularly large quake in 1819 formed a new scarp up to 6 m high and 80 km long, diverting the old channels of the Indus. It has become known as Allah's Bund – *God's embankment*. Another severe earthquake hit Gujarat on the morning of 26 January 2001 and claimed around 20,000 lives. With its epicentre near Bhuj, the tremors which hit 7.7 on the Richter scale virtually flattened the town and several nearby villages. Limbdi, Halvad and Morvi in Saurashtra were also badly damaged. **Saurashtra** is to the southeast of the Gulf of Kachchh, and between it and the Gulf of Khambhat (Cambay), is the **Kathiawad** peninsula. Rarely rising to more than 180 m, it is flanked by sandstones in the north. Over most of Kathiawad are great sheets of Deccan lavas, cut across by lava dykes. Around the ancient and holy city of Dwarka in the west and Bhavnagar in the east are limestones and clays, separated by a 50-km belt of alluvium, whose creamy-coloured soft stone is widely used as 'Porbandar stone'. **Northeast Gujarat** is a continuation of central Kachchh and is characterized by small plains and low hills. The railway line from Mumbai to Delhi runs through these hills which surround Ahmadabad. The **Western Ghats** extend into southeast Gujarat, the wettest region of the state.

**Climate** In Ahmadabad the maximum winter temperature is 27°C, although nights are cold and sub-zero cold spells have been recorded. In summer it is extremely hot and maximum temperatures can reach 48°C. Further south the winter temperatures never fall as far, and the summer temperatures are slightly more moderate. In the far south around Daman rainfall is still strongly affected by the southwest monsoon and totals often exceed 1,500 mm, nearly all between June and October. However, because Gujarat is marginal to the main rain-bearing winds the total amounts are highly variable, decreasing rapidly northwards. Ahmadabad normally receives about 900 mm a year while Kachchh, on the borders of the true desert, has recorded under 25 mm.

## History

Over the last one million years Gujarat has experienced alternating periods of greater and less rainfall. In these marginal areas some of India's earliest stone age settlements developed, for example at Rojadi near Rajkot and Adamgarh near the border with Madhya Pradesh. Other stone age settlements have been found around the Sabarmati and Mahi rivers in the south and east of the state.

**Indus Valley** and **Harappan** centres have been discovered at a number of sites, including **Lothal**, **Dhoravira**, **Rangpur**, **Amri**, **Lakhabaval** and **Rozdi**. Lothal, a remarkable Indus Valley site, is 10 km up the Gulf of Khambhat. In 1988 an exciting new Harappan discovery was made at **Kuntasi**, 30 km from Morvi. It has several apparently new features. Like Lothal, Kuntasi was a port, but it had a 'factory' associated with it. Its importance as a trading port is suggested by the discovery of a copper ring with a spiral motif very similar to that found in Crete. The unusual double fortifications seem to date from two periods (circa 2200 BC and 1900-1700 BC).

Rock edicts in the Girnar Hills indicate that Asoka extended his domain into Gujarat. The Sakas (Scythians; AD 130-390) controlled it after the fall of the Mauryan

## Cyclone hazard

Although cyclones are far more common on India's east coast than in the Arabian Sea hugely damaging storms can strike the Gujarat coast in the warmer months of the year. In 1998 the port of Kandla and the surrounding area was devastated by the high winds, torrential rain and storm surge which accompanied an early summer cyclone. At the end of May 2001 a similar cyclone moved towards the Kachchh and Saurashtra coasts, threatening further damage. In an area which has suffered three years of drought the rains are a mixed blessing, and when the same area has already been devastated by the earthquake, one official pointed out that "even the rains can be a nightmare as most people are living in tents and makeshift quake-damaged houses".



Empire. During the fourth and fifth centuries it formed part of the Gupta Empire. Gujarat attained its greatest territorial extent under the Solanki Dynasty, from the ninth century. The Vaghela Dynasty which followed was defeated by the Muslim Ala-ud-din Khalji, the King of Delhi. There then followed a long period of Muslim rule. Ahmad Shah I, the first independent Muslim ruler of Gujarat founded Ahmadabad in 1411.

The Mughal Humayun took Malwa and Gujarat in a brilliant campaign in 1534-1535 but soon lost them. His son, Akbar, reclaimed both in a similarly daring and inspired military operation, securing the region for the Mughals for nearly two centuries, a rule terminated by the Marathas in the mid-18th century.

In the scramble for trading bases the Dutch, English, French and Portuguese all established bases along the coast in the 17th century. The British East India Company's first headquarters in India was at Surat. It was later moved to Bombay. As British maritime supremacy became established all but the Portuguese at Daman and Diu withdrew. The state came under the control of the East India Company in 1818 and after the 1857 Mutiny (Rebellion), government authority was assumed by the Crown. The state was then divided into Gujarat province (25,900 sq km), with the rest comprising numerous princely states. Until Independence Kathiawad was one of the most highly fragmented regions of India, having 86 distinct political units. The largest, Junagadh, had an area of less than 9,000 sq km and a population of under 750,000 in 1947.

## Art and architecture

Gujarati provincial architecture flowered between 1300 and 1550. The new Muslim rulers made full use of the already highly developed skills of Hindu and Jain builders and craftsmen. The mosques and tombs that resulted reflect the new combination of Muslim political power and Hindu traditions. Thus, although the mosques obey strict Islamic principles they contain important features that are derived directly from Hindu and Jain precedents.

## Culture

About 15% of the **population** is tribal, the Bhil, Bhangi, Koli, Dhubla, Naikda and Macchi-Kharwa tribes all being represented. Gujarat is one of the modern strongholds of Jainism. Mahatma Gandhi was strongly influenced by Jain principles, including that of *ahimsa*, see page 1342. He found the deep divisions between high and low caste Hindus deeply repugnant. Renaming the former untouchables as 'Harijans' (God's people), he fought for their rights and dignity. Caste division remains a potent political force in Gujarat today. In the 19th century many Gujaratis went to East Africa and subsequently scattered to England, Canada and New Zealand. At home, Gujaratis are

### The Wild West

A visit to Gujarat can be rewarding but you must be prepared for slow and arduous journeys on public transport and be aware that English is rarely spoken outside the larger cities. A good option is to hire a car with driver or alternatively splash out and let the train take the strain.

The '*Royal Orient*' is Gujarat's answer to the famous 'Palace on Wheels'. It uses the metre-gauge carriages no longer needed in Rajasthan, and runs an eight-night tour from Delhi visiting Chittaurgarh, Udaipur, Junagadh, Somnath, Sasan Gir, Diu, Palitana, Ahmadabad and Jaipur. Contact The Royal Orient, A/6 Emporia Building, Baba Kharak Singh Marg, Delhi, T011 23364724, tcgl.del@rmt.sprintrpg.emvsnl.net.in.

Hotels, in atmospheric old palace and fort conversions, offer the unique opportunity to stay in off-the-beaten locations but they should be booked in advance. Tour operators such as North West Safaris, T079 6302019, ssibal@ad1.vsnl.net.in, specialize in visiting these unusual properties.

prominent in the business community. The majority of the people speak Gujarati, an Indo-Aryan **language** derived from Sanskrit. Maritime contacts with Persia, Arabia, Portugal and England led to the introduction of many words from these languages.

Whilst Gujarat has a long coastline and an almost endless supply of fish and shellfish, strict Jainism in the past and orthodox Hinduism today have encouraged the widespread adoption of a vegetarian diet. Gujaratis base their diet on rice, wholemeal *chapati*, a variety of beans and pulses rich in protein, and coconut and pickles; a *thali* would include all these, the meal ending with sweetened yoghurt. The dishes themselves are not heavily spiced, though somewhat sweeter than those of neighbouring states. Popular dishes include: *kadhi*, a savoury yoghurt curry with chopped vegetables and a variety of spices; *undhyoo*, a combination of potatoes, sweet potatoes, aubergines (egg plants) and beans cooked in an earthenware pot in the fire; Surat *paunk* made with tender kernels of millet, sugar balls, savoury twists and garlic chutney. Eating freshly prepared vegetable snacks from street vendors is popular. A large variety of *ganthia* or *farsan* (light savoury snacks prepared from chickpea and wheat flour), is a speciality in the state. Desserts are very sweet. Surat specializes in *gharis* made with butter, dried fruits and thickened milk and rich *halwa*. *Srikhand* is saffron-flavoured yoghurt with fruit and nuts.

## Modern Gujarat

At Independence in 1947, Gujarat proper was incorporated into Bombay state. In 1956 Saurashtra and Kachchh were added. On 1 May 1960 Bombay state was split into present day Maharashtra and Gujarat states and in 1961 India forcibly annexed Daman and Diu. After Partition the possession of the Rann of Kachchh was disputed by India and Pakistan. In 1965 they fought over it, and following the ceasefire on 1 July, division of the area was referred to an international tribunal. In 1968 the tribunal recommended that 90% should remain with India and 10% pass to Pakistan.

With the sole exception of 1977, Gujarat remained one of the Congress Party's chief strongholds throughout the period after Independence until 1989. It produced a number of national leaders after Mahatma Gandhi, including the first Prime Minister of the Janata Government in 1977, Morarji Desai. However, since the State Assembly elections of March 1995 the BJP has held control. In October 1999 the BJP bucked the national trend by winning 19 of the 26 Lok Sabha seats while the Congress (I) suffered further setbacks. The Lok Sabha results gave the Gujarat Chief Minister a breathing space in the internal strife within the state's BJP, where about 50 of the party's 117 Legislative Members had threatened to stage a revolt. In March 2002 clashes erupted between Hindus and Muslims in Gujarat directly related to the Hindu nationalist campaign to build a temple to Ram on the site of the Babri mosque at Ayodhya in Uttar Pradesh. Weeks of violence and riots followed and the Indian parliament was deadlocked by the opposition's determination to force Narendra Modi, Gujarat's BJP Chief Minister, out of office for failing to take any effective steps to protect the minority communities. The wily Modi managed to weather the storm, however, and is still in power today.

Gujarat is one of India's leading industrial states. Building on the cotton textile industry established in the 19th century, chemicals and petrochemicals, fertilizers and cement and engineering industries all have a major role. The state also has huge petrochemical complexes, Reliance's new factory at Jamnagar being one of the biggest oil-refining and petrochemical complexes in the world. Agriculture remains important, with cotton, tobacco and groundnut important cash crops and wheat and millets important cereals. Perhaps Gujarat's most striking agricultural development has been its dairy industry. India, now the world's largest milk producer, experienced a revolution in the dairy industry originating in Gujarat's dairy co-operatives' and their milk, butter and cheese now have India-wide markets. It is Gujarat's farmers who are the driving force behind the Indian Government's commitment to complete the Narmada dam projects, now in place and fully functional, albeit gaining height every year, after a succession of bitter legal disputes and the high profile opposition of the novelist Arundhati Roy and the social campaigner from Mumbai Medhar Patkar.



# Ahmadabad

→ *Phone code: 079. Colour map 2, C3. Population: 3.5 mn.*

*Ahmadabad, the former state capital (Gandhinagar is the new capital), is a very congested city which spreads out along both banks of the Sabarmati River in a chaotic fashion. The Old City, however, has a maze of narrow winding alleys with carved wooden house fronts and thriving bazars. The outstanding Calico Museum and Mahatma Gandhi's Sabarmati Ashram, as well as the culinary delights on offer, attract visitors though some find the city's noise and pollution a little offputting.* *⏩ For Sleeping, Eating and other listings, see pages 1237-1242.*

*Prohibition is in force. Ask for a 'liquor permit' on arrival in India at the airport tourist counter; getting one in the city is tortuous. Larger hotels may be authorized to issue 'spot' permits.*

## Ins and outs

**Getting there** The airport is 13 km northeast of town. Regular city buses collect passengers from the airport and arrive at Lal Darwaza, close to many budget hotels. Taxis charge Rs 180-230, and autos about Rs 90-100, to transfer. Train travellers arrive at the Junction Station to the east of the Old City, while long distance buses use the Rajpur Gate Terminus to the south. There are taxis and autos at both to get you to a hotel. *⏩ See Transport, page 1247, for further details.*

**Getting around** Ahmadabad is far too sprawling to be able to cover all the sights on foot so you will need to struggle with local buses or hire an auto-rickshaw or taxi.

## Background

Ahmadabad retains a highly distinctive feel born out of a long and continuously evolving social history. Recent developments in urban design have contributed important new experiments to its architectural tradition. It was founded in 1411 by **Ahmad Shah I**, then King of Gujarat. He made Asaval, an old Hindu town in the south, his seat of power, then expanded it to make it his capital. Almost constantly at war with the neighbouring Rajputs, fortifications were essential. The **Bhadra** towers and the square bastions of the royal citadel were among the first to be built. The city walls had 12 gates, 139 towers and nearly 6,000 battlements.

### Ahmadabad's 'pols'

The old parts of the city are divided into unique, self-contained *pols*, or quarters, fascinating to wander round. Huge wooden doors lead off from narrow lanes into a section of houses with decorative wooden screens and brackets where small communities of people practising a craft or skill once lived. Merchants, weavers, woodworkers, printers and jewellers – each had their *pol*, their houses along winding alleys which met in common courtyards and squares. Today, these old quarters are being developed rapidly, with tower blocks rising up from just inside the old city walls.



Although most of the **Old City** walls have gone, many monuments remain, some of them striking examples of Indian Islamic architecture. The **provincial Gujarati style** flourished from the mid-15th century, and in addition to the religious buildings many of the houses have façades beautifully decorated with wood carving. The Swami Narayan Temple, Kalipur, Rajani Vaishnav Temple and Harkore Haveli, near Manek Chowk as well as *havelis* on Doshiwadani Pol, illustrate traditional carving skills. Sadly, much of the old carving has been dismantled to be sold off to collectors.

The **'new' city**, lying on the west bank, has the site of Mahatma Gandhi's famous Sabarmati Ashram from where he began his historic Salt March in protest against the Salt Law in 1915. Modern Ahmadabad has its own share of showpieces designed by famous architects, among them Le Corbusier, Louis Kahn, Doshi and Correa. The School of Architecture, the National Institute of Design and the Indian Institute of Management (IIM) are national centres of learning.

With a long tradition in craftsmanship under Gujarati Sultans and Mughal Viceroys, Ahmadabad was one of the most brilliant Indian cities. Its jewellers and goldsmiths are renowned, copper and brassworkers produce very fine screens and carpenters produce fine *shisham* wood articles. There are skilled stonemasons, lacquer artists, ivory/bone carvers, hand-block printers and embroiderers producing exquisite pieces with beads and mirrors.

## Sights

In the Jami Masjid, Ahmadabad has one of the best examples of the second period of Gujarat's provincial architectural development. In 1411, Ahmad Shah I, the founder of a new dynasty, laid the foundations of the city which was to be his new capital. By 1423 the Jami Masjid, regarded by many as one of the finest mosques in India, was completed. He encouraged others to construct monumental buildings as well. Mahmud I Begarha (ruled 1459-1511) established the third phase of Gujarati provincial architecture, building some of India's most magnificent Islamic monuments.

### The central city

The citadel of the planned city formed a rectangle facing the river. A broad street was designed to run from Ahmad Shah's fortified palace in the citadel to the centre of the city, lying due east. The ancient citadel built by Ahmad Shah I in 1411, now known as the **Bhadra** (see above), lies between the Nehru and Ellis bridges. In the east face is the **Palace**, now the post office. **Sidi Sayid's Mosque** (circa 1570) formed part of the wall on the northeast corner but now stands isolated in a square. Ten windows of wonderful stone tracery depicting a branching tree are famous here, and have become the symbol of the city. Note particularly those on the west wall.

**Jami Masjid** The essential orientation of the Qibla wall to Mecca meant that the main entrance to the mosque itself had to be in its east wall. The mosque was aligned so that the present Mahatma Gandhi Road passed its north entrance. This is still the point at which you enter by a flight of steps. It is pleasantly quiet and peaceful inside. The vegetable and fruit market near the south entrance is worth visiting for the artistic display of stallholders' wares.

The beauty of the sanctuary is emphasized by the spacious courtyard paved in marble, with a tank in the middle. The façade has a screen of arches flanked by a pillared portico. The two 'shaking minarets', once 26 m high, were destroyed by earthquakes in 1819 and 1957. Over 300 graceful pillars are organized in 15 square bays. The whole rises from a single storey through the two-storeyed side aisles to the three-storey central aisle. The central octagonal lantern, rising through both storeys and covered by a dome, was also strikingly original.

**Teen Darwaza** is immediately to the east of the entrance to Ahmad Shah's mosque – the triumphal archway also known as the Tripolia (Triple gateway). Now crowded by shops, its effect is considerably diminished.

Northeast of the Astodia Gate and a short distance south of the railway station are **Sidi Bashir's Shaking Minarets**, two tall towers connected by a bridge which was once the entrance to the old mosque (now replaced by a modern one). The minarets were believed to 'shake' or vibrate in sympathy as they are cleverly built on a flexible sandstone base to protect against earthquake damage. **Bibi-ki-Masjid** (1454), Gomtipur, southeast of the railway station, also has a shaking minaret. If you climb up the 78 steps to a parapet 25 m high, and hold on to the minaret, your guide may be able to make it gently sway by putting his weight against it!



## Ahmadabad centre

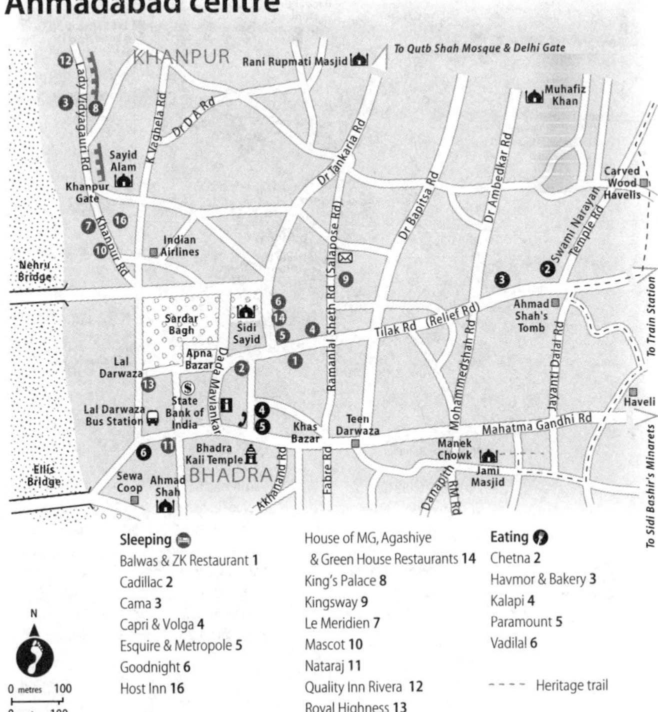

# Ahmadabad

Related map
A Ahmadabad centre, page 1233.

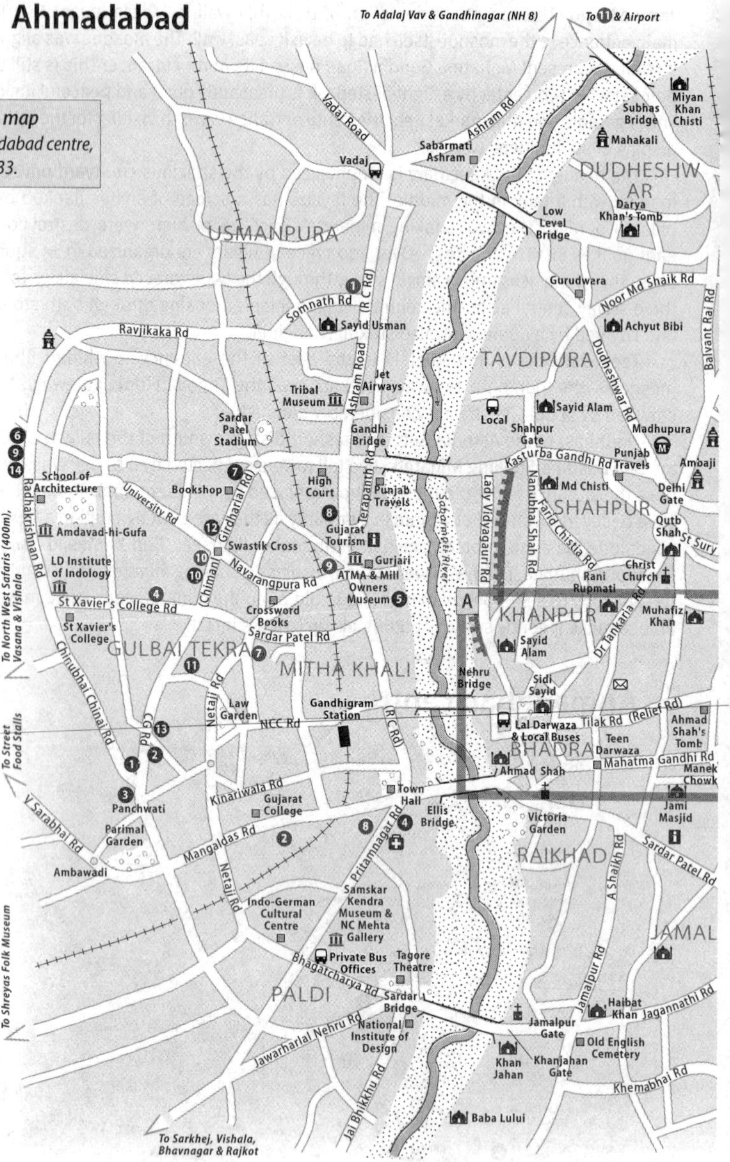

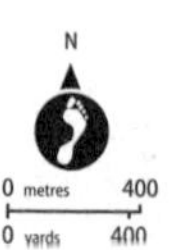


**Sleeping**

Comfort Inn Sunset **11**
Comfort Inn President **10**
Fortune Landmark **1**
Inder Residency **2**
Klassik Gold **4**
Moti Mahal **5**
Nalanda **7**
Panshikura & Toran Restaurant **8**
Poonam Palace **9**

**Eating**

Bhagwati Chaats & Havmor **1**
Black Knight **2**
Chills, Thrills & Spills **3**
Gopi & Mehta **4**
Havmor **5**
Khana Khazana **6**
Mirch Masala **7**
Purohit **8**
Rasrajan **9**
Sankalp **10**

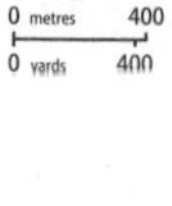

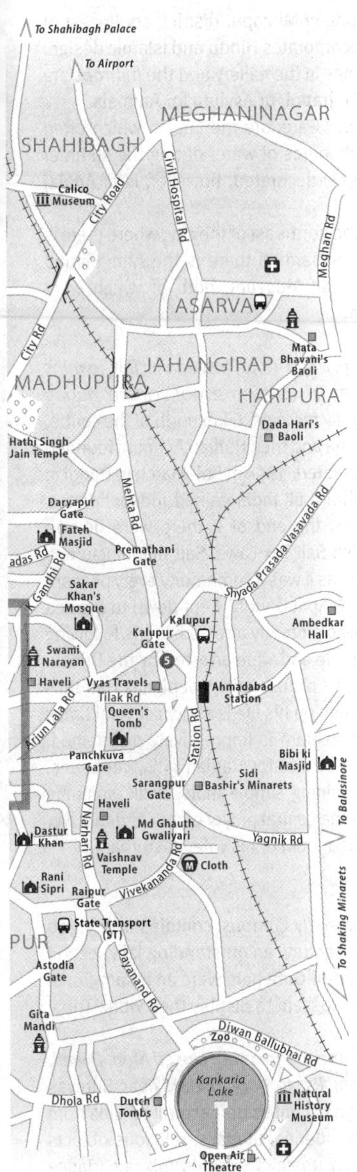


Sheeba 11
Ten & Colours of Spice 12
Tomato 13
Upper Crust 14



## The north

**Sayid Usman's mausoleum** is across the Gandhi bridge, immediately west of Ashram Road. The *rauza* (circa 1460) is one of the first examples of the Begarha style. Northwest of the Old City near Shahpur Gate, the **Mosque of Hasan Muhammad Chishti** (1565) has some of the finest tracery work in Ahmadabad.

Nearby, the **Calico Museum** ⓘ *except Wed and holidays, free, tours from 1030-1230 (secular textiles), 1445-1645, (religious textiles, plus superb collection of Cholas bronzes); report 15 mins before; they are different and complementary and the only way to see the museum, children under the age of 10 are not permitted to enter, guided tour of the garden is by appointment only*, a part of the Sarabhai Trust, is in an attractive old *haveli* in the botanically interesting Shahi Bagh gardens, 3 km north of Delhi Gate. It is one of the finest museums of its kind in the world. Some exhibits date from the 17th century and include rich displays of heavy brocades, fine embroideries, saris, carpets, turbans, Maharajahs' costumes and a royal Mughal tent. It illustrates weaving techniques but not weaving equipment. The setting is superb. The Religious section exhibits outstanding medieval Jain manuscripts, 14th- to 19th-century Jain icons, *pichhwais* and *pattachitras*. The Secular section contains Indian textiles that featured in trade, historic pieces of tie-and-dye, embroidery and beadwork from Gujarat, *phulkari* embroideries of Punjab, *patola* silk sarees from Patan, Pashmina shawls from Kashmir, Chamba *rumals* from Himachal, silks from Orissa and South India. It is also open for research. The guides are friendly and charming. **Moti Manor Hotel** is the only place nearby, for lunch.

There are several Jain temples in the city. The highly decorated, white marble **Hathi Singh Temple** (1848) just north of the Delhi Gate, dedicated to Dharamanath, the 15th Jain *Tirthankar*, is perhaps the most visited. Along the streets of Ahmadabad, it is quite common to see Jain *parabdis* (bird sanctuaries).

The **Rani Rupmati Masjid**, early 16th century, in Mirzapur district, southwest of Delhi Gate and just south of the **Grand Hotel**, incorporates Hindu and Islamic design. Rupmati was the Sultan's Hindu wife. The carvings in the gallery and the *mihrabs* are particularly attractive. To the southeast is the **Pinjrapol**, or Asylum for Animals.

At **Asarva**, about 1 km northeast of Daryapur Gate, are the *baolis*, which often serve a dual purpose of being a cool, secluded source of water during the summer and a place of religious sanctity. The most highly decorated, however, is at **Adalaj Vav**, 19 km away.

The British **Cantonment** lies about 4 km to the northeast of the city, where there is an Anglican Church. On the west bank of the Sabarmati there is the **Ahmadabad Textile Mill Owners' Association (ATMA)** and the **Museum**, both of which were designed by Le Corbusier, see further page 450.

**Sabarmati Ashram** ⓘ *0830-1900, 1 Apr-30 Sep, 0830-1830, last admission 30 mins before closing, free, Son et Lumière Sun, Wed, Fri (English 2100), closed during monsoons, Rs 5, donations for upkeep are gratefully received*, 6 km north of the centre, is Gandhi's Ashram, originally known as Satyagraha and then Harijan Ashram, founded in 1917. It was the starting point for Gandhi's celebrated, 385-km Salt March to Dandi in March 1930. He vowed not to return to the Ashram till India gained independence. Gandhi and 81 supporters began the march; by the end of it there were 90,000 protesters marching against the unpopular British Salt Tax Laws. Salt manufacture, a government monopoly, was chosen for the protest as it was a commodity every peasant used and could understand. At Dandi beach on 6 April Gandhi went down to the sea and made a small amount of salt, for which he was promptly arrested. In the following months, thousands of Indians followed his example and were arrested by the British. The **Sangrahalaya** includes a library, archives and a picture gallery depicting Gandhi's life in photographs and paintings. A five-minute film on his life is shown several times daily. The peace, quiet and simple style of the Ashram is impressively maintained. Some of the original ashram's work, such as a school for Harijan girls, continues. **Hridaya Kunj**, Gandhi's home for 15 years, containing simple mats, desk, spinning wheel and some personal belongings, overlooks the central prayer corner and the river and remains undisturbed, as does the unfurnished room of his wife, Kasturba.



## To the west

**LD Institute of Indology Museum** ⓘ *Gujarat University Campus*, contains over 3,300 pieces of medieval sculpture, many of 11th-13th century, an outstanding Jain section and archaeological finds. The 'caves' of **Amdavad-ni-Gufa** here were an inspirational venture by the architect Doshi and the artist MF Hussain to display their work. Tribal paintings and other works of art are being added.

**Shreyas Museum** ⓘ *winter, 1030-1730, summer 0830-1300, closed Mon, Diwali, Christmas and during school summer vacation, Rs 35 (foreigners)*, near Shreyas Railway Crossing, has a comprehensive collection of contemporary rural textiles from all parts of Gujarat – excellent beadwork, embroideries, utensils, religious objects and bullock cart accessories. Children's section upstairs exhibits folk art (dance costumes, masks, puppets). The guided tour also takes you around the campus.

**Sanskar Kendra Museum** ⓘ *museum 1030, gallery 1100, closed Mon, free*, an award-winning design by Le Corbusier, with ramps of steps leading up from a fountained pool, houses an excellent collection of old and contemporary art, superbly exhibited. The **NC Mehta Gallery** here, has a vast collection of miniatures from the Rajasthan, Mewar, Mughal, Kangra and other schools. The series of 150 paintings on the Gita Govinda theme and a set from the Gujarat Sultanate period are rare exhibits.

**Tribal Research Institute Museum** ⓘ *Gujarat Vidyapith, Ashram Rd, 1130-1930, Sat 1130-1430, closed Sun*, has re-creations of tribal hamlets of Gujarat, besides weapons, implements, wall art, terracotta figurines and textiles.

## South of the city

**Kamala Nehru Zoological Park** ⓘ *Satellite Rd, off M Dayanand Rd, Kankaria, except Mon*, was masterminded by the late Reuben David, a 'captive breeding' genius – note the albino porcupine, squirrel and deer here. **Sundervan** is a pleasant nature orientation park, snake demonstrations on their importance to the environment, walk-in aviary, library.

## Excursions

**Vishala**, 5 km away, is a purpose-built collection of traditional Gujarati village huts serving *thalis* at lunch and evening meal at 2100, accompanied by music (lunch Rs 80, dinner Rs 120). There is traditional dancing after dinner and light is provided in the evening entirely by lanterns. You sit cross-legged at low tables (low stools also provided), eat off green leaves or metal *thalis*, and drink from clay tumblers. Hospitable, friendly staff. Air-cooled seating for lunch and snacks. The Utensils Museumⓘ *Sarkhej Rd, Vasana, 1700-2300 weekdays, 1000-1300, 1700-2200 Sun, fix a return price with an auto*, renovated and expanded in a courtyard with a pool, has a very well-displayed collection of milking vessels (cattle, camel), Rajasthani pottery, Hindu prayer lamps, jewel boxes and betel nut crackers.

**Indroda Village Deer Park**, next to Sarita Udyan by Sabarmati River, has an interesting reptile collection and well marked nature trails through forests where you may spot nilgai, porcupine, jackal, crested honey buzzard, paradise fly-catcher etc. There is a tented campsite.

**Adalaj** is the hamlet where, in a garden setting, one of the finest step wells in India can be found. The Vav (*baoli*) shows a combination of Hindu, Muslim and Buddhist styles. A long flight of steps descends over 30 m to the water. It has four floors, each cooler than the one above. Ornately carved pillars, niches and cross beams create large octagonal landings (now inaccessible) which served as resting places. Remains of the bullock ramp used for drawing water are still visible. Queen Rupabai is believed to have had it built to provide the traveller with a cool and pleasant refuge from the summer heat. A visit is highly recommended. It is 17 km north of Ahmadabad near Gandhinagar cross-road (taxis charge around Rs 300 return). For a bite to eat on Gandhinagar Highway there is **Bageshree** for Gujarati *thalis* in lovely garden setting; and **Gokul** with a village theme, *havelis* and huts, folk concerts, Gujarati *thalis*. **Kathiawadi**, near crossroads, does highly spiced *thalis*.

## Sleeping

**Ahmadabad** *p1231, maps p1234 and p1233*
Most are near the centre, about 3 km from railway station. Budget travellers may not find any room with bath for under Rs 150. **D** grade hotels in Khanpur (centre) often have some a/c rooms with shower and TV. Those without restaurants provide good room service. Most **D** hotels on Tilak (Relief) Rd in between **Chetna Restaurant** and Sidi Sayid Mosque are similar in standard and facilities; most rooms have phone and bath with hot water, some a/c, though room sizes and prices differ.

**AL Taj Residency Ummed**, Airport Circle, Hansol, T079 2286 4444, www.tajhotels.com. 88 rooms and some expensive suites, tastefully decorated with traditional embroideries and art pieces, usual facilities, good pool, restaurant, hotel sometimes overbooked.

**AL-A Cama**, Khanpur Rd, T079 2560 1234, www.camahotelsindia.com. 50 a/c rooms, totally renovated and upgraded on 1st and 2nd floors with long bathrooms, some with riverview, less expensive rooms on 3rd floor, new restaurant, pool (not spotless), garden, good coffee shop, friendly management.

**AL-A Comfort Inn Sunset**, Airport Circle, T079 2286 2591, www.comfortinn.com. 33 rooms, usual modern facilities, airport pick up.

**AL-A Fortune Landmark**, Ashram Rd, T079 2755 2929, www.fortunelandmark.com. One of the best but on busy main road, massive, 96 varied rooms, good restaurants (buffet breakfast to set you up for the day), health club, Jacuzzi pool.

**AL-A Inder Residency**, Ellis Bridge, T079 2656 5222, www.inder-residency.com. 79 rooms, modern, very comfortable, very good Indian restaurant (avoid western), pool.

**AL-A Le Meridien**, Khanpur Rd near Nehru Bridge, T079 2550 5505, www.lemeridien.com. 63 rooms, good restaurants (**Waterfall** for buffets), dance floor, good indoor pool.

**A House of MG**, opposite Sidi Saiyad Mosque, Laldarwaja, T079 2550 6946, www.houseofmg.com. 10 beautifully decorated rooms in heritage hotel, centrally located with 2 excellent restaurants (see below), friendly, professional staff, recommended.

**B Comfort Inn President**, CG Rd, Swastik Char Rasta, T079 2646 7575, www.comfortinnpresident.com. 53 good rooms, friendly staff, average décor, excellent restaurants.

**B Klassik Gold**, CG Rd, T079 2644 5508, www.klassicgold.com. 33 rooms, excellent restaurant, efficient management, best in category.

**B Nalanda**, Mithakhali 6 Rds, T079 2646 8899, www.hotelnalanda.com. 38 clean rooms (standard rooms small; bath tubs and fridge in best), very good restaurant.

**B Mascot**, Khanpur Rd, T079 2550 3848, F2550 3221. Very comfortable, good value.

**B Quality Inn Rivera**, Khanpur Rd, T079 2560 1111, www.qualityinnrivera.com. 69 clean, comfortable rooms (some overlook river), restaurant, free airport transfer, lawn, quiet.

**C Host Inn**, opposite Le Meridien, Khanpur, T079 3022 6555. Very clean rooms in friendly, well-run hotel, no restaurant.

**C-D Dimple International**, Panchkuva, T079 2214 1849. 30 rooms with modern facilities.

**C-D King's Palace**, opposite Cama, T/F079 2550 0275. 37 very clean rooms, some a/c, good value, good restaurant, friendly staff.

**D Balwas**, 6751 Relief Rd, near Electricity House, T079 2550 7135. 26 clean rooms, 6 small at rear (side entrance), some economical non-a/c **E**, good restaurant attached but crowded, noisy area.

**D Goodnight**, Dr Tankaria Rd, opposite Sidi Sayid, Lal Darwaza, T079 25506997. 35 clean rooms, good restaurant, good service.

**D Kingsway**, near GPO, T079 25501215. 33 large rooms with fan, bath (hot water), modern, small breakfast menu and snacks.

**D Panshikura**, near Town Hall, Underbridge, Ellis Bridge. 24 a/c rooms, quieter at rear, excellent restaurant.

**D Poonam Palace**, off Ashram Rd, near Dipali Cinema. Good value rooms.

**D-E Metropole**, Hanuman Lane, opposite Electricity House, T079 2550 7988. 19 clean rooms (small singles) some a/c, good room service.

**E Esquire**, opposite Sidi Sayid Mosque. Clean and popular.

**E Nataraj**, Dada Mavlankar Rd, near Ahmad Shah Mosque. Simple rooms with bath, hostel-like but good value.

**E Swagat**, near Arya Samaj, Rajpur-Kankaria Rd. Rooms on 1st floor, practically windowless and claustrophobic, bit noisy, but very clean, shared shower, good room service from nearby restaurant, bus tickets, unused to foreigners but friendly, eager to please.

**E Volga**, near Electricity House, T079 2550 9497, Volga@icenet.net. Decent rooms, car rentals, internet.

**F Cadilac**, opposite Electricity House, Lal Darwaza, T079 2550 7558. Good value rooms with shared facilities, helpful travel desk.

## Eating

**Ahmadabad** *p1231, maps p1234 and p1233*

*Thalis* are around Rs 50 ('Kathiawadi' has more chilly and garlic, while 'Gujarati' is sweetened with sugar and jaggery).

**TTT Colours of Spice**, Swastik Crossroads. International (including Thai/Indonesian), pleasant a/c interior, courteous service, about Rs 300 each.

**TTT Fortune Landmark**, pleasant rooftop restaurant with city views, open after dark. Great atmosphere, live music, specialises in kebabs, tandoori, grills/roasts (Rs 500 each). Downstairs for good buffets. (Rs 200-275), enormous breakfast (Rs 175).

**TT Agashiye**, in **House of MG Hotel**, opposite Sidi Sayid Mosque, Lal Darwaja. Attractive Gujarati *thali* restaurant on the terrace of a 1920s heritage building. Unique atmosphere, local music, Gujarati *thalis* (Rs 170-200).

*For an explanation of the sleeping and eating price codes used in this guide, see inside the front cover. Other relevant information is found in Essentials pages 56-61.*

🍴🍴 **Bhagyodaya**, GPO Rd, opposite **Kingsway**. Good food, varied choice, pleasant outlook.
🍴🍴 **Black Knight**, CG Rd. Good Indian, Chinese, continental, medieval European theme decor.
🍴🍴 **China Town**, Stadium Circle. Good Chinese (including non-vegetarian). Try fish Manchurian or Chicken in hot garlic.
🍴🍴 **City Gold Multiplex**, Ashram Rd. The modern entertainment complexes have several adventurous outlets (Western, oriental) to which the young gravitate.
🍴🍴 **Food Inn**, at **Goodnight**, serves good Indian (unlimited *thali*) but freezing a/c.
🍴🍴 **Green House**, in House of MG Hotel I courtyard café selling wide range of Gujarati snacks , light meals and drinks..
🍴🍴 **HBM**, lounge here is cool (a/c) and attractive and ideal for relaxing, for Rs 70 cover charge, coffee and snacks available, books and TV.
🍴🍴 **Fun Republic**, Satellite Rd, and,
🍴🍴 **Mirch Masala**, CG Rd. Very spicy North Indian, Bollywood theme in Juhu beach-shack mock-up with filmland posters and music to match, also tempting and hygienic (usually forbidden!) 'street snacks'.
🍴🍴 **Paramount**, MG Rd near Bhadra. Indian. Famous for mutton/chicken biryanis, tikkas, a/c but lacks atmosphere.
🍴🍴 **Rajwadu**, Jivraj Park. A rural theme restaurant. Rajasthani/Gujarati dinner, delightful open-air setting, water courses, gardens, folk entertainment, large meals in brass/copper vessels, refills galore, a bit like a Bollywood film set but very pleasant, not quite as authentic as *Vishala* but more comfortable and accessible.
🍴🍴 **Sheebah**, opposite Telephone Exchange, Navrangpura. International, a/c, excellent north Indian (try fish, paneer or chicken *tikkas*), friendly. Continental and Chinese fast food counter (to avoid excess spices, request when ordering). Highly recommended.
🍴🍴 **Ten, the Restaurant**, Swastik Crossroads, CG Rd. Indian and continental, a/c, one of the best in town, ship-breakers yard décor, friendly, occasional live Indian music. Great fish meunière, fried fish, methi chicken, kebab platters, but avoid Chinese. For dessert try the '10-special pudding'. Good cake shop.
🍴🍴 **Tomato**, CG Rd. Western, a/c, 1950s American diner theme, Rock-and-Roll era decor and music, good atmosphere, young crowd; also Mexican/Italian. Coffee shop serves great coffee, nachos, tacos, sandwiches.
🍴 **Azad Halwai**, Revdi Bazar. North Indian sweets, try *Daal-Pakwan*, a Sindhi favourite.
🍴 **Cama Hotel** does excellent salads, club sandwiches and great value buffets (Rs 200-250).
🍴 **Chetna**, Krishna Cinema, Relief Rd (upstairs). Unlimited Gujarati *thalis*.
🍴 **Gopi**, Ashram Rd. A/c, mildly spiced *thalis* for foreigners, good service, family run.
🍴 **La-Bela**, Mirzapur. Mutton/chicken curry and other dishes cooked up by a family. Lady owner treats visitors like part of her family.
🍴 **Mehta**, Ellis Bridge, *thalis* and snacks.
🍴 **Navrang**, Vijay Crossroads. Punjabi *thalis*, a/c.
🍴 **New Swagath**, Babha Complex, near Gujarat Vidyapith. Good South Indian, *Puri-bhaji*.
🍴 **Sankalp**, CG Rd. South Indian, rooftop terrace garden with fountain, good *dosas*.
🍴 **Shiv Sagar** off CG Rd. Thalis (Rs 60), less spicy than elsewhere. Very cheap (under Rs 30) Indian meals and snacks are available at Bhatiar Gali, Law Garden, Raipur Gate, IIM Rd.
🍴 **Tulsi**, near Gujarat University. North Indian thalis and à la carte, a/c.
🍴 **Vallabha**, 1 Jeet Complex, opposite *'Shilip'*, C G Rd. Excellent Gujarati thalis.

### Cafés and fast food

Panchwati: **Bhagwati Chaats**, great Indian snacks and sweets, try *paneer tikkas, gulab jamuns* and *jalebis*.
**Chills, Thrills, Frills**. Veg/cheese burgers, excellent coffee, grilled and toasted sandwiches, ice creams, thick shakes, disappointing pizzas, young crowd (Rs 150 for 2).
**Dominos**, Stadium Circle. Good pizzas at a few tables outdoors (mainly takeaway), also desserts and side dishes.
**Periera Takeaways** and **Icy Pick**, both near Vijay Crossroads. Cold meats, kebabs, tikkas.
**Rasrajan**, Vijay Crossroads (a/c). Self service, a/c upstairs. good vegetarian salad bar, Indian and Chinese veg meals.
**Upper Crust**, Vijay Crossroads, (a/c). Good breads, cakes and desserts, *kathi kabab* rolls, sizzlers, Sun breakfast (Rs 50).

### Sweets

**Kamal**, Revdi Bazar, near the station. For excellent Indian sweets.
**Kamdhenu**, near VS Hospital. For good Gujarati sweets.

**Jai Sitaram**, near Paldi Railway Crossing. Delicious *kesar pedas* (saffron-flavoured milk sweets).

## Festivals and events

**Ahmadabad** *p1231, maps p1234 and p1233*
**14-15 Jan**: Makar Sankranti marks the end of winter. It is celebrated with kite flying by people of all ages, accompanied by colourful street markets and festivities Kites come in all colours, shapes and sizes, the best varieties reputedly being available in Manek Chowk and Tankshala, Kalupur. The flying continues after sunset, when the kites are lit with candles. **Sep/Oct**: Navratri, honouring Goddess Amba (*Shakti*), has special significance here and at Vadodara. Nine days of music and traditional '*Garba Ras*' dancing. The custom of women balancing clay pots while they dance is still practised.

## Shopping

**Ahmadabad** *p1231, maps p1234 and p1233*
Shops usually open from 0900-1900, most close on Sun. Manek Chowk is the main bazar. Other centres are Relief Rd, Ashram Rd, Lal Darwaza and Kapasia Bazar.

### Books

**Art Book Centre**, Madalpur, near Inder Residency.
**Book Shelf**, 16 City Centre, near 10-the Restaurant, CG Rd, Navrangpura. A/c.
**Books Plaza**, near Raymond show room, CG Rd. Also CDs.
**Crossword**, B6 Sri Krishna Centre, Mithakhali 6 Rds, T079 2642 5186. A/c, also CDs and café.
**Mapin**, Darpana Academy, Usmanpura, Ashram Rd. Specializes in Indian arts.
**Natraj**, Ashram Rd, with branches all over the city. Books and CDs.

### Handicrafts

Good bargains at **Satellite Rd**, where Kachchhi and Saurashtrian artisans sell embroideries, block prints and handicrafts – appliqué bedspreads, wall hangings etc, but bargain hard. Go to the huge **Sunday Market**, on the river bank at Ellis Bridge in the morning to pick up 'antiques', handicrafts and second-hand books.
**Garvi** and **Gujari**, Ashram Rd. Govt. Embroidered dresses, block-printed bed-spreads, lacquered furniture etc, well displayed, open 1030-1400, 1500-1900, closed Wed. Visit Law Gardens after 1600 to browse through stalls of artists and craftsmen.
**Honeycomb** at Cama Hotel.
**Kamdhenu** Ambawadi, has showrooms of several State Handicraft Co-ops.
**Shringar**, near **Honeycomb**, upmarket 'antiques'.
**Treasure**, near Judge's bungalow, Satellite Rd, is a gallery for art and handicrafts.
Brassware and wood carvings are sold at Manek Chowk.

### Textiles

Gujarat's famous embroideries, *bandhani* and block prints are sold at **Rani-no-Haziro** and **Dalgarwad** near Manek Chowk in the walled city. There are '*Khadi Bhandars*' and Handloom Housesfor textiles on Ashram Rd, between Gandhi Ashram and Natraj Theatre. **Revdi Bazar** and **Sindhi Market** have semi-wholesale textile shops. CG Rd is the upmarket shopping area for quality garments.
**Bhandej**, next to **Crosswords Bookshop**, T079 2642 2181, upmarket salon selling beautiful locally made clothes.
**Bhujodi**, Mithakhali Rd, T079 2640 0967, good range of ethnic-styled clothing and handicrafts.
**Sewa**, east of Ellis Bridge, is a commendable women's co-op producing very fine shadow embroidery and clothes.

## Activities and tours

**Ahmadabad** *p1231, maps p1234 and p1233*
**Ahmadabad Municipal Transport Service**, Lal Darwaza, T079 2658 9172, where you can reserve the following: **Tour 1** 0830-1830: Sidi Sayid mosque, Shaking minarets, Huteehsinh Jain temples, Gandhi Ashram, Gujarat Vidyapit, ISKCON temple, Sundarvan, Shreyas museum, Gandhinagar (also Akshardham) and Adalaj stepwell; Rs 160 a/c coach. **Tour 2** 0900-1700, slightly different, Rs 125 (non-a/c). **Tours 3, 4** 0930-1300, 1330-1730, split the sights; Rs 75, Rs 85 a/c. **Heritage Walking Tours** Mar-Aug 0730 to 1030, Sep-Feb 0800-1030. Excellent tour with qualified architects/conservationists; starts at

Swaminarayan temple, Relief Rd, Kalupur, of havelis, *pols*, artisans' workshops etc, for Rs 50. Check ahead at CRUTA, at the temple complex, T079 2539 1811 ext509. Highly recommended.
**Forican Tours**, opposite Electricity House, Lal Darwaza, T079 2550 6590, for bookings for Poshina.
**Sita**, Suflam Building, Mithakhali, Ashram Rd, T079 2656 9105.
**TCI**, near Natraj Theatre, behind Handloom House, Ashram Rd, T079 2658 7061.

## Transport

**Ahmadabad** *p1231, maps p1234 and p1233*
**Air**
Air India, Premchand House, near High Court, T079 2658 5622. **Air France**, T079 2644 2391. . **Lufthansa**, T079 2646 4122. **Singapore Airlines**, T079 2646 1335. **Swissair**, T079 2644 9149. International flights to **Abu Dhabi**, **Bangkok**, **Copenhagen**, **Dhaharan**, **Dubai**, **Geneva** and **Hong Kong**. Indian Airlines, Lal Darwaza, near Roopalee Cinema, T079 25503061. 1000-1315, 1415-1715. Airport T1400, www.indianairlines.nic.in. **Delhi**, **Mumbai**, **Calcutta**, **Kolkota** via **Bangalore**, **Hyderabad**, **Jaipur**. Jet Airways, Income Tax Char Rasta, Ashram Rd, T079 2754 3304, Airport T22866540, www.jetairways.com: **Mumbai**, **Delhi**. Also try new budget airline, Air Deccan, T079 3092 5213, www.air deccan.net, for cheap flights south.

**Bus**
**Local** City service available from main bus station, Lal Darwaza, railway station and all major points in the city.
**Long distance** Central Bus Station, Geeta Mandir, T079 2214 4764. Reservations 0700-1900. Advance booking for night services 1500-2300, luxury coach services 1030-1800. Arrive early to find your bus. ST buses to **Mehsana** (Rs 20) on very poor road, **Mumbai** (492 km, 11 hrs), **Palitana** 217 km, **Porbandar** 394 km, **Rajkot** 216 km, **Sasan Gir** 217 km, **Surat** 120 km, and **Vadodara** 113 km. **Udaipur** 287 km. Private operated coaches, from suburban stands, often run at night. **Punjab Travels**, K Gandhi Rd, Delhi Darwaza, and Embassy Market, Ashram Rd, T079 26589200. **Pawan**, Pritamnagar 1st Dhal, Ellis Bridge, T079 2657 5214. **Tanna**, Paldi, for **Bhavnagar**. **Shajanand**, Shefali Complex, Paldi, for buses to **Diu**; **Mt Abu**, 7 hrs (via Khed Brahma).

**Rickshaw**
Ask to see rate card as they inflate price for foreigners. Night charges are quite high.

**Taxi**
Tourist taxis for hire from **TCGL**, T079 2658 9683, **Sai**, 23 Aniket, Navrangpura; Rs 500 (4 hrs), Rs 900 (8 hrs), or Green Channel, T079 2656 0489.

**Train**
Always confirm from which station train departs. Ahmadabad is on a broad gauge line to Mumbai (Platforms 1-4, near the main entrance) and a metre gauge line to Delhi (Platforms 7-12). Platforms 5 and 6 serve both, according to demand, and has 3 rails! Ahmadabad Junction (Kalupur) Station, enquiries T131. Computerized reservations at Junction and Gandhigram stations: 1st Class 0800-1530, 2nd Class 0800-1430, 1500-2000, T135, enquiry T131. If you don't have a reservation, last-minute berths can be booked for some trains at a temporary counter on the platform; premium charged.
**Agra Cantt**: *Ahmadabad Gorakhpur Exp, 5045*, 0545, Tue, 25 hrs. **Ajmer**: *Ahmadabad Delhi Mail, 9105*, 0955, 10½ hrs (to Jaipur); *Ashram Exp 2915*, 1745, 7 hrs. **Bangalore**: *Ahmadabad Bangalore Exp*, 1800, Sun, 13¾ hrs. **Bhavnagar**: *Bhavnagar Exp 9936*, 0705, 5½ hrs; *Shetrunji Exp, 9910*, 1710, 5½ hrs. **Bhopal**: *Rajkot-Bhopal Jabalpur Exp, 1269/1263*, 1900, 14 hrs. **Chennai**: *Navjivan Exp, 6045*, 0630, 22¾ hrs. **Delhi (OD)**: *Ashram Exp, 2915*, 1745, 16½ hrs. **Jaipur**: *Aravali Exp, 9707*, 0620, 13¾ hrs; *Ashram Exp, 2915*, 1745, 11 hrs. **Kolkata (H)**: *Howrah Exp, 8033*, 0920, 20 hrs. **Jamnagar**: *Jamnagar Exp, 9153*, 1815, not Mon, 6 hrs; *Mumbai Porbandar Saurashtra Exp, 9215*, 2015, 7½ hrs; *Mumbai Okha Saurashtra Mail, 9005*, 0550, 7½ hrs (all stop at **Rajkot**, 2 hrs before Jamnagar). **Jodhpur**: *Ranakpur Exp, 4708*, 0030, 10 hrs (continues to **Bikaner**, 6 hrs). **Junagadh**: *Veraval Girnar Exp, 9946*, 2155, 8½ hrs; *Veraval Somnath Mail, 9924*, 2300, 10 hrs (both continue to **Veraval**, 2 hrs). **Mehsana**: *Aravali Exp, 9707*, 0620, 1¾ hrs; *Delhi Mail*,

9105, 0955, 2 hrs; *Ashram Exp, 2915,* 1745, 1½ hrs. **Mumbai Central**: *Shatabdi Exp, 2010,* 1435, not Fri, 7¼ hrs; *Gujarat Mail, 2902,* 2210, 8¾ hrs. **Porbandar**: *Mumbai Porbandar Saurashtra Exp, 9215,* 2015, 10½ hrs. **Udaipur City**: *DSR Express, 9944,* 2240, 9 hrs. **Vadodara**: *Gandhidham Vadodara Exp, 9104,* 0518, 2 hrs; *Ahmadabad Vadodara Exp, 9130,* 1445, 2½ hrs.

## Directory

**Ahmadabad** *p1231, maps p1234 and p1233*
**Banks** Bank of Baroda and **Andhra Bank**, Ashram Rd, Visa and TCs. Some on CG Rd and Ashram Rd, change TCs and currency. **Amex, Wall St Finance, Foreign Exchange Bureau**, all on CG Rd; **Thomas Cook**, near the High Court, involve less paper-work and open till late. **Cultural centres** West of Ellis Bridge, **Alliance Française**, behind Gujarat College. **British Library**, near Law Garden, T079 2646 4693, a/c; clean toilets. **Hospitals** Civil Hospital, Asarwa, T079 268 3721;Rajasthan T079 2286 6311;VS T079 2657 7621, Heart Foundation, T079 2657 5555. **Internet** Cyber Café, Shri Krishna Centre, Mithakhali. **Log-In**, 92 Kamdhenu Complex, Polytechnic Rd, Ambawadi, T079 2630 2019, also printouts. **Random Access**, Ambawadi, 10 terminals. **Post** GPO: off Relief Rd. Others at Navrangpura, Ellis Bridge, Gandhi Ashram, Gandhi Rd, Gujarat University, IIM, Madhavpura market, Polytechnic and Ambawadi – all with Speed Post. **Tourist offices** Gujarat (TCGL), HK House, opposite Bata, Ashram Rd, T079 26589172, www.gujarattourism.com; 1030-1830, closed Sun, 2nd and 4th Sat each month. Also at airport and railway station. **Goa**, Indata, Vaveli Building, Fantasa Pole, Gandhi Rd. **MP**, T079 2658 9172. **UP**, Smrutikunj Soc, opposite Asia Engineering School. **Useful addresses** Ambulance: T102. Fire: T101. Police: T100. **Foreigners' Regional Registration Office**: Police Commissioner's Office, Shahi Bagh.

# Around Ahmadabad

## North of Ahmadabad

**The fertile irrigated land immediately north of Ahmadabad becomes increasingly arid northwards towards Rajasthan. When approaching Mehsana there are signs of the growing economy, including natural gas, fertilizers, milk products and rape seed oil processing. There are some worthy trips in this area.** » *For Sleeping, Eating and other listings, see pages 1246-1248.*

### Gandhinagar → *Phone code: 02712 or 082 from Ahmadabad. Colour map 2, grid C3. Population: 195,900.*

When Bombay state was divided along linguistic lines into Maharashtra and Gujarat in 1960, a new capital city was planned for Gujarat named after Mahatma Gandhi. As with Chandigarh, Le Corbusier was instrumental in the design. The 30 residential sectors around the central government complex are similarly impersonal. Construction began in 1965 and the Secretariat was completed in 1970. It is now an established town with over a quarter of a million people. Gandhinagar, 23 km north of Ahmadabad, has become a popular place for day trippers from Ahmadabad with good multiplex theatre complexes and parks.

**Akshardham** ⓘ *Sector 20, 0900-1830 (Nov-Feb); 1000-2000 (Mar-Oct), part closed on Mon, Rs 25,* a temple with a cultural complex and entertainment park, is run by volunteers. The pink sandstone main building, floodlit at dusk, houses a 2-m gold leaf idol and some relics of Sri Swaminarayan, who led a Vedic revivalist movement 200 years ago. The three halls feature a variety of informative sound and light presentations relating to Sri Swaminarayan, the *Vedas* and the Hindu epics.

Sahajanabad Vun, the garden for meditation, is impressive and has 'singing fountains' and a restaurant. 

## Mehsana (Mahesana)

The town, 80 km north of Ahmadabad, has an impressive Jain temple, built in the 1980s but in the traditional architectural style. Mehsana is used by visitors to Modhera and Patan for an overnight stop. Women travellers have reported being hassled by men near the bus station.

## Modhera → *Colour map 2, grid C2.*

Virtually a deserted hamlet 25 km west of Mehsana, Modhera has the remains of one of the finest Hindu temples ⓘ *Rs 200 foreigners, video camera Rs 150*, in Gujarat. Quite off the beaten track, it retains a great deal of its atmosphere and charm. Visit early in the day as it get busy. The partially ruined **Surya** (Sun) **Temple** (1026), built during the reign of Bhimdev I and consecrated in 1026-1027, two centuries before the Sun Temple at Konark, is a product of the great Solanki period (eighth-13th centuries). Despite the temple's partial destruction by subsequent earthquakes which may have accounted for the collapse of its tower, it remains an outstanding monument, set against the backdrop of a barren landscape. Superb carvings of goddesses, birds, beasts and blossoms decorate the remaining pillars. Over the last 20 years the complex has undergone major restoration by the Archaeological Survey of India which is continuing as funds permit. Unlike the Temple at Konark, the main temple stands well above the surrounding land, raised by a high brick terrace faced with stone.

*A Classical Dance Festival is held in January.*

The **entrance** A rectangular pool (*kund*, now dry), over 50 m long and 20 m wide, with flights of steps and subsidiary shrines, faces the front of the temple. A remarkable structure, despite the damage caused by weathering it is still possible to gain an impression of the excellence of the carving. On the west side of the tank a steep flight of steps leads up to the main entrance of the east *mandapa* through a beautifully carved *torana*, of which only the pillars now remain. The **sabha mandapa**, a pillared hall, is 15 sq m. Note the cusped arches which became such a striking feature of Mughal buildings 600 years later. The corbelled roof of this entry hall, which has been reconstructed, is a low stepped pyramid. Beautiful columns and magnificent carvings decorate the hall. The western part of the oblong temple contains the raised **inner sanctuary**. The upper storeys have been completely destroyed, though it clearly consisted of a low pyramidal roof in front of the tall *sikhara* (tower) over the sanctuary itself. Surya's image in the sanctuary (now missing) was once illuminated by the first rays of the rising sun at each solar equinox (proof of the mathematical and astronomical knowledge of the designers). Images of Surya and Agni are among the better preserved carvings on the external walls which also contain some erotic scenes. The interior walls were plain other than for niches to house images of Surya.

## Patan

Little visited, Patan has over 100 beautifully carved Jain temples and many attractive traditionally carved wooden houses. It remains a centre for fine textiles, particularly silk *patola* saris produced by the characteristic *ikat* technique which involves tie-dyeing the warp threads before weaving to create designs on the finished fabrics. Only three extended families (at Salvivad and Fatipal Gate) can be seen at work on the highly prized double *ikat* weaving where both the warp and the weft threads are tie-dyed before being set on traditional looms – only to be found in Indonesia and Japan outside India. It takes three to six months to weave a sari, hence each sells at least Rs 50,000, samples are Rs 1,000. Patan is 35 km northwest of Mehsana and can be reached either by bus or train. Buses also run from Modhera.

The spectacular **Rani ki Vav** (late 11th century) ⓘ *Rs 200 foreigners; video camera Rs 150*, named after a Solanki queen, is one of the largest stepwells in India with superb carvings on seven storeys. Flights of steps lead down to the water level, lined by stringcourses of sculptured voluptuous women, Vishnu avatars and goddesses. The **Sahasralinga Talao** is a cluster of Solanki period (11th-12th century) shrines facing a small lake. Excavations are in progress. Site staff can be over-obtrusive.

## Vadnagar

The town, 40 km northeast of Mehsana, has the finest example of the *torana* arches that characterise North Gujarat. Beautiful sculptures decorate two of the original four 12th-century arched gateways on *kirti stambha* pillars. The Solanki period city gates are beautifully sculpted, the best being near the lake. The impressive 17th-century **Haktesvar temple**, the most important Siva temple in Gujarat, has fine carvings, erotic sculpture and a silver shrine. Tana-Riri, two poetess-singers from Vadnagar, are said to have saved Tansen from the burning effects of the Deepak Raga (Song of Fire) by singing the Maldaar Raga (Song of Rain). Akbar invited the sisters to sing in his court, but rather than refuse to sing for a Muslim emperor (which was against their custom) they immolated themselves. Their shrine can be seen at Vadnagar.



## Taranga

Named after Tara Devi, Taranga, 55 km northeast of Mehsana by bus, has a wonderful complex of well preserved, if somewhat over-restored, 12th-century Jain temples surrounded by spectacular hills. The large central sandstone temple to Adinatha is beautifully carved with sensual dancing figures, Hindu deities and Jain *Tirthankaras*. Inside is a bejewelled central statue carved out of a single piece of alabaster. There is a scenic trek from the main Adinath temple, passing some dramatic rock formations, to the hilltop Shilp Temple where one of the Jain saints meditated. Panthers have been sighted near the temple complex.

## Ambaji

Close to the Rajasthan border, en route to Mount Abu, Ambaji is known for its marble mines. You can see marble artisans at work at this temple town (and at Khedbrahma nearby) where *Bhadra Purnima* fair is held, with processions of flag bearing pilgrims followed by musicians and dancers. A picturesque rope-way goes to Gabbar hill, a holy pilgrimage for Hindus (Rs 40). Ahmadabad-Mt Abu buses stop at Ambaji.

The five 11th- and 12th-century Jain temples just east of Ambaji at **Kumbhariya** ⓘ *0630-1930; Aarti worship 0900-0930 and 1900, tea canteen, Jain thalis for Rs 12*, are worth visiting for their exquisite marble carvings, be sure to see the second temple; the main one has been largely rebuilt. Catch a jeep from Ambaji bus stand.

## Danta

Enroute from Taranga to Ambaji, the princely state of Danta was known for its cavalry. It is dominated by the medieval Parmara Rajput fort. The jungles and rocky hills harbour panther, nilgai and four-horned antelopes, and there is extensive birdlife. To explore, bicycles can be hired from in the village.

## Poshina

The small 15th-century Poshina fort, 45 km south of Abu Road, stands at the confluence of two holy rivers (Sai and Panhari) with views over the hills. It was the capital of the North Gujarat branch of Vaghela Rajputs. There are ancient Jain and Siva temples nearby as well as tribal villages where you can watch arrowmaking, basketwork, silversmiths and potters. The area is home to Bhils, colourful Garasias and Rabaris who herd camels, cattle and goats. The busy and interesting market centre is well worth stopping at; the last stretch of the approach road is very poor.

Ahmadabad-Ambaji buses stop at Kheroj from where it is possible to get shared jeeps to Poshina (12 km). **Chitra Vichitra Fair** is held a fortnight after **Holi** at **Gunbakhari,** 8 km away. It is attended by Bhils, Garasias and Rabaris (some of whom are now abandoning their traditional *dhotis* and turbans). The fair is very colourful with much revelry, dancing and singing, food stalls etc. Matchmaking is often followed by elopements. **Florican Tours** ⓣ *T079 2550 6590*, can arrange. Try staying in a tent (Gujarat Tourism) during fair. Delicious flavoured *lassi* near the village entrance but ask to prepare with your own mineral water.



### Palanpur and Balaram

The *maqbara* with fine mausolea in the old Nawabi capital of Palanpur stands rather neglected. The palace is now the court; look in to see the fabulous ceiling paintings and sandalwood carvings. The 1915 Kirti Stambha has the 700-year-long history of the Nawabs of Palanpur inscribed on it. Nearby Balaram has one of the best kept palace hotels in Gujarat, 3 km off the highway and 14 km north of Palanpur. About 20 km from there, the **Jessore Bear Sanctuary** in the Aravallis has sloth bear (occasionally spotted), panther, nilgai, sambhar, four-horned antelope etc, but these are best seen by climbing Jessore hill.



## South of Ahmadabad

### Vautha

Here the **Vautha Mela**, starting at **Kartik Purnima**, is held at the confluence of Sabarmati and Vatrak rivers, some 46 km south of Ahmadabad. Less colourful than Pushkar fair it is also far less touristy. About 4,000 donkeys, painted in vivid colours, and over 2,000 camels are traded. There is a great atmosphere on the river banks early in the morning, and in addition to the haggling over animals there are craft sales. Gujarat Tourism puts up twin bedded tents with catering.

### Nalsarovar Bird Sanctuary

The sanctuary, 65 km southwest of Ahmadabad, is noted for waterbirds including migratory ducks, flamingos and geese. The lake and the Surendranagar Reservoirs were declared a bird sanctuary in 1969. Uniquely in Saurashtra, Nalsarovar is surrounded by reed beds and marshes though the lake often dries out before the rains. Bharwad and Jat herdsmen and their water buffaloes live on the reed islands – you can get hot millet buttered chapatis and chutney with sweet tea or lassi from some shacks. Padhar fisherfolk who live around the lake are good artisans. **Forest Dept Bungalows** have two or three simple rooms and views of lake. The best time to visit is between November and February.

### Lothal 'Mound of the dead'

ⓘ *Closed on Fri.*

*❢ There is no shade and no proper drinks outlet. Carry bottled water.*

Southeast of Moenjodaro, 720 km as the crow flies, Lothal has some of the most substantial remains of the Harappan culture in India dating from circa 2500-1700 BC. Once a port sandwiched between the Sabarmati River and the Bhogavo River, it is now 10 km inland from the Gulf of Khambhat on a flat, often desolate looking plain. Thorn scrub and parched soils surround the site, and even in February a hot desiccating wind picks up flurries of dust. Lothal's location and function as a port have led most authorities to argue that it was settled by Harappan trading communities who came by sea from the mouths of the Indus. Others suggest that the traders came by an overland route. The site is surrounded by a mud-brick embankment 300 m north-south and 400 m east-west. Unlike the defensive walls at Harappa and Moenjodaro, the wall at Lothal enclosed the workers' area as well as the citadel. The presence of a dry dock and a warehouse further distinguish it from other major Harappan sites. Some visitors have found that the recent restoration work has made the walls look all too modern.

The massive excavated **dry dock** runs along the east wall of the city. A 12-m wide gap in the north side is believed to have been the entrance by which boats came into the dock, while a spillway over the south wall allowed excess water to overflow. The city wall at this point may have been a wharf for unloading. Excavations of the warehouse suggest that trade was the basis of Lothal's existence. The building at the southwest corner of the wharf had a high platform made of cubical mud-brick blocks, the gaps between them allowing ventilation. Over 65 Indus Valley seals discovered here show pictures of packing material, bamboo or rope, suggestive of trade; one from Bahrain is evidence of overseas trade. Excavations show a **planned city** in a grid pattern, with an underground drainage system, wells, brick houses with baths and fireplaces. The raised brick platform to the southeast may have been a kiln where seals and plaques were baked. Objects found include painted pottery, terracotta toys, ivory, shell, semi-precious stone items, bangles and even necklaces made of tiny beads of gold. Rice and millet were clearly in use, and there is some evidence that horses had been domesticated. The cemetery to the northwest had large funerary vessels indicating pit burials.



## Wadhwan

Wadhwan, northwest of Limbdi, was a princely state of the Jhalas, a Rajput clan. The fortified old township has plenty of interesting architecture including two old stepwells with attractive carvings, some fine 11th- to 16th century temples. It is an ideal place to watch and shop for *bandhani*, wood and stone carving, silver and brass work, and textiles.

The opulent 19th-century **Raj Mahal** (*Bal Vilas*) occupied by the royal family, surrounded by parkland, has a grand Durbar hall with chandeliers, frescoes, carved furniture, crystal and velvet curtains, and a Sheesh Mahal library and billiard room. The vast landscaped gardens have tennis courts, lily ponds and fountains. Maharajah Chaitanya Dev is a keen restorer of classic cars and has a personal vintage car collection.

## Sleeping

**Gandhinagar** *p1242*

**B Haveli**, Sector 11, opposite Sachivalaya, T079 2322 405124. 84 rooms, restaurants, exchange, car hire, free airport transfer, day rates available, rooms below standard.

**F Pathik Ashram**, Govt, Sector 11.

**F Youth Hostel**, Sector 16, T079 2322 2364. 2 rooms, 42 beds in 6-bed and 8-bed dorms, very good, no reservations.

**Mehsana** *p1243*

**A-C Water World Resort**, 25 mins' drive out of town, T02762 282351, www.waterworldresort.com. A/c cottages, modern, Mughal garden with a/c 'royal tents', vegetarian restaurant, wine shop, wave pool and sports complex, artificial lake.

**D-E Natraj**, 1 km from Bus Stand. 12 rooms ranging from basic dorm to comfortable a/c with bath, very good veg restaurant.

**D-E Vijay Guest House**, NH8, T02762-220041, near bus stop, on left going north. Good clean rooms with bath, some a/c, quieter at rear, friendly staff but no English spoken.

**E Apsara**, Janta Supermarket, opposite bus station, T02762-220027. Reasonable rooms, some a/c, *thali* meals.

**F Railway Retiring Rooms**, decent rooms (Rs 40) with bath.

**Patan** *p1243*

**E-F Neerav**, near bus and rly station. Rooms with bath (bucket hot water and room service, mornings only), some a/c with TV, clean, Gujarati *thali* and North Indian food, best but noisy area.

**F Navjivan**, GIDC Char Rasta. Rooms with bath (hot water), veg restaurant (Gujarati *thali* Rs 25-40; North Indian Rs 45-60).

**F Toran Tourist Bungalow**, Gujarat Tourism, 2 simple rooms, basic cafeteria, convenient for stepwell.

**Taranga** *p1244*
**B Bhavani Villa**, T02749 278705, on a hilltop, tourists welcomed like family guests. 4 new a/c rooms facing the hills, 2 private guest rooms in colonial period mansion, delicious Rajput meals, friendly hosts, great for nature lovers, game drives, riding (Rs 250 per hr), very good horse safaris (Rs 5000 per person).

**Poshina** *p1244*
**B Darbargarh** (Heritage Hotel), in 17th-century wing of the fort complex. Pleasant with open courtyards and hill views, old world charm, now renovated with antiques, Rajasthani miniatures and rare Tanjore paintings (rather haphazardly), 15 comfortable, air-cooled rooms (some complaints about cleanliness), spicy Indian meals, camel rides, folk entertainment, friendly hosts, owner is very knowledgeable about local tribes, crafts etc, good village safaris, advance reservations thorough Florican Tours, T079 2550 6590.

**Balaram** *p1245*
**A Balaram Palace Resort**, Chitrasani, splendid riverside location surrounded by hills. Impeccably restored 1930s palace, 17 a/c rooms (interiors too modern and characterless for some), choose between 4 colonial rooms with old fireplaces (some windowless) and rooms upstairs with views; Nawab Suite has huge arched windows, excellent terrace restaurants, lovely formal Nawabi garden, fountains, period swimming pool fed by natural cascading spring, good gym, bike hire. Recommended. Contact T079 26582191, bprhot@ad1.vsnl.net.in.

**Balasinore**
**A-B Balasinore Garden Palace**, 45 km from Kheda , T02690 262008. 6 refurbished rooms in an early 20th-century building, delicious Mughlai meals, one of few Nawab-family run heritage hotels, pleasant orchard garden, personal attention, tours of 650-million year old dinosaur site and tribal villages.

## Eating

**Gandhinagar** *p1242*
Sector 21 has street-side vendors who offer good snacks. Ask for the 'Bhatiar' couple who make *bajra ka rotla* (millet *chapatis*) and chicken curry, meat samosas and daal in a little shack, not too far from Akshardham.
TT **Chills, Thrills & Spills**, Sector-21 Shopping Centre. Pizzas, sandwiches, veg *thalis*.
TT **Premawati**, Akshardham Complex. Veg Gujarati food, Indian snacks, lime tea and delicious ice creams.
TT **Regent**, does good Indian.
TT **Relief**, excellent Indian and Continental.
TT **Torana**, Sector-28. Punjabi, South Indian snacks, in a garden.

**Mehsana** *p1243*
T **Kudarat**, near **Vijay** (Hindi sign with a triangular tree symbol), best of the highway cafés. South Indian and Punjabi. Open-air, so you may have a monkey for company.
T **Sher-e-Punjab**, by a petrol station, east of NH8, does good omelettes.

**Ambaji** *p1244*
T **Hotel Ambaji International**, highly recommended veg *thalis*.

## Transport

**Gandhinagar** *p1242*
Train and buses to Ahmadabad take 1 hr. ST Bus Station, Sector 11.

**Mehsana** *p1243*
Buses to **Ahmadabad** on a very poor road (2½ hrs) and **Patan**. To **Modhera**, buses leave from ST Bus Stand, ¾ hr, Rs 8; or bus from NH8/SH41 junction (Modhera Rd) but often full. Last return from Modhera, 1730 (sometimes delayed by up to 2 hrs). **Rajasthan** and **Delhi** bound trains from Ahmadabad stop at Mehsana.

**Palanpur** *p1245*
Ahmadabad and Delhi trains stop here. Direct buses go to **Mount Abu**; **Ambaji** (also share jeeps, Rs 20); **Poshina** through attractive countryside and tribal areas, 1200 (1 hr), Rs 7.

*For an explanation of the sleeping and eating price codes used in this guide, see inside the front cover. Other relevant information is found in Essentials pages 56-61.*

**Nalsarovar Bird Sanctuary** *p1245*
Direct buses from Ahmadabad (0700, 1500) take 2 hrs.

**Lothal** *p1245*
Trains and buses from Ahmadabad or Bhavnagar go close to Lothal. It can be a long, hard day, with not much to see at the end of it. Hiring a taxi or motorbike makes it easier.

**Bus**
There are a few buses from **Ahmadabad**; change at Dholka. Luxury and State buses can drop you at **Gundi** railway crossing; from there *chhakras* charge Rs 5 each for the drop to Lothal. Get back on the highway to get a bus back to Ahmadabad or Bhavnagar. Ideally hire a car from Ahmadabad (Rs 800-1000 ) for the 80 km drive to Lothal; travel 52 km to Bagodra on the NH8A, then turn left on SH1 towards Bhavnagar (73 km), go across the level crossing and immediately turn left. Lothal is signposted as 7 km (appalling section). From Bhavnagar follow the SH1 via Vallabhipur and Barwala. The turn off is 127 km from Bhavnagar.

**Train**
Some trains from Ahmadabad to Bhavnagar stop at **Lothal-Burkhi station**; shared motorbike trailers (*chhagras* or *chhakras*) drop you at Lothal or Utelia for a few rupees.



# Vadodara and the Old Forts

➔ *Colour map 2, grids C3/4.*

*The route south from Ahmadabad crosses the fertile alluvial plains of the Sabarmati and Mahi rivers before entering the Konkan region. The plains gradually give way south to broken hills while inland, parallel ridges reach between 500-600 m where strategically placed atmospheric old forts were sited. Rice dominates agriculture further south, but ragi (finger millet) and pulses are also common. A pleasant day trip by car from Vadodara could include the forts of Champaner in the foothills, Pawagadh on a hilltop and Dabhoi Fort.* ⏩ *For Sleeping, Eating and other listings, see pages 1254-1257.*

## Vadodara ➔ *Phone code: 0265. Colour map 2, C3. Population: 1.3 mn.*

Formerly Baroda, Vadodara was the capital of one of the most powerful princely states. It is now a rapidly expanding industrial town, yet the older part is pleasant and interesting to wander through. The Gaekwad stood high in the order of precedence among rulers, being one of only five to receive a 21-gun salute. He was reputedly so rich that he had a carpet woven of diamonds and pearls, and cannons cast in gold.

### Ins and outs

**Getting there** The airport, with flights from Ahmadabad, Delhi and Mumbai, is 9 km away with taxis (Rs 250, a/c Rs 350) and auto-rickshaws to town. Better hotels offer free airport transfer. Railway and the long-distance bus stations are to the northwest of town, close to hotels. From the railway station, walk under the bridge; then for five minutes. ⏩ *See Transport, page 1256, for further details.*
**Getting around** The local bus station is just opposite the railway station. There are taxis and autos to take you to the town centre and the sights.

### Sights

Much of the city's treasures, which can be seen in the palaces and museums reflect the wealth of the Gaekwads, a dynasty established by the powerful 18th-century Maratha General, Damaji. See page 1076.

The **Laxmi Vilas Palace** (1880-1890) ⓘ *Rs 100 (no photography)*, was built by RH Chisholm. The magnificent palace is somewhat neglected but the interiors are decorated with Venetian mosaic, Italian marble, porcelain, antique furniture, European stained glass, sculptures, a royal armoury etc. Nearby is the **Naulakhi Well**, a well-preserved *baoli* which has galleried levels.

Just to the south of the Palace is the **Maharajah Fateh Singh Museum** ⓘ *Nehru Rd, Laxmi Vilas Palace, 1000-1730 (1600-1900 Apr-Jun), closed Mon, Rs 15, guidebook Rs 35*, has a good display of royal state collection of European art (copies of some Murillo, Titian, Raphael, Rubens), a prized collection of paintings by the 19th-century Indian artist Raja Ravi Verma, and Chinese and Japanese statuary and porcelain, European porcelain. Further south, beyond the railway, the **Pratap Vilas** (circa 1910, known as Lalbagh Palace), with a baroque façade, is now the Railway Staff College; permission from Principal needed to visit the small rail museum. The beautiful **Shiv Mahal Palace**, near the race course, is being renovated.

In the town centre, the **Kirti Mandir** (early 20th century), the Gaekwad *samadhi* (memorial ground) has murals by Nandlal Bose and marble busts. The **Kothi** Building (late 19th century) is to the west and now houses the Secretariat. Across the road is the **Nyaya** (Law) **Mandir** (1896), not a temple but the High Court, in Mughal and Gothic styles. The **Jama Masjid** is next door.

Further along the road away from the lake is the **Mandvi** (1736), a Muslim Pavilion and the **Nazar Bagh Palace** (1721), which has a Shish Mahal (mirror palace), and is rather dilapidated now. The **College of Fine Art** is an institute of national renown.

Half-way down Raj Mahal Road are the remarkable buildings of the Khanderao Market. One of the old painted **havelis**, the four-storey Tambekarwada, residence of the Diwan of Vadodara (1849-1854), acquired by the Archaeological Survey, is well worth visiting. It is between Raopura Road and Dandia Bazar; rickshaw-wallahs appear not to know it so ask near the GPO and walk two minutes.

**Sayaji Bagh** is an extensive park, popular for evening strolls. **Kamnati Bagh** is also beautiful. There is a fairly interesting zoo and a planetarium. **Maharajah Sayajirao Museum** (Vadodara Museum) and **Art Gallery** ⓘ *in the Victoria Diamond*

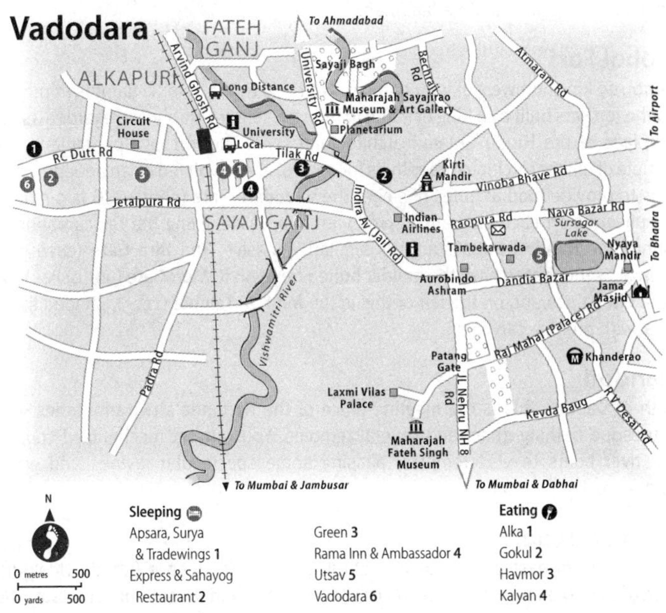


**Sleeping**
Apsara, Surya & Tradewings 1
Express & Sahayog Restaurant 2
Green 3
Rama Inn & Ambassador 4
Utsav 5
Vadodara 6

**Eating**
Alka 1
Gokul 2
Havmor 3
Kalyan 4

 *Jubilee Institute, Sayaji Bagh, 1000-1700, Sat 1000-1645*, designed by RF Chisholm. Archaeology, art, ethnology and ancient Jain sculptures; also Industrial arts, Mughal miniatures and European paintings. Nearby is the **Archaeology and Ancient History** ⓘ *MS University, 1400-1700, closed Sun and public holidays*. It contains Buddhist antiquities, archaeological finds from North Gujarat, and good pre-history of Gujarat.



# Around Vadodara

## Champaner

Champaner, 47 km northeast of Vadodara, stands at 880 m in the Girnar Hills. The fortress was the old capital of the local Rajputs who lost it in 1484 to Mahmud Beghara, who renamed it Muhammadabad and took 23 years to build his new city. In his campaign in Gujarat, the Mughal Emperor Humayun personally led a small team that scaled the walls of the city using iron spikes and then let the rest of the army in through the main gate. With the collapse of the Empire, Champaner passed to the Marathas.

In the **old city**, the remains of many 15th- and 16th-century mosques and palaces show a blend of Islamic and Jain traditions, a unique style encouraged by Champaner's relative isolation. The **Jami Masjid** (1523), a large, richly ornamented mosque is exemplary of the Gujarati style with interesting features such as oriel windows. Few older structures of the Chauhan Rajputs remain – **Patai Rawal** palace, the domed granary Makai Kota, the 11th- and 12th-century Lakulisha temple and some old wells.

Some 4 km southwest of Champaner **Pawagadh Fort** ⓘ *US$2*, dominates the skyline and is visible for miles around. According to myth Pavagadh was believed to have been part of the Himalaya carried off by the monkey god Hanuman. Occupying a large area, it rises in three stages; the ruined fort, the palace and middle fort, and finally the upper fort with Jain and Hindu temples, which are important places of pilgrimage. Parts of the massive walls still stand. The ascent is steep and passes several ruins including the Buria Darwaza (Gate), and the Champavati Mahal, a three-storey summer pavilion. The temple at the summit had its spire replaced by a shrine to the Muslim saint Sadan Shah.

## Dabhoi Fort

Dabhoi, 29 km southwest of Vadodara, was fortified by the Solanki Rajputs from 1100 and the fort was built by a King of Patan in the 13th century. Dabhoi is regarded as the birthplace of the Hindu Gujarati architectural style. The fort is a particularly fine example of military architecture with its four gates, a reservoir fed by an aqueduct and farms to provide food at times of siege. The **Vadodara Gate** (northwest) is 9-m high with pilasters on each side and carved with images depicting the reincarnation of Vishnu. The **Nandod Gate** (south) is similarly massive. The **Hira Gate** (east) with carvings, is thought to have the builder buried beneath it. **Mori Gate** (north) lies next to the old palace and on the left of this is the **Ma Kali Temple** (1225), shaped like a cross, with profuse carvings.

## Chandod

South of Dabhoi, this is the meeting place of the Narmada's two tributaries with picturesque bathing ghats and several temples. You can get mechanized country style river boats to visit temples, passing some spectacular ravines and water sculpted rocks.

## Chhota Udepur

Around 100 km east of Vadodara, picturesque Chhota Udepur (Chotta Udaipur), centred around a lake, was once the capital of a Chauhan Rajput princely state. The

### The oldest narrow gauge!

The Vadodara-Dabhoi-Chandod line is the world's oldest surviving narrow gauge railway. The 19th-century line was commissioned for bullock drawn locomotives in 1863. Later turned to steam, it is now run by a diesel engine. There are some vintage locomotives including steam engines in the Dabhoi station yard dating back to 1902. Take a ride on this line from Vadodara to Chandod via Dabhoi for the experience!

town has palaces and numerous colonial period buildings. It is the capital of a colourful tribal district where Bhils and Ratwas live in secluded hamlets of a handful of mud huts each. The huts are decorated with wall paintings called *pithoras* (tigers and other animals are favourite subjects) and protected from evil spirits by small terracotta devotionai figures.

There are colourful weekly tribal *haats* or **markets** in nearby villages which offer an insight into tribal arts, crafts and culture. (The one in town is held by the lake on Saturday.) The government-run tribal **museum** in Diwan Bungalow has interesting examples of *pithoras*, folk costumes, artefacts, aboriginal weapons and handicrafts, but the labelling is in Gujarati and the attendant knows little English. West of Chhota Udepur is the tribal institute at Tejgadh, which is working to document aboriginal languages and culture in the entire country.

The imposing Rajput **Kusum Vilas** palace, set in 40 acre grounds, though Mughal in architectural style, has some impressive European decorative features inside. The large Mughal-style gardens have fountains, ponds, European marble statuary, a colonnaded art deco swimming pool and tennis courts, while the garages have old cars and interesting carriages.

**Dasara Fair** here is famous. Other fairs held around **Holi** (March/April) in nearby villages like Kawant, with dancing, music, gymnastics and craft stalls, offer a glimpse of tribal life. **Bhagwati** is popular for Gujarati *thalis*.

## Surat and around

→ *Phone code: 0261. Colour map 5, A3. Population: 2.434 mn.*

Situated on the banks of the Tapti River, Surat was already an important trading centre by 1600 but went into decline in the 19th century. Today it is again a rapidly growing industrial and commercial city, but despite its historic significance there is nothing to attract a tourist.

The **museum** ⓘ *Wed-Sat 1045-1345, 1445-1745; Tue, Sun 1445-1745, Mon closed, photography prohibited*, near the castle, has an interesting collection of textiles, furniture, paintings, stamps, coins and ceramics. The tombs in the Dutch, English and Armenian **cemeteries**, however, are rather neglected and overgrown though some, like the Aungier and Oxinden mausolea, are imposing. The strong Muslim influence is evident in several 16th- and 17th-century mosques. There are two Parsi **Fire Temples** (1823) and the triple-domed Swami Narayan **Temple**. The Chintamani Jain temple, dating from the 15th century, has some fine wood carvings.

**Navsari**, 39 km from Surat, has a historic Parsi fire temple which is one of the most important Zoroastrian pilgrim places in India. You cannot enter the temple but the building and garden are worth seeing from outside. **Dandi**, 13 km from Navsari, where Gandhiji ended his Salt March from Ahmadabad to the south Gujarat coast, and picked up a handful of salt, see page 1236. A monument marks the spot and a photo gallery depicts events in Gandhi's life. **Karadi**, nearby, is where Gandhi was arrested after the Dandi March; his hut is still preserved. There is a small Gandhi

 Museum. Sleeping at the **Guest House**, very peaceful and friendly; contact '*Om Shanti*', Matwad (English spoken).

# Saputara → *Phone code: 02631. Colour map 5, grid A3. Altitude: 50-1083 m.*

Saputara, a pleasant hill resort created after independence in the Sahayadri hills, is Gujarat's only hill station. Set in a tribal region, there is an attractive lake and forests nearby. It is a relaxing place to enjoy walks, scenic places and folklore but it gets very crowded during weekends and holidays. » *For Sleeping, Eating and other listings, see pages 1254-1257.*

## Ins and outs

**Getting there** State buses run from Surat (135 km) and Nashik (Maharashtra, 80 km). Trains on the Mumbai-Ahmadabad line get you as far as Billimora (110 km), with buses to Saputara. » *See Transport, page 1257, for details.*
**Getting around** The resort is ideal for walking. Best season November to May.

## Sights

The name Saputara is derived from the snake deity which is worshipped here by the tribal people. The hub of activity at Saputara is the **lake** which has boating facilities and lake view eating places. The plateau is rather barren and not particularly appealing but there are some lovely walks around the hill resort. You could find attractive quartzite rocks, orchids and wild flowers on the trails.

Good views are to be had of the valley from Sunset Point, with a 10-minute ropeway service, and from Valley View Point which involves a strenuous 1.5-km climb. There are also some old Maratha hill forts which involve steep climbs – only recommended for serious trekkers. The Hatgadh fort offers superb views and a chance to see rock chats, martens and wolf snakes in cracks on the fort walls. Carry water.

The **Dangs** district comprises more than 300 villages with a population of over 150,000, more than 94% of them belonging to tribal communities. The Bhils, Kunbis, Warlis and Gamits depend on the forest for their livelihood, obtaining timber, honey and lac. They are known for their traditional musical instruments and vigorous dances performed wearing wooden masks. Most villages have a shrine to Wagha-Deva, the tiger God, sculpted on stone. The **Dangs Cultural and Ecological Museum**, with a stone serpent at the entrance, offers an insight into the tribal area and the natural history of the Dangs. There are interesting dioramas, folk costumes, tribal weaponry and musical instruments. The Artists' Village conducts workshops of bamboo crafts, *papier maché* and pottery.

## Excursion

**Dangs Darbar** held at Ahwa, 32 km north, is celebrated with a **tribal fair** around March/April. Tribal chieftains called Bhil Rajas and Kunbi Rajas, who still receive privy purses from the government, are honoured during this festival. For **Nag Panchami** tribal huts are decorated with paintings.

# Daman → *Phone code: 02636. Colour map 5, grid A3. Population: 35,700.*

Daman, on the coast, retains something of the atmosphere of its distinctive Portuguese inheritance which linked it both with Mediterranean Europe and Africa. A few people still use Portuguese in everyday speech. » *For Sleeping, Eating and other listings, see pages 1254-1257.*

## Ins and outs

**Getting there** The nearest railway station is at Vapi, 13 km southeast, on the Mumbai-Ahmadabad line. From there you can get taxis for transfer (Rs 20 entry fee) or walk about 600 m for a bus. Long-distance buses run from the major centres. They arrive at the main bus stand in Nani Daman. ▸▸ *See Transport, page 1257, for further details.*

**Getting around** The settlement north of the river, known as *Nani* (small) Daman, is where most of the accommodation is. To the south, *Moti* (large) Daman has a few colonial remains. Bicycle hire in Nani Daman bazar. Avoid the Indian holiday periods.

## History

The 380 sq km enclave of Daman, along with Diu and Goa, were Portuguese possessions until taken over by the Indian Government in 1961. Its association with Goa ceased when the latter became a 'State' in 1987. It is now a Union Territory with its own Pradesh Council. Daman developed at the mouth of the tidal estuary of the Daman Ganga River as a trading centre from 1531. Much of its early commerce was with the Portuguese territories in East Africa. Later (1817-1837), it was a link in the opium trade chain until this was broken by the British.

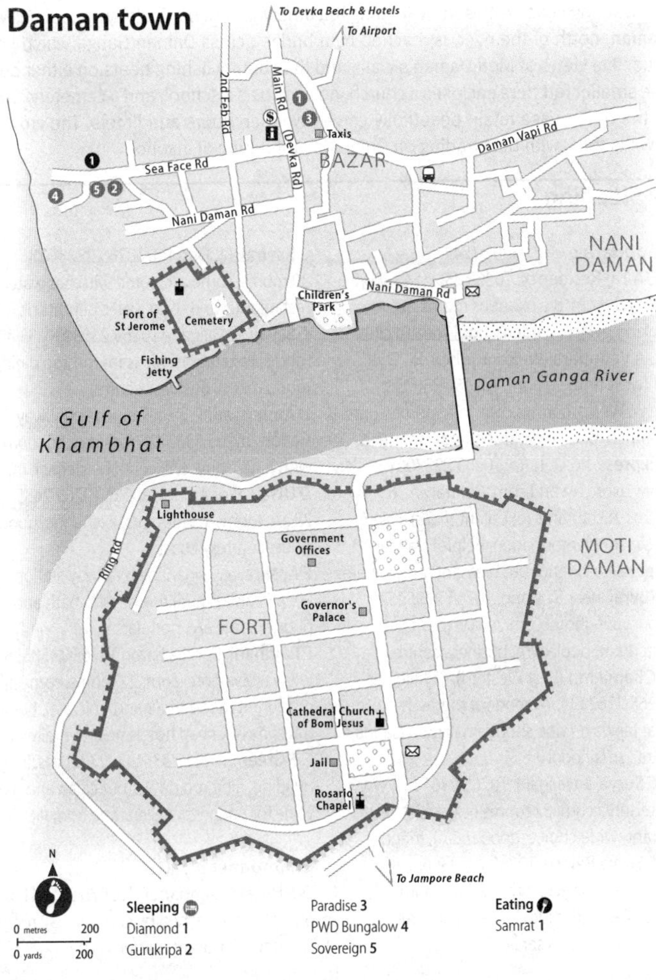

## Sights

**Moti Daman** retains something of the Portuguese atmosphere. The landward (east) side has a moat and drawbridge. The shaded main street inside the **fort** wall runs north-south between attractive arched gateways which have Portuguese arms carved on them. One shows a saint carrying a sword but the sculpted giants on the doorways are modelled on the guardian *dwarpalas* at entrances to Hindu temples.

The former **Governor's Palace** and other administrative buildings are along the main road while towards the south end is the old **Cathedral Church of Bom Jesus**, started in 1559 but consecrated in 1603. Large and airy when the main south door is open, the chief feature is its painted and gilt wooden altar reredos and pulpit. Much of the ornamentation, notably the gold crowns of the saints, have been stolen. On the west side of the small square is the old **jail**, still in use. To the south, against the fort wall, is the **Rosario Chapel**, formerly the Church of the Madre Jesus, with a unique feature in Indian churches of carved and gilded wooden panels illustrating stories from the life of Christ. These include the adoration of the Magi, Jesus teaching in the synagogue as a child, and Mary's ascension. The carved ceiling features charming cherubs.

**Jampore beach**, 3 km south of Moti Daman, is planted with casuarina groves and has a sandy beach with safe swimming but otherwise not particularly appealing. **Nani Daman**, north of the river, is reached by a bridge across Daman Ganga which gives attractive views of Moti Daman's walls and the country fishing boats on either bank. The smaller **fort** here encloses a church, now used as a school, and a cemetery. Some of the old houses retain beautifully carved wooden doors and lintels. The crowded town is thick with bars trading on Gujarat's prohibition of alcohol.

## Sleeping

### Vadodara *p1248, map p1249*

**AL-A Taj Residency**, T0265 235 4545, www.tajhotels.com. 84 luxurious rooms overlooking palace, gardens, pool , health club.

**AL-A Vadodara** (Welcomgroup), RC Dutt Rd (west from station), T0265 2330033, www. Welcomgroup.com. 134 rooms, some cramped, pool and gardens, golf arranged.

**B Express**, RC Dutt Rd, T0265 2337001, www.expressworld.com. Central a/c, 65 rooms, restaurants (excellent *thalis*), cake/sweet shop, information, helpful staff, unimpressive exterior but pleasant atmosphere.

**B Yuvraj**, near ST stand, T0265 2795252, www.yuvrajhotel.com. 45 a/c rooms, restaurant, pool, gym, business centre.

**B-C Rama Inn** (Best Western), Sayajiganj, T0265 2362831. 74 modern rooms, half a/c, near railway, 'wine shop', small gym (sauna extra), small pool.

**B-C Surya**, Sayajiganj, T0265 2361361, www.hotelsurya.com. 82 rooms (most a/c), restaurant (wide choice, good *thalis*), friendly.

**B-C Surya Palace**, T0265 2363366, www.suryapalace.com. 150 a/c rooms, extensive buffet lunch in a/c restaurant, efficient business services.

**C Kaviraj**, RC Dutt Rd, T0265 2323401. 30 rooms, some a/c, some with hot water, restaurant, wine shop issues permits til 1830.

**C Sayaji**, Sayajiganj, T0265 2363030. 53 a/c rooms, restaurants, pleasant rooftop dining (good *thalis*), business centre.

**D Ambassador**, Sayajiganj, near railway station, T0265 2362726. Good-sized rooms with bath, some a/c, could be cleaner, info.

**D Utsav**, Prof Amnekrao Rd, T0265 2435859. 28 a/c rooms, restaurants, exchange, good value, courtesy coach.

**E Apsara**, Sayajiganj near railway station, T0265 2362051. All rooms with bath and phone, some a/c, popular.

**E Rajdhani**, Dandia Bazar, T0265 24388383, www.revivalhotel.com. 22 rooms, some a/c, restaurant (good *thalis* and Chinese), helpful travel desk. Cheap hotels near the railway.

**E-F Green**, T0265 2336111. 22 rooms, in old building, a bit run down, but clean and good value for budget travellers, free from flies too.

### Champaner *p1250*

**D-E Hotel Champaner**, T02676 245641, is on a plateau reached by cable car, 32 rooms and dorm, pleasant garden.

**Chandod** *p1250*

**D-E Sarita Haveli**, 10 mins walk from the river, 19th-century, simple rooms, some a/c, dorm beds (Rs 150),library, period furniture, homecooked Indian food in courtyard, bullock cart tours of Juna Mandwa village, walking tours in the ravines, friendly, a bit shabby but good value.

**Chhota Udepur** *p1250*

**B-C Prem Bhuvan**. 7 rooms with bath (hot showers) in the renovated *Kusum Vilas* outhouse, modernized interiors (5 more are being renovated), pool, sports, set meals, (packages Rs 1500-2000).

**C Tribal Huts**, set beside a stream. Simple cottages designed along the lines of tribal huts but with aircooler and modern bathrooms, economical restaurant.

**Surat** *p1251*

**A Holiday Inn**, Athwa Lines, T0261 2226565, www.holidayinnsurat.com. 140 rooms, good restaurant (breakfast included), modern, attractive location, riverside pool, health club, efficient, courteous staff, the best.

**B-C Embassy**, Sufi Baug, near station, T0261 2443170, F2443173. 60 a/c rooms, some with tubs, popular restaurant (North Indian, Gujarati *thalis*), modern, pleasant.

**C Yuvraj**, opposite railway station, T0261 2413001, yuvraj_surat@hotmail.com. 55 rooms, central a/c, good restaurant, rooftop garden café, modern with business services.

**C-D Everyday Inn**, near Civil Court, T0261 2665154. 8 a/c doubles with bath (hot water) and TV in a house by the main road.

**F Vihar**, opposite the railway station, has rooftop views of the city, friendly and safe.

**Saputara** *p1252*

**B Patang**, T02631 237631, comfortable a/c rooms, the plushest in town.

**B-C Shavshanti Lake Resort**, Nageshwar Mahadev Rd, T02631 237292, www.sav shanti.com. 40 rooms, some a/c and overlooking lake, modern facilities.

**B-C Vaity**, Chimney Ropeway near Sunset Point, T02631 237210. Superbly situated on a hill with a panoramic views, clean, comfort- able rooms, lawn, friendly staff but 'unsophisticated' management, guides for surrounding excursions on weekdays.

**C-D Anando**, T02631 237202. 23 rooms with baths set on different levels facing the lake, vegetarian restaurant, good views.

**C-D Toran Hill Resort** (Gujarat Tourism), near Bus Stand T02631 237226, F237286. Cottages and log huts, dorms, restaurant (thalis Rs 25-35). Book at any Tourism office.

**D Chitrakut**, T02631 237221. Well situated with view of hills, average rooms with bath.

**E Shilpi**, T02631 237231. 10 rooms, clean and comfortable, attached baths, set back from main road towards the hills, restaurant (meals included). The restaurant **Vaity**, offers the widest choice including non-veg, and good views and outdoor seating.

**Daman** *p1252, map p1253*

There are plenty of cheap places on the seafront.

**B-C Cidade de Daman**, Devka Beach, T0260 2250590. 72 breezy, a/c rooms in impressive hotel, pool, popular for conferences.

**B-C Silver Sands**, Devka Beach, T0260 2254376, silversa@bom3. vsnl.net.in. 32 rooms, modern facilities, pool, bar, disco, across the road from the beach.

**C Dariya Darshan**, Devka Beach, T0260 2254476, dariyadarshan@vapi.wbbs.net. 38 modern a/c rooms, well fitted (TV, fridge), good outdoor restaurant (but piercingly loud Hindi film music heard throughout hotel), bar, pool, gym.

**C Miramar**, Devka Beach, T0260 2254971, www.miramarmirasol.com. 58 rooms (some a/c), some in cottages, sea-facing outdoor restaurant plays loud Indian film music, a/c indoors, discotheque, holiday camp style.

**C Princess Park**, Devka Beach, T0260 2254323, HPP@vapi.wbss.net. 27 rooms, some a/c, modern facilities, restaurant, good outlook facing the sea.

**C-D Gurukripa**, Nani Daman, T0260 225 5046, www.hotelgurukripa.com. 25 large a/c rooms with bath, good restaurant (wide choice of Punjabi, Gujarati, some Chinese), roof garden, car hire.

**C-D Sandy Resort**, Devka Beach, T/F 0260 2254644. 46 rooms, some a/c (best upstairs), restaurant, disco, pool, the quietest and most pleasant, across the road from the beach.

**D China Town**, Jampore Beach, T0260 2254920. 20 rooms (some a/c), few with sea view but short beds, shower and toilets could improve, friendly helpful staff, good restaurant serves Chinese/Indian food, bar does pinacoladas with fresh coconuts.

**D Sovereign**, T0260 2250236. 24 a/c rooms, clean, secure, friendly, veg restaurant (good Gujarati *thali*), chilled beer, travel desk.

**E Rahee Guest House** (PWD), Marwad Rd, between Nani Daman and Devka Beach, T0260 2254614. 15 rooms in neglected old building, some with bath and hot water, cheaper with Indian WCs.

**E Sanman**, Tin Batti, T0260 2255730. Rooms facing a busy main road, some a/c.

## Eating

**Vadodara** *p1248, map p1249*

**TTT Vadodara** has an extensive menu, polished service, plush, pricey, but try lunch buffet; alcohol against passport or permit.

**TT Goodies**, Race Course Rd. Parsee couple offer great baked goods.

**TT Kansa**, Sayajiganj. Gujarati and Rajasthani *thalis*. Traditional decor, turbaned waiters.

**TT Kwality**, Sayajiganj. Wide choice, good Italian and Peshwari dishes, garden seating.

**TT Oriental Spice**, Tilak Rd, Sayajiganj. Chinese.

**TT Pizza King**, Alkapuri. Italian, justly popular.

**TT Surya Palace** serves sumptous buffets. International, range of desserts, Rs 200.

**TT Volga**, Alankar Cinema, Sayajiganj. Good Mughlai kebabs and Chinese.

**T Gokul**, Kothi Char-rasta. Indian. Good Gujarati *thalis*, small place, large local clientele.

**T Sahayog**, 1st left past Express Hotel. Good South Indian *thalis* (Rs 45) and Punjabi.

**Surat** *p1251*

**TT Tex Palazzo**, wide choice, good *thalis* in revolving restaurant, views not spectacular.

**TT Yuvraj**. Rooftop garden café.

**T Saatvik** opposite railway station. Excellent, unlimited Gujarati *thalis*, Rs 45.

**Daman** *p1252, map p1253*

You can get fresh fish lunches/dinners at most hotels, also fish snacks at the bars.

**TT Duke**, Devka Beach. Parsi and *tandoori* food outdoors (also rooms to let in the old Parsi bungalow next door, Rs 400).

**TT Damanganga Lake Garden** on the Daman-Vapi Rd. Popular lake facing restaurant, with gardens and fountains. Unusual, though garish, bar has a Mughal theme with miniature paintings of royal drinking parties. Good atmosphere, ok food.

**TT Kadliya Lake Resort** is an island restaurant created by Daman Tourism, with lawns, gardens, cascades, fountains and boating facilities. The food upstairs is not bad and there is a bar and snacks downstairs by the lake. Service is slow and suffers an occasional scourge of flies and mosquitoes. Entry fee Rs 10, camera Rs 10, parking Rs 10.

**T Jampore Beach Resort**, cafeteria, bar, meals/snacks upstairs with view of sea, outdoor dining area, hammocks for relaxing.

**T Samrat**, Seaface Rd. Simple and clean, does excellent *thalis*.

## Festivals and events

**Vadodara** *p1248, map p1249*

**Ganesh Chaturthi** is celebrated by the large Maharashtrian population here.

**Navratri** is very colourful when local Garba, Dandia and Raas performances are held, and pilgrims head for Pawagadh.

## Shopping

**Vadodara** *p1248, map p1249*

Vadodara is a centre for **silver jewellery**. Shopping areas are Raopura, Mandvi, Teen Darwaza, National Plaza, Leheripura Mandir Bazar and Alkapuri Arcade.

**Khadi Bhandar**, Kothi Rd, for handlooms and local handicrafts.

## Activities and tours

**Vadodara** *p1248, map p1249*

**Swimming**

Lal Bagh and Sardar Bagh pools, Alkapuri; also at **Vadodara** and **Surya Palace** hotels.

**Tour operators**

**Prominent**, 7/12 Race Course Circle, T0265 2300120 Recommended for ticketing.

**Tradewings**, Sayajiganj, T0265 2327127, changes money (even on Sat).

## Transport

**Vadodara** *p1248, map p1249*

**Air**

**Indian Airlines**, Fatehgunj, T0265 2794747, 1000-1330, 1415-1700; Airport, T2466667, www.indianairlines.nic.in. **Mumbai**, **Delhi**. Jet Airways, 11 Panorama Complex, Alkapuri, T0265 2337051, Airport T0265 4823938.

**Bus**

**Local** From opposite the railway station. **Long distance** State Transport (SRTCs) to **Ujjain** (403 km), **Mumbai** (425 km), **Pune**, **Udaipur** and **Mount Abu**, among others. Central Bus Stand, opposite railway station, T0265 2327000. Reservations 0700-2200. Advance booking 0900-1300, 1330-1700.

**Taxi**

Tourist taxis from tourist office and travel agents. Non a/c Ambassador, Rs 6 per km, airport drop Rs 180, airport pick-up Rs 240, 80 km per 8 hrs, Rs 800-1000.

**Train**

Vadodara is on the Western Railways' Delhi-Mumbai broad gauge line. Sayajiganj Enquiries, T131. Reservations T135. 0800-2000 (2nd Class) and 0800-1800 (1st Class). **Ahmadabad**: many including *Gujarat Queen Exp, 9109*, 0813, 2¼ hrs; *Gujarat Exp, 9011*, 1303, 2¼ hrs; *Vadodara Ahmadabad Exp, 9129*, 1810, 2½ hrs. **Mumbai Central**: *Golden Temple Mail, 2904*, 2349, 6¼ hrs; *Kutch Exp, 9032*, 0508, 6½ hrs; *Paschim Exp, 2926*, 0852, 6¼ hrs. **New Delhi**: *Paschim Exp, 2925*, 1755, 16¾ hrs; *Rajdhani Exp, 2951*, 2153, 11 hrs. See narrow-gauge railway under Dabhoi. **Porbandar**: Mumbai *Porbandar Saurashtra Exp, 9215*, 1655, 14 hrs.

**Champaner** *p1250*

Shared jeeps and ST buses from Vadodara and Ahmadabad go to Machi where cable cars start for the ascent to the monuments on the hill; Rs 45 return (only hand baggage of 5 kg allowed), 0900-1300, 1400-1700.

**Surat** *p1251*

**Ahmadabad**: *Shatabdi Exp, 2009*, 0955, not Fri, 3½ hrs; *Gujarat Exp, 9011*, 1045, 4¾ hrs; **Mumbai Central**: *Kranti Rajdhani, 2954*, 0635, 3¾ hrs; *Paschim Exp, 2926*, 1055, 4¼ hrs. **New Delhi**: *Janata Exp, 9023*, 1325, 24 hrs; *Paschim Exp, 2925*, 1542, 19 hrs. **Porbandar**: *Mumbai Porbandar Saurashtra Exp, 9215*, 1408, 16½ hrs. **Rajkot** and **Jamnagar**: *Janata Exp, 9017*, 2132, 10½ hrs (Rajkot), 12½ hrs (Jamnagar).

**Saputara** *p1252*

From the NH8, the turn off for cars is at Chikhli to the west. Petrol is only available at Waghai (51 km northwest), and at a pump 40 km from Saputara, on the Nashik road. From Mumbai, there are private luxury buses (Modern Travels) on alternate days during the season. Train from Ahmadabad (400 km) or Mumbai (255 km) to **Billimora** and then local bus or taxi; or a narrow gauge train to **Waghai**.

**Daman** *p1252, map p1253*

For the **bus** stand: turn right out of Vapi station, walk 500 m along main road to a T-junction; the stand is nearby, on the left.

**Taxis** into Daman but shared with 8 others can be a squeeze (Rs 10 each); Rs 80 per taxi. By car, turn off the NH8 at Karmbeli between Bhilad and Vapi.

Not all **trains** stop at **Vapi** from Mumbai. *Gujarat Exp 9011*, 0545, 3 hrs; *Saurashtra Exp 9215*, 0745, 3½ hrs. From **Ahmadabad**: *Karnavati Exp 2934*, 0500, 5¼ hrs; *Shatabdi Exp*, 2010, 1435 (except Wed) 4¾ hrs.

## Directory

**Vadodara** *p1248, map p1249*

**Banks** Bank of Baroda, only Sayajiganj branch changes money; also Trade Wings on same street, fast and efficient. **Hospital** Sayaji Hospital, Sayajiganj; Maharani Jamunabai Hospital, Mandvi. **Post** GPO: Raopura. **Useful addresses** Forest office: T0265 2429748. Foreigners' Regional Registration Office: Collector's Office, Kothi Kacheri.

**Surat** *p1251*

**Banks** Exchange at State Bank of India, Chowk Rd. **Internet** Cyber Cafés, at Belgian Sq, Athwa Lines, Ambaji Rd and Bellevue Hotel, near the station.

**Daman** *p1252, map p1253*

**Banks** State Bank of India, Kabi Kabarda Rd. **Post** GPO: near bridge to Moti Daman.

# Saurashtra

*Around the coastal region of the Saurashtra peninsula are some of India's most remarkable religious sites, from Dwarka in the west to Palitana in the east, while the coastline itself is fringed with some attractive beaches which includes the former Portuguese territory of Diu. The historic town of Junagadh and the wildlife parks also draw visitors. Northern Saurashtra, with Rajkot at its centre, is one of the major groundnut growing regions of India. In January 2001, a massive earthquake left Limbdi, Halvad, Dhrangadra and Morvi severely damaged. Visitors should check before visiting these towns.* » *For Sleeping, Eating and other listings, see pages 1272-1282.*



## Rajkot → *Phone code: 0281. Colour map 2, grid C2. Population: 966,600.*

Rajkot is a bustling commercial city with a large number of shopping complexes and accompanying heavy road traffic but there are also some fine late 19th-century colonial buildings and institutions since the British Resident for the Western Indian States lived here. It has seen rapid industrialization in the last couple of decades, based especially in the processing of agricultural products.

Although there is an early Palaeolithic site at Rajkot, there is very little evidence of the settlement. Rajkot was the capital of the Jadejas, who ruled earlier from a place

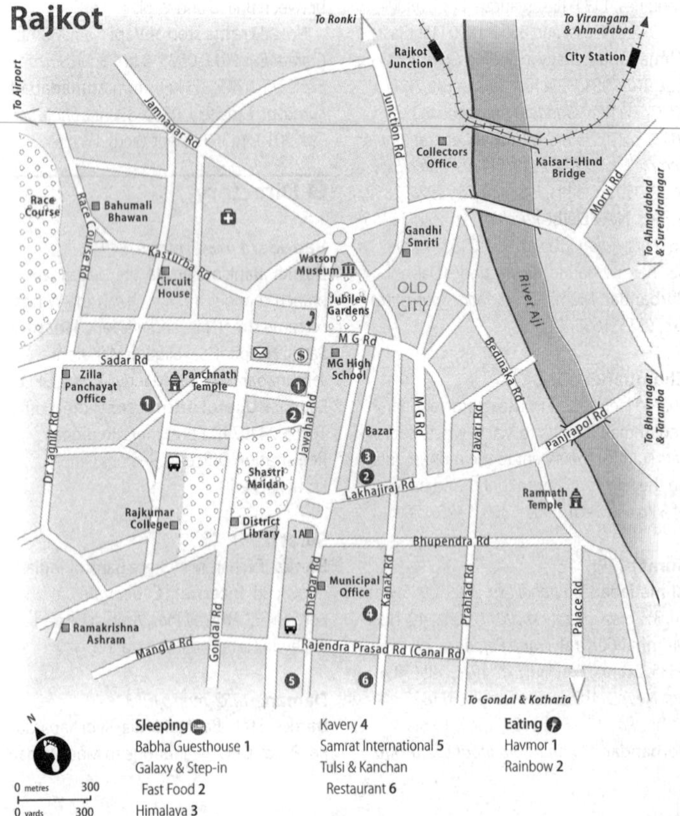

named Sardhar on the Rajkot-Bhavnagar road, and later set up this new city which became the headquarters of the British representatives in Saurashtra. The British impact can be seen in the impressive **Rajkumar College** in its vast grounds, a famous public school founded in 1870, and the richly endowed **Watson Museum** ⓘ *0900-1230, 1430-1800, closed Wed, 2nd and 4th Sat, each month, Rs 2, camera charges Rs 2 per photo, Jubilee Gardens*. It has exhibits from Indus Valley civilization, medieval sculpture, pottery and crafts, and colonial memorabilia. The **Memorial Institute** has the crumbling Lang Library in the Jubilee Gardens in the Old Civil Lines. Rajkot was the early home of Mahatma Gandhi. **Gandhi Smriti** (Kaba Gandhino Delo) is in Ghee Kanta Road, between MG Road and Lakahjiraj Road (rickshaw-wallahs know the way). **Gandhi Museum** ⓘ *Dharmandra Rd, 0900-1200, 1500-1800, closed Sun*, in the Gandhi family home (1880), contains photographs and a few personal effects. Descriptions are mainly in Hindi and Gujarati; guides speak no English. **Rashtriya Shala**, where Mahatma Gandhi went to school, is now trying to promote one of Gandhi's greatest ideals – handloom and handicrafts. Among the textiles being promoted is Patola style *ikat* silk weaving.



## Wankaner

On the bend of Machchu River, Wankaner (*wanka* – curve, *ner* – river), another capital of the Jhala Rajputs, was founded in 1605. The old ruler, Amar Sinhji was known for his flamboyant lifestyle but also introduced many wide-ranging reforms (in farmers' co-operatives, education, roads, tramways and internal security). He was also responsible for building the **Ranjitvilas Palace** (1907 extension to the 1880s British Residents' bungalow), visible for miles across the plains. It is built in a strange mix of styles (Venetian façades, a Dutch roof, *jarokha* balconies, a 'Mughal' pavilion, minarets, English clocktower etc) yet all is very well integrated. The garage has an interesting collection of models from the 1930s and 40s and a 1921 Silver Ghost, jeeps, wagons and old buggies. Kathiawadi horses in the stables. A part of the palace is now a **museum** brim full of royal memorabilia of a bygone lifestyle. There is an interesting stepwell with marble balustrade staircases, cool, subterranean chambers and marble statues of Vishnu and a fountain.

## Dhrangadra

The pretty little village town of Dhrangadra is the government Forest Department's headquarters for the **Little Rann of Kachchh Wild Ass Sanctuary** ⓘ *T02754-223016*. It was also the capital of a very progressive princely state, which had English and vernacular schools in 1855 and free education in the early 1900s. After it has recovered from the 2001 earthquake damage it should be possible to visit the Wild Ass Sanctuary from here. Full day jeep tour of Little Rann – wild asses, salt mining communities, bird sanctuary – is Rs 2,000 for two, including delicious home-cooked lunch.

## Bhavnagar → *Phone code: 0278. Colour map 5, grid A2. Population: 511,000.*

Bhavnagar was ruled by progressive rulers since it was founded in 1723. Surrounded by flat and richly cultivated land, it is now a major industrial town and cotton export centre, and is rapidly becoming one of India's most important ship-building ports. However, most of its character is preserved in the bazars of the Old City where you can pick your way through the crowded lanes amongst the old merchants' *havelis*.

The palace-like **Takhtsinghji Hospital** (1879-1883) was designed by Sir William Emerson. The 18th-century **Darbargadh** (Old Palace, extended 1894-1895), in the town centre, now has the State Bank but is scarcely visible in the incredibly overcrowded and dirty Darbargadh Bazar. **Barton Museum** (1895) ⓘ *0900-1300, 1400-1800, Rs 2*, in an impressive crescent-shaped building, has a collection of coins, carvings, geological and archaeological finds, farming implements, arms and armour, some handicrafts, miniature paintings and excellent bead and silk embroidery. The better known **Gandhi Smriti** ⓘ *0830-1230, 1500-1900, free*, is dedicated to Mahatma Gandhi (he was at university here; his old college is now an Ayurvedic education centre). Photographs portray his life and the freedom struggle. There are also letters and marksheets showing his scores at university. The unremarkable marble **Takhteshwar Temple** on a hillock has good views over the city and the distant coastline.

**Victoria Park**, 2 km from centre, is a former royal hunting preserve. Far removed from the image conveyed by its name of a manicured British city park, it has rolling scrub-forests and marshes rich in birdlife. Nilgai, hyena, jackal, jungle cat and monitor lizard can all be seen. A pleasant stroll from the Nilambagh Palace, it is a great place for walks. **Gaurishankar Lake**, a popular escape from the city with parks and steps along the embankments, is good for winter birdwatching when cranes, pelicans and ducks arrive. Plovers, terns etc nest on the islands.

## Velavadhar National Park

ⓘ *Foreigners US$5, still camera US$5; guide (some have no English), US$10 per trip, jeep US$25 per drive. Pay at Forest Range Office at park entrance.*

Some 10 km off the Bhavnagar-Vadodara Highway, the compact 36-sq km of flat grassland broken by dry open scrubland with some thorn forest was set up to protect the Indian blackbuck of which it has the largest population – about 1,000 within and another 1,000 which come in from the surrounding area. The Bhavnagar royal family came here for cheetah coursing, falconry and hunting, and also harvested grass for fodder for their cattle and horses. ▸▸ *For Sleeping, Eating and other listings, see pages 1272-1282.*

The blackbuck is the second largest of the antelopes and the fastest long distance runner of all animals. It can keep going at a steady 90 km per hour. The black and white dominant males sport spiral horns; the juvenile males are brown and white

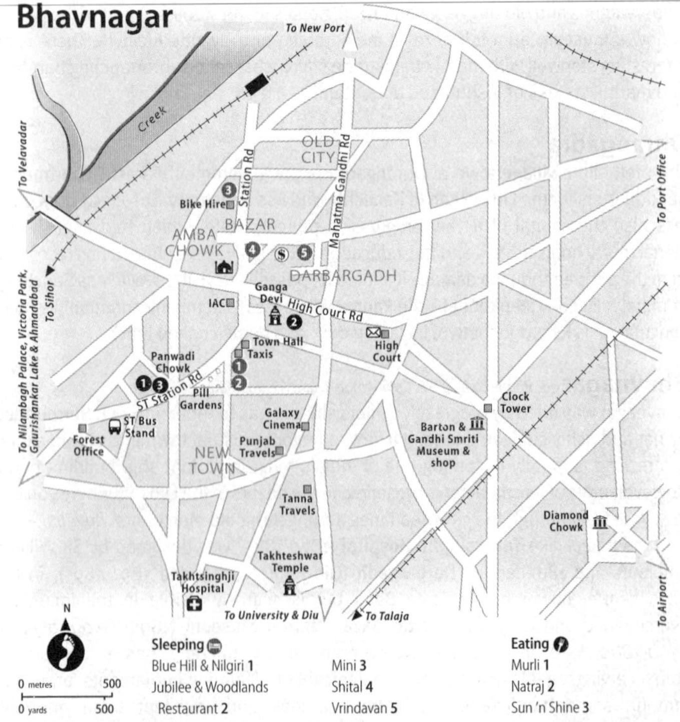

while the hornless females are brownish, with lighter parts. It is one of the most hunted animals in India, and so is an endangered species. Impressive males clash horns to establish territory and court females. Wolves, their prime predator, have been reduced to only two families, but they can still be seen. The park also contains a few sounders of wild boar in addition to 50-60 nilgai, usually seen near waterholes, jungle cat, which can be seen at dawn and dusk, and jackal. It has a rich birdlife with numerous birds of prey including the largest harrier roost in the world – some 1,500-2,000 of these light-bodied hawks gather here at sunset in November-December. During the monsoons the park is the best place in India for the lesser florican. In addition to the two rivers that border the park, there are three waterholes and three small pools which attract animals at midday.

## Sihor

Mid-way between Bhavnagar (27 km) and Palitana, the former Gohil Rajput capital has the 17th-century hilltop Darbargadh palace (now government offices). Though rather dilapidated, you can still see some intricate carved wooden balconies and pillars outside and 19th-century wall paintings inside. The Brahm **Kund**, 11th-12th century, 500 m to the south of the main road, about 2 km west of Sihor centre, is a deeply set stepped tank (now empty). It has around 100 sculpted images of deities in small niches, a few of which are still actively worshipped. There are also pillared galleries with rich carvings of musicians. In the village nearby brass utensils are produced as a cottage industry by rolling scrap from the Alang ship breaking yard and beating it into attractive water pots. Villagers are only too happy to show you around their workshops. The Khodiyar temple on the Bhavnagar-Sihor road has a pretty situation among hills.

## Palitana → *Phone code: 02848. Colour map 5, grid A2. Population: 51,900. Area: 13 sq km.*

Palitana is renowned for the extraordinary Jain temple complex on Shatrunjaya Hill which attracts domestic pilgrims as well as foreign visitors. No one is allowed to remain on the hill at night, but even during the day there is a peaceful serenity as you listen to the temple bells and pilgrims chanting in the City of the Gods. » *For Sleeping, Eating and other listings, see pages 1272-1282.*

Palitana was the capital of a small princely state founded by Shahji, a Gohel Rajput who belonged to the same clan as the Maharajah of Bhavnagar. The river bisects the town. The east bank has the hotels, eating places and shopping complexes and the bus and railway stations, while the west bank has the Willingdon Vegetable Market, vegetable vendors and some older Raj and royal buildings. The last ruler died leaving wives and sisters to fight over the royal palace and mansions which are now decaying but show signs of impressive architecture. The better houses are on Taleti Road. The busy little town is also known for diamond cutting and horse breeding. South African diamonds are imported from Belgium for cutting and polishing before being re-exported back to Belgium.

**The site** ⓘ *0700-1900, entry by free permit, camera Rs 40, visitors should wear appropriate, clean clothes, leather articles (even watch straps) and food or drink are not allowed in the temple area at the top of the hill, but can be left, along with shoes, at the entrance, take lots of water and a sun hat, arrive by dawn to join the pilgrims, and allow 2 hrs for the climb, and 4 to 5 hrs for the round trip, you can be carried up by a dhooli (string chair – Rs 500 return) but the hassle from aggressive touts in the early stages of the climb can be considerable (rates rise in summer, peaking during fairs and Mahavir Jayanti to Rs 1000)*, on **Shatrunjaya Hill**, is 3 km southwest. According to local tradition, Adinatha, the first Tirthankara, visited the hill several times and the first temple was erected by his son. Thereafter, the temple builders could not stop. Jains believe that Pundarika, the chief disciple of Adinatha, attained nirvana here.

Most of the temples are named after their founders and are mostly 16th century although the earliest may date from the 11th. It would appear that many others were destroyed by the Muslims in the 14th and 15th centuries, but later, when Jains obtained religious toleration they began rebuilding.

All the 863 temples are strung along the two ridges of the hill, with further temples in the hollow between, linking them. There are nine enclosures of fortifications (tuks) which provided defence. There are lovely views over the flat, cultivated black soils of the coastal plain, and on a clear day after the rains it is sometimes possible to see the Gulf of Khambat away to the east, and the Chamardi peak and the granite range of Sihor to the north.

There are two routes up the 600 m climb. The main route starts in the town of Palitana to the east of the hill, while a shorter and steeper route climbs up from the villages of Adpur to the west. Both are excellently made stepped paths. The main pilgrim route starts in Palitana. Over 3,500 steps, you will be told more by the *dhoolie* carriers at the bottom, lead up to the temples. There are two long flat stretches, but since some of the path is unshaded, even in winter it can get very hot.



Temples in this southern group include one of **Ramaji Gandharia** (16th century), and the **Bhulavani** (labyrinth, 18th century) which is a series of crypt-like chambers each surmounted with a dome. The **Hathiapol** (Elephant Gate, 19th century) faces southeast. The **Vimalavasi Tuk** occupies the west end of the south Ridge. In it is the **Adishvara Temple** (16th century) which dominates the site. It has a double-storey *mandapa* inside which is a large image of Rishabhanatha with crystal eyes and a gold crown of jewels. The **Vallabhai Temple** (19th century) with its finely clustered spires and the large **Motisah Temple** (1836) occupy the middle ground between the ridges.

The **Khartaravasi Tuk** is the largest and highest temple complex, stretched out along the northern Ridge and includes the **Adinatha Temple** (16th century). There are quadruple *Tirthankara* images inside the sanctuary.

If you wish to take the track down to Adpur turn left out of the complex entrance courtyard where you leave your shoes. Follow the sign to Gheti Pag gate.

## Alang

The beach at Alang has turned into the world's largest scrapyard for dead ships, the industry yielding rich pickings from the sale of salvaged metal (bronze, copper) and the complete range of ship's fittings from portholes to furniture, diesel engines and lifeboats. Alang village, 50 km south of Bhavnagar, has developed this surprising specialization because of the unusual nature of its tides. The twice monthly high tides are exceptional, reputedly the second highest in the world, lifting ships so that they can be beached well on shore, out of reach of the sea for the next two weeks. During this period the breakers move in unhindered. Labourers' 'huts' line the coast road though many workers commute from Bhavnagar.

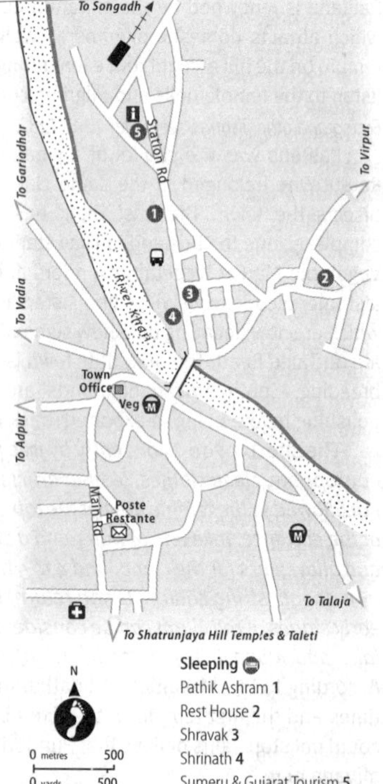

Even though entry to Alang port may not be available, the last few kilometres to the port are lined with the yards of dealers specialising in every item of ships' furniture. Valuable items are creamed off before the 'breaking' begins, but if you want 3 cm thick porthole glass, a spare fridge-freezer or a life jacket, this is the place to browse. However, customs officers always get first choice of valuables as they have to give permission for vessels to be beached, so don't expect too much. Some visitors have found the journey not worth the trouble since they couldn't enter the fenced off 'Lots'.

Alang is only open to tourists with **special permission** – obtained from the Gujarat Maritime Board at Sector 10A, opposite Air Force Station, Gandhinagar, T02842-235222 or Port Officer, New Port, Bhavnagar 5, T0278 2293090. Foreigners are finding it difficult to get permission to enter the beach/port area. Hotels in Bhavnagar may be able to help individuals gain entry but permits for groups are virtually impossible. Photography is not allowed. Strong shoes and modest dress are recommended.

## Mahuva and Gopnath

The fairly picturesque town (pronounced Mow-va), south of Palitana, was known for its historic port. Beautiful handcrafted furniture with lacquerwork and intricate hand-painting, is made here.

About 30 km northeast of Mahuva, Gopnath is where the 16th-century mystic poet, Narsinh Mehta is said to have attained enlightenment. Near the lighthouse, the 1940s mansion of late Maharajah Krishna Kumar Singhji of Bhavnagar was the summer home, a part of which is now a hotel. There are pleasant rocky, white-sand beaches – dangerous for swimming but good for walking– and a 700-year-old temple, a kilometre away.

## Gondal → *Phone code: 02825. Colour map 5, grid A1.*

The fascinating old town of Gondal, 38 km south of Rajkot, was the capital of one of the most progressive, affluent and efficient princely states during the British period. The exemplary state ruled by Jadeja Rajputs had an excellent road network, free compulsory education for all children including girls, sewage systems and accessible irrigation for farmers. The rulers rejected *purdah*, their palaces have no *zenanas*, and imposed no taxes on their subjects, instead earning revenue from rail connections between the port towns of Porbandar and Veraval with Rajkot and cities inland. The **Naulakha Palace** (1748) with a sculpted façade, pretty *jharoka* windows and carved stone pillars, has an impressive Darbar Hall and a museum of paintings, brass and silver. Silver items include caskets, models of buildings and scales used for weighing the Maharajah (he was weighed against silver and gold on his 25th and 50th birthday; the precious metals were then distributed to the poor). A gallery has toys from the 1930s and 1940s. The **Vintage and Classic Car Museum** is one of the finest in the country (1910 New Engine, 1920s Delage and Daimler, 1935-1955 models, horse-drawn carriages etc). Boating is possible on **Veri Lake** nearby, which attracts large numbers of rosy pelicans, flamingos, demoiselle and common eastern cranes and many others, particularly in January and February. You can visit the Bhuvaneshwari **Ayurvedic Pharmacy** founded in 1910 which still prepares herbal medicines according to ancient principles and runs a hospital which offers massages and treatment. There is also a horse and cattle stud farm. The early 20th-century **Swaminarayan temple** has painted interiors on the upper floors.

## Junagadh → *Phone code: 0285. Colour map 5, grid A1. Population: 168,700.*

The narrow winding lanes and colourful bazars of this small town, entered by imposing gateways, are evocative of earlier centuries. A large rock with 14 Asokan edicts, dating from 250 BC, stands on the way to the temple-studded Girnar Hill, believed to be a pre-Harappan site. Unfortunately the modern town is marred by ugly new buildings and dirty slums.

Established by the Mauryans in the fourth century BC, from the second to fourth centuries Junagadh was the capital of Gujarat under the **Kshattrapa** rulers. It is also associated with the **Chudasama Rajputs** who ruled from Junagadh from AD 875. The fort was expanded in 1472 by Mahmud Beghada, and again in 1683 and 1880. Sher Khan Babi, who took on the title of Nawab Bahadur Khan Babi, declared Junagadh an independent state in the 1700s. At the time of Partition the Nawab exercised his legal right to accede to Pakistan but his subjects were predominantly Hindu and after Indian intervention and an imposed plebiscite their will prevailed. The Nawab was exiled with his hundred dogs.

*You can tackle the town on foot allowing plenty of time for Uparkot. However, it's best to get an early start on Girnar Hill with the help of a rickshaw (around Rs 50 return).*

The old **Uparkot citadel** ⓘ *0700-1900*, on a small plateau is east of the town and was a stronghold in the Mauryan and Gupta Empires. The present walls are said to date from the time of the Chudasama Rajputs (ninth-15th century). The deep moat inside the walls is believe to have once had crocodiles. The Ottoman canons of Suleman Pasha, an ally of the Sultans, were moved here after the Muslim forces were unable to save Diu from Portuguese naval forces. The town was repeatedly under attack so there was a huge granary to withstand a long siege. The **Jama Masjid** was built from the remains of a Hindu palace. The 11th-century **Adi Chadi Vav**, a *baoli* with 172 steps and an impressive spiral staircase, is believed to commemorate two slave girls who were bricked up as sacrifice to ensure the supply of water. The 52-m deep Naghan Kuva is a huge 11th-century well which has steps down to the water level through the rocks, with openings to ventilate the path. The **Buddhist**



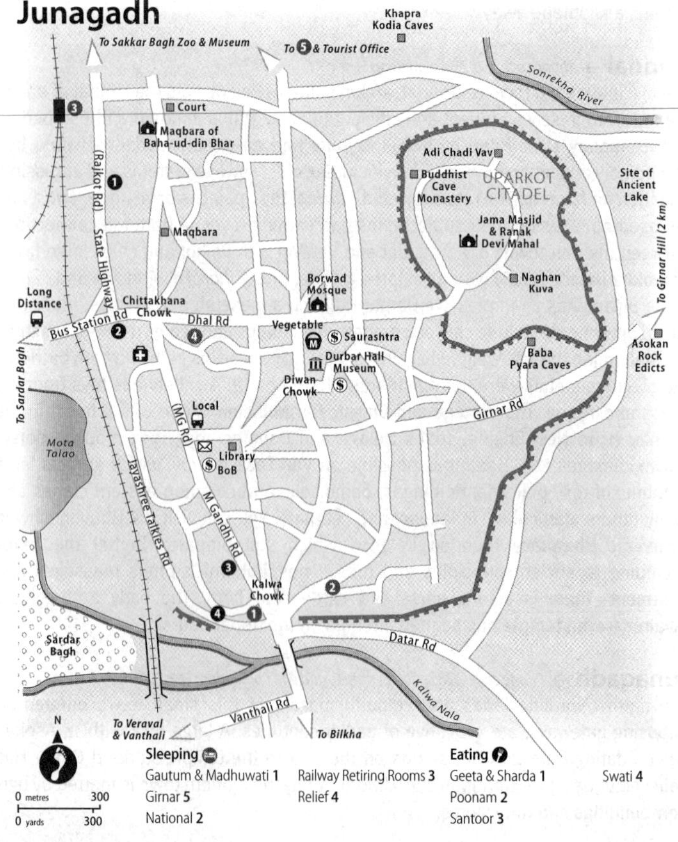

cave monastery in this fort complex dates from Asoka's time. Two of the three levels are open to visitors. The drainage system was very advanced as seen in the rainwater reservoir. The ventilation cleverly achieved a balance of light and cool breezes. Other Buddhist caves are hewn into the hillsides near the fort.

In the town, the late 19th-century **Mausolea** of the Junagadh rulers, not far from the railway station, are impressive. The **Maqbara** of Baha-ud-din Bhar with its silver doors and intricate, elaborate decoration, almost has a fairground flamboyance. The **Old Mausolea** at Chittakhana Chowk (opposite **Relief Hotel**, which has views of them from the roof), which were once impressive are now crumbling and overgrown.

**Durbar Hall Museum** ⓘ *Nawab's Palace, circa 1870, Janta Chowk, 0900-1215, 1500-1800, closed Wed, 2nd and 4th Sat of month, Rs 5 plus Rs 2 per photo, small but recommended*, houses royal memorabilia: portraits, palanquins, gem-studded carpets, costumes and weapons.

**Asokan rock edicts** ⓘ *0830-1100, 1400-1800, closed Wed and holidays*, carved in the Brahmi script on a large boulder is at the foot of the Girnar Hill, further east. The Emperor instructed his people to be gentle with women, to be kind to animals, to give alms freely and to plant medicinal herbs. The 13 edicts are summed up in the 14th.

**Girnar Hill**, rising 900 m above the surrounding plain, 3 km east of town, has been an important religious centre for the Jains from the third century BC. The climb up this worn volcanic cone by 10,000 stone steps takes at least two hours. You start just beyond Damodar Kund in teak forest; at the foot is the Asokan Edict while a group of 16 Jain temples surmounts the hill. The climb can be trying in the heat so is best started very early in the morning. You will find tea stalls en route and brazen monkeys. *Dhoolis* are available but are expensive. The charge depends on weight; Rs 1,500 for 60 kg!, to the first group of temples, which are the most interesting. There are good views from the top though the air is often hazy.

## Sasan Gir National Park → *Phone code: 02877. Colour map 5, grid A1.*

ⓘ *0700-1200, 1500-1730 from mid-Oct to mid-Feb; 0630-1100, 1600 to sunset from mid-Feb to mid-Jun (best season is Mar-May). Foreigners US$5, still camera US$5; video US$200; guide (some have no English), US$5 per trip; vehicle entry US$10; Jeep US$25 per 4-hr drive. Permits are only available from Sinh Sadan at Sasan. Permits are required. Temperature: 42-7°C. Rainfall: 1,000 mm.*

The sanctuary covers a total area of 1,412 sq km in the Saurashtra peninsula, of which 258 sq km at the core is the national park. As a result of over-grazing and agricultural colonization, only about 10% of the park is forest. However, much of the natural vegetation in the region was scrub jungle. The area has rocky hills and deep valleys with numerous rivers and streams, and there are extensive clearings covered with savannah-like fodder grasses.

The **Asiatic Lion** once had a wide range of natural territory running from North to West India through Persia to Arabia. It is now only found in the Gir forest; the last one seen outside India was in 1942, in Iran. Similar to its African cousin, the tawnier Asian is a little smaller and stockier in build with a skin fold on the belly, a thinner mane and a thicker tuft at the end of its tail. The 1913 census accounted for only 18 in the park. The lions' natural habitat was threatened by the gradual conversion of the forest into agricultural land and cattle herders grazing their livestock here. The conservation programme has been remarkably successful. In the mid-90s there were over 300 lions (some suggest, too many for this sanctuary). These, and 294 **panthers**, make Gir India's best Big Cat sanctuary. There have been attacks on villagers by park lions, these were probably 'provoked' as there are few reported 'maneaters'. Lions are more likely to be seen with the help of a tracker and guide (jeeps and guides available), but some visitors return disappointed. The Interpretation Zone's 'Safari Park' has a few lions. There are six routes in the park, between 22 and 50 km. Jeep (diesel, seats four), from **Sinh Sadan**, bookings between 0700-1100 or 1500-1700.

A **watch tower** camouflaged in the tree canopy at Kamleshwar overlooks an artificial reservoir harbouring wild crocodiles but it is poorly located and overcrowded with bus loads of noisy visitors at weekends. Other towers are at Janwadla and Gola. For **bird watching**, Adhodiya, Valadara, Ratnaghuna and Pataliyala, are good spots. A walk along Hiran River is also rewarding.

The Tulsishyam **hotsprings** in the heart of the forest (Tulsishyam is also a Krishna pilgrimage centre), and Kankai Mata **temple** dedicated to Bhim, the *Mahabharata* hero, and his mother Kunti, add interest. **Gir Interpretation Zone** ⓘ *rates as for the sanctuary – cheaper to take mini-bus tour*, at Devaliya, 12 km west of Sasan, is 16 sq km of Gir habitat fenced in as a 'Safari Park' to show a cross-section of wildlife; the four or five lions here can be easily seen in open scrubland in the area. Photographers will find this a good place to shoot lion behaviour as these lions are less shy than those in the sanctuary. Other Gir wildlife include spotted deer, sambar, nilgai, peafowl. Permits are available at the Reception here.

**Crocodile Rearing Centre** ⓘ *0800-1200, 1500-1800, free, near entrance to Sinh Sadan, and road leading to Lion Safari Lodge*, is full of marsh crocodiles, varying in size from a few centimetres to 1 m for restocking the population in the sanctuary. Eggs are collected in the park and taken to Junagadh for hatching under controlled conditions. Unfortunately, keepers prod the crocodiles to make them move.



## Veraval

Veraval is a noisy, unbearably smelly and unattractive town which provides a base for visiting the Hindu pilgrimage centre of Somnath at Prabhas Patan. Its importance now is as a fishing port – hence the stench. Sea-going *dhows* and fishing boats are still being built by the sea without the use of any modern instruments, traditional skills being passed down from father to son.

## Prabhas Patan (Somnath)

The **Somnath Temple** ⓘ *6km east of Veraval, puja at 0700, 1200 and 1900*, a major Hindu pilgrimage centre, is said to have been built out of gold by Somraj, the Moon God (and subsequently in silver, wood and stone). In keeping with the legend, the stone façade appears golden at sunset. Mahmud of Ghazni plundered it and removed the gates in 1024. Destroyed by successive Muslim invaders, it was rebuilt each time on the same spot. The final reconstruction did not take place until 1950 and is still going on. Unfortunately, it lacks character but it has been built to traditional patterns with a soaring 50 m high tower that rises in clusters. Dedicated to Siva, it has one of the 12 sacred *jyotirlingas*, see page 297.

Nearby is the ruined **Rudreshvara Temple** which dates from the same time as the Somnath Temple and was laid out in a similar fashion. The sculptures on the walls and doorways give an indication of what the original Somnath Temple was like.

**Krishna** was believed to have been hit by an arrow, shot by the Bhil, Jara, when he was mistaken for a deer at Bhalka Teerth nearby, and was cremated at Triveni Ghat, east of Somnath.

## Diu → *Phone code: 02875. Colour map 5, grid A1. Population: 21,600.*

The island of Diu has a fascinating history and a relaxed atmosphere with little traffic. The north side of the island has salt pans and marshes which attract wading birds, the south coast has some limestone cliffs and pleasant, sandy beaches. Although often compared to Goa, it is anywhere near as picturesque. The island is still visited by relatively few foreign travellers though its tavernas attract those deprived of alcohol from neighbouring Gujarat and the bars can get noisy especially at the weekend. It isn't a paradise island but if you are in the area, it does offer a welcome break from the rigours of travelling around Gujarat. » *For Sleeping, Eating and other listings, see pages 1272-1282.*

**Background** Like Daman across the gulf, Diu was a Portuguese colony until 1961. In 1987 its administration was separated from Goa (some 1,600 km away), which then became a State – Diu remains a Union Territory. From the 14th to 16th centuries the Sultans of Oman held the reins of maritime power here. The Portuguese failed to take Diu at their first attempt in 1531 but succeeded three years later. Like Daman, it was once a port for the export of opium from Malwa (Madhya Pradesh) but with the decline of Portugal as a naval power it became little more than a backwater.

*The night market is a great place to have a drink and to wander around.*

About 5,000 of the elders here (out of a population of 40,000), still speak fluent Portuguese. There are around 200 Catholic families and the local convent school teaches English, Gujarati, Portuguese and French. The Divechi people remain eligible for Portuguese passports and a few apply daily. Many families have a member working in Lisbon or former Portuguese Africa.

**Diu town** The small town is squeezed between the fort on the east and a large city wall to the west. With its attractively ornamented buildings and its narrow streets and squares, it has more of a Portuguese flavour than Daman. While some visitors find it quite dirty and decaying, and are disappointed by the number of liquor shops, others find Diu an enjoyable little place.

**St Paul's Church** (1601-1610), on Traveessa dos Hospital, the road running from the fort, has a fine baroque façade, impressive wood panelling and an attractive courtyard. At this church, take the left-hand on to Rua de Isabel Fernandes for the **Church of St Francis of Assisi** (1593), part of which is a hospital (a doctor is available at 0930 for a free consultation). On Rua de Torres Novas is **St Thomas's Church** ⓘ *0800-2000*, housing the museum with an interesting local collection. It has been renovated and now houses a collection including stone sculptures, wood carvings, and shadow clocks (as well as a café and pleasant rooms to let). These, and the fort, are floodlit at night.

**Diu Fort** (1535-1541) ⓘ *0700-1800*, considered one of the most important Portuguese forts in Asia, was built after the Mughal Emperor Humayun attacked the Sultan of Gujarat with the help of the Portuguese. Until 1960 it garrisoned 350 Portuguese soldiers. Skirted by the sea on three sides and a rock-cut canal on the fourth, it had two moats, one of which was tidal. The lighthouse stands at one end and parts of the central keep are still used as a jail but has few occupants. Some of the structures (walls, gateways, arches, ramps, bastions), though damaged, still give us an idea of the formidable nature of the defences. It is well worth allowing an hour for a visit.

Makata Lane or Panchwati, near the Zampa gate, has some impressive old mansions of rich Portuguese and Indian merchants ranging from Venetian-Gothic style bungalows to typical carved wooden or stone *havelis*.

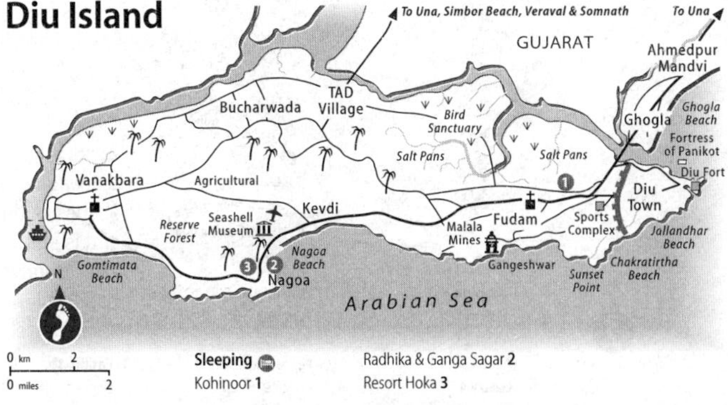

**Forte de Mar** Forte de Mar (Fortress of Panikot), built in 1535, was strategically important as an easily defended base for controlling the shipping lanes on the northeast part of the Arabian Sea. It has a lighthouse and a chapel to Our Lady of the Sea. It can be approached from Diu jetty when canoes or motor boats are available although landing is not permitted at present. The other fort at the eastern end of the island guarded the mint, while two others once guarded the west at Vanakbara and the bay to the south at Nagoa.

**Bird sanctuary** The creeks to the north of Diu island have been declared a bird sanctuary. There are watch towers to spot huge flocks of shore birds including oystercatchers, sanderlings, herons and plovers. Lots of herons and ibises, flamingos, pelicans, ducks etc visit seasonally. Jackals, foxes, jungle cat and porcupine are seen in the evening.

**Beaches** Several beaches on the south side of Diu Island are easy to get to from Diu town by cycle or auto-rickshaw. Beaches between Nagoa and Vanakbara are safe throughout the year except between May and July and are often empty, as is the beach along Ghogla. However, beware of the giant thorns which are hazardous to cycle tyres.

**Jallandhar Beach**, to the south, is pleasant and the nearest to Diu. There have been several reports of groups of teenage boys who not only come to watch and pester tourists but aggressively offer sex.



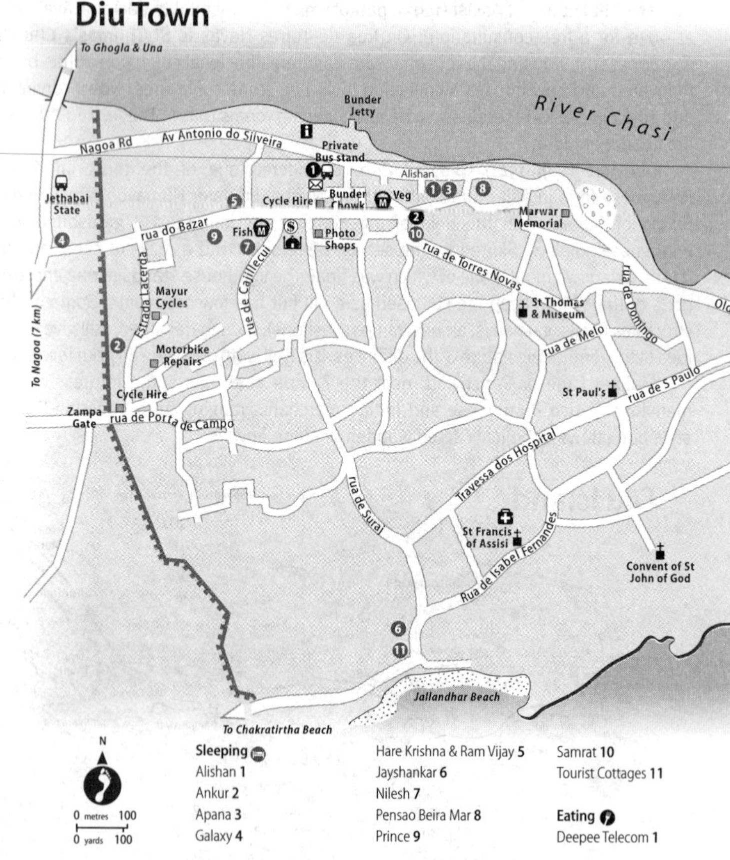

**Chakratirtha Beach**, just southwest, has a sunset view point, an open auditorium, and a small beach which is no longer the picture it was. This was a popular promenade for the townspeople until "ruined by the cabins which are, in a way, the beginning of the end of beautiful beaches like Chakratirth".

Just east of Diu Town, **Fudam** or Fofrara has the air of a Portuguese village with the crumbling Church of Our Lady of the Remedies. **Malala Mines** are limestone quarries off the Nagoa road. **Gangeshwar** temple nearby has an attractive *Nandi* and Siva *linga* washed by the sea at high tide.

About 7 km from town, facing the Arabian Sea, **Nagoa** offers the best location for a quiet stay away from Diu town. Its semi-circular palm-fringed beach suitable for swimming is popular with foreigners but also large numbers of Indian tourists who come to watch. There are quieter beaches nearby and the forests are pleasant for walks although the entire stretch from Nagoa is being landscaped for development. A **sea shell museum** ⓘ *Rs 10*, has opened on the road from the airport to Nagoa. It displays a large number of mollusc and crustacean shells, corals, fish and marine life from the world over collected by a retired merchant navy captain.

The fishing village of **Ghogla-Ahmedpur Mandvi** on the mainland is also part of Diu. Its name changes to Ahmedpur Mandvi on crossing to the Gujarat side of the border. The beach is good for swimming and it has splendid views of fishing villages and the fort and churches on Diu island. *Jyoti Watersports* and *Magico Do Mar* offer a variety of watersports here including parasailing, speed boating and waterskiing. Beware of the **rip tide** just a few metres out to sea which has claimed several lives.

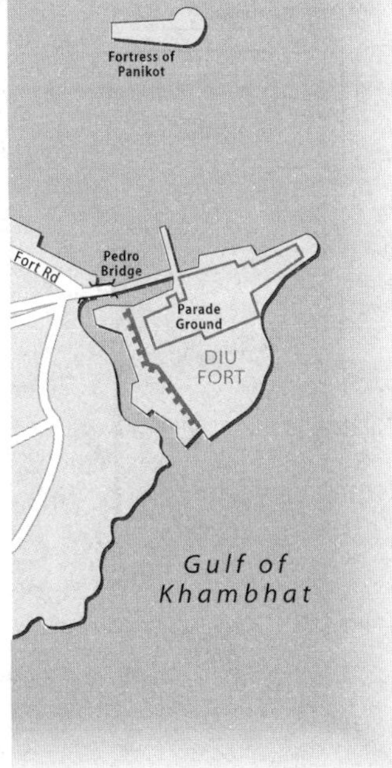


**Bucharwada**, to the north, lacks attractive beaches but has cheap spartan rooms in *Viswas* hotel. **Gomtimata**, a secluded white-sand beach to the west, is where a *Tourist Hostel* is expected to open. **Vanakbara**, the fishing village on the western tip of the island, has the Church of Our Lady of Mercy. Get to the early morning fish market and watch the colourful trawlers unload catches of shark, octopus and every kind of fish imaginable. The drying fish on "washing lines" and waterside activities provide photo opportunities. You can also watch traditional dhow building. There is a ferry service across to Gomtimata. **Simbor Beach** is a pleasant and little known beach. It is 27 km from Diu town, off the Una road, and can be reached in 45 minutes from Diu by hiring a moped or scooter. Carry food and water.

## Porbandar → *Phone code: 0286. Colour map 5, grid A1. Population 133,000.*

The former capital of the Jethwa Rajput petty princely state, Porbandar was previously named Sudamapuri, after Krishna's devoted friend, and has a temple dedicated to her. The tradition of dhow building which continues on the seashore to the present day reflects its maritime past when it traded with North Africa and Arabia. Today, Porbandar is closely associated with Mahatma Gandhi and is also known for its production of gold and silver trinkets, manufacture of fine quality silk and cotton and its chemical and cement factories.

Mahatma Gandhi was born in Porbandar in 1869. Next to the family home with its carved balconies is **Kirti Mandir** ⓘ *open from sunrise to sunset, but the guide takes a lunch break from 1300-1400*, a small museum that traces his life and contains memorabilia and a library. **Darbargadh**, a short walk from Kirti Mandir, the old palace of the Maharanas of Porbandar, built in the 1780s, is now deserted and has some intricate carvings and carved balconies. The rooms inside (if you can get in!) have interesting paintings. **Sartanji** (or Rana-no) **Choro** (1785 ), near the ST stand, is the beautiful pleasure pavilion of Maharajah Sartanji, a great poet, writer and music lover. The pavilion has domes, pillars and carved arches and its four sides represent the four seasons. The Maharana's deserted sprawling **Hazur Palace** is near the seafront. Ask for permission to visit the rooms inside at the office. **Daria Rajmahal**, the splendid turn-of-the-century palace of the Maharana of Porbandar, now a college, has intricate carvings, courtyards, fountains, carved arches and heavily embellished façades. The tower has excellent views of the seashore. **Chaya**, 2 km from Chowpatty sea face, is the old capital of the Jetwas. The Darbargadh Palace with a beautiful carved balcony, is believed to have secret tunnels and passages to temples and places of safety.

The **Bharat Mandir Hall** in Dayananda Vatika garden, is across the Jubilee (Jyubeeli) Bridge. It has a large marble relief map of India on the floor and bas reliefs of heroes from Hindu legends on the pillars. Nearby **Arya Kanya Gurukul** is an



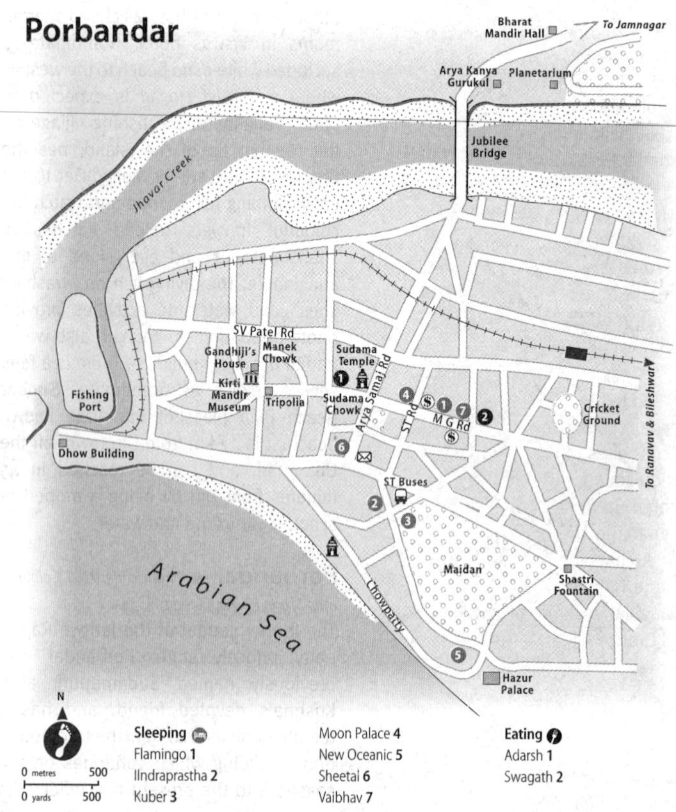

experiment in education for girls based on ancient Indian tradition. The dated **Planetarium** has shows in Gujarati only. The architecture incorporates different religious styles illustrating Gandhi's open mind.

**Jhavar Creek** attracts scores of waterbirds. Flamingos, pelicans, storks and heron can be seen from the road in the mangrove marshes. Fisheries have appeared around the creek where the fish put out to dry attract thousands of terns and gulls.

## Jamnagar and around → *Phone code: 0288. Colour map 2, grid C1. Population: 447,700.*

Jamnagar, now an expanding town, was a 16th-century pearl fishing centre with one of the biggest pearl fisheries in the world until the beginning of the 20th century. The famous cricketer Ranjitsinghji was its ruler from 1907-33. Although the January 2001 earthquake was strongly felt in the town there was no severe disruption.

**The walled city** is famous for its embroidery, silverware and *bandhani* (tie-and-dye) fabrics produced in workshops in the narrow lanes. Pirotan Island in the middle of the Ranmal lake in the Old City, reached by a stone bridge, has the **Lakhota Fort** and **Kotha Bastion** ⓘ *1030-1300, 1500-1730, closed Wed, 2nd and 4th Sun, no photography (unless tipped)*, with its arsenal. The fort museum has a collection of sculpture and pottery found in ruined medieval villages nearby. It is also a pleasant, cool and quiet spot just to relax while listening to the strains of '*Shri Ram, Jai Ram, Jai Jai Ram*' wafting across the lake from the **Bala Hanuman Temple**. The temple is worth a visit, especially early evening. The bastion has an old well from which water can be drawn by blowing into a small hole in the floor. The **Solarium** uses solar radiation to cure diseases.

The **Jain temples** in the Old City are profusely decorated with glass, gilding and mirrors. **Khijadia Lakes**, 10 km northeast of Jamnagar, are three freshwater lakes surrounded by salt pans and salt marshes. Entirely flooded in the wet season, the lakes remain fresh throughout the dry season, though they occasionally dry out completely. The lakes, a bird sanctuary, are an important staging post for migratory birds, including swallows, martins and wagtails, and many waterfowl. **Marine National Park** ⓘ *foreigners US$5,still camera US$5; video US$200; guide US$5*, 30 km away, offshore from the southern coast of the Gulf of Kachchh, comprises an archipelago of 42 islands noted for their coral reefs and mangroves. It is possible to see dolphins, finless porpoise and sea turtles and a variety of colourful tropical fish. The area also attracts a host of waterbirds. The best island to visit is 1½ sq km **Pirotan**. To get there hire motor boats for 15-45 people from Jamnagar jetty (or from Okha) and take a guide. Permit needed from the Director, Marine National Park, Jamnagar. Pirotan is uninhabited save for lighthouse staff.

## Dwarka → *Phone code: 02892. Colour map 2, grid C1. Population: 33,600.*

A small coastal town on the tip of the Kathiawad peninsula, Dwarka is one of the most sacred sites for Vaishnavite Hindus. It has the unique distinction of being one of Hinduism's four 'Holy Abodes' as well as one of its seven 'Holy Places'. Heavily geared up to receive pilgrims, the people are easy going, friendly and welcoming, even to the rarely seen tourist. The beach is good but without any palms for shade.

Archaeological excavations indicate that present day Dwarka is built on the sites of four former cities. Work in 1990 by the marine archaeologist SR Rao discovered triangular anchors weighing 250 kg similar to those used in Cyprus and Syria during the Bronze Age, suggesting that ships of up to 120 tonnes had used the port around the 14th century BC. Marine research in early 2002 revealed evidence of a substantial city off the coast over 100 m below current sea level, reviving the debate about the origins of Dwarka's offshore archaeological sites.

*Bala Hanuman temple is in the 'Guinness Book of Records' for continuous chanting (13,892 days – over 38 years).*

The present town is largely 19th century when the Gaekwad princes developed the town as a popular pilgrimage centre. Celebrated as Krishna's capital after his flight from Mathura, thousands come to observe Krishna's birthday, and also at Holi and Diwali.

The 12th-century **Rukmini Temple** has beautifully carved *mandapa* columns and a fine sanctuary doorway, but much else is badly weathered. The mainly 16th-century **Dwarkadisha Temple** ⓘ *0600-1200, 1700-2100,* was supposedly built in one night, and some believe that the inner sanctum is 2,500 years old. The sanctuary walls probably date from the 12th century. The exterior is more interesting. The soaring five-storey tower is supported by 60 columns. Non-Hindus may enter after completing a form to show some level of commitment to Hinduism and to Krishna, but no photography is allowed inside and cameras must be left at the entrance. Some visitors are approached for a 'minimum donation' of Rs 100. Good humoured lighthouse keepers may treat you to a free private guided tour in exchange for any foreign coin (they all 'collect') ⓘ *1600-1800 or 1 hr before sunset, whichever is earlier, Rs 1, no photography.* The views are beautiful – a very peaceful place to rest a while.

Outside Dwarka, the **Nageshwar Mandir** contains one of the 12 *jyotirlingas* in an underground sanctum. Work is in progress. It helps to be fairly agile if you wish to catch a glimpse. **Gopi Talav Teerth** is associated with Krishna (and Arjun) and contains several shrines in the complex.



## Okha

A small port at the head of the Gulf of Kachchh, Okha is 32 km north of Dwarka. You can visit the Marine National Park by hiring a motor boat from the jetty (see under Jamnagar). A pilgrimage to Dwarka is not complete until the island of **Beyt Dwarka** is visited off the coast from Okha. This is where Krishna is believed to have resided while Dwarka was his capital. The 19th-century temple complex contains several shrines and images of Krishna and his 56 consorts. Archaeological excavations have revealed Harappan artefacts dating from the second millennium BC.

## Sleeping

**Rajkot** *p1258, map p1258*

**B Kavery**, near GEB, Kanak Rd, T0281 223 9331, www.hotelkavery.com. 33 a/c rooms, modern facilities, good restaurants, exchange.

**B-C Aditya**, opposite Rajshri Cinema, T0281 2222003. 40 rooms, most with a/c, some dearer suites, restaurant, travel desk.

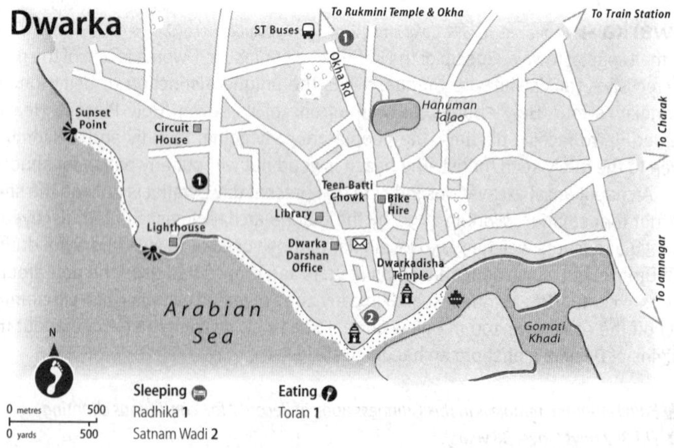

**C-D Galaxy**, Jawahar Rd, T0281 2222904, www.thegalaxyhotelrajkot.com. 37 very well furnished, clean rooms, most a/c, pleasant roof-garden, exchange (including TCs, credit cards), well run, courteous and efficient, no restaurant but excellent room service to bring in food, access by lift only. Recommended.
**C-D Samrat International**, 37 Karanpura, T0281 2222269. 32 decent rooms, some a/c, a/c vegetarian restaurant, exchange.
**D-E Babha Guest House**, Panchnath Rd, T0281 2220861, hotelbabha@rajkot.com. Small, good value rooms, some a/c, excellent veg *thalis*.
**D-E Himalaya**, Lakhajiraj Rd, T0281 2231736. Cleanish rooms with bath (bucket hot water), good value, very popular.
**D-E Railway Retiring Rooms** on 1st floor. 3 clean rooms (1 a/c), 4-bed dorm, reasonable veg restaurant, good value.

**Wankaner** *p1259*
**C-D Royal Oasis**, T02828-220000, F220002, guest house of the Ranjitvilas in large fruit orchards with original 1930s art deco features, interesting rooms but mosquitoes can be a problem, pool, meals at the palace (slow erratic service, "arrives cold") but worth it if presided over by Maharajah Pratap Singh in his 90s, who is a fund of historic anecdotes.

**Bhavnagar** *p1259, map p1260*
**A Neelambagh Palace**, Ahmadabad Rd, T0278 2429323, www.nilambagpalace.com 1850s palace, 27 upmarket a/c rooms, long bathrooms with tubs (main palace better than cottage annexe), lobby with intricate wood carving, chandeliers, royal portraits, grand banquet hall now restaurant, vast gardens with peacocks, beautiful stepped pool.
**B Dil Bahar**, Waghawadi Rd, opposite Victoria Park, T0278 2568391. 2 km out of town with extensive views. Former 1937 royal hunting lodge retaining art deco features, 4 a/c rooms, dated bathrooms, no TV or phone, period furniture (ask to see the 'Indian' room), home-cooked food (Indian, continental), pool (Apr-Jun), memorabilia, friendly staff, peaceful.
**B-C Blue Hill**, 500 m from bus, Pill Gardens, T0278 2426951, bluehillad1@sancharnet.in. 40 a/c rooms with bath, **A-B** suites (traditional Gujarati lacquered furniture, best with jacuzzi), a/c vegetarian restaurant, roof garden, popular with businessmen, comfortable hotel with a view of gardens (storks nest on the nearby trees in winter).
**B-C Sun 'n' shine**, Panwadi, T0278 2516131, F2516130. Attractive hotel with fountains in the lobby but located on busy main road. 46 comfortable rooms, popular vegetarian restaurant, health club (gym, sauna), travel desk, internet.
**C-D Jubilee**, next to **Blue Hill**, T0278 2430045. 33 a/c rooms, 10 newer dearer, **Woodlands** a/c restaurant (good for Indian), exchange, car hire.
**E-F Vrindavan**, Darbargadh, T0278 2519149, F2513022. Part of the old Darbargadh complex (18th-19th century) converted to a budget hotel, 100 rooms, some with baths but only a few have western toilets, some **D** a/c, also Rs 50 dorm beds, a/c Gujarati restaurant (*thali* Rs 50), rather noisy surroundings, helpful owner.
**F Mini**, Station Rd, T0278 2424415. Small hotel with clean rooms (some windowless), some a/c with TV (Rs 25), excellent value, very helpful and friendly manager, bus tickets, ISD phone, internet, good restaurant and cycle hire down the road.
**F Shital**, Amba Chowk, half-way between railway and bus station, entrance in alley at back, T0278 2428360. Some rooms with bath (bucket hot water), and men's dorm.

**Velavadhar National Park** *p1260*
**B Kaliyar Bhuvan Forest Lodge**, simple but adequate, 5 small rooms, reasonably furnished, but prohibitively priced. Reserve at Forest Office in Bhavnagar.

**Palitana** *p1261, map p1262*
Difficult to find cheap rooms but dormitory beds are Rs 20-50.
**B Vijay Vilas Palace** (Heritage Hotel), in Adpur, a cattle herders' village ringed by hills. 3 rooms in 1906 lodge (Italian country house feel), gradually being restored. Delicious homecooked Indian meals (non-residents Rs 250 with advance notice), 7 km from town (rickshaws Rs 50, shared

motorbike-rickshaws Rs 4). The shorter but steeper route to the Palitana temple complex starts a few hundred metres away at the temple in Adpur village (follow the milk maids carrying curd!). Book ahead through **North West Safaris**, T079-26302019, ssibal@ad1.vsnl.net.in.

**D-E Sumeru** (Gujarat Tourism), Station Rd, near Bus Stand, T02848 252327. 7 rooms, 3 a/c, 5 dorms (Rs 50) with cold water only, limited menu restaurant, Tourist Office, check-out 0900, several unfavourable reports.

**E Shravak**, opposite Central bus station, T02848 252428. 18 rooms with baths (western toilets, hot shower), cheaper with Indian wc, men's dorm but not too clean.

**F Patel House**, Station Rd, T02848 242441. Run by private farmer's trust, rather basic and impersonal but set around an open courtyard that shuts off some of the traffic noise, double rooms (cold taps, hot water in buckets, Indian toilet), some 4 and 6-bedded.

**Gopnath** *p1263*

**B-C Gopnath Bungalow**. Beautiful sea-views, 3 rooms in royal mansion, 4 clean, well-renovated rooms in the "English" bungalow (cheaper) in a rambling complex, great views of sea and cliffs, meals on request, pool, understaffed so expect inconveniences. Contact: Nilambagh Palace, Bhavnagar, T0278-2424241.

**Gondal** *p1263*

The heritage hotels are worth the experience.

**B Orchard Palace**, Palace Rd, near ST bus stand, T02825 224450. Overlooking mango and lime groves, 7 rooms in a wing, 2 a/c, with old- fashioned baths, attractive gardens, 35 vintage cars, pool (waiting to be filled), excellent dance performances, mosquito nuisance so burn rings, good food ("bland European dishes; order 'Indian' in advance every time"), good *kebabs* and Gujarati *thalis* but service can be slow (Rs 2,000 includes meals).

**B Riverside Palace** (19th century) by river Gondali, T02825 220002, www.gujarat.net/gondal. With a glassed-in terrace, 11 large, attractive rooms, 4-posters etc.

**B Royal Saloon**, standing in garden near Orchard Palace. Beautifully renovated suite in Maharaja's old train, with drawing and dining rooms and sit-outs on the platform, meals from the **Orchard Palace**. Sheer nostalgia.

**D Bhuvaneswari Rest House**, a/c rooms with western baths, Rs 350-700, simple but comfortable, *thali* meals. The Gondal family don't spend time with guests though "the Maharani is delightful company"; request high tea in their private drawing room (French gilt furniture, crystals, Lalique etc).

**Junagadh** *p1263, map p1264*

Rates double during Diwali (Oct- Nov) when large number of Indians visit Girnar.

**C-D Paramount**, Kalwa Chowk, T0285 2622119, F2650582. 31 rooms (some a/c) with TV and phone, attached baths, car rental, bus ticketing.

**C-D President**, opposite Railway Workshop, T0285 2626773. 15 clean rooms, 6 a/c (comfortable but short beds), all with hot water (winter only) and TV, 'deluxe' front rooms on busy road, noisy, those at rear with view of hills better.

**D-E Girnar**, Majwadi Darwaja, 2 km north, T0285 2621201 (Gujarat Tourism). 24 decent rooms, some a/c with bath, best with balcony, unattractive building but in good location, poor management.

**D-E Madhuwati**, Kalwa Chowk, T0285 2620087. 27 spacious rooms, some a/c, attached bath (hot showers in winter only), noisy location above a shopping complex, clean, comfortable, courteous staff.

**D-E National**, near Kalwa Chowk, T0285 2627891. 15 clean, comfortable rooms, 2 a/c dearer, some deluxe with TV, big discount for single, good value though several women visitors have complained of harassment, on noisy road.

**D-E Relief**, Dhal Rd, T0285 2620280. 14 rooms (some share bath), hot water, 2 a/c, snacks available, untrained but friendly staff, courteous owner can help with excursions.

**F Gautam**, Kalwa Chowk, T0285 2626432. Located on noisy intersection, small guest house with 12 simple rooms, most with shared bath, bucket hot water, cycle hire.

**F Railway Retiring Rooms** are clean and well maintained.

**Sasan Gir National Park** *p1265*

**AL-A Gir Lodge** (Taj), Sasan, T02877 285521, www.tajhotels.com. 27 comfortable rooms (better upstairs for views from balcony), 9

a/c, pleasant river-facing dining area but average meals at fixed times, slow service though friendly manager and chef, no pool, wildlife library and videos, jeep hire.
**A-B Maneland Jungle Lodge**, 2 km before Sasan, T02877 285555, www.maneland.com on edge of sanctuary. Well-appointed suites in bungalow (VIP faces jungle), and rooms in cottages resembling royal hunting lodges, restaurant with limited menu delightfully designed, jungle ambience, lions and panthers heard and occasionally spotted nearby, rich birdlife, wildlife videos. Recommended.
**B Sinh Sadan Forest Lodge** (Govt), T02877 285540, overpriced and run down rooms (foreigners US$30), with Indian toilets, better a/c chalets (US$50), tents with shared bath, 30-bed dorm (US$5), comfortable 2-bed tents, with shared toilet and cold shower - "fell asleep to the sound of a lion roaring nearby!", must order food in advance (mixed reports on quality). Book at least 1 week ahead.
**D Umeng**, T02877 285728. Near Sasan bus stop, backdrop of sanctuary but with crowded village on one side (calls from the mosque disturb the peace). 9 decent rooms with mediocre baths, rooftop dining room (order meal well ahead), jeep safaris, knowledgeable owner can help with visits to the sanctuary.

**Veraval** *p1266*
**D Park**, Veraval-Junagadh Rd, T02876 222701. Fairly well-appointed rooms, excellent location with spacious grounds, varied menu.
**D-E Madhuram**, Junagadh Rd, T02876 221938. Comfortable rooms, some a/c, taxis, travel desk, small cafeteria (limited menu), dorms, run down.

**Prabhas Patan** *p1266*
**D Mayuram**, Triveni Rd, T02876 231286. Acceptable rooms, good restaurant, clean.
**F Shri Somnath Guest House**, near Temple, T02876 220212. Has 20 very basic rooms.

**Diu** *p1266, maps p1267 and p1268*
Most are fairly basic. Some have a few a/c rooms with TV and charge double for the luxury, but offer good discounts when business is slow. High season: *Diwali*, Christmas/New Year and Apr-May.

**B Radhika Beach Resort**, Nagoa, close to the beach, , T02875 252555, www.radhika resort.com. 24 comfortable a/c rooms in modern 2-storey 'villas', excellent a/c restaurant, good pool in well tended garden, prompt service, small provisions store handy for beach. Recommended.
**B-C Kohinoor**, Fofrara, Diu-Nagoa Rd, Fudam, T02875 252209, www.hotelkohinoor diu.com. 28 clean, a/c rooms in ritzy resort (discounts possible), good restaurant serves Portuguese dishes, pool, gym-sauna, modern and pleasant rooms and amenities but no views, pastry shop and disco, gym, pool and water slide complex next door.
**B-C Magico do Mar**, Ghogla-Ahmedpur Mandvi, T02875 252116. Charming complex of 14 a/c huts with Saurashtrian decor, around a 1930s mansion of a Junagadh Nawab (best Nos 510-513), cheaper non a/c rooms in unimpressive bungalow needing renovation, fantastic views, some water sports, charming setting but poor service.
**B-C Suzlon Beach**, Ghogla-Ahmedpur Mandvi, T02875 252212. Cluster of attractive good sized bungalows, well appointed, clean a/c rooms, restaurant, bar, terrace opens onto beach and sea, lacks atmosphere.
**C Pensáo Beira Mar**, Fort Rd, T02875 *252342*. 6 rooms and suites in pleasant colonial house, sea-facing balcony, rooftop restaurant.
**C Prince**, near Fish Market, T02875 252265. 11 clean, well kept rooms (some deluxe), dorm (Rs 40), constant hot water, 1st floor rooms can be unbearably hot even at night, friendly staff.
**C-D Apana Guest House**, Old Fort Rd, T02875 252112. 29 clean rooms, 4 a/c, some with bath (best with TV, hot water, seaview and balcony) and dorm, can be noisy (mainly from Hindi films) especially at weekends, roadside terrace with restaurant and bar.
**C-D Samrat**, Collectorate Rd, T02875 *252354*. 12 clean rooms, 3 a/c, balconies, good restaurant, helpful manager. Recommended.
**D Galaxy**, next to bus station, T02875 253399. Clean rooms in newish 3 storey hotel, some a/c, restaurant, bar.
**D-E Hemal Garden**, opposite Sports Complex, T02875 252227. 10 simple cottage like rooms, bar, restaurant, family run, pleasant garden, rather basic but pleasant.

**D-E The Resort Hoka**, 100 m from the beach among Hoka palms and trees at Nagoa, T02875 253036, resort_hoka@hot mail.com. 10 decent rooms with bath, 3 with shared facilities, clean, pleasant garden restaurant serves excellent fresh fish, bar, laundry, travel, environment conscious and friendly management, discounts for long stays, not luxurious but pleasant and good value.
**E Jay Shankar Guest House**, 1 min from Jallandhar Beach, T02875 252424. 15 rooms, some with bath, small dorm (Rs 50).
**F Hare Krishna**, opposite Prince, T02875 252213. 9 rooms, basic (hard beds) but clean, some with balcony, friendly staff, popular restaurant, bar can be noisy.
**F Church Hostel**, in the old Fudam church. Simple rooms (Rs 100), use of kitchen, really quiet and pleasant.

**Porbandar** *p1269, map p1270*
**C Sheetal**, Arya Samaj Rd, opposite GPO, T/F0286 224 8341. Some a/c rooms with shower or tub, limited room service.
**C-D Kuber**, Bhavsinhji Park, near ST station, T0286 2241025. 19 rooms, most a/c, suites with fridge, good restaurant (residents only), friendly and helpful manager, free airport transfer. Highly recommended.
**C-D Indraprastha**, near ST Station, T0286 2242681. Large modern hotel, comfortable, some a/c, garden restaurant.
**D New Oceanic**, 8 Chowpatty, T0286 2242917. 17 rooms, some a/c, sea views, modern, good garden restaurant (western, Indian) but rather expensive.
**D-E Host**, Blvd Bhavsinhji Park, T0286 2241901. 14 rooms, some a/c, Indian veg meals on the terrace garden, restaurant too.
**D-E Moon Palace**, ST Rd, near Bhavsinhji Park, ST Rd, T0286 2241172, moonpalace@mail.com. Clean, cosy rooms with bath.

**Jamnagar** *p1271*
**B Express Hotel**, Motikhavdi, Sikka, T0288 2344416, www.expressworld.com. 93 centrally a/c rooms in modern hotel with good business facilities.
**B-C Aram** (Heritage Hotel), Pandit Nehru Rd, 3 km northwest from centre, T0288 2551701, www.hotelaram.com. Good a/c rooms in 1940s character mansion (bit garish), Raj memorabilia, pleasant veg garden restaurant, friendly, good service.
**C-D President**, Teen Batti, T0288 2557491, president@wilnetonline.net. 48 clean rooms, some a/c and balcony, relaxing a/c restaurant (wide menu, efficient service), internet.
**D-E Aashiana**, New Supermarket, Bedi Gate, 3rd floor, T0288 2559110. 34 rooms, 14 clean a/c rooms with TV, simple restaurant serving inexpensive Indian veg, good value.
**D-E Punit**, Pandit Nehru Marg, north of Teen Batti, T0288 2670560. Reasonable, clean rooms, some a/c, better at rear, good value.

**Dwarka** *p1271, map p1272*
Most hotels are poorly maintained.
**D-F Toran** (Gujarat Tourism), near Govt Guest House, T02892 234013. 6 clean, well-maintained rooms with nets, dorm, courteous service, checkout 0900, "dedicated and friendly manager". Recommended.
**F Meera**, near railway station, T02892 234031. Friendly, excellent *thalis*.
**F Satnam Wadi**, near the beach. Rooms with bath and sea view.

## Eating

**Rajkot** *p1258, map p1258*
**₹₹ Havmor**, Jawahar Rd, near Galaxy Hotel. Good non-veg food (varied menu, mainly Chinese), a/c.
**₹₹ Lakshmi Lodge** in road opposite Rainbow. Good *thalis*.
**₹₹ Royal Orchid**, Kalawad Rd. Good veg dishes.
**₹₹ Rainbow** Lakhajiraj Rd. Good South Indian, very busy in the evenings when you may have to queue outside.
**₹₹ Step-In**, Galaxy Centre, Jawahar Rd. Pizzas, Indian fast food and ice creams.

**Bhavnagar** *p1259, map p1260*
**₹₹₹ Nilambagh**, Banquet Hall (chandeliers, Belgian mirrors, Burma teak furniture). Wide choice. Good tandoori food. Garden restaurant at night is pleasant, except for loud Hindi film music.
**₹₹ Bageecha**, Waghawadi Rd. Wide choice of vegetarian in attractive garden setting, well appointed.
**₹₹ Greenland**, Krishnanagar, near Barton Museum. North Indian and ice creams in a pleasant garden setting.
**₹₹ Live-in**, Waghawadi Rd. Roof garden, Indian/Chinese vegetarian. Young people's hangout.

ƚƚ **Murli**, Panwadi Chowk, T431037. Excellent *thalis*.
ƚƚ **Nilgiri**, Blue Hill. Excellent Indian vegetarian (try *palak paneer* and cheese naan), also *idli, dosa* at tea time, a/c.
ƚ **Das**, near Nilambagh, **Ramkrishna**, near Piramal Chowk, and **Khatri**, on Waghawadi Rd, have melt-in-the mouth sweets (try *sangam*, a cashew nut candy, or the local *pedas*) and savoury snacks like the famous Bhavnagar *ganthias*.
ƚ **Evening Point**. Traditional Kathiawadi *thali* in a rustic setting.

**Palitana** *p1261, map p1262*
ƚ **Mansi Park**, Bhavnagar Rd. North Indian, Chinese. Pleasant open-air restaurant, tables on the lawn and in kiosks, hill views (main dishes Rs 35-50), also tea time treats (cheese toast, finger chips, *idli, dosa*).
Many eateries in Taleti Rd offer Gujarati *thali* as well as *pau-bhaji* and ice cream. Along Station Rd, *thalis* are Rs 10-15.

**Gopnath** *p1263*
ƚ **Jai Chamunda**, opposite Gopnath Bungalow, outdoor eating place though fairly clean, gets rather overcrowded and noisy on Sun. Good Kathiawadi veg *thalis* with unlimited refills (Rs 45), Rs 10 for local desserts; seafood at night to order (catch of the day lobster Rs 400, shrimps Rs 200 per kg).

**Junagadh** *p1263, map p1264*
ƚƚ **Garden Café**, Girnar Rd. Attractive outdoor restaurant with view of hills, among flowering plants and lawns, average food, good atmosphere and service; handy for visitors to the hill.
ƚ **Geeta** and **Sharda**, both near railway station. Good *thalis*.
ƚ **Poonam**, Dhal Rd, Chittakhana Chowk, 1st floor. Unlimited Gujarati *thalis* (Rs 35-60). Excellent food and service.
ƚ **Sagar**, offers similar fare to **Santoor**, see below. Great breakfasts also (poori-aloo, idli, vada, lassi. A/c.
ƚ **Sagar**, Jayshree Talkies Rd. Good Punjabi and Gujarati, veg, Indian breakfast (Rs 50).
ƚ **Santoor**, off MG Rd, near Kalwa Chowk, upstairs. Very good Indian and Chinese veg dishes, a/c, excellent value, 0945-1500, 1700-2300.
ƚ **Swati**, Jayshree Talkies Rd. Mainly Punjabi, some South Indian and Chinese, all veg. Good food and lassi, courteous, young enthusiastic staff, clean and comfortable (though smell of spices pervades), a/c, one of town's most popular restaurants.
Near Kalwa Chowk, try *Dal-Pakwana* (a Sindhi brunch), stuffed parathas, fruit juices. (Kesar mango from April to June). In Azad Chowk, try milk sweets, snacks and curds.

**Veraval** *p1266*
ƚ **Ali Baba**, near Park Hotel. Recommended for seafood.
ƚ **Sagar**, Riddhi-Siddhi Complex, 1st floor, between Bus Stand and clocktower. A/c, excellent service, veg Punjabi and South Indian.

**Diu** *p1266, maps p1267 and p1268*
Some Catholic homes serve traditional 'Portuguese' food to western travellers with an hour's notice (ask directions in the Christian locality near St Paul's Church).
ƚƚ **Apana**, Old Fort Rd. Large seafood platters (shark, lobster, kingfish, crab and veg), Rs 300, easily shared by 4-6. Recommended.
ƚƚ **Bom Appetite**, Mrs D'Souza's residence near St Paul's, T02875 253137. To order 'Portuguese' lunches.
ƚƚ **Martha's Place**, opposite the museum. Excellent home cooking, good views.
ƚƚ **Ram Vijay**, near State Bank of Saurashtra. Excellent 'home-made' ice creams, milk shakes and sodas, friendly.
ƚƚ **Uma Shakti**, near Samrat. Good food and service (try toasted cheese sandwiches).
ƚƚ -ƚ **Island Bar**, on Nagoa-Diu Rd, Nagoa. Varied, mid-range, cheap menu including Punjabi, Chinese, continental. Food can be excellent or indifferent, service can be slow.
ƚƚ -ƚ **Neelkant's Restaurant** Jallandhar Beach, serves delicious cheap *thalis*, new a/c for continental food, backpackers' meeting place, friendly, family run. Recommended.
ƚƚ -ƚ **Radhika Beach Resort**, Nagoa. Wide choice of Indian, Chinese, some continental. Well-prepared meals from spotless kitchen, pleasant a/c surroundings and attentive service.

**Porbandar** *p1269, map p1270*
Sudama Chowk near the ST Stand is where locals gather for *samosas, pakodas, bhel,*

*kachori, pau bhaji* etc in the evening.
**Adarsh**, MG Rd. A/c, Indian vegetarian and ice creams.
**Khana Khazana**, MG Rd. Open sunset to past midnight, is recommended for cheese/chutney sandwiches, cheese toasts, burgers and coffee; South Indian snacks (hot *idlis*) on Sun; also takeaway.
**Swagath**, MG Rd. Excellent *thalis*, pleasant. The bazar sells *khajli* (fried dough snack), *thabdi* and *peda* (milk sweets).

**Jamnagar** *p1271*
**Rangoli**, near Anupam Talkies, near Bedi Gate. A/c, good but more expensive veg Punjabi and South Indian, friendly, open lunch time and evening (except Wed).
**Kalpana**, near Teen Batti. Veg dishes.
**Urvee**, Supermarket, Town Hall Rd. Good Gujarati *thalis* at lunch time.

**Dwarka** *p1271, map p1272*
Poor choice of rather dirty eating places. **Dwarkeshwar** is best for tasty, hygienic *thalis* but slow service.

## Bars and clubs

**Diu** *p1266, maps p1267 and p1268*
The night market, near post office, very popular. Kingfisher, Turbo, London Pilsner, Rs 20-30 per bottle; tasty snacks from stalls too. Most bars close around 2130. **Nilesh** stays open until 2300.

## Festivals and events

**Palitana** *p1261, map p1262*
Teras Fair at Gheti (Adpur-Palitana, 4 km from town) 3 days before *Holi*. Thousands of Jain pilgrims attend, joined by villagers who come for free lunches!

**Junagadh** *p1263, map p1264*
**Feb-Mar**: Bhavnath Fair at Sivaratri at Damodar Kund near the Girnar foothills is very spectacular. Attended by *Naga Bawas* (naked sages), who often arrive on decorated elephants to demonstrate strange powers (including the strength of their penis), and colourful tribal people who come to worship and perform *Bhavai* folk theatre. **Nov-Dec**: a popular 10-day *Fair* is held at the Jain temples starting at **Kartik Purnima**.

**Dwarka** *p1271, map p1272*
**Aug/Sep**: Janmashtami, see page . Special worship and fair (Aug).

## Shopping

**Bhavnagar** *p1259, map p1260*
Textiles, locally embroidered cushion covers, shawls, *bandhni* and mock-silver jewellery are good buys. Try Vora Bazar, Radhanpuri Market, Amba Chowk, Darbargadh Lane and Talao fruit-and-veg market. Handlooms and handicrafts are best at **Khadi stores** in the Barton Museum building.

**Palitana** *p1261, map p1262*
Local handicrafts include embroidery (saris, dresses, purses, bags, wall hangings etc) and metal engraving. You can watch the craftsmen making harmonium reeds.

**Diu** *p1266, maps p1267 and p1268*
The night market is very lively in the evenings. Govt **Cottage Emporia** near the jetty sell local crafts of stone, metal and shell; **Jaysukh**, Sangaria Lane, has good shell crafts. Don't be tempted by star tortoise and turtle shell bangles and souvenirs; they are illegal under 'Wildlife Protection Act', severe penalties attached.

## Activities and tours

**Diu** *p1266, maps p1267 and p1268*
**Cruises**
Evening cruises from Bunder Chowk jetty to Nagoa Beach, with music, Rs 100 per person; times from tourist office.

**Tour operators**
**Oceanic**, Bunder Chowk, T02875 2521800.
**Reshma**, T/F02875 252241.

**Watersports**
At Nagoa and Ahmedpur-Mandvi: 8-seater speed boat (10-15 mins)/parasailing/wind surfing, each Rs 500; waterskiing Rs 100 (jet skiing at Nagoa beach). A pool/water slide complex is next to Kohinoor on the Diu-Nagoa road.

**Dwarka** *p1271, map p1272*
**Dwarka Darshan** a tour of 4 local pilgrimage sites (Nageshwar Mandir, Gopi Talav Teerth,

Beyt Dwarka, Rukmini Temple) by minibus, departs 0800, 1400, 5 hrs (can take 7!). Tickets Rs 30; book a day in advance for morning tour. Alternatively, visit only Beyt Dwarka for a worthwhile day spent with pilgrims.

## Transport

**Rajkot** *p1258, map p1258*

**Air**

Some 4 km northwest, airlines' buses run transfers to town. Indian Airlines, Angel's Hotel, Dhebar Chowk, T0281 2222295, airport T0281 2453313, www.indian-airlines.nic.in. Jet Airways, 7 Bilkha Plaza, Kasturba Rd, T0281 2479623, airport T0281 2454533, www.jetairways.com, flies to **Mumbai** daily.

**Bus**

The ST bus station is just south of the busy Dhebar Chowk at the centre, while more comfortable private long distance coaches arrive at the operators just behind it. ST buses to **Junagadh** (2 hrs), **Veraval** (5 hrs), **Jamnagar** (2 hrs) and **Dwarka** and **Ahna**. Eagle Travels run private luxury buses daily to **Ahmadabad** and **Mumbai**.

**Train**

Junction Station **Ahmadabad**: *Rajkot Ahmadabad Exp, 9154*, 0630, 4¼ hrs; *Saurashtra Exp*, 9216, 0050, 6½ hrs (continues to **Vadodara**, 3¾ hrs); *Janata Exp, 9018*, 1440, 5¼ hrs (continues to **Vadodara**, 2½ hrs). **Mumbai (Central)**: *Okha Mumbai Saurashtra Mail, 9006*, 1735, 14½ hrs; *Saurashtra Exp, 9216*, 0050, 18½ hrs. **Porbandar**: *Saurashtra Exp, 9215*, 0200, 4¾ hrs; *Porbandar Exp, 9264*, 0915, Mon, Thu, 5 hrs. **Vadodara**: same as Mumbai, 7¼-9 hrs. **Veraval**: *Rajkot-Veraval Mail 9838*, 1110, 5¼ hrs.

**Bhavnagar** *p1259, map p1260*

**Air**

The airport is 5 km southeast of town; auto-rickshaws to town insist on Rs 65-75. Indian Airlines, T0278 2439445, airport T0278 2493130, www.indian-airlines.nic.in, Jet Airways, Surat House, Waghawadi Rd, T0278 243 3371, airport T0278 2202004, www.jetairways.com, flies to **Mumbai**.

**Bus**

Frequent rickety ST buses to other main towns; **Palitana** (1¾ hrs, Rs 10); several to **Una for Diu** (6 hrs); **Velavadhar** (1 hr). Private operators: Tanna Travels, Waghawadi Rd, T0278 2420477, has luxury coaches (reclining seats) to/from **Ahmadabad**, almost hourly from 0600, 4½ hrs plus short tea break, recommended; to **Vadodara** 5½ hrs, 3 daily. Punjab Travels, Kalanala, T0278 2424582.

**Train**

The station in the Old City is about 3 km north of the ST Bus station in the New Town. **Ahmadabad**: a slow journey as the line takes a circuitous route to skirt the marshes. *Bhavnagar Ahmadabad Exp, 9935*, 1530, 5½ hrs; *Shetrunji Exp, 9909*, 0540, 5½ hrs; *Link Exp, 9947*, 2300, 7 hrs.

**Velavadhar National Park** *p1260*

A few buses from Bhavnagar; better to hire a car. Alternatively hire a Jeep/chhakra (motorbike trailer) from Vallabhipur. A new bridge being built near Bhavnagar port to Adhelai near the park will make access faster and easier.

**Palitana** *p1261, map p1262*

**Bus**

ST Bus (0800-1200, 1400-1800) to **Ahmadabad** (often with a change at Dhandhuka), deluxe from Ahmadabad (0700, 0800, 0900); to Bhavnagar (1½ hrs), **Jamnagar**, **Rajkot**, **Surat**, **Una**, **Vadodara**. Private deluxe coaches to **Surat** and **Mumbai** via **Vadodara**; surprisingly, none to Ahmadabad. Operators: Paras, Owen Bridge, T02848 252370. Opposite ST depot: Khodiar, T02848 252586 (to Surat) and Shah, T02848 252396.

**Taxi**

For up to 7, run between **Bhavnagar** (57 km by State Highway) and Palitana, Rs 15 each.

**Train**

To **Bhavnagar** about every 3 hrs. From **Ahmadabad**, change at Sihor: from Sihor to Palitana depart 0722, 1525, 1924; to Sihor 0900, 1805, 2030.

**Alang** *p1262*
from Bhavnagar: buses from ST Bus Stand, through the day from 0600 (last return 1800), 1¾ hrs, Rs 10. At Alang, tongas go up and down the beach front past the shipyards for Rs 5. Taxis take 1½ hrs, Rs 400-500 return, and auto-rickshaws Rs 300-400 (expect to bargain).

**Junagadh** *p1263, map p1264*
**Bycicle**
Hire from shops on Dhal Rd, near **Relief Hotel**; Rs 2 per hr, may need to bargain.

**Bus**
Regular buses to **Ahmadabad**, **Rajkot** (2 hrs), **Veraval**, **Porbandar** and **Sasan Gir** (2½ hrs).

**Train**
**Ahmadabad**: *Somnath Mail 9923*, 1902, 9¼ hrs; *Girnar Exp 9845*, 2120, 9 hrs. **Rajkot**: *Veraval Rajkot Mail 9837*, 1318, 5¼ hrs; *Fast Pass 341*, 0530, 3¼ hrs; *347*, 1000, 3¾ hrs; *349*, 1550, 3¾ hrs. **Veraval**: *Girnar Exp 9846*, 0623, 1¾ hrs. For **Sasan Gir**: take *Fast Pass* 352 to Delwada, 0605; a delightful journey.

**Sasan Gir National Park** *p1265*
**Air**
Nearest airport is Keshod (86 km).

**Bus**
Service to/from **Junagadh** (54 km), 2½ hrs, and **Veraval** (40 km), 2 hrs. Service to **Una** for Diu is unpredictable, morning dep 1100. Frequent buses from **Ahmadabad**.

**Train**
From **Junagadh** to Sasan Gir, *352*, 0650, 3 hrs, continues to **Delwada** near Diu; return to Junagadh, *351*, 1827, so possible to visit for the day. The route is very attractive. **Talala** is the last major station, 15 km before Sasan, so stock up with fruit, biscuits, liquids there. From **Veraval**, take *359* at 1039, or *353* at 1409, both bound for Khijadiya; return to **Veraval**, by *354* at 1138 or *360* at 1535.

**Veraval** *p1266*
**Somnath Travels**, Satta Bazar, will obtain tickets for long-distance journeys.

**Bicycle** hire from opposite bus station or railway station, some in poor condition (road between Veraval and Somnath is appalling).

**Buses** to **Keshod** (1 hr), **Diu**, **Porbandar** (2 hrs), **Bhavnagar** (9 hrs). Deepak Ramchand Taxis, T02876 222591 has non-a/c Ambassador taxis. To **Ahmedpur Mandvi** (via docks) and **Somnath** Rs 550, **Diu** Rs 600, tour of docks and Somnath Rs 250.

**Taxis** from Tower Rd and ST bus stands are cheaper than those at the railway station.

**Train** to **Ahmadabad**: *Somnath Mail 9923*, 1705, 11¼ hrs; *Girnar Exp 9845*, 1930, 10¾ hrs.

**Prabhas Patan** *p1266*
From **Veraval**, auto-rickshaw (bargain to Rs 30 return) or frequent bus.

**Diu** *p1266, maps p1267 and p1268*
Most visitors arrive by long distance buses either via Una or direct to the island, easiest from Ahmadabad via Bhavnagar.

**Air**
The airport is 6 km west of the town; auto-rickshaws charge around Rs 50 to transfer. **Jet Airways**, at the airport, Nagoa Rd, T02875 253542, www.jetairways.com, accepts credit card payment. **Mumbai**, daily (1050 and 1250 on alternate days), US$80.

**Bicycle**
Hire about Rs 50 per day. **A to Z**, near Vegetable Market, Panchwati Rd; **Shilpa**, Bunder Chowk; **Mayur**, past Ankur Hotel (across rough ground, then 20m along alley to left), excellent bikes; **Daud**, Zampa Gate, well maintained, new bikes; **Krishna Cycles** at Ghogla.

**Bus**
A road bridge connects Diu Town with Ghogla (frequent buses). ST buses operate from the Jethabai Bus Stand near the bridge to Ghogla. Local Bus Stand: to Nagoa 3 daily; frequent service to Bucharwada-Vanakbara and Una, Rs 4 (minibus Rs 6).

Most long-distance buses operate from the Jethabai Bus Stand just south of the bridge; enquire beforehand. ST services to **Ahmadabad** via Bhavnagar, 0700 (10 hrs); **Jamnagar** via Junagadh, 0600; **Porbandar**, 1300; **Rajkot**, several 0445-1725 (7 hrs); **Vadodara**, 1730; **Veraval**, several 0400-1300 (2½ hrs). Buses often leave 15-20 mins early. For **Bhavnagar** ask for 'direct bus' (departs 1035), as some go through Mahuva and are packed. Private agents in the Main Sq offer buses from the private bus stand to **Mumbai** (deluxe) at 1000, and towns in Gujarat which are more reliable than ST buses. To **Ahmadabad**, 1900; from Ahmadabad, a direct bus leaves from Paldi Chowrasta at 2100. Goa Travels runs buses to Bhavnagar, Junagadh (5 hrs), Palitana. A daily bus connects with **Mumbai** via Bhavnagar (20 hrs). **Una**, 30 mins from Diu (10 km), has more frequent buses to/from **Ahmadabad**, **Bhavnagar**, **Junagadh**, **Rajkot**, **Veraval** etc. Shiv Shakti, Sahajanand and Gayatri Travels run private buses from the main Bus Station to **Ahmadabad**, **Bhavnagar**, **Mumbai**, **Vadodara** etc. From Vanakbara, bus to **Okha**, 0700, 0800.

### Motorbike

Hire in the market area; about Rs 150 a day; Kismet has good new scooters Rs 100 per day, Rs 200 deposit, friendly service; repairs off Estrada Lacerda.

### Rickshaw

Auto-rickshaw: Rs 30 to Nagoa, Rs 25 to Ghogla.

### Train

Delwada, 8 km north is the nearest railhead just south of Una; auto-rickshaws demand Rs 100 from Diu to Una or Delwada. The station is a short walk from the centre of town – follow the locals! Slow train to **Junagadh** (stops at **Sasan Gir**) *351*, 1445. Veraval (90 km): to/from Ahmadabad, *Girnar Exp* and *Somnath Mail* take 12 hrs.

**Porbandar** *p1269, map p1270*
Jet Airways, T0286 2220974, www.jetairways.com, flies daily to Mumbai.

ST **buses** serve most centres of Gujarat. Bharat and Eagle Travels run regular private luxury buses to **Ahmadabad**, **Jamnagar**, **Junagadh**, **Rajkot** etc.

**Trains** are as follows: **Mumbai Central**: *Saurashtra Exp 9216*, 2000, 23½ hrs. Also to Rajkot and Ahmadabad.

**Jamnagar** *p1271*
Airport, 10 km west. Indian Airlines, T0288 2552911, www.indian-airlines.nic.in; to **Mumbai**.

STC **bus** services to **Rajkot** (frequent) and **Ahmadabad**; also **Dwarka** and **Porbandar**.

The railway station is 6 km northwest of town. **Ahmadabad**: *Saurashtra Exp 9216*, 2243, 7¼ hrs; *Saurashtra Mail 9006*, 1445, 7½ hrs. Both to **Mumbai Central**: 20¾ hrs and 17½ hrs via Rajkot: 1¾ hrs and 2¼ hrs. **Vadodara (and Ahmadabad)**: *Okha-Puri Exp*, 1115.

**Dwarka** *p1271, map p1272*
**Bus** to **Jamnagar**, **Porbandar** and **Somnath**. Private operators run to most major towns in Gujarat.

**Trains** to **Ahmadabad** and **Vadodara**: *Saurashtra Mail 9006*, 1215, 10 hrs, and **Mumbai Central**: 20 hrs. Also *Okha-Puri Exp*, 0835.

**Okha** *p1272*
From **Ahmadabad** by *Saurashtra Mail 9006*, 1120, 10¾ hrs. Local buses to Dwarka, 1 hr. Morning direct bus to Bhuj. From **Okha**, boats to Beyt Dwarka take 10-15, mins each way.

## Directory

**Bhavnagar** *p1259, map p1260*
**Banks** State Bank of Saurashtra, Darbargadh, changes currency and TCs. **Useful addresses** Forest office, near Nilambagh Palace, T0278 2428644.

**Palitana** *p1261, map p1262*
**Hospital** Mansinhji Govt Hospital, Main Rd; Shatrunjaya Hospital, Taleti Rd. **Post** GPO: Main Rd, with Poste Restante; PO, Bhairavnath Rd. **Tourist office** At Hotel Toran Sumeru.

**Junagadh** *p1263, map p1264*
**Banks** Bank of Baroda, near the town Post Office is very efficient and changes TCs; Bank of Saurashtra, changes currency.

**Sasan Gir National Park** *p1265*
The post office in the village has an excellent 'frank' for postcards and letters. Health Centre, Post Office and Bank at Sasan. Market at Talala.

**Diu** *p1266, maps p1267 and p1268*
**Banks** State Bank of Saurashtra, near Fish Market opposite *Nilesh hotel*, accepts TCs but

not foreign currency immediately (only encashed after notes are verified by HQ); very slow. Authorised dealers next to Reshma Travels and Alishan Hotel are more efficient for exchange (sterling and US$ TCs and currency). **Internet** Deepee Telecom and Cyber café, Bunder Chowk. **Medical store** Manesh Medical Store is a pharmacy with a doctor in the building. **Post** The main Post Office is on Bunder Chowk, the other is at Ghogla. **Tourist offices** At Tourist Complex, Ghogla. Mon-Fri, 0930-1315, 1400-1745. Information Asst, Diu jetty north of Bunder Chowk, T02875 252212.

**Porbandar** *p1269, map p1270*
**Banks** Bank of India, Kedareshwar Rd, and State Bank of India, MG Rd (and sometimes Bank of Baroda) change TCs of reputed companies. After frauds and fake notes, they are wary of currency.

**Jamnagar** *p1271*
**Post** Head Post Office at Chandni Chowk. Forestry Office, T0288 2552077. **Travel agents, exchange** and **internet** are around Teen Batti in the New Town Centre.



# Kachchh (Kutch)

*The scenic Maliya Miyana bridge, across salt marshes often filled with birds, gives a beguilingly attractive impression of the gateway to Kachchh. Yet perhaps this region is climatically the least appealing of Gujarat, and it is certainly the most sparsely populated. It is well and truly off the beaten tourist trail. The various communities such as Rabaris, Ahirs and Meghwals among others, each have a distinct dress and practise a particular craft.* *▸▸ For Sleeping, Eating and other listings, see pages 1288-1290.*

## Background

The region, the central peninsula, is surrounded by the seasonally flooded Great and Little Ranns. The Gulf of Kachchh to the south, a large inlet of the Arabian Sea, has a marine national park and sanctuary with 42 islands and a whole range of reefs, mudflats, coastal salt marsh and India's largest area of mangrove swamps.

The **Kachchh Peninsula** is relatively high, covered with sheets of volcanic lava but with often saline soil. Dry and rocky, there is little natural surface water though there are many artificial tanks and reservoirs. Intensive grazing has inhibited the development of the rich vegetation around the tanks characteristic of neighbouring Sindh in Pakistan, and there is only sparse woodland along the often dry river beds. The wetlands are severely over-exploited, but some of the lakes are important seasonal homes for migratory birds including pelicans and cormorants. The **Rann of Kachchh** in the north runs imperceptibly into the Thar desert. A hard smooth bed of dried mud in the dry season, some vegetation survives, concentrated on little grassy islands called *bets*, which remain above water level when the monsoons flood the mudflats.

With the arrival of the southwest monsoon in June the saltwater of the Gulf of Kachchh invades the Rann and the Rajasthan rivers pour freshwater into it. It then becomes an inland sea and Kachchh virtually becomes an island. From December to February, the Great Rann is the winter home of migratory **flamingos** when they arrive near **Khavda**. There are also sand-grouse, Imperial grouse, pelicans and avocets.

Local traditional **embroidery** and **weaving** is particularly prized. When the monsoons flooded vast areas of Kachchh, farming had to be abandoned and handicrafts flourished which not only gave expression to artistic skills but also provided a means of earning a living. Mirrorwork, Kachchh appliqué and embroidery with beads, *bandhani* (tie-and-dye), embroidery on leather, gold and silver jewellery, gilding and enamelling and colourful wool-felt *namda* rugs are available.

### The earthquake

The area around Bhuj was devastated by the severe earthquake which hit Gujarat on the morning of 26 January 2001 and claimed around 20,000 lives. With its epicentre near Bhuj, the tremors which hit 7.7 on the Richter scale virtually flattened the town and several nearby villages. Although a massive rebuilding programme began soon after much remains to be done. This section is an account of what existed prior to the earthquake. Check with the tourist office for up to date information. Visitors will be warmly welcomed and will play a big part in getting the town back on its feet.

## Bhuj → *Phone code: 02832. Colour map 2, grid C1. Population: 120,000.*

The devastating earthquake in January 2001 destroyed much of this old walled town with its tightly packed maze of narrow winding streets. Repairs and restoration are progressing. Most of the heritage buildings suffered extensive damage. It is hoped that some of the structures, as described below, will be restored by experts but many treasures have been lost permanently.

### Sights

Among the old buildings in the citadel is the palace of **Rao Lakha** (circa 1752), the fortunate patron of Ramsingh Malam, who after his European adventures became a master clockmaker, architect, glass-blower, tile-maker and much more. A large white mansion with carvings and fretwork, the palace contains a Darbar Hall, State Apartments and the noted **Aina Mahal** (Mirror Palace) which has suffered some damage but is restorable though items such as glass paintings have been destroyed. It has exquisite ivory inlaid doors (circa 1708), china floor tiles and marble walls covered with mirrors and gilt decorations.

The **Fuvara Mahal** (Music Room), next door, is a curiosity. Surrounded by a narrow walkway, the pleasure hall is a shallow tiled pool with a central platform where the Maharao sat in cool comfort to listen to music, watch dancers or recite his poetry. With its entrance shielded from the hot sun, the candlelit interior with embroidered wall hangings provided a welcome refuge. Ingenious pumps,, raised water to the tank above to feed the pool with sprinkling fountains. Some parts, especially the upper floors and roofs, were seriously damaged in January 2001.

**Rao Pragmalji's Palace** (1865) in red brick is across the courtyard. The elaborate anachronism was designed by the British engineer Colonel Wilkins (though some guides will say by an Italian architect). It contained a vast Darbar Hall, with verandahs, corner towers and *zenanas* all opulently decorated with carving, gilding, Minton tiles and marble. The upper floors suffered serious damage in the earthquake. It is used as Government offices. There are good views of the surrounding countryside from the tall clocktower connected to the palace by covered galleries. The colourful **Swaminarayan Temple** is behind the Palace and near the bazar.

The Italianate **Kachchh Museum** (1877), near Mahadev Gate, is the oldest in Gujarat. Exhibits include the largest collection of Kshatrap inscriptions (the earliest, of AD 89), textiles, weaponry, paintings and an anthropological section. Anyone interested in local traditional folk music and instruments may contact Mr UP Jadia here. Restoration is in progress with the help of Indo-Australian heritage experts.

**Bharatiya Sanskriti Darshan** ⓘ *Mandvi Rd, near Collector's Office*, is a small, delightful Folk Museum and Reference Library. The collection of 4,500 exhibits includes traditional handicrafts, textiles, weaponry, as well as artefacts of historic or artistic importance, and a recreated village of typical Kachchhi *bhungas* (huts) of different communities. *Kutch – People and their handicrafts* by PJ Jethi (Rs 100), and postcards for sale.

**Sarad Bagh Palace**, west of Hamirsar, the last residence of the Maharao (died 1991) is set in very lovely gardens. Exhibits include furniture and exotic ornaments. The **Maharaos' chatedis** (memorial tombs), further south, built of red sandstone were severely damaged in the 1819 earthquake and again in 2001. Some are beyond repair. **Ramkund**, nearby, has a stone lined tank with carvings of Hindu deities.

## Excursions

**Rudrani Dam** ⓘ *14 km north, 30-minute drive from Bhuj on the Sumrasar road,* has the colourful Rudramata Temple, originally 17th century, nearby. The goddess Sati's 'rudra' (frightening) aspect is believed to have fallen on this spot and is hence a place of pilgrimage, see page 1328.

**Qasab** is an outlet for KMVS (Kutch Mahila Vikas Sangathan), a collective of 1,200 craftswomen from 130 local villages who are practising their traditional skills to produce high quality clothes (Indian and western), home furnishings and some leather goods. The women market the products themselves, bypassing an intermediary, thus achieving a fairer deal for themselves and their producer group, see Shopping page 1289.



# Craft villages → *Colour map 2, grid C1. Population: 37,000.*

Handicrafts are a living tradition of Kachchh and the girls of various communities make beautifully embroidered garments for their own trousseaus while women produce attractive fabrics for a second income. Some visitors to villages near Bhuj are disappointed to find that the previously nomadic tribes are being housed in whitewashed urban housing in expanded older villages which are losing their traditional architecture. Cement and modern materials are replacing mud walls and cow dung. However, the handicrafts of these villages are still of a high standard.

## North of Bhuj

ⓘ *Buses from Bhuj go to the main villages from the ST stand, around 0800 (check time), but may involve a 15-min walk. It is better to arrange a taxi or hire a motorbike/scooter.*

The vast grasslands of **Banni** meet the Great Rann in the Khavda region, north of Bhuj. They are home to numerous pastoral nomadic, semi-nomadic and resident people who keep sheep, goats, camels, buffaloes and other livestock. The 40 or so hamlets here are best known for the minute detail of their embroidery. More recently, these villages have started focusing on selling handicrafts as their main source of income and there are signs of modernisation and commercialisation. The traditional thatched huts (*bhungas*) are made from mud plastered with cow dung which are often decorated with hand-painted floral patterns and inlaid with mirrors during festivals. Traditional utensils are still used for cooking, eating and storage in the houses. The area is known for its raptors: eagles, vultures and other birds of prey.

**Dhorodo**, 80 km north, is the centre for Jat embroidery, using chain stitches inset with small mirrors, leather embroidery as well as silver jewellery.

**Sumrasar**, 25 km northeast, is famous for its Ahir embroidery and Soof embroidery of the Sodhas, done without a plan but by counting the warp and weft of the material. Daya Nathani at Ami Baug is an award-winning artisan, and also an astute businesswoman (taxi-drivers are likely to know her house). Kala Raksha, Parkar Vas, Sumrasar Sheikh, near Collector's Office, T02832 277238, is a grassroots organization which maintains a small museum of heirloom textiles. It works with and

## A melting pot of tribes

Kachchh is a meeting point of Sindhi, Gujarati, Muslim and Rajasthani cultures; the local language is more Sindhi than Gujarati. The arid grasslands to the north, south and west of Bhuj are home to a number of pastoral tribes – the Bharwad shepherds and goat herds, the Rabari camel and cattle herders, Maldhars who keep buffaloes, Samra and Sindhi Muslim cameleers and others. The communities have the Lohan merchants, Langa musicians of the Indian desert and Kanbi Patel agriculturalists among them. They came from near and far – some, like the Sodha Rajputs, originated from the area neighbouring Rajasthan now in Pakistan, the Jats from Baluchistan, while the Sindhis claim Abyssinian descent.



trains 180 artisans to create contemporary pieces inspired by their own traditions. Now run by Judy Frater, the American author of *Threads of Identity*.

**Loria** (**Ludia**), 60 km away, has huts with painted and mirror inlaid walls, and is famed for its wood crafts.

**Zura**, 30 km, produces embroidered footwear and other leather crafts. Copper bells are also made in this village.

**Nirona**, 40 km northwest, has embroidery, lacquered wood crafts, wood carving and is the only home of highly skilful rogan-painting – fabrics painted using iron rods. Buses from Bhuj take about 1½ hours.

**Nakhtarana**, northwest in the heart of the craft village belt, produces some tie-and- dye work. There is a Chinkara Sanctuary at **Narayan Sarovar**, 75 km away.

**Charri Dund Lake**, a reservoir near Charri village, offers splendid birdwatching opportunities. Flamingoes, pelicans, cranes, storks, ducks etc gather in large numbers, specially in winter, while nearby grasslands are filled with passerine and ground dwelling birds. The Banni grasslands are known for their huge eagle and vulture congregations. Bombay Natural History Society and other organisations monitor bird migrations in the Banni region, and bird banding camps are set up around Charri lake. The grasslands are home to wolf, hyena, jackal, Indian and desert foxes and lesser wild cats but are imperilled by the government's decision to convert Banni into pastureland.

**Dholavira** is the site of excavation of a Harappan town (pre-2500BC) which some estimate to be larger than Moenjodaro, in Pakistan. It was only discovered in 1967 and excavation began in 1990. The drive to Khadir *beyt*, an oasis in the Great Rann, through dazzling salt flats is very scenic. Excavations show the complex to be on three levels (Citadel, Middle and Lower Towns) with pottery, stone cutting, coppersmithing, drainage systems and town planning at an advanced level. The fortifications with walls, bastions and double ramparts reflect danger from invasions or enemies. An inscribed tablet found here bears 10 letters in the Harappan script. The bus from Bhuj (via Rapar) takes seven hours.

## South of Bhuj

ⓘ *Buses to Rajkot or Ahmadabad can drop you off at most of the villages.*

There are a number of interesting villages south of Bhuj en route to Gandhidham. All require no permit – Mandvi, Mundra on the coast and Bachau, 84 km east. **Tunda Vandh** is a good place to see typical *bhungas* of Kachchh. Architecture students come to see, study and photograph the traditional architecture adapted to this hostile climate. The interiors have beautiful Rabari cupboards, chests, inlaid mirrors and paintings.

**Bhujodi**, 10 km southeast, off the main road and a 10-minute walk from the bus stand, is the centre for pitloom weaving. The weavers have now been organized into a co-operative. They produce colourful *galichas* (carpets), *durries* (rugs), *dhablos* (blankets), and other items from wool, camel/goat hair, cotton, and even synthetic fibres. Some embroidery and tie-and-dye can be seen here as well. Mr Vanka Kana Rabari has reasonably priced local embroidery etc, but not the most select quality. *Shrujan* sells upmarket embroideries and home furnishings.

**Padhdhar**, 22 km southeast of Bhujodi, produces Ahir embroidery using round mirrors with floral and geometrical patterns. **Dhaneti** is also a centre for Ahir and Rabari embroidery. Meet Govindbhai, a local entrepreneur, and his friendly family who will show you the embroidered and mirror inlaid fabrics made for their own use. There are some intricate hero stones (*pallias*) by the village lake.

**Dhamanka**, 50 km east of Bhuj, is famous for its block printed fabrics, table/bed linen, garments etc, using vegetable or chemical dyes. Used blocks can be bought here which make good decorative pieces.

**Anjar**, 22 km southeast, was an early Jadeja Rajput capital of Kachchh, founded 450 years ago. The Jesal-Toral shrine has a romantic tale of the reform of an outlaw prince through the love of a village girl. Anjar is also known for its metalcrafts, especially betel nut crackers and ornaments, *bandhni* and block printing. The 1818 Bungalow of Captain McMurdoch, the first European to settle in Kachchh, now government offices, has some Kamangari paintings on the ground floor.



## Mandvi

Mandvi, 54 km southwest of Bhuj, is a pretty little seaside town, with a reservoir in the centre and a river beyond. During the 18th century the town outclassed Bhuj in importance, the sea-faring people dominating the sea trade, taking cotton, rice, spices etc to the Persian gulf, Arabia and Zanzibar. The skill of building *dhows* and boats using simple tools is being revived along the river – worth watching.

The town is now a centre for handicrafts like *bandhni* tie-and-dyed fabrics, jewellery and shell toys. It is a desert town but important agricultural research for the Kachchh region is being carried out here in the Gujarat Agricultural University and the Vivekenand Research Institute, to improve farming in the often hostile environment. There is an 18th-century **palace** with an *Aina Mahal* (Mirror Hall) and music rooms which have remains of intricate stone carvings of Dutchmen, tigers and dancing girls and woodcarvings in the courtyard. The magnificent 1940s **Vijay Vilas palace** ⓘ *Rs 5, camera Rs 20, plus vehicle charge,* with huge domes, combines Indian and European styles. You can see the drawing room with royal memorabilia, and the attractive *jali* windows of the *zenana*. The terrace, reached by a spiral staircase, with excellent sea views, especially at sunset, is ideal for a picnic. The beaches on the town side are good for swimming and even camel or horse riding. A wind farm next to the beach is working hard to produce an alternative energy source. The *Maharao*'s pleasant private beach with few onlookers is open to visitors ⓘ *Rs 30 (worthwhile for women, to escape hassle from male onlookers).* Out of town, you can visit a magnificent new Jain temple.

## Bhuvad, Kandla and Gandhidham

On the Mundra Road, 19 km southwest of Anjar, Bhuvad has the ruined 13th-century temple of Bhuvaneshwar Mahadev. The *mandapa* (1289-1290) is supported by 34 unusual pillars (square base, octagonal middle and circular upper section). A local legend describes how the headless body of the chieftain Bhuvad, who was killed in battle about 1320, fought its way to the village. The District Gazetteer records that a shrine with a red headless figure is dedicated to him, while the nearby tall shrines commemorate warriors killed in the same battle. 

Further east along the coast is the port of **Kandla**, built to replace declining Mandvi. After independence, Kandla was further developed by the Government of India, to service the states in northwest India.

**Gandhidham**, 27 km north of Kandla, was founded by the Maharaos of Kachchh to accommodate refugees from Sindh in Pakistan after Partition in 1947. The enterprising community made a promising start and now the town is a prosperous business centre though the old handloom and embroidery co-operatives for refugees still exist. The town has developed with the increasing importance of Kandla as a port having lost Karachi sea port to Pakistan. The Institute of Sindhology here is researching on various aspects of Sindhi culture.

## Little Rann of Kachchh Sanctuary

→ *Colour map 2 grid C2.*



ⓘ *The southern part of the sanctuary is accessible. Forest Department fees, US$5 (foreigners), still camera US$5, at Bajana and Dhrangadhra. Temperature: maximum 42°C, minimum 7°C; Annual rainfall: 1,000 mm. Best season is late-Oct to mid-Mar.*

The 4,950 sq km Wild Ass Sanctuary of the Little Rann of Kachchh (created in 1973) and the 7,850 sq km desert wildlife sanctuary of the great Rann, together would comprise the largest contiguous tract of protected wildlife territory in India were it not divided by a road. The Little Rann is mostly a saline wilderness, broken by beyts – islands during the monsoon – covered with grass, bushes, acacia and thorn scrub. The area is under severe threat from the salt works, which clear the vegetation, release toxic effluents into the wetlands and pollute the air. A fast growing thorn scrub – *Prosopis juliflora* – is destroying most other vegetation.

### Sights

This is the last home of the **Asiatic wild ass** (locally called *khacchar* or *ghorker*), a handsome pale chestnut brown member of the wild horse family with a dark stripe down the back. Wild asses are usually seen as lone stallions, small groups of mares or harems of a male with mares. Large herds of 40-60 are sometimes seen but they are loosely knit. Males fight viciously, biting and kicking, for their females. Nilgai, antelope and chinkara (Indian gazelle) are other mammals seen, but the chinkara numbers have dwindled due to poaching. Blackbucks have become almost extinct in the Little Rann of Kachchh but are seen in villages nearby. Wolf is the primary predator, though not common. You might spot jackal, desert fox, jungle and desert cat on a drive. Birdlife is abundant. Houbara bustard, spotted and common Indian sand grouse, nine species of larks, desert warbler, desert wheatear, Indian and cream coloured courser, grey francolin and five species of quails are spotted at the *beyts*. The salt marshes teem with flamingos, pelicans, storks, ducks, herons and wading birds. Thousands of demoiselle and common eastern cranes spend the winter here.

### Excursions

The 13th-century **Jhinjwada fort**, on the edge of Little Rann west of Dasada, has majestic gateways. At the southeast corner of the Rann, **Kalaghoda**, southwest of Dasada on the way to Bajana Lake, is particularly interesting. The principal British salt trading post with an old village-pony express, it retains plenty of colonial architecture including Raj bungalows, a cricket pavilion and a bandstand. **Dasada** is a convenient base for visits to the Little Rann. The interesting village has an old fort with wood carvings, 15th-century tombs, potters, a shepherd's colony and nomadic settlements. The Malik Dynasty who received the 35-mile estate in return for military services to the sultan of Ahmadabad, now live in a 1940s mansion **Fatima Manzil**.

## Sleeping

**Bhuj** *p1283*
Several hotels have opened after rebuilding and repairs but check before arriving.
**B Garha Safari Lodge**, at Rudrani Dam, T079-26579672. An option for an out-of-town stay. 14 white-washed *bhungas* (local style huts), tribal furniture, hot water, 7 air-cooled, exchange, pool, atmospheric, good views of lake, jeep tours, mixed reports about food, cleanliness and service.
**B-D Prince**, Station Rd, T02832 220370, F250373. Rooms with bath, restaurant (varied menu), shops (books, clothes, tailoring, Qasab handicrafts), free airport transfer, guided tours of local villages Rs 1,500 per car, crowded area, no credit cards, 'spot' liquor permits.
**C-D Anam**, end of Station Rd, T02832 221390. Extensively damaged, due to re-open "in some time".
**C-D Lake View** Rajendra Park, T02832 253422, F250835. Non-a/c to deluxe a/c comfortable rooms, baths, fridges, garden restaurant, *thalis* indoors, gym, pool (open to non-residents, morning and afternoon), attractive location facing Hamirsar lake (birds in winter).
**D-E Abha International**, Siddharth Complex, Station Rd, T02832 254451, F251424. 31 rooms, with bath (hot water), can be noisy, some a/c (non-a/c very good value); veg restaurant.
**E-F Gangaram**, Darbargadh, T02832 224231. At intersection near Aina Mahal, extremely noisy. 15 clean, comfortable rooms with TV and baths (tiled floors and walls, showers), new a/c rooms, no restaurant, snacks served.
**F Annapurna**, Bhid Gate, T02832 220831. Clean rooms, noisy, friendly owners, great Kachchhi cuisine.
**F City Guest House**, Langa St, near Bazar, T02832 221067. 32 clean, quiet rooms, some with own shower, quiet garden for relaxing, cycle hire, helpful, well run, very good value, used by foreign backpackers.

**Mandvi** *p1286*
**D-E Holiday cottages**, on the beach, 5 small double bedroom cottages with bath (western toilets), some a/c, and tents (2 cots each, shared toilets), Indian-continental restaurant planned.
**F Vinayak**, in town, offers simple rooms (Rs 50).

**Gandhidham** *p1286*
**A-B Desert Palace (Sharma Resort)**, in Gandhidham-Anjar-Bhuj triangle, T02836-221823, www.sharmaresort.com. 60 a/c rooms, resort in local style huts with modern bath, TV, fridge, comfortable, good Punjabi food in outdoor restaurant, pool, gym, boating, ayurvedic treatments, free transfer from airports, good alternative base to Bhuj, reserve ahead.
**D Shiv**, 360 Ward 12-B (2 km from railway station), T02836221297, F20985. 39 rooms, some **C** a/c, wide menu restaurant.

**Little Rann of Kachchh Sanctuary** *p1287*
**B Camp Zainabad**, 9 km from Dasada. A cluster of 16 self contained *kooba* huts in a Eucalyptus grove (beds, hot shower, western toilet) (Rs 2000 each includes meals and safaris), recreating a local village, well located, atmospheric but small cots, hard mattresses and sometimes insipid food, owned and enthusiastically managed by former ruling family of Zainabad, well organized jeep safaris in the Little Rann, also camel/horse/village safaris, boating at nearby lake; contact Desert Coursers in Ahmedabad, T079 2675 2883.
**B Rann Riders**, comfortable air-cooled rooms in 15 spacious Kachchhi *bhungas* and Kathiawadi *koobas* (huts) amid plantation and farms, tiled hot showers, comfortable and relaxing, great atmosphere at night, home grown organic vegetables, fresh fish and poultry, delicious home-cooking (specially meat dishes), enthusiastic owner good jeeps for tours, contact **North West Safaris**, T079-26302019, ssibal@ad1.vsnl.net.in.
**C Fatima Manzil**, English cottage-style outhouse of 1940s mansion damaged by earthquake with renovated and improved rooms and baths. jeep safaris, Sarfraz Malik knows all about Rann wildlife, contact **North West Safaris**, T079- 26302019, ssibal@ad1.vsnl.net.in.
**E-F Guest Houses**, Govt, closer to the Rann, at Bajana and Dhrangadra where a jeep can be hired for visiting the Little Rann.

## Eating

**Bhuj** *p1283*

**Anando**. Excellent for Indian (including Gujarati) snacks. Friendly staff, a/c.

**Annapurna Guest House**, Bhid Gate. Kachchhi. Very cheap, authentic dishes, homely, allow you to sample each dish.

**Green**, Shroff Bazar. Punjabi. South Indian vegetarian. Well prepared food, friendly staff.

**Neelam**, Station Rd opposite **Prince**. North Indian (best paneer curries in town), some Chinese and continental. A/c, good variety and quality, friendly staff.

**Noor**, behind the bus station. Good, reasonably priced *biryani* and *chicken masala*.

**Omlette Centre**, near Bus Station. Popular for breakfast and snacks, excellent filled omelettes, sandwiches and 'English tea'.

**Tammu Fast Food**, between *Abha* and *Janataghar*, has good hot samosas, South Indian snacks and *batakawadas*.

**Toral**, at **Prince**, has good Gujarati, veg *thalis*; bit more expensive than elsewhere, but in a more comfortable setting.

### Snacks

Typical local *dhabelis* (spicy burger of peanuts and potatoes, in a roll), and *bhal* (nuts, gram, vegetables in a spicy sauce), can be sampled on Vaniyawad and Station Rd.

**Mandvi** *p1286*

**Rajneesh Osho**, near Azad Chowk, best value *thalis* in simple dining area. The bazar has fresh coconuts, biscuits, soft drinks and excellent local corn-on-the-cob. In the evening, hand-carts emerge with popular snacks.

## Festivals and events

**Bhuj** *p1283*

**Feb/Mar**: 4-day Rann Utsav (Kachchh Festival) organized by Gujarat Tourism during *Sivaratri* – tribal crafts, folk dances and music, and tours of nearby sights. Fairs in many villages in Feb-Mar (*Nag Panchami*), and around Janmashtami in **Aug-Sep**.

## Shopping

**Bhuj** *p1283*

Excellent folk embroidery, leather shoes, appliqué, mirrorwork, block-printed fabrics, painted pottery and local weaving are available. The market area stretches from Station Rd to the Darbargadh Palace complex, a maze of alleys specialising in different handicrafts. Most shops are closed from 1200 to 1500.

A number of NGOs have organized craft co-operatives for the benefit of artisans.

**Qasab**, 11 Nootan Colony, T02832 222124 and a small shop in Prince Hotel (see Excursions above).

**Shroff Bazar** has craft shops for hassle-free browsing, and clothes: Uday, T02832 224660, a talented designer (Rs 600 for trousers and top), interesting block-prints, excellent tailoring (made-to-measure in a few hours). In **Danda Bazar**: Al Md Isha for outstanding tie-and-dye; Khatri Daod for block-prints, embroideries.

**Kansara bazar**, for silver jewellery. Bandhini Ghar, for tie-and-dye. AA Wazir, opposite General Hospital, near High School, selection of old pieces of embroideries; some for sale.

## Activities and tours

**Little Rann of Kachchh Sanctuary** *p1287*

Naturalist guide Sarfraz Malik (see Fatima Manzil in Sleeping) is full of information on history and insights into the area. Tours of Little Rann wildlife sanctuary and nearby areas known for birds and blackbuck (including white mutant bucks) by jeep, charges Rs 500 per person per day, plus jeep hire Rs800 per day.

## Transport

**Bhuj** *p1283*

**Air**

Indian Airlines, T02832 222433, www.indian-airlines.nic.in, and Jet Airways, Prince Hotel, T02832 253671, www.jetairways.com, flies to **Mumbai**. Security is tight; pack cameras away in your checked baggage.

### Bus

Frequent service to **Ahmadabad**, 411 km. To **Mandvi, Rapar**; **Rajkot**, 5 hrs. Also to **Bhavnagar**; **Jaisalmer**, 8 hrs; **Jamnagar**, 0500, 2040, 2115; **Junagadh**, **Palitana**,1900; **Porbandar**, **Veraval** and **Somnath**. Most long distance buses are scheduled to arrive at sunrise or sunset, so times are changed seasonally. 'Luxury buses' with reclining seats, more leg room, comfort stops etc are strongly recommended. Many private operators cluster around the Bus Station, and run infrequent services to major towns in Gujarat.

### Train

From Mumbai *Bombay-Gandhidham Kutch Exp 9031*, 1710, 14¾ hrs (from Ahmadabad 0155, 6 hrs); then 2 hrs by bus or train to Bhuj. Trains also to **Kandla Port**. For **Rajasthan**: go to **Palanpur** *JPJ Pass*, 2020, 11½ hrs; trains from there to **Abu Rd**, **Ajmer**, **Jaipur** etc or bus; from Abu Rd, bus to **Udaipur**, 5 hrs.

### Mandvi *p1286*

Express bus from Bhuj, 1 hr; others very slow. From bus station, auto-rickshaws, Rs 50 for return trip to Palace (bargain). Possible to visit Mundra from Mandvi on same day, which also has direct services to Bhuj.

### Gandhidham *p1286*

The bus station is a 3-min walk – turn right from the railway station. Frequent buses to **Bhuj**, but very crowded.

Gandhidham is the principal railhead of Kachchh. **Mumbai Central**, *Kachchh Exp 9032* (excellent a/c sleeper and chair-car), 2045, 17 hrs via Vadodara. **Kandla Port**, *Fast Pass 177*, 0705; *173*, 0905; *175*, 1500: 30 mins. **Vadodara**, *Gandhidham Vadodara Exp 9104*, 2305, 7¾ hrs. *Nagercoil-Gandhidham Exp 6336* via Thiruvananthapuram, Kochi etc.

### Little Rann of Kachchh Sanctuary *p1287*

State **buses** from main towns in Gujarat; frequent from **Ahmadabad** (93 km), 2½ hrs; some continue to Zainabad. From **Dasada**, Sarfraz Malik arranges transfer; local buses to **Zainabad**. To **Bhuj**: short route by narrow road, 267 km; by NH8A, 400 km. **Dasada** is 33 km northwest of Viramgam station, which has **trains** from **Mumbai** and **Ahmadabad**. Hotels arrange transfer at extra cost on prior notice. Dhrangadra has trains from Mumbai.

## Directory

### Bhuj *p1283*

**Banks** State Bank of India, Station Rd changes Thomas Cook TCs, 1100-1500 weekdays, till 1300 Sat. **Bank of Baroda**, almost opposite changes Amex TCs (photocopy of passport needed).
**Post** Head PO: Lal Takri, 0700-1300, 1500-1800 (Mon-Sat). Sub-PO in the chowk at entrance to Aina Mahal. **Tourist offices** Gujarat Tourism, 416 Bahumali Building, T02832 224910. **Kachchh Explorer**, Aina Mahal, Bhuj. Mr Jethi there is very knowledgeable and enthusiastic, 0900-1200, 1500-1800, closed Sat. **Useful addresses** Fire:T02832 221490. Police: T02832 220892. Forestry Office: T02832 250600.

# Background

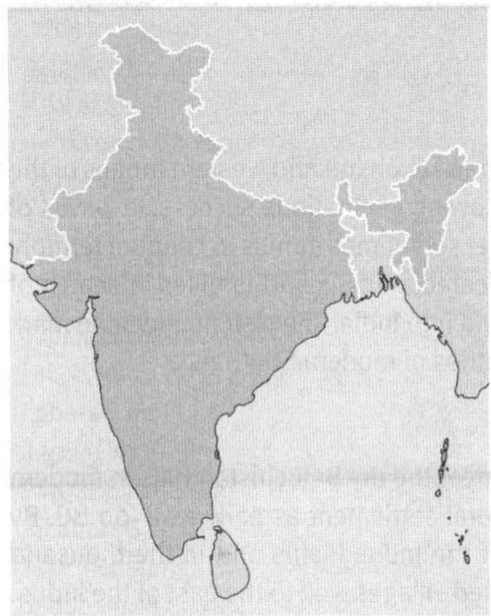



## Footprint features

# History

The first village communities in South Asia grew up on the arid western fringes of the Indus Plains 10,000 years ago. Over the following generations successive waves of settlers – sometimes bringing goods for trade, sometimes armies to conquer territory and sometimes nothing more than domesticated animals and families in search of land and peace – moved across the Indus and into India. They left an indelible mark on the landscape and culture of all the countries of modern South Asia.

## The first settlers

A site at Mehrgarh, where the Indus Plains meet the dry Baluchistan Hills in modern Pakistan, has revealed evidence of agricultural settlement as early as 8500 BC. By 3500 BC agriculture had spread throughout the Indus Plains and in the thousand years following there were independent settled villages well to the east of the Indus. Between 3000 BC and 2500 BC many new settlements sprang up in the heartland of what became the Indus Valley civilization.

Most cultural, religious and political developments during that period owed more to local development than to external influence, although India had extensive contacts with other regions, notably with Mesopotamia. At its height the Indus Valley civilization covered as great an area as Egypt or Mesopotamia. However, the culture that developed was distinctively South Asian. Speculation continues to surround the nature of the language, which is still untranslated.

## India from 2000 BC to the Mauryas

In about 2000 BC Moenjo Daro, widely presumed to be the capital of the Indus Valley Civilization, became deserted and within the next 250 years the entire Indus Valley civilization disintegrated. The causes remain uncertain: the violent arrival of new waves of Aryan immigrants (a theory no one now accepts), increasing desertification of the already semi-arid landscape, a shift in the course of the Indus and internal political decay have each been suggested as instrumental in its downfall. Whatever the causes, some features of Indus Valley culture were carried on by succeeding generations.

Probably from about 1500 BC northern India entered the Vedic period. Aryan settlers moved southeast towards the Ganga valley. Classes of rulers *(rajas)* and

| BC | Northern South Asia | Peninsular India | External events | BC |
|---|---|---|---|---|
| 900,000 | | | Earliest hominids in West Asia | |
| | | Earliest Palaeolithic sites - Narmada Valley; Karnataka; Tamil Nadu and Andhra. | First occupation of N China. | 450,000 |
| 500,000 | Lower Palaeolithic sites from NW to the Peninsula; Pre-Soan stone industries in NW. | | Origin of *homo sapiens* in Africa. | 150,000 |
| | | | *Homo sapiens* in East Asia. | 100,000 |
| | | | First human settlement in Americas (Brazil). | 30,000 |
| 10,000 | Beginning of Mesolithic period. | Continuous occupation of caves and riverside sites. | Earliest known pottery - Kukui, Japan. | 10,500 |
| | | | Ice Age retreats - Hunter gatherers in Europe. | 8,300 |
| 8,000 | First wheat and barley grown in Indus plains. | Mesolithic. | First domesticated wheat, barley in fertile crescent; first burials in North America. | 8,000 |
| 7,500 | Pottery at Mehrgarh; development of villages. | Increase in range of cereals in Rajasthan. | Agriculture begins in New Guinea. | 7,000 |
| 6,500 | Humped Indian cattle domesticated, farming develops. | Cultivation extends south. | Britain separated from Continental Europe by sea level. | 6,500 |

priests *(brahmins)* began to emerge. Grouped into tribes, conflict was common. In one battle of this period a confederacy of tribes known as the Bharatas defeated another grouping of 10 tribes. They gave their name to the region to the east of the Indus which is the official name for India today - Bharat.

The centre of population and of culture shifted east from the banks of the Indus to the land between the rivers Yamuna and Ganga, the doab (pronounced *doe-ahb*, literally 'two waters'). This region became the heart of emerging Aryan culture, which, from 1500 BC onwards, laid the literary and religious foundations of what ultimately became Hinduism, spreading to embrace the whole of India.

**The Vedas** The first fruit of this development was the Rig Veda, the first of four Vedas, composed, collected and passed on orally by Brahmin priests. While some scholars date the oral originsas early as the beginning of the second millennium BC, the date of 1300 BC to about 1000 BC still seems more probable. In the later Vedic period, from about 1000 BC to 600 BC, the Sama, Yajur and Artha Vedas show that the Indo-Aryans developed a clear sense of the Ganga-Yamuna *doab* as 'their' territory.

From the sixth to the third centuries BC the region from the foothills of the Himalaya across the Ganga plains to the edge of the Peninsula was governed under a variety of kingdoms or Mahajanapadhas - 'great states'. Trade gave rise to the birth of towns in the Ganga plains themselves, many of which have remained occupied to the present. Varanasi (Benaras) is perhaps the most famous example, but a trade route was established that ran from Taxila (20 km from modern Islamabad in Pakistan) to Rajgir 1,500 km away in what is now Bihar. It was into these kingdoms of the Himalayan foothills and north plains that both Mahavir, founder of Jainism and the Buddha, were born.



## The Mauryas

Within a year of the retreat of Alexander the Great from the Indus in 326 BC, **Chandragupta Maurya** established the first indigenous empire to exercise control over much of the subcontinent. Under his successors, that control was extended to all but the extreme south of peninsular India.

The centre of political power had shifted steadily east into wetter, more densely forested but also more fertile regions. The Mauryans had their base in the region known as Magadh (now Bihar) and their capital at Pataliputra, near modern Patna. Their power was based on massive military force and a highly efficient, centralized administration.

| BC | Northern South Asia | Peninsular India | External events | BC |
|---|---|---|---|---|
| 3,500 | Potter's wheel in use. Long distance trade. | | Sumeria, Mesopotamia: first urban civilization. | 3,500 |
| 3,000 | Incipient urbanization in the Indus plains. | First neolithic settlements in south Deccan (Karnataka). Ash mounds, cattle herding. | First Egyptian state; Egyptian hieroglyphics; walled citadels in Mediterranean Europe. | 3,100 |
| 2,500 | Indus valley civilization cities of Moenjo Daro, Harappa and many others. | Chalcolithic ('copper' age) in Rajasthan; Neolithic continues in south. | Great Pyramid of Khufu<br>China: walled settlements; European Bronze Age begins: hybridization of maize in South America. | 2,530<br>2,500 |
| 2,000 | Occupation of Moenjo Daro ends. | Chalcolithic in Malwa Plateau, Neolithic ends in south; in Karnataka and Andhra - rock paintings. | Earliest ceramics in Peru. Collapse of Old Kingdom in Egypt. Stonehenge in Britain. Minoan Crete. | 2,300<br>2,150 |
| 1,750 | Indus Valley civilization ends. | Hill-top sites in south India. | Joseph sold into Egypt - Genesis. | 1,750 |

## Indo-Aryans and Dravidians – distinct races?

Recent genetic research suggests that homo sapiens originated in Africa less than 150,000 years ago. Southern and northern Indian types developed distinct genetic characteristics less than 40,000 years ago as they moved out of their central Asian homeland, first into West Asia and then into India, disproving all ideas of racial purity. Early Mediterranean groups form the main component of the Dravidian speakers of the four South Indian states. Later Mediterranean types also seem to have come from the northwest and down the Indus Valley, but more important were the Indo-Aryans, who migrated from the steppes of Central Asia from around 2000 BC.

The greatest of the Mauryan emperors, **Asoka** took power in 272 BC. He inherited a full-blown empire, but extended it further by defeating the Kalingans in modern Orissa, before turning his back on war and preaching the virtues of Buddhist pacifism, see page 708. Asoka's empire stretched from Afghanistan to Assam and from the Himalaya to Mysore.

The state maintained itself by raising revenue from taxation - on everything, from agriculture, to gambling and prostitution. He decreed that 'no waste land should be occupied and not a tree cut down' without permission because all were potential sources of revenue for the state. The *sudras* (lowest of Hindu castes) were used as free labour for clearing forest and cultivating new land.

Asoka (described on the edicts as 'the Beloved of the Gods, of Gracious Countenance') left a series of inscriptions on pillars and rocks across the subcontinent. Over most of India these inscriptions were written in *Prakrit*, using the *Brahmi* script, although in the northwest they were in Greek using the *Kharoshti* script. They were unintelligible for over 2,000 years after the decline of the empire until James Prinsep deciphered the Brahmi script in 1837.

Through the edicts Asoka urged all people to follow the code of **dhamma** or dharma - translated by the Indian historian Romila Thapar as 'morality, piety, virtue and social order'. He established a special force of *dhamma* officers to try to enforce the code, which encouraged toleration, non-violence, respect for priests and those in authority and for human dignity.

However, Romila Thapar suggests that the failure to develop any sense of national consciousness, coupled with the massive demands of a highly paid

| BC | Northern South Asia | Peninsular India | External events | BC |
|---|---|---|---|---|
| 1,750<br>1,500 | Successors to Indus Valley. Aryans invade in successive waves. Development of Indo-Aryan language. | Copper Age spreads, Neolithic continues. Gram and millet cultivation. Hill terracing. Cattle, goats and sheep. | Anatolia: Hittite Empire. New Kingdom in Egypt. First metal working in Peru. First inscriptions in China; Linear B script in Greece, 1650. | 1,650<br>1,570<br>1,500<br>1,400 |
| 1,400 | Indo-Aryan spread east and south to Ganga – Yamuna doab. | Horses introduced into south. Cave paintings, burials. | Tutankhamun buried in Valley of Kings. | 1,337 |
| 1,200 | Composition of Rig Veda begins? | Iron age sites at Hallur, Karnataka. | Middle America: first urban civilization in Olmec; collapse of Hittite Empire, 1200. | 1,200 |
| 1,000 | Earliest Painted Grey Ware in Upper Ganga Valley; Brahmanas begin to be written. | Iron Age becomes more widespread across Peninsula. | Australia: large stone-built villages; David King of Israel, Kingdom of Kush in Africa. | |

bureaucracy and army, proved beyond the abilities of Asoka's successors to sustain. Within 50 years of Asoka's death in 232 BC the Mauryan Empire had disintegrated and with it the whole structure and spirit of its government.

## A period of fragmentation: 185 BC to AD 300

Beyond the Mauryan Empire other kingdoms had survived in South India. The Satavahanas dominated the central Deccan for over 300 years from about 50 BC. Further south in what is now Tamil Nadu, the early kingdoms of the Cholas and the Pandiyas gave a glimpse of both power and cultural development that was to flower over 1,000 years later. In the centuries following the break up of the Mauryan Empire these kingdoms were in the forefront of developing overseas trade, especially with Greece and Rome. Internal trade also flourished and Indian traders carried goods to China and Southeast Asia.

## The classical period - the Gupta Empire: AD 319-467

Although the political power of Chandra Gupta and his successors never approached that of his unrelated namesake nearly 650 years before him, the Gupta Empire which was established with his coronation in AD 319 produced developments in every field of Indian culture. Their influence has been felt profoundly across South Asia to the present.

Geographically the Guptas originated in the same Magadhan region that had given rise to the Mauryan Empire. Extending their power by strategic marriage alliances, Chandra Gupta's empire of Magadh was extended by his son, Samudra Gupta, who took power in AD 335, across North India. He also marched as far south as Kanchipuram in modern Tamil Nadu, but the heartland of the Gupta Empire remained the plains of the Ganga.

Chandra Gupta II reigned for 39 years from AD 376 and was a great patron of the arts. Political power was much less centralized than under the Mauryans and as Thapar points out, collection of land revenue was deputed to officers who were entitled to keep a share of the revenue, rather than to highly paid bureaucrats. Trade with Southeast Asia, Arabia and China all added to royal wealth.

That wealth was distributed to the arts on a previously unheard of scale. Some went to religious foundations, such as the Buddhist monastery at Ajanta, which produced some of its finest murals during the Gupta period. But Hindu institutions also benefited and some of the most important features of modern Hinduism date from this time. The sacrifices of Vedic worship were given up in favour of personal devotional worship, known as bhakti. Tantrism, both in its Buddhist and Hindu forms, with its emphasis on the female life force and worship of the Mother Goddess, developed. The focus of worship was increasingly towards a personalized and

| BC | Northern South Asia | Peninsular India | External events | BC |
|---|---|---|---|---|
| 800 | Mahabharata war – Bhagavad Gita; Aryan invaders reach Bengal. Rise of city states in Ganga plains, based on rice cultivation. | | First settlement at Rome. Celtic Iron Age begins in north and east of Alps. | 850<br>800 |
| 750 | | Megalithic grave sites. | Greek city states. | 750 |
| 700 | Upanishads begin to be written; concept of transmigration of souls develops; Panini's Sanskrit grammar. | | Iliad composed. | 700 |
| 600 | Northern Black Pottery. | | First Latin script; first Greek coins. | 600 |
| 599 | Mahavir born – founder of Jainism. | | First iron production in China; Zoroastrianism becomes official religion in Persia. | 550 |
| 563 | Gautama Buddha born. | | | |

monotheistic deity, represented in the form of either Siva or Vishnu. The myths of Vishnu's incarnations also arose at this period.

**The Brahmins**, the priestly caste who were in the key position to mediate change, refocused earlier literature to give shape to the emerging religious philosophy. In their hands the Mahabharata and the Ramayana were transformed from secular epics to religious stories. The excellence of contemporary sculpture both reflected and contributed to an increase in image worship and the growing role of temples as centres of devotion.

## Regional kingdoms and cultures

The collapse of Gupta power opened the way for successive smaller kingdoms to assert themselves. After the comparatively brief reign of **Harsha** in the mid-seventh century, which recaptured something both of the territory and the glory of the Guptas, the Gangetic plains were constantly fought over by rival groups, none of whom were able to establish unchallenged authority. Regional kingdoms developed, often around comparatively small natural regions.

**The Deccan** The Rashtrakutas controlled much of the central Peninsula between AD 700-950. However, the southern Deccan was dominated by the Chalukyas from the sixth century up to AD 750 and again in the 11th and 12th centuries. To their south the Pandiyas, Cholas and Pallavas controlled the Dravidian lands of what is now Kerala, Tamil Nadu and coastal Andhra Pradesh. The Pallavas, responsible for building the temples at Mamallapuram, just south of modern Madras (Chennai), flourished in the seventh century.

In the eighth century Kerala began to develop its own regional identity with the rise of the **Kulashekharas** in the Periyar Valley. Caste was a dominating feature of the kingdom's social organization, but with the distinctive twist that the **Nayars**, the most aristocratic of castes, developed a matrilineal system of descent.

It was the **Cholas** who came to dominate the south from the eighth century. Overthrowing the Pallavas, they controlled most of Tamil Nadu, south Karnataka and southern Andhra Pradesh from AD 850 to AD 1278. They often held the Kerala kings under their control. Under their kings **Rajaraja I** (984-1014) and **Rajendra** (1014-1044) the Cholas also controlled north Sri Lanka, sent naval expeditions to Southeast Asia and successful military campaigns north to the Ganga plains. They lavished endowments on temples and also extended the gifts of land to Brahmins instituted by the Pallavas and Pandiyas. Many thousands of Brahmin priests were brought

| BC | Northern South Asia | Peninsular India | External events | BC |
|---|---|---|---|---|
| 500 | Upanishads finished; Taxila and Charsadda become important towns and trade centres. | Aryans colonize Sri Lanka. Irrigation practised in Sri Lanka. | Wet rice cultivation introduced to Japan. | 500 |
| 326<br>321 | Alexander at Indus.<br>Chandragupta establishes Mauryan Dynasty. | Megalithic cultures. | Crossbow invented in China. | 350 |
| 300<br>297 | Sarnath and Sanchi stupas.<br>Mauryan power extends to Mysore. | First Ajanta caves in original form. | Mayan writing and ceremonial centres established. | 300 |
| 272-<br>250<br>232 | Asoka's Empire.<br>Brahmi script.<br>Death of Asoka. | Chola Pandiya, Chera kingdoms: earliest Tamil inscriptions. | Ptolemy.<br>First towns in Southeast Asia.<br>Rome captures Spain. | 285<br>250<br>206 |
| 185 | Shunga Dynasty, centred on Ujjain. | Megalithic cultures in hills of south. | Romans destroy Greek states. | 146 |

south to serve in major temples such as those in Chidambaram, and Rajendra wished to be remembered above all as the king who brought water from the holy Ganga all the way to his kingdom.

**The Rajputs** The political instability and rivalry that resulted from the ending of Gupta power in the north opened the way for new waves of immigrants from the northwest and for new groups and clans to seize power. Among these were the Rajputs (meaning '*sons of kings*') who claimed descent from a mythical figure who rose out of a sacrificial pit near Mount Abu.

From the seventh century AD Rajputs were always a force to be reckoned with in the northwest, albeit at a comparatively local level. The temples at Khajuraho in Central India, one of contemporary India's most remarkable sites, were built during the Rajput dynasty of the Chandelas (916-1203). However, the Rajputs never succeeded in forging a united front strong enough to establish either effective central government, control internally or protection from external attack. See page 281.

## The spread of Islamic power – the Delhi Sultanate

From about AD 1000 the external attacks which inflicted most damage on Rajput wealth and power came increasingly from the Arabs and Turks. Mahmud of Ghazni raided the Punjab virtually every year between 1000 and 1026, attracted both by the agricultural surpluses and the enormous wealth in cash, golden images and jewellery of North India's temples which drew him back every year. He sacked the wealthy centres of Mathura (UP) in 1017, Thanesar (Haryana) in 1011, Somnath (Gujarat) in 1024 and Kannauj (UP). He died in 1030, to the Hindus just another *mlechchha* ('impure' or sullied one), as had been the Huns and the Sakas before him, soon to be forgotten. Such raids were never taken seriously as a long-term threat by kings further east and as the Rajputs often feuded among themselves the northwest plains became an attractive prey.

Muslim political power was heralded by the raids of Mu'izzu'd Din and his defeat of massive Rajput forces at the Second Battle of Tarain in 1192. Mu'izzu'd Din left his deputy, Qutb u'd Din Aibak, to hold the territorial gains from his base at Indraprastha. Mu'izzu'd Din made further successful raids in the 1190s, inflicting crushing defeats on Hindu opponents from Gwalior to Benaras. The foundations were then laid for the first extended period of such power, which came under the Delhi sultans.

**Qutb u'd Din Aibak** took Lahore in 1206, although it was his lieutenant **Iltutmish** who really established control from Delhi in 1211. Qutb u'd Din Aibak consolidated Muslim dominion by an even-handed policy of conciliation and patronage. In Delhi he

| BC | Northern South Asia | Peninsular India | External events | BC |
|---|---|---|---|---|
| 100 | Kharavela King of Kalingans in Orissa. Final composition of Ramayana. | South Indian trade with Indonesia and Rome. Roman pottery and coins in South India. | Indian religions spread to Southeast Asia. Discovery of monsoon winds Introduction of Julian calendar. | 100 |

 converted the old Hindu stronghold of Qila Rai Pithora into his Muslim capital and began several magnificent building projects, including the Quwwat-ul-Islam mosque and the Qutb Minar, a victory tower. Iltutmish was a Turkish slave – a *Mamluk* – and the Sultanate continued to look west for its leadership and inspiration. However, the possibility of continuing control from outside India was destroyed by the crushing raids of **Genghis Khan** through Central Asia and from 1222 Iltutmish ruled from Delhi completely independently of outside authority. He annexed Sind in 1228 and all the territory east to Bengal by 1230.

A succession of dynasties followed, drawing on refugees from Genghis Khan's raids and from still further to the west to strengthen the leadership. In 1290 the first dynasty was succeeded by the Khaljis, which in turn gave way to the Tughluqs in 1320. **Mohammad bin Tughluq** (ruled 1324-1351) was described by the Moorish traveller Ibn Batuta as 'a man who above all others is fond of making presents and shedding blood'. Despite its periodic brutality, this period marked a turning point in Muslim government in India, as Turkish Mamluks gave way to government by Indian Muslims and their Hindu allies. The Delhi sultans were open to local influences and employed Hindus in their administration. In the mid-14th century their capital, Delhi, was one of the leading cities of the contemporary world but in 1398 their control came to an abrupt end with the arrival of the Mongol Timur.



**Timur's** limp caused him to be called Timur-i-leng (Timur the Lame, known to the west as Tamburlaine). This self-styled 'Scourge of God' was illiterate, a devout Muslim, an outstanding chess player and a patron of the arts. Five years before his arrival in India he had taken Baghdad and three years before that he had ravaged Russia, devastating land and pillaging villages. India had not been in such danger from Mongols since Genghis Khan had arrived on the same stretch of the Indus 200 years before.

After Timur, it took nearly 50 years for the Delhi Kingdom to become more than a local headquarters. Even then the revival was slow and fitful. The last Tughluqs were succeeded by an undistinguished line of Sayyids, who began as Timur's deputies who were essentially Afghan soldier/administrators. They later called themselves sultans and Lodi kings (1451-1526) and moved their capital to Agra. Nominally they controlled an area from Punjab to Bihar but they were, in fact, in the hands of a group of factious nobles.

## The Deccan Kingdoms

The Delhi Sultanate never achieved the dominating power of earlier empires or of its successor, the Mughal Empire. It exercised political control through crushing military raids and the exaction of tribute from defeated kings, but there was no real attempt to

| AD | North India | Peninsular India | External events | AD |
|---|---|---|---|---|
| | | Satavahanas control much of Peninsula up to 300 AD. Thomas brings Christianity to South India. *Tamil Sangram*. | Rome population of 1 mn. Pyramid of the sun at City of Teotihuacan, Mexico. | 50 |
| 78 | Kushan rulers in Northwest followed by Scythians. | | | |
| | | Arikamedu – trade with Rome. | | 68 |
| | | | Buddhism reaches China. | |
| 100 | Vaishnavism spreads to north and northwest. | | Paper introduced in China; first metal work in Southeast Asia. | 100 |
| | Lawbook of Manu Gandharan art. | Mahayana Buddhism spreads. Nagarjunakonda major centre in Andhra Pradesh. First cities on Deccan plateau. | Hadrian's wall in Britain. | 125 |
| 200 | Hinayana/Mahayana Buddhist split. | | | |

impose central administration. Power depended on maintaining vital lines of communication and trade routes, keeping fortified strongholds and making regional alliances. In the Peninsula to the south, the Deccan, regional powers contested for survival, power and expansion. The Bahmanis were the forerunners of a succession of Muslim dynasties, who sometimes competed with each other and sometimes collaborated against a joint external enemy.

Across West and South India today are the remains of the only major medieval Hindu empire – the Vijayanagar Empire – to resist effectively the Muslim advance. The ruins at Hampi demonstrate the power of a Hindu coalition that rose to power in the south Deccan in the first half of the 14th century, only to be defeated by its Muslim neighbours in 1565, see page 1011.

For over 200 years Vijayanagar (*'city of victory'*) kings fought to establish supremacy. It was an empire that, in the words of one Indian historian, made it 'the nearest approach to a war state ever made by a Hindu kingdom'. At times its power reached from Orissa in the northeast to Sri Lanka. In 1390 King Harihara II claimed to have planted a victory pillar in Sri Lanka. Much of modern Tamil Nadu and Andhra Pradesh were added to the core region of Karnataka in the area under Vijayanagar control.



## The Mughal Empire

In North India it is the impact of the Mughal rule that is most strikingly evident today. The descendants of conquerors, with the blood of both Tamburlaine (Timur) and Genghis Khan in their veins, they came to dominate Indian politics from Babur's victory near Delhi in 1526 to Aurangzeb's death in 1707. Their legacy was not only some of the most magnificent architecture in the world, but a profound impact on the culture, society and future politics of South Asia.

**Babur (the tiger)** Founder of the Mughal Dynasty, Babur was born in Russian Turkestan on 15 February 1483, the fifth direct descendant on the male side of Timur and 13th on the female side from Genghis Khan. He established the Mughal Empire by leading his cavalry and artillery forces to a stupendous victory over the combined armies of Ibrahim Lodi, last ruler of the Delhi Sultanate and the Hindu Raja of Gwalior, at **Panipat**, 80 km north of Delhi, in 1526. When he died four years later, the Empire was still far from secured, but he had not only laid the foundations of political and military power but had also begun to establish courtly traditions of poetry, literature and art which became the hallmark of subsequent Mughal rulers.

Babur, used to the delights of Persian gardens and the cool of the Afghan hills, was unimpressed by what he saw of India. In his autobiography he wrote: "Hindustan

| AD | North India | Peninsular India | External events | AD |
|---|---|---|---|---|
| 300 | | Rise of Pallavas. | Classic period of Mayan civilization. | 300 |
| 319 | Chandra Gupta founds Gupta Dynasty (Samudra 335, Chandra II 376, Kumara 415). | | Constantinople founded. | 330 |
| 454 | Skanda Gupta, the last imperial Gupta, takes power. Dies 467. | | End of Roman Empire. | 476 |
| | | | Teotihuacan, Mexico, population 200,000. | 500 |
| 540 | Gupta rule ends. | | Saint Sophia, Constantinople. | 532 |
| 550 | | First Chalukya Dynasty, | Buddhism arrives in Japan. | 550 |
| 578 | | Badami cave temple; last Ajanta paintings. | | |
| 600 | Period of small Indian states. | Bhakti movement. Chalukyan Dynasty in west | | |
| 629 | Hiuen Tsang travels India. | and central Deccan. | Death of Mohammad. | 632 |
| 630 | | Pallavas in Tamil Nadu. | | |

is a country that has few pleasures to recommend it. The people are not handsome. They have no idea of the charms of friendly society, of frankly mixing together, or of familiar intercourse. They have no genius, no comprehension of mind, no politeness of manner, no kindness or fellow-feeling, no ingenuity or mechanical invention in planning or executing their handicraft works, no skill or knowledge in design or architecture; they have no horses, no good flesh, no grapes or musk melons, no good fruits, no ice or cold water, no good food or bread in their bazars, no baths or colleges, no candles, no torches, not a candlestick".

Babur's depressing catalogue was the view of a disenchanted outsider. Within two generations the Mughals had become fully at home in their Indian environment and brought some radical changes. Babur was charismatic. He ruled by keeping the loyalty of his military chiefs, giving them control of large areas of territory.

**Humayun** However, their strength posed a problem for Humayun, his successor. Almost immediately after Babur's death Humayun was forced to retreat from Delhi through Sind with his pregnant wife. His son Akbar, who was to become the greatest of the Mughal emperors, was born at Umarkot in Sindh, modern Pakistan, during this period of exile, on 23 November 1542.



**Akbar** Akbar was only 13 when he took the throne in 1556. The next 44 years were one of the most remarkable periods of South Asian history, paralleled by the Elizabethan period in England, where Queen Elizabeth I ruled from 1558 to 1603. Although Akbar inherited the throne, it was he who really created the empire. He also gave it many of its distinguishing features.

Through his marriage to a Hindu princess he ensured that Hindus were given honoured positions in government, as well as respect for their religious beliefs and practices. He sustained a passionate interest in art and literature, matched by a determination to create monuments to his empire's political power and he laid the foundations for an artistic and architectural tradition which developed a totally distinctive Indian style. This emerged from the separate elements of Iranian and Indian traditions by a constant process of blending and originality of which he was the chief patron.

But these achievements were only possible because of his political and military gifts. From 1556 until his 18th birthday in 1560, Akbar was served by a prince regent, Bairam Khan. However, already at the age of 15 he had conquered Ajmer and large areas of Central India. Chittor and Ranthambore fell to him in 1567-1568, bringing most of what is now Rajasthan under his control. This opened the door south to Gujarat.

Afghans continued to cause his empire difficulties, including Daud Karrani, who declared independence in East India in 1574. That threat to Mughal power was finally crushed with Karrani's death in 1576. Bengal was far from the last of his conquests.

| AD | North India | Peninsular India | External events | AD |
|---|---|---|---|---|
| | | | Buddhism reaches Tibet. | 645 |
| 670 | Rajputs become powerful force in northwest. | Mahabalipuram shore temples. | | |
| 712 | Arabs arrive in Sind. | Nandivarman II in Tamil Nadu. Pandiyas in Madurai. | Muslim invasions of Spain. | 711 |
| 757 | | Rashtrakutas dominate central Peninsula. | | |
| 775 | | Kailasanath Temple, Ellora. | Charlemagne crowned. | 800 |
| | | Rise of Cholas. | Settlement of New Zealand. | 850 |
| | | | Cyrillic script developed. | 863 |
| 950 | Khajuraho temples started. | Rajendra Chola. | | |
| | | | Sung Dynasty in China. | 979 |
| 984 | | Rajaraja 1st. | | |

He brought Kabul back under Mughal control in the 1580s and established a presence from Kashmir, Sind and Baluchistan in the north and west, to the Godavari River on the border of modern Andhra Pradesh in the south.

Akbar deliberately widened his power base by incorporating Rajput princes into the administrative structure and giving them extensive rights in the revenue from land. He abolished the hated tax on non-Muslims *(jizya)*-ultimately reinstated by his strictly orthodox great grandson Aurangzeb-ceased levying taxes on Hindus who went on pilgrimage and ended the practice of forcible conversion to Islam.

**Artistic treasures** abound from Akbar's court - paintings, jewellery, weapons - often bringing together material and skills from across the known world. Akbar's eclecticism had a political purpose, for he was trying to build a focus of loyalty beyond that of caste, social group, region or religion. Like Roman emperors before him, he deliberately cultivated a new religion in which the emperor himself attained divinity, hoping thereby to give the empire a legitimacy which would last. While his religion disappeared with his death, the legitimacy of the Mughals survived another 200 years, long after their real power had almost disappeared.

**Jahangir** Akbar died of a stomach illness in 1605. He was succeeded by his son, Prince Salim, who inherited the throne as Emperor Jahangir ('*world seizer*'). He added little to the territory of the empire, consolidating the Mughals' hold on the Himalayan foothills and parts of central India but restricting his innovative energies to pushing back frontiers of art rather than of land. He commissioned works of art and literature, many of which directly recorded life in the Mughal court. Hunting scenes were not just romanticized accounts of rural life, but conveyed the real dangers of hunting lions or tigers; implements, furniture, tools and weapons were made with lavish care and often exquisite design.

From early youth Jahangir had shown an artistic temperament, but he also became addicted to alcohol and then to opium. In his autobiography, he wrote: "I had not drunk until I was 18, except in the time of my infancy two or three times my mother and wet nurses gave it by way of infantile remedy, mixed with water and rose water to take away a cough ... years later a gunner said that if I would take a glass of wine it would drive away the feeling of being tired and heavy ... After that I took to drinking wine... until wine made from grapes ceased to intoxicate me and I took to drinking arrack (local spirits). By degrees my potions rose to 20 cups of doubly distilled spirits, 14 during the daytime and the remainder at night".

**Nur Jahan** Jahangir's favourite wife, Nur Jahan, brought her own artistic gifts. Born the daughter of an Iranian nobleman, she had been brought to the Mughal court along with her family as a child and moved to Bengal as the wife of Sher Afgan, see page 158. She

| AD | North India | Peninsular India | External events | AD |
|---|---|---|---|---|
| 1001 | Mahmud of Ghazni raids Indus plains. Rajput dynasties grow. | Chola kings – navies sent to Southeast Asia: Chola bronzes. | Easter Island stone carvings. | 1000 |
| 1050 | Sufism in North India. Rajput dynasties in northwest. | | Norman conquest of England. | 1066 |
| | | | First European universities. | 1100 |
| 1110 | | Rise of Hoysalas. | | |
| 1118 | Senas in Bengal. | | | |
| | | | Angkor Wat, Cambodia; paper making spreads from Muslim world. | 1150 |
| 1192 | Rajputs defeated by Mu'izzu'd Din. | | Srivijaya Kingdom at its height in Java; Angkor Empire at greatest. | 1170 |

 made rapid progress after her first husband's accidental death in 1607, which caused her to move from Bengal to be a lady in waiting for one of Akbar's widows.

At the Mughal court in 1611, she met Jahangir. Mutually enraptured, they were married in May. Jahangir gave her the title Nur Mahal (Light of the Palace), soon increased to Nur Jahan (Light of the World). Aged 34, she was strikingly beautiful and had an astonishing reputation for physical skill and intellectual wit. She was a crack shot with a gun, highly artistic, determined yet philanthropic. Throughout her life Jahangir was captivated by her, so much so that he flouted Muslim convention by minting coins bearing her image.

By 1622 Nur Jahan effectively controlled the empire. She commissioned and supervised the building in Agra of one of the Mughal world's most beautiful buildings, the **I'timad ud-Daula** ('Pillar of government'), as a tomb for her father and mother. Her father, **Ghiyas Beg**, had risen to become one of Jahangir's most trusted advisers and Nur Jahan was determined to ensure that their memory was adequately honoured. She was less successful in her wish to deny the succession after Jahangir's death at the age of 58 to Prince Khurram. Acceding to the throne in 1628, he took the title of Shah Jahan (*Ruler of the World*) and in the following 30 years his reign represented the height of Mughal power.



**Shah Jahan** The Mughal Empire was under attack in the Deccan and the northwest when Shah Jahan became Emperor. He tried to re-establish and extend Mughal authority in both regions by a combination of military campaigns and skilled diplomacy. Akbar's craftsmen had already carved outstandingly beautiful *jalis* for the tomb of Salim Chishti in Fatehpur Sikri, but Shah Jahan developed the form further. Undoubtedly the finest tribute to these skills is found in the Taj Mahal, the tribute to his beloved wife Mumtaz Mahal, who died giving birth to her fourteenth child in 1631.

**Aurangzeb** The need to expand the area under Mughal control was felt even more strongly by Aurangzeb ('*The jewel in the throne*'), than by his predecessors, see page 1115. He had shown his intellectual gifts in his grandfather Jahangir's court when held hostage to guarantee Shah Jahan's good behaviour, learning Arabic, Persian, Turkish and Hindi. When he seized power at the age of 40, he needed all his political and military skills to hold on to an unwieldy empire that was in permanent danger of collapse from its own size.

Aurangzeb realized that the resources of the territory he inherited from Shah Jahan were not enough. One response was to push south, while maintaining his hold on the east and north. Initially he maintained his alliances with the Rajputs in the west, which had been a crucial element in Mughal strategy. In 1678 he claimed

| AD | North India | Peninsular India | External events | AD |
|---|---|---|---|---|
| 1198 | First mosque built in Delhi; Qutb Minar Delhi. | | Rise of Hausa city states in West Africa. | 1200 |
| 1206 | Delhi Sultanate established. | | Mongols begin conquest of Asia under Genghis Khan. | 1206 |
| 1206 | Turkish 'slave dynasty'. | Pandiyas rise. | | |
| | | | First Thai kingdom. | 1220 |
| 1222 | Iltutmish Sultan of Delhi. | | | |
| 1230 | | Konark, Sun Temple, Orissa | | |
| | | | Marco Polo reaches China. | 1275 |
| 1290 | Khaljis in Delhi; Jalal ud Din Khalji. | | | |
| 1320-24 | Ghiyas ud Din Tughluq. | | Black Death spreads from Asia to Europe. | 1348 |
| 1324-51 | Mohammad bin Tughluq. | | | |

## A monument to grief?

The grief that Mumtaz's death caused may have been the chief motivating force behind Shah Jahan's determination to build the Taj Mahal, a monument not just to his love for her, but also to the supremacy of Mughal refinement and power. However, that power had to be paid for and the costs were escalating. Shah Jahan himself had inherited an almost bankrupt state from his father. Expenditure on the army had outstripped the revenue collected by tribute from kings and from the chiefs given the rights and responsibility over territories often larger than European countries. Financial deficits forced Shah Jahan onto the offensive in order to guarantee greater and more reliable revenue.

Major reforms helped to reduce the costs of his standing army. However, maintaining the force necessary to control the huge territories owing allegiance to the emperor continued to stretch his resources to the full. By 1648, when he moved his capital to Delhi, the empire was already in financial difficulties and in 1657 the rumour that Shah Jahan was terminally ill immediately caused a series of battles for the succession between his four sons.

Aurangzeb, the second son and sixth child of Shah Jahan and Mumtaz Mahal – tough, intriguing and sometimes cruel, but also a highly intelligent strategist – emerged the winner, to find that Shah Jahan had recovered. Rather than run the risk of being deposed, Aurangzeb kept his father imprisoned in Agra Fort, where he had been taken ill, from June 1658 until his death in February 1666.



absolute rights over Jodhpur and went to war with the Rajput clans at the same time embarking on a policy of outright Islamisation. However, for the remaining 39 years of his reign he was forced to struggle continuously to sustain his power.

## The East India Company and the rise of British power

The British were unique among the foreign rulers of India in coming by sea rather than through the northwest and in coming first for trade rather than for military conquest. The ports that they established - Madras, Bombay and Calcutta - became completely new centres of political, economic and social activity. Before them Indian empires had controlled their territories from the land. The British dictated the emerging shape of the economy by controlling sea-borne trade. From the middle of the 19th century

| AD | North India | Peninsular India | External events | AD |
|---|---|---|---|---|
| 1336 | | Vijayanagar Empire established, Harihara I. | | |
| 1347 | | Ala-ud-Din sets up Bahmani dynasty, independent of Delhi, in Gulbarga. | | |
| 1351-88 | Firoz Shah Tughluq. | | Ming dynasty in China established. | 1368 |
| | | | Peking the largest city in the world. | 1400 |
| 1398 | Timur sacks Delhi. | | Ming sea-going expeditions to Africa. | 1405 |
| 1412 | End of Tughlaq Dynasty. | | | |
| 1414 | Sayyid Dynasty. | Bidar/Bahmani Kingdom in Deccan. | | 1428 |
| 1440 | Mystic Kabir born in Benaras. | | Aztecs defeat Atzcapatzalco. | 1438 |
| | | | Incas centralize power. | |
| 1451 | Afghan Lodi Dynasty established under Bahlul. | | Byzantine Empire falls to Ottomans. | 1453 |
| 1469 | Guru Nanak born in Punjab. | | | |
| | | | Columbus reaches the Americas; Arabs and Jews expelled from Spain. | 1492 |
| 1482 | | Fall of Bahmanis. | | |

railways transformed the economic and political structure of South Asia and it was those three centres of British political control, along with the late addition of Delhi, which became the foci of economic development and political change.

## The East India Company in Madras and Bengal

In its first 90 years of contact with South Asia after the Company set up its first trading post at **Masulipatnam**, on the east coast of India, it had depended almost entirely on trade for its profits. However, in 1701, only 11 years after a British settlement was first established at Calcutta, the Company was given rights to land revenue in Bengal.

The Company was accepted and sometimes welcomed, partly because it offered to bolster the inadequate revenues of the Mughals by exchanging silver bullion for the cloth it bought. However, in the south the Company moved further and faster towards consolidating its political base. Wars between South India's regional factions gave the Company the opportunity to extend their influence by making alliances and offering support to some of these factions in their struggles, which were complicated by the extension to Indian soil of the European contest for power between the French and the British.



**Robert Clive** The British established effective control over both Bengal and Southeast India in the middle of the 17th century. Robert Clive, in alliance with a collection of disaffected Hindu landowners and Muslim soldiers, defeated the new Nawab of Bengal, the 20-year-old Siraj-ud-Daula, in June 1757. At **Plassey** (Palashi), about 100 km north of Calcutta.

**Hastings and Cornwallis** The essential features of British control were mapped out in the next quarter of a century through the work of **Warren Hastings**, Governor-General from 1774 until 1785 and **Lord Cornwallis** who succeeded and remained in charge until 1793. Cornwallis was responsible for putting Europeans in charge of all the higher levels of revenue collection and administration and for introducing government by the rule of law, making even government officers subject to the courts.

## The decline of Muslim power

The extension of East India Company power in the Mughal periphery of India's south and east took place against a background of the rising power of Sivaji and his Marathas.

**Sivaji and the Marathas** Sivaji was the son of a Hindu who had served as a small-scale chief in the Muslim-ruled state of Bijapur. The weakness of Bijapur encouraged Sivaji to extend his father's area of control and he led a rebellion. The Bijapur general Afzal Khan, sent to put it down, agreed to meet Sivaji in private to

| AD | North India | Peninsular India | External events | AD |
|---|---|---|---|---|
| | | Vasco da Gama reaches India. | Inca Empire at its height. | 1498 |
| 1500 | | | Spanish claim Brazil; Safavid Empire founded in Persia. | 1500 |
| | | Vijayanagar dominates South India; | | |
| 1506 | Sikander Lodi founds Agra. | Krishnadevraya rules 1509-30. | | |
| | | Albuquerque seizes Goa; | | 1510 |
| | | Nizamshahis establish independent Ahmadnagar sultanate. | Ottomans capture Syria, Egypt and Arabia. | 1516 |
| 1526 | Babur defeats Ibrahim Lodi to establish Mughal power in Delhi. | Dutch, French, Portuguese and Danish traders. | Spaniards overthrow Aztecs in Mexico. | 1519 |
| | | | Potato introduced to Europe from South America. | 1525 |
| 1540 | Sher Shah forces Humayun into exile. | | | |

reach a settlement. In an act which is still remembered by both Muslims and Marathas, Sivaji embraced him with steel claws attached to his fingers and tore him apart. It was the start of a campaign which took Maratha power as far south as Madurai and to the doors of Delhi and Calcutta.

Although Sivaji himself died in 1680, Aurangzeb never fully came to terms with the rising power of the Marathas, though he did end their ambitions to form an empire of their own. While the Maratha confederacy was able to threaten Delhi within 50 years of Aurangzeb's death, by the early 19th century it had dissolved into five independent states, with whom the British ultimately dealt separately.

Nor was Aurangzeb able to create any wide sense of identity with the Mughals as a legitimate popular power. Instead, under the influence of Sunni Muslim theologians, he retreated into insistence on Islamic purity. He imposed Islamic law, the *sharia*, promoted only Muslims to positions of power and authority, tried to replace Hindu administrators and revenue collectors with Muslims and reimposed the *jizya* tax on all non-Muslims. By the time of his death in 1707 the empire no longer had either the broadness of spirit or the physical means to survive.

**Bahadur Shah** The decline was postponed briefly by the five year reign of Aurangzeb's son. Sixty-three when he acceded to the throne, Bahadur Shah restored some of its faded fortunes. He made agreements with the Marathas and the Rajputs and defeated the Sikhs in Punjab before taking the last Sikh guru into his service. Nine emperors succeeded Aurangzeb between his death and the exile of the last Mughal ruler in 1858. It was no accident that it was in that year that the British ended the rule of its East India Company and decreed India to be its Indian empire.

Mohammad Shah remained in his capital of Delhi, resigning himself to enjoying what Carey Welch has called "the conventional triad of joys: the wine was excellent, as were the women and for him the song was especially rewarding". The idyll was rudely shattered by the invasion of **Nadir Shah** in 1739, an Iranian marauder who slaughtered thousands in Delhi and carried off priceless Mughal treasures, including the Peacock Throne, see page 93.

## The East India Company's push for power

**Alliances** In the century and a half that followed the death of Aurangzeb, the British East India Company extended its economic and political influence into the heart of India. As the Mughal Empire lost its power India fell into many smaller states. The Company undertook to protect the rulers of several of these states from external attack by stationing British troops in their territory. In exchange for this service the rulers paid subsidies to the Company. The British extended their territory through the 18th century as successive regional powers were annexed and brought under direct Company rule.

| AD | North India | Peninsular India | External events | AD |
|---|---|---|---|---|
| 1542 | | St Francis Xavier reaches Goa. | | |
| 1555 | Humayun re-conquers Delhi. | | | |
| 1556 | Akbar Emperor. | | | |
| 1565 | | Vijayanagar defeated. | William Shakespeare born. | 1564 |
| | | First printing press in Goa. | | 1566 |
| | | | Dutch East India Co set up. | 1602 |
| 1603 | Guru Granth Sahib compiled. | | Tokugawa Shogunate in Japan. | 1603 |
| 1605 | Jahangir Emperor. | | First permanent English settlement in America. | 1607 |
| 1608 | | East India Co base at Surat. | | |
| | | | Telescope invented in Holland. | 1609 |

Background History

Progress to direct British control was uneven and often opposed. The Sikhs in Punjab, the Marathas in the west and the Mysore sultans in the south, fiercely contested British advances. **Haidar Ali** and **Tipu Sultan**, who had built a wealthy kingdom in the Mysore region, resisted attempts to incorporate them. Tipu was finally killed in 1799 at the battle of Srirangapatnam, an island fort in the Kaveri River just north of Mysore, where Arthur Wellesley, later the Duke of Wellington, began to make his military reputation.

The Marathas were not defeated until the war of 1816-18. Even then the defeat owed as much to internal faction fighting as to the power of the British-led army. Only the northwest of the subcontinent remained beyond British control until well into the 19th century. Thus in 1799 **Ranjit Singh** was able to set up a Sikh state in Punjab which survived until the late 1830s despite the extension of British control over much of the rest of India.

In 1818 India's economy was in ruins and its political structures destroyed. Irrigation works and road systems had fallen into decay and gangs terrorized the countryside. Thugs and dacoits controlled much of the open countryside in Central India and often robbed and murdered even on the outskirts of towns. The peace and stability of the Mughal period had long since passed. Between 1818 and 1857 there was a succession of local and uncoordinated revolts in different parts of India. Some were bought off, some put down by military force.



## A period of reforms

While existing political systems were collapsing, the first half of the 19th century was also a period of radical social change in the territories governed by the East India Company. **Lord William Bentinck** became Governor-General at a time when England was entering a period of major reform. In 1828 he banned the burning of widows on the funeral pyres of their husbands (**sati**) and then moved to suppress **thuggee** (the ritual murder and robbery carried out in the name of the goddess Kali). But his most far reaching change was to introduce education in English.

From the late 1830s massive new engineering projects began to be taken up; first canals, then railways. The innovations stimulated change and change contributed to the growing unease with the British presence. The development of the telegraph, railways and new roads, three universities and the extension of massive new canal irrigation projects in North India seemed to threaten traditional society, a risk increased by the annexation of Indian states to bring them under direct British rule. The most important of these was Oudh.

## The Rebellion

Out of the growing discontent and widespread economic difficulties came the Rebellion or 'Mutiny' of 1857. On 10 May 1857 troops in Meerut, 70 km northeast of Delhi, mutinied.

| AD | North India | Peninsular India | External events | AD |
|---|---|---|---|---|
| 1628 | Shah Jahan Emperor. | | Masjid-i-Shah Mosque in Isfahan. | 1616 |
| 1632-53 | Taj Mahal built. | | | |
| | | Fort St George, Madras, founded by East India Co. | | 1639 |
| | | | Manchus found Ch'ing Dynasty. | 1644 |
| | | | Tasman 'discovers' New Zealand. | 1645 |
| 1658 | Aurangzeb Emperor. | | | |
| | | | Louis XIV of France - the 'Sun King'. | 1653-1715 |

They reached Delhi the next day, where **Bahadur Shah**, the last Mughal Emperor, took sides with the mutineers. Troops in Lucknow joined the rebellion and for three months Lucknow and other cities in the north were under siege. Appalling scenes of butchery and reprisals marked the struggle, only put down by troops from outside.

## The Period of Empire

The 1857 rebellion marked the end not only of the Mughal Empire but also of the East India Company, for the British Government in London took overall control in 1858. Yet within 30 years a movement for self-government had begun and there were the first signs of a demand among the new western-educated élite that political rights be awarded to match the sense of Indian national identity.

**Indian National Congress** Established in 1885, this was the first all-India political institution and was to become the key vehicle of demands for independence. However, the educated Muslim élite of what is now Uttar Pradesh saw a threat to Muslim rights, power and identity in the emergence of democratic institutions which gave Hindus, with their built-in natural majority, significant advantages. Sir Sayyid Ahmad Khan, who had founded a Muslim University at Aligarh in 1877, advised Muslims against joining the Congress, seeing it as a vehicle for Hindu and especially Bengali, nationalism.

**The Muslim League** The educated Muslim community of North India remained deeply suspicious of the Congress, making up less than 8% of those attending its conferences between 1900-20. Muslims from UP created the All-India Muslim League in 1906. However, the demands of the Muslim League were not always opposed to those of the Congress. In 1916 it concluded the Lucknow Pact with the Congress, in which the Congress won Muslim support for self-government, in exchange for the recognition that there would be separate constituencies for Muslims. The nature of the future Independent India was still far from clear, however. The British conceded the principle of self-government in 1918, but however radical the reforms would have seemed five years earlier, they already fell far short of heightened Indian expectations.

**Mahatma Gandhi** Into a tense atmosphere Mohandas Karamchand Gandhi returned to India in 1915 after 20 years practising as a lawyer in South Africa. He arrived as the government of India was being given new powers by the British parliament to try political cases without a jury and to give provincial governments the right to imprison politicians without trial. In opposition to this legislation Gandhi proposed to call a *hartal*, when all activity would cease for a day, a form of protest still in widespread use. Such protests took place across India, often accompanied by riots.

On 13 April 1919 a huge gathering took place in the enclosed space of Jallianwala Bagh in Amritsar, see page 464. It had been prohibited by the government and General

| AD | North India | Peninsular India | External events | AD |
|---|---|---|---|---|
| 1677 | | **Shivaji** and Marathas. | Pennsylvania founded. | 1681 |
| 1690 | Calcutta founded. | | | |
| 1699 | Guru Gobind Singh forms Sikh Khalsa. | Regional powers dominate through 18th century: Nawabs of Arcot (1707); Maratha Peshwas (1714); Nizams of Hyderabad (1724). | Chinese occupy Outer Mongolia. | 1697 |
| 1703 | Nawabs of Bengal. | | Foundation of St Petersburg, capital of Russian Empire. | 1703 |
| 1707 | Death of Aurangzeb; Mughal rulers continue to rule from Delhi until 1858 Nawabs of Avadh. | | | |
| 1739 | The Persian Nadir Shah captures Delhi and massacres thousands. | | | |
| 1757 | Battle of Plassey; British power extended from East India. | East India Co strengthens trade and political power through 18th century. | US War of Independence. | 1775-8 |

## Mahatma Gandhi

Mohandas Karamchand Ghandi, a westernized, English educated lawyer, had lived outside India from his youth to middle age. He preached the general acceptance of some of the doctrines he had grown to respect in his childhood, which stemmed from deep Indian traditions – notably ahimsa, or non-violence. On his return the Bengali Nobel Laureate poet, Rabindranath Tagore, had dubbed him 'Mahatma' – Great Soul. From 1921 he gave up his Western style of dress and adopted the hand spun dhoti worn by poor Indian villagers. Yet, he was also fiercely critical of many aspects of traditional Hindu society. He preached against the discrimination of the caste system which still dominated life for the overwhelming majority of Hindus. Often despised by the British in India, his death at the hands of an extreme Hindu chauvinist in January 1948 was a final testimony to the ambiguity of his achievements: successful in contributing so much to achieving India's Independence, yet failing to resolve some of the bitter communal legacies which he gave his life to overcome.



Dyer ordered troops to fire on the people without warning, killing 379 and injuring at least a further 1,200. It marked the turning point in relations with Britain and the rise of Gandhi to the key position of leadership in the struggle for complete independence.

**The thrust for Independence** Through the 1920s Gandhi developed concepts and political programmes that were to become the hallmark of India's Independence struggle. Ultimately political Independence was to be achieved not by violent rebellion but by *satyagraha* - a "truth force" which implied a willingness to suffer through non-violent resistance to injustice.

In 1930 the Congress declared that 26 January would be Independence day – still celebrated as Republic Day in India today. Mohammad Iqbal, the Leader of the Muslim League, took the opportunity of his address to the League in the same year to suggest the formation of a Muslim state within an Indian Federation. Also in 1930 a Muslim student in Cambridge, **Chaudhuri Rahmat Ali**, coined a name for the new Muslim state **PAKISTAN**. The letters were to stand 'P' for Punjab, 'A' for Afghania, 'K' for Kashmir, 'S' for Sind with the suffix '*stan*', Persian for country. The idea still had little real shape however and waited on developments of the late 1930s and 1940s to bear fruit.

By the end of the Second World War the positions of the Muslim League, now under the leadership of **Mohammad Ali Jinnah** and the Congress led by **Jawaharlal Nehru**, were irreconcilable. While major questions of the definition of separate territories for a Muslim and non-Muslim state remained to be answered, it was clear to General Wavell, the British Viceroy through the last years of the war, that there was no alternative but to accept that independence would have to be given on the basis of separate states.

## Independence and Partition

One of the main difficulties for the Muslims was that they made up only a fifth of the total population were scattered throughout India. It was therefore impossible to define a simple territorial division which would provide a state to match Jinnah's claim of a '*two-nation theory*'. On 20 February 1947, the British Labour Government announced its decision to replace Lord Wavell as Viceroy with Lord Mountbatten, who was to oversee the transfer of power to new independent governments. It set a deadline of June 1948 for British withdrawal. The announcement of a firm date made the Indian politicians even less willing to compromise and the resulting division satisfied no one.

### The Indian flag

In 1921, the All Indian Congress considered a red and green flag to represent the two dominant religious groups (Hindu and Muslim); Gandhi suggested white be added to represent the other communities, as well as the charka (spinning wheel) symbolizing the Swadeshi movement, now centred in the party flag.

In 1931, the Indian National Congress adopted the tricolor as the national flag. This was intended to have no communal significance. The deep saffron denoted 'Courage and Sacrifice', the white 'Truth and Peace' and dark green 'Faith and Chivalry'. On the white stripe, the Dharma chakra represented the Buddhist Wheel of Law from Asoka's Lion capital at Sarnath.

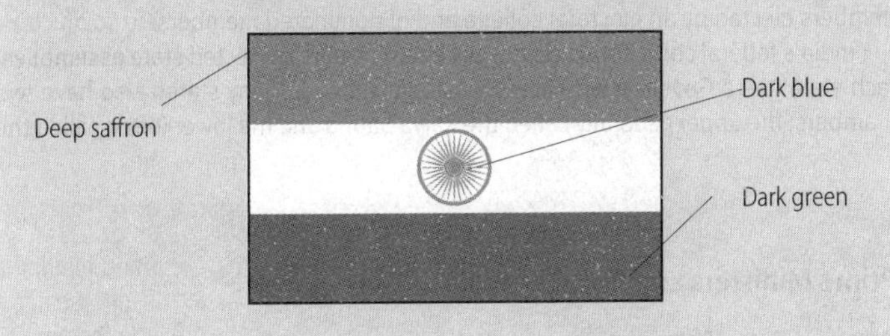


Independence arrived on 15 August for India and the 14 August for Pakistan because Indian astrologers deemed the 15th to be the most auspicious moment. Several key Princely States had still not decided firmly to which country they would accede. Kashmir was the most important of these, with results that have lasted to the present day.

# Modern India

India, with over one billion people in 2002, is the second most populated country in the world after China. That population size reflects the long history of human occupation and the fact that an astonishingly high proportion of India's land is relatively fertile. Sixty percent of India's surface area is cultivated today, compared with about 10% in China and 20% in the United States.

Although the birth rate has fallen steadily over the last 40 years, initially death rates fell faster and the rate of population increase has continued to be nearly 2% – or 18 million – a year. Today over 280 million people live in towns and cities.

## Politics and institutions

When India became Independent on 15 August 1947 it faced three immediate crises. Partition left it with a bitter struggle between Muslims on one side and Hindus and Sikhs on the other which threatened to tear the new country into pieces at birth. An estimated 13 million people migrated between the two new countries of India and Pakistan.

In the years since independence, striking political achievements have been made. With the two year exception of 1975-1977, when Mrs Gandhi imposed a state of emergency in which all political activity was banned, India has sustained a democratic system in the face of tremendous pressures. The General Elections of May 2004 saw the Congress Party return as the largest single party, though without an overall majority. They managed to forge alliances with some of the smaller parties and thus formed the new governmentunder the Prime Ministership not of the party's leader, Sonia Gandhi, but of ex-Finance Minister, Manmohan Singh.

## The constitution

Establishing itself as a sovereign democratic republic, the Indian parliament accepted Nehru's advocacy of a secular constitution. The President is formally vested with all executive powers exercised under the authority of the Prime Minister.

Parliament has a lower house (the *Lok Sabha*, or 'house of the people') and an upper house (the *Rajya Sabha* – Council of States). The former is made up of directly elected representatives from the 543 parliamentary constituencies (plus two nominated members from the Anglo-Indian community), the latter of a mixture of members elected by an electoral college and of nominated members.

India's federal constitution devolves certain powers to elected state assemblies. Each state has a Governor who acts as its official head. Many states also have two chambers, the upper generally called the Rajya Sabha and the lower (often called the



### Prime Ministers and Presidents since 1947

| Date | Prime Minister | Date | President |
|---|---|---|---|
| 1947-64 | Jawaharlal Nehru | 1948-50 | C Rajagopalachari |
| 1964-66 | Lal Bahadur Shastri | 1950-62 | Rajendra Prasad |
| 1966-77 | Indira Gandhi | 1962-67 | S Radhakrishnan |
| 1977-79 | Morarji Desai | 1967-69 | Zakir Hussain |
| 1979-80 | Charan Singh | 1969-74 | V V Giri |
| 1980-84 | Indira Gandhi | 1974-77 | Fakhruddin Ali Ahmed |
| 1984-89 | Rajiv Gandhi | 1977-82 | Neelam Sanjiva Reddy |
| 1989-90 | VP Singh | 1982-87 | Giani Zail Singh |
| 1990-91 | S Chandrasekhar | 1987-92 | R Venkataraman |
| 1991- 96 | PV Narasimha Rao | 1992-97 | Shankar Dayal Sharma |
| 1996 | Atal Behari Vaypayee | 1997-02 | K R Narayanan |
| 1996-97 | H D Deve Gowda | | |
| 1997-98 | Inder Kumar Gujral | | |
| 1998-04 | Atal Bihari Vajpayee | | |
| 2004 (May) | Manmohan Singh | 2002 | Abdul Kalam |

Vidhan Sabha) being of directly elected representatives. In practice many of the state assemblies have had a totally different political complexion from that of the Lok Sabha. Regional parties have played a far more prominent role, though in many states central government has effectively dictated both the leadership and policy of state assemblies.



**States and Union Territories** Union territories are administered by the President "acting to such an extent as he thinks fit". In practice Union territories have varying forms of self-government. Pondicherry has a legislative Assembly and Council of Ministers. The 69th Amendment to the Constitution in 1991 provided for a legislative assembly and council of Ministers for Delhi, elections for which were held in December 1993. The Assemblies of Union Territories have more restricted powers of legislation than full states. Some Union Territories – Dadra and Nagar Haveli, Daman and Diu, all of which separated from Goa in 1987 when Goa achieved full statehood - Andaman and Nicobar Islands and Lakshadweep, have elected bodies known as Pradesh Councils.

**Secularism** One of the key features of India's constitution is its secular principle. Some see the commitment to a secular constitution as under increasing challenge, especially from the Hindu nationalism of the Bharatiya Janata Party, the BJP.

**The judiciary** India's Supreme Court has similar but somewhat weaker powers to those of the United States. The judiciary has remained effectively independent of the government except under the Emergency between 1975-1977.

**The civil service** India continued to use the small but highly professional administrative service inherited from the British period. Renamed the Indian Administrative Service (IAS), it continues to exercise remarkable influence across the country. The administration of many aspects of central and regional government is in the hands of this élite body, who act largely by the constitutional rules which bind them as servants of the state. Many Indians accept the continuing efficiency and high calibre of the top ranking officers in the administration while believing that the bureaucratic system as a whole has been overtaken by widespread corruption.

**The police** India's police service is divided into a series of groups, numbering nearly one million. While the top ranks of the Indian Police Service are comparable to the IAS, lower levels are extremely poorly trained and very low paid. In addition to the domestic police force there are special groups: the Border Security Force, Central Reserve Police and others. They may be armed with modern weapons and are called in for special duties.

**The armed forces** Unlike its immediate neighbours, India has never had military rule. It has approximately one million men in the army – one of the largest armed forces in the world. Although they have remained out of politics the armed services have been used increasingly frequently to put down civil unrest especially in Kashmir, where there are currently around 400,000 troops.

**The Congress Party** The Congress won overall majorities in seven of the 10 general elections held before the 1996 election, although in no election did the Congress obtain more than 50% of the popular vote. In 1998 its popular support completely disappeared in some regions and fell below 30% nationally and in the elections of September- October 1999 Sonia Gandhi, Rajiv Gandhi's Italian born widow, failed to achieve the much vaunted revival in the Party's fortunes. Through 2001 into 2002 a sea change began with the BJP losing power in state assemblies in the north and becoming increasingly unpopular nationally, and the Congress picking up a wide measure of support, culminating in their victory in the May 2004 general election.

**The Non-Congress Parties** Political activity outside the Congress can seem bewilderingly complex. There are no genuinely national parties. The only alternative governments to the Congress have been formed by coalitions of regional and ideologically based parties. Parties of the left – Communist and Socialist – have never broken out of their narrow regional bases. The **Communist Party of India** split into two factions in 1964, with the Communist Party of India Marxist **(CPM)** ultimately taking power in West Bengal and Kerala. In the 1960s the **Swatantra Party** (a liberal party) made some ground nationally, opposing the economic centralization and state control supported by the Congress.

At the right of the political spectrum, the **Jan Sangh** was seen as a party of right wing Hindu nationalism with a concentrated but significant base in parts of the north, especially among higher castes and merchant communities. The most organized political force outside the Congress, the Jan Sangh merged with the **Janata Party** for the elections of 1977. After the collapse of that government it re-formed itself as the **Bharatiya Janata Party (BJP)**. In 1990-1991 it developed a powerful campaign focusing on reviving Hindu identity against the minorities. The elections of 1991 showed it to be the most powerful single challenger to the Congress in North India. In the decade that followed it became the most powerful single party across northern India and established a series of footholds and alliances in the South. Elsewhere a succession of regional parties dominated politics in several key states, including Tamil Nadu and Andhra Pradesh in the south and West Bengal and Bihar in the east.



**Recent developments** By mid-2001 the gloss had worn off the popularity of the BJP and it had suffered a series of scandals, but the Prime Minister had kept the core of the government together. In July 2001 Pakistan's military ruler General Pervez Musharraf visited New Delhi and Agra for talks at the Indian Government's invitation, but they ended in a shambles.

The attacks on New York and Washington on 11 September and the US-led "War on Terror" has had major repercussions iin India and Pakistan. While the Taliban's rapid defeat brought a new government to power in Afghanistan, the Kashmir dispute between India and Pakistan deepened. Both India and Pakistan sought political advantage from the war on terror, and when a terrorist attack was launched on the Indian parliament on 13 December 2001 the Indian government pushed massive reinforcements to the Pakistan border from Gujarat and Rajasthan to Kashmir. Demanding the return from Pakistan to India of twenty men wanted on terrorist charges, India also demanded that President Musharraf close down all camps and organisations which India claimed were the source of the attacks in Delhi and Kashmir. Although President Musharraf closed down *Lashkar e Taiba* and *Jaish e Mohammad*, two of the most feared groups operating openly in Pakistan, cross-border firing intensified along the Line of Control in Kashmir and attacks in Kashmir continued. On 16 May 2002 terrorists launched a devastating attack on an army camp in Jammu, killing at least 20 people, and Sonia Gandhi demanded that the Government translate rhetoric into action. Since the change of government in May 2004, however, things have improved dramatically, with the new Indian prime minister seeming to enjoy a genuinely warm rapport with Pakistan's Pervez Musharraf. During a speech in May 2005, Musharraf laid out fresh guidelines for a resolution to the Kashmir dispute, and expressed his wish to have the issue resolved within a year. While such good intentions have often lead to little positive action in the past, the situation at the time of writing is definitely more promising than it has been for some time.

# Economy

## Agriculture

Although agriculture now accounts for less than 30% of India's GDP, it remains the most important single economic activity. More than half of India's people depend directly on agriculture and its success has a crucial effect on the remainder of the economy.

Indian agriculture is enormously varied, reflecting the widely different conditions of climate, soil and relief. Cereal farming dominates most areas. Wheat, grown as a winter crop, is most important in western Uttar Pradesh through Haryana to Punjab. Rice, the most important single foodgrain, is concentrated in the wetter regions of the east and south. The total production of both crops has more than doubled in the last 20 years and 2001-2002 saw production of rice and wheat reach record levels.

Other cereal crops – sorghum and the millets – predominate in central India and unirrigated parts of the north. In addition to its cereals and a range of pulses, India produces important crops of tea, cotton and sugar cane. All have seen significant growth, tea and cotton manufacturers making important contributions to export earnings.

Between independence and the late 1960s most of the increase in India's agricultural output came from extending the cultivated area. In the last 20 years increasingly intensive use of land through greater irrigation and use of fertilizer, pesticides and high yielding varieties of seeds (HYVs) has allowed growth to continue. The area under irrigation has risen to over 35% in 2002, while fertilizer use has increased 25 times since 1961. Indian agriculture is dominated by small holdings. Only 20% of the land is farmed in units of more than 10 ha (compared with 31% 20 years ago), while nearly 60% of farms are less than one hectare.While the "Green Revolution" - the package of practices designed to increase farm output - has had its opponents, it has now transformed the agricultural productivity of many regions of India, allowing a population twice the size of that thirty years ago to be fed without recourse to imports or aid. Much of this has been achieved as the result of seed breeding and agricultural research in India's own agricultural research institutions.

## Resources and industry

India has extensive resources of iron ore, coal, bauxite and some other minerals. Reserves of coal at likely rates of use are estimated at well over 100 years (at least 30 billion tonnes, plus six billion tonnes of coking coal). Medium and high grade iron ore reserves (five billion tonnes) will last over 200 years at present extraction rates. Although iron ore is found widely across peninsular India, coal is largely restricted to West Bengal, Bihar and Orissa. India's coal output reached over 250 million tonnes in 2002 and iron ore 60 million tonnes, much of which was exported to Japan.

The search for oil intensified after the oil price rises of the 1970s and late 1980s. Development of the Bombay High, off the coast of Gujarat, has contributed to the total output of over 26 million tonnes. Oil, coal and gas provide the energy for just over half of India's 100 million kw electric generation capacity, 20 million kw being hydro and two million mw nuclear.

By 2002 India's power production had grown to over 470 billion kwh, but demand has risen so fast that many states continue to have power blackouts or 'loadshedding'. Firewood is estimated to provide nearly 30% of the total energy requirement, agricultural waste 9% and cow dung, a universal fuel in some poorer areas, 7%. A recent report highlights the health risk of the continuing dependence on traditional fuels for cooking, suggesting that because of the noxious fumes released in kitchens they are responsible for up to 500,000 deaths a year from cancers and related illnesses.

## India's Five Year Plans

In the early 1950s India embarked on a programme of planned industrial development. Borrowing planning concepts from the Soviet Union, the government tried to stimulate development through massive investment in the public sector, imposing a system of tight controls on foreign ownership of capital in India and playing a highly interventionist role in all aspects of economic policy. The private sector was allowed to continue to operate in agriculture and in a wide range of 'non-essential' industrial sectors.

Although significant achievements were made in the first two Five Year Plans (1951-1956, 1956-1961), the Third Five Year Plan failed catastrophically. Agriculture was particularly hard hit by three poor monsoons. After a period of dependence on foreign aid at the end of the 1960s, the economy started moving forward again. The 'Green Revolution' enabled Indian agriculture to increase production faster than demand and through the 1980s it was producing surplus foodgrains, enabling it to build up reserves.

### Achievements and problems

India today has a far more diversified industrial base than seemed imaginable at Independence. It produces goods, from aeroplanes and rockets to watches and computers, from industrial and transport machinery to textiles and consumer goods. The influence of India's manufacturing industry reaches every village. The most striking modern development is in the IT sector. According to the London *Financial Times* since the early 1990s India has become one of the world's leading centres for software development. With approximately seven million Indians on the net in 2002, India is rapidly transforming itself into a computer-based society. Yet despite the economic successes, many in India claim that the weaknesses remain profound. Perhaps half of the population continues to live in absolute poverty and despite surplus grain production many still lack an adequate diet.



# Culture

## Language

The graffiti written on the walls of any Indian city bear witness to the number of major languages spoken across the country, many with their own distinct scripts. In all the states of North and West India an Indo-Aryan language – the easternmost group of the Indo-European family – is predominant. Sir William Jones, the great 19th-century scholar, discovered the close links between Sanskrit (the basis of nearly all North Indian languages) German and Greek. He showed that they all must have originated in the common heartland of Central Asia, being carried west, south and east by the nomadic tribes who shaped so much of the subsequent history of both Europe and Asia.

**Sanskrit** As the pastoralists from Central Asia moved into South Asia from 2000 BC onwards, the Indo-Aryan languages they spoke were gradually modified. Sanskrit developed from this process, emerging as the dominant classical language of India by the sixth century BC, when it was classified in the grammar of **Panini**. It remained the language of the educated until about AD 1000, though it had ceased to be in common use several centuries earlier.

**Hindi and Urdu** The Muslims brought Persian into South Asia as the language of the rulers, where it became the language of the numerically tiny but politically powerful élite. The most striking example of Muslim influence on the earlier Indo-European languages is that of the two most important languages of India and Pakistan, Hindi and Urdu respectively. Most of the other modern North Indian languages were not written until the 16th century or after. Hindi developed into the language of the heartland of Hindu culture, stretching from Punjab to Bihar and from the foothills of the Himalaya to the marchlands of central India. 

**Bengali** At the east end of the Ganga plains Hindi gives way to Bengali (Bangla), the language today of over 50 million people in India, as well as more than 115 million in Bangladesh. Linguistically it is close to both Assamese and Oriya.

**Gujarati and Marathi** South of the main Hindi and Urdu belt of India and Pakistan is a series of quite different Indo-Aryan languages. Panjabi in both Pakistan and India (on the Indian side of the border written in the Gurumukhi script) and Gujarati and Marathi, all have common features with Urdu or Hindi, but are major languages in their own right.

**The Dravidian languages** The other major language family of South Asia today, Dravidian, has been in India since before the arrival of the Indo-Aryans. Four of South Asia's major living languages belong to this family group - Tamil, Telugu, Kannada and Malayalam, spoken in Tamil Nadu (and northern Sri Lanka), Andhra Pradesh, Karnataka and Kerala respectively.

Each has its own script. All the Dravidian languages were influenced by the prevalence of Sanskrit as the language of the ruling and educated élite. There have been recent attempts to rid Tamil of its Sanskrit elements and to recapture the supposed purity of a literature that stretches back to the early centuries BC. Kannada and Telugu were clearly established by AD 1000, while Malayalam, which started as a dialect of Tamil, did not develop its fully distinct form until the 13th century. Today the four main Dravidian languages are spoken by over 180 million people.



## Scripts

It is impossible to spend even a short time in India or the other countries of South Asia without coming across several of the different scripts that are used. The earliest ancestor of scripts in use today was **Brahmi**, in which Asoka's famous inscriptions were written in the third century BC. Written from left to right, a separate symbol represented each different sound.

**Devanagari** For about a 1,000 years the major script of northern India has been the Nagari or Devanagari, which means literally the script of the 'city of the gods'. Hindi, Nepali and Marathi join Sanskrit in their use of Devanagari. The Muslim rulers developed a right to left script based on Persian and Arabic.

**Dravidian scripts** The Dravidian languages were written originally on leaves of the palmyra palm. Cutting the letters on the hard palm leaf made particular demands which had their impact on the forms of the letters adopted. The letters became rounded because they were carved with a stylus. This was held stationary while the leaf was turned. The southern scripts were carried overseas, contributing to the form of the non-Dravidian languages of Thai, Burmese and Cambodian.

**Numerals** Many of the Indian alphabets have their own notation for numerals. This is not without irony, for what in the western world are called 'Arabic' numerals are in fact of Indian origin. In some parts of South Asia local numerical symbols are still in use, but by and large you will find that the Arabic number symbols familiar in Europe and the West are common.

# Literature

Sanskrit was the first all-India language. Its literature has had a fundamental influence on the religious, social and political life of the entire region. Its early literature was memorized and recited. The hymns of the Rig Veda probably did not reach their final form until about the sixth century BC.

## The Vedas

The Rig Veda is a collection of 1,028 hymns, not all directly religious. Its main function was to provide orders of worship for priests responsible for the sacrifices which were central to the religion of the Indo-Aryans. Two later texts, the Yajurveda and the Samaveda, served the same purpose. A fourth, the Atharvaveda, is largely a collection of magic spells.

**The Brahmanas** Central to the Vedic literature was a belief in the importance of sacrifice. At some time after 1000 BC a second category of Vedic literature, the Brahmanas, began to take shape. Story telling developed as a means to interpret the significance of sacrifice. The most famous and the most important of these were the Upanishads, probably written at some time between the seventh and fifth centuries BC.

**The Mahabharata** The Brahmanas gave their name to the religion emerging between the eighth and sixth centuries BC, Brahmanism, the ancestor of Hinduism. Two of it's texts remain the best known and most widely revered epic compositions in South Asia, the Mahabharata and the Ramayana.



## Dating the Mahabharata

Tradition puts the date of the great battle described in the Mahabharata at precisely 3102 BC, the start of the present era, and names the author of the poem as a sage, Vyasa. Evidence suggests however that the battle was fought around 800 BC, at **Kurukshetra.** It was another 400 years before priests began to write the stories down, a process which was not complete until 400 AD. The Mahabharata was probably an attempt by the warrior class, the Kshatriyas, to merge their brand of popular religion with the ideas of Brahmanism. The original version was about 3,000 stanzas long, but it now contains over 100,000 - eight times as long as Homer's Iliad and the Odyssey put together.

**Good and evil** The battle was seen as a war of the forces of good and evil, the **Pandavas** being interpreted as gods and the **Kauravas** as devils. The arguments were elaborated and expanded until about the fourth century AD by which time, as Shackle says, "Brahmanism had absorbed and set its own mark on the religious ideas of the epic and Hinduism had come into being". A comparatively late addition to the Mahabharata, the Bhagavad-Gita is the most widely read and revered text among Hindus in South Asia today.

## The Ramayana

Valmiki is thought of in India as the author of the second great Indian epic, the Ramayana, though no more is known of his identity than is known of Homer's. Like the Mahabharata, it underwent several stages of development before it reached its final version of 48,000 lines.

## Sanskrit literature

Sanskrit was always the language of the court and the élite. Other languages replaced it in common speech by the third century BC, but it remained in restricted use for over

## The story of Rama

Under Brahmin influence, Rama was transformed from the human prince of the early versions into the divine figure of the final story. Rama, the 'jewel of the solar kings', became deified as an incarnation of Vishnu. The story tells how Rama was banished from his father's kingdom. In a journey that took him as far as Sri Lanka, accompanied by his wife Sita and helper and friend Hanuman (the monkey-faced God depicted in many Indian temples, shrines and posters), Rama finally fought the king **Ravana**, again changed in late versions into a demon. Rama's rescue of Sita was interpreted as the Aryan triumph over the barbarians. The epic is widely seen as South Asia's first literary poem and is known and recited in all

Ravana, demon king of Lanka



1,000 years after that period. The remarkable Sanskrit grammar of Panini (see page 722) helped to establish grammar as one of the six disciplines essential to understanding the Vedas properly and to conducting Vedic rituals. The other five were phonetics, etymology, meter, ritual practice and astronomy. Sanskrit literature continued to be written in the courts until the Muslims replaced it with Persian, long after it had ceased to be a language of spoken communication. One of India's greatest poets, **Kalidasa**, contributed to the development of Sanskrit as the language of learning and the arts.

Literally 'stories of ancient times', the Puranas are about Brahma, Vishnu and Siva. They were not compiled until the fifth century AD. The stories are often the only source of information about the period immediately following the early Vedas. Each Purana was intended to deal with five themes: "the creation of the world (sarga); its destruction and recreation (pratisarga); the genealogy of gods and patriarchs (vamsa); the reigns and periods of the Manus (manvantaras); and the history of the solar and lunar dynasties".

## The Muslim influence

**Persian** In the first three decades of the 10th century AD Mahmud of Ghazni carried Muslim power into India. For considerable periods until the 18th century, Persian became the language of the courts. Classical Persian was the dominant influence, with Iran as its country of origin and Shiraz its main cultural centre, but India developed its own Persian-based style. Two poets stood out at the end of the 13th century AD, when Muslim rulers had established a sultanate in Delhi, Amir Khusrau, who lived from 1253 to 1325 and the mystic Amir Hasan, who died about AD 1328.

**Turki** The most notable of the Mughal sponsors of literature, Akbar (1556-1605) was himself illiterate. Babur left one of the most remarkable political autobiographies of any generation, the Babur-nama (History of Babur), written in Turki and translated into Persian. His grandson Akbar commissioned a biography, the Akbar-nama, which reflected his interest in all the world's religions. His son Jahangir left his memoirs, the Tuzuk-i Jahangiri, in Persian. They have been described as intimate and spontaneous and showing an insatiable interest in things, events and people.

### The Colonial Period

Persian was already in decline during the reign of the last great Muslim Emperor, **Aurangzeb** and as the British extended their political power so the role of English grew. There is now a very wide Indian literature accessible in English, which has thus become the latest of the languages to be used across the whole of South Asia.

In the 19th century English became a vehicle for developing nationalist ideals. However, notably in the work of **Rabindranath Tagore** , it became a medium for religious and philosophical prose and for a developing poetry. Tagore himself won the Nobel Prize for Literature in 1913 for his translation into English of his own work, Gitanjali. Leading South Asian philosophers and thinkers of the 20th century have written major works in English, including not only MK Gandhi and Jawaharlal Nehru, the two leading figures in India's Independence movement, but S Radhakrishnan, Aurobindo Ghose and Sarojini Naidu, who all added to the depth of Indian literature in English.

Several South Asian regional languages have their own long traditions of both religious and secular literature which are discussed in the relevant sections of this book.



## Science

**Views of the universe** Early Indian views of the universe were based on the square and the cube. The earth was seen as a square, one corner pointing south, rising like a pyramid in a series of square terraces with its peak, the mythical Mount Meru. The sun moved round the top of Mount Meru in a square orbit and the square orbits of the planets were at successive planes above the orbit of the sun. These were seen therefore as forming a second pyramid of planetary movement. Mount Meru was central to all early Indian schools of thought, Hindu, Buddhist and Jain.

However, about 200 BC the Jains transformed the view of the universe based on squares by replacing the idea of square orbits with that of the circle. The earth was shown as a circular disc, with Mount Meru rising from its centre and the Pole Star directly above it.

**The science of early India** By about 500 BC Indian texts illustrated the calculation of the **calendar**, although the system itself almost certainly goes back to the eighth or ninth century BC. The year was divided into 27 *nakshatras*, or fortnights, years being calculated on a mixture of lunar and solar counting.

**Technology** The only copy of Kautiliya's treatise on government (which was only discovered in 1909) dates from about 100 BC. It describes the **weapons** technology of catapults, incendiary missiles and the use of elephants, but it is also evident that gunpowder was unknown. Large scale **irrigation** works were developed, though the earliest examples of large tanks may be those of the Sri Lankan King Panduwasa at Anuradhapura, built in 504 BC. During the Gupta period dramatic progress was made in **metallurgy**, evidenced in the extraordinarily pure iron pillar which can be seen in the Qutb Minar in Delhi.

**Mathematics** Conceptions of the universe and the mathematical and geometrical ideas that accompanied them were comparatively advanced in South Asia by the time of the Mauryan Empire and were put to use in the rules developed for building temple altars. Indians were using the concept of zero and decimal points in the Gupta period. Furthermore in AD 499, just after the demise of the Gupta Empire, the astronomer Aryabhatta calculated Pi as 3.1416 and the length of the solar year as 365.358 days. He also postulated that the earth was a sphere rotating on its own axis and revolving around the sun and that the shadow of the earth falling on the moon caused lunar eclipses. The development of science in India was not restricted to the Gupta court. In South India, Tamil kings developed extensive contact with Roman and Greek thinkers during the first four centuries of the Christian era. Babylonian methods used for astronomy in Greece remained current in Tamil Nadu until very recent times. The basic texts of astronomy (the Surya Siddhanta) were completed by AD 400.



## Architecture

Over the 4,000 years since the Indus Valley civilization flourished, art and architecture have developed with a remarkable continuity through successive regional and religious influences and styles. The Buddhist art and architecture of the third century BC left few remains, but the stylistic influence on early Hindu architecture was profound. From the sixth century AD the first Hindu religious buildings to have survived into the modern period were constructed in South and East India.



### Hindu temple buildings

The principles of religious building were laid down by priests in the *Sastras*. Every aspect of Hindu, Jain and Buddhist religious building is identified with conceptions of the structure of the universe. This applies as much to the process of building - the timing of which must be undertaken at astrologically propitious times - as to the formal layout of the buildings. The cardinal directions of north, south, east and west are the basic fix on which buildings are planned. George Michell suggests that in addition to the cardinal directions, number is also critical to the design of the religious building. The key to the ultimate scale of the building is derived from the measurements of the sanctuary at its heart. Indian temples were nearly always built according to philosophical understandings of the universe. This cosmology, of an infinite number of universes, isolated from each other in space, proceeds by imagining various possibilities as to its nature. Its centre is seen as dominated by **Mount Meru** which keeps earth and heaven apart. The concept of *separation* is crucial to Hindu thought and social practice. Continents, rivers and oceans occupy concentric rings around the mountain, while the stars encircle the mountain in another plane. Humans live on the continent of **Jambudvipa**, characterized by the rose apple tree (*jambu*). For more information on temple architecture specific to the South, see Footprint's *South India*.

**Mandalas** The Sastras show plans of this continent, organized in concentric rings and entered at the cardinal points. This type of diagram was known as a **mandala**. Such a geometric scheme could be subdivided into almost limitless small compartments, each of which could be designated as having special properties or be devoted to a particular deity. The centre of the mandala would be the seat of the major god; they provided the ground rules for the building of stupas and temples across India and gave the key to the symbolic meaning attached to every aspect of religious buildings.

**Temple design** The focal point of the temple, its sanctuary, was the home of the presiding deity, the 'womb-chamber' (*garbhagriha*). A series of doorways, in large temples leading through a succession of buildings, allowed the worshipper to move towards the final encounter with the deity to obtain *darshan* – a sight of the god. Both Buddhist and Hindu worship encourage the worshipper to walk clockwise around the shrine, performing *pradakshina*.

The elevations are symbolic representations of the home of the gods. Mountain peaks such as Kailasa are common names for the most prominent of the towers. In North and East Indian temples the tallest of these towers rises above the *garbagriha* itself, symbolizing the meeting of earth and heaven in the person of the enshrined deity. In later South Indian temples the gateways to the temple come to overpower the central tower. In both, the basic structure is usually richly embellished with sculpture. When first built this would usually have been plastered and painted and often covered in gems. In contrast to the extraordinary profusion of colour and life on the outside, the interior is dark and cramped but here it is believed, lies the true centre of divine power.

## Muslim religious architecture

Although the Muslims adapted many Hindu features, they also brought totally new forms. Their most outstanding contribution, dominating the architecture of many North Indian cities, are the mosques and tomb complexes (*dargah*). The use of brickwork was widespread and they brought with them from Persia the principle of constructing the true arch. Muslim architects succeeded in producing a variety of domed structures, often incorporating distinctively Hindu features such as the surmounting finial. By the end of the great period of Muslim building in 1707, the Muslims had added magnificent forts and palaces to their religious structures, a statement of power as well as of aesthetic taste.

## European buildings

Nearly two centuries of architectural stagnation and decline followed the demise of Mughal power. The Portuguese built a series of remarkable churches in Goa that owed nothing to local traditions and everything to Baroque developments in Europe. Not until the end of the Victorian period, when British imperial ambitions were at their height, did the British colonial impact on public rather than domestic architecture begin to be felt. Fierce arguments divided British architects as to the merits of indigenous design. The ultimate plan for New Delhi was carried out by men who had little time for Hindu architecture and believed themselves to be on a civilizing mission, see page 89. Others at the end of the 19th century wanted to recapture and enhance a tradition for which they had great respect. They have left a series of buildings, both in formerly British ruled territory and in the Princely States, which illustrate this concern through the development of what became known as the Indo-Saracenic style.

In the immediate aftermath of the colonial period, Independent India set about trying to establish a break from the immediately imperial past, but was uncertain how to achieve it. In the event foreign architects were commissioned for major developments, such as Le Corbusier's design for Chandigarh and Louis Kahn's buildings in Dhaka and Ahmadabad. The latter, a centre for training and experiment, contains a number of new buildings such as those of the Indian architect Charles Correa.

# Music and dance

**Music** Indian music can trace its origins to the metrical hymns and chants of the Vedas, in which the production of sound according to strict rules was understood to be vital to the continuing order of the Universe. Through more than 3,000 years of development and a range of regional schools, India's musical tradition has been handed on almost entirely by ear. The chants of the **Rig Veda** developed into songs in the **Sama Veda** and music found expression in every sphere of life, reflecting the cycle of seasons and the rhythm of work.

Over the centuries the original three notes, which were sung strictly in descending order, were extended to five and then seven and developed to allow freedom to move up and down the scale. The scale increased to 12 with the addition of flats and sharps and finally to 22 with the further subdivision of semitones. Books of musical rules go back at least as far as the third century AD. Classical music was totally intertwined with dance and drama, an interweaving reflected in the term *sangita*.

At some point after the Muslim influence made itself felt in the north, North and South Indian styles diverged, to become Carnatic (Karnatak) music in the south and Hindustani music in the north. However, they still share important common features: *svara* (pitch), *raga* (the melodic structure) and *tala* or *talam* (metre).

**Hindustani music** probably originated in the Delhi Sultanate during the 13th century, when the most widely known of North Indian musical instruments, the *sitar*, was believed to have been invented. **Amir Khusrau** is also believed to have invented the small drums, the *tabla*. Hindustani music is held to have reached its peak under *Tansen*, a court musician of Akbar. The other important northern instruments are the stringed *sarod*, the reed instrument *shahnai* and the wooden flute. Most Hindustani compositions have devotional texts, though they encompass a great emotional and thematic range. A common classical form of vocal performance is the *dhrupad*, a four-part composition.

The essential structure of a melody is known as a **raga** which usually has five to seven notes and can have as many as nine (or even 12 in mixed ragas). The music is improvised by the performer within certain governing rules and although theoretically thousands of ragas are possible, only around a 100 are commonly performed. Ragas have become associated with particular moods and specific times of the day. Music festivals often include all night sessions to allow performers a wider choice of repertoire.

Carnatic (Karnatak) music, contemporary South Indian music, is traced back to Tyagaraja (1759-1847), Svami Shastri (1763-1827) and Dikshitar (1775-1835), three musicians who lived and worked in Thanjavur. They are still referred to as 'the Trinity'. Their music placed more emphasis on extended compositions than Hindustani music. Perhaps the best known South Indian instrument is the stringed *vina*, the flute being commonly used for accompaniment along with the violin (played rather differently to the European original), an oboe-like instrument called the *nagasvaram* and the drums, *tavil*.

**Dance** The rules for classical dance were laid down in the Natya shastra in the second century BC, which is still one of the bases for modern dance forms. The most common sources for Indian dance are the epics, but there are three essential aspects of the dance itself, Nritta (pure dance), Nrittya (emotional expression) and Natya (drama). The religious influence in dance was exemplified by the tradition of temple dancers, *devadasis*, girls and women who were dedicated to the deity in major temples. In South and East India there were thousands of *devadasis* associated with temple worship, though the practice fell into widespread disrepute and was banned in independent India. Various dance forms (for example Odissi, Manipuri, Bharat Natyam, Kathakali, Mohinyattam) developed in different parts of the country. India is also rich in folk dance traditions which are widely performed during festivals.

**The cinema** Film goers around the world are taking greater note of Indian cinema, both home-grown and that produced and directed by Indians abroad. Not all fall into the category of a Bollywood '*masala* movie' or 'curry western' churned out by the Mumbai (Bombay) film industry but many offer an insight into what draws millions to watch diverse versions of Indian life on the silver screen. A few titles, both all time favourites as well as new releases are listed here. Some of these are available on video or DVD.

Viewing: *Pather Panchali, Mother India; Titash Ekti Nadir Naam; Sholay; Bombay; Kuch Kuch Hota Hai; Lagaan; Kabhie Khushi Kabhie Cham; Monsoon Wedding; The Guru; The Warrior.*

# Religion

It is impossible to write briefly about religion in India without greatly oversimplifying. Over 80% of Indians are Hindu, but there are significant minorities. Muslims number about 125 million and there are over 23 million Christians, 19 million Sikhs, six million Buddhists and a number of other religious groups (see page 108). One of the most persistent features of Indian religious and social life is the caste system. This has undergone substantial changes since Independence, especially in towns and cities, but most people in India are still clearly identified as a member of a particular caste group. The Government has introduced measures to help the backward, or 'scheduled' castes, though in recent years this has produced a major political backlash.

## Hinduism



It has always been easier to define Hinduism by what it is not than by what it is. Indeed, the name 'Hindu' was given by foreigners to the peoples of the subcontinent who did not profess the other major faiths, such as Muslims or Christians. While some aspects of modern Hinduism can be traced back more than 4,000 years before that, other features are recent.

### Key ideas

According to the great Indian philosopher and former President of India, S Radhakrishnan, religion for the Hindu "is not an idea but a power, not an intellectual proposition but a life conviction. Religion is consciousness of ultimate reality, not a theory about God". There is no Hindu organization, like a church, with the authority to define belief or establish official practice. Not all Hindu groups believe in a single supreme God.In view of these characteristics, many authorities argue that it is misleading to think of Hinduism as a religion at all. Be that as it may, the evidence of the living importance of Hinduism is visible across India. Hindu philosophy and practice has also touched many of those who belong to other religious traditions, particularly in terms of social institutions such as caste, and in post-Independence India religious identity has become an increasingly politicized feature of national life.

**Darshan** One of Hinduism's recurring themes is 'vision', 'sight' or 'view' – **darshan**. Applied to the different philosophical systems themselves, such as *yoga* or *vedanta*, 'darshan' is also used to describe the sight of the deity that worshippers hope to gain when they visit a temple or shrine hoping for the sight of a 'guru' (teacher). Equally it may apply to the religious insight gained through meditation or prayer.

**The four human goals** Many Hindus also accept that there are four major human goals; material prosperity (*artha*), the satisfaction of desires (*kama*) and performing the duties laid down according to your position in life (*dharma*). Beyond those is the goal of achieving liberation from the endless cycle of rebirths into which everyone is locked (*moksha*). It is to the search for liberation that the major schools of Indian philosophy have devoted most attention. Together with dharma, it is basic to Hindu thought.

The *Mahabharata* lists 10 embodiments of **dharma**: good name, truth, self-control, cleanness of mind and body, simplicity, endurance, resoluteness of character, giving and sharing, austerities and continence. In *dharmic* thinking these are inseparable from five patterns of behaviour: non-violence, an attitude of equality, peace and tranquillity, lack of aggression and cruelty and absence of envy. Dharma, an essentially secular concept, represents the order inherent in human life.

## The four stages of life

Popular Hindu belief holds that an ideal life has four stages: that of the student, the householder, the forest dweller and the wandering dependent or beggar (sannyasi). These stages represent the phases through which an individual learns of life's goals and of the means of achieving them.

One of the most striking sights today is that of the saffron clad *sannyasi* (sadhu) seeking gifts of food and money to support himself in the final stage of his life. There may have been sadhus even before the Aryans arrived. Today, most of these have given up material possessions, carrying only a strip of cloth, a *danda* (staff), a crutch to support the chin during *achal* (meditation), prayer beads, a fan to ward off evil spirits, a water pot, a drinking vessel, which may be a human skull and a begging bowl. You may well see one, almost naked, covered only in ashes, on a city street.



**Karma** The idea of *karma*, 'the effect of former actions', is central to achieving liberation. As C Rajagopalachari put it: "Every act has its appointed effect, whether the act be thought, word or deed. The cause holds the effect, so to say, in its womb. If we reflect deeply and objectively, the entire world will be found to obey unalterable laws. That is the doctrine of karma".

**Rebirth** The belief in the transmigration of souls (*samsara*) in a never-ending cycle of rebirth has been Hinduism's most distinctive and important contribution to Indian culture. The earliest reference to the belief is found in one of the *Upanishads*, around the seventh century BC, at about the same time as the doctrine of *karma* made its first appearance.

**Ahimsa** AL Basham pointed out that belief in transmigration must have encouraged a further distinctive doctrine, that of non-violence or non-injury – *ahimsa*. The belief in rebirth meant that all living things and creatures of the spirit – people, devils, gods, animals, even worms – possessed the same essential soul. One inscription threatens that anyone who interferes with the rights of Brahmins to land given to them by the king will 'suffer rebirth for 80,000 years as a worm in dung'. Belief in the cycle of rebirth was essential to give such a threat any weight!

## Schools of philosophy

It is common now to talk of six major schools of Hindu philosophy. *Nyaya, Vaisheshika*, *Sankhya*, *Yoga*, *Purvamimansa* and *Vedanta*.

**Yoga** Yoga, can be traced back to at least the third century AD. It seeks a synthesis of the spirit, the soul and the flesh and is concerned with systems of meditation and self denial that lead to the realization of the Divine within oneself and can ultimately release one from the cycle of rebirth.

**Vedanta** These are literally the final parts of the Vedic literature, the *Upanishads*. The basic texts also include the Brahmasutra of Badrayana, written about the first century AD and the most important of all, the *Bhagavad-Gita*, which is a part of the epic the *Mahabharata*. There are many interpretations of these basic texts. Three are given here.

**Advaita Vedanta** holds that there is no division between the cosmic force or principle, *Brahman* and the individual Self, *atman* (also referred to as 'soul'). The fact

### Karma – an eye to the future

According to the doctrine of karma, every person, animal or god has a being or 'self' which has existed without beginning. Every action, except those that are done without any consideration of the results, leaves an indelible mark on that 'self', carried forward into the next life.

The overall character of the imprint on each person's 'self' determines three features of the next life: the nature of his next birth (animal, human or god), the kind of family he will be born into if human and the length of the next life. Finally, it controls the good or bad experiences that the self will experience. However, it does not imply a fatalistic belief that the nature of action in this life is unimportant. Rather, it suggests that the path followed by the individual in the present life is vital to the nature of its next life and ultimately to the chance of gaining release from this world.



that we appear to see different and separate individuals is simply a result of ignorance. This is termed *maya* (illusion), but Vedanta philosophy does not suggest that the world in which we live is an illusion. *Jnana* (knowledge) is held as the key to understanding the full and real unity of Self and Brahman. **Shankaracharya,** born at Kalady in modern Kerala, in the seventh century AD, is the best known Advaitin Hindu philosopher. He argued that there was no individual Self or soul separate from the creative force of the universe, or Brahman and that it was impossible to achieve liberation (*moksha*), through meditation and devotional worship, which he saw as signs of remaining on a lower level and of being unprepared for true liberation.

The 11-12th-century philosopher, **Ramanuja,** repudiated ideas of **Vishishtadvaita.** He transformed the idea of God from an impersonal force to a personal God and viewed both the Self and the World as real but only as part of the whole. In contrast to Shankaracharya's view, Ramanuja saw *bhakti* (devotion) as of central importance to achieving liberation and service to the Lord as the highest goal of life.

**Dvaita Vedanta** was developed by the 14th-century philosopher, Madhva. He believed that Brahman, the Self and the World are completely distinct. Worship of God is a key means of achieving liberation.

## Worship

**Puja** For most Hindus today, worship ('performing puja') is an integral part of their faith. The great majority of Hindu homes will have a shrine to one of the gods of the Hindu pantheon. Individuals and families will often visit shrines or temples and on special occasions will travel long distances to particularly holy places such as Benaras or Puri. Such sites may have temples dedicated to a major deity but may also have numerous other shrines in the vicinity dedicated to other favourite gods.

Acts of devotion are often aimed at the granting of favours and the meeting of urgent needs for this life – good health, finding a suitable wife or husband, the birth of a son, prosperity and good fortune. Puja involves making an offering to God and *darshan* (having a view of the deity). Hindu worship is generally, though not always, an act performed by individuals. Thus Hindu temples may be little more than a shrine on a river bank or in the middle of the street, tended by a priest and visited at special times when a darshan of the resident God can be obtained. When it has been consecrated, the image, if exactly made, becomes the channel for the godhead to work.

**Holy places** Certain rivers and towns are particularly sacred to Hindus. Thus there are seven holy rivers – the Ganga, Yamuna, Indus and mythical Sarasvati in the north and the Narmada, Godavari and Kaveri in the Peninsula. There are also seven holy places – Haridwar, Mathura, Ayodhya and Varanasi, again in the north, Ujjain, Dwarka and Kanchipuram to the south. In addition to these seven holy places there are four holy abodes: Badrinath, Puri and Ramesvaram, with Dwarka in modern Gujarat having the unique distinction of being both a holy abode and a holy place.

**Rituals and festivals** The temple rituals often follow through the cycle of day and night, as well as yearly lifecycles. The priests may wake the deity from sleep, bathe, clothe and feed it. Worshippers will be invited to share in this process by bringing offerings of clothes and food. Gifts of money will usually be made and in some temples there is a charge levied for taking up positions in front of the deity in order to obtain a darshan at the appropriate times.

Every temple has its special festivals. At festival times you can see villagers walking in small groups, brightly dressed and often high spirited, sometimes as far as 80-100 km.

## Hindu deities

Today three Gods are widely seen as all-powerful: Brahma, Vishnu and Siva. While Brahma is regarded as the ultimate source of creation, Siva also has a creative role alongside his function as destroyer. Vishnu in contrast is seen as the preserver or protector of the universe. Vishnu and Siva are widely represented have come to be seen as the most powerful and important. Their followers are referred to as Vaishnavite and Shaivites respectively and numerically they form the two largest sects in India.

**Brahma** Popularly Brahma is interpreted as the Creator in a trinity, alongside Vishnu as Preserver and Siva as Destroyer. In the literal sense the name Brahma is the masculine and personalized form of the neuter word Brahman.

In the early Vedic writing, *Brahman* represented the universal and impersonal principle which governed the Universe. Gradually, as Vedic philosophy moved towards a monotheistic interpretation of the universe and its origins, this impersonal power was increasingly personalized. In the *Upanishads*, Brahman was seen as a universal and elemental creative spirit. Brahma, described in early myths as having been born from a golden egg and then to have created the Earth, assumed the identity of the earlier Vedic deity Prajapati and became identified as the creator.

By the fourth and fifth centuries AD, the height of the classical period of Hinduism, Brahma was seen as one of the trinity of Gods – *Trimurti* – in which Vishnu, Siva and Brahma represented three forms of the unmanifested supreme being. It is from Brahma that Hindu cosmology takes its structure. The basic cycle through which the whole cosmos passes is described as one day in the life of Brahma – the *kalpa*. It equals 4,320 million years, with an equally long night. One year of Brahma's life – a cosmic year – lasts 360 days and nights. The universe is expected to last for 100 years of Brahma's life, who is currently believed to be 51 years old.

By the sixth century AD Brahma worship had effectively ceased (before the great period of temple building), which accounts for the fact that there are remarkably few temples dedicated to Brahma. Nonetheless images of Brahma are found in most temples. Characteristically he is shown with four faces, a fifth having been destroyed by the fire from Siva's third eye. In his four arms he usually holds a copy of the Vedas, a sceptre and a water jug or a bow. He is accompanied by the goose, symbolizing knowledge.

**Sarasvati** Seen by some Hindus as the 'active power' of Brahma, popularly thought of as his consort, Sarasvati has survived into the modern Hindu world as a far more important figure than Brahma himself. In popular worship Sarasvati represents the goddess of education and learning, worshipped in schools and colleges with gifts of fruit, flowers and incense. She represents 'the word' itself, which began to be deified

### How Sarasvati turned Brahma's head

Masson-Oursel recounts one myth that explains how Brahma came to have five heads. "Brahma first formed woman from his own immaculate substance and she was known as Sarasvati, Savitri, Gayatri or Brahmani. When he saw this lovely girl emerge from his own body Brahma fell in love with her. Sarasvati moved to his right to avoid his gaze, but a head immediately sprang up from the god. And when Sarasvati turned to the left and then behind him, two new heads emerged. She darted towards heaven and a fifth head was formed. Brahma then said to his daughter, 'Let us beget all kinds of living things, men, Suras and Asuras'. Hearing these words Sarasvati returned to earth, Brahma wedded her and they retired to a secret place where they remained together for a hundred (divine) years".



as part of the process of the writing of the Vedas, which ascribed magical power to words. The development of her identity represented the rebirth of the concept of a mother goddess, which had been strong in the Indus Valley Civilization over 1,000 years before and which may have been continued in popular ideas through the worship of female spirits.

In addition to her role as Brahma's wife, Sarasvati is also variously seen as the wife of Vishnu and Manu or as Daksha's daughter, among other interpretations. Normally white coloured, riding on a swan and carrying a book, she is often shown playing a vina. She may have many arms and heads, representing her role as patron of all the sciences and arts.

**Vishnu** Vishnu is seen as the God with the human face. From the second century a new and passionate devotional worship of Vishnu's incarnation as Krishna developed in the South. By 1,000 AD Vaishnavism had spread across South India and it became closely associated with the devotional form of Hinduism preached by **Ramanuja,** whose followers spread the worship of Vishnu and his 10 successive incarnations in animal and human form. For Vaishnavites, God took these different forms in order to save the world from impending disaster. AL Basham has summarized the 10 incarnations (see Table).

**Rama and Krishna** By far the most influential incarnations of Vishnu are those in which he was believed to take recognizable human form, especially as Rama (twice) and Krishna. As the Prince of Ayodhya, history and myth blend, for Rama was probably a chief who lived in the eighth or seventh century BC. Although Rama is now seen as an earlier incarnation of Vishnu than Krishna, he came to be regarded as divine very late, probably after the Muslim invasions of the 12th century AD. Rama (or Ram - pronounced to rhyme with *calm*) is a powerful figure in contemporary India. His supposed birthplace at Ayodhya became the focus of fierce disputes between Hindus and Muslims in the early 1990's which continue today. Krishna is worshipped extremely widely as perhaps the most human of the gods. His advice on the battlefield of the *Mahabharata* is one of the major sources of guidance for the rules of daily living for many Hindus today.

**Lakshmi** Commonly represented as Vishnu's wife, Lakshmi is widely worshipped as the goddess of wealth. Earlier representations of Vishnu's consorts portrayed her as Sridevi, often shown in statues on Vishnu's right, while Bhudevi, also known as Prithvi, who represented the earth, was on his left. Lakshmi is popularly shown in her own right as standing on a lotus flower, although eight forms of Lakshmi are recognized.

## Vishnu's ten incarnations

| Name | Form | Story |
|---|---|---|
| 1<br>*Matsya* | Fish | Vishnu took the form of a fish to rescue Manu (the first man), his family and the Vedas from a flood. |
| 2<br>*Kurma* | Tortoise | Vishnu became a tortoise to rescue all the treasures lost in the flood, including the divine nectar (Amrita) with which the gods preserved their youth. The gods put Mount Kailasa on the tortoise's back and when he reached the bottom of the ocean they twisted the divine snake round the mountain. They then churned the ocean with the mountain by pulling the snake. |
| 3<br>*Varaha* | Boar | Vishnu appeared again to raise the earth from the ocean's floor where it had been thrown by a demon, Hiranyaksa. The story probably developed from a non-Aryan cult of a sacred pig. |
| 4<br>*Narasimha* | Half-man, half lion | Having persuaded Brahma to promise that he could not be killed either by day or night, by god, man or beast, the demon Hiranyakasipu then terrorized everybody. When the gods pleaded for help, Vishnu appeared at sunset, when it was neither day nor night, in the form of a half man and half lion and killed the demon. |
| 5<br>*Vamana* | A dwarf | Bali, a demon, achieved supernatural power by asceticism. To protect the world Vishnu appeared before him in the form of a dwarf and asked him a favour. Bali granted Vishnu as much land as he could cover in three strides. Vishnu then became a giant, covering the earth in three strides. He left only hell to the demon. |
| 6<br>*Parasurama* | Rama with the axe | Vishnu was incarnated as the son of a Brahmin, Jamadagni as Parasurama and killed the wicked king for robbing his father. The king's sons then killed Jamadagni and in revenge Parasurama destroyed all male kshatriyas, 21 times in succession. |
| 7<br>*Rama* | The Prince of Ayodhya | As told in the Ramayana, Vishnu came in the form of Rama to rescue the world from the dark demon, Ravana. His wife Sita is the model of patient faithfulness while Hanuman, is the monkey-faced god and Rama's helper. |
| 8<br>*Krishna* | Charioteer of Arjuma<br>Many forms | Krishna meets almost every human need, from the mischievous child, the playful boy, the amorous youth to the Divine. |
| 9<br>The *Buddha* | | Probably incorporated into the Hindu pantheon in order to discredit the Buddhists, dominant in some parts of India until the 6th century AD. An early Hindu interpretation suggests that Vishnu took incarnation as Buddha to show compassion for animals and to end sacrifice. |
| 10<br>*Kalki* | Riding on a horse | Vishnu's arrival will accompany the final destruction of this present age, Kaliyuga, judging the wicked and rewarding the good. |

**Hanuman** The *Ramayana* tells how Hanuman, Rama's faithful servant, went across India and finally into the demon Ravana's forest home of Lanka at the head of his monkey army in search of the abducted Sita. He used his powers to jump the sea channel separating India from Sri Lanka and managed after a series of heroic and magical feats to find and rescue his master's wife. Whatever form he is shown in, he remains almost instantly recognizable.

**Siva** Professor Wendy Doniger O'Flaherty argues that the key to the myths through which Siva's character is understood, lies in the explicit ambiguity of Siva as the great ascetic and at the same time as the erotic force of the universe.

Siva is interpreted as both creator and destroyer, the power through whom the universe evolves. He lives on Mount Kailasa with his wife **Parvati** (also known as **Uma, Sati, Kali** and **Durga**) and two sons, the elephant-headed Ganesh and the six-headed

## Worship of Siva's linga

Worship of Siva's linga – the phallic symbol of fertility, power and creativeness – is universal across India. Its origins lie in the creation myths of the Hindu trinity and in the struggle for supremacy between the different Hindu sects. Saivite myths illustrate the supreme power of Siva and the variety of ways in which Brahma and Vishnu were compelled to acknowledge his supreme power.

One such story tells how Siva, Vishnu and Brahma emerged from the ocean, whereupon Vishnu and Brahma begged him to perform creation. Siva agreed – but then to their consternation disappeared for 1,000 celestial years. They became so worried by the lack of creation that Vishnu told Brahma to create, so he produced everything that could lead to happiness. However, no sooner had Brahma filled the universe with beings than Siva reappeared. Incensed by the usurping of his power by Brahma, Siva decided to destroy everything with a flame from his mouth so that he could create afresh.

As the fire threatened to consume everything Brahma acknowledged Siva's total power and pleaded with him to spare the creation that Brahma had brought forth. "But what shall I do with all my excess power?" "Send it to the sun", replied Brahma, "for as you are the lord of the sun we may all live together in the sun's energy."

Siva agreed, but said to Brahma "What use is this linga if I cannot use it to create?" So he broke off his linga and threw it to the ground. The linga broke through the earth and went right into the sky. Vishnu looked for the end of it below and Brahma for the top, but neither could find the end. Then a voice from the sky said "If the linga of the god with braided hair is worshipped, it will grant all desires that are longed for in the heart." When Brahma and Vishnu heard this, they and all the divinities worshipped the linga with devotion."



Karttikeya, known in South India as Subrahmanya. In sculptural representations Siva is normally accompanied by his 'vehicle', the bull (*Nandi* or *Nandin*).

Siva is also represented in Shaivite temples throughout India by the *linga*, literally meaning 'sign' or 'mark', but referring in this context to the sign of gender or phallus and *yoni*. On the one hand a symbol of energy, fertility and potency, as Siva's symbol it also represents the yogic power of sexual abstinence and penance. The *linga* has become the most important symbol of the cult of Siva. O'Flaherty suggests that the worship of the *linga* of Siva can be traced back to the pre-Vedic societies of the Indus Valley civilization (circa 2000 BC), but that it first appears in Hindu iconography in the second century BC. From that time a wide variety of myths appeared to explain the origin of *linga* worship. The myths surrounding the 12 **jyotirlinga** (*linga* of light) found at centres like Ujjain go back to the second century BC and were developed in order to explain and justify *linga* worship.

**Siva's alternative names** Although Siva is not seen as having a series of rebirths, like Vishnu, he none the less appears in very many forms representing different aspects of his varied powers. Some of the more common are:

**Chandrasekhara** – the moon (*chandra*) symboilizes the powers of creation and destruction.

**Mahadeva** – the representation of Siva as the god of supreme power, which came relatively late into Hindu thought, shown as the *linga* in combination with the *yoni*, or female genitalia.

**Nataraja** – the Lord of the Cosmic Dance. The story is based on a legend in which Siva and Vishnu went to the forest to overcome 10,000 heretics. In their anger the heretics attacked Siva first by sending a tiger, then a snake and thirdly a fierce black dwarf with a club. Siva killed the tiger, tamed the snake and wore it like a garland and then put his foot on the dwarf and performed a dance of such power that the dwarf and the heretics acknowledged Siva as the Lord.

**Rudra** – Siva's early prototype, who may date back to the Indus Valley Civilization.

**Virabhadra** – Siva created Virabhadra to avenge himself on his wife Sati's father, Daksha, who had insulted Siva by not inviting him to a special sacrifice. Sati attended the ceremony against Siva's wishes and when she heard her father grossly abusing Siva she committed suicide by jumping into the sacrificial fire. This act gave rise to the term *sati* (*suttee*, a word which simply means a good or virtuous woman). Recorded in the *Vedas*, the self immolation of a woman on her husband's funeral pyre probably did not become accepted practice until the early centuries BC. Even then it was mainly restricted to those of the Kshatriya caste.

**Nandi** – Siva's vehicle, the bull, is one of the most widespread of sacred symbols of the ancient world and may represent a link with Rudra, who was sometimes represented as a bull in pre-Hindu India. Strength and virility are key attributes and pilgrims to Siva temples will often touch the Nandi's testicles on their way into the shrine.

**Ganesh** One of Hinduism's most popular gods, Ganesh is seen as the great clearer of obstacles. Shown at gateways and on door lintels with his elephant head and pot belly, his image is revered across India. Meetings, functions and special family gatherings will often start with prayers to Ganesh and any new venture, from the opening of a building to inaugurating a company, will not be deemed complete without a Ganesh puja.

**Shakti, The Mother Goddess** Shakti is a female divinity often worshipped in the form of Siva's wife Durga or Kali. As Durga she agreed to do battle with Mahish, an *asura* (demon) who threatened to dethrone the gods. Many sculptures and paintings illustrate the story in which, during the terrifying struggle which ensued, the demon changed into a buffalo, an elephant and a giant with 1,000 arms. Durga, clutching weapons in each of her 10 hands, eventually emerges victorious. As Kali ('black') the mother goddess takes on her most fearsome form and character. Fighting with the chief of the demons, she was forced to use every weapon in her armoury, but every drop of blood that she drew became 1,000 new giants just as strong as he. The only way she could win was by drinking the blood of all her enemies. Having succeeded she was so elated that her dance of triumph threatened the earth. Ignoring the pleas of the gods to stop, she even threw her husband Siva to the ground and trampled over him, until she realized to her shame what she had done. She is always shown with a sword in one hand, the severed head of the giant in another, two corpses for earrings and a necklace of human skulls. She is often shown standing with one foot on the body and the other on the leg of Siva.

The worship of female goddesses developed into the widely practised form of devotional worship called Tantrism. Goddesses such as Kali became the focus of worship which often involved practices that flew in the face of wider Hindu moral and legal codes. Animal and even human sacrifices and ritual sexual intercourse were part of Tantric belief and practice, the evidence for which may still be seen in the art and sculpture of some major temples. Tantric practice affected both Hinduism and Buddhism from the eighth century AD; its influence is shown vividly in the sculptures of Khajuraho and Konark and in the distinctive Hindu and Buddhist practices of the Kathmandu Valley in Nepal.

**Skanda** The God of War, Skanda (known as Murugan in Tamil Nadu and by other regional names) became known as the son of Siva and Parvati. One legend suggests that he was conceived by the Goddess Ganga from Siva's seed.

## Hindu deities

| Deity | Association | Relationship |
|---|---|---|
| **Brahma** | Creator | One of Trinity |
| **Sarasvati** | Education and culture, "the word" | Wife of Brahma |
| **Siva** | Creator/destroyer | One of Trinity |
| **Bhairava** | Fierce aspect of Siva | |
| **Parvati** (Uma) | Benevolent aspect of female divine power | Consort of Siva, mother of Ganesh |
| **Kali** | The energy that destroys evil | Consort of Siva |
| **Durga** | In fighting attitude | Consort of Siva |
| **Ganesh/ Ganapati** | God of good beginnings, clearer of obstacles | Son of Siva |
| **Skanda** (Karttikkeya, Murugan, Subrahmanya) | God of War/bringer of disease | Son of Siva and Ganga |
| **Vishnu** | Preserver | One of Trinity |
| **Prithvi/ Bhudevi** | Goddess of Earth | Wife of Vishnu |
| **Lakshmi** | Goddess of Wealth | Wife of Vishnu |
| **Agni** | God of Fire | |
| **Indra** | Rain, lightning and thunder | |
| **Ravana** | King of the demons | |

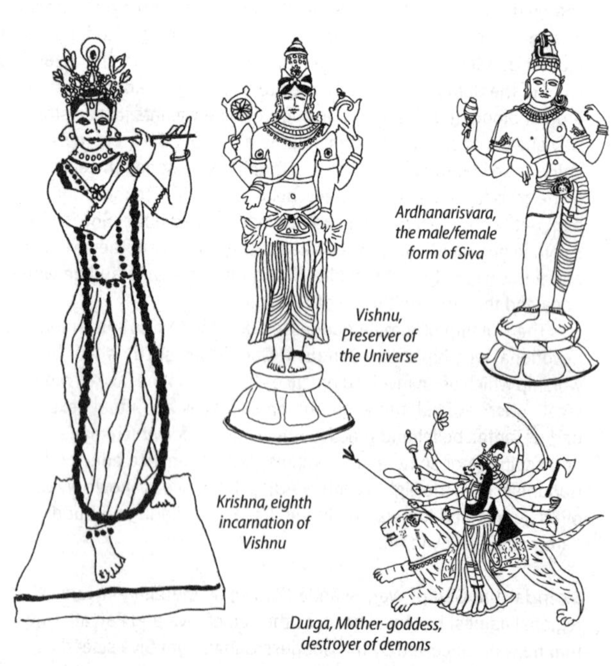

*Krishna, eighth incarnation of Vishnu*

*Vishnu, Preserver of the Universe*

*Ardhanarisvara, the male/female form of Siva*

*Durga, Mother-goddess, destroyer of demons*

| Attributes | Vehicle |
|---|---|
| 4 heads, 4 arms, upper left holds water pot and rosary or sacrificial spoon, sacred thread across left shoulder | Hamsa (goose/swan) |
| Two or more arms, vina, lotus, plam leaves, rosary | Hamsa |
| Linga; Rudra, matted hair, 3 eyes, drum, fire, deer, trident; Nataraja, Lord of the Dance | Bull - Nandi |
| Trident, sword, noose, naked, snakes, garland of skulls, dishevelled hair, carrying destructive weapons | Dog |
| 2 arms when shown with Siva, 4 when on her own, blue lily in right hand, left hand hangs down | Lion |
| Trident, noose, human skulls, sword, shield, black colour | Lion |
| 4 arms, conch, disc, bow, arrow, bell, sword, shield | Lion or tiger |
| Goad, noose, broken tusk, fruits | Rat/ mouse/ shrew |
| 6 heads, 12 arms, spear, arrow, sword, discus, noose cock, bow, shield, conch and plough | Peacock |
| 4 arms, high crown, discus and conch in upper arms, club and sword (or lotus) in lower | Garuda - mythical eagle |
| Right hand in abhaya gesture, left holds pomegranate, left leg on treasure pot | |
| Seated/standing on red lotus, 4 hands, lotuses, vessel, fruit | Lotus |
| Sacred thread, axe, wood, bellows, torch, sacrificial spoon | 2-headed ram |
| Bow, thunderbolt, lances | |
| 10 heads, 20 arms, bow and arrow | |

*Siva as Nataraj*

*Ganesh, bringer of prosperity*

*Parvati, wife of Siva*

*Kali, the "black" Mother-goddess*

 **Gods of the warrior caste** Modern Hinduism has brought into its pantheon over many generations gods who were worshipped by the earlier pre-Hindu Aryan civilizations. The most important is **Indra**, often shown as the god of rain, thunder and lightning. To the early Aryans, Indra destroyed demons in battle, the most important being his victory over Vritra, 'the Obstructor'. By this victory Indra released waters from the clouds, allowing the earth to become fertile. To the early Vedic writers the clouds of the southwest monsoon were seen as hostile, determined to keep their precious treasure of water to themselves and only releasing it when forced to by a greater power. Indra, carrying a bow in one hand, a thunderbolt in another and lances in the others and riding on his vehicle Airavata, the elephant, is thus the Lord of Heaven. His wife is the relatively insignificant **Indrani**.

**Mitra** and **Varuna** have the power both of gods and demons. Their role is to sustain order, Mitra taking responsibility for friendship and Varuna for oaths and as they have to keep watch for 24 hours a day Mitra has become the god of the day or the sun, Varuna the god of the moon.

**Agni**, the god of fire, is a god whose origins lie with the priestly caste rather than with the Kshatriyas, or warriors. He was seen in the Vedas as being born from the rubbing together of two pieces of dead wood and as Masson-Oursel writes "the poets marvel at the sight of a being so alive leaping from dry dead wood. His very growth is miraculous". Riding on a ram, wearing a sacred thread, he is often shown with flames leaping from his mouth and he carries an axe, wood, bellows or a fan, a torch and a sacrificial spoon, for he is the god of ritual fire.

The juice of the soma plant, the nectar of the gods guaranteeing eternal life, **Soma** is also a deity taking many forms. Born from the churning of the ocean of milk in later stories Soma was identified with the moon. The golden haired and golden skinned god **Savitri** is an intermediary with the great power to forgive sin and as king of heaven he gives the gods their immortality. **Surya**, the god of the sun, fittingly of overpowering splendour is often described as being dark red, sitting on a red lotus or riding a chariot pulled by the seven horses of the dawn (representing the days of the week). **Usha**, sometimes referred to as Surya's wife, is the goddess of the dawn, daughter of Heaven and sister of the night. She rides in a chariot drawn by cows or horses.

**Devas and Asuras** In Hindu popular mythology the world is also populated by innumerable gods and demons, with a somewhat uncertain dividing line between them. Both have great power and moral character and there are frequent conflicts and battles between them.

The **Rakshasas** form another category of semi-divine beings devoted to performing magic. Although they are not themselves evil, they are destined to cause havoc and evil in the real world.

The multiple-hooded cobra head often seen in sculptures represents the fabulous snake gods the **Nagas**, though they may often be shown in other forms, even human. In South India it is particularly common to find statues of divine Nagas being worshipped. They are usually placed on uncultivated ground under trees in the hope and belief, as Masson-Oursel puts it, that "if the snakes have their own domain left to them they are more likely to spare human beings". The Nagas and their wives, the **Naginis**, are often the agents of death in mythical stories.

## Hindu society

**Dharma** Dharma is seen as the most important of the objectives of individual and social life. But what were the obligations imposed by dharma? Hindu law givers, such as those who compiled the code of Manu (AD 100-300), laid down rules of family conduct and social obligations related to the institutions of caste and jati which were beginning to take shape at the same time.

## Auspicious signs

Some of Hinduism's sacred symbols are thought to have originated in the Aryan religion of the Vedic period.

**Om** The Primordial sound of the universe, 'Om' (or more correctly the three-in-one 'Aum') is the Supreme syllable. It is the opening and sometimes closing, chant for Hindu prayers. Some attribute the three constituents to the Hindu triad of Brahma, Vishnu and Siva. It is believed to be the cosmic sound of Creation which encompasses all states from wakefulness to deep sleep and though it is the essence of all sound, it is outside our hearing.

**Svastika** Representing the Sun and it's energy, the svastika usually appears on doors or walls of temples, in red, the colour associated with good fortune and luck. The term, derived from the Sanskrit 'svasti', is repeated in Hindu chants. The arms of the symbol point in the cardinal directions which may reflect the ancient practice of lighting fire sticks in the four directions. When the svastika appears to rotate clockwise it symbolizes the positive creative energy of the sun; the anti-clockwise svastika, symbolizing the autumn/winter sun, is considered unlucky.

**Six-pointed star** The intersecting triangles in the 'Star of David' symbol represents Spirit and Matter held in balance. A central dot signifies a particle of Divinity. The star is incorporated as a decorative element in some Muslim buildings such as Humayun's Tomb in Delhi.

**Lotus** The 'padma' or 'kamal' flower with it's many petals appears not only in art and architecture but also in association with gods and godesses. Some deities are seen holding one, others are portrayed seated or standing on the flower, or as with Padmanabha it appears from Vishnu's navel. The lotus represents purity, peace and beauty, a symbol also shared by Buddhists and Jains and as in nature stands away and above the impure, murky water from which it emerges. In architecture, the lotus motif occurs frequently.

Om

Svastika

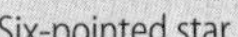

Six-pointed star

Lotus

**Caste** Although the word caste was given by the Portuguese in the 15th century AD, the main feature of the system emerged at the end of the Vedic period. Two terms – varna and jati – are used in India itself and have come to be used interchangeably and confusingly with the word caste.

**Varna**, which literally means colour, had a fourfold division. By 600 BC this had become a standard means of classifying the population. The fair-skinned Aryans distinguished themselves from the darker skinned earlier inhabitants. The priestly varna, the Brahmins, were seen as coming from the mouth of Brahma; the Kshatriyas (or Rajputs as they are commonly called in northwest India) were warriors, coming from Brahma's arms; the Vaishyas, a trading community, came from Brahma's thighs and the Sudras, classified as agriculturalists, from his feet. Relegated beyond the pale of civilized Hindu society were the untouchables or outcastes, who were left with the jobs which were regarded as impure, usually associated with dealing with the dead (human or animal) or with excrement.

## From liberal reform to a new fundamentalism

The first major reform movement was launched by the Bengali Brahmin, Ram Mohan Roy (1772-1833). He founded the **Brahmo Samaj**, the Society of God, in 1828, "to teach and to practise the worship of the one God". Services were modelled closely on those of the Unitarian Church, but he never broke with orthodox Hinduism. The Brahmo Samaj became very influential, particularly in Bengal, even though it divided and its numbers remained tiny.

In North India reform was carried out under the leadership of what one writer has called "the Luther of modern Hinduism", Dayananda Saraswati (1824-1883). Rejecting idolatry and many of the social evils associated with mid-19th century Hinduism, Dayananda Saraswati established the **Arya Samaj** (the Aryan Society). In the early 19th century the Arya Samaj launched a major attack on the caste system, through recruiting low caste Hindus and investing them with high caste status. At the same time they encouraged a movement for the reconversion of Christians and Muslims (the suddhi movement). By 1931 the Arya Samaj claimed about one million members. With a strongly Hindu nationalist political line, its programme underlay the rise in post-Independence India of the Jana Sangh Party and the present day BJP.



Many Brahmins and Rajputs are conscious of their varna status, but the great majority of Indians do not put themselves into one of the four varna categories, but into a **jati** group. There are thousands of different jatis across the country. None of the groups regard themselves as equal in status to any other, but all are part of local or regional hierarchies. These are not organized in any institutional sense and traditionally there was no formal record of caste status. While individuals found it impossible to change caste or to move up the social scale, groups would sometimes try to gain recognition as higher caste by adopting practices of the Brahmins such as becoming vegetarians. Many used to be identified with particular activities and occupations used to be hereditary. Caste membership is decided simply by birth. Although you can be evicted from your caste by your fellow members, usually for disobedience to caste rules such as over marriage, you cannot join another caste and technically you become an outcaste.

Right up until Independence in 1947 such punishment was a drastic penalty for disobeying one's dharmic duty. In many areas all avenues into normal life could be blocked, families would disregard outcaste members and it could even be impossible for the outcaste to continue to work within the locality.

Gandhi spearheaded his campaign for independence from British colonial rule with a powerful campaign to abolish the disabilities imposed by the caste system. Coining the term *Harijan* (meaning 'person of God'), which he gave to all former outcastes, Gandhi demanded that discrimination on the grounds of caste be outlawed. Lists – or 'schedules' – of backward castes were drawn up during the early part of this century in order to provide positive help to such groups. The term itself has now been widely rejected by many former outcastes as paternalistic and as implying an adherence to Hindu beliefs (Hari being a Hindu deity) which some explicitly reject and today the use of the secular term **'dalits'** – the 'oppressed' has been adopted in its place. There are several websites devoted to dalit issues, including www.dalits.org.

**Marriage**, which is still generally arranged by members of all religious communities, continues to be dictated almost entirely by caste and clan rules. Even in

### The sacred thread

The highest three varnas were classified as "twice born" and could wear the sacred thread symbolizing their status. The age at which the initiation ceremony (upanayana) for the upper caste child was carried out, varied according to class – 8 for a Brahmin, 11 for a Kshatriya and 12 for a Vaishya.

The boy, dressed like an ascetic and holding a staff in his hand, would have the sacred thread (yajnopavita) placed over his right shoulder and under his left arm. A cord of three threads, each of nine twisted strands, it was made of cotton for Brahmans, hemp for Kshatriyas or wool for Vaishyas. It was – and is – regarded as a great sin to remove it.

The Brahmin who officiated would whisper a verse from the Rig Veda in the boy's ear, the Gayatri mantra. Addressed to the old solar god Savitr, the holiest of holy passages, the Gayatri can only be spoken by the three higher classes. AL Basham translated it as: "Let us think on the lovely splendour of the god Savitr, that he may inspire our minds".

cities, where traditional means of arranging marriages have often broken down and where many people resort to advertising for marriage partners in the columns of the Sunday newspapers, caste is frequently stated as a requirement. Marriage is generally seen as an alliance between two families. Great efforts are made to match caste, social status and economic position, although the rules which govern eligibility vary from region to region. In some groups marriage between even first cousins is common, while among others marriage between any branch of the same clan is strictly prohibited.

## Hindu reform movements

In the 19th-century English education and European literature and modern scientific thought, alongside the religious ideas of Christian missionaries, all became powerful influences on the newly emerging western educated Hindu opinion. That opinion was challenged to re-examine inherited Hindu beliefs and practice.

Some reform movements have had regional importance. Two of these originated, like the **Brahmo Samaj**, in Bengal, see box. The **Ramakrishna Mission** was named after a temple priest in the Kali temple in Calcutta, Ramakrishna (1834-1886), who was a great mystic, preaching the basic doctrine that 'all religions are true'. He believed that the best religion for any individual was that into which he or she was born. One of his followers, **Vivekananda**, became the founder of the Ramakrishna Mission, which has been an important vehicle of social and religious reform, notably in Bengal, see page 595.

**Aurobindo Ghose** (1872-1950) links the great reformers from the 19th century with the post-Independence period. Educated in English – and for 14 years in England itself – he developed the idea of India as 'the Mother', a concept linked with the pre-Hindu idea of Shakti, or the Mother Goddess. For him 'nationalism was religion'. After imprisonment in 1908 he retired to Pondicherry, where his ashram became a focus of an Indian and international movement, see page 826.

**The Hindu calendar** While for its secular life India follows the Gregorian calendar, for Hindus, much of religious and personal life follows the Hindu calendar (see also Festivals). This is based on the lunar cycle of 29 days, but the clever bit comes in the way it is synchronized with the 365 day Gregorian solar calendar of the west by the addition of an 'extra month' (*adhik maas*), every 2½-3 years.

Hindus follow two distinct eras. The *Vikrama Samvat* which began in 57 BC (and is followed in Goa), and the *Salivahan Saka* which dates from 78 AD and has been the official Indian calendar since 1957. The *Saka* new year starts on 22 March and has the same length as the Gregorian calendar. In most of South India (except Tamil Nadu) the New Year is celebrated in the first month, *Chaitra* (corresponding to March-April). In North India (and Tamil Nadu) it is celebrated in the second month of *Vaisakh*.

The year itself is divided into two, the first six solar months being when the sun 'moves' north, known as the *Makar Sankranti* (which is marked by special festivals), and the second half when it moves south, the *Karka Sankranti*. The first begins in January and the second in June. The 29 day lunar month with its 'dark' (*Krishna*) and 'bright' (*Shukla*) halves based on the new (*Amavasya*) and full moons (*Purnima*), are named after the 12 constellations, and total a 354 day year. The day itself is divided into eight *praharas* of three hours each and the year into six seasons: *Vasant* (spring), *Grishha* (summer), *Varsha* (rains), *Sharat* (early autumn), *Hemanta* (late autumn), *Shishir* (winter).



**Hindu and corresponding Gregorian calendar months:**

| | | | |
|---|---|---|---|
| *Chaitra* | March-April | *Ashwin* | September-October |
| *Vaishakh* | April-May | *Kartik* | October-November |
| *Jyeshtha* | May-June | *Margashirsh* | November-December |
| *Aashadh* | June-July | *Poush* | December-January |
| *Shravan* | July-August | *Magh* | January-February |
| *Bhadra* | August-September | *Phalgun* | February-March |

## Islam

Even after partition in 1947 over 40 million Muslims remained in India and today there are around 120 million. Islamic contact with India was first made around AD 636 and then by the navies of the Arab Mohammad al Qasim in AD 710-712. These conquerors of Sindh made very few converts, although they did have to develop a legal recognition for the status of non-Muslims in a Muslim-ruled state. From the creation of the Delhi Sultanate in 1206, by Turkish rather than Arab power, Islam became a permanent living religion in India.

The victory of the Turkish ruler of Ghazni over the Rajputs in AD 1192 established a 500-year period of Muslim power in India. By AD 1200 the Turkish sultans had annexed Bihar in the east, in the process wiping out the last traces of Buddhism with the massacre of a Buddhist monastic order, sacked Varanasi and captured Gwalior. Within 30 years Bengal had been added to the Turkish empire and by AD 1311 a new Turkish dynasty, the Khaljis, had extended the power of the Delhi Sultanate to the doors of Madurai.

The early Muslim rulers looked to the Turkish ruling class and to the Arab caliphs for their legitimacy and to the Turkish élite for their cultural authority. From the middle of the 13th century, when the Mongols crushed the Arab caliphate, the Delhi sultans were left on their own to exercise Islamic authority in India. From then onwards the main external influences were from Persia. Small numbers of migrants, mainly the skilled and the educated, continued to flow into the Indian courts. Periodically their numbers were augmented by refugees from Mongol repression in the regions to India's northwest as the Delhi Sultanate provided a refuge for craftsmen and artists from the territories the Mongols had conquered from Lahore westwards.

**Muslim populations** Muslims only became a majority of the South Asian population in the plains of the Indus and west Punjab and in parts of Bengal. Elsewhere they formed important minorities, notably in the towns of the central

### Islamic patronage

The spread of Islam across India was achieved less by forcible conversion than by the patronage offered by the new rulers to Muslim saints and teachers. These were particularly influential in achieving mass conversions among the lower castes of Hindus.

Islam underwent important modifications as it became entrenched in India. From the outset the Muslim invaders had to come to terms with the Hindu majority population. If they had treated them as idolators they would have been forced, under Qur'anic law, to give them the choice of conversion or death. The political impossibility of governing as a tiny minority on those terms encouraged them to give Indian subjects the status of 'protected peoples'.

heartland such as Lucknow. The concentration at the east and west ends of the Ganga valley reflected the policies pursued by successive Muslim rulers of colonizing forested and previously uncultivated land. In the central plains there was already a densely populated, Hindu region, where little attempt was made to achieve converts.

**The Mughals** wanted to expand their territory and their economic base. To pursue this they made enormous grants of land to those who had served the empire and particularly in Bengal, new land was brought into cultivation. At the same time, shrines were established to Sufi saints who attracted peasant farmers. The mosques built in East Bengal were the centres of devotional worship where saints were venerated. By the 18th century many Muslims had joined the **Sunni** sect of Islam. The characteristics of Islamic practice in both these regions continues to reflect this background.

In some areas Muslim society shared many of the characteristic features of the Hindu society from which the majority of them came. Many of the Muslim migrants from Iran or Turkey, the élite **Ashraf** communities, continued to identify with the Islamic élites from which they traced their descent. They held high military and civil posts in imperial service. In sharp contrast, many of the non-Ashraf Muslim communities in the towns and cities were organized in social groups very much like the *jatis* of their neighbouring Hindu communities. While the élites followed Islamic practices close to those based on the Qur'an as interpreted by scholars, the poorer, less literate communities followed devotional and pietistic forms of Islam.

**Muslim beliefs** The beliefs of Islam (which means 'submission to God') could apparently scarcely be more different from those of Hinduism. Islam, often described as having "five pillars" of faith (see box) has a fundamental creed; 'There is no God but God; and Mohammad is the Prophet of God' (*La Illaha illa 'llah Mohammad Rasulu 'llah*). One book, the Qur'an, is the supreme authority on Islamic teaching and faith. Islam preaches the belief in bodily resurrection after death and in the reality of heaven and hell.

The idea of heaven as paradise is pre-Islamic. Alexander the Great is believed to have brought the word into Greek from Persia, where he used it to describe the walled Persian gardens that were found even three centuries before the birth of Christ. For Muslims, Paradise is believed to be filled with sensuous delights and pleasures, while hell is a place of eternal terror and torture, which is the certain fate of all who deny the unity of God.

Islam has no priesthood. The authority of Imams derives from social custom and from their authority to interpret the scriptures, rather than from a defined status within the Islamic community. Islam also prohibits any distinction on the basis of race or colour and most Muslims believe it is wrong to represent the human figure. It is

## The five pillars of Islam

In addition to the belief that there is one God and that Mohammed is his prophet, there are four obligatory requirements imposed on Muslims. Daily prayers are prescribed at daybreak, noon, afternoon, sunset and nightfall. Muslims must give alms to the poor. They must observe a strict fast during the month of Ramadan. They must not eat or drink between sunrise and sunset. Lastly, they should attempt the pilgrimage to the Ka'aba in Mecca, known as the Hajj. Those who have done so are entitled to the prefix Hajji before their name.

Islamic rules differ from Hindu practice in several other aspects of daily life. Muslims are strictly forbidden to drink alcohol (though some suggest that this prohibition is restricted to the use of fermented grape juice, that is wine, it is commonly accepted to apply to all alcohol). Eating pork, or any meat from an animal not killed by draining its blood while alive, is also prohibited. Meat prepared in the appropriate way is called Halal. Finally, usury (charging interest on loans) and games of chance are forbidden.



often thought, inaccurately, that this ban stems from the Qur'an itself. In fact it probably has its origins in the belief of Mohammad that images were likely to be turned into idols.

**Muslim sects** During the first century after Mohammad's death Islam split in to two sects which were divided on political and religious grounds, the Shi'is and Sunni's. The religious basis for the division lay in the interpretation of verses in the Qur'an and of traditional sayings of Mohammad, the Hadis. Both sects venerate the Qur'an but have different *Hadis*. They also have different views as to Mohammad's successor.

The **Sunnis** - always the majority in South Asia - believe that Mohammad did not appoint a successor and that Abu Bak'r, Omar and Othman were the first three caliphs (or vice-regents) after Mohammad's death. Ali, whom the Sunni's count as the fourth caliph, is regarded as the first legitimate caliph by the Shi'is, who consider Abu Bak'r and Omar to be usurpers. While the Sunni's believe in the principle of election of caliphs, Shi'is believe that although Mohammad is the last prophet there is a continuing need for intermediaries between God and man. Such intermediaries are termed Imams and they base both their law and religious practice on the teaching of the Imams.

Akbar, the most eclectic of Mughal emperors, went as far as banning activities like cow slaughter which were offensive to Hindus and celebrated Hindu festivals in court. In contrast, the later Mughal Emperor, Aurangzeb, pursued a far more hostile approach to Hindus and Hinduism, trying to point up the distinctiveness of Islam and denying the validity of Hindu religious beliefs. That attitude generally became stronger in the 20th century, related to the growing sense of the Muslim's minority position within South Asia and the fear of being subjected to Hindu rule.

**The Islamic calendar** The calendar begins on 16 July 622 AD, the date of the Prophet's migration from Mecca to Medina, the Hijra, hence AH (Anno Hejirae). *Murray's Handbook for travellers in India* gave a wonderfully precise method of calculating the current date in the Christian year from the AH date: "To correlate the Hijra year with the Christian year, express the former in years and decimals of a year, multiply by .970225, add 621.54 and the total will correspond exactly with the Christian year".

The Muslim year is divided into 12 lunar months, totalling 354 or 355 days, hence Islamic festivals usually move 11 days earlier each year according to the solar

(Gregorian) calendar. The first month of the year is *Moharram,* followed by *Safar, Rabi-ul-Awwal, Rabi-ul-Sani, Jumada-ul-Awwal, Jumada-ul-Sani, Rajab, Shaban, Ramadan, Shawwal, Ziquad* and *Zilhaj.* 

## Buddhism

India was the home of Buddhism, which had its roots in the early Hinduism, or Brahmanism, of its time. Today it is practised only on the margins of the subcontinent, from Ladakh, Nepal and Bhutan in the north to Sri Lanka in the south, where it is the religion of the majority Sinhalese community. Most are very recent converts, the last adherents of the early schools of Buddhism having been killed or converted by the Muslim invaders of the 13th century. However, India's Buddhist significance is now mainly as the home for the extraordinarily beautiful artistic and architectural remnants of what was for several centuries the region's dominant religion.

India has sites of great significance for Buddhists around the world. Some say that the Buddha himself spoke of the four places his followers should visit. **Lumbini**, the Buddha's birthplace, is in the Nepali foothills, near the present border with India. **Bodh Gaya**, where he attained what Buddhists term his 'supreme enlightenment', is about 80 km south of the modern Indian city of Patna; the deer park at **Sarnath**, where he preached his first sermon and set in motion the Wheel of the Law, is just outside Varanasi; and **Kushinagara**, where he died at the age of 80, is 50 km east of Gorakhpur. There were four other sacred places of pilgrimage – **Rajgir**, where he tamed a wild elephant; **Vaishali**, where a monkey offered him honey; **Sravasti**, associated with his great miracle; and **Sankasya**, where he descended from heaven. The eight significant events associated with the holy places are repeatedly represented in Buddhist art.

In addition there are remarkable monuments, sculptures and works of art, from Gandhara in modern Pakistan to Sanchi and Ajanta in central India, where it is still possible to see the vivid evidence of the flowering of Buddhist culture in South Asia. In Sri Lanka, Bhutan and Nepal the traditions remain alive.

**The Buddha's Life** Siddharta Gautama, who came to be given the title of the Buddha – the Enlightened One – was born a prince into the warrior caste in about 563 BC. He was married at the age of 16 and his wife had a son. When he reached the age of 29 he left home and wandered as a beggar and ascetic. After about six years he spent some time in Bodh Gaya. Sitting under the Bo tree, meditating, he was tempted by the demon Mara, with all the desires of the world. Resisting these temptations, he received enlightenment. These scenes are common motifs of Buddhist art.

The next landmark was the preaching of his first sermon on 'The Foundation of Righteousness' in the deer park near Benaras. By the time he died the Buddha had established a small band of monks and nuns known as the *Sangha* and had followers across North India. His body was cremated and the ashes, regarded as precious relics, were divided among the peoples to whom he had preached. Some have been discovered as far west as Peshawar, in Pakistan and at Piprawa, close to his birthplace.

**After the Buddha's death** From the Buddha's death, or *parinirvana*, to the destruction of Nalanda (the last Buddhist stronghold in India) in AD 1197, Buddhism in India went through three phases. These are often referred to as Hinayana, Mahayana and Vajrayana, though they were not mutually exclusive, being followed simultaneously in different regions.

**Hinayana** The Hinayana or Lesser Way insists on a monastic way of life as the only path to the personal goal of *nirvana*, see box page 1340, achieved through an austere life. Divided into many schools, the only surviving Hinayana tradition is the **Theravada**

## The Buddha's Four Noble Truths

The Buddha preached Four Noble Truths: that life is painful; that suffering is caused by ignorance and desire; that beyond the suffering of life there is a state which cannot be described but which he termed nirvana; and that nirvana can be reached by following an eightfold path.

The concept of nirvana is often understood in the west in an entirely negative sense – that of 'non-being'. The word has the rough meaning of 'blow out' or 'extinguish', meaning to blow out the fires of greed, lust and desire. In a more positive sense it has been described by one Buddhist scholar as "the state of absolute illumination, supreme bliss, infinite love and compassion, unshakeable serenity and unrestricted spiritual freedom". The essential elements of the eightfold path are the perfection of wisdom, morality and meditation.



**Buddhism**, which was taken to Sri Lanka by the Emperor Asoka's son Mahinda, where it became the state religion, and spread to southeast Asia as practised in Thailand, Myanmar, Cambodia and Laos today. Suffering, sorrow and dissatisfaction are the nature of ordinary life and can only be eliminated by giving up desire. In turn, desire is a result of the misplaced belief in the reality of individual existence. Theravada Buddhism taught that there is no soul and ultimately no God. *Nirvana* is a state of rest beyond the universe, once found never lost.

**Mahayana** In contrast to the Hinayana schools, the followers of the Mahayana school (the Great Way) believed in the possibility of salvation for all. They practised a far more devotional form of meditation and new figures came to play a prominent part in their beliefs and their worship – the **Bodhisattvas**, saints who were predestined to reach the state of enlightenment through thousands of rebirths. They aspired to Buddhahood, however, not for their own sake but for the sake of all living things. The Buddha is believed to have passed through numerous existences in preparation for his final mission. Mahayana Buddhism became dominant over most of South Asia and its influence is evidenced in Buddhist art from Gandhara in north Pakistan to Ajanta in Central India and Sigiriya in Sri Lanka.

**Vajrayana** A new branch of Buddhism, Vajrayana, or the Vehicle of the Thunderbold, appeared which began to lay stress on secret magical rituals and cults of female divinities. This new 'Diamond Way' adopted the practice of magic, yoga and meditation. It became associated with secret ceremonies, chanting of mystical 'mantras' and taking part in orgiastic rituals in the cause of spiritual gain in order to help others. The ideal of Vajrayana Buddhists is to be 'so fully in harmony with the cosmos as to be able to manipulate the cosmic forces within and outside himself'. It had developed in the north of India by the seventh century AD, matching the parallel growth of Hindu Tantrism. The magical

The Buddha in Bhumisparsha-mudra calling the earth to witness

power associated with Vajrayana requires instruction from a teacher or Lama, hence the Tibetan form is sometimes referred to as 'Lamaistic'. See also page 546.



**Buddhist beliefs** Buddhism is based on the Buddha's own preaching. However, when he died none of those teachings had been written down. He developed his beliefs in reaction to the Brahmanism of his time, rejecting several of the doctrines of Vedic religion which were widely held in his lifetime: the Vedic gods, scriptures and priesthood and all social distinctions based on caste. However, he did accept the belief in the cyclical nature of life and that the nature of an individual's existence is determined by a natural process of reward and punishment for deeds in previous lives - the Hindu doctrine of karma, see page 1323. In the Buddha's view, though, there is no eternal soul. He denied the identification of the Self with the everchanging Mind-Body (here, some see parallels in the Advaita Vedanta philosophy of Self-*Brahman* in Hinduism). In Buddhism, *Anatta* (no-Self), overcame the egoistical Self, given to attachment and selfishness.

Following the Buddha's death a succession of councils was called to try and reach agreement on doctrine. The first three were held within 140 years of the Buddha's death, the fourth being held at Pataliputra (modern Patna) during the reign of the Emperor Asoka (272-232 BC), who had recently been converted to Buddhism. Under his reign Buddhism spread throughout South Asia and opened the routes through Northwest India for Buddhism to travel into China, where it had become a force by the first century AD.

**Buddhism's decline** The decline of Buddhism in India probably stemmed as much from the growing similarity in the practice of Hinduism and Buddhism as from direct attacks. Mahayana Buddhism, with its reverence for Bodhisattvas and its devotional character, was more and more difficult to distinguish from the revivalist Hinduism characteristic of several parts of North India from the seventh to the 12th centuries AD. The Muslim conquest dealt the final death blow, being accompanied by the large scale slaughter of monks and the destruction of monasteries. Without their institutional support Buddhism faded away.



## Jainism

Like Buddhism, Jainism started as a reform movement of the Brahmanic religious beliefs of the sixth century BC. Its founder was a widely revered saint and ascetic, Vardhamma, who became known as **Mahavir** – 'great hero'. Mahavir was born in the same border region of India and Nepal as the Buddha, just 50 km north of modern Patna, probably in 599 BC. Thus he was about 35 years older than the Buddha. His family, also royal, were followers of an ascetic saint, Parsvanatha, who according to Jain tradition had lived 200 years previously.

Mahavir's life story is embellished with legends, but there is no doubt that he left his royal home for a life of the strict ascetic. He is believed to have received enlightenment after 12 years of rigorous hardship, penance and meditation. Afterwards he travelled and preached for 30 years, stopping only in the rainy season. He died aged 72 in 527 BC. His death was commemorated by a special lamp festival in the region of Bihar, which Jains claim is the basis of the now-common Hindu festival of lights, Diwali.

Unlike Buddhism, Jainism never spread beyond India, but it has survived continuously into modern India, claiming four million adherents. In part this may be because Jain beliefs have much in common with puritanical forms of Hinduism and are greatly respected and admired. Some Jain ideas, such as vegetarianism and reverence for all life, are widely recognized by Hindus as highly commendable, even

## The Jain spiritual journey

The two Jain sects differ chiefly on the nature of proper ascetic practices. The Svetambara monks wear white robes and carry a staff, some wooden pots and a woollen mop for sweeping the path in front of them, wool being the softest material available and the least likely to hurt any living thing swept away. The highest level of Digambara monks will go completely naked, although the lower levels will wear a covering over their genitalia. They carry a waterpot made of a gourd and peacock feathers to sweep the ground before they sit.

Jains believe that the spiritual journey of the soul is divided into 14 stages, moving from bondage and ignorance to the final destruction of all karma and the complete fulfilment of the soul. The object throughout is to prevent the addition of new karma to the soul, which comes mainly through passion and attachment to the world. Bearing the pains of the world cheerfully contributes to the destruction of karma.



by those who do not share other Jain beliefs. The value Jains place on non-violence has contributed to their importance in business and commerce, as they regard nearly all occupations except banking and commerce as violent. The 18 m high free-standing statue of Gommateshvara at Sravana Belgola near Mysore (built about AD 983) is just one outstanding example of the contribution of Jain art to India's heritage.

**Jain beliefs** Jains (from the word Jina, literally meaning 'descendants of conquerors') believe that there are two fundamental principles, the living (*jiva*) and the non-living (*ajiva*). The essence of Jain belief is that all life is sacred and that every living entity, even the smallest insect, has within it an indestructible and immortal soul. Jains developed the view of ahimsa - often translated as 'non-violence', but better perhaps as 'non-harming'. Ahimsa was the basis for the entire scheme of Jain values and ethics and alternative codes of practice were defined for householders and for ascetics.

**The five vows** may be taken both by monks and by lay people: not to harm any living beings (Jains must practise strict vegetarianism-and even some vegetables, such as potatoes and onions, are believed to have microscopic souls); to speak the truth; not to steal; to give up sexual relations and practice complete chastity; to give up all possessions-for the *Digambara* sect that includes clothes.

Celibacy is necessary to combat physical desire. Jains also regard the manner of dying as extremely important. Although suicide is deeply opposed, vows of fasting to death voluntarily may be regarded as earning merit in the proper context. Mahavir himself is believed to have died of self-starvation. The essence of all the rules is to avoid intentional injury, which is the worst of all sins. Like Hindus, the Jains believe in *karma*.

Jains have two main **sects**, whose origins can be traced back to the fourth century BC. The more numerous **Svetambaras** – the 'white clad' – concentrated more in eastern and western India, separated from the **Digambaras** – or 'sky-clad'– who often go naked. The Digambaras may well have been forced to move south by drought and famine in the northern region of the Deccan and they are now concentrated in the south of India.

Unlike Buddhists, Jains accept the idea of God, but not as a creator of the universe. They see him in the lives of the 24 **Tirthankaras** (prophets, or literally 'makers of fords' - a reference to their role in building crossing points for the spiritual journey over the river of life), or leaders of Jainism, whose lives are recounted in the Kalpsutra - the third century BC book of ritual for the Svetambaras. Mahavir is regarded as the last of these great spiritual leaders. Much Jain art details stories from these accounts and the Tirthankaras play a similar role for Jains as the Bodhisattvas do for Mahayana Buddhists. The first and most revered of the Tirthankaras, Adinatha, also known as Rishabnath, is widely represented in Jain temples.

## Sikhism

**Guru Nanak**, the founder of the religion was born just west of Lahore and grew up in what is now the Pakistani town of Sultanpur. His followers, the Sikhs, (derived from the Sanskrit word for 'disciples') form perhaps one of India's most recognizable groups. Beards and turbans give them a very distinctive presence and although they represent less than 2% of the population they are both politically and economically significant.

**Sikh beliefs** The first Guru, accepted the ideas of *samsara* – the cycle of rebirths – and *karma*, see page 1323, from Hinduism. However, Sikhism is unequivocal in its belief in the oneness of God, rejecting idolatry and any worship of objects or images. Guru Nanak believed that God is One, formless, eternal and beyond description.

Guru Nanak also fiercely opposed discrimination on the grounds of caste. He saw God as present everywhere, visible to anyone who cared to look and as essentially full of grace and compassion. Some of Guru Nanak's teachings are close to the ideas of the Benaras mystic **Kabir**, who, in common with the Muslim mystic sufis, believed in mystical union with God. Kabir's belief in the nature of God was matched by his view that man was deliberately blind and unwilling to recognize God's nature. He transformed the Hindu concept of *maya* into the belief that the values commonly held by the world were an illusion.

Guru Nanak preached that salvation depended on accepting the nature of God. If man recognized the true harmony of the divine order (*hookam*) and brought himself into line with that harmony he would be saved. Rejecting the prevailing Hindu belief that such harmony could be achieved by ascetic practices, he emphasized three actions; meditating on and repeating God's name (*naam*), 'giving', or charity (*daan*) and bathing (*isnaan*).

Many of the features now associated with Sikhism can be attributed to **Guru Gobind Singh**, who on 15 April 1699, started the new brotherhood called the *Khalsa* (meaning 'the pure', from the Persian word *khales*), an inner core of the faithful, accepted by baptism (*amrit*). The 'five ks' date from this period: *kesh* (uncut hair), the most important, followed by *kangha* (comb, usually of wood), *kirpan* (dagger or short sword), *kara* (steel bangle) and *kachh* (similar to 'boxer' shorts). The dagger and the shorts reflect military influence.

In addition to the compulsory 'five ks', the new code prohibited smoking, eating *halal* meat and sexual intercourse with Muslim women. These date from the 18th century, when the Sikhs were often in conflict with the Muslims. Other strict prohibitions include: idolatry, caste discrimination, hypocrisy and pilgrimage to Hindu sacred places. The Khalsa also explicitly forbade the seclusion of women, one of the common practices of Islam. It was only under the warrior king Ranjit Singh (1799-1838) that the idea of the Guru's presence in meetings of the Sikh community (the *Panth*) gave way to the now universally held belief in the total authority of the **Guru Granth**, the recorded words of the Guru in the scripture.

**Sikh worship** The meditative worship Guru Nanak commended is a part of the life of every devout Sikh today, who starts each day with private meditation and a recitation of the verses of Guru Nanak himself, the *Japji*. However, from the time of the third Guru, Sikhs have also worshipped as congregations in Gurudwaras ('gateways to the

**Sikhism's Gurus**

| Guru | Teachings and practice | Developments and events | External powers |
|---|---|---|---|
| 1 *Nanak* 1469-1539 | The life stories (**janam-sakhis**) of Guru Nanak, written between 50 and 80 years after his death, recorded wide travels, including Bengal and Mecca, studying different faiths. | Devotional and mystic tradition established by Guru Nanak, similar to that of Kabir. | Delhi sultanates |
| 2 *Angad* 1504-1538 | Special ceremonies and festivals began to augment individual devotions. | | |
| 3 *Amar Das* 1509-1574 | Introduction of worship in Gurudwaras. | | Portuguese make contact with India. |
| 4 *Ram Das* 1534-1581 | Built first lake temple in Amritsar; the first hereditary guru. Widening of congregational worship. | Tolerance for religious experiment. | Akbar |
| 5 *Arjan Dev* 1563-1606 | In 1603-4 collected hymns and sayings of the first 3 Gurus, of Sikh mystics and of his father's and his own in a single volume the Adi Granth (the Guru Granth Sahib). Started the Golden Temple at Amritsar. | The Adi Granth comprises nearly 6,000 hymns, 974 attributed to Guru Nanak. Written in Gurumukhi script, developed from Punjabi by the second Guru. | Akbar and Jahangir. Arjan Dev executed by Jahangir at Lahore |
| 6 *Har Gobind* 1595-1645 | Jat caste becomes dominant influence. Sikhs began to take up arms, largely to protect themselves against Mughal attacks. Har Gobind decided to withdraw to the Siwalik Hills. | The next 4 Gurus all spent much of their time outside Punjab in the Siwalik Hills, where they developed new martial traditions. | Jahangir and Shah Jahan |
| 7 *Har Rai* 1630-1661 | | | Shah Jahan |
| 8 *Har Krishna* 1656-1664 | | Died at Delhi. | Aurangzeb |
| 9 *Tegh Bahadur* 1622-1675 | | Executed by Aurangzeb. | Aurangzeb |
| 10 *Gobind Singh* 1666-1708 | Reformed Sikh government introduced the features now universally associated with Sikhism today. Assassinated at Nanded in Maharashtra. | The Khalsa was open to both men and women, who replaced their caste names with the names Singh (lion) and Kaur ('lioness' or 'princess') respectively. | Aurangzeb |

Guru'). The Golden Temple in Amritsar, built at the end of the 16th century, is the holiest site of Sikhism.

The present institutions of Sikhism owe their origins to reform movements of the 19th century. Under the Sikh Gurudwaras Act of 1925 all temples were restored to the management of a Central Gurudwara Management Committee, thereby removing them from the administrative control of the Hindus under which many had come. This body has acted as the religion's controlling body ever since. See also, Amritsar.

# Christianity

There are about 23 million Christians in India. Christianity ranks third in terms of religious affiliation after Hinduism and Islam and there are Christian congregations in all the major towns of India.

The great majority of the Protestant Christians in India are now members of the Church of South India, formed from the major Protestant denominations in 1947, or the Church of North India, which followed suit in 1970. Together they account for approximately half the total number of Christians. Roman Catholics make up the majority of the rest. Many of the church congregations, both in towns and villages, are active centres of Christian worship.

**Origins** Some of the churches owe their origin either to the modern missionary movement of the late 18th century onwards, or to the colonial presence of the European powers. However, Christians probably arrived in India during the first century after the birth of Christ. There is evidence that one of Christ's Apostles, **Thomas**, reached India in 52 AD, only 20 years after Christ was crucified. He settled in Malabar and then expanded his missionary work to China. It is widely believed that he was martyred in Tamil Nadu on his return to India in 72 AD and is buried in Mylapore, in the suburbs of modern Chennai. St Thomas' Mount, a small rocky hill just north of Chennai airport, takes its name from him. Today there is still a church of Thomas Christians in Kerala.

**The Syrian church** Kerala was linked directly with the Middle East, when Syrian Christians embarked on a major missionary movement in the sixth century AD. The Thomas Christians have forms of worship that show very strong influence of the Syrian church and they still retain a Syriac order of service. They remained a close knit community, coming to terms with the prevailing caste system by maintaining strict social rules very similar to those of the surrounding upper caste Hindus. They lived in an area restricted to what is now Kerala, where trade with the Middle East, which some centuries later was to bring Muslims to the same region, remained active.

**Roman Catholicism** The third major development took place with the arrival of the Portuguese. The Jesuit St Francis Xavier landed in Goa in 1542 and in 1557 Goa was made an Archbishopric, see page 1164. Goa today bears rich testimony to the Portuguese influence on community life and on church building. They set up the first printing press in India in 1566 and began to print books in Tamil and other Dravidian languages by the end of the 16th century.

**Northern missions** Protestant missions in Bengal from the end of the 18th century had a profound influence on cultural and religious development. On 9 November 1793 the Baptist missionary **William Carey** reached the Hugli River. Although he went to India to preach, he had wide-ranging interests, notably in languages and education and the work of 19th-century missions rapidly widened to cover educational and medical work as well. See page 595.

Converts were made most readily among the backward castes and in the tribal areas. The Christian populations of the tribal hill areas of Nagaland and Assam stem from such late 19th-century and 20th-century movements. But the influence of Christian missions in education and medical work was greater than as a proselytizing force. Education in Christian schools stimulated reformist movements in Hinduism itself and mission hospitals supplemented government-run hospitals, particularly in remote rural areas. Some of these Christian-run hospitals, such as that at Vellore, continue to provide high class medical care.

**Christian beliefs** Christian theology had its roots in Judaism, with its belief in one God, the eternal Creator of the universe. Judaism saw the Jewish people as the vehicle for God's salvation, the 'chosen people of God' and pointed to a time when God would send his Saviour, or Messiah. Jesus, whom Christians believe was 'the Christ' or Messiah, was born in the village of Bethlehem, some 20 km south of Jerusalem. Very little is known of his early life except that he was brought up in a devout Jewish family. At the age of 29 or 30 he gathered a small group of followers and began to preach in the region between the Dead Sea and the Sea of Galilee. Two years later he was crucified in Jerusalem by the authorities on the charge of blasphemy - that he claimed to be the son of God.

Christians believe that all people live in a state of sin, in the sense that they are separated from God and fail to do his will. They believe that God is personal, 'like a father'. As God's son, Jesus accepted the cost of that separation and sinfulness himself through his death on the cross. Christians believe that Jesus was raised from the dead on the third day after he was crucified and that he appeared to his closest followers. They believe that his spirit continues to live today and that he makes it possible for people to come back to God.

The New Testament of the Bible, which, alongside the Old Testament, is the text to which Christians refer as the ultimate scriptural authority, consists of four 'Gospels' (meaning 'good news') and a series of letters by several early Christians referring to the nature of the Christian life.



**Christian worship** Although Christians are encouraged to worship individually as well as together, most forms of Christian worship centre on the gathering of the church congregation for praise, prayer and the preaching of God's word, which usually takes verses from the Bible as its starting point. Different denominations place varying emphases on the main elements of worship, but in most church services today the congregation will take part in singing hymns (songs of praise), prayers will be led by the minister, priest or a member of the congregation, readings from the Bible will be given and a sermon preached. For many Christians the most important service is the act of Holy Communion (Protestant) or Mass (Catholic) which celebrates the death and resurrection of Jesus in sharing bread and wine, which are held to represent Christ's body and blood given to save people from their sin.

## Zoroastrianism

The first Zoroastrians arrived on the west coast of India in the mid-eighth century AD, forced out from their native Iran by persecution of the invading Islamic Arabs. Until 1477 they lost all contact with Iran and then for nearly 300 years maintained contact with Persian Zoroastrians through a continuous exchange of letters. They became known by their now much more familiar name, the **Parsis** (or Persians).

Although they are a tiny minority (approximately 100,000), even in the cities where they are concentrated, they have been a prominent economic and social influence, especially in West India. Parsis adopted westernized customs and dress and took to the new economic opportunities that came with colonial industrialization. Families in West India such as the Tatas continue to be among India's leading industrialists, just part of a community that in recent generations has spread to Europe and north America.

**Origins** Zoroastrians trace their beliefs to the prophet Zarathustra, who lived in Northeast Iran around the seventh or sixth century BC. His place and even date of birth are uncertain, but he almost certainly enjoyed the patronage of the father of Darius the Great. The passage of Alexander the Great through Iran severely weakened support for Zoroastrianism, but between the sixth century BC and the seventh century AD it was the major religion of peoples living from North India to central Turkey. The spread of Islam reduced the number of Zoroastrians dramatically and forced those who did not retreat to the desert to emigrate. 

**Parsi beliefs** The early development of Zoroastrianism marked a movement towards belief in a single God. **Ahura Mazda**, the Good Religion of God, was shown in rejecting evil and in purifying thought, word and action. Fire plays a central and symbolic part in Zoroastrian worship, representing the presence of God. There are eight Atash Bahram – major fire temples – in India; four are in Mumbai, two in Surat and one each in Navsari and Udwada. There are many more minor temples, where the rituals are far less complex – perhaps 40 in Mumbai alone.

Earth, fire and air are all regarded as sacred, while death is the result of evil. Dead matter pollutes all it touches. Where there is a suitable space therefore, dead bodies are simply placed in the open to be consumed by vultures, as at the Towers of Silence in Mumbai. However, burial and cremation are also common.



# Land and environment

## Geography

India falls into three major geological regions. The north is enclosed by the great arc of the Himalaya. Along their southern flank lie the alluvial plains of the Ganga and to the south again is the Peninsula. The island chains of the Lakshadweep and Minicoy off the west coast of India are coral atolls, formed on submarine ridges under the Arabian Sea.

### The origins of India's landscapes

Only 100 million years ago the Indian Peninsula was still attached to the great land mass of what geologists call 'Pangaea' alongside South Africa, Australia and Antarctica. Then as the great plates on which the earth's southern continents stood broke up, the Indian Plate started its dramatic shift northwards, eventually colliding with the Asian plate. As the Indian Plate continues to get pushed under the Tibetan Plateau so the Himalaya continue to rise.

**The Himalaya** The Himilaya dominate the northern borders of India, stretching 2,500 km from northwest to southeast. They are unparalleled anywhere in the world. Of the 94 mountains in Asia above 7,300 m, all but two are in the Himalaya. Nowhere else in the world are there mountains as high.

## Himalayan profile

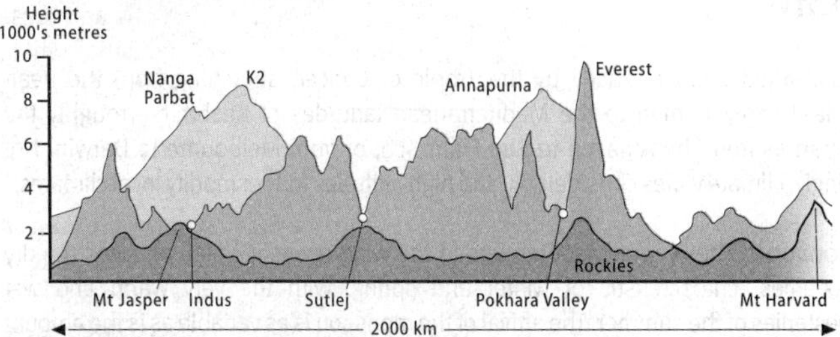

The Himalaya proper, stretching from the Pamirs in Pakistan to the easternmost bend of the Brahmaputra in Assam, can be divided into three broad zones. On the southern flank are the Shiwaliks, or Outer Ranges. To their immediate north run the parallel Middle Ranges of Pir Panjal and Dhauladhar and to the north again is the third zone, the Inner Himalaya, which has the highest peaks, many of them in Nepal.

The central core of the Himalayan ranges did not begin to rise until about 35 million years ago. The latest mountain building period, responsible for the Shiwaliks, began less than five million years ago and is still continuing, raising some of the high peaks by as much as 5 mm a year. Such movement comes at a price and the boundary between the plains and the Himalayan ranges is a zone of continuing violent earthquakes and massive erosion.

**The Gangetic Plains** As the Himalaya began their dramatic uplift, the trough which formed to the south of the newly emerging mountains was steadily filled with the debris washed down from the hills, creating the Indo-Gangetic plains. Today the alluvium reaches depths of over 3,000 m in places (and over 22 km at the mouth of the Ganga in Bangladesh), and contains some of the largest reserves of underground water in the world. These have made possible extensive well irrigation, especially in Northwest India, contributing to the rapid agricultural changes which have taken place.

The Indo-Gangetic plains are still being extended and modified. The southern part of Bengal only emerged from the sea during the last 5,000 years. The Ganga and the Indus have each been estimated to carry over one million tonnes of silt every year - considerably more than the Mississippi. The silts washed down from the Himalaya have made it possible for intensive rice cultivation to be practised continuously for hundreds of years, though they cause problems for modern irrigation development. Dams in the Himalayan region are being rapidly filled by silt, over 33 million tonnes being deposited behind the Bhakra Dam on the Sutlej River alone.

**The Peninsula** The crystalline rocks of the Peninsula are some of the oldest in the world, the **Charnockites** – named after the founder of Kolkata an enthusiastic amateur geologist, Job Charnock, see page 585 – being over 3,100 million years old. Over 60 million years ago, when India split from Madagascar, a mass of volcanic lava welled up through cracks in the earth's surface and covered some 500,000 sq km of northern Karnataka, Maharashtra, southern Gujarat and Madhya Pradesh.

The fault line which severed India from Africa was marked by a north-south ridge of mountains, known today as the Western Ghats, set back from the sea by a coastal plain which is never more than 80 km wide. In the south, the Nilgiris and Palanis are over 2,500 m high.

From the crest line of the **Western Ghats**, the Peninsula slopes generally eastwards, interrupted on its eastern edge by the much more broken groups of hills sometimes referred to as the **Eastern Ghats**. The east flowing rivers have created flat alluvial deltas which have been the basis of successive peninsular kingdoms.

## Climate

India is divided almost exactly by the Tropic of Cancer, stretching from the near-equatorial Kanniyakumari to the Mediterranean latitudes of Kashmir – roughly the same span as from the Amazon to San Francisco, or from Melbourne to Darwin. Not surprisingly, climate varies considerably and high altitudes further modify local climates.

**The monsoon** The term monsoon refers to the wind reversal which replaces the dry northeasterlies, characteristic of winter and spring, with the very warm and wet southwesterlies of the summer. The arrival of the monsoon is as variable as is the amount of rain which it brings. What makes the Indian monsoon quite exceptional is not its regularity but the depth of moist air which passes over the subcontinent. Over India, the highly unstable moist airflow is over 6,000 m thick compared with only 2,000 m over Japan, giving rise to the bursts of torrential rain which mark out the wet season.

**Winter** In winter, high pressure builds up over Central Asia. Most of India is protected from the cold northeast monsoon winds that result by the massive bulk of the Himalaya and daytime temperatures rise sharply in the sun. Right across the Ganga plains night temperatures fall to below 5°C in January and February. To the south the winter temperatures increase having a minimum temperature of around 20°C. Although much of North India often has beautiful weather from November through to March, there are periods when it is cool and overcast. Elsewhere, however, the winter is a dry season through nearly all of India. The low winter night temperatures coupled with increasing pollution in the larger cities such as Delhi and Kolkata, contribute to the growing problem of morning fog in December-January, a major health hazard as well as causing periodic travel chaos.

**Summer** From April onwards much of India becomes almost unbearably hot. Temperatures of over 50°C are not unknown. It is a time of year to get up to the hills. At the end of May very moist southwesterlies sweep across South India and the Bay of Bengal. They then double back northwestwards, bringing tremendously heavy rain first to the eastern Himalaya then gradually spreading northwestwards.

**The wet season** The monsoon season, which lasts from between three and five months depending on the region, brings an enveloping dampness which makes it very difficult to keep things dry. Many parts of the west coast get a three-month soaking and the Shillong plateau has received as much as 26 m in one year! If you are travelling in the wetter parts of India during the monsoon you need to be prepared for extended periods of torrential rain and major disruption to travel. However, many parts of India receive a total of under 1,000 mm a year, mainly in the form of heavy isolated showers. Rainfall generally decreases towards the Northwest, Rajasthan and northern Gujarat merging imperceptibly into genuine desert. Tamil Nadu in the southeast has an exceptional rainfall pattern, receiving most of its rain in the period of the retreating monsoon, October-December.

**Storms** Some regions of India suffer major storms. Cyclones may hit the east coast causing enormous damage and loss of life, the risk being greatest between the end of October and early December. In Northwest India, '*the Loo*', between April and June, brings dust storms and very hot winds. In Bengal Nor'westers can cause enormous damage in April-May

**Humidity** The coastal regions have humidity levels above 70% for most of the year which can be very uncomfortable. However, sea breezes often bring some relief on the coast itself. Moving north and inland, between December-May humidity drops sharply, often falling as low as 20% during the daytime.

## Vegetation and wildlife

### Vegetation

India's tropical location and its position astride the wet monsoonal winds ensured that 16 different forest types were represented in India. The most widespread was tropical dry deciduous forest. Areas with more than 1,700 mm of rainfall had tropical moist deciduous, semi-evergreen or wet evergreen forest, while much of the remainder had types ranging from tropical dry deciduous woodland to dry alpine scrub, found at high altitudes. However, today forest cover has been reduced to about 13% of the surface area, mainly the result of the great demand for wood as a fuel.

**Deciduous forest** Two types of deciduous tree remain particularly important, **Sal** (*Shorea robusta*), now found mainly in eastern India and **Teak** (*Tectona grandis*). Most teak today has been planted. Both are resistant to burning, which helped to protect them where man used fire as a means of clearing the forest. See also box below.

**Tropical rainforest** In wetter areas, particularly along the Western Ghats, you can still find tropical wet evergreen forest, but even these are now extensively managed. Across the drier areas of the peninsula heavy grazing has reduced the forest cover to little more than thorn scrub.

**Mountain forests and grassland** At between 1,000-2,000 m in the eastern hill ranges of India and in Bhutan, for example, wet hill forest includes evergreen oaks and chestnuts. Further west in the foothills of the Himalaya are belts of subtropical pine at roughly the same altitudes. Deodars (*Cedrus deodarus*) form large stands and moist temperate forest, with pines, cedars, firs and spruce, is dominant, giving many of the valleys a beautifully fresh, alpine feel.

Between 3,000-4,000 m alpine forest predominates. Rhododendron are often mixed with other forest types. Birch, juniper, poplars and pine are widespread.

There are several varieties of coarse grassland along the southern edge of the Terai and alpine grasses are important for grazing above altitudes of 2,000 m. A totally distinctive grassland is the bamboo (*Dendo calamus*) region of the eastern Himalaya.



## Trees

**Flowering trees** Many Indian trees are planted along roadsides to provide shade and they often also produce beautiful flowers. The **Silk Cotton Tree** (*Bombax ceiba*), up to 25 m in height, is one of the most dramatic. The pale greyish bark of this buttressed tree usually bears conical spines. It has wide spreading branches and keeps its leaves for most of the year. The flowers, which appear when the tree is leafless, are cup-shaped, with curling, rather fleshy red petals up to 12 cm long while the fruit produce the fine, silky cotton which gives it its name.

Other common trees with red or orange flowers include the Dhak (also called 'Flame of the forest' or *Palas*), the Gulmohur, the Indian coral tree and the Tulip tree. The smallish (6 m) deciduous **Dhak** (*Butea monosperma*), has light grey bark and a gnarled, twisted trunk and thick, leathery leaves. The large, bright orange and sweet pea-shaped flowers appear on leafless branches. The 8-9 m high umbrella-shaped **Gulmohur** (*Delonix regia*), a native of Madagascar, is grown as a shade tree in towns. The fiery coloured flowers make a magnificent display after the tree has shed its feathery leaves. The scarlet flowers of the **Indian Coral Tree** (*Erythrina indica*) appear when its branches with thorny bark are leafless. The tall **Tulip Tree** (*Spathodea campanulata*) (not to be confused with the North American one) has a straight, darkish brown, slender trunk. It is usually evergreen except in the drier parts of India. The scarlet bell-shaped, tulip-like, flowers grow in profusion at the ends of the branches from November to March.

Often seen along roadsides the **Jacaranda** (*Jacaranda mimosaefolia*), has attractive feathery foliage and purple-blue thimble-shaped flowers up to 40 mm long. When not in flower it resembles a Gulmohur, but differs in its general shape. The valuable **Tamarind** (*Tamarindus indica*), with a short straight trunk and a spreading crown, often grows along the roadside. An evergreen with feathery leaves, it bears small clusters of yellow and red flowers. The noticeable fruit pods are long, curved and swollen at intervals. In parts of India, the rights to the fruit are auctioned off annually for up to Rs 4,000 (US$100) per tree.

Of these trees the Silk cotton, the Dhak and the Indian coral are native to India. Others were introduced mostly during the last century: the Tulip tree from East Africa, the Jacaranda from Brazil and the Tamarind, possibly from Africa.

**Fruit trees** The familiar apple, plum, apricot and cherry grow in the cool upland areas of India. In the warmer plains tropical fruits flourish. The large, spreading **Mango** (*Mangifera indica*) bears the delicious, distinctively shaped fruit that comes in hundreds of varieties. The evergreen **Jackfruit** (*Artocarpus heterophyllus*) has dark green leathery leaves. The huge fruit (up to 90 cm long and 40 cm thick), growing from a short stem directly off the trunk and branches, has a rough, almost prickly skin and is almost sickly sweet. The **Banana** plant (*Musa*), actually a gigantic herb (up to 5 m high) arising from an underground stem, has very large leaves which grow directly off the trunk. Each large purplish flower produces bunches of up to 100 bananas. The **Papaya** (*Carica papaya*) grows to about 4 m with the large hand-shaped leaves clustered near the top. Only the female tree bears the fruit, which hang down close to the trunk just below the leaves.

**Palm trees** **Coconut Palms** (*Cocos nucifera*) are extremely common all round the coast of India. It has tall (15-25 m), slender, unbranched trunks, feathery leaves and large green or golden fruit with soft white flesh filled with milky water, so different from the brown fibre-covered inner nut which makes its way to Europe. The 10-15 m high **Palmyra palms** (*Borassus flabellifer*), indigenous to South and East India, have very distinctive fan-like leaves, as much as 150 cm across. The fruit, which is smaller than a coconut, is round, almost black and very shiny. The **Betel Nut Palm** (*Areca catechu*) resembles the coconut palm, its slender trunk bearing ring marks left by fallen leaf stems. The smooth, round nuts, only about 3 cm across, grow in large hanging bunches. **Wild Date Palms** (*Phoenix sylvestris*), originally came from North Africa. About 20-25 m tall, the trunks are also marked with the ring bases of the leaves which drop off. The distinctive leaflets which stick out from the central vein give the leaf a spiky appearance. Bunches of dates are only borne by the female tree.

All these palm trees are of considerable **commercial importance**. From the fruit alone the coconut palm produces coir from the outer husk, copra from the fleshy kernel from which coconut oil or coconut butter is extracted, in addition to the desiccated coconut and coconut milk. The sap is fermented to a drink called toddy. A similar drink is produced from the sap of the wild date and the palmyra palms which are also important for sugar production. The fruit of the betel nut palm is wrapped in a special leaf and chewed. The trunks and leaves of all the palms are widely used in building and thatching.

**Other trees** Of all Indian trees the **Banyan** (*Ficus benghalensis*) is probably the best known. It is planted by temples, in villages and along roads. The seeds often germinate in the cracks of old walls, the growing roots splitting the wall apart. If it grows in the bark of another tree, it sends down roots towards the ground. As it grows, more roots appear from the branches, until the original host tree is surrounded by a 'cage' which eventually strangles it. The famous one in Kolkata's Botanical Gardens is more than 400 m in circumference.

Related to the banyan, the **Pipal** or Peepul (*Ficus religiosa*), also cracks open walls and strangles other trees with its roots. With a smooth grey bark, it too is commonly found near temples and shrines. You can distinguish it from the banyan by the absence of aerial roots and its large, heart-shaped leaf with a point tapering into a pronounced 'tail'. It bears abundant 'figs' of a purplish tinge which are about 1 cm across.

The **Ashok** or **Mast** (*Polyalthia longifolia*) is a tall evergreen which can reach 15 m or more in height. One variety, often seen in avenues, is trimmed and tapers towards the top. The leaves are long, slender and shiny and narrow to a long point.

**Acacia** trees with their feathery leaves are fairly common in the drier parts of India. The best known is the **Babul** (*Acacia arabica*) with a rough, dark bark. The leaves have long silvery white thorns at the base and consist of many leaflets while the flowers grow in golden balls about 1 cm across.

The **Eucalyptus** or **Gum Tree** (*Eucalyptus grandis*), introduced from Australia in the 19th century, is now widespread and is planted near villages to provide both shade and firewood. There are various forms but all may be readily recognized by their height, their characteristic long, thin leaves which have a pleasant fresh smell and the colourful peeling bark.

The wispy **Casuarina** (*Casuarina*) grows in poor sandy soil, especially on the coast and on village waste land. It has the typical leaves of a pine tree and the cones are small and prickly to walk on. It is said to attract lightning during a thunder storm.

**Bamboo** (*Bambusa*) strictly speaking is a grass which can vary in size from small ornamental clumps to the enormous wild plant whose stems are so strong and thick that they are used for construction and for scaffolding and as pipes in rural irrigation schemes.

## Flowering plants

Common in the Himalaya is the beautiful flowering shrub or tree, which can be as tall as 12 m, the **Rhododendron** which is indigenous to this region. In the wild the commonest colour of the flowers is crimson, but other colours, such as pale purple occur too. From March to May the flowers are very noticeable on the hill sides. Another common wild flowering shrub is **Lantana**. This is a fairly small untidy looking bush with rough, toothed oval leaves, which grow in pairs on the square and prickly stem. The flowers grow together in a flattened head, the ones near the middle being usually yellowish, while those at the rim are pink, pale purple or orange. The fruit is a shiny black berry.

Many other flowering plants are cultivated in parks, gardens and roadside verges. The attractive **Frangipani** (*Plumeria acutifolia*) has a rather crooked trunk and stubby branches, which if broken give out a white milky juice which can be irritating to the skin. The big, leathery leaves taper to a point at each end and have noticeable parallel veins. The sweetly scented waxy flowers are white, pale yellow or pink. The **Bougainvillea** grows as a dense bush or climber with small oval leaves and rather long thorns. The brightly coloured part (which can be pinkish-purple, crimson, orange, yellow et cetera) which appears like a flower is not formed of petals, which are quite small and undistinguished, but by large papery bracts.

The unusual shape of the **Hibiscus**. The trumpet shaped flower, as much as 7 or 8 cm across, has a very long 'tongue' growing out from the centre and varies in colour from scarlet to yellow or white. The leaves are somewhat oval or heart-shaped with jagged edges. In municipal flowerbeds the commonest planted flower is probably the **Canna Lily**. It has large leaves which are either green or bronzed and lots of large bright red or yellow flowers. The plant can be more than 1 m high.

On many ponds and tanks the floating plants of the **Lotus** (*Nelumbo nucifera*) and the **Water Hyacinth** (*Eichornia crassipes*) are seen. Lotus flowers which rise on stalks above the water can be white, pink or a deep red and up to 25 cm across. The very large leaves either float on the surface or rise above the water. Many dwarf varieties are cultivated. The rather fleshy leaves and lilac flowers of the water hyacinth float to form a dense carpet, often clogging the waterways.

## Crops

Of India's enormous variety, the single most widespread crop is **rice** (commonly *Orysa indica*). This forms the most important staple in South and East India, though other cereals and some root crops are also important elsewhere. The rice plant grows in flooded fields called *paddies* and virtually all planting or harvesting is done by hand. Millets are favoured in drier areas inland, while wheat is the most important crop in the northwest.

There are many different sorts of millet, but the ones most often seen are finger millet, pearl millet (bajra) and sorghum (jowar). **Finger millet**, commonly known as ragi (*Eleusine corocana*), is so-called because the ear has several spikes which radiate out, a bit like the fingers of a hand. Usually less than 1 m high, it is grown extensively in the south. Both **pearl millet** (*Pennisetum typhoideum*, known as *bajra* in the north and *cumbu* in Tamil Nadu) and **sorghum** (*Sorghum vulgare*, known as *jowar* in the north and *cholam* in the south) look superficially similar to the more familiar maize though each can be easily distinguished when the seed heads appear. Pearl millet, mainly grown in the north, has a tall single spike which gives it its other name of bulrush millet. Sorghum bears an open ear at the top of the plant.

**Tea** (*Camellia sinensis*) is grown on a commercial scale in tea gardens in areas of high rainfall, often in highland regions. Over 90% comes from Assam and West Bengal in the Northeast and Tamil Nadu and Kerala in the South. Left to itself tea grows into a tree 10 m tall. In the tea gardens it is pruned to waist height for the convenience of the tea pluckers and forms flat topped bushes, with shiny bright green oval leaves.

**Coffee** (*Coffea*) is not as widely grown as tea, but high quality arabica is an important crop in parts of South India. Coffee is also a bush, with fairly long, shiny dark green leaves. The white, sweet smelling flowers, which yield the coffee berry, grow in groups along the stems. The coffee berries start off green and turn red when ripe.

**Sugar cane** (*Saccharum*) is another commercially important crop. This looks like a large grass which stands up to 3 m tall. The crude brown sugar is sold as jaggery and has a flavour of molasses.

Of the many spices grown in India, the two climbers pepper and vanilla and the grass-like cardamom are the ones most often seen. The **pepper** vine (*Piper Nigrum*) is indigenous to India where it grows in the warm moist regions. As it is a vine it needs support such as a trellis or a tree. It is frequently planted up against the betel nut palm and appears as a leafy vine with almost heart-shaped leaves. The peppercorns cluster along hanging spikes and are red when ripe. Both black and white pepper is produced from the same plant, the difference being in the processing.

**Vanilla** (*Vanilla planifolium*), which belongs to the orchid family, also grows up trees for support and attaches itself to the bark by small roots. It is native to South America, but grows well in India in areas of high rainfall. It is a rather fleshy looking plant, with white flowers and long slender pods.

**Cardamom** (*Elettaria cardomomum*) is another spice native to India and is planted usually under shade. It grows well in highland areas such as Sikkim and the Western Ghats. It is a herbaceous plant looking rather like a big clump of grass, with long leafy shoots springing out of the ground as much as 2-3 m in height. The white flowers grow on separate shoots which can be upright, but usually sprawl on the ground. It is from these flowers that the seed bearing capsules grow.

The **cashew nut** tree (*Anacardium occidentale*) was introduced into India, but now grows wild as well as being cultivated. It is a medium sized tree with bright green, shiny, rounded leaves. The nut grows on a fleshy fruit called a cashew apple and hangs down below this. **Cotton** (*Gossypium*) is important in parts of the west and south. The cotton bush is a small knee-high bush and the cotton boll appears after the flower has withered. This splits when ripe to show the white cotton lint inside.

The **castor oil** plant (*Ricinus Communis*) is cultivated as a cash crop and is planted in small holdings among other crops and along roads and paths. It is a handsome plant up to about 2 m in height, with very large leaves which are divided into some 12 'fingers'. The young stems are reddish and shiny. The well known castor oil is extracted from the bean which is a mottled brown in colour.

### Elephants – a future in the wild?

The Indian elephant (Elephas maximas), smaller than the African, is the world's second largest land mammal. Unlike the African elephant, the male rarely reaches a height of over 3 m; it also has smaller ears. Other distinguishing features include the high domed forehead, the rounded shape of the back and the smooth trunk with a single 'finger' at the end. Also the female is often tuskless or bears small ones called tushes and even the male is sometimes tuskless (makhnas). The Indian elephant has five nails on its front feet and four on the back (compared to the African's four and three respectively). There are approximately 6,500 elephants living in the wild in northern West Bengal, Assam and Bhutan. There are a further 2,000 in Central India and 6,000 in the three South Indian states of Kerala, Tamil Nadu and Karnataka.

The loss of habitat has made wild elephants an increasing danger to humans and about 300 people are killed every year by wild elephants, mainly in the northeast. The tribal people have developed skilled techniques for capturing and training wild elephants, which have been domesticated in India for about 5,000 years. They need a lot of feeding – about 18 hours a day. Working elephants are fed on a special diet, by hand straight at the mouth and they eat between 100 and 300 kg per day.



# Wildlife

India has an extremely rich and varied wildlife, though many species only survive in very restricted environments. Alarmed by the rapid loss of wildlife habitat the Indian Government established the first conservation measures in 1972, followed by the setting up of national parks and reserves. Some 25,000 sq km were set aside in 1973 for Project Tiger. Tigers have been reported to be increasing steadily in several of the game reserves but threats to their survival continue, notably through poaching. The same is true of other, less well known species. Their natural habitat has been destroyed both by people and by domesticated animals (there are some 250 million cattle and 50 million sheep and goats). There are now nearly 70 national parks and 330 sanctuaries in addition to programmes of afforestation and coastline preservation. Most parks and sanctuaries are open from October-March; those in the northeast are closed from April-September, while many in Madhya Pradesh and Uttar Pradesh close July-September.

## The animals

**The big cats** Of the three Indian big cats the Asiatic lion is virtually confined to a single reserve. The other two, the tiger and leopard, occasionally occur outside. The **tiger** (*Panthera tigris*), which prefers to live in fairly dense cover, is most likely to be glimpsed as it lies in long grass or in dappled shadow. The **asiatic lion** (*Panthera leo*) is now found only in the Gir National Park. Less sleek than the African lion, it has a more shaggy coat and a smaller, often black mane. The **leopard** or **panther** as it is often called in India (*Panthera pardus*), is far more numerous than the tiger, but is even more elusive. The all black form is not uncommon in areas of higher rainfall such as the Western Ghats and Northeast India, though the typical form is seen more often.

**Elephant and rhino** The **Indian elephant** (*Elephas maximus*) has been domesticated for centuries and today it is still used as a beast of burden. In the wild it inhabits

## Blackbuck and bishnois

The blackbuck is one of the handsomest antelopes with its elegant carriage and striking colour combination. Fleet footed, it often resorts to a bounding run across the countryside – the preferred habitat is grassland. The mature bucks are a deep brownish black with contrasting white underparts, and have spiralling horns, while juvenile males are brown and white. Does are fawn brown with white underparts, and are completely hornless. During the rutting season the bucks attain a remarkable sheen and they strut with heads raised and horns swept along their backs in a challenging stance. The rutting season varies locally but is generally around October and February-March.

Velavadhar National Park has one of the largest blackbuck populations among Indian sanctuaries. Gajner near Bikaner, the Sambhar Salt Lake, Tal Chappar in Shekhawati and Keoladeo Ghana National Park at Bharatpur are other good reserves for sightings. Blackbucks are held sacred by the Bishnois, the reason for their good numbers near Guda Bishnoi village of Jodhpur district.

hilly country with forest and bamboo, where it lives in herds which can number as many as 50 or more individuals. They are adaptable animals and can live in all sorts of forest, except those in the dry areas.Wild elephants are mainly confined to reserves, but occasionally move out into cultivation, where they cause great damage. The **great Indian one-horned rhinoceros** (*Rhinoceros unicornis*) has folds of skin which look like rivet covered armour plating. It stands at up to 170 cm at the shoulder.

**Deer, antelope, oxen and their relatives** Once widespread, these animals are now largely confined to the reserves. The male deer (stags) carry antlers which are branched, each 'spike' on the antler being called a tine. Antelopes and oxen, on the other hand, have horns which are not branched.

There are several deer species in India, mainly confined to very restricted ranges. Three species are quite common. The largest and one of the most widespread, is the magnificent **sambar** (*Cervus unicolor*) which can be up to 150 cm at the shoulder. It has a noticeably shaggy coat, which varies in colour from brown with a yellowish or grey tinge through to dark, almost black, in the older stags. The sambar is often found on wooded hillsides and lives in groups of up to 10 or so, though solitary individuals are also seen.

The **barasingha** or **swamp deer** (*Cervus duvauceli*), standing about 130 cm at the shoulder, is also quite common. The females are usually lighter and some are spotted, as are the young. The antlers are much more complex than those of the sambar, having as many as 20 tines, but 12 is more usual. Barasingha prefer swampy habitat, but are also seen in grassy areas, often in large herds.

The small **chital** or **spotted deer** (*Axis axis*), only about 90 cm tall, are seen in herds of 20 or so, in grassy areas. The bright rufous coat spotted with white is unmistakable; the stags carry antlers with three tines.

These animals live in open grasslands, never too far from water. The beautiful **blackbuck** or **Indian antelope** (*Antilope cervicapra*), up to 80 cm at the shoulder, occurs in large herds. The distinctive colouring and the long spiral horns make the stag easy to identify. The coat is chocolate brown above, very sharply demarcated from the white of the underparts. The females do not usually bear horns and like the young, have yellowish brown coats. The larger and heavier **nilgai** or **blue bull** (*Boselaphus tragocamelus*) is about 140 cm at the shoulder and is rather horse-like, with a sloping

## Tiger, tiger

At one time the tiger roamed freely throughout the sub-continent and at the beginning of this century the estimated population was 40,000 animals. Gradually, due mainly to increased pressure on its habitat by human encroachment and resulting destruction of the habitat, the numbers of this beautiful animal dwindled to fewer than 2,000 in 1972. This was the low point and alarmed at the approaching extinction of the tiger, concerned individuals with the backing of the Government and the World Wildlife Fund, set up Project Tiger in 1973. Initially nine parks were set up to protect the tiger and this was expanded over the years. However, despite encouraging signs in the first decade the latest tiger census suggests that there are still fewer than 2,500.



back. The male has a dark grey coat, while the female is sandy coloured. Both sexes have two white marks on the cheek, white throats and a white ring just above each hoof. The male carries short, forward-curving horns and has a tuft of long black hairs on the front of the neck. They occur in small herds on grassy plains and scrub land.

The very graceful **chinkara** or **Indian gazelle** (*Gazella gazella*) is only 65 cm at the shoulder. The light russet colour of the body has a distinct line along the side where the paler underparts start. Both sexes carry slightly S-shaped horns. Chinkara live in small groups in rather broken hilly countryside.

The commonest member of the oxen group is the **Asiatic wild buffalo** or water buffalo (*Bubalus bubalis*). About 170 cm at the shoulder, the wild buffalo, which can be aggressive, occurs in herds on grassy plains and swamps near rivers

## Major Indian wildlife parks

## Room at the park...

Booking accommodation in national parks can be very frustrating for independent travellers. In many parks it is essential to book in advance. Offices outside may tell you that it is fully-booked, even when outgoing tourists say that the accommodation is empty. This is because cancellation information is not relayed to all offices. The only way in is patient, friendly persistence, asking for just one day inside. This can then be extended once in. Be prepared for a lot of frustration, especially in Ramnagar (Corbett National Park). Where possible go to the park itself and book. You may prefer to try a specialist travel agent in one of the main towns in the region.

and lakes. The black coat and wide-spreading curved horns, carried by both sexes, are distinctive.

In the high Himalaya, the **yak** (*Bos grunniens*) is domesticated. The wild yak, found on bleak Himalayan hillsides has a shaggy, blackish brown coat and large horns; the domesticated animals are often piebald and the horns much smaller.

The **Indian bison** or **gaur** (*Bos gaurus*) can be up to 200 cm at the shoulder with a heavy muscular ridge across it. Both sexes carry curved horns. The young gaur is a light sandy colour, which darkens with age, the old bulls being nearly black with pale sandy coloured 'socks' and a pale forehead. Basically hill animals, they live in forests and bamboo clumps and emerge from the trees to graze.

The **bharal** or **blue sheep** (*Pseudois nayaur*) are found on the open slopes around Ladakh. About 90 cm at the shoulder, it has a grey-blue body and horns that curve backwards over the neck.

The rare **asiatic wild ass** (*Equus hemionus*) is confined to the deserts of the Little Rann of Kachchh. The fawn body has a distinctive dark stripe along the back. The dark mane is short and erect. The **wild boar** (*Sus scrofa*) has a mainly black body and a pig-like head; the hairs thicken down the spine to form a sort of mane. A mature male stands 90 cm at the shoulder and, unlike the female, bears tusks. The young are striped. Quite widespread, they often cause great destruction among crops.

One of the most important scavengers of the open countryside, the **striped hyena** (*Hyena hyena*) usually comes out at night. It is about 90 cm at the shoulder with a large head with a noticeable crest of hairs along its sloping back.

The **common giant flying squirrel** are common in the larger forests of India, except in the northeast (*Petaurista petaurista*). The body can be 45 cm long and the tail another 50 cm. They glide from tree to tree using a membrane stretching from front leg to back leg which acts like a parachute.

**In towns and villages** The **common langur** (*Presbytis entellus*), 75 cm, is a long-tailed monkey with a distinctive black face, hands and feet. Usually a forest dweller, it is found almost throughout India. The **rhesus macaque** (*Macaca mulatta*), 60 cm, is more solid looking with shorter limbs and a shorter tail. It can be distinguished by the orange-red fur on its rump and flanks.

**Palm squirrels** are very common. The **five-striped** (*Funambulus pennanti*) and the **three-striped palm squirrel** (*Funambulus palmarum*), are both about the same size (30 cm long, about half of which is tail). The five-striped is usually seen in towns.

The two bats most commonly seen in towns differ enormously in size. The larger so-called **flying fox** (*Pteropus giganteus*) has a wing span of 120 cm. These fruit-eating bats, found throughout, except in the driest areas, roost in large noisy colonies where they look like folded umbrellas hanging from the trees. In the evening they can be seen leaving the roost with slow measured wing beats. The much smaller **Indian pipistrelle** (*Pipistrellus coromandra*), with a wing span of about 15 cm, is an insect eater. It comes into houses at dusk, roosting under eaves and has a fast, erratic flight.

The **jackal** (*Canis aureus*), a lone scavenger in towns and villages, looks like a cross between a dog and a fox and varies in colour from shades of brown through to black. The bushy tail has a dark tip.

The **common mongoose** (*Herpestes edwardsi*) lives in scrub and open jungle. It kills snakes, but will also take rats, mice and chicken. Tawny coloured with a grey grizzled tinge, it is about 90 cm in length, of which half is pale-tipped tail.

The **sloth bear** (*Melursus ursinus*), about 75 cm at the shoulder, lives in broken forest, but may be seen on a lead accompanying a street entertainer who makes it 'dance' to music as a part of an act. They have a long snout, a pendulous lower lip and a shaggy black coat with a yellowish V-shaped mark on the chest.

If you take a boat trip on the Ganga or the Brahmaputra rivers, look out for the fresh water **gangetic dolphin** (*Platanista gangetica*) as it comes to the surface to breathe.

## Birds

**Town and village birds** Some birds perform a useful function scavenging and clearing refuse. One of the most widespread is the brown **pariah kite** (*Milvus migrans*, 65 cm). The more handsome chestnut and white **brahminy kite** (*Haliastur indus*, 48 cm) is largely confined to the waterside. The common brown **white-backed vulture** (*Gyps bengalensis*, 90 cm) looks ungainly and has a bare and scrawny head and neck. The smaller **scavenger vulture** (*Neophron percnopterus*, 65 cm) is mainly white, but often has dirty looking plumage and the bare head and neck of all vultures. In flight its wedge-shaped tail and black and white colouring are characteristic.

The **house crow** (*Corvus splendens*, 45 cm) on the other hand is a very smart looking bird with a grey body and black tail, wings, face and throat. It occurs in almost every town and village in India. The **jungle crow** (*Corvus macrorhynchos*, 50 cm) originally a bird of the countryside has started to move into populated areas and in the hill stations tends to replace the house crow. Unlike the house crow it is a glossy black all over and has a much deeper, hoarser caw.

The **feral pigeon**, or **blue rock dove** (*Columba livia*, 32 cm), found throughout the world, is generally a slaty grey in colour. It invariably has two dark bars on the wing and a white rump. The **little brown dove** (*Streptopelia senegalensis*, 25 cm) is bluey grey and brown above, with a pink head and underparts and a speckled pattern on the neck. The **collared dove** (*Streptopelia decaocto*, 30 cm) with a distinct half collar on the back of its neck, is common, especially in the drier parts of India.

Bulbuls are common in gardens and parks. The **red-vented bulbul** (*Pycnonotus cafer*, 20 cm), a mainly brown bird, can be identified by the slight crest and a bright red patch under the tail. The **house sparrow** (*Passer domesticus*, 15 cm) can be seen in towns throughout the mainland. The ubiquitous **common myna** (*Acridotheres tristis*, 22 cm), feeds on lawns, especially after rain or watering. Look for the white under the tail and the bare yellow skin around the eye, yellow bill and legs and in flight the large white wing patch.

A less common, but more striking bird also seen feeding in open spaces, is the **hoopoe** (*Upupa epops*, 30 cm), easily identified by its sandy plumage with black and white stripes and long thin curved bill. The marvellous fan-shaped crest is sometimes raised. Finally there is a member of the cuckoo family which is heard more often than seen. The **koel** (*Eudynamys scolopacea*, 42 cm), is commonly heard during the hot weather - kuoo-kuoo-kuoo, the double note starts off low and flute-like, rises in pitch and intensity, then suddenly stops, only to start all over again. The male is all black with a greenish bill and a red eye; the female streaked and barred.

**Water and waterside birds** The *jheels* (marshes or swamps) of India form one of the richest bird habitats in the world. Cormorants abound; the commonest, the **little cormorant** (*Phalacrocorax niger*, 50 cm) is found on most inland waters. An almost entirely black bird with just a little white on the throat, it has a long tail and a hooked bill. The **coot** (*Fulica atra*, 40 cm), another common black bird, seen especially in winter has a noticeable white shield on the forehead.

The magnificent **sarus crane** (*Grus antigone*, 150 cm) is one of India's tallest birds. It is widespread all year round across northern India, almost invariably in pairs. The bare red head and long red legs combined with its height and grey plumage make it easy to identify. The commonest migrant crane is probably the **common crane** (*Grus grus*, 120 cm), present only in winter, often in large flocks. It has mainly grey plumage with a black head and neck. There is a white streak running down the side of the neck and above the eye is a tuft of red feathers.

The **openbill stork** (*Anastomus oscitans*, 80 cm) and the **painted stork** (*Ibis leucocephalus*, 100 cm) are common too and are spotted breeding in large colonies. The former is white with black wing feathers and a curiously shaped bill. The latter, mainly white, has a pinkish tinge on the back and dark marks on the wings and a broken black band on the lower chest. The bare yellow face and yellow down-curved bill are conspicuous.

By almost every swamp, ditch or rice paddy up to about 1,200 m you will see the **paddy bird** (*Ardeola grayii*, 45 cm). An inconspicuous, buff-coloured bird, it is easily overlooked as it stands hunched up by the waterside. As soon as it takes off, its white wings and rump make it very noticeable. The **bronze-winged jacana** (*Metopidius indicus*, 27 cm) has very long toes which enable it to walk on the floating leaves of water-lilies and there is a noticeable white streak over and above the eye. Village ponds often have their resident bird.

The commonest and most widespread of the Indian kingfishers is the jewel-like **common kingfisher** (*Alcedo atthis*, 18 cm). With its brilliant blue upperparts and orange breast it is usually seen perched on a twig or a reed beside the water.

**Open grassland, light woodland and cultivated land** The **cattle egret** (*Bubulcus ibis*, 50 cm), a small white heron, is usually seen near herds of cattle, frequently perched on the backs of the animals. Equal in height to the sarus crane is the impressive, but ugly **adjutant stork** (*Leptopilos dubius*, 150 cm). This often dishevelled bird is a scavenger and is thus seen near rubbish dumps and carcasses. It has a naked red head and neck, a huge bill and a large fleshy pouch which hangs down the front of the neck.

The **rose-ringed parakeet** (*Psittacula krameri*, 40 cm) is found throughout India up to about 1,500 m while the **pied myna** (*Sturnus contra*, 23 cm) is restricted to northern and central India. The rose-ringed parakeet often forms huge flocks, an impressive sight coming in to roost. The long tail is noticeable both in flight and when the bird is perched. They can be very destructive to crops, but are attractive birds which are frequently kept as pets. The pied myna, with its smart black and white plumage is conspicuous, usually in small flocks in grazing land or cultivation. It feeds on the ground and on village rubbish dumps. The all black **drongo** (*Dicrurus adsimilis*, 30 cm) is almost invariably seen perched on telegraph wires or bare branches. Its distinctively forked tail makes it easy to identify.

Weaver birds are a family of mainly yellow birds, all remarkable for the intricate nests they build. The most widespread is the **baya weaver** (*Ploceus philippinus*, 15cm) which nest in large colonies, often near villages. The male in the breeding season combines a black face and throat with a contrasting yellow top of the head and the yellow breast band. In the non-breeding season both sexes are brownish sparrow-like birds.

**Hill birds** Land above about 1,500 m supports a distinct range of species, although some birds, such as the ubiquitous **common myna**, are found in the highlands as well as in the lower lying terrain.

The highland equivalent of the red-vented bulbul is the **white-cheeked bulbul** (*Pycnonotus leucogenys*, 20 cm) which is found in gardens and woodland in the Himalaya up to about 2,500 m and as far south as Mumbai. It has white underparts with a yellow patch under the tail. The black head and white cheek patches are distinctive. The crest varies in length and is most prominent in birds found in Kashmir, where it is very common in gardens. The **red-whiskered bulbul** (*Pycnonotus jocosus*, 20 cm) is widespread in the Himalaya and the hills of South India up to about 2,500 m. Its pronounced pointed crest, which is sometimes so long that it flops forward towards the bill, white underparts and red and white 'whiskers' serve to distinguish it. It has a red patch under the tail.

In the summer the delightful **verditer flycatcher** (*Muscicapa thalassina*, 15 cm) is a common breeding bird in the Himalaya up to about 3,000 m. It is tame and confiding, often builds its nest on verandahs and is seen perching on telegraph wires. In winter it is much more widely distributed throughout the country. It is an active little bird which flicks its tail up and down in a characteristic manner. The male is all bright blue green with somewhat darker wings and a black patch in front of the eyes. The female is similar, but duller.

Another species associated with man is the **white wagtail** (*Motacilla alba*, 21 cm), very common in the Himalayan summer up to about 3,000 m. It is found near water, by streams and lakes, on floating vegetation and among the house boats in Kashmir. Its black and white plumage and constantly wagging tail make it easy to identify.

Yet another species common in Kashmir and in other Himalayan hill stations is the **red-billed blue magpie** (*Urocissa erythrorhyncha*, 65 cm). With a long tail and pale blue plumage, contrasting with its black head, it is usually seen in small flocks as it flies from tree to tree. This is not so much a garden bird, but prefers tea gardens, open woodland and cultivation.

The highlands of India, especially the Himalaya, are the home of the ancestors of **domestic hens** and also of numerous beautiful **pheasants**. These are mainly forest dwellers and are not easy to see as they tend to be shy and wary of man.

Last but not least, mention must be made of India's national bird, the magnificent and well-known **Peafowl** (*Pavo cristatus*, male 210 cm, female 100 cm), which is more commonly known as the peacock. Semi-domesticated birds are commonly seen and heard around towns and villages, especially in the northwest of India. In the wild it favours hilly jungles and dense scrub.



## Reptiles and amphibians

India is famous for its reptiles, especially its snakes which feature in many stories and legends. In reality, snakes keep out of the way of people. One of the most common is the **Indian rock python** (*Python molurus*) a 'constrictor' which kills it's prey by suffocation. Usually about 4 m in length, they can be much longer. Their docile nature make them favourites of snake handlers.

The other large snakes favoured by street entertainers are cobras. The various species all have a hood which is spread when the snake draws itself up to strike. They are all highly venomous and the snake charmers prudently de-fang them to render them harmless. The best known is probably the **spectacled cobra** (*Naja naja*), which has a mark like a pair of spectacles on the back of its hood. The largest venomous snake in the world is the **king cobra** (*Ophiophagus hannah*) which is 5 m in length. It is usually brown, but can vary from cream to black and lacks the spectacle marks of the other. In their natural state cobras are generally inhabitants of forest regions.

Equally venomous, but much smaller, the **common krait** (*Bungarus caeruleus*) is just over 1 m in length. The slender, shiny, blue-black snake has thin white bands which can sometimes be almost indiscernible. They are found all over the country except in the northeast where the canniballistic **banded krait** with bold yellowish and black bands have virtually eradicated them.

In houses everywhere you cannot fail to see the **gecko** (*Hemidactylus*). This small harmless, primitive lizard is active after dark. It lives in houses behind pictures and curtain rails and at night emerges to run across the walls and ceilings to hunt the night flying insects which form its main prey. It is not usually more than about 14 cm long, with a curiously transparent, pale yellowish brown body. At the other end of the scale is the **monitor lizard** (*Varanus*), which can grow to 2 m in length. They can vary from a colourful black and yellow, to plain or speckled brown. They live in different habitats from cultivation and scrub to waterside places and desert.

The most widespread crocodile is the freshwater **mugger** or Marsh crocodile (*Crocodilus palustrus*) which grows to 3-4 m in length. The only similar fresh water species is the **gharial** (*Gavialis gangeticus*) which lives in large, fast flowing rivers. Twice the length of the mugger, it is a fish-eating crocodile with a long thin snout and, in the case of the male, an extraordinary bulbous growth on the end of the snout. The enormous, aggressive **estuarine** or **saltwater crocodile** (*Crocodilus porosus*) is now restricted to the brackish waters of the Sundarbans, on the east coast and in the Andaman and Nicobar Islands. It grows to 7 m in length and is much sleeker looking than the rather docile mugger.

# Books

The literature on India is as huge and varied as the subcontinent itself. India is a good place to buy English language books as foreign books are often much cheaper than the published price. There are also cheap Indian editions and occasionally reprints of out-of-print books. There are excellent bookshops in all the major Indian cities. Below are a few suggestions.

## Art and architecture

**T Richard Burton** *Hindu Art*, British Museum P. Well illustrated; a broad view of art and religion.
**Ilay Cooper and Barry Dawson** *Traditional Buildings of India*, Thames & Hudson.
**George Michell** *The Hindu Temple*, Univ of Chicago Press, 1988. An authoritative account of Hindu architectural development.
**Henri Sterlin** *Hindu India*. Köln, Taschen, 1998. Traces the development from early rock-cut shrines, detailing famous examples; clearly written, well illustrated.
**Giles Tillotson** *The Rajput Palaces*, Yale, 1987; *Mughal architecture*, London, Viking, 1990; *The tradition of Indian architecture*, Yale 1989. Superbly clear writing on development of Indian architecture under Rajputs, Mughals and the British.
**NS Ramaswami** *Temples of South India*, Chennai, Maps and Agencies, 1996.
**KR Srinivasan**'s *Temples of South India*, 3rd ed, New Delhi, National Book Trust, 1985, have good background information.

## Cities, sites and places

### Aurangabad

**C Berkson** *The caves of Aurangabad*, Mapin, Ahmadabad, 1986.

### Delhi

**Barton, G, and Malone, L** *Old Delhi: 10 easy walks*. Delhi, Rupa, 1988. An interesting companion with which to explore the old city, helpful maps.
**Kaul, H, Ed** *Historic Delhi: an anthology*. Delhi, OUP, 1985.
**Sainty, S** *Lost monuments of Delhi*. Delhi, Harper Collins, 1997. A booklet covering Islamic architecture in brief.
**Sharma, YD** *Delhi and its neighbourhood*. Delhi, ASI, 1972. History, architecture and site details.

### Dharamshala

**Avedon**, *In exile from the land of the snows*.
**Dalai Lama** *My land and my people* and *Freedom in Exile*.

**Norbu and Turnbull** *Tibet: Its history, religion and people*.
**Sogyal Rinpoche** *The Tibetan Book of Living and Dying*.

### Goa

**Anthony Hutt** *Goa: A Traveller's Historical and Architectural Guide*. An extensive, richly illustrated book.
**S Rajagopalan**, ASI's *Old Goa*.

### Gujarat

*Royal Families and Palaces of Gujarat*. Scorpion Cavendish,1998. £39 (paperback £29). Beautifully produced.
**SH Desai** *Junagadh and Girnar*.
**KV Soundara Rajan** *Junagadh*, an ASI booklet, 1985. Details the edicts and Buddhist caves on Uparkot.

### Hampi

**Longhurst**'s *Hampi Ruins*. Recommended.
**Settar**'s *Hampi* (both at *Aspirations Bookshop*, Hampi Bazar).

### Kanpur

**Manohar Malgaonkar** *The Devil's Wind: Nana Saheb's story*, 1988, New Delhi. Largely factual.
**George Otto Trevelyan** *Cawnpore*, 1992, Delhi.
**Andrew Ward** *Our bones are scattered*, 1996, New York.

### Khajuraho

**D Desai**'s *Religious Imagery of Khajuraho*. Good ASI booklet by Krishna Deva, Rs 5; detailed edition with colour plates, Rs 400. March 2000.
**Punja**'s *A Divine Ecstasy*, Viking (Penguin, India), 1992, carries an original interpretation.

### Kullu

**Penelope Chetwode** *Kulu, to the end of the habitable world*, John Murray, 1972. Chronicles her travels from Narkanda to Ani and over the Jalori Pass to Banjar and Aut in the Tirthan valley. Penelope Chetwode died a peaceful death near Khanag while travelling along this route during the early 1990s.

### Ladakh

**H Harres** *Ladakh*, Innsbruck, 1980.
**Andrew Harvey** *A Journey in Ladakh*, Cape, London, 1983.
**Helena Norberg-Hodge** *Ancient Futures: Learning from Ladakh*, Rider, London, 1992.
**Paldang** *Monasteries of Ladakh*.
**J Rizvi** *Ladakh, Crossroads of High Asia*, OUP, Delhi, 1983.
**Eric Shipton** *That Untravelled World*.
**M Singh** *Himalayan art*, UNESCO, 1971.
**DL Snellgrove and T Skorupski** *The Cultural Heritage of Ladakh*, Aris & Phillips, Delhi, 1977, 1980.

### Lucknow

**Rosie Llewellyn-Jones** *A fatal friendship: the Nawab, the British and the city of Lucknow*, 1992, OUP, Delhi. A lively guide to the city and its history. Her *A Very Ingenious Man* (1992, Delhi) follows the fortunes of Claude Martin.
**PJO Taylor** *A Companion to the Indian Mutiny of 1857*, 1996, OUP, Delhi. Includes an annotated bibliography.

Two books about the 'Uprising', particularly at Lucknow, are recommended:
**JG Farrell** *The Siege of Krishnapur*, a novel.
**Christopher Hibbert** *The Great Mutiny: India 1857*, Penguin. A factual history.

### Mahabalipuram

**Michael Lockwood** *Mahabalipuram and the Pandavas* Madras, Christian Literature Society, 1982.
**C Sivaramamurti** *Mahabalipuram* Fifth edition. New Delhi, Archaeological Survey of India, 1992.

### Sanchi

**Debala Mitra**, *Sanchi*, an Archaeological Survey of India Booklet.

### Shekhawati

**Ilay Cooper** *The painted towns of Shekhawati*, Mapin, Allahabad, 1994, has many colour photos and maps.
**P Rakesh and K Lewis** *Shekhawati: Rajasthan's painted houses*. Also well illustrated.

### Shimla

**JG Farrell**, *The Hill Station*. This last, unfinished novel describes colonial Shimla of 1871.
**Pamela Kanwar**'s Imperial Simla: the political culture of the Raj, OUP, New Delhi, 1990.
**Paul Scott** *Staying On*, Booker Prize winning novel set in post Independence Shimla.

### Varanasi

**GoI** *A Pilgrimage to Kashi*, Indica, 1999. Rs 275. An accessible cartoon strip - the city's

history and culture as discovered by modern day visitors.
**Jonathan P Parry** *Death in Banaras*, Cambridge UP, 1994.

### Zanskar

**Michel Peissel**, *Zanskar, the Hidden Kingdom.*
**Olivier Folloni** *Zanskar, a Himalayan Kingdom*, features superb photos.

## Current affairs and politics

**Patrick French** *Liberty or Death*, Harper Collins, 1997. Well researched and serious yet reads like a novel.
**Granta 57** *India: the Golden Jubilee* Superb edition devoted to India's 50th anniversary of Independence, twenty two international writers give brilliant snapshot accounts of India today.
**Sunil Khilnani** *The idea of India*, Penguin, 1997. Excellent introduction to contemporary India.
**Robert B Silver and Barbara Epstein** *India: a mosaic.* New York, NYRB, 2000. Distinguished essays on history, politics and literature including Amartya Sen on Tagore, Pankaj Mishra on nuclear India.
**Shashi Tharur** *India: from midnight to the millennium.* Viking, 1997.
**Mark Tully** *No full stops in India*, Viking, 1991. An often superbly observed but controversially interpreted view of contemporary India.

## History: medieval and modern

**John Beames** *Memoirs of a Bengal Civilian.* A readable insight into the British Raj in the post-Mutiny period, London, Eland, 1991.
**Michael Edwardes** *The Myth of the Mahatma.* Presents Gandhi in a whole new light.
**Rajmohan Gandhi** *The Good Boatman* Viking/Penguin 1995. An excellent biography by one of Gandhi's noted grandson's.
**Bamber Gascoigne** *The Great Moghuls*, London, Cape, 1987.
**John Keay** *India: a History*, Harper Collins, 2000. A major new popular history of the subcontinent.
**Jawaharlal Nehru** *The discovery of India*, New Delhi, ICCR, 1976.
**Francis Robinson** (ed) *Cambridge Encyclopaedia of India*, Cambridge, 1989. An introduction to many aspects of South Asian society.
**Percival Spear & Romila Thapar** *A history of India*, 2 vols, Penguin, 1978.
**Stanley Wolpert** *A new history of India*, OUP, 1990.

## History: pre-history and early history

**Bridget and Raymond Allchin** *Origins of a civilisation*, Viking, Penguin Books, 1997. The most authoritative up-to-date survey of the origins of Indian civilizations.
**AL Basham** *The Wonder that was India*, London, Sidgwick & Jackson, 1985. Still one of the most comprehensive and readable accounts of the development of India's culture.

## Language

**Rupert Snell and Simon Weightman** *Teach Yourself Hindi*. An excellent, accessible teaching guides with cassette tapes.
**H Yule and AC Burnell** (eds), *Hobson-Jobson*, 1886. New paperback edition, 1986. A delightful insight into Anglo-Indian words and phrases.

## Literature

**Upamanyu Chatterjee** *English August.* London, Faber, 1988. A wry account of a modern Indian Civil Servant's year spent in a rural posting.
**Nirad Chaudhuri** Four books give vivid, witty and often sharply critical accounts of India across the 20th century. *The autobiography of an unknown Indian*, Macmillan, London; *Thy Hand, Great Anarch!*, London, Chatto & Windus, 1987.
**Firdaus Kanga** *Trying to grow*, Bloomsbury, 1989; Mumbai life seen through the experiences of a Parsi family.
**Rohinton Mistry** *A fine balance.* Faber, 1995. A tale of the struggle to survive in the modern Indian city.
**VS Naipaul** *A million mutinies now*, Penguin, 1992. Naipaul's 'revisionist' account of India turns away from the despondency of his earlier two India books (*An Area of darkness* and *India: a wounded civilisation*).
**RK Narayan** has written many gentle and humorous novels and short stories of South

India. *The Man-eater of Malgudi* and *Under the Banyan tree and other stories*, *Grandmother's stories*, among many, London, Penguin, 1985.
**AK Ramanuja**: *The collected essays*. Ed by V Dhawadker. New Delhi, OUP, 1999. Brilliant essays on Indian culture and literature.
**Arundhati Roy** *The God of Small Things*. Indian Ink/Harper Collins, 1997. Excellent first novel about family turmoil in a Syrian Christian household in Kerala.
**Salman Rushdie** *Midnight's children*, London, Picador, 1981. A novel of India since Independence, offering at the same time funny and bitterly sharp critiques of South Asian life in the 1980s. *The Moor's Last Sigh*, Viking, 1996, is of particular interest to those travelling to Kochi and Mumbai.
**Paul Scott** *The Raj Quartet*, London, Panther, 1973; *Staying on*, Longmans, 1985. Outstandingly perceptive novels of the end of the Raj.
**Vikram Seth** *A Suitable Boy*, Phoenix House London, 1993. Prize winning novel of modern Indian life.
**Simon Weightman** (ed) *Travellers Literary Companion: the Indian Sub-continent*. An invaluable introduction to the diversity of Indian writing.

## Music and cinema

**Raghava R Menon** *Penguin Dictionary of Indian Classical Music*, Penguin New Delhi 1995.
**Lalit Mohan** *Bollywood, Popular Indian Cinema*, Joshi (Dakini).

## People

**Elisabeth Bumiller** *May you be the mother of one hundred sons*, Penguin, 1991. An American woman journalists' account of coming to understand the issues that face India's women today.
**Lakshmi Holmstrom** *The Inner Courtyard*, a series of short stories by Indian women, translated into English, Rupa, 1992.
**Norman Lewis** *A goddess in the stones*. An insight into tribal life in Orissa and Bihar.
**Sarah Lloyd** *An Indian Attachment*, London, Eland, 1992. A very personal and engaging account of time spent in an Indian village.

## Religion

**Wendy Doniger O'Flaherty** *Hindu Myths*, London, Penguin, 1974. A sourcebook translated from the Sanskrit.
**JP Jain** *Religion and Culture of the Jains*. 3rd ed. New Delhi, Bharatiya Jnanapith, 1981.
**IH Qureshi** *The Muslim Community of the Indo-Pakistan Sub-Continent 610-1947*, OUP, Karachi, 1977.
**Walpola Rahula** *What the Buddha Taught*.
**H Singh** *The heritage of the Sikhs*, 2nd ed. New Delhi, 1983.
**R Waterstone** *India, the cultural companion*, Duncan Baird, Winchester, 2002. India's spiritual traditions brought up to date, profusely illustrated.
**RC Zaehner** *Hinduism*, OUP.

## Travel

**William Dalrymple** *City of Djinns*, Indus/Harper Collins, 1993, paperback. Superb account of Delhi, based on a year living in the city. *The Age of Kali*, published in edited form in India as *In the court of the fish-eyed Goddess*, is his second anecdotal but insightful account.
**Trevor Fishlock** *Cobra Road*. London, John Murray, 1991. Impressions of a news journalist.
**Alexander Frater** *Chasing the monsoon*, London, Viking, 1990. A prize winning account of the human impact of the monsoon's sweep across India.
**John Hatt** *The tropical traveller: the essential guide to travel in hot countries*, Penguin, 3rd ed 1992. Wide ranging and clearly written common sense, based on extensive experience and research.
**John Keay** *Into India*. London, John Murray, 1999. Seasoned traveller's introduction to understanding and enjoying India.

## Trekking

**Bill Aitken** *The Nanda Devi Affair*, Penguin India, 1994.
**Chris Bonnington** *Annapurna South Face*, London, Cassell, 1971; Everest the hard way, London, Hodder & Stoughton, 1979.
**P Chabloz N Cremieu** *Hiking in Zanskar and Ladakh*, Geneva, Olizane, 1986.
**Justine Hardy** *The Ochre Border* 1995, Constable, London. An account of crossing

the Puri Parvati Pass from Kullu to Spiti.
**Edmund Hillary** *High Adventure*, New York, Dutton, 1955. Both classic accounts of Himalayan climbs.
**Harish Kapadia** *Spiti: Adventures in the Trans-Himalaya*, 1996, Indus.
**GD Khosla** *Himalayan Circuit*. 1989 OUP. An early account of travel into this then virtually unknown region of Kinnaur and Spiti.
**Charlie Loram** *Leh & Trekking in Ladakh* 1996. Trailblazer, Hindhead, Surrey.
**Audrey Salkeld** *The History of Great Climbs*, 1995 The Royal Geographical Society. A magnificently illustrated and written account of historic climbs.
**William Sax** *Mountain Goddess*, OUP, 1991; both about Nanda Devi.
**Dhanu Swadi and Deepak Sanan** *Exploring Kinnaur and Spiti in the Trans-Himalaya*, 1998, Indus.

More practical publications include:
**G Chand and M Puri** *Explore Himachal*, New Delhi, International Publishers, 1991. Descriptions of 110 routes and 27 detailed trekking maps.
**T Iozawa** *Trekking in the Himalayas*, Delhi, Allied Publishers, 1980. *Nest & Wings*, Post Box 4531, New Delhi 110016, T6442245: 'Trekking', 'Holiday & Trekking' and 'Trekking Map' titles (Rs 40-140) cover most trekking destinations in the Indian Himalaya; trekking itineraries are listed in brief but some booklets give additional insight into the history and culture of the area.
**Hugh Swift** *Trekking in Pakistan and India*, London, Hodder & Stoughton, 1990. Detailed practical guide, based on extensive first hand experience.

Also useful are:
**Himalayan Club's** *Himalayan Journal* (annual) from PO Box 1905, Mumbai 400001.
**Indian Mountaineering Foundation's** Indian Mountaineer (six-monthly) from Benito Juarez Rd, New Delhi 110021. *Peaks and passes of the Garhwal Himalaya* published by Alpinists Club, 1990.

## Wildlife and vegetation

**Salim Ali** *Indian hill birds*, OUP.
**Salim Ali and S Dillon Ripley** *Handbook of the birds of India & Pakistan* (compact ed).
**DV Cowen** *Flowering Trees and Shrubs in India*.
**Martin Ewans** *Bharatpur: Bird Paradise*, Lustre Press, Delhi.
**R Grimmet and C & T Inskipp** *Pocket guide to Birds of the Indian Sub-Continent*. 1999.
**Richard Ives** *Of tigers and men*, Doubleday, 1995.
**Krys Kazmierczak & Raj Singh** *A birdwatcher's guide to India*. Prion, 1998, Sandy, Beds, UK. Well researched and carrying lots of practical information for all birders.
**SM Nair** *Endangered animals of India*, New Delhi, NBT, 1992.
**O Polunin & A Stainton** *Flowers of the Himalaya*, OUP, 1984.
**SH Prater** *The Book of Indian Animals*.
**S Sippy and S Kapoor** *The Ultimate Ranthambhore Guide*, 2001. Informative, practical guide stressing conservation.
**Thapar and Rathore** *Wild tigers of Ranthambhore* OUP, 2000.

## Wildlife and vegetation

# Footnotes

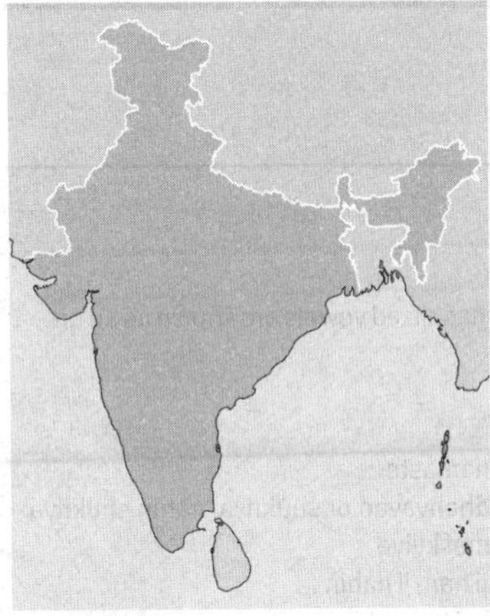

# Language

## Hindi words and phrases

### Pronunciation

a as in ah
o as in oh
i as in bee
u as oo in book
nasalized vowels are shown as an un

### Basics

| | |
|---|---|
| Hello, good morning, goodbye | namaste |
| Thank you/no thank you | dhanyavad or shukriya/nahin shukriya |
| Excuse me, sorry | maf kijiye |
| Yes/no | ji han/ji nahin |
| nevermind/that's all right | koi bat nahin |

### Questions

| | |
|---|---|
| What is your name? | apka nam kya hai? |
| My name is... | mera nam... Hai |
| Pardon? | phir bataiye? |
| How are you? | kya hal hai? |
| I am well, thanks, and you? | main thik hun, aur ap? |
| Not very well | main thik nahin hun |
| Where is the? | kahan hai? |
| Who is? | kaun hai? |
| What is this? | yeh kya hai? |

### Shopping

| | |
|---|---|
| How much? | Kitna? |
| That makes (20) rupees | (bis) rupaye |
| That is very expensive! | bahut mahanga hai! |
| Make it a bit cheaper! | thora kam kijiye! |

### The hotel

| | |
|---|---|
| What is the room charge? | kiraya kitna hai? |
| Please show the room | kamra dikhaiye |
| Is there an airconditioned room? | kya a/c kamra hai? |
| Is there hot water? | garam pani hai? |
| ... a bathroom/fan/mosquito net | ... bathroom/pankha/machhar dani |
| Is there a large room? | bara kamra hai? |
| Please clean it | saf karwa dijiye |
| Are there clean sheets/blanket? | saf chadaren/kambal hain? |
| Bill please | bill dijiye |

### Travel

| | |
|---|---|
| Where's the railway station? | railway station kahan hai? |
| How much is the ticket to Agra? | Agra ka ticket kitne ka hai? |
| When does the Agra bus leave? | Agra bus kab jaegi? |
| How much? | Kitna? |
| left/right | baien/dahina |
| go straight on | sidha chaliye |
| nearby | nazdik |

| | |
|---|---|
| Please wait here | yahan thahariye |
| Please come at 8 | ath bajai ana |
| quickly | jaldi |
| stop | rukiye |

## Restaurants

| | |
|---|---|
| Please show the menu | menu dikhaiye |
| No chillis please | mirch nahin dalna |
| ...sugar/milk/ice | ...chini/doodh/baraf |
| A bottle of water please | ek botal pani dijiye |
| sweet/savoury | mitha/namkin |
| spoon, fork, knife | chamach, kanta, chhuri |

## Time and days

| | | | |
|---|---|---|---|
| right now | abhi | month | mahina |
| morning | suba | year | sal |
| afternoon | dopahar | Sunday | ravivar |
| evening | sham | Monday | somvar |
| night | rat | Tuesday | mangalvar |
| today | aj | Wednesday | budhvar |
| tomorrow/yesterday | kal/kal | Thursday | virvar |
| day | din | Friday | shukravar |
| week | hafta | Saturday | shanivar |

## Numbers

| | | | |
|---|---|---|---|
| 1 | ek | 13 | terah |
| 2 | do | 14 | chaudah |
| 3 | tin | 15 | pandrah |
| 4 | char | 16 | solah |
| 5 | panch | 17 | satrah |
| 6 | chhai | 18 | atharah |
| 7 | sat | 19 | unnis |
| 8 | ath | 20 | bis |
| 9 | nau | 100/200 | sau/do sau |
| 10 | das | 1000/2000 | hazar/do hazar |
| 11 | gyara | 100,000 | lakh |
| 12 | barah | | |

## Basic vocabulary

Words such as airport, bank, bathroom, bus, doctor, embassy, ferry, hotel, hospital, juice, police, restaurant, station, stamp, taxi, ticket, train are used locally though often pronounced differently eg daktar, haspatal.

| | | | |
|---|---|---|---|
| and | aur | open | khula |
| big | bara | police station | thana |
| café/food stall | dhaba/hotel | road | rasta |
| chemist | dawai ki dukan | room | kamra |
| clean | saf | shop | dukan |
| closed | band | sick (ill) | bimar |
| cold | thanda | silk | reshmi/silk |
| day | din | small | chhota |
| dirty | ganda | that | who |

| | | | |
|---|---|---|---|
| English | angrezi | this | yeh |
| excellent | bahut achha | town | shahar |
| food/ to eat | khana | water | pani |
| hot (spicy) | jhal, masaledar | what | kya |
| hot (temp) | garam | when | kab |
| luggage | saman | where | kahan/kidhar |
| medicine | dawai | which/who | kaun |
| newspaper | akhbar | why | kiun |
| of course, sure | zaroor | with | ke sathh |

## Food and drink

Eating out is normally cheap and safe but menus can often be dauntingly long and full of unfamiliar names. Here are some Hindi words to help you. Pronunciation is explained on page 1368.

### Meat and fish

| | |
|---|---|
| gosht, mas | meat, usually mutton (sheep) |
| jhinga | prawns |
| macchli | fish |
| murgh | chicken |

### Vegetables (sabzi)

| | | | |
|---|---|---|---|
| aloo | potato | khumbhi | mushroom |
| baingan | aubergine | matar | peas |
| band gobi | cabbage | piaz | onion |
| bhindi | okra, ladies' fingers | phool gobi | cauliflower |
| gajar | carrots | sag | spinach |

### Styles of cooking

Many items on restaurant menus are named according to methods of preparation, roughly equivalent to terms such as 'Provençal' or 'sauté'.

**bhoona** in a thick, fairly spicy sauce
**chops** minced meat, fish or vegetables, covered with mashed potato,crumbed and fried
**cutlet** minced meat, fish, vegetables formed into flat rounds or ovals, crumbed and fried (eg prawn cutlet, flattened king prawn)
**do piaza** with onions (added twice during cooking)
**dumphuk** steam baked
**jhal frazi** spicy, hot sauce with tomatoes and chillies
**jhol** thin gravy (Bengali)
**Kashmiri** cooked with mild spices, ground almonds and yoghurt, often with fruit
**kebab** skewered (or minced and shaped) meat or fish; a dry spicy dish cooked on a fire
**kima** minced meat (usually 'mutton')
**kofta** minced meat or vegetable balls
**korma** in fairly mild rich sauce using cream /yoghurt
**masala** marinated in spices (fairly hot)
**Madras** hot
**makhani** in butter rich sauce
**moli** South Indian dishes cooked in coconut milk and green chilli sauce
**Mughlai** rich North Indian style
**Nargisi** dish using boiled eggs

**navratan curry** ('9 jewels') colourful mixed vegetables and fruit in mild sauce
**Peshwari** rich with dried fruit and nuts (Northwest Indian)
**tandoori** baked in a tandoor (special clay oven) or one imitating it
**tikka** marinated meat pieces, baked quite dry
**vindaloo** hot and sour Goan meat dish using vinegar

## Typical dishes

**aloo gosht** potato and mutton stew
**aloo gobi** dry potato and cauliflower with cumin
**aloo, matar, kumbhi** potato, peas, mushrooms in a dryish mildly spicy sauce
**bhindi bhaji** lady's fingers fried with onions and mild spices
**boti kebab** marinated pieces of meat, skewered and cooked over a fire
**dal makhani** lentils cooked with butter
**dum aloo** potato curry with a spicy yoghurt, tomato and onion sauce
**matar panir** curd cheese cubes with peas and spices (and often tomatoes)
**murgh massallam** chicken in creamy marinade of yoghurt, spices and herbs with nuts
**nargisi kofta** boiled eggs covered in minced lamb, cooked in a thick sauce
**rogan josh** rich, mutton/beef pieces in creamy, red sauce
**sag panir** drained curd (panir) sautéd with chopped spinach in mild spices
**sarson-ke-sag** and **makkai-ki-roti** mustard leaf cooked dry with spices served with maize four roti from Punjab
**shabdeg** a special Mughlai mutton dish with vegetables
**yakhni** lamb stew

## Rice

**bhat/sada chawal** plain boiled rice
**biriyani** partially cooked rice layered over meat and baked with saffron
**khichari** rice and lentils cooked with turmeric and other spices
**pulao/pilau** fried rice cooked with spices (cloves, cardamom, cinnamon) with dried fruit, nuts or vegetables. Sometimes cooked with meat, like a biriyani

## Roti – breads

**chapati (roti)** thin, plain, wholemeal unleavened bread cooked on a tawa (griddle), usually made from ata (wheat flour). Makkaikiroti is with maize flour.
**nan** oven baked (traditionally in a tandoor) white flour leavened bread often large and triangular; sometimes stuffed with almonds and dried fruit
**paratha** fried bread layered with ghi (sometimes cooked with egg or with potatoes)
**poori** thin deepfried, puffed rounds of flour

## Sweets

These are often made with reduced/thickened milk, drained curd cheese or powdered lentils and nuts. They are sometimes covered with a flimsy sheet of decorative, edible silver leaf.

**barfi** fudgelike rectangles/diamonds
**gulab jamun** dark fried spongy balls, soaked in syrup
**halwa** rich sweet made from cereal, fruit, vegetable, nuts and sugar
**khir, payasam, paesh** thickened milk rice/vermicelli pudding
**kulfi** coneshaped Indian ice cream with pistachios/almonds, uneven in texture
**jalebi** spirals of fried batter soaked in syrup
**laddoo** lentil based batter 'grains' shaped into rounds
**rasgulla (roshgulla)** balls of curd in clear syrup
**sandesh** dry sweet made of curd cheese

## Snacks

**bhaji, pakora** vegetable fritters (onions, potatoes, cauliflower etc) deep-fried in batter
**chat** sweet and sour fruit and vegetables flavoured with tama rind paste and chillis
**chana choor, chioora ('Bombay mix')** lentil and flattened rice snacks mixed with nuts and dried fruit
**dosai** South Indian pancake made with rice and lentil flour; served with a mild potato and onion filling (masala dosai) or without (ravai or plain dosai)
**idli** steamed South Indian rice cakes, a bland breakfast given flavour by spiced accompaniments
**kachori** fried pastry rounds stuffed with spiced lentil/ peas/potato filling
**samosa** cooked vegetable or meat wrapped in pastry triangles and deep fried
**utthappam** thick South Indian rice and lentil flour pancake cooked with spices/onions/tomatoes
**vadai** deep fried, small savoury lentil 'doughnut' rings. **Dahi vada** are similar rounds in yoghurt

# Glossary

Words in italics are common elements of words, often making up part of a place name

## A

**aarti** (arati) Hindu worship with lamps
**abacus** square or rectangular table resting on top of a pillar
***abad*** peopled
**acanthus** thick-leaved plant, common decoration on pillars, esp Greek
***achalam*** hill (Tamil)
**acharya** religious teacher
**Adi Granth** Guru Granth Sahib, holy book of the Sikhs
**Adinatha** first of the 24 Tirthankaras, distinguished by his bull mount
**agarbathi** incense
**Agastya** legendary sage who brought the Vedas to South India
**Agni** Vedic fire divinity, intermediary between gods and men; guardian of the Southeast
**ahimsa** non-harming, non-violence
**akhand path** unbroken reading of the Guru Granth Sahib
**alinda** verandah
**ambulatory** processional path
**amla/amalaka** circular ribbed pattern (based on a gourd) at the top of a temple tower
**amrita** ambrosia; drink of immortality
**ananda** joy
**Ananda** the Buddha's chief disciple
**Ananta** a huge snake on whose coils Vishnu rests
**anda** literally 'egg', spherical part of the stupa
**Andhaka** demon killed by Siva
**anicut** irrigation channel (Tamil)
**anna** (ana) one sixteenth of a rupee (still occasionally referred to)
**Annapurna** Goddess of abundance; one aspect of Devi
**antarala** vestibule, chamber in front of shrine or cella
**antechamber** chamber in front of the sanctuary
**apsara** celestial nymph
**apse** semi-circular plan
**arabesque** ornamental decoration with intertwining lines
**aram** pleasure garden
**architrave** horizontal beam across posts or gateways
**ardha mandapam** chamber in front of main hall of temple
**Ardhanarisvara** Siva represented as half-male and half-female
**Arjuna** hero of the Mahabharata, to whom Krishna delivered the Bhagavad Gita
**arrack** alcoholic spirit fermented from potatoes or grain
***aru*** river (Tamil)
**Aruna** charioteer of Surya, Sun God; Red
**Aryans** literally 'noble' (Sanskrit); prehistoric peoples who settled in Persia and North India
**asana** a seat or throne (Buddha's) pose
**ashram** hermitage or retreat
**Ashta Matrikas** The eight mother goddesses who attended on Siva or Skanda
**astanah** threshold
**atman** philosophical concept of universal soul or spirit
**atrium** court open to the sky in the centre In modern architecture, enclosed in glass
**aus** summer rice crop (Apr-Aug) Bengal
**Avalokiteshwara** Lord who looks down; Bodhisattva, the Compassionate
**avatara** 'descent'; incarnation of a divinity
**ayacut** irrigation command area (Tamil)
**ayah** nursemaid, especially for children

## B

**babu** clerk
**bada** cubical portion of a temple up to the roof or spire
**badgir** rooftop structure to channel cool breeze into the house (mainly North and West India)
**badlands** eroded landscape
**bagh** garden
**bahadur** title, meaning 'the brave'
**baksheesh** tip 'bribe'
**Balabhadra** Balarama, elder brother of Krishna
**baluster** (balustrade) a small column supporting a handrail
**bandh** a strike
**bandhani** tie dyeing (West India)
**Bangla** (Bangaldar) curved roof, based on thatched roofs in Bengal
**bania** merchant caste
**banian** vest
**baoli or vav** rectangular well surrounded by steps
**baradari** literally 'twelve pillared', a pavilion with columns
**barrel-vault** semi-cylindrical shaped roof or ceiling
**bas-relief** carving of low projection
**basement** lower part of walls, usually with decorated mouldings
**basti** Jain temple
**batter** slope of a wall, especially in a fort
**bazar** market
**bedi** (vedi) altar/platform for reading holy texts
**begum** Muslim princess/woman's courtesy title
**beki** circular stone below the amla in the finial of a roof
**belvedere** summer house; small room on a house roof
**bhabar** coarse alluvium at foot of Himalayas
**bhadra** flat face of the sikhara (tower)
**Bhadrakali** Tantric goddess and consort of Bhairav

**Bhagavad-Gita** Song of the Lord; section of the Mahabharata
**Bhagiratha** the king who prayed to Ganga to descend to earth
**bhai** brother
**Bhairava** Siva, the Fearful
**bhakti** adoration of a deity
**bhang** Indian hemp
**bharal** Himalayan blue sheep
**Bharata** half-brother of Rama
**bhavan** building or house
**bhikku** Buddhist monk
**Bhima** Pandava hero of the Mahabharata, famous for his strength
**Bhimsen** Deity worshipped for his strength and courage
**bhisti** a water-carrier
**bhogamandapa** the refectory hall of a temple
**bhumi** literally earth; a horizontal moulding of a sikhara
**bidi** (beedi) Indian cigarette, tobacco wrapped in tendu leaves
**bigha** measure of land – normally about one-third of an acre
**bo-tree** (or Bodhi) *Ficus religiosa*, pipal tree associated with the Buddha
**Bodhisattva** Enlightened One, destined to become Buddha
**bodi** tuft of hair on back of the shaven head (also *tikki*)
**Brahma** Universal self-existing power; Creator in the Hindu Triad.
**Brahmachari** religious student, accepting rigorous discipline (eg chastity)
**Brahman** (Brahmin) highest Hindu (and Jain) caste of priests
**Brahmanism** ancient Indian religion, precursor of modern Hinduism
**Buddha** The Enlightened One; founder of Buddhism
**bund** an embankment
**bundh** (literally closed) a strike
**burj** tower or bastion
**burqa** (burkha) over-dress worn by Muslim women observing purdah
**bustee** slum

## C

**cantonment** planned military or civil area in town
**capital** upper part of a column
**caryatid** sculptured human female figure used as a support for columns
**catamaran** log raft, logs (*maram*) tied (*kattu*) together (Tamil)
**cave temple** rock-cut shrine or monastery
**cella** small chamber, compartment for the image of a deity
**cenotaph** commemorative monument, usually an open domed pavilion
**chaam** Himalayan Buddhist masked dance
**chadar** sheet worn as clothing
**chai** tea
**chaitya** large arched opening in the façade of a hall or Buddhist temple
**chajja** overhanging cornice or eaves
**chakra** sacred Buddhist wheel of the law; also Vishnu's discus
**chala** Bengali curved roof
**Chamunda** terrifying form of the goddess Durga
**Chandra** Moon; a planetary deity
**chankramana** place of the promenade of the Buddha at Bodh Gaya
**chapati** unleavened Indian bread cooked on a griddle
**chaprassi** messenger or orderly usually wearing a badge
**char** sand-bank or island in a river
**char bagh** formal Mughal garden, divided into quarters
**char bangla** (char-chala) 'four temples' in Bengal, built like huts
**charan** foot print
**charka** spinning wheel
**charpai** 'four legs' – wooden frame string bed
**chatt(r)a** ceremonial umbrella on stupa (Buddhist)
**chauki** recessed space between pillars: entrance
**chaukidar** (chowkidar) night-watchman; guard
**chaultri** (choultry) travellers' rest house (Telugu)
**chaumukha** Jain sanctuary with a quadruple image, approached through four doorways
**chauri** fly-whisk, symbol for royalty
**chauth** 25% tax raised for revenue by Marathas
**cheri** outcaste settlement; slum (Tamil Nadu)
**chhang** strong mountain beer of fermented barley maize rye or millet or rice
**chhatri** umbrella shaped dome or pavilion
**chhetri** (kshatriya) Hindu warrior caste
**chikan** shadow embroidery on fine cotton (especially in Lucknow)
**chikki** nut crunch, a speciality of Lonavla
**chit sabha** hall of wisdom (Tamil)
**chitrakar** picture maker
**chlorite** soft greenish stone that hardens on exposure
**chogyal** heavenly king (Sikkim)
**choli** blouse
**chorten** Himalayan Buddhist relic shrine or memorial stupa
**chowk** (chauk) a block; open place in a city where the market is held
**chunam** lime plaster or stucco made from burnt seashells
**circumambulation** clockwise movement around a shrine
**clerestory** upper section of the walls of a building which allows light in
**cloister** passage usually around an open square
**coir** fibre from coconut husk
**corbel** horizontal block supporting a vertical structure or covering an opening
**cornice** horizontal band at the top of a wall
**crenellated** having battlements
**crewel work** chain stitching
**crore** 10 million

**cupola** small dome
**curvilinear** gently curving shape, generally of a tower
**cusp, cusped** projecting point between small sections of an arch

## D

**daal** lentils, pulses
**dacoit** bandit
**dada** (dadu) grandfather; elder brother
**dado** part of a pedestal between its base and cornice
**dahi** yoghurt
**dais** raised platform
**dak bungalow** rest house for officials
**dak** post
**dakini** sorceress
**Dakshineshvara** Lord of the South; name of Siva
**dan** gift
**dandi** wooden 'seat' carried by bearers
**darbar** (durbar) a royal gathering
**dargah** a Muslim tomb complex
**darshan** (darshana) viewing of a deity or spiritual leader
**darwaza** gateway, door
**Dasara** (dassara/dussehra/dassehra) 10 day festival (Sep-Oct)
**Dasaratha** King of Ayodhya and father of Rama
**Dattatraya** syncretistic deity; an incarnation of Vishnu, a teacher of Siva, or a cousin of the Buddha
**daulat khana** treasury
**dentil** small block used as part of a cornice
**deodar** Himalayan cedar; from *deva-daru*, the 'wood of the gods'
**dervish** member of Muslim brotherhood, committed to poverty
**deul** in Bengal and Orissa, generic name for temple; the sanctuary
**deval** memorial pavilion built to mark royal funeral pyre
**devala** temple or shrine (Buddhist or Hindu)
**devasthanam** temple trust
**Devi** Goddess; later, the Supreme Goddess
**dhaba** roadside restaurant (mainly North India) truck drivers' stop
**dhansak** Parsi dish made with lentils
**dharamshala** (dharamsala) pilgrims' rest-house
**dharma** moral and religious duty
**dharmachakra** wheel of 'moral' law (Buddhist)
**dhobi** washerman
**dhol** drums
**dhooli** (dhooli) swinging chair on a pole, carried by bearers
**dhoti** loose loincloth worn by Indian men
**dhyana** meditation
**digambara** literally 'sky-clad' Jain sect in which the monks go naked
***dighi*** village pond (Bengal)
**dikka** raised platform around ablution tank
**dikpala** guardian of one of the cardinal directions mostly appearing in a group of eight
**dikshitar** person who makes oblations or offerings
**dipdan** lamp pillar
**distributary** river that flows away from main channel
**divan (diwan)** smoking-room; also a chief minister
**Diwali** festival of lights (Oct-Nov)
**diwan-i-am** hall of public audience
**diwan-i-khas** hall of private audience
**diwan** chief financial minister
**do-chala** rectangular Bengali style roof
**doab** interfluve, land between two rivers
**dokra** tribal name for lost wax metal casting (cire perdu)
**dosai** (dosa) thin pancake
**double dome** composed of an inner and outer shell of masonry
**Draupadi** wife-in-common of the five Pandava brothers in the Mahabharata
***drug*** (*durg*) fort (Tamil, Telugu)
**dry masonry** stones laid without mortar
**duar** (dwar) door, gateway
**dun** valley
**dupatta** long scarf worn by Punjabi women
**Durga** principal goddess of the Shakti cult
**durrie** (dhurrie) thick handloom rug
**durwan** watchman
**dvarpala** doorkeeper
**dvipa** lamp-column, generally of stone or brass-covered wood

## E

**eave** overhang that shelters a porch or verandah
**ek** the number 1, a symbol of unity
**ekka** one horse carriage
**epigraph** carved inscription
***eri*** tank (Tamil)

## F

**faience** coloured tilework, earthenware or porcelain
**fakir** Muslim religious mendicant
**fan-light** fan-shaped window over door
**fenestration** with windows or openings
**filigree** ornamental work or delicate tracery
**finial** emblem at the summit of a stupa, tower, dome, or at the end of a parapet
**firman** edict or grant issued by a sovereign
**foliation** ornamental design derived from foliage
**frieze** horizontal band of figures or decorative designs

## G

**gable** end of an angled roof
**gadba** woollen blanket (Kashmir)
**gaddi** throne
**gadi/gari** car, cart, train
**gali** (galli) lane; an alley
**gana** child figures in art
**Gandharva** semi-divine flying figure; celestial musician
**Ganesh** (Ganapati) elephant-headed son of Siva and Parvati
**Ganga** goddess personifying the Ganges
***ganj*** market

**ganja** Indian hemp
***gaon*** village
**garbhagriha** literally 'womb-chamber'; a temple sanctuary
***garh*** fort
**Garuda** Mythical eagle, half-human Vishnu's vehicle
**Gauri** 'Fair One'; Parvati
**Gaurishankara** Siva with Parvati
**ghagra** (ghongra) long flared skirt
**ghanta** bell
**ghat** hill range, hill road; landing place; steps on the river bank
**ghazal** Urdu lyric poetry/love songs, often erotic
**ghee** clarified butter for cooking
**gherao** industrial action, surrounding home or office of politician or industrial manager
**giri** hill
**Gita Govinda** Jayadeva's poem of the Krishnalila
**godown** warehouse
**gola** conical-shaped storehouse
**gompa** Tibetan Buddhist monastery
**goncha** loose woollen robe, tied at waist with wide coloured band (Ladakh)
**Gopala** (Govinda) cowherd; a name of Krishna
**Gopis** cowherd girls; milk maids who played with Krishna
**gopuram** towered gateway in South Indian temples
**Gorakhnath** historically, an 11th-century yogi who founded a Saivite cult; an incarnation of Siva
**gosain** monk or devotee (Hindi)
**gram** chick pea, pulse
***gram*** village; gramadan, gift of village
**gudi** temple (Karnataka)
**gumbaz** (gumbad) dome
**gumpha** monastery, cave temple
**gur gur** salted butter tea (Ladakh)
**gur** palm sugar
**guru** teacher; spiritual leader, Sikh religious leader
**gurudwara** (literally 'entrance to the house of God'); Sikh religious complex

## H

**Haj** (Hajj) annual Muslim pilgrimage to Mecca
**hakim** judge; a physician (usually Muslim)
**halwa** a special sweet meat
**hammam** Turkish bath
**handi** Punjabi dish cooked in a pot
**Hanuman** Monkey devotee of Rama; bringer of success to armies
**Hara** (Hara Siddhi) Siva
**harem** women's quarters (Muslim), from 'haram', Arabic for 'forbidden by law'
**Hari** Vishnu Harihara, Vishnu- Siva as a single divinity
**Hariti** goddess of prosperity and patroness of children, consort of Kubera
**harmika** the finial of a stupa in the form of a pedestal where the shaft of the honorific umbrella was set
**hartal** general strike
**Hasan** the murdered eldest son of Ali, commemorated at Muharram
**hat** (haat) market
**hathi pol** elephant gate
**hathi** (hati) elephant
**hauz** tank or reservoir
**haveli** a merchant's house usually in Rajasthan
**havildar** army sergeant
**hawa mahal** palace of the winds
**Hidimba Devi** Durga worshipped at Manali
**hindola** swing
**hippogryph** fabulous griffin-like creature with body of a horse
**Hiranyakashipu** Demon king killed by Narasimha
**hiti** a water channel; a bath or tank with water spouts
**Holi** spring festival (Feb-Mar)
**hookah** 'hubble bubble' or smoking vase
**howdah** seat on elephant's back, sometimes canopied
**hundi** temple offering
**Hussain** the second murdered son of Ali, commemorated at Muharram
**huzra** a Muslim tomb chamber
**hypostyle** hall with pillars

## I

**lat** pillar, column
**icon** statue or image of worship
**Id** principal Muslim festivals
**Idgah** open space for the Id prayers
**idli** steamed rice cake (Tamil)
**ikat** 'resist-dyed' woven fabric
**imam** Muslim religious leader
**imambara** tomb of a Shiite Muslim holy man; focus of Muharram procession
**Indra** King of the gods; God of rain; guardian of the East
**Ishana** Guardian of the North East
**Ishvara** Lord; Siva
**iwan** main arch in mosque

## J

**jadu** magic
**jaga mohan** audience hall or ante-chamber of an Orissan temple
**Jagadambi** literally Mother of the World; Parvati
**Jagannath** literally Lord of the World; particularly, Krishna worshipped at Puri
**jagati** railed parapet
**jaggery** brown sugar, made from palm sap
**jahaz** ship: building in form of ship
**jali** literally 'net'; any lattice or perforated pattern
**jamb** vertical side slab of doorway
**Jambudvipa** Continent of the Rose-Apple Tree; the earth
**Jami masjid** (Jama, Jumma) Friday mosque, for congregational worship
**Jamuna** Hindu goddess who rides a tortoise; river
**Janaka** Father of Sita
**jangha** broad band of sculpture on the outside of the temple wall
**jarokha** balcony

**jataka stories** accounts of the previous lives of the Buddha
**jatra** Bengali folk theatre
**jauhar** (jauhar) mass suicide by fire of women, particularly in Rajasthan, to avoid capture
**jawab** literally 'answer,' a building which duplicates another to provide symmetry
**jawan** army recruit, soldier
**jaya stambha** victory tower
**jheel** (jhil) lake; a marsh; a swamp
**jhilmil** projecting canopy over a window or door opening
**-ji** (jee) honorific suffix added to names out of reverence and/or politeness; also abbreviated 'yes' (Hindi/Urdu)
**jihad** striving in the way of god; holy war by Muslims against non-believers
**Jina** literally 'victor'; spiritual conqueror or Tirthankara, after whom Jainism is named
**Jogini** mystical goddess
**jorbangla** double hut-like temple in Bengal
**Jyotirlinga** luminous energy of Siva manifested at 12 holy places, miraculously formed lingams

## K

**kabalai** (kavalai) well irrigation using bullock power (Tamil Nadu)
**kabigan** folk debate in verse
**kachcha** man's 'under-shorts' (one of five Sikh symbols)
**kacheri** (kutchery) a court; an office for public business
**kadal** wooden bridge (Kashmir)
**kadhi** savoury yoghurt curry (Gujarat/North India)
***kadu*** forest (Tamil)
**Kailasa** mountain home of Siva
**kalamkari** special painted cotton hanging from Andhra
**kalasha** pot-like finial of a tower
**Kali** literally 'black'; terrifying form of the goddess Durga, wearing a necklace of skulls/heads
**Kalki** future incarnation of Vishnu on horseback
**kalyanamandapa** marriage hall
**kameez** women's shirt
**kanga** comb (one of five Sikh symbols)
**kankar** limestone pieces, used for road making
**kantha** Bengali quilting
**kapok** the silk cotton tree
**kara** steel bracelet (one of five Sikh symbols)
**karma** impurity resulting from past misdeeds
**Kartikkeya** (Kartik) Son of Siva, God of war
**kashi-work** special kind of glazed tiling, probably derived from Kashan in Persia
**kati-roll** Muslim snack of meat rolled in a 'paratha' bread
**kattakat** mixed brain, liver and kidney (Gujarat)
**keep** tower of a fort, stronghold
***kere*** tank (Kanarese)
**keystone** central wedge-shaped block in a masonry arch
**khadi** woven cotton cloth made from home-spun cotton (or silk) yarn
**khal** creek; a canal
***khana*** suffix for room/office/place; also food or meal
**khanqah** Muslim (Sufi) hospice
**kharif** monsoon season crop
**khave khana** tea shop
**kheda** enclosure in which wild elephants are caught; elephant depot
***khet*** field
**khola** river or stream in Nepal
**khondalite** crudely grained basalt
**khukri** traditional curved Gurkha weapon
**kirpan** sabre, dagger (one of five Sikh symbols)
**kirti-stambha** 'pillar of fame,' free standing pillar in front of temple
**kohl** antimony, used as eye shadow
***konda*** hill (Telugu)
**kos minars** Mughal 'mile' stones
**kot** (kota/kottai/kotte) fort
**kothi** house
**kotla** citadel
***kovil*** (koil) temple (Tamil)
**Krishna** Eighth incarnation of Vishnu
**kritis** South Indian devotional music
**Kubera** Chief yaksha; keeper of the treasures of the earth, Guardian of the North
***kulam*** tank or pond (Tamil)
**kumar** a young man
**Kumari** Virgin; Durga
**kumbha** a vase-like motif, pot
**Kumbhayog** auspicious time for bathing to wash away sins
**kumhar** (kumar) potter
**kund** lake, well or pool
**kundan** jewellery setting of uncut gems (Rajasthan)
**kuppam** hamlet (Tamil)
**kurta** Punjabi shirt
**kurti-kanchali** small blouse
**kutcha** (cutcha/kacha) raw; crude; unpaved; built with sun-dried bricks
**kwabgah** bedroom; literally 'palace of dreams'

## L

***la*** Himalayan mountain pass
**lakh** 100,000
**Lakshmana** younger brother of Rama
**Lakshmi** Goddess of wealth and good fortune, consort of Vishnu
**Lakulisha** founder of the Pashupata sect, believed to be an incarnation of Siva
**lama** Buddhist priest in Tibet
**lassi** iced yoghurt drink
**lath** monolithic pillar
**lathi** bamboo stick with metal bindings, used by police
**lena** cave, usually a rock-cut sanctuary
**lingam** (linga) Siva as the phallic emblem
**Lingaraja** Siva worshipped at Bhubaneswar
**lintel** horizontal beam over doorway
**liwan** cloisters of a mosque
**Lokeshwar** 'Lord of the World', Avalokiteshwara to Buddhists and form of Siva to Hindus

**lunette** semicircular window opening
**lungi** wrapped-around loin cloth, normally checked

## M

**madrassa** Islamic theological school or college
**mahamandapam** large enclosed hall in front of main shrine
**maha** great
**Mahabharata** Sanskrit epic about the battle between the Pandavas and Kauravas
**Mahabodhi** Great Enlightenment of Buddha
**Mahadeva** literally 'Great Lord'; Siva
**mahal** palace, grand building
**mahalla** (mohulla) division of a town; a quarter; a ward
**mahant** head of a monastery
**maharaja** great king
**maharana** Rajput clan head
**maharani** great queen
**maharishi** (Maharshi) literally 'great teacher'
**Mahavira** literally 'Great Hero'; last of the 24 Tirthankaras, founder of Jainism
**Mahayana** The Greater Vehicle; form of Buddhism practised in East Asia, Tibet and Nepal
**Mahesha** (Maheshvara) Great Lord; Siva
**Mahisha** Buffalo demon killed by Durga
**mahout** elephant driver/keeper
**mahseer** large freshwater fish found especially in Himalayan rivers
**maidan** large open grassy area in a town
**Maitreya** the future Buddha
**makara** crocodile-shaped mythical creature symbolizing the river Ganga
**makhan** butter
***malai*** hill (Tamil)
**mali** gardener
**Manasa** Snake goddess; Sakti
**manastambha** free-standing pillar in front of temple
**mandala** geometric diagram symbolizing the structure of the Universe
***mandalam*** region, tract of country (Tamil)
**mandapa** columned hall preceding the temple sanctuary
***mandi*** market
**mandir** temple
**mani** (mani wall) stones with sacred inscriptions at Buddhist sites
**mantra** chant for meditation by Hindus and Buddhists
**maqbara** chamber of a Muslim tomb
**Mara** Tempter, who sent his daughters (and soldiers) to disturb the Buddha's meditation
**marg** wide roadway
**masjid** literally 'place of prostration'; mosque
**mata** mother
**math** Hindu or Jain monastery
**maulana** scholar (Muslim)
**maulvi** religious teacher (Muslim)
**maund** measure of weight about 20 kilos
**mausoleum** large tomb building
**maya** illusion
**medallion** circle or part-circle framing a figure or decorative motif
**meena** enamel work
**mela** festival or fair, usually Hindu
**memsahib** married European woman, term used mainly before Independence
**Meru** mountain supporting the heavens
**mihrab** niche in the western wall of a mosque
**mimbar** pulpit in mosque
**Minakshi** literally 'fish-eyed'; Parvati
**minar** (minaret) slender tower of a mosque
**mitthai** Indian sweets
**mithuna** couple in sexual embrace
**mofussil** the country as distinct from the town
**Mohammad** 'the praised'; The Prophet; founder of Islam
**moksha** salvation, enlightenment; literally 'release'
**momos** Tibetan stuffed pastas
**monolith** single block of stone shaped into a pillar
**moonstone** the semi circular stone step before a shrine (also chandrasila)
**mouza** (mowza) village; a parcel of land having a separate name in the revenue records
**mridangam** barrel-shaped drum (musical)
**muballigh** second prayer leader
**mudra** symbolic hand gesture
**muezzin** mosque official who calls the faithful to prayer
**Muharram** period of mourning in remembrance of Hasan and Hussain, two murdered sons of Ali
**mukha** mandapa, hall for shrine
**mullah** religious teacher (Muslim)
**mund** Toda village
**muqarna** Muslim stalactite design
**mural** wall decoration
**musalla** prayer mat
**muta** limited duration marriage (Leh)
**muthi** measure equal to 'a handful'

## N

**nadi** river
***nadu*** region, country (Tamil)
**Naga** (nagi/nagini) Snake deity; associated with fertility and protection
**nagara** city, sometimes capital
**nakkar khana** (naggar or naubat khana) drum house; arched structure or gateway for musicians
**nal mandapa** porch over a staircase
**nallah** (nullah) ditch, channel
**namaaz** Muslim prayers, worship
**namaste** common Hindu greeting (with joined palms) translated as: 'I salute all divine qualities in you'
**namda** rug
**Nandi** a bull, Siva's vehicle and a symbol of fertility
**nara durg** large fort built on a flat plain
**Narayana** Vishnu as the creator of life
**nata mandapa** (nat-mandir; nritya sala) dancing hall in a temple
**Nataraja** Siva, Lord of the cosmic dance
***nath*** literally 'place' eg Amarnath
**natya** the art of dance

**nautch** display by dancing girls
**navagraha** nine planets, represented usually on the lintel or architrave of the front door of a temple
**navaranga** central hall of temple
**navaratri** literally '9 nights'; name of the Dasara festival
**nawab** prince, wealthy Muslim, sometimes used as a title
**niche** wall recess containing a sculpted image or emblem, mostly framed by a pair of pilasters
**Nihang** literally 'crocodile': followers of Guru Gobind Singh (Sikh)
**nirvana** enlightenment; literally 'extinguished'
**niwas** small palace
**nritya** pure dance

## O

**obelisk** tapering and usually monolithic stone shaft
**oriel** projecting window

## P

**pada** foot or base
**padam** dance which tells a story
**padma** lotus flower, Padmasana, lotus seat; posture of meditating figures
**paga** projecting pilaster-like surface of an Orissan temple
**pagoda** tall structure in several stories
***pahar*** hill
**paisa** (poisa) one hundredth of a rupee
**palanquin** covered litter for one, carried on poles
***palayam*** minor kingdom (Tamil)
**pali** language of Buddhist scriptures
***palli*** village
**pan** leaf of the betel vine; sliced areca nut, lime and other ingredients wrapped in leaf for chewing
**panchayat** a 'council of five'; a government system of elected councils
**pandal** marquee made of bamboo and cloth
**pandas** temple priests
**pandit** teacher or wise man; a Sanskrit scholar
**pankah** (punkha) fan, formerly pulled by a cord
**parabdis** special feeding place for birds
**parapet** wall extending above the roof
**pargana** sub-division of a district usually comprising many villages; a fiscal unit
**Parinirvana** the Buddha's state prior to nirvana, shown usually as a reclining figure
**parishads** political division of group of villages
**Parsi** (Parsee) Zoroastrians who fled from Iran to West India in the eighth century to avoid persecution
**parterre** level space in a garden occupied by flowerbeds
**Parvati** daughter of the Mountain; Siva's consort
**pashmina** fine wool from a mountain goat
**Pashupati** literally Lord of the Beasts; Siva
**pata** painted hanging scroll
***patan*** town or city (Sanskrit)
**patel** village headman
**patina** green film that covers materials exposed to the air
**pattachitra** specially painted cloth (especially Orissan)
**pau** measure for vegetables and fruit equal to 250 grams
**paya** soup
**pediment** mouldings, often in a triangular formation above an opening or niche
**pendant** hanging, a motif depicted upside down
**peon** servant, messenger (from Portuguese *peao*)
**perak** black hat, studded with turquoise and lapis lazuli (Ladakh)
**peristyle** range of columns surrounding a court or temple
**Persian wheel** well irrigation system using bucket lift
**pettah** suburbs, outskirts of town (Tamil: *pettai*)
**pice** (old form) 1/100th of a rupee
**picottah** water lift using horizontal pole pivoted on vertical pole (Tamil Nadu)
**pida deul** hall with a pyramidal roof in an Orissan temple
**pida** (pitha) basement
**pietra dura** inlaid mosaic of hard, semi-precious stones
**pilaster** ornamental small column, with capital and bracket
**pinjra** lattice work
**pinjrapol** animal hospital (Jain)
**pipal** Ficus religiosa, the Bodhi tree
**pir** Muslim holy man
**pitha** base, pedestal
**pithasthana** place of pilgrimage
**podium** stone bench; low pedestal wall
**pokana** bathing tank (Sri Lanka)
**pol** fortified gateway
**porch** covered entrance to a shrine or hall, generally open and with columns
**portico** space enclosed between columns
**pradakshina** patha processional passage
**prakaram** open courtyard
**pralaya** the end of the world
**prasadam** consecrated temple food
**prayag** confluence considered sacred by Hindus
**puja** ritual offerings to the gods; worship (Hindu)
**pujari** worshipper; one who performs puja (Hindu)
**pukka** literally 'ripe' or 'finished'; reliable; solidly built
**punya** merit earned through actions and religious devotion (Buddhist)
**Puranas** literally 'the old' Sanskrit sacred poems
**purdah** seclusion of Muslim women from public view (literally curtains)
**pushkarani** sacred pool or tank

## Q

**qabr** Muslim grave
**qibla** direction for Muslim prayer
**qila** fort
**Quran** holy Muslim scriptures
**qutb** axis or pivot

## R

**rabi** winter/spring season crop
**Radha** Krishna's favourite consort
**raj** rule or government
**raja** king, ruler (variations include rao, rawal)
**rajbari** palaces of a small kingdom
**Rajput** dynasties of western and central India
**Rakshakas** Earth spirits
**Rama** Seventh incarnation of Vishnu
**Ramayana** Sanskrit epic – the story of Rama
**Ramazan** (Ramadan) Muslim month of fasting
**rana** warrior (Nepal)
**rangamandapa** painted hall or theatre
**rani** queen
**rath** chariot or temple car
**Ravana** Demon king of Lanka; kidnapper of Sita
**rawal** head priest
**rekha** curvilinear portion of a spire or sikhara (rekha deul, sanctuary, curved tower of an Orissan temple)
**reredos** screen behind an altar
**rickshaw** 3-wheeled bicycle-powered (or 2-wheeled hand-powered) vehicle
**Rig (Rg) Veda** oldest and most sacred of the Vedas
**Rimpoche** blessed incarnation; abbot of a Tibetan Buddhist monastery (gompa)
**rishi** 'seer'; inspired poet, philosopher
**rumal** handkerchief, specially painted in Chamba (Himachal Pradesh)
**rupee** unit of currency in India
**ryot** (rayat/raiyat) a subject; a cultivator; a farmer

## S

**sabha** columned hall (sabha mandapa, assembly hall)
**sabzi** vegetables, vegetable curry
**sadar** (sadr/saddar) chief, main especially Sikh
**sadhu** ascetic; religious mendicant, holy man
**safa** turban (Rajasthan)
**sagar** lake; reservoir
**sahib** title of address, like 'sir'
**sahn** open courtyard of a mosque
**Saiva** (Shaiva) the cult of Siva
**sal** a hall
**sal** hardwood tree of the lower slopes of Himalayan foothills
**salaam** literally 'peace'; greeting (Muslim)
**salwar** (shalwar) loose trousers (Punjab)
**samadh(i)** literally concentrated thought, meditation; a funerary memorial
**sambar** lentil and vegetable soup dish, accompanying main meal (Tamil)
**samsara** transmigration of the soul
**samudra** large tank or inland sea
**sangam** junction of rivers
**sangarama** monastery
**sangha** ascetic order founded by Buddha
**sangrahalaya** rest-house for Jain pilgrims
**sankha** (shankha) the conch shell (symbolically held by Vishnu); the shell bangle worn by Bengali women
**sanyasi** wandering ascetic; final stage in the ideal life of a man
**sarai** caravansarai, halting place
**saranghi** small four-stringed viola shaped from a single piece of wood
**Saraswati** wife of Brahma and goddess of knowledge
**sarkar** the government; the state; a writer; an accountant
**sarod** Indian stringed musical instrument
**sarvodaya** uplift, improvement of all
**sati** (suttee) a virtuous woman; act of self-immolation on a husband's funeral pyre
**Sati** wife of Siva who destroyed herself by fire
**satyagraha** 'truth force'; passive resistance
**sayid** title (Muslim)
**schist** grey or green finely grained stone
**seer** (ser) weight (about 1 kg)
**sepoy** (sepai) Indian soldier, private
**serow** a wild Himalayan antelope
**seth** merchant, businessman
**seva** voluntary service
**shahtush** very fine wool from the Tibetan antelope
**Shakti** Energy; female divinity often associated with Siva
**shala** barrel-vaulted roof
**shalagrama** stone containing fossils worshipped as a form of Vishnu
**shaman** doctor/priest, using magic, exorcist
**shamiana** cloth canopy
**Shankara** Siva
**sharia** corpus of Muslim theological law
**shastras** ancient texts defining temple architecture
**shastri** religious title (Hindu)
**sheesh mahal** palace apartment with mirror work
**shehnai** (shahnai) Indian wind instrument like an oboe
**sherwani** knee-length coat for men
**Shesha** (Sesha) serpent who supports Vishnu
**shikar** hunting
**shikara** boat (Kashmir)
**shisham** a valuable building timber
**sikhara** curved temple tower or spire
**shloka** (sloka) Sanskrit sacred verse
**shola** patch of forest or wood (Tamil)
**sileh khana** armoury
**sindur** vermilion powder used in temple ritual; married women mark their hair parting with it (East India)
**singh** (sinha) lion; Rajput caste name adopted by Sikhs
**sinha stambha** lion pillar
**sirdar** a guide who leads trekking groups
**Sita** Rama's wife, heroine of the Ramayana epic
**sitar** classical stringed musical instrument with a gourd for soundbox
**Siva** (Shiva) The Destroyer in the Hindu triad of Gods
**Sivaratri** literally 'Siva's night'; a festival (Feb-Mar)
**Skanda** the Hindu god of war; Kartikkeya
**soma** sacred drink mentioned in the Vedas
**spandrel** triangular space between the curve of an arch and the square enclosing it
**squinch** arch across an interior angle

**sri** (shri) honorific title, often used for 'Mr'; repeated as sign of great respect
**sridhara** pillar with octagonal shaft and square base
**stalactite** system of vaulting, remotely resembling stalactite formations in a cave
**stambha** free-standing column or pillar, often for a lamp or figure
**steatite** finely grained grey mineral
**stele** upright, inscribed slab used as a gravestone
***sthan*** place (suffix)
**stucco** plasterwork
**stupa** hemispheric Buddhist funerary mound
**stylobate** base on which a colonnade is placed
**subahdar** (subedar) the governor of a province; viceroy under the Mughals
**Subrahmanya** Skanda, one of Siva's sons; Kartikkeya in South India
**sudra** lowest of the Hindu castes
**sufi** Muslim mystic; sufism, Muslim mystic worship
**sultan** Muslim prince (sultana, wife of sultan)
**Surya** Sun; Sun God
**svami** (swami) holy man; a suffix for temple deities
**svastika** (swastika) auspicious Hindu/ Buddhist cross-like sign
**swadeshi** home made goods
**swaraj** home rule
**swatantra** freedom

## T

**tabla** a pair of drums
**tahr** wild goat
**tahsildar** revenue collector
**taikhana** underground apartments
**takht** throne
**talao** (*tal*, talar) water tank
**taluk** administrative subdivision of a district
**tamasha** spectacle; festive celebration
**tandava** (dance) of Siva
**tank** lake dug for irrigation; a masonry- lined temple pool with stepped sides
**tapas** (tapasya) ascetic meditative self-denial
**Tara** literally 'star'; a goddess
**tarkashi** Orissan silver filigree
**tatties** cane or grass screens used for shade
**Teej** Hindu festival
**tehsil** subdivision of a district (North India)
**tempera** distemper; method of mural painting by means of a 'body,' such as white pigment
**tempo** three-wheeler vehicle
**terai** narrow strip of land along Himalayan foothills
**teri** soil formed from wind blown sand (Tamil Nadu)
**terracotta** burnt clay used as building material
**thakur bari temple** sanctuary (Bengal)
**thakur** high Hindu caste; deity (Bengal)
**thali** South and West Indian vegetarian meal
**thana** a police jurisdiction; police station
**thangka** (thankha) cloth (often silk) painted with a Tibetan Mahayana deity
**thug** professional robber/murderer (Central India)
**tiffin** snack, light meal
**tika** (tilak) vermilion powder, auspicious mark on the forehead; often decorative
**tikka** tender pieces of meat, marinated and barbecued
**tillana** abstract dance
**tirtha** ford, bathing place, holy spot (Sanskrit)
**Tirthankara** literally 'ford-maker'; title given to 24 religious 'teachers', worshipped by Jains
**tonga** two-wheeled horse carriage
**topi** (topee) pith helmet
**torana** gateway; two posts with an architrave
***tottam*** garden (Tamil)
**tribhanga** triple-bended pose for standing figures
**Trimurti** the Hindu Triad, Brahma, Vishnu and Siva
**tripolia** triple gateway
**trisul** the trident chief symbol of the god Siva
**triveni** triple-braided
**tsampa** ground, roasted barley, eaten dry or mixed with milk, tea or water (Himalayan)
***tso*** lake (Ladakh)
**tuk** fortified enclosure containing Jain shrines
**tulsi** sacred basil plant
**tykhana** underground room for use in hot weather (North India)
**tympanum** triangular space within cornices

## U

**Uma** Siva's consort in one of her many forms
**untouchable** 'outcastes', with whom contact of any kind was believed by high caste Hindus to be defiling
**Upanishads** ancient Sanskrit philosophical texts, part of the Vedas
***ur*** village (Tamil)
**usta** painted camel leather goods
**ustad** master
**uttarayana** northwards

## V

**vahana** 'vehicle' of the deity
**vaisya** the 'middle-class' caste of merchants and farmers
**Valmiki** sage, author of the Ramayana epic
**Vamana** dwarf incarnation of Vishnu
***vana*** grove, forest
**Varaha** boar incarnation of Vishnu
**varam** village (Tamil)
**varna** 'colour'; social division of Hindus into Brahmin, Kshatriya, Vaishya and Sudra
**Varuna** Guardian of the West, accompanied by Makara (see above)
**Vayu** Wind god; Guardian of the North-West
**Veda** (Vedic) oldest known Hindu religious texts
**vedi** (bedi) altar, also a wall or screen
**verandah** enlarged porch in front of a hall
**vihara** Buddhist or Jain monastery with cells around a courtyard
**vilas** house or pleasure palace
**vimana** towered sanctuary containing the cell in which the deity is enshrined
**vina** plucked stringed instrument, relative of sitar

**Vishnu** a principal Hindu deity; the Preserver (and Creator)

**vyala** (yali) leogryph, mythical lion-like sculpture

## W

***-wallah*** suffix often used with a occupational name, eg rickshaw-wallah

**wav** (vav) step-well, particularly in Gujarat and western India (baoli)

**wazir** chief minister of a raja (from Turkish 'vizier')

**wazwan** ceremonial meal (Kashmir)

## Y

**yagya** (yajna) major ceremonial sacrifice

**Yaksha** (Yakshi) a demi-god, associated with nature

**yali** see vyala

**Yama** God of death, judge of the living

**yantra** magical diagram used in meditation; instrument

**yatra** pilgrimage

**Yellow Hat** Gelugpa Sect of Tibetan Buddhism – monks wear yellow headdress

**yeti** mythical Himalayan animal often referred to as 'the abominable snowman'

**yoga** school of philosophy stressing mental and physical disciplines; yogi

**yoni** a hole symbolising female sexuality; vagina

**yura** water channel (Ladakh)

## Z

**zamindar** a landlord granted income under the Mughals

**zari** silver and gold thread used in weaving or embroidery

**zarih** cenotaph in a Muslim tomb

**zenana** segregated women's apartments

**ziarat** holy Muslim tomb

**zilla** (zillah) district

# Index

Abbreviations used for state references: A&N = Andaman & Nicobar Islands; AP = Andhra Pradesh; Ar = Arunachal Pradesh; As = Assam; Bi = Bihar; Chh = Chhattisgarh; Goa = Goa; Guj = Gujarat; HP = Himachal Pradesh; J&K = Jammu & Kashmir; Jh = Jharkhand; Kar = Karnataka; Ke = Kerala; Mah = Maharashtra; Meg = Meghalaya; Miz = Mizoram; MP = Madhya Pradesh; Man = Manipur; Nag = Nagaland; Or = Orissa; P&H = Punjab & Haryana; Raj = Rajasthan; Sik = Sikkim; TN = Tamil Nadu; Tri = Tripura; UP = Uttar Pradesh; Utt = Uttaranchal; WB = West Bengal.

## A



## B

## C

## D

## E



## F



## G

## L



## M

## N

## O



## P

## Q



## R



## S

## W



## Y



## Z

# Map index

# Advertisers' index

# Map symbols

## Administration

- Capital city
- Other city/town
- International border
- Regional border
- Disputed border

## Roads and travel

- Motorway
- Main road (National highway)
- Minor road
- Track
- Footpath
- Railway with station
- Airport
- Bus station
- Metro station
- Cable car
- Funicular
- Ferry

## Water features

- River, canal
- Lake, ocean
- Seasonal marshland
- Beach, sandbank
- Waterfall

## Topographical features

- Contours (approx)
- Mountain
- Volcano
- Mountain pass
- Escarpment
- Gorge
- Glacier
- Salt flat
- Rocks

## Cities and towns

- Main through route
- Main street
- Minor street
- Pedestrianized street
- Tunnel
- One way-street
- Steps
- Bridge
- Fortified wall
- Park, garden, stadium
- Sleeping
- Eating
- Bars & clubs
- Building
- Sight
- Cathedral, church
- Chinese temple
- Temple
- Meru
- Mosque
- Stupa
- Synagogue
- Tourist office
- Museum
- Post office
- Police
- Bank
- Internet
- Telephone
- Market
- Hospital
- Parking
- Petrol
- Golf
- Detail map
- Related map

## Other symbols

- Archaeological site
- National park, wildlife reserve
- Viewing point
- Campsite
- Refuge, lodge
- Castle
- Diving
- Deciduous/coniferous/palm trees
- Hide
- Vineyard
- Distillery
- Shipwreck
- Historic battlefield

# Credits

**Footprint credits**
**Editor**: Stephanie Lambe
**Map editor**: Sarah Sorensen
**Picture editor**: Claire Benison

**Publisher**: Patrick Dawson
**Editorial**: Alan Murphy, Sophie Blacksell, Sarah Thorowgood, Claire Boobbyer, Felicity Laughton, Nicola Jones
**Cartography**: Robert Lunn, Claire Benison, Kevin Feeney, Angus Dawson, Esther Monzón García, Thom Wickes
**Series development**: Rachel Fielding
**Design**: Mytton Williams and Rosemary Dawson (brand)
**Sales and marketing**: Andy Riddle
**Advertising**: Debbie Wylde
**Finance and administration**: Sharon Hughes, Elizabeth Taylor

**Photography credits**
**Front cover**: Alamy (Taj Mahal)
**Back cover**: SuperStock (Painted storks)
**Inside colour section**: SuperStock, Travel Ink

**Print**
Manufactured in India by Nutech Photolithographers. Pulp from sustainable forests

**Footprint feedback**
We try as hard as we can to make each Footprint guide as up to date as possible but, of course, things always change. If you want to let us know about your experiences – good, bad or ugly – then don't delay, go to **www.footprintbooks.com** and send in your comments.

**Publishing information**
Footprint India
14th edition

October 2005

ISBN 1 904 777 43 0
CIP DATA: A catalogue record for this book is available from the British Library



**Published by Footprint**
6 Riverside Court
Lower Bristol Road
Bath BA2 3DZ, UK
T +44 (0)1225 469141
F +44 (0)1225 469461
discover@footprintbooks.com
www.footprintbooks.com

**Distributed in the USA by**
Publishers Group West



Neither the black and white nor coloured maps are intended to have any political significance.

Every effort has been made to ensure that the facts in this guidebook are accurate. However, travellers should still obtain advice from consulates, airlines etc about travel and visa requirements before travelling. The authors and publishers cannot accept responsibility for any loss, injury or inconvenience however caused.

# Acknowledgements

Firstly, grateful thanks to Robert and Roma Bradnock for the enormous amount of work they put in to compiling the previous thirteen editions of this book.

Matt Barrett would also like to thank the following for their help and support:
The Martin family, Delhi
Judith Kent & Peter Holland
Tutu at Diggi Palace, Jaipur
Gazi at Hotel Golden City, Jaisalmer
Roberto
Julie Moore
Jolyon Moore
Ed Bastin
Samit Sawhny
Rajesh at Maya, Agra
Thomas Verstraeten
Petra & Mustapha, somewhere in their van
Roberto & Karen, Jodphur
Hari at Regent Hotel, Bikaner
Melany Marker at URMUL
Alison Barrett, wife extraordinaire

Annie Dare would also like to thank the following for their help and support:
In Goa, thanks to Kennedy, John Douglas Coutinho of Ciaran's Camp, Jack Ajit Sukhija at Panjim Inn, Margaret Mascarenhas, Heta Pandit at Goa Heritage and Phil Dane at YogaMagic.
In Mumbai, the Gopalakrishnan family, Cyrus Oshidar and Piyush Pandey. In Karnataka, Mahesh V at O&M and Dr Hemlata Rao at the Institute for Social and Economic Change.
In Mysore, Holly & Tony in Gokulum and Manohar Hillel at the Green Hotel.
In Kerala, KS Bhagwaldas, CP Moosa, Thalia Kennedy, Malayala Manorama's Jacob Matthew, Pioneer Travels' PD Joseph, Vinesh Vidya and particularly Shine Aroor.
In Tamil Nadu, Victor Dey, Megha Abraham, Pleasant Tours' Ian Fernandez and Visalakshi Ramaswamy from the M Rm Rm Cultural Foundation.
In Andhra Pradesh, Hyderabadi-based tour guide B Harshavardhan.
In Delhi, Rajnish and KK Gupta at Paradise.
In England, Vivek Angra of India Tourism and Footprint's Stephanie Lambe, Sarah Thorowgood, Laura Dixon. And above all to David, Jilly, Jenny, Lucy & Matt.

Finally thanks to Dr David Snashall, Dr Martin Taylor, Dr Anthony Bryceson for Health.

# Author biographies

## Matt Barrett

Born and raised in London, Matt first came to India as a wide-eyed 18-year-old in 1990, and then spent the next 10 years looking for an excuse to return. A chequered career path saw him painting prisons in Australia, studying Arabic in Yemen, building a clinic in Angola and starting a carpet business in London. In 1998 Matt met his wife, Alison, who was then, as now, working for the British Council in Delhi, meaning that at last he had that excuse he'd been after, and moved permanently to India in 2001. Matt now works as a motorbike and mountain bike tour leader, writer and father.

## Annie Dare

Annie Dare is a freelance journalist based in London. She has travelled to India both on assignment and independently since first spending four months, chiefly in Jammu and Kashmir, in 1995. She studied Indian literature, politics and British Imperialism on the sub-continent as part of her English Literature degree from the School of African and Asian Studies at Sussex University, Brighton. Besides travel, she also writes about the international creative industries.

# Complete title listing

**Footprint publishes travel guides to over 150 destinations worldwide. Each guide is packed with practical, concise and colourful information for everybody from first-time travellers to travel aficionados. The list is growing fast and current titles are noted below. Available from all good bookshops and online at www.footprintbooks.com**

**(P) denotes pocket guide**

**Latin America and Caribbean**
Argentina
Antigua & Leeward Islands (P)
Barbados (P)
Belize, Guatemala & Southern Mexico
Bolivia
Brazil
Caribbean Islands
Central America & Mexico
Chile
Colombia
Costa Rica
Cuba
Cusco & the Inca Trail
Dominican Republic
Ecuador & Galápagos
Guatemala
Havana (P)
Mexico
Nicaragua
Patagonia
Peru
Peru, Bolivia & Ecuador
Rio de Janeiro (P)
South American Handbook
St Lucia (P)
Venezuela

**North America**
Vancouver (P)
New York (P)
Western Canada

**Africa**
Cape Town (P)
East Africa
Egypt
Libya
Marrakech (P)
Morocco
Namibia
South Africa
Tunisia
Uganda

**Middle East**
Dubai (P)
Israel
Jordan
Syria & Lebanon

### Australasia
Australia
East Coast Australia
New Zealand
Sydney (P)
West Coast Australia

### Asia
Bali
Bangkok & the Beaches
Bhutan
Cambodia
Goa
Hong Kong (P)
India
Indian Himalaya
Indonesia
Laos
Malaysia & Singapore
Nepal
Northern Pakistan
Rajasthan
South India
Sri Lanka
Sumatra
Thailand
Tibet
Vietnam

### Europe
Andalucía
Barcelona (P)
Belfast (P)
Berlin (P)
Bilbao (P)
Bologna (P)
Britain
Cardiff (P)
Copenhagen (P)
Costa de la Luz (P)
Croatia
Dublin (P)
Edinburgh (P)
England
Glasgow (P)
Ireland
Lisbon (P)
London
London (P)
Madrid (P)
Naples (P)
Northern Spain
Paris (P)
Reykjavík (P)
Scotland
Scotland Highlands & Islands
Seville (P)
Siena (P)
Spain
Tallinn (P)
Turin (P)
Turkey
Valencia (P)
Verona (P)
Wales

### Lifestyle guides
Surfing Britain
Surfing Europe

Also available:
Traveller's Handbook (WEXAS)
Traveller's Healthbook (WEXAS)
Traveller's Internet Guide (WEXAS)

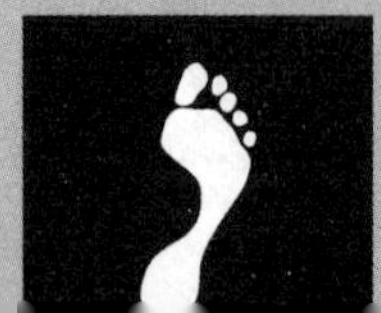

# What the papers say...

*"I carried the South American Handbook from Cape Horn to Cartagena and consulted it every night for two and a half months. I wouldn't do that for anything else except my hip flask."*
**Michael Palin, BBC Full Circle**

*"My favourite series is the Handbook series published by Footprint and I especially recommend the Mexico, Central and South America Handbooks."*
**Boston Globe**

*"If 'the essence of real travel' is what you have been secretly yearning for all these years, then Footprint are the guides for you."*
**Under 26 magazine**

*"Who should pack Footprint–readers who want to escape the crowd."*
**The Observer**

*"Footprint can be depended on for accurate travel information and for imparting a deep sense of respect for the lands and people they cover."*
**World News**

*"The guides for intelligent, independently-minded souls of any age or budget."*
**Indie Traveller**



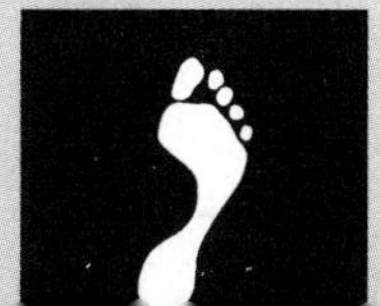

# The Footprint story: 1924-2005

**It was 1921**

Ireland had just been partitioned, the British miners were striking for more pay and the federation of British industry had an idea. Exports were booming in South America – how about a Handbook for businessmen trading in that far away continent? The *Anglo-South American Handbook* was born that year, written by W Koebel, the most prolific writer on Latin America of his day.

**1924**

Two editions later the book was 'privatized' and in 1924, in the hands of Royal Mail, the steamship company for South America, became *The South American Handbook*, subtitled 'South America in a nutshell'. This annual publication became the 'bible' for generations of travellers to South America and remains so to this day. In the early days travel was by sea and the Handbook gave all the details needed for the long voyage from Europe. What to wear for dinner; how to arrange a cricket match with the Cable & Wireless staff on the Cape Verde Islands and a full account of the journey from Liverpool up the Amazon to Manaus: 5898 miles without changing cabin!

**1939**

As the continent opened up, *The South American Handbook* reported the new Pan Am flying boat services, and the fortnightly airship service from Rio to Europe on the Graf Zeppelin. For reasons still unclear but with extraordinary determination, the annual editions continued through the Second World War.

**1970s**

From the 1970s, jet aircraft transformed travel. Many more people discovered South America and the backpacking trail started to develop. All the while the Handbook was gathering fans, including literary vagabonds such as Paul Theroux and Graham Greene (who once sent some updates addressed to **"The publishers of the best travel guide in the world, Bath, England"**.)

**1990s**

During the 1990s Patrick and James Dawson, the publishers of *The South American Handbook* set about developing a new travel guide series using this legendary title as the flagship. By 1997 there were over a dozen guides in the series and the Footprint imprint was launched.

**2000s**

In 2003, Footprint launched a new series of pocket format guides focusing on European short-break cities. By the end of 2004 there were over 100 Footprint travel guides covering more than 150 destinations around the world. In January 2004, *The South American Handbook* reached another milestone: 80 annual editions. Also in 2004, Footprint published its first activity guide, *Surfing Europe*, packed with 500 full-colour photographs and 70 maps and charts.

**The future**

A new range of full-colour guides was launched in 2005. There are also many other activity and travel guides in the pipeline. To keep up to date with the latest releases check out the Footprint website for all the latest news and information, **www.footprintbooks.com**.

# India

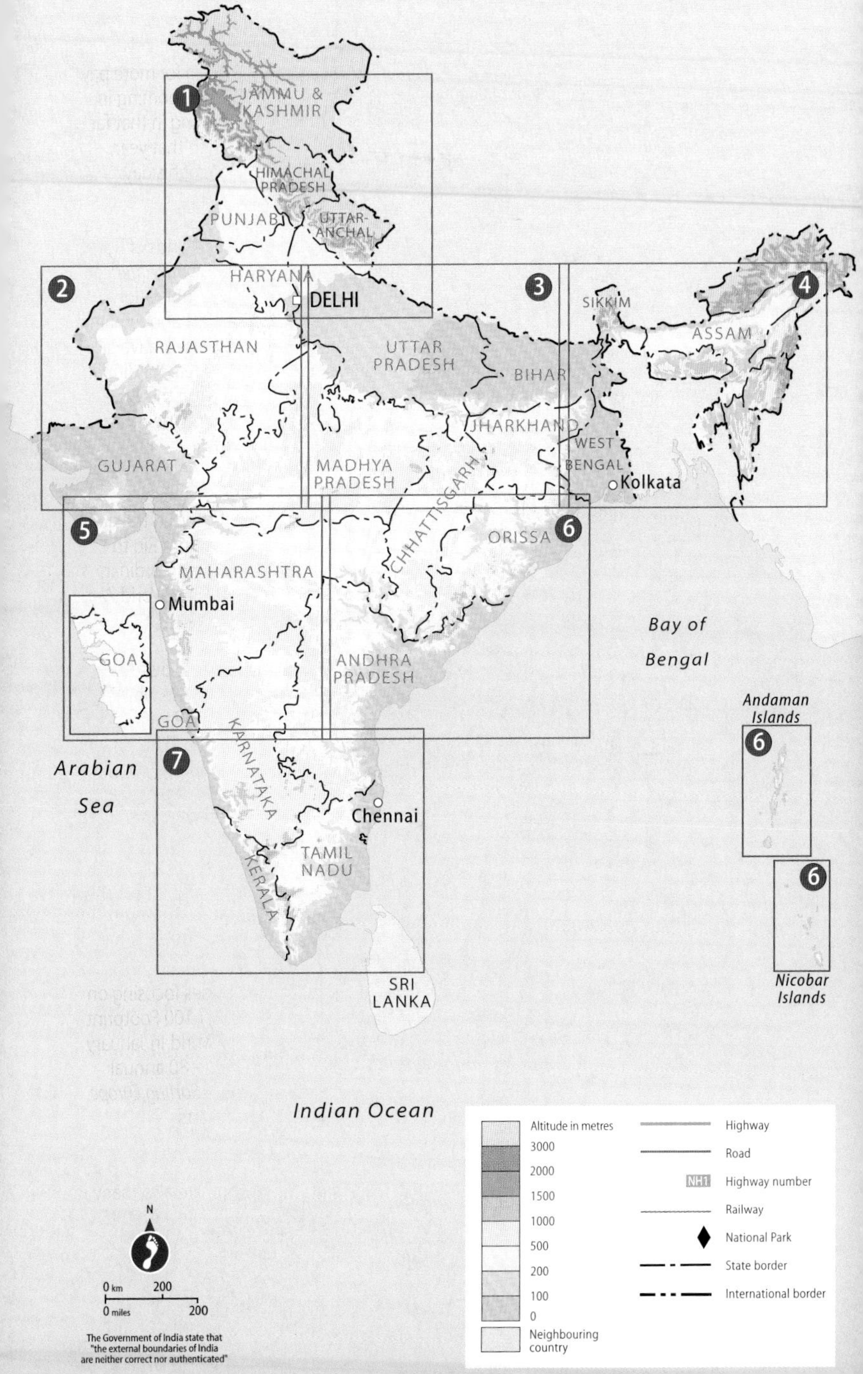

JAMMU &
KASHMIR
HIMACHAL
PRADESH
PUNJAB
UTTAR-
ANCHAL
HARYANA
DELHI
RAJASTHAN
UTTAR
PRADESH
BIHAR
SIKKIM
ASSAM
JHARKHAND
WEST
BENGAL
Kolkata
GUJARAT
MADHYA
PRADESH
CHHATTISGARH
ORISSA
MAHARASHTRA
Mumbai
GOA
ANDHRA
PRADESH
Bay of
Bengal
Andaman
Islands
Arabian
Sea
KARNATAKA
Chennai
TAMIL
NADU
KERALA
SRI
LANKA
Nicobar
Islands
Indian Ocean
1
2
3
4
5
6
7
Altitude in metres
3000
2000
1500
1000
500
200
100
0
Neighbouring
country
Highway
Road
NH1
Highway number
Railway
National Park
State border
International border
N
0 km
200
0 miles
200
The Government of India state that
"the external boundaries of India
are neither correct nor authenticated"

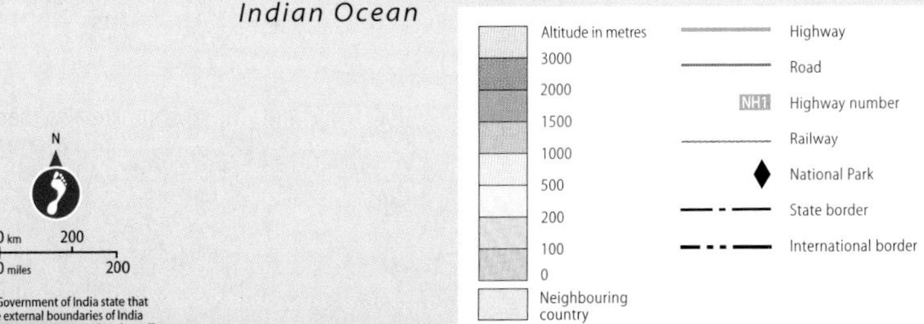

## Map 1

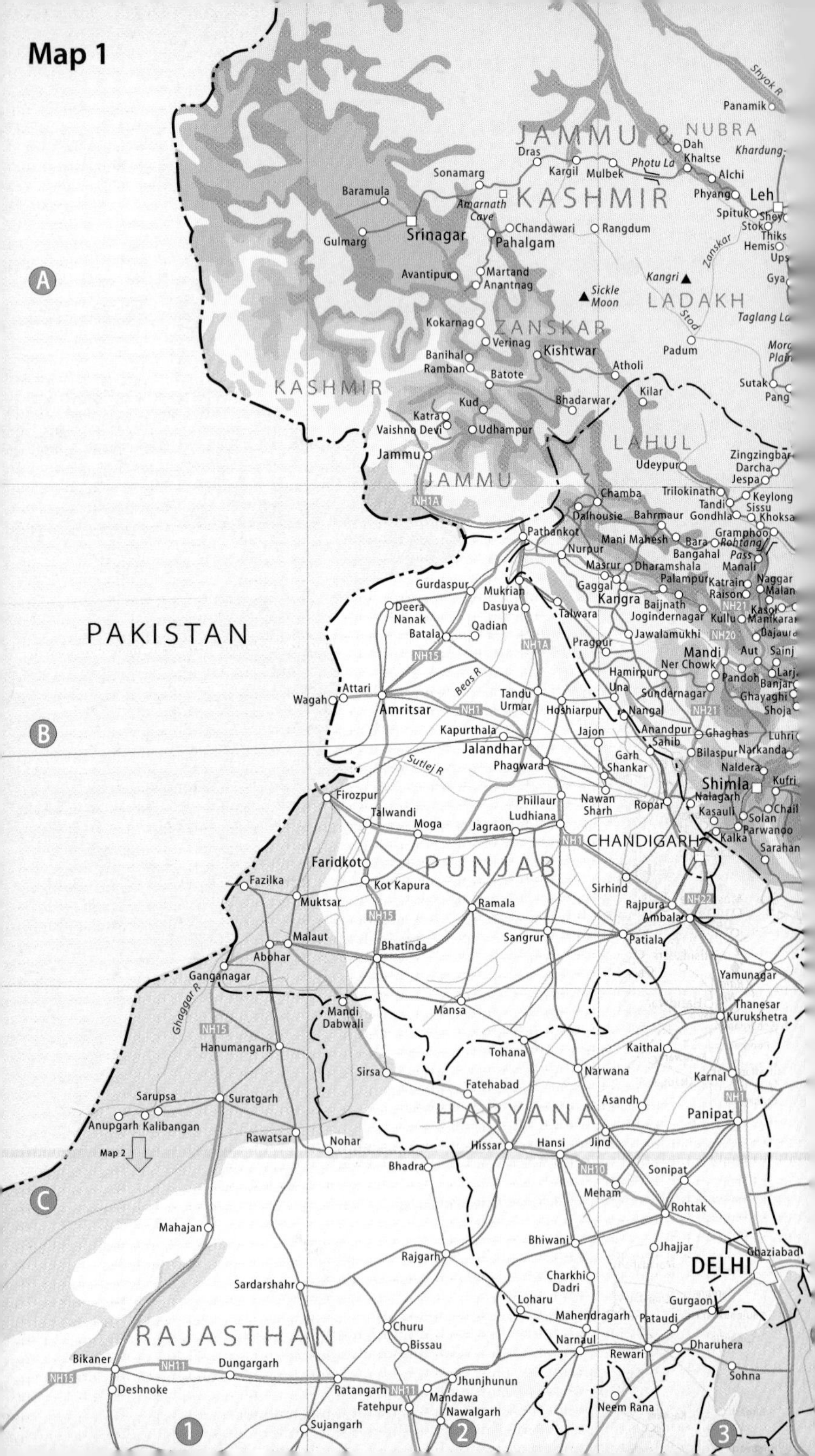

Map 1
Shyok R
Panamik
JAMMU & NUBRA
Dah
Dras
Khaltse
Kargil
Mulbek
Photu La
Alchi
Sonamarg
Baramula
Amarnath Cave
KASHMIR
Phyang
Leh
Spituk
Srinagar
Chandawari
Rangdum
Stok
Gulmarg
Pahalgam
Zanskar
Hemis
Avantipur
Martand
Anantnag
Kangri
A
Sickle Moon
LADAKH
Stod
Kokarnag
ZANSKAR
Verinag
Padum
Banihal
Kishtwar
Ramban
Atholi
Batote
Sutak
KASHMIR
Kilar
Kud
Bhadarwar
Katra
Vaishno Devi
Udhampur
LAHUL
Jammu
Udeypur
JAMMU
NH1A
Trilokinath
Chamba
Tandi
Keylong
Sissu
Dalhousie
Bahrmaur
Gondhla
Pathankot
Gramphoo
Mani Mahesh
Bara Bangahal
Rohtang Pass
Nurpur
Masrur
Dharamshala
Manali
Gurdaspur
Gaggal
Palampur
Katrain
Naggar
Mukrian
Kangra
Baijnath
Raison
Deera Nanak
Dasuya
Talwara
Jogindernagar
NH21
Kullu
PAKISTAN
Qadian
Jawalamukhi
NH20
Batala
NH1A
Pragpur
Mandi
Aut
NH15
Ner Chowk
Hamirpur
Pandoh
Beas R
Tandu Urmar
Una
Sundernagar
Ghayaghi
Attari
Wagah
Amritsar
NH1
Hoshiarpur
Nangal
NH21
Shoja
Kapurthala
Jajon
Anandpur Sahib
Ghaghas
B
Jalandhar
Garh Shankar
Bilaspur
Narkanda
Sutlej R
Phagwara
Naldera
Shimla
Kufri
Firozpur
Phillaur
Nawan Sharh
Ropar
Nalagarh
Chail
Talwandi
Ludhiana
Kasauli
Solan
Moga
Jagraon
Parwanoo
Kalka
NH1
CHANDIGARH
Sarahan
Faridkot
PUNJAB
Fazilka
Kot Kapura
Sirhind
Muktsar
Ramala
Rajpura
NH15
NH22
Ambala
Malaut
Sangrur
Patiala
Abohar
Bhatinda
Ganganagar
Yamunagar
Ghaggar R
Mandi Dabwali
Mansa
Thanesar
Kurukshetra
NH15
Hanumangarh
Tohana
Kaithal
Sirsa
Narwana
Karnal
Fatehabad
Sarupsa
Suratgarh
Asandh
NH1
Anupgarh
Kalibangan
HARYANA
Panipat
Rawatsar
Nohar
Hissar
Hansi
Jind
Map 2
Bhadra
NH10
Sonipat
C
Meham
Rohtak
Mahajan
Bhiwani
Jhajjar
Ghaziabad
Rajgarh
DELHI
Sardarshahr
Charkhi Dadri
Loharu
Gurgaon
Mahendragarh
Pataudi
Churu
RAJASTHAN
Narnaul
Rewari
Dharuhera
Bissau
Bikaner
Dungargarh
NH11
NH15
Sohna
Jhunjhunun
Deshnoke
Ratangarh
NH11
Mandawa
Fatehpur
Nawalgarh
Neem Rana
Sujangarh
1
2
3

TIBET
(CHINA)
NEPAL
HIMACHAL
PRADESH
UTTARANCHAL
UTTAR
PRADESH
RUPSHU
SPITI
Nubra R
Ladakh Range
Shyok
Tangtse
Lukung
Spangmik
Pangtong Tso
Indus R
Tashigong
Gardzong
Tso-Moriri
Sarchu
Bara Lacha Pass
Losar
Batal
Kibber
Kaza
Lalung
Dankar
Kungri Gompa
Tabo
Sumdo
Pin Valley NP
Gulling
Mudh
Sangam
Khabo
Puh
Wangtu
Kalpa
Jangi (Lippa)
Recong Peo
Sarahan
Sangla
Rampur Bushahr
Chitkul
Kailash
Yamunotri
Meru
Gangotri
Kedarnath
Badrinath
Hemkund
Barkot
Uttarkashi
Joshimath
Auli
Mussoorie
Tehri
Dehra Dun
Nanda Devi
Srinagar
Rishikesh
Deoprayag
Rudraprayag
Karnaprayag
Trisul
Byasi
Rajaji NP
Haridwar
Gwaldam
Larsho
Baijnath
Kausani
Saharanpur
Roorkee
Ranikhet
Pithorgarh
Kotdwara
Corbett NP
Almora
Muzaffarnagar
Nathjabad
Ramnagar
Nainital
Khatauli
Nagina
Bhowali
Kashipur
Kathgodam
Bijnor
Haldwani
Map 3
Tanakpur
Meerut
Lalkuan
Mahendranagar
Bilaspur
Banbassa
Kichha
Rampur
Pilibhit
Moradabad
Dudwa NP
Ramganga R
NH24
Hapur
Sambhal
Chandausi
Puranpur
Bulandshahr
Bareilly
Bisalpur
Mailani
Ghaghara R
Nepalganj Road
Khurja
Ganga R
Nanpara
Lakhimpur
Aligarh
Kasganj
Shahjahanpur
Vrindavan
A
B
C
4
5
6
N
0 km
50
0 miles
50
The Government of India state that "the external boundaries of India are neither correct nor authenticated"

## Map 2

PAKISTAN
A
B
C
1
2
3
N
0 km
50
0 miles
50
The Government of India state that "the external boundaries of India are neither correct nor authenticated"
Indira Gandhi Canal
Gajner NP
Kishangarh
Bhuttewal
Kolayat
NH15
Bap
Kakoo
Ramgarh
Ghotaru
Phalodi
Khichan
Jaisalmer
NH15
Pokaran
Sam
Thar Desert NP
Khuri
Osian
Dechhu
Balesar
Jodhpur
Shergarh (Garah)
Shiv
Luni
Gadra Road (Disused)
Barmer
Tilwara
Balotra
Basi
Samdari
Luni R
NH15
Jalor
Bhenswada
Ahor
Samdan
Daspan
Dhorimmana
Sheoganj
Bhinmal
Ramsen
NH14
Bera
Sirohi
Sanchore
Mt Abu
Abu Rd
Deesa
NH8
Balaram
Bhilari
Palanpur
Ambaji
Vav
Taranga
Lakhpat
Great Rann of Kachchh
Flamingo
NH15
NH14
Kakushi
Khavda
Suigem
Patan
Khedbrahma
Santalpur
Chanasma
Idar
Rapar
Sami
Visnagar
GUJARAT
NH15
Modhera
Mehsana
Himatnagar
Sabarmati
Nakhtrana
Rudrani Dam
Little Rann of Kachchh
Jinjwada
NH8
Naliya
Bhuj
NH8A
Dasada
Deshalpar
Samakhial
Kalaghoda
GANDHINAGAR
Patdi
Kalol
Bajana
NH8A
Wanku
Gandhidham
Viramgam
Kodai
Anjar
Kandla
Maliya
Halvad
Kapadvanj
Bhadreshwar
Dhangadra
Ahmadabad
Mandvi
Mundra
Nalsarovar NP
Morvi
Bavla
Gulf of Kachchh
Jodiya
Tarnetar
Kaira
Dakor
Wankaner
Surendranagar
Dholka
Okha Port
Dhrol
Bagodra
Nadiad
Jamnagar
Limbdi
NH8A
Lothal
Anand
Dwarka
Khambilaya
Chotila
Ranpur
Khambhat
Rajkot
Dhandhuka
Vadodara
Hingolgadh
Botad
Gop
Velavadhar NP
Karjan
Jasdan
Bhanvad
Gondal
NH8
Gadhada
Jambusar
Jetpur

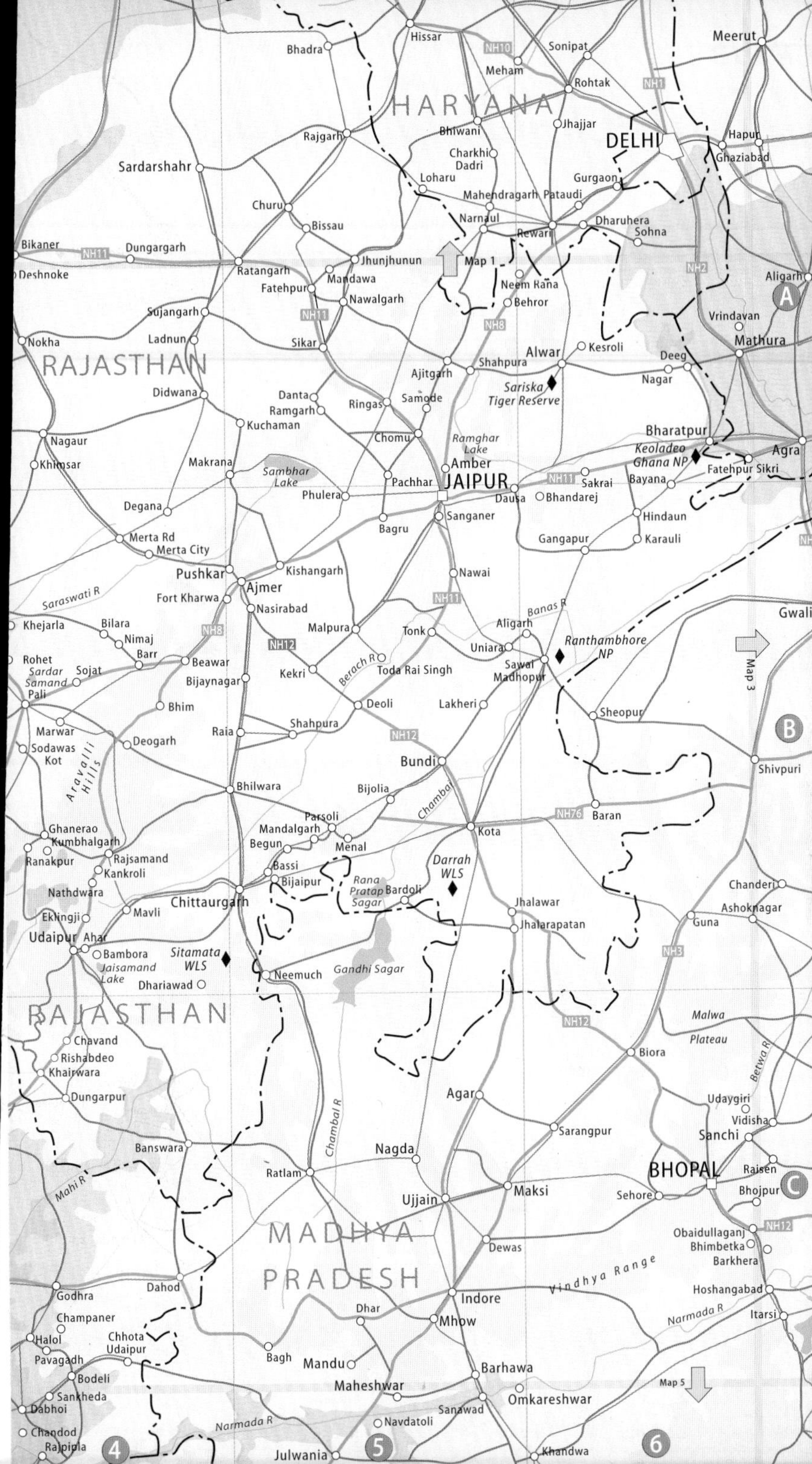
HARYANA
DELHI
RAJASTHAN
MADHYA PRADESH
JAIPUR
BHOPAL
Hissar
Bhadra
Sonipat
Meerut
Meham
Rohtak
Jhajjar
Bhiwani
Rajgarh
Hapur
Ghaziabad
Charkhi Dadri
Sardarshahr
Loharu
Gurgaon
Mahendragarh
Pataudi
Churu
Narnaul
Dharuhera
Sohna
Bissau
Rewari
Bikaner
Dungargarh
Deshnoke
Ratangarh
Jhunjhunun
Map 1
Fatehpur
Mandawa
Neem Rana
Aligarh
Nawalgarh
Behror
Sujangarh
Vrindavan
Mathura
Ladnun
Sikar
Alwar
Kesroli
Deeg
Nokha
Shahpura
Nagar
Ajitgarh
Sariska Tiger Reserve
Didwana
Danta
Ramgarh
Ringas
Samode
Kuchaman
Bharatpur
Nagaur
Chomu
Ramghar Lake
Keoladeo Ghana NP
Agra
Khimsar
Makrana
Sambhar Lake
Amber
Fatehpur Sikri
Pachhar
Sakrai
Bayana
Phulera
Dausa
Bhandarej
Degana
Sanganer
Hindaun
Bagru
Merta Rd
Merta City
Gangapur
Karauli
Pushkar
Kishangarh
Nawai
Ajmer
Fort Kharwa
Saraswati R
Nasirabad
Banas R
Gwalior
Khejarla
Bilara
Malpura
Aligarh
Nimaj
Tonk
Ranthambhore NP
Barr
Uniara
Rohet
Berach R
Sardar Samand
Sojat
Beawar
Sawai Madhopur
Toda Rai Singh
Map 3
Kekri
Pali
Bijaynagar
Deoli
Lakheri
Bhim
Sheopur
Marwar
Shahpura
Raia
Sodawas
Deogarh
Kot
Bundi
Shivpuri
Aravalli Hills
Bhilwara
Bijolia
Chambal
Baran
Parsoli
Kota
Ghanerao
Mandalgarh
Kumbhalgarh
Begun
Menal
Rajsamand
Ranakpur
Darrah WLS
Bassi
Kankroli
Bijaipur
Rana Pratap Sagar
Bardoli
Chanderi
Nathdwara
Chittaurgarh
Jhalawar
Ashoknagar
Mavli
Guna
Eklingji
Jhalarapatan
Udaipur
Ahar
Bambora
Sitamata WLS
Jaisamand Lake
Neemuch
Gandhi Sagar
Dhariawad
Malwa
Chavand
Plateau
Rishabdeo
Biora
Khairwara
Betwa R
Agar
Udaygiri
Dungarpur
Vidisha
Sarangpur
Sanchi
Chambal R
Banswara
Nagda
Raisen
Mahi R
Ratlam
Maksi
Sehore
Bhojpur
Ujjain
Obaidullaganj
Bhimbetka
Dewas
Barkhera
Vindhya Range
Godhra
Dahod
Indore
Hoshangabad
Champaner
Dhar
Narmada R
Itarsi
Halol
Mhow
Chhota Udaipur
Pavagadh
Bagh
Mandu
Bodeli
Barhawa
Sankheda
Maheshwar
Map 5
Omkareshwar
Dabhoi
Sanawad
Navdatoli
Narmada R
Chandod
Rajpipla
Julwania
Khandwa
NH1
NH2
NH3
NH8
NH10
NH11
NH12
NH76
A
B
C
4
5
6

# Map 3

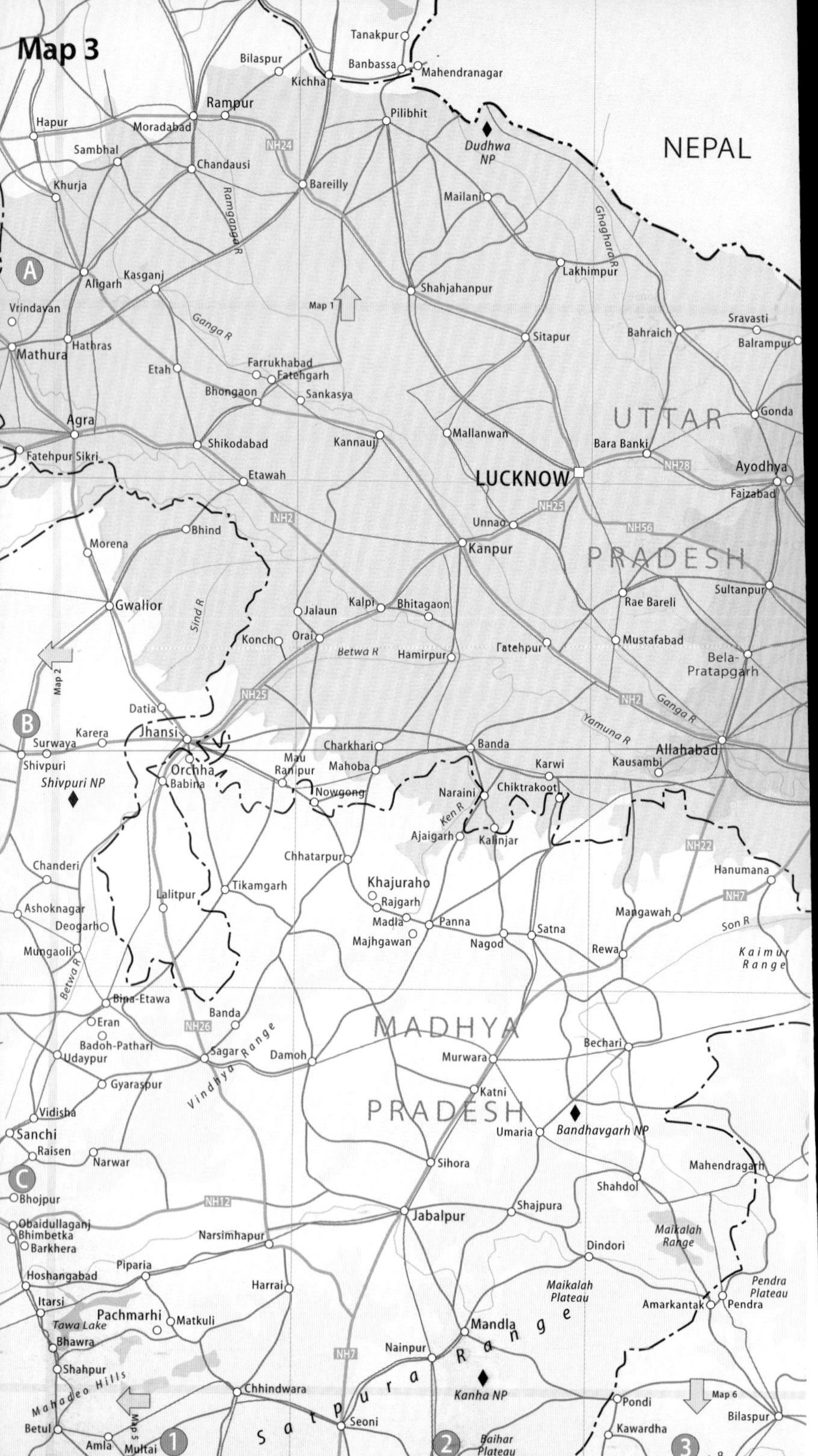

NEPAL
UTTAR
PRADESH
MADHYA
PRADESH
LUCKNOW
Tanakpur
Bilaspur
Banbassa
Mahendranagar
Kichha
Rampur
Pilibhit
Hapur
Moradabad
Dudhwa NP
Sambhal
Chandausi
Bareilly
Khurja
Mailani
Ramganga R
Ghaghara R
Lakhimpur
Aligarh
Kasganj
Shahjahanpur
Vrindavan
Map 1
Ganga R
Sitapur
Bahraich
Sravasti
Balrampur
Mathura
Hathras
Etah
Farrukhabad
Fatehgarh
Bhongaon
Sankasya
Gonda
Agra
Shikodabad
Kannauj
Mallanwan
Bara Banki
Ayodhya
Faizabad
Fatehpur Sikri
Etawah
NH24
NH28
NH25
NH2
NH56
Unnao
Bhind
Morena
Kanpur
Sultanpur
Rae Bareli
Gwalior
Sind R
Jalaun
Kalpi
Bhitagaon
Konch
Orai
Betwa R
Hamirpur
Fatehpur
Mustafabad
Bela-Pratapgarh
Map 2
Datia
Jhansi
Karera
Surwaya
Shivpuri
Shivpuri NP
Orchha
Babina
Mau Ranipur
Charkhari
Mahoba
Nowgong
Banda
Yamuna R
Allahabad
Kausambi
Karwi
Naraini
Chiktrakoot
Ken R
Ajaigarh
Kalinjar
NH22
Chanderi
Chhatarpur
Khajuraho
Rajgarh
Hanumana
Tikamgarh
Lalitpur
Ashoknagar
Deogarh
Madla
Panna
Majhgawan
Nagod
Satna
Mangawah
NH7
Son R
Rewa
Kaimur Range
Mungaoli
Bina-Etawa
Eran
NH26
Badoh-Pathari
Udaypur
Sagar
Damoh
Murwara
Bechari
Gyaraspur
Vindhya Range
Katni
Vidisha
Sanchi
Raisen
Narwar
Umaria
Bandhavgarh NP
Sihora
Mahendragarh
Shahdol
Bhojpur
NH12
Jabalpur
Shajpura
Obaidullaganj
Bhimbetka
Barkhera
Narsimhapur
Maikalah Range
Dindori
Hoshangabad
Piparia
Harrai
Maikalah Plateau
Pendra Plateau
Itarsi
Amarkantak
Pendra
Pachmarhi
Matkuli
Tawa Lake
Mandla
Bhawra
Nainpur
Satpura Range
Shahpur
Mahadeo Hills
Chhindwara
Kanha NP
Pondi
Map 6
Map 5
Seoni
Bilaspur
Betul
Kawardha
Amla
Multai
Baihar Plateau
A
B
C
1
2
3

N
0 km
50
0 miles
50
The Government of India state that "the external boundaries of India are neither correct nor authenticated"
A
B
C
4
5
6
Map 4
Sonauli 'crossing'
Nautanwa
Bagaha
Pharenda
Birganj
Raxaul
Sonbasa
Basopatti
Jaynagar
Laukaha
Basti
Gorakhpur
Kasia
Kusinagara
Dakha
Sitamarhi
Lauriya
Dumra
Gopalganj
Madhubani
Nimali
NH29
Deoria
NH28
Kishanpur
Akbarpur
Ghaghara R
Siwan
Gandak R
Darbhanga
Supaul
Kanti
Muzaffarpur
Kosi R
Vaishali
Pusa
Samastipur
Saharsa
Madhepura
Azamgarh
Mau
Chapra
Ghugri R
Shahganj
Sonepur
Hajipur
PATNA
Ganga R
Jaunpur
Maner
Khagarja
NH31
Damraon
Baraunì
Arrah
Monghyr
Saidpur
Buxar
Ghazipur
Sarnath
NH30
Arwal
Mokameh
Mughal Sarai
Pir
Jahanabad
Nalanda
Biharsharif
Luckaseeri
Varanasi
Bikramganj
Rajgir
Pawapuri
Bhimandh
Ramnagar
Sasaram
Belagunj
Sikandra
Son R
Daudnagar
Barabar Caves
Mirzapur
Bhabua Road
BIHAR
Nawala
Jha Jha
Katuria
Chunar
Gaya
Rajuali
NH2
Rohtasgarh
Bodh Gaya
Khajuri
Deoghar
Robertsganj
Sherghati
Madhupur
Dhanwar
Barhi
Giridi
Tilaiya Reservoir
Hazaribagh Road
Parsnath
Hazaribagh NP
Topchanchi Lake
Daltonganj
Singrauli
Pipri
Manika
Maithon Reservoir
Rihand (Pant Sagar)
Hazaribagh
Dumri
Chipadohar
Dhanbad
Kulti
NH33
Bokaro
Palamau Betla NP
Hundru Falls
Lodh Falls
Tori
Ramgarh
Kuru
Ghagri Falls
Lohardaga
Ranchi
Netarhat
Jonha Falls
Purulia
Deogarh Hills
Bero
Bundu
NH32
Sisai
Baikuntapur
Khunti
Dasam Falls
Balarampur
Surajpur
Ambikapur
Jashpur Hills
Gumla
Chandil
Sitapur
Tatanagar
Jamshedpur
JHARKHAND
CHHATTISGARH
Chaisbasa
NH23
Subarnarekha R
Birmitrapur
Pathalgaon
Gua
Rourkela
Jamda
Naomundi
Badampahar
Baripada
ORISSA
Talbandh
Bada Barabil
Joshipur
Sundargarh
Gobindpur
Bonai Hills
Barsua
Khiching
Brahmani R
Similipal NP
Hirakud Dam
Rawgarh
Jharsugada
NH6

Map 4
A
B
C
1
2
3
SIKKIM
Yumthang
Kangchendzonga NP
Lachung
Chemathang
Thangshing
Mangan
Dzongri
Phodong
Rumtek
Legship
Gangtok
Singtam
Naya Bazar
Rangpo
Sandakphu
Darjeeling
Kalimpong
Siliguri
Mirik
Bagdogra
New Jalpaiguri
BHUTAN
Jaldapara WLP
Manas NP
Nalbari
Bijni
Bongaigon
Saptagram
Barpeta Rd
Barpeta
Jalpaiguri
Coochbehar
Alipur Duar
NH31
Goalpara
River Brahmaputra
Krishnai
NH31B
Dhuburi
Boko
NH51
Phulbari
MEGHALAYA
Songsak
Darugiri
Singrimapi
Tura
Jadukata R
Jakrem
Siju
Burengapara
Jogbani
Forbesganj
Islampur
Kishanganj
Raniganj
Basantpur
Dalkola
Madhepura
Sarsi
Ghugri R
Mahanada R
Purnia
Katihar
NH34
WEST BENGAL
onghyr
Colgong
Bhagalpur
BIHAR
Pandua
Malda
Ingraz Bazar
Gaur
Berhait
Barahat
Bausi
Farakka
Katuria
Hausdiha
Dhulian
BANGLADESH
Deoghar
JHARKHAND
Jangipur
Hugli R
Madhupur
Murshidabad
Rampurhat
Tarapith
Baharampur
Maithon Reservoir
Suri
Sainthia
Bakresvar
Plassey
Dhanbad
Kulti
Asanol
Raniganj
Santiniketan
Bolpur
Durgapur
NH2
Krishnanagar
Nabadwip
Kalna
Barddhaman
Bankura
Damodar R
Naihati
Pandua
Map 3
Bangaon
Benapole
Bishnupur
Tarakeswar
NH35
Raipur
Arambagh
Serampore
WEST BENGAL
KOLKATA
NH6
Jaynagar
Diamond Harbour
Canning
Subarnarekha R
Haldia
Kakdwip
Baripada
Talbandh
Jaleswar
Sagardwip Island
Digha

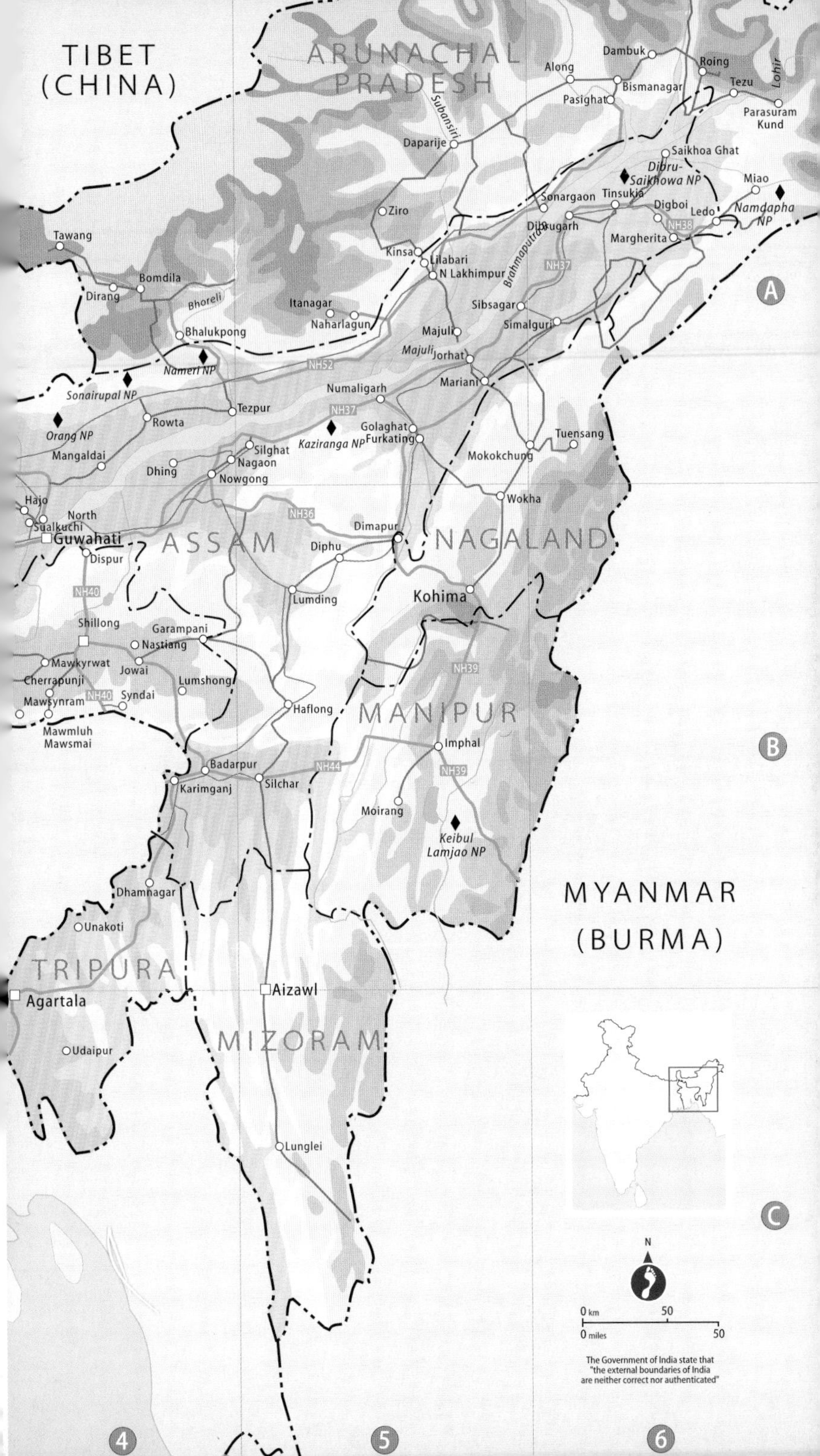

TIBET (CHINA)
ARUNACHAL PRADESH
Dambuk
Along
Roing
Bismanagar
Tezu
Lohit
Pasighat
Parasuram Kund
Subansiri
Daparije
Saikhoa Ghat
Dibru-Saikhowa NP
Miao
Sonargaon
Tinsukia
Ziro
Digboi
Ledo
Namdapha NP
Dibrugarh
NH38
Tawang
Margherita
Kinsa
Lilabari
N Lakhimpur
Brahmaputra
NH37
Bomdila
Dirang
Bhoreli
Itanagar
Sibsagar
Naharlagun
Simalguri
Majuli
Bhalukpong
Majuli
Jorhat
Nameri NP
NH52
Mariani
Sonairupal NP
Numaligarh
Tezpur
Rowta
NH37
Orang NP
Golaghat
Kaziranga NP
Furkating
Tuensang
Mangaldai
Silghat
Mokokchung
Nagaon
Dhing
Nowgong
Hajo
Wokha
North Sualkuchi
NH36
Dimapur
Guwahati
ASSAM
Diphu
NAGALAND
Dispur
NH40
Lumding
Kohima
Shillong
Garampani
Nastiang
Mawkyrwat
Jowai
NH39
Cherrapunji
Lumshong
Mawsynram
NH40
Syndai
Haflong
MANIPUR
Mawmluh Mawsmai
Imphal
Badarpur
NH44
NH39
Karimganj
Silchar
Moirang
Keibul Lamjao NP
Dhamnagar
MYANMAR (BURMA)
Unakoti
TRIPURA
Agartala
Aizawl
Udaipur
MIZORAM
Lunglei
N
0 km
50
0 miles
50
The Government of India state that "the external boundaries of India are neither correct nor authenticated"
A
B
C
4
5
6

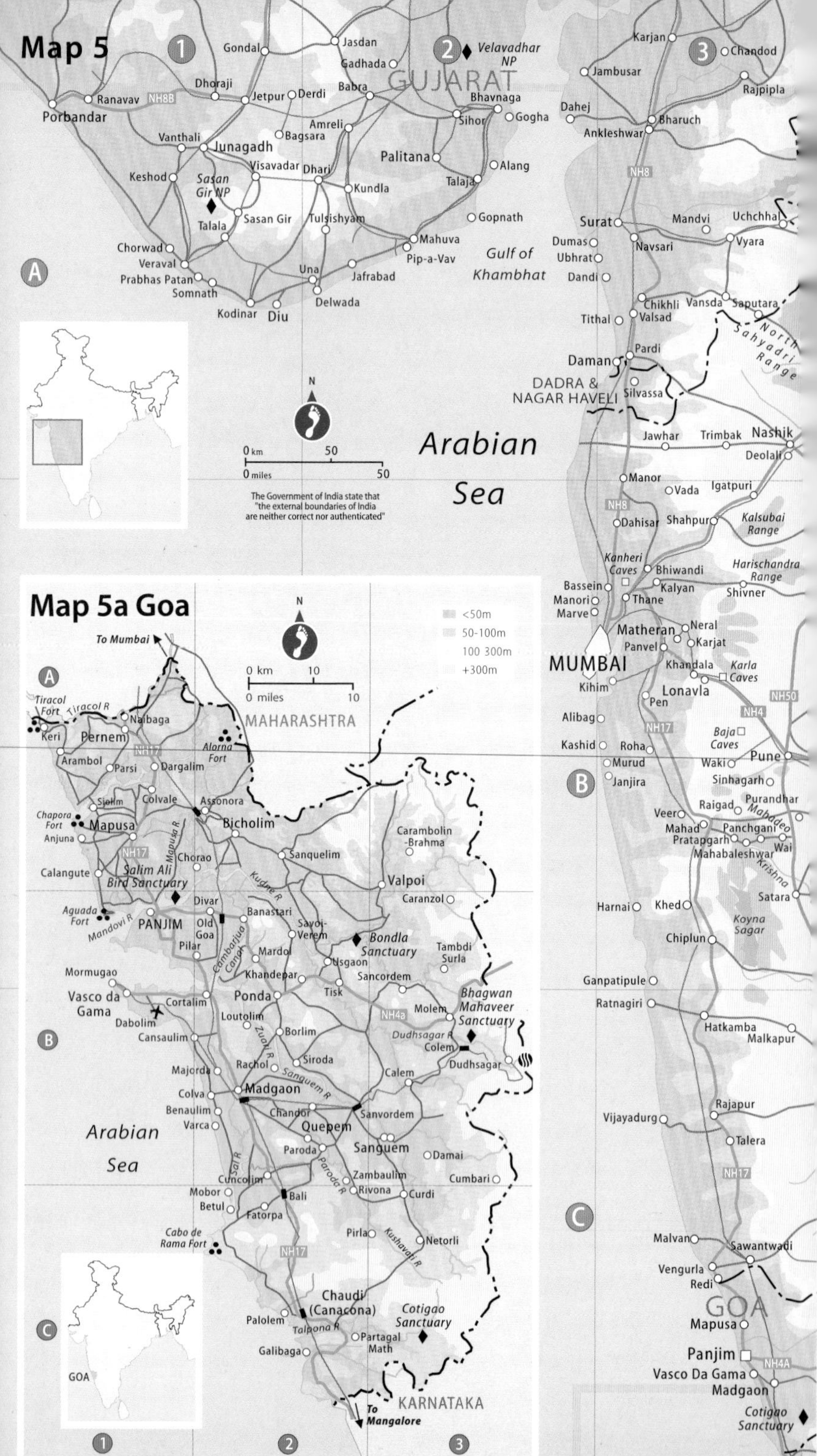

Map 5
GUJARAT
Porbandar
Ranavav
Gondal
Jasdan
Gadhada
Velavadhar NP
Dhoraji
Jetpur
Derdi
Babra
Bhavnaga
Gogha
Sihor
Amreli
Bagsara
Vanthali
Junagadh
Palitana
Alang
Keshod
Sasan Gir NP
Visavadar
Dhari
Kundla
Talaja
Talala
Sasan Gir
Tulsishyam
Gopnath
Chorwad
Veraval
Prabhas Patan
Somnath
Kodinar
Diu
Una
Delwada
Jafrabad
Mahuva
Pip-a-Vav
Gulf of Khambhat
Karjan
Chandod
Jambusar
Rajpipla
Dahej
Bharuch
Ankleshwar
Surat
Mandvi
Uchchhal
Vyara
Dumas
Navsari
Ubhrat
Dandi
Chikhli
Vansda
Saputara
Tithal
Valsad
North Sahyadri Range
Pardi
Daman
DADRA & NAGAR HAVELI
Silvassa
Arabian Sea
Jawhar
Trimbak
Nashik
Deolali
Manor
Vada
Igatpuri
Dahisar
Shahpur
Kalsubai Range
Kanheri Caves
Bhiwandi
Harischandra Range
Bassein
Kalyan
Shivner
Manori
Marve
Thane
Matheran
Neral
Panvel
Karjat
MUMBAI
Khandala
Karla Caves
Kihim
Lonavla
Pen
Alibag
Baja Caves
Kashid
Roha
Pune
Murud
Janjira
Waki
Sinhagarh
Raigad
Purandhar
Veer
Mahad
Mahadeo
Panchgani
Pratapgarh
Wai
Mahabaleshwar
Krishna
Satara
Harnai
Khed
Koyna Sagar
Chiplun
Ganpatipule
Ratnagiri
Hatkamba
Malkapur
Rajapur
Vijayadurg
Talera
Malvan
Sawantwadi
Vengurla
Redi
GOA
Mapusa
Panjim
Vasco Da Gama
Madgaon
Cotigao Sanctuary
NH8B
NH8
NH50
NH4
NH17
NH4A
0 km 50
0 miles 50
The Government of India state that "the external boundaries of India are neither correct nor authenticated"
Map 5a Goa
To Mumbai
<50m
50-100m
100 300m
+300m
0 km 10
0 miles 10
MAHARASHTRA
Tiracol Fort
Tiracol R
Keri
Naibaga
Pernem
Alorna Fort
Arambol
Parsi
Dargalim
Siolim
Colvale
Assonora
Chapora Fort
Mapusa
Bicholim
Anjuna
Mapusa R
Chorao
Sanquelim
Carambolin -Brahma
Calangute
Salim Ali Bird Sanctuary
Kudne R
Valpoi
Caranzol
Aguada Fort
Divar
Banastari
Mandovi R
PANJIM
Old Goa
Savoi-Verem
Bondla Sanctuary
Pilar
Cambarjua Canal
Mardol
Tambdi Surla
Usgaon
Mormugao
Khandepar
Sancordem
Vasco da Gama
Cortalim
Ponda
Tisk
Bhagwan Mahaveer Sanctuary
Dabolim
Loutolim
NH4a
Molem
Cansaulim
Zuari R
Borlim
Dudhsagar R
Colem
Siroda
Dudhsagar
Majorda
Rachol
Sanguem R
Calem
Colva
Madgaon
Benaulim
Chandor
Sanvordem
Varca
Quepem
Arabian Sea
Paroda
Sanguem
Damai
Sal R
Paroda R
Cuncolim
Zambaulim
Cumbari
Mobor
Rivona
Curdi
Betul
Bali
Fatorpa
Cabo de Rama Fort
Pirla
Kushavati R
Netorli
NH17
Chaudi (Canacona)
Cotigao Sanctuary
Palolem
Talpona R
Partagal Math
Galibaga
KARNATAKA
To Mangalore
GOA

Sanawad
Purnasa L
Mandhatta Gorge
Narmada R
Navdatoli
Narmada Gorge
Julwania
Khandwa
Map 2
Betul
Amla
Multai
Map 3
MADHYA PRADESH
Chikhaldara
Melghat WLS
Gawilgarh Hills
Achalpur
Nandurbar
Burhanpur
Akot
NH3
Tapti R
NH6
Map 6
A
Jalgaon
Sakri
Dhule
Bhusawal
Jamner
Malkapur
NH6
Tapti R
Murtajapur
Amravati
Wardha
Badnera
Sevagram
Akola
Fardapur
Ajanta Caves
Girna R
Malegaon
Buldana
Chandor
Chalisgaon
Shilod
Manmad
Ellora Caves
Ellora
Washim
Daulatabad
Pandharkawada
Lonar
Jalna
Aurangabad
Ellora Hills
Pandu Leni
Sangamner
Shrirampur
Shirdi
Hingol Hills
Hingol
Mahur
Kinwat WLS
Adilabad
Paithan
NH50
Nirmal
MAHARASHTRA
Godavari R
Basmath
Junnar
Ahmadnagar
Agargaon Range
Bid
Parbhani
Purna
Nanded
Pali
Godavari R
Balaghat Range
Armur
Jalgaon
Nizamabad
Bodham
Manjira R
B
Latur
Veshdi
Barsi
NH9
Dhond
Yellareddi
Udgir
Osmanabad
Kurduvadi
Kamareddi
Indapur
Medak
Bidar
Deura
Baramati
Vadgaon
Mohol
Pandharpur
Range
Zahirabad
Sangreddi
NH9
Solapur
Hotgi
Homanabad
Morangpalli
Aland
Secunderabad
Golconda
Karad
Gulbarga
Vikarabad
HYDERABAD
Sedam
Tandur
Ibrahimpatnam
NH4
Indi
Bhima R
Wadi
ANDHRA
Panhala
Miraj
Bijapur
Mahbubnagar
Badepalli
Kolhapur
Athni
KARNATAKA
Yadgir
Bagevadi
Jamkhandi
Nidgundi
Shorapur
Krishna R
PRADESH
NH4
Talikota
Hunsigi
Mudhol
Muddebihal
Raichur
Gadwal
C
Linsugur
Bagalkot
Gokak
Hungund
Krishna
Aihole
Alampur
Amboli
Tungabhadra
Atmakur
Ramdurg
Badami
Pattadakal
Belgaum
Kurnool
Mahakuta
NH13
Kushtagi
Nargund
Adoni
Dharwad
Nandyal
Alnavar
Gangawati
Gadag
Londa
Koppal
Hubli
Hampi
Dambal
Lakkundi
Map 7
Hospet
Ahobilam
Dandeli NP
Tungabhadra Dam
Bellary
Allagadda
Guntakal
Gooty
Mundgod
Shiggaon
Yellapur
4
Itiki
5
Swamihalli
6

Map 6
MADHYA PRADESH
MAHARASHTRA
CHHATTISGARH
ANDHRA PRADESH
Seoni
Kawardha
Bilaspur
Baihar Plateau
Maikala Range
Map 3
Seonath R
Mahanadi R
Katangi
Balaghat
Tirodi
Ramtek
Wainganga R
Raipur
Bhilai
NH6
Nagpur
Bhandara
Gonda
Durg
Rajnandgoan
Umer
Nawapura
Wardha
Sevagram
Dhamtari
Warsa
Nagbhir
Hinganghat
Sindewahi
Wainganga R
Kanker
Warora
Majri
Taroba NP
Tadali
Mul
Tel R
Pandharkawada
Ghugus
Chandarapur
Bastar Hills
Ballarpur
Adilabad
Kondagaon
Nirmal
Sirpur
Pappadahandi
Indravati Plateau
Indravati NP
Satmala Hills
Indravati R
Jagdalpur
NH43
Godavari R
Manchiraya
Jeypore
Telangana Plateau
Bijapur
Bailadila Hills
Kondhan
Ghanpur
Karimnagar
Palampet
Malkangiri
Laknavaram Lake
Pakhal Lake
Siddipett
Warangal
Sabari R
Sileru R
Jangaon
Bhongir
Yellandu
Ghatkesar
Kottagudem
Godavari R
Secunderabad
Golconda
HYDERABAD
NH5
Ibrahimpatnam
Khammam
Rajahmundry
NH9
Samalkot
Map 5
Tadepallegudem
Jaggayyapeta
Kakanada
Tanuku
Badepalli
Eluru
Mailepalli
Devarkonda
Kondapalli
Bhimavaram
Kolleru Lake
Amaravati
Vijayapuri
Vijayawada
Piduguralla
Nagarjunakonda
Macherla
Gudivada
Guntur
Narsapur
Krishna
Tenali
Vinnkonda
Srisailam
Bapatla
Krishna R
Atmakur
N
Podle
Cumbum
0 km 50
0 miles 50
Nandyal
Ongole
Singarayakonda
The Government of India state that "the external boundaries of India are neither correct nor authenticated"
Giddalur
Map 7
Ahobilam
Kanigi
Allagadda
Udayagiri
NH5
Kavali
A
B
C
1
2
3

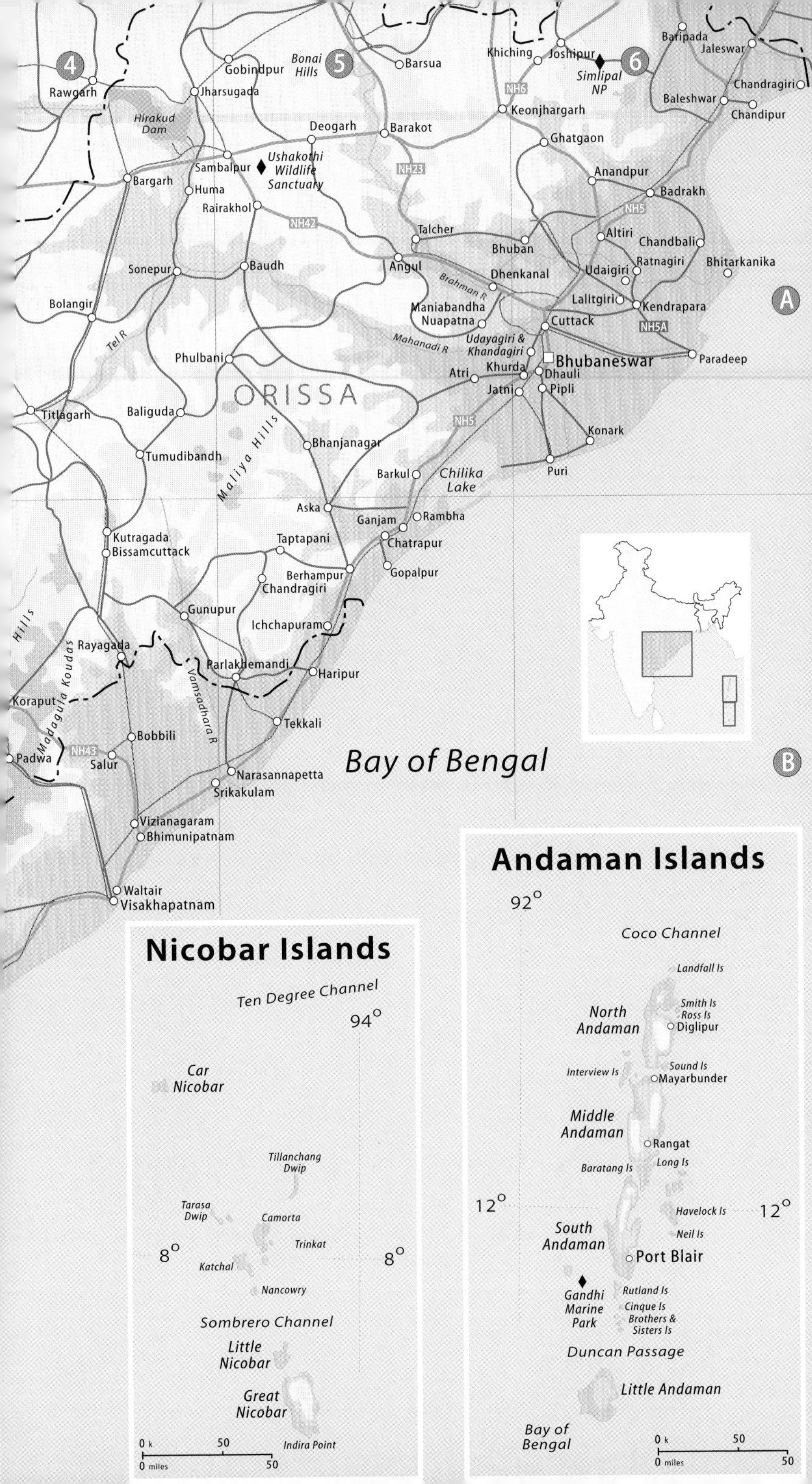

Rawgarh
Gobindpur
Bonai Hills
Barsua
Khiching
Joshipur
Simlipal NP
Baripada
Jaleswar
Chandragiri
Baleshwar
Chandipur
Jharsugada
Hirakud Dam
Deogarh
Barakot
Keonjhargarh
Ghatgaon
Sambalpur
Ushakothi Wildlife Sanctuary
Bargarh
Huma
Rairakhol
Anandpur
Badrakh
Talcher
Altiri
Chandbali
Bhuban
Ratnagiri
Bhitarkanika
Sonepur
Baudh
Angul
Udaigiri
Dhenkanal
Brahman R
Bolangir
Lalitgiri
Kendrapara
Maniabandha
Nuapatna
Cuttack
Tel R
Mahanadi R
Udayagiri & Khandagiri
Paradeep
Phulbani
Khurda
Bhubaneswar
Atri
Dhauli
Jatni
Pipli
ORISSA
Titlagarh
Baliguda
Konark
Bhanjanagar
Tumudibandh
Maliya Hills
Puri
Barkul
Chilika Lake
Aska
Rambha
Ganjam
Chatrapur
Kutragada
Bissamcuttack
Taptapani
Berhampur
Gopalpur
Chandragiri
Gunupur
Hills
Ichchapuram
Rayagada
Madagula Koudas
Parlakhemandi
Haripur
Vamsadhara R
Koraput
Tekkali
Bobbili
Padwa
Salur
Bay of Bengal
Narasannapetta
Srikakulam
Vizianagaram
Bhimunipatnam
Waltair
Visakhapatnam
NH6
NH23
NH42
NH5
NH5A
NH43
4
5
6
A
B
Andaman Islands
92°
Coco Channel
Landfall Is
Smith Is
Ross Is
North Andaman
Diglipur
Interview Is
Sound Is
Mayarbunder
Middle Andaman
Rangat
Baratang Is
Long Is
12°
Havelock Is
12°
South Andaman
Neil Is
Port Blair
Gandhi Marine Park
Rutland Is
Cinque Is
Brothers & Sisters Is
Duncan Passage
Little Andaman
Bay of Bengal
0 k 50
0 miles 50
Nicobar Islands
Ten Degree Channel
94°
Car Nicobar
Tillanchang Dwip
Tarasa Dwip
Camorta
Trinkat
8°
8°
Katchal
Nancowry
Sombrero Channel
Little Nicobar
Great Nicobar
Indira Point
0 k 50
0 miles 50

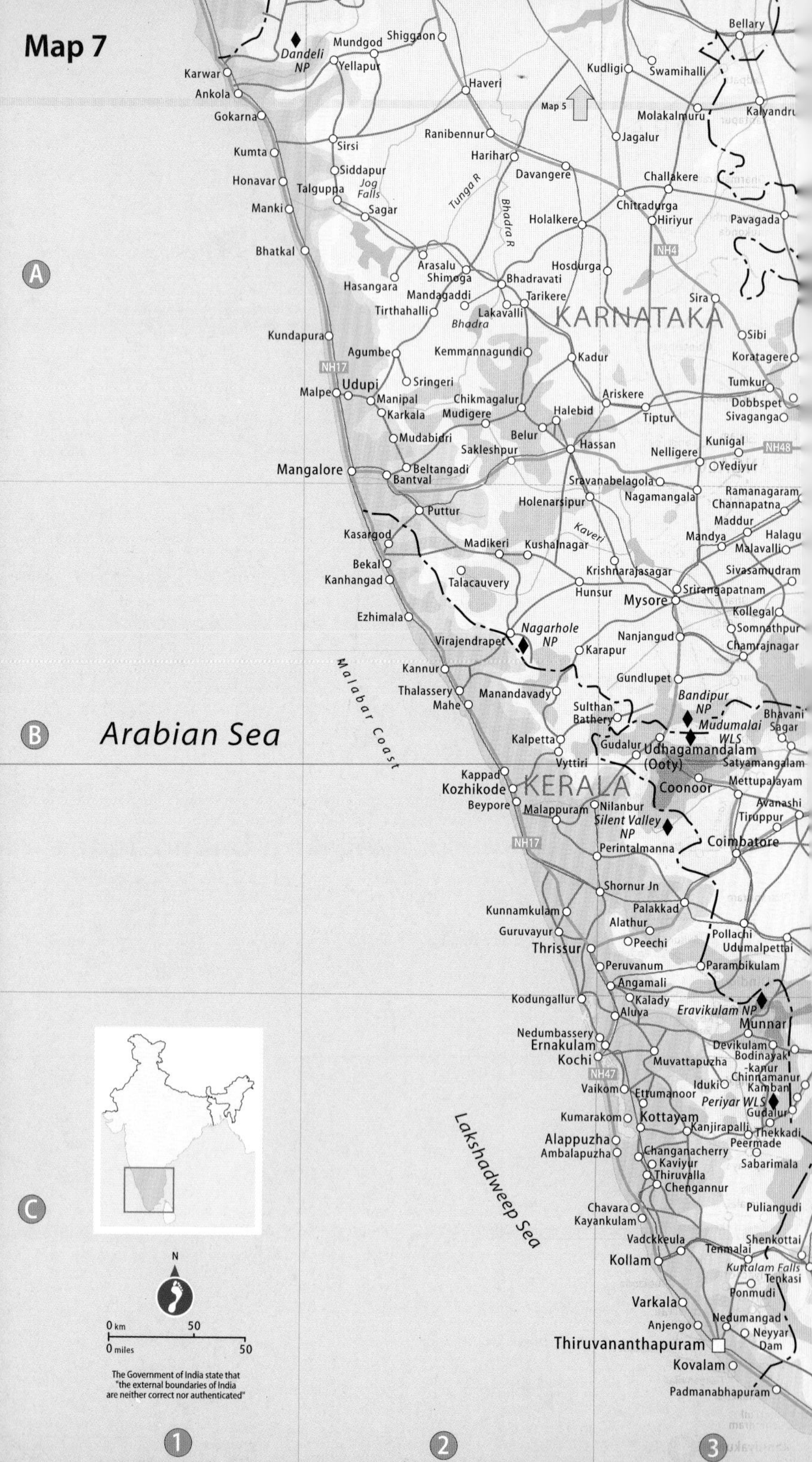
Map 7
Dandeli NP
Mundgod
Shiggaon
Yellapur
Karwar
Ankola
Gokarna
Haveri
Kudligi
Swamihalli
Bellary
Map 5
Molakalmuru
Kalyandru
Ranibennur
Jagalur
Sirsi
Kumta
Harihar
Siddapur
Jog Falls
Davangere
Challakere
Honavar
Talguppa
Tunga R
Bhadra R
Manki
Sagar
Chitradurga
Hiriyur
Holalkere
Pavagada
NH4
Bhatkal
A
Arasalu
Shimoga
Hosdurga
Hasangara
Bhadravati
Mandagaddi
Tarikere
Sira
Tirthahalli
Lakavalli
Bhadra
KARNATAKA
Kundapura
Sibi
Agumbe
Kemmannagundi
Kadur
Koratagere
NH17
Sringeri
Tumkur
Udupi
Malpe
Manipal
Chikmagalur
Ariskere
Dobbspet
Karkala
Mudigere
Halebid
Tiptur
Sivaganga
Belur
Mudabidri
Kunigal
Sakleshpur
Hassan
Nelligere
NH48
Yediyur
Mangalore
Beltangadi
Bantval
Sravanabelagola
Ramanagaram
Nagamangala
Channapatna
Holenarsipur
Puttur
Maddur
Kaveri
Kasargod
Madikeri
Kushalnagar
Mandya
Halagu
Malavalli
Bekal
Talacauvery
Krishnarajasagar
Sivasamudram
Kanhangad
Hunsur
Srirangapatnam
Mysore
Kollegal
Ezhimala
Nagarhole NP
Somnathpur
Nanjangud
Virajendrapet
Chamrajnagar
Karapur
Malabar Coast
Kannur
Gundlupet
Thalassery
Manandavady
Bandipur NP
Mahe
Bhavani Sagar
Sulthan Bathery
Mudumalai WLS
B
Arabian Sea
Kalpetta
Gudalur
Udhagamandalam (Ooty)
Vyttiri
Satyamangalam
Kappad
Mettupalayam
Kozhikode
KERALA
Coonoor
Beypore
Malappuram
Nilanbur
Avanashi
Silent Valley NP
Tiruppur
NH17
Coimbatore
Perintalmanna
Shornur Jn
Palakkad
Kunnamkulam
Alathur
Guruvayur
Pollachi
Peechi
Udumalpettai
Thrissur
Peruvanum
Parambikulam
Angamali
Kodungallur
Kalady
Aluva
Eravikulam NP
Nedumbassery
Munnar
Ernakulam
Devikulam
Kochi
Muvattapuzha
Bodinayak-kanur
NH47
Chinnamanur
Iduki
Vaikom
Ettumanoor
Kamban
Periyar WLS
Lakshadweep Sea
Kumarakom
Kottayam
Gudalur
Kanjirapalli
Thekkadi
Alappuzha
Peermade
Ambalapuzha
Changanacherry
Kaviyur
Sabarimala
Thiruvalla
Chengannur
C
Chavara
Puliangudi
Kayankulam
Vadckkeula
Shenkottai
N
Tenmalai
Kollam
Kuttalam Falls
Tenkasi
Ponmudi
Varkala
0 km
50
Nedumangad
Anjengo
0 miles
50
Neyyar Dam
Thiruvananthapuram
Kovalam
The Government of India state that "the external boundaries of India are neither correct nor authenticated"
Padmanabhapuram
1
2
3

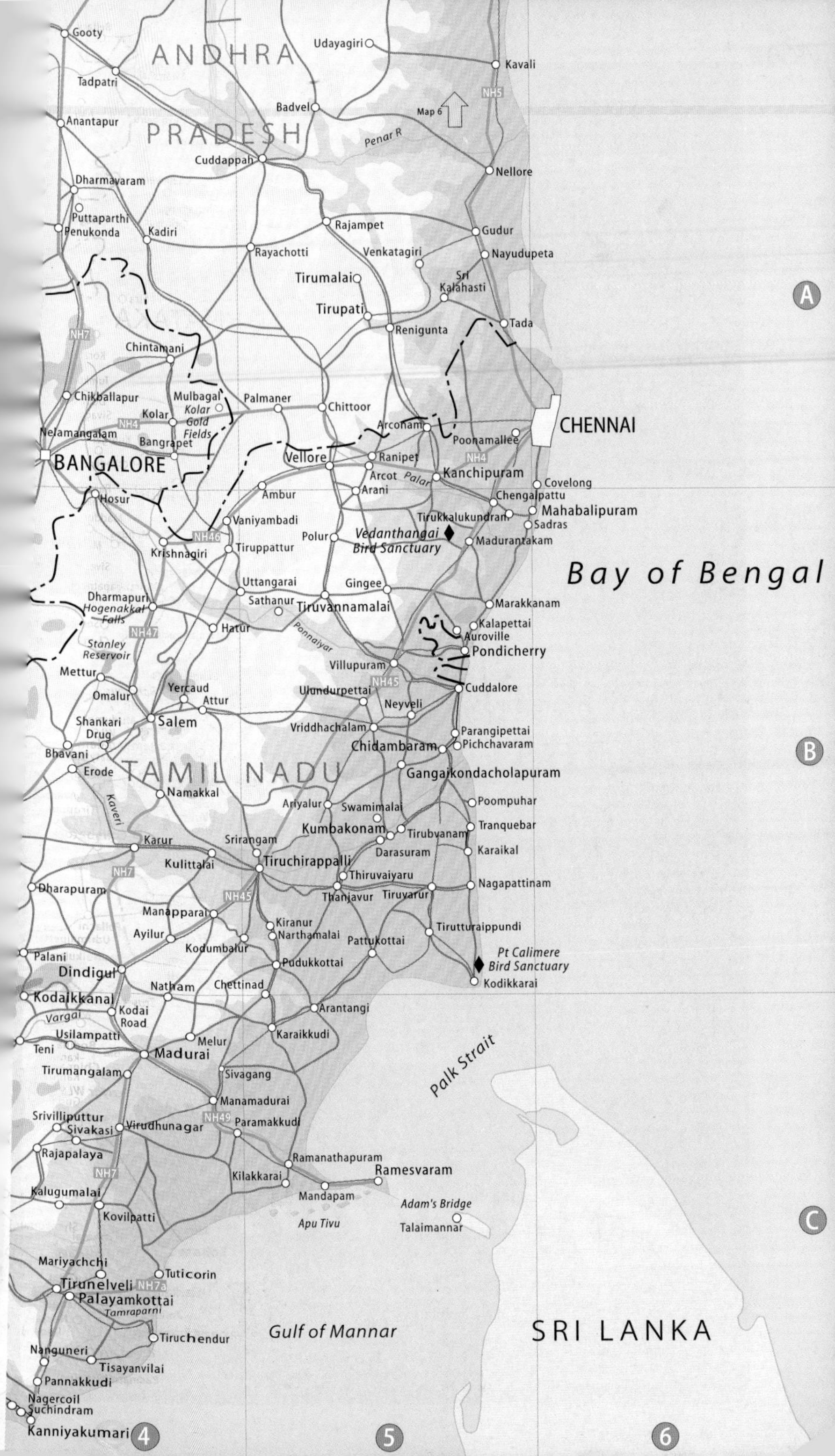

ANDHRA PRADESH
Gooty
Tadpatri
Anantapur
Udayagiri
Kavali
Badvel
Map 6
Penar R
Cuddappah
Nellore
Dharmavaram
Puttaparthi
Penukonda
Kadiri
Rajampet
Rayachotti
Venkatagiri
Gudur
Nayudupeta
Tirumalai
Sri Kalahasti
Tirupati
Renigunta
Tada
Chintamani
Chikballapur
Mulbagal
Kolar Gold Fields
Kolar
Palmaner
Chittoor
Nelamangalam
Bangrapet
Arconam
CHENNAI
Poonamallee
BANGALORE
Vellore
Ranipet
Arcot
Palar
Kanchipuram
Arani
Covelong
Hosur
Ambur
Chengalpattu
Mahabalipuram
Tirukkalukundram
Sadras
Vaniyambadi
Polur
Vedanthangai Bird Sanctuary
Madurantakam
Krishnagiri
Tiruppattur
Bay of Bengal
Uttangarai
Gingee
Dharmapuri
Hogenakkal Falls
Sathanur
Tiruvannamalai
Marakkanam
Hatur
Ponnaiyar
Kalapettai
Auroville
Stanley Reservoir
Pondicherry
Villupuram
Mettur
Cuddalore
Omalur
Yercaud
Ulundurpettai
Attur
Neyveli
Salem
Shankari Drug
Vriddhachalam
Parangipettai
Pichchavaram
Chidambaram
Bhavani
Erode
TAMIL NADU
Gangaikondacholapuram
Namakkal
Kaveri
Ariyalur
Swamimalai
Poompuhar
Kumbakonam
Tranquebar
Srirangam
Tirubvanam
Karur
Darasuram
Karaikal
Kulittalai
Tiruchirappalli
Thiruvaiyaru
Dharapuram
Thanjavur
Tiruvarur
Nagapattinam
Manapparai
Kiranur
Narthamalai
Tirutturaippundi
Ayilur
Pattukottai
Kodumbalur
Pt Calimere Bird Sanctuary
Palani
Dindigul
Pudukkottai
Kodikkarai
Natham
Chettinad
Kodaikkanal
Kodai Road
Arantangi
Vargai
Usilampatti
Melur
Karaikkudi
Teni
Madurai
Palk Strait
Tirumangalam
Sivagang
Manamadurai
Srivilliputtur
Sivakasi
Virudhunagar
Paramakkudi
Rajapalaya
Ramanathapuram
Ramesvaram
Kilakkarai
Kalugumalai
Mandapam
Adam's Bridge
Kovilpatti
Apu Tivu
Talaimannar
Mariyachchi
Tuticorin
Tirunelveli
Palayamkottai
Tamraparni
Gulf of Mannar
SRI LANKA
Tiruchendur
Nanguneri
Tisayanvilai
Pannakkudi
Nagercoil
Suchindram
Kanniyakumari
NH7
NH4
NH46
NH47
NH45
NH5
NH49
NH7a
A
B
C
4
5
6